ISBN 978-0-331-35590-1
PIBN 11110990

48

RE
ABS

, NUMBER
JULY 1, 1975

W75-06351 -- W75-06850
CODEN: SWRABW

SELECTED WATER RESOURCES ABSTRACTS is published semimonthly for the Water Resources Scientific Information Center (WRSIC) by the National Technical Information Service (NTIS), U.S. Department of Commerce. NTIS was established September 2, 1970, as a new primary operating unit under the Assistant Secretary of Commerce for Science and Technology to improve public access to the many products and services of the Department. Information services for Federal scientific and technical report literature previously provided by the Clearinghouse for Federal Scientific and Technical Information are now provided by NTIS.

SELECTED WATER RESOURCES ABSTRACTS is available to Federal agencies, contractors, or grantees in water resources upon request to: Manager, Water Resources Scientific Information Center, Office of Water Research and Technology, U.S. Department of the Interior, Washington, D. C. 20240.

SELECTED WATER RESOURCES ABSTRACTS is also available on subscription from the National Technical Information Service. Annual subscription rates are: To the SWRA Journal, $75 ($95 foreign); to the Journal & Annual Index, $100 ($125 foreign); to the Annual Index only, $50 ($65 foreign). Certain documents abstracted in this journal can be purchased from the NTIS at prices indicated in the entry. Prepayment is required.

SELECTED
WATER RESOURCES ABSTRACTS

A Semimonthly Publication of the Water Resources Scientific Information Center,
Office of Water Research and Technology, U.S. Department of the Interior

VOLUME 8, NUMBER 13
JULY 1, 1975

W75-06351 -- W75-06850

As the Nation's principal conservation agency, the Department of the Interior has responsibility for most of our nationally owned public lands and natural resources. This includes fostering the wisest use of our land and water resources, protecting our fish and wildlife, preserving the environmental and cultural values of our national parks and historical places, and providing for the enjoyment of life through outdoor recreation. The Department assesses our energy and mineral resources and works to assure that their development is in the best interests of all our people. The Department also has a major responsibility for American Indian reservation communities and for people who live in Island Territories under U.S. administration.

FOREWORD

Selected Water Resources Abstracts, a semimonthly journal, includes abstracts of current and earlier pertinent monographs, journal articles, reports, and other publication formats. The contents of these documents cover the water-related aspects of the life, physical, and social sciences as well as related engineering and legal aspects of the characteristics, conservation, control, use, or management of water. Each abstract includes a full bibliographical citation and a set of descriptors or identifiers which are listed in the **Water Resources Thesaurus.** Each abstract entry is classified into ten fields and sixty groups similar to the water resources research categories established by the Committee on Water Resources Research of the Federal Council for Science and Technology.

WRSIC IS NOT PRESENTLY IN A POSITION TO PROVIDE COPIES OF DOCUMENTS ABSTRACTED IN THIS JOURNAL. Sufficient bibliographic information is given to enable readers to order the desired documents from local libraries or other sources.

Selected Water Resources Abstracts is designed to serve the scientific and technical information needs of scientists, engineers, and managers as one of several planned services of the Water Resources Scientific Information Center (WRSIC). The Center was established by the Secretary of the Interior and has been designated by the Federal Council for Science and Technology to serve the water resources community by improving the communication of water-related research results. The Center is pursuing this objective by coordinating and supplementing the existing scientific and technical information activities associated with active research and investigation program in water resources.

To provide WRSIC with input, selected organizations with active water resources research programs are supported as "centers of competence" responsible for selecting, abstracting, and indexing from the current and earlier pertinent literature in specified subject areas.

Additional "centers of competence" have been established in cooperation with the Environmental Protection Agency. A directory of the Centers appears on inside back cover.

Supplementary documentation is being secured from established discipline-oriented abstracting and indexing services. Currently an arrangement is in effect whereby the BioScience Information Service of Biological Abstracts supplies WRSIC with relevant references from the several subject areas of interest to our users. In addition to Biological Abstracts, references are acquired from Bioresearch Index which are without abstracts and therefore also appear abstractless in SWRA. Similar arrangements with other producers of abstracts are contemplated as planned augmentation of the information base.

The input from these Centers, and from the 51 Water Resources Research Institutes administered under the Water Resources Research Act of 1964, as well as input from the grantees and contractors of the Office of Water Research and Technology and other Federal water resource agencies with which the

Center has agreements becomes the information base from which this journal is, and other information services will be, derived; these services include bibliographies, specialized indexes, literature searches, and state-of-the-art reviews.

Comments and suggestions concerning the contents and arrangements of this bulletin are welcome.

Water Resources Scientific Information Center
Office of Water Research and Technology
U.S. Department of the Interior
Washington, D. C. 20240

CONTENTS

SELECTED WATER RESOURCES ABSTRACTS

2. WATER CYCLE

2A. General

TEMPERATURE EFFECTS ON GREAT LAKES WATER BALANCE STUDIES,
State Univ. of New York, Buffalo. Dept. of Civil Engineering.
For primary bibliographic entry see Field 2H.
W75-06448

A SURROGATE-PARAMETER APPROACH TO MODELING GROUNDWATER BASINS,
Colorado State Univ., Fort Collins. Dept. of Civil Engineering.
For primary bibliographic entry see Field 2F.
W75-06449

DEVELOPMENT OF A STORM RUN-OFF PREDICTION MODEL WITH SIMULATED TEMPORAL RAINFALL DISTRIBUTION,
Meteorological Office, New Delhi (India).
For primary bibliographic entry see Field 2E.
W75-06453

A COMPARISON OF HYDROLOGIC AND HYDRAULIC CATCHMENT ROUTING PROCEDURES,
University Coll., Galway (Ireland).
For primary bibliographic entry see Field 2E.
W75-06456

RELATIONS BETWEEN PLANIMETRIC AND HYPSOMETRIC VARIABLES IN THIRD- AND FOURTH-ORDER DRAINAGE BASINS,
New Univ. of Ulster, Coleraine (Northern Ireland). School of Biological and Environmental Studies.
D. N. Wilcock.
Geological Society of America Bulletin, Vol 86, No 1, p 47-50, January 1975. 3 fig, 3 tab, 8 ref.

Descriptors: *Geomorphology, *Terrain analysis, *Drainage density, *Drainage patterns(Geologic), Streams, Drainage, Drainage systems, Watersheds(Basins), Hypsometric analysis, Foreign countries, Europe, Foreign research, Geology, Topography, Distribution, Networks.
Identifiers: *Stream frequency, Stream order, Stream planimetric variables, England, Scotland.

Analyses of relief distribution and drainage distribution within individual drainage basins suggested that relative density (stream frequency divided by the square of drainage density), a dimensionless variable describing a planimetric characteristic of stream organization in a basin, is related to the hypsometric integral (HI), a dimensionless variable describing the distribution of relief within a basin. The nature of this relation seems to be important in explaining much of the scatter in the graphical relations between stream frequency (F) and drainage density (D). The results suggested that, within any sample of drainage basins, the distribution of individual basin HI values about the sample mean HI value might influence the value of k in the relation of F equals a constant time D to the k power. (Lee-ISWS)
W75-06459

INTERNATIONAL HYDROLOGICAL DECADE REPRESENTATIVE AND EXPERIMENTAL BASINS IN THE UNITED STATES: CATALOG OF AVAILABLE DATA AND RESULTS, 1965-1972.
National Committee for the International Hydrological Decade, Washington, D.C.
Available from the National Technical Information Service, Springfield, Va 22161 as PB-237 002, $6.25 in paper copy, $2.25 in microfiche. NAS/IHD-74/01, July 1974. 149 p, 1 fig. NSF C310.

Descriptors: *Demonstration watersheds, *Data collections, *International Hydrological Decade, Basins, *Watersheds(Basins), Research and development, Information exchange, Watershed management.

The data collected in studies of the 60 International Hydrological Decade representative and experimental basins in the United States were briefly described. The main results were listed of the hydrological studies undertaken in those basins within the framework of, and as contributions to, the Decade. The report emphasized: (1) the objectives of studies in each area, (2) the significant results of the studies in each area, and (3) the data that are now available for exchange. There is a section on 'Reports Available Publicly' for each basin listed. (Jess-ISWS)
W75-06472

STATE OF THE SEA AROUND TROPICAL CYCLONES IN THE WESTERN NORTH PACIFIC OCEAN,
Environmental Prediction Research Facility (Navy), Monterey, Calif.
S. Brand, J. W. Blelloch, and D. C. Schertz.
Journal of Applied Meteorology, Vol 14, No 1, p 25-30, February 1975. 4 fig, 3 tab, 14 ref.

Descriptors: *Ocean waves, *Tropical cyclones, *Pacific Ocean, Waves(Water), Winds, Regression analysis, Forecasting, Meteorology, Oceanography, Typhoons, Storms.

The combined sea-height data for the year 1971 for the western North Pacific Ocean were examined to determine the sea-state characteristics around tropical storms and typhoons. The results showed that the areal extent about the storms of the combined sea height in the 9-15 ft range is primarily a function of storm duration, intensity (maximum sustained wind), and size. Equations derived by linear regression techniques were presented for describing the state of the sea about tropical cyclones. (Sims-ISWS)
W75-06495

A STUDY OF EDDY FLUXES OVER A FOREST,
Commonwealth Scientific and Industrial Research Organization, Aspendale (Australia). Div. of Atmospheric Physics.
For primary bibliographic entry see Field 2I.
W75-06498

A METHOD OF REMOVING LAMB WAVES FROM INITIAL DATA FOR PRIMITIVE EQUATION MODELS,
National Center for Atmospheric Research, Boulder, Colo.
For primary bibliographic entry see Field 2B.
W75-06499

ESTIMATING THE VARIANCE OF TIME AVERAGES,
Hawaii Univ., Honolulu. Dept. of Information and Computer Science.
For primary bibliographic entry see Field 7C.
W75-06502

ON PARAMETERIZATION OF TURBULENT TRANSPORT IN CUMULUS CLOUDS,
National Oceanic and Atmospheric Administration, Coral Gables, Fla. Experimental Meteorology Lab.
For primary bibliographic entry see Field 2B.
W75-06513

REPRESENTATIVENESS OF WATERSHED PRECIPITATION SAMPLES,
West Virginia Univ., Morgantown. Water Research Inst.
For primary bibliographic entry see Field 2B.
W75-06522

MARKOV MIXTURE MODELS FOR DROUGHT LENGTHS,
Harvard Univ., Boston, Mass. Graduate School of Business Administration.
B. B. Jackson.
Water Resources Research, Vol 11, No 1, p 64-74, February 1975. 6 fig, 5 tab, 12 ref.

Descriptors: *Droughts, *Markov processes, Streamflow, Synthetic hydrology, Probability, Dry seasons, Wet seasons, Model studies, Annual, Planning, *Massachusetts.
Identifiers: *Markov mixture models, *Quaboag River(Mass).

The generation of synthetic streamflow records for use in simulation studies of potential hydrologic designs was illustrated. Markov mixture models combined a Markov model for transitions between low and normal streamflow states with a mixture model blending to normal subpopulations. The models were particularly effective for generating synthetic streamflow records with long and severe droughts. They were used in a hypothetical planning problem to illustrate the application of a set of modeling precepts. (Roberts-ISWS)
W75-06545

BIRTH-DEATH MODELS FOR DIFFERENTIAL PERSISTENCE,
Harvard Unov., Boston, Mass. Graduate School of Business Administration.
For primary bibliographic entry see Field 2E.
W75-06546

ESTIMATING INFILTRATION FOR ERRATIC RAINFALL,
Oak Ridge National Lab., Tenn.
For primary bibliographic entry see Field 2G.
W75-06548

FORECASTING SNOWMELT RUNOFF IN THE UPPER MIDWEST,
Minnesota Univ., Minneapolis. Dept. of Civil and Mineral Engineering.
A. F. Pabst.
Available from the National Technical Information Service, Springfield, Va 22161, as PB-241 179, $6.25 in paper copy, $2.25 in microfiche. PhD Thesis, June 1973. 160 p, 46 fig, 11 tab, 68 ref. OWRT B-077-MINN(1), 14-31-0001-3902.

Descriptors: Flooding, Flood control, *Flood forecasting, *Runoff, *Mathematical models, Minnesota, *Model studies, Snowmelt, Watershed management, Frozen soils.
Identifiers: *Minnesota River Basin(Minn).

The performance of two mathematical runoff models, the SSARR model and HEC-1 model were evaluated with respect to their usefulness in computing snowmelt floods on a medium-sized Upper Midwest watershed. The continuous-accounting feature of the SSARR model makes it very valuable for simulating records containing a series of wet and dry periods. For snowmelt computations in the Midwest the SSARR model's ability to represent an area as a split basin with differing characteristics and to gradually change from one representation to the other is a marked advantage over HEC-1. With certain modifications either model will adequately perform snowmelt flood predictions in the Upper Midwest. As a result of applying these models to the Minnesota River Basin, certain conclusions can be drawn. The average water equivalent in the snowpack, the ex-

pected additional precipitation, the expected air temperatures, and the existing surface and frost conditions must all be known for a reliable forecast. If a glazed surface and tightly forzen ground conditions had existed in 1969, the peak discharge near the mouth of the Minnesota River could possibly have been 168,000 cfs--twice the observed peak. The type of frozen soil appears to have a greatef effect on controlling runoff than the thickness of the frozen layer. A relationship was developed, by multiple regression, which yields the volume of runoff between mid-March and April 30. With loss coefficients selected for each specific sub-basin, each year, the comprehensive streamflow model may predict flood runoff hydrographs more accurately.
W75-06648

2B. Precipitation

AGRICULTURAL DROUGH PROBABILITIES IN TENNESSEE,
Tennessee Univ., Knoxville. Dept. of Plant and Soil Science.
For primary bibliographic entry see Field 3F.
W75-06358

WEATHER MODIFICATION ACTIVITIES IN TEXAS, 1973,
Texas Water Development Board, Austin. Weather Modification and Technology Div.
For primary bibliographic entry see Field 3B.
W75-06464

A RADIOSONDE THERMAL SENSOR TECHNIQUE FOR MEASUREMENT OF ATMOSPHERIC TURBULENCE,
National Aeronautics and Space Administration, Greenbelt, Md. Goddard Space Flight Center.
J. L. Bufton.
Available from the National Technical Information Service, Springfield, Va 22161 as NASA TND-7867, $3.75 in paper copy, $2.25 in microfiche. NASA Technical Note D-7867, February 1975. 41 p, 12 fig, 3 tab, 28 ref.

Descriptors: *Instrumentation, *Radiosondes, *Turbulence, *Remote sensing, *Atmosphere, Eddies, Optical properties, Frequency, Distribution, Measurement.
Identifiers: *Thermosonde, Scintillation, Laser propagation.

A new system was developed to measure vertical profiles of microthermal turbulence in the free atmosphere. It combines thermal sensor technology with radiosonde balloon systems. The resultant data set from each thermosonde flight is a profile of the strength and distribution of microthermal fluctuations which act as tracers for turbulence. The optical strength of this turbulence is computed and used to predict optical and laser beam propagation statistics. A description of the flight payload, examples of turbulence profiles, and comparison with stimultaneous stellar observations were included. (Jones-ISWS)
W75-06476

METEOROLOGICAL INTERPRETATION OF SPACE PHOTOGRAPHS OF THE EARTH (QUANTITATIVE METHODS),
For primary bibliographic entry see Field 7C.
W75-06488

STATE OF THE SEA AROUND TROPICAL CYCLONES IN THE WESTERN NORTH PACIFIC OCEAN,
Environmental Prediction Research Facility (Navy), Monterey, Calif.
For primary bibliographic entry see Field 2A.
W75-06495

A PORTABLE AEROSOL DETECTOR OF HIGH SENSITIVITY,
State Univ. of New York, Albany. Atmospheric Sciences Research Center.
For primary bibliographic entry see Field 5A.
W75-06496

A METHOD OF REMOVING LAMB WAVES FROM INITIAL DATA FOR PRIMITIVE EQUATION MODELS,
National Center for Atmospheric Research, Boulder, Colo.
W. M. Washington, and D. P. Baumhefner.
Journal of Applied Meteorology, Vol 14 No 1, p 114-119, February 1975. 3 fig, 1 tab, 13 ref.

Descriptors: *Mathematical models, *Atmospheric pressure, *Winds, Forecasting, Numerical analysis, Model studies, Meteorology, Atmsophere, Atmospheric physics.
Identifiers: Geostrophic winds, Divergence, Convergence, Lamb waves.

A simple method of reducing the amplitude of Lamb waves in primitive equation model forecasts was proposed and tested. This method makes use of a Boussinesq-type approximation in which the vertical mean mass divergence is set equal to zero. It effectively reduces the Lamb waves by a factor of 3 in the example shown and does not degrade the forecast accuracy. The largest reduction in Lamb wave amplitude was found in the tropical regions. (Sims-ISWS)
W75-06499

CHLORIDES IN NATURAL AND ARTIFICIAL HAILSTONES,
Istituto di Fisica dell'Atmosfera, Verona (Italy). Osservatorio Scientifico.
F. Prodi.
Journal of Applied Meteorology, Vol 14, No 1, p 120-124, February 1975. 3 fig, 8 ref.

Descriptors: *Hail, *Precipitation(Atmospheric), *Chemistry of precipitation, *Cloud physics, *Chlorides, Salts, Membranes, Ice, Bubbles, Meteorology.
Identifiers: *Artificial hailstones, Growth of hailstones.

A membrane filter technique for precisely locating chlorides on any prepared ice surface was tested on hailstone cross sections. Chloride patterns, different in intensity in the various growth stages of the hailstones, were detected along the grain boundarics. To relate the environmental growth conditions of the hailstones to the chloride distributions, the filter technique was applied to deposits of ice grown by accretion in a wind tunnel from droplets of known NaCl concentrations. The results showed a dependence of the chloride distributions on time and temperature of storage: initially chlorides are uniformly distributed in the lattice structure and subsequently segregate to the grain boundaries during storage at temperatures close to 0C. It was suggested that the technique, especially when performed on freshly fallen hailstones, may contribute in inferring growth conditions of the hailstones in the parent cloud and their trajectories, provided that a realistic model of the chloride concentration in the liquid water of the hailcloud is outlined. (Sims-ISWS)
W75-06500

AN APT SIGNAL SIMULATOR,
New York State Coll. of Agriculture and Life Sciences, Ithaca. Div. of Atmospheric Sciences.
For primary bibliographic entry see Field 7B.
W75-06501

EMPIRICAL ESTIMATES OF THE STANDARD ERROR OF TIME-AVERAGED CLIMATIC MEANS,
National Center for Atmospheric Research, Boulder, Colo.
For primary bibliographic entry see Field 7C.
W75-06503

FREQUENCIES OF SHORT-PERIOD RAINFALL RATES ALONG LINES,
Illinois State Water Survey, Urbana.
A. L. Sims, and D. M. A. Jones.
Journal of Applied Meteorology, Vol 14, No 2, p 170-174, March 1975. 4 fig, 6 ref. AFCRL Contract F 19628-69-C-0070 and F 19628-72-C-0052.

Descriptors: *Rainfall intensity, *Precipitation(Atmospheric), *Frequency curves, Rainfall, Rates, Precipitation intensity, Meteorology, Climatology, Rain gages, Instrumentation, Radio communications systems, Precipitation gages, *Florida, *Illinois.
Identifiers: Thunderstorm Project.

Two-minute rainfall rates were measured along lines of recording raingages in Florida and Illinois. Knowledge of the frequencies of occurrence of short-duration rainfall rates is needed for estimating attenuation of radio communications and radars. Rainfall rate frequencies are also useful in estimating the erosion of high-speed devices by rain. Results were presented for one summer of data taken at each location. The Florida lines were 9.6 and 21.5 km in length and the Illinois lines 23.9 and 62.2 km. These line frequencies were compared with single gage frequencies at each location. The frequencies by which various rates are exceeded were shown for those that occur more than 0.001% of the time. Rain at rates greater than 0.1 mm/hr occurred less than 6% of the time at either location and for the longest line lengths. For similar line lengths, most rainfall rates have higher frequencies of occurrence in Florida than in Illinois. The rainfall rate frequencies were not significantly different for differing line orientations. (Sims-ISWS)
W75-06504

THE SPECTRAL REPRESENTATION OF MOISTURE,
Atmospheric Environment Service, Montreal (Quebec).
For primary bibliographic entry see Field 7C.
W75-06505 .

THE USE OF A VERTICALLY POINTING PULSED DOPPLER RADAR IN CLOUD PHYSICS AND WEATHER MODIFICATION STUDIES,
Washington Univ., Seattle. Dept. of Atmospheric Sciences.
For primary bibliographic entry see Field 3B.
W75-06507

PREDICTION AND MEASUREMENT OF THE ACCELERATED MOTION OF WATER DROPS IN AIR,
National Center for Atmospheric Research, Boulder, Colo.
J. D. Sartor, and C. E. Abbott.
Journal of Applied Meteorology, Vol 14, No 2, p 232-239, March 1975. 4 fig, 3 tab, 15 ref.

Descriptors: *Cloud physics, *Fluid mechanics, *Drops(Fluids), Numerical analysis, Drag, Movement, Turbulence, Analytical techniques, Measurement, Reynolds number, Equations, *Forecasting.
Identifiers: Acceleration, Drag coefficients, Navier-Stokes equation, Water drops, *Cloud droplets.

The lack of detailed information of the drag forces of cloud droplets during accelerated motion has made it necessary to assume that steady-state drag forces can be used to predict their motion at all times. This assumption is made implicitly in the calculations of collision efficiencies of cloud droplets even though theory and experiment demonstrate that drops accelerate while

hydrodynamically interacting. Interaction of droplets in turbulent motion should be particularly sensitive to discrepancies between accelerated drag and steady state. The motion of small water drops (Reynolds number R approximately less than 5) accelerating from rest in a still air chamber was observed. The drag coefficients of the accelerated motion of small droplets, obtained in this manner, were compared with observations of steady-state drag coefficients and were found to agree within experimental error. Using the steady-state drag coefficients obtained by Le Clair et al. from wind tunnel studies and numerical solutions to the Navier-Stokes equation of motion, the equations of motion (R approximately less than 5) for accelerating and decelerating drops were analytically integrated to obtain analytic prediction equations for their velocity and position as functions of time. Calculations from these equations were compared with observations and found to agree within experimental error, usually much less than 10%. (Jones-ISWS)
W75-06508

SUMMER ICE CRYSTAL PRECIPITATION AT THE SOUTH POLE,
State Univ. of New York, Albany. Atmospheric Sciences Research Center.
For primary bibliographic entry see Field 2C.
W75-06509

DUAL DOPPLER RADAR COORDINATION USING NOMOGRAMS,
Oklahoma Univ., Norman. Dept. of Meteorology.
G. M. Heymsfield.
Journal of Applied Meteorology, Vol 14, No 2, p 257-259, March 1975. 4 fig, 2 ref. NSF Grant GA-41844.

Descriptors: *Radar, *Remote sensing, *Storms, Instrumentation, Meteorology, Cloud physics, *Oklahoma, Data collections, Equations.
Identifiers: Nomograms, *Dual doppler radar.

A simple nomogram technique to facilitate dual Doppler radar data collection was presented. Equations and nomograms were developed for relating the position of a given target relative to two radars. The results were general, but application was made to the National Severe Storms Laboratory radars at Norman and the Cimarron site 40 km northwest of Norman. (Sims-ISWS)
W75-06510

RELATING RAINFALL RATE TO THE SLOPE OF RAINDROP SIZE SPECTRA,
National Hurricane Research Lab., Coral Gables, Fla.
F. J. Merceret.
Journal of Applied Meteorology, Vol 14, No 2, p 259-260, March 1975. 2 tab, 6 ref.

Descriptors: *Raindrops, *Regression analysis, Least squares method, Tropical regions, Precipitation(Atmospheric), Florida, Rainfall, On-site data collections, Clouds, Storms, Hurricanes, Distribution patterns.
Identifiers: *Raindrop spectra, *Marshall-Palmer distribution.

Tropical raindrop spectra were collected for several years by using airborne foil impactors in tropical cloud-lines, storms, and hurricanes. These data confirm the applicability of the exponential Marshall-Palmer distribution above ground in the tropics. They also confirm the validity of the form of the Marshall-Palmer equation for lambda, the slope term of the distribution, but only if lambda is computed from an intercept-constrained, least-squares fit to the drop-size distribution data. For spectra constraining N sub 0 to the classical value, the relation between lambda and R is close to the classical one. (Sims-ISWS)
W75-06511

WAVE-INDUCED INSTABILITIES IN AN ATMOSPHERE NEAR SATURATION,
Cooperative Inst. for Research in Environmental Sciences, Boulder, Colo.
F. Einaudi, and D. P. Lalas.
Journal of the Atmospheric Sciences, Vol 32, No 3, p 536-547, March 1975. 6 fig, 29 ref. NSF Grants GA-32604 and GA-40243.

Descriptors: *Computer models, *Mathematical models, *Cloud physics, *Gravity waves, Model studies, Atmosphere, Moisture content, Stability, Numerical analysis, Raindrops, Precipitation(Atmospheric), Latent heat, Saturation, Atmospheric physics.

The stability and the propagation characteristics of internal gravity waves that propagate in an atmosphere near saturation and, over some height range, create the appropriate thermodynamic conditions for condensation to occur for a fraction of the wave cycle are investigated. It was shown that if the atmosphere, over some height range, is close enough to saturation, a linear stability analysis is possible and results in a modified Richardson criterion, based on a new Brunt-Vaisala frequency, n sub ave, smaller than the corresponding n sub u with condensation effects neglected. Since (n sub ave) squared can become negative, even though the atmosphere is originally statically stable, the ability of gravity waves to trigger convective processes in a moist atmosphere was demonstrated. A numerical example was presented to illustrate the alterations of the characteristics of propagation. (Sims-ISWS)
W75-06512

ON PARAMETERIZATION OF TURBULENT TRANSPORT IN CUMULUS CLOUDS,
National Oceanic and Atmospheric Administration, Coral Gables, Fla. Experimental Meteorology Lab.
W. R. Cotton.
Journal of the Atmospheric Sciences, Vol 32, No 3, p 548-564, March 1975. 13 fig, 1 tab, 33 ref, 1 append.

Descriptors: *Computer models, *Mathematical models, *Air circulation, *Cloud physics, Model studies, Convection, Condensation, Clouds, Thunderstorms, Precipitation(Atmospheric), Entrainment, *Turbulence, Atmosphere, Moisture content, Eddies, Viscosity.
Identifiers: Liquid water content, Cumulus clouds, Turbulent transport.

A one-dimensional time-dependent cumulus model was developed and discussed. Data predicted by the model along with a bulk entrainment model were compared with a case study observation and Warner's mean profile of Q/Q sub A. While a great deal of the discrepancy between observed and predicted data could be attributed to the transient nature of convection, the consistent pattern of overprediction of such cloud properties as Q/Q/ sub A and vertical velocity was indeed disturbing. It was concluded that neither the entrainment model nor the scalar nonlinear eddy viscosity model can adequately treat the general problem of turbulent transport in convective clouds. There was, however, sufficient evidence suggesting that the models can be of practical value if their use is limited to dynamically active clouds and, in the case of the entrainment model, to a restricted portion of the cloud cycle life. Furthermore, there was little doubt that the entrainment coefficient is not a universal constant while the universality of the mixing length coefficients in the eddy viscosity models is still in question. (Sims-ISWS)
W75-06513

A SIMPLE STATISTICAL TREATMENT OF HIGHLY TURBULENT COUETTE FLOW,
National Center for Atmospheric Research, Boulder, Colo.
P. D. Thompson.
Journal of the Atmospheric Sciences, Vol 32, No 3, p 569-576, March 1975. 5 fig, 2 ref.

Descriptors: *Statistical methods, *Boundary layers, *Atmospheric physics, *Momentum transfer, *Turbulent flow, Reynolds number, Laboratory tests, Mathematical models, Velocity, Kinetics, Drag.
Identifiers: Couette flow.

From the integral conditions for momentum and kinetic energy balance in the state of fully developed turbulence, it was found possible to estimate the bulk statistical properties of highly turbulent Couette flow as functions of the Reynolds number. The average boundary shear, boundary layer thickness, and average momentum transport through the 'constant flux' layer were determined to within the value of a single nondimensional constant. The conclusions of this analysis were in quantitative agreement with laboratory measurements and were consistent with empirical formulas for the Reynolds stress over smooth surfaces. The significance of the results was discussed with specific reference to the problem of 'parameterizing' the statistical effects of turbulent momentum transport in terms of the large-scale average motion of the atmosphere. (Sims-ISWS)
W75-06514

RECOMBINATION LIMITS ON CHARGE SEPARATION BY HYDROMETEORS IN CLOUDS,
New Mexico Inst. of Mining and Technology, Socorro.
C. B. Moore.
Journal of the Atmospheric Sciences, Vol 32, No 3, p 608-612, March 1975. 2 fig, 7 ref. NSF Grant GI-33372 X.

Descriptors: *Thunderstorms, *Electricity, *Clouds, Meteorology, Hail, Raindrops, Precipitation(Atmospheric), New Mexico, Atmosphere, Electrical properties, Cloud physics.
Identifiers: Charge separation, Cloud droplets, *Hydrometeors, Charge transport, Space charge.

Several of the modern hypotheses that explain thundercloud electrification by charge transfers between particles in clouds do so by ignoring any recombination effects in subsequent interactions of the products of earlier charge separations. As this approach is unrealistic, solutions of the continuity relations for the concentrations of the neutral and of the charged cloud droplets were provided. These show that the concentrations of developed charged droplets are probably appreciably less than estimated in the hypotheses involving precipitation. Similarly, as shown by Colgate, recombination also limits the charge carried downward by falling hydrometeors. Accordingly, the sustained charge-separating ability of sedimenting precipitation is open to question. (Sims-ISWS)
W75-06515

REPRESENTATIVENESS OF WATERSHED PRECIPITATION SAMPLES,
West Virginia Univ., Morgantown. Water Research Inst.
M. Chang, and R. Lee.
Available from the National Technical Information Service, Springfield, Va 22161 as PB-241 058, $4.25 in paper copy, $2.25 in microfiche. Water Research Institute Bulletin 4, 1975. 46 p, 12 fig, 12 tab, 39 ref. (WRI-WVU-75-01). OWRT A-020-WVA(5).

Descriptors: *Local precipitation, *Topography, *Terrain analysis, *Gaging stations, *Spatial distribution, *Watersheds(Basins), *Statistical models, Sampling, Winds, Sites, Hydrologic data, Climatology, *West Virginia, Appalachian mountain region.
Identifiers: Representativeness, Precipitation samples, Topographic influence.

The representativeness of precipitation samples was investigated by examining the influences of topography and exposure in watersheds east and west of the Appalachian divide in West Virginia. The confusion between accuracy and representativeness was removed by evaluating gage errors as a function of directional wind speed during precipitation periods. Annual gage errors, in the network of 88 unshielded 8-inch gages, reduced the catch by about 5% of the observed mean. Elevation, and a geographic variable, accounted (statistically) for 60% of the spatial variability of precipitation. Small-scale terrain and slope parameters increased the predictability to about 75%. The inclusion of site and gage parameters in the covariance model raised the level of predietability to 90% both east and west of the divide, with standard errors 1.99 inches (east) and 2.07 inches (west). Representative values for each of the statistical parameters were estimated by independent analyses. The estimated true mean watershed precipitation was about 7.6 inches (21%) greater than the observed station mean (east), and about 5.3 inches (12%) greater (west).
W75-06522

CALCULATION OF SUPERSATURATION PROFILES IN THERMAL DIFFUSION CLOUD CHAMBERS,
Clarkson Coll. of Technology, Potsdam, N.Y. Dept. of Chemical Engineering; and Clarkson Coll. of Technology, Potsdam, N.Y. Inst. of Colloid and Surface Science.
J. L. Katz, and P. Mirable.
Journal of the Atmospheric Sciences, Vol 32, No 3, p 646-652, March 1975. 1 fig, 12 ref, 1 append. NSF Grant GK-34914.

Descriptors: *Supersaturation, *Profiles, Meteorology, Nucleation, *Temperature, Pressure, Vapor pressure, Laboratory equipment, Laboratory tests, Equipment, Diffusion.
Identifiers: *Thermal diffusion cloud chambers, *Cloud chambers.

The maximum supersaturation in a diffusion cloud chamber as a function of the temperature difference between the two plates was calculated under various conditions. It was shown that the assumption of linear profiles for the temperature and vapor pressure is a very good one, and that the effeet of thermal diffusion is negligible for a water-air mixture. An appendix contains a listing of a Fortran program used in the calculations. (Sims-ISWS)
W75-06530

MESOSCALE OBJECTIVE ANALYSIS OF THE WIND AND MOISTURE FIELD AROUND THE THUNDERSTORMS DEVELOPED OVER NSSL OBSERVATION NETWORK ON MAY 28, 1967,
Meteorological Research Inst., Tokyo (Japan).
K. Ninomiya.
Papers in Meteorology and Geophysics, Vol 25, No 2, p 81-97, June 1974. 12 fig, 3 tab, 14 ref.

Descriptors: *Thunderstorms, *Winds, *Moisture, Atmosphere, *Oklahoma, Analysis, Storms, On-site data collections, Discharge(Water), Temperature, Humidity, Water vapor, Meteorology, *Networks.
Identifiers: *Mesosystem, Mesoscale, Convergence, Diffluence, NSSL network.

A mesoscale objective analysis of the wind and moisture field around the thunderstorms which developed over the NSSL observation network on May 28, 1967, was made. The scheme of the objcetive analysis included the 'time to space conversion' of the observation relative to the mesosystems. The weighting function for the interpolation depends on both the distance between grid point and observation and the time difference between observation and analysis time. The distributions of wind and moisture obtained by the present analysis coincide fairly well with that obtained by subjective analysis. The morphological description of the change in the environmental situation of the thunderstorms was also attempted on the basis of the obtained wind and moisture field. The convergence line, which is formed along the northern boundary of the predominant low-level southerly winds, is simultaneously intensified with the thunderstorms' development. While the middle tropospheric wind field is not modified by the thunderstorms' development, a remarkable change of winds is found at the 250-mb level, where the upper outflow from the storms modifies the flow into a strong diffluence flow pattern. The analysis of the moisture field indicated that the storms' development is associated with the increase of moisture convergence in the lower layer. (Jones-ISWS)
W75-06535

SEA SALT PARTICLES TRANSPORTED TO THE LAND,
Hokkaido Univ., Sapporo (Japan). Dept. of Chemistry.
For primary bibliographic entry see Field 5B.
W75-06541

COULEE ALIGNMENT AND THE WIND IN SOUTHERN ALBERTA, CANADA,
Lethbridge Univ. (Alberta). Dept. of Geography.
For primary bibliographic entry see Field 2J.
W75-06543

RAIN--A WATER RESOURCE.
Department of the Interior, Washington, D.C.
For primary bibliographic entry see Field 3B.
W75-06586

AGRICULTURAL RESEARCH SERVICE PRECIPITATION FACILITIES AND RELATED STUDIES,
Agricultural Research Service, Washington, D.C.
D. M. Hershfield.
Soil and Water Conservation Research Division, Report ARS41-176, June 1971. 117 p, 37 tab, 48 fig, 73 ref.

Descriptors: *Rainfall, *Precipitation(Atmospheric), *Rainfall disposition, *Depth-area curves, *Rainfall intensity, Meteorology, Hydrologic cycle, On-site data collections, Rain.
Identifiers: *Rainfall distribution patterns.

The collection of current precipitation studies are primarily aimed at providing information about precipitation pertinent to research on the hydrology of specific agricultural watersheds. Although temporal and spatial variations of precipitation are obtained primarily from rural areas, the findings from the networks can also be taken as indicative of precipitation in urban settings, except for large metropolitan areas where local conditions may cause unique patterns. Researchers in the field of watershed hydrology realize that further development of this discipline will require the improvement of both observation and prediction methods. These studies were collected from 16 places in the United States. Specific objectives in these areas to study watershed hydrology include: (1) developing methods of evaluating rainfall; (2) determining frequency of storms and expectancies of amount and areal extent; (3) determining pertinent characteristics of rainfall with respect to runoff and sediment movement; (4) gaining a better understanding of the role of these areas and the influences of vegetation, climate and land management on the movement of water and sediment; (5) making hydrolic studies of surface and subsurface flows; and, (6) establishing rain gage networks to measure temporal and areal variations in precipitation, obtain basic data for rainfall variability over small areas, and to study depth-area relationships. (Poertner)
W75-06657

POTAMOLOGICAL STUDIES ON THE RIVER INA OF THE RIVER SYSTEM OF YODO: 1 (IN JAPANESE),
Osaka Kyoiku Univ. (Japan). Oceanography Lab.
For primary bibliographic entry see Field 5B.
W75-06701

DRAINAGE DENSITY AND EFFECTIVE PRECIPITATION,
Sri Lanka Univ., Peradeniya. Dept. of Geography.
For primary bibliographic entry see Field 4A.
W75-06704

ALMOST-PERIODIC, STOCHASTIC PROCESS OF LONG-RANGE CLIMATIC CHANGES,
Colorado State Univ., Fort Collins.
W. Q. Chin, and V. Yevjevich.
Scientific Series No. 39, 69 p, 1974, Environment Canada, Inland Waters Directorate, Ottawa, Canada. 61 fig, 83 ref.

Descriptors: *Climates, *Stochastic processes, *Mathematical studies, Research and development, Analytical techniques, Mathematics, Model studies, Mathematical models, Statistical models, Methodology, Analysis.
Identifiers: *Climatic change, Research.

A mathematical procedure for quantitative evaluation of long-term climatic changes as an almost-periodic stochastic process is described. The procedure relies on two basic hypotheses: (1) that long-term climatic changes are reflected in the fluctuations of the Oxygen-18 content measured in carbonate shells from deep-sea sediment cores and in the ice core from the Greenland ice sheet, and (2) that long-term almost-periodic variation in the distribution of incoming solar radiation at the top of the earth's atmosphere, as derived from the Milankovich theory of orbital and axial motions of the earth, is the basic deterministic process affecting long-term climatic changes. The background information necessary for a general appreciation of the nature of the oxygen-isotope data and the probable cause and effect of the Milankovich mechanism are outlined. The results show that the problems of long-term climatic changes are amenable to analyses and syntheses by a deterministic-stochastic approach, with the deterministic component being almost-periodic. Deterministic-stochastic models of several Oxygen-18 time series are presented. Parameters of the models have been estimated from which the generation of new samples of the process can be made. (Environment Canada)
W75-06739

2C. Snow, Ice, and Frost

AIRBORNE GAMMA RADIATION SURVEYS FOR SNOW WATER-EQUIVALENT RESEARCH-PROGRESS REPORT 1973,
EG and G, Inc., Las Vegas, Nev. Las Vegas Div.
For primary bibliographic entry see Field 5A.
W75-06411

WATER EQUIVALENT OF SNOW DATA FROM AIRBORNE GAMMA RADIATION SURVEYS - INTERNATIONAL FIELD YEAR FOR THE GREAT LAKES,
EG and G, Inc., Las Vegas, Nev. Las Vegas Div.
For primary bibliographic entry see Field 5A.
W75-06412

PORE WATER EXPULSION DURING FREEZING,
Hardy (R.M.) and Associates, Calgary (Alberta).
For primary bibliographic entry see Field 2G.
W75-06435

CARBON DIOXIDE PARTIAL PRESSURES IN ARCTIC SURFACE WATERS,
Alaska Univ., College. Forest Soils Lab.
For primary bibliographic entry see Field 2H.
W75-06442

SUMMER ICE CRYSTAL PRECIPITATION AT THE SOUTH POLE,
State Univ. of New York, Albany. Atmospheric Sciences Research Center.
A. W. Hogan.
Journal of Applied Meteorology, Vol 14, No 2, p 246-249, March 1975. 4 fig, 4 ref.

Descriptors: *Crystals, *Ice, *Precipitation(Atmospheric), *Antarctic, Radiosondes, Moisture, Clouds, Supersaturation, Meteorology.
Identifiers: *South Pole, Cirrus clouds.

Ice crystal precipitation was observed and the crystals replicated, at the South Pole during January and February 1974. The crystals were of columnar form. These columns were hollow or prismatic, and sometimes were in the form of combinations of bullets. These combinations were very fragile, disintegrating into individual bullets upon impaction. Smaller 'diamond dust' crystals were observed on two occasions. NOAA-NWS radiosonde data showed that the air was supersaturated with respect to ice at 650 to 600 mb (i.e., just above the surface) throughout the period. Ice crystal precipitation was only observed at the surface when cirrus bands were present at higher altitudes. It is likely that ice crystals, descending from the cirrus only a short distance above, grew to the larger columnar crystals while falling through the moist layer. As these layers were able to remain saturated, without precipitating or forming ice fogs or clouds at temperatures of -35C, heterogeneous freezing nuclei were probably absent at these levels throughout the period. (Jones-ISWS)
W75-06509

OBSERVATIONS OF POTENTIAL ICE NUCLEI,
Meteorological Research Inst., Tokyo (Japan).
For primary bibliographic entry see Field 3B.
W75-06536

PHOTOGRAMMETRIC DETERMINATION OF RELATIVE SNOW AREA,
Colorado State Univ., Fort Collins.
A. H. Barnes.
U.S. Forest Service, Rocky Mountain Forest and Range Experiment Station, June 1970. 14 p, 3 fig, 3 ta .

Descriptors: *Snow surveys, *Snow cover, *Snow management, *Photogrammetry, *Computer models, Computer simulation, Computer programs.

A photogrammetric and computer procedure for the evaluation of relative snow cover in a limited area of a drainage basin was developed. The primary goal was to provide a more precise and accurate evaluation than previously used. An additional benefit was to reduce the time required for each determination. The observational and computational procedures were based on several simplifying assumptions. Future applications of the basic procedure could include the effect of these assumptions. The photogrammetric principle, computational and measurement procedures are detailed in the report. A computer program was developed to accept the data as presented on the punch cards, identify the type of area (total area, gross snow area, or bare area within the gross snow area) compute the area, compute the percent snow, and output the significant values. The results of this limited evaluation indicate that the procedure can be used for the determination of percentage snow cover. The accuracy and precision of the procedure could be improved by consideration of several additional factors. These factors affect either the operator or the computations. No attempt was made to evaluate this procedure with other methods in use. These comparisons were considered outside the scope of this study. (Poertner)
W75-06670

DISTRIBUTION OF ISOTOPES IN SOME NATURAL WATERS IN THE REGION NORTH OF MT. JOLMO LUNGMA.
For primary bibliographic entry see Field 2K.
W75-06699

DETERMINATION OF THE MASS BALANCE ON SENTINEL GLACIER, BRITISH COLUMBIA, CANADA,
Department of the Environment, Ottawa (Ontario). Water Resources Branch.
O. Mokievsky-Zuboc.
Scientific Series No. 30, 35 p, 1973, Inland Waters Directorate. 9 fig, 11 ref, 6 tab.

Descriptors: *Photogrammetry, *Ablation, *Volumetric analysis, Glaciology, Water balance, Analytical techniques, Melting, Meltwater, Estimating, Methodology, Measurement, *Canada.
Identifiers: *Sentinel Glacier, *Mass balance, British Columbia, Retreat.

Mass balance for Sentinel Glacier was determined for the period 1966-1971. Two surface measurement methods were used for the entire glacier; terrestrial photogrammetry was used for the tongue area. Surface balance methods were compared to establish the degree of internal consistency and the magnitude of possible error. The terrestrial photogrammetry method gave the surface lowering of the exposed ice; changes in its elevation compared with surface ablation measurements gave the vertical component of ice flow for the lower part of the glacier. Sentinel Glacier showed four years with a positive mass balance and two years with a negative mass balance. The total loss, however, exceeded gain by 28 cm of water for the entire surface of the glacier. (Environment Canada)
W75-06732

ICE PILING ON LAKESHORES - WITH SPECIAL REFERENCE TO THE OCCURRENCES ON LAKE SIMCOE IN THE SPRING OF 1973,
Canada Centre for Inland Waters, Burlington (Ontario).
G. Tsang.
Scientific Series No. 35, 12 p, 1974, Inland Waters Directorate. 15 fig, 4 ref.

Descriptors: *Lake ice, *Iced lakes, Analysis, Analytical techniques, Mathematics, Equations, Mathematical studies, Lakes, Meteorology, Damages, *Canada.
Identifiers: *Ice piling, *Ice floes, *Lake Simcoe.

The piling of ice on lakeshores was studied. Ice piling is not a static but a dynamic event. Ice piling occurs when ice floes, which gather speed and momentum under the action of wind over an open-water fetch, ram onto the shore or onto shore-fastened ice. The kinetic energy of the ice floes is converted into the potential energy of the ice piles. A strong wind is not necessary for ice piling. Ice piles will occur under a wind of less than 6.75 m/s if other conditions are favorable. Meteorologically, a shift in wind direction from offshore to onshore is a necessary condition for ice piling. The fluctuation of wind strength and direction and the shifting of wind help to loosen the ice floes and promote ice piling. Ice piling occurs in above freezing temperatures only. Equations are derived that give the width of an openwater fetch required for ice piling, the speed of the ice floes for ice piling, the height of an ice pile, and the affecting factors. It is proposed that damage to shoreline properties may be avoided by accelerating the piling of ice at a distance offshore. Field data from the ice pilings on Lake Simcoe in the spring of 1973 are used in the study. (Environment Canada)
W75-06733

ANALYSIS OF MASS BALANCE VALUES AND THEIR ACCURACY FOR SENTINEL GLACIER, BRITISH COLUMBIA, CANADA,
Department of the Environment, Ottawa (Ontario). Water Resources Branch.
O. Mokievsky-Zubok.
Scientific Series No. 31, 4 p, 1974, Inland Waters Directorate. 12 ref, 2 fig, 1 tab.

Descriptors: *Measurement, Methodology, Volumetric analysis, Ice, Firn, Ablation, Analytical techniques, Glaciology, *Canada.
Identifiers: *Sentinel Glacier(BC), *Mass balance, British Columbia.

The accuracy of mass balance measurements for Sentinel Glacier was determined by comparison of (1) a method, based on determination of difference between measured winter and summer balances with (2) an alternate method, the difference between the volume of remaining snow cover and ice and firn ablation. The difference ranged from 0.2% to 8.8% as related to the thickness of the snow cover. The greatest difference was obtained for deeper snowpacks. Both methods provide acceptable results but, Method 1 is considered less accurate. (Environment Canada)
W75-06740

STUDY OF SENTINEL GLACIER, BRITISH COLUMBIA, CANADA WITHIN THE INTERNATIONAL HYDROLOGICAL DECADE PROGRAM - PROCEDURES AND TECHNIQUES,
Department of the Environment, Ottawa (Ontario). Water Resources Branch.
O. Mokievsky-Zuboc.
Technical Bulletin No. 77, 31 p, 1973, Inland Waters Directorate. 21 fig, 15 ref, 1 tab, 2 append.

Descriptors: *Glaciers, *Glaciology, *Investigations, *Surveys, International Hydrological Decade, Field work techniques, History, Equipment, Data collections, Ice, Measurement, Analytical techniques, *Canada.
Identifiers: *Sentinel Glacier, Data collection techniques, On-site investigations, British Columbia.

Sentinel Glacier, considered to be representative of many glaciers in the Mount Garibaldi area of British Columbia, is one of the glaciers studied as part of the Canadian contribution to the International Hydrological Decade (IHD) program. Situated in a maritime climate and subject to high winter precipitation, it presents many problems in obtaining the mass balance. Field work techniques and problems are discussed. (Environment Canada)
W75-06741

NEW BRUNSWICK FLOOD, APRIL-MAY 1973,
Environmental Protection Service, Halifax (Nova Scotia). Atlantic Region.
For primary bibliographic entry see Field 4A.
W75-06749

2D. Evaporation and Transpiration

COMPARED EVAPOTRANSPIRATION OF VARIOUS CROPS AND STUDY OF WATER-CONSUMPTION RATES,
Institut National de la Recherche Agronomique, Toulouse (France). Station d'Agronomie.
J. Puech, and M. Hernandez.
Ann Agron (Paris). Vol 24, No 4, p 437-455, 1973, Illus, (In French).

Identifiers: Crops, *Evapotranspiration, Fescue, Maize, Rates, Sorghum, Soya, Sunflower, Transpiration, *Consumptive use.

Maximum and actual evapotranspiration (ETM and ETR, respectively) of various crops (maize, sorghum, sunflower, soya, fescue) were compared and measured using evapotranspirometers and the neutron method. The water-consumption conditions of these crops in terms of climatic factors (measured potential evapotranspiration of reed fescue) was investigated, including the development of the ETM/ETR ratio in terms of the varieties of plants, soils, pedoclimatic factors, and the increasing contribution of the water reserves in the plants. The law of linear variation of the yield in terms of the ETR/ETM ratio was consistent. In some late-maturing plants, e.g., maize, sunflower, soya, the ETP measured with reed fescue was, over a given period, definitely increased.--Copyright 1974, Biological Abstracts, Inc.
W75-06728

A SENSITIVE RECORDING LYSIMETER,
Agricultural Research Inst., Cedara (South Africa).
R. Mottram, and J. M. De Jager.
Agrochemophysica. Vol 5, No 1, p 9-13, 1973, Illus.
Identifiers: Evapotranspiration, *Lysimeters, Transpiration, Instrumentation.

An economical and sensitive lysimeter for evaluating hourly water usage of crops was designed, constructed and tested. A cylindrical steel lysimeter of surface area 2.5457 sq m and soil depth of 0.4 rests on a mechanical balance system, having a resolution of 1 in 10,000. A precision strain gauge load beam of 0.1% accuracy and 20 kg capacity is incorporated in the balance lever system, and its output is recorded on a galvanometric strip chart recorder. The complete system provides measurement of evapotranspiration to within 0.1 mm of water.--Copyright 1974, Biological Abstracts, Inc.
W75-06729

2E. Streamflow and Runoff

DEVELOPMENT OF A STORM RUN-OFF PREDICTION MODEL WITH SIMULATED TEMPORAL RAINFALL DISTRIBUTION,
Meteorological Officé, New Delhi (India).
D. V. L. N. Rao, D. C. Mantan, and S. C. Hasija.
Nordic Hydrology, Vol 5, No 4, p 193-212, 1974. 10 fig, 5 tab, 5 ref.

Descriptors: *Excessive precipitation, *Rainfall-runoff relationship, *Hyetographs, *Hydrographs, Antécedent precipitation, Runoff, Precipitation(Atmospheric), Foreign countries, Asia, Foreign research, Unit hydrographs, Storm runoff, Surface runoff, Streamflow, Model studies, *Storm runoff, Precipitation excess.
Identifiers: *India(Yamuna Basin), Storm index, Antecedent precipitation index, Phi-index, Initial loss.

The Yamuna catchment up to Kalanur was studied. The representative character of limited pluviograph data was determined with the use of the storm index concept. After establishing a relationship between the limited pluviograph data and areal rainfall data, the possible effects of areal rainfall variation of the use of limited data were studied. A simulated temporal rainfall pattern for the area was then worked out and applied in the unit graph analysis, which led to the development of interesting relationships between rainfall intensity, antecedent precipitation index (API), and Phi-index, and the API-initial loss relationships. These two put together gave rise to a reasonable peak trend prediction diagram for the Yamuna catchment up to Kalanur. (Lee-ISWS)
W75-06453

ADAPTATION AND APPLICATION OF THE KARAZEV METHOD TO THE RATIONALIZATION OF QUEBEC'S HYDROMETRIC BASIC NETWORK,
National Inst. of Scientific Research, Quebec.
M. Leclerc, B. Bobee, and J. P. Villeneuve.
Nordic Hydrology, Vol 5, No 4, p 213-228, 1974. 3 fig, 3 tab, 3 ref.

Descriptors: *Hydrologic data, *Regional analysis, *Average runoff, *Networks, *Hydrometry, Stream-flow, *Canada, Surface waters, Regime, Runoff, Network design, Stations, Synoptic analysis, Gaging, Spatial distribution, Watersheds(Basins), Stream gages.
Identifiers: Quebec, *Karazev method, Rationalized method.

Certain principles inherent to the rational development of hydrometric networks were applied to the Quebec network. An application of a method specific to the development of a basic network was described. The method used to establish the number of stations required was based on the actual knowledge of the spatial distribution and time variability of the mean annual runoff. A modified version of Karazev's (1968) method, applied originally to a study of the hydrographic basins in the USSR, was found to be particularly suitable to regions of little hydrologic information and particularly to Quebec. (Lee-ISWS)
W75-06454

A COMPARISON OF HYDROLOGIC AND HYDRAULIC CATCHMENT ROUTING PROCEDURES,
University Coll., Galway (Ireland).
J. W. Porter.
Journal of Hydrology, Vol 24, No 3/4, p 333-349, February 1975. 8 fig, 1 tab, 12 ref.

Descriptors: *Simulation analysis, *Mathematical models, *Routing, *Rainfall-runoff relationships, Hydrology, Hydrologic systems, Hyetographs, Travel time, Time lag, Time of concentration, Watersheds(Basins), Hydraulics, *Australia.
Identifiers: *Catchment response, New South Wales, *Kinematic waves.

A comparative study of two nonlinear catchment routing techniques was presented. One technique was founded on hydrologic concepts of distributed storage, the other on hydraulic concepts of kinematic wave theory. Previously published data for storms recorded on the catchment of South Creek in New South Wales, Australia, were used. The hydrologic technique used was a modification of Laurensen's technique. The hydraulic technique was as formulated by Wooding. (Terstriep-ISWS)
W75-06456

RELATIONS BETWEEN PLANIMETRIC AND HYPSOMETRIC VARIABLES IN THIRD- AND FOURTH-ORDER DRAINAGE BASINS,
New Univ. of Ulster, Coleraine (Northern Ireland). School of Biological and Environmental Studies.
For primary bibliographic entry see Field 2A.
W75-06459

FLOODWAY DETERMINATION USING COMPUTER PROGRAM HEC-2,
Hydrologic Engineering Center, Davis, Calif.
For primary bibliographic entry see Field 7C.
W75-06481

APPLICATION OF THE HEC-2 BRIDGE ROUTINES,
Hydrologic Engineering Center, Davis, Calif.
For primary bibliographic entry see Field 7C.
W75-06482

SHALLOW LAMINAR FLOWS OVER ROUGH GRANULAR SURFACES,
University of the West Indies, St. Augustine (Trinidad). Dept. of Civil Engineering.
For primary bibliographic entry see Field 8B.
W75-06532

EFFECTS OF URBANIZATION ON CATCHMENT RESPONSE,
Puerto Rico Univ., Mayaquez. Dept. of Civil Engineering.
R. L. Bras, and F. E. Perkins.
Journal of the Hydraulics Division, American Society of Civil Engineers, Vol 101, No HY3, Proceedings Paper 11196, p 451-466, March 1975. 12 fig, 6 tab, 14 ref, 2 append.

Descriptors: *Hydraulics, Hydrology, *Simulation analysis, *Rainfall-runoff relationships, Mathematical models, Hyetographs, Urban drainage, Urban hydrology, Urban runoff, *Urbanization, *Puerto Rico, Urban renewal.
Identifiers: *Kinematic waves.

A mathematical model was utilized as an experimental tool to perform a series of controlled experiments on small hypothetical catchments characteristic of areas in Puerto Rico. The purpose of the experiments was to quantify the likely effects of typical urban developments on the hydrologic response characteristics of the hypothetical catchments, and to relate these effects to the separate physical changes introduced by urbanization. An important modeling issue also was investigated. Initially a very detailed model of the catchments was employed thus providing a fine spatial resolution but at relatively high cost. A simple scheme was developed in which the detailed model may be replaced by a much coarser and less expensive mathematical model with no significant loss of accuracy. (Terstriep-ISWS)
W75-06534

FLOW SEPARATION IN MEANDER BENDS,
Leeds Univ. (England). Dept. of Earth Sciences.
M. R. Leeder, and P. H. Bridges.
Nature, Vol 253, No 5490, p 338-339, January 31, 1975. 3 fig, 11 ref.

Descriptors: *Flow separation, *Meanders, *Froude number, *Deposition(Sediments), *River beds, River flow, Eddies, Sediment transport, Vortices, Erosion, Velocity, Tidal streams, On-site investigations.
Identifiers: Point bars, Bedforms, Scotland.

The occurrence of flow separation in natural meanders was investigated in channels from the intertidal zone of Solway Firth, Scotland. Flow separation in meander bends was experssed as a function of bend tightness and Froude number. The effects of flow separation were found to be: (1) decreased effective channel width and increased velocity and erosion rate along the outer bank, and (2) rapid deposition of suspended sediment in the inner part of the separation zone. An empirical criterion for predicting the onset of separation in meander bends was proposed. (Adams-ISWS)
W75-06539

CONFIDENCE LIMITS FOR DESIGN EVENTS,
Department of the Environment, Ottawa (Ontario). Water Resources Branch.
G. W. Kite.
Water Resources Research, Vol 11, No 1, p 48-53, February 1975. 1 fig, 5 tab, 13 ref.

Descriptors: *Design flow, *Frequency analysis, *Probability, *Statistical methods, Hydrology, *Design criteria, Distribution, Distribution patterns, Variability, Frequency, Statistical models, Statistics, Data processing, Analytical techniques.
Identifiers: Sample mean, Population mean, Standard deviation, Coefficient of skew, Random variables, Confidence limit, Variance, Log normal.

Frequency analysis is commonly used in hydrology to define flood plains, design hydraulic strue-tures, and aid in watershed planning and management. Although design event magnitudes may be determined analytically by using probability distributions, the analytical determination of cofidence limits for the design event is not easy. Using the alternate method of moments to determine confidence limits involves an assumption of normality of the distribution of design events. It was shown by data generation that this assumption is valid for quite small samples. Tables were given to compute confidence limits in this manner for several common probability distributions. (Dawes-ISWS)
W75-06544

BIRTH-DEATH MODELS FOR DIFFERENTIAL PERSISTENCE,
Harvard Unov., Boston, Mass. Graduate School of Business Administration.
B. B. Jackson.
Water Resources Research, Vol 11, No 1, p 75-95, February 1975. 20 fig, 1 tab, 11 ref, 1 append.

Descriptors: *Correlation analysis, *Planning, *Model studies, *Streamflow, *Statistical methods, Regression analysis, Statistical models, Persistence, Hydrologic systems, Hydrology, Maine, New Hampshire, Vermont, Massachusetts, Statistics, *New England.
Identifiers: Serial correlation, Correlation coefficient, Mean, Variance, Standard deviation.

Birth-death models can generate synthetic flow sequences that demonstrate differential persistence, i.e., sequences in which low flows show more persistence than high flows. A simple phenomenological model helped justify the assumption of differential persistence. The use of a birth-death model, together with a set of modeling precepts, showed that differential persistence is a phenomenon of considerable descriptive importance but, at least in some planning situations, does not carry corresponding prescriptive importance. (Dawes-ISWS)
W75-06546

MODERNIZATION OF NATIONAL WEATHER SERVICE RIVER FORECASTING TECHNIQUES,
National Weather Service, Silver Spring, Md.
For primary bibliographic entry see Field 4A.
W75-06562

FORECASTING SNOWMELT RUNOFF IN THE UPPER MIDWEST,
Minnesota Univ., Minneapolis. Dept. of Civil and Mineral Engineering.
For primary bibliographic entry see Field 2A.
W75-06648

CHENANGO RIVER, FLOOD PLAIN INFORMATION.
Army Engineer District, Baltimore, Md.
Broome County Legislature, Binghampton, New York, October, 1971. 27 p, 7 tab, 11 fig.

Descriptors: *Flood plains, *Flood frequency, *Historic floods, *River flow, *Flood forecasting, *Flood data, Flood profiles, Flood routing, Flood stages, Floods, Flood discharge, New York, Flood peak, Flood control.
Identifiers: Chenango River, Broome County(New York), Intermediate regional flood, Standard project flood.

The flood situation was analyzed along the Chenango River in the Towns of Chenango and Fenton, Broome County, New York. The information is based on rainfall, runoff, historical and current flood heights, and other technical data bearing upon the occurence and size of floods in the study area. Two significant phases of the flood problem are covered. First the largest known floods are discussed; second, probable future floods are considered. The report contains maps, profiles, and cross sections which indicate the extent of flooding that has been experienced and that which might occur in the future. This should prove helpful in planning the best use of the flood plains. From the maps, profiles, and cross sections the depth of probable flooding either by recurrence of the largest known floods or by occurrence of the Intermediate Regional or Standard Project Flood at any location may be learned. Plans for the solution of future floods are not included. It is intended to provide the basis for further study and planning on the part of local officials, and Broome County, in arriving at solutions to minimize vulnerability to flood damages. (Poertner)
W75-06677

SUSQUEHANA RIVER, FLOOD PLAIN INFORMATION.
Army Engineer District, Baltimore, Md.
Broome County Legislature, Binghampton, New York, June, 1970. 31 p, 20 fig, 8 tab.

Descriptors: *River flow, *Flood plains, *Flood frequency, *Historic floods, *Flood forecasting, *Flood data, Flood profiles, Flood routing, Flood stages, Floods, Flood discharge, New York, Flood control, Flood peak.
Identifiers: Susquehana River, Broome County(New York), Standard project flood, Intermediate regional flood.

The flood situation was analyzed along the 20-mile section of the Susquehana River in the Towns of Windsor and Colesville in eastern Broome County, New York. The information is based upon rainfall, runoff, historical and recent flood heights, and other technical data bearing upon the occurence and size of floods within the study area. Two significant phases of the flood situation are covered. First, the largest known floods of the past are discussed. Second, the probable future floods are considered. Included are maps, profiles, and selected cross sections which indicate the extent of flooding which might occur in the future within the study area. These materials should prove helpful in planning the best use of the flood plain. From the maps, profiles and cross sections, the depth of probably flooding, either by recurrence of the largest known flood or by occurrence of the Intermediate Regional or Standard Project Floods, at any location may be determined. Plans for the solution of future floods are not included. It is intended to provide the basis for further study and planning on the part of the Broome County Legislature in arriving at solutions to minimize vulnerability to flood damages. (Poertner)
W75-06678

SUSQUEHANNA AND CHENANGO RIVERS--FLOOD PLAIN INFORMATION.
Army Engineer District, Baltimore, Md.
Broome County Legislature, Binghampton, New York, December, 1969. 55 p, 17 tab, 26 fig.

Descriptors: *Historic floods, *River flow, *Flood plains, *Flood forecasting, *Flood data, *Flood control, Flood profiles, Flood routing, Flood frequency, Flood stages, Floods, Flood discharge, New York, Flood peak.
Identifiers: Susquehana River, Chenango River, Broome County(New York).

The flood situation was analyzed along the Susquehanna and Chenango Rivers in Broome County, New York. The information is based on rainfall, runoff, historical and current flood heights, and other technical data bearing upon the occurrence and size of floods. Two significant phases of the flood problem are covered. First, the largest known floods of the past are discussed and second, probable future floods are considered. Included are maps, profiles, and cross sections which indicate the extent of flooding that has been experienced and that which might occur in the future. This should prove helpful in planning the best use of the flood plains. From the maps, profiles, and cross sections, the depth of probable flooding either by recurrence of the largest known floods or by occurrence of the Intermediate Regional or Standard Project Flood at any location may be learned. Plans for the solution of future flood problems are not included. The information is intended to provide the basis for further study and planning on the part of local officials, and Broome County, in arriving at solutions to minimize vulnerability to flood damages. (Poertner)
W75-06679

PEAK FLOWS BY THE SLOPE-AREA METHOD,
Department of the Environment, Ottawa (Ontario). Water Resources Branch.
A. G. Smith.
Technical Bulletin No. 79, 31 p, 1974, Inland Waters Directorate. 13 fig, 8 ref, 5 tab.

Descriptors: *Peak discharge, *Measurement, *Slopes, Streamflow, Networks, Watersheds(Basins), Theoretical analysis, Hydraulics, Surveys, Floods, Flood data, Network design, Computer programs, *Canada.
Identifiers: *Slope-area method, Quesnel River, Regional studies, Columbia Basin.

Stream discharges are usually measured by the current meter method. During floods, however, it is frequently impossible or impractical to measure discharges by this means. Many peak discharges must be determined after the passage of the flood by indirect methods, such as the slope-area method. The indirect method of determining peak discharge is based on hydraulic equations, which relate the discharge to the water-surface profile and the geometry of the channel. A field survey is made to determine the water surface profile and the channel characteristics for a series of discharge measurements over a suitable range of stage. Values of the coefficient of roughness and the channel conveyance are calculated as a basis for computing the flood discharge. Detailed descriptions of the general procedures used in collecting field data and in computing discharge are given. The study for the Quesnel River, Station 08KH006, is used to illustrate the field and office procedures used in calculating peak flows. (Environment Canada)
W75-06745

NEW BRUNSWICK FLOOD, APRIL-MAY 1973.
Environmental Protection Service, Halifax (Nova Scotia). Atlantic Region.
For primary bibliographic entry see Field 4A.
W75-06749

FLOOD STAGES AND DISCHARGES FOR SMALL STREAMS IN TEXAS, 1972,
Geological Survey, Austin, Tex.
For primary bibliographic entry see Field 4A.
W75-06754

FLOOD HAZARD ANALYSES: FOX RUN, STARK AND WAYNE COUNTIES, OHIO.
Soil Conservation Service, Columbus, Ohio.
Prepared with Ohio Department of Natural Resources and Stark County, Ohio, February 1974. 7 p, 10 plates, 1 tab.

Descriptors: *Floods, *Flooding, *Flood profile, *Flood forecasting, Floodwater, Flood plain, *Ohio, Flood data.
Identifiers: *Fox Run(Ohio), 100-year flood, Stark County(Ohio), Wayne County(Ohio).

Fox Run, flowing eastward through Little Fox Lake in Wayne County on into Stark County where it joins the Tuscarawas River, drains 14.2 square miles. Established as a legal ditch in 1904, it

had been improved in 1968 by the Stark County Engineer and the Wayne Soil and Water Conservation District. Current use of gently sloping land is agricultural. Projections to 1990 estimate 65% of the area will be single family homes of 1/2 to 1 acre with the majority in Lawrence Township (Stark County). Flood projections indicate 225 acres (including stream channel and adjacent floodways) would be inundated by a 100-year flood which could reach an elevation as much as 6 feet over present low bank readings in some areas. Fox Run below Clays Park Lake is subject to backwater flooding from the Tuscarawas River. Comparable data are given for floods of 50 and 25 year intervals but these water surface elevations vary little from the 100-year flood. Plates show the extent of floods. This information is intended as a technical base for future local flood plain management decisions. (Park-North Carolina)
W75-06781

2F. Groundwater

HYDROLOGIC CHARACTERISTICS AND RESPONSE OF FRACTURED TILL AND CLAY CONFINING A SHALLOW AQUIFER,
Waterloo Univ. (Ontario). Dept. of Earth Sciences.
G. E. Grisak, and J. A. Cherry.
Canadian Geotechnical Journal, Vol 12, No 1, p 23-43, February 1975. 10 fig, 4 tab, 41 ref.

Descriptors: Hydrologic properties, *Fracture permeability, *Aquifer characteristics, *Aquitards, *Flow systems, Confined water, Aquifer system, Storage coefficient, Hydraulic conductivity, Groundwater movement, Porous media, Mathematical studies, Finite element analysis, Model studies, Steady flow, *Canada, Pumping, Tritium, Tracers, Flow nets.
Identifiers: Manitoba, *Fractured tills, Compression indices.

Fractures in glacial till and glaciolacustrine clay were observed in excavations up to 20 ft in depth and in drill cores in southeastern Manitoba. The fractures are characteristically coated with carbonate and oxide precipitates, which indicate groundwater movement through the fractures. The fractures impart an effective bulk hydraulic conductivity to the clay as evidenced by tritium tracer experiments and piezometer responses in the till and clay to pumping of an underlying sandy aquifer. The intergranular hydraulic conductivity of clay-loam till and glaciolacustrine clay in the Interior Plains, as determined from laboratory consolidation test data, is in the range 2 x 10 to the minus 10th power to 9 x 10 to the minus 11th power ft/s. The bulk hydraulic conductivity of the fractured clay-loam till at the study site, as determined from finite-element mathematical modeling, is about 6 x 10 to the minus 9th power ft/s. Analysis of piezometer drawdowns during a long-term pumping test indicated that rapid piezometer drawdowns in the confining layers can be accounted for by assigning specific storativity values in the range of 0.00001 to 0.000005/ft. (Prickett-ISWS)
W75-06434

A SURROGATE-PARAMETER APPROACH TO MODELING GROUNDWATER BASINS,
Colorado State Univ., Fort Collins. Dept. of Civil Engineering.
J. W. Labadie.
Water Resources Bulletin, Vol 11, No 1, p 97-114, February 1975. 5 fig, 13 ref.

Descriptors: *Parametric hydrology, *Mathematical models, *Groundwater basins, *Aquifer characteristics, Input-output analysis, Equations, Optimization, Hydrogeology, Least squares method, Model studies.
Identifiers: *Surrogate parameters, *Duality theory, Second-order gradient method, Nonconvex problems, Saddle-points, Lumped parameter systems.

A surrogate-parameter approach to modeling groundwater basins was presented, which has the following advantages over current simulation-type methods: (1) conducivness to modeling nonhomogeneous and nonisotropic basins; (2) there is no need to guess boundary conditions if accurate information is not available; (3) the model is amenable to systematic calibration or identification through the use of optimization techniques; and (4) compatibility with systematic algorithms for analyzing a wide range of management strategies. Since the parameter identification problem is large-scale and nonconvex, it was decomposed through application of generalized duality theory into several sub-problems of smaller size which were solved independently a number of times in order to achieve an overall solution. Results were presented for a hypothetical system of four interacting wells. (Visocky-ISWS)
W75-06449

NATURAL SOIL NITRATE: THE CAUSE OF THE NITRATE CONTAMINATION OF GROUND WATER IN RUNNELS COUNTY, TEXAS,
Texas Univ., Austin. Bureau of Economic Geology.
For primary bibliographic entry see Field 5B.
W75-06452

OXYGEN AND SULFUR ISOTOPIC COMPOSITION OF THE SULFATE IONS FROM MINERAL AND THERMAL GROUNDWATERS OF POLAND,
Comitato Nazionale per le Ricerche Nucleari, Pisa (Italy). Laboratorio di Geologia Nucleare.
For primary bibliographic entry see Field 5A.
W75-06455

EFFECT OF SOLUTE DISPERSION ON THERMAL CONVECTION IN A POROUS MEDIUM LAYER, 2,
Technion-Israel Inst. of Tech., Haifa. Faculty of Civil Engineering.
H. Rubin.
Water Resources Research, Vol 11, No 1, p 154-158, February 1975. 4 fig, 8 ref.

Descriptors: *Solutes, *Dispersion, *Convection, *Temperature, *Porous media, Heat transfer, Mathematical models, Boundaries(Surfaces), Equations, Currents(Water), Groundwater movement, Aquifers, Stratification, Salinity.
Identifiers: *Perturbations, Overstability, Cellular motion, Helical flow, Flow field, Instability, Parameters, Boussinesq approximation, Peclet number, Prandtl number, Rayleigh number, Schmidt number.

In some situations associated with geothermal activity, groundwater motions are affected by convection currents due to large temperature gradients. In such cases, usually saline hot water is located in the deep layers of the aquifer from which salt and heat are transferred to the upper layers. In part 1 - of this study the parameters of the two-dimensional flow field stability were determined. In part 2, further analysis of the phenomenon in three dimensions was presented. It was found that the convection cells have the shape of rolls whose axes are perpendicular to the steady state flow velocity. However, there is also a possibility of overstability of the flow field caused by rolls whose axes are parallel to the steady state velocity. The parameters of these two kinds of instability were determined. (See W73-13381) (Visocky-ISWS)
W75-06494

PUBLIC GROUNDWATER SUPPLIES IN MASON COUNTY,
Illinois State Water Survey, Urbana.
For primary bibliographic entry see Field 4B.
W75-06527

PUBLIC GROUNDWATER SUPPLIES IN STARK COUNTY,
Illinois State Water Survey, Urbana.
For primary bibliographic entry see Field 4B.
W75-06528

PUBLIC GROUNDWATER SUPPLIES IN PERRY COUNTY,
Illinois State Water Survey, Urbana.
For primary bibliographic entry see Field 4B.
W75-06529

PERMEABILITY AND EFFECTIVE STRESS,
Geological Survey, Menlo Park, Calif.
M. D. Zoback, and J. D. Byerlee.
American Association of Petroleum Geologists Bulletin, Vol 59, No 1, p 154-158, January 1975. 6 fig, 7 ref.

Descriptors: *Sandstones, *Permeability, *Effective stress, *Pore pressure, *Soil pressure, Model studies, Compacted soils, Interstices, Pores, Soil physical properties, Pore water, Hydrostatic pressure, *Stress, Overburden, Instrumentation, Reservoirs, Rocks.
Identifiers: Matrix pressure, Tectonic stress, Fluid pressure, Injection pressure, Berea sandstone.

Permeability of the Berea Sandstone was measured as a function of both confining pressure and pore pressure. As expected, permeability decreased with increased confining pressure and increased with increasing pore pressure. However, pore pressure had a significantly larger effect on permeability than did confining pressure. This behavior can be explained if the matrix through which the pore fluid flows has a higher compressibility than the granular framework which supports externally applied stresses. (Prickett-ISWS)
W75-06540

A THEORY OF THE COMBINED MOLE-TILE DRAIN SYSTEM,
Utah State Univ., Logan. Dept. of Agricultural and Irrigation Engineering.
K. Unhanand, and T. N. Kadir.
Water Resources Research, Vol 11, No 1, p 111-119, February 1975. 8 fig, 2 tab, 13 ref. AID/csd-2167.

Descriptors: *Mole drainage, *Tile drainage, *Unsteady flow, *Water table, *Equations, Groundwater movement, Theoretical analysis, Soils, Drainage, Hydraulic gradient, Mathematical models, Homogeneity, Isotropy, Hydraulic conductivity, Specific yield, Dupuit-Forchheimer theory, Darcys law, Laplaces equation.
Identifiers: Spacings.

A theory of water movement in the combined mole-tile drain system based on the transient state condition was developed. Two general equations were derived to describe the height of the water table at any location in the system at any elapsed time after the drainage process begins. One of the equations is applicable for the stage in which the water table is above the mole drains, and the other equation is for the stage in which the water table falls below the mole drains. The two general equations were simplified for the point located at midpoint between the tile drains and mole drains in the system. In the derivation, assumptions regarding the flow condition of groundwater and shape of the water table profile at certain boundaries were made. Field experiments were then conducted, and the test data were used in verifying the equation for the first stage. A reasonably good agreement between the theretical analysis and field data was obtained for this type of research. (Visocky-ISWS)
W75-06547

DRAINAGE OF GROUNDWATER RESTING ON A SLOPING BED WITH UNIFORM RAINFALL,
Agricultural Research Council, Cambridge (England). Unit of Soil Physics.
For primary bibliographic entry see Field 4B.
W75-06550

PROGRAM SOPH - SIMULATION OF TIME-VARIANT PIEZOMETRIC SURFACE IN A CONFINED AQUIFER SUBJECT TO PUMPING,
Department of the Environment, Ottawa (Ontario). Water Resources Branch.
For primary bibliographic entry see Field 4B.
W75-06737

GROUND-WATER LEVELS AND WELL RECORDS FOR CURRENT OBSERVATION WELLS IN IDAHO, 1922-73, PARTS A, B, AND C,
Geological Survey, Boise, Idaho.
For primary bibliographic entry see Field 4B.
W75-06753

GROUND-WATER DATA FOR MICHIGAN,
Geological Survey, Lansing, Mich.
For primary bibliographic entry see Field 7C.
W75-06756

EDWARDS AQUIFER, A STUDY OF EDWARDS RECHARGE ZONE REQUIREMENTS, AACOG WATER QUALITY PLANNING, PHASE 5,
Alamo Area Council of Governments, San Antonio, Tex.
For primary bibliographic entry see Field 4B.
W75-06761

THE HYDRO-MECHANICS OF THE GROUND WATER SYSTEM IN THE SOUTHERN PORTION OF THE KAIBOB PLATEAU, ARIZONA,
Arizona Univ., Tucson.
P. W. Huntoon.
PhD Dissertation, 1970. 247 p, 55 fig, 9 tab, 56 ref.

Descriptors: *Hydrology, *Areal hydrogeology, *Geohydrologic units, Regional analysis, Karst hydrology, Fracture permeability, Groundwater, *Arizona, Colorado River.
Identifiers: *Kaibob Plateau(Ariz), Grand Canyon(Ariz).

The Kaibob Plateau has an area of 880 square miles and lies north of the Grand Canyon of the Colorado River of Arizona. Marine Paleozoic sediments predominantly low permeability make up the 4000 foot sequence. The ground water system is controlled in two ways. The first is a lateral system defined by the stratigraphic sequency which controls forty percent of the plateau surface. It drains the upper 900 feet of section laterally toward fault zones or seep faces on the canyon wall. The fault zones are the second control and provide large capacity conduits both vertically and horizontally serving as flood drains for storm pulses. Fracturing also controls the development of extensive karst networks in limestones near the base of the Paleozoic section. Production from the large fault controlled drainage is also unattractive. Although the occurrence of water is certain, the large supplies are more than 2800 feet deep and exist in finite channels along the fault zone. Conventional drilling methods would be difficult to utilize. (Bradbeer-NWWA)
W75-06810

THE DISTRIBUTION OF MINOR ELEMENTS BETWEEN COEXISTING CALCITE AND DOLOMITE IN THE GASPORT MEMBER OF THE LOCKPORT FORMATION, LOCKPORT, NEW YORK,
State Univ. of New York, Buffalo.
For primary bibliographic entry see Field 2K.
W75-06811

HYDROSTRATIGRAPHIC UNITS OF THE SURFICIAL DEPOSITS OF EAST-CENTRAL ILLINOIS,
Illinois Univ., Urbana.
J. W. Vukovich.
MSc thesis 1967. 52 p, 13 fig, 2 tab, 25 ref.

Descriptors: *Glacial aquifer, *Groundwater, *Stratigraphy, *Illinois, Lithologic logs, Well data.
Identifiers: *Hydrostratigraphic, Mahomet Valley(Ill), McLean County(Ill), DeWitt County(Ill), Macon County(Ill), Piatt County(Ill), Ford County(Ill), Champaign County(Ill).

Surficial glacial deposits are the primary source of water in a region in east-central Illinois, that includes approximately 1200 square miles of counties, including McLean, DeWitt, Macon, Piatt, Ford and Champaign. Maps were made of lithologic or hydrostratigraphic units that would be useful to the future development of the water supply. The stratigraphy had to be worked out in detail. Correlation of the various till units was done by association of physical properties and their relative positions in the stratigraphy. Four units of permeable sand and gravel were defined as aquifers. The thickest was at the greatest depth and the units got progressively thinner upward toward the surface. Data for the stratigraphy were obtained from approximately 470 drillers logs. A differentiation of till sheets was made from the drillers logs. These till sheets are marked by weathered profiles, weathering zones of red-stained rock, and by rubble of till zones in the record. Cross-sections were made, three of which were almost perpendicular to the direction of movement of the Wisconsin glaciation which deposited most of the cover in the study area. The sand and gravel distributions are illustrated by four isolithic maps based on the hydrostratigraphic units previously determined. The buried Mahomet Valley runs along the bedrock surface and is filled, in the lowlands, with a sandy aquifer. Each of the hydrostratigraphic units is defined in detail and then distribution patterns are discussed. This study is compared with two recent studies of this area. (Bradbeer-NWWA)
W75-06817

2G. Water In Soils

SOIL AS A MEDIUM FOR THE RENOVATION OF ACID MINE DRAINAGE,
Pennsylvania State Univ., University Park. Dept. of Agronomy.
For primary bibliographic entry see Field 5D.
W75-06365

NEW CONCEPTS IN SOIL SURVEY INTERPRETATIONS FOR ON-SITE DISPOSAL OF SEPTIC TANK EFFLUENT,
Wisconsin Univ., Madison. Dept. of Soil Science.
For primary bibliographic entry see Field 5D.
W75-06402

DIFFUSION OF RADIOACTIVE FLUID THROUGH SOIL SURROUNDING A LARGE POWER-REACTOR STATION AFTER A CORE MELTDOWN ACCIDENT,
California Univ., Livermore. Lawrence Livermore Lab.
For primary bibliographic entry see Field 5B.
W75-06407

PORE WATER EXPULSION DURING FREEZING,
Hardy (R.M.) and Associates, Calgary (Alberta).
E. C. McRoberts, and N. R. Morgenstern.
Canadian Geotechnical Journal, Vol 12, No 1, p 130-141, February 1975. 6 fig, 3 tab, 15 ref, 1 append.

Descriptors: *Pore water, *Freezing, *Ice-water interfaces, *Frozen ground, *Porous media, Frost heaving, Soil types, Pore pressure, Saturated flow, Model studies, Finite element analysis, Numerical analysis, Interfaces, Moisture stress, Water storage, Laplaces equation, Analytical techniques, Thermal properties.
Identifiers: *Water expulsion.

When a freezing front advances through a saturated soil, water may either by expelled or attracted to the freezing front depending on soil type, stress level, and rate of freezing. Experiment evidence was considered which showed that coarse-grained sandy soils expel water under most conditions while fine grained soils can be made to expel water only at higher overburden pressures. A solution for the excess pore pressures that can be penetrated due to impeded drainage by pore water expulsion in an open system was presented. (Prickett-ISWS)
W75-06435

CONVERGENCE AND VALIDITY OF TIME EXPANSION SOLUTIONS: A COMPARISON TO EXACT AND APPROXIMATE SOLUTIONS,
Connecticut Agricultural Experiment Station, New Haven. Dept. of Ecology and Climatology.
J-Y. Parlange.
Soil Science Society of America Proceedings, Vol 39, No 1, p 3-6, January-February 1975. 1 fig, 12 ref.

Descriptors: *Mathematical studies, *Equations, *Diffusion, Saturated flow, Saturated soils, Porous media, Infiltration, Diffusivity, Boundaries(Surfaces), Absorption.
Identifiers: *Time expansion series, Spherical cavities, Convergence, Delta function solutions.

The convergence of series solutions for the diffusion equation by time expansion was discussed quantitatively, on the basis of the linear and delta function solutions for a spherical cavity. It was shown that convergence alone is a poor criterion to justify the validity of the series solutions. A counter example, diffusion in the presence of an impervious wall, showed that the series may converge for all times but be entirely erroneous. By comparison, an approximate integral technique yields a solution which agrees very well with the exact result. (Visocky-ISWS)
W75-06436

EFFECT OF APPLICATION RATE, INITIAL SOIL WETNESS, AND REDISTRIBUTION TIME ON SALT DISPLACEMENT BY WATER,
Punjab Agricultural Univ., Ludhiana (India). Dept. of Soils.
B. S. Ghuman, S. M. Verma, and S. S. Prihar.
Soil Science Society of America Proceedings, Vol 39, No 1, p 7-10, January-February 1975. 7 fig, 1 tab, 6 ref.

Descriptors: *Leaching, *Salts, *Soil moisture, *Infiltration, *Path of pollutants, Groundwater, Water pollution, Chlorides, Soil water movement, Percolation, Distribution patterns, Water distribution(Applied).
Identifiers: Salt spread, Salt peak, *Salt movement, Salt displacement.

Certain concepts regarding the displacement and profile-spread of surface-salts with applied water and the leaching efficiency of applied water were experimentally verified with soil columns. Treatments included different amounts and rates of water application and different initial soil water contents. Salt and water profiles were determined by destructive sampling in 2-cm depth intervals after variable times of redistribution. Salt front coincided with the water front in the initially dry soil and lagged behind it in the initially moist soil. Salt peak immediately after infiltration and after redistribution, for all initial soil water contents, occurred at a depth above which total water

storage equaled infiltration. But the salt spread in the profile increased as the initial water content increased. Immediately following infiltration, salt was displaced deeper with slower than with faster rates of water application. But when the application plus redistribution time was matched, the salt showed deeper movement with water added at faster than at slower rates. These results show that slower rates of water application may not increase the leaching efficiency of water under field conditions. (Sanderson-ISWS)
W75-06437

DETERMINATION OF SOIL WATER DIFFUSIVITY BY SORPTIVITY MEASUREMENTS,
Agricultural Research Service, Riverside, Calif. Salinity Lab.
C. Dirksen.
Soil Science Society of America Proceedings, Vol 39, No 1, p 22-27, January-February 1975. 6 fig, 2 tab, 11 ref.

Descriptors: *Soil moisture, *Moisture content, *Diffusion, *Absorption, *Hydraulic conductivity, Soil physical properties, Unsaturated flow, Soil water movement, Sorption, Numerical analysis, Soil water, Diffusivity.

A new method was proposed for determining the dependence of soil water diffusivity and conductivity on water content or pressure head in the tensiometer range. A weighted mean diffusivity is used to linearize the one-dimensional absorption problem. The resulting cumulative absorption is equated to that of the exact nonlinear solution to obtain an expression for the diffusivity in terms of sorptivity. To use this result, sorptivities must be measured for a series of step-function increases in the water content (pressure head) at the absorption interface. Such sorptivity measurements are quickly and easily made in situ. The method was tested on a numerical example with nearly perfect results. Also, sorptivity measurements were made on laboratory soil columns and the derived hydraulic conductivities compared well with those measured directly under steady state conditions. (Gibb-ISWS)
W75-06438

INFLUENCE OF SOIL MICROSTRUCTURE ON WATER CHARACTERISTICS OF SELECTED HAWAIIAN SOILS,
Hawaii Agricultural Experiment Station, Honolulu.
G. Y. Tsuji, R. T. Watanabe, and W. S. Sakai.
Soil Science Society of America Proceedings, Vol 39, No 1, p 28-33, January-February 1975. 7 fig, 2 tab, 12 ref. 211(d) Grant AID/csd-2833.

Descriptors: *Soil structure, *Soil physical properties, *Soil water, *Electronic equipment, Temperature, Retention, Soil texture, *Hawaii, Bulk density, Anisotropy, Montmorillonite, Kaolinite.
Identifiers: Scanning electron microscope, *Pore-size distribution, Oxisols, Ultisols, Vertisols, Inceptisols.

The higher water-holding capacity of Oxisols and Ultisols compared to that of the Vertisols and Inceptisols at 15 bars of suction was attributed to the presence of intraaggregate void spaces. Existence of such voids was verified with the aid of a scanning electron microscope. These voids were obvious in soils with kaolinitic and oxidic mineralogy but were not evident in soils of montmorillonitic or amorphous oxide composition. (Schict-ISWS)
W75-06439

LANDFORM-SOIL-VEGETATION-WATER CHEMISTRY RELATIONSHIPS, WRIGLEY AREA, N.W.T.: II. CHEMICAL, PHYSICAL, AND MINERALOGICAL DETERMINATIONS AND RELATIONSHIPS,
British Columbia Univ., Vancouver. Department of Soil Science.
M. E. Walmsley, and L. M. Lavkulich.
Soil Science Society of America Proceedings, Vol 39, No 1, p 89-93, January-February 1975. 3 tab, 18 ref.

Descriptors: *Soil-water-plant relationships, *Water chemistry, *Mineralogy, *Permafrost, *Canada, Geomorphology, Alpine, Grasslands, Colluvium, Bogs, Lakes, Streams, Soil formation, Clay minerals, Ice, Physical properties.
Identifiers: *Mackenzie Valley(Northwest Territories), Cryoturbation, Catenary sequence, Stone stripes, Stone rings, Coalescing fans, Polygonal bogs.

The relationship among five landforms in terms of chemical, physical, mineralogical, and water chemistry of lakes and the through flowing streams was presented. The landforms occur as a catenary sequence (toposequence) in the intermittent permafrost region of the Mackenzie Valley, Northwest Territories, Canada. The five landforms were identified as an alpine meadow, an area of stone stripe and stone ring formation, a colluvial slope, an area of coalescing fans, and an area of polygonal bog formation. Information collected on the chemical quality of a stream flowing through the area included pH, O2, Ca, Mg, Na, K, Cl, F and NO3. Chemical, physical, and mineralogical analyses of the soils occurring on these landforms illustrated the effect of climate on soil genesis. Cryoturbic action is the dominant process occurring in the stone stripe area while ice segregation is predominant in the area of polygonal bog formation. The limited decomposition of the soil organic matter is related to the harsh climate. Subdued pedogenic development of soils in the coalescing fan area is evident by their youthful profile differentiation. Water chemistry demonstrated the functional and integrated effect between dissolved load in the water and the landform through which the stream has flown. (Visocky-ISWS)
W75-06440

A NEW CERAMIC CUP SOIL-WATER SAMPLER,
Forest Service (USDA), La Crosse, Wis. Watershed Lab.
A. R. Harris, and E. A. Hansen.
Soil Science Society of America Proceedings, Vol 39, No 1, p 157-158, January-February 1975. 1 fig, 5 ref.

Descriptors: *Soil water, *Water sampling, *Instrumentation, Sampling, Water pollution.
Identifiers: *Porous ceramic cup, *Water sampler.

A newly designed soil-water sampler utilizing a miniature porous ceramic cup was suitable for either collecting large samples or for microtechniques. It eliminated sample transfer in the field and contamination from water channeling along sampler, and can be enclosed to discourage vandalism. It also permitted immediate preservation of the collected sample. (Schicht-ISWS)
W75-06441

EFFECT OF SOIL WATER POTENTIAL ON DISEASE INCIDENCE AND OOSPORE GERMINATION OF PYTHIUM APHANIDERMATUM,
Arizona Univ., Tucson. Dept. of Plant Pathology.
M. E. Stanghellini, and T. J. Burr.
Phytopathology. Vol 63, No 12, p 1496-1498, 1973, Illus.

Descriptors: Moisture uptake, *Soil water, *Germination, Plant growth, Alfalfa, *Plant diseases, Effects.
Identifiers: Pythium-aphanidermatum, Oospores, Spores.

Oospores of P. aphanidermatum germinated directly in asparagine-amended soils maintained at soil moisture levels ranging from saturation to -15 bars matric water potential. Percentage oospore germination and germ-tube growth rates were reduced at the lower soil moisture levels. Colonization of alfalfa seeds, sown in soil containing a natural population of 80 viable oospores of P. aphanidermatum/g soil, occurred at all soil moisture levels except -15 bars matric potential. Wet soil conditions favor the activity of Pythium by increasing nutrient availability for oospore germination.--Copyright 1974, Biological Abstracts, Inc.
W75-06447

EFFLUENT FOR IRRIGATION - A NEED FOR CAUTION,
Illinois State Water Survey, Urbana.
For primary bibliographic entry see Field 5D.
W75-06451

IN SITU SOIL WATER HOLDING CAPACITIES OF SELECTED NORTH DAKOTA SOILS,
North Dakota State Univ., Fargo. Dept. of Soils.
D. K. Cassel, and M. D. Sweeney.
Bulletin 495, 25 p, 7 fig, 3 tab, 18 ref.

Descriptors: *North Dakota, *Soil water, *Soil types, *Storage capacity, *Retention, Field capacity, Soil properties, Soil physical properties, Vegetation effects, Topsoil, Soil moisture, Soil texture, Bearing strength, Subsurface waters, On-site investigations.

Bulk density, particle size distribution (percent sand, silt, and clay), soil water characteristic, and in-situ field capacity were measured for each of 28 sites representing 26 soil types. Natural variation of all measured parameters was evident within a given soil series. Measured variation in in-situ field capacity for replicate sites of a given soil type ranged from three to five percentage units. No consistent relationship was observed between the measured in-situ field capacity and field capacity estimated by using 1/10 and 1/3 atmosphere pressure plate apparatus, irrespective of soil texture. For coarse to moderately coarse textured soils, in-situ field capacity was nearly always greater or less than the 1/10 atmosphere pressure plate extractor values, but rarely ever as low as the 1/3 atmosphere values. For medium to moderately fine textured soils, in-situ field capacity was either greater than or less than the 1/3 atmosphere value but did not exceed the water content at 1/10 atmosphere. (Sims-ISWS)
W75-06469

IMPLEMENTATION PACKAGE FOR A DRAINAGE BLANKET IN HIGHWAY PAVEMENT SYSTEMS,
Federal Highway Administration, Washington, D.C., Implementation Div.
For primary bibliographic entry see Field 4C.
W75-06470

EFFECT OF SOLUTE DISPERSION ON THERMAL CONVECTION IN A POROUS MEDIUM LAYER, 2,
Technion-Israel Inst. of Tech., Haifa. Faculty of Civil Engineering.
For primary bibliographic entry see Field 2F.
W75-06494

PREDICTION OF SEEPAGE THROUGH CLAY SOIL LININGS IN REAL ESTATE LAKES,
Arizona Water Resources Research Center, Tucson.
For primary bibliographic entry see Field 4A.
W75-06516

LAND TREATMENT OF MENHADEN WASTE WATER BY OVERLAND FLOW,
Louisiana State Univ., Baton Rouge. Dept. of Marine Science.
For primary bibliographic entry see Field 5D.

W75-06526

A THEORY OF THE COMBINED MOLE-TILE DRAIN SYSTEM,
Utah State Univ., Logan. Dept. of Agricultural and Irrigation Engineering.
For primary bibliographic entry see Field 2F.
W75-06547

ESTIMATING INFILTRATION FOR ERRATIC RAINFALL,
Oak Ridge National Lab., Tenn.
M. Reeves, and E. E. Miller.
Water Resources Research, Vol 11, No 1, p 102-110, February 1975. 14 fig, 1 tab, 11 ref, 2 append. NSF AG-199, 40-193-69.

Descriptors: *Infiltration, *Rainfall intensity, *Soil water movement, *Mathematical models, *Estimating, Groundwater movement, *Rainfall-runoff relationships, Runoff, Seepage, Simulated rainfall, Soil water, Infiltration rates, Hysteresis, Soil physical properties, Precipitation intensity, Hydrology, Watersheds(Basins), Storms.
Identifiers: Erratic rainfall, Cumulative infiltration, Soil crust.

To cheaply estimate the infiltration/runoff of typically unsteady rainfall events for purposes of watershed modeling, a method known as 'time compression' was tested against hysteretic Darcy computations. This method assumes that for a given soil the maximum infiltration rate is simply a function of the cumulative infiltration, regardless of the rainfall versus time history. The appraisal proved generally encouraging for application of this approximation to watershed modeling. The maximum infiltration rate was uniformly underestimated to a moderate degree in the early minutes of a downpour commencing late in an unsteady event. (Prickett-ISWS)
W75-06548

WATER TABLE POSITION AS AFFECTED BY SOIL AIR PRESSURE,
Agricultural Research Service, Reno, Nev.
For primary bibliographic entry see Field 4B.
W75-06549

DEPTH DISTRIBUTIONS OF GLOBAL FALLOUT SR90, CS137, AND PU239, 240 IN SANDY LOAM SOIL,
Health and Safety Lab. (AEC), New York.
For primary bibliographic entry see Field 5A.
W75-06795

REGIONAL UNIFORMITY OF CUMULATIVE RADIONUCLIDE FALLOUT,
Health and Safety Lab. (AEC), New York.
For primary bibliographic entry see Field 5A.
W75-06819

POROUS CERAMIC SOIL MOISTURE SAMPLERS, AN APPLICATION IN LYSIMETER STUDIES ON EFFLUENT SPRAY IRRIGATION,
Department of Agriculture, Lethbridge (Alberta). Research Station.
R. G. Bell.
N Z J Exp Agric, Vol 2 No 2 p 173-175, 1974. Illus.
Identifiers: Clays, Effluents, E-coli, Irrigation, *Lysimeters, Sampling, Soils, Yellow, *Soil moisture samplers, *Spray irrigation.

Porous ceramic soil moisture samplers were installed at 3 depths within a packed lysimeter. No leachate was produced, as the bottom 50 cm of the soil column was impervious yellow clay. Soil moisture samples were readily obtained from the porous ceramic samplers. The non-entry of the test organism Escherichia coli into the 1-bar samplers in the presence of clay suggests that cuch a sampling system cannot be usefully applied to studies requiring enumeration of the soil microflora or organisms intorduced by a soil-applied effluent, but can readily be applied to the study of mobile chemical substances.--Copyright 1974, Biological Abstracts, Inc.
W75-06843

2H. Lakes

PHYTOPLANKTON POPULATIONS IN RELATION TO DIFFERENT TROPHIC LEVELS AT WINNIPESAUKEE LAKE, NEW HAMPSHIRE, U.S.A.,
New Hampshire Univ., Durham. Dept. of Botany.
For primary bibliographic entry see Field 5C.
W75-06354

POPULATION DYNAMICS, BIOLOGY AND ESTIMATION OF PRODUCTION IN BENTHIC MOLLUSCA OF LAKE CHAD, (IN FRENCH),
Ecole Normale Superieure, Paris (France). Laboratoire de Zoologie.
For primary bibliographic entry see Field 2I.
W75-06360

THE EFFECTS OF ENVIRONMENTAL STRESS ON THE COMMUNITY STRUCTURE AND PRODUCTIVITY OF SALT MARSH EPIPHYTIC COMMUNITIES: PROGRESS REPORT,
City Coll., New York.
For primary bibliographic entry see Field 5C.
W75-06383

WIND-BLOWN DUST AS A SOURCE OF NUTRIENTS FOR AQUATIC PLANTS,
Canterbury Univ., Christchurch (New Zealand). Dept. of Zoology.
C. L. McLay.
Environ Pollut. Vol 5, No 3, p 173-180, 1973, Illus.

Descriptors: *Dusts, *Aquatic plants, Leaves, *Plant growth, Nutrients, Lakes.
Identifiers: Lemna-perpusilla, Scirpus-californicns, Duckweed.

The importance of natural and man-made dust accumulated on plant leaves, to the plant itself and to the surrounding vegetation, was investigated. The response of Lemna perpusilla to dust washed from the stems of Scirpus californicus which grows with the duckweed is reported. Duckweed growth was stimulated by the washings, and growth was stimulated by dust that accumulated on a concrete wall near the lake. Dust from both sources produced an immediate growth response by duckweed and probably contained soluble nutrients. Salts leached from the Scirpus stems may have been partially responsible for the increase in growth, and the utilization of nutrients from this source by aquatic plants may represent a previously unsuspected pathway in the nutrient cycle of a lake.--Copyright 1974, Biological Abstracts, Inc.
W75-06406

AIRBORNE GAMMA RADIATION SURVEYS FOR SNOW WATER-EQUIVALENT RESEARCH-PROGRESS REPORT 1973,
EG and G, Inc., Las Vegas, Nev. Las Vegas Div.
For primary bibliographic entry see Field 5A.
W75-06411

WATER EQUIVALENT OF SNOW DATA FROM AIRBORNE GAMMA RADIATION SURVEYS - INTERNATIONAL FIELD YEAR FOR THE GREAT LAKES,
EG and G, Inc., Las Vegas, Nev. Las Vegas Div.
For primary bibliographic entry see Field 5A.
W75-06412

EFFECTS OF SELECTED HERBICIDES ON BACTERIAL POPULATIONS IN FRESH AND TREATED WATER,
Clemson Univ., S.C. Dept. of Botany.
For primary bibliographic entry see Field 5C.
W75-06432

CARBON DIOXIDE PARTIAL PRESSURES IN ARCTIC SURFACE WATERS,
Alaska Univ., College. Forest Soils Lab.
P. I. Coyne, and J. J. Kelley.
Limnology and Oceanography, Vol 19, No 6, p 928-938, November 1974. 4 fig, 3 tab, 13 ref. DA-ENG-27021072-G33 and GV29343.

Descriptors: *Carbon dioxide, Water properties, *Pressure, *Instrumentation, *Alaska, Gases, Analytical techniques, Photosynthesis, Chemistry, Estimating, On-site tests, Physical properties, Vapor pressure, Cold regions, Supersaturation, Arctic, Surface waters, Atmosphere, Air-earth interfaces, Wind velocity, Water temperature, Sediments, Seasonal, Decomposing organic matter.
Identifiers: Partial pressures, *Infrared gas analysis, Evasion coefficient.

Seasonal changes in the CO2 partial pressure (PCO2) regime for an arctic freshwater pond and lake near Barrow, Alaska, were measured by infrared gas analysis by determining the CO2 concentration of air in equilibrium with the water. These waters were generally supersaturated in CO2 with respect to air throughout the period of open water and constitute a CO2 source to the arctic atmosphere. Meltwater standing on the bottom-fast ice of the lake in spring and water beneath the newly formed ice in fall also had CO2 partial pressures greater than ambient air. The seasonal mean CO2 partial pressure gradient between the water and the ambient air was 397 + or - 185 ppm for the pond and 115 + or - 83 ppm for the lake. PCO2 was inversely related to wind speed and water temperature but directly related to sediment temperature. Evasion rate coefficients calculated for the lake, based on in situ rate experiments, indicated an average transfer of 0.34 + or - 0.17 mg CO2/sq cm/atm/min to the atmosphere. (Henley-ISWS)
W75-06442

WIND STRESS ON NEARSHORE AND LAGOONAL WATERS OF A TROPICAL ISLAND,
Louisiana State Univ, Baton Rouge. Coastal Studies Inst.
For primary bibliographic entry see Field 2L.
W75-06445

TEMPERATURE EFFECTS ON GREAT LAKES WATER BALANCE STUDIES,
State Univ. of New York, Buffalo. Dept. of Civil Engineering.
D. D. Meredith.
Water Resources Bulletin, Vol 11, No 1, p 60-68, February 1975. 2 tab, 26 ref.

Descriptors: *Water temperature, *Great Lakes, *Water balance, Thermal expansion, Hydrology, Water level recorders, Precipitation(Atmospheric), Evaporation, Runoff, Groundwater, Analysis, Temperature, Profiles, Surface waters.

The Great Lakes constitute the earth's greatest expanse of fresh water and therefore represent an important natural resource. Because of the amount of precipitation on each lake, the amount of evaporation from the lake and the amount of surface runoff into the lake are difficult to determine. Management studies consider only the net basin supply, but such studies could be as much as 100% wrong because of temperature effects. Estimates were made of beginning-of-month water temperature profiles for each lake by using the cited literature. These water temperature profiles along with surface water temperatures were used to deter-

mine the effects of thermal expansion and contraction of water on the net basin supply values obtained from water balance studies that used end-of-month lake levels. Although the effect on lake levels was small, the effect on the net basin supply varied from zero for some months up to the same order of magnitude as the net basin supply value for that month. It was concluded that the thermal expansion and contraction of water should be considered when computing net basin supply values for each lake even though the effect on lake levels is small. (Roberts-ISWS)
W75-06448

GREAT LAKES WATER QUALITY, ANNUAL REPORT TO THE INTERNATIONAL JOINT COMMISSION, (1973).
International Joint Commission-United States and Canada. Great Lakes Water Quality Board.
For primary bibliographic entry see Field 5B.
W75-06474

SKYLAB STUDY OF WATER QUALITY,
Kansas Univ., Lawrence.
For primary bibliographic entry see Field 5A.
W75-06478

PREDICTION OF SEEPAGE THROUGH CLAY SOIL LININGS IN REAL ESTATE LAKES,
Arizona Water Resources Research Center, Tucson.
For primary bibliographic entry see Field 4A.
W75-06516

A LIMNOLOGICAL STUDY OF SILVERWOOD LAKE: IMPACT OF WATER TRANSPORT ON WATER QUALITY,
California State Polytechnic Univ., Pomona.
For primary bibliographic entry see Field 5A.
W75-06538

BIOLOGICAL, CHEMICAL AND RELATED ENGINEERING PROBLEMS IN LARGE STORAGE LAKES OF TASMANIA,
Hydro-Electric Commission, Tasmania (Australia). Civil Engineering Div.
For primary bibliographic entry see Field 4A.
W75-06556

REVIEW OF LAKE RESTORATION PROCEDURES,
Colorado Univ., Boulder.
For primary bibliographic entry see Field 5G.
W75-06566

LONG-TERM RECONSTRUCTION OF WATER LEVEL CHANGES FOR LAKE ATHABASCA BY ANALYSIS OF TREE RINGS,
Arizona Univ., Tucson. Lab. of Tree-Ring Research.
For primary bibliographic entry see Field 4A.
W75-06569

NUMERICAL MODELING OF THERMAL STRATIFICATION IN A RESERVOIR WITH LARGE DISCHARGE-TO-VOLUME RATIO,
Tennessee Valley Authority, Muscle Shoals, Ala. Air Quality Branch.
G. G. Park, and P. S. Schmidt.
Water Resources Bulletin, Vol 9, No 5, p 932-941, October 1973. 4 fig, 1 tab, 7 ref.

Descriptors: *Reservoirs, *Thermal stratification, *Lakes, *Water quality control, *Temperature, *Simulation analysis, *Texas, Behavior, Inflow, Outflow, Meteorological data, Flow, Effects, Epilimnion, Hypolimnion, Thermocline, Water resources, Planning, Depth, Convection, Diffusion, Southwest U.S., *Forecasting.
Identifiers: *Lyndon B. Johnson Lake(Texas), Sensitivity, Colorado River(Tex).

Thermal stratification in fresh-water reservoirs is a concern in water resources planning because of the strong dependence of many key chemical and biological parameters on temperature. In the southwestern United States, even relatively shallow reservoirs often exhibit significant stratification due to the long and intense warming period; Lake Lyndon B. Johnson, of primary concern in this study, typifies the characteristics of many reservoirs in this region. Described is a numerical model study of thermal stratification in a high discharge-to-volume reservoir. Predicted temperature profiles are compared with field data for two different years. The model accurately predicts the data of fall turnover and predicts degree of stratification and depth of the thermocline within about 20% for both years simulated. A parametric study of stratification mechanics for a high flow reservoir has indicated that diffusion was the predominant heat transport mechanism in the hypolimnion, while surface effects dominated the epilimnion. Flow effects for the particular case studied, in which all inflows and outflows occur in the epilimnion, did not significantly affect stratification behavior. (Bell-Cornell)
W75-06572

WHITE BEAR LAKE CONSERVATION DISTRICT (AS AMENDED).
For primary bibliographic entry see Field 6E.
W75-06603

FACTORS LIMITING PRIMARY PRODUCTIVITY IN TURBID KANSAS RESERVOIRS,
Kansas Water Resources Research Inst., Manhattan.
For primary bibliographic entry see Field 5C.
W75-06642

PHYTOPLANKTON OF THE WESTERN (KURTLI) POND IN 1967-1970 (IN RUSSIAN),
Acad. Sci. Turkm. SSR, Ashkhabad, Inst. Bot.
For primary bibliographic entry see Field 5C.
W75-06653

RESULTS OF TESTING CLEAN-FLO LAKE CLEANSER IN FLORIDA LAKES,
Florida State Game and Fresh Water Fish Commission, Lake City; and Clean-Flo Labs., Inc., Hopkins, Minn.
For primary bibliographic entry see Field 5D.
W75-06672

ON THE USE OF INDICATOR COMMUNITIES OF TUBIFICIDAE AND SOME LUMBRICULIDAE IN THE ASSESSMENT OF WATER POLLUTION IN SWEDISH LAKES,
Uppsala Univ. (Sweden). Inst. of Zoology.
For primary bibliographic entry see Field 5C.
W75-06698

COMPARATIVE STUDY OF THE NITROGEN LIFE-CYCLE IN THE PONDS (IN FRENCH),
Station d'Hydrobiologie Continentale, Biarritz (France).
For primary bibliographic entry see Field 5C.
W75-06702

DIURNAL VARIATION IN SAGAR LAKE, SAGAR (INDIA): I. STUDIES IN THE DEEP WATER AREA,
Saugar Univ., Sagar (India). Dept. of Botany.
For primary bibliographic entry see Field 5C.
W75-06705

PHYTOPLANKTON IN THE OLIGOHALINE LAKE, SELSO: PRIMARY PRODUCTION AND STANDING CROP,
Copenhagen Univ. (Denmark). Institut for Thallophyta.
For primary bibliographic entry see Field 5C.
W75-06708

LIFE IN A LAKE RESERVOIR: FEWER OPTIONS, DECREASED PRODUCTION,
Institute of Freshwater Research Drottningholm (Sweden).
For primary bibliographic entry see Field 5C.
W75-06712

A COMPARISON OF FRESH-WATER PROTOZOAN COMMUNITIES IN GEOGRAPHICALLY PROXIMATE BUT CHEMICALLY DISSIMILAR BODIES OF WATER,
Virginia Polytechnic Inst. and State Univ., Blacksburg. Dept. of Biology.
W. H. Yongue, Jr., J. Cairns, Jr., and H. Boatin, Jr.
Arch Protistenkd. Vol 115, No 2/3, p 154-161, 1973, Illus.
Identifiers: Bogs, *Michigan, *Ponds, *Protozoa, Hydrogen ion concentration, *Water hardness.

Twenty-eight protoxoan-free polyurethane foam substrates were placed in 2 ponds, about 100 m apart (Michigan), with markedly different pH and hardness. The protozoan species which colonized these substrates were studied 7 times at weekly intervals. Of the 202 spp. identified from the bog pond (pH 5.8-6.0, hardness 17.1-34.2 ppm) 112 occurred in more than 1 weekly harvest (or sampling). Of the 176 spp. from the pit pond (pH 8.0-9.0, hardness 102-154 ppm) 110 were recurring. Thirteen species were present continuously in both ponds from weeks 3 through 7 and 8 spp. occurred 50% or more of the time in one pond and did not appear at all in the other. Possible explanations for these similarities and differences are discussed.--Copyright 1974, Biological Abstracts, Inc.
W75-06715

THE BOTTOM FAUNA OF LAKE LILLE-JONSVANN, TRONDELAG, NORWAY,
Kongelige Norske Videnskabers Selskab, Trondheim. Museet.
For primary bibliographic entry see Field 5B.
W75-06716

THE BOTTOM FAUNA OF LAKE HUDDINGSVATN, BASED ON QUANTITATIVE SAMPLING,
Kongelige Norske Videnskabers Selskab, Trondheim. Museet.
For primary bibliographic entry see Field 5B.
W75-06717

THE EFFECT OF LIGHT INTENSITY ON THE AVAILABILITY OF FOOD ORGANISMS TO SOME LAKE BAIKAL FISHES,
Biologo-Geograficheskii Nauchno-Issledovatelskii Institut, Irkutsk (USSR).
L. A. Volkova.
Vopr Ikhtiol. Vol 13, No 4, p 709-722, 1973, Illus, (In Russian).
Identifiers: Coregonus-autumnalis-migratorius, Cottocomephorus-grewingki, Esox-lucius, Fishes, *Food organisms, Lakes, *Light intensity, Paracottus-kessleri, Phoxinus-phoxinus, *USSR(Lake Baikal).

Changes in the availability of food organisms as a function of light intensity were studied under experimental conditions with the following Lake Baikal fishes: Coregonus autumnalis migratorius and Cottocomephorus grewingki at various stages of ontogenesis and Paracottus kessleri, Phoxinus phoxinus and Esox lucius. The threshold levels of light intensity, lowest level of light intensity for initiation of active feeding and maximal intensity of these fish were determined. The role of vision in feeding was also investigated. The availability of food organisms for Baikal fishes of various ecological groups depends on the potential of their

receptors and the adaptive characteristics of the behavior in question.--Copyright 1974, Biological Abstracts, Inc.
W75-06723

ICE PILING ON LAKESHORES - WITH SPECIAL REFERENCE TO THE OCCURRENCES ON LAKE SIMCOE IN THE SPRING OF 1973,
Canada Centre for Inland Waters, Burlington (Ontario).
For primary bibliographic entry see Field 2C.
W75-06733

SUMMARY REPORT OF MICROBIOLOGICAL BASELINE DATA ON LAKE SUPERIOR, 1973,
Canada Centre for Inland Waters, Burlington (Ontario).
S. S. Rao, and J. Henderson.
Scientific Series No. 45, 8 p, 1974, Inland Waters Directorate. 9 fig, 3 ref, 5 tab.

Descriptors: *Lake Superior, *Microbiology, *Surveys, *Data collections, *Bacteria, Water quality, Coliforms, Pathogenic bacteria, Streptococcus, Water pollution, Microorganisms, Pollutant identification.

From May to November 1973, six Lake-wide cruises were made on Lake Superior to collect bacteriological data to establish baseline bacteriological levels and to develop criteria for non-degradative water quality standards. Samples were collected from 117 stations from depths of 1 m, 10 m, 50 m and bottom depths. They were immediately analyzed on board ship for total coliform, fecal coliform, fecal streptococcus and heterotrophic bacterial densities. Some monthly trends were observed in the coastal areas. Coliform densities increased throughout the sampling period. Fecal coliform populations fluctuated with peaks in May, July-August and November, and fecal streptococcus population densities decreased slightly from May-November. Maximum heterotrophic bacterial populations occurred during the July-August period. On a Lake-wide basis, coliforms increased to maximum levels during the September-October period and dropped during November to the levels found in the spring season. Fecal coliform, fecal streptococcus and heterotrophic bacterial populations exhibited trends similar to those observed in the coastal areas. At least 85% of the analyzed water samples showed fecal coliform and fecal streptococcus populations less than 1 per 100 ml. (Environment Canada)
W75-06738

SIMPLE COLOUR METER FOR LIMNOLOGICAL STUDIES,
Canada Centre for Inland Waters, Burlington (Ontario).
For primary bibliographic entry see Field 7B.
W75-06743

RADIONUCLIDE LEVELS IN THE GREAT LAKES WATERS - 1973,
Canada Centre for Inland Waters, Burlington (Ontario).
For primary bibliographic entry see Field 5A.
W75-06744

TRANSIENT RESPONSE OF SHALLOW ENCLOSED BASINS USING THE METHOD OF NORMAL MODES,
Canada Centre for Inland Waters, Burlington (Ontario).
D. B. Rao.
Scientific Series No. 38, 30 p, 1974, Inland Waters Directorate. 11 fig, 8 ref, 3 tab.

Descriptors: *Lakes, *Waves, Basins, Theoretical analysis, Analytical techniques, Model studies, Water circulation, Water levels, Equations, Forecasting.
Identifiers: *Wind stress, *Normal modes, Oscillations, Dynamic analysis.

Predicting the two-dimensional forced response (or the storm surge) of an arbitrary water body is discussed in terms of the normal mode expansion technique. Such an approach eliminates space dependence from the governing equations. Time-dependent aspects of the problem may then be solved either by a numerical evaluation of a form integral solution, which involves the normal mode functions and the wind stress field, or by a direct finite-difference integration in time alone by some explicit or implicit schemes. Hence the use of normal mode expansion procedure eliminates a complete numerical integration of the problem on a space-time finite difference grid, and offers certain advantages in avoiding such problems as computational stability, grid-dispersion, etc. A method is described for constructing the quasi-static normal modes for an arbitrary rotating basin and different methods are presented for obtaining the general solution for the forced response. Application of some of these procedures to two ideal cases is then considered. One case deals with the response of a non-rotating rectangular basin of uniform depth to a semi-infinite stress band propagating across the basin in a given direction; the other deals with the effect of an instantaneously imposed wind stress on a rotating rectangular basin of uniform depth. (Environment Canada)
W75-06746

COMPUTER ROUTINE FOR CALCULATING TOTAL LAKE VOLUME CONTENTS OF A DISSOLVED SUBSTANCE FROM AN ARBITRARY DISTRIBUTION OF CONCENTRATION PROFILES - A METHOD OF CALCULATING LAKEWIDE CONTENTS OF DISSOLVED SUBSTANCES,
Canada Centre for Inland Waters, Burlington (Ontario).
F. M. Boyce.
Technical Bulletin 83, 1973, 25 p, Inland Waters Directorate. 5 fig, 2 ref, 4 append.

Descriptors: *Computer programs, *Lakes, *Dissolved solids, Sampling, Theoretical analysis, Estimating, Bathymetry, Measurement, Hydrography, Mathematical studies, Data processing, Volumetric analysis, Algorithms, Lake Ontario, *Mapping.
Identifiers: Digital maps.

A computer program is described for calculating total lake volume of a dissolved substance using an arbitrary distribution of concentration profiles. The effects of bottom topography are taken into account in the calculations. The program was originally developed for the computation of lake total stored heat based on BT temperature profiles but has a wide range of applications. Adaptions of the technique have been developed to compute lake volume above or below any surface defined by an arbitrary distribution of measured depths. The method is useful for repeated surveys of the same lakes and adjusts to changes in sample pattern and lake water levels. Appendices explain the construction of digital maps of lake bathymetry assignation of algorithms to stations, and the data format. Appendix D contains the Fortran listing of splotch as coded for a CDC 6400 computer. (Environment Canada)
W75-06748

PHYTOPLANKTON OF THE NATRON-CONTAINING WATERS OF KANEM (CHAD): V. THE MESOHALINE LAKES (IN FRENCH),
Office de la Recherche Scientifique et Technique Outre-Mer, Fort-Lamy (Chad).
For primary bibliographic entry see Field 5C.
W75-06778

HYDROBACTERIOLOGICAL INVESTIGATIONS IN LAKE CONSTANCE: III. PROGRESSIVE GROWTH OF PLANKTON-DEPENDENT PRODUCTION OF BACTERIA AS AN INDICATION OF EUTROPHICATION, (IN GERMAN),
Staatliches Institut fuer Seenforschung und Seenbewirtschaftung, Langenargen (West Germany).
For primary bibliographic entry see Field 5C.
W75-06839

A PRELIMINARY PHYTOPLANKTON SURVEY OF TWELVE ADIRONDACK LAKES,
New York State Dept. of Environmental Conservation, Delmar. Wildlife Research Lab.
For primary bibliographic entry see Field 5C.
W75-06844

THE FLOATING LOG AND STUMP COMMUNITIES IN THE SANTEE SWAMP OF SOUTH CAROLINA,
South Carolina Univ., Columbia. Dept. of Biology.
For primary bibliographic entry see Field 2I.
W75-06845

PHYTOPLANKTON PERIODICITY OF SOME NORTH SHROPSHIRE MERES,
Freshwater Biological Association, Shrewsbury (England). Meres Lab.
C. S. Reynolds.
Br Phycol J, Vol 8, No 3, p 301-320, 1973. Illus.
Identifiers: England, *Meres(North Shropshire), Periodicity, Physicochemical studies, *Phytoplankton periodicity, Seasonal.

The seasonal succession of phytoplankton in 12 Shropshire (England) meres and pools is presented, together with notes on isolated collections from 8 others in the region. In the majority of the waters investigated, the annual periodicity conforms to a typical pattern. Departures from this established pattern are discussed in relation to differences in physico-chemical conditions of the water-bodies.--Copyright 1974, Biological Abstracts, Inc.
W75-06846

2I. Water In Plants

POPULATION DYNAMICS, BIOLOGY AND ESTIMATION OF PRODUCTION IN BENTHIC MOLLUSCA OF LAKE CHAD, (IN FRENCH),
Ecole Normale Superieure, Paris (France). Laboratoire de Zoologie.
C. Leveque.
Cah ORSTOM Ser Hydrobiol. Vol 7, No 2, p 117-147, 1973, Illus, English summary.

Descriptors: *Mollusks, *Lakes, *Benthic fauna, *Aquatic populations, Biomass, Aquatic animals, *Reproduction, Africa.
Identifiers: Bellamya, Lake Chad, Cleopatra, Corbicula, Melania.

In accordance with periodical samplings, populations of benthic mollusks from Lake Chad were observed for more than 1 yr in 3 localities (Samia, Bol et Baga Kawa). The evolution of the demographic structure (size structure) of the populations during successive samplings has provided the opportunity to study the biology of certain species and, more particularly, reproduction periods and longevity. Bellamya and Melania reproduce year round, but during the cool season there is a decrease in the birth rate. Corbicula have a heavy reproduction during this cool season. The normal 1 yr life span of Corbicula, can be extended (to 3 yr and more) under certain environmental conditions. After a brief explanation of 2 methods of production calculation in the case of cohorts (Bojsen Jensen method and method of instantaneous growth rate), 1 method is suggested which is available as well for populations with complex age structure. This method requires using both the average weight increase of 1 individual and the demographic structure of populations. With this

method, the instantaneous growth rate of the population (G) may be obtained and the instantaneous production estimated with the formula p = G X Biomass. This method was tested before it was applied to benthic mollusks populations from lake Chad. With the cohorts of Corbicula and Bellamya in experimental in situ rearings, the results with this method or with more classical ones are very similar. It is the same for the Bellamya populations in experimental rearings. The annual production (for dry organic weight and for shell weight) of natural populations of Melania, Cleopatra, Bellamya and Corbicula was estimated in localities where the studies of demography and dynamics were effected. The annual production/biomass (P/B) ratio was also calculated. According to the species and localities, it varies between 3 and 6. The use of instantaneous growth rate (G) of the population is discussed. The presence of a relation between G and the average weight of an individual of the population (W) is pointed out for different species. This relation is valid only within certain limits of W. On the other hand, another fairly good relation exists between G and average longevity for different species of aquatic molluscs.--Copyright 1974, Biological Abstracts, Inc.
W75-06360

WIND-BLOWN DUST AS A SOURCE OF NUTRIENTS FOR AQUATIC PLANTS,
Canterbury Univ., Christchurch (New Zealand). Dept. of Zoology.
For primary bibliographic entry see Field 2H.
W75-06406

SOME DIFFERENCES IN WATER REGIMEN OF ULMUS PUMILA L. OF DIFFERENT GEOGRAPHICAL ORIGIN,
Moscow State Univ. (USSR). Dept. of Plant Physiology.
F. Z. Borodulina, and T. A. Borisova.
Vestn Mosk Univ Ser 6 Biol Pochvoved. Vol 28, No 2, p 99-101, 1973.

Descriptors: *Trees, *Water storage, Transpiration, Leaves, Geographical regions.
Identifiers: *Ulmus-pumila.

The influence of U. pumila origin on water regimen of trees growing in equally favorable conditions of water supply was detected. Differences in water content of leaves, intensivity of transpiration and water retaining ability were observed.--Copyright 1974, Biological Abstracts, Inc.
W75-06480

A STUDY OF EDDY FLUXES OVER A FOREST,
Commonwealth Scientific and Industrial Research Organization, Aspendale (Australia). Div. of Atmospheric Physics.
B. B. Hicks, P. Hyson, and C. J. Moore.
Journal of Applied Meteorology, Vol 14, No 1, p 58-66, February 1975. 7 fig, 3 tab, 10 ref, append.

Descriptors: *Australia, *Heat flow, *Forests, *Micrometeorology, Temperature, Humidity, Winds, Eddies, Pine trees, Air temperature, Heat balance, Heat budget, Instrumentation, Momentum transfer.
Identifiers: Temperature gradients, Eddy-correlation equipment, Wind profiles, Heat storage, Mt. Gambier(Australia).

Eddy correlation instruments mounted above a plantation of Pinus radiata near Mt. Gambier, south Australia, were operated during two periods of intensive effort, in May and October 1972. Measurements of the Reynolds stress and of wind speed gradients showed that the zero plane for momentum is located at about d=0.8h (where h is the height of the trees), and that the roughness length of the surface is about 30% of the difference (h-d). Sensible heat fluxes and temperature gradients give a displacement length not significantly different from that applicable in the momentum case, but the roughness length for sensible heat transfer is smaller than that for momentum, by about a factor of 3. Advective effects were found to be important, particularly when the fetch across the canopy is less than about 0.8 km. Long-fetch cases allow an evaluation of the heat storage in the canopy and in the air below the height of eddy flux measurement. The rate of heat storage was found to be about 60 plus or minus 20 W/sq m/degree C/h of canopy temperature change (for a densely packed forest with trees about 13 m high), which is compatible with measurements of the biomass and assumed specific heats. The residual heat energy at about 6 m above the effective zero plane, unaccounted for by the various measured fluxes, was found to be related to the difference in net radiation over grassland and forest. (Sims-ISWS)
W75-06498

WATER-RETAINING ABILITY AND PROTEINS OF LEAVES AND CHLOROPLASTS IN PLANTS WITH DIFFERENT DROUGHT-RESISTANCE, (IN RUSSIAN),
Akademiya Nauk Moldavskoi SSR, Kishinev. Inst. of Plant Physiology and Biochemistry.
M. D. Kushnirenko, E. V. Kryukova, and S. N. Percherskaya.
Fiziol Rast Vol 20, No 3, p 582-589, 1973. Illus. English summary.

Descriptors: *Plants, *Water storage, Leaves, *Drought resistance, Plant physiology, *Drought tolerance, Beaus, Electrophoresis, Proteins.
Identifiers: Chlorophyll, Chloroplasts, Horse bean, Phaseolus-Sp, Cytoplasm.

Plants of Phaseolus and horse bean, hardened to drought before sowing by the method of P.A. Henckel (experimental) and non-hardened (control), were studied. Studies were made on the water-retaining ability (WA) of the leaves and chloroplasts, the hydrophilic nature (HN) of the air-dried leaves and chloroplasts and the state of chlorophyll-protein-lipid complex of the plastids. The proteins were conventionally subdivided into 2 fractions (high and low solubility), each consisting of many components. Both fractions were subjected to electrophoresis. WA of the leaves is lower than that of the chloroplasts. HN and WA of the leaves and chloroplasts of Phaseolus and horse bean, resistant to drought, is higher than in the control. The content of chlorophylls a and b is higher in the leaves of horse bean. However this pigment was bound stronger to the olipo-protein complex of the plastids in the drought-resistant plants of Phaseolus and horse bean. Soluble proteins of the leaves, cytoplasm and chloroplasts and more heterogenous and mobile during electrophoresis in the drought-resistant plants. The protein zones with the same electrophoretic mobility were detected in the leaves and chloroplasts of the drought-resistant plants of Phaseolus and bean. This water exchange of the chloroplasts may help to understand the regulatory mechanism of plant adaptation to drought.--Copyright 1974, Biological Abstracts, Inc.
W75-06560

IS DIARTHRON VESICULOSUM (THYMELAEACEAR) AN ECOLOGICAL PUZZLE: STUDIES ON THEROPHYTES ON STEPPE OF KABUL/AFGHANISTAN : II. THE EFFECT OF DROUGHT ON MINERAL RATIOS AND CARBOHYDRATE METABOLSIM, (IN GERMAN),
Bonn Univ. (West Germany). Pharmakognostisches Institut.
Siegmar-W. Breckle, and Ulrich Kull.
Bot Jahrb Syst Pflanzengesch Pflanzengeogr, Vol 93, No 4, p 539-561, 1973. Illus. English summary.
Identifiers: *Afghanistan(Kabul), Carbohydrates, *Diarthron-vesiculosum, Drought, *Ecological studies, *Metabolism, Minerals, Scabiosa-olivieri, Steppes, Therophytes, Thymelaceceae, Ziziphora-Tenuior.

D. vesiculosum (Fisch. et C.A. Mey.) Mey. is an annual which Korovin reported endures the dry summer in the deserts of Turkmenistan in living condition. In the surroundings of Kabul/Afghanistan, Ziziphora tenuior L. and Scabiosa olivieri Coult. were also studied in addition to Diarthron. Neither investigation of the phenological, morphological, and osmotic conditions (part I), nor studies of the mineral and carbohydrate contents gave any confirmation for the Russian observation. However, the 3 therophytes differ gradually in their behavior against drought. Diarthron shows the lowest mineral contents. In contrast to the 2 other annuals, in Diathron the content of carbohydrates and their portion is osmotically effective substances decrease during the ontogeny. The importance of slime-content in Diarthron remains obscure. Ziziphora wilts earlier and more rapidly than the other 2 spp., only a few days after the last rain. Scabiosa shows a behavior more similar to Diarthron, even more tolerant to drought. Suitable relations and measures are discussed, able to express the results of the analyzed substances. The concentrations of inorganic ions are expressed also as portions of the potential osmotic pressure of the cell sap. The composition of the plants during their ontogeny is also given.--Copyright 1974, Biological Abstracts, Inc.
W75-06561

COMPLEXES OF SOIL INVERTEBRATES IN SWAMPY FORESTS IN THE TAVDA-KUMA INTERRIVER REGION (IN RUSSIAN),
L. S. Kozlovskaya, and N. I. Shadrina.
Tr Inst Ekol Rast Zhivotn Ural Fil Akad Nauk SSSR. 83. p 182-193, 1972, Illus.

Descriptors: *Invertebrates, Soils, *Swamps, *Forests, Vegetation, Diptera, Insects, Nematodes, Rivers.
Identifiers: *USSR(Tavda-Kuma region), Acarina, Aulacomnium-palustre, Callus-palustris, Carex-appropinquata, Carex-globularis, Carex-limosa, Carex-rynchophysa, Carex-tenuiflora, Carex-vesicaria, Chaemedaphne-calyculata, Coleoptera, Collembola, Dryopteris-linnaeane, Enchytraeidae, Equisetum-palustre, Hylocomium-splendens, Ledum-palustre, Lumbricidae, Oxalis-Acetosella, Pleurozium, Russian-SFSR, Sphagnum-centrale, Tomenthyphum-nitens.

Group composition and number of soil invertebrates were studied in the Tavda-Kuma interriver region (Russian SFSR, USSR) in 1965-1966 to determine the biological activity of the soil and the prospects for increasing it. Data from geobotanical descriptions, chemical analyses of soil, observations at the level of soil ground waters and precipitation which characterize the ecology of the animals' habitat were used. Samples for study of microfauna were selected over the course of the vegetation period at the end of every month. Incidence of the following animal groups varied in different types of marshy forests: Acarina, Collembola, Enchytraidae, Diptera, Coleoptera, Nematodes, Lumbricidae. The following species of vegetation were observed: Carex appropinquata, C. globularis, C. limosa, Tomenthyphum nitens, Aulacomnium palustre, Carex vesi caria, Callus palustris, Sphagnum centrale, Ledum palustre, Chamaedaphne calyculata, Equisetum palustre, Carex tenuiflora, C. rynchophysa, Hylocomium splendens, Pleurozium, Dryopteris linnaeane, Oxalis acetosella. Larvae of the following families were observed: Yanthariddae, Carabidae, Sciaridae, Chironomidae, Tipulidae, Bibianidae, Muscidae, Cantharididae, Lithobiidae, Diptera, Tabanidae, Dolichopodidae, and Rhagionidae. Data revealed characteristic complexes of invertebrates in various soil types.--Copyright 1974, Biological Abstracts, Inc.
W75-06651

FOREST CONDITIONS IN THE CENTRAL PORTION OF THE TAVDA RIVER BASIN AND

THE TAVDA-KUMA INTERRIVER REGION (IN RUSSIAN),
B. P. Kolesnikov.
Tr Inst Ekol Rast Zhivotn Ural Fil Akad Nauk SSSR. 83. p 7-26, 1972, Illus.
Identifiers: Climates, Conifers, *Forests, Hardwood, Marshes, Morphology, Pine, Precipitation(Atmospheric), Rivers, Soils, *USSR(Transural region), *River basins.

Literature on forest conditions in the Transural region (USSR) is reviewed. Studies focused on the vicinity of the Tavda River basin and the Tavda-Kuma interriver region. Relief, surface structure, evolution of the surface, climate, soil conditions, precipitation, hydrological regime and vegetation covering are considered. Forest conditions are compared in the following region: Tavda right-bank pine forest region; Tavda left-bank marshy-pine forest region; and Tavda-Kuma interriver dark conifer-hardwood region, which may be divided into 2 regions from the standpoint of utilization of forest resources.--Copyright 1974, Biological Abstracts, Inc.
W75-06652

BUILDING STONES OF MODERN PHYSIOLOGY: ECOPHYSIOLOGY OF PLANTS,
K. Kreeb.
VEB Gustav Fischer Verlag: Jena, East Germany. 1974. 211 p, Illus.

Descriptors: Plants, Ecosystems, *Plant physiology, Solar radiation, Radiation, Temperature, Water balance, Water transfer, *Environmental effects.

Various aspects of plant ecophysiology are discussed. The 1st sections deal with ecology and ecophysiology and the importance of solar radiation. The next sections deal with radiation and temperature relationships, radiation and material production and the factor of water balance and transport. Further environmental factors such as pH, food, CO2, nitrogen and minerals, the combined effect of environmental factors and models of stomate regulation mechanisms and transpiration, growth and environmental protection are also discussed.--Copyright 1974, Biological Abstracts, Inc.
W75-06709

PERIPHYTON DYNAMICS IN LABORATORY STREAMS: A SIMULATION MODEL AND ITS IMPLICATIONS,
Oregon State Univ., Corvallis. Dept. of Botany.
C. D. Mcintire.
Ecol Monogr. Vol 43, No 3, p 399-420, 1973, Illus.
Identifiers: Grazing, Laboratory streams, Light, *Model studies, *Oregon, *Periphyton, Respiration, Seasons, Silt, Simulation analysis, Snails, Streams, Vegetation, *Lotic environment.

A simple and an expanded model of periphyton dynamics in lotic environments are described. The simple model includes 1 level variable, the biomass of the periphyton assemblage, and 4 rate variables: primary production, community respiration and 2 export fractions. In the expanded model 3 level variables and 8 rate variables are added to the simple model to introduce the effects of allochthonous organic matter and grazing activities by an aquatic snail. In general, computer output from the expanded model supports the hypothesis that the relatively low biomasses of periphyton observed in the small streams of western Oregon, are the result of grazing activities by aquatic animals, high silt loads during the fall and winter months and the effects of a dense canopy of terrestrial vegetation on light penetration. Furthermore, the model indicates that it is bioenergetically feasible for a periphyton biomass of about 10 g/sq m ash-free dry weight to support a consumer biomass of 150 g/sq m or more if the productive capacity of the system is sufficient. The simulation models provided an analytical way of synthesizing the results of a number of experiments with periphyton assemblages, identified weaknesses in the experimental data, and provided insights into the dynamics of periphyton assemblages that could not be obtained by intuition alone or by examining the results of individual experiments.--Copyright 1974, Biological Abstracts, Inc.
W75-06714

COMPARISON OF FEEDING AND BIODEPOSITION OF THREE BIVALVES AT DIFFERENT FOOD LEVELS,
Woods Hole Oceanographic Institution, Mass. Dept. of Biology.
K. R. Tenore, and W. M. Dunstan.
Mar Biol (Berl). Vol 21, No 3, p 190-195, 1973.
Identifiers: *Biodeposition, Bivalves, Crassostrea-virginica, Feeding, Food, Mercenaria-mercenaria, Mytilus-edulis, *Oysters, *Mussels.

Experiments on the edible mussel Mytilus edulis, the American oyster Crassostrea virginica, and the hard clam Mercenaria mercenaria, using flowing systems, showed that the feeding and biodeposition rates were affected by food concentration. At all levels of food concentration, the order of increasing feeding rate (both the percent of available particulate carbon and the actual amount of carbon removed) was: clam < oyster < mussel. All bivalves exhibited lower feeding rates (both percent and actual) at low food concentrations. However, the percent of available food removed quickly increased to a maximum at food coneentrations typical for the natural environment. This maximum remained constant for the mussel and oyster, but declined with increasing food coneentration for the clam. However, because this percentage was for increasing levels, the actual C removed continued to increase up to the highest food level for all 3 bivalves. In increasing order of biodeposition rate, the bivalves were: clam < oyster < mussel. The biodeposition rates of the 3 bivalves increased logarithmically with increased food concentration as a result of the production of pseudofecs. The feeding and biodeposition data were used to calculate assimilation rates, and this pointed out the higher efficiency of the oyster compared to the mussel and clam.--Copyright 1974, Biological Abstracts, Inc.
W75-06724

A LIMNOLOGICAL STUDY OF TASSHA-GAWA RIVER NEAR THE SADO MARINE BIOLOGICAL STATION OF NIIGATA UNIVERSITY,
Niigata Univ. (Japan). Dept. of Biology.
Y. Honma, T. Matsuki, N. Hokari, T. Oka, and Y. Sato.
Annu Rep Sado Mar Biol Stn Niigata Univ, 3 p 11-21, 1973. Illus.
Identifiers: Algae, *Biological studies, Crabs, Diatoms, Electrical conductivity, Fish, Insects, *Japan(Tassha-Gawa River), *Limnological studies, Marine, Protozoa, Rivers, Snails, Temperature, Hydrogen ion concentration.

Observations were made to elucidate several limnological conditions of Tassha-gawwa River, Japan, such as water temperature, pH, transparency and electric conductivity, and the benthic organisms collected quantitatively in the six stations were examined. In all, 19 spp. of aquatic insects, 59 spp. and varieties of diatoms, 18 spp. of blue-green algae, 12 spp. of green algae and 2 spp. of protozoan animals were identified. One species of freshwater crab and a snail were also obtained. In addition to these benthic organisms, 10 spp. of freshwater fishes were listed. As this river in the vicinity of the Sado Marine Biological Station is quite small, clean and rapid, the biotic communities are very scarce and simple.--Copyright 1974, Biological Abstracts, Inc.
W75-06836

PROGRESS REPORT OF RESEARCH WORK IN TASEK BERA, MALAYSIA,
Osaka Kyoiku Univ. (Japan). Lab. for Science Education.
T. Mizuno.
Mem Osaka Kyoiku Univ III Nat Sci Appl Sci, 21 p, 111-113, 1972. Illus.
Identifiers: *Biological studies, International Biological Program, *Malaysia(Tasek Bera), Phytoplankton, Zooplankton, *Aquatic animals, Asia(SE).

The production of freshwater organisms in SE Asia was studied as part of the researches of the International Biological Program. A general survey was carried out from Oct. 5, 1970-April 10, 1971. Zooplankton, phytoplankton, small attached animals and benthic animals were studied.--Copyright 1974, Biological Abstracts, Inc.
W75-06838

ELECTRON-MICROSCOPICAL INVESTIGATIONS ON WAX-COVERED STOMATAS, (IN GERMAN),
Universitaet Hohenheim (Landwirtschaftliche Hochschule)(West Germany) Laboratorium fuer Elektronenmikroskopie.
I. Rentschler.
Planta (Berl), Vol 117, No 2, p 153-161, 1974. Illus. English summary.
Identifiers: Brassica-napus, Chelidonium-majus, *Electron microscopy, Humidity, *Leaves, Nelumbo-nucifera, *Stomatas(Wax-covered), Transpiration, Tropaeolum-majns.

The wax structure of plant leaves (Brassica napus, Chelidonium majus, Tropaeolum majus, Nelumbo nucifera) was investigated by scanning electron microscopy and with the replica technique by transmission electron microscopy. In addition to replicas of the wax layer, replicas of the leaf surface after removal of the wax were examined. The wax layer is very thick and felt-like, especially when the plants were grown at low humidity. In this case the stomatas were also smaller than those of plants grown at high humidity. The amount of transpiration of leaves was correlated to the different formation of the wax layer. Thick and felt-like structure of the wax above the stomatas reduces the water loss considerably. On the other hand all water evaporates from leaves in a short time after removal of the wax.--Copyright 1974, Biological Abstracts, Inc.
W75-06842

THE FLOATING LOG AND STUMP COMMUNITIES IN THE SANTEE SWAMP OF SOUTH CAROLINA,
South Carolina Univ., Columbia. Dept. of Biology.
W. M. Dennis, and W. T. Batson.
Castanea, Vol 39, No 2, p 166-170, 1974.

Descriptors: Boehmeria-cylindrica, *Biological communities, Density, Floating logs, Frequency, Hypericum-walteri, Log, *South Carolina, Stump, *Swamps, Vitality, *Santee Swamp(SC).

A study was made of the floating log and stump communities of the Santee Swamp, Sumter County, South Carolina. The species inhabiting these communities were identified; percent frequency, mean density and vitality were determined; and the substrate was characterized as to species, degree of decay and position, as floating or attached. Twenty-four species were recorded in the 30 samples studied. The communities were homogeneous as to dominants with 2 spp., Hypericum walteri and Boehmeria cylindrica having frequency values in the 80-100% class and 19 spp. with frequency values in the 0-20% class.--Copyright 1974, Biological Abstracts, Inc.
W75-06845

AVAILABILITY OF AMINO ACIDS OF RATIONS WITH A PREDOMINANCE OF FISH

MEAL AND SPLEEN FOR TWO-YEAR-OLD RAINBOW TROUT SALMO IRIDEUS, (IN RUSSIAN),
Vsesoyuzni Nauchno-Issledovatelskii Institut Prudovogo Rybnogo Khoziaistva, Rybnoe (USSR).
M. A. Shcherbina, and S. P. Tryamkina.
Vopr Ikhtiol, Vol 14, No 1, p 128-133, 1974.
Identifiers: *Amino-acids, Availability, *Fish meal, *Rainbow trout, Rations, Salmo-irideus, Spleen, Trout, Fish foods.

The availability of amino acids was determined in 2 qualitatively different rations for pond-reared rainbow trout (S. irideus), one of which contained 55% spleen and 15% fish mean and the other 35% fish meal without spleen. Experimental data are given on the content of 9 indispensable amino acids (lysine, histidine, arginine, threonine, methionine, valine, phenylalanine, isoleucine and leucine), 6 nonessential amino acids (aspartic acid, serine, glycine, glutamic acid, alpha-alanine, tyrosine) in rations, the indices of their availability for 2-yr trout and the amino acid requirement of trout. Problems of the correspondence of the trout's requirements and the quantitative content of available amino acids in rations are discussed.--Copyright 1974, Biological Abstracts, Inc.
W75-06847

CESTODES IN FISH FROM A POND AT ILE-IFE, NIGERIA,
Ife Univ. (Nigeria). Dept. of Biological Sciences.
E. A. Aderounmu, and F. Aneniyi.
Afr J Trop Hydrobiol Fish, Vol 2, No 2, p 151-156, 1972.
Identifiers: Anomotaenia-sp, *Cestodes, Clarias-lazera, *Fish, Floods, Hemichromis-fasciatus, Heterobranchus-bidorsalis, Intestine, Lumen, *Nigeria(Ile-Ife), Polyonocobothrium-clarias, Ponds, Tilapia-nilotica.

About 55% of the fish examined at Ile-Ife, Nigeria, including Clarias lazera, Heterobranchus bidorsalis, Tilapia nilotica and Hemichromis fasciatus, were infected with endoparasites. Anomotaenia sp. (Cestoda) was found in the upper intestines of Hemichromis fasciatus and T. nilotica. This is the 1st record of this parasite in Nigeria and the 1st host record for H. fasciatus. Polyoncobothrium clarias (Cestoda) was found in the intestinal lumen of C. lazera. A lessening of infection from Nov. to Jan. in H. fasciatus and T. nilotica was noted; this decrease corresponded to the gradual subsiding of annual floods.--Copyright 1974, Biological Abstracts, Inc.
W75-06849

2J. Erosion and Sedimentation

THE REMOTE SENSING OF SUSPENDED SEDIMENT CONCENTRATIONS OF SMALL IMPOUNDMENTS,
Agricultural Research Service, Chickasha, Okla. Southern Great Plains Watershed Research Center.
For primary bibliographic entry see Field 7B.
W75-06399

JACKSON HOLE FLOOD CONTROL PROJECT,
Committee on Channel Stabilization (Army).
For primary bibliographic entry see Field 4A.
W75-06475

BEACH PROCESSES ON THE OREGON COAST, JULY, 1973,
Williams Coll., Williamstown, Mass.
For primary bibliographic entry see Field 2L.
W75-06493

BED FORM RESPONSE TO NONSTEADY FLOWS,
Army Engineer District, Sacramento, Calif.
D. M. Gee.
Journal of the Hydraulics Division, American Society of Civil Engineers, Vol 101, No HY3, Proceedings Paper 11195, p 437-449, March 1975. 7 fig, 2 tab, 8 ref, 2 append. NSF Grant GK-19907.

Descriptors: *Dunes, *Bed load, *Sand bars, *Sediment transport, *Flumes, Laboratory tests, Hydraulic roughness, Rivers, Flood flow, Sedimentation, Energy gradient, Hydraulics, Steady flow.
Identifiers: *Bed forms.

Sediment transport affects the stage-discharge relationship of an alluvial river during a flood event. Changes in bed form in response to changes in discharge and the response times were studied in laboratory flumes. A flood event was viewed as a series of discharges, all characterized by uniform flow at constant energy slope. The bed form response was studied by forcing a transition of bed forms between two distinct equilibrium states. The experiments were conducted in a long recirculating type flume in the Hydraulic Laboratory of the Unversity of California at Berkeley. The bed load transport rate varied during a transition. The response time was defined as that time required for 95% of the change from the initial to the final (the equilibrium) depth to occur. The generation of dunes appeared to proceed at a greater efficiency than the destruction of dunes. The mechanism by which the bar dimensions change is the transport of bed material as bed load. The bar roughness of a natural stream and the discharge may become out of equilibrium if the dischage changes more rapidly than the transport rate can alter the bar roughness. This disequilibrium may contribute to nonunique rating curves observed for some streams during flood events. (Singh-ISWS)
W75-06533

COULEE ALIGNMENT AND THE WIND IN SOUTHERN ALBERTA, CANADA,
Lethbridge Univ. (Alberta). Dept. of Geography.
C. B. Beaty.
Geological Society of America Bulletin, Vol 86, No 1, p 119-128, January 1975. 9 fig, 1 tab, 38 ref.

Descriptors: *Canada, *Geomorphology, *Winds, Joints(Geologic), Chinook, Recent epoch, Drainage patterns(Geologic), Erosion, Wind erosion, Canyons, Valleys, Distribution patterns, Dunes, Streams.
Identifiers: *Coulees, Alberta, Rose diagrams, Alignment patterns.

Study of the distincitive pattern of alignment and geographical distribution of more than 250 coulees in the plains of southern Alberta shows that (1) the coulees in question have a mean orientation of N 70 degrees E, and (2) their spatial distribution is not ubiquitous but rather displays a concentration in the area from Lethbridge west to the Rocky Mountain front. Several possible hypotheses of origin of the aligned coulees were considered, including subsurface structural control, the role of regional slope, the effect of lithologic differences, and wind action. Action of postglacial wind, operating to initiate surface furrows (by wind-driven snow or rain) that were enlarged by running water, accounts for the three outstanding characteristics of the aligned coulees: (1) their preferred orientation of N 70 degrees E, which approximates the mean direction of the strongest chinook winds in the southern Alberta plains; (2) their geographical distribution, which coincides with that part of the region experiencing the most pronounced chinooks; and (3) their almost exclusive location on windward topographic surfaces. No other hypothesis of origin is known that can satisfactorily explain all of these observed facts. (Visocky-ISWS)
W75-06543

THE COASTAL SEDIMENT COMPARTMENT,
Macquarie Univ., North Ryde (Australia). School of Earth Sciences.
For primary bibliographic entry see Field 2L.
W75-06551

BEACH EROSION CONTROL--TRUST FUND ACCOUNT.
For primary bibliographic entry see Field 6E.
W75-06597

STORM RUNOFF AND TRANSPORT OF RADIONUCLIDES IN DP CANYON, LOS ALAMOS COUNTY, NEW MEXICO,
Los Alamos Scientific Lab., N. Mex.
For primary bibliographic entry see Field 5B.
W75-06636

SEDIMENT SAMPLING NEAR MOUND LABORATORY - JULY 1974,
Health and Safety Lab. (AEC), New York.
For primary bibliographic entry see Field 5A.
W75-06800

2K. Chemical Processes

AUTOMATED ANALYSIS FOR CYANIDE,
Technicon Industrial Systems, Tarrytown, N.Y.
For primary bibliographic entry see Field 5A.
W75-06403

LANDFORM-SOIL-VEGETATION-WATER CHEMISTRY RELATIONSHIPS, WRIGLEY AREA, N.W.T.: II. CHEMICAL, PHYSICAL, AND MINERALOGICAL DETERMINATIONS AND RELATIONSHIPS,
British Columbia Univ., Vancouver. Department of Soil Science.
For primary bibliographic entry see Field 2G.
W75-06440

THE EFFECT OF INCREASES IN THE ATMOSPHERIC CARBON DIOXIDE CONTENT ON THE CARBONATE ION CONCENTRATION OF SURFACE OCEAN WATER AT 25C,
Liverpool Univ. (England). Donnan Labs.
G. Skirrow, and M. Whitfield.
Limnology and Oceanography, Vol 20, No 1, p 103-108, January 1975. 2 fig, 3 tab, 14 ref.

Descriptors: *Carbon dioxide, *Oceans, *Atmospheric pressure, Water properties, *Gases, Atmosphere, Inorganic compounds, Oxides, Carbonates, Bicarbonates, Calcite, Pressure, Physical properties, Sea water, Alkalinity, Temperature, Thermal properties, Stability, Supersaturation, Calcite, Climatology, Fossil fuels.
Identifiers: *Partial pressure, Oceanic mixed layer, Aragonite.

Equilibrium thermodynamics was used to assess the influence of predicted fossil carbon dioxide injections on the carbonate ion concentration in the oceanic mixed layer at 25C. The calculations indicated that a ten-fold increase is required in the atmospheric partial pressure of carbon dioxide to reduce the carbonate ion concentration to a level where calcite would begin to dissolve. This is at least three times the highest predicted partial pressure for atmospheric carbon dioxide. This result contradicts a number of recent claims that the calcite saturation level would be attained within the next 30 years. Such rapid removal of carbonate ions is only possible if the mixed layer is grossly out of equilibrium with the atmosphere. (Henley-ISWS)
W75-06444

OXYGEN AND SULFUR ISOTOPIC COMPOSITION OF THE SULFATE IONS FROM MINERAL AND THERMAL GROUNDWATERS OF POLAND,
Comitato Nazionale per le Ricerche Nucleari, Pisa (Italy). Laboratorio di Geologia Nucleare.

For primary bibliographic entry see Field 5A.
W75-06455

CHLORIDES IN NATURAL AND ARTIFICIAL HAILSTONES,
Istituto di Fisica dell'Atmosfera, Verona (Italy). Osservatorio Scientifico.
For primary bibliographic entry see Field 2B.
W75-06500

BACKGROUND SILVER CONCENTRATIONS IN ILLINOIS PRECIPITATION AND RIVER WATER,
Illinois State Water Survey, Urbana.
For primary bibliographic entry see Field 5A.
W75-06506

THE EFFECT OF ALCOHOLS ON THE CARBONIC ACID DEHYDRATION REACTION,
Oklahoma Univ,. Norman. Dept. of Chemistry.
For primary bibliographic entry see Field 5A.
W75-06521

STUDY OF THE PHYSICOCHEMISTRY OF A RIVER SYSTEM IN THE FRENCH MORVAN: I. HOURLY VARIATIONS, (IN FRENCH),
Institut National de la Recherche Agronomique, Thononles-Bains (France). Station d'Hydrobiologie Lacustre.
J. Feuillade.
Ann Hydrobiol. Vol 3, No 1, p 47-57, 1972, Illus.

Descriptors: *Rivers, Europe, *Water chemistry, *Water analysis, Solar energy.
Identifiers: *France(River Cure).

Variations of water physicochemistry, sunlight and air temperature were measured hourly during a day in May 1967, in the river Cure (French Morvan). The results are graphically discussed and with the help of a principal component analysis. Variations in water are not important over an hour. The statistical analysis points out the importance of sunlight over all other factors.--Copyright 1973, Biological Abstracts, Inc.
W75-06523

DISTRIBUTION OF ISOTOPES IN SOME NATURAL WATERS IN THE REGION NORTH OF MT. JOLMO LUNGMA.
Sci Sin. Vol 16, No 4, p 560-564, 1973, Illus.

Descriptors: Arctic, Ice, Glaciers, Snow, Rivers, Lakes, Oceans, Sea water, *Natural streams, Deuterium, Oxygen, *Isotope studies, Analytical techniques.
Identifiers: Mt. Jolmo Lungma, Oxygen-18, High altitudes, China.

Samples of glacial ice, pack snow and water from rivers, lakes and a spring at altitudes of 4550-7029 m in the region north of Mt. Jolmo Lungma show that the contents of deuterium and oxygen-18 are all lower than those in standard mean ocean water. In general, deuterium is comparatively less depleted in the solid than in the liquid phase. With regard to isotope altitude effect, age effect, profile isotopic composition and isotope concentration in the plateau-lake, the data observed are in conformity with the environmental factors.--Copyright 1974, Biological Abstracts, Inc.
W75-06699

THE SOLUBILITY OF SILICA IN CARBONATE WATERS,
L. R. Pittwell.
J Hydrol (Amst). Vol 21, No 3, p 299-300, 1974, Illus.

Descriptors: *Carbonates, *Silica, *Solubility, Silicates, Chemical reactions, Precipitates.
Identifiers: Bicarbonate.

The solubility of silica in water was determined by Vinogradov in 1966 and shown to be dependent on pH, but the alkaline side was not investigated, and there is also the problem of bicarbonates, which though mildly alkaline in pH, are potentially capable of reacting with silicates to form silica and a normal carbonate. Many natural waters exist which do contain appreciable amounts of silica and bicarbonate. It is therefore of interest to know just how close these may be to precipitating silica. This was determined experimentally.--Copyright 1974, Biological Abstracts, Inc.
W75-06703

BUILDING STONES OF MODERN PHYSIOLOGY: ECOPHYSIOLOGY OF PLANTS,
For primary bibliographic entry see Field 2I.
W75-06709

RELATIONS AMONG PH, CARBON DIOXIDE PRESSURE, ALAKLINITY, AND CALCIUM CONCENTRATION IN WATERS SATURATED WITH RESPECT TO CALCITE AT 25C AND ONE ATMOSPHERE TOTAL PRESSURE,
Wyoming Univ., Laramie. Dept. of Geology.
J. I. Drever.
Contrib Geol Univ Wyo. Vol 11, No 2, p 41-42, 1972, Illus.
Identifiers: *Alkalinity, Atmospheric pressure, *Calcite, *Calcium, *Carbon dioxide, Saturated waters, Hydrogen ion concentration.

Relations among pH, alkalinity, CO2 pressure and Ca concentration for calcite saturated water at 25C were calculated by computer and presented in the form of a graph. This graph allows various problems involving the carbonate system in natural waters to be solved by inspection, rather than by hand calculation.--Copyright 1974, Biological Abstracts, Inc.
W75-06711

DATA ON THE HYDROBIOLOGICAL RELATIONSHIPS OF THE BACKWATER OF THE BODROG RIVER NEAR SAROSPATAK: I. PRELIMINARY STUDIES ON THE DETERMINATION OF CHARACTERISTICS OF OXYGEN AND CARBON DIOXIDE BALANCE IN THE BACK-WATER,
Lajos Kossuth Univ., Debrecen (Hungary). Zoological Inst.
For primary bibliographic entry see Field 5A.
W75-06720

STUDY OF PRIMARY OXYGEN PRODUCTION IN THE HUNGARIAN SECTION OF THE DANUBE (DANUBIALIA HUNGARICA LVIII),
Magyar Tudomanyos Akademia, Budapest. Station for Danube Research.
For primary bibliographic entry see Field 5A.
W75-06721

INTERLABORATORY QUALITY CONTROL STUDY NO. 7 - MAJOR CATIONS AND ANIONS,
Canada Centre for Inland Waters, Burlington (Ontario).
D. J. McGirr, and R. W. Wales.
Report Series No. 30, 15 p, 1973, Inland Waters Directorate. 9 ref, 19 tab, append.

Descriptors: *Laboratory tests, *Quality control, *Cations, *Anions, Calcium, Magnesium, Sodium, Potassium, Alkalinity, Chloride, Sulfate, Nitrate, Hardness, Flame, Photometry, Evaluation.
Identifiers: Atomic absorption, Emission, Cadmium reduction, Titration.

Two synthetic samples and one natural water sample were distributed to twenty-two participating laboratories for determination of calcium, magnesium, sodium, potassium, alkalinity, chloride, sulfate and nitrate. The results for calcium, magnesium and alkalinity were good even though the natural sample was unstable for these three parameters. The precision for calcium and total hardness was much better by titration than by atomic absorption. Precision and accuracy were good for sodium and potassium, and precision was about the same whether atomic absorption or flame emission photometry was used. Precision for nitrate at low levels was only fair by any of the variety of methods used, although the cadmium reduction method was satisfactory at higher levels. Sulfate was also determined by a variety of methods, but precision was satisfactory for most of them. Chloride was determined with acceptable precision. The natural sample was supersaturated with carbonates and therefore was unstable with respect to calcium, magnesium and alkalinity. It was stable, however, with respect to the other parameters and the synthetic samples were stable with regard to all parameters tested over a three-month period of storage. Precision and accuracy were not seriously adversely affected by either sample instability or long-distance shipment. (Environment Canada)
W75-06747

AN ASSESSMENT OF AREAL AND TEMPORAL VARIATIONS IN STREAMFLOW QUALITY USING SELECTED DATA FROM THE NATIONAL STREAM QUALITY ACCOUNTING NETWORK,
Geological Survey, Reston, Va.
For primary bibliographic entry see Field 5B.
W75-06755

THE DISTRIBUTION OF MINOR ELEMENTS BETWEEN COEXISTING CALCITE AND DOLOMITE IN THE GASPORT MEMBER OF THE LOCKPORT FORMATION, LOCKPORT, NEW YORK,
State Univ. of New York, Buffalo.
P. J. Michalski.
MA Thesis 1969. 53 p, 14 fig, 5 tab, 21 ref, 2 append.

Descriptors: *Dolomite, *Calcite, *Magnesium, *Magnesium carbonate, *Diagenesis, Sedimentation, Rates, Sedimentation rate, *New York.
Identifiers: Gasport member, Lockport formation(N.Y.), Selective dolomitization.

Analysis of the carbonates (calcite and dolomite) in the Gasport Member of the Lockport Formation indicates that Fe and Mg contents are proportional to the dolomite concentration, and may be involved in the dolomitization process. The separate analysis of each of the coexisting carbonate phases indicates large amounts of Mg, Fe and Mn may substitute in calcite prior to or during dolomitization. Petrographic and chemical evidence indicates the incorporation of Mg, Fe and Mn in calcite may be an intermediate step in the formation of dolomite. The increased concentration of these elements in calcite as dolomitization proceeds may represent arrested stages of dolomitization. Selective dolomitization is known to proceed at different rates, and in many stages; it may begin as early as deposition of the carbonate muds and continue through diagenesis. Fossil material, consisting of principally calcite, swept into partially dolomitized carbonate muds would react slowly and have a lower final dolomite content than their matrix unless sufficient time was available for equilibrium to be achieved. (Bradbeer-NWWA)
W75-06811

2L. Estuaries

CONTRIBUTIONS OF TIDAL WETLANDS TO ESTUARINE FOOD CHAINS,
Maryland Univ., Prince Frederick. Center for Environmental and Estuarine Studies.
For primary bibliographic entry see Field 5C.
W75-06353

ESTUARINE POLLUTION IN THE STATE OF HAWAII, VOLUME 2: KANEOHE BAY STUDY,
Hawaii Univ., Honolulu. Water Resources Research Center.
For primary bibliographic entry see Field 5B.
W75-06362

A STUDY OF LAGOONAL AND ESTUARINE PROCESSES AND ARTIFICIAL HABITATS IN THE AREA OF THE JOHN F. KENNEDY SPACE CENTER,
Bethune-Cookman Coll., Dayton Beach, Fla.
P. Poonsi.
Available from the National Technical Information Service, Springfield, Va 22161 as N74-20718, $3.75 in paper copy, $2.25 in microfiche. Report NASA CR-137409, (1974). 31 p, 24 ref, 6 tab, 5 fig.

Descriptors: Habitats, *Reefs, *Biomass, *Estuaries, *Fish habitats, Biological communities, Trophic levels, Sport fish, Statistical models.
Identifiers: *Artificial habitats(Fish), Biodynamics, Tires.

The influence of an artificial habitat of discarded automobile tires upon the biomass in and around it was studied, using three sites on the Banana River. One site served as a control and the other two as locations for small tire reefs. Measurements and correlation studies of the biomasses and species indicate that the biodynamics of the sites are appreciably the same in the three cases, that there are probably adequate populations at the lower trophic levels, that there are perhaps reduced numbers of upper level carnivores and that it is likely that small artificial havens can contribute to an increase in populations of certain species of gamefish. (Katz)
W75-06395

PRIMARY AMINES IN CALIFORNIA COASTAL WATERS: UTILIZATION BY PHYTOPLANKTON,
California Univ., Irvine. Dept. of Developmental and Cell Biology.
For primary bibliographic entry see Field 5A.
W75-06443

THE EFFECT OF INCREASES IN THE ATMOSPHERIC CARBON DIOXIDE CONTENT ON THE CARBONATE ION CONCENTRATION OF SURFACE OCEAN WATER AT 25C,
Liverpool Univ. (England). Donnan Labs.
For primary bibliographic entry see Field 2K.
W75-06444

WIND STRESS ON NEARSHORE AND LAGOONAL WATERS OF A TROPICAL ISLAND,
Louisiana State Univ., Baton Rouge. Coastal Studies Inst.
S. A. Hsu.
Limnology and Oceanography, Vol 20, No 1, p 113-115, January 1975. 3 fig, 10 ref. ONR Contract N00014-69-A-0211-0003.

Descriptors: *Winds, *Ocean waves, Waves(Water), Lagoons, Tropical regions, Wind velocity, Shear, Stress, Shear stress, Oceans, Islands.
Identifiers: *Wind stress, *West Indies(Barbados).

Wind profiles were measured over a windward lagoon and a quasi-leeward area in Barbados, West Indies, under the prevailing trade winds. Relationships between shear and wind velocities for these environments were determined. Under average wind conditions the shear stress on these coastal waters is about 72% of that of an oceanic region. (Jones-ISWS)
W75-06445

RATIONAL PROTECTION OF WATER RESOURCES IN COASTAL ZONES THROUGH PLANNED DEVELOPMENT,
Florida Univ., Gainesville. Dept. of Civil and Coastal Engineering.
For primary bibliographic entry see Field 4B.
W75-06446

A THREE DIMENSIONAL WAVE MAKER, ITS THEORY AND APPLICATION,
Massachusetts Inst. of Tech., Cambridge. Dept. of Civil Engineering.
O. S. Madsen.
Journal of hydraulic Research, Vol 12, No 2, p 205-222, 1974. 2 fig, 11 ref. U. S. Army Contract DACW72-72-C-0023.

Descriptors: *Waves(Water), Theoretical analysis, *Laboratory tests, *Beaches, *Rip currents, Breakwaters, Surf, Sediment transport, Hydraulics, Flumes.
Identifiers: Progressive waves, *Three dimensional wavemaker, Incident waves.

A general wave maker theory was presented and used as a guide in the design of a new type of wave generator, the transverse-wave maker, a simple form of which was tested and found to generate waves in good agreement with theoretical predictions. The analogy between the wave motion generated by this type of wave maker and that of obliquely incident waves on a fully reflecting straight breakwater was noticed. The transverse-wave maker may be used to study the three dimensional wave motion and resulting wave induced currents occurring in the vicinity of a groin, jetty, or breakwater extending perpendicular to a gently sloping beach. Qualitative observations of the conditions in the surf zone during testing showed the formation of a very strong rip current in the center of the flume. This rip current tended to be diverted away from the centerline toward one side wall of the flume outside the surf zone. This type of transverse-wave maker may be modified to generate any desired mode of transverse waves by subdividing a plane wave maker into the appropriate number of separate flaps, the design being based on considerations of the sinusoidal variation across the flume of the desired transverse wave. (Bhowmik-ISWS)
W75-06457

PLUNGER-TYPE WAVEMAKERS: THEORY AND EXPERIMENT,
Tetra Tech, Inc., Pasadena, Calif.
S. Wang.
Journal of Hydraulic Research, Vol 12, No 3, p 357-388, 1974. 12 fig, 2 tab, 10 ref.

Descriptors: *Waves(Water), *Laboratory tests, *Mathematical models, *Deep water, Shallow water, Beaches, Theoretical analysis, Hydraulics, Flow.
Identifiers: *Plunger-type wavemakers, Irrotational flow, Oscillation, Conformal transformation.

The theory and the experimental results of a plunger-type wavemaker which generates waves by oscillating vertically in the water surface were described. A mathematical theory was presented, through which surface waves generated by a given form of plunger can be calculated as a function of plunger period and stroke. The theory was based upon the usual assumptions that the fluid is ideal, the flow is irrotational, and all motions are small. The water was considered deep, hence no effect of water depth entered into the analysis. While the theory is valid only for deep-water wave generation, results were shown applicable for laboratory channels of a finite depth. The effect of the plunger geometry was assumed to be governed solely by two parameters, the depth-width ratio and the sectional area coefficient. Experiments using triangular wedge-shape plungers of two different depth-width ratios were conducted in a wave tank. Results showed that the average scatter of the measured wave height about the theoretical prediction was 6.5%. It was considered that the theory can be used with confidence for the triangular-type plunger. No experiments for plungers of other form were conducted and no measurements of forces were included in the experiments. (Bhowmik-ISWS)
W75-06458

EVIDENCE OF SHOREFACE RETREAT AND IN-PLACE 'DROWNING' DURING HOLOCENE SUBMERGENCE OF BARRIERS, SHELF OFF FIRE ISLAND, NEW YORK,
Barnard Coll., New York. Dept. of Geology and Geography.
J. E. Sanders, and N. Kumar.
Geological Society of America Bulletin, Vol 86, No 1, p 65-76, January 1975. 12 fig, 1 tab, 46 ref. NSF Grant GA-25792.

Descriptors: *Shores, *Drowned(Submerged), *Submergence, Recent epoch, Dunes, Deposition(Sediments), Lagoons, Oceans, Sea level, Beaches, Coasts, Ocean waves, Environment, Sediments, Barrier islands, Sieve analysis, Continental shelf, *New York.
Identifiers: *Fire Island(NY), *Long Island(NY), In-place drowning, Shoreface retreat.

At different times within the Holocene period, the barriers on the shelf off Fire Island, Long Island, New York, have responded to submergency through the contrasting processes of in-place drowning and landward retreat. In-place drowning is indicated by evidence of a relict shoreline 7 km seaward of the present beach at a depth of -24 m. Based on published submergence curves, this inferred relict shoreline is tentatively dated at 8500 to 9000 yr B.P. Two cores collected seaward of the present beach in 14 to 16 m of water contain backbarrier saltmarsh peat which has been dated at 7750 + or -125 and 7585 + or -125 radiocarbon years. These cores are evidence that the -16 m barrier migrated continuously landward and eventually became the modern barrier. Inlet-filling sands can serve as indicators of former locations of barriers and as criteria for determining whether barriers have been drowned in place or have migrated landward. If a barrier migrates continuously landward, it should leave behind a blanket of inlet-filling sands. If a barrier drowns in place, inlet-filling sands should form only narrow, linear lenses parallel to the shore. (Visocky-ISWS)
W75-06460

ENVIRONMENTAL STUDIES (1973), JAMES BAY TERRITORY AND SURROUNDING AREA,
Department of the Environment, Hull (Quebec); and James Bay Development Corp., Montreal (Quebec).
For primary bibliographic entry see Field 6G.
W75-06467

BEACH PROCESSES ON THE OREGON COAST, JULY, 1973,
Williams Coll., Williamstown, Mass.
W. T. Fox, and R. A. Davis, Jr.
Available from the National Technical Information Service, Springfield, Va 22161 as AD-786 237, $4.75 in paper copy, $2.25 in microfiche. Technical Report 12, August 30, 1974. 85 p, 32 fig, 28 ref, 2 append. ONR Contract N00014-69-C-0151.

Descriptors: *Beach erosion, *Waves(Water), *Tides, *Weather, *Sand bars, *Winds, Upwelling, Rip currents, Surf, Oregon, Atmospheric pressure, Coasts, Fourier analysis.
Identifiers: *Longshore currents, Bar morphology.

During July and August 1973, a 45-day time-series study was undertaken on the central Oregon coast to relate weather and wave conditions to beach erosion and sand bar migration. The summer

weather pattern was dominated by the East-Pacific subtropical high which produced winds and waves from the northwest and extended periods of upwelling and coastal fog. When low pressure systems moved through, wind and waves shifted to the southwest. Waves were 1 to 3 meters high with periods of 5 to 9 seconds. Rip currents and southward flowing longshore currents reached 90 centimeters per second in the surf zone. Tide range was 2 to 4 meters. Three beaches were mapped at low tide to show changes in beach and bar morphology through time. At South Beach, Oregon, two sets of bars with intervening rip channels advanced shoreward at 1 to 5 meters per day and southward at 10 to 15 meters per day. At Beverly Beach, Oregon, a basalt ridge 700 meters offshore resulted in wave diffraction and sand deposition in the central portion of the beach. A rip channel at the south end of the beach moved 300 meters to the south. At Gleneden Beach, cusps 40 meters long were cut into the steep foreshore. A rhythmic topography with bars and rip channels existed in the nearshore. Sand bars advanced across the rip channels at 5 meters per day and welded onto the base of the foreshore. (Bhowmik-ISWS)
W75-06493

THE COASTAL SEDIMENT COMPARTMENT,
Macquarie Univ., North Ryde (Australia). School of Earth Sciences.
J. L. Davies.
Australian Geographical Studies, Vol 12, No 2, p 139-151, October 1974. 2 fig, 20 ref.

Descriptors: *Coasts, *Australia, *Sediment distribution, Seashores, *Beach erosion, Sedimentation, Dunes, Littoral, Quaternary period, Sea level, Waves(Water).
Identifiers: Coastal sediment compartment.

Definition of coastal sediment compartments appears necessary to the quantification of sediment budgets and the apparent general nature of such compartments and budgets in south eastern Australia is reviewed. The present situation, in which loss by deflation, inlet filling and offshore movement appears to balance or exceed gain from marine and subaerial erosion and onshore movement is contrasted with that in the mid-Holocene when it appears that many shores prograded. It is concluded that this progradation was related not to changes in sea level nor wave energy but to an excess of gain over loss due to an unusually large input from offshore. It may be possible to distinguish a broad cyclic pattern of budget progression through time within individual compartments. (Levick-CSIRO)
W75-06551

HEAVY METALS IN CULTIVATED OYSTERS (CRASSOSTREA COMMERCIALIS = SACCOSTREA CUCULLATA) FROM THE ESTUARIES OF NEW SOUTH WALES (AUSTRALIA),
Chief Secretary's Dept. , Sydney (Australia). New South Wales Fisheries Branch.
For primary bibliographic entry see Field 5B.
W75-06552

THE WESTERNPORT BAY ENVIRONMENTAL STUDY,
Victoria Ministry for Conservation, Melbourne (Australia). Westernport Bay Environmental Study.
For primary bibliographic entry see Field 6G.
W75-06555

THE UNCERTAIN SEARCH FOR ENVIRONMENTAL QUALITY,
Yale Univ., New Haven, Conn. School of Law.
For primary bibliographic entry see Field 5G.
W75-06557

MISSISSIPPI COASTAL ZONE MANAGEMENT APPLICATION 1974.
Mississippi Marine Resources Council, Long Beach.
For primary bibliographic entry see Field 6E.
W75-06575

PRESERVATION OF WETLANDS: THE CASE OF SAN FRANCISCO BAY,
Environmental Protection Agency, Washington, D.C. Office of Water Programs.
For primary bibliographic entry see Field 4A.
W75-06592

BISCAYNE BAY--AQUATIC PRESERVE.
For primary bibliographic entry see Field 6E.
W75-06598

ECOLOGICAL EFFECTS OF NUCLEAR STEAM ELECTRIC STATION OPERATIONS ON ESTUARINE SYSTEMS.
Maryland Univ., Prince Frederick. Center for Environmental and Estuarine Research.
For primary bibliographic entry see Field 5C.
W75-06621

AMMONIA EXCRETION BY ZOOPLANKTON AND ITS SIGNIFICANCE TO PRIMARY PRODUCTIVITY DURING SUMMER,
Washington Univ., Seattle. Dept. of Oceanography.
For primary bibliographic entry see Field 5C.
W75-06637

ELEMENTS IN A DECISION FRAMEWORK FOR PLANNING THE ALLOCATION OF COASTAL LAND AND WATER RESOURCES WITH ILLUSTRATION FOR A COASTAL COMMUNITY,
Massachusetts Univ., Amherst. Dept. of Agricultural and Food Economics.
For primary bibliographic entry see Field 6B.
W75-06645

DISSOLVED ORGANIC MATERIAL IN THE ST. LAWRENCE MARITIME ESTUARY: COMPARISON AND CHOICE OF METHODS (IN FRENCH),
For primary bibliographic entry see Field 5A.
W75-06706

LATE-STAGE PUBLIC MEETING STUDY OF THE NEW JERSEY COASTAL INLETS AND BEACHES FROM BARNEGAT INLET TO LONGPORT,
Army Engineer District, Philadelphia, Pa.
For primary bibliographic entry see Field 4D.
W75-06766

THE INTERCOASTAL WATERWAY: AN ECOLOGICAL PERSPECTIVE,
Florida Atlantic Univ., Boca Raton. Dept. of Biological Sciences.
For primary bibliographic entry see Field 5G.
W75-06776

COMPREHENSIVE LAND USE PLANNING-ITS DEVELOPMENT AND POTENTIAL IMPACT ON COASTAL ZONE MANAGEMENT,
Rhode Island Univ., Kingston. Marine Affairs Program.
For primary bibliographic entry see Field 4A.
W75-06787

COASTAL ZONE PLANNING: THE IMPACT OF REGIONAL EFFORTS IN NEW ENGLAND,
Woods Hole Oceanographic Institution, Mass.
For primary bibliographic entry see Field 6F.
W75-06790

DYE AND DROGUE STUDIES OF SPOIL DISPOSAL AND OIL DISPERSION,
Delaware Univ., Newark. Coll. of Marine Studies.
For primary bibliographic entry see Field 5B.
W75-06831

NEW INDICATOR SPECIES IN THE BALTIC ZOOPLANKTON IN 1972,
Wyzsza Szkola Rolnicza, Szczecin (Poland). Instytut Eksploatacji Zasobow Morza.
For primary bibliographic entry see Field 5B.
W75-06837

THE SEDIMENTARY ENVIRONMENTS OF TROPICAL AFRICAN ESTUARIES: FREETOWN PENINSULA, SIERRA LEONE,
University Coll., Cardiff (Wales). Dept. of Geology.
M. E. Tucker.
Geol Mijnbouw, Vol 52, No 4, p 203-215, 1973. Illus.
Identifiers: Africa, Bivalves, Crustaceans, Dry, Environment, *Estuaries, Mangroves, Peninsulas, River, Seas, Season, *Sierra-Leone(Freetown), Soils, Tropical zones, *Sediment transport.

Four main environments are described from tropical estuaries of the Freetown Peninsula, Sierra Leone: sand bars, channels, intertidal flats and mangrove swamps. The sand bars are predominantly well-sorted medium sands, and dunes as the main bed form. The channel sediments vary in grain size and bed form up the estuaries, but generally contain lag deposits (mostly of shell debris and laterite pebbles) coarser than the adjacent intertidal sediments. The intertidal flats are mostly muddy sands, commonly with scour pits and current lineation. The sedimentary structures are obliterated by infaunal bivalves and burrowing crustaceans. The mangroves, developed peripherally around the estuaries, are important in trapping and binding finer grades of sediment. Sierra Leone has an extreme 2 season climate, considerably affecting the estuarine sediments. During the dry season, a period of accretion, much sediment (mainly bed load) is taken into the estuaries from offshore. Crustaceans and bivalves increase in numbers and occupy a larger area of the intertidal flats. During the wet season, mud and plant debris are brought down by the rivers and some bed load is moved down or out of the estuaries. With rising sea level, the estuarine deposits are prograding landward, over fluviatile sediments and soils (laterite in this case), producing a coarsening upward sequence from rootlet beds through bioturbated muddy sands to well-sorted cross-bedded medium sands.--Copyright 1974, Biological Abstracts, Inc.
W75-06840

PRELIMINARY STUDY, WITH EMPHASIS ON PLANKTON, OF THE WATERS FROM THE TODOS OS SANTOS BAY, (IN PORTEGUESE),
Universidade Federal da Bahia, Salvador (Brazil). Inst. of Biology.
J. J. Santos.
Bol Zool Biol Mar (Nova Ser), 30 p 419-447, 1973. Illus. English summary.
Identifiers: *Bays, *Brazil plankton(Todos os Santos Bay), *Estuary, *Phytoplankton, Puerto Rico, Zooplankton.

A preliminary study of the waters in the 800 km2 area of the Baia de Todos os Santos (Brazil) includes an introductory survey of the literature on the plankton collected in the region, the methods used for obtaining information on some meteorological, hydrological and hydrographical data, and on the phytoplankton and the zooplankton of the area. The study of 17 plankton samples taken at different points inside the bay are discussed and compared with those obtained from other waters along the Brazilian coast and in Puerto Rico. The water in most of the bay is coastal water enriched by the nutrients drained from the

continent. The plankton is proportionally richer with smaller forms inside the bay than outside, off the coast. The bay contains a typically neritic planktonic structure in which the coastal forms predominate, together with estuarine species.--Copyright 1974, Biological Abstracts, Inc.
W75-06848

3. WATER SUPPLY AUGMENTATION AND CONSERVATION

3A. Saline Water Conversion

THE IMPORTANCE OF SALINITY IN URBAN WATER MANAGEMENT,
Culp, Wesner, Culp Clean Water Consultants, Corona Del Mar, Calif.
For primary bibliographic entry see Field 3C.
W75-06372

RECOMMISSIONING OF SEA WATER DEMINERALIZER, SERIAL NO. 204, U.S. COAST GUARD STATION, OCRACOKE, NORTH CAROLINA.
Ionics, Inc., Cambridge, Mass.
Available from the National Technical Information Service, Springfield, Va 22161 as AD-786 398, $3.25 in paper copy, $2.25 in microfiche. January 1965. 14 p, 1 tab, append. Coast Guard Contract Tcg-41774; CG-52, 149A.

Descriptors: *Demineralization, *Electrodialysis, *Waste water treatment, *Desalination processes, Water purification, Equipment, Desalination, Separation techniques, Dialysis, Sea water, Slime, Filters.

During August 1964, Ionics, Inc. received a request to restart the U.S. Coast Guard continuous flow sea water demineralizer located at Ocracoke, North Carolina. The demineralizer had not been operated since October 1962. At that time, an organic sliming problem was experienced in the stacks and demineralizer operation was suspended in order to perform analytical tests and to make a pretreatment study aimed at eliminating the problem. Subsequent pretreatment recommendations on the sliming problem have been closely followed. However, the raw water storage-flocculation tank provided has a smaller capacity than originally recommended and limits the continuous operation of the demineralizer to short runs of approximately nine hours. The pretreatment system was put into operation and the demineralizer operated satisfactorily on pretreated sea water with negligible stack sliming for the duration of the tests. The unit is supplying the station's potable water requirements and its operation should also provide valuable information for evaluations of sea water demineralization by electrodialysis. (Sims-ISWS)
W75-06479

SEA WATER DESALINATION BY REVERSE OSMOSIS, RECENT EXPERIENCE,
Societe Generale d'Epuration et d'Assainissement Degremont, Suresnes (France).
P. Treille, and J. M. Rovel.
Desalination, Vol 14, No 1, p 21-31, February 1974. 5 fig.

Descriptors: *Sea water, *Desalination, *Reverse osmosis, *Water quality control, Operating costs, Desalination plants, Installation, Water treatment, Reservoirs, Chlorides, Pumping, Measurement, Operation and maintenance, Management, *Waste water treatment.
Identifiers: Pumping stations, Clarification, Membrane efficiency, Optimum operation.

The sea water desalination plant at Houat, The Netherlands, in operation since July 1971, has a minimal capacity of 50 m3/day of water containing less than 250mg/l of chlorides. A description of the installation reveals the importance of the pretreatments required for proper operation and membrane conservation. The two-stage treatment has permitted suitable adaption to the variation in production which is a function of the season. Operating costs are analyzed. Optimum plant operation resulting in increased production of desalinated water as a consequence of higher conversion rates is discussed. (Bell-Cornell)
W75-06567

CONSTRUCTION AND INITIAL OPERATION OF THE VTE/MSF MODULE,
Office of Saline Water, Washington, D.C.
C. Grua.
Desalination, Vol 14, No 1, p 1-10, February 1974. (Presented at Fourth International Symposium on Fresh Water from the Sea, Heidelberg, September 1973). 3 ref.

Descriptors: *Water quality control, *Sea water, *Desalination plants, *California, *Design, *Water supply, Reclamation, Waste water(Pollution), Aquifers, Saline water intrusion, Construction, Water management(Applied), Injection wells, Planning, Water temperature, *Waste water treatment.
Identifiers: Environmental impact, Site selection, Cost savings, VTE/MSF module.

The VTE/MSF module being constructed at Fountain Valley, California as part of a supplemental water supply plant of advanced technology is considered. The plant combines waste water reclamation and sea water desalting to provide a good quality product water that will be injected into the Orange County aquifer as a barrier to sea water intrusion and for replenishment of the aquifer. The design of the desalting plant provides a highly adaptable test vehicle for the development of technology for the VTE/MSF process. The configuration of four VTE evaporative stages and six MSF preheat stages is designed to be expandable to a 12.5 mgd plant of sixteen evaporative stages and 30 stages of feed heating. Discussed is the environmental planning wherein assessment of the environmental impact of the entire project was undertaken. Considered was the impact on the environment of existing similar plants in terms of noise, appearance, odors, and outfall characteristics. The initial construction activity was the site preparation. To meet seismic design conditions, the top ten feet of soil was removed and recompacted to 95% Proctor. The initial operations are in the low temperature recycle mode. Finally, the management program in the Orange County Water District is described. (Bell-Cornell)
W75-06568

SYSTEM FOR DEMINERALIZING WATER BY ELECTRODIALYSIS,
For primary bibliographic entry see Field 5F.
W75-06685

EVAPORATION SYSTEM AS FOR THE CONVERSION OF SALT WATER,
E. H. Schwartzman.
U.S. Patent No. 3,869,351, 5 p, 4 fig, 3 ref; Official Gazette of the United States Patent Office, Vol 932, No 1, p 218, March 4, 1975.

Descriptors: *Patents, *Heat transfer, *Desalination, *Evaporation, Condensation, Refrigeration, Salt water, Fresh water, Evaporators.
Identifiers: Compressors.

A conversion system is described for evaporating salt water so as to produce fresh water. A quantity of salt water (liquid phase) is contained to receive heat and thereby evaporate a portion of such water to provide a gaseous phase. Heat is extracted from the gaseous phase resulting in condensed fresh water. The system transfers heat energy to a working fluid to power a compressor structure in a refrigeration cycle, and supplying heat to the liquid phase. Compressor structures are disclosed in the forms of an ejector and a turbine compressor. The same working fluid is employed in the power cycle and the refrigeration cycle. Specific structures are described for obtaining greater efficiency including an arrangement for staging individual systems. (Sinha-OEIS)
W75-06686

COLORADO RIVER SALINITY, NEW SOLUTIONS TO AN OLD PROBLEM.
For primary bibliographic entry see Field 5G.
W75-06774

3B. Water Yield Improvement

WEATHER MODIFICATION ACTIVITIES IN TEXAS, 1973,
Texas Water Development Board, Austin. Weather Modification and Technology Div.
Report 187, November 1974. 23 p, 1 tab.

Descriptors: *Weather modification, *Artificial rainfall, *Precipitation(Atmospheric), Meteorology, Cloud physics, Droughts, Cloud seeding, Hail, Rain, Silver iodide, Legal aspects, *Texas.
Identifiers: Hail suppression, Rainfall augmentation.

During calendar year 1973, nine weather modification projects were conducted in Texas. These projects inculded seven operational cloud seeding projects, one precipitation management research project, and one rain augmentation evaluation project. In all cases the objectives of the cloud seeding projects were to increase rainfall, to decrease hailfall, or both. In all operational cloud seeding projects silver iodide was the seeding agent used to stimulate rainfall and/or suppress hailfall. Sodium chloride was used in the research project. Two methods of cloud seeding were utilized in Texas during 1973. One method was to attempt to introduce the seeding material into clouds from ground-based generators. This method is based on the premise that the seeding material is transported from the ground to cloud base by the vertical component of the low level winds. The second cloud seeding method employed aircraft with silver iodide flares affixed to their wings to deliver the seeding material directly to the inflow region at cloud base. No attempt was made to analyze the degree of success of these activities. Clear-cut results are difficult to obtain and usually require that a given project continue for a number of years before quantifiable effects can be detected; however, there is great variability of natural weather phenomena in Texas. (Sims-ISWS)
W75-06464

BACKGROUND SILVER CONCENTRATIONS IN ILLINOIS PRECIPITATION AND RIVER WATER,
Illinois State Water Survey, Urbana.
For primary bibliographic entry see Field 5A.
W75-06506

THE USE OF A VERTICALLY POINTING PULSED DOPPLER RADAR IN CLOUD PHYSICS AND WEATHER MODIFICATION STUDIES,
Washington Univ., Seattle. Dept. of Atmospheric Sciences.
R. R. Weiss, and P. V. Hobbs.
Journal of Applied Meteorology, Vol 14, No 2, p 222-231, March 1975. 8 fig, 2 tab, 8 ref. NSF Grant GI-31759; AFCRL Contract F19628-74-C-0066.

Descriptors: *Radar, *Cloud physics, *Weather modification, Instrumentation, Cloud seeding, Precipitation(Atmospheric), Turbulence, Ice,

Rime, Water vapor, Radiosondes, Washington, Data processing.
Identifiers: *Doppler effect, Doppler radar, Fall speeds, Vapor deposition.

It was shown that Doppler radar measurements of the changes with height of the average fallspeeds of solid precipitation particles can be used together with radiosonde data to distinguish between growth of ice particles by riming and growth by deposition from the vapor phase. Under some conditions this information can be deduced from real-time observations, but generally, spectral broadening by turbulence requires that the velocity measurements be time-averaged. Examples of the use of this technique to deduce information on the modes of growth of ice particles in natural and in artificially seeded clouds were given. (Jones-ISWS)
W75-06507

OBSERVATIONS OF POTENTIAL ICE NUCLEI,
Meteorological Research Inst., Tokyo (Japan).
T. Kitagawa-Kitade, and H. Maruyama.
Papers in Meteorology and Geophysics, Vol 25, No 2, p 99-110, June 1974. 8 fig, 13 ref.

Descriptors: *Crystallization, *Instrumentation, Freezing, Lead, Iodine, On-site investigations, Measurement, Temperature, Ice, *Nucleation, *Weather modification.
Identifiers: *Ice nuclei, Lead iodide, Cold chamber, Millipore filter, Activation temperature, *Japan(Tokyo Karuizawa).

It was observed that potential ice nuclei, activated with the addition of iodine vapor to natural air, become highly active even at such a high temperature as minus 8C. Observations suggest that their concentration as well as that of natural ice nuclei increases exponentially along with the fall of activation temperature, although the former shows far steeper increase contrasted to the latter. The size of these potential ice nuclei is several 10th micron or less, which is observed by electron microscope. The Millipore filter was found to be much more useful than the cold chamber fór comparative observations, but it appears to take in iodine-activated nuclei at less than minus 12C, so due provisions have to be made for possible errors. The number of nuclei observed by means of the two methods is one order smaller for the filter method than for the cold chamber, this being ascribed probably to the nuclei of exteme small size. In both Tokyo and Karuizawa, the variation of ice nuclei concentrations is very high on some days and very low on others, and differs considerably by day and by hour, indicating little difference between the two locations under different atmospheric conditions. (Jones-ISWS)
W75-06536

RAIN--A WATER RESOURCE.
Department of the Interior, Washington, D.C.
Available from Superintendent of Documents, U.S. Govt. Printing Office, Washington, D.C. GPO:19730-525-709, for $0.25. 1973. 7 p, 3 fig, 2 tab.

Descriptors: *Rainfall disposition, *Runoff, *Precipitation intensity, *Water supply, Water resources, Water requirements, Vegetation effeets, Percolation, Overland flow, Groundwater, United States, Topography, Oceans, Lakes, Evapotranspiration, Evaporation, Water loss.

The amount of precipitation that falls around the world may range from less than 0.1 inch per year to more than 900 inches per year. What happens to water after it reaches the ground is dependent on the rate of precipitation, topography, soil, vegetation, temperature, and the extent of urbanization. Direct runoff in an urbanized area is relatively great due to impermeable pavements and storm sewer systems. Seventy percent of the precipitation in the United States returns to the atmosphere by evaporation and transpiration. The other thirty percent reaches a stream, lake, or ocean either by overland runoff or through the natural groundwater reservoir. Average annual streamflow in this country is approximately twelve-hundred billion gallons a day. Consumption runs about four hundred billion gallons a day. Atlanta, Georgia, for example, has some one-hundred and six billion gallons of precipitation each year. Water use is approximately twenty-six billion gallons yearly. Thus, if water from a year's precipitation could be collected and stored without evaporation loss, about four times the present population could be supplied. (Sperling-Florida)
W75-06586

ANALYSIS OF PUMPING WELL NEAR A STREAM,
Arizona Univ., Tucson.
For primary bibliographic entry see Field 4B.
W75-06809

3C. Use Of Water Of Impaired Quality

SALINITY IN WATER RESOURCES.
Proceedings of the 15th Annual Western Resources Conference, July 1973, edited by J. E. Flack and C. W. Howe, Merriman Publishing Company, Boulder, Colorado, 1974. $10.00. OWRT X-137(9081)(1).

Descriptors: *Salinity, *Irrigation water, *Saline soils, *Water quality, *Salt tolerance, *Economic efficiency, *Economics, Financing, Planning, Evaluation, Decision making, Agriculture, Conjunctive use, Conservation, Cost-benefit analysis, Farm management, Input-output analysis, Land resources, Prices, Project planning, Resource allocation, Water demand, Legislation, Irrigation effeets, Water rights, Irrigation efficiency, Optimization, Damages, *Colorado River Basin, *Model studies.

Current approaches to salinity control in the Colorado River are reviewed. New concepts regarding greatly increased irrigation efficiencies approaching one hundred percent are given. A model is described capable of evaluating water quantity and quality resulting from management strategies of an integrated stream-aquifer system. An optimizing model for timing, quantity, and quality of irrigation applications is described. A review of methods for measuring agricultural damages from salinity is presented, emphasizing farm management techniques to deal with increasing salinity. Damage to urban water systems is studied. The importance and types of economic incentives needed to induce water conservation and salinity reducing measures are studied, with recommendations for a water rights purchase program to reduce salinity and facilitate water transfers. The importance of cost-sharing arrangements to the selection of least-cost abatement programs is reviewed. The importance of spotting bottleneck gaps in knowledge and directing research to those issues is emphasized. (See W75-06367 thru W75-06375)
W75-06366

CURRENT APPROACHES AND ALTERNATIVES TO SALINITY MANAGEMENT IN THE COLORADO RIVER BASIN,
Bureau of Reclamation, Denver, Colo.
J. T. Maletic.
In: Proceedings of the 15th Annual Western Resources Conference, July, 1973, University of Colorado, Boulder, Merriman Publishing Co., Boulder, 1974. p 11-29, 3 fig, 3 tab, 10 ref.

Descriptors: *Colorado River Basin, *Salinity, *Watershed management, Arizona, Utah, Colorado, Wyoming, New Mexico, California, Nevada, Pollution abatement, Water pollution, Saline water, Irrigation, Irrigation practices, Economics.

Approaches currently being incorporated into plans for dealing with the salinity problem in the Colorado River Basin are summarized. Salinity control in the Colorado River Basin, when integrated into an over-all basin management plan, can prevent the costly increases in salinity anticipated from continuing economic growth in the basin. To be implementable, the plan will need to be socially, politically, economically, and ecologically acceptable as well as physically sound. In the Colorado River system, the basin management concept provides a more viable approach to salinity control than singular application of the complete water reuse concept. (See also W75-06366) (Bowden-Arizona)
W75-06367

IMPLICATIONS OF INCREASING FIELD IRRIGATION EFFICIENCY,
Agricultural Research Service, Riverside, Calif. Salinity Lab.
J. van Schilfgaarde.
In: Proceedings of the 15th Annual Western Resources Conference, July, 1973, University of Colorado, Boulder, Merriman Publishing Co., Boulder, 1974. p 30-35.

Descriptors: *Irrigation efficiency, *Salinity, *Leaching, *Water conservation, *Salt tolerance, Irrigation practices, Saline water, Pollution abatement, Costs, Soil management, Colorado River Basin, Evapotranspiration control, Economics, Crop response, Return flow.

Irrigated agriculture has been put on the defensive by the new national goals of ending discharge of pollutants into navigable streams by 1985, and by debate over whether such agricultural crop yields justify the national expense in water delivery systems and water quality projects. One way to lower the amount of salt in discharge water from irrigation fields is to lower the amount of water used in irrigating the fields. This will require developing plants with higher salt tolerance, exact monitoring of water delivery to the fields, and overall management of such agricultural tracts. Field experiments are now underway to test the validity of radically lowering leaching water in irrigated agriculture. This practice, by raising water efficiency, could significantly lengthen the life of irrigated fields, and perhaps even establish an equilibrium. (See also W75-06366) (Bowden-Arizona)
W75-06368

A WATER QUALITY MODEL TO EVALUATE WATER MANAGEMENT PRACTICES IN AN IRRIGATED STREAM-AQUIFER SYSTEM,
Geological Survey, Denver, Colo.
For primary bibliographic entry see Field 5G.
W75-06369

ECONOMIC ANALYSIS OF OPTIMAL USE OF SALINE WATER IN IRRIGATION AND THE EVALUATION OF WATER QUALITY,
Hebrew Univ., Jerusalem (Israel). Dept. of Agricultural Economics.
D. Yaron.
In: Proceedings of the 15th Annual Western Resources Conference, July, 1973, University of Colorado, Boulder, Merriman Publishing Co., Boulder, 1974. p 60-85, 40 ref, 1 tab, 7 fig.

Descriptors: *Salinity, *Economic justification, *Cost-benefit analysis, *Saline water, *Irrigation efficiency, Irrigation practices, Economics, Pollution abatement, Irrigation water quality, Water utilization.

While the biological and agricultural aspects of salinity have been extensively studied, little attention has been paid to the economic aspects of the

problem. The basic physical relationships involved in irrigation with saline water are reviewed, and an economic analysis is made on the microlevel (single crop, single farm) in the short and long run. An attempt is made to translate the implications of the analysis from the micro to the macro level. (See also W75-06366) (Bowden-Arizona)
W75-06370

EVALUATING AGRICULTURAL EFFECTS OF SALINITY ABATEMENT PROJECTS IN THE COLORADO RIVER BASIN: AGRONOMIC AND ECONOMIC CONSIDERATIONS,
Colorado State Univ., Fort Collins. Dept. of Economics.
For primary bibliographic entry see Field 5G.
W75-06371

THE IMPORTANCE OF SALINITY IN URBAN WATER MANAGEMENT,
Culp, Wesner, Culp Clean Water Consultants, Corona Del Mar, Calif.
G. M. Wesner.
In: Proceedings of the 15th Annual Western Resources Conference, July 1973, University of Colorado, Boulder, Merriman Publishing Co., Boulder, 1974. p 108-119, 3 fig, 1 tab, 1 ref.

Descriptors: *Colorado River, *Urban hydrology, *Desalination, *Saline water intrusion, *Water importing, Saline water, Groundwater, *California, Salinity, Groundwater mining, Overdraft, Groundwater recharge, Forecasting, Economic justification.
Identifiers: *Orange County(Calif).

Orange County, California, has a growing salinity problem in its water supply. Various options are examined which promise to alleviate this situation. In the past, excessive pumping of groundwater has led to a sea water intrusion. Current plans call for recharging the water table with higher quality water, and for a desalting facility to process Colorado River water. It is estimated that the adverse salt balance in Orange County will be corrected by 1990. In the interim, water quality improvement programs will upgrade water available to the public. (See also W75-06366) (Bowden-Arizona)
W75-06372

ECONOMIC INCENTIVES FOR SALINITY REDUCTION AND WATER CONSERVATION IN THE COLORADO RIVER BASIN,
Colorado Univ., Boulder. Dept. of Economics.
C. W. Howe, and D. V. Orr.
In: Proceedings of the 15th Annual Western Resources Conference, July 1973. University of Colorado, Boulder, Merriman Publishing Co., Boulder, 1974. p 120-138, 5 tab, 5 fig, 8 ref.

Descriptors: *Saline water, *Colorado River Basin, *Water allocation(Policy), *Water rights, Saline water, Arizona, Utah, Wyoming, Colorado, New Mexico, Nevada, California, Pollution abatement, Fossil fuels, Water demand, Economic efficiency, Water resources development, Water conservation.

The Colorado River Basin, particularly the Lower Basin, is facing future water shortages and a growing salinity level. Reductions in consumptive use and improvements in water quality in the Upper Basin would be desirable from the Lower Basin viewpoint. Whether such changes would be desirable from the Upper Basin viewpoint would depend on the methods used to accomplish such change, the incidence of costs of these methods, and the extent to which compensation might be paid. The more recent emergence of huge potential energy-related demands for water simply increases consumptive uses and salinity problems. Such developments increase the importance of finding additional steps in the Upper Basin for reducing salt and conserving water. The evaluation of alternative approaches to salinity and water quantity problems is considered, and economic incentives or disincentives are examined in light of their ability to induce water saving and salinity reduction. Concrete recommendations are made for a water rights purchase program which could greatly assist in the efficient reallocation of water and reduction of salinity. Preliminary estimates of the program's costs are made. (See also W75-06366) (Bowden-Arizona)
W75-06373

COST SHARING AND EFFICIENCY IN SALINITY CONTROL,
National Bureau of Standards, Washington, D.C. Building Economics Section.
H. E. Marshall.
In: Proceedings of the 15th Annual Western Resources Conference, July 1973, University of Colorado, Boulder, Merriman Publishing Co., Boulder, 1974. p 139-152, 1 fig, 14 ref.

Descriptors: *Colorado River Basin, *Salinity, *Cost sharing, *Economics, *Cost allocation, Arizona, New Mexico, Utah, California, Nevada, Colorado, Wyoming, Saline soils, Water pollution, Saline water, Irrigation water, Pollution abatement, Water quality control, Federal Project Policy.

There are no established cost-sharing rules for salinity control as a distinct project purpose. Unless such rules are legislated, cost-sharing is likely to be haphazard and unfair. One recommendation is that the federal government share the total life cycle costs (construction, operation, maintenance) of all salinity projects with a fixed contribution. This will force non-federal interests to select the cheapest feasible salinity control system. Beneficiaries of salinity control projects should pay in proportion to their benefits from the project. Upstream users must be charged in proportion to their pollution of water used by downstream users. Present state, federal, and institutional arrangements will complicate implementation of such charges. Also, such a distribution of salinity costs to those who benefit most from such abatement will result in high charges to irrigators. (See also W75-06366) (Bowden-Arizona)
W75-06374

FINDING KNOWLEDGE GAPS: THE KEY TO SALINITY CONTROL SOLUTIONS,
Colorado State Univ., Fort Collins. Environmental Resources Center.
For primary bibliographic entry see Field 5G.
W75-06375

PRELIMINARY STUDIES ON QUALITY OF UNDERGROUND WATERS ON GROWTH AND YIELD OF COCONUT (COCOS NUCIFERA),
Regional Research Station, Mudigere (India).
D. S. Kulkarni, P. A. Saranmath, and P. B. Shanthappa.
Mysore J Agric Sci Vol 7, No 1, p 122-124, 1973. Illus.

Descriptors: *Saline water, Effects, *Plant growth, Salinity, Sodium, Sulfates, *Water quality.
Identifiers: Coconut, Cocos-nucifera.

The effects of salinity and Na from 15 Indian coconut groves on coconut yield were tested. High sulfate coupled with high salt was harmful but no ill effects were noted with waters of moderate salinity.--Copyright 1974, Biological Abstracts, Inc.
W75-06466

PRACTICAL APPLICATIONS FOR REUSE OR WASTEWATER,
Los Angeles County Sanitation District, Calif.
J. D. Porkburst, C. W. Carry, A. N. Masse, and J. N. English.
In: Chemical Engineering Progress, Symposium Series, Vol 64, No 90, 1968. p 225-231, 4 tab, 1 fig.

Descriptors: *Sewage effluents, *Water reuse, *Water sources, *Recharge, *Waste water disposal, Water utilization, Reclaimed water, Tertiary treatment, Water conservation, California, Irrigation practices, Industries, Water supply.

In the foreseeable future the major reuse of renovated water will consist of groundwater recharge, irrigation, recreation, and industrial applications. Water of varying quality will be required in each of these applications, and tertiary treatment of the secondary effluent produced by activated sludge plants may be required in certain cases. Percolation of renovated water through the soil to a domestic groundwater supply has proved to adequately protect the public health. The small quantities of residual solids, organics, and bacteria remaining in the treated water are filtered and adsorbed by the first few feet of the soil layer. Secondary effluent of domestic origin is normally of acceptable quality for irrigation of field crops. As opposed to the water used for irrigating the land in recreational parks, water which would be reused in recreational lakes would require tertiary treatment. The use of renovated water for industrial purposes has proven more complex than other applications. The difficulty is due to widely varying quality requirements for specific industrial applications. To develop specific tertiary treatment processes for the removal of selected refractory components of secondary effluents, a research program has been conducted. The program has investigated both organic and inorganic removal. These methods include carbon adsorption, reverse osmosis, ion exchange, and electrodialysis. (Poertner)
W75-06659

ROLE OF VEGETATION IN THE PROCESSES OF SALT ACCUMULATION, (IN RUSSIAN),
Akademiya Nauk Kazakhskoi SSR, Alma-Ata. Institut Pochvovedeniya.
N. F. Mozhaytseva.
Izv Akad Nauk Kaz SSR Ser Biol. 1. p 10-15, 1973, Illus.
Identifiers: Aeluropus-sp, Calcium, Carbonates, Cenoses, Chlorides, Echinopsilon-sp, Halophytes, Ions, Magnesium, Potassium, Reeds, Roots, Salinity, *Salts, Saltwort, Sodium, Soil profiles, Sulfates, *Vegetation, Wormwood, Absorption, *Salt tolerance(Plants), *USSR(Syridar'i River delta).

Selective absorption of salt-forming elements by plants (Aerulgous sp., Echinopsilon sp., wormwood, salt wort, common weed) and participation of phytofactors in the redistribution of salts in the soil profile were studied in the Syridar'i River delta (Kazahkstan, USSR). Ca^{++}/Mg^{++}, K^{+}/Na^{+}, $Ca^{++} + Mg^{++}/K^{+} + Na^{+}$, $Cl/SO_4(-2)$, $Ca^{++} + Mg^{++}/Cl(-) + SO_4(-2)$, $Ca^{++} + Mg^{++}/HCO_3(-)$ were determined in 11 types of soil in the presence of numerous types of vegetation. Increased salinity of soils is accompanied by an increase in the percentage of water-soluble salts among salt-forming elements in vegetation. There is no direct proportionality among the various ions found in soil. The capacity of plants for selective accumulation is explained on the basis of biochemical characteristics: chemical properties of soil and ground water play a subordinate role. Aerial organs of plants differ significantly in qualitative composition of salt forming elements: the ratios between absorbed elements are characteristically stable in root systems. The main plant groups in the delta region do not alter the salinity of the soil by means of the biological cycle. Halophyte communities stabilize the concentrations of salt-forming elements to some extent. Grassy cenoses tend to accumulate Ca salts in the upper soil layers.--Copyright 1974, Biological Abstracts, Inc.
W75-06671

DIGESTED SLUDGE DISPOSAL AT SAN DIEGO'S AQUATIC PARK,
San Diego Dept. of Utilities, Calif.
For primary bibliographic entry see Field 5E.
W75-06674

3D. Conservation In Domestic and Municipal Use

FLOOD CONTROL IN COMMUNITY PLANNING,
California Univ., Berkeley. Dept. of Landscape Architecture.
For primary bibliographic entry see Field 6B.
W75-06429

THE EFFECTS OF DIMINISHED GROUND-WATER SUPPLIES ON SELECTED NEW HAMPSHIRE INDUSTRIES: AN ECONOMIC AND LEGAL EVALUATION,
New Hampshire Univ., Durham. Water Resource Research Center.
For primary bibliographic entry see Field 4B.
W75-06463

KALAMAZOO COUNTY, MICHIGAN, WATER QUALITY STUDY.
Jones and Henry, Toledo, Ohio.
For primary bibliographic entry see Field 5G.
W75-06759

MANAGEMENT IMPROVEMENT,
Jacksonville Dept. of Public Works, Fla. Water and Sewer Div.
For primary bibliographic entry see Field 5D.
W75-06760

WATER AND SEWER SYSTEMS PROGRAM AND DEVELOPMENT, FIVE-YEAR CAPITAL IMPROVEMENT PLAN: OCTOBER 1, 1972 - SEPTEMBER 30, 1977,
Jacksonville Dept. of Public Works, Fla.
For primary bibliographic entry see Field 5D.
W75-06762

CLEAN WATER . . . A NEW DAY FOR SOUTHEAST MICHIGAN,
Detroit Metro Water Dept., Mich.
For primary bibliographic entry see Field 5D.
W75-06763

PROSPECTUS FOR REGIONAL SEWER AND WATER PLANNING.
Southwestern Wisconsin Regional Planning Commission, Platteville.
For primary bibliographic entry see Field 5D.
W75-06782

URBAN SYSTEMS ENGINEERING DEMONSTRATION PROGRAM FOR HINDS, MADISON, RANKIN COUNTIES, MISSISSIPPI, VOLUME I: AREA-WIDE WATER SYSTEMS.
Clark, Dietz and Associates, Inc., Jackson, Miss
For primary bibliographic entry see Field 5D.
W75-06783

URBAN SYSTEMS ENGINEERING DEMONSTRATION PROGRAM FOR HINDS, MADISON, RANKIN COUNTIES, MISSISSIPPI, VOLUME II: AREA-WIDE SANITARY SEWER SYSTEM.
Clark, Dietz and Associates, Inc., Jackson, Miss.
For primary bibliographic entry see Field 5D.
W75-06784

URBAN SYSTEMS ENGINEERING DEMONSTRATION PROGRAM FOR HINDS, MADISON, RANKIN COUNTIES, MISSISSIPPI, VOLUME IV. AREA-WIDE STORM DRAINAGE AND FLOOD PLAIN MANAGEMENT STUDIES.
Clark, Dietz and Associates, Inc., Jackson, Miss.
For primary bibliographic entry see Field 5D.
W75-06785

3E. Conservation In Industry

THE WESTERNPORT BAY ENVIRONMENTAL STUDY,
Victoria Ministry for Conservation, Melbourne (Australia). Westernport Bay Environmental Study.
For primary bibliographic entry see Field 6G.
W75-06555

ENVIRONMENTAL CONTAMINANTS INVENTORY STUDY NO. 2 - THE PRODUCTION, USE AND DISTRIBUTION OF CADMIUM IN CANADA,
Canada Centre for Inland Waters, Burlington (Ontario).
For primary bibliographic entry see Field 5B.
W75-06742

3F. Conservation In Agriculture

AGRICULTURAL DROUGH PROBABILITIES IN TENNESSEE,
Tennessee Univ., Knoxville. Dept. of Plant and Soil Science.
J. M. Safley, Jr., and W. L. Parks.
Available from the National Technical Information Service, Springfield, Va 22161 as PB-240 977, $4.25 in paper copy, $2.25 in microfiche. University of Tennessee, Agricultural Experiment Station, Bulletin 533, August 1974. 65 p, 52 tab, 19 ref. OWRT A-017-TENN(4). 14-31-001-3843.

Descriptors: *Droughts, Precipitation(Atmospheric), *Weather data, *Tennessee, *Probability, *Drought resistance, Trees, *Crop response, Computer programs, Data collections, Crop production.

A long-term weather file consisting of sixty-seven select stations has been established for Tennessee. Precipitation probabilities for 1-, 2-, 3- and 4-week periods have been calculated using the incomplete gamma distribution; these data are being published. There are computer programs to calculate temperature extremes and means, to calculate psychrometric data, to calculate precipitation probabilities, weekly/monthly means, and intensity frequencies, to calculate evapotranspiration by a modified Thornthwaite model and by the Penman formula, and to calculate the Palmer Drought Index. Collection of statewide crop yield data is almost complete and the analysis of tree growth patterns by annual-ring width has begun. Work is in progress toward calculation of drought probabilities on a 1-week, 2-week, and a monthly basis for the State. Relation of crop yield data and tree growth to drought intensity will be performed by multiple regression techniques and yield predictors for the crops will be derived.
W75-06358

RECYCLING OF SEWAGE EFFLUENT BY IRRIGATION: A FIELD STUDY ON OAHU, SECOND PROGRESS REPORT FOR JULY 1972 TO JULY 1973,
Hawaii Univ., Honolulu. Water Resources Research Center.
For primary bibliographic entry see Field 5D.
W75-06361

ATTITUDES TOWARD WATER USE FRACTICES AMONG S.E. IDAHO FARMERS: A STUDY ON ADOPTION OF IRRIGATION SCHEDULING,
Idaho Univ., Moscow. Dept. of Agricultural and Forest Economics.
J. Carlson.
Idaho Water Resources Research Institute, Moscow, Technical Completion Report, January 1975. 39 p, 15 tab, 3 ref, append. Supported by Bureau of Reclamation.

Descriptors: *Irrigation practices, Management, *Water utilization, *Attitudes, Social values, *Idaho, Social aspects, Agriculture, Irrigation systems, Sprinkler irrigation.
Identifiers: *Irrigation scheduling.

Attitudes of Southern Idaho farmers toward the adoption of an irrigation scheduling program were measured. An interview survey of approximately 50% of the farmers in the A and B District provided data on the socioeconomic characteristics of farmers and attitudes toward their water use patterns. The findings pointed to several significant factors affecting the involvement of a farmer in the irrigation scheduling program. Those farmers having cooperative arrangements with relatives were less likely to utilize irrigation scheduling; while those who perceived that they had irrigation problems were more receptive. This finding suggests that unique social forces have an influence on the adoption of a new idea. Finally, farmers tended to feel that irrigation scheduling was appropriate for sprinkler irrigation systems but not for open ditch systems. While not entirely true, it suggests that irrigation scheduling fits into some farm operations better than others. This factor may be important in considering future areas for expansion of an irrigation scheduling program.
W75-06363

EFFECT OF SHELTER AND WATER-SPRINKLING DURING SUMMER AND AUTUMN ON SOME PHYSIOLOGICAL REACTIONS OF MURRAH BUFFALO HEIFERS,
Haryana Agricultural Univ., Hissar (India). Dept. of Livestock Production and Management.
N. S. R. Sastry, C. K. Thomas, V. N. Tripathi, R. N. Pal, and L. R. Gupta.
Indian J Anim Sci. Vol 43, No 2, p 95-99, 1973.

Descriptors: *Sprinkling, *Animal physiology, Effects, Stress, Tension stress relieving.
Identifiers: Buffalo, Shelter, Hot weather.

The effect of shelter and water-sprinkling during hot (April 1971-July 1971) and mild (end of April 1971-Oct. 1971) seasons on rectal temperature, pulse rate and respiration rate of growing Murrah buffalo heifers was investigated. Provision of shelter and water-sprinkling significantly reduced thermal strain experienced by the animals and aided them in maintaining a high metabolic rate as evidenced by rectal temperature and pulse rate at 9 am. The physiological apparatus of the animals was under greater stress during the hot than during the mild season. Buffalo heifers may be given protection from direct solar radiation by simple sunshades and may be sprinkled with water during hot summer and mild autumn seasons to alleviate the thermal stress from an adverse environment.--

W75-06401

THE QUANTITATIVE EFFECTS OF TWO METHODS OF SPRINKLER IRRIGATION ON THE MICROCLIMATE OF A MATURE AVOCADO PLANTATION,
Israel Meteorological Service, Bet-Dagan. Div. of Agricultural Meteorology.
J. Lomas, and M. Mandel.
Agric Meteorol. Vol 12, No 1, p 35-48, 1973, Illus.

Descriptors: *Sprinkler irrigation, Irrigation practices, Plants, *Weather modification, Arid climates.
Identifiers: *Avocado, Microclimatic modification, Sharav conditions.

The effects of above- and below-canopy irrigation on microclimatic amelioration of an avocado plantation during hot and dry (sharav) conditions were investigated. Above-canopy irrigation has the greatest effect on microclimatic modification reducing temperatures by 7C and increasing humidity by 27%. Below-canopy irrigation has a much lesser effect. The effect of irrigation on microclimatic modification is relatively short lived, both methods of irrigation showing similar results. Microclimatic modifications are themselves climatically dependent. The more extreme the 'sharav' conditions, the hotter and drier the ambient air, the greater the modifying effects. Practical considerations prevent large-scale irrigation above the tree-canopy and consequently below-canopy irrigation is practiced. Under field conditions the actual rate of cooling remains approximately 1/3 of the wet bulb depression.--Copyright 1974, Biological Abstracts, Inc.
W75-06428

EFFECT OF SOIL WATER POTENTIAL ON DISEASE INCIDENCE AND OOSPORE GERMINATION OF PYTHIUM APHANIDERMATUM,
Arizona Univ., Tucson. Dept. of Plant Pathology.
For primary bibliographic entry see Field 2G.
W75-06447

ECOLOGICAL AND PHYSIOLOGICAL IMPLICATIONS OF GREENBELT IRRIGATION, PROGRESS REPORT OF THE MALONEY CANYON PROJECT-1974,
California Univ., Riverside. Dept. of Plant Sciences.
For primary bibliographic entry see Field 5D.
W75-06461

RESEARCH ON WATER RESOURCES EVALUATION METHODOLOGY, A RIVER BASIN ECONOMIC AND FINANCIAL POST-AUDIT,
Little (Arthur D.), Inc., Cambridge, Mass.
For primary bibliographic entry see Field 6B.
W75-06524

WATER TABLE POSITION AS AFFECTED BY SOIL AIR PRESSURE,
Agricultural Research Service, Reno, Nev.
For primary bibliographic entry see Field 4B.
W75-06549

A PROTOTYPE OF THE MODERN SETTLING-RESERVOIR IN ANCIENT MESOPOTAMIA,
Illinois Univ., Urbana. World Hertiage Museum.
For primary bibliographic entry see Field 4A.
W75-06565

PROPELLING SHOE FOR USE IN AN IRRIGATION SYSTEM,
L. J. Dowd.
U.S. Patent No. 3,866,835, 5 p, 14 fig, 5 ref; Official Gazette for the United States Patent Office, Vol 931, No 3, p 1178, February 18, 1975.

Descriptors: *Patents, *Irrigation systems, *Water distribution(Applied), *Surface irrigation, Equipment, Distribution systems, Pipes, Application equipment, Conservation.
Identifiers: Propelling shoes.

An irrigation system includes an above ground, moving elongated water distribution pipe. The pipe is pivotally supported at one end, and spaced movable members support the pipe between the pivoted end and the opposite end. Drive means pivot the pipe about the support. The drive includes propelling shoes on the movable support and they engage the ground to assist in pivoting the pipe. Each shoe includes a planar lower plate having a surface which is slidable along the ground. An aperture is provided in the planar plate. A drive shaft is interconnected to the shoe and is pivotal relative to the shoe, between first and second angular positions. A drive cleat is interconnected to the drive shaft. The drive cleat includes a planar portion which is passed through the aperture in the planar plate of the shoe. The drive cleat is movable, in response to the movement of the drive shaft, between a ground disengaged position when the shaft is at the first angular position, and a maximum ground penetrating condition when the drive shaft is at the second angular position. (Sinha-OEIS)
W75-06697

THE RELATIONSHIP BETWEEN THE DM (DRY MATTER) CONTENT OF HERBAGE FOR SILAGE MAKING AND EFFLUENT PRODUCTION,
Hannah Dairy Research Inst., Ayr (Scotland).
For primary bibliographic entry see Field 5B.
W75-06725

NUTRIENT UPTAKE BY RICE UNDER DIFFERENT SOIL MOISTURE REGIMES,
Haryana Agricultural Univ., Hissar (India). Dept. of Soils.
S. M. Gorantiwar, I. K. Jaggi, and S. S. Khanna.
J Indian Soc Soil Sci. Vol 21, No 2, p 133-136, 1973.
Identifiers: Crops, Iron, *Nutrients, Phosphorus, Potassium, *Rice, Soil moisture, Sulfur, *Absorption, India.

A pot experiment was conducted in kharif 1969-70 to study the effect of 5 soil moisture levels on yield and uptake of nutrients by 3 varieties of rice in medium black soil of Jabalpur(India). The differences among the uptake values of P, K, S and Fe in the 3 varieties were non-significant. Differences in the yield and uptake of nutrients due to varying moisture regimes were significant. Rice grown under submergence yielded significantly more than at other moisture levels. There was no significant difference between the grain and straw yields under 4 cm and 7 cm of flooding. The uptake of P and K was significantly increased in 4 cm of submergence over all the other treatments and followed the order: 7 cm of submergence > 0 cm of water tension > 300 cm of water tension > 700 cm of water tension. The same trend was observed in the uptake of Fe and S but the difference between the uptake values of Fe and S was non-significant in 4 cm and 7 cm of submergence. The residual availability of P, K and S in soil at post harvest was found more in 300 and 700 cm of water tension as compared to 0 cm of water tension and submergence. The reverse trend was found with the residual availability of Fe.--Copyright 1974, Biological Abstracts, Inc.
W75-06726

EFFECT OF MIDTERM DRAINAGE ON YIELD AND FERTILIZER NITROGEN USE EFFICIENCY ON TWO HIGH YIELDING VARIETIES OF RICE,
Indian Agricultural Research Inst. New Delhi. Nuclear Research Lab.
G. S. Upadhya, and N. P. Datta.
J Indian Soc Soil Sci. Vol 21, No 2, p 219-226, 1973.
Identifiers: Ammonium sulfate, Drainage, *Fertilizer, Flooding, *Nitrogen, *Rice, Urea, *Crop yield, India.

A field experiment was carried out in kharif season at the Indian Agricultural Research Institute farm, New Delhi, to assess the effect of midterm drainage on yield and fertilizer N use efficiency on rice using 15N labeled sources on 2 high yielding varieties of rice (Padma and IR-22). (NH4)2SO4 and urea were similar in their effect on grain and straw yield. Continuous flooding was better than midterm drainage treatment. Varietal differences were significant in yield. Percentage utilization of fertilizer N was more under continuous flooding than under midterm drainage. It was more in (NH4)2SO4 than in urea treatment. Varieties differed in their utilization of fertilizer N. Utilization of fertilizer N was more at primordial initiation stage than at transplanting.--Copyright 1974, Biological Abstracts, Inc.
W75-06727

COMPARED EVAPOTRANSPIRATION OF VARIOUS CROPS AND STUDY OF WATER-CONSUMPTION RATES,
Institut National de la Recherche Agronomique, Toulouse (France). Station d'Agronomie.
For primary bibliographic entry see Field 2D.
W75-06728

A SENSITIVE RECORDING LYSIMETER,
Agricultural Research Inst., Cedara (South Africa).
For primary bibliographic entry see Field 2D.
W75-06729

CHANGE IN THE MICROCLIMATE OF THE AIR LAYER NEAR THE SOIL FOLLOWING SPRINKLING COTTON WITH WATER,
A. I. Efanova.
Izv Akad Nauk Tadzh SSR Otd Biol Nauk. 2, p 14-18, 1973, Illus. (In Russian).
Identifiers: Air, Climates, *Cotton, Humidity, *Microclimates, Soils, *Sprinkling irrigation, Temperature, *USSR(Tadzhikistan-Gissar Valley).

Experiments were carried out in the Gissar valley of Tadzhikistan (USSR) in 1964-1966 to establish the optimal rate of water when sprinkling cotton and to study the effect of irrigation on the microclimate of the surface boundary layer and yield. The relative humidity of the surface boundary layer from overhead watering of the plants increased both with respect to individual observations during the day and to periods of development within limits from 4 to 19%. Sprinkling at a rate of 1500 and 2000 l/ha/sprinkling at the phase of budding, mass flowering, and fruit formation lowered the air temperature at the level of the plants in the early afternoon (1-2 p.m.) an h after sprinkling by 0.5-4.3C in July and Aug. and increased it by 0.9-2.7 deg in the evening hours. Overhead watering of cotton during critical periods created a favorable microclimate at the level of the plants, which promoted an increase of prefrost harvests by 1.5-4.9 cent/ha and total yield by 1.3-2.3 cent/ha. The best rate for 3-fold sprinkling is 1500 l/ha/sprinkling. On the average for the 3 yr the increment of the prefrost harvest was 4.9 cent/ha and of the total harvest 2.3 cent/ha.--Copyright 1974, Biological Abstracts, Inc.
W75-06730

ANALYSIS OF PUMPING WELL NEAR A STREAM,
Arizona Univ., Tucson.
For primary bibliographic entry see Field 4B.
W75-06809

DYNAMICS OF CONTENT OF CAROTENOIDS AND CHLOROPHYLLS IN THE UPPER LEAVES OF WHEAT AND BARLEY DURING THE CRITICAL PERIOD OF WATER DEFICIENCY IN SOILS, (IN RUSSIAN),
Vsesoyuznyi Institut Rastenievodstva, Leningrad (USSR).
O. B. Motkalyuk.
Fiziol Rast. Vol 20, No 6, p 1242-1247, 1973. Illus.
Identifiers: *Barley, *Carotenoids, *Chlorophylls, Dynamics, Embryo, Leaves, Meiosis, Mitosis, Phytochrome, Soils, Spores, Stamen, Vegetation, Water deficiencies, *Wheat.

The development of the embryonic ear during 7 vegetative periods was studied. Earlier data on the presence of an early maximum of phytochrome accumulation (at the beginning of active growth and on a decrease of phytochrome content during the reproductive period were confirmed. The 1st maximum of the pigment content in the leaves was registered prior to a period critical to water deficiency in soil, during the stamen formation or the formation of pollen parent cells in them. A decrease in the content of phytochromes coincides with 2 moments in the critical period: the appearance and differentiation of pollen parent cells before meiosis; the formation and vacuolization of mononuclear microspores before the 1st mitosis.--

W75-06841

4. WATER QUANTITY MANAGEMENT AND CONTROL

4A. Control Of Water On The Surface

LAND-USE ISSUES: PROCEEDINGS OF A CONFERENCE.
Virginia Polytechnic Inst. and State Univ., Blacksburg. Water Resources Research Center.
Available from the National Technical Information Service, Springfield, Va 22161 as PB-240 974, $5.75 in paper copy, $2.25 in microfiche. Publication 629, Cooperative Extension Service, November 1974. 112 p. Edited by M. J. Foxton and P. M. Ashton.

Descriptors: *Land use, *Virginia, Land management, Standards, Water quality, Flood plains, Legislation, Planning, Water policy, Attitudes, Zoning, Legal aspects, Urbanization, Land resources, Institutional constraints.

Fifteen papers presented before a conference on land-use issues in Virginia, plus two additional papers, are included in this Virginia-oriented publication. The in-place land-use legislation, the planning process, the approaches to land-use policy, the application of land-use controls, water and water quality policy, and the impact of citizen attitudes on land use are discussed. Special issues treated include standards for implementing comprehensive plans, alternatives to zoning, rural and urban conflicts, flood-plain management, impacts of new communities, and methods of designating land for special purposes, such as agricultural and environmental districts.
W75-06359

HYDROGEOLOGY AND WATER QUALITY MANAGEMENT,
Moody and Associates, Inc., Harrisburg, Pa. Environmental Services Div.
For primary bibliographic entry see Field 5G.
W75-06400

REPORT TO THE SONOMA CREEK ADVISORY COMMITTEE, SONOMA, CALIFORNIA,
California Univ., Berkeley. Dept. of Landscape Architecture.
For primary bibliographic entry see Field 6B.
W75-06430

CHARACTERISTICS OF WYOMING STOCK-WATER PONDS AND DIKE SPREADER SYSTEMS,
Wyoming Univ., Laramie. Water Resources Research Inst.
V. E. Smith.
Water Resources Series No. 47, July 1974. 41 p, 8 fig, 2 tab, 16 ref.

Descriptors: *Stock water, Ponds, Streamflow, *Beneficial use, Dikes, Evaporation, Hydrology, Precipitation(Atmospheric), Runoff, Water rights, *Wyoming.
Identifiers: Capacity curves, *Dike spreaders.

Based on information from available studies, an evaluation was made of the characteristics and hydrologic processes related to Wyoming stock-water ponds and dike spreader systems. Capacity curves for various configurations of stock-water ponds were developed and maps of average annual evaporation, precipitation and runoff were compiled. The amount of water constituting beneficial use was examined and recommendations relative to water rights administration were presented.
W75-06433

TEMPERATURE EFFECTS ON GREAT LAKES WATER BALANCE STUDIES,
State Univ. of New York, Buffalo. Dept. of Civil Engineering.
For primary bibliographic entry see Field 2H.
W75-06448

DEVELOPMENT OF A STORM RUN-OFF PREDICTION MODEL WITH SIMULATED TEMPORAL RAINFALL DISTRIBUTION,
Meteorological Office, New Delhi (India).
For primary bibliographic entry see Field 2E.
W75-06453

ADAPTATION AND APPLICATION OF THE KARAZEV METHOD TO THE RATIONALIZATION OF QUEBEC'S HYDROMETRIC BASIC NETWORK,
National Inst. of Scientific Research, Quebec.
For primary bibliographic entry see Field 2E.
W75-06454

A COMPARISON OF HYDROLOGIC AND HYDRAULIC CATCHMENT ROUTING PROCEDURES,
University Coll., Galway (Ireland).
For primary bibliographic entry see Field 2E.
W75-06456

RELATIONS BETWEEN PLANIMETRIC AND HYPSOMETRIC VARIABLES IN THIRD- AND FOURTH-ORDER DRAINAGE BASINS,
New Univ. of Ulster, Coleraine (Northern Ireland). School of Biological and Environmental Studies.
For primary bibliographic entry see Field 2A.
W75-06459

RESERVATION, RESERVOIR AND SELF-DETERMINATION: A CASE STUDY OF RESERVOIR PLANNING AS IT AFFECTS AN INDIAN RESERVATION,
Mississippi State Univ, Mississippi State. Dept. of Anthropology.
For primary bibliographic entry see Field 6B.
W75-06462

SAN LUIS UNIT, TECHNICAL RECORD OF DESIGN AND CONSTRUCTION - VOLUME II, DESIGN, SAN LUIS DAM AND PUMPING-GENERATING PLANT, O'NEILL DAM AND PUMPING PLANT,
Bureau of Reclamation, Denver, Colo.
For primary bibliographic entry see Field 8A.
W75-06468

LONG-RANGE WATER SUPPLY PROBLEMS, PHASE I.
Kansas Water Resources Board, Topeka.
For primary bibliographic entry see Field 6D.
W75-06473

JACKSON HOLE FLOOD CONTROL PROJECT.
Committee on Channel Stabilization (Army).
Available from the National Technical Information Service, Springfield, Va 22161 as AD-777 796, $3.25 in paper copy, $2.25 in microfiche. Technical Report 11, March 1974. 13 p.

Descriptors: *Flood control, *Stream stabilization, *Levees, Flood plains, Riprap, Erosion, Sedimentation, Braiding, Bank stability, Channels, Rivers, *Wyoming.
Identifiers: Snake River, Jackson Hole(Wyo).

At the 28th meeting of the Committee on Channel Stabilization, held in Vicksburg, Mississippi, on May 22-23, 1973, a representative of the U.S. Army Engineer District, Walla Walla, described the Jackson Hole Flood Control Project on the Snake River in Wyoming, and requested the advice of the Committee on certain aspects of the project. At its 29th meeting, held in Jackson, Wyoming, on September 18-19, 1973, the Committee inspected and further discussed various aspects of the project. Specific questions that were submitted in writing by the District representative at the May meeting were given, followed in each case by the respective response of the Committee as initially prepared after the May meeting and modified after the September inspection and meeting. To clearly identify the Jackson Hole Flood Control Project, the authorized project description extracted from the reports supplied by the district was briefly summarized. Committee recommendations were presented. (Sims-ISWS)
W75-06475

FLOODWAY DETERMINATION USING COMPUTER PROGRAM HEC-2,
Hydrologic Engineering Center, Davis, Calif.
For primary bibliographic entry see Field 7C.
W75-06481

PROCEDURES MANUAL FOR DETECTION AND LOCATION OF SURFACE WATER USING ERTS-1 MULTISPECTRAL SCANNER DATA, VOLUME I - SUMMARY.
National Aeronautics and Space Administration, Houston, Tex. Lyndon B. Johnson Space Center.
For primary bibliographic entry see Field 7C.
W75-06484

PREDICTION OF SEEPAGE THROUGH CLAY SOIL LININGS IN REAL ESTATE LAKES,
Arizona Water Resources Research Center, Tucson.
G. Sposito.
Available from the National Technical Information Service, Springfield, Va 22161 as PB-241 063, $3.75 in paper copy, $2.25 in microfiche. Completion Report, 1975. 36 p, 3 fig, 1 tab, 26 ref, append. OWRT A-055-ARIZ (1). 14-31-0001-5003.

Descriptors: *Seepage control, Water conservation, Clays, *Southwest US, Lakes, *Artificial lakes, Soil water, Leakage, *Underseepage, Equations, Water loss, Infiltration, *Reservoir leakage, *Linings, Forecasting.
Identifiers: *Clay liners.

The rapid expansion in the development of real estate lakes in the Southwest has produced a somewhat haphazard use of clay soils or clays in attempts to seal these lakes against seepage losses. This situation is further aggravated by the fact that very little basic information exists on the equilibrium and movement of water in a swelling clay soil, which is the type of natural lining material of direct relevance to seepage control. New results are presented in the theory of swelling clay soils, including a description of the equilibrium moisture profile and the steady flow of water in a submerged, saturated, natural clay soil liner. The theory then is applied to develop an equation for the rate of seepage (the rate of lowering of the

water surface) through a swelling liner in a real estate lake of simple trapezoidal configuration. This equation is compared to the standard results for the seepage rate, as calculated on the classical theory of water flow through non-swelling soils, and is applied to estimate the seepage rate from an experimental reservoir studied by Rollins and Dylla (1970). The principal conclusions are: (a) the major effect of swelling in the liner, except for very shallow lakes, is to cancel the contribution of gravity to the seepage rate, (b) the most important factor determining seepage loss is likely to be the soil water tension in the pervious soil surrounding the lake and liner, and (c) the seepage equation can provide a useful estimate of the rate of loss when the important geometric and soil water parameters for the lake, the liner, and the surrounding soil are available.
W75-06516

REDESIGNING FLOOD MANAGEMENT - PROJECT AGNES PHASE I,
New York State Coll. of Agriculture and Life Sciences, Ithaca. Dept. of Agricultural Economics.
For primary bibliographic entry see Field 6F.
W75-06520

RESEARCH ON WATER RESOURCES EVALUATION METHODOLOGY, A RIVER BASIN ECONOMIC AND FINANCIAL POST-AUDIT,
Little (Arthur D.), Inc., Cambridge, Mass.
For primary bibliographic entry see Field 6B.
W75-06524

ANALYSIS OF RELIEF WELLS IN EMBANKMENTS,
Osmania Univ., Hyderabad (India). Dept. of Civil Engineering.
For primary bibliographic entry see Field 4B.
W75-06537

A LIMNOLOGICAL STUDY OF SILVERWOOD LAKE: IMPACT OF WATER TRANSPORT ON WATER QUALITY,
California State Polytechnic Univ., Pomona.
For primary bibliographic entry see Field 5A.
W75-06538

MARKOV MIXTURE MODELS FOR DROUGHT LENGTHS,
Harvard Univ., Boston, Mass. Graduate School of Business Administration.
For primary bibliographic entry see Field 2A.
W75-06545

BIRTH-DEATH MODELS FOR DIFFERENTIAL PERSISTENCE,
Harvard Unov., Boston, Mass. Graduate School of Business Administration.
For primary bibliographic entry see Field 2E.
W75-06546

A THEORY OF THE COMBINED MOLE-TILE DRAIN SYSTEM,
Utah State Univ., Logan. Dept. of Agricultural and Irrigation Engineering.
For primary bibliographic entry see Field 2F.
W75-06547

UNIQUE WATER SUPPLY PROBLEMS IN THE NORTH WEST OF SOUTH AUSTRALIA,
South Australian Dept. of Health, Adelaide.
For primary bibliographic entry see Field 6D.
W75-06553

BIOLOGICAL, CHEMICAL AND RELATED ENGINEERING PROBLEMS IN LARGE STORAGE LAKES OF TASMANIA,
Hydro-Electric Commission, Tasmania (Australia). Civil Engineering Div.
H. H. McFie.
Water (Journal of the Australian Water and Wastewater Association) Vol 1, No 4, p 14-17, December 1974. 1 fig, 1 tab, 1 ref.

Descriptors: *Lakes, *Reservoir operation, *Hydroelectric plants, *Biological properties, *Water chemistry, *Australia, Limnology, Stratification, Thermal properties, Chemical properties, Corrosion, Hydraulic structures, Concrete structures, Fish populations, Dams.
Identifiers: Great Lake(Tas), Lake St. Clair(Tas), Lake Rowallan(Tas), Lake Pedder(Tas), Lake Gordon(Tas).

The Tasmanian Hydro-Electric Commission Australia, has seven man-made lakes with capacities of greater than 124,000,000 cu m, and an additional three under construction. The general features of these lakes, in terms of stratification, aquatic ecology and water chemistry are briefly described. Problems encountered in maintaining three of the existing lakes, and related features of two of those being completed, are discussed in more detail, with particular reference to fish populations and deterioration of structures. (Levick-CSIRO)
W75-06556

MODERNIZATION OF NATIONAL WEATHER SERVICE RIVER FORECASTING TECHNIQUES,
National Weather Service, Silver Spring, Md.
W. T. Sittner.
Water Resources Bulletin, Vol 9, No 4, p 655-659, August 1973. 7 ref.

Descriptors: *River forecasting, *River systems, Hydrology, Mathematical models, Computers, Runoff, Precipitation, Simulation analysis, Parametric hydrology, Systems analysis, River basin development, Technology, *Forecasting.
Identifiers: *National Weather Service, Catchment models, Parameter optimization, Data requirements.

The National Weather Service, which has the responsibility for making and issuing river and flood forecasts throughout the United States, is nearing the conclusion of a five year period of transition from index type catchment modeling to the use of conceptual hydrologic models. The decision to make this technological change was based on an extensive research project in which various catchment models were tested in a wide variety of basins and their strong and weak points ascertained. This project is described. Some of the problems involved in the changeover include practical parameter optimization methods, computer requirements for the more complex technology, data requirements, fitting of the catchment model to major river systems, training of personnel, and staffing. (Bell-Cornell)
W75-06562

SYSTEM FOR REGULATION OF COMBINED SEWAGE FLOWS,
Municipality of Metropolitan Seattle, Wash.
For primary bibliographic entry see Field 5D.
W75-06563

A PROTOTYPE OF THE MODERN SETTLING-RESERVOIR IN ANCIENT MESOPOTAMIA,
Illinois Univ., Urbana. World Hertiage Museum.
S. T. Kang.
Water Resources Bulletin, Vol 9, No 3, p 577-582, June 1973. 1 fig, 18 ref.

Descriptors: *Irrigation systems, *Canals, *Reservoirs, *Settling basins, *History, *Deserts, Flood control, Water supply, Agriculture, Weirs, Outlets, Inlets(Waterways), Water utilization, Regulated flow.
Identifiers: *Iraq(Ancient Mesopotania), Settling reservoir.

In Iraq, the area once served by an ancient canal system is now abandoned to desert. The Ur III texts would indicate that the Sumerian irrigation system allowed the raising of good crops of grain, vegetables and fruits in an area now completely barren except for an occasional thorn-bush. The Sumerian term nag-ku5, a key word referring to the ancient Sumerian canal and irrigation systems, is discussed. Ur III material suggests that the nag-ku5 may have served a role similar to that of the modern settling-reservoir. The nag-ku5 was probably a place where silt could settle out of the canal water before it left by the kun (tail) or outlet. Umma texts indicate that the nag-ku5 provided the means for regulation of the rate and amount of water flow to the fields. In addition to being a regulatory device, it was also critical for daily life, serving as a trough of clear water for men and animals. The aim of this study is the hope that knowledge of the past can help this desert bloom once more. (Bell-Cornell)
W75-06565

REVIEW OF LAKE RESTORATION PROCEDURES,
Colorado Univ., Boulder.
For primary bibliographic entry see Field 5G.
W75-06566

LONG-TERM RECONSTRUCTION OF WATER LEVEL CHANGES FOR LAKE ATHABASCA BY ANALYSIS OF TREE RINGS,
Arizona Univ., Tucson. Lab. of Tree-Ring Research.
C. W. Stockton, and H. C. Fritts.
Water Resources Bulletin, Vol 9, No 5, p 1006-1027, October 1973. 6 fig, 5 tab, 19 ref.

Descriptors: *Dendrochronology, *Lakes, *Water levels, *Canada, Rivers, Dams, Deltas, Variability, Hydraulics, Hydrology, Sampling, Waterways, Trees, Water resources, Management, Ecology, Channels, Levees, Data collections.
Identifiers: *Water level reconstruction, Canonical analysis, *Tree-ring data, White Spruce.

A study of past changes in lake levels demonstrates that dendrochronology can be a useful tool in water resources management. Recent closure of the gates on the W.A.C. Bennett Dam on the Peace River in British Columbia caused a drop in water levels of Lake Athabasca. Since the ecology of the lake and adjacent delta region had depended on the now lessened snow-melt flooding from the Upper Peace River Basin, it became necessary to consider artificially inducing this annual inundation. It was necessary to determine the long-term water level changes affecting the present ecology. Water levels in the channels could be correlated with lake levels. Using canonical analysis and 10-day mean lake levels for three different subperiods in the known 33-year record of lake level changes, along with tree-ring series from appropriately chosen stands of white spruce (reflecting the water stages in the channels), reconstructions were made of the long-term record for late May, early July, and late September. Results show May lake levels have been three times as variable in the past as in the period of historical record (1935-1967), July levels twice as variable, and September levels 10% less variable. However, the mean water level for each of the three subperiods for the long-term record is very close to the means for the period of historical record. (Bell-Cornell)
W75-06569

WATER QUALITY MANAGEMENT: THE CASE FOR RIVER BASIN AUTHORITIES,
Ohio Univ., Athens. Dept. of Civil Engineering.
For primary bibliographic entry see Field 5G.
W75-06571

NUMERICAL MODELING OF THERMAL STRATIFICATION IN A RESERVOIR WITH LARGE DISCHARGE-TO-VOLUME RATIO,
Tennessee Valley Authority, Muscle Shoals, Ala. Air Quality Branch.
For primary bibliographic entry see Field 2H.
W75-06572

PRESERVATION AND ENHANCEMENT OF THE AMERICAN FALLS AT NIAGARA--FINAL REPORT TO THE INTERNATIONAL JOINT COMMISSION.
American Falls International Board, Buffalo, N.Y.
For primary bibliographic entry see Field 6G.
W75-06574

RAIN--A WATER RESOURCE.
Department of the Interior, Washington, D.C.
For primary bibliographic entry see Field 3B.
W75-06586

CALIFORNIA SURFACE WATER LAW,
I. M. Goldman.
Hastings Law Journal, Vol 17, p 826-834, May 1966. 45 ref.

Descriptors: *Judicial decisions, *Natural flow doctrine, *Reasonable use, *California, *Surface waters, Surface runoff, Legal aspects, Land tenure, Water rights, Common law, Repulsion(Legal aspects), Riparian rights, Riddance(Legal aspects), Overland flow, Urban runoff, Civil law, Adjacent land owners, State jurisdiction, Runoff.
Identifiers: Comparative law, Water rights(Nonriparians).

A seeming confusion exists in the courts of California as to what the California law of surface waters is. This confusion is apparent in two conflicting decisions handed down recently by different state appellate courts. In the case of Keys v. Nomley, it was held that the common law doctrine of reasonable use governed surface water rights in urban areas. In Pagliotti v. Acquistapace, another court ruled that the law of California as to surface waters in urban, as well as rural, areas is the 'civil law' doctrine of natural flow. These two cases are evaluated and other California decisions concerning surface waters are also discussed. It is concluded that the civil law doctrine is and has been the law of California, but there is a trend toward adoption of the reasonable use rule. The two doctrines are compared and it is suggested that the reasonable use doctrine is the better rule, particularly for urban areas. (Sperling-Florida)
W75-06591

PRESERVATION OF WETLANDS: THE CASE OF SAN FRANCISCO BAY,
Environmental Protection Agency, Washington, D.C. Office of Water Programs.
R. A. Luken.
Natural Resources Journal, Vol 14, p 139-152, January 1974.

Descriptors: *Shore protection, *Interfaces, *Wetlands, *Bays, Conservation, Dredging, Dikes, Zoning, Government, Environmental control, Land development, reclamation, Economic justification, Economic impact, Weather patterns, Income analysis.
Identifiers: *Private interest groups, *State policy.

The extensive conversion of wetlands in the San Francisco Bay area has resulted in the creation of the San Francisco Bay Conservation and Development Commission. The Commission is authorized to regulate areas subject to Bay dredging, diking and filling and to control zoning within a shoreline band one-hundred feet deep from the landward limit of the Bay. Pressure for wetland conversion is attributable to commercial and governmental efforts directed towards economic development. This impetus can be overcome only if such Commissions maintain the support of those parties who are adversely affected by their endeavors. In particular, private property owners are subject to rental loss and communities face decreased tax revenue. Legal devices, acquisition and taxation controls, and transfer payments are all potential institutional devices which are capable of sustaining the support of such concerned interest groups. Measured against effectiveness, equity, and efficiency the legal and taxation techniques best minimize expense and promote effectiveness and equity, while the transfer payments best nullify community proclivity for development. (Gagliardi-Florida)
W75-06592

WATER: SUPPLY, DEMAND AND THE LAW,
Resources for the Future, Inc., Washington, D.C.
For primary bibliographic entry see Field 6D.
W75-06594

NEW WATER LAW PROBLEMS AND OLD PUBLIC LAW PRINCIPLES,
New Mexico Univ., Albuquerque.
For primary bibliographic entry see Field 6E.
W75-06595

PROVIDENCE RIVER AND HARBOR, RHODE ISLAND (FINAL ENVIRONMENTAL IMPACT STATEMENT).
Corps of Engineers, Waltham, Mass. New England Div.
For primary bibliographic entry see Field 5G.
W75-06615

INTERFERENCE WITH THE FLOW OF SURFACE WATER,
For primary bibliographic entry see Field 6E.
W75-06620

ORGANIZATIONAL PROBLEM-SOLVING,
Kansas Water Resources Research Inst., Manhattan.
For primary bibliographic entry see Field 6B.
W75-06643

ELEMENTS IN A DECISION FRAMEWORK FOR PLANNING THE ALLOCATION OF COASTAL LAND AND WATER RESOURCES WITH ILLUSTRATION FOR A COASTAL COMMUNITY,
Massachusetts Univ., Amherst. Dept. of Agricultural and Food Economics.
For primary bibliographic entry see Field 6B.
W75-06645

FORECASTING SNOWMELT RUNOFF IN THE UPPER MIDWEST,
Minnesota Univ., Minneapolis. Dept. of Civil and Mineral Engineering.
For primary bibliographic entry see Field 2A.
W75-06648

BACTERIOLOGY OF STREAMS AND THE ASSOCIATED VEGETATION OF A HIGH MOUNTAIN WATERSHED,
Wyoming Univ., Laramie. Water Resources Research Inst.
For primary bibliographic entry see Field 5B.
W75-06650

STUDY OF ALTERNATIVE DIVERSIONS. REPORT ON THE HYDROLOGICAL STUDIES OF MANITOBA HYDRO SYSTEM.
Underwood, McLellan and Associates Ltd., Winnipeg (Manitoba).
For primary bibliographic entry see Field 8B.
W75-06664

CHENANGO RIVER, FLOOD PLAIN INFORMATION.
Army Engineer District, Baltimore, Md.
For primary bibliographic entry see Field 2E.
W75-06677

SUSQUEHANA RIVER, FLOOD PLAIN INFORMATION.
Army Engineer District, Baltimore, Md.
For primary bibliographic entry see Field 2E.
W75-06678

SUSQUEHANNA AND CHENANGO RIVERS--FLOOD PLAIN INFORMATION.
Army Engineer District, Baltimore, Md.
For primary bibliographic entry see Field 2E.
W75-06679

METHOD OF EXCAVATING TO FORM OR ENLARGE A WATERWAY,
L. N. Smith.
U.S. Patent No. 3,867,772, 5 p, 9 fig, 7 ref; Official Gazette of the United States Patent Office, Vol 931, No 4, p 1471, February 25, 1975.

Descriptors: *Patents, *Water resources development, *Dredging, Reclamation, Earth handling equipment, Eutrophication, Lakes.

A method of enlarging an underwater basin or body of water having an earth bank with trees, brush, and roots growing on it, is to move a material collecting dredge element in a generally horizontal path below the water level to collect earth material from the bank. A rotating chipper disc having knife mechanism for reducing the trees, brush and roots to chips and fragments is also moved in a horizontal path at water level. Both the chipped material and earth material are removed by the dredge in slurry form. The object is to provide a method for economically reclaiming atrophied lakes and making new shorelines available at reasonable prices. (Sinha-OEIS)
W75-06689

REMOVAL OF MARINE GROWTHS FROM LAKES, WATERWAYS, AND OTHER BODIES OF WATER,
For primary bibliographic entry see Field 5G.
W75-06696

DRAINAGE DENSITY AND EFFECTIVE PRECIPITATION,
Sri Lanka Univ., Peradeniya. Dept. of Geography.
C. M. Madduma Bandara.
J Hydrol (Amst). Vol 21, No 2, p 187-190, 1974, illus.

Descriptors: *Precipitation(Atmospheric), *Drainage density, Evaporation, Water loss.
Identifiers: Sri-Lanka, *Ceylon.

Recently in a study of the morphometry of dissection in the central hills of Sri Lanka, it was found that the relationship between drainage density and effective precipitation in this area is significantly positive. This result when considered in combination with other findings could be interpreted as an indication that above a certain critical level of effective precipitation (i.e., 80-90) the relationship between drainage density and P/E index turns positive. Such a conclusion is in agreement with the results of recent work by Langbein and Schumm (1958) and Hadley and Schumm (1961), who demonstrated that sediment yield reaches a maximum under grassland conditions and possibly reaches another peak where the impeding effect of vegetation cannot be increased by further increase of precipitation.--Copyright 1974, Biological Abstracts, Inc.
W75-06704

WELLAND CANAL WATER QUALITY CONTROL EXPERIMENTS (PHASE II),
Department of the Environment, Ottawa (Ontario). Wastewater Technology Centre.
For primary bibliographic entry see Field 5G.
W75-06736

PEAK FLOWS BY THE SLOPE-AREA METHOD,
Department of the Environment, Ottawa (Ontario). Water Resources Branch.
For primary bibliographic entry see Field 2E.
W75-06745

NEW BRUNSWICK FLOOD, APRIL-MAY 1973.
Environmental Protection Service, Halifax (Nova Scotia). Atlantic Region.
Technical Bulletin No. 81, 114 p, 1974. 40 fig, 11 ref, 48 tab.

Descriptors: *Flooding, *Floods, *Snowmelt, *Runoff, *Rainfall, *Forecasting, Flood forecasting, Damages, Flood damage, Control, Flood control, Flood stages, Hydrographs, *Canada.
Identifiers: *Snow accumulation, Forecasting techniques.

During the latter part of April and early part of May 1973, extreme flood conditions occurred in most parts of New Brunswick. These conditions were caused by rainfall combined with heavy snowmelt. The most seriously affected part of the province was the flood plain of the Lower Saint John River in the Fredericton area and in the agricultural lands a few miles downstream of Fredericton. Damages in these two areas accounted for about 60 per cent of the total economic cost of the flood. During the 1973 flood, forecasting and emergency measures activities were successful in avoiding more serious personal hardship and greater economic losses. Warning provided through weather and streamflow forecasting permitted some advance planning to react to the emergency while the Emergency Measure Organization proved its worth in directing the disaster activities. In spite of this, the flood caused an estimated $2.5 million in damage to moveable property. Continuation and improvement of flood forecasting and emergency measures programs are clearly desirable. (Environment Canada)
W75-06749

FLOOD STAGES AND DISCHARGES FOR SMALL STREAMS IN TEXAS, 1972,
Geological Survey, Austin, Tex.
E. E. Schroeder.
Geological Survey open-file report, 1974. 283 p, 1 fig, 3 tab, 11 ref.

Descriptors: *Floods, *Texas, *Small watersheds, *Stage-discharge relations, *Basic data collections, Peak discharge, Gaging stations, Hydrologic data.

Basic hydrologic data that may be used to define the magnitude and frequency of floods for drainage areas of less than 20 square miles in Texas are compiled. A network of 150 crest-stage partial-record gages was established. These gages are distributed throughout the State to sample all hydrologic areas and flood-frequency regions. Each gage site is equipped with one or more crest-stage gages and a stage-rainfall recorder. Theoretical stage-discharge ratings have been computed for 142 stations utilizing the culvert geometry and slope in a computer program. The stage-discharge relation for the other eight gages, which are located at bridges, can be defined by current-meter measurements or by indirect methods such as slope-area, contracted-opening, slope-conveyance, flow-over-roadway embankment, or other special studies. (Knapp-USGS)
W75-06754

A SURVEY OF THE WATER RESOURCES OF ST. CROIX, VIRGIN ISLANDS,
Geological Survey of Puerto Rico, San Juan.
D. G. Jordan.
Geological Survey open-file report (Caribbean District), 1973. 131 p, 29 fig, 6 tab, 17 ref.

Descriptors: *Water resources, *Surface waters, *Groundwater, *Virgin Islands, Hydrologic data, Water yield, Water quality, Rainfall-runoff relationships.
Identifiers: *St. Croix(VI).

St. Croix, V. I., consists of two mountainous volcanic rock cores separated by a graben containing clays with minor limestone and conglomerate that is overlain by about 300 feet of marl and limestone. Predominantly fine-grained alluvium mantles much of the limestone and marl area and fills overdeepened south-trending valleys to depths of as much as 100 feet. Rainfall follows an orographic pattern ranging from about 30 inches in eastern St. Croix to 55 inches in the northwestern mountains. Storm runoff from individual storms seldom exceeds 5 percent of the rainfall. The low proportion of storm runoff is attributed to the capability of the soil zone to accept large volumes of water and deficient soil moisture most of the year. The retention of large volumes of rainfall in the soil zone from which it is evaporated and transpired by plants greatly reduces the water available for recharge to the aquifers of the island. Estimates of effective recharge to the aquifers range from less than 0.5 inch in some volcanic and marl rocks to 5 inches annually in more porous limestone and alluvium. Most areas where major groundwater supplies are available, principally in central St. Croix, have already been developed. The Castle Coakley area, with a potential yield of 400,000 gpd, is the only major groundwater area still undeveloped. Advancements in desalination have made the brackish groundwater in the Kingshill Marl (estimated at 35 billion recoverable gallons) a potential source of water. (Knapp-USGS)
W75-06757

HANDBOOK FOR A FLOOD PLAIN MANAGEMENT STRATEGY,
East-West Gateway Coordinating Council, St. Louis, Mo.
For primary bibliographic entry see Field 6F.
W75-06764

EVALUATION OF FOUR COMPLETED SMALL WATERSHED PROJECTS: SOUTH CAROLINA, MARYLAND, IDAHO-NEVADA, AND WEST VIRGINIA,
Economic Research Service, Washington, D.C.
For primary bibliographic entry see Field 4D.
W75-06765

FLOOD PLAIN INFORMATION: MILL CREEK, KOOSKOOSKIE AND VICINITY, WALLA WALLA COUNTY, WASHINGTON.
Army Engineer District, Walla Walla, Wash.
Prepared for Walla Walla County, Washington, May, 1972. 22 p, 6 fig, 3 tab, 13 plates, glossary.

Descriptors: *Flooding, *Floods, *Flood plain, Flood control, Flood protection, Levees, Historic flood, *Washington.
Identifiers: *Mill Creek(Wash), *Kooskooskie(Wash), Intermediate Regional Flood, Standard Project Flood.

Mill Creek slopes at 78 feet per mile and the channel averages 94 feet wide and 4.2 feet deep. The topography is extremely rugged and has been classed as the watershed for Walla Walla's water supply, which limits man's access and activities. The flood plain in the vicinity of Kooskooskie is mainly agricultural with some rural residences. Warm winds and rain cause a large winter runoff during December and January. Spring runoff caused by rainfall and snowmelt occurs in March and April. A stream gage at Kooskooskie and newspaper files provided data. Mill Creek is subject to short duration flash floods but not to sustained floods. Three of four bridges over the creek obstruct flood flow. A small diversion dam near Kooskooskie has no flood control capacity. A few small privately constructed levees offer little protection against a large flood. The greatest known flood occurred on December 23, 1964 cresting at 19.3 feet, where 16 feet marks the bankfull stage. The most recent flood on January 6, 1969, crested at 18.3 feet. Flood stages for an Intermediate Regional Flood would be 20.9 feet and for a Standard Project Flood would be 24.6 feet. Both supercede the largest known flood and, therefore, are capable of causing great damage and health hazards. Areas that would be flooded are detailed. (Salzman-North Carolina)
W75-06767

FLOOD PLAIN INFORMATION: BLACKSNAKE CREEK, ST. JOSEPH, MISSOURI.
Army Engineer District, Kansas City, Mo.
Prepared for the City of St. Joseph, Missouri and the Missouri Water Resources Board, April, 1971. 30 p, 8 fig, 3 tab, 7 plates.

Descriptors: Floods, Flooding, *Flood control, *Flood protection, *Flood plains, *Flood profiles, Farmponds, *Missouri.
Identifiers: *Blacksnake Creek(Mo), St. Joseph(Mo).

Blacksnake Creek, a small left bank tributary of the Missouri River, flows through St. Joseph to join the river. The watershed, with a drainage area of 8.6 square miles, has an elongated elliptical shape about 6 miles long and 2 miles wide. Channel dimensions are about 40 feet wide and 10 feet deep with a slope of 43 feet/mile. Lower channel is enclosed in a deteriorating conduit of varying sizes constructed to carry storm water and afford greater utilization of the lower flood plain area. Development in the flood plain averaging 400 feet wide consists of aged warehouses, commercial and industrial structures. Agricultural areas dominate portions of the flood plain north of St. Joseph. Most floods are caused by short duration thunderstorms having high intensity rainfall. Flood damage prevention measures include 8 flood detention structures and 9 farmponds which together control only the headwaters which is about 12% of the drainage area above the conduit. During the largest recorded flood in May, 1962, flood waters rose approximately 7 feet in half an hour and remained out of banks for over an hour. An Intermediate Regional Flood (IRF) and Standard Project Flood (SPF) would cause inundation of the flood plain with estimated peak discharges of 6400 cfs and 13,900 cfs with flows out of banks about six hours. Areas and depths of flooding are shown. (Salzman-North Carolina)
W75-06768

FLOOD PLAIN INFORMATION: NACHES RIVER, CITY OF NACHES AND VICINITY, WASHINGTON,
Army Engineer District, Seattle, Wash.
Prepared for Yakima County, May, 1972. 24 p, 8 fig, 6 tab, 13 plates.

Descriptors: *Flood plains, *Planning, *Flood plain zoning, *Flood profiles, Flood damage, Obstruction to flow, Historic floods, Flood data, Land use, *Washington.
Identifiers: *Naches River(Wash), Naches(Wash), Flood plain management, Standard Project Flood, Intermediate Regional Flood.

The narrow flood plain of the Naches River, a major tributary of the Yadkin River, is primarily agricultural with some commercial development. Valley hills are used for orchards, leaving only the lowlands adjacent to the river for future expansion of the city of Naches. Average river slope in the study reach is 30.8 feet/mile. Winter and spring

floods caused by heavy rainfall or snowmelt or a combination generally rise slowly and stay out of banks for long periods. Greatest recorded flood occurred in December, 1933. Due to insufficient data for this flood, the more recent flood of May, 1948 is used for comparison purposes. Peak discharge of the May, 1948 flood was 12,600 cfs with an elevation of 1567.5 feet, mean sea level datum. An Intermediate Regional Flood (IRF) would be 4.5 feet higher and would produce 33,500 cfs. Main channel velocity would average 12 to 15 feet/second and cause severe stream-bank erosion. A Standard Project Flood (SPF) would be another 4.5 feet higher with a peak discharge of 83,000 cfs. Levees along both banks at Naches and two irrigation storage reservoirs on upper tributaries have beneficial effects in reducing flooding in the flood plain area. The Comprehensive Land Use Plan for this area should be revised to reflect the flood plain and flood hazard information presented. (Diefendorf-North Carolina)
W75-06769

FLOOD PLAIN INFORMATION: LITTLE BLUE RIVER, EAST FORK, WHITE OAK BRANCH, JACKSON COUNTY, MISSOURI,
Army Engineer District, Kansas City, Mo.
Prepared for the Jackson County Court and the Missouri Water Resources Board, May, 1970. 33 p, 13 fig, 4 tab, 24 plates.

Descriptors: *Floods, *Flooding, *Flood control, *Flood plains, Flood protection, Levees, *Missouri.
Identifiers: *Jackson County(Mo), Little Blue River(Mo), East Fork(Mo), White Oak Branch(Mo).

Little Blue River, originating in north-central Cass County, Missouri, flows northward through Jackson County to join the Missouri River. With its tributaries, East Fork and White Oak Branch, the river drains an area of 270.2 square miles, 90% of which lies in Jackson Conty. Elevations range from 1000 feet, mean sea level (msl) in the headwaters to 700 feet msl at its mouth. The basin (overall length of 33 miles, maximum width of 13 miles) contains numerous impoundments including recreation lakes and private and public ponds. The flood plain lies along the southeastern fringe of Kansas City as well as portions of Independence with many of the developed residential and commercial properties unprotected. Much of the land is still in agricultural use. Downstream from East Fork, the river slopes 2.3 feet per mile with a channel width ranging from 30 to 80 feet and banks 18 to 24 feet high. Above East Fork, the stream slopes at 2.8 feet per mile with a channel width of 18 feet and bank height of 10 feet. Manmade encroachments including 27 bridges obstruct flood flow. Comprehensive flood damage prevention measures include an improved and enlarged channel in conjunction with the construction of the Atherton Levee, located in the lower flood plain. The largest known flood occurred on September 14, 1961 with a peak discharge of 9,460 cfs, cresting at 27.94 feet compared to the flood stage elevation of 18.0 feet. The most recently recorded flood on June 15, 1968 crested at 20.92 feet. An Intermediate Regional Flood and Standard Project Flood would have estimated peak discharges of 27,500 cfs and 52,000 cfs, respectively. Both would cause damages in excess of $40 million. (Salzman-North Carolina)
W75-06770

SPECIAL FLOOD HAZARD INFORMATION: MILL CREEK, UMATILLA COUNTY, OREGON.
Army Engineer District, Walla Walla, Wash.
Prepared for Umatilla County Oregon, February 1972. 10 p, 4 fig, 1 tab, 8 plates.

Descriptors: Floods, Flooding, *Flood plains, *Flood control, *Levees, Flood protection, *Washington, *Oregon.
Identifiers: *Mill Creek(Wash), Umatilla County(Wash), Henry Canyon(Ore), Intermediate Regional Flood, Standard Project Flood.

Mill Creek with a study reach of 1.6 miles extends from Oregon-Washington State line upstream to the mouth of Henry Canyon with most of the flood plain devoted to summer homes and cabins. The average stream slope is 84 feet per mile; its channel averages 73 feet in width and 4.4 feet in depth. Flooding on Mill Creek is frequent, occurring 29 times in the past 36 years. Floods on Mill Creek are of short duration and flood stages rise and recede rapidly. Road bridge approach fills for 5 bridges and brush in the channel restrict flood flows. A levee, between sections 102 and 103, reduces high flows somewhat, but it is vulnerable to failure due to construction material, lack of adequate bank protection, and existing channel alignment which directs flow at the levee. The largest known flood occurred on March 31, 1931. An Intermediate Regional Flood would have an estimated discharge of 3000 cfs at the state line, while a Standard Project Flood resulting from severe rainfall plus snowmelt would result in a discharge of 8250 cfs. (Salzman-North Carolina)
W75-06771

FLOOD PLAIN INFORMATION: YAKIMA RIVER, CITY OF SELAH AND VICINITY, WASHINGTON.
Army Engineer District, Seattle, Wash.
Prepared for Yakima County and City of Selah, June 1973. 26 p, 9 fig, 7 tab, 10 plates.

Descriptors: *Flood plains, *Flood plain zoning, *Land use, Planning, Flood damage, Flood data, Flood profiles, Obstruction to flow, Reservoirs, Dams, Levees, *Washington, Historic floods.
Identifiers: *Yakima River(Wash), Selah(Wash), Yakima Valley(Wash), Flood plain management, Standard Project Flood, Intermediate Regional Flood.

Hills adjacent to Yakima Valley are used extensively for orchards, leaving the less fertile valley floor relatively undeveloped, and a convenient site for future expansion of Selah. Selah Valley is about 4 miles long and 1 1/2 miles wide; the section of the Yakima River described covers a reach of approximately 8 miles with flood plain primarily agricultural land and irrigated pasture with some commercial, industrial, and residential development. Highest flood flow recorded was in November 1906 although the December 1973 discharge would have been greater had crests not been materially reduced by operation of upstream reservoirs. Winter floods from rainfall may be expected in November and December. Spring floods are caused primarily by snowmelt. Extensive levees along both banks and floatable materials stored on the flood plain create a constricting effect during floods. As compared to the peak discharge of 41,000 cfs at Umtanum gage in 1906, peak discharge of an Intermediate Regional Flood (IRF) would be 35,000 cfs and of a Standard Project Flood (SPF) 60,000 cfs. Main channel velocity of flow would average 8 to 10 feet/second for an IRF causing severe erosion and transporting large objects. Both types of flood would result in inundation of developed land, causing considerable damage. (Diefendorf-North Carolina)
W75-06772

SPECIAL FLOOD HAZARD INFORMATION REPORT: BAYOU SARA, BAYOU SARA CREEK, NORTON CREEK, HELLS SWAMP BRANCH, VICINITY OF SARALAND, ALABAMA.
Army Engineer District, Mobile, Ala.
Prepared for City of Saraland, August 1972. 23 p, 10 fig, 6 tab, 8 plates.

Descriptors: *Flood forecasting, *Flood control, *Flood plains, *Flood damage, *Flood profiles, Flood data, Historic floods, Obstruction to flow, Flash floods, Land use, Planning, *Alabama, Hurricanes, Thunderstorms, Tidal effects.
Identifiers: Bayou Sara(Ala), Bayou Sara Creek(Ala), Norton Creek(Ala), Hells Swamp Branch(Ala), Saraland(Ala), Mobile Bay, U.S. Highway No. 43(Ala), Standard Project Flood, Intermediate Regional Flood, Flood plain management.

In the vicinity of Saraland in southwest Alabama, numerous residential, industrial, and commercial developments are subject to flooding and have been damaged by past floods. Norton Creek, a tributary of Bayou Sara Creek, traverses the city with 12 bridges creating obstructions to flow. Parts of Norton Creek and Hells Swamp Branch channels are completely clogged by debris. Floods resulting from tropical storms occur mostly during August and September, from frontal type storms during winter, and in summer from thunderstorms. Hurricane tidal surges in Mobile Bay also create critical floods. The largest recorded flood occurred in April 1955 from phenomenal rainfall resulting in flash flooding. Peak discharges at U.S. Highway No. 43 on Bayou Sara Creek for the 1955 flood was 15,000 cfs compared to 14,400 cfs for an Intermediate Regional Flood (IRF) and 20,900 cfs for a Standard Project Flood (SPF). Above Craft Highway approximately 2,900 acres would be flooded by an IRF with 3,850 acres being flooded by an SPF. Both floods would create hazardous conditions. A system of levees, floodwalls, and diversion channel to protect urban development was considered but not recommended as annual cost would have exceeded annual benefit. However, a channel enlargement and clearing project on Norton Creek has been completed. (Diefendorf-North Carolina)
W75-06773

REMOTE SENSING,
Bureau of Reclamation, Washington, D.C.
For primary bibliographic entry see Field 7B.
W75-06775

FLOOD PLAIN INFORMATION: SPRING BRANCH, INDEPENDENCE, MISSOURI.
Army Engineer District, Kansas City, Mo.
Prepared for the City of Independence, Missouri, February 1973. 25 p, 16 fig, 4 tab, 8 plates.

Descriptors: Floods, *Flooding, *Flood control, *Flood plain, *Flood protection, Flood flow, *Flood profiles, *Missouri, Velocity.
Identifiers: *Spring Branch(Mo), Independence(Mo), Intermediate Regional Flood(IRF), Standard Project Flood(SPF).

Spring Branch Basin drains a 10.75 square mile area in northeastern Independence. The channel slopes at an average of 24 feet/mile with a width of 30 feet. Flood plain has a sewage treatment plant plus agricultural land interspersed with residential and industrial areas. No gaging station exists. Newspaper files, historical documents and records provided information. Flood producing storms occur from April through October causing floods of high peaks, high velocities, short duration and relatively small run-off. Channel debris and continued encroachment on flood plain impede flood flow. Although no planned flood damage program exists for Spring Branch, Independence is planning a recreational dam and reservoir on one of the stream's small tributaries, but it will have little effect on flood flow. According to newspaper accounts the greatest flooding occurred on September 14, 1961 as a result of intense rainfall in a 24 hour period and created problems of overflow near the sewer treatment plant. Plant floods have been of minor magnitude on Spring Branch. However, based on analysis of flow records of nearby streams, an Intermediate Regional Flood (IRF) or Standard Project Flood (SPF) would inundate the flood plain with possible velocities of flow as much as 16.9 feet/second and 20.3 feet/second respectively in the channel. An SPF could rise at

the rate of 3 feet/hour and be above bankfull for approximately 8 hours. Release of raw sewage caused by inability of sewage treatment plant to handle high discharges would create a health hazard for the entire community. (Salzman-North Carolina)
W75-06779

KEY LAND USE ISSUES FACING EPA.
Harbridge House, Inc., Boston, Mass.
For primary bibliographic entry see Field 5G.
W75-06780

FLOOD HAZARD ANALYSES: FOX RUN, STARK AND WAYNE COUNTIES, OHIO.
Soil Conservation Service, Columbus, Ohio.
For primary bibliographic entry see Field 2E.
W75-06781

URBAN SYSTEMS ENGINEERING DEMONSTRATION PROGRAM FOR HINDS, MADISON, RANKIN COUNTIES, MISSISSIPPI, VOLUME I: AREA-WIDE WATER SYSTEMS.
Clark, Dietz and Associates, Inc., Jackson, Miss
For primary bibliographic entry see Field 5D.
W75-06783

URBAN SYSTEMS ENGINEERING DEMONSTRATION PROGRAM FOR HINDS, MADISON, RANKIN COUNTIES, MISSISSIPPI, VOLUME IV. AREA-WIDE STORM DRAINAGE AND FLOOD PLAIN MANAGEMENT STUDIES.
Clark, Dietz and Associates, Inc., Jackson, Miss.
For primary bibliographic entry see Field 5D.
W75-06785

COMPREHENSIVE LAND USE PLANNING-ITS DEVELOPMENT AND POTENTIAL IMPACT ON COASTAL ZONE MANAGEMENT,
Rhode Island Univ., Kingston. Marine Affairs Program.
R. A. Sinta.
Marine Affairs Journal, Number 1, p 9-32, December 1973.

Descriptors: *Planning, *Coasts, *Land use, *Land management, *Land resources, *Legislation, *Rhode Island, Zoning, Natural resources, Local governments, State governments, Federal governments.
Identifiers: *Coastal zone management, *Coastal Resource Management Council, Office of Regional Planning, *Land use policy, Jackson Land Use Bill, Muskie Land Use Bill.

Due to inadequate management practices of local, state and regional governments, the federal government has become involved in comprehensive land use policies. Developed from the Jackson, Muskie and Nixon Administration Bills, federal policy supports state participation in areas of regional and/or statewide impact. Local governments are also authorized to develop, implement and regulate land use plans. On the national level the Office of Regional Planning within the Department of Interior is already involved with coastal zone activities with increased responsibility for coastal areas of environmental concern likely in the future. Rhode Island's coastal zone management stems from a statewide land use plan which considers the factors of urban sprawl, population growth, inadequate protection of water supplies, inadequate protection for estuarine and marine fisheries and inadequate provision for future recreation uses. Existing state laws exercise land use control through zoning, land acquisition, and other regulations. Adoption of a comprehensive system whereby local governments must conform to local imposed zoning is urged. The Coastal Resources Management Council should be organized with the State Department of Natural Resources with competent experts in coastal zone affairs. (Salzman-North Carolina)
W75-06787

SPECIAL FLOOD HAZARD INFORMATION REPORT: GALLAGHER CREEK, MERIDIAN, LAUDERDALE COUNTY, MISSISSIPPI.
Army Engineer District, Mobile, Ala.
Prepared for Mississippi Research and Development Center, June 1972. 13 p, 2 tab, 11 plates.

Descriptors: *Floods, *Flooding, *Flood plain, *Flood control, *Flood profiles, Flood protection, Flash floods, *Mississippi, Flood damages, Velocity.
Identifiers: *Gallagher Creek(Miss), Meridian(Miss), Lauderdale County(Miss), Intermediate Regional Flood(IRF), Greater Probable Flood(GPF).

Gallagher Creek, having a slope of 21 feet/mile, flows south through Meridian for 7 miles before emptying into Sowashee Creek. Its narrow drainage basin (average width of one mile) is about 75% urbanized with much residential property in the flood plain. Since it is ungaged, data were limited in compiling historical information as well as forecasting future flood information. Floods in winter and spring are caused by frontal type storms lasting 2 to 4 days and covering large areas. Summer thunderstorms with a high intensity over small areas may cause flash flooding. To reduce flood crests, Meridian has replaced some of smaller culverts with larger bridges and cleared the channel of trees and undergrowth in some places. No flood regulation measures exist. One of the largest floods occurred on July 30, 1971 with an estimated peak discharge of 4500 cubic feet per second and caused damages of about $1.5 million. An Intermediate Regional Flood (IRF) and a Greater Probable Flood (GPF) which has an average frequency of occurrence once in 500 years would be of equal or greater magnitude than previous floods. An IRF could result in inundation of 500 acres of residential and commercial sections of Meridian including private and public utilities with about 600 acres damaged by a GPF. Main channel velocities can be expected of 4 to 11 feet/second for an IRF, slightly higher during a GPF. (Salzman-North Carolina)
W75-06792

FLOOD PLAIN INFORMATION: LOS PENASQUITOS DRAINAGE AREA, SAN DIEGO COUNTY, CALIFORNIA.
Army Engineer District, Los Angeles, Calif.
Prepared for San Diego County and the City of San Diego, May 1967. 26 p, 6 fig, 31 plates, append.

Descriptors: *Flood, *Flood plain, *Flood profile, *Flood damage, Flood water, *California.
Identifiers: San Diego County(Calif), Soledad Canyon(Calif), Carmel Valley(Calif), *Los Penasquitos Creek(Calif), Intermediate Regional Flood, Standard Project Flood.

Los Penasquitos area, mostly in an undeveloped part of San Diego County, is about 15 miles north of the City of San Diego. This study includes parts of the flood plains of Soledad Canyon, Carmel Valley, Los Penasquitos Creek, Poway Creek, Rattlesnake Creek, and Pomerado Valley. A special problem area is Poway Valley, 3.5 miles long with a total drainage area of about 4.4 miles, where project-housing developments have been built with some homes and roads in the flood plain, and some of the flood-control channels constructed are inadequate for large floods. Steady growth continues in manufacturing, government, and tourism, the major industries, with rapid increases in population and in urban and industrial development. Since the land is semiarid with streamflows generally occurring only during storms, flood hazards are often not apparent. Areas along downstream reaches of streams are most vulnerable to flood damage. Channels are poorly defined and adequate to accommodate only minor flows. Nature and extent of flood problems for San Diego County, Los Penasquitos area and each sub-area are given. Storms lasting several days occurring from December through March cause most floods. Plates show the extent of flooding in the various areas for a Standard Project Flood, an Intermediate Regional Flood (100-year flood), and a lesser flood (50-year). The overflow area of the Intermediate Regional Flood has been selected by local interests to be used in flood plain planning and regulation. (Park-North Carolina)
W75-06793

4B. Groundwater Management

SUBSURFACE WASTE DISPOSAL BY INJECTION IN HAWAII: A CONCEPTUAL FORMULATION AND PHYSICAL MODELING PLAN,
Hawaii Univ., Honolulu. Water Resources Research Center.
For primary bibliographic entry see Field 5B.
W75-06351

THE IMPORTANCE OF SALINITY IN URBAN WATER MANAGEMENT,
Culp, Wesner, Culp Clean Water Consultants, Corona Del Mar, Calif.
For primary bibliographic entry see Field 3C.
W75-06372

HYDROGEOLOGY AND WATER QUALITY MANAGEMENT,
Moody and Associates, Inc., Harrisburg, Pa. Environmental Services Div.
For primary bibliographic entry see Field 5G.
W75-06400

ECONOMIC AND ENVIRONMENTAL EVALUATION OF NUCLEAR WASTE DISPOSAL BY UNDERGROUND IN SITU MELTING,
California Univ., Livermore. Lawrence Livermore Lab.
For primary bibliographic entry see Field 5B.
W75-06413

HYDROLOGIC CHARACTERISTICS AND RESPONSE OF FRACTURED TILL AND CLAY CONFINING A SHALLOW AQUIFER,
Waterloo Univ. (Ontario). Dept. of Earth Sciences.
For primary bibliographic entry see Field 2F.
W75-06434

EFFECT OF APPLICATION RATE, INITIAL SOIL WETNESS, AND REDISTRIBUTION TIME ON SALT DISPLACEMENT BY WATER,
Punjab Agricultural Univ., Ludhiana (India). Dept. of Soils.
For primary bibliographic entry see Field 2G.
W75-06437

RATIONAL PROTECTION OF WATER RESOURCES IN COASTAL ZONES THROUGH PLANNED DEVELOPMENT,
Florida Univ., Gainesville. Dept. of Civil and Coastal Engineering.
B. A. Christensen.
Water Resources Bulletin, Vol 9, No 6, p 1201-1209, December 1973. 8 fig, 7 ref.

Descriptors: *Planning, *Land management, *Groundwater, *Water resources, Saline water intrusion, Comprehensive planning, Future, Planning(Projected), Alternative planning, Conservation, Interfaces, Coasts, Preservation, *Florida.

A study was described from a purely groundwater resources standpoint, dealing with the establishment of methods for identification of areas which are suitable development and of areas where complete preservation or controlled and limited

development should be encouraged. A graphic methodology was proposed. Required data input is available from most federal and state agencies involved with water resources inventories or development. The procedure was said to be usable by the nontechnically trained user. (Jess-ISWS)
W75-06446

A SURROGATE-PARAMETER APPROACH TO MODELING GROUNDWATER BASINS,
Colorado State Univ., Fort Collins. Dept. of Civil Engineering.
For primary bibliographic entry see Field 2F.
W75-06449

PICKLING LIQUORS, STRIP MINES, AND GROUND-WATER POLLUTION,
Ohio State Univ., Columbus. Dept. of Geology and Mineralogy.
For primary bibliographic entry see Field 5B.
W75-06450

NATURAL SOIL NITRATE: THE CAUSE OF THE NITRATE CONTAMINATION OF GROUND WATER IN RUNNELS COUNTY, TEXAS,
Texas Univ., Austin. Bureau of Economic Geology.
For primary bibliographic entry see Field 5B.
W75-06452

THE EFFECTS OF DIMINISHED GROUND-WATER SUPPLIES ON SELECTED NEW HAMPSHIRE INDUSTRIES: AN ECONOMIC AND LEGAL EVALUATION,
New Hampshire Univ., Durham. Water Resource Research Center.
R. H. Forste.
Available from the National Technical Information Service, Springfield, Virginia 22161, as PB-241 127, $4.25 in paper copy, $2.25 in microfiche. Bulletin No 5, June 1973, 71 p, 15 fig, 27 tab, 26 ref. OWRT A-028-NH(3), 14-31-0001-3529.

Descriptors: *Water management(Applied), *Water utilization, *Groundwater, *Reasonable use, Competing uses, Legal aspects, Water rights, Resource allocation, Economics, Water law, *New Hampshire, Water supply, Institutional constraints, Withdrawal, Water allocation(Policy), Industries, Water sources.

Increasing withdrawals of groundwater for industrial and residential uses in New Hampshire present allocation problems involving legal and economic equity. Legal issues have been based on the rule of reasonable use. To deal with groundwater allocation the economic damages/losses resulting from diminished groundwater should be considered and estimated. The New Hampshire courts haven't had these estimates, or a methodology for determining them. The objectives of this study were to (1) estimate the costs incurred by industrial groundwater users if supply constraints are imposed; (2) outline a methodological framework to guide decisions on resource allocations; (3) assess the impact on selected industrial groundwater users in the short-run and project long-run adjustments under supply contraints. Four firms were selected for analysis. Cost structure of the firms was related to their industrial processes. The groundwater law and equity were examined. Several implications may be drawn from the findings: (1) research on the availability of groundwater supplies is necessary; (2) ownership of groundwater rests in the public and should be utilized accordingly; (3) the premise of societal ownership implies regulation and management of the resource by the State; (4) regulatory commissions and courts should have the economic implications of alternatives available when faced with a groundwater dispute. The partial budgeting simulations developed provide an example of one technique that would be feasible, useful and expeditious in this context. (Wakefield-New Hampshire)
W75-06463

PRELIMINARY STUDIES ON QUALITY OF UNDERGROUND WATERS ON GROWTH AND YIELD OF COCONUT (COCOS NUCIFERA),
Regional Research Station, Mudigere (India).
For primary bibliographic entry see Field 3C.
W75-06466

IMPLEMENTATION PACKAGE FOR A DRAINAGE BLANKET IN HIGHWAY PAVEMENT SYSTEMS,
Federal Highway Administration, Washington, D.C., Implementation Div.
For primary bibliographic entry see Field 4C.
W75-06470

PUBLIC GROUNDWATER SUPPLIES IN MASON COUNTY,
Illinois State Water Survey, Urbana.
D. M. Woller, and J. P. Gibb.
Available from the National Technical Information Service, Springfield, Va 22161 as PB-241 131, $3.25 in paper copy, $2.25 in microfiche. Bulletin 60-12, 1975, 9 p.

Descriptors: *Water supply, *Illinois, *Groundwater resources, *Well data, Unconsolidated aquifers, Gravels, Sand aquifers, Groundwater, Groundwater availability, Hydrology, Hydrogeology, Water resources, Water quality, Water wells, Municipal water, Water yield, Water properties, Hardness(Water), Chemical properties, Shallow wells, Deep wells, Geology.
Identifiers: Mason County(Ill), Dissolved minerals, Water bearing formations.

All available information is reported on production wells used for public groundwater supplies in Mason County, Illinois. The definition of public water supply as contained in the Environmental Protection Act of 1970 was used to determine those water systems and wells to be included. Sand and gravel deposits in the unconsolidated materials above bedrock are tapped as the sources for municipal water supplies. There are 11 municipal production and standby wells tapping these aquifers to depths ranging from 78 to 222 ft. Reported yields range from 60 to 1000 gpm depending primarily upon the type of well constructed and the permeability, thickness, and areal extent of the sand and gravel unit tapped by each well. The iron content of these wells ranges from 0.0 to 4.6 mg/1, and the hardness from 140 to 341 mg/1. A description for each production well includes the aquifer tapped, date drilled, depth, driller, legal location, elevation in feet above mean sea level, log, construction features, yield, pumping equipment, and chemical analyses. (Humphreys-ISWS)
W75-06527

PUBLIC GROUNDWATER SUPPLIES IN STARK COUNTY,
Illinois State Water Survey, Urbana.
D. M. Woller, and J. P. Gibb.
Available from the National Technical Information Service, Springfield, Va 22161 as PB-241 132, $3.25 in paper copy, $2.25 in microfiche. Bulletin 60-11, 1975. 10 p, 1 fig.

Descriptors: *Water supply, *Illinois, *Groundwater resources, *Well data, Aquifers, Bedrock, Sandstones, Dolomite, Groundwater, Groundwater availability, Hydrology, Hydrogeology, Water resources, Water quality, Water wells, Municipal water, Water yield, Water properties, Hardness(Water), Chemical properties, Deep wells, Geology, Sulfates, Chlorides.
Identifiers: *Stark County(Ill), Dissolved minerals, Water bearing formations.

All available information is reported on production wells used for public groundwater supplies in Stark County, Illinois. The definition of public water supply as contained in the Environmental Protection Act of 1970 was used to determine those water systems and wells to be included. Unconsolidated sand and gravel deposits generally do not provide adequate water for municipal use and have not been tapped by any municipalities. Underlying bedrock units are tapped for water supplies. Seven wells, ranging in depth from 758 to 2082 ft, have reported yields from 52 to 320 gpm. Analyses of water they produce indicate the iron content ranges from 0.0 to 2.4 mg/1, hardness from 55 to 324 mg/1, sulfates from 60 to 350 mg/1, chlorides from 200 to 600 mg/1, and total dissolved minerals from 900 to 1900 mg/1. A description for each well includes the aquifer or aquifers tapped, date drilled, depth, driller, legal location, elevation in feet above mean sea level, log, construction features, yield, pumping equipment, and chemical analyses. (Humphreys-ISWS)
W75-06528

PUBLIC GROUNDWATER SUPPLIES IN PERRY COUNTY,
Illinois State Water Survey, Urbana.
D. M. Woller.
Available from the National Technical Information Service, Springfield, Va 22161 as PB-241 133, $3.25 in paper copy, $2.25 in microfiche. Bulletin 60-13, 1975. 5 p.

Descriptors: *Water supply, *Illinois, *Groundwater resources, *Well data, Groundwater, Groundwater availability, Hydrology, Hydrogeology, Water resources, Water quality, Water wells, Municipal water, Water yield, Water properties, Hardness(Water), Chemical properties, Deep wells, Aquifers, Geology, Bedrock, Sandstones.
Identifiers: *Perry County(Ill), Dissolved minerals, Water bearing formations.

All available information is reported on production wells used for public water supplies in Perry County, Illinois. The definition of public water supply as contained in the Environmental Protection Act of 1970 was used to determine those water systems and wells to be included. Consolidated bedrock aquifers are tapped as the primary source of municipal water supply. Two wells tap Pennsylvanian sandstones at depths of 550 and 575 ft. Their reported yields are 33 and 130 gpm. Past and recent analyses of water they produce indicate that the iron content ranges from 0.0 to 0.7 mg/l and the hardness ranges from 166 to 186 mg/l. Pennsylvanian sandstone and underlying Mississippian limestone are tapped by two wells 550 and 557 ft deep. Their reported yields are 40 and 90 gpm. Their iron content ranges from 0.4 to 1.4 mg/l and their hardness ranges from 183 to 220 mg/l. Water from the shallower Pennsylvanian rocks including thin coals is fairly highly mineralized in most of Perry County. For this reason, these rocks have been cased from the well and the deeper sandstone and limestone units containing less mineralized water are tapped for municipal supplies. A description for each production well includes the aquifer tapped, date drilled, depth, driller, legal location, elevation in feet above mean sea level, log, construction features, yield, pumping equipment, and chemical analyses. (Humphreys-ISWS)
W75-06529

ANALYSIS OF RELIEF WELLS IN EMBANKMENTS,
Osmania Univ., Hyderabad (India). Dept. of Civil Engineering.
D. B. Rao.
Indian Geotechnical Journal, Vol 4, No 3, p 271-277, July 1974. 3 fig, 2 tab, 5 ref.

Descriptors: *Groundwater, *Seepage, *Embankments, *Pressure head, *Dewatering, Unsteady flow, Levees, Alluvial aquifers, Mathe-

matical studies, Theis equation, Well spacing, High pressure, Analytical techniques, Equations, Confined water, Drawdown, Hydrostatic pressure, Surface-groundwater relationships, Earth dams, Sand boils.
Identifiers: *Relief wells.

Seepage under earth dams and levees through pervions foundations is a serious problem. Relief wells are particularly effective to control the seepage and hydrostatic pressures. Available formulas and design methods pertain to steady state seepage; however, this does not truly represent the actual response during early stages of pumping. Analytical and graphical results were given to assess the parameters involved in the analysis of transient seepage flow for pressure relief problems. (Prickett-ISWS)
W75-06537

WATER TABLE POSITION AS AFFECTED BY SOIL AIR PRESSURE,
Agricultural Research Service, Reno, Nev.
D. R. Linden, and R. M. Dixon.
Water Resources Research, Vol 11, No 1, p 139-143, February 1975. 6 fig, 8 ref.

Descriptors: *Drainage, *Irrigation, *Border irrigation, *Water table, *Recharge, Groundwater, Piezometers, Atmospheric pressure, Groundwater recharge, Infiltration, On-site investigations.
Identifiers: *Soil air pressure, Hydraulic head.

Air pressure in the unsaturated soil and hydraulic heads beneath a shallow water table were measured during border irrigations. Air pressures rose during the irrigation, thereby increasing the hydraulic heads. The increased hydraulic heads were not uniformly distributed under the border strip but varied in the cross-slope and with-slope directions and thus caused groundwater redistribution. Cross-slope and with-slope variations in air pressures also caused variations in infiltration and groundwater recharge. (Schicth-ISWS)
W75-06549

DRAINAGE OF GROUNDWATER RESTING ON A SLOPING BED WITH UNIFORM RAINFALL,
Agricultural Research Council, Cambridge (England). Unit of Soil Physics.
G. D. Towner.
Water Resources Research, Vol 11, No 1, p 144-147, February 1975. 3 fig, 1 tab, 5 ref.

Descriptors: *Drainage, *Groundwater, *Water table aquifers, *Rainfall, *Ditches, Steady flow, Hydraulic conductivity, Watersheds(Divides), Equations, Water table, Height, Slopes, Surface-groundwater relationships.
Identifiers: *Sloping aquifer.

The differential equation derived by Childs for groundwater flow over a sloping bed, the streamlines being assumed to be parallel to the slope, is integrated for the case of ditches and uniform rainfall. Experssions are obtained for the maximum vertical water table height, the location of this maximum and of the watershed, and the water table shape. Calculated water table heights are in much better agreement with previously published experimental data than those calculated from an earlier theory based on the assumption that streamlines are horizontal. Thus Childs' revised assumption is confirmed. An approximate solution for the form of the water table under small rainfall rates is also derived. (Visocky-ISWS)
W75-06550

UNIQUE WATER SUPPLY PROBLEMS IN THE NORTH WEST OF SOUTH AUSTRALIA,
South Australian Dept. of Health, Adelaide.
For primary bibliographic entry see Field 6D.
W75-06553

ADMINISTRATION OF GROUND WATER AS BOTH A RENEWABLE AND NONRENEWABLE RESOURCE,
Idaho Bureau of Mines and Geology, Moscow.
D. R. Ralston.
Water Resources Bulletin, Vol 9, No 5, p 908-917, October 1973. 4 fig, 6 ref.

Descriptors: *Groundwater, *Management, *Water law, *Administration, *Idaho, Water rights, Hydraulics, Annual, Recharge, Discharge(Water), Aquifers, Water levels, Water storage, Wells, Pumping, Rates, Stock water, Flow, *Water resources, River basins.
Identifiers: *Raft River Basin(Idaho).

Groundwater is intended to be administered in many western states as a flow or renewable resource. In Idaho, this administration is based on the appropriation doctrine of water rights. Two generalizations may be made concerning groundwater. First, water artificially discharged from an aquifer system must deplete the total resource by that amount; water consumptively pumped from a well must be derived from either increased recharge, decreased discharge, or a decrease of water in storage. Second, the annual rate of recharge to a groundwater system is often only a small percentage of the total resource in storage. Groundwater may be divided into flow and stock portions. In those basins where the second generalization is true, most groundwater may be classified as stock. However, only the flow portion of groundwater may be developed if utilization of the resource is to be enjoyed over an infinite period. Data from the Raft River Basin in Idaho indicate that the flow and stock characteristics of groundwater are time dependent. The resource exhibits the characteristics of both a renewable and nonrenewable resource. As a result, present administrative techniques do not provide for effective management of the resource. (Bell-Cornell)
W75-06570

GROUNDWATER POLLUTION: CASE LAW THEORIES FOR RELIEF,
Missouri Univ., Columbia.
For primary bibliographic entry see Field 5B.
W75-06589

PROGRAM SOPH - SIMULATION OF TIME-VARIANT PIEZOMETRIC SURFACE IN A CONFINED AQUIFER SUBJECT TO PUMPING,
Department of the Environment, Ottawa (Ontario). Water Resources Branch.
A. Vanden Berg.
Inland Waters Directorate, 1974. 56 p, 10 fig, 2 ref, 9 tab, append.

Descriptors: *Aquifers, *Piezometry, *Computer programs, *Pump testing, *Groundwater, Simulation analysis, Aquifer characteristics, Wells, Operations research, Synthetic hydrology, Dynamic programming, Model studies, Computers, Theoretical analysis.

The necessary documentation is provided for the application of computer program SOPH (Simulation of Piezometric Head). SOPH employs the alternating direction implicit procedure (ADIP) to calculate the time-variant piezometric-head distribution in a two-dimensional aquifer which is subjected to pumping and/or recharging. The preparation of the input card deck is described in detail and further clarified by working out an example. A listing of the FORTRAN program is given in the appendix. (Environment Canada)
W75-06737

SUBSURFACE DISPOSAL OF WASTE IN CANADA - II, DISPOSAL-FORMATION AND INJECTION-WELL HYDRAULICS,
Department of the Environment, Ottawa (Ontario). Water Resources Branch.
For primary bibliographic entry see Field 5E.
W75-06750

SUBSURFACE DISPOSAL OF WASTE IN CANADA - III - REGIONAL EVALUATION OF POTENTIAL FOR UNDERGROUND DISPOSAL OF INDUSTRIAL LIQUID WASTES,
Water Resources Branch.
For primary bibliographic entry see Field 5E.
W75-06751

GROUND-WATER LEVELS AND WELL RECORDS FOR CURRENT OBSERVATION WELLS IN IDAHO, 1922-73, PARTS A, B, AND C,
Geological Survey, Boise, Idaho.
H. G. Sisco.
Geological Survey Basic-Data Release (3 volumes), September 1974. Total pages 1234 (vol 1-309; vol 2-495; and vol 3-430).

Descriptors: *Basic data collections, *Idaho, *Hydrologic data, Water levels, *Water wells, Withdrawal, *Observation wells.

The groundwater-level data presented were collected to provide the basic data needed by agencies and individuals interested in developing, managing, and administering the groundwater resources in Idaho. The development of Idaho's groundwater resources has expanded at a very rapid rate in recent years. A large part of the agricultural water supply, as well as most municipal, industrial, and domestic supplies, is derived from wells. Use of groundwater has been accompanied by a decline of local and, in some cases, regional groundwater levels. The operation of this statewide observation-well network also provides data that can be used to: (1) indicate changes in the amount of groundwater in storage and thereby suggest the water-supply outlook for the future; (2) identify areas in which groundwater levels are at or are approaching land surface, or are declining toward current or foreseeable limits of economic lift; (3) forecast changes in the base flow of streams; and (4) provide long-term records for use in water-resource investigations. (Knapp-USGS)
W75-06753

GROUND-WATER DATA FOR MICHIGAN,
Geological Survey, Lansing, Mich.
For primary bibliographic entry see Field 7C.
W75-06756

A SURVEY OF THE WATER RESOURCES OF ST. CROIX, VIRGIN ISLANDS,
Geological Survey of Puerto Rico, San Juan.
For primary bibliographic entry see Field 4A.
W75-06757

KALAMAZOO COUNTY, MICHIGAN, WATER QUALITY STUDY.
Jones and Henry, Toledo, Ohio.
For primary bibliographic entry see Field 5G.
W75-06759

EDWARDS AQUIFER, A STUDY OF EDWARDS RECHARGE ZONE REQUIREMENTS, AACOG WATER QUALITY PLANNING, PHASE 5,
Alamo Area Council of Governments, San Antonio, Tex.
W. F. Wilson.
1970. 25 p, 12 fig.

Descriptors: *Spring waters, *Aquifer management, *Groundwater, Water yield, *Saline water intrusion, Water sources, Water storage, Aquifer characteristics, Groundwater reservoirs, Groundwater recharge, Natural recharge, Safe yield, Water supply, Water pollution, Waste water treatment, Sewage effluents, *Texas, *Recharge.
Identifiers: *San Antonio(Tex), *Edwards Aquifer(Tex).

Both the quantity and quality of water discharged from the Edwards Aquifer around San Antonio and the Alamo Area Council of Governments (AACOG) region, supplying 90% of its water. Since 1950 the annual accumulated discharge has exceeded the accumulated recharge 78% of the time. If pumpage from the Edwards continues to increase as it has this deficit will increase, reducing pressure in the fresh water zone and allowing salt water intrusion to the area's wells. Alternative sources of water must be developed or consumption decreased: at the present growth rate in the region the projected water needs by 2000 exceed the combined resources of the Edwards Aquifer, Applewhite Lake, Cibolo Lake, even if the Aquifer were pumped so much that the natural springs in the area stopped flowing. This is perhaps a clear case of population growth limited by water supply. A related problem is water quality. The 28,000 square miles of attractive rolling topography where the Edwards outcrops to the north of San Antonio is under increasing pressures of urbanization. A regional water treatment system is needed on the Edwards recharge area to prevent disastrous contamination of this fresh water source from a dispersed arrangement of small treatment plants. (Herr-North Carolina)
W75-06761

ANALYSIS OF ELECTRICAL RESISTIVITY MEASUREMENTS OF SHALLOW DEPOSITS,
Iowa State Univ., Ames.
D. W. Tarman.
MSc thesis, 1967. 96 p, 22 fig, 1 tab, 26 ref, append.

Descriptors: *Electrical well-logging, *Resistivity, Geophysics, Borehole geophysics, Shallow wells, Data processing, Documentation, *Iowa.
Identifiers: Gish-Rooney method.

The widespread occurrence of glacial drift in the region of central Iowa requires that geologic data be obtained in ways other than from bedrock exposures. Methods available are borehole investigations, correlation between isolated outcrops and geophysical methods. Of the geophysical methods the electrical resistivity method is the fastest and least expensive, potentially. A resistivity survey was conducted over a pre-established grid on a till covered area and over a series of cross sections in a small alluvium-filled valley. The resistivity data were analyzed using several methods including the Gish-Rooney method, the Werner method, the Moore method, the Hummel method, the Tagg method, Roman's method and the Mooney-Wetzel method. The results were compared to values obtained on the geologic control which consisted of actual cores. The Gish-Rooney method gave results within 10 percent of the control depth approximately 75 per cent of the time. The other methods are qualitatively analyzed and a set of suggested procedures for well log surveys is presented. A detailed description of the measuring instruments is included. Recommendations include determination of the instruments' sensitivity from a well logged hole, determination of the electrical drift on the machine through the laboratory, determination of the soil profile and water table effects. (Bradbeer-NWWA)
W75-06808

ANALYSIS OF PUMPING WELL NEAR A STREAM,
Arizona Univ., Tucson.
S. A. Bhatti.
MSc thesis, 1967. 103 p, 17 fig, 13 tab, 23 ref.

Descriptors: *Aquifer testing, *Methodology, *Testing procedures, Drawdown, Irrigation, Irrigation design, Saline water intrusion.
Identifiers: Indus River, *Pakistan(Indus River), Waterlogging.

When pumping of a well begins, the tubewell obtains most of its water from the immediate vicinity, but as the cone of influence expands, it receives a part of its water from the nearby stream until the entire amount of water from the stream is drawn. This time will depend on the aquifer characteristics, the tubewell discharge, the distance between the well and the stream, and the infiltration regimen of the stream. The test data were collected from an aquifer test on the Sangla Hill Scheme Tubewell Number 2 in Pakistan. It had a depth of 280 feet with a 121 foot screen of 10 inches in diameter. Fifty observation wells were used and their stratigraphic information is provided. Six methods of analysis were used including, (1) the Theis Modified Method by Rorboughs, (2) the Theis Modified Method by Stallman, (3) the Inflection Point Method by Hantush, (4) assumption that the leaky aquifer was in steady state condition which allows estimation of the coefficient of transmissibility, (5) the percentage contribution of the stream was found by comparison of the coefficient of storage obtained when the stream was dry and full respectively, and (6) the Image Theory by Glover and Balmer. These methods were compared. The image method and the inflection point method were easy and accurate compared to the Theis Modified Curves. Yet no single method is recommended as this will depend on the field conditions encountered. (Bradbeer-NWWA)
W75-06809

THE HYDRO-MECHANICS OF THE GROUND WATER SYSTEM IN THE SOUTHERN PORTION OF THE KAIBOB PLATEAU, ARIZONA,
Arizona Univ., Tucson.
For primary bibliographic entry see Field 2F.
W75-06810

GROUND WATER POLLUTION FROM SUBSURFACE EXCAVATIONS PART VI - DISPOSAL WELLS.
Environmental Protection Agency, Washington, D.C.
For primary bibliographic entry see Field 5D.
W75-06812

GROUND WATER POLLUTION FROM SUBSURFACE EXCAVATIONS, PART VII, PITS AND LAGOONS.
Environmental Protection Agency, Washington, D.C.
For primary bibliographic entry see Field 5D.
W75-06813

THE SORPTION OF FLUORIDE ION WITH SPECIAL REFERENCE TO FLUORIDE REMOVAL FROM POTABLE WATERS,
North Dakota Univ., Grand Forks.
For primary bibliographic entry see Field 5F.
W75-06815

HYDROSTRATIGRAPHIC UNITS OF THE SURFICIAL DEPOSITS OF EAST-CENTRAL ILLINOIS,
Illinois Univ., Urbana.
For primary bibliographic entry see Field 2F.
W75-06817

4C. Effects On Water Of Man's Non-Water Activities

IMPLEMENTATION PACKAGE FOR A DRAINAGE BLANKET IN HIGHWAY PAVEMENT SYSTEMS,
Federal Highway Administration, Washington, D.C., Implementation Div.
Available from the National Technical Information Service, Springfield, Va 22161, as PB-236 395, \$3.75 in paper copy, \$2.25 in microfiche. Report 72-1, May 1972. 25 p, 3 fig, 7 ref, 1 append.

Descriptors: *Highways, *Subsurface drainage, *Hydrogeology, *Soil mechanics, *Subsurface drains, Hydraulics, Soil compaction, Soil filters, Soil investigations, Soil strength, Soil water, Soils, Groundwater, Seepage, Paving, Design.
Identifiers: *Drainage blanket, *Subgrade design.

This user package presents guidelines for the use of a two-layer drainage blanket to handle groundwater seepage from under highway pavements. Positive removal of the Water is considered essential in order to minimize the problems of subgrade softening and weakening of pavement structures. A supplemental or companion report closely coordinated with this package provides additional information on guidelines for design of the two-layer system. Title of the report is 'Development of Guidelines for the Design of Subsurface Drainage Systems for Highway Pavement Structural Sections.' It was prepared for the Federal Highway Administration by Cedergren/KOA, a Joint Venture Consulting Firm of Sacramento and Long Beach, California. (Terstriep-ISWS)
W75-06470

EFFECTS OF URBANIZATION ON CATCHMENT RESPONSE,
Puerto Rico Univ., Mayaquez. Dept. of Civil Engineering.
For primary bibliographic entry see Field 2E.
W75-06534

MISSISSIPPI COASTAL ZONE MANAGEMENT APPLICATION 1974.
Mississippi Marine Resources Council, Long Beach.
For primary bibliographic entry see Field 6E.
W75-06575

CALIFORNIA SURFACE WATER LAW,
For primary bibliographic entry see Field 4A.
W75-06591

IMPACT OF HUMAN ACTIVITIES ON THE QUALITY OF GROUNDWATER AND SURFACE WATER IN THE CAPE COD AREA,
Massachusetts Univ., Amherst. Water Resources Research Center.
For primary bibliographic entry see Field 5B.
W75-06644

EDWARDS AQUIFER, A STUDY OF EDWARDS RECHARGE ZONE REQUIREMENTS, AACOG WATER QUALITY PLANNING, PHASE 5,
Alamo Area Council of Governments, San Antonio, Tex.
For primary bibliographic entry see Field 4B.
W75-06761

4D. Watershed Protection

INTERNATIONAL HYDROLOGICAL DECADE REPRESENTATIVE AND EXPERIMENTAL BASINS IN THE UNITED STATES: CATALOG OF AVAILABLE DATA AND RESULTS, 1965-1972.
National Committee for the International Hydrological Decade, Washington, D.C.
For primary bibliographic entry see Field 2A.
W75-06472

PRESERVATION AND ENHANCEMENT OF THE AMERICAN FALLS AT NIAGARA--FINAL REPORT TO THE INTERNATIONAL JOINT COMMISSION.
American Falls International Board, Buffalo, N.Y.
For primary bibliographic entry see Field 6G.
W75-06574

MAN'S ACTIVITIES IN WATERSHED AREAS--A NEED FOR PLANNING,
L. P. Wilson.
Environmental Law, Vol 4, p 229-250, Winter 1974.

Descriptors: *Lumbering, *Natural resources, *Watershed management, *Recreation, *Oregon, Land management, Water quality control, Planning, Multiple-purpose projects, Environmental effects, Environmental sanitation, Legal aspects, Water quality, Water pollution, Soils, Forest management, Federal government, Watersheds(Basins), Watersheds(Divides).

The increasing demand for timber resources and recreation areas has caused federal forest managers to consider previously overlooked areas for development. Especially in the western states municipal watersheds have offered promising possibilities. The use of the watershed and other previously unused areas allows for the dilution of overall forest impacts resulting in a minimization of localized environmental damage. Watershed areas where water and soil are the principal resources differ from forest areas where timber and recreation are the primary resources. Despite a lack of research into multiple-uses of watersheds, exploitation of these areas has already begun. The current legal action to halt logging within the Bull Run Forest Reserve is illustrative of the controversy that can arise when the multiple use of a previously single use watershed area commences without a complete environmental impact report by the agency. The outcome of this case will hopefully decide critical planning issues, and provide minimum standards valuable to both the Forest Service and to communities having municipal watersheds. The elements that should be contained within any watershed planning standard are discussed. (Sperling-Florida)
W75-06588

CROSS CREEK WATERSHED PROJECT, WASHINGTON COUNTY, PENNSYLVANIA (FINAL ENVIRONMENTAL IMPACT STATEMENT).
Soil Conservation Service, Washington, D.C.
For primary bibliographic entry see Field 8A.
W75-06616

DECOMPOSITION OF FOUR SPECIES OF LEAF MATERIAL IN THREE REPLICATE STREAMS WITH DIFFERENT NITRATE INPUT,
Oregon State Univ, Corvallis. Dept. of Fisheries and Wildlife.
For primary bibliographic entry see Field 5B.
W75-06649

EVALUATION OF FOUR COMPLETED SMALL WATERSHED PROJECTS: SOUTH CAROLINA, MARYLAND, IDAHO-NEVADA, AND WEST VIRGINIA,
Economic Research Service, Washington, D.C.
J. D. Sutton.
Agricultural Economic Report No 271, November, 1974. 54 p, 5 fig, 33 tab, 15 ref.

Descriptors: Watershed Protection and Flood Prevention Act of 1954, *Watershed management, *Watersheds(Basins), *South Carolina, *Idaho, *West Virginia, *Maryland, Water control, *Planning, Economic impact, Economic prediction, Flood control, Drainage effects, Drainage programs, *Small watershed.
Identifiers: Cedar Creek(Idaho), Twin Falls County(Idaho), Peck's Run(West Virginia), Upshur County(West Virginia), Coonfoot Branch(Maryland), Worcester County(Maryland), Big Creek(South Carolina), Saluda River(South Carolina).

The purpose was to determine the efficacy of Soil Conservation planning procedures used in four small (watershed of 250,000 acres of less) projects initiated under the Watershed Protection and flood Prevention Act of 1954 (P.L. 83-566). The evaluation compared qualitative appraisals of interviewees (residents and officials), perceived costs and benefits to average annual values estimated in the work plan of the projects. Generally, the desired physical manipulation of the water resources--flood decrease, increased supply for irrigation, municipal use, and recreation--was achieved, but projected economic effects such as crop yields weren't always generated. In the Big Creek Watershed Project, 13,279 acres, in rural Piedmont South Carolina, water supply increased and flooding decreased but flood plain usage was lower than expected. The Coonfoot Branch Watershed Project, 3,752 acres in rural Worcester County, Maryland, improved drainage, reduced flood damage, and produced improved crop yields. The Cedar Creek Watershed Project, 5,300 acres, in Twin Falls County, Idaho, produced actual costs less than planned, decreased crop yield, damages, provided additional acreage, and increased community income. In the Peck's Run Watershed Project, 8,210 acres, in Upshur and Barbour Counties, West Virginia, Flood damage reduction was as planned, land was freed for use, costs were higher than expected for installation and lower for maintenance, and different land usages and lower yields than expected were produced. (Park-North Carolina)
W75-06765

LATE-STAGE PUBLIC MEETING STUDY OF THE NEW JERSEY COASTAL INLETS AND BEACHES FROM BARNEGAT INLET TO LONGPORT,
Army Engineer District, Philadelphia, Pa.
Transcript of proceedings held March 19, 1974, at Stockton State College, Pomona, New Jersey, March, 1974. 55 p, 2 append.

Descriptors: Coasts, *Coastal engineering, Erosion, *Erosion control, *Beach erosion, Beaches, Navigation, Storms, Jetties, Dune, Dune sands, Groins, Shore protection, Shores, *New Jersey.
Identifiers: *Barnegat Inlet(New Jersey), Long Beach Island(New Jersey), Brigantine Island(New Jersey), Absecon Island(New Jersey), Longport(New Jersey).

The public hearing was held to assess opinion on proposals to remedy navigation, beach erosion control, and storm protection problems of the area from Barnegat Inlet to Longport. Solutions included rebuilding key jetties, dredging channels, removing material deposits, construction of groins and berms, raising the beach level, and additional smaller erosion control projects in various locations. Major Rogge of Brigantine questioned the siphon effect of the littoral drift project and the funding share figures (26.3 million Federal, 24 million local). Mr. Thompson, Surf City Councilman, was concerned with storm protection capabilities and dune protection. Mr. Moore, Supervisor of the Office of Shore Protection, endorsed the project. Mr Barrasso, City Engineer of Atlantic City, discussed the erosion control project, beach restoration, and installation of a submerged breakwater. Other issues included the impact of the projects on private beach ownership, storm warning and protection, dune preservation, and the placement of a breakwater for a proposed offshore nuclear plant. (Park-North Carolina)
W75-06766

5. WATER QUALITY MANAGEMENT AND PROTECTION

5A. Identification Of Pollutants

SENSITIVITY OF VERTEBRATE EMBRYOS TO HEAVY METALS AS A CRITERION OF WATER QUALITY - PHASE II BIOASSAY PROCEDURES USING DEVELOPMENTAL STAGES AS TEST ORGANISMS,
Kentucky Water Resources Inst., Lexington.
W. J. Birge, J. J. Just, A. G. Westerman, J. A. Black, and O. W. Roberts.
Available from the National Technical Information Service, Springfield, Va 22161 as PB-240 978, $3.75 in paper copy, $2.25 in microfiche. Research Report No 84, March 1975. 36 p, 5 fig, 3 tab, 98 ref. OWRT B-039-KY(1). 14-31-0001-4088.

Descriptors: *Bioassay, *Bioindicators, *Heavy metals, *Water quality, *Pollutant identification, *Embryonic growth stage, *Toxicity, Trace elements, Monitoring, Analytical techniques, Cultures, Water pollution effects.
Identifiers: *Vertebrate embryos.

Chick, amphibian and fish embryos were evaluated as bioassay and bioindicator organisms. Test procedures were developed by which embryonic stages may be used (1) in bioassay systems to evaluate the toxicity of particular metallic or metal-containing trace contaminants, and (2) as bioindicators to monitor the quality of natural water resources. A bioassay technique was devised in which metallic toxicants were administered to chick embryos by 'needle tract' injection into the yolk sac. This provided more uniform distribution of test metals throughout the yolk mass than can be obtained by conventional yolk sac injection methods, and gave more sensitivity and uniformity of test results. Metals such as arsenic, cadmium, mercury, lead and zinc are easily detectable at a level of 1 ppb. An in vitro culture technique was developed by which embryos of aquatic vertebrates may be 'maintained' for bioassay and bioindicator purposes. Five test species were identified, suitable synthetic culture water was formulated, and culture monitoring procedures were determined. Most toxic metals (e.g., mercury) may be detected at 1 ppb or less with the use of more sensitive embryonic species (e.g., trout). Early cleavage stages of the leopard frog (Rana pipiens) proved more sensitive to cadmium than older embryos, similar to results obtained in Phase I with mercury treatment of trout and frog embryos. (See also W74-03206) (Grieves-Kentucky)
W75-06352

THE REMOTE SENSING OF SUSPENDED SEDIMENT CONCENTRATIONS OF SMALL IMPOUNDMENTS,
Agricultural Research Service, Chickasha, Okla. Southern Great Plains Watershed Research Center.
For primary bibliographic entry see Field 7B.
W75-06399

AUTOMATED ANALYSIS FOR CYANIDE,
Technicon Industrial Systems, Tarrytown, N.Y.
A. Conetta, J. Jansen, and J. Salpeter.
Pollution Engineering, Vol 7, No 1, p 36-37, January 1975. 3 fig, 1 tab.

Descriptors: *Pollutant identification, *Water analysis, *Automation, *Organic compounds, *Instrumentation, *Analytical techniques, Chemical analysis, Evaluation, Colorimetry, Chemistry, Color reactions, Laboratory tests, Water properties, Nitrogen compounds, Testing procedures, Specifications.
Identifiers: *Cyanide, Ultraviolet digestor, Fractionation.

An automated procedure for the determination of cyanide in water was described. The metal cyanide complexes are broken down with ultraviolet radiation. Continuous distillation is by flash steam. The performance specifications of the system with aqueous standards are: range = 10 to 500 micrograms/liter, analysis rate = 30 samples/hour, detection limit = 10 micrograms/liter, replication at 300 micrograms/liter = + or -0.27%. (Henley-ISWS)
W75-06403

DIFFUSION OF RADIOACTIVE FLUID THROUGH SOIL SURROUNDING A LARGE POWER-REACTOR STATION AFTER A CORE MELTDOWN ACCIDENT,
California Univ., Livermore. Lawrence Livermore Lab.
For primary bibliographic entry see Field 5B.
W75-06407

AIR SAMPLING FOR IODINE-125,
Atomic Energy of Canada Ltd., Chalk River (Ontario). Chalk River Nuclear Labs.
R. M. Holford.
Available from the National Technical Information Service, Springfield, Va 22161 as Rept. No. AECL-4598, $4.00 in paper copy, $2.25 in microfiche. Report No. AECL-4598, February 1974. 14 p, 4 fig, 3 tab, 6 ref, 3 append.

Descriptors: *Pollutant identification, *Radioisotopes, *Monitoring, *Iodine, Absorption, Filters, Sampling, Radioactivity, Analytical techniques, Coals, Instrumentation, Measurement.
Identifiers: Charcoal.

In monitoring for air-borne I125, self absorption in the filter on which iodine is collected is a problem because of the low energy of the emitted radiation. Therefore recommended techniques for air sampling at the production facility and the processing laboratory require the use of charcoal-containing filters made of low Z materials. Provided self absorption is not excessive, absolute disintegration rates for I125 can be calculated directly from pulse-height spectra by a method using the coincidence properties of the radiation. (Houser-ORNL)
W75-06408

CESIUM-137 FALLOUT IN RED DESERT BASIN OF WYOMING, USA,
Dow Chemical Co., Golden, Colo. Rocky Flats Div.
D. E. Michels.
Available from the National Technical Information Service, Springfield, Va 22161 as Rept. RFP-2164, $4.00 in paper copy, $2.25 in microfiche. Report No. RFP-2164, July 1974. 10 p, 2 fig, 1 tab.

Descriptors: *Radioisotopes, *Radioactivity, *Fallout, *Cesium, *Wyoming, Winds, Snow, Distribution, Soil contamination, Basins, Correlation analysis, Precipitation(Atmospheric), Topography, Research and development, Vegetation, Public health.
Identifiers: *Red Desert basin(Wyo).

High variability characterizes fallout cesium-137 in the Red Desert Basin of Wyoming. Correlations between fallout levels and factors of climate, topography, and vegetation suggest that bare soil more readily captures fallout from wind than does sagebrush; that wet fallout processes are of little significance in this arid place; that association between cesium-137 and snow is weak, hence drifting of snow is not a significant factor in the distribution of fallout; and that impingement of fallout particles directly on soils by wind action may be the dominant mechanism of fallout deposition in the Basin. Analysis was not conclusive when the data were sorted according to a single parameter, either mean annual precipitation or topography or vegetation. However, significant differences between average values and smaller values for standard deviations result when sorting is done according to two parameters, topography and vegetation. Highest levels of cesium-137 were found on barren ridges which, in the Basin, are exposed to persistent synoptic winds. (Houser-ORNL)
W75-06409

ENVIRONMENTAL RADIOACTIVITY AT THE NATIONAL NUCLEAR RESEARCH CENTRE, PELINDABA,
Atomic Energy Board, Pelindaba, Pretoria (South Africa). Isotopes and Radiation Div.
D. Van As, and C. M. Vleggaar.
Available from the National Technical Information Service, Springfield, Va 22161 as Rept. No. PEL-229, $4.00 in paper copy, $2.25 in microfiche. Report No. PEL-229, November 1973. 20 p, 16 tab, 11 ref, append.

Descriptors: *Monitoring, *Surveys, *Radioactivity, *Effluents, *Nuclear wastes, Path of pollutants, Rivers, Radioisotopes, Strontium, Iodine, Public health, Fish, Water, Nuclear explosions, Testing, Fallout.
Identifiers: *Gamma radiation, *Critical path, *Critical radionuclide, Crocodile River.

A revised environmental survey program, introduced during 1970 with the emphasis on monitoring of the critical paths of exposure of the general public, was continued in 1972. Results of determinations of both gross radioactivity and individual nuclides in samples of fish and water (which are critical materials for liquid effluent releases) from the Hartbeespoort Dam and from the Crocodile River are given and discussed. Results of gamma-spectrometric, I 131 and Sr 90 analyses of milk, the critical material for releases to the atmosphere, are presented. Results are given of regular investigations of the composition of effluent releases. These investigations are performed in order to be able to detect other possible critical nuclides. Levels of deposited and airborne activity from nuclear bomb tests are reported. (Houser-ORNL)
W75-06410

AIRBORNE GAMMA RADIATION SURVEYS FOR SNOW WATER-EQUIVALENT RESEARCH-PROGRESS REPORT 1973,
EG and G, Inc., Las Vegas, Nev. Las Vegas Div.
A. E. Fritzsche, and Z. G. Burson.
Available from NTIS, Springfield, Va 22161 as Rept. No. EGG-1183-1623, $5.45 in paper copy, $2.25 in microfiche. Report No. EGG-1183-1623, December 1973. 52 p, 22 fig, 8 tab, 6 ref.

Descriptors: Surveys, *Radioactivity, Hydrology, *Snow cover, *Melt water, *Water equivalent, *Air pollution, Aircraft, Remote sensing, Data collections, Great Lakes, Minnesota, Research and development, Technology, Altitude, Meteorology, Soil contamination, Aerial sensing, *Lake Ontario.

The areal average of water equivalent of snow cover was measured by airborne surveys of natural terrestrial gamma radiation for 28 survey lines in the Lake Ontario Basin as a part of the International Field Year for the Great Lakes. Measurements over selected calibration lines compared well with ground-based data. Errors (plus or minus 0.9 to 1.3 cm) from airborne measurements in the results represent uncertainties in soil moisture effects, sampling statistics and airborne radioactivity contributions. Examination of methods to account for airborne randon daughter contributions concentrated on dual-detector systems in which one detector preferentially 'looked' up. Such systems can be used to separate the airborne radioactivity, but the accuracy of the resulting ground component is limited to about plus or minus 4%. A 4% error in the gamma data produces a 0.7 cm error in the water equivalent. Since at least half of the weight allotment must be dedicated to the shield and additional detectors, and because of the difficulty of obtaining precise values of all constants, an unshielded detector system is recommended at this time for airborne surveys of the water equivalent of snow cover. (Houser-ORNL)
W75-06411

WATER EQUIVALENT OF SNOW DATA FROM AIRBORNE GAMMA RADIATION SURVEYS - INTERNATIONAL FIELD YEAR FOR THE GREAT LAKES,
EG and G, Inc., Las Vegas, Nev. Las Vegas Div.
Z. G. Burson, and A. E. Fritzsche.
Available from NTIS, Springfield, Va 22161 as Rept. No. EGG-1183-1622, $5.45 in paper copy, $2.25 in microfiche. Report No. EGG-1183-1622, December 1973. 59 p, 3 fig, 9 tab, 6 ref, 6 append.

Descriptors: *Surveys, Aircraft, *Radioactivity, *Snow cover, *Water equivalent, *Remote sensing, *Lake Ontario, New York, Great Lake Region, Measurement, Gamma rays, Data collections, Research and development, Aerial sensing.

Areal determinations of the water equivalent of snow in the Lake Ontario drainage basin in New York State were made from an airborne platform as part of the International Field Year for the Great Lakes (IFYGL) program. About 350 line miles representing the area surrounding Rochester and Syracuse, New York, were surveyed during the fall and winter of 1973. The attenuation by the snow cover of the natural gamma radiation from the soil served as the measurement technique. This method requires surveys both before and after snow covers the ground in order to observe the attenuation of the gamma intensity. Separate measurements of the total photon flux and two specific energy components comprise three water equivalent determinations for each survey line. Results of the airborne areal water equivalent determinations are listed. (Houser-ORNL)
W75-06412

TRANSURANICS AT PACIFIC ATOLLS I. CONCENTRATIONS IN THE WATERS AT ENEWETAK AND BIKINI,
California Univ., Livermore. Lawrence Livermore Lab.
V. E. Noshkin, K. M. Wong, R. J. Eagle, and C. Gatrousis.
Available from NTIS, Springfield, Va 22161 as Rept. No. UCRL-51612, $4.00 in paper copy, $2.25 in microfiche. Report No. UCRL-51612, June 1974. 33 p, 15 fig, 11 tab, 12 ref.

Descriptors: *Radioisotopes, *Radioactivity, *Nuclear explosions, Testing, *Pacific Ocean, *Lagoons, *Atolls, Monitoring, Measurement, Assessment, Hazards analysis, Human population, Water pollution, Public health.
Identifiers: Pacific Atolls, Enewetak, Bikini, Transuranics.

Concentrations and distributions of Pu 239, 240 and other transuranic radionuclides in the lagoon waters of Enewetak and Bikini Atolls are described. The data are derived from a series of samples collected during the period October-December 1972. The samples are being radiochemically processed and analyzed for specific radionuclides; the available results for Sr90, Cs137, Np237, Pu238, 239, 240, 241 and Am241 in specific water samples are presented and discussed. (Houser-ORNL)
W75-06414

BIOLOGICAL DOSE AND RADIOLOGICAL ACTIVITY FROM NUCLEAR REACTOR OR NUCLEAR WEAPON FISSION PRODUCTS,
Oak Ridge National Lab., Tenn.
R. O. Chester.
Available from NTIS, Springfield, Va 22161 as Rept. No. ORNL-4996, $5.45 in paper copy, $2.25 in microfiche. Report No. ORNL-4996, December 1974. 92 p, 9 fig, 4 append.

Descriptors: *Nuclear powerplants, *Reactors, *Radioactivity, *Nuclear explosions, *Computer programs, *Model studies, Dispersion, Fallout, Biology, Human population, Radioisotopes, Bioassay, Pollutant identification, Food chains.
Identifiers: Yields, Dose calculations.

The use of a computer code, YIELDS is described. It performs rapid, accurate calculation of dose and activity from the fission products in a nuclear reactor core or from a nuclear weapon. For example, if a dispersal model is assumed, calculations can be made of contaminated area, dose from inhaled or ingested fission products to each part of a biological system, or dose from external fission products, from a dispersed reactor core, or nuclear weapon fallout. Individual beta and gamma ray energies for each isotope are included, permitting detailed calculation of biological dose or other functions of these energies vs time. The calculation method facilitates the handling of complicated radiological decay chains coupled with multisection biological systems. The option of sorting the output by isotopes or chemical species is available. (Houser-ORNL)
W75-06419

HEALTH AND SAFETY LABORATORY FALLOUT PROGRAM QUARTERLY SUMMARY REPORT, MARCH 1, 1974 THROUGH JUNE 1, 1974,
Health and Safety Lab. (AEC), New York.
E. P. Hardy, Jr.
Available from NTIS, Springfield, Va 22161 as Rept. No. HASL-284, $13.60 in paper copy, $2.25 in microfiche. Report No. HASL-284, July 1974. 249 p, 19 fig, 23 tab, 95 ref.

Descriptors: *Monitoring, *Fallout, *Data collections, *Radioactivity, Nuclear explosions, *Soil contamination, *Water pollution, *Air pollution, Diets, Precipitation(Atmospheric), Environment, Milk, Air, Domestic water, Radioisotopes, Strontium, Carbon, Bibliography, Nuclear power plants, Effluents.
Identifiers: Weapons testing, Deposition.

Current data are presented from the Health and Safety Laboratory Program, the Swedish National Defense Research Institute, the Air Dynamics Laboratory of NOAA and the Radiological and Environmental Research Division of Argonne National Laboratory. Interpretive reports and notes are presented on radioactivity from nuclear tests in air and precipitation in Sweden; strontium 90 in diet during 1973; surface deposition in the United States; carbon 14 measurements in the stratosphere during 1971-73; and environmental radiation measurements in the vicinity of a boiling water reactor. A bibliography of recent publications related to radionuclide studies is also presented. (See W75-06421 thru W75-06427) (Houser-ORNL)
W75-06420

RADIOACTIVITY FROM NUCLEAR WEAPONS IN AIR AND PRECIPITATION IN SWEDEN FROM MID-YEAR 1968 TO MID-YEAR 1972,
Research Inst. of National Defence, Stockholm (Sweden).
B. Bernstrom.
In: Report No. HASL-284, p I-2-33, July 1974. 8 fig, 6 tab, 11 ref.

Descriptors: *Radioactivity, *Measurement, Nuclear explosions, *Air pollution, *Precipitation(Atmospheric), Fallout, Water pollution, Cesium, Barium, Monitoring, Radioisotopes, Sampling, Analysis, Pacific Ocean, Data collections, Underground, Testing.
Identifiers: *Sweden, China, USSR.

The concentrations of various fission products in ground level air and precipitation from mid-year 1968 to mid-year 1972 are reported. Since 1963 the cesium-137 concentration in surface air decreases each year to 1967. After a small increase in 1968 the air concentration of cesium-137 remains on the same level to 1971 and decreases during 1972 to the lowest level reported since the measurements started. Short-lived barium-140 was detected in ground level air after the Chinese explosions in December 1968, November 1971, January 1972, and March 1972. After the Chinese tests in September 1969 and October 1970 the concentration of barium-140 was below the detection level. (See also W75-06420) (Houser-ORNL)
W75-06421

STRONTIUM-90 IN THE DIET. RESULTS THROUGH 1973,
Health and Safety Lab. (AEC), New York.
B. G. Bennett.
In: Report No. HASL-284, p I-34 - I-48, July 1974. 3 fig, 4 tab, 5 ref.

Descriptors: *Diets, *Strontium, *Surveys, *Census, *Data collections, Data processing, Statistical methods, Food chains, Soil contamination, Path of pollutants, Fallout, New York, California.
Identifiers: *New York City, *San Francisco(Calif).

Estimates of Sr 90 intake via the total diet in New York City and San Francisco have been made since 1960 from quarterly food samplings and average consumption statistics. The dietary intakes of Sr 90 have been decreased from the maximum levels attained during 1963-64, but the declines have become more gradual in recent years due to the continuing small amounts of Sr 90 deposition and the little-changing cumulative deposit of Sr 90 in soil. The annual intake in 1973 averaged 9.7 pCi/day in New York and 3.2 pCi/day in San Francisco, slight decreases from the previous year. (See also W75-06420) (Houser-ORNL)
W75-06422

SURFACE DEPOSITION IN THE UNITED STATES,
National Oceanographic and Atmospheric Administration, Silver Spring, Md. Air Resources Labs.
A. J. Miller, R. J. List, and J. D. Mahlman.
In: Report No. HASL-284, p I-49 - I-63, July 1974. 4 fig, 10 ref.

Descriptors: *Fallout, *Strontium, *Tritium, *United States, *Geographical regions, Regions, Great Plains, Southwest US, Ion exchange, Tracking techniques, Tracers, Radioactive tracers, Model studies, Ion transport, *Utah.
Identifiers: Surface deposition, Salt Lake City.

Comparison is made of the surface deposition patterns over the United States as depicted by observations of Strontium 90 in soil, tritium rainout and Strontium 90 in pot and ion-exchange collectors versus the results generated by the general circulation tracer model from the Geophysical Fluid Dynamics Laboratory. The following three observed data sets exhibit certain common characteristics: (1) A general maximum in the Great Plains states, (2) A general minimum in the Southwest, and (3) A relatively high value, if not an absolute maximum, in the Salt Lake City area. The results of the general circulation tracer model calculations present a reasonable 'first depiction' of the details of surface deposition and are very encouraging as an indicator of the transport of such conservative trace substances. (See also W75-06420) (Houser-ORNL)
W75-06423

CARBON-14 MEASUREMENTS IN THE STRATOSPHERE FROM A BALLOON-BORNE MOLECULAR SIEVE SAMPLER (1971-1973),
Argonne National Lab., Ill.
R. E. Sowl, J. Gray, Jr., T. E. Ashenfelter, and K. Telegadas.
In: Report No. HASL-284, p I-64 - I-76, July 1974. 1 tab, 7 ref.

Descriptors: *Carbon, *Measurement, *Air pollution, *Pollutant identification, *Fallout, Atmospheric pollution, Path of pollutants, Public health, Nuclear explosions, Sampling, Analysis, Laboratory equipment, Analytical techniques, Apparatus.
Identifiers: Weapons testing, *Molecular sieve sampler.

The U.S. Government has conducted an extensive atmospheric program of whole air collection in the troposphere and stratosphere since 1953. These atmospheric samples were analyzed for C14 collected in the form of CO2. Excess C14 (C14 due to nuclear testing) data have been derived and the results made available (Hagemann, et al., 1965; ESSA, 1966, 1967, 1969; NOAA, 1971). Beginning in mid-1970, molecular sieve samples designed to replace the whole air samplers were flown operationally on the USAEC balloon flights in the northern and southern hemispheres. The results from mid-1970 to mid-1971 have been reported (Telegadas et al., 1972). This report contains the Carbon 14 measurements from the balloon-borne molecular sieve sampler since mid-1971. A complete description of the molecular sieve sampler is given by Ashenfelter et al., (1972). (See also W75-06420) (Houser-ORNL)
W75-06424

ENVIRONMENTAL RADIATION MEASUREMENTS IN THE VICINITY OF A BOILING WATER REACTOR: HASL DATA SUMMARY,
Health and Safety Lab. (AEC), New York.
G. de P. Burke.
In: Report No. HASL-284, p I-77 - I-88, July 1974. 1 fig, 7 tab, 7 ref.

Descriptors: *Monitoring, *Nuclear power plants, *Effluents, *Measurement, Environment, Model studies, Gases, Data collections, Publications, Analysis, Xenon, Krypton, Sampling, Fallout.
Identifiers: *Plume exposure, *Noble gases.

Environmental radiation measurements were made over a three-year period in the vicinity of a boiling water power reactor. Contributions to total radiation exposures resulting from the gaseous effluents are calculated from a plume exposure model and compared with values determined from ionization chamber and TLD measurements. In almost all cases, exposures attributable to the plant are less than 10 mR/year. Gas sample analyses are also presented. (See also W75-06420) (Houser-ORNL)
W75-06425

PROJECT AIRSTREAM,
Health and Safety Lab. (AEC), New York.
P. W. Krey, L. E. Toonkel, and M. Schonberg.
In: Report No. HASL-284, p II-7 - II-139, July 1974. 5 fig, 14 tab, 52 ref.

Descriptors: *Atmosphere, *Monitoring, Measurement, *Air pollution, *Fallout, Aircraft, *Radioisotopes, Sampling, *Radiochemical analysis, Data collections, Altitude, Analysis, Strontium, Cesium, Cerium, Filters, Equipment, Quality control, Polonium, Lead, Standards, Beryllium, Plutonium.

Project Airstream is the Health and Safety Laboratory's study of radioactivity in the lower stratosphere employing the RB-57F aircraft as a sampling platform. This project is a continuation of the Defense Atomic Support Agency's Project Stardust except that Airstream's sampling missions are limited to only one per season. Radiochemical data are presented from the missions flown in January, September and November 1973 and in January 1974. (See also W75-06420) (Houser-ORNL)
W75-06426

CESIUM-137 IN VARIOUS CHICAGO FOODS (COLLECTION MONTH APRIL 1974),
Argonne National Lab., Ill.
J. O. Karttunen.
In: Report No. HASL-284, p III-2 - III-5, July 1974. 2 tab, 5 ref.

Descriptors: *Diets, *Food chains, *Cesium, *Potassium, *Measurement, Fruit crops, Vegetable crops, Milk, Fish, Analysis, Assay, Assessment, Fallout, Path of pollutants, Cities, *Illinois.
Identifiers: *Chicago(Ill), Infant diets, Adult diets.

Since April 1961, the 137Cs and potassium content of the Chicago portion of Tri-City Diet Sampling Program has been determined in bulk food samples by gamma ray spectrometry using a 4 in x 4 in NaI (Tl) crystal. Each variety of food (all fresh vegetables, all fresh fruits, etc.) is composited before measurement, and each sample is counted 400-1000 minutes. From these measurements composite daily and yearly food intakes are obtained. The results for the April 1974 semi-annual are tabulated. (See also W75-06420) (Houser-ORNL)
W75-06427

PRIMARY AMINES IN CALIFORNIA COASTAL WATERS: UTILIZATION BY PHYTOPLANKTON,
California Univ., Irvine. Dept. of Developmental and Cell Biology.
B. B. North.
Limnology and Oceanography, Vol 20, No 1, p 20-27, January 1975. 3 fig, 2 tab, 27 ref. NSF Grant GA 33904X.

Descriptors: *Pollutant identification, *Amino acids, Organic compounds, *Phytoplankton, Analytical techniques, *Primary productivity, Proteins, Ammonia, Nitrogen compounds, Nitrogen, Evaluation, Instrumentation, Marine plants, Aquatic plants, Fluorescence, *California, Sea water, Coasts, Organic matter, Ecosystems, Peptides.
Identifiers: *Fluorescamine, *Fluorometric measurement, *Newport Bay(Calif), Catalina Channel, Glycine.

A new reagent, fluorescamine, provides a simple, rapid fluorometric measurement of primary amino compounds in seawater. The reagent detects as little as 0.2 micromoles (glycine equivalents) directly in 2 ml of seawater. Fluorescamine-positive primary amines in the region of Newport Bay, California, range from about 0.3 micromoles in nearshore waters to 14 micromoles in bay sediments. About half the fluorescamine-positive material in Newport Bay water can be taken up rapidly by photoplankton, and thus, may be an important nitrogen source. The half not taken up probably occurs as peptides. Fluorescamine should be invaluable for studies on microbial nutrition and cycling of organic matter in aquatic ecosystems. (Henley-ISWS)
W75-06443

THE EFFECT OF INCREASES IN THE ATMOSPHERIC CARBON DIOXIDE CONTENT ON THE CARBONATE ION CONCENTRATION OF SURFACE OCEAN WATER AT 25C,
Liverpool Univ. (England). Donnan Labs.
For primary bibliographic entry see Field 2K.
W75-06444

PICKLING LIQUORS, STRIP MINES, AND GROUND-WATER POLLUTION,
Ohio State Univ., Columbus. Dept. of Geology and Mineralogy.
For primary bibliographic entry see Field 5B.
W75-06450

OXYGEN AND SULFUR ISOTOPIC COMPOSITION OF THE SULFATE IONS FROM MINERAL AND THERMAL GROUNDWATERS OF POLAND,
Comitato Nazionale per le Ricerche Nucleari, Pisa (Italy). Laboratorio di Geologia Nucleare.
G. Cortecci, and J. Dowgiallo.
Journal of Hydrology, Vol 24, No 3/4, p 271-282, 1975. 4 fig, 4 tab, 28 ref.

Descriptors: *Pollutant identification, *Oxygen isotopes, *Sulfur, Isotope studies, *Sulfur bacteria, *Analytical techniques, Oxygen, Radioisotopes, Sulfates, Sulfur compounds, Deuterium, Hydrogen, Saline water, Salinity, Chemical properties, Water quality, Geologic time, Mineralogy, Radiochemical analysis, *Groundwater, Meteoric water, Mineral water, Thermal water.
Identifiers: *Poland, Carpathians, Sudety Mountians, Bacterial fractionation, Graphite-reduction technique.

The 018 and S34 contents were given of the sulfate dissolved in some mineral and thermal groundwaters in northwest Poland, in the Carpathians, in the Carpathian foredeep, and in the Sudety Mountains. The oxygen isotopic composition of sulfate ions were compared with the 018/016 and D/H ratios of the environmental waters. From the results obtained, the oxygen and sulfur isotopic composition of the sulfate ions seems generally due to a sulfate bacterial metabolic activity, which has enriched the residual sulfate in the heavy isotopes. No correlation exists between the delta 018(SO4--) values and the other parameters, such as depth and age of aquifers, outflow temperature, total salinity, sulfate concentration, delta 018, and delta D values of the environmental waters, except for the (SO4--) water pairs with delta 018(H20) greater than 0. In this case there is a positive delta 018(SO4--) - delta 018(H2O) correlation which proves a partial isotopic equilibration and excludes for these waters an admixture with relatively recent infiltration waters. The positive 018 contents of some waters (from +3.0 to +6.7 parts per thousand) analyzed and discussed previously by Dowgiallo (1973) were newly examined in the light of experimental results recently published on the oxygen and hydrogen isotopic fractionation in the ultrafiltration process of water (or aqueous colution) by compacted clay. (Henley-ISWS)
W75-06455

SKYLAB STUDY OF WATER QUALITY,
Kansas Univ., Lawrence.
J. R. McCauley.
Available from the National Technical Information Service, Springfield, Va 22161 as N74-32764, $3.25 in paper copy, $ 2.25 in microfiche. Progress Report, June-August 1974. 9 p, 3 fig, 2 ref. NASA Contract NAS 9-13271.

Descriptors: *Remote sensing, *Data processing, *Water quality, Satellites(Artificial), Lakes, Suspended solids, Photography, Infrared radiation, *Kansas, Reservoirs, Correlation analysis.
Identifiers: *Skylab.

Earth Resources Environmental Program (EREP) data products thus far received for the September 18, 1973, SL3 pass over southeast Kansas include S-190A positive transparencies. These photos cover three lakes: Toronto, Fall River, and Elk City Reservoirs. Concurrent with satellite overflight, field crews were on all three lakes collecting water samples. These samples were analyzed for concentrations of bicarbonate, carbonate, calcium, magnesium, potassium, sodium, sulfate, and chloride. In addition, total solids, total heat-stable solids, suspended solids, heat-stable suspended solids, and pH were determined. The four black and white S-190A products were analyzed quantitatively with a Macbeth EP-1000 macrodensitometer. Five locations were selected on Fall River and Toronto Reservoirs, and four on Elk City Reservoir. Each density measurement was centered as nearly as possible over one or more ground truth sampling station. Attempts were then made to relate film density to corresponding water quality parameters. The analysis established a strong linear correlation between the red/green radiance ratio and suspended solids. This result compared quite favorably to ERTS MSS CCT results. (Sims-ISWS)
W75-06478

A PORTABLE AEROSOL DETECTOR OF HIGH SENSITIVITY,
State Univ. of New York, Albany. Atmospheric Sciences Research Center.
A. Hogan, W. Winters, and G. Gardner.
Journal of Applied Meteorology, Vol 14, No 1, p 39-45, February 1975. 2 fig, 3 tab, 21 ref. NOAA contract 044022 and NSF Grant GA32502.

Descriptors: *Pollutant identification, *Aerosols, *Atmosphere, *Instrumentation, *Air pollution, *On-site tests, Dusts, Fog, Clouds, Meteorology, Water vapor, Meteoric water, Analytical techniques, Measurement, Condensation, Nucleation, Calibrations, Suspension.
Identifiers: Diffuser-denuder, Marine atmosphere, *Greenland, Aitken nuclei, Counters.

A portable photoelectric nucleus counter, with similar sensitivity to the Pollak photoelectric nucleus counter with convergent light beam, was developed and calibrated. This instrument was incorporated into a packaged measurement system which allows the experimenter to determine the effective diffusion coefficient and fraction charged, of the natural aerosol, in uncontaminated areas. The photoelectric counter has comparable accuracy to the absolute (Aitken, Scholz) counters in the concentration range of interest, and is capable of determining the concentration once per minute. Field tests of the prototype instrument were conducted near sea level in Greenland. The concentration of natural aerosol in this area ranged from 150 to 200 particles/cu cm. The instrumentation had sufficient sensitivity to detect a gradual increase in particle size at this low concentration. (Henley-ISWS)
W75-06496

CALIBRATION OF THE POLLAK COUNTER WITH MONODISPERSE AEROSOLS,
Minnesota Univ., Minneapolis. Particle Technology Lab.
B. Y. H. Liu, D. Y. H. Pui, A. W. Hogan, and T. A. Rich.
Journal of Applied Meteorology, Vol 14, No 1, p 46-51, February 1975. 3 fig, 28 ref, 1 append. NSF Grant GA32502 and EPA Grant 801301.

Descriptors: *Pollutant identification, *Aerosols, *Calibrations, *Instrumentation, *Atmosphere, *Air pollution, Measurement, Dusts, Fog, Mist, Evaluation, Testing, Analytical techniques, Testing procedures, Electronic equipment, Standards, Nucleation.
Identifiers: Pollack counter, Monodisperse aerosols.

The photoelectric condensation nucleus counter of Pollak with convergent light beam was compared with an electrical aerosol detector by using monodisperse aerosols with particle diameters between 0.025 and 0.15 micrometers, particle concentrations between 127 and 260,800/cu cm, and particles of two different chemical constituencies, e.g., NaCl and material volatilized from a heated nichrome wire. Very good agreement was obtained. The discrepancy between these two methods was found to be less than 9% at concentration levels below 10,000 particles/cu cm and 17% at 250,000 particles/cu cm. This discrepancy is well within the combined uncertainties in the two independent aerosol concentration measuring methods. (Henley-ISWS)
W75-06497

CHLORIDES IN NATURAL AND ARTIFICIAL HAILSTONES,
Istituto di Fisica dell'Atmosfera, Verona (Italy). Osservatorio Scientifico.
For primary bibliographic entry see Field 2B.
W75-06500

BACKGROUND SILVER CONCENTRATIONS IN ILLINOIS PRECIPITATION AND RIVER WATER,
Illinois State Water Survey, Urbana.
D. F. Gatz.
Journal of Applied Meteorology, Vol 14, No 2, p 217-221, March 1975. 2 fig, 3 tab, 18 ref. Contract INT D-7197; AEC Contract AT(11-1)-1199.

Descriptors: *Pollutant identification, *Silver iodide, *Cloud seeding, *Precipitation(Atmospheric), *Rivers, On-site investigations, Sampling, Water chemistry, Analytical techniques, Chemical analysis, Chemistry, *Illinois.
Identifiers: Dry deposition.

Work was undertaken to measure background silver in Illinois precipitation in the absence of any known seeding operations in or near Illinois. The rainfall-weighted mean concentration in samples from several stations was 73 ng/l. This is somewhat higher than has been found in unseeded precipitation in other parts of North America, but not high enough to preclude wind-blown soil dust as a primary source. (Sims-ISWS)
W75-06506

IDENTIFICATION AND DETERMINATION OF TRACE AMOUNTS OF ORGANIC AND INORGANIC CONTAMINANTS IN THE DELAWARE RIVER AND BAY,
Delaware State Coll., Dover. Dept. of Chemistry.
G. R. Seidel.
Available from the National Technical Information Service, Springfield, Va 22161 as PB-241 059, $3.75 in paper copy, $2.25 in microfiche. Completion Report, November 1974, 26 p. OWRT A-019-DEL(1).

Descriptors: *Delaware River, Organic Compounds, *Insecticides, Inorganic compounds, *Trace elements, *Pollutant identification, *Chlorinated hydrocarbon pesticides, *Pesticide residues, Polychlorinated biphenyls, Mass spectroscopy.
Identifiers: *Delaware Bay, Metallic ions.

The waters and bottoms of Delaware River, Bay, and a number of fresh water bodies were analyzed for chlorinated insecticides and metallic ions. These are reported and reflect the health or lack of it of these water resources. A research gas chromatograph (Micro-Tek, Model 220) equipped with an electron capture detector and all glass system was used for determining the chlorinated insecticides; a dual beam atomic absorption spectrophotometer (Jarrell Ash Model 810) was used for measuring the content of metallic ions. Data have been obtained which might become a starting point for: (1) further analyses to determine whether or not the bodies of water studied are becoming more or less contaminated, (2) to serve as an incentive to study additional lakes, rivers and tidal areas to measure their extent of contamination.
W75-06517

THE EFFECT OF ALCOHOLS ON THE CARBONIC ACID DEHYDRATION REACTION,
Oklahoma Univ., Norman. Dept. of Chemistry.
G. Atkinson, R. C. Patel, and R. J. Boe.
Available from the National Technical Information Service, Springfield, Va 22161 as PB-241 130, $4.25 in paper copy, $2.25 in microfiche. Completion Report, (March 1975). 53 p, 12 fig, 4 tab, 5 ref. OWRT A-045-OKLA(1). 14-31-0001-4036.

Descriptors: *Dehydration, Kinetics, Carbon dioxide, Activation energy, Chemical reactions, Ions, Ion exchange.
Identifiers: *Carbonic acid, Debye-Huckel theory, MgCl2-NaHCO3 mixtures.

The carbonic acid dehydration kinetics have been studied by the stopped-flow technique in CH3OH/H2O and t-BuOH2O mixtures. Precise values of the activation parameters delta G(++), delta H(++), and delta S(++) have been obtained. CH3OH has a very minor effect on the dehydration process except in the very low organic range. The addition of t-BuOH has a marked effect on the process with delta H(++) showing a maximum near Xo=0.06 and delta S(++) going from negative to positive at the same concentration. The chemical interactions of Mg+2 with carbonate and bicarbonate in the presence of the Na+ ion have been studied as a function of temperature ranging from 0-30C and of ionic strength varying from 0.15 to 0.64 M. In the case of MgCO3 ion pair formation, a constant enthalpy of reaction was observed in the temperature range investigated. In the case of MgHCO3+ ion pair formation, the association constant shows a minimum around 20C. Within experimental error, the effect of ionic strength on the ion pair formation processes is in line with the Debye-Huckel theory in its extended form. The NaCO3- and NaHCO3 ion pair formation constants in the absence of the Mg+2 ion have been determined at 20C. The values are 0.5 M-1 with an ionic strength of 0.36 M and 4.4 M-1 at 0.19 M, respectively. The calculations were based on the EMF measurements using the glass and the ion-selective electrodes.
W75-06521

PUBLIC GROUNDWATER SUPPLIES IN MASON COUNTY,
Illinois State Water Survey, Urbana.
For primary bibliographic entry see Field 4B.
W75-06527

PUBLIC GROUNDWATER SUPPLIES IN STARK COUNTY,
Illinois State Water Survey, Urbana.
For primary bibliographic entry see Field 4B.
W75-06528

PUBLIC GROUNDWATER SUPPLIES IN PERRY COUNTY,
Illinois State Water Survey, Urbana.
For primary bibliographic entry see Field 4B.
W75-06529

A LIMNOLOGICAL STUDY OF SILVERWOOD LAKE: IMPACT OF WATER TRANSPORT ON WATER QUALITY,
California State Polytechnic Univ., Pomona.
R. Kubomoto, J. Miller, and R. Wothington.
American Water Works Association Journal, Vol 66, No 11, p 663-667, November 1974. 4 fig, 3 tab, 8 ref.

Descriptors: *Limnology, *Lakes, *Water quality, Physical properties, Chemical properties, Biological properties, *Water transfer, Multiple-purpose reservoirs, Turbidity, Dissolved oxygen, Temperature, Pollutants, *Pollutant identification, Algae, Fish, Recreation, Reservoirs, *California.
Identifiers: *Silverwood Lake*Calif).

When state agencies involved with the California Water Project realized the major need for more recreational areas in southern California, they designed Silverwood Lake, located near the headwaters of the west fork of the Mojave River, as a multipurpose reservoir. The water-quality study of Silverwood Lake was undertaken to determine (1) if there was a significant deterioration of water quality as the northern water moved to the south, (2) if the movement of northern water to the south was introducing different species of phytoplankton into the southern California water system, (3) if the use of the lake as a recreational area was significantly affecting the quality of the water, and (4) if there was a possibility that the lake would develop a monomictic or dimictic pattern of stratification. The period of testing extended from October 1972 through February 1973. Samples were obtained from three locations on the lake. No major detriments due to importation of water are obvious, and the effects of recreational use of the reservoir are negligible. If maintained at the current level of use and quality of imported water, Silverwood Lake will provide many years of recreational use and water supply. (Sims-ISWS)
W75-06538

SEA SALT PARTICLES TRANSPORTED TO THE LAND,
Hokkaido Univ., Sapporo (Japan). Dept. of Chemistry.
For primary bibliographic entry see Field 5B.
W75-06541

FUNDAMENTALS OF AQUATIC BIOASSAYS,
Ministry for Conservation, Melbourne (Australia). Westernport Bay Environmental Study.
D. S. Negilski.
Proceedings of the Royal Australian Chemical Institute, Vol 42, No 2, p 50-54, February 1975. 4 fig, 24 ref.

Descriptors: *Bioassay, *Toxicity, *Water pollution effects, *Testing procedures, Aquatic animals, Water quality, Laboratory tests, Fish, Graphical analysis, Analytical techniques, Water analysis, Water pollution control, *Pollutant identification.

A review is presented of the principles and methods of bioassays in application to pollution control and environmental monitoring. Both acute and chronic toxicity tests, conducted in static and flowing water, are considered; the selection and handling of test animals, requirements for equipment, methods of analysis and presentation of results are discussed. It is emphasized that accepted standards for procedures, analysis and reporting are necessary if the information is to be efficiently used by water-resource managers and policy makers. (Levick-CSIRO)
W75-06554

STEADY-STATE WATER QUALITY MODELING IN STREAMS,
Cornell Univ., Ithaca, N.Y. School of Civil and Environmental Engineering.
For primary bibliographic entry see Field 5B.
W75-06564

AERIAL RADIOLOGICAL MEASURING SURVEY OF THE MAINE YANKEE ATOMIC POWER PLANT SEPTEMBER 1971.
EG and G, Inc., Las Vegas, Nev.
Available from NTIS, Springfield, Va 22161 as Rept. No. ARMS-71.65, $4.00 in paper copy, $2.25 in microfiche. Atomic Energy Commission, Divison of Operational Safety Report No. ARMS-71.6.5, August 1974. 22 p, 3 fig, 3 tab, 3 ref.

Descriptors: *Surveys, *Monitoring, *Measurement, *Radioactivity, *Remote sensing, Aerial sensing, Aircraft, Nuclear powerplants, Data collections, Sites, Background radiation, Fallout, Public health, Maine.
Identifiers: *Maine Yankee Atomic Power Plant, Gamma Radiation.

The Aerial Radiological Measuring System (ARMS) was used to survey the area surrounding the Maine Yankee Atomic Power Plant during September 1971, prior to reactor start-up. The survey measured terrestrial gamma radiation. A high sensitivity detection system collected gamma-ray spectral and gross-count data. The data were then computer processed into a map of 530 square mile area showing isoexposure contours three feet above the ground. Exposure rates and isotopes identified are consistent with normal terrestrial background radiation. (Houser-ORNL)
W75-06630

AERIAL RAIOLOGICAL MEASURING SURVEY OF THE FORT ST. VRAIN NUCLEAR GENERATING STATION OCTOBER 1971,
EG and G, Inc., Las Vegas, Nev.
Available from the National Technical Information Service, Springfield, Va 22161, as Rept. No ARMS-72.6.9, $4.00 in paper copy, $2.25 in microfiche. Atomic Energy Commission, Division of Operational Safety Report No ARMS-72.6.9, August 1974. 22 p, 3 fig, 3 tab, 3 ref.

Descriptors: *Colorado, *Radioactivity, *Measurement, *Surveys, *Remote sensing, *Aerial sensing, Aircraft, Assessment, Background radiation, Data collections, Radioisotopes, Nuclear powerplants, Effluents, Fallout, Public health.
Identifiers: *Fort St. Vrain Nuclear Generating Station(Colo), Gamma radiation.

The Aerial Radiological Measuring System (ARMS) was used to survey the area surrounding the Fort St. Vrain Nuclear Generating Station during October, 1972, prior to reactor start-up. The survey measured terrestrial gamma radiation. A high-sensitivity detection system collected gamma-ray spectral and gross-count data. The data were then computer processed into a map of a 670 square mile area showing isoexposure contours three feet above the ground. Exposure rates and isotopes identified are consistent with normal terrestrial background radiation. (Houser-ORNL)
W75-06631

AERIAL RADIOLOGICAL MEASURING SURVEY OF THE PRAIRIE ISLAND NUCLEAR GENERATING PLANT SEPTEMBER 1971,
EG and G, Inc., Las Vegas, Nev.
Available from the National Technical Information Service, Springfield, Va 22161, as Rept No ARMS-71.6.2, $4.00 in paper copy, $2.25 in microfiche. Atomic Energy Commission, Division of Operational Safety Report No ARMS-71.6.2, August 1974. 22 p, 3 fig, 3 tab, 3 ref.

Descriptors: *Minnesota, *Surveys, *Monitoring, *Measurement, *Nuclear powerplants, *Effluents, *Radioactivity, Remote sensing, Aerial sensing, Aircraft, Sampling, Data collections, Sites, Fallout, Public health, Background radiation.
Identifiers: *Prairie Island Nuclear Generating Plant(Minn), Gamma radiation.

The Aerial Radiological Measuring System (ARMS) was used to survey the area surrounding the Prairie Island Nuclear Generating Plant during September 1971, prior to reactor start-up. The survey measured terrestrial gamma radiation. A high-sensitivity detection system collected gamma-ray spectral and gross-count data. The data were then computer processed into a map of an 800 square mile area showing isoexposure contours three feet above the ground. Exposure rates and isotopes identified are consistent with normal terrestrial background radiation. (Houser-ORNL)
W75-06632

AERIAL RADIOLOGICAL MEASURING SURVEYS OF THE TURKEY POINT STATION APRIL 1972,
EG and G, Inc., Las Vegas, Nev.
Available from the National Technical Information Service, Springfield, Va 22161, as Rept No ARMS-72.6.2, $4.00 in paper copy, $2.25 in microfiche. Atomic Energy Commission, Division of Operational Safety Report No ARMS-72.6.2, July 1974. 22 p, 3 fig, 3 tab, 3 ref.

Descriptors: *Florida, *Radioactivity, *Measurement, *Remote sensing, *Surveys, *Aerial sensing, Aircraft, Assessment, Radioisotopes, Background radiation, Data collection, Nuclear powerplants, Effluents, Public health, Background radiation.
Identifiers: *Turkey Point Nuclear Power Station(Fla), Gamma radiation.

The Aerial Radiological Measuring System (ARMS) was used to survey the area surrounding the Turkey Point nuclear power station during April 1972, prior to reactor start-up. The survey measured terrestrial background gamma radiation. A high-sensitivity detection system collected gamma-ray spectral and gross-count data. The data were then computer processed into a map of a 175 square mile area showing isoexposure contours three feet above the ground. Exposure rates and isotopes identified are consistent with normal terrestrial background radiation. (Houser-ORNL)
W75-06633

AERIAL RADIOLOGICAL MEASURING SURVEY OF THE PILGRIM STATION SEPTEMBER 1971,
EG and G, Inc., Las Vegas, Nev.
Available from the National Technical Information Service, Springfield, Va 22161, as Rept No ARMS-71.6.4, $4.00 in paper copy, $2.25 in microfiche. Atomic Energy Commission, Division of Operational Safety Report No ARMS-71.6.4, August 1974. 22 p, 3 fig, 3 tab, 3 ref.

Descriptors: *Massachusetts, *Radioactivity, *Measurement, *Assessment, *Surveys, *Remote sensing, Aerial sensing, Aircraft, Nuclear powerplants, Effluents, Fallout, Public health, Background radiation.
Identifiers: *Pilgrim Nuclear Power Station(Mass), Gamma radiation.

The Aerial Radiological Measuring System (ARMS) was used to survey the area surrounding the Pilgrim nuclear power station during September 1971, prior to reactor start-up. The survey measured terrestrial background gamma radiation. A high-sensitivity detection system collected gamma-ray spectral and gross-count data. The data were then computer processed into a map of 230 square mile area showing isoexposure contours three feet above the ground. Exposure rates and isotopes identified are consistent with normal terrestrial background radiation. (Houser-ORNL)
W75-06634

AERIAL RADIOLOGICAL MEASURING SURVEY OF THE INDIAN POINT STATION AUGUST 1969,
EG and G, Inc., Las Vegas, Nev.
Available from the National Technical Information Service, Springfield, Va 22161, as Rept No ARMS-69.6.4, $4.00 in paper copy, $2.25 in microfiche. Atomic Energy Commission, Division of Operational Safety Report No ARMS-69.6.4, July 1974. 22 p, 3 fig, 3 tab, 3 ref.

Descriptors: *New York, *Radioactivity, *Measurement, *Surveys, *Assessment, *Remote sensing, Aerial sensing, Aircraft, Nuclear powerplants, Effluents, Fallout, Public health, Gases, Background radiation.
Identifiers: *Plume track, *Indian Point Station(NY), Gamma radiation.

The Aerial Radiological Measuring System (ARMS) was used to survey the area surrounding the Indian Point Station during August 1969. The survey measured terrestrial background gamma radiation and included an attempt to detect stack release gases. A high-sensitivity detection system collected gamma-ray spectral and gross-count data. The data were then computer processed into a map of 625 square mile area showing isoexposure contours three feet above the ground. Exposure rates and isotopes identified in the area survey are generally consistent with normal terrestrial background. A single point source of low energy photons, possibly an x-ray machine, was observed near the edge of the area. The plume assay revealed no radioactivity other than normal background. (Houser-ORNL)
W75-06635

EVALUATION OF METHODS FOR DETECTING COLIFORMS AND FECAL STREPTOCOCCI IN CHLORINATED SEWAGE EFFLUENTS,
Illinois State Water Survey, Urbana.
S. D. Lin.
Report of Investigation No. 78, 1974. 23 p, 13 fig, 10 tab, 41 ref, 4 append.

Descriptors: *Sewage effluents, *Sewage bacteria, *Coliforms, *E. coli, *Streptococcus, Water pollution effects, Microbiology, Evaluation, Chlorination, Sewage treatment, Sanitary engineering, Laboratory tests, Environmental engineering, *Pollutant identification.
Identifiers: *Chlorinated sewage, *Secondary sewage effluents, Detection methods.

Total coliform (TC), fecal coliform (FC), and fecal streptococcus (FS) recoveries in chlorinated secondary sewage effluents were investigated by the membrane filter (MF) and multiple-tube (most probable number, MPN) methods. The LES two-step MF method was found to be comparable to the MPN procedure for determining TC. The TC detection was 1.5 times greater by the LES two-step technique than that obtained by the M-Endo one-step MF procedure. Fecal coliform recovery by the M-FC MF procedure was lower than the recovery obtained by the MPN method. Azide-dextrose broth, brain-heart infusion broth, and peptone yeast-extract casitone used separately with the M-Enterococcus agar MF2 (2-day incubation) procedure were not satisfactory for the recovery of FS. The M-Enterococcus agar procedure with bile broth enrichment (MF2) or prolonged incubation for 3 days (MF3) significantly increased FS recovery and both were comparable to the MPN method. The results cited should be useful in assessing the efficiency of disinfection practices for waste treatment plants employing effluent chlorination. (Poertner)
W75-06654

MEASUREMENT OF MANGANESE IN NATURAL WATERS BY ATOMIC ABSORPTION,
Mississippi State Univ., Mississippi State.
L. R. Robinson, R. A. Dixon, and E. D. Breland.
Water and Sewage Works, February 1968. p 80-82, 1 tab, 8 ref.

Descriptors: *Spectroscopy, *Chemical analysis, *Analytical techniques, *Moss spectrometry, *Qualitative analysis, *Pollutant identification, Inorganic compounds, Instrumentation, Water analysis, Manganese.
Identifiers: Atomic absorption spectroscopy.

Atomic absorption spectroscopy provides a rapid, reproducible, sensitive method to quantitatively measure manganese. Atomic absorption measures energy as it is absorbed by an atomic vapor. As a sample is sprayed into a flame and atomized, a light beam, with a resonance wave length identical to that of the element to be measured, is directed through the flame, into a monochromator, and then into a detector. The detector measures the final intensity of the beam. The amount of light absorbed, or the decrease in light intensity reaching the detector, is proportional to the concentration of the element in the sample. Techniques for quantitating manganese were found to be rapid, simple, and reproducible. The technique is outlined and all steps, such as reagents, sample collection, concentration, and measurement, are described. Where manganese concentrations are below the minimum sensitivity of the instrument used, a concentration technique can be used to produce satisfactory results. (Poertner)
W75-06658

POTAMOLOGICAL STUDIES ON THE RIVER INA OF THE RIVER SYSTEM OF YODO: 1 (IN JAPANESE),
Osaka Kyoiku Univ. (Japan). Oceanography Lab.
For primary bibliographic entry see Field 5B.
W75-06701

DISSOLVED ORGANIC MATERIAL IN THE ST. LAWRENCE MARITIME ESTUARY: COMPARISON AND CHOICE OF METHODS (IN FRENCH),
D. Cauchois, and M. Khalil.
J Fish Res Board Can. Vol 31, No 2, p 133-139, 1974, Illus, English summary.

Descriptors: *Estuaries, *Pollutants, Analytical techniques, *Separation techniques, Hydrocarbons, *Sea water, Chlorine compounds, Organic wastes, Chemical wastes.
Identifiers: *St-Lawrence estuary.

To study quantitatively and qualitatively the dissolved organic matter in the St. Lawrence maritime estuary, a comparison between the different extracting methods was undertaken. Two of them are proposed; 1 based on liquid-liquid extraction, the 2nd by adsorption on a resin (Amberlite XAD-2). The methods used remove different spectrums of organic compounds from sea water. Hydrocarbons were found to constitute the major part of the extracts varying between 3 and 5 mg/l. None of the methods used extracts more than 20% of the total organic matter present. The concentration of the organic chloro-compounds in the water column is in the order of 80 ppb.--Copyright 1974, Biological Abstracts, Inc.
W75-06706

THE USE OF A MODIFIED GULF V PLANKTON SAMPLER FROM A SMALL OPEN BOAT,
Ministry of Agriculture, Fisheries and Food, Lowestoft (England). Fisheries Lab.
For primary bibliographic entry see Field 7B.
W75-06707

AN AIR-LIFT FOR QUANTITATIVE SAMPLING OF THE BENTHOS,
Hull Univ. (England). Dept. of Zoology.
For primary bibliographic entry see Field 7B.
W75-06713

MARINE ALPHA-RADIOACTIVITY OFF SOUTHERN AFRICA: 3. POLONIUM-210 AND LEAD -210,
Department of Industries, Cape Town (South Africa). Div. of Sea Fisheries.
L. V. Shannon.
S Afr Div Sea Fish Invest Rep. 100. p 1-34, 1973, Illus.
Identifiers: *Africa(Cape of Good Hope), Chemicals, *Electro deposition, Fish, Food, *Lead-210, Marine organisms, Oceanographic studies, Phytoplankton, *Polonium-210, *Radioactivity, Salinity, Tracers, Zooplankton, *Solvent extraction, *Pollutant identification, Sea water.

A method is outlined for the determination of Pb-210 and Po-210 in sea-water by solvent extraction followed by electrodeposition and alpha-counting. The mean activities of Pb-210 and Po-210 in sea-water samples collected at a depth of 20 m in the sea around the Cape of Good Hope during March 1969, were 38 x 10 to the 15 power Ci/l and 20 x 10 to the minus 15 power Ci/l, respectively. Variations in the concentrations of these nuclides could in part be ascribed to different water masses and current systems. Unsupported Po-210 in 387 samples of marine organisms, collected from 1967-1969 within 1000 miles of Southern Africa was determined by repeated total alpha-counting. In addition, Pb-210 and Po-210 in 13 zooplankton, 4 phytoplankton and 6 pelagic fish samples collected during 1969 were determined by chemical extraction, electrodeposition and alpha-counting. The mean values for lead-210 and polonium-210 in the zooplankton samples were 31 pCi/kg wet material and 380 pCi/kg wet material, respectively. In zooplankton the Pb-210 activity was on the average 1/12 of the Po-210 activity. The concentration of Po-210 in marine life increased along the food chain. Po-210 in sea-water and plankton appears to be closely related to the distribution of salinity and the possible utility of Po-210 as a natural oceanographic tracer is discussed.--Copyright 1974, Biological Abstracts, Inc.
W75-06718

DATA ON THE HYDROBIOLOGICAL RELATIONSHIPS OF THE BACKWATER OF THE BODROG RIVER NEAR SAROSPATAK: I. PRELIMINARY STUDIES ON THE DETERMINATION OF CHARACTERISTICS OF OXYGEN AND CARBON DIOXIDE BALANCE IN THE BACK-WATER,
Lajos Kossuth Univ., Debrecen (Hungary). Zoological Inst.
G. Devai, I. Devai, K. Horvath, I. Bancsi, and M. Toth.
Acta Biol Debrecina. 7/8. p 210-222, 1969/70(1971), Illus, English summary.

Descriptors: *Rivers, *Water analysis, *Backwater, Aquatic life, *Oxygen, *Carbon dioxide, Europe, Ecology.
Identifiers: *Hungary(Bodrog River), Hydrobiological relationships, Sarospatak.

This 1st part of a series of hydro-ecological papers is concerned with water analysis of the backwater of the river Bodrog, near Sarospatak (NE-Hungary). The purpose of this paper is to demonstrate that even in those backwaters that are characterized by a regular hydro-dynamism there are many trends which may be due to the periodical activity of living organisms. Necessity of simultaneous measurements of O2 and CO2 data is shown.--Copyright 1973, Biological Abstracts, Inc.
W75-06720

STUDY OF PRIMARY OXYGEN PRODUCTION IN THE HUNGARIAN SECTION OF THE DANUBE (DANUBIALIA HUNGARICA LVIII),
Magyar Tudomanyos Akademia, Budapest. Station for Danube Research.
Z. T. Dvihally.
Ann Univ Sci Budap Rolando Eotvos Nominatae Sect Biol. 13, p 33-43, 1971, Illus.

Descriptors: *Rivers, Europe, *Oxygen, Analytical techniques, *Flow rates, *Primary productivity, *Pollutant identification.
Identifiers: Austria, *Danube River(Humgary).

Measurements of O2 production potential in laboratory and in situ in the Hungarian section of the Danube river are described. The differences observed in the O2 production potentials of the Austrian and Hungarian sections of the river appear to be due to differences in the flow speeds. The primary O2 production of the water was inversely proportional to the flow speed. The differences between the maxima and minima of the daily O2 production as obtained from 24-hr-measurements ranged from 3.2 mg/l to 7.5 mg/l in different months.--Copyright 1973, Biological Abstracts, Inc.
W75-06721

SUMMARY REPORT OF MICROBIOLOGICAL BASELINE DATA ON LAKE SUPERIOR, 1973,
Canada Centre for Inland Waters, Burlington (Ontario).
For primary bibliographic entry see Field 2H.
W75-06738

RADIONUCLIDE LEVELS IN THE GREAT LAKES WATERS - 1973,
Canada Centre for Inland Waters, Burlington (Ontario).
R. W. Durham.
Scientific Series No. 48, 5 p, 1974, Inland Waters Directorate. 2 fig, 5 ref, 2 tab.

Descriptors: *Great Lakes, *Surveys, *Radioactivity, Radioactive wastes, Monitoring, Sampling, Measurement, Cesium, Testing procedures, Lake Huron, *Canada, *Pollutant identification.
Identifiers: *Radionuclides, Nuclear power, Spectrometry, Antimony, Douglas Point(Ont), Pickering(Ont).

The only artificially produced radionuclides detected in the waters of the Great Lakes by gamma ray spectrometry using a large volume Ge(Li) detector were 137CS and 125SB. The radioactivity levels of these radionuclides in the open waters of the lakes were measured during the spring and summer of 1973. Similar measurements were made at the plume-lake interface of the Ontario Hydro nuclear generating stations at Douglas Point and Pickering. The results of all the measurements were quite low with a range of 14-87 PCI/cu. m. for 137CS and 41-124 PCI/cu. m. for 125SB. (Environment Canada)
W75-06744

INTERLABORATORY QUALITY CONTROL STUDY NO. 7 - MAJOR CATIONS AND ANIONS,
Canada Centre for Inland Waters, Burlington (Ontario).
For primary bibliographic entry see Field 2K.
W75-06747

AN ASSESSMENT OF AREAL AND TEMPORAL VARIATIONS IN STREAMFLOW QUALITY USING SELECTED DATA FROM THE NATIONAL STREAM QUALITY ACCOUNTING NETWORK,
Geological Survey, Reston, Va.
For primary bibliographic entry see Field 5B.
W75-06755

REMOTE SENSING,
Bureau of Reclamation, Washington, D.C.
For primary bibliographic entry see Field 7B.
W75-06775

HEALTH AND SAFETY LABORATORY FALLOUT PROGRAM, QUARTERLY SUMMARY REPORT (JUNE 1, 1974 THROUGH SEPTEMBER 1, 1974),
Health and Safety Lab. (AEC), New York.
E. P. Hardy, Jr.
Available from NTIS, Dept. of Comm., Springfield, Va 22161 as Rept. No. HASL-286, $7.60 in paper copy, $2.25 in microfiche. Report No. HASL-286, October 1974. 176 p, 39 fig, 55 tab, 19 ref, 5 append.

Descriptors: *Fallout, *Surveys, *Monitoring, *Radioactivity, *Data collections, Publications, Laboratories, Air pollution, Soil contamination, Depth, Distribution, Background, Radiation, Human population, Public health, Diets, Sediments, Oceans, Land, Cesium, Strontium, Plutonium, Milk, Domestic water, Bibliographies.
Identifiers: *Taiwan, *New Zealand.

Current data are presented from the Health and Safety Laboratories Program, the Institute of Nuclear Science in Taiwan, and the National Radiation Laboratory in New Zealand. Interpretive reports and notes are presented on depth distribution of artificial radionuclides in soil, alpha contribution to beta background, global deposition of Sr 90 through 1973, fallout plutonium in diet, strontium 90 in human bone, sediment sampling near Mound Laboratory, Miamisburg, Ohio and ocean vs. land strontium 90 fallout. Tabulations are included of radionuclide levels in fallout, surface air, milk, diet, and tap water. A bibliography of recent publications related to radionuclide studies is also presented. (See W75-06795 thru W75-06807) (Houser-ORNL)
W75-06794

DEPTH DISTRIBUTIONS OF GLOBAL FALLOUT SR90, CS137, AND PU239, 240 IN SANDY LOAM SOIL,
Health and Safety Lab. (AEC), New York.
E. P. Hardy, Jr.
In: Report No. HASL-286, p I-2 - I-10, October 1974. 1 fig, 4 tab, 5 ref.

Descriptors: *Soil contamination, *Radioactivity, Depth, *Profiles, Analysis, Strontium, Cesium, Plutonium, Migration, *Distribution, Radioisotopes, Movement, Sampling, *Massachusetts, Path of pollutants.
Identifiers: *Cape Cod(Mass).

The first of a series of depth profile soil samples taken at an undisturbed site on Cape Cod have been analyzed for Sr90, Cs137, and Pu239, 240. Cesium 137 shows the least tendency to migrate downward followed by Pu239, 240 and Sr90, in that order. The objective of this experiment is to measure the depth distributions of these isotopes on a bi-annual basis to estimate rate of movement. (See also W75-06794) (Houser-ORNL)
W75-06795

ALPHA CONTRIBUTION TO BETA BACKGROUND—A FOLLOW-UP STUDY,
Health and Safety Lab. (AEC), New York.
I. M. Fisenne, and H. W. Keller.
In: Report No. HASL-286, p I-11 - I-16, October 1974. 2 tab, 3 ref.

Descriptors: *Background radiation, *Measurement, Instrumentation.
Identifiers: Low level radiation, *Yttrium.

Contributions to low level background have been investigated in an attempt to pinpoint the sources. Of primary interest is the reduction of the beta scintillation counter background used for yttrium 90 measurements. (See also W75-06794) (Houser-ORNL)
W75-06796

WORLDWIDE DEPOSITION OF SR 90 THROUGH 1973,
Health and Safety Lab. (AEC), New York.
H. L. Volchok, and L. Toonkel.
In: Report No. HASL-286, p I-17 - I-35, October 1974. 4 fig, 4 tab, 12 ref.

Descriptors: *Fallout, *Strontium, *Radioactivity, *Measurement, Sampling, Radiochemical analysis, Analytical techniques, Evaluation, Surveys, Seasonal, Data collections, Nuclear explosions, Testing.

The total Sr 90 fallout on the earth's surface in 1973 was 63 kilocuries. This is the lowest since the Health and Safety Laboratory program began in 1958. The seasonal and latitudinal variations have remained as before. Approximately double this amount of Sr 90 is anticipated to be deposited in 1974. Data collected by the United States and the United Kingdom are compared. (See also W75-06794) (Houser-ORNL)
W75-06797

FALLOUT PU 239, 240 IN DIET,
Health and Safety Lab. (AEC), New York.
B. G. Bennett.
In: Report No. HASL-286, p I-36 - I-52, October 1974. 6 tab, 13 ref.

Descriptors: *Fallout, *Plutonium, *Measurement, *Assay, *Diets, Food chains, Human population, Public health, Digestion, Sampling, Foods, Fish, Milk, Path of pollutants, Potatoes, Soil contamination, Drinking water, Vegetable crops, Grains(Crops).

Ingestion intake of fallout Pu 239, 240 in New York in 1972 has been determined from a complete diet sampling. Concentration of plutonium in the 19 food categories ranged from .01 pCi/kg in shell fish to below the minimum detection level in milk. Annual intake in total diet is estimated to have been 1.5 pCi in 1972. Further analyses of Pu in wheat have been completed, and an uptake estimate is made for Pu in potatoes. Recent results for Pu in tap water are also reported. (See also W75-06794) (Houser-ORNL)
W75-06798

STRONTIUM-90 IN THE HUMAN BONE, 1973 RESULTS FOR NEW YORK CITY AND SAN FRANCISCO,
Health and Safety Lab. (AEC), New York.
B. G. Bennett.
In: Report No. HASL-286, p I-53 - I-70, October 1974. 5 fig, 5 tab, 15 ref.

Descriptors: *Strontium, Human population, *Assessment, *Assay, Biology, Absorption, Food chains, Model studies, Growth stages, Diets, Surveys, Behavior, Retention, *California, New York.
Identifiers: *New York City, *San Francisco, *Human bone, Young, Adult.

Results are presented of determinations of Sr 90 content of 229 specimens of human vertebrae obtained during 1973 in New York City and San Francisco. The average Sr 90 to Ca ratios for adult vertebrae are 1.35 pCi/gCa in New York and .80 pCi/gCa in San Francisco, about 3% less than the average values of the previous year. Average Sr 90 concentrations in children's bone are now little different from the adult values. A two compartment bone model, which accounts for both short and long term retention of Sr 90 in bone, is used to describe the variations of Sr 90 content of bone and provide correlation with dietary Sr 90 intake. Regression analysis of the 13 years of survey data provides values of the relative retention of dietary Sr 90 and the effective bone turnover rates. The bone model gives satisfactory description of observed Sr 90 levels and allows reliable assessment of the long-term behavior of Sr 90 in man. (See also W75-06794) (Houser-ORNL)
W75-06799

SEDIMENT SAMPLING NEAR MOUND LABORATORY - JULY 1974,
Health and Safety Lab. (AEC), New York.
H. L. Volchok, and J. C. Burke.
In: Report No. HASL-286, p I-71 - I-81, October 1974. 1 fig, 2 tab, 2 ref.

Descriptors: *Sediments, *Sampling, Analysis, *Plutonium, *Ponds, Canals, Freshwater, Behavior, Evaluation, Public health, Water pollution, *Ohio.
Identifiers: *Mound Laboratory(Ohio).

Eight large diameter sediment cores and 16 water samples were taken from local water bodies in the vicinity of Mound Laboratory, Miamisburg, Ohio: The North and South Ponds and the Miami-Erie Canal. These samples will be analyzed for plutonium and other chemical and physical properties to determine the geochemical behavior of plutonium in a fresh water system. (See also W75-06794) (Houser-ORNL)
W75-06800

IS THERE EXCESS SR90 FALLOUT IN THE OCEANS,
Health and Safety Lab. (AEC), New York.
H. L. Volchok.
In: Rept. No. HASL-286, p I-82 - I-89, October 1974. 16 ref.

Descriptors: *Fallout, *Strontium, *Oceans, *Measurement, *Radioactivity, *Atlantic Ocean, Depth, Profiles, Data collections, Assessment, Evaluation, Research and development.

Atlantic Ocean concentration depth profiles continue to suggest greater Sr90 deposition, per unit area, than for adjacent land bodies. Extrapolating from this to all oceans results in much more Sr90 than was reportedly produced. The pertinent land, atmospheric and oceanic evidence are reviewed hopefully to stimulate research toward a resolution to the problem. (See also W75-06794) (Houser-ORNL)
W75-06801

ENVIRONMENTAL RADIOACTIVITY SURVEYS FOR NUCLEAR POWER PLANTS IN NORTH TAIWAN,
National Taiwan Univ., Taipei. Health Physics Section.
P-S. Weng, T-C. Chu, C-S. Hsu, H-T. Chang, and K-L. Pang.
In: Report No. HASL-286, p III-2 - III-24, October 1974. 16 fig, 15 tab, 1 ref.

Descriptors: *Monitoring, *Radioactivity, *Nuclear powerplants, Construction, *Background radiation, *Nuclear explosions, Testing, Fallout, Sampling, Air pollution, Sites, Water wells, Ground water, Rain, Meteorology, Silts, Vegetation, Vegetables, Soil contamination, Oceans, Aquatic life, Biota.
Identifiers: China, *Taiwan, Dosimetry.

This report is the continuation of environmental radioactivity monitoring for the nuclear power plants in North Taiwan which are under construction. During this monitoring period, the fifteenth nuclear weapon test was held at Lop Nor of mainland China on June 27, 1973 and caused significant increase in radioactivity. Several thermoluminescent dosimeters monitoring stations have been established as compared with the previous years, and low volume air samples were added to monitor airborne particulates in addition to the gummed films and pots. (See also W75-06794) (Houser-ORNL)
W75-06802

ENVIRONMENTAL RADIOACTIVITY ANNUAL REPORT 1973 (NEW ZEALAND).
National Radiation Lab., Christchurch (New Zealand). Dept. of Health.
In: Report No. HASL-286, p III-25 - III-66, October 1974. 12 fig, 15 tab.

Descriptors: *Monitoring, Environment, *Radioactivity, Measurement, *Nuclear explosions, *United States, Testing, Fallout, Strontium, Cesium, Bioindicators, Bioassay, Milk.
Identifiers: *New Zealand, *France, *USSR.

During 1973, country-wide average deposition of strontium 90 on New Zealand was the lowest since measurements commenced in 1960. A maximum country-wide average level of 3.6 millicuries per square kilometre was deposited in 1964 following the large scale U.S.S.R. and U.S.A. nuclear tests in 1961 and 1962. Annual deposits thereafter decreased to a minimum of 0.8 mCi/sq km in 1968. Smaller increases reaching a maximum annual deposit of 1.4 mCi/sq km occurred in the next few years as a result of French nuclear tests in the South Pacific. During 1973, however, the country-wide average deposit decreased to 0.3 mCi/sq km, less than one-tenth the 1964 maximum. It is estimated that at the end of 1973 about 20% of the total strontium 90 deposition on New Zealand had come from French tests in the South Pacific. The concentration of strontium 90 and cesium 137 in milk reflect the changes in fallout deposition. The average levels during 1973 were the lowest since measurements commenced. (See also W75-06794) (Houser-ORNL)
W75-06803

APPENDIX TO HEALTH AND SAFETY LABORATORY FALLOUT PROGRAM, QUAR-

TERLY SUMMARY REPORT (JUNE 1, 1974 THROUGH SEPTEMBER 1, 1974).
Health and Safety Lab. (AEC), New York.
Available from NTIS, Dept. of Comm., Springfield, Va 22161 as Rept. No. HASL-286, $10.60 in paper copy, $2.25 in microfiche. Report No. HASL-286, Appendix, October 1974. 474 p, 4 fig, 5 tab, 7 ref.

Descriptors: *Fallout, *Data collections, *Strontium, Sites, *Monitoring, Radioisotopes, Lead, Air pollution, Milk, Potable water, *Path of pollutants.
Identifiers: Deposition, Conversion factors, Elements, Isotopes.

Data are reported from monthly monitoring sites in the United States and in other countries as follows: Sr 90 and Sr 89 in monthly deposition at World land sites; Radionuclides and lead in surface air; and Radiostrontium in milk and tap water. (See W75-06794 and W75-06805 thru W75-06807) (Houser-ORNL)
W75-06804

STRONTIUM 90 AND STRONTIUM 89 IN MONTHLY DEPOSITION AT WORLD LAND SITES,
Health and Safety Lab. (AEC), New York.
E. P. Hardy, Jr.
In: Report No. HASL-286, Appendix, p a-2 - 334, October 1974. 2 fig, 1 tab.

Descriptors: *Monitoring, *Fallout, *Sites, *Measurement, *Radioactivity, *Strontium, Data collections, Publications, Data processing, Data storage and retrieval, Radioisotopes, Sampling, Analysis.
Identifiers: Deposition.

At present, there are 34 monthly monitoring sites in the United States and 82 in other countries. The collections are made using either high-walled stainless steel pots with exposed areas of 0.076 square meters or plastic funnels with exposed areas of 0.072 square meters to which are attached ion-exchange columns. To facilitate the accurate storage, retrieval, and handling of the data generated from the monthly fallout collection network, all data have been transcribed to punched cards. The data printed out from the punched cards are presented in tables. Monthly Sr90 deposition values for New York City since 1954 are shown in graph form. (See also W75-06804) (Houser-ORNL)
W75-06805

RADIONUCLIDES IN LEAD AND SURFACE AIR,
Health and Safety Lab. (AEC), New York.
H. L. Volchok, L. Toonkel, and M. Shonberg.
In: Report No. HASL-286, Appendix, p B-1 - 131, October 1974. 1 tab, 7 ref.

Descriptors: *Monitoring, Measurement, *Radioisotopes, *Sampling, Sites, *Fallout, Data collections, Analytical techniques, Radiochemical analysis, Gamma rays, Atlantic Ocean, Beryllium, Zirconium, Nuclear experiments, Cesium, Cerium, Manganese, Iron, Strontium, Cadmium, Plutonium, Lead, Quality control.
Identifiers: Gross gamma, *China, *France.

The primary objective of this program is to study the spatial and temporal distribution of nuclear weapons debris and lead in the surface air. Other special studies of surface air contamination have been added over the course of the program. Many of the original NRL sites, which grouped roughly along the 80th Meridian (West), have been continned in the current program. Since 1963 a number of other sites were added to investigate the possible effects of longitude, elevation and proximity to coastlines, and from late 1965 through March 1969, samplers were placed on four Atlantic Ocean weather ships to extend the surface air study over the marine environment. The present network extends from about 76 deg North to 90 deg South. A table lists the sampling stations along with their coordinates and elevations. (See also W75-06804) (Houser-ORNL)
W75-06806

RADIOSTRONTIUM IN MILK AND TAP WATER,
Health and Safety Lab. (AEC), New York.
E. P. Hardy, Jr.
In: Rept. No. HASL-286, Appendix, p C-1 - 7, October 1974. 2 fig, 3 tab.

Descriptors: *Fallout, *Radioactivity, *Strontium, *Cesium, *Monitoring, Measurement, *Milk, *Potable water, Food chains, Data collections, Publications, New York.
Identifiers: *New York City(NY).

In 1954, the Health and Safety Laboratory began monitoring liquid whole milk in New York City for strontium-90 in order to estimate the dietary contribution from the ingestion of this radionuclide from this source. During the same year, tap water sampling was begun on a routine basis at the laboratory which receives its supply from one of the main reservoirs servicing New York City. Although a more complete study of the strontium-90 content of the diets in three major U.S. cities was started in March 1960, milk and tap water analyses in New York City have been continued in order to provide a detailed and continuous history of the contamination levels of these staples. Some additional data of Cesium 137 to Strontium 90 ratio are given. (See also W75-06804) (Houser-ORNL)
W75-06807

HEALTH AND SAFETY LABORATORY FALLOUT PROGRAM QUARTERLY SUMMARY REPORT, (SEPTEMBER 1, 1974 THROUGH DECEMBER 1, 1974),
Health and Safety Lab. (AEC), New York.
E. P. Hardy, Jr.
Available from NTIS, Springfield, Va. 22161 as Rept. No. HASL-288, $7.60 in paper copy, $2.25 in microfiche. Report No. HASL-288, January 1975. 172 p, 9 fig, 30 tab, 42 ref, 1 bib.

Descriptors: *Fallout, *Radioactivity, *Radioisotopes, *Monitoring, Measurement, *Assay, *Data collections, Data processing, Publications, Documentation, Sampling, Analysis, Analytical techniques, Strontium, Cesium, Plutonium, Lead, Diets, Milk, Air pollution, Water pollution, Potable water, Soil contamination, Food chains.
Identifiers: Human bone.

This report presents current data from the Health and Safety Laboratory Program. The initial section consists of interpretive reports and notes on the regional uniformity of cumulative radionuclide fallout, analyses of quality control samples at HASL and a contractor laboratory in 1974, and quality control results for the HASL surface air samples in 1973. Subsequent sections include tabulations of radionuclide levels in fallout, surface air, stratospheric air, milk, diet, and tap water. A bibliography of recent publications related to radionuclide studies is also presented. Detailed data are tabulated in HASL-288-Appendix. (See W75-06819 thru W75-06826) (Houser-ORNL)
W75-06818

REGIONAL UNIFORMITY OF CUMULATIVE RADIONUCLIDE FALLOUT,
Health and Safety Lab. (AEC), New York.
E. P. Hardy, Jr.
In: Report No. HASL-288, p I-2 - 9, January 1975, 2 fig, 2 tab, 8 ref.

Descriptors: *Fallout, *Cesium, *Strontium, *Plutonium, *Radioisotopes, Surveys, Monitoring, Assay, *Nuclear explsions, Testing, Cities, Bays, Sampling, Analysis, Soil contamination, Regional analysis, Precipitation(Atmospheric), Uniformity coefficient.
Identifiers: *New york City, *San Francisco Bay.

Integrated deposits of Cs 137, Sr 90, and Pu 239, 240 from atmospheric nuclear testing were determined in the New York and San Francisco areas by analyzing soil samples collected at a number of sites. Higher fallout levels in New York reflected heavier mean annual precipitation but the variability within each area was less than 15 percent. (See also W75-06818) (Houser-ORNL)
W75-06819

ANALYSES OF QUALITY CONTROL SAMPLES AT HASL AND A CONTRACTOR LABORATORY DURING 1974,
Health and Safety Lab. (AEC), New York.
E. P. Hardy, Jr.
In: Report No. HASL-288, p I-10 - 32, January 1975. 5 tab, 1 ref.

Descriptors: *Sampling, *Analysis, *Quality control, Laboratories, *Assay, *Fallout, Diets, Drinking water, Ion exchange, Resins, Calcium compounds, Phosphates, Cation exchange, Vegetation, Incineration.
Identifiers: *Human bone, Ash.

Samples of biological material and fallout, analyzed at HASL and by a contractor laboratory include quality control samples which are submitted as blinds. These checks consist of blanks, reference samples analyzed repeatedly over a period of years, replicates or splits of unknowns, spikes, and duplicate samplings. Quality control data are summarized for ashed bone, diet, tap water, and fallout samples analyzed for Sr 90, Cs 137, and Ca during 1974. (See also W75- 06818) (Houser-ORNL)
W75-06820

HASL SURFACE AIR SAMPLING PROGRAM - THE QUALITY OF ANALYSIS - 1973,
Health and Safety Lab. (AEC), New York.
L. Toonkel, M. Schonberg, and H. Volchok.
In: Report No. HASL-288, p I-33 - 60, January 1975. 6 tab, 6 ref.

Descriptors: *Analytical techniques, Analysis, *Sampling, *Quality control, Evaluation, *Radioactivity, *Reliability, Variability, *Air pollution, Water pollution, Soil contamination, Strontium, Plutonium, Beryllium, Zirconium, Cesium, Cerium, Radioisotopes.
Identifiers: Surface air.

In general the quality of the analyses in the Surface Air Sampling program in 1973 was satisfactory. The accuracy averaged within 15% and the mean precision was within plus or minus 15% in most cases. There was an inexplicable tendency toward a small negative bias for a number of the substances analyzed. (See also W75-06818) (Houser-ORNL)
W75-06821

PROJECT AIRSTREAM,
Health and Safety Lab. (AEC), New York.
P. W. Krey, L. E. Toonkel, and M. Schonberg.
In: Report No. HASL-288, p II-7 - 96, January 1975. 6 fig, 7 tab, 24 ref.

Descriptors: *Surveys, *Monitoring, *Radioactivity, Aircraft, *Air pollution, Sampling, Analysis, Radiochemical analysis, Data collections, Seasonal, Sulphur, Strontium, Lead, Polonium, Plutonium, Beryllium, *Remote sensing.
Identifiers: *Lower stratosphere.

Project Airstream is HASL's study of radioactivity in the lower stratosphere employing the WB-57F aircraft as a sampling platform. This project is a continuation of the Defense Atomic Support

Agency's Project Stardust except that Airstream's sampling missions are limited to only one per season. Radiochemical data from the missions flown in January, June and November 1973 and in April 1974 are presented. (See also W75-06818) (Houser-ORNL)
W75-06822

APPENDIX TO HEALTH AND SAFETY LABORATORY FALLOUT PROGRAM QUARTERLY SUMMARY REPORT, (SEPTEMBER 1, 1974 THROUGH DECEMBER 1, 1974),
Health and Safety Lab. (AEC), New York.
E. P. Hardy, Jr.
Available from NTIS, Springfield, Va. 22161 as Rept. No. HASL-288-Appendix. Report No. HASL-288-Appendix, January 1975. 474 p.

Descriptors: *Fallout, *Radioactivity, *Data collections, *Sites, Sampling, Analysis, Publications, Public health, Laboratories, Strontium, Air pollution, Water pollution, Milk, Potable water.

Data are reported from monthly monitoring sites in the United States and in other countries as follows: Sr 90 and Sr 89 in monthly deposition at World land sites; Radionuclides and lead in surface air, and Radiostrontium in milk and tap water. (Houser-ORNL) (See W75-06818 and W75-06826)
W75-06823

SR 90 AND SR 89 IN MONTHLY DEPOSITION AT WORLD LAND SITES.
Health and Safety Lab. (AEC), New York.
In: Rept. No. HASL-288-Appendix, p A-1 - A-333, January 1975. 2 fig.

Descriptors: *Surveys, *Monitoring, Measurement, Assay, *Fallout, *Strontium, Sites, Data collections, Data processing, Publications, Sampling, Analysis, Public health, Laboratories, Precipitation(Atmospheric), Administration, Coordination.
Identifiers: *New York City.

At present, there are 34 monthly monitoring sites in the United States and 82 in other countries. The collections are made using either high-walled stainless steel pots which exposed areas of 0.076 square meters or plastic funnels with exposed areas of 0.072 square meters to which are attached ion-exchange columns. The data printed out from the punched cards are presented in tables. All ratios of Sr89 to Sr90 have been extrapolated to the midpoint of the sampling month. Calculated values of the concentration of Sr90 in precipitation are given in units of pCi of Sr90 per liter. The total precipitation in centimeters and the Sr90 deposition in millicuries per square kilometer for data available during a calendar year are listed. The groups or organizations responsible for the sampling are also identified on the individual site data sheets. Monthly Sr90 deposition values for New York City since 1954 are shown in graph form. (See also W75-06823) (Houser-ORNL)
W75-06824

RADIONUCLIDES AND LEAD IN SURFACE AIR,
Health and Safety Lab. (AEC), New York.
H. L. Volchok, L. Toonkel, and M. Schonberg.
In: Report No. HASL-288-Appendix, p B-1 - 131, January 1975. 1 tab, 7 ref.

Descriptors: *Monitoring, *Air pollution, *Fallout, *Oceans, *Sea breezes, Atlantic Ocean, Meteorology, Strontium, Lead, Radioisotopes, Water pollution, Sites, Sampling, Radiochemical analysis, Gamma rays, Public health.

The primary objective of this program is to study the spatial and temporal distribution of nuclear weapons debris and lead in the surface air. Other special studies of surface air contamination have been added over the course of the program. Many of the original NRL sites, which grouped roughly along the 80th Meridian (West), have been continned in the current program. Since 1963 a number of other sites were added to investigate the possible effects of longitude, elevation and proximity to coastlines, and from late 1965 through March 1969, samplers were placed on four Atlantic Ocean weather ships to extend the surface air study over the marine environment. The present network extends from about 76 degrees North to 90 degrees South. Table 2a lists the sampling stations along with their coordinates and elevations. (See also W75-06823) (Houser-ORNL)
W75-06825

RADIOSTRONTIUM IN MILK AND TAP WATER.
Health and Safety Lab. (AEC), New York.
In: Report No. HASL-288-Appendix, p C-1 - C-7, January 1975. 1 fig, 2 tab.

Descriptors: *Monitoring, *Radioactivity, *Measurement, *Strontium, *Cesium, *Milk, *Drinking water, New York, Cities, Diets, Public health, Absorption, Food chains, Data collections, Data processing, Publications, Sampling, Analysis.
Identifiers: *Ingestion, *New York City.

In 1954, the Health and Safety Laboratory began monitoring liquid whole milk in New York City for Strontium 90 in order to estimate the dietary contribution from the ingestion of this radionuclide from this source. During the same year, tap water sampling was begun on a routine basis at the laboratory which receives its supply from one of the main reservoirs servicing New York City. Although a more complete study of the Strontium 90 content of the diets in three major U.S. cities was started in March 1960, milk and tap water analyses in New York City have been continued in order to provide a detailed and continuous history of the contamination levels of these staples. (See also W75-06823) (Houser-ORNL)
W75-06826

SYSTEM FOR DETECTING PARTICULATE MATTER,
Princeton Electronic Products, Inc., North Brunswick, N.J. (assignee).
S. R. Hofstein.
U.S. Patent 3,830,969. Issued August 20, 1974. Official Gazette of the United States Patent Office, Vol 925, No 3, p 1000, August, 1974. 1 fig.

Descriptors: *Patents, *Waste identification, Liquids, Analyzers, Sampling, Matter, Particles, *Pollutant identification.
Identifiers: *Particulate matter, *Television image.

A system and method for detecting and graphically visualizing particulate matter present in a fluid sample were described. The liquid sample is held in a transparent container and agitated by spinning the container for a limited time period. This places the particles in transient motion relative to the then stationary container. A television camera forms a time continuous image of the illuminated container and scattered points of light from the moving particles. This television image is processed by a signal converter tube. The processed image, now retaining only the light points corresponding to the moving particles, can be displayed on CRT equipment. The processed image signal may also be furnished to an electronic particle detector and analyzer, which will examine the particulate matter for characteristics such as movement, distribution, dimensions, and number or concentration. (Prague-FIRL)
W75-06833

HYDROBACTERIOLOGICAL INVESTIGATIONS IN LAKE CONSTANCE: III. PROGRESSIVE GROWTH OF PLANKTON-DEPENDENT PRODUCTION OF BACTERIA AS AN INDICATION OF EUTROPHICATION, (IN GERMAN),
Staatliches Institut fuer Seenforschung und Seenbewirtschaftung, Langenargen (West Germany).
For primary bibliographic entry see Field 5C.
W75-06839

POROUS CERAMIC SOIL MOISTURE SAMPLERS, AN APPLICATION IN LYSIMETER STUDIES ON EFFLUENT SPRAY IRRIGATION,
Department of Agriculture, Lethbridge (Alberta). Research Station.
For primary bibliographic entry see Field 2G.
W75-06843

5B. Sources Of Pollution

SUBSURFACE WASTE DISPOSAL BY INJECTION IN HAWAII: A CONCEPTUAL FORMULATION AND PHYSICAL MODELING PLAN,
Hawaii Univ., Honolulu. Water Resources Research Center.
F. L. Peterson, and L. S. Lau.
Available from the National Technical Information Service, Springfield, Va 22161 as PB-240 982, $3.25 in paper copy, $2.25 in microfiche. Technical Memorandum Report No 41, November 1974. 14 p, 4 fig, 4 ref. OWRT B-038-HI(1). 14-31-0001-5068.

Descriptors: *Hawaii, *Model studies, *Path of pollutants, *Waste water disposal, Aquifers, *Groundwater movement, *Injection wells, Hydraulics, Hydrogeology, Water pollution sources.
Identifiers: Hawaiian groundwater system, Density-stratified fluids, *Hele-Shaw models, *Sandbox models, Injection hydrodynamics.

Emphasis on water pollution control and stringent regulations on waste water disposal into surface and coastal waters has focused attention on subsurface disposal as an alternative in Hawaii. The need exists to ascertain the mechanics of injection well systems and the fate and effects of the injected fluid in the aquifer. A laboratory study was begun to examine the hydromechanics of waste injection into Hawaiian density stratified groundwater systems using both a sandbox model and a vertical Hele-Shaw model. The sandbox model is constructed to allow use of a variety of aquifer fluids, movement of dyed injection fluids will be followed by visual observation, liquid sampling, and photography.
W75-06351

CONTRIBUTIONS OF TIDAL WETLANDS TO ESTUARINE FOOD CHAINS,
Maryland Univ., Prince Frederick. Center for Environmental and Estuarine Studies.
For primary bibliographic entry see Field 5C.
W75-06353

STOCHASTIC VARIATIONS IN WATER QUALITY PARAMETERS,
Rutgers - the State Univ., New Brunswick, N. J. Bureau of Engineering Research.
R. C. Ahlert.
Available from the National Technical Information Service, Springfield, Va 22161 as PB-240 980, $3.25 in paper copy, $2.25 in microfiche. Water Resources Research Institute, New Brunswick, Rutgers University, February 1975. 6 p, 13 ref. OWRT A-035-NJ(3). 14-31-0001-4030.

Descriptors: *Simulation analysis, *Mathematical models, *Statistical models, *Stochastic processes, Water quality, Temperature, Dissolved oxygen, Biochemical oxygen demand, Oxygen demand, Ammonia, Reservoir operation, *Model studies, New Jersey, Optimization, Discharge(Water), Organic loading.

Identifiers: Passaic River Basin(NJ), Passaic Valley Water Commission, Combined deterministic-stochastic models, Quality prediction, Pollutant loading.

A combined form of deterministic-stochastic modeling has been applied to the simulation of water quality parameters. The objective was to identify an optimum means of dynamic simulation for the purpose of water quality prediction and management. Consistent with earlier experience, discharge records for watersheds of various sizes (Passaic River Basin) are easily modeled. Temperature is modeled extremely well, also. Simulations of BOD (carbonaceous), dissolved oxygen, oxygen deficit and ammonia-N concentrations were relatively poor. A simple linear correlation between annual BOD loading (carbonaceous) and annual rainfall was observed. This led to successful deterministic-stochastic models of BOD (carbonaceous) loading. Ammonia-N loading models were not as successful, however, primarily because of significant gaps in reported data and the necessity of employing weekly averages as the basis of analysis.
W75-06355

AN INVENTORY AND SENSITIVITY ANALYSIS OF DATA REQUIREMENTS FOR AN OXYGEN MANAGEMENT MODEL OF THE CARSON RIVER,
Nevada Univ., Reno. Dept. of Civil Engineering.
R. G. Orcutt, and J. G. Gonzales.
Available from the National Technical Information Service, Springfield, Va 22161 as PB-241 099, $3.75 in paper copy, $2.25 in microfiche. Nevada University Desert Research Institute, Reno, Center for Water Resources Research, Cooperative Report Series Publication No EN-1, September 1972. 53 p, 16 fig, 1 tab, 36 ref, 4 append. OWRT A-044-NEV(1).

Descriptors: *Oxygen demand, *Computer models, Model studies, Water management(Applied), Water quality control, *Nevada, Evaluation, *Waste assimilative capacity, Biodegradation, Rivers, *Low-flow augmentation, Organic loading, Dissolved oxygen, Sewage, Path of pollutants.
Identifiers: *Carson River(Nev), Oxygen management models, *Sensitivity analysis.

An assessment of the need for developing more specific data on the capacity of the Carson River to assimilate biodegradable wastes is given. In order to provide this assessment, the effects of different degrees of low flow augmentation and residual waste loads on the oxygen levels of the River were estimated. Results indicate that the oxygen levels in the Carson River would be most sensitive to dissolved oxygen levels of entering waste water and to the dilution effect of low flow augmentation. Computed oxygen levels are less sensitive to assumed benthal deposits and increased sewage loading and relatively insensitive to the organic concentrations of entering wastes and to reasonable variations of the physical features of the low flow model chosen to simulate the Carson River.
W75-06356

ESTUARINE POLLUTION IN THE STATE OF HAWAII, VOLUME 2: KANEOHE BAY STUDY,
Hawaii Univ., Honolulu. Water Resources Research Center.
D. C. Cox, P. R. Fan, K. E. Chave, R. I. Clutter, and K. R. Gundersen.
Technical Report No 31, November 1973. 444 p, 75 fig, 78 tab, append.

Descriptors: Hydrogeology, *Hawaii, *Estuaries, *Path of pollutants, Oceanography, Ecology, Biota, Water quality, Phosphorus, Recreation, Sedimentation, Microbiology, Nitrogen, Sewage disposal, Economics, Rainfall, Wind velocity, Coliforms, Water temperature, Plankton, Organic wastes, Lagoons.
Identifiers: *Kaneohe Bay(HI).

Kaneohe Bay, a combination coastal-plain estuary and lagoon, is used extensively for recreation and as a fishery. Fresh water discharges to the bay, principally from perennial streams, originally totaled about 97 mgd, but have been reduced by diversions by about 38 percent. Only 8 percent of the exchange transport with ocean water affects the southeastern part of the bay, which comprises 27 percent of the bay volume. Into this southeastern part of the bay is discharged nearly 3 mgd of sewage effluents, mostly after secondary treatment. During floods, both perennial and intermittent streams discharge large amounts of sediments, one stream discharging an estimated 9470 tons in a single 24-hour storm period. High concentrations of total coliforms and fecal coliforms occurred in the stream mouths and in the vicinity of sewer outfalls; however, most of the bay water met the state standards for the highest water quality class. Nitrogen concentrations offshore, in streams, and the bay were found generally to exceed standards, indicating unreasonably restrictive standards. Phosphorus concentrations in streams and at outfalls exceeded standards but decreased rapidly away from points of discharge. Plankton studies indicated a high productivity in the south decreasing to lower productivity to the north. Trends toward eutrophication, decreasing diversity, and stability have been documented. Among alternatives for reducing the pollution of the bay by sewage effluents, the diversion of the effluents by force main to the open ocean east of Kaneohe Bay was found to be the most economical.
W75-06362

A WATER QUALITY MODEL TO EVALUATE WATER MANAGEMENT PRACTICES IN AN IRRIGATED STREAM-AQUIFER SYSTEM,
Geological Survey, Denver, Colo.
For primary bibliographic entry see Field 5G.
W75-06369

A CRITICAL APPRAISAL OF THE WATER POLLUTION PROBLEM IN INDIA IN RELATION TO AQUACULTURE,
Central Inland Fisheries Research Inst., Barrackpore (India).
V. G. Jhingran.
In: Indo-Pacific Fisheries Council Proceedings, 15th Session, Wellington, New Zealand. Oct. 18-27, 1972. Section II, Coastal Aquaculture and Environment. Bangkok, 1974, p 45-50. 2 tab, 16 ref.

Descriptors: *Water pollution sources, *Sewage effluents, *Aquiculture, Industrial wastes, Biochemical oxygen demands, Estuaries, Freshwater, Fertilizers, Waste water treatment, Pesticides, Activated sludge, DDT, Herbicides.
Identifiers: *India.

The major sites of freshwater pollution in India lie along the important river systems. Estuaries, in general, are not yet severely affected, although there is evidence of adverse effects of organic and industrial effluents in certain areas. There is no significant marine pollution as yet but the rapid development of industrial programs poses a threat for the future. Pollutants that threaten aquaculture are listed and discussed. Little information is available on the toxicity of various pesticides to endemic fish species and additional research is required before control measures can be formulated. (Katz)
W75-06378

THE CHEMICAL TOXICITY OF ELEMENTS,
Battelle-Pacific Northwest Labs., Richland, Wash. Water and Land Resources Dept.
For primary bibliographic entry see Field 5C.
W75-06381

DIFFUSION OF RADIOACTIVE FLUID THROUGH SOIL SURROUNDING A LARGE POWER-REACTOR STATION AFTER A CORE MELTDOWN ACCIDENT,
California Univ., Livermore. Lawrence Livermore Lab.
J. H. Pitts, B. R. Bowman, R. W. Martin, and J. P. McKay.
Available from the National Technical Information Service, Springfield, Va 22161 as Rept. No. UCRL-51494, $4.00 in paper copy, $2.25 in microfiche. Report No. UCRL-51494, December 1973. 24 p, 15 fig, 7 ref.

Descriptors: *Path of pollutants, *Nuclear powerplants, *Accidents, *Hazards analysis, *Radioactivity, *Diffusion, *Soil contamination, Liquids, Gases, Model studies, Clays, Assessment, Sands, Flow, Flow rates, Heat transfer, Cooling, Heating, Melting.
Identifiers: Core meltdown.

The flow of fluids through the soil surrounding a large power-reactor station after a core meltdown accident was analyzed. Fracture of, or penetration through, a portion of the containment floor was assumed so that radioactive gases would be driven through the soil by pressure within the containment shell. Results for both one-dimensional ideal gas and multiphase flow were obtained using dimensionless variables so that results are applicable for all soil conditions. Two-dimensional results are included for a specific case where permeability of the soil varies spatially. These calculations show that the time required for radioactive gases to permeate to the ground surface are years for silty-type clays and about 10 h for sand-type soil. Heat transfer calculations that estimate the amount of steam generated should the core melt penetrate the containment floor and contact wet soil show that cooling systems must be in operation within four or five days in order to prevent overpressurization of the containment shell. (Houser-ORNL)
W75-06407

CESIUM-137 FALLOUT IN RED DESERT BASIN OF WYOMING, USA,
Dow Chemical Co., Golden, Colo. Rocky Flats Div.
For primary bibliographic entry see Field 5A.
W75-06409

ENVIRONMENTAL RADIOACTIVITY AT THE NATIONAL NUCLEAR RESEARCH CENTRE, PELINDABA,
Atomic Energy Board, Pelindaba, Pretoria (South Africa). Isotopes and Radiation Div.
For primary bibliographic entry see Field 5A.
W75-06410

ECONOMIC AND ENVIRONMENTAL EVALUATION OF NUCLEAR WASTE DISPOSAL BY UNDERGROUND IN SITU MELTING,
California Univ., Livermore. Lawrence Livermore Lab.
J. J. Cohen, R. L. Braun, L. L. Schwartz, and H. A. Tewes.
Available from NTIS, Springfield, Va 22161 as Rept. No. UCRL-51713, $4.00 in paper copy, $2.25 in microfiche. Report No. UCRL-51713, November 1974. 17 p, 6 fig, 2 tab, 19 ref, append.

Descriptors: *Radioactive waste disposal, *Underground waste disposal, *Heating, *Melting, Evaluation, Management, Reviews, Environmental effects, Economics, Geological formations, Comparative benefits, Comparative costs, Public health.

Disposal of high-level nuclear waste by the Deep Underground Melt Process (DUMP) is reviewed and evaluated relative to other proposed methods for waste management. Although the potential en-

vironmental impact (population exposure to radiation) for the DUMP concept was found to be lower than that for alternative disposal methods, the difference is of small significance. The economic advantages, however, were substantial. A potential 80% cost savings relative to other geologic disposal methods is indicated. (Houser-ORNL)
W75-06413

TRANSURANICS AT PACIFIC ATOLLS I. CONCENTRATIONS IN THE WATERS AT ENEWETAK AND BIKINI,
California Univ., Livermore. Lawrence Livermore Lab.
For primary bibliographic entry see Field 5A.
W75-06414

SOURCES OF POTENTIAL BIOLOGICAL DAMAGE FROM ONCE-THROUGH COOLING SYSTEMS OF NUCLEAR POWER PLANTS,
Oak Ridge National Lab., Tenn.
C. P. Goodyear, C. C. Coutant, and J. R. Trabalka.
Available from NTIS, Springfield, Va 22161 as Rept. No. ORNL-TM-4180, $5.50 in paper copy, $2.25 in microfiche. Report No. ORNL-TM-4180, July 1974. 48 p, 6 fig, 98 ref.

Descriptors: *Nuclear powerplants, Effluents, Environmental effects, Sites, Ecosystems, Biological communities, Ecology, *Temperature, *Cooling water, Water pollution sources, Assessment, Toxicity, Radiation, Dissolved oxygen.
Identifiers: Biocides.

A general introduction is presented to pertinent biological and ecological information related to predicting the environmental effects of operating a nuclear power plant equipped with once-through, open circuit cooling of steam turbine condensers. Information of this nature forms the basis (along with detailed, site-specific data) for assessments of ecological impacts of nuclear power plants. Assessments include temperature changes, mechanical and pressure changes, impingement on intake screens, chemical toxicity of biocides, changes in dissolved oxygen, induced circulation, radiation, and combinations of all of these. Other sources of damage may arise at particular power plant sites. All of these need to be carefully considered and their effects predicted when making power plant environmental impact assessments. (Houser-ORNL)
W75-06415

DRAFT ENVIRONMENTAL STATEMENT HTGR FUEL REFABRICATION PILOT PLANT AT THE OAK RIDGE NATIONAL LABORATORY.
Oak Ridge National Lab., Tenn.
Available from NTIS, Springfield, Va 22161 as Rept. No. WASH-1533, $11.00 in paper copy, $2.25 in microfiche. Report No. WASH-1533, January 1974. 161 p, 25 fig, 16 tab, 28 ref, 5 append.

Descriptors: *Nuclear powerplants, *Temperature, *Coolants, Construction, *Environmental effects, *Uranium, Thorium, Design, Design criteria, Operations, Research and development, Pilot plants, Technology.
Identifiers: Chemical processing plant, *Thorium fuel cycle, *Environmental impact statements.

A proposed project to demonstrate the technology for refabrication of uranium-233 for use in high-temperature gas-cooled reactors (HTGR) operating on the thorium fuel cycle. The proposed project, with a projected cost of $10 million, includes the design, construction, and operation of an integrated pilot plant to develop and demonstrate the HTGR fuel fabrication technology. This project is coordinated with the HTGR fuel reprocessing pilot plant that is planned for installation in the Idaho Chemical Processing Plant (ICPP) at the National Reactor Testing Station (NRTS) in Idaho Falls, Idaho. These projects complement each other in the development of HTGR fuel recycle technology. (Houser-ORNL)
W75-06417

BIOLOGICAL DOSE AND RADIOLOGICAL ACTIVITY FROM NUCLEAR REACTOR OR NUCLEAR WEAPON FISSION PRODUCTS,
Oak Ridge National Lab., Tenn.
For primary bibliographic entry see Field 5A.
W75-06419

HEALTH AND SAFETY LABORATORY FALLOUT PROGRAM QUARTERLY SUMMARY REPORT, MARCH 1, 1974 THROUGH JUNE 1, 1974,
Health and Safety Lab. (AEC), New York.
For primary bibliographic entry see Field 5A.
W75-06420

RADIOACTIVITY FROM NUCLEAR WEAPONS IN AIR AND PRECIPITATION IN SWEDEN FROM MID-YEAR 1968 TO MID-YEAR 1972,
Research Inst. of National Defence, Stockholm (Sweden).
For primary bibliographic entry see Field 5A.
W75-06421

STRONTIUM-90 IN THE DIET. RESULTS THROUGH 1973,
Health and Safety Lab. (AEC), New York.
For primary bibliographic entry see Field 5A.
W75-06422

SURFACE DEPOSITION IN THE UNITED STATES,
National Oceanographic and Atmospheric Administration, Silver Spring, Md. Air Resources Labs.
For primary bibliographic entry see Field 5A.
W75-06423

CARBON-14 MEASUREMENTS IN THE STRATOSPHERE FROM A BALLOON-BORNE MOLECULAR SIEVE SAMPLER (1971-1973),
Argonne National Lab., Ill.
For primary bibliographic entry see Field 5A.
W75-06424

ENVIRONMENTAL RADIATION MEASUREMENTS IN THE VICINITY OF A BOILING WATER REACTOR: HASL DATA SUMMARY,
Health and Safety Lab. (AEC), New York.
For primary bibliographic entry see Field 5A.
W75-06425

PROJECT AIRSTREAM,
Health and Safety Lab. (AEC), New York.
For primary bibliographic entry see Field 5A.
W75-06426

CESIUM-137 IN VARIOUS CHICAGO FOODS (COLLECTION MONTH APRIL 1974),
Argonne National Lab., Ill.
For primary bibliographic entry see Field 5A.
W75-06427

EFFECT OF APPLICATION RATE, INITIAL SOIL WETNESS, AND REDISTRIBUTION TIME ON SALT DISPLACEMENT BY WATER,
Punjab Agricultural Univ., Ludhiana (India). Dept. of Soils.
For primary bibliographic entry see Field 2G.
W75-06437

PICKLING LIQUORS, STRIP MINES, AND GROUND-WATER POLLUTION,
Ohio State Univ., Columbus. Dept. of Geology and Mineralogy.
W. A. Pettyjohn.
Ground Water, Vol 13, No 1, p 4-10, January-February 1975. 3 fig, 5 tab.

Descriptors: *Path of pollutants, *Water pollution sources, *Strip mines, *Liquid wastes, Industrial wastes, Acidic water, Spoil banks, Pollutant identification, Groundwater, Surface waters, *Ohio, Waste disposal, Hydrogeology, Geochemistry, On-site data collections.
Identifiers: Pickling liquors.

In 1964 a waste disposal firm began dumping neutralized spent pickling liquors into an abandoned strip mine in eastern Ohio. In 1970 the disposal pit was enlarged and shortly thereafter significant water pollution problems began to occur. Highly mineralized fluids began to leak from the disposal pit into the surrounding spoil material and eventually into streams and ponds. These solutions are characterized by a low pH and excessive concentrations of dissolved solids, hardness, sulfate, chloride, nitrate, iron, fluoride, aluminum, chromium, nickel, and zinc. In addition to the contamination by steel mill wastes, acid-mine drainage from surrounding areas degrades both ground and surface water. Acid-mine drainage is characterized by a low pH, and high concentrations of dissolved solids, hardness, sulfate, and iron. Geohydrologic and geochemical data clearly illustrate that abandoned strip mines should not be used for the storage of toxic liquid or semiliquid materials. (Gibb-ISWS)
W75-06450

EFFLUENT FOR IRRIGATION - A NEED FOR CAUTION,
Illinois State Water Survey, Urbana.
For primary bibliographic entry see Field 5D.
W75-06451

NATURAL SOIL NITRATE: THE CAUSE OF THE NITRATE CONTAMINATION OF GROUND WATER IN RUNNELS COUNTY, TEXAS,
Texas Univ., Austin. Bureau of Economic Geology.
C. W. Kreitler, and D. C. Jones.
Ground Water, Vol 13, No 1, p 53-61, January-February 1975. 11 fig, 1 tab, 13 ref.

Descriptors: *Groundwater, *Water pollution sources, *Nitrates, *Soil surveys, *Water quality, Subsurface waters, Pollutants, Soil water, Leaching, Animal wastes(Wildlife), Cattle, Feed lots, Soil tests, Isotope studies, Water pollution, Spectrometers, *Texas, Nitrogen, Fertilizers.
Identifiers: Natural soil nitrate, *Anoxia, Runnels County(Tex).

The groundwaters of Runnels County, Texas, are highly contaminated with nitrate. The average nitrate concentration of 230 water samples was 250 mg.l NO3. The natural variations of the stable nitrogen isotopes N14 and N15 identified natural soil nitrate as the predominant source. Nitrate from animal wastes was of minor importance. The delta N15 range of natural soil nitrate was +2 to +8 parts per thousand, whereas the delta N15 range of animal waste nitrate was +10 to +20 parts per thousand. (Atmospheric nitrogen was used as a standard for mass spectrometric analysis. Experimental error for sample preparation and isotopic analysis was + or -1 part per thousand.) More than 66% of the groundwater nitrates analyzed were in the delta N15 range of natural soil nitrates. Dryland farming since 1900 caused the oxidation of the organic nitrogen in the soil to nitrate. Minimal fertilizer has been used because of the lack of suitable water for irrigation. During the period 1900-1950, nitrate was leached below the root zone but not to the water table. Extensive terracing

after the drought in the early 1950's raised the water table approximately 6 meters and leached the nitrate into the groundwater. Tritium dates indicate that the groundwater is less than 20 years old. (Prickett-ISWS)
W75-06452

GREAT LAKES WATER QUALITY, ANNUAL REPORT TO THE INTERNATIONAL JOINT COMMISSION, (1973).
International Joint Commission-United States and Canada. Great Lakes Water Quality Board.
Available from the National Technical Information Service, Springfield, Va 22161 as PB-233 188, $9.25 in paper copy, $2.25 in microfiche. April 1973. 315 p, 36 fig, 12 tab.

Descriptors: *Great Lakes, *Water quality, Water pollution sources, Pollutants, Lakes, Limnology, Thermal pollution, Water pollution, Eutrophication, Ships, Rivers, Legal aspects, Water law, Water policy, Canada, United States, Federal government, State governments.

A current assessment of water quality in the boundary waters of the Great Lakes and of the control program involved in the improvement of water quality was presented. (Sims-ISWS)
W75-06474

LAND TREATMENT OF MENHADEN WASTE WATER BY OVERLAND FLOW,
Louisiana State Univ., Baton Rouge. Dept. of Marine Science.
For primary bibliographic entry see Field 5D.
W75-06526

SEA SALT PARTICLES TRANSPORTED TO THE LAND,
Hokkaido Univ., Sapporo (Japan). Dept. of Chemistry.
S. Tsunogai.
Tellus, Vol 27, No 1, p 51-58, 1975. 4 fig, 5 tab, 13 ref.

Descriptors: *Salts, *Monsoons, *Typhoons, Saline water, Coasts, Pacific coast region, *Chlorides, Rivers, Sea water, Sedimentation, Precipitation(Atmospheric), Soil contamination, Fallout, Sediment transport, Path of pollutants.
Identifiers: Salt transport, Salt particle intrusion, *Japan, *Chloride deposition(Rains).

Large quantities of sea salt particles are suddently transported to the land by the discrete events of a violent storm. In Japan these events are the typhoon in summer on the Pacific coast region and the north-west monsoon in winter on the Japan Sea coastal region. The share of sedimentation, one of the mechanisms of the transport of sea salt particles to the land, is only about 20% of precipitation over various parts of Japan. The contribution of impaction with surface obstacles is negligibly small, as observed in the example of the Ogochi Basin. This conclusion was also confirmed by analyzing the concentration of chloride in rivers undisturbed by other sources. Moreover, the analysis revealed the following facts. The half-decrease distance of the concentration is about 20 km from the coast in both coastal regions in Japan. The total deposition of sea salt was calculated to be 2,700,000 metric tons per year in the whole of Japan (area 370,000 square kilometers) and the mean concentration of chloride in rain to be 2.4 ppm over Japan as a whole, but the concentration is about 3 times larger over the Japan Sea coastal region than over the Pacific coast region, owing to the violent north-west monsoon in winter. (Lee-ISWS)
W75-06541

HEAVY METALS IN CULTIVATED OYSTERS (CRASSOSTREA COMMERCIALIS = SACCOSTREA CUCULLATA) FROM THE ESTUARIES OF NEW SOUTH WALES (AUSTRALIA),
Chief Secretary's Dept. , Sydney (Australia). New South Wales Fisheries Branch.
N. J. Mackay, R. J. Williams, J. L. Kacprzac, M. N. Kazacos, and A. J. Collins.
Australian Journal of Marine and Freshwater Research, Vol 26, No 1, p 31-46, March 1975. 9 fig, 5 tab, 17 ref.

Descriptors: *Heavy metals, *Oysters, *Australia, *Estuaries, *Path of pollutants, Water pollution effects, Sampling, Monitoring, Variability, Zinc, Cadmium, Copper, Arsenic compounds, Mollusks, Lead, Aging(Biological).
Identifiers: *New South Wales(Australia), Crassostrea commercialis, Georges River(NSW).

Results are reported of a survey of copper, zinc, cadmium, lead and arsenic levels in the Sydney rock oyster from 19 estuaries along the coast of New South Wales. Metal concentrations were generally low, and represented little or no health risk to consumers. Evidence indicates that metal levels decrease with increasing age and wet weight of the oysters. In one estuary (Georges River) a gradient of increasing metal concentration in oysters with increasing distance upstream from the sea was found, which may suggest an effect of pollution, through this needs verification. The variability of metal concentrations is discussed in relation to a suggested sampling method for future monitoring of metal levels in this species. (Levick-CSIRO)
W75-06552

STEADY-STATE WATER QUALITY MODELING IN STREAMS,
Cornell Univ., Ithaca, N.Y. School of Civil and Environmental Engineering.
R. Willis, D. R. Anderson, and J. A. Dracup.
Journal of the Environmental Engineering Division, American Society of Civil Engineers, Vol 101, No EE2, Proceedings paper No 11246, p 245-258, April 1975.

Descriptors: *Environmental engineering, *Rivers, *Dissolved oxygen, *Simulation analysis, *Water quality, *Mathematical models, Management, Water distribution(Applied), Streams, Advection, Dissolved oxygen, Biochemical oxygen demand, California, Nevada, Planning, Systems analysis, *Path of pollutants.
Identifiers: Mass transport, Input data.

A general mathematical model for simulation of conservative and nonconservative constituents in streams and rivers is developed. Mass transport of constituents is accomplished by advection and biochemical reactions. The models simulate the interaction of the dissolved-oxygen resources of the water system with the nitrogen cycle, chlorophyll a, and carbonaceous biochemical oxygen demand. Also, conservative substances and phosphorous uptake by algae and coliforms are simulated by the model. The results of applying the model to the Truckee River system in northern California and Nevada are presented. The system's reservoirs, natural streams sewage treatment plants, and irrigation diversions are described. The model demonstrates the ability to simulate historical water quality conditions and to be a flexible, easily adaptable planning tool. Planners can assess the impact of alternate water quality control measures on the river system by varying treatment levels at each discharge point and the quality and quantity conditions at each headwater in the system. Also, the model can estimate the volume of dilution water required to meet dissolved oxygen target levels in the system. The validity of any simulation, however, rests on the quality of the input data. (Bell-Cornell)
W75-06564

NUMERICAL MODELING OF THERMAL STRATIFICATION IN A RESERVOIR WITH LARGE DISCHARGE-TO-VOLUME RATIO,
Tennessee Valley Authority, Muscle Shoals, Ala. Air Quality Branch.
For primary bibliographic entry see Field 2H.
W75-06572

GROUNDWATER POLLUTION: CASE LAW THEORIES FOR RELIEF,
Missouri Univ., Columbia.
P. N. Davis.
Missouri Law Review, Vol 39, No 2, p 117-163, Spring 1974. 3 tab, 164 ref, 3 append.

Descriptors: *Groundwater resources, *Water pollution, *Judicial decisions, *Legal aspects, Groundwater movement, Groundwater availability, Groundwater, Water supply, Industrial wastes, Water pollution sources, Water resources development, Water management(Applied), Negligence, Risks, Water law.
Identifiers: Nuisance.

One-quarter of the earth's supply of fresh water lies underground. Traditionally, shallow wells have tapped this underground resource for domestic and livestock watering purposes. With the increase in industrial technology the uses of groundwater have multiplied and total withdrawals from wells have increased. This increased tapping of the supply has caused both shortages and pollution problems. Courts in many states have been faced with the resolution of these problems. In the majority of cases dealing with pollution of percolating groundwater courts employ the law of negligence or private nuisance. According to negligence theory, a groundwater user is liable for his pollution if he knew or should have known of the injury which occurred. Nuisance law on the other hand does not look toward the comparative reasonableness of a person's conduct, but addresses itself to the nature of the injurious consequences. Two states use the restatement of torts rule concerning interferences with the use of land, and eleven jurisdictions have imposed strict liability for certain types of percolating groundwater pollution. Eastern states tend to recognize the hydrologic relationship between surface watercourses and groundwater and grant relief for the pollution of one by an activity affecting the other. (Proctor-Florida)
W75-06589

WATER REGULATIONS--OIL POLLUTION PREVENTION.
For primary bibliographic entry see Field 5G.
W75-06600

POINT SOURCES COVERED BY NPDES AND PROCEDURES.
For primary bibliographic entry see Field 5G.
W75-06617

EFFLUENT GUIDELINES ARE ON THE WAY,
For primary bibliographic entry see Field 5G.
W75-06619

ECOLOGICAL EFFECTS OF NUCLEAR STEAM ELECTRIC STATION OPERATIONS ON ESTUARINE SYSTEMS.
Maryland Univ., Prince Frederick. Center for Environmental and Estuarine Research.
For primary bibliographic entry see Field 5C.
W75-06621

ANALYSIS OF CALVERT CLIFFS REFERENCE STATION MEASUREMENTS (TEMPERATURE, SALINITY, AND DISSOLVED OXYGEN),
Martin Marietta Labs., Baltimore, Md.
H. Obremski.
In: Report No. ORO-4328-3, pIII-1 - III-37, June 1974, 8 fig, 7 tab, 4 ref.

Descriptors: *Maryland, *Temperature, *Salinity, *Dissolved oxygen, Profiles, Sites, Nuclear power plants, Surveys, Monitoring, Environment, Measurement, *Chesapeake Bay, Aquatic environment, Water pollution, Thermal pollution, Standards, Data collections, Seasonal.
Identifiers: *Calvert Cliffs Site(Md).

Permit requirements for new power plants call for pre-operational field studies to determine environmental baselines from which to evaluate post-operational environmental changes. This presently is being attempted by characterizing the physical, chemical, and biological conditions at a site through intensive field sampling before and during plant construction and after plant operation begins. This approach, however, does not provide a clearcut comparison of pre- and post-operational environmental conditions. Physical, chemical, and biological parameters at a site can fluctuate significantly from one year to another making it difficult to attribute observed environmental changes unambiguously to the addition of a power plant. To eliminate this ambiguity, the Reference Station Method, a statistical technique for comparing pre- and post-operational environmental conditions at a power plant site, was developed. This method is being field tested for temperature, salinity, and dissolved oxygen measurements at the Baltimore Gas and Electric Company's Calvert Cliffs nuclear power plant on the Chesapeake Bay. (See also W75-06621) (Houser-ORNL)
W75-06622

RADIOCHEMISTRY--GAMMA ANALYSIS: CALVERT CLIFFS SEDIMENT RADIOACTIVITIES BEFORE AND AFTER TROPICAL STORM AGNES,
National Aeronautics and Space Administration, Washington, D.C. Planatology Branch.
P. J. Cressy, Jr.
In: Report No. ORO-4328-3, p IV-1 - IV-11, June 1974, 6 fig.

Descriptors: *Maryland, Nuclear power plants, Effluents, *Chesapeake Bay, *Monitoring, Measurement, *Assay, *Radioactivity, Sediments, Tropical cyclones, Storms, Environmental effect, Aquatic environment, Distribution, Analytical techniques, Radiochemistry.
Identifiers: *Calvert Cliffs Site(Md), *Tropical storm Agnes.

A preliminary report is presented of a cooperative study of surface sediments near the Calvert Cliffs Nuclear Power Plant Site. The general purpose of this investigation is to establish base levels and correlations of natural and man-made, gamma-ray emitting radionuclides prior to operation of the power plant. The first sets of samples examined under this program were acquired some six weeks before and six weeks after Tropical Storm Agnes. Measured radioactivities in these samples were analyzed to determine what effect, if any, Agnes had on radionuclide and sediment distributions. The effect of Agnes on radionuclide distribution was relatively small. (See also W75-06621) (Houser-ORNL)
W75-06623

PHYTOPLANKTON: CONTINUING STUDIES ON PRIMARY PRODUCTIVITY AND STANDING CROP OF PHYTOPLANKTON AT CALVERT CLIFFS, CHESAPEAKE BAY,
Maryland Univ., Prince Frederick. Center for Environmental and Estuarine Research.
For primary bibliographic entry see Field 5C.
W75-06624

ZOOPLANKTON: PROGRESS REPORT TO THE U.S. ATOMIC ENERGY COMMISSION ZOOPLANKTON STUDIES AT CALVERT CLIFFS,
Maryland Univ., Prince Frederick. Natural Resources Inst.
For primary bibliographic entry see Field 5C.
W75-06625

EFFECT OF TROPICAL STORM AGNES ON STANDING CROPS AND AGE STRUCTURE OF ZOOPLANKTON IN MIDDLE CHESAPEAKE BAY,
Maryland Univ., Prince Frederick. Natural Resources Inst.
For primary bibliographic entry see Field 5C.
W75-06626

MEROPLANKTON,
Maryland Univ., Prince Frederick. Center for Environmental and Estuarine Studies.
For primary bibliographic entry see Field 5C.
W75-06627

BENTHIC ANIMAL-SEDIMENT,
Maryland Univ., Prince Frederick. Center for Environmental and Estuarine Studies.
For primary bibliographic entry see Field 5C.
W75-06628

BENTHIC-HEAVY METALS,
Federal City Coll., Washington, D.C.
For primary bibliographic entry see Field 5C.
W75-06629

STORM RUNOFF AND TRANSPORT OF RADIONUCLIDES IN DP CANYON, LOS ALAMOS COUNTY, NEW MEXICO,
Los Alamos Scientific Lab., N. Mex.
W. D. Purtymun.
LA-5744, October 1974. 9 p, 1 fig, 7 tab, 7 ref. AEC Contract W-7405-ENG.36.

Descriptors: *Radioactive wastes, *Sediments, *Sediment transport, *Storm runoff, Sediment discharge, *New Mexico, Effluents, Waste treatment, Suspended load, Radioactivity, Precipitation(Atmospheric).
Identifiers: DP Canyon(Los Alamos County NM).

Investigations were made to determine runoff volumes, suspended sediment loads, and amounts of radioactivity carried out of DP Canyon by storm runoff. Radionuclides contained in the waste treatment plant effluent at Los Alamos Scientific Laboratory's Technical Area 21 are discharged to the canyon where they are bound to stream channel sediments which are later carried away by storm runoff. Twenty-three runoff events, during the summer of 1967, carried off approximately 88,000 kilograms of suspended sediment in approximately 36,800 cubic meters of water. Less than 74 microcuries of gross alpha and approximately 40,100 microcuries of gross beta were transported out of the canyon in solution. Suspended sediments carried approximately 70 microcuries of gross alpha and 11,300 microcuries of gross beta. About 31,000 microcuries of Strontium-90, 5.9 microcuries of Plutonium-238, 7.0 microcuries of Plutonium-239, and 9.1 microcuries of Americium-241 left the canyon in solution. (Harmeson-ISWS)
W75-06636

IMPACT OF HUMAN ACTIVITIES ON THE QUALITY OF GROUNDWATER AND SURFACE WATER IN THE CAPE COD AREA,
Massachusetts Univ., Amherst. Water Resources Research Center.
K. H. Deubert.
Available from the National Technical Information Service, Springfield, Va 22161, as PB-241 137, $4.25 in paper copy, $2.25 in microfiche. Completion Report, FY-74-6, Publication No 42, (1974). 56 p, 4 fig, 18 tab, 10 ref. OWRT A-043-MASS(1).

Descriptors: *Massachusetts, *Path of pollutants, Water quality, Environmental effects, *Groundwater, Surface waters, *Waste disposal, *Craneberries, Urbanization, Industrial wastes, Water supply, City planning, Septic tanks, Cesspools, Water pollution sources, Distribution patterns.
Identifiers: *Cape Cod(Mass), *Automobile traffic pollutants.

The effects of human activities on water quality were investigated. The disposal of waste causes the most adverse impact on water quality--groundwater in particular. Neither automobile traffic nor cranberry production appears to have a measurable impact on quality of water. These conclusions refer only to regular conditions. Irregular occurrences causing accidental pollution, such as spillage, direct application of chemicals to water, leaching from stockpiles, etc., require separate consideration. To preserve water quality in the Cape Cod area, planning activities should concentrate on the disposal of waste. Disposal through cesspools and septic tanks was adequate when the population figures were small, but rapid growth of towns without changes in the methods of waste disposal may lead to groundwater problems. Areas not served by public water supplies will probably be the first ones to be affected.
W75-06644

DECOMPOSITION OF FOUR SPECIES OF LEAF MATERIAL IN THREE REPLICATE STREAMS WITH DIFFERENT NITRATE INPUT,
Oregon State Univ., Corvallis. Dept. of Fisheries and Wildlife.
F. J. Triska, and J. R. Sedell.
Available from the National Technical Information Service, Springfield, Va 22161, as PB-241 139, $3.75 in paper copy, $2.25 in microfiche. Oregon Water Resources Research Institute, Corvallis, Completion Report WRRI-29, February 1975. 35 p, 7 fig, 2 tab, 43 ref. OWRT A-021-ORE(1).

Descriptors: *Nitrates, Streams, *Decomposing organic matter, Leaves, *Litter, Solid wastes, *Small watersheds, Fertilization, Lumbering, Chemical oxygen demand, *Nutrient requirements, Water pollution sources.
Identifiers: *Leaf material, Replicate streams, Allochthonous debris.

Inputs of leaf litter and other allochthonous debris constitute the biological energy base of small watershed streams. The relationship of decompositon rate to nitrate inputs of a 3 - 4 fold magnitude was tested in three replicate experimental streams. Such a magnitude of nitrate inputs simulated possible input effects of nitrogen fertilization or logging, two common forest practices. At the levels tested, no significant increase in decomposition rate was observed on any of four litter species as a result of nitrate addition. Common parameters measured included weight loss, changes in carbon quality, absolute changes in nitrogen content, and microbial respiration measured as oxygen consumption. Results were partially confounded by growth of filamentous green algae during spring. As a result of chemical oxygen demand or leaf pack envelopment by the decaying algal mat, approximately one-third of the total oxygen consumption was not related to litter decomposition. Phosphate in conjunction with nitrate addition was not tested since phosphate did not appear limiting. Although not related to increases in nitrate concentration in water, decomposing litter did exhibit a twofold increase in nitrogen content following initial leaching. The mechanism of this increase, whether by biological or chemical means, remains to be investigated. Also, the impact of nutrient chemistry in such refractory materials as wood and bark should be the subject of future experimentation.
W75-06649

BACTERIOLOGY OF STREAMS AND THE ASSOCIATED VEGETATION OF A HIGH MOUNTAIN WATERSHED,
Wyoming Univ., Laramie. Water Resources Research Inst.
Q. D. Skinner.
Available from the National Technical Information Service, Springfield, Va 22161, as PB-241 140, $3.25 in paper copy, $2.25 in microfiche. Completion Report, December 1974. 6 p, 5 ref. OWRT A-012-WYO(1).

Descriptors: *Wyoming, Watershed management, *Range management, *Bacteria, Water pollution sources, Vegetation, *Water quality, Monitoring, *Bioindicators, Streams.
Identifiers: *Nash Fork stream(Wyo), Mountain watershed, Nitrate reducing bacteria.

The major objective was to relate variations of bacteria count with (1) vegetative types; (2) range conditions; (3) and various uses of the watershed. Three summers and two winters were spent monitoring the water quality of the Nash Fork watershed on a weekly basis with selected bacteria tests. Results show that the range conditions of the Nash Fork study area can be classified as being in good condition. There exists a seasonal variation in the various bacteriological groups monitored. Total coliforms, fecal coliforms and entercocci reach peak concentrations in late summer. The main source of pollution appears to be animals rather than humans. There existed little difference in variations of bacteria counts between vegetation types, with the exception of nitrate reducing bacteria which had higher counts below wet meadows. The ski area had an effect on bacteria counts during the operating season. Although effluent was chlorinated and fecal organisms killed off, there existed a rise in counts of nitrate and sulfate reducing bacteria below the ski area. Possibilities for combining the sciences of range management and bacteriology are many. However, research must continue for determining the ecological significance of different vegetation types as related to numbers and various populations of bacteria found in streams draining the vegetated areas.
W75-06650

A SURVEY OF BACKGROUND WATER QUALITY IN MICHIGAN STREAMS.
Michigan, Department of Natural Resources, Detroit, Michigan, November 1970. 47 p, 18 fig, 2 tab, 9 ref, 3 append.

Descriptors: *Water quality, *On-site date collections, *Water analysis, *Michigan, *Natural streams, Chemical analysis, Biological properties, Physical properties, Sampling, Water chemistry, Water pollution effects.
Identifiers: *Michigan streams.

To help protect and conserve its water resources, the State of Michigan has adopted objectives for implementing and enforcing selected chemical, physical and biological water characteristics. To achieve these objectives, water samples were collected at 154 stations on streams thru-out the state from August 1967 to January 1968. Analyses were made of 22 different parameters. The Upper Peninsula of the state has exceptionally good water quality. A combination of favorable soil and drainage characteristics, extensive forest cover and relatively little human perturbation account for this high level of quality. The southeastern part of the Lower Peninsula has unfavorable soil types, poor drainage and sparse vegetation, as well as cultural activities of a synergistic nature, which compound the negative influence of water quality. The northern half of the Lower Peninsula, with its sandy soils, fairly heavy vegetative cover and only moderate development, benefits from water of a quality which, for the most part, approaches that of the Upper Peninsula waters. The pressures of population, economic activity and recreational uses are beginning to cause concern in some parts of this region, however, and future growth patterns will be significant in determining the fate of its waters. Much of the agricultural activity of the state is centered in the southern Lower Peninsula due to favorable soil conditions and climate. (Poertner)
W75-06662

LANE COUNTY PRELIMINARY GENERAL PLAN-WATER QUALITY REPORT.
Lane Council of Governments, Eugene, Oreg.
January, 1974. 138 p, 8 tab, 106 fig.

Descriptors: *Water quality, *Planning, *Reservoirs, *Water utilization, *Water pollution sources, *Dissolved oxygen, Biological oxygen demand, Turbidity, Temperature, Sediments, Rivers, Oregon, On-site investigations, Water quality control, Hydrologic data, Governments.
Identifiers: Lane County(Oregon).

A detailed examination was made of the existing quality of water resources in Lane County, Oregon. Sections of this report deal with hydrology, water quality parameters, water use, and pollution sources in Lane County. The water quality of four main areas was studied. These areas are: the Middle Fork Willamette sub-basin, the Coast Fork Willamette sub-basin, the McKenzie sub-basin, and the Main Stem Willamette sub-basin. Graphs indicating parameters such as B.O.D., pH, temperature, turbidity, bacterial loads, and dissolved oxygen are given for each of these areas. The water quality of Lane County was found to be quite high. This was attributed to three factors: numerous streams, high rates of flow, and the origination of streams in uninhabited mountain regions. Major problems occur on those streams that are relatively sluggish and pass through areas where human activity is concentrated. The Mohawk, Long Tom, and portions of the Coast Fork and Main Stem Willamette have slow meandering reaches and are affected by extensive development. Other chronic water quality problems are related primarily to the prevalence of clay soils, various land use influences, and the effect of the many reservoirs. (Poertner)
W75-06681

DISTRIBUTION OF ISOTOPES IN SOME NATURAL WATERS IN THE REGION NORTH OF MT. JOLMO LUNGMA.
For primary bibliographic entry see Field 2K.
W75-06699

POTAMOLOGICAL STUDIES ON THE RIVER INA OF THE RIVER SYSTEM OF YODO: 1 (IN JAPANESE),
Osaka Kyoiku Univ. (Japan). Oceanography Lab.
Masao Kobayashi, and Akikazu Nakamura.
Mem Osaka Kyoiku Univ III Nat Sci Appl Sci. 21, p 135-159, 1972, Illus, English summary.

Descriptors: Asia, *Rivers, *Rainfall, Precipitation(Atmospheric), *Potamology, Water quality, *Water pollutants, Chemical analysis.
Identifiers: Japan(Ina River), Yodo.

Two kinds of observations one consecutive at a few stations and another itinerant along the River Ina (Japan) were made. The data were collected a few days after rainfalls. The variations of water temperature and the quality of river water at 3 stations was measured hourly for 24 h or 7 h (10:00 17:00). Water temperature is influenced by atmospheric conditions. pH is comparatively high at day time and rather low at night, and a diurnal variation of 4.3 alkalinity is similar to pH. Very low chlorinity is observed with heavy precipitation and small values of chemical oxygen (COD) and SiO2 and slightly large values of Ca2+ are measured when the precipitation is low. The variations of Cl, COD and SiO2 are very large and complicated. At the confluence near the Golf Bridge, the main course shows large values of pH, 4.3 alkalinity and Ca2+ and small values of COD and SiO2, while the tributary shows a small value of 4.3 alkalinity, a large value of SiO2 and almost constant values of pH and Ca2+ even when the amount of precipitation is large. Comparisons between 7-h and 24-h observations and of these components suggest that 24-h means may be estimated by 7-h means of water temperature, pH and 4.3 alkalinity.--Copyright 1974, Biological Abstracts, Inc.
W75-06701

THE SOLUBILITY OF SILICA IN CARBONATE WATERS,
For primary bibliographic entry see Field 2K.
W75-06703

THE BOTTOM FAUNA OF LAKE LILLE-JONSVANN, TRONDELAG, NORWAY,
Kongelige Norske Videnskabers Selskab, Trondheim. Museet.
J. O. Solem.
Norw J Zool. Vol 21, No 3, p 227-261, 1973, Illus.
Identifiers: Autumn, Bivalvia, *Bottom fauna, Coleoptera, Gastropoda, Heteroptera, Hirudinea, Insects, Lakes, Migration, Mollusks, *Norway(Lake Lille-Jonsvann), Oligochaeta, Oviposition, Trichoptera, Trondelag.

Quantitative bottom fauna investigations covering the littoral and sublittoral zones in the mesotrophic lake Lille-Jonsvann (62 deg 23 minutes N, 10 deg 33 minutes E), Trondheim, are presented. Higher taxa particularly treated are Oligochaeta, Hirudinea, Heteroptera, Trichoptera, Coleoptera, Gastropoda, and Bivalvia (Sphaeriidae). Of the total fauna, the insects represent 62% of the number of specimens and 39% of the biomass in the depth range 0.2-10 m. The corresponding values of the mollusks are 27% and 47%, respectively. The insects and the mollusks are by far the dominating animal groups. Three of the species treated clearly showed migration to deeper water in autumn and factors affecting the migration are discussed. A correlation between the depth distribution of the caddis larvae and the oviposition procedure of the females is discussed.--Copyright 1974, Biological Abstracts, Inc.
W75-06716

THE BOTTOM FAUNA OF LAKE HUDDINGSVATN, BASED ON QUANTITATIVE SAMPLING,
Kongelige Norske Videnskabers Selskab, Trondheim. Museet.
B. Sivertsen.
Norw J Zool. Vol 21, No 4, p 305-321, 1973, Illus.
Identifiers: *Bottom fauna, Chironomidae, Gammarus-lacustris, Insects, Lakes, *Norway(Lake Huddingsvatn), Oligochaeta, Peloscolex-ferox, *Sampling, Trondheim.

Bottom samples taken from Lake Huddingsvatn during the years 1965-1968 were analyzed. In the lake, about 300 km northeast of Trondheim, Norway, Chironomidae and Oligochaeta were the predominant groups, followed by Gammarus lacustris. Of the Chironomidae, Chironomini were predominant where the bottom was rich in organic detritus. On poorer bottom substrate Orthocladiinae predominated. Of the Oligochaeta, Peloscolex ferox alone accounted for 77%. The faunal variation between the different years was small, with the insect groups showing the greatest variation. The mean values of abundance showed similar variation during a 4-yr period in Lake Huddingsvatn and a lake situated 10 km away in the same watercourse.--Copyright 1974, Biological Abstracts, Inc.
W75-06717

EFFECT OF WATER POLLUTION ON ICHTHYOFAUNA: PART I. TOXICITY OF

METALS AND THEIR SALTS AND OF INORGANIC SUSPENSIONS (IN POLISH),
Wyzsza Szkola Rolnicza, Krakow (Poland).
For primary bibliographic entry see Field 5C.
W75-06719

THE STRUCTURE OF ECOSYSTEMS,
Illinois Univ., Urbana. Center for Advanced Computation.
For primary bibliographic entry see Field 6G.
W75-06722

THE RELATIONSHIP BETWEEN THE DM (DRY MATTER) CONTENT OF HERBAGE FOR SILAGE MAKING AND EFFLUENT PRODUCTION,
Hannah Dairy Research Inst., Ayr (Scotland).
M. E. Castle, and J. N. Watson.
J Br Grassl Soc. Vol 28, No 3, p 135-138. 1973, Illus.
Identifiers: Bacteria, *Dry matter, *Effluents, Equations, Geotrichum-candidum, *Herbage, Pollution, Crop production, Regression equations, Scotland, *Silage, Wilting.

A study of 16 silages made at the Hannah Research Institute, Scotland, and 22 silages made at the Grassland Research Institute showed highly significant positive relationships between the dry matter (DM) percentages of the material ensiled and the resultant silage. Regression equations derived from this data and from a record of the presence or absence of effluent were used. The average minimum DM content of herbage for ensiling which would produce no effluent was 22.9%. To ensure a margin of safety against production of effluent, a minimum DM content of 24.7% in the herbage was calculated from the confidence limits. To obtain this DM content, herbage will normally require wilting; effluent production should then be negligible. Most silage effluent is regarded as undesirable in drains, streams and rivers. Silage effluent provides all the essential nutrients for certain water-horne bacteria and a fungus (Geotrichum candidum) which can grow in drains.--Copyright 1974, Biological Abstracts, Inc.
W75-06725

ENVIRONMENTAL CONTAMINANTS INVENTORY STUDY NO. 2 - THE PRODUCTION, USE AND DISTRIBUTION OF CADMIUM IN CANADA,
Canada Centre for Inland Waters, Burlington (Ontario).
D. B. Lymburner.
Report Series No. 39, 71 p, 1974, Environment Canada, Inland Waters Directorate, Ottawa, Canada. 7 fig, 110 ref, 13 tab, append.

Descriptors: *Cadmium, *Environmental effects, *Data collections, *Canada, Pollutants, Toxicity, Economics, Metals, Disposal, Distribution, *Path of pollutants, Water pollution sources.
Identifiers: Production, Environmental levels.

Preliminary information is presented on cadmium occurrence, characteristics, production process, global economic significance and major uses. The structure of cadmium production and use in Canada is then analyzed using quantitative data on production, consumption by end use, imports and exports. This information is illustrated by a material flow chart, and maps detailing the distribution of establishments involved in the production and consumption of cadmium are included. Throughout the analysis, environmental inputs are computed where possible. Occupations entailing potential exposure to cadmium are listed and a selected bibliography of references on cadmium toxicity is provided. (Environment Canada)
W75-06742

COMPUTER ROUTINE FOR CALCULATING TOTAL LAKE VOLUME CONTENTS OF A DISSOLVED SUBSTANCE FROM AN ARBITRARY DISTRIBUTION OF CONCENTRATION PROFILES - A METHOD OF CALCULATING LAKEWIDE CONTENTS OF DISSOLVED SUBSTANCES,
Canada Centre for Inland Waters, Burlington (Ontario).
For primary bibliographic entry see Field 2H.
W75-06748

SUBSURFACE DISPOSAL OF WASTE IN CANADA - II, DISPOSAL-FORMATION AND INJECTION-WELL HYDRAULICS,
Department of the Environment, Ottawa (Ontario). Water Resources Branch.
For primary bibliographic entry see Field 5E.
W75-06750

SUBSURFACE DISPOSAL OF WASTE IN CANADA - III - REGIONAL EVALUATION OF POTENTIAL FOR UNDERGROUND DISPOSAL OF INDUSTRIAL LIQUID WASTES,
Water Resources Branch.
For primary bibliographic entry see Field 5E.
W75-06751

AN ASSESSMENT OF AREAL AND TEMPORAL VARIATIONS IN STREAMFLOW QUALITY USING SELECTED DATA FROM THE NATIONAL STREAM QUALITY ACCOUNTING NETWORK,
Geological Survey, Reston, Va.
T. D. Steele, E. J. Gilroy, and R. O. Hawkinson.
Geological Survey open-file report 74-217, August 1974. 210 p, 10 fig, 9 tab, 31 ref, 8 append.

Descriptors: *Water quality, *Variability, *Statistics, Hydrologic data, Fourier analysis, *Data collections, Statistical methods, Water temperature, Networks.
Identifiers: Harmonic analysis.

Streamflow chemical-quality data and stream-temperature data at 88 stations throughout the United States and Puerto Rico were analyzed to develop and to evaluate methodologies for the general assessment of the variation of the Nation's streamflow quality conditions. Lowest harmonic amplitudes, which are indicative of little seasonal variability in stream temperature, were observed in Florida, along the eastern Gulf coast, and along the Pacific coast. Greatest annual variations in stream temperatures exist in the Souris, Red (of the North), and Missouri River basins. Trends in stream temperature were found to exist in the Atlantic coast above Florida; Florida and the eastern Gulf; the Souris River, Red River of the North, and Missouri River basins; the Texas Gulf and Rio Grande area; the Colorado River basin; and the Pacific coast area. Significant trends were found in the long-term streamflow chemical quality record at 15 of 88 stations analyzed. Of these stations, 10 showed an increase in levels of specific conductances while 5 showed a decrease. Trends were indicated for water-quality data in the Atlantic coast above Florida; the Souris River, Red River of the North, and Missouri River basin; the Arkansas and Red River basins; the Texas Gulf and Rio Grande area; the Colorado River basin; and the Pacific coast area. (Knapp-USGS)
W75-06755

REPORT ON THE CHARLES RIVER: A STUDY OF WATER POLLUTION,
Massachusetts Water Resources Commission, Boston. Div. of Water Pollution Control.
W. R. Jobin, and A. F. Ferullo.
March 1971. 48 p, 13 fig, 10 tab, 17 ref, 4 append.

Descriptors: *Water quality standards, *Water quality control, Water pollution, *Water pollution control, *Water pollution sources, River flow, Biochemical oxygen demand, Phosphates, *Massachusetts.
Identifiers: *Charles River(Mass), Boston(Mass), Milford(Mass), Waterton(Mass).

Although assigned a C classification by the Water Quality Standards of 1967 a survey indicated that the entire lower basin of the Charles River was below the acceptable standards. Proposals recommend raising the river to Class B standards, suitable for bathing. The study investigated tributary streams; combined sewer overflows (the major sources of pollution); water quality (bacteria, dissolved oxygen, algae, salinity, and bottom deposits); a storm detention and chlorination facility; present and proposed projects for enhancement of water quality, river flow, phosphate and BOD discharges; and the assimilative capacity of the river. The cost of raising the river to a C classification is $32 million, $5 million for a detention and chlorination facility for sewer overflows and $27 million for a new dam decreasing saline intrusions to the basin. The best method of raising the river to B classification is a proposed deep tunnel requiring $500 million and 5 to 10 years but which would remove pollution from Boston Harbor as well as the basin. Other alternatives are presented: separating the combined sewers, $51 million; another stormwater detention facility, $10 million; and careful pollution control management, but results would be less beneficial along with the lesser costs. (Park-North Carolina)
W75-06777

SOLID WASTE DISPOSAL AND OCEAN DUMPING,
Naval War Coll., Newport, R.I.
J. W. Sellers.
Marine Affairs Journal, Number 1, p 52-77, December 1973.

Descriptors: *Oceans, *Waste disposal, *Solid wastes, *Water pollution sources, Water pollution, Sludge, Water management, Planning, Legislation.
Identifiers: Ocean dumping, Solid waste disposal.

Legislation and control to harness pollution sources must be tempered with astute research, planning, analyses and management of waste disposal in a manner most beneficial or, at the worst, least harmful to the environment and to man. The solid waste problem is examined and the marine environment as a depository for wastes as compared with alternative methods of disposal is discussed. The physical and biological nature of the oceans is discussed especially in terms of assimilative capacity. Most problems are generated locally and could be resolved through control. EPA presently administers the policy on ocean dumping issuing permits for waste transportation and dredge dumping. EPA is currently developing guidelines to implement legislation which seeks to diminish dumping of toxic materials. Solid wastes have been identified, yet absolute control is constrained by several factors including uncertainties and effects of pollutants, data availability, future potential (recycling), problem perception and affluence. Solution to the solid wastes problem rests with how best to utilize the marine environment and/or to determine the utility of all disposal methods based on benefit-cost analysis. These alternatives include recycling, landfill, burning, and life style changes; each generates new kinds of problems. Research is necessary to determine permissible level of ocean dumping; meanwhile management must consider solid waste disposal in terms of economic, conservation, social, and psychological needs and environmental goals. (Salzman-North Carolina)
W75-06789

HEALTH AND SAFETY LABORATORY FALLOUT PROGRAM, QUARTERLY SUMMARY REPORT (JUNE 1, 1974 THROUGH SEPTEMBER 1, 1974),
Health and Safety Lab. (AEC), New York.
For primary bibliographic entry see Field 5A.
W75-06794

DEPTH DISTRIBUTIONS OF GLOBAL FALLOUT SR90, CS137, AND PU239, 240 IN SANDY LOAM SOIL,
Health and Safety Lab. (AEC), New York.
For primary bibliographic entry see Field 5A.
W75-06795

FALLOUT PU 239, 240 IN DIET,
Health and Safety Lab. (AEC), New York.
For primary bibliographic entry see Field 5A.
W75-06798

SEDIMENT SAMPLING NEAR MOUND LABORATORY - JULY 1974,
Health and Safety Lab. (AEC), New York.
For primary bibliographic entry see Field 5A.
W75-06800

ENVIRONMENTAL RADIOACTIVITY ANNUAL REPORT 1973 (NEW ZEALAND).
National Radiation Lab., Christchurch (New Zealand). Dept. of Health.
For primary bibliographic entry see Field 5A.
W75-06803

APPENDIX TO HEALTH AND SAFETY LABORATORY FALLOUT PROGRAM, QUARTERLY SUMMARY REPORT (JUNE 1, 1974 THROUGH SEPTEMBER 1, 1974).
Health and Safety Lab. (AEC), New York.
For primary bibliographic entry see Field 5A.
W75-06804

STRONTIUM 90 AND STRONTIUM 89 IN MONTHLY DEPOSITION AT WORLD LAND SITES,
Health and Safety Lab. (AEC), New York.
For primary bibliographic entry see Field 5A.
W75-06805

HEALTH AND SAFETY LABORATORY FALLOUT PROGRAM QUARTERLY SUMMARY REPORT, (SEPTEMBER 1, 1974 THROUGH DECEMBER 1, 1974),
Health and Safety Lab. (AEC), New York.
For primary bibliographic entry see Field 5A.
W75-06818

REGIONAL UNIFORMITY OF CUMULATIVE RADIONUCLIDE FALLOUT,
Health and Safety Lab. (AEC), New York.
For primary bibliographic entry see Field 5A.
W75-06819

ANALYSES OF QUALITY CONTROL SAMPLES AT HASL AND A CONTRACTOR LABORATORY DURING 1974,
Health and Safety Lab. (AEC), New York.
For primary bibliographic entry see Field 5A.
W75-06820

APPENDIX TO HEALTH AND SAFETY LABORATORY FALLOUT PROGRAM QUARTERLY SUMMARY REPORT, (SEPTEMBER 1, 1974 THROUGH DECEMBER 1, 1974),
Health and Safety Lab. (AEC), New York.
For primary bibliographic entry see Field 5A.
W75-06823

SR 90 AND SR 89 IN MONTHLY DEPOSITION AT WORLD LAND SITES.
Health and Safety Lab. (AEC), New York.
For primary bibliographic entry see Field 5A.
W75-06824

RADIONUCLIDES AND LEAD IN SURFACE AIR,
Health and Safety Lab. (AEC), New York.
For primary bibliographic entry see Field 5A.
W75-06825

RADIOSTRONTIUM IN MILK AND TAP WATER.
Health and Safety Lab. (AEC), New York.
For primary bibliographic entry see Field 5A.
W75-06826

DYE AND DROGUE STUDIES OF SPOIL DISPOSAL AND OIL DISPERSION,
Delaware Univ., Newark. Coll. of Marine Studies.
V. Klemas, D. Maurer, W. Leatham, P. Kinner, and W. Treasure.
Journal of the Water Pollution Control Federation, Vol 46, No 8, p 2026-2034, August, 1974. 18 fig, 12 ref.

Descriptors: *Dredging, *Dye, *Currents(Water), Sediments, Estuaries, Circulation, Oil pollution, Dispersion, Path of pollutants, Water pollution sources, Waste disposal.
Identifiers: *Hydrographic circulation, Drogue, Surface water movement, Aquatic frontal system, Tidal flow, *Delaware Bay.

As part of a study to determine short-term consequences of dredging and dumping on benthic invertebrate colonies near the mouth of the Delaware Bay, a sampling grid for geological and biological stations was designed before dredging commenced. Dye and drogue studies were made to map the general hydrographic circulation in order to establish these stations, and a dye study was also made of surface water movement at a suggested off-shore oil terminal location. The procedures used and results obtained from these studies, which utilized aircraft-boat, radio-coordinated teams, are presented. (Nelson-FIRL)
W75-06831

NEW INDICATOR SPECIES IN THE BALTIC ZOOPLANKTON IN 1972,
Wyzsza Szkola Rolnicza, Szczecin (Poland). Instytut Eksploatacji Zasobow Morza.
T. Radziejewska, J. Chojnakci, and J. Maslowski.
Mar Biol (Berl), Vol 23, No 2, p 111-113, 1973. Illus.
Identifiers: Aetideus-armatus, *Baltic Sea, Centropages-typicus, Ectopleura-dumortieri, Electra-pilosa, Eucalanus-elongatus, Hydrographic studies, Metridia-Lucens, Plankton, Rosacea-plicata, Tomopteris-kefersteini, *Zooplankton, *Bioindications, *Saline water intrusion.

The occurrence of zooplankton species, indicating a saline-water influx from the North Sea into the Baltic Sea in 1972, is described. Particular attention is paid to 8 spp. so far unknown in this region (Ectopleura dumortieri, Rosacea plicata, Tomopteris kefersteini, Aetideus armatus, Centropages typicus, Eucalanus elongatus, Metridia lucens, Electra pilosa). The appearance of these zooplankters in the Southern Baltic Sea is discussed in relation to the hydrographic changes taking place in this area in 1972. Assessments are made regarding the intensity of dynamic exchange processes in the Baltic and North Atlantic waters in 1972.--Copyright 1974, Biological Abstracts, Inc.
W75-06837

5C. Effects Of Pollution

SENSITIVITY OF VERTEBRATE EMBRYOS TO HEAVY METALS AS A CRITERION OF WATER QUALITY - PHASE II BIOASSAY PROCEDURES USING DEVELOPMENTAL STAGES AS TEST ORGANISMS,
Kentucky Water Resources Inst., Lexington.
For primary bibliographic entry see Field 5A.
W75-06352

CONTRIBUTIONS OF TIDAL WETLANDS TO ESTUARINE FOOD CHAINS,
Maryland Univ., Prince Frederick. Center for Environmental and Estuarine Studies.
D. R. Heinle, D. A. Flemer, J. F. Ustach, and R. A. Murtagh.
Available from the National Technical Information Service, Springfield, Va 22161 as PB-240 975, $3.75 in paper copy, $2.25 in microfiche. Maryland Water Resources Research Center, College Park, Technical Report No 29 (1975). 34 p, 1 fig, 4 tab, 21 ref, append. OWRT B-019-MD(1). 14-31-0001-4091.

Descriptors: *Detritus, *Nutrients, *Marshes, Food chains, Estuaries, *Maryland, Wetlands, Carbon, Production.
Identifiers: Carbon balance, *Patuxent estuary(Md), Adenosine triphosphate.

Flows of detritus and nutrients from stable marshes in the upper Patuxent estuary subjected to low tidal amplitude were slight. The quantity of particulate carbon flowing from the marsh to the estuary was less than 10% of annual production. By contrast, a portion of the marshes subjected to scouring by ice lost virtually all of its above ground biomass to the estuary and contributed over half of the annual carbon budget to the system. An appendix entitled 'Problems with Adenosine Triphosphate Measurements in the Patuxent River Marshes' concluded that this technique is a poor biomass indicator for the marshes.
W75-06353

PHYTOPLANKTON POPULATIONS IN RELATION TO DIFFERENT TROPHIC LEVELS AT WINNIPESAUKEE LAKE, NEW HAMPSHIRE, U.S.A.,
New Hampshire Univ., Durham. Dept. of Botany.
H. W. Yeo, and A. C. Mathieson.
Available from the National Technical Information Service, Springfield, Va 22161 as PB-240 981, $6.25 in paper copy, $2.25 in microfiche. New Hampshire Water Resources Research Center, Durham, Completion Report, February, 1973. 155 p, 77 fig, 9 tab, 49 ref. OWRT A-019-NH(1).

Descriptors: *Phytoplankton, *New Hampshire, *Trophic level, Lakes, Phosphates, Nitrates, Silicates, Nitrogen, *Nutrients, Cyanophyta, *Eutrophication, *Mesotrophy, Period of growth, Plant groupings, Water pollution effects.
Identifiers: Lake Winnipesaukee(NH), Myxophycean plankton, Newfound Lake(NH), Lake Winnisquam(NH).

Composition, abundance, and seasonal periodicity of phytoplankton at Lake Winnipesaukee were determined. Trophic levels were evaluated for the entire lake and for eight individual stations. The study also compared the trophic levels of Lake Winnipesaukee with Newfound and Winnisquam Lakes. Samples of phytoplankton were taken from three to six depths at eight stations with a 4-liter Van Dorn water sampler. Water samples were also taken for nutrient analyses of orthophosphate, total phosphates, nitrate-nitrogen and silicon dioxide. The response of phytoplankton to nutrient enrichments of nitrates, phosphates and silicates was evaluated. The differences in phytoplankton numbers (cell/ml) and nutrient levels were compared with previous records at Winnisquam and Newfound Lakes. The nutrient levels at Winnipesaukee were in excess of those previously found at Newfound and Winnisquam Lakes. The species diversity at Winnipesaukee Lake was much greater than at either of the other two lakes. The blue-green algae were the dominant phytoplankters. The concept of phytoplankton associations was useful in evaluating the trophic level of Lake Winnipesaukee. Although dominated by a Eutrophic Myxophycean Plankton, oligotrophic phytoplankton associations also are evident. The application of the phytoplankton quotient concept, to the individual stations provided a mesotrophic

rating for four stations while four other stations were categorized as eutrophic. A collective interpretation of the representative phytoplankton associations also indicated mesotrophy as the trophic level of the overall lake.
W75-06354

THE CHRONIC EFFECTS OF COPPER AND ZINC ON FISHES,

Oklahoma State Univ., Stillwater. Dept. of Biological Sciences.
M. R. Curd, and H. R. Jarrell.

Stillwater, Oklahoma Water Resources Research Institute, Termination Report (March 1975). 3 p. OWRT A-033-OKLA(1). 14-31-0001-4036.

Descriptors: Water pollution effects, Toxicity, Fish, Perch, *Sunfishes, Channel catfish, *Zinc, *Copper, Growth rates, Histopathology, *Lethal limit, *Growth stages, *Juvenile growth stage, Fish eggs.
Identifiers: *Sublethal concentrations, *Logperch.

Initial objectives were to determine effects of sublethal concentrations of copper and zinc on eggs and juvenile stages of logperch Percina caprodes and the longear sunfish Lepomis megalotis, to determine effects of sublethal amounts of zinc on the growth rates and to determine the synergestic effects, if any, of sublethal mixtures of zinc and copper. The fourth objective was to determine the histological differences, if any, between controls and fishes subject to treatment as above. Because copper levels as low as 0.1 ppm (the minimum level tested) proved to be lethal to eggs and juvenile stages, sufficient numbers of fish could not be raised to obtain the original objectives. Subsequent research with channel catfish fry was attempted but disease and continued extraneous substrate toxicity of both control and experimental aquaria prevented obtaining results of other than highly questionable value.
W75-06364

EFFECTS OF BORON-WATER ON RATS,

Nevada Univ., Reno. Coll. of Agriculture.
G. H. Green, M. D. Lott, and H. J. Weeth.

Proceedings, Western Section, American Society of Animal Science, Vol 24, p 254-258, 1973. 1 fig, 3 tab, 10 ref. OWRT A-053-NEV(1).

Descriptors: *Boron, *Bioassay, *Growth rates, Inhibition.
Identifiers: *Subtoxic effects, Rats, *Tissue analysis.

Two experiments were conducted on growing rats to determine subtoxic effects of boron in the drinking water. One experiment tested the effects of 300 mg B/liter and determined this level to cause subtoxic responses. The other experiment tested the ability of the testes to recover from four levels of boron (0, 75, 150, and 300 mg B/liter) and determined that levels above 150 mg B/liter caused irreversible testis damage. Levels less than 75 mg B/liter seemed to have no significant effects. (Katz)
W75-06376

EFFECT OF POLYCHLORINATED BIPHENYLS (PCB'S) ON SURVIVAL AND REPRODUCTION OF DAPHNIA, GAMMARUS, AND TANYTARSUS,

National Water Quality Lab., Duluth, Minn.
A. V. Nebeker, and F. A. Puglisi.

Transactions of the American Fisheries Society, No 4, p 722-728, 1974. 9 tab, 15 ref.

Descriptors: *Polychlorinated biphenyls, *Reproduction, *Bioassay, *Aroclor, Analytical techniques, Toxicants, Lethal limit, Midges, Growth rates, *Water pollution effects.
Identifiers: *Gammarus pseudolimneaus, *Daphnia magna, *Tanytarsus dissimilis.

Continuous-flow and static bioassays were conducted at 18C, with survival and reproduction as measures of relative toxicity of eight PCB's. Three PCB-mixture bioassays were also conducted. Aroclor 1248 was the most toxic to Daphnia magna of the eight Aroclors tested in static tests; the 3-wk LC50 was 25 microgram/liter. Aroclor 1254 was the most toxic PCB to Daphnia under continuous-flow conditions with a 3-wk LC50 of 1.3 microgram/liter. Ninety-six-hr LC50 values for Aroclor 1242 (A-1242) and A-1248 on Gammarus pseudolimnaeus in continuous-flow tests were 73 and 20 microgram/liter. Reproduction and survival of young were good at 2.8 microgram/liter A-1242 and 2.2 microgram/liter 1248. The midge Tanytarsus dissimilis did not emerge in abundance above 5.1 microgram/liter A-1248 or 3.5 microgram/liter A-1254. The 3-wk LC50 for Aroclor 1254 was 0.65 microgram/liter for larvae and 0.45 microgram/l for pupae. Tissue residues for G. pseudolimnaeus ranged from 4.0 microgram/g A-1254 in control animals to 552 microgram/g A-1248 in scuds held for 60 days in water containing 5.1 microgram/liter A-1248. (Katz)
W75-06377

THE EFFECTS OF LEAD ON ALGAE, I: EFFECTS OF PB ON VIABILITY AND MOTILITY OF PLATYMONAS SUBCORDIFORMUS (CHLOROPHYTA:VOLVOCALES),

Scripps Institution of Oceanography, La Jolla, Calif.
A. Hessler.

Water, Air and Soil Pollution, Vol 3, No 3, p 371-385, 1974. 8 fig, 3 tab, 16 ref.

Descriptors: *Lead, *Reproduction, *Viability, *Algae, *Growth rates, Movement, Primary productivity, Heavy metals, Water pollution sources, *Water pollution effects, Biological properties.
Identifiers: *Platymonas subcordiformis, *Sublethal effects, Flagella.

The effects of lethal and sublethal concentrations of PbCl2 on reproduction, viability, and motility of a marine unicellular green flagellate alga, Platymonas subcordiformis, were studied under controlled laboratory conditions. The severity of the effects depended primarily upon the coneentration of Pb++ and the duration of treatment. Log phase cells were most sensitive than stationary phase cells. Sublethal amounts of Pb (2.5 and 10 mg/liter Pb++) tended to retard population growth delaying cell division and daughter cell separation. A lethal amount of Pb (60 mg/liter Pb++) caused inhibition of growth and cell death. Various intracellular abnormalities resulted from Pb treatment. The flagella were shed or altered in a variety of ways, depending on Pb concentration; motility was least affected by low Pb and completely impaired by high Pb. Normal wild-type cells appeared to be more sensitive to Pb than mechanically sheared (flagella-less) cells and cells of a non-flagellate mutant of Platymonas. Exposure of cells to Pb in non-growth conditions of dark and cold (2 degrees C) had little negative effect. (Katz)
W75-06379

THE EFFECT OF ULTRA LOW VOLUME AERIAL DISPERSAL OF NALED ON AN AQUATIC HABITAT, EHL(K)74-25, OCTOBER 1974,

Environmental Health Lab., Kelly AFB, Tex.
J. M. Livingston, and J. T. Goodwin.

Available from the National Technical Information Service, Springfield, Va 22161 as AD-787 653, $3.25 in paper copy, $2.25 in microfiche. October 1974. 15 p, 1 fig, 5 tab, 6 ref.

Descriptors: *Insecticides, *Aquatic habitats, *Insect control, *Water pollution effects, Pesticides, Aquatic insects, Mosquitoes, Pest control, Pesticide toxicity, Fish, Mortality.
Identifiers: *Dibrom, *Naled, *Acetylcholinesterase.

Ultra low volume aerial applications of naled (Dibrom 14) at 0.7 and 1.5 oz per acre were made at Robins AFB Ga. on 31 July, 1974. The effects of the spray on non target aquatic organisms were monitored utilizing caged fish, shoreline sampling, drift traps, drop traps, acetylcholinesterase levels in fish brain and other observations. Acetylcholinesterase activity in fish brains was depressed in the treated areas but no significant mortality of fish was noted. No gross effect on the normal fauna was observed. From this test it is concluded that no extensive monitoring activities are required for routine spray missions using conventional rates of naled, but closely spaced, multiple applications may require monitoring. (Katz)
W75-06380

THE CHEMICAL TOXICITY OF ELEMENTS,

Battelle-Pacific Northwest Labs., Richland, Wash. Water and Land Resources Dept.
G. W. Dawson.

June 1974. 25 p, 1 tab, 28 ref.

Descriptors: *Toxicity, *Chemical properties, *Elements(Chemical), *Radioactive wastes, *Water pollution sources, Water quality standards, Radioactive waste disposal, Water pollution effects.

The inherent chemical hazards of the materials found in radioactive wastes should be understood and considered when dealing with the management of these wastes. Acceptable threshold levels for the 104 known elements in air and water intended for potable supply, propagation of aquatic life and irrigation purposes are delineated. A final data point was added to indicate a limiting marine level beyond which edible species could concentrate elements to hazardous levels in their flesh. Many values are estimations or extrapolations from acute effect data or from chemical similitude to other elements. (Katz)
W75-06381

GROWTH RESPONSE OF A MARINE PHYTOPLANKTON COCCOLITHUS HUXLEYI, TO VARIOUS CHEMICAL FORMS OF COBALT,

Oregon State Univ., Corvallis. School of Oceanography.
H. L. Longaker.

Available from the National Technical Information Service, Springfield, Va 22161 as RLO 2227-T-1244, $6.25 in paper copy, $2.25 in microfiche. M.S. Thesis, June 1974. 52 p, 3 fig, 11 tab, 43 ref, append.

Descriptors: *Nutrient requirements, *Growth rates, *Phytoplankton, *Cobalt metals, Trace elements, Statistical methods, Primary productivity, Water pollution effects.
Identifiers: *Cocculithus huxleyi, *EDTA, *Vitamin B12.

Two experiments were performed on Coccolithus huxleyi, a marine phytoplankton, to determine if Co(III)-EDTA is more efficacious in stimulating growth than Co(II)-EDTA. One experiment had cobalt concentrations of 10 and 1 micro g/l; the other had concentrations of 1 and 0.1 micro g/l. In both experiments there were no observed differences in specific growth rates between treatments of Co(III)-EDTA with 0.000001 M additional EDTA and Co(II) with 0.000001 M EDTA. Both resulted in specific growth rates larger than controls without added EDTA or cobalt. It is not possible to measure the amount of Co(II)-EDTA that is oxidized to Co(III)-EDTA at these experimental concentrations. (Katz)
W75-06382

THE EFFECTS OF ENVIRONMENTAL STRESS ON THE COMMUNITY STRUCTURE AND PRODUCTIVITY OF SALT MARSH EPIPHYTIC COMMUNITIES: PROGRESS REPORT,

City Coll,. New York.

J. J. Lee.
Available from the National Technical Information Service, Springfield, Va 22161 as COO-3254-20, $10.00 in paper copy, $2.25 in microfiche. August 1974. 138 p, 17 tab, 51 fig. AEC Contract No. AT(11-1)3254.

Descriptors: *Environmental effects, *Salt marshes, *Stress, *Food chains, *Productivity, Nutrient requirements, Nematodes, Trophic levels, Technology, Water pollution effects.
Identifiers: *Epiphyte communities, Microcosm experiments.

Progress is reported on various projects related to a study of the effects of environmental stress on the community structure and productivity of salt marsh epiphytic communities. An apparatus has been developed that can be used for in situ experiments with aufwuchs communities and perhaps can be used in estuarine water quality assessments. A second major advance was the demonstration of information processing in food web transformations. The report includes material that are part of 18 published or submitted manuscripts. Synopses of these papers are included. (Katz)
W75-06383

MARINE RADIOECOLOGY: A SELECTED BIBLIOGRAPHY OF NON-RUSSIAN LITERATURE,
Environmental Protection Agency, Boise, Idaho.
E. Edmundson, Jr., V. Schultz, and A. W. Klement, Jr.
1974. 52 p.

Descriptors: *Reviews, *Bibliographies, Radioecology, *Sea water, Radioactivity effects, *Marine biology, Water pollution effects.
Identifiers: *Marine radioecology.

References to the literature available on the subject of marine radioecology are found in this bibliography. Reports of laboratory and field studies are included as were those of salt and brackish water and anadromous and catadromous species. Bibliographies are also listed. (Katz)
W75-06384

A REVIEW OF THE LITERATURE ON THE USE OF DIURON IN FISHERIES,
Bureau of Sport Fisheries and Wildlife, Columbia, Mo. Fish-Pesticide Research Lab.
W. W. Johnson, and A. M. Julin.
Available from the National Technical Information Service, Springfield, Va 22161 as PB-235 446, $5.25 in paper copy, $2.25 in microfiche. July 1974. 81 p, 2 tab, 27 ref.

Descriptors: *Herbicides, *Aquatic weed control, *Aquiculture, *Reviews, Bibliographies, Algae, Pesticides, Algicides, Metabolism, Mode of Action, Photosynthesis, Pesticide residues, Analytical techniques, Toxicity, Fish, Water pollution effects.
Identifiers: *Diuron, Karmex(R).

Diuron is a major phenylurea herbicide produced by duPont. It was introduced experimentally in 1951, registered for industrial weed control in 1953 under the trade name 'Karmex', and for agricultural use in 1954. It has been extensively studied and used in aquatic environments. Diuron shows good potential as a broad-spectrum, aquatic herbicide as it controls most algal species and many vascular hydrophytes. Factors affecting the efficacy of diuron include light, temperature and water quality. It is also strongly adsorbed by organic matter and some clays. Diuron acts primarily on the light reaction of photosynthesis by strongly inhibiting the 'Hill reaction'. It is persistent in the aquatic environment and evidence indicates that low levels of accumulation may occur in non-target organisms so that chronic effects may be significant. A review of the literature on the use of diuron in fisheries is presented. (Katz)
W75-06385

A REVIEW OF THE LITERATURE ON THE USE OF SQUOXIN IN FISHERIES,
Bureau of Sport Fisheries and Wildlife, Cook, Wash. Western Fish Nutrition Lab.
G. J. Crowley.
Available from the National Technical Information Service, Springfield, Va 22161 as PB-235 456, $3.75 in paper copy, $2.25 in microfiche. March 1974. 24 p, 3 tab, 37 ref.

Descriptors: *Piscidides, *Aquiculture, Selectivity, Sport fish, *Pest control, Freshwater fishes, *Reviews, Bibliographies, Water pollution effects, Salmonids, Chemical analysis, Bioassay, Toxicity, Laboratory tests, Pesticide residues, Mode of Action.
Identifiers: *Squoxin, *Squawfish, Ptychocheilus oregonensis, Ptychocheilus umpqua.

The piscicide Squoxin is highly selective against two species of squawfish, Ptychocheilus oregonensis and P. umpqua. Extensive field testing in Idaho and Oregon has demonstrated the effectiveness of the chemical in controlling squawfish while not harming sympatric fish species, especially salmonids, and invertebrates. The use of Squoxin as an invention to promote fish culture by squawfish population eradication has been patented in the United States and Canada. The compound is not yet registered. However, efforts toward this end are under way as part of the Squoxin Development Project. Collaborators in this project are presently compiling available information for application to Environmental Protection Agency, anticipated in early 1974. Literature concerning the use of Squoxin in fisheries is reviewed. (Katz)
W75-06386

A REVIEW OF THE LITERATURE ON THE USE OF COPPER SULFATE IN FISHERIES,
Bureau of Sport Fisheries and Wildlife, Marion, Ala. Southeastern Fish Cultural Lab.
G. A. Jackson.
Available from the National Technical Information Service, Springfield, Va 22161 as PB-235 445, $4.75 in paper copy, $2.25 in microfiche. March 1974. 91 p, 2 tab, 216 ref.

Descriptors: *Copper sulfate, *Algicides, *Pesticides, *Reviews, *Aquiculture, *Bibliographies, Pest control, Piscicides, Toxicity, Mode of Action, Water quality, Water pollution effects.

Copper sulfate is currently registered by the Environmental Protection Agency as an algicide and has been given a tolerance of 1.0 ppm in potable waters. This chemical is commonly employed for other aquatic purposes such as a therapeutant, piscicide and molluscicide and future clearance of copper sulfate for these applications is dependent on a thorough evaluation of its efficacy on target species and its toxicity to non-target organisms. In the past, failure to recognize variations in water quality, especially water hardness and alkalinity, has often resulted in undesirable consequences. When properly administered, however, with a full consideration of the various water quality parameters and biota present, copper sulfate is one of the most efficient and versatile chemicals available to the aquatic biologist. The literature concerning copper sulfate's use in fisheries is reviewed. (Katz)
W75-06387

A REVIEW OF THE LITERATURE ON THE USE OF ROTENONE IN FISHERIES,
Bureau of Sport Fisheries and Wildlife, LaCrosse, Wis. Fish Control Lab.
R. A. Schnick.
Available from the National Technical Information Service, Springfield, Va 22161 as PB-235 454, $4.25 in paper copy, $2.25 in microfiche. May 1974. 130 p, 3 tab, 315 ref.

Descriptors: *Reviews, *Rotenone, *Fish control agents, *Pest control, *Piscicides, *Bibliographies, Pesticides, Freshwater fish, Aquiculture, Fish management, Regulation, Toxicity, Water pollution effects, Organic compounds.
Identifiers: Fishery reclamation, Noxfish(R), Pro-Noxfish(R), Chem-Fish(R).

Rotenone has been used for 40 years as a piscicide in the United States and Canada. It is effective in low concentrations (0.05 to 2 mg/l of the commercial formulations) against most life stages of many species of freshwater and marine fishes, but with a range of specificity among species. Other desirable characteristics of rotenone include less persistence in water than organochlorine pesticides, low toxicity to birds and mammals, and rapid toxicity to fish. If needed, it can be detoxified easily by potassium permanganate or chlorine and removed by activated carbon. The activity of rotenone is limited by high pH, hardness, alkalinity, and low temperatures. Several methods are available for determining the amount of rotenone in the water, milk, plants, and fish. Twenty degradation products have been observed after rotenone was exposed to light; this observation may pose a problem in the tolerance registration of rotenone. A review is presented of the literature concerning rotenone's use in fisheries. (Katz)
W75-06388

A REVIEW OF THE LITERATURE ON THE USE OF ENDOTHALL IN FISHERIES,
Bureau of Sport Fisheries and Wildlife, Denver, Colo. Fish Pesticide Research Lab.
J. G. Armstrong.
Available from the National Technical Information Service, Springfield, Va 22161 as PB-235 447, $3.25 in paper copy, $2.25 in microfiche. March 1974. 22 p, 1 tab, 26 ref.

Descriptors: *Herbicides, *Pest control, *Aquiculture, *Algicides, *Reviews, Aquatic weed control, Fish, Fisheries, Toxicity, Chemical degradation, Water pollution effects.
Identifiers: *Endothall.

Endothall is an organic contact herbicide and algicide used in lakes and ponds. It is used on terrestrial seed crops as a pre-harvest desiccant and is registered for use as a pre- and post-emergent herbicide. It is registered for use in lakes and ponds as a herbicide and algicide. It is of value to those concerned with a fishery because it does not persist in the environment and the levels required to control aquatic vegetation do not seem to be harmful to either fishes or fish-food organisms. It is relatively safe to the applicator and economical. A control program, using endothall would be both ethical and defensible. Literature concerning Endothall's use in fisheries is reviewed. (Katz)
W75-06389

A REVIEW OF THE LITERATURE ON THE USE OF MASOTEN IN FISHERIES,
Bureau of Sport Fisheries and Wildlife, Stuttgart, Ark. Fish Farming Experiment Station.
J. E. Ellis.
Available from the National Technical Information Service, Springfield, Va 22161 as PB-235 453, $4.25 in paper copy, $2.25 in microfiche. (March 1974). 62 p, 102 ref.

Descriptors: *Reviews, *Pesticides, *Aquiculture, *Freshwater fish, *Organophosphorus pesticides, Organophosphorus compounds, Impounded waters, Parasites, Toxicity, Bibliographies, Water pollution effects.
Identifiers: *Trichlorofon, *Masoten(R), *Parasiticide.

Trichlorfon is the common name of the active ingredient in Masoten (R). It is an organic phosphate parasiticide originated by Bayer AG in Germany and developed by Chemagro in the United States.

Its first use in fisheries was to control ectoparasites. It was recently registered under the trade name Masoten for use in impounded waters (aquariums and ponds) for fish not used as food (goldfish and bait fish). It is an effective therapeutant for the control of anchorworms Lernaea sp., fish lice Argulus sp., and gill flukes Cleidodiscus sp., Dactylogyrus sp., and Gyrodactylus sp. In Europe it is approved for use on the same target organisms including treatment of food fish such as carp, eel, and trout. Literature concerning Masoten's use in fisheries is reviewed. (Katz)
W75-06390

A REVIEW OF THE LITERATURE ON THE USE OF LIME (CA(OH)2, CAO, CACO3) IN FISHERIES,
Bureau of Sport Fisheries and Wildlife, Warm Springs, Ga. Southeastern Fish Control Lab.
J. B. Sills.
Available from the National Technical Information Service, Springfield, Va 22161 as PB-235 449, $3.75 in paper copy, $2.25 in microfiche. February 1974. 30 p, 53 ref.

Descriptors: *Calcium compounds, *Lime, *Aquiculture, *Reviews, *Pesticides, Bibliographies, Calcium carbonate, Ponds, Fish farming, Fish parasites, Fisheries, Water pollution effects.
Identifiers: Calcium hydrate, Pond care.

The literature concerning lime's use in fisheries is reviewed. Liming is a form of multi-purpose pond care. Properly applied, lime kills free swimming and bottom dwelling organisms that are harmful to fish, produces a favorable pH in acid waters and increases the alkaline reserve in water and mud which buffers against extreme changes in pH. Lime is considered to be a relatively safe industrial chemical and since it is generally recognized as a safe food ingredient by the U.S. Food and Drug Administration, its use in fish ponds should cause little concern to regulatory agencies. (Katz)
W75-06391

A REVIEW OF THE LITERATURE ON THE USE OF BETADINE IN FISHERIES,
Bureau of Sport Fisheries and Wildlife, Seattle, Wash. Western Fish Disease Lab.
N. C. Nelson.
Available from the National Technical Information Service, Springfield, Va 22161 as PB-235 443, $3.75 in paper copy, $2.25 in microfiche. March 1974. 48 p, 2 tab, 71 ref.

Descriptors: *Reviews, *Aquiculture, *Pesticides, *Fish eggs, *Toxicity, Bibliographies, Freshwater fishes, Fish diseases, Pest control, Bactericides, Salmon, Trout, Pathogenic bacteria, Fungi, Water quality, Water pollution effects.
Identifiers: *Betadine.

Many bacterial and viral fish diseases can be transmitted on eggs from carrier brood fish. In 1969, Betadine (providone-iodine), a non-selective organie iodine germicide, was found to be an effective egg surface disinfectant. This literature review was written to support FDA registration for Betadine Solution on food fish eggs. It is virucidal and bactericidal to common fish pathogens at levels which are non-toxic to salmonid eggs. The effectiveness and safety of Betadine Solution make it a likely candidate for successful registration. (Katz)
W75-06392

A REVIEW OF THE LITERATURE ON THE USE OF FORMALIN-MALACHITE GREEN IN FISHERIES,
Bureau of Sport Fisheries and Wildlife, Seattle, Wash. Western Fish Disease Lab.
N. C. Nelson.
March 1974. 31 p, 2 tab, 42 ref.

Descriptors: *Reviews, *Aquiculture, *Fish parasites, *Pesticides, Toxicity, Freshwater fish, Fish diseases, Pest control, Water pollution effects.
Identifiers: *Formalin, *Malachite green.

This literature review was written to support initiation of FDA registration procedures for use of the formalin-malachite green mixture as a therapeutant in fish culture. This mixture of chemicals is used to treat external parasites, particularly Icthyophthirius, of coldwater and warmwater fishes. It is a very effective medicament with a lower toxicity than that of either chemical used individually, but additional data on toxicity to nontarget organisms will probably have to be gathered before registration can be obtained. (Katz)
W75-06393

A REVIEW OF THE LITERATURE ON THE USE OF MALACHITE GREEN IN FISHERIES,
Bureau of Sport Fisheries and Wildlife, Seattle, Wash. Western Fish Disease Lab.
N. C. Nelson.
Available from the National Technical Information Service, Springfield, Va 22161 as PB-235 450, $4.75 in paper copy, $2.25 in microfiche. March 1974. 79 p, 5 tab, 124 ref.

Descriptors: *Fungicide, *Pesticides, *Reviews, *Fish diseases, Bibliographies, Fish eggs, Fish hatcheries, Pest control, Toxicity, Fish parasites, Aquiculture, Mode of Action, Water pollution effects.
Identifiers: *Malachite green.

Malachite green is used extensively in fish batcheries as a fungicide on both eggs and fish, and is also effective against certain external protozoan and bacterial infections. It can be applied as an aqueous solution in tanks, troughs, raceways, and ponds for fixed or extended treatment, used as a dip, or applied topically. At present, malachite green is not registered with the FDA for use on food fishes. Since it has been implicated as a mutagen, carcinogen and teratogen, safety will have to be demonstrated before registration is possible. This literature review was written as the first step in the drug clearance process. (Katz)
W75-06394

INTERACTION OF SELECTED PESTICIDES WITH MARINE MICROORGANISMS,
Syracuse University Research Corp., N.Y.
H. C. Sikka, and C. P. Rice.
Available from the National Technical Information Service, Springfield, Va 22161 as AD-785 079, $4.75 in paper copy, $2.25 in microfiche. Office of Naval Research, Final Report, September 1974. 76 p, 7 fig, 15 tab, 52 ref.

Descriptors: *Chlorinated hydrocarbon pesticides, *Marine algae, *DDT, *Dieldrin, *Environmental effects, DDE, Growth rates, Photosynthesis, Metabolism, Laboratory tests, Bacteria, Fungi, Primary productivity, Inhibitors, Toxicity, Water pollution effects.
Identifiers: *Bioaccumulation, Methoxychlor, Carbaryl, l-Naphthol.

The effects of some persistent chlorinated hydrocarbon pesticides on six species of marine algae were tested. Carbaryl and l-naphthol, a degradation product, were investigated in terms of uptake, metabolism, growth and photosynthesis by the algae. Uptake and metabolism of dieldrin, DDT and methoxychlor by the six species of algae were examined. Dieldrin, DDT and methoxychlor were concentrated by the algae to levels much higher than the original concentration in the medium. Growth was inhibited, to differing degrees, by methoxychlor, carbaryl and l-naphthol. (Katz)
W75-06396

AEROBIC DIGESTION OF EXTRACELLULAR MICROBIAL POLYSACCARIDES,
Oklahoma State Univ., Stillwater. Bioenvironmental Engineering Labs.
For primary bibliographic entry see Field 5D.
W75-06405

SOURCES OF POTENTIAL BIOLOGICAL DAMAGE FROM ONCE-THROUGH COOLING SYSTEMS OF NUCLEAR POWER PLANTS,
Oak Ridge National Lab., Tenn.
For primary bibliographic entry see Field 5B.
W75-06415

FISH PARASITES OCCURRING IN THIRTEEN SOUTHERN CALIFORNIA RESERVOIRS,
California State Univ., San Diego.
For primary bibliographic entry see Field 8I.
W75-06416

DRAFT ENVIRONMENTAL STATEMENT HTGR FUEL REFABRICATION PILOT PLANT AT THE OAK RIDGE NATIONAL LABORATORY.
Oak Ridge National Lab., Tenn.
For primary bibliographic entry see Field 5B.
W75-06417

A COMPILATION OF AUSTRALIAN WATER QUALITY CRITERIA,
Caulfield Inst. of Tech., (Australia).
For primary bibliographic entry see Field 5G.
W75-06418

EFFECTS OF SELECTED HERBICIDES ON BACTERIAL POPULATIONS IN FRESH AND TREATED WATER,
Clemson Univ., S.C. Dept. of Botany.
N. D. Camper, and J. M. Shively.
Available from the National Technical Information, Service, Springfield, Va 22161 as PB-240 972, $3.25 in paper copy, $2.25 in microfiche. South Carolina Water Resources Research Institute , Clemson, Report No. 49, November 1974. 10 p, 1 fig, 3 tab, 4 ref. S-047-SC.

Descriptors: *Herbicides, Degradation(Decomposition), Microorganisms, Water pollution effects, Eutrophication, Monitoring, *Bacteria, Lakes, Ponds, Diquat.
Identifiers: Diuron, Dichlobenil.

Bacterial populations in untreated and herbicide-treated waters were subjected to three different herbicides. Diuron, dichlobenil, and diquat were added (100 mg/l) to water samples from two fresh water lakes and two herbicide-treated ponds. Total numbers of bacteria were monitored. Bacterial populations in fresh lake water decreased initially after herbicide additions; however, final populations were significantly greater than the controls. Similar observations were recorded for bacteria in dichlobenil- and diuron-treated water. Selective enrichment is implicated by the results of these experiments.
W75-06432

POPULATION DYNAMICS OF HUNTERELLA NODULOSA (CESTOIDEA:CARYOPHYLLIDEA) IN ALBERTA,
Calgary Univ. (Alberta). Dept. of Biology.
For primary bibliographic entry see Field 8I.
W75-06465

THE EFFECTS OF PCB'S AND SELECTED HERBICIDES ON THE BIOLOGY AND GROWTH OF PLATYMONAS SUBCORDIFORMIS AND OTHER ALGAE,
Maine Univ., Orono. Dept. of Botany and Plant Pathology.
R. L. Vadas.

Available from the National Technical Information Service, Springfield, Va 22161 as PB-241 056, $3.75 in paper copy, $2.25 in microfiche. Report 2-74 Environmental Studies Center, University of Maine, Orono, (1974). 35 p, 8 fig, 4 tab, 27 ref. OWRT A-027-ME(1).

Descriptors: *Polychlorinated biphenyls, *Herbicides, Water pollution effects, *Algae, *Growth rates, *Carrying capacity, Inhibition, Organophosphorus pesticides, Chlorinated hydrocarbon pesticides.
Identifiers: *Playtomonas subcordiformis, Aroclor 1254, Organophosphates, Malathion, Algal growth.

Growth rates and carrying capacities for Platymonas subcordiformis were determined using various concentrations of the PCB, Aroclor 1254, and the Organophosphate, Malathion. Growth was slightly and completely inhibited by 100 and 1000 ppb respectively of Aroclor 1254. With Malathion growth inhibition was temporary or complete at 50 ppm or greater. At alkaline pH's the recovery of growth, especially at 50 ppm, took 3 to 5 days. At higher concentrations of Malathion, recovery took longer if occurring at all. The inhibitory effects of Malathion, Aroclor, and chlorinated hydrocarbons are modified by inoculum densities, phase of algal growth at which the substance is added and in the case of the former possibly by the pH of the media.
W75-06518

HEAVY METALS IN CULTIVATED OYSTERS (CRASSOSTREA COMMERCIALIS = SACCOSTREA CUCULLATA) FROM THE ESTUARIES OF NEW SOUTH WALES (AUSTRALIA),
Chief Secretary's Dept. , Sydney (Australia). New South Wales Fisheries Branch.
For primary bibliographic entry see Field 5B.
W75-06552

FUNDAMENTALS OF AQUATIC BIOASSAYS,
Ministry for Conservation, Melbourne (Australia). Westernport Bay Environmental Study.
For primary bibliographic entry see Field 5A.
W75-06554

ECOLOGICAL EFFECTS OF NUCLEAR STEAM ELECTRIC STATION OPERATIONS ON ESTUARINE SYSTEMS.
Maryland Univ., Prince Frederick. Center for Environmental and Estuarine Research.
Available from the NTIS, Springfield, Va 22161 as Rept. No. ORO-4328-3, $10.60 in paper copy, $2.25 in microfiche. Report No. ORO-4382-2, June 1974. 359 p, 100 fig, 61 tab, 72 ref.

Descriptors: *Maryland, *Chesapeake Bay, *Nuclear power plants, *Environmental effects, *Ecosystems, *Estuarine environment, Operations, Investigations, Surveys, Sampling, Pollutant identification, Radioactivity, Thermal pollution, Data collections, Biota, Water quality, Radiochemical analysis, Metals, Aquatic animals, Plankton, Benthic fauna, Sediments.
Identifiers: *Calvert Cliffs Site(Md).

This is the third progress report dealing with studies pertaining to a segment of the estuarine environment located at the western shore zone of the Chesapeake Bay in Calvert County, Maryland. The investigations, which are basically field oriented, began in 1971. The first objective, 'to obtain adequate pre-operational base line environmental and biotic data in order to characterize an estuarine area which is to be used as a nuclear steam electric station site', has remained as the primary objective during this pre-operational phase. Ojbective No. 2 is as follows: 'to determine the effects of a nuclear S.E.S. operation on an estuarine environment and associated biota by appropriate post-operational field studies'. This latter objective is scheduled to be met during the second phase of the work when the nuclear S.E.S. becomes operational. Estimates for start-up of unit No. 1 range from September 1974 to January 1975 which will allow at least three years of continuous sampling before any S.E.S. induced changes occur. (See W75-06622 thru W75-06629). (Houser-ORNL)
W75-06621

ANALYSIS OF CALVERT CLIFFS REFERENCE STATION MEASUREMENTS (TEMPERATURE, SALINITY, AND DISSOLVED OXYGEN),
Martin Marietta Labs., Baltimore, Md.
For primary bibliographic entry see Field 5B.
W75-06622

RADIOCHEMISTRY--GAMMA ANALYSIS: CALVERT CLIFFS SEDIMENT RADIOACTIVITIES BEFORE AND AFTER TROPICAL STORM AGNES,
National Aeronautics and Space Administration, Washington, D.C. Planatology Branch.
For primary bibliographic entry see Field 5B.
W75-06623

PHYTOPLANKTON: CONTINUING STUDIES ON PRIMARY PRODUCTIVITY AND STANDING CROP OF PHYTOPLANKTON AT CALVERT CLIFFS, CHESAPEAKE BAY,
Maryland Univ., Prince Frederick. Center for Environmental and Estuarine Research.
D. A. Flemer, and L. W. Beaven.
In: Report No. ORO-4328-3, p V-1 - V-102, June 1974. 7 fig, 6 tab, 24 ref.

Descriptors: *Maryland, *Monitoring, Environment, Sites, Nuclear power plants, *Phytoplankton, *Aquatic plants, *Chesapeake Bay, Absorption, Carbon radioisotopes, Chlorophyll, Nitrogen, Sampling, Crop production, Standing crops, Analytical techniques, Organic matter, Carbon, Dissolved solids, Cruises, Ships, Grazing.
Identifiers: *Calvert Cliffs Site(Md).

Field data on primary productivity and the standing crop of phytoplankton of Calvert Cliffs from September 1971 to May 1974 are summarized. Three months data are lacking to complete a third annual cycle. A descriptive overview is presented of the material in hand and a statistical analysis is proposed for a later time. Some statistical interpretations are available on the combined sampling and analytical error for several factors. Data presented include: 14C-uptake by phytoplankton, chlorophyll a, particulate carbon (PC), particulate nitrogen (PN), and dissolved organic carbon (DOC). Several experiments were conducted in an effort to determine whether grazing substantially affects the outcome of sample incubation in light and dark bottles using the 14C-uptake procedure. A specific diel study was conducted in November 1973 to determine if grazing was measurable at the level of primary productivity and phytoplanktonic standing crop. (See also W75-06621) (Houser-ORNL)
W75-06624

ZOOPLANKTON: PROGRESS REPORT TO THE U.S. ATOMIC ENERGY COMMISSION ZOOPLANKTON STUDIES AT CALVERT CLIFFS,
Maryland Univ., Prince Frederick. Natural Resources Inst.
D. R. Heinle, and H. S. Millsaps.
In: Report No. ORO-4328-3, p VI-1 - VI-14, June 1974. 6 fig, 1 tab, 8 ref.

Descriptors: *Maryland, *Surveys, Aquatic environment, *Zooplankton, *Copepods, *Chesapeake Bay, *Environmental effects, *Nuclear powerplants, Effluents, Data colleetions, Distribution, Census, Speciation, Fluorescence, Chlorophyll.
Identifiers: *Calvert Cliffs Site(Md).

Patchiness of Zooplankton was determined by sampling a crossed pattern with a plankton pump in Chesapeake Bay near Calvert Cliffs. Relative fluorescence of chlorophyll was measured to correlate changes in fluorescence with changes in zooplankton densities. Coefficients were calculated for each species along each transect based on total counts. Data collected are reported. (See also W75-06621) (Houser-ORNL)
W75-06625

EFFECT OF TROPICAL STORM AGNES ON STANDING CROPS AND AGE STRUCTURE OF ZOOPLANKTON IN MIDDLE CHESAPEAKE BAY,
Maryland Univ., Prince Frederick. Natural Resources Inst.
D. R. Heinle, H. S. Millsaps, and C. V. Millsaps.
In: Report No. ORO-4328-3, p VI-15 - VI-41, June 1974. 12 fig, 7 ref.

Descriptors: *Maryland, *Surveys, Aquatic environment, *Zooplankton, *Chesapeake Bay, *Tropical cyclones, Environmental effects, *Standing crops. Aging(Physical), Durability, Storms, Damages, Data collections, Speciation, Seasonal, Salinity, Copepods.
Identifiers: *Calvert Cliffs(Md), *Tropical storm Agnes.

General magnitude of densities and the age structures of populations of dominant summer species, particularly Acartia tonsa, were not affected by 'Agnes'. Salinities at mid-Bay did not drop below the range tolerated by A. tonsa. Species with requirements for higher salinities, e.g., Olthona brevicornis, disappeared after 'Agnes'. They were detected again in late August or early September but failed to achieve densities recorded in other years. (See also W75-06621) (Houser-ORNL)
W75-06626

MEROPLANKTON,
Maryland Univ., Prince Frederick. Center for Environmental and Estuarine Studies.
L. Lubbers, J. E. Cooper, and J. A. Mihursky.
In: Report No. ORO-4328-3, p VII-1 - VII-24, June 1974. 2 fig, 15 tab, 5 ref.

Descriptors: *Maryland, *Environmental effects, *Surveys, *Census, Sites, *Chesapeake Bay, Aquatic animals, Fish, Larvae, Life cycles, Distribution, Population, Animal population, Aquatic population, Nuclear power plant, Effluents.
Identifiers: *Meroplankton, Eggs, *Calvert Cliffs Site(Md).

Report covers 29 regular sampling dates over a 20 month period which is somewhat longer than the previous report, 22 dates in 13 months. Similar trends in distribution and relative abundance do occur although total numbers of organisms found in this study period are considerably less. Greatest numbers of eggs and larvae appear in the warmer months. During the winter months, however, the highest concentration of larvae are found in the deeper zones, the same zones scheduled as the source of condenser water supply for the Steam Electric Station. The Calvert Cliffs plant is expected to use 2.4 million gallons of water per minute. The volume of water within the study segment is 3.5 x 10(8) cu m. It would take about .7 days for the S.E.S. to pump that volume of water. A table presents the total number of fish eggs and larvae expected in that water mass each month based on averages from the fish eggs and larvae collections between 1971 and 1974. (See also W75-06621) (Houser-ORNL)
W75-06627

BENTHIC ANIMAL-SEDIMENT,
Maryland Univ., Prince Frederick. Center for Environmental and Estuarine Studies.
N. K. Mountford, P. E. Prere, and J. A. Mihursky.
In: Report No. ORO-4328-3, p VIII-1 -VIII-112, June 1964. 64 fig, 31 tab, 20 ref.

Descriptors: *Maryland, *Surveys, Aquatic environment, *Chesapeake Bay, *Water pollution, Sites, Nuclear power plants, Effluents, *Environmental effects, Aquatic animals, Temperature, *Sediments, Salinity, Benthic fauna, Biomass, Hydrography, Depth, Size, Speciation.
Identifiers: *Calvert Cliffs Site(Md).

Data are reported from a benthic animal-sediment study. Some benthic data from other studies are included for comparison as the end of the third year approaches for pre-operative data collection. The major future comparison will be between the present pre-operational and future post-operational data obtained after the Calvert Cliffs Nuclear Steam Electric Station is under operation with both the first and eventually the second unit on line. Information is presented on the (1) Hydrographic data, (2) Benthic infauna data, and (3) Comparison of data by location. (See also W75-06621) (Houser-ORNL)
W75-06628

BENTHIC-HEAVY METALS,
Federal City Coll., Washington, D.C.
H. Phelps.
In: Rept. No. ORO-4328-3, p IX-1 - IX-11, June 1974. 5 fig, 1 tab, 5 ref.

Descriptors: *Maryland, *Surveys, *Heavy metals, *Chesapeake Bay, Water pollution sources, *Nuclear powerplants, Effluents, Copper, Cadmium, Zinc, Lead, Nickel, Sediments, Aquatic life, Sediment load, Absorption, Environmental effect.
Identifiers: *Calvert Cliffs Site(Md.).

The purpose of this study is to determine whether any changes in concentrations of heavy metals, specifically copper, cadmium, zinc, lead, and nickel, will occur in sediments and benthic organisms near the Calvert Cliffs Nuclear Powerplant. A pre- and post-plant operative sampling design is scheduled. Plant operations were tentatively scheduled to start towards the end of 1974. Laboratory work has centered on the metal loading capacity of the sediments which are reported here. The methods and procedures are given for sampling and analysis. (See also W75-06621) (Houser-ORNL)
W75-06629

AMMONIA EXCRETION BY ZOOPLANKTON AND ITS SIGNIFICANCE TO PRIMARY PRODUCTIVITY DURING SUMMER,
Washington Univ., Seattle. Dept. of Oceanography.
M. Jawed.
Mar Biol (Berl) Vol 23, No 2, p 115-120, 1973. Illus.
Identifiers: *Ammonia, Columbia River, Diffusion, Excretion, Jellyfishes, Plankton, Plumes, *Primary productivity, Rivers, Summer, *Zoo plankton, Oregon, Washington.

Excretion rates of ammonia were determined for zooplankton off the coasts of Washington and Oregon. Rates varied from 0.16-0.60 microgram-atoms NH_4^+-N/mg dry weight/day for most planktonic animals and from 0.02-0.06 for jellyfishes. Ammonia concentration in seawater was low in offshore regions. Ammonia released by zooplankton was studied in relation to primary productivity during summer. In the Columbia River plume offshore, excreted ammonia contributed about 90% of the total N requirements of observed production rates. The ammonia-N contribution was 36% in oceanic waters and was relatively unimportant in the inshore region. The significance of eddy diffusivity in offshore waters and upwelling in inshore waters is also discussed.--Copyright 1974, Biological Abstracts, Inc.
W75-06637

FACTORS LIMITING PRIMARY PRODUCTIVITY IN TURBID KANSAS RESERVOIRS,
Kansas Water Resources Research Inst., Manhattan.
W. J. O'Brien.
Available from the National Technical Information Service, Springfield, Va 22161, as PB-241 135, $3.75 in paper copy, $2.25 in microfiche. KWRRI Contribution No 156, January 1975. 34 p, 11 fig, 2 tab, 29 ref, append. OWRT A-052-KAN(1), 14-31-0001-3516.

Descriptors: *Turbidity, *Limiting factors, *Phosphorus, Phytoplankton, Reservoirs, Primary productivity, Thermal stratification, Lakes, Water pollution effects, *Kansas, *Nutrient requirements, *Light penetration, *Mixing.
Identifiers: *Reservoir morphometry.

To learn more about the nature of eastern Kansas lakes, four reservoirs, varying in size from 175 acres to 12,200 acres, were studied over a 2-year period. Measurements taken at each lake included temperature, light intensity, nutrient and oxygen concentration, pH, alkalinity, primary productivity and a nutrient limitation bioassay. Use of the common carbon-14 technique for assaying nutrient limitation revealed the existence of a previously unrecognized lag between the addition of the added limiting nutrient and the response of increased carbon uptake. This technique was carefully documented while a modified laboratory bioassay was employed in the study of nutrient limitation of the lakes. Two distinct types of reservoirs occur in eastern Kansas; smaller lakes thermally stratify during the warmer months while the larger reservoirs only occasionally do so. Those reservoirs which stratify were found to have lower turbidity and lower dissolved nutrients than did the generally unstratified lakes where mixing to the bottom occurs throughout the summer. In phytoplankton growth the turbidity and complete mixing to the bottom were found to be quite critical. The results suggest that phosphorus additions to large reservoirs may not be as critical as in more northern areas. Nutrient additions to either type of lake are likely to be ineffective in promoting increased fish production because increased plant production simply falls to the lower oxygen poor area of these lakes. Recreational value of future reservoirs could be increased with greater emphasis on the size, depth and configuration of the basin.
W75-06642

DECOMPOSITION OF FOUR SPECIES OF LEAF MATERIAL IN THREE REPLICATE STREAMS WITH DIFFERENT NITRATE INPUT,
Oregon State Univ., Corvallis. Dept. of Fisheries and Wildlife.
For primary bibliographic entry see Field 5B.
W75-06649

PHYTOPLANKTON OF THE WESTERN (KURTLI) POND IN 1967-1970 (IN RUSSIAN),
Acad. Sci. Turkm. SSR, Ashkhabad, Inst. Bot.
Sh. I. Kogan, and L. V. Kudimova.
Izv Akad Nauk Turkm SSR Ser Biol Nauk. 3. p 12-20, 1973, Illus. (English summary).
Identifiers: Algae, *Phytoplankton, Ponds, *USSR(Western Kurtli), *Cyanophyta.

Algal species, varieties and forms (238) have been recorded in the phytoplankton (at this USSR locality) in the process of investigations. The increase has been established of the number and importance of blue-green algae during the investigated years.--Copyright 1974, Biological Abstracts, Inc.
W75-06653

EVALUATION OF METHODS FOR DETECTING COLIFORMS AND FECAL STREPTOCOCCI IN CHLORINATED SEWAGE EFFLUENTS,
Illinois State Water Survey, Urbana.
For primary bibliographic entry see Field 5A.
W75-06654

ON THE USE OF INDICATOR COMMUNITIES OF TUBIFICIDAE AND SOME LUMBRICULIDAE IN THE ASSESSMENT OF WATER POLLUTION IN SWEDISH LAKES,
Uppsala Univ. (Sweden). Inst. of Zoology.
G. Milbrink.
Zoon. Vol 1, No 2, p 125-139, 1973, Illus.

Descriptors: *Water pollution, *Water pollution effects, Eutrophication, Lakes, Aquatic life, *Tubificids, Europe.
Identifiers: Chaetae, Lumbriculidae, Tubifex-tubifex, Tubificidae, *Sweden.

Ecological details from all available sources on the subject are summarized for ecologically important aquatic oligochaetes. Tubificidae (22 spp.) and 2 Lumbriculidae recorded from Swedish lakes are treated in order of tolerance to different degrees of eutrophication. The different species are placed in the specific communities in which they are generally found in those lakes. It is the specific composition of tolerant and sensitive species in a community which has an indicator value. The ecological demands of Tubifex tubifex are especially discussed partly because several other tubificids with hair chaetae used to be classified as T. tubifex--and thus some ecological reports must be considered dubious--and partly because the species is generally found in both the most polluted Swedish waters and in the cleanest, which is unique among tubificid species in Sweden.--Copyright 1974, Biological Abstracts, Inc.
W75-06698

PHYTOPLANKTON OF THE LOWER IRTYSH IN JULY, 1968, (IN UKRAINIAN),
Tyumenskii Gosudarstvennyi Meditsinskii Institut (USSR). Dept. of Biology.
Y. I. Yurova.
Ukr Bot Zh. Vol 30, No 3, p 385-386, 1973, English summary.
Identifiers: Algae, Melosira-distans, Melosira-italica-ssp-subarctica, *Phytoplankton, *USSR(Lower Irtysh), *Cyanophyta, Eutrophication.

A description is presented of phytoplankton of the lower Irtysh (USSR) on the basis of processing samples taken in July, 1968. The character of the lower Irtysh phytoplankton is found to be similar to that of the middle reaches. A blue-green algae bloom was observed which was not observed in the middle reaches and the presence of some forms (Melosira italica spp. subarctica M. distans var. alpigena and others) not found in the middle reaches are 2 differences noted. In all, 95 spp. represented were detected.--Copyright 1974, Biological Abstracts, Inc.
W75-06700

COMPARATIVE STUDY OF THE NITROGEN LIFE-CYCLE IN THE PONDS (IN FRENCH),
Station d'Hydrobiologie Continentale, Biarritz (France).
M. Laurent, and J. Badia.
Ann Hydrobiol. Vol 4, No 1, p 77-102, 1973, Illus, English summary.

Descriptors: *Ponds, Ecology, Bacteria, *Nitrogen, *Nitrogen compounds, Mathematical analysis, Muds, Nitrification, Ammonification.
Identifiers: Heterotrophic nitrification.

A comparative study of 2 ponds under very different ecological conditions was carried out: physico-chemical measures, counting of bacteria in mud and in water during an annual cycle; N and nitrogenous compounds were particularly studied. The interpretation of results in worked out by classical graphic analysis and of mathematical analysis (factor analysis and principal component analysis,

factor analysis of correspondances and harmonic analysis). The opposition between the temperature and the number of ammonifying germs on one hand and the ammoniacal N content on the other hand is pointed out. The existence of heterotrophic nitrification in muds is suggested. The mathematical analysis allows a much finer interpretation of data than the classical analysis, for showing the opposition between ammonifying germs and ammoniacal nitrogen as well as for heterotrophic nitrification; it seems necessary for studying seasonal variations of ecological factors in natural environments.--Copyright 1974, Biological Abstracts, Inc.
W75-06702

DIURNAL VARIATION IN SAGAR LAKE, SAGAR (INDIA): I. STUDIES IN THE DEEP WATER AREA,
Saugar Univ., Sagar (India). Dept. of Botany.
S. B. Saksena, and A. D. Adoni.
Hydrobiologia. Vol 43, No 3/4, p 535-543, 1973, Illus.

Descriptors: *Lakes, Asia, Freshwater, Plankton, *Chemical properties, Chlorides, Carbonates, Oxygen, Crustaceans, Rotifers, Microorganisms, Diurnal.
Identifiers: *India(Sagar Lake), Microcystis, Trachelomonas.

A diurnal study of an inland freshwater lake was made with respect to physical and chemical properties and of the plankton. Chlorides have followed the total carbonates while dissolved O2 and pH have shown no relationship. Microcystis has followed no definite pattern of diurnal movement. All crustaceans, some of the rotifers and Trachelomonas perform considerable diurnal movement in the course of a 24 h period.--Copyright 1974, Biological Abstracts, Inc.
W75-06705

PHYTOPLANKTON IN THE OLIGOHALINE LAKE, SELSO: PRIMARY PRODUCTION AND STANDING CROP,
Copenhagen Univ. (Denmark). Institut for Thallophyta.
K. Woldike.
Ophelia. Vol 12, No 1/2, p 27-44, 1973, Illus.

Descriptors: *Phytoplankton, *Lakes, Europe, Nutrients, Aquatic algae, Growth rates, Environmental effects.
Identifiers: Chlorophyll, Crop, *Denmark, Haline, Lake, Nitrate, Oligo, pH, Phosphate, Phyto, Plankton, Primary, Production, Salinity, Selso, Silicon, Standing.

The variations in the phytoplankton were measured during 1 yr in the oligohaline Danish lake, Selso. Measurements were made of the variations in volume of total phytoplankton and in volumes of the different algal groups. The amount of chlorophyll-a was measured, and the primary production determined, as the maximum rate of gross production. Among the more important environmental factors measurements were made of temperature, transparency, conductivity, salinity, pH, alkalinity, O2 content and the nutrients nitrate, phosphate and silicon. The relations between the variations in the photoplankton volume and the variations in pH, alkalinity and the content of nutrients are discussed. A comparison is made with other, earlier investigated Danish inshore waters.--Copyright 1974, Biological Abstracts, Inc.
W75-06708

LIFE IN A LAKE RESERVOIR: FEWER OPTIONS, DECREASED PRODUCTION,
Institute of Freshwater Research Drottningholm (Sweden).
T. Lindstrom.
Ambio. Vol 2, No 5, p 145-153, 1973, Illus.

Identifiers: Aquatic animals, *Ecosystem, Fish, Fishing, Lakes, Options, Plankton, *Production, Reservoirs, Zooplankton, *Sweden.

The joint efforts of several research units were directed towards 4 levels in the ecosystems of lake reservoirs: The physicochemical environment, the plants, the bottom animals and zooplankton and the fish. Information from some recent Swedish studies is compiled. The overall effect of the transformations is a decrease in the production capacity and a simplification of the ecosystems of lake reservoirs. Fishing can be maintained, if based mainly on the production in the pelagic block of the ecosystem.--Copyright 1974, Biological Abstracts, Inc.
W75-06712

A COMPARISON OF FRESH-WATER PROTOZOAN COMMUNITIES IN GEOGRAPHICALLY PROXIMATE BUT CHEMICALLY DISSIMILAR BODIES OF WATER,
Virginia Polytechnic Inst. and State Univ., Blacksburg. Dept. of Biology.
For primary bibliographic entry see Field 2H.
W75-06715

EFFECT OF WATER POLLUTION ON ICHTHYOFAUNA: PART I. TOXICITY OF METALS AND THEIR SALTS AND OF INORGANIC SUSPENSIONS (IN POLISH),
Wyzsza Szkola Rolnicza, Krakow (Poland).
P. Epler.
Postepy Nauk Roln. Vol 18, No 3, p 71-94, 1971, Illus.

Descriptors: Water pollution, Pollutants, Oxygen, Fish, Rainbow trout, *Water pollution effects, Chemical analysis, Metals, Salts, Inorganic compounds, Bioindicators, *Toxicity, *Metals.

Water pollutants alter the physical, chemical and sanitary properties of H2O, change the quantity and quality of organisms on which fish live and have an immediate toxic effect on fish. The concentration of pollutants is relevant. Toxicity is less under adequate O2 levels. Detailed laboratory investigations covered the most important chemical elements, with rainbow trout used as the test organism.--Copyright 1974, Biological Abstracts, Inc.
W75-06719

ENVIRONMENTAL CONTAMINANTS INVENTORY STUDY NO. 2 - THE PRODUCTION, USE AND DISTRIBUTION OF CADMIUM IN CANADA,
Canada Centre for Inland Waters, Burlington (Ontario).
For primary bibliographic entry see Field 5B.
W75-06742

PHYTOPLANKTON OF THE NATRON-CONTAINING WATERS OF KANEM (CHAD): V. THE MESOHALINE LAKES (IN FRENCH),
Office de la Recherche Scientifique et Technique Outre-Mer, Fort-Lamy (Chad).
A. Iltis.
Cah O R S T O M (Off Rech Sci Tech Outre-Mer) Ser Hydrobiol. Vol 5, No 1, p 73-84, 1971, Illus.

Descriptors: *Phytoplankton, *Lakes, *Seasonal, Analysis, Africa, Cyanophyta, Diatoms.
Identifiers: *Chad(Kanem), Diatomophyceae, *Mesohaline Lakes, *Natron, Oscillatoria-platensis-var-minor.

The seasonal variation of phytoplankton was studied for 15 mo. in 2 natroned mesohaline lakes Equatorial Africa. Cyanophyceae and Diatomophyceae are dominant in the phytoplankton having the same characteristics as the polyhaline lakes. Oscillatoria platensis var. minor Rich is the characteristic and generally the most abundant species of these media.--Copyright 1973, Biological Abstracts, Inc.
W75-06778

OSMOREGULATORY RESPNSES TO DDT AND VARYING SALINITIES IN SALMO GAIRDNERI - I. GILL NA-K-ATPASE,
Idaho State Univ., Pocatello. Dept. of Biology.
T. P. Leadem, R. D. Campbell, and D. W. Johnson.
Comparative Biochemistry and Physiology, Vol 49A, No. 1, p 197-205, September 1, 1974. 4 fig, 29 ref.

Descriptors: *Laboratory tests, *DDT, *Rainbow trout, Freshwater, Sea water, Enzymes, Salt tolerance, *Water pollution effects.
Identifiers: *Osmoregulatory response.

DDT inhibited activity of Na-K-ATPase and Mg-ATPase in gills of rainbow trout adapted to freshwater, one-third sea water, and sea water. A negative correlation was found between gill Na-K-ATPase and serum sodium in treated fish in sea water. Enzyme activity was inhibited in fresh water fish but no osmoregulatory impairment was found, indicating a minor or non-existent role for gill Na-K-ATPase in fresh water osmoregulation. Enzyme activity was inhibited in trout acclimated to sea water. (Sandoski-FIRL)
W75-06829

HYDROBACTERIOLOGICAL INVESTIGATIONS IN LAKE CONSTANCE: III. PROGRESSIVE GROWTH OF PLANKTON-DEPENDENT PRODUCTION OF BACTERIA AS AN INDICATION OF EUTROPHICATION, (IN GERMAN),
Staatliches Institut fuer Seenforschung und Seenbewirtschaftung, Langenargen (West Germany).
J. Deufel.
Int Rev Gesamten Hydrobiol, Vol 57, No 1, p 153-156, 1972. English summary.

Descriptors: *Lakes, *Eutrophication, *Bacteria, Plankton, Europe, Water pollution effects, Bioindicators, Pollutant identification.
Identifiers: *Lake Constance(West Germany).

Within the last 10 yr the number of bacteria in the pelagic region of Lake Constance (Bodensee)(West Germany), counted during the circulation period, increased almost 10 fold. This growth agrees completely with other biological and chemical results, and indicates a progressive eutrophication of the lake.--Copyright 1973, Biological Abstracts, Inc.
W75-06839

A PRELIMINARY PHYTOPLANKTON SURVEY OF TWELVE ADIRONDACK LAKES,
New York State Dept. of Environmental Conservation, Delmar. Wildlife Research Lab.
N. B. Reynolds, and L. M. Mercer.
NY Fish Game J, Vol 21, No 1, p 58-66, 1974. Illus.
Identifiers: *Adirondack lakes, *Eutrophication, Hurricane Agnes, *Lakes, *Phytoplankton, Surveys, *New York, Water pollution effects.

This investigation was conducted to evaluate the relationships between composition and abundance of phytoplankton in 12 lakes in the Adirondack region of New York (USA). Possible differences in eutrophication are also considered. Five divisions and 60 taxa were cataloged. All the lakes were found to be oligotrophic and dystrophic althought there was some indication of pollution. Possible effects of Hurricane Agnes in 1972 are discussed.--Copyright 1974, Biological Abstracts, Inc.
W75-06844

5D. Waste Treatment Processes

RECYCLING OF SEWAGE EFFLUENT BY IRRIGATION: A FIELD STUDY ON OAHU,

soils absolute amount and differences noted in renovating capacity are a function of their physical and chemical properties. The Rayne rapidly declined in its renovating capacity in the latter stages of the study. This could have been prevented by liming treatments. (Sink-Penn State)
W75-06365

NEW CONCEPTS IN SOIL SURVEY INTERPRETATIONS FOR ON-SITE DISPOSAL OF SEPTIC TANK EFFLUENT,
Wisconsin Univ., Madison. Dept. of Soil Science.
J. Bouma.
Soil Science Society of America Proceedings, Vol 38, No 6, p 941-946, November-December 1974. 2 fig, 22 ref. EPA Grant 802874-01-0.

Descriptors: *Septic tanks, *Sewage disposal, *Soil disposal fields, *Soil surveys, *Land use, Soil types, Water pollution sources, Waste water disposal, Waste disposal, Waste treatment, Sewage treatment, Soil investigations, Permeability, Zoning, Land development, Land classification, Land management, Land resources, On-site tests, Planning.
Identifiers: Purification.

Soil survey interpretations for on-site disposal of septic tank effluent were made in terms of soil limitations by using existing technology. New technology, based on a detailed analysis of liquid movement and associated purification, can be used to overcome severe and very severe limitations and to reduce slight and moderate limitations. Experimental data obtained and technology derived from single experimental innovative disposal systems are relevant only if extrapolations can be made to other soils shown to be identical. Three procedures of extrapolation were discussed: (1) detailed on-site spot checks of key properties, (2) on-site taxonomic soil classifications, and (3) taxonomic soil classifications at the experimental site followed by extrapolation to mapping units named after the same soil series. Largely unknown variability of key properties for liquid waste disposal in soil series or in mapping units may reduce the practical value of the latter two procedures but potential advantages are (1) reductions of expensive on-site inspections and (2) use of soil maps for showing potential changes in land-use patterns following introduction of innovative technology. This approach emphasizes soil potential rather than soil limitations. (Sanderson-ISWS)
W75-06402

AEROBIC DIGESTION OF EXTRACELLULAR MICROBIAL POLYSACCARIDES,
Oklahoma State Univ., Stillwater. Bioenvironmental Engineering Labs.
A. W. Obayashi, and A. F. Gaudy.
Research Report, 1972. 32 p, 5 fig, 2 tab, 30 ref. (Presented at 27th Industrial Waste Conference, Purdue University, May 2-4, 1972). OWRT A-035-OKLA(1).

Descriptors: *Oxidation, *Microorganisms, *Sludge, *Waste water treatment, Aerobic treatment, Aeration, Bacteria, Organic matter, *Aeration.
Identifiers: Total oxidation, Extended aeration, Polysaccharides, Slime layer.

The extended aeration, or total oxidation, sludge process is based on the premise that the increase in biological solids resulting from metabolism of the incoming waste is balanced by the decrease in biological solids due to their aerobic digestion. The question about this method is whether all the organic constituents of the cell, such as those in the cytoplasm, the walls and membrane and the capsular slime layer, can be metabolized and converted to carbon dioxide. The slime layer is usually complex heteropolysaccharides. This investigation was made to determine whether extracellular heteropolysaccharides of microorganisms can be used as sources of organic carbon for the growth of other microorganisms. The results show that extracellular polysaccharide cannot be considered biologically inert material and that it can metabolized. These results support the idea of total oxidation of biological solids. (Orr-FIRL)
W75-06405

EFFLUENT FOR IRRIGATION - A NEED FOR CAUTION,
Illinois State Water Survey, Urbana.
W. H. Walker.
Ground Water, Vol 13, No 1, p 11-16, January-February 1975. 24 ref.

Descriptors: *Water pollution, *Water pollution control, *Soil contamination, *Sludge disposal, *Sewage effluents, Liquid wastes, Waste water disposal, Municipal wastes, Legal aspects, Economics, Irrigation.

Most municipal waste treatment systems receive, treat, and eventually discard to some segment of the environment storm runoff and liquid wastes from all industrial, commercial, and domestic areas and establishments in the community. Existing pollution protection laws prohibit surface-water dilution of these effluents and sludges. Drying, burning, or distilling them is very costly, causes air pollution, and produces potentially hazardous chemical residues which still must be diposed of in some nonpolluting fashion. There are no 'technologically feasible, economically reasonable' alternative methods of effectively treating these wastes to an acceptable quality level for discharge to streams. For these reasons, land disposal of sewage effluent and sludges now is being widely promoted and employed as the best available method of treatment. Most operating facilities for land disposal of effluents are not monitored adequately to provide required data to quantitatively evaluate the total buildup and possible subsequent release of toxic chemicals in contiguous soil, plant, and water environments. Considering the potential danger to public health which may result if widespread use of this particular waste disposal practice is employed, it is imperative that all such permitted sites be monitored and evaluated in detail for all possible adverse effeets, and the results of these findings then considered in the design and operation of future installations. Concurrent with this work, research must be expedited and greatly expanded to develop effective alternative treatment methods to employ where land disposal of effluent probes to be impracticable. (Gibb-ISWS)
W75-06451

ECOLOGICAL AND PHYSIOLOGICAL IMPLICATIONS OF GREENBELT IRRIGATION, PROGRESS REPORT OF THE MALONEY CANYON PROJECT-1974,
California Univ., Riverside. Dept. of Plant Sciences.
V. B. Younger, and T. E. Williams.
Available from the National Technical Information Service, Springfield, Va 22161, as PB-241 101, $5.25 in paper copy, $2.25 in microfiche. Progress Report, California Water Resources Center, Contribution 148, 1974, (California Water Resources Center Project UCAL-WRC-W-374). 114 p, 11 fig, 20 tab, 40 ref. OWRT B-161-CAL(1).

Descriptors: *Waste water teatment, Irrigation, Environmental effects, *Irrigation effects, *Vegetation effects, Water pollution effects, *Water reuse, Water quality, Reclaimed water, *California.
Identifiers: *Maloney Canyon(Calif), *Greenbelt irrigation.

The multipurpose nature of a waste water irrigated greenbelt such as Maloney Canyon dictates the establishment of extensive research into the responses of components of plant, soil, and water systems to the application of effluent irrigation.

The feasibility of such a greenbelt in terms of beneficial responses versus potential environmental degradation was investigated. The clarification of both factors in all studies is essential for the design to be effective. Research at Maloney Canyon over the past 5 years has centered along two basic lines. The first is aimed primarily at the effects which effluent irrigation has upon native chaparral and introduced vegetation types as related to the selection of suitable species or entire vegetation types for establishment in a fire suppressing greenbelt. The second is concerned with examination of the components of the applied waste water, as both nutrients and potential pollutants, in their effects upon plant, soil, water systems, and the response of those systems in a 'living filter' renovation process. (Synder-California, Davis)
W75-06461

RECLAMATION OF ENERGY FROM ORGANIC WASTES,
Illinois Univ., Urbana. Dept. of Civil Engineering.
J. T. Pfeffer.
Available from the National Technical Information Service, Springfield, Va 22161 as PB-231 176, $5.75 in paper copy, $2.25 in microfiche. Environmental Protection Agency, Cincinnati, Ohio, EPA-670/2-74-016, March 1974. 128 p, 27 fig, 34 tab, 48 ref, 5 append. EPA Grant R-800766.

Descriptors: *Waste disposal, *Fermentation, *Solid wastes, *Gases, *Organic wastes, Methane, Natural gas, Fuels, Energy, Wastes, Cellulose, *Anaerobic digestion, Methodology, Cost analysis, *Waste water treatment, Nutrient requirements, Economics.
Identifiers: *Resource recovery, Substrates.

The anaerobic fermentation process was applied to the production of methane from the organic fraction of urban refuse. Shredded domestic refuse from which the inorganic fraction was separated was used as a substrate. Raw sewage sludge was added to the substrate in proportion to the rate at which it is produced by a population producing a given quantity of refuse. The quantity and quality of gas produced, the rate of gas production, the solids reduction, nutritional requirements, and operating problems were evaluated in a laboratory system operating at temperatures ranging from 35 to 60C. The results of the laboratory study together with published data on both capital and operating costs of refuse shredding, refuse separation, reactor volume, reactor mixing, reactor heating, and residue dewatering were used to analyze the economics of the process. (Sims-ISWS)
W75-06471

RECLAMATION OF ACID RINSE WATER,
General Electric Co, Lynn, Mass. Direct Energy Conversion Programs.
R. M. Dempsey, and A. B. LaConti.
Available from the National Technical Information Service, Springfield, Va 22161 as AD-784 445, $3.75 in paper copy, $2.25 in microfiche. (1974). 43 p, 12 fig, 15 tab, 4 ref. Army Contract DAAK02-73-C-0407.

Descriptors: *Membranes, *Reverse osmosis, *Acids, *Waste water treatment, Chemical wastes, Osmosis, Films, Ion exchange, Chemistry, Laboratory tests, Membrane processes, Separation techniques, Waste treatment, Semipermeable membranes.

A possible limitation of most commercial reverse osmosis membranes is marginal stability during continuous operation in strong acid media (pH less than or equal to 1.5). A modified membrane designated sulfonated P30 that is readily solvent cast and exhibits good film forming characteristics was developed and appears promising for use as a reverse osmosis membrane in strong acid media. It was successfully used for fuel cell applications in contact with strong acid electrolytes for thousands of hours. During preliminary feasibility tests with this membrane, it was demonstrated that a 0.5 mil (0.0005 in.) knife-cast membrane exhibited approximately 90% rejection when evaluated for reverse osmosis renovation of a 3000 ppm acid feed simulating rinse water from a military nitrocellulose plant. A program was conducted to develop production techniques for fabricating composite films and spiral wound modules of the membrane system for reverse osmosis application of recovering acid rinse water. Three trial modules were developed and tested, and twelve production type spiral modules were fabricated, tested, and delivered. (Sims-ISWS)
W75-06477

RECOMMISSIONING OF SEA WATER DEMINERALIZER, SERIAL NO. 204, U.S. COAST GUARD STATION, OCRACOKE, NORTH CAROLINA.
Ionics, Inc., Cambridge, Mass.
For primary bibliographic entry see Field 3A.
W75-06479

LAND TREATMENT OF MENHADEN WASTE WATER BY OVERLAND FLOW,
Louisiana State Univ., Baton Rouge. Dept. of Marine Science.
M. Meo.
Available from the National Technical Information Service, Springfield, Va 22161 as PB-241 062, $5.25, in paper copy, $2.25 in microfiche. Ms Thesis, December 1974. 98 p, 9 fig, 20 tab, 39 ref, 2 append. OWRT A-033-LA(2). NOAA Contract 04-3-158-19.

Descriptors: *Waste water treatment, *Overland flow, *Nutrient removal, Waste treatment, Industrial wastes, Organic wastes, Water chemistry, Marine fish, Fish handling facilities, Spoil banks, Spraying, Vegetation effects, Groundwater, Infiltration, Pollutants, Path of pollutants.
Identifiers: Gulf menhaden, Stickwater, Fish meal, Fish oil.

From April through August 1974, menhaden processing wastewater from an industrial plant near Dulac, Louisiana, was partially reclaimed with the use of land treatment by overland flow. The waste was pumped from a primary treatment pond after screening, and was spray-discharged at a rate of 5.08 cm per week onto a naturally vegetated spoil bank of clay soil material (6% slope, 30 m long). The effluent flowed unevenly through the plant cover and litter layer. The effluent, with total organic carbon, nitrogen, and phosphorus concentrations of 800, 600, and 50 mg/l, respectively, was purified by the action of the soil-plant system, reducing the waste nutrient load an average of 58% for carbon, 51% for nitrogen, and 53% for phosphorus. Roseau cane, the dominant plant on the slope, increased in live standing crop by 55%, in nitrogen by 47%, and in phosphorus by 13%. Levels of groundwater nitrogen just exceeded 10 mg/l at a depth of 30 cm after five months. Waste total coliform MPN was diminshed by 66% over the slope. (Sims-ISWS)
W75-06526

ANALYSIS OF MULTIPLE OBJECTIVES IN WATER QUALITY,
Case Western Reserve Univ., Cleveland, Ohio. Systems Engineering Div.
Y. Y. Haimes, and W. A. Hall.
Journal of the Hydraulics Division, American Society of Civil Engineers, Vol 101, HY4, Proceedings paper No 11234, p 387-400, April 1975. 1 fig, 19 ref.

Descriptors: *Water quality, *Planning, *Management, *Thermal pollution, Hydraulics, Methodology, Biochemical oxygen demand, Dissolved oxygen, Waste water treatment, Optimization, Constraints, Algae, Temperature, Mathematical models, Systems analysis, Equations, Streams, Treatment facilities.
Identifiers: Multiple objectives, *Surrogate Worth Tradeoff method, Cost minimization, Streeter-Phelps equation, Multilevel optimization, Problem decomposition, Lagrange multipliers.

Water quality planning is characterized by multiple and often noncommensurable goals and objectives. Needed are mathematical models which are susceptible to multiple objective functions in their noncommensurable forms and units. Herein, a number of water quality objectives and goals, classified as primary and secondary objectives, are introduced. The concepts of noninferior (Parento optimum) solution, indifference band, and preferred solution are defined. A general multiobjective model for water quality planning and management is developed. Specific multiple objectives and constraints associated with biological oxygen demand, dissolved oxygen, thermal pollution, and algae bloom are introduced and examined. An example wastewater treatment problem is presented werein three noncommensurable objectives are considered: minimizing the total treatment cost, minimizing changes in temperature, and minimizing the maximum algae concentration for all reaches. The Surrogate Worth Tradeoff (SWT) method is reviewed and its application to the water quality model is analyzed. In particular, basics in the derivation of the trade-off functions and the surrogate worth functions are given. The SWT method permits accurate treatment of noncommensurate objectives in multiple objective systems. The method recognizes that optimization theory is usually more concerned with the relative value of additional increments of the various goals than with their absolute values. (Bell-Cornell)
W75-06559

SYSTEM FOR REGULATION OF COMBINED SEWAGE FLOWS,
Municipality of Metropolitan Seattle, Wash.
C. V. Gibbs, S. M. Alexander, and C. P. Leiser.
Journal of the Sanitary Engineering Division, American Society of Civil Engineer, Vol 98, No SA6, p 951-972, December 1972. 9 fig, 3 tab, 6 ref.

Descriptors: *Combined sewers, Flow, *Regulation, Computers, Hydrology, *Runoff, Overflow, *Control systems, Pumping stations, Flood routing, Water quality, Telemetry, Operations, Storage, Mathematical models, *Washington.
Identifiers: *Automatic control, Rule curve technique, Control equipment, Real-time computations, *Seattle(Wash).

The Municipality of Metropolitan Seattle has installed a computer directed control system which provides centralized control of regulator and pumping stations on trunk and interceptor sewers. The system will represent a procedure for regulation of combined sewage flows through use of available storage in trunk and interceptor sewer to reduce or eliminate overflows. The equipment includes the computer based central facility and automatic controls for 36 remote pumping and regulator stations. A procedure has been developed for automatic control using the rule curve technique. The central facilitiy includes an operator oriented console and facilities for background data processing. Communication with remote stations is over leased telephone lines. The equipment at each remote station is designed for failsafe operation to return to local control in an orderly manner in the event of failure of the central station equipment or communication lines. (Bell-Cornell)
W75-06563

SEA WATER DESALINATION BY REVERSE OSMOSIS, RECENT EXPERIENCE,
Societe Generale d'Epuration et d'Assainissement Degremont, Suresnes (France).
For primary bibliographic entry see Field 3A.
W75-06567

CONSTRUCTION AND INITIAL OPERATION OF THE VTE/MSF MODULE,
Office of Saline Water, Washington, D.C.
For primary bibliographic entry see Field 3A.
W75-06568

WATER REGULATIONS--AREAWIDE WASTE TREATMENT MANAGEMENT PLANNING AREAS AND RESPONSIBLE PLANNING AGENCIES.
For primary bibliographic entry see Field 5G.
W75-06599

WATER REUSE, A BIBLIOGRAPHY, VOLUME 3,
Office of Water Research and Technology, Washington, D.C.
Available from the National Technical Information Service, Springfield, Va 22161, as PB-241 171, $11.25 in paper copy, $2.25 in microfiche. Water Resources Scientific Information Center Report OWRT/WRSIC 75-204-VOL 3, March 1975, 444 p.

Descriptors: Artificial recharge, Desalination, Filtration, Groundwater, Industrial wastes, Ion exchange, Irrigation water, Municipal wastes, Pollution abatement, Potable water, Recirculated water, *Reclaimed water, Return flow, Reverse osmosis, *Sewage treatment, *Tertiary treatment, Waste disposal, *Waste water treatment, Water conservation, Water purification, Water quality, *Water treatment, *Bibliographies.

This report, containing 291 abstracts, is another in a series of planned bibliographies in water resources to be produced from the information base comprising SELECTED WATER RESOURCES ABSTRACTS (SWRA). At the time of search for this bibliography, the data base had 80,488 abstracts covering SWRA through January 15, 1975 (Volume 8, Number 2). Author and subject indexes are included. (See also W75-06639, W73-11701 and W75-11702)
W75-06638

WATER REUSE, A BIBLIOGRAPHY, VOLUME 4,
Office of Water Research and Technology, Washington, D.C.
Available from the National Technical Information Service, Springfield, Va 22161, as PB-241 172, $11.25 in paper copy, $2.25 in microfiche. Water Resources Sceintific Information Center Report OWRT/WRSIC 75-204-Vol. 4, March 1975, 448 p.

Descriptors: Aritificial recharge, Desalination, Filtration, Groundwater, Industrial wastes, Ion exchange, Irrigation water, Municipal wastes, Pollution abatement, Potable water, Recirculated water, *Reclaimed water, Return flow, Reverse osmosis, *Sewage treatment, *Tertiary treatment, Waste disposal, *Waste water treatment, Water conservation, Water purification, Water quality, *Water treatment, *Bibliographies.

This report, containing 297 abstracts, is another in a series of planned bibliographies in water resources to be produced from the information base conprising SELECTED WATER RESOURCES ABSTRACTS (SWRA). At the time of search for this bibliography, the data base had 80,488 abstracts covering SWRA through January 15, 1975 (Volume 8, Number 2). Author and subject indexes are included. (See also W75-06638, W73-11701 and W73-11702.)
W75-06639

PRACTICAL APPLICATIONS FOR REUSE OR WASTEWATER,
Los Angeles County Sanitation District, Calif.
For primary bibliographic entry see Field 3C.
W75-06659

AUTOMATION OF SCUM SKIMMERS, CALUMET TREATMENT WORKS, PRELIMINARY SETTLING TANKS.
Greeley and Hansen, Chicago, Ill.
The Metropolitan Sanitary District of Greater Chicago, Chicago, Illinois, September 1971. 9 p, 9 fig, 2 tab.

Descriptors: *Automation, *Scum, *Settling basins, *Sewage treatment, *Treatment facilities, *Primary treatment, Secondary treatment, Sludge disposal, Illinois, Waste water treatment.
Identifiers: Scum removal, Scum skimming, Preliminary settling tanks, Metropolitan Sanitary District of Greater Chicago, Chicago(Illinois).

The Calumet Treatment Works provides facilities for primary and secondary treatment and sludge disposal. The primary portion of the treatment plant consists of a pumping station, grit chambers and 20 preliminary settling tanks. The existing scum removal and handling facilities are limited to the preliminary settling tanks and include manually operated scum tipping troughs on each of the preliminary settling tanks. A mixture of scum and water discharged in to the scum troughs flows by gravity to a scum pump that pumps the mixture to the scum concentration tank. Three methods of automating the preliminary settling tank scum skimming operation were investigated. These were electric motor operation, pneumatic cylinder operation and replacement of the tipping troughs by chain and flight-type scum cross collectors to beach scum into a scum box. It was concluded that any method of automation would require the rehabilitation of the troughs for proper operation. It is recommended that the existing troughs and bearings and bearing supports be rehabilitated and that an arrangement using pneumatic cylinders to be provided to operate the tipping troughs. The cost was estimated at $117,000. (Poertner)
W75-06665

SCUM REMOVAL FACILITIES, NORTH SIDE TREATMENT WORKS, FINAL SETTLING TANKS.
Greeley and Hansen, Chicago, Ill.
The Metropolitan Sanitary District of Greater Chicago, Chicago, Illinois, May 1971. 16 p, 10 fig, 2 tab.

Descriptors: *Treatment facilities, *Scum, *Sewage treatment, *Primary treatment, *Secondary treatment, *Settling basins, Pumping stations, Illinois, Waste water treatment.
Identifiers: Scum removal, Final settling tanks, Scum concentration tanks, Metropolitan Sanitary District of Greater Chicago, Chicago(Illinois).

The North Side Treatment Works provides facilities for primary and secondary sewage treatment. The secondary portion of the treatment plant comprises Batteries A, B, C and D. Batteries A, B and C each comprise 12 aeration tanks and 14 final settling tanks. Battery D comprises 6 aeration tanks and final settling tanks. Studies of the final settling tanks have been made to outline alternative scum removal systems. Three methods of collecting scum that floats to the surface of the square final settling tanks in Batteries A, B and C have been investigated. These methods all involve scum tipping pipes and scum baffles. Each circular final settling tank in Batteries A, B, C and D would be provided with scum collecting facilities comprising scum skimming blades, scum baffles, scum troughs and scum withdrawal piping. The scum from the final settling tanks would be conveyed to the proposed scum concentration facilities. It is recommended that studies be made to determine the effect of the increased overflow rate on effluent quality of the final settling tanks. Torque flow type pumps to pump the scum and water directly to the scum concentration tanks are recommended for the square final settling tanks for Batteries A, B and C. (Poertner)
W75-06666

SCUM REMOVAL FACILITIES, WEST-SOUTHWEST TREATMENT WORKS, BATTERIES A, B, AND C.
Greeley and Hansen, Chicago, Ill.
The Metropolitan Sanitary District of Chicago, Chicago, Illinois, July 1971. 14 p, 10 fig, 2 tab, 1 append.

Descriptors: *Scum, *Sewage treatment, *Treatment facilities, *Primary treatment, *Secondary treatment, Pumping stations, Piping systems(Mechanical), Settling basins, Illinois, Waste water treatment.
Identifiers: Scum removal, Final settling tanks, Scum concentration tanks, Scum piping, Metropolitan Sanitary District of Greater Chicago, Chicago(Illinois).

The West-Southwest Treatment Works operated by the Metropolitan Sanitary District of Greater Chicago provides facilities for primary and secondary treatment and sludge disposal. The secondary portion of the plant consists of batteries A, B and C which are each comprised of eight aeration tanks and 24 final settling tanks. The existing scum removal and handling facilities are limited to the preliminary tanks and include scum skimming mechanisms on each of the preliminary tanks that deliver a mixture of scum and water to collector troughs. In order to improve the overall plant capture of scum, a scum removal system will be installed in the final settling tanks. Each final tank will be arranged with scum collecting facilities comprising scum skimming blades, scum baffles, scum troughs and scum withdrawal piping. Studies of alternative arrangements of pumping units, pumping stations, and scum piping were made. The pumping unit types considered were centrifugal torque flow, centrifugal rotary piston, plunger, pneumatic ejector and progressing cavity pumps. Two types of pumping stations were considered: on-site construction and pre-fabricated package units. Various types of piping materials for scum piping were investigated. Two alternative locations for discharging the scum collected in the final tanks were studied. Cost estimates for all alternatives are given and recommendations are given for modifications and new construction. (Poertner)
W75-06667

SCUM REMOVAL FACILITIES, NORTH SIDE TREATMENT WORKS, PRELIMINARY SETTLING TANKS.
Greeley and Hansen, Chicago, Ill.
The Metropolitan Sanitary District of Greater Chicago, Chicago, Illinois, July 1971. 13 p, 7 fig, 3 tab.

Descriptors: *Scum, *Treatment facilities, *Sewage treatment, *Settling basins, *Primary treatment, Secondary treatment, Pumping stations, Illinois, Waste water treatment.
Identifiers: Scum removal, Preliminary settling tanks, Scum concentration tanks, Metropolitan Sanitary District of Greater Chicago, Chicago(Illinois).

The North Side Treatment Works provides facilities for primary and secondary sewage treatment. The primary portion of the treatment plant consists of a pumping station, grit chambers and 8 preliminary settling tanks. Studies of the preliminary settling tanks have been made to outline alternative scum removal systems. Four methods of collecting scum that floats to the surface of the preliminary settling tanks have been investigated. Two methods of conveying the scum that floats to the surface of the preliminary settling tanks to the effluent side of the tank where scum removal facilities would be located were considered. In order to further dewater the scum from the preliminary settling tanks, scum concentration tanks will be provided. It was recommended that the preliminary tanks be provided with scum colleeting facilities consisting of a chain and flight type scum cross collector, scum beach, scum box, and scum baffle. Two onsite constructed pumping

stations, a 6-inch scum line to transfer the scum to the concentration tanks, and two scum concentration tanks were also recommended. (Poertner)
W75-06668

SCUM REMOVAL FACILITIES, CALUMET TREATMENT WORKS, FINAL SETTLING TANKS.
Greeley and Hansen, Chicago, Ill.
The Metropolitan Sanitary District of Greater Chicago, Chicago, Illinois August 1971. 14 p, 6 fig, 1 tab.

Descriptors: *Sewage treatment, *Treatment facilities, *Primary treatment, *Secondary treatment, *Scum, Settling basins, Illinois, Waste water treatment, Sludge treatment.
Identifiers: Scum skimming, Final settling tanks, Metropolitan Sanitary District of Greater Chicago, Calumet Treatment Works.

The Calumet Treatment Works provides facilities for primary and secondary treatment and sludge disposal. The secondary portion of the treatment process consists of Batteries A, B and C. Batteries A and B are comprised of 11 aeration tanks and 8 final settling tanks each. Battery C is comprised of 6 aerations tanks and 8 final settling tanks. The existing scum removal and handling facilities are limited to the preliminary settling tanks. Studies of alternative scum removal systems for the final settling tanks have been made to outline needed additions required to collect scum. Three methods of collecting scum that floats to the surface of the square final settling tanks in Batteries A and B have been investigated. Each circular final settling tank in Battery C would be provided with scum collecting facilities comprising scum skimming blades, scum baffles, scum boxes and scum withdrawal piping. The scum and water collected on the surface of the final settling tanks at Batteries A, B and C would be conveyed to the existing scum concentration tank. Recommendations were also made for the provision of scum-skimming facilities consisting of probing arms, scum troughs, scum baffles, and scum withdrawal piping for the square final settling tanks at Batteries A and B. (Poertner)
W75-06669

RESULTS OF TESTING CLEAN-FLO LAKE CLEANSER IN FLORIDA LAKES,
Florida State Game and Fresh Water Fish Commission, Lake City; and Clean-Flo Labs., Inc., Hopkins, Minn.
L. Trent, and B. McArthur.
Hyacinth Control Journal, Vol 12, p 44-45, May 1974. 2 tab, 3 ref.

Descriptors: *Water treatment, *Nutrient removal, *Phosphates, *Aquatic algae, *Chemical precipitation, *Algal control, Cyanophyta, Lakes, Florida.
Identifiers: Filamentous algae, Lemna minor, Duckweed.

A study was made of efficacy and observable toxicity in Florida lakes of a new product formulation comprising an admixture of soluble calcium, aluminum and sodium cations, and a buffering agent. The intended purpose of the compound is to remove phosphate from natural waters by precipitation, thereby causing a natural decline of aquatic flora. Eight impoundments were treated with quantities ranging from 5 ppm to 20 ppm, and visual results noted. The results of the pilot study indicate the effectivness of Clean-Flo Lake Cleanser (patent pending) in controlling certain aquatic weeds in Florida. No dead fish were detected and, in earlier laboratory studies, fish survived in concentrations up to 1000 ppm with no noticeable deleterious effects. Further studies emphasizing more accurate chemical analysis and more complete algae tests are warranted. More studies dealing with aquatic animals native to Florida waters are also recommended. (Poertner)
W75-06672

PROCESS FOR THE EXTRACTION OF PHENOL FROM WASTE WATERS IN THE FORM OF UREA-FORMALDEHYDE-PHENOL CONDENSATES,
Societa Italiana Resine S.p.A., Milan (Italy). (assignee)
S. Vargiu, S. S. Giovanni, G. Mazzoleni, and S. Pezzoli.
U.S. Patent No. 3,869,387, 5 p, 3 tab, 4 ref; Official Gazette of the United States Patent Office, Vol 932, No 1, p 229, March 4, 1975.

Descriptors: *Separation techniques, *Patents, *Waste water treatment, *Phenols, *Pollutant abatement, Water pollution control, Water quality control, Ureas, Hydrogen ion concentration.
Identifiers: Formaldehyde.

Phenol is extracted from waste waters in the form of urea-formaldehyde-phenol condensates. These synthetic resin products can be used as adhesives and binding agents. Formaldehyde, urea, and a waste water containing phenol in a concentration of about 0.01 to 5 wt.% are reacted for about 15 to 60 minutes at temperatures of about 60 to 95 deg C and a pH of about 9.5, the molar ratio of formaldehyde to phenol being from 2500:1 to about 100:1 and that of formaldehyde to urea about 2:1 to 2.7:1. A first reaction product is obtained with a viscosity of about 20 to 35 seconds measured at 25 deg C in a No. 4 Ford cup. The first reaction product is thereafter kept at temperatures of about 60 deg to 95 deg C and at a pH of about 4.0 to 5.5 for about 4 to 10 minutes to obtain a second reaction product. The second reaction product is thereafter reacted with additional urea and waste water containing phenol for about 60 to 240 minutes at temperatures of about 60 deg to 95 deg C and at a pH of about 5.7 to 6.8. The third reaction product is thereafter brought to a pH of about 8 and the urea-formaldehydephenol condensate formed is isolated. (Sinha-OEIS)
W75-06682

TREATMENT OF WASTEWATER,
Autotrol Corp., Milwaukee, Wis. (assignee)
W. N. Torpey.
U.S. Patent No. 3,869,380, 6 p, 7 fig, 1 tab, 9 ref; Official Gazette of the United States Patent Office, Vol 932, No 1, p 227, March 4, 1975.

Descriptors: *Patents, *Oxidation, *Waste water treatment, *Biological treatment, Pollution abatement, Water pollution control, Carbon, Nitrogen, Slime, Denitrification.

Process and apparatus are described for the oxidation of carbonaceous and nitrogeneous matter in wastewater by use of a mixture of biologically active slimes attached to partially submerged rotating contactors. The biological contactors are mounted in a single-stage treatment unit and are supplied with wastewater at a controlled rate relative to the surface of the contactors and distributed evenly over the contactor surface. A denitrifying unit, located upstream from the single-stage treatment unit is supplied with wastewater and recirculated effluent from the single-stage treatment unit. The denitrifying unit utilizes biologically active slimes attached to rotating biological contactors for the removal of carbonaceous matter from the wastewater supported by nitrate oxygen from the recirculated effluent. (Sinha-OEIS)
W75-06684

PROCESS FOR THE PURIFICATION OF SULFUR AND NITROGEN CONTAINING WASTE WATER AND WASTE GAS,
Deutsche Gold- und Silber-Scheidesnstalt A.G., Frankfurt-am-Mein (West Germany).
F. Geiger, T. Lussling, and W. Igert.
U.S. Patent No. 3,867,509, 4 p, 3 fig, 5 ref; Official Gazette of the United States Patent Office, Vol 931, No 3, p 1370, February 18, 1975.

Descriptors: *Patents, *Waste water treatment, *Gases, *Waste treatment, Sulfur, Nitrogen, *Water purification, Temperature, Alkalis(Bases), Hydrogen ion concentration.
Identifiers: *Waste gases, Alkaline earths, Chlorites.

Waste waters and waste gases which contain oxidizable compounds can be quickly and quantitatively deodorized and detoxified, even in the presence of ammonia, free or as a compound, by treatment with alkali or alkaline earth chlorites in an acid medium. The treated waste water and waste gas can be emptied subsequently without further treatment into streams or the atmosphere. In general the waste water or waste gas is treated at the temperature at which it occurs. However, it is suitable to carry out the reaction at elevated temperatures, e.g., at about 80 deg C. The process can be carried out either discontinuously or continuously in the usual stirring vessels. Any reactor can be used which guarantees a sufficiently thorough mixing, either by forced circulation or corresponding fixed immovable installations. For commercial processes the continuous forms of carrying out the invention are of primary interest since the process permits the establishment of a constant pH value by employing customary measuring and regulating devices and the supply of a fixed amount of chlorite dependent upon the condition of the waste gas and waste water. (Sinha-OEIS)
W75-06690

PROCESS RM FOR PURIFYING INDUSTRIAL WASTE WATERS CONTAINING DIISOPROPYL AMINE,
Zimmer A.G., Frankfurt am Main (West Germany). (assignee)
H. Jakob.
U.S. Patent No. 3,867,287, 4 p, 1 fig, 4 ref; Official Gazette of the United States Patent Office, Vol 931, No 3, p 1316, February 18, 1975.

Descriptors: *Patents, *Industrial wastes, *Waste water treatment, Pollution abatement, Water pollution control, Separation techniques, *Water purification.
Identifiers: Diisopropyl amine, Amines, Air-liquid mixture, Air stream.

A process for purifying industrial waste water containing undesired amounts of diisopropyl amine by the removal of the amine comprises contacting the waste water, in finely divided form, with a continuously renewed stream of air, and subsequently separating the resultant air and liquid mixture in a separation zone to produce a purified waste water. The waste water is passed through a multi-chamber container, each chamber provided with liquid jet air washers, several parallel waste water cycles are maintained through each chamber and the air flow is successively guided through liquid jet air washers provided for each individual chamber. (Sinha-OEIS)
W75-06691

WATER TREATMENT WITH NITROGEN DIOXIDE,
Kappe Associates, Inc., Rockville, Md. (assignee)
S. E. Kappe, and D. S. Kappe.
U.S. Patent No. 3,867,284, 6 p, 3 ref; Official Gazette of the United States Patent Office, Vol 931, No 3, p 1315, February 18, 1975.

Descriptors: *Patents, *Waste water treatment, *Sewage treatment, Nitrogen compounds, *Organic matter, *Oxidation, Pollution abatement, Water purification, Water pollution control, Domestic wastes, Treatment.
Identifiers: *Nitrogen dioxide.

A method of treating domestic sewage waste water comprises dissolving an effective amount of nitrogen dioxide in domestic sewage waste water containing as organic materials: bacteria, other

microorganisms, fats, alcohols, aldehydes, ketones, carbohydrates with aldehyde ends, organie acids, ammonia, ammonium compounds, cellulose, primary amines, amino acids and urea. The effective amount of nitrogen dioxide is from 1 milligram to 50 grams per gram of organic material. The treated domestic sewage waste water is then discharged into a waterway. During the reaction, the pollutant is oxidized by the nitrogen dioxide. For example, nitrous oxide is generally not as powerful as nitric oxide as an oxidizing agent. Therefore, less nitric oxide will be required to oxidize the same pollutant. To treat the same pollutant, less nitrogen dioxide (NO2) is needed than if nitric oxide (NO) were used. Fourteen examples of the method are presented. (Sinha-OEIS)
W75-06693

METHOD AND APPARATUS FOR PREVENTING THERMAL POLLUTION,
Computer Sciences Corp., Los Angeles, Calif. (assignee)
J. A. Labond, and D. L. Orphal.
U.S. Patent No. 3,851,495, 4 p, 2 fig, 6 ref; Official Gazette of the United States Patent Office, Vol 929, No 1, p 63, December 3, 1974.

Descriptors: *Patents, *Pollution abatement, *Waste water treatment, *Thermal pollution, *Water pollution control, *Cooling towers, Heated water, Water cooling, Electric powerplants, Industrial plants, Nuclear powerplants, Reservoirs.

Thermal pollution from industrial manufacturing and electric generating plants is avoided by incorporating in the water cooling system of such plants an underground water storage and heat dissipation space as formed by nuclear explosion. The system incorporates a wet type water cooling system (primarily because of its lower cost) and one or more nuclear chimneys below the level of the local aquifer or water table so that makeup water for water lost through evaporation in the wet type cooling unit is added by water draining or leaching to the nuclear chimney from the aquifer level. To prevent thermal pollution a large underground reservoir is formed. It has greater vertical dimension than horizontal dimension. The upper level of the reservoir is connected to the cooling unit to receive water. The lower end is connected to the industrial facility. Excess heat energy remaining in the water issuing from the cooling unit is dissipated in the earth. (Sinha-OEIS)
W75-06694

CONTINUOUS BIOLOGICAL DENITRIFICATION OF WASTEWATER,
McMaster Univ., Hamilton (Ontario).
P. M. Sutton, K. L. Murphy, and R. N. Dawson.
Technology Development Report EPS 4-WP-74-6, 242 p, August 1974, Environment Canada, Environmental Protection Service, Water Pollution Control Directorate. 44 fig, 88 ref, 40 tab, 4 append.

Descriptors: *Denitrification, *Nitrates, *Feasibility studies, Pilot plants, Laboratory tests, Analytical techniques, *Waste water treatment, Evaluation, *Biological treatment.
Identifiers: Packed column reactors, Stirred tank reactors, Temperature effects, Processes.

The feasibility of using continuous microbial denitrification for nitrate removal from municipal waste-water over a wide range of temperatures is examined. Both pilot plant upflow packed column reactors and a stirred tank reactor were investigated. Low temperature effects on the process were of major concern. The temperature dependency of the denitrification rate was shown to follow on Arrhenius relationship between 5C and 25C in both the packed column and stirred tank reactor systems. At 5C, 10-12 mg/l of nitrate as N were removed from a municipal nitrified sewage effluent provided a minimum sludge age of 6 days was maintained in the stirred tank reactor. The nitrate removal in the packed column units was defined as a function of detention time and packing surface area available for bacterial growth and was found to exhibit a slightly less temperature sensitivity compared to the stirred tank system. Unit denitrification rates determined from batch, stirred tank reactor studies were not significantly different from rates arrived at during continuous flow studies at the same sludge age. Solids yields from the stirred tank system did not vary at the 3 day and 6 day sludge ages. It was demonstrated that closed nitrogen balances could be performed on both the stirred tank and packed column reactors to account for the bacterial conversion of nitrate to nitrogen gas. (Environment Canada)
W75-06734

OPERATIONAL EXPERIENCE WITH A BASE METAL MINE DRAINAGE PILOT PLANT,
Department of the Environment, Ottawa (Ontario). Wastewater Technology Centre.
P. M. Huck, B. P. Le Clair, and P. W. Shibley.
Technology Development Report EPS 4 WP-74-8, 34 p, September 1974, Water Pollution Control Directorate. 7 ref, 3 fig, 10 tab.

Descriptors: *Waste water treatment, *Flocculation, Heavy metals, Technology, Pilot plants, Effluent quality, Research and development, Pollution abatement, Lead, Zinc, Copper, Iron, Equipment, Operations, Mine wastes.
Identifiers: *Base metals, *Sludge handling, *Effluent polishing, New Brunswick, Mining industry.

The development and effectiveness of waste treatment processes for base metal mining wastes are described. The establishment of a pilot plant at Brunswick Mining and Smelting Corporation's No. 12 Mill in Northeastern New Brunswick is detailed and the results of tests using three minewaters of varying strength are reported. Polymeric flocculation, sludge recycling, and various polishing techniques were utilized. The strength of the influent had little effect on effluent quality. Effluent metal concentrations attained were: 0.3 MG/L for lead, 0.6 MG/L for zinc, 0.1 MG/L for copper, and 0.6 MG/L for iron. (Environment Canada)
W75-06735

MANAGEMENT IMPROVEMENT,
Jacksonville Dept. of Public Works, Fla. Water and Sewer Div.
Team report, March 20, 1972. 101 p, 6 fig, 11 append.

Descriptors: *Sewerage, *Urban drainage, Sewage disposal, *Water distribution(Applied), Water districts, *Drainage systems, Planning, Combined sewers, Water management(Applied), *Florida, Water control.
Identifiers: *Jacksonville(Fla).

Conversion of Jacksonville's obsolete water and sewer works into an efficient system meeting ecological standards and laws may cost $400 million by 1990. After a thorough inventory of the system and present facilities, publications, contracts, ordinances and past studies relating to the control of the system and the funding process, this study sets forth recommendations for management, operations and development of an efficient program. One proposal is to designate one activity and one individual in the Director's office to have responsibility of monitoring all financial transactions. Other recommendations include the stabilization of the newly altered organizational structure of the Public Works Department. With a more effective management, improvements to the system are facilitated. This includes (1) conversion of a 5-year capital improvement plan to a more viable planning document, (2) publication of quarterly reports, (3) increased dissemination of information and formalized record keeping, (4) creation of a permanent industrial waste control activity, (5) bimonthly billing, (6) upgrading of acquired facilities, and (7) the employment of qualified water and sewer system managers. (Salzman-North Carolina)
W75-06760

WATER AND SEWER SYSTEMS PROGRAM AND DEVELOPMENT, FIVE-YEAR CAPITAL IMPROVEMENT PLAN: OCTOBER 1, 1972 - SEPTEMBER 30, 1977,
Jacksonville Dept. of Public Works, Fla.
March, 1972. 93 p.

Descriptors: *Sewerage, *Water management(Applied), *Drainage systems, Water works, Water distribution, Bond issues, *Costs, *Government finance, Participating funds, Grants, *Florida, Water control, Economic efficieney.
Identifiers: *Jacksonville(Fla), Tributary laterals, Trunk systems.

An improvement of the plan of 1971, this report forms a basis for shaping a master municipal system serving the entire Jacksonville area and provides for project enumeration to the year 2000 with an ultimate construction cost of $2.2 billion. Funds for construction of individual projects are requested for the year cash payments will be dispersed, with reimbursement expected from the federal government in later stages of the plan. Due to the greater cost in installation of tributary laterals (individual connections), this plan provides studies to implement trunk (group) treatment sewerage systems in the unsewered areas of Jacksonville. Program flexibility is hindered by constraints imposed by the pollution requirements of the Florida Administration Codes. Recommendations for project financing are by revenue bonds and special assessments. The water and acquisition programs, compared to the sewer, are limited in nature. The sewer programs are detailed, listing specific improvements to present facilities, acquisition of other facilities and construction of new facilities. (Salzman-North Carolina)
W75-06762

CLEAN WATER . . . A NEW DAY FOR SOUTHEAST MICHIGAN,
Detroit Metro Water Dept., Mich.
F. R. Janeczk.
Detroit Metro Water Department, December, 1973. 16 p, 9 fig, 4 tab, 11 plates.

Descriptors: *Michigan, *Waste water treatment, *Water quality, *Sewage treatment, *Water pollution, Oxidation, Aeration, Municipal wastes, Industrial wastes, Waste treatment, Waste disposal, Reaeration, Settling basins, Water reuse, Phosphorous.
Identifiers: *Detroit(Mich), Ferrous chloride.

Since 1966, $239 million of the $700 million improvement program of the Detroit Metro Water Department (DMWD) has been completed so that Michigan and federal water quality standards can be met. Forty-one miles of regional interceptors, storm-water overflow control facilities, and waste-water treatment plant expansion have been completed, providing a 1200 mgd capacity. Ferrous chloride, a steel processing waste, is used to precipitate phosphorous. Oxygen, preduced in an on-site cryogenic process plant, is used in deep covered activated sludge tanks which are more than twice as fast as conventional tanks. Secondary clarifiers are of a patented high-overflow peripheral inflow and discharge design. Scum from primary clarifiers is burned in a water hearth furnace. Dewatered sludge is incinerated in a large multiple-hearth furnace. Air pollution control in both furnaces uses reclaimed process water. Over 60 firms have installed pretreatment facilities at their plants to reduce the load the pollutants sent on to DMWD facilities so that hazardous and toxic wastes are no longer being dumped into the river

by these firms. DMWD results include 80% removal of solids, BOD, oil, and phosphorous, and 70% removal of phenols. After chlorination, treated water of swimming beach quality is discharged to the Detroit River. There has been a significant increase in sport fishing in the area and decreasing eutrophication of Lake Erie. (Herr-North Carolina)
W75-06763

COLORADO RIVER SALINITY, NEW SOLUTIONS TO AN OLD PROBLEM.
For primary bibliographic entry see Field 5G.
W75-06774

PROSPECTUS FOR REGIONAL SEWER AND WATER PLANNING.
Southwestern Wisconsin Regional Planning Commission, Platteville.
Available from the National Technical Information Service, Springfield, Va 22161 as PB-231 712, $10.00 in paper copy, $2.25 in microfiche. Technical Report No. 2, January 1971. 20 p, 1 tab, append. CPA-1003-720-77.

Descriptors: *Sewers, *Sewage, *Waste water disposal, *Drainage systems, *Water requirements, Waste disposal, Planning, *Wisconsin, Water quality.
Identifiers: Grant County(Wis), Green County(Wis), Iowa County(Wis), Lafayette County(Wis), Richland County(Wis).

Purpose is to establish the need for an areawide sewer and water planning program, recommend the most effective method for establishing, organizing and accomplishing the required work elements, and provide enough data to permit development of an initial budget for rural Grant, Green, Iowa, Lafayette and Richland Counties in Southwestern Wisconsin with a combined population of about 126,000. Except for Grant, each county is losing population. Platteville City with 9,615 is the largest population center. Only Iowa and Lafayette Counties have prepared water and sewer plans within the past few years. Some communities still have no public systems and major improvements are needed for others. Lack of adequate facilities points to need for a regional sewer and water plan to critically evaluate the inventory of existing facilities and coordinate their improvement with proposed systems. The extent of deterioration of surface water quality, potential development of small private systems, determination of costs of replacing septic tanks with public sewers and need to coordinate facility construction are discussed. Objectives need to be selected and then translated into standards for system and facility design and water quality management. To provide a regional inventory, maps, background studies, analysis of soils data, economic activity and existing water and sewer systems, and forecasts of economic activity and population must be undertaken. Alternative staffing arrangements to carry out the proposed study should be explored. A planning period of two or three years is anticipated. (Hufschmidt-North Carolina)
W75-06782

URBAN SYSTEMS ENGINEERING DEMONSTRATION PROGRAM FOR HINDS, MADISON, RANKIN COUNTIES, MISSISSIPPI, VOLUME I: AREA-WIDE WATER SYSTEMS.
Clark, Dietz and Associates, Inc., Jackson, Miss
Prepared for Hinds, Madison, Rankin, Capital City Council of Governments and Pearl River Basin Development District, Final Report, No. USE-COG-73-1, June, 1973. 150 p, 11 fig, 26 plates, 40 tab, 9 append. USE-MS-04-25-0003. USE-MS-04-25-0003, USE-MS-04-00-0002.

Descriptors: *Mississippi, *Water supply, *Water storage, *Water requirements, *Water management(Applied), City planning, Water distribution(Applied), Water quality, Water treatment, Water rates, Water demand.
Identifiers: *Jackson(Miss), Urban demonstration programs, Hinds County(Miss), Madison County(Miss), Rankin County(Miss), Water systems, Capital City Council of Governments(Miss), Pearl River(Miss), Ross Barnett Reservoir(Miss).

The goal of the three county area is to conserve water resources by the most efficient and cost-effective method of supplying water to meet anticipated needs (1971 through 1991). Water supply consists of five major aquifers and the Pearl and Big Black Rivers. Jackson uses the Pearl River, currently appropriating 72,000,000 gallons per day, and the smaller areas are served by wells. Normal maximum demands are expected to increase from 59.3 million gallons/day (MGD) in 1976 to 89.9 MGD in 1991 in the Jackson urban area system. Rural and smaller systems pose no problems but consolidation is proposed for the systems in the Jackson urban area with primary purpose to treat water of the Pearl River and distribute it to the individual system as its needs require. Facilities construction projects would cost $36,640,000, over twenty years, consisting of a 30 MGD water treatment plant, a major transmission main, completion of 24-, 20-, and 16-inch loop lines in western Rankin County, two 5,000,000 gallon ground storage tanks, two high level systems with booster pumps and 1,000,000 gallon elevated storage tanks. The City of Jackson is recommended to implement the plans, and revenue bonds are proposed as the funding mechanism. (Park-North Carolina)
W75-06783

URBAN SYSTEMS ENGINEERING DEMONSTRATION PROGRAM FOR HINDS, MADISON, RANKIN COUNTIES, MISSISSIPPI, VOLUME II: AREA-WIDE SANITARY SEWER SYSTEM.
Clark, Dietz and Associates, Inc., Jackson, Miss.
Prepared for Hinds, Madison, Rankin, Capital City Council of Governments and Pearl River Basin Development District, Final Report, No. USE-COG-73-2, June 1973. 122 p, 7 fig, 20 plates, 45 tab, 4 append. USE-MS-04-25-0003. USE-MS-04-25-0003, USE-MS-04-00-0002.

Descriptors: *Waste water treatment, *Waste water disposal, *Sanitary engineering, *Sewage disposal, Treatment facilities, *Sewage treatment, *Sewerage, Sewers, Sewage lagoons, Sewage districts, Sewage effluents, *Mississippi, Bio-chemical oxygen demand, Activated sludge, Aerated lagoons.
Identifiers: *Jackson(Miss), Rankin County(Miss), Madison County(Miss), Hinds County(Miss), Capital City Council of Governments(Miss), Pearl River(Miss), Urban Demonstration Programs, Contact stabilization.

Present practices and alternative plans to meet future sanitary sewer needs of the three counties composing the Jackson Metropolitan Area are analyzed including an inventory of existing facilities, present and future waste flows (seven basins in the cities of Jackson and Clinton will increase substantially), description of water quality standards and uses, different wastewater treatment techniques and costs, and sewer system analysis. Proposals are divided into collection and transport and treatment sections. Estimated costs of proposed projects, i.e. extending interceptor lines and building a 1 MGD treatment plant plus one 5.0 MGD pump station and a 1.0 MGD pump station, in the two collection areas (East and West Bank Sewer Districts) are divided into four five year increments (1971-1991) totalling $21,412,000. Transport and treatment costs along both banks of the Pearl River were developed with three alternatives. Alternate I using present interceptors is considered the most cost-effective plan, having the advantage that it can be phased so that more areas can be served during the earlier years of the study period. Financing proposals consider local revenue bonds, and State and Federal (72% funding) grants. The City of Jackson was suggested as the single implementation agency. (Park-North Carolina)
W75-06784

URBAN SYSTEMS ENGINEERING DEMONSTRATION PROGRAM FOR HINDS, MADISON, RANKIN COUNTIES, MISSISSIPPI, VOLUME IV. AREA-WIDE STORM DRAINAGE AND FLOOD PLAIN MANAGEMENT STUDIES.
Clark, Dietz and Associates, Inc., Jackson, Miss.
Prepared for Hinds, Madison, Rankin, Capital City Council of Governments and the Pearl River Basin Development District, Final report No. USE-COG-73-4, June 1973. 175 p, 74 fig, 150 tab. USE-MS-04-25-0003. USE-MS-04-25-0003, USE-MS-04-00-0002.

Descriptors: *Storm drains, *Storm runoff, *Storm water, Flood plains, *Flood plain zoning, *Flood protection, Drainage districts, *Drainage systems, Drainage, Drainage area, Drainage water, *Mississippi.
Identifiers: *Jackson(Miss), Hinds County(Miss), Madison County(Miss), Rankin County(Miss), Capital City Council of Governments(Miss), Pearl River(Miss).

Based on inventories of existing facilities and prevailing conditions and analysis of needs to 1992, requirements to provide adequate drainage are given for each basin and town along with cost estimates. Four of the eighteen basins and one town, Canton, would have substantial damage in a 50 year flood due to inadequate facilities. Plans call for channel improvements, and maintenance erosion control, right-of-way acquisition, and upgraded or new drainage structures. Staging of program is suggested in four five year increments to 1993. Flood information studies have been conducted for five basins, Purple Creek (1968), Lynch Creek (1971), Cany Creek (1969), Richland Creek (1967), and Town Creek (1969). Greatest floods on record occurred in 1953 and 1961. The plan recommends studies of all waterways as present studies are an inadequate basis for an area-wide management program. A flood plain ordinance is presented as well as implementation measures involving the extensive costs of easements acquisition for drainage courses. Since local government units cannot now require developers and builders to dedicate necessary easements, enabling legislation should be enacted. A Storm Drainage Commission composed of citizens representing units of local government is suggested to coordinate area-wide proposals. (Park-North Carolina)
W75-06785

GROUND WATER POLLUTION FROM SUBSURFACE EXCAVATIONS PART VI - DISPOSAL WELLS.
Environmental Protection Agency, Washington, D.C.
Water Well Journal, Vol 38, No 9, p 83-87, September, 1974.

Descriptors: *Injection, *Pollutant identification, *Water pollution, Groundwater recharge, Path of pollutants, Pollutants, Thermal pollution, Arizona, California, Idaho, New York.
Identifiers: Snake River Plain(Idaho), Long Island(N.Y).

Many thousands of the estimated fifteen million fresh water wells in the United States are for disposal of brines, chemical wastes or domestic sewage effluent, which are pollutants of fresh water. Initially, injection of contaminated liquids through wells into fresh water aquifers causes degradation of the chemical and bacteriological quality of the ground water in the immediate vicinity of the injection site. Eventually, the degradation spreads and may reach surface waters hydraulically connected to the contaminated aquifer. Cooling water, storm-water runoff, industrial wastes and domestic sewage are the principal contaminants. The rate of injection is governed by the parameters for withdrawal rates, plus the effect of the chemical compatibility of the injected

fluid with the native ground water. The first step to control potential ground water pollution is a detailed hydrogeologic investigation, then, a monitoring system should be designed and implemented to provide continuing surveillance of polluted water and of the efficiency of any control measures. (See W75-06813 and W75-06814) (Bradbeer-NWWA)
W75-06812

GROUND WATER POLLUTION FROM SUBSURFACE EXCAVATIONS, PART VII, PITS AND LAGOONS.
Environmental Protection Agency, Washington, D.C.
Water Well Journal, Vol 28, No 10, p 53-55, October, 1974.

Descriptors: *Lagoons, *Pits, *Water pollution sources, Seepage, Leakage, Permeability, Watertight, Legal aspects, Regulation, Cadmium, Waste disposal, *Waste water treatment.
Identifiers: Nassau County(NY), Public Law 92-500, Pretreatment of waste.

Data by which to evaluate the existing scope of the problem of municipal and industrial waste lagoons and similar open excavations in relation to ground water quality have not been assembled and analyzed. The need for such an assessment will become greater with time. A continuously inundated soil soon clogs to the extent that the infiltration rate is reduced below the minimum for an acceptable infiltration system, so that resting of sewage ponds is necessary. Clogging can also happen when the ground surface water is too close to the lagoon bottom and surface tension supports the water column and resists drainage. Percolating liquids from industrial pits have a greater potential to degrade ground water than does domestic sewage, and few storage ponds have been designed with proper consideration to water tightness. In many cases knowledge of the pollution does not come until a natural ground water discharge area is reached by the waste water plume. Methods of control include the pretreatment of wastes, better lining techniques, use of barrier wells, banning the use of pits, or localizing the approach to individual pits. Monitoring is essential to any such regulations. (See also W75-06812) (Bradbeer-NWWA)
W75-06813

GROUND WATER POLLUTION FROM SUBSURFACE EXCAVATIONS, PART VIII SEPTIC SYSTEMS.
Environmental Protection Agency, Washington, D.C.
Water Well Journal, Vol 28, No 11, p 53-56, November, 1974.

Descriptors: *Septic tanks, *Cesspools, *Waste disposal, Sewage treatment, Domestic wastes, Groundwater, Water pollution, *Hawaii, Disposal, Protection, Water law, Water policy, Political constraints, *Wastewater treatment.

Septic systems are prevalent throughout the United States, the heaviest concentration being in suburban subdivisions developed following World War II and in recreational lake development. The predominant type of system is the individual household septic tank. Although the septic tank with an associated subsurface percolation system is the most commonly used type, raw sewage is still discharged directly from the plumbing system into cesspools dug in the ground. The practice is no longer approved for new installations. The basis design of a septic tank is described and regional (climatic) variations are exemplified. Two categories of environmental effects which bear on control measures were identified as: (1) those which lead to restrictions on the use of septic systems, and (2) those which are inherent in a properly designed and well-functioning system in suitable soil. The failure of percolation systems, the direct discharge of waste to ground water through natural drainage systems and the location of a shallow biological zone which can be completely missed in the placement of septic systems are three of the situations in the first category. Control methods are divided into three situations, (1) those for existing systems, (2) new installations, and (3) where no practical alternative is feasible. Methods of dealing with these three categories are described. (See also W75-06812) (Bradbeer-NWWA)
W75-06814

SET PROBE OF POLLUTION CONTROL AMENDMENTS.
For primary bibliographic entry see Field 5G.
W75-06827

AERATING EFFLUENT AND KEEPING SLUDGE IN SUSPENSION.
Netherlands Patent 57251V/32. Issued July 31, 1974. Derwent Netherlands Patents Reports, Vol 5, No 33, p 2, September 24, 1974.

Descriptors: *Waste water treatment, *Patents, Equipment, *Aeration, *Effluents, Sludge, Suspension, Jets, Flow, Activated sludge, Sludge treatment, Suspended load, Suspended solids.

Effluent is aerated and activated sludge is maintained in suspension by jets of water obliquely striking the surface. The vessel is circular, elliptical, or polygonal in shape and of constant cross-section through the greater part of its height. The jets strike the surface at not more than 60 degrees, preferably 10 to 20 degrees to the surface with a speed of 3 to 12 m/sec. The horizontal component of the tangent is in the general direction of flow. (Prague-FIRL)
W75-06832

SOLID BOWL CENTRIFUGAL SEPARATOR,
W. H. Peck, and S. A. Collier.
U.S. Patent 3,829.009. Issued August 13, 1974, Official Gazette of the United States Patent Office, Vol 925, No 2, p 514, August, 1974. 1 fig.

Descriptors: *Patents, *Centrifuges, *Slurries, *Solids, Equipment, *Waste water treatment, Separation techniques.

A centrifugal separator for the removal of solids from slurry was described. A high speed bowl rotates about a vertical axis and is centrally fed with slurry in its upper region. A circular ceiling plate above the level of slurry feed establishes a narrow annulus with the cylindrical upper rim section of the bowl. This becomes sealed with sludge as the solid constituents build up in the vicinity. A series of plows advance slowly around the annulus and through the sludge seal and elevate the sludge above the ceiling plate, into the path of a series of rotatable buckets. These buckets assume outside ecliptic positions where they scoop wads of sludge from the sludge seal, and assume inside ecliptic positions where their directional relationship is reversed so that centrifugal force dislodges the wads, causing them to be flung radially over the rim of the bowl. The liquid constituent of the slurry is then forced out through an outlet in the bowl bottom wall. (Prague-FIRL)
W75-06835

POROUS CERAMIC SOIL MOISTURE SAMFLERS, AN APPLICATION IN LYSIMETER STUDIES ON EFFLUENT SPRAY IRRIGATION,
Department of Agriculture, Lethbridge (Alberta). Research Station.
For primary bibliographic entry see Field 2G.
W75-06843

5E. Ultimate Disposal Of Wastes

SUBSURFACE WASTE DISPOSAL BY INJECTION IN HAWAII: A CONCEPTUAL FORMULATION AND PHYSICAL MODELING PLAN,
Hawaii Univ., Honolulu. Water Resources Research Center.
For primary bibliographic entry see Field 5B.
W75-06351

NEW CONCEPTS IN SOIL SURVEY INTERPRETATIONS FOR ON-SITE DISPOSAL OF SEPTIC TANK EFFLUENT,
Wisconsin Univ., Madison. Dept. of Soil Science.
For primary bibliographic entry see Field 5D.
W75-06402

ECONOMIC AND ENVIRONMENTAL EVALUATION OF NUCLEAR WASTE DISPOSAL BY UNDERGROUND IN SITU MELTING,
California Univ., Livermore. Lawrence Livermore Lab.
For primary bibliographic entry see Field 5B.
W75-06413

RECLAMATION OF ENERGY FROM ORGANIC WASTES,
Illinois Univ., Urbana. Dept. of Civil Engineering.
For primary bibliographic entry see Field 5D.
W75-06471

DEVELOPMENT OF CRITERIA TO CONTROL OCEAN DUMPING - EXECUTIVE SUMMARY.
Interstate Electronics Corp., Anaheim, Calif. Oceanics Div.
Available from the National Technical Information Service, Springfield, Va 22161 as PB-233 018, $3.25 in paper copy, $2.25 in microfiche. (1974). IEC 4460C1612. 16 p, 4 fig. EPA Contract 68-01-0796.

Descriptors: *Waste disposal, *Oceans, *Reviews, Atlantic Ocean, Pacific Ocean, Gulf of Mexico, Maps, Bibliographies, Waste dumps, *Water quality standards.
Identifiers: *Ocean dumps.

Brief summaries of eight reports previously published under this contract were presented. These reports all concern ocean waste disposal, and have the following titles: 'Directory of Managers, Engineers and Scientists in Ocean Waste Disposal and Related Environmental Science Fields'; 'A Bibliography on Ocean Waste Disposal'; 'Ocean Waste Disposal in Selected Geographic Areas'; 'Ocean Waste Disposal in the New York Bight'; 'Ocean Waste Disposal Practices in Metropolitan Areas of California'; 'An Atlas of Ocean Waste Disposal Sites'; 'Navigation Aids for Ocean Waste Disposal Control'; 'Guidelines for Development of Criteria for Control of Ocean Waste Disposal.' (Sims-ISWS)
W75-06486

STORM RUNOFF AND TRANSPORT OF RADIONUCLIDES IN DP CANYON, LOS ALAMOS COUNTY, NEW MEXICO,
Los Alamos Scientific Lab., N. Mex.
For primary bibliographic entry see Field 5B.
W75-06636

IMPACT OF HUMAN ACTIVITIES ON THE QUALITY OF GROUNDWATER AND SURFACE WATER IN THE CAPE COD AREA,
Massachusetts Univ, Amherst. Water Resources Research Center.
For primary bibliographic entry see Field 5B.
W75-06644

DIGESTED SLUDGE DISPOSAL AT SAN DIEGO'S AQUATIC PARK,
San Diego Dept. of Utilities, Calif.
R. E. Graham, and R. E. Dodson.
Paper presented at 41st Annual Conference of the Water Pollution Control Federation, Chicago, Illinois, September 22-27, 1968. 16 p, 5 ref.

Descriptors: *Sludge disposal, *Land reclamation, *Agricultural engineering, *Sludge digestion, *Sludge treatment, *Waste water disposal, Sludge, Waste water treatment, Liquid wastes, Waste dumps, Waste disposal, Sewage treatment, California, Irrigation practices, Soil management, Land development, Soil conservation.
Identifiers: San Diego(California).

Field studies and large-scale production programs at San Diego over the past 13 years have proven the effectiveness of soil building by the application of liquid digested sludge to potential growing areas, which are basically sand, both for farm production and for park development. The rapid creation of a heavily used park in sterile sand had been particularly effective. Most major problems were due to the engineering failures in the transmission facilities, and with proper handling of the liquid sludge at the disposal sites. Odor control has been a problem because of the growing population pressures surrounding the disposal area. Present practice is to spread the liquid sludge on leveled sand beds in lifts of not over 1 to 2 in. (2.5 to 5 cm), to flush the delivery pipeline with supernate after every day's pumping, and to pump the accumulated supernate to a trunk sewer for return to the treatment plant. Odor is controlled by the use of a systemic masking agent and by cessation of pumping during occasional adverse wind conditions. Insects are controlled by working the disposal area and by use of insecticide sprays. On a dry weight basis cost was $6.76/ton or $4,730/acre. (Poertner)
W75-06674

SUBSURFACE DISPOSAL OF WASTE IN CANADA - II, DISPOSAL-FORMATION AND INJECTION-WELL HYDRAULICS,
Department of the Environment, Ottawa (Ontario). Water Resources Branch.
R. O. Van Everdingen.
Technical Bulletin 78, Inland Waters Directorate, 1974. 12 fig, 10 tab, 15 ref, 30 p.

Descriptors: *Waste disposal, *Injection wells, *Underground waste disposal, Hydraulics, Model studies, Permeability, Aquifers, Pressure, Equations, Mathematical studies, Base flow, Flow rates, *Canada.
Identifiers: Fracturing.

Injection-well and disposal-formation hydraulics are examined as they relate to the selection of sites for subsurface disposal of liquid wastes. Pressure build-up in the disposal formation may cause reactivation of abandoned oil, gas, or water wells and an increased rate of discharge which may result in the eventual discharge of the waste materials, perhaps even after the injection well is no longer operating. Models using computers can be used to predict the effects of subsurface disposal and several mathematical models are described. Equations useful for determining pressure build-up are developed and factors which can affect the build-up are discussed. (See also W75-06751) (Environment Canada)
W75-06750

SUBSURFACE DISPOSAL OF WASTE IN CANADA - III - REGIONAL EVALUATION OF POTENTIAL FOR UNDERGROUND DISPOSAL OF INDUSTRIAL LIQUID WASTES,
Water Resources Branch.
R. O. van Everdingen.
Technical Bulletin No 82, 42 p, 1974, Inland Waters Directorate, 7 fig, 27 ref, 6 tab.

Descriptors: *Industrial wastes, *Underground waste disposal, *Waste disposal, Injection wells, Geology, Hydrodynamics, Liquid wastes, *Canada.
Identifiers: *Site evaluation, *Site selection, Hydrochemistry, Criteria, Waste classification.

A regional analysis of potential sites for underground disposal of industrial wastes is presented. The criteria to be used in site selection are discussed. These include geology, hydrodynamics, hydrochemistry, man-made hazards, and separation from underground resources such as groundwater or minerals. The criteria are then used to identify regions in Canada that should not be used for subsurface disposal and to indicate certain regions that hold potential for safe injection of noxious wastes. Eight areas ranging from the Maritime plain to the Arctic lowlands are designated as potentially suitable for injection wells. (See also W75-06750) (Environment Canada)
W75-06751

CLEAN WATER . . . A NEW DAY FOR SOUTHEAST MICHIGAN,
Detroit Metro Water Dept., Mich.
For primary bibliographic entry see Field 5D.
W75-06763

SOLID WASTE DISPOSAL AND OCEAN DUMPING,
Naval War Coll., Newport, R.I.
For primary bibliographic entry see Field 5B.
W75-06789

GROUND WATER POLLUTION FROM SUBSURFACE EXCAVATIONS PART VI - DISPOSAL WELLS.
Environmental Protection Agency, Washington, D.C.
For primary bibliographic entry see Field 5D.
W75-06812

GROUND WATER POLLUTION FROM SUBSURFACE EXCAVATIONS, PART VII, PITS AND LAGOONS.
Environmental Protection Agency, Washington, D.C.
For primary bibliographic entry see Field 5D.
W75-06813

GROUND WATER POLLUTION FROM SUBSURFACE EXCAVATIONS, PART VIII SEPTIC SYSTEMS.
Environmental Protection Agency, Washington, D.C.
For primary bibliographic entry see Field 5D.
W75-06814

DYE AND DROGUE STUDIES OF SPOIL DISPOSAL AND OIL DISPERSION,
Delaware Univ., Newark. Coll. of Marine Studies.
For primary bibliographic entry see Field 5B.
W75-06831

5F. Water Treatment and Quality Alteration

REMOVAL OF IRON AND MANGANESE FROM LOW ALKALINITY WATERS,
Mississippi State Univ., Mississippi State.
L. R. Robinson, and E. D. Breland.
Public Works, February 1968. p 72-76, 1 fig, 4 tab, 16 ref.

Descriptors: *Iron, *Manganese, *Municipal water, *Water treatment, *Alkaline water, *Oxidation-reduction potential, Water quality control, Water pollution treatment, Iron oxides, Bicarbonates, Alkalinity, Aeration, Sedimentation, Filtration, Water supply, Treatment facilities, Water purification, Pilot plants.
Identifiers: *Iron removal, *Manganese removal.

Iron removal from low alkalinity waters have proven difficult. Oxidation rates for the ferrous iron are so slow that it is economically impossible to design treatment plants using only aeration. Chemical treatment must also be used. A major study was conducted to find the factors which retard the rate of oxidation of ferrous iron and manganese in ground water supplies in Mississippi and Alabama. Pilot plant and oxidation studies were set up. Researchers found that iron removal by aeration, sedimentation, and filtration is difficult in water having bicarbonate alkalinities of less than 50 mg/l as CACO3. The apparent cause if the failure of ferrous iron to oxidize. Ferrous iron oxidation rates can be increased by raising the bicarbonate alkalinities by the addition of soda ash. The increases in oxidation rates in these studies were due almost entirely to the increases in bicarbonate alkalinity. Raising the pH of the water above 8.5 by adding lime permits satisfactory iron removal. Increases in bicarbonate alkalinities increase oxidation rates and removal of manganese slightly. Effective oxidation and removal of manganese can be accomplished by aeration, sedimentation and filtration if the pH is raised to above 9.0 with the addition of lime. Organic material has no apparent effect on oxidation rates of ferrous iron and manganese. (Poertner)
W75-06660

PHOTOSYNTHETIC DIFFICULTIES IN AN IRON REMOVAL PLANT,
Irwin and Summerford, Hot Springs, Ark.
C. R. Summerford, and L. R. Robinson.
Water and Sewage Works, September 1970. p 311-318, 2 tab, 7 fig, 8 ref.

Descriptors: *Iron, *Water treatment, *Municipal water, *Photosynthetic bacteria, *Water quality control, *Iron oxides, Photosynthesis, Filtration filters, Chlorination, Water pollution treatment, Treatment facilities, Photosynthetic oxygen.
Identifiers: *Iron removal.

Persistent biological growths in the aerator, contact basin and filters have caused considerable difficulties in the operation of the iron removal plant for the city of West Helena, Arkansas. The study of the water treatment plant had three objectives. The first was to study the causes of the persistent biological growths. The second was to examine several possible methods of controlling these growths. Finally, the third was to determine if the organic growths were interfering with the primary plant function of iron removal. Both the West Helena water treatment plant and a pilot plant were used. The pilot plant was used to see if biological growth would develop in a clean plant at the same rate as the main plant. In the main plant, the experimental modification consisted of covering one filter with a block plastic and applying air with the backwash water to another filter. All the alterations which were tried seemed to aid in controlling the biological growths, but not one single method nor any combination, eliminated the growths. The present control practice of superchlorination was required in addition to all the alterations made for the purpose of this study. After this study, it appears that the most effective way to eliminate the biological growths would be to cover all the exposed processes. (Poertner)
W75-06661

IRON REMOVAL IN HIGH SILICA GROUNDWATERS,
Jordon and Associates, Camp Hill, Pa. Environmental Engineering Div.
L. R. Robinson.
Paper presented at a Specialty Conference on Environmental Engineering Research, Development and Design, Pennsylvania State University, University Park, July 9, 1974. 22 p, 10 tab.

Descriptors: *Hardness(Water), *Water chemistry, *Iron, *Groundwater, *Silica, *Water quality control, Water pollution treatment, Iron oxides, Alkalinity, Bicarbonates, Alkaline water, Iron compounds, Chemical engineering, Chemical precipitation.
Identifiers: *Iron removal.

Aeration and filtration processes use oxygen in oxidizing ferrous iron to the insoluble ferric state. This oxidation and ensuing precipitation forms the basis for most iron removal processes. Aeration, to provide the oxygen required for iron oxidation, reaction time and sedimentation, followed by filtration provides the nucleus for most groundwater iron removal plants. This basic scheme, however, does not always provide for satisfactory iron removal efficiencies. In water which contain organie matter, iron removal interference has been attributed to the presence of humic acids. In waters where organic concentrations are insignificant, the oxygen concentration, alkalinity and/or pH are factors which are frequently mentioned as those which have the greatest effect on iron oxidation, precipitation and removal. Recent studies have indicated that interference with iron oxidation and removal is frequently attributable to low pH and low alkalinity concentrations. Other reports have indicated that high concentrations of silica can catalyze ferrous iron oxidation and retard hydrolysis of ferric iron and thus hinder sedimentation and filtration. This study indicates that silica interference with iron removal is apparently silica reacting in alkalinity determinations to indicate sufficiently high bicarbonate alkalinity concentrations to insure rapid ferrous iron oxidation. Lime or soda can promote iron removal. (Poertner)
W75-06663

SYSTEM FOR DEMINERALIZING WATER BY ELECTRODIALYSIS,
A. R. Tejeda.
U.S. Patent No. 3,869,376, 9 p, 7 fig, 2 ref; Official Gazette of the United States Patent Office, Vol 932, No 1, p 226, March 4, 1975.

Descriptors: *Patents, *Demineralization, *Ion exchange, *Water treatment, *Electrodialysis, *Permselective membranes, Distillation, Membranes, Separation techniques, Effluent, Desalination, Waste water treatment.
Identifiers: Flow patterns, Soft water.

The electrodialytic demineralization of water is achieved by passing soft water through a treating chamber defined by a pair of permselective membranes of which the one closer to the cathode of the cell is cationic permselective and the one closer to the anode is anionic permselective. The chamber is charged with an ion exchange material. The effluent from the treating chamber may be passed through a second treating chamber. The ion exchange materials with which the cell or cells are charged may be cationic, anionic, both cationic and anionic, or cationic in one chamber and anionic in another chamber where more than one treating chamber is employed. The particular types of ion exchange materials selected will depend upon the flow pattern and arrangement of chambers in different electrodialytic cells. (Sinha-OEIS)
W75-06685

THE SORPTION OF FLUORIDE ION WITH SPECIAL REFERENCE TO FLUORIDE REMOVAL FROM POTABLE WATERS,
North Dakota Univ., Grand Forks.
P. W. West.
MSc thesis 1936, 24 p, 10 fig, 2 tab, 19 ref.

Descriptors: Water quality, Chemical analysis, Chemical wastes, *Potable water, *Fluoride, *North Dakota, *Waste treatment.
Identifiers: Fluoride removal.

The significance of fluorides in drinking water, particularly from the artesian waters of North Dakota, is discussed from the standpoint of the occurrence of mottled enamel. Analytical methods for the determination of small concentrations of fluorides are reviewed and criticized, and a method is defined. Zeolites will remove fluoride but the capacity is too small to be practical. The same is true of zeolites treated with manganese, nickel, zirconium, cobalt and chromium. In low pH conditions, activated charcoal will remove fluoride. Other useful methods of removal are delineated and the difficulties described. The most successful, though, was a lead filter which in itself is toxic. (Bradbeer-NWWA)
W75-06815

SOLID BOWL CENTRIFUGAL SEPARATOR,
For primary bibliographic entry see Field 5D.
W75-06835

5G. Water Quality Control

STOCHASTIC VARIATIONS IN WATER QUALITY PARAMETERS,
Rutgers - the State Univ., New Brunswick, N. J. Bureau of Engineering Research.
For primary bibliographic entry see Field 5B.
W75-06355

AN INVENTORY AND SENSITIVITY ANALYSIS OF DATA REQUIREMENTS FOR AN OXYGEN MANAGEMENT MODEL OF THE CARSON RIVER,
Nevada Univ., Reno. Dept. of Civil Engineering.
For primary bibliographic entry see Field 5B.
W75-06356

ESTUARINE POLLUTION IN THE STATE OF HAWAII, VOLUME 2: KANEOHE BAY STUDY,
Hawaii Univ., Honolulu. Water Resources Research Center.
For primary bibliographic entry see Field 5B.
W75-06362

SOIL AS A MEDIUM FOR THE RENOVATION OF ACID MINE DRAINAGE,
Pennsylvania State Univ., University Park. Dept. of Agronomy.
For primary bibliographic entry see Field 5D.
W75-06365

SALINITY IN WATER RESOURCES.
For primary bibliographic entry see Field 3C.
W75-06366

A WATER QUALITY MODEL TO EVALUATE WATER MANAGEMENT PRACTICES IN AN IRRIGATED STREAM-AQUIFER SYSTEM,
Geological Survey, Denver, Colo.
L. F. Konikow, and J. D. Bredehoeft.
In: Proceedings of the 15th Annual Western Resources Conference, July, 1973, University of Colorado, Boulder, Merriman Publishing Co., Boulder, 1974. p 36-59, 14 fig, 2 tab, 10 ref.

Descriptors: *Model studies, *Mathematical models, *Salinity, *Watershed management, *Colorado, Saline water, Return flow, Irrigation efficiency, Crop response, Irrigation practices, Groundwater, Economics, Forecasting, Projections, Irrigation.
Identifiers: Arkansas River.

The complex water-quality variations which exist in an irrigated stream-aquifer system can be simulated with a digital model that couples a finite-difference technique, used to solve the flow equations, with the method of characteristics used to solve the transport (dispersion) equations. This modeling technique was successfully applied to an 11-mile stretch of the Arkansas River Valley in southeastern Colorado for a one year period. Once verified, the model can be used to predict the effeets of changes in management or irrigation praetices on the quality and quantity of ground and surface water. Three tests were run to demonstrate the types of problems to which the model might be applied. Analysis of the tests indicated that initial or short-term responses to changes in irrigation practices are strongly related to antecedent conditions and do not necessarily reflect actual long-term responses to these changes. Perhaps the greatest value of the model is its capability to be utilized for predicting future long-term results. The model can be applied to other irrigated areas where the required data are available or can be collected. Although the cost of initiating and maintaining a satisfactory data collection network may be considered high, it is believed that these can be justified in many areas by the potential benefits that can be derived from a calibrated model. With a few programming modifications, the technique can be used for many problems in which it is desired to predict the rates and directions of movement of contaminants through a saturated porous medium. (See also W75-06366) (Bowden-Arizona)
W75-06369

ECONOMIC ANALYSIS OF OPTIMAL USE OF SALINE WATER IN IRRIGATION AND THE EVALUATION OF WATER QUALITY,
Hebrew Univ., Jerusalem (Israel). Dept. of Agricultural Economics.
For primary bibliographic entry see Field 3C.
W75-06370

EVALUATING AGRICULTURAL EFFECTS OF SALINITY ABATEMENT PROJECTS IN THE COLORADO RIVER BASIN: AGRONOMIC AND ECONOMIC CONSIDERATIONS,
Colorado State Univ., Fort Collins. Dept. of Economics.
R. A. Young, W. T. Franklin, and K. C. Nobe.
In: Proceedings of the 15th Annual Western Resources Conference, July 1973, University of Colorado, Boulder, Merriman Publishing Co., Boulder, 1974. p 86-107, 29 ref.

Descriptors: *Colorado River Basin, *Salinity, *Water pollution sources, *Cost-benefit analysis, *Economic justification, Saline water, Saline soils, Arizona, Colorado, Utah, Wyoming, California, Nevada, New Mexico, Pollution abatement, Water pollution, Soil profiles, Salt tolerance, Crop response.

Agronomic, economic and other considerations for evaluating effects of salinity on irrigated cropping regions are reviewed. Salinity abatement benefits in crop yield are compared with salinity costs. However, estimates of yields from saline waters are difficult because the data base, derived from studies at the U.S. Salinity Laboratory, Riverside, California, is of questionable validity. Present methods of predicting the average soil profile salinity are subject to gross errors. Also, farm methods can drastically effect salinity damage, and thus make estimates difficult. It is questionable if secondary and indirect economic impacts from salinity in the Colorado River Basin are pertinent since such effects are likely to be offset elsewhere in the national economy. In view of these facts, and because of the large public investment (up to $500 million) salinity abatement projects would require in the basin, a new reassessment of salinity damages is called for. (See also W75-06366) (Bowden-Arizona)
W75-06371

ECONOMIC INCENTIVES FOR SALINITY REDUCTION AND WATER CONSERVATION IN THE COLORADO RIVER BASIN,
Colorado Univ., Boulder. Dept. of Economics.
For primary bibliographic entry see Field 3C.
W75-06373

COST SHARING AND EFFICIENCY IN SALINITY CONTROL,
National Bureau of Standards, Washington, D.C. Building Economics Section.
For primary bibliographic entry see Field 3C.
W75-06374

FINDING KNOWLEDGE GAPS: THE KEY TO SALINITY CONTROL SOLUTIONS,
Colorado State Univ., Fort Collins. Environmental Resources Center.
N. H. Evans.
In: Proceedings of the 15th Annual Western Resources Conference, July 1973, University of Colorado, Boulder, Merriman Publishing Co., 1974. p 153-159, 4 ref.

Descriptors: *Regional analysis, *Colorado River Basin, *Saline soils, *Saline water, *Salinity, *Research priorities, Colorado, Arizona, Wyoming, New Mexico, Utah, Nevada, California, Water pollution, Desalination, Water pollution sources, Irrigation water, Research facilities.

Science has not totally solved the salinity problem and irrigators are not using what improved techniques now exist. Also, the nature of the salinity problem has changed from one of simply maintaining the proper field environment for plant growth to the new complication of not discharging highly saline waters for use by downstream farmers. Three possible alternative solutions present themselves. One can control irrigation return flow, control point sources of salt, and control natural sources of salt. The water resources research centers of the Colorado River Basin are now moving to attack the problem together. This will help identify research which must be done, and will integrate this research. (See also W75-06366) (Bowden-Arizona)
W75-06375

HYDROGEOLOGY AND WATER QUALITY MANAGEMENT,
Moody and Associates, Inc., Harrisburg, Pa. Environmental Services Div.
R. A. Landon.
Journal of the Hydraulics Division, American Society of Civil Engineers, Vol 101, No HY2, Proceedings paper 11137, p 285-289, February 1975.

Descriptors: *Management, *Hydrogeology, *Water quality, Aquifer management, Environmental effects, Land use, Topography, Soils, Geology, Geochemistry, Surface-groundwater relationships, Groundwater movement, Discharge(Water), Model studies, Methodology, Geologic mapping, Maps, *Pennsylvania, Hydraulics.
Identifiers: Static systems, Dynamic systems.

Numerous environmental and water quality investigations were completed which are largely two-dimensional in that the environmental and land-use factors were evaluated from a surficial standpoint only, with minimum concern given to the third dimension of depth, and therefore, the majority of the hydrogeologic framework lying below land surface. An integral part of Comprehensive Water Quality Management Planning (COWAMP) program for Pennsylvania is a definition of the hydrogeologic framework that controls the occurrence of ground water, as well as data describing the quantity and quality of that resource. Recognition of the fact that the environment is a complex interweaving of many variables, and the strong control exerted by the natural physical components comprising the hydrogeologic framework can be expected to minimize or avoid the deleterious and sometimes catastrophic results of the omission of such recognition. (Visocky-ISWS)
W75-06400

POLICY AND RESEARCH IMPLICATIONS OF THE NATIONAL WATER COMMISSION'S RECOMMENDATIONS,
Wisconsin Univ., Madison. Dept. of Agricultural Economics.
For primary bibliographic entry see Field 6E.
W75-06404

A COMPILATION OF AUSTRALIAN WATER QUALITY CRITERIA,
Caulfield Inst. of Tech., (Australia).
B. T. Hart.
Australian Water Resources Council, Technical Paper No. 7, 1974. 349 p. Published by Australian Government Publishing Service, Camberra.

Descriptors: Water quality, *Water quality control, *Water quality standards, Water resources, *Planning, *Governments, Legislation, *Management, Social aspects, Evaluation, Documentation, Public health, Aquatic life, Ecosystems, Domestic water, Crop production, Irrigation, Livestock, Industrial water, Aesthetics, Recreation, Bioassay.
Identifiers: *Australia.

The environmental assessment process can be considered to have two dimensions: (1) planning to ensure environmental compatability; this will be achieved by the development of an environmental assessment methodology designed as far as possible to fulfill three requirements, namely, (a) identify potential beneficial and adverse impacts arising from a range of alternative actions; (b) measure the magnitude of all impacts; (c) evaluate the importance of all impacts; (2) the formal documentation of expected environmental impacts. This planning process generally involves the input of information supplied from surveys to provide baseline data, from citizen participation, and from documented environmental criteria. The problem is most obvious in the field of water quality control. The efficient management of Australia's water resources depends, among other things, upon adequate baseline data and a comprehensive collection of water quality criteria for all beneficial uses of water. (Houser-ORNL)
W75-06418

SURFACE WATER QUALITY IN MINNESOTA: THE TRANSLATION OF GOALS AND POLICIES INTO RESULTS,
Minnesota Univ., St. Paul. Water Resources Research Center.
J. J. Waelti.
Available from the National Technical Information Service, Springfield, Va 22161 as PB-241 016, $4.75 in paper copy, $2.25 in microfiche. Bulletin No. 72, February 1975, 70 p. OWRT B-054-Minn(8). 14-31-0001-3601.

Descriptors: *Water quality, *Water pollution, *Water resources, Administration, *Minnesota, Planning, Economics, Water policy, Alternative planning, Legislation, Legal aspects, State governments, Water pollution control, Government finance.
Identifiers: Zero discharge.

The study focuses on problems of translating public policy goals relating to surface water quality into reality. Surface water pollution is seen as a result of economic incentives. Broad policy alternatives for addressing surface water pollution are examined. Judicial measures for dealing with water pollution problems are discussed, along with their limitations and the necessity for specific legislation. Water quality legislation at the Federal and State (Minnesota) level is reviewed. The mechanics of water quality administration are discussed, with emphasis on the Minnesota Pollution Control Agency. Problems and progress under the Water Pollution Control Act Amendments of 1972 are discussed. Changes in enforcement tools are emphasized. Other problems relating to surface water pollution control are discussed including the funding gap and the zero-discharge controversy.
W75-06431

ECOLOGICAL AND PHYSIOLOGICAL IMPLICATIONS OF GREENBELT IRRIGATION, PROGRESS REPORT OF THE MALONEY CANYON PROJECT-1974,
California Univ., Riverside. Dept. of Plant Sciences.
For primary bibliographic entry see Field 5D.
W75-06461

ENVIRONMENTAL STUDIES (1973), JAMES BAY TERRITORY AND SURROUNDING AREA,
Department of the Environment, Hull (Quebec); and James Bay Development Corp., Montreal (Quebec).
For primary bibliographic entry see Field 6G.
W75-06467

GREAT LAKES WATER QUALITY, ANNUAL REPORT TO THE INTERNATIONAL JOINT COMMISSION, (1973).
International Joint Commission-United States and Canada. Great Lakes Water Quality Board.
For primary bibliographic entry see Field 5B.
W75-06474

DEVELOPMENT OF CRITERIA TO CONTROL OCEAN DUMPING - EXECUTIVE SUMMARY.
Interstate Electronics Corp., Anaheim, Calif. Oceanics Div.
For primary bibliographic entry see Field 5E.
W75-06486

WATER QUALITY STANDARDS AND INTERNATIONAL DEVELOPMENT.
Agency for International Development, Washington, D.C. Office of Science and Technology.
Available from the National Technical Information Service, Springfield, Va 22161 as PB-204 408, $3.75 in paper copy, $2.25 in microfiche. TA/OST/71-4, October 1971. 27 p, 15 ref, append.

Descriptors: *Water quality standards, *Water quality control, Water supply, United States, Surface waters, Water resources, Public health, Economics, Water quality, Water pollution control.
Identifiers: Developing countries.

The development of water quality criteria and standards in the United States was traced and water supply problems and water standards in the developing countries of the world were assessed. The World Health Organization was credited as the major force in introducing drinking water standards in developing countries and in promoting techniques to increase the availability of safe community water supplies. Unease was expressed over the delicate and difficult balance of simultaneously achieving pollution abatement and economic development. Inadequate policies, laws, and institutions were cited as responsible, in large part, for limited progress in improving community water supplies and in economic development. Specific steps for overcoming such deficiencies were given. A summary of selected criteria from 'International Standards for Drinking Water' (WHO, second edition, 1963) was appended. (Harmeson-ISWS)
W75-06487

THE WESTERNPORT BAY ENVIRONMENTAL STUDY,
Victoria Ministry for Conservation, Melbourne (Australia). Westernport Bay Environmental Study.
For primary bibliographic entry see Field 6G.
W75-06555

THE UNCERTAIN SEARCH FOR ENVIRONMENTAL QUALITY,
Yale Univ., New Haven, Conn. School of Law.
B. A. Ackerman, S. Rose-Ackerman, J. W. Sawyer, Jr., and D. W. Henderson.
The Free Press, A Division of Macmillan Publishing Co, Inc, New York, NY, 1974. 386 p, 12 fig, 10 tab, 219 ref, 5 append.

Descriptors: *Water pollution control, *Water policy, United States, *Economics, *Political aspects, *Legal aspects, *Regulation, *Delaware River Basin Commission, Costs, Benefits, Marginial costs, Cost-benefit analysis, Dissolved oxygen, Biochemical oxygen demand, Zoning, Mathematical models, Systems analysis.
Identifiers: *Environmental quality, *Delaware Estuary Comprehensive Study, Cost minimization, Regulation models, Technocratic approach, Market model, Activist approach, Legal orders.

The scientific, economic, political and legal foundations of the water pollution policy currently being pursued in the United States are analyzed in depth. Extensive study is made of the Delaware River Basin Commission's program to clean-up the highly polluted Delaware Estuary flowing past Philadelphia. Through the Delaware example, the failings of the present national program are exemplified; shown is how policymakers have been led to fight the wrong war against environmental degredation--a multi-billion dollar war generating pitifully meager results. Advanced technocratic methods and creative institutional engineering have proved inadequate for environmental tasks. Analyzed are the use of cost-benefit analysis as an environmental policy tool and the Delaware Estuary Comprehensive Study (DECS) approach to benefit estimation. Three models of regulation are available for an agency considering a cost-minimization strategy: legal orders, market model, and activist approach. A new set of policy objectives and institutional mechanisms is proposed. Three levels of recommendations include: (1) substantive environmental policy, calling for a more self-conscious effort to set priorities; (2) institutional reconstruction, which advocates central control for coherent development while not giving a single agency unlimited power to define and resolve a given pollution problem; and (3) policy implementation, wherein the limitations of innovation within the traditional model of regulation through legal orders are explored, and a discriminating incorporation of market and activist models of control are proposed. (Bell-Cornell)
W75-06557

COMPREHENSIVE WATER QUALITY MANAGEMENT PLANNING,
Pennsylvania Dept. of Environmental Resources, Harrisburg. Office of Comprehensive Water and Wastewater Management Planning.
K. A. Bartal, and L. V. Gutierrez, Jr.
Journal of the Hydraulics Division, American Society of Civil Engineers, Vol 101, No HY4, Proceedings paper No 11263, p 371-386, April 1975. 3 fig, 2 tab.

Descriptors: *Water quality, *Water management(Applied), *Comprehensive planning, *Regions, *Social participation, *Pennsylvania, Hydraulics, Water resources, Computer models, Alternative planning, Economics, Design, Operation and maintenance, Groundwater, Simulation analysis, Mathematical models.
Identifiers: *Data systems, Environmental factors, Environmental planning, Federal legislation, Statewide, Management criteria, Nonpoint source management.

The comprehensive water quality management planning (COWAMP) program being undertaken by the Commonwealth of Pennsylvania responds to the latest Federal legislation and regulations, as well as to state requirements. The study program has been divided into nine separate local studies and represents a statewide effort to establish a valid water quality management plan that responds to alternative environmental futures and features a precedent-setting degree of public participation. The Pennsylvania COWAMP program is not typical; it is a multidisciplinary attack on the complex problem of creating realistic yet aggressive water quality management criteria, based not only on the technological but also on the social, economic, and land-use aspects of environmental planning. By articulating and incorporating environmental amenities unique to Pennsylvania, the program will be tailored specifically to the Commonwealth's needs. To provide consistency among the statewide water quality management studies, the consultants will use two computer modeling tools. ECOFIN accomplishes the preliminary design of system components to obtain total present-worth costs of construction, replacement, operation, and maintenance over specific planning periods. UDOM is intended to provide a comprehensive water quality simulation model based on the modified Streeter-Phelps equations for DO and BOD. (Bell-Cornell)
W75-06558

ANALYSIS OF MULTIPLE OBJECTIVES IN WATER QUALITY,
Case Western Reserve Univ., Cleveland, Ohio. Systems Engineering Div.
For primary bibliographic entry see Field 5D.
W75-06559

REVIEW OF LAKE RESTORATION PROCEDURES,
Colorado Univ., Boulder.
C. J. Boyter, and M. P. Wanielista.
Water Resources Bulletin, Vol 9, No 3, p 499-511, June 1973. 1 tab, 33 ref.

Descriptors: *Lakes, *Water quality control, Bottom sediments, Aquatic plants, Oxygen, Management, Sewage, Nurtients, Water pollution, Florida, Water treatment, Oxygenation, Dredging, Drawdown, Costs, Destratification.
Identifiers: *Resotration procedures(Lakes), Displacement, Water hyacinths, Literature review.

Results are reported of a search to find what restoration procedure to use for a given lake condition. The restoration procedures considered are applicable to water, bottom sediments, and aquatic plant impovement. Thirteen suggested methods of restoration are reviewed. The techniques which apply to water include: (1) the elimination of pollutants entering the water from controllable sources; (2) replacing the water with high quality water; and (3) direct treatment of the existing water. Methods to control pollutional releases from the bottom sediments have been divided into three categories: sediment covering, oxygenation, and dredging. Techniques for removal or control of undesirable plants or plant productivity with the goal of restoring the natural balance are categorized as chemical, mechanical, biological, and physical. Discussion of these procedures and methods should provide pollution control and water management agencies with some additional information for making the choice of the appropriate restoration technique. (Bell-Cornell)
W75-06566

WATER QUALITY MANAGEMENT: THE CASE FOR RIVER BASIN AUTHORITIES,
Ohio Univ., Athens. Dept. of Civil Engineering.
J. L. Thomas.
Water Resources Bulletin, Vol 9, No 5, p 884-891, October 1973. 17 ref.

Descriptors: *Water management(Applied), *Water pollution control, *River basin commissions, *Planning, Waste water treatment, Regions, Comprehensive planning, Economics, Operations, Water policy, Federal government, State governments.
Identifiers: *Environmental quality.

There is a lamentable absence of comprehensive planning in the current crusade to improve water quality. A serious shortcoming is the lack of evaluation of the effects of waste water treatment upon environmental quality. State efforts to secure adequate pollution control have been ineffective for several reasons, including lack of money, trained personnel, and political strength. On the federal level, current interpretation of official policy encourages only a superficial plan in order to qualify for federal money. The nature of pollution in a river basin demands a coordinated attack against it. Engineering and economic criteria suggest that a properly empowered river basin authority would be the logical organization to plan and operate a water quality management system. Several forms of such authorities have operated effectively and efficiently for many years in the United States and other industrialized countries. Examples of successful river basin authorities and their advantages and methods of operation are discussed. By utilizing the economies of scale available through comprehensive planning and coordinated operation over a large region, the river basin authority should give the taxpayer more for his money; moreover, the authority should be more flexible and stable. (Bell-Cornell)
W75-06571

NUMERICAL MODELING OF THERMAL STRATIFICATION IN A RESERVOIR WITH LARGE DISCHARGE-TO-VOLUME RATIO,
Tennessee Valley Authority, Muscle Shoals, Ala. Air Quality Branch.
For primary bibliographic entry see Field 2H.
W75-06572

MISSISSIPPI COASTAL ZONE MANAGEMENT APPLICATION 1974.
Mississippi Marine Resources Council, Long Beach.
For primary bibliographic entry see Field 6E.
W75-06575

WATER REGULATIONS--TOXIC POLLUTANT EFFLUENT STANDARDS.
Pollution Control Guide, Vol 2, paragraph 8950, p 9385-9388, 1973.

Descriptors: *Water quality standards, *Federal government, *Toxins, *Water pollution control, *Pollutant identification, Water law, Administrative agencies, Water pollution, Water quality, Water quality control, Legislation, Legal aspects, Pollutants, Federal Water Pollution Control Act, Water Quality Act, Regulation, Poisons, Water pollution effects, Water pollution sources, Public health.
Identifiers: Hazardous substances(Pollution), Effluent limitations, FWPCA Amendments of 1972, Administrative regulations, Mercury pollution, Environmental policy.

The criteria to be used by the Environmental Protection Agency (EPA) in the selection of toxic pollutants for which specific effluent standards will be established are presented. These criteria were established by the EPA pursuant to section 307(a) of the Federal Water Pollution Control Act Amendments of 1972. Specific provisions require the application of the following basic criteria: (1) Available data indicate that the pollutant could, if discharged into water, constitute a serious environmental threat; (2) the pollutant is discharged, or can be discharged, from point sources; (3) data are available to establish effluent standards meeting the requirements of the Act; and (4) abatement actions under other provisions of the Act are not commensurate with the nature and seriousness of the pollution problem. The following pollutants are included as toxic pollutants and others may be added in the future: aldrin; dieldrin; benzidine; cadmium; cyanide; DDD; DDE; DDT; endrin; mercury; polychlorinated biphenyls; toxaphene. (Deckert-Florida)

W75-06576

WATER REGULATIONS--PRETREATMENT STANDARDS.
Pollution Control Guide, Vol 2, paragraph 8941-8945, p 9381-9382, 1973.

Descriptors: *Water quality standards, *Industrial water, *Federal government, *Regulation, *Administrative agencies, Water law, Waste water(Pollution), Water pollution, Water pollution control, Water pollution treatment, Water quality control, Legislation, Water quality, Federal Water Pollution Control Act, Pollutants, Legal aspects, Regulation.
Identifiers: Effluent limitations, Administrative regulations, FWPCA Amendments of 1972, Environmental policy.

Regulations were established by the Environmental Protection Agency implementing section 307(b) of the Federal Water Pollution Control Act Amendments of 1972. These regulations set forth standards for pretreatment of pollutants introduced into publicly owned treatment works. The standards apply to all non-domestic users of public treatment works, with special provision applicable to major contributing industries as defined in this part. These regulations do not affect any state or local pretreatment standards not in conflict with federal standards. Specific provisions limit the quantity and quality of incompatible pollutants which may be introduced into publicly owned treatment works, with further provision calling for compliance with specific effluent limitation guidelines for specific industry categories as such guidelines are promulgated. Compliance must be attained not later than three years from the date of final promulgation of such standards. (Deckert-Florida)
W75-06579

ENVIRONMENTAL DEFENSE FUND V. TENNESSEE VALLEY AUTHORITY.
For primary bibliographic entry see Field 6E.
W75-06580

STATE OF WISCONSIN V. CALLAWAY (ACTION FOR INJUNCTIVE RELIEF ON DREDGING ACTIVITIES ON MISSISSIPPI RIVER).
For primary bibliographic entry see Field 6E.
W75-06581

STATE EX REL. DEPARTMENT OF HEALTH V. NORTH JERSEY DISTRICT WATER SUPPLY COMMISSION (ACTION SEEKING MANDATORY INJUNCTION ON REQUIRING COMPLIANCE WITH ORDER TO IMPROVE, ADD TO, OR ALTER WATER TREATMENT PLANT).
For primary bibliographic entry see Field 6E.
W75-06582

STATE LAND USE PLANNING.
For primary bibliographic entry see Field 6E.
W75-06583

ENVIRONMENTAL LAW--PUBLIC TRUST--INJURY TO PUBLIC TRUST IS BASIS FOR AWARD OF DAMAGES,
W. L. Christian.
Seton Hall Law Review, Vol 5, p 394-408, Winter 1974. 121 ref.

Descriptors: *Judicial decisions, *New Jersey, *Nuclear powerplants, *Thermal pollution, Bays, Rivers, Intertidal areas, Waste water disposal, Legal aspects, Level review, Aquatic life, Damages, Wildlife conservation, Common law, Land tenure.
Identifiers: *Public trust doctrine.

In State v. Jersey Central Power and Light Co., the defendant company operated an atomic power plant which used water from the Forked River for cooling and discharged the heated water into Oyster Creek and Barnegat Bay, both tideland areas. An unscheduled shutdown of the plant resulted in a ten degree temperature drop in Oyster Creek. This led to the death of approximately five hundred thousand fish, mostly menhaden, from thermal shock. The State sued on several counts, one of which was a common law action for recovery of damages by the State as parens patriae for injury to wildlife. The court held the State had the right and the fiduciary duty to collect damages for the destruction of wildlife, a part of the corpus of the public trust. (Sperling-Florida)
W75-06584

ENVIRONMENTAL LAW--JUDICIAL REVIEW UNDER NEPA,
J. Holtmann.
Missouri Law Review, Vol 38, p 658-664, Fall 1973. 45 ref.

Descriptors: *Federal jurisdiction, *Arkansas, *Legal aspects, *Decision making, Construction, Dams, Adoption of practices, Administration, Legal review, Environmental effects, Planning, Recreation, Water supply, Natural flow, Water allocation(Policy), Water requirements, Flood protection.
Identifiers: National Environmental Policy Act, Environmental Impact Statement.

In Environmental Defense Fund v. Corps of Engineers, the plaintiff sought to halt construction of a dam. The district court entered a temporary injunction which was to be vacated when the Corps of Engineers complied with the provisions of the National Environmental Policy Act by preparing an environmental impact statement. It was required that the statement detail the environmental consequences of the project and the possible alternatives to the proposed course of action. The court found that construction of the dam would deprive the area of a free flowing stream. In addition, the court noted that although other dams already provided an abundance of recreational waters, the proposed dam would provide needed flood control and water supply benefits. The balancing of interests was irrelevant, however, since there could be no judicial review of the merits of an agency decision to continue construction of the dam. The decision was affirmed on appeal with a modification allowing for limited review of the merits of agency decisions. (Sperling-Florida)
W75-06585

MAN'S ACTIVITIES IN WATERSHED AREAS--A NEED FOR PLANNING,
For primary bibliographic entry see Field 4D.
W75-06588

FEDERAL WATER POLLUTION CONTROL STATUTES IN THEORY AND PRACTICE,
Illinois Univ., Chicago.
L. M. Wenner.
Environmental Law, Vol 4, p 251-293, Winter 1974. 154 ref.

Descriptors: *Federal government, *Water pollution control, *Water quality, *Administration, *Legal aspects, *Federal Water Pollution Control Act, Abatement, Judicial decisions, Legislation, Legal review, Law enforcement, State governments, Water resources, Waste water treatment, Waste assimilative capacity, Waste dilution, Navigable waters, Conservation.
Identifiers: Federal Water Pollution Control Amendments of 1972, Standing(Legal aspects), Refuse Act of 1899, National Environmental Policy Act.

Until fairly recently, federal legislative efforts toward the abatement of water pollution have been designed to influence, indirectly, the vigor with which states enforced their own laws. Since 1965 there has been a shift toward greater direct federal involvement in enforcement. In the face of initial opposition by the states, the change in emphasis has been accomplished gradually. In the 1972 Amendments of the Federal Water Pollution Control Act the attempt to shift the main responsibility of dealing with water pollution to the federal agencies fell short. The 1972 Amendments project as an ultimate goal for 1985 'a no discharge policy', or complete treatment of wastes before discharge into waterways. While final approval of state discharge permit plans vests in the Environmental Pollution Agency, initial enforcement of effluent standards is to be left in the states where that power has long resided. While the new law resolves some old problems such as the concept of navigable waters, standing to sue, and group actions, other questions, such as the attitudes of administrators of the new law and the appropriate role of the federal government in water pollution control remain. (Sperling-Florida)
W75-06590

HANDLING OF AIR AND WATER POLLUTION CASES BY THE PLAINTIFF,
R. E. Cartwright.
Forum, Vol 9, p 639-648, Spring 1974. 5 ref.

Descriptors: *Legal aspects, *Judicial decisions, *Water pollution, *Water quality control, *Common law, Institutional constraints, Law enforcement, Legal review, Negligence, Water law, Trespass, Natural flow doctrine, Relative rights, Water rights, Prescriptive rights, Preferences(Water rights).

Historically, the courts and the economy in both the products liability and environmental law fields have been more concerned with helping industry grow than they have been with the protection of individuals who might be injured in the process. Industrial progress, employment, and the promise of extra tax revenues have always seemed to outweigh the protection of individuals and the imposition of great social costs. In the face of this inertia various legal theories have evolved to assist private plaintiffs. The negligence theory is adequate particularly where the plaintiff has sustained actual property or personal injury damages. The trespass theory is applicable where the defendant has caused an entry onto the plaintiff's property, even if the intrusion was caused by a gas. The nuisance theory is most widely used in environmental actions, and the theory of strict liability for ultra-hazardous activities has been succesfully used in cases dealing with drifting crop sprays and the escape of lethal exterminating gases. In addition, federal, state and local enactments in the pollution field have come to the aid of plaintiffs. (Sperling-Florida)
W75-06593

NEW WATER LAW PROBLEMS AND OLD PUBLIC LAW PRINCIPLES,
New Mexico Univ., Albuquerque.
For primary bibliographic entry see Field 6E.
W75-06595

RED TIDE RESEARCH.
For primary bibliographic entry see Field 6E.
W75-06596

BISCAYNE BAY--AQUATIC PRESERVE.
For primary bibliographic entry see Field 6E.
W75-06598

WATER REGULATIONS--AREAWIDE WASTE TREATMENT MANAGEMENT PLANNING

AREAS AND RESPONSIBLE PLANNING AGENCIES.
Pollution Control Guide, Vol 2, paragraph 8938-38N, p 9375-9378, 1974.

Descriptors: *Water pollution treatment, *Regional development, *Comprehensive planning, *Federal government, *Administrative agencies, Urbanization, Water law, Waste water(Pollution), Water pollution, Water pollution control, Community development, Water quality control, Legislation, Water quality, Federal Water Pollution Control Act, Legal aspects, Regulation, State governments, Local governments, Governmental interrelations.
Identifiers: Administrative regulations, Environmental policy, FWPCA Amendments of 1972.

Regulations were established by the Environmental Protection Agency (EPA) pursuant to section 208(a) of the Federal Water Pollution Control Act Amendments (FWPCA) of 1972. These regulations are designed to serve as guides for state and local officials in identifying areas which, as a result of urban-industrial concentrations or other factors, have substantial water quality control problems which require an areawide approach to planning for the implementing of corrective action. Procedures and criteria are also set forth for designating agencies which are capable of developing waste treatment management plans for such areas. Within 180 days after issuance of this part the Governor of each state shall notify the EPA of his actions regarding designation of 208 planning areas and agencies. Only those agencies designated under this part shall be eligible for assistance under section 208(f),(l),(g) and (h) of the FWPCA Amendments of 1972. (Deckert-Florida)
W75-06599

WATER REGULATIONS--OIL POLLUTION PREVENTION.
Pollution Control Guide, Vol 2, paragraph 8720-8727, p 9215-9219, 1974.

Descriptors: *Water pollution, *Oil wastes, *Navigable waters, *Water pollution sources, Wastes, Chemical wastes, Industrial wastes, Oil, Oil spills, Waste water(Pollution), Waste water disposal, Water pollution, Disasters, Water law, Water resources development, Water quality control, Water quality standards, Pollution abatement, Enforcement, Administration, Regulation, Environmental control.
Identifiers: State policy, Administrative regulations.

Regulations establish procedures, methods, and equipment and other requirements for equipment to prevent the discharge of oil from non-transportation-related onshore and offshore facilities. The regulations generally apply to oil pollution of navigable waters of the United States or adjoining shorelines. Actual or potential polluters are required to prepare and implement spill prevention control and countermeasure plans. These plans must be prepared in accordance with good engineering practices to include containment equipment for possible oil discharges. Bulk storage installations and dike containment areas must be sufficiently impervious to contain spilled oil. Alternative containment systems are required to provide for emergency in-plant catch basins or holding ponds. Civil penalties are set forth for non-compliance of provisions. (Proctor-Florida)
W75-06600

WATER REGULATIONS--POLICIES AND PROCEDURES FOR STATE CONTINUING PLANNING PROCESS.
Pollution Control Guide, Vol 2, paragraph 8960-8986, p 9391-9397, 1974.

Descriptors: *Comprehensive planning, *Federal government, *State governments, *Administrative agencies, *Water quality control, Discharge(Water), Future planning(Projected), Watersheds(Basins), Basins, Planning, Water resources development, Water pollution control, Administration, Coordination, Long-term planning, Governmental interrelations, Inter-agency cooperation, Water quality standards, Water law, Water quality control, Federal Water Pollution Control Act, Water Quality Act, Control, Hydrologic systems.
Identifiers: Administrative regulations, Environmental policy, National Pollutant Discharge Elimination System, Effluent limitations, FWPCA Amendments of 1972.

Regulations were established by the Environmental Protection Agency pursuant to section 303(e) of the Federal Water Pollution Control Act, as amended in 1972. These regulations specify procedural and other requirements for the submission and approval of state continuing planning processes. The state continuing planning process is directed toward the attainment of water quality standards established under section 303 of the Act which are designed to achieve the goals set forth in the Act. The process provides a mechanism for developing an annual state strategy for directing resources, establishing priorities, scheduling actions, and reporting progress. Included are regulations pertaining to the scope and purpose of the processes, definitions, general requirements, specific requirements for basin plans and annual state strategies, submission and approval of planning processes and reports, and the relationship of the processes to state participation in the National Pollutant Discharge Elimination System. (Deckert-Florida)
W75-06601

ADOPTED STANDARDS (WATER QUALITY).
Pollution Control Guide, Vol 1, paragraph 581-588, p 577-580, February 1974.

Descriptors: *Administrative agencies, *Water quality standards, *Federal Water Pollution Control Act, *State governments, *Adoption of practices, Decision-making, Administration, Water law, Legislation, Water quality control, Water pollution control, Legal aspects, Federal government, Water quality, Water treatment, Regulation, Governmental interrelations, Water policy, Law enforcement, Jurisdiction, Federal-state water rights conflicts.
Identifiers: FWPCA Amendments of 1972, Administrative regulations, Environmental policy, State policy.

Any water quality standard adopted by any state awaiting approval or approved by the Environmental Protection Agency (EPA) on October 18, 1972, will remain in effect unless the state is notified of any required changes. The 18th of October is the date of enactment of the Amendments to the Federal Water Pollution Control Act. If the state failed to adopt the required changes within ninety days the agency would be required to promulgate the necessary changes. Any state that had not adopted intrastate water quality standards by October 18, 1972, was required to adopt and submit such standards to the EPA Regional Administrator by April 16, 1973. The Agency may establish water quality standards for a state that fails to adopt or revise adequate standards by calling a conference of federal departments and agencies, interstate agencies, states, municipalities and industries affected by the standards. Following the conference, the Agency may establish such standards pursuant to procedures set forth in the Act. (Sperling-Florida)
W75-06602

POWER AUTHORITY OF STATE OF NEW YORK V. DEPT. OF ENVIRONMENTAL CONSERVATION OF STATE OF NEW YORK (SEEKING DECLARATORY AND INJUNCTIVE RELIEF AS TO WHETHER DEPARTMENT WAS WITHOUT AUTHORITY IN ISSUING CERTIFICATE FOR POWERPLANT WATER DISCHARGE).
For primary bibliographic entry see Field 6E.
W75-06606

U.S. V. W.B. ENTERPRISES, INC. (SUIT TO RECOVER CIVIL PENALTY ASSESSED FOR LEAKAGE OF OIL FROM BARGE).
For primary bibliographic entry see Field 6E.
W75-06607

COMMONWEALTH OF PENNSYLVANIA V. BARNES AND TUCKER CO. (ACTION TO REQUIRE OWNER OF CLOSED MINE TO TREAT ACID MINE DRAINAGE DISCHARGING FROM MINE).
For primary bibliographic entry see Field 6E.
W75-06609

ARKANSAS ENVIRONMENTAL QUALITY ACT OF 1973.
For primary bibliographic entry see Field 6E.
W75-06610

U.S. V. LEWIS (INJUNCTION ACTION BASED ON VIOLATION OF RIVERS AND HARBORS ACT.
For primary bibliographic entry see Field 6E.
W75-06612

U.S. V. STOECO HOMES, INC. (APPEAL FROM INJUNCTION FOR VIOLATIONS OF RIVERS AND HARBORS ACT).
For primary bibliographic entry see Field 6E.
W75-06613

WATER REGULATIONS--LIABILITY LIMITS FOR SMALL ONSHORE STORAGE FACILITIES.
Pollution Control Guide, Vol 2, paragraph 8730-8735, p 9221-9223, 1973.

Descriptors: *Oil pollution, *Water pollution, *Legislation, *Water quality control, United States, Governments, Oil spills, Oil wastes, Oil industry, Drilling, Water pollution sources, Industrial wastes, Oily water, Water law.
Identifiers: *Waste discharge, *On-shore storage facilities.

Subpart A establishes size classifications and associated liability limits for small onshore oil storage facilities with a fixed capacity of 1,000 barrels or less, Liability for discharge of oil into the waters of the United States from such facilities unless removal is performed by the United States government is limited by this subpart. Unless the United States can demonstrate willful negligence or willful misconduct within the privity and knowledge of the owner, liability is assessed according to the barrel capacity and the above ground or below ground location of the facility. (Proctor-Florida)
W75-06614

PROVIDENCE RIVER AND HARBOR, RHODE ISLAND (FINAL ENVIRONMENTAL IMPACT STATEMENT).
Corps of Engineers, Waltham, Mass. New England Div.
Available from the National Technical Information Service, Springfield, Va. 22161 as EIS-RI-73-1663-F. October 17, 1973. 173p.

Descriptors: *Water pollution sources, *Navigation, *Channel improvement, *Dredging, Water pollution, Waste disposal, Channels, Rivers, *Rhode Island, Aquatic habitat, Benthic fauna, Benthic flora, Biochemical oxygen demand, Chemical oxygen demand, Oil spills, Commercial fishing, Ships, Oceans, Environmental effects.

Identifiers: *Environmental Impact Statements, *Providence River(R.I.), Ocean dumping.

A navigation improvement project to remove shoals in the Providence River in areas opposite the Fuller Rock Light, adjacent to Ponham Beacon, and an extensive area southeast of Coninicut Light will complete the Providence River project to deepen the channel from 35 to 40 feet. The dumpsite is the ocean disposal site 4.6 miles from Brenton Reef Light in water 100-108 feet deep used in the original dredging. Adverse environmental effects are those associated with dredging and ocean disposal, including increased turbidity, increased BOD and COD, and disruption of benthic communities. Particularly in the spoil area, the fishery and benthic environment has not returned to normal within a year of dumping. To minimize further damage, disposal at the original site is recommended. Two out of three of the areas to be dredged are located near sewage outfalls and the environmental quality is consequently in a stressed condition. Recent dredging during the original project also requires an assumption that no benthic organisms of value exist, even in the area least affected by pollutants. This disruption of the environment by turbidity during dredging will be minimal, and temporary. Alternatives proved unfeasible, and completion of this project assures the efficient and safe passage of deep-draft vessels, together with accompanying economic benefits to local industries and businesses using the port. (Ostapoff-Florida)
W75-06615

POINT SOURCES COVERED BY NPDES AND PROCEDURES.
Pollution Control Guide, Vol 1, paragraph 1505-1523, p 1512-1527, 1973.

Descriptors: *Discharge(Water), *Permits, *Water pollution control, *Regulation, *Federal government, Waste water(Pollution), Water quality control, Federal Water Pollution Control Act, Water Quality Act, Water law, Effluents, Water pollution sources, Administrative agencies, Control, Law enforcement, Legal aspects, Administration, Inter-agency cooperation, Water pollution treatment.
Identifiers: National Pollution Discharge Elimination System, Administrative regulations, Licenses, Effluent limitations, Certification, FWPCA Amendments of 1972.

Although all discharges from point sources into navigable waters are regulated by the system of effluent limitations established under the Federal Water Pollution Control Act, not all dischargers must obtain NPDES permits for the discharge of pollutants. Some dischargers are required to obtain a different permit; others need not obtain any permit. Provisions are presented that detail persons required to obtain an NPDES permit and the procedures for acquiring a permit. Specific areas covered are: requirements for submission of applications, including information and state certification requirements, application fees, and deadlines; notice to other governmental agencies; public participation requirements; environmental impact statements; power of the Regional Administrator to issue a final decision; public hearing requirements; and rules governing the conduct of adjudicatory hearings concerning proposed permit applications. (Deckett-Florida)
W75-06617

POLLUTION--REGULATION.
For primary bibliographic entry see Field 6E.
W75-06618

EFFLUENT GUIDELINES ARE ON THE WAY,
H. M. Malin, Jr.
Environmental Science and Technology, Vol 6, No 9, p 786-787, September 1972.

Descriptors: *Effluents, *Wastes, *Water pollution sources, *Industrial pollution, Industrial wastes, Waste water(Pollution), Waste water disposal, Water pollution, Regulations, Water law, Water resources development, Water quality control, Water quality, Pollution abatement, Administration, Administrative decisions, Environmental control, Enforcement, Regulation, Federal government.
Identifiers: Administrative regulations, Environmental policy, Effluent limitations.

In its efforts to control industrial water pollution, the Environmental Protection Agency (EPA) has adopted a tactiv used by its Office of Air Programs to halt air pollution from stationary sources. The EPA's Office of Water Programs has been restructured to provide a framework for developing effluent guidelines and performance standards. The EPA's previous effluent control strategy, based on water quality standards oriented to the receiving waters, proved too costly and cumbersome. Moreover, remedies for the enforcement of these water quality standards were virtually devoid of clout. Legal authority to operate the effluent guidelines program will soon be forthcoming from Congress, and the EPA is already progressing with the program's development. The guidelines will identify both the best practicable technology currently available and the best available demonstrated technology. By 1976 all industrial waste sources would be required to meet the 'best practicable' guidelines. Within 15 months of the passage of the law the EPA will promulgate performance standards for new sources or all old sources which undergo 'major modification'. Such sources would have to incorporate the 'best available demonstrated techology.' The EPA will also publish a toxic substances list, effluent standards for each toxic substance, and effluent pretreatment guidelines. (Proctor-Florida)
W75-06619

RESULTS OF TESTING CLEAN-FLO LAKE CLEANSER IN FLORIDA LAKES,
Florida State Game and Fresh Water Fish Commission, Lake City; and Clean-Flo Labs., Inc., Hopkins, Minn.
For primary bibliographic entry see Field 5D.
W75-06672

LANE COUNTY PRELIMINARY GENERAL PLAN-WATER QUALITY MANAGEMENT PLAN.
Lane Council of Governments, Eugene, Oreg.
March, 1974. 51 p, 4 fig, 39 tab, 1 append.

Descriptors: *Water quality control, *Management, *Administration, *Waste water(Pollution), *Planning, *Industrial effluents, *Water quality standards, Water resources development, Water pollution sources, Oregon long-term planning, Operations.
Identifiers: Lane County(Oregon), Eugene(Oregon).

Actions, target dates and estimated costs involved in controlling domestic and industrial sources of water pollution in the Willamette Basin portion of Lane County, Oregon are specified in this plan. Maps are included to show the planning area, river basin relationships and population distribution. A table specifies the wastewater pollution sources studied. The water quality management plan is organized by river basins. It shows present and future treatment technology for each significant domestic and industrial wastewater source. Public costs (in terms of 1972 dollars) and timing are shown for each public domestic wastewater project, and timing for funding and construction are indicated for industrial ventures. The plan itself, in complete detail, is contained in the tables and maps presented in the latter portion of this document. The appendix to the plan contains goals, policies, and recommendations extracted from the 'County-Wide Policies' document that may have an impact on water quality. Recommendations are made for the adoption of the water quality management plan as the basis for water pollution control in Lane County. (Poertner)
W75-06680

PROCESS FOR CONTAINING OIL SPILLS,
Secretary of Agriculture, Washington, D.C. (assignee)
W. L. Stanley, and A. G. Pittman.
U.S. Patent No 3,869,385, 6 p, 10 ref:; Official Gazette of the United States Patent Office, Vol 932, No 1, p 229, March 4, 1975.

Descriptors: *Patents, *Oil spills, *Oil pollution, *Pollution abatement, Water quality control, Water pollution control, Coagulation, *Separation techniques.
Identifiers: *Chemical treatment, Polyisocyanate, Polyamines.

A process is described for containing an oil spill on a body of water. A polyisocyanate and a polyamine are applied to the oil spill in such amounts as to furnish free isocyanate groups in approximately equimolar proportion to amino groups. Both the polyisocyanate and the polyamine have a density less than that of the water and are at least partially miscible with oil but essentially immiscible with water. The process is not based on absorbance but on the principle of containing the oil by a thickening or coagulating effect, with the result that relatively small proportions of the reagents are effective. For example, in many cases the use of about 1 to 3 parts of polyisocyanate plus polyamine per 100 parts of oil is sufficient to attain the desired containment effect. (Sinha-OEIS)
W75-06683

MODULAR OIL CONTAINMENT BOOM,
Murphy-Pacific Marine Salvage Co., New York. Merritt Div. (assignee)
R. K. Thurman.
U.S. Patent No. 3,868,824, 5 p, 3 fig, 7 ref; Official Gazette of the United States Patent Office, Vol 932, No 1, p 49, March 4, 1975.

Descriptors: *Patents, *Oil spills, *Oil pollution, *Pollution abatement, Water pollution control, Water quality control, Equipment, *Separation techniques.
Identifiers: Wave action, *Oil containment booms.

A floating oil containment boom is formed of a multiplicity of modules which may easily be connected and disconnected while afloat. The modules include a vertical barrier, on both sides of which are connected a pair of foam-filled drums. A flexible waterproof panel having a zipper on each end is secured to the barrier by use of battens fastened to the barrier over the panel and outside a welt formed on the panel edges where the panel overlaps the barrier. A piping is formed adjacent and parallel to the zipper on the end of the panel for use in connection with a slotted tube as an auxiliary means for fastening adjacent panel ends together. A set of chains is provided for interconnecting the top and bottom end corners of adjacent barriers together to prevent excessive vertical and angular displacement between adjacent modules to prevent stressing of the flexible panel by heavy wave action. (Sinha-OEIS)
W75-06687

OIL-WATER SEPARATION PROCESS,
H. F. Keller, Jr.
U.S. Patent No. 3,867,285, 8 p, 9 tab, 2 ref; Official Gazette of the United States Patent Office, Vol 931, No 3, p 1315, February 18, 1975.

Descriptors: *Patents, *Oil wastes, *Oil pollution, *Pollution abatement, Water pollution control, *Filtration, *Separation techniques, Filters, Organic matter, Solid wastes.
Identifiers: Particulate solids, Acidification.

A filtration method for treating fluid systems containing oil, water and particulate solids to produce clarified water, solids-free oil and oil-free solids is disclosed. It uses an improved filter media which permits more rapid and efficient filtration treatment of such fluid systems. The fluid system containing oil having an API Gravity value from about 11 to about 70, water and particulate solids is filtered through a finely divided oil and water insoluble filter media to retain particulate solids and oil within the filter media and pass an effluent of either clarified water or a mixture of solids-free oil and water which separates into defined layers of solids-free oil and clarified water, with the mixture being attained when the oil content of the fluid system is in excess of about 1% by weight. When the fluid system contains acid insolubilizing, water soluble, organic material, the fluid system, prior to filtration, is acidified with a non-toxic acid to a pH below about 4.8 to convert the organic material to a water insoluble, adsorbable oil. The filter media is periodically regenerated by stripping oil therefrom and then backwashing the media to remove entrained solids. The products produced by the method include clarified water, solids-free oil and oil-free solids. (Sinha-OEIS)
W75-06692

METHOD AND APPARATUS FOR PREVENTING THERMAL POLLUTION,
Computer Sciences Corp., Los Angeles, Calif. (assignee)
For primary bibliographic entry see Field 5D.
W75-06694

FLOTATION TYPE WATER SWEEP BOOM AND METHODS,
C. H. Rudd.
U.S. Patent No. 3,852,965, 6 p, 11 fig, 5 ref; Official Gazette of the United States Patent Office, Vol 929, No 2, p 530, December 10, 1974.

Descriptors: *Separation techniques, *Patents, *Oil spills, *Oil pollution, *Flotsam, Water quality control, *Pollution abatement, *Water pollution control, Equipment.

A floating boom apparatus is adapted to collect floating material and elements, such as oil, in water by being towed laterally through the water from each end of the boom. A curtain extends downward in the water from a floating surface barrier with the upper portion of the curtain being impervious and the lower portion being open for the passage of water. The boom is towed by two lines, one extending through the floating surface barrier and the other connected along the lower extremity of the curtain, and the lower line is pulled in advance of the upper line. (Sinha-OEIS)
W75-06695

REMOVAL OF MARINE GROWTHS FROM LAKES, WATERWAYS, AND OTHER BODIES OF WATER,
D. A. Meyer.
U.S. Patent No. 3,866,396, 9 p, 22 fig, 6 ref; Official Gazette of the United States Patent Office, Vol 931, No 3, p 1034, February 18, 1975.

Descriptors: *Aquatic weed control, *Harvesting of algae, *Patents, Lakes, Rivers, *Water quality, *Quality control, Water resources, Bodies of water, Eutrophication, Water supply, River flow, Aquatic plants, Marine plants, Submerged plants.

A novel device for selectively removing various types of marine growths from lakes, rivers, canals and other waterways has a rotary cutter placed in a housing which is closed except at its forwardmost portion. The cutter includes a rotatable drum having helical cutter blades arranged to cut encountered growths into short lengths. A portion of adjacent cutter blades extend into the housing while the remaining portion of these blades are passing past the opening in the housing. The housing is submerged below the water surface from a suitable floating structure such as a barge, with a suction pump mounted on the barge connected to the housing for bringing about a suction condition. The suction extends to the space between adjacent blades passing past the opening in the housing causing encountered growths to move and be held in contact with the blades in an optimum position for cutting. The suction also serves to remove the growths from the housing and deliver them to a traveling screen belt on the barge. There water is removed from the cut growths, and the growths, now semi-dried, are packaged in an appropriate manner. (Sinha-OEIS)
W75-06696

WELLAND CANAL WATER QUALITY CONTROL EXPERIMENTS (PHASE II),
Department of the Environment, Ottawa (Ontario). Wastewater Technology Centre.
E. E. Shannon, F. J. Ludwig, D. T. Vachon, and I. F. Munawar.
Technology Development Report EPS 4-WP-74-10, 59 p, October 1974, Water Pollution Control Directorate. 12 fig, 15 ref, 10 tab, 3 append.

Descriptors: *Water quality control, Water chemistry, Algae, Biomass, Nutrients, Phosphorus, Chlorophyll, Sampling, Monitoring, Phytoplankton, Zooplankton, Data collections, *Feasibility studies.
Identifiers: *Welland Canal, *Alum, Flocculants, Turbidity, Treatment costs.

Feasibility studies on the utilization of alum for water quality control in the Fourth Welland Canal were described in an earlier Phase I report by Shannon and Vachon (1973). This report details the results of the full scale alum treatment (dosage of 2.5 mg/l as Al) of the Fourth Canal. The continuing program on the experimental basins is also described. The biological, chemical, and physical characteristics of the Fourth Canal were monitored weekly from April 1973 to March 1974. On the basis of the chlorophyll, total phosphorus, turbidity and water transparency data it was concluded that alum treatment was successful in maintaining acceptable water quality in the central and southerly reaches of the canal. The average water quality in the Central reach was equal to, and in some respects superior to, the water quality in the flow-through northerly reach. Because of suspected phosphorus inputs, higher total phosphorus and chlorophyll levels were evident in the southerly reach. Consequently, it was recommended that alum treatment be repeated in this reach in May 1974. The cost of treating the Fourth Canal in 1973 was $16,470, or approximately $90/acre of water surface. Special algal enumeration and identification studies in the experimental basins revealed that the alum treatment was effective in controlling algal biomass. Zooplankton data collected in the experimental basins suggested that alum or sodium aluminate treatments at realistic application levels will not adversely affect natural zooplankton populations. (Environment Canada)
W75-06736

PUBLIC PERCEPTIONS OF WATER QUALITY AND THEIR EFFECT ON WATER-BASED RECREATION,
Department of the Environment, Ottawa (Ontario). Water Planning and Management Branch.
For primary bibliographic entry see Field 6B.
W75-06752

KALAMAZOO COUNTY, MICHIGAN, WATER QUALITY STUDY,
Jones and Henry, Toledo, Ohio.
Available from the National Technical Information Service, Springfield, Va 22161, as PB-235 670, $5.25 in paper copy, $2.25 in microfiche. Prepared for Kalamazoo Metropolitan County Planning Commission, Kalamazoo, Michigan, August, 1974. 100 p, 30 fig, 3 tab, 19 ref, 4 append. CPA-MI-05-28-0354.

Descriptors: *Water quality control, *Water pollution control, Water resources, *Eutrophication, *Water demand, *Planning, Water quality standards, Water policy, Groundwater resources, Subsurface water, Water distribution, Sewers, Urban drainage, *Michigan.
Identifiers: Observation wells, Kalamazoo River(Mich), Portage Creek(Mich).

With an abundance of well-distributed water resources, Kalamazoo undertook a study to determine existing water quality information to assist the county in developing a comprehensive water management plan. Relying heavily on existing data, reports, and surveys of the hydrologic and geologic conditions, this report analyzes and evaluates this information, and examines the relationship of water quality to water use and water quality standards. Although ground water is of good quality, the surface water has shown degraded water quality resulting from industrial and agricultural effluent. Present water quality requirements vary significantly from industry to industry, as well as for household uses. Increasing eutrophication in lakes and pollution in the Kalamazoo River and Portage Creek, has led to the following recommendations for improving water quality through management: (1) continual sampling and analysis--including expansion of the monitoring system; (2) completion of sanitary sewer projects; (3) designation of observation wells in all land disposal or land storage areas; (4) reduction of withdrawals of water in upper aquifers to prevent salt water intrusion, (5) flushing or urban run-off; and (6) establishment of a county agency responsible for water quality control to hear complaints, administer and coordinate sampling projects and conduct water quality surveys. (Salzman-North Carolina)
W75-06759

EDWARDS AQUIFER, A STUDY OF EDWARDS RECHARGE ZONE REQUIREMENTS, AACOG WATER QUALITY PLANNING, PHASE 5,
Alamo Area Council of Governments, San Antonio, Tex.
For primary bibliographic entry see Field 4B.
W75-06761

COLORADO RIVER SALINITY, NEW SOLUTIONS TO AN OLD PROBLEM.
Reclamation ERA, Vol 60, No 4, p 1-7, Autumn 1974. 6 fig.

Descriptors: *Colorado River Basin, *Mexican Water Treaty, *Salinity, *Water management(Applied), Water resources development, Colorado River, *Mexico, Water resources, Colorado, Irrigation.
Identifiers: Imperial Dam, Bureau of Reclamation, Paradox Valley Unit(Colo), Grand Valley Basin Unit(Colo), Crystal Geyser Unit(Utah), Las Vegas Wash Unit(Nev).

Water quality on the Colorado River will be enhanced due to recent passage of Federal legislation authorizing a $280.6 million program aimed at controlling the river's salinity. A formal protest from Mexico started a series of negotiations and agreements intended to reduce river salinity at the border and provided basis for the legislation. Users in both United States and Mexico will benefit. It also authorizes $125 million for salinity control projects upstream from Imperial Dam to improve water quality in the Lower Basin. Bureau of Reclamation is the primary agency constructing facilities to carry out the salinity program. Present regional economic loss is estimated at $53 million due to crop failures, poor soil and other results of high saline concentrations. Almost 10 million tons of salts and other minerals are picked up by the river as it flows from its headwaters to Mexico. Salinity levels range from less than 50 parts per

million at headwaters to an average of about 850 million parts per million at Imperial Dam near Yuma, Arizona. A large desalting complex will be built near Yuma plus facilities to manage, treat and dispose of drainage return flows from the Wellton-Mohawk Irrigation District, a significant salinity source. Funds will also provide a protective pumping well field, repairs to 49 miles of Coachella Canal to reduce conveyance losses, and salinity control measures at Paradox Valley Unit, Colo., Grand Valley Basin Unit, Colo., Crystal Geyser Unit, Utah, and Las Vegas Wash Unit, Utah. (Salzman-North Carolina)
W75-06774

THE INTERCOASTAL WATERWAY: AN ECOLOGICAL PERSPECTIVE,
Florida Atlantic Univ., Boca Raton. Dept. of Biological Sciences.
G. A. Marsh.
Florida Environmental and Urban Issues, Vol II, No 2, p 6-7, 13-15, November, 1974. 1 fig.

Descriptors: *Saline water, Fresh water, Interfaces, *Estuaries, *Encroachment, Water resource management, *Marine animals, Water pollution control, Water quality control, *Florida, Ecology.
Identifiers: South Florida's Atlantic Intracoastal Waterway(ICWW), Palm Beach County(Fla), Broward County(Fla), Dade County(Fla).

South Florida's Atlantic Intracoastal Waterway (ICWW) interconnects a series of natural lakes, bays and lagoons which are separated from the ocean by islands and peninsulas which form the Gold Coast. ICWW provides a protected boating passage linking the coastal municipalities and serves the recreational, drainage and waste disposal needs of Palm Beach, Broward and Dade Counties. Environmentally degrading changes to inland marine waters have resulted from population growth. Water quality has declined and demand for waterfront acreage has brought devastation to natural shoreline vegetation and proliferation of finger canal development adjoining the waterway. Despite pollution, ICWW remains a habitat for many forms of marine and estuarine life. Fresh water is added to waterways by increased urban run-off and land drainage thereby reducing saline content and killing marine and estuarine species. Control facilities to treat effluent of partially or non-treated solutions and surface run-off, both agricultural and urban, have been implemented. Pathogenic microorganisms are evident, which underlines the urgent need for water chemistry analysis, guidelines, and legislation for regulatory design criteria for future canal development. (Salzman-North Carolina)
W75-06776

REPORT ON THE CHARLES RIVER: A STUDY OF WATER POLLUTION,
Massachusetts Water Resources Commission, Boston. Div. of Water Pollution Control.
For primary bibliographic entry see Field 5B.
W75-06777

KEY LAND USE ISSUES FACING EPA.
Harbridge House, Inc., Boston, Mass.
Available from the National Technical Information Service, Springfield, Va 22161 as PB-235 345, $10.25 in paper copy, $2.25 in microfiche. Environmental Protection Agency, Washington, D.C., Office of Planning and Evaluation Report EPA 230/3-74-011, February 1974. 371 p, 13 fig, 8 tab, 7 append. BOA-68-01-1561.

Descriptors: *Land use, *Planning, *Environmental quality, Land management, Natural resources, Air pollution, Water pollution, Thermal pollution, Environmental effects, Water pollution control.
Identifiers: Land use planning, Locational siting, Agricultural land use, Industrial siting.

Land use issues of concern to EPA policy makers either because of projected trends, patterns, timing, and/or magnitude of their environmental impact are identified and assessed. First divided into major categories like transportation or agriculture, land use issues are analyzed by growth and development patterns and siting of key facilities (location). Focus is four-fold: (1) identify current land use problems, (2) determine trends and projections impacting future land use problems, (3) develop methodology for assessing relative importance of the issues in light of EPA's concerns and responsibilities, and (4) identify gaps in information and/or policy that prohibit a complete assessment. Data include nationwide patterns of land use, environmental impacts on air, water and land, and present land use projects and programs. Each land use issue is viewed in terms of its direct pollution impact and indirect effects of future use. The direct link between man's use of the land and total environmental quality is underscored as the full-cycle of the cause-effect relationship is examined. Coordination between planning, review and implementation of policies affecting land use involving all political jurisdictions is necessary. (Salzman-North Carolina)
W75-06780

A REVIEW OF THE PRESENT AND ANNOUNCED FUTURE CAPABILITIES FOR COMMERCIAL OIL RECOVERY BEYOND THE 656 FOOT ISOBATH,
State Univ. of New York, Stony Brook. Marine Sciences Research Center.
L. C. Leopold.
Marine Affairs Journal, Number 1, p 91-97, December 1973.

Descriptors: Oil, *Oil fields, Exploitation, *Oil industry, *Drilling, *Exploration, *Secondary recovery(Oil), *Economic efficiency, *Investment, International waters, Oil wells, Legislation.
Identifiers: Submersible Production System, Rigs, Drilling.

This is a brief look at the commitment of the oil industry to deep offshore exploitation. A tabulation inventory of drilling rigs was undertaken to illustrate what the usage level was at the time of the counts. Considering that no growth in 600 plus foot group has occurred until now, the 38 new rigs reflect the conclusion that 600 plus foot water is now an economically justified depth. The latter part of the article is a synthesis of reports which help to define the degree of commitment and present capabilities to economic oil recovery beyond 656 feet. ESSO's Submersible Production System is just one of several methods which proves the feasibility of drilling for oil at these depths. As new shore basins are discovered, new deep-water production systems generated and oil demand continues, deep drilling in coastal areas will continue. The only foreseeable deterrents are the regulation in natural gas prices and the shortage of construction equipment. Continual capital and manpower investment points to the oil industry's interest in deep-well drilling. (Salzman-North Carolina)
W75-06791

SET PROBE OF POLLUTION CONTROL AMENDMENTS.
Engineering News and Record, Vol 193, No 7, p 24, August 8, 1974.

Descriptors: *Waste treatment, *Costs, *Industrial wastes, *Municipal wastes, Pulp and paper industry, Chemical industry, *Administrative agencies, Economic impact, Federal Water Pollution Control Act.
Identifiers: 1972 Amendments.

Five contracts have been awarded by the National Commission on Water Quality for studies of the impact of the Federal Water Pollution Control Act Amendments of 1972. The studies are on the cost to municipalities and industries of meeting the effluent limitations of the law and possible sources of local funding for municipalities building waste treatment plants; and studies on petroleum refining, iron and steel, pulp and paper, and organic chemicals industries which include examinations of alternative methods of waste treatment and associated costs, quality of effluent with various methods and materials and energy requirements. (Orr-FIRL)
W75-06827

LINKS WITH WATER RESOURCES AND LAND USE PLANNING STRESSED AT CORNELL CONFERENCE.
Civil Engineering-ASCE, Vol 44, No. 8, p 92-94, August, 1974.

Descriptors: *Conferences, *Water quality, *Planning, *Alternative planning, Future planning(Projected), Project planning, Sewers, Water pollution sources, Land use, Management.

Highlights of the first water quality planning conference held at Cornell University in June 1974 are outlined. Points discussed include the implementing of plans, better planning of river basins, water quality linked with land use, sewers as a dominant factor in controlling urban growth, Pennsylvania's systematic approach to planning, and the significance of non-point source pollution. (Sandoski-FIRL)
W75-06828

EXPERIMENTAL OIL SKIMMER.
Mechanical Engineering, Vol 96, No 8, p 48, August, 1974. 1 fig.

Descriptors: *Oils spills, *Oceans, *Oil skimmers, Recovery, Equipment, California, Separation techniques, Pollution abatement.
Identifiers: Oil-recovery capacities, Survival test(Equipment).

A test was run on an oil skimmer which could be used for emergency oil spills at high seas. This system built by Lockheed Missiles and Space Company, was tested by riding it (with Coast Guard escorts) through a storm off the northern California coast. The oil-recovery capacities are up to 1000 gallons of oil per minute. A disc-drum revolves in an oil-water mix, oil adheres to the discs and free water runs off, and the oil is carried past wipers that direct it to a hollow axle. Oil then is pumped from the machine to storage containers. The machine is designed to be carried to an airport near an oil-spill site, assembled in an hour, and towed or carried on a buoy tender to the work area. (Prague-FIRL)
W75-06830

NINE MILLION GALLONS PER MINUTE DOWN THE DRAIN, FEDERAL GUIDELINES PRESENT A TOUGH CHALLENGE,
Canadian Petroleum, Vol 15, No 7, p 40-42, July, 1974.

Descriptors: *Water quality control, *Industrial water, *Canada, *Industries, Industrial wastes, Environmental control, Waste water treatment, Water quality standards, Effluents, Heavy metals.

With their introduction of water quality guidelines in 1973, Environment Canada has emphasized the reduction of effluent BOD and the elimination of such contaminants as cyanides. The federal standards are not nearly as precise on the tolerable levels of heavy metals since not enough is known about the interaction of various metals. A description of various industrial pollutants, their effects, industrial problems, and treatment methods and materials is provided. (Sandoski-FIRL)
W75-06834

6. WATER RESOURCES PLANNING

6A. Techniques Of Planning

STOCHASTIC VARIATIONS IN WATER QUALITY PARAMETERS,
Rutgers - the State Univ., New Brunswick, N. J. Bureau of Engineering Research.
For primary bibliographic entry see Field 5B.
W75-06355

CONFIDENCE LIMITS FOR DESIGN EVENTS,
Department of the Environment, Ottawa (Ontario). Water Resources Branch.
For primary bibliographic entry see Field 2E.
W75-06544

BIRTH-DEATH MODELS FOR DIFFERENTIAL PERSISTENCE,
Harvard Unov., Boston, Mass. Graduate School of Business Administration.
For primary bibliographic entry see Field 2E.
W75-06546

COMPREHENSIVE WATER QUALITY MANAGEMENT PLANNING,
Pennsylvania Dept. of Environmental Resources, Harrisburg. Office of Comprehensive Water and Wastewater Management Planning.
For primary bibliographic entry see Field 5G.
W75-06558

ANALYSIS OF MULTIPLE OBJECTIVES IN WATER QUALITY,
Case Western Reserve Univ., Cleveland, Ohio. Systems Engineering Div.
For primary bibliographic entry see Field 5D.
W75-06559

STEADY-STATE WATER QUALITY MODELING IN STREAMS,
Cornell Univ., Ithaca, N.Y. School of Civil and Environmental Engineering.
For primary bibliographic entry see Field 5B.
W75-06564

ECONOMIC FORECASTING FOR VIRGINIA'S WATER RESOURCE PROGRAMS,
Virginia State Water Control Board, Richmond.
For primary bibliographic entry see Field 6B.
W75-06573

URBAN SYSTEMS ENGINEERING DEMONSTRATION PROGRAM: INFORMATION SUMMARY FOR WATERWORKS, SANITARY SEWERAGE, SOLID WASTE MANAGEMENT, STORM DRAINAGE AND FLOOD PLAIN MANAGEMENT,
Diversified Consultants, Inc., Jackson, Miss.
J. A. Elliott, R. L. Waters, and A. P. Desmarais.
The Gulf Regional Planning Commission, Gulfport, Mississippi, 1973. 59 p, 16 tab. MS-04-25-1001. MS-04-2501001.

Descriptors: *Comprehensive planning, *Mississippi, *Urbanization, *Regional analysis, Sewerage, Surveys, Urban drainage, Forecasting, Solid wastes, Data collections, Water supply, Flood plains, Storm water.

A comprehensive plan was developed for the four-county region of the Gulf Regional Planning Commission. The plan dealt with the subjects of waterworks, sanitary sewerage, solid waste management, storm drainage, and flood plan management. A five-volume report of the study was prepared. This report summarizing these volumes. The study area had a 1970 population of 268,000. Total land area is 2,600 acres and land use forecasts do not predict large scale development of presently undeveloped areas. The area's economy is helped by an abundance of natural resources. Tourism, government, agriculture and manufacturing are four major components of the economic base. Six general objectives were formulated for the study, including: (1) reliable projections and data on future and existing services in each of the fields studies, (2) the development of short-range and long-range plans, (3) development of regional public policies for orderly development, (4) encouragement of consolidation of small utility systems, (5) development and/or refinement of tools to implement the plan, and (6) periodic review of local regulations and policies to insure that they are in accordance with the overall objectives. Requirements for each area of the program are outlined up to year 1990. Total cost of the programs is estimated at $204.2 million with sanitary sewerage being the most expensive ($147.1 million) and solid waste management the least expensive ($1.0 million). (Poertner)
W75-06673

6B. Evaluation Process

LAND-USE ISSUES: PROCEEDINGS OF A CONFERENCE.
Virginia Polytechnic Inst. and State Univ., Blacksburg. Water Resources Research Center.
For primary bibliographic entry see Field 4A.
W75-06359

ATTITUDES TOWARD WATER USE PRACTICES AMONG S.E. IDAHO FARMERS: A STUDY ON ADOPTION OF IRRIGATION SCHEDULING,
Idaho Univ., Moscow. Dept. of Agricultural and Forest Economics.
For primary bibliographic entry see Field 3F.
W75-06363

SALINITY IN WATER RESOURCES.
For primary bibliographic entry see Field 3C.
W75-06366

CURRENT APPROACHES AND ALTERNATIVES TO SALINITY MANAGEMENT IN THE COLORADO RIVER BASIN,
Bureau of Reclamation, Denver, Colo.
For primary bibliographic entry see Field 3C.
W75-06367

ECONOMIC ANALYSIS OF OPTIMAL USE OF SALINE WATER IN IRRIGATION AND THE EVALUATION OF WATER QUALITY,
Hebrew Univ., Jerusalem (Israel). Dept. of Agricultural Economics.
For primary bibliographic entry see Field 3C.
W75-06370

EVALUATING AGRICULTURAL EFFECTS OF SALINITY ABATEMENT PROJECTS IN THE COLORADO RIVER BASIN: AGRONOMIC AND ECONOMIC CONSIDERATIONS,
Colorado State Univ., Fort Collins. Dept. of Economics.
For primary bibliographic entry see Field 5G.
W75-06371

FINDING KNOWLEDGE GAPS: THE KEY TO SALINITY CONTROL SOLUTIONS,
Colorado State Univ, Fort Collins. Environmental Resources Center.
For primary bibliographic entry see Field 5G.
W75-06375

HYDROGEOLOGY AND WATER QUALITY MANAGEMENT,
Moody and Associates, Inc., Harrisburg, Pa. Environmental Services Div.
For primary bibliographic entry see Field 5G.
W75-06400

POLICY AND RESEARCH IMPLICATIONS OF THE NATIONAL WATER COMMISSION'S RECOMMENDATIONS,
Wisconsin Univ., Madison. Dept. of Agricultural Economics.
For primary bibliographic entry see Field 6E.
W75-06404

A COMPILATION OF AUSTRALIAN WATER QUALITY CRITERIA,
Caulfield Inst. of Tech., (Australia).
For primary bibliographic entry see Field 5G.
W75-06418

FLOOD CONTROL IN COMMUNITY PLANNING,
California Univ., Berkeley. Dept. of Landscape Architecture.
M. K. B. Robinson.
Available from the National Technical Information Service, Springfield, Va 22161 as PB-240 973, $5.75 in paper copy, $2.25 in microfiche. Masters Thesis, June 1972. 139 p, 21 fig, 55 ref. (California Water Resources Center Project UCAL-WRC-W-289). OWRT-B-128-CAL(2).

Descriptors: *Flood control, *Water management(Applied), *Flood protection, Streamflow, *California, Planning, *Community development, Project planning, Water demands.
Identifiers: *Sonoma Valley(Calif).

In the semi-arid west, of which central California is a part, natural free flowing streams are in shorter supply than they are in more humid climates, and therefore they are more precious. A large population in the State and extensive development of irrigated agriculture have made great demands on the limited water supply. Consequently, the dam and reservoir are becoming quite characteristic of California. In the Sonoma Valley urban pressures have not been great because the valley is by-passed by the freeway system. The population in the valley has grown slowly through the last few decades. A new highway and a new increase in housing construction is sure to come, most likely in this decade. In the meanwhile, options are still open in the Sonoma Valley to plan now for a future which includes the natural, freeflowing streams and use them for many purposs, including flood control, which will not destroy them. Several possible means of managing flood waters in the valley are analyzed, values of the natural waterways are described, and a program is proposed to reduce the problems associated with Sonoma Creek by utilizing its values rather than destroying them. (Snyder-California, Davis)
W75-06429

REPORT TO THE SONOMA CREEK ADVISORY COMMITTEE, SONOMA, CALIFORNIA,
California Univ., Berkeley. Dept. of Landscape Architecture.
M. K. Robinson.
Available from the National Technical Information Service, Springfield, Va 22161 as PB-241 015, $3.75 in paper copy, $2.25 in microfiche. Research Report, February, 1971. 35 p, 6 fig, 17 ref. (California Water Resources Center Project UCAL-WRC-W-289). OWRT-B-128-CAL(1).

Descriptors: *Water management(Applied), *Flood control, *Streamflow, *California, Streams, *Social values, Economics, Floods, Management, Environment, Programs, Project planning.
Identifiers: *Sonoma Valley(Calif).

A creek is seen differently by different people. To some it is primarily the source of floods and conditions which inhibit the economic development of the basin. Others feel equally strongly that the beauty and refreshment that a natural waterway brings to the environment adds a value to the lives of the people in the community which outweighs possible economic returns if the creek were destroyed. Several possible means of managing flood waters in the valley are analyzed, values of the natural waterways are described, and a program is proposed to reduce the problems associated with Sonoma Creek by utilizing its values rather than destroying them. (Snyder-California, Davis)
W75-06430

SURFACE WATER QUALITY IN MINNESOTA: THE TRANSLATION OF GOALS AND POLICIES INTO RESULTS,
Minnesota Univ., St. Paul. Water Resources Research Center.
For primary bibliographic entry see Field 5G.
W75-06431

CHARACTERISTICS OF WYOMING STOCK-WATER PONDS AND DIKE SPREADER SYSTEMS,
Wyoming Univ., Laramie. Water Resources Research Inst.
For primary bibliographic entry see Field 4A.
W75-06433

RATIONAL PROTECTION OF WATER RESOURCES IN COASTAL ZONES THROUGH PLANNED DEVELOPMENT,
Florida Univ., Gainesville. Dept. of Civil and Coastal Engineering.
For primary bibliographic entry see Field 4B.
W75-06446

RESERVATION, RESERVOIR AND SELF-DETERMINATION: A CASE STUDY OF RESERVOIR PLANNING AS IT AFFECTS AN INDIAN RESERVATION,
Mississippi State Univ., Mississippi State. Dept. of Anthropology.
J. H. Peterson, Jr.
Available from the National Technical Information Service, Springfield, Va 22161, as PB-241 100, $3.75 in paper copy, $2.25 in microfiche. Mississippi Water Resources Research Institute, Mississippi State, Completion Report, 1975. 36 p, 15 ref. OWRT A-076-MISS(1).

Descriptors: Water resources development, Social values, *Indian reservations, Reservation Doctrine, Reservoirs, *Mississippi, Planning, Attitudes, *Social change, *Social impact, Public lands, Federal reservations.
Identifiers: *Choctaw-Indians, Edinburg Dam(Miss).

A case study is presented of Indian tribal government and relationships between the tribe and various governmental agencies, with respect to water resources development and augmentation of income for the tribe. Specifically, the reaction of the Mississippi Choctaw Indians to the proposed Edinburg dam and reservoir, which will inundate some of the tribal lands, is discussed. There appears to be the possibility that the tribe might benefit from increased recreational activities in the area and from increased tourism, upon completion of the reservoir project. (Priest-Mississippi State)
W75-06462

THE EFFECTS OF DIMINISHED GROUND-WATER SUPPLIES ON SELECTED NEW HAMPSHIRE INDUSTRIES: AN ECONOMIC AND LEGAL EVALUATION,
New Hampshire Univ., Durham. Water Resource Research Center.
For primary bibliographic entry see Field 4B.
W75-06463

REDESIGNING FLOOD MANAGEMENT - PROJECT AGNES PHASE I,
New York State Coll. of Agriculture and Life Sciences, Ithaca. Dept. of Agricultural Economics.
For primary bibliographic entry see Field 6F.
W75-06520

RESEARCH ON WATER RESOURCES EVALUATION METHODOLOGY, A RIVER BASIN ECONOMIC AND FINANCIAL POST-AUDIT,
Little (Arthur D.), Inc., Cambridge, Mass.
J. M. Wilkinson.
Available from the National Technical Information Service, Springfield, Va 22161 as PB-241 061, $7.25 in paper copy, $2.25 in microfiche. Completion Report, March 31, 1975. 202 p, 51 tab, 123 ref. OWRT C-5126(4228)(1). 14-31-0001-4228.

Descriptors: *Evaluation, *Methodology, *Cost-benefit analysis, *Water resources development, *Planning, *Operations, *Investments, Economics, *Financing, Hydrology, Flood control, Hydroelectric power, Irrigation, Navigation, Recreation, Water supply, Fish, Wildlife, Legal aspects, *Project post-evaluation, Missouri River.
Identifiers: *Post-audit analysis.

Benefit-cost analysis has long been relied upon as a tool for planning and justifying river-basin programs. Almost no record is kept of actual benefit accruals to compare with planning expectations. This postaudit of the Pick-Sloan Missouri Basin Program attempted to quantify the 30-year performance of multipurpose programs in dollar terms. Applying current evaluation Principles and Standards of the Water Resources Council on an ex-post basis, the objective was to determine how much physical and dollar realities have differed from original plans, why they have differed, and what are the implications for future planning. Because benefit estimating procedures remain so imperfect, a wide range of values could be quantified; however, it appears that flood control and electric power program performance far exceeded plan, while that for irrigation and navigation programs fell far short of plan. Benefits could be double or half most of those estimated in this post-audit, depending on value assumptions. Also, external forces have radically altered original plans. Together, these uncertainties and imperfections render benefit-cost analysis and long range planning of questionable utility and very misleading as measures for program justification. A rigorous financial test of project worth is recommended.
W75-06524

ATTITUDES OF IDAHO RESIDENTS TOWARD FREE FLOWING RIVERS AS A WATER USE IN IDAHO,
Idaho Univ., Moscow. Dept. of Sociology and Anthropology.
J. E. Carlson.
Available from the National Technical Information Service, Springfield, Va 22161 as PB-241 453, $4.25 in paper copy, $2.25 in microfiche. Idaho Water Resources Research Institute, Moscow, Completion Report, Scenic Rivers Study Report No. 12, October 1974. 55 p, 3 fig, 14 tab, 8 ref, append. OWRT C-3342(3718)(5).

Descriptors: *Idaho, *Water utilization, *Attitudes, Social values, *Wild rivers, Running waters, Natural resources, Social aspects, Land use, Surveys, *Priorities, Classification.

This study was designed to determine: (1) the relative position of natural resources among other areas of concern to the people of Idaho, and (2) the relative importance of wild rivers as a water use in Idaho. There was a 91 percent return rate for the interviewer administered questionnaire. Idaho residents rank various natural resource uses high in priority. These high priority uses tend to be both in the areas of utilization and preservation suggesting that Idaho residents tend to approach resource use from a balanced perspective. The highly controversial area of wild and scenic river classification is supported by the study in that attitudes toward having more wild rivers in Idaho tend to be somewhat polarized at the extremes of the response categories. Attitudinal questions should not be taken at face value but must be considered in light of the person's overall priority rankings regarding resource use. Looking only at attitudes may provide misleading results.
W75-06525

COMPREHENSIVE WATER QUALITY MANAGEMENT PLANNING,
Pennsylvania Dept. of Environmental Resources, Harrisburg. Office of Comprehensive Water and Wastewater Management Planning.
For primary bibliographic entry see Field 5G.
W75-06558

WATER QUALITY MANAGEMENT: THE CASE FOR RIVER BASIN AUTHORITIES,
Ohio Univ., Athens. Dept. of Civil Engineering.
For primary bibliographic entry see Field 5G.
W75-06571

ECONOMIC FORECASTING FOR VIRGINIA'S WATER RESOURCE PROGRAMS,
Virginia State Water Control Board, Richmond.
C. P. Becker, A. M. Griffin, Jr., and C. S. Lown.
Water Resources Bulletin, Vol 9, No 5, p 963-975, October 1973. 3 fig, 4 ref.

Descriptors: *Economics, *Forecasting, *Water resources, *Virginia, Planning, Population, Projections, Unemployment, Insurance, Statistics, Projects, Water quality, Management, Data collections, Computers, Regions.
Identifiers: Industrial activity, Payroll data, Economic data, Hydrologic area, Exponential forecasting, Employment records.

Water resource and water quality management planning depend, to a large degree, on forecasts of industrial activity and population projections. A flexible economic data base is important where planning follows varying formats of geographical and industrial detail. Records of employment and payroll collected in the administration of Unemployment Insurance (U.I.) programs are available from State Employment Agencies. Many years of record are available on punched cards or magnetic tape and may be arrayed and manipulated by computer. This basic approach has been followed in Virginia. Historical U.I. payroll and employment records for 1956-1970 were procured on magnetic tape. The data were arrayed by major hydrologic area and by regional planning district. Projections of manufacturing activity were then generated by fitting several exponential equations to annual payroll data in two-digit Standard Industrial Classifications. Then these exponentials were extrapolated to provide a range of industrial projections. Other parameters of manufacturing activity were then correlated to the payroll data to generate projections of indexes such as employment, value-added, and gross manufacturing output. U.I. payroll data are now being correlated to parameters in non-manufacturing categories. Projections for industries such as trade and services will link extrapolated payroll data with benchmark correlations of payroll and sales receipts. (Bell-Cornell)
W75-06573

MAN'S ACTIVITIES IN WATERSHED AREAS--A NEED FOR PLANNING,
For primary bibliographic entry see Field 4D.
W75-06588

AESTHETICS OF WILD AND SCENIC RIVERS A METHODOLOGICAL APPROACH,
Idaho Univ., Moscow. Dept. of Agricultural and Forest Economics.
E. L. Michalson.
Available from the National Technical Information Service, Springfield, Va 22161, as PB-241 134, $5.75 in paper copy, $2.25 in microfiche. Idaho Water Resources Research Institute, Moscow, Completion Report, Scenic Rivers Study No 11, October 1974, 139 p, 9 tab, 10 ref, 2 append. OWRT C-3342(No 3718)(5).

Descriptors: *Idaho, *Aesthetics, *Wild rivers, Methodology, Evaluation, Recreation demand, Social values, Attitudes, Social aspects, Psychological aspects.
Identifiers: *Scenic rivers, *Salmon River(Idaho), Consumer surplus.

The specific objectives were to define outstandingly scenic areas of the Salmon River, and to evaluate methods of establishing values for aesthetic experiences. Two attempts were made to use the slides developed in the inventory process of the Salmon River to obtain audience response from a slide showing. The responses from the audiences were neither consistent nor did they form a concensus of opinion. The next procedure used was to develop recreational demand equations for several areas of Idaho. As a part of the demand analysis the consumer surplus was estimated for each area and the value of aesthetics was related to the amount of consumer surplus in each area. This was done by designing a scaling questionnaire which allowed the recreational users interviewed to rank a bundle of recreational experiences. These rankings were then summed and a summated Likert-Type scale analysis was used to develop a distribution which ranked the experiences. The Likert-Type scale, as developed for this study, indicates the way recreationists would distribute the value of their experiences among the several categories. While the Likert-Type scale analysis most likely underestimates the value of aesthetics, it is a useful approximation of the quantification of aesthetic value.
W75-06641

ORGANIZATIONAL PROBLEM-SOLVING,
Kansas Water Resources Research Inst., Manhattan.
R. L. Swinth.
Available from the National Technical Information Service, Springfield, Va 22161, as PB-241 136, $17.00 in paper copy, $2.25 in microfiche. Contribution No 148. November, 1974. 182 p. OWRT B-026-KAN(1).

Descriptors: To carry out its planning activities an organization will often follow an authority approach. This traditional method has significant limitations. Yet, planning and problem-solving can be dealt with differently. On the other hand organizations can effectively solve novel and complex tasks by organizational joint problem-solving. This approach is characterized by a set of propositions formulated to describe how responsibility is distributed and how search and coordination are facilitated. These procedures have been evaluated jointly by field study and laboratory study. An analysis was conducted to establish the relationship between the performance of various project groups, such as the Corps of Engineers, and their use of various problem-solving techniques. People were aided and trained in the use of organizational joint problem-solving procedures to assess whether their performance was better than those who were not.
W75-06643

ELEMENTS IN A DECISION FRAMEWORK FOR PLANNING THE ALLOCATION OF COASTAL LAND AND WATER RESOURCES WITH ILLUSTRATION FOR A COASTAL COMMUNITY,
Massachusetts Univ., Amherst. Dept. of Agricultural and Food Economics.
R. N. Allbee, and D. A. Storey.
Available from the National Technical Information Service, Springfield, Va 22161, as PB-241 138, $4.75 in paper copy, $2.25 in microfiche. Massachusetts Water Resources Research Center, Completion Report FY-74-3, Publication No 36, 1973. 78 p. OWRT A-046-MASS(1).

Descriptors: *Massachusetts, *Decision making, *Planning, Land use, Coasts, *Water allocation(Policy), Community development, Water resources development, *Optimization, Coastal marshes, State governments, Social values, Systems analysis, *Feasibility studies, Urbanization, Management, Multiple purpose projects, *Economic impact, Regional analysis.
Identifiers: *Coastal zone management, *Ipswich(Mass).

Analytical methodologies are considered under two broad headings: optimality analysis and feasibility analysis. Optimization techniques include mathematical programming, which is very precise but not highly capable of handling multiple objcetives and intangibles, and simulation, better suited to the problem but very expensive. Feasibility analysis techniques do not necessarily reveal the best or optimal allocation but give procedures for choosing among alternatives being analyzed. A matrix approach which relates possible or projected changes in different human activities to the set of multiple objectives through measurement of tangible and intangible impacts is developed and illustrated. A suggested supplement would further break down the impacts among different groups of citizens. Illustration of the decision framework is provided for Ipswich, Massachusetts, a community of roughly 11,000 people with extensive salt marshes and clam flats, a large quasi-public beach area (Crane's Beach) and relatively little waterfront development except for one residential cluster. The illustration is based mainly on secondary data. Primary data requirements and analytical procedures are suggested. In order to account for the full range of social values associated with coastal resources, much of the public planning should take place at a higher level of government than the local community, chiefly at the state level.
W75-06645

PROCEEDINGS OF CONFERENCE ON 'TRENDS IN WATER MANAGEMENT',
Minnesota Univ., St. Paul. Water Resources Research Center.
For primary bibliographic entry see Field 6E.
W75-06647

WATER RESOURCES APPRAISAL FOR HYDROELECTRIC LICENSING, SANTEE RIVER BASIN, SOUTH CAROLINA-NORTH CAROLINA.
Federal Power Commission, Washington, D.C. Bureau of Power.
1970. 127 p, 82 fig, 36 tab.

Descriptors: *Hydroelectric project licensing, *South Carolina, *North Carolina, *Hydroelectric plants, *River basin development, River systems, Water resources development, River basins, Rivers and Harbors Act.
Identifiers: *Santee River Basin.

The major headwater tributaries of the Santee River, the Wateree-Catawba, the Broad, and the Saluda, rise in the Blue Ridge mountain region of northwestern South Carolina and central North Carolina. Most of the flow of the Santee River is diverted 87 miles above its mouth into the Cooper River, a short coastal stream, which is used for the tail canal of the Pinopolis power plant, and empties into the Atlantic Ocean at Charleston. It is expected that by the year 2000 the basin population will be about 4,370,000. Approximately 19 percent of the area in the Santee River Basin, with 9 percent of the population, has been classed as eligible for assistance under the 1965 Public Works and Economic Development Act (PL 89-136). Of the basin sites studied for future development of water and related land resources, only four offer possibilities for favorable economic development using Federal financing. These are the Saluda (Green River), Clinchfield, Greater Lockhart (with either conventional or pumped storage capacity), and Blairs projects. The redivision of Santee River waters from the Cooper River through a proposed powerhouse at St. Stephen has been authorized by the River and Harbor Act of 1968 (PL 90-483). (Poertner)
W75-06655

WATER RESOURCE APPRAISAL FOR HYDROELECTRIC LICENSING, WISCONSIN RIVER BASIN, WISCONSIN.
Federal Power Commission, Washington, D.C. Bureau of Power.
Appraisal Report, 1969. 98 p, 28 tab, 62 fig.

Descriptors: *Hydroelectric plants, *Wisconsin, *Hydroelectric project licensing, *River basin development, Utilities, River systems, Water resources development, Recreation, Flood control, Water supply, Water quality control, Erosion control, Fish and wildlife, River basins.
Identifiers: *Wisconsin River Basin.

The electric power needs of the 11,728 square mile Wisconsin River Basin are supplied by three privately-owned utilities. The basin has potential for development and utilization of its water resources in the interest of flood control, water supply, water quality control, recreation, cooling water for steam-electric generating plants, and scenic river areas. Future development is being studied and utilization of the basins water resources are under consideration for either relicensing or Federal takeover by eleven existing hydroelectric projects. The eleven projects are in reasonable good condition and should be capable of being operated efficiently for an extended period after their licenses expire. Some additional recreational facilities should be provided at all existing projects under consideration to satisfy future demands. Future improvement of water quality in the Wisconsin River below Rhinelander would expand and increase the opportunities for recreational use. The quality of the water is satisfactory for recreational activities at the two upstream existing projects under consideration, Otter Rapids and Rhinelander. (Poertner)
W75-06676

LANE COUNTY PRELIMINARY GENERAL PLAN-WATER QUALITY REPORT.
Lane Council of Governments, Eugene, Oreg.
For primary bibliographic entry see Field 5B.
W75-06681

PUBLIC PERCEPTIONS OF WATER QUALITY AND THEIR EFFECT ON WATER-BASED RECREATION,
Department of the Environment, Ottawa (Ontario). Water Planning and Management Branch.
J. G. M. Parkes.
Social Science Series No 8, 53 p, 1973, (Inland Waters Directorate, available in English and French.) 6 fig, 34 tab, 20 ref, 2 append.

Descriptors: *Water quality, *Recreation, *Psychological aspects, Surveys, Planning, Water pollution effects, Pollution abatement, Costs, Social aspects, Attitudes, *Canada.
Identifiers: *Public perception, Questionnaires, Water quality improvement, Saskatchewan, Quebec, Nova Scotia, Environmental perception.

This study was part of the Department of the Environment's summer student shoreline survey program. The objectives were to examine the public's perception of water quality, the influence of water quality on water-oriented recreation, and the willingness of the public to pay for improvement. The areas selected for study represent three distinct recreational environments: The Maritime Coast of Nova Scotia, The Eastern Township Area of Quebec, and the Plains of Saskatchewan. The data gathered concerning recreational use patterns and population characteristics at these sites are intended to be used for future planning. (Environment Canada)
W75-06752

SOCIAL IMPACT ASSESSMENT: AN ANALYTIC BIBLIOGRAPHY,
Brown Univ., Providence, R.I.
M. A. Shields.
Prepared for Army Engineer Institute for Water Resources, Fort Belvoir, Virginia. IWR Paper 74-P6, Oct., 1974, 129 p, 40 ref, 3 append.

Descriptors: *Bibliographies, Social impact, *Research and development, *Planning, Social aspects, Water resources development, Information retrieval, Publications, Information exchange.
Identifiers: *Social Impact Assessment(SIA), Information systems, Programmatic essay.

Intent was to organize and evaluate the existing knowledge base gained through social science research in order to identify research gaps and create the basis for a working bibliography intended for both scholars and practitioners. Three sources of reference, Office of Water Resources Research abstracts, authors' citations, and references from colleagues were used to develop both a raw and annotated bibliography, lists of descriptors, identifiers and locators, and methological approaches to social impact assessment. Social Impact Studies(SIA), required by the Corps of Engineers as part of their planning process, fall into several categories: demographic, institutional, economic, community, cohesion, lifestyles, displacement and relocation. These topics are given expository analysis using significant studies to illustrate important points. Methodological approaches to social impact assessment are presented in tabular form. As SIA gains in importance as an operational function in the government planning process, this reference which can be continually updated and revised can serve as a valuable aid to planners in making better decisions regarding the impacts of public works projects. (Salzman-North Carolina)
W75-06758

EVALUATION OF FOUR COMPLETED SMALL WATERSHED PROJECTS: SOUTH CAROLINA, MARYLAND, IDAHO-NEVADA, AND WEST VIRGINIA,
Economic Research Service, Washington, D.C.
For primary bibliographic entry see Field 4D.
W75-06765

PROSPECTUS FOR REGIONAL SEWER AND WATER PLANNING.
Southwestern Wisconsin Regional Planning Commission, Platteville.
For primary bibliographic entry see Field 5D.
W75-06782

SOVEREIGNTY OF THE SEAS AND THE EFFECT UPON NAVAL STRATEGY,
Naval War Coll., Newport, R.I.
For primary bibliographic entry see Field 6E.
W75-06786

COMPREHENSIVE LAND USE PLANNING-ITS DEVELOPMENT AND POTENTIAL IMPACT ON COASTAL ZONE MANAGEMENT,
Rhode Island Univ., Kingston. Marine Affairs Program.
For primary bibliographic entry see Field 4A.
W75-06787

ORGANIZING NEW ENGLAND COMMERCIAL FISHERMEN AT THE REGIONAL LEVEL,
Rhode Island Univ., Kingston.
For primary bibliographic entry see Field 6E.
W75-06788

SOLID WASTE DISPOSAL AND OCEAN DUMPING,
Naval War Coll., Newport, R.I.
For primary bibliographic entry see Field 5B.
W75-06789

COASTAL ZONE PLANNING: THE IMPACT OF REGIONAL EFFORTS IN NEW ENGLAND,
Woods Hole Oceanographic Institution, Mass.
For primary bibliographic entry see Field 6F.
W75-06790

A REVIEW OF THE PRESENT AND ANNOUNCED FUTURE CAPABILITIES FOR COMMERCIAL OIL RECOVERY BEYOND THE 656 FOOT ISOBATH,
State Univ. of New York, Stony Brook. Marine Sciences Research Center.
For primary bibliographic entry see Field 5G.
W75-06791

6C. Cost Allocation, Cost Sharing, Pricing/Repayment

ECONOMIC INCENTIVES FOR SALINITY REDUCTION AND WATER CONSERVATION IN THE COLORADO RIVER BASIN,
Colorado Univ., Boulder. Dept. of Economics.
For primary bibliographic entry see Field 3C.
W75-06373

COST SHARING AND EFFICIENCY IN SALINITY CONTROL,
National Bureau of Standards, Washington, D.C. Building Economics Section.
For primary bibliographic entry see Field 3C.
W75-06374

RESEARCH ON WATER RESOURCES EVALUATION METHODOLOGY, A RIVER BASIN ECONOMIC AND FINANCIAL POST-AUDIT,
Little (Arthur D.), Inc., Cambridge, Mass.
For primary bibliographic entry see Field 6B.
W75-06524

WATER AND SEWER SYSTEMS PROGRAM AND DEVELOPMENT, FIVE-YEAR CAPITAL IMPROVEMENT PLAN: OCTOBER 1, 1972 - SEPTEMBER 30, 1977,
Jacksonville Dept. of Public Works, Fla.
For primary bibliographic entry see Field 5D.
W75-06762

A REVIEW OF THE PRESENT AND ANNOUNCED FUTURE CAPABILITIES FOR COMMERCIAL OIL RECOVERY BEYOND THE 656 FOOT ISOBATH,
State Univ. of New York, Stony Brook. Marine Sciences Research Center.
For primary bibliographic entry see Field 5G.
W75-06791

6D. Water Demand

FLOOD CONTROL IN COMMUNITY PLANNING,
California Univ., Berkeley. Dept. of Landscape Architecture.
For primary bibliographic entry see Field 6B.
W75-06429

LONG-RANGE WATER SUPPLY PROBLEMS, PHASE I.
Kansas Water Resources Board, Topeka.
Kansas State Water Plan Studies, October 1974. 107 p, 39 fig, 19 tab, 49 ref.

Descriptors: *Kansas, *Water supply, Flood control, Irrigation, Water quality, Water resources, Recreation, Municipal water, Industrial water, Minerals, Agriculture, Land resources, Groundwater, Economics, Water management(Applied), *Water demand, Planning, *Long-term planning.
Identifiers: Water plan studies, Long-range problems.

Kansas has extensive water, mineral, and land resources which can be utilized to provide economic opportunities. However, in many sections of the state it has become increasingly apparent that an adequate quantity of fresh water is not an inexhaustable resource. The gross water used in 1965 was 3.3 million acre-feet. Of this quantity, agriculture used 2.35 million acre-feet while industry and people used the remaining 0.95 million acre-feet. By the beginning of the 21st century, the gross water requirement for agriculture was expected to be 10.9 million acre-feet while people and industry were expected to account for 1.5 million acre-feet. The fact that irrigation development in the western third of the state was pumping groundwater out of some areas faster than it was being replaced by natural recharge was discussed. A significant number of counties in western Kansas were expected to face major depletion of groundwater supplies before the 21st century. The future water supply situation for Kansas was shown graphically in several figures which illustrated the total projected demands, the present and potential available groundwater in storage, and the potential undeveloped surface water yields. (Roberts-ISWS)
W75-06473

UNIQUE WATER SUPPLY PROBLEMS IN THE NORTH WEST OF SOUTH AUSTRALIA,
South Australian Dept. of Health, Adelaide.
O. Fuller, and R. Shepherd.
Water (Journal of the Australian Water and Wastewater Association) Vol 1, No 4, p 19-20,22, December 1974. 2 tab.

Descriptors: *Australia, *Water demand, *Water supply, *Arid lands, Water requirements, Dependable supply, Groundwater availability, Groundwater resources, Exploration, Water sources.
Identifiers: South Australia, Aboriginal reserves.

The North West Area of South Australia includes an Aboriginal Reserve of some 33,000 square miles, on which are located five settlements with a combined population of nearly 1,200. Recent developments in administration of such settlements, and in particular an influx of funds from governments, are expected to result in extensive building schemes, with attendant demands for reticulated water supplies and waste disposal systems. Rainfall in the area is low and erratic, surface water supplies are not reliable, and such data as are presently available indicate that safe yield from underground basins is limited. Investigations currently under way at each settlement are described. (Levick-CSIRO)
W75-06553

6E. Water Law and Institutions

LAND-USE ISSUES: PROCEEDINGS OF A CONFERENCE.
Virginia Polytechnic Inst. and State Univ., Blacksburg. Water Resources Research Center.
For primary bibliographic entry see Field 4A.
W75-06359

SALINITY IN WATER RESOURCES.
For primary bibliographic entry see Field 3C.
W75-06366

POLICY AND RESEARCH IMPLICATIONS OF THE NATIONAL WATER COMMISSION'S RECOMMENDATIONS,
Wisconsin Univ., Madison. Dept. of Agricultural Economics.
D. W. Bromley, W. R. Butcher, and S. C. Smith.
Land Economics, Vol L, No 1, p 15-34, February 1974. 2 tab. OWRR B-057-WIS(5).

Descriptors: *Federal government, *National Water Commission, *Planning, *Water management, *Water rights, Water resources, Water resources development, Conservation, Environmental control.
Identifiers: Water Resource Information System.

A National Water Commission was created in 1968 to analyze the nation's water problems and needs, and to generate water policy. In a report published in June 1973, emphasis centered on ways to improve utilization, allocation and management of existing water supplies without Cassandra-like projections regarding future water requirements. Institutional reform coupled with public participation would provide solutions to the nation's water problems. Initially, the Water Resource Council should move to the Executive Office of the President to improve land use and river basin planning and to determine planning grants for states. Through a series of policy changes such as local government financing and support of transferability of water rights, water management would be enhanced. With some emphasis on conservation policies, the report reflects a utilitarian point of view and middle of the road position recommending water quality standards for receiving waters only and suggesting that the quality of the environment is not an absolute to be protected at any cost. Recommendations include recreation uses and pollution control measures. Report does not address goals and objectives of water policies, but it does approve of multiple objective planning calling for price incentives, and underlines the need for water management to meet economic demands and environmental criteria. Besides setting guidelines for management (although failing to articulate an overall flow management framework), and a Water Resources Information System, the Commission offers at least 8 specific recommendations for the implementation of public participation in the planning and evaluation process. A broad concept of water resource management with a logically consistent institutional structure is needed. (Salzman-North Carolina)
W75-06404

SURFACE WATER QUALITY IN MINNESOTA: THE TRANSLATION OF GOALS AND POLICIES INTO RESULTS,
Minnesota Univ., St. Paul. Water Resources Research Center.
For primary bibliographic entry see Field 5G.
W75-06431

CHARACTERISTICS OF WYOMING STOCK-WATER PONDS AND DIKE SPREADER SYSTEMS,
Wyoming Univ., Laramie. Water Resources Research Inst.
For primary bibliographic entry see Field 4A.
W75-06433

RESERVATION, RESERVOIR AND SELF-DETERMINATION: A CASE STUDY OF RESERVOIR PLANNING AS IT AFFECTS AN INDIAN RESERVATION,
Mississippi State Univ., Mississippi State. Dept. of Anthropology.
For primary bibliographic entry see Field 6B.
W75-06462

THE EFFECTS OF DIMINISHED GROUND-WATER SUPPLIES ON SELECTED NEW HAMPSHIRE INDUSTRIES: AN ECONOMIC AND LEGAL EVALUATION,
New Hampshire Univ., Durham. Water Resource Research Center.
For primary bibliographic entry see Field 4B.
W75-06463

INTERNATIONAL HYDROLOGICAL DECADE REPRESENTATIVE AND EXPERIMENTAL BASINS IN THE UNITED STATES: CATALOG OF AVAILABLE DATA AND RESULTS, 1965-1972.
National Committee for the International Hydrological Decade, Washington, D.C.
For primary bibliographic entry see Field 2A.
W75-06472

GREAT LAKES WATER QUALITY, ANNUAL REPORT TO THE INTERNATIONAL JOINT COMMISSION, (1973).
International Joint Commission-United States and Canada. Great Lakes Water Quality Board.
For primary bibliographic entry see Field 5B.
W75-06474

WATER QUALITY STANDARDS AND INTERNATIONAL DEVELOPMENT.
Agency for International Development, Washington, D.C. Office of Science and Technology.
For primary bibliographic entry see Field 5G.
W75-06487

ROLE OF THE SCIENTIST TECHNICIAN IN WATER POLICY DECISIONS AT THE COMMUNITY LEVEL: A STUDY IN PURPOSIVE COMMUNICATION,
Minnesota Univ., St. Paul. Dept. of Rural Sociology.
R. E. Rickson, P. J. Tichenor, G. A. Donohue, and C. E. Olien.
Available from the National Technical Information Service, Springfield, Va 22161 as PB-241 122, $4.25 in paper copy, $2.25 in microfiche. Minnesota, Water Resources Research Center, St. Paul, Bulletin Number 79, January 1975. 51 p, 14 tab, 6 ref, append. OWRT B-067-Minn(2). 14-31-0001-3900.

Descriptors: *Community development, *Attitudes, Sociology, *Water policy, *Decision making, Communication, Information exchange, Scientific personnel.
Identifiers: *Scientific applications.

The objective is to increase understanding of how scientific knowledge may be most effectively applied to community problem-solving. The report focuses on: how certain community characteristics affect public perspective of science and the role of the scientist in solving water resource problems; and the degree of consensus between perspectives and local leaders about science and the role of the scientist in defining and solving water problems. (Waelti-Minnesota)
W75-06519

THE UNCERTAIN SEARCH FOR ENVIRONMENTAL QUALITY,
Yale Univ., New Haven, Conn. School of Law.
For primary bibliographic entry see Field 5G.
W75-06557

ADMINISTRATION OF GROUND WATER AS BOTH A RENEWABLE AND NONRENEWABLE RESOURCE,
Idaho Bureau of Mines and Geology, Moscow.
For primary bibliographic entry see Field 4B.
W75-06570

MISSISSIPPI COASTAL ZONE MANAGEMENT APPLICATION 1974.
Mississippi Marine Resources Council, Long Beach.
1974. 146 p, 6 fig, 1 tab, 3 append.

Descriptors: *Planning, *Mississippi, *Federal government, *State governments, *Grants, Administrative agencies, Governmental interrelations, Budgeting, Water resources development, Water policy, Water law, Financing, Government finance, Shores, Zoning, Land management, Land use, Water utilization, Coasts, Coastal marshes, Coastal plains, Estuaries, Gulf coastal plain, Bayous, Comprehensive planning, Federal government, Cost sharing.
Identifiers: *Coastal zone management, Coastal waters, Environmental policy.

The revised application of the Mississippi Marine Resources Council requesting federal assistance for its statewide Coastal Zone Management Development Program was submitted to the Office of Coastal Environment of the Department of Commerce. It conforms to the final regulations and procedures set forth in the federal guidelines of November 29, 1973. The program is designed to be consistent with the requirements of the Coastal Zone Management Act of 1972 and involves the development of a statement setting forth objectives, policies, and standards to guide the use of lands and waters in the coastal zone. The cost of this first year effort is estimated to be $152,346 for which a grant of $101,564 is being requested. Included is a summary of the state's past coastal zone management activities as well as the specific activities and goals of the proposed program. (Deckert-Florida)
W75-06575

WATER REGULATIONS--TOXIC POLLUTANT EFFLUENT STANDARDS.
For primary bibliographic entry see Field 5G.
W75-06576

UNITED STATES V. 295.90 ACRES OF LAND, MORE OR LESS, IN THE COUNTY OF LEE, STATE OF FLORIDA, AND CARL A. NORBERG, ET AL. (ACTION ON EMINENT DOMAIN PROCEEDING).
368 F. Supp. 1301 (M.D. Fla. 1974).

Descriptors: *Accretion, *Bodies of water, *Florida, *Judicial decisions, *Meanders, Land tenure, Surveys, Mapping, Riparian rights, Water law, Legal aspects, Eminent domain, Condemnation.
Identifiers: *Wilderness areas.

An eminent domain proceeding was instituted by the United States to acquire certain lands on Sanibel Island for use as part of a national wildlife refuge. The Government contended that it already owned a major portion of the subject lands prior to the institution of the suit due to an error in the original survey. The general rule is that when lands are patented according to an official survey showing meander lines along a body of water any excess land outside the meander line is apportioned to the patentee and his title is extended to the water's edge in accord with the intent of the surveyor. Where, however, the meander line is shown to be grossly erroneous and tantamount to fraud, then any land beyond the meander line is to be treated as unsurveyed land, with title remaining in the government. The court held that despite the fact that no water bottom existed in the area indicated, it was enough that some water bottom existed in the section to preclude a finding of gross and palpable error tantamount to fraud. (Proctor-Florida)
W75-06577

COUNTY WATER MANAGEMENT–JURISDICTION (AS AMENDED).
Minnesota Sess. Laws, Vol 4, Ch. 392, S.F. No. 2822, p 631-632, approved April 5, 1974 (1974).

Descriptors: *Minnesota, *Legislation, *Local governments, *Jurisdiction, *Water utilization, Water law, Governments, State governments, Governmental interrelations, Regulation, Administration, Suburban areas, Legal aspects, Zoning, Control, Water policy, Bodies of water, Water resources development, Planning, Surface waters, Water rights, Inter-agency cooperation.
Identifiers: Water rights(Non-riparians), State policy.

Certain provisions of the Minnesota Statutes are hereby amended in order to clarify the jurisdiction of counties and lake conservation districts over certain bodies of water. Minnesota Statutes, 1973 Supplement, Section 378.31, is amended to provide that every county board shall have the power set forth in that section with respect to waters situated wholly or partly within the county and not situated entirely within any city, village, borough, or lake conservation district. All programs undertaken pursuant to such powers shall be consistent with statewide and/or regional water and related land resources plans. No body of water shall be improved under this section unless public access is provided to the shoreline thereof. County boards may regulate the surface use of waters within this jurisdiction, except that where a body of water lies in more than one county, such regulation must be approved by all the county boards having jurisdiction over that body of water or placed into effect by order of the commissioner of natural resources. Where a body of water lies partially within a city, village, or borough, further restrictions are established to assure compatibility between state, county, and local surface use regulations. (Deckert-Florida)
W75-06578

WATER REGULATIONS–PRETREATMENT STANDARDS.
For primary bibliographic entry see Field 5G.
W75-06579

ENVIRONMENTAL DEFENSE FUND V. TENNESSEE VALLEY AUTHORITY.
371 F. Supp. 1004 (E.D. Tenn. 1973).

Descriptors: *Dam construction, *Judicial decisions, Legislation, Construction, Project planning, Benefits, Water quality control, Recreation, Agriculture, Project purposes, *Tennessee Valley Authority, Optimum development plans, Water resources development, Tennessee.
Identifiers: *Environmental Impact Statements, *National Environmental Policy Act, Injunctive relief, Tellico Dam project(Tenn).

Suit was brought to enjoin the Tennessee Valley Authority (TVA) from completing the construction of the Tellico Dam Project. The Tellico Project is a multi-purpose water resource and regional development plan which contemplates the inundation of acreage upon completion of the reservoir. This acreage consists of agricultural land, recreational areas, and important historical and archaeological landmarks. The project was subject to the National Environmental Policy Act (NEPA), which requires the inclusion of an environmental impact statement relating to any federal action significantly affecting the quality of the human environment. Plaintiffs attacked the sufficiency of the statement's discussion of various areas, including historical and archaeological impact, family relocation, and ecological effect. The court held that TVA had compiled with NEPA in issuing a statement which disclosed the significant impacts to result from the project and discussed the reasonable alternatives available. Moreover, the court found that TVA reached its decision through a good faith consideration and balancing of environmental factors. (Proctor-Florida)
W75-06580

STATE OF WISCONSIN V. CALLAWAY (ACTION FOR INJUNCTIVE RELIEF ON DREDGING ACTIVITIES ON MISSISSIPPI RIVER).
371 F. Supp. 807 (W.D. Wis. 1974).

Descriptors: *Dredging, *Landfills, *Channel improvement, Legal aspects, Channel erosion, Rivers, Channels, *Wisconsin, *Mississippi River.
Identifiers: *Environmental Impact Statements, *Administrative regulations, Injunctive relief.

An action was brought by the State of Wisconsin in the District Court for injunctive relief with respect to dredging activities in that part of the Mississippi River which forms a boundary of the State of Wisconsin. As an aid to navigation in the upper Mississippi River, the defendant Army Corps of Engineers operated and maintained a system of locks and dams with a nine-foot channel. The channel was maintained at a depth of nine feet by the defendants through a yearly dredging program which resulted in the deposit of the spoil on lands near the dredging site. The court held that the dredging process significantly affected the environment requiring the preparation of an environmental impact statement. The court enjoined continued dredging until submission of the environmental impact statement, with a proviso for a petition for modification of the injunction in emergency situations. (Proctor-Florida)
W75-06581

STATE EX REL. DEPARTMENT OF HEALTH V. NORTH JERSEY DISTRICT WATER SUPPLY COMMISSION (ACTION SEEKING MANDATORY INJUNCTION ON REQUIRING COMPLIANCE WITH ORDER TO IMPROVE, ADD TO, OR ALTER WATER TREATMENT PLANT).
317 A.2d 86 (N.J. Ct. App. 1974).

Descriptors: *Water supply development, *Public health, *Water treatment, *Filtration, Treatment facilities, Treatment, Bond issues, Water districts, Water resources, Conservation, Reservoirs, Capital costs, *New Jersey, Water supply, Water management, Water quality.
Identifiers: Injunctive relief, Inverse condemnation, State policy.

An injunction was issued requiring the North Jersey Water Supply District to effect immediate compliance with a State Department of Health order requiring the District to improve the water treatment plant located at a particular reservoir. Two participating communities in the District, Passaic Valley and Newark, appealed from that portion of the order requiring them to participate in the proposed filtration construction and to contribute a proportionate share of its cost, alleging that the order was unreasonable. The court reasoned that the State's overriding concern and obligation is to safeguard the public health and that water supplies should be pure in quality and economically and prudently managed for the benefit of the public. As a necessary adjunct, an implied power resides in the District not only to repair and maintain existing facilities, but also to construct additional facilities at the joint expense of the participating municipalities. The court held that such action did not constitute inverse condemnation of Passaic Valley's soon to be abandoned filtration plant, and that exercise of the State's police power does not give rise to a right of compensation, even though the value of the pro-

W75-06593

WATER: SUPPLY, DEMAND AND THE LAW,
Resources for the Future, Inc., Washington, D.C.
For primary bibliographic entry see Field 6D.
W75-06594

NEW WATER LAW PROBLEMS AND OLD PUBLIC LAW PRINCIPLES,
New Mexico Univ., Albuquerque.
R. E. Clark.
Rocky Mountain Law Review, Vol 32, p 437-451, 1960. 61 ref.

Descriptors: *Water law, *Legislation, *Judicial decisions, *Water pollution, *Water quality control, Groundwater, Management, Runoff, Flood plains, Oklahoma, Arizona, Utah, Flood control, Regulation, Overflow, Water resources development, Cities.

The modern era has added complicating factors to the age-old community problem of an adequate and potable water supply. Goals such as improved development allocation, and distribution of water supplies, flood plain development, and pollution controls have been established. Recent legislative changes in water law display a concern for the public interest, recognition of the useful role that scientific methods and technical data must play in water resources policy and management, and a general awareness of changing community preferences with respect to actual uses. Decisions construing this legislation focus on the public nature of water problems. Court decisions in various western states have dealt with legislation as it applies to ground water management and balancing the varigated land-water interests among individuals, communities and states. The unifying community characteristic of the West is anxiety over water resources, their scarcity and their destructive excesses. The dominant water law institutions of the West have been greatly modified through piecemeal legislation which has recognized the inherent limitation of private litigation to protect water rights. The West is a pioneer in the anticipation through law and administrative procedures of the water resources future of the Nation. (Sperling-Florida)
W75-06595

RED TIDE RESEARCH.
Florida Sess Laws, Vol 3, Ch 74-123, p 294-295, approved June 9, 1974, effective July 1, 1974 (1974).

Descriptors: *Red tide, *Water pollution sources, *Legislation, *Florida, Aquatic life, Marine biology, Mortality, Public health, Water law, Water pollution, Fish toxins, Marine algae, Marine animals, Marine plants, Aquatic environment, Aquatic microbiology, Fish kill.

An ad hoc council within the Florida Department of Natural Resources is created for red tide research. It shall consist of three to seven members comprised of representatives of the Department of Natural Resources and the Department of Health and Rehabilitation Services. These members may appoint not more than four additional members to serve at their pleasure. The Council will evaluate and coordinate all the red tide research activities within the State of Florida and report annually to the Legislature on its activities during the preceeding year. (Sperling-Florida)
W75-06596

BEACH EROSION CONTROL--TRUST FUND ACCOUNT.
Florida Sess Laws, Vol 2, Ch 74-102, p 165-168, approved May 30, 1974, effective July 1, 1974 (1974).

Descriptors: *Legislation, *Florida, *Beach erosion, *Weathering, Waves(Water), Storms, Running waters, Impact(Rainfall), Erosion rates, Wind erosion, Financing, Economics, Budgeting, Capital, Costs, Financial feasibility, Water law.
Identifiers: Erosion control accounts.

The Florida Department of Natural Resources is authorized to pay up to 75% of non-federal construction and miantenance costs of specified beach erosion control projects. The use of funds for beach restoration where there is no public access is prohibited. For an area to qualify for state funding, local interests must provide permanent public access to project areas. The Department is authorized to expend funds from the erosion control trust fund account in order to alleviate emergency conditions related to shoreline stability. Expenses for other erosion controls, beach preservation, and hurricane protection are provided. The Department is also authorized to initiate, construct, and pay the entire costs of projects which involve shoreline whose upland owner is the State of Florida. (Sperling-Florida)
W75-06597

BISCAYNE BAY--AQUATIC PRESERVE.
Florida Sess Laws, Vol 3, Ch 74-171, p 364-366, approved June 11, 1974, effective--same date (1974).

Descriptors: *Legislation, *Florida, Bays, Riparian rights, Legal aspects, Water law, Competing uses, Water pollution, Water rights, Water quality control, Water resources development, Water policy, Water management(Applied), Water allocation(Policy), State governments, Waste water(Pollution), Waste water disposal, Waste water treatment.
Identifiers: *Environmental policy, *Biscayne Bay(Fla).

Biscayne Bay in Dade and Monroe Counties, Florida is established as an aquatic preserve. The preserve will operate within the scope of the powers, duties, and responsibilities of the Trustees of the Internal Improvement Trust Fund. Restrictions are imposed on the sale and use of lands and waters in the preserve. The riparian rights of upland owners within or adjacent to the preserve are delineated. Wastes and effluents are prohibited from being discharged into the preserve to the extent that such discharges substantially interfere with the purpose of the legislation. Bulkhead lines are also to be relocated to enhance the preserve. The enactment further provides for enforcement, application of existing law, severability and an effective date. (Sperling-Florida)
W75-06598

WATER REGULATIONS--AREAWIDE WASTE TREATMENT MANAGEMENT PLANNING AREAS AND RESPONSIBLE PLANNING AGENCIES.
For primary bibliographic entry see Field 5G.
W75-06599

WATER REGULATIONS--OIL POLLUTION PREVENTION.
For primary bibliographic entry see Field 5G.
W75-06600

WATER REGULATIONS--POLICIES AND PROCEDURES FOR STATE CONTINUING PLANNING PROCESS.
For primary bibliographic entry see Field 5G.
W75-06601

ADOPTED STANDARDS (WATER QUALITY).
For primary bibliographic entry see Field 5G.
W75-06602

WHITE BEAR LAKE CONSERVATION DISTRICT (AS AMENDED).
Minnesota Sess Laws, Vol 2, Ch 111, H.F. No 2703, p 151-152, approved March 13, 1974 (1974).

Descriptors: *Minnesota, *Legislation, *Regulation, *Lakes, *Water conservation, Administration, Administrative agencies, State governments, Inter-agency cooperation, Local governments, Lake shores, Land use, Water resources development, Water quality control, Law enforcement, Legal aspects, Water law, Water policy, Boating regulations, Management, Non-structure alternatives, Water rights, Water utilization, Adoption of practices.
Identifiers: Public trust doctrine, Environment policy, Water rights(Non-riparians), State policy, White Bear Lake(Minn).

The White Bear conservation district is granted specific regulatory powers with respect to the use of boats and motors on the lake, the maintenance and policing of public facilities for access to the lake, the construction and maintenance of permanent and temporary docks and moorings, the construction and use of mechanical and chemical means of de-icing the lake and removing weeds and algae, the construction and maintenance of commercial marinas, and any other construction or lakeshore use on any land abutting the shoreline of the lake. The district also has the power to contract with other governmental bodies or agencies to perform any of the functions of the district, to receive financial assistance from other governmental agencies, and to petition without bond any watershed district within which the lake conservation district may be situated for improvements. The expenses of the district shall be borne by the municipalities in proportion to the assessed value of each municipality. (Deckert-Florida)
W75-06603

HJELLE V. BROOKS (ACTION TO ENJOIN ENFORCEMENT OF ALASKAN REGULATION OF CRAB FISHING IN THE BERING SEA SHELLFISH AREA).
377 F. Supp. 430 (D. Alaska 1974).

Descriptors: *Alaska, *Judicial decisions, *State jurisdiction, *Commercial fishing, *Constitutional law, Commercial shellfish, Crabs, Administrative agencies, Federal jurisdiction, Legal aspects, Water rights, Water law, Federal-state water rights conflicts, Regulation, Oceans, International law, Jurisdiction, International waters, Control, Fish conservation, Resources, Fish harvest, Law enforcement, State governments.
Identifiers: Injunctive relief, Territorial seas(Jurisdiction), Administrative regulations, Coastal waters, Contiguous zone, Water rights(Non-riparians), Standing(Legal), Declaratory judgments.

Plaintiff Washington crab fishermen brought suit seeking declaratory and injunctive relief before a three-judge district court in Alaska. The plaintiffs immediately sought a preliminary injunction barring the defendant, an Alaskan state agency, from enforcing certain regulation pertaining to crab fishing in the Bering Sea. The plaintiffs contended that the defendant's attempt to regulate crab fishing in waters outside the territorial waters of Alaska violated the due process and commerce clauses of the federal constitution. The defendants argued that the court lacked jurisdiction, that the plaintiffs had adequate recourse through the state courts and the federal court should therfore abstain, that the state may unilaterally extend its maritime boundaries to the territorial limits so long as it does not conflict with federal or international law, and that the state regulations may be applied extraterritorially if necessary to protect state interests. The court held that it had jurisdiction and, finding that the plaintiffs showed a reasonable likelihood of succeeding and would suffer considerable harm if the injunction was not issued, granted the preliminary injunction. (Deckert-Florida)
W75-06604

GRAND CANYON DORRIES, INC. V. WALKER (SEEKING DECLARATORY INJUNCTIVE RELIEF CONCERNING DISCHARGES OF WATER FROM DAM).
500 F. 2d 588 (10th Cir. 1974).

Descriptors: *Judicial decisions, United States, *Colorado River, *Streamflow, *Dams, Economic aspects, Federal government, Water demand, Reservoir operation, Legal aspects, Administrative agencies, Adoption of practices, Safety, Administration, Decision making, Utah, Water distribution(Applied), Water allocation(Policy), Reservoir releases, Administrative decisions, Adjudication procedure, Regulation.
Identifiers: Injunctive relief, NEPA, Environmental impact statement, Licenses, Declaratory judgments, Navigation obstructions.

On appeal before the United States Court of Appeals for the Tenth Circuit the operators of commercial float trips on the Colorado River below the Glen Canyon dam sought to enjoin the director of the National Park Service from intermittently reducing the flow of water from the dam and thereby impairing the safe conduct of appellants' trips. The District Court in Utah had denied relief and that judgment was affirmed on appeal. The Circuit Court held that even if contractual obligations arose from the appellants' concession licenses, injunctive relief was not available in a contract action. The Court also found that the application of the National Environmental Policy Act to the ongoing operation of a dam was not ripe for a judicial determination in the absence of an administrative determination of the matter. (Sperling-Florida)
W75-06605

POWER AUTHORITY OF STATE OF NEW YORK V. DEPT. OF ENVIRONMENTAL CONSERVATION OF STATE OF NEW YORK (SEEKING DECLARATORY AND INJUNCTIVE RELIEF AS TO WHETHER DEPARTMENT WAS WITHOUT AUTHORITY IN ISSUING CERTIFICATE FOR POWERPLANT WATER DISCHARGE).
379 F. Supp. 243 (N.D. N.Y. 1974).

Descriptors: *New York *Judicial decisions, *Legal aspects, *Electric power production, *Waste water disposal, Regulation, United States, Jurisdiction, Administrative agencies, Administration, Decision making, Adoption of practices, Standards, Legislation, Water policy, Water law, Electric power plants, Thermal pollution, Adjudication procedure, Administrative decisions.
Identifiers: Notice, Injunctive relief, Declaratory relief, FWPCA Amendments of 1972.

Action was brought in a United States district court in New York by the Power Authority of the State of New York against the New York Department of Environmental Conservation. The Power Authority sought mandatory, injunctive, and declaratory relief to restrain the Department from holding hearings on the Authority's certification for water discharge from a proposed powerplant. The court held that it lacked jurisdiction since the issuance of notice for hearing and a single day of hearings was insufficient administrative action for jurisdiction to attach. None-the-less, the Department has the authority under the Federal Water Pollution Control Act to hold hearings on the Certification of Water discharges to determine if these discharges comply with various sections of the 1972 Amendments to the Federal Water Pollution Control Act. (Sperling-Florida)
W75-06606

U.S. V. W.B. ENTERPRISES, INC. (SUIT TO RECOVER CIVIL PENALTY ASSESSED FOR LEAKAGE OF OIL FROM BARGE).
378 F. Supp. 420 (S.D. New York 1974).

Descriptors: *Judicial decisions, *Oil spills, *Legal aspects, *Federal Water Pollution Control Act, United States, *New York, Water quality control, Rivers, Oil wastes, Water pollution, Water pollution sources, Water pollution effects, Legislation, Waste water discharge, Environmental sanitation, Administration, Oil pollution, Enforcement, Adjudication procedure.
Identifiers: Hazardous substances(Pollution), Non-point source(Pollution).

Suit was brought by the United States to recover a five hundred dollar civil penalty assessed against a barge owner. The assessment was made by the Coast Guard district commander for the alleged violation of the Federal Water Pollution Control Act by leakage of some twenty-five to thirty gallons of oil into the East River. The Southern District Court of New York held that since the Coast Guard is charged with execution of the statute, great weight must be given to its interpretation of the statute. The provision in the Act proscribing discharge of oil and hazardous substances is aimed at preventing any discharges, and not just those discharges which are not removed. In this case, since the discharge created a sheen or discoloration of the water's surface, the defendant violated the Act, and the imposition of a civil penalty was not limited only to compensatory damages. (Sperling-Florida)
W75-06607

WARM SPRINGS DAM TASK FORCE V. GRIBBLE (SEEKING INJUNCTION TO DELAY AWARDING CONTRACT FOR CONSTRUCTION OF MAJOR SECTION OF PROPOSED DAM AND RESERVOIR PROJECT).
378 F. Supp. 240 (N.D. Cal. 1974).

Descriptors: *California, *Federal government, *Judicial decisions, *Construction, *Dams, Reservoirs, Legal aspects, Environmental effects, Contract Administration, Adoption of practices, Planning, Administrative agencies, Conservation, Water resources development, Decision making, Administrative decisions, Adjudication procedure, Equity, Preservation.
Identifiers: Injunctive relief, Environmental Impact Statements, National Environmental Policy Act.

Suit was brought in the Northern District of California by an unincorporated association against Corps of Engineers of the United States Army. The suit seeks a preliminary injunction to delay the award of a contract for the construction of a major segment of a proposed dam and reservoir project until alleged deficiencies in the environmental impact statement were remedied. The court held that the archeological element of the environmental impact statement was not deficient despite obvious shortcomings. The Secretary of Interior's determination that the archaeological district within the area of the proposed project might be eligible for inclusion in the National Register of Historic Places compelled the Corps to reconsider the project. If the Corps proposed to substantially alter the property, it should not act until the Advisory Council on Historical Preservation had an opportunity to comment. However, the Corps was only restricted from disturbing known or suspected sites, not from disturbing any portion at all within the district. (Sperling-Florida)
W75-06608

COMMONWEALTH OF PENNSYLVANIA V. BARNES AND TUCKER CO. (ACTION TO REQUIRE OWNER OF CLOSED MINE TO TREAT ACID MINE DRAINAGE DISCHARGING FROM MINE).
319 A 2d 871 (Pa 1974).

Descriptors: *Pennsylvania, *Acid mine water, *Water pollution control, *Regulation, *Judicial decisions, Legislation, Industrial wastes, Waste water treatment, Conservation, Environmental ef-

Legal rview, Water rights, Planning, Water policy, Water resources development, Adoption of praetices.
Identifiers: *Coastal waters, *Coastal zone management, Environmental policy, State policy.

There is hereby created the Alabama Coastal Area Board, composed of eight designated officials from various agencies of state and local governments. The Board shall develop and implement a comprehensive coastal area administration program consistent with the national policy expressed in the Coastal Zone Management Act of 1972 and the goals of the state legislature as expressed herein. The Board shall have the authority to control certain 'regulated activities', as defined in the Act, as it deems necessary for the preservation and development of coastal areas. Unless permissible under the administration program to be developed, the following activities may not be conducted without permit of the Board: excavation or dumping of any kind in any coastal areas; killing or materially damaging any flora or fauna in any coastal area; and the creation of any structure affecting the ebb and flow of the tide in any coastal area. Procedures for issuing such permits are set forth in the Act. Decisions of the board concerning the permits are subject to judicial review and criminal and civil sanctions may be imposed for violation of the Act's provisions. (Deckert-Florida)
W75-06611

U.S. V. LEWIS (INJUNCTION ACTION BASED ON VIOLATION OF RIVERS AND HARBORS ACT.
355 F. Supp. 1132 (S.D. Ga. 1973).

Descriptors: *Navigable waters, *Judicial decisions, *Road construction, *Marshes, Highway effeets, Environment, Environmental effects, Roads, Rivers and Harbors Act, Legislation, *Georgia, Permits, Water law, Water resources development, Waste disposal, Sludge disposal, Water quality control, Damages.
Identifiers: *Injunctive relief.

The United States brought suit in the Southern District of Georgia seeking to enjoin construction of a causeway across tidal marsh. The court held the marshlands were navigable waters for purposes of the exercise of federal jurisidiction. In addition the construction of a causeway without a permit from the Army Corps of Engineers was held to violate the 'obstruction' section of the Rivers and Harbors Act, and the unauthorized deposit of refuse matter into navigable water was a violation of 33 U.S.C. Section 407. (Proctor-Florida)
W75-06612

U.S. V. STOECO HOMES, INC. (APPEAL FROM INJUNCTION FOR VIOLATIONS OF RIVERS AND HARBORS ACT).
498 F. 2d 597 (3d Cir. 1974).

Descriptors: *New Jersey, *Judicial decisions, *Regulation, *Tidal marshes, *Rivers and Harbors Act, Dredging, Permits, Legislation, Water law, Administrative agencies, Legal aspects, Land tenure, Excavation, Federal jurisdiction, Federal government, Wetlands, Administration, Navigable waters, Legal review, Land development, Landfills, Land management, Silting, Water pollution sources, Water quality control.
Identifiers: Navigational servitude, Navigability tests, Fill permits, Administrative regulations, Coastal zone management, Injunctive relief, FWPCA Amendments of 1972, Navigation obstructions.

The federal government, alleging violations of the Rivers and Harbors Appropriation Act of 1899, sought to permanently enjoin the defendant development corporation from engaging in any further dredge, fill, or construction operations on its property, without the prior recommendation of the Army Corps of Engineers and approval of the Secretary of the Army. The government alleged that the defendant's operations were resulting in the unauthorized discharge of dredge fill into the adjacent navigable lagoons. It further contended that the entire parcel of property was within the navigable waters of the United States and thus excavation of the lagoons without a permit was in violation of the act. The lower court granted the injunction and the defendant appealed. The Court of Appeals for the Third Circuit held that the lagoons were navigable waters under the Act, but those portions of the defendant's property which were above the mean high tide were no longer subject to the government's navigational servitude. Accordingly, the court sustained the injunction to the extent that it prohibited hydraulic dredging, but remanded the case for the entry of a modified injunction in accordance with this opinion. (Deckert-Florida)
W75-06613

WATER REGULATIONS--LIABILITY LIMITS FOR SMALL ONSHORE STORAGE FACILITIES.
For primary bibliographic entry see Field 5G.
W75-06614

POINT SOURCES COVERED BY NPDES AND PROCEDURES.
For primary bibliographic entry see Field 5G.
W75-06617

POLLUTION--REGULATION.
Minnesota Sess. LAAWS, Vol 4, Ch 483, H.F. No 1662, p 942-947, approved April 11, 1974 (1974).

Descriptors: *Minnesota, *Legislation, *Environmental control, *Regulation, *Administrative agencies, Waste disposal, Water law, Legal aspects, State governments, Administration, Permits, Standards, Air pollution, Pollution abatement, Quality control, Wastes, Solid wastes, Water quality standards.
Identifiers: Environmental policy, Administrative regulations.

The director of the Minnesota state pollution control agency is hereby authorized to appoint a deputy director and an assistant director. The director may designate the depty director to act in his stead as a member of any agency, board, committee or commission that the director is made a member of by law. The statutory meaning of 'solid waste' is expanded to include garbage, refuse, and other discharded solid materials, including solids and sludges resulting from industrial, commercial and agricultural operations, and from community activities, but does not include animal waste used as fertilizer, earthenfill, rocks, or certain types of common water pollutants. The pollution control agency is directed to establish air quality and noise pollution standards and is authorized to establish regulations relating to air and noise pollution. The agency is provided permit authority to govern noise pollution and is granted power to regulate the storage of solid waste. The statutory definition of 'junk yard' is expanded. (Deckert-Florida()
W75-06618

EFFLUENT GUIDELINES ARE ON THE WAY,
For primary bibliographic entry see Field 5G.
W75-06619

INTERFERENCE WITH THE FLOW OF SURFACE WATER,
T. H. Burnett.
Kentucky Law Journal, Vol 50, No 1, p 254-257, 1961. 17 ref.

Descriptors: *Surface waters, *Judicial decisions, *Runoff, *Surface runoff, *Reasonable use,

Water resources, Drainage water, Overland flow, Rain water, Highway, Storm runoff, Landfills, Water law, Water resources development, Negligence, Legal aspects, Adjudication procedure, Kentucky, Water management(Applied).
Identifiers: Liability(Legal aspects), Water rights(Non-riparians), State policy, Common enemy.

Plantiff and defendant own land on opposite sides of a highway. The natural surface drainage is northwesterly across plaintiff's land, under an abandoned fill, under the highway, and onto defendant's land. Defendant constructed a fill across a creek on his land six hundred feet northwest of the highway and installed several large drainpipes. During an unprecedented rainfall, water backed up behind defendant's fill and onto plantiff's land, damaging a tenanat's house and other property. The issue was submitted to the jury under instructions based on negligence in the construction of the fill. In affirming judgment for the plaintiff, the court held that the civil law rul of absolute liability for obstruction of surface waters applied. The judicial rule prohibits interference with the natural flow of surface water that causes an invasion of another's interests in the use and enjoyment of his land. The relative merits are discussed of the common enemy rule, the civil law rule and the reasonable use doctrine in determining liability for interference with the flow of surface waters. The adoption of the reasonable use doctrine in Kentucky is recommended. (Proctor-Florida)
W75-06620

INTERSTATE WATER COMPACTS, A BIBLIOGRAPHY,
Office of Water Research and Technology, Washington, D.C.
Available from the National Technical Information Service, Springfield, Va 22161, as PB-241 170, $12.00 in paper copy, $2.25 in microfiche. Water Resources Scientific Information Center, Report OWRT/WRSIC 75-205, March 1975, 488 p. Edited by Frank E. Maloney, College of Law, University of Florida.

Descriptors: *Interstate compacts, *Bibliographies, *Interstate commissions, Legislation, Legal aspects, *Water rights, *Water law, *River basin commissions, Water pollution control, Water resources development, Abstracts, Administrative agencies, Federal government, State governments, Flood control.

This report, containing 306 abstracts, is another in a series of planned bibliographies in water resources to be produced from the information base conprising SELECTED WATER RESOURCES ABSTRACTS (SWRA). At the time of search for this bibliography, the data base had 80,488 abstracts covering SWRA through January 15, 1975 (Volume 8, Number 2). Author and subject indexes are included.
W75-06640

ORGANIZATIONAL PROBLEM-SOLVING,
Kansas Water Resources Research Inst., Manbattan.
For primary bibliographic entry see Field 6B.
W75-06643

PROCEEDINGS OF CONFERENCE ON 'TRENDS IN WATER MANAGEMENT',
Minnesota Univ., St. Paul. Water Resources Research Center.
Available from the National Technical Information Service, Springfield, Va 22161, as PB-241 158, $4.25 in paper copy, $2.25 in microfiche. Bulletin No 80, January 1975, 49 p. OWRT A-999-MINN(35), 14-31-0001-5023.

Descriptors: *Water policy, Planning, *Water management(Applied), *Minnesota, *Conferences, Administrative agencies, *Project planning, State government, Reviews, Operations.

The program of the Conference consisted of presentations of representatives of the U.S. Army Corps of Engineers, the Soil Conservation Service, the Upper Mississippi River Basin Commission, the Minnesota Pollution Control Agency, the Department of Natural Resources, and the State Planning Agency. The papers addressed questions of how the agency perceives its role as a water manager; how that perception is reflected in its operation. A review of current programs are comments on anticipated changes or new programs in the next few years, also were presented. (Waelti-Minnesota)
W75-06647

SOVEREIGNTY OF THE SEAS AND THE EFFECT UPON NAVAL STRATEGY,
Naval War Coll., Newport, R.I.
E. L. Gallup.
Marine Affairs Journal, Number 1, p 1-8, December 1973.

Descriptors: *Oceans, *Territorial seas, *Military aspects, *International waters, Navigable waters, International law.
Identifiers: *Military strategy, *Naval strategy, *National sovereignty claims, *Marine sovereignty, *Freedom of the seas.

Limitations upon the use of the ocean imposed by various nationalities must have some effect upon naval strategy. Effects of alterations in the freedom of the seas concept upon naval strategies of major powers under varying conditions and levels of international conflict are explored. Since World War II, national sovereignty claims have increased over internal waters, special zones, seabed, territorial seas and the airspace above these areas. Sea claims during past wars and crises have necessitated an international agreement to reduce naval conflicts as well as define boundaries of naval, fishing and other activities. It would appear that world acceptance of a 12-mile territorial sea is most probable although a greater limit is possible. Regardless of whether the intended purpose of zones is to control pollution, to regulate fishing or avoid collision with offshore oil wells, the net result is a decreasing freedom of the seas. Naval strategy will be affected by the increasing restriction on the use of the ocean in inverse proportion to the level of intensity of the conflict. The greatest impact of extension of marine sovereignty will occur in those situations least damaging to the national interests of the maritime powers or under conditions most amenable to alternate solutions. (Salzman-North Carolina)
W75-06786

ORGANIZING NEW ENGLAND COMMERCIAL FISHERMEN AT THE REGIONAL LEVEL,
Rhode Island Univ., Kingston.
W. H. MacKenzie.
Marine Affairs Journal, Number 1, p 33-51, December 1973.

Descriptors: *Marine fisheries, *Fisheries, *Fish management, *New England, *Trade associations, Commercial fishing, Governments, Organizations.
Identifiers: New England Fisheries Steering Committee(NEFSC), Atlantic Offshore Fish and Lobster Association(AOFLA), *200 mile fishing zone.

New England commercial fishermen are organizing to resolve problems among themselves and to influence fishing-related decisions at all levels of government. This study details the formation, growth and operating procedures of the two regional New England efforts, Atlantic Offshore Fish and Lobster Association (AOFLA) and the New England Fisheries Steering Committee (NEFSC). The movement to organize grew in response to increasing international interests in fisheries combined with differences on coastal state rights. AOFLA has enlisted 53 fishermen and lobstermen as well as an executive secretary who hopes to solve off-shore gear conflicts and to fight for a 200 mile fishing zone. Unincorporated, AOFLA has only a draft set of by-laws, meager financial support and a weak political force. NEFSC also supports the 200 mile fishing zone. Comprised of fishing organizations and industries, as well as members of the government and science communities, NEFSC claims to be the regional spokesman, although no substantial evidence exists to support any kind of political or legal action. Organizing fishermen is not an easy task. If regional efforts become stronger, the next step may be affiliation with the National Federation of Fishermen. (Salzman-North Carolina)
W75-06788

SET PROBE OF POLLUTION CONTROL AMENDMENTS.
For primary bibliographic entry see Field 5G.
W75-06827

NINE MILLION GALLONS PER MINUTE DOWN THE DRAIN, FEDERAL GUIDELINES PRESENT A TOUGH CHALLENGE,
For primary bibliographic entry see Field 5G.
W75-06834

6F. Nonstructural Alternatives

LAND-USE ISSUES: PROCEEDINGS OF A CONFERENCE.
Virginia Polytechnic Inst. and State Univ., Blacksburg. Water Resources Research Center.
For primary bibliographic entry see Field 4A.
W75-06359

REDESIGNING FLOOD MANAGEMENT - PROJECT AGNES PHASE I,
New York State Coll. of Agriculture and Life Sciences, Ithaca. Dept. of Agricultural Economics.
D. J. Allee.
Available from the National Technical Information Service, Springfield, Va 22161 as PB-241 064, $4.25 in paper copy, $2.25 in microfiche. Completion Report, New York Water Resources and Marine Sciences Center, Ithaca, September 1976, 61 p. OWRT A-045-NY(2). 14-31-0001-4032.

Descriptors: *Flood control, *Flood protection, Flood recurrance interval, Non-structural alternatives, Flood forecasting, Water policy, Flood plains, Design flood, *Management, Risks, Local governments, Regional analysis, Evaluation, Land use, Warning systems, Flood plain zoning, Planning.
Identifiers: *Susquehanna River basin, *Flood risks.

Four studies--a part of a larger program of flood related research--are reported here. Flood risk management has emphasized dams and channel modification. Also an elaborate set of relief programs has evolved. Now the harder to deal with tactics of inducing local governments to regulate flood plain use plus efforts to make development more flood sensitive are being more seriously addressed. These studies provide a background for this evolution of a broader mix of public programs. Evaluation of water resources planning in the Susquehanna River Basin suggests that a marked difference in perception of flood risk by planners and local leaders was not overcome and probably led to less acceptance of the planners proposals. Regional analysis techniques can provide a basis for restructuring flood relief payments so that the result is a more vigorous as well as a more flood sensitive, rebuilt community. Furthermore, environmental analysis techniques that relate resource capacity to the requirements of land use

FLOOD PLAIN INFORMATION: LITTLE BLUE RIVER, EAST FORK, WHITE OAK BRANCH, JACKSON COUNTY, MISSOURI,
Army Engineer District, Kansas City, Mo.
For primary bibliographic entry see Field 4A.
W75-06770

SPECIAL FLOOD HAZARD INFORMATION: MILL CREEK, UMATILLA COUNTY, OREGON.
Army Engineer District, Walla Walla, Wash.
For primary bibliographic entry see Field 4A.
W75-06771

FLOOD PLAIN INFORMATION: YAKIMA RIVER, CITY OF SELAH AND VICINITY, WASHINGTON.
Army Engineer District, Seattle, Wash.
For primary bibliographic entry see Field 4A.
W75-06772

SPECIAL FLOOD HAZARD INFORMATION REPORT: BAYOU SARA, BAYOU SARA CREEK, NORTON CREEK, HELLS SWAMP BRANCH, VICINITY OF SARALAND, ALABAMA.
Army Engineer District, Mobile, Ala.
For primary bibliographic entry see Field 4A.
W75-06773

FLOOD PLAIN INFORMATION: SPRING BRANCH, INDEPENDENCE, MISSOURI.
Army Engineer District, Kansas City, Mo.
For primary bibliographic entry see Field 4A.
W75-06779

URBAN SYSTEMS ENGINEERING DEMONSTRATION PROGRAM FOR HINDS, MADISON, RANKIN COUNTIES, MISSISSIPPI, VOLUME IV. AREA-WIDE STORM DRAINAGE AND FLOOD PLAIN MANAGEMENT STUDIES.
Clark, Dietz and Associates, Inc., Jackson, Miss.
For primary bibliographic entry see Field 5D.
W75-06785

COASTAL ZONE PLANNING: THE IMPACT OF REGIONAL EFFORTS IN NEW ENGLAND,
Woods Hole Oceanographic Institution, Mass.
S. H. Anderson.
Marine Affairs Journal, Number 1, p 78-90, December 1973.

Descriptors: *Planning, *Coasts, *New England, *Coordination, Land use, Natural resources, Management.
Identifiers: *Regional planning, *Coastal zone management.

Development of coastal zone planning in New England has benefited from regional efforts to induce information sharing and cooperative planning. Although no regional government structure exists, a number of private and public regional organizations can provide significant inputs to comprehensive coastal resource planning. Some of these organizations are described, followed by an analysis of the means by which a regional perspective may be further encouraged through citizen involvement. Six organizations have provided planners with means to develop alternative plans for coastal zone use, but at present, the actual coordination among the region's states and regional organizations is fragmented. Ultimately, adherence to a plan is dependent on citizen support. To involve the public, defined by their occupational relationship to the coastal zone as well as specific interest groups, planners must provide public forums (town meetings), public surveys, workshops and citizens advisory boards. These channels, coupled with educational activities in schools, through promotional and research publications, and over the mass media will bring the public into the planning process and help develop a regional perspective in planning of the New England marine region. (Salzman-North Carolina)
W75-06790

SPECIAL FLOOD HAZARD INFORMATION REPORT: GALLAGHER CREEK, MERIDIAN, LAUDERDALE COUNTY, MISSISSIPPI.
Army Engineer District, Mobile, Ala.
For primary bibliographic entry see Field 4A.
W75-06792

FLOOD PLAIN INFORMATION: LOS PENASQUITOS DRAINAGE AREA, SAN DIEGO COUNTY, CALIFORNIA.
Army Engineer District, Los Angeles, Calif.
For primary bibliographic entry see Field 4A.
W75-06793

6G. Ecologic Impact Of Water Development

SOME PERSPECTIVES ON THE STATUS OF AQUATIC WADING BIRDS IN SOUTH FLORIDA,
Bureau of Sport Fisheries and Wildlife, Atlanta, Ga.
J. P. Crowder.
Available from the National Technical Information Service, Springfield, Va 22161 as PB-235 216, $3.25 in paper copy, $2.25 in microfiche. South Florida Environmental Project: Ecological Report No. DI-SFEP-74-29, Feb. 1974. 13 p, 16 ref.

Descriptors: *Ecology, *Wading birds, *Environmental effects, *Florida, Nests, Waterfowl, National Parks.
Identifiers: *Bird populations, *Everglades National Park(Fla), Breeding, Nesting, Wood Storks, White Ibis, Cattle Egret.

Relationships between wading birds, water levels, and other biota of the south Florida wetlands ecosystem are discussed. Data from other studies are consolidated to present information on wading birds in the Everglades National Park and the remainder of Florida south of Lake Okeechobee. A total of 35,000 breeding pairs of wading birds (excluding 22,500 pairs of cattle egrets) are all that is left of a once larger population of about 2.5 million in 1870. The effects of wetlands drainage on nesting success and broader implications of feeding and other ecological relationships of wading birds are discussed with emphasis on population size, feeding efficiency, predator-prey relationships, and stress. Particular emphasis is placed on wood stork, white ibis, and cattle egrets. Recommendations for preserving these birds are presented with a discussion of artificial feeding habitat. (Katz)
W75-06397

THE EXOTIC VERTEBRATES OF SOUTH FLORIDA,
Bureau of Sport Fisheries and Wildlife, Atlanta, Ga.
J. P. Crowder.
Available from the National Technical Information Service, Springfield, Va 22161 as PB-235 214, $3.75 in paper copy, $2.25 in microfiche. South Florida Environmental Project: Ecological Rept No. DI-SFEP-74-30, Feb. 1974. 38 p.

Descriptors: *Ecology, *Florida, *Fishes, Animal groupings.
Identifiers: *Exotic animals, *Tropical fish, Knight anole, Marine toad, Cuban treefrog, Walking catfish, Native wildlife, Cichlids.

Species of introduced exotic vertebrates of south Florida (Lake Okeechobee southward) are identified and described. The principal factors responsible for their introductions are explored

and recommendations are made for alleviation of current problems caused by exotics and for prevention of further harmful introductions. Major problems were determined to be (1) the rapid spread of exotic tropical fishes, principally cichlids and the walking catfish (Clarias batrachus) and their displacement of native sunfishes, and (2) the presence of a number of exotic psittacine birds with potential for depredations of fruit and grain crops, and (3) three species of giant herptiles (knight anole, marine toad, cuban treefrog) that prey upon their smaller native counterparts. (Katz)
W75-06398

DRAFT ENVIRONMENTAL STATEMENT HTGR FUEL REFABRICATION PILOT PLANT AT THE OAK RIDGE NATIONAL LABORATORY.
Oak Ridge National Lab., Tenn.
For primary bibliographic entry see Field 5B.
W75-06417

REPORT TO THE SONOMA CREEK ADVISORY COMMITTEE, SONOMA, CALIFORNIA,
California Univ., Berkeley. Dept. of Landscape Architecture.
For primary bibliographic entry see Field 6B.
W75-06430

ENVIRONMENTAL STUDIES (1973), JAMES BAY TERRITORY AND SURROUNDING AREA,
Department of the Environment, Hull (Quebec); and James Bay Development Corp., Montreal (Quebec).
69 p, 22 fig, 101 ref.

Descriptors: *Environment, *Canada, *Ecosystems, *Cold regions, Air environment, Climatology, Hydrography, Hydrometry, Oceanography, Geology, Terrain analysis, Sedimentology, Water-fowl, Wetlands, Wildlife, Big game, Aquatic animals, Marine animals, Estuarine environment, Lakes, Rivers.
Identifiers: *James Bay(Canada).

Studies and biophysical inventories carried out in 1973 under the terms of the agreement signed between the James Bay Development Corportation and Environment Canada were reported. Studies in the following subjects were discussed: (1) atmospheric environment, (2) hydrography and oceanography, (3) terrain studies, (4) waterfowl and wetlands habitat, (5) wildlife, (6) aquatic fauna, (7) classification of ecological systems, (8) hydrometry, (9) water quality, and (10) man's activities in the territory. (Sims-ISWS)
W75-06467

ATTITUDES OF IDAHO RESIDENTS TOWARD FREE FLOWING RIVERS AS A WATER USE IN IDAHO,
Idaho Univ., Moscow. Dept. of Sociology and Anthropology.
For primary bibliographic entry see Field 6B.
W75-06525

THE WESTERNPORT BAY ENVIRONMENTAL STUDY,
Victoria Ministry for Conservation, Melbourne (Australia). Westernport Bay Environmental Study.
M. A. Shapiro.
Water (Journal of the Australian Water and Wastewater Association) Vol 1, No 4, p 9-13, December 1974.

Descriptors: *Baseline studies, *Regional development, *Environmental effects, *Australia, Surveys, Investigations, Harbors, Industries, Bays, Watersheds(Basins), Economic impact, Social impact, Wildlife habitats, Recreation facilities, Comprehensive planning.
Identifiers: *Westernport Bay(Vic).

The Westernport Bay area in southern Victoria (Australia) is noted for the wildlife it shelters, and provides a major recreational facility for metropolitan Melbourne. It is also one of only a few locations on the Australian coast which possess the factors of markets, labor, deep water, land quality and land availability required in a suitable site for the development of an industrial port complex. A cooridinated multidisciplinary study involving basic and applied research activities is under way, with the responsibility for developing the comprehensive knowledge of the Bay and its catchment necessary for a balanced approach to planning its development. The projects involved within the structure of the Study are listed and briefly described. They range from studies of climate, geology and hydrology, through marine and littoral ecology to history, economics and sociology. The study is jointly financed by government and industry, and a major report is to be submitted in late 1974. (Levick-CSIRO)
W75-06555

THE UNCERTAIN SEARCH FOR ENVIRONMENTAL QUALITY,
Yale Univ., New Haven, Conn. School of Law.
For primary bibliographic entry see Field 5G.
W75-06557

PRESERVATION AND ENHANCEMENT OF THE AMERICAN FALLS AT NIAGARA--FINAL REPORT TO THE INTERNATIONAL JOINT COMMISSION.
American Falls International Board, Buffalo, N.Y.
June 1974. 78 p, 44 fig, 9 tab, 7 append.

Descriptors: *Erosion control, *Waterfalls, *Aesthetics, *Great Lakes Region, *International Joint Commission, Economic feasibility, Economic impact, Environmental effects, Canada, United States, International Commissions, Scenery, Water resources development, Evaluation, Geology, Erosion, Engineering, Rivers, Engineering geology, Future planning(Projected), Forecasting, Alternative planning, Water management(Applied), Governmental interrelations.
Identifiers: *Environmental policy, *Niagara Falls.

A study was undertaken at the request of the United States and Canadian governments to investigate and report upon measures necessary to preserve or enhance the beauty of the American Falls at Niagara. The study was subsequently expanded to include aspects of public safety at the American Falls and at the Goat Island flank of the Horseshoe Falls. Extensive geological investigations were conducted to determine what measures might be taken to control the erosion occurring at the crests of the Falls. Alternative measures were evaluated in terms of their aesthetic, economic, and environmental effects and proposals of varying cost are presented. It was concluded that the process of erosion and recession should be accepted as a dynamic part of the natural condition of the Falls and should not be interrupted. However, specific measures should be taken to restore the level of the Maid-of-the-Mist Pool and to protect the safety of visitors to the Falls. (Deckert-Florida)
W75-06574

ENVIRONMENTAL DEFENSE FUND V. TENNESSEE VALLEY AUTHORITY.
For primary bibliographic entry see Field 6E.
W75-06580

ENVIRONMENTAL LAW--JUDICIAL REVIEW UNDER NEPA,
For primary bibliographic entry see Field 5G.
W75-06585

7. RESOURCES DATA

7A. Network Design

ADAPTATION AND APPLICATION OF THE KARAZEV METHOD TO THE RATIONALIZATION OF QUEBEC'S HYDROMETRIC BASIC NETWORK,
National Inst. of Scientific Research, Quebec.
For primary bibliographic entry see Field 2E.
W75-06454

MESOSCALE OBJECTIVE ANALYSIS OF THE WIND AND MOISTURE FIELD AROUND THE THUNDERSTORMS DEVELOPED OVER NSSL OBSERVATION NETWORK ON MAY 28, 1967,
Meteorological Research Inst., Tokyo (Japan).
For primary bibliographic entry see Field 2B.
W75-06535

7B. Data Acquisition

THE REMOTE SENSING OF SUSPENDED SEDIMENT CONCENTRATIONS OF SMALL IMPOUNDMENTS,
Agricultural Research Service, Chickasha, Okla. Southern Great Plains Watershed Research Center.
H. B. Pionke, and B. J. Blanchard.
Water, Air and Soil Pollution, Vol 4, No 1, p 19-32, March 1975. 2 fig, 1 tab, 10 ref. NASA S-70251-AG, Task No. 5.

Descriptors: *Remote sensing, *Sediment transport, *Water pollution, Path of pollutants, Suspended solids, Aerial sensing, Analytical techniques, *Oklahoma.

The suspended sediment concentrations of 14 Oklahoma impoundments were related to bands of reflected light as measured from an aircraft-borne multispectral scanner. Suspended sediment concentrations (Y) were curvilinearly related to reflectance (X) where the exponent on X exceeds one. The best relationships, upon consideration of sensitivity, range, and precision, appeared in the bands defined by 588 to 643 and 650 to 690 nm wavelength. The latter was less precise. The measured range in sediment concentration was 13 to 232 mg/liter. (ARS)
W75-06399

DETERMINATION OF SOIL WATER DIFFUSIVITY BY SORPTIVITY MEASUREMENTS, .
Agricultural Research Service, Riverside, Calif. Salinity Lab.
For primary bibliographic entry see Field 2G.
W75-06438

A NEW CERAMIC CUP SOIL-WATER SAMPLER,
Forest Service (USDA), La Crosse, Wis. Watershed Lab.
For primary bibliographic entry see Field 2G.
W75-06441

PRIMARY AMINES IN CALIFORNIA COASTAL WATERS: UTILIZATION BY PHYTOPLANKTON,
California Univ, Irvine. Dept. of Developmental and Cell Biology.
For primary bibliographic entry see Field 5A.
W75-06443

A RADIOSONDE THERMAL SENSOR TECHNIQUE FOR MEASUREMENT OF ATMOSPHERIC TURBULENCE,
National Aeronautics and Space Administration, Greenbelt, Md. Goddard Space Flight Center.
For primary bibliographic entry see Field 2B.
W75-06476

PROCEDURES MANUAL FOR DETECTION AND LOCATION OF SURFACE WATER USING ERTS-1 MULTISPECTRAL SCANNER DATA, VOLUME I - SUMMARY.
National Aeronautics and Space Administration, Houston, Tex. Lyndon B. Johnson Space Center.
For primary bibliographic entry see Field 7C.
W75-06484

A PORTABLE AEROSOL DETECTOR OF HIGH SENSITIVITY,
State Univ. of New York, Albany. Atmospheric Sciences Research Center.
For primary bibliographic entry see Field 5A.
W75-06496

CALIBRATION OF THE POLLAK COUNTER WITH MONODISPERSE AEROSOLS,
Minnesota Univ., Minneapolis. Particle Technology Lab.
For primary bibliographic entry see Field 5A.
W75-06497

AN APT SIGNAL SIMULATOR,
New York State Coll. of Agriculture and Life Sciences, Ithaca. Div. of Atmospheric Sciences.
W. W. Knapp, and P. S. Sanik.
Journal of Applied Meteorology, Vol 14, No 1, p 132-135, February 1975. 3 fig, 1 ref.

Descriptors: *Instrumentation, *Remote sensing, *Satellites(Artificial), Infrared radiation, Electronic equipment, Electrical engineering, Testing procedures.
Identifiers: *Signal simulators, Scanning radiometers, Automatic picture transmission.

An inexpensive device designed to simulate video signals produced by the scanning radiometer system used on current NOAA series satellites was described. The simulator features independent control of both visible and infrared channel video levels during periods corresponding to the earth scan portions of each scan line. The known and adjustable signal levels provided by this simulator unit simplify the tasks of calibration, adjustment, and servicing APT display systems. (Sims-ISWS)
W75-06501

THE USE OF A VERTICALLY POINTING PULSED DOPPLER RADAR IN CLOUD PHYSICS AND WEATHER MODIFICATION STUDIES,
Washington Univ., Seattle. Dept. of Atmospheric Sciences.
For primary bibliographic entry see Field 3B.
W75-06507

DUAL DOPPLER RADAR COORDINATION USING NOMOGRAMS,
Oklahoma Univ., Norman. Dept. of Meteorology.
For primary bibliographic entry see Field 2B.
W75-06510

AERIAL RADIOLOGICAL MEASURING SURVEY OF THE MAINE YANKEE ATOMIC POWER PLANT SEPTEMBER 1971.
EG and G, Inc., Las Vegas, Nev.
For primary bibliographic entry see Field 5A.
W75-06630

AERIAL RAIOLOGICAL MEASURING SURVEY OF THE FORT ST. VRAIN NUCLEAR GENERATING STATION OCTOBER 1971,
EG and G, Inc., Las Vegas, Nev.
For primary bibliographic entry see Field 5A.
W75-06631

AERIAL RADIOLOGICAL MEASURING SURVEY OF THE PRAIRIE ISLAND NUCLEAR GENERATING PLANT SEPTEMBER 1971,
EG and G, Inc., Las Vegas, Nev.
For primary bibliographic entry see Field 5A.
W75-06632

AERIAL RADIOLOGICAL MEASURING SURVEYS OF THE TURKEY POINT STATION APRIL 1972,
EG and G, Inc., Las Vegas, Nev.
For primary bibliographic entry see Field 5A.
W75-06633

AERIAL RADIOLOGICAL MEASURING SURVEY OF THE PILGRIM STATION SEPTEMBER 1971,
EG and G, Inc., Las Vegas, Nev.
For primary bibliographic entry see Field 5A.
W75-06634

AERIAL RADIOLOGICAL MEASURING SURVEY OF THE INDIAN POINT STATION AUGUST 1969,
EG and G, Inc., Las Vegas, Nev.
For primary bibliographic entry see Field 5A.
W75-06635

THE USE OF A MODIFIED GULF V PLANKTON SAMPLER FROM A SMALL OPEN BOAT,
Ministry of Agriculture, Fisheries and Food, Lowestoft (England). Fisheries Lab.
S. J. Lockwood.
J Cons Cons Int Explor Mer. Vol 35, No 2, p 171-174, 1974, Illus.

Descriptors: Sampling, *Plankton, *Equipment, Seston.
Identifiers: *Gulf V Plankton Sampler, Samplers.

The sampler is made from marine grade aluminum, is 50 cm in diameter, 213 cm long and weighs 30 kg in air when fully rigged. It had been used successfully from an 8 m Yorkshire cable in depths considerably less than 10 m as well as in greater depths. Two davits were wedged in the boat's side to carry the sampler in a position which reduced handling to a minimum. The warp was paid away and hauled either by a manual winch or with the aid of a crab-pot hauler. Towing speed was set by reference to the engine tachometer but the external flowmeter reading gave an accurate measure of consistency. The coefficient of variation was less than 10% of the mean. By comparison the coefficient of variation rose as high as 46% when the sampler was towed by a 15 m keel boat.--Copyright 1974, Biological Abstracts, Inc.
W75-06707

AN AIR-LIFT FOR QUANTITATIVE SAMPLING OF THE BENTHOS,
Hull Univ. (England). Dept. of Zoology.
R. G. Pearson, M. R. Litterick, and N. V. Jones.
Freshwater Biol. Vol 3, No 4, p 309-315, 1973, Illus.
Identifiers: *Air-lift sampling, *Benthos, Fauna, Quantitative samplers, *Sampling, Surber sampler, Allan grab.

A new air-lift which quantitatively samples the fauna from a variety of substrate at a range of water depths, and which is operated by 1 person, is described. Performance of the sampler under different conditions is discussed and comparisons are made between the air-lift and a Surber sampler and an Allan grab.--Copyright 1974, Biological Abstracts, Inc.
W75-06713

ANALYSIS OF MASS BALANCE VALUES AND THEIR ACCURACY FOR SENTINEL GLACIER, BRITISH COLUMBIA, CANADA,
Department of the Environment, Ottawa (Ontario). Water Resources Branch.
For primary bibliographic entry see Field 2C.
W75-06740

SIMPLE COLOUR METER FOR LIMNOLOGICAL STUDIES,
Canada Centre for Inland Waters, Burlington (Ontario).
K. P. B. Thomson, J. Jerome, and H. W. MacPhail.
Scientific Series No. 49, 13 p, 1974, Inland Waters Directorate. 12 fig, 5 ref, 2 tab.

Descriptors: *Water analysis, *Color, *Measurement, Organoleptic properties, Instrumentation, Tracking techniques, Water circulation, Turbidity, Research and development, Remote sensing, Canada, Lake Superior.
Identifiers: *Irradiance, *Color meters, Meters.

A simple in situ irradiance meter for objective measurement of water color has been designed and built by the Remote Sensing Section at Canada Centre for Inland Waters. The principle of the instrument is to measure the upwelling natural irradiance close to the surface at two selected wavelengths and express these as a ratio or color index. Experiments carried out with this instrumentation in Lake Superior have shown that the color indices can be used as water-mass tracers with midlake and near-shore regions being clearly identified. Results also show that the color indices provide a useful measurement of the relative turbidity characteristics of large lakes. (Environment Canada)
W75-06743

PEAK FLOWS BY THE SLOPE-AREA METHOD,
Department of the Environment, Ottawa (Ontario). Water Resources Branch.
For primary bibliographic entry see Field 2E.
W75-06745

TRANSIENT RESPONSE OF SHALLOW ENCLOSED BASINS USING THE METHOD OF NORMAL MODES,
Canada Centre for Inland Waters, Burlington (Ontario).
For primary bibliographic entry see Field 2H.
W75-06746

REMOTE SENSING,
Bureau of Reclamation, Washington, D.C.
R. R. Ledzian.
Reclamation ERA, Vol 60, No 4, p 8-18, Autumn 1974. 11 fig.

Descriptors: *Remote sensing, *Analytical techniques, *Radar, *Water management(Applied), *Water supply, *Planning, *Groundwater availability, Water resources development, Water resources.
Identifiers: *Earth Resources Technology Satellite(ERTS), *Earth Resources Observation Systems(EROS), Data Collective Platform(DCP), Multispectral scanner(MSS), Return beam vidicon(RBV).

Remote sensing is the acquisition of data from a distant platform for detecting the nature of an object without actually touching it. This technology which increases man's knowledge of his finite resources ranges from very short wave lengths at which gamma rays are emitted to the comparatively long wavelengths at which radar operates. Earth Resources Technology Satellite (ERTS) orbits the earth in 103 minutes, crossing the same spot at the same time every 18 days, permitting comparison of images with the same sun angle. Two imaging systems sense and record radiation in several visible and near-infrared bands. Multispectral analysis, change detection analysis, and pattern recognition techniques are used to translate spectral, temporal and spatial characteristics of the satellite data into a valuable tool for planning and management of natural resources. Some uses of remote sensing are: to monitor environment during construction; to delineate area of shallow groundwater on agricultural lands; to forecast run-off; to take inventory of irrigated lands and cropping patterns to determine changes in area for improved water use; to aid in flood plain mapping in demonstrating that the Mississippi Basin could be mapped for less than $20,000 to determine the extent of inundation, to assess regional effectiveness of flood control measures, and to identify areas where significant changes may be required to avoid disasters; to provide data on discharge of industrial waste effluents into lakes and streams, turbidity patterns and oil slick patterns which indicate pollution tracks; to locate water impoundments under the national dam inspection program. (Salzman-North Carolina)
W75-06775

ELECTRON-MICROSCOPICAL INVESTIGATIONS ON WAX-COVERED STOMATAS, (IN GERMAN),
Universitaet Hohenheim (Landwirtschaftliche Hochschule)(West Germany) Laboratorium fuer Elektronenmikroskopie.
For primary bibliographic entry see Field 2I.
W75-06842

7C. Evaluation, Processing and Publication

AGRICULTURAL DROUGH PROBABILITIES IN TENNESSEE,
Tennessee Univ., Knoxville. Dept. of Plant and Soil Science.
For primary bibliographic entry see Field 3F.
W75-06358

A WATER QUALITY MODEL TO EVALUATE WATER MANAGEMENT PRACTICES IN AN IRRIGATED STREAM-AQUIFER SYSTEM,
Geological Survey, Denver, Colo.
For primary bibliographic entry see Field 5G.
W75-06369

A COMPILATION OF AUSTRALIAN WATER QUALITY CRITERIA,
Caulfield Inst. of Tech., (Australia).
For primary bibliographic entry see Field 5G.
W75-06418

INTERNATIONAL HYDROLOGICAL DECADE REPRESENTATIVE AND EXPERIMENTAL BASINS IN THE UNITED STATES: CATALOG OF AVAILABLE DATA AND RESULTS, 1965-1972.
National Committee for the International Hydrological Decade, Washington, D.C.
For primary bibliographic entry see Field 2A.
W75-06472

SKYLAB STUDY OF WATER QUALITY,
Kansas Univ., Lawrence.
For primary bibliographic entry see Field 5A.
W75-06478

FLOODWAY DETERMINATION USING COMPUTER PROGRAM HEC-2,
Hydrologic Engineering Center, Davis, Calif.
V. R. Bonner.
Training Document No. 5, May 1974. 38 p, 1 fig, 5 ref, 3 append.

Technology Satellite (ERTS-1) in conjunction with ancillary data in the form of topographic and highway maps and meteorological data summaries. The procedure is divided into several distinct phases. A five-volume manual was prepared to instruct potential users of the procedure. This first volume of the procedures manual summarizes the total computer-aided procedure, presents the resource requirements for implementation, and discusses operational use of the information derived from the procedure. (Sims-ISWS)
W75-06484

METEOROLOGICAL INTERPRETATION OF SPACE PHOTOGRAPHS OF THE EARTH (QUANTITATIVE METHODS),
D. M. Sonechkin.
Available from the National Technical Information Service, Springfield, Va 22161 as NASA TTF-786, $5.75 in paper copy, $2.25 in microfiche. NASA Technical Translation F-786, February 1975. 138 p, 26 fig, 10 tab, 175 ref, append. Translated from Meteorologicheskoye Deshifrirovaniye kosmicheskikh Snimkov Zemli (Kolichestvennyye Metody), Hydrometerological Press, Leningrad (USSR), 1972, 130 p.

Descriptors: *Remote sensing, *Satellites(Artificial), *Meteorology, *Translations, Infrared radiation, Cloud cover, Photography, Automation, Data processing, Telemetry.
Identifiers: Television, Geographic control.

A systematic exposition is presented of the procedures and results of meteorological interpretation of television and infrared images of the earth, obtained with the aid of satellites. Main attention was devoted to quantitative methods. Modern techniques of pattern recognition as the methodical basis of quantitative interpretation of earth photographs were surveyed. (Sims-ISWS)
W75-06488

ESTIMATING THE VARIANCE OF TIME AVERAGES,
Hawaii Univ., Honolulu. Dept. of Information and Computer Science.
R. H. Jones.
Journal of Applied Meteorology, Vol 14, No 2, p 159-163, March 1975. 12 ref. Contract AFOSR-72-2405A.

Descriptors: *Mathematical studies, *Climatology, Average, *Time series analysis, Statistical methods, Mathematics, Markov processes, Meteorology, Equations, *Estimating.
Identifiers: Variance, Weighted averages.

The variance of a time average of a stationary time series depends on the spectral density near frequency zero rather than on the variance of the process. Equations were given for estimating the variance of a time average by fitting a low-order autoregression to the data. Details were given for selecting the order of the autoregression. An example was presented which uses an analysis of variance approach for testing for climatic trends, allowing for diurnal and annual variability and serial correlation. (Sims-ISWS)
W75-06502

EMPIRICAL ESTIMATES OF THE STANDARD ERROR OF TIME-AVERAGED CLIMATIC MEANS,
National Center for Atmospheric Research, Boulder, Colo.
R. Madden, and W. Sadeh.
Journal of Applied Meteorology, Vol 14 No 2, p 164-169, March 1975. 2 fig, 2 tab, 11 ref.

Descriptors: *Mathematical studies, *Climatology, *Time series analysis, *Atmospheric pressure, Statistical methods, Markov processes, Average, Meterology, Seasonal, Statistics.
Identifiers: Standard errors, Time-averaged means.

The standard error of yearly and seasonally time-averaged station pressure values was estimated directly from a 49-year time series. The results compare well with similar estimates inferred from the autocorrelation of the pressure data. The effect of seasonal variability in the autocorrelation on this standard error was indicated and a possible implication for numerical climatic-change experiments was proposed. (Sims-ISWS)
W75-06503

THE SPECTRAL REPRESENTATION OF MOISTURE,
Atmospheric Environment Service, Montreal (Quebec).
I. Simmonds.
Journal of Applied Meteorology, Vol 14, No 2, p 175-179, March 1975. 4 fig, 5 tab, 4 ref.

Descriptors: *Moisture, *Humidity, *Dew point, *Model studies, Computer models, Mathematical studies, Numerical analysis, Atmosphere, Water vapor.
Identifiers: *Dew point depression, Mixing ratio.

Some experiments were performed, which were designed to compare the representation efficiency of dew point depression, relative humidity, and mixing ratio, with a view to incorporating moisture into a spectral model. A score was defined based on the ability of a finite spherical harmonic series for a given variable to reconstitute the grid-point fields of dew point depression, relative humidity, and mixing ratio. Based on this measure, the conclusion was reached that a finite series of dew point depression is slightly superior to a similar series of relative humidity in being able to represent the grid-point structure of the three fields, and a great deal better than mixing ratio. (Jones-ISWS)
W75-06505

REPRESENTATIVENESS OF WATERSHED PRECIPITATION SAMPLES,
West Virginia Univ., Morgantown. Water Research Inst.
For primary bibliographic entry see Field 2B.
W75-06522

COMPREHENSIVE WATER QUALITY MANAGEMENT PLANNING,
Pennsylvania Dept. of Environmental Resources, Harrisburg. Office of Comprehensive Water and Wastewater Management Planning.
For primary bibliographic entry see Field 5G.
W75-06558

MODERNIZATION OF NATIONAL WEATHER SERVICE RIVER FORECASTING TECHNIQUES,
National Weather Service, Silver Spring, Md.
For primary bibliographic entry see Field 4A.
W75-06562

LONG-TERM RECONSTRUCTION OF WATER LEVEL CHANGES FOR LAKE ATHABASCA BY ANALYSIS OF TREE RINGS,
Arizona Univ., Tucson. Lab. of Tree-Ring Research.
For primary bibliographic entry see Field 4A.
W75-06569

AUTOMATED DATA PROCESSING TECHNIQUES IN THE WATER SURVEY OF CANADA,
Department of the Environment, Ottawa (Ontario). Water Resources Branch.
W. J. Ozga.
Technical Bulletin No. 84, 29 p, 1974, Inland Waters Directorate, Ottawa, 15 fig.

Descriptors: *Canada, *Hydrologic data, Equipment, Technology, *Data processing, Computers, Streamflow, *Automation, Data storage and retrieval, Publications, Surveys, Computer programs.
Identifiers: Hydrometrics.

Automated data processing techniques were introduced in the Water Survey of Canada in 1966 along two fronts: (a) computation of streamflow data using a digitizer, and (b) storage of hydrometric data on magnetic tape. General procedures for the collection, computation and publication of basic hydrometric data are explained. However, the main purpose is to summarize the events leading to automation and the factors and problems involved in the selection and implementation of the system as it now exists. (Environment Canada)
W75-06731

PROGRAM SOPH - SIMULATION OF TIME-VARIANT PIEZOMETRIC SURFACE IN A CONFINED AQUIFER SUBJECT TO PUMPING,
Department of the Environment, Ottawa (Ontario). Water Resources Branch.
For primary bibliographic entry see Field 4B.
W75-06737

SUMMARY REPORT OF MICROBIOLOGICAL BASELINE DATA ON LAKE SUPERIOR, 1973,
Canada Centre for Inland Waters, Burlington (Ontario).
For primary bibliographic entry see Field 2H.
W75-06738

ALMOST-PERIODIC, STOCHASTIC PROCESS OF LONG-RANGE CLIMATIC CHANGES,
Colorado State Univ., Fort Collins.
For primary bibliographic entry see Field 2B.
W75-06739

COMPUTER ROUTINE FOR CALCULATING TOTAL LAKE VOLUME CONTENTS OF A DISSOLVED SUBSTANCE FROM AN ARBITRARY DISTRIBUTION OF CONCENTRATION PROFILES - A METHOD OF CALCULATING LAKEWIDE CONTENTS OF DISSOLVED SUBSTANCES,
Canada Centre for Inland Waters, Burlington (Ontario).
For primary bibliographic entry see Field 2H.
W75-06748

GROUND-WATER LEVELS AND WELL RECORDS FOR CURRENT OBSERVATION WELLS IN IDAHO, 1922-73, PARTS A, B, AND C,
Geological Survey, Boise, Idaho.
For primary bibliographic entry see Field 4B.
W75-06753

FLOOD STAGES AND DISCHARGES FOR SMALL STREAMS IN TEXAS, 1972,
Geological Survey, Austin, Tex.
For primary bibliographic entry see Field 4A.
W75-06754

AN ASSESSMENT OF AREAL AND TEMPORAL VARIATIONS IN STREAMFLOW QUALITY USING SELECTED DATA FROM THE NATIONAL STREAM QUALITY ACCOUNTING NETWORK,
Geological Survey, Reston, Va.
For primary bibliographic entry see Field 5B.
W75-06755

GROUND-WATER DATA FOR MICHIGAN,
Geological Survey, Lansing, Mich.
G. C. Huffman.
Geological Survey Data Report, 1974. 86 p, 34 fig, 2 tab, 43 ref.

Descriptors: *Data collections, *Hydrologic data, *Groundwater, *Michigan, Water levels, Water wells, Water yield, Aquifers, Drawdown, Water quality.

Records of water levels in principal aquifers of Michigan through 1973 and other related data, such as records of groundwater pumage, are presented. Also included are data on municipal, public, and industrial water-supply facilities. Records of water levels in areas of heavy pumpage and in areas where changes are principally due to natural influences are illustrated or tabulated to allow comparison between these types of water-level fluctuations. Numerous hydrographs are included to illustrate changes in water levels. Shown in summary form are supplementary data on the yield of wells, pumpage, storage facilities, treatment, quality of water, and trends of groundwater levels for 1973 and for part of the previous record. (Knapp-USGS)
W75-06756

A SURVEY OF THE WATER RESOURCES OF ST. CROIX, VIRGIN ISLANDS,
Geological Survey of Puerto Rico, San Juan.
For primary bibliographic entry see Field 4A.
W75-06757

FLOOD PLAIN INFORMATION: MILL CREEK, KOOSKOOSKIE AND VICINITY, WALLA WALLA COUNTY, WASHINGTON.
Army Engineer District, Walla Walla, Wash.
For primary bibliographic entry see Field 4A.
W75-06767

FLOOD PLAIN INFORMATION: BLACKSNAKE CREEK, ST. JOSEPH, MISSOURI.
Army Engineer District, Kansas City, Mo.
For primary bibliographic entry see Field 4A.
W75-06768

FLOOD PLAIN INFORMATION: NACHES RIVER, CITY OF NACHES AND VICINITY, WASHINGTON,
Army Engineer District, Seattle, Wash.
For primary bibliographic entry see Field 4A.
W75-06769

FLOOD PLAIN INFORMATION: LITTLE BLUE RIVER, EAST FORK, WHITE OAK BRANCH, JACKSON COUNTY, MISSOURI,
Army Engineer District, Kansas City, Mo.
For primary bibliographic entry see Field 4A.
W75-06770

SPECIAL FLOOD HAZARD INFORMATION: MILL CREEK, UMATILLA COUNTY, OREGON.
Army Engineer District, Walla Walla, Wash.
For primary bibliographic entry see Field 4A.
W75-06771

FLOOD PLAIN INFORMATION: YAKIMA RIVER, CITY OF SELAH AND VICINITY, WASHINGTON.
Army Engineer District, Seattle, Wash.
For primary bibliographic entry see Field 4A.
W75-06772

SPECIAL FLOOD HAZARD INFORMATION REPORT: BAYOU SARA, BAYOU SARA CREEK, NORTON CREEK, HELLS SWAMP BRANCH, VICINITY OF SARALAND, ALABAMA.
Army Engineer District, Mobile, Ala.
For primary bibliographic entry see Field 4A.
W75-06773

FLOOD PLAIN INFORMATION: SPRING BRANCH, INDEPENDENCE, MISSOURI.
Army Engineer District, Kansas City, Mo.
For primary bibliographic entry see Field 4A.
W75-06779

SPECIAL FLOOD HAZARD INFORMATION REPORT: GALLAGHER CREEK, MERIDIAN, LAUDERDALE COUNTY, MISSISSIPPI.
Army Engineer District, Mobile, Ala.
For primary bibliographic entry see Field 4A.
W75-06792

FLOOD PLAIN INFORMATION: LOS PENASQUITOS DRAINAGE AREA, SAN DIEGO COUNTY, CALIFORNIA.
Army Engineer District, Los Angeles, Calif.
For primary bibliographic entry see Field 4A.
W75-06793

8. ENGINEERING WORKS

8A. Structures

SAN LUIS UNIT, TECHNICAL RECORD OF DESIGN AND CONSTRUCTION - VOLUME II, DESIGN, SAN LUIS DAM AND PUMPING-GENERATING PLANT, O'NEILL DAM AND PUMPING PLANT,
Bureau of Reclamation, Denver, Colo.
November 1974. 375 p, 203 fig, 7 tab, 9 append.

Descriptors: *Dams, *Dumping plants, *Powerplants, *Central Valley Project, Electric powerplants, Hydroelectric plants, Dam design, Dam construction, Earth dams, Reserovirs, Design flood, Spillways, Outlet works, Electrical equipment, Cranes, Construction equipment, *California, Hydraulics.

Volume II discusses in considerable detail the design of the San Luis dam and pumping-generating plant and the O'Neill dam and pumping plant. These facilities are part of the San Luis unit, a major addition to the Central Valley Project. The unit is a storage facility for excess water from the delta area, fed by streams of the Sierra Range during winter and spring runoff, that would normally waste into the Pacific Ocean. The design of the two dams was described in detail with many drawings and photographs. Also described were the spillway and outlet works, the pumping and generating plants, and the electrical switchyard facilities. (Sims-ISWS)
W75-06468

JACKSON HOLE FLOOD CONTROL PROJECT.
Committee on Channel Stabilization (Army).
For primary bibliographic entry see Field 4A.
W75-06475

APPLICATION OF THE HEC-2 BRIDGE ROUTINES,
Hydrologic Engineering Center, Davis, Calif.
For primary bibliographic entry see Field 7C.
W75-06482

BASIC UNDERSTANDING OF EARTH TUNNELING BY MELTING, VOLUME I - BASIC PHYSICAL PRINCIPLES,
Westinghouse Astronuclear Lab., Pittsburgh, Pa.
D. L. Black.
Available from the National Technical Information Service, Springfield, Va 22161 as PB-235 084, $7.00 in paper copy, $2.25 in microfiche. DOT-TSC-OST-74-6.I, July 1974. 155 p, 45 fig, 8 tab, 53 ref. DOT-TSC-591.

Descriptors: *Flood protection, *Watershed management, *Erosion control, *Dam construction, Recreation facilities, *Pennsylvania, Erosion, Sedimentation, Dams, Flood control, Flood recurrence interval, Flooding, Floods, Streams, Sediments, Recreation, Recreation demand, Lakes, Parks, Water supply, Water storage, Fish, Fishing, Fish passages, Flood plains.
Identifiers: *Environmental Impact Statements, *Crosscreek Watershed Project(Penn).

The program entails construction of a watershed protection and flood prevention project for the Cross Creek Watershed in Washington County, Pennsylvania. Land treatment measures will be applied to control erosion and reduce stream sedimentation. Four dams will be built to provide flood protection from a 100-year frequency storm. One dam will also create a recreation lake and store millions of gallons of water for municipal use. The lake and accompanying recreation facilities will form the nucleus of a 7500 acre county park. The environmental impact of the project will provide for the following beneficial effects: reduction of flood damage by 92 percent; reduction of soil erosion by 27 percent; reduction of sediment yield from the watershed by 46 percent; provide facilities for 150,000 annual visitor days of recreation; and provide adequate water supply for the present population plus supplies for an additional 500 families and industrial growth. Adverse environmental effects include temporary impairment of stream quality and fishery during construction; inundation of covering of 14,370 feet of stream by dams, sediment pools, or other permanent impoundments; construction pollution; and restriction of fish passages by the dams. Alternatives include land treatment only, land treatment and acquisition of flood plain properties, land treatment and recreation only, land treatment and water supply only, or no action. (Gagliardi-Florida)
W75-06616

EXPERIENCE WITH HYDROELECTRIC PROJECT ENVIRONMENTAL RELATIONSHIPS IN SOUTHEASTERN UNITED STATES,
Army Engineer District, Savannah, Ga.
C. C. Brown, C. L. Carter, and F. H. Posey.
U.S. Army Engineering District, Planning Board, Savannah, Georgia, (1970) 32 p. 8 fig, 1 tab, 16 ref.

Descriptors: *Environmental effects, *Hydroelectric plants, *Reservoir management, *Reservoir design, *Reservoir silting, Thermal stratification, Aeration, Water quality, Chemical wastes, Iron, Manganese, Flood control, Hydroelectric power, Dissolved oxygen, Destratification, Environmental engineering.
Identifiers: Environmental impacts.

The Corps of Engineers is charged with the responsibility for minimizing any adverse effect on the environment resulting from the construction and operation of its reservoirs. Many of the environmental problems so far identified are of thermal, chemical, or operational origin. Thermal stratification occurs in many reservoirs because of the detention time required for water to flow through the impoundment and the rate of heat exchange between the reservoir waters and the atmosphere. Seasonal changes in iron and manganese concentrations have been observed in large reservoirs. Increases in these metallic concentrations are apparently related to the decrease in dissolved oxygen. Operational requirements of reservoirs in the southeastern United States must consider many purposes, including: flood control, navigation, hydroelectric power, domestic and industrial water supply, fish and wildlife enhancement, recreation, and water quality control. Limited observations of specific tests show that turbine aeration is one means by which dissolved oxygen content of discharges can be improved. The early experience with destratification systems such as the air diffuser system under investigation at the Allatoona Project is encouraging. Evaluation of effects on iron and manganese concentrations, and pH are considered inconclusive because of differences discovered in early sampling and analysis techniques. (Poertner)
W75-06675

8B. Hydraulics

A THREE DIMENSIONAL WAVE MAKER, ITS THEORY AND APPLICATION,
Massachusetts Inst. of Tech., Cambridge. Dept. of Civil Engineering.
For primary bibliographic entry see Field 2L.
W75-06457

PLUNGER-TYPE WAVEMAKERS: THEORY AND EXPERIMENT,
Tetra Tech, Inc., Pasadena, Calif.
For primary bibliographic entry see Field 2L.
W75-06458

HYDRAULIC MODEL STUDIES OF PLUNGE BASINS FOR JET FLOW,
Bureau of Reclamation, Denver, Colo. Engineering and Research Center.
P. L. Johnson.
Available from the National Technical Information Service, Springfield, Va 22161 as PB-235 659, $3.25 in paper copy, $2.25 in microfiche. REC-ERC-74-9, June 1974. 16 p, 9 fig, 9 ref.

Descriptors: *Scour, *Riprap, *Design criteria, *Laboratory tests, *Outlet works, Model studies, Jets, Tailwater, Hydraulic design, Hydraulic models, Basins.
Identifiers: *Plunge basins, Velocity head, Stilling basins.

Model studies were conducted to develop design guidelines for riprap-lined plunge basins. Depressions scoured by free jets dropping into water-covered gravel beds were measured to determine basin dimensions. Design values of the criteria were selected so that further scour would not occur. The depth, length, and width of the plunge basin were found to be functions of the following parameters: (1) height of the outlet above tailwater surface, (2) pressure head on outlet, (3) outlet size, (4) tailwater depth, and (5) size of riprap. (Adams-ISWS)
W75-06492

WALL JET ANALOGY TO HYDRAULIC JUMP,
Manchester Univ. (England). Inst. of Science and Technology.
R. Narayanan.
Journal of the Hydraulics Division, American Society of Civil Engineers, Vol 101, No HY3, Proceedings Paper 11172, p 347-359, March 1975. 11 fig, 16 ref, 2 append.

Descriptors: *Hydraulic jump, *Hydraulics, *Open channels, *Turbulence, *Boundary processes, Velocity, Continuity equation, Reynolds number, Froude number, Momentum equation, Shear stress, Jets, Flow.
Identifiers: Blasius equation, Displacement thickness.

Hydraulic jump on horizontal bed of a rectangular channel was treated as a plane turbulent wall jet of an incompressible fluid of finite width in adverse pressure gradient. Momentum integral techniques were applied to determine the longitudinal variations of the parameters characterizing the assumed mean velocity distribution. The kinematic constraint arising from the requirement of continuity was imposed. The idealized wall jet was modified to take into account the mean velocity distribution ahead of the jumps that is typical of most of the experimental situations. The mean flow properties of jumps at high Froude numbers, e.g., the maximum velocity, surface velocity, and depth profile, were predicted and compared with experimental results. The characteristics such as the lengths of the roller and the extent of the jump can also be predicted. However, the length characteristics were found to be sensitive to the turbulent kinematic stress. Further improvement to the theory can be made through a clearer understanding of turbulent stresses in a hydraulic jump. The theory brings out the scale effects arising from the Reynolds number and the upstream conditions of the flow. (Singh-ISWS)
W75-06531

SHALLOW LAMINAR FLOWS OVER ROUGH GRANULAR SURFACES,
University of the West Indies, St. Augustine (Trinidad). Dept. of Civil Engineering.
H. O. Phelps.
Journal of the Hydraulics Division, American Society of Civil Engineers, Vol 101, No HY3, Proceedings Paper 11166, p 367-384, March 1975. 8 fig, 4 tab, 24 ref, 2 append.

Descriptors: *Laminar flow, *Boundary layers, *Roughness coefficient, *Instrumentation, *Drag, Laboratory tests, Velocity, Flow, Hydraulics, Reynolds number, Shear, Friction.
Identifiers: Nusselt equation.

Several investigations have established that at high values of relative roughness mean depths of liquid in laminar shear flow over rough surfaces are greater than the corresponding depths on a smooth surface. In this investigation the nature of the flow field in the vicinity of isolated roughness elements fixed to a smooth base was demonstrated with a flow visualization technique. Velocity profiles measured with an optical velocity meter were shown to be governed by the Nusselt equation, but surface velocity is a function of relative roughness and is less than the corresponding value for a smooth surface. An analytical model was proposed to explain an empirical relationship between friction coefficient, relative roughness, and Reynolds number. The equation developed was used to calculate the product of the coefficient of drag of a sphere resting on a plane surface and the tip Reynolds number and also to demonstrate the influence of velocity distribution on the drag coefficient. (Sinh-ISWS)
W75-06532

BED FORM RESPONSE TO NONSTEADY FLOWS,
Army Engineer District, Sacramento, Calif.
For primary bibliographic entry see Field 2J.
W75-06533

FLOW SEPARATION IN MEANDER BENDS,
Leeds Univ. (England). Dept. of Earth Sciences.
For primary bibliographic entry see Field 2E.
W75-06539

TURBULENT FLOW OF INELASTIC NON-NEWTONIAN FLUIDS IN PIPES,
Banaras Hindu Univ., Varanasi (India). Inst. of Tech.
S. N. Gupta, and P. Mishra.
Indian Journal of Technology, Vol 12, No 5, p 181-185, May 1974. 4 fig, 16 ref.

Descriptors: *Turbulent flow, *Reynolds number, *Fluid friction, *Non-Newtonian flow, *Fluid mechanics, Analysis, Theoretical analysis, Equations, Viscosity, Flow, Friction, *Pipe flow, Pipes.
Identifiers: *Fluid properties.

Several theories of turbulent momentum transport for non-Newtonian fluids flowing in pipes were discussed. The Gill-Scher theory was compared with data on power law, nonpower law, and Bingham plastic types of non-Newtonian fluids. It was shown that Newtonian turbulent theory was applicable to non-Newtonian fluids if the proper

constant and the differential viscosity were used. (Adams-ISWS)
W75-06542

CONFIDENCE LIMITS FOR DESIGN EVENTS,
Department of the Environment, Ottawa (Ontario). Water Resources Branch.
For primary bibliographic entry see Field 2E.
W75-06544

MARKOV MIXTURE MODELS FOR DROUGHT LENGTHS,
Harvard Univ., Boston, Mass. Graduate School of Business Administration.
For primary bibliographic entry see Field 2A.
W75-06545

DRAINAGE OF GROUNDWATER RESTING ON A SLOPING BED WITH UNIFORM RAINFALL,
Agricultural Research Council, Cambridge (England). Unit of Soil Physics.
For primary bibliographic entry see Field 4B.
W75-06550

STUDY OF ALTERNATIVE DIVERSIONS. REPORT ON THE HYDROLOGICAL STUDIES OF MANITOBA HYDRO SYSTEM.
Underwood, McLellan and Associates Ltd., Winnipeg (Manitoba).
Manitoba Hydro, Winnipeg, Manitoba, Canada, February 12, 1970. 136 p, 67 tab, 32 fig, 4 ref, 4 append.

Descriptors: *Diversion, *Hydroelectric plants, *Diversion structures, *Hydrologic data, *Water data, *River regulation, *Mathematical studies, Hydroelectric power, Reservoir management, Canada, Routing, Systems analysis, River forecasting, River systems.
Identifiers: Manitoba Hydro System, Manitoba(Canada), Churchill River.

A hydrologic study was originated in connection with a systems study of the Manitoba Hydro system conducted during the period October 1969 to February 1970. Realizing the importance of the hydrologic data and its effect on the future planning and operation of Manitoba Hydro, it was decided that a documentation of the hydrologic data that have been collected for use in the systems study is necessary. These hydrologic data were used for various design and system study analysis. Therefore, the hydrological data presented is suitable for use in further conduct of these different analyses. The collection and analysis of the hydrologic data were principally oriented to the broad objective of systems study. Included are the hydrologic data collected and the deterministic and probalistic analysis of system firm energy. The statistical analysis of the monthly flows is also presented. These were done to determine the season variations of flow and find the probability distribution of the flows corresponding to different seasons for the major rivers in the project area. The objective of the study was to develop a suitable method of applying the storage-utilization technique for the study of the relation between the reservoir system and firm energy. (Poertner)
W75-06664

BLAST HOLE BIT TECHNOLOGY.
Dresser Industries, Inc., Dallas, Tex. Mining Services and Equipment Div.
For primary bibliographic entry see Field 8C.
W75-06816

8C. Hydraulic Machinery

SAN LUIS UNIT, TECHNICAL RECORD OF DESIGN AND CONSTRUCTION - VOLUME II, DESIGN, SAN LUIS DAM AND PUMPING-GENERATING PLANT, O'NEILL DAM AND PUMPING PLANT,
Bureau of Reclamation, Denver, Colo.
For primary bibliographic entry see Field 8A.
W75-06468

THE DEVELOPMENT OF A CONTINUOUS DRILL AND BLAST TUNNELING CONCEPT, PHASE II,
Rapidex, Inc., Peabody, Mass.
For primary bibliographic entry see Field 8H.
W75-06485

SYSTEM FOR REGULATION OF COMBINED SEWAGE FLOWS,
Municipality of Metropolitan Seattle, Wash.
For primary bibliographic entry see Field 5D.
W75-06563

AUTOMATION OF SCUM SKIMMERS, CALUMET TREATMENT WORKS, PRELIMINARY SETTLING TANKS.
Greeley and Hansen, Chicago, Ill.
For primary bibliographic entry see Field 5D.
W75-06665

SCUM REMOVAL FACILITIES, NORTH SIDE TREATMENT WORKS, FINAL SETTLING TANKS.
Greeley and Hansen, Chicago, Ill.
For primary bibliographic entry see Field 5D.
W75-06666

SCUM REMOVAL FACILITIES, WEST-SOUTHWEST TREATMENT WORKS, BATTERIES A, B, AND C.
Greeley and Hansen, Chicago, Ill.
For primary bibliographic entry see Field 5D.
W75-06667

SCUM REMOVAL FACILITIES, NORTH SIDE TREATMENT WORKS, PRELIMINARY SETTLING TANKS.
Greeley and Hansen, Chicago, Ill.
For primary bibliographic entry see Field 5D.
W75-06668

SCUM REMOVAL FACILITIES, CALUMET TREATMENT WORKS, FINAL SETTLING TANKS.
Greeley and Hansen, Chicago, Ill.
For primary bibliographic entry see Field 5D.
W75-06669

BLAST HOLE BIT TECHNOLOGY.
Dresser Industries, Inc., Dallas, Tex. Mining Services and Equipment Div.
Bulletin No. BHBT/2-73/5C. 1973, 23 p.

Descriptors: *Drilling equipment, Drilling, Borehole, *Design criteria, Materials engineering, Technology, *Materials testing, *Quality control, Specifications, Evaluation, Testing, Instrumentation.
Identifiers: Bit design, Journal angle, Drillability testing, Testing equipment, Blast hole bit.

The limited amount of space that contains the blast hole bit, the angle of the journal on the arm of the bit (the journal angle or pin angle), the conical angles on the cutters, the length of the bit teeth, the hardfacing of the bit teeth, and the cutter design on the bit are related to the hardness of the formation, the depth to be drilled and the diameter and shape of the hole. The materials and properties of the rock bit components and their metallurgical control are discussed (as well as quality control procedures in the Dresser Company). Dull bit evaluation and the causes of rapid drilling are illus-

At Lost Creek Dam at Trail, Oregon, on May 13-18, 1973, lean 3-inch maximum size aggregate (MSA) concrete mixtures were designed to be compacted by vibratory rollers. The control mix contained 235 pounds cement per cubic yard while other mixtures had a portion of the total volume of cement replaced with pozzolan, either fly ash or a locally available calcined shale. These mixes contained from 99 to 275 pounds cementitious materials per cubic yard. In addition, two other mixtures (1-1/2-inch MSA and 3/4-inch MSA) were designed and used as a 3-inch starter or bedding mix off the hardened horizontal lift joint. Each layer, except bedding layers, was approximately 8-inches thick after compaction. It was concluded that properly proportioned roller compacted concrete can be effectively placed by soils compaction methods using a vibratory roller. The results of tests on drilled core specimens indicate that permeability and bond test results are similar to conventionally placed lean mass concrete values. The quality of the hardened lift joint is improved with the use of bedding mixtures. A modified Vebe apparatus can be used for control testing and for molding concrete central cylinders. (Sims-ISWS)
W75-06491

8G. Materials

PERMEABILITY AND EFFECTIVE STRESS,
Geological Survey, Menlo Park, Calif.
For primary bibliographic entry see Field 2F.
W75-06540

THE WATER UTILITIES LOOK AT ELECTRICAL GROUNDING,
East Bay Municipal Utility District, Oakland, Calif.
L. B. Hertzberg.
In: IEEE Transactions on Industry and General Applications, Vol IGA-6, No 3, May/June 1970, Baltimore, Maryland. p 278-281, 6 ref.

Descriptors: *Corrosion control, *Water distribution(Applied), *Municipal water, *Electrical grounding, *Electrolysis, *Metal pipes, Plastic pipes, Pipelines, Water supply, Water conveyance, Corrosion, Deterioration.
Identifiers: *Non-metallic materials, Anodic protection.

Engineers engaged in design of grounding protection are alerted to the need for development of new, independent, and reliable electrical grounding techniques. The only metal in the water supply distribution system in the early 1950's consisted of isolated fittings and valves. In 1968, the National Electrical Code (NEC) was revised because of the decreasing reliability of water pipe as an electrical ground. The NEC then described a new type of 'made electrode' which could be used where the water piping system or other local metallic underground system was not available. The new grounding electrode, 'Ufer System', used not less than 20 feet of bare copper conductor, encased along the bottom of a concrete foundation footing which is in direct contact with the earth. Steel and cast iron mains are being replaced with discontinuous (or non-metallic) piping because rising copper prices are forcing water utilities to install plastic service laterals. Better corrosion control practices are resulting in insulation of galvanically dissimilar metals, and corrosive soil conditions are leading to use of non-metallic materials for underground piping. This will help supply safe water in adequate amounts for fire protection and all other public needs. (Poertner)
W75-06656

ANALYSIS OF ELECTRICAL RESISTIVITY MEASUREMENTS OF SHALLOW DEPOSITS,
Iowa State Univ., Ames.
For primary bibliographic entry see Field 4B.
W75-06808

8H. Rapid Excavation

THE DEVELOPMENT OF A CONTINUOUS DRILL AND BLAST TUNNELING CONCEPT, PHASE II,
Rapidex, Inc., Peabody, Mass.
C. R. Peterson.
Available from the National Technical Information Service, Springfield, Va 22161 as PB-234 204, $3.75 in paper copy, $2.25 in microfiche. DOT-TSC-OST-74-10, May 1974. 76 p, 19 fig, 8 tab, 17 ref. DOT-TSC-611.

Descriptors: *Tunneling, *Tunneling machines, *Excavation, Drilling, Drilling equipment, Rock excavation, Automation, Equipment, Explosives, Construction equipment, Tunnel construction.
Identifiers: Blasting.

A spiral drilling pattern was described which offers high efficiency drill and blast tunneling via frequent small blasts rather than occasional large blasts. Design work was presented for a machine which would stay at the face to provide essentially continuous drilling, loading, blasting, and mucking. Field tests proving the concept were described and photos of the spiral tunnel advance were provided. Successful testing of a suitable blast shield is also described and photos provided. Advance rates of four times conventional drill and blast practice were projected at about half the conventional cost per foot. (Sims-ISWS)
W75-06485

BASIC UNDERSTANDING OF EARTH TUNNELING BY MELTING, VOLUME I - BASIC PHYSICAL PRINCIPLES,
Westinghouse Astronuclear Lab., Pittsburgh, Pa.
For primary bibliographic entry see Field 8A.
W75-06489

BASIC UNDERSTANDING OF EARTH TUNNELING BY MELTING, VOLUME II - EARTH STRUCTURE AND DESIGN SOLUTIONS,
Westinghouse Astronuclear Lab., Pittsburgh, Pa.
For primary bibliographic entry see Field 8A.
W75-06490

8I. Fisheries Engineering

FISH PARASITES OCCURRING IN THIRTEEN SOUTHERN CALIFORNIA RESERVOIRS,
California State Univ., San Diego.
R. L. Miller, A. C. Olson, Jr., and L. W. Miller.
Calif Fish Game. Vol 59, No 3, p 196-206, 1973.

Descriptors: Fish, *Fish parasites, *Fish management, Fisheries, Reservoirs, *California.
Identifiers: Acanthocephala, Cestoda, Digenea, Hirudinea, Monogenea, Nematoda.

Fishes (480) representing 13 freshwater species from 7 genera and 4 families were collected from 13 reservoirs and examined for metazoan parasites. Dorosoma petenense, Cyprinus carpio, Notemigonus crysoleucas, Ictalurus catus, I. melas, I. natalis, I. nebulosus, I. punctatus, Lepomis cyanellus, L. macrochirus, Micropterus salmoides, Pomoxis annularis, and P. nigromaculatus were infected with 1 or more helminths. Parasites found were Digenea: Hysteromorpha triloba, Posthodiplostomum minimum, Uvulifer ambloplitis, and Clinostomum marginatum; Monogenea: Dactylogyrus extensus, Cleidodiscus pricei, Urocleidus dispar, U. ferox, U. furcatus, U. principalis, and Actinocleidus fusiformis; Cestoda: Corallobothrium fimbriatum, C. giganteum, Proteocephalus ambloplitis, Proteocephalus sp., and Bothriocephalus claviceps; Nematoda: Contracaecum sp. and Eustrongylides sp.; Acanthocephala: Southwellina hispida; and Hirudinea: Myzobdella moorei. Of these 20 parasites, 4 are new records for California. This survey will provide some baseline data for fisheries management in San Diego County and southern California.--Copyright 1974, Biological Abstracts, Inc.
W75-06416

POPULATION DYNAMICS OF HUNTERELLA NODULOSA (CESTOIDEA:CARYOPHYLLIDEA) IN ALBERTA,
Calgary Univ. (Alberta). Dept. of Biology.
D. R. Mudry, and H. P. Arai.
Can J Zool Vol 51, No 7: p 787-792, 1973. Illus.

Descriptors: *Infection, *Fish diseases, Fish populations, *Canada, *Worms.
Identifiers: Caryophyllidea, Catostomus-commersoni, Cestoidea, Hunterella-nodulosa.

Incidence, intensity, and population size distribution of 5669 individuals of H. nodulosa from 646 Catostomus commersoni were examined. Incidence of infection increased with fish weight up to about 50 g. In fish above 50 g the incidence remained fairly constant at about 70%. Intensity of infection was directly proportional to fish weight. No seasonal changes in incidence and intensity were observed. Seasonal changes in frequency distribution of worm size classes indicated a seasonal infection cycle.--Copyright 1974, Biological Abstracts, Inc.
W75-06465

WATER INTAKE AND FISH RETURN SYSTEM,
Envirex, Inc., Waukesha, Wis. (assignee)
R. F. Taylor, D. A. Strow, and H. Mansouri.
U.S. Patent No. 3,868,324, 4 p, 5 fig, 9 ref; Official Gazette of the United States Patent Office, Vol 931, No 4, p 1647, February 25, 1975.

Descriptors: *Patents, *Fish barriers, *Fish passages, *Screens, Fish, Rivers, Water levels, Water quality.
Identifiers: *Fisheries engineering, Fish screens.

The water intake structure is located alongside a natural watercourse. A number of travelling water screen units are arranged in a straight line between support columns and the screens are flush with the columns. The line extends at a sharp angle across and downstream of the channel to a gate opening into a holding channel so that the intake stream from the watercourse approaches the screens at a sharp angle. The fish are unobstructed in moving sideward to avoid successively the several screens until reaching the gate which opens into a fish holding channel. Periodically the gate is closed and the fish are screened or flushed into the watercourse. Other suitable means of returning the fish to natural waters may also be provided. Both the travelling water screen units and the fish holding channel and return apparatus may be of whatever height is required to accommodate the fluctuations which must be expected in the water level of the watercourse. (Sinha-OEIS)
W75-06688

BENTHIC FAUNA OF PONDS OF THE KARAMET-NIYAZ FISH-BREEDING FARM,
Akademiya Nauk Turkmenskoi SSR, Ashkhabad. Institut Zoologii i Parazitologii.
R. E. Muravleva, and O. V. Zhitnikova.
Izv Akad Nauk Turkm SSR Ser Biol Nauk. 4, p 45-51, 1973, Illus, (In Russian).
Identifiers: *Benthic fauna, *Fish hatcheries, Insects, Invertebrates, Ponds, Productivity, *USSR(Karamet-Niyaz).

Benthic invertebrates rapidly colonize the ponds (Karamet-Niyaz, USSR). The formation of benthic fauna occurs because of oviposition by insects from the nearby ponds and because of invertebrates brought in by the water from the canal supply system. Productivity of zoobenthosis on the stage of the formation is low.--Copyright 1974, Biological Abstracts, Inc.
W75-06710

PARASITIC FAUNA AND DISEASES OF JUVENILE CARP REARED IN HATCHERIES AND IN SPAWNING PONDS, (IN RUSSIAN),
Akademiya Nauk Litovkkoi SSR, Vilnius. Institut Zoologii i Parazitologii.
V. P. Kyamezha, and A.-D. Y. Zhalyunene.
Liet Tsr Mokslu Akad Darb Ser C, 3 p 69-76, 1973. English summary.
Identifiers: *Carp, Cyprinus-carpio, Fauna, *Hatcheries, Juveniles, *Parasitic infection(Fish), Spawning ponds, *Fish parasites, *Fish diseases.

The larvae of hatchery reared carp (Cyprinus carpio) are not infected by parasites, but when reared in epizootically unfavorable ponds they are liable to parasite infection. If proper sanitary conditions are provided in ponds the hatchery method of carp reproduction can be recommended as a sufficiently effective remedy for fighting carp infection diseases. (More than 20 parasite spp. are given.)--Copyright 1974, Biological Abstracts, Inc.
W75-06850

9. MANPOWER, GRANTS AND FACILITIES

9A. Education (Extramural)

TENTH ANNUAL REPORT, PROGRAM ACTIVITIES, FISCAL YEAR, 1974,
Massachusetts Univ., Amherst. Water Resources Research Center.
For primary bibliographic entry see Field 9D.
W75-06646

9D. Grants, Contracts, and Research Act Allotments

LAND AND WATER RESEARCH, ANNUAL REPORT 1974,
Pennsylvania State Univ., University Park. Inst. for Research on Land and Water Resources.
M. S. Archer.
Available from the National Technical Information Service, Springfield, Va 22161, as PB-240 976, $3.75 in paper copy, $2.25 in microfiche. Information Report No 73, December 1974. 41 p. OWRR A-999-PA(3).

Descriptors: *Water pollution, *Waste water treatment, *Economic impact, *Social impact, *Tourism, *Acid mine, *Hydrology, *Reservoirs, *Solid wastes.
Identifiers: *New land uses, *Acquisition practices, *Soil productivity, *Roadside ecology, *Economic data systems, *Hydrogeologic studies, *Sewage information retrieval.

This publication supplements Information Report Number 72, the Fiscal Year '74 Annual Report. This publication, which includes photographs and narrative sections, highlights activities of the Water Resources Research Center, the Land Resources Research Center and the Regional Analysis Center in scholarly research and involvement in public affairs. As an indication of the interdisciplinary nature of the Institute, the work of 181 University personnel, representing 8 colleges and 26 academic departments at Penn State is featured. Sections describing research projects are grouped as follows: (1) Projects completed during Fiscal Year 1974; (2) Projects continued during Fiscal Year 1974; (3) Projects initiated during Fiscal Year 1974; (4) Projects initiated during Fiscal Year 1975. Numerous broad lines of research are reported with concentrations in such areas as: water pollution control; renovation of waste water; management of watersheds; control of aquatic plant growth; development of water supply and waste water systems to meet regional needs; the economic impact of highways; land use planning; social impact of water reservoir development; biological and engineering studies of land and water resources; economic efficiency studies; acid mine water neutralization; soil productivity; roadside ecology; and solid waste disposal. (Sink-Penn State)
W75-06357

TENTH ANNUAL REPORT, PROGRAM ACTIVITIES, FISCAL YEAR, 1974,
Massachusetts Univ., Amherst. Water Resources Research Center.
Available from the National Technical Information Service, Springfield, Va 22161, as PB-241 152, $5.25 in paper copy, $2.25 in microfiche. (1974), 94 p, 12 ref. OWRT A-999-MASS(11).

Descriptors: *Water Resources Institute, *Massachusetts, *Universities, Colleges, Education, Training, *Programs, Projects, *Research and development, Grants, Contracts, Water Resources Research Act.

During the 1974 fiscal year the Massachusetts Water Resources Research Center supported a total of 29 new and continuing projects. Of this total, 20 projects were supported in part under Section 100 of the Water Resources Research Act of 1974 (allotment grant), 6 under Section 101 (matching grant), and 3 under Title II. Forty-two faculty members in 18 University departments were engaged, in otherwise associated with, Center-supported research. A total of 68 students, most of them graduate students, worked on these research projects.
W75-06646

10. SCIENTIFIC AND TECHNICAL INFORMATION

10C. Secondary Publication And Distribution

MARINE RADIOECOLOGY: A SELECTED BIBLIOGRAPHY OF NON-RUSSIAN LITERATURE,
Environmental Protection Agency, Boise, Idaho.
For primary bibliographic entry see Field 5C.
W75-06384

RESOURCE CONSERVATION GLOSSARY.
Soil Conservation Society of America, Ankeny, Iowa, 1970. 52 p.

Descriptors: Information exchange, Classification, Documentation, *Conservation, *Resources, *Thesauri, Agronomy, Biology, Ecology, Economics, Engineering, Forestry, Geology, Hydrology, Ranges, Recreation, Soils, Watersheds(Basins), Indexing.
Identifiers: *Glossaries.

Terms were included that are regularly used in the selected technologies of agronomy, biology, conservation, ecology, economics, engineering, forestry, geology, hydrology, range, recreation, soils, and watersheds. The glossary was intended to serve as a reference for professionals and laymen as well as students. (Humphreys-ISWS)
W75-06483

WATER REUSE, A BIBLIOGRAPHY, VOLUME 3,
Office of Water Research and Technology, Washington, D.C.
For primary bibliographic entry see Field 5D.
W75-06638

WATER REUSE, A BIBLIOGRAPHY, VOLUME 4,
Office of Water Research and Technology, Washington, D.C.
For primary bibliographic entry see Field 5D.
W75-06639

INTERSTATE WATER COMPACTS, A BIBLIOGRAPHY,
Office of Water Research and Technology, Washington, D.C.
For primary bibliographic entry see Field 6E.
W75-06640

SOCIAL IMPACT ASSESSMENT: AN ANALYTIC BIBLIOGRAPHY,
Brown Univ., Providence, R.I.
For primary bibliographic entry see Field 6B.
W75-06758

10E. Translations

METEOROLOGICAL INTERPRETATION OF SPACE PHOTOGRAPHS OF THE EARTH (QUANTITATIVE METHODS),
For primary bibliographic entry see Field 7C.
W75-06488

10F. Preparation Of Reviews

A REVIEW OF THE LITERATURE ON THE USE OF DIURON IN FISHERIES,
Bureau of Sport Fisheries and Wildlife, Columbia, Mo. Fish-Pesticide Research Lab.
For primary bibliographic entry see Field 5C.
W75-06385

A REVIEW OF THE LITERATURE ON THE USE OF SQUOXIN IN FISHERIES,
Bureau of Sport Fisheries and Wildlife, Cook, Wash. Western Fish Nutrition Lab.
For primary bibliographic entry see Field 5C.
W75-06386

A REVIEW OF THE LITERATURE ON THE USE OF COPPER SULFATE IN FISHERIES,
Bureau of Sport Fisheries and Wildlife, Marion, Ala. Southeastern Fish Cultural Lab.
For primary bibliographic entry see Field 5C.
W75-06387

A REVIEW OF THE LITERATURE ON THE USE OF ROTENONE IN FISHERIES,
Bureau of Sport Fisheries and Wildlife, LaCrosse, Wis. Fish Control Lab.
For primary bibliographic entry see Field 5C.
W75-06388

A REVIEW OF THE LITERATURE ON THE USE OF ENDOTHALL IN FISHERIES,
Bureau of Sport Fisheries and Wildlife, Denver, Colo. Fish Pesticide Research Lab.
For primary bibliographic entry see Field 5C.
W75-06389

A REVIEW OF THE LITERATURE ON THE USE OF MASOTEN IN FISHERIES,
Bureau of Sport Fisheries and Wildlife, Stuttgart, Ark. Fish Farming Experiment Station.
For primary bibliographic entry see Field 5C.
W75-06390

A REVIEW OF THE LITERATURE ON THE USE OF LIME (CA(OH)2, CAO, CACO3) IN FISHERIES,
Bureau of Sport Fisheries and Wildlife, Warm Springs, Ga. Southeastern Fish Control Lab.
For primary bibliographic entry see Field 5C.
W75-06391

A REVIEW OF THE LITERATURE ON THE USE OF BETADINE IN FISHERIES,
Bureau of Sport Fisheries and Wildlife, Seattle, Wash. Western Fish Disease Lab.

For primary bibliographic entry see Field 5C.
W75-06392

A REVIEW OF THE LITERATURE ON THE USE OF FORMALIN-MALACHITE GREEN IN FISHERIES,
Bureau of Sport Fisheries and Wildlife, Seattle, Wash. Western Fish Disease Lab.
For primary bibliographic entry see Field 5C.
W75-06393

A REVIEW OF THE LITERATURE ON THE USE OF MALACHITE GREEN IN FISHERIES,
Bureau of Sport Fisheries and Wildlife, Seattle, Wash. Western Fish Disease Lab.
For primary bibliographic entry see Field 5C.
W75-06394

SUBJECT INDEX

AUTHOR INDEX

ORGANIZATIONAL INDEX

ACCESSION NUMBER INDEX

ABSTRACT SOURCES

)URCE	ACCESSION NUMBER	TOTAL
. CENTERS OF COMPETENCE		
Cornell University, Policy Models for Water Resources Systems	W75-06557--06559 06562--06573	15
ERDA Oak Ridge National Laboratory, Nuclear Radiation and Safety	W75-06407--06415 06417--06427 06621--06635 06794--06807 06818--06826	58
Franklin Institute (FIRL), Municipal Wastewater Treatment Technology	W75-06405 06827--06835	10
Illinois State Water Survey, Hydrology	W75-06400 06402--06403 06434--06446 06448--06460 06464 06467--06479 06481--06515 06526--06550 06636	104
National Water Well Association, Water Well Construction Technology	W75-06808--06817	10
University of Arizona, Arid Land Water Resources	W75-06367--06375	9
University of Florida, Eastern U. S. Water Law	W75-06574--06620	47
University of North Carolina, Metropolitan Water Resources Planning and Management	W75-06404 06758--06777 06779--06793	36

ABSTRACT SOURCES

SOURCE	ACCESSION NUMBER	TO
B. STATE WATER RESOURCES RESEARCH INSTITUTES	W75-06351--06359 06361--06365 06429--06433 06461--06463 06516--06522 06642--06650	
C. OTHER		
Agricultural Research Service	W75-06399	
BioSciences Information Service	W75-06360, 06401 06406, 06416 06428, 06447 06465--06466 06480 06560--06561 06637 06651--06653 06671 06698--06730 06778 06836--06850	
Commonwealth Scientific and Industrial Research Organization, Australia	W75-06551--06556	
Effects of Pollutants on Aquatic Life (Katz)	W75-06376--06398	
Engineering Aspects of Urban Water Resources (Poertner)	W75-06654--06670 06672--06681	
Environment Canada	W75-06731--06752	
Ocean Engineering Information Service (Patents)	W75-06682--06697	

ABSTRACT SOURCES

JRCE	ACCESSION NUMBER	TOTAL
OTHER (CONTINUED)		
Office of Water Research and Technology	W75-06366 06523--06525 06638--06641	8
U. S. Geological Survey	W75-06753--06757	5

CENTERS OF COMPETENCE AND THEIR SUBJECT COVERAGE

- Ground and surface water hydrology at the Illinois State Water Survey and the Water Resources Division of the U.S. Geological Survey, U.S. Department of the Interior.
- Metropolitan water resources planning and management at the Center for Urban and Regional Studies of University of North Carolina.
- Eastern United States water law at the College of Law of the University of Florida.
- Policy models of water resources systems at the Department of Water Resources Engineering of Cornell University.
- Water resources economics at the Water Resources Center of the University of Wisconsin.
- Eutrophication at the Water Resources Center of the University of Wisconsin.
- Water resources of arid lands at the Office of Arid Lands Studies of the University of Arizona.
- Water well construction technology at the National Water Well Association.
- Water-related aspects of nuclear radiation and safety at the Oak Ridge National Laboratory.
- Water resource aspects of the pulp and paper industry at the Institute of Paper Chemistry.

Supported by the Environmental Protection Agency in cooperation with WRSIC

- Effect on water quality of irrigation return flows at the Department of Agricultural Engineering of Colorado State University.
- Agricultural livestock waste at East Central State College, Oklahoma.
- Municipal wastewater treatment technology at the Franklin Institute Research Laboratories.

Subject Fields

1 NATURE OF WATER

2 WATER CYCLE

3 WATER SUPPLY AUGMENTATION AND CONSERVATION

4 WATER QUANTITY MANAGEMENT AND CONTROL

5 WATER QUALITY MANAGEMENT AND PROTECTION

6 WATER RESOURCES PLANNING

7 RESOURCES DATA

8 ENGINEERING WORKS

9 MANPOWER, GRANTS, AND FACILITIES

10 SCIENTIFIC AND TECHNICAL INFORMATION

INDEXES

SUBJECT INDEX

AUTHOR INDEX

ORGANIZATIONAL INDEX

ACCESSION NUMBER INDEX

ABSTRACT SOURCES

U.S. DEPARTMENT OF COMMERCE
National Technical Information Service
5285 Port Royal Road
Springfield, VA 22161

SELECTED WATER RESOURCES ABSTRACTS

VOLUME 8, NUMBER 14
JULY 15, 1975

W75-06851 -- W75-07350
CODEN: SWRABW

SELECTED WATER RESOURCES ABSTRACTS is published semimonthly for the Water Resources Scientific Information Center (WRSIC) by the National Technical Information Service (NTIS), U.S. Department of Commerce. NTIS was established September 2, 1970, as a new primary operating unit under the Assistant Secretary of Commerce for Science and Technology to improve public access to the many products and services of the Department. Information services for Federal scientific and technical report literature previously provided by the Clearinghouse for Federal Scientific and Technical Information are now provided by NTIS.

SELECTED WATER RESOURCES ABSTRACTS is available to Federal agencies, contractors, or grantees in water resources upon request to: Manager, Water Resources Scientific Information Center, Office of Water Research and Technology, U.S. Department of the Interior, Washington, D. C. 20240.

SELECTED WATER RESOURCES ABSTRACTS is also available on subscription from the National Technical Information Service. Annual subscription rates are: To the SWRA Journal, $75 ($95 foreign); to the Journal & Annual Index, $100 ($125 foreign); to the Annual Index only, $50 ($65 foreign). Certain documents abstracted in this journal can be purchased from the NTIS at prices indicated in the entry. Prepayment is required.

SELECTED
WATER RESOURCES ABSTRACTS

A Semimonthly Publication of the Water Resources Scientific Information Center,
Office of Water Research and Technology, U.S. Department of the Interior

VOLUME 8, NUMBER 14
JULY 15, 1975

W75-06851 -- W75-07350

As the Nation's principal conservation agency, the Department of the Interior has responsibility for most of our nationally owned public lands and natural resources. This includes fostering the wisest use of our land and water resources, protecting our fish and wildlife, preserving the environmental and cultural values of our national parks and historical places, and providing for the enjoyment of life through outdoor recreation. The Department assesses our energy and mineral resources and works to assure that their development is in the best interests of all our people. The Department also has a major responsibility for American Indian reservation communities and for people who live in Island Territories under U.S. administration.

FOREWORD

Selected Water Resources Abstracts, a semimonthly journal, includes abstracts of 'current and earlier pertinent monographs, journal articles, reports, and other publication formats. The contents of these documents cover the water-related aspects of the life, physical, and social sciences as well as related engineering and legal aspects of the characteristics, conservation, control, use, or management of water. Each abstract includes a full bibliographical citation and a set of descriptors or identifiers which are listed in the **Water Resources Thesaurus.** Each abstract entry is classified into ten fields and sixty groups similar to the water resources research categories established by the Committee on Water Resources Research of the Federal Council for Science and Technology.

WRSIC IS NOT PRESENTLY IN A POSITION TO PROVIDE COPIES OF DOCUMENTS ABSTRACTED IN THIS JOURNAL. Sufficient bibliographic information is given to enable readers to order the desired documents from local libraries or other sources.

Selected Water Resources Abstracts is designed to serve the scientific and technical information needs of scientists, engineers, and managers as one of several planned services of the Water Resources Scientific Information Center (WRSIC). The Center was established by the Secretary of the Interior and has been designated by the Federal Council for Science and Technology to serve the water resources community by improving the communication of water-related research results. The Center is pursuing this objective by coordinating and supplementing the existing scientific and technical information activities associated with active research and investigation program in water resources.

To provide WRSIC with input, selected organizations with active water resources research programs are supported as "centers of competence" responsible for selecting, abstracting, and indexing from the current and earlier pertinent literature in specified subject areas.

Additional "centers of competence" have been established in cooperation with the Environmental Protection Agency. A directory of the Centers appears on inside back cover.

Supplementary documentation is being secured from established discipline-oriented abstracting and indexing services. Currently an arrangement is in effect whereby the BioScience Information Service of Biological Abstracts supplies WRSIC with relevant references from the several subject areas of interest to our users. In addition to Biological Abstracts, references are acquired from Bioresearch Index which are without abstracts and therefore also appear abstractless in SWRA. Similar arrangements with other producers of abstracts are contemplated as planned augmentation of the information base.

The input from these Centers, and from the 51 Water Resources Research Institutes administered under the Water Resources Research Act of 1964, as well as input from the grantees and contractors of the Office of Water Research and Technology and other Federal water resource agencies with which the

Center has agreements becomes the information base from which this journal is, and other information services will be, derived; these services include bibliographies, specialized indexes, literature searches, and state-of-the-art reviews.

Comments and suggestions concerning the contents and arrangements of this bulletin are welcome.

Water Resources Scientific Information Center
Office of Water Research and Technology
U.S. Department of the Interior
Washington, D. C. 20240

CONTENTS

FOREWORD iii

SUBJECT FIELDS AND GROUPS

(Use Edge Index on back cover to Locate Subject Fields and Indexes in the journal.)

01 NATURE OF WATER
Includes the following Groups: Properties; Aqueous Solutions and Suspensions

02 WATER CYCLE
Includes the following Groups: General; Precipitation; Snow, Ice, and Frost; Evaporation and Transpiration; Streamflow and Runoff; Groundwater; Water in Soils; Lakes; Water in Plants; Erosion and Sedimentation; Chemical Processes; Estuaries.

03 WATER SUPPLY AUGMENTATION AND CONSERVATION
Includes the following Groups: Saline Water Conversion; Water Yield Improvement; Use of Water of Impaired Quality; Conservation in Domestic and Municipal Use; Conservation in Industry; Conservation in Agriculture.

04 WATER QUANTITY MANAGEMENT AND CONTROL
Includes the following Groups: Control of Water on the Surface; Groundwater Management; Effects on Water of Man's Non-Water Activities; Watershed Protection.

05 WATER QUALITY MANAGEMENT AND PROTECTION
Includes the following Groups: Identification of Pollutants; Sources of Pollution; Effects of Pollution; Waste Treatment Processes; Ultimate Disposal of Wastes; Water Treatment and Quality Alteration; Water Quality Control.

06 WATER RESOURCES PLANNING
Includes the following Groups: Techniques of Planning; Evaluation Process; Cost Allocation, Cost Sharing, Pricing/Repayment; Water Demand; Water Law and Institutions; Nonstructural Alternatives; Ecologic Impact of Water Development.

07 RESOURCES DATA
Includes the following Groups: Network Design; Data Acquisition; Evaluation, Processing and Publication.

08 ENGINEERING WORKS
Includes the following Groups: Structures; Hydraulics; Hydraulic Machinery; Soil Mechanics; Rock Mechanics and Geology; Concrete; Materials; Rapid Excavation; Fisheries Engineering.

09 MANPOWER, GRANTS, AND FACILITIES
Includes the following Groups: Education—Extramural; Education—In-House; Research Facilities; Grants, Contracts, and Research Act Allotments.

10 SCIENTIFIC AND TECHNICAL INFORMATION
Includes the following Groups: Acquisition and Processing; Reference and Retrieval; Secondary Publication and Distribution; Specialized Information Center Services; Translations; Preparation of Reviews.

SUBJECT INDEX

AUTHOR INDEX

ORGANIZATIONAL INDEX

ACCESSION NUMBER INDEX

ABSTRACT SOURCES

Descriptors: *Model studies, *Mathematical models, *Hydraulic models, Hydraulic similitude, Rivers, Estuaries, Hydraulics, Froude number, Reynolds number, Equations, Scaling, Flow characteristics, Calibrations, Computer models.
Identifiers: Fixed bed models, Movable bed models.

Comparisons and common aspects between physical and mathematical models were discussed. Use of both types of models has been proved important for design purposes as well as for the understanding of physical problems in rivers. Both types may be used for fixed bed and movable bed models. Common aspects include: (1) schematization of the prototype problem; (2) solving the engineering problem for the model and translating this solution into the solution for prototype problem; (3) model calibration using prototype data from an existing situation; and (4) scale effects. Physical models require a new model for every prototype, are less flexible than mathematical models, are not easily stored, and can provide more detail of flow pattern for such problems as bed configuration due to a three-dimensional flow pattern. Mathematical models are more flexible, do not require a new model for every prototype, are more easily stored, are suitable when a large reach has to be covered and only few details of flow phenomena are required, and require a relatively large amount of computer time for determining detail flow patterns. Both model types are possible for many problems and an example was discussed where the models were complementary. (See also W75-07038) (Humphreys-ISWS)
W75-07040

APPLICATION OF A CATCHMENT MODEL IN SOUTHEASTERN AUSTRALIA,
Monash Univ., Clayton (Australia). Dept. of Civol Engineering.
J. W. Porter, and T. A. McMahon.
Journal of Hydrology, Vol 24, No 1/2, p 121-134, January 1975. 4 fig, 2 tab, 11 ref.

Descriptors: *Synthetic hydrology, *Mathematical models, *Computer models, Hydrology, *Watersheds(Basins), Model studies, Hydrographs, Instrumentation, Climates, *Australia.

Some results of the application of a computer catchment model to catchments in southeastern Australia were presented and discussed. Problems that were pertinent to model development and application were outlined. These include preparation time prior to application, the requirement for expertise in model use, inadequacies in hydrologic physics, difficulties of modeling in arid regions, and special aspects such as stream transmission losses. (Jess-ISWS)
W75-07054

RAINFALL AND SNOWMELT RUNOFF FROM INTERMEDIATE ELEVATION WATERSHEDS,
M. Molnau, D. J. Davis, L. Druffel, and R. S. C. Lee.
Available from the National Technical Information Service, Springfield, Va 22161 as PB-241 502, $3.25 in paper copy, $2.25 in microfiche. Idaho Water Resources Research Institute, Moscow, Completion Report, September 1973. 13 p, 7 ref. OWRT A-029-IDA(1).

Descriptors: *Water balance, Snowmelt, Runoff, *Erosion, Evapotranspiration, *Mathematical models, *Agricultural watersheds, Forest watersheds, *Pacific Northwest US, Rainfall-runoff relationships, *Model studies.

Many low and intermediate elevation watersheds in the Pacific Northwest receive both rain and snow precipitation during the winter months. This results in winter runoff events that are damaging to agricultural land and can also decrease the snow water storage limiting water availability in late spring and early summer. The winter and spring runoff from forested lands was studied at a snow research site where melt from the rain and snow events could be measured. Predictable lags occurred between time of melt and time of peak in stream hydrographs. The Kentucky Watershed Model was also used to evaluate the effects of precipitation type and amount of runoff patterns. Runoff in the early winter was not satisfactorily modeled. An agricultural watershed was used to study runoff and erosion resulting from rain on snow and rain on frozen ground. Soil loss was found to depend mainly on amounts of precipitation since runoff began, volume of runoff, change in snow cover and soil moisture conditions. Rain on frozen ground produced less erosion than comparable amounts of rain on bare unfrozen soil. A study of the water balance showed that precipitation was distributed approximately 27 percent to runoff, 57 percent to evapotranspiration and 16 percent to deep percolation. It also showed the Penman method of computing evapotranspiration was satisfactory when compared to soil moisture changes.
W75-07101

PROCEDURES FOR EVALUATING THE SURFACE WATER BALANCE OF GRAN CANARIA,
United Nations Development Program, Las Palmas de Gran Canaria (Spain),
For primary bibliographic entry see Field 2D.
W75-07194

EVAPOTRANSPIRATION AND PLANT PRODUCTION DIRECTLY RELATED TO GLOBAL RADIATION,
Royal Veterinary and Agriculture Coll., Copenhagen (Denmark). Hydrotechnical Lab.
For primary bibliographic entry see Field 2D.
W75-07195

URBAN STORM RAINFALL-RUNOFF-QUALITY INSTRUMENTATION,
Geological Survey, Reston, Va.
For primary bibliographic entry see Field 5A.
W75-07202

HISTORY OF HYDROLOGY--A BRIEF SUMMARY,
Geological Survey, Raleigh, N.C.
R. L. Nace.
Nature and Resources, Vol 10, No 3, p 2-9, July-September 1974. 2 fig.

Descriptors: *Hydrology, *Hydrologic cycle, *History, Data collections.
Identifiers: *History of hydrology.

Hydrology is a set of concepts about the role and behavior of water in the earth system. The central concept of hydrology is the hydrological cycle--the continual circulation of water through the system ocean-atmosphere-land-biosphere. The world ocean is both the source of all water in the system and the final destination of its circulation. The full-fledged concept of the hydrological cycle was born only about 300 years ago and it was not fully and clearly stated for another 100 years. During the latter part of the nineteenth century and early in the twentieth, scientists in nearly every European country made significant contributions to groundwater hydrology. A succession of brilliant investigations, based largely on laboratory studies with relatively little field observation, had led to formulation of ever more elegant mathematical expressions. In the latter part of the nineteenth century prominence in the whole field of hydrology began to shift to the United States. In the United States emphasis for many years was on the collection of basic data. The United States Geological Survey began systematic stream gaging in 1889. Within 75 years the national network of observation stations grew to about 25,000, including

streamflow, groundwater levels, chemical quality of water, and the suspended solid load of streams. The International Hydrological Decade (IHD) program gave a great impetus to study of all prinicipal aspects of hydrology, including large-scale water balances. (Knapp-USGS)
W75-07227

ANOTHER EXPLANATION OF THE OBSERVED CYCLONIC CIRCULATION OF LARGE LAKES,
Massachusetts Inst. of Tech., Cambridge.
For primary bibliographic entry see Field 2H.
W75-07246

NEARSHORE LAKE CURRENTS MEASURED DURING UPWELLING AND DOWNWELLING OF THE THERMOCLINE IN LAKE ONTARIO,
Canada Centre for Inland Waters, Burlington (Ontario).
For primary bibliographic entry see Field 2H.
W75-07251

EFFECT OF ARABIAN SEA-SURFACE TEMPERATURE ANOMALY ON INDIAN SUMMER MONSOON: A NUMERICAL EXPERIMENT WITH THE GFDL MODEL,
National Oceanic and Atmospheric Administration, Princeton, N.J. Geophysical Fluid Dynamics Lab.
For primary bibliographic entry see Field 2B.
W75-07255

RAINFALL-INDUCED RUNOFF COMPUTED FOR FALLOW FIELDS,
Agricultural Research Service, Durant, Okla. Water Quality Management Lab.
V. L. Hauser, and E. A. Hiler.
Transactions of American Society of Agricultural Engineers, Vol 18, No 1, p 122-125, January-February 1975. 5 fig, 1 tab, 13 ref.

Descriptors: Hydrology, *Great Plains, *Agriculture, *Equations, *Rainfall-runoff relationships, Runoff, Agricultural runoff, Surface runoff, Rainfall intensity, Rainfall, Solar radiation, Sheet erosion, Suspended load, Texas, Kansas, Iowa, Forecasting, *Runoff forecasting.

There are no long-term runoff records available that could be used to determine the needed runoff amount of return-frequency information for the western Great Plains; however, management of this water can increase yields. Rainfall amount and intensity, runoff, and soil water were measured on 3 terraced fields for 12 years. The soil was clay loam and had a slowly permeable layer; the average land slope was 1.5%. The fields were cropped in a wheat-sorghum-fallow sequence which gave 22 months of fallow for each 36-month period. Stubble mulch tillage was used to control wind and water erosion. A set of equations was developed to compute rainfall-induced runoff from fallow land with the use of daily rainfall, maximum 1-hr rainfall for the day, and computed soil water content. Equations were computed for three conditions (1) soil water content greater than field capacity, (2) fallow-after-wheat from June to January, and (3) fallow-after-sorghum plus after wheat January to June. About 15% more runoff was computed than was measured on a fallow period basis; however, a linear correction reduced the error to 4.6%. The following conclusions were drawn from the study: (1) the equations for soil water can be used to compute runoff from rainfall records; (2) soil water content may be computed and used successfully in runoff equations; (3) daily runoff can be computed accurately with inputs of daily rainfall, computed soil water content, and maximum 1-hr rainfall for the day; and (4) the use of computed soil water content permits the equation set to compute runoff for the whole year. (Dawes-ISWS)
W75-07261

COASTAL MORPHOLOGY,
Louisiana State Univ., Baton Rouge.
For primary bibliographic entry see Field 2L.
W75-07270

MODEL DEVELOPMENT AND SYSTEMS ANALYSIS OF THE YAKIMA RIVER BASIN: HYDRAULICS OF SURFACE WATER RUNOFF,
Washington State Univ., Pullman. Dept. of Civil and Environmental Engineering.
H. D. Copp, and D. T. Higgins.
Available from the National Technical Information Service, Springfield, Va., 22161, as PB-241 531, $6.25 in paper copy, $2.25 in microfiche. Washington Water Research Center, Pullman, Report No. 17B, November 1974. 150 p, 43 fig, 8 tab, 12 ref, 2 append. OWRT B-036-WASH(4) B-043-WASH(3), and B-050-WASH(3).

Descriptors: *Computer models, *Systems analysis, Runoff, *Washington, Probability, Model studies, Planning, Watershed management, Forecasting, *Simulation analysis, *Hydraulic models.
Identifiers: *Yakima River basin(Wash).

A computer model is described that is an accounting of water quality in the Yakima River that flows from upper watershed areas into and through predefined stream reaches to the watershed outlet. The model adds tributary streams at confluences, and subtracts withdrawals from the stream. The model is deterministic; water quantities must be specified. However, with (a) separate analyses to define water runoff at various levels of probability and (b) model use with these runoff quantities, future probabilistic events and their consequences can be analyzed. Model development recognized the flexibility which water planning must have. Accordingly, the user has considerable freedom in establishing (1) watershed description, (2) the stream system, (3) quantities of flow in the streams, (4)positions and quantities of withdrawals and/or return flows, (5) location and operation rules of storage-reservoirs, and (6) flow quantities needed to meet above-mentioned requirements. The model is thus capable of simulating many water management plans, existing or envisioned, and a wide range of water quatity regimes.
W75-07278

2B. Precipitation

DOPPLER RADAR OBSERVATIONS OF A HAILSTORM,
Arizona Univ., Tucson. Inst. of Atmospheric Physics.
L. J. Battan.
Journal of Applied Meteorology, Vol 14, No 1, p 98-108, February 1975. 4 fig, 3 tab, 22 ref. NSF Grants GA-24134 and GA-37825X.

Descriptors: *Radar, *Hail, *Air circulation, Remote sensing, *Arizona, Storms, Meteorology, Analysis, Instrumentation, On-site data collections.
Identifiers: *Doppler shift, Radar reflectivity, Hailstones, Hailstreaks.

A severe hailstorm, occurring on 10 August 1966, passed over a zenith pointing, X-band, pulsed-Doppler radar located on a mountain in southeastern Arizona. An analysis was made of measurements of radar reflectivity, mean Doppler velocity, variance of the Doppler spectrum, and calculated updraft velocity. The vertical air motions and characteristics of the hydrometeors within the storm were highly variable over distances of a few hundred meters to a few kilometers. The storm consisted of a series of updraft cores containing a number of discrete volumes, 1-2 km in diameter, of rapidly rising air with smaller accompanying eddies. The updraft cores were separated by regions of weak updrafts or downdrafts. For the most part, the highest reflectivities were outside the updraft cores. It was visualized that the hailstone growth was initiated within the updraft, not as a continuous process, but rather as pockets of hailstones within the fast-rising, distinct volumes. This process could account for the layers of clear and opaque ice within large stones by allowing them to pass through several rising volumes. It might also account for brief bursts of hail and short hailstreaks observed at the ground. (Jones-ISWS)
W75-07049

EXPERIMENTAL RESULTS WITH A RAIN ANALYZER,
Massachusetts Inst. of Tech., Cambridge. Research Lab. of Electronics.
J. Sander.
Journal of Applied Meteorology, Vol 14, No 1, p 128-131, February 1975. 2 fig, 2 tab, 9 ref.

Descriptors: *Instrumentation, *Rainfall intensity, *Raindrops, Raingages, Measurement, Attenuation, Correlation analysis, On-site data collections, Precipitation(Atmospheric).
Identifiers: *Rain analyzer, Microwave attenuation.

The rain analyzer is an instrument with which the main part of the raindrop size spectrum can be determined. During measurements of the rain attenuation of millimeter waves, rainfall was recorded both with rain analyzers and with standard rain gages. The observed millimeter-wave attenuation was somewhat more directly related to rainfall rates obtained with the analyzer than to those measured with rain gages. The average drop-size distribution measured during the experiment was similar to that of Laws and Parsons. (Jones-ISWS)
W75-07050

EMPIRICAL FOG DROPLET SIZE DISTRIBUTION FUNCTIONS WITH FINITE LIMITS,
Northwestern Univ., Evanston, Ill. Interdisciplinary Atmospheric Sciences Research Group.
J. V. Mallow.
Journal of the Atmospheric Sciences, Vol 32, No 2, p 440-443, February 1975. 1 fig, 1 tab, 11 ref.

Descriptors: *Drops(Fluids), *Fog, Numerical analysis, Radar, Distribution patterns, Equations, Theoretical analysis.
Identifiers: *Size distribution, Lidar.

The Deirmendjian-Chu-Hogg fog droplet size distribution function N(a) = Ca to the alpha power exp (- (alpha/gamma) a to the gamma power) restricts the parameters alpha and gamma to be positive. A procedure for calculating realistic fog distributions, including appropriate normalization, was outlined. It was shown that actual distributions are described by both positive and negative alpha and gamma. (Jones-ISWS)
W75-07051

HAIL AND RAINDROP SIZE DISTRIBUTIONS FROM A SWISS MULTICELL STORM,
Eidgenoessische Technische Hochschule, Zuerich (Switzerland).
B. Federer, and A. Waldvogel.
Journal of Applied Meteorology, Vol 14, No 1, p 91-97, February 1975. 6 fig, 1 tab, 23 ref.

Descriptors: *Hail, *Rainfall, Thunderstorms, *Instrumentation, Remote sensing, Radar, Distribution patterns, Raindrops, Storms, Measurement.
Identifiers: Liquid water content, Hailstreaks, *Switzerland.

Time-resolved hail and raindrop size distributions measured simultaneously during a multicellular hailstorm were presented. The time variation of the size distributions allowed a detailed analysis of the structure of the hailswath. It consisted of four

hail cells with a duration of 2-3 min each. The number density of the hailstones increased and the mean diameter decreased during the lifetime of a cell. The contributions of liquid water and ice water content to the total water W was about equal; W was never larger than 5 g/cu m. The size distributions were well approximated by an exponential law. The mean distribution was given by N sub H (D) = 12 exp(-0.42D). The distributions were compared with measurements and calculations of other authors and the differences were discussed. (Jones-ISWS)
W75-07056

STATIONARITY OF MESOSCALE AIRFLOW IN MOUNTAINOUS TERRAIN,
Utah State Univ., Logan. Dept. of Soil Science and Biometeorology.
G. L. Wooldridge, and R. I. Ellis.
Journal of Applied Meteorology, Vol 14, No 1, p 124-128, February 1975. 5 fig, 1 tab, 12 ref.

Descriptors: *Winds, *Mountains, Velocity, Turbulence, Turbulent flow, *Utah, On-site data collections.
Identifiers: *Mesoscale, Superpressure balloons, Double theodolites, *Cache Valley(Utah).

Criteria for stationarity of turbulent atmospheric flow were examined for the mesoscale in a mountain valley in northeastern Utah. Data from four sequences of superpressure balloon flights were used. It was shown that the horizontal components of the Lagrangian velocities at levels below the ridges of the surrounding mountains are only weakly stationary; the vertical component fits the criteria better. Above the ridge levels all components of the velocities exhibit reasonable stationarity in the turbulent flow. (Jones-ISWS)
W75-07061

GEOPHYSICAL MONITORING FOR CLIMATIC CHANGE, NO. 2, SUMMARY REPORT 1973.
National Oceanic and Atmospheric Administration, Boulder, Colo. Environmental Research Labs.
For primary bibliographic entry see Field 7C.
W75-07076

SEVERE RAINSTORM AT ENID, OKLAHOMA OCTOBER 10, 1973,
National Severe Storms Lab., Norman, Okla.
L. P. Merritt, K. E. Wilk, and M. L. Weible.
NOAA Technical Memorandum ERL NSSL-73, November 1974. 50 p, 24 fig, 3 tab, 14 ref.

Descriptors: *Storms, *Precipitation(Atmospheric), *Floods, Rainfall, Weather forecasting, Cyclones, Forecasting, *Oklahoma.
Identifiers: *Severe storms, *Convective rainstorms, Synoptic conditions, Precipitation forecasting, Enid(Okla).

On October 10, 1973, a convective rainstorm devastated Enid, Oklahoma, and resulted in extensive flood damage over five counties in north central Oklahoma. Meteorological analyses at synoptic, subsynoptic, and mesoscales indicate that (1) evolution of the storm system was governed largely by conditions and events at the synoptic scale; (2) concentrated convective rainfall in north central Oklahoma occurred in conjunction with, and in all likelihood significantly enhanced development of a major extratropical cyclone; and (3) the most outstanding feature of the storm system was the formation of a stationary and well-defined region of sustained convective activity wherein individual cells formed repeatedly and moved northward, reaching maturity, in most instances, as they passed over the Enid area. Although the rarity of the Enid storm precluded anticipating its occurrence, it is likely that short-term forecasting of precipitation amounts and flash flood potential could have been significantly improved with detailed hourly analyses of subsynoptic surface data and digital radar data using objective techniques. (NOAA)
W75-07077

SUMMARY OF SYNOPTIC METEOROLOGICAL OBSERVATIONS FOR GREAT LAKES AREAS: VOLUME 2, LAKE HURON AND GEORGIAN BAY.
National Climatic Center, Asheville, N.C.
Summary of Synoptic Meteorological Observations for Great Lakes Areas; Volume 2, Lake Huron and Georgian Bay, January 1975, 250 p.

Descriptors: *Climatology, *Atmospheric circulation, Climates, *Weather, *Precipitation(Atmospheric), Temperature, Wind, Cloud cover, Humidity, Weather observations, Wind direction, Wind velocity, Velocity measurement, Wind pressure, Pressure, Water waves, Lake waves, Visibility, Fog, *Great Lakes, *Lake Huron.
Identifiers: *Georgian Bay(Lake Huron).

This volume is one in a series of four intended to serve as a large scale climatic guide to thirteen major Great Lakes areas. Consisting entirely of tables, this volume contains data on weather occurrence by wind direction and hour; mean wind speed by direction and hour; mean cloud amounts by wind direction; ceiling heights; cloud amounts; visibility; relative humidity by air temperature; wind direction by air temperature; means, extremes and percentiles of air temperature; occurrence of fog; sea height; wave height versus wave period; monthly and annual percent frequencies, and means of sea surface temperature; and monthly and annual sea level pressures. (NOAA)
W75-07079

MANUALLY DIGITIZED RADAR GRIDS: A COMPARISON OF RESOLUTION CAPABILITIES FOR A HEAVY RAINFALL SITUATION,
National Weather Service, Fort Worth, Tex. Southern Region.
J. D. Belville.
NOAA Technical Memorandum NWS SR-80, February 1975, 16 p.

Descriptors: *Radar, *Rainfall intensity, *Rainfall-runoff relationships, Depth-area-duration analysis, Meteorology, Precipitation(Atmospheric), Precipitation intensity, Rain, Rainfall, Rainfall disposition, Hydrology, Hydrologic properties, Hydrologic data, Flood control, Texas.
Identifiers: *Manually Digitized Radar Program, Pecos River Storm(Tex).

The National Weather Service (NWS) hydrologic and radar programs must improve techniques in accurately locating and quickly identifying heavy rainfall patterns to prevent loss of life. One approach to this problem was the introduction of the Manually Digitized Radar (MDR) Program. This system enabled forecasters and hydrologists to keep track of rainfall patterns by using a quantitative index. Refinement of this system is necessary in order to increase its reliability. In this paper, a higher resolution grid, about 20 n mi (37km) on a side, is used in an attempt to locate a rainfall pattern with more precision than is possible with the present system. Use of the smaller grid also provides a better basis for estimating the magnitude of the rainfall in areas where rainfall data are sparse. (NOAA)
W75-07081

JUMBO TORNADO OUTBREAK OF 3 APRIL 1974,
Chicago Univ., Ill. Dept. of the Geophysical Sciences.
T. T. Fujita.
Weatherwise, Vol 27, No 3, p 116-126, June 1974. 17 fig, 1 tab, 10 ref. NESS 0404-158-1, NASA NGR 14-001-008.

Descriptors: *Tornadoes, *Meteorological data, Maps, Storms, Cyclones, Wind(Meteorology), Aerial surveys, *Aerial photography, Topography, United States.
Identifiers: *Severe storms, Tornado paths, Tornado cyclone.

Following the Jumbo tornado outbreak, an extensive aerial survey was performed in cooperation with the National Severe Storms Laboratory and the University of Oklahoma. The aerial survey revealed that the total path length of tornadoes in the eleven-state area was in excess of 2000 miles. Statistics during the past three years indicate that the total path mileage of U.S. tornadoes is approximately 4000 miles per year. Just about one-half of this total path mileage occurred within an 18-hour period beginning at 1400 CDT on 3 April. Tornado paths were found in unexpected locations such as in deep canyons, and on steep slopes of mountains. The Jumbo outbreak of tornadoes on 3-4 April 1974 in terms of the total number and the path mileage was more extensive than all known outbreaks. Besides, the tornado characteristics included many important aspects such as multiple suction vortices, family tornadoes, and cousin tornadoes spawned from interacting tornado cyclones. (NOAA)
W75-07082

RESEARCH NEEDS RELATED TO HYDROMETEOROLOGIC ASPECTS OF FUTURE ENERGY PRODUCTION,
National Oceanic and Atmospheric Administration, Oak Ridge, Tenn. Air Resources Atmospheric Turbulence and Diffusion Lab.
For primary bibliographic entry see Field 6D.
W75-07094

1973 WATER RESOURCES DATA FOR OREGON, SURFACE WATER RECORDS, PRECIPITATION RECORDS,
Oregon State Water Resources Board, Salem.
For primary bibliographic entry see Field 7C.
W75-07150

PRELIMINARY RESULTS OF THE COMPARISON OF THE AMOUNT OF ARTIFICIAL PRECIPITATION AND WATER RESERVES OF SEEDED FRONTAL CLOUDS,
For primary bibliographic entry see Field 3B.
W75-07163

INFRARED EMISSIVITY, SHORT-WAVE ALBEDO, AND THE MICROPHYSICS OF STRATIFORM WATER CLOUDS,
Commonwealth Scientific and Industrial Research Organization, Aspendale (Australia). Div. of Atmospheric Physics.
G. W. Paltridge.
Journal of Geophysical Research, Vol 79, No 27, p 4053-4058, September 20, 1974. 6 fig, 2 tab, 17 ref.

Descriptors: *Infrared radiation, *Solar radiation, *Physics, *Clouds, Albedo, Radiation, Thermal radiation, Absorption, Drops(Fluids), Particle size, Entrainment.
Identifiers: *Infrared emissivity, *Short-wave albedo, Stratocumulus, Liquid water content, Drop-size distribution, Black body radiation, Mean free path.

Simultaneous measurements of the microphysics and solar and thermal radiation fields of stratocumulus clouds were reported. It was shown that the mass absorption coefficient a sub o for window infrared radiation should be almost independent of position in these clouds because of the manner in which liquid water content and drop size distribution vary with height. Its theoretical value is of the

order of 650 sq cm/g. Measured values of total emissivity yield an a sub o in the range 150-800 sq cm/g. Such clouds must be at least 500 m thick in order to be optically black to longwave radiation. Neiburger's (1949) result that the two-stream approximation overestimates the shortwave albedo of thin clouds was not supported by the present work. His discrepancy between observation and theory can be largely eliminated by taking specific account of the increase in liquid water content with height. (Jones-ISWS)
W75-07196

EFFECTIVENESS OF CONTROLLED CONVECTION IN PRODUCING PRECIPITATION,
Massachusetts Inst. of Tech., Cambridge. Dept. of Meteorology.
For primary bibliographic entry see Field 3B.
W75-07199

ESTIMATES OF TEMPERATURE AND PRECIPITATION FOR NORTHEASTERN UTAH,
Geological Survey, Salt Lake City, Utah.
For primary bibliographic entry see Field 4A.
W75-07241

THE JANUARY GLOBAL CLIMATE SIMULATED BY A TWO-LEVEL GENERAL CIRCULATION MODEL: A COMPARISON WITH OBSERVATION,
RAND Corp., Santa Monica, Calif.
W. L. Gates.
Journal of the Atmospheric Sciences, Vol 32, No 3, p 449-477, March 1975. 41 fig, 1 tab, 27 ref. ARPA Contract DAHC15-73-C-0181.

Descriptors: *Climates, *Computer models, *Circulation, Atmospheric pressure, Winds, Temperature, Moisture, Clouds, Precipitation(Atmospheric), Evaporation, Heat balance, Climatology, Model studies, Meteorology.

The mean global distributions of pressure, temperature, wind, moisture, cloudiness, precipitation, evaporation, and surface heat balance simulated for January by the two-level Mintz-Arakawa atmospheric general circulation model were compared with the corresponding observed fields. Although there were a number of shortcomings, in general the large-scale distribution of global climate was reasonably well portrayed by the model, in spite of its limited vertical resolution. The model simulates the semi-permanent cyclones and anticyclones of both the tropics and higher latitudes in approximately their correct positions, together with the associated large-scale temperature and circulation fields of the middle and lower troposphere. In comparison with models of greater resolution, these results suggest that with further selective improvements in the physical parameterizations, relatively coarse global models (of correspondingly lower computational demands) are useful tools in the study of many aspects of climate. The most prominent errors of the present model simulations were in the portrayal of processes related to the transfer of moisture. The simulated cloudiness was about half that observed (in the Northern Hemisphere), and the average precipitation rate was about twice that observed and extends over too broad a zone in the tropics. (Jones-ISWS)
W75-07253

EFFECT OF ARABIAN SEA-SURFACE TEMPERATURE ANOMALY ON INDIAN SUMMER MONSOON: A NUMERICAL EXPERIMENT WITH THE GFDL MODEL,
National Oceanic and Atmospheric Administration, Princeton, N.J. Geophysical Fluid Dynamics Lab.
J. Shukla.
Journal of the Atmospheric Sciences, Vol 32, No 3, p 503-511, March 1975. 10 fig, 1 tab, 20 ref.

Descriptors: *Monsoons, *Temperature, *Oceans, Computer models, Atmospheric pressure, Statistical analysis, Precipitation(Atmospheric), Winds, Evaporation, Moisture, Model studies, Summer, *Indian Ocean.
Identifiers: *Sea temperature anomaly, *Arabian Sea, Somali coast.

The global general circulation model of the Geophysical Fluid Dynamics Laboratory was integrated with and without a cold sea surface temperature (SST) anomaly over the Somali coast and the western Arabian Sea. The temperature anomaly is -3C near the Somali coast and linearly decreases eastward having zero anomaly at about 1500 km east of the coast. Comparison of the mean of the two model states indicates that the rainfall over India and the adjoining region is drastically reduced due to the colder SST anomaly over the western Arabian Sea. The other associated features due to the cold anomaly are an increase in sea surface pressure over the Arabian Sea, a decrease in local evaporation, and a reduction in the cross equatorial component of the wind at the surface and hence a reduction in the cross equatorial moisture flux. Statistical analysis of the results was done by comparing the difference between the two mean states (signal) and the standard deviation of the errors (noise) in estimating the mean due to the finiteness of the averaging period. It was found that the results of the present numerical experiment are statistically significant. (Jones-ISWS)
W75-07255

DEVELOPMENT OF BANDED STRUCTURE IN A NUMERICALLY SIMULATED HURRICANE,
National Weather Service, Silver Spring, Md.
M. B. Mathur.
Journal of the Atmospheric Sciences, Vol 32, No 3, p 512-522, March 1975. 8 fig, 1 tab, 22 ref. NSF Grant GA35093.

Descriptors: *Hurricanes, *Computer models, *Storms, *Simulation analysis, Latent heat, Convection, Numerical analysis, Atmosphere, Heating, Meteorology.
Identifiers: *Cloud bands, Vertical motion.

The developments of the propagating and the stationary bands in a three-dimensional model of a hurricane (Isbell, 1964) were investigated. Propagating bands in the vertical motion fields in the middle and the upper troposphere form in the regions of strong heating in the upper troposphere and weak cooling in the middle troposphere. The structures of the wind, temperature, and pressure fields in these bands are similar to those observed in the outer radar bands of hurricanes. Strong, nearly stationary bands form close to the center in the intense storm stage. Results of two experiments, one (M1) in which the so-called nonconvective release of latent heat in the upper troposphere was included and the other (M2) in which this heating was not incorporated, were compared. Convective release of latent heat was included in both experiments. The stationary bands which formed in M1, also developed in M2. The propagating bands which formed in M1, however, did not develop in M2. The rate of intensification of the simulated storm in M1 was nearly the same as observed by Isbell; it was, however, significantly weaker in M2. It was shown that the inclusion of nonconvective release of latent heat in M1 enhanced the upper tropospheric outflow which induced strong zones of convergences in the boundary layer. The resulting increase in the upward motion at the top of the boundary layer augmented the convective release of latent heat and led to a rapid intensification of the disturbance. (Jones-ISWS)
W75-07256

ICE CLOUDS AT THE SUMMER POLAR MESOPAUSE,
National Oceanic and Atmospheric Administration, Boulder, Col. Aeronomy Lab.
G. C. Reid.
Journal of the Atmospheric Sciences, Vol 32, No 3, p 523-535, March 1975. 7 fig, 22 ref, 1 append.

Descriptors: *Clouds, *Ice, *Cloud physics, Summer, Satellites(Artificial), Water vapor, Computer models, *Polar regions, Arctic, Solar radiation, Sublimation, Eddies, Diffusion, Equations.
Identifiers: *Mesopause, Noctilucent clouds, Mixing ratio, Sublimination nuclei.

Recent satellite observations showed the existence of a persistent layer of light-scattering particles in the vicinity of the polar mesopause during the summer. The suggestion was made that this layer consists of ice particles, and that noctilucent clouds are a sporadic manifestation of the layer near its low-latitudes edge. The consequences of this proposal in terms of the water vapor content of the mesosphere were explored through the development of a model for such a cloud, in which the water vapor mixing ratio was assumed to be 1 to 10 ppm at 60 km, and the temperature was assumed to drop to values well below 140 K at the mesopause. Water vapor is transported upward by eddy diffusion, and is photodissociated by solar ultraviolet radiation. Sublimation nuclei of radius 10 angstrom were assumed to exist in the vicinity of the mesopause, and the growth of the ice particles and their terminal speed of descent were calculated from simple kinetic theory considerations. The results indicate that radii of order 1000 angstrom cannot be attained by spherical cloud particles unless there is much more water vapor in the mesosphere than current estimates suggest, or unless there is a substantial and persistent upward motion of the mesosphere as a whole. Nonspherical shapes were also considered, however, and it was found that needle-shaped and disc-shaped particles can readily grow to linear dimensions of order 1000 angstrom. (Jones-ISWS)
W75-07257

TRANSFER OF PARTICLES IN NONISOTROPIC AIR TURBULENCE,
Istituto di Fisica dell-Atmosfera, Bologna (Italy).
M. Caporaloni, F. Tampieri, F. Trombetti, and O. Vittori.
Journal of the Atmospheric Sciences, Vol 32, No 3, p 565-568, March 1975. 3 fig, 12 ref.

Descriptors: *Mathematical models, *Atmospheric physics, *Particle size, *Velocity, Turbulence, Turbulent flow, Numerical analysis, Diffusion, Atmosphere.
Identifiers: *Dry deposition, Brownian diffusion, Eddy diffusion.

The inertia of particles is the basis of the present model of particle 'dry deposition' from a turbulent fluid. The basic physical concepts of particle thermal motion as described by Einstein were extended to describe the particle motion in nonisotropic turbulence in terms of a 'turbophoretic' velocity. The particle transfer from the turbulent fluid to a collecting black surface was therefore given in terms of a differential motion describing the chain of 'inertial flights' undergone by the particle under the gradient of turbulence velocity component in the direction of the collecting surface. The model of dry deposition shows satisfactory agreement with experimental values of particle deposition velocity as a function of particle size. (Sims-ISWS)
W75-07258

MEASUREMENT OF GROWTH RATE TO DETERMINE CONDENSATION COEFFICIENTS FOR WATER DROPS GROWN ON NATURAL CLOUD NUCLEI,
Missouri Univ., Rolla. Graduate Center for Cloud Physics Research.
A. M. Sinnarwalla, D. J. Alofs, and J. C. Carstens.
Journal of the Atmospheric Sciences, Vol 32, No 3, p 592-599, March 1975. 9 fig, 1 tab, 18 ref. NSF Grant GA-30876.

Descriptors: *Nucleation, *Drops(Fluids), *Growth rates, *Cloud physics, Measurement, *Missouri, Condensation, Meteorology, Diffusion, Laboratory tests, Size, Velocity.
Identifiers: Thermal diffusion chamber, Error analysis, *Rolla(Mo).

Growth rate measurements were made for water drops grown on nuclei in atmospheric air samples taken in Rolla, having a population of 15,000 and very little industry, is relatively free of urban pollutants. The measurements were made in a vertical flow thermal diffusion chamber of supersaturations of 0.5 and 1%. The time to grow from near dry radius to the final radius (6 to 7.5 micrometers) was measured. If one assumes the thermal aecommodation coefficient is unity, the measurements indicate an average value of 0.026 for the condensation coefficient. The temperature ranged from 22.5 to 25.7C. (Jones-ISWS)
W75-07259

THREE MODELS FORTHE COALESCENCE GROWTH OF CLOUD DROPS,
Naval Weapons Center, China Lake, Calif.
D. T. Gillespie.
Journal of the Atmospheric Sciences, Vol 32, No 3, p 600-607, March 1975. 6 ref.

Descriptors: *Coalescence, *Model studies, *Drops(Fluids), *Cloud physics, Computer models, Stochastic processes, Clouds, Statistical methods, Statistical models, Physical properties, Growth rates, Meteorology, Model studies.
Identifiers: *Cloud drops, Stochastic coalescence equation.

In an attempt to resolve the confusion over the 'stochastic completeness' of the stochastic coalescence equation, an analysis was made of an idealized cloud consisting of a number of large 'drops' falling through very many small, equal-size 'droplets' with a constant drop-droplet collection kernel. It was shown how three superficially equivalent physical interpretations of the drop-droplet collection kernel lead to three quite different models for the growth of the drops. The implications of and relationships between the model were drawn out in detail. The stochastic completeness controversy was apparently a consequence of a failure to distinguish clearly between two of these three conceptual approaches. The three models are (1) the continuous model, (2) the quasi-stochastic model, and (3) the pure stochastic model. (Jones-ISWS)
W75-07260

THE INFLUENCE OF SNOWCOVER ON THE ATMOSPHERIC CIRCULATION AND ITS ROLE IN CLIMATIC CHANGE: AN ANALYSIS BASED ON RESULTS FROM THE NCAR GLOBAL CIRCULATION MODEL,
National Center for Atmospheric Research, Boulder, Colo.
J. Williams.
Journal of Applied Meteorology, Vol 14, No 2, p 137-152, March 1975. 17 fig, 1 tab, 45 ref.

Descriptors: *Atmosphere, *Circulation, *Computer models, Glaciers, *Snow cover, *Climates, Monsoons, Oceans, Temperature, Winds, Clouds, Moisture, Kinetics, Energy.
Identifiers: Little Ice Age, July.

The NCAR global circulation model was used with boundary conditions representing those of a glacial period July, except that areas in North America, Europe, Asia, and South America, which formerly were glaciated, have no orography change but have an albedo change equivalent to covering the areas with snow. The resuls of the snowcover experiment were compared with those of a July control and a July ice-age case. Reduction of global mean eddy kinetic energy, elimination of the tropical easterly jet, and changes in other climatic variables suggest a weakening of the Northern Hemisphere summer monsoon in the snowcover case compared with the control case. Over North America is a ridge of high mean sea level pressure giving northerly flow over the Hudson Bay-Great Lakes area. At 6 km is a trough of low pressure over eastern North America and a somewhat weaker trough over the British Isles and western Europe. The pole-to-equator temperature gradient increased in the snowcover case when compared with the control case. The Northern Hemisphere jet stream, in zonal average, is stronger and farther south. Cloudiness increased over the snowcover areas compared with the control case; precipitation decreased but not as much as in the ice age case. Results suggest that changes in albedo and ocean surface temperature influence the simulated atmospheric circulation more than changes in orography caused by glaciation. The July snowcover experiment reproduced many of the atmospheric circulation features in the Northern Hemisphere associated with extensive snowcover in summer months, hypotheses regarding the inception of glacierization, and the reconstructed climate of the Little Ice Age (1550-1850 AD). (Jones-ISWS)
W75-07267

OPTICAL LEVITATION OF LIQUID DROPS BY RADIATION PRESSURE,
Bell Labs., Holmdel, N.J.
A. Ashkin, and J. M. Dziedzic.
Science, Vol 187, No 4181, p 1073-1075, March 21, 1975. 2 fig, 4 ref.

Descriptors: *Drops(Fluids), *Radiation, Optical properties, Cloud physics, Aerosols, Light, Electric fields, Clouds, Instrumentation, Coalescence, Fluid mechanics.
Identifiers: *Laser beams, *Levitation, Fluid dynamics, Radiation pressure, Scattering(Light).

Charged and neutral liquid drops in the diameter range from 1 to 40 microns can be stably levitated and manipulated with laser beams. The levitation technique was extended toward smaller particles (about 1 micron), lower laser power (less than 1 milliwatt), and deeper traps (greater than ten times the particle's weight). The technique developed have particular importance in cloud physics, aerosol science, fluid dynamics, and optics. The interactions of the drops with light, the electric field, the surrounding gas, and one another can be observed with high precision. (Jones-ISWS)
W75-07269

THE IMPACTS OF SNOW ENHANCEMENT: TECHNOLOGY ASSESSMENT OF WINTER OROGRAPHIC SNOWPACK AUGMENTATION IN THE UPPER COLORADO RIVER BASIN.
Stanford Research Inst., Menlo Park, Calif.
For primary bibliographic entry see Field 3B.
W75-07333

SNOWPACK, CLOUD-SEEDING, AND THE COLORADO RIVER: A TECHNOLOGY ASSESSMENT OF WEATHER MODIFICATION,
Stanford Research Inst., Menlo Park, Calif.
For primary bibliographic entry see Field 3B.
W75-07334

2C. Snow, Ice, and Frost

DOPPLER RADAR OBSERVATIONS OF A HAILSTORM,
Arizona Univ., Tucson. Inst. of Atmospheric Physics.
For primary bibliographic entry see Field 2B.
W75-07049

THE ELECTRICAL ANISOTROPY OF SEA ICE IN THE HORIZONTAL PLANE,
Geophysical Survey Systems, Inc., North Billerica, Mass.
K. J. Campbell, and A. S. Orange.
Journal of Geophysical Research, Vol 79, No 33, p 5059-5063, November 20, 1974. 6 fig, 7 ref.

Descriptors: *Sea ice, *Ice, Measurement, Instrumentation, Radar, *Anisotropy, Ice-water interfaces, Physical properties, *Canada, *Arctic, Electrical properties.
Identifiers: *Electrical anisotropy.

Sea ice electrical anisotropy in the horizontal plane was observed with an impulse radar technique under development for profiling ice thickness. The radar technique used can be considered the electromagnetic equivalent of acoustic subbottom profiling methods. The anisotropy phenomenon was characterized by a marked change in amplitide of the vertically propagated signal reflected from the sea ice/water interface as the linerarly polarized antenna was rotated in the horizontal plane on or above the ice surface. Anisotropy for both first-year and multiyear sea ice was observed in several areas of the Canadian Arctic. Additional experimental work is necessary to determine the nature of the anisotropy mechanism. (Sims-ISWS)
W75-07055

HAIL AND RAINDROP SIZE DISTRIBUTIONS FROM A SWISS MULTICELL STORM,
Eidgenoessische Technische Hochschule, Zuerich (Switzerland).
For primary bibliographic entry see Field 2B.
W75-07056

ICE SHELVES AND ICE FLOW,
Scott Polar Research Inst., Cambridge (England).
G. de Q. Robin.
Nature, Vol 253, No 5488, p 168-172, January 17, 1975. 2 fig, 16 ref.

Descriptors: *Glaciers, *Ice cover, Movement, *Velocity, *Antarctic, Remote sensing, Aircraft, Radar, Surveys, Measurement, Glaciology, Icebergs.
Identifiers: Ice shelves, Ice flow, *Ross Ice Shelf.

Of the 13,800,000 sq km of ice covering Antarctica, some 12,100,000 sq km lie on a rock base, while about 1,500,000 sq km are in the form of floating slabs of ice round the periphery of the continent. The largest of these is the Ross Ice Shelf. To provide the first data for planning the Ross Ice Shelf Project, extensive airborne soundings of the ice shelf were made. A new map of the thickness of the Ross Ice Shelf was based on profiling of the ice thickness by radio echo sounding from aircraft. Streamlines of ice flow were deduced from the thickness pattern and extrapolation of velocities upstream by the assumption of mass continuity. These data provide an insight into the importance of the momentum with which an ice stream enters the shelf for the overall velocity field. (Sims-ISWS)
W75-07059

RAINFALL AND SNOWMELT RUNOFF FROM INTERMEDIATE ELEVATION WATERSHEDS,
For primary bibliographic entry see Field 2A.
W75-07101

TEMPERATURE FIELD AND HEAT FLOW IN SNOW COVER,
M. A. Dolov, and M. Ch. Zalikhanov.
Available from the National Technical Information Service, Springfield, Va 22161 as TT-71-51011, $3.25 in paper copy, $2.25 in microfiche. TT 71-51011, 1974, 16 p, 3 fig, 5 tab, 7 ref. Translated from Trudy Nauchno-Issledovatelskogo Gidrometeorologicheskogo Instituta, No 22, p 178-186, 1966.

Descriptors: *Snow cover, *Temperature, *Heat flow, Snow, Snowpacks, Heat transfer, Thermal conductivity, Thermal properties.

Temperature distribution in snow cover and heat exchange of snow with the surrounding medium were studied for dry and wet snow. A very thick snow layer was broken into two and the temperature distribution and heat flow under these conditions were studied separately. The influence of the density of snow on its heat exchange with the surrounding medium was studied by molecular heat conductivity. Heat exchange between the snow cover and air actually depends on the density of snow and the range of temperature variation of the snow surface. Comparison of the heat flow of dry and wet snow of the same densities and temperature variations on the snow surface showed that heat flow in dry snow is approximately 20-30% less than that in wet snow. (Sims-ISWS)
W75-07170

ICE CLOUDS AT THE SUMMER POLAR MESOPAUSE,
National Oceanic and Atmospheric Administration, Boulder, Col. Aeronomy Lab.
For primary bibliographic entry see Field 2B.
W75-07257

THE INFLUENCE OF SNOWCOVER ON THE ATMOSPHERIC CIRCULATION AND ITS ROLE IN CLIMATIC CHANGE: AN ANALYSIS BASED ON RESULTS FROM THE NCAR GLOBAL CIRCULATION MODEL,
National Center for Atmospheric Research, Boulder, Colo.
For primary bibliographic entry see Field 2B.
W75-07267

THE IMPACTS OF SNOW ENHANCEMENT: TECHNOLOGY ASSESSMENT OF WINTER OROGRAPHIC SNOWPACK AUGMENTATION IN THE UPPER COLORADO RIVER BASIN,
Stanford Research Inst., Menlo Park, Calif.
For primary bibliographic entry see Field 3B.
W75-07333

2D. Evaporation and Transpiration

AN INSTRUMENT SYSTEM FOR ESTIMATION OF EVAPOTRANSPIRATION BY THE EDDY CORRELATION METHOD,
Idaho Univ., Moscow. Coll. of Forestry, Wildlife, and Range Sciences.
G. H. Belt, J. King, and E. Bailey.
Idaho Forest, Wildlife and Range Experiment Station, Station Paper Nov. 19, 16 p, December, 1974. 12 fig, 2 tab, 5 ref.

Descriptors: *Evapotranspiration, *Instrumentation, *On-site data collections, *Eddies, *Meteorological data, Anemometers, Humidity, Air temperature, Data collections, Forests, Calibrations, Electronic equipment, Remote sensing, Condensation, Hygrometry, On-site tests, Wind velocity, Air circulation.
Identifiers: Gill-type propeller anemometers, Brady-array humidity sensors, Metro-Data digital tape recorder.

A fast-response meteorological instrument system for measuring parameters used in calculating evapotranspiration above a forest stand is described. Comprised of Gill-type propeller anemometers, Brady-array humidity sensors, thermistor air-temperature sensors, and a Metro-Data digital tape recorder, the system was designed to measure eddy fluctuations in the range from 1 to 0.005 cycles/second. Details of signal conditioning circuitry for the Brady-array are presented along with a discussion of apparatus and techniques employed to calibrate the sensors as part of the instrument system. Problems with electrical noise and condensation within instrument packages which occurred during field trials are also discussed. (Witt-IPC)
W75-06894

THE EFFECT OF CONIFERS ON THE CHEMISTRY AND MASS BALANCE OF TWO LARGE LYSIMETERS IN CASTRICUM (THE NETHERLANDS),
Food and Agriculture Organization of the United Nations, Kitale (Kenya). Turkana Irrigation Project.
H. Ryckborst.
Journal of Hydrology, Vol 24, No 1/2, p 77-87, January 1975. 10 fig, 1 tab, 6 ref.

Descriptors: *Conifers, Chemistry, *Lysimeters, Drainage water, Dune sands, Rainfall, Vegetation, Infiltration, Evapotranspiration, Hydrogen ion concentration, Rain water, Water balance.
Identifiers: *Netherlands(Castricum).

A comparison of the quality of drainwater from dunesand in a bare lysimeter and in a lysimeter with growing conifers showed significant differences. Over a period of 16 years the vegetated lysimeter plot intercepted 24% more Cl(-), SO4(-) and Na(+) + K(+) ions from rainwater and aerosols than the bare plot. On the other hand, the conifers reduced the average output of Ca(++) and Mg(++) in drainwater by 13% and the total amount of NO3(-) in drainwater was reduced by a factor of 20. The pH value of drainwater decreased during periods of rainfall, while large amounts of Ca(++) and HC):(-) were leached out. The percentage of the rainfall that infiltrated through the bare sandy soil remained constant at 80% during 16 years. In contrast, the vegetated lysimeter drained 62% of the rain during its first year of operation. Thereafter a continuing decrease occurred over a period of 7 years, coinciding with increased growth and evapotranspiration of the conifers. After 7 years, the decrease in volume of recharged rainwater leveled off to 25% of the rainfall. From that period, the conifers did not grow nearly as well as the surrounding trees with free access to groundwater. (Roberts-ISWS)
W75-07052

EFFECTS OF ROOT MEDIUM AND WATERING ON TRANSPIRATION, GROWTH AND DEVELOPMENT OF GLASSHOUSE CROPS: III. EFFECT OF WATERING-FACTOR AND VOLUME OF ROOT MEDIUM ON YIELD AND QUALITY OF GREENHOUSE TOMATOES,
State Experiment Station Landvik, Grimstad (Norway).
G. Guttormsen.
Plant Soil. Vol 40, No 3, p 479-492. 1974, Illus.

Descriptors: *Tomatoes, Crops, Field crops, *Plant growth, Water greenhouses, *Water requirements, Peat, *Soil amendments, *Plant growth regulators, *Soil-water-plant relationships.

The effect of various watering factors and of peat volume on the growth and development of greenhouse tomatoes was investigated in 2 factorial experiments. The water-factors were determined on the basis of evaporation from a free water surface, where mm of water added/mm of evaporation = watering-factor. The watering-factors 1, 1.5, 2, 3 and 4.5 were combined with 14, 28 and 42 dm3 of peat/plant. The plants were grown under conditions which gave relatively much drainage water. An additive effect of watering-factor and volume was observed. The total yield and the size of the fruit were greatest with watering-factor 2-3. The effect of increase in volume was greatest between 14 and 28 dm3 of peat/plant. The main tendency was to a positive correlation between the total yield or fruit weight and the number of fruits with blotchy ripening or brown vascular bundles. The number of fruits with imperfect form was positively correlated with the number of hollow fruits and with the weight of the fruits. There was a positive correlation between weight of the fruit and hollowness. Moreover, there was a negative correlation between the number of perfect fruits and the total production, and between perfect friuts and the weight of the fruits. It was possible to use automated watering and peat in a standardized growing

by a decrease in leaf area density. The removal of the flower clusters increased both the vegetative growth and the root growth. It had no significant effect on E sub T. The influence of the plant factors on transpiration is of relatively minor importance in regard to the relationship between optimal water supply and E sub e, when cultivation is carried out in porous media with a sufficient supply of water, and under glasshouse conditions.--Copyright 1974, Biological Abstracts, Inc.
W75-07153

PROCEDURES FOR EVALUATING THE SURFACE WATER BALANCE OF GRAN CANARIA,
United Nations Development Program, Las Palmas de Gran Canaria (Spain),
L. E. Ahlgren, and H. J. Van Der Zel.
Nordic Hydrology, Vol 5, No 4, p 229-246, 1974. 10 fig, 3 tab, 4 ref.

Descriptors: *Surface waters, *Evapotranspiration, *Water balance, Precipitation(Atmospheric), Runoff, Hydrology, Geologic formations, Recharge, Evaluation, Atlantic Ocean.
Identifiers: *Gran Canaria, Potential evapotranspiration, Class A pan evaporation.

Standard procedures were modified to fit local conditions in order to evaluate the surface water balance in Gran Canaria, a volcanic island 200 km off the west coast of Africa at latitude 28 degrees N. With a bookkeeping method, the terms of the balance equation were calculated on a daily basis. Precipitation was based on data from a limited number of representative stations. Runoff data were extrapolated by quantifying the characteristics of the geological formations by the SCS curve number method. Potential evapotranspiration data based on Class A pan measurements or Penman calculations were extrapolated by using the Blaney-Criddle method. Real evapotranspiration was calculated by using the Thornthwaite-Mather hypothesis. The results of this simplified procedure coincided well with the results of an independent evaluation of the recharge. (Roberts-ISWS)
W75-07194

EVAPOTRANSPIRATION AND PLANT PRODUCTION DIRECTLY RELATED TO GLOBAL RADIATION,
Royal Veterinary and Agriculture Coll., Copenhagen (Denmark). Hydrotechnical Lab.
H. C. Aslyng.
Nordic Hydrology, Vol 5, No 4, p 247-256, 1974. 5 fig, 16 ref.

Descriptors: *Evapotranspiration, *Radiation, Plant breeding, Regression analysis, Productivity, Plant growth, Latent heat, Lysimeters, Soil-water-plant-relationships, Vegetation.
Identifiers: *Global radiation, Net radiation.

This paper was based on the thesis that when sun radiation is not in excess and advected energy supply can be neglected, then for periods of plant cover and growth, both evapotranspiration and plant production are linearly and strongly related to global radiation. The regression coefficients will depend also on plant, soil, and other climatic factors, but global radiation is the dominating factor for potential evapotranspiration and potential plant production in given regions. Under comparable conditions different plant species and strains will result in different regression coefficients due to differences in genetic abilities. Potential evapotranspiration determined by a soil water balance study of well-developed and growing crops and by the Penman method was found to be strongly correlated even for daily values. The dry matter yield of a grass crop was found to be a linear function of global radiation throughout the growth period May to October. For each cutting, about 5 kcal/sq cm was found to be ineffective due to insufficient leaf cover. Cutting intervals of 4 weeks gave a lower total yield than intervals of 6 weeks. (Roberts-ISWS)
W75-07195

EVAPORATION DUE TO SPRAY,
Delaware Univ., Newark. Coll. of Marine Studies.
J. Wu.
Journal of Geophysical Research, Vol 79, No 27, p 4107-4109, September 20, 1974. 1 fig, 1 tab, 8 ref.

Descriptors: *Evaporation, *Sprays, *Drops(Fluids), Winds, Waves(Water), Wind velocity, Laboratory tests, Heat balance, Boundary layers, Laminar flow, Turbulent flow, Humidity.
Identifiers: *Wind-wave tank, Laser, Phototransistor.

Evaporation due to spray produced in a laboratory wind-wave tank was calculated from the measured droplet concentration and was found to increase drastically with wind velocity. A laser and phototransistor unit was used with a tank 1.5 m wide and 14 m long. An axial flow fan was installed at the upwind end and a permeable wave absorber located at the downwind end. The test section was at the middle length position. The tank was covered for the first 8 m to provide a 0.35-m deep air passage above 1.2-m deep water. The wind velocity near the water surface was found to vary logarithmically with the elevation above the mean water surface. The airflow boundary layer completed its transition from laminar to turbulent at the wind velocity of 2 m/s and became aerodynamically rough when the wind velocity in the tunnel was 14 m/s; intensive spray was initiated at a wind velocity of 9 m/s. The contribution of water vapor in the atmosphere surface layer from spray evaporation increased by more than 2 orders of magnitude over the narrow velocity range of the experiment. It appeared that evaporation would be mainly from droplets when the wind velocity is greater than 15 m/s. (Roberst-ISWS)
W75-07197

ESTIMATES OF TEMPERATURE AND PRECIPITATION FOR NORTHEASTERN UTAH,
Geological Survey, Salt Lake City, Utah.
For primary bibliographic entry see Field 4A.
W75-07241

A MEASUREMENT OF ALBEDO CHANGES RESULTING FROM AFFORESTATION FRACTICES,
Institute of Hydrology, Wallingford (England).
A. J. B. Baty, J. C. Rodda, and R. F. Templeman.
Hydrological Sciences Bulletin, Vol 18, No 4, p 451-458, December 1973. 3 fig, 2 tab, 12 ref.

Descriptors: *Albedo, *Evaporation, *Forest management, Radiation, Heat balance, Environmental effects, Meteorology, Instrumentation, Electronic equipment, Solar radiation, Watersheds(Basins), Forest watersheds, On-site investigations, Small watersheds.
Identifiers: Solarimeters, *United Kingdom(England).

The measurement of albedo by portable battery-powered recorders before and after the ploughing of drainage ditches by the Forestry Commission on a small catchment in northern England was described. The change in the evaporation brought about by the reduction of the mean basin albedo from 15.2 plus or minus 0.7% to 13.1 plus or minus 0.8% would not in itself produce a significant change in the basin's hydrological behaviour. (Sims-ISWS)
W75-07265

2E. Streamflow and Runoff

MEAN ANNUAL RUNOFF IN THE SAN FRANCISCO BAY REGION, CALIFORNIA, 1931-70,
Geological Survey, Menlo Park, Calif.
For primary bibliographic entry see Field 7C.
W75-06936

THE USE OF STREAMFLOW MODELS IN PLANNING,
Harvard Univ., Boston, Mass. Graduate School of Business Administration.
For primary bibliographic entry see Field 6A.
W75-06949

RIVER AND ESTUARY MODEL ANALYSIS, VOLUME 3.
Proceedings of the International Association for Hydraulic Research Symposium on River Mechanics (4 Vol.), Bangkok, Thailand, January 9-12, 1973. Asian Institute of Technology, Bangkok, Thailand. 488 p. (1973).

Descriptors: *Conferences, *Hydraulic models, *Mathematical models, *Model studies, Rivers, Channels, Sediment transport, Estuaries, Floods, Flood plains, Hydrology, Water quality, Flood routing, Analog models, Inlets(Waterways), Surface waters, Flow Dispersion, Numerical analysis, Unsteady flow, Tidal streams, Tidal waters.
Identifiers: *River mechanics, Fixed bed models, Movable bed models.

River mechanics was discussed at a symposium held at Bangkok in 1973. The two broad topics discussed in Volume 3 were: (1) hydraulic modeling, and (2) mathematical modeling. (See W75-06999 thru W75-07037) (Humphreys-ISWS)
W75-06998

SIMULATION OF SEDIMENT TRANSPORT IN HYDRAULIC MODELS,
Technische Universitaet, Obernach (West Germany). Versuchsanstalt fuer Wasserbau-Oskar von Miller-Institut.
For primary bibliographic entry see Field 2J.
W75-06999

RIVER MODELS WITH A MOVABLE BED,
Queen's Univ., Kingston (Ontario). Dept. of Civil Engineering.
For primary bibliographic entry see Field 2J.
W75-07000

THE TIDAL REGIME OF THE ELBE-RIVER, HYDRAULIC MODEL WITH MOVABLE BED,
Bundesanstalt fur Wasserbau, Hamburg (West Germany).
For primary bibliographic entry see Field 2L..
W75-07001

A SMALL SCALE HYDRAULIC MODEL IN MARINE TRANSPORTATION STUDIES,
Canadian Marine Transportation Administration, Ottawa (Ontario).
For primary bibliographic entry see Field 2L.
W75-07002

STUDIES FOR CHALNA PORT IN THE DELTA OF GANGES RIVER,
Institut za Vodoprivredu Jaroslav Cerni, Belgrade (Yugoslavia). Hydraulic Lab.
For primary bibliographic entry see Field 8B.
W75-07003

LARGE MATERIAL MODELS IN WATERSHED HYDROLOGY RESEARCH,
Agricultural Research Service, Fort Collins, Colo.
For primary bibliographic entry see Field 2A.
W75-07004

COMBINATION OF A PHYSICAL AND A MATHEMATICAL RIVER MODEL WITH FIXED BED,
Bundesanstalt fuer Wasserbau, Karlsruhe (West Germany).
H. Dorer.
In: River and Estuary Model Analysis, Volume III; Proceedings of the International Association for Hydraulic Research Symposium on River Mechanics (4 Vol.), Bangkok, Thailand, January 9-12, 1973. Asian Institute of Technology, Bangkok, Thailand, p 75-83. (1973). 5 fig.

Descriptors: *Model studies, *River regulation, *River training, Hydraulic models, Mathematical models, Equations, Rivers, Navigation, Roughness coefficient.
Identifiers: *Federal Republic of Germany(River Rhine), Fixed bed model.

By combining a physical and a mathematical model, it is possible to do the model investigations in a shorter time and with lower costs than by using a physical model only. With a part of the River Rhine as an example, the mathematical model was described. The results both of the mathematical and the physical model were given for two examples. The mathematical model based upon the one-dimensional equation for gradually varied steady flow proved to be a useful method of investigation, even in cases of complicated flow conditions. By combining a mathematical and a physical model the efficiency of the model investigations, concerning a part of the Rhine with the aim of obtaining better conditions for navigation, was improved. It was possible to study a number of possible solutions of the river geometry in the mathematical model more quickly and at much lower costs than in the physical model. The solution obtained by the mathematical model proved to be quite near the final solution, only some little improvements being necessary in the physical model. (See also W75-06998) (Humphreys-ISWS)
W75-07005

RIVER SIMULATION BY CHANNEL NETWORK ANALYSIS,
Asian Inst. of Tech., Bangkok (Thailand). Div. of Water Science and Engineering.
N. L. Ackermann, and C-K. Chang.
In: River and Estuary Model Analysis, Volume III; Proceedings of the International Association for Hydraulic Research Symposium on River Mechanics (4 Vol.), Bangkok, Thailand, January 9-12, 1973. Asian Institute of Technology, Bangkok, Thailand, p 85-96. (1973). 6 fig, 1 tab, 3 ref.

Descriptors: *Model studies, *Rivers, *Analytical techniques, *Simulation analysis, Mathematical models, Open channels, Channel improvement, Stream improvement, Numerical analysis, Discharge(Water), Roughness coefficient, Networks, Navigation, Hydraulics.
Identifiers: *Laos(Mekong River), Channel network analysis.

An iteration procedure, somewhat similar to that used in the analysis of pipe networks, was developed to predict flow conditions in a system of interconnecting open channels. This procedure was used to study the flow in the Mekong River throughout a broad, shallow reach 2 kilometers in length where the river flows around numerous islands and submerged rock formations. The river was modeled as a system of interconnecting channels, the geometry of which was determined from data obtained from hydrographic surveys. Changes in the river geometry which were required to produce improved navigation conditions could be simulated in the model by making corresponding mathematical changes to the geometry of the channel network. The effects of planned channel improvements were computed and compared to results obtained from a hydraulic model investigation. The hydraulic characteristics of a broad shallow reach of the Mekong River was simulated by a system of interconnecting channels. (See also W75-06998 (Humphreys-Isws))
W75-07006

DETERMINATION OF DISCHARGE SCALE FOR A TIDAL MODEL OF A COMPLEX RIVER,
Irrigation and Power Research Station, Poondi (India).
For primary bibliographic entry see Field 2L.
W75-07007

SOME NOTES ON HYDRAULIC MODEL TESTS OF RIVER CHANNELS,
Public Works Research Inst., Kashima (Japan). Kashima Hydraulics Lab.
K. Suga.
In: River and Estuary Model Analysis, Volume III; Proceedings of the International Association for Hydraulic Research Symposium on River Mechanics (4 Vol.), Bangkok, Thailand, January 9-12, 1973. Asian Institute of Technology, Bangkok, Thailand, p 109-120. (1973). 5 fig, 2 tab, 4 ref.

Descriptors: *Hydraulic models, *Rivers, *Hydraulic similitude, Model studies, Calibrations, Channels, Scour, Sediment transport, River training, Channel improvement, Laboratory tests, Analytical techniques.
Identifiers: Fixed bed models, Movable bed models, Distorted models.

The problem of similarity laws for fixed and movable beds, new examination methods for verification of physical modeling, the methods for experiment planning, and other important matters obtained from experiences were described. For example, the special care in which the surface velocity distribution measured by aerial photography during a large flood was used for verification of the model, determination method for time scales of movable bed models by measuring the rates of sediment transport both at actual river and fundamental two dimensional channel, fundamental study on the effects of distortion of the models especially at curved reaches, and the effect of roughness of sidewall on the local erosion were discussed. From the view point of actual performance of model tests, general experimental techniques developed at Kashima Hydraulics Laboratory were presented. The results of experiments have been applied to the designs of actual river channels with favorable results. Studies on development of new bed materials and experiment methods for rivers which have few fields data were recommended. (See also W75-06998) (Humphreys-ISWS)
W75-07008

MODELING AND ANALYSIS OF FLOODS THROUGH FLOOD PLAINS,
California State Univ., Sacramento. Dept. of Civil Engineering.
A. L. Prasuhn.
In: River and Estuary Model Analysis, Volume III; Proceedings of the Internationl Association for Hydraulic Research Symposium on River Mechanics (4 Vol.), Bangkok, Thailand, January 9-12, 1973. Asian Institute of Technology, Bangkok, Thailand, p 121-132. (1973). 5 fig, 3 tab, 1 ref.

Descriptors: *Model studies, *Flood plains, *Rivers, Flood stages, Overflow, River flow, Overland flow, Banks, Flood flow, Hydraulic models, Hydraulics, Laboratory tests, Roughness coefficient, Orchards, Trees, Analysis, Roughness(Hydraulic), Land use, *California.
Identifiers: Hedgerows.

A model study was undertaken to evaluate the hydraulic effects of increased tree concentrations in orchards planted on the overbank portions of river systems. Procedures were developed to predict the resulting river depth and resistance adjustments based on the flood plain model data. It was

Descriptors: *Model studies, *Design, *Rivers, *Estuaries, *Systems analysis, Mathematical models, Equations, Computer models, Forecasting, Floods, Water pollution, Water quality, Distribution patterns, Water management(Applied), River basins, Flow, *Computer programs.
Identifiers: One-dimensional flow, One-layer fluid.

A design system is an ensemble of computer routines organized into a single program-documentation entity that can build any model of a particular type and run this model when presented only with the topographical description of the model and the initial and boundary data. The System 11, 'Siva,' of the Computational Hydraulics Centre in Copenhagen, is such a design system, capable of constructing mathematical models of any one-dimensional flow of a one-layer (vertically homogeneous) fluid. It can be used to model rivers, estuaries, fjords, certain lakes, and similar bodies of water, with the objectives of forecasting floods or pollution levels or for various other purposes of river basin management. Partial differential equations upon which System 11 is based were given. Applications of System 11, 'Siva' were discussed. (See also W75-06998)
(Humphreys-ISWS)
W75-07016

THE APPLICATION OF RIVER SYSTEM MECHANICS,
Hawaii Univ., Honolulu. Dept. of Civil Engineering.
Y-S. Fok.
In: River and Estuary Model Analysis, Volume III; Proceedings of the International Association for Hydraulic Research Symposium on River Mechanics (4 Vol.), Bangkok, Thailand, January 9-12, 1973. Asian Institute of Technology, Bangkok, Thailand, p 215-226, (1973). 15 ref.

Descriptors: *River systems, *Systems analysis, *Model studies, Dynamics, Channel morphology, Erosion, Rivers, River basins, Meanders, Travel time.
Identifiers: *River mechanics, Statics, Kinematics, Hydraulic geometry, Stream order.

River system mechanics offers a systematic classification of the important parameters of a river system based on the basic dimensions involved. Equations of the statics, kinematics, and dynamics of the river system mechanics were presented in this sequence so that the nature of applications of these three areas of studies can be understood. All the equations presented were developed from a statistical method, therefore, each equation has its empirical constants which can be evaluated from measured data. The usefulness of the frequency of occurrence as an index to show the flow conditions in time was shown in many examples of application of the kinematics and dynamics of river system mechanics. However, since the frequency of occurrence is derived from the probabilistic process of the hydrological data, the sequential characteristics of such data were ignored. It was suggested that the stochastic process of hydrological data should be used to replace the probabilistic process, so that a time series may be incorporated to the kinematic or dynamic equations and the flow conditions can be predicted. Examples of river system studies discussed included: (1) stream-ordering systems for statics; (2) time of travel, and reaeration capacity for kinematics; and (3) river meanders, erosion rate, and dissolved load for dynamics. (See also W75-06998)
(Humphreys-ISWS)
W75-07017

ANALOG, DIGITAL AND HYBRID SIMULATION OF WATER LEVEL DISTRIBUTION IN OCCURRENCES OF FLOODS IN A SYSTEM RIVER FLOOD PLAIN,
Technische Universitaet, Hanover (West Germany). Institut fuer Wasserwirtschaft, Hydrologie und Landwirtschaftlichen Wasserbau.
P. Homagk, and R. Mull.
In: River and Estuary Model Analysis, Volume III; Proceedings of the International Association for Hydraulic Research Symposium on River Mechanics (4 Vol.), Bangkok, Thailand, January 9-12, 1973. Asian Institute of Technology, Bangkok, Thailand, p 227-237, (1973). 5 fig, 7 ref.

Descriptors: *Model studies, *Flood stages, *Hybrid computers, Rivers, Floods, *Water levels, Analog models, *Computer models, Theoretical analysis, Flood plains, Simulation analysis, Distribution.

Manning's formula was applied to simulation of water flow in a quasi one-dimensional system of a river and its flood plain. The greatest deviation between the simulated water level distribution by analog and digital procedures was about 10 cm. There were two main reasons for the differences: (1) the mesh size (40 m) of the digital procedure was half the size used in the analog model (80 m) and (2) on the analog network all resistances were changed only 5 times, whereas 13 steps were necessary for the digital procedure with an over-relaxation factor 1.41 to get a difference of less than 1 cm between the calculated water levels of the 13th and 14th step. A better result was expected with variable mesh sizes. As a result of these investigations, a hybrid simulator was constructed to solve steady and nonsteady flow problems. The computer is an RC-network of variable resistances and capacitances. A processor adjusts the units according to a given characteristic. To measure voltages and to change resistances, an adequate interface connects the analog and the digital components. (See also W75-06998)
(Humphreys-ISWS)
W75-07018

DESIGNING BY OBJECTIVES, A SIMULATION STUDY ON THE RIVER YOM IN NORTHERN THAILAND,
MacDonald (Murdoch) and Partners, London (England).
For primary bibliographic entry see Field 4A.
W75-07019

THE STOCHASTIC METHOD IN RIVER MECHANICS,
Pittsburgh Univ., Pa. Dept. of Civil Engineering.
C-L. Chiu, and T. S. Lee.
In: River and Estuary Model Analysis, Volume III; Proceedings of the International Association for Hydraulic Research Symposium on River Mechanics (4 Vol.), Bangkok, Thailand, January 9-12, 1973. Asian Institute of Technology, Bangkok, Thailand, p 251-262, (1973). 2 fig, 9 ref. NFS Grant GK 30845.

Descriptors: *Model studies, *Stochastic processes, *River beds, Statistical models, Mathematical models, Equations, Shape, Rivers, Simulation analysis, Sediment transport, Roughness(Hydraulic), Velocity, Depth, Cross-sections, Hydrographs.
Identifiers: *Transport processes, River mechanics, River geometry.

A stochastic method of analyzing, modeling, and simulating irregular cross sections of a river was reported, which has proved adequate in case studies. A parameter, K, found from the stochastic analysis and case studies, was presented as the roughness index of irregular bed forms of a river and as the generator of the variances, for given simulation intervals, of stochastic variables which are building blocks of irregular river cross sections to be simulated. K was defined as K squared = 1/2 of 'diffusion coefficient' in one-dimensional diffusion equation or K = h sub w/square root of L, where L sub w is height of bed form and L is length of bed form. Emphasized was the concept of using quantities associated with the stochastically simulated river cross sections as inputs to the deterministic, hydrodynamic systems (equations)

of transport processes. Such a coupling of the stochastic and deterministic techniques enables the utilization of their combined strength while complementing their individual weaknesses. (See also W75-06998) (Humphreys-ISWS)
W75-07020

FLOOD-ROUTING IN NON-PRISMATIC CHANNELS USING AN IMPLICIT METHOD OF SOLUTION,
Liverpool Univ. (England). Dept. of Civil Engineering.
A. R. Halliwell, and M. Ahmed.
In: River and Estuary Model Analysis, Volume III; Proceedings of the International Association for Hydraulic Research Symposium on River Mechanics (4 Vol.), Bangkok, Thailand, January 9-12, 1973. Asian Institute of Technology, Bangkok, Thailand, p 263-274, (1973). 5 fig, 4 ref.

Descriptors: *Flood routing, *Gradually varied flow, *Open channel flow, Mathematical studies, Equations, Unsteady flow, Finite element analysis, Analysis, Analytical techniques, Continuity equation, Momentum equation, Numerical analysis, Open channels, Flood stages, Flood profiles.
Identifiers: Nonprismatic channels, Implicit method.

The one-dimensional equations of gradually-varied unsteady flow in nonprismatic open channels were presented and discussed. The equations were numerically integrated with the aid of an implicit scheme. Approximations to the equations were made with a centered finite-difference technique which resulted in a series of nonlinear simultaneous equations. These were solved by the generalized iteration method of Newton. In order to study the passage of flood waves along a number of different channels, a program was written in Fortran for use with the KDF 9 electronic digital computer. Simple prismatic channels were considered to test the program and the numerical scheme. Examples of converging and diverging channels were given. When compared with water depths in prismatic channels, the depth increased for converging channels and decreased for diverging channels. (See also W75-06998) (Humphreys-ISWS)
W75-07021

MATHEMATICAL MODEL OF MEKONG RIVER NEAR VIENTIANE AND NONGKHAI,
Asian Inst. of Tech., Bangkok (Thailand). Div. of Water Science and Engineering.
S. Pinkayan, N. L. Ackermann, and T. Tingsanchali.
In: River and Estuary Model Analysis, Volume III; Proceedings of the International Association for Hydraulic Research Symposium on River Mechanics (4 Vol.), Bangkok, Thailand, January 9-12, 1973. Asian Institute of Technology, Bangkok, Thailand, p 291-302, (1973). 7 fig, 1 ref.

Descriptors: *Model studies, *Floods, *Rivers, *Mathematical models, Hydrographs, Calibrations, Overflow, Flood plains, River flow, Flood stages, Numerical analysis, Return flow, Water levels.
Identifiers: *Mekong River(Laos-Thailand).

The water surface elevations produced by flood flows in the Mekong River near Vientiane, Laos, and Nongkhai, Thailand, were mathematically simulated. The flow in the main channel was determined by a numerical solution of the unsteady free surface flow equations. Spatially varied discharges resulting from overbank flows both into and out of the main channel were considered. The overbank spill into the flood plain was determined by using a modified weir equation in which the lateral discharge was proportional to the 3/2 power of the difference in the elevations between the water level in the main channel and the river bank. The return flow was considered as a function of the storage in the flood plain. This functional relationship which characterized the flood plain was determined empirically from model calibration. Flows resulting from severe floods in the Mekong River which occurred in 1966 and 1971 were simulated. A reasonable agreement existed between the computed and observed water surface elevations. (See also W75-06998) (Humphreys-ISWS)
W75-07023

MODELING RIVER AND ESTUARY UNSTEADY FLOW SYSTEMS,
Utah State Univ., Logan. Dept. of Civil Engineering.
C-L. Chen, and M-S. Chu.
In: River and Estuary Model Analysis, Volume III; Proceedings of the International Association for Hydraulic Research Symposium on River Mechanics (4 Vol.), Bangkok, Thailand, January 9-12, 1973. Asian Institute of Technology, Bangkok, Thailand, p 303-314, (1973). 2 fig, 25 ref.

Descriptors: *Rivers, *Estuaries, *Model studies, *Finite element analysis, Numerical analysis, Mathematical models, Equations, Flow, *Unsteady flow, Bores, Surges, Dam failure, Rupturing, Dry beds, Streambeds, Flood waves, Waves(Water), Beaches.
Identifiers: Breaking waves, Explicit method.

Mathematical models of river and estuary unsteady flow systems, which consists of both gradually varied and rapidly varied unsteady flow equations, were solved in finite difference form. An explicit finite difference scheme with specified rectangular grid intervals based on the method of characteristics was formulated for numerical solution. A technique was developed for tracing bores or surges for which the method of characteristics fails to hold because characteristics cross each other. A simplifying assumption was introduced to overcome the singularity problem that is inherent at the leading tip of a wavefront moving on a dry bed. Several typical computer results were obtained by solving the dam-breaking problem and coastal breaking wave problem. It was demonstrated how the proposed numerical techniques can validly be applied to many practical problems of similar nature. Completion of this computer modeling of unsteady flow systems was believed to be very useful to the future study of dispersion and flushing of pollutant in rivers and homogeneous estuaries. (See also W75-06998) (Humphreys-ISWS)
W75-07024

MATHEMATICAL INVESTIGATION OF A TIDAL RIVER,
Calcutta Port Commissioners (India). Hydraulic Study Dept.
For primary bibliographic entry see Field 2L.
W75-07025

THEORETICAL STUDIES OF LONG WAVE PROPAGATION IN ESTUARIES OF FINITE LENGTH,
Birmingham Univ. (England). Dept. of Civil Engineering.
For primary bibliographic entry see Field 2L.
W75-07026

FLOOD ROUTING FOR URBAN RIVER NETWORK,
Osaka Univ. (Japan). Dept. of Civil Engineering.
A. Murota, T. Kanda, and T. Eto.
In: River and Estuary Model Analysis, Volume III; Proceedings of the International Association for Hydraulic Research Symposium on River Mechanics (4 Vol.), Bangkok, Thailand, January 9-12, 1973. Asian Institute of Technology, Bangkok, Thailand, p 339-350, (1973). 7 fig.

Descriptors: *Flood routing, *Model studies, *Mathematical models, *Tidal streams, Simulation analysis, Finite element analysis, Tidal effects,

For primary bibliographic entry see Field 5B.
W75-07032

MATHEMATICAL MODELLING FOR SHORT-TERM TRANSPORT IN VERTICALLY MIXED ESTUARIES,
Madras Univ., Guindy (India). Dept. of Hydraulic Engineering.
For primary bibliographic entry see Field 2L.
W75-07033

CHARACTERISTICS OF THE INTERFACIAL REGION OF A TWO-LAYER FLOW SYSTEM,
Melbourne Univ., Parkville (Australia). Dept. of Civil Engineering.
For primary bibliographic entry see Field 2L.
W75-07034

A MATHEMATICAL MODEL TO PREDICT DISCHARGE VARIATIONS IN AN ESTUARY WITH SHALLOW WATER AND A LARGE TIDAL RANGE,
Ente Nazionale per l'Energia Elettrica, Milan (Italy).
For primary bibliographic entry see Field 2L.
W75-07035

FINITE ELEMENT NUMERICAL MODELLING OF FLOW AND DISPERSION IN ESTUARIES,
University Coll. of Swansea (Wales). Dept. of Civil Engineering.
For primary bibliographic entry see Field 2L.
W75-07036

UNSTEADY FLOW IN OPEN CHANNEL WITH MOVABLE BED,
National Taiwan Univ., Taipei.
C. M. Wu.
In: River and Estuary Model Analysis, Volume III; Proceedings of the International Association for Hydraulic Research Symposium on River Mechanics (4 Vol.), Bangkok, Thailand, January 9-12, 1973. Asian Institute of Technology, Bangkok, Thailand, p 477-488, (1973). 2 fig, 1 tab, 8 ref, 1 append.

Descriptors: *Model studies, *Unsteady flow, *Sediment transport, Open channels, Channel morphology, Beds, Sediments, Streambeds, Flow, Channel flow, Fluid mechanics, Mathematical studies, Theoretical analysis, Mathematics, Equations.
Identifiers: *Movable bed.

A mathematical model for simulating the joint mechanism of unsteady sediment and water flow was presented. This model is based on a treatment of the basic set of partial differential equations for one-dimensional, unsteady, movable bed open-channel flow with homogeneous density. The method of characteristics transforms the basic set of partial differential equations into a set of ordinary differential equations with three different sets of slope. These three new equations are subsequently treated as finite difference equations, and solutions of the unsteady problem are readily possible with the aid of the known boundary or previous conditions. (See also W75-06998) (Sims-ISWS)
W75-07037

GENERAL REPORTS, DISCUSSIONS, LECTURES, VOLUME 4.
For primary bibliographic entry see Field 2J.
W75-07038

THE INTERACTION OF VELOCITY DISTRIBUTION AND SUSPENDED LOAD IN TURBULENT STREAMS,
Massachusetts Inst. of Tech., Cambridge. Ralph M. Parsons Lab. for Water Resources and Hydrodynamics.
For primary bibliographic entry see Field 2J.
W75-07039

APPLICATION OF PHYSICAL AND MATHEMATICAL MODELS FOR RIVER PROBLEMS,
Waterloopkundig Laboratorium, Delft (Netherlands).
For primary bibliographic entry see Field 2A.
W75-07040

1973 WATER RESOURCES DATA FOR OREGON, SURFACE WATER RECORDS, PRECIPITATION RECORDS,
Oregon State Water Resources Board, Salem.
For primary bibliographic entry see Field 7C.
W75-07150

INFLUENCE OF FLOOD WAVES OF MOUNTAIN RIVERS ON DRIFT DISCHARGE,
A. F. Mandych.
Available from the National Technical Information Service, Springfield, Va 22161 as TT-72-51105, $3.25 in paper copy, $2.25 in microfiche. TT 72-51105, 1974, 6 p, 1 fig, 2 tab, 5 ref. Translated from Meteorologiya i Gidrologiya, Vol 2, p 41-43, 1966.

Descriptors: *Rivers, *Flood waves, *Erosion, *Turbidity, Surges, River flow, Runoff, Fluvial sediments, Sediment discharge, Sediments, Flood discharge, Potamology.
Identifiers: USSR.

Violent, fast-moving floods resulting from heavy showers in summer and autumn in mountain rivers Adzhariya and Guriya are very close in hydraulic properties to positive forward-traveling displacement waves, the peculiarities of which have been studied with reference to the sudden rush of water into the tail bays of hydroelectric powerplants. A steep head front is inherent to a forward-traveling displacement wave; in the region of this front, the velocities of the current and particularly the bottom velocities attain maximum values. Consequently, the river flow in the zone of wave front has a highly increased washing and transporting ability. The turbidity of water, and consequently the drift discharge, increase appreciably due to the movement of the wave resulting from the inflow of water. (Sims-ISWS)
W75-07164

THE CHARACTER OF CHANNEL MIGRATION ON THE BEATTON RIVER, NORTHEAST BRITISH COLUMBIA, CANADA,
Simon Fraser Univ., Burnaby (British Columbia). Dept. of Geography.
For primary bibliographic entry see Field 2J.
W75-07191

FLASH FLOOD POTENTIAL FROM CHANNEL MEASUREMENTS,
Geological Survey, Reston, Va.
For primary bibliographic entry see Field 4A.
W75-07203

A METHOD FOR ESTIMATING MAGNITUDE AND FREQUENCY OF FLOODS IN SOUTH DAKOTA,
Geological Survey, Huron, S. Dak.
For primary bibliographic entry see Field 4A.
W75-07211

A HYDROLOGIC ASSESSMENT OF THE SEPTEMBER 14, 1974, FLOOD IN ELDORADO CANYON, NEVADA,
Geological Survey, Carson City, Nev.
P. A. Glancy, and L. Harmsen.
Open-file report 75-14, December 1974. 69 p, 26 fig, 5 tab, 9 ref.

Descriptors: *Flash floods, *Thunderstorms, *Nevada, *Disasters, Sediment transport, Erosion, Flood damage, Peak discharge, Flood waves.
Identifiers: *Eldorado Canyon(Nev).

A devastating flash flood of thundershower origin struck Eldorado Canyon, a 22.9 square-mile drainage with a past flooding history, in southern Nevada at about 2:30 p.m., September 14, 1974. The severe runoff resulted from intense basinwide rain and hail at rates up to 3 inches of precipitation per half hour. The storm moved downbasin and generally increased in intensity with time, which compounded runoff rates. Peak discharge was estimated to be 76,000 cfs just upstream from the developed area near the canyon mouth. About 2,000 acre-feet of runoff reached Lake Mohave, the canyon terminus. Runoff dumped an estimated 70,000 cu yd (about 100,000 tons) of inorganic sediment in Lake Mohave and throughout the lowermost canyon reach. It also delivered an estimated 4 acre-feet of organic or floating debris to Lake Mohave. Although the recurrence interval for this magnitude runoff is great, a similar event could occur in any given year. With proper understanding and informed planning, the risk of damage from similar floods in the future can be greatly reduced. (Knapp-USGS)
W75-07214

INDEX OF FLOOD MAPS FOR CALIFORNIA PREPARED BY THE U.S. GEOLOGICAL SURVEY THROUGH 1974,
Geological Survey, Menlo Park, Calif.
For primary bibliographic entry see Field 7C.
W75-07216

FLOODS OF SEPTEMBER-OCTOBER 1967 IN SOUTH TEXAS AND NORTHEASTERN MEXICO,
Geological Survey, Reston, Va.
E. E. Schroeder, R. U. Grozier, D. C. Hahl, and A. E. Hulme.
Available from Supt. of Documents, GPO, Washington, D.C. 20402, for $3.55. (paper cover) Water-Supply Paper 1880-B, 1974. 52 fig, 3 plate, 17 tab, 8 ref.

Descriptors: *Floods, *Hurricanes, *Texas, *Mexico, Groundwater, Storm runoff, Water levels, Rainfall, Flood data, Hydrological data, Floodwater, Historic floods, Streamflow.

Floods produced by Hurricane Beulah during September and October 1967 in Texas and Mexico were outstanding because of the magnitude of the stage and discharge and because of the number of river basins affected. Previously known maximum stages were exceeded, at the downstream station, in five river basins in Texas by amounts ranging from 2.7 feet at Guadelupe River near Tivoli to 9.2 feet at Aransas River near Skidmore. The greatest relative maximum discharge recorded during the storm occurred at Medio Creek near Beeville, where the peak discharge was 4.1 times the previous maximum since 1919 and 6.0 times the magnitude of a regional 50-year flood. Because of the large volume of fresh-water inflow to bays and estuaries along the Texas coast, the salinity of the water was greatly reduced. Hurricane Beulah caused significant rises in water levels in shallow wells by percolation of rainfall and ponded waters and by the cascading of floodwaters directly into numerous inundated wells. Flooding along the Rio Grande and its floodways below Falcon Dam was the greatest since the American floodway system was completed in 1926. Flooding along the Mexican floodways destroyed all stream-gaging equipment. A 4,000-square-mile area of south Texas having no defined drainage system contains thousands of shallow wind-formed depressions. These normally dry depressions were inundated by the storm runoff, which produced a vast amount of ponded water. Rainfall measurements of 25 inches during the period September 19-25, 1967, were common in Texas, and as much as 35 inches was measured in Mexico. (Knapp-USGS)

W75-07219

SURFACE WATER FEATURES OF FLORIDA,
Geological Survey, Tallahassee, Fla.
For primary bibliographic entry see Field 7C.
W75-07221

INDEX OF SURFACE WATER STATIONS IN TEXAS, OCTOBER 1974.
Geological Survey, Austin, Tex.
For primary bibliographic entry see Field 7C.
W75-07224

PHYSIOGRAPHIC MAP OF THE OKALOACOOCHEE SLOUGH IN COLLIER COUNTY, FLORIDA,
Geological Survey, Miami, Fla.
For primary bibliographic entry see Field 7C.
W75-07225

FLOOD MAPPING IN CHARLOTTE AND MECKLENBURG COUNTY, NORTH CAROLINA,
Geological Survey, Charlotte, N.C.
For primary bibliographic entry see Field 4A.
W75-07230

WATER RESOURCES INVESTIGATIONS IN FLORIDA, 1974.
Geological Survey, Reston, Va.
For primary bibliographic entry see Field 7C.
W75-07231

STREAMFLOW CHARACTERISTICS IN NORTHEASTERN UTAH AND ADJACENT AREAS,
Geological Survey, Salt Lake City, Utah.
For primary bibliographic entry see Field 7C.
W75-07232

HYDROLOGIC UNIT MAP--1974, STATE OF WEST VIRGINIA.
Geological Survey, Reston, Va.
For primary bibliographic entry see Field 7C.
W75-07234

HYDROLOGIC UNIT MAP--1974, STATE OF INDIANA.
Geological Survey, Reston, Va.
For primary bibliographic entry see Field 7C.
W75-07235

HYDROLOGIC UNIT MAP--1974, STATE OF PENNSYLVANIA.
Geological Survey, Reston, Va.
For primary bibliographic entry see Field 7C.
W75-07236

HYDROLOGIC UNIT MAP--1974, STATE OF OHIO.
Geological Survey, Reston, Va.
For primary bibliographic entry see Field 7C.
W75-07237

MAP SHOWING DRAINAGE AREAS, MIDDLETOWN QUADRANGLE, CONNECTICUT,
Geological Survey, Hartford, Conn.
For primary bibliographic entry see Field 7C.
W75-07239

FRICTIONAL EFFECTS IN SIDE CHANNEL SPILLWAYS WITH INCREASING DISCHARGE,
Connecticut Univ., Storrs. Inst. of Water Resources.
For primary bibliographic entry see Field 8B.
W75-07274

2F. Groundwater

A SURROGATE-PARAMETER APPROACH TO MODELING GROUNDWATER BASINS,
Colorado State Univ., Fort Collins. Dept. of Civil Engineering.
J. W. Labadie.
Water Resources Bulletin, Vol 11, No 1, p 97-114, February 1975. 5 fig, 13 ref.

Descriptors: *Groundwater basins, *Management, *Simulation analysis, *Methodology, *Model studies, Water demand, Evaluation, Optimization, Pumping, Wells, Constraints, Storage, Equations, Systems analysis, *Hydrogeology.
Identifiers: Parameter identification, Surrogate-parameter approach, Least squares error criterion, Problem decomposition, Finite difference models, Duality theory, Gradient method, Transmissibility.

A surrogate-parameter approach to modeling groundwater basins can be efficiently utilized for systematic evaluation of management alternatives. How such a model can be calibrated or identified using optimization techniques is illustrated. A least-squares error criterion is used in formulating the mathematical programming problem for parameter identification; since the problem is large-scale and nonconvex, it is subsequently decomposed via duality theory into several smaller subproblems. A hypothetical problem involving four interacting wells is solved, where transmissibility coefficients are assumed known and storage coefficients determined through solution of the resulting dual problem. A second-order gradient method is used for the nonconvex subproblems so that globality of subproblem solutions during intermediate iterations of the dual problems cannot be guaranteed. In spite of this, results show that convergence to a saddle-point is rapid. The surrogate-parameter approach has the following advantages over current simulation approaches to groundwater basin modeling: (1) conduciveness to modeling nonhomogeneous and nonisotropic basins; (2) less arbitrariness; (3) model amenability to systematic calibration or identification through the use of optimization techniques; and (4) compatibility with systematic algorithms for analyzing a wide range of management strategies. (Bell-Cornell)
W75-06960

EFFECT OF MINING OPERATIONS ON GROUNDWATER LEVELS IN THE NEW LEAD BELT MISSOURI,
Missouri Univ., Rolla. Dept. of Geological Engineering.
For primary bibliographic entry see Field 4B.
W75-06986

SEDIMENTOLOGY OF AQUIFERS OF THE TONGUE RIVER FORMATION, NORTH DAKOTA,
North Dakota Univ., Grand Forks. Dept. of Geology.
For primary bibliographic entry see Field 4B.
W75-06993

GROUNDWATER OF SOUTHEASTERN VIRGINIA.
Virginia State Water Control Board, Richmond. Bureau of Water Control Management.
For primary bibliographic entry see Field 4B.
W75-07044

GEOTHERMAL DRILLING IN KLAMATH FALLS, OREGON,
Storey (E. E.) Well Drilling, Klamath Falls, Oreg.
For primary bibliographic entry see Field 8B.
W75-07146

OPTIMUM DEVELOPMENT OF GROUND WATER FROM THE COASTAL AQUIFERS OF DELAWARE; WHERE, HOW MUCH, AND FOR HOW LONG CAN WE SAFELY PUMP OUR COASTAL AQUIFERS,
Delaware Univ., Newark. Water Resources Center.
For primary bibliographic entry see Field 4B.
W75-07149

MAJOR AND HISTORICAL SPRINGS OF TEXAS,
Texas Water Development Board, Austin.
For primary bibliographic entry see Field 4B.
W75-07152

RATE OF SULFURIC-ACID PRODUCTION IN YELLOWSTONE NATIONAL PARK,
Wisconsin Univ., Madison. Dept. of Bacteriology.
For primary bibliographic entry see Field 2K.
W75-07189

ERTS IMAGERY FOR GROUND-WATER INVESTIGATIONS,
Geological Survey, Bay Saint Louis, Miss. Gulf Coast Hydroscience Center.
For primary bibliographic entry see Field 7B.
W75-07208

SIMULATED DRAWDOWN FOR SELECTED WELL FIELDS IN THE OHIO RIVER ALLUVIAL AQUIFER,
Geological Survey, Louisville, Ky.
For primary bibliographic entry see Field 4B.
W75-07209

HYDROLOGIC- AND SALT-BALANCE INVESTIGATIONS UTILIZING DIGITAL MODELS, LOWER SAN LUIS REY RIVER AREA, SAN DIEGO COUNTY, CALIFORNIA,
Geological Survey, Menlo Park, Calif.
For primary bibliographic entry see Field 5B.
W75-07212

GROUND-WATER DATA, 1973, INDIAN WELLS VALLEY, CALIFORNIA,
Geological Survey, Menlo Park, Calif.
For primary bibliographic entry see Field 4B.
W75-07215

QUALITY OF THE GROUND WATER IN BASALT OF THE COLUMBIA RIVER GROUP, WASHINGTON, OREGON, AND IDAHO,
Geological Survey, Reston, Va.
For primary bibliographic entry see Field 2K.
W75-07217

GROUND-WATER WITHDRAWALS IN THE UPPER PEACE AND UPPER ALAFIA RIVER BASINS, FLORIDA,
Geological Survey, Tallahassee, Fla.
For primary bibliographic entry see Field 7C.
W75-07222

ANNUAL REPORT ON GROUND WATER IN ARIZONA--WITH EMPHASIS ON GILA BEND BASIN, MCMULLEN VALLEY, AND THE SOUTHEAST PART OF THE HARQUAHALA PLAINS--SPRING 1973 TO SPRING 1974.
Geological Survey, Phoenix, Ariz.
For primary bibliographic entry see Field 4B.
W75-07223

HYDROLOGY AND GEOLOGY OF DEEP SANDSTONE AQUIFERS OF PENNSYLVANIAN AGE IN PART OF THE WESTERN COAL FIELD REGION, KENTUCKY,
Geological Survey, Louisville, Ky.
R. W. Davis, R. O. Plebuch, and H. M. Whitman.

Kentucky Geological Survey, University of Kentucky, Lexington, Series 10, Report of Investigations 15, 1974. 26 p, 9 fig, 11 plate, 1 tab, 17 ref.

Descriptors: *Hydrogeology, *Kentucky, *Water yield, *Aquifer characteristics, Mathematical models, Recharge, Sandstones, Coal mines, Mining, Water resources, Borehole geophysics.
Identifiers: Western Coal Field region(Ky).

Sandstone aquifers of Early Pennsylvanian age in the Western Coal Field region of Kentucky yield fresh water from wells as deep as 1,000 feet. The aquifer sands were deposited within valleys cut on the Late Mississippian surface and as deltaic and barrier-bar deposits that overlie both the Mississippian and earlier Pennsylvanian valley-filling deposits. Most of the aquifers have low transmissivity and storage properties, no perciptible recharge from the surface, and steadily declining water levels in the vicinity of centers of pumping. These characteristics were confirmed by a digital computer model. One aquifer which is not presently developed may have a potential yield as much as 300 gpm to individual wells and probably can receive recharge from the surface. Because of their poor hydrologic characteristics, the deep Pennsylvanian aquifers do not seem capable of supplying water for any large-scale economic development of the region. (Knapp-USGS)
W75-07228

HYDROLOGY OF THE SAND-AND-GRAVEL AQUIFER IN CENTRAL AND SOUTHERN ESCAMBIA COUNTY, FLORIDA, PRELIMINARY REPORT--NOVEMBER 1973,
Geological Survey, Tallahassee, Fla.
For primary bibliographic entry see Field 4B.
W75-07229

WATER RESOURCES INVESTIGATIONS IN FLORIDA, 1974.
Geological Survey, Reston, Va.
For primary bibliographic entry see Field 7C.
W75-07231

MAP SHOWING DEPTH TO WATER, ANCHORAGE AREA, ALASKA,
Geological Survey, Anchorage, Alaska.
For primary bibliographic entry see Field 7C.
W75-07238

CONTOUR MAP OF THE BEDROCK SURFACE, MOUNT HOLYOKE QUADRANGLE, MASSACHUSETTS,
Geological Survey, Boston, Mass.
For primary bibliographic entry see Field 7C.
W75-07240

DELINEATION OF BURIED GLACIAL-DRIFT AQUIFERS,
Geological Survey, Denver, Colo.
T. C. Winter.
Available from Supt. of Documents, GPO, Washington, D.C. 20402, $3.15 single copy. Journal of Research of the US Geological Survey, Vol 3, No 2, p 137-148, March-April 1975. 12 fig, 1 tab, 21 ref.

Descriptors: *Glacial aquifers, *Stratigraphy, *Aquifers, *Mapping, *Statistical methods, Hydrogeology, Glacial drift, Glacial sediments.

Locating and delineating buried glacial-drift aquifers poses one of the major problems to hydrogeologists working in glacial terrain. To show the vertical and horizontal boundaries of aquifers, most techniques require a multiple set of maps, a fence diagram, or a combination of maps and sections. Calculations of the first two moments (mean and standard deviation) of a discontinuous distribution result in values that represent the center of gravity (mean position) and spread (standard deviation) of all the sand units in a drill hole. Data for the moment method consist of depth to center point and thickness of each sand unit. A 2,600 sq mi area in northwestern Minnesota that contained 71 test holes drilled to bedrock was used to test the usefulness of the moment method in glacial terrain. Plots of relative position of center of gravity and relative spread showed three groupings for relative center of gravity (shallow, 0-26 percent, medium, 30-55, and deep 58-72) and three for spread of sand units (narrow, 1-5 percent, medium, 8-19, and wide, 22-38). The resulting vertical-variability pattern map shows the areas of each of the nine combinations of these two factors. Because the vertical-variability map does not show quantity of sand, the map is most informative if the total thickness of sand, or percent sand of total drift thickness, is recorded by each hole location on the map. The center or gravity is useful for describing the vertical position of the principal sand in a drill hole because it lies within the principal sand unit in 34 of the 63 holes that contained sand, and it is within 15 percent (based on total drift thickness) of the principal sand unit in 22 of the remaining 29 holes. (Knapp-USGS)
W75-07242

GEOLOGIC SETTING AND CHEMICAL CHARACTERISTICS OF HOT SPRINGS IN WEST-CENTRAL ALASKA,
Geological Survey, Anchorage, Alaska.
T. P. Miller, I. Barnes, and W. W. Patton, Jr.
Available from Supt. of Documents, GPO, Washington, D.C. 20402, $3.15 single copy. Journal of Research of the US Geological Survey, Vol 3, No 2, p 149-162, March-April 1975. 1 fig, 5 tab, 60 ref.

Descriptors: *Hot springs, *Geothermal studies, *Alaska, *Geochemistry, Thermal water, Mineral water, Water temperature, Water chemistry, Hydrogeology.

Numerous hot springs occur in a variety of geologic provinces in west-central Alaska. Granitic plutons are common to all the provinces, and the hot springs are spatially associated with the contacts of these plutons. Of 23 hot springs whose bedrock geology is known, all are within 4.8 km of a granitic pluton. The occurrence of hot springs, however, appears to be independent of the age, composition, or magmatic history of the pluton. Most of the analyzed hot springs appear to have chemical and isotopic compositions indicating that they were derived from deeply circulating meteoric water. About 25 percent of the analyzed hot springs show a distinct saline character with high concentrations of chloride, sodium, potassium, and calcium indicating either much more complex water-rock reactions that in the other hot springs or the addition of another type of water. Chemical geothermometers suggest subsurface temperatures in the general range of 70 deg to 160 deg C. If the hot spring waters have derived their heat solely from deep circulation, they must have reached depths of 2 to 5 km, assuming geothermal gradients of 30 deg to 50 deg C/km. If a shallow igneous heat source exists in the area or if dilution or mixing has occurred, these depths may be shallower. The geologic and chemical data, although preliminary, suggest that most of the hot springs of west-central Alaska have relatively low subsurface temperatures and limited reservoir capacities in comparison with geothermal areas presently being utilized for electrical power generation. The springs may, however, have some potential for limited power generation locally, if and when heat-exchange technology becomes available, as well as for space heating and agricultural uses. (Knapp-USGS)
W75-07243

THE USE OF THE DIGITAL SIMULATION LANGUAGE PDEL IN HYDROLOGIC STUDIES,
Wayne State Univ., Detroit, Mich. Dept. of Mathematics.
W. C. Tam, and W. J. Karplus.
Water Resources Bulletin, Vol 9, No 6, p 1100-1111, December 1973. 6 fig, 5 ref. OWRR B-150-CAL(12). NSF Grant GK31463X.

Descriptors: *Simulation analysis, *Computer programs, *Numerical analysis, *Groundwater movement, *Groundwater recharge, Aquifers, Dupuit-Forchheimer theory, Percolation, Analytical techniques, Equations, Hydrologic systems, Digital computers, Programming languages.
Identifiers: *Partial differential equations, PDEL computer program, Parabolic equations.

Digital simulation languages have become popular means for the simulation and analysis of systems on a digital computer. However, the use of these languages for the simulation of systems characterized by partial differential equations has been very limited. In hydrologic studies, mathematical models involving elliptic and parabolic partial differential equations are most common. The application of the digital simulation language PDEL to analyze problems in hydrologic studies was described. PDEL is designed specifically to solve partial differential equations of the elliptic, parabolic, and hyperbolic types. The language provides convenient and easy-to-learn statements for the description of problem to the computer. A computer program is automatically generated to solve the problem and the numerical solution printed and plotted. Two important hydrologic problems were used for illustration. The first was the analysis of groundwater table recession in large unconfined aquifers and the second was the growth of groundwater mounds in response to uniform percolation. (Singh-ISWS)
W75-07254

REPORT ON WATER SUPPLY, FORT HUACHUCA AND VICINITY, ARIZONA.
Army Engineer District, Los Angeles, Calif.
For primary bibliographic entry see Field 4B.
W75-07332

A RELATION BETWEEN GAMMA RADIATION AND PERMEABILITY, DENVER-JULESBERG BASIN,
Shell Oil Co., Denver, Colo.
For primary bibliographic entry see Field 4B.
W75-07335

2G. Water In Soils

CONTRIBUTIONS TO THE KNOWLEDGE OF BROWN ALLUVIAL SOILS IN THE LOWER FLOODPLAIN OF THE JIU RIVER,
Institutul de Studii si Cercetari Pedologie, Bucharest (Rumania).
I. Nitu, A. Ghita, and E. Ursuleac.
An Inst Stud Cercet Pedol, 39, p 295-311, 1971, Illus, English summary.

Descriptors: Europe, Soils, *Brown soils, *Flood plains, Alluvium, Soil(Physical properties), Soil(Chemical properties), *Soil analysis, Soil classification.
Identifiers: *Romania(Jiu River).

A characterization of natural conditions determining the development of brown alluvial soil in the lower flood-plain of the Jiu river (Romania) is presented. An important role in the development of these soils is displayed by the relief which, escaping the influence of flood, favors the continuity of the pedogenetic process. From the analysis of morphologic features and physico-chemical data an evident difference between brown alluvial soils and other alluvial soils was revealed. The

evolution of these soils towards the zonal ones is indicated by certain features as: depth of soils existence of certain horizons well defined by their color and structure, carbonate leaching, as well as humus distribution along the soil profile.--Copyright 1974, Biological Abstracts, Inc.
W75-06982

BACTERIAL METHANE OXIDATION AND ITS INFLUENCE IN THE AQUATIC ENVIRONMENT,
Ohio State Univ., Columbus. Dept. of Microbiology.
For primary bibliographic entry see Field 5B.
W75-06987

EARTH MANUAL, A WATER RESOURCES TECHNICAL PUBLICATION.
Bureau of Reclamation, Denver, Colo. Engineering and Research Center.
For primary bibliographic entry see Field 8D.
W75-07046

CHEMICAL ANALYSIS FOR EVALUATION OF SOIL SORPTION PROPERTIES,
Ontario Ministry of the Environment, Toronto. Pollution Control Branch.
For primary bibliographic entry see Field 5B.
W75-07058

THE DEPENDENCE OF BARE SOIL ALBEDO ON SOIL WATER CONTENT,
Agricultural Research Service, Phoenix, Ariz. Water Conservation Lab.
S. B. Idso, R. D. Jackson, R. J. Reginato, B. A. Kimball, and F. S. Nakayama.
Journal of Applied Meteorology, Vol 14, No 1, p 109-113, February 1975. 7 fig, 10 ref.

Descriptors: *Albedo, *Remote sensing, *Solar radiation, *Infrared radiation, *Soil moisture, Loam, Soil moisture meters, Gravity, Drainage, Air-earth interfaces, Soil water movement, Measurement, Evaporation.
Identifiers: *Microwave radiometers, *Zenith angle.

Simple albedo measurement may prove useful for sensing surface soil water content and as a research tool in the study of evaporation of water from soil. Intensive concurrent measurements of the albedo and soil water content of a drying bare soil indicated that albedo, normalized for sun zenith angle effects, is a linear function of the soil water content of a very thin surface layer (less than 0.2 cm thick) over a sizeable vilumetric water content range (0.00 to 0.18 for an Avondale loam). Albedo is also well correlated with the average soil water content of greater soil thicknesses. Measurements to a depth of 10 cm indicated that the relation is relatively independent of season. (Schicht-ISWS)
W75-07062

INFLUENCE OF SAMPLE DISTURBANCE AND TEST METHOD ON KEY ENGINEERING PROPERTIES OF MARINE SOILS,
Lehigh Univ., Bethlehem, Pa. Dept. of Civil Engineering.
M. Perlow, Jr.
Master's Thesis, June 1974. 65 p, 11 fig, 1 tab, 46 ref, 2 append. SG-NG-2-72, NSF-GA-37079, ONR N00014-67-A-370-005.

Descriptors: *Bulk density, *Environmental effects, Shear strength, Sediments, Gulf of Mexico, Bottom sediments, Ocean environments, Coasts, Engineering, Sampling, *Soils, *Testing.
Identifiers: *Vane shear strength, *Environmental impact, San Diego Trough, Wilkinson Basin, Abyssal Plain, Mississippi Delta, Marine soils, Gulf of Maine, Sediment properties.

Detailed measurements of bulk density and vane shear strength were made in situ and on gravity cores in the San Diego Trough, Wilkinson Basin, and Abyssal Plain and Mississippi Delta areas of the Gulf of Mexico. Comparisons of in situ and laboratory measurements were made to evaluate the influence of sample disturbance and test method on bulk density and vane shear strength. Location differences between in situ and gravity core locations and the associated areal variation of bulk density and vane shear strength were described in detail for all comparisons. The influence of sample disturbance on vane strength was difficult to evaluate because of differences in vane rotation rate and vane size between in situ and laboratory vane measurements. Large strength differences resulted from the great differences in angular shear velocity at the vane blade edges between in situ and laboratory vane measurements. A direct linear relationship between vane strength and angular shear velocity was found to exist in the Wilkinson Basin and San Diego Trough Test Areas. Comparison of in situ and laboratory vane strengths at a standar shear velocity, rather than a standard rotation rate, is proposed to eliminate uncertainties associated with rotation rate and vane size differences. A vane test procedure for both in situ and laboratory vane tests based on angular shear velocity is outlined. (NOAA)
W75-07074

MASS PHYSICAL PROPERTIES, SLIDING AND ERODIBILITY OF EXPERIMENTALLY DEPOSITED AND DIFFERENTLY CONSOLIDATED CLAYEY MUDS,
Tuebingen Univ. (West Germany). Geologisch-Palaontologisches Institut.
For primary bibliographic entry see Field 2J.
W75-07266

2H. Lakes

THE HELME-RESERVOIR NEAR KELBRA (KYFFHAEUSER, DDR): III. THE PLANKTON DURING 1967-1970 (IN GERMAN),
Martin Luther-Universitaet, Halle-Wittenberg (East Germany). Hygiene Institut.
Hermann Heynig.
Arch Protistenkd. Vol 114, No 1/2, p 14-33, 1972, Illus, English summary.

Descriptors: *Reservoirs, *Plankton, Europe, *Water quality.
Identifiers: *East Germany(Kelbra).

Some information about the reservoir near Kelbra (district of Halle) (East Germany) is given. Some aspects of the water quality and some general data about the plankton are given. The list of all organisms found in the plankton from 1967-1970 is followed by taxonomical and ecological observations on some interesting plankton organisms.--Copyright 1973, Biological Abstracts, Inc.
W75-06937

ON THE EFFICIENT ALLOCATION OF ENVIRONMENTAL ASSIMILATIVE CAPACITY: THE CASE OF THERMAL EMISSIONS TO A LARGE BODY OF WATER,
California Univ., Los Angeles. Dept. of Engineering Systems.
For primary bibliographic entry see Field 5B.
W75-06950

WATER MANAGEMENT--A GENERAL REPORT,
Illinois State Water Survey, Urbana.
For primary bibliographic entry see Field 4A.
W75-06953

MENTUM, AND WATER VAPOR OVER LAKE ONTARIO DURING IFYGL,
National Oceanic and Atmospheric Administration, Boulder, Colo. Environmental Research Labs.
For primary bibliographic entry see Field 2D.
W75-07080

WATER DEVELOPMENT OF THE NORTH DAKOTA POTHOLE REGION FOR FISH PRODUCTION,
North Dakota State Univ., Fargo. Dept. of Zoology.
J. J. Peterka.
Available from the National Technical Information Service, Springfield, Va 22161 as PB-241 471, $3.25 in paper copy, $2.25 in microfiche. Research Report No. WI-221-022-74, November, 1974. 6 p, 3 ref. OWRT A-032-NDAK(2).

Descriptors: *Ecology, *Fish, *Wetlands, *Rainbow trout, Benthos, Invertebrates, Plankton, Salamanders, Wildlife, Water chemistry, Ducks, Population, Feeding habits, Estimating, *North Dakota.

To determine the feasibility of growing rainbow trout commercially in south central North Dalota, three prairie pothole lakes were stocked with 500 trout per ha. Mortality in all lakes was high from May to June, ranging from 23 to 85 percent. Two lakes summerkilled in August when decay of Aphanizomenon caused dissolved oxygen levels to drop below 1.0 mg/l. On the two lakes that did not summerkill, only 4.4 percent of the 1971 stock and 0.1 percent in 1972 was harvested in October in the 24 ha lake; 0.8 percent was harvested in the 4 ha lake in 1971. Dissolved oxygen lows in these lakes were 2.4 mg/l (4 ha lake) and 4.5 mg/l (24 ha lake), respectively; maximum phytoplankton blooms were 19 mm3/l and 7 mm 3/l. Maximum surface temperature for all lakes was 25 C; alkalinity ranged from 226 to 552 mg/l as CaCO3; soluble phosphates from 0.27 to 3.02 mg/l; nitrate-nitrite nitrogen from 0.00 to 0.79 mg/l; total hardness from 452 to 1,084 mg/l as CaCO3; specific conductance from 1,220 to 2,800 micromhos cm-3 at 25 C; and pH from 7.7 to 9.7. Amphipods, Chaoborus and chironomids comprised 29.8, 29.7 and 15.1 percent by volume of total food consumed by trout from June to October. Populations of tiger salamanders (Ambystoma tigrinum) ranged from 150/ha to 1,030/ha in the four lakes. Trout can reach a commercially useful size in one season; however, without special management, it is not feasible to grow them in the prairie pothole lakes studied.
W75-07103

CAN THE BALTIC SEA BE TURNED INTO A FRESHWATER LAKE,
For primary bibliographic entry see Field 4A.
W75-07165

SEASONAL NITRATE CYCLING AS EVIDENCE FOR COMPLETE VERTICAL MIXING IN LAKE TAHOE, CALIFORNIA-NEVADA,
California Univ., Davis. Inst. of Ecology; and California Univ., Davis. Div. of Environmental Studies.
For primary bibliographic entry see Field 5C.
W75-07198

CHEMICAL AND BIOLOGICAL QUALITY OF LAKE DICIE AT AUSTIS, FLORIDA, WITH EMPHASIS ON THE EFFECTS OF STORM RUNOFF,
Geological Survey, Tallahassee, Fla.
For primary bibliographic entry see Field 5C.
W75-07213

HYDROLOGY OF THE OKLAWAHA LAKES AREA OF FLORIDA,
Geological Survey, Tallahassee, Fla.
For primary bibliographic entry see Field 7C.
W75-07220

PHYSIOGRAPHIC MAP OF THE OKALOACOOCHEE SLOUGH IN COLLIER COUNTY, FLORIDA,
Geological Survey, Miami, Fla.
For primary bibliographic entry see Field 7C.
W75-07225

ANOTHER EXPLANATION OF THE OBSERVED CYCLONIC CIRCULATION OF LARGE LAKES,
Massachusetts Inst. of Tech., Cambridge.
J. R. Bennett.
Limnology and Oceanography, Vol 20, No 1, p 108-110, January 1975. 3 fig, 6 ref.

Descriptors: *Water circulation, *Lakes, *Upwelling, *Winds, Bodies of water, Surface waters, Advection, Circulation, Thermal stratification, Stratified flow, Limnology, Drag, Stress, Currents(Water).
Identifiers: *Cyclonic circulation, Lake circulation theory, Lake static stability, Lake surface stress.

Two classical explanations of the lake surface circulation are well known. First, Emery and Csanady explain that as warm surface water is advected to the right of the prevailing wind, increased wind drag over this warm water results in a cyclonic wind stress that drives a cyclonic surface flow. Wunsch explains that cyclonic flow as the Lagrange drift induced by internal Kelvin waves. A third mechanism was shown to be as important as the two classical ones. This mechanism was explained by the variation of lake static stability caused by wind induced upwelling. (Lee-ISWS)
W75-07246

NEARSHORE LAKE CURRENTS MEASURED DURING UPWELLING AND DOWNWELLING OF THE THERMOCLINE IN LAKE ONTARIO,
Canada Centre for Inland Waters, Burlington (Ontario).
J. O. Blanton.
Journal of Physical Oceanography, Vol 5, No 1, p 111-124, January 1975. 8 fig, 3 tab, 14 ref.

Descriptors: *Currents(Water), *Lake Ontario, *Thermocline, Lake basins, Upwelling, Cycles, Shores, Winds, Great Lakes, Measurement, Bottom sediments, Temperature, Time series analysis, Coasts, Kinetics, Energy.
Identifiers: *Downwelling, Kelvin wave, Bottom profiles.

The upwelling-downwelling cycles observed along the north shore of Lake Ontario had periods of about 12 to 16 days in length. Currents associated with the downwelling cycle were typically stronger. The periods of the cycles were at least a factor of 2 larger than were periods expected from cyclone movements across the Great Lakes. Although the upwelling-downwelling cycles are generally a response to the wind, this discrepancy suggested a tendency for a more wave-like periodic response. The kinetic energy in currents near the theoretical inertial period clearly delineated a nearshore zone of about 8 km in width. Internal wave periods observed were 14 and 17 h, but no 14 h periods were observed beyond 8 km. Most of the upwelling and downwelling was confined to this zone. The sloping shore model of Csanady (1971a) gave a width near 6 km measured from the point where the equilibrium thermocline intersected the bottom. This point was located at depths between 10 and 20 m from July to October, or roughly about 1 to 3 km from shore, yielding a total theoretical width of about 7 to 9 km. (Roberts-ISWS)
W75-07251

SHORT-PERIOD VARIATIONS IN A GREAT LAKES COASTAL CURRENT BY AERIAL PHOTOGRAPHY,
Wisconsin Univ., Madison. Marine Studies Center.
L. A. Yeske, and T. Green.
Journal of Physical Oceanography, Vol 5, No 1, p 125-135, January 1975. 19 fig, 1 tab, 28 ref. NSF Grant 33140, NASA, Grant NGL 50-002-127.

Descriptors: Great Lakes, *Current(Water), *Coasts, *Photogrammetry, *Lake Superior, *Aerial photography, Shear, Eddies, On-site data collections, Measurement, Remote sensing.
Identifiers: Keweenaw Current, Draft cards, Countercurrents.

Measurements of the surface velocity structure off the Keweenaw Peninsula of Lake Superior were obtained in 1971 and 1972 with the use of aerial photography to track surface drift cards. Variations in the current structure were described at 9-min intervals, over a 45-min period of one experiment, by streamlines and isotachs extending across the entire coastal region. Speed contour irregularities and eddies of about 100 m diameter could be traced in some of the aerial sequences. Speed fluctuations of 25% of the mean flow occurred frequently. The horizontal divergence and relative vorticity structure for each sequence was also calculated; magnitudes of each were up to three times that of the local Coriolis parameter. Both inshore and offshore countercurrents were observed. The region of anticyclonic shear was typically twice as wide as the cyclonic shear region. Cross-stream velocity gradients were about three times larger than those measured in the Gulf Stream. Rossby numbers ranged from 0.5 to 0.8, and inertial accelerations appeared to be larger than local accelerations at least 25% of the time. Horizontal eddy viscosity coefficients ranged from + or -1000 to + or -100,000 sq cm/s. Geostrophic calculations based on bathythermograph sections, airborne radiometer flights, and meteorological data were also discussed. (Roberts-ISWS)
W75-07252

MICROBIAL TRANSFORMATIONS OF MERCURY IN AQUATIC ENVIRONMENTS,
Purdue Univ., Lafayette, Ind. Dept. of Agronomy.
For primary bibliographic entry see Field 5B.
W75-07275

LAKE ERIE INTERNATIONAL JETPORT MODEL FEASIBILITY INVESTIGATION; REPORT 1, SCOPE OF STUDY AND REVIEW OF AVAILABLE DATA,
Army Engineer Waterways Experiment Station, Vicksburg, Miss.
D. G. Outlaw, and D. L. Durham.
Available from the National Technical Information Service, Springfield, Va., 22161, as Ad-783 463, $4.25 in paper copy, $2.25 in microfiche. Army Engineer Waterways Experiment Station, Vicksburg, Mississippi. Technical Report H-74-6, Report 1, July 1974. 69 p, 7 tab, 48 ref.

Descriptors: *Seiches, *Waves(Water), *Airports, *Lake Erie, *Hydraulic models, Model studies, Hydraulics, Feasibility studies, Data collections, Reviews, *Seiches, Tides, Water quality, Refraction(Water waves), Lakes.
Identifiers: *Mass circulation(Lakes), Wave diffraction(Lakes).

The scope of the U.S. Army Engineer Waterways Experiment Station's (WES) investigation of the proposed Lake Erie International Jetport is described and data obtained from the literature and private individuals are summarized. The objectives of the investigation, Part I, include a review of the literature concerning wave activity (wind waves, seiches, and tides) and mass circulation in Lake Erie, preliminary design of necessary hydraulic models, and preliminary application of

analytical and/or numerical models to seiching and mass circulation. The investigation is separated into five tasks: (a) review of the literature, (b) seiche analysis, (c) wave refraction and diffraction analyses, (d) mass circulation analysis, and (e) preliminary model design. Existing lake geology, climate, bottom and shoreline characteristics, water balance, water temperature, lake levels, lake currents, wave regime, shore erosion, and water quality data in the central basin of Lake Erie near Cleveland, Ohio, are summarized in Part II. (WES)
W75-07286

EXTREME FLUCTUATIONS IN WATER QUALITY OF EUTROPHIC FISH KILL LAKES: EFFECT OF SEDIMENT MIXING,
Fisheries Research Board of Canada, Winnipeg (Manitoba). Freshwater Inst.
For primary bibliographic entry see Field 5C.
W75-07290

PERIPHYTON COLONIZATION AND PRODUCTIVITY IN THE REACTOR COOLING RESERVOIR--PAR POND,
Du Pont de Nemours (E. I.) and Co., Aiken, S.C. Savannah River Lab.
For primary bibliographic entry see Field 5C.
W75-07292

AMCHITKA BIOENVIRONMENTAL PROGRAM. LIMNOLOGY OF AMCHITKA ISLAND, ALASKA,
Battelle Columbus Labs., Ohio.
For primary bibliographic entry see Field 5A.
W75-07293

NUTRIENTS IN ICE. SOME DATA FROM A HIGH MOUNTAIN LAKE,
For primary bibliographic entry see Field 5C.
W75-07301

DIEL PERIODICITY IN THE PHYTOPLANKTON COMMUNITY OF THE OLIGOTROPHIC LAKE PAAJARVI, SOUTHERN FINLAND. I. PHYTOPLANKTONIC PRIMARY PRODUCTION AND RELATED FACTORS,
Helsinki Univ. (Finland). Dept. of Botany.
For primary bibliographic entry see Field 5C.
W75-07302

GAMMARUS PREDATION AND THE POSSIBLE EFFECTS OF GAMMARUS AND CHAOBORUS FEEDING ON THE ZOOPLANKTON COMPOSITION IN SOME SMALL LAKES AND PONDS IN WESTERN CANADA,
Calgary Univ. (Alberta). Dept. of Biology.
For primary bibliographic entry see Field 5C.
W75-07309

CRUSTACEAN PLANKTON COMMUNITIES OF 340 LAKES AND PONDS IN AND NEAR THE NATIONAL PARKS OF THE CANADIAN ROCKY MOUNTAINS,
Calgary Univ., Alberta. Dept. of Biology.
For primary bibliographic entry see Field 5C.
W75-07310

PHOSPHORUS DYNAMICS IN PONDS,
Alabama Agricultural Experiment Station, Auburn.
For primary bibliographic entry see Field 5C.
W75-07316

LAKE TUUSULA DESTRATIFICATION AND AERATION TEST, WINTER 1972/73,
National Water Board of Finland, Helsinki.
For primary bibliographic entry see Field 5C.
W75-07317

WATER QUALITY, NUTRIENTS, AND NET PLANKTON ANALYSIS OF SUMMERSVILLE LAKE,
West Virginia Univ., Morgantown. Dept. of Biology.
For primary bibliographic entry see Field 5C.
W75-07319

SPATIAL AND SEASONAL VARIATIONS IN PHYTOPLANKTONIC PRIMARY PRODUCTION AND BIOMASS IN THE OLIGOTROPHIC LAKE PAAJARVI, SOUTHERN FINLAND,
Helsinki Univ (Finland). Dept. of Botany.
For primary bibliographic entry see Field 5C.
W75-07323

NATURAL RESOURCES MANAGEMENT IN THE GREAT LAKES BASIN,
Cornell Univ., Ithaca, N.Y. Water Resources and Marine Sciences Center.
For primary bibliographic entry see Field 6E.
W75-07344

2I. Water In Plants

THE RELATION OF TEMPERATURE AND LEAF WETNESS TO THE DEVELOPMENT OF LEAF BLIGHT OF WHEAT,
Indian Agricultural Research Inst., New Delhi. Div. of Mycology and Plant Pathology.
For primary bibliographic entry see Field 3F.
W75-06943

THE EFFECTS OF HUMIDITY AND CYTOKININ ON GROWTH AND WATER RELATIONS OF SALT-STRESSED BEAN PLANTS,
Ceara Univ., Fortaleza (Brazil). Departmente de Bioquimica y Biologia Molecula.
For primary bibliographic entry see Field 3C.
W75-07022

THE EFFECT OF CONIFERS ON THE CHEMISTRY AND MASS BALANCE OF TWO LARGE LYSIMETERS IN CASTRICUM (THE NETHERLANDS),
Food and Agriculture Organization of the United Nations, Kitale (Kenya). Turkana Irrigation Project.
For primary bibliographic entry see Field 2D.
W75-07052

DESERT BIOLOGY, VOL. 2.
G. W. Brown (ed.) 601 p. Illus. Academic Press, Inc.: New York, N.Y., London, England, 1974, Pr. $45.00.

Descriptors: *Deserts, *Biology, Africa, United States, Soils, Arid regions, Vegetation, Algae, Lichens, Fungi, Arthropods, Fish, *Water requirements, *Desert plants.
Identifiers: *Saudi Arabia, *Sahara Desert, *Sonoran Desert, Pimian Indians.

This volume continues the study begun in the 1st volume on the physical and biological aspects of desert structure. Hydrogeology of deserts, desert soils and physical environment and vegetation of the Sahara desert (North Africa) are examined in the opening chapters. Another article focused on the algae, lichens and fungi found in deserts while others study the arthropods and fishes of arid regions and their adaptations to this type of environment are discussed. Included is a paper on water relations and ecophysiology of desert plants. Man's relationship to the desert is explored in the 2 concluding articles which deal with the Pimian Indians of the Sonoran Desert (USA) and with those living in areas north of Jiddah in Saudi Arabia. Each article contains numerous literature references and illustrations. Systematic, author

RIVER MODELS WITH A MOVABLE BED,
Queen's Univ. Kingston (Ontario). Dept. of Civil Engineering.
M. S. Yalin.
In: River and Estuary Model Analysis, Volume III; Proceedings of the International Association for Hydraulic Research Symposium on River Mechanics (4 Vol.), Bangkok, Thailand, January 9-12, 1973. Asian Institute of Technology, Bangkok, Thailand, p 11-24. (1973) 3 fig, 5 ref.

Descriptors: *Hydraulic similitude, *Hydraulic models, *Alluvial channels, Theroretical analysis, Equations, Rivers, Velocity, Bottom sediments, River beds, Movement, Shape, Dunes, Ripple marks, Streambeds.
Identifiers: *Movable bed, *Dimensionless variables.

The determination of scales for river models with a movable bed was discussed, with special emphasis on the geometrically similar reproduction of large-scale bed features (dunes). The velocity scales were determined from a generalized friction equation which took into account the energy losses due to both skin friction and the geometry of sand waves (ripples and dunes). Application of the analysis was illustrated with four numerical examples. (See also W75-06998) (Humphreys-ISWS)
W75-07000

SOME NOTES ON HYDRAULIC MODEL TESTS OF RIVER CHANNELS,
Public Works Research Inst., Kashima (Japan). Kashima Hydraulics Lab.
For primary bibliographic entry see Field 2E.
W75-07008

HYDRAULIC PROBLEMS OF THE MEKONG RIVER IN THE QUATRE-BRAS REACH,
Vyzkumny Ustav Vodohospodarsky, Bratislava (Czechoslovakia).
For primary bibliographic entry see Field 2E.
W75-07012

THE APPLICATION OF RIVER SYSTEM MECHANICS,
Hawaii Univ., Honolulu. Dept. of Civil Engineering.
For primary bibliographic entry see Field 2E.
W75-07017

UNSTEADY FLOW IN OPEN CHANNEL WITH MOVABLE BED,
National Taiwan Univ, Taipei.
For primary bibliographic entry see Field 2E.
W75-07037

GENERAL REPORTS, DISCUSSIONS, LECTURES, VOLUME 4.
Proceedings of the International Association for Hydraulic Research Symposium on River Mechanics (4 Vol.), Bangkok, Thailand, January 9-12, 1973. Asian Institute of Technology, Bangkok, Thailand. 433 p. (1973).

Descriptors: *Conferences, *Sediment transport, *Sediment yield, *Hydraulic models, *Mathematical models, *Floods, *River beds, Sediment control, Deposition(Sediments), Scour, Flood damage, Flood control, Warning systems, Sediment discharge, Streamflow, Bed load, Suspended load, Channels, Estuaries, Watersheds(Basins), Peak discharge, Flood flow, Hydrology.
Identifiers: *River mechanics.

River mechanics was discussed at a symposium held at Bangkok, Thailand in 1973. The nine broad subject areas discussed in Volume 4 were: (1) sediment yield and deposition; (2) sediment control and scour prevention; (3) sediment transportation; (4) river bed form; (5) flow and sediment measurement; (6) hydraulic modeling; (7) flood computation; (8) flood damage, warning, and control; and (9) mathematical modeling. Volume 4 contains the proceedings, general reports, and discussions for the twelve technical sessions and two special lectures. (See W75-07039 and W75-07040) (Humphreys-ISWS)
W75-07038

THE INTERACTION OF VELOCITY DISTRIBUTION AND SUSPENDED LOAD IN TURBULENT STREAMS,
Massachusetts Inst. of Tech., Cambridge. Ralph M. Parsons Lab. for Water Resources and Hydrodynamics.
A. T. Ippen.
In: General Reports, Discussions, Lectures, Vol. IV; Proceedings of the International Association for Hydraulic Research Symposium on River Mechanics (4 Vol.), Bangkok, Thailand, January 9-12, 1973. Asian Institute of Technology, Bangkok, Thailand, p 341-369, (1973). 17 fig, 2 tab, 23 ref.

Descriptors: *Sediment transport, *Suspended load, *Analytical techniques, *Reviews, Turbulent flow, Particle size, Sediments, Suspended solids, Equations, Mathematical studies, Model studies, Suspension, Resistance, Hydraulics, Alluvial channels, Velocity, Flow, Movement, Fluid friction, Sediment distribution, Distribution patterns, Dispersion, Mixing.
Identifiers: *Concentration-distribution function, Sediment mixtures.

The material presented was intended to summarize the present state of knowledge in the field of suspended load transport in turbulent streams. This knowledge is limited to the steady and uniform two-dimensional flow over a 'flat' bottom with granular particles suspended in various concentrations. Subjects discussed were: (1) historical perspective of problem; (2) analytical approach to suspended load transport including formulation of basic dispersion relation and derivation of basic concentration-distribution function; (3) experimental modifications of basic equations for effect of sediment on velocity distribution, modification of concentration-distribution, and concentration phenomena near the bottom; (4) evaluation of total transport in suspension for single-size particles and mixtures of sediments; and (5) effect of suspensions on hydraulic resistance. Research of the experimental-analytical type provides important insight and will continue to do so, but engineering problems are in the field and all research must be directed to their solution. The continued exploration of all sedimentation aspects is vital to the development of water resources in all countries. Only further progress and full utilization of research capabilities in the laboratory and the field will give assurance that the necessary use of water resources by man will be planned in harmony with the natural environment. (See also W75-07038) (Humphreys-ISWS)
W75-07039

STATISTICAL PROPERTIES OF WAVE-CURRENT FORCE,
North Carolina State Univ., Raleigh. Dept. of Civil Engineering, and North Carolina State Univ., Raleigh. Dept. of Geosciences.
For primary bibliographic entry see Field 2L.
W75-07070

STABILIZATION OF COASTAL DREDGE SPOIL WITH SPARTINA ALTERNIFLORA,
North Carolina State Univ., Raleigh. Dept. of Botany; and North Carolina State Univ., Raleigh. Dept. of Soil Science.
For primary bibliographic entry see Field 2L.
W75-07071

SEDIMENT MOVEMENT IN TUBBS INLET, NORTH CAROLINA,
North Carolina State Univ., Raleigh. Center for Marine Coastal Studies.
For primary bibliographic entry see Field 2L.
W75-07072

A NEW TECHNIQUE FOR BEACH EROSION CONTROL,
North Carolina State Univ., Raleigh. Center for Marine Coastal Studies.
T. J. French, J. L. Machemehl, and N. E. Huang.
North Carolina University Sea Grant Reprint No. 52. Reprint from North Carolina State University Center for Marine and Coastal Studies Report No. 74-3, July 1974. 81 p, 10 fig, 2 tab, 6 ref, 3 append.

Descriptors: *Beach erosion, *Shore protection, *Erosion control, Water table, Coasts.
Identifiers: *Filtering system, Beach profiles, Coastal processes, Wave action, Beach accretion.

An experimental study of a new technique for beach erosion control was conducted in a wave channel facility. The primary objective was to determine the effects of a sub-sand filtering system on the stability of a beach profile. The filter system was designed, constructed and placed in the beach section 4 in. to 6 in. below the sand surface. The effects of waves on the beach section (filtered/unfiltered) were evaluated. The sub-sand filtering system was used to control the flow conditions at the sediment boundary. In the off-shore zone, the filters had a stabilizing effect on the overlying material (measurements indicated a substantial difference between filtered and unfiltered profiles). In the breaker zone, the filters had little effect on breaker scour. The sediment eroded from the breaker zone was stored in the foreshore zone. In the fore-shore zone, the filters were a tremendous aid in speeding accretion. The filter system generated rapid and large accretion. The filter system was very effective in building/replacing a fore-shore berm. (NOAA)
W75-07073

THE EFFECT OF SEDIMENT ON RESERVOIR WATER QUALITY,
Virginia State Water Control Board, Richmond.
For primary bibliographic entry see Field 5C.
W75-07116

OYSTER REEF SEDIMENTATION, BILOXI BAY, MISSISSIPPI,
University of Southern Mississippi, Hattiesburg. Dept. of Geology.
For primary bibliographic entry see Field 2L.
W75-07148

INFLUENCE OF FLOOD WAVES OF MOUNTAIN RIVERS ON DRIFT DISCHARGE,
For primary bibliographic entry see Field 2E.
W75-07164

OBSERVATIONS ON HILLSLOPE EROSION IN TOWER KARST TOPOGRAPHY OF BELIZE,
Louisiana State Univ., Baton Rouge. Dept. of Geography.
R. C. McDonald.
Geological Society of America Bulletin, Vol 86, No 2, p 255-256, February 1975. 3 fig.

Descriptors: *Karst, *Geomorphology, *Talus, Sinks, Karst hydrology, Carbonate rocks, Subsurface drainage, Land forming, Runoff, Lakes, Erosion, Dolomite, Springs, Topography.
Identifiers: *Karst towers, *Central America(Belize), Hillslope erosion.

Differential erosion in karst topography of Belize forms closed basins around karst towers. Ephemeral lakes that collect in the basins are active in removing talus and undermining hillslope support by corrosion. Channel incision establishes more rapid drainage of the basins that surround towers, resulting in less active hillslope erosion. Tower karst topography of coastal Belize is in the process of changing from a landscape characterized by rapid talus removal and undermining to a landscape characterized by slow talus removal and little slope undermining. As the drainage continues to improve around karst towers, steep tower hillslopes become more obscured at their bases by the accumulation of talus. (Sanderson-ISWS)
W75-07190

THE CHARACTER OF CHANNEL MIGRATION ON THE BEATTON RIVER, NORTHEAST BRITISH COLUMBIA, CANADA,
Simon Fraser Univ., Burnaby (British Columbia). Dept. of Geography.
E. J. Hickin, and G. C. Nanson.
Geological Society of America Bulletin, Vol 86, No 4, p 487-494, April 1975. 9 fig, 1 tab, 11 ref.

Descriptors: *Dendrochronology, *Meanders, *Forests, Age, Channel erosion, Flood plains, Alluvial channels, Deposition(Sediments), Geomorphology, Willow trees, *Canada, Channel morphology, Gradients(Streams), Streamflow, Aerial photography, Regression analysis, Mathematical models.
Identifiers: *British Columbia(Beatton River), *Channel migration, Channel curvature, Point bars, Scroll bars, Lateral migration, Poplar, Spruce, Alder.

Dendrochronological surveys on ten point-bar complexes on the Beatton River, northeast British Columbia, provided the basis for measurement of lateral migration and incision during the last 250 years. The rate of channel-bend migration reaches a maximum value where the ratio, radius of channel curvature to stream width (r sub m/w sub m), approximates 3.0. The rate of channel migration rapidly declines for bends with values of r sub m/w sub m greater or less than 3.0. In addition, the spacing of flood-plain ridges (d) increases with increasing rates of bend migration. Equations for predicting the migration rate (M, meters/year) on the study showed M as a power function of both r sub m/w sub m and d. Two sets of coefficients and exponents for r sub m/w sub m were used, depending on whether r sub m/w sub m fell in the range 1.3 to 2.9 or the range 2.9 to 7.9. (Visocky-ISWS)
W75-07191

EVALUATION OF THE CAUSES OF LEVEE EROSION IN THE SACRAMENTO-SAN JOAQUN DELTA, CALIFORNIA,
Geological Survey, Menlo Park, Calif.
J. T. Limerinos, and W. Smith.
Available from the National Technical Information Service, Springfield, Va. 22161 as PB-239 796, $4.25 in paper copy, $2.25 in microfiche. Water-Resources Investigations 28-74, January 1975. 30 fig, 10 tab, 9 ref.

Descriptors: *Erosion, *Levees, *California, *Boating, Stream erosion, Waves(Water), Bank erosion.
Identifiers: *Sacramento-San Joaquin Delta(Calif).

Erosion was studied in two typical channels in the Sacramento-San Joaqun Delta, California to determine the relative amount of damage caused by natural forces and by waves generated by boats. In a typical narrow channel, subject to winter floodflow and heavy boat traffic, about 20 percent of the annual energy dissipated against the levees could be attributed to boat-generated waves, about 10 percent to wind-generated waves, and 70 percent to tractive shear stress. In a channel relatively unaffected by winter floodflows, energy dissipation from boat-generated waves was shown to range from about 45 to 80 percent of the total, depending upon wind movement assumptions made in the computations. (Knapp-USGS)

X-ray studies have been performed on both LiCl solutions and on pure water. The larger angle measurements made on the salt solutions were used to determine the radius of the first hydration shell surrounding the foreign ions. It was also shown that the temperature dependence of the hydration radius was in agreement with the Debye-Huckel Theory. Sufficient data were not obtained to definitely establish the degree to which the results were affected by error. Small angle X-ray measurements were made on water in the temperature range from 0 to 92 degrees Centigrade. No evidence for a mixture model for water was found. The temperature dependence of the zero angle scattering agreed with what was theoretically expected for a simple, one-component fluid. The hydration or solvation layer around foreign ions in aqueous solution gives water the ability to hold large amounts of impurities in solution. If the solvation layer could be greatly reduced or removed the impurities in the solution would precipitate out. The X-ray method used gives a means of measuring the solvation layer and as such would be useful if a study were undertaken to modify or remove the hydration shell.
W75-06997

COPPER IN SURFACE WATERS SOUTH OF NEW ZEALAND,
Massachusetts Inst. of Tech., Cambridge. Dept. of Earth and Planetary Sciences.
E. Boyle, and J. M. Edmond.
Nature, Vol 253, No 5487, p 107-109, January 10, 1975. 2 fig, 1 tab, 10 ref.

Descriptors: *Copper, *Sea water, *Oceanography, *Surface waters, Silicates, Phosphates, Salinity, Nitrates, Alkalinity, Ships, Oceans, Pacific Ocean, Upwelling, Ocean circulation, Sampling.
Identifiers: New Zealand.

The sampling of the transition metals, including copper, in the ocean has so far produced unsatisfactory results. For copper, contamination during sampling has been suggested as one source of error, and this was overcome by sampling surface waters in regions of marked horizontal gradients in chemical properties. Samples were collected on station from the bow of the ship. The sampler was a 4-l polyethylene jerry jug which had been leached with 0.1 N hydrochloric acid for 24 h, rinsed four times with very pure distilled water, and stored in a polyethylene bag. The jug was filled at a depth of at least 3 m. It was definitely established that relative to lower latitudes, copper is enriched in the surface waters of the Antarctic upwelling areas, and, by extension, in the deep waters of the ocean. If the correlation with nitrate is valid, then copper can be classified as a limiting nutrient. The levels in the surface water in low and midlatitudes should be very close to zero (less than 0.1 nmol per kg) and the maximum values in the deep Pacific should not exceed 5 nmol per kg. (Sims-ISWS)
W75-07060

CUMULATIVE CHEMICAL LIGHT METER,
Westinghouse Research Labs., Pittsburgh, Pa.
For primary bibliographic entry see Field 5A.
W75-07063

MAJOR AND HISTORICAL SPRINGS OF TEXAS,
Texas Water Development Board, Austin.
For primary bibliographic entry see Field 4B.
W75-07152

EXAMINATION OF WATERS: EVALUATION OF METHODS FOR SELECTED CHARACTERISTICS,
Australian Water Resources Council, Canberra (Australia).
For primary bibliographic entry see Field 5A.
W75-07154

AN EVALUATION OF NEW METHODS FOR THE DETERMINATION OF AMMONIA IN WATER,
Brisbane City Council (Australia).
For primary bibliographic entry see Field 5A.
W75-07157

INSTRUMENTAL METHODS FOR THE DETERMINATION OF TRACE METALS IN WATER,
New South Wales Dept. of Mines, Sydney (Australia). Chemical Lab.
For primary bibliographic entry see Field 5A.
W75-07159

THE AUTOMATION OF ROUTINE COLORIMETRIC ANALYSIS OF WATER,
New South Wales Dept. of Mines, Sydney (Australia). Chemical Lab.
For primary bibliographic entry see Field 5A.
W75-07162

THERMAL ALTERATION OF ORGANIC MATTER IN RECENT MARINE SEDIMENTS. II ISOPRENOIDS,
California Univ., Los Angeles. Dept. of Geophysics and Planetary Physics.
For primary bibliographic entry see Field 5B.
W75-07168

GEOCHEMICAL ANALYSIS OF STREAM SEDIMENTS AS A TOOL FOR ENVIRONMENTAL MONITORING: A PIGYARD CASE STUDY,
Brock Univ., St. Catharines (Ontario). Dept. of Geological Sciences.
For primary bibliographic entry see Field 5A.
W75-07188

RATE OF SULFURIC-ACID PRODUCTION IN YELLOWSTONE NATIONAL PARK,
Wisconsin Univ., Madison. Dept. of Bacteriology.
T. D. Brock, and J. L. Mosser.
Geological Society of America Bulletin, Vol 86, No 2, p 194-198, February 1975. 2 fig, 4 tab, 14 ref. NSF Grant GB-35046.

Descriptors: *Acidic water, *Acid bacteria, *Thermal springs, Tracers, Volume, Seepage, Ponds, Hydrothermal studies, Hydrogen sulfide, Water table, Leaching, Hydrogen ion concentration, Sulfur bacteria, Acidic soils, Thermometers, Chemical analysis, Sodium chloride.
Identifiers: *Yellowstone National Park, *Sulfuric acid, Dilution rate.

Production of sulfuric acid in vapor-dominated hydrothermal systems is primarily a bacterial process. The rate of production of sulfuric acid was measured in springs in several acid-altered areas in Yellowstone National Park. Most of these springs lack surface water flow, but water enters and leaves these springs at approximately constant rates via underground seepage. The rate of water exchange in these steady-state systems was measured by enriching the springs with sodium chloride and measuring the rate at which the chloride ion was diluted. In all cases, the added chloride was diluted at an exponential rate. The rate at which sulfuric acid was being produced was calculated from a knowledge of the dilution rate and volume of the springs and from measurement of the sulfuric-acid concentrations of the waters. Water in acid springs enters as cold, acid groundwater which is steam heated within the source pool. In springs with pool volumes of 2000 liters or less, most of the sulfuric acid was produced outside the spring, probably by bacteria present in the nearby acid-altered soil. In springs with pool volumes around 1,000,000 liters most of the sulfuric acid was produced in situ by resident bacterial populations. (Visocky-ISWS)
W75-07189

PRINCIPAL-COMPONENT ANALYSIS OF STREAMFLOW CHEMICAL QUALITY DATA,
Geological Survey, Reston, Va.
For primary bibliographic entry see Field 5B.
W75-07200

QUALITY OF THE GROUND WATER IN BASALT OF THE COLUMBIA RIVER GROUP, WASHINGTON, OREGON, AND IDAHO,
Geological Survey, Reston, Va.
R. C. Newcomb.
Available from Supt. of Documents, GPO, Washington DC 20402, for 75 cents. Water-Supply Paper 1999-N, 1972. 71 p, 9 fig, 1 plate, 3 tab, 29 ref.

Descriptors: *Water chemistry, *Water quality, *Basalts, *Groundwater, Washington, Oregon, Idaho, Geochemistry, Hydrogeology, Hot springs, Bicarbonates, Calcium, Sodium, Columbia River.
Identifiers: *Columbia River aquifer.

The groundwater within the 50,000-square-mile area of the layered basalt of the Columbia River Group in Washington, Oregon, and Idaho is a generally uniform bicarbonate water having calcium and sodium in nearly equal amounts as the principal cations. The water contains a relatively large amount of silica. The sodium water is more common beneath the floors of the main synclinal valleys; the calcium water, elsewhere. In addition to the prevalent type, five special types form a small part of the groundwater; four of these are natural and one is artificial. The four natural special types are: (1) calcium sodium chloride waters that rise from underlying sedimentary rocks west of the Cascade Range, (2) mineralized water at or near warm or hot springs, (3) water having unusual ion concentrations, especially of chloride, near sedimentary rocks intercalated at the edges of the basalt, and (4) more mineralized water near one locality of excess carbon dioxide. The one artificial kind of special groundwater has resulted from unintentional artificial recharge incidental to irrigation in parts of central Washington. Carbon-14 determinations indicate that the water has been underground for periods ranging from modern times to several tens of thousands of years. (Knapp-USGS)
W75-07217

GEOLOGIC SETTING AND CHEMICAL CHARACTERISTICS OF HOT SPRINGS IN WEST-CENTRAL ALASKA,
Geological Survey, Anchorage, Alaska.
For primary bibliographic entry see Field 2F.
W75-07243

AN AUTOMATED TECHNIQUE FOR TOTAL DISSOLVED FREE AMINO ACIDS IN SEAWATER,
Oregon State Univ., Corvallis. School of Oceanography.
For primary bibliographic entry see Field 5A.
W75-07247

2L. Estuaries

POLLUTIONAL EFFECTS OF PULP AND PAPER MILL WASTES IN PUGET SOUND.
For primary bibliographic entry see Field 5C.
W75-06881

THE DISTRIBUTION OF MERCURY IN SEDIMENT CORES FROM BELLINGHAM BAY, WASHINGTON,
Washington Univ., Seattle. Dept. of Oceanography.
For primary bibliographic entry see Field 5B.
W75-06901

ECOLOGICAL VARIABILITY OF PIKE-PERCH IN LITHUANIAN WATER. (3. NOURISHMENT OF PIKE-PERCH IN THE LAGOON OF KURIS.HES-HAFF.)), (IN RUSSIAN),
Akademiya Nauk Litovkkoi SSR, Vilnius. Institut Zoologii i Parazitologii.
A. B. Gyarulaitis.
Liet Tsr Moksiu Akad Darb Ser B. 4 p 97-110, 1972. English summary.

Descriptors: *Fish, *Pike, *Perch, *Ecosystems, Lagoons, Europe, Ecology.
Identifiers: Acerina-cemua, *Lithuania, Lucioperca-lucioperca, Osmerus-eperlanus, Perca-fluviatilis, Rutilus-rutilus.

The composition of food of young and older fish (Lucioperca lucioperca), the dependence of nourishment upon the age of the predator, the quantity of food components, the proportion of body length of the victim and the predator, the dimensional-age and seasonal pecularities were studied. In the Kursiu Marios Lagoon (USSR) pike-perch become predatory between 5.1-6.0 cm in length and in the open sea they live mostly on European small smelt (Osmerus eperlanus m. spirinchus Pallas). Matured pike-perch live mostly on roach (Rutilus rutilus (L.)), ruff (Acerina cernia (L.)), perch (Perca fluviatilis L.), European small smelt, European big smelt (O. eperlanus (L.)) and its youngsters. The composition of food and the intensity of feeding in different years and in different parts of the sea is different and depends upon seasonal changes of food base. Younger pike-perch feed on European small smelt, ruff and perch, while older ones eat roach, European big smelt and the youngsters of pike-perch. Pike-perch live mostly on fish of small dimensions or on the youngsters of bigger fish. The body length of victims ranges from 2-18 cm and on the average constitutes 9.7-61.6% of the pike-perch body length.--Copyright 1973, Biological Abstracts, Inc.
W75-06961

RIVER AND ESTUARY MODEL ANALYSIS, VOLUME 3.
For primary bibliographic entry see Field 2E.
W75-06998

THE TIDAL REGIME OF THE ELBE-RIVER, HYDRAULIC MODEL WITH MOVABLE BED,
Bundesanstalt fur Wasserbau, Hamburg (West Germany).
E. Giese, J. Teichert, and H. Vollmers.
In: River and Estuary Model Analysis, Volume III; Proceedings of the International Association for Hydraulic Research Symposium on River Mechanics (4 Vol.), Bangkok, Thailand, January 9-12, 1973. Asian Institute of Technology, Bangkok, Thailand, p 25-36. (1973). 10 fig, 3 ref.

Descriptors: *Model studies, *Tidal streams, *Sediment transport, Rivers, Estuaries, Instrumentation, Hydraulic similitude, River training, Hydraulic models, Alluvial channels.
Identifiers: Movable bed models.

An estuary tidal model of the Elbe River was used for schemes of suitable actions in regard to enlargement and maintenance of required navigable water depth and width for high capacity ships. The horizontal scale of the model is 1:800 and the vertical scale 1:100. Discussed were similarity considerations, hydrological and morphological information, model construction, instrumentation, control for dynamical and morphological similarity, and model tests conducted to determine stabilization effects of the navigation channel northwest of Cuxhaven. Tests determined that alignment of a training wall combined with widening and deepening of the center channel was the most satisfactory scheme investigated. (See also W75-06998) (Humphreys-ISWS)
W75-07001

kept at the mean high water level. Effect of tsunami breakwaters at the bay mouth to the flow profile was estimated experimentally and numerically to determine piling up of water in the bay. Effects of tsunami breakwaters at the bay mount to transformation of tsunami and to river discharge were estimated from the result of the experiment and to that of the past researches concerning the interaction between wave and current. It was found that the effect of the tsunami breakwaters was much less when river discharges exist. When the amount of the river discharges was equal to the design flood discharges, the tsunami wave height decrements were similar (1) when the river discharges existed and the tsunami breakwaters were not constructed and (2) when the river discharges did not exist and the tsunami breakwaters were constructed. (See also W75-06998) (Humphreys-ISWS)
W75-07014

SYSTEM 11 'SIVA', A DESIGN SYSTEM FOR RIVERS AND ESTUARIES,
Technische Hogeschool, Delft (Netherlands). International Courses in Hydraulics.
For primary bibliographic entry see Field 2E.
W75-07016

MODELING RIVER AND ESTUARY UNSTEADY FLOW SYSTEMS,
Utah State Univ., Logan. Dept. of Civil Engineering.
For primary bibliographic entry see Field 2E.
W75-07024

MATHEMATICAL INVESTIGATION OF A TIDAL RIVER,
Calcutta Port Commissioners (India). Hydraulic Study Dept.
A. K. Chatterjee.
In: River and Estuary Model Analysis, Volume III; Proceedings of the International Association for Hydraulic Research Symposium on River Mechanics (4 Vol.), Bangkok, Thailand, January 9-12, 1973. Asian Institute of Technology, Bangkok, Thailand, p 315-326, (1973). 5 fig, 3 ref.

Descriptors: *Model studies, *Tidal streams, *Tidal effects, Mathematical models, Equations, Finite element analysis, Numerical analysis, Tides, Rivers, Channels, Water levels, Discharge(Water), Streamflow, Analytical techniques.
Identifiers: *India(Rupnarain River), Explicit method.

A mathematical model was given for the simulation of the propagation of tides in long irregular channels, incorporating the bed slope in the schematization process which varies from reach to reach and the friction factor varying from reach to reach as well as with time. In several solutions, the bed slope term was neglected and its effect was compensated as far as possible by adjustment of the friction factor (a constant value of the Chezy's C). The method of solution was the explicit finite difference scheme with diamond grids. The computed tidal curves at Dhanipur and Gopinathpur on the Rupnarain River agree within plus or minus 4% of the prototype water levels. This discrepancy was felt to be due to nonsimulation of the correct bed slope. The noticeable influences of the slope term were the lowering of the ebb arm of the tide curves and the increase in the volume of the ebb flow. (See also W75-06998) (Humphreys-ISWS)
W75-07025

THEORETICAL STUDIES OF LONG WAVE PROPAGATION IN ESTUARIES OF FINITE LENGTH,
Birmingham Univ. (England). Dept. of Civil Engineering.
D. W. Knight.
In: River and Estuary Model Analysis, Volume III; Proceedings of the International Association for Hydraulic Research Symposium on River Mechanics (4 Vol.), Bangkok, Thailand, January 9-12, 1973. Asian Institute of Technology, Bangkok, Thailand, p 327-338, (1973). 8 fig, 6 tab, 1 ref.

Descriptors: *Mathematical studies, *Estuaries, *Theoretical analysis, *Tidal effects, Waves(Water), Tides, Water levels, Equations, Tidal waters, Water level fluctuations, Hydraulic models, Continuity equation, Momentum equation, Mathematics.

Proudman's (1957) analytical solution was described and amplified for the problem of tidal propagation in an idealized estuary which is a horizontal channel of constant rectangular section, closed at one end and open at the other to a periodic influence. The motion was considered to be one dimensional and the solution includes the effect of both the convective acceleration and the friction terms. Equations were presented giving the amplification of the tide as it progresses up the estuary, the times of high and low water, and the heights of high and low water. The influence of various dimensionless groups was demonstrated by a graphical presentation of the results. A comprehensive set of numerical results were tabulated for comparison with other analytical solutions to the same problem and for comparison with experimental results. (See also W75-06998) (Humphreys-ISWS)
W75-07026

FLOOD ROUTING FOR URBAN RIVER NETWORK,
Osaka Univ. (Japan). Dept. of Civil Engineering.
For primary bibliographic entry see Field 2E.
W75-07027

CIRCULATION IN SHALLOW ESTUARIES,
Texas Univ., Austin. Dept. of Civil Engineering.
F. D. Masch, and N. J. Shankar.
In: River and Estuary Model Analysis, Volume III; Proceedings of the International Association for Hydraulic Research Symposium on River Mechanics (4 Vol.), Bangkok, Thailand, January 9-12, 1973. Asian Institute of Technology, Bangkok, Thailand, p 371-381, (1973). 4 fig, 2 tab, 4 ref.
OWRR C-1158(No 1591)(4).

Descriptors: *Estuaries, *Model studies, *Circulation, *Texas, Mathematical models, Tidal effects, Shallow water, Numerical analysis, Currents(Water), Velocity, Tidal waters, Water quality, *Path of pollutants.
Identifiers: *Galveston Bay(Tex), Tidal models.

Results were presented for a numerical tidal simulation model for the analysis and evaluation of circulation patterns in shallow homogeneous estuaries such as those found along the Gulf Coast of the United States. Basic model output consists of the time history of tidal amplitudes and component tidal velocities under vertically integrated conditions. The velocity components for each grid element are resolved vectorially and plotted on an overlay of the bay system to illustrate circulation patterns. Such plots involving net (time averaged over a tidal cycle) velocity vectors are representative of the overall circulation patterns while plots utilizing instantaneous velocities or velocities at different phases during a tidal cycle (i.e., flood, ebb, and slack conditions) provide a more detailed description of the local circulation. These circulation patterns are all fundamental to the analysis of transport characteristics including salinity and water quality in estuaries. After calibration with actual prototype data, the model was operated for an intermediate inflow condition in order to establish baseline circulation patterns in Galveston Bay, Texas. Two practical examples in which shell reefs were removed were then simulated to show the effects of dredging on established circulation. Further analysis of the circulation patterns per-

mitted estimates to be made of the physical exchange across the dredged areas and in other parts of the bay system. (See also W75-06998) (Humphreys-ISWS)
W75-07030

MATHEMATICAL MODELLING FOR SHORT-TERM TRANSPORT IN VERTICALLY MIXED ESTUARIES,
Madras Univ., Guindy (India). Dept. of Hydraulic Engineering.
M. Narayanan.
In: River and Estuary Model Analysis, Volume III; Proceedings of the International Association for Hydraulic Research Symposium on River Mechanics (4 Vol.), Bangkok, Thailand, January 9-12, 1973. Asian Institute of Technology, Bangkok, Thailand, p 429-440, (1973). 5 fig, 7 ref. OWRR C-1158(No 1591)(3).

Descriptors: *Estuaries, *Model studies, *Tidal waters, *Dispersion, *Texas, Mathematical models, Path of pollutants, Effluents, Waste disposal, Water pollution, Tides, Pollutants, Hydraulics, Numerical analysis, Equations, Dissolved solids, Salinity.
Identifiers: *Matagorda Bay(Tex).

A two-dimensional convective-dispersion transport model was described which provides spatial and temporal variations in the concentration of a conservative constituent introduced into a shallow well-mixed estuary. The solution was accomplished through a multistage implicit method and the model used as basic input instantaneous tidal velocities, depths, and dispersion coefficients computed from an operational mathematical tidal hydrodynamics model. The application of the model was demonstrated by slug and continuous releases of conservative materials into high and low tidal velocity areas in Matagorda Bay, Texas. (See also W75-06998) (Sims-ISWS)
W75-07033

CHARACTERISTICS OF THE INTERFACIAL REGION OF A TWO-LAYER FLOW SYSTEM,
Melbourne Univ., Parkville (Australia). Dept. of Civil Engineering.
R. J. Vass.
In: River and Estuary Model Analysis, Volume III; Proceedings of the International Association for Hydraulic Research Symposium on River Mechanics (4 Vol.), Bangkok, Thailand, January 9-12, 1973. Asian Institute of Technology, Bangkok, Thailand, p 441-451, (1973). 4 fig, 8 ref.

Descriptors: *Saline water-freshwater interfaces, *Model studies, *Estuaries, *Density stratification, Mathematical models, Laboratory tests, Boundaries(Surfaces), Flow, Freshwater, Saline water, Density, Velocity, Rivers, Fluid mechanics, Hydraulic models, Transition flow.
Identifiers: *River mechanics.

A study was presented of the behavior of the interfacial region occurring between two fluids of slightly differing densities (fresh and salt water) under various hydraulic conditions. The configuration resembles the central position of an arrested saline wedge that might occur where a freshwater river enters a sea. The prime aim of the study was to investigate the development of the 'transition' region at the interface with distance along the interface under variations of density and upper layer velocities. An approximation method was used to simplify equations and a numerical solution was given for (1) the development of the transition region and (2) the velocity profiles at any point along the interface. Laboratory experiments were conducted to test the theoretical analyses for density differences ranging from 0.15 to 0.75% and for upper layer velocities up to approximately 6 cm/sec. The results presented for one test show reasonable agreement with the theory. (See also W75-06998) (Sims-ISWS)
W75-07034

A MATHEMATICAL MODEL TO PREDICT DISCHARGE VARIATIONS IN AN ESTUARY WITH SHALLOW WATER AND A LARGE TIDAL RANGE,
Ente Nazionale per l'Energia Elettrica, Milan (Italy).
F. Ferrari.
In: River and Estuary Model Analysis, Volume III; Proceedings of the International Association for Hydraulic Research Symposium on River Mechanics (4 Vol.), Bangkok, Thailand, January 9-12, 1973. Asian Institute of Technology, Bangkok, Thailand, p 453-464, (1973). 3 fig, 2 tab, 14 ref.

Descriptors: *Estuaries, *Tidal effects, *River flow, *Model studies, Rivers, Deltas, Mathematical models, Continuity equation, Flow, Discharge(Water), Streamflow forecasting, Powerplants, Thermal powerplants, Cooling water.
Identifiers: *Italy(Po River), Adriatic Sea.

The river Po enters the Adriatic sea with a delta; the Po di Pila branch is the main branch of the delta network. A bars band partially obstructs the river mouth. The tidal effects propagate for about 50 km upstream of the mouth. Given the average daily discharge of the Po in an upstream section at which the tidal effects can be neglected, it is desired to assess the variations of the instantaneous discharge in the branch of the Po di Pila caused by the tide in the sea area in front of the delta. The flow in this branch of the river was studied with a simplified mathematical model based on the hydraulic scheme of a cylindrical channel with large-sill submerged weir. The continuity equation takes into consideration the prism shape of the backwater in the river and the flow through the large-sill weir. The verification of the given method was carried out by using the results of 7 field records of the instantaneous discharge made from 1970 to 1971 in the channel of the Po di Pila. The range of the data for daily average discharge extends from 500 cu m/sec to 2300 cu m/sec. The results are satisfactory as far as the evaluation of the minimum and maximum values of instantaneous discharge and the maximum variation of discharge during the tidal cycle is concerned. (See also W75-06998) (Sims-ISWS)
W75-07035

FINITE ELEMENT NUMERICAL MODELLING OF FLOW AND DISPERSION IN ESTUARIES,
University Coll. of Swansea (Wales). Dept. of Civil Engineering.
C. Taylor, and J. Davis.
In: River and Estuary Model Analysis, Volume III; Proceedings of the International Association for Hydraulic Research Symposium on River Mechanics (4 Vol.), Bangkok, Thailand, January 9-12, 1973. Asian Institute of Technology, Bangkok, Thailand, p 465-476, (1973). 4 fig, 8 ref.

Descriptors: *Estuaries, *Model studies, *Dispersion, *Finite element analysis, Effluents, Mathematical studies, Equations, Waste disposal, Pollutants, Tidal effects, Numerical analysis, Hydraulics, Mathematical models, Estuarine environment.

The finite element numerical method was used to formulate, in matrix form, the equations governing the dispersion of effluent within a bounded tidal domain. The relevant equations were those depicting conservation of momentum and mass and the advective diffusion equation for each effluent species. Each equation was assembled in matrix form and subsequently solved, either coupled or uncoupled, with appropriate iterative implicit techniques. The applicability of the technique was tested by comparison with known analytic solutions and other physical or numerical models. Experience with the tidal model showed that the finite element method offers distinct advantages in reproducing physical processes. A particular mesh can be refined in a region of interest and actual boundary geometry is more easily followed. (See also W75-06998) (Sims-ISWS)
W75-07036

A WATER-QUALITY SIMULATION MODEL FOR WELL MIXED ESTUARIES AND COASTAL SEAS: VOL. VI, SIMULATION, OBSERVATION, AND STATE ESTIMATION,
New York City-Rand Inst., N.Y.
For primary bibliographic entry see Field 5B.
W75-07042

ESTIMATION OF SEA SURFACE TEMPERATURE FROM REMOTE SENSING IN THE 11- TO 13-MICROMETER WINDOW REGION,
National Aeronautics and Space Administration, Greenbelt, Md. Goddard Space Flight Center.
For primary bibliographic entry see Field 7B.
W75-07043

COPPER IN SURFACE WATERS SOUTH OF NEW ZEALAND,
Massachusetts Inst. of Tech., Cambridge. Dept. of Earth and Planetary Sciences.
For primary bibliographic entry see Field 2K.
W75-07060

SUMMARY AND ANALYSIS OF PHYSICAL OCEANOGRAPHY DATA COLLECTED IN THE NEW YORK BIGHT APEX DURING 1969-70,
National Oceanic and Atmospheric Administration, Boulder, Colo. Marine Ecosystems Analysis Program.
R. L. Charnell, and D. V. Hansen.
Available from NTIS, Springfield, Va 22161 as COM-75-10358, $375 in paper copy, $2.25 in microfiche. MESA Report No. 74-3, August 1974, 49 p.

Descriptors: *Oceanography, *Circulation, *Water flow, *Stratification, Ocean currents, Oceans, Temperature, Salinity, Seasonal variations, Estuaries, Bottom water, Runoff, Water masses, Tidal currents, Turbidity currents, Hudson River, New York.
Identifiers: *Physical oceanography, *New York Bight, Hudson River discharge, Water movement.

An analysis is presented of physical oceanography data collected on a monthly basis in the apex of the New York Bight during 1969 and early 1970. Data include temperature and salinity values, recovery information on surface and seabed drifters, and current meter observations. Hudson River discharge and wind data from Ambrose light station are also included. The data show apex water to be stratified three-fourths of the year caused by high river runoff and insolation. During winter, heat loss and wind mixing destroy and impede reformation of stratification. There is a strong northward flow of water in the lower layers along the axis of the Hudson shelf channel; some of this bottom water flows into the Hudson estuary and part turns eastward to flow parallel to Long Island. Eventually, this eastward flow turns and joins the southwest flow of shelf water, suggesting that an anticyclonic circulation exists in the apex most of the year. Surface flow exhibits high seasonality in response to surface winds, with northward flow during spring and summer and southeast movement during fall and winter. Surface flow from Raritan Bay flows south along the New Jersey coast most of the year. (NOAA)
W75-07069

STATISTICAL PROPERTIES OF WAVE-CURRENT FORCE,
North Carolina State Univ., Raleigh. Dept. of Civil Engineering, and North Carolina State Univ., Raleigh. Dept. of Geosciences.
Chi C. Tung, and N. E. Huang.
North Carolina University Sea Grant Reprint No. 53, 15 p. Reprint from: Journal of the Waterways

Identifiers: Coastal processes, Tidal currents, *Littoral transport, Tubbs Inlet(NC), Fluorescent tracers, Sea Grant Program, Bypassing.

A pattern of sediment movement and sediment transport rate into the estuary through Tubbs Inlet was established by mapping bedform and sedimentary structure orientation, analysis of tidal-current direction and velocity throughout a complete tidal cycle, and analysis of fluorescent tracer sand movement. The generalized sediment transport pattern indicated movement into the estuary across the intertidal sand flats of the inlet by flood-tidal currents. During flood tide waves are refracted around the ebb-tidal delta and focused toward the inlet. Breaking waves place sediment into suspension which is then transported by tidal currents. Sediment is moved landward through the main channel; however, net movement through the gorge is seaward. Current velocities in the main channel are maximum during ebb flow. Flood currents in the gorge range from 50 cm/sec to 75 cm/sec. Sediment is moved seaward, primarily through the main channel, and reintroduced into the littoral transport system bypassing the inlet. Concentrated zones of tracer sand were detected as the 'sand mass' moved along the recurved spit on the eastern side of the inlet. The rate of net transport of these zones was approximately 0.6 cm/sec. The movement rate of the concentrated zones was much less than the rates calculated for individual tracer grains. (NOAA)
W75-07072

A NEW TECHNIQUE FOR BEACH EROSION CONTROL,
North Carolina State Univ., Raleigh. Center for Marine Coastal Studies.
For primary bibliographic entry see Field 2J.
W75-07073

COASTAL ZONE MANAGEMENT: THE PROCESS OF PROGRAM DEVELOPMENT,
Coastal Zone Management Inst., Sandwich, Mass.
J. Armstrong, H. Bissell, R. Davenport, J. Goodman, and M. Hershman.
November 1974. 390 p, 10 fig, 5 tab, 376 ref, 3 append. $10.00. NOAA 3-37157.

Descriptors: *Coasts, *Planning, *Management, *Boundaries(Property), Estuaries, Legislation, Information exchange, Legal aspects, Water law, Boundary disputes, Bibliographies.
Identifiers: *Coastal zone management, Land and water uses, Geography, Public performance, *Sanctuaries.

A technical guide is presented for use by state and local officials involved in the development and implementation of coastal zone management programs. It has been organized in such a way as to parallel the requirements for management program development which are contained in the Coastal Zone Management Act of 1972 and the Section 305 regulations published November 29, 1973, in the Federal Register (15 CFR 920). Additional information on the design of a management program consistent with the Act's requirements is contained in the criteria for management program approval published in draft form August 21, 1974, in the Federal Register (15 CFR 923). The Coastal Zone Management Act of 1972 is reproduced in the appendix. A bibliography is organized according to geographical areas. (NOAA)
W75-07075

PLANNING FOR SHORELINE AND WATER USES.
For primary bibliographic entry see Field 6B.
W75-07086

THE LIMNOBIOLOGY OF DEVILS LAKE CHAIN, NORTH DAKOTA,
North Dakota Univ., Grand Forks. Dept. of Biology.
For primary bibliographic entry see Field 5B.
W75-07102

OYSTER REEF SEDIMENTATION, BILOXI BAY, MISSISSIPPI,
University of Southern Mississippi, Hattiesburg. Dept. of Geology.
C. M. Hoskin.
Southeastern Geology, Vol 16, No 1, p 41-57, August 1974. 7 fig, 32 ref. OWRT A-051-MISS(3).

Descriptors: *Sedimentology, *Bays, *Reefs, *Oysters, Estuaries, Banks, Shellfish, Deposition(Sediments), Sediment transport, Silts, Clays, Sands, Gravels, Suspended solids, *Mississippi.
Identifiers: *Biloxi Bay(Miss), Shells.

Size-frequency distributions were determined for bottom sediments, collected by grab, from three living oyster reefs (27 samples) and from two non-reef sites (33 samples). Oyster reef sediments were found to contain 10% gravel (shells), about 60% sand (mixture of fragmented shells and quartz), 15% silt, and 15% clay. Nearby non-reef sediment contained only traces of gravel, about 35% sand, 28% silt, and 38% clay. Size-frequency distributions of reef sediment were leptokurtic, and those for non-reef sediments were platykurtic. Grainsize parameters of mean size, standard deviation and skewness did not distinguish between reef and non-reef sediments. Measured current velocities ranged up to 0.94 ft/sec at the surface, and near bottom currents met the threshold velocity of 0.5 ft/sec for erosion and transport of fine sand. Suspended sediment loads ranged between 58 and 183 mg/l, tending to be greater downwind in both reef and non-reef environments. Suspended sediment load varies with the wind, decreasing with decreasing wind velocity. (Sims-ISWS)
W75-07148

THERMAL ALTERATION OF ORGANIC MATTER IN RECENT MARINE SEDIMENTS. I PIGMENTS,
California Univ., Los Angeles. Inst. of Geophysics and Planetary Physics.
For primary bibliographic entry see Field 5B.
W75-07167

THERMAL ALTERATION OF ORGANIC MATTER IN RECENT MARINE SEDIMENTS. III ALIPHATIC AND STEROIDAL ALCOHOLS,
California Univ., Los Angeles. Inst. of Geophysics and Planetary Physics.
For primary bibliographic entry see Field 5B.
W75-07169

TIDAL AND DIURNAL EFFECTS ON ZOOPLANKTON SAMPLE VARIABILITY IN A NEARSHORE MARINE ENVIRONMENT,
Bedford Inst., Dartmouth (Nova Scotia).
D. D. Sameoto.
Journal of the Fisheries Research Board of Canada, Vol 32, No 3, p 347-366, March 1975. 5 fig, 6 tab, 17 ref.

Descriptors: *Zooplankton, *Sampling, *Variability, *Estuarine environment, Copepods, Fluctuations, Correlation analysis, Tides, Tidal effects, Diurnal, Oceanography, Nets, Statistical analysis, Biomass, Aquatic life, *Canada.
Identifiers: St. Margaret's Bay(Canada), Nova Scotia.

Two 26-h series of duplicate and replicate vertical zooplankton samples taken at two stations at two different times of the year showed that a periodic fluctuation correlated to the tide was present in the biomass of zooplankton and in the numbers of animals of several copepod species. Diurnally migrating species of zooplankton did not show a tidal correlation. The hour to hour fluctuations in zooplankton were generally more important than the difference between stations 1.6 km apart.

Similar relations were found between the zooplankton and the tide in May and August even though there were significant differences in the composition of the zooplankton community during the two periods. Correlation coefficients between all species in all samples showed the presence of a diurnally migrating predator community and a ıonmigrating prey community consisting of opepods. An experiment using sample data suggested that to obtain a reasonably accurate estimate of the mean numbers of a given species, at .ast two vertical tows should be made on a station at a 6-h interval. (Sims-ISWS)
W75-07179

AN APPLICATION OF THE METHOD OF CHARACTERISTICS TO TIDAL CALCULATIONS IN (X-Y-T) SPACE,
University of Strathcylde, Glasgow (Scotland). Dept. of Civil Engineering.
J. M. Townson.
Journal of Hydraulic Research, Vol 12, No 4, p 499-523, 1974. 14 fig, 29 ref.

Descriptors: *Estuaries, *Circulation, *Tides, *Analytical techniques, *Fluid mechanics, Model studies, Density currents, Boundary processes, Coriolis force, Dispersion, Computers, Equations, Numerical analysis, Waves(Water), Currents(Water).
Identifiers: *Method of characteristics, Bicharacteristics.

In (x-y-t) space, the characteristic surfaces were defined by two so-called bicharacteristics obtained from the eigenvalues of the coefficient matrix of the long wave equations presented. The method of characteristics was shown as a basic tool in the (x-y-t) tidal situation. The method deals with all variables at the same point and, thus, represents some advantage over staggered grid methods. Results obtained by applying the method to a relatively coarse representation of an estuary were in broad agreement with measurements taken from a physical model. However, numerical models of the long wave equations along may not reproduce such effects as circulations in hydraulic models. An explicit version of the convective diffusion equation was coupled with the long wave system and certain features of float movement were reproduced by the action of the convective terms alone. The method of characteristics was suggested as a convenient framework for the manipulation of data on estuary processes. (Singh-ISWS)
W75-07182

EVALUATION OF THE CAUSES OF LEVEE EROSION IN THE SACRAMENTO-SAN JOAQUN DELTA, CALIFORNIA,
Geological Survey, Menlo Park, Calif.
For primary bibliographic entry see Field 2J.
W75-07210

TIDAL DISCHARGE ASYMMETRY IN A SALT MARSH DRAINAGE SYSTEM,
Virginia Inst. of Marine Science, Gloucester Point.
J. D. Boon, III.
Limnology and Oceanography, Vol 20, No 1, p 71-80, January 1975. 7 fig, 1 tab, 21 ref.

Descriptors: *Tidal waters, *Tidal streams, *Tidal marshes, Discharge(Water), *Virginia, Currents(Water), Channel flow, Suspended solids, Hydraulics, Marshes, Salt marshes, Drainage systems, On-site investigations, Measurement, Model studies.
Identifiers: *Tidal cycles, Current speed, Wachapreague(Va), Little Fool Creek(Va).

Tidal discharge and area-averaged current speed were measured over complete tidal cycles at the entrance to a salt marsh drainage system near Wachapreague, Virginia. A pronounced asymmetry in curves of discharge and current speed through time was observed which can be simulated by a model incorporating semidiurnal tides and 'overtides' in conjunction with marsh and channel storage relationships. As a persistent feature in marsh channel flow relationships, the asymmetry, along with an apparent difference in flood and ebb maxima, may have a systematic, long-term influence on the net transport of suspended matter entering and leaving natural marshes. (Lee-ISWS)
W75-07244

AN AUTOMATED TECHNIQUE FOR TOTAL DISSOLVED FREE AMINO ACIDS IN SEAWATER,
Oregon State Univ., Corvallis. School of Oceanography.
For primary bibliographic entry see Field 5A.
W75-07247

A COMPARISON OF VERTICAL DRIFT-ENVELOPES TO CONVENTIONAL DRIFT-BOTTLES,
Michigan Univ., Ann Arbor. Dept. of Atmospheric and Oceanic Science.
E. C. Monahan, B. J. Higgins, and G. T. Kaye.
Limnology and Oceanography, Vol 20, No 1, p 141-147, January 1975. 3 fig, 2 tab, 10 ref.

Descriptors: *Currents(Water), *Drift bottles, *Water circulation, Ocean currents, Oceanography, Drifting(Aquatic), Winds, Seiches, On-site investigations, Laboratory tests, *Massachusetts.
Identifiers: *Vertical drift-envelopes, Nantucket Sound(Mass), Cape Cod(Mass).

A comparison of the recovery sites of vertical drift-envelopes and of ballasted drift-bottles released simultaneously at common locations in Nantucket Sound off Cape Cod substantiates a preliminary conclusion, based on small tank experiments and simple calculations, that vertical envelopes move more rapidly through the water due to direct wind influence than do ballasted bottles. The bottles therefore provide a truer indication of surface currents than do the envelopes. (Jess-ISWS)
W75-07248

SEASONAL VARIATION OF THE ALONGSHORE VELOCITY FIELD OVER THE CONTINENTAL SHELF OFF OREGON,
Department of the Environment, Ottawa (Ontario). Marine Sciences Directorate.
A. Huyer, R. D. Pillsbury, and R. L. Smith.
Limnology and Oceanography, Vol 20, No 1, p 90-95, January 1975. 8 fig, 17 ref. NSF Grants GX-28746, GX-33502.

Descriptors: *Ocean currents, *Currents(Water), *Coasts, Water circulation, *Continental shelf, Rip currents, Oceanography, *Oregon, Seasonal, Velocity.

The seasonal variation in the alongshore velocity field was inferred from direct current observations made over the Oregon continental shelf at various locations and irregular intervals since 1965. Monthly mean currents were computed and compared with earlier studies to give a description of the seasonal variation in the alongshore currents. In winter, the alongshore flow is generally northward and independent of depth. In spring, flow is southward at all depths but stronger near the surface. In summer, surface flow is southward and deep flow is northward; the southward surface flow forms a coastal jet and the deep northward velocity increases with distance offshore. (Jess-ISWS)
W75-07249

A COMPARISON OF OBSERVED AND NUMERICALLY SIMULATED CIRCULATION IN THE CAYMAN SEA,
National Oceanic and Atmospheric Administration, Miami, Fla. Atlantic Oceanographic and Meteorological Lab.
R. L. Molinari.
Journal of Physical Oceanography, Vol 5, No 1, p 51-62, January 1975. 17 fig, 13 ref. NSF Grant GA 20569; IDOE Grant AG-253.

Descriptors: *Circulation, *Currents(Water) *Oceans, Anticyclones, Eddies, Numerical analysis, Model studies, On-site investigations, Topography, Advection, Friction, Flow.
Identifiers: *Cayman Sea, *Yucatan Current.

An observational and numerical study of the circulation in the Cayman Sea was presented. Data taken in three different years suggested a common February to May circulation pattern. A well-developed current crosses 85W south of the Cayman Ridge. An anticylonic eddy in the central basin appeared to be a common feature of this season's circulation. The data from these cruises consistently portrayed significant accelerations occurring in the vicinity of Cozumel Island where the flow merges with the Yucatan Current. A different pattern was inferred from data collected in July and August. The north component of the flow over the western edge of the Cayman Ridge appeared to determine the type of flow regime observed. The numerical model was based on predictive equations for the voricities in a two-layer ocean on a beta-plane, and included topographic, advective, and friction effects. The model was driven by lateral input boundary conditions derived from an April-May 1968 observational study. The baroclinic western boundary current of the numerical model developed in response to eastern input boundary conditions, while the barotropic current was constrained to intensify and flow along the continental slopes. (Roberts-ISWS)
W75-07250

COASTAL MORPHOLOGY,
Louisiana State Univ., Baton Rouge.
H. J. Walker.
Soil Science, Vol 119, No 1, p 3-19, January 1975. 4 fig, 40 ref.

Descriptors: *Seashores, *Geomorphology, *Coasts, *Tidal effects, *Beach erosion, Lagoons, Estuaries, Deltas, Dunes, Reefs, Coral, Ocean waves, Barriers, Oceans, Ocean currents.
Identifiers: *Coastal morphology, Coastal processes, Cliffs, Coastal forms, Subaerial processes, Subaqueous processes.

The coast, i.e., the zone where land, sea, and atmosphere meet, is one of earth's most varied and variable environments. Its tectonic and climatic history have produced a configuration which is being altered by physical, chemical, and biological processes. Because these processes operate at different intensities in various parts of the world, the degree of alteration varies greatly. Coastal processes cause both erosion and deposition but the overall effect is a tendency toward smoothing out the coastline. Some of the most common forms along coasts of today are cliffs, beaches, lagoons, estuaries, deltas, dunes, and reefs. Many of these are ephemeral and are present today mainly because coatal processes are operating at a level only recently reached by a rising sea. Even though stillstand has prevailed only 3000-5000 years, there already has been a major reduction in the size and variety of many of these forms and also a major reduction in the quantity of sand available for the nourishment of the world's beaches and coastal dunes. As long as stillstand continues, variety in coastal forms is destined to be reduced even more. (Lee-ISWS)
W75-07270

TYPE 16 FLOOD INSURANCE STUDY: TSUNAMI PREDICTIONS FOR PACIFIC COASTAL COMMUNITIES,
Army Engineer Waterways Experiment Station, Vicksburg, Miss.
For primary bibliographic entry see Field 6F.
W75-07283

UNSTEADY SALINITY INSTRUSION IN ESTUARIES; PART I: ONE-DIMENSIONAL, TRANSIENT SALINITY INTRUSION WITH VARYING FRESHWATER INFLOW; PART II: TWO-DIMENSIONAL ANALYSIS OF TIME-AVERAGED SALINITY AND VELOCITY PROFILES,
Massachusetts Inst. of Tech., Cambridge. Ralph M. Parsons Lab. for Water Resources and Hydrodynamics.
J. S. Fisher, D. R. F. Harleman, and M. L. Thatcher.
Available from the National Technical Information Service, Springfield, Va., 22161, as AD-782 804, $3.75 in paper copy, $2.25 in microfiche. Committee on Tidal Hydraulics, Corps of Engineers, US Army, Technical Bulletin No. 20, July 1974. 41 p, 14 fig, 2 tab, 12 ref. DA-22-079-CIVENG-65-20.

Descriptors: *Estuaries, *Salinity, *Saline water intrusion, Inflow, Hydraulics, Mathematical models, Hydraulic models, Model studies, Tidal water, Forecasting, Distribution patterns, Equations, Flow profiles, Unsteady flow, *Correlation analysis.
Identifiers: *Velocity distribution.

A study concerned with transient salinity intrusion is described in two parts. In Part I a one-dimensional numerical model is developed for the prediction of transient salinity intrusion under conditions of varying freshwater inflow. The model couples the one-dimensional continuity and momentum equation for unsteady tidal motion in a variable area estuary with the mass transport equation for salinity. In Part II a two-dimensional analytical model is developed for the prediction of vertical distributions of velocity and salinity, averaged over a tidal period. The results of the numerical model described in Part I are used to determine the longitudinal salinity gradient which, for partially and well-mixed estuaries, is assumed to be independent of depth. The governing equations of the two-dimensional model are the vertical and longitudinal equations of motion, the equations of continuity and salt conservation, and an equation of state relating salinity and density. Dimensionless correlations, between mean vertical mass and momentum transfer coefficients and gross estuary characteristics, based on previous experimental data are pesented. These correlations are used to predict vertical velocity and salinity profiles for the WES salinity flume for the 25 tidal cycle test with decreasing freshwater inflow. Comparisons of predicted and observed salinity and velocity profiles are given. (WES)
W75-07284

REMEDIAL PLANS FOR PREVENTION OF HARBOR SHOALING, PORT ORFORD, OREGON; HYDRAULIC MODEL INVESTIGATION,
Army Engineer Waterways Experiment Station, Vicksburg, Miss.
For primary bibliographic entry see Field 8B.
W75-07285

STA-POND STABILITY TESTS; HYDRAULIC MODEL INVESTIGATION,
Army Engineer Waterways Experiment Station, Vicksburg, Miss.
For primary bibliographic entry see Field 8B.
W75-07287

A COMPARATIVE STUDY OF PRIMARY PRODUCTION AND STANDING CROPS OF PHYTOPLANKTON IN A PORTION OF THE UPPER CHESAPEAKE BAY SUBSEQUENT TO TROPICAL STORM AGNES,
Johns Hopkins Univ., Baltimore, Md. McCollum-Pratt Inst.
For primary bibliographic entry see Field 5C.
W75-07291

AUTECOLOGY OF VAGILE AND HEMISESSILE SPECIES ON PILES OVERGROWN WITH VEGETATION AND ANIMALS: MACROFAUNA. 5. MOLLUSKS,
L. Schutz.
Available from the National Technical Information Service, Springfield, Va 22161 as AD-784 653, $3.25 in paper copy, $2.25 in microfiche. NOO T-22, 1974. 17 p, 51 ref. Translated from Internationale Revue der Gesamten Hydrobiologie, Vol 54, p 581-592, 1969.

Descriptors: *Benthic fauna, *Ecological distribution, *Life cycles, *Mollusks, Mussels, Salinity, Crustaceans, Brackish water, Growth rates, Diets, Reproduction.
Identifiers: *Motile species, Salinity gradient, Mytilus edulis, Congeria cochleata, Embletonis pallida.

The life cycles of many motile micro- and macroanimals show that euryhaline animals alter their life rhythm when they leave the sea and migrate into brackish water. The stronger the limnic influence, the more retarded are development and growth. The environment influences the overall regulation and coordination system of development. The extremely euryhaline mussel, Mytilus edulis, adapts its life rhythm to salinity variations. The species Congeria has representatives generally in tropic-subtropic brackish waters. Congeria cochleata appears mainly in Beta-mesohaline and in Alpha-oligohaline areas of the Baltic Canal. In the boreal zone, C. cochleata is relatively insensitive to waste water contamination. It attaches itself to piles, stones, and even aquatic plants, as well as to mud bottom. The opistobranchian, Embletonia pallids, appears in brackish waters in the boreal zone. The easternmost encounter was in the Baltic Sea near Helsinki, northernmost encounter was near Kalmar. The distribution, habitats, food habits, life cycles and reproduction of these mollusks are described. (Jones-Wisconsin)
W75-07296

THE SEAWEEDS OF THE MURMANSK REGION IN THE VICINITY OF THE MALYY OLENIY (NEMETSKIY) ISLAND,
For primary bibliographic entry see Field 5C.
W75-07297

EFFECT OF INTERACTIONS BETWEEN TEMPERATURE AND NITRATE SUPPLY ON THE CELL-DIVISION RATES OF TWO MARINE PHYTOFLAGELLATES,
California Univ., San Diego, La Jolla. Inst. of Marine Resources.
For primary bibliographic entry see Field 5C.
W75-07322

INFORMATION FOR BUYERS AND OWNERS OF COASTAL PROPERTY IN NORTH CAROLINA.
North Carolina State Univ., Raleigh. Center for Marine and Coastal Studies.
For primary bibliographic entry see Field 6E.
W75-07350

3. WATER SUPPLY AUGMENTATION AND CONSERVATION

3A. Saline Water Conversion

MULTICOMPONENT FIXED-BED ION-EXCHANGE: THEORY, PRACTICAL SIMPLIFICATIONS, AND PROCESS APPLICATIONS,
California Univ., Berkeley. Sea Water Conversion Lab.
G. Klein, and T. Vermeulen.
SWCL Report 74-1, July 1974. 51 p, 2 fig, 2 tab, 67 ref. OSW Grants 14-01-0001-358, 14-01-0001-737, 14-01-0001-1698.

Descriptors: *Desalination, *Desalination processes, *Ion exchange, Separation techniques, Water treatment, Sea water, Resins, Cation exchange, Anion exchange, Chemical reactions, Chemical precipitation, Theoretical analysis, Laboratory tests.
Identifiers: Deionization, Fixed-bed ion exchange, Column dynamics.

The general theory of fixed-bed separations for ion exchange and adsorption was reviewed, with emphasis on extensions contributed by this study. Findings based on the equilibrium model were discussed, as applied to single stepwise feed-composition changes. Mathematical methods for calculating composition-path grids, phase equilibria, and composition-velocity eigenvalues were reviewed and amplified for both mass-action and constant-separation-factor systems, and an improved version for complete calculation of equilibrium performance of ternary ion-exchange systems was provided. A survey was given on ion-exchange accompanied by chemical reaction -- i.e., complexing and precipitation. Also, experimental and theoretical work on column dynamics of multicomponent ion exchange was surveyed with consideration of cyclic operations. (Sims-ISWS)
W75-07045

3B. Water Yield Improvement

A CASE STUDY OF TWO STORMFURY CLOUDLINE SEEDING EVENTS,
National Oceanic and Atmospheric Administration, Boulder, Colo. Weather Modification Program Office.
R. C. Sheets, and S. C. Pearce.
NOAA Technical Memorandum ERL WMPO-21, February 1975, 55 p.

Descriptors: *Cloud seeding, *Clouds, Weather modification, Cloud physics, Atmospheric physics, Meteorology, Atmosphere, Convection, Climatology, Radar, Weather patterns, Temperature, Water vapor, Atmospheric pressure, Wind pressure.
Identifiers: *Cloudline seeding, Project STORMFURY, Cloud structure, Vertical velocities, Equivalent potential temperature, Cloud environment.

Two cloudline seeding cases were selected for study from the Project STORMFURY cloudline exercises. One case involved clouds in a rather active convective environment while the other case was more isolated. Both cases show that the seeded clouds grew more than the surrounding clouds but no unbiased control clouds were monitored. The temperature at the 550 mb level in the disturbed area were approximately 1C colder than ambient temperatures. This temperature drop is attributed to evaporative cooling in an extremely dry layer which existed at this level. No significant temperature change was noted at the 350 mb level, but at least a temporary increase in the broad scale water vapor content at this level was observed. The duration of these changes is undetermined. (NOAA)
W75-07078

PRELIMINARY RESULTS OF THE COMPARISON OF THE AMOUNT OF ARTIFICIAL PRECIPITATION AND WATER RESERVES OF SEEDED FRONTAL CLOUDS,
B. N. Leskov.
Available from the National Technical Information Service, Springfield, Va 22161 as AD-782 066, $3.25 in paper copy, $2.25 in microfiche. FTD-HT-23-1177-74, June 26, 1974. 7 p, 1 fig, 1 tab, 7 ref. Translated from Trudy Ukrainskiy Nauchno-Iss-

ledovatel'skiy Gidrometeorologicheskiy Institut. Issledovaniya Protsessov Oblako- i Osadkoobrazovaniya, No. 106, p 37-41, 1971.

Descriptors: *Weather modification, *Artificial precipitation, *Cloud seeding, *Precipitable water, Precipitation(Atmospheric), Cloud physics, Storms, Meteorology, Rain, Clouds, Fronts(Atmospheric).
Identifiers: Frontal clouds.

For estimating the degree of washout of seeded layers by artificial precipitation, it is of interest to compare their water reserves with the amount of artificial precipitation. Analysis of the compared values showed that, in the majority of cases, they differ greatly from each other; in addition, the actual amount of artificial precipitation sometimes exceeds the total water reserves of the precipitation layers. It is impossible to consider frontal clouds as reservoirs of possible additional moisture. They are generators of natural precipitation. Upon introducing additional nuclei of precipitation particles into the cloud, the cloud continues to work as a generator causing the growth and release of artificial precipitation particles. Frontal cloud modification should lead not to a redistribution but to an absolute increase in precipitation. (Sims-ISWS)
W75-07163

CAN THE BALTIC SEA BE TURNED INTO A FRESHWATER LAKE,
For primary bibliographic entry see Field 4A.
W75-07165

EFFECTIVENESS OF CONTROLLED CONVECTION IN PRODUCING PRECIPITATION,
Massachusetts Inst. of Tech., Cambridge. Dept. of Meteorology.
V. P. Starr, D. A. Anati, and D. A. Salstein.
Journal of Geophysical Research, Vol 79, No 27, p 4047-4052, September 20, 1974. 2 fig, 2 tab, 9 ref, 1 append. NSF Grant GA-1310X.

Descriptors: *Convection, *Precipitation(Atmospheric), Water vapor, Mining, Thunderstorms, Entrainment, Atmosphere, Energy, Buoyancy, Condensation, Saturation, Dry seasons, Radiosondes, Computer programs, Analysis, Shafts(Excavations), Density, Stability.
Identifiers: *Controlled atmospheric convection, Aerological accelerator, Lapse rate.

The effectiveness of controlled atmospheric convection was analyzed in comparison to natural precipitation at five different locations on the globe. The aerological accelerator, a vertical tube of large height and diameter, presents a method for removal of water vapor from air by vertical convection. The question of whether a period of low precipitation is a period of favorable or unfavorable conditions for production of water by the aerological accelerator was examined. In addition, a prototype of the device was presented, namely, a deep mine shaft that produces water upon condensation in forced vertically rising air. (Jones-ISWS)
W75-07199

PREDICTING REDUCTION IN WATER LOSSES FROM OPEN CHANNELS BY PHREATOPHYTE CONTROL,
Agricultural Research Service, Phoenix, Ariz. Water Conservation Lab.
H. Bouwer.
Water Resources Research, Vol 11, No 1, p 96-101, February 1975. 7 fig, 2 tab, 16 ref.

Descriptors: Phreatophytes, *Water loss, *Open channels, Channels, Seepage, Water tables, *Flood plains, Streams, Evapotranspiration, Groundwater, Vegetation, Evaporation.
Identifiers: *Phreatophytic control, Water savings, Step functions, Salt cedar.

A procedure was presented for calculating seepage from a stream due to uptake of groundwater by vegetation or evaporation from soil in the floodplain. The calculation required that the relation between evapotranspiration rate and water table depth be known. When these relations were available for a given floodplain before and after removal of phreatophytes, the reduction in seepage losses from the stream due to phreatophyte removal could be computed. To simplify the calculation process, the curves relating evapotranspiration rate and water table depth, which are generally sigmoid (curved in two directions), could be approximated by step functions of the same area. Potential water savings by phreatophyte control were calculated for step functions that were representative of deep-rooted vegetation, shallow rooted vegetation, and bare soil In addition to the depth from which groundwater could be evaporated before and after phreatophyte removal, the water savings were affected by the vertical distance between the water level in the stream and the floodplain. (Roberts-ISWS)
W75-07264

THE IMPACTS OF SNOW ENHANCEMENT: TECHNOLOGY ASSESSMENT OF WINTER OROGRAPHIC SNOWPACK AUGMENTATION IN THE UPPER COLORADO RIVER BASIN.
Stanford Research Inst., Menlo Park, Calif.
University of Oklahoma Press, Norman, 1974. 624 p, 100 tab, 33 fig, 294 ref, 7 append. Compiled by L. W. Weisbecker.

Descriptors: *Colorado River Basin, *Weather modification, *Artificial precipitation, *Arid lands, *Snow management, Cloud seeding, Colorado, Arizona, Utah, California, Nevada, Water shortage, Environmental effects, Snowpacks, Water yield improvement, Legal aspects.
Identifiers: *Technology assessment.

The Winter Orographic Snowpack Augmentation program (WOSA) offers an inexpensive method of increasing the water supply in the Colorado River Basin. For a cost of $5.4 million per annum, the project will generate about 2.3 million acre feet of runoff within the Basin and 1.2 million outside it. The environmental, economic and social impacts of WOSA on the high mountain areas where it will be operated are almost uniformly negative. The impacts are of moderate intensity and can be compensated, controlled and monitored for an additional $5.0 million per year. The water produced in the mountains would be of no benefit to local residents but would be used by downstream desert states. A major problem facing WOSA is the development of law and policy to deal with the implications of this new technology; new guidelines must be formulated to deal with it. (See also W75-07334) (Bowden-Arizona)
W75-07333

SNOWPACK, CLOUD-SEEDING, AND THE COLORADO RIVER: A TECHNOLOGY ASSESSMENT OF WEATHER MODIFICATION,
Stanford Research Inst., Menlo Park, Calif.
L. W. Weisbecker.
University of Oklahoma Press, Norman, 1974. 86 p, 16 fig, append.

Descriptors: *Cloud seeding, *Snowpacks, *Colorado River Basin, *Weather modification, Snow, Mountains, Runoff, Streamflow, Water quality, Silver iodide, Environmental effects, Avalanches, Floods, Meteorology, Legal aspects, Orography.
Identifiers: Snowpack augmentation, *Technology assessment.

A technology assessment was made of winter orographic snowpack augmentation in the Colorado River Basin. The assessment consisted of: (1) a cost/effectiveness analysis based on the state-of-the-art in snowpack augmentation; (2) an estimate of improved cost/benefit ratios that might be achieved over a five-year period through improvements in the state-of-the-art of snowpack augmentation, (3) an assessment of the impact of snowpack augmentation on the economic, social, and environmental systems; (4) an assessment of public attitudes toward snowpack augmentation; (5) an assessment of the legal and jurisdictional consequences of snowpack augmentation and of potential public policies regarding its implementation; and (6) comparison of snowpack augmentation with other alternative means of alleviating water problems in the area. This book is a condensation of a 624-page technical report. (See also W75-07333) (Sims-ISWS)
W75-07334

3C. Use Of Water Of Impaired Quality

QUALITY OF PULP INDUSTRY WASTE WATERS AND THEIR USE FOR CROP IRRIGATION (IZSLEDVANE NA KACHESTVATA NA OTPAL'CHNITE VODI OT TSELULOZNATA PROMISHLENOST I IZPOLZUVANETO IM ZA NAPOYAVANE NA SELSKOSTOPANSKI KULTURI),
For primary bibliographic entry see Field 5D.
W75-06895

THE EFFECTS OF HUMIDITY AND CYTOKININ ON GROWTH AND WATER RELATIONS OF SALT-STRESSED BEAN PLANTS,
Ceara Univ., Fortaleza (Brazil). Departmente de Bioquimica y Biologia Molecula.
J. T. Prisco, and J. W. O'Leary.
Plant Soil. Vol 39, No 2, p 263-276, 1973.

Descriptors: *Plant growth, *Humidity, Salinity, Water loss.
Identifiers: Hormone balance, Benzyl adenine, Kinin, *Cytokinin.

Salinity inhibited growth of plants in both low and high humidities when compared to control plants grown under the same conditions. However, salt-treated plants grew better under high humidity when compared to salt-stressed plants grown under low humidity. Benzyl adenine (B.A.) sprays did not have any effect on growth of salt-treated plants grown in low humidity. However, when plants were grown in high humidity, B.A. either had no effect or inhibited the growth of the plants. Salinity increased leaf resistance to water vapor loss (R sub L) in both low and high humidity, and B.A. decreased R sub L of salt-treated plants in both humidities. The effects of salinity on decreasing root permeability were the same in both humidities studied, and they were not reversed by B.A. applications. The results do not support the idea that growth inhibition due to salinity is simply the result of impaired cytokinin metabolism and/or transport. Rather, the growth inhibition probably is due to the effect of salinity on the balance of hormones and could be acting at several different steps.--Copyright 1974, Biological Abstracts, Inc.
W75-07022

WASTE WATER RECLAMATION: THE STATE-WIDE PICTURE,
California State Dept. of Water Resources, Sacramento.
For primary bibliographic entry see Field 5D.
W75-07118

HEALTH ASPECTS OF WATER REUSE,
Los Angeles County Sanitation District, Calif.
F. D. Dryden, and H. J. Ongerth.
Typescript paper presented at the 47th Annual Conference of the Water Pollution Control Federation, Denver, Colorado, October 7, 1974. 15 p, 18 ref.

Descriptors: *Water reuse, *Public health, *Water quality, *Water purification, *Hazards, *Organic wastes, Organic compounds, Reclaimed water, Pesticide toxicity, Heavy metals, Safety factors. Identifiers: Health aspects.

The degree of health risk from reclaimed water is roughly proportional to the type and degree of human contact with the water and the adequacy and reliability of the treatment processes. The heterogeneous nature of wastewater and the wide ranges in concentrations of organic and inorganic constituents combine to make it a difficult flow stream for which to provide treatment that will reliably achieve a uniform end product. The contaminants in sewage and reclaimed water which are of health concern may be broadly classed as biological agents and chemical agents. Waterborne bacteria and parasitic disease outbreaks of epidemic proportions have been largely eliminated. Increasing attention has been given to the transmission of viral diseases through the water route. For uses of reclaimed water where ingestion is likely, control of chemical contaminants is a necessity. The chemical agents of health concern which may be present in reclaimed water include a wide variety of toxic organic and inorganic chemicals, such as heavy metals and pesticides. Four types of research be conducted: studies of the health of populations subject to percentages of wastewater in their water supplies; bioassays on a variety of wastewater types and degrees of treatment; improved procedures for the identification of organic compounds; and the construction of pilot plants. (Poertner)
W75-07129

HYDROPHYSICAL PROPERTIES, SALT RESERVES AND SOIL DESALINATION PROCESSES IN THE ATREK RECENT DELTA AREAS,
Desert Inst., Ashkhabad (USSR).
A. P. Lavrov, E. V. Larin, S. A. Sanin, and I. G. Tolstolytkin.
Probl Osvoeniya Pustyn'. 5, p 36-40, 1972.

Descriptors: Crops, Agronomic crops, *Rice, Cereal crops, Field crops, *Water requirements, *Soil-water-plant relationships, Deltas, Saline soils.
Identifiers: *USSR(Atrek Delta).

For the cultivation of agricultural crops (rice) in these areas of the USSR the following water dosages are recommended: 1100-1200 m3/ha for meadow soils, 1000-1100 for takyr-like soils and approximately 1000 m3/ha for typical solonchakes (after their improvement).--Copyright 1974, Biological Abstracts, Inc.
W75-07262

3D. Conservation In Domestic and Municipal Use

METROPOLITAN WATER SUPPLY ALLOCATION AND OPERATION,
Northwestern Univ., Evanston, Ill. Dept. of Civil Engineering.
D. L. Hey, and R. S. Gemmell.
Available from the National Technical Information Service, Springfield, Va 22161, as PB-241 260, $5.75 in paper copy, $2.25 in microfiche. University of Illinois Water Resources Center, Urbana-Champaign Research Report No 83, March 1974. 124 p, 17 fig, 14 tab, 55 ref, 2 append. OWRT B-059-ILL(1), UILU-WRC-74-0083.

Descriptors: *Water management(Applied), *Water supply, *Water distribution, *Water allocation, *Water costs, *Regional analysis, Planning, Water utilization, Water demand, Optimum development plans, Distribution systems.
Identifiers: *Geometric programming, *Regional systems, *Municipal water supply industry.

Presently allocation and distribution of water is determined by the supply and demand market, and therefore is geopolitically dictated and inefficient in balancing the supply in a multi-system region. The problem of efficient service districts for water supply systems is examined. Economic efficiency generates conditions which provide a rationale for choosing treatment and transportation facilities from a set of alternatives which will optimize utilization. The major problem is to minimize the total cost of providing a multiple plan and regional water supply system. To achieve maximum use and minimum cost, the capability of each system element must be assessed, and then optimally employed by determining the marginal costs of production and transportation. A methodology is presented for creating an objective function which incorporates production and transportation costs as well as constraints at meeting water demands and capacity limitations. Using data from the physical facilities, treatment processes and existing water supply problems of Chicago, a regional function is constructed and minimization demonstrated. (Salzman-North Carolina)
W75-06851

INSTITUTIONAL INTERACTION IN METROPOLITAN WATER RESOURCE PLANNING,
Metropolitan Council, St. Paul, Minn. Comprehensive Planning Dept.
For primary bibliographic entry see Field 6E.
W75-06939

CROSS-IMPACT SIMULATION IN WATER RESOURCE PLANNING,
Stanford Research Inst., Menlo Park, Calif.
For primary bibliographic entry see Field 6A.
W75-06940

REGIONAL IMPACT OF WATER RESOURCE INVESTMENTS IN A DEVELOPING AREA,
Geological Survey, Reston, Va. Water Resources Div.
For primary bibliographic entry see Field 6A.
W75-06948

VARIATION OF URBAN RUNOFF QUALITY AND QUANTITY WITH DURATION AND INTENSITY OF STORMS--PHASE III,
Texas Tech Univ., Lubbock. Water Resources Center.
For primary bibliographic entry see Field 5B.
W75-06975

INTEGRATION OF HYDROLOGIC, ECONOMIC, ECOLOGIC, SOCIAL, AND WELL-BEING FACTORS IN PLANNING FLOOD CONTROL MEASURES FOR URBAN STREAMS,
Georgia Inst. of Tech., Atlanta. Environmental Resources Center.
For primary bibliography entry see Field 6F.
W75-06980

THE HANLON CREEK STUDY: AN ECOLOGICAL APPROACH TO URBAN PLANNING,
Guelph Univ. (Ontario). Dept. of Land Resource Science.
For primary bibliographic entry see Field 6B.
W75-07067

WATER AND SEWERAGE DEVELOPMENT PLAN - KANSAS CITY METROPOLITAN REGION.
Metropolitan Planning Commission-Kansas City Region, Mo.
For primary bibliographic entry see Field 5D.
W75-07083

BIBLIOGRAPHY AND INDEX OF GEOLOGY AND HYDROLOGY, FRONT RANGE URBAN CORRIDOR, COLORADO,
Colorado Univ., Boulder. Dept. of Geological Sciences.
F. Chronic, and J. Chronic.
Available from Sup Doc, GPO, Washington, DC 20402, price $1.15. (paper cover) Geological Survey Bulletin 1306, 1974. 102 p, 1,810 ref.

Descriptors: *Colorado, *Bibliographies, *Water resources, *Hydrology, *Geology, Urbanization, Environment.
Identifiers: *Front Range Urban Corridor(Colo).

This bibliography describes geological and hydrological information about the Front Range Urban Corridor of Colorado. The Front Range Urban Corridor is one of the fastest growing areas in the Nation. With Denver, Colo. as its geographic, commercial, cultural, and population nucleus, the urban corridor covers about 4,500 square miles and extends north to south about 140 miles along the Front Range of the Rocky Mountains in a belt about 40 miles across. Broad open spaces still exist within this area. In fact, most of the area is rural; but urbanization is accelerating at the fringes of all major communities, and in many places whole new satellite towns are springing up within commuter distance of the larger centers. Urbanization is spreading across the piedmont and into the mountains, giving rise to environmental problems,. (Knapp-USGS)
W75-07218

3E. Conservation In Industry

A NOVEL BLEACHING PROCESS FOR REMOVAL OF COLOR AND TOXICITY FROM BLEACH PLANT EFFLUENT,
MacMillan Bloedel Ltd., Vancouver (British Columbia).
For primary bibliographic entry see Field 5D.
W75-06861

ENVIRONMENTAL PROTECTION AND ITS EFFECTS ON PRODUCTION CONDITIONS IN THE PULP AND PAPER INDUSTRY (UMWELTSCHUTZ UND SEINE AUSWIRKUNGEN AUF DIE PRODUKTIONSBEDINGUNGEN IN DER),
For primary bibliographic entry see Field 5D.
W75-06878

ZURN-ATTISHOLZ SYSTEM IS CHOSEN BY WAUSAU (PAPER MILLS CO.) FOR PULP MILL EFFLUENT.
For primary bibliographic entry see Field 5D.
W75-06879

THE SSVL (STIFTELSEN SKOGSINDUSTRIERNAS VATTEN OCH LUFTVARDSFORSKING) ENVIRONMENTAL CARE PROJECT (OF THE SWEDISH FOREST PRODUCTS INDUSTRY): TECHNICAL SUMMARY.
For primary bibliographic entry see Field 5D.
W75-06880

PAPER AND PAPERBOARD MANUFACTURING. (2). WATER SUPPLIES,
For primary bibliographic entry see Field 5F.
W75-06889

IN-PLANT REDUCTION OF SUSPENDED SOLIDS AT (EDDY FOREST PRODUCTS LTD.) ESPANOLA (ONTARIO),
Eddy Forest Products Ltd., Espanola (Ontario).
For primary bibliographic entry see Field 5D.
W75-06892

WATER REUSE FROM THE BLEACHERY TO THE RECOVERY SYSTEM,
For primary bibliographic entry see Field 5D.
W75-06893

BLEACH PLANT WATER REDUCTION,
For primary bibliographic entry see Field 5D.
W75-06932

FORECASTING INDUSTRIAL WATER UTILIZATION IN THE PETROLEUM REFINING SECTOR: AN OVERVIEW,
New York State Coll. of Agriculture and Life Sciences, Ithaca, N.Y. Dept. of Agricultural Economics.
T. H. Stevens, and R. J. Kalter.
Water Resources Bulletin, Vol 11, No 1, p 155-163, February 1975. 3 tab, 22 ref.

Descriptors: *Forecasting, *Industrial water, *Water utilization, *Water demand, Water resources, *Management, *Oil industry, Demand, Supply, Legislation, Technology, Prices, Energy, Alternative planning, Simulation analysis, Impact, Effluents, Control, Standards, Mathematical models, Systems analysis.
Identifiers: Petroleum refining, *Public policy, Environmental quality, Water recirculation, Petroleum consumption, Refinery location.

Petroleum refining is a major water using industry. At a time when the nation is evaluating energy policy alternatives, attention should be devoted to the relation between these alternatives and water resources management issues. Various factors which affect the utilization of and demand for water in the petroleum refining industry are: water price, environmental quality legislation, and technological elements. Each factor is related to relevant public policy issues. A general overview is presented of the principal water resources management policy issues which must be considered in any analysis of future water utilization; moreover, several empirical estimates of the potential impact of policy alternatives are given. The relationship of the above factors to the degree of water recirculation is presented. Next, alternative petroleum consumption forecasts and refinery location scenarios are developed. A parametric model of fossil fuel markets is utilized. The model is a market simulation framework which is used to forecast the demand and supply of oil, natural gas, and coal. A series of alternative water utilization forecasts for the domestic petroleum refining sector are developed and compared to those presented by others. In general, results obtained from the parametric model fall in the low end of the range of results from other forecasts. (Bell-Cornell)
W75-06944

REGIONAL IMPACT OF WATER RESOURCE INVESTMENTS IN A DEVELOPING AREA,
Geological Survey, Reston, Va. Water Resources Div.
For primary bibliographic entry see Field 6A.
W75-06948

POWER SHORTAGE CONTINGENCY PROGRAM FOR THE PACIFIC NORTHWEST, LEGISLATIVE, REGULATORY AND INSTITUTIONAL ASPECTS,
Kell, Alterman, Runstein and Thomas, Portland, Oreg.
For primary bibliographic entry see Field 6E.
W75-06977

WATER USE AND COAL DEVELOPMENT IN EASTERN MONTANA: WATER AVAILABILITY, WATER DEMANDS AND ECONOMIC IMPACTS,
Montana State Univ., Missoula. Bureau of Business and Economic Research.
For primary bibliographic entry see Field 6D.
W75-06978

WATER USE AND COAL DEVELOPMENT IN EASTERN MONTANA: WATER AVAILABILITY AND DEMANDS,
Montana State Univ., Bozeman. Dept. of Economics and Agricultural Economics.
For primary bibliographic entry see Field 6D.
W75-06979

EFFECT OF MINING OPERATIONS ON GROUNDWATER LEVELS IN THE NEW LEAD BELT MISSOURI,
Missouri Univ., Rolla. Dept. of Geological Engineering.
For primary bibliographic entry see Field 4B.
W75-06986

PROCEEDINGS OF THE WORKSHOP ON RESEARCH NEEDS RELATED TO WATER FOR ENERGY.
Illinois Univ., Urbana. Water Resources Center.
For primary bibliographic entry see Field 6D.
W75-07089

COAL CONVERSION: PROCESSES, RESOURCE REQUIREMENTS, AND ENVIRONMENTAL IMPACT.
Illinois Univ., Urbana. Inst. for Environmental Studies.
For primary bibliographic entry see Field 6D.
W75-07090

WATER REQUIREMENTS FOR A SYNTHETIC FUELS INDUSTRY BASED ON COAL,
Office of Coal Research, Washington, D.C.
For primary bibliographic entry see Field 6D.
W75-07091

LEGAL ASPECTS OF WATER FOR COAL GASIFICATION,
Virginia Polytechnic Inst. and State Univ., Blacksburg. Water Resources Research Center.
For primary bibliographic entry see Field 6E.
W75-07092

RESEARCH NEEDS RELATED TO HYDROLOGIC ASPECTS OF WATER FOR ENERGY FROM LARGE ENERGY COMPLEXES,
Minnesota Dept. of Natural Resources, St. Paul.
For primary bibliographic entry see Field 6D.
W75-07093

RESEARCH NEEDS ON ECONOMIC AND RESOURCE MANAGEMENT ASPECTS FOR COAL GASIFICATION/LIQUEFACTION,
Tennessee Univ., Knoxville. Appalachian Resources Project.
For primary bibliographic entry see Field 6B.
W75-07097

HYDROLOGY AND GEOLOGY OF DEEP SANDSTONE AQUIFERS OF PENNSYLVANIAN AGE IN PART OF THE WESTERN COAL FIELD REGION, KENTUCKY,
Geological Survey, Louisville, Ky.
For primary bibliographic entry see Field 2F.
W75-07228

INDUSTRIAL WATER DEMAND FORECASTING,
Department of the Environment, Ottawa (Ontario). Water Planning and Management Branch.
For primary bibliographic entry see Field 6D.
W75-07346

3F. Conservation In Agriculture

RESEARCH ON CROP ROTATIONS, FERTILIZATION AND IRRIGATION IN VENETO: III. YIELDS OF ANNUAL BIENNAL AND 6-YR ROTATIONS; 1964-1969, (IN ITALIAN),
Padua Univ. (Italy). Istituto di Agronomia Generale e Coltivazioni Erbacee ed Arboree.
L. Giardini.
Riv Agron. Vol 6, No 2, p 89-103. 1972.

Descriptors: *Crops, *Plant growth, Planting management, *Fertilizers, Rainfall intensity, Irrigation, Alfalfa, Maize, Wheat, Ryegrass, Beets, Europe.
Identifiers: *Italy(Veneto), *Crop rotations.

Three types of rotations were carried out in dry and irrigated conditions (6-year rotation: autumn-spring herbage crops followed by maize, beet, autumn-spring herbage crops followed by maize, wheat and a catch crop of forage maize, alfalfa, alfalfa; biennal: autumn-spring herbage crops and maize, wheat and catch crop of forage maize; annual rotation: Italian ryegrass and maize). In each rotation 3 levels of fertilization were tested: manure, manure plus mineral fertilizer (60 kg/ha of N/crop except for alfalfa + 60 kg/ha of P_2O_5/yr + 75 kg/ha of K_2O/yr), manure plus double mineral fertilizer. The rainfall conditions affected the data on irrigation effects. Mineral fertilization was efficient even in the presence of heavy manuring. The strong responsiveness of the Italian ryegrass-maize rotation contrasted with the results of the 6-yr rotation. The preceding crops influenced the yields of the successive crops, especially in relation to manuring. The heavily fertilized Italian ryegrass-maize rotation showed best results with respect to the average annual dry matter yields and to the nutritive values per unit area.—Copyright 1973, Biological Abstracts, Inc.
W75-06899

WATER MANAGEMENT IN CHINA, TOP PRIORITY FOR 2500 YEARS,
Northern Illinois Univ., De Kalb. Dept. of Geography.
C. J. Loeser.
Water Resources Bulletin, Vol 9, No 1, p 145-154, February 1973. 2 fig, 8 ref.

Descriptors: *Water management(Applied), *Water resources development, *River systems, *History, *Projects, Irrigation, Flood control, Agriculture, Hydrology, Dams, Lakes, Streams, Regional analysis.
Identifiers: *China, Geography, Water plans, Drainage basins.

The civilization of China has evolved as a result of interplay between irrigated regions in the higher reaches and flood prone lower basins of two major rivers, the Hwand and the Yangtze. The importance of the problems of water control has remained central throughout the history of China. Discussed are exceptional circumstances in the physical geography of China which are responsible for the dependence of Chinese civilization on man's capacity to control the behavior of water. Early projects are described which involved men who, as hydrological engineers, became and remain culture heroes to hundreds of millions of Chinese. Modern projects are described which promise to fulfill the most ancient ambitions in the organization of these river systems. Primary considerations include irrigation and flood control. Discussed also are river and canal transport. (Bell-Cornell)
W75-06942

THE RELATION OF TEMPERATURE AND LEAF WETNESS TO THE DEVELOPMENT OF LEAF BLIGHT OF WHEAT,
Indian Agricultural Research Inst., New Delhi. Div. of Mycology and Plant Pathology.
A. S. Prabhu, and Ved Prakash.

Plant Dis Rep. Vol 57, No 12, p 1000-1004, 1973, Illus.

Descriptors: *Wheat, Temperature, *Blights, *Plant diseases, Plant pathology, Pathogenic fungi, Humid climates.
Identifiers: Alternaria-triticina.

Infection and further development of leaf blight fungus, Alternaria triticina, were related to temperature and relative humidity data from sheltered hygrothermographs at the 1-ft level in wheat plots inoculated with A. triticina at different dates. Parallel inoculations on 81-day-old plants in pots were conducted to identify temperature requirements for infection at a given duration and number of wet periods. Leaf wetness greater than or equal to 10 h for 4 consecutive days following inoculation with coincident average temperature minima 50-54F were associated with moderate to high blight intensities. A day was favorable if there were greater than or equal to 10 h of leaf wetness with coincident temperature minima greater than or equal to 50F. Disease incidence and intensity were related to the frequency of favorable infection days. The average minimum temperature and the number of favorable infection days determined the infection rate.--Copyright 1974, Biological Abstracts, Inc.
W75-06943

A DYNAMIC MODEL FOR WATER AND RELATED LAND RESOURCE PLANNING,
Hawaii Univ., Honolulu. Dept. of Agricultural Engineering.
For primary bibliographic entry see Field 6D.
W75-06958

EFFECT OF WATER REGIME ON SOME PHYSIOLOGICAL PROCESSES AND PRODUCTIVITY OF COTTON, (IN RUSSIAN),
Tashkent Agricultural Inst. (USSR).
A. R. Rakhimov.
Fiziol Biokhim Kul't Rast. Vol 5, No 3, p 313-317, 1973, English summary.

Descriptors: *Cotton, Agronomic crops, Crops, Field crops, *Water requirements, *Plant growth, Productivity, Crop production, *Plant physiology, Available water, Water supply, Bound water.
Identifiers: Gossypium-barbadense, Gossypium-hirsutum, Free water.

With varying degrees of water supply a ratio of free to bound wáter changes in the early maturing varieties (C-3210, C-3506) of Gossypium hirsutum L.: with optimal humidity (80% of soil total moisture capacity) the ratio may be in favor of free water. The value of its activity is significant. In the late maturing fine-fibered varieties (2850, C-6002) of G. barbadense L. under severe conditions of water-supply (40% of soil total moisture capacity) the ratio is in favor of bound water. Due to water bound osmotically, the factors of tension (osmotic pressure, suction power, etc) may be higher than in the standard variety 108 phi and in the control (60% of soil total moisture capacity). The same regularity is observed in cotton productivity.--Copyright 1974, Biological Abstracts, Inc.
W75-06976

INCREASING WATER USE EFFICIENCY THROUGH IMPROVED ORFICE DESIGN AND OPERATIONAL PROCEDURES FOR SUB-IRRIGATION SYSTEMS,
Texas A and M Univ., College Station. Water Resources Inst. Office of Water Research and Technology.
O. C. Wilke, and E. A. Hiler.
Available from the National Technical Information Service, Springfield, Va 22161 as PB-241 344. $3.75 paper copy, $2.25 microfiche. Technical Report No 63, February, 1975. 37 p, 1 tab, 10 fig, 12 ref, append. OWRT B-080-TEX (5) 14-31-0001-3338.

Descriptors: *Irrigation efficiencies, *Mathematical models, *Subsurface irrigation, Orifices, Design, *Water utilization, Operations.
Identifiers: *Drip irrigation.

Two mathematical models describing one-dimensional flow from buried sources and in unsaturated soils were developed. One considered the consumption of water by roots. For the assumed distribution of the root consumption with time and depth, the 10-cm (4-in.) deep source provided better water distribution than did 20- and 30-cm (8- and 12-in.) deep sources. Irrigation from zero depth, as in the case of trickle irrigation, appeared to be the best system for the given conditions. Plugging of emitters by particulate materials decreased as the cross-sectional area of the emitter opening was increased. Less than 0.06 atm (1 psig) vacuum had little effect on the flow of emitters tested. Higher vacuum amounts caused the reopening of plugged orifice emitters, but caused plugging of labyrinth emitters. Vacuum-induced plugging of labyrinth emitters resulted from accumulation of silt and fine sand within the flow path. Operation at higher pressures caused limited flow recovery. A theory was proposed for determining pressure distributions in drip laterals where water is uniformly distributed along the lateral's length. The theory provided acceptable design in two tests. Computer-derived design curves were developed. Because 1000 or more emitters may be required for subirrigation of each acre, emitters need to be both inexpensive and resistant to plugging. Four experimental emitters were designed and constructed. A modification of one microtube emitter is being produced commercially. Two moveable drip systems were proposed. Drip irrigation lines successfully trailed a center-pivot irrigation system. Also a tractor-irrigation lines successfully trailed a center-pivot irrigation system. Also a tractor-mounted impement was developed for moving individual drip irrigation laterals.
W75-06991

MODELING AND ANALYSIS OF FLOODS THROUGH FLOOD PLAINS,
California State Univ., Sacramento. Dept. of Civil Engineering.
For primary bibliographic entry see Field 2E.
W75-07009

EFFECTS OF ROOT MEDIUM AND WATERING ON TRANSPIRATION, GROWTH AND DEVELOPMENT OF GLASSHOUSE CROPS: III. EFFECT OF WATERING-FACTOR AND VOLUME OF ROOT MEDIUM ON YIELD AND QUALITY OF GREENHOUSE TOMATOES,
State Experiment Station Landvik, Grimstad (Norway).
For primary bibliographic entry see Field 2D.
W75-07053

EFFECTS OF IRRIGATION DEVELOPMENT ON TRADE PATTERNS AND INCOME GENERATION,
North Dakota State Univ., Fargo. Dept. of Agricultural Economics.
For primary bibliographic entry see Field 6B.
W75-07104

EFFECT OF ROOT MEDIUM AND WATERING ON TRANSPIRATION, GROWTH AND DEVELOPMENT OF GLASSHOUSE CROPS: II. THE RELATIONSHIP BETWEEN EVAPORATION PAN MEASUREMENTS AND TRANSPIRATION IN GLASSHOUSE CROPS,
State Experiment Station Landvik, Grimstad (Norway).
For primary bibliographic entry see Field 2D.
W75-07153

RAINFALL-INDUCED RUNOFF COMPUTED FOR FALLOW FIELDS,
Agricultural Research Service, Durant, Okla. Water Quality Management Lab.
For primary bibliographic entry see Field 2A.
W75-07261

NOTE ON THE EFFECT OF DIFFERENT WATER REGIMES ON GROWTH AND YIELD OF THREE VARIETIES OF RICE (ORYZA SATIVA L.),
Jawaharlal Nehru Agricultural Univ., Jabalpur (India). Dept. of Soil Science and Agricultural Chemistry.
S. M. Gorantiwar, and I. K. Jaggi.
Indian J Agric Sci, Vol 42, No 9, p 866-867, 1972. Illus.

Descriptors: *Rice, *Plant growth, Moisture stress, Moisture tension, Aquatic soils, *Water requirements.
Identifiers: Oryza-Sativa.

The 3 cultivars were 'IR 8,' 'Padma' and 'Jaya' and the 5 levels of moisture were 700, 300 and 0 cm (height) of water tension, and 4 cm and 7 cm of standing water. Tensiometer readings were recorded daily, and water was added to the pots to maintain a required tension of 300 plus or minus 50 and 700 plus or minus 50 cm of water column throughout the experimental period. The treatments of 300 and 700 cm water tension resulted in a reduction in the number of effective tillers per plant, panicle development, number of fertile grains and weight of individual grains. Plants grown on continuously submerged soil were larger, tillered more profusely and yield more. 'Jaya' responded to flooding to a greater extent. High grain yields in the submergence treatments may be attributed to an increase in the availability of P and N to the plant. But the high soil-moisture stress in the treatment of 300 and 700 cm of water adversely affected the yield.--Copyright 1974, Biological Abstracts, Inc.
W75-07263

PRODUCTIVITY INCREASE OF AGRICULTURAL ECOSYSTEMS OF DANUBIAN LOWLANDS BY DAMMING AND BY DRAINAGE, (IN FRENCH),
Academia de Stiinte Agricole si Silvice, Bucharest (Rumania).
N. Petrescu.
Bull Acad Sci Agric For. 1 p, 71-83. 1972 Illus.

Descriptors: Crops, Plant growth, *Ecosystems, Agriculture, *Productivity, *Irrigation practices, River Basins, Europe, Control systems, Regulated flow, Drainage, Controlled Drainage, Drainage practices, River basins, Europe.
Identifiers: *Romania(Danube River Basin), Damming, Lowlands.

Crop analysis demonstrates the higher productivity of ecosystems in the Danubian basin than those of adjacent lowland zones. Certain technical measures must be instituted to maximize the potential yield of these ecosystems. Irrigation prevents crop yield fluctuations due to drought. The maximal, average, and minimal crop yield of corn in an irrigated culture was 8249, 5907, and 2342 kg/ha respectively as against 4832, 3348, and 1475 kg/ha for non-irrigated cultures.--Copyright (c) 1974, Biological Abstracts, Inc.
W75-07279

NUTRITIVE VALUE OF OATS AND SUDAN GRASS GROWN AT CONTROLLED TEMPERATURES,
Commonwealth Scientific and Industrial Research Organization, Canberra (Australia). Div. of Plant Industry.
R. W. Downes, K. R. Christian, and M. Freer.
Australian Journal of Agricultural Research, Vol 25, No 1, p 89-97, January 1974. 1 fig, 3 tab, 44 ref.

Descriptors: *Plant growth, *Photosynthesis, *Water utilization, *Forage grasses, *Oats, Temperature control, Crop production, Nutrients, Temperate, Tropical regions, Digestion.
Identifiers: *Sudan grass.

Fodder oats and Sudan grass were grown in pots in glasshouses with day/night temperatures of 27/22 and 21/16C. Plants were harvested at the emergence of each leaf and at various stages after anthesis. Growth rates and changes in dry matter content, nitrogen cellulose and in vitro digestibility in oats were similar under both temperature regimes, but more primary leaf and less panicle were formed at the high temperatures. Sudan grass development was much more rapid at the high temperatures, but production of dry matter was consistently lower than at the low temperatures. Sudan grass produced much more dry matter than oats. Differences in composition were small, but stem digestibility remained higher in Sudan grass after anthesis. Because of their efficiency of photosynthesis and water use, tropical species warrant further study of their nutritive value as forage crops. (Mastic-Arizona)
W75-07330

AN INPUT-OUTPUT MODEL OF THE LOWER RIO GRANDE REGION OF TEXAS,
Pan American Univ., Edinburg, Tex. School of Business Administration.
For primary bibliographic entry see Field 6A.
W75-07348

4. WATER QUANTITY MANAGEMENT AND CONTROL

4A. Control Of Water On The Surface

METROPOLITAN WATER SUPPLY ALLOCATION AND OPERATION,
Northwestern Univ., Evanston, Ill. Dept. of Civil Engineering.
For primary bibliographic entry see Field 3D.
W75-06851

ECONOMIC CRITERIA FOR FRESHWATER WETLAND POLICY IN MASSACHUSETTS,
Massachusetts Univ., Amherst. Dept. of Food and Resource Economics.
For primary bibliographic entry see Field 6B.
W75-06896

PUERTO RICO WATER RESOURCES PLANNING MODEL PROGRAM DESCRIPTION,
Geological Survey, Reston, Va.
For primary bibliographic entry see Field 7C.
W75-06934

A SUMMARY VIEW OF WATER SUPPLY AND DEMAND IN THE SAN FRANCISCO BAY REGION, CALIFORNIA,
Geological Survey, Menlo Park, Calif.
For primary bibliographic entry see Field 6D.
W75-06935

MEAN ANNUAL RUNOFF IN THE SAN FRANCISCO BAY REGION, CALIFORNIA, 1931-70,
Geological Survey, Menlo Park, Calif.
For primary bibliographic entry see Field 7C.
W75-06936

WATER MANAGEMENT IN CHINA, TOP PRIORITY FOR 2500 YEARS,
Northern Illinois Univ., De Kalb. Dept. of Geography.
For primary bibliographic entry see Field 3F.
W75-06942

FACTOR ANALYSIS OF SHORELINE PHYSIOGRAPHY AND PERCEPTION OF WATER LEVEL DRAWDOWN BY RESERVOIR SHORELINE RESIDENTS,
Toronto Univ. (Ontario). Faculty of Forestry.
R. Jaakson.
Water Resources Research, Vol 9, No 1, p 81-92, February 1973. 3 fig, 3 tab, 12 ref.

Descriptors: *Water level fluctuations, *Reservoirs, *Recreation, *Lakes, *Drawdown, Analytical techniques, Storage capacity, Evaluation, Beaches, Slopes, Variability, Data collections, Summer, Planning, Mathematical models, Systems analysis, *Canada.
Identifiers: Factor analysis, Shoreline physiography, Trent Canal(Ontario), Perceptions, Shoreline residents, Visitation, Enjoyment, Interviews, Dimension models.

Factor analysis is used to examine the relationship between variations in shoreline physiography and perception of water level fluctuation by reservoir recreation users. Three elements of perception are studied: frequency of objection to water level fluctuation; frequency with which users feel that recreation enjoyment is reduced by water level fluctuation; and, as an element that may reflect perception, user days of recreation. A test of the relation between factors and water level fluctuation is made by correlating factor scores with storage capacity on 11 reservoirs and three control lakes. Five factors are identified and evaluated in terms of their significance to recreation. The factor analysis consists of a modified principal component techniques, with orthogonal Varimax rotation. From the Ontario Recreation Land Inventory data, five physical shoreline variables have been used: (1) wet beach slope; (2) wet beach material; (3) wet beach cliff height; (4) backshore slope; and (5) backshore material. In considering the above elements of perception, water level fluctuation refers to water drawdown and dropping water levels during the summer recreation season. Considered as a descriptive model of existing conditions on lakes, the shoreline physiography dimensions may be used in planning new reservoirs or as a guide for an overview of existing reservoirs. (Bell-Cornell)
W75-06945

A PROGRAMING MODEL FOR THE DESIGN OF MULTIRESERVOIR FLOOD CONTROL SYSTEMS,
Natal Univ, Durban (South Africa). Dept. of Civil Engineering.
J. S. Windsor.
Water Resources Research, Vol 11, No 1, p 30-36, February 1975. 4 fig, 9 ref.

Descriptors: *River basin development, *Reservoirs, *Project planning, *Flood control, Design, *Linear programming, Optimization, Hydrographs, Decision making, Methodology, Variability, Storage capacity, Flood routing, Reservoir releases, Spillways, Constraints, Equations, Mathematical models, Systems analysis.
Identifiers: Mixed integer programming, Cost minimization, Multireservoir systems, Damage centers, Mass balance.

A methodology is presented for determining the optimal size, number, and location of flood control reservoirs in a river basin development. The flood control system may involve one or more potential damage centers. The method of solution employed is mixed integer programming, a modified form of linear programming. At this level of optimization, it is assumed that the nonlinear cost functions for the reservoirs and damage centers are known and may be approximated by a set of piecewise linear segments. Temporal and spatial flood variability at all significant points within the drainage basin is accounted for by using a representative range of recorded or synthetically derived flood hydrographs, along with the probable maximum flood, as input data to the model. Each potential flood combination is routed in turn through the proposed river basin development by using a decision policy that automatically minimizes the expected total costs of the system and at the same time provides a reasonably high degree of assurance against hydraulic failure. The inclusion of probable maximum flood input data ensures that floods are controlled even under the most adverse conditions. This approach offers a potentially powerful method in the analysis of integrated systems where a large number of interdependent variables are involved. (Bell-Cornell)
W75-06951

WATER MANAGEMENT--A GENERAL REPORT,
Illinois State Water Survey, Urbana.
W. C. Ackermann.
Hydrological Sciences Bulletin, Vol 19, No 1, p 119-130, March 1974 (From: International Symposium on the Hydrology of Lakes, Helsinki, Finland, July 1973). 10 ref.

Descriptors: *Water management(Applied), *Lakes, *Hydrology, *Model studies, Data collections, Remote sensing, Numerical analysis, Water balance, Temperature, Ice, Water quality, Simulation, Thermal pollution, Erosion, Sedimentation, Eutrophication, Great Lakes, Dissolved oxygen, Bacteria, Fisheries, Ecology, Food chains, Systems analysis.
Identifiers: Lake restoration, Chemical effects, Heat discharge.

Water management of both natural and man-made lakes is the most advanced step of the scientific-engineering processes relating to these bodies of water. Programs of observation and analyses of how these complex lake systems operate would enable management to optimize the lake's behavior so as to gain multiple benefits. In managing lakes, one must consider the on-site and off-site purposes to be served, all characteristics of the water body, and the upstream and downstream effects. This report is a product of a July 1973 lake symposium focusing on the hydrological-hydraulic elements of geophysics. A state-of-the-art paper, it summarizes the major developments which have occurred in lake studies since the Garda symposium in 1966. The emphasis at that time was on hydrological measurements and balances directed at understanding and proper design, but with only a slight attention given to management aspects. Understanding is enhanced today, but all the questions at the time of Garda are still important. Described are the areas in which principal advances have been made over the past seven years in the ability to manage lakes: (1) The International Field Year for the Great Lakes; (2) use of remote sensing as a tool for management; (3) the progress and status of numerical modelling for understanding, identification of data gaps, and for management; and (4) lake restoration as a deliberate attempt to reverse the processes of lake degradation. (Bell-Cornell)
W75-06953

INTEGRATION OF HYDROLOGIC, ECONOMIC, ECOLOGIC, SOCIAL, AND WELL-BEING FACTORS IN PLANNING FLOOD CONTROL MEASURES FOR URBAN STREAMS,
Georgia Inst. of Tech., Atlanta. Environmental Resources Center.
For primary bibliographic entry see Field 6F.
W75-06980

EFFECT OF DIVERTING MISSISSIPPI RIVER WATER TO TEXAS ON SEDIMENTATION IN THE RIVER,
Louisiana Water Resources Research Inst., Baton Rouge.

For primary bibliographic entry see Field 2J.
W75-06983

OWNERSHIP AND USE RIGHTS IN WATER WITHIN NORTH DAKOTA,
North Dakota Univ., Grand Forks. School of Law.
For primary bibliographic entry see Field 6E.
W75-06995

MODELING AND ANALYSIS OF FLOODS THROUGH FLOOD PLAINS,
California State Univ., Sacramento. Dept. of Civil Engineering.
For primary bibliographic entry see Field 2E.
W75-07009

MODEL SIMULATION OF THE DOWNSTREAM EFFECTS OF OPERATING THE SIRIKIT POWER STATION,
Electricity Generating Authority of Thailand, Nonthaburi. Planning Dept.
For primary bibliographic entry see Field 8B.
W75-07015

ANALOG, DIGITAL AND HYBRID SIMULATION OF WATER LEVEL DISTRIBUTION IN OCCURRENCES OF FLOODS IN A SYSTEM RIVER FLOOD PLAIN,
Technische Universitaet, Hanover (West Germany). Institut fuer Wasserwirtschaft, Hydrologie und Landwirtschaftlichen Wasserbau.
For primary bibliographic entry see Field 2E.
W75-07018

DESIGNING BY OBJECTIVES, A SIMULATION STUDY ON THE RIVER YOM IN NORTHERN THAILAND,
MacDonald (Murdoch) and Partners, London (England).
R. F. Stoner, and J. B. Downs.
In: River and Estuary Model Analysis, Volume III; Proceedings of the International Association for Hydraulic Research Symposium on River Mechanics (4 Vol.), Bangkok, Thailand, January 9-12, 1973. Asian Institute of Technology, Bangkok, Thailand, p 239-250, (1973). 2 fig, 4 tab, 4 ref.

Descriptors: *Model studies, *River basin development, *Planning, Floods, Forecasting, Flood discharge, Peak discharge, Flood recurrence interval, Flood stages, Flooding, River flow, Evaporation, Hydrologic aspects, Rainfall, Runoff, Flood plains, Agriculture, Irrigation, Flood protection, Analysis.
Identifiers: *Thailand(River Yom).

The simulation model used when planning the development of the River Yom Basin was discussed. The main objective of the Yom Basin study was to provide a plan for the overall development of the basin's water resources and it was divided into three parts to examine: (1) the irrigation potential and make recommendations for likely cropping patterns, cultivation intensities, and area to be developed; (2) the river flood problem and make outline proposals for flood alleviation measures; and (3) the hydro-electric potential of the basin. The simulation model used inputs for river flow, rainfall, and evaporation which actually occurred in a single year, and was run for each year on record. Outputs related to meeting study objectives were analyzed on a probability basis. Tabulated results of the simulation study showed that the development plan for flood control will substantially reduce dam peak discharges and area flooded for return periods from 2 to 10 years. (See also W75-06998) (Humphreys-ISWS)
W75-07019

MATHEMATICAL MODEL OF MEKONG RIVER NEAR VIENTIANE AND NONGKHAI,
Asian Inst. of Tech., Bangkok (Thailand). Div. of Water Science and Engineering.
For primary bibliographic entry see Field 2E.
W75-07023

MODELING RIVER AND ESTUARY UNSTEADY FLOW SYSTEMS,
Utah State Univ., Logan. Dept. of Civil Engineering.
For primary bibliographic entry see Field 2E.
W75-07024

FLOOD ROUTING FOR URBAN RIVER NETWORK,
Osaka Univ. (Japan). Dept. of Civil Engineering.
For primary bibliographic entry see Field 2E.
W75-07027

THE PASSAGE OF A FLOOD WAVE THROUGH A JUNCTION,
Sri Lanka Univ., Peradeniya. Dept. of Civil Engineering.
For primary bibliographic entry see Field 2E.
W75-07028

A MATHEMATICAL MODEL TO PREDICT DISCHARGE VARIATIONS IN AN ESTUARY WITH SHALLOW WATER AND A LARGE TIDAL RANGE,
Ente Nazionale per l'Energia Elettrica, Milan (Italy).
For primary bibliographic entry see Field 2L.
W75-07035

GENERAL REPORTS, DISCUSSIONS, LECTURES, VOLUME 4.
For primary bibliographic entry see Field 2J.
W75-07038

STABILIZATION OF COASTAL DREDGE SPOIL WITH SPARTINA ALTERNIFLORA,
North Carolina State Univ., Raleigh. Dept. of Botany; and North Carolina State Univ., Raleigh. Dept. of Soil Science.
For primary bibliographic entry see Field 2L.
W75-07071

FLOOD PLAIN INFORMATION: AGUA HEDIONDA CREEK, PACIFIC OCEAN TO BUENA, SAN DIEGO COUNTY, CALIFORNIA.
Army Engineer District, Los Angeles, Calif.
Prepared for San Diego County, July, 1973. 24 p, 11 fig, 6 tab, 16 plates.

Descriptors: *Floods, *Flood data, *Flooding, *Flood damage, Flow, Historic floods, Maximum Probable Flood, Flood water, Flood recurrence interval, Flood frequency, *California, Runoff, Velocity.
Identifiers:, *San Diego County(Calif), Agua Hedionda Creek(Calif), Buena Creek(Calif), Carlsbad(Calif), Intermediate Regional Flood, Standard Project Flood.

The drainage area of Agua Hedionda Creek and its tributary, Buena Creek, covers 29 square miles from Buena to the Pacific Ocean. A very broad flood plain runs from El Camino Real to Agua Hedionda Lagoon which provides considerable flood storage during large floods. Development is largely agricultural or undeveloped; only 5% of the 700 acres in the flood plain are developed as ranches with a mobile park and golf course upstream from El Camino Real. Agua Hedionda Lagoon at the Pacific Ocean has been improved as a water sports area. Because of steep banks, residences flanking the shores are outside the flood plain. The City of Carlsbad projects that the highly developed area just outside the Lagoon flood plain will continue to grow rapidly. Storms critical for the watershed produce high peak flows of short duration and relatively small volumes. Snow is not an important runoff factor. Several reaches of improved channel and construction of a concrete weir act as flood damage reduction measures. Major floods occurred since 1862 on an irregular basis. Future floods expected from severe local storms are projected as the Intermediate Regional Flood (IRF) with peak flows of 10,500 cubic feet/second (cfs) and 15,000 cfs for a Standard Project Flood (SPF) at the Lagoon entrance with lesser discharges upstream. Flood velocities reaching 8 feet/second (fps) on the overbank for an IRF upstream from El Camino Real would create substantial damage and erosion. Residential damage would be small since most development is outside the flood plain. Severe erosion can occur in steep canyon areas with possible velocities of 22 fps. (Park-North Carolina)
W75-07087

FLOOD HAZARD ANALYSIS: FOUR MILE AND EIGHT MILE CREEKS, BUTLER COUNTY, KANSAS.
Soil Conservation Service, Salina, Kans.
Prepared for Butler County Planning Commission, November, 1974. 42 p, 11 plates, 6 tab.

Descriptors: *Floods, *Flooding, *Flood plains, *Flood profile, *Flood data, Flood damage, Flood plain zoning, Flood discharge, Flood flow, Maximum probable flood, *Kansas.
Identifiers: Four Mile Creek(Kansas), Eight Mile Creek(Kansas), Butler County(Kansas), Wichita(Kansas), Intermediate Regional Flood, 500-year flood.

Drainage patterns and runoff in the Four Mile and Eight Mile Creek areas east of Wichita are changing as increasing population and housing density impinge upon the agricultural lands. Urbanization is expected to increase from the present 13% to 32% for Four Mile Creek watershed (73.43 sq. mi.), and from 5% to 14% for the Eight Mile Creek watershed (34.82 sq. mi.), based upon present growth patterns. High intensity spring and summer thunderstorms cause small floods several times a year with larger floods occurring at irregular yearly intervals. Mean annual precipitation is 30 inches; annual mean runoff approximately 5 inches. An adequate and dependable water supply necessary for major development is lacking in the study area. The major flood of record in April 1944 caused damage to crops, livestock, machinery, railroads, roads and bridges. Flood discharges and elevations for projected 10-year, 25-year, 50-year, 100-year, and 500-year frequency floods for 30 points along Four Mile Creek and for 35 stations along Eight Mile Creek are given. A flood plain management program based on the data supplied is suggested as an alternative to control by dams as encroachments have preempted available sites and by channel work which would require substantial financing. Local flood plain regulations and ordinances must be approved by the Chief Engineer, Kansas Division of Water Resources, prior to building. Minimum standards prohibit human habitation unless adequately protected within the flood plain zone based on the 100-year frequency flood and require suitable flood proofing of new construction to an elevation level approved by the chief engineer. Other important factors to be considered for efficient flood plain management are suggested. (Park-North Carolina)
W75-07088

STUDY OF TRACE ELEMENTS IN WATERS OF TWO ALASKAN RESERVOIR SITES,
Alaska Univ., College. Inst. of Water Resources.
For primary bibliographic entry see Field 5B.
W75-07100

SUMMARY OF THE BAYLANDS SALT WATER FLOOD CONTROL PLANNING STUDY.
Tudor Engineering Co., San Francisco, Calif.

Santa Clara County Flood Control and Water District, San Jose, California, January 1973. 26 p, 11 fig.

Descriptors: *Saline water-freshwater interfaces, *Diversion structures, *Flood protection, *Planning, *Bays, Levees, Saline water barriers, Alternative planning, California, Check structures, Dikes, Flood control.
Identifiers: Santa Clara County(California), San Francisco Bay, Baylands.

The basic flood problems presently handled by the Santa Clara County Flood Control and Water district are caused by fresh water flowing in the major streams of the County from near their headwaters to their outfalls into San Francisco Bay. In July, 1971 the District initiated a study of the problems of salt water flooding along the Bay front and in the Baylands area of the County. The purpose of the study was to develop information that will assist in a determination of whether the Flood Control and Water District should expand its responsibilities to include protection of the Baylands from salt water flooding and how this may be accomplished. Flooding has become a problem of increasing concern because intensive utility, military, industrial and residential activities have located in portions of the low-lying Baylands. The existing levees in the Baylands were constructed primarily to enclose the salt ponds. They are of mixed earthwork construction. Three basic alternative plans were analyzed. The first plan is a 'do-nothing' alternative. The second alternative is the Inboard Levee Plan. This would consist of perimeter levees utilizing in part the existing alignment of the inboard system. The third alternative is the Outboard Levee Plan, utilizing for the most part the alignment of the existing outboard levee system on the Bay side of the salt ponds and on the channels. Design factors, construction costs, assessed values, tax cost, and comparative costs are given for all alternatives. (Poertner)
W75-07136

AN OVERVIEW OF URBAN HYDROLOGY AND RUNOFF MANAGEMENT,
H. G. Poertner.
In: Proceedings, National Symposium on Urban Rainfall and Runoff and Sediment Control, University of Kentucky, Lexington, July 29-31, 1974. p 25-31.

Descriptors: *Urban hydrology, *Urban runoff, *Administration, *Flood control, *Institutional constraints, *Cities, Storm drains, Flood plains, Flood plain zoning, Water policy, Planning, Drainage engineering, Urbanization, Regional development, Management.
Identifiers: *Runoff control, Stormwater management.

One alternative to the present unsatisfactory state of runoff control and flood plain management is to establish a modern program of management responsive to all segments of the population. Major limitations of present practices in engineering and design are: deficiencies in knowledge of urban hydrology, lack of analyses of accumulated data, and ineffective use of data for producing optimum designs of integrated drainage systems. Problems of urban drainage are primarily institutional. Enabling legislation is needed for management of water on a watershed basis, in entire metropolitan areas, by a single authority. A regional entity can produce a more uniform approach to the solution of water problems and replace present piece-meal and ineffective procedures with coordinated and competent planning, engineering, construction, and management. Action programs should be developed on federal, state and local levels to improve drainage systems and correct deficiencies within existing flood plains. This would be beneficial to existing communities as well as those that may emerge in the surrounding areas. Such programs should be flexible and should be integrated. Research in both management and engineering now demands full-time attention. (Poertner)
W75-07141

DEVELOPMENT OF A COMPUTER PROGRAM TO ROUTE RUNOFF IN THE MINNEAPOLIS-ST. PAUL INTERCEPTOR SEWERS,
Minnesota Univ., Minneapolis. St. Anthony Falls Hydraulic Lab.
For primary bibliographic entry see Field 5D.
W75-07143

REAL-TIME ESTIMATION OF RUNOFF IN THE MINNEAPOLIS-ST. PAUL METROPOLITAN AREA,
Minnesota Univ., Minneapolis. St. Anthony Falls Hydraulic Lab.
For primary bibliographic entry see Field 5G.
W75-07144

THE REAL-TIME COMPUTATION OF RUNOFF AND STORM FLOW IN THE MINNEAPOLIS-ST. PAUL INTERCEPTOR SEWERS,
Minnesota Univ., Minneapolis. St. Anthony Falls Hydraulic Lab.
For primary bibliographic entry see Field 5G.
W75-07145

1973 WATER RESOURCES DATA FOR OREGON, SURFACE WATER RECORDS, PRECIPITATION RECORDS,
Oregon State Water Resources Board, Salem.
For primary bibliographic entry see Field 7C.
W75-07150

CAN THE BALTIC SEA BE TURNED INTO A FRESHWATER LAKE,
A. Meclewski.
Available from the National Technical Information Service, Springfield, Va 22161 as AD-779 006, $3.25 in paper copy, $2.25 in microfiche. NRL Translation 1291, April 26, 1974. 5 p. Translated from Poseidon (East German publication), No 3, p 104-107, 1973.

Descriptors: *Oceans, *Sea water, *Dikes, Salinity, Saline water, Freshwater, Fishing, Climatology, Oceanography, Evaporation, Runoff, Hydraulic structures, Hydrology.
Identifiers: *Baltic Sea.

An interview with Stanislaw Hueckel, Director of the Institute of Hydroengineering of the Polish Academy of Sciences in Gdansk was presented. Professor Hueckel explained that he was not the originator of the proposal to turn the Baltic into a freshwater lake, but rather that he only wanted to call attention to a concept which had been developed earlier. If the sporadic penetration of salt water from the North Sea can be prevented, the Baltic could be converted into a freshwater sea within 25 years. Greater quantities of potable fresh water could then be obtained. Technical difficulties would not be greater than in the diking of the Zuyder Zee in Holland. All the Baltic countries could begin the study of the problem on the basis of a joint agreement. (Sims-ISWS)
W75-07165

IMPACT ANALYSIS: HINDSIGHT AND FORESIGHT IN SASKATCHEWAN,
Saskatchewan Fisheries Lab., Saskatoon.
For primary bibliographic entry see Field 6G.
W75-07171

HYDROELECTRIC DEVELOPMENT OF THE NELSON RIVER SYSTEM IN NORTHERN MANITOBA,
Manitoba Hydro, Winnipeg.
For primary bibliographic entry see Field 6G.
W75-07172

ENVIRONMENTAL IMPACT OF THE CHURCHILL FALLS (LABRADOR) HYDROELECTRIC PROJECT: A PRELIMINARY ASSESSMENT,
Waterloo Univ. (Ontario). Dept. of Biology.
For primary bibliographic entry see Field 6G.
W75-07173

ASSESSMENT OF THE IMPACT OF HYDRO-DAMS,
British Columbia Univ., Vancouver. Inst. of Animal Resource Ecology.
For primary bibliographic entry see Field 6G.
W75-07178

FLASH FLOOD POTENTIAL FROM CHANNEL MEASUREMENTS,
Geological Survey, Reston, Va.
H. C. Riggs.
In: Flash Floods; Proceedings of the Paris Symposium, September 1974: International Association of Hydrological Sciences Publication No 112, p 52-56, 1974. 4 fig, 6 ref.

Descriptors: *Flash floods, *Channel morphology, *Alluvial channels, Peak discharge, Flow characteristics, Streamflow, Design flood, Measurement.

Discharge measurements of flash floods add to hydrological knowledge and provide information needed for protection from future floods. But planning for protection cannot be postponed until a serious flood has occurred at each site. Thus method of estimating flood potential at ungaged sites are needed. A promising method utilizes (1) a relation between a flood characteristic and stream channel size based on data at gaging stations, and (2) channel size measurements at ungaged sites at which flood characteristics are to be estimated. The method is described and demonstrated using data on ephemeral and perennial streams. The flood characteristics used are the 10-year or the 50-year floods. Channel size is represented by the top width of a cross section; the top of the cross section is variously defined by channel bars, by breaks in bank slope, or by the lower limit of permanent vegetation. In semiarid regions this method produces better results than regression of basin characteristics. Floods of higher recurrence intervals can be approximated as a multiple of the 10-year flood. (Knapp-USGS)
W75-07203

A METHOD FOR ESTIMATING MAGNITUDE AND FREQUENCY OF FLOODS IN SOUTH DAKOTA,
Geological Survey, Huron, S. Dak.
L. D. Becker.
Available from NTIS, Springfield, Va 22161 as PB-239 831/As, $4.75 in paper copy, $2.25 in microfiche. Water-Resources Investigations 35-74, August 1974. 78 p, 23 fig, 4 tab, 15 ref.

Descriptors: *Floods, *South Dakota, *Flood frequency, Flood recurrence interval, Rainfall-runoff relationships, Flood forecasting, Peak discharge, Flood data.

A general flood-frequency analysis provides a method for estimating flood magnitudes and frequencies in South Dakota. The State is divided into two hydrologic regions. For each region, the 2-, 5-, 10-, 25-, 50-, and 100-year floods are related to basin and climatic characteristics by regression equations. Indices based on contributing drainage area size, elevation, and mean annual precipitation are the most useful variables. Relationships based on these variables can be used to estimate floods of selected frequency at most ungaged sites where peak flows are not significantly affected by regulation or other manmade works. Equations and graphs are applicable to drainage basins with areas approximately from 0.1 sq mi to 4,000 sq mi in the Eastern Region and from 0.1 sq mi to 9,000 sq mi in the Western Region. Flood characteristics are

tabulated for 130 gaging stations. Maximum flood peaks determined at 188 gaging stations and 52 miscellaneous sites are compared with regional flood relationships. (Knapp-USGS)
W75-07211

A HYDROLOGIC ASSESSMENT OF THE SEPTEMBER 14, 1974, FLOOD IN ELDORADO CANYON, NEVADA,
Geological Survey, Carson City, Nev.
For primary bibliographic entry see Field 2E.
W75-07214

INDEX OF FLOOD MAPS FOR CALIFORNIA PREPARED BY THE U.S. GEOLOGICAL SURVEY THROUGH 1974,
Geological Survey, Menlo Park, Calif.
For primary bibliographic entry see Field 7C.
W75-07216

FLOODS OF SEPTEMBER-OCTOBER 1967 IN SOUTH TEXAS AND NORTHEASTERN MEXICO,
Geological Survey, Reston, Va.
For primary bibliographic entry see Field 2E.
W75-07219

SURFACE WATER FEATURES OF FLORIDA,
Geological Survey, Tallahassee, Fla.
For primary bibliographic entry see Field 7C.
W75-07221

INDEX OF SURFACE WATER STATIONS IN TEXAS, OCTOBER 1974.
Geological Survey, Austin, Tex.
For primary bibliographic entry see Field 7C.
W75-07224

FLOOD MAPPING IN CHARLOTTE AND MECKLENBURG COUNTY, NORTH CAROLINA,
Geological Survey, Charlotte, N.C.
W. G. Stamper.
Open-file report, 1974. 21 p, 5 fig, 1 tab, 7 ref.

Descriptors: *Floods, *Maps, *North Carolina, Flood profiles, Flood data, Stage-discharge relations, Backwater, Flood plain zoning, Maximum probable flood, Design flood, Mapping.
Identifiers: *Flood maps, *Charlotte(NC), *Mecklenburg, County(NC).

Development on the flood plains of streams in Charlotte and Mecklenburg County, North Carolina has created a serious flood hazard. A flood map series is being compiled to include 286 miles of streams in the city and county. Impervious cover, drainage area, channel length, and channel slope were computed for each drainage basin to determine the 100-year flood discharge. The cross-sections for 286 miles of streams at approximately 500-foot intervals were obtained from aerial photographs using photogrammetric methods. The hydraulic geometry of over 200 bridges and culverts was measured. The Manning roughness coefficients were picked at selected locations in the field and then interpolated using aerial photographs. The 100-year flood elevations were computed using the step-backwater method. The computed floodway district encroachment lines and floodway fringe boundaries are presented on a series of topographic maps with insets showing a tabulation of the data. (Knapp-USGS)
W75-07230

STREAMFLOW CHARACTERISTICS IN NORTHEASTERN UTAH AND ADJACENT AREAS,
Geological Survey, Salt Lake City, Utah.
For primary bibliographic entry see Field 7C.
W75-07232

WATER-RESOURCES INVESTIGATIONS IN WISCONSIN, 1975 FISCAL YEAR,
Geological Survey, Madison, Wis.
For primary bibliographic entry see Field 7C.
W75-07233

MAP SHOWING DRAINAGE AREAS, MIDDLETOWN QUADRANGLE, CONNECTICUT,
Geological Survey, Hartford, Conn.
For primary bibliographic entry see Field 7C.
W75-07239

ESTIMATES OF TEMPERATURE AND PRECIPITATION FOR NORTHEASTERN UTAH,
Geological Survey, Salt Lake City, Utah.
F. K. Fields, and D. B. Adams.
Available from Sup. of Documents, GPO, Washington, D.C. 20402, $3.15 single copy. Journal of Research of the US Geological Survey, Vol 3, No 2, p 131-136, March-April 1975. 7 fig, 3 ref.

Descriptors: *Temperature, *Precipitation(Atmospheric), *Utah, Estimating, Forecasting, Computer programs, Data processing, Statistical methods, Regression analysis, Data collections.

Estimates of temperature and precipitation were made for northeastern Utah from information that was collected at 67 locations. The variable-length records were converted to the common-time base of 1941-70; then general relations were developed to extend the converted point values to unsampled sites. Regression techniques were used to fill voids in the temperature-data base. Incomplete precipitation records were adjusted to the 1941-70 average on the assumption that the ratio of concurrent data is directly proportional to the ratio of the respective 1941-70 average annual values at nearby sites. Equations were developed in a computer program to express the relationship of temperature and precipitation with altitude and location and to extend the information to unsampled sites. Two-thirds of the observed and estimated average annual temperature and precipitation values are within plus or minus 1.5 deg F and 2.08 in., respectively, of the calculated averages. Schematic diagrams, plotted by computer, were prepared to show variations of altitude, temperature, and precipitation; and maps, also plotted by computer, show lines of equal altitude, precipitation, and temperature. (Knapp-USGS)
W75-07241

RAINFALL-INDUCED RUNOFF COMPUTED FOR FALLOW FIELDS,
Agricultural Research Service, Durant, Okla. Water Quality Management Lab.
For primary bibliographic entry see Field 2A.
W75-07261

PREDICTING REDUCTION IN WATER LOSSES FROM OPEN CHANNELS BY PHREATOPHYTE CONTROL,
Agricultural Research Service, Phoenix, Ariz. Water Conservation Lab.
For primary bibliographic entry see Field 3B.
W75-07264

KONA DAM VS. KONATOWN: A SOCIOLOGICAL INTERPRETATION OF SELECTED IMPACTS OF RESERVOIR DEVELOPMENT ON A COMMUNITY FIELD,
East Texas State Univ., Commerce. Dept. of Sociology and Anthropology.
For primary bibliographic entry see Field 6B.
W75-07271

CAPACITY EXPANSION MODEL OF WATER RESOURCE FACILITIES FOR A MAJOR RIVER SYSTEM,
Texas Univ. at Austin. Coll. of Engineering.
For primary bibliographic entry see Field 6A.
W75-07277

MODEL DEVELOPMENT AND SYSTEMS ANALYSIS OF THE YAKIMA RIVER BASIN: HYDRAULICS OF SURFACE WATER RUNOFF,
Washington State Univ., Pullman. Dept. of Civil and Environmental Engineering.
For primary bibliographic entry see Field 2A.
W75-07278

COMPUTER-CALCULATED GEOMETRIC CHARACTERISTICS OF MIDDLE-MISSISSIPPI RIVER SIDE CHANNELS; VOLUME 1: PROCEDURES AND RESULTS; VOLUME 2: SIDE CHANNEL CONTOUR MAPS,
Army Engineer Waterways Experiment Station, Vicksburg, Miss.
S. J. Winfrey, and V. E. LaGarde.
Army Engineer Waterways Experiment Station, Vicksburg, Mississippi. Technical Report M-74-5, June 1974. Vol 1: 110 p, 19 tab, 18 pl, 4 ref. Vol 2: 23 p, 1 tab, 1 fig, 24 map.

Descriptors: *River basins, *Open channels, Ecology, Streams, *Mississippi River Basin, *Computer models, Computer programs, Maps, Contours, Topographic mapping, Hydraulics, Model studies.
Identifiers: *Hydraulic geometry, Middle Mississippi River, *Side channels(Mississippi River).

Several geometric characteristics of water-basin regimes, including basin size and shape, area underwater at specific water depth, and cross-sectional area, are commonly associated with benthic, plankton, and fish community population structures, although little quantitative data are available to support the association. This two-volume report describes a general procedure that was developed to calculate values of selected parameters used to define the above-mentioned geometric characteristics of any water-basin regime. The procedure was successfully applied to yield quantitative information for those parameters for 18 side channels of the Middle Mississippi River. Which of the parameters selected as quantitative descriptors of the characteristics are best indicators of animal community population structures is expected to be determined as a result of other projects currently under way at the U.S. Army Engineer Waterways Experiment Station. Volume I contains a description of the procedure and the results of implementing it. Volume II contains a set of computer-plotted contour maps for the 18 side channels. (WES)
W75-07282

GILA RIVER BASIN, NEW RIVER AND PHOENIX CITY STREAMS, ARIZONA: ALTERNATIVE PLANS FOR FLOOD CONTROL AND RECREATIONAL DEVELOPMENT.
Army Engineer District, Los Angeles, Calif.
April, 1974. 57 p, 2 tab, maps.

Descriptors: *Arizona, *Floodwater, Engineering structures, Floodplain zoning, *Cost-benefit ratio, Historic floods, Bypasses, Diversion structures, Canals, Flood recurrence interval, Recreation, Recreation facilities, *Flood control, *Alternative planning.
Identifiers: *Gila River Basin(Ariz), Phoenix(Ariz).

An assessment is made of feasible alternatives for providing flood control in the Phoenix area. The study area, slightly over 2600 square miles, has had increasing flood problems because urban growth has placed housing on the floodplains. Since this growth is expected to continue, flood problems can be expected to worsen. Also, ur-

banization, by paving the land surface, increases runoff. Five alternative actions are presented to alleviate the danger of flooding. Environmental and social considerations have entered into the plans. With the exception of the alternative to take no action, all proposed plans have some unavoidable consequences for riparian vegetation and archeological sites. All proposed actions have favorable benefit-to-cost ratios. (Bowden-Arizona)
W75-07331

REPORT ON WATER SUPPLY, FORT HUACHUCA AND VICINITY, ARIZONA.
Army Engineer District, Los Angeles, Calif.
For primary bibliographic entry see Field 4B.
W75-07332

THE CALIFORNIA STATE WATER PROJECT IN 1970.
California State Dept. of Water Resources, Sacramento.
For primary bibliographic entry see Field 6B.
W75-07347

AN INPUT-OUTPUT MODEL OF THE LOWER RIO GRANDE REGION OF TEXAS,
Pan American Univ., Edinburg, Tex. School of Business Administration.
For primary bibliographic entry see Field 6A.
W75-07348

4B. Groundwater Management

A SURROGATE-PARAMETER APPROACH TO MODELING GROUNDWATER BASINS,
Colorado State Univ., Fort Collins. Dept. of Civil Engineering.
For primary bibliographic entry see Field 2F.
W75-06960

EFFECT OF MINING OPERATIONS ON GROUNDWATER LEVELS IN THE NEW LEAD BELT MISSOURI,
Missouri Univ., Rolla. Dept. of Geological Engineering.
D. L. Warner.
Available from the National Technical Information Service, Springfield, Va 22161 as PB-241 343, $4.75 in paper copy, $2.25 in microfiche. Completion Report, December 1974. 85 p, 13 fig, 3 tab, 28 ref. OWRT A-060-MO(2). 14-31-0001-3825-4025.

Descriptors: *Missouri, Mining, Dewatering, Pumping, Groundwater, *Water levels, *Aquifers, Lead, *Mine water.
Identifiers: *New Lead Belt(Mo), *Lead mining, *Mine dewatering, *Groundwater levels.

Lead deposits of the Viburnum Trend or New Lead Belt of southeast Missouri were discovered in the 1950's. The district has since become the world's largest lead producer. The mining area is in a narrow north-south band about 50 miles long. There are presently eight operating underground mines. Ore deposits are in the Cambrian age Bonneterre Formation, a carbonate unit about 275 feet thick. The Bonneterre and the underlying Lamotte Formation comprise the deep groundwater aquifer of the area and are overlain by the Davis Formation, a shale aquitard. Formations above the Davis comprise an unconfined aquifer. In order to work the underground mines of the New Lead Belt, it is necessary to dewater the Bonneterre Formation. This requires pumpage of several hundred to several thousand gpm, depending on the mine location. The effect of this pumping on groundwater levels was evaluated. The study showed that it is probable that mine pumping does not affect groundwater levels in the deep aquifer beyond a distance of about five miles from any of the mines. Major areas of influence are still more restricted. As mining continues, the area influenced will extend further from north to south, but will probably not expand much east-west. The little information available indicates that no general decline in water levels in the shallow unconfined aquifer has resulted. It appears that the Davis Formation is an effective aquitard and only where it is fractured is interaquifer leakage likely to be rapid enough to cause a major decline in the water table of the shallow aquifer.
W75-06986

INCREASING WATER USE EFFICIENCY THROUGH IMPROVED ORFICE DESIGN AND OPERATIONAL PROCEDURES FOR SUB-IRRIGATION SYSTEMS,
Texas A and M Univ., College Station. Water Resources Inst. Office of Water Research and Technology.
For primary bibliographic entry see Field 3F.
W75-06991

SEDIMENTOLOGY OF AQUIFERS OF THE TONGUE RIVER FORMATION, NORTH DAKOTA,
North Dakota Univ., Grand Forks. Dept. of Geology.
A. F. Jacob.
Research Report No. WI-221-023-74, November, 1974, 4 p, 3 ref. OWRT A-033-NDak (1).

Descriptors: *Groundwater, Aquifers, *Sedimentology, Lignite, *North Dakota, *Sand aquifers, Mapping, Distribution, Forecasting.
Identifiers: *Lignite aquifers, *Tongue River Formation(NDak).

Much groundwater is taken from aquifers in Tertiary sediments and sedimentary rock in the Williston Basin area of North Dakota. These aquifers occur in the Tongue River Formation and are of two types: sand bodies and lignite beds. The most important sand aquifers are linear sand and sandstone bodies up to about 1,000 feet wide, 60 feet thick and many miles long. The sand was deposited in streams that flowed eastward from the ancient Rocky Mountains into the Williston Basin area during the Paleocene Epoch. Lignite aquifers occur in areas adjacent to the sand bodies. They are beds that are laterally extensive and usually not greater than about 20 feet thick. They formed from organic matter that originated in swamps adjacent to the main streams. Fine-grained sediment (silt and clay) surrounds the sand and lignite aquifers. In some places where the Tongue River Formation is present at the earth's surface, erosion has exposed the sand bodies as buttes. Here the sand bodies can be mapped on air photos to determine the pattern of the depositing streams. This pattern can be projected into areas where the Tongue River Formation is buried, enabling the prediction of the location of at least some sand and lignite aquifers in the subsurface.
W75-06993

GROUNDWATER OF SOUTHEASTERN VIRGINIA.
Virginia State Water Control Board, Richmond. Bureau of Water Control Management.
Planning Bulletin 261-A, August 1974. 33 p, 13 fig, 1 tab, 10 ref.

Descriptors: *Groundwater, *Aquifers, *Hydrogeology, *Virginia, Groundwater resources, Groundwater recharge, Dewatering, Water table, Water levels, Groundwater movement, Water quality, Pollutants, Chlorides, Water level fluctuations, Withdrawal, Artesian heads, Pumping, Drawdown, Computer models, Subsurface waters, Water supply.
Identifiers: Water level declines.

From 1941 to 1974, large industrial withdrawals of groundwater in the Franklin area produced a cone of depression approximately 32 km in diameter and 55 m deep. Withdrawals at Franklin and elsewhere in southeastern Virginia have raised concern over current and future development and utilization of groundwater. The southeastern Virginia study area includes all of Isle of Wight, Prince George, Southampton, and Surry counties, parts of Dinwiddie, Greensville, and Sussex Counties, and cities of Chesapeake, Emporia, Franklin, Hopewell, Norfolk, Petersburg, Portsmouth, Suffolk, and Virginia Beach. The availability of groundwater in southeastern Virginia presently is good because pumpage in the area has not been increased in recent years. The quality of groundwater in the area also is very good. However, if pumpage is increased above the present rate, groundwater levels may decline to a point below the top of the Lower Cretaceous aquifers; in this manner dewatering of the principal aquifers would begin. Increased pumpage also may cause the high chloride-water wedge(s) to move westward resulting in the contamination of freshwater wells. (Sims-ISWS)
W75-07044

GOALS, POLICIES AND MANAGEMENT OF WATER RESOURCES IN THE RIO GRANDE VALLEY (APJ-1).
Middle Rio Grande Council of Governments of New Mexico, Albuquerque; and Herkenhoff (Gordon) and Associates, Albuquerque, N. Mex.
Special Report No. 34, January, 1971. 38 p, 2 fig, 12 ref.

Descriptors: *Groundwater resources, *Groundwater recharge, Water resources, *Water supply, *Rio Grande River, Water treatment, Water table, Water table aquifers, Water rights, Water demand, Irrigation, Water, Water delivery, Wells, Water levels, Water sources, Water wells, Geology formations, Hydrologic properties, *New Mexico.
Identifiers: Rio Grande Valley(NM), *Albuquerque(NM), *Santa Fe formation(NM), Bernalillo County(NM), Valencia County(NM), Sandoval County(NM), San Juan-Chama Project(NM), Coefficient of storage.

The area involved (APJ-1) contains 1450 square miles in Bernalillo, Valencia, and Sandoval Counties in New Mexico. It is rapidly urbanizing around the City of Albuquerque. General goals and policies for efficient management and maintenance of the water supply are given. All municipal, industrial, and domestic water supply is presently drawn from underground sources. The San Juan-Chama project under construction (total diversion 110,000 acre-feet per year) will divert water into the Rio Grande watershed and will provide storage points for imported water. The water table elevations in the less urbanized areas should remain constant to year 2000. Near Albuquerque, the water table may recede as much as 85 feet causing the city to use its share of the San Juan-Chama diversion to recharge its groundwater supply. Geologic conditions and hydrology are described. Use in Albuquerque is presently averaging 200 gallons/capita/day with the largest loss due to irrigation (70% lost to evapotranspiration). It is recommended that the primary future water source for the area should be deep wells that produce from the Santa Fe formation. All feasible water sources, including sewage treatment plant effluent and storm runoff, should be exploited as recharge or direct uses. Well construction is not greatly dependent upon location in the study area with the favored design being the gravel wall well which provides maximum production of water from unconsolidated sands and gravels. Treatment criteria for municipal supplies, criteria for distribution storage (fire storage, equalizing storage, transfer storage) and pumping equipment problems are discussed. (Park-North Carolina)
W75-07084

ALAMITOS BARRIER PROJECT,
Los Angeles County Flood Control District, Calif.
E. Alves, Jr., and D. B. Hunt.

Report 68-69, 1969. 72 p, 24 fig, 11 tab, 1 append.

Descriptors: *Saline water jntrusion, *Saline water-freshwater interfaces, *Saline water barriers, *California, *Injection, *Recharge, Groundwater barriers, Groundwater movement, Separation techniques, Flooding, Sea water, Geohydrologic units, Aquicludes.
Identifiers: *Los Angeles(California), *Alamitos barrier.

Fresh water injection and salt water extraction operations in the Alamitos Barrier Project during the 1968-69 fiscal year were relatively trouble free and marked by successful maintenance activities. The majority of the redevelopments took place near the central and easterly portions of the barrier in an effort to increase injection where the greatest difficulty in achieving protective elevations in the I zone was experienced. As pointed out in the 1967-68 report, the trapped saline wedge continued to migrate slowly inland, being gradually dissipated as it mixed with fresher water. Analysis of groundwater data indicates that the highest groundwater elevations occurred during December, 1968. The record rainfall in January and February reduced inland pumping requirements and injection rates were correspondingly reduced, reaching a minimum in February which was held with slight change through June. Changes in water quality during the year are illustrated by Fall, 1968 and Spring, 1969 isochlor maps. There were major changes in the configuration of the recent aquifer isochlors. Supplemental chlorination of the barrier ceased July 6, 1967. Shock chlorination was used during 1967-68; however, it was not used during 1968-69. A record 5530 acre-feet of fresh water was injected at a total cost of $53.11/AF (not including amortization of capital expenditures) of which $24.00/AF was the price of water. In addition, 1823.8 acre-feet of saline water was extracted from the recent aquifer at a cost of $27.78/AF. (Poertner)
W75-07131

A PROGRAM FOR WATER RECLAMATION AND GROUNDWATER RECHARGE, ENVIRONMENTAL IMPACT STATEMENT.
Jenks and Adamson, Palo Alto, Calif.
Santa Clara County Flood Control and Water District, San Jose, California, April 1973. 26 p, 5 fig, 3 tab, 3 append.

Descriptors: *Water reuse, *Water conservation, *Environmental effects, *Groundwater, *Recharge, *Saline water intrusion, Monitoring, Artificial recharge, Environmental control, Injection wells, Pollution, California, Water quality control.
Identifiers: Santa Clara County(California), Waste water reclamation, Environmental Impact Statements.

A water reclamation plant is to be located at the existing Palo Alto Subregional Water Quality Control Plant, together with a ground water well injection and monitoring system. The results of an environmental impact study are reported. The project will not in any significant way alter the existing terrestrial environment. However, the project will impact to a significant extent both the ground water and surface water environment in the affected area. The primary purpose of the proposed project is to prevent further salt water intrusion to the underground water resource supply. In addition, the project will reduce pollution to the receiving waters of San Francisco Bay. Thus, the significant impact of the project will be positive both in respect to quality and quantity of the natural water resource. The adverse effects from the plant will be noise and air pollution. The project was adopted for implementation after consideration and evaluation of five basic alternatives to meet the water supply needs of the affected area. Two alternatives involve importation of water. One alternative involves desalination of San Francisco Bay water, and the remaining two alternatives involve use of reclaimed wastewater to either (1) percolate into the ground water basin, or (2) inject into the ground water basin. (Poertner)
W75-07137

GEOTHERMAL DRILLING IN KLAMATH FALLS, OREGON,
Storey (E. E.) Well Drilling, Klamath Falls, Oreg.
For primary bibliographic entry see Field 8B.
W75-07146

OPTIMUM DEVELOPMENT OF GROUND WATER FROM THE COASTAL AQUIFERS OF DELAWARE; WHERE, HOW MUCH, AND FOR HOW LONG CAN WE SAFELY PUMP OUR COASTAL AQUIFERS,
Delaware Univ., Newark. Water Resources Center.
R. D. Varrin, and A. Salam.
Transactions of the Delaware Academy of Science-1970 and 1971, p 63-76, 1973. 10 fig. OWRT A-004-DEL(6).

Descriptors: *Groundwater, *Saline water intrusion, *Drawdown, *Aquifers, Coasts, *Delaware, Pumping, Aquifer management, Freshwater, Saline water, Interfaces, Saline water-freshwater interfaces, Subsurface waters, Wells, Water levels.

Overdevelopment of the groundwater in coastal areas causes salt water from the sea to intrude into the freshwater aquifers, thus polluting it. Any change in the water table causes the boundary or interface between the fresh and salt water to move. If the water table is lowered, the salt tongue may move several thousand feet inland. Using a model, the position of the freshwater/salt water interface before and after it is affected by man can be studied. The principal activity that affects the freshwater/salt water balance is pumping. Pumping lowers the groundwater table and causes the salt water to move inland. An optimum scheme of location was developed and experiments were conducted to find an optimum pumping. The wells were placed at variable depths in such a way that they were equi-distant from the interface profile. Under pumping at a rate of 200 gallons per minute per square mile, the water table rose to an average of 15 feet and the interface profile was pushed back about 1/2 mile seaward. (Sims-ISWS)
W75-07149

MAJOR AND HISTORICAL SPRINGS OF TEXAS,
Texas Water Development Board, Austin.
G. Brune.
Report 189, March 1975. 95 p, 58 fig, 2 tab, 76 ref.

Descriptors: *Springs, *Texas, *History, *Hydrogeology, Spring waters, Water sources, Water supply, Artesian aquifers, Artesian wells, Groundwater movement, Groundwater, Geology, Discharge(Water).

Springs have been very important to Texas from the time of its first inhabitants. Texas originally had 281 major and historically significant springs, other than saline springs. Sixty-three springs, many with important historical backgrounds, have completely failed. Of the 281 springs studied, 139 issue from 2 underground reservoirs. Although total flow of the springs discussed has declined, it still amounts to about 1,150,000 acre-feet per year, and if all the smaller springs are included, the total annual flow probably exceeds 3,000,000 acre-feet. The underground reservoirs from which springs arise may be cavernous limestone or gypsum, sand, gravel, or other permeable formations. Although a large number of water analyses were obtained and studied, no progressive trend toward contamination of spring waters could be found. The decline of spring flows probably began soon after the first colonization of Texas by Spain. Clearing of forest land and heavy grazing of pastures probably reduced recharge. In the middle 1800's, the drilling of many flowing wells greatly reduced the artesian pressure on springs. Detailed informaton was given separately for each spring, including the location, geologic setting, historical background, and discharge. (Sims-ISWS)
W75-07152

GROUND-WATER QUALITY BENEATH SOLID-WASTE DISPOSAL SITES AT ANCHORAGE, ALASKA,
Geological Survey, Anchorage, Alaska.
For primary bibliographic entry see Field 5B.
W75-07204

INVESTIGATING GROUND-WATER POLLUTION FROM INDIANAPOLIS' LANDFILLS--THE LESSONS LEARNED,
Geological Survey, Indianapolis, Ind.
For primary bibliographic entry see Field 5B.
W75-07205

MONITORING REGIONAL EFFECTS OF HIGH PRESSURE INJECTION OF INDUSTRIAL WASTE WATER IN A LIMESTONE AQUIFER,
Geological Survey, Tallahassee, Fla.
For primary bibliographic entry see Field 5B.
W75-07206

GROUND-WATER CONTAMINATION IN THE SILURIAN DOLOMITE OF DOOR COUNTY, WISCONSIN,
Geological Survey, Madison, Wis.
For primary bibliographic entry see Field 5B.
W75-07207

ERTS IMAGERY FOR GROUND-WATER INVESTIGATIONS,
Geological Survey, Bay Saint Louis, Miss. Gulf Coast Hydroscience Center.
For primary bibliographic entry see Field 7B.
W75-07208

SIMULATED DRAWDOWN FOR SELECTED WELL FIELDS IN THE OHIO RIVER ALLUVIAL AQUIFER,
Geological Survey, Louisville, Ky.
H. F. Grubb.
Available from the National Technical Information Service, Springfield, Va. 22161 as PB-239 163 $3.75 in paper copy, $2.25 in microfiche. Water-Resources Investigations 2-74, January 1975. 38 p, 24 fig, 1 tab, 17 ref, append.

Descriptors: *Drawdown, *Simulation analysis, *Ohio River, *Alluvial channels, Aquifers, *Kentucky, Withdrawal, Mathematical models, Surface-groundwater relationships, Well spacing.

Drawdown caused by pumping was simulated for three sites in the alluvial aquifer adjacent to the Ohio River by digital modeling. Two well-field arrangements were studied at each site. The initial well-field arrangement at each site consisted of three wells located in a line parallel to the Ohio River. The simulated wells were 350 feet apart and 500 feet from the river. Pumping was simulated at a rate of 1,500 gpm for 256 days. The second well-field arrangement allowed comparison drawdown between the initial well-field arrangement and (a) wells located 350 feet nearer the river, (b) additional wells, located between the initial well field and the bedrock valley wall and (c) wells located on a line perpendicular to the river rather than parallel to the river. A verification procedure for the digital model based on observed aquifer response to a flood on the Ohio River is included. (Knapp-USGS)
W75-07209

HYDROLOGIC- AND SALT-BALANCE INVESTIGATIONS UTILIZING DIGITAL MODELS, LOWER SAN LUIS REY RIVER AREA, SAN DIEGO COUNTY, CALIFORNIA,
Geological Survey, Menlo Park, Calif.
For primary bibliographic entry see Field 5B.
W75-07212

GROUND-WATER DATA, 1973, INDIAN WELLS VALLEY, CALIFORNIA,
Geological Survey, Menlo Park, Calif.
R. L. Banta.
Open-file report, December 1974. 9 p, 4 fig, 1 tab, 3 ref.

Descriptors: *Groundwater, *California, *Water quality, *Water levels, Basic data collections, Arsenic compounds, Withdrawal, Hydrologic data.
Identifiers: *Indian Wells Valley(Calif).

Water-level measurements were made in about 110 wells in Indian Wells Valley, California in October 1973. The average water-level decline was 1.2 feet in six wells in the intermediate area between October 1972 and October 1973. This decline was 2.3 feet less than the average decline during the previous year. The average water level in the Inyokern area remains about the same between October 1972 and October 1973. The average water-level decline was 2.0 feet in four wells in the Ridgecrest area between October 1972 and October 1973. The total pumpage from Indian Wells Valley during 1973 was about 14,900 acre-feet, a decrease of about 2 percent from 1972. During 1972 five arsenic determinations ranged from 10 to 15 micrograms per litre. (Knapp-USGS)
W75-07215

GROUND-WATER WITHDRAWALS IN THE UPPER PEACE AND UPPER ALAFIA RIVER BASINS, FLORIDA,
Geological Survey, Tallahassee, Fla.
For primary bibliographic entry see Field 7C.
W75-07222

ANNUAL REPORT ON GROUND WATER IN ARIZONA--WITH EMPHASIS ON GILA BEND BASIN, MCMULLEN VALLEY, AND THE SOUTHEAST PART OF THE HARQUAHALA PLAINS--SPRING 1973 TO SPRING 1974.
Geological Survey, Phoenix, Ariz.
Arizona Water Commission, Phoenix, Bulletin 9, February 1975. 45 p, 16 fig.

Descriptors: *Groundwater, *Arizona, *Basic data collections, *Hydrologic data, Withdrawal, Water yield, Water supply, Water wells.

The geologic and hydrologic data necessary to evaluate the groundwater resources of Arizona, 1973-1974 are compiled. Maps show potential well production by areas, depth to water in selected wells in spring 1974, and change in well levels in selected wells from 1969 to 1974. In areas where groundwater development has taken place the potential well-production values are based on the actual measured production of existing wells. In other areas the potential well-production values are based on the extrapolation of the known production of a few wells that penetrate the several water-bearing units and on the inferred hydrologic characteristics of the units. The report also contains maps showing detailed hydrologic conditions in the Gila Bend basin, McMullen Valley, and the southeast part of the Harquahala Plains. The groundwater reservoirs furnish about two-thirds of the water used in Arizona. The largest use of water is for irrigation; however, more water is being withdrawn each year for municipal and industrial uses. For the 21st consecutive year, the withdrawal of groundwater exceeded 4 million acre-feet. In 1973 the withdrawal of groundwater was nearly 4.8 million acre-feet; through 1973, nearly 149 million acre-feet of groundwater had been withdrawn from the groundwater reservoirs in Arizona. (Knapp-USGS)
W75-07223

HYDROLOGY AND GEOLOGY OF DEEP SANDSTONE AQUIFERS OF PENNSYLVANIAN AGE IN PART OF THE WESTERN COAL FIELD REGION, KENTUCKY,
Geological Survey, Louisville, Ky.
For primary bibliographic entry see Field 2F.
W75-07228

HYDROLOGY OF THE SAND-AND-GRAVEL AQUIFER IN CENTRAL AND SOUTHERN ESCAMBIA COUNTY, FLORIDA, PRELIMINARY REPORT--NOVEMBER 1973,
Geological Survey, Tallahassee, Fla.
H. Trapp, Jr.
Open-file report FL-74027, 1975. 64 p, 11 fig, 1 tab, 15 ref.

Descriptors: *Hydrogeology, *Water resources, *Groundwater, *Florida, *Aquifer characteristics, Groundwater movement, Hydrologic data, Water levels.
Identifiers: *Pensacola(Fla), *Escambia County(Fla).

The sand-and-gravel aquifer is the only fresh-water aquifer in the Pensacola area of Florida. Problems related to development of the aquifer include maximum safe yield, local contamination, local salt-water intrusion, corrosiveness of the water, areas of high iron concentration, and increasing nitrate concentration. Although the thickness of the aquifer locally exceeds 1,000 feet, most of the clean sand layers are no more than 450 feet below land surface. The highest head is at the north edge of the area; the head is drawn down below sea level in areas of heavy pumping. Groundwater moves southward from the northern half of the county to be intercepted near Cantonment. Almost all groundwater discharged south of Cantonment derives from local precipitation. The report contains maps showing concentrations of carbon dioxide, nitrate, and iron in water from the aquifer, potentiometric maps, geohydrologic sections, and lithologic and radioactive logs of test holes. (Knapp-USGS)
W75-07229

WATER-RESOURCES INVESTIGATIONS IN WISCONSIN, 1975 FISCAL YEAR,
Geological Survey, Madison, Wis.
For primary bibliographic entry see Field 7C.
W75-07233

MAP SHOWING DEPTH TO WATER, ANCHORAGE AREA, ALASKA,
Geological Survey, Anchorage, Alaska.
For primary bibliographic entry see Field 7C.
W75-07238

CONTOUR MAP OF THE BEDROCK SURFACE, MOUNT HOLYOKE QUADRANGLE, MASSACHUSETTS,
Geological Survey, Boston, Mass.
For primary bibliographic entry see Field 7C.
W75-07240

DELINEATION OF BURIED GLACIAL-DRIFT AQUIFERS,
Geological Survey, Denver, Colo.
For primary bibliographic entry see Field 2F.
W75-07242

GEOLOGIC SETTING AND CHEMICAL CHARACTERISTICS OF HOT SPRINGS IN WEST-CENTRAL ALASKA,
Geological Survey, Anchorage, Alaska.
For primary bibliographic entry see Field 2F.
W75-07243

REPORT ON WATER SUPPLY, FORT HUACHUCA AND VICINITY, ARIZONA.
Army Engineer District, Los Angeles, Calif.
March 29, 1974. 2 vols.

Descriptors: *Watershed management, *Water resources, *Water sources, *Groundwater, *Water supply development, *Arizona, Water levels, Aquifers.
Identifiers: Fort Huachuca(Ariz), San Pedro River(Ariz).

Adequate groundwater is available in the upper San Pedro River basin to support present and foreseeable future growth at Fort Huachuca and in surrounding areas. Production wells can be located in the East Range of Fort Huachuca. The capital costs of modifying the existing water supply system to meet present deficiencies of the system, plus inclusion of provisions for future expansion, were estimated at $920,000 (1974 prices). The total capital cost of modifying the existing water supply system to meet present deficiencies and of expanding the Post's water supply system to meet assumed daytime Post populations of 25,000 and 50,000 are estimated at $2,330,000 and $6,180,000 respectively. An alternative supply of water could result from construction of Charleston Reservoir, as authorized under the Central Arizona Project. However, the Bureau of Reclamation has assigned a low priority to this work. (Bowden-Arizona)
W75-07332

A RELATION BETWEEN GAMMA RADIATION AND PERMEABILITY, DENVER-JULESBERG BASIN,
Shell Oil Co., Denver, Colo.
C. L. Rabe.
Journal of Petroleum Technology, February, p 65-67, 1957. 6 fig, 1 ref.

Descriptors: *Radioactivity, *Permeability, Gamma radiation, Clay, Radioactive well logging, Clay minerals, Adsorption, Cements, Marking techniques, *Colorado, *Sandstones.
Identifiers: Dakota Sandstone, Muddy Sandstone, Bentonite marker beds.

A relation does exist between permeability and gamma radiation for clay-bonded Muddy and Dakota sands of the Denver-Julesberg Basin, Colorado. In order to apply this relation, gamma ray surveys must be adjusted to a common scale, and proper correction made for thin bed effects. The relation is limited to clay-bonded sands, as calcareous or siliceous cementing materials, which are sometimes encountered and reduce permeability, would not be expected to increase gamma radiation above the clay-free line. Therefore, examination of cores or cuttings is necessary. For the best results where thin beds are involved, the logging speed and time constant should be so chosen that the 'drag' has a value of about 1 foot. Interpretation can also be improved if statistical variation is recorded at a high and low level of radiation and at a chart speed comparable to that of the logging speed. (Bradbeer-NWWA)
W75-07335

4C. Effects On Water Of Man's Non-Water Activities

CATION CONCENTRATIONS OF SMALL STREAMS DRAINING MATCHED FORESTED AND CLEARCUT WATERSHEDS IN WESTERN MONTANA,
Montana Univ., Missoula. School of Forestry.
G. T. Foggin, III, and L. K. Forcier.
Available from the National Technical Information Service, Springfield, Va 22161, as PB-241 309, $4.25 in paper copy, $2.25 in microfiche. Research Report No 58, Montana University Joint Water Resources Research Center, Bozeman, December

1974. 54 p, 5 fig, 12 tab, 54 ref. OWRT A-069-MONT(1).

Descriptors: *Forest management, *Watersheds(Basins), *Land use, *Clearcutting, *Water quality, *Sediment control, *Cations, *Montana, Watershed management, *Small watersheds, Forest watersheds, Land management, Conductance, Water chemistry.

The effects of land management practices on stream water quality in western Montana are not well known. To adress this issue, 15 small clearcut basins were randomly chosen within 50 km of Missoula and their morphometric characteristics determined. Based on this analysis, 15 forested watersheds were selected that were morphometrically similar to the clearcut basins. During the spring and summer of 1974, stream water samples were collected and analyzed for (Ca++), (Mg++), (Na+), (K+) and specific conductance. In basins thought to be on non-calcareous bedrock, specific conductance was quite low compared to that of watersheds assumed to be underlain by calcareous material. The relative concentrations of the four cations were not the same between these two groups of watersheds. Clearcut basins generally had greater stream flow than forested areas. Despite this potential for dilution, average nutrient concentrations on the clearcut basins indicate a greater dissolved nutrient release from the clearcuts. The magnitude of the increase between clearcut and forested basins is substantially less than the increase between basins on calcareous and non-calcareous parent material. Vegetative recovery following forest disturbance was expected to affect stream chemistry. The average time sine clearcutting in the random sample, 9.3 years, may account for the deviation of the western Montana results from some published studies. However, contradictory trends are noted when comparing the cationic concentrations of the two most recently logged watersheds with their forested counterparts.
W75-06853

THE HANLON CREEK STUDY: AN ECOLOGICAL APPROACH TO URBAN PLANNING,
Guelph Univ. (Ontario). Dept. of Land Resource Science.
For primary bibliographic entry see Field 6B.
W75-07067

URBAN STORM RAINFALL-RUNOFF-QUALITY INSTRUMENTATION,
Geological Survey, Reston, Va.
For primary bibliographic entry see Field 5A.
W75-07202

BIBLIOGRAPHY AND INDEX OF GEOLOGY AND HYDROLOGY, FRONT RANGE URBAN CORRIDOR, COLORADO,
Colorado Univ., Boulder. Dept. of Geological Sciences.
For primary bibliographic entry see Field 3D.
W75-07218

A MEASUREMENT OF ALBEDO CHANGES RESULTING FROM AFFORESTATION PRACTICES,
Institute of Hydrology, Wallingford (England).
For primary bibliographic entry see Field 2D.
W75-07265

EFFECTS OF RESERVOIR CLEARING ON WATER QUALITY IN THE ARCTIC AND SUBARCTIC,
Alaska Univ., College. Inst. of Water Resources.
For primary bibliographic entry see Field 5C.
W75-07272

4D. Watershed Protection

CATION CONCENTRATIONS OF SMALL STREAMS DRAINING MATCHED FORESTED AND CLEARCUT WATERSHEDS IN WESTERN MONTANA,
Montana Univ., Missoula. School of Forestry.
For primary bibliographic entry see Field 4C.
W75-06853

TYPES OF EROSION AND DEPOSITION OF SEDIMENTS IN LAKE ASHTABULA AND THE CONTROLLING PROCESSES,
North Dakota Univ., Grand Forks. Dept. of Geology.
For primary bibliographic entry see Field 2J.
W75-06996

LARGE MATERIAL MODELS IN WATERSHED HYDROLOGY RESEARCH,
Agricultural Research Service, Fort Collins, Colo.
For primary bibliographic entry see Field 2A.
W75-07004

APPLICATION OF A CATCHMENT MODEL IN SOUTHEASTERN AUSTRAILIA,
Monash Univ., Clayton (Australia). Dept. of Civol Engineering.
For primary bibliographic entry see Field 2A.
W75-07054

RAINFALL AND SNOWMELT RUNOFF FROM INTERMEDIATE ELEVATION WATERSHEDS,
For primary bibliographic entry see Field 2A.
W75-07101

5. WATER QUALITY MANAGEMENT AND PROTECTION

5A. Identification Of Pollutants

CATION CONCENTRATIONS OF SMALL STREAMS DRAINING MATCHED FORESTED AND CLEARCUT WATERSHEDS IN WESTERN MONTANA,
Montana Univ., Missoula. School of Forestry.
For primary bibliographic entry see Field 4C.
W75-06853

A PRELIMINARY REVIEW OF ANALYTICAL METHODS FOR THE DETERMINATION OF SUSPENDED SOLIDS IN PAPER INDUSTRY EFFLUENTS FOR COMPLIANCE WITH EPA-NPDES PERMIT TERMS,
National Council of the Paper Industry for Air and Stream Improvement, Inc., New York.
J. J. McKeown, H. S. Costa, and D. B. Buckley.
National Council of the Paper Industry for Air and Stream Improvement, Special Report No 75-01, 34 p, January, 1975. 3 fig, 12 tab, 8 ref, 2 appendices.

Descriptors: *Water analysis, *Pollutant identification, *Suspended solids, *Permits, *Pulp and paper industry, Effluents, Water pollution sources, Analytical techniques, Industrial wastes, Wastes, Pulp wastes, Pollutants, Waste identification, Filters, Filtration, Testing procedures, Reviews, Data collections, Inter-Agency cooperation, Governments, Discharge(Water), Regulation, Legislation.

It is shown that variation in analytical testing procedures permitted under Environmental Protection Agency-National Pollutant Discharge Elimination System regulations can account for widely varying measured suspended solids contents of pulp and paper mill effluents. As a consequence, the utility of much of the data available on suspended solids is said to be of questionable value for defining discharge permit conditions unless complete descriptions of procedures used accompany the data. Significant variations in results were found to be related to the filtering media and systems employed, volume of effluent filtered, and post-filtration washing procedure. It is recommended that the various agencies concerned collaborate to develop a uniform test procedure, and that this procedure then be applied to generate a data base on solids discharge which can be used as a reliable basis for establishing permit requirements. (Hansen-IPC)
W75-06865

RAPID MONITORING OF MILL EFFLUENT QUALITY,
T. E. Howard, C. C. Walden, and J. R. Munro.
Canadian Pulp and Paper Association, Technical Section, Air and Stream Improvement Conference, Montreal, September 23-25, 1974, Preprinted Proceedings (Montreal, P.Q.), p 71-74, 2 fig, 2 tab.

Descriptors: *Water analysis, *Oxygen demand, *Pulp wastes, Effluents, Pulp and paper industry, Bioassay, *Monitoring, Biological properties, Analytical techniques, Industrial wastes, Waste water treatment, Quality control, Water quality control, Biochemical oxygen demand, Operations, Toxicity, Fish.

The 96-hour bioassay and 5-day BOD tests commonly applied to industrial effluents are useful in meeting the requirements of regulatory agencies and in evaluating long-term aspects of treatment plant performance. They are not well adapted to short-term process control, and do not contribute to immediate application of remedial measures when operating problems arise. There is a need for rapid methods to assess biological characteristics of effluent quality. Several tests are discussed which may have value for rapid monitoring of treatment plant functioning. These include continuous in situ bioassay, test of thermal tolerance in fish, residual oxygen bioassay, and measurement of oxygen uptake rates in treated effluents. The latter test is regarded as particularly promising and is discussed in some detail. This test can be completed in less than 8 hours, sufficiently short for remedial action to deal with operational problems. Preliminary data indicate that effluents with an oxygen uptake rate of less than 1 mg/liter/hr are nontoxic. Effluents with higher uptake rates are generally toxic. (Hansen-IPC)
W75-06870

THE DETERMINATION OF CHROMIUM (VI) IN NATURAL WATERS BY DIFFERENTIAL PULSE POLAROGRAPHY,
Tennessee Univ., Knoxville. Dept. of Chemistry.
Analytica Chimica Acta, Vol 75, No 1, p 199-205, March, 1975. 2 fig, 3 tab, 22 ref.

Descriptors: *Water analysis, *Chromium, *Polarographic analysis, Analytical techniques, Copper, Iron, Ammonium compounds, Trace elements, Water pollution sources, Pollutants, Chemical analysis, Metals, Inorganic compounds, *Pollutant identification.

A method utilizing differential pulse polarography for the determination of Cr(VI) in natural water is described. Additions of 0.62 microgram Cu(II)/ml and 0.55 microgram Fe(III)/ml did not interfere with the determination of 0.050 microgram Cr (VI)/ml. The natural water samples containing Cr(VI) were buffered to approximately pH 7 with 0.1 molar ammonium acetate and 0.005 molar ethylenediamine and analyzed. Natural water samples of chromium content from 0.035 microgram/ml to 2.0 microgram/ml may be analyzed directly without further preparation. The detection limit is 0.010 microgram/ml. (Witt-IPC)
W75-06874

POLLUTIONAL EFFECTS OF PULP AND PAPER MILL WASTES IN PUGET SOUND.
For primary bibliographic entry see Field 5C.
W75-06881

POLLUTION LOAD FACTORS FOR BLEACH PLANT EFFLUENTS,
Hooker Chemicals and Plastics Corp., Niagara Falls, N.Y.
Tappi, Vol 58, No 2, p 134, February, 1975. 1 tab.

Descriptors: *Bleaching wastes, *Pulp wastes, *Suspended solids, *Organic loading, Water pollution control, Equations, Mathematics, Effluents, Water pollution, Chemical analysis, Suspensions, Fibers(Plant), *Pollutant identification.
Identifiers: Pollution load, Conversion factors.

Cinversion factors are tabulated for changing analytically determined effluent pollution loads (ppm) into the more practical lb per ton (of unbleached oven-dry pulp) expression. A mathematical formula for appropriate calculations at other than listed fiber concentrations (1-15%) is also given. (Brown-IPC)
W75-06884

TRACE ANALYSIS OF PHENOLS IN WATER BY GAS CHROMATOGRAPHY,
Fisheries and Marine Service, Winnipeg (Manitoba).
Journal of the Fisheries Research Board of Canada, Vol 32, No 2, p 292-294, February, 1975. 1 tab, 7 ref.

Descriptors: *Water analysis, *Gas chromatography, *Phenols, *Pollutant identification, Analytical techniques, Pollutants, Water pollution sources, Water properties, Water quality, Water, Water chemistry, Organic compounds, Organic matter, Aromatic compoounds, Chemicals, Industrial wastes, Chemical wastes, Chemical analysis, Chromatography.
Identifiers: Cresols, Xylenols.

A method for the analysis of low concentrations of phenols, cresols, and xylenols in water samples was developed. Ortho-xylene is added as an internal standard and the sample is extracted one with chloroform to remove a portion of the total organic material present. The phenols are converted to their trimethylysilyl derivatives and analyzed by gas chromatography. The method is rapid and requires a minimum of sample manipulation. The lower limit od detection is 0.100 mg/liter for phenol, 0.025 mg/liter for cresols, and 0.050 mg/liter for xylenols. (Witt-IPC)
W75-06890

MERCURY IN THE WESTERN ENVIRONMENT.
Proceedings of a Workshop, Portland, Oregon, February 25-26, 1971. Continuing Education Publications, Corvallis, Oregon, 1973, D.R. Buhler, Editor, 360 pages, 82 fig, 98 tab, 390 ref.

Descriptors: *Mercury, *Toxicity, *Public health, *Conferences, Organic compounds, Inorganic compounds, Surface waters, Pollutants, Water pollution, Fish, Aquatic life, Food chains, Sediments, Oysters, Biology, Lead, Animal physiology, Analytical techniques, Spectroscopy, Chromatography, *Path of pollutants, Pollutant identification, Heavy metals.

A compilation of information on the sources and effects of mercury in the western environment is presented. The book is divided into four sections (Mercury in the Aquatic Environment, Mercury in the Terrestrial Environment, Analysis of Mercury and Methylmercury, and Toxicity of Mercury Compounds) and includes a discussion at the end of each section. The book is based on proceedings of a workshop organized to bring together individuals concerned with the sources and distribution of mercury in the western United States and Canada, the effects of mercury contamination on fish and wildlife; the analysis of mercury; and the nature and occurrence of mercury-related damage to man. It also provided, to a degree, a status report of contemporary research on mercury pollution and toxicity. (See W75-06898 thru W75-06930)
W75-06897

SOURCES AND PRESENT STATUS OF THE MERCURY PROBLEM,
Hope Coll., Holland, Mich. Dept. of Chemistry.
For primary bibliographic entry see Field 5B.
W75-06898

MERCURY IN THE STATE OF WASHINGTON,
Environmental Protection Agency, Seattle, Wash. Region X.
For primary bibliographic entry see Field 5B.
W75-06900

THE DISTRIBUTION OF MERCURY IN SEDIMENT CORES FROM BELLINGHAM BAY, WASHINGTON,
Washington Univ., Seattle. Dept. of Oceanography.
For primary bibliographic entry see Field 5B.
W75-06901

MERCURY CONCENTRATIONS IN FISH,
Bureau of Sport Fisheries and Wildlife, Washington, D.C.
C. Henderson, and W. E. Shanks.
In: Mercury in the Western Environment, Continuing Education Publications, Corvallis, Oregon, p 45-58, 1973. 1 fig, 5 tab, 3 ref.

Descriptors: *Mercury, *Fish, *Sampling, *Distribution, Toxicity, Monitoring, Data collections, Regions, Analytical techniques, Spectroscopy, *Pollutant identification, Heavy metals.

As a part of the National Pesticide Monitoring Program, mercury analyses were conducted on composite fish samples collected by the U.S. Bureau of Sport Fisheries and Wildlife (BSFW) in the fall of 1969 and 1970. Three composite samples, each of a different species and consisting of three to five adult fish, were collected at each of 50 monitoring stations in 1969 and at each of 100 monitoring stations in 1970 located on major rivers and lakes throughout the United States. In 39 composite samples from 14 stations collected in 1969 in BSFW Region 1 (Pacific) and Alaska, detectable levels were found in all samples with values ranging from 0.06-1.25 ppm. In the fall of 1970, all 84 composite samples from 23 stations in BSFW Region 1 and Alaska contained mercury residues with values ranging from 0.05-1.7 ppm. Mean (0.26 ppm) and median (0.17 ppm) values were slightly higher than in other BSFW regions. (See also W75-06897) (Jernigan-Vanderbilt)
W75-06902

MERCURY IN AQUATIC SPECIES FROM THE PACIFIC NORTHWEST,
Oregon State Univ., Corvallis. Environmental Health Sciences Center.
D. R. Buhler, R. R. Claeys, and W. E. Shanks.
In: Mercury in the Western Environment, Continuing Education Publications, Corvallis, Oregon, p 59-75, 1973. 1 fig, 7 tab, 18 ref. USPHS (ES 00210).

Descriptors: *Distribution, *Mercury, *Fish, *Pacific Northwest U.S., Aquatic animals, Freshwater, Estuaries, Rivers, Lakes, Bays, Data collections, Idaho, Oregon, Washington, Analytical techniques, Spectroscopy, Laboratory tests, Sampling, Toxicity, *Pollutant identification, Heavy metals.

Freshwater and estuarine organisms were collected from various rivers, lakes and bays in Idaho, Oregon, Washington and northern California and the muscle tissue then analyzed for mercury via flameless atomic absorption. Mercury was present in all samples tested with the highest concentration 1.98 ppm, occurring in a northern squawfish taken from the Snake River. At least 80-90% of the mercury found in the muscle tissue was in the methylmercury form. The mercury content of the fishes varied appreciably according to species. Approximately 85% of the brown bullhead, 77% of the northern squawfish, 54% of the channel catfish, 47% of the largemouth bass, and 11% of the white sturgeon examined contained mercury concentrations that exceeded the 0.5 ppm guidelines value set by the U.S. Food and Drug Administration. Other freshwater fish species showed lower mercury levels and anadromous fishes such as adult chinook and coho salmon, collected in freshwater had the lowest mercury content. The sampling location had considerable influence on the mercury concentrations found in a given fish species. Fish from the Coast Fork of the Willamette River and Antelope Reservoir in Oregon and the Snake River in Idaho, Oregon and Washington contained especially high mercury levels. (See also W75-06897) (Jernigan-Vanderbilt)
W75-06903

MERCURY RESIDUES IN IDAHO FISHES - 1970,
Idaho Dept. of Fish and Game, Boise.
S. Gebhards, J. Cline, F. Shields, and L. Pearson.
In: Mercury in the Western Environment, Continuing Education Publications, Corvallis, Oregon, p 76-80, 1973. 1 fig, 2 tab, 3 ref.

Descriptors: *Fish, *Mercury, *Idaho, *Distribution, Toxicity, Public Health, Sampling, Analytical techniques, Spectroscopy, Rivers, Foods, Mining, Mining wastes, Water pollution, *Pollutant identification, Heavy metals.
Identifiers: *Snake River(Idaho).

A total of 160 fish samples, representing 19 species were collected from 18 areas in Idaho. Mercury residues were determined by neutron activation analysis. Detectable mercury was found in 98% of the samples with the highest residue, 1.7 ppm found in a Squawfish. A total of 19% of the fish tested contained or exceeded the 0.5 ppm U.S. Food and Drug Administration guideline for mercury residues in human foods. Data suggested that channel catfish, yellow perch, and suckers accumulate higher mercury levels than other species taken from the same waters. Fish from reservoir sections of the Snake River contained higher mercury levels than those collected from free-flowing river sections. Large quantities of quicksilver lost during mining activities in the late 1860's may be responsible for the elevated mercury residue in fish from Jordan Creek, Idaho. (See also W75-06897) (Jernigan-Vanderbilt)
W75-06904

FDA'S PROGRAM OF MERCURY IN FOODS,
Food and Drug Administration, Seattle, Wash.
For primary bibliographic entry see Field 5G.
W75-06905

THE RATE OF LOSS OF MERCURY BY PACIFIC OYSTERS,
Washington Univ., Seattle. Coll. of Fisheries.
For primary bibliographic entry see Field 5C.
W75-06906

MERCURY IN FUR SEALS,
National Marine Fisheries Service, Seattle, Wash. Marine Mammal Biological Lab.
For primary bibliographic entry see Field 5C.
W75-06907

MERCURY LEVELS IN CALIFORNIA SEA LIONS,
Oregon State Univ., Corvallis. Environmental Health Sciences Center.
For primary bibliographic entry see Field 5C.
W75-06908

THE GENERAL AND COMPARATIVE BIOLOGY OF TOXIC METALS AND THEIR DERIVATIVES: MERCURY AND LEAD,
Hawaii Univ., Honolulu. Environmental Center.
For primary bibliographic entry see Field 5C.
W75-06909

MERCURY CONTAMINATION IN CALIFORNIA'S FISH AND WILDLIFE,
California State Dept. of Fish and Game, Sacramento.
For primary bibliographic entry see Field 5C.
W75-06910

PRELIMINARY STUDIES OF MERCURY TISSUE LEVELS FROM GAME BIRDS AND FISH IN UTAH,
Utah State Univ., Logan. Dept. of Toxicology.
For primary bibliographic entry see Field 5C.
W75-06911

MERCURY-WILDLIFE STUDIES BY THE DENVER WILDLIFE RESEARCH CENTER,
Bureau of Sport Fisheries and Wildlife, Denver, Colo. Denver Wildlife Research Center.
For primary bibliographic entry see Field 5C.
W75-06912

MERCURY IN PHEASANTS AND OTHER BIRDS FROM EASTERN WASHINGTON,
Washington State Dept. of Game, Olympia.
For primary bibliographic entry see Field 5C.
W75-06913

MERCURY LEVEL STUDIES IN MIGRATORY WATERFOWL,
Reed Coll., Portland, Oreg. Dept. of Chemistry.
For primary bibliographic entry see Field 5C.
W75-06914

MERCURY IN HUNGARIAN PARTRIDGE AND IN THEIR NORTH CENTRAL MONTANA ENVIRONMENT,
Montana Fish and Game Dept., Choteau.
For primary bibliographic entry see Field 5C.
W75-06915

AN ANALYSIS OF MERCURY RESIDUES IN IDAHO PHEASANTS,
Idaho State Dept. of Health, Boise.
For primary bibliographic entry see Field 5C.
W75-06916

SEASONAL VARIATIONS IN MERCURY CONTENT OF OREGON PHEASANTS,
Oregon State Univ., Corvallis. Environmental Health Sciences Center.
For primary bibliographic entry see Field 5C.
W75-06917

PHEASANT FEEDING STUDY USING SEEDS TREATED WITH METHYL AND PHENYLMERCURY,
Bureau of Sport Fisheries and Wildlife, Boise, Idaho. Div. of River Basin Studies.
For primary bibliographic entry see Field 5C.
W75-06918

INTRODUCTION TO THE ANALYTICAL METHODS FOR THE DETERMINATION OF MERCURY COMPOUNDS,
Oregon State Univ., Corvallis. Environmental Health Sciences Center.
R. R. Claeys.
In: Mercury in the Western Environment, Continuing Education Publications, Corvallis, Oregon, p 229-233, 1973. 1 fig, 10 ref.

Descriptors: *Mercury, Organic compounds, Inorganic compounds, *Analytical techniques, Colorimetry, Spectroscopy, Chromatography, Research and development, *Reviews, *Pollutant identification, Heavy metals.

Various methods for the determination of mercury and its compounds were described briefly. The development of the analytical methods used for the analysis of mercury in the environment was summarized. Colorimetry, atomic absorption, neutron activation, and gas chromatography were discussed, and general comparisons of the methods were made. (See also W75-06897) (Jernigan-Vanderbilt)
W75-06919

NONFLAME METHODS FOR MERCURY DETERMINATION BY ATOMIC ABSORPTION: A REVIEW,
Perkin-Elmer Corp., Burlingame, Calif.
A. A. Koch, and D. C. Manning.
In: Mercury in the Western Environment, Continuing Education Publications, Corvallis, Oregon, p 234-241, 1973. 43 ref.

Descriptors: *Mercury, *Analytical techniques, *Spectroscopy, Research and development, Laboratory tests, Testing procedures, *Reviews, *Pollutant identification, Heavy metals.
Identifiers: *Atomic absorption spectroscopy.

A summary was presented of the published work on the determination of mercury at trace concentrations by nonflame atomic absorption spectroscopy. These methods involved either the reduction of the mercury to elemental form and subsequent determination of the free mercury in an absorption cell or the deposition of mercury onto a base metal from the sample solution and subsequent thermal release of the mercury into an absorption cell. Detection limits of less than 0.001 micrograms were possible using these procedures. The cold vapor stannous chloride method for atomic absorption was substantially more sensitive than the standard solution nebulization sampling techniques. It is relatively easy to convert a standard flame atomic absorption instrument to determine mercury by this method. (See also W75-06897) (Jernigan-Vanderbilt)
W75-06920

SEMI-AUTOMATED DETERMINATION OF MERCURY IN FISH TISSUE,
Fisheries Research Board of Canada, Winnipeg (Manitoba). Freshwater Inst.
F. A. J. Armstrong, and J. F. Uthe.
In: Mercury in the Western Environment, Continuing Education Publications, Corvallis, Oregon, p 242-249, 1973. 4 fig, 2 tab, 4 ref.

Descriptors: *Mercury, *Fish, Animal physiology, *Analytical techniques, Research and development, *Automation, *Pollutant identification, Heavy metals.

An automated method for determination of mercury was described. Samples of the tissue were digested with nitric and sulphuric acids, oxidized with potassium permanganate and cleared with hydrogen peroxide. Mercury was then reduced with hydroxylamine sulfate and stannous sulfate and the vapor equilibrated with air using Technicon Auto Analyzer equipment and determined by flameless atomic absorption spectrometry at a rate of 30 samples per hour. The standard deviation of the methods is plus or minus 0.04 at the 0.5 ppm level. The automated method is rapid and may be completed in under eight hours, although routine analysis usually takes 24 hours. For inspection work it is therefore to be preferred over neutron activation analysis. Precision and accuracy are adequate for most inspection and research purposes. (See also W75-06897) (Jernigan-Vanderbilt)
W75-06921

AN INSTRUMENTAL NEUTRON ACTIVATION METHOD FOR THE DETERMINATION OF MERCURY: WITH COMPARISONS TO ATOMIC ABSORPTION SPECTROPHOTOMETRY,
Oregon State Univ., Corvallis. Radiation Center.
P. J. Mellinger, and V. N. Smith.
In: Mercury in the Western Environment, Continuing Education Publications, Corvallis, Oregon, p 250-256, 1973. 1 fig, 3 tab, 4 ref.

Descriptors: *Mercury, *Analytical techniques, *Instrumentation, Radioisotopes, Tracers, Spectroscopy, Colorimetry, *Neutron activation analysis, *Pollutant identification, Heavy metals.
Identifiers: Atomic absorption spectrophotometry.

An instrumental neutron activation analysis method using the Hg196 (n, gamma) Hg197 and the Hg202 (n, gamma) Hg 203 reaction was described for the determination of trace quantities of mercury in biological tissue. Samples were irradiated for three hours in a thermal neutron flux of 1.2 x 10 to the 12th power neutrons per sq cm/sec and allowed to decay for 10 days prior to measurement with a 30 cu cm Ge(Li) detector (resolution of 2.5 kev) coupled to a 2,048 channel gamma ray analyzer. Interlaboratory comparisons were made using flameless atomic absorption spectrophotometry and colorimetry with good agreement. (See also W75-06897) (Jernigan-Vanderbilt)
W75-06922

NEUTRON ACTIVATION ANALYSIS FOR THE DETERMINATION OF MERCURY IN ENVIRONMENTAL SAMPLES,
Washington State Univ., Pullman. Nuclear Radiation Center.
R. H. Filby, A. I. Davis, and K. R. Shah.
In: Mercury in the Western Environment, Continuing Education Publications, Corvallis, Oregon, p 257-264, 1973. 1 fig, 2 tab, 17 ref.

Descriptors: *Mercury, *Analytical techniques, *Neutron activation analysis, Evaluation, Instrumentation, Radioisotopes, Tracers, Spectroscopy, *Pollutant identification, Heavy metals.

An instrumental neutron activation analysis procedure using the Hg202 (n, gamma) Hg203 reaction was described for the determination of mercury in biological tissues, water, and other environmental materials. Reactor irradiation at a thermal neutron flux of 5 x 10 to the 12th power neutrons/sq cm/sec was followed by a six-week decay period and measurement of Hg203 using a Ge(Li) spectrometer system. The method was precise and the sensitivity varied with sample matrix. For mammalian blood, the detection limit was 3.0 ppb mercury. The advantages and disadvantages of activation analysis compared with atomic absorption, spectrophotometric methods, and emission spectrography were discussed. (See also W75-06897) (Jernigan-Vanderbilt)
W75-06923

A RAPID SEMIMICRO METHOD FOR METHYLMERCURY RESIDUE ANALYSIS IN FISH BY GAS CHROMATOGRAPHY,
Fisheries Research Board of Canada, Winnipeg (Manitoba). Freshwater Inst.
J. Solomon, and J. F. Uthe.

In: Mercury in the Western Environment, Continuing Education Publications, Corvallis, Oregon, p 265c272, 1973. 3 fig, 2 tab, 6 ref.

Descriptors: *Mercury, *Fish, *Analytical techniques, Chromatography, Organic compounds, Animal physiology, Laboratory tests, Research and development, Spectroscopy, *Pollutant identification, Heavy metals, *Gas chromatography.
Identifiers: Gas liquid chromatography, *Methylmercury.

A rapid gas chromatographic method for the determination of the methylmercury content of fish tissues was described. This semimicro method eliminated evaporation steps and lowered the handling dangers for the chemist. Dimethylmercury and other mercurials did not interfere with monomethylmercury in this method. It worked well for the determination of methylmercury, and duplicate analysis of samples gave values that agreed within 2%. Atomic absorption and thin-layer chromatography were used to confirm the presence of methylmercury in the final extracts. Analysis of fish from many areas with this method indicates that the mercury present in fish is essentially all methylated. (See also W75-06897) (Jernigan-Vanderbilt)
W75-06924

THE HUMAN HEALTH HAZARDS OF METHYLMERCURY,
Mayo Clinic, Rochester, Minn. Dept. of Medical Statistics, Epidemiology and Population Genetics.
For primary bibliographic entry see Field 5C.
W75-06925

EXPERIMENTAL PORCINE METHYLMERCURIALISM,
Washington State Univ., Pullman. Dept. of Veterinary Pathology.
For primary bibliographic entry see Field 5C.
W75-06926

THE HUMAN MORPHOLOGICAL LESIONS OF METHYLMERCURY INJURY,
Washington Univ., Seattle. Dept. of Pathology.
For primary bibliographic entry see Field 5C.
W75-06927

METHYLMERCURY TOXICITY: A PROBABILISTIC ASSESEMENT,
California Univ., Berkeley. School of Public Health.
For primary bibliographic entry see Field 5C.
W75-06928

MERCURY CONTAMINATION-PRIBILOF ISLANDS,
Center for Disease Control, Atlanta, Ga.
For primary bibliographic entry see Field 5C.
W75-06929

THE PHARMACODYNAMICS OF MERCURY AND ITS COMPOUNDS WITH EMPHASIS ON THE SHORT-CHAIN ALKYLMERCURIALS,
Rochester Univ., N.Y. Dept. of Radiation Biology and Biophysics.
For primary bibliographic entry see Field 5C.
W75-06930

EFFECTS OF CERTAIN CHEMICAL POLLUTANTS ON SMALL AQUATIC ANIMALS,
Kansas Water Resources Research Inst., Manhattan.
E. C. Bovee.
Available from the National Technical Information Service, Springfield, Va 22161 as PB-241 336, $3.25 in paper copy, $2.25 in microfiche. KWRRI Contribution No. 157, January 1975. 11 p, 4 fig, 9 ref. OWRT A-058-KAN(1). 14-31-0001-3816.

Descriptors: *Cadmium, Calcium, *Protozoa, Water pollution effects, *Bioassay, Cations, *Pollutant identification, Heavy metals, *Toxicity, *Bioindicators, Thermal pollution.
Identifiers: *Photomicrography, Tetrahymena pyriformis.

A quick, accurate, photomicrographic method has been developed for bioassaying the presence and concentration of heavy-metals pollutants in water. The method detects toxic levels of pollutants and for a single toxic metal will detect one part of metal in one billion parts of water. The animal used, the ciliated protozoan, Tetrahymena pyriformis, is easily and cheaply raised in the laboratory and is poisoned by about the same levels of metals as the blue-gill sunfish. The bioassay is run in less than half a day, including developing and analysis of films of the locomoting animal on which the assay depends. With reference-graphs of the pollutants, the method is potentially of practical use to laboratories interested in detecting presence and amounts of pollutants in a water source or plant-effluent. In 'hard' waters calcium, especially, and other non-toxic cations, e.g., sodium, potassium, magnesium, partly inhibit toxic effects of heavy metals. 'Hard' waters can therefore carry a slightly larger burden of toxic metals than can 'soft' waters which have little or no mineral content. At higher temperatures in water, toxic effect of heavy metals, e.g., cadmium, is noticeably increased. This suggests that waters heated by thermal pollution can carry a lesser burden of toxic pollutants than cooler waters, and less in summer months than in cooler months.
W75-06981

LIGHT INITIATED REACTIONS IN WATER CONTAINING CHELATED METAL IMPURITIES,
North Dakota State Univ., Fargo. Dept. of Chemistry.
For primary bibliographic entry see Field 2K.
W75-06994

ACID PRECIPITATION IN THE NORTHEASTERN UNITED STATES,
Cornell Univ., Ithaca, N.Y. Section of Ecology and Systematics.
For primary bibliographic entry see Field 5B.
W75-07057

COPPER IN SURFACE WATERS SOUTH OF NEW ZEALAND,
Massachusetts Inst. of Tech., Cambridge. Dept. of Earth and Planetary Sciences.
For primary bibliographic entry see Field 2K.
W75-07060

CUMULATIVE CHEMICAL LIGHT METER,
Westinghouse Research Labs., Pittsburgh, Pa.
G. D. Dixon, D. H. Davies, and J. D. Voytko.
Environmental Science and Technology, Vol 9, No 3, p 234-237, March 1975. 6 fig, 5 ref.

Descriptors: *Pollutant identification, *Light intensity, *Photoactivation, *Instrumentation, *Photoperiodism, Analytical techniques, Light, Photosynthesis, Solar radiation, Radiation, Chemistry, Spectrophotometry, Chlorophyll, Energy conversion, Primary productivity, Measurement, Viscosoty.
Identifiers: *Chemical light meter, *Actinometers, Photoisomerization, Photochemical degradation, Gardner-Holdt viscosity tube, Chemical actinometer.

A cumulative light meter was devised based on the light-induced degradation of aqueous polymer solutions. The viscosity of the solution can be related to the total amount of incident light absorbed. The system possesses a number of significant advantages over competitive actinometers. It is very cheap, needs no extra equipment or skilled personnel, and can be simply modified to respond to any desired spectral region. (Henley-ISWS)
W75-07063

INSTRUMENTS FOR WATER QUALITY MEASUREMENTS,
California Univ., Berkeley. Lawrence Berkeley Lab.
S. L. Phillips, and D. A. Mack.
Environmental Science and Technology, Vol 9, No 3, p 214-220, March 1975. 5 tab.

Descriptors: *Pollutant identification, *Instrumentation, *Analytical techniques, *Measurement, *Water quality, *Water analysis, Chemical analysis, Chromatography, On-site tests, Water measurement, Evaluation, Laboratory tests, Trace elements, Water chemistry, Nutrients, Quality control, Testing, Colorimetry, Testing procedures, Pesticides, Monitoring, Metals, Carbon, Mineralogy, Automation.
Identifiers: AutoAnalyzer, Gas membrane electrodes.

Techniques were discussed that form the basis of current commercial or developing techniques for measuring metals, nutrients, pesticides, and oxygen demand in water supplies. The discussion gives a general picture of the instrumentation available. Listings of instrument manufacturers were included. (Henley-ISWS)
W75-07065

STUDY OF TRACE ELEMENTS IN WATERS OF TWO ALASKAN RESERVOIR SITES,
Alaska Univ., College. Inst. of Water Resources.
For primary bibliographic entry see Field 5B.
W75-07100

ADVANCED PLANNING OF FLOOD CONTROL PROJECTS,
Santa Clara County Flood Control and Water District, San Jose, Calif.
For primary bibliographic entry see Field 6B.
W75-07139

EXAMINATION OF WATERS: EVALUATION OF METHODS FOR SELECTED CHARACTERISTICS.
Australian Water Resources Council, Canberra (Australia).
Technical Paper No. 8, 1974. 109 p. J. A. McGlynn, compiler.

Descriptors: *Water quality, *Analytical techniques, *Water analysis, *Laboratory tests, Water pollution, Water chemistry, Sampling, Testing, Trace elements, Chemical analysis, Instrumentation, Nitrates, Phosphorus, Colorimetry, Ions, Electrodes, Chemical properties, Metals, Oily water, Oil wastes, Oil pollution, Mercury, Freshwater, Sea water, Standards, Methodology, Testing procedures, *Pollutant identification.
Identifiers: *Standard methods, Mineral oil.

The eight papers presented provide up-to-date information on analytical techniques to aid in the selection and practical implementation of new and improved methods and to give increased precision and accuracy of laboratory data as well as increased productivity and improved laboratory efficiency. Subjects included: (1) a review of methods for the determination of nitrate in waters, (2) methods for determination of phosphorus in waters, (3) an evaluation of new methods for the determination of ammonia in water, (4) a review of mercury analysis and sampling techniques, (5) instrumental methods for the determination of trace metals in water, (6) determination of mineral oil in water, (7) a review of techniques for the characterization and identification of oil spillages, and (8) the automation of routine analysis of water. Recommendations were given for future research into improvement of water quality assessment

techniques. (See W75-07155 thru W75-07162) (Humphreys-ISWS)
W75-07154

A REVIEW OF METHODS FOR THE DETERMINATION OF NITRATE IN WATERS,
Chemical and Bacteriological Labs., Melbourne (Australia).
J. R. Huxley, and D. Wisel.
In: Examination of Waters: Evaluation of Methods for Selected Characteristics; Australian Water Resources Council Technical Paper No. 8, p 13-20, 1974. 1 tab, 39 ref.

Descriptors: *Chemical analysis, *Nitrates, *Pollutant identification, *Analytical techniques, *Reviews, Nitrogen compounds, Chemical wastes, Spectrophotometry, Ultraviolet radiation, Ions, Electrodes, Reduction(Chemical), Chemical reactions, Nitrites, Inorganic compounds, Pollutants.
Identifiers: Ultraviolet spectrophotometry, Ion-selective electrode methods.

Methods for the determination of nitrate in water and wastewater were reviewed and compared as to range and potential interferences. Poor results obtained from inter-laboratory trials carried out by other workers revealed the generally unsatisfactory nature of commonly used methods, particularly at concentrations below a few mg/l NO3-N. Methods discussed include phenoldisulphonic acid, brucine, UV spectrophotometry, selective-ion electrode, and those based on reduction to nitrite. For use at concentrations between 1 and 10 mg/l NO3-N, the automated hydrazine method appeared marginally the most precise and subject to the least interferences. No method could be recommended in severely polluted water except perhaps the selective ion electrode method if the alkalinity and chloride are low, the ionic strength does not vary significantly from sample to sample, and the nitrate concentration is above 2 mg/l NO3-N. For determination at extremely low concentrations, the choice was between the two cadmium reduction methods, although these may be subject to interference in some situations. (See also W75-07154) (Sims-ISWS)
W75-07155

METHODS FOR DETERMINATION OF PHOSPHORUS IN WATERS,
Western Australia Government Chemical Labs., Perth.
N. Platell, and P. N. Jack.
In: Examination of Waters: Evaluation of Methods for Selected Characteristics; Australian Water Resources Council Technical Paper No. 8, p 21-25, 1974. 30 ref.

Descriptors: *Chemical analysis, *Phosphorus, *Pollutant identification, *Analytical techniques, Chemical wastes, Pollutants, Oxidation, Digestion, Nutrients, Colorimetry, Color reactions, Laboratory tests.
Identifiers: Interferences(Chemical).

Marine and freshwater biologists have traditionally studied water phosphorus levels. The more widespread interest has come with the increased interest in pollution and it is pertinent to consider what to look for and to revise available methods. Examination of recent reviews and articles indicated that total phosphorus is the only definite measurable phosphorus form, that perchloric acid oxidation/digestion is the most satisfactory method of measurement, and that, except for arsenic 5+, interferences are negligible in the molybdenum blue method. After conversion to orthophosphate, automatic methods could be applied. The recommended methods is that of Murphy and Riley (1962), with modifications in regard to sample preparation, i.e., digestion, sample size, and reagent preparation. (See also W75-07154) (Sims-ISWS)
W75-07156

AN EVALUATION OF NEW METHODS FOR THE DETERMINATION OF AMMONIA IN WATER,
Brisbane City Council (Australia).
J. Kennewell, and N. Long.
In: Examination of Waters: Evaluation of Methods for Selected Characteristics; Australian Water Resources Council Technical Paper No. 8, p 27-41, 1974. 11 tab, 22 ref.

Descriptors: *Chemical analysis, *Ammonia, *Pollutant identification, *Analytical techniques, Chemical wastes, Pollutants, Laboratory tests, Testing procedures, Colorimetry, Methodology, Automation.
Identifiers: Phenol hypochlorite methods, Ion-selective electrode methods.

Two new developments in the ammonia determination for waters were reviewed. One concerns two variations of the colorimetric 'indophenol blue' methods, (1) the method of Solorzano (1969) for natural waters through to saline waters and wastewater and (2) the method of Harwood and Kuhn (1970) for natural waters and wastewater. The other concerns developments based on the principle of the application of an ammonia selective-ion electrode. Although much of the information in the review relied on appraisal of the available literature, data were included and conclusions drawn from laboratory investigation of the methods under review. Comparison of the methods was made on sewage samples but most results relied on spike recoveries. All three methods appear more than satisfactory alternatives to traditional methods. (See also W75-07154) (Sims-ISWS)
W75-07157

A REVIEW OF MERCURY ANALYSIS AND SAMPLING TECHNIQUES,
Western Australia Government Chemical Labs., Perth.
N. Platell, and T. Webb.
In: Examination of Waters: Evaluation of Methods for Selected Characteristics; Australian Water Resources Council Technical Paper No. 8, p 43-51, 1974. 67 ref.

Descriptors: *Chemical analysis, *Sampling, *Mercury, *Pollutant identification, *Analytical techniques, Chemical wastes, Pollutants, Laboratory tests, Testing procedures, Methodology, Adsorption, Filtration, Spectroscopy, Colorimetry, Chromatography, Fluorescence, Neutron activation analysis.
Identifiers: Atomic adsorption spectrometry, Amalgamation, Interferences(Chemical).

In the last decade, mercury as an environmental pollutant has received a great deal of attention. In the field of water pollution in particular, this attention has shown that exceedingly low levels of mercury are of considerable significance. As a result, better sampling and analysis techniques have been required. This review deals briefly with mercury forms and significant levels, and in more detail, with sampling losses and methods of analysis. These methods include colorimetric, flameless atomic absorption with various concentration techniques and interferences, neutron activation, atomic fluorescence and gas chromatography. (See also W75-07154) (Sims-ISWS)
W75-07158

INSTRUMENTAL METHODS FOR THE DETERMINATION OF TRACE METALS IN WATER,
New South Wales Dept. of Mines, Sydney (Australia). Chemical Lab.
J. A. McGlynn.
In: Examination of Waters: Evaluation of Methods for Selected Characteristics; Australian Water Resources Council Technical Paper No. 8, p 53-78, 1974. 10 tab, 64 ref.

Descriptors: *Chemical analysis, *Trace elements, *Pollutant identification, *Analytical techniques, *Metals, Spectroscopy, Polarographic analysis, Methodology, Sampling, Laboratory tests, Water chemistry, Instrumentation, Electrodes, Ion exchange, Chemical wastes, Pollutants.
Identifiers: Atomic absorption spectrometry, Anodic stripping voltammetry, Concentration techniques, Interferences(Chemical), Trace metals.

Instrumental methods for the determination of trace metals in water at or below typical water supply standards were reviewed. Discussion included the application of methods based on atomic absorption spectrometry, differential pulse polarography, and anodic stripping voltammetry. Techniques for concentration of metals to allow adequate sensitivities for the various methods were also discussed. The need for care both in selection of pretreatment technique to ensure measurement of total metal content, and in control of calibration by standard addition was emphasized. Anodic stripping voltammetry was recommended for those metals suited to it, or direct flame atomic absorption spectrometry if concentrations and salinity permit. (See also W75-07154) (Sims-ISWS)
W75-07159

DETERMINATION OF MINERAL OIL IN WATER,
Victoria Dept. of Agriculture (Australia). Div. of Agricultural Chemistry.
R. S. Belcher.
In: Examination of Waters: Evaluation of Methods for Selected Characteristics; Australian Water Resources Council Technical Paper No. 8, p 79-83, 1974. 12 ref.

Descriptors: *Chemical analysis, *Oil, *Pollutant identification, *Analytical techniques, Oily water, Sea water, Oil pollution, Water pollution, Pollutants, Separation techniques, Infrared radiation, Ultraviolet radiation, Spectrophotometry, Chromatography, Gravimetry, Fluorescence, Absorption, Evaporation, Water chemistry, Oil spills.
Identifiers: Atomic absorption spectrometry, Fluorescence spectrography.

Methods in use for determination of low-level mineral oil contamination of water were reviewed and some limitations on efficiency of extraction of the oil, separation of natural substances, and measurement of levels of pollution were noted. A method involving infrared spectrophotometry and a new extraction procedure developed by the Division of Agricultural Chemistry was given in detail and its advantages and disadvantages were discussed. This topic, while currently of special interest for the examination of sea water for residues from oil contamination is also potentially important in the investigation of oil pollution of freshwater bodies and streams. (See also W75-07154) (Sims-ISWS)
W75-07160

A REVIEW OF TECHNIQUES FOR THE CHARACTERISATION AND IDENTIFICATION OF OIL SPILLAGES,
New South Wales Dept. of Mines, Sydney (Australia). Chemical Lab.
J. A. McGlynn.
In: Examination of Waters: Evaluation of Methods for Selected Characteristics; Australian Water Resources Council Technical Paper No. 8, p 85-89, 1974. 21 ref.

Descriptors: *Chemical analysis, *Pollutant identification, *Oil, *Oil spills, Analytical techniques, Spectrometry, Water pollution sources, Absorption, Oil pollution, Infrared radiation, Ultraviolet radiation, Chromatography, Metals, Fluorescence, Separation techniques.
Identifiers: Infrared absorption spectrometry, Ultraviolet absorption spectrometry, Ultraviolet fluorescence, Trace metals.

The value of a wide range of techniques to match oil spill samples with oil from possible sources was discussed. Techniques include infrared absorbance, ultraviolet fluorescence, ultraviolet absorbance, paper chromatography, trace metal ratios, and specification properties such as sulphur, viscosity, and specific gravity. An addendum included techniques which were considered most useful for comparison of oil spillages to possible sources. (See also W75-07154) (Sims-ISWS)
W75-07161

THE AUTOMATION OF ROUTINE COLORIMETRIC ANALYSIS OF WATER,
New South Wales Dept. of Mines, Sydney (Australia). Chemical Lab.
J. A. McGlynn.
In: Examination of Waters: Evaluation of Methods for Selected Characteristics; Australian Water Resources Council Technical Paper No. 8, p 91-97, 1974. 2 fig, 1 tab, 21 ref.

Descriptors: *Colorimetry, *Automation, Cost-benefit analysis, *Chemical analysis, Analytical techniques, Pollutant identification, Digestion, Distillation, Economics, Cost-benefit ratio, Instrumentation, Laboratory tests, Testing procedures.
Identifiers: Interferences(Chemical), Cross contamination.

The value of automated colorimetry for analysis of routine water samples was examined. Operational considerations and limitations were discussed together with an approximate cost-benefit analysis based on labor and capital costs for equipment. Subject to limitations, the use of automatic analyzer techniques was recommended where economically justified. (See also W75-07154) (Sims-ISWS)
W75-07162

THERMAL ALTERATION OF ORGANIC MATTER IN RECENT MARINE SEDIMENTS. I PIGMENTS, .
California Univ., Los Angeles. Inst. of Geophysics and Planetary Physics.
For primary bibliographic entry see Field 5B.
W75-07167

THERMAL ALTERATION OF ORGANIC MATTER IN RECENT MARINE SEDIMENTS. II ISOPRENOIDS,
California Univ, Los Angeles. Dept. of Geophysics and Planetary Physics.
For primary bibliographic entry see Field 5B.
W75-07168

THERMAL ALTERATION OF ORGANIC MATTER IN RECENT MARINE SEDIMENTS. III ALIPHATIC AND STEROIDAL ALCOHOLS,
California Univ., Los Angeles. Inst. of Geophysics and Planetary Physics.
For primary bibliographic entry see Field 5B.
W75-07169

GEOCHEMICAL ANALYSIS OF STREAM SEDIMENTS AS A TOOL FOR ENVIRONMENTAL MONITORING: A PIGYARD CASE STUDY,
Brock Univ., St. Catharines (Ontario). Dept. of Geological Sciences.
G. R. Alther.
Geological Society of America Bulletin, Vol 86, No 2, p 174-176, February 1975. 8 fig, 2 tab, 2 ref.

Descriptors: *Geochemistry, *Sediments, *Environmental effects, *Monitoring, Analysis, Feed lots, Farm wastes, Chemical analysis, *Canada, Streambeds, Magnesium, Calcium, Sodium, Potassium, Zinc, Copper, Lead, Cobalt, Nickel, Iron, Manganese, Statistical methods, Flame photometry, Water pollution, Pollutant identification.
Identifiers: *St. Catharines(Ontario), Pigs, Chi-square test, Atomic absorption.

A geochemical analysis of 11 chemical elements in stream sediments in the vicinity of a pig farm shows that geochemical exploration methods can be used for regional environmental monitoring of organic pollution. In a 5-sq mi area in southern Ontario, contaminated stream sediments showed definite increases in Mg, Ca, Na, K, and Zn. Changes in Cu content were inconclusive; Pb, Co, Ni, Fe, and Mn showed background averages. The study showed that stream sediments are affected by large-scale agricultural operations within a short period of time. It is conclusive that groundwater will be affected as contamination continues. (Visocky-ISWS)
W75-07188

PRINCIPAL-COMPONENT ANALYSIS OF STREAMFLOW CHEMICAL QUALITY DATA,
Geological Survey, Reston, Va.
For primary bibliographic entry see Field 5B.
W75-07200

URBAN STORM RAINFALL-RUNOFF-QUALITY INSTRUMENTATION,
Geological Survey, Reston, Va.
G. F. Smoot, J. Davidian, and R. H. Billings.
In: Flash Floods; Proceedings of Paris Symposium, September 1974: International Association/Hydrological Sciences Publication No 112, p 44-47, 1974. 2 fig.

Descriptors: *Instrumentation, *Urban hydrology, *Urban runoff, Storm runoff, Rainfall-runoff relationships, Sampling, Water quality, Sewers, Stream gages, Data collections, Precipitation gages, Data processing.

A project was initiated to develop the necessary instrumentation to study urban runoff and has resulted in an intergrated system, including precipitation gages, a sewer flow measuring device, automatic sampler, clock, recorder, and necessary logic. The precipitation gages are the tipping bucket type having a readability of 0.25 mm. The flow measuring device functions within the sewer under both open-channel and pressure flow conditions, the meter is a venturi flume whose constricted bottom forces subcritical depths to form upstream, with the flow passing through critical depth at the throat. In pipes having very steep slopes, the flow remains supercritical both upstream from and through the constriction. The device is a modified venturi meter for pressure flows. In the transition between open-channel and pressure flows, the upstream pipe is full whereas the throat and downstream pipe are partly full. The water sampler collects 24 two-litre samples at predetermined time intervals, holding them refrigerated until they are analyzed. Data are recorded on a single recorder along with time so that all parameters are time correlated. Presently, these instrumentation systems are being installed in several sewered catchment basins throughout the United States. (Knapp-USGS)
W75-07202

GROUND-WATER DATA, 1973, INDIAN WELLS VALLEY, CALIFORNIA,
Geological Survey, Menlo Park, Calif.
For primary bibliographic entry see Field 4B.
W75-07215

QUALITY OF THE GROUND WATER IN BASALT OF THE COLUMBIA RIVER GROUP, WASHINGTON, OREGON, AND IDAHO,
Geological Survey, Reston, Va.
For primary bibliographic entry see Field 2K.
W75-07217

AN AUTOMATED TECHNIQUE FOR TOTA DISSOLVED FREE AMINO ACIDS IN SEA WATER,
Oregon State Univ., Corvallis. School of Oceanography.
D. D. Coughenower, and H. C. Curl, Jr.
Limnology and Oceanography, Vol 20, No 1, p 128-131, January 1975. 1 fig, 3 tab, 8 ref. NOAA Contract 2-35187.

Descriptors: *Pollutant identification, *Amino acids, *Sea water, *Automation, *Colorimetry *Analytical techniques, Analysis, Spectroscopy Chemistry, Color reactions, Evaluation, Instrumentation, Testing, Testing procedures, Measurement, Salinity, Organic compounds, Estuaries, Nitrogen compounds, Nutrients.
Identifiers: *Ninhydrin solution, Hydrazine sulfate, Salt effect, Proline, Cystine, Arginine, Histidine.

An automated method for total dissolved free amino acid in seawater, using an air-stable ninhydrin solution, is most suitable as a field method providing real time information. Data taken in two estuaries were presented to show the distribution of total amino acid. (Henley-ISWS)
W75-07247

MICROBIAL TRANSFORMATIONS OF MERCURY IN AQUATIC ENVIRONMENTS,
Purdue Univ., Lafayette, Ind. Dept. of Agronomy.
For primary bibliographic entry see Field 5B.
W75-07275

LAKE ERIE INTERNATIONAL JETPORT MODEL FEASIBILITY INVESTIGATION; REPORT 1, SCOPE OF STUDY AND REVIEW OF AVAILABLE DATA,
Army Engineer Waterways Experiment Station, Vicksburg, Miss.
For primary bibliographic entry see Field 2H.
W75-07286

AMCHITKA BIOENVIRONMENTAL PROGRAM. LIMNOLOGY OF AMCHITKA ISLAND, ALASKA,
Battelle Columbus Labs., Ohio.
R. D. Burkett.
Available from the National Technical Information Service, Springfield, Va 22161 as BMI-171-153, $4.00 in paper copy, $2.25 in microfiche. Final Summary Report and Progress Report, March 1974. 37 p, 4 fig, 13 tab, 19 ref, 2 append. AEC AT(26-1)-171.

Descriptors: *Environmental effects, *Alaska, *Nuclear explosions, Aquatic environment, Aquatic habitats, Biota, Plankton, Biological communities.
Identifiers: *Amchitka Island(Alaska).

Perturbations to the biota and aquatic environment resulting from the underground nuclear tests, Milrow and Cannikin, and their necessary support activities were investigated. Changes observed in lakes following Milrow were slight, most being attributed to manifestations of seasonal fluctuation and not to Milrow. Natural shifts in physical and chemical parameters plus changes in rates of metabolic parameters (heterotrophy and primary productivity) were not noticeably altered. No elimination of planktonic species or dramatic change in plankton community structure was noted. Longer term post-Cannikin reconnaisance has not produced evidence to indicate that any significant changes in chemical and biological parameters occurred due to the Cannikin ground shock wave. Several aquatic habitats were seriously altered as a result of drilling operations and general support activities. These water bodies might recover their predisturbance status following evacuation of the Island. Three lakes were partially drained due to ground-surface displacement following Milrow, and one, Heart Lake, sustained

gross morphological changes. The Cannikin detonation resulted in gross morphological changes in several lakes near SZ, rupture of a dike in a drill- and containment pond, and formation of Cannikin Lake in the Cannikin subsidence crater, which, as of 1972, contains the largest water volume on the island. (Jones-Wisconsin)
W75-07293

WORKSHOP ON SAMPLE PREPARATION TECHNIQUES FOR ORGANIC POLLUTANT ANALYSIS HELD AT DENVER, COLORADO ON 2-4 OCTOBER 1973.
National Field Investigations Center-Denver, Colo.
Available from the National Technical Information Service, Springfield, Va 22161 as PB-232 015, $3.75 in paper copy, $2.25 in microfiche. November 1973. 40 p.

Descriptors: *Analytical techniques, *Sampling, *Organic compounds, *Pollutant identification, Industrial wastes, Chemicals, Quality control, Separation techniques, Distillation, Chromatography.
Identifiers: Resin-column samplers, Sample preservation.

Various sampling methods and analytical techniques of industrial organic chemicals discharged into surface waters are discussed. Many techniques are currently used to analyze industrial effluents, natural waters, bottom sediments, and aquatic biota for industrial and agricultural organic-chemical pollutants. Sample contamination is discussed in detail. Considerable interest is shown in macroreticular resins for integrated sampling. Petroleum-containing samples are preserved by the addition of sulfuric acid, while formalin was suggested for PCB-containing samples. Tissue- and bottom-sediment samples are preserved by freezing. Extraction procedures cover a wide variety of techniques whereby the organie pollutant(s) of interest are transferred from the inorganic or biological matrix and usually concentrated prior to chemical characterization. Samples that are too complex to be separated under normal gas chromatographic conditions are usually subjected to some form of fractionation during, or after, extraction. Thin-layer chromatography is a recommended technique in view of its low cost and the visual impact it can have in a courtroom. Probably the most promising cleanup technique is some form of automated gel-permeation chromatography. The qualitative and quantitative aspects of quality control in the organic laboratory are prescribed. (Jones-Wisconsin)
W75-07295

THE BOD5/DO RATIO. A NEW ANALYTICAL TOOL FOR WATER QUALITY EVALUATION,
Environmental Protection Agency, Philadelphia, Pa. Region III.
N. W. Melvin, and R. H. Gardner.
Available from the National Technical Information Service, Springfield, Va 22161 as PB-230 358, $3.75 in paper copy; $2.25 in microfiche. Report EPA-903/9-73-009 (1973). 46 p, 14 fig, 1 tab.

Descriptors: *Biochemical oxygen demand, *Dissolved oxygen, *Analytical techniques, *Water quality, Streams, Water pollution, Measurement, Computer programs, Methodology, Classification, Sewage effluents, *Pollutant identification.
Identifiers: *BOD5/DO ratio, Case studies.

The two paramters, BOD and DO, are used to determine the ratio between them at each site and for each sample taken. Postulation are demonstrated and illustrated by the various situations actually occurring at stream stations across the United States. The BOD5/DO ratio is shown to be useful in evaluating the general health of streams. Assignment of ratio scales to streams can assist workers in the water pollution field to understand the actual reaction of a stream to clean-up efforts as well as to monitor any progressive changes being imposed by man-made pollution sources. Data presented indicate the ratio works well in differing stream types and can be used to evaluate the net ecological activity in streams. It can also be shown that streams exhibit varying ratios with both time and season. Those streams which are relatively clean exhibit only minor fluctuations about a central mode; conversely, degraded streams show a much larger fluctuation amplitude and the BOD5/DO trace is generally arratic. Evaluation of the long-term trend slope of the ratio trace will give a good indication of the net effect of pollution-abatement efforts. (Jones-Wisconsin)
W75-07329

5B. Sources Of Pollution

INTERRELATIONSHIPS OF VARIOUS BIOASSAY PROCEDURES FOR PULP AND PAPER EFFLUENTS,
B.C. Research, Vancouver (British Columbia).
For primary bibliographic entry see Field 5C.
W75-06867

WORLD FOCUS ON POLLUTION (ENFOQUE GLOBAL DE LA CONTAMINACION),
Investigacion y Tecnica del Papel, Vol 11, No 42, p 947-966, October, 1974.

Descriptors: *Air pollution, *Water pollution, *Industrial wastes, *Municipal wastes, Pulp and paper industry, Foreign countries, Europe, Research and development, Water pollution sources, Waste water(Pollution), Wastes, Pollutants, *Pulp wastes.
Identifiers: *Spain.

World-wide polluting activity of both industry and the general populace is briefly reviewed, and air and water contaminants emitted by Spanish industries, including the pulp and paper industry, are discussed. Although the pollution problem in Spain is not as severe as in some equally developed countries, technical investigations are being conducted to determine means of reducing industrial pollution loads before contamination diminishes the quality of life sustained by industry and the environment. (Sykes-IPC)
W75-06873

WOODY SOLIDS DISCHARGED INTO WATER COURSES BY THE FOREST PRODUCTS INDUSTRY.
For primary bibliographic entry see Field 5C.
W75-06882

MERCURY IN THE WESTERN ENVIRONMENT.
For primary bibliographic entry see Field 5A.
W75-06897

SOURCES AND PRESENT STATUS OF THE MERCURY PROBLEM,
Hope Coll., Holland, Mich. Dept. of Chemistry.
D. H. Klein.
In: Mercury in the Western Environment, Continuing Education Publications, Corvallis, Oregon, p 3-15, 1973. 3 fig, 13 ref. FWQA (16040 FRL).

Descriptors: *Mercury, *Great lakes, *Industrial wastes, *Air pollution, Surface runoff, Mining, Fossil fuels, Lead, Zinc, Copper, Legal aspects, Path of pollutants, Heavy metals.

The levels of mercury in segments of the uncontaminated environment are relatively low. Mercury contents of wildlife and sediments from much of the Great Lakes region are elevated well above these natural levels, and approach those previously observed in Sweden and Japan. Very high levels of mercury in fish are due primarily to discharge of waste mercury to the waters. However, the few data available indicate that much more mercury enters the atmosphere by voltalization, where it may be transported by winds and subsequently rained out. Analysis of the tabulated uses of mercury shows that about 3,000 tons of mined and refined mercury are wasted to the atmosphere yearly, and about half that much to the waters. Combustion of fossil fuels also contributes a few thousand tons to the atmosphere. The smelting of ores, especially of lead, zinc, and copper, is a third major source of atmospheric mercury. Urban soils are remarkably enriched in mercury, as a result of fallout from other, as yet undefined, sources. (See also W75-06897) (Jernigan-Vanderbilt)
W75-06898

MERCURY IN THE STATE OF WASHINGTON,
Environmental Protection Agency, Seattle, Wash. Region X.
R. A. Lee.
In: Mercury in the Western Environment, Continuing Education Publications, Corvallis, Oregon, p 29-35, 1973. 2 fig, 2 ref.

Descriptors: *Mercury, *Industrial wastes, Rivers, *Distribution, *Washington, Municipal wastes, Sediments, Analytical techniques, Spectroscopy, Mining, *Path of pollutants, *Pollutant identification, Heavy metals.

Mercury levels in selected industrial and municipal wastewaters and from environmental sources were collected to determine the occurrences and distribution of mercury in the state of Washington, in accordance with state regulation and control of unnatural mercury discharges. The amount of mercury lost to waterways by each of two mercury cell chloralkali plants exhibited a dramatic decrease between April and December of 1970. Sediment samples from Bellingham Bay in an area immediately adjacent to a chloralkali plant outfall contained high mercury levels when compared to samples taken in other areas of the bay. Substantial amounts of mercury were also found to be distributed naturally in major streams and rivers. (See also W75-06897) (Jernigan-Vanderbilt)
W75-06900

THE DISTRIBUTION OF MERCURY IN SEDIMENT CORES FROM BELLINGHAM BAY, WASHINGTON,
Washington Univ., Seattle. Dept. of Oceanography.
M. H. Bothner, and D. Z. Piper.
In: Mercury in the Western Environment, Continuing Education Publications, Corvallis, Oregon, p 36-44, 1973. 8 fig, 9 ref.

Descriptors: *Mercury, *Sediments, *Washington, Industrial wastes, Sampling, Analytical techniques, Spectroscopy, Cores, Carbon, On-site data collections, Distribution, Bays, *Path of pollutants, *Pollutant identification, Heavy metals.
Identifiers: Bellingham Bay(Wash).

Cores of undisturbed surface sediment and gravity cores up to 75 cm long were collected from Bellingham Bay in Puget Sound for mercury analysis. Samples of bulk sediments were freeze-dried and analyzed instrumentally by neutron activation utilizing the Hg203 photopeak. Within a sediment core the mercury concentration was generally homogeneous in the top 5 cm probably due to biological and/or tidal mixing of the surface sediment. The mercury concentration decreased rapidly with depth from high values in the upper 5 cm to uniformly low values of less than 0.5 ppm below 15 cm. Surface values decreased with distance away from a major industrial outfall. Total carbon concentrations were measured for the same samples analyzed for mercury. The data suggested that both the carbon content of sedi-

ment and distance from the industrial outfall may be important factors in controlling the distribution of mercury in the surface sediment. There did not seem to be a strong correlation between mercury and total carbon concentrations with depth in the sediment. (See also W75-06897) (Jernigan-Vanderbilt)
W75-06901

THE PHARMACODYNAMICS OF MERCURY AND ITS COMPOUNDS WITH EMPHASIS ON THE SHORT-CHAIN ALKYLMERCURIALS,
Rochester Univ, N.Y. Dept. of Radiation Biology and Biophysics.
For primary bibliographic entry see Field 5C.
W75-06930

THE HELME-RESERVOIR NEAR KELBRA (KYFFHAEUSER, DDR): III. THE PLANKTON DURING 1967-1970 (IN GERMAN),
Martin Luther-Universitaet, Halle-Wittenberg (East Germany). Hygiene Institut.
For primary bibliographic entry see Field 2H.
W75-06937

PROBABILISTIC METHODS IN STREAM QUALITY MANAGEMENT,
Washington Univ., Seattle. Dept. of Civil Engineering.
S. J. Burges, and D. P. Lettenmaier.
Water Resources Bulletin, Vol 11, No 1, p 115-130, February 1975. 6 fig, 3 tab, 12 ref.

Descriptors: Streams, *Water quality, *Management, *Probability, *Stochastic processes, *Simulation analysis, Dissolved oxygen, Biochemical oxygen demand, Monte Carlo methods, Sampling, Estimating, Equations, Model studies, Temperature, Travel time, Reaeration, Systems analysis, *Risks.
Identifiers: First order analysis, Streeter-Phelps equations, Prediction, Sensitivity analysis.

Recent advances in water quality modelling have shown the need for stochastic models to simulate the probabilistic nature of water quality. However, often all that is needed is an estimate of the uncertainty in predicting water quality variables. First order analysis is a simple method of providing an estimate of the uncertainty in a deterministic model due to uncertain parameters. The method is applied to the simplified Streeter-Phelps equations for DO and BOD; a more complete Monte Carlo simulation is used to check the accuracy of the results. An analysis of the sensitivity of the DO and BOD estimates to varying levels of parameter and input variable uncertainty is given. Results of the uncertainty analyses are discussed in terms of water quality management objectives, and the feasibility of mathematical models for management is assessed. The first order analysis is found to give accurate estimates of means and variances of DO and BOD up to travel times exceeding the critical time. Uncertainty in travel time and the BOD decay constant are most important for small travel times; uncertainty in the reaeration coefficient dominates near the critical time. Uncertainty in temperature is a negligible source of uncertainty in DO for all travel times. (Bell-Cornell)
W75-06946

ON THE EFFICIENT ALLOCATION OF ENVIRONMENTAL ASSIMILATIVE CAPACITY: THE CASE OF THERMAL EMISSIONS TO A LARGE BODY OF WATER,
California Univ., Los Angeles. Dept. of Engineering Systems.
C. R. Scherer.
Water Resources Research, Vol 11, No 1, p 180-181, February 1975. 3 fig, 9 ref.

Descriptors: *Economic efficiency, *Thermal capacity, *Lakes, *Water quality control, *Temperature, Standards, Environment, Heated water, Effluents, Flow rate, Costs, Ports, Size, Cooling towers, Powerplants, Marginal costs, Mathematical models, Systems analysis, Methodology, *Waste assimilative capacity, *Thermal pollution.
Identifiers: Environmental quality, Thermal emissions.

Considered is the economically efficient level of environmental assimilative capacity in the case of thermal electric rejected heat discharges to large lakes subject to temperature standards. A mathematical model relating heated effluent flow rate and 'near-field' temperature is used to determine maximum diffusor port size. Diffusor costs are developed as a function of discharge velocity, port size being given. Cooling tower costs are also developed for comparison with diffusor costs in selecting an optimal level of thermal assimilative capacity. The relationship between this selection process and optimal power plant siting models is outlined. It is shown that arbitrarily fixing discharge velocity at some 'practical' level will tend to bias the results of these siting models toward overly conservative use of thermal assimilative capacity. This means, available capacity will not be fully exploited, and the cost of a given level of power output will be greater than is necessary. (Bell-Cornell)
W75-06950

VARIATION OF URBAN RUNOFF QUALITY AND QUANTITY WITH DURATION AND INTENSITY OF STORMS--PHASE III,
Texas Tech Univ., Lubbock. Water Resources Center.
G. B. Thompson, D. M. Wells, R. M. Sweazy, and B. J. Claborn.
Available from the National Technical Information Service, Springfield, Va 22161 as PB-241 406, $4.25 in paper copy, $2.25 in microfiche. Completion Report WRC-74-2, August, 1974. 56 p, 7 fig, 13 tab, 28 ref. OWRT B-177-TEX(1). 14-31-0001-4130.

Descriptors: *Texas, *Urban runoff, *Water quality, *Storm runoff, Watershed management, Water pollution sources, *Precipitation intensity, *Biochemical oxygen demand, *Chemical oxygen demand, Low flow, Dry seasons, *Storm sewers.
Identifiers: *Lubbock(Tex).

In the 1,499 acre watershed in Lubbock, Texas, thirty-five percent of the total precipitation appeared as direct runoff. From storm to storm, runoff pollutant concentrations varied widely in average and extreme values. COD and BOD washoff from the watershed equaled, respectively, 16.7 and 1.75 pounds/acre-inch of rainfall. There was a continuous, though highly variable, discharge during dry weather from the 26th Street storm sewer, totaling approximately two million gallons per year. Quality of the dry weather flow was considerably poorer than that of untreated domestic sewage. The yearly amount of COD in the dry weather discharge was equal to 15 percent of the mean annual COD in storm runoff. Discharges resulting from efforts to fight major fires contained significant quantities of pollutants. A facility should be constructed to provide interception and storage of the storm sewer discharge. Such a holding pond should trap all dry weather flow, and all flows resulting from unusual events.
W75-06975

BACTERIAL METHANE OXIDATION AND ITS INFLUENCE IN THE AQUATIC ENVIRONMENT,
Ohio State Univ., Columbus. Dept. of Microbiology.
P. R. Dugan, and T. L. Weaver.
Available from the National Technical Information Service, Springfield, Va 22161 as PB-241 345, $5.75 in paper copy, $2.25 in microfiche. Ohio Water Resources Center, Columbus, Partial Completion Report, August 1974. 133 p, 52 fig, 21 tab, 137 ref. OWRT A-027-OHIO(2).

Descriptors: *Bacteria, *Oxidation, *Methane bacteria, Clays, Methane, Membranes, Enzymes, Soils, Suspended solids, Oxygenation, Water pollution sources.
Identifiers: *Methane oxidation, Cytoplasm.

Suspended clay particles enhance bacterial methane oxidation by decreasing the lag phase of growth, increasing total methane oxidized, and by increasing the rate of methane oxidation. Bacterial methane oxidation enhancement increases with increasing clay concentrations up to 4.0%. The clay types kaolinite, illite, vermiculite, and bentonite equally stimulated bacterial methane oxidation. Clay particles less than 2 micrometers in size elicit a greater stimulation of methane oxidation than particles greater than 2 micrometers in size. The silicious remains of diatoms slightly enhance bacterial methane oxidation. Calcium phosphate and calcium carbonate in suspension almost completely inhibit bacterial methane oxidation. Anacystis nidulans produces an extracellular substance that inhibits bacterial methane oxidation. Chlorella vulgaris and Anabaena variabilis inhibit bacterial methane oxidation when exposed to light. Increased methane utilization rates increase rates of dissolved oxygen composition. Methylosinus trichosporium is one of the bacteria responsible for methane oxidation. A variety of amino acids, organic acids, pentoses, and hexoses enhance methane oxidation by this bacterium. The bacterium fixes about 50% of the methane it oxidizes into cell material and one oxygen atom is consumed at each oxidative step during methane oxidation which is consistent with a monooxygenase. Intracytoplasmic membranes are organelles of electron transport and energy entrapment in this bacterium; methane is fixed into cell material by the cytoplasmic enzyme serine hydroxymethyl transferase. The bacterium has a specific formaldehyde dehydrogenase in the cytoplasm. ATPase was observed in both cytoplasm and membranes.
W75-06987

STUDIES ON THE HYDROLYSIS AND PRECIPITATION OF ALUMINUM (III),
Ohio State Univ., Columbus. Dept. of Civil Engineering.
For primary bibliographic entry see Field 5D.
W75-06988

CIRCULATION IN SHALLOW ESTUARIES,
Texas Univ., Austin. Dept. of Civil Engineering.
For primary bibliographic entry see Field 2L.
W75-07030

MATHEMATICAL MODELLING OF WATER QUALITY IN A RIVER SYSTEM,
Melbourne Univ., Parkville (Australia). Dept. of Civil Engineering.
J. D. Lawson, and R. J. Vass.
In: River and Estuary Model Analysis, Volume III; Proceedings of the International Association for Hydraulic Research Symposium on River Mechanics (4 Vol.), Bangkok, Thailand, January 9-12, 1973. Asian Institute of Technology, Bangkok, Thailand, p 401-414, (1973). 6 fig, 29 ref.

Descriptors: *Path of pollutants, *Model studies, *Water quality, *Rivers, *Effluents, Dissolved oxygen, Biochemical oxygen demand, Mathematical models, Simulation analysis, Pollutants, Water pollution, Thermal pollution, Powerplants, Watersheds(Basins), *Australia.
Identifiers: *Latrobe River(Australia).

The concepts related to the development of a mathematical simulation model for the Latrobe River Basin in Victoria, Australia, were investigated. The relevant parameters affecting natural stream purification, their interdependence, and the subsequent development of suitable mathematical equations were outlined. The model comprises a series of cells each of which is assumed to contain fully mixed water. Effluents are

introduced as point sources. Account is taken of the conservative or decaying nature of the effluent. The unsteady nature of fresh water throughout may be reproduced from hydrological records. A case study of the Latrobe River was presented. Historical records for water quality were reproduced together with the results of simulation studies in the river for biochemical oxygen demand and dissolved oxygen deficit. The problem of obtaining reliable and sufficient data was also considered. (See also W75-06998) (Sims-ISWS)
W75-07031

MATHEMATICAL MODELS FOR THE PLANNING AND MANAGEMENT OF THE SAINT JOHN RIVER SYSTEMS,
Department of the Environment, Ottawa (Ontario). Ecological Systems Research Div.
A. K. Biswas, and P. J. Reynolds.
In: River and Estuary Model Analysis, Volume III; Proceedings of the International Association for Hydraulic Research Symposium on River Mechanics (4 Vol.), Bangkok, Thailand, January 9-12, 1973. Asian Institute of Technology, Bangkok, Thailand, p 415-428, (1973). 5 fig, 10 ref.

Descriptors: *Model studies, *Water quality, *Rivers, *Effluents, Dissolved oxygen, Biochemical oxygen demand, Mathematical models, Computer programs, Simulation analysis, Linear programming, Pollutants, Water pollution, Management, Comprehensive planning, Watersheds(Basins), *Canada.
Identifiers: *Saint John River(Canada).

Models add one more dimension to the decision-making process by better understanding of the system in consideration, by broadening of the information base, by predicting the consequences of several alternative courses of action, and by selecting a suitable course of action which will accomplish a prescribed result. For the Saint John River System in Canada, two complementary models were developed: a linear programming model for the preliminary screening of alternative designs and operating policies to be followed by a simulation model for more detailed analyses of select few designs and operating policies. The development and use of these two models were discussed as planning and management tools for the Saint John River Basin. (See also W75-06998) (Sims-ISWS)
W75-07032

MATHEMATICAL MODELLING FOR SHORT-TERM TRANSPORT IN VERTICALLY MIXED ESTUARIES,
Madras Univ., Guindy (India). Dept. of Hydraulic Engineering.
For primary bibliographic entry see Field 2L.
W75-07033

CHARACTERISTICS OF THE INTERFACIAL REGION OF A TWO-LAYER FLOW SYSTEM,
Melbourne Univ., Parkville (Australia). Dept. of Civil Engineering.
For primary bibliographic entry see Field 2L.
W75-07034

A MATHEMATICAL MODEL TO PREDICT DISCHARGE VARIATIONS IN AN ESTUARY WITH SHALLOW WATER AND A LARGE TIDAL RANGE,
Ente Nazionale per l'Energia Elettrica, Milan (Italy).
For primary bibliographic entry see Field 2L.
W75-07035

FINITE ELEMENT NUMERICAL MODELLING OF FLOW AND DISPERSION IN ESTUARIES,
University Coll. of Swansea (Wales). Dept. of Civil Engineering.
For primary bibliographic entry see Field 2L.
W75-07036

THE INTERACTION OF VELOCITY DISTRIBUTION AND SUSPENDED LOAD IN TURBULENT STREAMS,
Massachusetts Inst. of Tech., Cambridge. Ralph M. Parsons Lab. for Water Resources and Hydrodynamics.
For primary bibliographic entry see Field 2J.
W75-07039

A WATER-QUALITY SIMULATION MODEL FOR WELL MIXED ESTUARIES AND COASTAL SEAS: VOL. VI, SIMULATION, OBSERVATION, AND STATE ESTIMATION,
New York City-Rand Inst., N.Y.
J. J. Leendertse, and S-K. Liu.
Report R-1586-NYC, September 1974. 103 p, 69 fig, 1 tab, 9 ref, 4 append.

Descriptors: *Model studies, *Water quality, *Urban runoff, *Estuarine environment, Computer models, Overflow, Pollutants, Storm runoff, Storm drains, Urban drainage, Coliforms, Sewage bacteria, Bays, Estuaries, Tides, Simulation analysis, New York.
Identifiers: *Jamaica Bay(NY), *New York City.

The water-quality simulation of post-rainstorm coliform bacteria distributions in Jamaica Bay, New York was described by use of models of the drainage basins surrounding the bay and a water-quality simulation of the bay itself. A stochastic analysis method was introduced into the investigation to assess the behavior and resolving power of the water-quality simulation model and to derive an optimal estimate of missing input data. The estimates obtained by simulation agree well with those obtained by field measurements, except near Bergen Basin where an unknown source of coliform bacteria exists. The origin and extent of this input should be determined from new field surveys. Since the response to a rainstorm of all major components of this urban estuarine system can be determined, the models described provide the basis for the optimal design and management of an auxiliary treatment system for sewer overflows of the drainage basins around the bay. (Sims-ISWS)
W75-07042

GROUNDWATER OF SOUTHEASTERN VIRGINIA,
Virginia State Water Control Board, Richmond. Bureau of Water Control Management.
For primary bibliographic entry see Field 4B.
W75-07044

ACID PRECIPITATION IN THE NORTHEASTERN UNITED STATES,
Cornell Univ., Ithaca, N.Y. Section of Ecology and Systematics.
C. V. Cogbill, and G. E. Likens.
Water Resources Research, Vol 10, No 6, p 1133-1137, December 1974. 5 fig, 1 tab, 32 ref.

Descriptors: *Air pollution, *Precipitation(Atmospheric), *Acidic water, *Water pollution sources, Water pollution, Pollutants, *Path of pollutants, Acids, *Northeast U.S, Anions, Cations, Industrial wastes, Hydrogen ion concentration, Pollutant identification.
Identifiers: Acid precipitation.

Analysis of recent precipitation samples from the northeastern United States showed a consistent pH of less than 4.4, when the expected pH based upon equilibrium with CO_2 would be 5.6. A stoichiometric formation process being assumed, some 65% of the acidity is due to H_2SO_4, 30% to HNO_3, and less than 5% to HCl. The pH values may be predicted from chemical content and generally agree to within 0.1 pH unit with the observed pH. The distribution of acid precipitation encompasses most of the northeastern United States. This pattern apparently has existed since about 1950-1955, but the intensity of acid deposition, especially that due to HNO_3, has increased since then. Analysis of prevailing winds indicated that much of the acidity originates as a general source over industrial areas in the Midwest. (Sims-ISWS)
W75-07057

CHEMICAL ANALYSIS FOR EVALUATION OF SOIL SORPTION PROPERTIES,
Ontario Ministry of the Environment, Toronto. Pollution Control Branch.
G. D. Zarnett.
Research Paper S2040, October 1974. 18 p, 1 fig, 4 ref.

Descriptors: *Chemical analysis, *Soils, *Adsorption, Sampling, Moisture content, Salts, Phosphates, Ion exchange, Sorption, Analytical techniques, Pollutants, Waste water treatment, Soil disposal fields, Septic tanks, Tile drains, *Path of pollutants.

The movement of contaminants through soil poses a major difficulty in the design and planning of private waste treatment systems. The problems connected with waste treatment by tile field systems require knowledge of the capacity or degree of uptake of specific contaminants by the soil, the effect of concentration, and the rate of movement. Analyses and techniques were described which will be useful in evaluating the capabilities of soils for contaminant removal. The soil adsorption isotherm determination is the most informative for determining soil capacities for single and multi species systems and the concomitant effects of varying concentration. The rate of contaminant movement can then be calculated with the use of the isotherm parameters. (Sims-ISWS)
W75-07058

CRUDE OIL SPILLS, DISAPPEARANCE OF AROMATIC AND ALIPHATIC COMPONENTS FROM SMALL SEA-SURFACE SLICKS,
Argonne National Lab., Ill.
W. Harrison, M. A. Winnik, P. T. Y. Kwong, and D. Mackay.
Environmental Science and Technology, Vol 9, No 3, p 231-234, March 1975. 1 fig, 13 ref.

Descriptors: *Path of pollutants, *Oil spills, Oceans, *Weathering, *Aromatic compounds, Mathematical models, Model studies, On-site investigations, *Oil pollution, *Oil wastes, Oily water, Evaporation.

Experimental data were presented for the weathering of five small (1.04 cu m) ocean spills of South Louisiana crude oil. The oil was spiked with cumene and the concentrations of cumene and several alkanes were measured for up to 5 hr after the spill. Comparison of the rates of loss of cumene and nonane, which have similar volatilities but different solubilities, was made in an attempt to quantify the relative rates of evaporation and dissolution. An approximate model of the evaporation-dissolution process was derived which suggests that cumene is lost principally by evaporation. The effects of whitecapping and the existence of different weathering rates in the same spill were described. (Sims-ISWS)
W75-07064

DISPERSION OF FLOATABLES IN LAKE CURRENTS,
Canada Centre for Inland Waters, Burlington (Ontario).
For primary bibliographic entry see Field 2H.
W75-07068

SUMMARY AND ANALYSIS OF PHYSICAL OCEANOGRAPHY DATA COLLECTED IN THE NEW YORK BIGHT APEX DURING 1969-70,
National Oceanic and Atmospheric Administration, Boulder, Colo. Marine Ecosystems Analysis Program.
For primary bibliographic entry see Field 2L.
W75-07069

RESEARCH NEEDS RELATED TO HYDROMETEOROLOGIC ASPECTS OF FUTURE ENERGY PRODUCTION,
National Oceanic and Atmospheric Administration, Oak Ridge, Tenn. Air Resources Atmospheric Turbulence and Diffusion Lab.
For primary bibliographic entry see Field 6D.
W75-07094

RESEARCH NEEDS RELATED TO HEAT DISSIPATION FROM LARGE POWER PLANTS,
Iowa Univ., Iowa City. Inst. of Hydraulic Research.
T. E. Croley, II, and J. F. Kennedy.
In: Proceedings of the Workshop on Research Needs Related to Water for Energy, Water Resources Center, University of Illinois at Urbana-Champaign, Research Report No. 93, p 111-133, November, 1974. 1 fig, 1 tab, 33 ref.

Descriptors: Water resources, *Water requirements, *Energy conversion, *Thermal pollution, *Water cooling, *Cooling towers, *Research prioritics, Environmental effect, Economic impact, Power plants, Lakes.
Identifiers: *Cooling ponds, Spray cooling, Once-through cooling, Closed cycle cooling.

As demand for electrical power continues to increase, the power industry is attempting to meet these needs by building more and larger power plants. Operating with large thermal inefficiencies, great amounts of waste heat were generated and discarded in natural water bodies. Due to recent legislation which reqires cooling methods to circumvent the natural water sources, other means for transferring heat directly to the atmosphere and/or into space have been developed. Cooling towers, cooling ponds and lakes, spray cooling and once-through cooling are described briefly with corresponding research needs outlined. Design criteria and procedures of open-cycling cooling (once-through), cheapest and most environmentally damaging, are explained. Because of recent legislation, once-through cooling will be used in the future only where it can be demonstrated convincingly that no adverse environmental impact will be produced. Research will be needed on problems arising from economic, thermodynamic and human factors of alternative methods. Cooling ponds and lakes are being considered as alternatives. Heat rejection rates depend upon pond temperature, area depth, air temperature, wind speed, overall heat exchange factors and other factors. Studies for heat balance considerations are cited. Research needs are summarized for cooling lakes and ponds, spray cooling, and cooling towers (in terms of physical data), systems relationships models, economic assessment (cost-benefit analyses) and the measurement of indirect effects (social, political). Research is needed to make selection of a combination of the above processes integrating the design with economic-thermodynamic studies. (See also W75-07089) (Salzman-North Carolina)
W75-07095

STUDY OF TRACE ELEMENTS IN WATERS OF TWO ALASKAN RESERVOIR SITES,
Alaska Univ., College. Inst. of Water Resources.
D. W. Smith, and M. J. Hayes.
vailable from the National Technical Information Service, Springfield, Va 22161 as PB-241 470, $4.75 in paper copy, $2.25 in microfiche. Alaska Institute of Water Resources, Fairbanks, Report No. IWR-57, January, 1975. 82 p, 39 fig, 14 tab, 75 ref. OWRT A-044-ALAS(1).

Descriptors: *Alaska, *Reservoir sites, *Trace elements, *Metals, Reservoirs, Water sampling, Spectroscopy, Calcium, Iron, Cadmium, Chromium, Copper, Manganese, Nickel, Cobalt, Zinc, Impoundments, *Reservoir construction, *Reservoir design, *Pre-impoundment, Water pollution sources, Water quality.
Identifiers: *Ship Creek reservoir(Alas), Monashka Creek reservoir(Alas).

The occurrence of trace metals in the waters of Ship and Monashka Creeks reservoirs in Alaska was investigated. Water samples have been collected over a period from late March through mid-October, 1974. The samples have been analyzed for fourteen biologically important metals using both flame and flameless atomic absorption spectroscopy. Ship Creek has greater concentrations of calcium, iron, potassium, zinc, cadmium, cobalt, copper, and nickel than does Monashka Creek. The concentrations of most of these elements are greater in water from the lower regions of the Ship reservoir than in the influent waters. The level of cadmium in Ship Creek reservoir (and iron and manganese during some seasons of the year) exceeds the tolerance limit for water supplies set by the US Public Health Service. Although the concentrations of metals in Monashka Creek are usually low, there is some indication that iron and manganese levels may exceed the US Public Health Service's recommended levels in some seasons. Concentration of these metals will increase due to the lack of clearing prior to impoundment. If a larger impoundment is constructed at Ship Creek, the problems associated with increased metal concentrations may become severe. Reservoir clearing, multiple outlets, and aeration systems should be considered in the design and construction of such a structure. Since the waters of Monashka Creek were impounded prior to clearing, a system of multiple outlets or an aeration system should be considered in the final design to minimize treatment costs.
W75-07100

THE LIMNOBIOLOGY OF DEVILS LAKE CHAIN, NORTH DAKOTA,
North Dakota Univ., Grand Forks. Dept. of Biology.
J. K. Neel.
Available from the National Technical Information Service, Springfield, Va 22161 as PB-241 460, $3.25 in paper copy, $2.25 in microfiche. Research Report No. WI-221-026-74, November, 1974. 17 p, 1 fig, 5 tab, 4 ref. OWRT A-026-NDAK(1).

Descriptors: *Water quality control, *Lakes, *North Dakota, *Phytoplankton, *Limnology, Biota, Lake basins, Benthos, Cyanophyta.
Identifiers: *Lake restoration, Limnobiology(Lakes), *Devils Lake(NDak).

The two lakes isolated from general surface runoff had highest mineral concentration and least varied biotas. Increased runoff into the chain (1969-1972) has so far increased volume only in Devils Lake where dilution of dissolved compounds and mineral pickup from dried lake beds have both occurred. There was no shortage of phosphorus and nitrogen in the system, and phosphorus availability was noted over wide areas, including groundwater, almost simultaneously in 1972. Phytoplankton was dominated by blue-green algae except in the Stump Lakes. Benthos of East Stump consisted of two salt tolerant forms, but that of West Stump contained groups common to the general area except molluscs. Volume restoration to date has improved water quality in affected areas and benefited fish, wildlife, and recreational resources.
W75-07102

DISTRIBUTION AND ECOLOGY OF RIVER MOLLUSKS IN CENTRAL AND WESTERN NORTH DAKOTA,
North Dakota Univ., Grand Forks. Dept. of Geology.
A. M. Cvancara.
Available from the National Technical Information Service, Springfield, Va 22161 as PB-241 473, $3.25 in paper copy, $2.25 in microfiche. Research Report No. WI-221-029-75, January, 1975. 5 p, 3 ref. OWRT A-013-NDAK(1).

Descriptors: *Mollusks, Ecology, *North Dakota, Water quality, Clams, *Snails, Distribution, *Bioindicators, Water pollution.
Identifiers: *Pill clams, Souris River(NDak).

At least 44 species of aquatic mollusks inhabit North Dakota--13 mussels, 9 pill clams and 22 snails--and most of these can be found in the central and western parts of the state (except for the Red River Valley in the eastern part of the state). The most frequently occurring mussel, pill clam, and snail are Anodonta grandis Say, Pisidium compressum Prime, and Physa gyrina Say. These mollusks are distributed within three molluscan provinces in the state: Northeastern, Intermediate and Southwestern. The Intermediate province (corresponding to the Missouri Coteau) trends northwest through the central part of the state and contains 23 species. The Northeastern and Southwestern provinces contain 41 and 26 species. Individual species distributions are cosmopolitan, sporadic or restricted. Ecological factors limiting the occurrence of one or more groups of mollusks are: (1) size and relative permanency of water body; (2) bottom instability; (3) possibly high turbidity; (4) possibly high total chlorides; (5) high total sulfates; (6) lack of suitable fish (for mussels only); and, (7) man's activities, such as alteration or destruction of habitat, drainage changes, and water pollution. Mollusks can serve as useful biological indicators of poor water quality and they suggest a pollution problem on the Souris River downstream from the city of Minot.
W75-07105

THERMAL ALTERATION OF ORGANIC MATTER IN RECENT MARINE SEDIMENTS. I PIGMENTS,
California Univ., Los Angeles. Inst. of Geophysics and Planetary Physics.
R. Ikan, Z. Aizenshtat, M. J. Baedecker, and I. R. Kaplan.
Available from the National Technical Information Service, Springfield, Va 22161 as N74-30838, $3.75 in paper copy, $2.25 in microfiche. Publication 1243, (1974). 27 p, 8 fig, 2 tab, 36 ref.

Descriptors: Marine geology, *Analytical techniques, *Sediments, *Pigments, *Organic matter, Analysis, Chromatography, Mass spectrometry, Evaluation, Instrumentation, Contineutal shelf, Sedimentation, *California, Organic compounds, Spectroscopy, Chlorophyll, Lipids, Solvent extractions, Photosynthesis.
Identifiers: *Tanner Basin(Calif), *Carotenes, Chlorins, Alpha-ionene, Prophyrins, Bandaras Bay, Carotenoids.

Sediment from Tanner Basin, the outer continental shelf off southern California, was analyzed for photosynthetic pigments and their derivatives, namely carotines and chlorins. Samples of the sediment were also exposed to raised temperatures (65C, 100C, 150C) for various periods of time (1 week, 1 month, 2 months). Analysis of the heat-treated sediment revealed the presence of alpha-ionene and 2,6-dimethylnapthalene, thermal-degradation products of beta-carotene. Chlorins were converted to nickel porphyrins of both DPEP and etio series. Possible mechanisms of these transformations were presented. (See W75-07168 and W75-07169) (Henley-ISWS)
W75-07167

THERMAL ALTERATION OF ORGANIC MATTER IN RECENT MARINE SEDIMENTS. II ISOPRENOIDS,
California Univ., Los Angeles. Dept. of Geophysics and Planetary Physics.
R. Ikan, M. J. Baedecker, and I. R. Kaplan.

Available from the National Technical Information Service, Springfield, Va 22161 as N74-30839, $3.75 in paper copy, $2.25 in microfiche. Publication 1244, (1974). 20 p, 3 fig, 2 tab, 31 ref.

Descriptors: *Sediments, *Organic matter, *Analytical techniques, Marine geology, *Organic compounds, Chromatography, Mass spectrometry, Evaluation, Instrumentation, Sedimentation, *California, Spectroscopy, Solvent extractions, Continental shelf, Chlorophyll, Analysis, Marine biology, Organic wastes.
Identifiers: *Isoprenoids, *Tanner Basin(Calif), Hexane, Benzene, Methanol, Phytol, Chlorins, Ketone, Phytanic acid, Pristanic acid.

A series of isoprenoid compounds were isolated from a heat-treated marine sediment (from Tanner Basin) which were not present in the original sediment. Among the compounds identified were: phytol, dihydrophytol, C sub 18-isoprenoid ketone, phytanic and pristanic acids, C sub 19- and C sub 20-monoolefines, and the alkanes pristane and phytane. The significance and possible routes leading to these compounds were discussed. (See also W75-07167) (Henley-ISWS)
W75-07168

THERMAL ALTERATION OF ORGANIC MATTER IN RECENT MARINE SEDIMENTS. III ALIPHATIC AND STEROIDAL ALCOHOLS,
California Univ., Los Angeles. Inst. of Geophysics and Planetary Physics.
R. Ikan, M. J. Baedecker, and I. R. Kaplan.
Publication 1245, (1974). 24 p, 1 fig, 4 tab, 28 ref.

Descriptors: *Organic matter, *Sediments, Marine geology, *Analytical techniques, *Alcohols, Chromatography, Mass spectrometry, Evaluation, Instrumentation, Sedimentation, *California, Organie compounds, Spectroscopy, Solvent extractions, Continental shelf, Analysis, Chemicals, Organic wastes, Marine biology, Carbon.
Identifiers: *Tanner Basin(Calif), *Aliphatic alcobols, Bandaras Bay(Calif), Isoprenoids, Sterols, Stanols.

Recent sediments from Tanner Basin and Bandaras Bay were analyzed for normal, isoprenoid, and steroidal alcohols by using chromatographic (column, GLC, TLC), and spectroscopic (UV, IR, MS) methods prior to and after heat-treatment (from 65 to 150C). Normal saturated alcohols (C sub 14-C sub 24) and some monounsaturated alcohols were identified as well as the isoprenoid alcohols phytol and dihydrophytol. Two series of sterols Delta (5) and Delta (7) were found in Tanner Basin sediment, and Delta (5)-sterols and triterpenes in Bandaras Bay sediment. Sterols from both sediments also contained the corresponding stanols. GLC and MS study of branched-cyclic hydrocarbons revealed the presence of steranes and sterenes (intermediates in sterane formation). (See also W75-07167) (Henley-ISWS)
W75-07169

AN APPLICATION OF THE METHOD OF CHARACTERISTICS TO TIDAL CALCULATIONS IN (X-Y-T) SPACE,
University of Strathcylde, Glasgow (Scotland). Dept. of Civil Engineering.
For primary bibliographic entry see Field 2L.
W75-07182

WATER QUALITY DIMENSIONS OF WATER RESOURCES PLANNING,
North Carolina Water Resources Research Inst., Raleigh.
For primary bibliographic entry see Field 5G.
W75-07185

GEOCHEMICAL ANALYSIS OF STREAM SEDIMENTS AS A TOOL FOR ENVIRONMENTAL MONITORING: A PIGYARD CASE STUDY,
Brock Univ., St. Catharines (Ontario). Dept. of Geological Sciences.
For primary bibliographic entry see Field 5A.
W75-07188

SEASONAL NITRATE CYCLING AS EVIDENCE FOR COMPLETE VERTICAL MIXING IN LAKE TAHOE, CALIFORNIA-NEVADA,
California Univ., Davis. Inst. of Ecology; and California Univ., Davis. Div. of Environmental Studies.
For primary bibliographic entry see Field 5C.
W75-07198

PRINCIPAL-COMPONENT ANALYSIS OF STREAMFLOW CHEMICAL QUALITY DATA,
Geological Survey, Reston, Va.
T. D. Steele, and N. C. Matalas.
In: Mathematical Models in Hydrology; Proceedings of Warsaw Symposium, July 1971: International Association of Hydrological Sciences Publication No 100, p 355-363, 1974. 1 fig, 4 tab, 6 ref.

Descriptors: *Water quality, *Statistics, *Variability, Water chemistry, Correlation analysis, Water pollution sources, Pollutant identification.
Identifiers: *Principal component analysis.

Principal components were computed from various matrix combinations of annual mean concentrations of the major solutes in streamflow. For data from eight sampling stations in the United States with periods of records extending from 20 to 30 years, between 56 and 84 percent of the variability of the major ions was explained by the first principal component, and an additional 12 to 34 percent was explained by the second principal component. Annual mean specific conductances correlated highly with the first principal component, indicating that conductance may serve as an index reflecting the variability inherent in salinity conditions in streamflow. Additional sensitivity analysis was carried out to evaluate the effect on the first principal component of dropping one or two relatively minor chemical constituents from the data correlation matrix from which the principal components were derived. (Knapp-USGS)
W75-07200

GROUND-WATER QUALITY BENEATH SOLID-WASTE DISPOSAL SITES AT ANCHORAGE, ALASKA,
Geological Survey, Anchorage, Alaska.
C. Zenone, D. E. Donaldson, and J. J. Grunwaldt.
Ground Water, Vol 13, No 2, p 182-190, March-April 1975. 8 fig, 2 tab, 9 ref.

Descriptors: *Alaska, *Landfills, *Water pollution sources, *Path of pollutants, Hydrogeology, Water table, Water quality, Waste disposal, Garbage dumps.
Identifiers: *Anchorage(Alaska).

At three solid-waste disposal sites in the Anchorage areas of Alaska, differences in local geohydrologic conditions influence groundwater quality. Leachate was detected in groundwater within and beneath two sites where the water table is very near land surface and refuse is deposited either at or below the water table in some parts of the filled areas. No leachate was detected in groundwater beneath a third site where waste disposal is well above the local water table. (Knapp-USGS)
W75-07204

INVESTIGATING GROUND-WATER POLLUTION FROM INDIANAPOLIS' LANDFILLS--THE LESSONS LEARNED,
Geological Survey, Indianapolis, Ind.
W. G. Weist, Jr., and R. A. Pettijohn.
Ground Water, Vol 13, No 2, p 191-196, March-April 1975. 2 fig, 5 ref.

Descriptors: *Water pollution sources, *Path of pollutants, *Landfills, *Indiana, *Groundwater, Sampling, Water wells, Test wells, Observation wells, Monitoring.
Identifiers: *Indianapolis(Ind).

In Indianapolis, the nature and extent of water pollution resulting from the operation of seven landfills in or near the city was studied using 10 to 36 observation wells, ranging from 14 to 170 feet deep, installed in and around each landfill. After the wells were completed and developed, water samples were collected from selected wells for detailed chemical analysis. Every month the water levels are measured and field determination of four chemical and physical water parameters are made. (Knapp-USGS)
W75-07205

MONITORING REGIONAL EFFECTS OF HIGH PRESSURE INJECTION OF INDUSTRIAL WASTE WATER IN A LIMESTONE AQUIFER,
Geological Survey, Tallahassee, Fla.
G. L. Faulkner, and C. A. Pascale.
Ground Water, Vol 13, No 2, p 197-208, March-April 1975. 7 fig, 2 tab, 13 ref.

Descriptors: *Path of pollutants, *Florida, *Waste disposal wells, *Injection wells, *Monitoring, Industrial wastes, Aquifers, Artesian aquifers, Limestones, Hydrogeology, Water pollution sources.
Identifiers: *Pensacola(Fla).

More than 10 billion gallons of acid industrial waste has been injected under high pressure into a saline-water-filled part of a limestone aquifer of low transmissivity 1,400 feet below land surface near Pensacola, Florida. A similar waste disposal system is planned for the same zone at a site about 8.5 miles to the east. The injection zone is the lower limestone of the Floridan aquifer. The lower limestone is overlain by a confining layer of plastic clay at the injection site and underlain by another confining layer of shale and clay. The injection system consists of two injection wells about a quarter of a mile apart and three monitor wells. Three more monitor wells in the injection zone activated in early 1974 at sites 17 miles northeast, 22 miles east and 33 miles northeast of the injection site. No change in pressure or water quality due to injection was, by mid-1974, evident in the upper limestone at the injection site, but static pressures in the lower limestone at the site has increased 8-fold since injection began in 1963. Diluted waste arrived at the south monitor well in 1973. By mid-1974 pressure effects from waste injection were calculated to extend radially more than 40 miles from the injection site. No effects were measured at the well 33 miles away. Less than 20 miles northeast of the active injection site, the lower limestone contains fresh water. Changes in the pressure regime due to injection indicate a tendency for northeastward movement of the freshwater/salt-water interface in the lower limestone. (Knapp-USGS)
W75-07206

GROUND-WATER CONTAMINATION IN THE SILURIAN DOLOMITE OF DOOR COUNTY, WISCONSIN,
Geological Survey, Madison, Wis.
M. G. Sherrill.
Ground Water, Vol 13, No 2, p 209-213, March-April 1975. 6 fig, 11 ref.

Descriptors: *Water pollution sources, *Groundwater, *Wisconsin, *Septic tanks, *Industrial wastes, Karst, Dolomite, Path of pollutants, Hydrogeology.
Identifiers: *Door County(Wis).

Door County, a recreational and fruit-growing area bordering Lake Michigan in northeastern Wisconsin, has had a long history of groundwater contamination from surface and near-surface sources. Contamination is most severe in late summer when the influx of tourists and fruit-canning operations create additional wastes. Thin soil cover and well-fractured dolomitic bedrock give easy entry to groundwater contaminants throughout large parts of Door County. Many contaminants enter the dolomite by surface or near-surface seepage. There is little attenuation of contamination concentrations in the well-jointed dolomite, and contaminants may travel long distances underground in a relatively short time. The major source of groundwater contamination is bacterial, from individual waste-disposal systems, agricultural, industrial, and municipal sources. The contaminated areas include only a small percentage of the total groundwater system and are separated by large areas of groundwater free of contamination. Tests based on indicator bacteria suggest that the periods of highest contamination potential occur during or immediately following rapid groundwater recharge periods. Increasing the depth of casing and pressure grouting the casing into firm bedrock are two well-construction procedures that reduce the contamination potential in wells. (Knapp-USGS)
W75-07207

HYDROLOGIC- AND SALT-BALANCE INVESTIGATIONS UTILIZING DIGITAL MODELS, LOWER SAN LUIS REY RIVER AREA, SAN DIEGO COUNTY, CALIFORNIA,
Geological Survey, Menlo Park, Calif.
J. A. Moreland.
Available from NTIS, Springfield, Va 22161 as PB-239 697/As, $4.25 in paper copy, $2.25 in microfiche. Water Resources Investigations 24-74, October 1974. 66 p, 19 fig, 8 tab, 14 ref.

Descriptors: *Water balance, *Salinity, *Path of pollutants, *Mathematical models, *California, Planning, Groundwater basins, Hydrologic budget, Groundwater movement, Water management(Applied), Water quality, Watershed management.
Identifiers: *San Luis Rey River(Calif), *San Diego County(Calif).

Hydrologic and salt balances were computed for the Pauma, Pala, Bonsall, and Mission groundwater basins of the San Luis Rey River watershed, California. Hydrologic budgets were tested for compatibility with known hydrologic parameters by constructing and verifying near-steady-state and transient-state models. Near-steady-state inflow and outflow were calculated to be 3.7 cubic hectometres per year for Pauma basin, 3.1 cu hm per year for Pala basin, 6.6 cu hm per year for Bonsall basin, and 8.3 cu hm per year for Mission basin. In 1972 annual net difference between inflow and outflow was -2.8 cu hm per year for Pauma, -1.0 cu hm for Pala, +0.1 cu hm per year for Bonsall, and +1.5 cu hm per year for Mission. Salt-balance calculations for 1972 indicate that salt inflow exceeded salt outflow by 2,000 tonnes per year in Pauma basin, 640 tonnes per year in Pala basin, 2,400 tonnes per year in Bonsall basin, and 3,800 tonnes per year in Mission basin. (Knapp-USGS)
W75-07212

CHEMICAL AND BIOLOGICAL QUALITY OF LAKE DICIE AT AUSTIS, FLORIDA, WITH EMPHASIS ON THE EFFECTS OF STORM RUNOFF,
Geological Survey, Tallahassee, Fla.
For primary bibliographic entry see Field 5C.
W75-07213

HYDROLOGY OF THE OKLAWAHA LAKES AREA OF FLORIDA,
Geological Survey, Tallahassee, Fla.
For primary bibliographic entry see Field 7C.
W75-07220

A WASTE ASSIMILATIVE CAPACITY MODEL FOR A SHALLOW, TURBULENT STREAM,
Marquette Univ., Milwaukee, Wis.
V. Novotny, and P. A. Krenkel.
Water Research, Vol 9, No 2, p 233-241, 1975. 9 fig, 1 tab, 16 ref.

Descriptors: *Mathematical models, *Nitrification, *Oxygen requirements, *Reaeration, *Waste assimilative capacity, *Water quality, Dissolved oxygen, Waste water treatment, Water pollution control, *Tennessee, Model studies, Streams.
Identifiers: *Holston River(Tenn).

A mathematical water quality model (DOSAGI) for self-purification of small streams was modified and applied for the waste assimilative capacity determination of a shallow turbulent stream in Tennessee. The model is a steady state dissolved oxygen balance model which solves simultaneously the three basic equations for deoxygenation, nitrification, and dissolved oxygen concentration. Verification of the model, with the data from two water quality surveys, demonstrated that the model can be successfully applied (excluding the effect of photosynthesis by aquatic weeds). The model requires determination of deoxygenation and degree of treatment. The solution matrix includes temperature, the deoxygenation coefficient, streamflow, wastewater loads, stream depth, and the reaeration coefficient as vectors for the waste assimilative capacity determination. (Harmeson-ISWS)
W75-07268

MICROBIAL TRANSFORMATIONS OF MERCURY IN AQUATIC ENVIRONMENTS,
Purdue Univ., Lafayette, Ind. Dept. of Agronomy.
L. E. Sommers, and M. Floyd.
Available from the National Technical Information Service, Springfield, Va. 22161 as PB-241 486, $4.75 in paper copy, $2.25 in microfiche. Purdue University Water Resources Research Center, Lafayette, Technical Report No. 54 December 1974. 80 p, 8 fig, 20 tab, 76 ref. OWRT A-023-IND (1).

Descriptors: *Mercury, *Aquatic microorganisms, *Lake sediments, Analytical techniques, Water pollution sources, Sediments, Sediment-water interfaces, Microbiology, *Pollutant identification.
Identifiers: *Alkylmercury, *Monoalkylmercury, *Flameless atomic absorption.

A procedure was developed for determining total mercury in soils and sediments. Also a simple steam distillation - flameless atomic absorption procedure was developed and evaluated for extraction and quantitation of organic mercury in sediments. Experiments were conducted to determine the fate of mercuric chloride and methyl mercuric chloride in lake sediments incubated under laboratory and field conditions. The results indicated that CH3Hg+ is unstable in sediments and may be converted into dialkylmercury or possibly Hg2+. The necessity for microbial activity in mercury transformations was established using sediments sterilized with autoclaving or by exposure to gamma radiation. The rates of mercury conversions were enhanced by increasing temperatures, amending sediments with organic carbon, and increasing mercury concentrations. The field study indicated that nonalkylmercury can be formed under natural conditions and that CH3Hg+ introduced into sediments may be degraded. In general, the rates for mercury transformations were greater under laboratory conditions than during in situ incubation.
W75-07275

WATER QUALITY MODEL OF THE LOWER FOX RIVER, WISCONSIN,
Environmental Protection Agency, Washington, D.C. Office of Enforcement and General Counsel.
D. Crevensten, A. Stoddard, and G. Vajda.
Available from the National Technical Information Service, Springfield, Va. 22161 as PB-230 269, $4.25 in paper copy, $2.25 in microfiche. Report EPA-905-73-001, August 1973. 68 p, 10 fig, 9 tab, 17 ref.

Descriptors: Rivers, *Water pollution control, *Model studies, *Dissolved oxygen, Municipal wastes, Pulp wastes, Sewage treatment, Computer programs, Biochemical oxygen demand, Water quality standards, Forecasting, *Lake Michigan, *Wisconsin.
Identifiers: *Fox River(Wis), Green Bay(Lake Michigan).

Gross water pollution has existing in the Lower Fox River and Green Bay, Wisconsin, for a number of years. Concentrated in this basin are eight urban areas and nineteen pulp and paper manufacturers that make intensive use of the river for disposal and assimilation of wastes. The lower river, approximately 40 miles long, flows northeasterly through a series of 18 locks and dams. A mathematical model describing the interrelationship between the dissolved oxygen concentration of a river and its various sources and sinks has been adapted for use in a study of the river. The analysis assumes a steady-state condition and describes the longitudinal distribution of dissolved oxygen from Neenah-Menash to Green Bay, a distance of approximately 40 miles. The model was verified for various conditions of waste loading, river temperature, and river flow. It was then used to evaluate the implementation of interim best practicable control technology on effluent limitations for industrial dischargers and 90% BOD removal from municipal waste sources, as an estimate of treatments levels. The study indicated that implementation of the effluent limits will result in significant improvement of water quality. (Jones-Wisconsin)
W75-07327

THE NITROGEN-TO-PHOSPHORUS RATIO IN THE PHOTIC ZONE OF THE SEA AND THE ELEMENTAL COMPOSITION OF PLANKTON,
Washington Univ., Seattle, Dept. of Oceanography.
For primary bibliographic entry see Field 5C.
W75-07328

THE BOD5/DO RATIO. A NEW ANALYTICAL TOOL FOR WATER QUALITY EVALUATION,
Environmental Protection Agency, Philadelphia, Pa. Region III.
For primary bibliographic entry see Field 5A.
W75-07329

THE FATE AND BEHAVIOR OF CRUDE OIL ON MARINE LIFE,
Massachusetts Univ., Gloucester. Marine Station.
For primary bibliographic entry see Field 5C.
W75-07339

5C. Effects Of Pollution

BACTERIAL DEGRADATION OF ARYLSULFONATES IN TREATMENT OF WASTEWATER,
Maryland Univ., College Park. Dept. of Microbiology.
For primary bibliographic entry see Field 5D.
W75-06852

INTERRELATIONSHIPS OF VARIOUS BIOASSAY PROCEDURES FOR PULP AND PAPER EFFLUENTS,
B.C. Research, Vancouver (British Columbia).

C. C. Walden, D. J. McLeay, and D. D. Monteith.
Canadian Pulp and Paper Association, Technical Section, Air and Stream Improvement Conference, Montreal, September 23-25, 1974. Preprinted Proceedings (Montreal, P.Q.), p 1-8, 11 fig, 3 tab, 16 ref.

Descriptors: *Bioassay, *Pulp wastes, *Toxicity, *Water analysis, Water pollution sources, Pulp and paper industry, Fish, Water pollution effects, Wastes, Industrial wastes, Analytical techniques, Water quality standards, Storage, Stability, Anaerobic conditions, Legislation, Fishkill, Water pollution, Temperature, Water quality, Water temperature, Water properties.

Bioassay procedures for pulp and paper mill effluents were investigated in order to develop a method which measures only inherent toxicity. This procedure was used to establish relationships between various current procedures and regulatory requirements. Flow-through solution replacement and complete physical exchange of the solutions in the same time interval were shown to be equivalent. Maximum stability of toxicity in bioassay solutions was achieved by solution replacement every 24 hr, where exposure periods were 72 hr or longer, and fish loading was 0.5 g/liter. With exchange every 12 hr, fish loadings up to 2 g/liter could be accommodated with minimal loss in toxicity, even for shorter-term exposures. Storage with complete exclusion of air is the most important safeguard for stabilizing sample toxicity. Storage at low temperatures achives little more, except where anaerobiosis may occur. The toxicity of some samples during storage presented an anomalous behavior. The conversion into toxic units provided a basis for direct comparison of bioassay data. Examination of regulatory requirements showed that the present Federal legal requirement is about twice as stringent as the static monitoring bioassay and other regulatory guidelines. Monitoring bioassay procedures, with exposure times of 24 or 48 hr, can be designed which have the same sensitivity for measuring effluent toxicity as the present gamut of regulatory procedures, and are considerably simpler. (Witt-IPC)
W75-06867

POLLUTIONAL EFFECTS OF PULP AND PAPER MILL WASTES IN PUGET SOUND.
Washington State Pollution Control Commission (Olympia, Wash.), 503 p, March, 1967.

Descriptors: *Pulp wastes, *Water pollution effects, Organizations, Industrial wastes, Wastes, Water pollution sources, Pulp and paper industry, Waste water(Pollution), Effluents, Water quality, Dispersion, Surface waters, Pacific Northwest U.S., *Washington, Aquatic life, On-site tests, Laboratory tests, Analytical techniques, Water pollution control, Water pollution treatment, Waste water treatment, Water analysis, Water pollution, Sulfite liquors.
Identifiers: *Puget Sound(Wash).

This report presents the work and findings of a cooperative study by the Washington State Pollution Control Commission and the Federal Water Pollution Control Administration on the pollutional effects of pulp and paper mill effluents in Puget Sound. The effluents are discharged by 7 pulp and paper mills (6 sulfite pulp, paper, and paperboard mills and 1 kraft pulp and paper mill) located at Bellingham, Anacortes, Everett, and Port Angeles, Washington. The comprehensive study program consisted of in-plant surveys to determine the amounts and characteristics of the wastes discharged; waste distribution and water quality studies to determine the transport and dispersion of mill wastes in the receiving stream and to assess their effects on water quality; and biological studies to determine the effects of the dispersed wastes and degraded water quality on marine life. Methods and procedures employed in many of the field and laboratory studies are described briefly. The major findings of the studies are summarized and recommendations are made on how to reduce or eliminate pollution from each of the mills. (Witt-IPC)
W75-06881

WOODY SOLIDS DISCHARGED INTO WATER COURSES BY THE FOREST PRODUCTS INDUSTRY.
Paperi ja Puu, Vol 56, No 12, p 1013-1016, 1019-1025, December, 1974. 6 fig, 1 tab, 7 ref.

Descriptors: *Wood wastes, *Pulp wastes, *Water pollution, *Bottom sediments, *Degradation(Decomposition), Water pollution sources, Pulp and paper industry, Wastes, Industrial wastes, Pollutants, Fibers(Plant), Bark, Lignins, Sludge, Water pollution, Water quality, Organic matter, Clays, Sands, Inorganic compounds, Gases, Porosity, Structure, Hydrogen ion concentration, Temperature, Humus, Decomposing organic matter, Foreign countries, Europe.
Identifiers: Fillers, Mechanical pulp fibers, Chemical pulp fibers, *Kymi River(Finland).

In 1972 the Finnish forest industry discharged daily 5.6 million cu m of waste water containing 822 tons of solids. More efficient mechanical purification methods reduced this load to about 500 tons/day by the start of 1974. Fibers and bark fragments comprise the bulk of these solids. Fillers and sludge are minor components. These solids form rather thick sediments especially in discharge areas close to mills. A study of the disintegration of wood wastes in natural sediments was performed below the Kuusankoski mills on the Kymi River. Slow disintegration occurred in acidic (pH 4-5) and oxygen-poor or oxygen-free sediments. Deposits rich in organic matter (silt clay and fine sand gyttja) showed faster decay than those comprising mainly inorganic matter (coarse and fine sands), since the evolution of a gases from the former loosened their structure and increased their porosity. Water penetration and reduced gas formation caused a pH rise and promoted the disintegration of deeper layers. All processes were favored in the warmer seasons. A part of the fibers in top sediment layers disintegrated or were lifted by gas bubbles and floated with the stream. After 4 years, the decomposition of deeper layers appeared as erosion of the fiber surface and sometimes of the inner secondary wall layers, embrittlement and rupture of fibers, and formation of holes penetrating all fiber layers. Mechanical pulp (groundwood) fibers riçher in lignin and containing shive-like bundles were more resistant to decomposition than lignin-poorer chemical pulp fibers. Bark decomposed into a finely dispersed humus-like material. (Brown-IPC)
W75-06882

DANGER, . CARRYOVER FROM TALL OIL PERILS FISH, SHOULD BE CONTROLLED,
SCM Corp., Jacksonville, Fla. Glidden-Durkee Div.
Pulp and Paper, Vol 49, No 2, p 116-118, February, 1975. 2 tab, 22 ref.

Descriptors: *Chemicals, *Pulp wastes, Toxicity, *Fish, Sulfur compounds, Fish food organisms, Lethal limit, Toxins, Water pollution sources, Industrial wastes, Wastes, Pollutants, Inorganic compounds, Organic compounds, Effluents, Chemical wastes, Water pollution effects, Economics.
Identifiers: *Tall oil, Rosins, Fatty acids, Kraft mills.

Chemicals found in waste streams of kraft pulp mills and tall oil plants, notably sulfur compounds, as well as rosins and fatty acids, are known to be toxic to fish and fish food organisms. Control and improved recovery of tall oil is suggested as a financially attractive solution for the toxicity problem. Tables indicate minimum concentrations lethal to fish of several contaminants found in kraft pulp mill and tall oil plant effluents. (Sykes-IPC)
W75-06883

MERCURY IN THE WESTERN ENVIRONMENT.
For primary bibliographic entry see Field 5A.
W75-06897

MERCURY CONCENTRATIONS IN FISH,
Bureau of Sport Fisheries and Wildlife, Washington, D.C.
For primary bibliographic entry see Field 5A.
W75-06902

MERCURY IN AQUATIC SPECIES FROM THE PACIFIC NORTHWEST,
Oregon State Univ., Corvallis. Environmental Health Sciences Center.
For primary bibliographic entry see Field 5A.
W75-06903

MERCURY RESIDUES IN IDAHO FISHES - 1970,
Idaho Dept. of Fish and Game, Boise.
For primary bibliographic entry see Field 5A.
W75-06904

THE RATE OF LOSS OF MERCURY BY PACIFIC OYSTERS,
Washington Univ., Seattle. Coll. of Fisheries.
A. H. Seymour.
In: Mercury in the Western Environment, Continuing Education Publications, Corvallis, Oregon, p 85-90, 1973. 2 fig, 2 tab, 6 ref. FWQA (16040 EDG).

Descriptors: *Mercury, *Oysters, *Radioisotopes, Tracers, Biology, Aquatic waters, Sea water, Marine organisms, Discharge, Pollutant identification, Path of pollutants, Heavy metals.

A radioisotope of mercury (Hg203) with a 47-day half-life was used to estimate the rate of loss of mercury by individual oysters. After the oysters, Crassostrea gigaes had accumulated Hg203C12 directly from seawater in a laboratory aquarium, they were transferred to fresh seawater for nine days and then returned to their natural bed. Measurements of Hg203 in the oysters were made daily for the first nine days and at fortnightly intervals, thereafter, until the experiment was terminated in July, 1970 at 133 days. The rates of loss of Hg203 were approximately exponential for four periods (days 1-2, 2-9, 9-32 and 32-133). The average values for the total rate of loss by both radiological decay and biological turnover were estimated for the four periods, and from these estimates the biological half-life values were calculated. For the four periods, the biological half-life values for mercury, when added to water as mercuric chloride, were 4.9, 9.8, 21 and 44 days, respectively. (See also W75-06897) (Jernigan-Vanderbilt)
W75-06906

MERCURY IN FUR SEALS,
National Marine Fisheries Service, Seattle, Wash. Marine Mammal Biological Lab.
R. E. Anas.
In: Mercury in the Western Environment, Continuing Education Publications, Corvallis, Oregon, p 91-96, 1973. 4 fig, 7 ref.

Descriptors: *Mercury, *Marine animals, *Alaska, *Distribution, Mammals, Animal physiology, Sampling, Analytical techniques, Spectroscopy, Data collections, Testing procedures, *Pollutant identification, Heavy metals.
Identifiers: *Pribilof Islands(Alas), *Fur seals.

Samples of liver and muscle tissue from pulp, young male, and adult female fur seals (Callorhinus ursinus) and brain tissue from adult female fur seals that were collected on the Pribilof Islands, Alaska and off the coast of Washington in 1970, were analyzed for mercury. All of the samples contained mercury with mercury levels higher in the liver than in muscle and brain. The mean values for liver tissues analyzed by flameless atomic absorption were 0.20 ppm for 10 pups, 10.8 ppm for 29 males, two and three years old, and 67.2 ppm for 29 females ages 5-19. The highest value obtained was 172 ppm in the liver of a 19-year-old female. The mean values for muscle tissues, also analyzed for flameless atomic absorption, were 0.06 ppm for five pups, 0.25 ppm for 29 young males and 0.26 ppm for 10 adult females. Increased levels of mercury in liver were significantly correlated with age, but levels in muscle could not be similarly correlated. The mean value for brain tissue analyzed by neutron activation analysis (NAA) was 0.22 ppm for seven adult females. Values from NAA were 52, 20, and 97% higher than those from atomic absorption for samples of liver from three adult females. (See also W75-06897) (Jernigan-Vanderbilt)
W75-06907

MERCURY LEVELS IN CALIFORNIA SEA LIONS,
Oregon State Univ., Corvallis. Environmental Health Sciences Center.
D. R. Buhler, and B. R. Mate.
In: Mercury in the Western Environment, Continuing Education Publications, Corvallis, Oregon, p 97-102, 1973. 3 tab, 4 ref.

Descriptors: *Mercury, *Toxicity, Mammals, *Marine animals, *Food chains, Carnivores, Animal pathology, Animal physiology, Analytical techniques, Chromatography, Correlation studies, Organic compounds, Inorganic compounds, *Pollutant identification, Heavy metals.
Identifiers: *California sea lions.

An attempt was made to correlate the levels of mercury with the occurrence of a disease outbreak among California sea lions (Zalophus californianus). Analyses of mercury levels in ten sick or recently dead animals showed that these animals (which are the top carnivores of their marine food chain) accumulated very high levels in their tissues. There was, however, no correlation between the severity of the disease symptoms and mercury residues in the animals. The liver contained the highest concentrations of mercury, averaging 137 ppm. Only a small portion of the mercury present in the liver of these animals was in the form of methylmercury. (See also W75-06897) (Jernigan-Vanderbilt)
W75-06908

THE GENERAL AND COMPARATIVE BIOLOGY OF TOXIC METALS AND THEIR DERIVATIVES: MERCURY AND LEAD,
Hawaii Univ., Honolulu. Environmental Center.
S. M. Siegel, A. Eshleman, I. Umeno, N. Puerner, and C. W. Smith.
In: Mercury in the Western Environment, Continuing Education Publications, Corvallis, Oregon, p 119-134, 1973. 8 fig, 7 tab, 31 ref. NASA (NGR-012-001-042).

Descriptors: *Mercury, *Lead, *Toxicity, *Growth rates, Correlation studies, *Heavy metals, Ions, Laboratory tests, Testing procedures, Analytical techniques, Spectroscopy, *Pollutant identification.

A program of comparative studies with heavy metals was carried out as part of a general survey of the ecological significance of environmental contaminants. More than 20 species of plants, invertebrates and unicellular forms were examined for their responses to mercury and its derivatives. Comparative studies were also conducted with lead compounds because of many similarities in the behavior of this metal and that of mercury in the environment. (See also W75-06897) (Jernigan-Vanderbilt)
W75-06909

MERCURY CONTAMINATION IN CALIFORNIA'S FISH AND WILDLIFE,
California State Dept. of Fish and Game, Sacramento.
W. H. Griffith.
In: Mercury in the Western Environment, Continuing Education Publications, Corvallis, Oregon, p 135-139, 1973. 1 tab.

Descriptors: *Mercury, *Toxicity, *Game birds, *Fish, Public health, Foods, Seeds, Research and evaluation, Laboratory tests, Analytical techniques, Organic compounds, Inorganic compounds, Mining wastes, Industrial wastes, Effluents, *California, *Pollutant identification, Heavy metals.

Mercury contamination in pheasants originated from their ingestion of mercury-treated seed grain. Laboratory findings revealed that virtually all of the mercury in pheasants is methylmercury. The mercury contamination of the aquatic environment in California appeared to originate from urban and industrial effluents, mercury mines, and mercury lost during California's mining era. As a result of evaluations made in 1970, these three notices were issued to the public: (1) California pheasants were safe to eat throughout the state during the 1970 season as a result of prompt action taken by the California Department of Agriculture that restricted the use of mercurial fungicides and the treated seeds to application by permit only; (2) large striped bass and catfish from the Sacramento-San Joaquin Delta and San Francisco Bay areas should not be eaten more than once a week and pregnant women should not eat them at all; (3) mercury-treated seed should not be used as human or animal feed. (See also W75-06897) (Jernigan-Vanderbilt)
W75-06910

PRELIMINARY STUDIES OF MERCURY TISSUE LEVELS FROM GAME BIRDS AND FISH IN UTAH,
Utah State Univ., Logan. Dept. of Toxicology.
F. A. Smith.
In: Mercury in the Western Environment, Continuing Education Publications, Corvallis, Oregon, p 140-165, 1973. 5 tab, 1 ref.

Descriptors: *Mercury, *Game birds, *Fish, *Utah, Toxicity, Laboratory tests, Analytical techniques, Spectroscopy, Testing procedures, *Pollutant identification, Heavy metals.

Mercury analyses were performed on 25 pheasants, 20 chukars and 18 fish collected in Utah. Results showed 9% of the pheasants to contain 0.5 ppm or more of mercury while 89% of the fish exceeded 0.5 ppm mercury. Walleye pike contained the highest concentrations of mercury, with levels up to 3.89 ppm. All chukar partridge examined had mercury levels well below 0.5 ppm. Analyses for DDT, DDE and dieldrin are also reported on 18 of the 25 pheasants and 13 of the 20 chukars that were analyzed for mercury. (See also W75-06897) (Jernigan-Vanderbilt)
W75-06911

MERCURY-WILDLIFE STUDIES BY THE DENVER WILDLIFE RESEARCH CENTER,
Bureau of Sport Fisheries and Wildlife, Denver, Colo. Denver Wildlife Research Center.
L. C. McEwen, R. K. Tucker, J. O. Ells, and M. A. Haegele.
In: Mercury in the Western Environment, Continuing Education Publications, Corvallis, Oregon, p 146-156, 1973. 3 fig, 6 tab, 7 ref.

Descriptors: *Mercury, *Wildlife, *Game birds, *Toxicity, Colorado, Laboratory tests, Laboratory animals, Analytical techniques, Spectroscopy, Testing procedures, *Pollutant identification, Heavy metals.

Several studies have been undertaken to determine mercury-wildlife effects and relationships. These studies have included investigations of: (1) the acute oral toxicity of some common mercury-containing fungicides to mallard ducks and other captive birds; (2) mercury residues in tissues of gray partridges fed wheat treated with Ceresan L(trademark), (3) effects of daily Ceresan M(trademark) doses on pheasant reproduction and of single doses of Ceresan M(trademark) to mallard and coturnix quail on eggshell thickness; and (4) acute oral toxicity of Ceresan M(trademark) to wild pheasants in a natural habitat. (See also W75-06897) (Jernigan-Vanderbilt)
W75-06912

MERCURY IN PHEASANTS AND OTHER BIRDS FROM EASTERN WASHINGTON,
Washington State Dept. of Game, Olympia.
J. B. King, and J. B. Lauckhardt.
In: Mercury in the Western Environment, Continuing Education Publications, Corvallis, Oregon, p 157-166, 1973. 5 tab, 3 ref.

Descriptors: *Mercury, *Game birds, *Washington, *Distribution, Birds, Analytical techniques, Animal physiology, Toxicity, Data collections, *Pollutant identification.
Identifiers: Pheasants.

A total of 81 game birds were analyzed for mercury by the Washington State Game Department. Analysis was done by neutron activation at Washington State University Reactor Center. Of 27 winter road-killed and spring-collected pheasants, three birds were found with an excess of 0.5 ppm mercury in liver tissue. Liver samples from two birds were below ! ppm, but one exceeded 4 ppm. Breast tissue from only one bird contained more than 0.5 ppm mercury. Experimental birds provided with seeds that had been treated with an ethyimercury-type fungicide refused to consume any appropriate quantities of the seed. The maximum concentration of mercury achieved in the birds was 2.6 ppm in liver tissue. (See also W75-06897) (Jernigan-Vanderbilt)
W75-06913

MERCURY LEVEL STUDIES IN MIGRATORY WATERFOWL,
Reed Coll., Portland, Oreg. Dept. of Chemistry.
L. S. Arighi.
In: Mercury in the Western Environment, Continuing Education Publications, Corvallis, Oregon, p 167-171, 1973. 3 fig, 2 tab.

Descriptors: *Mercury, *Waterfowl, *Oregon, Game birds, Ducks, Sampling, Analytical techniques, Radioisotopes, *Distribution, *Pollutant identification, Heavy metals.

Neutron activation analysis was used to determine the concentration of mercury in migratory waterfowl, primarily ducks, taken at the Sauvies Island Game Management area in Oregon during the 1970-71 hunting season. The study was conducted on a small sample of four prominent species of the area: mallard, pintail, widgeon and greenwing teal. Gamma spectra from the initial samples showed the presence of Se75 as well as Hg203. This caused some difficulty in determining mercury levels and limited the mercury determinations. (See also W75-06897) (Jernigan-Vanderbilt)
W75-06914

MERCURY IN HUNGARIAN PARTRIDGE AND IN THEIR NORTH CENTRAL MONTANA ENVIRONMENT,
Montana Fish and Game Dept., Choteau.
J. P. Weigand.

In: Mercury in the Western Environment, Continuing Education Publications, Corvallis, Oregon, p 172-185, 1973. 2 fig, 8 tab, 13 ref.

Descriptors: *Mercury, *Game birds, *Montana, Data collections, Animal physiology, *Food chains, On-site data collections, Analytical technique, Spectroscopy, Seeds, Grain, *Pollutant identification, Heavy metals.
Identifiers: *Hungarian partridge.

From October, 1969 through October, 1970, 69 Hungarian partridge collectively representing both sex and age classes were collected from north central Montana. Mercury was detected in breast muscle of each specimen. The mean mercury contents in muscle tissue from males and females were 0.17 ppm and 0.13 ppm, and for adults and juveniles, 0.16 ppm and 0.15 ppm. Maximum concentrations of mercury in breast muscle occurred in December, February and July, whereas the lowest level occurred in April and May. Mercury concentrations in two of three eggs extracted from oviducts exceeded the levels found in the breast muscle of the hens. Mercury levels in breast muscle of partridges five and seven weeks old were less than that found in eggs. Of 39 soil samples, 34 (87%) contained less than 0.10 ppm mercury. Breast muscle from 58% of the partridge tested exceeded the 0.10 ppm mercury soil background. Two of three harvested barley samples that were spilled contained less than 0.05 ppm mercury and the third had 0.10 ppm mercury. Two wheat samples each tested 0.09 ppm mercury. Limited sampling indicates mercury levels in partridge from north central Montana are not high enough to result in widespread mortality nor in interference with reproduction. (See also W75-06897) (Jernigan-Vanderbilt)
W75-06915

AN ANALYSIS OF MERCURY RESIDUES IN IDAHO PHEASANTS,
Idaho State Dept. of Health, Boise.
D. W. Brock, F. Shields, III, E. R. Norberg, and J. E. Cline.
In: Mercury in the Western Environment, Continuing Education Publications, Corvallis, Oregon, p 186-198, 1973. 1 fig, 5 tab, 7 ref.

Descriptors: *Mercury, *Game birds, *Idaho, *Seasonal, Spring, Sampling, Animal populations, Analytical techniques, Spectroscopy, Chromatography, Seeds, Toxicity, Pollutant identification, Heavy metals.
Identifiers: Pheasants.

Mercury residues in Idaho pheasants were determined. The study was also designed to evaluate seasonal variations of mercury levels and to compare results obtained with various analytical methods. A total of 246 pheasants were tested over a period of approximately 1 1/2 years. Six sets of samples were collected from areas where high pheasant population and heavy hunting pressures occur. The samples were tested for mercury by neutron activation, dithizone, and gas liquid chromatography procedures. The results showed that the highest levels of mercury occurred in the spring, indicating that the chief source of pheasant contamination is mercury-treated seed grain planted during that time of the year. They also demonstrated that comparative results can be obtained using different analytical methods. (See also W75-06897) (Jernigan-Vanderbilt)
W75-06916

SEASONAL VARIATIONS IN MERCURY CONTENT OF OREGON PHEASANTS,
Oregon State Univ., Corvallis. Environmental Health Sciences Center.
D. R. Buhler, R. R. Claeys, and H. J. Rayner.
In: Mercury in the Western Environment, Continuing Education Publications, Corvallis, Oregon, p 199-211, 1973. 6 fig, 4 tab, 13 ref.

Descriptors: *Mercury, *Game birds, *Oregon, *Seasonal, Data collections, Regions, Seeds, Sampling, Animal physiology, Organic compounds, Inorganic compounds, Toxicity, Regulations, Pollutant identification, Heavy metals.
Identifiers: Pheasants.

One hundred and eighty-seven ring-necked pheasants were collected for mercury analysis in April, August, October and December, 1970 from three agricultural areas of Oregon, including Malheur County, Umatilla County and the Willamette Valley (Benton, Lane, Linn, Marion, Polk and Yamhill counties). The major source of mercury contamination in Oregon pheasants appeared to be from mercury fungicides used in the treatment of seeds for agriculture. The mercury content of the birds, therefore, varied appreciably according to season and location, reflecting the crops grown in the area and the dates of sampling and planting. Pheasants from Malheur County, Umatilla County and the Willamette Valley contain mean mercury concentrations in breast muscle of 0.189, 0.007 and 0.246 ppm, respectively. The mercury content of muscle tissue ranged between 0.001 and 6.33 ppm mercury with 14 of the 187 birds examined exceeding the 0.5 ppm U.S. Food and Drug Administration guideline value. Most of the mercury present in the tissues of the pheasants was in the methylmercury form. A high ratio of mercury concentration in the liver to that in muscle was found in many birds and was apparently associated with recent consumption of the mercury-treated seeds. (See also W75-06897) (Jernigan-Vanderbilt)
W75-06917

PHEASANT FEEDING STUDY USING SEEDS TREATED WITH METHYL AND PHENYLMERCURY,
Bureau of Sport Fisheries and Wildlife, Boise, Idaho. Div. of River Basin Studies.
E. R. Norberg, D. W. Brock, F. Shields, III, and J. E. Cline.
In: Mercury in the Western Environment, Continuing Education Publications, Corvallis, Oregon, p 212-218, 1973. 1 fig, 3 tab, 5 ref.

Descriptors: *Mercury, *Organic compounds, *Seeds, *Game birds, On-site tests, Analytical techniques, Chromatography, Toxicity, *Absorption, Pollutant identification, Heavy metals.

Groups of ring-necked pheasants (Phasianus colchicus torguatus) were fed wheat treated with phenylmercuric acetate or methylmercury dicyandiamide fungicides. The birds failed to accumulate appreciable amounts of the phenylmercury compound but significant retention occurred when pheasants were fed the wheat treated with the methylmercury derivative. A differential rate of buildup and decline (after removal of the treated feed) was noted between male and female birds. Male birds tended to accumulate mercury more rapidly than females and mercury levels in the males remained at a high level throughout the entire exposure and recovery period. The buildup of mercury in hens, however, tended to occur more slowly but reached a higher peak and started to decrease more rapidly than with the male birds. (See also W75-06897) (Jernigan-Vanderbilt)
W75-06918

SEMI-AUTOMATED DETERMINATION OF MERCURY IN FISH TISSUE,
Fisheries Research Board of Canada, Winnipeg (Manitoba). Freshwater Inst.
For primary bibliographic entry see Field 5A.
W75-06921

THE HUMAN HEALTH HAZARDS OF METHYLMERCURY,
Mayo Clinic, Rochester, Minn. Dept. of Medical Statistics, Epidemiology and Population Genetics.
L. T. Kurland.
In: Mercury in the Western Environment, Continuing Education Publications, Corvallis, Oregon, p 283-297, 1973. 1 fig, 35 ref.

Descriptors: *Mercury, *Organic compounds, *Public health, *Human pathology, Toxicity, Animal pathology, Fish, Animal physiology, Human physiology, Analytical techniques, Pollutant identification, Heavy metals.
Identifiers: *Methylmercury.

The findings of a special committee of the U.S. Public Health Service were discussed. The purpose of the Committee was: (1) to review events of mercury poisoning in human and animal populations; (2) to clarify the sources and risks of mercury and especially the reported high levels of mercury in fish; and (3) to make recommendations for the further studies of the effects of mercury and its compounds aimed at providing better methods of control. The report includes sections on the medical implications of mercury ingestion, microbial transformation of mercury in the environment, ecological effects of methylmercury contamination including the effects on fish and wildlife, and analytical methods for mercury compounds. The recommended allowable daily intake (ADI) was 0.03 mg methylmercury for a 70 kg mass. (See also W75-06897) (Jernigan-Vanderbilt)
W75-06925

EXPERIMENTAL PORCINE METHYLMERCURIALISM,
Washington State Univ., Pullman. Dept. of Veterinary Pathology.
R. C. Piper, V. L. Miller, and E. O. Dickinson.
In: Mercury in the Western Environment, Continuing Education Publications, Corvallis, Oregon, p 298-310, 1973. 3 tab, 17 ref.

Descriptors: *Mercury, *Organic compounds, *Toxicity, *Hogs, Testing procedures, Laboratory tests, Laboratory animals, Animal physiology, Animal pathology, Analytical techniques, *Pollutant identification, Heavy metals.
Identifiers: *Methylmercury.

Toxicity, symptomatology, clinical course, and distribution of mercury in tissues were determined and correlated in pigs given single and daily oral doses of methylmercury dicyandiamide (MMD) for 30 consecutive days or until death or euthanasia in extremis. The minimal fatal oral dose of MMD to pigs was 20 mg MMD/kg body weight. Signs of toxicosis were observed in pigs given single doses as low as 5 mg MMD/kg but not in pigs given 2.5 mg MMD/kg. The minimal fatal repetitive oral dose of MMD was 0.65 mg MMD/kg after 26 or 30 daily doses. Single large doses of MMD caused a severe gastroenteritis that progressed rapidly to shock, coma and death 12-28 hours after dosage. Signs of toxicity, tissue concentrations and distribution of mercury differed among pigs that survived the initial oral dose for at least five days. Neurological disturbances were the most characteristic clinical signs. Mercury was widely distributed throughout the body. Concentrations of mercury were highest in the renal cortex with the second highest levels in the liver. Moderately large concentrations were also present in the renal medulla and skeletal muscles. Concentrations of mercury in the skeletal muscles and brain were much higher than those reported in experimental porcine inorganic and arylmercurialism. (See also W75-06897) (Jernigan-Vanderbilt)
W75-06926

THE HUMAN MORPHOLOGICAL LESIONS OF METHYLMERCURY INJURY,
Washington Univ., Seattle. Dept. of Pathology.
N. K. Mottet.
In: Mercury in the Western Environment, Continuing Education Publications, Corvallis, Oregon, p 311-319, 1973. 5 fig, 14 ref.

Descriptors: *Mercury, *Organic compounds, *Human pathology, *Cytology, Toxicity, Human physiology, Public health, Inorganic compounds, *Pollutant identification, Heavy metals.
Identifiers: *Methylmercury.

A review of the relatively few well-documented human autopsy case reports dealing with the effects of methylmercury compounds in chronic mercury intoxication was presented. The lesions of adults who died within two months of intoxication differed in several important respects from those who died several months or years after the injury. Deaths that occurred within two months of exposure revealed the accumulation of edema fluid in the brain and turbid, edematous meninges. Those cases that survived longer had fibrous thickening of the meninges and decrease in brain size (atrophy) with a compensatory increase in fluid. Acute lesions were also found in the skin, liver, kidneys and cardiovascular system. The blood vessels of the control nervous system and elsewhere in the body had perivascular dilatation and edema and in long-standing cases there were capillary proliferation and thickening of the vessel wall. Slight intimal thickening was seen in the small arteries. A catarrhal type of acute inflammatory change occurred in the mucous membrane of the digestive tract, especially in the duodenum. Fatty change, degeneration and necrosis were frequently observed in the liver and kidneys. (See also W75-06897) (Jernigan-Vanderbilt)
W75-06927

METHYLMERCURY TOXICITY: A PROBABILISTIC ASSESEMENT,
California Univ., Berkeley. School of Public Health.
R. C. Spear, and E. Wei.
In: Mercury in the Western Environment, Continuing Education Publications, Corvallis, Oregon, p 320-327, 1973. 4 fig, 2 tab, 7 ref.

Descriptors: *Mercury, *Toxicity, *Statistics, *Mathematical models, Organic compounds, Mathematical studies, Probability, Fish, Public health, Foods, *Food chains, Pollutant identification, Heavy metals.
Identifiers: *Methylmercury.

Methylmercury intake via contaminated foodstuffs was assessed in a probabilistic context. The statistical variables considered included the degree of contamination, the quality of food consumed and the consumption frequency. The results indicated that computer simulation techniques can relate consumption patterns to the proportion of an exposed population at risk. (See also W75-06897) (Jernigan-Vanderbilt)
W75-06928

MERCURY CONTAMINATION-PRIBILOF ISLANDS,
Center for Disease Control, Atlanta, Ga.
F. Hochberg, and S. Sherman.
In: Mercury in the Western Environment, Continuing Education Publications, Corvallis, Oregon, p 328-331, 1973. 1 fig, 1 tab, 4 ref.

Descriptors: *Mercury, *Toxicity, *Human pathology, *Alaska, Contaminants, Public health, Organic compounds, Human physiology, Correlation studies, On-site data collections, Laboratory tests, Analytical techniques, Sampling, Pollutant identification, Heavy metals.
Identifiers: *Pribilof Islands(Alas).

An effort was made to determine the potential for neurologic dysfunction in individuals with chronic low-level mercury exposure. The residents of St. Paul Island, the largest of the Pribilof Islands, were studied because of their consumption of seal meat and liver, which is high in mercury content. 30% of the households surveyed contained at least one individual with neurologic symptoms. However, clinical evaluation of all those diagnosed or symptomatic cases failed to reveal evidence suggesting that neurologic disease was related to mercury exposure. Neutron activation analysis of hair samples obtained from the residents of St. Paul revealed mean mercury levels of 4.45 ppm. (See also W75-06897) (Jernigan-Vanderbilt)
W75-06929

THE PHARMACODYNAMICS OF MERCURY AND ITS COMPOUNDS WITH EMPHASIS ON THE SHORT-CHAIN ALKYLMERCURIALS,
Rochester Univ., N.Y. Dept. of Radiation Biology and Biophysics.
T. W. Clarkson.
In: Mercury in the Western Environment, Continuing Education Publications, Corvallis, Oregon, p 332-354, 1973. 11 fig, 9 tab, 41 ref. AEC(W 7401-Eng-49)/NIH (GM105190-04).

Descriptors: *Mercury, *Absorption, *Mammals, *Distribution, *Metabolism, Organic compounds, Inorganic compounds, Foods, Animal physiology, Resins, *Pollutant identification, Heavy metals.

Short-chain alkylmercurials were compared with other classes of mercury compounds in respect to rates of absorption from food, patterns of distribution and deposition in the mammalian body, rates of biotransformation to inorganic mercury and pathways of excretion. Recent findings on the mechanisms of fecal excretion of methylmercury were discussed. Preliminary findings were presented on the use of new mercury binding resins to facilitate excretion. (See also W75-06897) (Jernigan-Vanderbilt)
W75-06930

EFFECTS OF CERTAIN CHEMICAL POLLUTANTS ON SMALL AQUATIC ANIMALS,
Kansas Water Resources Research Inst., Manhattan.
For primary bibliographic entry see Field 5A.
W75-06981

BIOLOGICAL EFFECTS OF METHYL MERCURY IN AQUATIC SYSTEMS ON MALLARDS AND SCAUP,
Michigan State Univ., East Lansing. Dept. of Fisheries and Wildlife.
J. R. Ford, and H. H. Prince.
Available from the National Technical Information Service, Springfield, Va 22161 as PB-241 383, $4.75 in paper copy, $2.25 in microfiche. Completion Report, Michigan Institute of Water Research, East Lansing, March 1975. 73 p, 9 fig, 16 tab, 63 ref. OWRT A-052-MICH(1). 14-31-0001-3522.

Descriptors: *Mercury, *Reproduction, *Ducks(Domestic), Water pollution effects, Waterfowl, *Mallard ducks, Lethal limit, Toxicity, Food and cover crops.
Identifiers: *Methyl mercury, Survival, *Scaup, Hatchability, Ducklings, Food consumption.

The effect of mercury contamination in an aquatic system on the survival and reproduction of two waterfowl species was evaluated. Mallards (Anas platyrhyncos) and scaup (Aythya spp.), during October and November, were estimated to have daily total mercury consumption rates of 0.008 and 0.681 mg, respectively. Scaup, during March, were estimated to consume 0.175 mg total mercury daily. Feeding experiments with mallards indicate that consumption of methyl mercury can lower both survival and reproduction. Lethal effects were observed after both male and female mallards consumed 60.3 plus or minus 13.4 mg of methyl mercuric chloride at varied doses above 0.5 mg per day over a 120 day period. Reductions in hatchability of eggs and survival of ducklings were observed at doses less than 0.5 mg per day. Time, sex and reproductive status affected the decline of total mercury levels in breast, brain, liver and kidney tissues of mallards after a single 8 mg dose. It took from 30 to more than 90 days for mercury levels in tissues to decline below 1 ppm after a 8 mg dose.
W75-06985

BACTERIAL METHANE OXIDATION AND ITS INFLUENCE IN THE AQUATIC ENVIRONMENT,
Ohio State Univ., Columbus. Dept. of Microbiology.
For primary bibliographic entry see Field 5B.
W75-06987

LETHAL AND SUBLETHAL EFFECTS OF HERBICIDES ON ZOOPLANKTON SPECIES,
Tennessee Univ., Knoxville. Dept. of Zoology.
D. L. Bunting, and E. B. Robertson, Jr.
Available from the National Technical Information Service, Springfield, Va 22161 as PB-241 337, $3.75 in paper copy, $2.25 in microfiche. Tennessee Water Resources Research Center, Knoxville, Report No. 43, April 1975. 35 p, 14 tab, 29 ref, $3.00. OWRT A-028-TENN(1).

Descriptors: *Zooplankton, *Herbicides, Aquatic life, Daphnia, Water pollution effects, *Lethal limit, Diptera, Copepods, 2-4-D, Rotifers, *Toxicity, 2-4-5-T.
Identifiers: *Sublethal effects, Amitroles.

Nauplii, 0-4 hours old, of the copepod Cyclops vernalis were exposed to concentration ranges of amitrole, amitrole-T, and the free acid and alkanolamine salt of 2,4-D. LD50, LT50, and incipient lethal levels were calculated and discussed. Adult Cyclops vernalis, Mesocyclops edax, and Macrocyclops albidus were exposed to amitrole and the 2,4-D salt to provide comparative data. Third and fourth instar larvae of Chaoborus punctipennis, a planktonic dipteran, were subjected to static tests of the commercial herbicides containing 2,4-D, ammonium sulfamate, and amitrole. Fifty percent responses were calculated for each herbicide, and an emergence-suppression threshold was noted for amitrole. Data were obtained for three rotifers, Keratella cochlearis, K. americana, and Brachionus angularis, relative to the acute toxicity of six water soluble or water emulsifiable forms of 2,4,5-T. Technical 2,4,5-T was also assayed against K. cochlearis. Data on the effects of food level on LT50, and food level, dose, and exposure time on LC50 were given. The effects of temperature, exposure time, and concentration of aminotriazole on Daphnia pulex females and males were measured. LT50 data were presented along with a discussion of sublethal effects and information from preliminary tests using forms of 2,4-D and 2,4,5-T.
W75-06989

MUSSELS AND POLLUTION IN THE RED RIVER DRAINAGE, NORTH DAKOTA AND MINNESOTA,
North Dakota Univ., Grand Forks. Dept. of Geology.
A. M. Cvancara.
Research Report No. WI-221-019-74, November, 1974, 3 p, 4 ref.

Descriptors: *North Dakota, *Minnesota, *Mussels, Ecology, Distribution, River flow, Water pollution, Turbidity, Drainage.
Identifiers: *Red River Valley(NDak).

Thirteen species of mussels inhabit the Red River of the North and 18 of its tributaries in eastern North Dakota and western Minnesota. Eight mussel species have been collected from the Red River, and 1-13 species from each of its tributaries. The four most common species are Lasmigona complanata, Anodonta grandis, Anodontoides ferussacianus and Lampsilis siliquoidea. Five species, Amblema costata, Quadrula quadrula, Proptera alata, Ligumia recta latissima and Lampsilis ventricosa, are generally characteristic of the larger rivers in the Red River Valley. Lasmigonia

compressa and Anodontoides ferussacianus are generally indicative of smaller rivers in the Valley. The mussel fauna of the Red River Valley, which is part of the Hudson Bay drainage, originated from that of the Mississippi River system. The Valley fauna, however, constitutes only 26 percent of that of the Mississippi. Four ecological factors are presumably of primary importance in restricting the distribution of mussels in the Red River Valley. These are: prolonged lack of river flow, high chloride content, water pollution and possibly high turbidity.
W75-06992

DISTRIBUTION AND ECOLOGY OF RIVER MOLLUSKS IN CENTRAL AND WESTERN NORTH DAKOTA,
North Dakota Univ., Grand Forks. Dept. of Geology.
For primary bibliographic entry see Field 5B.
W75-07105

THE WATER POLLUTION POTENTIAL OF REPRESENTATIVE PESTICIDES IN SELECTED ENVIRONMENTS,
Virginia Polytechnic Inst. and State Univ., Blacksburg.
P. H. King, H. H. Yeh, and C. W. Randall.
Paper presented at the Second Annual Environmental Engineering and Science Conference, University of Lousiville, Lousiville, Kentucky, April 1, 1972. 18 p, 11 fig, 7 ref.

Descriptors: *Water pollution effects, *Environmental effects, *Pesticides toxicity, *Pollutant identification, *Persistence, *Organic compounds, Algae, Algal toxins, Pesticide kinetics, Carbamate pesticides, Organic pesticides, Food chains, Euglena, Chlorella, Pesticides, Pesticide residues.
Identifiers: Lindane, Parathion, Chloroisopropyl carbonate.

An understanding of the distribution and persistence of pesticides in selected aquatic environments is a key to evaluation of their pollution potential as well as determining the ultimate fate of these materials. An experimental basis for predicting the impact of selected pesticides on the general environment by means of studies of their distribution and persistence in selected specific environments is described. Laboratory investigations were carried out to study the fate of three representative pesticides, lindane, parathion and chloroisopropyl carbamate (CIPC), in aquatic systems containing large concentrations of algal cells. The results are compared with data previously reported for uptake on inorganic sorbents. Persistence studies showing pesticide degradation in similar algae laden systems are also described. The algae used in the experimental work were of the genera Euglena and Chlorella. The uptake of pesticides from water solution by algae illustrates one possible means by which pesticides may be introduced into the food chain and thus eventually be concentrated in higher animals such as fish. (Poertner)
W75-07114

THE EFFECT OF SEDIMENT ON RESERVOIR WATER QUALITY,
Virginia State Water Control Board, Richmond.
Y. Samuel, and C. W. Randall.
A paper presented at the AICHE/EPA Second National Conference on Complete Water Reuse: Water's Interface with Energy, Air, and Solids, Chicago, Illinois, May 4-8, 1975. 36 p, 6 tab, 5 fig, 10 ref.

Descriptors: *Sediments, *Phosphates, *Water quality, *Reservoirs, *Sewage treatment, *Eutrophication, Sediment-water interfaces, Sedimentation, Silting, Interfaces, Deposition(Sediments), Phosphorus.
Identifiers: Reservoir water quality.

The quality of water in the Occoquan Reservoir has deteriorated considerably during recent years. This was largely the result of sewage treatment discharges to Bull Run and its tributaries. The treated effluents contain large quantities of nitrogen and phosphorus which add to the Reservoir nutrient load and accelerate eutrophication. The relationship among silt, sediment, and water quality in the Reservoir as measured by phosphorus concentration was defined. A primary concern was how phosphates are released from sediment to the overlying water under different conditions, and whether sediment acts principally as a source or sink for phosphates. The assay procedure was evaluated and once the accuracy was established it was possible to study the effect of selected parameters on phosphate release. The rate of release of phosphates was found to be unaffected by pH changes, depth of sediment, and the depth of overlying water. The rate of release of phosphates was enhanced by anaerobic conditions, concentration of phosphates in the sediment, and a rise in temperature. Other nutrients such as carbon and nitrogen are also released with phosphates. The sediment may act as a sink or source for phosphates, depending on the phosphate concentration in the overlying water. (Poertner)
W75-07116

SOCIAL AND ECONOMIC IMPACTS OF WASTE WATER MANAGEMENT IN THE MERRIMACK BASIN,
Abt Associates, Inc., Cambridge, Mass.
M. Eigerman.
In: The Merrimack: Design for a Clean River, American Society of Civil Engineers, National Meeting, Session No. 17, Washington, D.C., January 30, 1973. 6 p.

Descriptors: *Administration, *Alternate planning, *Water pollution control, *Planning, *Regional analysis, Social impact, *Waste water treatment, Tertiary treatment, Management, Effects, Forecasting, Economic impact, Environmental effects, Water quality control, New Hampshire, Massachusetts.
Identifiers: *Merrimack River Basin, Matrix analysis.

In the study of the Merrimack River Basin, the task was to identify and, wherever possible, quantify significant social and economic changes resulting from alternative advance wastewater treatment processes marshalled into alternative management schemes. The single objective was maximum feasible purity of major point-source waste discharges. Social impacts were addressed by using a two-dimensional matrix handling fifteen impact categories and six sub-areas of the Merrimack Basin. By applying the matrix to each of seven Corps alternative plans and to a 'baseline scenario' represented by the States' implementation plans, three determinations for each cell were made; whether there were significant impact, whether the direction of change was upward, downward, or stable and finally, whether the change so characterized would have generally positive or negative effects. The economic side of the analysis concerned itself chiefly with quantifying the agricultural, industrial and manpower implications of water-disposal versus land-disposal alternatives. The Merrimack exercise demonstrated that social and economic impact assessment can be enormously useful planning input even at the feasibility level. Not only did it stretch the engineering mind into new and exciting territory, but it also will make some response to the planning jurisdiction's own aspirations practically inevitable. (Poertner)
W75-07121

WASTE WATER MANAGEMENT - A REGIONAL PROBLEM,
Corps of Engineers, New York. North Atlantic Div.
H. E. Schwarz.
In: The Merrimack: Design for a Clean River, American Society of Civil Engineers, National Meeting, Session No. 17, Washington, D.C., January 30, 1973. 5 p.

Descriptors: *Regional analysis, *Administration, *Water pollution control, *River basins, *Planning, Water quality control, Waste water treatment, Alternate planning, Effects, Impaired water quality, Environmental control, Ecology, Social impact, Management, New Hampshire, Massachusetts.
Identifiers: *Merrimack River Basin, Waste water management.

The Northeastern United States Water Supply Study, or NEWS Study, was initiated by the North Atlantic Division of the Corps of Engineers in 1966. Waste management as a problem intimately linked to water supply came to the foreground. The Merrimack, already identified as a candidate for restoration as a water supply source, was selected as one of the test cases. The Merrimack River, now grossly polluted, previously had been thoroughly studied for conventional waste treatment. Maximum feasible purity of waste discharges and the reclamation of waste water and some of its pollutants for beneficial uses was the goal. A task force was assembled in the New England Division office of the Corps of Engineers at Waltham that integrated people from several Corps offices, from other Federal agencies, from Universities and from private consulting firms into a single study team. Their task was to prepare a feasibility report in six months that would: (1) determine the nature and extent of the Merrimack River's pollution problem; (2) develop and screen alternative technical solutions to that problem, and (3) analyze the changes that the most likely of these solutions might have on the ecologic, hygienic, aesthetic, social and economic character of the Merrimack Basin. (Poertner)
W75-07124

IMPACT ANALYSIS: HINDSIGHT AND FORESIGHT IN SASKATCHEWAN,
Saskatchewan Fisheries Lab., Saskatoon.
For primary bibliographic entry see Field 6G.
W75-07171

HYDROELECTRIC DEVELOPMENT OF THE NELSON RIVER SYSTEM IN NORTHERN MANITOBA,
Manitoba Hydro, Winnipeg.
For primary bibliographic entry see Field 6G.
W75-07172

ENVIRONMENTAL IMPACT OF THE CHURCHILL FALLS (LABRADOR) HYDROELECTRIC PROJECT: A PRELIMINARY ASSESSMENT,
Waterloo Univ. (Ontario). Dept. of Biology.
For primary bibliographic entry see Field 6G.
W75-07173

ECOLOGICAL CONSEQUENCES OF THE PROPOSED MORAN DAM ON THE FRASER RIVER,
Simon Fraser Univ., Burnaby (British Columbia). Dept. of Biological Sciences.
For primary bibliographic entry see Field 6G.
W75-07174

DEVELOPMENT OF JAMES BAY: THE ROLE OF ENVIRONMENTAL IMPACT ASSESSMENT IN DETERMINING THE LEGAL RIGHT TO AN INTERLOCUTORY INJUNCTION,
McGill Univ., Montreal (Quebec). Dept. of Geography.
For primary bibliographic entry see Field 6G.
W75-07175

ECOLOGICAL CHANGES DUE TO HYDROELECTRIC DEVELOPMENT ON THE SAINT JOHN RIVER,
Fisheries and Marine Service, Halifax (Nova Scotia). Resource Development Branch.
For primary bibliographic entry see Field 6G.
W75-07176

IMPACT OF THE BENNETT DAM ON THE PEACE-ATHABASCA DELTA,
Canadian Wildlife Service, Edmonton (Alberta).
For primary bibliographic entry see Field 6G.
W75-07177

SEASONAL NITRATE CYCLING AS EVIDENCE FOR COMPLETE VERTICAL MIXING IN LAKE TAHOE, CALIFORNIA-NEVADA,
California Univ., Davis. Inst. of Ecology; and California Univ., Davis. Div. of Environmental Studies.
H. W. Paerl, R. C. Richards, R. L. Leonard, and C. R. Goldman.
Limnology and Oceanography, Vol 20, No 1, p 1-8, January 1975. 2 fig, 1 tab. NSF-RANN Grant GI-22.

Descriptors: *Limnology, *Nitrogen cycle, *Lake morphometry, Nitrates, Bacteria, Lakes, Mixing, Freshwater, Bodies of water, Turnover, Euphotic zone, Nitrification, Detritus, *California, Nevada.
Identifiers: *Nitrate cycling, *Lake Tahoe(Calif-Nev).

A study of annual nitrate cycling in Lake Tahoe provided evidence that the lake is both oligotrophic and holomictic. Beginning with the spring phytoplankton bloom, a sequence of biological nitrogen transformations is responsible for formation of a nitrate gradient, characterized by a distinct 'nitracline.' The main processes responsible are nitrate depletion by phytoplankton uptake and deep water nitrification by bacteria. Sinking detritus appeared to be the main source of reduced nitrogen available for nitrification. As cooling proceeded during fall and winter 1972, depression of the nitracline revealed the process of vertical mixing and eventual turnover of the water mass. (Jess-ISWS)
W75-07198

CHEMICAL AND BIOLOGICAL QUALITY OF LAKE DICIE AT AUSTIS, FLORIDA, WITH EMPHASIS ON THE EFFECTS OF STORM RUNOFF,
Geological Survey, Tallahassee, Fla.
A. G. Lamonds.
Available from NTIS, Springfield, Va 22161 as PB-239 014/As, $4.25 in paper copy, $2.25 in microfiche. Water-Resources Investigations 36-74, December 1974. 61 p, 7 fig, 9 tab, 12 ref, append.

Descriptors: *Eutrophication, *Algae, *Biological properties, *Lakes, *Florida, Chemical analysis, Data collections, Water analysis, Water quality, *Storm runoff, Water pollution sources, Storm drains, Limnology, Water pollution effects.
Identifiers: *Lake Dicie(Fla), *Lake County(Fla).

After a storm drain was constructed to carry runoff from part of the city of Eustis, Florida, into Lake Dicie, algal blooms occurred in the lake. Street runoff contains high concentrations of nitrogen, phosphorus, and lead, as well as other trace metals. The quantity of inorganic nitrogen and orthophosphate carried into the lake during the course of the investigation (March 1971 to June 1973) was equivalent to about 3,500 pounds of commercial 6-6-6 fertilizer and was more than sufficient to support large populations of phytoplankton. Algal blooms occurred in the winter when the lake slowly 'turned over,' mixing the nutrient-rich bottom water with water from the upper part of the lake. An experiment in which lake samples were fertilized with nitrogen and phosphorus indicated that the explosive growth of phytoplankton was related to the abundance of inorganic nitrogen which was available to the phytoplankton during the winter when the lake was not stratified. (Woodward-USGS)
W75-07213

EFFECTS OF RESERVOIR CLEARING ON WATER QUALITY IN THE ARCTIC AND SUBARCTIC,
Alaska Univ., College. Inst. of Water Resources.
D. W. Smith, and S. R. Justice.
Available from the National Technical Information Service, Springfield, Va. 22161 as PB-241 853, $3.25 in paper copy, $2.25 in microfiche. Report No. IWR-58, January 1975. 15 p, 1 fig, 4 ref. OWRT A-043-ALAS (1).

Descriptors: *Reservoirs, *Leaching, *Pre-impoundment, Surveys, Water quality, Soil classification, Economic justification, Water chemistry, Oxygen, Nutrients, Color, *Alaska, Hydrogen ion concentration, Alkalinity, Iron, Managanese, Temperature, Carbon, Conductivity, Soil moisture, Arctic, Subarctic.
Identifiers: Moose Creek(Alas), Kotzebue, Ship Creek, Monashka Creek, Barrow, Leaching columns, Leachate, Tannin/Lignin, Total organic carbon, Soil organic content, *Reservoir clearing.

A research project examining the advisability of clearing reservoirs in the Arctic and subarctic is described. Soil samples were collected from five Alaskan reservoir sites, classified as to particle size and organic content, leached in sealed six-inch diameter columns, and changes in electrical conductivity, alkalinity, tannin/lignin, dissolved oxygen, color, nitrate plus nitrite, ammonia, total orgaic carbon, iron, and manganese were determined on the leachate. Clearing was found to be advisable for reservoir sites at Mosse Creek, Ship Creek and Barrow, and was recommended, pending scour studies, for Monashka Creek. It was not found to be advisable for the Kotzebue reservoir site. An approach to the evaluation of the most economical depth of reservoir clearing, considering water treatment costs and clearing costs, is presented.
W75-07272

EXTREME FLUCTUATIONS IN WATER QUALITY OF EUTROPHIC FISH KILL LAKES: EFFECT OF SEDIMENT MIXING,
Fisheries Research Board of Canada, Winnipeg (Manitoba). Freshwater Inst.
J. Barica.
Water Research, Vol. 8, No. 11, p 881-888, 1974. 7 fig, 2 tab, 15 ref.

Descriptors: *Oxygen sag, *Lake sediments, *Sagponds, Fish farming, Cycling nutrients, Nitrogen compounds, Phosphorus compounds, Dissolved oxygen, Canada, Anaerobic conditions, Rainbow trout, Eutrophication, Fishkill, Upwelling, Cyanophyta.
Identifiers: Aphanizomenon flos-aquae, Erickson(Manitoba).

The pothole lakes, located in southwestern Manitoba, represent a great economic potential for summer fish farming. However, their periodic sedimentary nutrient releases and recurring anoxic conditions preclude successful aquaculture. Ice and snow cover during 5-6 months reduces biological nutrient assimilation and is replaced by decomposition and anaerobic conditions. The lakes are re-aerated by a complete turnover after ice break up. Nearly pure cultures of Aphanizomenon flos-aquae blooms occur in mid-June; after their collapse in midsummer, bacterial decomposition of the dead algae cells is accompanied by a drop in dissolved oxygen, resulting in total fish kills. Decomposition releases substantial amounts of ammonia-N and orthophosphate-P, providing nutrients for another algal cycle. One of the possible triggering mechanisms for the collapse of algal blooms and fish kills is the upwelling of anoxic bottom water, apparently caused by heavy winds or stirred-up lake sediments. Test results demonstrated that even a short contact of lake water with upwelled sediments caused an immediate drop of DO and enrichment by ammonia to concentrations over 1 mg/l. Most of these lakes have already reached the eutrophic stage. The sediments are the major nutrient reservoir and are also the major source of BOD. Several restoration measures offer promise. (Auen-Wisconsin)
W75-07290

A COMPARATIVE STUDY OF PRIMARY PRODUCTION AND STANDING CROPS OF PHYTOPLANKTON IN A PORTION OF THE UPPER CHESAPEAKE BAY SUBSEQUENT TO TROPICAL STORM AGNES,
Johns Hopkins Univ., Baltimore, Md. McCollum-Pratt Inst.
M. E. Loftus, and H. H. Seliger.
Available from the National Technical Information Service, Springfield, Va 22161 as COO-3278-23, $4.00 in paper copy, $2.25 in microfiche. Report COO-3278-2. (Undated). 32 p, 5 fig, 3 tab, 19 ref. AEC AT(11-1)3278, NSF FI 32110.

Descriptors: *Primary productivity, *Standing crops, *Phytoplankton, *Chesapeake Bay, Dinoflagellates, Salinity, Nutrients, Temperature, Light, Phosphates, Oxygen, Bacteria, Bottom sediments, Tropical cyclones.
Identifiers: *Upper Chesapeake Bay, *Hurricane Agnes.

Natural phytoplankton communities in Rhode River, West River and an adjacent section of Chesapeake Bay have been studied since June, 1969. There are statistically significant comparisons of baseline data from which both short-term and long-term effects of Hurricane Agnes (June 21, 1972) on phytoplankton populations can be evaluated. There was immediate dramatic change in relative species composition to favor large dinoflagellates and a 3-fold increase in man total phytoplankton standing crop during 1973. The rapidly increased phytoplankton crop was composed of an algal species endemic during the summer season. The bloom after the storm continued through the salinity recovery and nutrient depletion until the fall decline in temperature. The observations that standing crops of phytoplankton in 1973 equalled or surpassed the previous year's post-Agnes levels, that a 4-fold elevation of dissolved organic phosphate levels occurred in 1973 river samples above those observed in pre-Agnes samples and post-Agnes bay water, and that oxygen depletion in bottom waters in 1973 was associated with high bacterial levels are consistent with hypothesis that the amplification of normal species densities in 1973 resulted from utilization of organic material deposited in the bottom sediments by Agnes in the preceding year. (Jones-Wisconsin)
W75-07291

PERIPHYTON COLONIZATION AND PRODUCTIVITY IN THE REACTOR COOLING RESERVOIR--PAR POND,
Du Pont de Nemours (E. I.) and Co., Aiken, S.C. Savannah River Lab.
L. J. Tilly.
Available from the National Technical Information Service, Springfield, Va 22161 as DP-MS-7367, $4.00 in paper copy, $2.25 in microfiche. Report DP-MS-73-67 (Undated). 9 p, 2 fig, 1 tab, 2 ref. AEC AT(07-2)-1.

Descriptors: *Periphyton, *Productivity, *Cooling water, Nuclear power plants, Standing crops, Plant growth, Biological communities, Heated water, Regression analysis, Correlation analysis.
Identifiers: *Par Pond(SC), Artificial substrates.

The influence of thermal effluents upon periphyton are of interest because this component is often quantitatively important in aquatic food

chains and because its growth integratively reflects conditions in a fixed location. Glass microscope slides colonized by periphyton are being collected at six different locations at Par Pond, a reactor cooling reservoir on the Savannah River Plant in South Carolina, with varying thermal effluents for determinations of dry-weight standing crop, chlorophyll, species composition, and C14 productivity. Standing crops and productivity differ with proximity to the thermal discharge, and also by season, so that zones of maximum growth shift with time. Periphyton community characteristics are discussed in relation to limnological characteristics of the stations studied. In 19 of 25 experiments analyzed for 1973, a significant or highly significant relationship between periphyton production and mean growing temperature was found. When data from all experiments were composited for regression and correlation analysis, the evidence for temperature dependence vanished. If all such data are reduced to means for temperature and standing crop, and these are examined statistically, a highly significant relationship between average periphyton accumulation and growing temperature is found. (Jones-Wisconsin)
W75-07292

THE SEAWEEDS OF THE MURMANSK REGION IN THE VICINITY OF THE MALYY OLENIY (NEMETSKIY) ISLAND,
A. D. Zinova.
Available from the National Technical Information Service, Springfield, Va 22161 as AD-784 715, $3.25 in paper copy, $2.25 in microfiche. NOO T-18, 1974. 14 p, 1 tab. Translated from Gosudarstvennyy Gidrologicheskiy Institut, Leningrad, No 21, p 88-97, 1935.

Descriptors: *Marine algae, *Distribution, Systematies, Biological communities, Iodine, Harvesting of algae.
Identifiers: *Sea weeds, Malyy Oleniy Island(USSR), Murmansk(USSR).

The growth, distribution, and abundance of sea weed in the region of Malyy Oleniy (Nemetskiy) Island in the Murmansk vicinity was investigated to determine the quantity of harvestable algae for the iodine industry. It was established that algae grow along the coasts of this island and continent and the width of the distribution belt reached 1-1.5 km along the island's northern coast, on its southern coast and on the continent, this width varied from 1 to 50 m. The seaweed concentrations on the Malyy Oleniy Island and those of the continental shore are listed according to their locations and species on the different types of shoreline. The total quantity of sea weeds torn loose during the 5-day observation period comprised 538.9 cubic meters, or 269.45 tons. Harvesting is hampered by lack of good roads and communications, as well as prevailing heavy surf and breakers and lack of moorings. (Jones-Wisconsin)
W75-07297

FISH AND WATER QUALITY CRITERIA.
Water Pollution Research Lab., Stevenage (England).
Notes on Water Pollution No 65, June 1974. 4 p, 3 fig, 1 tab, 11 ref.

Descriptors: *Toxins, *Water quality standards, *Fish, Hydrogen ion concentration, Ammonia, Heavy metals, Poisons, Copper, Nickel, Zinc, Cadmium, Calcium, Phenol, Toxicity, Bioindicators.
Identifiers: Hydrogen cyanide, Organic complexing substances.

Water quality, presence of multiple poisons and species differences of fish are important in the selection of water quality criteria. The toxicity of hydrogen cyanide and ammonia can be altered by the effects of pH, toxicity of heavy metals can be changed by water hardness, zinc by suspended solids, and copper by organic complexing substances. Physiological responses of fish to different calcium concentrations in water may affect the toxicity of heavy metals. Often mixtures of toxicants are present in polluted water. Also the effects of phenol, copper, and radioactive cadmium vary with fish species. The response rate of fish to a single poison normally differs from species to species and must be tested for a period long enough to permit determination of the concentration at which relative homeostasis occurs. To establish water quality standards for the protection of fisheries, the concentration of toxins in which fish can survive for a prolonged period of time, remain in good health, show good growth, and reproduce must be determined. Examples are given for survival of rainbow trout exposed to ammonia and zine; phenol; or cadmium, copper, or nickel in hard water; roach exposed to cadmium; and rudd to ammonia or zinc and hard water. (Buchanan-Davidson-Wisconsin)
W75-07298

STREAM POLLUTION BY FARM ANIMALS,
Louisiana Tech Univ., Ruston. Dept. of Agricultural Engineering.
J. W. D. Robbins.
In: 2nd Annual Environmental and Science Conference, April 20-21, 1972, University of Louisville, Kentucky, p 673-706. 5 tab, 4 ref.

Descriptors: *Streams, *Water pollution sources, *Domestic animals, Farm wastes, Agricultural runoff, North Carolina, Management, Soil disposal fields, Nitrates, Farm lagoons, Waste disposal, Groundwater pollution.
Identifiers: Land spreading.

The actual and potential importance of animal wastes in agricultural land runoff were investigated by quantifying factors governing timing, volume and concentration of waste discharges. The natural pollution load on streams draining agricultural basins free of farm animals and with appreciable rainfall and runoff, should be considered in water quality management. Pollution indices for streams receiving land drainage parallel stream hydrographs with extended drag-out on cessation of surface runoff. Soil provides natural treatment of animal wastes, thus land spreading is very effective in preventing water pollution. However, high applications of animal wastes per unit area may cause nitrate contamination of groundwater. Exclusive use of anaerobic lagoons for treating animal wastes is unsatisfactory in areas where rainfall exceeds evaporation. Dumping fresh animal wastes directly into streams should be prohibited. Although satisfactory estimating equations of general applicability for predicting waste contributions to surface waters based on animal number, temperature, and stream flow rate could not be developed from this short-term study, predictive relationships held quite well. Groundwater problems associated with properly located and managed animal production sites were minimal. Extent of water pollution caused by animal production units is almost entirely dependent upon production and waste management practices rather than on the volume of wastes involved. (Jones-Wisconsin)
W75-07299

ON THE THEORY OF NATURAL SELF-PURIFICATION OF RESERVOIRS,
G. B. Melnikov, F. P. Riabov, A. K. Stolbunov, and N. M. Karpushin.
Verhandlungen Internationale Vereinigung Limnologie, Vol 18, p 1320-1325, 1973. 5 ref.

Descriptors: *Self-purification, *Reservoirs, *Organic matter, *Oxidation, Bacteria, Denitrification, Rivers, Enzymes, Microorganisms, Turhulence.
Identifiers: Reservoirs(Dnieper River), USSR, Proteolytic bacteria.

Two ways of solving the pressing problem of clean water most practicable are regulating self-purification of natural bodies, and intensification of waste and sewage treatment. The combination of these measures is based on the fact that an exact estimation of natural self-purification rate and depth makes it possible to determine whether to let a basin destroy pollutants itself or to subject it to special treatment. The results obtained during 1960-1970 on two Dnieper River cascade reservoirs, Dneprodzerzhinsk and Lenin are reported. The aim was to disclose some peculiarities of natural self-purification of flat-country cascade reservoirs. The fact that a reservoir represented a complex system in which the opposite processes of natural pollution and natural self-purification occurred simultaneously was considered. When developing the general theory of cascade reservoir self-purification the following must be taken into account: the maximal rate of natural self-purification in downstream near-dam areas; the character of the biological agents of self-purification (denitrifying, phenol-destructive and proteolytic bacteria), facultative biochemical activities which facilitate mineralization of organic solutes in changeable environmental conditions; and estimation of pollution and self-purification rates using not only numbers but also the enzyme activities of microorganisms as agents of self-purification. (Jones-Wisconsin)
W75-07300

NUTRIENTS IN ICE. SOME DATA FROM A HIGH MOUNTAIN LAKE,
O. Groterud.
Verhandlungen Internationale Vereinigung Limnologie, Vol 18, p 327-333, 1972. 2 fig, 7 tab, 2 ref.

Descriptors: *Nutrients, *Lake ice, *Lakes, *Altitude, Snow, Phosphates, Nitrates, Nitrites, Ammonia, Height.
Identifiers: *Mountain lakes, Lake Ovre Heimdalsvatn(Norway).

The relationship between the nutrients in ice and in lake water was studied in a Norwegian lake, 1090 m above sea level. Snow and ice samples were collected from Lake Ovre Heimdalsvatn in polyethylene vessels, melted and tapped into polyethylene bottles. In order to avoid pollution, both the samples of ice and snow were taken with a plastic spoon. Analyses indicated a relatively high content of nutrients (phosphates, nitrates + nitrites, and ammonia) in the ice, and the most surprizing feature was the content of phosphates and its irregular, vertical as well as horizontal, distribution. Freezing experiments in the laboratory showed that lake waters increased in phosphate content after completely freezing in a sample bottle. The experiments indicated that phosphate can be released from some organic substances during the freezing process, and that this phenomenon also applies to the ice frozen on the lake. On the basis of hydrographical research just after the spring thaw, the relatively great amount of phosphate in the lake ice (and probably also in the ice of the drainage area) seems to have a great influence on the phosphate content of the water masses. (Jones-Wisconsin)
W75-07301

DIEL PERIODICITY IN THE PHYTOPLANKTON COMMUNITY OF THE OLIGOTROPHIC LAKE PAAJARVI, SOUTHERN FINLAND. I. PHYTOPLANKTONIC PRIMARY PRODUCTION AND RELATED FACTORS,
Helsinki Univ. (Finland). Dept. of Botany.
V. Ilmavirta.
Annales Botanici Fennici, Vol 11, No 2, p 136-177, 1974. 31 fig, 18 tab, 66 ref.

Descriptors: *Diurnal, *Phytoplankton, *Oligotrophy, *Primary productivity, Vertical migration, Biomass, Hydrology, Meteorology, Radiation, Thermal stratification, Algae, Light penetration, Light intensity, Environmental ef-

fects, On-site investigations, Respiration, Photosynthesis, Distribution, Suspended solids.
Identifiers: Lake Paajarvi(Finland).

Diurnal variations in productivity of phytoplankton in the oligotrophic Lake Paajarvi in Finland were strongly influenced by meteorological and hydrological conditions. Radiation was the most important environmental factor. Chemical factors varied with time, depth, and thermal stratification. Migration of algae from the surface occurred during periods of high light intensity. Distribution of non-motile specimens was determined by water movements. Surface inhibition of production and decrease of production with depth caused by light absorption were apparent in the production to biomass ratio. The difference between primary production in long exposures and the sum of short exposures varied; it was most pronounced in June and decreased in August. The effect of length of exposure decreased as the trophic status of the water rose. The composition and total volume of phytoplankton showed diurnal variations. Phytoplankton production was affected by dark fixation, respiration, and liberation of extracellular products. Primary production could be correlated to total radiation, but correlation to biomass and environmental factors was poor. The best parameter explaining plankton primary production and its diurnal variations was the production to biomass ratio, but production efficiency and the shape of the production depth curve showed no well defined relation to production. (Buchanan-Davidson-Wisconsin)
W75-07302

EFFICIENCY OF THE UTILIZATION OF NANNOPLANKTON PRIMARY PRODUCTION BY COMMUNITIES OF FILTER FEEDING ANIMALS MEASURED IN SITU,
Z. M. Gliwicz, and A. Hillbricht-Ilkowska.
Verhandlungen Internationale Vereinigung Limnologie, Vol 18, p 197-203, 1972. 1 tab, 14 ref.

Descriptors: *Secondary productivity, *Nannoplankton, *Primary productivity, *Zooplankton, *Grazing, Energy transfer, Bacteria, Tripton, Copepods, Oligotrophy, Dystrophy, Eutrophication.
Identifiers: *Filter feeding zooplankton, Calanoid copepods.

This discussion deals with the efficiency (ratio of food quantity ingested by consumer to the food quantity produced) as applied to the lake phytoplankton-zooplankton trophic system, or, more specifically, to the filter feeding zooplankton (filtrators and sedimentators) on the one hand, and to nannophytoplankton on the other. The method applied in this experiment of nannoplankton consumption involved comparison of the numbers of algae, bacteria cells and tripton particles in natural lake water in two containers with the same densities of zooplankters but the animals in one being inhibited and unable to graze. The anaesthetizing reagent (Physostigminum salicylicum) strongly affected the animal's neural system, but was totally neutral in relation to algae and bacteria. Gross primary production was measured as oxygen production (dark and light bottles) from which the net phytoplankton was removed by filtration through bolting cloth. Dominance of macrofiltrators, especially calanoid copepods, within the community of filter feeders results in very effective utilization of plankton net primary production by zooplankton. Nannoplankton growth and production are limited mainly by zooplankton grazing in oligotrophic and dystrophic lakes, while in more eutrophic lakes other factors seem to be more important in limiting these phenomena. (Jones-Wisconsin)
W75-07303

THE PRESENT CONDITION OF LAKE WASHINGTON,
W. T. Edmondson.
Verhandlungen Internationale Vereinigung Limnologie, Vol 18, p 284-291, 1972. 5 fig, 11 ref.

Descriptors: *Rehabilitation, *Lake Washington, *Pollution abatement, Washington, Water pollution control, Carbon dioxide, Oxygen, Nutrients, Plankton, Biological communities, Alkalinity, Phosphates, Nitrates, Chlorophyll, Light penetration.
Identifiers: *Sewage diversion.

During the period of 1941-1963 Lake Washington received increasing amounts of effluent from secondary sewage treatment plants. During 1963-1968 the sewage was diverted step-wise, and after February 1968 the effluents were halted. The lake's condition improved rapidly and sensitively with the changes in nutrient input. In the summer of 1971, the transparency has in fact exceeded that observed in 1950, and the hypolimnetic oxygen concentrations toward the end of summer 1969 were close to those of 1950. Thus lake has conformed to predictions. Nevertheless, the lake's condition is not yet identical to that of 1950; in particular plankton has not yet returned to its 1950 condition and appears to be still in transition. Since 1950 the watersheds have changed considerably--large areas have been deforested for urbanization with resultant environmental modifications. Nitrate and alkalinity are now higher than in 1950. However, the lake showed that it was able to accept a rather large increase in nutrients before it deteriorated, and that it could rapidly revert when relieved of that stress. (Jones-Wisconsin)
W75-07304

AN ECOLOGICAL STUDY OF THE KSC TURNING BASIN AND ADJACENT WATERS.
Florida Inst. of Tech., Melbourne.
Available from the National Technical Information Service, Springfield, Va 22161 as N74-26905, $3.75 in paper copy, $2.25 in microfiche. Special Report No 6 to the John F. Kennedy Space Center, Florida, January 1974. 37 p, 23 fig, 2 tab. NASA NGR 10-015-008.

Descriptors: *Baseline studies, *Chemical properties, *Biological properties, *Physical properties, Florida, Hydrogen sulfide, Heavy metals, Benthic fauna, Benthic flora, Biological communities, Bacteria, Sulfates, Bottom sediments, Nutrients, Canals, Dredging, Basins, Borrow pits.
Identifiers: *Kennedy Space Center(Fla), *Turning Basin, Merritt Island(Fla), Banana River(Fla), Indian River(Fla).

This baseline investigation of the conditions existing in the waters and bottoms of the Kennedy Space Center Turning Basin near the Vertical Assembly Building, the borrow pit near Pad 39A and the Barge Canal connecting them, was to determine the various parameters of chemical, biological and microbiological significance as they existed prior to the proposed construction of new checkout facilities on the banks of the Turning Basin. The waters of the Turning Basin, barge canal, and borrow pit are quite similar to those of the Banana River and Indian River. They are, in general, well mixed and well oxygenated. A few deep pockets in the uneven bottom terrain approach anoxic conditions, and a mud sample from one of these areas had a strong hydrogen sulfide odor, indicating that it was anoxic. The absence of response in the tests for heavy metal ions is considered an indication that there was no industrial pollution present. The microbiological tests did not demonstrate E. coli, an indication that there is no waste pollution of these waters. The low diversity and low total populations of the benthic community are characteristic of the recent origin of these waters. (Jones-Wisconsin)
W75-07305

CHLOROPHYLL CONCENTRATIONS, WATER QUALITY, AND NUTRIENT CONCENTRATIONS IN CHEAT LAKE, WEST VIRGINIA,
West Virginia Univ., Morgantown. Dept. of Biology.
J. W. Yahnke.
Proceedings West Virginia Academy of Science, Vol 45, No 2, p 155-163, 1973. 4 fig, 1 tab, 3 ref.

Descriptors: *Chlorophyll, *Lakes, *Nutrients, *West Virginia, Alkalinity, Chemical properties, Backwater, Phosphates, Seasonal, Sulfates, Hydrogen ion concentration.
Identifiers: *Cheat Lake(W Va).

Data on concentrations of primary nutrients and water quality variables in Cheat Lake, West Virginia are provided. Relationships between these variables are examined along with their effects on algal biomass, indicated by concentration of chlorophyll in the algal assemblage. Multivariate discriminant analysis was used to test whether there was a statistically significant difference between stations based upon chemical variables and chlorophyll concentrations. Based on the chemical environment, the lake and its two backwaters constitute three distinct systems, with Morgan Run intermediate between the lake and Ruble's Run. The chemical environment was found much more variable in the backwaters than in the lake due to incursions of lakewater into the backwaters, which were more frequent and more intense in Morgan Run than in Ruble's Run. Chlorophyll concentrations were much greater in the lake than in either of the backwaters; chlorophyll concentrations in both backwaters were similar. Chlorophyll concentrations were greater in the lake due to the greater stability of the chemical environment. Chlorophyll and dissolved phosphate showed marked seasonality falling to their lowest levels following onset of thermal stratification. (Jones-Wisconsin)
W75-07306

THE TROPHIC-DYNAMIC ASPECTS OF ECOSYSTEM MODELS,
Ohio State Univ., Columbus. Dept. of Civil Engineering.
R. M. Sykes.
International Association Great Lakes Research, Proceedings 16th Conference Great Lakes Research, p 977-988, 1973. 3 fig, 3 tab, 11 ref.

Descriptors: *Trophic level, *Ecosystems, *Model studies, Biological communities, Nutrients, Food chains, Distribution, Dominant organisms, Equations, Succession.
Identifiers: Ecosystem trophic-dynamics.

A preliminary critique of the hypothesis that species in natural communities may be partitioned into trophic levels is discussed. The mathematical formulation employed in ecosystem models are statements of the trophic level concept and only indirectly, if at all, are they models of real ecosystems. The analysis of several common formulations of the supposition shows that the law of conservation of mass places certain restrictions upon the biomass in each trophic level and the mass fluxes between levels. These restrictions may be regarded as properties of the trophic level hypothesis. If the behavior of a particular community can be shown to conform to these restrictions, its species may be partitioned into trophic levels. Conversely, if the community's behavior does not conform to the derived restrictions, the trophic level assumption is not applicable. Interesting properties of the hypothesis concern the steady-state distribution of nutrients among the trophic levels. Changes in the nutrient input rate affect principally the top predator and alternate levels beneath it. Because of this, systems of trophic levels have parity. Removal or addition of a top predator level changes the system's parity and, therefore, the responses of all levels beneath. (Jones-Wisconsin)
W75-07307

PLANT NUTRIENTS IN SWEDISH LAKE AND RIVER WATERS,
T. Ahl.
Verhandlungen Internationale Vereinigung Limnologie, Vol 18, p 302-309, 1972. 5 fig, 1 tab, 5 ref.

Descriptors: *Nutrients, *Lakes, *Rivers, Nitrogen, Phosphorus, Municipal wastes, Industrial wastes, Land use, Urbanization, Watersheds(Basins), Agricultural runoff, Fertilizers, Annual.
Identifiers: *Sweden, Lake Vanern(Sweden), Lake Vattern(Sweden), Lake Malaren(Sweden), Lake Hjalmaren(Sweden), River Fyrisan(Sweden), River Skelleftealven(Sweden).

Variations of nitrogen and phosphorus in Swedish lakes and rivers and the nutrient loadings of Lake Vanern, Lake Vattern, Lake Malaren, and Lake Hjalmaren are presented. Many of the rivers flowing to the four large Swedish lakes had, in 1969, a mean concentration of total nitrogen between 1.5 and 4 mg/l, and contained from 0.08 to 0.24 mg/l of total P. There was an increasing N/P ratio in many rivers. The following N yield had been calculated for the catchment areas of Lake Malaren and Lake Hjalmaren, Lake Vanern, and Lake Vattern: 5.8, 3.5, and 2.9 kg/ha year, respectively. The yield of P is 0.50, 0.25, and 0.45 kg/ha year, respectively. These figures include N and P from nearshore municipal and industrial sources. To reach the admissible level, the nutrient load of Lake Malaren and Lake Hjalmaren should be reduced by 80-90% and 70-80%, respectively. With the present rate of urbanization and agricultural land use it is doubtful if this level can be reached. (Jones-Wisconsin)
W75-07308

GAMMARUS PREDATION AND THE POSSIBLE EFFECTS OF GAMMARUS AND CHAOBORUS FEEDING ON THE ZOOPLANKTON COMPOSITION IN SOME SMALL LAKES AND PONDS IN WESTERN CANADA,
Calgary Univ. (Alberta). Dept. of Biology.
R. S. Anderson, and L. G. Raasveldt.
Canadian Wildlife Service Occasional Paper No 18, 1974. 23 p, 4 fig, 7 tab, 51 ref.

Descriptors: *Amphipoda, *Diets, *Crustaceans, Diptera, Larvae, Fish food organisms, Competition, Midges, Canada, Copepods, Predation, Zooplankton.
Identifiers: Gammarus lacustris lacustris, Chaoborus americanus, Alberta, British Columbia.

The food and predatory feeding habits of Gammarus lacustris lacustris, Chaoborus americanus, and copepod species were studied in small lakes and ponds of the Alberta prairies and mountain lakes and ponds in western Alberta and eastern British Columbia to determine their importance in the food web of the aquatic community. Fish introduction may not immediately or permanently affect the population of the food organisms, such as Gammarus, but continuous stocking of large numbers of fish may. Gammarus adults capture and eat a variety of aquatic invertebrates of the same size or smaller with which they commonly co-occur. The intensity of predation probably affects the abundance of certain plankton species; low densities of certain species in oligotrophic lakes were probably due to Gammarus, Chaoborus, and Diaptomus. Experiments and data from 52 aquatic communities suggested that Gammarus predation may be an important reason why it rarely co-occurs with anostracans and why co-occurrence of Gammarus and Chaoborus was uncommon. The relative abundance of these two genera and their diurnal limnetic occurrence in fish-free lakes influenced the abundance of certain aquatic invertebrates and species composition of invertebrate communities. (Buchanan-Davidson-Wisconsin)
W75-07309

CRUSTACEAN PLANKTON COMMUNITIES OF 340 LAKES AND PONDS IN AND NEAR THE NATIONAL PARKS OF THE CANADIAN ROCKY MOUNTAINS,
Calgary Univ., Alberta. Dept. of Biology.
R. S. Anderson.
Journal Fisheries Research Board of Canada, Vol 31, No 5, p 855-869. 1 fig, 8 tab, 43 ref.

Descriptors: *Crustaceans, *Distribution, Zooplankton, Canada, Copepods, Cladocera, Predation, Competition, Salinity, Water temperature, Lakes, Ponds, Surveys, Varieties.
Identifiers: Prairie lakes, Alpine lakes, Alpine ponds, Anostracans, Alberta, British Columbia.

A total of 97 crustacean plankton species were found in 340 lakes and ponds in southern Alberta and southeastern British Columbia, which ranged between 660-2455 m in elevation, had areas of less than 0.1-3940 hectares, were 0.5-136 m deep, and had saline concentrations of 2-29,000 ppm. Of these, 32 were copepods, 50 cladocerans, and 9 anostracans. Predator-prey relationships, competition, permanence of water body, heat, and extremes in salinity were the most important factors influencing distribution of species. Only two species were present in more than half the lakes and ponds. The number of species per community increased with complexity of habitat. The most common and abundant species tolerated a wide range of conditions and showed up to a five-fold variation in generation time. High alpine lakes and ponds and highly saline prairie lakes had few crustacean species but similar genera. (Buchanan-Davidson-Wisconsin)
W75-07310

EH STATUS OF LAKE SEDIMENT-WATER SYSTEMS IN RELATION TO NITROGEN TRANSFORMATIONS,
Wisconsin Univ., Madison. Dept. of Soil Science.
D. A. Graetz, D. R. Keeney, and R. B. Aspiras.
Limnology and Oceanography, Vol 18, No 6, p 908-917, 1973. 2 fig, 5 tab, 33 ref, EPA 16010 EHR.

Descriptors: *Oxidation-reduction potential, *Lake sediments, *Sediment-water interfaces, *Nitrogen, Ammonia, Nitrification, Nitrates, Denitrification, Wisconsin, Cycling nutrients.
Identifiers: Lake Mendota(Wis), Lake Wingra(Wis), Lake Tomahawk(Wis).

The results of this investigation indicate that in situ Eh measurements in sediment-water systems will give a reliable qualitative description of the overall oxidizing-reducing conditions in the systems. Large Plexiglas columns were used to evaluate the changes in the forms and amounts of nitrogen in the bottom waters and sediments of three freshwater lakes during stratified (anoxic) and turnover (aerated) conditions. Sampling ports and permanently placed black Pt electrodes were installed so that water and sediment phases could be monitored Sediment Eh declined rapidly from -150 to -250 mV and remained at this level irrespective of the oxygen concentration in the overlying water. During anoxic conditions, ammonium-nitrogen was released to the water at a relatively constant rate. Aeration affected rapid nitrification. Nitrate in the overlying water decreased with time, possibly due to diffusion into the highly reduced sediment and subsequent denitrification. Although the concentrations of a particular ionic species in these sediments was not enough to have controlling effect on the Eh, the presence of large amounts of oxidized Fe did seem to slow the rate of decrease, as noted in Tomahawk and Mendota sediments. (Jones-Wisconsin)
W75-07311

EFFECT OF MAN'S ACTIVITIES ON DISTRIBUTION OF TRACE ELEMENTS IN SUB-BOTTOM SEDIMENTS OF LAKE GEORGE, NEW YORK,
Rensselaer Polytechnic Inst., Troy, N.Y. Fresh Water Inst.
M. Schoettle, and G. M. Friedman.
Sedimentology, Vol 21, p 473-478, 1974. (FWI Report No 73-14, Contribution No 164 from the Eastern Deciduous Forest Biome, IBP, November 1974). 5 fig, 3 ref. NSF AG-199, AEC 40-193-69.

Descriptors: *Bottom sediments, *Distribution, *Trace elements, Carbon, Copper, Zinc, Chromium, Iron, Sedimentology, Mesotrophy, Oligotrophy, Organic matter.
Identifiers: *Lake George(NY).

To determine the effects of man's activities on the lake bottom sediments of Lake George, cores were removed from the southern mesotrophic basin and from the northern oligotrophic basin. The southern core did not reach relict glacial sediment, indicating a thicker layer of organic rich clay; there the concentration of trace elements was lower, and all the trace elements were concentrated near the top of the core. The increased trace elements in the southern core sediments was not paralleled by an increase in organic carbon. In the northern core, the concentration of trace elements (copper, zinc, chromium, and iron) was almost constant throughout the core with the exception of manganese, which was concentrated near the core surface. Relict glacial clays contained much less organic carbon than modern clays. Man's activities in the watershed surrounding the southern basin caused increased concentrations of the trace elements studied in the newly deposited bottom sediments. The greater concentration of trace elements in the northern basin was probably caused by differences in the bedrock. Organic matter in Lake George sediments was much higher than in Lake Michigan sediments. (Buchanan-Davidson-Wisconsin)
W75-07312

CLEANER, THE LAKE GEORGE MODEL,
Rensselaer Polytechnic Inst., Troy, N.Y. Fresh Water Inst.
R. A. Park, D. Scavia, and N. L. Clesceri.
IBP, Eastern Deciduous Forest Biome Contribution No 186. (Undated). 31 p, 13 fig, 1 tab, 23 ref.

Descriptors: *Ecosystems, *Computer models, Trophic level, Competition, Planning, Nutrients, Lakes, Nannoplankton, Aquatic animals, Fish food organisms, Insects, Aquatic plants, Aquatic algae, Fish, Sediments, Organic matter, Biomass, Nitrogen, Phosphates, Phytoplankton, Zooplankton.
Identifiers: CLEANER Model, Lake George(N.Y.).

CLEANER (Comprehensive Lake Ecosystem Analyzer for Environmental Resources), an ecosystem model based on the International Biological Program model CLEAN, can be used for environmental management. It represents functional physiological and ecologic relationships for major ecosystem compartments (blue-green algae, nannophytoplankton, herbivorous cladocerans, nutrients, net phytoplankton, herbivorous copepods, omnivorous zooplankton, bluegill-like fish, bass-like fish, carp-like fish, benthic insects, decomposers, macrophytes, suspended organic matter, and sedimented organic matter), with disaggregation of trophic levels for study of competition among dissimilar forms. The choice of compartments modeled was based on a consideration of the principal modes of resource utilization and ecologic interaction found in the Lake George, New York ecosystem. It is easily calibrated, has a broad scope, few data requirements, and interactive capability with user-oriented output. It is a one dimensional model without physical mixing terms, but can be coupled with hydrodynamic models. CLEANER can be used to study ecological relationships, guide data collection, provide scenarios, extract relationships between pollutants and ecosystem effects, educate, examine environmental trade-offs and impacts, and determine critical values of pollutants. CLEANER can eventually be combined with other models (WTRSHD, POPUL, and economic models) to predict nutrient loading and tourist response, permitting simulation of long range environmental, social, and economic impacts. (Buchanan-Davidson-Wisconsin)
W75-07313

LAKE KEURUSSELKA, PHYSICAL AND CHEMICAL PROPERTIES OF WATER, PHYTOPLANKTON, ZOOPLANKTON AND FISHES,
Jyvaskyla Univ. (Finland). Dept. of Biology.
P. Eloranta.
Aqua Fennica, p 18-43, 1973. 28 fig, 7 tab, 34 ref.

Descriptors: *Physical properties, *Chemical properties, *Phytoplankton, *Zooplankton, *Fisheries, Biological communities, Domestic wastes, Eutrophication, Humus, Color, Biomass, Limiting factors, Light intensity, Vertical migration.
Identifiers: *Lake Keurusselka(Finland).

The water quality of Lake Keurusselka, Finland is especially affected by the water discharging from bog areas at the lake's northern end and by the domestic wastes from Keuruu and Kolho. Thus, many zones can be delineated in the lake on the basis of the physical and chemical properties. The phytoplankton studies show that great areas of the lake are eutrophic due to domestic waste effluents. The high humic content and the darkness of the waters result in a reduction in the number of species in spite of eutrophication. The zooplankton biomass was very great although most of the species were indicative of oligotrophy or were indifferent to the trophic degree. The large biomass of Limnocalanus macrurus throughout the summer attests to the absence of predators especially vendace. It was difficult to determine clear diurnal vertical migrations of zooplankton as a result of different light intensities. The fish studies indicated great variations in the structure and mean sizes of the fish stock as well as differences in the compositions of the size and age classes in some areas of the lake. (Jones-Wisconsin)
W75-07314

PHOSPHORUS SOURCES AND TRANSPORT IN AN AGRICULTURAL RIVER BASIN OF LAKE ERIE,
Heidelberg Coll., Tiffin, Ohio. Dept. of Biology.
D. B. Baker, and J. W. Kramer.
In: Proceedings 16th Conference Great Lakes Research, p 858-871, 1973. 6 fig, 6 tab, 14 ref.

Descriptors: *Water pollution sources, *Phosphorus, *Agricultural runoff, *River basins, *Lake Erie, Ohio, Eutrophication, Land use, Measurement, Nutrient removal.
Identifiers: Sandusky River(Ohio), Point sources, Diffuse sources.

The contribution of phosphorus from point sources and diffuse sources to the Sandusky River were examined. The mean annual export of total phosphorus from a portion of the Sandusky River Basin was determined to be 454 metric tons. Annual point source inputs of phosphorus within the study area were observed to be 118 metric tons. Assuming all point source phosphorus leaves the system, a minimum diffuse source component of the output would be 336 metric tons or 74% of the total output. This represents a diffuse phosphorus loading coefficient of 103 kg/yr/sq km, a value 2.4 times as large as the 44 kg/yr/sq km which is used to calculate rural runoff in much of Lake Erie Basin. It is suggested that the diffuse source loading coefficient should represent a eutrophication index related to land use. The reduction of phosphorus loading into Lake Erie from diffuse sources will require comprehensive land use planning and implementation in the entire Lake Erie Basin. Reduced values for the diffuse phosphorus loading coefficient, corrected for annual variations in runoff, would provide a measure of progress towards less eutrophic land use management. (Jones-Wisconsin)
W75-07315

PHOSPHORUS DYNAMICS IN PONDS,
Alabama Agricultural Experiment Station, Auburn.
C. E. Boyd.
In: Proceedings of 25th Annual Conference of the Southeastern Association of Game and Fish Commissioners, p 418-426, 1971. 1 fig, 53 ref.

Descriptors: *Phosphorus, *Farm ponds, *Fish farming, Cycles, Absorption, Cycling nutrients, Fertilization, Bottom sediments, Aquatic plants, Food chains.
Identifiers: *Fish ponds.

The sources and sinks of phosphorus are discussed in relation to the fertility of fish ponds. Particular attention is given to phosphorus dynamics, P forms in water, P depletion, phosphorus availability in sediment, utilization of sediment phosphorus by macrophytes, phosphorus accumulation by aquatic plants, trophic transfers, and phosphorus losses. A qualitative model of the phosphorus dynamics in a fish pond is presented. Most ofthe possible inputs, transfers, and losses are likely important in infertile, unfertilized ponds. The sediments probably regulates the phosphorus status of most unfertilized ponds. Furthermore, the native fertility of ponds is directly related to the fertility of underlaying and surrounding soil. Fertilization is probably the only significant phosphorus input to well-managed ponds and where the sediment acts as a phosphorus sink. The use of fertilization in controlling macrophytes by encouraging phytoplankton which release P more quickly is advocated. Phosphorus transfers from water to phytoplankton and finally to fish are of major significance. Considerable P losses from fertilized ponds are due to sediment uptake, seepage, and fish harvest. Once sediments become saturated with phosphorus, equilibrium concentrations will probably increase to a level where the fertilization rates can be lowered. (Jones-Wisconsin)
W75-07316

LAKE TUUSULA DESTRATIFICATION AND AERATION TEST, WINTER 1972/73,
National Water Board of Finland, Helsinki.
J. Keto, and P. Seppanen.
Aqua Fennica, p 126-136, 1973. 6 fig, 3 tab, 4 ref.

Descriptors: *Water pollution treatment, *Destratification, *Aeration, Sewage effluents, Oxygen sag, Hypolimnion, Nutrients, Technology, Agricultural runoff, Phosphorus, Mechanical equipment, Estimated costs, Freezing, Oxygenation, Turbidity, Nitrogen.
Identifiers: *Lake Tuusula(Finland).

Study of the present state and prospects for improvement of Lake Tuusula, Finland indicates that the primary long-term requirement is to stop flow of all sewage and farming effluents into it. Owing to its critical oxygen state in late winter, either the lake must be aerated, or else hypolimnion water rich in nutrients must be drained as a short-term remedy. The typical N and P load is aggrevated by intensive cultivation in the watershed and sewage effluents released directly into the lake. The first aeration test in Lake Tuusula was made in winter 1969-70 by aerating the water and returning it to the desired depth without destratifying the lake. The purpose of the trials described was to test equipment and to prepare cost estimates. As the test proceeded, the vertical differences in oxygen were found to grow; by mid-March the difference of oxygen content between the surface and bottom averaged 0.5 mg oxygen per liter. The test seems to have been very successful in increasing the quantity of oxygen in Lake Tuusula. Even in a very cold winter, the equipment can be expected to sustain a good oxygen state. (Jones-Wisconsin)
W75-07317

SECRETION OF DISSOLVED ORGANIC CARBON AND NITROGEN BY AQUATIC MACROPHYTES,
R. G. Wetzel, and B. A. Manny.
Verhandlungen Internationale Vereinigung Limnologie, Vol 18, p 162-170, 1972. 8 fig, 2 tab, 14 ref.

Descriptors: *Carbon, *Nitrogen, *Aquatic plants, Organic matter, Adsorption, Eutrophication, Metabolism, Submerged plants, Floating plants, Michigan, Hardness(Water).
Identifiers: *Dissolved organic carbon, Dissolved organic matter, Lawrence Lake(Michigan), Najas flexilis, Lemna perpusilla.

Cyclic interactions of dissolved organic matter with inorganic nutrients are important in regulation of pelagic productivity and eutrophication. Preliminary studies examined the dissolved organic carbon and nitrogen components of secreted dissolved organic matter by a submersed and a floating-leaved macrophyte. An ultraviolet combustion technique was used to fractionate the dissolved organic carbon and dissolved organic nitrogen into UV-labile and UV-refractory components. Macrophytic sources of dissolved organic carbon and dissolved organic nitrogen are discussed and compared with estimates of allochthonous sources entering hardwater Lawrence Lake, Michigan. Najas flexilis and axenic Lemna perpusilla were used. The C/N ratio and secreted organic matter was 11:4 for total dissolved organic carbon and dissolved organic nitrogen produced by Najas in bicarbonate buffered media. This ratio was used in estimates of dissolved organic nitrogen produced by submersed littoral flora. Secretion of organic substrates by Lemna perpusilla was very low when the carbon sources was atmospheric carbon dioxide or aqueous carbonic acid. Lemna perpusilla utilizes both atmospheric and aqueous carbon. Decomposition rates of dissolved organic carbon secreted by Lemna were slower and contained more UV-refractory organic compounds than dissolved organic carbon secreted by Najas. (Jones-Wisconsin)
W75-07318

WATER QUALITY, NUTRIENTS, AND NET PLANKTON ANALYSIS OF SUMMERSVILLE LAKE,
West Virginia Univ., Morgantown. Dept. of Biology.
B. D. Lorenz.
Proceedings West Virginia Academy of Science, Vol 45, No 2, p 146-154, 1973. 5 fig, 1 tab, 15 ref.

Descriptors: *Chemical properties, *Nutrients, *Plankton, West Virginia, Nitrates, Phosphates, Reservoirs, Seasonal, Distribution, Copepods, Crustaceans, Rotifers, Algae, Daphnia, Mesotrophy.
Identifiers: *Summersville Lake(West Virginia), *Net plankton.

Concentrations and seasonal variation in the levels of nitrate and molybdate reactive orthophosphate, species composition and seasonal abundance of net plankton populations, and the trophic status of Summerville Lake were determined. Sampling was conducted on a semimonthly basis at a point near the dam. Chemical analysis involved the determination of nitrate and molybdate reactive orthophosphate. Net plankton samples were counted and identified to the species level. The mean concentration of nitrate in the top twenty meters during the stratification period was 2.1 mg/l. The mean concentration of molybdate reactive orthophosphate in the top twenty meters during the same period was 8.5 microgram/l. The net plankton community consisted primarily of copepods, cladocerans, rotifers, and non-filamentous green algae with copepods constituting the major portion. Seasonal alternation was apparent between the cyclopoid copepods, Cyclops bicuspidatus thomasi and Mesocyclops edax, the latter becoming common during early summer. Seasonal succession of four species of Daphnia was also observed during the investigation. Flood conditions resulting from Hurricane Agnes exerted an obvious effect on all biological and chemical parameters investigated. On the basis of nutrient concentrations and species composition, Summersville Lake appears to be mesotrophic. (Jones-Wisconsin)
W75-07319

BIOTIC INTERACTIONS BETWEEN DIFFERENT SPECIES OF ALGAE,

Auburn Univ., Alabama. Dept. of Fisheries and Allied Aquaculture.
C. E. Boyd.

Journal of the Weed Science Society of America, Vol 21, No 1, p 32-37, 1973. 7 tab, 22 ref.

Descriptors: *Algae, *Inhibitors, Chlorophyta, Cyanophyta, Plant growth, Anabaena.
Identifiers: Oscillatoria rubescens, Anabaena flos-aquae, Microcystis aeruginosa, Coccochloris peniocystis.

Circumstantial evidence indicates that inhibitory substances of algal origin likely play an important role in development of algal flora in many natural waters. Influence of one species upon growth of a second species was evaluated by procedure used by Proctor and Vance. Two species were grown in combination and individually. Any significant increase or decrease in growth of one species in a two-species combination, as compared to its growth in a single-species culture, was attributed to influence of the second species. Species of green algae seldom grew as well in two-species cultures with other green algae, or with blue-green algae, as when cultured alone. Several species of algae apparently excreted one or more substances into the medium which inhibited growth of the second species. Inhibition of growth of green algae was particularly great in two-species cultures with the blue-green algae, Oscillatoria rubescens, Anabaena flos-aquae, Microcystis aeruginosa, and Coccochloris peniocystis. Green algae failed to grow at normal rates in media prepared from filtrates of water from ponds which contained blue-green algae blooms. Inhibitory substances are apparently an important factor in development and persistence of relatively unialgal blooms of various species. (Jones-Wisconsin)
W75-07320

SEASONAL DISTRIBUTION, COMPOSITION, AND ABUNDANCE OF ZOOPLANKTON IN ONTARIO WATERS OF LAKE ST. CLAIR,

Lake Erie Fisheries Research Station, Wheatly (Ontario).
J. H. Leach.

International Association Great Lakes Research, Proceedings 16th Conference Great Lakes Research, p 54-64, 1973. 6 fig, 6 tab, 22 ref.

Descriptors: *Seasonal, *Distribution, *Zooplankton, *Lake Ontario, Rotifers, Copepods, Eutrophication, Crustaceans, Biological communities, Daphnia, Protozoa, Varieties, Water temperature.
Identifiers: *Lake St. Clair(Ontario).

Information collected between April and November 1972 on the distribution, abundance, and species composition of zooplankton in the Ontario waters of Lake St. Clair is reported. Zooplankton samples were collected twice monthly by oblique hauls from near bottom to the surface from 12 stations. Rotifers were numerically dominant with Keratella cochlearis and Polyarthra vulgaris the most numerous species. Four cyclopoid and eight calanoid copepods species were found. Cyclops bicuspidatus thomasi was the most abundant copepode, but it was exceeded by Cyclops vernalis in the most eutrophic area. Diaptomus ashlandi and Diaptomus minutus were the dominant calanoid copepods. Twenty-two species of cladocerans were found with Bosmina longirostris and Daphnia retrocurva the most abundant. Mean zooplankton abundance increased from 160 individuals/l in the northwest to almost 1000 individuals/l in the southeastern part of the lake and was related to both temperature and chlorophyll-a content. The distribution of phaeopigments was not significantly related to that of total zooplankton, although a relationship between phaeopigments and both rotifers and cladocerans was evident. In shallow Lake St. Clair it is likely that resuspended sediments are contributing to phaeopigment content. (Jones-Wisconsin)
W75-07321

EFFECT OF INTERACTIONS BETWEEN TEMPERATURE AND NITRATE SUPPLY ON THE CELL-DIVISION RATES OF TWO MARINE PHYTOFLAGELLATES,

California Univ., San Diego, La Jolla. Inst. of Marine Resources.
W. H. Thomas, and A. N. Dodson.

Marine Biology, Vol 24, No 3, p 213-217, 1974. 3 fig, 1 tab, 18 ref. NSF GA 32529X.

Descriptors: *Temperature, *Nitrates, *Reproduction, *Dinoflagellates, Nutrients, Gymnodinium, Marine algae, Growth rates.
Identifiers: Dunaliella.

Because sea water temperature varies horizontally and vertically, interactions between temperature and a limiting nutrient may have important ecological consequences on the growth of marine phytoplankton, Dunaliella and Gymnodinium splendens. Growth curves for Dunaliella showed a lag in cell division at 15C, but exponential growth occurred at 25C the first day following nitrate inoculation. Growth of G. splendens was erratic: exponential growth occurred immediately at 18C, but at 25C growth rates were difficult to calculate at low nitrate levels; nevertheless there was a growth response to nitrate concentration. Half saturation constants and maximum cell division rates were determined at two temperatures for nitrate limited growth of these phytoflagellates, using batch culture techniques. The half saturation constant increased with increasing temperature. Cells growing at a higher temperature have higher requirements for a limiting nutrient. Maximum cell division rates increased with increasing temperature in G. splendens but not in Dunaliella. The results suggest that changes in the half saturation constant with temperature impose a double stress on these phytoplankton when they grow in nitrate-depleted, high-temperature water. The success of dinoflagellates compared to diatoms in offshore water may be due to their vertical motility, to high nitrate and low temperature water. (Buchanan-Davidson-Wisconsin)
W75-07322

SPATIAL AND SEASONAL VARIATIONS IN PHYTOPLANKTONIC PRIMARY PRODUCTION AND BIOMASS IN THE OLIGOTROPHIC LAKE PAAJARVI, SOUTHERN FINLAND,

Helsinki Univ (Finland). Dept. of Botany.
K. Ilmavirta, and A.-L. Kotimaa.

Annales Botanici Fennici, Vol 11, No 2, p 112-120, 1974. 6 fig, 43 ref.

Descriptors: *Primary productivity, *Variability, *Seasonal, *Phytoplankton, Biomass, Lakes, Oligotrophy, Diatoms, Pyrrophyta, Spatial distribution, Dominant organisms.
Identifiers: *Lake Paajarvi(Finland), Cryptophyceae.

The chemistry, primary production, and phytoplankton biomass were studied in the mesohumic, oligotrophic Lake Paajarvi, Finland, from 1970-1971. Chemical variations were negligible. During the ice-free period there was no marked decrease in inorganic carbon and no increase in oxygen saturation, but during thermal stratification the hypolimnetic oxygen concentration decreased slightly, however, the oxygen depth curve remained orthograde. When ice-covered, the oxygen saturation percentage dropped in the 12-14 m layer. When primary production was low during the winter, the coneentration of inorganic carbon was higher and hydrogen ion concentration values lower than in summer. Small phytoplankton biomasses during winter caused low potassium permanganate values and slightly higher nitrogen concentrations. Production decreased during ice cover, and maximum production occurred when stratification was most stable in July and August. The biomass began to increase after the break-up of ice, reaching a maximum in May-July and could be correlated with phytoplankton production. Biomass levels below the ice were low. The dominant phytoplankton group was Pyrrophyta; the Cryptophyceae species, Chroomonas acuta and Cryptomonas erosa most abundant. Seasonal variations of biomass showed that Cryptophyceae dominated in winter, spring, and early summer; Diatomae in autumn; and Chlorophyta and Cyanophyta remained low all year. (Buchanan-Davidson-Wisconsin)
W75-07323

STUDIES ON THE EFFECT OF ETHYLENEDIAMINE TETRAACETIC ACID (EDTA) ON THE METAL NUTRITION OF MARINE ALGAE,

Johns Hopkins Univ., Baltimore, Md. Chesapeake Bay Inst.
W. R. Taylor, and J. L. Taft.

Progress report September 1, 1972 - June 30, 1973. 24 p, 6 fig, 1 tab, 27 ref.

Descriptors: *Chemical reaction, *Acids, *Nutrient requirements, *Marine algae, Chelation, Trace elements, Cations.
Identifiers: *Ethylenediaminetetraacetic acid, Monochrysis lutheri, EDTA.

Algal trace metal requirements and algal growth enhancement with the metal chelator ethylenediaminetetraacetic acid (EDTA) were examined in a chelate-free defined medium, CF-1, using Monochrysis lutheri in axenic batch cultures. This study attempted to test the validity of a previously developed model and to further investigate the role of EDTA in algal nutrition. Results indicate an initial uptake of carbon-14 by the organisms and a subsequent dilution of the label with respect to nitrogen. To test the hypothesis that EDTA incorporation is concentration dependent, a series of duplicate cultures were prepared. Cells grew in all cultures except those containing 1860 micromoles EDTA. The uptake rate was highest during the first two hours. A constant, but lower, uptake rate was observed after 22 and 94 hours. Results indicate that Cu is not toxic to M. lutheri in the complexed form and confirms, for this organism, that growth is enhanced with EDTA when a metal is present in toxic concentrations. The significance of EDTA in algal growth enhancement has been attributed to its metal buffering capacity. However, EDTA induced alterations in cell membrane permeability may cause physiological alterations as yet unreported for planktonic algae. (Jones-Wisconsin)
W75-07324

THE FEEDING BEHAVIOR OF THE COPEPODS IN THE CHESAPEAKE BAY,

Johns Hopkins Univ., Baltimore, Md. Chesapeake Bay Inst.
S. E. Storms, and W. R. Taylor.

Progress report September 1, 1972 - June 30, 1973. 20 p, 6 fig, 1 tab, 8 ref.

Descriptors: *Feeding rates, *Copepods, *Chesapeake Bay, Zooplankton, Digestion, Herbivores, Food webs, Algae.
Identifiers: Acartia tonsa, Acartia clausi, Eurytemora effinis.

Two copepod species, Acartia tonsa and A. clausi, form a major portion of the Chesapeake Bay zooplankton: A. tonsa predominates most of the year, but during the winter months A. clausi also becomes numerous. As herbivores, these copepods represent an important link in the estuarine food web, and because of their abundance, are suspected of being the dominant organisms in their trophic level. Feeding experiments were run on stations along the main channel including one approximately 10 miles from mouth. Ingestion rates for mid-bay stations in December

1972 were highest in the 8-16 micron dimeter range of algal cells, which coincided with the range in which the highest cell concentrations occurred. Acartia tonsa was the only copepod present in the December experiments. Ingestion rates were generally lower during experiments run in February 1973. At the upper bay station, the phytoplankton concentration was greatest in the 6 micron range, and Eurytemora affinis displayed its highest ingestion rate in that size range, although ingestion remained high in the 6-12 micron range. Using regression equation for converting cell volume to cell organic carbon content in phytoplankton other than diatoms, the mean organic carbon ingestion rate was 0.83 micrograms carbon/animal/day. (Jones-Wisconsin)
W75-07325

THE RECYCLING OF PHOSPHORUS IN THE CHESAPEAKE BAY ESTUARY,
Johns Hopkins Univ., Baltimore, Md. Chesapeake Bay Inst.
J. L. Taft, and W. R. Taylor.
Progress report September 1, 1972 - June 30, 1973. 19 p, 6 fig, 1 tab, 9 ref.

Descriptors: *Cycling nutrients, *Phosphorus, *Chesapeake Bay, *Estuaries, Phytoplankton, Zooplankton, Detritus.

The rate of phosphorus exhange between soluble reactive (DIP), particulate, dissolved organic (DOP) and poly (POLY P) phosphorus nutrient pools in Chesapeake Bay was investigated. Preliminary results are reported. Methods used for determination of DIP, DOP, and POLY P were adaptations of those in Strickland and Parsons (1968). Data were collected concurrently for nitrogenous plant nutrients, particulate nitrogen, silicate, alkalinity, oxygen, chlorophyll, temperature, pH, salinity and incident radiation. At three stations in February, experiments were conducted to estimate the rate and nature of phosphorus release by freshly captured zooplankton. Transport coefficients for P-32 into the particulate fraction were computed to eliminate the contribution of detrital phosphorus and to permit comparison with nitrogen transport and carbon assimilation. Two patterns of phosphorus exchange predominate. DIP-32 was assimilated into the particulate fraction at a constant rate. After 23 hours 70% of the P-32 was particulate. At the same station in February, DIP-32 was assimilated rapidly during the first five hours and more slowly thereafter. After 22 hours, 90% of the P-32 was particulate. Only 5% or less of the P-32 was contained in DOP or POLY P fractions at the end of each experiment. (Jones-Wisconsin)
W75-07326

THE NITROGEN-TO-PHOSPHORUS RATIO IN THE PHOTIC ZONE OF THE SEA AND THE ELEMENTAL COMPOSITION OF PLANKTON,
Washington Univ., Seattle, Dept. of Oceanography.
K. Banse.
Available from the National Technical Information Service, Springfield, Va. 22161 as RLO 2225T2618, $4.00 in paper copy; $2.25 in microfiche. (1972), 11 p, 1 fig, 18 ref. AT(45-1)-2225.

Descriptors: *Phosphates, *Nitrogen, *Euphotic zone, *Sea water, Absorption, *Phytoplankton, Nitrogen compounds, Suspended load, Seston, Zooplankton.
Identifiers: Nitrogen:phosphorus ratio.

The ratio of disappearance of inorganic nitrogen and phosphate from the photic layer of sea water cannot be expected to be correlated with the elemental ratio of uptake or assimilation by newly formed phytoplankton or suspended particulate matter. The ratio of nitrogen and phosphate ion disappearance from water represents the net result of removal into various particulate pools (phytoplankton, zooplankton, and non-living particulate matter (seston) and pools of dissolved organie nitrogen and phosphorus, and release from any of these pools into the inorganic pools of these elements. Only some of the rates of these processes can be correlated. The ratio of net removal of the elements from the water may not necessarily represent the ratio of uptake or assimilation by the phytoplankton or flux into the other seston pools. Also the ratio of concentrations of the elements in water mixed into the upper layer from below may shift and change the ratio of net change in the upper layer. (Buchanan-Davidson-Wisconsin)
W75-07328

AMCHITKA BIOENVIRONMENTAL PROGRAM: FRESHWATER VERTEBRATE AND INVERTEBRATE ECOLOGY OF AMCHITKA ISLAND, ALASKA. FINAL SUMMARY REPORT AND PROGRESS REPORT,
Utah State Univ., Logan.
J. M. Neuhold, W. T. Helm, and R. A. Valdez.
Available from the National Technical Information Service, Springfield, Va 22161 as BMI-171-154, $5.45 in paper copy, $2.25 in microfiche. Batelle, Columbus Laboratories, Ohio, Report BMI-171-154, June 1974. 43 p, 13 fig, 11 tab, 33 ref, append.

Descriptors: *Environmental effects, *Nuclear explosions, *Ecosystems, Underground, Food chains, Ponds, Streams, Aquatic animals, Aquatic plants, Salmonids, Sculpin, Pink salmon, Sockeye salmon, Sticklebacks, Primary productivity, Anadramous fish.
Identifiers: *Amchitka Island(Alaska), *Dolly Varden.

Dolly Varden and threespine stickleback were the most abundant and well-distributed of the six freshwater species of fishes encountered on Amchitka. There were small runs of pink salmon and a limited distribution of coho salmon and freshwater Aleutian sculpin. Two underground nuclear tests affected local populations of fishes with deaths in threespine stickleback due to test-induced pressure changes occurring within 2,000 m from site zero (SZ). The only loss of Dolly Varden resulted from watershed and pond alterations that drained streams and ponds. More widespread and persistent effects on freshwater biota resulted from pretest construction and drilling activities. Detectable changes in fish and invertebrate populations resulted in four streams near the four drill sites from increased siltation and from the release of drilling residue. (Katz)
W75-07338

THE FATE AND BEHAVIOR OF CRUDE OIL ON MARINE LIFE,
Massachusetts Univ., Gloucester. Marine Station.
C. S. Yentsch, E. S. Gilfillan, and J. R. Sears.
Available from the National Technical Information Service, Springfield, Va 22161 as AD-786 584, $4.25 in paper copy, $2.25 in microfiche. June 1973. 62 p, 34 fig, 2 tab, 10 ref. DOT-CG-13992-A.

Descriptors: *Crude oil, *Bioindicators, *Respiration, *Monitoring, *Marine animals, *Marine plants, Water quality, Water pollution effects, Metabolism, Oil, Chemical analysis, Mussels, Algae, Salinity, Stress, Animal physiology, Feeding rates, Clams, Emulsions, Dehydration.
Identifiers: *Mytilus edulis, *Carbon budget.

The objective was to evaluate the feasibility of using physiological responses of marine organisms as quantitative indicators of low petroleum hydrocarbon concentrations. Results indicate that physiological responses of selected test organisms to low level petroleum concentrations are not suitable for monitoring purposes. None of the crude oils used were acutely toxic to selected marine plants and animals, but responses of the animals indicate that sea-water extracts of crude oils can have severe metabolic effects. Plants were found to be more resistant to oil pollution than animals. (Katz)
W75-07339

STUDY OF IMPORTANCE OF BACKWATER CHUTES TO A RIVERINE FISHERY,
Southern Illinois Univ., Carbondale. Fisheries Research Lab.
H. L. Schramm, Jr., and W. M. Lewis.
Available from the National Technical Information Service, Springfield, Va 22161 as AD-786 544, $6.25 in paper copy, $2.25 in microfiche. Prepared for Army Engineer Waterways Experiment Station, August 1974. 144 p, 3 fig, 13 tab, 153 ref.

Descriptors: *Reviews, *Rivers, Physiochemical properties, Fishes, River systems, *Mississippi River, *Backwater, *Environmental effects, Mississippi River Basin, Turbidity, Dissolved oxygen, Channels, Freshwater fish, Benthos, Bass, Catfishes, Sunfishes.
Identifiers: *Environmental effects, *Side channels.

A comprehensive review was made of the literature to determine the environmental impact of the loss of backwater areas in connection with proposed changes in the channel of the Mississippi River between St. Louis, Missouri, and Cairo, Illinois. The review covered two general areas: literature pertaining to the physical, chemical and biotic factors of larger rivers, and literature pertaining to the biology of the fishes recorded as present in the section of concern in the Mississippi River. Only a limited amount of data has been published. The direct effects of the physiochemical factors (current, turbidity, substrate, and dissolved oxygen were examined. Based on the literature, it was concluded that extra-channel areas provided the most favorable conditions of existence for the fishes recorded as present in the study area. (Extra-channel areas include the complex of habitats classified as side-channels, river lakes and ponds, and sloughs.) Identification is made of those specific fish that would and those that would not be affected by the hypothetical physiochemical conditions that would prevail following the loss or alteration of the extra-channel areas. (Katz)
W75-07340

RESPONSE OF SALT MARSH BIVALVES TO ENRICHMENT WITH METAL-CONTAINING SEWAGE SLUDGE AND RETENTION OF LEAD, ZINC, AND CADMIUM BY MARSH SEDIMENTS,
Marine Biological Lab., Woods Hole, Mass. Boston Univ. Marine Program.
I. Valiela, M. D. Banus, and J. M. Teal.
Environmental Pollution, Vol 7, No 2, p 149-157, September 1974. 1 fig, 6 tab, 21 ref.

Descriptors: *Lead, *Cadmium, *Zinc, *Sewage sludge, *Salt marshes, *Mussels, Heavy metals, Tidal marshes, Mollusks, Shellfish, Benthos, Oysters, Commercial shellfish, Environmental effects, Growth rates, Fertilizers, Absorption, Water pollution effects.
Identifiers: *Mercenaria mercenaria, *Crassostrea virginica, *Modiolus demissus, Bioaccumulation.

Growth in Mercenaria mercenaria and Crassostrea virginica, bivalves found in tidal creeks in salt marshes on the coast of the NW Atlantic, was not affected by experimental additions of metal-containing sewage sludge and urea fertilizers to salt marsh plots. Modiolus demissus, a mussel inhabiting the marsh surface itself, did grow better under the same fertilizer treatments. All three species of shellfish showed no increases in lead or zinc contents, but all showed increased cadmium contents related to the sludge fertilizer treatments. Increases in zinc, and particularly in cadmium, but not lead, were detected in the creek bottom detritus downstream from the plots. The surface

sediment of the marsh plots shows significant accumulation of all three metals. The calculation of input-output budgets shows that lead was trapped in the sediments with virtually no losses to deeper waters. Zinc and cadmium also accumulated in the sediments but there is some transport away from the salt marsh surface, especially in the case of cadmium. (Katz)
W75-07341

FORMALIN AS A THERAPEUTANT IN FISH CULTURE,
Bureau of Sport Fisheries and Wildlife, La Crosse, Wis. Fish Control Lab.
R. A. Schnick.
Available from the National Technical Information Service, Springfield, Va 22161 as PB-237 198, $5.75 in paper copy, $2.25 in microfiche. Fish and Wildlife Service, April 1973. 131 p, 7 tab, 222 ref.

Descriptors: *Aquiculture, *Fungicides, *Fish eggs, *Fish diseases, Fish parasites, Pesticides, Standards, Toxicity, Pesticide residues, Trematodes, Crustaceans, *Reviews, *Bibliographies.
Identifiers: *Formalin.

Formalin is the most effective and widely used therapeutant and prophylactant for the control of fungus on fish eggs and external parasites on fish. It has not been registered for these uses by the regulatory agencies. Fish culturists cannot legally use this chemical on fish consumed for food. This paper was written to support the initiation of the registration procedure for formalin. Literature from 1909 was analyzed for information on the efficacy, toxicity and residues of formalin in connection with its use in the aquatic environment. There is evidence that formalin is safe for use on some marine and many freshwater fishes and is effective in controlling and preventing fungus on fish eggs and certain external parasites on fish. Used properly, formalin is not a hazard to applicators nor harmful to fish. A method is available to detect residues in fish. (Katz)
W75-07342

5D. Waste Treatment Processes

BACTERIAL DEGRADATION OF ARYLSULFONATES IN TREATMENT OF WASTEWATER,
Maryland Univ., College Park. Dept. of Microbiology.
T. M. Cook, K. I. Braunschweiger, and L. A. More.
Available from the National Technical Information Service, Springfield, Va 22161, as PB-241 280, $4.75 in paper copy, $2.25 in microfiche. Maryland Water Resources Research Center, College Park, Technical Report No 31, (1975). 73 p, 14 fig, 3 tab, 24 ref, 5 append. OWRT A-020-MD(1), 14-31-0001-3520.

Descriptors: *Detergents, *Biodegradation, *Waste water treatment, *Linear alkylate sulfonates, *Maryland, Respiration, Bacteria, Sewage treatment, *Biological treatment, Sulfonates, Alkylbenzene sulfonates, Pseudomonas.
Identifiers: River die-away test, Bacterial respiration, *Patuxent River(Md), Arylsulfonates, Moraxella species.

The river die-away test was used to study biodegradation of linear alkylbenzene sulfonates (LAS) detergents in natural waters. Samples of water from the Patuxent River at various seasons of the year contained organisms capable of degrading sodium dodecylbenzene sulfonate (DBS). Two pure cultures of LAS degraders were isolated; the culture from sewage was tentatively identified as a moraxella species and the culture from river water as a Pseudomonas species. The two cultures were shown to produce greater than 95% degradation of LAS added to culture media. Both cultures degraded dodecylbenzene sulfonate; they were also able to degrade the non-aromatic surfactant, sodium dodecylsulfate, but not the branched-chain ABS detergent. The two LAS degraders produced significant growth with butyl-, pentyl-, hexyl- and heptylbenzene sulfonate; colorimetric tests showed degradation of the octyl-, dodecyl-, tridecyl-, tetradecyl- and pentadecylbenzene sulfonates. In the shake-flask procedure using a medium containing yeast extract and LAS, the detergent was degraded by 96% in 8 days. In a mineral salts medium with LAS (10 microgram/ml), degradation of 75% or more occurred in 2 days. Cells grown on acetate or glutamate oxidized hexylbenzene sulfonate or DBS at rates comparable to that of cells grown on hexylbenzene sulfonate. With hexylbenzene sulfonate as substrate there was no detectable accumulation in the medium of either sulfite or sulfate. Cells grown on hexylbenzene sulfonate showed oxygen uptake with hexylbenzene sulfonate of DBS, but not catechol. Comparison of the amount of growth produced on hexylbenzene sulfonate and acetate indicated a 1 to 2 mole relationship.
W75-06852

A NOVEL BLEACHING PROCESS FOR REMOVAL OF COLOR AND TOXICITY FROM BLEACH PLANT EFFLUENT,
MacMillan Bloedel Ltd., Vancouver (British Columbia).
W. A. Moy, K. Sharpe, and R. G. Betz.
Canadian Pulp and Paper Association, Technical Section, Air and Stream Improvement Conference, Montreal, September 23-25, 1974, Preprinted Proceedings (Montreal, P.Q.), p 75-80, 11 tab, 23 ref.

Descriptors: *Color, *Toxicity, *Bleaching wastes, *Pulp wastes, Water pollution sources, Industrial wastes, Wastes, Water consumption, Pulp and paper industry, Water costs, Costs, Steam, Chemicals, Effluents, Sodium compounds, Calcium compounds, Water conservation, Chlorine compounds, Chlorine, *Waste water treatment.
Identifiers: Semibleached pulp, Kraft pulp, Newsprint, Sodium hypochlorite, Calcium hypochlorite.

A bleaching sequence capable of producing semibleached kraft pulp suitable for use in newsprint is discussed. It includes a sodium hypochlorite first stage, followed by a mild caustic extraction, and a calcium hypochlorite third stage. Through use of this sequence, instead of the more typical chlorine/hot caustic extraction stages, effluent color was reduced by 90%. The effluent was nontoxic, and fresh water usage was reduced. Improvement of pulp yield and reduced water and steam costs are said to offset increased chemical cost. The modified bleaching sequence was a superior alternative to other systems for effluent color reduction. (Hansen-IPC)
W75-06861

THE IMPLEMENTATION OF A POLLUTION CONTROL SYSTEM AT THE ONTARIO PAPER COMPANY LIMITED,
J. T. Charlton, W. F. Fell, and A. Y. Yau.
Canadian Pulp and Paper Association, Technical Section, Air and Stream Improvement Conference, Montreal, September 23-25, 1974, Preprinted Proceedings (Montreal, P.Q.), p 47-53, 3 fig, 1 tab, 2 ref.

Descriptors: Pollution abatement, *Sulfite liquors, *Waste water treatment, *Pulp wastes, Industrial wastes, Water pollution sources, Foaming, Color, *Biochemical oxygen demand, *Evaporators, Water quality control, *Incineration, Wastes, Capital costs, Costs, Pollutants, Treatment facilities, *Canada.
Identifiers: Copeland recovery process, Eimco belt washers.

A system was designed and installed at Ontario Paper Co. Ltd.'s Thorold, Ontario, mill to collect and incinerate waste liquors from the sulfite pulping and chemical recovery operations. The sulfite liquor recovery system employs horizontal-type belt washers (also known as 'Extractors') supplied by Eimeo Envirotech Ltd. (Toronto), and the incineration system consists of evaporators, a Copeland fluidized-bed reactor, and auxiliary equipment. The primary purpose of the $8,270,000 system is to eliminate the foam and color originating at this mill and to reduce the 5-day BOD loading. Although these objective have not yet been completely reached, there has been a significant improvement. Some light foam still forms in the receiving stream but does not persist. It probably is caused by the remaining spent sulfite liquor not yet processed. The 5-day BOD in the evaporator condensate averages about 500 mg/liter. The BOD remaining in the effluent is, however, still 40% of that generated in the pulping process, its bulk being spent sulfite liquor not yet recovered or burned. The problem of evaporator instability when using mixed alcohol plant effluent and spent sulfite liquor needs to be solved before the objectives of BOD reduction can be reached. (Witt-IPC)
W75-06862

ORGANIZING FOR TODAY'S EFFLUENT CONTROL NEEDS,
Intercontinental Pulp Co. Ltd., Prince George (British Columbia).
G. A. Decker, and S. Louie.
Canadian Pulp and Paper Association, Technical Section, Air and Stream Improvement Conference, Montreal, September 23-25, 1974, Preprinted Proceedings (Montreal, P.Q.), p 133-137, 5 fig, 2 tab, 2 ref.

Descriptors: *Water pollution control, *Pulp wastes, *Bleaching wastes, *Air pollution, Water reuse, Water pollution sources, Industrial wastes, Sewage treatment, Biological treatment, Pulp and paper industry, Odor, Labor, Personnel, Education, Operation and maintenance, Monitoring, Effluents, Oxidation, *Waste water treatment, *Canada.
Identifiers: Evaporator condensates, Turpentine, Black liquor, Precipitators, Kraft mills.

Antipollution systems and equipment installed at Intercontinental Pulp Co.'s mill in British Columbia are described briefly. The mill, a joint venture by Canadian Forest Products of Vancouver, British Columbia, the Reed Paper Group of London, England, and Feldmuehle AG. of West Germany, produces about 600 tons/day of kraft pulp. In-plant measures include equipment for maximum reuse of process waters, fiber and chemical reclaim systems, and monitoring of effluent quality. Mill and bleach plant effluents are subjected to secondary treatment by a biological process. Air pollution control equipment includes a pre-oxidizer scrubber for foul evaporator condensates, turpentine decanter underflow and blow line vents; a weak black liquor oxidation system in conjunction with an odor control unit for gases scrubbed from bleach plant effluents and a wet bottom precipitator on the rocovery stack. It is emphasized that systems such as these will not produce the desired results unless they are operated properly, and instances of operator failure are cited. The steps taken to educate employees in the correct use of the facilities are discussed. (Hansen-IPC)
W75-06863

PROBLEMS OF WASTE WATER PURIFICATION IN DIFFERENT PH RANGES (PROBLEME DER ABWASSERREINIGUNG IN UNTERSCHIEDLICHEN PH-BEREICHEN),
C. H. Mobius.
Translation available from IPC, Appleton at $7.50. English translation of Wochenblatt fur Papierfabrikation, Vol 102, No 23/24, p 897-900, December 15, 1974. 2 fig, 26 ref.

Descriptors: *Waste water treatment, *Pulp wastes, *Flocculation, *Hydrogen ion concentration, Zeta potential, Coagulation, Neutralization, Colloids, Acidity, Alkalinity, Organic matter, Clays, Montmorillonite, Biological treatment, Water purification, Water pollution sources, Water pollution treatment, Pulp and paper industry, Wastes, Industrial wastes, Waste treatment, Water quality control, Effluents.
Identifiers: Alum, Alkaline sizing, Paper coating effluents, Paper sizing effluents.

This discussion is restricted to chemical flocculation. The effect of pH on zeta-potential is discussed, as well as coagulation by charge neutralization. The destabilization of protective colloids (e.g., starch) is considered. Acid effluents (pH 4.5-6.5) are easily coagulated. Neutral effluents (pH 6.5-7.5) frequently occur in paper and board manufacture and can be treated like acid effluents, using more alum. Basic effluents (pH over 7.5) arise from coating operations and from alkaline sizing. These can not always be coagulated simply with alum; the difficulty here is frequently the presence of protective colloids, and special techniques are discussed. Dissolved organic materials can be partly removed by addition of absorptive substances like sodium montmorillonite, but further biological or physical purification treatments are usually needed. (Ward-IPC)
W75-06864

A PRELIMINARY REVIEW OF ANALYTICAL METHODS FOR THE DETERMINATION OF SUSPENDED SOLIDS IN PAPER INDUSTRY EFFLUENTS FOR COMPLIANCE WITH EPA-NPDES PERMIT TERMS,
National Council of the Paper Industry for Air and Stream Improvement, Inc., New York.
For primary bibliographic entry see Field 5A.
W75-06865

THE TREATMENT OF EFFLUENT IN THE PAPER INDUSTRY. SOME CONSIDERATIONS ON THE EQUIPMENT USED,
H. Verbrugge.
Translation available from IPC, Appleton at $7.50. English translation of La Technique de l'Eau, No 310, p 23-26, October, 1972. 13 fig, 1 tab.

Descriptors: *Pulp wastes, *Waste water treatment, Equipment, *Treatment facilities, Sewage treatment, Screens, Pulp and paper industry, Activated sludge, Biological treatment, Aeration, Aerated lagoons, Sludge treatment, Dewatering, Filtration, Centrifugation, Incineration, Settling basins, Reviews, Translations.
Identifiers: Sand remover, Surface aerators, Rotary brush, Grab screen.

The principal processes and equipment used in treating paper industry effluents are reviewed. Both primary treatment (screening, sand removal, primary settling) and secondary treatment (activated sludge treatment with aeration plus secondary settling, aerated lagoon treatment, and sludge thickening, filtration, centrifugation, and incineration) and covered. Detailed diagrams and illustrations are included of a rectangular sand remover, grab screen, primary settling tanks, an activated sludge system, aerated lagoon treatment, floating surface aerator, vortex surface aerator, rotary brush, secondary settling tank, and a sludge thickener. (Speckhard-IPC)
W75-06866

PRIMARY EFFLUENT TREATMENT AT NORTHWOOD (PULP AND TIMBER LTD.),
Northwood Pulp and Timber Ltd., Prince George (British Columbia).
W. G. Lim.
Canadian Pulp and Paper Association, Technical Section, Air and Stream Improvement Conference, Montreal, September 23-25, 1974, Preprinted Proceedings (Montreal, P.Q.), p 109-111, 1 fig, 1 tab.

Descriptors: *Waste water treatment, *Pulp wastes, *Treatment facilities, *Sewage treatment, Waste treatment, Pulp and paper industry, Water purification, Filters, Sludge, Sludge disposal, Performance, Pumping, Operations, Water pollution sources, Filtration, Industrial wastes, Design criteria, Industrial plants, Canada.
Identifiers: Eimco clarifier, Eimcobelt gravity filters, Rietz sludge press.

A bleached softwood kraft mill in British Columbia started up in mid-1966 with only secondary effluent treatment. Despite the design features which were incorporated in the mill to minimize losses to the sewers, secondary treatment alone was inadequate, and it was necessary to add primary treatment facilities. The design criteria and physical layout of this system, which includes pumping station, Eimeo clarifier, Eimcobelt gravity filters, Rietz sludge press, and sludge disposal, are described. Performance data and operating problems, along with their solutions, are given. (Hansen-IPC)
W75-06868

OPERATING PERFORMANCE OF WASTE TREATMENT SYSTEMS FOR A LINERBOARD MILL,
A. Graham.
Canadian Pulp and Paper Association, Technical Section, Air and Stream Improvement Conference, Montreal, September 23-25, 1974, Preprinted Proceedings (Montreal, P.Q.), p 63-70, 3 fig.

Descriptors: *Waste water treatment, *Pulp wastes, *Treatment facilities, *Operations, Sewage treatment, Aerated lagoons, Biochemical oxygen demand, Suspended solids, Industrial wastes, Water pollution control, Waste treatment, Pulp and paper industry, Water pollution sources, Water pollution treatment, Performance, *Canada.
Identifiers: Linerboard, Board mills, Kraft mills.

An effluent treatment system installed at an integrated high-yield kraft linerboard mill is described in detail. It provides for primary and secondary treatment of combined effluents, followed by final treatment in aerated lagoons. Data for 18 months of operation are given. BOD reduction has averaged about 75%, and suspended solids reduction about 25%. (Hansen-IPC)
W75-06869

TOXICITY REMOVAL FROM KRAFT BLEACHERY EFFLUENT USINAG A TWO-STAGE ACTIVATED SLUDGE SYSTEM,
Environmental Protection Service, Burlington, (Ontario). Wastewater Technology Centre.
Canadian Pulp and Paper Association, Technical Section, Air and Stream Improvement Conference, Montreal, September 23-25, 1974, Preprinted Proceedings (Montreal, P.Q.), p 125-131. 4 fig, 5 tab, 6 ref.

Descriptors: *Bleaching wastes, *Activated sludge, *Toxicity, *Waste water treatment, Water pollution sources, Industrial wastes, Pulp and paper industry, Waste treatment, Rainbow trout, Fish, Biochemical oxygen demand, Legislation, Pulp wastes, Wastes, Pilot plants, Treatment facilities, Water quality, Water pollution treatment, Biological treatment, Solids contact processes, *Canada.

A pilot-scale two-stage activated sludge system was used to treat kraft bleachery effluent at Eddy Forest Products Ltd., Espanola, Ontario. For comparison, a conventionally loaded single-stage system was operated in parallel with the two-stage system. Emphasis was placed on assessment and comparison of the capabilities of the activated sludge systems for the reduction of acute toxicity to juvenile rainbow trout. Process efficiencies were determined and engineering design parameters developed. The pilot-scale results showed that the two-stage system was capable of greater toxicity reduction than the single-stage system. At similar volumetric loadings the two-stage system also provided greater BOD reduction than the single-stage system. Effluents from neither system met toxicity requirements of the 1971 Canadian Pulp and Paper Effluent Regulations, but areas where further research is appropriate are identified, and recommendations for additional work are given. (Hansen-IPC)
W75-06871

OPERATING CHARACTERISTICS OF A PAPER MILL PRIMARY CLARIFIER,
Scott Paper Co., Westbrook, Maine. S. D. Warren Div.
Canadian Pulp and Paper Association, Technical Section, Air and Stream Improvement Conference, Montreal, September 23-25, 1974, Preprinted Proceedings (Montreal, P.Q.), p 31-35. 7 fig.

Descriptors: *Pulp wastes, *Treatment facilities, Pulp and paper industry, *Operations, Waste water treatment, Water purification, Water pollution sources, Industrial wastes, Wastes, Waste treatment, Sludge, Settling velocity, Suspended solids, Chemical precipitation, Flocculation, Effluents, Industrial plants, Pollution abatement, Water pollution control, *Maine, New England.
Identifiers: Dorr-Oliver clarifier, *Presumpscot River(Maine).

The treatment of effluents from S. D. Warren Co.'s Westbrook, Maine, integrated pulp and paper mill is discussed. The mill produces about 300 tons/day of bleached kraft pulp and 600 tons/day of coated printing and specialty papers. Effluents from the paper mill are treated in a 180-ft diameter Dorr-Oliver primary clarifier with a clay and sand bottom. It is designed to treat 15 million gal/day and is presently treating 9 million gal/day with a surface settling rate of 354 gal/sq ft/day, a weir overflow rate of 16,000 gal/ft/day, a retention time of 8.5 hr, and sludge removal rate of 540 gal/min at an average consistency of 2.5-3.0% solids. Treatment efficiencies have averaged better than 99% removal of settleable solids, and 85% removal of suspended solids. Flocculants have been evaluated, and when used, have increased the suspended solids removal efficiency to as much as 99%. The fiber content of the sludge is presently 40-45%. Major problems encountered have been associated with sludge withdrawal, principally due to the size and location of the sludge lines. Effluents are presently being discharged to the Presumpscot River, but will eventually be treated, in compliance with current regulations, in an activated sludge secondary treatment plant now under construction. (Witt-IPC)
W75-06872

DEWATERING OF EXCESS ACTIVATED SLUDGE AT THE SYASYA INTEGRATED PULP AND PAPER MILL (OBEZVOZHIVANIE IZBYTOCHNOGO ILA NA SYAS'KOM KOMBINATE),
Syasskii Lesokhimicheskii Kombinat (USSR).
Bumazhnaya Promyshlennost, No 11, p 23-24, November, 1974.

Descriptors: *Activated sludge, *Dewatering, Treatment facilities, *Sludge treatment, Coagulation, Lime, Filtration, Filters, Fertilizers, Crops, Industrial wastes, Wastes, Sludge disposal, *Waste water treatment, Water pollution sources, Water pollution control, Pollutants, Aeration, Mixing, Foreign countries, Landfills.
Identifiers: Ferric chloride, Vacuum filters, USSR.

A description is given of the sludge dewatering process at the Syasya pulp and paper mill. Excess sludge from the aeration tank, at a concentration of 5-7 g/liter, is transferred to two thickeners

where it is concentrated within 8-12 hr to 20-30 g/liter. The sludge is then transferred to an aerated blow-off chamber, where it remains 2-3 hr. The sludge is then pumped to a pressure tank and then to a mixing chamber where it is treated with coagulants (ferric chloride and lime). It is then filtered on vacuum filters. The dewatered sludge, containing 80-83% water, is disposed of in a landfill or used for fertilization of agricultural crops. The installation is not yet fully completed (it lacks a blender tank, primary sedimentation tanks, etc.), so that it is presently overloaded. However, its general performance has been satisfactory, and its efficiency should improve with some suggested modifications. (Stapinski-IPC)
W75-06875

INTEGRATED PURIFICATION OF EFFLUENTS FROM VISCOSE RAYON PRODUCTION USING ION EXCHANGE AND ELECTRODIALYSIS (K VOPROCU O KOMPLEKSNOI OCHISTKE STOCHNYKH VOD VISKOZNYKH PROIZVODSTV S PROMOSHCHIYU IONNOGO OBMENA I ELEKTRODIALIZA),
Vsesoyuznyi Nauchno-Issledovatelskii Institut Iskusstvennogo Volokna, Leningrad (USSR). Leningradskii Filial.
Khimicheskie Volokna, No 4, p 70-71, 1974.

Descriptors: *Waste water treatment, *Ion exchange, *Electrodialysis, Textiles, Industrial wastes, Water pollution sources, Suspended solids, Gases, Cation adsorption, Calcium, Iron, Zinc, Metals, Sodium, Alkali metals, Alkaline earth metals, Organic matter, Sodium sulfate, Waste treatment, Wastes, Water pollution control, Pollution abatement, Water purification, Separation techniques, Water quality control, Sulfates.
Identifiers: *Viscose rayon, *USSR.

On the basis of an intensive study of the effluents from viscose rayon production, an integrated 5-stage process is recommended for the purification of such effluents. The acidic wastes are subjected to mechanical purification to remove suspended particles and dissolved gases, then are purified with ion-exchange resins. Zn, Ca, Fe, and other polyvalent cations are removed first. Resins in the H form are then used to remove Na ions. The third stage involves the removal of sulfate ions, the fourth stage the removal of organic material. The last stage is to remove those Na ions which are introduced during the regeneration of anion-exchange resins. A mixture of the eluates from the 2nd, 3rd, and 5th stages is sent to a unit for the recovery of sodium sulfate by electrodialysis. The first-stage eluate is used for Zn recovery, while the fourth-stage eluate is sent to biochemical purification. (Chern-IPC)
W75-06876

TWO-STAGE BIOLOGICAL PURIFICATION OF EFFLUENTS (L'EPURATION BIOLOGIQUE DES EAUX RESIDUAIRES EN DEUX PHASES),
Informations Chimie, No 112, p 75-79, October, 1972. 2 fig, 1 tab.

Descriptors: *Pulp wastes, *Biological treatment, *Treatment facilities, Bacteria, Fungi, Protozoa, Construction costs, Operating costs, Electric power demand, Flocculation, Suspended solids, Phosphates, Fibers(Plant), Biochemical oxygen demand, Water pollution sources, Wastes, Industrial wastes, Water pollution control, Pollution abatement, Foreign countries, Europe, Sedimentation, *Waste water treatment.
Identifiers: *Attisholz activated sludge process, Pollution load.

A description is given of the Attisholz system, developed by the Swiss Attisholz mill, for the biological purification of effluents. The system is based on different requirements of bacteria and fungi on one hand, and of protozoa on the other. In the first stage, a bacterial sludge is used, while a protozoan sludge used in the second stage serves to eliminate the bacteria and the remaining organic matter. The advantages of the process are compactness of the installation, low construction and operating costs, insensitivity to variations in the pollution load, low power consumption (especially at high degrees of purification), and considerable reduction of excess activated sludge. If necessary, the biological treatment is followed by chemical treatment to flocculate the remaining suspended solids and insoluble phosphates. The Attisholz process was studied at the Biberist mill under pilot-plant conditions in 1966, and an industrial installation was put into operation in 1967 for treatment of papermaking and paper coating effluents. In this installation (which is described) a third biological stage has been added, as well as a presedimentation tank for the recovery of fibers. The 5-day BOD reduction exceeds 90%. (Stapinski-IPC)
W75-06877

ENVIRONMENTAL PROTECTION AND ITS EFFECTS ON PRODUCTION CONDITIONS IN THE PULP AND PAPER INDUSTRY (UMWELTSCHUTZ UND SEINE AUSWIRKUNGEN AUF DIE PRODUKTIONSBEDINGUNGEN IN DER),
Allgemeine Papier-Rundschau, No 42, p 1174, 1176, 1178, 1180, 1182-1183, October 21, 1974.

Descriptors: *Pulp and paper industry, *Water reuse, *Industrial production, Corrosion, Deposition(Sediments), Recirculated water, Impaired water quality, Water conservation.

This discussion on environmental problems in the pulp and paper industry attempts to point out the need for a greater degree of closing of circulation systems and to examine, in particular, the complex nature of resulting deposit and corrosion problems. Processes leading to deposits and corrosion are considered along with counter measures. Emphasis is on the need for avoiding a one-sided approach in dealing with such problems. Only intensive cooperation of all the participants and consideration of all the factors involved will give an optimum solution. Precise recognition of the problems involved is especially important. (Speckhard-IPC)
W75-06878

ZURN-ATTISHOLZ SYSTEM IS CHOSEN BY WAUSAU (PAPER MILLS CO.) FOR PULP MILL EFFLUENT.
Paper Trade Journal, Vol 159, No 4, p 29-30, January 27, 1975. 1 fig, 1 tab.

Descriptors: *Treatment facilities, *Waste water treatment, *Pulp wastes, Water pollution sources, Industrial wastes, Wastes, Waste treatment, Sludge treatment, Sludge disposal, Activated sludge, Biological treatment, Water purification, Pollution abatement, Water pollution control, Effluents, Dewatering, Filtration, Landfills, Wisconsin.
Identifiers: *Zurn-Attisholz activated sludge process, *Wisconsin River(Wis.), Magnefite pulping, Vacuum filters.

A $4 million effluent treatment facility featuring a paper mill effluent clarifier and a Zurn-Attisholz (2-stage high-rate activated slude) system for treating pulp mill effluents will be installed by Wausau Paper Mills Co., Brokaw, Wis. The company produces 330 tons/day of fine papers and 186 tons/day of Magnefite hardwood pulp. The pH of the pulp mill sewer will be adjusted and the flow screened and pumped to the Zurn-Attisholz system. Sludge recycle equipment will be identical for the first and second stages. Sludge pits at the settler inlet will collect part of the sludge which is pumped to the aeration tank by air lifts; sludge from the main part of the tank will be removed by a suction scraper traveling bridge mechanism. Combined primary and secondary sludge will be dewatered on two vacuum filters, and filtrate and thickener overflow is piped to the Zurn-Attisholz influent sump. Filter cake will be disposed of as landfill, and effluent flows discharged to the Wisconsin River. (Sykes-IPC)
W75-06879

THE SSVL (STIFTELSEN SKOGSINDUSTRIERNAS VATTEN OCH LUFTVARDSFORSKING) ENVIRONMENTAL CARE PROJECT (OF THE SWEDISH FOREST PRODUCTS INDUSTRY): TECHNICAL SUMMARY.
Stiftelsen Skogsindustriernas Vatten och Luftvardsforsking (Stockholm), 1974, 286 p, 3 appendices.

Descriptors: *Pollution abatement, *Europe, *Pulp and paper industry, Water pollution control, Research and development, Air pollution, Foreign research, Foreign countries, Evaporation, Discharge(Water), Accidents, Sludge treatment, Sludge disposal, Chemical degradation, Biological treatment, Water pollution sources, Industrial wastes, Wastes, Water quality control, Waste treatment, Waste water treatment, Pulp wastes, Sulfite liquors.
Identifiers: *Forest products industry, Stiftelsen Skogsindustriernas Vatten och Luftvardsforsking, Pulp washing, Pulp screening, Bleach plants, Condensates, Kraft pulp mills, Sulfite pulp mills, Neutral sulfite semichemical pulp mills, Fiberboard mills.

During 1970-73, a survey of environmental pollution loads discharged by the Swedish pulp, paper, and fiberboard industries (which revealed the magnitude of the abatement problem) was followed by a review of available control technologies and several sub-project research and development studies on promising and economical emission reduction approaches. These investigations, summaries of which are appended, dealt with closure of paper mill water circuits and of the cooking-washing-screening system, the operation of bleach plants, evaporation and treatment of condensates, temporary and accidential discharges, sludge handling and disposal, biological and chemical effluent treatments, and air pollution problems. Water and atmospheric quality protection measures recommended for bleached and unbleached kraft, sulfite, and neutral sulfite semichemical pulp mills, as well as for paper and fiberboard mills, are discussed in the light of the various findings. (Brown-IPC)
W75-06880

MECHANISM OF LIGNIN REMOVAL IN ACTIVATED SLUDGE TREATMENT OF PULP MILL EFFLUENTS,
Toronto Univ. (Ontario).
Water Research, Vol 8, No 11, p 857-862, November, 1974. 5 fig, 3 tab, 4 ref.

Descriptors: *Pulp wastes, *Activated sludge, *Lignins, *Biological treatment, Sorption, Chemical reactions, Oxidation, Biodegradation, Microgial degradation, Water pollution sources, Industrial wastes, Wastes, *Waste water treatment, Proteins, Organic compounds, Pollutants, Water pollution treatment, Water purification, Sulfite liquors.
Identifiers: Alkali lignin, Lignosulfonates, Molecular weight.

Maximum lignin removals by activated sludge treatment of pulp mill effluents amounted to 15% for lignosulfonates and 70% for alkali lignin. The lower molecular weight lignosulfonates were preferentially removed, whereas alkali lignins of all molecular weights were removed rather uniformly. Only the high molecular weight fractions of both lignosulfonates and alkali lignin were sorbed on the protein zein. It is concluded that lignin removal during activated sludge treatment may occur by physical sorption, chemical oxidation and condensation, and biological degradation. (Buchanan-IPC)
W75-06885

(NOVA SCOTIA FOREST INDUSTRIES) PILOTS UNOX SYSTEM FOR SECONDARY TREATMENT (OF SULFITE AND NEWSPRINT MILL EFFLUENTS),
Nova Scotia Forest Industries, Port Hawkesbury.
Pulp and Paper Canada, Vol 76, No 2, p 67-72 (T32-36), February, 1975. 7 fig, 4 tab, 1 ref.

Descriptors: *Pulp wastes, *Waste water treatment, *Oxygen, *Biological treatment, *Sewage treatment, Pilot plants, Effluents, Sulfite liquors, Toxicity, Legislation, Sludge, Biochemical oxygen demand, Hydrogen ion concentration, Dissolved oxygen, Costs, Maintenance costs, Capital costs, Pulp and paper industry, Waste treatment, Water pollution sources, Fish, Aerobic conditions, Aerobic treatment, Water pollution control, Odor, Chemical oxygen demand.
Identifiers: *UNOX process.

UNOX is a high-rate biological process in which pure oxygen is used in place of air in a closed reactor under slight pressure. It was adopted for treating waste water from the Port Hawkesbury mill, because of its apparent advantages over conventional secondary treatment plants, such as reduced capital and maintenance costs, flexibility of operation, elimination of odor, and low space requirements. The system removed an average of 91% of the effluent's 5-day BOD and 40% of the COD, but the final effluent failed fish toxicity tests, partly because of heavy metal concentrations present and partly because of the need to raise the ammonia nutrient level from 6-8 to 40 ppm at times. (Gotman-IPC)
W75-06886

PHOTOCHEMICAL DECOLORIZATION OF PULP MILL EFFLUENTS,
Institute of Paper Chemistry, Appleton, Wis.
Tappi, Vol 58, No 2, p 130-133, February, 1975. 1 fig, 4 tab, 15 ref.

Descriptors: *Pulp wastes, *Color, *Ultraviolet radiation, Effluents, Waste water treatment, Sulfite liquors, Oxygen, Osication, Costs, Economics, Operating costs, Biochemical oxygen demand, Sodium compounds, Kinetics, Chemical reactions, Radiation, Solar radiation, Industrial wastes, Pollutants, Wastes, Water pollution sources, Water pollution control, Water quality control, Bleaching wastes.
Identifiers: Total organic carbon, Ketones, N-Bromosuccinimide, Hydrogen peroxide, Sodium hypochlorite, Bromine compounds, Oxidants.

The method of color removal described involves the oxidation of color bodies with oxygen in the presence of UV light. Reductions of BOD demand and total organic carbon occurred during the decolorization of unbleached kraft decker effluent, caustic extract from kraft pulp bleaching, and neutral sulfite semichemical pulp washings. Of the additives used to increase the process efficiency (such as ketones, N-bromo-succinimide, hydrogen peroxide, and NaOC1) the hypochlorite as the most effective. It extended the active wavelength range to 300 nm and longer, thus allowing the use of sunlight in lieu of mercury lamps. The addition of 0.1% NaOC1 enhanced the rate of decolorization by a factor of about 50 when using a medium-pressure mercury lamp. The method is capable of complete (100%) irreversible decolorization under laboratory conditions. It poses no chemical recovery or sludge handling problems, and its cost may be comparable to other new methods of color removal. (Gotman-IPC)
W75-06887

CHEMICAL SEDIMENTATION OF FOREST INDUSTRY WASTE WATERS (KEMISK FALLNING AV SKOGSINDUSTRIELLA AVLOPPSVATTEN),
Kemisk Tidskrift, Vol 86, No 7/8, p 54-56, 59, 1974. 8 fig, 3 tab.

Descriptors: *Pulp wastes, *Chemical precipitation, *Waste water treatment, Water purification, Separation techniques, Biological treatment, Waste treatment, Water pollution treatment, Wastes, Sludge, Industrial wastes, Pulp and paper industry, Chemicals, Flocculation, Water quality control, Aluminum, Sulfates.
Identifiers: Boliden AVR.

Processes and techniques used in the purification of pulp and paper mill effluents via chemical sedimentation are reviewed. Results obtained with an iron-containing aluminum sulfate preparation (Boliden AVR') are emphasized, including combination of the process with biological purification. Sludge handling is also discussed. (Speckhard-IPC)
W75-06888

BLEACHERY EFFLUENT TREATMENT,
K. V. Nayak, F. M. A. Nicolle, and J. A. Histed.
Canadian Pulp and Paper Association, Technical Section, Air and Stream Improvement Conference, Montreal, September 23-25, 1974, Preprinted Proceedings (Montreal, P.Q.), p 19-25. 4 fig, 5 tab, 9 ref.

Descriptors: *Bleaching wastes, *Color, *Pulp and paper industry, *Waste water treatment, Water pollution sources, Industrial wastes, Wastes, Chemical precipitation, Lime, Calcium compounds, Sludge, Temperature, Lignins, Organic compounds, Pulp wastes, Effluents, Waste treatment, Pollutants, Pollution abatement, Chlorine, Chlorination.

Experiments on color removal from bleachery effluents are reported. It was found that when alkaline extraction stage effluent was mixed with concentrated chlorination effluent (obtained by extensive recycling of chlorination filtrate), a lignin-like precipitate was formed, with concurrent color reduction in the supernatant liquid. A 3-stage process involving this initial precipitation step, lime treatment of the supernatant liquid, and subsequent carbonation to remove excess lime, resulted in significant color reduction of the final effluent, with fairly rapid settling rates in the various stages. The treatment of combined effluents in the volume range of 1500 to 1720 gal/ton produced the best response with respect to decolorization efficiency. Increasing the temperature in the lime treatment stage improved the sludge settling rate. Under preferred conditions about 91% reduction in color was obtained with a lime consumption of about 20 lb (as CaO) per ton of pulp. (Hansen-IPC)
W75-06891

IN-PLANT REDUCTION OF SUSPENDED SOLIDS AT (EDDY FOREST PRODUCTS LTD.) ESPANOLA (ONTARIO),
Eddy Forest Products Ltd., Espanola (Ontario).
R. Thompson, P. J. Savage, and C. Y. Chai.
Canadian Pulp and Paper Association, Technical Section, Air and Stream Improvement Conference, Montreal, September 23-25, 1974, Preprinted Proceedings (Montreal, P.Q.), p 9-11. 6 fig.

Descriptors: *Pulp wastes, *Suspended solids, *Pollution abatement, Biochemical oxygen demand, Water pollution sources, Effluents, Industrial wastes, Wastes, *Waste water treatment, Pollutants, Water quality control, Pulp and paper industry, *Canada.
Identifiers: Woodrooms, Spills, Pulp washing, White water(Paper machine), Kraft mills, Fiber recovery.

In-plant measures have been initiated at a Canadian bleached kraft pulp and paper mill to reduce the amount of suspended solids in the mill effluent. Equipment was installed to reduce suspended solids in the woodroom effluent, recover spills from the brown stock washers, and recover fiber from the paper machine drain water as well as from the wet ends of the pulp machines. Flow diagrams of the woodroom effluent treatment system, brown stock washer drain system, and fiber recovery system are given. Suspended solids have been reduced to 25% of their former amount, and the BOD load has been halved. (Witt-IPC)
W75-06892

WATER REUSE FROM THE BLEACHERY TO THE RECOVERY SYSTEM,
F. M. A. Nicolle, and J. A. Histed.
Candian Pulp and Paper Association, Technical Section, Air and Stream Improvement Conference, Montreal, September 23-25, 1974, Preprinted Proceedings (Montreal, P.Q), p 113-119. 6 fig, 7 tab, 15 ref.

Descriptors: *Bleaching wastes, *Water reuse, *Pulp and paper industry, Water conservation, Industrial wastes, Wastes, Laboratory tests, Recirculated water, Industrial water, Chemical precipitation, Calcium, Water pollution sources, Pollution abatement, Waste disposal, Chlorine, Chlorination.
Identifiers: Kraft pulp, Pulp screening, Pulp washing, Chlorine dioxide, Chemical recovery, Countercurrent processes.

Laboratory tests demonstrated the feasibility of using bleachery effluents for pulp screening and kraft brown stock washing. Countercurrent washing and extensive recycling of chlorination filtrate in the bleaching of softwood pulp by the D(C)EDED sequence was used to produce the concentrated effluents required for simulation of the effluent-free mill. Problems were encountered due to formation of a precipitate when chlorination filtrate was made alkaline. The cause of this precipitate has since been traced to an unusually high ash and calcium content in the unbleached pulp. Because of this precipitate the original flow system intended for simulation had to be modified to permit use of bleachery effluent on the brown stock washers. A workable flow system is presented, along with recommendations for disposal of excess bleachery effluents in other parts of the recovery process. (Hansen-IPC)
W75-06893

QUALITY OF PULP INDUSTRY WASTE WATERS AND THEIR USE FOR CROP IRRIGATION (IZSLEDVANE NA KACHESTVATA NA OTPAL'CHNITE VODI OT TSELULOZNATA PROMISHLENOST I IZPOLZUVANETO IM ZA NAPOYAVANE NA SELSKOSTOPANSKI KULTURI),
S. Sev, and I. Papazov.
Godishnik Visshiya Inzhenerno-Stroitelen Institut, Vol 23, No 1, p 75-84, 1971. 2 fig, 2 tab, 5 ref.

Descriptors: *Pulp wastes, *Irrigation water, *Crops, *Waste water disposal, *Water reuse, Industrial wastes, Wastes, Suspended solids, Sulfur compounds, Hydrogen sulfide, Chemical oxygen demand, Biochemical oxygen demand, Crop production, Crop response, Soils, Color, Toxicity, Lethal limit, Waste dilution, Sedimentation, Aeration, Oxidation, Potatoes, Sugar beets.
Identifiers: *Bulgaria.

Potatoes and feed beets were irrigated with unpurified effluents from the St. Kiradzhiev kraft mill. The effluents consisted of waste from kraft pulp manufacture, pulp screening and washing, and the kraft paper machine.They contained, on the average, 198.42 g/cu m of suspended solids, 420.56 g/liter dry solids, 13.04 g/liter sulfur compounds (methyl sulfide, dimethyl disulfide, hydrogen sulfide, and methyl mercaptan), and had a COD of 310.35 g/liter and a 5-day BOD of 143.74 g/liter. During the first season, irrigation increased the crop yield. However, continuous irrigation over a 3 year period caused a gradual reduction of the crop yield and a visible discoloration of the soil. This was apparently due to the presence of sulfur

compounds in the effluents and their gradual accumulation in the soil to toxic levels, and was more pronounced in heavy soils than in light sandy soils. The mill effluents can be used for irrigation provided their content of sulfur compounds is reduced to nontoxic levels either by suitable dilution or by passage through a horizontal sedimentation tank, a cascade aerator, and a sedimentation pond (this process results in oxidation of a large fraction of the sulfur compounds). (Stapinski-IPC)
W75-06895

CLARIFIER INSTALLATION IN AN INTEGRATED SULFITE AND NEWSPRINT MILL,
P. Veilleux.
Canadian Pulp and Paper Association, Technical Section, Air and Stream Improvement Conference, Montreal, September 23-25, 1974, Preprinted Proceedings (Montreal, P.Q.), p 27-29. 3 fig.

Descriptors: *Water purification, *Treatment facilities, *Pulp wastes, Sulfite liquors, Pulp and paper industry, Wood wastes, Lime, Neutralization, Sludge treatment, Sludge disposal, Filtration, Dewatering, Incineration, Water pollution sources, Industrial wastes, Wastes, *Waste water treatment, Waste treatment, Pollution abatement, Water pollution control, Water quality control, *Canada, Landfills.
Identifiers: Woodrooms, Sulfite pulp mills, Newsprint mills.

The clarifier and related equipment installed at the Alma newsprint mill of Price Co. (Canada) is described. The effluent to be handled includes the combined discharges from the woodroom, sodium-base sulfite pulp mill, and paper mill, and includes some discharge from the mill sanitary sewers. The system provides for lime neutralization of wastes before clarification, and for thickening of sludge in a continuous filter, with final dewatering in a vertical V-press. The dewatered sludge is disposed of by trucking to a landfill site, with incineration in bark-burning boilers as a possible alternative. (Hansen-IPC)
W75-06931

BLEACH PLANT WATER REDUCTION,
O. K. Aschim, and K. C. Wiest.
Canadian Pulp and Paper Association, Technical Section, Air and Stream Improvement Conference, Montreal, September 23-25, 1974, Preprinted Proceedings (Montreal, P.Q.), p 101-102. 4 tab.

Descriptors: *Water conservation, *Pulp and paper industry, *Bleaching wastes, Water consumption, Temperature, Foaming, Treatment facilities, Operations, Water quality control, Water pollution sources, Industrial water, *Canada, Chlorine, Chlorination.
Identifiers: *Bleach plants, Kraft pulp mills.

By raising the operating temperature in the chlorination stage from 70F to 120-130F, Prince Albert Pulp Co. was able to reduce fresh water consumption from 50,300 to 32,300 gal/ton at its softwood bleached kraft mill. Except that the more closed system resulted in increased defoamer requirements, no adverse effects have been observed. The reduction in water consumption has resulted in improved operation of the effluent treatment facilities. (Hansen-IPC)
W75-06932

CONSOLIDATED-BATHURST IN-PLANT POLLUTION ABATEMENT CONTROL SCHEME,
C. Dionne, M. Fraser, K. Godin, and G. A. Menier.
Canadian Pulp and Paper Association, Technical Section, Air and Stream Improvement Conference, Montreal, September 23-25, 1974, Preprinted Proceedings (Montreal, P.Q.), p 81-84. 6 fig.

Descriptors: *Pollution abatement, *Pulp wastes, *Suspended solids, *Biochemical oxygen demand, Legislation, Water reuse, Bark, Fibers(Plant), Pulp wastes, Effluents, Water pollution sources, Industrial wastes, Water pollution control, Reclamation, Industrial water, Recirculated water, Pollutants, *Canada.
Identifiers: White water, Spills, Fiber recovery.

The approaches used and projected by Consolidated-Bathurst Ltd. at several of its mills to control effluent suspended solids and BOD to meet Canadian Provincial and Federal Government Regulations are described. Areas in which substantial improvements have been made are white water reuse, bark fines reduction, centrifugal cleaner rejects reclamation, and spill recovery. Flow diagrams for the latter three systems are given. (Hansen-IPC)
W75-06933

EXPANDING WASTE WATER TREATMENT CONSIDERATIONS AT CORPS OF ENGINEERS RECREATION AREAS,
Army Engineer District, St. Louis, Mo.
E. E. Middleton.
Water Resources Bulletin, Vol 9, No 1, p 155-159, February 1973.

Descriptors: *Waste water treatment, *Recreation, *Projects, Operations, Lakes, Wastes, *Illinois, Engineering, Design, Waste treatment, Filtration, *Treatment facilities.
Identifiers: Extended aeration, Plant operators.

Through its recreation program, the Corps of Engineers is becoming more involved in the design and operation of waste water treatment plants. Over the past few years, there have been many changes in the waste water treatment requirements at St. Louis District Corps of Engineers projects. Discussed are the methods considered for treating these wastes. Septic tanks and oxidation pond or lagoon are among several possible methods, but extended aeration plant, followed by filtration, is the process used in most of the areas. The treatment plant operators have become key members of the project operation team. A discussion of the District's operator training program is presented along with the operator's job requirements. Through a Spring inspection of all treatment plants in the District, a mechanism has been provided for encouraging feedback to the design engineer from the operator. (Bell-Cornell)
W75-06941

A PRESENT VALUE-UNIT COST METHODOLOGY FOR EVALUATING MUNICIPAL WASTEWATER RECLAMATION AND DIRECT REUSE,
Army Mobility Equipment Research and Development Center, Fort Belvoir, Va. Sanitary Sciences Div.
V. J. Ciccone, M. L. Granstrom, S. L. Yu, and J. J. Seneca.
Water Resources Bulletin, Vol 11, No 1, p 21-32, February 1975. 4 fig, 4 tab, 16 ref.

Descriptors: *Water supply, *Water demand, Waste water(Pollution), *Reclamation, *Water reuse, *Alternative planning, *Methodology, *Cost analysis, Evaluation, Capital costs, Operating costs, Unit costs, Economies of scale, Value, Optimization, Waste water treatment, Comprehensive planning, Municipal water, Constraints, Decision making, Recycling, Mathematical models, Equations, Systems analysis, Water users.
Identifiers: Cost minimization.

A least cost evaluation model based on the Present Value-Unit Cost (PVUC) method is developed and applied to a hypothetical municipal water supply-wastewater treatment problem. Two basic considerations are involved: (1) meeting projected water demand over the planned horizon by construction and operation of a conventional storage and distribution facility, supplementing existing water sources by importation or new source development; and (2) instituting a dual system by recycling wastewaters for direct reuse to meet nonpotable projected demands and satisfy potable requirements from existing and secondary sources. A discriminant, which is the PVUC difference between the two alternatives, yields a decision input easily calculated. When applied over selected planning horizons, the discriminant predicts a cost equivalency of the two alternatives at some future point in time. The strategy employs given water demands, sources, geophysical parameters, and available selected advance wastewater treatment methods to evaluate the alternatives in a system which permits reclamation of treated wastewaters to desired quality. The reclaimed wastewaters are subsequently distributed to selected users categorized as industrial, commercial, and public. The projected water demands are exogenous constraints which must be satisfied. The cost functions which include capital and operating costs are constructed to reflect economies of scale. This approach is designed to permit a flexible and comprehensive analysis of alternative sources of water supply, allowing for a decision based upon least cost solutions to be made. (Bell-Cornell)
W75-06947

A GEOMETRIC PROGRAMMING MODEL FOR OPTIMAL ALLOCATION OF STREAM DISSOLVED OXYGEN,
Rensselaer Polytechnic Inst., Troy, N.Y.
J. G. Ecker.
Management Science, Vol 21, No 6, p 658-668, February 1975. 6 tab, 18 ref.

Descriptors: *Water quality control, *Dossolved oxygen, *Standards, *Streams, *Water policy, *Waste water treatment, *Pollution abatement, Annual costs, *Hudson River, Treatment facilities, Economics, Reach(Streams), Design, Equations, Constraints, Mathematical models, Systems analysis, Biochemical oxygen demand.
Identifiers: Geometric programming, Nonlinear programming, Waste discharge, Cost minimization, Continuous variables, Posynomial programming.

A nonlinear model is developed for allocating treatment requirements along a stream so as to meet stream dissolved oxygen standards at each point in the stream while minimizing the total annual cost of all discharging activities. An application of the model to several reaches of the Upper Hudson River is considered, and some alternative pollution abatement policies are analyzed. The crucial variables in the model are the removal rates of the individual processes which act in series to form the treatment plant. The actual design of the treatment plants as well as the total removal rate determined by the individual process removal rates are considered. Insight is given into the fixed charge aspect of the problem in that solutions to the model will be useful in determining whether or not certain processes should be included in the treatment plant design. However, the basic use of the model will be to determine the optimal operating levels for individual treatment processes in a fixed system design. Also, the model is particularly useful for sensitivity analyses involving changes in the characteristics of the stream and changes in stream standards. (Bell-Cornell)
W75-06954

A KINETIC MODEL FOR DESIGN OF COMPLETELY-MIXED ACTIVATED SLUDGE TREATING VARIABLE-STRENGTH INDUSTRIAL WASTEWATERS,
Associated Water and Air Resources Engineers, Inc., Nashville, Tenn.
C. E. Adams, W. W. Eckenfelder, and J. C. Hovious.
Water Research, Vol 9, No 1, p 37-42, January 1975. 4 fig, 1 tab, 5 ref.

Descriptors: Kinetics, *Industrial wastes, Waste water(Pollution), *Waste water treatment, *Water pollution control, *Activated sludge, Mathematical models, Equations, Biochemical oxygen demand, *Design, Operation and maintenance, Effluents, Organic loading, Systems analysis, *Treatment facilities.
Identifiers: Prediction, Influents.

A mathematical model is effectively employed to predict the performance of high and variable strength industrial wastes. The equation logically states that the overall removal rate decreases as the fraction of BOD remaining to be removed decreases. The rationale for this rests in the fact that the more readily removable compounds are exhausted, those yet to be removed result in a decreasing removal rate. This model and the supporting data infer that variations in influent organic strength will result in variations in effluent quality with a constant organic loading whereas existing models indicate little effect of influent on effluent. Consequently, a lower-than-normal organic loading will be necessitated at higher-than-average influent concentrations in order to maintain consistent effluent quality. The feasibility of operating such lightly loaded systems as well as the economic impact resulting from such a design will require evaluation for each concentrated waste. Proper use of the equation will not only allow optimization of the design, including delineating equalization requirements, but will also enable more effective operation by providing a method of calculating the required organic loading to maintain consistent effluent. (Bell-Cornell)
W75-06955

COST OF TRICKLING FILTER RECIRCULATION PART I,
C. R. Lee.
Water and Sewage Works, Vol 122, No 1, p 57-59, January 1975. 5 fig, 23 ref, append.

Descriptors: *Waste water treatment, *Trickling filters, *Cost analysis, *Design, Optimization, Operation and maintenance, Amortization, Annual, Pumping, Equations, Mathematical models, Systems analysis.
Identifiers: Recirculation flow, Recirculation ratio.

The trickling filter has been one of the most commonly used processes for wastewater treatment. Many mathematical models capable of designing the desired effluent have been developed. Problems still arise in designing the recirculation flow configuration and ratio using these methods. The recirculation ratio of the trickling filter ranges from 0.5 to 3.0. Questions arise in the optimal design concerning costs, sensitivity of design variables, and improvement of treatment efficiency. Discussed are design formulae for flow configurations and treatment conditions proposed by Eckenfelder and by the National Research Council. Shown are Eckenfelder's plug-flow type formula and complete-mixing type formula. Reviewed are cost analyses of waste treatment. Operation and maintenance (O.M.) cost is taken as an evaluation of the optimum design. The O.M. cost here is the sum of the annual operation and maintenance cost and the amortization cost. The models used to calculate the costs of trickling filter and pumping systems are shown in the appendix. From these models, the total O.M. cost and the optimum design cost for various cases may be found. Results indicate the optimal cost will be compromised by the two opposite trends of the pumping cost and the filter cost, when the recirculation ratio increases. (See also W75-06957) (Bell-Cornell)
W75-06956

COST OF TRICKLING FILTER RECIRCULATION PART II,
C. R. Lee, and T. Takamatsa.
Water and Sewage Works, Vol 122, No 2, p 64-66, February 1975. 3 fig, 1 tab, 23 ref, append.

Descriptors: *Waste water treatment, *Trickling filters, *Design, Cost analysis, Optimization, Flow rates, Wastes, Temperature, Operation and maintenance, Effects, Pumping, Equations, Mathematical models, Systems analysis, *Operating costs, *Maintenance costs.
Identifiers: Removal efficiency, Recirculation ratio.

The total operation and maintenance (O.M.) cost of a trickling filter with a recirculation system is taken as an evaluation of the optimum design. The total O.M. cost calculated by using Eckenfelder's formula is generally lower than that calculated by the National Research Council formula. The recirculation ratio, which makes the required volume of the filter minimal, will not be the optimal design, when pumping cost is taken into consideration. The optimal designs of the two formulas show quite a discrepancy due to the recirculation ratio and the flow rate. By Eckenfelder's formula, the deeper filter is more economical than the shallower filter, within 10 ft. depth. The temperature effect is greater at higher removal efficiency, and the differences of the total O.M. cost due to the temperature variations are greater at lower temperatures. In most cases, the recirculation will improve the filter performances but will not necessarily be an economical design if the total O.M. cost is considered. Especially, by Eckenfelder's formula, when a high degree of treatment is required, the recirculation will not improve the filter performance, until the recirculation ratio increases beyond the critical zone. (See also W75-06956) (Bell-Cornell)
W75-06957

VARIATION OF URBAN RUNOFF QUALITY AND QUANTITY WITH DURATION AND INTENSITY OF STORMS--PHASE III,
Texas Tech Univ., Lubbock. Water Resources Center.
For primary bibliographic entry see Field 5B.
W75-06975

CORRESPONDENCE CONFERENCE ON REMOVAL OF NITROGEN FROM MUNICIPAL WASTEWATER,
Massachusetts Univ., Amherst. Water Resources Research Center.
B. B. Berger.
Available from the National Technical Information Service, Springfield, Va 22161 as PB-241 378, $3.25 in paper copy, $2.25 in microfiche. Publication No. 48 - Completion Report FY-75-3, March 1975, 18 p. OWRT A-059-MASS(1). 14-31-0001-4021.

Descriptors: *Education, *Conferences, Methodology, *Waste water treatment, *Nitrogen, Training, Municipal water, *Information exchange.
Identifiers: Correspondence conferences, *Information transfer.

This project had three objectives: a test of the effectiveness of information transfer through a correspondence 'at home' conference, the gaining of experience for preparation of guides utilizing correspondence conferences in a long-term program of continuing education, and more specifically in this case a transfer of knowledge on new and emerging techniques in removal of nitrogen from municipal wastewaters. This proposed technique of information transfer seeks to avoid the major expense and inconvenience of conventional specialty conference attendance, while enabling the participants to extract a maximum of benefit through personal participation in such conferences. A set of six papers, each dealing with an important phase of nitrogen removal from municipal wastewater and each prepared by an authority in the field was sent to 67 registrants. Each registrant was given an opportunity to direct two series of questions through the conference staff to each author. The major conclusions are that correspondence conferences can provide an effective way to transfer information and they can be considered as a desirable supplement to conventional specialty conferences.
W75-06984

STUDIES ON THE HYDROLYSIS AND PRECIPITATION OF ALUMINUM (III),
Ohio State Univ., Columbus. Dept. of Civil Engineering.
A. J. Rubin, and P. L. Hayden.
Available from the National Technical Information Service, Springfield, Va 22161 as PB-241 318, $5.25 in paper copy, $2.25 in microfiche. Completion Report No. 364X, April 1973. 91 p, 20 fig, 19 tab, 108 ref. OWRT A-016-OHIO(1).

Descriptors: *Chemistry of precipitation, *Aluminum, *Waste water treatment, *Hydrolysis, *Coagulation, Aqueous solutions, Metals, Alkalis(Bases).

Results are described of an extensive and systematic investigation of the aqueous chemistry of aluminum(III). Hydrolytic species were identified and their formation constants determined using computed analysis of potentiometric data. Aluminum hydroxide precipitates were defined by several experimental techniques including precipitate boundary analysis of light scattering data. Crystal structures were identified by x-ray diffraction measurements. A hydrosol formed in acid solutions up to OH/Al ratios of 3.0. Precipitation experiments conducted in nitrate, chlorine, sulfate and phosphate media indicated that the solubility and colloidal stability of the condensed phase is greatly affected by the type and concentration of anion present as well as solution age. Comparison of pH-concentration limits of solubility and stability with published coagulation data indicates a very close agreement. Apparently, precipitation of insoluble hydroxide is an important factor in the chemical coagulation process when using hydrolyzing metals such as aluminum(III).
W75-06988

DEVELOPMENT OF MICRO-SCALE LABORATORY FILTRATION TECHNIQUES,
Tennessee Univ., Knoxville. Dept. of Civil Engineering.
J. C. Burdick, III, W. A. Drewry, and L. D. Watson.
Available from the National Technical Information Service, Springfield, Va 22161 as PB-241 334, $3.75 in paper copy, $2.25 in microfiche. Tennessee Water Resources Research Center, Knoxville, Research Report No. 41, December 1974. 32 p, 10 fig, 8 tab, 9 ref, append. $3.00. OWRT A-033-TENN(1). 14-31-0001-4043.

Descriptors: *Filtration, *Analytical techniques, *Laboratory tests, *Waste water treatment, *Sludge treatment, Equipment, Design, Activated sludge, *Filters.
Identifiers: *Micro-scale filtration procedures.

The need exists for developing micro-scale techniques in order to investigate vacuum filtration in the laboratory to provide design parameters for full-scale plant use. The results of tests conducted indicate that similar values for the mean specific resistance and filter yields can be obtained by using small scale units; consequently, the volume of sludge required for determining these parameters can be greatly reduced to amounts that can be obtained from laboratory activated sludge units. The practical limit for the filter leaf area appears to be above 0.004 sq ft to obtain consistently reliable results. This is due to the observation that a significant difference occurred between the mean filter yields of the standard leaf apparatus and the 0.004 sq ft leaf apparatus for the Third Creek conditioned sludge. Variables that need to be more closely controlled include sludge temperature, vacuum, filter area, and the time of filtration

after the addition of $FeCl_3$. Based upon these preliminary results, detailed consideration on micro-scale procedures for water plant sludges appears to offer a valuable alternative to existing procedures.
W75-06990

A WATER-QUALITY SIMULATION MODEL FOR WELL MIXED ESTUARIES AND COASTAL SEAS: VOL. VI, SIMULATION, OBSERVATION, AND STATE ESTIMATION,
New York City-Rand Inst., N.Y.
For primary bibliographic entry see Field 5B.
W75-07042

CHEMICAL ANALYSIS FOR EVALUATION OF SOIL SORPTION PROPERTIES,
Ontario Ministry of the Environment, Toronto. Pollution Control Branch.
For primary bibliographic entry see Field 5B.
W75-07058

WATER AND SEWERAGE DEVELOPMENT PLAN - KANSAS CITY METROPOLITAN REGION.
Metropolitan Planning Commission-Kansas City Region, Mo.
1971. 130 p, 21 fig, 26 tab.

Descriptors: *Sewerage, Drainage systems, Water control, Utilities, *Water management(Applied), *Planning, *Urban drainage, Basins, Water resources development, *Land use, Water quality, Project planning, Zoning, *Missouri, *Kansas, Regional development, Cities.
Identifiers: *Kansas City Metropolitan Region(Mo-Kan).

Policies, plans and implementation tactics of water and sewerage systems in the eight county region of metropolitan Kansas City are described. To meet the regional goal of sufficient utilities for all present and potential users, a water and sewerage plan is developed which meets desired quality standards, uses watershed as basis for systems, identifies areas of future growth and suggests adequate facilities to meet demands, encourages adoption and enforcement of zoning and subdivision regulations and recommends the control of supply by central water distribution systems. A detailed inventory of natural physical data in the area provides the constraints and criteria for establishing facility priorities. As the demands and future growth patterns of each county are assessed, water and sewerage facilities can be planned to be coordinated with land use development for a workable regional program. Success of facilities and systems plans requires intergovernmental and interagency cooperation as well as support of the general public. Maps for each county detail separately a general water plan and a general sewer plan. (Salzman-North Carolina)
W75-07083

REPORT ON REGIONAL POLLUTION CONTROL: HALIFAX-DARTMOUTH METROPOLITAN AREA.
Halifax-Dartmouth Metropolitan Area Planning Committee (Nova Scotia). Task Group on Water Supply and Waste Disposal.
Prepared for Metropolitan Area Planning Committee, Halifax-Dartmouth, Nova Scotia, November, 1971. 14 p, 1 tab, 3 append.

Descriptors: *Sewerage, *Sewage treatment, *Sewage districts, *Pollution control, *Construction costs, *Cost analysis, Sewers, Planning, *Canada, Regional development.
Identifiers: *Halifax-Dartmouth Metropolitan Area(Nova Scotia), Regional sewerage system.

Alternatives for pollution control of the Halifax-Dartmouth Metropolitan Area and recommendations for a regional sewage collection and treatment system for the city of Halifax, part of Dartmouth, and the Herring Cove area of Halifax County are presented. Basic assumptions are presented for time horizon to year 2000; treatment requirements by type of waste, and outflow location (65% BOD for Halifax Harbour sanitary waste), and tunnel capacity (4 times dry weather flow in year 2000). Sewage treatment alternatives are broken down into area subsections. Seven sewage treatment plant sites are reviewed for the regional system resulting in eight combined alternatives. Costs are based on E.N.R. Index of 1300 and thus not representative of today's costs but are viable for comparison purposes. Estimates for alternatives are given. While 3 alternatives are equal in capital costs, 2 have high operating costs, $8.41 and $9.35 million versus $6.6 million, resulting in the recommendation of a single plant coordinated system possibly at the Hen and Chickens shoal for the regional system instead of a fragmented system requiring 4 plants. Investigation of potential effects on the harbour is also recommended. (Park-North Carolina)
W75-07085

RESEARCH NEEDS RELATED TO HYDROMETEOROLOGIC ASPECTS OF FUTURE ENERGY PRODUCTION,
National Oceanic and Atmospheric Administration, Oak Ridge, Tenn. Air Resources Atmospheric Turbulence and Diffusion Lab.
For primary bibliographic entry see Field 6D.
W75-07094

RESEARCH NEEDS RELATED TO HEAT DISSIPATION FROM LARGE POWER PLANTS,
Iowa Univ., Iowa City. Inst. of Hydraulic Research.
For primary bibliographic entry see Field 5B.
W75-07095

EFFLUENT TREATMENT AND ITS COST FOR THE SYNTHANE COAL-TO-SNG PROCESS,
Bureau of Mines, Pittsburgh, Pa.
J. P. Strakey, Jr., A. J. Forney, W. P. Haynes, and K. D. Plants.
In: Proceedings of the Workshop on Research Needs Related to Water for Energy, Water Resources Center, University of Illinois at Urbana-Champaign, Research Report No. 93, p 169-178, November, 1974. 4 tab, 6 ref.

Descriptors: *Coals, *Environmental effects, *Energy, *Environmental control, *Waste treatment, Energy conversion, Sulfur, Nitrogen compounds, Ponding, Recycling, Air pollution, *Costs.
Identifiers: SYNTHANE Coal-to-SNG process, Gasifier, Scrubbers, Precipitators.

In an effort to convert coal into substitute-natural gas (SNG) in an environmentally acceptable manner, the gasification plant will require extensive controls to prevent the release of large quantities of pollutants to the environment. Data collected in a small gasifier is used to project environmental impact of a full-scale plant employing the synthane process (one of four new coal-to-SNG processes), and to estimate the cost of controls. Various emissions including sulfur, nitrogen oxides, assorted gases, and solid effluents like ash and lime sludge are discussed and related to possible control options. These include desulfurization before combustion, redesigning processes to reduce emissions, means to reduce particulate matter and harmful gaseous material and the use of precipitators and scrubbers. Ponding for solid and liquid disposal, recycling of uncontaminated water, and treatment of polluted water downstream from gasifier are other alternatives for treatment of effluents generated in SYNTHANE process. Estimates of cost of pollution controls are listed. This study indicates that gaseous, solid and liquid wastes from a full-scale SYNTHANE plant can be controlled in an acceptable manner at an acceptable cost. (See also W75-07089) (Salzman-North Carolina)
W75-07098

TREATMENT OF A MUNITIONS-MANUFACTURING WASTE BY THE FIXED ACTIVATED SLUDGE PROCESS,
Virginia State Water Control Board, Richmond.
R. C. Albert, R. C. Hoehn, and C. W. Randall.
Typescript paper prepared for the 27th Annual Purdue Industrial Waste Conference, Purdue University, Lafayette, Indiana, May 2-4, 1972. 36 p, 12 fig, 5 tab, 13 ref.

Descriptors: *Activated sludge, *Waste treatment, *Treatment facilities, *Bacteria, *Biochemical oxygen demand, *Chemical oxygen demand, Effluents, Organic compounds, Aerobic bacteria, Aerobic treatment, Biological treatment, Flocculation, Microbial degredation, Sludge digestion, Sludge treatment.
Identifiers: *Munitions manufacturing wastes, Filamentous bacteria, Fixed activated sludge.

The mode of treatment differed from conventional activated sludge processes in that attached, filamentons microorganisms, rather than suspended, flocculent biomasses, were the active biota. The waste, the treatment process, and the treatment unit are described in detail. The utilization of organic substrate in the fixed activated sludge (FAS) treatment unit, expressed as a percentage of the influent concentration, was assessed in terms of three parameters: total organic carbon, biochemical oxygen demand, and chemical oxygen demand. Substrate utilization then was expressed as a function of three variables: the influent organic strength, the dilution of the raw waste, and the screen area in contact with the waste during its passage through the treatment unit. The treatment of the munitions-manufacturing waste by the FAS process is not only feasible, but the efficiency and kinetic parameters compared favorably to values reported in the literature for treatment of other wastes by conventional activated sludge. (Poertner)
W75-07106

THE TREATABILITY OF A MUNITIONS-MANUFACTURING WASTE, WITH ACTIVATED CARBON,
Rummel, Klepper and Kahl, Baltimore, Md.
G. R. Schulte, R. C. Hoehn, and C. W. Randall.
Paper presented at the 28th Annual Purdue Industrial Waste Conference, Purdue University, West Lafayette, Indiana, May 2-4, 1973. 35 p, 5 tab, 9 fig, 13 ref.

Descriptors: *Activated carbon, *Nitrates, *Sulfates, *Organic wastes, *Lime, *Waste water treatment, Water pollution treatment, Adsorption, Trickling filters, Nitrogen compounds, Organic compounds, Color reactions.
Identifiers: *Munitions manufacturing wastes, Trinotrotoluene(TNT), Color removal, Nitroaromatic compounds.

The extent was studied to which color and nitroaromatic compounds (including TNT and its isomers) could be removed from a munitions-manufacturing waste with one type of activated carbon. The effect of pH on the adsorption characteristics also was evaluated. Adsorptive properties of the activated carbon for the particular waste in question, and for pure a-TNT, were determined by Freundlich isotherm analysis and by breakthrough curves. The waste used in this study was high in solids, nitrates, and sulfates; was extremely acidic; and contained many nitroaromatic compounds in addition to trinitrotoluene (TNT). The color of the waste was yellow to orange, and the intensity was pH dependent. Both batch studies and column studies were conducted to determine the adsorbability of color and aromatic nitrobodies by activated carbon. Treatment with activated carbon for the removal of nitroaromatic compounds

and color in wastes originating from the manufacture of TNT is technically feasible. Nitroaromatic compounds, including TNT, that react to produce color with the Silas-Mason test, are best adsorbed by carbon when the waste is strongly acidic. Color removal also is best accomplished from an acidic medium. The TNT-manufacturing wastes should not be neutralized with lime prior to treatment with carbon. (Poertner)
W75-07107

FACTORS THAT AFFECT ACTIVATED SLUDGE PHOSPHATE RELEASE,
Virginia Polytechnic Inst., Blacksburg.
C. W. Randall, B. S. Hulcher, and P. H. King.
Journal of the American Water Resources Association, Water Resources Bulletin, Volume 6, No 4, p 648-660, August, 1970, 11 fig, 1 tab, 13 ref.

Descriptors: *Sanitary engineering, *Activated sludge, *Phosphates, *Biological treatment, *Chemical reactions, *Nutrient removal, Oxidation-reduction potential, Dissolved oxygen, Aerobic treatment, Sludge, Microbial degradation, Sludge treatment, Biodegradation, Oxygen demand, Laboratory tests.

The activated sludge process can remove significant amounts of phosphorus from sewage, but the removal efficiency is usually significantly reduced by the release of phosphate back to solution during subsequent treatment steps. Soluble phosphate release from activated sludge was studied with emphasis on defining the factors that affect such release and the actual release mechanisms. Laboratory units were used for experimental purposes. The experiments were designed to study the relationship between soluble phosphate release and various environmental factors such as redox potential (ORP), dissolved oxygen (DO), pH, solids concentration, solids destruction, and sulfate salt addition. The effect of substrate utilization on phosphate uptake and the relationship between uptake characteristics and subsequent phosphate release were also studied. The results show that some phosphate storage occurs during aerobic substrate utilization. Following substrate utilization, activated sludge phosphate release is dierectly related to the amount of biological stress the organisms are subjected to, and the mechanism of,release is primarily cell lysis. The phosphate released per unit sludge under anoxic conditions is relatively constant. Under normal environmental conditions, neither ORP or pH change have a significant affect on phosphate release. (Poertner)
W75-07108

WASTE WATER TREATMENT WORKS DATA BOOK.
Illinois State Environmental Protection Agency, Springfield.
January 1972. 118 p, 4 tab.

Descriptors: *Waste water treatment, *Data storage and retrieval, *Sewage treatment, *Treatment facilities, *Drainage districts, *Illinois, Data collections, Treatment, Public utilities, Utilities, Water pollution control, Information retrieval, Governments, Data processing.
Identifiers: Waste water treatment works, Sewage treatment plants.

Data are tabulated on waste water treatment works discharging to Illinois waters and on treatment works under construction permit from the Environmental Protection Agency or its predecessor, the Sanitary Water Board. Since the design data and plans for any given plant must be coded for computer storage, the processes and equipment stated for a given plant may only represent approximations to actual processes or equipment in use, or may be generic names used where a more appropriate code is not available. The data are for informational purposes only, and do not necessarily describe fully the processes and equipment considered prior to issuance of a construction permit or operating permit to the owner of the treatment works. Information is presented on: population data; treatment works, listed by ownership types; new treatment works under construction or operating permit, by ownership type; and treatment works, organized by process employed. Data are also given on specific facilities including the name of the owner, drainage basin, type of treatment, and the treatment facilities. (Poertner)
W75-07109

BIOLOGICAL TREATMENT OF HIGH THIOSULFATE INDUSTRIAL WASTE WATER,
Virginia Polytechnic Inst., Blacksburg.
W. C. Kreye, P. H. King, and C. W. Randall.
Paper presented at the 28th Annual Industrial Waste Conference, Purdue University, Lafayette, Indiana, May 1973. 26 p, 4 tab, 8 fig, 7 ref.

Descriptors: *Sulfates, *Biological treatment, *Reduction(Chemical), *Industrial wastes, *Organic wastes, *Activated sludge, Chemical oxygen demand, Oxidation, Nitrogen, Phosphorus, Waste treatment, Biochemical oxygen demand.
Identifiers: Thiosulfate removal.

A biological system was studied capable of achieving a high degree of thiosulfate removal from a typical industrial wastewater. In addition removal of organic matter was another goal of the total treatment process. Although the concentration of organics in the wastewater selected was low, organic removal in the presence of a high concentration of thiosulfate was monitored since it seemed desirable to develop a biological system that would be capable of treating a mixed industrial thiosulfate waste and domestic sewage in one unit. Since thiosulfate has a very high biochemical oxygen demand (BOD), thiosulfate must be oxidized or reduced by either a chemical or a biological process to remove the B.O.D. from the wastewater. An activated sludge unit can be acclimated to successfully oxidize high concentrations of thiosulfate. In the process the system may lose its ability to oxidize organic material. Thiosulfate oxidation is best accomplished at a low mixed liquor pH. Rising pH levels are an early indication of an impending failure of the system. The nitrogen and phosphorus requirement of biological thiosulfate oxidation systems is very low. (Poertner)
W75-07110

COLUMNAR DENITRIFICATION OF A MUNITIONS MANUFACTURING WASTEWATER,
Environmental Protection Agency, Manassas, Va. Advanced Waste Treatment Research Lab.
D. O. Tucker, C. W. Randall, and P. H. King.
Paper presented at the 29th Annual Purdue Industrial Waste Treatment Conference, Purdue University, Lafayette, Indiana, May 7-9, 1974. 18 p, 2 fig, 3 tab, 19 ref.

Descriptors: *Waste water treatment, *Industrial wastes, *Nitrates, *Organic compounds, *Activated carbon, *Denitrification, Organic wastes, Trickling filters, Tertiary treatment, Solids contact processes, Nutrient removal, Adsorption.
Identifiers: *Munitions manufacturing wastes, Columnar denitrification.

The possibility was studied of treating two industrial wastes from a denitrification unit. One waste is high in nitrates and low in organic matter; the other high in organic matter and low in nitrates. The experiments were also designed to provide information concerning rapid denitrification in a columnar unit. The wastes were mixed to the desired proportions and subjected to columnar denitrification. Two bench-scale denitrification columns were constructed and used to investigate the feasibility of columnar denitrification of the industrial nitrate waste, to determine the amount of organic carbon waste needed for denitrification, and to define the detention time necessary for efficient operation of the columns. Throughout the entire period of operation of the activated carbon column, very good denitrification results were achieved. Never in the course of the experiment did the total nitrogen removal fall below 98.3%. Removal efficiencies as high as 99.3% were observed with an average removal of 98.9%. These figures demonstrate the stability of operation and high removal efficiencies possible at an average packed column detention time of 157.5 minutes. The organic carbon removal efficiency fluctuated more than did the total nitrogen removal efficiencies. The highest removal efficiency noted was 74.6% while the lowest was 42.6% with an average of 61.2%. (Poertner)
W75-07111

COMPARATIVE EFFECTIVENESS OF SELECTED PRECIPITANTS FOR PHOSPHORUS REMOVAL IN TERTIARY TREATMENT,
Virginia Polytechnic Inst. and State Univ., Blacksburg.
P. H. King, J. D. Jenkins, R. C. Hoehn, and C. W. Randall.
Paper presented at the Fourth Annual Environmental Engineering and Science Conference, University of Louisville, Louisville, Kentucky, March 4-5, 1974. 15 p, 3 tab, 11 fig, 12 ref.

Descriptors: *Nutrient removal, *Phosphorus, *Tertiary treatment, *Chemical precipitation, *Waste water treatment, *Sewage treatment, Trickling filters, Effluents, Lime, Flocculation, Coagulation, Dewatering, Sludge, Suspended solids, Comparative benefits.
Identifiers: *Precipitants.

The performance was determined of add-on tertiary treatment units designed for substantial phosphorus removal from the effluent of a conventional trickling filter sewage treatment plant. Precipitants selected for study were lime, alum, sodium aluminate, and ferric sulfate. In each case dosage of the coagulant was sufficient to achieve a residual total phosphorus concentration of less than 0.3 mg/l. In addition to chemical dosage in terms of required cation to phosphorus molar ratio, optimum pH level and flocculation time were determined, concurrent suspended solids and total organic carbon removal efficiencies were defined, and the general dewatering properties of the remaining sludge were qualitatively described. The required dosages show that substantially higher dosages of lime are required than for either alum, sodium aluminate or ferric sulfate. Phosphorus removal using lime is strongly pH dependent. One of the most important aspects of selecting an appropriate precipitant for phosphorus removal in tertiary treatment is the quantity and quality of the sludge produced. Lime treatment yielded the largest volume of sludge, but the dewatering properties were excellent. In each of the systems tested, the concurrent suspended solids removal was excellent, providing a significant benefit for the type of add-on tertiary treatment being investigated. (Poertner)
W75-07113

CONSIDERATIONS FOR ANALYSIS OF INFILTRATION-INFLOW,
Edison Water Quality Research Lab., N.J.
R. Field, and D. J. Cesareo.
A paper presented at the 1974 International Public Works Congress and Equipment Show, Toronto, Ontario, Canada, September 16, 1974. 27 p, 1 fig, 2 tab, 11 ref.

Descriptors: *Infiltration, *Inflow, *Sewerage, *Rainfall-runoff relationships, *Sewers, Groundwater movement, Infiltration rates, Runoff, Simulated rainfall, Combined sewers, Data collections, Cost-benefit analysis, On-site data collections, Annual costs, Maintenance costs, Operating costs.
Identifiers: *Sanitary sewers, Extraneous flows, Surcharge.

The U.S. Environmental Protection Agency (EPA) has developed basic guidelines to follow in developing a thorough cost-effective infiltration/inflow evaluation and correction program. Infiltration/Inflow is defined as the total quantity of water from both infiltration and inflow without distinguishing the source. Excessive Infiltration/Inflow is defined as the quantities of infiltration/inflow which can be economically eliminated from a sewer system by rehabilitation. Infiltration and inflow countermeasures can be divided into two parts: prevention of excessive extraneous flows, and correction of conditions already imposed on existing sewer systems. The EPA proposes an initial survey to determine if the infiltration/inflow is excessive and if it is, then a sewer system evaluation survey should be made. This survey is the systematic examination of the sewer system to determine the specific location, flow rate and rehabilitation costs of each infiltration/inflow source or sources. The evaluation survey is outlined as a series of five consecutive parts consisting of the physical survey, the rainfall simulation, preparatory cleaning, internal inspection, and the survey report. Cost analyses are given for both the infiltration/inflow analysis and the sewer system evaluation. Case studies are described. (Poertner)
W75-07117

WASTE WATER RECLAMATION: THE STATEWIDE PICTURE,
California State Dept. of Water Resources, Sacramento.
J. R. Teerink.
Typescript paper presented at a meeting of the Water Section of the Commonwealth Club, San Francisco, California, May 2, 1974. 13 p.

Descriptors: *Water reuse, *Return flow, *Groundwater recharge, *Water utilization, *Reclaimed water, *Water supply, Water allocation(Policy), Water conservation, Water demand, Water quality control, California, Artificial recharge, Water yield improvement, Irrigation water, Waste water treatment.
Identifiers: Waste water reclamation, Agricultural waste water.

Waste water reclamation appears to be the most promising method of developing a supplemental source of water. Reclaimed water can be used after ground water recharge for almost any purpose. It can be used directly for agricultural and other irrigation, recreation, and industrial purposes, including use as cooling water. Waste water reclamation is defined as 'the planned renovation of waste water with the intent of producing usable water for a specific beneficial purpose.' Much of the water used in California is returned to the freshwater cycle, either directly after its use or following treatment. This includes 95 percent of the irrigation return waters from nearly 9 million acres of irrigated land and the treated wastes from inland cities, particularly in the Central Valley. Although reclamation (demineralization) of these waters would tend to enhance water quality, it would not create a new supply. Waste water reclamation possibilities in the San Francisco Bay area have recently been studied by the Department of Water Resources and the State Water Resources Control Board. The study has shown that a large amount of waste water, perhaps 500,000 acre-feet, can be reclaimed by the year 1980. This source of water could present an attractive opportunity for meeting future demands for power plant cooling, an option that becomes increasingly important. The use of reclaimed agricultural waste water in the power plant cooling process would not only satisfy water supply needs but assist in solving waste disposal needs as well. (Poertner)
W75-07118

REGIONAL SEWAGE TREATMENT NEEDS FOR EUGENE-SPRINGFIELD URBAN AREA.
CH2M/Hill, Corvallis, Oreg.
Eugene, Oregon, February, 1975. 160 p, 21 fig, 25 tab, 19 ref, 4 append.

Descriptors: *Waste water treatment, *Planning, *Sewerage, *Oregon, *Regional development, Waste water disposal, Sewers, Sewage districts, Sewage treatment, Sanitary engineering, Cities, Flood protection, Alternate planning.
Identifiers: *Eugene(Oregon), *Springfield(Oregon).

Two governmental bodies provide sewerage services: Eugene and Springfield, Oregon through the Springfield Utility Board. Recently passed local legislation places all responsibility for Springfield sewage collection and treatment on the City of Springfield forces. Based on evaluation of costs and related factors, regional sewage treatment for the metropolitan Eugene-Springfield urban area will be accomplished by separate expansion and upgrading of the existing Eugene and Springfield facilities. Two regional sewage treatment plans have been analyzed. Plan A, the 'Dual Regional Plant Plan,' assumes separate and parallel expansion and upgrading of the existing Eugene and Springfield facilities. Plan B, the 'Single Regional Plant Plan,' considered abandonment of existing Springfield facilities; expansion and upgrading of the Eugene facilities; and construction of a 72-inch diameter connecting interceptor sewer. An evaluation and ranking process was used to analyze each plan. This included monetary cost effectiveness, implementation capability, financial equity and cost allocation, compatability with local planning, utilization of existing facilities, energy consumption, comparative environmental compatability, and comparative reliability and flexibility. It is recommended that both the City of Eugene and the City of Springfield undertake work remaining to: complete federal facilities planning requirements, review and update user ordinances, authorize detailed predesign work, and explore methods of financing. (Poertner)
W75-07119

WASTE WATER MANAGEMENT - IMPLICATIONS FOR REGIONAL PLANNING,
For primary bibliographic entry see Field 8A.
W75-07120

WASTE WATER MANAGEMENT - ALTERNATIVES FOR THE MERRIMACK RIVER,
Corps of Engineers, New York. North Atlantic Div.
F. M. McGowan.
In: The Merrimack: Design for a Clean River, American Society of Civil Engineers, National Meeting, Session No. 17, Washington, D.C, January 30, 1973. 7 p, 20 fig.

Descriptors: *Waste water treatment, *Tertiary treatment, *Water pollution control, *Alternate planning, *Regional analysis, Multiple-purpose projects, Optimization, Water quality control, Costs, Management, Planning, Annual costs, Capital costs, Administration, Waste water management, New Hampshire, Massachusetts.
Identifiers: *Merrimack River Basin.

The regional solutions suggested for the Merrimack River pollution abatement program are based on: high water quality, reuse of treated wastewaters, advanced technologies, alternative systems, and coordinated basin and metropolitan area wastewater management. In examining regional solutions, inspection shows pollution to be coming primarily from: (1) recreational areas at the headwaters of the Merrimack: the Laconia-Franklin area; (2) New Hampshire State capital area - the City of Concord; (3) heavily industrialized cities of Manchester, New Hampshire; (4) Nashua, New Hampshire; (5) Fitchberg-Leominster area in Massachusetts; and (6) the Lowell-Lawrence and Haverhill area in Massachusetts. Solutions for the Merrimack could be developed depending on the objectives of the people and their representatives. The land and water technologies could be mixed, for example, so that the secondary-tertiary treatment system would function in the non-irrigation season and the secondary portion combined with land could take over then, in the remainder of the year. During the irrigation season, the tertiary system, with its high operating costs, could be shut down and the land scheme used. The approach also combines many of the benefits and opportunities discussed for the two individual technologies. A cost estimate for such an approach would be about $1 billion in capital expenditures and $100 million in annual operating costs. (Poertner)
W75-07122

TECHNIQUES OF WASTE WATER MANAGEMENT,
Vanderbilt Univ., Nashville, Tenn. Dept. of Environmental and Water Resources Engineering.
W. W. Eckenfelder, Jr.
In: The Merrimack: Design for a Clean River, American Society of Civil Engineers, National Meeting, Session No. 17, Washington, D.C., January 30, 1973. 19 p, 2 fig, 2 tab, 22 ref.

Descriptors: *Tertiary treatment, *Waste water treatment, *Water pollution control, *Optimization, *Regional analysis, Industrial wastes, *Municipal wastes, Water quality control, Treatment facilities, Sewage treatment, Administration, Management, New Hampshire, Massachusetts.
Identifiers: *Merrimack River Basin, Waste water management.

In tertiary treatment of wastewater, it is essential to optimize the biological process in order to effect optimal performance and economics from the tertiary system. It is possible to estimate the average effluent quality from a secondary treatment facility as design input for tertiary treatment design; however, variation in secondary effluent quality can exert a profound effect on tertiary performance. In recent years, a number of biological process modifications have been developed to enhance the treatment efficiency and to provide a more uniform effluent, such as: (1) high purity oxygen in which dissolved oxygen levels of 10 mg/l are maintained in the aeration basin; and, (2) powdered activated carbon added to aeration basins. There are a number of process combinations including biological, physical and chemical which are technically feasible to produce an effluent of any desired quality. The selection of the optimum process combination to yield the least cost will depend upon the volume and characteristics of the wastewaters being treated and upon the availability and cost of chemicals and equipment. As regional and combined treatment systems increase in use several considerations are necessary to insure optimal and consistent effluent quality. If physical-chemical treatment is to be considered, pretreatment of many of the industrial wastewaters that are poorly adsorbed on carbon and could lead to high biological growths on the carbon and bed clogging. Equalization of the industrial wastewaters and to some degree the municipal wastewaters is important to insure uniform effluent quality. Where the activated sludge process is to be employed, optimization of the process to minimize effluent COD, N and P is essential for optimal and economic operation. (Poertner)
W75-07123

HEALTH ASPECTS OF WATER REUSE,
Los Angeles County Sanitation District, Calif.
For primary bibliographic entry see Field 3C.
W75-07129

A SMALL SCALE SWIRL CONCENTRATOR FOR STORM FLOW,
Wisconsin Univ., Milwaukee.
R. A. White.
MS thesis, May 1974. 55 p, 25 fig, 10 tab, 15 ref, 2 append.

Descriptors: *Sewerage, *Water pollution control, *Flood control, *Model studies, *Storm runoff, *Combined sewers, Sewage, Sewage treatment, Sewers, Conveyance structures, Storm surge, Wisconsin, Storm drains, Storm water, Overflow.
Identifiers: *Swirl concentrator, Sewer backups.

An investigation was made of operational characteristics of the swirl concentrator, a new device which was developed for the regulation of suspended matter in combined sewer flows. This device has been shown to be very effective in removing solids quickly. It has no moving parts, and can be made of concrete and put underground. This should allow for some treatment of the sewage before discharge into the storm water during heavy seasonal rains. The swirl concentrator would need no attention during storm flow operation. Further, the apparatus is small and inexpensive to justify its temporary use in developed residential areas. Historically the swirl concentrator has been fed by gravity sewers. In this study, it was necessary to adapt pumped sewage discharge to the concentrator. It was shown by scaled model study that a swirl concentrator could be devised on a small scale for use with small pumps in relieving surcharged sewers. The modification made for this special application was found to be applicable to, and improving upon normal scale swirl concentrators. (Poertner)
W75-07130

REGIONAL WATER QUALITY MANAGEMENT PLAN, 1973,
Bay Area Sewage Services Agency, Berkeley, Calif.
For primary bibliographic entry see Field 5G.
W75-07132

LAND APPLICATION ALTERNATIVES FOR WASTEWATER MANAGEMENT.
Army Engineer District, San Francisco, Calif.
For primary bibliographic entry see Field 5G.
W75-07135

A PROGRAM FOR WATER RECLAMATION AND GROUNDWATER RECHARGE, ENVIRONMENTAL IMPACT STATEMENT.
Jenks and Adamson, Palo Alto, Calif.
For primary bibliographic entry see Field 4B.
W75-07137

RECLAMATION OF WASTEWATER IN SANTA CLARA COUNTY: A LOOK AT THE POTENTIAL.
Consoer, Townsend and Associates, San Jose, Calif; and Bechtel Corp., San Francisco, Calif.
Santa Clara Valley Water District, San Jose, California, October 1973. 18 p, 11 fig, 3 tab.

Descriptors: *Water reuse, *Water utilization, *Artificial recharge, *Recharge, *Reclaimed water, Water allocation(Policy), Water conservation, Water demand, Water quality control, California.
Identifiers: Santa Clara County(California).

In 1970, in response to the growing concern about water sources and water management a long range plan for wastewater disposition was begun. One facet was a study to determine the potential benefits or disadvantages of reclaiming and reusing wastewater rather than discharging it into San Francisco Bay. There will be a critical need for augmented water supplies both in Santa Clara County and throughout the large San Felipe Service Area starting in 1978. In looking at the markets for reclaimed wastewater in the area to be served by the proposed San Felipe Project, it was found that by far the major market or use for reclaimed wastewater would be groundwater recharge in north Santa Clara County. Another large market for reclaimed water would be farms and orchards in the area. Present wastewater quality was compared to present and projected water supplies. Alternative programs using reclaimed wastewater were studied. Four of these plans use reclaimed water rather than importation, and the fifth alternative combines reclamation and importation. A system combining importing water and reclamation would be cheaper than reclamation and reuse alone. (Poertner)
W75-07138

MATHEMATICAL MODELS OF MAJOR DIVERSION STRUCTURES IN THE MINNEAPOLIS-ST. PAUL INTERCEPTOR SEWER SYSTEM,
Minnesota Univ., Minneapolis. St. Anthony Falls Hydraulic Lab.
G. S. Harris.
Memorandum No. 120, December 1968. 21 p, 28 fig, 2 tab, 5 ref, 1 append.

Descriptors: *Combined sewers, *Water pollution control, *Mathematical models, *Diversion structures, *Computer models, *Interceptor sewers, Sewers, Hydraulic structures, Minnesota, Computer models, Mississippi River, Sanitary engineering.
Identifiers: Minneapolis(Minnesota), St. Paul(Minnesota).

The hydraulic characteristics are described of 19 different diversion structures, which comprise 6 types in the Minneapolis St. Paul interceptor sewer system. No two diversion structures are the same, but some are quite similar in their geometry. From the general hydraulic description of the diversion structures, it is possible to arrive at equations which describe the flow diverted to the interceptor sewer in terms of the flow entering the diversion and the settings of the gates and Fabridams. A computer program has been written to calculate the flow diverted to the interceptor at each of the 19 main diversion structures which fall into the six types. The program has as input for a particular diversion structure the fixed constants such as orifice width, diameter of gate, discharge coefficients, the gate and Fabridam heights, and the inflow to the diversion structure. Each diversion structure type has a subroutine which accepts the appropriate information and solves the flow diverted to the interceptor. From the mathematical description of the diversion structures and the computer program it has been possible to derive a set of operating graphs for the diversion structures. For a given inflow the flow which is diverted to the interceptor depends on the Fabridam and gate settings. (Poertner)
W75-07142

DEVELOPMENT OF A COMPUTER PROGRAM TO ROUTE RUNOFF IN THE MINNEAPOLIS-ST. PAUL INTERCEPTOR SEWERS,
Minnesota Univ., Minneapolis. St. Anthony Falls Hydraulic Lab.
G. S. Harris.
Memorandum No. 121, December 1968. 18 p, 29 fig, 1 tab, 13 ref, 1 append.

Descriptors: *Routing, *Water quality control, *Computer programs, *Rainfall-runoff relationships, *Interceptor sewers, Sewers, Data storage and retrieval, Programs, Minnesota, Runoff, Mississippi River, Combined sewers, Hydraulics.
Identifiers: Minneapolis(Minnesota), St. Paul(Minnesota), Method of characteristics.

The development is described of a program to route storm runoff through the Minneapolis-St. Paul combined interceptor sewer system. Because of the complicated nature of the pipe layout, a computer program was required to simulate the flow. The program considers the flow which enters the system at 15 major points, which handle 80 per cent of the flow. As there was concern over the applicability of normal flood routing methods in this system, it was decided to solve the equations governing unsteady flow in open channels and compare the results of this solution with conventional routing methods. The method of characteristics is used to determine the flow velocity and depth at increasing intervals of time starting from known or assumed initial conditions in an open channel in which there is insteady flow. The most important result of this phase of the investigation was the conclusion that the average-lag method of routing produces the same results as the method of characteristics if the appropriate routing constants are chosen. As a consequence of this result the whole of flood hydrographs entering the Twin Cities interceptor sewer system can be quickly evaluated to a sufficient degree of accuracy in real time by the progressive average-lag method. (Poertner)
W75-07143

A SIMPLE SYSTEM FOR FREEZE DRYING,
New Hampshire Univ., Durham. Inst. of Natural and Environmental Resources.
For primary bibliographic entry see Field 7B.
W75-07245

THE CHARACTERISTICS AND ULTIMATE DISPOSAL OF WASTE SEPTIC TANK SLUDGE,
Alaska Univ., College. Inst. of Water Resources.
T. Tilsworth.
Available from the National Technical Information Service, Springfield, Va. 22161 as PB-241 488, $3.75 in paper copy, $2.25 in microfiche. Completion Report No. IWR-56, November 1974. 30 p, 2 fig, 7 tab, 41 ref, append. OWRT A-039-ALAS (1), 14-31-0001-3802, 14-31-0001-4002.

Descriptors: *Septic tanks, Sludge, Anaerobic conditions, *Alaska, Cold climate, Aerobic conditions, Economics, Aerobic digestion, *Waste water treatment, Waste disposal, *Ultimate disposal, Waste identification, Biochemical oxygen demand, Chemical oxygen demand, Domestic wastes, Sewage treatment, Treatment facilities, Cost analysis.
Identifiers: Fairbanks(Alas).

Individual household treatment of domestic sewage has been accomplished, in part, by the use of septic tanks. These treatment units are still being widely used in urban and rural areas where sewers and sewage treatment facilities are nonexistant. Periodic removal of waste septic tank sludge can result in environmental damage unless adequate provision has been made for processing this sludge for ultimate disposal. Septage samples were obtained from the Fairbanks, Alaska locale and were characterized as to BOD, COD, solids and others. Several experiments were performed on the septic sludge including aeration and digestion studies. Methods of treatment and ultimate disposal were discussed as well as cost analyses.
W75-07273

EFFECTS OF HYDROLIGIC REGIME ON NUTRIENT REMOVAL FROM WASTEWATER USING GRASS FILTRATION FOR FINAL TREATMENT,
Pennsylvania State Univ., University Park. Dept. of Agricultural Engineering.
E. A. Myers, and R. M. Butler.
Available from the National Technical Information Service, Springfield, Va. 22161 as PB-241 487, $475 in paper copy, $2.25 in microfiche. Pennsylvania Institute for Research on Land and Water Resources University Park, Research Publication 88, December 1974. 65 p, 13 fig, 33 tab, 21 ref, append. OWRT B-054-PA (3). 14-31-0001-3931.

Descriptors: *Overland flow, *Rates of application, *Waste water treatment, *Filters, *Sewage treatment, Seasonal, Effluents, Nitrates, Phosphates, *Nutrient removal, Design criteria, Laboratory tests, On-site tests.

Identifiers: *Nitrate removal, *Phosphate removal, *Grass filtration system, Application frequency, Long contact time.

Grass filtration has been proposed as a method for final treatment of secondary treated sewage effluent. The effectiveness of grass filtration or overland flow wastewater systems, however, has not been tested adequately. Thus, a field study was conducted to determine the effects of wastewater application rate, flow distance, application frequency, and season of the year on nitrate and phosphate removal. The removal of phosphate and nitrate, however, increased as the application frequency was decreased. However, in all the field tests, the reduction in phosphate and nitrate was very small, zero to approximately 20 percent. Laboratory tests, undertaken because of the small nitrogen removals in the field, were conducted. Five to six hours were required in the laboratory to achieve a 90 percent reduction in nitrate concentration from an effluent with an initial NO3-N concentration of 12 mg/l. The field and laboratory studies indicate that obtaining a sufficiently long contact time is the most important consideration in designing a grass filtration system. (Sink-Penn State)
W75-07276

ECONOMIC IMPACT STUDY OF THE POLLUTION ABATEMENT EQUIPMENT INDUSTRY,
Little (Arthur D.), Inc., Cambridge, Mass.
For primary bibliographic entry see Field 5G.
W75-07345

COST-EFFECTIVE DESIGN OF WASTEWATER TREATMENT FACILITIES BASED ON FIELD DERIVED PARAMETERS.
Saint Louis Metropolitan Sewer District, Mo.
Available from the National Technical Information Service, Springfield, Va 22161 as PB-234 356, $5.25 in paper copy, $2.25 in microfiche. Environmental Protection Agency, Cincinnati, Ohio, Report No. EPA-670/2/-74-062, July 1974. 100 p, 20 fig, 13 tab, 12 ref, 3 append. 1BB043. 11060 GVT.

Descriptors: *Sewage treatment, *Economic efficiency, Facilities, *Design, *Waste water treatment, Pilot plants, Cost-benefit ratio, Peak loads, Mathematical models, Annual costs, *Missouri, *Treatment facilities, Cost analysis.
Identifiers: Metropolitan St. Louis Sewer Dist., *St. Louis(Mo).

The Metropolitan St. Louis Sewer District is currently expanding its two major primary treatment facilities for secondary treatment equivalence. These plants process about 100 mgd and characterize the extremes encountered in municipal wastewater treatment. Bissell Point receives a strong wastewater dominated by industrial discharges; Lemay receives highly diluted wastewater. Both plants are less than five years old. A variety of special plant, pilot plant, and laboratory investigations were conducted to develop cost-effective mathematical models to describe optimum design conditions (and costs) for secondary treatment and waste solids handling as a function of the required design reliability, establish the optimum point of design reliability as a function of facility expenditure for each plant, and compare the cost differential between the two plants to illustrate the influence of wastewater quality upon facility costs and optimum design configurations. The optimum point of design reliability for both plants was 97.6%. Increasing reliabilities resulted in a gradual decline of the benefit/cost ratio to about 90% of optimum at 99.91% reliability. It is recommended that all systems be designed for rationally defined boundary conditions and peaking factors. Computer programs were developed to solve the optimum design configuration as a function of design reliability. (Auen-Wisconsin)
W75-07349

5E. Ultimate Disposal Of Wastes

DEWATERING OF EXCESS ACTIVATED SLUDGE AT THE SYASYA INTEGRATED PULP AND PAPER MILL (OBEZVOZHIVANIE IZBYTOCHNOGO ILA NA SYAS'KOM KOMBINATE),
Syasskii Lesokhimicheskii Kombinat (USSR).
For primary bibliographic entry see Field 5D.
W75-06875

LAND APPLICATION ALTERNATIVES FOR WASTEWATER MANAGEMENT.
Army Engineer District, San Francisco, Calif.
For primary bibliographic entry see Field 5G.
W75-07135

PRELIMINARY REVIEW OF USED LUBRICATING OILS IN CANADA,
Environmental Protection Service, Ottawa (Ontario).
For primary bibliographic entry see Field 5G.
W75-07151

GROUND-WATER QUALITY BENEATH SOLID-WASTE DISPOSAL SITES AT ANCHORAGE, ALASKA,
Geological Survey, Anchorage, Alaska.
For primary bibliographic entry see Field 5B.
W75-07204

INVESTIGATING GROUND-WATER POLLUTION FROM INDIANAPOLIS' LANDFILLS—THE LESSONS LEARNED,
Geological Survey, Indianapolis, Ind.
For primary bibliographic entry see Field 5B.
W75-07205

GROUND-WATER CONTAMINATION IN THE SILURIAN DOLOMITE OF DOOR COUNTY, WISCONSIN,
Geological Survey, Madison, Wis.
For primary bibliographic entry see Field 5B.
W75-07207

THE CHARACTERISTICS AND ULTIMATE DISPOSAL OF WASTE SEPTIC TANK SLUDGE,
Alaska Univ., College. Inst. of Water Resources.
For primary bibliographic entry see Field 5D.
W75-07273

5F. Water Treatment and Quality Alteration

PAPER AND PAPERBOARD MANUFACTURING. (2). WATER SUPPLIES,
Paper, Vol 183, No 2, p 81-82, 85, 87, January 20, 1975. 4 fig.

Descriptors: *Industrial water, *Pulp and paper industry, *Water supply, *Water treatment, *Water utilization, *Water softening, *Water pollution, Rain water, Surface waters, Groundwater, Boiler feed water, Solvents, Bicarbonates, Sulfates, Nitrates, Chlorides, Calcium, Magnesium, Suspended solids, Color, Flocculation, Coagulation, Chemical precipation, Ion exchange, Lime, Separation techniques, Iron compounds, Salts.

This general discussion of water covers water supplies (rain, surface, and ground waters); uses of water in paper and board manufacture (including boiler makeup water, condensing water, pulp washing, dilution and transport of papermaking stock, solution of chemicals, washing media for wires, felts, etc.); chemical impurities in water (calcium and magnesium bicarbonates, sulfates, chlorides, and nitrates, and iron salts); removal of suspended matter and color from water by flocculation, coagulation, sedimentation, and filtration; and water softening by the lime-soda and ion-exchange processes. (Sykes-IPC)
W75-06889

HIGH-RATE WATER TREATMENT: A REPORT ON THE STATE OF THE ART,
American Society of Civil Engineers, New York. Subcommittee on High-Rate Water Treatment.
P. H. King, R. L. Johnson, C. W. Randall, and G. W. Rehberger.
Typescript, July, 1974. 20 p, 9 tab, 4 fig, 5 ref.

Descriptors: *Municipal water, *Water treatment, *Water purification, *Filtration, *Flocculation, *Water quality control, *Sedimentation, Settling basins, Coagulation, Water softening, Lime, Treatment, Data collections.
Identifiers: High-rate water treatment, Hydraulic loading, High-rate filtration.

The ASCE-EED Committee on Water Purification recently conducted a survey of State regulatory agencies to determine the prevailing concept of 'high-rate' water treatment and to ascertain their attitude toward the various methods currently being employed. A second phase of the Committee's work was concerned with an analysis of operating data from several high-rate water treatment plants in Virginia. In considering the results of this study, the Committee concluded that while the general understanding of the term 'high-rate treatment' usually pertains to higher hydraulic loading rates on filtration units, a broader based concept of high-rate treatment that includes other units as well needs to be propogated. The entire system, from rapid mix to final stabilization and disinfection, should be handled as a single entity to arrive at the optimum and most economical solution for each case. The data cited in this paper clearly indicate that the propriety of utilizing high-rate treatment processes in many municipal water treatment facilities has been adequately demonstrated. Finally, the Committee concluded that there are economic advantages inherent in high-rate treatment and these are gained without sacrificing water quality. (Poertner)
W75-07112

PREVENTIVE MAINTENANCE,
East Bay Municipal Utility District, Oakland, Calif.
For primary bibliographic entry see Field 8C.
W75-07115

A SIMPLE SYSTEM FOR FREEZE DRYING,
New Hampshire Univ., Durham. Inst. of Natural and Environmental Resources.
For primary bibliographic entry see Field 7B.
W75-07245

5G. Water Quality Control

ORGANIZING FOR TODAY'S EFFLUENT CONTROL NEEDS,
Intercontinental Pulp Co. Ltd., Prince George (British Columbia).
For primary bibliographic entry see Field 5D.
W75-06863

A PRELIMINARY REVIEW OF ANALYTICAL METHODS FOR THE DETERMINATION OF SUSPENDED SOLIDS IN PAPER INDUSTRY EFFLUENTS FOR COMPLIANCE WITH EPA-NPDES PERMIT TERMS,
National Council of the Paper Industry for Air and Stream Improvement, Inc., New York.
For primary bibliographic entry see Field 5A.
W75-06865

FDA'S PROGRAM OF MERCURY IN FOODS,
Food and Drug Administration, Seattle, Wash.
F. D. Clark.
In: Mercury in the Western Environment, Continuing Education Publications, Corvallis, Oregon, p 81-84, 1973. 2 ref.

Descriptors: *Mercury, *Foods, *Regulations, *Public health, Toxicity, Analytical techniques, Spectroscopy, Heavy metals, *Standards, Pollutant identification.

The history of the U.S. Food and Drug Administration's (FDA) current interest concerning mercury in foods, with emphasis on fish and shellfish was traced. The toxicological basis for the guideline figure of 0.5 ppm was discussed, as well as the relationship of this figure to available methodology. The results of the surveys on the mercury content of several foods were reported, and available details and results on current surveys of fish and shellfish for mercury were provided as well as a general description of the present FDA program for mercury in foods. (See also W75-06897) (Jernigan-Vanderbilt)
W75-06905

THE HUMAN HEALTH HAZARDS OF METHYLMERCURY,
Mayo Clinic, Rochester, Minn. Dept. of Medical Statistics, Epidemiology and Population Genetics.
For primary bibliographic entry see Field 5C.
W75-06925

THE NEED FOR A COMPREHENSIVE APPROACH IN THE MANAGEMENT OF ENVIRONMENTAL RESOURCES,
North Carolina State Univ., Raleigh. Dept. of Civil Engineering.
For primary bibliographic entry see Field 6G.
W75-06938

PROBABILISTIC METHODS IN STREAM QUALITY MANAGEMENT,
Washington Univ., Seattle. Dept. of Civil Engineering.
For primary bibliographic entry see Field 5B.
W75-06946

ON THE EFFICIENT ALLOCATION OF ENVIRONMENTAL ASSIMILATIVE CAPACITY: THE CASE OF THERMAL EMISSIONS TO A LARGE BODY OF WATER,
California Univ., Los Angeles. Dept. of Engineering Systems.
For primary bibliographic entry see Field 5B.
W75-06950

WATER MANAGEMENT--A GENERAL REPORT,
Illinois State Water Survey, Urbana.
For primary bibliographic entry see Field 4A.
W75-06953

A GEOMETRIC PROGRAMMING MODEL FOR OPTIMAL ALLOCATION OF STREAM DISSOLVED OXYGEN,
Rensselaer Polytechnic Inst., Troy, N.Y.
For primary bibliographic entry see Field 5D.
W75-06954

SIMULATION AS AN AID TO DECISION MAKING IN A WATER UTILITY,
Puerto Rico Aqueduct and Sewer Authority, Santurce. Planning Area.
For primary bibliographic entry see Field 6A.
W75-06959

VANVOOREN V. JOHN E. FOGARTY MEMORIAL HOSPITAL (ACTION FOR DAMAGES AND RELIEF FROM POLLUTION OF ARTESIAN WELL).
For primary bibliographic entry see Field 6E.
W75-06962

STATE BOARD'S DISCRETIONARY POWER TO PENALIZE POLLUTERS DECLARED INVALID.
For primary bibliographic entry see Field 6E.
W75-06964

SMITH V. JACKSON PARISH SCHOOL BOARD (ACTION FOR DAMAGES TO POND CAUSED BY DEFECTIVE SEWAG SYSTEM).
For primary bibliographic entry see Field 6E.
W75-06965

AMERICAN PAPER INSTITUTE V. TRAIN (ACTION SEEKING REVIEW OF WATER POLLUTION EFFLUENT LIMITATION GUIDELINES FOR THE PAPER INDUSTRY).
For primary bibliographic entry see Field 6E.
W75-06966

ILLINOIS SUPREME COURT OK'S PCB'S POWER TO FINE POLLUTERS.
Pollution Control Guide, Vol 3, paragraph 19820, p 19473-19474, 1974.

Descriptors: *Illinois, *Judicial decisions, *Penalties(Legal), *Law enforcement, *Water pollution control, Jurisdiction, Governments, Water law, Water resources development, Administrative agencies, Water pollution, Adjudication procedure, Regulation, Administration, Legal aspects, Legislation, Decision making.
Identifiers: Environmental policy, State policy.

Specified sections of the Illinois Environmental Protection Act conferring authority on the Illinois Pollution Control Board to impose discretionary, variable, monetary civil penalties on polluters, have recently been held constitutional by the Illinois Supreme Court. The court ruled that the penalty power granted to the Board is not an unconstitutional delegation of judicial power in violation of the separation of powers provisions of the constitutions of either the state of Illinois or the United States. The key factor in considering the question of improper delegation of power is the presence or absence of judicial power. In supporting the Board's power to impose civil penalties the court noted that the U.S. Supreme Court has never found judicial power to have been improperly vested in an administrative agency. The court concluded that the trend in state decisions is to allow administrative agencies to impose discretionary civil penalties. (Sperling-Florida)
W75-06968

BROWN V. RUCKELSHAUS (AND COMPANION CASE) (CHALLENGE TO EXECUTIVE IMPOUNDMENT).
1 Pollution Control Guide, Vol 3, paragraph 15015, p 15147-15156, 1973.

Descriptors: *Judicial decisions, *California, *Allotments, *Federal government, *Administrative agencies, Legal aspects, Legal review, Water law, Political constraints, Federal jurisdiction, Administration, Governmental interrelations, Legislation, project planning, Waste water treatment, Political aspects, Water policy, Financing, Water treatment, Federal Water Pollution Control Act, Adjudication procedure.
Identifiers: Class action suits, *FWPCA Amendments of 1972, Sovereign immunity, Standing(Legal), Administrative regulations, Declaratory judgments, Injunctive relief.

Plaintiff Congressman brought action on behalf of himself and all other citizens of California challenging the defendant Environmental Protection Agency Administrator's impoundment of funds authorized under the Federal Water Pollution Control Act Amendments of 1972. The plaintiff municipality brought suit shortly therafter, and the two actions were consolidated. The plaintiffs contended that the Administrator exceeded his statutory authority in impounding the authorized funds. The defendant argued that the actions were bared by the doctrine of sovereign immunity, that there was no justiciable controversy, that the plaintiffs lacked standing to sue, and that the defendant's actions were within the scope of his discretionary powers under the Act. The United States District Court ruled that both plaintiffs had failed to demonstrate that the defendant's actions had injured or would injure them in any way, and therefore, they lacked standing to sue. The court also ruled that the provision of the Act authorizing citizens to sue on their own behalf did not permit the maintenance of class action suits to challenge the actions of the administrator. Granting the defendant's motion for dismissal, the court went on the state that the impoundment of funds was not beyond the scope of executive discretion. (Deckert-Florida)
W75-06969

CAMPAIGN CLEAN WATER, INC. V. RUCKELSHAUS (CITIZENS SUIT ON IMPOUNDMENT OF FWPCA FUNDS.)
1 Pollution Control Guide, Vol 3, paragraph 15009, p 15108-15116, 1973.

Descriptors: *Judicial decisions, *Virginia, *Allotments, *Federal government, *Waste water treatment, Administrative agencies, Legal aspects, Political constraints, Legal review, Federal jurisdiction, Water law, Governmental interrelations, Administration, Legislation, Project planning, Federal budget, political aspects, Water policy, Financing, Water treatment, Federal Water Pollution Control Act.
Identifiers: Class action suits, *FWPCA Amendments of 1972, Sovereign immunity, Standing(Legal), Administrative regulations, Declaratory judgments, Injunctive relief.

The plaintiff environmental group brought class action seeking declaratory and injunctive relief to compel the defendant federal administrator to allow the full sums authorized by Section 207 of the Federal Water Pollution Control Act Amendments of 1972. The plaintiff challenged the defeudant's announced policy with respect to the impoundment of $6 billion of the designated $11 billion authorized by the Act for construction of waste treatment facilities. The defendant sought dismissal of the action on the following grounds: (1) the plaintiff lacked standing to sue; (2) this action was rendered moot by virtue of City of New York v. Ruckelshaus; (3) the doctrine of sovereign immunity; (4) no case or controversy. The United States District Court rejected the defendant's motion and ruled that the challenged policy of impoundment of funds constituted an abuse of discretion and declaring that policy null and void, granted the plaintiffs motion for summary judgment. Recognizing that the Act granted the executive some discretion with respect to appropriations, the court refused to grant injunctive relief and limited the scope of its declaratory judgment to those interests represented by the plaintiff organization. (Deckert-Florida)
W75-06970

THE CITY OF NEW YORK, ET AL. V. RUCKELSHAUS (IMPOUNDMENT OF FEDERAL WATER POLLUTION CONTROL ACT FUNDS).
1 Pollution Control Guide, Vol. 3, paragraph 15008, p 15100-15108, 1974.

Descriptors: *Judicial decisions, *Allotments, *Federal government, *Administrative agencies, *Waste water treatment, Legal aspects, Political constraints, Federal jurisdiction, Legal review,

Water law, Governmental interrelations, Administration, Legislation, Project planning, Political aspects, Water policy, Financing, Water treatment, Federal Water Pollution Control Act.
Identifiers: *Class action suits, *FWPCA Amendments of 1972, Sovereign immunity, Standing(Legal), Administrative regulations, Declaratory judgments, Injunctive relief.

The plaintiff municipality, on behalf of itself and other similarly situated municipalities in the State of New York, brought class action against the defendant Administrator of the Environmental Protection Agency. The plaintiff sought a declaratory judgment and mandamus compelling the defendant to comply with the Federal Water Pollution Control Act Amendments of 1972. Whereas the Act authorized the sums of $5 billion for 1973 and $6 billion in 1974 for the construction of publicly owned sewage treatment works, the defendant had alloted only $2 billion and $3 billion respectively for those periods. The defendant argued that the wording of the Act granted him the discretion to decide how much of the authorization to utilize in granting the plaintiff's motion for summary judgment, the United States District Court for the District of Columbia, while expressly not ruling on the power of the executive concerning the 'obligation' of such sums, ruled that the Administrator must allocate the full amount authorized by Congress. The court rejected the defendant's jurisdiction and standing arguments, and ordered the full amount to be allocated. However, the court stayed the effectiveness of its order pending expedited appeal to the United States, Court of Appeals for the District of Columbia. (Deckert-Florida)
W75-06971

CALVERT CLIFFS COORDINATING COMMITTEE, INC., ET AL. V. UNITED STATES ATOMIC ENERGY COMM'N., ET AL. (ENFORCEMENT OF THE NATIONAL ENVIRONMENTAL POLICY ACT).
For primary bibliographic entry see Field 6G.
W75-06972

TOWARD CLEANER WATER.
Environmental Protection Agency, Washington, D.C.
Available from Superintendent of Documents, U.S. Govt. Printing Office, Washington, D.C. January 1974. 33 p, 7 append.

Descriptors: *Federal Water Pollution Control Act, *Permits, *Pollution abatement, *Water pollution control, Water pollution treatment, Water pollution standards, Water pollution, Effluents, Legislation, Federal government, Jurisdiction, State governments, State jurisdiction.
Identifiers: *FWPCA Amendments of 1972, Effluent limitations, Administrative regulations.

The National Pollutant Discharge Elimination System (NPDES) is a new national permit program designed to control the discharge of pollutants into the Nation's waters. The NPDES, created by the Federal Water Pollution Control Act Amendments of 1972 is an attempt to prevent, reduce, and eliminate water pollution by means of establishing standards of permissible effluent discharge, through the issuance of permits. The NPDES permit, in essence, is a contract between a discharger and the government. A discharger who violates the conditions of the permit or makes illegal discharges without a permit is subject to criminal sanctions of fine or imprisonment. Permanent permit authority may be delegated to a state only if the state meets the requirements of the law and regulations published by the Environmental Protection Agency (EPA). The EPA has authority to veto a proposed state permit if the permit does not comply with the law or EPA regulations. The EPA and the states are required to make public information on the permit system and provide for a public hearing before issuing or denying a permit. (Denvir-Florida)
W75-06973

CORRESPONDENCE CONFERENCE ON REMOVAL OF NITROGEN FROM MUNICIPAL WASTEWATER,
Massachusetts Univ., Amherst. Water Resources Research Center.
For primary bibliographic entry see Field 5D.
W75-06984

MATHEMATICAL MODELLING OF WATER QUALITY IN A RIVER SYSTEM,
Melbourne Univ., Parkville (Australia). Dept. of Civil Engineering.
For primary bibliographic entry see Field 5B.
W75-07031

MATHEMATICAL MODELS FOR THE PLANNING AND MANAGEMENT OF THE SAINT JOHN RIVER SYSTEMS,
Department of the Environment, Ottawa (Ontario). Ecological Systems Research Div.
For primary bibliographic entry see Field 5B.
W75-07032

ENVIRONMENTAL CONSIDERATIONS FOR CONSTRUCTION PROJECTS.
Agency for International Development, Washington, D.C. Office of Science and Technology.
For primary bibliographic entry see Field 6G.
W75-07047

REPORT ON REGIONAL POLLUTION CONTROL: HALIFAX-DARTMOUTH METROPOLITAN AREA.
Halifax-Dartmouth Metropolitan Area Planning Committee (Nova Scotia). Task Group on Water Supply and Waste Disposal.
For primary bibliographic entry see Field 5D.
W75-07085

PLANNING FOR SHORELINE AND WATER USES.
For primary bibliographic entry see Field 6B.
W75-07086

PROCEEDINGS OF THE WORKSHOP ON RESEARCH NEEDS RELATED TO WATER FOR ENERGY.
Illinois Univ., Urbana. Water Resources Center.
For primary bibliographic entry see Field 6D.
W75-07089

RESEARCH NEEDS RELATED TO THE ENVIRONMENTAL ASPECTS OF COAL GASIFICATION/LIQUEFACTION,
Hittman Associates, Inc., Columbia, Md.
For primary bibliographic entry see Field 6D.
W75-07099

THE LIMNOBIOLOGY OF DEVILS LAKE CHAIN, NORTH DAKOTA,
North Dakota Univ., Grand Forks. Dept. of Biology.
For primary bibliographic entry see Field 5B.
W75-07102

ALAMITOS BARRIER PROJECT,
Los Angeles County Flood Control District, Calif.
For primary bibliographic entry see Field 4B.
W75-07131

REGIONAL WATER QUALITY MANAGEMENT PLAN, 1973,
Bay Area Sewage Services Agency, Berkeley, Calif.
D. F. Murphy.
December 5, 1973. 20 p, 2 tab.

Descriptors: *Planning, *Wastewater pollution, *Drainage water, *Bays, *Water management(Applied), *Water quality control, Water quality standards, Water policy, Water demand, Water allocation(Policy), California, Wastewater disposal, Salt marshes, Administration, Regional development, Impaired water quality, Sewage effluents, Multiple-purpose projects.
Identifiers: *San Francisco Bay.

Formation of the Bay Area Sewage Services Agency (BASSA) was authorized by the Legislature and approved by the Governor in 1971. The enabling legislation requires BASSA to adopt a regional water quality management plan 'not later than January 1, 1974'. The development of the BASSA regional plan is closely related to the development of the Water Quality Management Plan for San Francisco Bay Basin (Basin Plan). The Basin Plan which is being managed by the State Water Resources Control Board will cover some of the principle subjects which BASSA's regional plan must cover. Therefore, to minimize duplication of State-BASSA planning and to preclude divergence of our plans, BASSA will not undertake its regional plan until the Basin Plan is more fully developed. This document contains two distinct parts: (1) BASSA's initial (1973) regional plan; and (2) BASSA's operating policies. The former is intended to satisfy BASSA's legislative mandate until the full regional plan is adopted. The latter is necessary to provide cohesion in the Agency's operations and to permit close coordination with other agencies. The authorization and the purpose of the plan are discussed. It is intended that this 1973 initial BASSA Plan serve as a guide for ongoing planning, including development of the Basin Plan. It is also the Agency's intention that the completed Basin Plan supersede this document. Specific features of the 1973 initial BASSA plan are listed. (Poertner)
W75-07132

REGIONAL SERVICES PROGRAM, FISCAL YEAR 1974-75,
Bay Area Sewage Services Agency, Berkeley, Calif.
P. C. Soltow, Jr., and D. F. Murphy.
March, 1974. 9 p, 1 tab.

Descriptors: *Administration, *Discharge water, *Water quality control, *Water management(Applied), *Water reuse, *Wastewater treatment, Runoff, Infiltration, Inflow, Monitoring, Urban runoff, Coordination, Data storage and retrieval, California, Regional development, Bays.
Identifiers: *San Francisco Bay, Regional services.

The regional services program has set as its goal the assistance of local and subregional agencies in the development and adoption of water quality management programs which will adequately protect the environment, be cost-effective and efficient, and reclaim and reuse wastewater and residuals. The proposed regional services of first priority for the fiscal year 1974-75 are described. These programs include a revision of all self-monitoring programs for waste dischargers, the implementation of wastewater reclamation plans, operator training, regional evaluation of residuals management, and project coordination. Proposed regional services of a second priority are given also. These include control of industrial wastes at their sources, review the new techniques that improve efficiency of wastewater management, the development of an information data bank, management of unsewered areas, investigations of urban runoff, and the assistance of local agencies in the solution of infiltration/inflow problems. The manpower needs and the activities chart for the planning department are shown. The appendix contains a table of the responsibilities of water quality agencies and a chart of the interrelationships of water quality plans. (Poertner)
W75-07133

LAND APPLICATION ALTERNATIVES FOR WASTEWATER MANAGEMENT.
Army Engineer District, San Francisco, Calif.
December 1973. 21 p, 17 fig, 5 tab, 1 append.

Descriptors: *Water reuse, *Sludge disposal, *Environmental control, *Social aspects, *Sewage treatment, *Sludge treatment, Sewage disposal, Waste disposal, Comprehensive planning, Alternative planning, California.
Identifiers: *Land application of wastewater.

In November of 1971, the United States Congress requested that the Corps of Engineers conduct a study of water quality and waste disposal problems related to wastewater management in the San Francisco Bay and Sacramento - San Joaquin Delta Region. Specific tasks assigned the Corps were the development of land application alternatives for treatment processes, disposal of sludge, wastewater reclamation and reuse. These tasks were to be carried out with considerations for the environmental quality, social well-being and regional development. The alternatives presented are comprised of combinations of land application and conventional sewage treatment plants. The land treatment process utilizes the entire biosystem, including the soil and its vegetative cover, to purify the wastewater. The wastewater is renovated primarily by three basic internal mechanisms operating within the soil, namely plant uptake; filtration, cation exchange and fixation; and reactions with soil microorganisms. The Corps found that land application alternatives could produce an effluent comparable to tertiary treatment. The method could also be used for ultimate disposal of sludge. No adverse, major socio-ecological or economic factors were identified that would negate wastewater management by land application. The reclaimed water could be put to beneficial uses. (Poertner)
W75-07135

MATHEMATICAL MODELS OF MAJOR DIVERSION STRUCTURES IN THE MINNEAPOLIS-ST. PAUL INTERCEPTOR SEWER SYSTEM,
Minnesota Univ., Minneapolis. St. Anthony Falls Hydraulic Lab.
For primary bibliographic entry see Field 5D.
W75-07142

DEVELOPMENT OF A COMPUTER PROGRAM TO ROUTE RUNOFF IN THE MINNEAPOLIS-ST. PAUL INTERCEPTOR SEWERS,
Minnesota Univ., Minneapolis. St. Anthony Falls Hydraulic Lab.
For primary bibliographic entry see Field 5D.
W75-07143

REAL-TIME ESTIMATION OF RUNOFF IN THE MINNEAPOLIS-ST. PAUL METROPOLITAN AREA,
Minnesota Univ., Minneapolis. St. Anthony Falls Hydraulic Lab.
G. S. Harris.
Memorandum No. 119, December 1968. 10 p, 4 tab, 4 fig, 14 ref.

Descriptors: *Water pollution control, *Rainfall-runoff relationships, *Interceptor sewers, *Computer programs, *Hydrographs, *Urban hydrology, Diversion structures, Mathematical models, Routing, Minnesota, Runoff, Combined sewers.
Identifiers: Real-time computations, Runoff hydrographs, St. Paul(Minnesota), Minneapolis(Minnesota).

The problem of computing runoff from the rain gage readings and the method which has been initially adopted for computing runoff in real time are discussed for the Minneapolis-St. Paul area. The mathematical model involves three basic components: (a) runoff, (b) diversion, and (c) routing of storm runoff. The runoff analysis, involving urban hydrology, was the main subject of the study. At the present time the runoff analysis is incomplete in that it does not include an evaluation of the rainfall losses. Due to the fact that very little information was available on the hydrologic characteristics of the catchments in the Twin City area and because the 'real time' analysis requires short computation time, it was decided to use a rather simple and direct approach for part of this initial hydrologic computation. The triangular unit hydrograph was selected with this in mind. A computer program has been written to evaluate the runoff hydrographs in the 15 main catchments using rainfall excess. Basically, the program reads the input data which include area, Thiessen polygon factors, time base, and time-to-peak for each unit hydrograph. The program then reads the rain gages and computes the hydrographs at the downstream ends of the 15 catchments. (Poertner)
W75-07144

THE REAL-TIME COMPUTATION OF RUNOFF AND STORM FLOW IN THE MINNEAPOLIS-ST. PAUL INTERCEPTOR SEWERS,
Minnesota Univ., Minneapolis. St. Anthony Falls Hydraulic Lab.
C. E. Bowers, G. S. Harris, and A. F. Pabst.
Memorandum No. M-118, December 1968. 23 p, 20 fig, 2 tab, 14 ref.

Descriptors: *Combined sewers, *Water pollution control, *Rainfall-runoff relationships, *Computer programs, *Data storage and retrieval, *Data processing, Computers, Sewers, Minnesota, Interceptor sewers, Runoff, Mississippi River, Sanitary engineering, Sewerage, Hydrology.
Identifiers: Real-time computation, Minneapolis(Minnesota), St. Paul(Minnesota).

Modern techniques and methods of analysis were applied to an existing combined sewer system in Minneapolis and St. Paul. The goal was to find ways to increase the effectiveness of the system in collecting sewage and reduce the amount of pollution of the Mississippi River. The analytical studies were initially concerned with the theoretical concepts involved in computing the amount of water from rainfall which enters the sewer system and in determining the way in which the consequent flood hydrographs travel through the system. The method developed involves an electronic computer to read the rain gages and compute the runoff, including an evaluation of the loss of rainfall due to infiltration and other losses. It will then compute the amount of flow which is diverted to the interceptor sewers at the diversion structures. To do this the program requires information on the heights of the various gates and Fabridams in the system. Finally the program must check whether the flow depth or rate exceeds certain predetermined levels. If it does, gate settings must be adjusted and certain parts of the computation must be repeated. The theories which govern the rainfall runoff relationship, the diversion structures and the routing are discussed. In most areas some confirmation is needed using field data. (Poertner)
W75-07145

OPTIMUM DEVELOPMENT OF GROUND WATER FROM THE COASTAL AQUIFERS OF DELAWARE; WHERE, HOW MUCH, AND FOR HOW LONG CAN WE SAFELY PUMP OUR COASTAL AQUIFERS,
Delaware Univ., Newark. Water Resources Center.
For primary bibliographic entry see Field 4B.
W75-07149

PRELIMINARY REVIEW OF USED LUBRICATING OILS IN CANADA,
Environmental Protection Service, Ottawa (Ontario).
D. J. Skinner.
Report EPS 3-WP-74-4, June 1974. 112 p, 64 ref, append.

Descriptors: *Oil, *Oil pollution, *Oil wastes, Water pollution control, Soil contamination, Pollutants, Oil industry, Fuels, Chemical wastes, Heavy metals, Natural resources, Recycling, Legal aspects, *Canada.

The problem of waste lubricating oil is one that shares many features with the major resource and environmental concerns of our time. A survey of the present situation in Canada was presented including overall volumes, chemical compositions, current and end-uses and disposal methods, and a brief look at existing legislation. The shortcomings of present methods were examined and promising areas of investigation were highlighted. A need at all levels of government was recognized for comprehensive and effective regulations covering oil and other liquid wastes both to minimize health and environmental hazards and to rationalize the storage and transportation of such wastes. (Sims-ISWS)
W75-07151

WATER QUALITY DIMENSIONS OF WATER RESOURCES PLANNING,
North Carolina Water Resources Research Inst., Raleigh.
D. H. Howells.
Journal of the Hydraulics Division, American Society of Civil Engineers, Vol 101, No HY2, Proceedings Paper 11146, p 277-284, February 1975. 9 ref, 1 append.

Descriptors: *Hydrologic cycle, *Land use, *Water quality, *Water resources, *Planning, Agricultural watersheds, Hydrology, Low-flow augmentation, Nitrogen, Phosphorus, Precipitation(Atmospheric), Sediments, Soil erosion, Storm runoff, Streamflow, Land resources, Water pollution.
Identifiers: National Environmental Policy Act.

The traditional and unnatural separation of water quality planning from water resource planning was pointed to as a major obstacle to the achievement of integrated and economical solutions of land and water resources management problems. Principles of the hydrologic cycle were used as a prespective on opportunities for more imaginative treatment of water quality in land and water resources than are presently utilized. Management of pollution from non-point sources should focus on available land-water management techniques rather than end-of-the-line treatment of polluted runoff. The magnitude of the water quality problem and the limited resources available to deal with it rule against arbitrary positions by regulatory agencies restricting the range of socially acceptable alternatives for water quality management. All means, including low streamflow augmentation, should be considered in order to reach least-cost solutions. Land use, water quality, and water resources planning remain badly fragmented at high cost to the public. (Harmeson-ISWS)
W75-07185

A WASTE ASSIMILATIVE CAPACITY MODEL FOR A SHALLOW, TURBULENT STREAM,
Marquette Univ., Milwaukee, Wis.
For primary bibliographic entry see Field 5B.
W75-07268

EFFECTS OF RESERVOIR CLEARING ON WATER QUALITY IN THE ARCTIC AND SUBARCTIC,
Alaska Univ., College. Inst. of Water Resources.
For primary bibliographic entry see Field 5C.
W75-07272

ENVIRONMENTAL INVENTORY AND ASSESSMENT, ILLINOIS WATERWAY; 12-FOOT CHANNEL NAVIGATION PROJECT,
Army Engineer Waterways Experiment Station, Vicksburg, Miss.
For primary bibliographic entry see Field 8B.
W75-07288

ON THE THEORY OF NATURAL SELF-PURIFICATION OF RESERVOIRS,
For primary bibliographic entry see Field 5C.
W75-07300

WATER QUALITY MODEL OF THE LOWER FOX RIVER, WISCONSIN,
Environmental Protection Agency, Washington, D.C. Office of Enforcement and General Counsel.
For primary bibliographic entry see Field 5B.
W75-07327

FORMALIN AS A THERAPEUTANT IN FISH CULTURE,
Bureau of Sport Fisheries and Wildlife, La Crosse, Wis. Fish Control Lab.
For primary bibliographic entry see Field 5C.
W75-07342

ECONOMIC IMPACT STUDY OF THE POLLUTION ABATEMENT EQUIPMENT INDUSTRY.
Little (Arthur D.), Inc., Cambridge, Mass.
Available from the National Technical Information Service, Springfield, Va 22161 as PB-225 841, $8.75 in paper copy, $2.25 in microfiche. Environmental Protection Agency, Washington, D.C., Report 230/9-73-030, December 1972. 283 p, 20 fig, 62 tab, 24 ref. EPA 68-01-0553.

Descriptors: *Pollution abatement, *Industries, *Equipment, *Economic impact, Air pollution, Water pollution control, Standards, Instrumentation, Chemicals, Waste water treatment, Profit, Marketing.

The demand and impact analyses of the pollution abatement industry are performed under assumptions of three alternative futures for the 1972-80 period. (1) Baseline--extrapolates pollution abatement activity from a base year predating major environmental legislation, (2) Federal Compliance Schedule--simulates on-time enforcement of existing standards, and, (3) Expected Compliance Schedule--reflects the contractors' forecast of what may alternatively occur. The industries analyzed include air pollution control equipment (for particulate and gaseous emissions from stationary sources), water pollution control equipment, instrumentation for air and water pollution abatement, and chemicals for water pollution control. The industry is analyzed by its structure, its markets, and its performance. The demand is examined for air pollution control, municipal sewage treatment, industrial sewage treatment, and water and wastewater chemicals. The industry's impact analysis is based on supply curves, price effects, and employment effects. In all of the industrial sectors except water and wastewater chemicals, the Federal Compliance Schedule threatens to create a booming industry through 1975 or 1976, thereafter quickly falling to a situation of low operating rates, low profits, and venture failures. (Auen-Wisconsin)
W75-07345

6. WATER RESOURCES PLANNING

6A. Techniques Of Planning

PUERTO RICO WATER RESOURCES PLANNING MODEL PROGRAM DESCRIPTION,
Geological Survey, Reston, Va.
For primary bibliographic entry see Field 7C.
W75-06934

INSTITUTIONAL INTERACTION IN METROPOLITAN WATER RESOURCE PLANNING,
Metropolitan Council, St. Paul, Minn. Comprehensive Planning Dept.
For primary bibliographic entry see Field 6E.
W75-06939

CROSS-IMPACT SIMULATION IN WATER RESOURCE PLANNING,
Stanford Research Inst., Menlo Park, Calif.
P. G. Kruzic.
IWR Contract Report 74-12, Army Engineer Institute for Water Resources, Fort Belvoir, Virginia, November 1974. 20 p, 7 fig, 6 tab, 14 ref, append.

Descriptors: *Water resources, *Alternative planning, *Simulation analysis, Computer programs, Forecasting, Mathematical models, Projects, Assessment, *Methodology, Effects, Regional development, Systems analysis, Equations, *Long-term planning, *Cities, Urbanization.
Identifiers: *Cross-impact simulation, Long-range changes, Long-term impact.

Described is KSIM, a computerized simulation planning procedure, and its application to a water resources problem. The procedure allows structuring and analyzing relationships among broadly-defined variables in large socio-economic systems. It enables, first, definition and structuring of a set of variables describing a perceived problem, and then calculation and display of the changes in the variables over time. By observing the changes and then making modifications, a model can be developed to test various alternatives and improve problem understanding. KSIM aids water resource planners in identifying problems, formulating alternatives, and assessing the impacts and long-term consequences of those alternatives. Discussed is the application of KSIM to an urban water planning problem of assessing the effects of water resources development upon such urban considerations as provision of services, employment patterns, and changes in residential preferences. Seven interacting variables are defined in terms of perceived growth or decline levels. A cross-impact matrix is completed to establish the relationship between each pair of variables. An on-line computer program is used to project future conditions of the regional system. (Bell-Cornell)
W75-06940

FACTOR ANALYSIS OF SHORELINE PHYSIOGRAPHY AND PERCEPTION OF WATER LEVEL DRAWDOWN BY RESERVOIR SHORELINE RESIDENTS,
Toronto Univ. (Ontario). Faculty of Forestry.
For primary bibliographic entry see Field 4A.
W75-06945

PROBABILISTIC METHODS IN STREAM QUALITY MANAGEMENT,
Washington Univ., Seattle. Dept. of Civil Engineering.
For primary bibliographic entry see Field 5B.
W75-06946

REGIONAL IMPACT OF WATER RESOURCE INVESTMENTS IN A DEVELOPING AREA,
Geological Survey, Reston, Va. Water Resources Div.
E. Attanasi.
Water Resources Bulletin, Vol 11, No 1, p 69-76, February 1975. 2 tab, 7 ref, append.

Descriptors: *Impact, *Water resources development, *Investment, *Regional development, *Regression analysis, *Puerto Rico, Multiple-purpose projects, Income distribution, Economics, Mathematical models, Systems analysis.
Identifiers: Public investments, Regional industrialization, Developing economies, Location, Industrial patterns.

The process and pattern of regional economic growth in a developing area are intimately associated with new plant and industrial location decisions. Regional development and industrialization patterns are investigated and related via regression analysis to water resource investments for the island of Puerto Rico. Growth measures for the nine year period considered include the change in income generated by the local manufacturing sector and the change in the municipio's (analogous to U.S. counties) share of annual island income. Although study results indicate water resource investments have little immediate or short-term impact, significant relationships and variations in regional responses appear over longer periods of time. This is shown by applying a variation of Zellner's method of performing seemingly unrelated regressions jointly. By this method, subsets of parameter coefficients of specific economic variables were restricted across regional equations while unrestricted coefficients were interpreted as explaining systematic regional variations in response to public investment. Regional differences, obtained by using this method, are frequently neglected when simply examining the overall development process. In terms of policy implications, results show an apparent, significant relationship, over the period considered, between changes in the distribution of income and the pattern of water resource development. (Bell-Cornell)
W75-06948

THE USE OF STREAMFLOW MODELS IN PLANNING,
Harvard Univ., Boston, Mass. Graduate School of Business Administration.
B. B. Jackson.
Water Resources Research, Vol 11, No 1, p 54-63, February 1975. 1 tab, 53 ref.

Descriptors: *Streamflow, *Model studies, *Planning, *Synthetic hydrology, Simulation analysis, Equations, Systems analysis, Rivers, Dams, Design, Hydrologic data, Monte Carlo methods, Markov processes, Optimum development plans, Decision making.
Identifiers: *Hydrologic models, Model construction.

A large and growing number of models are available for generating synthetic streamflow traces for use in planning. A survey of these techniques suggests some general precepts for the construction and use of hydrologic models in planning. The first portion of this paper is a brief overview of some of the major families of models for synthetic hydrology; the second part attempts some generalizations on the basis of the experience to date with such streamflow models. Considered are: early work, and Rippl's mass curve analysis; the Hurst phenomenon; lag 1 Markov and related models; fractional noise models; and the broken line models. A distinction is drawn between descriptive models, which are intended to provide insights into the actual workings of some system, and prescriptive models, which are intended for use in planning and which need not mirror the actual workings of a system exactly. Data evaluation, model construction, the use of phenomenological arguments, and model testing and uses are discussed. Eight steps are suggested for the construction of new hydrologic models for planning. To illustrate the application of these principles in different planning situations, two other articles by B. B. Jackson consider the optimal design and operation of a single reservoir on a single stream, where the decision makers have different objective functions. (See W75-06545 and W75-06546) (Bell-Cornell)
W75-06949

A PROGRAMING MODEL FOR THE DESIGN OF MULTIRESERVOIR FLOOD CONTROL SYSTEMS,
Natal Univ., Durban (South Africa). Dept. of Civil Engineering.
For primary bibliographic entry see Field 4A.
W75-06951

A GEOMETRIC PROGRAMMING MODEL FOR OPTIMAL ALLOCATION OF STREAM DISSOLVED OXYGEN,
Rensselaer Polytechnic Inst., Troy, N.Y.
For primary bibliographic entry see Field 5D.
W75-06954

A KINETIC MODEL FOR DESIGN OF COMPLETELY-MIXED ACTIVATED SLUDGE TREATING VARIABLE-STRENGTH INDUSTRIAL WASTEWATERS,
Associated Water and Air Resources Engineers, Inc., Nashville, Tenn.
For primary bibliographic entry see Field 5D.
W75-06955

A DYNAMIC MODEL FOR WATER AND RELATED LAND RESOURCE PLANNING,
Hawaii Univ., Honolulu. Dept. of Agricultural Engineering.
For primary bibliographic entry see Field 6D.
W75-06958

SIMULATION AS AN AID TO DECISION MAKING IN A WATER UTILITY,
Puerto Rico Aqueduct and Sewer Authority, Santurce. Planning Area.
R. E. Filardi, and W. J. O'Brien.
Water Resources Bulletin, Vol 11, No 1, p 131-147, February 1975. 5 fig, 4 tab, 11 ref.

Descriptors: *Water supply, *Decision making, *Simulation analysis, *Management, Time series analysis, Water distribution(Applied), Water treatment, Planning, Water quality, Water quantity, Water policy, Environment, Surface waters, Reservoirs, Computers, Mathematical models, Systems analysis.
Identifiers: *Water utilities, Regression equations, Simulation language.

Water utility managers would find their decision making activities greatly enhanced if provided with a set of techniques having the following characteristics: (1) the ability to procure information and knowledge about real-life systems; (2) the ability to promote analysis of the real-life system; and (3) the capacity of gauge the impact of decisions. A model/simulation is presented, having the capability to mime operational aspects of water supply systems. The simulation produces time series of what are considered relevant operational variables. These series are amenable to analysis of both static and dynamic effects of alternative policies, changing environmental conditions and varying parametric specifications. Because of its modular structure and the ad hoc programming language utilized, it offers great flexibility. The model is used to simulate a hypothetical water supply utility which is broken down into three logical sub-systems: water source, water treatment, and water distribution. The simulation model allows extensions, deletions, and modifications without consequent reformulation or extensive reprogramming. It performs a number of statistical tests useful for its own verification and validation. Discussed are possible uses of the model for planning, design and operation. The model could be used for optimization by stochastic approximation or search for optimal responses. (Bell-Cornell)
W75-06959

A SURROGATE-PARAMETER APPROACH TO MODELING GROUNDWATER BASINS,
Colorado State Univ., Fort Collins. Dept. of Civil Engineering.
For primary bibliographic entry see Field 2F.
W75-06960

CAPACITY EXPANSION MODEL OF WATER RESOURCE FACILITIES FOR A MAJOR RIVER SYSTEM,
Texas Univ. at Austin. Coll. of Engineering.
D. M. Himmelblau, and W. G. Lesso.
Available from the National Technical Information Service, Springfield, Va., 22161, as PB-241 500, $7.50 in paper copy, $2.25 in microfiche. Completion Report, April, 1975, 224 p, 2 tab, 40 fig, 8 ref, 3 append. OWRT A-022-TEX(2) 14-31-0001-3844, 14-31-0001-4044.

Descriptors: *Mathematical models, *Linear programming, Water resources, Planning, *Optimization, *Texas, Flooding, Reservoirs, Recreation, Construction, Model studies, River basins.
Identifiers: *Trinity River basin(Tex), Sensitivity analysis, Water resource systems, Nonlinear programming.

The objective has been to develop a practical and effective strategy for the optical expansion of a complex water resources system. Certain linear and nonlinear programming techniques have been combined and extended so that they can serve as tools to improve the planning, design, evaluation, and management of complex water resources systems. An efficient computer code has been prepared to carry out some of the required numerical calculations. A mathematical model of the components of a river basin that is compatible with the optimization strategy has been prepared. Practical optimization requires suitable mathematical models of the system. An integral relationship exists between the models and the effectiveness of the scheme to optimize the system.
W75-07277

MODEL DEVELOPMENT AND SYSTEMS ANALYSIS OF THE YAKIMA RIVER BASIN: HYDRAULICS OF SURFACE WATER RUNOFF,
Washington State Univ., Pullman. Dept. of Civil and Environmental Engineering.
For primary bibliographic entry see Field 2A.
W75-07278

AN INPUT-OUTPUT MODEL OF THE LOWER RIO GRANDE REGION OF TEXAS,
Pan American Univ., Edinburg, Tex. School of Business Administration.
J. C. Murrell, R. B. Geenens, and R. N. McMichael.
Texas Interindustry Project Report, April 1972. 175 p, 16 tab, 36 ref, 2 append. HUD Sec. 701.

Descriptors: *Economic impact, *Planning, *Input-output analysis, *Texas, Regions, Methodology, Data collections, Agriculture, Labor supply, Export, Tourism, Foreign trade, Mexico, Oil industry, Employment, Import, Commerciai shellfish, *Rio Grande River, Model studies.
Identifiers: Lower Rio Grande Region(Tex).

The development, functions, and use of an input-output model prepared for the Lower Rio Grande Region of Texas are explained. The model consists of five tables: (1) the Transactions Table, built by estimating dollar transactions in and outside the region, (2) a Direct Coefficients Table, derived by dividing the total industry purchase into each dollar amount, (3) the Direct and Indirect Effects Table is essentially a mathematical solution of the second table, i.e., a group of simultaneous equations is solved, (4) the Labor Coefficients Table which estimates the labor requirements, and (5) the Closed Model, which includes the households within the processing section and measures the interaction of the households with the original 71 industries in the processing section. The model provides a necessary tool for the choice of three possible alternatives facing the region, (a) some form of planned development must be substituted to change the natural development of the area, (b) the natural development can be influenced in other directions, and (c) manpower development can be used to reduce the social cost by producing changes within human resources that are consistent with the natural development of the economy. (Auen-Wisconsin)
W75-07348

6B. Evaluation Process

PROCEEDINGS - CONFERENCE ON PUBLIC PARTICIPATION IN WATER RESOURCES PLANNING AND MANAGEMENT.
North Carolina Water Resources Research Inst., Raleigh.
Available from the National Technical Information Service, Springfield, Va. 22161 as PB241 276, $6.25 in paper copy, $2.25 in microfiche.Conference sponsored by Water Resources Research Institutes of Al, Fl, Ga, Ms, NC, SC, Tn, and Va, June 19-20, 1974. Report No UNC-WRRI-74-95, June, 1974, 194 p, Edited by James M. Stewart. OWRT A-999-NC(41).

Descriptors: *Social participation, *Planning, *Management, *Education, *Reviews, *Information exchange, Legal aspects, Social aspects, Institutions, Decision making, Research priorities, Public rights.
Identifiers: *Public participation.

The conference reviewed (1) the state of the art and (2) research needs in public participation in water resource planning and management. Papers and discussions were presented on 'Identification of Publics in Water Resource Planning,' 'Information Response and Interaction - Dialogue Aspects of Public Participation,' 'Accountability of Public Water Resource Agencies: Legal Institutions for Public Interaction,' 'Education of Planners and Managers for Effective Public Participation,' 'Education of Publics for Participation in Water Resource Policy and Decision-Making,' and 'Analysis of Public Participation Problem and Research Needs.' (See W75-06555 thru W75-06860) (McJunkin-North Carolina State)
W75-06854

IDENTIFICATION OF PUBLICS IN WATER RESOURCES PLANNING,
Georgia Inst. of Tech., Atlanta. Environmental Resources Center; and Georgia Inst. of Tech., Atlanta Dept. of City Planning.
G. E. Willeke.
In: Proceedings, Conference on Public Participation in Water Resources Planning and Management, Report No UNC-WRRI-74-95, p 3-18, 1974.

Descriptors: *Social aspects, *Project planning, *Methodology, *Public rights, Flanning, Administration, Environmental effects, Professional personnei.
Identifiers: *Public participation, Publics, Community leaders, Interest groups.

It is futile to expect to fully identify all publics relevant to a water resources planning study, but necessary to strive for a suitable approximation appropriate to the planning task. Segments of a population (publics) should be identified, including: (1) major governmental units, (2) special interest groups, (3) local public interest groups, and (4) the 'unreachables' who have a stake in water resources planning but chose not to participate or to be informed. It is important to realize that individuals may be in more than one group, but the operation dynamics of each group should be understood. Does the leader adequately represent the group. What is their role. Frequently groups identify themselves, and this can be enhanced by asking participants to identify themselves and their affiliation(s). Publics can also be identified by a third

party such as a citizen committee which assists the planning agency by locating concerned publics. Planning staff can also identify those groups which must be considered in a particular project from lists of associations, maps showing affected geographic areas, and field interviews. Demographic analysis, especially from census data, is expecially helpful in locating publics who may not tend to be vocal but most be considered. Finally, historical analyses of past projects may help the planning staff to generate a list of concerned parties including those who may gain or lose from projects. Multiple channels of communication to the public should be employed in order to reach as many of these publics as possible. (See also W75-06854) (Herr-North Carolina)
W75-06855

INFORMATION RESPONSE AND INTERACTION - DIALOGUE ASPECTS OF PUBLIC PARTICIPATION,
North Carolina State Univ., Raleigh. Dept. of Sociology and Anthropology.
A. C. Davis.
In: Proceedings Conference on Public Participation in Water Resources Planning and Management, Report No UNC-WRRI-74-95, p 19-50, 1974. 11 fig, 7 ref.

Descriptors: *Structural models, *Project planning, *Social aspects, Management, Planning, Administration, Public rights, Professional personnel, Information exchange.
Identifiers: *Public participation, Public meetings, Information services, Interaction techniques.

Analysis of citizen participation techniques indicates a range of possible activities from an elitist authoritarian approach to various 'democratic' participatory approaches. Models are proposed to show variations in types of participation, timing, procedures, and groups involved. Information-response models, in which the planner generates plans and then seeks public reaction, tend to be one-way communication. Public hearings are usually employed. Cost is relatively low, but so is public representation. As more feedback is allowed and included in the planning process, more time and energy are consumed but the resulting plans should be a better representation of public needs and desires. Interaction-dialogue models involve a somewhat different role for the planner. He gathers information from relevant publics, formulates alternative plans, and subjects them to continuous review. The planner may act as coordinator and catalyst between various publics using workshops or other small group techniques. An ombudsman, representing the publics, may work with the planner. Or a process of plural planning may be used with each interested public offering its own plan and ultimately reaching a solution through compromise or the efforts of a hearing officer appointed to arbitrate. A state-of-the-art survey of water resources agency personnel shows that nearly all preferred personal contact as their primary source of input from others and nearly 3/4 preferred public meetings or hearings as the primary way to disseminate information. (See also W75-06854) (Herr-North Carolina)
W75-06856

ACCOUNTABILITY OF PUBLIC WATER RESOURCE AGENCIES: LEGAL INSTITUTIONS FOR PUBLIC INTERACTION,
Virginia Polytechnic Inst. and State Univ., Blacksburg. Water Resources Research Center.
P. M. Ashton.
In: Proceedings Conference on Public Participation in Water Resources Planning and Management, Report No UNC-WRRI-74-95, p 51-75, 1974. 74 ref.

Descriptors: *Legal aspects, *Judicial decisions, *Legal review, Regulation, Equity, Constitutional law, Civil law, Common law, Public rights, Administration, Legislation, Project planning, Social aspects.
Identifiers: *Public participation, Administrative Procedures Act of 1966, Public trust doctrine.

Administrative agencies are substantially insulated from public intervention by national legal institutions. The courts have found no inherent public right to be involved in agency decision processes except as specifically allowed by law. Substantial problems are involved in seeking to force accountability through court action, including problems of standing, injury, judicial review, and statutory jurisdiction. Enabling legislation has established these regulatory and administrative agencies to isolate decision making and control from the political arena into efficient decision making units which are relatively free from the time consuming requirements of citizen participation. The Administrative Procedures Act of 1966 allows agencies considerable freedom in applying their own statutory requirements regarding who may intervene on a given matter. The public has little right to be involved unless a member of the public has substantial interest in the proceedings. Standing to seek judicial review is granted only where 'injury in fact' (in excess of $10.000 damage) of a specific plaintiff can be demonstrated. Agency actions may be reversed by the courts for being arbitrary and capricious, contrary to constitutional right, in excess of statutory jurisdiction, taken without compliance to procedural rules, or unsupported by substantial evidence. Potential improvements are discussed, including the public trust doctrine, common law remedies, a constitutional amendment, and an environmental court. (See also W75-06854) (Herr-North Carolina)
W75-06857

EDUCATION OF PLANNERS AND MANAGERS FOR EFFECTIVE PUBLIC PARTICIPATION,
Clemson Univ., S.C.
B. C. Dysart, III.
In: Proceedings, Conference on Public Participation in Water Resources Flanning and Management, Report No UNC-WRRI-74-95, p 77-127, 1974. 7 tab, 3 append.

Descriptors: *Social aspects, *Education, *Training, Leadership, Professional personnel, Project planning, Methodology.
Identifiers: *Public participation, On-the-job education.

A mail questionnaire survey was used to assess the educational needs of water resource planners and managers in their development of public participation programs. Research in the 10-state South Atlantic-Gulf-Tennessee region identified approximately 20 key water resource people per state with representation from government agencies, private industry, and concerned citizen groups. Statistical analysis of responses revealed that individuals with an engineering background working for business or industry were more likely to have a poor attitude toward public participation than individuals with a non-engineering background. Public agencies, particularly at the state and federal levels, were more involved in public participation programs, apparently because these are needed to comply with requirements. At all levels a lack of sufficient technical capabilities was not seen as a problem. Areas of weakness include a need for better communication skills, lack of willingness to consider input from 'nonprofessionals', insufficient 'sensitivity' to changing goals of society, and 'attitudinal' maters in general. Educational programs to rectify these problems were proposed. Traditional lecture-type short courses were rejected. Attractive alternatives include: a seminar approach, a weekend retreat combining several groups, one-to-one visit with successful organizers of citizen participation, and self-study programs. The limited time available to members of the target audience must be recognized in any educational endeavor. (See also W75-06854) (Herr-North Carolina)
W75-06858

EDUCATION OF PUBLICS FOR PARTICIPATION IN WATER RESOURCE POLICY AND DECISION-MAKING,
Mississippi State Univ., Mississippi State. Social Science Research Center.
P. J. Ross.
In: Proceedings Conference on Public Participation in Water Resources Planning and Management, Report No UNC-WRRI-74-95, p 129-164, 1974. 2 tab, 2 fig, 36 ref.

Descriptors: *Social aspects, *Project planning, Administration, Methodology, Public rights, Planning, Decision making.
Identifiers: *Public participation, Public meetings, *Information programs, Mass media, Communication, Army Corps of Engineers.

A study of agency public participation programs, especially those of the U.S. Army Corps of Engineers, reveals a shift from dealing with the public as 'informed observer' to 'citizen participant.' In the 1960's the public was involved through hearings which were often poorly publicized and so late in the planning process that they served more as review sessions than active participation in plan formulation. In the '70's efforts have been made to involve the public early in the project problem analysis phase. Meetings latter present alternative solutions as they are worked out and the solution ultimately selected before the report is finalized. Standard reports have been supplemented with various innovations including brochures outlining pros and cons of each alternative and a mail-in feedback portion, distributed at public meetings and to interested groups. Other education/information mechanisms include the media, printed materials, public meetings and hearings, small group discussions, and personal contacts. Of these, the media provide the widest coverage but personal contacts are probably used most for input from interests outside the agency. Although efforts have been made to increase public participation they have resulted mainly in generating public interest and involvement but not in mustering support of public acceptance of agency proposals. More involvement throughout the planning process is needed; specific suggestions for types of involvement at each step of the planning process are given. (See also W75-06854) (Herr-North Carolina)
W75-06859

ANALYSIS OF PUBLIC PARTICIPATION PROBLEMS AND RESEARCH NEEDS.
In: Proceedings, Conference on Public Participation in Water Resources Planning and Management, Report No UNC-WRRI-74-95, p 185-189, 1974.

Descriptors: *Research and development, *Conflicts, *Project planning, Analytical techniques, Economics, Planning, Management, Methodology, Social aspects, Research priorities.
Identifiers: *Public participation, Public access to information.

Increased public involvement holds much promise for better public policies and programs, but broad public participation in water resources planning and management is still largely untried in a systematic way, in part because this is a relatively recent phenomenon. Several types of programs to increase public participation are listed and possible consequences identified. Planners, managers and various publics would be educated by the process. Various publics, both accepting and hostile, would be identified. Public participation would increase but so might problems of maintaining a properly balanced and concerned relationship. With the increasing responsiveness and accountability of these programs come higher agency costs in time and resources. For all of these assorted outcomes to be sufficiently predictable under various geographical and situational conditions further research will be required. Empirical study is also necessary to establish guidelines as to

what experts and activists include in their judgments of 'meaningful and effective' public participation. Criteria and guidelines for the design and evaluation (including cost effectiveness) of public participation programs are needed. Research could include ex post facto studies of public participation programs and cooperative studies with agencies through design of programs to meet operational as well as research objectives. Research should seek to minimize public frustration, conflict, and delay of water resource projects. (See also W75-06854) (Herr-North Carolina)
W75-06860

ECONOMIC CRITERIA FOR FRESHWATER WETLAND POLICY IN MASSACHUSETTS,
Massachusetts Univ, Amherst. Dept. of Food and Resource Economics.
T. R. Gupta, and J. H. Foster.
American Journal of Agricultural Economics, Vol 57, No.1, p 40-45. February 1975, 4 tab, 12 ref. OWRT B-023-MASS(13), 14-31-0001-3596.

Descriptors: *Wetlands, *Economics, *Wildlife, *Aesthetics, *Flood control, *Evaluation, Northeast United States, *Massachusetts, Benefits, Costs, Preservation, Decision making, Water policy, Cost-benefit analysis.

The value of wildlife, visual-cultural benefits, water supply and flood control benefits of wetlands (varied by benefit productivity levels) are determined with help from appropriate scientists. Comparison of benefit value with opportunity cost of wetland preservation is demonstrated as the basis for decisions concerning permits for wetland alteration. The analysis suggests that 90% of the wetlands in the state of Massachusetts should be preserved. (Larson-Massachusetts)
W75-06896

THE NEED FOR A COMPREHENSIVE APPROACH IN THE MANAGEMENT OF ENVIRONMENTAL RESOURCES,
North Carolina State Univ., Raleigh. Dept. of Civil Engineering.
For primary bibliographic entry see Field 6G.
W75-06938

WATER MANAGEMENT IN CHINA, TOP PRIORITY FOR 2500 YEARS,
Northern Illinois Univ., De Kalb. Dept. of Geography.
For primary bibliographic entry see Field 3F.
W75-06942

FORECASTING INDUSTRIAL WATER UTILIZATION IN THE PETROLEUM REFINING SECTOR: AN OVERVIEW,
New York State Coll. of Agriculture and Life Sciences, Ithaca, N.Y. Dept. of Agricultural Economics.
For primary bibliographic entry see Field 3E.
W75-06944

A PRESENT VALUE-UNIT COST METHODOLOGY FOR EVALUATING MUNICIPAL WASTEWATER RECLAMATION AND DIRECT REUSE,
Army Mobility Equipment Research and Development Center, Fort Belvoir, Va. Sanitary Sciences Div.
For primary bibliographic entry see Field 5D.
W75-06947

AN ECONOMIC ANALYSIS OF WATER RESOURCE INVESTMENTS AND REGIONAL ECONOMIC GROWTH,
Wisconsin Univ., Madison. Dept. of Economics.
C. J. Cicchetti, V. K. Smith, and J. Carson.
Water Resources Research, Vol 11, No 1, p 1-6, February 1975. 7 tab, 14 ref.

Descriptors: Water resources, *Investment, *Regional economics, *Multiple-purpose projects, *Southwest U.S., *Economic impact, Estimating, Human population, Measurement, Cost allocation, Behavior, Equations, Arid lands, Systems analysis.
Identifiers: Economic analysis, Economic growth, Economic subregions, Cobb-Douglas function, Production function, Sensitivity, Change, Pooled data.

Effects are analyzed of the Bureau of Reclamation's water resource projects over the period 1930-70 on regional economic growth in the southwestern United States. The overall five-state area selected for analysis is one of general, or at least seasonal, water shortage. Thus, water management is expected to have greater influence on regional economic activity there than in less arid regions. The unit of observation for analysis is an economic subregion, consistent with the specific projects involved and theoretical models of growth centers. Behavioral relationships are more closely tied to the body of economic theory developed for modeling regional economic growth. With the use of composite computer mapping techniques, three characteristics have been utilized to define the economic regions: population density, irrigated croplands, and highway accessibility. The effects of water investments are examined in two ways: studying the determinants of the level of economic activity in a subregion at a given time; and focusing on the measured changes in the level of economic activity over time. Conventional economic analysis is performed to derive production functions. Results show that water resource investments have an impact on regional economic growth. The extent of the effect depends on the nature of the water investment, the state of the regional economy, and the amount and nature of other investments. (Bell-Cornell)
W75-06952

WATER MANAGEMENT--A GENERAL REPORT,
Illinois State Water Survey, Urbana.
For primary bibliographic entry see Field 4A.
W75-06953

SIMULATION AS AN AID TO DECISION MAKING IN A WATER UTILITY,
Puerto Rico Aqueduct and Sewer Authority, Santurce. Planning Area.
For primary bibliographic entry see Field 6A.
W75-06959

THE HANLON CREEK STUDY: AN ECOLOGICAL APPROACH TO URBAN PLANNING,
Guelph Univ. (Ontario). Dept. of Land Resource Science.
E. E. Mackintosh.
Journal of Soil and Water Conservation, Vol 29, No 5, p 277-280, November-December 1974. 5 fig, 6 ref.

Descriptors: *Small watersheds, *City planning, *Water conservation, *Ecology, Ecosystems, Watersheds(Basins), Urbanization, Groundwater recharge, Natural recharge, Streamflow, Runoff, Water table, Recreation facilities, Social needs, Parks, *Canada.
Identifiers: *Hanlon Creek(Ont).

Hanlon Creek, a small watershed on the southern fringe of Guelph, Ontario, drains an area of 7300 acres. At the moment, the watershed is predominantly agricultural. The city annexed part of the watershed in response to forecasted expansion of industry and housing. Location of an expressway within the watershed boundaries precipitated the events leading up to the investigation being undertaken. The study was undertaken to determine the effect of the Hanlon Expressway on the ecology of Hanlon Creek, and to determine the effect of long-range urbanization on the ecology of Hanlon Creek. Based on the inventory analysis, a series of recommendations can be generated that allows development to proceed within a framework that assures the preservation of natural systems. Most importantly, the procedure assures urban dwellers of adequate open space and recreational activities. (Sims-ISWS)
W75-07067

COASTAL ZONE MANAGEMENT: THE PROCESS OF PROGRAM DEVELOPMENT,
Coastal Zone Management Inst., Sandwich, Mass.
For primary bibliographic entry see Field 2L.
W75-07075

WATER AND SEWERAGE DEVELOPMENT PLAN - KANSAS CITY METROPOLITAN REGION.
Metropolitan Planning Commission-Kansas City Region, Mo.
For primary bibliographic entry see Field 5D.
W75-07083

REPORT ON REGIONAL POLLUTION CONTROL: HALIFAX-DARTMOUTH METROPOLITAN AREA.
Halifax-Dartmouth Metropolitan Area Planning Committee (Nova Scotia). Task Group on Water Supply and Waste Disposal.
For primary bibliographic entry see Field 5D.
W75-07085

PLANNING FOR SHORELINE AND WATER USES.
Available from the National Technical Information Service, Springfield, Va 22161 as COM-74-11667, $3.25 in paper copy, $2.25 in microfiche. A Report on the Third Marine Recreation Conference, B. J. Cole, ed., Marine Advisory Service, University of Rhode Island, Kingston, Rhode Island, 1974. 20 p, append.

Descriptors: *Coasts, *Planning, *Water management(Applied), *Water demand, *Marinas, Shore protection, Recreation, Waste disposal, Water pollution control, *Northeast US.
Identifiers: *Coastal zone management.

One concern to coastal management and recreation interest groups is the role of government in coastal zone planning. To receive federal grants for coastal zone planning, states must meet federal criteria including coastal zone definition, areas of special environmental concern, and consideration of national interests as well as individual state objectives. Rhode Island is attacking coastal management problems one-at-a-time beginning with barrier beach development and progressing to sand and gravel industry regulations. Maine is formulating management plans on an area-by-area basis beginning with Penobscot Bay. A strong argument is presented to make recreation another objective of coastal zone management and to allow the marine recreation community to participate in discussions and hearings. Summaries of 'Planning, Politics and the Public' papers present the need of planning to control resource demands, population growth and commercial development. In an increasingly crowded and polluted environment, new methods must be found to compensate land owners for severe restrictions on the use of their property. The importance of the marina industry on the economy of the New England region, where New Hampshire alone reported $11.2 million total sales of boats, supplies and services, was emphasized. The effects of resin and fuel shortages are beginning to reduce boat building and use of marine recreation facilities. Charging for pumping of boat waste holding tanks into tank trucks, cooperation among several marinas to build a single waste treatment facility and leak-and-rust-proof gas and diesel storage tanks are suggested to improve marinas. Proposals were made for considering water user fees for marinas

and other marine facilities to help finance new facilities and/or coastal zone management. (Salzman-North Carolina)
W75-07086

PROCEEDINGS OF THE WORKSHOP ON RESEARCH NEEDS RELATED TO WATER FOR ENERGY.
Illinois Univ., Urbana. Water Resources Center.
For primary bibliographic entry see Field 6D.
W75-07089

RESEARCH NEEDS RELATED TO HYDROLOGIC ASPECTS OF WATER FOR ENERGY FROM LARGE ENERGY COMPLEXES,
Minnesota Dept. of Natural Resources, St. Paul.
For primary bibliographic entry see Field 6D.
W75-07093

RESEARCH NEEDS ON SOCIAL, POLITICAL AND INSTITUTIONAL ASPECTS OF COAL UTILIZATION,
Kentucky Univ., Lexington. Center for Developmental Change.
For primary bibliographic entry see Field 6D.
W75-07096

RESEARCH NEEDS ON ECONOMIC AND RESOURCE MANAGEMENT ASPECTS FOR COAL GASIFICATION/LIQUEFACTION,
Tennessee Univ., Knoxville. Appalachian Resources Project.
S. L. Carroll.
In: Proceedings of the Workshop on Research Needs Related to Water for Energy, Water Resources Center, University of Illinois at Urbana-Champaign. Research Report No. 93, p 156-165, November, 1974. 1 fig, 64 ref.

Descriptors: Economics, Benefits, Costs, *Economic efficiency, Coals, Oil, *Oil industry, Energy, *Energy conversion, *Cost-benefit analysis, *Econometrics, Economic impacts, Transportation, Demand, *Research priorities.
Identifiers: *Coal gasification/liquefaction, Systems approach, General equilibrium overview, Industrial organization analyses, Econometric demand and supply analysis.

To replace oil importation by gasification of coal, annual new coal production must exceed 725,000,000 tons and will cost nearly 6 times as much as energy derived from Mideast oil. Types of magnitudes that are involved in large-scale coal gasification are reviewed, and recommendations for economic research to make this process feasible in supplanting oil are outlined. The following areas suggest means to assess the industry: a systems approach to the establishment of a coal gasification industry, a general equilibrium overview of such as industry, and extensive industrial organization analysis. Central feature of the systems analysis outlined by a chart dealing with coal production in Appalachia is the use of the cost-benefit criterion for evaluation of various abatement strategies. In the general equilibrium overview, an eclectic approach to the energy industry uses econometric demand and supply analysis as well as programming techniques to determine efficient methods of transportation. Industrial organization analysis demands studies of the behavior, structure, distribution of resources and ownership, and future performance of the coal gasification industry. A bibliography covering various techniques to coal gasification and the economic impact is included. (See also W75-07089) (Salzman-North Carolina)
W75-07097

EFFECTS OF IRRIGATION DEVELOPMENT ON TRADE PATTERNS AND INCOME GENERATION,
North Dakota State Univ., Fargo. Dept. of Agricultural Economics.
T. A. Hertsgaard.
Available from the National Technical Information Service, Springfield, Va 22161 as PB-241 472, $3.75 in paper copy, $2.25 in microfiche. Research Report No. WI-222-004-74, November, 1974. 23 p, 1 fig, 6 tab, 3 ref. OWRT B-003-NDAK(3).

Descriptors: Economics, *Economic impact, Benefits, Community development, *Input-output analysis, *Irrigation, *North Dakota, *Income analysis, Model studies, Cost analysis, Industry, Farm management.

Expenditures data were collected from a sample of farms, nonfarm, firms, households, and local units of government in a seven-county area in northeastern North Dakota. Input-output technical coefficients and interdependence coefficients were computed from these data and were not found to differ significantly from those obtained in a previous study of southwestern North Dakota. Interdependence coefficients were applied to levels of output of the basic sectors of each region and the state for the years since 1958. The resulting estimates of personal income were compared with those developed by the Bureau of Economic Analysis, U.S. Department of Commerce, to determine the degree of validity of the input-output model for estimating gross outputs of the respective sectors in the state. The comparisons indicated the input-output model provided estimates of personal income that averaged within about 4.8 percent of Department of Commerce estimates at the state level. Estimates at the regional level were less reliable, especially for those regions in which petroleum mining is an important sector. However, the model appeared to be satisfactory for estimating the economic effects of irrigation or coal resource development.
W75-07104

REGIONAL SEWAGE TREATMENT NEEDS FOR EUGENE-SPRINGFIELD URBAN AREA.
CH2M/Hill, Corvallis, Oreg.
For primary bibliographic entry see Field 5D.
W75-07119

WASTE WATER MANAGEMENT - IMPLICATIONS FOR REGIONAL PLANNING,
For primary bibliographic entry see Field 8A.
W75-07120

ADVANCED PLANNING OF FLOOD CONTROL PROJECTS,
Santa Clara County Flood Control and Water District, San Jose, Calif.
G. Korbay, J. Richardson, M. Burns, C. Church, and E. Ferguson.
December 1970. 35 p, 37 tab, 1 append.

Descriptors: *Planning, *Flood control, *Cost comparisons, *Project planning, *Priorities, *Alternative planning, Project feasibility, Project purposes, Furure_planning(Projected), Net income, Construction costs, California, Financing, Scheduling.
Identifiers: Santa Clara County(California).

In the past the Flood Control District's staff has recognized the need for a five-year advance construction schedule, and proposed schedules have been drawn up for each of the five flood control zones. Each zone schedule was submitted to the appropriate zone Advisory Committee for review and comment. The Committee-approved schedules have been submitted to the Board of Supervisors (formerly the governing body of the Flood Control District) and more recently the Board of Directors for adoption as District policy. The zone schedules were prepared by a staff 'Task Force'. The activities of the Task Force fall within three general categories; Procedure, Methods of Financing and Recommendations. Procedure includes the mechanics of determining the net funds available for construction in each fiscal year. A detailed description of the procedure and methodology used to establish the net income, project priorities and scheduling of the high priority projects is contained in the Appendix. Secondly, the alternative methods of financing flood control projects were investigated and are summarized in the Appendix. The Task Force recommends a five-year construction schedule for each zone for consideration by the Flood Control Zone Advisory Committees under an adopted policy framework by the District Board of Directors. (Poertner)
W75-07139

HYDROELECTRIC DEVELOPMENT OF THE NELSON RIVER SYSTEM IN NORTHERN MANITOBA,
Manitoba Hydro, Winnipeg.
For primary bibliographic entry see Field 6G.
W75-07172

WATER QUALITY DIMENSIONS OF WATER RESOURCES PLANNING,
North Carolina Water Resources Research Inst., Raleigh.
For primary bibliographic entry see Field 5G.
W75-07185

KONA DAM VS. KONATOWN: A SOCIOLOGICAL INTERPRETATION OF SELECTED IMPACTS OF RESERVOIR DEVELOPMENT ON A COMMUNITY FIELD,
East Texas State Univ., Commerce. Dept. of Sociology and Anthropology.
R. N. Singh.
Available from the National Technical Information Service, Springfield, Va. 22161 as PB-241 489, $7.00 in paper copy, $2.25 in microfiche. Completion Report, February 1975, 175 p., 6 fig, 2 maps, 24 tabl, 51 ref, 4 append. OWRT C-4059 (no. 9011) (1).

Descriptors: Social aspects, *Environmental effects, Ecology, Institutional constraints, Economic impact, Projects, Evaluation, *Alternative planning, Multiple-purpose reservoirs, *Social impact, Social values, Social needs, Community development.
Identifiers: *Environmental impact, Delphi procedures, Public projects.

The study was aimed at identifying a set of procedures useful for the delineation of environmental impacts of a public project from a sociological perspective. The research process included three major procedures: (1) analysis of Kona Dam as an action process in terms of its major phases, activities and behaviors involved during its history; (2) identification of Konatown as a community field in terms of its major constituent elements at ecological, institutional, and social levels of analysis; and (3) study of an interaction between Kona Dam and Konatown, mainly in terms of the impacts of the former on the latter. By using an 'action guide', it was possible to collect systematically in a historical manner selected data concerning Kona Dam Project. The action project was discussed in terms of major phases, namely: (1) initiation, (2) organization of sponsorship, (3) goal setting or planning, (4) implementation of plans, and (5) evaluation of the project. Delphi procedures were used during action analysis to identify and rank the dam's goals, environmental impacts, and alternatives. The procedures identified and ranked systematically eleven goals of the project, forty-four of its environmental impacts (past and future), and eleven plausible alternatives to it. After the selected characteristics of the community field of Konatown were identified, it was possible to see which of those charac-

teristics had already been, or might in the future be, affected by the dam project.
W75-07271

GILA RIVER BASIN, NEW RIVER AND PHOENIX CITY STREAMS, ARIZONA: ALTERNATIVE PLANS FOR FLOOD CONTROL AND RECREATIONAL DEVELOPMENT.
Army Engineer District, Los Angeles, Calif.
For primary bibliographic entry see Field 4A.
W75-07331

NATURAL RESOURCES MANAGEMENT IN THE GREAT LAKES BASIN,
Cornell Univ., Ithaca, N.Y. Water Resources and Marine Sciences Center.
For primary bibliographic entry see Field 6E.
W75-07344

INDUSTRIAL WATER DEMAND FORECASTING,
Department of the Environment, Ottawa (Ontario). Water Planning and Management Branch.
For primary bibliographic entry see Field 6D.
W75-07346

THE CALIFORNIA STATE WATER PROJECT IN 1970.
California State Dept. of Water Resources, Sacramento.
Bulletin 132-70, June 1970. 244 p, 8 fig, 17 tab, 4 append.

Descriptors: *California, *Water resources development, *Projects, Financing, Bond issues, Interest rates, Recreation, Wildlife, Fisheries, Hydroelectric plants, Dams, Power marketing, Aqueducts, Flood control, Right-of-way, Canals, Pumping plants, Alternative planning, Agricultural runoff, Cost repayment, Water reuse, Water storage, Irrigation, Contracts, Income, Capital costs, Operation and maintenance, Water allocation(Policy), Cost allocation.

This eighth annual Project report documents progress during 1969; it updates long-range financial projections and provides data and computations to support those charges to be assessed water service contractors during 1971. Project management centered on alleviating an immediate financial problem induced by the inability to market $600 million in general obligation bonds within the statutory 5% interest ceiling. Ninety percent of those facilities required to fulfill initial water delivery commitments in 1973 were either completed or under contract; those declared operational in 1969 triggered guaranteed minimum payments of $16.15 million annually. Operations included 284,246 acre-feet of water delivered from project facilities; 1,554,800 recreation days provided by project lakes, and 2,614,000,000 kilowatt-hours of electric energy generated at project powerplants. As of 1970, estimated capital costs to be incurred for the entire Project (1952-1985) totaled $2,837 million, exclusive of future costs to be financed by revenue bonds. Of this estimation, $1,676 million had been incurred to 1970. Assuming legislative approval to raise the statutory interest ceiling on general obligation bonds, sufficient funds should be available to complete the '1973 Project Facilities.' Water charges to be assessed during 1971 will total about $55 million; through 1971, payments will have totaled about $228 million. (Auen-Wisconsin)
W75-07347

6C. Cost Allocation, Cost Sharing, Pricing/Repayment

METROPOLITAN WATER SUPPLY ALLOCATION AND OPERATION,
Northwestern Univ., Evanston, Ill. Dept. of Civil Engineering.
For primary bibliographic entry see Field 3D.
W75-06851

A PRESENT VALUE-UNIT COST METHODOLOGY FOR EVALUATING MUNICIPAL WASTEWATER RECLAMATION AND DIRECT REUSE,
Army Mobility Equipment Research and Development Center, Fort Belvoir, Va. Sanitary Sciences Div.
For primary bibliographic entry see Field 5D.
W75-06947

AN ECONOMIC ANALYSIS OF WATER RESOURCE INVESTMENTS AND REGIONAL ECONOMIC GROWTH,
Wisconsin Univ., Madison. Dept. of Economics.
For primary bibliographic entry see Field 6B.
W75-06952

COST OF TRICKLING FILTER RECIRCULATION PART I,
For primary bibliographic entry see Field 5D.
W75-06956

COST OF TRICKLING FILTER RECIRCULATION PART II,
For primary bibliographic entry see Field 5D.
W75-06957

WATER USE AND COAL DEVELOPMENT IN EASTERN MONTANA: WATER AVAILABILITY, WATER DEMANDS AND ECONOMIC IMPACTS,
Montana State Univ., Missoula. Bureau of Business and Economic Research.
For primary bibliographic entry see Field 6D.
W75-06978

EFFLUENT TREATMENT AND ITS COST FOR THE SYNTHANE COAL-TO-SNG PROCESS,
Bureau of Mines, Pittsburgh, Pa.
For primary bibliographic entry see Field 5D.
W75-07098

THE CHARACTERISTICS AND ULTIMATE DISPOSAL OF WASTE SEPTIC TANK SLUDGE,
Alaska Univ., College. Inst. of Water Resources.
For primary bibliographic entry see Field 5D.
W75-07273

LIFE HISTORY, ECOLOGY, AND MANAGEMENT OF THE SMALLMOUTH BUFFALO, ICTIOBUS BUBALUS (RAFINESQUE), WITH REFERENCE TO ELEPHANT BUTTE LAKE,
New Mexico Agricultural Experiment Station, University Park.
D. B. Jester.
Available from the National Technical Information Service, Springfield, Va 22161 as COM-74-10265, $5.25 in paper copy, $2.25 in microfiche. Research Report 261, September 1973. 111 p, 26 fig, 43 tab, 119 ref.

Descriptors: *Fish management, *Buffalo fish, *Commercial fish, Life history studies, Ecological distribution, Growth rates, Spawning, Fish diets, Fish populations, Fish diseases, Fish harvest, Fishing gear, Systematics, Reservoirs, Pounds fish per acre, Carp, Carpsucker, *New Mexico.
Identifiers: *Elephant Butte Lake(NM), Smallmouth buffalo fish.

Investigations of smallmouth buffalo fish in a New Mexico reservoir are combined with available literature, to include life history, population ecology, commercial value, and management methods. Reported range of the species is modified to extend the western boundary into Montana, New Mexico, and west of the Continental Divide into central Arizona. Age-growth studies revealed a large increase in growth rates as a direct result of reduced population density, or indirectly, the result of commercial harvest. While buffalo required two to 11 years to reach a weight of 1,000 grams in nine waters, time required to reach this weight decreased from nine years to six in Elephant Butte Lake after three years of commercial fishing. Spawning habitat and behavior, sex ratios, maturity, fecundity, and food and feeding habits are discussed. The smallmouth buffalo has a market value adequate to justify small commercial fishing operations on a sustained yield basis. Market expansion is possible with development of a distribution system which will allow supplying buffalo to areas where demand appears to be consistent but is too small for a single fisherman to schedule regular deliveries. Buffalo are sold primarily as whole, dressed fish by Los Angeles' retailers at prices ranging from 26 cents/lb to 35 cents/lb. (Auen-Wisconsin)
W75-07343

ECONOMIC IMPACT STUDY OF THE POLLUTION ABATEMENT EQUIPMENT INDUSTRY.
Little (Arthur D.), Inc., Cambridge, Mass.
For primary bibliographic entry see Field 5G.
W75-07345

AN INPUT-OUTPUT MODEL OF THE LOWER RIO GRANDE REGION OF TEXAS,
Pan American Univ., Edinburg, Tex. School of Business Administration.
For primary bibliographic entry see Field 6A.
W75-07348

COST-EFFECTIVE DESIGN OF WASTEWATER TREATMENT FACILITIES BASED ON FIELD DERIVED PARAMETERS.
Saint Louis Metropolitan Sewer District, Mo.
For primary bibliographic entry see Field 5D.
W75-07349

6D. Water Demand

A SUMMARY VIEW OF WATER SUPPLY AND DEMAND IN THE SAN FRANCISCO BAY REGION, CALIFORNIA,
Geological Survey, Menlo Park, Calif.
S. E. Rantz.
San Francisco Bay Region Environment and Resources Planning Study Basic Data Contribution 47 (U.S. Geological Survey open-file report), 1972. 41 p, 4 fig, 16 tab, 7 ref.

Descriptors: *Water supply, *Water demand, *California, Water resources development, Water yield, Water utilization, Safe yield, Consumptive use.
Identifiers: *San Francisco Bay area(Calif).

The water-supply situation in the nine counties that comprise the San Francisco Bay region, California is summarized. Water data are based on 1970 conditions. Firm water supply is tabulated for each subregion by source--ground water, surface water, and imported water. Water demand in 1970 is tabulated for each subregion by type of use or demand--public supply, rural self-supply, irrigation, self-supplied industrial water, and thermoelectric power generation. The San Francisco Bay region is dependent to a large degree on imported water. Under 1970 conditions of develop-

ment, the firm water supply is 2.2 million acre-feet per year; of that quantity, almost 1 million acre-feet per year is imported water. The water demand in 1970 was 1.9 million acre-feet, about half of which was consumed. Under 1970 conditions of water development and use, a series of dry years would probably necessitate some curtailment of irrigation activities in four of the subregions, where the bulk of the demand is for irrigation water. Under those same conditions there is generally ample water for municipal and industrial use throughout the region. Although the firm water supply of the San Francisco Bay region, including imported water, is generally adequate to meet present needs, supplemental supply would be required to meet increased demand. The expansion of existing surface-water facilities and the construction of new surface-water projects, now considered feasible, could provide a combined firm supplemental yield of slightly more than 1 million acre-feet per year. (Knapp-USGS)
W75-06935

FORECASTING INDUSTRIAL WATER UTILIZATION IN THE PETROLEUM REFINING SECTOR: AN OVERVIEW,
New York State Coll. of Agriculture and Life Sciences, Ithaca, N.Y. Dept. of Agricultural Economics.
For primary bibliographic entry see Field 3E.
W75-06944

A DYNAMIC MODEL FOR WATER AND RELATED LAND RESOURCE PLANNING,
Hawaii Univ., Honolulu. Dept. of Agricultural Engineering.
T. Liang, and W-y. Huang.
Water Resources Bulletin, Vol 11, No 1, p 33-48, February 1975. 14 fig, 13 ref.

Descriptors: *Water resources, *Planning, *Demand, *Supply, Natural resources, *Land resources, *Dynamic programming, Storage, Control, Model studies, Constraints, Optimization, Feasibility studies, Water utilization, Evaluation, Agriculture, Land development, Planting management, Reservoirs, Equations, Systems analysis, Cost analysis, *Hawaii.
Identifiers: Resource demand, Multiple cropping, Natural resource capacity, Hawaii, Truck crops, Environmental quality.

By the control or selection of types and levels of activities, resource activity demands can be modified to best suit the storage-modified fluctuating resource supply. Manipulation of the supply: demand relation decreases resource waste and reduces the need for, and construction of, large and expensive storage facilities. Planning an optimal system of activities for generating economic goods and services within an existing natural resource capacity is a difficult problem to solve. A dynamic programming model with the capacity to check multiple resource demand and supply compatibility over many time periods has been developed for solution of this type of problem. The characteristics of natural resource supply and the demand of activities have been utilized to reduce the number of time periods and to minimize the loss of the dynamic reality of the problem. Reduction in the number of time periods extends the capability of the model to the solution of complex resource planning problems without oversimplification. The model has been applied to the town of Kamuela on the island of Hawaii, where a small reservoir has been constructed for the purpose of developing vacant land into a vegetable producing area. The model is useful in studying the feasibility of developing the unused land. (Bell-Cornell)
W75-06958

WATER USE AND COAL DEVELOPMENT IN EASTERN MONTANA: WATER AVAILABILITY, WATER DEMANDS AND ECONOMIC IMPACTS,
Montana State Univ., Missoula. Bureau of Business and Economic Research.
P. E. Polzin.
Available from the National Technical Information Service, Springfield, Va 22161 as PB-241 331, $7.50 in paper copy, $2.25 in microfiche. Montana University Joint Water Resources Research Center, Bozeman, Report No. 57, November 1974. 223 p, 2 fig, 70 tab, append. OWRT C-5258(No. 4217)(1).

Descriptors: *Strip mines, *Coal mines, *Water requirements, *Economic impact, Economic predictions, *Montana, *Water demands, Great plains, Energy, Costs.
Identifiers: Northern Great Plains(Mont), Coal-water relationships, Coal-energy production.

A one-year study was conducted to assess Montana's role in the national energy picture (particularly from the standpoint of strip-coal mining development); to describe the region in terms of economy, agriculture, water use and people, with a section on the Indian population; and to project the impact of coal-related development in terms of coal mining, electrical generation and gasification. Included in the projected impact were studies of future levels of coal development, coal-related employment and earnings, total employment, population and income, and water use increases. Findings were classified according to two alternative projections for coal development in Montana for 1980 and 1985 (Alternative 1 - no gasification) and (Alternative 2 - with gasification). Under alternative 1, Montana coal production was projected to be 49 million tons per year (1980) and 61 million tons (1985). Under alternative 2, production was projected to be 57 million tons per year (1980) and 77 million tons (1985). Additional water demand for the seven-county impact area studied was for alternative 1: 38,470 acre-feet (1980) and 57,670 acre-feet per year (1985). For alternative 2: 49,610 acre-feet (1980) and 80,020 acre-feet per year (1985). The study concludes that this water is available, but that reservoir storage may have to be provided to assure a stable supply.
W75-06978

WATER USE AND COAL DEVELOPMENT IN EASTERN MONTANA: WATER AVAILABILITY AND DEMANDS,
Montana State Univ., Bozeman. Dept. of Economics and Agricultural Economics.
R. L. Stroup, and S. B. Townsend.
Available from the National Technical Information Service, Springfield, Va 22161 as PB-241 332, $4.75 in paper copy, $2.25 in microfiche. Montana University Joint Water Resources Research Center, Bozeman, Completion Report No. 59, December 1974. 89 p, 1 fig, 36 tab, 13 ref. OWRT C-5258(No. 4217)(2).

Descriptors: *Coal mines, *Strip mines, *Water supply, *Water requirements, *Water demand, *Competing uses, Water allocation(Policy), *Montana, *Water availability, *Water utilization, Costs.
Identifiers: *Coal development, Fort Union Formation(Mont), Coal gasification, Mine-mouth generation.

A one-year, two-phase study was undertaken to assess the availability and demand for water in the coal region of eastern Montana. The physical availability of surface and ground water was treated, as were the legal problems associated with coal development, broken down by type of development. Data presented indicate that sufficient groundwater is available in eastern Montana to permit substantial amounts of coal development. Use of this water would not be without cost, however. Direct costs of impoundment and delivery, and foregone opportunities for using the water instream must be considered. Increased costs and decreased availability of irrigation water, problems caused for aquatic ecosystems, reduced availability of water for some types of recreation, loss of hydropower downstream, possible shortening of the navigation schedule, and the increased need for sewage treatment are all potential problems to be considered when deciding how much water should be used for coal development. The demand for water in coal development will depend in part on the cost of water to developers. For any given type of coal conversion plant which might be proposed, there is considerable flexibility in the extent of water use. Information on the location, size, and timing of coal development and water demands is of great concern to planners. But much more data must be developed if accurate forecasts are to be made. (Williams-Montana State)
W75-06979

GOALS, POLICIES AND MANAGEMENT OF WATER RESOURCES IN THE RIO GRANDE VALLEY (APJ-1).
Middle Rio Grande Council of Governments of New Mexico, Albuquerque; and Herkenhoff (Gordon) and Associates, Albuquerque, N. Mex.
For primary bibliographic entry see Field 4B.
W75-07084

PROCEEDINGS OF THE WORKSHOP ON RESEARCH NEEDS RELATED TO WATER FOR ENERGY.
Illinois Univ., Urbana. Water Resources Center.
Available from NTIS, Springfield, Va 22161 as PB-241 346, $8.75 PC, $2.25 MF. Workshop held in Indianapolis, Ind, Oct 20-22, 1974. Sponsored by Water Resources Center, Univ. of Ill. at Urbana-Champaign. Research Rept. No. 93. Nov. 1974. 297 p, 12 fig, 19 tab, 207 ref, append. Glenn E. Stout, ed. OWRT X-147(No 4271)(1).

Descriptors: *Energy budget, *Energy dissipation, *Energy conversion, *Research and development, Water resources, *Environmental effects, *Water requirements, Hydrologic aspects, Waste water treatment, *Research priorities, Social aspects, Legal aspects, Thermal pollution, Pollution, Economic impact.
Identifiers: *Coal gasification, *Coal liquefaction, *Coal conversion.

Development of large scale energy conversion facilities and their impact on water resources in the Ohio River, Great Lakes and Upper Mississippi River basins was studied at an interdisciplinary workshop. Within limits determined by available water resources and minimization of environmental impact, participants identified areas in which research will be needed if energy conversion facilities are developed. Coal gasification and liquefaction received special emphasis. Included are 2 papers on coal conversion processes and related water requirements, 9 papers with commentaries related to main topic and reports of discussion groups which identify research needs and rank them in importance. A summary of research needs includes: determination of availability and quality of water with respect to legal, social and environmental implications; study of character, transport, rate and environmental impact of coal conversion waste products; development of waste treatment; and a budget study to ensure optimum utilization and conservation. Papers provide information concerning technical, social, political, legal, institutional and environmental aspects of energy related water use and coal conversion technology. (See W75-07090 thru W75-07099) (Salzman-North Carolina)
W75-07089

COAL CONVERSION: PROCESSES, RESOURCE REQUIREMENTS, AND ENVIRONMENTAL IMPACT.
Illinois Univ., Urbana. Inst. for Environmental Studies.

In: Proceedings of the Workshop on Research Needs Related to Water for Energy, Water Resources Center, University of Illinois at Urbana-Champaign, Research Report No. 93, p 3-50, November, 1974. 8 fig, 9 tab, 39 ref.

Descriptors: *Energy conversion, Water resources, *Water supply, *Water requirements, Pollution, *Coals, *Economic impact, Economics, Environmental effect, *Research priorities.
Identifiers: *Coal conversion, High Btu gasification processes.

Coal, one of the nation's most abundant energy resources, is costly and requires extensive air quality controls because of its high sulfur content. Available information on the processes for gasifying and liquefying coal, the products and the possible consequences of coal conversion on resources, environmental quality and the economy has been condensed and assembled. An overview of coal production processes, followed by an assessment of the processes currently under development for the production of high and low Btu, are presented. Processes for converting coal to liquid and solid fuels are discussed complete with an analysis of factors influencing design and location of conversion plants. These factors are determined by availability of adequate resources and the effect of the plant on the whole environment. Each coal conversion process is reviewed by its process, state of development, water requirements, operation and its estimated costs. In the analysis of the various coal conversion processes such as High Btu gasification process (HYGAS), Koppers-Totzek process, Char Oil Energy Development conversion process and modified Lurgi process, water consumption needs and requirements as well as wastewater effluents and water losses are identified. The most efficient level of water utilization for a given facility at a given site should be based on relative supply and demand for water resources at the site. (See also W75-07089) (Salzman-North Carolina)
W75-07090

WATER REQUIREMENTS FOR A SYNTHETIC FUELS INDUSTRY BASED ON COAL,
Office of Coal Research, Washington, D.C.
E. Schmetz, and G. A. Mills.
In: Proceedings of the Workshop on Research Needs Related to Water for Energy, Water Resources Center, University of Illinois at Urbana-Champaign, Research Report No. 93, p 69-79, November, 1974. 4 tab, 7 ref.

Descriptors: *Water demand, *Water requirements, Research and development, Design, Coals, Energy, *Energy conversion, Pollution, Coal mines, Coal mine wastes, Effluents, *Research priorities.
Identifiers: *Coal gasification process, *Coal liquefaction process, Substitute natural gas(SNG), Coal conversion plants.

The Office of Coal Research (OCR) is working with industry to develop technology for maximum utilization of coal to alleviate the nation's energy problem in an environmentally acceptable manner. OCR's endeavors to develop the production of substitute natural gas (SNG) as well as fuel produced through liquefaction, and the subsequent water requirements of these processes are outlined. Water uses relate to the needs for gasification and liquefaction processes and to the effect of pollutants on water utilized in the conversion process and that associated with mining operations. Water needs for gasification of coal include inputs for cooling and clean-up of gases and by-products, and for the production of hydrogen. Three designs of gasifiers are used to produce SNG including the stirred fixed-bed gasifier, where oxygen and steam are passed through coal which sits on a grate; the entrained-flow gasifier (Koppers-Totzek), where pulverized coal is entrained in a stream of oxygen and steam through a nozzle into the gasifier where gasification of the coal occurs; and the fluid bed type, where a bed of pulverized coal is fluidized by the process gas. Water requirements for a 250,000,000 scf/day SNG-plant and time-frame and water needs for the first 90 SNG plants are given. Conversion of coal to liquid or low melting boiler fuels employs three processes: liquid-phase hydrogenative extraction of coal, liquid phase catalytic hydrodesulfurization and gas-phase fluidized-bed carbonization. Water requirements for liquefaction plants to the year 2000 are projected. Coal conversion plants require more research to develop a water treatment scheme to reuse waste water, to treat polluted water, and to introduce new technology to possibly change the production process. (Salzman-North Carolina)
W75-07091

RESEARCH NEEDS RELATED TO HYDROLOGIC ASPECTS OF WATER FOR ENERGY FROM LARGE ENERGY COMPLEXES,
Minnesota Dept. of Natural Resources, St. Paul.
G. H. Hollenstein.
In: Proceedings of the Workshop on Research Needs Related to Water for Energy, Water Resources Center, University of Illinois at Urbana-Champaign, Research Report No. 93, p 99-100, November, 1974.

Descriptors: *Hydrologic data, *Energy conversion, Energy, Power plants, Pollution, *Water utilization, *Water reuse, Costs, *Optimization, Water shortage, *Water demand, Weather modification, Precipitation(Atmospheric), Research and development, Technology, Water policy, Economics, *Research priorities.
Identifiers: Hydrometeorology.

Some research needs related to the solution of practical problems of large energy complexes are discussed. Proximity to energy sources requires development of a systematic program for evaluating the general availability and distribution plus the hydrologic characteristics of available water supplies involved in the siting of any major complex. To increase water uses yet conserve, new technology and innovative methodologies must be applied to water reuse; i.e., new methods to integrate present uses and wastewater discharges with energy water needs, to recapture and reuse water lost through evaporation and other processes, and to recycle and store groundwater supplies. Atmospheric weather modification to supplement water supplies is another area where new methods and techniques to analyze possible results should be developed. One of major research needs is to develop rational, functional programs which will integrate greater and more efficient production of energy with as little hydrologic and environmental impairment as possible by the most economical means. (See also W75-07089) (Salzman-North Carolina)
W75-07093

RESEARCH NEEDS RELATED TO HYDROMETEOROLOGIC ASPECTS OF FUTURE ENERGY PRODUCTION,
National Oceanic and Atmospheric Administration, Oak Ridge, Tenn. Air Resources Atmospheric Turbulence and Diffusion Lab.
S. R. Hanna.
In: Proceedings of the Workshop on Research Needs Related to Water for Energy, Water Resources Center, University of Illinois at Urbana-Champaign, Research Report No. 93, p 102-107, November, 1974. 19 ref.

Descriptors: Energy, *Energy dissipation, Heat, *Heat flow, *Dispersion, Atmosphere, Clouds, Fog, *Meteorology, *Thermal pollution, Water cooling, Thermal power plants, Research and development, Model studies, Air pollution, Path of pollutants, Cooling towers, *Research priorities.
Identifiers: Cooling ponds, *Coal gasification, Power parks.

Increasing use of water in cooling waste heat has generated greater thermal pollution as well as demands for more water. The environmental modification by cooling towers and ponds is reevaluated. Although cooling towers cause the development of small cumulus clouds and contribute to intense fog, atmospheric effects of waste heat dissipation are currently observed to be of only slight significance. Because increases in waste heat are expected, more research is needed to evaluate its environmental effects. Waste heat from coal gasification, power plants, and from large energy centers is evaluated in relation to its dissipation and effect on the atmosphere. Specific calculations help determine the environmental impact of these emissions dealing with plume rise, cloud formation, ground cover fog and drift deposition. Recommended research, listed by priorities, includes: the study of cloud formation by multiple cooling tower plumes; the testing of a cloud-growth model; development of dispersion theory to calculate fog increases; the measuring of drift deposition; and development of models of plumes from cooling towers and heat rejections from cooling ponds for observation of heat budget terms. (See also W75-07089) (Salzman-North Carolina)
W75-07094

RESEARCH NEEDS RELATED TO HEAT DISSIPATION FROM LARGE POWER PLANTS,
Iowa Univ., Iowa City. Inst. of Hydraulic Research.
For primary bibliographic entry see Field 5B.
W75-07095

RESEARCH NEEDS ON SOCIAL, POLITICAL AND INSTITUTIONAL ASPECTS OF COAL UTILIZATION,
Kentucky Univ., Lexington. Center for Developmental Change.
S. Johnson, and A. Randall.
In: Proceedings of the Workshop on Research Needs Related to Water for Energy, Water Resources Center, University of Illinois at Urbana-Champaign, Research Report No. 93, p 137-153, November, 1974. 2 fig, 24 ref, 1 append.

Descriptors: Coals, *Energy conversion, *Economic impacts, Social aspects, *Social impact, Community development, Employment opportunities, Area redevelopment, *Cost-benefit analysis, Research and development, Legislation, Human resources, Regional economics, Political aspects, Institutions, Governments, Environmental impacts, Environmental control, *Research priorities.
Identifiers: *Coal gasification.

The value of a natural resource is determined by the interactions of scarcity, technology and human value systems. The impact of the development of coal conversion processes in the more humid eastern half of the United States is discussed. Intending to provide a perspective on requirements needed to achieve a desirable balance between energy supply, environmental protection and the social and economic well-being of people affected by the coal complex, past experience and the present situation of the coal mining industry are outlined. Cost-benefit analysis serves as an important tool to measure the impact of the coal-mining industry on the regional economic activity. The introduction of large scale coal conversion and increased mining activity will result in an increased population as well as other consequences to rural areas. Land speculation, an inevitable result, forces those newly employed and those displaced because of site selection, to pay higher prices for building costs and land sites. Demand for public and private services far exceeds the ability and revenue sources of the community to provide them. To estimate these and other possible effects, a coal gasification plant planned for Western Kentucky was analyzed. Research must be directed toward creating temporary systems to handle stress in construction phase, to develop laws and

regulations, to identify policy incentives for coal industry to behave in the interest of the community, and finally, to assess the impacts of industrial expansion on environmental protection, economic diversity, and problems of rapid growth. (See also W75-07089) (Salzman-North Carolina)
W75-07096

RESEARCH NEEDS ON ECONOMIC AND RESOURCE MANAGEMENT ASPECTS FOR COAL GASIFICATION/LIQUEFACTION,
Tennessee Univ., Knoxville. Appalachian Resources Project.
For primary bibliographic entry see Field 6B.
W75-07097

EFFLUENT TREATMENT AND ITS COST FOR THE SYNTHANE COAL-TO-SNG PROCESS,
Bureau of Mines, Pittsburgh, Pa.
For primary bibliographic entry see Field 5D.
W75-07098

RESEARCH NEEDS RELATED TO THE ENVIRONMENTAL ASPECTS OF COAL GASIFICATION/LIQUEFACTION,
Hittman Associates, Inc., Columbia, Md.
C. W. Mallory, T. R. Mills, and D. Emerson.
In: Proceedings of the Workshop on Research Needs Related to Water for Energy, Water Resources Center, University of Illinois at Urbana-Champaign. Research Report No. 93, p 184-196, November, 1974. 2 tab.

Descriptors: *Coal mines, Coals, *Energy conversion, *Environmental effects, *Sites, *Research and development, Energy, Reclamation, Waste treatment.
Identifiers: *Coal gasification, Coal refineries, Coal liquefaction, Appalachia, Eastern Interior, Fort Union, Powder River, Four Corners.

Under the auspices of the Office of Coal Research, a study of the environmental aspects associated with the siting, construction and operation of large scale coal refineries was conducted to identify environmental effects and to define the magnitude of these effects. Approaches used to mitigate adverse environmental consequences are defined. Five major coalbearing regions (Appalachia, Eastern Interior, Fort Union, Powder River and 4 Corners) having reserves adequate to support a number of large scale coal refineries were considered. Major environmental issues considered in planning and siting of large scale coal refinery complexes include creation of new industrial areas, influx of population, commitment of large quantities of water, land disturbance, modification of natural drainage, generation of waste products, and destruction of terrestrial and aquatic habitats. Each issue is detailed in terms of the environmental, economic, and social ramifications of the coal plant on an area. For example, a coal refinery and power plant requires large amounts of cooling water as well as water for consumptive uses resulting from increased population. This water need will necessitate the siting of coal complexes with regard to the long term commitment to fill all water requirements. Although major environmental issues have been defined, basic and applied research will be needed to develop approaches, strategies and policy options that will be required. (See also W75-07089) (Salzman-North Carolina)
W75-07099

THE CALIFORNIA WATER PLAN, OUTLOOK IN 1974,
California State Dept. of Water Resources, Sacramento.
C. A. McCullough, and J. D. Voyder.
Bulletin No. 160-74, November, 1974. 64 p, 10 fig, 21 tab.

Descriptors: *Planning, *Water supply development, *Water quality, *Conservation, *Potential water supply, Projections, Water allocation(Policy), Water conservation, Water requirements, Water supply, Water utilization, California, Long-term planning, Water resources development, Alternate planning.
Identifiers: *California water plan.

In California, the status of developed and available water supplies compared to present demands for water is still favorable. The situation affords time for consideration of all alternative sources for future water supply, including techniques for more efficient use of water to reduce demands. This outlook is premised on completion of Auburn Dam on the American River, New Melones Dam on the Stanislaus River, and Warm Springs Dam on Dry Creek in the Russian River Basin, and the Peripheral Canal being constructed and in operation by 1980. How long this condition lasts depends on the completion of additional water conveyance facilities needed to deliver already regulated supplies. No new water projects that would develop additional supplies of any significance have been authorized. The quality of the State's water supply is generally quite satisfactory, with the significant exception of the Colorado River and some localized ground water problems. The quality is expected to be maintained and improved as the result of the basin plans for water quality management currently being developed by the State Water Resources Control Board. While the urban areas of the State should experience no significant or extensive water shortages during the next 20 years, the outlook for any large expansion is not optimistic. (Poertner)
W75-07134

DAVIS COUNTY COMPREHENSIVE STUDY, 1972 UPDATE CULINARY WATER, PRESSURE IRRIGATION WATER, SANITARY SEWERAGE.
Davis County, Salt Lake City, Utah.
1972. 27 p.

Descriptors: *Domestic water, *Water supply, *Irrigation systems, *Sewerage, *Utah, *Water distribution(Applied), *Potable water, Water allocation(Policy), Water quality, Municipal water, Comprehensive planning, Cities.
Identifiers: Davis County(Utah).

The inventory for the years of 1971 and 1972 of all water systems in Davis County, Utah, has been updated. This includes the culinary water system, pressure irrigation water system and the sanitary sewerage system. Also, the supply, storage and distribution of each water system has been evaluated. Statements of present adequacy and projections are based upon this evaluation. Each system has been evaluated in light of its own situation and in relation to the Weber Basin Project which is a country-wide system. For each city in Davis County, data is given on the growth of the city in terms of residential units, commercial or industrial expansion, and a projection of the population by 1990. The inventory and any projected plans for the supply, storage and distribution of water are given for each city. Also included is information on whether grants have been used or applied for. Weber Basin should be able to furnish water to the cities, districts and private companies as the needs arise. Weber Basin has applied for a grant to HUD for construction of a 6,000,000 gallon reservoir to serve several cities in Davis County and Weber County. This project will enable Weber Basin to meet increasing demands as the area continues to grow. (Poertner)
W75-07140

INDUSTRIAL WATER DEMAND FORECASTING,
Department of the Environment, Ottawa (Ontario). Water Planning and Management Branch.
D. M. Tate, and R. Robichaud.
Social Science Series No. 10, 1973. 23 p, 4 fig, 1 tab, 16 ref.

Descriptors: *Model studies, *Industrial water, *Water demand, *Forecasting, Water costs, Water consumption, Comprehensive planning, Water management(Applied), Water conservation, Municipal water, Water shortage, Capital costs, Evaluation, Water supply, Water users, Water distribution, Water rates, Competing uses, Recreation.

A simulation model was developed to forecast industrial water demand in Canada in order to avoid severe water shortages, anticipate conflicting water demands, increase the scope of comprehensive water resource planning, and evaluate the effects of government policy in the water management field. Water-use coefficients and water pricing and cost were judged to be unsatisfactory techniques for forecasting water demands. The water-use coefficients lose accuracy when applied to regional areas and water pricing and cost rely on a circular argument. The proposed simulation model, however, utilizes a module approach, emphasizing flexibility in the number of factors included, and the precision of the relationships. The model is discussed in terms of its verification, versatility, responsiveness to government policy, expandability, information requirements, and limitations. A lack of background information on several important parameters of the model, and on water cost as it affects demand, limits the specific application of the model for high precision uses. Several sample applications of the model were analyzed, and the extension of the model to some industrial sectors and to the municipal sector is demonstrated. (Becker-Wisconsin)
W75-07346

6E. Water Law and Institutions

PROCEEDINGS - CONFERENCE ON PUBLIC PARTICIPATION IN WATER RESOURCES PLANNING AND MANAGEMENT.
North Carolina Water Resources Research Inst., Raleigh.
For primary bibliographic entry see Field 6B.
W75-06854

ACCOUNTABILITY OF PUBLIC WATER RESOURCE AGENCIES: LEGAL INSTITUTIONS FOR PUBLIC INTERACTION,
Virginia Polytechnic Inst. and State Univ., Blacksburg. Water Resources Research Center.
For primary bibliographic entry see Field 6B.
W75-06857

EDUCATION OF PUBLICS FOR PARTICIPATION IN WATER RESOURCE POLICY AND DECISION-MAKING,
Mississippi State Univ., Mississippi State. Social Science Research Center.
For primary bibliographic entry see Field 6B.
W75-06859

FDA'S PROGRAM OF MERCURY IN FOODS,
Food and Drug Administration, Seattle, Wash.
For primary bibliographic entry see Field 5G.
W75-06905

INSTITUTIONAL INTERACTION IN METROPOLITAN WATER RESOURCE PLANNING,
Metropolitan Council, St. Paul, Minn. Comprehensive Planning Dept.
L. T. Ball.
Water Resources Bulletin, Vol 9, No 3, p 529-537, June 1973. 4 ref.

Descriptors: *Water resources, *Management, *Planning, *Minnesota, *Water policy,

Watershed(Basins), Local governments, Regional analysis, Political aspects, Coordination, Institutions, Cities.
Identifiers: *Metropolitan planning, *Institutional coordination, Political interaction, Behavioral sciences, *Minneapolis-St. Paul(Minn).

Methods of institutional coordination derived from the applied behavioral sciences have been useful in determining the policy planning and implementation responsibilities that must be shared between local governments, water districts, and a regional planning body in the Minneapolis-St. Paul area. The confines of the traditional behavioral science models of organizations and institutional change process, and the realities of administrative systems imbedded in political processes at both the local and state levels, have created conflicts between regional planners, watershed district staff and consultants, and municipal administrators. Recently, there has been a sharp curtailment of watershed district powers. Reported is a recently completed study on the Twin Cities area which considered the major institutional problem areas. A conceptual framework was developed and applied to two watershed districts, and the results evaluated for other research purposes as well as for policy development for the 1973 Minnesota legislative session. Needed are increased flexibility and adaptation to change, less formality, and consideration of a wide range of public interests in the formulation of public policy for water resource management. The conceptual framework provides an alternative to the traditional Weberian bureaucratic model, characterized by an emphasis on rationality, a strict hierarchical system of authority, efficiency, and formal rules. (Bell-Cornell)
W75-06939

VANVOOREN V. JOHN E. FOGARTY MEMORIAL HOSPITAL (ACTION FOR DAMAGES AND RELIEF FROM POLLUTION OF ARTESIAN WELL).
321 A,2d 100 (R.I. 1974).

Descriptors: *Rhode Island, *Judicial decisions, *Oil pollution, *Artesian wells, *Legal aspects, Water law, State jurisdiction, damages, equity, Oily water, Water pollution, Water pollution sources, Oil, Land tenure, Adjacent land owners, Subsurface waters, Groundwater, Water rights, Overlying proprietor, Legal review, Water pollution effects, Water quality, Potable water, Adjudication procedure, Water quality control.
Identifiers: *Liability(Legal aspects).

The plaintiff landowner sought equitable relief and money damages from an adjoining landowner and a corporation, both defendants herein. The plaintiff alleged that the defendants were negligent in the manner in which they repaired a fuel oil leak in the adjacent landowners furnace. The lower court directed verdicts in favor of both defendants and the plaintiff appealed. The Supreme Court of Rhode Island held that the evidence failed to show that the corporate defendant had any duty to the plaintiff to replace soil saturated with spilled oil after it had repaired the oil leak. The court further held that the evidence did present a jury question as to whether the adjacent landowner had exercised reasonable care in attempting to prevent contamination of the well. Accordingly, the judgment as to the corporate defendant was affirmed and the judgment as to the adjacent landowner was reversed and the case remanded for further proceedings. (Deckert-Florida)
W75-06962

HENDRICKSON V. WILSON (ACTION TO ENJOIN HARBOR EXPANSION PENDING IMPACT STATEMENT).
374 F Supp 865 (W.D. Mich 1973).

Descriptors: *Harbors, *Engineering structures, *Shore protection, Environmental quality, *Recreation, Aesthetics, Natural resources, Recreation demand, Recreation facilities, Social aspects, Social impact, Judicial decisions, Bodies of water, Marinas, Regulation, Water resources development, Michigan, Water law.
Identifiers: *Environmental Impact Statements, NEPA.

Action was brought by property owners to enjoin state agencies and the Army Corps of Engineers from proceeding with the contemplated expansion of a harbor until an environmental impact statement could be filed in accordance with federal and state law. Plaintiffs alleged that the harbor construction with its boat launching and docking facilities had precipitated a breakdown of the area's septic systems and had caused the pollution of the surrounding environment. They contended that the expansion involved both federal and state action and that the plan would affect the surrounding human environment. The United States District Court upheld the determination of the Corps of Engineers that the proposed construction of additional offshore mooring facilities in the harbor was not major federal action significantly affecting the quality of the human environment. Therefore, no environmental impact statement was required prior to construction. (Proctor-Florida)
W75-06963

STATE BOARD'S DISCRETIONARY POWER TO PENALIZE POLLUTERS DECLARED INVALID.
Pollution Control Guide, Vol 3, paragraph 19913, p 19725-19726, 1974.

Descriptors: *Illinois, *Judicial decisions, *Adjudication procedure, *Legislation, *Administrative agencies, Administration, Adoption of practices, Legal aspects, State governments, Standards, Water pollution sources, Legal review, Water pollution control, Water law, Law enforcement, Regulation, Penalties(Legal), Jurisdiction, Water quality control, Water quality standards, Constitutional law.
Identifiers: Injunctive relief, Liability(Legal aspects), Administrative regulations.

The Illinois Fifth District Appellate Court has recently ruled that the Illinois Pollution Control Board has the power to determine if the state's Environmental Protection Act has been violated, but may not impose penalties on parties found to be in violation of the standards. Provisions of the Act which gave the Board unfettered discretionary power to set penalties effected an unconstitutional delegation of legislative and judicial authority. The lack of standards to guide the Board was the fatal weakness in the statutory plan. In one of two decisions, the court said that an administrative agency's imposition of a discretionary penalty constituted an unconstitutional exercise of judicial power which violated the Illinois Constitution's doctrine of separation of powers. Although it determined that the Pollution Control Board could not penalize the manufacturer, the court did not discuss other enforcement powers of the Board such as the authority to enjoin any person who violates a provision of the Act. (Sperling-Florida)
W75-06964

SMITH V. JACKSON PARISH SCHOOL BOARD (ACTION FOR DAMAGES TO POND CAUSED BY DEFECTIVE SEWAG SYSTEM).
300 So 2d 252 (La App 1974).

Descriptors: *Water pollution, *Judicial decisions, *Water pollution sources, Ponds, *Louisiana, Sewage disposal, Sewers, Sewage, Engineering structures, Negligence, Legal aspects, Water quality control, Water law.
Identifiers: *Nuisance, *Contamination.

Plaintiff, owner of a pond adjacent to a school, brought suit against the School Board seedking injunctive and monetary relief for injury caused by a defective sewage system on School Board Property. The trial court awarded money damages and enjoined the School Board from further contaminating plaintiff's pond. On appeal the trial court was affirmed as to the measure of damages, but reversed as to the grant of permanent injunctive relief. The court held that since the contamination had ceased it was improper to order the Board to prevent acts which were no longer occurring. (Proctor-Florida)
W75-06965

AMERICAN PAPER INSTITUTE V. TRAIN (ACTION SEEKING REVIEW OF WATER POLLUTION EFFLUENT LIMITATION GUIDELINES FOR THE PAPER INDUSTRY).
381 F Supp 553 (D D C 1974).

Descriptors: *Judicial decisions, *Legal review, *Water quality standards, *Water pollution control, *District of Columbia, Water pollution sources, Effluents, Regulation, Water law, Water pollution, Adoption of practices, Administrative agencies, Federal Water Pollution Control Act, Permits, Administration, Standards, Adjudication procedure, Legal aspects, Water quality control, Federal jurisdiction.
Identifiers: *FWPCA Amendments of 1972, Administrative regulations, Effluent limitations, Environmental policy, Standing(Legal).

A paper manufacturer brought action in federal district court seeking review of water pollution effluent limitation guidelines promulgated by the Environmental Protection Agency. The court held that if the challenged regulations were guidelines, and as such only aids in establishing standards of performance for the issuance of permits, the paper company was not adversely affected by the issuance of the regulations and thus could not seek judicial review. If the regulations were limitations, which the court held them to be, review could only be by a United States Court of Appeals. The 1972 Ammendments to the Federal Water Pollution Control Act provide that judicial review of the limitations be by United States Courts of Appeal. When Congress has specified a procedure for judicial review of administrative action, courts will not make non-statutory remedies available without a showing of patent violation of agency authority. (Sperling-Florida)
W75-06966

STATE OF NEW YORK V. BISHOP (ACTION BY STATE ON TRESPASS FOR FILLING BELOW HIGH WATER MARK OF BAY).
359 N Y S 2d 817 (S Ct 1974).

Descriptors: *Riparian rights, *Erosion, *New York, Judicial decisions, Land tenure, Soil erosion, Waves(Water), Tides, Shores, Navigable waters, Bays, Bodies of water, Trespass, Public rights, Public access, Water pollution.
Identifiers: *Mean high water mark, Nuisance(Legal aspects).

An action was brought by the State of New York alleging trespass by defendant property owner in filling in property below the high water mark of the bay on gounds that the area was not owned by defendant but constituted underwater land owned and held in trust by the town's trustees. The complaint also alleged that the defendant had created and maintained a public nuisance, and had polluted the waters of the state. The court held a 1950 title registration judgment did not bind the state to the location of the mean high water mark described therin since defendant held a title diminishable in extent by erosion and consequent influx of the tide. Also held that the erosion of defendant's parcel carried with it all incidents of ownership, including the right of reclamation. (Proctor-Florida)
W75-06967

ILLINOIS SUPREME COURT OK'S PCB'S POWER TO FINE POLLUTERS.
For primary bibliographic entry see Field 5G.
W75-06968

BROWN V. RUCKELSHAUS (AND COMPANION CASE) (CHALLENGE TO EXECUTIVE IMPOUNDMENT).
For primary bibliographic entry see Field 5G.
W75-06969

CAMPAIGN CLEAN WATER, INC. V. RUCKELSHAUS (CITIZENS SUIT ON IMPOUNDMENT OF FWPCA FUNDS.)
For primary bibliographic entry see Field 5G.
W75-06970

THE CITY OF NEW YORK, ET AL. V. RUCKELSHAUS (IMPOUNDMENT OF FEDERAL WATER POLLUTION CONTROL ACT FUNDS).
For primary bibliographic entry see Field 5G.
W75-06971

CALVERT CLIFFS COORDINATING COMMITTEE, INC., ET AL. V. UNITED STATES ATOMIC ENERGY COMM'N., ET AL. (ENFORCEMENT OF THE NATIONAL ENVIRONMENTAL POLICY ACT).
For primary bibliographic entry see Field 6G.
W75-06972

TOWARD CLEANER WATER.
Environmental Protection Agency, Washington, D.C.
For primary bibliographic entry see Field 5G.
W75-06973

VANCE V. KASSAB (SUIT TO RESTRAIN DEFENDANT FROM CONSTRUCTING DRAIN PIPE WHICH WOULD DISCHARGE ON PETITIONER'S LAND).
325 A.2d 924 (Common Ct. Pa. 1974).

Descriptors: *Pennsylvania, *Conduits, *Waste water disposal, *Administrative agencies, *Judicial decisions, Pipelines, Remedies, Construction, Adjacent landowner, Roads, State jurisdiction, Constitutional law, Equity.
Identifiers: Injunctive relief(Legal aspects), Sovereign immunity, Statutes.

An action was brought to enjoin the Pennsylvania Department of Transportation and a roadbuilder from constructing a pipe to drain water from a township road. The court held that the Secretary of Transportation had specific statutory authority to arrange for construction of a pipe to drain water from a township road. If construction of the pipe caused a discharge of water onto the plaintiff's land, the state would be obligated to file a declaration of taking. The plaintiffs then would have the right to file objections to the power or right of the state to appropriate property. Since an adequate statutory remedy was available equitable relief was denied. (Sperling-Florida)
W75-06974

POWER SHORTAGE CONTINGENCY PROGRAM FOR THE PACIFIC NORTHWEST, LEGISLATIVE, REGULATORY AND INSTITUTIONAL ASPECTS,
Kell, Alterman, Runstein and Thomas, Portland, Oreg.
L. Jourolmon, L. B. Day, C. P. Thomas, L. D. Kell, and J. F. Adamson.
Available from the National Technical Information Service, Springfield, Va 22161 as PB-241 323, $10.50 in paper copy, $2.25 in microfiche. Completion Report, 1975. 370 p, 5 fig, 19 tab, 147 ref, append. OWRT C-5049(No. 4226)(1).

Descriptors: *Columbia River, Legal aspects, *Pacific Northwest US, *Electric power production, *Legislation, *Nuclear energy, Regulation, Treaties, Streamflow, Federal Power Act, Energy, Institutions, *Hydroelectric power, Public utility districts, River basin development, Public utilities.
Identifiers: Public utility commissions, Federal Power Commission, Solar power, Power shortages, *Power curtailment, Power rationing.

The potential electric power shortage threatened by the critical regional streamflows in the season of 1973 was studied. It was assumed that the region could experience a series of crises which could not be met by the combined regional power capability. The Pacific Northwest is served by a hydroelectric system owned by the Federal Government, privately owned utilities, public agencies, municipalities, cooperatives and public utility districts throughout the Columbia River Basin. As the hydroelectric sites on the Columbia River system have become exhausted, the pool of proprietary utilities is initiating a hydro-thermal generating system. A series of legislative and contractual recommendations designed to establish priorities for continuation of essential electric service are made. Strong recommendations are given for development of solar electric plants and nuclear power plants, based on fission reactors of contemporary design and the future technologies of breeder and fusion reactors. By the year 2075 the world's population will require 10 to 15 Q's of energy annually. A 'Q' is the equivalent of 2.9 kw hrs times 10 to the 14th power or 2.90 quadrillion kilowatt hours.
W75-06977

WATER USE AND COAL DEVELOPMENT IN EASTERN MONTANA: WATER AVAILABILITY AND DEMANDS,
Montana State Univ., Bozeman. Dept. of Economics and Agricultural Economics.
For primary bibliographic entry see Field 6D.
W75-06979

OWNERSHIP AND USE RIGHTS IN WATER WITHIN NORTH DAKOTA,
North Dakota Univ., Grand Forks. School of Law.
R. E. Beck.
Research Report No. WI-221-025-74, November, 1974, 3 p. OWRT A-035-NDak (1).

Descriptors: *North Dakota, Legal aspects, Common law, *Equitable apportionment, Federal-state water rights conflicts, Judicial decisions, Overlying proprietor, Permits, *Public rights, Reservation doctrine, Riparian waters, Usufructuary rights, *Water law, Water permits, *Water rights, Prescriptive rights, Prior appropriation, Riparian rights, Legislation.

No significant planning for the conservation, preservation, and development of a state's water resource can take place without identifying and analyzing the law relating to five broad areas of ownership and use rights: private rights; public rights; federal rights; Indian rights; and international rights, including claims of other states. Essentially there are three categories of private rights in North Dakota: appropriation under North Dakota statutes, groundwater through application to beneficial use at least before 1955; and surface waters under the riparian doctrine while it still subsisted in North Dakota. In general, the public own the waters within North Dakota subject to appropriation under state statute for beneficial use. Indians water rights have not been quantified nor has their ultimate theoretical scope been defined. The federal government has at least three bases for claiming rights; as riparian owner, as permittee under the state system and as proprietor of a superior navigation easement. Basic constitutional law doctine and compacts control much of the international and interstate situation. Equitable apportionment must take place but has not with reference to North Dakota.
W75-06995

LEGAL ASPECTS OF WATER FOR COAL GASIFICATION,
Virginia Polytechnic Inst. and State Univ., Blacksburg. Water Resources Research Center.
W. R. Walker, and W. E. Cox.
In: Proceedings of the Workshop on Research Needs Related to Water for Energy, Water Resources Center, University of Illinois at Urbana-Champaign, Research Report No. 93, p 82-92, November, 1974. 18 ref.

Descriptors: *Legal aspects, Easements, Eminent domain, Equity, *Federal-state water rights conflicts, Water permits, *Public rights, Riparian water, Usufructuary right, *Riparian rights, *Water law, Natural Flow Doctrine, Legislation, *Water allocation(Policy), Research and development, Common law, Regulation, Zoning, Supply contracts.
Identifiers: *Coal gasification, Riparian Doctrine, Appropriative Doctrine, Diffused Surface Water Doctrine.

Since water is a necessary aspect of the conversion processes, the acquisition of the legal right to the requisite water is a significant factor. Laws and regulations throughout the United States which apply to water rights, ownership and control of utilization are explored. Private water rights for both surface water and groundwater have been the principal method of allocating water among competing users. Although federal control extends over navigable waters and inter- and intra-state streams which affect those waters, state legislation is the primary source of control. Complexity and uncertainty of water rights develop from environmental quality constraints as well as the obscure Western 'reserved water rights' legislation. Private water rights can be categorized into the Riparian Doctrine, Appropriative Doctrine and Diffused Surface Water Doctrine. These doctrines are discussed in relation to coal gasification or liquefaction in operation. State water laws often contrain the quantity of water needed for coal gasification and liquefaction and may also impose constraints on water quality alteration. Federal acts to protect the environment may conflict with industrial water applications. Legal problems involve altering use of stored water to meet needs of energy conversion. (See also W75-07089) (Salzman-North Carolina)
W75-07092

RESEARCH NEEDS ON SOCIAL, POLITICAL AND INSTITUTIONAL ASPECTS OF COAL UTILIZATION,
Kentucky Univ., Lexington. Center for Developmental Change.
For primary bibliographic entry see Field 6D.
W75-07096

DEVELOPMENT OF JAMES BAY: THE ROLE OF ENVIRONMENTAL IMPACT ASSESSMENT IN DETERMINING THE LEGAL RIGHT TO AN INTERLOCUTORY INJUNCTION,
McGill Univ., Montreal (Quebec). Dept. of Geography.
For primary bibliographic entry see Field 6G.
W75-07175

NATURAL RESOURCES MANAGEMENT IN THE GREAT LAKES BASIN,
Cornell Univ., Ithaca, N.Y. Water Resources and Marine Sciences Center.
J. A. Burkholder.
Available from the National Technical Information Service, Springfield, Va 22161 as COM-73-11943, $7.00 in paper copy, $2.25 in microfiche. New York State Sea Grant Program, Great Lakes Management Problems Series, May 1973. 172 p, 3 fig, 44 ref.

Descriptors: *Great Lakes, Management, *Institutions, Social aspects, Political aspects, Economics, *International commissions, Systems analysis, *Natural resources, *Canada, *United States.

Notwithstanding the 1972 Water Quality Agreement between the U.S. and Canada for the Great Lakes, each country's interest could be better served with a broader agreement, integrating bilateral concerns. A two-phase plan is devised. All new features agreed to by the two governments under the Water Quality Agreement would be extended to specifically encompass air quality, fishery, lake levels, and navigation, as well as water quality concerns. To this, new functions, responsibilities and concepts have been added. The use of 'international technical boards' would be continued with five single central Great Lakes boards--air and water quality board, fishery board, lake levels board, navigation board, and a research advisory board. Regional offices would be utilized--a central administration office in the first phase with addition of four Lake-Basin offices under the second. The basic roles of the IJC/Great Lakes arrangements would be that of coordination and oversight (surveillance and guidance) in five major task areas: (1) A Basin-wide policy guidance function, (2) development of a central Great Lakes Basin information system, (3) a comprehensive research advisory function, (4) a basin planning function, including development of a Basin-wide (international) framework plan, and (5) measures to facilitate implementation and review of joint programs. (Auen-Wisconsin)
W75-07344

THE CALIFORNIA STATE WATER PROJECT IN 1970.
California State Dept. of Water Resources, Sacramento.
For primary bibliographic entry see Field 6B.
W75-07347

INFORMATION FOR BUYERS AND OWNERS OF COASTAL PROPERTY IN NORTH CAROLINA.
North Carolina State Univ., Raleigh. Center for Marine and Coastal Studies.
Available from the National Technical Information Service, Springfield, Va 22161 as COM-74-10959, $3.25 in paper copy, $2.25 in microfiche. (1974). 4 p.

Descriptors: *North Carolina, *Coasts, *Urbanization, *Land use, Community development, Erosion, Inlets(Waterways), Soil types, Storms, Dunes, Vegetation, Permits, Boundaries(Property), Septic tanks, Zoning, Insurance, Building codes.
Identifiers: Real estate development.

This brochure describes areas of awareness for prospective purchasers of coastal property in North Carolina to avoid depreciation or loss of investment. (1) Do not build in areas subject to beach erosion; (2) Avoid sites susceptible to inlet migration, (3) Do not build or buy in locations subjcet to flooding and high winds. Other areas to be considered are suitable soil type for septic tank effluents, sand fill over marsh areas, and the protection of dunes and coexisting vegetation. Federal, state, and local permits are required for shore erosion control, dredging, filling, dune alteration, agricultural drainage, diking, various waste discharges, and sanitation. Purchasers of land adjacent to dredged canals should assure that the canals are designed for adequate flushing. Boundary descriptions should be verified by competent representatives, and proposed land use should be compatible with local zoning regulations. Compliance with special building provisions often in effeet for areas subject to flooding and wind storm damage is required to obtain insurance. (Auen-Wisconsin)
W75-07350

6F. Nonstructural Alternatives

INTEGRATION OF HYDROLOGIC, ECONOMIC, ECOLOGIC, SOCIAL, AND WELL-BEING FACTORS IN PLANNING FLOOD CONTROL MEASURES FOR URBAN STREAMS,
Georgia Inst. of Tech., Atlanta. Environmental Resources Center.
L. D. James, A. C. Benke, and H. L. Ragsdale.
Available from the National Technical Information Service, Springfield, Va 22161 as PB-241 385, $7.25 in paper copy, $2.25 in microfiche. Report No. ERC-0375, February 1975. 203 p, 23 fig, 58 tab, 93 ref, 3 append. OWRT B-082-GA(1). 14-31-0001-4070.

Descriptors: *Non-structural alternatives, Flood control, *Flood plain zoning, *Floodproofing, Urban hydrology, Urban sociology, Urbanization, *Social aspects, *Vegetation, Ecosystems, Land management, *Project planning, Parks, Aesthetics, *Georgia, City planning, *Channel improvement.

A well-planned flood control program requires coordinated implementation of a number of structural and nonstructural measures selected through the evaluation of a variety of hydrologic, economic, ecologic, social preference, and community well-being information. This study employed regional hydrologic analysis, a computer program for maximizing net benefits, field surveys of the flood plain environment, a questionnaire to learn the perceptions and the preferences of the concerned public, and an analysis of the relationship between flood plain land use and the well-being of the community and integrated all five types of information into the formulation of flood control programs for four small urban watersheds in Metropolitan Atlanta. The needed information of all five types is outlined in detail, and procedures for collecting and analyzing it are explained. The study strategy was to present the framework of information needs and procedures for collection and analysis to a class of graduate students containing several experienced planners, select four case study flood plains, divide the class into five teams (one for each information category), have the students collect the data, and formulate a course of action through group discussion. Plans combining channelization, flood proofing existing homes and businesses, building codes to require flood proofing of new construction, land use restrictions on new flood plain development, and preservation of identified valuable ecological areas are proposed. A 17-step procedure for use in formulating flood control programs for urban or urbanizing areas is outlined.
W75-06980

FLOOD PLAIN INFORMATION: AGUA HEDIONDA CREEK, PACIFIC OCEAN TO BUENA, SAN DIEGO COUNTY, CALIFORNIA.
Army Engineer District, Los Angeles, Calif.
For primary bibliographic entry see Field 4A.
W75-07087

FLOOD HAZARD ANALYSIS: FOUR MILE AND EIGHT MILE CREEKS, BUTLER COUNTY, KANSAS.
Soil Conservation Service, Salina, Kans.
For primary bibliographic entry see Field 4A.
W75-07088

TYPE 16 FLOOD INSURANCE STUDY: TSUNAMI PREDICTIONS FOR PACIFIC COASTAL COMMUNITIES,
Army Engineer Waterways Experiment Station, Vicksburg, Miss.
A. W. Garcia, and J. R. Houston.
Available from the National Technical Information Service, Springfield, Va., 22161, as AD-785 533, $5.75 in paper copy, $2.25 in microfiche. Army Engineer Waterways Experiment Station, Vicksburg, Mississippi. Technical Report H-74-3, May 1974. 128 p, 79 fig, 1 tab, 35 ref, append.

Descriptors: *Flood forecasting, *Tsunamis, Coasts, *California, *Alaska, Insurance, Seismic design, Ocean waves, Forecasting, Tidal effects, Non-structural alternatives, Pacific coast region.
Identifiers: *Wave runup, *Flood insurance(Coasts).

Calculations of runup due to seismic sea waves (tsunamis) of distant origin are made for 15 coastal communities within the State of California and 3 coastal communities within the State of Alaska. The values given are interpreted as being equaled or exceeded on the average of once per 100 or once per 500 years, whichever is indicated. The combined effects of astronomical tides and tsunamis are incorporated into the analysis as well as local resonance effects where judged significant. The methodology is discussed. Analysis of the error attributed to each of the various steps in the procedure results in an estimated maximum average error of about plus or minus 40 percent for the southern California communities and plus or minus 75 percent for the Alaskan communities. It is essential that these runup predictions be reviewed approximately every five years in the light of advancements in the theory of tsunami generation, propagation, and runup. Significant future developments should be incorporated into the predictions performed and flood insurance rates adjusted accordingly. (WES)
W75-07283

GILA RIVER BASIN, NEW RIVER AND PHOENIX CITY STREAMS, ARIZONA: ALTERNATIVE PLANS FOR FLOOD CONTROL AND RECREATIONAL DEVELOPMENT.
Army Engineer District, Los Angeles, Calif.
For primary bibliographic entry see Field 4A.
W75-07331

6G. Ecologic Impact Of Water Development

ECONOMIC CRITERIA FOR FRESHWATER WETLAND POLICY IN MASSACHUSETTS,
Massachusetts Univ., Amherst. Dept. of Food and Resource Economics.
For primary bibliographic entry see Field 6B.
W75-06896

THE NEED FOR A COMPREHENSIVE APPROACH IN THE MANAGEMENT OF ENVIRONMENTAL RESOURCES,
North Carolina State Univ., Raleigh. Dept. of Civil Engineering.
D. S. Airan.
Water Resources Bulletin, Vol 9, No 3, p 421-432, June 1973. 6 fig, 1 tab, 31 ref.

Descriptors: *Comprehensive planning, *Management, Environment, Resources, *Pollution abatement, *Water quality control, Constraints, Air, Land resources, Limiting factors, Ecology, Feasibility, Waste disposal, Groundwater, Sewage, Solid wastes, Pesticides, Surface waters, Oceans, Decision making, Rivers.
Identifiers: Environmental quality, *Environmental impact, Radioactive wastes, Human wastes.

Environmental resources can be managed properly only by adopting a comprehensive approach. The whole environment must be considered as a single system, and prior to any action, all types of environmental impacts caused by it should be studied in detail. The close relationship between different environmental problems is emphasized; existing management patterns are analyzed; and new alternatives whenever applicable are proposed. Water resources is sub-divided

into ground, surface and sea water. Considered are: groundwater pollution; finding a quality parameter better than BOD; flushing of human waste in municipal sewers; sewer overloading by ground garbage; water quality management in rivers; and pollution in, and radioactive waste disposal into, the sea. Air pollution due to different processes is discussed, and problems in the management of land resources are considered, including disposal of solid wastes and the use of pesticides. The different constraints which must be considered in the decision-making process while developing a plan are discussed. Efforts neglecting the interaction among different aspects of the environment do not upgrade the quality of water, air, and land to any appreciable degree. Since it is impossible to satisfy all constraints in any system, a plan must be an optimal compromise consisting of those feasible alternatives which allow attainment of the maximum objectives with the minimum expenditure of resources. Limiting factors in environmental resource management include: economical, environmental, political, social, engineering/technical feasibility, resources, and needs. (Bell-Cornell)
W75-06938

HENDRICKSON V. WILSON (ACTION TO ENJOIN HARBOR EXPANSION PENDING IMPACT STATEMENT).
For primary bibliographic entry see Field 6E.
W75-06963

CALVERT CLIFFS COORDINATING COMMITTEE, INC., ET AL. V. UNITED STATES ATOMIC ENERGY COMM'N., ET AL. (ENFORCEMENT OF THE NATIONAL ENVIRONMENTAL POLICY ACT).
1 Pollution Control Guide (Vol. 3), paragraph 15004, p 15046-15062, 1973.

Descriptors: *Environmental effects, *Judicial decisions, *Administrative decisions, *Federal government, *Federal Water Pollution Control Act, Radioactivity effects, Legal aspects, Legal review, Water law, Permits, Regulation, Administration, Administrative agencies, Federal project policy, Evaluation, Decision making, Legislation, Nuclear powerplants, Inter-agency cooperation, Adjudication procedure.
Identifiers: Administrative regulations, *National Environmental Policy Act, Citizen suits, Licenses, Environmental policy.

The petitioners, an environmental group, brought action in the United States Court of Appeals for the District of Columbia, seeking review of an order of the Atomic Energy Commission (AEC). The petitioners argued that certain rules recently adopted by the Commission to govern consideration of environmental factors through its review processes failed to satisfy the requirements of the National Environmental Policy Act (NEPA) of 1969. Specifically challenged were rules relating to the consideration of environmental factors by hearing boards, implementation of the NEPA review standards, and application of environmental standards to projects approved before the NEPA standards took effect. The Commission contended that the vagueness of the NEPA mandate left much room for agency discretion and that the challenged rules fell well within the broad language of the Act. The court ruled that while the Act granted discretionary powers concerning substantive matters, the procedural directives of the Act were specific and had not been followed by the Commission. The court ordered the AEC rules revised in accordance with the NEPA requirement that environmental factors be considered to the fullest extent possible, and that environmental issues be considered at every stage where a balancing of environmental and nonenvironmental factors is appropriate. (Deckert-Florida)
W75-06972

ENVIRONMENTAL CONSIDERATIONS FOR CONSTRUCTION PROJECTS.
Agency for International Development, Washington, D.C. Office of Science and Technology.
Available from the National Technical Information Service, Springfield, Va 22161 as PB-203 326, $3.75 in paper copy, $2.25 in microfiche. Report TA/OST/71-1, July 1971. 31 p, 55 ref.

Descriptors: *Construction, *Environmental effects, Road construction, Harbors, Airports, Irrigation systems, Dam construction, Powerplants, Industries, Mining, Mineral industry, Pulp and paper industry, Fertilizers, Sewage treatment.

Environmental considerations for twelve categories of construction projects were presented in the form of key questions designed to serve as general points of departure for analyzing the potential environmental consequences of proposed projects. Projects discussed were: road construction, port and harbor development, airports, irrigation systems, dam construction, power plants, petroleum-petrochemical industry, mining, smelting, pulp and paper industry, fertilizer plants, and sewage treatment. (Sims-ISWS)
W75-07047

THE HANLON CREEK STUDY: AN ECOLOGICAL APPROACH TO URBAN PLANNING,
Guelph Univ. (Ontario). Dept. of Land Resource Science.
For primary bibliographic entry see Field 6B.
W75-07067

COAL CONVERSION: PROCESSES, RESOURCE REQUIREMENTS, AND ENVIRONMENTAL IMPACT.
Illinois Univ., Urbana. Inst. for Environmental Studies.
For primary bibliographic entry see Field 6D.
W75-07090

RESEARCH NEEDS RELATED TO THE ENVIRONMENTAL ASPECTS OF COAL GASIFICATION/LIQUEFACTION,
Hittman Associates, Inc., Columbia, Md.
For primary bibliographic entry see Field 6D.
W75-07099

SOCIAL AND ECONOMIC IMPACTS OF WASTE WATER MANAGEMENT IN THE MERRIMACK BASIN,
Abt Associates, Inc., Cambridge, Mass.
For primary bibliographic entry see Field 5C.
W75-07121

WASTE WATER MANAGEMENT - A REGIONAL PROBLEM,
Corps of Engineers, New York. North Atlantic Div.
For primary bibliographic entry see Field 5C.
W75-07124

HANLON CREEK ECOLOGICAL STUDY, PHASE A,
Guelph Univ. (Ontario).
J. D. Milliken, R. J. Brooks, P. Chisholm, D. Elrick, and R. R. Forster.
Guelph University, Center for Resources Development, Ontario, Canada, Publication No. 50, September 1971. 66 p, 12 fig, 9 tab.

Descriptors: *Ecology, *Land use, *Urban sociology, *On-site data collections, *Watersheds(Basins), Water, Quality control, Drainage patterns(Geologic), Runoff, Canada, Environmental control, Storage, Aquatic environment.
Identifiers: Runoff retention ponds, Guelph, Ontario(Canada).

The existing micro-drainage system of the Hanlon Expressway Corridor in the vicinity of Hanlon Creek at Guelph, Ontario was identified and analyzed in relationship to the effect of proposed expressway works. The highway as proposed may interfere with sub-surface drainage in some locations resulting in ponding and high water tables. Rerouting of surface drainage in some areas as proposed may be expected to result in soil erosion during construction particularly and an increase in the sediment load reaching the stream. An increase in levels of sodium and chloride in the water of the Hanlon Creek may be expected from de-icing salts used on the Expressway. Existing high nitrate levels if supported by relatively small increases in phosphate will induce heavy algal blooms. Deforestation either directly associated with construction or resulting from changes in water tables and exposure will increase solar heating of the stream and threaten desirable aquatic species. The plans should consider erosion control, storm runoff retention ponds, minimum destruction of existing vegetation, and maintenance of all environmental protection measures. Monitoring systems should be established and further research should be initiated. (See also W75-07128) (Poertner)
W75-07127

HANLON CREEK ECOLOGICAL STUDY, PHASE B, VOL. 1,
Guelph Univ. (Ontario).
J. D. Milliken, R. J. Brooks, E. A. Cebotarev, P. Chisholm, and E. E. Mackintosh.
Guelph University, Center for Resources Development, Ontario, Canada, Publication No. 51, April 1972. 71 p, 13 fig, 1 tab.

Descriptors: *Urbanization, *Urban sociology, *Land use, *Ecology, *On-site data collections, *Social aspects, Aesthetics, Recreation facilities, Recreation demand, Soil management, Alternative planning, Conservation, Canada, Ecological distribution, Physiological ecology, Plant ecology, Water quality control.
Identifiers: Guelph, Ontario(Canada), Hanlon Creek Watershed.

The Hanlon Creek watershed in the City of Guelph, Ontario was studied in concert with the projected environmental impact of a multiplicity of urban land uses. A substantial volume of base data is given which depicts the present terrestrial and aquatic environment of the Hanlon Creek and its watershed. These data have provided the basis for projecting and testing development opportunities and constraints. In addition, this inventory is sufficiently comprehensive to establish a base plane for measurement of change as urbanization takes place in the vicinity. Recommendations are made concerning municipal development and change, stream biology considerations, terrestrial wildlife and vegetation, landscape quality control, and social concerns. Data and discussions are included on soil and water resources, biological conditions in Hanlon Creek, terrestrial wildlife and vegetation, landscape esthetics and sociological aspects. The study guidelines included development policies which identified several alternative boundaries for lands deemed undesirable for urban development, yet desirable for conservation or 'greenbelt' purposes. These alternative policies are studied with the emphasis on conservation, recreation, development, and servicing capability. (See also W75-07127) (Poertner)
W75-07128

REGIONAL SERVICES PROGRAM, FISCAL YEAR 1974-75,
Bay Area Sewage Services Agency, Berkeley, Calif.
For primary bibliographic entry see Field 5G.
W75-07133

IMPACT ANALYSIS: HINDSIGHT AND FORESIGHT IN SASKATCHEWAN,
Saskatchewan Fisheries Lab., Saskatoon.

F. M. Atton.
Journal of the Fisheries Research Board of Canada, Vol 32, No 1, p 101-105, January 1975. 2 fig, 2 tab.

Descriptors: *Hydroelectric project licensing, *Reservoirs, *Environment, *Environmental effects, Shoreline cover, Shore protection, Terrain analysis, Erosion rates, Sedimentation, Pakolimnology, Limnology, *Canada, Ecology, Water quality, Fisheries.
Identifiers: *Saskatchewan(Canada).

Three hydro-developments in Saskatchewan were described. A fourth reservoir proposal is under study and is to be reviewed for a decision in 1975. This appears to be the first project where impact analysis is being carried out before implementation is decided upon. A brief resume of information on these impoundments includes limnology, aquatic ecology, and water quality. This enabled broad description of the impact of impoundment and inundation rather than consideration of the fishery resource only. Particular attention was given to the need for shoreline mapping, terrain description, forest clearing, erosion prediction, permafrost discovery, and mitigation of effects on fishery resources. The discussion emphasized the practical approach. (Dawes-ISWS)
W75-07171

HYDROELECTRIC DEVELOPMENT OF THE NELSON RIVER SYSTEM IN NORTHERN MANITOBA,
Manitoba Hydro, Winnipeg.
I. W. Dickson.
Journal of the Fisheries Research Board of Canada, Vol 32, No 1, p 106-116, January 1975. 3 fig.

Descriptors: *Hydroelectric project licensing, *Ecology, *Environment, *Environmental effects, Shoreline cover, Terrain analysis, Erosion rates, Sedimentation, Paleolimnology, Limnology, Economic impact, Social impact, Social values, Social adjustment, Flow, Recreation, Wildlife, *Canada, Aesthetics, Earth-water interfaces.
Identifiers: *Nelson River System(Manitoba).

Manitoba Hydro plans to divert the Churchill River at Southern Indian Lake to the Nelson River via the Rat-Burntwood Rivers. Combined flows of the Churchill and Nelson Rivers would generate more than 7 mil kw at 14 power generating sites along the Nelson River system. Regulation of Lake Winnipeg is required to provide storage to augment flows in the Nelson River. Impacts to beaches, marshes, recreation, and wildlife are important aspects of Lake Winnipeg regulation. The level and flow pattern of Outlet Lakes at Lake Winnipeg will also be altered by regulation. Life styles and cultural values of residents in the Cross Lake community may be affected by the project. Diversion of 30,000 cfs from the Churchill to the Nelson River may reduce flows which have historically ranged from 20,500 to 92,000 cfs to minimum winter and summer flows of 1500 and 500 cfs, respectively. Altered levels, flows, and associated ice regime may be expected to significantly alter the aesthetic qualities of the river. Raising Southern Indian Lake level may cause major changes to the appearance of the landscape and the use of associated resources. Storage and release of waters from impoundments along the Rat-Burntwood diversion route will significantly alter the characteristics of the land-water interface. Flows increased from 4000 to 34,000 cfs and flooding will have a major impact on availability and use of associated resources. Notigi Lake control for Churchill River diversion will cause flooding of about 40,500 hectares. Additional flooding of approximately the same area below the Notigi Control can be anticipated following diversion and the development of Wuskwatim and Manasan sites on the Burntwood River. (Dawes-ISWS)
W75-07172

ENVIRONMENTAL IMPACT OF THE CHURCHILL FALLS (LABRADOR) HYDROELECTRIC PROJECT: A PRELIMINARY ASSESSMENT,
Waterloo Univ. (Ontario). Dept. of Biology.
H. C. Duthie, and M. L. Ostrofsky.
Journal of the Fisheries Research Board of Canada, Vol 32, No 1, p 117-125, January 1975. 4 fig, 3 tab, 6 ref.

Descriptors: *Hydroelectric project licensing, *Ecology, *Environment, *Environmental effects, Shoreline cover, Shore protection, Terrain analysis, Erosion rates, Sedimentation, Pakolimnology, Limnology, Chemical properties, Ecological distribution, *Canada, Flooding, Water chemistry, Planning, Biomass.
Identifiers: *Labrador(Churchill Falls).

The Churchill Falls hydroelectric project in western Labrador involved the creation of reservoirs totalling 6650 sq km in area and the diversion of two rivers: the Churchill and the Naskaupi. A considerable area of forest and muskeg was inundated. Flooding began in 1971 and full pond was expected in 1974. The nominal installed capacity of the scheme is 5.23 million kw, most of which will be transmitted via three 735-kv lines to the Hydro Quebec grid. The entire project will be completed by 1975. The original feasibility studies for the project concentrated on a cataloging of fish and wildlife. Downstream effects of flow regulation were considered. Before hydroelectric development, the area was practically uninhabited and was given very little economic attention. A unique feature of ecological importance affected by the scheme is the vegetation of the spray zone around the falls. A study of the effect on this vegetation of closing the falls is in progress. A study of the impact of flooding on water quality and biology was begun before damming and will be continued indefinitely after impoundment. Preliminary findings show little evidence for humification or oxygen deficiency even in newly flooded areas, but conductivity and many dissolved ions have increased. Populations of both phytoplankton and zooplankton have generally increased and changed qualitatively with impoundment, particularly in shallow water. The primary productivity of the phytoplankton has increased significantly in flooded areas. The ecological impact on the Naskaupi River of the loss of its headwaters is being investigated. Other ongoing ecological studies at Churchill Falls include investigations on fisheries, wildlife, and forests. (Dawes-ISWS)
W75-07173

ECOLOGICAL CONSEQUENCES OF THE PROPOSED MORAN DAM ON THE FRASER RIVER,
Simon Fraser Univ., Burnaby (British Columbia). Dept. of Biological Sciences.
G. H. Geen.
Journal of the Fisheries Research Board of Canada, Vol 32, No 1, p 126-135, January 1975. 1 fig, 20 ref.

Descriptors: *Dams, *Environmental effects, *Salmon, *Rivers, Fish barriers, Fish handling facilities, Fish ladders, Commercial fishing, Anadromous fish, Reservoirs, Lakes, Ecology, Hydroelectric plants, Damsites, Effects, Migration patterns, Fish migration, Fish behavior, *Canada.
Identifiers: Ecological effects, *Fraser River(Canada).

The details of a high-head dam often proposed for the Fraser River were presented. The anticipated effects of such a development were considered. Changes in temperature, flow, and turbidity regimes would likely reduce the growth or survival of young salmon in both the lower river and the Strait of Georgia. Nitrogen supersaturation would affect both adults and young salmonids for a considerable distance below the dam. Satisfactory and

Nitrogen, Supersaturation, Sludge worms, Bloodworms, *Canada.
Identifiers: *Saint John River(Canada).

Most of the available head of the Saint John River is utilized for hydroelectric development by a series of dams located from the headwaters almost to tidewater. Seven of these hydroelectric dams were described in terms of location, power generation, size of impoundment, operating schedule, and fish passage facilities. Access to upstream spawning areas by Atlantic salmon (Salmo salar) and other anadromous species has been impeded, while ecological changes in the impoundments have favored such species as the alewife (Alosa pseudoharengus) and the white sucker (Catostomus commersoni). Hydroelectric developments on the main stem of the river have reduced the capacity of the river to assimilate organic wastes and have resulted in a reduction of dissolved oxygen content. Fish kills have occurred due to low dissolved oxygen in the headponds and to supersaturation of nitrogen below the lowermost dam. The combination of impoundments and high pollution load results in the heterotrophic food chain dominating the biological carbon flow. (Sims-ISWS)
W75-07176

IMPACT OF THE BENNETT DAM ON THE PEACE-ATHABASCA DELTA,
Canadian Wildlife Service, Edmonton (Alberta).
G. H. Townsend.
Journal of the Fisheries Research Board of Canada, Vol 32, No 1, p 171-176, January 1975.

Descriptors: Dams, *Environmental effects, *Wetlands, *Habitats, Wildlife habitats, Wildlife, Marshes, Aquatic habitats, Ecology, Soil-water-plant relationships, Marsh plants, Plant morphology, Fish, Waterfowl, Spawning, Weirs, *Canada.
Identifiers: Perched basins, *Peace-Athabasca delta(Canada).

The Peace-Athabasca Delta Project was an intergovernmental study group assembled to assess possible downstream effects of the W.A.C. Bennett Dam on the Peace-Athabasca delta and Lake Athabasca. Low water levels on the delta coincided with the upstream filling of the Williston Reservoir during 1968-1970, exposing thousands of acres of marsh and lake bottom, advancing plant succession (toward the less desirable willow communities), threatening access of migrating fish to the delta's spawning lakes, and reducing nesting habitat for waterfowl and overwinter habitat for muskrats. The resultant drastic decline in the muskrat population affected the economy of Fort Chipewyan and the lifestyle of its native people because of their dependency on trapping. The long-term effects of the changed regime were predicted to decrease important shoreline of perched basins by approximately 50%, to cause plant succession to proceed uninterrupted for longer periods of time, thereby accelerating the ageing of the delta, to shift plant zones to lower elevations around lake margins, and to reduce the vertical ranges and area of early successional plant communities by as much as 50%. Waterfowl production is expected to decline by 20-25%, and muskrat populations will decrease by 40-65%. Bison grazing meadows will suffer losses although moose habitat is expected to improve. A number of remedial alternatives were examined to seek a solution to restoration of water levels. A fixed-crest weir on an outlet channel of Lake Athabasca was selected to satisfactorily restore the natural regime. (Sims-ISWS)
W75-07177

ASSESSMENT OF THE IMPACT OF HYDRODAMS,
British Columbia Univ., Vancouver. Inst. of Animal Resource Ecology.
I. E. Efford.
Journal of the Fisheries Research Board of Canada, Vol 32, No 1, p 196-209, January 1975. 2 ref, 1 append.

Descriptors: Dams, *Hydroelectric plants, *Hydroelectric project licensing, *Environmental effects, Political aspects, Planning, Project planning, Damsites, Dam design, Pipelines, Decision making, *Canada.
Identifiers: *Environmental impact statement, Case studies.

At present, assessments of the impact of a dam are becoming part of the design process but they are still not completed early enough to affect the overall decision to construct a particular dam at a particular site. Thus, their real value is lost because attempts to correct social and environmental problems are made after rather than before the problem has arisen. Impact statements at the moment assess only alternatives to the design of a dam. They ought to include analyses of alternative uses of the valley, the long-term value of delaying the decision, the relative merits of generating power by other means, and finally the merits of reducing energy demands by rationing or raising prices. The assessment of impact should be considered a positive contribution to helping the decision-maker rather than an annoying complication preventing him from getting on with his job. In today's increasingly complex world we must proceed more cautiously because the synergistic interactions, resulting from major undertakings like dams, pipelines, etc., are many and frequently not obvious. Public access to impact assessments is an essential aspect of the democratic process and will help to anticipate some of these problems. An appendix lists 80 large dams having capacities of more than 100 MW as well as various characteristics of the projects. (Sims-ISWS)
W75-07178

KONA DAM VS. KONATOWN: A SOCIOLOGICAL INTERPRETATION OF SELECTED IMPACTS OF RESERVOIR DEVELOPMENT ON A COMMUNITY FIELD,
East Texas State Univ., Commerce. Dept. of Sociology and Anthropology.
For primary bibliographic entry see Field 6B.
W75-07271

COMPUTER-CALCULATED GEOMETRIC CHARACTERISTICS OF MIDDLE-MISSISSIPPI RIVER SIDE CHANNELS; VOLUME 1: PROCEDURES AND RESULTS; VOLUME 2: SIDE CHANNEL CONTOUR MAPS,
Army Engineer Waterways Experiment Station, Vicksburg, Miss.
For primary bibliographic entry see Field 4A.
W75-07282

LAKE ERIE INTERNATIONAL JETPORT MODEL FEASIBILITY INVESTIGATION; REPORT 1, SCOPE OF STUDY AND REVIEW OF AVAILABLE DATA,
Army Engineer Waterways Experiment Station, Vicksburg, Miss.
For primary bibliographic entry see Field 2H.
W75-07286

ENVIRONMENTAL INVENTORY AND ASSESSMENT, ILLINOIS WATERWAY; 12-FOOT CHANNEL NAVIGATION PROJECT,
Army Engineer Waterways Experiment Station, Vicksburg, Miss.
For primary bibliographic entry see Field 8B.
W75-07288

MATHEMATICAL MODEL STUDY OF A FLOW CONTROL PLAN FOR THE CHESAPEAKE AND DELAWARE CANAL,
Army Engineer Waterways Experiment Station, Vicksburg, Miss.
For primary bibliographic entry see Field 8B.
W75-07289

AMCHITKA BIOENVIRONMENTAL PROGRAM: FRESHWATER VERTEBRATE AND INVERTEBRATE ECOLOGY OF AMCHITKA ISLAND, ALASKA. FINAL SUMMARY REPORT AND PROGRESS REPORT,
Utah State Univ., Logan.
For primary bibliographic entry see Field 5C.
W75-07338

7. RESOURCES DATA

7A. Network Design

HISTORY OF HYDROLOGY--A BRIEF SUMMARY,
Geological Survey, Raleigh, N.C.
For primary bibliographic entry see Field 2A.
W75-07227

HYDROLOGIC UNIT MAP--1974, STATE OF WEST VIRGINIA.
Geological Survey, Reston, Va.
For primary bibliographic entry see Field 7C.
W75-07234

HYDROLOGIC UNIT MAP--1974, STATE OF INDIANA.
Geological Survey, Reston, Va.
For primary bibliographic entry see Field 7C.
W75-07235

HYDROLOGIC UNIT MAP--1974, STATE OF PENNSYLVANIA.
Geological Survey, Reston, Va.
For primary bibliographic entry see Field 7C.
W75-07236

HYDROLOGIC UNIT MAP--1974, STATE OF OHIO.
Geological Survey, Reston, Va.
For primary bibliographic entry see Field 7C.
W75-07237

7B. Data Acquisition

AN INSTRUMENT SYSTEM FOR ESTIMATION OF EVAPOTRANSPIRATION BY THE EDDY CORRELATION METHOD,
Idaho Univ., Moscow. Coll. of Forestry, Wildlife, and Range Sciences.
For primary bibliographic entry see Field 2D.
W75-06894

DEVELOPMENT OF MICRO-SCALE LABORATORY FILTRATION TECHNIQUES,
Tennessee Univ., Knoxville. Dept. of Civil Engineering.
For primary bibliographic entry see Field 5D.
W75-06990

ESTIMATION OF SEA SURFACE TEMPERATURE FROM REMOTE SENSING IN THE 11- TO 13-MICROMETER WINDOW REGION,
National Aeronautics and Space Administration, Greenbelt, Md. Goddard Space Flight Center.
C. Prabhakara, G. Dalu, and V. G. Kunde.
Journal of Geophysical Research, Vol 79, No 33, p 5039-5044, November 20, 1974. 5 fig, 4 tab, 26 ref.

Descriptors: *Remote sensing, *Satellites(Artificial), *Temperature, *Oceans, Estimating, Data collections, Radiation, Humidity, Measurement, Water vapor, Absorption, Sea water.

The Nimbus 3 and 4 Iris spectral data in the 11- to 13-micrometer water vapor window region were analyzed to determine the sea surface temperature (SST). The high spectral resolution data of Iris were averaged over approximately 1-micrometer-wide intervals to simulate channels of a radiometer to measure the SST. Three such channels in the 775- to 960-cm (12.9-10.5 micrometer) region were utilized to measure the SST over cloud-free oceans. However, two of these channels were sufficient in routine SST determination. The differential absorption properties of water vapor in the two channels enabled the determination of the water vapor absorption correction without detailed knowledge of the vertical profiles of temperature and water vapor. The feasibility of determining the SST was demonstrated globally with Nimbus 3 data, where cloud-free areas can be selected with the help of albedo data from the medium-resolution infrared radiometer experiment on board the same satellite. The SST derived from this technique agrees with the measurements made by ships to about 1C. (Sims-ISWS)
W75-07043

DOPPLER RADAR OBSERVATIONS OF A HAILSTORM,
Arizona Univ., Tucson. Inst. of Atmospheric Physics.
For primary bibliographic entry see Field 2B.
W75-07049

EXPERIMENTAL RESULTS WITH A RAIN ANALYZER,
Massachusetts Inst. of Tech., Cambridge. Research Lab. of Electronics.
For primary bibliographic entry see Field 2B.
W75-07050

THE ELECTRICAL ANISOTROPY OF SEA ICE IN THE HORIZONTAL PLANE,
Geophysical Survey Systems, Inc., North Billerica, Mass.
For primary bibliographic entry see Field 2C.
W75-07055

HAIL AND RAINDROP SIZE DISTRIBUTIONS FROM A SWISS MULTICELL STORM,
Eidgenoessische Technische Hochschule, Zuerich (Switzerland).
For primary bibliographic entry see Field 2B.
W75-07056

STATIONARITY OF MESOSCALE AIRFLOW IN MOUNTAINOUS TERRAIN,
Utah State Univ., Logan. Dept. of Soil Science and Biometeorology.
For primary bibliographic entry see Field 2B.
W75-07061

THE DEPENDENCE OF BARE SOIL ALBEDO ON SOIL WATER CONTENT,
Agricultural Research Service, Phoenix, Ariz. Water Conservation Lab.
For primary bibliographic entry see Field 2G.
W75-07062

CUMULATIVE CHEMICAL LIGHT METER,
Westinghouse Research Labs., Pittsburgh, Pa.
For primary bibliographic entry see Field 5A.
W75-07063

INSTRUMENTS FOR WATER QUALITY MEASUREMENTS,
California Univ., Berkeley. Lawrence Berkeley Lab.
For primary bibliographic entry see Field 5A.
W75-07065

INFLUENCE OF SAMPLE DISTURBANCE AND TEST METHOD ON KEY ENGINEERING PROPERTIES OF MARINE SOILS,
Lehigh Univ., Bethlehem, Pa. Dept. of Civil Engineering.
For primary bibliographic entry see Field 2G.
W75-07074

JUMBO TORNADO OUTBREAK OF 3 APRIL 1974,
Chicago Univ., Ill. Dept. of the Geophysical Sciences.
For primary bibliographic entry see Field 2B.
W75-07082

TIDAL AND DIURNAL EFFECTS ON ZOOPLANKTON SAMPLE VARIABILITY IN A NEARSHORE MARINE ENVIRONMENT,
Bedford Inst., Dartmouth (Nova Scotia).
For primary bibliographic entry see Field 2L.
W75-07179

A TEST OF AN EXPERIMENTAL POLAR-ORBITING SATELLITE SYSTEM FOR RELAYING HYDROLOGICAL DATA,
Geological Survey, Reston, Va.
R. W. Paulson.
In: Flash Floods; Proceedings of the Paris Symposium, September 1974: International Association of Hydrological Sciences Publication No. 112, p 23-28, 1974. 4 fig, 6 ref.

Descriptors: *Data collections, *Data transmission, *Telemetry, *Satellites(Artificial), Hydrologic data, Water wells, Floods, Water levels, Water quality, Gaging stations, Monitoring.
Identifiers: *ERTS.

The U.S. Geological Survey is testing an experimental polar-orbiting satellite communications system that relays hydrological data from remote ground-based radios to central data-reception sites. Hydrological stations at several test sites across the United States were instrumented with small battery-operated radios that transmit data several times daily to the Earth Resources Technology Satellite (ERTS), which re-broadcasts the data to central data-reception sites. The most commonly transmitted hydrological variable is rever stage, but rainfall, snow depth, groundwater level, and a wide variety of water quality parameters are also transmitted. Although the availability of data from a hydrological station is presently restricted to 3-6 opportunities per day with the experimental ERTS satellite, a system of several polar-orbiting satellites is technically feasible and satellite-relayed data could be made available in a timely fashion for monitoring hydrological conditions and for flood warning. The Data Collection System is being tested by the Geological Survey in cooperation with the Earth Resources Observation System (EROS) program of the U.S. Department of the Interior, the National Aeronautics and Space Administration (NASA), and numerous water resources management agencies. (Knapp-USGS)
W75-07201

URBAN STORM RAINFALL-RUNOFF-QUALITY INSTRUMENTATION,
Geological Survey, Reston, Va.
For primary bibliographic entry see Field 5A.
W75-07202

ERTS IMAGERY FOR GROUND-WATER INVESTIGATIONS,
Geological Survey, Bay Saint Louis, Miss. Gulf Coast Hydroscience Center.
G. K. Moore, and M. Deutsch.
Ground Water, Vol 13, No 2, p 214-226, March-April 1975. 6 fig, 12 ref.

Descriptors: *Remote sensing, *Water resources, *Mapping, *Satellites(Artificial), *Groundwater, Hydrogeology, Investigations, Exploration, Surveys, Terrain analysis.
Identifiers: *ERTS.

ERTS imagery offers an opportunity to apply moderately high-resolution satellite data to the nationwide study of water resources. This imagery is both a tool and a form of basic data. The main advantage of its use is to reduce the need for field work. In addition, broad regional features may be seen easily on ERTS imagery, whereas they would be difficult or impossible to see on the ground or on low-altitude aerial photographs. Some present and potential uses of ERTS imagery are to locate new aquifers, to study aquifer recharge and discharge, to estimate groundwater pumpage for irrigation, to predict the location and type of aquifer management problems, and to locate and monitor strip mines which commonly are sources for acid mine drainage. In many cases, boundaries which are gradational on the ground appear to be sharp on ERTS imagery. Initial results indicate that the accuracy of maps produced from ERTS imagery is adequate for many purposes. (Knapp-USGS)
W75-07208

A SIMPLE SYSTEM FOR FREEZE DRYING,
New Hampshire Univ., Durham. Inst. of Natural and Environmental Resources.
B. M. Kilcullen, and R. D. Harter.
Journal of Chemical Education, Vol 51, p 590, September 1974. 1 fig. OWRT A-020-NH(11).

Descriptors: *Freeze drying, *Laboratory equipment, *Drying, Equipment, Laboratories, Design, Waste water treatment, Water treatment.

A simple system to freeze dry small quantities of material was described. The apparatus is similar to the series of vacuum traps routinely used for vacuum distillation. Most of the equipment should be readily available in the laboratory. The system was constructed so that simultaneous freeze drying of two samples is possible. However, the design is readily adaptable to available equipment. Standard separable vacuum traps are used throughout. (Sims-ISWS)
W75-07245

A COMPARISON OF VERTICAL DRIFT-ENVELOPES TO CONVENTIONAL DRIFT-BOTTLES,
Michigan Univ., Ann Arbor. Dept. of Atmospheric and Oceanic Science.
For primary bibliographic entry see Field 2L.
W75-07248

OPTICAL LEVITATION OF LIQUID DROPS BY RADIATION PRESSURE,
Bell Labs., Holmdel, N.J.
For primary bibliographic entry see Field 2B.
W75-07269

7C. Evaluation, Processing and Publication

PUERTO RICO WATER RESOURCES PLANNING MODEL PROGRAM DESCRIPTION,
Geological Survey, Reston, Va.
D. W. Moody, T. Maddock, III, M. R. Karlinger, and J. J. Lloyd.
Geological Survey open-file report, June 1973. 126 p, 3 fig, 3 tab, 9 ref, 5 append.

Descriptors: *Planning, *Mathematical models, *Puerto Rico, *Computer programs, Data processing, Systems analysis, Water resources development.

The Model Definition and Control Program (MODCOP) is intended to assist a planner in preparing input data for the Puerto Rico Water Resources Planning Model. The model utilizes a mixed-integer mathematical program to identify a minimum present cost set of water resources projects (diversions, reservoirs, groundwater fields, desalinization plants, water treatment plants, and interbasin transfers of water) which will meet a set of future water demands and to determine their sequence of construction. While MODCOP was specifically written to generate input data for the planning model (described in this report), the program can be easily modified to reflect changes in the model's mathematical structure. (Knapp-USGS)
W75-06934

A SUMMARY VIEW OF WATER SUPPLY AND DEMAND IN THE SAN FRANCISCO BAY REGION, CALIFORNIA,
Geological Survey, Menlo Park, Calif.
For primary bibliographic entry see Field 6D.
W75-06935

MEAN ANNUAL RUNOFF IN THE SAN FRANCISCO BAY REGION, CALIFORNIA, 1931-70,
Geological Survey, Menlo Park, Calif.
S. E. Rantz.
San Francisco Bay Region Environment and Resources Planning Study Basic Data Contribution 69 (Geological Survey Miscellaneous Field Studies Map MF-613), 1974. 24 p, 2 map, 3 tab, 2 ref.

Descriptors: *Runoff, *California, *Maps, Rainfall-runoff relationships, Data collections, Hydrologic data.
Identifiers: *San Francisco Bay region(Calif).

This map shows the areal distribution of mean annual runoff in the San Francisco Bay region, California. The report area includes the nine counties that are collectively referred to as the San Francisco Bay region, and adjacent area. The values of mean annual runoff shown on the map represent natural flow, or that part of the precipitation that would appear in water courses or stream channels where, or if, human activity had negligible effect on runoff. The 76 gaging-station records used in developing the runoff map were therefore, those for streams that are either virtually undeveloped or, if developed, have records whose annual discharges can be adjusted for such manmade effects as diversion, storage, and import of water. For consistency, mean annual runoff figures for all gaging stations were adjusted to cover a common 40-year time base, 1931-70; the dearth of long-term runoff records made it impractical to use a base period longer than 40 years. Mean annual precipitation for the period 1931-70 is virtually identical with the long-term mean annual precipitation, thereby confirming the representativeness of the 40-year study period. (Knapp-USGS)
W75-06936

CROSS-IMPACT SIMULATION IN WATER RESOURCE PLANNING,
Stanford Research Inst., Menlo Park, Calif.
For primary bibliographic entry see Field 6A.
W75-06940

SYSTEM 11 'SIVA', A DESIGN SYSTEM FOR RIVERS AND ESTUARIES,
Technische Hogeschool, Delft (Netherlands). International Courses in Hydraulics.
For primary bibliographic entry see Field 2E.
W75-07016

ANALOG, DIGITAL AND HYBRID SIMULATION OF WATER LEVEL DISTRIBUTION IN OCCURRENCES OF FLOODS IN A SYSTEM RIVER FLOOD PLAIN,
Technische Universitaet, Hanover (West Germany). Institut fuer Wasserwirtschaft, Hydrologie und Landwirtschaftlichen Wasserbau.
For primary bibliographic entry see Field 2E.
W75-07018

SOC73, A ONE-DIMENSIONAL WAVE PROPAGATION CODE FOR ROCK MEDIA,
California Univ., Livermore. Lawrence Livermore Lab.
For primary bibliographic entry see Field 8E.
W75-07041

AN ANALYSIS OF THE GROUND MOTION FROM RIO BLANCO,
California Univ., Livermore. Lawrence Livermore Lab.
L. S. Germain.
Report UCRL-51668, September 30, 1974. 16 p, 20 fig, 8 tab, 6 ref. AEC Contract W-7405-Eng-48.

Descriptors: *Colorado, *Seismic studies, *On-site data collections, Evaluation, Analysis, Seismology, Movement, Velocity, Seismic waves, Nuclear explosions, Underground.
Identifiers: *Rio Blanco project, *Ground motion.

Project Rio Blanco is a government-industry gas-reservoir stimulation experiment using three 30-kt (125-TJ) nuclear explosives detonated simultaneously in a single well bore, at depths of 1780, 1900, and 2040 m. The detonation occurred at approximately 10:00 a.m. Mountain Daylight Time on May 17, 1973. As a part of the project, 36 locations were instrumented for ground motion by the U.S. Geological Survey, Seismic Engineering Branch. Data resulting from these measurements were published by the Environmental Research Corporation. In particular, distance, bearing, and peak amplitudes for acceleration, velocity, and displacement were given for each station. These data, and similar data from the other gas stimulation experiments, Gasbuggy and Rulison, were subjected to further analysis. High-accuracy estimates of ground motion for such events is beyond the current state of the art and will remain so until an explanation for the 50% variation in station response can be found. (Humphreys-ISWS)
W75-07048

APPLICATION OF A CATCHMENT MODEL IN SOUTHEASTERN AUSTRAILIA,
Monash Univ., Clayton (Australia). Dept. of Civol Engineering.
For primary bibliographic entry see Field 2A.
W75-07054

SUMMARY AND ANALYSIS OF PHYSICAL OCEANOGRAPHY DATA COLLECTED IN THE NEW YORK BIGHT APEX DURING 1969-70,
National Oceanic and Atmospheric Administration, Boulder, Colo. Marine Ecosystems Analysis Program.
For primary bibliographic entry see Field 2L.
W75-07069

GEOPHYSICAL MONITORING FOR CLIMATIC CHANGE, NO. 2, SUMMARY REPORT 1973.
National Oceanic and Atmospheric Administration, Boulder, Colo. Environmental Research Labs.
December 1974, 110 p. John M. Miller, editor.

Descriptors: Measurement, *Gases, *Aerosols, *Meteorology, *Solar radiation, Carbon dioxide, Ozone, Instrumentation, Calibrations, Chemical precipitation, Data collections, Data storage and retrieval, *Monitoring, Geophysics, Climates.
Identifiers: *Observatory facilities, Mauna Loa, South Pole, Barrow(AK), Samoa, Freon-11, Aitken nuclei concentration, Data acquisition systems.

During 1973, there was a shift from the previous emphasis in the program objectives of the Geophysical Monitoring for Climatic Change from establishing observatories to developing uniform operating and reporting procedures. The amount of data has increased and this has led to the design of centralized data handling methods to cope with the information expected in 1974 and 1975. Major physical changes within the observatory network occurred with the completion of the total ozone observational dome at Point Barrow, preparatory design work for major additions to the South Pole program, and construction of a sampling tower at Samoa. Details of augmented programs are included such as measurement programs, flask sampling for freon and carbon tetrachloride, lidar system development, Aitken data collection, and solar radiation monitoring programs. The year saw staff assigned to 3 new observatories; acquisition and installation of new measurement programs; and establishment of initial support facilities and staff for data quality control and processing and for analyses. (NOAA)
W75-07076

SUMMARY OF SYNOPTIC METEOROLOGICAL OBSERVATIONS FOR GREAT LAKES AREAS: VOLUME 2, LAKE HURON AND GEORGIAN BAY.
National Climatic Center, Asheville, N.C.
For primary bibliographic entry see Field 2B.
W75-07079

MANUALLY DIGITIZED RADAR GRIDS: A COMPARISON OF RESOLUTION CAPABILITIES FOR A HEAVY RAINFALL SITUATION,
National Weather Service, Fort Worth, Tex. Southern Region.
For primary bibliographic entry see Field 2B.
W75-07081

FLOOD PLAIN INFORMATION: AGUA HEDIONDA CREEK, PACIFIC OCEAN TO BUENA, SAN DIEGO COUNTY, CALIFORNIA.
Army Engineer District, Los Angeles, Calif.
For primary bibliographic entry see Field 4A.
W75-07087

FLOOD HAZARD ANALYSIS: FOUR MILE AND EIGHT MILE CREEKS, BUTLER COUNTY, KANSAS.
Soil Conservation Service, Salina, Kans.
For primary bibliographic entry see Field 4A.
W75-07088

RESEARCH NEEDS RELATED TO HYDROLOGIC ASPECTS OF WATER FOR ENERGY FROM LARGE ENERGY COMPLEXES,
Minnesota Dept. of Natural Resources, St. Paul.
For primary bibliographic entry see Field 6D.
W75-07093

WASTE WATER TREATMENT WORKS DATA BOOK.
Illinois State Environmental Protection Agency, Springfield.
For primary bibliographic entry see Field 5D.
W75-07109

1973 WATER RESOURCES DATA FOR OREGON, SURFACE WATER RECORDS, PRECIPITATION RECORDS,
Oregon State Water Resources Board, Salem.
C. L. Wheeler.
1973. 246 p, 3 fig.

Descriptors: *Data collections, *Streamflow, *Precipitation(Atmospheric), Rivers, Streams, Water resources, Surface waters, Surface runoff, Stream gages, Gaging stations, Rainfall, Rain gages, Basic data collections, Hydrologic data, Meteorological data, Climatic data, Meteorology, Hydrology.

The surface water records for the 1973 water year (October 1, 1972, through September 30, 1973) for gaging stations and miscellaneous sites within Oregon were given. The base data collected at gaging stations consists of records of stage and measurements of discharge. In addition, observations of factors affecting the stage-discharge relation, weather records, and other information, were used to supplement base data in determining daily flow. The records of stage were primarily obtained from water-stage records that give a continuous record of fluctuations. A few records of stage were obtained from direct readings on nonrecording gages. Measurements of discharge were made with a current meter by the general methods outlined in standard textbooks on the measurement of stream discharge. Daily discharge was tabulated for 188 gaging stations, along with supporting information concerning the station. A section was included covering the precipitation data from storage precipitation stations operated by the Stage Engineer under a cooperative program with the National Oceanic and Atmospheric Administration and from storage precipitation stations operated by the U.S. Forest Service. Daily precipitation amounts were reported for 127 locations. Descriptions of the gages, their operation, and the data were provided. The period of record for the rainfall data is also from October 1, 1972 through September 30, 1973. (Sims-ISWS)
W75-07150

A TEST OF AN EXPERIMENTAL POLAR-ORBITING SATELLITE SYSTEM FOR RELAYING HYDROLOGICAL DATA,
Geological Survey, Reston, Va.
For primary bibliographic entry see Field 7B.
W75-07201

SIMULATED DRAWDOWN FOR SELECTED WELL FIELDS IN THE OHIO RIVER ALLUVIAL AQUIFER,
Geological Survey, Louisville, Ky.
For primary bibliographic entry see Field 4B.
W75-07209

INDEX OF FLOOD MAPS FOR CALIFORNIA PREPARED BY THE U.S. GEOLOGICAL SURVEY THROUGH 1974,
Geological Survey, Menlo Park, Calif.
J. R. Crippen.
Open-file report, March 1975. 29 p.

Descriptors: *Maps, *Floods, *California, Flood data, Flood plains, Flood plain zoning, Floodways.
Identifiers: *Flood maps, *Flood-prone areas.

An index is presented of quadrangle flood maps prepared by the U.S. Geological Survey in California through 1974. The maps are listed alphabetically for the entire State as well as by county. The index was prepared from a computer file of such maps. A similar, but more comprehensive, national file includes these maps with others for the entire Nation. A program is available for the national file that can retrieve map data by land-line location or by State and county. Both the file presented here and the national file are designed to be periodically updated. (Knapp-USGS)
W75-07216

HYDROLOGY OF THE OKLAWAHA LAKES AREA OF FLORIDA,
Geological Survey, Tallahassee, Fla.
P. W. Bush.
Florida Bureau of Geology, Tallahassee, Map Series No 69, 1974. 1 sheet, 9 fig, 11 ref.

Descriptors: *Eutrophication, *Limnology, *Water pollution sources, *Florida, Farm wastes, Fertilizers, Industrial wastes, Hydrogeology, *Maps.
Identifiers: *Oklawaha lakes(Fla).

Lakes Apopka, Carlton, Beauclair, Dora, Eustis, Harris, Little Harris, Griffin, and Yale are part of a chain of lakes that is the most prominent feature of the upper Oklawaha River drainage basin in central Florida. The main use of the lakes is recreation, but the desirability of most of the lakes for recreation has decreased in recent years. Land-use practices have caused the lake water quality to deteriorate. The main cause of cultural eutrophication in the Oklawaha lakes is muck farming of the reclaimed marsh and wetlands along the north shore of Lake Apopka. To maintain optimum water levels while growing crops, water is pumped from the farms to Lake Apopka and to Apopka-Beauclair Canal when water is in excess, and allowed to flow by gravity from the lake to the farms when water is deficient. Water from the farms is rich in nutrients dissolved from the highly organic muck and from fertilizers. Since Lake Apopka and Apopka-Beauclair Canal are at the head of the chain of lakes, nutrient-rich water flows to the downstream lakes. Other sources of the nutrients that enter the lakes are sewage treatment plants and industrial plants, primarily citrus processing plants. (Knapp-USGS)
W75-07220

SURFACE WATER FEATURES OF FLORIDA,
Geological Survey, Tallahassee, Fla.
L. J. Snell, and W. E. Kenner.
Florida Bureau of Geology, Tallahassee, Map Series No 66, 1974. 1 sheet, 1 map, 2 tab, 5 ref.

Descriptors: *Surface waters, *Florida, Streams, Lakes, Springs, Swamps, Wetlands, *Maps.

The variety of surface-water features of Florida is the result of the State's location in the subtropical zone between the Atlantic Ocean and the Gulf of Mexico, its average rainfall of 53 inches, its relatively flat terrain, and the nature of the its soils and underlying rocks. The surface-water features include extensive marshes and swamps, many streams, lakes, and ponds in certain parts of the State, few streams in the Central Highlands, and the extensive network of ditches and canals, particularly in the southeastern part. The great marshes and swamps and the other wetlands throughout the State are the most typical and outstanding surface-water features. These wetlands, which have been the habitat of subtropical and tropical wildlife in Florida, are altered by the works of man through the vast networks of ditches and canals for the development of land for citrus and other crops and for residential and recreational uses. Another prominent surface-water feature is the large number of lakes and ponds, 7,712 that are 10 or more acres in area and 19 larger than 6,400 acres (10 square miles). Lake Okeechobee is the largest freshwater lake in the United States wholly within a single State. Some lakes are connected to the deep artesian aquifer and are called 'sinkhole' lakes; some occupy depressions that were shallow marine basins or bays in past geologic time; others are underlain by peat or clay and are not well connected with water-bearing formations. Most streams have low gradients and their flow is sluggish because of the relatively flat terrain and low altitudes characteristic of Florida. (Knapp-USGS)
W75-07221

GROUND-WATER WITHDRAWALS IN THE UPPER PEACE AND UPPER ALAFIA RIVER BASINS, FLORIDA,
Geological Survey, Tallahassee, Fla.
A. F. Robertson, and L. R. Mills.
Florida Bureau of Geology, Tallahassee, Map Series No 67, 1974. 1 sheet, 9 fig, 1 tab, 7 ref.

Descriptors: *Groundwater, *Withdrawal, *Florida, Industrial water, Irrigation water, Municipal water, Water levels, Drawdown, Aquifers, Groundwater basins, *Maps.
Identifiers: *Peace River(Fla), *Alafia River(Fla).

In 1971, 120 billion gallons of groundwater was withdrawn from the Floridan Aquifer in the upper Peace and upper Alafia River bains, Florida. Withdrawals increased from 22 billion gallons in 1935 to 143 billion gallons in 1968. Industries associated with phosphate mining and production and with citrus processing used about 76 billion gallons in 1971. Withdrawals for irrigation were 33 billion gallons and for municipal supplies were 11.6 billion gallons in 1971. The decrease in total water withdrawals since 1968 is caused mainly by the decrease in industrial withdrawals. Posphate mining operations, using more recirculated water from holding ponds, have reduced their withdrawals from the aquifer for make-up water. Increased annual withdrawals have resulted in declines of water levels in the Floridan Aquifer of more than 40 feet since 1949. Seasonal variations in groundwater withdrawals are reflected in seasonal water-level fluctuations of as much as 20 feet over the central and southern parts of the area of investigation. (Knapp-USGS)
W75-07222

ANNUAL REPORT ON GROUND WATER IN ARIZONA--WITH EMPHASIS ON GILA BEND BASIN, MCMULLEN VALLEY, AND THE SOUTHEAST PART OF THE HARQUAHALA PLAINS--SPRING 1973 TO SPRING 1974.
Geological Survey, Phoenix, Ariz.
For primary bibliographic entry see Field 4B.
W75-07223

INDEX OF SURFACE WATER STATIONS IN TEXAS, OCTOBER 1974.
Geological Survey, Austin, Tex.
Texas District report, 1974. 21 p, 1 plate, 2 tab.

Descriptors: *Water measurement, *Texas, *Gaging stations, Stream gages, Discharge measurement, Surface waters, Water quality, Peak discharge, Flood data, Reservoirs, Tides, Sediments, Pesticides.

This index of surface-water measuring stations in Texas shows the station number and name, type of record collected, and the office at which the basic data are permanently filed. A permanent numerical designation for gaging stations has been adopted on a nationwide basis; stations are numbered and listed in downstream order. As of October 1, 1974, 471 stream-gaging, 81 reservoir-content, 12 stage, 15 flood-hydrograph partial-record, 8 flood-profile partial-record, 103 low-flow partial-record, 46 crest-stage partial-record, 48 tide-level, 11 periodic water-quality, 128 daily chemical-quality, 28 continuous-recording water-quality, 73 periodic chemical-quality, 145 periodic organic-quality, 95 pesticide, 8 sediment, 53 periodic sediment, 58 periodic biological, and 57 reservoir-inventory stations were in operation. (Knapp-USGS)
W75-07224

PHYSIOGRAPHIC MAP OF THE OKALOACOOCHEE SLOUGH IN COLLIER COUNTY, FLORIDA,
Geological Survey, Miami, Fla.
B. F. McPherson, and H. J. McCoy.
Open-file map, April 1974. 1 sheet.

Descriptors: *Wetlands, *Swamps, *Florida, *Maps, Photogrammetry, Terrain analysis, Geomorphology, Physiography.
Identifiers: *Physiographic maps, *Okaloacoochee Slough(Fla).

This map shows the physiographic boundaries of the Okalacoochee Slough within the Big Cypress Area of critical State concern, Collier County, Florida. It also shows the major wetland extensions of the slough and the direction of flow from the slough into these areas. Islands of higher land occur in the slough, and diking and other agricultural development are evident in places. (Knapp-USGS)
W75-07225

SEDIMENT YIELDS OF STREAMS IN THE UMPQUA RIVER BASIN, OREGON,
Geological Survey, Portland, Oreg.
D. A. Curtiss.
Open-file report, 1975. 1 sheet, 1 map, 1 tab, 8 ref.

Descriptors: *Sediment yield, *Suspended load, *Bed load, *Oregon, Sediment discharge, Discharge(Water).
Identifiers: *Umpqua River(Oreg).

Sediment data were collected at 11 sites in the Umpqua River basin, Oregon, from 1956 to 1973. Bedload was estimated to be 3 percent of the mean annual suspended-sediment yield, except for the Cow Creek basin, where bedload was estimated to be 5 percent. A regionalized map provides a visual generalization of discharge-weighted concentrations. The estimated mean annual suspended-sediment yields from the 11 sites in the Umpqua River basin ranged from 260 tons per square mile on Olalla Creek near Tenmile to 1,900 tons per square mile on Lookingglass Creek near Brockway. These values represent a long-term average and may differ greatly from year to year depending on hydrologic conditions in a given year. (Knapp-USGS)
W75-07226

HISTORY OF HYDROLOGY--A BRIEF SUMMARY,
Geological Survey, Raleigh, N.C.
For primary bibliographic entry see Field 2A.
W75-07227

FLOOD MAPPING IN CHARLOTTE AND MECKLENBURG COUNTY, NORTH CAROLINA,
Geological Survey, Charlotte, N.C.
For primary bibliographic entry see Field 4A.
W75-07230

WATER RESOURCES INVESTIGATIONS IN FLORIDA, 1974.
Geological Survey, Reston, Va.
Water Resources Investigations Folder for Florida, 1974. 1 sheet, 1 map.

Descriptors: *Water resources, *Investigations, *Florida, Data collections, Hydrologic data, Surveys, Water quality, Groundwater, Surface waters.

The water-resources program of the U.S. Geological Survey in Florida consists of the collection of basic information through its hydrologic-data stations, areal hydrologic and interpretive studies, and research projects. The basic data collected, the results of the areal studies, and the research findings are presented mainly in publications of the U.S. Geological Survey and State agencies, but some appear also in technical journals, open-file reports, and other publications. This folder contains a brief description of the water-resources investigations in Florida in which the U.S. Geological Survey participates, and a list of selected references. (Knapp-USGS)
W75-07231

STREAMFLOW CHARACTERISTICS IN NORTHEASTERN UTAH AND ADJACENT AREAS,
Geological Survey, Salt Lake City, Utah.
F. K. Fields.
Utah Department of Natural Resources, Salt Lake City, Basic-Data Release No 25, 1975. 190 p, 1 fig, 2 tab.

Descriptors: *Basic data collections, *Hydrologic data, *Utah, *Streamflow, Surface waters, Gaging stations, Peak discharge, Low flow, Duration curves.

This report contains statistical summaries of streamflow records from 74 gaging stations, which are mostly in northeastern Utah. Low-flow, high-flow, and flow-duration summaries were compiled from daily discharge values; and flows of each month are compared through correlation with flows of 1, 2, and 12 months in the future. (Knapp-USGS)
W75-07232

WATER-RESOURCES INVESTIGATIONS IN WISCONSIN, 1975 FISCAL YEAR,
Geological Survey, Madison, Wis.
R. A. Lansing.
Wisconsin District report, February 1975. 46 p.

Descriptors: *Investigations, *Water resources, *Data collections, *Hydrologic data, *Wisconsin, Federal government, Water yield, Surface waters, Groundwater, Water quality.

The water-resources investigations of the Wisconsin District of the U.S. Geological Survey, Water Resources Division, consist of the collection of basic records through the hydrologic-data network, interpretive studies, and research projects. Much of the work of the U.S. Geological Survey is a cooperative effort in which planning and financing are shared by state and local governments or other Federal agencies. This report describes the water-resources projects and activities of the U.S. Geological Survey in Wisconsin for the 1975 fiscal year (July 1, 1974 to June 30, 1975). The included map shows the locations of areal studies (other than statewide); statewide basic-record sites; low-flow, partial-record sites; and crest-stage, partial-record sites. The report also contains a listing of all publications that have been prepared or contributed to by the Wisconsin District. (Knapp-USGS)
W75-07233

HYDROLOGIC UNIT MAP--1974, STATE OF WEST VIRGINIA.
Geological Survey, Reston, Va.
For Sale by USGS, Nat'l Center, 12201 Sunrise Valley Dr., Reston, Va. 22092, $1.00. Hydrologic Unit Map of West Virginia, 1974. 1 sheet, 1 map.

Descriptors: *Maps, *Hydrology, *West Virginia, Water resources, Data collections, Planning, *Networks.
Identifiers: *Hydrologic unit maps.

This map and accompanying table show Hydrologic Units in West Virginia that are basically hydrographic in nature. The Cataloging Units shown will supplant the Cataloging Units previously used by the U.S. Geological Survey in its Catalog of Information on Water Data (1966-72). The Regions, Subregions and Accounting Units are aggregates of the Cataloging Units. The Regions and Subregions are currently (1974) used by the U.S. Water Resources Council for comprehensive planning, including the National Assessment, and as a standard geographical framework for more detailed water and related land-resources planning. The Accounting Units are those currently (1974) in use by the U.S. Geological Survey for managing the National Water Data Network. (Knapp-USGS)
W75-07234

HYDROLOGIC UNIT MAP--1974, STATE OF INDIANA.
Geological Survey, Reston, Va.
For sale by USGS, Nat'l Center, 12201 Sunrise Valley Dr., Reston, Va. 22092, $1.00. Hydrologic Unit Map of Indiana, 1974. 1 sheet, 1 map.

Descriptors: *Maps, *Hydrology, *Indiana, Water resources, Data collections, Planning, *Networks.
Identifiers: *Hydrologic unit maps.

This map and accompanying table show Hydrologic Units in Indiana that are basically hydrographic in nature. The Cataloging Units shown will supplant the Cataloging Units previously used by the U.S. Geological Survey in its Catalog of Information on Water Data (1966-72). The Regions, Subregions and Accounting Units are aggregates of the Cataloging Units. The Regions and Subregions are currently (1974) used by the U.S. Water Resources Council for comprehensive planning, including the National Assessment, and as a standard geographical framework for more detailed water and related land-resources planning. The Accounting Units are those currently (1974) in use by the U.S. Geological Survey for managing the National Water Data Network. (Knapp-USGS)
W75-07235

HYDROLOGIC UNIT MAP--1974, STATE OF PENNSYLVANIA.
Geological Survey, Reston, Va.
For sale by USGS, National Center, 12201 Sunrise Valley Dr., Reston, Va. 22092, $1.00. Hydrologic Unit Map of Pennsylvania, 1974. 1 sheet, 1 map.

Descriptors: *Maps, *Hydrology, *Pennsylvania, Water resources, Data collections, Planning, *Networks.
Identifiers: *Hydrologic unit maps.

This map and accompanying table show Hydrologic Units in Pennsylvania that are basically hydrographic in nature. The Cataloging Units shown will supplant the Cataloging Units previously used by the U.S. Geological Survey in its Catalog of Information on Water Data (1966-72). The Regions, Subregions and Accounting Units are aggregates of the Cataloging Units. The Regions and Subregions are currently (1974) used by the U.S. Water Resources Council for comprehensive planning, including the National Assessment, and as a standard geographical framework for more detailed water and related land-resources planning. The Accounting Units are those currently (1974) in use by the U.S. Geological Survey for managing the National Water Data Network. (Knapp-USGS)
W75-07236

HYDROLOGIC UNIT MAP--1974, STATE OF OHIO.
Geological Survey, Reston, Va.
For sale by USGS, Nat'l Center, 12201 Sunrise Valley Dr., Reston, Va. 22092, $1.00. Hydrologic Unit Map of Ohio, 1974. 1 sheet, 1 map.

Descriptors: *Maps, *Hydrology, *Ohio, Water resources, Data collections, Planning, *Networks.
Identifiers: *Hydrologic unit maps.

This map and accompanying table show Hydrologic Units in Ohio that are basically hydrographic in nature. The Cataloging Units shown will supplant the Cataloging Units previously used by the U.S. Geological Survey in its Catalog of Information on Water Data (1966-72). The Regions, Subregions and Accounting Units are aggregates of the Cataloging Units. The Regions and Subregions are currently (1974) used by the U.S. Water Resources Council for comprehensive planning, including the National Assessment, and as a standard geographical framework for more detailed water and related land-resources planning. The Accounting Units are those currently (1974) in use by the U.S. Geological Survey for managing the National Water Data Network. (Knapp-USGS)
W75-07237

MAP SHOWING DEPTH TO WATER, ANCHORAGE AREA, ALASKA,
Geological Survey, Anchorage, Alaska.
G. W. Freethey, J. W. Reeder, and W. W. Barnwell.
Open-file report, 1974. 1 sheet, 1 map.

Descriptors: *Water table, *Alaska, *Maps, Hydrologic data, Water wells, Water levels.
Identifiers: *Anchorage(Alaska).

This generalized map shows the approximate depth from land surface to the top of the saturated zone near Anchorage, Alaska. The depths were determined from boring and well data collected from 1955 to 1973. The configuration of the depth units displays the effect of the irregular topography in the Anchorage Area. (Knapp-USGS)
W75-07238

MAP SHOWING DRAINAGE AREAS, MIDDLETOWN QUADRANGLE, CONNECTICUT,
Geological Survey, Hartford, Conn.
M. P. Thomas, and J. E. Palmer.
Miscellaneous Field Studies Map MF-639 A (Connecticut Valley Urban Area Project), 1975. 1 sheet, 1 map, 1 ref.

Descriptors: *Drainage area, *Connecticut, Streamflow, Watersheds(Basins).
Identifiers: *Middletown(Conn).

This map shows stream systems and drainage areas that contribute streamflow to selected sites on streams in the Middletown Quadrangle, Connecticut. Drainage areas shown have not been adjusted for the manmade changes in the natural regimens such as storm sewers, diversion dams, canals, and tunnels. (Knapp-USGS)
W75-07239

CONTOUR MAP OF THE BEDROCK SURFACE, MOUNT HOLYOKE QUADRANGLE, MASSACHUSETTS,
Geological Survey, Boston, Mass.
C. J. Londquist.
Miscellaneous Field Studies Map MF-640 A (Connecticut Valley Urban Area Project Contribution 121), 1975. 1 sheet, 1 map, 3 ref.

Descriptors: *Bedrock, *Massachusetts, *Subsurface mapping, Subsurface investigations, *Contours, Aquifers, Geologic mapping, *Maps.
Identifiers: *Mt. Holyoke(Mass).

Contours show the altitude of the bedrock surface in the Mt. Holyoke quadrangle, Massachusetts. The position of the contours is based largely on data from wells and test holes, geophysical studies, and the published geologic map supplemented by knowledge of the geologic history of the region. The map shows the configuration of the bedrock surface if all unconsolidated earth materials were removed. (Knapp-USGS)
W75-07240

ESTIMATES OF TEMPERATURE AND PRECIPITATION FOR NORTHEASTERN UTAH,
Geological Survey, Salt Lake City, Utah.
For primary bibliographic entry see Field 4A.
W75-07241

DELINEATION OF BURIED GLACIAL-DRIFT AQUIFERS,
Geological Survey, Denver, Colo.
For primary bibliographic entry see Field 2F.
W75-07242

THE JANUARY GLOBAL CLIMATE SIMULATED BY A TWO-LEVEL GENERAL CIRCULATION MODEL: A COMPARISON WITH OBSERVATION,
RAND Corp., Santa Monica, Calif.
For primary bibliographic entry see Field 2B.
W75-07253

THE USE OF THE DIGITAL SIMULATION LANGUAGE PDEL IN HYDROLOGIC STUDIES,
Wayne State Univ., Detroit, Mich. Dept. of Mathematics.
For primary bibliographic entry see Field 2F.
W75-07254

MODEL DEVELOPMENT AND SYSTEMS ANALYSIS OF THE YAKIMA RIVER BASIN: HYDRAULICS OF SURFACE WATER RUNOFF,
Washington State Univ., Pullman. Dept. of Civil and Environmental Engineering.
For primary bibliographic entry see Field 2A.
W75-07278

COMPUTER-CALCULATED GEOMETRIC CHARACTERISTICS OF MIDDLE-MISSISSIPPI RIVER SIDE CHANNELS; VOLUME 1: PROCEDURES AND RESULTS; VOLUME 2: SIDE CHANNEL CONTOUR MAPS,
Army Engineer Waterways Experiment Station, Vicksburg, Miss.
For primary bibliographic entry see Field 4A.
W75-07282

MATHEMATICAL MODEL STUDY OF A FLOW CONTROL PLAN FOR THE CHESAPEAKE AND DELAWARE CANAL,
Army Engineer Waterways Experiment Station, Vicksburg, Miss.
For primary bibliographic entry see Field 8B.
W75-07289

WATER QUALITY MODEL OF THE LOWER FOX RIVER, WISCONSIN,
Environmental Protection Agency, Washington, D.C. Office of Enforcement and General Counsel.
For primary bibliographic entry see Field 5B.
W75-07327

THE BOD5/DO RATIO. A NEW ANALYTICAL TOOL FOR WATER QUALITY EVALUATION,
Environmental Protection Agency, Philadelphia, Pa. Region III.
For primary bibliographic entry see Field 5A.
W75-07329

8. ENGINEERING WORKS

8A. Structures

EARTH MANUAL, A WATER RESOURCES TECHNICAL PUBLICATION.
Bureau of Reclamation, Denver, Colo. Engineering and Research Center.
For primary bibliographic entry see Field 8D.
W75-07046

ENVIRONMENTAL CONSIDERATIONS FOR CONSTRUCTION PROJECTS.
Agency for International Development, Washington, D.C. Office of Science and Technology.
For primary bibliographic entry see Field 6G.
W75-07047

CONSIDERATIONS FOR ANALYSIS OF INFILTRATION-INFLOW,
Edison Water Quality Research Lab., N.J.
For primary bibliographic entry see Field 5D.
W75-07117

WASTE WATER MANAGEMENT - IMPLICATIONS FOR REGIONAL PLANNING,
P. D. Spreiregen.
In: The Merrimack: Design for a Clean River, American Society of Civil Engineers, National Meeting, Session No. 17, Washington, D.C., January 30, 1973. 11 p, 1 fig.

Descriptors: *Alternate planning, *Administration, *Water pollution control, *Regional analysis, *Aesthetics, *Architecture, Waste water treatment, Social impact, Effects, Environmental effects, Environmental engineering, New Hampshire, Massachusetts, Multiple-purpose projects.
Identifiers: *Merrimack River Basin, Management implications.

Possible parameters for evaluating development proposals, regional planning and development proposals, regional planning and development sequence for wastewater treatment are discussed. These evaluations would start with a regional ecological inventory focusing on identifying the three domains of nature: wilderness, rural and urban. Various patterns of geology, climate, vegetation and wildlife would be identified as well as various degrees of intervention and alteration to begin a regional ecological inventory. Site analysis would include evaluating the results of man-made changes by rating the quality of cultivated areas, outdoor recreation places, towns and cities. This process would help discern the compatability of a site's characteristics with the site's actual usage. The second facet of wastewater management would involve design. This includes evaluating landscapes from a visual standpoint, and then determining the appropriate character of engineering or architectural works in each sort of landscape. The three ranges of landscapes are: (1) visually weak landscapes with visually strong structures; (2) visually strong landscapes with visually weak structures; and (3) visually moderate landscapes with visually moderate structures. Therefore, in the management of wastewater using the element of design, it is necessary to emulate the scale, rhythmn, and massing in a completely contemporary way. In the case of the Merrimack River Basin wastewater management study, some of the ponderables considered were: how worn urban waterfronts could be revitalized and humanized, how a flow augmentation outfall could be handled as an esthetic landscape element, how carbon absorption columns could be deployed, or how aeration or storage lagoons could be designed and tailored to landscape. (Poertner)
W75-07120

CAN THE BALTIC SEA BE TURNED INTO A FRESHWATER LAKE,
For primary bibliographic entry see Field 4A.
W75-07165

ANALYSIS OF LONGITUDINAL BEHAVIOUR OF BURIED PIPES,
Sydney Univ. (Australia).
For primary bibliographic entry see Field 8D.
W75-07166

DEVELOPMENT OF JAMES BAY: THE ROLE OF ENVIRONMENTAL IMPACT ASSESSMENT IN DETERMINING THE LEGAL RIGHT TO AN INTERLOCUTORY INJUNCTION,
McGill Univ., Montreal (Quebec). Dept. of Geography.
For primary bibliographic entry see Field 6G.
W75-07175

ECOLOGICAL CHANGES DUE TO HYDROELECTRIC DEVELOPMENT ON THE SAINT JOHN RIVER,
Fisheries and Marine Service, Halifax (Nova Scotia). Resource Development Branch.
For primary bibliographic entry see Field 6G.
W75-07176

IMPACT OF THE BENNETT DAM ON THE PEACE-ATHABASCA DELTA,
Canadian Wildlife Service, Edmonton (Alberta).
For primary bibliographic entry see Field 6G.
W75-07177

ASSESSMENT OF THE IMPACT OF HYDRO-DAMS,
British Columbia Univ., Vancouver. Inst. of Animal Resource Ecology.
For primary bibliographic entry see Field 6G.
W75-07178

STABILITY OF STRUCTURES WITH INTERMEDIATE FILTERS,
Uttar Pradesh Irrigation Research Inst., Roorkee (India). Ground Water Div.
A. S. Chawla.
Journal of the Hydraulics Division, American Society of Civil Engineers, Vol 101, No HY2, Proceedings Paper 11139, p 223-241, February 1975. 10 fig, 11 ref, 2 append.

Descriptors: *Seepage, *Hydraulic structures, *Potential flow, *Uplift pressure, Drainage, Dam design, Foundations, Analysis, Equations, Stability, Filters, Seepage control, Design data, Soil mechanics, Permeability.
Identifiers: *Conformal mapping, Complex variables.

A seepage problem of a horizontal plane of drainage located between two cutoff walls was investigated. The problem was solved exactly by use of conformal mapping. Equations for the seepage discharge to the filter and for the uplift pressures on the base were given. These equations were solved numerically for pressures at key points. The results were presented in charts of design curves. Uplift pressures were found to reduce considerably along the entire length of the structure even if a very short filter was provided. Various lengths and locations of the filter were investigated to determine the best results. It was found that the filter should be located such as to minimize the total uplift on the base downstream of the gateline. Increasing the depth of the downstream cutoff resulted in increased uplift pressure downstream of the filter. (Adams-ISWS)
W75-07183

DISCHARGE OVER POLYGONAL WEIRS,
Technische Hochschule, Aachen (West Germany). Inst. for Water Resources Development.
For primary bibliographic entry see Field 8B.
W75-07187

LAKE MICHIGAN INTAKES: REPORT ON THE BEST AVAILABLE TECHNOLOGY,
Lake Michigan Cooling Water Intake Technical Committee, Chicago, Ill.
Available from the National Technical Information Service, Springfield, Va 22161 as PB-236 112, $5.75 in paper copy, $2.25 in microfiche. Report August 1973. 140 p, 19 fig, 8 tab, 75 ref.

Descriptors: *Lake Michigan, *Intakes, *Technology, Aquatic life, Monitoring, Entrainment, Fish, Bypasses, Screens, Cooling water, Industrial water, Municipal water, Hydroelectric plants, Design, Environmental effects, Installation, Intakes structures.
Identifiers: Fish protection.

In view of the various ecological situations, no generic type intake structure or system can be recommended. Each proposed and existing intake should be considered independently utilizing the best technology for protecting aquatic life. The single most important factor is the intake location. The adequacy of existing intake facilities must be determined by a monitoring program measuring the daily and seasonal variations in numbers, size and weight of all life stages of fish species entrapped in the intake system. Areas where fish concentrate should be determined and avoided. The intake structure should not serve as an attractant to immature and adult fish either by physical alteration of the environment, by providing shelter or by the influence of heated discharge water, unless deicing is essential for maintenance of water flow. In the absence of other adequate fish-protection devices, intake water velocities should not exceed the fish escape velocities. Fish should be returned undamaged from the forebay area to a physical environment approximating that at point of withdrawal through a well designed return system. Horizontal traveling screens and louver screens appear to have the greatest potential as fish-protection devices where fish bypasses are required. Intake designs, exclusion devices, bypass and fish removal systems, and infiltration systems are detailed. (Jones-Wisconsin)
W75-07294

8B. Hydraulics

INCREASING WATER USE EFFICIENCY THROUGH IMPROVED ORFICE DESIGN AND OPERATIONAL PROCEDURES FOR SUB-IRRIGATION SYSTEMS,
Texas A and M Univ., College Station. Water Resources Inst. Office of Water Research and Technology.
For primary bibliographic entry see Field 3F.
W75-06991

RIVER AND ESTUARY MODEL ANALYSIS, VOLUME 3.
For primary bibliographic entry see Field 2E.
W75-06998

SIMULATION OF SEDIMENT TRANSPORT IN HYDRAULIC MODELS,
Technische Universitaet, Obernach (West Germany). Versuchsanstalt fuer Wasserbau-Oskar von Miller-Institut.
For primary bibliographic entry see Field 2J.
W75-06999

THE TIDAL REGIME OF THE ELBE-RIVER, HYDRAULIC MODEL WITH MOVABLE BED,
Bundesanstalt fur Wasserbau, Hamburg (West Germany).
For primary bibliographic entry see Field 2L.
W75-07001

STUDIES FOR CHALNA PORT IN THE DELTA OF GANGES RIVER,
Institut za Vodoprivredu Jaroslav Cerni, Belgrade (Yugoslavia). Hydraulic Lab.
M. Vojinovic, and J. Muskatirovic.
In: River and Estuary Model Analysis, Volume III; Proceedings of the International Association for Hydraulic Research Symposium on River Mechanics (4 Vol.), Bangkok, Thailand, January 9-12, 1973. Asian Institute of Technology, Bangkok, Thailand, p 49-61. (1973). 5 fig.

Descriptors: *Model studies, *Tidal streams, *Deltas, *Harbors, Alluvial channels, Hydraulic models, Rivers, Tidal waters, River flow, Navigable rivers, Regime, River regulation, Currents(Water), Discharge(Water), Freshwater, Tidal effects.
Identifiers: *India(Pussur River), *India(Ganges River), Fixed bed model, Movable bed model.

In the delta of the Ganges River the construction of a new big Chalna Port on the Pussur River is anticipated. For this purpose, observations and measurements of the behavior of the Pussur River and hydraulic model studies were performed. The regime of the Pussur River and its natural development and influence of regulation works on tidal and fresh water regime were analyzed. Velocity and discharge measurements and observation of flow patterns were presented. Studies on a physical model of the present flow conditions and the effect of the Chalna Port on the flow conditions of the Pussur River were analyzed. It was concluded that with construction of the Chalna Port natural stability of the reach will not be disturbed. (See also W75-06998) (Humphreys-ISWS)
W75-07003

COMBINATION OF A PHYSICAL AND A MATHEMATICAL RIVER MODEL WITH FIXED BED,
Bundesanstalt fuer Wasserbau, Karlsruhe (West Germany).
For primary bibliographic entry see Field 2E.
W75-07005

RIVER SIMULATION BY CHANNEL NETWORK ANALYSIS,
Asian Inst. of Tech., Bangkok (Thailand). Div. of Water Science and Engineering.
For primary bibliographic entry see Field 2E.
W75-07006

DETERMINATION OF DISCHARGE SCALE FOR A TIDAL MODEL OF A COMPLEX RIVER,
Irrigation and Power Research Station, Poondi (India).
For primary bibliographic entry see Field 2L.
W75-07007

SOME NOTES ON HYDRAULIC MODEL TESTS OF RIVER CHANNELS,
Public Works Research Inst., Kashima (Japan). Kashima Hydraulics Lab.
For primary bibliographic entry see Field 2E.
W75-07008

HYDRAULIC MODELING OF UNSTEADY FLOWS OF THE MEKONG RIVER,
Asian Inst. of Tech., Bangkok (Thailand), Div. of Water Science and Engineering.
For primary bibliographic entry see Field 2E.
W75-07010

AN APPROACH TO THE MODELING OF THE MEKONG AT PHNOM PENH,
Makerere Univ., Kampala (Uganda). Faculty of Technology.
For primary bibliographic entry see Field 2E.
W75-07011

THE INFLUENCE OF TIDAL INLET CURRENTS ON THE PROPAGATION OF WAVE ENERGY INTO ESTUARIES - PHYSICAL MODEL INDICATIONS,
Army Engineer Waterways Experiment Station, Vicksburg, Miss.
For primary bibliographic entry see Field 2L.
W75-07013

ON AN EFFECT OF RIVER DISCHARGE TO TSUNAMI IN A MODEL OF URADO BAY,
Kyoto Univ. (Japan). Disasters Prevention Research Inst.
For primary bibliographic entry see Field 2L.
W75-07014

MODEL SIMULATION OF THE DOWNSTREAM EFFECTS OF OPERATING THE SIRIKIT POWER STATION,
Electricity Generating Authority of Thailand, Nonthaburi. Planning Dept.
S. Aphaiphuminart, and J. E. Cowley.
In: River and Estuary Model Analysis, Volume III; Proceedings of the International Association for Hydraulic Research Symposium on River

Mechanics (4 Vol.), Bangkok, Thailand, January 9-12, 1973. Asian Institute of Technology, Bangkok, Thailand, p 195-206, (1973). 4 fig, 1 tab.

Descriptors: *Model studies, *Rivers, *Diversion dams, *Hydroelectric plants, Hydraulic models, Calibrations, Laboratory tests, Evaluation, Water level fluctuations, Streamflow, Downstream.
Identifiers: *Thailand(Nan River).

The design, construction, and operation were described of a scale model of a 300-kilometer length of the Nan River. The results of simulation of an extensive series of situations in which the Sirikit power station was operated in conjunction with the two diversion structures planned for this reach were presented. From detailed simulation of a wide range of conditions, it was shown that up to four 125 MW generating units can be used at the Sirikit power station, in any pattern of peaking, without compromising downstream interests. The only provision attached to this conclusion is that the total volume of water released each day be sufficient to meet the average flow from the reservoir needed downstream. (See also W75-06998) (Humphreys-ISWS)
W75-07015

THE APPLICATION OF RIVER SYSTEM MECHANICS,
Hawaii Univ., Honolulu. Dept. of Civil Engineering.
For primary bibliographic entry see Field 2E.
W75-07017

THE STOCHASTIC METHOD IN RIVER MECHANICS,
Pittsburgh Univ., Pa. Dept. of Civil Engineering.
For primary bibliographic entry see Field 2E.
W75-07020

FLOOD-ROUTING IN NON-PRISMATIC CHANNELS USING AN IMPLICIT METHOD OF SOLUTION,
Liverpool Univ. (England). Dept. of Civil Engineering.
For primary bibliographic entry see Field 2E.
W75-07021

SUBMERGENCE COMPUTATIONS UPSTREAM OF CHANNEL OBSTRUCTIONS,
Indian Inst. of Science, Bangalore. Dept. of Civil and Hydraulic Engineering.
N. S. L. Rao, and K. Sridharan.
In: River and Estuary Model Analysis, Volume III; Proceedings of the International Association for Hydraulic Research Symposium on River Mechanics (4 Vol.), Bangkok, Thailand, January 9-12, 1973. Asian Institute of Technology, Bangkok, Thailand, p 361-370, (1973). 11 fig, 3 ref.

Descriptors: *Flow profiles, *Open channels, *Backwater, Froude number, Length, Gradually varied flow, Estimating.
Identifiers: M1 type, S1 type, Nondimensional, Rectangular channels, Trapezoidal channels, Triangular channels, Parabolic channels.

Using normal flow Froude number as a reference parameter, computations had been made for generalised nondimensional backwater profiles of M1 and S1 type for several common channel shapes including rectangular, trapezoidal, triangular, and parabolic. The results were presented in terms of the nondimensional profile length for different pool elevations at the downstream end. The figures presented can be used to obtain a quick estimate of the backwater profile lengths. (See also W75-06998) (Humphreys-ISWS)
W75-07029

UNSTEADY FLOW IN OPEN CHANNEL WITH MOVABLE BED,
National Taiwan Univ., Taipei.
For primary bibliographic entry see Field 2E.
W75-07037

GENERAL REPORTS, DISCUSSIONS, LECTURES, VOLUME 4.
For primary bibliographic entry see Field 2J.
W75-07038

APPLICATION OF PHYSICAL AND MATHEMATICAL MODELS FOR RIVER PROBLEMS,
Waterloopkundig Laboratorium, Delft (Netherlands).
For primary bibliographic entry see Field 2A.
W75-07040

STATISTICAL PROPERTIES OF WAVE-CURRENT FORCE,
North Carolina State Univ., Raleigh. Dept. of Civil Engineering, and North Carolina State Univ., Raleigh. Dept. of Geosciences.
For primary bibliographic entry see Field 2L.
W75-07070

A NEW TECHNIQUE FOR BEACH EROSION CONTROL,
North Carolina State Univ., Raleigh. Center for Marine Coastal Studies.
For primary bibliographic entry see Field 2J.
W75-07073

STUDY OF TRACE ELEMENTS IN WATERS OF TWO ALASKAN RESERVOIR SITES,
Alaska Univ., College. Inst. of Water Resources.
For primary bibliographic entry see Field 5B.
W75-07100

MATHEMATICAL MODELS OF MAJOR DIVERSION STRUCTURES IN THE MINNEAPOLIS-ST. PAUL INTERCEPTOR SEWER SYSTEM,
Minnesota Univ., Minneapolis. St. Anthony Falls Hydraulic Lab.
For primary bibliographic entry see Field 5D.
W75-07142

DEVELOPMENT OF A COMPUTER PROGRAM TO ROUTE RUNOFF IN THE MINNEAPOLIS-ST. PAUL INTERCEPTOR SEWERS,
Minnesota Univ., Minneapolis. St. Anthony Falls Hydraulic Lab.
For primary bibliographic entry see Field 5D.
W75-07143

REAL-TIME ESTIMATION OF RUNOFF IN THE MINNEAPOLIS-ST. PAUL METROPOLITAN AREA,
Minnesota Univ., Minneapolis. St. Anthony Falls Hydraulic Lab.
For primary bibliographic entry see Field 5G.
W75-07144

THE REAL-TIME COMPUTATION OF RUNOFF AND STORM FLOW IN THE MINNEAPOLIS-ST. PAUL INTERCEPTOR SEWERS,
Minnesota Univ., Minneapolis. St. Anthony Falls Hydraulic Lab.
For primary bibliographic entry see Field 5G.
W75-07145

GEOTHERMAL DRILLING IN KLAMATH FALLS, OREGON,
Storey (E. E.) Well Drilling, Klamath Falls, Oreg.
D. M. Storey.
Presented at The Oregon Institute of Technology Geothermal International Conference, October 8, 1974. 10 p.

Descriptors: *Wells, *Thermal water, *Drilling, Heat exchangers, Geology, Heating, Drilling equipment, Economics, Geothermal studies, *Oregon, Costs.
Identifiers: *Geothermal wells, *Klamath Falls(Ore).

The drilling of geothermal wells in the Klamath Falls area is done by two methods. The most widely used is the percussion or cable rig. The other method used is the air-rotary. The construction of geothermal wells can be classed into two types of wells: those serving commercial facilities and those for residential use. The geothermal commercial well is constructed approximately the same as any other large well with the exception of installing casing. A string of casing may have to be set in the hole and cemented in to case off a flow of cold water. The depths of commercial wells will vary from 400 to 1805 feet. Residential wells will vary from 150 to 1000 feet in depth. They consist of drilling a 10 inch diameter hole to a depth where 'live' or moving hot water is encountered. This hot water ranges anywhere from 140 to 250+F. Two strings of 2-inch steel coils are set in the well to a depth determined by the depth of well and the water temperatures. City water is used to flow in the coils in the well. As heat is needed, water is moved through the coils by a circulating pump. The cost of a residential geothermal well ranges from $3000 to $10,000. A commercial geothermal well will cost up to $30,000 or more. (Sims-ISWS)
W75-07146

TURBULENT PRESSURE FIELD BENEATH A HYDRAULIC JUMP,
Indian Inst. of Tech., Madras. Hydraulic Engineering Lab.
M. H. A. Khader, and K. Elango.
Journal of Hydraulic Research, Vol 12, No 4, p 469-489, 1974. 7 fig, 4 tab, 19 ref.

Descriptors: *Turbulence, *Pressure, *Laboratory tests, *Hydraulic jump, *Open channel flow, Statistical methods, Hydraulics, Froude number, Hydraulic structures, Analysis, Data processing, Flumes.
Identifiers: *Spectral analysis, Stilling basins, Autocorrelation.

Statistical characteristics of the fluctuating pressure on the flume floor beneath a classical hydraulic jump were estimated by analog and digital analyses of data obtained in a laboratory flume. A relatively high intensity of pressure fluctuation equal to 0.085 times the initial dynamic pressure was obtained. This was due to the stage of flow development in the supercritical stream flowing over an Ogee weir. The characteristics evaluated showed little variation from the initial Froude number which ranged from 4.7 to 6.6. The structure of the turbulent pressure field was discussed in terms of moments of the probability density histograms, shape of the autocorrelation and spectral density functions, and the estimated time-microscales. (Adams-ISWS)
W75-07180

IMPROVEMENT OF THE 'BASELESS' PROPORTIONAL WEIR,
Indian Inst. of Science, Bangalore. Dept. of Civil and Hydraulic Engineering.
N. S. L. Rao, and D. Chandrasekaran.
Journal of Hydraulic Research, Vol 12, No 4, p 491-498, 1974. 4 fig, 1 tab, 4 ref.

Descriptors: *Weirs, *Discharge(Water), *Discharge measurement, *Discharge coefficients, Hydraulics, Flow, Depth, Velocity, Hydrometry, Hydraulic structures.
Identifiers: *Baseless proportional weir, *Discharge-head relation, Relative errors.

Maintenance of accuracy in the measurements of different hydraulic quantities such as depth of flow, velocity, and discharge is an important

aspect of hydrometry. Improvements for a baseless weir already published were presented. This modification should reduce the errors in the measurement of discharges over the baseless weir. This is particularly true for small discharges over the weir. (Bhowmik-ISWS)
W75-07181

REMOVAL OF AIR FROM WATER LINES BY HYDRAULIC MEANS,
MacLaren (James F.) Ltd., Willowdale (Ontario). Hydrologic Sciences Div.
For primary bibliographic entry see Field 8C.
W75-07184

LOW-HEAD AIR-REGULATED SIPHONS,
Tana River Development Authority, Nairobi (Kenya).
For primary bibliographic entry see Field 8C.
W75-07186

DISCHARGE OVER POLYGONAL WEIRS,
Technische Hochschule, Aachen (West Germany). Inst. for Water Resources Development.
H. Indlekofer, and G. Rouve.
Journal of the Hydraulics Division, American Society of Civil Engineers, Vol 101, No HY3, Proceedings Paper 11178, p 385-401, March 1975. 12 fig, 5 tab, 13 ref, 2 append.

Descriptors: *Discharge coefficient, Hydraulics, *Hydraulic models, *Weirs, *Spillways, Hydraulic structures, Discharge(Water), Overflow, Spillways, Flow, Mathematics.
Identifiers: *Polygonal weirs, *Corner weirs.

Intake towers and weirs in reservoirs with small water depth (less than or equal to 30.0 m = 98.4 ft) and small floods (less than or equal to 100 cu m/s = 3500 cfs) can be designed with polygon in plan in several cases. The polygon is easier to construct compared to the circle in plan, but the hydraulic computation is more complicated. The influence of an individual corner of the polygonal weir on the discharge coefficient and therefore on the discharge capacity was shown. The independent variable hydraulic and geometric parameters, e.g., corner angle, weir height, and overfall head influenced the flow at the weir and over the weir crest in different ways. All the results of this basic investigations showed that a simple mathematical relation between disturbing effect of the corner and the overfall head can be assumed. A simplified two-dimensional flow theory was developed to make the hydraulic computation of the discharge capacity of polygonal weirs possible. (Bhowmik-ISWS)
W75-07187

TURBULENCE AND DIFFUSION INVESTIGATIONS IN A SUBMERGED AXISYMMETRIC WATER JET,
Ebasco Services, Inc., New York.
N. S. Shashidhara, and E. L. Bourodimos.
Water Resources Bulletin, Vol 11, No 1, p 77-96, February 1975. 14 fig, 6 tab, 41 ref.

Descriptors: *Jets, *Velocity, *Shear stress, *Turbulence, *Diffusion, Fluid mechanics, Equilibrium, Entrainment, Laboratory tests, Analytical techniques, Hydraulics.
Identifiers: *Submerged water jet, Mixing length, Self-preservation, Geometrical similarity.

The normalized mean velocity profile across the axis of a submerged water jet reaches self-preservation at a distance of 8-10 jet diameters downstream. The profile is gaussian and the velocity deceleration along the axis follows a hyperbolic pattern. Self-preservation implies that a given flow field with its components in dynamic equilibrium becomes geometrically similar at all sections. The mixing length is not a function of the axial distance but it does show a variation in radial direction. Self-preservation for turbulence intensities was noted at about 45 jet diameters distance and beyond. Radial variation of turbulence intensities did not show self-preservation even at 100 jet diameters distance downstream. The normalized turbulent shear stress had a minimum value of 0 at the axis. Variation of the efflux velocities (8, 10, or 12 ft/sec) did not have any appreciable effect on the overall characteristics of the jet. (Singh-ISWS)
W75-07192

THE USE OF THE DIGITAL SIMULATION LANGUAGE PDEL IN HYDROLOGIC STUDIES,
Wayne State Univ., Detroit, Mich. Dept. of Mathematics.
For primary bibliographic entry see Field 2F.
W75-07254

FRICTIONAL EFFECTS IN SIDE CHANNEL SPILLWAYS WITH INCREASING DISCHARGE,
Connecticut Univ., Storrs. Inst. of Water Resources.
V. E. Scottron.
Available from the National Technical Information Service, Springfield, Va. 22161 as PB-241 480, $3.25 in paper copy, $2.25 in microfiche. Completion Report, December 1974. 6 p, 4 fig, 21 ref, append. OWRT A-051-CONN (1) 14-31-0001-3807.

Descriptors: *Open channel flow, Discharge(Water), Spillways, Friction.
Identifiers: *Spatially varied flow, *Side-channel spillways, *Frictional effects, Roof gutters, Street gutters, Dam spillways.

A detailed experimental study of the frictional effects in side channel spillways with increasing discharge was conducted using a model of the convergence of two wide channels as a test case. Careful reworking of the analysis showed that a single momentum equation as used in the past was not sufficient to explain certain anomalies. Additional equations were developed for energy and mixing losses. These equations proved satisfactory in matching experimental results. (de Lara-Connecticut)
W75-07274

VAN BUREN REACH, ARKANSAS RIVER NAVIGATION PROJECT; HYDRAULIC MODEL INVESTIGATION,
Army Engineer Waterways Experiment Station, Vicksburg, Miss.
L. J. Shows, and J. J. Franco.
Available from the National Technical Information Service, Springfield, Va., 22161, as AD-784 091, $10.25 in paper copy, $2.25 in microfiche. Army Engineer Waterways Experiment Station, Vicksburg, Mississippi. Technical Report H-74-7, July 1974. 83 p, 4 tab, 30 pl.

Descriptors: *Hydraulic models, *Navigation, River training, Hydraulics, Arkansas, Model studies, Dikes, *Channel improvement, *River beds.
Identifiers: Arkansas River Navigation Project, *Arkansas River(Ark), Van Buren(Ark), Vane dikes.

The Van Buren reach of the Arkansas River is in Lock and Dam No. 13 pool near Van Buren, Ark., about river mile 353. The reach is characterized by three relatively flat bends and is crossed by three existing or proposed bridges. The location of the navigation spans of the two existing bridges could cause considerable difficulties in navigating the reach and in maintaining a channel of adequate dimensions based on the alignment of the navigation spans. A hydraulic model was constructed to an undistorted scale of 1:120. Originally the model was of the semifixed-bed type for the navigation studies. It was later converted to the movable-bed type. The investigation revealed: a. The channel had a natural tendency to develop in a sinuous alignment with the channel crossing first toward the right bank and then back toward the left bank, b. The best alignment for the channel insofar as navigation is concerned is along the left or convex side of the bend. c. Development of a channel along the left side would require considerable contraction and training structures. d. A system of vane dikes could be developed which would practically eliminate the need for maintenance dredging. (WES)
W75-07280

GEOMORPHOLOGY OF THE MIDDLE MISSISSIPPI RIVER,
Colorado State Univ., Fort Collins. Engineering Research Center.
S. A. Schumm, M. A. Stevens, and D. B. Simons.
Available from the National Technical Inofrmation Service, Springfield, Va., 22161, as AD-783 424. $5.25 in paper copy, $2.25 in microfiche. Army Engineer Waterways Experiment Station, Vicksburg, Mississippi, Contract Report Y-74-2, July 1974. 110 p, 29 fig, 7 tab, 21 ref, 2 append.

Descriptors: *Channel Improvements, *Geomorphology, *Hydraulic models, Hydraulic structures, Hydraulics, *Mississippi River, River training, Illinois, Missouri, Channel morphology, Model studies, Flood protection, Flood stages, Dikes.
Identifiers: Side channels(Mississippi River), Middle Mississippi River, Notched dikes.

A comprehensive study of the historical geomorphology of the Middle Mississippi River was made to determine the physical impact of river contraction works on river morphology and behavior, and subsequent effects on the side channels. The studies included physical model studies of the river and side channels, the combined effects of navigation improvement structures and flood protection works on flood stages, and a review of the history of development and modification of the Middle Mississippi River. Based on the laboratory model studies, it was concluded that in nearly all field situations, the inlet to the side channel formed by dike fields is located in a position to receive unusually high quantities of sediment. Consequently, the life of these side channels can be increased if the intakes are closed soon after formation of the side channel. It is also possible to realign the river so that the intake to a side channel is in a favorabel position and alignment to obtain clear water and very little sediment. However, this would require massive structures to resist the forces of the main channel and would be extremely expensive. The use of notched dikes might help in extending the life of a few side channels. (WES)
W75-07281

COMPUTER-CALCULATED GEOMETRIC CHARACTERISTICS OF MIDDLE-MISSISSIPPI RIVER SIDE CHANNELS; VOLUME 1: PROCEDURES AND RESULTS; VOLUME 2: SIDE CHANNEL CONTOUR MAPS,
Army Engineer Waterways Experiment Station, Vicksburg, Miss.
For primary bibliographic entry see Field 4A.
W75-07282

UNSTEADY SALINITY INSTRUSION IN ESTUARIES; PART I: ONE-DIMENSIONAL, TRANSIENT SALINITY INTRUSION WITH VARYING FRESHWATER INFLOW; PART II: TWO-DIMENSIONAL ANALYSIS OF TIME-AVERAGED SALINITY AND VELOCITY PROFILES,
Massachusetts Inst. of Tech., Cambridge. Ralph M. Parsons Lab. for Water Resources and Hydrodynamics.
For primary bibliographic entry see Field 2L.
W75-07284

REMEDIAL PLANS FOR PREVENTION OF HARBOR SHOALING, PORT ORFORD, OREGON; HYDRAULIC MODEL INVESTIGATION,
Army Engineer Waterways Experiment Station, Vicksburg, Miss.
C. E. Chatham, Jr., and M. L. Giles.
Available from the National Technical Information Service, Springfield, Va., 22161, as Ad-781 483, $7.00 in paper copy, $2.25 in microfiche. Army Engineer Waterways Experiment Station, Vicksburg, Mississippi. Technical Report H-74-4, June 1974. 178 p, 26 tab, 98 photo, 12 pl, 10 ref.

Descriptors: Harbors, *Hydraulic models, *Shoals, *Waves(Water), *Oregon, Model studies, *Breakwaters, Hydraulic structures, Channel improvement, Optimum development plans, Hydraulics.
Identifiers: *Port Orford(Ore), *Harbor shoaling prevention.

A 1:100-scale undistorted hydraulic model of Port Orford, Oregon and sufficient offshore area to permit generation of the required test waves was used to develop and test several plans of improvement proposed to eliminate harbor shoaling without adversely affecting wave heights at the existing pier. Improvement plans consisted of (a) removal of portions of the existing breakwater, (b) realignment or lengthening of the existing breakwater, and (c) construction of new breakwater structures in the vicinity of Fort Point and Battle Rock. A 54-ft-long wave machine, electrical wave height measuring and recording apparatus, and coal and nylon tracer materials were used in the model. Tests were conducted with prebreakwater and existing breakwater conditions, and the results were compared to determine the causes and sources of harbor shoaling. Improvement plans were then tested and compared with existing prototype conditions. Of the plans tested, the optimum configuration appears to be a 600 ft extension of the basic planned breakwater structure, which would prevent material from entering the harbor and stabilize material already in the harbor. (WES)
W75-07285

STA-POND STABILITY TESTS; HYDRAULIC MODEL INVESTIGATION,
Army Engineer Waterways Experiment Station, Vicksburg, Miss.
D. D. Davidson.
Army Engineer Waterways Experiment Station, Vicksburg, Mississippi. Miscellaneous Paper H-74-7, August 1974. 39 p, 1 fig, 18 photo, 7 pl.

Descriptors: *Breakwaters, *Groins(Structures), *Hydraulic models, Stability, Waves(Water), Model studies, Hydraulics, Testing, Hydraulic structures, Groins(Structures), Testing procedures.
Identifiers: *Armor units(Hydraulics), *Stability tests.

Model tests were conducted on STA-POD armor units used on selected groin-type structures, subjected to the largest waves that can attack the units when placed in the surf zone in a water depth equal to the height of the unit. One preliminary test also was conducted to obtain an indication of the stability of STA-PODS when used on a breakwater slope (1:1.5). All tests were conducted in a wave flume 110 ft long, 4 ft wide, and 4 ft deep. The surf zone tests utilized a 1:25 model to prototype scale, while the breakwater slope tests used only model values. It was concluded from results of the surf zone tests, where the model STA-PODS were tested on a hard-surface slope, that 5-ton STA-PODS used as a groin or samll jetty type structure in the prototype would be stable for wave heights in excess of the 7.5 ft tested on the model. A small area of STA-PODS tested on a 1:1.5 breakwater slope indicated that random-placed STA-PODS interlocked and provided good stability characteristics. The use of STA-PODS as a breakwater unit would be practical, provided their structural stamina were sufficient to endure forces during prototype construction and storm action, and provided additional research indicated their damage coefficient was sufficiently large to make STA-PODS economically feasible. (WES)
W75-07287

ENVIRONMENTAL INVENTORY AND ASSESSMENT, ILLINOIS WATERWAY; 12-FOOT CHANNEL NAVIGATION PROJECT,
Army Engineer Waterways Experiment Station, Vicksburg, Miss.
W. P. Emge, H. H. Allen, G. H. Hughes, G. S. Wilhelm, and J. H. Zimmerman.
Army Engineer Waterways Experiment Station, Vicksburg, Mississippi. Miscellaneous Paper Y-74-1, April 1974. 421 p, 136 ref, 19 append.

Descriptors: *Dredging, *Inland waterways, *Environmental effects, Illinois, Hydraulics, Channels, Navigation, Surveys, *Alternative planning, Water quality, Biota, Channel improvement.
Identifiers: *Illinois Waterway(Ill), *Navigation channels.

An environmental inventory was made of the Illinois Waterway, and environmental assessments were made of the four proposed alternatives to reach a 12-ft minimum navigation channel from an existing 9-ft minimum navigation channel on the Waterway. The proposed alternatives were: (1) raising the existing normal pool level by 3 ft, (2) dredging the channel 3 ft and transporting the dredged material to land disposal sites or depositing it in the open water, (3) raising the pool level 1.5 ft and dredging the channel 1.5 ft, and (4) no action. It was found that the Illinois Waterway varies significantly in its environmental quality from the upper reaches near Chicago where it is highly polluted to its lower reaches at Grafton, Illinois, where it is fairly diverse in biota. Particular areas on the Waterway deemed to have special environmental values were delineated and discussed relative to the various alternatives. (WES)
W75-07288

MATHEMATICAL MODEL STUDY OF A FLOW CONTROL PLAN FOR THE CHESAPEAKE AND DELAWARE CANAL,
Army Engineer Waterways Experiment Station, Vicksburg, Miss.
B. H. Johnson.
Army Engineer Waterways Experiment Station, Vicksburg, Mississippi. Miscellaneous Paper H-74-10, September 1974. 38 p, 1 tab, 4 ref, 2 append.

Descriptors: *Canals, *Control structures, *Flow control, *Open channel flow, Hydraulics, *Mathematical models, Model studies, Hydraulic models, *Delaware, *Environmental control, Unsteady flow, Planning, Feasibility studies.
Identifiers: *Sea level canals, *Chesapeake and Delaware Canal(Del).

In 1954 Congress authorized an enlargement of the sea level canal connecting the Delaware River and the Chesapeake Bay. This enlargement was to provide a 35-ft by 450-ft channel section instead of the 27-ft by 250-ft channel which existed at that time. As of 1974, about 90 percent of the project has been physically completed. Extensive studies to define the ecological effects of channel enlargement have not thus far indicated any significant adverse effect which would warrant flow control in the canal. However, it was considered advisable to investigate the feasibility of flow control schemes in case such control ever became desirable. Of the various flow control schemes considered, a navigation lock and dam in the main canal, along with a small bypass canal was selected as the best flow control plan. A mathematical model, called SOCHMJ, for the computation of unsteady flows in a system composed of an unlimited number of open channels has been employed to determine the feasibility of such a flow control plan. The results from the mathematical model study indicate that the proposed flow control plan is feasible. (WES)
W75-07289

A RELATION BETWEEN GAMMA RADIATION AND PERMEABILITY, DENVER-JULESBERG BASIN,
Shell Oil Co., Denver, Colo.
For primary bibliographic entry see Field 4B.
W75-07335

UNIFIED FORMULATION OF WALL TURBULENCE,
Ebasco Services Inc., New York.
G-T. Teh.
Journal of the Hydraulics Division, American Society of Civil Engineers, Vol 98, No HY12, p 2263-2271, December, 1972. 3 fig, 23 ref.

Descriptors: Hydraulics, *Turbulence, *Viscosity, *Roughness, Movement, *Roughness coefficient, Turbulent flow, Turbulent boundary layers, Hydraulic structures, Linings.
Identifiers: *Wall effects, Wall smoothness, Restricted flow.

In most analyses of the wall turbulence under neutral conditions, two assumptions have been made for the rear-wall region: (1) the mixing length is proportional to the distance from the wall and (2) the turbulent shear stress is constant over the region of interest. These two assumptions resulted in a logarithmic velocity profile valid in the near wall region. Because of the nature of this logarithmic function, the zero velocity condition at the wall cannot be specified. To determine the integration constant in the equation, an artificial distinctiog between the smooth and rough surface was introduced. By incorporating the effect of the viscosity into the roughness length model, allowing the total shear stress to vary linearly, and modifying the mixing length, the present theory gives good results for the entire flow region. The resulting equation covers the smooth wall as well as the rough wall flow. The equation also provides a single formula to describe the velocity profile in the three near-wall regions for a smooth surface. (Bradbeer-NWWA)
W75-07336

CAVITATION, A NOVEL DRILLING CONCEPT,
Mobil Research and Development Corp., Dallas, Tex. Field Research Lab.
F. A. Angona.
International Journal of Rock Mechanics, Mineralogical Sciences and Geomechanical Abstracts, Vol 11, p 115-119, 1974. 10 fig, 5 ref.

Descriptors: *Cavitation, *Corrosion, *Scour, *Fluid mechanics, *Drilling, Drilling fluids, Drilling equipment, Rotary drilling, Celerity, Erosion.
Identifiers: *Cavitation drilling, Lueders limestone.

An experimental investigation of cavitation erosion as a possible drilling mechanism is described. Cavitation is the phenomenon associated with the formation and violent collapse of bubbles in a liquid. The energy associated with the collapse of a single bubble is small, but the spherical convergence of the collapsing bubble generates an energy density sufficient to erode materials with strengths as high as that of tungsten. A focusing acoustic system enclosed in a pressure chamber permitted the sound pressure and the hydrostatic pressure to be independently varied over the range of 1-20 atmospheres. The intensity of cavitation, as measured by the erosion rate of Lenders limestone and aluminum, was found to increase as the third power of hydrostatic pressure. Experimental results obtained in this pressure range correlate

with published Soviet data taken at pressures up to 75 atmospheres. Extrapolation of data to 10,000 foot drilling conditions indicates penetration rates higher than those for rotary drilling provided a borehole transducer with an acoustic output in excess of 100 horsepower can be developed. (Bradbeer-NWWA)
W75-07337

8C. Hydraulic Machinery

POWER SHORTAGE CONTINGENCY PROGRAM FOR THE PACIFIC NORTHWEST, LEGISLATIVE, REGULATORY AND INSTITUTIONAL ASPECTS,
Kell, Alterman, Runstein and Thomas, Portland, Oreg.
For primary bibliographic entry see Field 6E.
W75-06977

PREVENTIVE MAINTENANCE,
East Bay Municipal Utility District, Oakland, Calif.
J. S. Harnett.
Journal American Water Works Association, Vol 61, No 8, August 1969. p 398-400.

Descriptors: *Maintenance, *Water districts, *Utilities, *Inspection, *Municipal water, *Operation and maintenance, Rehabilitation, Reliability, Repairing, Monitoring, Water supply, California, Facilities.
Identifiers: *Preventive maintenance, San Francisco Bay area.

Preventive maintenance is an absolute necessity in all water systems. The preventive maintenance program may be divided into three categories: the local distribution system; the water production system; and the dams in both systems that come under the jurisdiction of the state Department of Water Resources. 'Maintenance' is defined as the upkeep of district facilities with goals of efficient operation, a minimum of breakdowns, good appearance, reasonable costs, extended useful life, and safety. Maintenance can be classified in three categories: routine maintenance, emergency repairs and regular inspections. The East Bay Municipal Utility District of California has three major maintenance programs. The first program is concerned with the dams, seven of which impound surface runoff and 24 which hold treated water. The responsibility for inspection, maintenance and repair of aqueduct transmission facilities is the second program. The third and largest program pertains to the local distribution system. The goal of the district's maintenance, inspection, and surveillance programs is safe, efficient, uninterrupted operation. Preventive maintenance programs on all facilities of storage, transmission, and distribution must be well organized, well equipped and well manned in order to be effective. An overview of the District's inspection and maintenance program is given. (Poertner)
W75-07115

A SMALL SCALE SWIRL CONCENTRATOR FOR STORM FLOW,
Wisconsin Univ., Milwaukee.
For primary bibliographic entry see Field 5D.
W75-07130

REMOVAL OF AIR FROM WATER LINES BY HYDRAULIC MEANS,
MacLaren (James F.) Ltd., Willowdale (Ontario). Hydrologic Sciences Div.
P. E. Wisner, F. N. Mohsen, and N. Kouwen.
Journal of the Hydraulics Division, American Society of Civil Engineers, Vol 101, No HY2, Proceedings Paper 11142, p 243-257, February 1975. 16 fig, 1 tab, 9 ref, 2 append.

Descriptors: *Air entrainment, Hydraulics, *Dimensional analysis, *Pipe flow, Pipelines, Flow, Hydraulic similitude, Model studies, Velocity, Water, Mechanical equipment, Froude number, Bubbles.
Identifiers: *Air removal, Pipeline summits.

Removal of air from water lines by mechanical devices or by hydraulic action of flowing water was described. Published results on the hydraulic removal of air were discussed. A dimensional analysis was performed for stable air pockets in a pipe. An experimental setup of 10-inch pipe was made to test removal of air pockets from a summit or high point in the pipe line. Test results were presented and compared with previously available data. It was concluded that: (1) no similitude was found for the time of clearance of isolated air pockets in water lines, (2) results of model tests gave conservative estimates for the time of clearance if scaled by the Froude law, and (3) for pipe under 1 ft diameter clearance of air pockets was found to require very high velocities. Mechanical air removal devices were recommended for cases in which hydraulic removal was not possible or was too slow. (Adams-ISWS)
W75-07184

LOW-HEAD AIR-REGULATED SIPHONS,
Tana River Development Authority, Nairobi (Kenya).
C. R. Head.
Journal of the Hydraulics Division, American Society of Civil Engineers, Vol 101, No HY3, Proceedings Paper 11155, p 329-345, March 1975. 10 fig, 14 ref, 2 append.

Descriptors: *Siphons, *River regulation, *Flow control, *Spillways, *Water control, Design, Discharge(Water), Weirs, Model studies, Froude number, Hydraulic structures, Hydraulics, Hydraulic similitude, Water levels, Air entrainment, Flood control, Hydraulic models.
Identifiers: Discharge characteristics, Air-regulated siphons.

The development of air-regulated low-head siphons for river control works was discussed. This type of siphon has a very flat stage-discharge curve which has been found desirable. If the strueture was designed for the head, an air-regulated siphon would flow full at higher heads. Typical section and design details were shown. The several flow phases were discussed. Combined spillways with siphons and weirs were described and discharge curves were presented for them. A design method was described. The need for Froude law model studies to complete most designs was mentioned. The models were needed because important design details such as the inlet lip, crest, nappe deflector, and outlet lip cannot be determined by analytical means. (Adams-ISWS)
W75-07186

UNIFIED FORMULATION OF WALL TURBULENCE,
Ebasco Services Inc., New York.
For primary bibliographic entry see Field 8B.
W75-07336

8D. Soil Mechanics

EARTH MANUAL, A WATER RESOURCES TECHNICAL PUBLICATION.
Bureau of Reclamation, Denver, Colo. Engineering and Research Center.
Second Edition, 1974. 810 p, 135 fig, 6 tab, append.

Descriptors: *Publications, *Soil mechanics, *Soil physical properties, *Earthworks, *Soil classification, *Soil engineering, *Soil investigations, Documentation, Soil compaction, Construction, Earth dams, Earth materials, Foundations, Soil tests, Testing, Laboratory tests, Sampling, Instrumentation, On-site tests, On-site investigations, Analytical techniques, Exploration, Canals, Pipelines, Soil stabilization, Soil groups, Engineering, Subsurface investigations.

The following subjects were discussed: (1) properties of soils including identification and classification, index properties, and engineering properties; (2) investigations including stages of investigations, principles of investigations, exploratory methods, and recording and reporting of data; and (3) control of earth construction including principles of construction control, earthwork, foundations, rolled earth dams, canals, pipelines, miscellaneous construction features and stabilized soils. An extensive appendix presents procedures for sampling, classification, laboratory and field tests of soils, and instrument installations. Although the Manual is primarily geared to the Reclamation organization, engineers and technicians of other governmental agencies, foreign governments, and private firms can, with modifications, utilize the information as a guide to their individual investigations, control of earth construction, and laboratory testing since emphasis is upon practical applications rather than upon complex theory. Users should recognize that certain recommendations and values are the result of experience and cannot always be mathematically proved. The Manual has been written as a guide and aid for the construction of a safe and stable structure with utmost concern for the safety of lives. (Humphreys-ISWS)
W75-07046

INFLUENCE OF SAMPLE DISTURBANCE AND TEST METHOD ON KEY ENGINEERING PROPERTIES OF MARINE SOILS,
Lehigh Univ,. Bethlehem, Pa. Dept. of Civil Engineering.
For primary bibliographic entry see Field 2G.
W75-07074

ANALYSIS OF LONGITUDINAL BEHAVIOUR OF BURIED PIPES,
Sydney Univ. (Australia).
H. C. Poulos.
Available from the National Technical Information Service, Springfield, Va 22161 as PB-231 685, $3.75 in paper copy, $2.25 in microfiche. December 1973. 35 p, 17 fig, 23 ref, append.

Descriptors: *Pipelines, *Soil mechanics, *Movement, Pipes, Conduits, Steel pipes, Culverts, Engineering structures, Piping systems(Mechanical), Pipe foundations, Structural analysis, Deflection, Deformation, Structural design, Structural behavior.

The longitudinal behavior of a buried pipeline was analyzed in relation to two cases: (1) a pipeline beneath a loaded area and (2) a pipeline situated in a swelling or shrinking soil. The effects of various factors such as the relative flexibility of the pipe, the depth of embedment, and the magnitude of the soil movement were investigated for each case. The relative flexibility of a pipeline is characterized by a dimensionless factor, K sub R, and it was shown that large moments and end-reactions may be developed in relatively stiff pipelines in which K sub R is greater than or equal to 0.01. A limited number of comparisons between measured and theoretical behavior of pipelines showed that the theory is capable of predicting the order of magnitude of pipeline moments and deflections. (Sims-ISWS)
W75-07166

STABILITY OF STRUCTURES WITH INTERMEDIATE FILTERS,
Uttar Pradesh Irrigation Research Inst., Roorkee (India). Ground Water Div.
For primary bibliographic entry see Field 8A.
W75-07183

EVALUATION OF THE CAUSES OF LEVEE EROSION IN THE SACRAMENTO-SAN JOAQUN DELTA, CALIFORNIA,
Geological Survey, Menlo Park, Calif.
For primary bibliographic entry see Field 2J.
W75-07210

MASS PHYSICAL PROPERTIES, SLIDING AND ERODIBILITY OF EXPERIMENTALLY DEPOSITED AND DIFFERENTLY CONSOLIDATED CLAYEY MUDS,
Tuebingen Univ. (West Germany). Geologisch-Palaontologisches Institut.
For primary bibliographic entry see Field 2J.
W75-07266

8E. Rock Mechanics and Geology

SOC73, A ONE-DIMENSIONAL WAVE PROPAGATION CODE FOR ROCK MEDIA,
California Univ., Livermore. Lawrence Livermore Lab.
J. F. Schatz.
Report UCRL-51689, November 5, 1974. 35 p, 26 fig, 26 ref. AEC Contract W-7405-Eng-48.

Descriptors: *Mathematical models, *Computer models, *Rock mechanics, Explosives, Rock properties, Excavation, Rock excavation, Rocks, Deformation, Stress, Physical properties, Geology.

SOC73 is a highly modified version of SOC, a computer program that numerically simulates mechanical wave propagation in geologic media. Innovation in SOC73 lies mainly in the constitutive modeling of solid media. New models were introduced in which the pressure-volume behavior and the behavior of brittle, ductile, and tensile failure are more continuous and representative of laboratory and field observations than before. There are also new methods of low-pass compressional filtering and high-pass distorsional filtering that are more physically and numerically satisfying. The concept of failure-associated strain was also introduced. It allows an estimate of the damage caused to the medium by an inelastic stress wave. (Sims-ISWS)
W75-07041

8G. Materials

REPORT ON CONDITION OF CAST IRON PIPE,
Toronto Dept. of Public Works (Ontario).
M. J. Long, M. F. Oster, and F. T. Booth.
(1970) 7 p, 4 fig, 1 tab.

Descriptors: *Maintenance, *Inspection, *Water conveyance, *Pipes, *Water distribution(Applied), *Metal pipes, Distribution systems, Linings, Canada, On-site investigations, Testing, Flow friction, Roughness coefficient, Strength of materials.
Identifiers: Toronto(Ontario-Canada), Water pipe survey, Cast iron pipe.

Because the water distribution system of Toronto, Ontario, Canada was, for the most part, constructed between 1870 and 1942, the Department of Public Works felt the need to evaluate the system. From the information obtained from the two methods of examination, hydraulic tests and the physical tests, it was possible to choose the type of improvement programme best suited to overcome inadequacies, such as reconstruction of existing mains, cleaning and cement mortar lining, or construction of additional mains. The measured 'C-values' (roughness coefficient) indicated that there is a correlation between the age of the main and the coefficient of friction, in that the older the main the lower the value of 'C'. Pictures of the interior of the pipe show that there is no great reduction in cross-sectional area, but the surface of the cast iron is very rough and produces excessive head losses. The ring tests indicated that the strength of a cast iron pipe is not materially affected by age. Where areas of pressure and flow are unsatisfactory under current and expected future rates of flow, a cleaning and cement mortar lining programme will be considered. Future pipe will be installed with a cement lining. (Poertner)
W75-07125

REPORT ON CLEANING AND CEMENT MORTAR LINING OF SMALL DIAMETER WATERMAINS.
Toronto Dept. of Public Works (Ontario).
(1970) 15 p, 1 tab.

Descriptors: *Water conveyance, *Protective linings, *Cement grouting, *Metal pipes, *Water distribution(Applied), *Cleaning, Descaling, Linings, Canada, Maintenance, Flow friction, Roughness coefficient.
Identifiers: *Cement mortar lining, Water mains, Toronto(Ontario-Canada), Cast iron pipe, Pipeline maintenance.

As a result of a survey of the water distribution system in the City of Toronto, it was found that the capacity of the system was considerably reduced due to tuberculation of the mains which caused low flow coefficients. Consequently, it was decided to embark on a programme of cleaning and cement mortar lining of the mains. Prior to any cleaning and lining being undertaken, temporary by-pass piping was laid on the surface of the street and the water services of any consumer affected were connected to it. Cleaning of the pipe was carried out by either hydraulic or drag cleaning. When the main had been satisfactorily cleaned, a squeegee was dragged through several times to completely de-water the pipe. The lining equipment consisted of a power plant, mixer, mortar pump, hose, lining machine and pulling unit with variable speed drive. After the mortar has set for a minimum of twenty-four hours, the nipples are replaced and the main charged and chlorinated and flushed. The services are returned to normal use, the by-pass removed and the excavation backfilled. It was concluded that an air operated lining machine is more reliable than electric in small diameter pipe. A small diameter main can be cleaned and lined for as little as 1/3 the cost of a new main. Cleaning and cement mortar lining improved existing flow capacity as much as 2 1/2 times for less than half of the cost of a new main. (Poertner)
W75-07126

CAVITATION, A NOVEL DRILLING CONCEPT,
Mobil Research and Development Corp., Dallas, Tex. Field Research Lab.
For primary bibliographic entry see Field 8B.
W75-07337

8H. Rapid Excavation

SOC73, A ONE-DIMENSIONAL WAVE PROPAGATION CODE FOR ROCK MEDIA,
California Univ., Livermore. Lawrence Livermore Lab.
For primary bibliographic entry see Field 8E.
W75-07041

8I. Fisheries Engineering

ECOLOGICAL CONSEQUENCES OF THE PROPOSED MORAN DAM ON THE FRASER RIVER,
Simon Fraser Univ., Burnaby (British Columbia). Dept. of Biological Sciences.
For primary bibliographic entry see Field 6G.
W75-07174

LIFE HISTORY, ECOLOGY, AND MANAGEMENT OF THE SMALLMOUTH BUFFALO, ICTIOBUS BUBALUS (RAFINESQUE), WITH REFERENCE TO ELEPHANT BUTTE LAKE,
New Mexico Agricultural Experiment Station, University Park.
For primary bibliographic entry see Field 6C.
W75-07343

9. MANPOWER, GRANTS AND FACILITIES

9A. Education (Extramural)

BETTER WATER FOR BETTER LIFE.
Michigan State Univ., East Lansing. Inst. of Water Research.
For primary bibliographic entry see Field 9D.
W75-07147

9D. Grants, Contracts, and Research Act Allotments

BETTER WATER FOR BETTER LIFE.
Michigan State Univ., East Lansing. Inst. of Water Research.
(1974). 40 p, 38 ref. OWRT A-999-MICH(2).

Descriptors: *Water Resources Institute, *Universities, *Facilities, Organizations, Contracts, Grants, Projects, Water Resources Research Act, Water resources, Water resources development, Water quality, Water pollution, Pollutants, Management, Personnel, Planning, Michigan.

The history and activities of the Institute of Water Research (IWR) at Michigan State University were described. The IWR was established in 1961. It is presently supported by the University, industrial grants, private foundations, federal grants and contracts, and funding from the Office of Water Resources Research. Research projects involving lakes and streams, pollution, and management of water quality were briefly reviewed. The teaching and service activities of the IWR were described, and biographical information was provided for the current staff. A list of publications was included. (Sims-ISWS)
W75-07147

10. SCIENTIFIC AND TECHNICAL INFORMATION

10C. Secondary Publication And Distribution

BIBLIOGRAPHY AND INDEX OF GEOLOGY AND HYDROLOGY, FRONT RANGE URBAN CORRIDOR, COLORADO,
Colorado Univ., Boulder. Dept. of Geological Sciences.
For primary bibliographic entry see Field 3D.
W75-07218

10F. Preparation Of Reviews

CORRESPONDENCE CONFERENCE ON REMOVAL OF NITROGEN FROM MUNICIPAL WASTEWATER,
Massachusetts Univ., Amherst. Water Resources Research Center.
For primary bibliographic entry see Field 5D.
W75-06984

THE INTERACTION OF VELOCITY DISTRIBUTION-AND SUSPENDED LOAD IN TURBULENT STREAMS,
Massachusetts Inst. of Tech., Cambridge. Ralph M. Parsons Lab. for Water Resources and Hydrodynamics.
For primary bibliographic entry see Field 2J.
W75-07039

EXAMINATION OF WATERS: EVALUATION OF METHODS FOR SELECTED CHARACTERISTICS.
Australian Water Resources Council, Canberra (Australia).
For primary bibliographic entry see Field 5A.
W75-07154

FORMALIN AS A THERAPEUTANT IN FISH CULTURE,
Bureau of Sport Fisheries and Wildlife, La Crosse, Wis. Fish Control Lab.
For primary bibliographic entry see Field 05C.
W75-07342

SUBJECT INDEX

POLLUTANT IDENTIFICATION

POLLUTION ABATEMENT

POLLUTION CONTROL

POLYGONAL WEIRS

PORT ORFORD (ORE)

POTABLE WATER

POTENTIAL FLOW

POTENTIAL WATER SUPPLY

POWER CURTAILMENT

PRE-IMPOUNDMENT

PRECIPITABLE WATER

PRECIPITANTS

PRECIPITATION (ATMOSPHERIC)

AUTHOR INDEX

ORGANIZATIONAL INDEX

ACCESSION NUMBER INDEX

ABSTRACT SOURCES

Source	Accession Number	Total
A. Centers of Competence		
Cornell University, Policy Models for Water Resources Systems	W75-06938 -- 06942 06944 -- 06960	22
Illinois State Water Survey, Hydrology	W75-06998 -- 07021 07023 -- 07052 07054 -- 07065 07067 -- 07068 07146 -- 07152 07154 -- 07192 07194 -- 07199 07244 -- 07261 07264 -- 07270 07334	146
Institute of Paper Chemistry, Water Pollution from Pulp and Paper Industry	W75-06861 -- 06895 06931 -- 06933	38
National Water Well Association, Water Well Construction Technology	W75-07335 -- 07337	3
University of Arizona, Arid Land Water Resources	W75-07330 -- 07333	4
University of Florida, Eastern U. S. Water Law	W75-06962 -- 06974	13
University of North Carolina, Metropolitan Water Resources Planning and Management	W75-06855 -- 06860 07083 -- 07099	23
University of Wisconsin, Eutrophication	W75-07290 -- 07329	40
University of Wisconsin, Water Resources Economics	W75-07343 -- 07350	8
B. State Water Resources Research Institutes	W75-06851 -- 06854 06836 06975 06980 -- 06997 07100 -- 07105 07272 -- 07278	
C. Other		
Army Engineer Waterways Experiment Station	W75-07280 -- 07289	10
BioSciences Information Service	W75-06899, 06937 06943, 06961 06976 07022, 07053 07066, 07153 07193 07262 -- 07263 07279	13

ABSTRACT SOURCES

Source	Accession Number	Total
C. Other (Cont'd)		
Effects of Pollutants on Aquatic Life (Katz)	W75-07338 -- 07342	5
Engineering Aspects of Urban Water Resources (Poertner)	W75-07106 -- 07145	40
National Oceanic and Atmospheric Administration	W75-07069 -- 07082	14
Office of Water Research and Technology	W75-06977 -- 06979 07271	4
U. S. Geological Survey	W75-06934 -- 06936 07200 -- 07243	47
Vanderbilt University, Metals Pollution	W75-06897 -- 06898 06900 -- 06930	33

☆ U. S. GOVERNMENT PRINTING OFFICE : 1975 O - 210-951 (27)

CENTERS OF COMPETENCE AND THEIR SUBJECT COVERAGE

- Ground and surface water hydrology at the Illinois State Water Survey and the Water Resources Division of the U.S. Geological Survey, U.S. Department of the Interior.
- Metropolitan water resources planning and management at the Center for Urban and Regional Studies of University of North Carolina.
- Eastern United States water law at the College of Law of the University of Florida.
- Policy models of water resources systems at the Department of Water Resources Engineering of Cornell University.
- Water resources economics at the Water Resources Center of the University of Wisconsin.
- Eutrophication at the Water Resources Center of the University of Wisconsin.
- Water resources of arid lands at the Office of Arid Lands Studies of the University of Arizona.
- Water well construction technology at the National Water Well Association.
- Water-related aspects of nuclear radiation and safety at the Oak Ridge National Laboratory.
- Water resource aspects of the pulp and paper industry at the Institute of Paper Chemistry.

Supported by the Environmental Protection Agency in cooperation with WRSIC

- Effect on water quality of irrigation return flows at the Department of Agricultural Engineering of Colorado State University.
- Agricultural livestock waste at East Central State College, Oklahoma.
- Municipal wastewater treatment technology at the Franklin Institute Research Laboratories.

Subject Fields

- 1 NATURE OF WATER
- 2 WATER CYCLE
- 3 WATER SUPPLY AUGMENTATION AND CONSERVATION
- 4 WATER QUANTITY MANAGEMENT AND CONTROL
- 5 WATER QUALITY MANAGEMENT AND PROTECTION
- 6 WATER RESOURCES PLANNING
- 7 RESOURCES DATA
- 8 ENGINEERING WORKS
- 9 MANPOWER, GRANTS, AND FACILITIES
- 10 SCIENTIFIC AND TECHNICAL INFORMATION

INDEXES

- SUBJECT INDEX
- AUTHOR INDEX
- ORGANIZATIONAL INDEX
- ACCESSION NUMBER INDEX
- ABSTRACT SOURCES

U.S. DEPARTMENT OF COMMERCE
National Technical Information Service
5285 Port Royal Road
Springfield, VA 22161

OFFICIAL BUSINESS

PRINTED MATTER

John Littlewood
Documents Division
220 D Library
Champaign Ill. 61822

SELECTED WATER RESOURCES ABSTRACTS

VOLUME 8, NUMBER 15
AUGUST 1, 1975

W75-07351 -- W75-07850
CODEN: SWRABW

SELECTED WATER RESOURCES ABSTRACTS is published semimonthly for the Water Resources Scientific Information Center (WRSIC) by the National Technical Information Service (NTIS), U.S. Department of Commerce. NTIS was established September 2, 1970, as a new primary operating unit under the Assistant Secretary of Commerce for Science and Technology to improve public access to the many products and services of the Department. Information services for Federal scientific and technical report literature previously provided by the Clearinghouse for Federal Scientific and Technical Information are now provided by NTIS.

SELECTED WATER RESOURCES ABSTRACTS is available to Federal agencies, contractors, or grantees in water resources upon request to: Manager, Water Resources Scientific Information Center, Office of Water Research and Technology, U.S. Department of the Interior, Washington, D. C. 20240.

SELECTED WATER RESOURCES ABSTRACTS is also available on subscription from the National Technical Information Service. Annual subscription rates are: To the SWRA Journal, $75 ($95 foreign); to the Journal & Annual Index, $100 ($125 foreign); to the Annual Index only, $50 ($65 foreign). Certain documents abstracted in this journal can be purchased from the NTIS at prices indicated in the entry. Prepayment is required.

Rev. Oct. 1974

SELECTED
WATER RESOURCES ABSTRACTS

A Semimonthly Publication of the Water Resources Scientific Information Center,
Office of Water Research and Technology, U.S. Department of the Interior

VOLUME 8, NUMBER 15
AUGUST 1, 1975

W75-07351 -- W75-07850

As the Nation's principal conservation agency, the Department of the Interior has responsibility for most of our nationally owned public lands and natural resources. This includes fostering the wisest use of our land and water resources, protecting our fish and wildlife, preserving the environmental and cultural values of our national parks and historical places, and providing for the enjoyment of life through outdoor recreation. The Department assesses our energy and mineral resources and works to assure that their development is in the best interests of all our people. The Department also has a major responsibility for American Indian reservation communities and for people who live in Island Territories under U.S. administration.

FOREWORD

Selected Water Resources Abstracts, a semimonthly journal, includes abstracts of current and earlier pertinent monographs, journal articles, reports, and other publication formats. The contents of these documents cover the water-related aspects of the life, physical, and social sciences as well as related engineering and legal aspects of the characteristics, conservation, control, use, or management of water. Each abstract includes a full bibliographical citation and a set of descriptors or identifiers which are listed in the **Water Resources Thesaurus.** Each abstract entry is classified into ten fields and sixty groups similar to the water resources research categories established by the Committee on Water Resources Research of the Federal Council for Science and Technology.

WRSIC IS NOT PRESENTLY IN A POSITION TO PROVIDE COPIES OF DOCUMENTS ABSTRACTED IN THIS JOURNAL. Sufficient bibliographic information is given to enable readers to order the desired documents from local libraries or other sources.

Selected Water Resources Abstracts is designed to serve the scientific and technical information needs of scientists, engineers, and managers as one of several planned services of the Water Resources Scientific Information Center (WRSIC). The Center was established by the Secretary of the Interior and has been designated by the Federal Council for Science and Technology to serve the water resources community by improving the communication of water-related research results. The Center is pursuing this objective by coordinating and supplementing the existing scientific and technical information activities associated with active research and investigation program in water resources.

To provide WRSIC with input, selected organizations with active water resources research programs are supported as "centers of competence" responsible for selecting, abstracting, and indexing from the current and earlier pertinent literature in specified subject areas.

Additional "centers of competence" have been established in cooperation with the Environmental Protection Agency. A directory of the Centers appears on inside back cover.

Supplementary documentation is being secured from established discipline-oriented abstracting and indexing services. Currently an arrangement is in effect whereby the BioScience Information Service of Biological Abstracts supplies WRSIC with relevant references from the several subject areas of interest to our users. In addition to Biological Abstracts, references are acquired from Bioresearch Index which are without abstracts and therefore also appear abstractless in SWRA. Similar arrangements with other producers of abstracts are contemplated as planned augmentation of the information base.

The input from these Centers, and from the 51 Water Resources Research Institutes administered under the Water Resources Research Act of 1964, as well as input from the grantees and contractors of the Office of Water Research and Technology and other Federal water resource agencies with which the

Center has agreements becomes the information base from which this journal is, and other information services will be, derived; these services include bibliographies, specialized indexes, literature searches, and state-of-the-art reviews.

Comments and suggestions concerning the contents and arrangements of this bulletin are welcome.

Water Resources Scientific Information Center
Office of Water Research and Technology
U.S. Department of the Interior
Washington, D. C. 20240

CONTENTS

SELECTED WATER RESOURCES ABSTRACTS

1. NATURE OF WATER

1B. Aqueous Solutions and Suspensions

COOPERATIVE PHENOMENA IN ISOTOPIC HYDRODYNAMIC DISPERSION,
Nevada Univ., Reno. Desert Research Inst.
For primary bibliographic entry see Field 5B.
W75-07725

2. WATER CYCLE

2A. General

NONSTATIONARY MODEL OF THE TRANSFORMATION OF EFFECTIVE PRECIPITATION INTO RUNOFF,
S. A. Rusin.
Soviet Hydrology, Selected Papers No. 4, p 289-300, 1973. 6 fig, 8 ref. Translated from Transactions of the State Hydrologic Institute (Trudy GGI), No. 211, p 88-104, 1973.

Descriptors: *Rainfall-runoff relationships, *Runoff, *Mathematical models, Mathematical studies, Surface runoff, Precipitation(Atmospheric), Basins, Model studies, Hydrographs, Optimization, Floods.
Identifiers: Volkha-Verkhniy basin(USSR), Glukhovka-Mostovoy basin(USSR).

Optimization methods were used in solving the so-called inverse problem, i.e., the function describing how precipitation is transformed into runoff given effective precipitation and an outlet hydrograph. The solution involved construction of a direct runoff velocity curve during a flood period. Data from the Volkha-Verkhniy and Glukhovka-Mostovoy basins show the curve of direct runoff speed to be fairly stable for a specific drainage area. It increased to a maximum value (in advance of maximum discharge) before decreasing to form a tail or recession limb. (Jess-ISWS)
W75-07437

A GLOBAL OCEAN-ATMOSPHERE CLIMATE MODEL. PART I. THE ATMOSPHERIC CIRCULATION,
National Oceanic and Atmospheric Administration, Princeton, N.J. Geophysical Fluid Dynamics Lab.
S. Manabe, K. Bryan, and M. J. Spelman.
Journal of Physical Oceanography, Vol 5, No 1, p 3-29, January 1975. 19 fig, 1 tab, 40 ref, 1 append.

Descriptors: *Model studies, *Climates, *Atmospheric physics, *Oceans, Water balance, Temperature, Heat balance, Circulation, Fourier analysis, Time, Radiation, Convection, Condensation, Hydrology, Momentum transfer, Equations, Mixing, Finite element analysis, Precipitation(Atmospheric).
Identifiers: Global grid, Heat exchange, Momentum exchange, Water exchange, Zonal wind, Meridonal circulation, Sea level pressure.

A joint ocean-atmosphere model covering the entire globe was constructed at the Geophysical Fluid Dynamics Laboratory of NOAA. This model differed from the earlier version of the joint model of Bryan and Manabe both in global domain and inclusion of realistic rather than idealized topography. The structure of the atmospheric portion of the joint model was described and the atmospheric circulation and climate that emerged from the time integration of the model was discussed. The primitive equations of motion were incorporated in a spherical coordinate system. The numerical problems associated with the treatment of mountains were minimized by using the 'sigma' coordinate system in which pressure, normalized by surface pressure, was the vertical coordinate. For vertical finite differencing, nine levels were chosen to represent the planetary boundary layer and the stratosphere as well as the troposphere. In order to identify the effect of the ocean currents upon climate, the joint model climate was compared with another climate obtained from the time integration of an 'A-model' in which oceanic regions were occupied by wet swampy surfaces without any heat capacity. The results showed that the total poleward transport of energy was affected little by the oceanic heat transport. Further comparison between the two models indicated that ocean currents significantly affect not only the horizontal distribution of surface temperature of both oceans and continents but also the global distribution of precipitation. (See also W75-07447) (Roberts-ISWS)
W75-07446

A GLOBAL OCEAN-ATMOSPHERE CLIMATE MODEL. PART II. THE OCEANIC CIRCULATION,
National Oceanic and Atmospheric Administration, Princeton, N.J. Geophysical Fluid Dynamics Lab.
K. Bryan, S. Manabe, and R. C. Pacanowski.
Journal of Physical Oceanography, Vol 5, No 1, p 30-46, January 1975. 12 fig, 6 tab, 34 ref, 2 append.

Descriptors: *Numerical analysis, *Oceans, *Atmosphere, *Climates, Stratification, Heat balance, Sea ice, Surface waters, Water balance, Temperature, *Model studies, Circulation, Atmospheric physics, Fourier analysis, Time, Radiation, Convection, Condensation, Hydrology, Momentum transfer, Salinity, Distribution, Equations, Mixing, Finite element analysis, Topography.
Identifiers: Poleward, Pack ice, Zonal wind, Trade wind belt, Ekman drift, Global grid, Radiative transfer, Heat exchange, Momentum exchange, Water exchange, Meridonal circulation, Sea level pressure, Thermohaline.

A numerical experiment was carried out with a joint model of the ocean and atmosphere. The 12-level model of the world ocean predicted the fields of horizontal velocity, temperature, and salinity. It included the effects of bottom topography and a simplified model of polar pack ice. The numerical experiment allowed the joint ocean-atmosphere model to seek an equilibrium over the equivalent of 270 years in the ocean time scale. The initial state of the ocean was uniform stratification and complete rest. Although the final temperature distribution was more zonal than it should be, the major western boundary currents and the equatorial undercurrent were successfully predicted. The calculated salinity field had the correct observed range, and correctly indicated that the Atlantic is more salty than the Pacific. The poleward heat transport of the model was very sensitive to the strength of the circulation in the vertical-meridonal plane. The heat transport was strongest in the trade wind belt where Ekman drift and thermohaline forces acted together to cause a net flow of surface water toward the poles. The results suggested that seasonal effects must be included in any future studies to test the full potential of a joint atmosphere-ocean climate model. (See also W75-07446) (Roberts-ISWS)
W75-07447

VERIFICATION OF NUMERICAL MODELS OF LAKE ONTARIO. II. STRATIFIED CIRCULATIONS AND TEMPERATURE CHANGES,
Canada Centre for Inland Waters, Burlington (Ontario).
For primary bibliographic entry see Field 2H.
W75-07462

WATER RESOURCES,
National Aeronautics and Space Administration, Greenbelt, Md. Goddard Space Flight Center.
For primary bibliographic entry see Field 7B.
W75-07501

HYDROLOGIC IMPACT OF WATER MODIFICATION,
Agricultural Research Service, Chickasha, Okla.
For primary bibliographic entry see Field 3B.
W75-07505

SOME SEDIMENT ASPECTS OF TROPICAL STORM AGNES,
Geological Survey, Reston, Va.
For primary bibliographic entry see Field 2J.
W75-07557

A SPECIAL PLANNING TECHNIQUE FOR STREAM-AQUIFER SYSTEMS,
Geological Survey, Denver, Colo.
C. T. Jenkins, and O. J. Taylor.
Open-file report No 74-242, 1974. 16 p, 4 fig, 1 tab, 20 ref.

Descriptors: *Surface-groundwater relationships, *Mathematical models, *Planning, Model studies, Water yield, Aquifer characteristics, Water management(Applied), Conjunctive use, Analog models, Computer models.
Identifiers: *Stream-aquifer systems.

The potential effects of water-management plans on stream-aquifer systems may be simulated using electric-analog or digital-computer models. Many of the electric-analog models require large amounts of hardware. Digital-computer models require no special hardware preparation but often they require so many repetitive solutions of equations that they result in calculations that are unduly unwieldy and expensive, even on the latest generation of computers. Further, the more detailed digital models require a vast amount of core storage. A concept that offers a solution to these problems is that the effects on streamflow of groundwater withdrawal or recharge (stress) at any point in such a system can be approximated using two classical equations and a value of time that reflects the integrated effect of the following: irregular impermeable boundaries; stream meanders; aquifer properties and their areal variations; distance of the point from the stream; and imperfect hydraulic connection between the stream and the aquifer. The value of time is called the stream depletion factor (sdf). Results of a relatively few tests on detailed models can be summarized on maps showing lines through points of equal sdf. Simple arithmetic, using only a slide rule and charts or tables of dimensionless values, will be sufficient for many calculations. If a large digital computer is available, detailed description of the system and its stresses will require only a fraction of the core storage, leaving the greater part of the storage available for sophisticated analyses, such as optimization. (Knapp-USGS)
W75-07584

PROJECT AQUA NORWEGIAN IB (INTERNATIONAL BIOLOGICAL PROGRAM)/PF, (IN NORWEGIAN),
Zoologisk Museum, Oslo (Norway).
L. Lien.
Fauna (Oslo). Vol 26, No 2, p 104-111. 1973, Illus, English summary.

Descriptors: Fresh water, Europe, Brackish water, *Geographical areas.
Identifiers: Project Aqua, *Norway, Inland waters.

The purpose of Project Aqua is to prepare an international list of freshwater and brackish water areas which are of importance for research and

education. A preliminary list of Norwegian Project Aqua-sites is given, and their geographical location is shown. The Norwegian list is based on information given by institutions and scientists working with problems connected with inland waters.--Copyright 1974, Biological Abstracts, Inc.
W75-07749

2B. Precipitation

WATER RESOURCE OBSERVATORY WIND AND SOLAR RADIATION DATA WATER YEARS 1973 AND 1974,
Wyoming Univ., Laramie. Water Resources Research Inst.
For primary bibliographic entry see Field 7C.
W75-07354

A COMPARISON OF INFRARED IMAGERY AND VIDEO PICTURES IN THE ESTIMATION OF DAILY RAINFALL FROM SATELLITE DATA,
National Environmental Satellite Service, Washington, D.C.
Available from the National Technical Information Service, Springfield, Va. 22161. NOAA Technical Memorandum NESS 62, January 197.

Descriptors: *Precipitation(Atmospheric), *Rainfall intensity, Meteorology, Precipitation intensity, Rain, Rates, Rainfall disposition, Distribution patterns, Satellites(Artificial), Data collections, *Remote sensing, Weather forecasting, Southeast U.S.
Identifiers: *Infrared imagery, *Video pictures, *Rainfall estimation techniques.

An empirical method of estimating 24-hr rainfall in the tropics and subtropics us5. 14 p, 10 fig, 7 tab, 3 ref. (NOAA-75031102)ing both satellite video pictures and infrared imagery was tested to determine whether comparable results could be obtained. This method was tested for Alabama, Georgia, and South Carolina for the months of July, August, and September 1973. The infrared data set provided approximately the same degree of accuracy as the video data set, and the mean of the estimates from the two data sets provided additional accuracy. Seven-day-running totals of these mean estimates coincided closely with 7-day-running totals of observed rainfall. The rainfall estimation technique applies best to humid tropical convective storm areas. (NOAA)
W75-07422

COMPATIBILITY OF LOW-CLOUD VECTORS AND RAWINS FOR SYNOPTIC SCALE ANALYSIS,
National Environmental Satellite Service, Washington, D.C.
L. F. Hubert, and L. F. Whitney, Jr.
Available from Superintendent of Documents, U.S. Gov't Printing Office Washington, D.C. 20402, as C55.13:NOAA TR NESS 70, for $0.75. NOAA Technical Report NESS 70, October 1974. 26 p, 9 fig, 3 tab, 10 ref. (NOAA-74121804)

Descriptors: *Meteorological data, *Clouds, *Weather data, Pacific Ocean, Satellites(Artificial).
Identifiers: *Meteorological satellites, *Synoptic scale analysis, *Cloud vectors, Geosynchronous satellite data, Rawin observations, Wind data.

Low-cloud motions derived by both manual and computer techniques from geosynchronous satellite data and rawin observations are analyzed in various combinations for a two-part analysis compatability experiment. Since the true air motion is unknown, compatibility rather than absolute accuracy of these three data sets was examined. Two important points were brought out: (1) Increased density and better distribution of wind data provided by geosynchronous satellites control analyses so that severe editing is unnecessary (i.e., good data distribution and density overcome the effect of a few bad data), and (2) the analyses illustrate a shortcoming of these satellite wind data. Since low-cloud vectors are obtained only at the periphery and not within disturbances, the intensity of disturbances is under-estimated. Availability of infrared data from geosynchronous satellites will increase the number of middle- or high-cloud vectors in or near these disturbances. These additional vectors may aid in better depicting the intensity of disturbances. (NOAA)
W75-07424

DROUGHT IN THE SAHARA: A BIOGEOPHYSICAL FEEDBACK MECHANISM,
Massachusetts Inst. of Tech., Cambridge. Dept. of Meteorology.
J. Charney, P. H. Stone, and W. J. Quirk.
Science, Vol 187, No 4175, p 434-435, February 7, 1975. 2 fig, 7 ref.

Descriptors: *Droughts, *Albedo, Rainfall, Subsidence, Climates, Grazing, Biology, Geophysics, Vegetation.
Identifiers: *Sahara, Biosphere.

Two integrations of a global circulation model, differeing only in the prescribed surface albedo in the Sahara, showed that an increase in albedo resulting from a decrease in plant cover caused a decrease in rainfall. Thus any tendency for plant cover to decrease would be reinforced by a decrease in rainfall, and could initiate or perpetuate a drought. The amount of overgrazing was correlated with the droughts in the southern region of the Sahara. Thus a decrease in plant cover may be accompanied by an increase in surface albedo. This would lead to a decrease in the net incoming radiation and an increase in the radiative cooling of the air. As a consequence, the air would sink to maintain thermal equilibrium by adiabatic compression, and cumulus convection and its associated rainfall would be suppressed. (Roberts-ISWS)
W75-07430

A GLOBAL OCEAN-ATMOSPHERE CLIMATE MODEL. PART I. THE ATMOSPHERIC CIRCULATION,
National Oceanic and Atmospheric Administration, Princeton, N.J. Geophysical Fluid Dynamics Lab.
For primary bibliographic entry see Field 2A.
W75-07446

ICE FALLOUT IN CONVECTIVE STORMS,
Commonwealth Scientific and Industrial Research Organization, Aspendale (Australia). Div. of Atmospheric Physics.
For primary bibliographic entry see Field 2C.
W75-07456

THE TOTAL WATER CONTENT OF CLOUDS IN THE SOUTHERN HEMISPHERE,
F. Loewe.
Australian Meteorological Magazine, Vol 22, No 1, p 19-20, March 1974. 3 tab, 1 ref.

Descriptors: *Clouds, *Water balance, *Precipitable water, Atmosphere, Water vapor, Ice, Water, Cloud cover.
Identifiers: *Southern Hemisphere, Cloud thickness, *Water content(Clouds).

Starting from estimates of the precipitable water held in the Southern Hemisphere as given by Newton, an estimate was made of the amount of water substance held as ice and liquid water in clouds. Cloud cover and thickness estimates also came from Newton. The calculations resulted in an estimate of 146 megatons of water substance contained in the clouds over the Southern Hemisphere. This is only 2.7% of the total water vapor content, 5400 megatons, and is considered negligible in large-scale considerations of the atmospheric water balance. (Jones-ISWS)
W75-07457

THE LIFE CYCLE OF VALLEY FOG. PART I: MICROMETEOROLOGICAL CHARACTERISTICS,
Calspan Corp., Buffalo, N.Y.
R. J. Pilie, E. J. Mack, W. C. Kocmond, C. W. Rogers, and W. J. Eadie.
Journal of Applied Meteorology, Vol 14, No 3, p 347-363, April 1975. 18 fig, 2 tab, 20 ref.

Descriptors: *Fog, *Valleys, *Meteorology, Temperature, Dew point, Towers, Winds, Radiation, Dew, Evaporation, Aircraft, Heat transfer, Circulation, Saturation, *New York.
Identifiers: *Ground fog, *Valley fog, Visibility, Divergence, Inversion, *Chemung River Valley(NY).

Extensive measurements were made of micrometeorological variables associated with eleven fogs in the Chemung River Valley near Elmira, New York. Temperature was measured at five levels on a 17 m tower, dew point at three levels, wind speed and direction at two levels, and net radiation and vertical wind at one level. Visibility was measured at three locations, and dew deposition and evaporation at one location near the surface. Vertical temperature distributions were also measured with use of an aircraft. To explain observed temperature behavior (maximum cooling rate near 100 m in the 6 h preceeding fog) and the initial formation of a thin fog layer slightly below that level, it seemed necessary to invoke Defant's model of valley circulation. Radiation divergence at the fog layer aloft then produces an inversion near the fog top and unstable conditions at lower levels. The fog base therefore propagates downward. Dew deposition is responsible for formation of a low-level dew point inversion before fog forms, a necessary condition for initial fog formation aloft. The inversion breaks as fog forms and dew weight is constant from that time until sunrise. Evaporation of dew after sunrise maintains saturation throughout the fog depth as fog temperature increases, and is therefore responsible for fog persistence. (See also W75-07460) (Jones-ISWS)
W75-07459

THE LIFE CYCLE OF VALLEY FOG. PART II: FOG MICROPHYSICS,
Calspan Corp., Buffalo, N.Y.
R. J. Pilie, E. J. Mack, W. C. Kocmond, W. J. Eadie, and C. W. Rogers.
Journal of Applied Meteorology, Vol 14, No 3, p 364-374, April 1975. 13 fig, 1 tab, 7 ref.

Descriptors: *Fog, *Valleys, *Cloud physics, *Meteorology, Haze, Saturation, Supersaturation, Turbulence, Diffusion, Drops(Fluids), Particle size, Nucleation, Clouds, Moisture content, *New York.
Identifiers: *Ground fog, *Valley fog, Visibility, Drop-size distribution, *Chemung River Valley(NY).

Extensive measurements were made of the microphysics of valley fog in the Chemung River Valley near Elmira, New York. Data on drop size distributions, drop concentrations, liquid water contents, and haze and cloud nucleus concentrations obtained on eight fog nights were discussed. Shallow ground fog usually occurs prior to the formation of deep valley fog. The data show that ground fog is characterized by droplet concentrations of 100 to 200 per cu cm in the 1 to 10 micrometer radius range with mean radii of 2 to 4 micrometers. As deep fog forms aloft, droplet concentration near the surface decreases to less than 2 per cu cm and the mean radius increases from 6 to 12 micrometers. Droplets of radii less than 3

micrometers disappear. Droplet concentration and liquid water content increase gradually until the first visibility minimum at the surface when typical values range from 12 to 25 per cu cm and 50 to 150 mg per cu m, respectively. The small droplets reappear at first visibility minimum. Bimodal drop size distributions occur in approximately half of the fogs with one mode at 2-3 micrometer radius and a second mode between 6 and 12 micrometers. Aloft, drop size distributions become narrower and the mean radius decreases with increasing altitude and increasing age of fog. The cloud nucleus concentration active at S = 3% is usually between 800 and 1000 per cu cm near the surface and decreases to 500-800 per cu cm at 300 m. (See also W75-07459) (Jones-ISWS)
W75-07460

A NEW HOT-WIRE LIQUID CLOUD WATER METER,
National Hurricane Research Lab., Coral Gables, Fla.
F. J. Merceret, and T. L. Schricker.
Journal of Applied Meteorology, Vol 14, No 3, p 319-326, April 1975. 5 fig, 10 ref.

Descriptors: *Instrumentation, *Clouds, *Moisture content, Drops(Fluids), Thermal conductivity, Viscosity, Water, Evaporation, Temperature, Electricity, Raindrops, Calibrations, Particle size.
Identifiers: *Hot-wire meter, Vaporization heat.

The National Hurricane Research Laboratory has developed and flight tested a new airborne liquid water meter for cloud physics measurements. The sensor is maintained at constant temperature rather than at constant current, and the operating temperature is held well below the in-situ boiling point. These two changes from previous instruments, such as the popular Johnson-Williams meter, permit accurate response over a wider range of drop sizes and finer spatial resolution. Flight tests on NOAA Research Flight Facility aircraft showed the new unit to be more sensitive, more stable, and more rapidly responding than the J-W and Levine instruments presently on board. (Jones-ISWS)
W75-07461

ESTIMATING EVAPOTRANSPIRATION BY HOMOCLIMATES,
Geological Survey, Lubbock, Tex.
For primary bibliographic entry see Field 2D.
W75-07576

FORMULATING CONVERSION TABLES FOR STICK-MEASURE OF SACRAMENTO PRECIPITATION STORAGE GAGES,
Forest Service (USDA), Fort Collins, Colo. Rocky Mountain Forest and Range Experiment Station.
For primary bibliographic entry see Field 7B.
W75-07654

PROBABILITY OF SEQUENCES OF WET AND DRY DAYS FOR TENNESSEE,
Tennessee Univ., Knoxville. Dept. of Plant and Soil Science.
J. M. Safley, Jr., H. A. Fribourg, J. V. Vaiksnoras, and R. H. Strand.
Available from the National Technical Information Service, U.S. Dept. of Commerce, Springfield, Va 22161. NOAA Technical Memorandum EDS 22, December 1974. 73 p, 1 fig, 67 tab, 8 ref.

Descriptors: *Precipitation(Atmospheric), *Rainfall, *Probability, Climates, *Tennessee, Seasonal.
Identifiers: *Precipitation patterns, Initial probabilities, Transitional probabilities, Seasonal precipitation, Long-term weather observations, Daily forecasts, Frequencies of occurrence.

Probabilities of sequences of wet and dry days can be used in evaluating probable gains or losses related to many activities. Both initial and transitional probabilities can be calculated from past, long-term weather observations. Initial probabilities indicate the likelihood that any day during a week will be dry, without reference to rainfall on previous days. Transition probabilities predict the probability of a day being dry if the previous day was also dry or if the previous day was wet. Tables of these probabilities are presented for sixty-seven locations in Tennessee for five levels of daily precipitation, ranging from 0.01 to 0.50 inch per day. (NOAA)
W75-07721

THE RAINFALL INTERCEPTION PROCESS AND MINERAL CYCLING IN A MONTANE RAIN FOREST IN EASTERN PUERTO RICO,
Puerto Rico Nuclear Center, San Juan. Terrestrial Ecology Program.
For primary bibliographic entry see Field 2K.
W75-07727

A KINEMATIC ANALYSIS OF TROPICAL STORM BASED ON ATS CLOUD MOTIONS,
Chicago Univ., Ill. Dept. of the Geophysical Sciences.
T. T. Fujita, and J. J. Tecson.
SMRP Research Paper No. 125, August 1974. 20 p, 11 fig, 2 tab, 9 ref. SMRP Research Paper No. 125. NOAA Grant 04-3-022-8.

Descriptors: *Hurricanes, *Storm structure, *Tropical cyclones, *Cloud physics, *Wind velocity, Atlantic Ocean, Wind pressure, Air circulation, Weather patterns, Tropical regions, *Remote sensing.
Identifiers: *Applications Technology Satellite(ATS III), *Tropical storm Anna, Cross-equatorial flow, North Hemisphere trades.

The asymmetric structure of an incipient storm in the Atlantic Ocean is determined, using low-cloud velocities computed from the Applications Technology Satellite (ATS III) picture sequences. The investigation concerns the kinematic analysis of tropical storm Anna during July 26, 27, and 28, 1969 when it intensified into tropical storm stage in the vicinity of 10 deg N and 35 deg W, reportedly late on the 27th. The cross-equatorial flow from the southern hemisphere was responsible for providing the inflow to the storm while the northern hemisphere trades supplied the major contribution to the circulation around the storms. The inflow from the southern sector of the disturbance and the over-all circulation increased as the storm intensified. (NOAA)
W75-07824

LAKE ONTARIO BASIN: OVERLAND PRECIPITATION, 1972-73,
National Oceanic and Atmospheric Administration, Ann Arbor, Mich. Great Lakes Environmental Lab.
D. C. Norton.
NOAA Technical Memorandum ERL GLERL-1, March 1975, 18 p.

Descriptors: *Precipitation(Atmospheric), *Precipitation gages, *Lake Ontario, Isohyets, Mapping, Probable maximum precipitation, Rainfall, Sleet, Snowfall, Climatology, Great Lakes.
Identifiers: *Thiessen polygon procedure, Hourly values, Accumulated value.

Daily precipitation values were derived for the United States portion of the Lake Ontario land basin for 1972 and 1973. The daily precipitation values were generated using a Thiessen polygon procedure and National Weather Service station data. Isohyetal maps are provided for 1972 and 1973. (NOAA)
W75-07831

2C. Snow, Ice, and Frost

ENVIRONMENTAL STUDIES OF AN ARCTIC ESTUARINE SYSTEM--FINAL REPORT,
Alaska Univ., College. Marine Science Inst.
For primary bibliographic entry see Field 2L.
W75-07417

POTENTIAL VALUE OF EARTH SATELLITE MEASUREMENTS TO OCEANOGRAPHIC RESEARCH IN THE SOUTHERN OCEAN,
National Environmental Satellite Service Washington, D.C.
E. P. McClain.
NOAA Technical Memorandum NESS 61, January 1975. 18 p, 6 fig, 1 tab, 35 ref, append. NOAA-75021904.

Descriptors: *Oceanographic surveys, *Mapping, *Temperature gradients, *Geodesy, Maps, Microwaves, Equipment, Communication, *Antarctic.
Identifiers: Ice pack concentrations, Satellite observations, Sea-ice, Sea surface temperature, Southern Ocean.

Data from NOAA operational satellites as well as from NASA research and development satellites such as Nimbus and the Earth Resources Technology Satellite (ERTS) have increasing operational and research use in oceanography. Methods are being developed to improve the mapping and monitoring of icepack concentration, character, and condition from satellite observations in the visible, near-infrared, and thermal infrared parts of the spectrum. Techniques also have been developed to map sea-surface temperatures and temperature gradients on regional and hemispheric scales from space. Recently acquired NOAA and ERTS measurements are higher in spectral and spatial resolution than those previously available, and the newest Nimbus carries the first passive microwave imager in space. Examples of some of this newly available data and their applications are presented, future sensor systems are discussed briefly. (NOAA)
W75-07421

SNOW DEPTH AND SNOW EXTENT USING VHRR DATA FROM THE NOAA-2 SATELLITE,
National Environmental Satellite Service, Washington, D.C.
D. F. McGinnis, Jr., J. A. Pritchard, and D. R. Wiesnet.
Available from the National Technical Information Service, Springfield, Va. 22161 NOAA Technical Memorandum NESS 63, February 1975. 10 p, 7 fig, 5 ref. (NOAA-75032701).

Descriptors: Satellites(Artificial), *Snow, Data collections, *Remote sensing, Meteorology, Density, Reflectance, *Regression analysis, Southeast U.S.
Identifiers: *NOAA-2 Environmental Satellite, *Spectral bands, Parabolic regression analysis, *Very high resolution, Radiometer(VHRR), Densitometer, Thermal spectral bands, Visible spectral bands, *Snow depths.

The NOAA-2 environmental satellite provides daily coverage of the Earth in the visible (0.6-0.7 micrometers) and thermal (10.5-12.5 micrometers) spectral bands. The ground resolution of the Very High Resolution Radiometer (VHRR) is 1 km at nadir. This improved resolution in the visible region permits more detailed observation of snow features than was possible with previous operational satellites. A densitometer examination of a visible-band image from Feb. 11, 1973, which shows heavy snow cover in considerable detail over areas extending from Alabama to North Carolina, indicates that, in general, there is direct correlation between increasing brightness and increasing snow depths. Digitized reflectance data from the study area were compared with prestorm

bare-ground digitized reflectance data of Feb. 6, 1973, to determine the relation of snow reflectivity to snow depths. A parabolic regression analysis of greatest satellite brightness versus greatest snow depth for 211 data pairs produced a correlation coefficient of 0.84. (NOAA)
W75-07423

SEASONAL CHANGE OF ANTARCTIC SEA ICE COVER,
Lamont-Doherty Geological Observatory, Palisades, N.Y.
A. L. Gordon, and H. W. Taylor.
Science, Vol 187, No 4174, p 346-347, January 31, 1975. 2 fig, 14 ref.

Descriptors: *Sea ice, *Ice cover, *Ice, *Antarctic, Antarctic Ocean, Winds, *Seasonal, Heat balance.

The winter expansion of the sea ice surrounding Antarctica and the subsequent retreat of the ice in summer may be linked with the wind stress acting on the Southern Ocean in conjunction with the heat exchange in open water regions within the ice fields. Calculations suggested a probability that the curl of the wind stress and the associated Ekman divergence, in conjunction with the heat balance, may account for the immense expansion of the Antarctic sea ice in winter. The rapid decay of the ice in summer would also be related to these factors, when the generation of open water acts as a heat source for the ocean. (Sims-ISWS)
W75-07431

LANDFORM-SOIL-VEGETATION-WATER CHEMISTRY RELATIONSHIPS, WRIGLEY AREA, N.W.T.: I. MORPHOLOGY, CLASSIFICATION, AND SITE DESCRIPTION,
British Columbia Univ., Vancouver. Dept. of Soil Science.
For primary bibliographic entry see Field 2K.
W75-07435

COASTAL BREAKUP IN THE ALASKAN ARCTIC,
Louisiana State Univ., Baton Rouge. Coastal Studies Inst.
A. D. Short, and W. J. Wiseman, Jr.
Geological Society of America Bulletin, Vol 86, No 2, p 199-202, February 1975. 6 fig, 19 ref. ONR Contract N00014-69-A-0211-0005.

Descriptors: *Ice breakup, *Coasts, *Rivers, *Arctic, Sedimentation, Marine geology, On-site investigations, Melting, Deltas, Seashores, Snow, Ice, Beaches, Geomorphology, Beach erosion, Deposition(Sediments), *Alaska.
Identifiers: *Alaskan Arctic Coast.

During observations of breakup along the Alaskan Arctic Coast, river flooding of the frozen nearshore zone, sea ice breakup, and beach thaw were examined. Spring river flooding, generated by earlier inland melt, accompanies arrival of temperatures above 0 C on the coast. The extent of flooding over the nearshore ice is related to total flood discharge and coastal morphology. Along wave-controlled barrier-island coasts, flooding and bed load are confined to lagoons, whereas on fluvial-dominated coasts, floodwater and sediment spread across lobate delta fronts and offshore shoals. During this time, marine influence is minimal as a result of protection afforded by sea ice cover. Sea ice melt continues through summer, and the final coastal sea ice breakup and ice dispersion depend on offshore Ekman transport, breakup of the offshore pack ice, and local bathymetry. The coastal ice breaks up 4 to 8 weeks after initiation of melt. Melt of ice and snow within the beach generates beach collapse and resultant unique arctic beach features, whereas flow of tundra snowmelt across the beach produces micro-fans and micro-deltas. (Sims-ISWS)
W75-07445

ICE FALLOUT IN CONVECTIVE STORMS,
Commonwealth Scientific and Industrial Research Organization, Aspendale (Australia). Div. of Atmospheric Physics.
F. A. Berson.
Australian Meteorological Magazine, Vol 22, No 1, p 1-17, March 1974. 6 fig, 4 tab, 25 ref.

Descriptors: *Clouds, *Ice, *Convection, *Storms, *Australia, Radar, Mass, Cyclones, Satellites(Artificial), Thunderstorms, Graupel, Hail, Dew point, Reflectance, Refractivity, Hydrologic budget, Crystals.
Identifiers: Cumulonimbus, Rayleigh scattering, Echoes, Trajectories, Backscatter, Crystal concentration.

Layer-type 10 cm radar echoes from apparently 'clear air,' extending to large distances ahead of conventive storm clouds were examined for their origin and spatial dimensions. The echoes were attributed to Rayleigh scattering from ice crystals originating in the tops of cumulonimbus and anvil clouds. The quantity of ice in the echo volume was assessed from the measured reflectivity factor with the use of mass-reflectivity relationships deduced from size and concentration of crystals sampled by others in clear air and nonraining clouds. The calculated amount of one to two million tons of ice contained in the average echo volume associated with moderate to severe storms compares favorably with an estimate from considerations of water substance continuity, obtained by applying the convective precipitation model of Kessler. The crystal concentrations in the layer have not yet been established by in situ sampling in the vicinity of storms, but there is indirect evidence for particles in the diameter range 100 to 500 microns to be sufficiently concentrated to play a part in natural seeding of middle level clouds. (Jones-ISWS)
W75-07456

REPORT ON THE CANADIAN ERTS PROGRAM,
Canada Centre for Remote Sensing, Ottawa (Ontario).
For primary bibliographic entry see Field 7C.
W75-07485

ENVIRONMENTAL SURVEYS IN ALASKA BASED UPON ERTS DATA,
Alaska Univ., College.
For primary bibliographic entry see Field 7B.
W75-07486

WATER RESOURCES,
National Aeronautics and Space Administration, Greenbelt, Md. Goddard Space Flight Center.
For primary bibliographic entry see Field 7B.
W75-07494

USE OF TIME-LAPSE PHOTOGRAPHY TO ASSESS POTENTIAL INTERCEPTION IN ARIZONA PONDEROSA PINE,
Arizona Univ., Tucson. Dept. of Watershed Management.
L. C. Tennyson, P. F. Ffolliott, and D. B. Thorud.
Water Resources Bulletin, Vol 10, No 6, p 1246-1254, December, 1974. 3 fig, 16 ref.

Descriptors: Snow, *Snowmelt, *Snow management, *Ponderosa pine trees, *Water yield improvment, Snowcover, Snowpacks, Canopy, Evaporation, Sublimation, *Interception, Streamflow, Wind erosion.
Identifiers: *Time lapse photography.

The behavior of intercepted snow on a stand of uneven-aged ponderosa pine was studied using a super 8 mm time-lapse movie camera to determine the significance of snowfall interception to water yield from this type of forest. A snow load index was developed to estimate interception storage for 2 trees in the field of view for discrete time periods. The rate of snow accumulation was nonlinear with initial storage being rapid, then slowing with time. Most of the intercepted snow eventually reached the snowpack on the ground by snowmelt, snowslide, or wind. Some water was lost by evaporation of meltwater or sublimation of canopy snow, but these losses appeared to be minor. The knowledge of intercepted snow behavior in these areas is prerequisite to formation of water yield improvement programs involved with snow resources. (Mastic-Arizona)
W75-07547

NASA REMOTE SENSING OF SEA ICE IN AIDJEX,
Geological Survey, Tacoma, Wash.
W. J. Campbell.
In: Means of Acquisition and Communication of Ocean Data, Vol 2, Surface, Sub-surface and Upper-air Observations; Proc of WMO Technical Conference, Tokyo, Oct 2-7, 1972: World Meteorological Organization Report No 7, p 56-66, 1973. 13 ref.

Descriptors: *Remote sensing, *Sea ice, *Arctic, Data collections, Ice cover, Heat flow, Aircraft, Satellites(Artificial).
Identifiers: *AIDJEX.

AIDJEX (Arctic Ice Dynamics Joint Experiment) is an international and interdisciplinary study of the sea ice of the Arctic Ocean. The objective of AIDJEX is to reach a fundamental understanding of the dynamics and thermodynamic interaction between the sea ice and its environment. The AIDJEX Committee and Principal Investigators view remote sensing as a necessary and integral part of any investigation of sea ice, and great efforts are being made to utilize all available aircraft and satellite support. (Knapp-USGS)
W75-07564

EXTENDED AERATION SEWAGE TREATMENT IN COLD CLIMATES,
Environmental Protection Agency, College, Alaska. Arctic Environmental Research Lab.
For primary bibliographic entry see Field 5D.
W75-07608

HYDROLOGICAL AND EROSION INFLUENCES OF SHELTERBELTS, (IN RUSSIAN),
For primary bibliographic entry see Field 4D.
W75-07651

2D. Evaporation and Transpiration

A CALCULATION OF SUMMARY EVAPORATION OF AN OBSERVATION OF AN IRRIGATION REGIME OF SALINE SOILS,
Vsesoyuznyi Nauchno-Issledovatelskii Institut Gidrotekhniki i Melioratsii, Moscow (USSR).
S. I. Vanichkina, and E. K. Karimov.
Dokl Vses Ord Lenina Akad S-Kh Nauk Im V I Lenina. 5, p 44-45. 1973.

Descriptors: *Saline soils, *Irrigation practices, *Evaporation, *Cotton, Corn(Field), Soil-water-plant relationships, Heat balance, Moisture availability, Soil water, Moisture uptake.
Identifiers: Summary evaporation.

Methods of calculation of summary evaporation from cotton fields using biological curves of water usage and evaporation from cotton, summary radiation and deficit of air moisture were used. The results were compared with materials of heat-balancing observations of the evaporation during a course of a year. The results of calculations of summary evaporation of corn fields from the biological curves of this culture, from the dependance of summary evaporation on the active

water reserves of the soil and from the relationship of average daily output of water to the vegetation with the yield of green mass of the corn are also included.--Copyright 1974, Biological Abstracts, Inc.
W75-07415

DROUGHT IN THE SAHARA: A BIOGEOPHYSICAL FEEDBACK MECHANISM,
Massachusetts Inst. of Tech., Cambridge. Dept. of Meteorology.
For primary bibliographic entry see Field 2B.
W75-07430

STABLE ISOTOPE FRACTIONATION DUE TO EVAPORATION AND ISOTOPIC EXCHANGE OF FALLING WATERDROPS: APPLICATIONS TO ATMOSPHERIC PROCESSES AND EVAPORATION OF LAKES,
Pennsylvania Univ., Philadelphia. Dept. of Geology.
M. K. Stewart.
Journal of Geophysical Research, Vol 80, No 9, p 1133-1146, March 20, 1975. 13 fig, 7 tab, 31 ref. NSF Grant GA-33860.

Descriptors: *Isotope fractionation, *Isotope studies, *Evaporation, Atmosphere, Vapor pressure, Humidity, Equilibrium, Condensation, Kinetics, Humidity, Deuterium, Ventilation, Drops(Fluids), Lakes.
Identifiers: *Isotope exchange, Kinetic fractionation.

Drops of water were allowed to evaporate or exchange water with surrounding air while being freely suspended on vertical streams of N_2, Ar, or He gas and confined in a uniformly tapered glass tube with relative humidities of 0, 50, and 100%. The purpose was to determine the effects of evaporation and isotopic exchange on the deuterium and oxygen-18 contents of the drops. Equilibrium fractionation was found to exist between a drop and vapor at its surface even during rapid evaporation in zero humidity atmospheres. A kinetic fractionation occurred during diffusive transport of the vapor species (H_2O, HDO, and H_2O18) between the surface of the drop and the free atmosphere. In dry atmospheres the kinetic fractionation was given by D/D prime to the nth power, where D/D prime is the ratio of the diffusion coefficients of H_2O and HDO or H_2O16 and H_2O18 in the particular gas used. The exponent n was found to be in good agreement with the value obtained from studies of evaporation rates of falling drops by previous authors ($n = 0.58$). In moist atmospheres the kinetic fractionation depended also on the relative humidity and isotope composition of the atmospheric vapor. Exchange adjustment times for isotopic equilibration of drops with saturated atmospheres were measured and found to be in agreement with theoretical predictions. Applications of the results to the study of atmospheric processes and isotopic fractionation during evaporation of lakes were discussed. (Roberts-ISWS)
W75-07473

ESTIMATING EVAPOTRANSPIRATION BY HOMOCLIMATES,
Geological Survey, Lubbock, Tex.
T. E. A. Van Hylckama.
Geographical Review, Vol 65, No 1, p 37-48, January 1975. 4 fig, 1 tab, 31 ref.

Descriptors: *Evapotranspiration, *Southwest U.S., *Arid lands, *Climatology, Meteorology.
Identifiers: *Homoclimates.

Climates are often characterized by graphs in which temperature and precipitation or evapotranspiration and precipitation are combined. Stations having similar climatic diagrams are called homoclimes. An example of the applicability of the method of using homoclimates to estimate potential evapotranspiration is taken from the semiarid southwestern United States. Two comparisons are made: one between evapotranspiration rates measured in evapotranspirometers near Buckeye, Arizona, and those computed with microclimatological data available from a homoclimatic area about 50 kilometers to the east, near Tempe, Arizona; the other between rates computed with data from both places. (Knapp-USGS)
W75-07576

HEAT EXCHANGE BETWEEN OCEAN AND ATMOSPHERE IN THE EASTERN NORTH PACIFIC FOR 1961-71,
National Marine Fisheries Service, La Jolla, Calif. Southwest Fisheries Center.
N. E. Clark, L. Eber, R. M. Laurs, J. A. Renner, and J. F. T. Saur.
Available from Superintendent of Documents, U.S. Govt. Printing Office, Washington, DC 20402, as C55.13: NMFS SSRF-682. Technical Report NMFS SSRF-682, December 1974. 108 p.

Descriptors: *Oceanography, *Heat flux, Climate changes, Heat transfer, *Pacific Ocean.
Identifiers: *Heat exchange, *Ocean's thermal structure, *Air-sea interaction, Total heat exchange values, Sensible heat transfer, Incoming solar radiation, Effective back radiation, Fisheries prediction, Heat exchange computations.

Summaries of large-scale heat exchange between ocean and atmosphere in the eastern North Pacific Ocean are presented for the period 1961 through 1971. The summaries are based on computations made from synoptic marine radio weather reports and include (1) monthly values of total heat exchange and departures from a long-term mean; (2) long-term monthly mean values of the total heat exchange, incoming solar radiation, effective back radiation, and evaporative and sensible heat transfer and (3) annual cycles of total heat exchange for selected areas. Outstanding spatial and temporal features of the heat exchange values are discussed. Comparisons are made between the total heat exchange values and those given in two other reports. Discrepancies between values given in this report and those published in the other reports are attributed to differences in the empirical equations used to make the heat exchange computations, differences in data processing techniques, differences in the observed data used in the computations due to different methods of acquisition, and the possibility of ocean climate changes. (NOAA)
W75-07714

2E. Streamflow and Runoff

A GLOBAL OCEAN-ATMOSPHERE CLIMATE MODEL. PART II. THE OCEANIC CIRCULATION,
National Oceanic and Atmospheric Administration, Princeton, N.J. Geophysical Fluid Dynamics Lab.
For primary bibliographic entry see Field 2A.
W75-07447

FLOODS IN AND NEAR THE CHARLOTTE AMALIE AREA, ST. THOMAS, U.S. VIRGIN ISLANDS,
Geological Survey of Puerto Rico, San Juan.
For primary bibliographic entry see Field 7C.
W75-07550

TIME-OF-TRAVEL STUDY, LAKE ERIE-NIAGARA RIVER BASINS,
Geological Survey, Albany, N.Y.
For primary bibliographic entry see Field 5B.
W75-07554

EFFECT OF PORT ORANGE BRIDGE-CAUSEWAY ON FLOW OF HALIFAX RIVER, VOLUSIA COUNTY, FLORIDA,
Geological Survey, Tallahassee, Fla.
For primary bibliographic entry see Field 4C.
W75-07555

COMPUTING BACKWATER AT OPEN CHANNEL CONSTRICTIONS,
Geological Survey, Bay Saint Louis, Miss. Gulf Coast Hydroscience Center.
For primary bibliographic entry see Field 8B.
W75-07558

HYDROLOGIC DATA OF THE HOOSIC RIVER BASIN, MASSACHUSETTS,
Geological Survey, Boston, Mass.
B. P. Hansen, F. B. Gay, and L. G. Toler.
Massachusetts Water Resources Commission, Boston, Hydrologic-Data Report No 15 (U S Geological Survey open-file report), 1974. 33 p, 1 fig, 14 tab, 18 ref.

Descriptors: *Basic data collections, *Surface waters, *Groundwater, *Massachusetts, Hydrologic data, Streamflow, Water quality, Water wells, Springs, Sediment load.
Identifiers: *Hoosic River basin(Mass).

The Hoosic River has its headwaters in northwestern Massachusetts and southern Vermont and flows northwestward through southern Vermont into New York, where it is tributary to the Hudson River. This report contains hydrologic data for that part inside Massachusetts and includes all, or parts of, the towns of Adams, Cheshire, Clarksburg, Dalton, Florida, Hancock, Lanesborough, New Ashford, North Adams, Savoy, Williamstown, and Windsor. Data presented include selected information on wells, test borings, springs, seismic surveys, streamflow records, chemical analyses of surface water and groundwater and of rainfall, and suspended-sediment concentrations of surface water. (Knapp-USGS)
W75-07565

HYDROLOGIC RECORDS FOR LAKE COUNTY, FLORIDA, 1972-73,
Geological Survey, Tallahassee, Fla.
C. P. Laughlin, and D. M. Hughes.
Open-file report FL-74018, 1974. 77 p, 38 fig, 25 tab, 7 ref.

Descriptors: *Basic data collections, *Hydrologic data, *Florida, Groundwater, Surface waters, Lakes, Streamflow, Water levels, Water wells, Water quality.
Identifiers: *Lake County(Fla).

This report contains selected basic data on the water resources of Lake County, Florida and summarized hydrologic conditions during 1972-73. Records of water levels in wells and lakes, and chemical and bacteriological analyses are reported for May 1972 to May 1973. Stream discharge records are reported for October 1, 1971 to September 30, 1972, the 1972 water year. (Knapp-USGS)
W75-07566

EXTENT AND FREQUENCY OF FLOODS ON SCHUYLKILL RIVER NEAR PHOENIXVILLE AND POTTSTOWN, PENNSYLVANIA,
Geological Survey, Harrisburg, Pa.
For primary bibliographic entry see Field 4A.
W75-07567

WATER RESOURCES OF THE CURLEW VALLEY DRAINAGE BASIN, UTAH AND IDAHO,
Geological Survey, Salt Lake City, Utah.
For primary bibliographic entry see Field 4A.
W75-07570

DYE-DISPERSION STUDY ON LAKE CHAMPLAIN, NEAR CROWN POINT, NEW YORK,
Geological Survey, Albany, N.Y.
For primary bibliographic entry see Field 5B.
W75-07571

VELOCITY AND DEPTH MEASUREMENTS FOR USE IN THE DETERMINATION OF REAERATION COEFFICIENTS,
Geological Survey, Trenton, N.J.
J. S. Zogorski, P. W. Anderson, and O. O. Williams.
Open-file report, 1973. 31 p, 6 fig, 3 tab, 29 ref.

Descriptors: *Reaeration, *Streamflow, Velocity, Depth, Discharge(Water), Water quality.
Identifiers: *Reaeration coefficients.

Empirical computation of reaeration coefficients generally requires knowledge of mean velocity and mean depth of a stream. A practical method for obtaining this knowledge is described. The method involves time-of-travel, streamflow, and cross-sectional measurements, the development of discharge-velocity curves, streamflow profiles, and the computation of cross-sectional areas. Values for mean velocity and mean depth are determined and related to mean discharge. (Knapp-USGS)
W75-07572

MAGNITUDE AND FREQUENCY OF FLOODS IN KANSAS--UNREGULATED STREAMS,
Geological Survey, Lawrence, Kans.
For primary bibliographic entry see Field 4A.
W75-07581

EFFECTS OF THE MAY 5-6, 1973, STORM IN THE GREATER DENVER AREA, COLORADO,
Geological Survey, Reston, Va.
W. R. Hansen.
Circular 689, 1973. 20 p, 19 fig, 9 ref.

Descriptors: *Floods, *Colorado, *Rainfall-runoff relationships, *Storm runoff, Urban hydrology, Erosion, Sedimentation, Flood damage, Urban runoff.
Identifiers: *Denver(Colo).

The Greater Denver area, Colorado, has had a long history of intensive rainstorms and infrequent but destructive floods. Rain began falling on the Greater Denver area the evening of Saturday, May 5, 1973, and continued through most of Sunday, May 6. Below about 7,000 feet altitude, the precipitation was mostly rain; above that altitude, it was mostly snow. Although the rate of fall was moderate, at least 4 inches of rain or as much as 4 feet of snow accumulated in some places. Sustained precipitation falling at a moderate rate thoroughly saturated the ground and by midday Sunday sent most of the smaller streams into flood stage. The South Platte River and its major tributaries began to flood by late Sunday evening and early Monday morning. Damage was generally most intense in areas where man had modified the landscape--by channel constrictions, paving, stripping of vegetation and topsoil, and oversteepening of hillslopes. Roads, bridges, culverts, dams, canals, and the like were damaged or destroyed by erosion and sedimentation. Streambanks and structures along them were scoured. Thousands of acres of croplands, pasture, and developed urban lands were coated with mud and sand. Flooding was intensified by inadequate storm sewers, blocked drains, and obstructed drainage courses. Saturation of hillslopes along the Front Range caused rockfalls, landslides, and mudflows as far west as Berthoud Pass. (Knapp-USGS)
W75-07582

WATER-RESOURCES INVESTIGATIONS IN TEXAS, FISCAL YEAR 1975,
Geological Survey, Austin, Tex.
For primary bibliographic entry see Field 7C.
W75-07583

RIVER FORECASTS PROVIDED BY THE NATIONAL WEATHER SERVICE, VOLUME 1, 1972,
National Weather Service, Office of Hydrology. Silver Spring, Md.
For primary bibliographic entry see Field 4A.
W75-07717

THE INITIAL WATER CIRCULATION AND WAVES INDUCED BY AN AIRFLOW,
National Oceanic and Atmospheric Administration, Boulder, Colo. Environmental Research Lab.
W. L. McLeish, and G. E. Putland.
Available from Superintendent of Documents, U.S. Govt Printing Office, Washington DC 20402. Report ERL 316-AOML 16, February 1975. 45 p, 21 fig, 1 tab, 8 ref.

Descriptors: *Air flow, Laminar flow.
Identifiers: *Wind-generated water current, *Water circulation, *Water waves, *Wind-water tunnel, Circulation pattern, Capillary-gravity waves, Capillary waves, Gravity waves, Wave energy, Ocean surface, Air-sea interactions, Mechanisms of transport, Water-velocity profiles.

The early water circulation and waves under an airflow were examined in laboratory experiments. At a particular fetch or time, a waterflow undergoes a laminar-turbulent transition through an intermediate circulation pattern. Simultaneously the first, capillary-gravity waves undergo a correlated characteristic transition leading to separate capillary and gravity waves, and the wave energy increases markedly. Some of the energy of the current is transferred to the waves during the transition. A viscous sublayer lies at the surface above a turbulent flow, but is thinner than a corresponding sublayer at a solid boundary. (NOAA)
W75-07718

THREE DIMENSIONAL TURBULENT DIFFUSION FROM POINT SOURCES OF POLLUTION IN AN OPEN CHANNEL,
Delaware Univ, Newark. Dept. of Chemical Engineering.
For primary bibliographic entry see Field 5B.
W75-07723

HYDROLOGICAL AND PHYSICAL-CHEMICAL INVESTIGATIONS ON THE PO RIVER AT POLESELLA: 2. JULY 1970-JUNE 1973, (IN ITALIAN),
Istituto di Biologia del Mare, Venice (Italy).
For primary bibliographic entry see Field 5B.
W75-07741

HYDROLOGICAL AND PHYSICAL-CHEMICAL INVESTIGATIONS ON THE ADIGE RIVER AT BOARA PISANI: 2. JULY 1970-JUNE 1972, (IN ITALIAN),
Istituto di Biologia del Mare, Venice (Italy).
For primary bibliographic entry see Field 5B.
W75-07742

WATER CURRENT OR TIDE DIRECTION-OF-FLOW INDICATOR,
For primary bibliographic entry see Field 7B.
W75-07823

THE WINDS, CURRENTS AND WAVES AT THE SITE OF THE FLOATING CITY OFF WAIKIKI,
Hawaii Univ., Honolulu. Dept. of Ocean Engineering.
For primary bibliographic entry see Field 4A.
W75-07826

DIGITAL RADAR DATA AND ITS APPLICATION IN FLASH FLOOD FORECASTING,
National Weather Service Forecast Office, Pittsburgh, Pa.
For primary bibliographic entry see Field 4A.
W75-07832

CLIMATOLOGY OF LAKE ERIE STORM SURGES AT BUFFALO AND TOLEDO,
National Weather Service, Silver Spring, Md. Techniques Development Lab.
For primary bibliographic entry see Field 2H.
W75-07834

MAP SHOWING DRAINAGE AREAS, HADDAM QUADRANGLE, CONNECTICUT,
Geological Survey, Hartford, Conn.
For primary bibliographic entry see Field 7C.
W75-07839

MAP SHOWING DRAINAGE AREAS, GUILFORD QUADRANGLE, CONNECTICUT,
Geological Survey, Hartford, Conn.
For primary bibliographic entry see Field 7C.
W75-07840

MAP SHOWING DRAINAGE AREAS, BRANFORD QUADRANGLE, CONNECTICUT,
Geological Survey, Hartford, Conn.
For primary bibliographic entry see Field 7C.
W75-07841

MAP SHOWING DRAINAGE AREAS, NEW-HAVEN-WOODMONT QUADRANGLES, CONNECTICUT,
Geological Survey, Hartford, Conn.
For primary bibliographic entry see Field 7C.
W75-07842

MAP SHOWING DRAINAGE AREAS, NIANTIC QUADRANGLE, CONNECTICUT,
Geological Survey, Hartford, Conn.
For primary bibliographic entry see Field 7C.
W75-07843

MAP SHOWING DRAINAGE AREAS, OLD LYME QUADRANGLE, CONNECTICUT,
Geological Survey, Hartford, Conn.
For primary bibliographic entry see Field 7C.
W75-07844

WATER AVAILABILITY AND GEOLOGY OF WALKER COUNTY, ALABAMA,
Geological Survey, Tuscaloosa, Ala.
For primary bibliographic entry see Field 7C.
W75-07846

2F. Groundwater

FLOW PATTERNS OF RAINWATER THROUGH SLOPING SOIL SURFACE LAYERS AND THE MOVEMENT OF NUTRIENTS BY RUNOFF,
Iowa State Univ., Ames. Dept. of Agronomy.
For primary bibliographic entry see Field 5B.
W75-07395

HYDROLOGY AND GEOCHEMISTRY OF KARST TERRAIN, UPPER LOST RIVER DRAINAGE BASIN, INDIANA,
Indiana Univ., Bloomington. Dept. of Geology.
J. L. Bassett.
Available from the National Technical Information Service, Springfield, Va 22161 as PB-241 714, $5.25 in paper copy, $2.25 in microfiche. MA Thesis, June 1974, 102 p, 30 fig, 6 tab, 40 ref, 4 append. OWRT C-3122(No. 3689)(1).

Descriptors: *Hydrology, *Geochemistry, *Karst hydrology, *Indiana, Areal hydrogeology, Hydrogeology, Streamflow, Watersheds(Basins), Chemistry, Geology, Water chemistry, Carbonate rocks, Karst, Groundwater, Limestones, Sinks, Subsurface drainage.
Identifiers: *Lost River(Ind).

The upper Lost River drainage basin of south-central Indiana has long been regarded as one of the classic karst areas of the United States. Several large sinking streams and two large karst springs are known in the basin. Stream tracing with fluorescent dye proved the existence of two major independent karst drainage systems. The karst springs respond very rapidly to rainfall, and quantitative dye tracing showed that flow velocities as great as 5.5 miles per day exist in subsurface drainage conduits. Waters sampled from the Orangeville Rise have a dominate $CaCO_3$ composition at moderate to high flow rates, but at low flow rates contain appreciable Mg and SO_4. The Ca/Mg molar ratios are inversely related to SO_4 concentration. Waters entering swallow holes along the eastern margin of the sinkhole plain are consistently supersaturated with respect to calcite and have equilibrium CO_2 pressures about an order of magnitude lower than those at the Orangeville Rise. Two principal forms of spring flow recharge occur in the basin: (1) direct and rapid recharge from open swallow holes and (2) diffuse infiltration from the sinkhole plain. (Sims-ISWS)
W75-07398

SURFACE PLUGGING DURING BASIN RECHARGE OF TURBID WATER,
Southwestern Great Plains Research Center, Bushland, Tex.
For primary bibliographic entry see Field 4B.
W75-07439

EARTH RESISTIVITY SURVEYS - A METHOD FOR DEFINING GROUND-WATER CONTAMINATION,
Geraghty and Miller, Port Washington, N.Y.
For primary bibliographic entry see Field 5B.
W75-07440

WATER LEVEL FLUCTUATIONS DUE TO EARTH TIDES IN A WELL PUMPING FROM SLIGHTLY FRACTURED CRYSTALLINE ROCK,
Du Pont de Nemours (E.I.) and Co., Aiken, S.C. Savannah River Lab.
For primary bibliographic entry see Field 5B.
W75-07463

ANALYSIS OF FLOW TO AN EXTENDED FULLY PENETRATING WELL,
Pahlavi Univ., Shiraz (Iran).
For primary bibliographic entry see Field 4B.
W75-07464

NEW EQUATIONS FOR DETERMINING THE FORMATION CONSTANTS OF AN AQUIFER FROM PUMPING TEST DATA,
Sheffield Univ. (England). Dept. of Civil and Structural Engineering.
For primary bibliographic entry see Field 4B.
W75-07465

NUMERICAL ANALYSIS OF VERTICAL WATER MOVEMENT IN A BOUNDED PROFILE,
New South Wales Univ., Kensington (Australia). School of Civil Engineering.
For primary bibliographic entry see Field 2G.
W75-07521

GEOHYDROLOGY OF BACA AND SOUTHERN PROWERS COUNTIES, SOUTHEASTERN COLORADO,
Geological Survey, Denver, Colo.
For primary bibliographic entry see Field 7C.
W75-07551

COASTAL SALINITY RECONNAISSANCE AND MONITORING SYSTEM--SOUTH COAST OF PUERTO RICO,
Geological Survey of Puerto Rico, San Juan.
For primary bibliographic entry see Field 5A.
W75-07553

VIBRATORY COMPACTION IN THE LABORATORY OF GRANULAR MATERIALS IN LONG COLUMNS,
Geological Survey, Reston, Va.
A. I. Johnson, and D. A. Morris.
Reprint of Paper from American Society for Testing Materials Special Technical Publication 523, p 171-181, 1973. 6 fig, 1 tab, 10 ref.

Descriptors: *Porous media, *Laboratory tests, *Compaction, Density, Packed beds, Flow, Specific yield, Groundwater movement, *Drainage.
Identifiers: *Vibratory compaction.

For a laboratory study of the drainage of long columns of porous media, a maximum density, uniformly distributed throughout the column, was required. A mechanical technique was developed for the packing of drainage columns, as much as 60 inches long, with glass beads and natural sands of various particle sizes. A vibratory packer used to pack these columns (1 to 8 inches in diameter) provided good reproducibility of dry unit weight and porosity between duplicate columns as well as a vertical uniformity of these properties within the same or duplicate columns. The standard method of packing columns is based on the effects of time, amplitude, and surcharge weight on the uniformity and reproducibility of results. The technique was standardized at a packing period of 10 seconds and a vibratory amplitude of 0.09 cm. (Knapp-USGS)
W75-07559

GEOHYDROLOGIC CONSIDERATIONS IN THE MANAGEMENT OF RADIOACTIVE WASTE,
Geological Survey, Reston, Va.
For primary bibliographic entry see Field 5B.
W75-07562

HYDROLOGIC DATA OF THE HOOSIC RIVER BASIN, MASSACHUSETTS,
Geological Survey, Boston, Mass.
For primary bibliographic entry see Field 2E.
W75-07565

FIELD TRIP GUIDE BOOK FOR HYDROGEOLOGY OF THE TWIN CITIES ARTESIAN BASIN,
Geological Survey, Denver, Colo.
For primary bibliographic entry see Field 4B.
W75-07573

TECTONIC STRESS DETERMINATIONS, NORTHERN PICEANCE CREEK BASIN, COLORADO,
Geological Survey, Reston, Va.
R. G. Wolff, J. D. Bredehoeft, W. S. Keys, and F. Shuter.
In: Energy Resources of the Piceance Creek basin, Colorado: Guidebook, 25th Field Conference, Rocky Mountain Association of Geologists, Denver, p 193-197, 1974. 6 fig, 1 tab, 15 ref.

Descriptors: *Groundwater basins, *Colorado, *Stress, *Geophysics, Borehole geophysics, Fractures(Geologic).
Identifiers: *Tectonic stress, *Hydraulic fracturing, *Piceance Creek basin(Colo).

A study of the groundwater hydrology of the northern portion of the Piceance Creek basin provided the opportunity to determine the regional state of tectonic stress of the area. Uncased holes were logged with a borehole televiewer to select fracture-free zones. Specially designed equipment permitted the hydraulic fracturing of all preselected zones during one trip into the hole. Fracturing pressures and instantaneous shut-in pressures were used to determine the magnitude of the principal horizontal stresses. Post-fracturing televiewer logging revealed the dip and strike of induced fractures. Comparision of the orientation and magnitude of stresses, as determined from the fracturing and televiewer logging data, agrees well with surface indications of the tectonic state of stress. The approach can be used to obtain meaningful state of stress measurements. (Knapp-USGS)
W75-07574

SIMULATED WATER-LEVEL CHANGES RESULTING FROM PROPOSED CHANGES IN GROUND-WATER PUMPING IN THE HOUSTON, TEXAS, AREA,
Geological Survey, Houston, Tex.
For primary bibliographic entry see Field 7C.
W75-07575

WATER-RESOURCES INVESTIGATIONS IN TEXAS, FISCAL YEAR 1975,
Geological Survey, Austin, Tex.
For primary bibliographic entry see Field 7C.
W75-07583

A SPECIAL PLANNING TECHNIQUE FOR STREAM-AQUIFER SYSTEMS,
Geological Survey, Denver, Colo.
For primary bibliographic entry see Field 2A.
W75-07584

STOCHASTIC MODELING OF GROUNDWATER SYSTEMS,
Massachusetts Inst. of Tech., Cambridge. Dept. of Civil Engineering.
L. W. Gelhar, P. K. Ko, H. H. Kwai, and J. L. Wilson.
Available from the National Technical Information Service, Springfield, Va 22161 as PB-241 740, $9.25 paper copy, $2.25 microfiche. Ralph M. Parsons Laboratory for Water Resources and Hydrodynamics, Report No 189, September 1974. 313 p, 121 fig, 12 tab, 48 ref, 4 append. $5.00. OWRT C-4119(No 9022)(2).

Descriptors: *Groundwater, *Aquifer testing, *Stochastic processes, Surface-groundwater relationships, Aquifers, Mathematical models, Groundwater recharge, *Kansas, Model studies, Estimating, Time series analysis, Analytical techniques.
Identifiers: *Spectral analysis, Aquifer parameters estimation.

Important new research results are developed on the use of spectral analysis techniques to evaluate groundwater resources. The linear theory of aquifer spectral response in the frequency domain is developed, including effects of aquifer slope, vertical flow, and variable transmissivity. Numerical simulations of the nonlinear effects in the spectral domain are developed and show that the nonlinear effects are typically quite small, thus making the simple linear theory applicable for most field situations. Additional features explored are the effects of spatial variability of hydraulic conductivity and the influence of transient flow in the partially saturated zone above the water table. Through spectral analysis in the wave number domain, an error criterion is established for a simple observation network which is used to measure

groundwater flow. The effects of storage in the partially saturated zone on the frequency spectrum of groundwater fluctuations are estimated and found to be negligible in most cases. The theoretical results are applied to evaluate, through spectral analysis, time series of groundwater levels, precipitation and stream stage for a site in Kansas. Using a procedure based on the linear spectral theory, estimates of aquifer transmissivity and storativity are developed. The procedure yields parameter estimates which are in agreement with those obtained from pumping tests. The results should be applicable under specified conditions to the estimation of aquifer parameters from natural fluctuations of groundwater level.
W75-07595

SYSTEM IDENTIFICATION AND MULTI-LEVEL OPTIMIZATION OF INTEGRATED GROUND WATER SYSTEMS,
California Univ., Los Angeles. Dept. of Engineering Systems.
J. A. Dracup.
Available from the National Technical Information Service, Springfield, Va 22161 as PB-241 924, $3.25 paper copy, $2.25 microfiche. Completion Report, February 1974. 3 p, 3 ref. OWRT A-033-CAL(4).

Descriptors: *Optimization, *Conjunctive use, *Surface-ground water relationships, Mathematical models, *Model studies, Forecasting, *Aquifer characteristics, *Optimum development plans, *Groundwater.
Identifiers: System identification, Multi-level optimization.

Conjunctive surface water and ground water systems are analyzed using the techniques of system identification and multi-level optimization. Mathematical models describing the behavior of the ground water regime are developed. Given historic ground water levels and aquifer parameters, transfer functions of the model are determined. Given any input, future responses of the system are predicted. Aquifer characteristics are determined for each subsystem in the first-level optimization. A general model for optimal development and operation of an integrated ground water basin is developed in the second-level optimization.
W75-07722

COOPERATIVE PHENOMENA IN ISOTOPIC HYDRODYNAMIC DISPERSION,
Nevada Univ., Reno. Desert Research Inst.
For primary bibliographic entry see Field 5B.
W75-07725

HYDROGEOLOGICAL MAPS OF THE ALLUVIAL AQUIFER IN AND ADJACENT TO THE ROCKY MOUNTAIN ARSENAL, COLORADO,
Geological Survey, Denver, Colo.
For primary bibliographic entry see Field 7C.
W75-07836

AVAILABILITY OF GROUND WATER IN THE SACO RIVER BASIN, EAST-CENTRAL NEW HAMPSHIRE,
Geological Survey, Concord, N.H.
For primary bibliographic entry see Field 7C.
W75-07837

MAPS OF SAN GORGONIO PASS-UPPER COACHELLA VALLEY AREA, CALIFORNIA, SHOWING WATER-LEVEL CONTOURS, 1936 AND 1966-17,
Geological Survey, Menlo Park, Calif.
For primary bibliographic entry see Field 7C.
W75-07838

GEOLOGIC MAP OF WALKER COUNTY, ALABAMA,
Geological Survey, Tuscaloosa, Ala.
For primary bibliographic entry see Field 7C.
W75-07845

WATER AVAILABILITY AND GEOLOGY OF WALKER COUNTY, ALABAMA,
Geological Survey, Tuscaloosa, Ala.
For primary bibliographic entry see Field 7C.
W75-07846

2G. Water In Soils

EFFECT OF SOIL ENRICHMENT WITH MINERAL ELEMENTS AND FERTILIZERS ON SURFACE WATER AND PLANTS,
Ghent Rijksuniversiteit (Belgium). Faculteit Landbouwwetenschappen.
For primary bibliographic entry see Field 5B.
W75-07368

EFFECTS OF SURFACE MOISTURE SUPPLY ON THE SUBSOIL NUTRITIONAL REQUIREMENTS OF LUCERNE (MEDICAGO SATIVA L.),
Commonwealth Scientific and Industrial Research Organization, Canberra (Australia). Div. of Plant Industry.
J. R. Simpson, and J. Lipsett.
Australian Journal of Agricultural Research, Vol 24, No 2, p 199-209, March 1973. 6 tab, 1 fig, 22 ref.

Descriptors: *Moisture availability, *Subsoil, *Drought tolerance, *Nutrient requirements, *Crop production, *Soil profiles, Phosphorus, Lime, Root distribution, Fertilizers.
Identifiers: Monocalcium phosphate, Sodium borate, Fertilizer placement, *Lucerne(Medicago sativa L.).

Lucerne plants (Medicago sativa L.) were grown in deep (85 cm.) reconstituted profiles of granitic soils under glasshouse conditions. The plants were subjected to controlled degrees of drought in surface layers, while a water table was maintained at 85 cm. depth. The effect of monocalcium phosphate, sodium borate, and calcium carbonate (lime) at a 55 cm. depth was compared with an application to the surface layers, either frequently moistened or dry. Deep placement of monocalcium phosphate increased the phosphorus content and yield of the droughted plants, but the effects were greatly enhanced when the phosphate band was amended with lime and borate. This combination of phosphate, lime and borate was particularly effective because of a marked increase in lateral root proliferation within the amended layer. The results show the importance of subsoil nutritional characteristics in stabilizing lucerne yields over intermittently wet and dry periods. (Mastic-Arizona)
W75-07393

STRUCTURAL PROBLEMS OF INDONESIAN SOILS,
Lembaga Penelitian Tanah, Bogor (Indonesia).
D. Muljadi.
Meded Fac Landbouwwet Rijksuniv Gent. Vol 37, No 3, p 1062-1065, 1972.

Descriptors: Soils, *Soil stabilization, Polymers, *Construction, Erosion control, Moisture intake, Water loss, Sands, Clays.
Identifiers: Andosols, *Indonesia, Volcanic sand.

Suitable soil conditioners or polymers must be found for the improvement of the soil physical conditions of specific problem soils such as: volcanic sand, especially to improve: soil structure, aggregate stability, water holding capacity, and nutrient holding capacity; eroded soils of high clay content (montmorillonite and illite), to improve: aggregate stability, water intake rate, and to reduce erosion and surface runoff; andosol, to improve soil structure and stability of aggregates and to reduce erosion and surface runoff.--Copyright 1974, Biological Abstracts, Inc.
W75-07394

FLOW PATTERNS OF RAINWATER THROUGH SLOPING SOIL SURFACE LAYERS AND THE MOVEMENT OF NUTRIENTS BY RUNOFF,
Iowa State Univ., Ames. Dept. of Agronomy.
For primary bibliographic entry see Field 5B.
W75-07395

SOIL MOISTURE TRANSPORT IN ARID SITE VADOSE ZONES,
Atlantic Richfield Hanford Company, Richland, Wash. Research Dept.
For primary bibliographic entry see Field 5B.
W75-07403

MULTIPLE REGRESSION EQUATIONS ESTIMATING WATER HOLDING CAPACITIES WITH TEXTURAL COMPOSITION AND ORGANIC MATTER OF UPLAND SOILS IN KOREA (IN KOREAN),
Institute of Plant Environment, Suwon (Republic of Korea).
D. Y. Cha, and M. E. Park.
Res Rep Off Rural Dev (Plant Environ) (Suwon). 15. p 29-36, 1973. English summary.

Descriptors: Moisture tension, *Field capacity, *Estimating, Wilting point, *Retention, *Estimating equations, Mathematical studies, *Regression analysis, *Soils, Silt, Water availability, Soil surfaces, Subsoil.
Identifiers: *Korea, Upland soils.

Formulas to estimate the water holding capacity of Korean upland soil are proposed as follows: field moisture capacity % = 7.0922 + (0.2474 x silt %) + (0.3069 x clay %) + (1.1236 x 0.M. (organic matter) %); wilting point moisture % = 2.6687 + (0.0319 x silt %) + (0.3109 x clay %) + (0.4175 0.M. %); available moisture % = 4.5406 + (0.2121 x silt %) - (0.0014 x clay %) + (0.716 0.M. %). The water holding capacity has a positive correlation with silt, clay, and organic matter and a negative correlation with the sand fraction. Silt content greatly influences field moisture capacity and clay also has some effect on wilting point moisture. Surface soils are slightly higher than subsoils in available moisture. With an increase of 1% organic matter, field moisture capacity increases in 0.46-1.74%, wilting point moisture. 0.08-0.73%, available moisture, 0.02-0.26%.--Copyright 1974, Biological Abstracts, Inc.
W75-07406

A CALCULATION OF SUMMARY EVAPORATION OF AN OBSERVATION OF AN IRRIGATION REGIME OF SALINE SOILS,
Vsesoyuznyi Nauchno-Issledovatelskii Institut Gidrotekhniki i Melioratsii, Moscow (USSR).
For primary bibliographic entry see Field 2D.
W75-07415

SOIL WATER HYSTERESIS IN A FIELD SOIL,
Agricultural Research Service, Phoenix, Ariz. Water Conservation Lab.
K. K. Watson, R. J. Reginato, and R. D. Jackson.
Soil Science Society of America Proceedings, Vol 39, No 2, p 242-246, March-April 1975. 5 fig, 11 ref.

Descriptors: *Soil water, *Hysteresis, On-site investigations, *Soil moisture, *Soil physical properties, Soil, Soil tests, Soil investigations, Moisture, Moisture content, Moisture availability, Soil moisture meters, Instrumentation, Soil density, Water pressure, Tensiometers, Bulk density.

Identifiers: *Unsaturated soils, *Undisturbed soil cores.

The requirements for the measurement in the field of the hysteresis characteristics of the soil water pressure (h)-water content (theta) relationship were discussed and details given of the method whereby an undisturbed hexagonal monolith of soil was isolated from the surrounding soil. The instrumentation used in measuring the soil water movement in this monolith, with particular reference to h and theta measurements at points in the soil profile, was described. The shapes of typical theta-time and h-time curves were discussed in relation to possible hysteresis, and the actual h(theta) relationship for soil at the 8- to 9-cm depth was determined. (Prickett-ISWS)
W75-07428

MICROCOMBUSTION METHOD FOR THE DETERMINATION OF CARBON-14-LABELED PESTICIDE RESIDUES IN SOIL,
Agricultural Research Service, Fort Collins, Colo.
For primary bibliographic entry see Field 5A.
W75-07432

LANDFORM-SOIL-VEGETATION-WATER CHEMISTRY RELATIONSHIPS, WRIGLEY AREA, N.W.T.: I. MORPHOLOGY, CLASSIFICATION, AND SITE DESCRIPTION,
British Columbia Univ., Vancouver. Dept. of Soil Science.
For primary bibliographic entry see Field 2K.
W75-07435

EFFECT OF STONES ON THE HYDRAULIC CONDUCTIVITY OF RELATIVELY DRY DESERT SOILS,
California Univ., Riverside. Dept. of Soil Science and Agricultural Engineering.
G. R. Mehuys, L. H. Stolzy, J. Letey, and L. V. Weeks.
Soil Science Society of America Proceedings, Vol 39, No 1, p 37-42, January-February 1975. 8 fig, 4 tab, 13 ref. NSF Subcontract No. 539.

Descriptors: *Soil water, *Soil water movement, *Bulk density, *Hydraulic conductivity, Laboratory tests, Tensiometers, Volumetric analysis, Gravimetric analysis, Deserts, Soils.
Identifiers: *Stony soils, *Soil columns, Matric potential, Thermocouple psychrometers.

The objective was to determine whether moisture transmission properties of stony soils could be evaluated using samples of the same soil in which the stony fraction (greater than 2 mm) had been excluded. Experiments were conducted in the laboratory on soil columns with and without stones. Unsaturated hydraulic conductivity was measured with a transient outflow method over the matric potential range of -0.05 to -50 bars by using tensiometers and soil psychrometers. On a weight basis, the soils studied contained up to 40% stones greater than 2 mm in diameter. If expressed as a function of matric potential, hydraulic conductivity values were similar, with or without stones. Soil water potential as measured by tensiometers or by thermocouple psychrometers was not affected by stones because these instruments respond to moisture changes in the soil portion only. When unsaturated hydraulic conductivity was expressed as a function of volumetric water content, the apparent conductivities were higher for a given water content when stones were present. A simple correction of water contents of stone-free samples, based on the stone volume of each soil, adequately accounted for differences observed when water contents were computed on a total volume basis. (Schicht-ISWS)
W75-07436

SOIL ERODIBILITY AS DETERMINED BY RAINDROP TECHNIQUE,
International Inst. of Tropical Agriculture, Ibadan (Nigeria).
For primary bibliographic entry see Field 2J.
W75-07448

FIELD DETERMINATION OF HYSTERESIS IN SOIL-WATER CHARACTERISTICS,
Universite Scientifique et Medicale de Grenoble (France). Institut de Mecanique.
J. M. Royer, and G. Vachaud.
Soil Science Society of America Proceedings, Vol 39, No 2, p 221-223, March-April 1975. 3 fig, 12 ref.

Descriptors: *Soil water, *Hysteresis, On-site investigations, *Soil moisture, *Soil physical properties, Soils, Soil tests, Soil investigations, Moisture, Moisture content, Moisture availability, Soil moisture meters, Instrumentation, Soil density, Water pressure.
Identifiers: *Soil water suction, *Unsaturated soils.

It is still a common practice to infer field values of soil water content (or of soil water suction) from the measurement of the soil water suction (or the soil water content) and the use of 'representative' soil water characteristics. A series of independent measurements of changes in water content and in soil suction were conducted on two watersheds during one year. It was shown on both sites that hysteresis is too important to be neglected, and that considerable errors will result from the determination of both water content and soil suction with the use of a single sensor. (Prickett-ISWS)
W75-07451

DRYING OF LAYERED SOIL COLUMNS UNDER NONISOTHERMAL CONDITIONS,
Volcani Inst. of Agricultural Research, Bet-Dagan (Israel).
A. Hadas.
Soil Science, Vol 119, No 2, p 143-148, February 1975. 6 fig, 1 tab, 16 ref.

Descriptors: *Soils, *Evaporation, *Soil water, *Laboratory tests, *Diffusivity, Soil profiles, Soil properties, Heat flow, Heterogeneity, Cultivation, Flow.
Identifiers: *Soil columns, Aggregate size classes, Vapor transfer, Nonisothermal conditions.

An experiment was carried out to clarify the effects of steady and fluctuating nonisothermal conditions on evaporation from soil profiles having an aggregated top layer of different thicknesses and aggregate sizes. It was found that there are optimal ranges of aggregate size and depth of the top layer which result in reduced evaporation losses from layered soils. These results differ from theoretical predictions and the discrepancies were discussed and explained. Under fluctuating nonisothermal conditions the water losses were reduced to a larger extent than under steady nonisothermal conditions. These results showed that employing an isothermal diffusion model to nonisothermal evaporation will introduce large errors into the predictions. Furthermore, any evaporation experiment carried out to check or evaluate the process under field conditions, should be carried out under simulated field conditions. It was suggested that to conserve water in the soil profile by tillage operations, the soil should be tilled prior to the introduction of the water into the soil. (Schicht-ISWS)
W75-07452

USE OF AXISYMMETRIC INFILTRATION MODEL AND FIELD DATA TO DETERMINE HYDRAULIC PROPERTIES OF SOILS,
Utah State Univ., Logan. Dept. of Civil Engineering.
R. W. Jeppson, W. J. Rawls, W. R. Hamon, and D. L. Schreiber.
Water Resources Research, Vol 11, No 1, p 127-138, February 1975. 13 fig, 3 tab, 26 ref.

Descriptors: *Soil water movement, *Infiltration, *Soil moisture meters, *Infiltrometers, *Hydraulic conductivity, Simulated rainfall, Field capacity, Pore pressure, Hydrologic properties, Saturated flow, Permeability, *Idaho.
Identifiers: *Reynolds Creek Experimental Watershed(Idaho), Burdine equation.

A numerical model was described for solving axisymmetric infiltration problems. The model uses saturation-capillary pressure data and a modified Burdine equation to develop reasonable estimates of relative hydraulic conductivity. A specially designed infiltrometer and a field data collection system, which provide infiltration capacity, saturation-time, and saturation-capillary pressure data, were also described. The numerical solutions were fitted to the field data to define the hydraulic properties of the soil. Close agreement was found between the numerical model solutions and the field measurements for two sites on the Reynolds Creek Experimental Watershed in southwestern Idaho. A feasible method was developed for determining the hydraulic properties of surface soils under natural conditions. (Gibb-ISWS)
W75-07466

THEORY OF WATER MOVEMENT IN SOILS: 11. CONCLUSION AND DISCUSSION OF SOME RECENT DEVELOPMENTS,
Connecticut Agricultural Experiment Station, New Haven. Dept. of Ecology and Climatology.
J-Y. Parlange.
Soil Science, Vol 119, No 2, p 158-161, February 1975. 1 tab, 15 ref.

Descriptors: *Soils, *Analytical techniques, *Absorption, *Diffusion, *Diffusivity, Moisture content, *Soil water movement, Soil water.

Recent research has extended some of the analytical tools developed in the present series of papers on the theory of water movement in soils. Various corrections were discussed and compared in the case of one-dimensional diffusion. It was shown that the suggestion by Cisler to correct earlier results by simply multiplying by a constant numerical factor was a significant improvement, particularly when the diffusivity does not vary too rapidly with water content. (See also W73-12600, W73-05099, W73-08341, W73-05098, W73-05097, W73-04225, W73-04106, and W72-02728) (Schicht-ISWS)
W75-07482

SEASONAL TRENDS AND VARIABILITY OF SOIL MOISTURE UNDER TEMPERATE PASTURE ON THE NORTHERN TABLELANDS OF NEW SOUTH WALES (AUSTRALIA),
University of New England, Armidale (Australia). Dept. of Agronomy and Soil Science.
R. C. G. Smith, and G. G. Johns.
Australian Journal of Experimental Agriculture and Animal Husbandry, Vol 15, No 73, p 250 - 255, April 1975. 6 fig, 16 ref.

Descriptors: *Water balance, *Model studies, *Moisture availability, *Soil moisture, *Seasonal, *Pastures, Soil-water-plant relationships, Dry seasons, Pasture management, Planting management, Meteorological data, Evaporation, Rainfall, Australia.
Identifiers: Northern Tablelands(N.S.W.).

A water balance model predicting changes in soil moisture at Armidale, New South Wales (Australia) was developed and tested against soil moisture measurements over a two-year period. The model accounted for 96% of the variance in observed soil moisture. It was then used to predict the expected soil moisture pattern using long-term records for daily rainfall and pan evaporation. The predicted seasonal patterns are described, and

their consequences for the establishment of new pasture species and forage crops are discussed. The need for soil moisture data in interpreting the results of field experiments is stressed. (CSIRO)
W75-07520

NUMERICAL ANALYSIS OF VERTICAL WATER MOVEMENT IN A BOUNDED PROFILE,
New South Wales Univ., Kensington (Australia). School of Civil Engineering.
K. K. Watson, and A. A. Curtis.
Australian Journal of Soil Research, Vol 13, No 4, p 1 - 11, April 1975. 10 fig, 13 ref.

Descriptors: *Soil water movement, *Numerical analysis, *Infiltration, *Air, Mathematical studies, Porous media, Drainage, Computer models, Soil profiles, Sands, Unsaturated flow, Darcys law, Equations.

The usual assumption made in soil water studies that the effect of the air phase on the flow process is negligible is discussed in relation to certain profile configurations where such an assumption is not valid. A computer-based numerical solution of the equation describing water movement in an unsaturated soil is then modified by the inclusion of a time-dependent boundary condition, thus allowing the modelling of the air compression effect during infiltration. This analysis also satisfactorily models the drainage along primary draining scanning curves which occurs in the upper part of the profile as the air pressure increases. The analysis is limited to the Darcy flow regime which, for the system considered, terminates when the excess air pressure equals the air entry value of the porous material. Detailed results are presented for a sand and a sandy loam. (CSIRO)
W75-07521

REDISTRIBUTION OF WATER FOLLOWING PRECIPITATION ON PREVIOUSLY DRY SANDY SOILS,
Commonwealth Scientific and Industrial Research Organization, Wembley (Australia). Div. of Land Resources Management.
B. A. Carbon.
Australian Journal of Soil Research, Vol 13, No 4, p 13-19, April 1975. 4 fig, 2 tab, 8 ref.

Descriptors: *Soil water movement, *Sands, *Field capacity, Infiltration, Soil moisture, Diffusion, Moisture tension, Moisture content, Mathematical studies, Laboratory tests, Wetting, Germination, Clovers, Soil-water-plant relationships.

Theoretical and experimental evidence is provided to show that the redistribution of a given amount of water some days after infiltration into a previously dry soil can be predicted, provided that the relationship between soil water potential and soil water content is known. The capillary potential at the wetting front during infiltration into the dry soil is also required. In sandy soils an increase in amount of applied water leads to a decrease in the soil moisture content at the soil surface. This change in 'field capacity' as a function of applied water is shown to strongly influence seedling emergence. (CSIRO)
W75-07522

SIMULATION OF THE WATER BALANCE FOR PLANTS GROWING ON COARSE-TEXTURED SOILS,
Commonwealth Scientific and Industrial Research Organisation, Wembley (Australia). Div. of Land Resources Management.
For primary bibliographic entry see Field 2I.
W75-07523

AN EVALUATION OF THE USE OF WASTE HEAT FOR SOIL WARMING IN THE SOUTHEAST,
North Carolina State Univ., Raleigh. Dept. of Biological and Agricultural Engineering.
For primary bibliographic entry see Field 3C.
W75-07599

DISTRIBUTION AND PERSISTENCE OF 1,2-DIBROMO-3-CHLOROPROPANE IN SOIL AFTER APPLICATION BY INJECTION AND IN IRRIGATION WATER,
California Univ., Davis. Dept. of Nematology.
For primary bibliographic entry see Field 5B.
W75-07609

THE EFFECT OF SLAKED-LIME AND STRAW ON THE SOIL PH IN THE FLOODED AND UPLAND CONDITION (IN KOREAN),
Office of Rural Development, Suwon (Republic of Korea). Crop Experiment Station.
S. B. Ahn, M. H. Lee, and W. K. Oh.
Res Rep Off Rural Dev (Plant Environ) (Suwon). 15. p 67-71, 1973, English summary.

Descriptors: *Soils, *Alkalinity, Soil properties, Soil chemical properties, Lime, Flood plains, Flooding, *Hydrogen ion concentration, Rice.
Identifiers: *Slaked-lime, *Straw, Upland.

Rice straw was applied at 3 levels, 0, 0.3 and 0.6% of soil and slaked-lime at 0, 0.15 and 0.3%. Soil pH was affected by both straw and slaked-lime in the flooded condition, but only slaked-lime affected the soil pH in the upland condition. The following formulas were given: in the flooded condition; pH = 5.5293 + 8.6007x sub 1 + 2.7836x sub 2- 6.7422x sub 1 sup 2-1.8522x sub 2 sup 2 - 7.000x sub 1 x sub 2 and in the upland condition; pH = 5.29 + 0.613x sub 1 - 0.00912x sub 1 sup 2 (x sub 1 = slaked lime, x sup 2 = straw). When basic materials were not supplied and the concentration of CO sub 2 was high, soil pH was affected by (H) sup + ions, but when basic materials were supplied continuously and concentration of CO sub 2 was low, soil pH was affected by (OH) -ions.--Copyright 1974, Biological Abstracts, Inc.
W75-07645

DECREASE OF THE LOSS OF SOIL NUTRIENTS AND RICE HARVEST DURING EARLY PRESOWING FLOODING OF THE RICE FIELD, (IN RUSSIAN),
Akademiya Nauk Kazakhskoi SSR, Alma-Ata. Inst. of Microbiology and Virology.
A. N. Ilyaletdinov, I. Zh. arAstanov, M. K. Kanatchinova, and S. I. Suleimenova.
Izv Akad Nauk Kaz SSR Ser Biol. Vol 6, p 38-44, 1973, Illus.

Descriptors: *Nutrients, Soil microorganisms, *Organic matter, *Rice, Nitrogen.
Identifiers: Anaerobiosis, *Soil nutrients.

The readily soluble organic matter of soil passing into a weakly alkaline extract is decomposed by soil microorganisms within several weeks. In the case of aerobic decomposition of the organic matter of soil the N of readily hydrolyzed compounds (protein) is lost along with the readily soluble C compounds. The losses of gaseous ammonia from calcareous meadow-bog soils are inversely proportional to the degree of saturation of the soil with water, being minimum in flooded soil. Ammonium is lost in noticeable quantities from moderately wet soil. Early flooding, promoting an earlier onset of anaerobiosis and decrease of losses of nutrients from the soils of rice fields, increases the yield of rice.--Copyright 1974, Biological Abstracts, Inc.
W75-07731

Descriptors: --*Lake Ontario, *Circulation, *Hydraulic models, *Numerical analysis, Mathematical studies, Water circulation, Temperature, Heat budget, Mixing, Currents(Water), Lakes, Great Lakes, *Model studies, Mathematical models, *Water temperature.
Identifiers: *Stratified circulations, 1972 International Field Year on Lake Ontario.

Data from the 1972 International Field Year on Lake Ontario were used to test the performance of three-dimensional hydrodynamic models of large lakes. This study is a sequel to a previous report concerning the quasi-homogeneous model simulation of an episode associated with tropical storm Agnes during the latter part of June 1972, and it is concerned with the stratified model simulation of the circulation of Lake Ontario during and after a storm on August 9, 1972. In addition, the temperature predictions and heat content changes for both episodes were discussed. With regard to time scales greater than the inertial period, the water levels and currents computed under stratified conditions agreed with observations to the same extent as under homogeneous conditions. Stratification appeared to exert an appreciable effect on the circulation, but it was difficult to separate baroclinic and barotropic effects because of their interactions. For intermediate time scales, the quality of temperature predictions appeared acceptable with reference to advective heat transports. Longer term mechanisms of thermocline formation, maintenance, and erosion were not considered in view of the proposed use of this model in conjunction with an operational monitoring program. Short-term dynamical effects with the associated phenomena of internal waves were not well simulated in the experiments because of the choice of model parameters. (See also W75-01987) (Jess-ISWS)
W75-07462

THE EFFECTS OF GEOLOGY AND LAND USE ON THE EXPORT OF PHOSPHORUS FROM WATERSHEDS,
Toronto Univ. (Ontario). Dept. of Zoology.
For primary bibliographic entry see Field 5B.
W75-07470

STABLE ISOTOPE FRACTIONATION DUE TO EVAPORATION AND ISOTOPIC EXCHANGE OF FALLING WATERDROPS: APPLICATIONS TO ATMOSPHERIC PROCESSES AND EVAPORATION OF LAKES,
Pennsylvania Univ., Philadelphia. Dept. of Geology.
For primary bibliographic entry see Field 2D.
W75-07473

WAVE-INDUCED NEARSHORE CIRCULATION,
Tetra Tech, Inc., Pasadena, Calif.
For primary bibliographic entry see Field 2L.
W75-07476

AGE DETERMINATION AND YEAR-CLASS FLUCUTATIONS OF CISCO, COREGONUS ALBULA L., IN THE MJOSA HYDROELECTRIC RESERVOIR, NORWAY,
Ministry of Agriculture, Oslo (Norway).
P. Aass.
Rep Inst Freshwater Res Drottningholm. 52p 5-22, 1972, Illus.

Descriptors: *Fish, *Aging(Biological), *Cisco, Herring, Analyses, Europe, Reservoirs.
Identifiers: Coregonus-Albula, Mjosa, Hydroelectric reservoir, *Norway.

The reliability of cisco aging techniques was tested by examining scales and otoliths from 2068 fish caught on the spawning run during the years 1966-71. Disagreements between scale and otolith ages occur at all age levels, but increase markedly beyond otolity age 3+. In nearly all cases of disagreement, otolith age is higher than scale age and the difference may be as great as 7 yr. Age compositions and length-frequency distributions together with tagging results demonstrate that cisco ages can be determined more accurately from otoliths than from scales. Otoliths show that most ciscoes mature at an age of 2+. Fish up to ages 7+--8+ are important for the commercial fishery. The oldest specimens identified were of the age 12+. The recruitment is very uneven. Only every 3rd yr does a rich year class arise. The intervening year classes are insignificant and may fail altogether to appear in the catches. The fluctuations are probably not caused by river regulations or lake impoundments, nor by climatic factors. Intraspecific food competition is probably responsible for the population fluctuations. At the present time there is no need for fishery regulations or artificial stocking of cisco in Mjosa.--Copyright 1974, Biological Abstracts, Inc.
W75-07560

WATER-QUALITY RECONNAISSANCE OF SURFACE INFLOW TO UTAH LAKE,
Geological Survey, Salt Lake City, Utah.
For primary bibliographic entry see Field 5A.
W75-07586

PHOSPHORUS CYCLING IN LAKES,
North Carolina Univ., Chapel Hill. Dept. of Environmental Sciences and Engineering.
For primary bibliographic entry see Field 5B.
W75-07597

FUTURE DREDGING QUANTITIES IN THE GREAT LAKES,
Eastern Michigan Univ., Ypsilanti. Dept. of Geography and Geology.
For primary bibliographic entry see Field 5G.
W75-07603

PHYTOPLANKTON COMPOSITION AND ABUNDANCE IN LAKE ONTARIO DURING IFYGL,
Michigan Univ., Ann Arbor. Great Lake Research Div.
For primary bibliographic entry see Field 5C.
W75-07604

EUTROPHICATION OF SURFACE WATER - LAKE TAHOE'S INDIAN CREEK RESERVOIR,
Lake Tahoe Area Council, South Lake Tahoe, Calif.
For primary bibliographic entry see Field 5C.
W75-07605

EUTROPHICATION OF LAKE TAHOE EMPHASIZING WATER QUALITY,
California Univ., Davis. Inst. of Ecology.
For primary bibliographic entry see Field 5C.
W75-07691

MATHEMATICAL MODELING OF PHYTOPLANKTON IN LAKE ONTARIO I. MODEL DEVELOPMENT AND VERIFICATION,
Manhattan Coll., Bronx. N.Y. Environmental Engineering and Science Program.
For primary bibliographic entry see Field 5C.
W75-07700

ECOLOGICAL STUDIES ON FRY AND JUVENILE OF FISHES AT AQUATIC PLANT AREAS IN A BAY OF LAKE BIWA: III. RELATIONSHIP OF THE FOOD HABITS TO THE HABITAT OF NIGOROBUNA (CARASSIUS CARASSIUS GLANDOCULUS) LARVAE, (IN JAPANESE),
Kanazawa Univ. (Japan). Biology Inst.
K. I. Hirai.
Jap J Ecol, Vol 22, No 2, p 69-93, 1972, Illus. English summary.

Descriptors: *Fry, Fish food organisms, Fish behavior, Larvae, Ecology.
Identifiers: Carassius, Chydorus, Nigorobuna, *Japan(Lake Biwa).

The relationship of the food habits to the habitat of nigorobuna larvae was investigated at Yamanoshita Bay in the south basin of Lake Biwa (Japan) from 1964 to 1968. Quantitative analyses of feeding of larvae were studied for significance of the aquatic plant belt as a habitat of the larvae. Though the larvae are more or less distributed throughout the aquatic plant belt, they are very abundant in the submerged plant belt. The more abundant floating plant materials present, the higher is the density of the larvae. There is a fairly good quantity of plankters available for the nigorobuna larvae in the aquatic plant belt, and their amount increases in relation to that of the floating plant materials. The nigorobuna larvae devoured small crustaceans and chironomid larvae which are commonly found in the aquatic plant belts; they eat Chydorus intensively. The bulk of the gut contents of the larvae increase in relation to plankter density. The food habits of the nigorobuna larvae is discussed in relation to their habitat preference. A submerged plant belt with abundant floating plant materials where numerous small cladocerans flourish is the most favorable site for development of the nigorobuna larvae.--Copyright 1973, Biological Abstracts, Inc.
W75-07729

SEASONAL OCCURRENCE OF SEVERAL GROUPS OF HETEROTROPHIC BACTERIA IN TWO RESERVOIRS,
Caskoslovanska Ademie Ved, Prague. Hydrobiologicka Laborator.
For primary bibliographic entry see Field 5A.
W75-07732

CORRELATION BETWEEN TROPHIC STRUCTURE, SPECIES DIVERSITY AND BIOMASS OF ZOOPLANKTON OF NORTHERN LAKES, (IN RUSSIAN),
Moscow State Univ. (USSR). Faculty of Biology and Soil Science.
A. M. Gilyarov, and T. A. Gorelova.
Zool Zh. Vol 53, No 1, p 25-34, 1974, Illus, English summary.

Descriptors: *Biomass, *Zooplankton, Lakes.
Identifiers: USSR, Species diversity.

The ratio of carnivore biomass to herbivore biomass (Bc/Bh) was used as an index of trophic structure. Species diversity (H) was estimated by the Shannon formula using biomass values. A positive correlation was found between the total biomass (B) and Bc/Bh both by the average data for all lakes and for individual lakes. A negative correlation was found between B and H for individual lakes. Bc/Bh and H are negatively correlated as well. To estimate the correlation between 2 indices and not take into account the 3rd one, coefficients of partial correlation were used. There is no correlation between Bc/Bh and H, the value of B being constant. A correlation between Bc/Bh and B exists, the value of H being constant. All coefficients attain significant values only for communities in sufficiently deep water. The importance of lake depth remains as yet unclear since B and Bc/Bh correlate positively with the depth whereas no correlation is observed between B nd Bc/Bh, the depth being constant.--Copyright 1974, Biological Abstracts, Inc.
W75-07734

FOOD OF WHITE CATFISH, ICTALURUS CATUS (LINN.) (ICTALURIDAE) STOCKED IN FARM PONDS,
University of Agricultural Sciences, Bangalore (India). Dept. of Fish Culture.

K. V. Devaraj.
Int Rev Gesamten Hydrobiol. Vol 59, No 1, p 147-151. 1974.

Descriptors: *Catfishes, *Fish food organisms, *Alabama.

Stomach contents of 124 white catfish, I. catus, ranging from 51-431 mm collected from farm ponds of Auburn University, Auburn, Alabama were examined. Fishes in these ponds were given supplemental food 6 days/wk. Juvenile catfish below 100 mm fed more actively on a variety of food items than larger fish. White catfish measuring 201 mm and above preferred dipterans to other natural food items. In all size groups supplemental feed occupied a dominant position when compared to other food items. Other food items present in the stomachs in varying quantities included detritus, microcrustaceans, trichipterans, fish remains and miscellaneous items, thus indicating the omnivorous feeding of white catfish.--Copyright 1974, Biological Abstracts, Inc.
W75-07737

ENERGY BALANCE AND EXCHANGE IN A LAKE: EXAMPLE OF A MATHEMATICAL ANALYSIS OF LIMNOLOGICAL PROCESSES, (IN GERMAN),
Max-Planck-Institut fuer Limnologie zu Ploen (West Germany).
H. J. Krambeck.
Arch Hydrobiol. Vol 73, No 2, p 137-192. 1974, Illus. English-summary.

Descriptors: *Lakes, *Water temperature, *Energy budget, Limnology, *Mathematical models.

Long term measurements of water temperature at short intervals at several depths of a lake is a powerful tool in solving some limnological problems. They make possible the investigation of the frequency and amplitudes of internal seiches and the evaluation of the exchange constant which is responsible for the transport of dissolved matter in the lake. These studies in connection with measurements of solar radiation and air temperature make possible the construction of a thermal model which describes the physical energy balance of a lake.--Copyright 1974, Biological Abstracts, Inc.
W75-07738

DYNAMICS AND PRODUCTIVITY OF PHYTOPLANKTON AND PELAGIC BACTERIA IN A HIGH MOUNTAIN LAKE (ANTERIOR FINSTERTAL LAKE, AUSTRIA), (IN GERMAN),
Innsbruck Univ. (Austria). Inst. of Zoology.
For primary bibliographic entry see Field 5C.
W75-07745

ROLE OF CRUCIAN CARP IN TRANSMISSION OF ENTERIC PATHOGENS, (IN KOREAN),
Catholic Medical Coll., Seoul (Republic of Korea). Dept. of Preventive Medicine.
For primary bibliographic entry see Field 5B.
W75-07747

LIMNOLOGICAL TRANSPORT AND FOODSTUFF MODELS (IN GERMAN,
For primary bibliographic entry see Field 5C.
W75-07751

MITES ASSOCIATED WITH AQUATIC AND SEMI-AQUATIC DIPTERA FROM SAN MATEO COUNTY, CALIFORNIA (ACARINA: HYGROBATIDAE, UNIONICOLIDAE, PIONIDAE, ASCIDAE AND DIPTERA: CHIRONOMIDAE, TIPULIDAE, PSYCHODIDAE),
San Mateo County Mosquito Abement District, Burlingame, Calif.
R. H. Whitsel, and R. F. Schoeppner.
Proc Entomol Soc Wash. Vol 75, No 1, p 71-77, 1973.

Descriptors: *Diptera, *Mites, Reservoirs, Aquatic insects, *California.
Identifiers: Acarina, Ascidae, Chironomidae, Hygrobatidae, Phaenopsectra-profusa, Pionidae, Psychodidae, Tipulidae, Unionicolidae.

Light trap collections near a reservoir in San Mateo County, California, included many aquatic and semi-aquatic Diptera (Chironomidae, Tipulidae, Psychodidae) with attached mites (Acarina: Hygrobatidae, Unionicolidae, Pionidae, Ascidae). Insects and associated mites, their abundance and some observations on their biology are listed. Weekly tabulation of mite incidence on Phaenopsectra profusa (Townes) is presented--Copyright 1973, Biological Abstracts, Inc.
W75-07755

LAKE ONTARIO BASIN: OVERLAND PRECIPITATION, 1972-73,
National Oceanic and Atmospheric Administration, Ann Arbor, Mich. Great Lakes Environmental Lab.
For primary bibliographic entry see Field 2B.
W75-07831

CLIMATOLOGY OF LAKE ERIE STORM SURGES AT BUFFALO AND TOLEDO,
National Weather Service, Silver Spring, Md. Techniques Development Lab.
N. A. Pore, H. P. Perrotti, and W. S. Richardson.
NOAA Technical Memorandum NWS TDL-54, March 1975. 27 p, 18 fig, 4 tab, 2 ref.

Descriptors: *Storm surge, *Lake Erie, *Storms, Storm water, Damages, Surface waters, Water measurement, Water levels, *New York, Ohio.
Identifiers: *Water surface, *Lake level, *Extratropical storms, Buffalo(NY), Toledo(Ohio).

Extratropical storms frequently cause the water surface of Lake Erie to become distorted with high water in one end of the lake and low water in the other. The abnormal water levels are called storm surges and are defined to be the effect of meteorological disturbance on the lake level. Storm surges can be either positive or negative. The climatological monthly frequencies of storm surges of various heights at the eastern and western ends of Lake Erie are presented. Thirty-three years of lake level data for Buffalo, N.Y. and Toledo, Ohio have been processed. The occurrenees of storm surges greater than two feet, both positive and negative, have been put into classes at half-foot intervals for each month of the year. This information should be useful in determining the probabilities of specific storm surge heights and lake levels in the future. (NOAA)
W75-07834

PEARL RIVER BOATWAY, ROSS BARNETT RESERVOIR TO JACKSON AREA,
Geological Survey, Jackson, Miss.
For primary bibliographic entry see Field 7C.
W75-07847

PEARL RIVER BOATWAY MAP, MORGANTOWN TO SANDY HOOK, COLUMBIA AREA, MISSISSIPPI,
Geological Survey, Jackson, Miss.
For primary bibliographic entry see Field 7C.
W75-07848

PEARL RIVER BOATWAY MAP, MONTICELLO TO MORGANTOWN, MISSISSIPPI,
Geological Survey, Jackson, Miss.
For primary bibliographic entry see Field 7C.
W75-07849

PEARL RIVER BOATWAY MAP, GEORGETOWN TO MONTICELLO, MISSISSIPPI,
Geological Survey, Jackson, Miss.
For primary bibliographic entry see Field 7C.
W75-07850

2I. Water In Plants

LITTORAL DISTRIBUTION AND DRIFT OF SELECTED RIFFLE INSECTS,
Idaho Cooperative Fishery Unit, Moscow.
For primary bibliographic entry see Field 81.
W75-07356

COMPETITIVE INTERACTION OF GRASSES WITH CONTRASTING TEMPERATURE RESPONSES AND WATER STRESS TOLERANCES,
University of New England, Armidale (Australia). Dept. of Agronomy.
For primary bibliographic entry see Field 3F.
W75-07363

SALT TOLERANCE IN THE WILD RELATIVES OF THE CULTIVATED TOMATO: WATER BALANCE AND ABSCISIC ACID IN LYCOPERSICON ESCULENTUM AND L. PERUVIANUM UNDER LOW AND HIGH SALINITY,
Negev Inst. for Arid Zone Research, Beersheba (Israel). Div. of Life Sciences.
For primary bibliographic entry see Field 3C.
W75-07364

PRODUCTIVITY OF VEGETABLE CROPS IN A REGION OF HIGH SOLAR INPUT, I. GROWTH AND DEVELOPMENT OF THE POTATO (SOLANUM TUBEROSUM L.), II. YIELDS AND EFFICIENCIES OF WATER USE AND ENERGY,
Commonwealth Scientific and Industrial Research Organization, Griffith (Australia). Div. of Irrigation Research.
For primary bibliographic entry see Field 3F.
W75-07366

THE BUFFALO GOURD (CUCURBITA FOETIDISSIMA) HBK: A POTENTIAL CROP FOR THE PRODUCTION OF PROTEIN, OIL, AND STARCH ON ARID LANDS,
Arizona Univ., Tucson.
W. P. Bemis, L. C. Curtis, C. W. Weber, J. W. Berry, and J. M. Nelson.
Agriculture Technology for Developing Countries, Technical Series Bulletin No. 15, Office of Agriculture, Technical Assistance Bureau, Agency for International Development, Washington, D.C. January 1975. 20 p, 9 tab, 28 ref.

Descriptors: *Arid lands, *Vegetable crops, *Drought tolerance, *Nutrients, *Proteins, *Water requirements, North America, Plant growth, Plant breeding, Irrigation effects.
Identifiers: *Buffalo gourd, Cucurbita foetidissima.

The world wide food shortage is exacerbated in arid lands because crop production is uncertain because rainfall is uncertain. The feral xerophytic Buffalo gourd, Cucurbita foetidissima, has evolved in the semiarid regions of western North America and is well adapted to desert environments. The plant has abundant yields of seeds rich in edible oil and protein and large carbohydrate reserves in the form of starch in the large storage roots. This wild perennial has the potential of becoming a major food crop in arid regions. Its low water needs constitute an important asset. The Buffalo gourd's history, morphology, genetical and botanical characteristics are reviewed. (Bowden-Arizona)
W75-07371

ALKALOID CONTENT OF ROEMERIA REFRACTA (IN RUSSIAN),
Akademiya Nauk Uzbekskoi SSR, Tashkent. Institut Botaniki.
S. A. Salikhov, and U. A. Akhmedov.
Uzb Biol Zh. Vol 17, No 3, p 34-36, 1973.

Descriptors: *Plant morphology, Semiarid climates, *Desert plants.
Identifiers: *Alkaloid content(Plants), *Romeria-refracta, USSR, Semideserts.

Plants grown under semidesert conditions contain a greater quantity of alkaloids than plants from irrigated areas. Their maximum content was found in plants growing in lower foothills at a height of 600-800 m above sea level and the minimum at a height of 1100-1200 m. A clear-cut relation between accumulation of alkaloids and slope exposure was not established, but apparently southwestern slopes are the most favorable.--Copyright 1974, Biological Abstracts, Inc.
W75-07454

UTILITY OF ERTS FOR MONITORING THE BREEDING HABIT OF MIGRATORY WATERFOWL,
Environmental Research Inst. of Michigan, Ann Arbor.
For primary bibliographic entry see Field 7B.
W75-07492

REDISTRIBUTION OF WATER FOLLOWING PRECIPITATION ON PREVIOUSLY DRY SANDY SOILS,
Commonwealth Scientific and Industrial Research Organization, Wembley (Australia). Div. of Land Resources Management.
For primary bibliographic entry see Field 2G.
W75-07522

SIMULATION OF THE WATER BALANCE FOR PLANTS GROWING ON COARSE-TEXTURED SOILS,
Commonwealth Scientific and Industrial Research Organisation, Wembley (Australia). Div. of Land Resources Management.
B. A. Carbon, and K. A. Galbraith.
Australian Journal of Soil Research, Vol 13, No 4, p 21-31, April 1975. 4 fig, 4 tab, 15 ref.

Descriptors: *Computer models, *Water balance, *Soil-water-plant relationships, Computer programs, Simulation analysis, Interception, Infiltration, Soil water movement, Evaporation, Meteorological data, Drainage, Water storage, Throughfall, Sands, Simulation analysis.

A computer simulation model for the water balance of plants growing on a coarse soil is described, in which the flux of water between atmosphere, plant and soil compartments is determined by a rate-limiting process. The inputs required by the program are measurable physical parameters, and wherever possible calculations are performed according to established physical principles; no mathematical optimisation procedures are used. Subroutines are included for interception (optional); throughfall (added directly to the first soil compartment); redistribution between soil compartments; and evaporation. As most field meteorological data are not available on a better than daily basis, simulation is performed on a daily time scale. From tests showing close agreement between simulated and observed results, it is suggested that evaporation, soil water storage and deep drainage may be satisfactorily predicted. (CSIRO)
W75-07523

THE COMPARED BIOLOGY OF CERCOSPORIOSIS AND HELMINTHOSPORIOSIS IN GUINEA GRASS (PANICUM MAXIMUM), (IN FRENCH),
Centre de Recherches Agronomiques des Antilles et de la Guyane, Petit Bourg (Guadeloupe).
P. Pauvert, and G. Jacqua.
Ann Phytopathol. Vol 4, No 3, p 245-256. 1972, Illus, (English summary).

Descriptors: *Plant diseases, *Parasitism, Humidity, Environmental effects, Rain, Wind, *Grasses.
Identifiers: Cercospora-Fusimaculans, Cercosporiosis, Helminthosporiosis, Helminthosporium-Spp, Panicum-Maximum.

Two diseases of P. maximum are described: helminthosporiosis caused by several undetermined Helminthosporium spp. and cercosporiosis caused by Cercospora fusimaculans Atk. A comparative study of their epidemiology was done. The 2 parasites can sporulate on dead leaves where they live saprophytically. Sporulation does not occur without high humidity. Both are wind and rain dispersed, but wind dispersal is not effective for C. fusimaculans because of the poor preservation of spores at the low humidity which prevails for dissemination. Helminthosporium spores are highly resistant to desiccation and can travel far without alteration of their viability. Spash dissemination is effective for C. fusimaculans. Rainfalls over 2 mm exhaust Helminthosporium fructification, and washing of contaminated leaves occurs. Free water is necessary for spore germination of Cercospora, not for Helminthosporium. Symptoms of Helminthosporiosis may appear 12 hr after pollution, 7 days for C. fusimaculans. Under the climate of the West Indies helminthosporiosis is a more important disease than cercosporiosis.--Copyright 1974, Biological Abstracts, Inc.
W75-07552

FLUCTUATIONS OF AQUATIC AND TERRESTRIAL INVERTEBRATES IN DRIFT SAMPLES FROM CONVICT CREEK, CALIFORNIA,
Missouri Univ., Columbia. School of Forestry.
T. M. Hinckley, and H. D. Kennedy.
Northwest Sci. Vol 46, No 4, p 270-276. 1972, Illus.

Descriptors: *California, *Insects, *Aquatic insects, *Mayflies, Diurnal, Ponds.
Identifiers: Chironomids, Terrestrial insects, Crane flies, *Diurnal drift patterns, Riffles, Convict Creek(Calif).

The experimental stream sections at the Sierra Nevada Aquatic Research Laboratory, Bishop, California, were used for a study of the diurnal drift patterns of aquatic and terrestrial insects in both patterns of aquatic and terrestrial insects in both a riffle and a pool. Observations were made of changes of drift abundance and type by artificially altering the water flow and velocity through these areas. A peak in aquatic drift organisms occurred around sunset. Mayflies were the dominant aquatic organisms while chironomids and crane flies were the most common terrestrial ones.--Copyright 1974, Biological Abstracts, Inc.
W75-07563

THREE TYPES OF REMOTE-READING DENDROGRAPHS,
Geological Survey, Reston, Va.
For primary bibliographic entry see Field 7B.
W75-07577

THE EFFECT OF MOISTURE DEFICIT ON CARBOHYDRATE METABOLISM OF DESERT PLANTS,
Akademiya Nauk Uzbekskoi SSR, Tashkent. Institut Botaniki.
I. L. Zakhar'Yants, N. P. Oshanina, and B. S. Sabirov.
Uzb Biol Zh, Vol 16, No 6, p 32-35. 1972.

Descriptors: *Soil moisture, Plant physiology, Carbohydrates, Arid climates, Arid lands, *Desert plants, Metabolism.
Identifiers: Artemisia-diffusa, Haloxylon-aphyllum, Haloxylon-persicum, Kochia-prostrata, Pectin, Salsola-orientalis, Sucrose.

Under the influence of low soil moisture (20% of the full soil moisture) an increase in the carbohydrate retention was noted in the leaves of 6 taxa studied: Kochia prostrata var. villosissima Bong. et May., K. prostrata var. virescens Fenzl, Salsola orientalis S. G. Gmel., Haloxylon aphyllum (Minkw.), H. persicum Bge. and Artemisia diffusa H. Krasch. A higher carbohydrate retention was caused by an accumulation of components as sucrose, hemicellulose and pectin.--Copyright 1974, Biological Abstracts, Inc.
W75-07602

TAXONOMY AND ECOLOGY OF STENONEMA MAYFILES (HEPTAGENIIDAE:EPHEMEROPTERA),
National Environmental Research Center, Cincinnati, Ohio.
For primary bibliographic entry see Field 5C.
W75-07694

REPRODUCTION AND DEVELOPMENT OF THE BAIKAL WHITEFISH COREGONUS LAVARETUS BAICALENSIS DYB. IN CONNECTION WITH THE PROBLEM OF ITS ARTIFICIAL BREEDING, (IN RUSSIAN),
For primary bibliographic entry see Field 8I.
W75-07711

PLANT-WATER-USE EFFICIENCY WITH GROWTH REGULATORS AND TRANSPIRATION SUPPRESSANTS,
Delaware Univ., Newark. Dept. of Plant Science.
For primary bibliographic entry see Field 3C.
W75-07724

MEASUREMENT AND CONTROL OF WATER POTENTIAL IN A SOIL-PLANT SYSTEM,
New Hampshire Univ., Durham. Inst. of Natural and Environmental Resources.
G. W. Gee, W. Liu, H. Olvang, and B. E. Janes.
Soil Sci, Vol 115, No 5, p 336-342. 1973.

Descriptors: *Soil water, Soil moisture, *Root zone, Soil-water-plant relationships.
Identifiers: Polyethylene glycol, *Pepper plant.

Water potential gradients were measured in soil-grown pepper plants. In one test where plants were equilibrated at low water potentials, the root zone water potential agreed well with water potential measurements in the plant stem and plant leaves. On the other hand it was found that the water potential in root-free soil adjecent to the root zone was higher than that in the root zone and that the observed gradient increased with decreasing root zone water potential. This increased gradient was attributed to decreased soil water conductivity in the root-free soil and to increased flow resistance across a millipore membrane separating the root-free soil and the root zone. In another test the total water potential in the root zone was controlled at 3 different levels by adding polyethylene glycol solution directly to the root zone. In this test the water potentials and water potential gradients responded in a reasonable fashion to the applied osmotic stress indication that control of water potentials in soil-plant systems is possible with polyethylene glycol.--Copyright 1974, Biological Abstracts, Inc.
W75-07730

PERFORMANCE OF FLOOD-RESISTANT AND DEEP-WATER RICE IN RELATION TO GROWTH AND YIELD UNDER DIFFERENT CULTURAL PRACTICES,
Rice Research Station, Chinsura (India).

S. K. Datta, and B. Banerji.
Indian J Agric Sci. Vol 42, No 8, p 664-670, 1972, Illus.

Descriptors: *Rice, *Crop production, Soil moisture, Growth rates.
Identifiers: *India.

Three cultivars of rice (Oryza sativa L.)--2 deep-water types, viz. 'Baku' and 'Kalakhersail,' and a flood-resistant type, 'FR 43B'--were studied under deep-water and usual field conditions. The deep-water cultivars showed a significantly better performance for growth habit (plant height, stem length, number of internodes, number of nodal tillers, etc.) and yield attributes (panicle number and length, grains/panicle, grain and straw) under deep-water conditions than under usual field conditions, showing their distinct water-tolerant nature. The flood-tolerant cultivar showed better results under field conditions in most of the characters (number of main tillers, number of panicles, grain and straw yields). The deep-water cultivars can be cultivated in the low-lying areas likely to be under prolonged submergence. Nodal tillers contributed considerably to the production of grain and straw. Most of the nodal tillers arose from some specific active nodes (viz. 7th, 8th and 9th); their formation depended upon the level of water.--Copyright 1973, Biological Abstracts, Inc.
W75-07752

ESTIMATES OF ABUNDANCE OF FISHES IN THE OLSAVA CREEK, WITH RESPECT TO A LONG WINTER,
Ceskoslovenska Akademie Ved, Brno. Ustav pro Vyskum Obratlovcu.
J. Libosvarsky, and E. Wohlgemuth.
Zool Listy. Vol 22, No 1, p 78-83. 1973.

Descriptors: Fish population, Biomass, Environmental effects, Seasonal, Fisheries management.
Identifiers: *Czechoslovakia(Olsova Creek), Godio-Gobio, Leuciscus-cephalus, Noemacheilus-barbatulus, Phoxinus-phoxinus.

The size and species composition of the fish stock was investigated by successive removal of fish from 4 sections of the stream (in Czechoslovakia) by electro-fishing gear. The reliability of the data obtained was examined by computing coefficients of variation of both parameters of the method - the probability of capture and the estimate. The assumption of equal probability of capture of fish of different weight was charged with a systematic error. Thirteen species of fishes were captured: the total biomass varied between 23 and 1180 kg/ha; the numbers varied between 2.3 and 26.2 thousand fish/ha. Leuciscus cephalus, Noemacheilus barbatulus, Gobio gobio and Phoxinus phoxinus were aboundant by both weight and number. Following the long winter of 1961-1962, the number of fishes especially N. barbatulus and G. gobio decreased rapidly. The causes of the decrease are discussed. The zonation of the fishes is examined in the light of Huet's 'Regle des pentes.'--Copyright 1974, Biological Abstracts, Inc.
W75-07791

2J. Erosion and Sedimentation

NUTRIENT AND SEDIMENT PRODUCTION FROM FORESTED WATERSHEDS,
Nevada Agricultural Experiment Station, Reno.
For primary bibliographic entry see Field 5B.
W75-07353

SOME USES OF SOIL STABILIZERS IN THE USA,
Agricultural Research Service, Ames, Iowa. Soil and Water Conservation Research Div.
W. C. Moldenhauer, and D. M. Gabriels.
Meded Fac Landbouwwet Rijksuniv Gent. Vol 37, No 3, p 1076-1085, 1972.

Descriptors: *Soil stabilization, *Erosion control, Asphalt, United States, *Alcohols, Road construction, Construction.
Identifiers: Polyethylene film, *Polyvinyl alcohol, Straw.

Stabilizers are now being used particularly in highway and other construction projects where costs are less of a factor. Asphalt has some advantages over straw and polyethylene film for erosion prevention in such circumstances with respect to labor costs. Polyvinyl alcohol is very effective for controlling soil erosion in the field but has 1 disadvantage. It is only very slightly soluble so that the dry form is almost unusable. Dissolving and sealing the solution near the area of application may be feasible if the area is large enough. At the present costs of conditioners for erosion control are within acceptable range for highway, building, and military uses. For partial coverage of the soil surface on high-value crops their use is also economic. At the present application rates deemed necessary they are still far out of range for large-scale agriculture.--Copyright 1974, Biological Abstracts, Inc.
W75-07374

STRUCTURAL PROBLEMS OF INDONESIAN SOILS,
Lembaga Penelitian Tanah, Bogor (Indonesia).
For primary bibliographic entry see Field 2G.
W75-07394

AMOUNTS AND HYDROLYSIS OF PYROPHOSPHATE AND TRIPOLYPHOSPHATE IN SEDIMENTS,
Missouri Univ., Columbia. Dept. of Agronomy.
For primary bibliographic entry see Field 5A.
W75-07399

RECONNAISSANCE OF BOTTOM SEDIMENTS ON THE INNER AND CENTRAL NEW JERSEY SHELF (MESA DATA REPORT),
National Oceanic and Atmospheric Administration, Boulder, Colo. Marine Ecosystems Analysis Program.
For primary bibliographic entry see Field 2L.
W75-07425

DETERMINATION OF SAND ROUGHNESS FOR FIXED BEDS,
Queen's Univ., Kingston (Ontario). Dept. of Civil Engineering.
For primary bibliographic entry see Field 8B.
W75-07434

SOIL ERODIBILITY AS DETERMINED BY RAINDROP TECHNIQUE,
International Inst. of Tropical Agriculture, Ibadan (Nigeria).
E. Bruce-Okine, and R. Lal.
Soil Science, Vol 119, No 2, p 149-157, February 1975. 5 fig, 5 tab, 24 ref.

Descriptors: *Erosion rates, *Raindrops, *Soil moisture, *Africa, Tropic, Clay minerals, Clay loam, Sands, Rating curves, Soil texture, Water temperature, *Soil erosion.
Identifiers: *Raindrop technique, *Nigeria, Raindrop energy, Ped size, Soil moisture potential.

Aggregates of two tropical soils from western Nigeria were used to investigate the possibility of using the raindrop technique to determine the soil erodibility index as compared with soil behavior towards erosion under natural field conditions. Aggregate size, initial soil moisture potential, and raindrop temperature were tested for their effect on structural stability of the soils. High soil moisture potential (more negative) significantly increased the erodibility of a clayey soil containing expanding lattice clay minerals. The erodibility index of a sandy clay loam soil containing kaolinitic clay minerals and amorphous iron and aluminum oxides was slightly decreased when at high moisture potential. The increase in water temperature increased the erodibility of both soils. Erodibility was found to vary directly with sand and inversely with clay content. A routine laboratory method of evaluating the erodibility of a soil with a rating curve was proposed. (Lee-ISWS)
W75-07448

HUMIC MATTER IN NATURAL WATERS AND SEDIMENTS,
Fisheries Research Board of Canada, Winnipeg (Manitoba). Freshwater Inst.
For primary bibliographic entry see Field 5B.
W75-07453

SUSPENDED MARINE CLAY MINERAL IDENTIFICATION BY SCANNING ELECTRON MICROSCOPY AND ENERGY-DISPERSIVE X-RAY ANALYSIS,
Texas A and M Univ., College Station. Dept. of Oceanography.
N. J. Bassin.
Limnology and Oceanography, Vol 20, No 1, p 133-137, January 1975. 5 fig, 2 tab, 9 ref.

Descriptors: *Clays, *Electron microscopy, *X-ray analysis, *Suspended solids, *Marine geology, Analytical techniques, Clay minerals, Inorganic compounds, Mineralogy, Particle size, Silts, Water quality, X-ray diffraction, Microscopy, Non-destructive tests, Geomorphology.
Identifiers: *Caribbean Sea.

A technique enabling qualitative identification of clay mineral species commonly found in marine environments, on a particle-by-particle basis, permits electron microscopic and X-ray analysis examination of specific clay particles, without affecting either their morphology or association, on membrane ultrafilters containing as little as 0.2 mg of particulate matter. (Henley-ISWS)
W75-07472

GULLY EROSION, NORTHWESTERN COLORADO: A THRESHOLD PHENOMENON,
Texas Univ. at Austin. Dept. of Geological Sciences.
P. C. Patton, and S. A. Schumm.
Geology, Vol 3, No 2, p 88-90, February 1975. 2 fig, 7 ref.

Descriptors: *Gully erosion, *Sedimentation, *Geomorphology, Gullies, Erosion, Soil erosion, Valleys, Sediments, Alluvial fans, Arid lands, *Colorado.
Identifiers: *Discontinuous gullies, Piceance Creek(Colo), Yellow Creek(Colo).

The widespread occurrence of discontinuous gullies in the oil-shale region of northwestern Colorado is of particular concern because of the resulting progressive destruction of the valley floors. Furthermore, the integration of a semi-arid drainage network can cause a rapid increase in the sediment yield of the basin, with subsequent harmful effects downstream. Field work in the Piceance Creek and Yellow Creek drainage basins indicates that these discontinuous gullies developed on oversteepened segments of the valley floors. Although the critical slope of entrenchment is probably related to magnitude of runoff, discharge measurements are not available; therefore, drainage-basin area was selected as the most representative measure of discharge. An inverse relation between drainage-basin area and critical slope of entrenchment applies, and the lower limit of scatter of the data establishes a critical slope-area relation, which can be used to identify potentially unstably valley floors. This relation can help the land manager determine areas of instability where preventive measures can most economically and successfully be undertaken. It was stressed that this particular quantitative relation is

applicable only to the Piceance Creek and Yellow Creek drainage basins. In more heterogeneous basins, other variables will need to be included in the analysis; however, the general theory of valley stability will remain applicable. (Sims-ISWS)
W75-07477

BOTTOM CURRENT MEASUREMENTS IN THE LABRADOR SEA,
Lamont-Doherty Geological Observatory, Palisades, N.Y.
For primary bibliographic entry see Field 2L.
W75-07478

SEDIMENT IN IRRIGATION AND DRAINAGE WATERS AND SEDIMENT INPUTS AND OUTPUTS FOR TWO LARGE TRACTS IN SOUTHERN IDAHO,
Agricultural Research Service, Kimberly, Idaho. Snake River Conservation Research Center.
For primary bibliographic entry see Field 5G.
W75-07546

SOME SEDIMENT ASPECTS OF TROPICAL STORM AGNES,
Geological Survey, Reston, Va.
H. P. Guy, and T. L. Clayton.
ASCE Proceedings, Journal of the Hydroulics Division, Vol 99, No HY9, p 1653-1658, September 1973. 4 fig, 2 tab.

Descriptors: *Sediment yield, *Hurricanes, *Peak discharge, *Floods, *Virginia, Sedimentation, Erosion, Rainfall-runoff relationships, Storm runoff, Urban hydrology.
Identifiers: *Stave Run(Va).

Storms of unusual magnitude are of interest to scientists, engineers, governments, and certainly no less to the general populace. In June, 1972, tropical storm Agnes resulted in a large amount of rainfall over an unusually large area. This note documents the runoff and sediment aspects of this storm on the drainage basin of Stave Run at Reston, Va., on which a substantial part of the national headquarters building of the U.S. Geological Survey is located. Agnes caused an unusual amount of runoff and sediment to be conveyed by Stave Run, even though the peak intensity of runoff was relatively low. The low runoff intensity resulted from the relatively low precipitation intensity for small drainage areas. Of the 492 tons of sediment transported by the streamflow from the basin, 94% was silt-and-clay-sized particles. A computed 961 tons of sediment was eroded in the basin, of which 469 tons was deposited. The deposited material was estimated to contain an insignificant amount of clay, 43% silt-sized particles, 45% sand, and 12% gravel. (Knapp-USGS)
W75-07557

EFFECTS OF THE MAY 5-6, 1973, STORM IN THE GREATER DENVER AREA, COLORADO,
Geological Survey, Reston, Va.
For primary bibliographic entry see Field 2E.
W75-07582

A DIVER-OPERATED DREDGE FOR COLLECTING QUANTITATIVE BENTHIC SAMPLES IN SOFT SEDIMENTS,
Rice Univ., Houston, Tex.
A. A. Ekdale, and J. E. Warme.
J Paleontol, Vol 47, No 6 p 1119-1121, 1973. Illus.

Descriptors: *Sampling, Analytical techniques, Benthos, *Dredging, *Bottom sampling, Sediments.
Identifiers: Water-lift suction dredge.

A diver-operated water-lift suction dredge allows an investigator to collect underwater samples directly, maintain uniform samples size in soft sediments and overcome problems of shoveling or scooping underwater.--Copyright 1974, Biological Abstracts, Inc.
W75-07614

A MODEL FOR PREDICTING EROSION AND SEDIMENT YIELD FROM SECONDARY FOREST ROAD CONSTRUCTION,
Forest Service (USDA), Fort Collins, Colo. Rocky Mountain Forest and Range Experiment Station.
For primary bibliographic entry see Field 4C.
W75-07653

SEDIMENT AND EROSION CONTROL DESIGN CRITERIA,
Maryland Dept. of Natural Resources, Annapolis. Water Resources Administration.
For primary bibliographic entry see Field 4D.
W75-07672

PROCESS DESIGN MANUAL FOR SUSPENDED SOLIDS REMOVAL.
Hazen and Sawyer, New York.
For primary bibliographic entry see Field 5D.
W75-07712

BEACH FORMS AND COASTAL PROCESSES,
Columbia Univ., New York. Teachers Coll.
For primary bibliographic entry see Field 2L.
W75-07715

STUDIES ON SOIL EROSION CONTROL: 4. THE HYDRAULIC STUDIES OF WATER FLOW IN SLOPED LAND (IN JAPANESE),
Obihiro Zootechnical Univ. (Japan). Lab. of Agricultural and Civil Engineering.
For primary bibliographic entry see Field 4A.
W75-07756

BEACH EROSION CONTROL IMPROVEMENTS, WAIKIKI BEACH, OAHU, HAWAII (KAPAHULU STORM DRAIN TO THE ELKS CLUB) (FINAL ENVIRONMENTAL IMPACT STATEMENT),
Corps of Engineers, Honolulu, Hawaii. Pacific Ocean Div.
For primary bibliographic entry see Field 8A.
W75-07780

DOES CANOEING INCREASE STREAMBANK EROSION,
Forest Service (USDA), St. Paul, Minn. North Central Forest Experiment Station.
E. A. Hansen.
North Central Forest Experiment Station, Research Note NC-186, 1975, 4 p, 3 fig, 1 tab, 6 ref.

Descriptors: *Bank stabilization, Stream erosion, *Stream improvement, Vegetation establishment, Boating, Camping, Recreation, *Michigan, Bank erosion.
Identifiers: *Streambank erosion, *Canoeing.

An increase in canoeists from 13,000 in 1966 to 64,000 in 1973 has not measurably accelerated streambank erosion. During this period as many streambanks healed naturally as there were new points of erosion. Many other banks were revegetating naturally. Most erosion was considered natural but people sliding and camping on the banks caused some erosion. To minimize streambank erosion, management efforts should be directed towards restricting streambank traffic and use rather than canoeing per se. (Forest Service)
W75-07792

FLUORIDE: GEOCHEMICAL AND ECOLOGICAL SIGNIFICANCE IN EAST AFRICAN WATERS AND SEDIMENTS,
Michigan Univ., Ann Arbor. Dept. of Zoology.
For primary bibliographic entry see Field 5B.
W75-07802

INDUSTRIALIZATION AFFECTS HEAVY METAL AND CARBON ISOTOPE CONCENTRATIONS IN RECENT BALTIC SEA SEDIMENTS,
Kiel Univ. (West Germany). Institut fuer Reine und Angewandte Kernphysik.
For primary bibliographic entry see Field 5B.
W75-07803

METHOD OF PROTECTION FOR SLOPES AND CRESTS OF RIVERS, CHANNELS, AND THE LIKE,
For primary bibliographic entry see Field 8F.
W75-07819

BEACH EROSION INVENTORY OF CHARLESTON COUNTY, SOUTH CAROLINA: A PRELIMINARY REPORT,
South Carolina Univ., Columbia. Dept. of Geology.
M. F. Stephen, B. J. Brown, D. M. FitzGerald, D. K. Hubbard, and M. O. Hayes.
South Carolina Sea Grant Technical Report Number 4, March 1975. 79 p, 36 fig. Tech. Report No 4. NOAA Grant SC-SG-75-4.

Descriptors: *Beach erosion *Deposition(Sediments), *Sediments, Aerial photography, *South Carolina.
Identifiers: *Shoreline changes, *Erosion trends, Morphological variations, Tidal inlets, Set back lines, Erosion-deposition graphs, Transgressive barrier islands, State-wide beach profile, Erosional inventory reports, Coastal counties, *Charleston County(SC).

Rates of shoreline change measured from vertical aerial photographs between the years 1939 and 1973 allow classification of the Charleston County, South Carolina, coastline into four categories: areas of long term erosion, which have undergone relatively continuous erosion over the study interval; areas of long term accretion, which have undergone relatively continuous deposition over the study interval; unstable areas, with fluctuations in position of the shoreline greater than 50 feet over the study interval; and stable areas, with fluctuations in position of the shoreline of less than 50 feet over the study interval. Beach erosion and deposition trends are closely tied to the occurrence and morphological variations of tidal inlets. Shoreline sediment type and modifications made by man also strongly affect erosion and deposition trends. Limits for set back lines and areas suitable and unsuitable for development can be defined directly from the erosion-deposition graphs presented. (NOAA)
W75-07833

SHORELINE PROTECTION GUIDE FOR PROPERTY OWNERS,
New York Sea Grant Advisory Service, Albany.
For primary bibliographic entry see Field 8A.
W75-07835

2K. Chemical Processes

REAGENTS FOR DETERMINATIONS OF TRACE IMPURITIES IN WATER, PHASE II,
Southern Illinois Univ., Carbondale. Dept. of Chemistry and Biochemistry.
For primary bibliographic entry see Field 5A.
W75-07352

SOME CHEMICAL OBSERVATIONS ON THE UPPER SALT RIVER AND ITS TRIBUTARIES,
Arizona State Univ., Tempe.
M. R. Sommerfeld, R. D. Olsen, and T. D. Love.

Journal of the Arizona Academy of Science, Vol 9, No 3, p 78-81, October 1974. 1 fig, 3 tab, 7 ref.

Descriptors: *Chemical analysis, *Salts, *Water sampling, *Water chemistry, Rivers, Tributaries, Sodium chloride, *Arizona, Banks, Water types, Sodium, Potassium, Calcium, Magnesium.
Identifiers: *Salt River(Ariz).

Chemical characteristics were determined on water samples collected at several sites on the Salt River and its major tributaries in Arizona. The data confirmed that the Salt River has a high specific conductance and can be described as sodium chloride water. The analysis revealed that neither the salt banks and adjacent springs located beneath the Salt River Canyon bridge nor the four tributaries, Carrizo Creek, Cedar Creek, and the White and Black Rivers are the major source of the high dissolved salt content of the Salt River. Considerable differences among the major tributaries were revealed in the chemical analyses. The source of the large quantities of dissolved salts is confined either to the lower reaches of the major tributaries or a fairly inaccessible twenty mile stretch of the Salt River above U.S. Highway 60. (Mastic-Arizona)
W75-07369

WATER SUPPLY IN CENTRAL AND SOUTHERN APACHE COUNTY,
Arizona Water Commission, Phoenix.
For primary bibliographic entry see Field 4B.
W75-07370

HYDROLOGY AND GEOCHEMISTRY OF KARST TERRAIN, UPPER LOST RIVER DRAINAGE BASIN, INDIANA,
Indiana Univ., Bloomington. Dept. of Geology.
For primary bibliographic entry see Field 2F.
W75-07398

AMOUNTS AND HYDROLYSIS OF PYROPHOSPHATE AND TRIPOLYPHOSPHATE IN SEDIMENTS,
Missouri Univ., Columbia. Dept. of Agronomy.
For primary bibliographic entry see Field 5A.
W75-07399

MARINE POLLUTION MONITORING: STRATEGIES FOR A NATIONAL PROGRAM,
Scripps Institution of Oceanography, La Jolla, Calif.
For primary bibliographic entry see Field 5A.
W75-07418

CHANGE IN THE PHYSIOCOCHEMICAL COMPOSITION OF WATER UNDER THE EFFECT OF FELLINGS,
Severo-Kavkazskaya Lesnaya Opytnaya Stantsiya, Maykop (USSR).
For primary bibliographic entry see Field 5B.
W75-07429

NITRATE MEASUREMENTS USING A SPECIFIC ION ELECTRODE IN PRESENCE OF NITRITE,
Oak Ridge National Lab., Tenn.
For primary bibliographic entry see Field 5A.
W75-07433

LANDFORM-SOIL-VEGETATION-WATER CHEMISTRY RELATIONSHIPS, WRIGLEY AREA, N.W.T.: I. MORPHOLOGY, CLASSIFICATION, AND SITE DESCRIPTION,
British Columbia Univ., Vancouver. Dept. of Soil Science.
M. E. Walmsley, and L. M. Lavkulich.
Soil Science Society of America Proceedings, Vol 39, No 1, p 84-88, January-February 1975. 3 fig, 1 tab, 12 ref.

Descriptors: *Soil-water-plant relationships, *Water chemistry, *Permafrost, *Canada, Geomorphology, Alpine, Soil types, Soil horizons, Regolith, Bogs, Lichens, Vegetation, Arctic.
Identifiers: *Mackenzie Valley(Northwest Territories), Cryoturbation, Stone stripes, Krummholz vegetation, Histic epipedon, Polygonal bogs, Toposequence.

Five landforms occurring in the intermittent permafrost region of the Mackenzie Valley were described. The five landforms, consisting of distinct soil and vegetative characteristics occur on a transect from the 1170 m ASL (above sea level) position at the summit of Cap Mountain, Wrigley area, Northwest Territories, to approximately 500 m ASL at the base of the slope. Two soils meet the requirement of a histic epipedon. An area of stone stripe and stone ring formation was encountered at approximately 1000 m ASL and an extensive area of lichen-covered polygonal bogs occurred at approximately 500 m ASL. The soils were described in relation to environmental factors and the processes of cryoturbation causing intermittent horizons were discussed. (Visocky-ISWS)
W75-07435

HUMIC MATTER IN NATURAL WATERS AND SEDIMENTS,
Fisheries Research Board of Canada, Winnipeg (Manitoba). Freshwater Inst.
For primary bibliographic entry see Field 5B.
W75-07453

A CONTINUOUS TURBIDITY MONITORING SYSTEM FOR COASTAL SURFACE WATERS,
Old Dominion Univ., Norfolk, Va. Inst. of Oceanography.
For primary bibliographic entry see Field 5A.
W75-07471

SUSPENDED MARINE CLAY MINERAL IDENTIFICATION BY SCANNING ELECTRON MICROSCOPY AND ENERGY-DISPERSIVE X-RAY ANALYSIS,
Texas A and M Univ., College Station. Dept. of Oceanography.
For primary bibliographic entry see Field 2J.
W75-07472

THE DETERMINATION OF AMMONIA IN SEAWATER,
Marine Biological Association of the United Kingdom, Plymouth (England). Plymouth Lab.
M. I. Liddicoat, S. Tibbitts, and E. I. Butler.
Limnology and Oceanography, Vol 20, No 1, p 131-132, January 1975. 4 ref.

Descriptors: *Ammonia, *Sea water, *Analytical techniques, Analysis, *Estimating, Chemistry, Spectrophotometry, Color reactions, Evaluation, Testing, Instrumentation, Laboratory tests, Testing procedures, Nitrogen compounds, Oceans, Ammonium compounds, Ultraviolet radiation.
Identifiers: *Phenolhypochlorite method, Indophenol, Potassium ferrocyanide.

A simple phenolhypochlorite method for the estimation of ammonia in seawater obeys Beer's Law over the concentration range 0-20 microgram-atoms NH3-N/liter; the standard deviation on a set of samples containing 4 microgram-atoms NH3-N/liter is 0.04. (Henley-ISWS)
W75-07474

TEMPERATURE MEASUREMENTS IN THE UPPER 10 M WITH MODIFIED EXPENDABLE BATHYTHERMOGRAPH PROBES,
Woods Hole Oceanographic Institution, Mass.
For primary bibliographic entry see Field 7B.
W75-07475

CHEMISTRY IN THE AQUATIC ENVIRONMENT,
Victoria Ministry for Conservation, Melbourne (Australia). Westernport Bay Environmental Study.
For primary bibliographic entry see Field 5A.
W75-07524

CHEMICAL QUALITY OF GROUND WATER IN HAWAII,
Geological Survey, Honolulu, Hawaii.
For primary bibliographic entry see Field 5A.
W75-07585

WATER-QUALITY RECONNAISSANCE OF SURFACE INFLOW TO UTAH LAKE,
Geological Survey, Salt Lake City, Utah.
For primary bibliographic entry see Field 5A.
W75-07586

DETERMINATION OF SMALL QUANTITIES OF CARBON DIOXIDE IN NATURAL WATERS,
Nagoya Univ. (Japan). Water Research Lab.
For primary bibliographic entry see Field 5A.
W75-07588

THE DETERMINATION OF NITRATE IN WATERS AT LOW PPM LEVELS BY AUTOMATIC DISCRETE-SAMPLE ANALYSIS,
Beckman Instruments, Inc., Irvine, Calif.
For primary bibliographic entry see Field 5A.
W75-07637

THE EFFECT OF SLAKED-LIME AND STRAW ON THE SOIL PH IN THE FLOODED AND UPLAND CONDITION (IN KOREAN),
Office of Rural Development, Suwon (Republic of Korea). Crop Experiment Station.
For primary bibliographic entry see Field 2G.
W75-07645

DEVELOPMENT OF A METHOD FOR THE EXTRACTION AND DETERMINATION OF NON-POLAR, DISSOLVED ORGANIC SUBSTANCES IN SEA WATER,
For primary bibliographic entry see Field 5A.
W75-07650

AUTOMATED ION-SELECTIVE ELECTRODE METHOD FOR DETERMINING FLUORIDE IN NATURAL WATERS,
Geological Survey, Denver, Colo.
For primary bibliographic entry see Field 5A.
W75-07657

LIQUID CHROMATOGRAPHIC DETERMINATION OF NITROGLYCERIN PRODUCTS IN WASTE WATERS,
Radford Army Ammunition Plant, Va.
For primary bibliographic entry see Field 5A.
W75-07659

MARINE ALGAL ASSAY PROCEDURE BOTTLE TEST,
Pacific Northwest Environmental Research Lab., Corvallis, Ore.
For primary bibliographic entry see Field 5A.
W75-07686

HANDBOOK OF RADIOCHEMICAL ANALYTICAL METHODS,
National Environmental Research Center, Las Vegas, Nev. Technical Support Lab.
For primary bibliographic entry see Field 5A.
W75-07697

Descriptors: Documentation, *Bibliographies, *Model studies, Mathematical models, *Mathematical studies, Mathematics, *Tidal waters, *Estuaries, Information exchange, Data collections, Publications, Reviews, Technical writing, Statistical models, Analytical techniques, Estimating, Theoretical analysis, Numerical analysis, Indexing.
Identifiers: Catalogs, Deterministic models, Statistical models, *Coastal waters, Tidal rivers, KWIC index, Author index, Corporate index, Inverted index.

This document catalogs 164 items of literature available in the field of numerical modeling for tidal rivers, estuaries, and coastal waters. Included models are of both a deterministic and statistical nature. The deterministic models in this classification use such forcing functions as tidal height, wind stress, density gradients, etc. in determining the velocity field. A limited number of models have been included which do not fit this description. Included are a document listing, a selected review and four indices: (a) keyword-in-context (KWIC) index, (b) author index, (c) corporate index, and (d) inverted index. (NOAA)
W75-07409

PORT DESIGN AND ANALYSIS METHODOLOGY,
Massachusetts Inst. of Tech., Cambridge. Sea Grant Project Office.
For primary bibliographic entry see Field 8A.
W75-07410

TEACHING COASTAL ZONE MANAGEMENT: AN INTRODUCTORY COURSE SYLLABUS,
Massachusetts Inst. of Tech., Cambridge. Dept. of Civil Engineering.
D. W. Ducsik.
Sea Grant Report No. MITSG 75-1, September 30, 1974. Index No. 75-101-Cdi. 14 p, 4 fig, 20 ref, append. (NOAA-74121605) NOAA Grant NG-43-72.

Descriptors: *Management, *Education, *Water resources, Resources, Coasts, Ecology, Economics, Law of the sea, Environment.
Identifiers: *Coastal zone management, *Syllabus.

The experience of developing and teaching a graduate level subject in coastal zone management at M.I.T. during the 1973-1974 academic year is reported. The objective of the subject is to introduce students with a variety of backgrounds to the wide range of problems and policy issues surrounding human use of the land-sea interface. The primary emphasis is on the allocation of shorelands, where the range of competing uses is the greatest and the possibilities for conflict most pronounced. Discussions include the physical and ecological processes characteristic of shoreland areas; the human activities placing demands on the coastal resources base; the incidence and magnitude of adverse affeets on ecological and amenity values; the institutional setting of coastal decision making; recent legislative developments; and special problem areas and critical policy issues. (NOAA)
W75-07411

INVESTIGATIONS ON CONCENTRATIONS, DISTRIBUTIONS, AND FATES OF HEAVY METAL WASTES IN PARTS OF LONG ISLAND SOUND,
Connecticut Univ., Groton. Marine Sciences Inst.
For primary bibliographic entry see Field 5B.
W75-07412

TOXAPHENE INTERACTIONS IN ESTUARINE ECOSYSTEMS,
Georgia Univ., Savannah. Marine Extension Center.
For primary bibliographic entry see Field 5C.
W75-07414

ENVIRONMENTAL STUDIES OF AN ARCTIC ESTUARINE SYSTEM--FINAL REPORT,
Alaska Univ., College. Marine Science Inst.
Environmental Studies of an Arctic Estuarine System-Final Report; IMS Report R74-1; Sea Grant Report No. 73-16, 1974, 539p. (NOAA-75022106) EPA 16100EDM NOAA Grant OSG 04-3-158-41.

Descriptors: *Estuarine environment, *Arctic, *Alaska, Polar regions, Lagoons, Waves(Water), Currents(Water), Winds, Beaches, Geomorphology, Sedimentology, Sedimentation, Mineralogy, Geochemistry, Ice, Nutrients, Chemical analysis, Phytoplankton, Aquatic life, Aquatic plants, Benthos, Estuarine fisheries, Birds, Fish, Benthic fauna.
Identifiers: *Arctic estuarine system, *Colville River(AK), Fast ice, Beaufort Sea(AK), Arctic birds.

The Colville River estuarine system was studied with respect to physical, chemical, geomorphological and biological factors over a period of four years. A detailed account is given of wind, waves, and currents in a lagoon; beach morphology and sedimentology in a lagoon; aspects of size distributions, mineralogy and geochemistry of deltaic and adjacent shallow marine sediments of North Arctic Alaska; fast ice on the northern coast of Alaska; seasonal variations in the nutrient chemistry and conservative constituents in coastal Alaskan Beaufort Sea waters; primary productivity and phytoplankton organisms in the Colville River system; nearshore benthos; and Colville River delta fisheries research. A summary of observations of birds at Oliktok Point and notes on birds observed along the Colville River are included. (NOAA)
W75-07417

MARINE POLLUTION MONITORING: STRATEGIES FOR A NATIONAL PROGRAM,
Scripps Institution of Oceanography, La Jolla, Calif.
For primary bibliographic entry see Field 5A.
W75-07418

ENGINEERING CONSIDERATIONS FOR MARINAS IN TIDAL MARSHES,
Delaware Univ., Newark. Dept. of Civil Engineering.
College of Marine Studies, Sea Grant Publication DEL-SG-9-74, November 1974. 114 p, 18 fig, 20 tab, 22 ref. NOAA Contract 04-3-158-30.

Descriptors: *Estuaries, *Tidal marshes, *Marinas, Engineering, Management, Recreation facilities, Environmental engineering, Water resources, Economics, Design criteria, *Coastal engineering.
Identifiers: Environmental impact, Coastal zone management, Commercial fisheries.

Design guidelines have been developed to incorporate the desirable qualities of the marsh in a marina, thereby reducing the environmental impact. When a marina displaces marshland, the most important quality which must be maintained is biological production. The methods suggested and recommended for the preservation of this quality are: flush the marina to promote water circulation which cycles nutrients and prevents eutrophication; use dredge spoils from the marsh to establish new productive marshes elsewhere; provide contact area within the marina so fouling communities, an organic food source, can prosper and multiply; control water quality so that estuarine species can thrive in the marina; and provide an equal amount of organic food in the marina to make up for the loss of food from displaced marshland. To indicate how a complementary marina-marsh system could be achieved, an example of a composite design using these guidelines is also presented. (NOAA)
W75-07420

RECONNAISSANCE OF BOTTOM SEDIMENTS ON THE INNER AND CENTRAL NEW JERSEY SHELF (MESA DATA REPORT),
National Oceanic and Atmospheric Administration, Boulder, Colo. Marine Ecosystems Analysis Program.
W. L. Stubblefield, M. Dickon, and J. P. Swift.
Available from the Superintendent of Documents, U.S. Gov't Printing Office, Washington, D.C. 20402. NOAA Environmental Research Laboratories Marine Ecosystems Analysis Program MESA Report No. 1, July 1974. 39 p, 6 fig, 4 tab, 8 ref. (NOAA-74111811).

Descriptors: *Continental shelf, *Bottom sediments, *Waste disposal, Coasts, Sediments, Petrography, Resources, Fisheries, Sediment transport, Data collections, *New Jersey.
Identifiers: *Environmental impact, *Grain-size distribution, Mineral resources, Food supply.

The petrography of samples from two areas on the New Jersey Shelf was analyzed to resolve the relation between surficial grain-size distribution, hydraulic regime, and bathymetry. Determination of this relation is essential to understanding of the sediment flux in these areas and is a critical parameter for environmental impact problems. The sample localities are presently undergoing, or are being considered for, a variety of conflicting usages, including food resources (fishing), mineral resources (beach borrow), and waste disposal (dredge spoil and sewage). The samples were examined for grain-size distribution in quarter-phi intervals and for related statistical parameters which include mean grain size, standard deviation, skewness, and kurtosis. A mean grain-size distribution map for each area suggests a relation between bathymetry and grain-size distribution which, in turn, defines certain features of a hydraulic regime. Selected samples were further examined for relative percent of detritus, clay pebbles, fauna content, and heavy mineral concentrations. The individual metrographical parameters are presented in tabular form. (NOAA)
W75-07425

TIDES AND TIDAL CURRENTS OF NARRAGANSETT BAY,
Rhode Island Univ., Kingston. Dept. of Ocean Engineering.
M. Spaulding, and C. Swanson.
Marine Technical Report Number 35, 1974. 40 p, 27 fig, 13 tab. (NOAA-74122701).

Descriptors: *Tides, *Charts, *Rhode Island, Recreation, Data collections.
Identifiers: *Tidal currents, *Oceanographic data, *Tidal heights, *Narragansett Bay(RI).

The tidal current and height charts for Narragansett Bay have been created primarily for the recreational user, notably the sailor. The charts show the hourly velocity to the nearest tenth of a knot, and direction of the tidal currents by means of arrows. A series of hourly tidal height charts shows the height to the nearest tenth of a foot above mean sea level throughout the bay. Also included is a table, on which the charts are based, which gives the time and range of the tides at Newport, Rhode Island, from 1975 to 1984. This table is divided into one month per page and subdivided into columns of times and ranges for each year. The time is based on a 24-hour clock, Eastern Standard Time (EST), and the range is the difference in feet between high water at the time shown and the next low water. The charts were generated under the assumption of no wind, constant river flow, and no atmospheric pressure gradient over the bay, i.e. no storm. There is one tidal current chart and one tide height chart for each hour after high tide at Newport giving a total of 13 current and height charts covering one tidal cycle. Included is a table of factors for correcting velocity and height for various tidal ranges. (NOAA)
W75-07426

BISCAYNE BAY: ENVIRONMENTAL AND SOCIAL SYSTEMS.
Miami Univ., Coral Gables, Fla.
University of Miami Sea Grant Special Report Number 1, March 1975, Susan U. Wilson (ed). 51 p, 9 fig, ref, 3 append. (NOAA-75040203) $3.00. Special Report No. 1 NOAA Grant OSG 04-5-158-14.

Descriptors: *Bays, *Estuaries, *Florida, Inlets(Waterways), Shores, Aquatic environment, Coastal plains, Intertidal areas, Geology, Geologic formations, Geomorphology, Environmental effects, Climatology, Climatic data, Weather, Weather data, Currents(Water), Water circulation, Waves, Water quality, Water quality control, Biota, Political aspects, Area redevelopment, Jurisdiction, Water resources development, Land use, Industries, Recreation, Transportation, Utilities.
Identifiers: *Biscayne Bay(Fl), *Environmental systems, *Social systems, Political jurisdications, Residential land use, Commerce, Miami(Fl).

Described are Biscayne Bay, its uses, and how man has modified it and its shores. The various environmental systems are described in detail including geology, climate and weather, tides and currents, water quality, and biota. Social systems are also addressed, including political jurisdictions, residential land use, industry and commerce, recreation, public land use, and transportation and utilities. (NOAA)
W75-07427

COASTAL BREAKUP IN THE ALASKAN ARCTIC,
Louisiana State Univ., Baton Rouge. Coastal Studies Inst.
For primary bibliographic entry see Field 2C.
W75-07445

NEARSHORE CURRENT PATTERNS ALONG THE CENTRAL CALIFORNIA COAST,
California Univ., Santa Cruz. Div. of Applied Sciences.
G. B. Griggs.
Estuarine and Coastal Marine Science, Vol 2, No 4, p 395-405, October 1974. 4 fig, 4 tab, 15 ref.

Descriptors: *Ocean currents, *Coasts, *California, *Pacific Ocean, Currents(Water), Oceanography, Ocean circulation, Seasonal.
Identifiers: *Nearshore ocean currents.

Sea surface and seabed drifters indicated that nearshore current patterns change seasonally along the central California coast in the Monterey Bay area. The winter months are characterized by a well-defined northward flow (Davidson Current) with average monthly speeds of 3 to 11 km/day. During the spring, surface flow reverses and the southward flowing California current dominates with average nearshore speeds of 4 to 10 km/day. Drift during the summer and fall is quite variable with occasional reversals of direction. These fluctuations seem to be partly due to the presence of eddies associated with the California Current system and partially to local wind patterns. Although near bottom drift varies, a northward flow predominates throughout the year with average speeds of 0.3 to 0.6 km/day. Although offshore currents do appear to flow in and out of Monterey Bay, circulation in the bay is much slower than that in the offshore area thereby making it highly susceptible to pollutant accumulation. (Jess-ISWS)
W75-07449

PHYSICAL AND BIOLOGICAL CHARACTERISTICS OF AN UPWELLING AT A STATION OFF LA JOLLA, CALIFORNIA DURING 1971,
Dalhousie Univ., Halifax (Nova Scotia). Dept. of Oceanography.
D. Kamykowski.

CONSTITUTIONAL RESTRICTIONS ON COASTAL LAND USE,
Oregon State Land Conservation and Development Commission, Portland.
For primary bibliographic entry see Field 6E.
W75-07515

WATER QUALITY PLANNING FOR THE DELAWARE ESTUARY - AN EXAMPLE,
Rutgers - the State Univ., New Brunswick, N.J. Water Resources Research Inst.
For primary bibliographic entry see Field 5G.
W75-07519

COASTAL SALINITY RECONNAISSANCE AND MONITORING SYSTEM--SOUTH COAST OF PUERTO RICO,
Geological Survey of Puerto Rico, San Juan.
For primary bibliographic entry see Field 5A.
W75-07553

EFFECT OF PORT ORANGE BRIDGE-CAUSEWAY ON FLOW OF HALIFAX RIVER, VOLUSIA COUNTY, FLORIDA,
Geological Survey, Tallahassee, Fla.
For primary bibliographic entry see Field 4C.
W75-07555

WATER QUALITY OF TAMPA BAY, FLORIDA: DRY-WEATHER CONDITIONS, JUNE 1971,
Geological Survey, Tallahassee, Fla.
For primary bibliographic entry see Field 5A.
W75-07556

DYE-DISPERSION STUDY ON LAKE CHAMPLAIN, NEAR CROWN POINT, NEW YORK,
Geological Survey, Albany, N.Y.
For primary bibliographic entry see Field 5B.
W75-07571

THE SEASONAL CYCLE OF GROWTH AND PRODUCTION IN THREE SALT MARSHES ADJACENT TO THE SAVANNAH RIVER,
Skidaway Inst. of Oceanography, Savannah, Ga.
G. L. McIntire, and W. M. Dunstan.
Technical Report Series No 75-2, (1975). 18 p, 6 fig, 3 tab, 13 ref. NOAA Grant OSG R/EE-2(04-3-158-6).

Descriptors: *Salinity, *Detritus, Food chains, Effluents, *Salt marshes, *Productivity, *Georgia, *Growth rates, Growth stages.
Identifiers: *Seasonal cycle, Spartina alterniflora, Growth parameters, *Savannah River marsh(GA), Total dry weight, Ash-free dry weight, Environmental perturbations.

Three geographically similar Spartina alterniflora marshes near Savannah, Georgia were studied monthly during 1974. Production levels, percent ash, and other growth parameters were measured. While general growth trends were similar at all three sites, the levels of production varied significantly with the marsh on the Savannah River showing the greatest production. Measurements of standing dead Spartina revealed a ready supply of detrital energy which is available to the adjacent estuarine regions throughout the year. The Savannah River marsh demonstrated that studies of river systems with high levels of industrial and municipal effluents must consider increased plant production as well as inhibitory or toxic effects. This study is a first step towards a 'condition index' for coastal salt marshes which would enable industrial and governmental agencies to determine the effects of environmental perturbations on these important natural resources. (NOAA)
W75-07713

BEACH FORMS AND COASTAL PROCESSES,
Columbia Univ., New York. Teachers Coll.
W. E. Yasso, and Elliott M. Hartman, Jr.
Beach Forms and Coastal Processes, MESA New York Bight Atlas, Monograph 11, January 1975. 51 p, 37 fig, 3 tab, 49 ref.

Descriptors: *Geomorphology, *Landforms, *Coasts, Headlands, Estuaries, Islands, Littoral drift, Jetties, Groins, Beach erosion, New York.
Identifiers: *Barrier spit, *Barrier bars, *Ocean facing shorelines, Wave refraction, *New York Bight Coast(NY).

Headlands, estuaries, a barrier spit, and barrier bars and islands separated from the mainland by shallow lagoons are the major landforms of the New York Bight coast. Bight beaches are subject to both annual and long-term changes in shape and position typical of ocean-facing shorelines. Wave refraction causes littoral drift of beach sand in a predominantly westward direction along the south sore of Long Island. Northward littoral drift predominates along the New Jersey coast north of Dover Township. South of Dover Township the drift is predominantly southward. Jetties and groins temporarily block littoral drift; they do not stop beach erosion entirely. Coastal storms and man's encroachment onto beaches amplify the normal erosion of waves, wind, and tide. Many people fail to learn from storms and from natural erosion that building on beaches and dunes should be avoided. (NOAA)
W75-07715

PROCEEDINGS OF A CONFERENCE ON MANAGEMENT OF DREDGE ISLANDS IN NORTH CAROLINA ESTUARIES,
North Carolina Univ., Wilmington. Dept. of Biology.
J. F. Parnell, and R. F. Soots.
Report UNC-SG-75-01, May 1974. 142 p, 18 fig, 2 tab. NOAA Grant OSG 04-3158-40.

Descriptors: *Management, *Estuaries, *Wildlife, Dikes, *North Carolina, Environmental effects, Fish population, Birds, *Habitats.
Identifiers: *Dredge islands(NC), Estuarine ecosystem, Coastal birds, Colonial birds, Dredge material, Bird population, *Spoil.

The process of removing substrate materials from navigation channels has resulted in the creation of many small estuarine islands. While the dredging process that creates these islands is generally considered detrimental to estuarine ecosystems, recent research has shown that dredge islands are valuable as nesting sites for many coastal birds. This conference was designed to bring the results of this research to the attention of the agencies and organizations with responsibilities and interests in the estuaries and to explore the possibilities and problems of managing these islands for wildlife, particularly nesting colonial birds. Speakers were selected to cover the major aspects of management and to represent the views of the agencies that would be directly or indirectly involved in such a management program. The conference brought together over 70 people from 24 state or federal agencies and private organizations. (NOAA)
W75-07716

THE WATER QUALITY AND TIDAL FLUSHING CHARACTERISTICS OF THREE SMALL BOAT BASINS; DES MOINES MARINA, EDMONDS HARBOR, AND NEWPORT SHORES,
Washington Univ., Seattle. Dept. of Civil Engineering.
For primary bibliographic entry see Field 5B.
W75-07726

POPULATION AND BIOMASS DYNAMICS OF ZOOBENTHOS OF THE SOUTHERN ARAL SEA REGION AND CHANGE IN THE FOOD BASE OF BOTTOM-FEEDING FISH, (IN RUSSIAN).
Interdisciplinary Inst. of Natural Sciences, Nukus (USSR).

B. Bekmurzaev.
Uzb Biol Zh. Vol 17, No 6, p 49-51. 1973.

Descriptors: *Biomass, *Benthos, *Bottom fish, Fish food organisms, Bays.
Identifiers: *Aral Sea, USSR.

Quantitative data are presented on the zoobenthos and its seasonal changes in the Sarbas, Abbas and Dzhaltyrbas Bays of the Aral Sea (Uzbek SSR, USSR). In 1962-1968, 110 benthic forms and species were found in the coastal part of the southern Aral. Sarbas and Abbas Bays were the richest in number of species and forms, 68 and 57 respectively. The quantitative composition of Dzhaltyrbas Bay was poorer (48). The change in the zoobenthos is intimately related with a reduction of the runoff of the Amu-Darya River and of the coastal regions of the sea. As a result of this runoff, the total biomass of food invertebrates has decreased.--Copyright 1974, Biological Abstracts, Inc.
W75-07733

POSSIBILITIES FOR THE USE AND EVALUATION OF BRINY ZONES (ESTUARIES, LAGOONS ETC.) IN PARTICULAR BY AQUACULTURE, (IN FRENCH),
Paris-7 Univ. (France). Lab. of Physics of Biological Structures.
M. Petitjean.
Trav Mus Hist Nat Grigore Antipa. Vol 13, p 109-136. 1973, Illus.

Descriptors: *Aquiculture, Estuaries, Lagoons.
Identifiers: *Myxohaline zones.

Various myxohaline aquatic zones are discussed with respect to their use in aquaculture as a means of combating the current worldwide protein shortage. The productivity of these bodies of water is superior to that of both marine and freshwater areas. Also stressed is the greater sensitivity of these waters to external influences and the need for careful detailed study of the harmful effects involved in using these regions as food sources.--Copyright 1974, Biological Abstracts, Inc.
W75-07739

PHYSICO-CHEMICAL STUDY OF THE WATERS AND SEDIMENTS OF THE BRACKISH WATER POND OF BAGES-SIGEAN, (IN FRENCH).
Arago Lab., Banyuls-sur-Mer (France).
M. Fiala.
Vie Milieu Ser B Oceanogr. Vol 23, No 1, p 21-50, 1972/1973, Illus, English summary.

Descriptors: *Lagoons, Water chemistry, Phytoplankton, *Salinity, *Sediments, Nutrients, *Brackish water.
Identifiers: *France(Bages-Sigean).

A 1 yr study was conducted on the lagoon of Bages-Sigean to determine its main physico-chemical characteristics. Its connection with the sea brings an increasing gradient of salinity from north (8%) to south (36%). Under mediterranean climatic conditions, the surface waters show sudden variations of temperature and salinity. Another particularity is the richness of compounds in the waters and in the sediments, necessary to the life of microorganisms. The surface waters hold an average of 3 mg/l glucose, from 0.1-0.8 mg/l nitrate and 8-10 microgram/l phosphate. The large variations during the year seem to be in connection with the strong freshening. This richness in mineral nutritive salts gives rise to the development of abundant phytoplankton. The sediments are richer than the waters in glucose (10 times) and phosphates (about 20 times). They are also characterized by their instability.--Copyright 1974, Biological Abstracts, Inc.
W75-07743

DISTRIBUTION OF COLIFORM BACTERIA IN THE COASTAL WATER, (IN JAPANESE),
Tokai Univ., Tokyo (Japan). Coll. of Marine Science and Technology.
For primary bibliographic entry see Field 5B.
W75-07744

NORMATIVE ASPECTS OF SCIENTIFIC RESEARCH IN THE OCEANS, THE CASE OF MEXICO,
Rhode Island Univ., Kingston. Law of the Sea Inst.
For primary bibliographic entry see Field 6E.
W75-07775

STUDIES ON EFFECTS OF THERMAL POLLUTION IN BISCAYNE BAY, FLORIDA,
Rosenstiel School of Marine and Atmospheric Science, Miami, Fla.
For primary bibliographic entry see Field 5C.
W75-07790

CLAVICEPS PURPUREA ON SPARTINA IN COASTAL MARSHES,
Gulf Coast Research Lab., Ocean Springs, Miss.
For primary bibliographic entry see Field 5C.
W75-07827

CONTRIBUTION OF FUNGI TO BIODEGRADATION OF SPARTINA AND OTHER BRACKISH MARSHLAND VEGETATION,
Louisiana State Univ., Baton Rouge. Dept. of Food Science.
For primary bibliographic entry see Field 5C.
W75-07828

BEACH EROSION INVENTORY OF CHARLESTON COUNTY, SOUTH CAROLINA: A PRELIMINARY REPORT,
South Carolina Univ., Columbia. Dept. of Geology.
For primary bibliographic entry see Field 2J.
W75-07833

3. WATER SUPPLY AUGMENTATION AND CONSERVATION

3A. Saline Water Conversion

WATER DESALTING IN HAWAII,
Holmes and Narver, Inc., Anaheim, Calif. Nuclear and Systems Sciences Group.
J. M. Duncan, and B. J. Garrick.
Available from the National Technical Information Service, Springfield, Va. 22161, as PB-241 706, $5.25 in paper copy, $2.25 in microfiche. OSW Report INT-OSW-RDPR-75-1001, June 1974, 93 p, 40 fig, 9 tab, 33 ref, 2 append. (Hawaii Department of Land and Natural Resources Report R50). OSW 14-30-3093.

Descriptors: Desalination, *Desalination plants, Municipal water, *Water supply, Water costs, *Hawaii, *Bracksih water, Planning, Reverse osmosis, Electrodialysis, Ion exchange, Cost comparisons, Alternative costs, *Cost analysis.

Possible applications were studied for water desalting in Hawaii. General water supply features of the islands are discussed. The areas most appropriate for the study of desalting were the Kihei-Makena (Maui) and the Kibola (Hawaii) sectors. There is little need for seawater desalting in the islands in view of the abundance of brackish waters of moderate salinity. This study was limited to the brackish waters and the electrodialysis, reverse osmosis, and ion exchange processes. Electrodialysis and reverse osmosis are the most economical desalting methods for potential use. For Maui island, water from a 1-million gallon per day electrodialysis plant operating at 50 percent plant factor and producing a water quality of 500 parts per million total dissolved solids (TDS) from brackish feed water of about 1,000 parts per million TDS would cost between 100 and 117 cents per 1,000 gallons. If a 90-percent plant factor can be achieved, the cost of this water would be reduced to between 67 and 78 cents per 1,000 gallons. By comparison current water rates in Hawaii average less than 40 cents per 1,000 gallons. No costing of alternative fresh water supplies is provided. Desalted waters would have only limited promise since the fresh water alternatives are more economical. The importance is emphasized of this information as input to the on-going Hawaii Water Resources Regional Study.
W75-07506

RESEARCH ON PIEZODIALYSIS - FOURTH REPORT,
Ionics, Inc., Watertown, Mass.
F. Leitz, J. Shorr, K. Sims, S. Spencer, and D. Carlson.
Available from the National Technical Information Service, Springfield, Va 22161, as PB-236 613, $5.25 in paper copy, $2.25 in microfiche. Report INT-OSW-RDPR-74-988, May 1973. 110 p, 28 fig, 14 tab, 7 ref, 2 append. 14-01-0001-2333.

Descriptors: *Desalination, *Membrane processes, *Membranes, *Dialysis, *Electro-osmosis, Separation techniques, Waste water treatment, Measurement.
Identifiers: *Piezodialysis, *Mosaic membranes, Charge-mosaic membranes, Latex-polyelectrolyte membranes, Composite membranes, Salt flux.

Considerable progress has been made both in theoretical treatment of piezodialysis and in development of appropriate membranes for this process since the last status report (See W73-11154). The theoretical treatment has been expanded. Overall flux coefficients have been defined for a composite membrane and related to the flux coefficients for the component resins. These relationships provide considerable insight into the piezodialysis process. Equivalent symmetrical coefficients were derived for unsymmetrical membranes. Techniques have been developed for measurement of conductivity and water transport factors of component resins in a composite membrane. These measurements were made on a very good example of latex-poly-electrolyte membrane. The agreement between calculated and measured salt and water fluxes was good, considering the wide divergence between the structure of the idealized model and the likely membrane morphology. Divergences between calculated and measured permeate concentration suggest some possible changes in morphology under flow conditions. Membrane development work was concentrated on the latex-polyelectrolyte membrane. This type of membrane consists of a styrenebutadiene film which is permeated with high molecular weight linear polystyrene sulfonate. The styrene portions of the film are converted to an anion-exchange resin. The variables in this process were studied extensively. Very substantial interactions between variables were discovered. By combining the results of several local optimizations a substantially improved membrane was produced. Operating at a production rate of 6 to 7 GFD. Thus, piezodialysis is on the verge of being a practical desalting process. (See also W75-07622) (OWRT)
W75-07621

RESEARCH ON PIEZODIALYSIS - FIFTH REPORT,
Ionics, Inc., Watertown, Mass.
F. Leitz, J. Shorr, S. Spencer, and N. Denno.
Available from the National Technical Information Service, Springfield, Va 22161, as PB-236 614, $4.75 in paper copy, $2.25 in microfiche. Report

INT-OSW-RDPR-74-989, December 1973. 73 p, 16 fig, 16 tab, 8 ref. OWRT Contract 14-01-0001-2333.

Descriptors: *Desalination, *Membrane process, Membranes, *Dialysis, *Electro-osmosis, Separation techniques, Reviews, *Waste water treatment, Mathematical models.
Identifiers: *Piezodialysis, *Mosaic membranes, Charge-mosaic membranes, Latex-polyelectrolyte membranes, Composite membranes, Salt flux.

A review of the piezodialysis program is presented. This shows the advantages and possible performance of the process and the rate of development of mosaic membranes appropriate for piezodialysis. The mathematical model developed for piezodialysis is summarized. The relationship of parameters in this model to the Kedem, Katchalsky, Weinstein and Caplan model for a parallel element mosaic is shown. A very simple approximate equation for permeate concentration is presented. An ambiguity in the meaning of optimum membrane performance is at least partially resolved. A further investigation was made of variables in the lates-polyelectrolyte method of mosaic method fabrication. In addition to providing relationships between fabrication variables and membrane performance, this investigation provided the first overall hypothesis of how membrane performance relates to membrane morphology. In addition a good deal of the ambiguity of earlier data was explained. A new route to a latex-polyelectrolyte membrane which avoids chloromethylation is evaluated. Significant advantages in the process of latex-polyelectrolyte optimization result from the much greater reproducibility and predictability of membrane properties in this new procedure. A closer look at membrane morphology was provided by a group of transmission electron micrographs. Clear structural differentiations were obtained between self-enriching and non-salt-enriching membranes. (See also W75-07621) (OWRT)
W75-07622

TUBULAR REVERSE OSMOSIS MEMBRANE RESEARCH,
Philco-Ford Corp., Newport Beach, Calif. Aeronutronic Div.
J. L. Richardson, R. H. Williams, G. Segovia, H. Parker-Jones, and F. Ju.
Available from the National Technical Information Service, Springfield, Va 22161, as PB-236 943, $8.50 in paper copy, $2.25 in microfiche. Report INT-OSW-RDPR-74-993, (1974). 206 p, 75 fig, 63 tab, 25 ref, 3 append. OWRT Contract 14-30-2884.

Descriptors: *Reverse osmosis, *Desalination, *Membrane processes, *Ultrafiltration, *Pretreatment(Water), Sea water, Gels, Waste water treatment.
Identifiers: *Tubular membranes, Membrane fabrication, *Composite membranes, Porous polysulfone support, Crosslinking, Gelation.

A principal objectiv was the development of tubular NS-100 ultrathin composite membranes capable of demonstrating single-pass seawater desalination while contained within flexible braided pressure supports. An additional objective was to demonstrate the potential of ultrafiltration as pretreatment for the reverse osmosis desalination of seawater. Results are reported of the program which was organized into four tasks: Development of Improved Flexible Tubular Pressure Supports; Substrate Extrusion-Gelation; Advanced Tubular Composite Mebranes for Seawater Desalination; and Tubular Ultrafiltration Membranes for the Pretreatment of Seawater. (OWRT)
W75-07623

DEVELOPMENT OF IMPROVED PBI MEMBRANE SYSTEMS FOR WASH WATER RECYCLING AT PASTEURIZATION TEMPERATURES,
Celanese Research Co., Summit, N.J.
For primary bibliographic entry see Field 5D.
W75-07624

OPERATION AND EVALUATION OF ALUMINUM TUBED MSF-VTE-HTE PILOT PLANT AT WRIGHTSVILLE BEACH TEST FACILITY,
Reynolds Metals Co., Richmond, Va.
D. A. Fauth, R. I. Lindberg, and L. M. Coggins.
Available from the National Technical Information Service, Springfield, Va. 22161, as PB-235 835, $4.25 in paper copy, $2.25 in microfiche. Report INT-OSW-RDPR-74-986, March 1973. 36 p, 6 fig, 1 append, 2 charts. OWRT Contract 14-30-3057.

Descriptors: *Desalination plants, Desalination processes, Aluminum alloys, Distillation, Corrosion, *Flash distillation, *Evaporators, Heat transfer, *Pilot plants, *Operations, *North Carolina, Tubes, Treatment facilities, Waste water treatment, Scaling.
Identifiers: Detaclad aluminum steel, Remedial anti-pitting devices, Passivated film attack, Wrightsville Beach Test Facility(NC), MSF-VTE-HTE pilot plants.

Aluminum alloys were tested as heat transfer tubes and for vessel construction in a 54,000 gpd MSF-VTE-HTE, (multi-stage flash-rectical tube effect-horizontal tube effect), pilot plant utilizing two scale preventive pretreatments. The sulfuric acid treated portion of the plant operated at a 250F terminal temperature, and a threshold chemical treated portion operated at a 190F terminal temperature. The plant consisted of one all-aluminum evaporator-condenser, three combination steel-aluminum evaporator-condensers, two all-aluminum brine heaters, three all-aluminum vertical tube effects, one all-aluminum horizontal tube effect, and other components of aluminum. Alloy 3004 performed excellently for vessel construction and heat transfer tubing, and alloy 3003 performed excellently as heat transfer tubing. A slight amount of pitting occurred in the tubes in the heat reject vessel. Some exterior chemical attack occurred on the brine heater tubes. Both of these minor problems could easily be remedied. (OWRT)
W75-07625

DEVELOPMENT OF FORCED FLOW ELECTRODESALINATION SEPARATOR MATERIALS,
Aqua-Chem, Inc., Milwaukee, Wis.
R. M. Ahlgren, and B. Schneider.
Available from the National Technical Information Service, Springfield, Va. 22161, as PB-236 616, $4.25 in paper copy, $2.25 in microfiche. Report INT-OSW-RDPR-74-990, June 1974. 66 p, 11 photo, 12 graphs, append. OWRT Contract 14-30-3089.

Descriptors: *Desalination, *Electrodialysis, *Membranes, Fabrication, Waste water treatment, Separation techniques, Brackish water, Sea water.
Identifiers: *Thin-cell separators, Forced flow, *Elastomers, Electrodialysis stack, Silk screen technique, Cell pairs.

An improved concept of operating electrodialysis stacks with ultra-thin spacing between membranes has been developed. Thin separators (0.5 mm) utilize a formed-in-place elastomer gasket in a thin plastic mesh. A limited volume thin cell separator production method was developed. A demonstration stack utilizing about two thousand five hundred square feet of membrane (150 cell pair) was constructed. This stack was operated on simulated brackish water (3000 ppm) and seawater (35,000 ppm). Electrical power consumption was about one kilowatt hour per one thousand gallons per one thousand parts per million salt removed. The production capacity of the stack was over one hundred thousand gallons per day on brackish water and between five and ten thousand gallons per day on seawater. The estimated production cost of this type of electrodialysis separator is about one half of the cost of standard separators. (OWRT)
W75-07626

REVERSE OSMOSIS FOR SPACECRAFT WASH WATER RECYCLING, MEMBRANE COUPON AND MODULE EVALUATIONS,
McDonnell-Douglas Astronautics Co. West, Huntington Beach, Calif.
For primary bibliographic entry see Field 5D.
W75-07627

REVERSE OSMOSIS FOR SPACECRAFT WASH WATER RECYCLING, HIGH PRESSURE PUMP DEFINITION,
McDonnell Douglass Astronautics Co.-West, Huntington Beach, Calif.
For primary bibliographic entry see Field 8C.
W75-07628

MANAGEMENT, OPERATION AND MAINTENANCE BRACKISH WATER TEST FACILITY - ANNUAL REPORT 1973 ROSWELL, NEW MEXICO MAY 1, 1972 - OCTOBER 31, 1973,
Burns and Roe Construction Corp., Paramus, N.J.
A. R. Bernardi.
Available from the National Technical Information Service, Springfield, Val 22161, as PB-237 172, $5.75 in paper copy, $2.25 in microfiche. Report INT-OSW-RDPR-74-991, June 1974. 127 p, 27 fig, 8 tab. OWRT Contract 14-30-3012.

Descriptors: Equipment, *Operations, Management, Corrosion control, *Maintenance, Waste disposal, *New Mexico, Brackish water, *Desalination plants, Waste water treatment, *Treatment facilities.
Identifiers: Roswell Test Facility(NMex).

This report covers work performed at the Roswell Test Facility, Roswell, New Mexico, for the period May 1, 1972, through October 31, 1973. Work consisted of maintaining the Roswell Test Facility in the best and safest possible condition in accordance with the best established industrial practices and to provide the supporting effective development, test and evaluation program to advance the state of the art of water conversion. (OWRT)
W75-07629

APPRAISAL OF SALINE WATER IN OKLAHOMA AND ITS FUTURE DEVELOPMENT THROUGH DESALTING,
Oklahoma Water Resources Board, Oklahoma City.
F. Nelson.
Available from the National Technical Information Service, Springfield, Va. 22161, as PB-239 396, $7.00 in paper copy, $2.25 in microfiche. Report INT-OSW-RDPR-75-997, May 1974. 164 p, 47 fig, 7 tab, 40 ref. OWRT Contract 14-30-3176.

Descriptors: Desalination, *Desalination plants, *Water supply, *Electrodialysis, *Municipal water, Water costs, *Oklahoma, Planning, Brackish water, Brine disposal, Desalination processes, Waste water treatment.
Identifiers: Foss Reservoir plant(Okla).

Initially, a survey was made to identify communities using brackish water supplies in selected areas. Based on initial screening, 5 counties in North central Oklahoma and 11 counties in the southwest corner of the state were selected for further study. Water analyses on the supplies of these areas were brought up-to-date. Data on over a hundred of these communities is included in the Appendix. Extensive discussion of the 3 mgd electrodialysis plant at Foss Reservoir is given, including bid costs, water costs, pretreatment and brine disposal. It is concluded that most communities presently using brackish water can best meet their water problem through alternate fresh water

sources. However, it is further concluded that in the future, as the alternatives become more limited, there will be increasing need for desalting. Any immediate plans for desalting in the areas considered will await the results from the Foss Reservoir plant which is about to start operation. (OWRT)
W75-07630

ECONOMIC FEASIBILITY OF DESALTING SYSTEMS FOR MUNICIPAL WATER SUPPLY IN IOWA,
Dewild Grant Reckert and Associates, Des Moines, Iowa.
D. L. Laverentz.
Available from the National Technical Information Service, Springfield, Va 22161 as PB-239 359, $9.25 in paper copy, $2.25 in microfiche. Report INT-OSW-RDPR-74-998, June 1974. 274 p, 59 fig, 100 tab, 93 ref. OWRT Contract 14-30-3120.

Descriptors: Desalination processes, Desalination plants, *Water supply, *Municipal water, Water costs, *Iowa, Brackish water, *Economic feasibility, Cities, Waste water treatment.

The economic feasibility of using desalting methods for improving water quality in Iowa communities was determined. Ten communities were chosen for the study: Adair, Estherville, Grundy Center, Holstein, Le Claire, Leon, Oakland, Oxford, Sibley and Washington. The population of the cities ranged from 666 to 6317. The salinity of the existing city water supplies ranged from 970 ppm to 2774 ppm. The cost analyses made for desalting included the complete system charges -- pretreatment, desalting plant, storage, transmission and brine disposal. The most applicable processes were electrodialysis, reverse osmosis, and ion exchange. Costs for the entire desalting system varied from 58 cents per 1000 gallons to 261 cents per 1000 gallons. Size of the community, salinity of the feed water and pretreatment required have effects on final cost of desalting. Calculations were also made of possible economic benefits that may be derived from desalting as compared to the use of the untreated brackish water source. (OWRT)
W75-07631

POSSIBLE OPTIONS FOR REDUCING THE SALINITY OF THE COLORADO RIVER WATERS FLOWING TO MEXICO (FINAL ENVIRONMENTAL IMPACT STATEMENT),
Department of State, Washington, D.C.
Available from the National Technical Information Service, U.S. Dept. of Commerce, Springfield, Va. 22161, as EIS-NM-73-1516-F, $9.50 in paper copy, $2.25 in microfiche. September 26, 1973. 329 p, 12 tab, 41 map, 4 graph.

Descriptors: *Salinity, *Colorado River, *Mexican Water Treaty, *Desalination, Environmental effects, Rio Grande River, Deserts, Farms, Brines, Saline water, Construction, Brine disposal, Colorado River Basin, Seepage canals, Colorado, Mexico, Vegetation, Wildlife, Desalination processes, Desalination wastes, Water resources, Wastes, Weather modification.
Identifiers: *Environmental Impact Statements, International agreements.

Summarized are the anticipated environmental effects of a variety of proposed means of further reducing the salinity of the Colorado River waters being delivered to Mexico pursuant to the 1944 U.S.-Mexican Treaty for utilization of waters of the Colorado and Tijuana Rivers and of the Rio Grande. The environmental effects vary widely, depending upon the various options considered. The predicted adverse effects are primarily transitory and those normally associated with the period of construction and use of heavy construction equipment. Moderate amounts of desert, vegetation, farm lands and wildlife would be destroyed in the course of construction along the right of way. All of the desalting options have the inherent advantage of conserving scarce water resources in the area, but necessitate the taking of measures to dispose of the waste brine that is inevitably produced in the process. A favored possibility is to transport the brine along a 53 mile concrete land drain to the Santa Clara Slough. Alternatives considered include nine different desalting projects, relining canals to salvage water presently being lost through seepage, using weather modification techniques to augment available water resources, or placing a moratorium on all future federally supported development projects in the Colorado Basin. (Gagliardi-Florida)
W75-07782

HEAVY METALS REMOVAL BY THERMAL PROCESSES,
Princeton Univ., N.Y. Center for Environmental Studies.
For primary bibliographic entry see Field 5D.
W75-07798

METHOD OF STERILIZING REVERSE OSMOSIS WATER TREATMENT UNITS,
Culligan, Inc., Northbrook, Ill. (assignee).
For primary bibliographic entry see Field 5D.
W75-07806

3B. Water Yield Improvement

HYDROLOGIC IMPACT OF WATER MODIFICATION,
Agricultural Research Service, Chickasha, Okla.
E. H. Seely, and D. G. DeCoursey.
American Water Resources Bulletin, Vol 11, No 2, p 365-369, April 1975. 9 ref.

Descriptors: *Weather modification, Hydrology, *Rainfall, *Model studies, *Great Plains, *Risks, Agriculture, Agroclimatology, Water supply, Forecasting, Estimating.
Identifiers: *Hydrologic impact.

Weather modification is being proposed as a routine method of augmenting agricultural water supplies in the Southern Great Plains. Some of the potential hydrologic impacts of weather modification are discussed. Previous work in assessing hydrologic impact is reviewed; the conclusion is drawn that the work is insufficient. An approach based on hydrologic models, is suggested that can consider undertainties about the effect of weather modification on rainfall and some uncertainties about the effect of model error on impact conclusions. (ARS)
W75-07505

USE OF TIME-LAPSE PHOTOGRAPHY TO ASSESS POTENTIAL INTERCEPTION IN ARIZONA PONDEROSA PINE,
Arizona Univ., Tucson. Dept. of Watershed Management.
For primary bibliographic entry see Field 2C.
W75-07547

THE EFFECT OF MOISTURE DEFICIT ON CARBOHYDRATE METABOLISM OF DESERT PLANTS,
Akademiya Nauk Uzbekskoi SSR, Tashkent. Institut Botaniki.
For primary bibliographic entry see Field 2I.
W75-07602

WATERSHED MANAGEMENT IN ARIZONA'S MIXED CONIFER FORESTS: THE STATUS OF OUR KNOWLEDGE,
Forest Service (USDA), Fort Collins, Colo. Rocky Mountain Forest and Range Experiment Station.
For primary bibliographic entry see Field 4C.
W75-07648

RUNOFF AND EROSION AFTER BRUSH SUPPRESSION ON THE NATURAL DRAINAGE WATERSHEDS IN CENTRAL ARIZONA,
Arizona State Univ., Tempe.
P. A. Ingebo, and A. R. Hibbert.
U.S. Department of Agriculture, Forest Service, Research Note RM-275, 7 p, December, 1974. 2 fig, 2 tab, 5 ref.

Descriptors: *Chaparral, *Brush control, *Water yield improvement, *Erosion, *Watershed management, Brushlands, Streamflow, Sediment transport, Grasses, Shrubs, *Arizona, Southwest U.S., Arid lands, Range management, Runoff, Storm runoff, Surface runoff, Watersheds(Basins).

Brush cover on two small watersheds totaling 26 acres in central Arizona was chemically suppressed in 1954-1955. Annual streamflow subsequently increased 22% (0.36 area-inch), much less than on other treated chaparral watersheds. Most of the increase in streamflow occurred during the winter season. Annual sediment movement from the treated watersheds was reduced by and about 1 cu ft/acre. Grasses, forbs, and half-shrubs, which were not sprayed, increased after the chemical treatment. (Witt-IPC)
W75-07655

OPPORTUNITIES FOR INCREASING WATER YIELDS AND OTHER MULTIPLE USE VALUES ON PONDEROSA PINE FOREST LANDS,
Forest Service (USDA), Fort Collins, Colo. Rocky Mountain Forest and Range Experiment Station.
H. E. Brown, M. B. Baker, Jr., J. J. Rogers, W. P. Clary, and J. L. Kovner.
U.S. Department of Agriculture, Forest Service, Research Paper RM-129, 40 p, December, 1974. 23 fig, 11 tab, 69 ref.

Descriptors: *Water yield improvement, *Forest management, *Multiple purpose, *Ponderosa pine trees, Watershed management, *Arizona, Southwest U.S., Lumber, Water, Wildlife, Floods, Sedimentation, Water quality, Land management, Livestock, Grazing, Land clearing, Costs, Lumbering, Environmental effects, Coniferous forests, Recreation, Aesthetics, Model studies, Grasses, Pine trees, Lumbering.
Identifiers: Beaver Creek(Arizona).

Multiple use productivity is described for watershed lands in the ponderosa pine type of Arizona, with special emphasis on the Beaver Creek Pilot Watershed near Flagstaff. Yields of timber, herbage, and water under past management are reported, along with information on wildlife values, esthetics, flood and sedimentation hazards, and water quality. Changes in productivity and environmental quality are then described following five experimental land treatments including livestock grazing and various levels of forest thinning and clearing. Preliminary analytical procedures for predicting treatment responses and costs allow the user to estimate the tradeoffs in production and environmental quality. Some further research need for bringing these and other response models to operational capability is described. (Witt-IPC)
W75-07660

3C. Use Of Water Of Impaired Quality

SALT TOLERANCE IN THE WILD RELATIVES OF THE CULTIVATED TOMATO: WATER BALANCE AND ABSCISIC ACID IN LYCOPERSICON ESCULENTUM AND L. PERUVIANUM UNDER LOW AND HIGH SALINITY,
Negev Inst. for Arid Zone Research, Beersheba (Israel). Div. of Life Sciences.
M. Tal, and U. Gavish.
Australian Journal of Agricultural Research, Vol 24, No 3, p 353-361, May 1973. 5 tab, 2 fig, 16 ref.

Descriptors: *Salinity, *Transpiration, *Tomatoes, *Salt tolerance, Stress, Stomata, Osmotic pressure, Flow resistance, Adaptation, Saline water.
Identifiers: Abscisic acid.

Transpiration of whole plants and detached leaves, stomatal density and opening, and abscisic acid level were measured for the cultivated tomato and the more salt tolerant wild species grown under control and saline conditions. Transpiration was higher in the wild species, but decreased under more salinity. Wild plants had fewer stomata per unit leaf area, but these opened wider in the control and closed more in the saline solution as compared with the cultivated plants. Root resistance to water flow was higher in wild plants. The abscisic acid level was higher in the cultivated plants and increased in both plants under salinity. The results suggest that the higher osmotic pressure produced in the leaves of the wild plants grown in saline solution enables them to absorb more water from this solution. In addition, better stomatal control and a greater increase in mesophyll resistance to water flow under salinity appear to be significant in the superior adaptation of wild species to stress. (Mastic-Arizona)
W75-07364

EFFICIENT USE OF WATER - POLICY AND PROBLEMS,
Ministry of Agriculture, Tel-Aviv (Israel). Water Commission.
For primary bibliographic entry see Field 6D.
W75-07401

ISRAEL'S WATER ECONOMY AND ITS PROBLEMS IN THE EARLY SEVENTIES,
Tahal Consulting Engineers Ltd, Tel-Aviv (Israel). Long Range Planning Section.
For primary bibliographic entry see Field 6D.
W75-07402

AN EVALUATION OF THE USE OF WASTE HEAT FOR SOIL WARMING IN THE SOUTHEAST,
North Carolina State Univ., Raleigh. Dept. of Biological and Agricultural Engineering.
R. W. Skaggs, D. C. Sanders, and C. R. Willey.
Available from the National Technical Information Service, Springfield, Va 22161 as PB-241 739, $5.25 in paper copy, $2.25 in microfiche. North Carolina Water Resources Research Institute, Raleigh, UNC-WRRI Report No 103, March 1975. 100 p, 34 fig, 28 tab, 30 ref, append. OWRT A-060-NC(1). 14-31-0001-4033.

Descriptors: *Heat transfer, Surface irrigation, Subsurface irrigation, Cooling water, *Heated water, *Soil temperature, *Southeast U.S., *Horticultural crops, *Mathematical models, North Carolina, Evaluation.
Identifiers: *Soil warming, Waste heat.

A field experiment was conducted to evaluate the use of waste heat for soil warming in the southeast. The water was heated to 100F (38C) and circulated through a network of one-inch diameter, 18 ft. long plastic pipes buried at a depth of 20 inches and spaced 20 inches apart. Soil temperature and heat flux measurements determined the effect of soil warming in combination with surface and subsurface irrigation on the soil temperature regime and on the amount of heat that can be transferred. The growth, development and yield of six horticultural crops were evaluated. Heat could be transferred to the soil system at rates ranging from 11.9 Btu/ft2 during hot periods to greater than 43.7 Btu/ft2 hr during cold periods. Heat transfer rates were increased 4 percent during summer months by subirrigation. Low volume sprinkler irrigation increased heat transfer rates by 16% and when both were used the heat transfer was increased 24%. During cool periods soil warming increased soil surface temperature by 9-12F and at the 8-inch depth by 15-20F. The mathematical model of Kendrick and Havens was used to project the heat flux measurements to prototype scale systems. A soil warming system of the type studied would require approximately 16,000 acres in the summer and 3,800 acres in the winter to handle the waste heat from a 1000 megawatt plant in North Carolina. The soil warming system will not now be economically competitive with conventational cooling methods in the Southeast. (Stewart-North Carolina State)
W75-07599

MINIMIZING THE SALT BURDENS OF IRRIGATION DRAINAGE WATERS,
Agricultural Research Service, Riverside, Calif. Salinity Lab.
For primary bibliographic entry see Field 5G.
W75-07620

LAND APPLICATION OF WASTEWATER AT COLORADO SPRINGS,
Colorado Springs Dept. of Public Utilities, Colo. Wastewater Div.
For primary bibliographic entry see Field 5G.
W75-07670

PLANT-WATER-USE EFFICIENCY WITH GROWTH REGULATORS AND TRANSPIRATION SUPPRESSANTS,
Delaware Univ., Newark. Dept. of Plant Science.
D. J. Fieldhouse.
Available from the National Technical Information Service, Springfield, Va 22161 as PB-241 897, $3.25 in paper copy, $2.25 in microfiche. Completion Report, August 1972. 6 p, 3 ref. OWRT A-010-DEL(1). 14-01-0001-1627.

Descriptors: *Growth rates, *Transpiration, *Retardants, Irrigation, Tomatoes, Tobacco, Seed treatment, Fruit Germination, Mature growth stage, *Water utilization.
Identifiers: Pepper, Water stress, Transplants.

Water stress in plants may be minimized by the use of cultural practices that stimulate early growth, reduce water loss, restrict vegetative growth, control fruit set, and/or hasten maturity, thus reducing the need for irrigation. Tomato and pepper seeds germinated sooner and produced more rapid early growth when soaked in salt solutions at some time prior to planting. The response was not reduced by drying and storing the seeds for several months after treatment. Gibberellic acid at low concentrations on very young seedlings increased the rate of growth at below optimum temperatures. These treatments would speed up early growth so that young seedling would reach a more drought resistance stage sooner. A wax base transpiration suppressant was effective for reducing water loss from tomato, pepper, tobacco and sweet potato transplants. Applications could be made as a spray or as a plant dip. Proper selection of a surfactant was essential with the dip application. Alar (succinic acid 2,2-dimethyl hydrazide) and Ethrel (2-chloroethanephosphonic acid) were effective on tomatoes and peppers for reducing late vegetative growth and fruit set, thus, providing increased water-use efficiency.
W75-07724

EFFECTS OF BRACKISH IRRIGATION WATER AND FERTILIZERS ON MILLET AND CORN,
Hebrew Univ., Rehovoth (Israel).
S. Ravikovitch.
Exp Agric. Vol 9, No 2, p 181-188, 1973, Illus.

Descriptors: *Irrigation water, *Brackish water, Crop production, *Corn(Field), Millet, *Fertilizers, Nitrogen, Phosphorus.

Millet irrigated with water of EC (electrical conductivity) 3.30 mmho/cm produced yields 79-93% of the control (tap water of 0.61 mmho/cm), depending on the N and P treatment applied. With water of EC 5.05 mmho/cm yields equivalent to 52-72% were obtained. Corn yields were 78-90% of the control with irrigation water of 4.60 mmho/cm and 55-64% when irrigated with water of 7.06 mmho/cm. The N and P contents were mostly higher in plants grown on plots irrigated with brackish water.--Copyright 1973, Biological Abstracts, Inc.
W75-07754

WASTEWATER IRRIGATION: ITS LEGAL IMPACT,
Virginia Polytechnic Inst. and State Univ., Blacksburg. Water Resources Research Center.
For primary bibliographic entry see Field 6E.
W75-07766

THE FEASIBILITY OF PENAEID SHRIMP CULTURE IN BRACKISH PONDS RECEIVING TREATED SEWAGE EFFLUENT,
North Carolina State Univ., Raleigh. Sea Grant Program.
W. L. Rickards.
UNC Sea Grant Reprint No. 58, (1974). 10 p. Reprinted from: Wastewater Use in the Production of Food and Fiber-Proceedings, 1974. U.S. Environmental Protection Agency, Environmental Protection Technology Series EPA-660/2-74-041, p 504-512. NOAA Grant OSG 2-35178.

Descriptors: *Aquiculture, *Aeration, *Shrimp, *Cultures, Environment, Sewage effluents, Brackish water, Impaired water quality, Aerobic treatment, Aerobic conditions, Oxygen, Oxygen requirements, Dissolved oxygen, Growth rates, Environmental effects, Size.
Identifiers: *Penaeid shrimp, *Treated sewage effluent ponds.

A study was conducted as an extension of a previous project where penaeid shrimp had been stocked in control and treated sewage ponds -- shrimp grew in control ponds but failed to survive in treated sewage ponds. It had been concluded in the earlier project that low levels of dissolved oxygen in the water at night and wide diurnal pH fluctuations were responsible for shrimp failure. The subsequent project was designed to modify oxygen and pH regimes in a sewage pond and subsequently stock it with shrimp to determine whether or not factors in addition to oxygen and/or pH had been responsible for the previous shrimp mortalities. Shrimp were able to survive and grow in the aerated sewage pond. New studies can proceed involving penaeid shrimp food chains utilizing treated domestic effluent and production dynamics in aquacultural applications. (NOAA)
W75-07830

3D. Conservation In Domestic and Municipal Use

THE CENTRAL ARIZONA PROJECT, A STAFF REPORT TO THE METROPOLITAN UTILITIES MANAGEMENT AGENCY BOARD AND THE MAYOR AND COUNCIL OF THE CITY OF TUCSON,
Tucson Metropolitan Utilities Management Agency Board, Ariz.
For primary bibliographic entry see Field 4B.
W75-07372

FIELD TRIP GUIDE - BOOK FOR HYDROGEOLOGY OF THE TWIN CITIES ARTESIAN BASIN,
Geological Survey, Denver, Colo.
For primary bibliographic entry see Field 4B.
W75-07573

EFFECTS OF THE MAY 5-6, 1973, STORM IN THE GREATER DENVER AREA, COLORADO,
Geological Survey, Reston, Va.
For primary bibliographic entry see Field 2E.
W75-07582

CHARACTERIZATION AND TREATMENT OF URBAN LAND RUNOFF,
North Carolina Water Resources Research Inst., Raleigh.
For primary bibliographic entry see Field 5D.
W75-07607

TEN COUNTIES INVESTIGATION: MUNICIPAL, INDUSTRIAL AND ARGICULTURAL WATER DEMAND IN COLUSA, GLENN, HUMBOLDT, LAKE, MARIN, MENDOCINO, NAPA, SOLANO, SONOMA, AND YOLO COUNTIES,
California State Dept. of Water Resources, Sacramento.
For primary bibliographic entry see Field 6D.
W75-07611

URBAN STORMWATER MANAGEMENT AND TECHNOLOGY: AN ASSESSMENT,
Metcalf and Eddy, Inc., Palo Alto, Calif.
For primary bibliographic entry see Field 5D.
W75-07692

3E. Conservation In Industry

METHODS OF COMMUNICATING ACTIVITIES IN POLLUTION ABATEMENT BY FIVE HUNDRED MAJOR INDUSTRIAL CORPORATIONS IN THE UNITED STATES,
Texas A and M Univ., College Station. Environmental Quality Program.
For primary bibliographic entry see Field 5G.
W75-07359

TEXAS WATERBORNE COMMERCE COMMODITY FLOW STATISTICS,
Texas Transportation Inst., College Station.
For primary bibliographic entry see Field 6B.
W75-07376

JAPAN: A SURVEY OF PORTS, DEEP WATER TERMINALS, AND VESSELS,
Army Engineer District, San Francisco, Calif. Economics Branch.
For primary bibliographic entry see Field 6C.
W75-07379

SOUTHWEST ENERGY STUDY. SUMMARY REPORT.
Southwest Energy Federal Task Force.
For primary bibliographic entry see Field 6B.
W75-07380

AN EVALUATION OF THE SUITABILITY OF ERTS DATA FOR THE PURPOSES OF PETROLEUM EXPLORATION,
Earth Satellite Corp., Washington, D.C.
For primary bibliographic entry see Field 7B.
W75-07488

AUTOMATED STRIP MINE AND RECLAMATION MAPPING FROM ERTS,
Ohio State Univ., Columbus.
For primary bibliographic entry see Field 7B.
W75-07491

MINERAL RESOURCES, GEOLOGICAL STRUCTURE, AND LANDFORM SURVEYS,
National Aeronautics and Space Administration, Greenbelt, Md. Goddard Space Flight Center.
For primary bibliographic entry see Field 7C.
W75-07500

FOSSIL FUELS AND POWER GENERATION IN THE COLORADO RIVER BASIN,
Brigham Young Univ., Provo, Utah. Dept. of Botany and Range Science.
K. T. Harper.
In: Environmental Management in the Colorado River Basin, October 15-16, 1973, Salt Lake City, Utah, Utah State University Press, Logan, 1974, p 164-173, 1 tab, 21 ref.

Descriptors: *Colorado River Basin, *Energy conversion, *Environmental effects, *Oil shales, Arizona, New Mexico, Utah, Colorado, Wyoming, Nevada, California, Strip mines, Fossil fuels, *Pollution abatement, Powerplants, Cost-benefit analysis.
Identifiers: Environmental management.

The Colorado River Basin has vast reserves of fossil fuels, particularly coal and oil shale. Energy needs nationwide and the cost of importing petroleum will force development of the basin's resources. Environmental impacts associated with coal fueled power generating plants will be diverse. Disruption can be exported in connection with mining, transportation, power generation, and power conveyance. The magnitude of any impact will depend upon the size of the industry, attention given impact mitigating practices and unforeseen technological advances. Studies are necessary if these energy resources are to be exploited in a manner compatible with the environment. Better methods of strip mining and of land rehabilitation must be found. More thought should be given to the economic and social change inherent in the eventual abandonment of the strip-mine-powerplant complexes. Finally, there is a real need for an accurate assessment of the actual cost of pollution controls now being forced on the power industry. These costs are probably more than consumers are actually willing to pay for the results derived. (See also W75-07525) (Bowden-Arizona)
W75-07537

POWER GENERATION AND THE COLORADO RIVER BASIN,
Utah Power and Light Co., Salt Lake City.
V. A. Finlayson.
In: Environmental Management in the Colorado River Basin, October 15-16, 1973, Salt Lake City, Utah, Utah State University Press, Logan, 1974, p 174-189, 3 fig, 3 tab, 21 ref.

Descriptors: *Colorado River Basin, *Energy conversion, *Geothermal studies, Water resources, *Water utilization, Arizona, Utah, New Mexico, Colorado, Wyoming, Nevada, California, Powerplants, Strip mines, Oil shales, Fossil fuels, Oil, Natural gas, Nuclear powerplants, *Long-term planning, Environmental effects.
Identifiers: Environmental management.

Utah Power and Light Company's projected energy needs and resources are outlined. The company is committed to finding fossil fuel substitutes. However, shortages of oil and natural gas and delays in the nuclear power program make coal the key fuel for at least the next decade. Particulates emitted by coal fired electric plants can be removed; it is questionable whether sulfur removal is worth the costs in energy and money. Water supply in the basin is adequate for energy development provided the states allocate water for such use. Alternative energy sources are assessed. Geothermal power may be on line in the 1980's, and nuclear plants are a definite alternative for that decade. Coal gasification, oil shale, and tar sands are all handicapped by large water needs. Solar energy conversion will not be commercially available until the year 2000. (See also W75-07525) (Bowden-Arizona)
W75-07538

TRANSPORTATION AND REGIONAL ENVIRONMENTAL MANAGEMENT,
Wyoming Univ., Laramie. Dept. of Economics; and Div. of Business and Economic Research.
For primary bibliographic entry see Field 6B.
W75-07539

A STUDY OF THE DYEING OF NYLON 6 WITH DISPERSE DYES FROM CHLORINATED HYDROCARBON SOLVENTS,
Auburn Univ., Ala. Dept. of Textile Engineering.
W. S. Perkins, and D. M. Hall.
Textile Research Journal, Vol 44, No 7, July 1974, p 528-531, 3 fig, 2 tab, 14 ref. OWRT A-033-ALA(1).

Descriptors: *Dyes, *Plastics, Solvents, Sorption, Solubility.
Identifiers: *Chlorinated hydrocarbons, *Dispersive dyes, Partition coefficients.

Dyeing of nylon 6 (polycaprolactam) film from trichlorethylene and perchloroethylene with several purified dyes is reported. Rate curves and diffusion data indicate that the sorption of disperse dyes by nylon from these solvents is slower by 50-100 times their sorption by polyester. Dyes with polar substituents give higher partition coefficients, probably due to their lower solubility in the solvents and higher solubility in nylon 6 than in very nonpolar dyes. Very few of the dyes studied have partition coefficients which would make exhaust dyeing desirable; however, the possibility of synthesizing dyes or finding dyes which would have application to nylon does appear to exist.
W75-07589

RECOVERY AND REUSE OF COAGULANTS FROM TREATMENT OF WATER AND WASTEWATER,
Virginia Polytechnic Inst. and State Univ., Blacksburg. Dept. of Civil Engineering.
For primary bibliographic entry see Field 5D.
W75-07600

TEN COUNTIES INVESTIGATION: MUNICIPAL, INDUSTRIAL AND ARGICULTURAL WATER DEMAND IN COLUSA, GLENN, HUMBOLDT, LAKE, MARIN, MENDOCINO, NAPA, SOLANO, SONOMA, AND YOLO COUNTIES,
California State Dept. of Water Resources, Sacramento.
For primary bibliographic entry see Field 6D.
W75-07611

STUDY OF THE RELATION BETWEEN RESIDUAL SODA AND WATER-EXTRACTABLE COMPONENTS OF VACUUM DRUM WASHED KRAFT PULP AND OF REPULPED CORRUGATED CONTAINER EFFLUENT CHARACTERISTICS,
National Council of the Paper Industry for Air and Stream Improvement, Inc., New York.
For primary bibliographic entry see Field 5B.
W75-07634

MEMBRANE PROCESSES FOR FRACTIONATION AND CONCENTRATION OF SPENT SULFITE LIQUORS,
Institute of Paper Chemistry, Appleton, Wis.
For primary bibliographic entry see Field 5D.
W75-07638

PROSPECTS FOR THE APPLICATION OF REVERSE OSMOSIS IN THE PULP AND PAPER INDUSTRY (PERSPEKTIVY PUZITIA REVERZNEJ OSMOZY V CELULOZOPAPIERENSKOM PRIEMYSLE),
Vyskumny Ustav Papiern a Celulozy, Bratislava (Czechoslovakia).
For primary bibliographic entry see Field 5D.
W75-07639

GULF STATES (PAPER CORPORATIONS'S TUSCALOOSA, ALABAMA) NEW MULTI-HEARTH FURNACE WASTE TREATMENT SYSTEM,
Gulf States Paper Corp., Tuscaloosa, Ala.
For primary bibliographic entry see Field 5D.
W75-07641

ENVIRONMENTAL PROTECTION AND ECONOMIC ASPECTS OF INTERNAL WATER CIRCULATION SYSTEMS IN THE PULP AND PAPER INDUSTRY (UMWELTFREUNDLICHE UND WIRTSCHAFTLICHE ASPEKTE INNERER WASSERKREISLAUEFE IN DER PAPIER- UND ZELLSTOFF-INDUSTRIE),
For primary bibliographic entry see Field 5D.
W75-07643

PILOT SCALE TREATMENT OF WINE STILLAGE,
California State Dept. of Agriculture, San Francisco. Wine Advisory Board.
For primary bibliographic entry see Field 5D.
W75-07699

ULTRA PURE WATER PROCESS AND APPARATUS,
Aqua Media, Sunnyvale, Calif. (assignee).
For primary bibliographic entry see Field 5F.
W75-07810

CONDENSED WATER DECHLORINATION APPARATUS,
Hitachi Ltd., Tokyo (Japan). (assignee)
For primary bibliographic entry see Field 5D.
W75-07813

3F. Conservation In Agriculture

EFFECT OF DIFFERENT IRRIGATION PRACTICES ON THE GROWTH AND YIELD OF GRAPES (IN RUSSIAN),
A. I. Nasimov.
Uzb Biol Zh. Vol 17, No 1, p 17-19, 1973.

Descriptors: *Irrigation practices, *Plant growth, Fruit crops, Sprinkler irrigation, Soil-water-plant relationships, Furrow irrigation, Subsurface irrigation.
Identifiers: Grapevines.

Overhead sprinkling and subsoil irrigation increased the yield and quality of grapes and improved the growth and development of the plants. The 4-yr average yield (1967-1970) on 10-13-yr grapevines with subsoil irrigation was 174 cent/ha, with overhead sprinkling 131 cent/ha, and in the control (furrow irrigation) 103 cent/ha; on 3-6-yr grapevines the yield with subsoil irrigation was 187 cent/ha and in the control 122. The weight of the berries and clusters increased with overhead sprinkling. A more intense accumulation of sugar was noted with subsoil irrigation.--Copyright 1974, Biological Abstracts, Inc.
W75-07358

COMPETITIVE INTERACTION OF GRASSES WITH CONTRASTING TEMPERATURE RESPONSES AND WATER STRESS TOLERANCES,
University of New England, Armidale (Australia). Dept. of Agronomy.
W. Harris, and A. Lazenby.
Australian Journal of Agricultural Research, Vol 25, No 2, p 227-246, March 1974. 9 tab, 29 ref.

Descriptors: *Grasses, *Arid lands, *Drought tolerance, *Crop production, *Irrigated land, *Plant growth, Pastures, Stress, Competition.
Identifiers: Lolium perenne, Lolium perenne x multiflorum, Phalaris tuberosa, Festuca arundinacea, Paspalum dilatatum.

Grass species grown for two years in monoculture and two-species mixtures were studied under dryland and irrigated treatments. Competition effects were described with the use of diallel analysis and the aggressivities of the grass species were shown. Phalaris tuberosa in monoculture produced the highest yield under dryland conditions. Although appearing to assist survival of this species in mixture, marked dominance of Lolium perenne x multiflorum was detrimental in that it suppressed P. tuberosa, F. arundinacea, and P. dilatatum and thus restricted the potential of these species to produce in dryland conditions. This study confirmed the values of cool season growth and the high digestibility of the ryegrasses. However, the ability of P. tuberosa and F. arundinacea to grow and survive under conditions of water stress and overgrazing is of longer-term value to pastures of the region (Armidale, N.S.W.). Including only a small amount of ryegrass in seed mixtures would not only reduce the effects of ryegrass suppression, but would also reduce inter-ryegrass competition allowing development of larger ryegrass plants which may survive longer and contribute more to pasture production. (Mastic-Arizona)
W75-07363

HYDRAULIC DESIGN OF TWIN-CHAMBER TRICKLE IRRIGATION LATERALS,
Hawaii Univ., Honolulu. Dept. of Agricultural Engineering.
I-P. Wu, and D. D. Fangmeier.
University of Arizona, Tucson, Agricultural Experiment Station, Technical Bulletin 216. December 1974. 11 p, 14 fig, 7 ref.

Descriptors: *Trickle irrigation, *Hydraulic design, *Hydraulic models, *Irrigation engineering, Model studies, Computer programs, Tubes, Orifices, Orifice flow, Pressure.
Identifiers: Twin-chamber tubing, Single-chamber tubing.

Twin chamber tubing is a special tubing developed for trickle irrigation and consists of a main chamber and a secondary chamber. The ratio of numbers of orifices in the main to the secondary chamber controls the pressure differences between the two chambers. Water is discharged from orifices in the wall of the main chamber into the secondary chamber which discharges water for irrigation. The main advantages of twin-chamber tubing are that larger orifices can be used without increasing discharge and longer lengths of tubing can be used with a more uniform orifice discharge than with single-chamber tubing. The purposes of this study were to develop a simple model for computer simulation of twin-chamber tubing, and to develop design curves from the computed data. Hydraulic analysis of twin-chamber irrigation tubing was made by considering the main chamber to be the supply tube and the secondary chamber to be the distribution tube. By doing so, hydraulic analysis of a single chamber irrigation tube can be used to determine both pressure and discharge distribution along a twin-chamber irrigation tube. Development of design charts and procedures of engineering applications are described. (Mastic-Arizona)
W75-07365

PRODUCTIVITY OF VEGETABLE CROPS IN A REGION OF HIGH SOLAR INPUT, I. GROWTH AND DEVELOPMENT OF THE POTATO (SOLANUM TUBEROSUM L.), II. YIELDS AND EFFICIENCIES OF WATER USE AND ENERGY,
Commonwealth Scientific and Industrial Research Organization, Griffith (Australia). Div. of Irrigation Research.
P. J. M. Sale.
Australian Journal of Agricultural Research, Vol 24, No 5, p 733-749; 751-762, September 1973. 11 fig, 9 tab, 39 ref.

Descriptors: *Potatoes, *Solar radiation, *Crop production, *Irrigation, *Water utilization, *Irrigation effects, Plant growth, Photosynthesis.
Identifiers: Shading.

Details are given of yields and size gradings of three potato crops grown under conditions of high solar input, high temperature and varying irrigation treatments. The first part of this study describes the growth and development of the potato under three different levels of solar input and two levels of irrigation. The second part describes the final yields and efficiency of water use and energy by the potato crops under the different levels of treatment. Total yields were up to 50 t ha(-1). Differences resulting from different irrigation treatments were surprisingly small. Water use was about 300 g for each 1 g dry weight produced and efficiency was slightly greater in the wetter irrigation treatments. Reductions of 21 percent and 34 percent of the solar input markedly reduced yields. Tuber moisture percentage at harvest was not affected by irrigation treatment differences, but was reduced as shading increased. It is suggested that an increase in plant density and encouragement of early haulm growth may increase the yield by increasing the numbers of tubers which develop per unit area. (Mastic-Arizona)
W75-07366

PERFORMANCE OF BLUE GRAMA, SIDEOATS GRAMA, AND ALKALI SACATON ACCESSIONS UNDER IRRIGATION NEAR LAS CRUCES, NEW MEXICO,
New Mexico State Univ., University Park. Dept. of Agronomy.
F. A. Quinones.
Agricultural Experiment Station, New Mexico State University, Research Report No. 289, November 1974. 8 p, 7 tab, 3 ref.

Descriptors: *Irrigation, *Grama grasses, *New Mexico, *Plant growth, *Alkaline soils, *Crop production, Range management, Varieties, Agronomy, Seeds, Arid lands, Forage grasses, Germination, Adaptation.
Identifiers: Alkali sacaton, Alkaline soils, Seed production, Blue grama, Sideoats grama.

Blue grama, sideoats grama, and alkali sacaton are important grasses on the New Mexico rangelands. Blue grama and sideoats grama are warm season perennial grasses that are palatable to all livestock and maintain a high nutritive value. Alkali sacaton is also a warm season perennial grass that is relatively palatable and provides spring and summer grazing in alkaline areas. The yield and agronomic characteristics of various accessions of these grasses were evaluated in comparison with the cultivars or accessions commonly used for range reseedings. A test of four blue grama grass varieties shows the Lovington variety to be satisfactory in most traits. PMNM-118 was much the same, and did produce seed under unfavorable conditions when other strains yielded poorly. A sideoats grama test with four varieties showed the Vaughn to be a desirable cultivar, but PMNM-28 exhibited many favorable traits and should be evaluated further as a possible replacement for areas to which Vaughn is not adapted. The evaluation of alkali sacaton indicated A-920 to be a good forage producer; better methods or locations for producing seed should be investigated. The alkali sacaton accession PMC-14 was found to be desirable for use in mixtures for reseeding New Mexico ranges. (Mastic-Arizona)
W75-07367

THE EFFECT OF LEVEL OF WATER INTAKE ON SOME ASPECTS OF DIGESTION AND NITROGEN METABOLISM OF THE 'DESERT SHEEP' OF THE SUDAN,
Khartoum Univ. (Sudan). Faculty of Agriculture.
H. E. Osman, and B. Fadlalla.
Journal of Agricultural Science, Cambridge, Vol 82, part 1, p 61-69, February 1974. 10 tab, 24 ref.

Descriptors: *Water consumption, *Water requirements, *Digestion, *Grazing, *Arid lands, *Sheep, Hay, Water shortage, Proteins, Nitrogen, Dry seasons, Metabolism.
Identifiers: *Sudan desert sheep, Organic matter.

Five trials were conducted on eight adult rams (Sudan desert sheep) to study the effect of water intake restriction on some aspects of digestion and nitrogen metabolism. Feeds used were berseem hay (Medicago sativa), lubia hay (Dolichos lablab), maize hay (Zea mais), a concentrate mixture, and a mixture of desert grasses. Restriction of water did not affect digestibility of organic matter, crude protein, or crude fiber significantly. Increases in rumen ammonia and blood urea nitrogen coneentration were reduced by water restriction except when the desert grasses were fed. Restriction of water intake also slightly increased the rate of fermentation of rumen contents which is taken as a measure of microbial activity in the rumen, and retention of nitrogen. The results are interpreted as indicative of more efficient nitrogen utilization under water restriction conditions. To understand the nutritional status of the Sudan desert sheep it is necessary to study the levels of feed intake, water consumption, and grazing habits during the dry season. This will help in assessing the effect of a drinking water shortage on the protein metabolism of desert sheep. (Mastic-Arizona)
W75-07373

PREHISTORIC SOIL AND WATER CONTROL IN THE AMERICAN SOUTHWEST: A CASE STUDY,
Northern Arizona Univ., Flagstaff. Dept. of Anthropology.
D. Brooks.
M.A. Thesis, May 1974. 59 p, 9 fig, 5 tab, 2 plates, 33 ref.

Descriptors: *Utah, *Arid lands, *Dams, *Agriculture, *Irrigation systems, *Soil-water-plant relationships, Corn(Field), Runoff, Soil moisture, *Southwest U.S.
Identifiers: Prehistoric Agriculture, Indians(American).

Although prehistoric water control systems have long been noted in the American Southwest, scholars have displayed little interest in how the systems actually worked. One type of system, check dams, on Horse Flats, a high plateau on the western periphery of Elk Ridge in southeastern Utah, is described. At an elevation of 8,000 feet, the area seems uninviting for agriculture, partienlarly corn. Yet thirty surviving check dams indicate that the Flats were cropped. Several tentative conclusions about how the system worked are offered. The dams were filled by natural sedimentation, not human transport. Evidence suggests that the system grew from lower dams upward. Corn seems to have been the main crop. The site seems to have been exploited between 1000 A.D. and 1300 A.D. It remains to be discovered just how productive such techniques are in utilizing runoff for agriculture. (Bowden-Arizona)
W75-07375

EFFECTS OF SURFACE MOISTURE SUPPLY ON THE SUBSOIL NUTRITIONAL REQUIREMENTS OF LUCERNE (MEDICAGO SATIVA L.),
Commonwealth Scientific and Industrial Research Organization, Canberra (Australia). Div. of Plant Industry.
For primary bibliographic entry see Field 2G.
W75-07393

WILDLIFE, ECOLOGY, AND PLANNING IN A PROPOSED IRRIGATION DEVELOPMENT IN NORTH DAKOTA,
North Dakota State Univ., Fargo.
For primary bibliographic entry see Field 6G.
W75-07400

THE EFFECT OF YOUNG FIELD SHELTERBELTS ON THE ELEMENTS OF MICROCLIMATE AND ON THE YIELD OF AGRICULTURAL CROPS,
E. V. Antonov.
Tr Kaz Nauchno-Issled Inst Lesn Khoz. 7. p 109-114, 1970.

Descriptors: *Shelterbelts, *Agronomic crops, *Soil-water-plant relationships, Corn, Environmental effects, Microclimatology, Wheat, Snow cover, Wind velocity, Chernozems, Grasslands.
Identifiers: Betula-verrucosa, Populus-balsamifera, USSR, Poplars, Steppes.

The investigations were conducted on the permanent study areas for the improvement of agriculture by forestry measures in the State farms of the Kokchetav Region (USSR) on ordinary and southern heavy loamy slightly solonetzic chernozems, where field shelterbelts (FSB) were established with the spacing of planting places of 1.0-1.5 x 1.5-3.0 m. The main tree species were Populus balsamifera and Betula verrucosa. The effeet of 3-4-yr-old strips on the reduction of wind velocity and on the snow distribution is felt at a distance 25-30 times the strip heights, whereas the effect of the 5-6-yr-old ones, as regards the increase of density, is felt at a distance 15-20 times the strip heights. Under the protection of 3-yr-old FSB of poplar, the yield of the corn herbage in the zone up to 70 m from the stands was 1500-8100 kg/ha higher than in the open steppe. Under the effeet of the 4-yr-old FSB of poplar, increase of yield of the 'Lyutestsens 167' spring wheat was observed up to a distance of 15-25 heights. On the whole, the yield increment due to FSB, in comparison with the open steppe, is 50-450 kg/ha in cereals, and 1500-8100 kg/ha in corn. Indexes are presented of the effect of FSB on the reduction of wind velocity, on evaporation from the open water surface, on air temperature and on distribution of snow.--Copyright 1974, Biological Abstracts, Inc.
W75-07408

A CALCULATION OF SUMMARY EVAPORATION OF AN OBSERVATION OF AN IRRIGATION REGIME OF SALINE SOILS,
Vsesoyuznyi Nauchno-Issledovatelskii Institut Gidrotekhniki i Melioratsii, Moscow (USSR).
For primary bibliographic entry see Field 2D.
W75-07415

ALKALOID CONTENT OF ROEMERIA REFRACTA (IN RUSSIAN),
Akademiya Nauk Uzbekskoi SSR, Tashkent. Institut Botaniki.
For primary bibliographic entry see Field 2I.
W75-07454

AGRICULTURE, FORESTRY, RANGE RESOURCES,
National Aeronautics and Space Administration, Houston, Tex., Lyndon B. Johnson Space Center.
For primary bibliographic entry see Field 7C.
W75-07493

AGRICULTURE, FORESTRY, RANGE RESOURCES,
National Aeronautics and Space Administration, Houston, Tex., Lyndon B. Johnson Space Center.
For primary bibliographic entry see Field 7C.
W75-07498

WATER QUALITY IN EASTERN OREGON,
Oregon State Univ., Corvallis. Dept. of Soil Science.
For primary bibliographic entry see Field 5B.
W75-07517

SEASONAL TRENDS AND VARIABILITY OF SOIL MOISTURE UNDER TEMPERATE PASTURE ON THE NORTHERN TABLELANDS OF NEW SOUTH WALES (AUSTRALIA),
University of New England, Armidale (Australia). Dept. of Agronomy and Soil Science.
For primary bibliographic entry see Field 2G.
W75-07520

AN EXAMINATION OF THE ENVIRONMENTAL CARRYING CAPACITY CONCEPT FOR THE AGRICULTURAL SECTOR OF THE COLORADO RIVER BASIN,
New Mexico State Univ., University Park.
G. W. Thomas.
In: Environmental Management in the Colorado River Basin, October 15-16, 1973, Salt Lake City, Utah, State University Press, Logan, 1974, p 119-148, 6 fig, 2 tab, 32 ref.

Descriptors: *Colorado River Basin, *Carrying capacity, *Environmental effects, *Agriculture, Arizona, New Mexico, Colorado, Utah, Wyoming, Nevada, California, Air pollution, Water pollution, *Long-term planning, Farm wastes, Fertilizers, Productivity, Fossil fuels.
Identifiers: Environmental management.

The resource base will limit man's ability to supply food and fiber to an ever increasing population. While the capacity of the environment for absorbing pollution will also intervene, the finite nature of resources will prove more important. Population control is essential in all countries. To feed the world in the year 2000, it will be necessary to double yields, increase acreage by at least 50 percent, introduce exotic foods such as insects, and destroy much wildlife and recreational lands. Innovations in crops and farming technology tend to reduce the land and water requirements per capita but require large energy subsidies. Organic farming, if practiced on a wide scale, will increase per capita land and water requirements because acre yields will drop. A vegetarian diet requires less land than a diet dependent on meat products, because humans move closer to the producers in the food chains. The substitution in recent decades of many foods for cereals and potatoes has increased per capita land and water requirements. Use of processed foods in the United States has increased pressure on land and water resources. The Colorado River Basin is rich in agricultural resources with water and fossil fuels as the major limiting factors in the region's carrying capacity. Growing populations will put more pressure on the region necessitating the forging of new energy technologies and better knowledge of the region's ecosystems. (See also W75-07525) (Bowden-Arizona)
W75-07535

AGRICULTURE'S MANAGEMENT OF THE ENVIRONMENT IN THE COLORADO RIVER BASIN,
American Farm Bureau Federation, Salt Lake City, Utah. Natural Resources Dept.
L. H. Johnson.
In: Environmental Management in the Colorado River Basin, October 15-16, 1973, Salt Lake City, Utah, Utah State University Press, 1974, p 149-162, 27 ref.

Descriptors: *Colorado River Basin, *Agriculture, *Droughts, *Water allocation(Policy), *Irrigation, Arizona, New Mexico, Utah, Colorado, Wyoming, Nevada, California, Flood damage, Erosion control, Salinity, Legal aspects.
Identifiers: Environmental management.

Agricultural efforts to manage the environment in the Colorado Basin constitute activities to manage six enemies: flood, drought, erosion, fire, disease and insects. The conservation of water resources in order to protect topsoils, stop floods, and mitigate droughts is perhaps agriculture's most distinguished accomplishment in the basin. Untamed rivers are truly wild, and periodically, such streams kill and destroy. Today, the basin holds

number of rainy days had any relationship with yield. In 30% of the total experimental period no rainfall was received during the growth period of 51-65 days of the crop, and there was no rain in nearly 50% of the total period during 66-80 days of the crop growth. In general, only once in 3 yr was the distribution of rainfall favorable for bunch groundnut in Saurashtra. Rainfall from the full pegging to the pod development (51-80 days) stage significantly correlated with yield. The most critical period was the week from full pegging to early pod development (51-57 days). A decrease in 1 mm rainfall during this week reduced the yield by 3.27 kg/ha.--Copyright 1973, Biological Abstracts, Inc.
W75-07753

MICROBIOLOGICAL AND ENZYMIC ACTIVITY OF IRRIGATED AND FERTILIZED SOIL (IN RUSSIAN),
Khersonskii Selskokhozyaistvennyi Institut (USSR).
K. F. Kiver.
Mikrobiol Zh (KYYIV). Vol 35, No 2, p 149-153, 1973, English summary.

Descriptors: *Irrigation practices, Irrigation efficiency, *Fertilization, Timing, Farm management, Fertilizers, Organic matter, Soil moisture, *Soil management, Microorganisms, Rhizosphere, Soil microorganisms.
Identifiers: Enzymic, Fertilization, Irrigation, Microbiological, Microorganisms, Soil, Tomato, Under.

Autumn irrigation during the vegetation period in combination with application of organic fertilizers improves moisture conditions and the nutrient regime of the soil and increases the total amount of microorganisms. The microbiological and enzymic processes are most intensive in rhizosphere soil. With improved biological activity of soil yield of tomatoes increased.--Copyright 1974, Biological Abstracts, Inc.
W75-07764

PORTABLE PEDESTAL MOUNTED TOWER IRRIGATOR,
Alco Standard Corp., Valley Forge, Pa. (assignee)
S. D. Newell.
U.S. Patent No. 3,870,235, 6 p, 25 fig, 12 ref; Official Gazette of the United States Patent Office, Vol 932, No 2, p 516, March 11, 1975.

Descriptors: *Patents, *Irrigation systems, *Water distribution(Applied), Equipment, Conservation, Agriculture, Conveyance structures.

A portable, rotatable, pedestal or column supported irrigating or liquid dispensing apparatus has a pair of oppositely balanced, cable tensioned and supported, horizontally extending, truss arm spray assemblies. They are mounted on a support base which is carried by a wheeled truck or car. The car is adapted to be moved from one operating location to another as required after an overlapping spray pattern has been effected at one area. The lower part of the construction includes a connector pipe that is mounted within a triangular-shaped lower support frame and provided with coupling means for connection to fluid inlet piping. A pipe extends centrally vertically upward from the lower pipe along and within the lower support frame and an upper rotatable support frame. The upper pipe is rotatably carried and driven and serves as a through-extending support for the upper frame and its truss assemblies. (Sinha-OEIS)
W75-07822

4. WATER QUANTITY MANAGEMENT AND CONTROL

4A. Control Of Water On The Surface

INFLUENCES OF WASTEWATER MANAGEMENT ON LAND USE: TAHOE BASIN 1950-1972,
California Univ., Santa Cruz.
For primary bibliographic entry see Field 5D.
W75-07362

PREHISTORIC SOIL AND WATER CONTROL IN THE AMERICAN SOUTHWEST: A CASE STUDY,
Northern Arizona Univ., Flagstaff. Dept. of Anthropology.
For primary bibliographic entry see Field 3F.
W75-07375

WATER RIGHTS,
Wisconsin Univ., Madison. School of Law.
For primary bibliographic entry see Field 6E.
W75-07378

WATER SUPPLY AND WASTEWATER DISPOSAL IN RURAL AREAS OF INDIA,
Greenleaf/Telesca, Miami, Fla. Environmental Sciences Dept.
D. S. Airan.
Water Resources Bulletin, Vol 9, No 5, p 1035-1040, October 1973. 14 ref.

Descriptors: *Water supply, *Waste water disposal, *Environmental sanitation, *Rural areas, Human population, Planning, Projects, Public utilities, Public health, Design standards.
Identifiers: *India, *Environmental hygiene, Developing countries, Urban centers, Case study, Beri(India), Economic aspects.

Piped water supply and sewerage have been taken almost for granted in developed countries. The provision of safe water supplies and sanitary disposal of wastes is extremely important for sound health and balanced progress of any society. However, less than one tenth of the population in developing countries enjoy these facilities at present. This paper reviews the importance, background and current status of water and wastewater facilities in India. The relative situation in urban centers and in rural areas, conventional practices in environmental hygiene, the programs for improvement, and the problems involved with possible solutions are discussed. Problems such as population, poverty, and uneven rainfall distribution combine to stall any progress in India. About three-fourths of the total population lives in rural areas where there are no good roads, safe water supplies, or dependable waste disposal arrangements; moreover, some rural areas do not even have electric power. In the cities, migrations are causing an increasing population growth rate, so that public health utilities such as hospitals and water supply systems fall short of requirements soon after they are installed. The main problem in planning such utilities is financing. Mutual cooperation between residents, local administration, and state government is recommended. Despite aid from various international organizations since 1947, India has a long way to go before satisfactory standards are attained. (Bell-Cornell)
W75-07381

LINEAR DECISION RULE IN RESERVOIR MANAGEMENT AND DESIGN, 4. A RULE THAT MINIMIZES OUTPUT VARIANCE,
Johns Hopkins Univ., Baltimore, Md. Dept. of Geography and Environmental Engineering.
C. ReVelle, and J. Gundelach.

Water Resources Research, Vol 11, No 2, p 197-203, April 1975. 2 tab, 31 equ, 4 ref.

Descriptors: *Reservoir operation, *Design, *Linear programming, *Reservoir releases, Constraints, Management, Reservoir storage, Costs, Equations, Mathematical models, Systems analysis.
Identifiers: *Output variance, Historical data, Minimization, Reservoir capacity.

A linear decision rule (LDR) in reservoir management and design is reviewed and then transformed. A generalized formulation of a new LDR is presented, and the necessary steps to implement it are carried out for a particular form of the new rule. The proposed rule permits further minimization of expected losses arising from deviations of releases from prespecified target levels. The use of the rule also makes possible a larger minimum commitment of water. The problem is solved for historical data from the Gunpowder River in Maryland under both the previous and the new form of the LDR. Results obtained are compared for the two cases. The new form of the LDR allows a higher minimum release level than the maximum possible under the previous rule. In comparison of the original rule and the new rule with the same minimum flow constraints, the minimum size reservoir under the new rule is 16.3% greater than the one required with the previous LDR. This difference is compensated for by a 23.2% decrease in the variance of the average release. (See also W75-07384) (Bell-Cornell)
W75-07383

LINEAR DECISION RULE IN RESERVOIR MANAGEMENT AND DESIGN, 5. A GENERAL ALGORITHM,
Johns Hopkins Univ., Baltimore, Md. Dept. of Geography and Environmental Engineering.
J. Gundelach, and C. ReVelle.
Water Resources Research, Vol 11, No 2, p 204-207, April 1975. 4 tab, 4 equ, 3 ref.

Descriptors: *Reservoir operation, *Design, *Linear programming, Algorithms, Constraints, Reservoir storage, Reservoir releases, Management, Equations, Mathematical models, Systems analysis.
Identifiers: Chance-constrained programming, Capacity, Decision constants.

For the chance-constrained reservoir model introduced by ReVelle et al. (1969), a rapid algorithm is derived that determines the capacity and decision constants for a reservoir to be operated by use of the linear decision rule. The new algorithm supplants the earlier technique, which was fitted to a specialized problem format. The solution is achieved without resorting to the usual linear programming solution techniques, and the algorithm is simple enough to be carried out merely by hand computation. The chance-constrained reservoir model seeks the smallest reservoir that satisfies constraints on freeboard, minimum storage, and minimum release. The new algorithm will serve for any feasible formulation of a reservoir operating by the linear rule. (See also W75-07383) (Bell-Cornell)
W75-07384

DECISION ANALYSIS FOR THE RIVER WALK EXPANSION IN SAN ANTONIO, TEXAS,
Texas Univ., San Antonio. Dept. of Environmental Studies.
For primary bibliographic entry see Field 6B.
W75-07387

A SCREENING MODEL FOR WATER RESOURCES PLANNING,
Nebraska Univ., Lincoln. Water Resources Research Inst.
For primary bibliographic entry see Field 6A.
W75-07388

PIMA COUNTY MOVES ON GEOLOGIC HAZARDS,
Arizona Bureau of Mines, Tucson.
For primary bibliographic entry see Field 6F.
W75-07392

FLOW PATTERNS OF RAINWATER THROUGH SLOPING SOIL SURFACE LAYERS AND THE MOVEMENT OF NUTRIENTS BY RUNOFF,
Iowa State Univ., Ames. Dept. of Agronomy.
For primary bibliographic entry see Field 5B.
W75-07395

AQUATIC PLANT HARVESTING: DEVELOPMENT OF HIGH-SPEED HARVESTERS AND PROCESSING AND UTILIZATION OF HARVESTED VEGETATION,
Wisconsin Univ., Madison. Dept. of Agricultural Engineering; and Wisconsin Univ., Madison. Dept. of Mechanical Engineering.
D. F. Livermore, R. G. Koegel, H. D. Bruhn, S. H. Sy, and H. F. Link.
Available from the National Technical Information Service, Springfield, Va 22161 as PB-241 715, $4.25 in paper copy, $2.25 in microfiche. Wisconsin Water Resources Center, Madison, Technical Report WIS WRC 75-02, March 1975. 47 p, 16 fig, 8 tab, 15 ref, append. OWRT B-078-WIS(2) and GI 39193 (NSF/RANN). 14-31-0001-3947 and GI 39193.

Descriptors: *Wisconsin, *Aquatic weed control, *Aquatic vegetation, *Rooted aquatic plants, *Water harvesting, *Productivity, Costs, Mulching, *Mechanical equipment, Treatment, Feeds.
Identifiers: Dane County(Wisc).

Research was conducted to reduce the cost of aquatic plant harvesting by increasing harvester productivity through high-speed harvesting, by reducing the handling costs of the harvested vegetation, and/or by improving the potential for economic utilization of the vegetation. Also described are the design, construction, and testing of a craft for concentrating and collecting pre-cut, floating aquatic vegetation at speeds several times those of conventional harvesters. Recommendations are made for increasing the mechanical efficiency of this machine. A moisture prediction function was developed for aquatic vegetation subjected to pressure. Presented are data on the chemical constituents of the vegetation which were compared to conventional forage materials. Possible uses of the cut vegetation are enumerated.
W75-07397

WILDLIFE, ECOLOGY, AND PLANNING IN A PROPOSED IRRIGATION DEVELOPMENT IN NORTH DAKOTA,
North Dakota State Univ., Fargo.
For primary bibliographic entry see Field 6G.
W75-07400

NONSTATIONARY MODEL OF THE TRANSFORMATION OF EFFECTIVE PRECIPITATION INTO RUNOFF,
For primary bibliographic entry see Field 2A.
W75-07437

STREAM GAGING INFORMATION, AUSTRALIA -- SUPPLEMENT 1973.
Australian Water Resources Council, Canberra.
For primary bibliographic entry see Field 7C.
W75-07480

GEOLOGIC EVALUATION AND APPLICATIONS OF ERTS-1 IMAGERY OVER GEORGIA,
Georgia State Geological Survey, Atlanta.
For primary bibliographic entry see Field 7B.

W75-07530

THE FUTURE OF REGIONAL PLANNING IN THE UNITED STATES,
Council on Environmental Quality, Washington, D.C.
For primary bibliographic entry see Field 6B.
W75-07531

CRITERIA FOR THE DETERMINATION OF RECREATIONAL CARRYING CAPACITY IN THE COLORADO RIVER BASIN,
Forest Service (USDA), Missoula, Mont. Northern Forest Fire Lab.
For primary bibliographic entry see Field 6B.
W75-07533

STRATEGIES FOR ENVIRONMENTAL PLANNING IN THE UPPER COLORADO RIVER REGION,
California Univ., Berkeley. Dept. of Landscape Architecture.
For primary bibliographic entry see Field 6B.
W75-07534

AN EXAMINATION OF THE ENVIRONMENTAL CARRYING CAPACITY CONCEPT FOR THE AGRICULTURAL SECTOR OF THE COLORADO RIVER BASIN,
New Mexico State Univ., University Park.
For primary bibliographic entry see Field 3F.
W75-07535

TRANSPORTATION IN THE COLORADO RIVER BASIN,
Boston Aschmann Associates, San Jose, Calif.
For primary bibliographic entry see Field 6B.
W75-07540

URBANIZATION IN THE COLORADO RIVER BASIN,
Utah State Univ., Logan. Dept. of Political Science.
For primary bibliographic entry see Field 4C.
W75-07541

CONCEPTS OF CARRYING CAPACITY AND PLANNING IN COMPLEX ECOLOGICAL SYSTEMS,
Colorado State Univ., Fort Collins. Dept. of Sociology and Anthropology.
For primary bibliographic entry see Field 6A.
W75-07544

THE DEVELOPMENT AND ENVIRONMENTAL PROTECTION OF THE COLORADO RIVER BASIN,
Utah Agricultural Experiment Station, Logan.
For primary bibliographic entry see Field 6B.
W75-07545

FLOODS IN AND NEAR THE CHARLOTTE AMALIE AREA, ST. THOMAS, U.S. VIRGIN ISLANDS,
Geological Survey of Puerto Rico, San Juan.
For primary bibliographic entry see Field 7C.
W75-07550

TIME-OF-TRAVEL STUDY, LAKE ERIE-NIAGARA RIVER BASINS,
Geological Survey, Albany, N.Y.
For primary bibliographic entry see Field 5B.
W75-07554

COMPUTING BACKWATER AT OPEN CHANNEL CONSTRICTIONS,
Geological Survey, Bay Saint Louis, Miss. Gulf Coast Hydroscience Center.
For primary bibliographic entry see Field 8B.
W75-07558

VIBRATORY COMPACTION IN THE LABORATORY OF GRANULAR MATERIALS IN LONG COLUMNS,
Geological Survey, Reston, Va.
For primary bibliographic entry see Field 2F.
W75-07559

EXTENT AND FREQUENCY OF FLOODS ON SCHUYLKILL RIVER NEAR PHOENIXVILLE AND POTTSTOWN, PENNSYLVANIA,
Geological Survey, Harrisburg, Pa.
W. F. Busch, and L. C. Shaw.
Open-file report, September 1973. 29 p, 9 fig, 3 tab, 12 ref.

Descriptors: *Floods, *Pennsylvania, Flood frequency, Flood recurrence interval, Hydrologic data, Flood data, Stage-discharge relations, Flood profiles.
Identifiers: *Schuylkill River(Penn), Pottstown(Penn).

The extent and frequency of inundation are given for the Schuylkill River in the vicinity of Phoenixville and Pottstown, Pennsylvania. Streamflow data for the Schuylkill River are probably as abundant as those for any stream in the State. Records of peak gage heights and discharge on the Schuylkill River at Reading extend back to 1757. From 1757 to 1894, 19 floods were recorded. A record of annual flood peaks since 1928 is available for the Schuylkill River at Pottstown. A continuous record is also available for Philadelphia from 1932 to the present. By use of relations presented in this report, the extent, depth, and frequency of flooding can be estimated for any site along the reach of the Schuylkill River from Oaks to Pottstown. These flood data are presented so that regulatory agencies, organizations, and individuals may have a technical basis for making decisions on the use of flood-prone areas. (Knapp-USGS)
W75-07567

WATER RESOURCES DATA FOR GEORGIA, 1974.
Geological Survey, Doraville, Ga.
For primary bibliographic entry see Field 7C.
W75-07569

WATER RESOURCES OF THE CURLEW VALLEY DRAINAGE BASIN, UTAH AND IDAHO,
Geological Survey, Salt Lake City, Utah.
C. H. Baker, Jr.
Utah Department of Natural Resources Technical Publication No 45, 1974. 91 p, 9 fig, 5 plate, 9 tab, 27 ref.

Descriptors: *Water resources, *Groundwater basins, *Surface waters, *Idaho, *Utah, Groundwater, Hydrogeology, Hydrologic data, Basic data collections.
Identifiers: *Curlew Valley(Idaho-Utah).

The Curlew Valley drainage basin covers about 1,200 square miles in northern Utah and southern Idaho. Locomotive Springs are in the southern end of the basin. Runoff in this semiarid region is scanty, and the drainage basin includes only two small perennial streams. No water leaves the drainage basin in either of these streams. The principal aquifers in Curlew Valley are in valley-fill deposits that include unconsolidated deposits and volcanic rocks. Three major groundwater flow systems have been distinguished that contain water of suitable chemical quality for irrigation, and each is tapped locally by large-capacity wells. A fourth flow system, which contains hot, saline water, is present at depth in the western part of the valley. Comparison of the available measurements of the discharge at Locomotive Springs suggests that the discharge during 1969-72 was less than that mea-

sured in 1939 and 1967. This apparent decrease in spring discharge paralleled a period when withdrawals from wells were substantially increasing in Curlew Valley. (Knapp-USGS)
W75-07570

VELOCITY AND DEPTH MEASUREMENTS FOR USE IN THE DETERMINATION OF REAERATION COEFFICIENTS,
Geological Survey, Trenton, N.J.
For primary bibliographic entry see Field 2E.
W75-07572

HAS WISCONSIN ENOUGH WATER,
Geological Survey, Madison, Wis.
For primary bibliographic entry see Field 6D.
W75-07580

MAGNITUDE AND FREQUENCY OF FLOODS IN KANSAS--UNREGULATED STREAMS,
Geological Survey, Lawrence, Kans.
P. R. Jordan, and T. J. Irza.
Kansas Water Resources Board, Topeka, Streamflow Characteristics Technical Report No 11, February 1975. 34 p, 9 fig, 6 tab, 17 ref.

Descriptors: *Floods, *Kansas, *Flood frequency, Flood data, Peak discharge, Water yield, Hydrologic data, Flood recurrence interval.

Flood magnitudes for selected recurrence intervals for unregulated streams in Kansas are related most significantly to the contributing drainage area and the 2-year 24-hour rainfall. Equations are provided for estimating flood peaks for selected recurrence intervals at ungaged sites or at gaging stations having short records. The accuracy of 100-year floods calculated from the equation is equivalent to the accuracy that would be obtained from about 12 years of record of flood peaks at the site. Floods are most common May through August in western Kansas and from April through July in eastern Kansas. Maximum known floods on an envelope curve for western Kansas range from 2,440 cubic feet per second for 1.6 square miles to 178,000 cfs for 6,770 square miles. Maximum known floods on an envelope curve for eastern Kansas range from 7,080 cfs for 2.06 square miles to 436,000 cfs for 3,818 square miles. (Knapp-USGS)
W75-07581

ALTERNATIVE INFORMATION AND INTERACTION APPROACHES TO PUBLIC PARTICIPATION IN WATER RESOURCES DECISION MAKING - A STATE-OF-THE-ARTS REPORT,
North Carolina State Univ., Raleigh. Dept. of Sociology and Anthropology.
For primary bibliographic entry see Field 6B.
W75-07598

TEACHING WATER RESOURCE MANAGEMENT WITH THE AID OF A COMPUTER-IMPLEMENTED STIMULATOR,
Virginia Polytechnic Inst. and State Univ., Blacksburg. Dept. of Fisheries and Wildlife Sciences.
For primary bibliographic entry see Field 6B.
W75-07601

REGIONAL GROWTH AND WATER RESOURCE INVESTMENT,
Utah State Univ., Logan. Dept. of Economics.
For primary bibliographic entry see Field 6B.
W75-07615

EEL RIVER DEVELOPMENT ALTERNATIVES, APPENDIX,
California State Dept. of Water Resources, Sacramento.

Descriptors: *California, *Water resources development, *Alternate planning, *Estimated costs, Water supply, Flood control, Recreation, Direct costs, Cost allocation, Damsites, Project planning, Project feasibility.
Identifiers: *Eel River(Calif), Dos Rios Project(Calif).

The criteria and procedures used to evaluate various alternatives to the Eel River Dos Rios Project are detailed. The various developments were limited to direct projects costs, with the total cost of each project to be allocated among the various project purposes--flood control, recreation, and water supply. Water supply capabilities of each alternative were based on meeting the projected water needs in the Sacramento-San Joaquin Delta to maintain the contractual commitments of the existing State Water Project. A criterion was developed which allowed matching the amount of total active storage capacity in a reservoir system to the net water supply which would be available on a long-term basis. Project staging was based upon plans which would allow dams and tunnels to be constructed as late as possible. Each system should also be capable of meeting possible initial demands in 1986. Major cost items were estimated for anadronous fish preservation and recreation use. Costs of off peak pumping power were calculated on an annual capacity of $2.00/kw and an energy charge of 2.00 mills/kw/hr. The corresponding values for continuous pumping power were $26.50/kw and 1/00/kw/hr. The average annual costs represent an average annual equivalent of the capitalized costs, based on a 5% interest rate over the 100-year period. (Auen-Wisconsin)
W75-07616

SNOW ACCUMULATION AND MELT ALONG BORDERS OF A STRIP CUT IN NEW MEXICO,
Forest Service (USDA), Fort Collins, Colo. Rocky Mountain Forest and Range Experiment Station.
H. L. Gary.
U.S. Department of Agriculture, Forest Service, Research Note RM-279, 8 p, December, 1974. 4 fig, 1 tab, 9 ref.

Descriptors: *Clear-cutting, *Watershed management, *Water yield improvement, *Snowmelt, Forest management, Snowfall, Snow management, Snow, Runoff, New Mexico, Southwest U.S., Rocky Mountain Region, Melting, Snowpacks, Mountain forests, Water sources.

Snowfall amounts were similar along the sunny and shady borders of an east-west oriented clearcut strip in New Mexico. Maximum snow accumulation was greater along both borders than in the adjacent forest. Periodic melting along the sunny border reduced the snowpack, but winter melt losses were somewhat balanced by melt crusts which prevented blowing snow. Snow disappeared 5 to 6 weeks earlier along the sunny border than along the shady border or forest interior. Melt rates along the shady border were 30-40% greater than those observed in the forest interior, but times of complete melt were the same. (Witt-IPC)
W75-07656

MONTEREY COUNTY MASTER DRAINAGE PLAN, SANTA RITA CREEK WATERSHED.
Monterey County Surveyors, Inc., Salinas, Calif; and McCreary-Koretsky-International, Salinas, Calif.
Monterey County Flood Control and Water Conservation District, Salinas, California, August 1972. 40 p, 1 fig, 4 tab, 2 ref, 1 addendum.

Descriptors: *Regional analysis, *Drainage engineering, *Runoff, *Flood control, *Surface drainage, *Planning, Long-term planning, California, Design criteria, Engineering design, Environmental control, Drainage districts, Drainage programs, Drainage systems, Environmental engineering.
Identifiers: *Monterey County(California), *Santa Rita Creek Watershed, *Master drainage plan.

plan, it is suggested that a Watershed Zone Advisory Committee be established. The Committee would: evaluate planning progress, consolidate efforts of the region, advise the District on priorities for construction, recommend operation and maintenance programs. (Poertner)
W75-07662

MONTEREY COUNTY MASTER DRAINAGE PLAN, CARMEL VALLEY WATERSHEDS.
Monterey County Surveyors, Inc., Salinas, Calif; and Koretsky King Associates, Inc., Salinas, Calif.
Monterey County Flood Control and Water Conservation District, Salinas, California, June 1973. 47 p, 2 fig, 5 tab, 6 ref.

Descriptors: *Regional analysis, *Drainage engineering, *Runoff, *Flood control, *Surface drainage, *Planning, Long-term planning, California, Design criteria, Engineering design, Environmental control, Drainage districts, Drainage programs, Drainage systems, Environmnental engineering.
Identifiers: *Master drainage plan, *Monterey County(California), *Carmel Valley(California).

Carmel Valley encompasses a total area of approximately 12 square miles, and consists of 36 adjacent, but independent, watersheds. In order to evaluate the capacity of existing surface drainage and flood control structures and to prepare requirements for future structures, peak streamflow rates were determined at all critical locations. This master drainage plan was prepared for the following purposes: (1) to prepare a Watershed Master Drainage Plan for the Carmel Valley Watersheds as one step in establishing an overall County Drainage Plan, so the future development and future flood control works might proceed in an orderly and reasonable manner; (2) to establish design criteria for all future flood control works to be constructed within Monterey County; (3) using these criteria, to assess the adequacy of the existing major drainage facilities within the study area to pass the design flows under present and future planned development; (4) to determine the basic pattern of drainage and to indicate size, location, capacity and significant hydraulic characteristics of the required major facilities; and (5) to provide recommendations for such legal instruments necessary to implement and control this Master Drainage Plan. To implement the Master Drainage Plan, it was suggested that a Watershed Zone Advisory Committee be established. The purpose is to evaluate planning progress, consolidate efforts of the entire region, advise the District on priorities for construction of primary and secondary drainage facilities, recommend an operation and maintenance program, and keep the District informed on conditions of the Watershed Zone. (Poertner)
W75-07663

BANK AND CHANNEL PROTECTIVE LINING DESIGN PROCEDURES.
New York State Dept. of Transportation, Albany. Bureau of Soil Mechanics.
Soils Design Procedure, SDP-2, August, 1971. 65 p, 35 fig, 9 ref.

Descriptors: *Erosion control, *Channel erosion, *Bank protection, *Bank erosion, *Drainage engineering, *Channel improvement, Highways, Roads, Runoff, Soil types, Soil properties, Stream erosion, Soil mechanics, Storm runoff, Drainage effects, Drainage practices, Linings, Flow, Erosion, Erosion rate, Soil erosion, Engineering design, Design standards, New York.

Procedures and guidelines are presented for the design of bank and channel protective linings. The purpose is to present alternative methods for preventing detrimental erosion caused by runoff and stream flows along banks and in channels of natural or man-made watercourses. Because soil properties are a factor in erosion, the effects of soil type on protection requirements are discussed. Various types of bank and channel protection are described along with their limitations and advantages as determined from construction experience and field performance. The manual is profusely illustrated with photographs, sketches and design aids in the form of standard graphs and nomographs. Personnel of the New York State Department of Transportation are requested to use this manual in the design of all channels on all current and future projects. (Poertner)
W75-07665

FLOOD CONTROL IN COOK COUNTY,
League of Women Voters of Chicago, Ill.
November, 1972. 26 p, 4 fig, 2 tab, 10 ref.

Descriptors: *Waste water(Pollution), *Flood control, *Detention reservoir, *Combined sewers, *Illinois, *Lake Michigan, Flood flow, Flood discharge, Flood protection, Sewers, Storm water, Flood peak, Urbanization, Runoff, Overflow, Water pollution control, Tunnels, Underground storage.
Identifiers: *Cook County(Illinois).

Flood control in suburban Cook County involves solving present flooding problems and preventing future ones. Channelization and dredging can facilitate the removal of storm waters from an area. Construction of retention basins and ponds to hold water temporarily during peak flows can mitigate downstream flooding problems. While storm water is presently discharged to Lake Michigan, no new permits for outfalls to the lake have been granted since 1969. Prevention of future problems can be achieved by zoning to prohibit development on vulnerable flood plains and by requiring developers to provide storm water retention equal to the increased run-off caused by construction. The primary agency in Cook County which deals with waste water is the Metropolitan Sanitary District of Greater Chicago. Other agencies involved are the Cook County Forest Preserve District, the Division of Water Resources Management of the Illinois State Department of Transportation, the Northeastern Illinois Planning Commission, the Army Corps of Engineers, and the United States Soil Conservation Service. A proposed three billion dollar Chicago Underflow Plan is expected to take ten years for implementation. Sources of funding include all federal, state and local funds that could possibly be obtained for the abatement of water pollution. (Poertner)
W75-07674

RATTLESNAKE CREEK STUDY,
Wichita Water Dept., Kans.
G. J. Stramel.
January 1967. 31 p, 11 fig, 4 tab.

Descriptors: *Water quality, *Water quality control, *Diversion, *Runoff, *Subhumid climates, *Geology, Topography, Precipitation(Atmospheric), Irrigation, Infiltration, Aquifer characteristics, Aquifers, Aquifer testing, Hydrographs, Diversion structures, Closed conduits, Water rights, Groundwater, Hydraulics, Kansas.
Identifiers: Rattlesnake Creek(Kansas).

The Wichita Water Department conducted a reconnaissance survey to determine whether or not the good quality water flowing in Rattlesnake Creek can be salvaged by diversion to Cheney Reservoir. The survey showed that good quality water existed at all stages in the upper reaches of Rattlesnake Creek and that it might be relatively easy to divert the creek water from Rattlesnake Creek Basin to the North Fork of the Ninnescah River and on the Cheney Reservoir. Good quality water flowing into the lower reaches of the Rattlesnake Creek drainage basin mixed with natural high chloride water and was polluted. Most of the waters of Rattlesnake Creek will ultimately be consumed by irrigation and the Quivira Wildlife Refuge. Existing water rights and an anticipated growth in the establishment of additional water rights will leave little, if any water for out-of-basin diversion. Rattlesnake Creek alone offers no immediate help to the City of Wichita. The possibility exists of to diverting water from the Arkansas River into the Rattlesnake Creek basin, and thence to Cheney Reservoir. (Poertner)
W75-07676

USE OF MODELING FOR PLANNING STORM WATER STRATEGIES,
Florida Univ., Gainesville.
For primary bibliographic entry see Field 5G.
W75-07677

ECONOMICS OF COMBINED SEWAGE DETENTION FACILITIES,
San Francisco City and County Dept. of Public Works, Calif.
For primary bibliographic entry see Field 5G.
W75-07680

APPLICATION AND TESTING OF THE EPA STORMWATER MANAGEMENT MODEL TO GREENFIELD, MASSACHUSETTS,
Massachusetts Univ., Amherst. Dept. of Civil Engineering.
For primary bibliographic entry see Field 5G.
W75-07681

LANDSCAPE TENDING AND NATURE CONSERVATION AS PARTIAL TASKS FOR SOCIALISTIC LAND DEVELOPMENT,
L. Bauer, and H. Weinitschke.
VEB Gustav Fischer Verlag: Jena, East Germany. 1973. 3rd Ed 382 p, Illus. Maps.

Descriptors: *Conservation, *Forest management, *Pollution control, Soil conservation, Lakes, Regulation, Legal aspects.
Identifiers: Forestation.

This 3rd edition, intended for nature conservationists, consists of sections concerning the basics of landscape care, including forests, water balance, terrain and soil problems; reforestation, forest-field disturbution, care of lakes, air, disposal of refuse, noise pollution, biocidal effects and construction; nature protection as a contribution to landscape care; legal regulations; and the activities of the International Union for Conservation of Nature and Natural Resources. A bibliography, an index, 144 illustrations and 47 tables are included.--Copyright 1974, Biological Abstracts, Inc.
W75-07707

RIVER FORECASTS PROVIDED BY THE NATIONAL WEATHER SERVICE, VOLUME 1, 1972.
National Weather Service, Office of Hydrology. Silver Spring, Md.
Available from National Climatic Center, Asheville, NC 28801, for $0.75. 1973, 62 p.

Descriptors: Rivers, *Forecasting, *Flood forecasting, Hydrology, Tables(Data), Warning systems, Floods, Water supply, Data acquisition, Surface waters, Flood control, United States, *River forecasting, *Hydrologic data.

River forecasts and warnings, as well as other National Weather Service hydrologic services are described and information is given on: Hydrologic operations, forecasts and services; River Forecast Centers; NWS Field Offices; Data Acquisition Networks; Flash Flood Warning Program; Water Supply Forecasting Program; Highest stages at National Weather Service gages; and Record high stages prior to gage records. Indexes are arranged by states, stations, and rivers. A list of water supply forecast points is included. Illustrations in-

cluded are: Map of River Centers, Map of Local NWS Offices, Map of Radar Network, Hydrologic Forecast System Chart, and Operations Chart-River and Flood Forecast and Warning Program. (NOAA)
W75-07717

STUDIES ON SOIL EROSION CONTROL: 4. THE HYDRAULIC STUDIES OF WATER FLOW IN SLOPED LAND (IN JAPANESE),
Obihiro Zootechnical Univ. (Japan). Lab. of Agricultural and Civil Engineering.
Y. Matsuda.
Res Bull Obihiro Zootech Univ Ser I. Vol 7, No 4, p 688-703, 1973, English summary.

Descriptors: *Soil erosion, Open channel flow, *Impact(Rainfall), Raindrops.

Water flow which erodes soil of fields is primarily attributable to rainfall, in which case part of the raindrops flow to a lower level, infiltrating the soil as they flow. This process is, therefore distinguished from general open channels because flow in the latter case permits lateral inflow and outflow. However, because water passages soon occur, rainfall cannot flow uniformly over the land. However, if ideal flow conditions are assumed, theoretical solutions for water surface profile may be derived and compared with experimental values. Variations of the general equation were combined and each water head and velocity in a given elevation was calculated. Each shearing force, which was equivalent to the tractive force on the base, was calculated using another equation. From the 2 equations, the effects of slope, infiltration rate and the roughness coefficient were evaluated and it was concluded that the effect of the roughness coefficient was the most significant.--Copyright 1973, Biological Abstracts, Inc.
W75-07756

A TURNING POINT,
Department of Housing and Urban Development, Washington, D.C.
For primary bibliographic entry see Field 6F.
W75-07765

MAINTENANCE OF BAY RIDGE AND RED HOOK CHANNELS, NEW YORK NAVIGATION PROJECT (FINAL ENVIRONMENTAL IMPACT STATEMENT),
Army Engineer District, New York.
For primary bibliographic entry see Field 8A.
W75-07784

THE MENDOTA WATERSHED PROJECT, LASALLE AND BUREAU COUNTIES, ILLINOIS (FINAL ENVIRONMENTAL IMPACT STATEMENT),
Soil Conservation Service, Champaign, Ill.
For primary bibliographic entry see Field 4D.
W75-07785

PEACOCK CREEK, LIBERTY COUNTY, GEORGIA (FINAL ENVIRONMENTAL IMPACT STATEMENT),
Army Engineer District, Savannah, Ga.
Available from the National Technical Information Service, U.S. Dept. of Commerce, Springfield, Va. 22161, as EIS-GA-73-0416-F, $4.25 in paper copy, $2.25 in microfiche. November 1972. 70 p, 9 tab, 4 map.

Descriptors: *Flood control, *Flood protection, *Channel improvement, Standing waters, Oxygen, Channels, Environmental effects, Turbidity, Georgia, Surface waters, Water temperature, Flooding, Hardwood, Storms, Floods, Biota, Wildlife, Fish.
Identifiers: *Environmental Impact Statements, *Peacock Creek(Geo), Liberty County(Geo).

The project involves initiation of flood control measures on Peacock Creek, Liberty County, Georgia and consists of improving channel dimensions, snagging, and clearing of the creek. The environmental impact of the project will be to provide flood protection, afford the orderly removal of standing surface water, stimulate area development, and enhance the environment for human habitation. The adverse environmental effects include removal of hardwoods and other biota from project right-of-way, possible increase in water temperature, probable decrease in dissolved oxygen, and temporary turbidity during construction. The following alternatives were considered: snag and clear channels only, provide flood protection from 5 to 10 year storm frequencies, and no action. (Gagliardi-Florida)
W75-07788

UPPER SALT CREEK WATERSHED, COOK, LAKE AND DUPAGE COUNTIES, ILLINOIS (FINAL ENVIRONMENTAL IMPACT STATEMENT),
Soil Conservation Service, Washington, D.C.
For primary bibliographic entry see Field 8A.
W75-07789

THE WINDS, CURRENTS AND WAVES AT THE SITE OF THE FLOATING CITY OFF WAIKIKI,
Hawaii Univ., Honolulu. Dept. of Ocean Engineering.
M. St. Denis.
Report UNIHI-Seagrant-CR-75-01. December 1974. 95 p. Hawaii's Floating City (Development Program). NOAA Grant OSG 04-5-158-17.

Descriptors: *Engineering structures, *Offshore platforms, *Forecasting, Estimating, Evaluation, Future planning(Projected), Projections, Risks, Winds, Cyclones, Tropical cyclones, Waves(Water), Ocean waves, Currents(Water), Water circulation, Ocean circulation, Ocean currents, *Hawaii.
Identifiers: *Floating City(HA), *Floating platforms, *Waikiki(HA), Trade winds, Kona winds, Tidal currents, Wind drift, Ekman drift, Oceanic flow.

Long-term forecasts are presented of winds, currents and waves at a station some three miles off Waikiki selected as a possible site for a floating platform to house a community of oceanic denizens. The forecasts are to be used to design the platform. Detailed information is given on wind types (trade and Kona winds); Kona storms; and tropical cyclones. The general circulation, tidal currents, Ekman or wind drift, and large scale oceanic flow is described as are wave patterns, swells, cyclonic waves and long-term wave trends common to the area. (NOAA)
W75-07826

FLOOD CONTROL, SEABROOK MARINE LABORATORY, TEXAS,
Texas Parks and Wildlife Dept., Austin.
For primary bibliographic entry see Field 8A.
W75-07829

DIGITAL RADAR DATA AND ITS APPLICATION IN FLASH FLOOD FORECASTING,
National Weather Service Forecast Office, Pittsburgh, Pa.
D. D. Sisk.
Available from National Technical Information Service, U.S. Department of Commerce, Sills Bldg 5285 Port Royal Road, Springfield, Va 22161.

Descriptors: *Flood forecasting, *Flash floods, *Instrumentation, *Warning systems, *Radar, Digital computers, Forecasting, Estimating, Measurement, Probability, Programs, Forecasting.
Identifiers: *Digital radar data, D/RADEX.

Digitized Radar Experiments (D/RADEX) were designed to assist in the development, testing and evaluation of techniques for automatic processing and presentation of weather radar data in real-time for operational applications. A minicomputer and its related processing and interface equipment are used to take over control of the radar for approximately twenty seconds to collect radar video returns for archiving and printout displays. A case study is presented that illustrates how D/RADEX can assist in determining areas of potential flash flooding. The D/RADEX hydrological printout is used and illustrated. (NOAA)
W75-07832

MAP SHOWING DRAINAGE AREAS, HADDAM QUADRANGLE, CONNECTICUT,
Geological Survey, Hartford, Conn.
For primary bibliographic entry see Field 7C.
W75-07839

MAP SHOWING DRAINAGE AREAS, GUILFORD QUADRANGLE, CONNECTICUT,
Geological Survey, Hartford, Conn.
For primary bibliographic entry see Field 7C.
W75-07840

MAP SHOWING DRAINAGE AREAS, BRANFORD QUADRANGLE, CONNECTICUT,
Geological Survey, Hartford, Conn.
For primary bibliographic entry see Field 7C.
W75-07841

MAP SHOWING DRAINAGE AREAS, NEW HAVEN-WOODMONT QUADRANGLES, CONNECTICUT,
Geological Survey, Hartford, Conn.
For primary bibliographic entry see Field 7C.
W75-07842

MAP SHOWING DRAINAGE AREAS, NIANTIC QUADRANGLE, CONNECTICUT,
Geological Survey, Hartford, Conn.
For primary bibliographic entry see Field 7C.
W75-07843

MAP SHOWING DRAINAGE AREAS, OLD LYME QUADRANGLE, CONNECTICUT,
Geological Survey, Hartford, Conn.
For primary bibliographic entry see Field 7C.
W75-07844

PEARL RIVER BOATWAY, ROSS BARNETT RESERVOIR TO JACKSON AREA,
Geological Survey, Jackson, Miss.
For primary bibliographic entry see Field 7C.
W75-07847

PEARL RIVER BOATWAY MAP, MONTICELLO TO MORGANTOWN, MISSISSIPPI,
Geological Survey, Jackson, Miss.
For primary bibliographic entry see Field 7C.
W75-07849

PEARL RIVER BOATWAY MAP, GEORGETOWN TO MONTICELLO, MISSISSIPPI,
Geological Survey, Jackson, Miss.
For primary bibliographic entry see Field 7C.
W75-07850

4B. Groundwater Management

WATER SUPPLY IN CENTRAL AND SOUTHERN APACHE COUNTY,
Arizona Water Commission, Phoenix.
P. S. Osborne, and P. C. Briggs.
June 1974. 12 p, 8 fig, 4 ref.

Descriptors: *Water supply development, *Water quality, *Wells, *Aquifer systems, *Groundwater resources, Depth, Groundwater availability, *Arizona, Geologic units.
Identifiers: Apache County(Ariz).

Rapid growth in the number of subdivisions within Apache County has prompted the need for increased water supplies. Summaries are presented of information regarding groundwater supplies to aid in deciding whether further subdivision should be approved. Figures provide information such as depth of water, potential well yields, and water quality. The availability and suitability of water in several aquifer systems are described. The most heavily used aquifers at present are the Kaibab-Coconino and the recent alluvium. The Cretaceous rocks appear to have the most potential for future development. Depth of water ranges from less than 200 feet to 500 feet. Maximum yield reported from this system is 130 gpm, and water quality is good with the total dissolved solids content ranging from 300-500 ppm. (Mastic-Arizona)
W75-07370

THE CENTRAL ARIZONA PROJECT, A STAFF REPORT TO THE METROPOLITAN UTILITIES MANAGEMENT AGENCY BOARD AND THE MAYOR AND COUNCIL OF THE CITY OF TUCSON,
Tucson Metropolitan Utilities Management Agency Board, Ariz.
J. McGill, and H. Holub.
October 1974. 133 p, 17 fig, 27 ref.

Descriptors: *Groundwater resources, *Water law, *Colorado river, *Water costs, *Water supply, Groundwater mining, Subsidence, Irrigation, Water demand, Aqueducts, *Arizona, Irrigation water, Population, Water quality.
Identifiers: *Central Arizona Project(CAP), Tucson(Ariz), Farm land retirement.

The Central Arizona Project (CAP) consists of an aqueduct system to carry water from Lake Havasu on the Colorado River to the Phoenix and Tucson areas of Central Arizona in order to supplement the rapidly diminishing groundwater supplies. Presented are a history and description of CAP, and a discussion of the effects of CAP on Arizona and particularly on the City of Tucson. Costs for the project and the water it will supply are discussed. A primary objective was to present information for making the decision of whether or not the City of Tucson should contract for CAP water. Problems include the possibility of subsidence as groundwater supplies are used up, Tucson's projected population growth, retirement of irrigated farm land, the relatively high cost of CAP water, and the need for water law reform. Recommendations call for contracting small amounts of CAP water in the initial years particularly if no attempt is made to check population growth in the City, and to continue retirement of farm land while pursuing water law reforms to change the financing methods of the CAP. (Mastic-Arizona)
W75-07372

WATER RIGHTS,
Wisconsin Univ., Madison. School of Law.
For primary bibliographic entry see Field 6E.
W75-07378

SURFACE PLUGGING DURING BASIN RECHARGE OF TURBID WATER,
Southwestern Great Plains Research Center, Bushland, Tex.
O. R. Jones, D. W. Goss, and A. D. Schneider.
Transactions of the American Society of Agricultural Engineers, Vol 17, No 6, p 1011-1019, November-December 1974. 7 fig, 2 tab, 9 ref.

Descriptors: *Artificial recharge, *Pit recharge, *Groundwater recharge, *Suspended solids, Infiltration rates, Playas, *Texas, Basins.
Identifiers: *Ogallala aquifer, Recharge rates.

Three experimental recharge basins were excavated to determine if artificial recharging of playa water on the Southern High Plains to the Ogallala aquifer is practical. To establish guidelines and standards for the operation of such basins, it is necessary to develop relationships between the permeability of the Pleistocene sediments that overlie the Ogallala aquifer, suspended solids content of the water supply, and quantity of playa water that can be recharged before plugging limits recharge to critically low rates. Most suspended solids in playa water were deposited on or near the surface during basin recharge, except where cracking of the basin surface allowed sediment deposition at undetermined depths. Although plugging was related to the amount of suspended solids introduced into the basin with the recharge water, the total amount of suspended solids required to cause plugging varied by an order of magnitude between tests. The major factor limiting recharge of turbid water through excavated basins was plugging on or near the surface. While substantial quantities of turbid water can be recharged, pretreatment to remove part of the suspended solids load should improve basin performance. (Gibb-ISWS)
W75-07439

INVESTIGATION AND REHABILITATION OF A BRINE-CONTAMINATED AQUIFER,
Engineering Enterprises, Inc., Norman, Okla.
For primary bibliographic entry see Field 5B.
W75-07441

THIRTY-FIVE YEARS OF CONTINUOUS DISCHARGE OF SECONDARY TREATED EFFLUENT ONTO SAND BEDS,
Rensselaer Polytechnic Inst., Troy, N.Y. Dept. of Environmental Engineering.
For primary bibliographic entry see Field 5B.
W75-07442

THE CONFIGURATION OF CONTAMINATION ENCLAVES FROM REFUSE DISPOSAL SITES ON FLOODPLAINS,
Iowa State Univ., Ames. Dept. of Earth Sciences.
For primary bibliographic entry see Field 5B.
W75-07443

WATER LEVEL FLUCTUATIONS DUE TO EARTH TIDES IN A WELL PUMPING FROM SLIGHTLY FRACTURED CRYSTALLINE ROCK,
Du Pont de Nemours (E.I.) and Co., Aiken, S.C. Savannah River Lab.
For primary bibliographic entry see Field 5B.
W75-07463

ANALYSIS OF FLOW TO AN EXTENDED FULLY PENETRATING WELL,
Pahlavi Univ., Shiraz (Iran).
I. Javandel, and N. Zaghi.
Water Resources Research, Vol 11, No 1, p 159-164, February 1975. 10 fig, 10 ref.

Descriptors: *Groundwater, *Water wells, *Potential flow, Hydraulics, Groundwater potential, Fourier analysis, Groundwater movement, Water yield, Safe yield, Discharge(Water).
Identifiers: Radially extended wells.

An analytic solution was derived yielding the potential distribution in a bounded confined aquifer pumped by a well that was radially extended at the bottom. An exact solution for the rate of discharge was found by which the effect of local radial extension on the increase of the pumping rate was studied. Solutions were evaluated numerically, and the results were presented graphically in terms of dimensionless parameters. The results showed that production rate is doubled in some cases by extending the bottom of the well. (Gibb-ISWS)
W75-07464

NEW EQUATIONS FOR DETERMINING THE FORMATION CONSTANTS OF AN AQUIFER FROM PUMPING TEST DATA,
Sheffield Univ. (England). Dept. of Civil and Structural Engineering.
N. S. Boulton, and T. D. Streltsova.
Water Resources Research, Vol 11, No 1, p 148-153, February 1975. 2 fig, 5 tab, 11 ref, 1 append.

Descriptors: *Groundwater, *Pumping, *Aquifer testing, Confined water, Aquicludes, Permeability, Drawdown, Storage coefficient, Transmissivity, Hydraulics, Hydrologic properties, Equations, Sandstones.
Identifiers: Partial penetrating wells, Type curve solutions, *Great Britain, Bunter sandstone.

New equations were given, based on an extended theory, that take into account the following factors: the compressibility and anisotropy of the main aquifer; the partial penetration of the abstraction well; the depth at which the drawdown in an observation well is measured; the existence of a low-permeability layer, called 'the aquitard,' above the aquifer; and the saturated and unsaturated zones above the water table. A practical method of evaluating the formation constants for an aquifer from pumping test data was fully discussed. Type curves based on the new equations were used to analyze data from a pumping test in the thick Bunter sandstone formation of Shropshire (Great Britain). A correction for the water derived from storage within the abstraction well was found to be necessary. (Gibb-ISWS)
W75-07465

AN EVALUATION OF THE SUITABILITY OF ERTS DATA FOR THE PURPOSES OF PETROLEUM EXPLORATION,
Earth Satellite Corp., Washington, D.C.
For primary bibliographic entry see Field 7B.
W75-07488

MINERAL RESOURCES, GEOLOGICAL STRUCTURE, AND LANDFORM SURVEYS,
National Aeronautics and Space Administration, Greenbelt, Md. Goddard Space Flight Center.
For primary bibliographic entry see Field 7C.
W75-07500

OREGON'S APPROACH TO GROUNDWATER INVESTIGATIONS,
Oregon State Engineer's Office, Salem.
J. R. Illian.
In: Land and Water Use in Oregon; Seminar conducted by Oregon State University, Spring Quarter 1974, Water Resources Research Institute, Corvallis, Oregon, p 97-112, July 1974. 12 fig.

Descriptors: *Groundwater, *Oregon, *Model studies, Hydrogeology, Hydrologic cycle, Recharge, Discharge(Water), Aquifers, Groundwater resources, Underground streams, Underflow, Water quality, Dissolved solids, Temperature, Pumping, Drawdown.

The Oregon State Engineer's Office, in cooperation with the Oregon State Water Resources Board, expanded the Ground-Water Basins Investigation Program in June 1972. This statewide program is intended to determine the general extent and characteristics of each groundwater basin and to ascertain the degree to which groundwater may serve as an alternative to surface water supplies. A description of the origin, purpose, procedures, and progress of this program was presented. A general conceptual model of the groundwater resources of Oregon was described. This conceptual model will be used as a basis for the development of a mathematical model which will make possible the investigation of the effects of various assumed stresses. With this capability, the optimum scheme of development can be identified prior to large scale development. (See also W75-07507) (Sims-ISWS)

W75-07516

GEOHYDROLOGY OF BACA AND SOUTHERN PROWERS COUNTIES, SOUTHEASTERN COLORADO,
Geological Survey, Denver, Colo.
For primary bibliographic entry see Field 7C.
W75-07551

HYDROLOGIC RECORDS FOR LAKE COUNTY, FLORIDA, 1972-73,
Geological Survey, Tallahassee, Fla.
For primary bibliographic entry see Field 2E.
W75-07566

WATER RESOURCES DATA FOR GEORGIA, 1974.
Geological Survey, Doraville, Ga.
For primary bibliographic entry see Field 7C.
W75-07569

WATER RESOURCES OF THE CURLEW VALLEY DRAINAGE BASIN, UTAH AND IDAHO,
Geological Survey, Salt Lake City, Utah.
For primary bibliographic entry see Field 4A.
W75-07570

FIELD TRIP GUIDE BOOK FOR HYDROGEOLOGY OF THE TWIN CITIES ARTESIAN BASIN,
Geological Survey, Denver, Colo.
T. C. Winter, and R. F. Norvitch.
Paper prepared for Annual Meeting of the Geological Society of America and Associated Societies, Minneapolis, Minn: Minnesota Geological Survey, 1972. 35 p, 13 fig, 1 tab, 10 ref. (Available from the Minnesota Geological Society) $3.00.

Descriptors: *Hydrogeology, *Minnesota, Water supply, Aquifers, *Groundwater, Water yield, Water quality, Water utilization, Cities, Artesian aquifers.
Identifiers: *Minneapolis-St. Paul(Minn), *Twin Cities(Minn).

This field trip guide focuses on several of the significant aspects of the hydrogeology of the Minneapolis-St. Paul (Twin Cities) area. Emphasis is placed on the principal bedrock aquifer and the role of glacial drift in the hydrology. Stops include field examination of the Jordan-Prairie du Chien aquifer, a well-screen manufacturing plant and its research well field, views of surface expression of partly buried bedrock valleys, an artificial-recharge site where experiments were run on deep-well water injection into the Prairie du Chien Group (carbonate rock), and a site where groundwater discharges as a large spring from the Prairie du Chien Gruoup. Although much glacial geology is seen along the trip route, emphasis is placed on the drift-filled bedrock valleys. The Twin Cities supply themselves and 13 surrounding municipalities with water from the Mississippi River. Water from a large number of wells within the cities is used mainly for industry and air conditioning. In addition, most suburban communities use groundwater to the extent that groundwater now exceeds surface water as a source of supply. Total groundwater use in 1970 in the metropolitan area was 194 mgd; 48 mgd was for domestic purposes, 75 mgd for air conditioning, 100 mgd for industrial and commercial purposes, and 38 mgd for irrigation. The amount of groundwater that can be developed in the metropolitan area on a sustained basis is about 845 mgd. (Knapp-USGS)
W75-07573

SIMULATED WATER-LEVEL CHANGES RESULTING FROM PROPOSED CHANGES IN GROUND-WATER PUMPING IN THE HOUSTON, TEXAS, AREA,
Geological Survey, Houston, Tex.
For primary bibliographic entry see Field 7C.
W75-07575

HAS WISCONSIN ENOUGH WATER,
Geological Survey, Madison, Wis.
For primary bibliographic entry see Field 6D.
W75-07580

A SPECIAL PLANNING TECHNIQUE FOR STREAM-AQUIFER SYSTEMS,
Geological Survey, Denver, Colo.
For primary bibliographic entry see Field 2A.
W75-07584

CHEMICAL QUALITY OF GROUND WATER IN HAWAII,
Geological Survey, Honolulu, Hawaii.
For primary bibliographic entry see Field 5A.
W75-07585

STOCHASTIC MODELING OF GROUNDWATER SYSTEMS,
Massachusetts Inst. of Tech., Cambridge. Dept. of Civil Engineering.
For primary bibliographic entry see Field 2F.
W75-07595

POLLUTED GROUNDWATER: ESTIMATING THE EFFECTS OF MAN'S ACTIVITIES,
General Electric Co., Santa Barbara, Calif. Center for Advanced Studies.
For primary bibliographic entry see Field 5B.
W75-07698

RATIONALE AND METHODOLOGY FOR MONITORING GROUNDWATER POLLUTED BY MINING ACTIVITIES,
General Electric Co., Santa Barbara, Calif. Center for Advanced Studies.
For primary bibliographic entry see Field 5B.
W75-07710

SYSTEM IDENTIFICATION AND MULTI-LEVEL OPTIMIZATION OF INTEGRATED GROUND WATER SYSTEMS,
California Univ., Los Angeles. Dept. of Engineering Systems.
For primary bibliographic entry see Field 2F.
W75-07722

GROUND-WATER PROTECTION IN PENNSYLVANIA, A MODEL STATE PROGRAM,
Geraghty and Miller, Port Washington, N.Y.
August 1974. 15 p, 2 tab, 1 map.

Descriptors: *Groundwater resources, *Water resources, *Pennsylvania, *Water pollution, Water pollution sources, Groundwater, Groundwater availability, Subsurface waters, Water supply, Water demand, Water resources development, Water law, Water sources, Subsurface waters, Runoff.

Many states are in the process of updating laws and regulations to facilitate the correction and control of serious ground-water pollution. Pennsylvania has a program with clearly stated objectives and backed by a well-informed technical and legal staff with legislative support for enforcement procedures. Groundwater is to a large extent quality controlled by activities of man on the land. Most industrial and urban undertakings capable of affecting Pennsylvania's groundwater are covered by regulations requiring reports detailing the anticipated effects. Groundwater is highly susceptible to pollution and carries a high potential for polluting surface water. During the drier months, Pennsylvania streamflow may be composed of as much as 100% ground-water discharge. Groundwater pollution may be irreparable for hydrogeologic or economic reasons. Pennsylvania regulations accordingly discourage the growth of potentially damaging activities such as subsurface waste disposal wells. A graph and map are included. (Proctor-Florida)
W75-07777

GEOTHERMAL LEASING PROGRAM, VOL IV, APPENDIX I, COMMENTS ON DRAFT IMPACT STATEMENT AND PROPOSED REGULATIONS (FINAL ENVIRONMENTAL IMPACT STATEMENT),
Department of the Interior, Washington, D.C.
For primary bibliographic entry see Field 8B.
W75-07781

AVAILABILITY OF GROUND WATER IN THE SACO RIVER BASIN, EAST-CENTRAL NEW HAMPSHIRE,
Geological Survey, Concord, N.H.
For primary bibliographic entry see Field 7C.
W75-07837

MAPS OF SAN GORGONIO PASS-UPPER COACHELLA VALLEY AREA, CALIFORNIA, SHOWING WATER-LEVEL CONTOURS, 1936 AND 1966-17,
Geological Survey, Menlo Park, Calif.
For primary bibliographic entry see Field 7C.
W75-07838

GEOLOGIC MAP OF WALKER COUNTY, ALABAMA,
Geological Survey, Tuscaloosa, Ala.
For primary bibliographic entry see Field 7C.
W75-07845

WATER AVAILABILITY AND GEOLOGY OF WALKER COUNTY, ALABAMA,
Geological Survey, Tuscaloosa, Ala.
For primary bibliographic entry see Field 7C.
W75-07846

4C. Effects On Water Of Man's Non-Water Activities

SOME USES OF SOIL STABILIZERS IN THE USA,
Agricultural Research Service, Ames, Iowa. Soil and Water Conservation Research Div.
For primary bibliographic entry see Field 2J.
W75-07374

CHANGE IN THE PHYSIOCOCHEMICAL COMPOSITION OF WATER UNDER THE EFFECT OF FELLINGS,
Severo-Kavkazskaya Lesnaya Opytnaya Stantsiya, Maykop (USSR).
For primary bibliographic entry see Field 5B.
W75-07429

THE EFFECTS OF GEOLOGY AND LAND USE ON THE EXPORT OF PHOSPHORUS FROM WATERSHEDS,
Toronto Univ. (Ontario). Dept. of Zoology.
For primary bibliographic entry see Field 5B.
W75-07470

TRANSPORTATION IN THE COLORADO RIVER BASIN,
Boston Aschmann Associates, San Jose, Calif.
For primary bibliographic entry see Field 6B.
W75-07540

URBANIZATION IN THE COLORADO RIVER BASIN,
Utah State Univ., Logan. Dept. of Political Science.
C. W. Hübner.
In: Environmental Management in the Colorado River Basin, October 15-16, 1973, Salt Lake City, Utah, Utah State University Press, Logan, 1974, p 216-240, 19 ref, 11 tab, 1 fig, 3 append.

Descriptors: *Colorado River Basin, *Urbanization, *Ecosystems, *Land use, Water resourses, *Water pollution, *Long-term planning, Human population, Arizona, Utah, Colorado, New Mexico, California, Nevada, Wyoming, Pollutants, Air pollution.
Identifiers: Environmental management.

The recent urbanization process in the Colorado River Basin and its relationship to agriculture, recreation, transportation and energy are examined. The concept of a 'carrying capacity' can be applied to man-made, man-dominated urban systems, which, like natural ecosystems, have resource pollution limits. The 11 states having jurisdiction in the Colorado River Basin have 25 urbanized areas (population over 50,000). Basically, the region is empty with scattered urban centers. This highly urbanized area will become more so in the future. Over the past 20 years, 43 percent of the region's growth has come from migration and many of the rural counties have suffered population declines. This movement to the cities has brought a conflict between agricultural and urban use of the scarce good land and water. Another problem facing the basin is that the relatively unpopulation and politically impotent area might be used as a sink for urban waste products. At present, the states of the basin lack the political power to control the use of the basin's environment. (See also W75-07525) (Bowden-Arizona)
W75-07541

URBANIZATION WITH OR WITHOUT ENVIRONMENTAL QUALITY,
United States International Univ., San Diego, Calif.
T. A. MacCalla.
In: Environmental Management in the Colorado River Basin, October 15-16, 1973, Salt Lake City, Utah, Utah State University Press, Logan, 1974, p 241-259, 20 ref, 1 fig, append.

Descriptors: *Colorado River Basin, *Human population, *Land use, *Urban impact, Arizona, Utah, Wyoming, Colorado, Nevada, California, New Mexico.
Identifiers: Environmental management.

Taking urbanization as the process and environmental quality as the product, the growth of cities as seen as irreversible and the real question is what kind of environmental quality is probable or possible in this future growth. A five point urban forecast is made for the United States: (1) Blacks and other minorities will dominate 13 central cities by 1985 and the school systems of 11 more; (2) the working age population (20-64) will rise from 106 million in 1970 to 136 million by 1985; (3) the biggest population growth between 1970 and 1985 will be the addition of 26 million apartment dwellers ages 25-54; (4) the number of people over 65 will double to 31 million; (5) people under 25 will constitute 45 percent of the population in 1985. This urban growth makes the adoption of an environmental conscience mandatory for human survival. Since the urban growth cannot be stopped, comprehensive planning is essential to ensure environmental quality. With such densities of humans, the environment will not be a luxury but a necessity for the health of communities. (See also W75-07525) (Bowden-Arizona)
W75-07542

EFFECT OF PORT ORANGE BRIDGE-CAUSEWAY ON FLOW OF HALIFAX RIVER, VOLUSIA COUNTY, FLORIDA,
Geological Survey, Tallahassee, Fla.
W. C. Bridges.
Open-file report 72005, 1972. 19 p, 5 fig, 1 tab.

Descriptors: *Streamflow, *Bridges, *Florida, Profiles, Flow profiles, Backwater, Regime, Tides, Lagoons, Water levels.
Identifiers: *Halifax River(Fla).

The effects of the Port Orange bridge-causeway on the flow of the Halifax River, Florida, are described. Flood-tide profiles indicate a small degree of restriction of streamflow. Part of this may be caused by oyster bars and part by the bridge-causeway. Differences in water-surface elevations of 0.30 foot at the relief culvert represent the maximum effect on the river by the bridge-causeway. The maximum velocity measured on the ebb tide was 2.26 fps. (Knapp-USGS)
W75-07555

WATERSHED MANAGEMENT IN ARIZONA'S MIXED CONIFER FORESTS: THE STATUS OF OUR KNOWLEDGE,
Forest Service (USDA), Fort Collins, Colo. Rocky Mountain Forest and Range Experiment Station.
L. R. Rich, and J. R. Thompson.
U.S. Department of Agriculture, Forest Service, Research Paper RM-130, 18 p, December 1974. 3 fig, 3 tab, 45 ref.

Descriptors: *Watershed management, *Arizona, *Forest management, *Mixed forests, *Water yield improvement, Vegetation, Land clearing, Evapotranspiration, Soil moisture, Snow cover, Snowmelt, Coniferous forests, Wildlife, Aesthetics, Southwest U.S., Water yield, Clear-cutting, Streamflow, Forest watersheds.

Removing mixed conifer forest vegetation has increased water yields approximately in proportion to the percent of the area in cleared openings. Most of the yield increase can be accounted for by the reduction in evapotranspiration. Reduced soil-moisture deficit and increased snow accumulation and melt rates in the cut openings contribute to these increases. When fitted to the timber-stand structure, patchcutting is compatible with recommended mixed conifer silviculture, beneficial to wildlife, and esthetically pleasing. Although mixed conifer areas make up only 0.4% of the total land area of Arizona, they contribute 6% of the State's water yield. Intensive management of these forest lands could increase annual streamflow 36,500 acre-feet/year, roughly 12 billion gallons of water/year. (Witt-IPC)
W75-07648

A MODEL FOR PREDICTING EROSION AND SEDIMENT YIELD FROM SECONDARY FOREST ROAD CONSTRUCTION,
Forest Service (USDA), Fort Collins, Colo. Rocky Mountain Forest and Range Experiment Station.
C. F. Leaf.
U.S. Department of Agriculture, Forest Service, Research Note RM-274, 4 p, December, 1974. 2 fig, 1 tab, 7 ref.

Descriptors: *Forests, *Roads, *Sediment yield, *Erosion, Soil erosion, *Colorado, Rocky Mountain Region, Mountain forests, Lumbering, Access routes, Road construction, Forest watersheds, Mathematical models, Sediments, Water quality.

One of the more visible and controversial environmental impacts associated with timber harvesting and development in central Colorado is road construction. Better tools are needed to quantify the effect of soil disturbance on erosion onsite, and the subsequent yield of sediment downstream. This note summarizes available data and proposes a preliminary model for predicting an index of onsite erosion and downstream sediment yield. (Witt-IPC)

W75-07653

RUNOFF AND EROSION AFTER BRUSH SUPPRESSION ON THE NATURAL DRAINAGE WATERSHEDS IN CENTRAL ARIZONA,
Arizona State Univ., Tempe.
For primary bibliographic entry see Field 3B.
W75-07655

PEARL RIVER BOATWAY MAP, MORGANTOWN TO SANDY HOOK, COLUMBIA AREA, MISSISSIPPI,
Geological Survey, Jackson, Miss.
For primary bibliographic entry see Field 7C.
W75-07848

4D. Watershed Protection

NUTRIENT AND SEDIMENT PRODUCTION FROM FORESTED WATERSHEDS,
Nevada Agricultural Experiment Station, Reno.
For primary bibliographic entry see Field 5B.
W75-07353

STRUCTURAL PROBLEMS OF INDONESIAN SOILS,
Lembaga Penelitian Tanah, Bogor (Indonesia).
For primary bibliographic entry see Field 2G.
W75-07394

THE EFFECTS OF GEOLOGY AND LAND USE ON THE EXPORT OF PHOSPHORUS FROM WATERSHEDS,
Toronto Univ. (Ontario). Dept. of Zoology.
For primary bibliographic entry see Field 5B.
W75-07470

GULLY EROSION, NORTHWESTERN COLORADO: A THRESHOLD PHENOMENON,
Texas Univ. at Austin. Dept. of Geological Sciences.
For primary bibliographic entry see Field 2J.
W75-07477

SEDIMENT IN IRRIGATION AND DRAINAGE WATERS AND SEDIMENT INPUTS AND OUTPUTS FOR TWO LARGE TRACTS IN SOUTHERN IDAHO,
Agricultural Research Service, Kimberly, Idaho. Snake River Conservation Research Center.
For primary bibliographic entry see Field 5G.
W75-07546

WATERSHED MANAGEMENT IN ARIZONA'S MIXED CONIFER FORESTS: THE STATUS OF OUR KNOWLEDGE,
Forest Service (USDA), Fort Collins, Colo. Rocky Mountain Forest and Range Experiment Station.
For primary bibliographic entry see Field 4C.
W75-07648

HYDROLOGICAL AND EROSION INFLUENCES OF SHELTERBELTS, (IN RUSSIAN),
G. P. Surmach.
Dokl Vses Ord Lenina Akad S-Kh Nauk Im V I Lenina, 3, p 28-29, 1973.

Descriptors: *Erosion control, Thawing, Flow characteristics.
Identifiers: Forest belts.

Quantitative characteristics of the flow of thawed water from plow-lands and arable lands in a zonal cut and characteristics of water absorption and anti-erosion activity of water belts are given. The necessity of a combination of forest belts and simple hydrotechnological systems is established.

New formulas for calculation of distances between additional water-regulatory forest belts are included.--Copyright 1974, Biological Abstracts, Inc.
W75-07651

A MODEL FOR PREDICTING EROSION AND SEDIMENT YIELD FROM SECONDARY FOREST ROAD CONSTRUCTION,
Forest Service (USDA), Fort Collins, Colo. Rocky Mountain Forest and Range Experiment Station.
For primary bibliographic entry see Field 4C.
W75-07653

RUNOFF AND EROSION AFTER BRUSH SUPPRESSION ON THE NATURAL DRAINAGE WATERSHEDS IN CENTRAL ARIZONA,
Arizona State Univ., Tempe.
For primary bibliographic entry see Field 3B.
W75-07655

SEDIMENT AND EROSION CONTROL DESIGN CRITERIA,
Maryland Dept. of Natural Resources, Annapolis. Water Resources Administration.
M. A. Ports.
In: The APWA Reporter, Vol 42, No 5, May 1975, p 18-19, 2 fig.

Descriptors: *Sediment control, *Sediment load, *Soil erosion, *Maryland, *Sediment yield, *Erosion control, Sedimentation rates, Erosion, Soil engineering, Soil investigations, Soil management, Soil surfaces, Surface runoff, Storm runoff, Drainage engineering, Agricultural engineering.
Identifiers: *Siltation.

In an effort to control erosion and sediment caused by human activity, the Maryland Legislature adopted, in 1970, the Statewide Sediment Control Law. All erosion and sediment control plans are considered on the basis of qualitative judgement of each plan's effectiveness. Since existing in-stream water quality standards for sediment loadings are unworkable during peak runoff periods, proposed design and analysis procedures must provide for calculation of the sediment yield prior to a rainstorm event. Because natural erosion rates range between 0.1 to 1.0 tons/acre/year, erosion rates below 1 ton/acre/year should not be considered to produce sediment pollution. With the use of watershed systems to protect water and land resources, sediment yields above 15 tons/acre/year should be established as sediment pollution for urban construction sites. It is recommended that sediment yields above 5 tons/acre/year be established as sediment pollution for agriculturally related activities. No attempt has been made to set criteria for construction directly within stream channels, lakes, tidal estuaries, or for the Atlantic Shoreline. The Universal Soil Loss Equation as developed by the USDA Agricultural Research Service provides a method for determining the combinations of control practices needed to meet the maximum allowable sediment yield. (Poertner)
W75-07672

LANDSCAPE TENDING AND NATURE CONSERVATION AS PARTIAL TASKS FOR SOCIALISTIC LAND DEVELOPMENT,
For primary bibliographic entry see Field 4A.
W75-07707

STUDIES ON SOIL EROSION CONTROL: 4. THE HYDRAULIC STUDIES OF WATER FLOW IN SLOPED LAND (IN JAPANESE),
Obihiro Zootechnical Univ. (Japan). Lab. of Agricultural and Civil Engineering.
For primary bibliographic entry see Field 4A.
W75-07756

THE MENDOTA WATERSHED PROJECT, LASALLE AND BUREAU COUNTIES, ILLINOIS (FINAL ENVIRONMENTAL IMPACT STATEMENT),
Soil Conservation Service, Champaign, Ill.
Available from the National Technical Information Service, U.S. Dept. of Comerce, Springfield, Va. 22161, as EIS-IL-73-1834-F, $3.75 in paper copy, $2.25 in microfiche. November 26, 1973. 49 p, 3 map, 1 photo.

Descriptors: *Watershed Protect. and Flood Prev. Act, *Flood protection, *Channel improvement, Flood damage, Vegetation effects, Watershed management, Flood control, Floods, Land management, Retardance, Channels, Erosion, Runoff, Nutrients, Land use, *Illinois.
Identifiers: *Environmental Impact Statements, LaSalle County(Ill), Bureau Counties(Ill), *Mendota watershed(Ill).

The purpose of the project is watershed protection and flood prevention. The project will include land treatment measures supplemented by five floodwater retarding structures and 0.9 miles of channel modification. The environmental impact of the land treatment program will reduce average annual upland erosion by 40 percent, reduce runoff and nutrient losses, improve land use, and create public awareness of remaining flood hazards. Combined land treatment and structural measures will reduce overall flood damages 86.5 percent. Approximately 52 acres of water surface will provide the basis for an estimated 56,000 average annual visitor days of recreation. The main adverse effect is that the vegetative cover on 50 acres required for spoil areas, construction areas and areas required for temporary storage will be temporarily disturbed. Agricultural production on 119 acres will also be lost or diminished as a result of acquisition of land rights. Five alternatives were considered: land treatment only; two floodwater retarding structures; channel modification only; flood plain management and land treatment; and no project. The State of Illinois and the U.S. Army, Departments of Health, Education and Welfare, Interior, and Transportation, and the Environmental Protection Agency submitted comments. (Gagliardi-Florida)
W75-07785

UPPER SALT CREEK WATERSHED, COOK, LAKE AND DUPAGE COUNTIES, ILLINOIS (FINAL ENVIRONMENTAL IMPACT STATEMENT),
Soil Conservation Service, Washington, D.C.
For primary bibliographic entry see Field 8A.
W75-07789

DOES CANOEING INCREASE STREAMBANK EROSION,
Forest Service (USDA), St. Paul, Minn. North Central Forest Experiment Station.
For primary bibliographic entry see Field 2J.
W75-07792

5. WATER QUALITY MANAGEMENT AND PROTECTION

5A. Identification Of Pollutants

REAGENTS FOR DETERMINATIONS OF TRACE IMPURITIES IN WATER, PHASE II,
Southern Illinois Univ., Carbondale. Dept. of Chemistry and Biochemistry.
A. L. Caskey, R. J. Antepenko, and J. C. L. Swan.
Available from the National Technical Information Service, Springfield, Va 22161 as PB-241 516, $5.25 in paper copy, $2.25 in microfiche. Illinois Water Resources Center, Urbana, Research Report No. 100, April 1975. 110 p, 29 tab, 13 fig, 17 ref. OWRT A-049-ILL(1). 14-31-0001-3513.

Descriptors: *Trace elements, Analytical techniques, *Pollutant identification, *Nitrates, *Nitrites, Sulfonates, Research and development, Groundwater, *Spectrophotometry, Water analysis.
Identifiers: *Reagents.

Determinations of trace impurities in water are often complicated. Sensitive, specific, stable, water-soluble reagents are needed for rapid, spectrophotometric determinations of trace impurities in water. A new method for the determination of nitrate in water is described which uses zinc 1-naphthol-4-sulfonate, an easily prepared, readily purified, stable, water-soluble reagent; the reagent is much better than 1-napthol-4-sulfonic acid, which is satisfactory only under carefully controlled conditions. The same reagent, zinc 1-naphthol-4-sulfonate, also has been proposed for the rapid, specific, sensitive determination of nitrite in natural waters. Nitrite can be determined at ppm levels in the presence of several thousand fold excess of nitrate. The methods can be applied to such diverse systems as lakes where agricultural fertilizer run-off may be significant, to effluents from plants in the food-preparation industry, and to natural-water systems in highly mineralized areas. (See also W72-07354).
W75-07352

OSCILLOPOLAROGRAPHIC DETERMINATION OF CU(II), CD(II), PB(II), ZN(II), NI(II), MN(II) AND CR(VI) IN WASTE WATERS (IN ITALIAN),
Pavia Univ. (Italy). Istituto di Chimica Generale.
C. Bertoglio Riolo, T. Fulle Soldi, and G. Spini.
Ann Chim. Vol 62, No 11/12, p 730-739, 1972, English summary.

Descriptors: *Waste water, Analytical techniques, *Polarographic analysis, Cadmium, Chromium, Copper, Lead, Manganese, Nickel, Zinc, *Pollutant identification.
Identifiers: Absorption, Atomic, Oscillo polarographic analysis.

Experimental conditions were investigated for the determination of Cu(II), Cd(II), Pb(II), Zn(II), Ni(II), Mn(II) and Cr(VI) in waste waters by osscillographic polarography. For all of these elements, analytical sensitivity and precision of this method are reported. The influence of the most common agents which cause interference is also reported. Results are in good agreement with atomic absorption spectroscopic analysis and confirm that the oscillopolarography is a suitable and reliable method for routine determinations in waste water.--Copyright 1974, Biological Abstracts, Inc.
W75-07361

AMOUNTS AND HYDROLYSIS OF PYROPHOSPHATE AND TRIPOLYPHOSPHATE IN SEDIMENTS,
Missouri Univ., Columbia. Dept. of Agronomy.
D. C. Riego.
Available from the National Technical Information Service, Springfield, Va 22161 as PB-241 698, $7.00 in paper copy, $2.25 in microfiche. PhD Dissertation, August 1974. 175 p, 31 fig, 9 tab, 150 ref, append. OWRT B-051-MO(2).

Descriptors: Chemistry, *Sediments, *Phosphates, *Hydrolysis, Fertilizers, Phosphorus, Phosphorus compounds, Water pollution sources, Analytical techniques, Soil chemistry, Soil chemical properties, Chemical analysis, Nutrients, Chemical wastes, Rivers.
Identifiers: Pyrophosphate, Tripolyphosphate.

A method to determine pyrophosphate (PP) and tripolyphosphate (TPP) in sediments was developed. The limit of detection was 0.5 microgram P/g sediment. Fourteen sediments were tested and the highest TPP found was 1.8 micrograms P/g sediment. Thirteen of the sediment sam-

ples contained less than 1 microgram P/g as TPP. Only 3 of 14 samples contained more than 1 microgram P/g as PP. The highest level of PP found in a sediment was 8.5 micrograms P/g from an animal waste lagoon. The rates of hydrolysis of TPP and PP in sediments were determined. The influence of temperature, biological activity, and pH on the rate of TPP and PP hydrolysis was investigated. The rate of TPP and PP hydrolysis increased with increasing temperature. TPP and PP were hydrolyzed faster in nonsterile sediment than in sediment which had been sterilized. The rate of PP hydrolysis increased as the pH was increased. (Sims-ISWS)
W75-07399

AUTOMATED ANALYSIS OF INDIVIDUAL REFRACTORY ORGANICS IN POLLUTED WATER,
Oak Ridge National Lab., Tenn.
W. W. Pitt, R. L. Jolley, and S. Katz.
For sale by the Superintendent of Documents, U.S. Government Printing Office, Washington, D.C. 20402, $1.75. Environmental Protection Agency report number, EPA-660/2-74-076, August 1974. 98 p, 32 fig, 17 tab, 17 ref. 16ACG 03. 14-12-833.

Descriptors: *Pollutant identification, *Sewage effluents, *Chromatography, *Organic compounds, *Chlorination, Water analysis, Water pollution, Pollutants, Municipal wastes, Carbohydrates, Analytical techniques, Separation techniques, Instrumentation, Chemical oxygen demand, Gas chromatography, Spectrometry, Photometry, Fluorometry, Ion exchange, Radioactive tracers, Chlorine, Sewage treatment, Waste water treatment.
Identifiers: High-resolution liquid chromatography, Primary effluent, Secondary effluent, Ultraviolet-absorbing constituents, Chlorine-containing organics, Oxidizable constituents, Cerate oxidimetry, Chlorine-36.

Residual organic compounds present in municipal sewage treatment plant effluents at microgram-per-liter levels were analyzed using high-resolution anion-exchange chromatography. Effluents were concentrated 50- to 3000-fold by vacuum evaporation and freeze-drying and then analyzed by liquid chromatographs capable of detecting uv-absorbing, oxidizable (with sulfatoceric acid), or carbohydrate constituents. Using techniques such as uv spectroscopy, gas chromatography, and mass spectrometry, 56 organic compounds were identified in primary effluent and 13 organic compounds in secondary effluent. Some of these constituents were quantified. Chromatographic procedures, coupled with radioactive tracer chlorination, were applied to the analysis of chlorinated primary and secondary effluents. More than 60 peaks containing chlorine were found, and specific chlorinated compounds were tentatively identified by cochromatography and quantified at the 0.5- to 4-microgram/liter level. A detector system for liquid chromatography based on cerate oxidimetry was adapted as a rapid, sensitive continuous monitor for measuring the COD of waters. The effects of column geometry and operating parameters on chromatographic resolution were studied. Two high-resolution, ion exchange chromatographs (UV-Analyzers) were constructed for U.S. Environmental Protection Agency research laboratories, and are being used in the analysis of treated sewage effluents and other polluted waters. (EPA)
W75-07404

INVESTIGATIONS ON CONCENTRATIONS, DISTRIBUTIONS, AND FATES OF HEAVY METAL WASTES IN PARTS OF LONG ISLAND SOUND,
Connecticut Univ., Groton. Marine Sciences Inst.
For primary bibliographic entry see Field 5B.
W75-07412

MARINE POLLUTION MONITORING: STRATEGIES FOR A NATIONAL PROGRAM,
Scripps Institution of Oceanography, La Jolla, Calif.
Marine Pollution Monitoring: Strategies for a National Program, Deliberations of a workshop held at Santa Catalina Marine Biological Laboratory of the University of Southern California Allan Hancock Foundation, October 25-28, 1972, 203 p. (NOAA 75030307).

Descriptors: *Monitoring, *Chemcontrol, *Analytical techniques, *Sea water, Marine animals, *Sampling, *Chemical analysis, Pollutants, Water pollution, Chemical wastes, Wastes, Heavy metals, *Pollutant identification, Control systems, Data collections, Data transmission, Measurement.
Identifiers: Marine pollution monitoring, Chemical identification, Marine organisms, Marine water, Transport paths, Analysis aids.

Twenty-six scientists assembled at Santa Catalina Marine Station under NOAA sponsorship to develop strategies for initiation of monitoring programs for chemical pollutants in the marine environment. Topics discussed include the sampling of marine waters, estuaries, marine organisms, and transport paths; analytical techniques for selected inorganic species, and selected organic compounds; and various aids to analysis of marine organisms for heavy content. Recommendations include the establishment of a national marine monitoring program for chemical pollution; establishment of a technical group in NOAA to plan and implement such a program; establishment of an advisory panel to recommend policies; and the convening of workships to consider all aspects of marine pollution monitoring. (NOAA)
W75-07418

APPLICATION OF X-RAY EMISSION SPECTROMETRY TO THE DETERMINATION OF MERCURY IN BIOLOGICAL SAMPLES,
National Inst. of Environmental Health Sciences, Research Triangle Park, N.C.
P. Walsh, P. Hamrick, and N. Underwood.
Rev Sci Instrum, Vol 44, No 8, p 1019-1020, 1973.

Descriptors: *X-ray spectroscopy, *Mercury, Blood, Kidneys, Urine, *Sampling, *Analytical techniques, X-ray analysis, *Pollutant identification.

The application of x-ray emission spectrometry to quantitative determination of mercury in biological samples is described. Mercury was measured in blood, water, kidney and urine. Matrix effects were detectable but not critical.--Copyright 1974, Biological Abstracts, Inc.
W75-07419

MICROCOMBUSTION METHOD FOR THE DETERMINATION OF CARBON-14-LABELED PESTICIDE RESIDUES IN SOIL,
Agricultural Research Service, Fort Collins, Colo.
W. E. Beard, and W. D. Guenzi.
Soil Science Society of America Proceedings, Vol 39, No 1, p 63-65, January-February 1975. 1 fig, 2 tab, 5 ref.

Descriptors: Pesticides, *Soil analysis, *Tagging, *Soil tests, *Analytical techniques, Carbon dioxide, Chemical analysis, Evaluation, Gas chromatography, Radioactivity techniques, Instrumentation, Testing, DDT, Analysis, Chemistry, Testing procedures, Solvent extractions, *Pesticide residues, *Pollutant identification.
Identifiers: *Carbon-14, *Microcombustion method, Nitrogen analyzers, Picloram, Lindane, Scintillation counting techniques, Degradation products.

A dry combustion procedure commonly used for total carbon analysis was modified and used to determine the concentration of C-14-labeled pesticides in soil. Modifications included replacement of the Ascarite CO2 trap with a solution of an organic base compatible with liquid scintillation solvents, and minor carrier gas flow changes. Recovery of three pesticides from four soils ranged from 83 to 99% and averaged 94%. (Henley-ISWS)
W75-07432

NITRATE MEASUREMENTS USING A SPECIFIC ION ELECTRODE IN PRESENCE OF NITRITE,
Oak Ridge National Lab., Tenn.
C. W. Francis, and C. D. Malone.
Soil Science Society of America Proceedings, Vol 39, No 1, p 150-151, January-February 1975. 2 fig, 1 tab, 9 ref.

Descriptors: *Nitrates, *Nitrogen compounds, *Analytical techniques, *Instrumentation, *Measurement, Inorganic compounds, Chemicals, Denitrification, Nitrites, Water quality, Colorimetry, Analysis, Estimating, Evaluation, Ions, Electrodes, *Pollutant identification.
Identifiers: *Sulfanilamide, *Nitrite interference, Nitrite complexing.

The presence of the nitrite anion NO2(-) may lead to a significant error in measuring NO3-N concentrations with a specific ion electrode. Interference by nitrite was eliminated by complexing the nitrite with sulfanilamide in 0.01 N H2SO4. In this manner, nitrate levels can be read directly in concentrations ranging from 10 to 5000 ppm NO3-N. The method is particularly useful in denitrification studies where HCO3(-) and CO3(--) anions as well as NO2(-) preclude direct NO3-N measurements. (Henley-ISWS)
W75-07433

EARTH RESISTIVITY SURVEYS - A METHOD FOR DEFINING GROUND-WATER CONTAMINATION,
Geraghty and Miller, Port Washington, N.Y.
For primary bibliographic entry see Field 5B.
W75-07440

THE LINEAR MEAN GRADIENT MODEL FOR TWO-PARTICLE TURBULENT DIFFUSION,
National Center for Atmospheric Research, Boulder, Colo.
M. L. Thiebaux.
Journal of the Atmospheric Sciences, Vol 32, No 1, p 92-101, January 1975. 9 ref.

Descriptors: *Air pollution, *Diffusion, *Model studies, Mathematics, *Statistics, Energy dissipation, Turbulent flow, Probability, Mixing, Dispersion, *Pollutant identification.
Identifiers: *Diffusivity tensor, Linear mean gradient model, Relative diffusivity.

A two-particle description of turbulent diffusion provides the information required to determine certain kinds of shape characteristics of cloud contaminants. The concept of scale-dependent relative diffusivity for the spreading of contaminant clouds is implicit in the two-particle description. The linear mean gradient model was applied to the diffusion of a pair of particles passively advected by an inhomogeneous, nonstationary ensemble of velocity fields. The central result was a differential equation satisfied by a model joint probability density function of the particle positions, approximating that of the real ensemble. Phenomenologically determined coefficients appeared in the equation. One of these was the one-particle effective eddy diffusivity tensor while the other was a tensor quantity representative of the correlation between the motions of the particles. Conditions on the tensor coefficients were found to ensure that the one-particle model was properly embedded in the two-particle model. The separation into a center-of-mass diffusion model and a relative diffusion model was accomplished. Corresponding diffusivi-

ty tensors were derived and specialized to the case of homogeneous turbulence. A method was suggested for determining the required diffusivity tensors from observations of the statistical properties of tracer trajectories. (Singh-ISWS)
W75-07444

A CONTINUOUS TURBIDITY MONITORING SYSTEM FOR COASTAL SURFACE WATERS,
Old Dominion Univ., Norfolk, Va. Inst. of Oceanography.
W. W. Berg, Jr., P. Fleischer, G. R. Freitag, and E. L. Bryant.
Limnology and Oceanography, Vol 20, No 1, p 137-141, January 1975. 4 fig, 4 ref.

Descriptors: *Turbidity, Water properties, *Monitoring, *On-site tests, *Water analysis, Instrumentation, Analytical techniques, Measurement, Physical properties, Optical properties, Turbidity currents, Water quality, Water, Testing, Opacity, Salinity, Data collections, Oceans, Coasts, Surface waters, Suspended solids.
Identifiers: *Turbidimeter, *Optical transmissometer, Particulate matter, Santa Barbara Channel, Chesapeake Bay.

A continuous, time-referenced turbidity monitoring system utilizes a keel mounted optical transmissometer with a modified strip chart recorder. It allows detailed study of the distribution of suspended particles in surface waters. (Henley-ISWS)
W75-07471

SUSPENDED MARINE CLAY MINERAL IDENTIFICATION BY SCANNING ELECTRON MICROSCOPY AND ENERGY-DISPERSIVE X-RAY ANALYSIS,
Texas A and M Univ., College Station. Dept. of Oceanography.
For primary bibliographic entry see Field 2J.
W75-07472

THE DETERMINATION OF AMMONIA IN SEA-WATER,
Marine Biological Association of the United Kingdom, Plymouth (England). Plymouth Lab.
For primary bibliographic entry see Field 2K.
W75-07474

THE PREVALENCE OF HUMAN DENTAL CARIES AND WATER-BORNE TRACE METALS,
Forsyth Dental Center, Boston, Mass.
R. L. Glass, K. J. Rothman, F. Espinal, H. Velez, and N. J. Smith.
Arch Oral Biol. Vol 18, No 9, p 1099-1104, 1973, Illus.

Descriptors: *South America, Human diseases, Water pollution, *Metals, Fluorides, *Trace elements, Water analysis, Calcium, Magnesium, Molybdenum, Copper, Iron, Vanadium, Spectroscopy, Pollutant identification, Public health, Potable water.
Identifiers: *Colombia, *Dental caries, Spectroscopic analysis.

Marked differences in the prevalence of dental caries were observed in 2 isolated villages in Colombia, South America. These differences approximate those observed between areas of minimal and optimal fluoride ingestion, although each village has less than 0.1 ppm fluoride in the drinking water. Dietary histories reveal remarkedly similar dietary practices. Samples of drinking water were collected from these villages, and analyzed by emission spectroscopy for the concentrations of 21 trace elements. In the case of 13 elements, concentrations were at or below the threshold of detection or showed minimal variability. Concentrations of Ca, Mg, Mo and V were higher in the water samples from the village with the low caries prevalence, while concentrations of Cu, Fe and Mg were higher in the samples from the village with the higher prevalence. These differences were highly significant. The caries prevalence in the high caries village was typical of the country as a whole.--Copyright 1974, Biological Abstracts, Inc.
W75-07479

TOXICITY OF THE FLESH OF COMMON FISH TO THE WHITE MOUSE (MUS MUSCULUS VAR. ALBA),
Poitiers Univ. (France). Laboratoire de Microbiologie et Biologie Maritime.
For primary bibliographic entry see Field 5C.
W75-07483

ENVIRONMENT SURVEYS,
National Aeronautics and Space Administration, Langley Station, Va. Langley Research Center.
For primary bibliographic entry see Field 7B.
W75-07503

CHEMISTRY IN THE AQUATIC ENVIRONMENT,
Victoria Ministry for Conservation, Melbourne (Australia). Westernport Bay Environmental Study.
M. A. Shapiro, and D. W. Connell.
Proceedings of the Royal Australian Chemical Institute, Vol 42, No 5, p 113 - 118, May 1975. 4 fig, 2 tab, 23 ref.

Descriptors: *Reviews, *Water quality, *Water analysis, *Aquatic environment, Water chemistry, Environmental control, Environmental effects, Sampling, Analytical techniques, *Pollutant identification, Water pollution, *Path of pollutants.

Chemical evaluations are basic to understanding and managing the aquatic environment; and in many investigations the chemist must work as part of an interdisciplinary team, at least to the extent that he is fully aware of the implications of his work in the broader field which includes physical, ecological and social aspects. A review of the role of the chemist in such studies is presented, with emphasis on three critical areas: clarification of the impact of various substances on aquatic ecology; determination of the manner of degradation and distribution of contaminants in an ecological context; and development of sensitive analytical techniques suitable for large numbers of samples. The definition of water 'quality' in environmental terms is of the utmost importance in attempts to develop targeted methodology to solve existing problems. (CSIRO)
W75-07524

COASTAL SALINITY RECONNAISSANCE AND MONITORING SYSTEM--SOUTH COAST OF PUERTO RICO,
Geological Survey of Puerto Rico, San Juan.
J. R. Diaz.
Open-file report 74-1, 1974. 28 p, 15 fig, 8 tab, 2 ref.

Descriptors: *Saline water intrusion, *Puerto Rico, *Groundwater, *Aquifers, Saline water-freshwater interfaces, Water quality, Sampling, Sea water, Coasts.

Sea-water intrusion and other salinity conditions in the alluvial aquifer in the coastal areas of Guanica, Guayanilla-Yauco, Tallaboa, Juana Diaz, and Jobos, Puerto Rico, are described. The criteria for the water classification consider the dissolved solids content and other quality-of-water factors of particular importance for the use of water for domestic, irrigation, and industrial purposes. An increase in chloride ion and other significant changes in the chemical composition of the water in the alluvial aquifer were considered reliable indications of salt-water intrusion into the aquifer. Active zones of sea-water intrusion were detected in the southwestern sections of the Guayanilla-Yauco and Tallaboa areas. This intrusion is caused by overpumping of wells and by the penetration of sea water through old streambed channels and open sea-water canals. Small areas subjected to possible salt-water intrusion were found around Boca Chica in the Juana Diaz area in the southwestern section of the Salinas fan in the Jobos area. (Knapp-USGS)
W75-07553

WATER QUALITY OF TAMPA BAY, FLORIDA: DRY-WEATHER CONDITIONS, JUNE 1971,
Geological Survey, Tallahassee, Fla.
C. R. Goodwin, J. S. Rosenshein, and D. M. Michaelis.
Open-file report FL 74026, 1974. 85 p, 2 fig, 10 tab, 4 ref.

Descriptors: *Bays, *Florida, *Water quality, *Sampling, *Data collections, Hydrologic data, Basic data collections, Water analysis, Estuaries, Water pollution.
Identifiers: *Tampa Bay(Florida).

Two intensive water-quality sampling efforts were made in Tampa Bay, Florida, during critical hydrologic conditions. One was made during June 1971, an exceptionally dry weather period; another was made in October 1971, a moderately wet-weather period. The bay also was sampled periodically at selected sites during the 3-year investigation. Samples were collected from parts of Tampa Bay in Hillsborough, Manatee, and Pinellas Counties covering about 350 square miles of the bay system. These sampling efforts were made to provide information necessary for calibration and verification of a digital computer model that accurately simulates hydrodynamic and water-quality conditions in the bay. In addition, many of the data were gathered to provide a wide range of benchmark water-quality information. This report contains, in tabular form, data on 48 parameters from water samples collected from 105 sites in Tampa Bay. (Knapp-USGS)
W75-07556

HYDROLOGIC RECORDS FOR LAKE COUNTY, FLORIDA, 1972-73,
Geological Survey, Tallahassee, Fla.
For primary bibliographic entry see Field 2E.
W75-07566

WATER RESOURCES DATA FOR GEORGIA, 1974.
Geological Survey, Doraville, Ga.
For primary bibliographic entry see Field 7C.
W75-07569

WATER-QUALITY STUDIES TODAY AND TOMORROW,
Geological Survey, Menlo Park, Calif.
J. D. Hem.
In: Hydrology and Water Resources in Arizona and the Southwest, Vol 3; Proceedings of the 1973 Meetings of the Arizona Section of American Water Resources Association and the Hydrology Section, Arizona Adademy of Science, May 4-5, 1973, Tucson, p 44-49, 1973.

Descriptors: *Water quality, *Instrumentation, *Water analysis, Automation, Path of pollutants, Data collections, Waste disposal, Waste disposal wells, Saline water, Measurement.

Development of better instruments for analysis and automation have greatly increased the available information on quality of water during the past decade. There remains a need for further research on relationships between dissolved material and the solids in contact with water in order to cope with existing or potential problems in water quality such as the extent to which lead from automobile

hausts may contaminate water supplies, or the fety of disposal of toxic wastes into deep saline uifers. (Knapp-USGS)
75-07579

HEMICAL QUALITY OF GROUND WATER HAWAII,
eological Survey, Honolulu, Hawaii.
. A. Swain.
awaii Division of Water and Land Development, onolulu, Report R48, May 1973. 54 p, 5 fig, 12 ate, 2 tab, 24 ref, append.

escriptors: *Water quality, *Hawaii, Groundwater, Basic data collections, Hydrologic ata, Water chemistry, Water pollution sources.

roundwater quality is described for the five ajor islands of Hawaii. In general, the water uality of each island is a function of the environ- ent and of man's activities. The environmental ctors are rainfall, geology, and sea-water intru- on. Man's activities that affect quality are gricultural pumping and return irrigation water, dustrial wastes, and domestic wastes. The pur- ose of the study was to identify present ground- ater quality conditions, both natural and as af- ected by usage, to show readily identifiable hanges in quality with time and usage, and to re- ate water-quality conditions to the development f groundwater supplies. (Knapp-USGS)
V75-07585

VATER-QUALITY RECONNAISSANCE OF URFACE INFLOW TO UTAH LAKE,
Geological Survey, Salt Lake City, Utah.
. C. Mundorff.
Jtah Department of Natural Resources, Salt Lake City, Technical Publication No 46, 1974. 96 p, 16 ig, 3 plate, 20 tab, 35 ref.

Descriptors: *Water quality, *Utah, *Surface waters, Irrigation water, Lakes, Dissolved ox- ygen, Water chemistry, Water pollution sources, Sediment yield.
Identifiers: *Utah Lake(Utah).

Water-quality reconnaissance in the drainage basin of Utah Lake covered an area of about 2,180 square miles, mostly, in Wasatch and Utah Coun- ies, Utah. Altitudes in the area range from about 4,490 to 11,943 feet and normal annual precipita- ion (1931-60) ranged from about 10 to 60 inches. Most of the water available for use within the study area is derived from snowmelt in sparsely populated areas at higher altitudes where water use is small. The Provo River and its tributaries upstream from Hailstone had dissolved-solids con- centrations of less than 200 mg/litre. The flow of the Provo River downstream from Deer Creek Reservoir is largely regulated. Although a large part of the flow is diverted near the mouth of Provo Canyon during the irrigation season, the dis- solved-solids concentration of the water that en- tered Utah Lake was nearly always between 200 and 300 mg/litre. The water available for irrigation from the Provo River at the canyon mouth had a low- or medium-salinity hazard and a low-sodium hazard. Dissolved-solids concentrations of inflow to Utah Lake from Spanish Fork kuring February 1971 to September 1972 ranged from about 270 mg/litre during high flow to 1,110 mg/litre during low flow. Dissolved-oxygen concentrations mea- sured at the Provo River and Spanish Fork near or upstream from the canyon mouths ranged from about 9 to 11 mg/litre. At the Provo River near Provo and at Spanish Fork near Utah Lake, pronounced diurnal fluctuation in dissolved-ox- ygen concentrations (6.4-17.2 mg/litre for the Provo River and 5.4-14.8 mg/litre for Spanish Fork) resulted from greatly depleted flow and from dense algal growth in the reaches of depleted flow. (Knapp-USGS)
W75-07586

DETERMINATION OF SMALL QUANTITIES OF CARBON DIOXIDE IN NATURAL WATERS,
Nagoya Univ. (Japan). Water Research Lab.
K. Satake, Y. Saijo, and H. Tominaga.
Jap J Limnol, 16-20, 1972. Illus.

Descriptors: *Analytical techniques, *Chemical analysis, *Water analysis, *Fresh water, Benthos, Zooplankton, Microorganisms, *Carbon dioxide.

This technique is highly sensitive; concentrations of CO_2 as low as 0.2 mg CO_2-C/l are easily deter- mined. It takes 4 min for the determination of each sample and only 1 ml of sample. This technique can be employed not only for CO_2 measurement in 14C photosynthesis experiments, but can also be applied to many other ecological of physiological studies of aquatic organisms. In fresh water where the CO_2 concentration is low, it is possible to determine the rate of photosynthesis and respira- tion by measuring CO_2 concentration in situ or in light and dark bottles. Application can also be made to the study of respiration of individual or small groups of organisms such as benthos or zooplankton.--Copyright 1974, Biological Ab- stracts, Inc.
W75-07588

DISTRIBUTION AND PERSISTENCE OF 1,2-DIBROMO-3-CHLOROPROPANE IN SOIL AFTER APPLICATION BY INJECTION AND IN IRRIGATION WATER,
California Univ., Davis. Dept. of Nematology.
For primary bibliographic entry see Field 5B.
W75-07609

A DIVER-OPERATED DREDGE FOR COL- LECTING QUANTITATIVE BENTHIC SAM- PLES IN SOFT SEDIMENTS,
Rice Univ., Houston, Tex.
For primary bibliographic entry see Field 2J.
W75-07614

REVERSE OSMOSIS FOR SPACECRAFT WASH WATER RECYCLING, MEMBRANE COUPON AND MODULE EVALUATIONS,
McDonnell-Douglas Astronautics Co. West, Huntington Beach, Calif.
For primary bibliographic entry see Field 5D.
W75-07627

THE DETERMINATION OF NITRATE IN WATERS AT LOW PPM LEVELS BY AUTO- MATIC DISCRETE-SAMPLE ANALYSIS,
Beckman Instruments, Inc., Irvine, Calif.
J. Ramirez-Munoz.
Analytica Chimica Acta, Vol 72, No 2, p 437-442, October 1974. 2 fig, 3 tab, 3 ref.

Descriptors: *Nitrates, *Pollutant identification, *Water analysis, *Analytical techniques, Labora- tory equipment, Automatic control, *Ultraviolet radiation, Testing procedures, Water pollution sources, Chemical analysis, Operations, Equip- ment, Reliability, Performance.

The adaptation of the UV technique to an auto- matic discrete-sample system, the AMA-40 System (Beckman Automated Materials Analyzer), is described. Automatic handling of samples provides several advantages in the UV measurement, for example, rapid sample prepara- tion (addition of reagents and dilution processes), elimination of personal errors in manual handling, and standardization of the whole process with identical conditions (which leads to improved precision). The operating conditions are discussed, and the experimental setup is illustrated. The addi- tion of 0.25 molar HCl resulted in better repeata- bility in comparison with tests performed at higher acidity. Filtration is mandatory for turbid samples. The experimental setup is simple and can be pro- grammed to provide a reading every minute. It is easily applicable to routine determinations of nitrate in water. In routine work only single readings/sample should be scheduled; for optimal accuracy, duplicate or triplicate readings are recommended for low nitrate concentrations. (Witt-IPC)
W75-07637

DEVELOPMENT OF A METHOD FOR THE EX- TRACTION AND DETERMINATION OF NON- POLAR, DISSOLVED ORGANIC SUBSTANCES IN SEA WATER,
C. Osterroht.
Journal of Chromatography, Vol 101, No 2, p 289- 298, December 18, 1974. 5 fig, 5 tab, 27 ref.

Descriptors: *Sea water, *Organic compounds, *Water analysis, *Pesticides, Analytical techniques, Adsorption, Laboratory equipment, Sampling, Testing procedures, Gas chromatog- raphy, DDT, DDE, Aldrin, Chlorinated hydrocar- bon pesticides, *Pollutant identification, Water pollution sources, Polychlorinated biphenyls, *Separation techniques.
Identifiers: Lindane, Benzene hex- achloride(Hexachlorocyclohexane), Dichlorodiphenyltrichloroethane, Dichlorodiphen- yldichloroethylene, Pristane, 2-6-10-14- Tetramethylpentadecane, Phenanthrene, 2- Chlorobiphenyl, n-Hexadecane, Amberlite XAD.

A method for extracting sea water by sorption on Amberlite XAD is described. The apparatus, sam- pling technique, work-up procedure, and deter- mination by gas chromatography are described. Recovery tests with DDT, DDE, lindane, aldrin, 2- chlorobiphenyl, phenanthrene, pristane, and n- hexadecane demonstrated the applicability of the method to non-polar substances. The recoveries were about 80%. Gas chromatograms of two sam- ples are shown. (Witt-IPC)
W75-07650

THE EXTRACTION AND RECOVERY OF CHLORINATED INSECTICIDES AND POLYCHLORINATED BIPHENYLS FROM WATER USING POROUS POLYURETHANE FOAMS,
Bristol Univ. (England). Dept. of Inorganic Chemistry.
P. R. Musty, and G. Nickless.
Journal of Chromatography, Vol 100, No 1, p 83- 93, November 13, 1974. 2 fig, 9 tab, 8 ref.

Descriptors: *Insecticides, *Polychlorinated biphenyls, *Water analysis, Analytical techniques, Adsorption, Pollutants, Water pollution sources, Trace elements, Water properties, Water quality, Organic compounds, Chromatography, Gas chro- matography, Chemical analysis, *Pollutant identification, Water pollution, *Separation techniques.
Identifiers: *Polyurethane, Foam plastics.

Porous polyurethane foams were used for the ex- traction and recovery of chlorinated insecticides and polychlorinated biphenyls from water. One liter of tap water was doped at the ppb level and elution of the adsorbed compounds was complete with 50 ml of acetone and 100 ml of n-hexane. Quantitative recoveries were obtained for the thir- teen insecticides used, at a water flow rate of 100 ml/min. The recoveries for polychlorinated biphenyls were 40-99% at 100 ml/min. The amount of methylene blue absorbed from aqueous solution by the foams was correlated with the efficiencies of six forms, of different surface areas and bulk densities, for adsorbing chlorinated insecticides and polychlorinated biphenyls from water. (Witt- IPC)
W75-07652

AUTOMATED ION-SELECTIVE ELECTRODE METHOD FOR DETERMINING FLUORIDE IN NATURAL WATERS,
Geological Survey, Denver, Colo.
D. E. Erdmann.

Environmental Science and Technology, Vol 9, No 3, p 252-253, March, 1975. 5 tab, 3 ref.

Descriptors: *Fluorides, *Water analysis, *Pollutant identification, Analytical techniques, Trace elements, Natural streams, Ions, Electrodes, Aluminum, Chemical analysis, Water chemistry, Water properties, Water quality, Halides, Inorganic compounds, Instrumentation.
Identifiers: AutoAnalyzer, *Ion selective electrode method.

An automated fluoride method which uses AutoAnalyzer modules in conjunction with a fluoride ion-selective electrode was evaluated. The results obtained on 38 natural water samples agreed well with those determined by a similar manual method (average difference 0.026 mg/liter). An average fluoride concentration of 0.496 mg/liter was found when several natural water samples were spiked with 0.50 mg/liter fluoride. Aluminum is the only significant interfering substance, and it can be easily tolerated if its concentration does not exceed 2 mg/liter. Thirty samples were analyzed/hour over a concentration range of 0-2 mg/liter. (Witt-IPC)
W75-07657

LIQUID CHROMATOGRAPHIC DETERMINATION OF NITROGLYCERIN PRODUCTS IN WASTE WATERS,
Radford Army Ammunition Plant, Va.
C. D. Chandler, G. R. Gibson, and W. T. Bolleter.
Journal of Chromatography, Vol 100, No 1, p 185-188, November 13, 1974. 3 fig, 9 ref.

Descriptors: *Chromatography, *Nitrates, *Water analysis, *Pollutant identification, *Waste water(Pollution), Nitrogen compounds, Analytical techniques, Chemical analysis, Water pollution sources, Pollutants, Inorganic compounds, Chemical wastes, Water quality, *Industrial wastes, Chemical industry, *Explosives, Laboratory equipment.
Identifiers: Glycerol nitrates.

A high-pressure liquid chromatographic procedure is described for the quantitative determination of nitrate esters such as trinitroglycerin (glycerol trinitrate). The technique is free from interference by inorganic or other organic nitrates that can cause error in the determination of trinitroglycerin by spectrophotometric or titrimetric methods. It is also more quantitative than the thin-layer chromatographic method, and the nitrate esters are not subject to thermal decomposition as in the gas chromatographic technique. Concentrations as low as 10 ppm of either tri- or dinitroglycerin in water samples were conveniently determined. The primary use of the procedure has been in the analysis of waste water samples from the trinitroglycerin purification process. The data show a high degree of sensitivity and specificity for the various nitrated compounds. (Witt-IPC)
W75-07659

MARINE ALGAL ASSAY PROCEDURE BOTTLE TEST,
Pacific Northwest Environmental Research Lab., Corvallis, Ore.
Available from the National Technical Information Service, Springfield, Va. 22161, as PB-239 709, $4.25 in paper copy, $2.25 in microfiche. Report EPA-660/3-75-006, December 1974. 43 p, 10 fig, 2 tab, 49 ref.

Descriptors: Eutrophication, Phytoplankton, *Bioassay, Phosphates, *Marine algae, Estuaries, *Pollutant identification, Estuarine environment, Nitrates, Nurtients, Limiting factors, Algae, Nitrogen compounds, Chlorophyta, Oceans, Salt tolerance, *Analytical techniques.
Identifiers: Algal assay procedure, *Dunaliella tertiolecta.

Described is protocol for a standardized primary producer nutrient bioassay for assessment of the effect of cultural eutrophication in estuarine and coastal marine areas. The green biflagellate unicellular alga Dunaliella tertiolecta Butcher (DUN clone) was selected as the bioassay organism because of its wide salinity tolerance, sensitivity to incremental additions and natural levels of critical or limiting nutrients, excellent replication and simple evaluation characteristics. (EPA)
W75-07686

HANDBOOK OF RADIOCHEMICAL ANALYTICAL METHODS,
National Environmental Research Center, Las Vegas, Nev. Technical Support Lab.
Available from the National Technical Information Service, Springfield, Va. 22161, as PB-240 621, $5.75 in paper copy, $2.25 in microfiche. Report EPA-680/4-75-001, February 1975. 140 p, 14 fig, F. B. Johns, editor.

Descriptors: *Chemical analysis, *Analytical techniques, *Radiochemical analysis, *Pollutant identification, *Radioactivity techniques, *Strontium radioisotopes.

This manual is a compilation of the chemical procedures used at the National Environmental Research Center-La Vegas for determining stable elements and radionuclides in environmental surveillance samples. It supersedes 'Southwestern Radiological Health Laboratory Handbook of Radiochemical Analytical Methods' published as Report No. SWRHL-11 in March 1970. The procedures in the current compilation are intended for use in processing relatively large numbers of samples in the shortest possible time for environmental radiological surveillance and, therefore, in some cases represent a compromise between precise analytical determination and adequate determination for surveillance purposes. For historical purposes, two methods for radiostrontium in milk are included since large numbers of samples were analyzed by these methods. An appendix provides instructions for preparing reagents listed for each method. It does not provide instructions for preparing solutions normally found in chemistry laboratories. (EPA)
W75-07697

PILOT SCALE TREATMENT OF WINE STILLAGE,
California State Dept. of Agriculture, San Francisco. Wine Advisory Board.
For primary bibliographic entry see Field 5D.
W75-07699

APPLICATION AND PROCUREMENT OF AUTOMATIC WASTEWATER SAMPLERS,
National Environmental Research Center, Cincinnati, Ohio.
R. P. Lauch.
Available from the National Technical Information Service, Springfield, Va. 22161, as PB-241 085, $3.75 in paper copy, $2.25 in microfiche. Report EPA-670/4-75-003, April 1975. 23 p, 1 tab, 25 ref. 1H327; ROAP 24ALE; Task 04

Descriptors: *Sampling, Water pollution, *Water sampling, *Automation, *Instrumentation, Water quality standards.
Identifiers: Water sampler application, Water sampler procurement, *Waste water samplers, Effluent sampler application, Automatic wastewater samplers.

Application and procurement of automatic sampling devices are discussed. Different sampler characteristics including compositing, proportionality, perservation, lift, and power are described. Manufacturers are listed. Application is discussed with reference to compliance with the National Pollutant Discharge Elimination System permit program, treatment plant control, and other

Ardea herodias), sandhill crane (Grus canadensis), common loon (Gavia immer) and largemouth bass (Micropterus salmoides). Hemorrhagic enteritis was found in association with E. tarda in some of the species presented.--Copyright 1974, Biological Abstracts, Inc.
W75-07735

THE ENUMERATION OF AEROBIC ACTINOMYCETES IN WATER SAMPLES, (IN FRENCH),
Institut Pasteur, Lille (France). Laboratoire d'Hydrobiologie.
C. Eak-Hour, and H. Leclerc.
Ann Microbiol (Paris). Vol 124, No 4, p 533-546. 1973 English Summary.

Descriptors: *Actinomycetes, *Aerobic bacteria, *Sampling, *Pollutant identification, Water sampling.

A practical method for the quantification of actinomycetes in water and in sediments was sought. A number of factors were investigated: suppression of bacteria and of fungi by the use of antibiotics, the purification, concentration and homogenization of samples and the comparative efficiency of different culture media. Techniques for different types of water samples are suggested.--Copyright 1974, Biological Abstracts, Inc.
W75-07740

EFFECT OF HYDROGEN ION CONCENTRATION ON THE DETERMINATION OF LEAD BY SOLVENT EXTRACTION AND ATOMIC ABSORPTION SPECTROPHOTOMETRY,
Purdue Univ., Lafayette, Ind., Dept. of Biochemistry.
R. J. Everson, and H. E. Parker.
Analytical Chemistry, Vol 46, No 13, p 1966-1970, November, 1974, 3 fig, 4 tab, 17 ref.

Descriptors: *Spectrophotometry, *Chelation, *Lead, *Solvent extractions, *Hydrogen ion concentration, Analytical techniques, Heavy metals, Testing procedures, Separation techniques, *Pollutant identification.
Identifiers: *Atomic absorption method.

The effect of hydrogen ion concentration on the chelating agents ammonium pyrrolidine carbodithioate (APCD) and sodium diethyldithiocarbamate (DDC) on the extraction of lead by these ligands, and on the stability of the lead chelates in the organic phase following extraction was studied. At low pH values, both chelating agents were decomposed, with APCD being the more stable. However, when the extraction of the lead chelate followed quickly after the addition of the chelating agent, there appeared to be little effect of pH on the extraction by APCD and effects on the DDC extraction only at pH values below 3. It appeared that APCD can extract lead quantitatively from pH 0.25 to 8.0 and DDC can above pH 3.25. Following extraction, the lead chelates appeared stable in the organic phase for at least one hour even though the pH of the aqueous phase varied from 2 to 8. (Pulliam-Vanderbilt)
W75-07793

COMPARISON OF ANALYTICAL TECHNIQUES FOR INORGANIC POLLUTANTS,
Laboratory of the Government Chemist, London (England).
R. F. Coleman.
Analytical Chemistry, Vol 46, No 12, p 989A-996A, October, 1974, 1 fig, 3 tab, 25 ref.

Descriptors: *Analytical techniques, *Testing procedures, Pollutants, Spectrophotometry, Microscopy, Electron microscopy, Mass spectrometry, X-ray spectroscopy, Neutron activation analysis, Electrochemistry, *Pollutant identification.

This paper discussed various analytical methods which are applied to inorganic pollutants found in food, water, or collected on air filters from the atmosphere. It aimed to provide some background data to assist in the selection of the appropriate technique for current and future problems. Advantages and disadvantages of various analytical methods and guides when to use each were discussed. Comparisons between the methods were also made. The methods considered were: Microscopy (optical and electron); atomic spectroscopy (flame and flameless A.A.S., atomic fluorescence, and atomic emission); mass spectrometry (spark and plasma source); x-ray spectrometry (wavelength and energy dispersive); neutron activation analysis; and electrochemical methods (anodic stripping voltammetry). (Pulliam-Vanderbilt)
W75-07794

REJECTION OF TRACE METALS FROM COAL DURING BENEFICIATION BY AGGLOMERATION,
National Research Council of Canada, Ottawa (Ontario). Div. of Chemistry.
C. E. Capes, A. E. McIlhinney, D. S. Russell, and A. F. Sirianni.
Environmental Science and Technology, Vol 8, No 1, p 35-38, January, 1974, 1 fig, 2 tab, 10 ref.

Descriptors: *Coals, *Heavy metals, *Electric powerplants, *Beneficiation, Separation techniques, Electric power costs, Mercury, *Pollutant identification, *Air pollution.
Identifiers: Oil agglomeration.

The rejection of trace quantities of heavy metals from coals during the process of fine grinding followed by selective oil agglomeration of the carbonaceous constituents was examined. Six different steam and coking coals, mainly from Canadian and U.S. sources, were treated. The level of most heavy elements was low but, in light of the large throughputs of power plants, the potential environmental hazard may be significant, especially for those elements which are volatile or may form volatile compounds when fired. Many of the trace metals were substantially removed during agglomerative beneficiation of the coal. Some which are apparently in organic association in the coal remained in the agglomerated product. Analytical methods used in the study were atomic absorption, optical emission spectroscopy, and spark source mass spectroscopy. Problems deriving from the ash content in untreated coals may be alleviated by such treatment. There is also the possibility of recovering appreciable amounts of metals with commercial value from the tailings. (Pulliam-Vanderbilt)
W75-07795

SYNTHESIS OF A SULPHONATED FERROIN REAGENT FOR CHELATING IRON (II) IN STRONG ACID SPECTROPHOTOMETRIC DETERMINATION OF THE OXIDATION STATE OF IRON IN SILICATES,
Australian National Univ., Canberra. Research School of Earth Sciences.
E. Kiss.
Analytica Chimica Acta, Vol 72, No 1, p 127-144, September, 1974, 3 fig, 3 tab, 25 ref.

Descriptors: *Analytical techniques, *Iron, *Spectrophotometry, *Rocks, *Heavy metals, Iron oxides, Chelation, Silicates, Mineralogy, Testing procedures, Soil tests, Pollutant identification.

The relatively easy accessibility of the ferroin chromogen 3-(4-phenyl-2-pyridyl)-5,6-diphenyl-1,2,4-triazine (PPDT) and its diammonium disulphonate derivative (PPDT-DAS) was described via an 8-step total synthesis. The extreme sensitivity and good selectivity of PPDT-DAS was comparable to terrosite. PPDT-DAS showed extreme resistance to thermal and oxidative degradation and also formed the tris-chelate with iron (II) ions in molar acid concentrations. Maximum color was formed in the pH range 3-8 with a molar absorptivity of 29,300 at 570m. Only fluoride (more than 500 ppm), EDTA, cyanide and comparable amounts of Cu(I) and Co(II) interfered. PPDT-DAS was successfully applied to the spectrophotometric microdetermination of mg quantities of Fe (II) oxide in silicate samples. The novel feature of this application was the simultaneous chelate formation with the release of Fe (II) from the silicate matrix in the cold by a solution of PPDT-DAS in hydrofluoric and sulphuric acids. Air oxidation problems were completely eliminated, but some resistant minerals were left largely undecomposed. More refractory materials were decomposed in PTFE bombs. (Pulliam-Vanderbilt)
W75-07796

METHYLMERCURY POISONING IN IRAQ,
Baghdad Univ. (Iraq).
For primary bibliographic entry see Field 5C.
W75-07797

DETERMINATION OF TRACE ELEMENTS IN COAL BY INSTRUMENTAL NEUTRON ACTIVATION ANALYSIS,
Ghent Rijksuniversiteit (Belgium). Instituut voor Nukleaire Wetenschappen.
C. Block, and R. Dams.
Analytica Chimica Acta, Vol 68, No 1, p 11-24, January, 1974, 9 tab, 2 fig, 13 ref.

Descriptors: *Trace elements, *Coals, *Analytical techniques, *Neutron activation analysis, Fossil fuels, Spectroscopy, Radioisotopes, Air pollution, Instrumentation, *Pollutant identification.

Neutron activation analysis by means of Ge (Li) gamma-spectrometry and computer-assisted data reduction is described for the simultaneous determination of 43 elements in coal samples in concentrations ranging from a few per cent down to 1 ppb. Its analytical possibilities are discussed. Two neutron irradiations and 3-5 gamma-spectrometric measurements were performed for each sample. The overall standard deviation for nearly all elements was determined by the counting statistics. (Jernigan-Vanderbilt)
W75-07799

FLUORIDE: GEOCHEMICAL AND ECOLOGICAL SIGNIFICANCE IN EAST AFRICAN WATERS AND SEDIMENTS,
Michigan Univ., Ann Arbor. Dept. of Zoology.
For primary bibliographic entry see Field 5B.
W75-07802

MICROBIOLOGICAL FOULING AND ITS CONTROL IN COASTAL WATER AND THE DEEP OCEAN,
Woods Hole Oceanographic Institution, Mass.
S. C. Dexter.
Technical Report WHOI-74-64, September 1974. 57 p. ONR H-83609-A, Amendment No. 3 and H-801 B.

Descriptors: *Fouling, *Toxicity, *Calibration, Water pollution control, Damages, Measurement, *Pollutant identification.
Identifiers: *Microbiological fouling, *Electron microscopy, Savonius rotor, Woods Hole(Mass), Sargasso Sea.

The rates of microfouling film formation on various toxic and nontoxic substrates exposed to natural sea water have been measured using scanning electron microscopy. Exposure conditions for the test samples ranged from four days in shallow coastal water at Woods Hole to over 400 days at depths to 5000 meters in the Sargasso Sea. The results are discussed in terms of the surface energy of the substrate, and are applied to the problem

of preventing the Savonius rotor speed sensor of oceanographic current meters from loss of calibration due to fouling. The conditions in terms of time and depth of exposure under which fouling preventative measures need to be undertaken are defined. Materials selection is discussed for a current meter to make near surface measurements under severe fouling conditions. (NOAA)
W75-07825

5B. Sources Of Pollution

NUTRIENT AND SEDIMENT PRODUCTION FROM FORESTED WATERSHEDS,
Nevada Agricultural Experiment Station, Reno.
J. Brown, W. Howe, and C. Skau.
Available from the National Technical Information Service, Springfield, Va 22161 as PB-241 524, $3.75 in paper copy, $2.25 in microfiche. Cooperative Report Series Publication No. AG-1, 1973. 33 p, 1 fig, 10 tab, 49 ref, 3 append. ASAE Paper No. 73-201. OWRT A-043-NEV(1), and B-047-NEV(1).

Descriptors: *Nutrients, Sediments, *Land use, *Forest watersheds, Watersheds(Basins), *Water quality, Nitrogen, Nitrates, Dissolved solids, Suspended solids, Phosphates, *Sediment discharge, Correlation analysis, Regression analysis, Energy, Phosphorus, Water pollution sources.
Identifiers: *Lake Tahoe(Nev-Calif), *Truckee River(Nev-Calif), Orthophosphates.

An effort to determine and quantify relationships between drainage basin characteristics and certain water quality parameters is reported. Beginning August 1970, monthly concentrations of suspended sediments, nitrate nitrogen, organic nitrogen, and dissolved orthophosphate were determined for 25 forested watersheds of the Lake Tahoe-Truckee River System. Quantified watershed characteristics of soils, geology, geomorphology, vegetation, and land use for each watershed are assumed to act in combination to determine nutrient and sediment discharges from a drainage area. Correlation and regression analyses were used to test this assumption. Suspended sediment production is largely dependent upon two criteria: (1) sources of sediment and (2) energy to move it. Energy is evidently more important in this region, with overland slope and stream discharge dominating the relationship. Nitrogen production exhibits excessive seasonal variability and is apparently determined by watershed characteristics which reflect sources of nitrogen and influence of watershed drainage patterns throughout the year. Phosphorus production, on the other hand, is much more uniform and is primarily determined by factors affecting base flow relations, regardless of season. (Schulke-Nevada)
W75-07353

ENVIRONMENTAL QUALITY AND SAFETY, VOL. 2. GLOBAL ASPECTS OF CHEMISTRY, TOXICOLOGY AND TECHNOLOGY AS APPLIED TO THE ENVIRONMENT.
For primary bibliographic entry see Field 6G.
W75-07355

EFFECT OF SOIL ENRICHMENT WITH MINERAL ELEMENTS AND FERTILIZERS ON SURFACE WATER AND PLANTS,
Ghent Rijksuniversiteit (Belgium). Faculteit Landbouwwetenschappen.
A. Cottenie.
Qual Plant Mater Veg. Vol 22, No 1, p 37-53, 1972.

Descriptors: *Surface waters, *Vegetation, Pollutants, *Soil amendments, *Fertilizers, *Water pollution sources, Soil treatment, Nutrients.
Identifiers: *Mineral elements, Soil enrichment.

Observations indicate that intensive use of solid fertilizers may result in a certain accumulation of nutrient elements in the soil and an enrichment of soil water with these elements. This type of contamination, however, is less important than soil and plant pollution with external sources of trace elements, which can lead to toxic accumulations in plants and yield depressions. An accurate identification of such situation is possible using simple pot experiment techniques. The most effective way for immobilizing an excess of unwanted trace elements in light textured soils, is a consistant increase of soil pH by liming.--Copyright 1974, Biological Abstracts, Inc.
W75-07368

SOME CHEMICAL OBSERVATIONS ON THE UPPER SALT RIVER AND ITS TRIBUTARIES,
Arizona State Univ., Tempe.
For primary bibliographic entry see Field 2K.
W75-07369

A GENERAL LINEAR APPROACH TO STREAM WATER QUALITY MODELING,
IBM Federal Systems Div., Gaithersburg, Md.
M. Arbabi, and J. Elzinga.
Water Resources Research, Vol 11, No 2, p 191-196, April 1975. 1 fig, 3 tab, 20 equ, 14 ref.

Descriptors: *Water quality control, *Streams, *Linear programming, Standards, Dissolved oxygen, Biochemical oxygen demand, Optimization, Reach(Streams), Costs, Methodology, Mathematical models, Systems analysis, Model studies.
Identifiers: *Linear constraints, Constraint elimination, Balance equations, Relaxation technique, Willamette River(Oregon).

The problem of meeting stream dissolved oxygen standards while optimizing some objective is considered. New properties of the oxygen sag equation allow the constraint set of such mathematical programs to be described to a high degree of accuracy by linear inequalities; except for upper and lower bounds on pollutant discharges, three linear constraints at most are required per reach. Constraint elimination techniques are developed that can further reduce the number of constraints necessary. As a means of highlighting the potential power of these techniques to large-scale models, they are applied to the Willamette River in Oregon and Liebman's seven-reach example. A further reduction in the size of the mathematical program to be solved can be realized by employing the technique of relaxation. This technique, coupled with constraint elimination, should allow the efficient solution of large water quality problems. (Bell-Cornell)
W75-07382

WATER QUALITY MODELING BY MONTE CARLO SIMULATION,
Maine Univ., Orono. Dept. of Civil Engineering.
W. F. Brutsaert.
Water Resources Bulletin, Vol 11, No 2, p 229-236, April 1975. 6 fig, 1 tab, 10 equ, 4 ref.

Descriptors: *Water quality control, *Simulation analysis, *Monte Carlo method, *Stochastic processes, *Probability, Streams, Equations, Biochemical oxygen demand, Dissolved oxygen, Mathematical models, Systems analysis, Optimum development plans, Design, Wastes.
Identifiers: *Streeter-Phelps model, Frequency distributions, Triangular probability density function, Confidence level.

The applicability of Monte Carlo simulation to water quality modeling is demonstrated using a simple Streeter-Phelps model. The model accounts for the stochasticity of the input parameters. Triangular probability density functions are shown to be useful in case insufficient information is available to define meaningful frequency distributions of input parameters. The model output is presented as probability distributions of stream quality parameters. To demonstrate the usefulness of the technique, a simple, critical DO-deficit problem is set up. The technique is applicable to optimizing design and operation of wastewater treatment systems. (Bell-Cornell)
W75-07386

STOCHASTIC WATER QUALITY CONTROL BY SIMULATION,
Texas Univ., San Antonio. Div. of Environmental Studies.
C. S. Shih.
Water Resources Bulletin, Vol 11, No 2, p 256-266, April 1975. 5 fig, 6 tab, 6 equ, 11 ref.

Descriptors: *Water quality control, *Stochastic processes, *Simulation analysis, *Reliability, *River basins, *Management, Probability, Computers, Optimization, Water policy, Standards, Regional analysis, Return flow, Effluents, Treatment facilities, Streams, Decision making, Biochemical oxygen demand, Dissolved oxygen, Costs, Systems analysis, Equations, Mathematical models, *Texas.
Identifiers: Chance-constrained quadratic programming, Sensitivity, *San Antonio River basin(Tex).

In order to handle the probabilistic nature of treated waste effluent characteristics, the reliability associated with a basin-wide quality management goal has been included in the modeling process. Meanwhile, the quantitative and qualitative variations of the irrigation return flows and the urban runoff also exhibit a probabilistic nature in terms of both temporal and spatial measurements. Computer simulation has been utilized in analyzing the reliability and sensitivity of a river basin quality management. A simulation-optimization scheme for the determination of policies in regional water quality management has been developed subject to specific water quality standards. Stochastic quadratic programming techniques were used in the optimization analysis, the objective function consisting of minimizing a convex quadratic cost function including the operating cost, the amortization of capital expenditures and maintenance costs. A series of simulation models describing the statistical water quality control phenomena was developed. Meanwhile, a simulation analysis for the description of the probabilistic nature of the stream quality was developed for the control strategies of the return flows in the regional management system. As an illustration of the applicability of this water quality control approach, the major wastewater treatment facilities in the San Antonio River basin were analyzed. The sensitivity analysis was conducted to assess the most satisfying strategies for a regional water quality management system subject to probabilistic standards. (Bell-Cornell)
W75-07389

FLOW PATTERNS OF RAINWATER THROUGH SLOPING SOIL SURFACE LAYERS AND THE MOVEMENT OF NUTRIENTS BY RUNOFF,
Iowa State Univ., Ames. Dept. of Agronomy.
N. L. Powell, and D. Kirkham.
Available from the National Technical Information Service, Springfield, Va 22161 as PB-241 713, $3.75 in paper copy, $2.25 in microfiche. Completion Report No. 64, Iowa State Water Resources Research Institute, Ames, October 1974. 45 p, 10 fig, 2 tab, 40 ref. OWRT A-044-IA(4), 14-31-0001-4015, 14-31-0001-3515, 14-31-0001-3015.

Descriptors: *Runoff, *Groundwater movement, Slopes, Rainfall-runoff relationships, *Saturated flow, Fertilizers, Flow, Water pollution sources, *Nitrates, Nutrients, *Path of pollutants, Model studies, Seepage, *Flow nets, Tile drains.
Identifiers: LaPlace's Equation Solutions.

A modified Gram-Schmidt method gave the mathematical solution for two boundary value problems of agricultural drainage in saturated, sloped soil bedding. In the first problem, seepage

patterns of rainfall flowing through the bedding to a tile drain on a barrier were found. In the second problem, seepage patterns of rainfall through soil underlain by a barrier at great depth, with no tile drain, were found. Solutions were obtained by solving LaPlace's equation subject to boundary conditions. Flow nets and other flow characteristics were determined. For the first problem, 16 to 100 percent of the minimum saturating rainfall passed through the medium to the tile. For the second problem, 13 to 77 percent of the minimum saturating rainfall flowed into the medium above a critical point on the surface and out of the medium below the critical point. Several geometries were investigated. Laboratory studies with a sand tank model showed agreement between calculated streamlines and dye streaks. In the same model packed with soil, nitrate solutions were injected into the soil both above and below the critical point. At regular intervals, the runoff water was analyzed for nitrate. Nitrate injection upslope gave lower concentrations but the runoff contained nitrate for a longer time.
W75-07395

SOIL MOISTURE TRANSPORT IN ARID SITE VADOSE ZONES,
Atlantic Richfield Hanford Company, Richland, Wash. Research Dept.
R. E. Isaacson, L. E. Brownell, and J. C. Hanson.
October, 1974. 95 p, 32 fig, 9 tab, 39 ref, 6 append. AEC AT(45-1)-2130.

Descriptors: *Radioactive waste disposal, *Nuclear wastes, *Radioactive wastes, *Water pollution sources, *Arid lands, *Soil contamination, *Washington, Water table, Soil dynamics, Soil water, Vadose water, Percolation, Soil moisture, Columbia River, Groundwater.
Identifiers: Richland(Wash), Vadose zones.

Radioactive wastes have been buried in backfilled trenches at the Hanford site. Whether or not the aridity of this site will prevent the wastes from percolating to the water table has been questioned. An analysis of the physical processes that affect the rate and direction of moisture movement in the vadose zone of the dry soils at Hanford is described. The depth of penetration of meteoric precipitation has been determined by profiling fallout tritium at two locations where the water table is about 90 meters below ground surface. In situ temperatures and water potentials were measured with temperature transducers and thermocouple psychrometers at one of these locations to obtain thermodynamic data for identifying the factors influencing soil-moisture transport. Neutron probes are being used to monitor soil moisture changes in two lysimeters, three meters in diameter by 20 meters deep. The lysimeters are also equipped to measure pressure, temperature, and water potential as a function of depth and time. Nonisothermal soil moisture transport processes are being studied. A thermal pump that moves water towards the surface exists as a result of annual sinusoidal oscillation of temperature in the upper nine meters of soil. A partially desiccated zone exists at a depth between 9 to 16 meters. (Bowden-Arizona)
W75-07403

REPORT TO THE CONGRESS ON OCEAN POLLUTION, OVERFISHING, AND OFFSHORE DEVELOPMENT; JULY 1973 THROUGH JUNE 1974.
National Oceanic and Atmospheric Administration, Washington, D.C.
Available from Superintendent of Documents, U.S. Government Printing Office, Washington, D.C. 20402, for $1.45. Report to Congress on Ocean Pollution, Overfishing, and Offshore Development; July 1973 through June 1974, issued January 1975. 77 p, 10 fig, 3 tab, 2 append. (NOAA 75040305). PL 92-532.

Descriptors: *Oceans, *Water pollution, *Water pollution sources, *Oil pollution, *Environmental effects, *Environmental control, Pollutants, Pollution abatement, Oil spills, Oil wastes, Waste water(Pollution), Chemical wastes, Animal physiology, Genetics, Fish conservation, Fish management, Fish harvest, Fishing, Fisheries, Commercial fishing.
Identifiers: Marine pollution, Marine pollution research, Overfishing, Offshore development, Petroleum hydrocarbons, Synthetic hydrocarbons, Offshore deepwater ports, Offshore powerplants, Ocean mining, Offshore oil development, Offshore gas development.

Accomplishments and other aspects of U.S. marine research efforts directed at long-range effects of pollution, overfishing, and other man-induced changes of ocean ecosystems are described in this annual report to Congress. Areas addressed include research activities of the government and private sector concerning marine pollution by petroleum hydrocarbons, heavy metals, and synthetic hydrocarbons; offshore development (deepwater ports, powerplants, ocean mining, and oil and gas development); regional studies on marine pollution; and various overfishing developments. (NOAA)
W75-07405

A BIBLIOGRAPHY OF NUMERICAL MODELS FOR TIDAL RIVERS, ESTUARIES AND COASTAL WATERS,
Rhode Island Univ., Kingston. Dept. of Ocean Engineering.
For primary bibliographic entry see Field 2L.
W75-07409

INVESTIGATIONS ON CONCENTRATIONS, DISTRIBUTIONS, AND FATES OF HEAVY METAL WASTES IN PARTS OF LONG ISLAND SOUND,
Connecticut Univ., Groton. Marine Sciences Inst.
P. Dehlinger, W. F. Fitzgerald, D. F. Paskausky, R. W. Garvine, and W. F. Bohlen.
Marine Sciences Institute Final Report, October 1974. 161 p, 36 fig, 31 tab, 78 ref, 2 append. (NOAA-74121601).

Descriptors: *Water pollution, *Waste disposal, *Estuaries, *Sounds, *Oysters, *Metals, Coasts, Zinc, Copper, Mercury, Manganese, Nickel, Water circulation, Cadmium, Pollutants, Connecticut, New York.
Identifiers: Data(Tables), *New York Bight, *Long Island Sound, Heavy metal wastes, Flushing.

A two-year investigation was conducted on heavy metal wastes in Long Island Sound, with emphasis on the eastern Sound and the Connecticut coast. The program consisted of five integrated projects with the ultimate objective being to determine a preliminary budget of these wastes. The projects were concerned with the concentrations, distributions, and fates of heavy metals in the water column, water circulation patterns and water renewal times in the Sound, the structure and outflow of the Connecticut River into the Sound, the transport of suspended materials in the Sound, and the uptake of metals in oysters at various locations along the Connecticut coast. The names of the projects are as follows: Heavy Metal Wastes in Eastern Long Island Sound--Trace Metal Speciation; Circulation and Renewal of Waters in Eastern L.I.S.; Connecticut River Discharge in L.I.S.; Suspended Material Transport in Eastern L.I.S.; and Determinations of Heavy Metals in Shellfish in L.I.S. (NOAA)
W75-07412

TOXAPHENE INTERACTIONS IN ESTUARINE ECOSYSTEMS,
Georgia Univ., Savannah. Marine Extension Center.
For primary bibliographic entry see Field 5C.
W75-07414

RECONNAISSANCE OF BOTTOM SEDIMENTS ON THE INNER AND CENTRAL NEW JERSEY SHELF (MESA DATA REPORT),
National Oceanic and Atmospheric Administration, Boulder, Colo. Marine Ecosystems Analysis Program.
For primary bibliographic entry see Field 2L.
W75-07425

CHANGE IN THE PHYSIOCOCHEMICAL COMPOSITION OF WATER UNDER THE EFFECT OF FELLINGS,
Severo-Kavkazskaya Lesnaya Opytnaya Stantsiya, Maykop (USSR).
A. A. Drobikov.
Soviet Hydrology, Selected Papers No. 3, p 267-273, 1973, 4 tab, 11 ref. Translated from Forestry (Lesovedeniye), No. 3, p 3-9, 1973.

Descriptors: *Water quality, *Forest management, Rivers, *Water pollution sources, Watersheds(Basins), *Lumbering, Physicochemical properties, Chemical properties, Biological properties, Water pollution, Cutting management, Forests, Water temperature, Biochemical oxygen demand, Coliforms, Dissolved oxygen, Chlorides, Ammonia, Sulfates, Suspended solids, *Clear-cutting.
Identifiers: USSR.

The change in some physiocochemical characteristics of river water and in the number of microorganisms in it under the effect of forest felling, discharge, and seasons was examined. It was established that the strongest creek pollution occurs when the water crosses a clear-cut area. Selective group cuttings reduced to a minimum the negative effects of felling on river water quality. Seasonal (winter and summer) physicochemical property values were tabulated for the runoff after passing through a clear-cut area, a gradually cut area, a selectively group-cut area, and virgin forests. The investigations were performed in three drainage basins ranging in size from 5.3 to 5.7 hectares. (Humphreys-ISWS)
W75-07429

EARTH RESISTIVITY SURVEYS - A METHOD FOR DEFINING GROUND-WATER CONTAMINATION,
Geraghty and Miller, Port Washington, N.Y.
R. L. Stollar, and P. Roux.
Ground Water, Vol 13, No 2, p 145-150, March-April 1975. 4 fig, 10 ref.

Descriptors: *Groundwater, *Water pollution, *Electrical resistance, *Pollutant identification, *Conductivity, On-site investigations, Water pollution sources, Resistivity, Pollutants, Groundwater movement.
Identifiers: Case histories, *Pollution plume, Specific conductance.

An important part of every investigation of groundwater pollution is to locate and define the extent of the contaminated body of groundwater. Because earth resistivity is inversely proportional to groundwater conductivity, the location of groundwater that has been contaminated by a relatively high concentration of conductive industrial wastes, for example, may be quickly and accurately traced. For the resistivity method to give useful results, resistivity contrasts must exist in the subsurface. For example, if the contaminant does not have a significantly greater conductivity than the natural groundwater, the method may not work. In addition, if depth to water is too great, the thickness of the unsaturated sediments can mask any contrasts between contaminated and natural groundwater. The geologic environment must be relatively uniform so that the resistivity values and profiles can be compared with one another. Four case histories of industrial and landfill sites were discussed. The areas underlain by the contaminated groundwater bodies ranged from 25 to 100 acres. The depths to the contaminated water

were relatively shallow, ranging from 5 to about 60 feet below land surface. In three of the cases, the results of the earth resistivity studies, which were verified by installing test wells in and around the area being investigated, proved to be remarkably accurate. In the fourth study, the conditions mentioned were not met, and the survey was unsuccessful. (Prickett-ISWS)
W75-07440

INVESTIGATION AND REHABILITATION OF A BRINE-CONTAMINATED AQUIFER,
Engineering Enterprises, Inc., Norman, Okla.
J. S. Fryberger.
Ground Water, Vol 13, No 2, p 155-160, March-April 1975. 4 fig, 1 tab, 7 ref.

Descriptors: *Groundwater, *Water pollution, *Oil fields, *Brines, *Rehabilitation, Pollution abatement, Cost-benefit analysis, Brine disposal, Economics, Alluvial aquifers, Disposal fields, Cost analysis, Decision making, Investigations, Saline water intrustion, *Arkansas, Ponds, Disposal, Waste water(Pollution).
Identifiers: *Evaporation pits, *Disposal pits.

Faulty disposal of oil field brine through an 'evaporation' pit and later through a faulty disposal well resulted in the contamination of one square mile of an alluvial aquifer in southwestern Arkansas. The physical parameters of the contamination were defined, and some of the chemical changes that occur as the brine moved through the aquifer were explained. In addition, alternate methods of aquifer rehabilitation were explored, and the costs of rehabilitation were compared with potential benefits. It was concluded that rehabilitation is not now economically justified. (Prickett-ISWS)
W75-07441

THIRTY-FIVE YEARS OF CONTINUOUS DISCHARGE OF SECONDARY TREATED EFFLUENT ONTO SAND BEDS,
Rensselaer Polytechnic Inst., Troy, N.Y. Dept. of Environmental Engineering.
D. B. Aulenbach, and T. J. Tofflemire.
Ground Water, Vol 13, No 2, p 161-166, March-April 1975. 6 fig, 1 tab, 5 ref.

Descriptors: *Groundwater, *Water pollution, *Sewage effluents, *Sewage treatment, *Aerobic treatment, Nitrates, Phosphates, Trickling filters, Sands, Wells, *New York.
Identifiers: *Lake George Village(NY).

The Lake George Village sewage treatment plant has been discharging trickling filter effluent onto natural delta sand beds for 35 years. The applied sewage apparently appears near the banks of West Brook approximately 600 m from the lower sand beds. Wells were placed between the recharge beds and the appearance of the seepage at West Brook. The quality of the water in the wells was evaluated for slightly over one year. The groundwater appeared to be aerobic at all times indicating that the oxygen demand of the applied effluent was adequately reduced before it reached the groundwater. This should afford adequate and proper tertiary treatment for the applied effluent. The phosphorus concentration was significantly reduced at the first well downstream (groundwater) approximately 150 m from the sand beds. The phosphorus in well 2 approximately 600 m from the lower sand beds reached a high value of 150 micrograms/liter during the late fall but was less than 100 micrograms/liter during the rest of the year. Some of the nitrogen in the applied effluent was apparently oxidized to nitrate which was very little removed by the sand system. The highest nitrate concentration found was 14 mg N/l in well 3C during spring, whereas well 3A had almost consistently the lowest concentration of nitrate. (Gibb-ISWS)
W75-07442

THE CONFIGURATION OF CONTAMINATION ENCLAVES FROM REFUSE DISPOSAL SITES ON FLOODPLAINS,
Iowa State Univ., Ames. Dept. of Earth Sciences.
R. Palmquist, and L. V. A. Sendlein.
Ground Water, Vol 13, No 2, p 167-181, March-April 1975. 12 fig, 6 tab, 15 ref.

Descriptors: *Groundwater, Water pollution, Wastes, *Water pollution sources, *Water pollution control, Subsurface flow, Leachate, *Path of pollutants, Wells, *Iowa, Hydrogeology, Monitoring, Water quality.
Identifiers: *Contamination enclaves, Malenclaves.

The theoretical shape of a zone of contaminated groundwater (an enclave) can be predicted from a knowledge of the three-dimensional, groundwater flow pattern. The reasoning in other investigators suggests that the horizontal shape of the enclave is a flame-like plume extending from the source, parallel to the groundwater flow lines, in a downflow direction. According to LeGrand, the ultimate size of the enclave will depend upon the relative rates of decay, diffusion, dilution, and absorption of the contaminants. Similar reasoning suggests that, in vertical section, the boundaries of the enclave will follow the groundwater flow lines between contamination source and groundwater discharge site. This reasoning suggests that the three-dimensional shape of an enclave is that of a tongue-like lobe, the length, width, and depth of which increases with increasing distance from and increasing height above the discharge site. Studies made in Iowa indicate that the size and shape of the contamination enclave resulting from refuse disposal sites can be predicted from the initial geohydrologic conditions and that it may become possible to estimate the concentrations within the enclave at any point in time and space. These possibilities open the way toward a strategy of minimizing potential contamination of aquifers through selective refuse site placement on the floodplain. (Gibb-ISWS)
W75-07443

HUMIC MATTER IN NATURAL WATERS AND SEDIMENTS,
Fisheries Research Board of Canada, Winnipeg (Manitoba). Freshwater Inst.
T. A. Jackson.
Soil Science, Vol 119, No 1, p 56-64, January 1975. 78 ref.

Descriptors: *Humus, *Freshwater, *Sea water, *Sediments, *Organic matter, Chemical properties, Podzols, Aquatic life, Soils, Ecology, Geology, Economics.

The natural hisotory of aquatic and sedimentary humic substances in both marine and freshwater environments was reviewed. The ecological, geological, and economic importance of these compounds was discussed, and attention was drawn to problems requiring further research. The humic matter of natural waters and sediments is partly allochthonous (leached or eroded from soil and transported to lakes and oceans by streams and groundwater) and partly autochthonous (formed from the cellular constituents and exudates of indigeneous aquatic organisms). The highest proportions of allochthonous material occur in certain inland waters and coastal marine environments. Indigenous aquatic humic substances are essentially similar to the humic substances of soils, but tend to exhibit characteristic differences owing to the differences in source material and environment of formation. In general, the character of humic matter varies with the biological source material. The abundance and nature of humic substances in natural waters and sediments show marked geographical variability. The humic matter of ocean water is concentrated in coastal regions, especially near the mouths of rivers. One of the principal reasons for the geochemical and economic importance of humification is that the process causes the carbon and nitrogen of biochemical compounds to be partially shunted into relatively inert humic substances instead of being completely mineralized and recycled. As in soil, the beneficial effects of humic matter in aquatic systems can probably be ascribed largely to its metal-binding and cation-exchange properties. (Sims-ISWS)
W75-07453

WATER LEVEL FLUCTUATIONS DUE TO EARTH TIDES IN A WELL PUMPING FROM SLIGHTLY FRACTURED CRYSTALLINE ROCK,
Du Pont de Nemours (E.I.) and Co., Aiken, S.C. Savannah River Lab.
I. W. Marine.
Water Resources Research, Vol 11, No 1, p 165-173, February 1975. 10 fig, 1 tab, 16 ref. AEC Contract AT(07-2)-1.

Descriptors: *Radioactive wastes, *Radioactive waste disposal, *Water level fluctuations, *Tides, Wells, Permeability, Porosity, Transmissivity, Storage coefficient, Pump testing, Aquifer testing, Barometric efficiency, Metamorphic rocks, Crystalline rocks, Gravity, Coastal plains, Sediments, Injection, *South Carolina.
Identifiers: *Earth tides, Triassic basin(Buried), Packer tests, Elastic moduli, Specific storage, Barometric fluctuations.

At the Savannah River plant of the Atomic Energy Commission near Aiken, South Carolina, there are three distinct groundwater systems: the coastal plain sediments, the crystalline metamorphic rocks, and a buried Triassic basin. The coastal plain sediments include several Cretaceous and Tertiary granular aquifers and aquicludes, the total thickness being about 305 m. Below these sediments, water occurs in small fractures in crystalline metamorphic rock. Water level fluctuations due to earth tides were recorded in the crystalline metamorphic rock system and in the coastal plain sediments. No water level fluctuations due to earth tides were observed in wells in the Triassic rock because of the very low permeability. The water level fluctuations due to earth tides in the crystalline rock were about 10 cm, and those in the sediments were about 1.8 cm. The use of water level fluctuations due to earth tides to calculate porosity appeared to present practical difficulties both in the crystalline metamorphic rock system and in the coastal plain sediments. In a 1-yr pumping test on a well in the crystalline metamorphic rock the flow was controlled to within 0.1% of the total discharge, which was 0.94 l/s. The water level fluctuations due to earth tides in the pumping well were 10 cm, the same as when this well was not being pumped. (Schicht-ISWS)
W75-07463

INTERACTION OF MULTIPLE JETS WITH AMBIENT CURRENT,
General Electric Co., Philadelphia, Pa. Re-entry and Environmental Systems Div.
R. R. Boericke.
Journal of the Hydraulics Division, American Society of Civil Engineers, Vol 101, No HY4, Proceedings Paper 11247, p 357-370, April 1975. 7 fig, 16 ref, 2 append.

Descriptors: *Jets, *Circulation, *Model studies, *Velocity, *Mixing, Numerical analysis, Lakes, *Thermal pollution, Currents(Water), Diffusion, Entrainment, Fluid mechanics, Hydraulics, Outlets, Cooling water, Path of pollutants.
Identifiers: Streamlines, Multiple jets.

Numerical calculation of the interaction between a cooling water discharge and an ambient current in a lake was described. The calculations were done by an explicit predictor-corrector method. The calculated flow patterns compared favorably with those obtained by dye studies in a physical model. Results were presented for three values of ambient

current. For an ambient velocity of 1 fps (0.3 m/s), the cooling water is transported directly downstream. For ambient current velocities of 0.5 fps (0.2 m/s) and 0.2 fps (0.1 m/s), a large recirculation region develops in which discharge flow is reentrained in the circulatory flow. When this occurs, the temperature decrease along the discharge jet will be reduced due to the increased temperature of the entrained water. (Adams-ISWS)
W75-07467

THE APPLICATION OF REGIONAL GEOCHEMICAL RECONNAISSANCE SURVEYS IN THE ASSESSMENT OF WATER QUALITY AND ESTUARINE POLLUTION,
Imperial Coll. of Science and Technology, London (England). Applied Geochemistry Research Group.
S. R. Aston, and I. Thornton.
Water Research, Vol 9, No 2, p 189-195, February 1975. 3 fig, 3 tab, 9 ref.

Descriptors: *Regional analysis, *Geochemistry, *Estuarine environment, *Water pollution effects, Water pollution sources, Water quality, Surveys, Mapping, Heavy metals, Trace elements, Spectroscopy, Colorimetry, Analytical techniques, Sediments, Arsenic compounds, Sulfides, Cadmium, Zinc, Lead, Copper, Nickel, Industrial wastes, Rivers, Monitoring, Drainage, Correlation analysis, Salinity.
Identifiers: *England, *Wales, Aquaculture.

Preliminary studies on the application of regional geochemical reconnaissance data, based on stream sediment sampling, to the assessment of water quality and estuarine pollution were encouraging. The use of the trace metal composition of tributary drainage sediments for the prediction of the upper limits of the trace metal concentration ranges in associated waters was demonstrated. This suggested that the available reconnaissance data may be a useful ancillary aid in the location of water monitoring sites in potential problem areas for potable water abstraction. The close association between the trace metal status of estuarine waters and sediments and their respective tributary drainage sediments allowed the use of regional geochemical reconnaissance data in the selection of estuaries for aquaculture and other amenities. Regional geochemical reconnaissance data, although a useful guide to the trace metal status of potable and estuarine waters, does require more detailed follow-up studies in selected areas, especially for temporal studies to establish seasonal variations in surface drainage systems. The extension of the present investigation, involving areas of fairly well known characteristics and relatively small climatic and environmental scope, to lesser known areas and regions of greater natural variations could well prove useful. (Visocky-ISWS)
W75-07469

THE EFFECTS OF GEOLOGY AND LAND USE ON THE EXPORT OF PHOSPHORUS FROM WATERSHEDS,
Toronto Univ. (Ontario). Dept. of Zoology.
P. J. Dillon, and W. B. Kirchner.
Water Research, Vol 9, No 2, p 135-148, February 1975. 6 tab, 77 ref.

Descriptors: *Path of pollutants, *Phosphorus, *Watersheds(Basins), *Geologic control, *Land use, Lakes, Algae, Nutrients, Eutrophication, Domestic wastes, Model studies, *Canada, Soil types, Streamflow, Discharge(Water), Population, Density, Forests, Grazing, Igneous rocks, Bedrock, Soil chemical properties, Urbanization.
Identifiers: *Ontario, *Canadian Shield, Flushing rate, Export coefficient.

The export of total phosphorus from 34 watersheds in southern Ontario was measured over a 20-month period. The annual average export for igneous watersheds (i.e., those of the Canadian Shield) that were forested was 4.8 mg/sq m/yr, significantly different from the average (11.0 mg/sq m/yr) for watersheds that included pasture as well as forest. Similarly, on sedimentary rock, the mean export from forested watersheds (10.7 mg/sq m/yr) differed significantly from those with forest and pasture (28.8 mg/sq m/yr). The differences between watersheds of different geology but similar land use were also highly significant. Additional data from the literature supported these conclusions. Other forested igneous watersheds of plutonic origin averaged 4.2 mg/sq m/yr of total phosphorus exported; forested igneous watersheds of volcanic origin, however, averaged 72 mg/sq m/yr. The overall average export from each type of watershed as classified by geology and land use was very similar to that for the same classification found in this study. The effects of agriculture and urbanization were to greatly increase the total phosphorus exported. Wide ranges of values probably reflect the intensity of land use. (Visocky-ISWS)
W75-07470

WATER QUALITY IN EASTERN OREGON,
Oregon State Univ., Corvallis. Dept. of Soil Science.
V. Van Volk.
In: Land and Water Use in Oregon; Seminar conducted by Oregon State University, Spring Quarter 1974, Water Resources Research Institute, Corvallis, Oregon, p 113-130, July 1974. 12 tab.

Descriptors: *Water quality, *Irrigation, *Oregon, Return flow, Nutrients, Salts, Sediment load, Biological properties, Turbidity, Irrigation effects, Furrow irrigation, Nitrates, Phosphorus compounds, Eutrophication, Analytical techniques, On-site investigations, Sampling.
Identifiers: Snake River(Ore), Malheur River(Ore), Owyhee(Ore).

An irrigation runoff water quality study was initiated in northern Malheur County in eastern Oregon in the spring of 1971. The area surrounding Ontario, Oregon, was selected for the initial study. Samples were collected on a weekly basis from May through September 1971 and thereafter on a monthly basis through 1972 and 1973. With this sampling frequency, trends in nutrient constituents, salt levels, and sediment loads could be seen as the cropping season progressed. All elements and sediments measured increased in the water as the water passed from its source through irrigated fields and into the Snake River. The orthophosphate level in the Owyhee River source water averaged 0.07 ppm, which exceeded the phosphorus level shown to cause eutrophication in lakes provided no other elemental deficiency exists. Orthophosphate levels in the surface runoff waters increased, sometimes slightly exceeding 0.2 ppm PO4-P. Thus, orthophosphate levels are sufficiently high to cause eutrophication in lakes under the right conditions. The nitrate nitrogen levels observed in the surface drains did not exceed 3 ppm during the irrigation season. However, water samples collected from surface drains in the winter months reflected a sizable increase in the nitrate nitrogen levels, a reflection of the increased percentage of percolation as opposed to surface runoff in the drainage water. (See also W75-07507) (Sims-ISWS)
W75-07517

CHEMISTRY IN THE AQUATIC ENVIRONMENT,
Victoria Ministry for Conservation, Melbourne (Australia). Westernport Bay Environmental Study.
For primary bibliographic entry see Field 5A.
W75-07524

FATE OF INSECTICIDES IN AN IRRIGATED FIELD; AZINPHOSMETHYL AND TETRADIFON CASES,
Agricultural Research Organization, Bet-Dagan (Israel). Inst. of Soils and Water.
B. Yaron, H. Bielorai, and L. Kliger.
Journal of Environmental Quality, Vol 3, No 4, October-December, 1974. p 413-417, 7 fig, 7 ref.

Descriptors: *Organophosphorus pesticides, *Insecticides, *Irrigation water, *Pesticide residues, Soil moisture, Percolation, Irrigation, Potatoes, *Path of pollutants, Water pollution sources.
Identifiers: Organchlorine pesticides, *Tetradifon, *Azinphosmethyl, Israel.

The effects and persistence of an organophosphorus (azinphosmethyl) and an organochlorine insecticide (tetradifon) in an irrigated potato field was studied. After two amounts of irrigation water were applied, the kinetics of persistence and the downward movement of the two pesticides were followed during the irrigation season. The azinphosmethyl remained in the upper layers of the soil after irrigation and disappeared from the field 30 days after application. The tetradifon was found in trace amounts in the deeper layer of the soil and persisted throughout the irrigation season. Tetradifon persistence was not affected by the irrigation treatments, but it transport into the soil was affected by the amount of water applied. Some residue of the tetradifon was found in the potato peel, but no trace of azinphosmethyl was found in the potato plant or leaves despite two applications. Differences in irrigation treatments did not affect the amount of tetradifon residue in the peel, therefore its presence may be due only to a process of direct contact. (Mastic-Arizona)
W75-07548

COASTAL SALINITY RECONNAISSANCE AND MONITORING SYSTEM--SOUTH COAST OF PUERTO RICO,
Geological Survey of Puerto Rico, San Juan.
For primary bibliographic entry see Field 5A.
W75-07553

TIME-OF-TRAVEL STUDY, LAKE ERIE-NIAGARA RIVER BASINS,
Geological Survey, Albany, N.Y.
B. Dunn.
Open-file report, January 1975. 41 p, 28 fig, 4 tab.

Descriptors: *Travel time, *New York, *Path of pollutants, Rivers, Streams, Duration curves, Discharge(Water), Lake Erie, Great Lakes.
Identifiers: *Lake Erie basin(NY), *Niagara River basin(NY).

In the Lake Erie-Niagara River basins in New York, time of travel was determined for 80.54 stream miles on Cattaraugus, Cayuga, Ellicott, Murder, and Tonawanda Creeks; Cazenovia Creek basin; and the Buffalo River. Time-of-travel data for several subreaches are depicted in a series of graphs that show time-distance relationships for several discharge rates. Flow-duration curves and minimum average consecutive 7-day discharges for a 10-year return period were determined for one site each on Cattaraugus, Cayuga, and Murder Creeks, and for two sites on Tonawanda and Ellicott Creeks. The 7-day frequency data were also developed for a site on Buffalo River. Effluent discharge was measured at nine treatment plants. Considerable fluctuation in discharge was recorded at some of the plants. Time-of-travel data are shown in graphic form depicting the time-distance relationships for the three major reaches in the Cazenovia Creek basin for several discharge rates. (Knapp-USGS)
W75-07554

GENERALIZED STREAM TEMPERATURE ANALYSIS SYSTEM,
Geological Survey, Bay Saint Louis, Miss. Gulf Coast Hydroscience Center.
D. P. Bauer, H. E. Jobson, and M. E. Jennings.
Reprint from Proceedings of the 21st Annual Hydraulics Division Specialty Conference, Bozeman, Montana, August 15-17, 1973: American Society of Civil Engineers Publication, p 167-177, 1973. 1 fig, 1 tab, 14 ref.

Descriptors: *Water temperature, *Thermal pollution, *Path of pollutants, *Mathematical models, Heated water, Model studies, Jets, Computer programs, Water pollution control.

A rationale is given for linking three existing temperature excess prediction models into a generalized stream temperature analysis system. Using the linkage concept, the output from one temperature model becomes the input to the next model. These models are a two-dimensional surface jet model for near region analysis; a two-dimensional stream-tube model for intermediate region analysis; and a one-dimensional surface exchange model for far region analysis. The linked stream excess temperature models are coded into a computer programming system in such a way that the programs can be used individually or in sequence depending on the problem at hand. An example problem is used to illustrate the calculations. (Knapp-USGS)
W75-07561

GEOHYDROLOGIC CONSIDERATIONS IN THE MANAGEMENT OF RADIOACTIVE WASTE,
Geological Survey, Reston, Va.
G. D. DeBuchananne.
Nuclear Technology, Vol 24, p 356-361, December 1974. 10 ref.

Descriptors: *Radioactive waste disposal, *Nuclear wastes, *Path of pollutants, *Hydrogeology, Climates, Groundwater movement, Aquifer characteristics, Underground waste disposal, Forecasting, Model studies.

Nongaseous radioactive wastes occur as liquids containing high-level concentrations of radionuclides, liquids containing low concentrations of radionuclides, and solids contaminated by radioactivity. Whether released by accident or design into the earth or onto the earth's surface, only water is capable of transporting signficant quantities of radionuclides away from burial sites. Geohydrologic information that must be determined to predict the velocity and direction of waste movement from a site include climate, hydrology, detailed subsurface geology, permeability, porosity, sorptive potential, seismic potential, and geologic history of the area. Since the late 1960's mathematical models have been used to make predictions of waste transport in some hydrologic systems. Intensive field investigations at each site are needed before these models can be used. (Knapp-USGS)
W75-07562

FLUCTUATIONS OF AQUATIC AND TERRESTRIAL INVERTEBRATES IN DRIFT SAMPLES FROM CONVICT CREEK, CALIFORNIA,
Missouri Univ., Columbia. School of Forestry.
For primary bibliographic entry see Field 2I.
W75-07563

DYE-DISPERSION STUDY ON LAKE CHAMPLAIN, NEAR CROWN POINT, NEW YORK,
Geological Survey, Albany, N.Y.
P. H. Hamecher, and L. A. Wagner.
Open-file report 74-355, January 1975. 16 p, 11 fig, 1 ref.

Descriptors: *Path of pollutants, *Dispersion, *Lakes, *New York, Pulp wastes, Fluorescent dye, Tracers, Dye dispersion, Dye releases.
Identifiers: *Lake Champlain(NY).

A dye-dispersion study near the subsurface diffuser pipe of International Paper Company's waste-treatment plant on Lake Champlain near Crown Point, N.Y., October 18, 1973, was intended to define the dispersion pattern of treated effluent discharged into the lake and to determine the volume of diluted effluent in an area adjacent to the diffuser pipe after a period of time. A 20% solution of Rhodamine-WT dye was injected into effluent in the Parshall flume at an average rate of 130 millilitres per minute for 4 hours. Maximum dye concentration of near-surface samples of water in a 114- x 244-metre rectangle downstream from the diffuser pipe was 32 micrograms per litre. Average depth of the dye-colored water in the rectangle was 3.69 metres; volume of that water was 102,800 cubic metres. The dispersion patterns (dye clouds) formed by injected dye are outlined on a map of the study area. (Knapp-USGS)
W75-07571

VELOCITY AND DEPTH MEASUREMENTS FOR USE IN THE DETERMINATION OF REAERATION COEFFICIENTS,
Geological Survey, Trenton, N.J.
For primary bibliographic entry see Field 2E.
W75-07572

WATER-QUALITY STUDIES TODAY AND TOMORROW,
Geological Survey, Menlo Park, Calif.
For primary bibliographic entry see Field 5A.
W75-07579

EFFECT OF STREAM TURBULENCE ON HEATED WATER PLUMES,
Geological Survey, Menlo Park, Calif.
J. Weil, and H. B. Fischer.
ASCE Proceedings, Journal of the Hydraulics Division, Vol 100, No HY7, Paper 10674, p 951-970, July 1974. 11 fig, 1 tab, 19 ref, append.

Descriptors: *Jets, *Path of pollutants, *Thermal pollution, Heated water, Mixing, Turbulence, Density, Open channel flow.
Identifiers: *Heated water plumes.

A heated water surface jet flowing at the mean local velocity in open channel flow was studied in a recirculating flume. The jet contains no excess momentum that can cause mixing by relative motion of parallel streams. Downstream behavior is determined by buouancy and ambient flow turbulence. The independent variables are a distance ratio, a depth ratio, a friction factor, and a densimetric Froude number. In the range of study, the axis temperature is independant of depth ratio and Froude number, and only weakly dependent on friction factor. Mixing is significant, but dilution is less than for momentum jets in still water. Mixing and spread of the plume are determined by buoyant.motion and turbulence, but not by jet excess momentum. The insensitivity of axis temperature dilution to initial temperature difference is unexpected because another measure of plume behavior, the plume half width, is predictably dependent on source temperature. (Knapp-USGS)
W75-07587

PHOSPHORUS CYCLING IN LAKES,
North Carolina Univ., Chapel Hill. Dept. of Environmental Sciences and Engineering.
C. R. O'Melia.
Available from the National Technical Information Service, Springfield, Va 22161 as PB-214 745, $3.75 in paper copy, $2.25 in microfiche. North Carolina Water Resources Research Institute, Raleigh, UNC-WRRI Report No 97, December 1974. 45 p, 8 fig, 4tab, 42 ref. OWRT A-074-NC(2). 14-31-0001-4033.

Descriptors: *Phosphorus, Lakes, *Model studies, Computer models, Nutrients, *Cycling nutrients, Retention, Hypoliminon, Forecasting, Estimating. Identifiers: *Predictive models, Phosphorus concentration, Nutrient loading, Phosphorus cycling, Oxic hypolimnetic waters.

A predictive model for phosphorus in lakes has been developed and verified. The model shows excellent agreement between observed and predicted average phosphorus concentrations for lakes with a wide range of hydraulic detection times (1 to 700 years) and mean depths (14 to 313 meters). At present the model should be applied only to lakes with oxic hypolimnetic waters. The model has been verified for conditions of constant nutrient loadings. The model provides an explanation for the effects of mean lake depth on water quality noted by several limnologists. Vertical exchange of phosphorus forms across the thermocline and natural aggregation within the lake are important processes for the transport and deposition of phosphorus in lakes. The significance of these processes increases with lake depth. Nomographs are presented which summarize model calculations and permit the model to be used for predictive purposes. Required information includes mean lake depth and areal hydraulic loading. Predictions of permissible phosphorus loadings can be made for lakes which meet the conditions assumed in formulating the model. (Stewart-North Carolina State)
W75-07597

FUTURE DREDGING QUANTITIES IN THE GREAT LAKES,
Eastern Michigan Univ., Ypsilanti. Dept. of Geography and Geology.
For primary bibliographic entry see Field 5G.
W75-07603

THE SIGNIFICANCE AND CONTROL OF WASTEWATER FLOATABLES IN COASTAL WATERS,
California Univ., Berkeley. Sanitary Engineering Research Lab.
For primary bibliographic entry see Field 5G.
W75-07606

CHARACTERIZATION AND TREATMENT OF URBAN LAND RUNOFF,
North Carolina Water Resources Research Inst., Raleigh.
For primary bibliographic entry see Field 5D.
W75-07607

DISTRIBUTION AND PERSISTENCE OF 1,2-DIBROMO-3-CHLOROPROPANE IN SOIL AFTER APPLICATION BY INJECTION AND IN IRRIGATION WATER,
California Univ., Davis. Dept. of Nematology.
L. R. Hodges, and B. Lear.
Nematologica, Vol 19, No 2, p 146-158, 1973, Illus.

Descriptors: *Pesticides, *Soil contamination effects, Loam, Sands, Irrigation, Chemical analysis, *Soil contamination, Pollutant identification.
Identifiers: Meloidogyne-incognita, Nematocide, 1,2-dibromo-3-chloropropane, Soil pollution.

Applications of 1,2-dibromo-3-chloropropane (DBCP) were made to mini-field plots of Yolo sandy loam by means of injection, flooding and sprinkler irrigation. Soil samples were removed at various depths and time intervals, processed to extract the chemical and the amount determined by gas chromatography and correlated to the degree of kill of Meloidogyne incognita. Deepest penetration in soil occurred by injection. Application of water to injected plots moved the chemical deeper into the soil than no irrigation. In flood applications most of the chemical was retrained near the soil surface with only small quantities reaching a depth of 15 cm. Application by sprinkler resulted

in shallow penetration. Excellent correlation between depths of chemical penetration and nematode kills were obtained.--Copyright 1974, Biological Abstracts, Inc.
W75-07609

STUDY OF THE RELATION BETWEEN RESIDUAL SODA AND WATER-EXTRACTABLE COMPONENTS OF VACUUM DRUM WASHED KRAFT PULP AND OF REPULPED CORRUGATED CONTAINER EFFLUENT CHARACTERISTICS,
National Council of the Paper Industry for Air and Stream Improvement, Inc., New York.
D. E. Fowler, W. L. Carpenter, and H. F. Berger.
NCASI Technical Bulletin, No. 277, 61 p, October 1974. 22 fig, 14 tab, 16 ref.

Descriptors: *Pulp wastes, *Sodium, *Biochemical oxygen demand, *Chemical oxygen demand, *Color, Industrial wastes, Water pollution sources, Wastes, Sodium sulfate, Sodium compounds, Laboratory tests, Effluents, Model studies, Pollutants, Water reuse, Recycling.
Identifiers: Pulp washing, Chemical losses, Kraft mills, Repulping, Corrugated boxes, Waste paper.

Spent cooking liquor remaining in washed pulp and later diffused into a paper mill's waste water system may account for as much as 70-80% of the total effluent BOD, and 50% of the mill's sodium sulfate (saltcake) losses. Pulp leaching studies were conducted to simulate additional leaching that occurs in a mill system beyond the washing operation. Washed pulps from kraft mills were extracted with hot deionized water, and the extracts analyzed for sodium, BOD, COD, and color. Linear relationships are shown to exist between extractable sodium and BOD and COD. A less precise relationship exists between extractable sodium and color. The correlations of BOD, COD, and color to saltcake losses at the washers may be used to predict reductions of these parameters which would result from improved washer operation. In a short study of repulping of printed and unprinted corrugated containers, no significant differences were noted in water-extractable BOD, COD, and color. (Hansen-IPC)
W75-07634

SPECIFIC WASTEWATER DISCHARGE AND SPECIFIC POLLUTION LOAD OF PAPER MILLS (UEBER DEN SPEZIFISCHEN ABWASSERANFALL UND DIE SPEZIFISCHE SCHMUTZFRACHT VON PAPIERFABRIKEN),
Technische Universitaet, Darmstadt (West Germany). Wasser- und Abwasserforschungsstelle.
H-L. Dalpke, and L. Gottsching.
Wochenblatt fur Papierfabrikation, Vol 102, No 19, p 721-728, 730, October 15, 1974. 2 fig, 7 tab, 19 ref.

Descriptors: Pulp and paper industry, Europe, *Pollutants, *Pulp wastes, *Surveys, *Water pollution sources, *Industrial wastes, Effluents, Suspended solids, Biochemical oxygen demand, Chemical oxygen demand, Water purification, Mechanical equipment, Biological treatment, Foreign countries, Treatment facilities, Efficiencies, Wastes, Waste water treatment, Waste water(Pollution).
Identifiers: *West Germany.

This report by the Water and Waste Water Research Center at the Institute of Paper-making of the Technological University, Darmstadt, gives the results of a survey of 106 German paper mills with a total production in 1973 of about 5 million tons of paper and board. The data are classified according to type of product and include the amount of effluent, settleable solids, BOD, and COD. The clarifying efficiency of mechanical and biological treatment plants is evaluated by data taken before and after treatment. The ratios of BOD to COD are analyzed. The tables in this report summarize the data, giving mean, minimum, and maximum values for each type of mill. (Ward-IPC)
W75-07640

OIL SPILL AND OIL POLLUTION REPORTS JULY 1974 - OCTOBER 1974,
California Univ., Santa Barbara. Marine Science Inst.
For primary bibliographic entry see Field 5G.
W75-07689

CRANKCASE DRAINAGE FROM IN-SERVICE OUTBOARD MOTORS,
Southwest Research Inst., San Antonio, Tex. Dept. of Emissions Research.
C. T. Hare, and K. J. Springer.
Available from the National Technical Information Service, Springfield, Va. 22161, as PB-240 691, $5.75 in paper copy, $2.25 in microfiche. Environmental Protection Agency, Cincinnati, Ohio. Report EPA-670/2-74-092, December 1974. 115 p, 48 fig, 18 tab, 25 ref. 1BB038; ROAP 21APO; Task 08 EHS 70-108.

Descriptors: Boats, *Oil pollution, *Oil water, Gasoline, Texas, Lakes, *Water pollution control, Measurement, *Water pollution sources.
Identifiers: *Outboard motors, *Crankcase drainage, San Antonio(Tex).

Crankcase drainage from 35 outboard motors was measured during normal operation on two lakes in the San Antonio area. The motors included a variety of sizes and brand names, and they were tested under prolonged constant-speed conditions as well as cyclic speed conditions designed to simulate user operation in the field. Four engines of the same group were also tested with a drainage intercepting and recirculating device. Drainage was measured by both mass and volume, and results were also computed in mass per unit time (g/hr) and percentage of fuel consumed by weight and by volume. Analysis of some fuel samples was conducted by gas chromatograph, including a few in which drainage was mixed with fuel by the recirculating device mentioned above. Photographic documentation of the test engines, the drainage systems, and test/measurement techniques was also obtained. Based on measurements obtained and estimations of the current outboard motor population, a range for the national total crankcase drainage emissions was estimated. The major causes of variation in drainage rates were engine type, engine operating speed, and differences from one engine to another of the same type (or a similar type). (EPA)
W75-07696

POLLUTED GROUNDWATER: ESTIMATING THE EFFECTS OF MAN'S ACTIVITIES,
General Electric Co., Santa Barbara, Calif. Center for Advanced Studies.
J. F. Karubian.
Available from the National Technical Information Service, Springfield, Va. 22161, as PB-241 078, $5.75 in paper copy $2.25 in microfiche. Environmental Protection Agency, Report EPA 680/4-74-002, July 1974. 99 p, 12 fig, 41 tab, 29 ref. GE74TMP-17 1HA328. EPA 68-01-9759, Tasks 1, 3.

Descriptors: *Farm wastes, *Industrial wastes, Waste water(Pollution), *Water pollution control, *Water pollution sources, Federal Water Pollution Control Act, *Groundwater, Liquid wastes, Management, Organic wastes, Pollutants, *Water pollution, Water pollution effects, Water pollution treatment, Feed lots, Fertilizer.
Identifiers: Petroleum refining(Pollution), Phosphate Mining(Pollution).

A method is presented for estimating kinds, amounts, and trends of groundwater pollution caused by man's activities. Preliminary research is described for a number of examples: unlined earthen basins and lagoons used by the pulp and paper industry, petroleum refining, and primary metals industries; phosphate mining wastewater ponds; agricultural fertilizer use; and beef cattle feedlots. Sources of information are primarily census data, other statistical data, and descriptions of production processes. Estimates are made of past and projected volumes and areas covered by potential pollutants so that geohydrological analysis can be used to estimate the infiltration potential of pollutants. Results are not definitive but are intended only to illustrate use of the methodology for geographical areas of interest. (EPA)
W75-07698

MATHEMATICAL MODELING OF PHYTOPLANKTON IN LAKE ONTARIO 1. MODEL DEVELOPMENT AND VERIFICATION,
Manhattan Coll., Bronx, N.Y. Environmental Engineering and Science Program.
For primary bibliographic entry see Field 5C.
W75-07700

CHARACTERIZATION OF VESSEL WASTES IN DULUTH-SUPERIOR HARBOR,
Environmental Quality Systems, Inc., Rockville, Md.
G. D. Gumtz, D. M. Jordan, and R. Waller.
Available from the National Technical Information Service, Springfield, Va. 22161, as PB-241 081, $4.25 in paper copy, $2.25 in microfiche. Environmental Protection Agency, Cincinnati, Ohio, Report EPA-670/2-74-097, December 1974. 51 p, 12 tab, 9 ref. 1BB038; ROAP 21-BBU R-802772.

Descriptors: Ships, *Minnesota, Lake Superior, Harbors, *Wastes, *Oil pollution, Water pollution sources, Waste identification.
Identifiers: *Duluth-Superior Harbor(Minn), *Vessel wastes, *Waste characterization.

Five wastes from United States, Canadian, and foreign commercial vessels were studied at the Duluth-Superior Harbor during late 1973: bilge water, non-oily ballast water, sewage, garbage/refuse, and dunnage. Vessels generate bilge water at about 6,650 liters/hour with an average oil content of about 225 milligrams/liter. Waste oil which is apparently discharged to bilges (about 600 grams/hour) appears more consistent than either of these two parameters. Bilge water is a substantial pollution problem: on the average about 40 liters (10 gallons) of oil may be discharged during each day a vessel spends in the harbor. Although containing about twice the common water quality contaminants as the harbor waters, ballast water is not a significant environmental problem. Large quantities are, however, discharged: about 9,000 metric tons/visit by lake and bulk carriers. Sewage is apparently generated onboard vessels consistent with accepted design rates (100 gallons/man/day). Although largely under control, sewage may impact wastewater treatment facilities by being significantly stronger than typical municipal wastewaters. Chemical additives commonly found in vessel sewage may adversely affect wastewater treatment facilities and harbor receiving waters. (EPA)
W75-07701

THE EFFECTS OF AIR AND WATER POLLUTION CONTROLS ON SOLID WASTE GENERATION, 1971-1985, EXECUTIVE SUMMARY,
Stone (Ralph) and Co., Inc., Los Angeles, Calif.
R. Stone.
Available from the National Technical Information Service, Springfield, Va. 22161, as PB-240 739, $4.75 in paper copy, $2.25 in microfiche. Environmental Protection Agency. Report EPA-670/2-74-095a, December 1974. 73 p, 14 fig, 15 tab, 22 ref. 1DB314; ROAP 09ABF; Task 03. 68-03-0244.

Descriptors: *Air pollution, *Water pollution control, *Industrial wastes, Waste disposal, Water

treatment,, Residues, Wastes, *Pollution abatement, Waste water treatment.
Identifiers: Pollution control, Solid waste residues, Intermedia transfer.

The affects of air and water pollution controls on solid waste generation were evaluated. The solid wastes from pollution control were identified for individual industrial sectors by their original air or water pollutant constituents, and the treatment process applied. The wastes were categorized by type and by location (rural or urban). Total solid wastes from pollution control activities were estimated for 1971 and projected for 1985. Particulates and sulfur oxides were identified as the major air pollutants capable of generating solid wastes when treated; suspended solids and biological oxygen demand were identified as the principal means of estimating the impact of water pollution control on solid wastes. Important sectors generating solid wastes included power plants (SIC 491), paper and pulp (SIC 26), chemicals (SIC 28), cement and clay (SIC 324-326), steel furnaces (SIC 331), nonferrous smelting and refining (SIC 333, 334), sewerage systems (SIC 4952), and hazardous wastes from uranium mining (SIC 10). Mine tailing ponds were estimated to be a greater source than all the above sources but were not seen to be a landfill disposal problem. This publication is a summary of the more extensive report 'Forecasts of the Effects of Air and Water Pollution Controls on Solid Waste Generation' (EPA-670/2-74-095b). (EPA)
W75-07705

STATE-OF-THE-ART FOR THE INORGANIC CHEMICALS INDUSTRY: INDUSTRIAL INORGANIC GASES,
Illinois Inst. of Tech., Chicago. Dept. of Environmental Engineering.
J. W. Patterson, and R. A. Minear.
Available from the National Technical Information Service, Springfield, Va. 22161, as PB-240 961, $7.25 in paper copy, $2.25 in microfiche. Environmental Protection Agency Report EPA-600/2-74-009c, March 1975. 50 p, 7 fig, 13 tab, 2 ref. PE 1BB036 R/T 21 AZQ29, R-800857.

Descriptors: *Gases, *Chemical industry, *Industrial wastes, Inorganic compounds, *Air pollution, *Pollution abatement, Reviews, Effluents, Cooling water, Waste water treatment.
Identifiers: *Inorganic gases, Scrubber solutions.

A literature and field study of the inorganic gas industry revealed that the industry is dominated by (1) air separation plants producing argon, nitrogen and/or oxygen, (2) hydrogen plants and (3) carbon dioxide plants. The major effluent of the industry is cooling water, which may be contaminated with raw product condensates, oil and grease, and water supply and cooling water treatment chemicals. Spent scrubber solutions from product purification may also constitute a significant waste, although newer production technology eliminates this aspect, as well as oil and grease. (EPA)
W75-07708

STATE-OF-THE-ART FOR THE INORGANIC CHEMICALS INDUSTRY: INORGANIC PESTICIDES,
Illinois Inst. of Tech., Chicago. Dept. of Environmental Engineering.
J. W. Patterson.
Available from the National Technical Information Service, Springfield, Va. 22161, as PB-240 959, $4.25 in paper copy, $2.25 in microfiche. Environmental Protection Agency Report EPA-600/2-74-009a, March 1975. 63 p, 12 fig, 16 tab, 11 ref. PE 1BB036 R/T 21 AZR 06, R-800857.

Descriptors: *Pesticides, *Inorganic compounds, Chemicals, Chemical wastes, *Agricultural chemicals, *Chemical industry, *Inorganic pesticides, Reviews, Water pollution control, Waste identification, Water pollution sources, *Industrial wastes.
Identifiers: Waste characteristics.

A literature and field study of the manufacture of inorganic pesticides revealed that many inorganic formulations are still widely used for agricultural purposes. The inorganic pesticide industry is a small but distinct segment of the total agricultural chemical industry. Its manufacturing processes and wastewaters contrast sharply with those associated with organic pesticides. The inorganic pesticide market is dominated by eight products, each of which is discussed with respect to its manufacturing effluent characteristics and applicable pollution control technology. Field studies demonstrated that five of the eight products can be manufactured without generating any process wastewater. Aqueous effluents from the manufacture of the remaining three inorganic pesticides appear to be directly controllable by previously demonstrated in-plant control and/or wastewater treatment technologies. (EPA)
W75-07709

RATIONALE AND METHODOLOGY FOR MONITORING GROUNDWATER POLLUTED BY MINING ACTIVITIES,
General Electric Co., Santa Barbara, Calif. Center for Advanced Studies.
D. L. Warner.
Available from the National Technical Information Service, Springfield, Va. 22161, as PB-241 402, $4.75 in paper copy, $2.25 in microfiche. Environmental Protection Agency, EPA 680/4-74-003, July 1974. 75 p, 25 fig, 78 ref. 1HA326, EPA 68-01-0759, Task 3.

Descriptors: *Groundwater movement, Legal aspects, *Mine acids, *Mine wastes, *Mine water, *Solid wastes, *Water pollution control, *Water pollution sources, Water pollution, Mining, Monitoring.
Identifiers: *Groundwater monitoring, *Mining pollution.

The rationale and related methodology for monitoring groundwater pollution caused by mining and mineral processing are discussed. Some mines and waste-disposal areas will continue to be pollution sources long after the mines have closed. Because of the broad range of mining activities and diversity of geologic and hydrologic settings, monitoring programs for mineral operations must be individually considered. Technology for at-source control of water pollution from mining is reviewed. Some methods used to improve surface water quality may cause deterioration in groundwater quality. Existing State and Federal laws and regulations for control of mine drainage pollution and the inability of most to influence the design, permitting, or abandonment of underground mines on the basis of water pollution considerations are discussed. (EPA)
W75-07710

THREE DIMENSIONAL TURBULENT DIFFUSION FROM POINT SOURCES OF POLLUTION IN AN OPEN CHANNEL,
Delaware Univ., Newark. Dept. of Chemical Engineering.
M. R. Samuels.
Available from the National Technical Information Service, Springfield, Va 22161 as PB-241 909, $3.75 in paper copy, $2.25 in microfiche. Termination Report, (1974). 24 p, 14 fig, 6 tab, 4 ref. OWRT A-015-DEL(1).

Descriptors: *Diffusion, *Turbulence, Momentum transfer, Pollutants, Heat transport, Eddies, Hydraulics, *Flow rates, River flow, *Open channel flow, Model studies, Flumes, Jets, Path of pollutants, *Flow profiles, Temperature, Velocity, Water pollution sources.
Identifiers: Eddy diffusivities, *Temperature profiles, *Velocity profiles.

A recirculating open channel water flume was used to study momentum and thermal transfer in turbulent channel flows, as a prelude to development of tools for simulating and predicting turbulent diffusion in river flows. The velocity profiles were measured at two different flow rates. Each profile was composed of 90 point velocities measured by means of a calibrated hot film anemometer at regularly spaced points throughout one lateral half of the channel. Temperature profiles were measured downstream from a 'point' source of hot water injected into the main channel flow. The same two water flow rates and channel slopes were used as in the velocity profile studies. Techniques have been developed for determining eddy diffusivities for both momentum and heat transport from the measured velocity and temperature profiles. The momentum diffusivity model developed yields a scalar diffusivity which is a function of position. The thermal diffusivity model yields average vertica and lateral diffusivities. Although quantitative comparison of the momentum and thermal diffusivities determined from the experimental data is not possible, their relationship is in qualitative agreement with that expected from the Reynolds analogy.
W75-07723

COOPERATIVE PHENOMENA IN ISOTOPIC HYDRODYNAMIC DISPERSION,
Nevada Univ., Reno. Desert Research Inst.
C. M. Case, and C. L. Carnahan.
Available from the National Technical Information Service, Springfield, Va. 22161 as PB-241 896, $4.75 in paper copy, $2.25 in microfiche. Nevada Water Resources Research Center, Reno, Project Report No 30, April 1975. 83 p, 19 fig, 7 tab, 19 ref, append. OWRT A-048-NEV(1). 14-31-0001-3828.

Descriptors: *Hydrology, Statistical methods, *Dispersion, Hydrodynamics, *Path of pollutants, *Isotope studies, Tritum, *Diffusion, ,*Molecular structure, Water structure.

This study theoretically examines the effects on the rate of hydrodynamic dispersion of two types of dispersing material - isotopic (tritium) and suspended - as an example of cooperative phenomena using statistical mechanics. By these means a preliminary formula describing hydrodynamic dispersion in relation to pollutants in water was developed. For clusters with higher binding energy, corresponding either to a higher concentration of isotopes or larger atomic numbers, e.g., tritium versus deuterium, more thermal energy is required to achieve a given level of dispersion. For removal of water molecules from the cluster, the curves of entropy versus temperature lie below each other as successive configurations contain fewer and fewer radioactive isotopes. Lower concentrations of radioactive isotopes mean lower binding energy in the cluster and hence less energy is necessary to go from one configuration to the next. A tetrahedral picture for liquid water is at best only approximately correct, and a systematic examination of the effect of vacancies in and distortions of the tetrahedral lattice should be carried out. The relative values of Helmholz free energy and entropy are of use in describing the diffusion of deuterium and tritium in water. The next important step is to calculate the diffusion coefficient for radioactive water in water using the model developed. (Fallon-Nevada)
W75-07725

THE WATER QUALITY AND TIDAL FLUSHING CHARACTERISTICS OF THREE SMALL BOAT BASINS; DES MOINES MARINA, EDMONDS HARBOR, AND NEWPORT SHORES,
Washington Univ., Seattle. Dept. of Civil Engineering.
C. R. Knoll.
Available from the National Technical Information Service, Springfield, Va 22161 as PB-241 913, $5.75 in paper copy, $2.25 in microfiche. M S Thesis, 1974. 119p, 31 fig, 1 tab, 67 ref, 2 append. OWRT A-064-WASH(1). 14-31-0001-4048.

Descriptors: *Washington, Tidal waters, Tidal effects, *Water quality, Biology, Hydraulic models, Harbors.
Identifiers: Des Moines Marina(Wash), Edmonds Harbor(Wash), Newport Shores(Wash), *Tidal flushing.

Tide induced circulation patterns and gross flushing characteristics of Des Moines Marina, Edmonds Harbor, and Newport Shores are compared with field observations of current and water quality within the marinas. As a general rule, no gross pollution problems within boat basins were noticeable. In considering water quality versus relative stagnation of harbor waters, water quality seemed to be related to circulation characteristics. The greater the circulation, the less difference in water quality between the waters inside and outside of the boat basin. The fresh water site, Newport Shores, seems to have more of a potential eutrophication problem than the marine sites of Des Moines Marina and Edmonds Harbor but it is not critical now. A sampling procedure is suggested for obtaining standardized descriptions of the quality of water within a marina as compared to the quality of ambient waters. The suggested approach incorporates sampling at that time on the tidal cycle when spatial variations in local exchange and water quality within the marina basin are minimum.
W75-07726

HYDROLOGICAL AND PHYSICAL-CHEMICAL INVESTIGATIONS ON THE PO RIVER AT POLESELLA: 2. JULY 1970-JUNE 1973, (IN ITALIAN),
Istituto di Biologia del Mare, Venice (Italy).
V. U. Fossato.
Arch Oceanogre Limnol. Vol 18, No 1, p 47-58. 1973, Illus, English summary.

Descriptors: *Nutrients, Rivers, *Water chemistry.
Identifiers: *Po river, Adriatic sea, *Italy.

The research begun in 1968 on the waters of the Po river at Polesella is continued. The results, not withstanding the variability of the physical-chemical and hydrological conditions of the river, make evident the seasonal character of the variations of some chemical parameters and allow the contribution of nutrients by the river to the Adriatic sea to be estimated.--Copyright 1974, Biological Abstracts, Inc.
W75-07741

HYDROLOGICAL AND PHYSICAL-CHEMICAL INVESTIGATIONS ON THE ADIGE RIVER AT BOARA PISANI: 2. JULY 1970-JUNE 1972, (IN ITALIAN),
Istituto di Biologia del Mare, Venice (Italy).
V. U. Fossato.
Arch Oceanogr Limnol. Vol 18, No 1, p 59-70. 1973, Illus, English summary.

Descriptors: *Nutrients, Rivers, *Water chemistry.
Identifiers: Adriatic sea, *Adige river, *Italy.

Results obtained in the preceding research biennium are confirmed and the physical-chemical characteristics of the waters of the Adige river (Italy) at various seasons and different flow levels outlined. From these data it is possible to estimate the quantity of N, P and Si soluble salts brought by the river to the Adriatic Sea and utilized by phytoplankton.--Copyright 1974, Biological Abstracts, Inc.
W75-07742

DISTRIBUTION OF COLIFORM BACTERIA IN THE COASTAL WATER, (IN JAPANESE),
Tokai Univ., Tokyo (Japan). Coll. of Marine Science and Technology.
K. Ogawa.
J Oceanogr Soc Jpn. Vol 29, No 5, p 203-208. 1973, Illus, English summary.

Descriptors: *Coliforms, Rivers, Estuaries, Bays, Harbors, Distribution, *Bacteria.
Identifiers: *Aerobacter-Aerogenes, *Escherichia-Coli, *Escherichia-Freundii, *Japan, Orido Bay, Shimizu Harbor.

Distribution of coliform bacteria was surveyed monthly during July-1968 through Dec.-1969 in Shimizu Harbor and Orido Bay, Japan. Among 3 significant rivers flowing into the coastal region, the water of Tomoe River was most microbiologically polluted. Throughout the period of investigation horizontal distribution of the bacterial density was highest at the estuary of the Tomoe River, and its density decreased toward Shimizu Harbor and Orido Bay. The bacterial density decreased from surface to deeper layer. High density of bacteria was observed in the bottom deposits in winter. The bacterial distribution might be disturbed by currents caused by geographical features. Various types of coliforms were isolated in the surveyed areas. All types of Escherichia coli, E. freundii and Aerobacter aerogenes appeared in the area of estuaries, and only limited types occurred offshore. Bacterial number increased from upper stream toward the mouth of each river. The bacterial density differed from river to river. In the rivers flowing through the city the bacterial density changed with water temperature, whereas in the river running through agricultural districts it might be affected by rainfall.--Copyright 1974, Biological Abstracts, Inc.
W75-07744

ROLE OF CRUCIAN CARP IN TRANSMISSION OF ENTERIC PATHOGENS, (IN KOREAN),
Catholic Medical Coll., Seoul (Republic of Korea). Dept. of Preventive Medicine.
P. K. Lee.
J Cath Med Coll. Vol 23, p 379-386. 1972, English summary.

Descriptors: *Carp, *Enteric bacteria, Pathogenic bacteria, *Fish diseases, Salmonella, Shigella, Vibrio.
Identifiers: *South Korea(Han River).

Crucian carp can carry and transmit enteric pathogens such as Salmonella, Shigella or Vibrio. Enteric pathogens were isolated from Han river water samples, and crucian carp gills and intestinal contents. The duration of survival of these pathogens in fish gut and the role of crucian carp as a vector were studied. At water temperatures of 24-27C the duration of survival of S. typhi and Sh. dysenteriae (A-1) in the gut of the crucian carp was from 5-6 days after feeding. At water temperatures of 1-5C, it was from 6-7 days in the fish gut. Duration of survival of V. eltor (Ogawa type) and V. parahaemolyticus (K-3 type) was similar. Sûrvival of these pathogens in water was twice as long as that in the fish gut.--Copyright 1973, Biological Abstracts, Inc.
W75-07747

MICROBIOLOGICAL AND ENZYMIC ACTIVITY OF IRRIGATED AND FERTILIZED SOIL (IN RUSSIAN),
Khersonskii Selskokhozyaistvennyi Institut (USSR).
For primary bibliographic entry see Field 3F.
W75-07764

RENOVATION OF WASTES BY MINE TAILINGS PONDS,
Idaho Univ, Moscow.
L. L. Mink, R. E. Williams, A. T. Wallace, and L. M. McNay.
Mining Engineering, Vol 25, No 7, p 81-88, July, 1973. 8 tab, 5 fig, 16 ref.

Descriptors: *Mine wastes, *Pollution abatement, *Metals, Mining engineering, Cadmium, Copper, Lead, Zinc, Effluents, Mine drainage, Ponds, Water pollution control, Water pollution sources.

Samples were collected from the wastes disposal operations of seven major mines in the Coeur d'Alene district. The supernatant of the samples was analyzed for cadmium, copper, lead, antimony and zinc, using an atomic absorption spectrophotometer. The quantities of heavy metal ions in the water at the inflow and outflow points. are described. These data reflect the immediate impact tailings pond effluent may have on the environment. Design and operation of the tailings pond have an obvious effect on the quality of water discharged from the pond. Most ponds which discharge acceptable water are utilizing a form of peripheral discharge for the inflow and a decent system for the outflow. (Jernigan-Vanderbilt)
W75-07800

EFFECT OF DIETARY SELENIUM AND AUTOXIDIZED LIPIDS ON THE GLUTATHIONE PEROXIDASE SYSTEM OF GASTROINTESTINAL TRACT AND OTHER TISSUES IN THE RAT,
California Univ., Davis. Dept. of Food Science and Technology.
For primary bibliographic entry see Field 5C.
W75-07801

FLUORIDE: GEOCHEMICAL AND ECOLOGICAL SIGNIFICANCE IN EAST AFRICAN WATERS AND SEDIMENTS,
Michigan Univ., Ann Arbor. Dept. of Zoology.
P. Kilham, and R. E. Hecky.
Limnology and Oceanography, Vol 18, No 6, p 932-945, November, 1973, 4 tab, 2 fig, 48 ref, Contract NSF (GB-8328X).

Descriptors: *Fluoride, *Sediments, Rivers, Chloride, Rocks, Chemical reactions, Lakes, Aquatic life, Geochemistry, Distribution, *Africa.
Identifiers: *East Africa, *Tanzania.

The geochemistry of fluoride in East African lakes and rivers was examined to elucidate processes of fluoride acquisition, concentration, removal, and diagenesis in inland waters in a region relatively little influenced by man. The range of fluoride concentrations (0.02-1,627 mg/liter) is the greatest found anywhere. A strong correlation was found between the concentration of fluoride in the predominant crystalline rocks of each particular drainage basin and the F:Cl ratio in surface waters. Because fluoride-rich volcanic rocks are common in East Africa very high fluoride concentrations, the products of chemical weathering, are often observed. Fluoride removal from surface waters is not significant; concentration by evaporation proceeds until saturation with respect to villiaumite is reached. Fluoride: Chloride ratios for the interstitial waters of a 7-m core from Small Momela Lake, Tanzania, indicate that in sedimentary environments fluoride may be removed from pore waters as fluoride and possibly fluorapatite. Geographical evidence suggests that the high fluoride concentrations may influence the distribution of man, livestock, zooplankton, phytoplankton, and higher aquatic plants. (Jernigan-Vanderbilt)
W75-07802

INDUSTRIALIZATION AFFECTS HEAVY METAL AND CARBON ISOTOPE CONCENTRATIONS IN RECENT BALTIC SEA SEDIMENTS,
Kiel Univ. (West Germany). Institut fuer Reine und Angewandte Kernphysik.
H. Erlenkeuser, E. Suess, and H. Willkomm.
Geochimica et Cosmochimica Acta, Vol 38, No 61, p 823-842 June, 1974. 5 fig, 4 tab, 62 ref.

Descriptors: *Industrial wastes, *Heavy metals, *Sediments, Radioisotopes, Tracers, Seawater, Cadmium, Lead, Zinc, Copper, Iron, Manganese, Nickel, Cobalt, Fossil fuels, Water pollution, Distribution.
Identifiers: *Baltic Sea.

Recent sediment cores of the western Baltic Sea were analyzed for heavy metal and carbon isotope contents. The sedimentation rate was determined from radio-carbon dates to be 1.4mm/yr. The 'recent age' of the sediment was about 850 yr. Within the upper 20 cm of sediment, certain heavy metals became increasingly enriched towards the surface; Cd, Pb, Zn and Cu increased 7-, 4-, 3-, and 2-fold, respectively, whereas Fe, Mn, Ni and Co remained unchanged. Simultaneously, the radiocarbon content decreased by about 14 per cent. The enrichment in heavy metals as well as the decrease in the C14 concentration during the last 130 plus or minus 30 yr parallels industrial growth as reflected in European fossil fuel consumption within that same period of time. The near-surface sediments are affected by residues released from fossil fuels at the rate of about 30 g/sq m yr for the past two decades. The residues have a pronounced effect on the heavy metal and carbon isotope composition of the most Recent sediments allowing estimates to be made for sedimentation, erosion and heavy metal pollution. (Jernigan-Vanderbilt)
W75-07803

HYDROGEOLOGICAL MAPS OF THE ALLUVIAL AQUIFER IN AND ADJACENT TO THE ROCKY MOUNTAIN ARSENAL, COLORADO,
Geological Survey, Denver, Colo.
For primary bibliographic entry see Field 7C.
W75-07836

5C. Effects Of Pollution

ENVIRONMENTAL QUALITY AND SAFETY, VOL. 2. GLOBAL ASPECTS OF CHEMISTRY, TOXICOLOGY AND TECHNOLOGY AS APPLIED TO THE ENVIRONMENT.
For primary bibliographic entry see Field 6G.
W75-07355

INTERACTING CARBON AND LIGHT LIMITS TO ALGAL GROWTH,
Missouri Univ., Columbia. Dept. of Sanitary Engineering.
R. E. King.
Available from the National Technical Information Service, Springfield, Va 22161 as PB-241 517, $4.75 in paper copy, $2.25 in microfiche. MS thesis, 1974. 82 p, 32 fig, 6 tab, 14 ref. OWRR A-071-MO(1).

Descriptors: *Photosynthesis, *Carbon, *Light, *Algae, *Plant growth, Light intensity, Scenedesmus, Anabaena, Chlamydomonas, Growth rates, Limiting factors, Carbon dioxide, Hydrogen ion concentration, Equations.
Identifiers: Pediastrum biradiatum, Scenedesmus acutiformis, Anabaena variabilis, Phormidium olivacea.

Two separate investigations were conducted, the first was to evaluate the differences of algae ability to extract carbon from a single concentration of carbonate-bicarbonate alkalinity under different light intensities and, the second, to evaluate the ability of algae to extract carbon from different carbonate-bicarbonate alkalinities at a single constant light intensity. The test algae were Pediastrum biradiatum, Scenedesmus acutiformis, Anabaena variabilis, and Phormidium olivacea. The free carbon dioxide concentration at which the algae became carbon limited varied with both light intensity and type of algae. Pediastrum biradiatum was able to fix carbon from the carbonate-bicarbonate alkalinity to a lower free carbon dioxide value with increasing alkalinity at a light intensity of 130 foot candles but not at 42 foot candles. Scenedesmus acutiformis could fix carbon from the carbonate-bicarbonate alkalinity only to a maximum pH of 10.80. The relations of the specific algal growth rate to light intensity follows the Monod equation reasonably well. The relations of the specific growth rate to free carbon dioxide concentration follows the Monod equation only at high concentrations of free carbon dioxide. The interactions imposed on the specific growth rate of algae by simultaneous limitation of carbon availability and light intensity is multiplicative. (Jones-Wisconsin)
W75-07357

EFFECT OF SOIL ENRICHMENT WITH MINERAL ELEMENTS AND FERTILIZERS ON SURFACE WATER AND PLANTS,
Ghent Rijksuniversiteit (Belgium). Faculteit Landbouwwetenschappen.
For primary bibliographic entry see Field 5B.
W75-07368

ECOLOGY OF THE PLANKTON OF PRUDHOE BAY, ALASKA,
Alaska Univ., College. Inst. of Marine Science.
R. A. Horner, K. O. Coyle, and D. R. Redburn.
IMS Report No. R74-2; Sea Grant Report No. 73-15, August 1974. 95 p, 4 fig, 14 tab, 96 ref, append. (NOAA-75022105). OSG 04-3-1581-41, ONR N00014-67-A-0317-003.

Descriptors: *Phytoplankton, *Algae, *Zooplankton, Diatoms, *Alaska, Arctic, Polar regions, Aquatic microorganisms, Marine algae, Marine plants, Aquatic plants, Aquatic life, Aquatic animals, Ecosystems, Aquatic productivity, Food webs, Harvesting of algae, Water temperature, Salinity, Water pollution effects, Nutrients.
Identifiers: *Prudhoe Bay(AK), Pennate diatoms, Species composition, Ice algae, Water transparency, Nutrient concentration.

Basic quantitative data are presented on the phytoplankton of the Prudhoe Bay area. The phytoplankton community was selected for study because phytoplankton are the primary energy source upon which the marine food web is based and any major changes in the phytoplankton composition might affect the entire ecosystem. The phytoplankton community is described in terms of species composition and relative numbers of individuals present. Primary productivity; contribution of ice algae to primary production; and major environmental parameters influencing primary productivity, such as temperature, salinity, nutrient concentrations, and water transparency are discussed. A section on zooplankton describes the spatial variability in community compositon and the relative abundance of species present; and the relationship of observed variability to hydrographic conditions existing at station locations. (NOAA)
W75-07407

THERMOREGULATORY BEHAVIOR AND DIEL ACTIVITY PATTERNS OF BLUEGILL, LEPOMIS MACROCHIRUS, FOLLOWING THERMAL SHOCK,
Wisconsin Univ., Madison. Lab. of Limnology.
T. L. Beitinger.
Available from Superintendent of Documents C55.13:72/4, Washington, D.C. 20402, for $2.75. Fishery Bulletin, Vol 72, No 4, p 1087-1093, October 1974. 3 fig, 1 tab, 29 ref, (NOAA 74120905-9).

Descriptors: *Thermal pollution, *Animal behavior, *Heated water, Electric powerplants, Fish, Diurnal distribution, Diel migration, Wisconsin, Water pollution effects, *Sunfishes.
Identifiers: *Thermal shock, *Thermoregulation, Centrarchidae, Locomotion.

Individual bluegill were allowed to thermoregulate for 3 days in a temperature-preference apparatus and then were exposed for 30 min to one of three temperature treatments: 21.0 deg., 31.0 deg., or 36.1 deg. C. Fish exposed to 31 deg C served as controls for handling procedures. Thermoregulatory performance of surviving fish was monitored for an additional 3 days. Pretreatment results indicated mean lower and upper avoidance temperatures of 29.3 deg and 33.1 deg, and 31.2 deg. C as the midpoint of the preferred range. All 20 fish exposed to 21 deg and 31 deg C survived treatment and demonstrated no significant differences between pretreatment and posttreatment thermoregulatory performance. Thirty-five percent of fish (7 of 20) exposed to 36.1 deg. C died during treatment. Fish surviving the 36.1 deg C. treatment retained the ability to thermoregulate; however, their mean lower and upper avoidance temperature increased 0.6 deg. and 0.7 deg C, respectively. Activity patterns were typically diurnal, but variable, in all three treatment groups. Immediately after treatment, the activity of fish exposed to 21 deg and 36.1 deg. C was markedly decreased. Thereafter, activity tended to be higher in the 21 deg C group and lower in the 36.1 deg C group then during the pretreatment period. (NOAA)
W75-07413

TOXAPHENE INTERACTIONS IN ESTUARINE ECOSYSTEMS,
Georgia Univ., Savannah. Marine Extension Center.
Robert J. Reimold.
Marine Science Center, Technical Report Series Number 74-6, 1974. 80 p, 11 fig, 7 tab, 6 ref, 2 append. (NOAA-74121103).

Descriptors: *Water pollution sources, *Ecosystems, Estuaries, Grasses, Industrial wastes, *Georgia, Monitoring, Pollutants, Bioindicators, Ecology, Coasts, *Water pollution effects.
Identifiers: *Toxaphene, *Species diversity, Pollution sources, Spartina alterniflora, Cordgrasses, Anchovy, Flushing, Duplin Estuary(Geo), Terry Creek(Geo), Brunswick East Estuary(Geo).

During 1973-1974, the toxaphene concentration in effluent from a Brunswick manufacturing plant continued to decrease from around 30 ppb to near 6 ppb. Concurrent with this was an increase in the species diversity of organisms in waters receiving the effluent. During 1973-1974 the diversity index, H Bar, was 1.9977 in the Duplin Estuary (considered to be undisturbed and free from any toxaphene contamination) contrasted with a higher index of 2.2577 in Terry Creek (which receives effluent containing toxaphene). Experiments to follow the movement of toxaphene from the substrate into the salt marsh cordgrass, Spartina alterniflora, using 36Chlorine labeled toxaphene were initiated. Spartina alterniflora was grown in sea water media for 26 and 100 days in a controlled environmental chamber. The greatest uptake was found in the roots and rhizomes. The least uptake was found in the leaves. Continued monitoring of toxaphene in the fauna of Terry Creek suggests as before that the oyster is not as good a biological monitoring organism as is the common anchovy. Toxaphene concentrations in the white shrimp are higher in the head and thorax than in the abdomen although the concentrations are much lower than found in preceding years. (NOAA)
W75-07414

PROBLEMS AND POTENTIALS OF RECYCLING WASTES FOR AQUACULTURE,
Massachusetts Inst. of Tech., Cambridge. Sea Grant Project Office.
For primary bibliographic entry see Field 5D.
W75-07416

THE APPLICATION OF REGIONAL GEOCHEMICAL RECONNAISSANCE SUR-

VEYS IN THE ASSESSMENT OF WATER QUALITY AND ESTUARINE POLLUTION,
Imperial Coll. of Science and Technology, London (England). Applied Geochemistry Research Group.
For primary bibliographic entry see Field 5B.
W75-07469

THE PREVALENCE OF HUMAN DENTAL CARIES AND WATER-BORNE TRACE METALS,
Forsyth Dental Center, Boston, Mass.
For primary bibliographic entry see Field 5A.
W75-07479

TOXICITY OF THE FLESH OF COMMON FISH TO THE WHITE MOUSE (MUS MUSCULUS VAR. ALBA),
Poitiers Univ. (France). Laboratoire de Microbiologie et Biologie Maritime.
J. Brisou.
C R Seances Soc Biol Fil. Vol 165, No 3, p 679-682, 1971, Illus.

Descriptors: Fish, Herrings, Saline water fish, Freshwater fish, Water pollution, *Pollutant identification, *Fish toxins, *Rodents, Laboratory animals, Toxicity.
Identifiers: Carassius-auratus, Clupea-harengus, Clupea-pilchardus, Cod, Gadus-lusens, Goldfish, Herring, Mackerel, Mus-musculus-var-alba, Sardine, Scomber-scombrus, *White mice, *Mice.

Toxicity of the flesh of common fish to the white mouse was studied. The species of fish included cod (Gadus luscus), mackerel (Scomber scombrus), sardines, (Clupea pilchardus), herring (C. harengus) as representatives of salt water fishes. The fresh water fish were the goldfish (Carassius auratus) and the silver colored variant (Carassius carassius). The food supply in fresh condition, was given to the mice each day, along with a supply of water. The observation period lasted up to 3 wk. Symptoms of intoxication usually appeared between the 5th and 10th day. The mouse is extremely sensitive to acute intoxication by the flesh of fish of many countries including those of temperate zones and of common human consumption. These findings suggest reservations in the use of the method of biological detection of toxic pollutants in water involving observing the effect of chemical contamination on the food chain.--Copyright 1974, Biological Abstracts, Inc.
W75-07483

MERCENARIA MERCENARIA (MOLLUSCA: BIVALVIA): TEMPERATURE-TIME RELATIONSHIPS FOR SURVIVAL OF EMBRYOS AND LARVAE,
Maryland Univ., Solomons. Natural Resources Inst.
V. S. Kennedy, W. H. Roosenburg, M. Castagna, and J. A. Mihursky.

Descriptors: *Clams, *Mollusks, *Cooling water, *Electric powerplants, *Mortality, Survival, Shellfish, Embryos, Larvae, Water temperature, Entrainment, Water pollution effects, *Thermal pollution.
Identifiers: Mercenaria mercenaria(L.), Bivalvia, Hard clam, Temperature tolerance.

To estimate the effects of entrainment of Mercenaria mercenaria embryos and larvae in the cooling-water systems of steam-electric power plants, a thermal gradient apparatus was used. Cleavage stages, trochophore larvae and straight-hinge veliger larvae were subjected to 11 different temperatures for 8 different time periods. There was a direct relationship of mortality with temperature increase and, at higher temperatures, with increase in time exposure. As the clams aged, temperature tolerance increased, with cleavage stages most sensitive to higher temperature and straight-hinge larvae least sensitive. Multiple regression analyses of percentage mortality on temperature and time produced estimating equations that allow prediction of percentage mortality under different conditions of temperature and time exposure. Entrainment of M. mercenaria embryos and larvae in cooling systems of power plants should be as short as possible if mortality is to be held to a minimum. (NOAA)
W75-07549

PHOSPHORUS CYCLING IN LAKES,
North Carolina Univ., Chapel Hill. Dept. of Environmental Sciences and Engineering.
For primary bibliographic entry see Field 5B.
W75-07597

PHYTOPLANKTON COMPOSITION AND ABUNDANCE IN LAKE ONTARIO DURING IFYGL,
Michigan Univ., Ann Arbor. Great Lake Research Div.
E. F. Stoermer, M. M. Bowman, J. C. Kingston, and A. L. Schaedel.
Environmental Protection Agency, Report EPA-660/3-75-004, February 1975. 373 p, 61 fig, 7 tab, 65 ref. 1BA026. R800605.

Descriptors: Algae, *Phytoplankton, *Lake Ontario, Nusiance algae, *Seasonal, *Succession, Lakes, *Lake stages, Diatoms, Nutrients, Cyanophyta, Chlorophyta, Distribution, *Eutrophication, Water pollution effects, Halophytes, Aquatic plants.
Identifiers: International field, Year for the Great Lakes.

Based on samples collected during the International Field Year for the Great Lakes, the phytoplankton assemblage of Lake Ontario is dominated by taxa indicative of degraded water quality, including many potentially nusiance producing species. Many taxa characteristic of the offshore waters of the upper Great Lakes are either absent from the flora or very rare. Compared to the upper lakes, the flora of Lake Ontario undergoes extreme seasonal succession, with diatoms predominating during the winter and early spring, green algae becoming abundant during the summer, blue-green algae showing a distinct fall peak. Various species of microflagellates are a relatively important element of the flora during all seasons. Succession during the spring bloom appears to be controlled by the thermal bar, and the data suggest control by depletion of essential nutrients following stratification. Striking differences were apparent in samples collected on comparable dates in the spring of two successive years. These differences apparently result from exceptional weather conditions which prevailed during the first sampling period. The distribution of species particularly tolerant of disturbance appeared to be controlled by both proximity to major population centers and lake morphometry. The abundance of halophilic species in most productive areas suggests effects of conservative ion contamination as well as nutrient enrichment. (EPA)
W75-07604

EUTROPHICATION OF SURFACE WATER - LAKE TAHOE'S INDIAN CREEK RESERVOIR,
Lake Tahoe Area Council, South Lake Tahoe, Calif.
P. H. McGauhey, D. B. Porcella, and G. L. Dugan.
Environmental Protection Agency, Report EPA-660/3-75-003, February 1975. 188 p, 31 fig, 10 tab, 33 ref. EPA, WQO Grant Nos 16010 DNY, 16010 DSW.

Descriptors: *Eutrophication, *Nitrification, *Denitrification, *Reclaimed wastes, *Aquatic productivity, Density, *Bioassay, Limnology, *Cycling nutrients, *Benthos, Aquatic microorganisms, Algae, Vascular plants, Fish population, Tertiary treatment, Nutrients, Biomass, Cyanophyta, Phosphorus, Water pollution effects, California.
Identifiers: *Indian Creek Reservoir(Calif), *Sewage export, Lake Tahoe area(Calif).

From April 1969 to October 1974 field and laboratory analyses and observations were made at approximately weekly intervals to evaluate the relationship between the quality of water impounded at Indian Creek Reservoir (ICR) and the reclaimed water exported by the South Tahoe Public Utility District. The reclaimed water comprised from 70 to 80 per cent of the annual impoundment. On the average the reclaimed water contained 0.1 to 0.2 mg/l of phosphorus and 15-24 mg/l of ammonia, the latter making it toxic to fish implanted in ICR. However, as the reservoir matured, nitrification-denitrification removed most of the nitrogen from the system and by March 1970 the reservoir had become a excellent trouth fishery. Excess N is comparison with P evidently precluded blooms of blue green algae but low phosphorus did not prevent the impoundment from becoming typical of a highly productive environment, with vascular plants invading to considerable depths because of the high degree of clarity of the reclaimed water. By 1974 the biosystem was at an approximately steady state. This state may not remain because of the appearance of epiphytic blue green algae which caused taste and odor problems in the water and in the fish. It is concluded that the reservoir responds to more complex factors than are measurable by analysis of reclaimed water. The results show why a system of wastewater reclamation must be designed on the basis of the natural as well as the man-controlled components of the system, and points the way to the necessary parameters and institutional concepts if water is to be reclaimed for a specific purpose. (EPA)
W75-07605

THE EFFECTS OF EFFLUENT FROM THE CANADIAN TEXTILE INDUSTRY ON AQUATIC ORGANISMS: A LITERATURE REVIEW,
Fisheries and Marine Service, Winnipeg (Manitoba).
B. Thompson.
Technical Report No. 489, 108 p, 1974. 3 fig, 26 tab, 155 ref.

Descriptors: *Textiles, *Water pollution effects, *Reviews, *Industrial wastes, *Toxicity, *Aquatic life, Water pollution sources, Effluents, Wastes, Waste water(Pollution), Industries, Canada, Foreign countries, Publications, Detergents, Dyes, Acids, Salts, Chemical wastes, Chemicals, Phenols, Organic compounds, Metals, Properties, Biochemical oxygen demand, Chemical oxygen demand, Suspended solids, Dissolved solids, Hydrogen ion concentration, Color, Odor.

Production figures for the Canadian textile industry are presented and the distribution of the industry, particularly in the provinces of Ontario and Quebec, is discussed. Processes used in textile manufacture are explained and the general properties (BOD, COD, suspended solids, dissolved solids, pH, color, and odor) of textile effluents are described, followed by the properties of waste from individual processes (scouring, dyeing, washing, neutralization, and bleaching). The toxicity to aquatic organisms of synthetic detergents, dyes, dye carriers, acids, salts, and various other process chemicals is evaluated in detail. Finally, it is pointed out that important areas for future research are the toxicity of dyes, dye carriers, and other phenolic compounds, and their toxicity when mixed with other components of the effluent. (Witt-IPC)
W75-07644

MARINE ALGAL ASSAY PROCEDURE BOTTLE TEST,
Pacific Northwest Environmental Research Lab., Corvallis, Ore.
For primary bibliographic entry see Field 5A.
W75-07686

IMPACT OF THE USE OF MICROORGANISMS ON THE AQUATIC ENVIRONMENT,
Environmental Protection Agency, Gulf Breeze, Fla. Gulf Breeze Environmental Research Lab.
Available from the National Technical Information Service, Springfield, Va. 22161, as PB-240 159, $8.50 in paper copy, $2.25 in microfiche. Report EPA-660/3-75-001, January 1975, 226 p. (Proceedings of Workshop-Symposium held at Pensacola Beach, FL. April, 1974 edited by A.W. Bourquin, S.P. Meyers, and D.G. Ahearn). 1EA077/010/25AJN.

Descriptors: *Microorganisms, *Insect control, Bacteria, Aquatic weed control, Aquatic environment, Viruses, Fungi, Protozoa, Water pollution control, Pathogenic bacteria, Arctic, Oil wastes, Louisiana, Salt marshes.
Identifiers: *Hydrocarbon degrading microorganisms.

Proceedings are presented of a symposium-workshop sponsored by the EPA Gulf Breeze Environmental Research Laboratory to determine the possible impact of artificially introducing microbial insect control agents or oil-degrading agents into the aquatic environment. The efficacy and safety testing, especially against non-target aquatic organisms, for use of bacteria, viruses, fungi, and protozoa to control aquatic insect pests is discussed with remarks of panel members representing government, academic, and industry. Special attention is given to persistence of pathogens in aquatic environments as well as control of aquatic weeds and other non-insect pests. The use of microorganisms to clean up oil spills in aquatic environments is discussed by industrial, academic, and governmental scientists. Special considerations are given to selection of hydrocarbonoclastic microorganisms and use of these microorganisms in special environments--Arctic regions and Louisiana salt marshes. Summary papers are presented for each panel concerned with microbial pesticides and one summary for the session on microbial degradation of oil. Bibliographies are presented with each paper and discussion. (EPA)
W75-07687

EUTROPHICATION OF LAKE TAHOE EMPHASIZING WATER QUALITY,
California Univ., Davis. Inst. of Ecology.
C. R. Goldman.
Available from the National Technical Information Service, Springfield, Va. 22161, as PB-240 318, $11.25 in paper copy, $2.25 in microfiche. Environmental Protection Agency Report EPA-660/3-74-034, December 1974. 408 p, 77 fig, 36 tab, 164 ref. 1BA031 16010 DBU.

Descriptors: *Eutrophication, *Primary productivity, *Synoptic analysis, *Bioassay, *Remote sensing, *Detergents, Water pollution sources, Aquatic productivity, Zooplankton, Discharge(Water), Periphyton, Aquatic bacteria, Limiting factors, Crayfish, Geomorphology, Sediment transport, Nutrients.
Identifiers: *Lake Tahoe(Calif-Nev), Pacifastacus leniusculus, Mysis relicta.

A 4 1/2-year study on the rate and factors affecting the cultural eutrophication of oligtrophic Lake Tahoe is reported. Primary productivity has increased alarmingly with a steady shift in the seasonal maximum from early spring to late summer. Productivity increased 25.6% from 1968 to 1971. Using the 1959-1960 data from earlier studies, the increase to 1971 was 51%. Diatoms dominate the phytoplankton population and the maximum zone of phytoplankton photosynthesis may be as deep as 50-70 m. The extent of winter mixing is important in the nutrient budget of the lake and bacteria associated with stream-borne nutrients facilitate nutrient regeneration. The littoral zone, although extremely important visually to the lake, contributes only 10% of the total primary production. Great variability in fertility of the lake has been demonstrated by synoptic studies and aerial remote sensing. Highest productivity is found in the lake near tributaries which drain disturbed land. Nutrients associated with road building, housing, and lumbering are major causes of eutrophication in Tahoe. In bioassay studies NTA was found to stimulate primary productivity. Drainage from a sewage land disposal site continues to yield high levels of nitrate, and marinas may serve as nutrient and sediment traps or as eutrophic, isolated systems. Daphnia, an important cladoceran component of the zooplankton population has virtually disappeared from the lake and predation by the introduced zooplankter Mysis relicta and the kokanee salmon are suspect. (EPA)
W75-07691

TAXONOMY AND ECOLOGY OF STENONEMA MAYFILES (HEPTAGENIIDAE:EPHEMEROPTERA),
National Environmental Research Center, Cincinnati, Ohio.
P. A. Lewis.
Available from the National Technical Information Service, Springfield, Va. 22161, as PB-241 235, $4.75 in paper copy, $2.25 in microfiche. Report EPA-670/4-74-006, December 1974. 80 p, 203 fig, 4 tab, 60 ref.

Descriptors: *Systematics, *Bioindicators, *Aquatic insects, *Mayflies, Distribution, Water pollution, Benthos, Insects, Limnology, Life cycles, *Ecology.
Identifiers: Insect ecology, *Stenonema mayflies, *Pollution tolerance, Environmental requirements.

Keys and descriptions are provided of all North American species of Stenonema mayflies and information from the leterature is consolidated on their ecology, environmental requirements, and pollution tolerance. Accounts of each species include synonymy, nymphal description, collection records, and a distribution map. The 31 species described and keyed include three recently described species, four new synonyms, two resurrected species, and new combinations involving three additional species and subspecies. Twelve species and one subspecies are classified as intolerant to organic pollution, eight species as tolerant of mild pollution, and seven species and two subspecies as tolerant to moderate pollution. (EPA)
W75-07694

MATHEMATICAL MODELING OF PHYTOPLANKTON IN LAKE ONTARIO 1. MODEL DEVELOPMENT AND VERIFICATION,
Manhattan Coll., Bronx. N.Y. Environmental Engineering and Science Program.
R. V. Thomann, D. M. DiToro, R. P. Winfield, and D. J. O'Connor.
Available from the National Technical Information Service, Springfield, Va. 22161, as PB-241 046, $7.00 in paper copy, $2.25 in microfiche. Environmental Protection Agency, Report EPA 660/3-75-005, March 1975. 177 p, 58 fig, 15 tab, 9 ref. 1BA026 R800610.

Descriptors: *Mathematical models, Computer models, Eutrophication, Water quality, Nutrients, Cycling nutrients, Dispersion, Mass transfer, Simulation analysis, Lakes, *Lake Ontario, Great Lakes, *Phytoplankton, Chlorophyll.

The basic mathematical structure for describing the dynamics of phytoplankton in Lake Ontario is presented. Data on chlorophyll and principal nutrients are reviewed and summarized and the mathematical modeling strategy is detailed. The modeling strategy begins with the construction of a horizontally completely mixed lake with vertical layers, LAKE 1. This spatially simplified model is used to develop the interactions and kinetic behavior of the various components of each subsystem. A more detailed 3-dimensional model is then used to describe open lake and near shore variations in phytoplankton biomass. Ten biological and chemical variables are used in both models and include four trophic levels above the phytoplankton, chlorophyll a as a measure of phytoplankton biomass, two phosphorus components and three nitrogen components. Under reasonable sets of model parameters as reported in the literature, the Lake 1 model output compared favorably with observed data on the dependent variables. Spring growth and peak chlorophyll concentrations are related primarily to increasing light and temperature. The model indicates that growth ceases due to phosphorus limitation. The results to date indicate that the mathematical model of phytoplankton in Lake Ontario as developed herein is a reasonable first approximation to observed data. As such, the model can form a basis for preliminary estimates of the effects of nutrient reduction programs on Lake Ontario. (EPA)
W75-07700

THE SEASONAL CYCLE OF GROWTH AND PRODUCTION IN THREE SALT MARSHES ADJACENT TO THE SAVANNAH RIVER,
Skidaway Inst. of Oceanography, Savannah, Ga.
For primary bibliographic entry see Field 2L.
W75-07713

PERIODICITY, IDENTIFICATION, AND CONTROL OF ALGAE IN MANAGED PONDS,
University of Southern Mississippi, Hattiesburg. Coll. of Science and Technology.
A. N. Fleming.
Publication No MSCP-73-019, August 1973. 171 p, 9 fig, 16 tab, ref. (Master's Thesis). NOAA Grant OSG 2-35362.

Descriptors: *Algae, *Nuisance algae, *Phytoplankton, *Chlorophyta, Aquatic life, Algal control, Aquatic weed control, Aquatic algae, Algal toxins, Algal poisoning, Algicides, Copper sulfate, Aquatic life, Aquatic plants, Diatoms, Fish farming, Fish hatcheries, Fisheries, Life cycles, Growth rates, Growth stages.
Identifiers: *Seasonal variations, *Periodicity.

The seasonal variation, periodicity, and relative abundance of six divisions of algae occurring at a commercial and federal fish hatchery were investigated every two weeks from April, 1971 through May, 1972. Chemical and physical factors, which include dissolved oxygen, pH, hardness, temperature, phosphorus, and nitrogen were correlated with phytoplankton production, periodicity, and seasonal variation. A temperature differential of 4 to 5C between the hatcheries did not reflect any major differences in phytoplankton diversity, although phytoplankton periodicity was directly related to temperature. The majority of phytoplankton found at the hatcheries consisted of green algae with diatoms and other chrysophytes, usually the co-dominant algae. (NOAA)
W75-07719

ISOLATION OF EDWARDSIELLA TARDA FROM AQUATIC ANIMAL SPECIES AND SURFACE WATERS IN FLORIDA,
Florida Univ., Gainesville. Dept. of Veterinary Science.
For primary bibliographic entry see Field 5A.
W75-07735

DISTRIBUTION OF COLIFORM BACTERIA IN THE COASTAL WATER, (IN JAPANESE),
Tokai Univ., Tokyo (Japan). Coll. of Marine Science and Technology.
For primary bibliographic entry see Field 5B.
W75-07744

DYNAMICS -- AND PRODUCTIVITY OF PHYTOPLANKTON AND PELAGIC BACTERIA IN A HIGH MOUNTAIN LAKE (ANTERIOR FINSTERTAL LAKE, AUSTRIA), (IN GERMAN),
Innsbruck Univ. (Austria). Inst. of Zoology.
M. Tilzer.
Arch Hydrobiol Supplementb. Vol 40, No 3, p 201-273. 1972, Illus, English summary.

Descriptors: *Phytoplankton, *Biomass, Lakes, *Primary productivity.
Identifiers: Pelagic bacteria, *Austria.

The phytoplankton was dominated by motile nannoplanktonic algae; Gymnodinium uberrimum was the most important species during 1970 comprising an average of 57% of the biomass. Phytoplankton fresh weight was lowest in spring and highest in summer. Pelagic bacterial biomass was unexpectedly high, following the fluctuations of the phytoplankton biomass with a lag of 4-6 wk. The most important pre-selections for phytoplankton were low nutrient requirements and high adaptability of changing light intensities and partly by phototactic vertical migrations. Perennation is due to endurance of photosynthesis below ice, low metabolism and probably storage of nutrients. Primary productions rates (mean: 4 mgC.m-3 . d-1) vary in a wide range (0.07 in Mar., 19 mgC . m-3 . d-1 in Sept.). Light inhibition in early summer is considerable and causes downward migration of the motile species whereas immobile forms prefer low light periods. Bacteria seem to be the only heterotrophic producers in winter. The ratio heterotrophic to autotrophic CO_2 uptake varies from 3:1 (Mar.) to 0.03:1 (early summer). Internal and external losses of biomass are increased with the absolute values of production rates. Plankton tends to an equilibrium between assimilation on the one, consumption and decomposition on the other side. Compared with Lake Erken (Sweden) metabolic processes are slowed down by the factor 5.--Copyright 1973, Biological Abstracts, Inc.
W75-07745

ROLE OF CRUCIAN CARP IN TRANSMISSION OF ENTERIC PATHOGENS, (IN KOREAN),
Catholic Medical Coll., Seoul (Republic of Korea). Dept. of Preventive Medicine.
For primary bibliographic entry see Field 5B.
W75-07747

LIMNOLOGICAL TRANSPORT AND FOODSTUFF MODELS (IN GERMAN,
D. M. Imboden.
Schweiz Z Hydrol. Vol 35, No 1, p 29-68, 1973, Illus, English summary.

Descriptors: *Lakes, Limnology, *Mathematical models, *Eutrophication, Epilimnion, Hypolimnion, Nutrients.

Physical and biochemical processes have a significant influence on the material balance of a lake. Mathematical concepts are developed to treat transport phenomena with which a comparison of different lakes is possible. A 2-box model consisting of the subsystems epilimnion and hypolimnion, for lakes with 1 specific limiting nutrient factor (e.g., phosphorus) is employed to evaluate eutrophication processes. In particular, a theoretical basis for Vollenweider's empirical relation between specific P loading and the trophic state is presented. The heterogenous O_2-consumption in the deep part of the lake during summer stagnation is calculated with diffusion theory.--Copyright 1974, Biological Abstracts, Inc.
W75-07751

STUDIES ON EFFECTS OF THERMAL POLLUTION IN BISCAYNE BAY, FLORIDA,
Rosenstiel School of Marine and Atmospheric Science, Miami, Fla.
M. A. Roessler, and D. C. Tabb.
For sale by the Superintendent of Documents, U. S. Government Printing Office, Washington, D.C. 20402, Price $5.75 in paper copy, $2.25 in microfiche from NTIS as PB-239 328. Environmental Protection Agency, Ecological Research Series Report EPA-660/3-74-014. August 1974. 145 p, 37 fig, 16 tab, 73 ref, append. EPA Grant WP-0135-01A, Project 18080 DFU.

Descriptors: *Thermal pollution, *Water pollution effects, *Environmental effects, *Estuaries, Heated water, *Florida.
Identifiers: Waste heat, Biscayne Bay(Fla).

Field studies on the effects of thermal additions from the Florida Power and Light Company's discharge at Turkey Point have been conducted to determine the effects of this effluent on the macroinvertebrates and fishes of the area. Replicate samples with a 3 m (10 foot) otter trawl lined with .63 mm (1/4 in.) bar mesh were obtained monthly at 20 stations. Data on temperature, salinity and oxygen were collected during each sampling period. Additional chemical data were collected when opportunity existed. The experimental results suggest that maximum summer discharge temperatures should not exceed 33C in order to avoid deterimental changes in the environment. Intermittent flow of discharge water is not as damaging as constant flow. Card Sound appears to be as productive as Biscayne Bay and temperatures exceeding 33C will also cause damage in Card Sound. (EPA)
W75-07790

METHYLMERCURY POISONING IN IRAQ,
Baghdad Univ. (Iraq).
F. Bakir, S. F. Damluji, L. Amin-Zaki, M. Murtadha, and A. Khalidi.
Science, Vol 181, p 230-240, July, 1973, 7 fig, 4 tab, 15 ref. NSF (RANN) (GI-300978) NIGMS (GM-15190) and (GM-01781).

Descriptors: *Mercury, *Poisoning, *Human pathology, *Wheat, Constraints, Fish, Exposure, Water pollution, Epidemics, Toxicity, Distribution, Regression analysis, Tissues, Urine, Ingestion, Analytical techniques, Laboratory tests, Mortality, Spectroscopy, Environmental effects, Laboratory animals.
Identifiers: *Methylmercury, *Iraq, Hair, Inhalation.

The effect on humans of the epidemic of methylmercury poisoning by contaminated grin in Iraq was studied. Urine, hair, tissue extracts and blood samples were examined for mercury content. Comparisons were made of infants, born and unborn, males and females, children and adults. Urine measurement for mercury concentration is of no value as a guide to the amount of mercury to which a person had been exposed. The concentration of methylmercury in the blood is the best indicator of the body burden in people exposed to methylmercury. The measurement of mercury content in the hair is the best means for determining the history of exposure. The rate of blood clearances from mercury contamination varies individually. Methylmercury is transferred into milk at a concentration equal to 3 per cent that of blood. The clearance of mercury from blood may be accelerated by oral administration of D penicillamine and thiol resin. Methylmercury was identified as the causative agent of poisoning. Constraints are outlines to avoid further epidemics. (Rowe-Vanderbilt)
W75-07797

EFFECT OF DIETARY SELENIUM AND AUTOXIDIZED LIPIDS ON THE GLUTATHIONE PEROXIDASE SYSTEM OF GASTROINTESTINAL TRACT AND OTHER TISSUES IN THE RAT,
California Univ., Davis. Dept. of Food Science and Technology.
K. Reddy, and A. L. Tappel.
Journal of Nutrition, Vol 104, No 8, p 1069-1078, August, 1974. 2 fig, 5 tab, 39 ref.

Descriptors: *Toxins, *Lipids, *Path of pollutants, *Animal metabolism, *Animal pathology, Environmental effects, Metals, Pollutants.
Identifiers: *Selenium.

The effect of dietary selenium on the detoxification of dietary peroxides via the glutathione peroxidase system was studied. Rats were fed Torula yeast-based selenium-deficient diets with either 15% fresh tocopherol-stripped corn oil or 15% autoxidized corn oil with a peroxide value of 692 mEq/kg. Rats fed these two diets were further divided into groups that were fed either 0 or 2 ppm selenium as selenomethionine. Body weight gain of the two groups of rats fed the autoxidized oil was significantly lower than that of the two groups fed fresh corn oil. The specific activity of glutathione peroxidase in various regions of the gastrointestinal tract, liver, blood and adipose from selenium-supplemented rats was significantly higher than in these tissues from the non-supplemented rats. In the rats not supplemented with selenium, blutathione peroxidase activity was significantly increased in the group fed autoxidized corn oil; increased activity was not observed in tissues of selenium-supplemented rats fed peroxides. With few exceptions, glutathione reductase activity was the same in tissues from each of the four dietary groups. Significantly more peroxide accumulated in the adipose of the peroxide-fed rats not supplemented with selenium than in the adipose of the other three groups. (Pulliam-Vanderbilt)
W75-07801

MICROBIOLOGICAL FOULING AND ITS CONTROL IN COASTAL WATER AND THE DEEP OCEAN,
Woods Hole Oceanographic Institution, Mass.
For primary bibliographic entry see Field 5A.
W75-07825

CLAVICEPS PURPUREA ON SPARTINA IN COASTAL MARSHES,
Gulf Coast Research Lab., Ocean Springs, Miss.
L. N. Eleuterius, and S. P. Meyers.
Reprinted from Mycologia, Vol LXVI, No 6, p 978-986, Nov.-Dec. 1974.

Descriptors: *Fungi, *Plant diseases, Marsh plants, Aquatic plants, *Marshes, *Parasitism, Ecosystems, Estuaries, Estuarine environment, Germination.
Identifiers: *Claviceps purpurea, *Spartina alterniflora, *Ergot, *Marsh grass, Marshland vegetation, Sclerotia, Infection intensity, Gulf Coast, Spartina patens, Spartina cynosuroides.

The ergot fungus Claviceps purpurea was found on Spartina alterniflora throughout Gulf and Atlantic coastal marshes. Spartina patens and Spartina cynosuroides were also collected bearing sclerotia of C. purpurea. Observations on the intensity of infection are reported, with notably heavy infection apparent in regions of spoil deposits. Conditions for germination of sclerotia are given along with some details of stromal morphology. Implications of C. purpurea in salt marsh ecosystems are discussed. (NOAA)
W75-07827

CONTRIBUTION OF FUNGI TO BIODEGRADATION OF SPARTINA AND OTHER BRACKISH MARSHLAND VEGETATION,
Louisiana State Univ., Baton Rouge. Dept. of Food Science.
S. P. Meyers.
Reprinted from Veroff. Inst. Meeresforsch. Bremerh. Suppl. 5. p 357-375, 1974. NOAA Grant OSG 2-35231.

Descriptors: *Biodegradation, *Microbial degradation, Marsh plants, *Fungi, Marshes, Molds, Yeasts, Aquatic plants, Plant diseases, Detritus, Ecosystems, Estuaries, Estuarine environment, Growth stages, Deterioration, Degradation(Decomposition), *Louisiana, *Coastal marshes.
Identifiers: *Spartina alterniflora, Marshland vegetation, *Marsh grass, Mycota, Fusarium, Cephalosporium, Lulworthia, Leptosphaeria, Fungal attack, Pichia spartinae, Kluyveromyces drosophilarum.

Transformation of marsh grass, Spartina alterniflora, to detritus is an initial energy transfer step in the coastal Louisiana estuarine ecosystem. Spartina is systematically attacked by a selective mycota throughout its development and decomposition. Fungi include, among others, species of Fusarium and Cephalosporium as well as representatives of the marine taxa Lulworthia and Leptosphaeria. Molds colonizing external plant surfaces differ from those isolated within the culm. Fungal attack is correlated with seasonal development and subsequent decomposition of the plant. A large yeast biomass, notably sporogenous taxa Pichia spartinae and Kluyveromyces drosophilarum, is prevalent in the oxidized portions of the Spartina rhizosphere and within the peripheral tissue and intercellular spaces of the culm. These species, with strong B-glucosidase activity, reach maximal populations during dieback of Spartina. A mutualistic yeast/mold association in turnover of plant substrates is suggested. (NOAA)
W75-07828

5D. Waste Treatment Processes

USE OF ENVIRONMENTAL ANALYSES ON WASTEWATER FACILITIES BY LOCAL GOVERNMENT,
Teknekron, Inc., Washington, D.C. Applied Research Div.
J. C. Fensterstock, and D. M. Speaker.
For sale by the Superintendent of Documents, U.S. Government Printing Office, Washington, D.C. 20402 Price $2.70. Environmental Protection Agency, Report EPA-600/5-74-015, July 1974. 193 p, 10 fig, 7 append. EPA Program Element HA095, R/T21 ART-06. Contract 68-01-1898.

Descriptors: Analysis, Evaluation, *Institutional constraints, Administrative agencies, Water resources development, On-site investigations, *Waste water treatment, *Local governments, *Treatment facilities, Environment.

Environmental analyses (assessments, impact statements, negative declarations, appraisals, etc.) on wastewater treatment facilities to be constructed in four case study areas were reviewed. Environmental analyses reflected Council of Environmental Quality (CEQ) and EPA guidelines in force during 1970 and 1972. Case examples were selected to ensure representation of jurisdictional patterns, settings, and availability of environmental analyses. The study reviewed decision-making processes of local and state governments. The study identified and detected several types of problems, both substantive and procedural. They were: inadequate environmental orientation of staffs; exclusion of lay public input; intra/inter-organizational conflicts; inadequate guidelines; and timing of environmental analyses for local consideration of consequences. Recommendations included: legislative changes; Federal funding for staff training programs; definitive guidelines for organizational structuring; and suggestions to increase lay public participation during the planning and decision-making processes. (Scherer-EPA)
W75-07360

INFLUENCES OF WASTEWATER MANAGEMENT ON LAND USE: TAHOE BASIN 1950-1972,
California Univ., Santa Cruz.
J. E. Pepper, and R. Jurgenson.
For sale by the Superintendent of Documents, U.S. Government Printing Office, Washington, D.C. 20402 Price $2.50. Environmental Protection Agency, Report EPA-600/5-74-019, October 1974. 167 p, 18 fig, 46 tab, 267 ref, 5 append. EPA Program Element IHA095, R/T 21AZC/03. Contract No. 68-01-1842.

Descriptors: *Treatment facilities, *Waste water treatment, *Land use, California, Nevada, Water quality control, *Management, Water pollution effects.
Identifiers: *Lake Tahoe basin(Nev-Calif).

Statistical analysis indicates that wastewater infrastructure projects have had a significant influence on the land use pattern in the Lake Tahoe Basin. Land use densities have increased immediately following the expansion of plant capacities in areas serviced by three of the four major wastewater treatment facilities. The subdivision approval rate of raw land was also found to be a function of anticipated treatment capacity. Federal and state water quality agencies played an active and central role in wastewater management programs designed to remove the threat of water pollution at Lake Tahoe. Cooperation among all levels of government led to expeditious resolution of the water quality problem in spite of the numerous geographic, economic and political constraints in the region. However, the provision of sewerage facilities also removed land development constraints. Local governments, acting without coordinated land use policies, permitted intensive land uses which could not have occurred with septic tank treatment. These increases in land use have subsequently produced major environmental problems in the Tahoe Basin. Thus, the singular focus on water quality led to unforeseen environmental impacts resulting from the land use changes made possible by the provision of extensive sewerage systems. (Kibby-EPA)
W75-07362

WATER QUALITY MODELING BY MONTE CARLO SIMULATION,
Maine Univ., Orono. Dept. of Civil Engineering.
For primary bibliographic entry see Field 5B.
W75-07386

STOCHASTIC WATER QUALITY CONTROL BY SIMULATION,
Texas Univ., San Antonio. Div. of Environmental Studies.
For primary bibliographic entry see Field 5B.
W75-07389

DYNAMIC PROGRAMMING FOR OPTIMAL CAPACITY EXPANSION OF WASTEWATER TREATMENT PLANTS,
Case Western Reserve Univ., Cleveland, Ohio. Systems Engineering Div.
M. A. Kaplan, and Y. Y. Haimes.
Water Resources Bulletin, Vol 11, No 2, p 278-293, April 1975. 4 fig, 1 tab, 13 equ, 15 ref.

Descriptors: *Waste water treatment, *Long-term planning, *Operation and maintenance, *Dynamic programming, Optimization, Costs, Capital costs, Scheduling, Methodology, Constraints, Equations, Computer programs, Mathematical models, Systems analysis, Treatment facilities, *Ohio.
Identifiers: *Capacity expansion, *Cost minimization, *Miami River basin(Ohio).

Presented is a dynamic programming procedure for the planning and operation of a wastewater treatment plant over a long period of time. In order to meet increased demands for wastewater treatment in the future, the expansion of existing plants is considered. Dynamic programming is used to determine the optimal schedule of expansion at each plant, simultaneously deriving an optimal operating policy (treatment level). The planning objective is to minimize the long-term cost of wastewater treatment, the present value of construction costs along with operating, maintenance, and replacement costs and effluent charges, if any. It is assumed that the capacity of any plant is monotonic non-decreasing and that the capacity of treatment plants may be expanded only by adding discrete increments. The optimal timing of capacity expansion at each plant depends on: (1) the shape of the projected wastewater demand function; (2) the interest rate used; (3) the locations and capacities of the facilities available; and (4) the rates of increase of the costs of construction, labor, chemicals, and electric power. An example illustrating the use of the procedure is presented. (Bell-Cornell)
W75-07390

AUTOMATED ANALYSIS OF INDIVIDUAL REFRACTORY ORGANICS IN POLLUTED WATER,
Oak Ridge National Lab., Tenn.
For primary bibliographic entry see Field 5A.
W75-07404

PROBLEMS AND POTENTIALS OF RECYCLING WASTES FOR AQUACULTURE,
Massachusetts Inst. of Tech., Cambridge. Sea Grant Project Office.
J. Kildow, and J. E. Huguenin.
Report No. MITSG 74-27, December 30, 1974, 170 p, 3 fig, 10 tab, 149 ref, 5 append. NOAA OSG NG-43-72.

Descriptors: *Aquaculture, *Effluents, *Wastes, *Sewage, *Recycling, Feeds, Waste disposal, Food chains, Carcinogens, Fishing, Seafood, Tolerances, Toxic tolerances, Public health, Contamination, Management analysis, Law, Food adulteration, Food contamination, Marketing, Product development.
Identifiers: Secondary sewage, Thermal waste, Thermal effluents, Delaney Amendment, Consumer attitudes, Product design.

The potentialities and problems of using thermal effluents and/or secondary sewage as inputs to a marine aquaculture system are described. The demand on Coastal Zones for both waste disposal and food production is complimented by the rising feed cost for raising fish and farm animals. In examining the advantages of a waste-food recycle system, current and foreseeable problems, especially those dealing with biological, social, political and legal matters, become more recognizable and solutions obtainable. Economic planning, institutions, consumer acceptance of waste-grown seafoods and marketing strategies are discussed. (NOAA)
W75-07416

THIRTY-FIVE YEARS OF CONTINUOUS DISCHARGE OF SECONDARY TREATED EFFLUENT ONTO SAND BEDS,
Rensselaer Polytechnic Inst., Troy, N.Y. Dept. of Environmental Engineering.
For primary bibliographic entry see Field 5B.
W75-07442

THE SEPTIC TANK'S ROLE IN LAND USE,
Oregon State Dept. of Environmental Quality, Portland.
R. D. Jackman.
In: Land and Water Use in Oregon; Seminar conducted by Oregon State University, Spring Quarter 1974, Water Resources Research Institute, Corvallis, Oregon, p 69-75, July 1974. 2 fig, 7 ref.

Descriptors: *Septic tanks, *Waste water treatment, *Administrative agencies, *Cities, City planning, Planning, Legislation, Legal aspects, Community development, Sewers, Sewage treatment, Disposal, Domestic wastes, Soil disposal fields, Water pollution sources, *Oregon.

The septic tank system, or subsurface sewage disposal system, is the method most commonly used for individual household disposal of domestic sewage where no community sewerage system is available. Until now, we have miserably failed to recognize the low-density limitations of septic-tank systems. They have been permitted in the past in high density suburban developments on tiny lots without adequate replacement areas and no real hope for sewers. The septic tank has been the excuse for procrastination in implementing strong land use planning and zoning in Oregon. The Legislature enacted 1973 House Bill 2786 to authorize the Department of Environmental Quality (DEQ) to develop rules and regulations for alternative systems to the septic tank system. DEQ is administering the subsurface sewage program of 25 counties by memoranda of agreement and of 11 counties directly through DEQ's five Regions and three Branch Offices. Oregon is beginning to plan ahead and not by default. DEQ works with developers and, for a fee, investigates the development for sewage disposal and provides a report so the applicant may have his subdivision approved and sell lots. (See also W75-07507) (Sims-ISWS)
W75-07514

REDUCTION OF WASTEWATER FOAMING BY PROCESS CHEMICAL SUBSTITUTION,
Virginia Polytechnic Inst. and State Univ., Blacksburg.
C. W. Randall.
Environmental Protection Agency, Washington, D.C., Technology Transfer Program. Paper presented at the Industry Seminars for Pollution Control, Atlanta, Georgia, September 25-26, 1973. pp 111-117, 3 tab.

Descriptors: *Industrial wastes, *Textiles, *Foaming, *Waste water treatment, *Activated sludge, *Aerated lagoons, Settling basin, Chemical properties, Aeration, Aerobic bacteria, Bacteria, Biological treatment, Flocculation, Sludge treatment.
Identifiers: Process chemical substitution.

One of the most commonly occurring problems associated with the treatment of textile dyeing and finishing wastewaters is excessive foaming. Excessive foaming may seriously affect the efficiency of wastewater treatment when biological processes, such as activated sludge, that require a large amount of agitation and aeration are used. A case history is given of a waste treatment situation wherein excessive foaming problems had to be solved by in-plant process chemical change before reliable operation and treatment could be accomplished. In an attempt to provide treatment in compliance with pollution control regulations, an extended aeration activated sludge system was designed and installed. As the biological solids grew in the lagoon, the major portion became entrapped in the generating foam, were floated to the surface, and eventually dumped in a circular pile on the apron surrounding the lagoon. The initial attempt at solving the problem consisted of hosing the biological solids back into the lagoon. The second solution attempted was the use of defoaming agents. To achieve a reduction of the foaming during wastewater treatment through process chemical substitution, it was necessary to reduce the high foaming materials in the dye bath. Not only did the chemical changes solve the spotting and foaming problems, they also decreased the chemical costs. (Poertner)
W75-07591

TREATING FINISHING WASTE CHEMICALLY AND BIOLOGICALLY,
Virginia Polytechnic Inst. and State Univ., Blacksburg.
C. W. Randall, and P. H. King.
American Dyestuff Reporter, June 1973, p 63-87. 8 fig, 2 tab, 7 ref.

Descriptors: *Textiles, *Dyes, *Color reactions, *Industrial wastes, *Biological treatment, *Waste water treatment, *Effluents, Coagulation, Flocculation, Organic wastes, Treatment facilities, Neutralization, Aerated logoons, Settling basin, Sludge, Dissolved oxygen.
Identifiers: Color removal, Textile manufacturing wastes.

Full-scale plant operating data are presented that illustrate the efficacy of a combined chemical-biological treatment process for removal of both color and organic matter from a concentrated textile dyeing and finishing waste. The basic premise in operating the waste treatment plant is that chemical treatment is best for color removal and biological treatment is optimum for reduction of organic matter. The combination of the two types of processes results in a high degree of treatment and the discharges of an effluent which is esthetically acceptable and does not cause a stress on the oxygen resources of the receiving stream. The operating data indicate that the use of excess lime as a primary coagulant for color removal is entirely satisfactory provided attention is given to the need for some chemical aid to condition the floc, and thus enable it to be separated out in a sedimentation basin. A long-chain anionic polyelectrolyte is the optimum floc conditioning chemical for lime floes. The performance of aerated lagoons for removal of organic matter from industrial wastes is temperature dependent. In designing these units, consideration should be given to this problem. (Poertner)
W75-07592

DEVICES FOR ONBOARD TREATMENT OF WASTES FROM VESSELS,
Thiokol Chemical Corp., Brigham City, Utah. Wasatch Div.
T. J. O'Grady, and P. E. Lakomski.
Environmental Protection Agency, Report EPA-670/2-74-091, December 1974. 117 p, 30 fig, 13 tab, 2 append. 1BB038; ROAP 21APK; Task 18. EPA Contract 68-01-0115.

Descriptors: *Sewage treatment, *Waste water treatment, Sludge disposal, Tertiary treatment, Ships, Recycling, *Filtration, Water quality standards, *Incineration, Chlorination, Cost analysis.
Identifiers: *Zero discharge waste treatment, Physical/chemical treatment, *Filter-incinerator, Waste water recycle.

A program involving the demonstration of a pleasure craft zero discharge, physical/chemical waste treatment system employing a unique filter-incinerator device was conducted. Extensive test data from laboratory and shipboard demonstration tests of the system are presented. Data on manufacture and installtion costs for the pleasure craft are also presented. The program demonstrated the ability to zero discharge waste and comply with the 23 June 1972 EPA no-discharge standard. A device combining two unit operations (filtration and incineration) will effectively and safely remove and destroy sewage sludge. With minor modifications, the pleasure craft waste treatment system will meet Coast Guard requirements for commercial vessels. (EPA)
W75-07594

RECOVERY AND REUSE OF COAGULANTS FROM TREATMENT OF WATER AND WASTEWATER,
Virginia Polytechnic Inst. and State Univ., Blacksburg. Dept. of Civil Engineering.
P. H. King, G. H. H. Chen, and K. R. Weeks, Jr.
Available from the National Technical Information Service, Springfield, Va. 22161 as PB-241 742, $4.25 in paper copy, $2.25 in microfiche. Virginia Water Resources Research Center, Blacksburg. VPI-WRRC-Bulletin 77, March 1975, 58 p, 20 fig, 1 tab, 29 ref. OWRT A-040-VA(3).

Descriptors: *Water treatment, Coagulation, Sludge disposal, *Waste water treatment, Water reuse, Aluminum, Iron compounds, Computer models, Capital costs, Metals, Chemical precipitation, Dewatering, Separation techniques.
Identifiers: Alum recovery, *Chemical reuse, *Coagulant recovery, *Iron salts.

In laboratory experiments, procedures were tested for economical recovery of hydrolyzed metallic coagulants used in treatment of polluted surface waters and selected wastewater discharges. Investigations focused on treatment systems using aluminum and iron salts as coagulants and precipitants. The experiments sought answers to how much coagulant can be recovered, what is the best means of separating and dewatering the remaining solids, and how effective is the recovered coagulant during reuse. An economic analysis estimated the capital cost of implementing the process, and determined what savings may be expected in chemical costs. A computer model was developed for determining the economic break-even point with reference to treatment plant capacity. Research findings indicate that recovery of both aluminum and iron salts is technically feasible, though the potential for aluminum recovery appears greater. Among additional benefits from the process described are large reductions in sludge volume and improved settleability and filterability of the remaining sludge. Laboratory tests indicate that the efficiency of recovered metal in coagulating suspended solids is not materially reduced from that of fresh coagulant.
W75-07600

CHARACTERIZATION AND TREATMENT OF URBAN LAND RUNOFF,
North Carolina Water Resources Research Inst., Raleigh.
N. V. Colston, Jr.
Environmental Protection Agency, Cincinnati, Ohio, Report EPA-670/2-74-096, December 1974. 157 p, 70 fig, 73 tab, 8 ref. 1BB034/ROAP:21-ATB/TASK:014. 11030 HJP.

Descriptors: Runoff, Surface drainage, *Water pollution sources, Flocculants, *Waste water treatment, Water quality, Coagulation, Computers, *Urban runoff, *Storm runoff, Storm water, *Urban drainage, Model studies, *North Carolina, Regression analysis.
Identifiers: Storm water management model, Durham(NC).

Urban land runoff from a 1.67 square-mile urban watershed in Durham North Carolina, was characterized with respect to annual pollutant yield. Regression equations were developed to relate pollutant strength to hydrograph characteristics. Urban land runoff was a significant source of pollution when compared to the raw municipal waste generated within the study area. On an annual basis, the urban runoff yield of COD was equal to 91 percent of the raw sewage yield, the BOD yield was equal to 67 percent, and the urban suspended solids yield was 20 times that contained in raw municipal wastes for the same area. Downstream water quality was controlled by urban land runoff 20 percent of the time. In urban drainage basins, investments in upgrading secondary municipal waste treatment plants without concomitant steps to moderate the adverse effects of urban land runoff are questionable in view of the apparent relative impact of urban land runoff on receiving water quality. (EPA)
W75-07607

EXTENDED AERATION SEWAGE TREATMENT IN COLD CLIMATES,
Environmental Protection Agency, College, Alaska. Arctic Environmental Research Lab.
H. J. Coutts, and C. D. Christianson.
Report EPA-660/2-74-070, December 1974. 80 p, 26 fig, 15 tab, 36 ref 1 BB044.

Descriptors: *Waste water treatment, *Sewage treatment, Biological treatment, Temperature, Activated sludge, Cold regions, Aeration, Subarctic, Alaska, Domestic sewage, Coliforms, Nutrients.
Identifiers: Extended aeration, Clarification, Organics.

In an effort to develop design criteria for biological treatment of low temperature domestic sewages, two parallel low temperature extended aeration units were designed and operated near Fairbanks, Alaska. The two units has exposed aeration basins utilizing submerged aerators and were differentiated by type of clarifier. One unit had conventional horizontal flow clarifier while the other had a modified upflow clarifier with tube settlers. The liquid temperature varied from 0C to 19C. In addition, 0.5 MGD subarctic, oxidation ditch and low temperature bench scale units were studied. Organic loading was the parameter most seriously affected by low temperatures. BOD removals above 80% at liquid temperatures below 7C could generally be maintained at loadings of 0.08 Kg BOD/Kg MLSS/Day or less. As in warmer climates, intentional sludge wastage was required. Low temperature solids accumulation rates indicated that standard wastage criterion of 0.5 Kg SS/Kg BOD is usually adequate. Other parameters investigated and reported were: (1) aeration for oxygen transfer and mixing; (2) comparative clarifier performance; (3) nutrient and total coliform removals. (EPA)
W75-07608

DEVELOPMENT OF AN APPROACH TO IDENTIFICATION OF EMERGING TECHNOLOGY AND DEMONSTRATION OPPORTUNITIES,
Battelle Columbus Labs., Ohio.
For primary bibliographic entry see Field 5G.
W75-07617

RESEARCH ON PIEZODIALYSIS - FOURTH REPORT,
Ionics, Inc., Watertown, Mass.
For primary bibliographic entry see Field 3A.
W75-07621

RESEARCH ON PIEZODIALYSIS - FIFTH REPORT,
Ionics, Inc., Watertown, Mass.
For primary bibliographic entry see Field 3A.
W75-07622

TUBULAR REVERSE OSMOSIS MEMBRANE RESEARCH,
Philco-Ford Corp., Newport Beach, Calif. Aeronutronic Div.
For primary bibliographic entry see Field 3A.
W75-07623

DEVELOPMENT OF IMPROVED PBI MEMBRANE SYSTEMS FOR WASH WATER RECYCLING AT PASTEURIZATION TEMPERATURES,
Celanese Research Co., Summit, N.J.
J. E. Poist, and F. S. Model.
Available from the National Technical Information Service, Springfield, Va 22161, as PB-236 939, $4.25 in paper copy, $2.25 in microfiche. Report INT-OSW-RDPR-74-995, July 1974. 52 p, 14 tab, 18 fig, 5 ref. OWRT Contract 14-30-3112.

Descriptors: *Reverse osmosis, *Membranes, *Separation techniques, Pressure, Semipermeable membranes, Filters, Filtration, Permeability, *Recycling, Waste water treatment, Desalination, *Water reuse.
Identifiers: *Wash water, Polybenzimidazole membranes, *Pasteurization, Sterilization, Urea rejection, Detergent rejection, Soap rejection, Lactic acid rejection, Spiral wound module, Flat sheet tests.

The important variables in preparation of asymmetric RO flat sheets of PBI membrane have been identified and optimized. The resultant preparative procedure has been scalled up to yield production sheets (11.5 in x 36 in x .008 in) of this PBI membrane. Finally, the large PBI sheets have been fabricated successfully in-house into prototype spiral wound modules capable of processing wash water feed at 75C. (OWRT)
W75-07624

OPERATION AND EVALUATION OF ALUMINUM TUBED MSF-VTE-HTE PILOT PLANT AT WRIGHTSVILLE BEACH TEST FACILITY,
Reynolds Metals Co., Richmond, Va.
For primary bibliographic entry see Field 3A.
W75-07625

DEVELOPMENT OF FORCED FLOW ELECTRODESALINATION SEPARATOR MATERIALS,
Aqua-Chem, Inc., Milwaukee, Wis.
For primary bibliographic entry see Field 3A.
W75-07626

REVERSE OSMOSIS FOR SPACECRAFT WASH WATER RECYCLING, MEMBRANE COUPON AND MODULE EVALUATIONS,
McDonnell-Douglas Astronautics Co. West, Huntington Beach, Calif.
G. W. Wells, and R. E. Shook.
Available from the National Technical Information Service, Springfield, Va. 22161, as PB-236 941, $6.25 in paper copy, $2.25 in microfiche. Report INT-OSW-RDPR-74-999, July 1974. 159 p, 31 fig, 31 tab, 5 ref. OWRT Contract 14-30-3062.

Descriptors: *Reverse osmosis, *Membranes, *Separation techniques, *Desalination, *Filtration, Water quality standards, Pollutant identification, Recycling, Water reuse, *Waste water treatment.
Identifiers: *Composite membranes, Cellulose acetate, Pasteurization, Sterilization, Ethyl cellulose, Plasma-formed membranes, Urea rejection, Lactic acid rejection, *Wash water.

An 80 gpd RO module was evaluated in a 12-week test program; it successfully recovered water meeting National Academy of Sciences and National Research Council standards from simulated space mission water. The results of the membrane coupon tests indicated that the composite membranes appeared to be most promising for use in spacecraft wash water recovery at 165F. (OWRT)
W75-07627

REVERSE OSMOSIS FOR SPACECRAFT WASH WATER RECYCLING, HIGH PRESSURE PUMP DEFINITION,
McDonnell Douglass Astronautics Co.-West, Huntington Beach, Calif.
For primary bibliographic entry see Field 8C.
W75-07628

MANAGEMENT, OPERATION AND MAINTENANCE BRACKISH WATER TEST FACILITY - ANNUAL REPORT 1973 ROSWELL, NEW MEXICO MAY 1, 1972 - OCTOBER 31, 1973,
Burns and Roe Construction Corp., Paramus, N.J.
For primary bibliographic entry see Field 3A.
W75-07629

APPRAISAL OF SALINE WATER IN OKLAHOMA AND ITS FUTURE DEVELOPMENT THROUGH DESALTING,
Oklahoma Water Resources Board, Oklahoma City.
For primary bibliographic entry see Field 3A.
W75-07630

ECONOMIC FEASIBILITY OF DESALTING SYSTEMS FOR MUNICIPAL WATER SUPPLY IN IOWA,
Dewild Grant Reckert and Associates, Des Moines, Iowa.
For primary bibliographic entry see Field 3A.
W75-07631

DEVELOPMENT OF A COAL-BASED SEWAGE-TREATMENT PROCESS.
Office of Coal Research, Washington, D.C.
For Sale by: Superintendent of Documents, U.S. Government Printing Office, Wash., D.C. 20402 - Price $5.75. Final Report, OCR Research and Development Report No. 55, (1975). 488 p, 56 fig, 77 tab. 14-01-0001-483.

Descriptors: *Waste water treatment, *Sewage treatment, Waste treatment, Suspended solids, *Filtration, *Incineration, Coals, Pilot plants, Tertiary treatment, Effluents, Design data, Treatment facilities, Costs, Industrial water.
Identifiers: *Coal-based sewage treatment, *Coal filtration, Chemical treatment.

Coal has been found to be valuable as a medium for sewage-treatment. Suspended solids can be removed by coal filtration, with partial removal of dissolved matter by physical and chemical reactions on coal. The coal-sewage wastes are incinerated directly with the recovery of heat. A coal-sewage treatment process has been developed through the pilot plant stage and is recommended for post, or 'tertiary' treatment of secondary sewage plant effluent and for industrial use. Design data and cost estimates are given. The average filter flow rate in the treatment of raw sewage is 0.35 gallons per square foot of filter per minute at 15 feet of head. At this flow rate, the tank area required for a given flow of sewage is approximately half that required for normal secondary treatment. The filter flow rate in the post-treatment of secondary treatment plant effluent is 1.0 gallon per square foot per minute at 16 feet of head. In the treatment of raw sewage the consumption of sized filter bed coal, including the filter bed residue, is approximately 9.20 tons per million gallons. In the post-treatment of secondary effluent the coal consumption is approximately 1.32 tons per million gallons.
W75-07632

EFFLUENT TREATMENT IS SPECIALIST'S WORK,
Van Luven Consultants Ltd., Montreal (Quebec).
R. Van Soest.
Pulp and Paper Canada, Vol 76, No 1, p 70-71, January 1975. 2 fig, 2 ref.

Descriptors: *Pulp wastes, *Waste water treatment, *Treatment facilities, Biological treatment, Pulp and paper industry, Canada, Foreign countries, North America, Europe, United States, Industrial wastes, Waste treatment, Pollution abatement, Water pollution control.
Identifiers: *Zurn-Attisholz process, Switzerland.

The acceptance by the Canadian pulp and paper industry of the Zurn-Attisholz process (a two-stage high-rate biological system developed by Cellulose Attisholz AG in Switzerland) for treating pulp and paper mill wastes, is discussed. A brief description of the process is included. It has as yet not been accepted in Canada, but has been used successfully in Europe and the U.S.A. (Sykes-IPC)
W75-07633

STUDY OF THE RELATION BETWEEN RESIDUAL SODA AND WATER-EXTRACTABLE COMPONENTS OF VACUUM DRUM WASHED KRAFT PULP AND OF REPULPED CORRUGATED CONTAINER EFFLUENT CHARACTERISTICS,
National Council of the Paper Industry for Air and Stream Improvement, Inc., New York.

For primary bibliographic entry see Field 5B.
W75-07634

DEWATERING OF SEWAGE SLUDGE (ENTWAESSERUNG VON KLAERSCHLAMM),
Lurgi Apparate-Technik G.m.b.H., Frankfurt am Main (West Germany).
G. Thomas.
English translations of Chemie-Ingenieur-Technik, Vol 46, No 11, p 471-476, 1974. 11 fig, 18 ref.

Descriptors: *Sewage sludge, *Sludge treatment, *Dewatering, *Reviews, Filtration, Centrifugation, Aluminum, Equipment, Sludge, Heat treatment, Chemicals, Lime, Iron compounds, Salts, Polyelectrolytes, Water purification, Water quality control, Incineration, Water pollution treatment, Filters, *Waste treatment.
Identifiers: Aluminum compounds.

This is a review of the status of sludge dewatering techniques, including thickening, vacuum and pressure filtration, and centrifugation. Also covered are the recovery of aluminum compounds and a comparison of dewatering devices. The need for conditioning of sludges through thermal treatment or addition of chemicals (lime, iron salts, aluminum salts, polyelectrolytes, ash) to attain good filtration and centrifugation properties shows how important it is not to view dewatering as a closed process, but rather as part of effluent and sludge treatment, including incineration. (Speckhard-IPC)
W75-07635

STUDIES ON COAGULATION TREATMENT OF SPENT WATER FROM PULPING PROCESS. (1). COAGULATION CHARACTERISTICS OF LIGNOSULFONATE (IN JAPANESE),
Tokyo Univ. (Japan).
M. Jo, G. Meshitsuka, and J. Nakano.
Japan Tappi, Vol 28, No 12, p 604-610, December 1974. 9 fig, 1 tab, 12 ref. English summary.

Descriptors: *Coagulation, *Bleaching wastes, *Pulp wastes, Pulp and paper industry, *Lignins, *Waste water treatment, Chlorination, Chlorine, Separation techniques, Water pollution sources, Chemical reactions, Chemical precipitation, Aluminum, Sulfates, Hydrogen ion concentration, Waste water treatment, Sulfonates, Foreign research.
Identifiers: *Japan.

The coagulation of lignin residues in pulp mill bleach plant effluents was studied, using a commercial lignosulfonate as a lignin model compound, which was purified by gel chromatography and treated with chlorine (alone or plus NaOH) under conditions simulating pulp bleaching. Chlorination markedly increased the number of functional groups (COOH, phenolic OH and CO) and decreased the molecular weight of the lignosulfonate. The presence of NaOH did not alter this result significantly, except to produce a larger number of phenolic OH groups. Aluminum sulfate at pH 4.5-5.0 effectively coagulated untreated, Cl-treated, and Cl/NaOH-treated lignosulfonate, but the efficiency of coagulation dropped markedly with increased amount of added Cl. The efficiency was better when coagulant was added before, rather than after, pH adjustment of the effluent. (Brown-IPC)
W75-07636

MEMBRANE PROCESSES FOR FRACTIONATION AND CONCENTRATION OF SPENT SULFITE LIQUORS,
Institute of Paper Chemistry, Appleton, Wis.
I. K. Bansal, and A. J. Wiley.
Tappi, Vol 58, No 1, p 125-130, January 1975. 3 fig, 6 tab, 11 ref.

Descriptors: *Sulfite liquors, *Pulp wastes, *Reverse osmosis, *Waste water treatment, Water pollution sources, Industrial wastes, Pulp and paper industry, Water pollution treatment, Membrane processes, Separation techniques, Organic compounds, Lignins, Sulfonates, Wastes, Waste treatment, Costs, Membranes, Filtration, Pressure, Temperature, Energy, Liquid wastes, Carbohydrates, Evaporation.
Identifiers: *Ultrafiltration, Cellulose acetate, Sugars, Reducing sugars, Wood sugars, Fractionation, Concentration, Calcium-base liquors.

Commercially available ultrafiltration and reverse osmosis modules equipped with cellulose acetate membranes were effectively employed to fractionate and concentrate marketable wood chemicals from spent sulfite liquors. Fractionation of calcium-base spent sulfite liquors was conducted in the ultrafiltration modules operated at 300 psig and elevated temperatures. The feed with 28% reducing sugar on solids was converted to permeates with 62% sugar on solids. Spent sulfite liquors were concentrated from 103 to 309 g/liter of solids with an overall average flux rate of 20.7 gal/sq ft/day. Concentration of the lower molecular weight organics (mainly reducing sugars) contained in the ultrafiltration permeates were carried to 206 g/liter of total solids, with use of reverse osmosis 'tight' membranes operated at 30-35 C and 700 psig. Recovery of wood sugars in the final concentrate averaged 87%, with an overall average flux rate of about 5.5 gal/sq ft/day. Under some conditions, it may be possible to directly utilize or market the ultrafiltration concentrate of the high molecular weight lignosulfonates at the 30% solids concentration and also the reverse osmosis concentrate containing reducing sugars at the 20% total solids level. A modified flow sheet is proposed for combining the membrane systems with evaporation units. Tables indicating projected cost savings and thermal energy savings obtained with such a combination are included. (Sykes-IPC)
W75-07638

PROSPECTS FOR THE APPLICATION OF REVERSE OSMOSIS IN THE PULP AND PAPER INDUSTRY (PERSPEKTIVY PUZITIA REVERZNEJ OSMOZY V CELULOZOPAPIERENSKOM PRIEMYSLE),
Vyskumny Ustav Papieru a Celulozy, Bratislava (Czechoslovakia).
L. Balhar.
Papir a Celuloza, Vol 29, No 11, p 257-259, 1974. 5 fig, 3 ref.

Descriptors: *Reverse osmosis, *Pulp wastes, *Bleaching wastes, *Waste water treatment, Separation techniques, Sulfite liquors, Industrial wastes, Water pollution sources, Osmotic pressure, Membrane processes, Pressure, Water quality control, Water pollution treatment, Membranes, Wastes, Waste treatment, Filtration, Strength, Liquid wastes, Laboratory tests, Foreign countries, Pulp and paper industry.
Identifiers: Czechoslovakia.

Reverse osmosis has shown promise in treating pulp and paper mill effluent. The reverse osmosis rate depends on the quality of the membrane and on the difference between the osmotic pressure of the thickened solution and the reverse osmosis pressure used. Laboratory data are given showing the osmotic pressure of spent pulping liquor solutions and bleachery effluents of various coneentration. The data show that the osmotic pressure of bleachery effluents increases with increasing concentration more steeply than that of effluents containing spent liquors and consequently that reverse osmosis pressures of 40 and 84 kg/sq cm would be needed to concentrate effluents containing spent liquor and bleachery effluent, respectively, considering that the reverse osmosis pressure has to be about 30 kg/sq cm higher than the osmotic pressure of the concentrated liquid to achieve an acceptably high rate. Since the use of high pressure is limited by membrane strength, the possibility of concentrating the bleachery effluent to only 25 g/liter and the use of more permeable membranes retaining only organic molecules are discussed. (Trubacek-IPC)
W75-07639

SPECIFIC WASTEWATER DISCHARGE AND SPECIFIC POLLUTION LOAD OF PAPER MILLS (UEBER DEN SPEZIFISCHEN ABWASSERANFALL UND DIE SPEZIFISCHE SCHMUTZFRACHT VON PAPIERFABRIKEN),
Technische Universitaet, Darmstadt (West Germany). Wasser- und Abwasserforschungsstelle.
For primary bibliographic entry see Field 5B.
W75-07640

GULF STATES (PAPER CORPORATIONS'S TUSCALOOSA, ALABAMA) NEW MULTI-HEARTH FURNACE WASTE TREATMENT SYSTEM,
Gulf States Paper Corp., Tuscaloosa, Ala.
R. R. Fuller.
Southern Pulp and Paper Manufacturer, Vol 37, No 12, p 22-25, December 1974. 4 fig, 2 tab.

Descriptors: *Pulp wastes, *Waste water treatment, *Tertiary treatment, *Incineration, Water purification, Pulp and paper industry, Organic compounds, Dewatering, Suspended solids, Oxygen demand, Color, Water pollution sources, Waste treatment, Industrial wastes, Effluents, Industrial plants, Treatment facilities, Oxygen, Oxidation, Biological treatment, Chemical precipitation, Coagulation, Aluminum, Sulfates.
Identifiers: Nichols-Herreshoff furnace, Aluminum sulfate, Chemical recovery.

The tertiary treatment system described includes a four-stage bio-oxidation system and an Elmco reactor-clarifier where alum mud is added to react with residual organic compounds. Insoluble materials are thickened and then dewatered. Dewatered solids are conveyed to a Nichols-Herreshoff multiple-hearth furnace where they are burned to an ash which is treated with sulfuric acid to recover alum mud for reuse. Effluent treatment system equipment vendors are listed. (Sykes-IPC)
W75-07641

JET AERATION IN DEEP CHANNEL CIRCLING CLARIFIER IS WORKING WELL FOR K-C MILL,
Kimtech, Inc., Neenah, Wis.
A. R. LeCompte.
Paper Trade Journal, Vol 159, No 1, p 1 (cover), 28-32, January 6, 1972. 8 fig, 9 ref.

Descriptors: *Pulp and paper industry, *Waste water treatment, *Aeration, *Treatment facilities, Industrial wastes, Water purification, Water pollution treatment, Channel flow, Channels, Jets, Sulfite liquors, Clays, Water pollution sources, Oxygenation, Water quality control, Air, Air entrainment, Pulp wastes, Pollution abatement, Pumps, *Massachusetts.
Identifiers: Starch, Clarifiers, Hemp, Paper mills, Kraft mills, NSSC pulp mills.

A jet aeration system was installed at Kimberly-Clark (K-C), Corporation's Lee, Massachusetts mill to treat pulp mill wastes from kraft and neutral sulfite cooks of hemp, and paper mill waste consisting of significant amounts of clay and starch (used in the production of coated business papers). The aeration equipment consists of seven 8-jet manifolds, each served by a submersible pump. Air is provided by two centrifugal blowers, and a ring manifold distributes the air around the channel. The jet manifold system is housed in a circular channel concentric with the final clarifier. In the aeration process, a primary fluid is directed through a nozzle into a mixing chamber. Air enters the chamber and is sheared into minute bubbles when entrained in the primary fluid. The combined mixture is jetted into the aeration channel, which

forms a plume that travels horizontally while spreading through the flow before rising to the surface. Capacities of the system are outlined. (Sykes-IPC)
W75-07642

ENVIRONMENTAL PROTECTION AND ECONOMIC ASPECTS OF INTERNAL WATER CIRCULATION SYSTEMS IN THE PULP AND PAPER INDUSTRY (UMWELTFREUNDLICHE UND WIRTSCHAFTLICHE ASPEKTE INNERER WASSERKREISLAUEFE IN DER PAPIER- UND ZELLSTOFF-INDUSTRIE),
W. Lutz.
Das Oesterreichische Papier, Vol 11, No 9, p 19-22, September 1974. 2 fig.

Descriptors: *Pulp wastes, *Pulp and paper industry, *Water reuse, *Costs, *Water conservation, Waste water treatment, *Pollution abatement, Water consumption(Except consumptive use), Economics, Effluents, Industrial wastes, Reclaimed water, Water purification, Recirculated water, Treatment facilities.
Identifiers: *Attisholz process, Ruthner clarifier.

Recirculated water is increasingly used to reduce water consumption in the paper industry, and some of its aspects are discussed. A diagram is given of the Attisholz process for the water treatment system of sulfite pulp mills, and a sketch is included of the Ruthner rapid clarifier for purifying effluent. Some statistics on the costs of different purification processes for the effluents of various types of paper mills are presented. (Ward-IPC)
W75-07643

MERCURY CLEANUP ROUTES--I,
M. D. Rosenzweig.
Chemical Engineering, Vol 82, No 2, p 60-61, January 20, 1975. 2 fig.

Descriptors: *Mercury, *Waste water treatment, *Pollution abatement, Activated carbon, Ion exchange, Water pollution sources, Industrial wastes, Chemical wastes, Metals, Water pollution control, Waste treatment, Foreign research, Separation techniques.
Identifiers: Chlor-alkali plants, *Akzo TMR process, *BMS process, *TNO process.

Brief descriptions are given of processes developed by Billingsfors Bruks AB. (Sweden), the Organization for Applied Scientific Research (TNO) in the Netherlands, and Akzo Zout Chemie Nederland B.V. (Netherlands), for removing mercury from waste waters, particularly waste waters from chlor-alkali plants. Both the Billingsfors Bruks BMS process and the TNO process use specially activated carbons to absorb mercury, while the Akzo process uses a resin in which thiol groups are attached to a chemically inert and mechanically strong matrix (a macroporous styrene/divinylbenzene copolymer). Flow diagrams of the Billingsfors BMS and the Akzo Imae TMR processes are included. (See also W75-07647) (Witt-IPC)
W75-07646

MERCURY CLEANUP ROUTES -- II,
N. R. Iammartino.
Chemical Engineering, Vol 82, No 3, p 36-37, February 3, 1975. 2 fig, 1 tab.

Descriptors: *Mercury, *Waste water treatment, *Pollution abatement, Water pollution sources, Industrial wastes, Chemical wastes, Metals, Waste treatment, Wastes, *Separation techniques, Water pollution control, Iron, Oxidation, Chemical precipitation.
Identifiers: *Re-elixirization process, Japan, Magnetic ferrites.

Brief descriptions are given of three commercial techniques, developed by Nippon Electric Co. (Tokyo, Japan), Georgia-Pacific Corp. (Bellingham, Washington), and FMC Corp. (New York), for removing mercury from waste waters. Nippon's batch orcontinuous process purges mercury and other heavy metals from various effluents such as offgas-scrubbing liquor from municipal waste incineration, and waste water from electroplating of metals. The other two processes remove mercury from chlor-alkali plant wastes. (See also W75-07646) (Witt-IPC)
W75-07647

BIODEGRADATION BY THE ACTIVATED SLUDGE SYSTEM OF STEAM PROCESS WATER IN THE TIMBER INDUSTRY,
M. Reinbold, and M. Mallevialle.
Water Research, Vol 9, No 1, p 87-93, January 1975. 7 fig, 7 tab, 7 ref.

Descriptors: *Waste water treatment, *Activated sludge, *Biodegradation, *Wood wastes, Steam, Organic matter, Biochemical oxygen demand, Chemical oxygen demand, Water pollution sources, Laboratory tests, Nitrogen, Phosphorus, Nutrients, Color, Phenols, Bacteria, Drying, *Industrial wastes, Waste treatment, Pollution abatement, Pine trees, Carbohydrates, Organic loading, Biological treatment, Drying, Economics.
Identifiers: *Plywood industry, *Veneer industry, Total organic carbon, Polysaccharides, Tannins, Humus, Pentosans, Sugars, Corynebacterium.

Waste water resulting from the steam drying of pinewood peeler logs contains a large amount of organic matter. Treatments by coagulation or flocculation are inadequate for removing this material, and incineration is too expensive. Laboratory studies are described which show that this material can be removed by the activated sludge process. If sufficient N and P nutrient elements are added, a high level of efficiency is achieved: 98% of the 5-day BOD, 70% of the COD, and 66% of the total organic carbon are removed. Most of the remaining nonbiodegradable products, which are responsible for the color of the water, are polysaccharide compounds. During treatment, the tannins, pseudo-humic matter, phenols, polyphenols, and certain pentosans and simple sugars disappear completely. Biological purification is effected predominantly through the action of bacteria of the genus Corynebacterium. (Witt-IPC)
W75-07649

THE AKZO PROCESS FOR THE REMOVAL OF MERCURY FROM WASTE WATER,
Akzo Zout Chemie Nederland B.V., Hengelo (Netherlands).
G. J. De Jong, and C. J. N. Rekers.
Journal of Chromatography, Vol 102, p 443-450, December 31, 1974. 5 fig, 1 tab.

Descriptors: *Mercury, *Waste water treatment, *Ion exchange, *Pollution abatement, Oxidation, Hydrogen ion concentration, Filtration, Chlorine, Sodium compounds, Iron compounds, Activated carbon, Bonding, Water pollution sources, Industrial wastes, Metals, Water pollution control, Waste treatment, Foreign research, Resins, Separation techniques, Wastes, Chemical wastes.
Identifiers: *Akzo process, Chlorine compounds, Sodium hypochlorite, Imac TMR ion exchange resin, Chlor-alkali plants.

A Dutch process for the removal of mercury from waste water, particularly from chlor-alkali plants, consists of (1) oxidation of the metallic mercury to ionic mercury with chlorine or sodium hypochlorite, (2) control of the waste water pH at about 3 to keep iron in solution, (3) filtration in a sand or cloth filter to remove solids, (4) dechlorination of the liquid with activated carbon, and (5) removal of the mercury on the Imae TMR ion-exchange resin. The latter is a polymeric mercaptan in which thiol groups are attached to a chemically and mechanically inert matrix. The affinity of this thiol resin towards mercury is very high; the strength of the resin-mercury bond is comparable to that of the mercury-sulfur bond in HgS. The resin can be regenerated with concentrated HCl. The process guarantees a low coneentration of mercury (less than 5 ppb) in the effluent even under strongly fluctuating conditions. The mercury is recycled into the electrolysis process. The Akzo process is competitive with other processes for the removal of mercury from waste water. (Witt-IPC)
W75-07658

CONSIDERATIONS FOR ANALYSIS OF INFILTRATION-INFLOW,
National Environmental Research Center, Cincinnati, Ohio. Advanced Waste Treatment Research Lab.
D. J. Cesareo, and R. Field.
September 16, 1974. 27 p, 2 tab, 1 fig, 11 ref.

Descriptors: *Inflow, *Infiltration, *Sewerage, *Waste water disposal, *Water pollution control, *Combined sewers, Sewers, Leakage, Maintenance, Operation and maintenance, Municipal wastes, Water pollution control, Overflow, Engineering design, Sanitary engineering, Environmental engineering.

The impacts of raw wastewater diversion at treatment facilities, the incidence and duration of sewage overflows, and adverse sanitary and health conditions and inconveniences caused by surcharged sewers and flooding constitute serious problems in many urban areas. This necessitates careful operation of waste water collection and treatment facilities and reduction of infiltration and inflow to public and private sewer systems. Infiltration and inflow countermeasures can be divided into two parts; prevention of excessive extraneous flows, and correction of conditions already imposed on existing sewer systems. Prevention of excessive infiltration into new sewer systems depends on effective design; choice of materials; rigid limitations on infiltration allowances; and diligent inspection and testing of construction projects. Correction of excessive infiltration in existing sewer systems involves evaluation and interpretation of sewage flow conditions to determine the presence and extent of the problem, the location and gauging of such infiltration flows, a cost-effective engineering evaluation to optimize corrective methods, and the elimination of these flows by various repair and replacement methods. (Poertner)
W75-07664

CONTROL OF FILAMENTOUS MICROORGANISMS DURING ACTIVATED SLUDGE TREATMENT OF A COMPLEX INDUSTRIAL WASTE,
Virginia Polytechnic Inst. and State Univ., Blacksburg.
C. W. Randall, P. H. King, and R. C. Hoehn.
Paper presented at the WWEMA Industrial Water and Pollution Control Conference and Exposition, Conrad Hilton Hotel, Chicago, Illinois, March 14-16, 1973. 27 p, 11 fig, 3 tab, 5 ref.

Descriptors: *Activated sludge, *Sludge treatment, *Waste water treatment, *Microorganisms, *Oil wastes, Industrial wastes, Effluent, Treatment facilities.
Identifiers: Activated Sludge treatment, Filamentous microorganisms, Filamentous overgrowth, Nylon.

Although highly treatable, waste finishing oil from a nylon manufacturing process, when added to wastewater flow from biological treatment, has some unusual properties that cause the activated sludge system to repeatedly become filamentous. Activated sludge treatment of the wastewater without finishing oils did not produce filaments. Sludge bulk due to overgrowth of the filamentous

forms caused systems failure. Investigation revealed that sludge bulking was stimulated by three different conditions. A small deficiency of nitrogen stimulated proliferation and was prevented by adding both nitrogen and phosphorus to the waste prior to treatment. A mixed liquor pH below 6 produced bulking and subsequent wide fluctuation in pH values. Although pH adjustments were made, the sludge still bulked when the dissolved oxygen concentration dropped below 1 mg/l. Bulking was caused by the activated sludge flocs becoming brush-shaped due to low oxygen tension. Improvment in the settling properties occurred when the dissolved oxygen concentration was raised above 1 mg/l. Also, the 'food-to-microorganisms' ratio affected the settling properties. BOD5 values above .9 should not be used. Once these factors were controlled the substrate removal rate was greater than typical domestic sewage values, oxygen requirements were moderate, and sludge production was low. (Poertner)
W75-07666

LINCOLN TRAIL AREA DEVELOPMENT DISTRICT COMPREHENSIVE WATER AND SEWER PLAN.
Schimpeler-Corradino Associates, Louisville, Ky.
Lincoln Trail Area Development District, Elizabethtown, Kentucky, June 1973. 538 p, 43 tab, 26 fig, 7 append.

Descriptors: *Planning, *Land use, *Sewerage, *Water supply development, *Urbanization, *Kentucky, Long-term planning, Comprehensive planning, Water resources development, Regional development, Regional analysis, Cities, Water quality control.
Identifiers: *Lincoln Trail Area Development District.

The planning philosophy of Lincoln TRAIL Area Development is based on an understanding that land use patterns are shaped by the availability of water and sewer utilities. The importance of utilities to an industry and/or commercial location must be considered in developing an effective program, as well as the realization that there exists a minimum population density upon which water and/or sewer facilities can be established. Detailed analyses of existing facilities, administrative jurisdictions, water resources, capabilities and quality, and fiscal resources constitute elements for this planning process. There are nine objectives to be fulfilled to make a water/sewer plan effective: (1) provide a realistic projection of socio-economic factors; (2) relate land use planning to water and sewer development; (3) provide orderly development of all water and sewer systems; (4) establish optimum service areas; (5) make best use of public money; (6) provide a definitive guide, for regional review, for water and sewer; (7) establish a system of priorities for water and sewer facilities; (8) provide annual estimates of funds from federal agencies; and (9) provide estimated total annual capital requirements for each area development district. The allocation of scare resources toward the development of water and sewer systems is a fundamental part of the planning for utilities. (Poertner)
W75-07667

GREATER TAMPA UTILITY GROUP-STANDARD UTILITIES LOCATION,
Greater Tampa Utility Group, Fla.
For primary bibliographic entry see Field 8A.
W75-07668

SECONDARY TREATMENT AND BEST PRACTICABLE TECHNOLOGY,
Kalamazoo Dept. of Public Works, Mich.
D. H. Swets.
Paper presented at APWA International Congress and Equipment Show, Denver, Colorado, September 18, 1973. 6 p.

Descriptors: *Federal Water Pollution Control Act, *Tertiary treatment, *Waste water treatment, *Sewage treatment, Sludge, Domestic waste, Effluents, Water pollution control, Treatment facilities, Water quality control, Water Quality Act, Water quality standards, Waste water disposal, Waste water(Pollution), Sanitary engineering.
Identifiers: *Secondary treatment, *Effluent quality, *Best practicable technology, Combined sewers, Wastewater effluent.

Enforcing the Federal Water Pollution Control Act Amendments of 1972 is directly linked to the true meaning of the terms 'secondary treatment' and 'best practicable technology'. Although defined as 'treatment of wastewater by biological methods after primary treatment by sedimentation', secondary treatment as practiced today can achieve a wide variety of degrees in removal of pollutants depending on the extent, efficiency, and effectiveness of the facilities provided. Using suspended values of 15 mg/l of BOD5 and 20 mg/l suspended solids, most plants already constructed would not be adequate. Plants using the trickling filter and activated sludge process can be expected to produce, consistently, only 70% to 90% removal instead of the proposed 92% removal. Regulations now state an intent to achieve 85% removal. Secondary treatment plants may be upgraded by construction of additional aeration or trickling filtering capacity and final settling facilities. Effluent standards applicable to wastewater treatment using best practicable technology will become more restrictive. It appears that the ultimate oxygen demand (considering the ultimate BOD, ammonia nitrogen concentration and dissolved oxygen in the effluent) will be a factor, as will the chemical oxygen demand. More testing and analysis of wastewater effluent components will be necessary. (Poertner)
W75-07669

A BIOLOGICAL ABSORPTION SYSTEM FOR THE TREATMENT OF COMBINED SEWER OVERFLOW,
Envirex, Inc., Milwaukee, Wis. Environmental Sciences Div.
R. W. Agnew, C. A. Hansen, O. F. Nelson, W. H. Richardson. and L. Holt.
Paper presented at 1974 International Public Works Congress and Equipment Show, Toronto, Ontario, Canada, September 16, 1974. 40 p, 12 fig, 8 tab.

Descriptors: *Biological treatment, *Sewage treatment, *Combined sewers, *Overflow, Lake Michigan, Water quality control, Water pollution control, Sludge, Storm runoff, Water pollution, Waste water treatment, Wisconsin.
Identifiers: *Sewer overflow, Kenosha(Wisconsin), Contact stabilization, Biological absorption.

The Kenosha Demonstration project has demonstrated the engineering feasibility of utilizing a high rate biological absorption process to treat combined sewer overflow. Essentially a high rate contact stabilization process, the project consisted of the construction, operation, and evaluation of a 20 MGD treatment system added to an existing 23 MGD conventional activated sludge plant. During 46 overflow events, 164.52 million gallons of potential combined sewer overflow were treated. Results indicate an average removal of 93% in suspended solids, 83% total BOD5, and 68% of dissolved BOD5. On the basis of weighted mean concentrations, raw and final, of measured parameters it was determined that the systems concept was sound and that effluent quality was approximately equivalent to conventional secondary treatment. Stabilization time was shown to adversely affect effluent quality. In all cases, the time of storage in biosolid reservoirs should be limited to five days or less. In the new treatment systems built in future years, it is recommended that the mixed liquor suspended solids range between 1700-5000 mg/l, contact time and between 10-20 minutes, reaeration time between 1-3 hours, and one-third of the dissolved oxygen supply be allocated to the contact basin and two-thirds to the stabilization process. (Poertner)
W75-07678

POLYMER AIDED ALUM COAGULATION OF TEXTILE DYEING AND FINISHING WASTES,
Virginia Polytechnic Inst. and State Univ., Blacksburg.
W. C. Kreye, P. H. King, and C. W. Randall.
Paper presented at 27th Annual Industrial Wastes Conference, Purdue University, West Lafayette, Indiana, May, 1972. 22 p, 10 fig, 2 tab, 7 ref.

Descriptors: *Textiles, *Waste water treatment, *Polymers, *Coagulation, *Dyes, Flocculation, Aluminum, Water quality control, Industrial wastes, Color, Virginia, Sludge, Water pollution control.
Identifiers: *Alum, Textile dyeing waste, Polyelectrolytes, United Piece Dye Works, Bluefield(Virginia).

A chemical treatment system utilizing (either) alum (alone or in combination) with a properly selected polyelectrolyte is highly efficient in removing a high percentage of color from a representative textile dyeing and finishing waste, as well as being effective in removing a substantial fraction of organic matter. Polymer usage decreases the alum demand to below 270 ppm. Flocculation time decreases to two to three minutes and settling time to five to ten minutes depending upon the polymer used. Sludge volume was in the two percent range for all systems. Removal of color and organic matter was largely independent of the polymer used. Polymer conditioning alleviates the problems associated with a voluminous, poorly settling floc and results in an overall process that may well find increasing application in the context of increasingly rigid water quality standards. (Poertner)
W75-07682

PLASTIC PIPE IN COLDER CLIMATES,
Winnipeg Waterworks, Waste and Disposal Div. (Manitoba).
For primary bibliographic entry see Field 5F.
W75-07683

CHEMICAL CONTROL OF ROOTS,
Sacramento County Dept. of Public Works, Calif.
N. R. Townley.
Septermber 1973. 19 p, 3 fig, 1 tab, 2 ref.

Descriptors: *Root systems, *Sewerage, *Clogging, *Chemcontrol, *Root development, *Sewers, Pipelines, Herbicides, California, Maintenance, Public utilities, Operation and maintenance, Pipes, Waste water disposal.
Identifiers: *Roots, *Root kills, Metham, Dichlobenil, Endothal, Sacramento(California).

Removal of root growth from sewer collection systems constitutes a significant portion of the sewer maintenance budget. Although effective when used at scheduled intervals, mechanical cleaning does not inhibit root regrowth. Chemicals, when properly used, will kill the roots and discourage their return. From preliminary laboratory tests, the chemicals Metham, Dichlobenil, and Endothal emerged as candidates for field testing. From 1969 to 1972, about 447,000 feet of 6 in. diameter vitrified clay pipe were treated at a current cost figure of 16 cents per foot. Down-stream manholes were blocked with inflatable plugs and one gallon of chemical for each one hundred gallons of water was dumped into an upstream manhole. After two years, post-television inspection of treated lines indicated positive results. Tabulations from the years 1966 to 1972 give data on the steady decline in root stoppages, mainly since 1969, Metham proved to be an effective root killer, capable of killing beyond the point of actual treat-

ment. Dichlobenil also kills roots and acts as an inhibitor for regrowth. To achieve the average root kill of 75%, careful consideration must be given to application procedures. (Poertner)
W75-07685

LIMESTONE AND LIMESTONE-LIME NEUTRALIZATION OF ACID MINE DRAINAGE,
Environmental Protection Agency, Rivesville, W. Va. Crown Mine Drainage Control Field Site.
R. C. Wilmoth.
For sale by the Superintendent of Documents, U. S. Government Printing Office, Washington, D. C. 20402 Price $1.40. Environmental Protection Agency, Cincinnati, Ohio, Report EPA-670/2-74-051, June 1974. 91 p, 15 fig, 47 tab, 32 ref.

Descriptors: *Limestone, *Mine drainage, Iron, *Calcium hydroxide, Excavation, *Neutralization, *Waste water treatment, Sludge, Cost comparisons, Water pollution control, Surface drainage, *West Virginia.
Identifiers: *Coal mine drainage, *Ferric iron.

The critical parameters affecting neutralization of ferric-iron acid mine waters were characterized in comparative studies using hydrated lime, rock-dust limestone, and a combination of the two as neutralizing agents. The advantages and disadvantages of each of these neutralizing agents were noted. On the ferric-iron test water, combination limestone-lime treatment provided a better than 25-percent reduction in materials cost as compared to straight lime or limestone treatment. Significant reduction in sludge production was noted by the use of rock-dust limestone and by the use of combination treatment as compared to hydrated-lime treatment. Emphasis on optimizing limestone utilization efficiencies resulted in an increase from approximately 35- to 50-percent utilization. Studies using limestone that had been ground to pass a 400-mesh screen resulted in utilization efficiencies near 90 percent. (EPA)
W75-07688

MINE DRAINAGE POLLUTION CONTROL DEMONSTRATION GRANT PROCEDURES AND REQUIREMENTS,
NUS Corp., Rockville, Md.
For primary bibliographic entry see Field 5G.
W75-07690

URBAN STORMWATER MANAGEMENT AND TECHNOLOGY: AN ASSESSMENT,
Metcalf and Eddy, Inc., Palo Alto, Calif.
J. A. Lager, and W. G. Smith.
Available from the National Technical Information Service, Springfield, Va. 22161, as PB-231 345, $3.25 in paper copy, $2.25 in microfiche. Environmental Protection Agency, Cincinnati, Ohio. Report EPA-670/2-74-040, December 1974. 447 p, 83 fig, 85 tab, 308 ref. 1BB034/ROAP 21ASZ/Task 1 EPA Contract 68-03-0179.

Descriptors: Disinfection, Drainage, Water pollution, *Waste water treatment, *Sewage treatment, Surface runoff, Runoff, Sewage, Water quality, Cost analysis, Storage tanks, *Storm sewers, *Overflow, *Combined sewers, Hydraulics, *Mathematical models, Remote control, *Urban runoff, *Storm water.
Identifiers: Physical-chemical treatment.

A comprehensive investigation and assessment of promising, completed, and ongoing urban stormwater projects, representative of the state-of-the-art in abatement theory and technology, has been accomplished. The results, presented in textbook format, provide a compendium of project information on management and technology alternatives within a framework of problem identification, evaluation procedures, and program assessment and selection. Essentially every metropolitan area of the United States has a stormwater problem, whether served by a combined sewer system (approximately 29 percent of the total sewered population) or a separate sewer system. However, the tools for reducing stormwater pollution, in the form of demonstrated processes and devices, do exist and provide many-faceted approach techniques to individual situations. These tools are constantly being increased in number and improved upon as a part of a continuing nationwide research and development effort. The most promising approaches to date involve the integrated use of control and treatment systems with an areawide, multidisciplinary perspective. (EPA)
W75-07692

EVALUATION OF ALTERNATIVE METHODS FOR FINANCING MUNICIPAL WASTE TREATMENT WORKS,
Meta Systems, Inc., Cambridge, Mass.
R. J. deLucia, L. M. Koppel, D. F. Luecke, S. Robinson, and P. Schaefer.
Available from the National Technical Information Service, Springfield, Va. 22161, as PB-241 045, $7.25 in paper copy, $2.25 in microfiche. Environmental Protection Agency, Report EPA-600/5-75-001, March 1975. 190 p, 11 fig, 371 tab, 52 ref, 6 append. EPA Contract 68-01-2411.

Descriptors: *Waste water treatment, *Treatment facilities, *Financing, Costs, Evaluation, *Alternative costs, Projects, Programs.

This is part of a continuing investigation by the EPA of alternative financing programs for treatment plant facilities undertaken in response to Section 317 of The Water Pollution Control Act Amendments of 1972. Findings and recommendations regarding alternative financing programs are presented. Current programs are reviewed, criteria for the evaluation of financing programs are described and some differences of current programs in light of these criteria are discussed. Important features of alternative financing programs are discussed and an analysis of features that could be changed to improve program preference according to the criteria is presented. (EPA)
W75-07693

SYSTEM ALTERNATIVES IN OXYGEN ACTIVATED SLUDGE,
District of Columbia Dept. of Environmental Services, Washington.
J. B. Stamberg, D. F. Bishop, S. M. Bennett, and A. B. Hais.
Available from the National Technical Information Service, Springfield, Va. 22161, as PB-241 310, $4.25 in paper copy, $2.25 in microfiche. Environmental Protection Agency, Cincinnati, Ohio. Report EPA-670/2-75-008, April 1975. 59 p, 22 fig, 6 tab, 26 ref. 1BB043 ROAP 21-ASR Task-015 68-01-0162.

Descriptors: Oxygen, Sedimentation, *Waste water treatment, *Activated sludge, Centrifuges, Dewatering, Filtration, Suspended solids, *Settling basins, Alternative planning, Aerobic bacteria.
Identifiers: *Oxygen activated sludge.

An oxygen activated sludge system with co-current contacting of oxygen and mixed liquor in a plug flow reactor was operated on District of Columbia primary effluent during a two-year period over a wide range of loading (F/M 0.26 to 2.0) with Solids Retention Times (SRT) from 2.0 to 13.0 days at the EPA-DC Pilot Plant. The reactor detention times varied from a nominal 1.5 to over 3.0 hours with the mixed liquor suspended solids between 2700 and 8100 mg/l. The clarifier overflow rates varied between 300 and 1960 gpd/ft2 depending on the mixed liquor particle shape (the intensity of filamentous growth) and water temperature. The average underflow solids varied between 1.0% and 2.4% depending on clarifier volume and recycle rate. The total solids production varied from 0.35 to 1.0 pound of solids produced per pound of BOD5. The undigested underflow solids thickened to 4-5% by either gravity or air floatation without chemical additives and dewatered by vacuum filtration to 8-12% with polymers and 13-21% with lime and ferric chloride addition. (EPA)
W75-07695

PILOT SCALE TREATMENT OF WINE STILLAGE,
California State Dept. of Agriculture, San Francisco. Wine Advisory Board.
E. D. Schroeder.
Available from the National Technical Information Service, Springfield, Va 22161 as PB-240 996, $5.75 in paper copy, $2.25 in microfiche. Environmental Protection Agency, Corvallis, Oregon. Report EPA-660/2-75-002, February 1975. 118 p, 25 fig, 42 tab, 22 ref. 1BB037. 12060 HPC.

Descriptors: *Centrifugation, *Industrial wastes, *Waste identification, *Biological treatment, Separation techniques, *Waste water treatment, Farm wastes, Pilot plants, *Aerobic treatment, Lagoons.
Identifiers: *Winery waste water, Anaerobic packed towers.

Pilot and laboratory scale studies were run on aerobic and anaerobic biological treatment of winery stillage over a two year period. The pilot scale studies included work with aerobic lagoons and anaerobic packed towers. Laboratory systems studied were aerobic reactors without recycle and batch fed anaerobic processes. Because suspended solids removal was a key factor in successful biological treatment, centrifugation, detartration, coagulation and flocculation, and combinations of these methods were included in the studies. Centrifugation was the best method of removing solids prior to biological treatment. Solids removal in combination with an aerobic treatment process can be expected to produce final filtrate chemical oxygen demands of about 700 mg/l and a final filtrate BOD of about 75 mg/L. Anaerobic processes studied did not operate well but produced effluents with chemical oxygen demands of the order of 4000 mg/L. (EPA)
W75-07699

THE EFFECTS OF AIR AND WATER POLLUTION CONTROLS ON SOLID WASTE GENERATION, 1971-1985, EXECUTIVE SUMMARY,
Stone (Ralph) and Co., Inc., Los Angeles, Calif.
For primary bibliographic entry see Field 5B.
W75-07705

FEASIBILITY OF 5 GPM DYNACTOR/MAGNETIC SEPARATOR SYSTEM TO TREAT SPILLED HAZARDOUS MATERIALS,
Industrial Bio-Test Labs., Inc., Northbrook, Ill.
R. G. Sanders, S. R. Rich, and T. G. Pantazelos.
Available from the National Technical Information Service, Springfield, Va. 22161, as PB-241 080, $3.75 in paper copy, $2.25 in microfiche. Environmental Protection Agency, Cincinnati, Ohio, Report EPA-670/2-75-004, April 1975. 32 p, 11 fig, 4 tab, 3 ref. 68-01-0123.

Descriptors: Design, Operations, *Water treatment, *Activated carbon, Water pollution treatment, *Separation techniques, Neutralization, Chemical precipitation, *Waste water treatment.
Identifiers: Hazardous materials spill control, Hazardous chemical spills, Dynamic reactors, *Magnetic separators.

Design and operating details are given for a new type of continuous flow thin-film, gas-liquid-particulate contact device called the Dynactor. The device is used as a continuous flow short-time contact reactor to effectively decontaminate water contaminated with spilled hazardous materials. The decontamination is effectively achieved by one or more processes involving oxidation,

neutralization, precipitation or adsorption on powdered carbon. Contaminated water is processed by the pilot plant model Dynactor at 100 psi and at a rate of 5 gpm; stoichiometric quantities of decontaminating agents in the form of gases, liquids, slurries or powders are metered into the continuously flowing liquid configuration. The device is portable, lightweight polypropylene construction, has no moving parts, requires a pump for liquid motive power and can be scaled up to process 250 gpm of contaminated water. Design and operating details are given for continuous flow magnetic separation to remove flocculated carbon and precipitates from the Dynactor effluent after decontamination of hazardous materials. Experimental data on successful decontamination of heavy metals by precipitation, acids and bases by neutralization, phenol, chlorine and pesticides by powdered carbon adsorption and other selected hazardous compounds are presented. (EPA)
W75-07706

PROCESS DESIGN MANUAL FOR SUSPENDED SOLIDS REMOVAL.
Hazen and Sawyer, New York.
Environmental Protection Agency, Technology Transfer Office, Washington, D.C., January 1975. 263 p, 81 fig, 36 tab, 249 ref.

Descriptors: *Suspended solids, *Waste water treatment, *Sedimentation, *Filtration, *Flocculation, *Coagulation, *Chemical reactions, Operations, Maintenance, Waste treatment, Sewage treatment, Solids contact processes, Separation techniques, Cost analysis, Flotation, Filters, Suspension, Solid wastes, Waste disposal, Trickling filters, Tertiary treatment.

A new source of information is presented for use by engineers and industry in the planning, design and operation of present and future wastewater treatment facilities. Much of the information presented is based on the evaluation and operation of pilot, demonstration and full scale plants. The design criteria thus generated represent typical values. The manual surveys current practice in the removal of suspended solids in both traditional and advanced treatment of municipal wastewater. Specific processes are described, design considerations are discussed and results are illustrated by data from actual installations. Included are processes such as sedimentation, straining and granular media filtration which affect physical separation of solids as well as coagulation and flocculation processes which alter solids characteristics to facilitate such separation. Detailed information is also provided concerning handling and application of coagulant chemicals. Aspects of operation and maintenance pertinent to design are discussed and estimated costs of construction and operation are provided for particular processes. (Poertner)
W75-07712

WASTEWATER IRRIGATION: ITS LEGAL IMPACT,
Virginia Polytechnic Inst. and State Univ., Blacksburg. Water Resources Research Center.
For primary bibliographic entry see Field 6E.
W75-07766

FORT LAUDERDALE, FLORIDA (FINAL ENVIRONMENTAL IMPACT STATEMENT),
Environmental Protection Agency, Atlanta, Ga. Region IV.
Available from the National Technical Information Service, U.S. Dept. of Commerce, Springfield, Va. 22161, as EIS-FL-73-1100-F, $8.50 in paper copy, $2.25 in microfiche. July 1973. 253 p, 2 map, 15 tab, 4 graph, 2 diagram.

Descriptors: *Federal Water Pollution Control Act, *Waste water treatment, *Filtration, *Nitrification, *Chlorination, Deep wells, Irrigation, Shallow wells, Effluents, Disinfection, Septic tanks, Injection wells, Waste water(Pollution), Waste water treatment, Discharge(Water), Canals, Landfills, Incineration, Lagoons, *Florida water supply, Water shortage, Water siltation, Sludge disposal, Biological treatment.
Identifiers: *Environmental Impact Statements, *Ft. Lauderdale(Fla), Federal Water Pollution Control Act Amendments of 1972.

The proposed action consists of federal grants assistance to the City of Ft. Lauderdale, Florida, as authorized by the Federal Water Pollution Control Act. The City applied for federal funds to aid in construction of a larger and more advanced water collection and treatment system. The assistance will be utilized to improve multi-media filtration, nitrification, and (breakpoint) chlorination. Facilities necessary to insure the attainment of secondary treatment standards will also be constructed, as will be a deep well for effluent disposal. The projects beneficial environmental impacts consist of a decrease in the quantity of oxygen demanding and biostimulating materials currently being discharged into Ft. Lauderdal's waters; the improvement of chlorination, allowing better disinfection of the wastewater effluent; and the potential for population growth without the accompanying water quality degradation that would occur if the project is not built. Various alternatives considered include biological, physical, chemical, and biologication-physical-chemical hybrid treatments; ocean outfall; canal or intracoastal waterway discharge; deep well, and disposal; irrigation; septic tank; shallow well and Everglade discharge; effluent disposal methods and land surface application; land fill; ocean disposal; injection well; incineration; protein source; building material; composting; and lagooning sludge disposal methods. Comments were received from various agencies and organizations. (Gagliardi-Florida)
W75-07783

RESEARCH DEMONSTRATION PILOT STUDY OF MUNICIPAL WASTE COMPOSTING (FINAL ENVIRONMENTAL STATEMENT),
Agricultural Research Service, Washington, D.C.
T. W. Edminster.
Available from the National Technical Information Service, U.S. Dept. of Commerce, Springfield, Va. 22161, as EIS-MD-74-0148-F, $3.75 in paper copy, $2.25 in microfiche. November 20, 1973. 26 p, 3 fig.

Descriptors: *Sewage treatment, *Sewage sludge disposal, Diseases, Environmental control, Habitats, Microenvironment, Environmental sanitation, Water law, Air pollution, *Maryland.
Identifiers: *Environmental Impact Statements, *Beltsville(Md), Federal agencies, Composting.

A proposal was made to establish and operate a site to test the composting of sewage sludge and organic refuse. The project will be undertaken by the Agricultural Research Service and the Maryland Environmental Service. The compost will be used for both research and land development. Among the deleterious environmental effects of the project are the building of a large crushed-rock surface which would have to be removed for subsequent agricultural use; the use of heavy machinery; and the possible production of undesirable odors through anaerobic decomposition, and possible pathogenic contamination of surface and ground waters. Alternatives to the composting project range from no action to conducting a smaller scale operation of the same site or moving to a different site. In addition, alternatives to composting sludge are suggested such as a trenching system of sludge use on land and spreading fresh sludge on the land surface and plowing in. No long term environmental impacts will result from the pilot study since it is a temporary demonstration. In the event, however, that the project results in satisfactory composting procedure, it would have very favorable and significant environmental effects. (Proctor-Florida)
W75-07786

NORTH BROWARD COUNTY, FLORIDA (FINAL ENVIRONMENTAL IMPACT STATEMENT),
Environmental Protection Agency, Atlanta, Ga. Region IV.
Available from the National Technical Information Service, U.S. Dept. of Commerce, Springfield, Va. 22161, as EIS-FL-73-0516-F, $6.25 in paper copy, $2.25 in microfiche. March 20, 1973. 163 p, 7 tab, 3 map.

Descriptors: *Waste water disposal, *Waste water treatment, *Water pollution treatment, *Water pollution control, Water pollution sources, Water pollution, Waste water(Pollution), Construction, Oceans, Outfall sewers, Sewage, Sewage disposal, Sewage treatment, Canals, *Florida.
Identifiers: *Environmental Impact Statements, *Broward County(Fla).

The project consists of the construction of wastewater pumping stations, forcemains, treatment plant, and water treatment plant ocean outfall in North Broward County, Florida. The primary unavoidable adverse effects are those related to actual construction such as noise, traffic, stripping of trees and foliage, and soil erosion. The project will be of benefit in establishing authority in one governmental body responsible for sewage treatment, eliminating the continued construction of small plants throughout the area. The project will make possible the exercise of tighter control as to the timing and nature of new additions to the system and as to the nature of the water discharged to the system. It will also eliminate many discharges into inland waters which result in violations of water quality standards. Alternatives considered include ocean outfalls, deep well disposal, septic tanks and doing nothing. Additionally, alternative plant sites and collection systems were considered. (Denvir-Florida)
W75-07787

HEAVY METALS REMOVAL BY THERMAL PROCESSES,
Princeton Univ., N.Y. Center for Environmental Studies.
R. T. Probstein.
In: Proceedings of the Conference 'Traces of Heavy Metals in Water: 'Removal Processes and Monitoring', November 15-16, 1973, Princeton University, Princeton, New Jersey. 24 p, 5 fig, 19 ref.

Descriptors: *Heavy metals, Removal, *Thermal properties, *Evaporation, *Freezing, *Waste water treatment, Concentrations, Scaling, Corrosion, Electrodialysis, Reverse osmosis, Effluent, Reclamation, Precipitation, Latent heat, Condensation, Heat transfer, Compression, Desalination, *Distillation, Laboratory tests.
Identifiers: Metal plating, Fluorocarbons.

Rapidly increasing world energy costs have reduced the attractiveness of standards flash and boiling distillation systems because of their low thermal performance and correspondingly high energy consumption. Thermal processes with relatively low energy consumption are vapor compression distillation and freezing. Vapor compression, although not a new process, has not been developed for the specific purpose of handling heavy metal wastewaters. Some development, pilot plant and demonstration work is required to enable the method to treat reliably the highly corrosive and scale forming waters with corrosive distillates using efficient high volume compressors and enhanced heat transfer surfaces. Freezing also appears to be quite promising, particularly since it minimizes the corrosion and scale problem. However, freezing is still in an embryonic stage from a commercial viewpoint and requires much more development and testing on heavy metal wastewaters before its potential for this application can be properly evaluated. (Rowe-Vanderbilt)
W75-07798

DEVELOPMENT AND APPLICATION OF THE WASTE-PLUS-WASTE PROCESS FOR RECOVERING METALS FROM ELECTROPLATING AND OTHER WASTES,
Bureau of Mines, Rolla, Mo. Rolla Metallurgy Research Center.
A. A. Cochran, and L. C. George.
Bureau of Mines, Report No. RI 7877, Washington, D.C., May, 1974. 18 pages, 9 fig, 10 tab, 24 ref.

Descriptors: *Heavy metals, *Waste water treatment, *Industrial wastes, *Neutralization, Economics, Resources, Cadmium, Chromium, Copper, Nickel, Zinc.
Identifiers: *Waste-plus-waste process, *Electroplating.

Laboratory-scale research was conducted to develop a new process for treating electroplating and other wastes. Various acid and alkaline cyanide wastes were combined under controlled conditions to neutralize the wastes and to almost completely precipitate the metals and cyanides. The metals were subsequently recovered for recycling: the cyanides can also be easily recycled. The process was successfully used to treat the major types of electroplating and etching wastes, containing Cd, Cr, Cu, Ni, and Zn and to treat both concentrated and dilute wastes. The economic aspects of treating concentrated electroplating, etching, and anodizing wastes are especially attractive because of the low cost of mixing two wastes, the high value of the recovered metals, and the simplicity of the recovery procedures. The filtrates from the waste-plus-waste step were relatively harmless compared with the original wastes and met Public Health Service standards for free cyanide content. Free cyanide ions were not detected in most of the filtrates; the limit of detection was 0.03 ppm. Only small amounts of HCN were produced during the neutralization; the HCN was collected and neutralized. (Pulliam-Vanderbilt)
W75-07804

SEPARATOR FOR LIQUIDS OF DIFFERENT DENSITIES,
P. Preus, and J. J. Gallagher.
U.S. Patent No. 3,862,040, 4 p, 4 fig, 3 ref; Official Gazette of the United States Patent Office, Vol 930, No 3, p 1332, January 21, 1975.

Descriptors: *Patents, *Skimming, *Waste water treatment, *Water treatment, Pollution abatement, Water pollution control, Separation techniques, Equipment, Liquid wastes.
Identifiers: *Decanting, *Gravity separation, Separators.

A separator for liquids of different densities includes a skimmer for separating the liquids, a separating tank for holding the more dense liquid from the skimmer and a concentrating tank to receive the less dense liquid from the skimmer. (Sinha-OEIS)
W75-07805

METHOD OF STERILIZING REVERSE OSMOSIS WATER TREATMENT UNITS,
Culligan, Inc., Northbrook, Ill. (assignee).
C. E. Lyall.
U.S. Patent No. 3,850,797, 3 p, 1 fig, 3 ref; Official Gazette of the United States Patent Office, Vol 928, No 4, p 1698, November 26, 1974.

Descriptors: *Patents, *Semipermeable membranes, *Reverse osmosis, *Waste water treatment, *Filtration, Membranes, Equipment, *Desalination, Hydrogen ion concentration.
Identifiers: Sterilization.

A method is disclosed for treating a reverse osmosis water treatment unit and particularly the semipermeable membrane used therein in such a manner both to sterilize and to extend the life of the membrane of the unit. This method comprises: passing an aqueous solution having a pH in the range of from 4.5 to 6 and containing formaldehyde or the like and an acid selected from the group consisting of acetic, formic, citric, fumaric and boric into the water treatment unit and through the membrane of the unit during a period of unit 'down time' and maintaining the solution in the unit and in contact with the membrane for as long a period of time as is reasonably possible and preferably until such time as the unit must again be activated. (Sinha-OEIS)
W75-07806

CONNECTION FITTING FOR WATER TREATMENT APPARATUS,
For primary bibliographic entry see Field 5F.
W75-07808

SKIMMING BLADE,
FMC Corp., Chicago, Ill. (assignee)
W. C. Bishop.
U.S. Patent No. 3,872,017, 4 p, 3 fig, 4 ref; Official Gazette of the United States Patent Office, Vol 932, No 3, p 1080, March 18, 1975.

Descriptors: *Patents, *Pollution abatement, *Water pollution control, *Waste water treatment, Skimming, Equipment, Water quality control.
Identifiers: Water clarification, Settling tanks.

A skimming blade is used in a liquid clarification tank which has longitudinally extending weir boxes that define the outlet for receiving clarifying liquid. The skimming blade is supported on a bridge that is reciprocated above the tank along a path parallel to the direction of flow of liquid within the tank and has cutouts having bases located above the lower edge of the blade. The skimming blade is maintained in a first skimming position where the bases of the cutouts are above the liquid level while the bridge is traversing the box area of the tank and a second skimming position where the bases of the cutouts and the lower edge of the blade are located below the liquid level. (Sinha-OEIS)
W75-07812

CONDENSED WATER DECHLORINATION APPARATUS,
Hitachi Ltd., Tokyo (Japan). (assignee)
T. Teranishi, and O. Takita.
U.S. Patent No. 3,872,011, 3 p, 1 fig, 7 ref; Official Gazette of the United States Patent Office, Vol 932, No 3, p 1079, March 18, 1975.

Descriptors: *Patents, *Thermal powerplants, *Nuclear powerplants, *Water quality control, Water treatment, Resins, Dissolved oxygen, Chlorination, Condensation, Recycling, *Waste water treatment, *Water reuse.
Identifiers: *Dechlorination, Steam condensers, Vacuum degassing.

In a condensed water dechlorination apparatus for a thermal power plant or a nuclear power plant, the performance of resin in dechlorination towers usually deteriorates after use of about one week. For this reason, it is usually necessary to regenerate the resin in each of the dechlorination towers. A system is provided for recycling the blow water to a steam condenser instead of discharging the water outwardly, the dissolved oxygen being removed by a vacuum degassing effect in the steam condenser. A control valve and an auxiliary pump, and optionally an auxiliary tank are also provided in the line from the dechlorination tower to the steam condenser so as to ensure a safe and stable operation. In order to facilitate the vacuum degassing effect in the steam condenser, it may be possible to discharge the blow water through spray nozzles into the steam condenser. (Sinha-OEIS)
W75-07813

REMOVAL OF HEAVY METAL POLLUTANTS FROM AQUEOUS MEDIA,
Celanese Corp., New York. (assignee)
H. J. Davis, and L. A. Lee.
U.S. Patent No. 3,872,001, 4 p, 5 fig, 4 ref; Official Gazette of the United States Patent Office, Vol 932, No 3, p 1075, March 18, 1975.

Descriptors: *Waste water treatment, *Patents, *Pollution abatement, *Water pollution control, Metals, Cations, *Heavy metals, Chelation, Mercury(Metal), Polymers, Films.
Identifiers: *Polymeric films.

A process for removing pollutant heavy metal cations from an aqueous media is comprised of passing the pollutant-containing aqueous media through a substantially water insensitive, flexible base, porous polymeric film thereby forming a complex with the pollutant metal cations to be removed. The film is prepared from a polymer containing from about 0.01 to 3.0 free hydroxyl groups per gram of polymer which has been reacted with a polyfunctional carboxylic or sulfonic acid or anhydride to produce an acid-containing polymer and is subsequently contacted with a divalent metal chelate which is not subject to water degradation. (Sinha-OEIS)
W75-07815

REMOVAL OF POLLUTANTS FROM WASTEWATER,
Autotrol Corp., Milwaukee, Wis. (assignee)
W. N. Torpey.
U.S. Patent No. 3,871,999, 6 p, 6 fig, 5 ref; Official Gazette of the United States Patent Office, Vol 932, No 3, p 1074, March 18, 1975.

Descriptors: *Patents, *Waste water treatment, *Pollution abatement, *Water pollution control, *Biological treatment, Domestic wastes, Oxidation, Denitrification, Microorganisms, Organic wastes.
Identifiers: Ammonia nitrogen, Carbonaceous matter.

A biological method is described for effecting removal of substantially all of the ammonia nitrogen as well as 85 to 95% of the carbonaceous matter present in normal domestic wastewater. The process can include a first stage which oxidizes a minor portion of the ammonia present to nitrates and a second stage that provides denitrification of remaining nitrogenous compounds. The second stage is operated in a manner excluding molecular oxygen to encourage the growth of microorganisms that use nitrate oxygen for respiration and ammonia as an energy source. (Sinha-OEIS)
W75-07816

AERATING APPARATUS HAVING BALLAST MEANS THEREFOR,
Environmental Products Inc., Richmond, Va. (assignee)
R. C. Dively.
U.S. Patent No. 3,871,581, 4 p, 4 fig, 14 ref; Official Gazette of the United States Patent Office, Vol 932, No 3, p 948, March 18, 1975.

Descriptors: *Patents, *Waste water treatment, *Aeration, *Pollution abatement, *Water pollution control, *Sewage treatment, *Industrial wastes, Equipment.

An aerating apparatus for use in sewage and industrial waste treatment systems utilizes a top-mounted motor with a submerged ballast capable of providing a stable unit. The ballast is combined with means for establishing a low loss fluid flow into a propeller driven by the motor. Water which is lifted by the propeller then engages a deflector which deflects the water substantially radially of the apparatus in order to be aerated. In a preferred form of the invention, the ballast is carried by the means utilized to establish the low loss fluid flow and is toroidal in cross section. (Sinha-OEIS)

W75-07817

WATER QUALITY ANALYSIS SYSTEM WITH MULTICIRCUIT SINGLE SHELL HEAT EXCHANGER,
Beckman Instruments, Inc., Fullerton, Calif. (assignee)
E. A. Houser, and B. W. Schwindt.
U.S. Patent No. 3,871,444, 8 p, 14 fig, 6 ref; Official Gazette of the United States Patent Office, Vol 932, No 3, p 902, March 18, 1975.

Descriptors: *Patents, *Water quality, *Electric powerplants, *Steam, *Heat exchangers, Equipment, Powerplants, Thermal pollution, Waste water treatment.
Identifiers: Power generation plants.

A modular water quality analysis system for steam electric power generating plants includes a novel single shell multicircuit heat exchanger having means to individually vary the rate of flow of cooling water through each of the multiple circuits therein. The single heat exchanger can simultaneously cool a plurality of samples entering it at widely differing high inlet temperatures to the same lower range of outlet temperatures. The heat exchanger can be mounted on top of the system rack which contains a plurality of modules of apparatus for accepting water or steam samples from various test points in the power generating system, reducing the pressure and temperature thereof, directing and metering the flow of samples, and performing analyses for such water characteristics as pH, specific or cation conductivity, dissolved oxygen, and sodium content. Flexibility of design in the modular system also permits the same basic apparatus to be adapted to a large variety of different sizes and types of power generating plants having different analysis requirements thereby providing a custom installation for each plant which nonetheless retains all of the advantages of standardized design and equipment. (Sinha-OEIS)
W75-07818

MARINE SEWAGE TREATMENT SYSTEM FOR WATER CRAFT,
F. Humphrey.
U.S. Patent No. 3,870,634, 8 p, 7 fig, 5 ref; Official Gazette of the United States Patent Office, Vol 932, No 2, p 637, March 11, 1975.

Descriptors: *Patents, *Sewage treatment, *Waste water treatment, *Pollution abatement, *Water pollution control, Waste disposal, Equipment.
Identifiers: Marine wastes, Water craft.

A marine sewage treatment system has a digestor unit which includes a first tank receiving the sewage effluent, a secondary treatment unit including a second tank receiving the fluid discharged from the first tank and a final filter receiving the fluid discharged from the second tank. The first and second tanks include baffles controlling the flow of fluid within the tanks. The first and second tanks each are supported via a guide and anchor assembly for automatically leveling and agitating the fluid within the first and second tanks. (Sinha-OEIS)
W75-07820

SELF-CONTAINED TERTIARY FILTER PLANT AND CHLORINATION UNIT,
W. R. Setterstrom.
U.S. Patent No. 3,870,633, 5 p, 5 fig, 12 ref; Official Gazette of the United States Patent Office, Vol 932, No 2, p 637, March 11, 1975.

Descriptors: *Patents, *Water pollution control, *Pollution abatement, *Tertiary treatment, *Waste water treatment, Equipment, Chlorination, Filters, Filtration.

A self-contained enclosure includes vertical and horizontal partitions defining a storage chamber for the sewage treatment plant effluent, and sand filter bed, a chlorination unit, a backwash storage chamber with check valves between chambers which are otherwise fluid connected for control of gravity flow. Air under pressure through ejectors force controlled fluid flow through the treatment chambers and backwash material return to the upstream primary sewage treatment plant. (Sinha-OEIS)
W75-07821

5E. Ultimate Disposal Of Wastes

WATER SUPPLY AND WASTEWATER DISPOSAL IN RURAL AREAS OF INDIA,
Greenleaf/Telesca, Miami, Fla. Environmental Sciences Dept.
For primary bibliographic entry see Field 4A.
W75-07381

THE CONFIGURATION OF CONTAMINATION ENCLAVES FROM REFUSE DISPOSAL SITES ON FLOODPLAINS,
Iowa State Univ., Ames. Dept. of Earth Sciences.
For primary bibliographic entry see Field 5B.
W75-07443

GEOHYDROLOGIC CONSIDERATIONS IN THE MANAGEMENT OF RADIOACTIVE WASTE,
Geological Survey, Reston, Va.
For primary bibliographic entry see Field 5B.
W75-07562

DEVICES FOR ONBOARD TREATMENT OF WASTES FROM VESSELS,
Thiokol Chemical Corp., Brigham City, Utah. Wasatch Div.
For primary bibliographic entry see Field 5D.
W75-07594

DESIGNING LANDFILLS TO MINIMIZE LEACHATE,
Waste Age Magazine, West Chester, Pa.
R. W. Eldredge.
Paper presented at International Public Works Congress and Equipment Show, Denver, Colorado, September 15-20, 1973. 13 p, 5 fig, 7 ref.

Descriptors: *Solid wastes, *Municipal wastes, *Environmental sanitation, *Leaching, *Leachate, *Landfills, Organic wastes, Water pollution control, Liquid wastes, Sludge disposal, Waste water treatment, Waste water(Pollution), Environmental engineering.
Identifiers: *Sanitary landfills, Leachate treatment, Landfill design.

Landfill designs minimize leaching potential by diverting surface waters, separating the fill from gound waters, and limiting the liquid content of materials placed in the fill. Care should be taken that leaching will not occur so rapidly, or in so concentrated a form, as to impair that part of the environment where the leachate flows. To solve the problem of diversion of surface and flowing sources within the site, ditches, swales, and beams are constructed on undisturbed earth. On refuse filled areas, asphalt or plastic linears with gas venting mechanisms are provided. Excavated areas, exposed springs or seeps may be tiled or guided to a surface drain, avoiding passage through the refuse. Also, daily refuse cell construction should be as compact as possible--normally six inches thick. Planting vegetation on landfills at an early stage can help eliminate percolation. It is impractical to construct an impenetrable capsule for refuse, but reducing the association of water with solid waste will reduce the amount of leachate produced. (Poertner)
W75-07679

FORT LAUDERDALE, FLORIDA (FINAL ENVIRONMENTAL IMPACT STATEMENT),
Environmental Protection Agency, Atlanta, Ga. Region IV.
For primary bibliographic entry see Field 5D.
W75-07783

NORTH BROWARD COUNTY, FLORIDA (FINAL ENVIRONMENTAL IMPACT STATEMENT),
Environmental Protection Agency, Atlanta, Ga. Region IV.
For primary bibliographic entry see Field 5D.
W75-07787

5F. Water Treatment and Quality Alteration

RECOVERY AND REUSE OF COAGULANTS FROM TREATMENT OF WATER AND WASTEWATER,
Virginia Polytechnic Inst. and State Univ., Blacksburg. Dept. of Civil Engineering.
For primary bibliographic entry see Field 5D.
W75-07600

LINCOLN TRAIL AREA DEVELOPMENT DISTRICT COMPREHENSIVE WATER AND SEWER PLAN.
Schimpeler-Corradino Associates, Louisville, Ky.
For primary bibliographic entry see Field 5D.
W75-07667

PLASTIC PIPE IN COLDER CLIMATES,
Winnipeg Waterworks, Waste and Disposal Div. (Manitoba).
J. M. MacBride.
Presented at AFWA International Congress and Equipment Show, Toronto, Ontario, Canada, September 14-19, 1974. 6 p.

Descriptors: *Plastic pipes, *Cold regions, *Pipelines, *Conveyance structures, *Hydraulic structures, *Canada, Hydraulic conduits, Water distribution(Applied), Water supply, Municipal water, Materials testing, Subarctic.
Identifiers: Polyvinyl chloride pipes, Polybutylene pipes, Winnipeg(Manitoba-Canada).

The Waterworks, Waste and Disposal Division of the City of Winnipeg is responsible for the supply of potable water to all users and the treatment and disposal of their sewage. The climate in Winnipeg is relatively dry. Summer temperatures in the 90's (Farenheit) are not uncommon; neither are winter extremes of more than 30 degrees below zero uncommon. Because of the cost, shortage of materials and other factors, Winnipeg's use of plastics for piping is increasing rapidly. Sewage syphons and forcemains across Winnipeg's rivers have been constructed of polyethelene in sizes varying from 18 in. to 32 in. This work was done in temperatures ranging from 10 F to 30 F. The pipe maintained an amazing amount of flexibility under these cold weather conditions. Polyvinyl chloride (PVC) pipe has so far only been used on test for water distribution mains in the city PVC pipe is also used in the transmission of chlorine solutions for water and sewage treatment. Polybutylene pipe is now being used as a service pipe in residential areas as an alternative to Type K copper. Recent impact tests carried out by the independent test laboratory for the City of Winnipeg indicates that while PVC becomes more rigid at temperatures of 0 F., it still exhibits impact strengths equal to or greater than asbestos cement pipe. All three materials, polyethelene, polyvinyl chloride, and polybutylene seem suited for use in cold weather. (Poertner)
W75-07683

AN ARCTIC WATER SUPPLY SYSTEM,
Directorate of Construction Engineering and Design Engineering, Ottawa (Ontario).
E. G. Taylor.
Paper presented to the Canadian Section Conference, American Waterworks Association, April 22, 1968. 45 p, 28 fig, 2 tab, 9 append.

Descriptors: *Water distribution(Applied), *Cold weather construction, *Cold regions, *Arctic, *Pipelines, *Water supply, Water conveyance, Water utilization, Control systems, Automatic control, Instrumentation, Monitoring, Remote control, Construction, Aluminum, Hydraulic structures, Conveyance structures, Hydraulic conduits, Canada, Tunnel construction, Consumptive use.
Identifiers: *Alert(Northwest Territories-Canada), Utilidors.

An unusual water supply and distribution system has been in operation at Alert, Northwest Territories, since the fall of 1965. The source of supply is a lake that covers some 900 acres having an average depth of about 25 feet. The water is of quite good quality. Aluminum pipe was chosen for its light weight, its corrosion resistance, and its small thermal expansion. Freezing of the water is prevented by heating the water in boilers and heating and insulating the water distribution network. Above-ground utilidors housing both water supply lines and a sewer pipeline were used in the camp area. The system was designed to provide 50 gallons per capita daily, and each pump was capable of delivering the entire day's supply. The Moyno pump is a screw-type positive displacement pump which is well suited to pumping small quantities of water against high heads. The pipeline from the lake pumphouse to the camp water house is approximately 8,000 feet long and consists of 2-inch aluminum pipe in 25-foot lengths joined with Victualic couplings. The camp water house contains facilities for metering chlorinating, filtrating, heating and storing water received from the lake. It is also the focal point of the camp distribution system and contains the pressure tank, heating system and circulating pumps. Elaborate remote control and monitoring devices have been provided. (Poertner)
W75-07684

FEASIBILITY OF 5 GPM DYNACTOR/MAGNETIC SEPARATOR SYSTEM TO TREAT SPILLED HAZARDOUS MATERIALS,
Industrial Bio-Test Labs., Inc., Northbrook, Ill.
For primary bibliographic entry see Field 5D.
W75-07706

PROCESS DESIGN MANUAL FOR SUSPENDED SOLIDS REMOVAL.
Hazen and Sawyer, New York.
For primary bibliographic entry see Field 5D.
W75-07712

CONNECTION FITTING FOR WATER TREATMENT APPARATUS,
R. Dujardyn.
U.S. Patent No. 3,861,418, 3 p, 5 fig, 9 ref; Official Gazette of the United States Patent Office, Vol 930, No 3, p 1138, January 21, 1975.

Descriptors: *Patents, *Water treatment, Equipment, Water softening, Waste water treatment.
Identifiers: Fittings.

A connection fitting for water treatment apparatus is designed in such a way that it comprises all the required connections and can be fitted, as is, to the apparatus of which it becomes an integral part. The connection fitting comprises a body having a top wall, a bottom wall and a side wall and with first, second and third passages. The first passage extends eccentrically between the bottom and top walls of the body and is adapted to receive a closure plug which can be removed. The second and third passages are parallel and L-shaped. (Sinha-OEIS)
W75-07808

ULTRA PURE WATER PROCESS AND APPARATUS,
Aqua Media, Sunnyvale, Calif. (assignee).
T. L. Faylor, and R. W. Martin.
U.S. Patent No. 3,870,033, 6 p, 6 fig, 4 ref; Official Gazette of the United States Patent Office, Vol 932, No 2, p 451, March 11, 1975.

Descriptors: *Patents, *Water purification, *Heat exchangers, *Water treatment, Equipment, Tubes, Water quality, Quality control.
Identifiers: *Deionization.

A method and apparatus are described which produce hot deionized water having a temperature of about 170 deg F. and a deionized purity equivalent to about 18 megohm electrical resistivity at 25C. The water purification system produces ultra pure water in production quantities for industrial and commercial uses. It combines a large capacity storage tank with a pretreatment circuit and an ultra pure water recirculation loop in a way that has a number of significant advantages. The heat exchanger includes a tank at least partially filled with liquid, a coiled tube of inert plastic tubing immersed in the liquid in the tank and having an inlet connected to the inlet supply and having an outlet connected to the outlet means and a heating element disposed within and spaced from the coil for direct heating of the liquid in the tank and for indirect heating of the deionized water in the interior of the tubing. (Sinha-OEIS)
W75-07810

BACTERICIDAL WATER PURIFIER FOR DECHLORINATED WATER,
Matsushita Electric Industrial Co. Ltd., Osaka (Japan). (assignee)
A. Nishino, Y. Iura, M. Kubo, and M. Tateisi.
U.S. Patent No. 3,872,013, 4 p, 7 fig, 4 ref; Official Gazette of the United States Patent Office, Vol 932, No 3, p 1079, March 18, 1975.

Descriptors: *Patents, *Membranes, *Bactericides, *Water purification, *Water quality control, Activated carbon, Calcium carbonate, Filtration, Heavy metals, Filters, Biological membranes, Potable water, *Water treatment.
Identifiers: Dechlorination, Sterilization.

A water purifier for drinking water has one or more bactericidal membranes which inhibit the propagation of bacteria in the purifier after removal of chlorine or its derivatives from the supplied water. Porous sheets of a water insoluble material such as a synthetic fiber are coated with a bactericidal substance such as a sparingly soluble halide of a Group IB heavy metal. These are placed between the activated carbon layer and outlet of a water purifier. Additional provision of calcium carbonate granules in the purifier is effective in improving the bactericidal efficiency. (Sinha-OEIS)
W75-07811

5G. Water Quality Control

METHODS OF COMMUNICATING ACTIVITIES IN POLLUTION ABATEMENT BY FIVE HUNDRED MAJOR INDUSTRIAL CORPORATIONS IN THE UNITED STATES,
Texas A and M Univ., College Station. Environmental Quality Program.
C. A. Quinn.
EQN Note 16. April 1974. 86 p, 19 tab, 7 ref. Price: $3.00.

Descriptors: *Industries, *Pollution abatement, *Communication, Administrative costs, Surveys, Attitudes, Social aspects, *Water pollution control, Water quality control.
Identifiers: *Public relations, *Advertising, Major corporations.

The extent to which the top 500 United States industrial corporations (as determined according to sales by Fortune magazine, May 1972) have established and implemented public relations programs to inform their various publics of their pollution abatement activities was investigated by a questionnaire sent to the chief executive officer of each firm. The areas examined included (1) company characteristics, (2) type of pollution abatement public relations program, (3) the programs' personnel characteristics, finances, and effectiveness, and (4) the company executives' attitudes toward the communication of pollution abatement activities. The responses indicated that large firms (sales of two billion dollars or more) and pollution prone industries (chemicals, foods, paper and wood products, petroleum refining, metal manufacturing, rubber, and motor vehicles and parts) were most likely to have established a pollution abatement public relations program, with the percentage of companies with programs declining for smaller firms and in industries less pollution prone. Generally, pollution abatement public relations programs utilized traditional mass media and were integrated in the general public relations activities. A majority of responding company executives believed such programs to be important, but these private beliefs had little effect on the size of their company's program. (Becker-Wisconsin)
W75-07359

INFLUENCES OF WASTEWATER MANAGEMENT ON LAND USE: TAHOE BASIN 1950-1972,
California Univ., Santa Cruz.
For primary bibliographic entry see Field 5D.
W75-07362

THE INTERRELATIONSHIP OF ECONOMIC DEVELOPMENT AND ENVIRONMENTAL QUALITY IN THE UPPER COLORADO RIVER BASIN: AN INTERINDUSTRY ANALYSIS,
Colorado Univ., Boulder. Dept. of Economics.
For primary bibliographic entry see Field 6B.
W75-07377

SOUTHWEST ENERGY STUDY. SUMMARY REPORT.
Southwest Energy Federal Task Force.
For primary bibliographic entry see Field 6B.
W75-07380

A GENERAL LINEAR APPROACH TO STREAM WATER QUALITY MODELING,
IBM Federal Systems Div., Gaithersburg, Md.
For primary bibliographic entry see Field 5B.
W75-07382

AQUATIC PLANT HARVESTING: DEVELOPMENT OF HIGH-SPEED HARVESTERS AND PROCESSING AND UTILIZATION OF HARVESTED VEGETATION,
Wisconsin Univ., Madison. Dept. of Agricultural Engineering; and Wisconsin Univ., Madison. Dept. of Mechanical Engineering.
For primary bibliographic entry see Field 4A.
W75-07397

EFFICIENT USE OF WATER - POLICY AND PROBLEMS,
Ministry of Agriculture, Tel-Aviv (Israel). Water Commission.
For primary bibliographic entry see Field 6D.
W75-07401

REPORT TO THE CONGRESS ON OCEAN POLLUTION, OVERFISHING, AND OFFSHORE

DEVELOPMENT; JULY 1973 THROUGH JUNE 1974,
National Oceanic and Atmospheric Administration, Washington, D.C.
For primary bibliographic entry see Field 5B.
W75-07405

ENVIRONMENTAL STUDIES OF AN ARCTIC ESTUARINE SYSTEM–FINAL REPORT,
Alaska Univ., College. Marine Science Inst.
For primary bibliographic entry see Field 2L.
W75-07417

INVESTIGATION AND REHABILITATION OF A BRINE-CONTAMINATED AQUIFER,
Engineering Enterprises, Inc., Norman, Okla.
For primary bibliographic entry see Field 5B.
W75-07441

WATER RESOURCES,
National Aeronautics and Space Administration, Greenbelt, Md. Goddard Space Flight Center.
For primary bibliographic entry see Field 7B.
W75-07494

LAND AND WATER USE IN OREGON,
Oregon State Univ., Corvallis. Water Resources Research Inst.
For primary bibliographic entry see Field 6B.
W75-07507

THE PRACTICAL LIMITS OF POLLUTION CONTROL TECHNOLOGY,
Oregon State Univ., Corvallis. Dept. of Civil Engineering.
F. D. Schaumburg.
In: Land and Water Use in Oregon; Seminar conducted by Oregon State University, Spring Quarter 1974, Water Resources Research Institute, Corvallis, Oregon, p 1-7, July 1974.

Descriptors: *Environmental control, *Legal aspects, *Water quality standards, *Management, Regulation, Water quality control, Government finance, Legislation, Water law, Water policy, Political aspects, Environmental effects, Balance of nature, Environmental engineering, Water pollution, Administrative agencies, Water treatment, Water pollution control, Environment, Water quality act, Ecology, Economic feasibility, Economics.

The need for a more coordinated approach to environmental problems was stressed. It was argued that our present laws and procedures tend to divide the environment into water, land, and air problems. Solutions to water pollution problems, for instance, are attempted without regard to the effects of the water treatment on the land and air. It was pointed out that the 1972 Amendments of the Water Pollution Control Act set up goals that are impossible to achieve thermodynamically, technologically, and economically. Greater technological input in the decision-making process is needed. Too many of the positions of authority have gone to nontechnical persons, most of them lawyers. More input from industry and the public is needed in environmental management. State and federal agencies should not force industries of municipalities past the point where justifiable environmental good is achieved. More cooperation is needed, rather than the largely adversary procedure that now exists. (See also W75-0750) (Sims-ISWS)
W75-07508

WILLAMETTE RIVER PARKS SYSTEM,
Willamette River Parks System, Salem, Oreg.
For primary bibliographic entry see Field 6B.
W75-07513

WATER QUALITY PLANNING FOR THE DELAWARE ESTUARY - AN EXAMPLE,
Rutgers - the State Univ., New Brunswick, N.J. Water Resources Research Inst.
W. Whipple, Jr.
Water Resources Bulletin, Vol 11, No 2, p 300-350, April 1975. 1 tab, 7 ref.

Descriptors: Water resources, *Planning, *Water quality control, Water pollution sources, Water pollution treatment, Municipal wastes, Reaeration, *Water Quality Act, *Urban runoff, Estuaries.
Identifiers: Non-point pollution sources, *Instream aeration, *Instream oxygenation, *Delaware estuary.

The Delaware Estuary has been intensively studied but the planning for water quality control is very unsatisfactory, including the most recent interagency plan. Earlier planning by the FWPCA and the Delaware River Basin Commission was better; but this planning appears to have been halted and perhaps superseded by the provisions of PL 92-500. The Tocks Island reservoir planned to maintain minimum flows may never be built on account of environmental objections; but the consequences of such a decision are not being faced. Meanwhile recent research indicates that urban runoff will be a major influence possibly adding a load of as much as 500,000 lbs. of BOD in a single storm. Unit costs of treating urban runoff pollution are very high, due to its extreme variability. Artificial aeration or oxygenation may provide a more economical means of improving the dissolved oxygen regimen, as compared to primary treatment of urban runoff, or tertiary treatment of effluents. In any event planning on a regional basis is desirable in the Delaware and elsewhere, and PL 92-500 may need to be changed to facilitate it.
W75-07519

FUTURE DIRECTIONS IN ENVIRONMENTAL LEGISLATION,
For primary bibliographic entry see Field 6E.
W75-07532

FOSSIL FUELS AND POWER GENERATION IN THE COLORADO RIVER BASIN,
Brigham Young Univ., Provo, Utah. Dept. of Botany and Range Science.
For primary bibliographic entry see Field 3E.
W75-07537

POWER GENERATION AND THE COLORADO RIVER BASIN,
Utah Power and Light Co., Salt Lake City.
For primary bibliographic entry see Field 3E.
W75-07538

TRANSPORTATION AND REGIONAL ENVIRONMENTAL MANAGEMENT,
Wyoming Univ., Laramie. Dept. of Economics; and Div. of Business and Economic Research.
For primary bibliographic entry see Field 6B.
W75-07539

RESOURCE ALLOCATION AND MANAGEMENT IN THE COLORADO RIVER BASIN,
Utah State Univ., Logan. Dept. of Political Science.
For primary bibliographic entry see Field 6E.
W75-07543

SEDIMENT IN IRRIGATION AND DRAINAGE WATERS AND SEDIMENT INPUTS AND OUTPUTS FOR TWO LARGE TRACTS IN SOUTHERN IDAHO,
Agricultural Research Service, Kimberly, Idaho. Snake River Conservation Research Center.
M. J. Brown, D. L. Carter, and J. A. Bondurant.
Journal of Environmental Quality, Vol 3, No 4, p 347-351, October-December, 1974. 1 fig, 3 tab, 10 ref.

Descriptors: *Irrigation water, *Sediment control, *Sediment transport, *Surface runoff, *Irrigation operation and maintenance, Erosion, Drainage water, Infiltration, *Idaho.
Identifiers: *Sediment retention ponds, Snake River(Idaho).

Sediment inputs from Snake River irrigation water and sediment losses back to the river were measured from two large irrigated tracts in Southern Idaho. A net sediment accumulation of 0.69 metric tons/ha onto the Northside tract was determined, but a net loss of 0.46 metric tons/ha occurred on the Twin Falls tract. Much of the difference was the result of a drainage system constructed to grade on the Northside tract whereas most drains on the Twin Falls tract are natural channels with steeper gradients. Erosion loss from farms could be reduced by more careful water use and construction of on-farm sediment retention ponds. These ponds would not only reduce the amount of sediment returning to the river, but would also reduce the costs of sediment removal from drains and canals. The sediment retention ponds could provide fill for low areas and for landscaping, and additional benefits could include nitrogen removal by phytoplankton, and recreation such as water sports and fishing. (Mastic-Arizona)
W75-07546

GENERALIZED STREAM TEMPERATURE ANALYSIS SYSTEM,
Geological Survey, Bay Saint Louis, Miss. Gulf Coast Hydroscience Center.
For primary bibliographic entry see Field 5B.
W75-07561

ENERGY FROM COAL: GUIDELINES FOR THE PREPARATION OF ENVIRONMENTAL IMPACT STATEMENTS,
Battelle Columbus Labs., Ohio.
For primary bibliographic entry see Field 6G.
W75-07590

AN EVALUATION OF THE USE OF WASTE HEAT FOR SOIL WARMING IN THE SOUTHEAST,
North Carolina State Univ., Raleigh. Dept. of Biological and Agricultural Engineering.
For primary bibliographic entry see Field 3C.
W75-07599

FUTURE DREDGING QUANTITIES IN THE GREAT LAKES,
Eastern Michigan Univ., Ypsilanti. Dept. of Geography and Geology.
C. N. Raphael, E. Jaworski, C. F. Ojala, and D. S. Turner.
Environmental Protection Agency, Report EPA-660/3-74-029, December 1974. 219 p, 20 fig, 78 tab, 55 ref. R-801062.

Descriptors: *Great Lakes, *Dredging, Disposal, Lakes, Water policy, Sedimentation, Navigation, Water levels, *Projections, United States, Canada, Water pollution control.
Identifiers: Lake levels, *Disposal sites(Lakes).

Based on historical records, an overview and projection of U.S. and Canadian dredging quantities in the Great Lakes are presented. Using current pollution criteria, future quantities of polluted maintenance dredging are estimated for each lake. Recent environmental policies have influenced dredging and particularly disposal practices. These policies, as well as sedimentation, lake levels, and economic factors are discussed in relation to dredging. During the next decade, maintenance and private dredging volumes will not change significantly, whereas new work will decrease. As in

the past, most maintenance dredging will occur in U.S. projects, particularly in Lake Erie. A factor which will determine future U.S. maintenance dredging is the availability of confined disposal sites. If the 62 sites are completed for commercial harbors as planned, 300,000 of the 6.45 million cubic yards of annual projected polluted spoil will not have disposal facilities. Where pollution elimination systems are in use, shoaling in some industrial harbors may be decreasing. Although long-term lake levels are not predictable, an inverse relationship between maintenance dredging and lake levels is evident. (EPA)
W75-07603

PHYTOPLANKTON COMPOSITION AND ABUNDANCE IN LAKE ONTARIO DURING IFYGL,
Michigan Univ., Ann Arbor. Great Lake Research Div.
For primary bibliographic entry see Field 5C.
W75-07604

THE SIGNIFICANCE AND CONTROL OF WASTEWATER FLOATABLES IN COASTAL WATERS,
California Univ., Berkeley. Sanitary Engineering Research Lab.
R. E. Selleck, L. W. Bracewell, and R. Carter.
Environmental Protection Agency, Report EPA 660/3-74/016, January 1974. 119 p, 31 fig, 29 tab, 19 ref. 1BA025. 800373.

Descriptors: *Water pollution control, Waste water disposal, Methodology, *California, Sampling, Regulation, Path of pollutants.
Identifiers: *Ocean outfalls, Surface pollution, Southern California Bight, Surface floatables, Surface films, Surface slicks.

Significance of flotage derived from submerged primary effluent plumes in the Southern California Bight is evaluated in terms of three components: particulates greater than or equal to 0.5 mm in size, particulates less than or equal to 0.1 mm in size, and surface film materials. The sampling methods utilized to collect the flotage from the surface are described in detail. The surface film and micro-particulates were captured by fabric screen samplers developed during the study. The large particulates penetrated the ocean thermocline and gathered on the surface in profusion. The grease and wax portions of the particulates could be measured reliably with hexane extraction, with the mass of HEM of sewage origin being in the order of a metric ton on the water surface within the study area. Such particulates contained considerable numbers of coliform bacteria but little PCB compunds or pesticides. The surface film materials and/or micro-particulates contained significant concentrations of coliform organisms and PCB compounds, but not pesticides. The HEM derived from this type of flotage may have amounted to 300 kg on the water surface within the study area in July 1973. Regulations for controlling the concentration of flotage on the ocean surface are suggested after considerable discussion. (EPA)
W75-07606

FORMAL PLANNING AND REPORTING SYSTEM: PROCEDURAL MANUAL,
Environmental Protection Agency, Washington, D.C. Office of Resources Management.
Available from the National Technical Information Service, Springfield, Va 22161, as PB-227 114, $5.75 in paper copy, $2.25 in microfiche. February 1973. 137 p, 8 append.

Descriptors: *Project planning, *Administration, *Regions, Budgeting, *Federal project policy, Pollution abatement, State governments.
Identifiers: Reporting, *Decentralization, Program guidance decisions, Procedure manual.

Convinced that a decentralized organization will most effectively implement programs, the responsibilities of both the headquarters and the regional Environmental Protection Agency offices are prescribed. The headquarters must communicate its objectives and strategy to the regions and the regions must show that they understand the strategy and are getting the job done. An output-oriented planning and reporting system that obtains commitments to specific outputs and reports progress and problems in a timely fashion is proposed as the communications and feedback mechanism between the headquarters and regional EPA offices. The system delineates procedures for long-term budgetary resources allocation and program guidance decisions, for annual and mid-term program and accomplishment plans, for sweeping resource allocation changes, and for coordination and reporting within and between levels. The roles of assistant and regional administrators in the planning and reporting system are described. For the evaluation of an output-oriented system, the precision of output measures is a limitation of a system not based on profits. The proxies used by EPA as indicators of ultimate public welfare are ambient air and water quality. Although they are important indicators, these output measures cannot be used as the final measure for making allocation and program guidance decisions. (Becker-Wisconsin)
W75-07612

DEVELOPMENT OF AN APPROACH TO IDENTIFICATION OF EMERGING TECHNOLOGY AND DEMONSTRATION OPPORTUNITIES,
Battelle Columbus Labs., Ohio.
H. Nack, K. Murthy, E. Stambaugh, H. Carlson, and G. R. Smithson.
Available from the National Technical Information Service, Springfield, Va 22161, as PB-233 646, $8.50 in paper copy, $2.25 in microfiche. EPA Report No. EPA-650/2-74-049, May 1074. 270 p, 26 fig, 7 tab, 12 ref.

Descriptors: *Pollution abatement, *Air pollution, *Environmental effects, *Government supports, *Industrial wastes, Industrial production, *Technology, Metallurgy, Oil industry, Pilot plants, Systems analysis.
Identifiers: *New process technology, *Petroleum refining industry, *Secondary nonferrous metal industry, Process profiles, Industry trends, Government-industry joint projects.

The petroleum refining and the secondary nonferrous metals industries were studied to develop an approach appropriate for the assessment of environmental effects associated with their activities and for the identification of new technology which could be used to minimize adverse environmental effects. A new methodology for characterizing major industries from the standpoint of their present environmental impact and for assessing the probable effect of 'emerging process technology' on environmental considerations is viewed by the EPA as the basis for selecting industries that need help in air pollution control. The approach developed includes (1) a process profile for each industry, noting the companies of importance, raw materials used, processes employed, and their products and wastes, (2) an examination of the profiles by experts from each industry in order to verify the accuracy and completeness of the profiles and to identify trends of the industry, (3) an assessment of emerging technology (potential for helping to abate existing environmental problems), and identification of candidate demonstration projects, and an examination of the feasibility of jointly sponsored government-industry projects. The role of industry esperts is important to this approach. Since the two industries studied here have substantially different characteristics, this approach has general applicability. (Becker-Wisconsin)
W75-07617

MINIMIZING THE SALT BURDENS OF IRRIGATION DRAINAGE WATERS,
Agricultural Research Service, Riverside, Calif. Salinity Lab.
J. D. Rhodes, J. D. Oster, R. D. Ingvalson, J. M. Tucker, and M. Clark.
Journal of Environmental Quality, Vol 3, No 4, p 311-316, October-December, 1974. 7 tab, 7 ref.

Descriptors: *Irrigation water, *Drainage water, *Alfalfa, *Water quality, *Irrigation efficiency, Leaching, Salts, Soil profiles, Salt balance, Water pollution, Water pollution control, Soil water movement, Weathering, Lysimeters.

Irrigation of alfalfa using waters synthesized to represent eight important river waters of the western U.S. was carried out in a controlled lysimeter experiment. Results showed that minimizing the quantity of drainage water gives the smallest possible return of applied salts in the return flow. Reasons for this effect are: (1) it maximizes the precipitation of carbonate minerals and gypsum in the soil, (2) it minimizes soil mineral weathering and the dissolution of salts previously deposited in the soil, and (3) it maximizes the amount of soluble salt diverted in the water that is retained in storage in the soil profile and not returned in the drainage water. These results point out the inadequacy of the assumption of salt balance used as the basis of many irrigation management and water quality evaluation practices. In addition, reducing the leaching fraction by increasing irrigation efficiency reduces the salt burden of drainage waters and minimizes their pollution effects. (Mastic-Arizona)
W75-07620

CONSIDERATIONS FOR ANALYSIS OF INFILTRATION-INFLOW,
National Environmental Research Center, Cincinnati, Ohio. Advanced Waste Treatment Research Lab.
For primary bibliographic entry see Field 5D.
W75-07664

LAND APPLICATION OF WASTEWATER AT COLORADO SPRINGS,
Colorado Springs Dept. of Public Utilities, Colo. Wastewater Div.
B. A. Kocerha.
Paper presented at the APWA International Congress and Equipment Show, Denver, Colorado, September 1973. 4 p.

Descriptors: *Wastewater, *Waste water treatment, *Water conservation, *Irrigation water, *Waste water disposal, *Colorado, Water demand, Droughts, Water resources development, Sanitary engineering.
Identifiers: *Colorado Springs, *Land application of waste water.

Due to severe drought in the late 1950's, the City of Colorado Springs, Colorado, considered developing its wastewater treatment plant for irrigation purposes. In 1960 a non-potable water treatment system was installed at the plant to supplant the potable supply. The non-potable treatment plant, supplied by the secondary-treated and disinfected wastewater treatment plant effluent, consisted fo pressure-type rapid sand filters followed by chlorination. This treatment was intended to reduce the BOD and suspended solid levels and was designed to treat between 250,000 and 2 million gallons of water per day to be used for land irrigation. Concurrent with the construction of a tertiary treatment plant in 1970, four dual-media (coal and sand) gravity filters were installed to replace the pressure-sand filters. The total cost for non-potable water at Colorado Springs is 11 cents per 1000 gallons. This includes the cost of secondary treatment, sand filtration and chlorination. In 1966, Colorado College analyzed soil samples taken from irrigated land area for pH, phosphates, nitrogen, and plugging conditions.

Nothing was found which could be considered harmful with respect to irrigation by reclaimed wastewater. (Poertner)
W75-07670

IS THE REFUSE ACT PERMIT PROGRAM LEGAL AND LOGICAL,
Rust Engineering Co., Pittsburgh, Pa.
L. R. Robinson.
In: Water and Sewage Works, January 1972. p 50-53, 5 ref.

Descriptors: *Water quality, *Water quality control, *Discharge(Water), *Water Quality Act, *Rivers and Harbors Act, *Navigable rivers, Navigable waters, Navigation, Pollutants, Pollution abatement, Pollutant identification, Water pollution, Federal Water Pollution Control Act, Environmental control, Federal government, Water law, Waste water disposal.

In July 1970, President Nixon established the Environmental Protection Agency (EPA) to set and enforce standards for air and water quality. Three months later, he transferred primary authority for industrial wastewater control from the EPA to the Secretary of the Army. President Nixon based his action on the United States River and Harbors Act of 1899 and established the Refuse Act Permit Program. This law, interpreted by the President, had a definite bearing on water pollution and the permit program would stop the discharge of refuse matter in specific cases unless the Army Corps of Engineers provided a permit. The obvious intent of the Congress in 1899 was to prevent obstructions to navigation when it wrote the Rivers and Harbors Act. That adequate Federal water pollution statutes had not yet been enacted led Congress to pass the Water Quality Act of 1965. The Refuse Act Permit Program should be cancelled. If standards established under the Water Quality Act of 1965 are insufficient and if additional enforcement mechanisms are needed, the EPA should be given additional authority by the Congress. (Poertner)
W75-07671

WATER QUALITY CONTROL PLAN: SAN FRANCISCO BAY BASIN, CALIFORNIA,
Water Resources Engineers, Inc., Walnut Creek, Calif; and Yoder, Trotter, Orlob and Associates, Walnut Creek, Calif.
State Water Resources Control Board, Sacramento, California, November, 1974. 62 p, 28 fig, 15 tab.

Descriptors: *Water pollution control, *Water quality control, *Bays, *Water policy, *California, *Planning, Water resources, Effluents, Land use, Population, Basic data collection, Waste water treatment, Environmental control, Environmental effects, Wetlands, Environmental engineering, Water resources development, Oil spills, Federal Water Pollution Control Act.
Identifiers: *San Francisco Bay Basin, Water quality control plan.

The basic purpose of the State Board's basin planning effort is to ascertain future direction of water quality control management for protection of California's waters. Water quality objectives recommended here for the protection of beneficial uses were developed from data reviewed during this study and from the literature, including published and unpublished reports. An assessment of existing and anticipated water quality problems involves identifying and quantifying point and diffuse (nonpoint) waste loads, evaluating by mathematical modeling techniques, the relative effect of future waste loads on the aquatic environment, and classifying basin receiving water segments in regard to pollution problems. Although municipal wastewater treatment and disposal facility improvements are emphasized, additional control measures are recommended for industrial wastewaters, urban runoff, agricultural systems, construction activities and dredging operations within the Basin. Further control actions for the State and Regional Boards as well as other agencies associated with water pollution control are recommended, including a surveillance program for measuring the effect of the Basin Plan. (Poertner)
W75-07673

FLOOD CONTROL IN COOK COUNTY,
League of Women Voters of Chicago, Ill.
For primary bibliographic entry see Field 4A.
W75-07674

RATTLESNAKE CREEK STUDY,
Wichita Water Dept., Kans.
For primary bibliographic entry see Field 4A.
W75-07676

USE OF MODELING FOR PLANNING STORM WATER STRATEGIES,
Florida Univ., Gainesville.
W. C. Huber.
Presented at the 1974 International Public Works Congress and Equipment Show, Toronto, Ontario, Canada, September 1974. 10 p, 6 fig, 3 tab, 19 ref.

Descriptors: *Storm water, *Runoff, *Mathematical models, *Planning, *Design, *Operations, Infiltration, Urban runoff, Storm runoff, Snowmelt, Effective precipitation, Average runoff, Surface runoff, Model studies, Computer models, Synthetic hydrology, Storage, Drainage engineering.

The overall objective of urban runoff models is to serve as aids to decision making for abatement of water quantity and quality problems due to urban storm water and combined sewer runoff. An urban runoff model is simply a group of mathematical expressions that simulate the physics of conversion of rainfall to runoff. Superimposed upon this process may be the related processes of dry weather flow and infiltration, snow melt, treatment and storage, and, of course, generation of water quality parameters. The modeling process may usually be subdivided into three modeling objectives: planning, design, and operation. Planning models are used for an overall assessment of the urban runoff problem as well as estimates of the effectiveness and costs of abatement procedures. Design models are oriented toward the detailed simulation of a single storm event. They provide a complete description of flow and pollutant routing from the point of rainfall through the entire urban runoff system and often into the receiving waters as well. Operational models are used to produce actual control decisions during a storm event. Rainfall is entered from telemetered stations and the model is used to predict system responses a short time into the future. Modeling offers a useful and cost-effective means of planning for storm water control. (Poertner)
W75-07677

ECONOMICS OF COMBINED SEWAGE DETENTION FACILITIES,
San Francisco City and County Dept. of Public Works, Calif.
R. T. Cockburn.
Prepared for the APWA Urban Drainage Workshop, San Francisco, California, January 22-23, 1975. 31 p, 21 fig, 6 ref.

Descriptors: *Waste water treatment, *Storm runoff, *Storm surge, *Water quality, *Water quality control, *Combined sewers, Overflow, Sewage treatment, Mathematical models, Sewage, Storage, Discharge(Water), California.
Identifiers: San Francisco(California).

The City and County of San Francisco (CCSF) operates three waste water treatment plants with a combined sanitary capacity of 100 mgd and an interceptor system of approximately 300 mgd to service 43 separate combined sewer districts. The system has two major inadequacies. The dry weather interception, collection, treatment and disposal system, is inadequate to handle the wet weather flows occurring in the system. Effluent from the City's three treatment plants violates existing standards and quality levels required by State and Federal policy. After careful study of the San Francisco system it was determined that San Francisco should retain the combined sewer system which, when adequately controlled by sufficient storage and treatment capacity, provides a higher level of water quality protection than a separate system. Separation would result in little or no benefit at great cost. Total elimination of degradation of the waters contiguous to San Francisco cannot be attained solely by control of discharges from San Francisco. Control of 90% of the volumes now overflowing will reduce the present 82 overflows to 81 annually; the receiving water bacterial violations will be reduced from 170 days/year to 60 days. Treatment of weather discharges must provide substantially complete removal of settleable and floatable materials plus sufficient removal to meet requirements of water contact sports standards on the beaches. (Poertner)
W75-07680

APPLICATION AND TESTING OF THE EPA STORMWATER MANAGEMENT MODEL TO GREENFIELD, MASSACHUSETTS,
Massachusetts Univ., Amherst. Dept. of Civil Engineering.
T. K. Jewell, P. A. Mangarella, and F. A. DiGiano.
In: Proceedings of National Symposium on Urban Rainfall and Runoff and Sediment Control, University of Kentucky, Lexington, July 29-31, 1974. p 61-71, 7 fig, 4 ref.

Descriptors: *Storm water, *Runoff, *Mathematical models, *Planning, *Design, *Operations, Infiltration, Urban runoff, Storm runoff, Effective precipitation, Average runoff, Surface runoff, Model studies, Computer models, Synthetic hydrology, Massachusetts.
Identifiers: *Greenfield(Massachusetts).

The Storm Water Management Model (SWMM) was used to predict quantity and suspended solids content of urban storm water runoff from a 547 acre test basin in Greenfield, Massachusetts. A sensitivity analysis of the input parameters for the runoff portion of the simulation program has been made. Initial comparison was made utilizing synthetic rainfall data. An evaluation of the predictive capability of the three grids, compared with measured quantity and quality, is now in progress. Tentative guidelines have been developed that will assist potential users of this type of urban storm water runoff model. The program cannot itself design drainage systems or treatment facilities. It can perform many repetitive calculations to predict and route storm water and pollutants. If accurate input data is provided and the proper interpretation is made of the output, the SWMM can provide very accurate data upon which engineering design decisions can be made. (Poertner)
W75-07681

IMPACT OF THE USE OF MICROORGANISMS ON THE AQUATIC ENVIRONMENT,
Environmental Protection Agency, Gulf Breeze, Fla. Gulf Breeze Environmental Research Lab.
For primary bibliographic entry see Field 5C.
W75-07687

LIMESTONE AND LIMESTONE-LIME NEUTRALIZATION OF ACID MINE DRAINAGE,
Environmental Protection Agency, Rivesville, W. Va. Crown Mine Drainage Control Field Site.
For primary bibliographic entry see Field 5D.
W75-07688

OIL SPILL AND OIL POLLUTION REPORTS JULY 1974 - OCTOBER 1974,
California Univ, Santa Barbara. Marine Science Inst.
F. A. DeWitt, Jr., and P. Melvin.
Available from the National Technical Information Service, Springfield, Va. 22161, as PB-240 719, $7.25 in paper copy, $2.25 in microfiche. Environmental Protection Agency Cincinnati, Ohio. Report EPA-670/2-75-003, March 1975. 205 p, 437 ref. R-803063.

Descriptors: *Bibliographies, *Oil pollution, *Oil spills, Oil wastes, Patents, *Water pollution control, Documentation, Research and development.

The July 1974 - October 1974 Oil Spill and Oil Pollutiou Reports is the first quarterly compilation of oil spill events and oil pollution report summaries. Presented are: (a) summaries of oil spill events; (b) summaries and bibliographic literature citations; (c) summaries of current research projects; and (d) patent summaries. (EPA)
W75-07689

MINE DRAINAGE POLLUTION CONTROL DEMONSTRATION GRANT PROCEDURES AND REQUIREMENTS,
NUS Corp., Rockville, Md.
F. J. Zaval, and R. A. Burns.
Available from the National Technical Information Service, Springfield, Va. 22161, as PB-230 709, $12.25 in paper copy, $2.25 in microfiche. Environmental Protection Agency, Cincinnati, Ohio. Report EPA-670/2-74-003, October 1974. 99 p, 15 fig. 68-03-0268.

Descriptors: *Grants, *Mine drainage, Financing, *Water polluton control, Mining engineering, Reclamation.
Identifiers: *Mine drainage pollution.

Procedures and requirements are provided for use by all individuals considering or participating in Section 107 grant demonstration projects authorized by Federal Water Pollution Control Act Amendments of 1972. The report provides an interpretation of Section 107, defines the procedures and requirements for grant applicants, and discusses all phases of deomonstration projects, including monitoring requirements and reports. (EPA)
W75-07690

URBAN STORMWATER MANAGEMENT AND TECHNOLOGY: AN ASSESSMENT,
Metcalf and Eddy, Inc., Palo Alto, Calif.
For primary bibliographic entry see Field 5D.
W75-07692

CRANKCASE DRAINAGE FROM IN-SERVICE OUTBOARD MOTORS,
Southwest Research Inst., San Antonio, Tex. Dept. of Emissions Research.
For primary bibliographic entry see Field 5B.
W75-07696

POLLUTED GROUNDWATER: ESTIMATING THE EFFECTS OF MAN'S ACTIVITIES,
General Electric Co., Santa Barbara, Calif. Center for Advanced Studies.
For primary bibliographic entry see Field 5B.
W75-07698

CHARACTERIZATION OF VESSEL WASTES IN DULUTH-SUPERIOR HARBOR,
Environmental Quality Systems, Inc., Rockville, Md.
For primary bibliographic entry see Field 5B.
W75-07701

STATE-OF-THE-ART FOR THE INORGANIC CHEMICALS INDUSTRY: INDUSTRIAL INORGANIC GASES,
Illinois Inst. of Tech., Chicago. Dept. of Environmental Engineering.
For primary bibliographic entry see Field 5B.
W75-07708

STATE-OF-THE-ART FOR THE INORGANIC CHEMICALS INDUSTRY: INORGANIC PESTICIDES,
Illinois Inst. of Tech., Chicago. Dept. of Environmental Engineering.
For primary bibliographic entry see Field 5B.
W75-07709

RATIONALE AND METHODOLOGY FOR MONITORING GROUNDWATER POLLUTED BY MINING ACTIVITIES,
General Electric Co., Santa Barbara, Calif. Center for Advanced Studies.
For primary bibliographic entry see Field 5B.
W75-07710

THE WATER QUALITY AND TIDAL FLUSHING CHARACTERISTICS OF THREE SMALL BOAT BASINS; DES MOINES MARINA, EDMONDS HARBOR, AND NEWPORT SHORES,
Washington Univ., Seattle. Dept. of Civil Engineering.
For primary bibliographic entry see Field 5B.
W75-07726

GOVERNMENT VIEWS ON WATER POLLUTION CONTROL,
Federal Water Pollution Control Administration, Washington, D.C.
K. Biglane.
Journal of Petroleum Technology, Vol 23, p 829-831, July 1971.

Descriptors: *Oil industry, *Water pollution sources, *Oil pollution, *Oil spills, *Federal Water Pollution Control Act, *Federal government, Water pollution, Water law, Environmental effeets, Law enforcement, Legal aspects, Waste water disposal, Legislation, Disasters.

The federal government is anxious to assist in the creation and operation of pollution control programs and facilities, but expects the cost of clean water to be shared by both public and private interests. Damage to the environment by increasing amounts of oil pollution must be ameliorated. This may be accomplished by minimizing the risks of accidental oil spills through the use of adequate prevention measures and prosecution of careless polluters. The amount of oil discharged in normal operations must be reduced by using new procedures and equipment. A law providing for aggressive federal oil pollution control was contained in amendments to the Federal Water Pollution Control Act entitled the Water Quality Improvement Act of 1970. The act prohibits the discharge of harmful quantities of oil. Civil and criminal penalties, and the costs of any oil spill cleanup are to be borne by the discharger. One of the most significant provisions of the Act is that preventive regulations be issued. The regulations will require that failsafe design concepts, operations control procedures, and safety and sensor mechanisms be applied to the oil industry. (Sperling-Florida)
W75-07760

UNITED STATES V. RESERVE MINING CO. (ACTION ON REMAND FROM EIGHTH CIRCUIT ON SUIT TO ENJOIN MINING CO FROM DISCHARGING CARCINOGENICS INTO INTERSTATE WATERS).
380 F. Supp. 11 (D. Minn. 1974).

Descriptors: *Minnesota, *Lake Superior, *Public health, *Mine wastes, *Asbestos, United States, Judicial decisions, Industrial wastes, Legal aspects, Mining, Chemical wastes, Mineral industry, Water pollution sources, Water pollution effects, Water quality, Safety, Federal Water Pollution Control Act, Common law, Economic aspects, Remedies.
Identifiers: Nuisance(Legal aspects), Injunctive relief, Hazardous substances(Pollution).

Plaintiffs sought an injunction against defendant's continuing discharge of taconite tailings into the intrastate and interstate waters of Lake Superior. Defendant operated a taconite mining and processing plant on the shore of Lake Superior, and discharged 67,000 short tons of suspended solids into Lake Superior daily. These solids included amosite asbestos, a known human carcinogen. Plaintiffs contended that the amosite asbestos detected in the drinking water and air of surrounding communities was traceable to defendant's discharges, and that the discharges constituted a common law nuisance and a violation of the Federal Water Pollution Control Act. Defendant denied these allegations and contended that it has no alternative means of disposal of the tailings, and that an injunction of its operation would have severe adverse consequences on the economy of the area. The District Court held that the discharges violated the Federal Water Pollution Control Act and constituted a common law nuisance, and that in view of the demonstrated threat to the public health and defendant's intransigent refusal to dispose of the failings by safer alternative means, an injunction of further discharges was justified. On appeal to the 8th Circuit, the injunction was stayed and the cause remanded. (Sperling-Florida)
W75-07761

SCENIC HUDSON PRESERVATION CONFERENCE V. CALLAWAY (SUIT BY CONSERVATIONISTS TO ENJOIN HYDRO-ELECTRIC PLANT CONSTRUCTION).
For primary bibliographic entry see Field 6E.
W75-07762

CABIN CREEK, AN ACCUMULATION OF UNPAID SOCIAL AND ENVIRONMENTAL COSTS IN APPALACHIA,
Army Engineer District, Huntington, W. Va.
R. G. Baumgardner, and D. E. Steiner.
Water Spectrum, Vol 6, No 2, p 32-38 (1974). 7 photo, 3 map.

Descriptors: *Acid mine water, *Mine wastes, *Water quality control, *Water pollution sources, *West Virginia, Navigable waters, Water conservation, Environmental sanitation, Reclamation, Planning, Data collections, Ohio River, Reservoirs, Flood damage, Flood protection, Wastes, Treatment facilities, Environmental effects, Legislation, Water law, Safety.
Identifiers: *Watershed protection, Flood plain management.

Cabin Creek is a watershed in West Virginia which presents vistas of deep-mine refuse and strip mined coal fields. Section 223 of the Flood Control Act of 1970 authorized the Army Corps of Engineers to review the effects of strip mining operations upon navigable waters and their tributaries and recommend appropriate measures to alleviate the adverse conditions found. Congress asked for a pilot demonstration of a reclamation project that might be undertaken by the Corps. The Corps selected the Huntington District of the Ohio River Division for the assignment. The Huntington Division recommended the drainage basin of Cabin Creek in the Appalachian region as a representative problem area suffering from strip mining effects. The study group found that reservoir storage, flood plain management, and channel rehabilitation afforded opportunities for flood damage prevention. It proposed, among other al-

ternatives, an attack on water quality problems which could include waste collection and treatment systems coupled with eliminating acid mine drainage problems at their source. Six basic categories of projects and measures for rehabilitation are outlined. Finally, the benefits which could be achieved by implementing these projects are discussed. (Sperling-Florida)
W75-07767

WATER QUALITY-BASED EFFLUENT LIMITATIONS.
Pollution Control Guide, Vol 1, paragraph 601-623, p 601-606, 1973. 6 p.

Descriptors: *Standards, *Water quality, *Federal Water Pollution Control Act, *Effluents, Public health, Technology, Fish, Shellfish, Wildlife conservation, Legislation, Water quality control, Water treatment, Waste water disposal, Pollutants, Water law, State governments.
Identifiers: *FWPCA Amendments of 1972.

Water quality standards are the quantitative embodiment of the goals of the 1972 Amendments to the Federal Water Pollution Control Act. They specify the physical, chemical and biological characteristics of water necessary to protect the public health and welfare and provide for the propagation of fish, shellfish, and wildlife. Experience with other legislation has shown that water quality standards form a cumbersome basis for pollution control, due to the difficulty in establishing a direct relationship between the quantity and quality of pollutant discharges and the resulting quality of the receiving water. The 1972 Act, however, requires that the relationship between discharges and water quality be explicitly established where possible. Complementing the water quality standards program is an independent system of effluent limitations that will be applied without reference to the quality of the receiving water. Even though water quality standards are not the sole basis of the program, they still play an important role in the overall process. Each state is required to develop a water quality management program each portion of which must be reviewed and approved by the Environmental Protection Agency. (Sperling-Florida)
W75-07769

DISCHARGE LIMITATIONS--FEDERAL FACILITIES.
Pollution Control Guide, Vol 1, paragraph 950-592, p 916-921, 1973.

Descriptors: *Discharge(Water), *Federal project policy, *Water pollution control, *Water pollution treatment, *Regulation, Waste water(Pollution), Federal government, Jurisdiction, Federal jurisdiction, Control, Water quality standards, Water quality control, Water law, Federal Water Pollution Control Act, Water Quality Act, Effluents, Water pollution sources, Administrative agencies, Law enforcement, Legal aspects, Administration, Inter-agency cooperation, Governmental interrelations, Project planning, Permits, Reservoir storage.
Identifiers: *National Pollutant Discharge Elimination System, FWPCA Amendments of 1972, Administrative regulations, Effluent limitations, Licenses, Certification.

Summarized are the policies of the Environmental Protection Agency (EPA) pertaining to discharge limitations applicable to federal facilities and guidelines for planning storage reservoirs. Every discharger under the jurisdiction of any federal agency must comply with federal, state, interstate, and local pollution control requirements, including the payment of reasonable service charges. The President may, subject to certain limitations, exempt any agency of the executive branch for a period not to exceed one year. Only the EPA is authorized to issue National Pollutant Discharge Elimination System (NPDES) permits to federal dischargers and no state agency is authorized to enter, inspect or monitor a federal facility. Federal dischargers are also exempt from the requirement that all EPA NPDES permit applicants obtain state certification of compliance with applicable limitations and standards. The storage reservoir planning guidelines reflect the EPA policy prohibiting the use of water storage reservoirs as substitutes for adequate waste treatment or other methods for controlling waste at the source. The guidelines applicable to federal projects cover the following areas: adequate treatment or control at the source; the need for storage for water quality control; environmental assessment; assessment of the value of water quality control storage; identification of beneficiaries; and assessment of other benefits. (Deckert-Florida)
W75-07770

WATER REGULATIONS--WATER QUALITY STANDARDS.
Pollution Control Guide, Vol 2, paragraph 8800-8810, p 9241-9249, 1973.

Descriptors: *Water quality, *Water quality standards, *Regulation, *Legislation, *Federal Water Pollution Control Act, United States, Governments, Water pollution, Water law, Public rights, Water policy.

Part 120--Water Quality Standards identifies and describes state adopted water quality standards which the Administrator of the Environmental Protection Agency has determined meet the criteria of the Federal Water Pollution Control Act. Water quality standards consist of water quality criteria and plans for the enforcement and implementation of such criteria. State-adopted water quality standards which are approved by the Administrator are available for inspection at the Regional Offices of the Environmental Protection Agency and at its Washington, D.C. address. (Proctor-Florida)
W75-07771

WATER REGULATIONS--STATE PROGRAM ELEMENTS NECESSARY FOR PARTICIPATION IN THE NATIONAL POLLUTANT DISCHARGE ELIMINATION SYSTEM.
Pollution Control Guide, Vol 2, paragraph 8890-8903, p 9311-9331, 1974.

Descriptors: *Federal Water Pollution Control Act, *Water pollution sources, *Discharge(Water), United States, Waste disposal, Water quality control, Waste identification, Permits, Waste treatment, Sewage effluents, Oceans, Bodies of water.
Identifiers: *Waste discharge, *Vessels.

Part 124, State Program Elements necessary for participation in the National Pollutant Discharge Elimination System (NPDES) establishes guidelines specifying procedural and other elements which must be present in a state or interstate program in order to obtain NPDES permits for specific pollutant discharges. Activities excluded from the provisions are set forth. Public notice of every complete application for an NPDES permit will be circulated in a manner designed to inform interested persons of the proposed discharge and appropriate governmental agencies will be notified to provide opportunity to submit their written views and recommendations. Public hearings will be held with reference to specific applications. Once authorized by permits, discharges will be monitored periodically to insure compliance with the conditions of the permit. Any state or interstate agency participating in the program has the capability for the enforcement of the permit requirements. (Proctor-Florida)
W75-07772

WATER REGULATIONS--NPDES.
Pollution Control Guide, Vol 2, paragraph 8910-8936, p 9351-9371, 1973.

Descriptors: *Water pollution, *Water pollution sources, *Permits, *Federal Water Pollution Control Act, *Discharge(Water), Navigable waters, United States, Waste disposal, Water quality control, Waste identification, Waste treatment, Sewage effluents, Oceans, Bodies of water.
Identifiers: *Waste discharge.

Part 125, National Pollutant Discharge Elimination System prescribes the policy and procedures to be followed in connection with applications for federally issued permits authorizing discharges into navigable waters, waters of the contiguous zone, and the oceans. Exceptions to the applicability of the provisions are noted. All discharges of pollutants from all point sources into navigable waters, the waters of the contiguous zone or ocean are unlawful unless the discharger has a permit or is specifically exempted by law or regulation. Average and maximum daily quantitative limitations for the level of pollutants will be specified. Public notice of every complete application for a permit will be given, as well as an opportunity for public hearing before grant or denial of a permit application. (Proctor-Florida)
W75-07773

WATER REGULATIONS--PREPARATION OF WATER QUALITY MANAGEMENT BASIN PLANS.
Pollution Control Guide, Vol 2, paragraph 8987-8991, p 9401-9408, 1974. 8 p.

Descriptors: *Basins, *Water quality control, *Comprehensive planning, *State governments, *Federal government, Future planning(Projected), Watersheds(Basins), Planning, Water resources development, Water pollution control, Long-term planning, Administration, Coordination, Governmental interrelations, Administrative agencies, Inter-agency, Cooperation, Water quality standards, Water Quality Act, Federal Water Pollution Control Act, Water law, Regional development, Hydrologic systems.
Identifiers: Administrative regulations, *National Pollutant Discharge Elimination System, Environmental policy, Effluent limitations, FWPCA Amendments of 1972.

Presented are regulations established by the Environmental Protection Agency pursuant to section 303 (e) of the Federal Water Pollution Control Act, as amended in 1972. These regulations specify procedural and other requirements for the preparation of basin plans pursuant to state continuing planning processes approved in accordance with section 303 (e) of the Act. A basin plan is a management document which identifies the water quality problems of a particular basin and sets forth an effective remedial program. The plan should be designed to provide for orderly water quality management by identifying problems, assessing needs and priorities, scheduling actions to be taken, and coordinating planning. Included are regulations pertaining to the scope and purpose of basin planning, preparation for basin planning, basin plan methodology and contents, monitoring and surveillance, completion and review of basin plans, and the relation of basin plans to certain grants and permits. (Deckert-Florida)
W75-07774

WATER REGULATIONS--CRITERIA FOR THE EVALUATION OF PERMIT APPLICATIONS.
Pollution Control Guide, Vol 2, paragraph 9138-9165, p 9551-9557, 1973.

Descriptors: *Water pollution, *Water pollution sources, *Water quality control, *Water management, Sewage treatment, Water law, Pollutant identification, Data collections, Path of pollutants, Toxins, Water quality, Pollution abatement, Regulation.

Criteria are presented for the evaluation of permit applications for the dumping or discharge of materials in quantities which would adversely affect human or marine health into ocean waters. Application for permits should be evaluated on the basis of the impact of the materials on the marine environment and marine ecosystems. The disposal of some types of waste materials is strictly regulated to minimize known or potential adverse effects on the aquatic environment. Regulation of containerized wastes, materials containing living organisms, solid wastes, and disposal of dredged material is described. Material which is determined to be unpolluted may be dumped at approved sites. Test procedures for determining the nature and quantity of pollutants are revised as applicable knowledge develops. In order to limit possible concentrations of pollutants in specific areas, release and mixing zones have been developed. (Proctor-Florida)
W75-07776

GROUND-WATER PROTECTION IN PENNSYLVANIA, A MODEL STATE PROGRAM,
Geraghty and Miller, Port Washington, N.Y.
For primary bibliographic entry see Field 4B.
W75-07777

ENVIRONMENTAL CONCERN AND POLITICAL ELITES: A STUDY OF PERCEPTIONS BACKGROUNDS AND ATTITUDES,
California Univ., Davis. Inst. of Governmental Affairs.
For primary bibliographic entry see Field 6G.
W75-07779

RESEARCH DEMONSTRATION PILOT STUDY OF MUNICIPAL WASTE COMPOSTING (FINAL ENVIRONMENTAL STATEMENT),
Agricultural Research Service, Washington, D.C.
For primary bibliographic entry see Field 5D.
W75-07786

REJECTION OF TRACE METALS FROM COAL DURING BENEFICIATION BY AGGLOMERATION,
National Research Council of Canada, Ottawa (Ontario). Div. of Chemistry.
For primary bibliographic entry see Field 5A.
W75-07795

RENOVATION OF WASTES BY MINE TAILINGS PONDS,
Idaho Univ., Moscow.
For primary bibliographic entry see Field 5B.
W75-07800

SEPARATOR FOR LIQUIDS OF DIFFERENT DENSITIES,
For primary bibliographic entry see Field 5D.
W75-07805

OIL BOOM,
Shell Oil Co., Houston, Tex. (assignee).
R. R. Ayers.
U.S. Patent No. 3,859,797, 3 p, 1 fig, 5 ref; Official Gazette of the United States Patent Office, Vol 930, No 2, p 623, January 14, 1974.

Descriptors: *Patents, *Oil spills, *Oil pollution, *Pollution abatement, Water pollution control, *Separation techniques, Equipment, Flotsam.
Identifiers: *Oil booms.

A boom for deployment on a water surface comprises: an upright corrugated skirt with the axes of corrugations running from top to bottom of the skirt; support for the skirt having at least one pair of V-shaped outriggers having floats attached to its extremities and inverted over the upper edge of the skirt and attached to it; tandem cables for carrying boom tension attached near the water line on opposite sides of the skirt; and bafffles spaced in front of the skirt. (Sinha-OEIS)
W75-07807

LAKE RAKING APPARATUS,
U.S. Patent No. 3,863,237, 3 p, 3 fig, 5 ref; Official Gazette of the United States Patent Office, Vol 930, No 4, p 1977, January 28, 1975.

Descriptors: *Patents, *Pollution abatement, *Water pollution control, *Water quality control, Ponds, *Lakes, Equipment, Dredging.
Identifiers: Debris.

A hand operated apparatus removes stones, weeds, debris and the like from the bottom of ponds and lakes. The apparatus is comprised of a rigid foraminious box-like structure having one open side and a handle attached to one edge of the open side and a rigid cutting edge attached to the edge of the open side opposite the handle. In operation the take is grasped by the cross bar and open end of the rigid receptable, pulled across the area of lake bottom to be cleaned with the cutting edge in contact with the lake bottom. The debris present will be urged up into the receptacle and retained therein. (Sinha-OEIS)
W75-07809

SKIMMING BLADE,
FMC Corp., Chicago, Ill. (assignee)
For primary bibliographic entry see Field 5D.
W75-07812

APPARATUS FOR TAKING FLOATING AND SOLID MATERIALS OUT OF CHANNELS,
G. Abel.
U.S. Patent No. 3,872,006, 4 p, 5 fig, 9 ref; Official Gazette of the United States Patent Office, Vol 932, No 3, p 1077, March 18, 1975.

Descriptors: *Patents, *Flotsam, *Water pollution control, Water quality control, *Pollution abatement, Equipment, *Separation techniques, Solid wastes.

An apparatus is described for taking floating and solid materials out of channels, especially channels of clarification plants. The apparatus includes an inclined grate that is transmissible for liquids and extends to the bottom of a channel, the grate changing over into a conveyor chute leading to a discharge outlet. Driven elevator chains are provided with blades passing along the inclined conveyor chute and adjoining grate to remove floating and solid materials from the channel in which the grate is positioned. These elevator chains are guided by lower and upper sprockets, the lower sprockets being mounted in independent suspension on side walls pivotally arranged about the axis of the upper sprockets thereby providing the blades with better mobility. The apparatus may also be used in the textile or leather manufacturing industries for removing fibers and fiber-like materials from liquids. (Sinha-OEIS)
W75-07814

THE FEASIBILITY OF PENAEID SHRIMP CULTURE IN BRACKISH PONDS RECEIVING TREATED SEWAGE EFFLUENT,
North Carolina State Univ., Raleigh. Sea Grant Program.
For primary bibliographic entry see Field 3C.
W75-07830

6. WATER RESOURCES PLANNING

6A. Techniques Of Planning

THE INTERRELATIONSHIP OF ECONOMIC DEVELOPMENT AND ENVIRONMENTAL QUALITY IN THE UPPER COLORADO RIVER BASIN: AN INTERINDUSTRY ANALYSIS,
Colorado Univ., Boulder. Dept. of Economics.
For primary bibliographic entry see Field 6B.
W75-07377

WATER SUPPLY AND WASTEWATER DISPOSAL IN RURAL AREAS OF INDIA,
Greenleaf/Telesca, Miami, Fla. Environmental Sciences Dept.
For primary bibliographic entry see Field 4A.
W75-07381

A GENERAL LINEAR APPROACH TO STREAM WATER QUALITY MODELING,
IBM Federal Systems Div., Gaithersburg, Md.
For primary bibliographic entry see Field 5B.
W75-07382

LINEAR DECISION RULE IN RESERVOIR MANAGEMENT AND DESIGN, 4. A RULE THAT MINIMIZES OUTPUT VARIANCE,
Johns Hopkins Univ., Baltimore, Md. Dept. of Geography and Environmental Engineering.
For primary bibliographic entry see Field 4A.
W75-07383

LINEAR DECISION RULE IN RESERVOIR MANAGEMENT AND DESIGN, 5. A GENERAL ALGORITHM,
Johns Hopkins Univ., Baltimore, Md. Dept. of Geography and Environmental Engineering.
For primary bibliographic entry see Field 4A.
W75-07384

A REVIEW AND EVALUATION OF MULTIOBJECTIVE PROGRAMMING TECHNIQUES,
Johns Hopkins Univ., Baltimore, Md. Dept. of Geography and Environmental Engineering.
J. L. Cohon, and D. H. Marks.
Water Resources Research, Vol 11, No 2, p 208-220, April 1975. 5 fig, 5 tab, 51 equ, 48 ref.

Descriptors: *Water resources, *Planning, *Evaluation, Decision making, Constraints, Optimization, Systems analysis, Mathematical models, *Reviews.
Identifiers: *Multiobjective programming techniques, Vector optimization, Trade-offs.

The recent proliferation of methods for solving vector optimization problems has left little time for considering some highly important issues related to the multiobjective analysis of public investment alternatives. Presented is a discussion of these issues and an evaluation of the utility of multiobjective programming techniques for water resource planning. Three criteria are established for such evaluation: (1) computational efficiency; (2) explicitness of trade-offs among objectives; and (3) the amount of information generated for decision making. The multiobjective approaches are classified, and the methods in the various classes are reviewed and evaluated in terms of the hypothesized criteria. The classes, and their methods considered, are: (1) generating techniques, including weighting and constraint methods; (2) techniques which rely on prior articulation of preferences: noninterative methods, including goal programming, utility functions and optimal weights, the electre method, and the surrogate worth trade-off method; and (3) techniques which rely on progressive articulation of

preferences, including the step method. The evaluations are then used in establishing conclusions about the applicability of the multiobjective approaches to water resource problems. (Bell-Cornell)
W75-07385

WATER QUALITY MODELING BY MONTE CARLO SIMULATION,
Maine Univ., Orono. Dept. of Civil Engineering.
For primary bibliographic entry see Field 5B.
W75-07386

DECISION ANALYSIS FOR THE RIVER WALK EXPANSION IN SAN ANTONIO, TEXAS,
Texas Univ., San Antonio. Dept. of Environmental Studies.
For primary bibliographic entry see Field 6B.
W75-07387

A SCREENING MODEL FOR WATER RESOURCES PLANNING,
Nebraska Univ., Lincoln. Water Resources Research Inst.
W. Viessman, Jr., G. L. Lewis, I. Yomtovian, and N. J. Viessman.
Water Resources Bulletin, Vol 11, No 2, p 245-255, April 1975. 2 fig, 3 tab, 3 ref.

Descriptors: Water resources, *Planning, *Linear programming, *Economic efficiency, *Simulation analysis, *Flood control, Optimization, Regional development, Management, Streamflow, Costs, Benefits, Flood damage, Alternative planning, Surface waters, Water utilization, Reservoir storage, Recreation, Constraints, Evaluation, Hydrologic aspects, Mathematical models, Systems analysis, *Nebraska.
Identifiers: *Screening models, *Elkhorn River basin(Neb), Cost minimization, Benefit maximization.

Optimization and simulation are combined in a procedure to select the most efficient arrangement of components for regional water resources development and management policy. The technique is applied to the Elkhorn River basin in Nebraska, which extends over 7,000 square miles and includes 184 proposed reservoirs. Structure sizes, locations and operating policies are selected for optimal plans based on economic efficiency and regional development. Model input consists of an historical or simulated sequence of unregulated annual and within-year period streamflows at each water use or management site. The proposed model is intended as a preliminary screening tool; it is easy to apply, has minimal data requirements, and has a sound physical base. Use of the model, which utilizes linear programming, in decision making for flood control is considered in detail. Objectives employed in evaluating alternatives include both net annual benefit maximization and annual cost minimization. Results indicate that substantial savings in time and costs over conventional planning techniques are effected. Agreement between model output and agency design values was noted.
W75-07388

STOCHASTIC WATER QUALITY CONTROL BY SIMULATION,
Texas Univ., San Antonio. Div. of Environmental Studies.
For primary bibliographic entry see Field 5B.
W75-07389

DYNAMIC PROGRAMMING FOR OPTIMAL CAPACITY EXPANSION OF WASTEWATER TREATMENT PLANTS,
Case Western Reserve Univ., Cleveland, Ohio. Systems Engineering Div.
For primary bibliographic entry see Field 5D.
W75-07390

MATHEMATICAL MODELLING OF WATER RESOURCES SYSTEMS,
Israel Inst. of Tech., Haifa.
N. Buras.
Hydrological Sciences Bulletin, Vol 19, No 4, p 393-400, December 1974. 80 ref.

Descriptors: *Water resources, *Planning, *Mathematical models, Computers, *Operations research, Dynamic programming, Linear programming, Environmental effects, Cost-benefit analysis, Regional development, *Model studies.
Identifiers: *Systems engineering, Systems synthesis, Trade-offs.

Mathematical models are becoming increasingly important in water resources systems engineering. Systems engineering can be viewed as a sequence of steps which lead from the formulation of the problem, to the design of the various components, to their construction, and finally to their operation. Computers facilitate and expedite analysis at almost any level of accuracy. However, the limitations of the available computer capability often determine that level. The application of mathematical models to the central problem in water resources enables a more incisive insight into the nature of the problem. The use of mathematical models, however, depends heavily on the amount and quality of the data available because the results of analysis are only as good as the data used and the assumptions underlying the mathematical models. There are two broad areas in mathematical modelling of water resources systems which now receive increased attention. One area, in which the emphasis is in natural sciences, has to do with environment impacts of those systems. The other area, where social sciences carry more weight, is that of relating the economy to demand for and benefits from water and water derived outputs. (Singh-ISWS)
W75-07438

HYDROLOGIC IMPACT OF WATER MODIFICATION,
Agricultural Research Service, Chickasha, Okla.
For primary bibliographic entry see Field 3B.
W75-07505

COMPUTER SIMULATION OF LAND USE DYNAMICS,
Oregon State Univ., Corvallis. Willamette Simulation Unit.
C. C. Calligan.
In: Land and Water Use in Oregon; Seminar conducted by Oregon State University, Spring Quarter 1974, Water Resources Research Institute, Corvallis, Oregon, p 9-25, July 1974. 9 fig, 6 ref.

Descriptors: *Computer models, *Land use, *Model studies, *Oregon, Urbanization, Mathematical models, Land management, Land classification, Land resources, Forests, Agriculture, Cities, Industries, Valleys.
Identifiers: *Willamette Valley(Ore).

The land use model described is one component of the larger Willamette Simulation Model. Various inputs into the model describe policy variables whose values the policy maker (the model user) can directly influence and scenario variables that can be changed frequently in order to create different 'what if' scenarios such as interest rates. Data variables are fixed inputs whose values are determined initially by the modeler, but which can be changed if better data becomes available. Dynamic inputs are variables that come from other components of the model; their values are updated at each time step (e.g., demand for industrial land from the economic component). Dynamic outputs are variables that are calculated at each time step in the land use component; some are information outputs only and some feed back to other components as inputs (e.g., speculative land value to the economic component). The use of the model was illustrated by a discussion of its use in predicting the demand for residential land and land market speculation. The model helped to identify the key variables and to determine how they are interconnected. It also can help to find elusive 'critical points of intervention.' (See also W75-07507) (Sims-ISWS)
W75-07509

ENVIRONMENTAL CARRYING CAPACITY: AN INTEGRATIVE MANAGEMENT CONCEPT,
Environmental Protection Agency, Washington, D.C. Office of Research and Development.
P. W. House.
In: Environmental Management in the Colorado River Basin, October 15-16, 1973, Salt Lake City, Utah, Utah State University Press, Logan, 1974, p 37-58. 4 fig.

Descriptors: *Model studies, *Colorado River Basin, *Computer models, *Long-term planning, *Environmental effects, *Land use, Arizona, New Mexico, Utah, Colorado, Wyoming, Nevada, California, Regional analysis, Resource allocation.
Identifiers: Environmental management.

A State of the System Model can be designed to measure and evaluate a region's resources. Such a model can be used to test a region's current allocation of resources or a comprehensive plan for the future. Feasibility of a proposal is demonstrated if the desired growth can be achieved without violating any of the side conditions initially built into the model, such as development of industry without exceeding a predetermined maximum permissible pollution level. The State of the System Model has four basic components: (1) Sectors of growth; (2) Production component output; (3) Limitations and constraints; and (4) Long term goals of society. Since the model has many adjustment loops, it is particularly adept at incorporating the variables of a region. Thus, the model addresses questions such as whether or not a region has the capability of arriving at desired goals given the existing problems and the area-specific adjustment processes. (See also W75-07525) (Bowden-Arizona)
W75-07529

CONCEPTS OF CARRYING CAPACITY AND PLANNING IN COMPLEX ECOLOGICAL SYSTEMS,
Colorado State Univ., Fort Collins. Dept. of Sociology and Anthropology.
D. M. Freeman, and P. J. Brown.
In: Environmental Management in the Colorado River Basin, October 15-16, 1973, Salt Lake City, Utah, Utah State University Press, Logan, 1974, p 281-297, 17 ref.

Descriptors: *Colorado River Basin, *Planning, *Decision making, *Regional development, *Carrying capacity, Arizona, Utah, Colorado, New Mexico, Wyoming, California, Nevada, Alternative planning.
Identifiers: Environmental management.

The concept of carrying capacity is examined for its utility in analyzing resource allocation problems in ecosystems as complex as the Colorado River Basin. The key to solving a problem is to formulate it usefully. Carrying capacity is too limited a concept to be useful, i.e., it sets limits of numbers but fails to clarify distribution. Planning should focus instead on alternative futures. Actions taken should be at the lowest possible cost in resources and the highest possible number of options should be kept open for the future. The social sciences can help fabricate learning systems for planning decisions. Benefits could be: (1) to allow for decentralized decision making with the discipline of preserving and expanding the contexts of choice; (2) to allow flexibility in decision making with a defense against all decisions that foreclose future options. (See also W75-07525) (Bowden-Arizona)
W75-07544

PUERTO RICO WATER RESOURCES PLANNING MODEL STUDY,
Geological Survey, Reston, Va.
D. W. Moody, E. D. Attanasi, E. R. Close, T. Maddock, III, and M. A. Lopez.
Open-file report, July 1973. 114 p, 10 fig, 8 tab, 77 ref.

Descriptors: *Model studies, *Planning, *Systems analysis, *Puerto Rico, *Water resources development, *Data collections, Basic data collections, Water demand, Water supply, Economics, Costs, Mathematical models.

The Puerto Rico Water Resources Planning Model Study, in addition to developing analytical tools for Commonwealth planners, was designed to provide an opportunity to evaluate the adequacy of data collection programs in terms of water resources development, and some of the water problems facing Commonwealth planners are reviewed. Some of the systems analysis techniques available to water resources planners and planning models proposed for use in Puerto Rico, are described. The availability of data used in the planning models and the steps required to implement the techniques are summarized. (Knapp-USGS)
W75-07568

A SPECIAL PLANNING TECHNIQUE FOR STREAM-AQUIFER SYSTEMS,
Geological Survey, Denver, Colo.
For primary bibliographic entry see Field 2A.
W75-07584

MONTEREY COUNTY MASTER DRAINAGE PLAN, SANTA RITA CREEK WATERSHED.
Monterey County Surveyors, Inc., Salinas, Calif; and McCreary-Koretsky-International, Salinas, Calif.
For primary bibliographic entry see Field 4A.
W75-07661

MONTEREY COUNTY MASTER DRAINAGE PLAN EL TORO CREEK WATERSHED.
Monterey County Surveyors, Inc., Salinas, Calif.; and Koretsky King Associates, Inc., Salinas, Calif.
For primary bibliographic entry see Field 4A.
W75-07662

MONTEREY COUNTY MASTER DRAINAGE PLAN, CARMEL VALLEY WATERSHEDS.
Monterey County Surveyors, Inc., Salinas, Calif; and Koretsky King Associates, Inc., Salinas, Calif.
For primary bibliographic entry see Field 4A.
W75-07663

WATER QUALITY CONTROL PLAN: SAN FRANCISCO BAY BASIN, CALIFORNIA,
Water Resources Engineers, Inc., Walnut Creek, Calif; and Yoder, Trotter, Orlob and Associates, Walnut Creek, Calif.
For primary bibliographic entry see Field 5G.
W75-07673

SYSTEM IDENTIFICATION AND MULTI-LEVEL OPTIMIZATION OF INTEGRATED GROUND WATER SYSTEMS,
California Univ., Los Angeles. Dept. of Engineering Systems.
For primary bibliographic entry see Field 2F.
W75-07722

6B. Evaluation Process

ECONOMIC IMPLICATION OF PUBLIC WATER POLICY IN ARIZONA,
Arizona Univ., Tucson. Dept. of Agricultural Economics.
For primary bibliographic entry see Field 6E.
W75-07351

METHODS OF COMMUNICATING ACTIVITIES IN POLLUTION ABATEMENT BY FIVE HUNDRED MAJOR INDUSTRIAL CORPORATIONS IN THE UNITED STATES,
Texas A and M Univ., College Station. Environmental Quality Program.
For primary bibliographic entry see Field 5G.
W75-07359

WATER SUPPLY IN CENTRAL AND SOUTHERN APACHE COUNTY,
Arizona Water Commission, Phoenix.
For primary bibliographic entry see Field 4B.
W75-07370

TEXAS WATERBORNE COMMERCE COMMODITY FLOW STATISTICS,
Texas Transportation Inst., College Station.
J. T. Lamkin, and W. R. Lowery.
Available from the National Technical Information Service, Springfield, Va 22161 as COM-74-10083, $5.25 in paper copy, $2.25 in microfiche. TAMU-SG-73-207, June 1973. 115 p, 17 fig, 89 tab, 3 append. NOAA 04-30-158-18.

Descriptors: *Texas, *Inland waterways, *Transportation, *Harbors, Economic impact, Coasts, Employment, Import, Export.
Identifiers: *Waterborne commerce.

Information compiled on tonnage reflects commodity movements at Texas ports and waterways in 1965 and 1970 and highlights the role of waterborne commerce to the Texas economy. Total tonnage moving in foreign trade increased by 4 million tons in 1970 over 1965 while domestic coastwise traffic declined by a corresponding amount during the same period. Intracoastal waterway traffic increased by almost 8 million tons. However, despite this absolute increase in Texas' share of foreign tonnage, domestic coastwide and internal tonnage declined in relation to the rest of the Nation. Several of the major ports in the State have serious traffic imbalances. The data illustrates the close connection between most ports and waterways in the state and the petroleum and chemical industries. Texas ports and waterways were utilized by the State's industries to ship and receive over 190 million tons of goods in 1970, representing 12.6% of total activity at all U.S. ports in that year. Domestic movements represent 78.8% of the Texas total while coastwise and inland water traffic represents 32.8% and 15.0% respectively, of the U.S. total in these categories. Major commodities making up the flow are identified. The loss of 4 million tons in coastwide trade is of special concern to the State. (Auen-Wisconsin)
W75-07376

THE INTERRELATIONSHIP OF ECONOMIC DEVELOPMENT AND ENVIRONMENTAL QUALITY IN THE UPPER COLORADO RIVER BASIN: AN INTERINDUSTRY ANALYSIS,
Colorado Univ., Boulder. Dept. of Economics.
B. Udis, C. W. Howe, and J. F. Kreider.
Available from the National Technical Information Service, Springfield, Va 22161 as COM-73-11970, $15.25 in paper copy, $2.25 in microfiche. Report No. EDA-OER-73-122, July 1973. 651 p, 55 fig, 190 tab, 102 ref. OER-351-G-71-8.

Descriptors: *Computer programs, *Computer models, *Regional economics, *Environmental effects, *Air pollution, *Hydrologic systems, *Colorado River Basin, *River basin development, Input-output analysis, Water supply, Water quality, Salinity, Economic impact, Water management(Applied), Forestry, Agriculture, Recreation, Mining, Electric power, Oil shales, Water pollution, Industrial production.
Identifiers: *Air diffusion models, *Hydrologic-salinity models, Colorado River sub-basin, Green River sub-basin, San Juan River sub-basin, Fortran.

To permit planners to test some of the environmental implications of alternative growth patterns for the three sub-basins of the Upper Colorado River, a set of compatible models relating economic activities, present and prospective, to air quality and water quality and quantity resulting from economic patterns of activity were developed. The Upper Main Stem, the Green and the San Juan sub-basins contain great potential for further recreational and industrial development, and therefore provide an opportunity to identify the results of inconsistent planning. Each sub-basin model contains three major components: (1) an economic input-output model supplemented by coefficients of air- and waterborne waste residuals for each industry; (2) an air diffusion model; and (3) a hydrologic-salinity model to trace monthly surface and groundwater and salt flows through the system. Although originally the feasibility of water and air quality models for such large and complex regions was questionable, results have been encouraging. It is anticipated that similar models will be applied to analyze major environmental impacts of such critical developments as increasing agricultural water uses, development of a major shale oil industry, and continued diversions of water from the Upper Main Stem sub-basin to the eastern slope of the Rocky Mountains. (Becker-Wisconsin)
W75-07377

JAPAN: A SURVEY OF PORTS, DEEP WATER TERMINALS, AND VESSELS,
Army Engineer District, San Francisco, Calif. Economics Branch.
For primary bibliographic entry see Field 6C.
W75-07379

SOUTHWEST ENERGY STUDY. SUMMARY REPORT.
Southwest Energy Federal Task Force.
Available from the National Technical Information Service, Springfield, Va 22161 as PB-232 096, $8.75 in paper copy, $2.25 in microfiche. November 1972. 253 p, 28 fig, 25 tab.

Descriptors: *Energy, *Fossil fuels, *Colorado River Basin, *Southwest U.S., *Environmental effects, Coal mines, Economic impact, Electric power production, Electric power demand, Strip mine wastes, Energy conversion, Indian reservations, Public lands, Electric powerplants, Social impact, Air pollution, Strip mines, Land reclamation, Transmission lines, Transportation, Natural resources, Water supply, Future planning(Projected), Spoil banks, Leases, Pipelines.
Identifiers: *Coal reserves, *Coal-fired electric power.

Based on observations and inspections by the Southwest Energy Study team, the information presented in work group reports, information furnished by contributors to the study, and comments received on the April 1972 draft of the report on the Southwest Energy Study, conclusions were evolved concerning existing and proposed coal-fired steam-electric generating plants in the Southwestern United States. Also examined were projected needs for electric energy, alternative means for supplying it, and the resulting environmental effects. Four different energy production levels (Phases I-IV) were assumed in order to represent horizons against which to judge impacts and needed controls on the use of Colorado River

Basin coal. The study findings are grouped under six categories: (1) Energy Need and Supply, (2) Resources Available, (3) Impacts, (4) Mitigation of Impacts, (5) Alternatives, and (6) Information Needs. Sufficient coal and water exist within the area to meet the need for 30,000 mw of coal-fired steam-electric energy. This power generation is predicted, according to diffusion model analysis, to create sulphur dioxide concentrations exceeding short-term national air quality standards in the vicinity of all plants included in Phase I, the lowest level of energy production. Significant information shortages exist in many important areas of the study. (Becker-Wisconsin)
W75-07380

A REVIEW AND EVALUATION OF MULTIOBJECTIVE PROGRAMMING TECHNIQUES,
Johns Hopkins Univ., Baltimore, Md. Dept. of Geography and Environmental Engineering.
For primary bibliographic entry see Field 6A.
W75-07385

DECISION ANALYSIS FOR THE RIVER WALK EXPANSION IN SAN ANTONIO, TEXAS,
Texas Univ., San Antonio. Dept. of Environmental Studies.
J. H. Dean, and C. S. Shih.
Water Resources Bulletin, Vol 11, No 2, p 237-244, April 1975. 3 fig, 2 equ, 3 ref.

Descriptors: Water resources development, *Decision making, *Intangible benefits, *Methodology, Evaluation, Rivers, Simulation analysis, Monte Carlo methods, Recreation, Tangible benefits, Management, Planning, Systems analysis, Equations, Mathematical models, Reliability, Economics, Assessment, *Texas.
Identifiers: *San Antonio River Walk(Texas), Decision analysis, *Multiattribute utility theory, Alternatives, Sensitivity analysis, Urban areas, Ranking, Optimum choice-making.

The San Antonio River Walk, a unique tourist attraction and urban rejuvenation catalyst, is of great social and economic value to that city. Its success has led to plans for expansion of the present River Walk. It is held that the expansion decision should not be evaluated merely on a benefit-cost ratio. The Water Resources Council has recommended that intangible attributes such as recreational values and social impacts be considered as well as tangible attributes such as cost. This has prompted the application of decision analysis techniques with multiattribute utility ratings. Decision analysis is a systematic solution procedure which can be used to crystallize a complicated decision problem into manageable subproblems by ranking the decision alternatives in accordance with cardinal utility values attached to their consequences. Recent advances in multiattribute utility theory allow a decision maker to weigh utility assessment over tangible and intangible attributes according to their relative importance. This insures that the intangible attributes will receive due consideration in the final decision-making. Moreover, sensitivity analysis embedded with Monte-Carlo simulation can add extra dimensions of reliability to the decision analysis results. (Bell-Cornell)
W75-07387

A SCREENING MODEL FOR WATER RESOURCES PLANNING,
Nebraska Univ., Lincoln. Water Resources Research Inst.
For primary bibliographic entry see Field 6A.
W75-07388

ANALYSIS OF NEW TECHNIQUES FOR PUBLIC INVOLVEMENT IN WATER PLANNING,
Stanford Univ., Calif. Dept. of Civil Engineering.
T. P. Wagner, and L. Ortolano.
Water Resources Bulletin, Vol 11, No 2, p 329-344, April 1975. 40 ref.

Descriptors: *Water resources, *Planning, *Simulation analysis, Computers, Communication, Forecasting, Decision making, Alternative planning, Evaluation, Priorities, Mathematical models, Systems analysis, Washington.
Identifiers: *Public involvement, Gaming, Delphi method, Public brochures, Priority evaluation game, Predicting, Policy, Ranking, Impact, Seattle(Wash), Inland Lakes Project.

Growing demands by the public for a more active role in water planning have recently generated considerable interest among researchers and planners in the subject of public involvement techniques. Numerous surveys have found, however, that standard public participation techniques (e.g., public hearings) by themselves are considered inadequate. Several techniques having potential for overcoming some of the limitations of standard public involvement methods have recently been developed. Several of these new techniques are described and analyzed in terms of their potential utility in water resources planning. Delphi inquiries, KSIM, gaming simulations, the priority evaluation game, computer based communication systems, and public brochures with feedback are examined in terms of ease of implementation, numbers of affected publics who can participate, kinds of results which can be expected in field level planning situations, and the kinds of planning activities with which the techniques can be used. The activities include problem definition, formulation of alternative actions, impact analysis, and the ranking of alternative actions. Of all the new techniques examined, the use of public information brochures with feedback currently has the greatest potential for meaningfully involving publics in field level water planning. (Bell-Cornell)
W75-07391

ISRAEL'S WATER ECONOMY AND ITS PROBLEMS IN THE EARLY SEVENTIES,
Tahal Consulting Engineers Ltd., Tel-Aviv (Israel). Long Range Planning Section.
For primary bibliographic entry see Field 6D.
W75-07402

TEACHING COASTAL ZONE MANAGEMENT: AN INTRODUCTORY COURSE SYLLABUS,
Massachusetts Inst. of Tech., Cambridge. Dept. of Civil Engineering.
For primary bibliographic entry see Field 2L.
W75-07411

MATHEMATICAL MODELLING OF WATER RESOURCES SYSTEMS,
Israel Inst. of Tech., Haifa.
For primary bibliographic entry see Field 6A.
W75-07438

LAND AND WATER USE IN OREGON,
Oregon State Univ., Corvallis. Water Resources Research Inst.
Available from the National Technical Information Service, Springfield, Va. 22161, as PB-241 709, $5.75 in paper copy, $2.25 in microfiche. Seminar, Spring Quarter 1974, July 1974. 130 p. OWRT A-999-ORE(17).

Descriptors: *Conferences, *Land use, *Water utilization, *Oregon, Model studies, Computer models, Land classification, Economics, Social aspects, Demand, Industries, Urbanization, Flood plains, Flood protection, Flood plain insurance, Water law, Adjudication procedure, Administrative agencies, Legislation, Parks, Natural resources, Recreation, Legal aspects, Waste treatment, Septic tanks, Planning, Public access, Coasts, Groundwater, Aquifer systems, Groundwater basins, Water quality.
Identifiers: Consumer protection, *Willamette River(Ore).

Oregon land and water problems were discussed in a series of 10 weekly seminars. Subjects included: (1) the practical limits of pollution control technology, (2) computer simulation of land use dynamics, (3) evolving patterns of flood plain use, (4) adjudication in landwater disputes, (5) consumer protection and land use, (6) Willamette River parks system, (7) the septic tank's role in land use, (8) constitutional restrictions on coastal land use, (9) Oregon's approach to groundwater investigation, and (10) water quality in eastern Oregon. (See W75-07508 thru W75-07517) (Humphreys-ISWS)
W75-07507

THE PRACTICAL LIMITS OF POLLUTION CONTROL TECHNOLOGY,
Oregon State Univ., Corvallis. Dept. of Civil Engineering.
For primary bibliographic entry see Field 5G.
W75-07508

COMPUTER SIMULATION OF LAND USE DYNAMICS,
Oregon State Univ., Corvallis. Willamette Simulation Unit.
For primary bibliographic entry see Field 6A.
W75-07509

EVOLVING PATTERNS OF FLOOD PLAIN USE,
Oregon State Univ., Corvallis. Dept. of Geography.
For primary bibliographic entry see Field 6F.
W75-07510

ADJUDICATION IN LAND-WATER DISPUTES,
Oregon Div. of State Lands, Salem.
For primary bibliographic entry see Field 6E.
W75-07511

CONSUMER PROTECTION AND LAND USE,
Oregon Real Estate Div., Salem.
H. H. Hargreaves.
In: Land and Water Use in Oregon; Seminar conducted by Oregon State University, Spring Quarter 1974, Water Resources Research Institute, Corvallis, Oregon, p 51-54, July 1974.

Descriptors: *Land use, *Land development, *Zoning, *Legislation, *Oregon, Real property, Regulation, Planning, Social aspects, Legal aspects, Comprehensive planning.
Identifiers: *Real estate agents, *Consumer protection, Real estate, Disclosure statements, Warranties.

The forces for consumer protection and land use planning are in tension with the traditional conduct of the real estate and building businesses. Consumer protection legislation was built into House Bill 2607, which was repealed in the 1974 special legislative session. It required the developer to disclose all relevant information to the consumer about the purchase. This included information about the land, water, sewage, planned improvements or lack of same, schools, fire protection, etc. Confusion about the warranty aspect of full disclosure in House Bill 2607 was a major factor in its repeal. The agent or developer provides service to both seller and purchaser. In order to serve the seller he must know the product as intimately as possible; it is simply not possible to provide adequate representation without knowing the property. The agent or the seller cannot execute a responsible sale unless available information about land use is offered the purchaser. The responsible agent, for instance, thinks in economic and environmental terms and he is probably more informed than planners about personal and social relationships in a given area. Responsible agents can aid the efforts to plan wisely, but to gain their interest, they must be forced into the process it-

self. Disclosure laws can serve to stimulate their involvement. (See also W75-07507) (Sims-ISWS)
W75-07512

WILLAMETTE RIVER PARKS SYSTEM,
Willamette River Parks System, Salem, Oreg.
G. W. Churchill.
In: Land and Water Use in Oregon; Seminar conducted by Oregon State University, Spring Quarter 1974, Water Resources Research Institute, Corvallis, Oregon, p 55-67, July 1974.

Descriptors: *Parks, *Rivers, *River basin development, Recreation facilities, Scenery, Scenic highways, Legislation, Legal aspects, Administrative agencies, Natural resources, Public access, Water policy, Water quality control, Water pollution control, Pulp wastes, Pulp and paper industry, *Oregon.
Identifiers: *Willamette River(Ore).

The history and present status of the Willamette River Parks System was discussed. The system was established by a law passed in 1967. Presently, 69.5 miles of river frontage are owned by the state or by local governments as part of the parks system. The pollution of the river has been reduced, to an important extent by the reduction of paper mill wastes discharged into the river. The effects of recent amendments to the 1967 law were described. Significant amendments were reproduced as part of the paper. (See also W75-07507) (Sims-ISWS)
W75-07513

THE SEPTIC TANK'S ROLE IN LAND USE,
Oregon State Dept. of Environmental Quality, Portland.
For primary bibliographic entry see Field 5D.
W75-07514

CONSTITUTIONAL RESTRICTIONS ON COASTAL LAND USE,
Oregon State Land Conservation and Development Commission, Portland.
For primary bibliographic entry see Field 6E.
W75-07515

OREGON'S APPROACH TO GROUNDWATER INVESTIGATIONS,
Oregon State Engineer's Office, Salem.
For primary bibliographic entry see Field 4B.
W75-07516

WATER QUALITY IN EASTERN OREGON,
Oregon State Univ., Corvallis. Dept. of Soil Science.
For primary bibliographic entry see Field 5B.
W75-07517

ENVIRONMENTAL MANAGEMENT IN THE COLORADO RIVER BASIN.
Proceedings of Conference, October 15-16, 1973, Salt Lake City, Utah, Utah State University Press, Logan, 1974. 313 p. Crawford, A. B., Peterson, D. F., eds.

Descriptors: *Colorado River Basin, *Environmental effects, *Salinity, *Agriculture, *Urbanization, Arizona, New Mexico, Utah, Wyoming, California, Colorado, Nevada, Planning, Recreation, Powerplants, Energy conversion, Transportation, Legislation.

The Colorado River Basin is characterized by aridity and by the limited assimilative capacity of the region's environment. Background for considering environmental management in the basin is provided by surveys of the problems confronting basin-wide planning, and by the use of environmental indices and the concept of carrying capacity in planning. Topics considered individually are recreation, agriculture, energy development, transportation, and urbanization. Also, the international implications of salinity, the future of regional planning in the United States, the prospects for environmental legislation in the United States and future research needs are considered. (See W75-07526 thru W75-07545) (Bowden-Arizona)
W75-07525

MANAGEMENT OBJECTIVES IN THE COLORADO RIVER BASIN: THE PROBLEM OF ESTABLISHING PRIORITIES AND ACHIEVING COORDINATION,
Bureau of Reclamation, Salt Lake City, Utah. Upper Colorado Region.
D. L. Crandall.
In: Environmental Management in the Colorado River Basin, October 15-16, 1973, Salt Lake City, Utah, Utah State University Press, Logan, 1974, p 17-23.

Descriptors: *Coordination, Research priorities, *Priorities, Colorado River, *Colorado River Basin, *Resource allocation, *Water supply, *Water demand, *Arizona, Utah, New Mexico, Colorado, Wyoming, California, Nevada, Urbanization, Agriculture, Energy Conversion, Powerplants, Regional analysis.
Identifiers: *Central Arizona Project(CAP), Environmental management.

Since 1900 the flow of the Colorado River has been thoroughly committed to uses such as hydroelectric power, mining, irrigated agriculture, cities and recreation. Future uses such as coal gasification, coal fired electric plants, the Central Arizona Project, the Navajo Project and various Utah projects will place water requirements beyond the river's current flow and may necessitate restricting Lower Basin uses for the benefit of Upper Basin development. Also, settlement of Indian claims may place a new and heavy demand on the river's flow. Environmental planning has always been a part of past efforts to manage the Colorado. For example, water is released from Lake Powell at times to enhance bass spawning in Lake Mead. The overcommitment of the river's water will make future management and environmental planning more difficult. It will be necessary for priorities to be set by citizens acting through local, state, and federal bodies. (See also W75-07525) (Bowden-Arizona)
W75-07527

THE ROLE OF ENVIRONMENTAL INDICES IN REGIONAL MANAGEMENT,
Resources for the Future, Inc., Washington, D.C.
J. C. Davies, III.
In: Environmental Management in the Colorado River Basin, October 15-16, 1973, Salt Lake City, Utah, Utah State University Press, Logan, 1974, p 24-36. 1 ref.

Descriptors: Environment, *Colorado River Basin, *Long-term planning, *Environmental effects, *Regional analysis, Arizona, New Mexico, Utah, Wyoming, California, Nevada, Colorado.
Identifiers: *Environmental indices, Environmental management.

An index is a quantitative summary of data and relates to a particular purpose or problem. Indices are easier to use than computers and less mystifying to most people. They are particularly helpful in trade-off considerations, and in evaluating a program's performance. However, despite these advantages, environmental indices are not made or used enough. One obstacle to use is limited understanding of the nature of the environment; thus, environmental problems change and evolve. Also, it is not always easy to convert change as measured in an index to values such as good or bad. There are simple data limitations in many environmental areas. And finally, there is a reluctance by some to use indices because indices evaluate their programs. These obstacles must and will be overcome for indices are a useful tool in assessing environmental change. (See also W75-07525) (Bowden-Arizona)
W75-07528

ENVIRONMENTAL CARRYING CAPACITY: AN INTEGRATIVE MANAGEMENT CONCEPT,
Environmental Protection Agency, Washington, D.C. Office of Research and Development.
For primary bibliographic entry see Field 6A.
W75-07529

COLORADO RIVER MANAGEMENT AND INTERNATIONAL LAW,
International Law Association, Mexico City.
For primary bibliographic entry see Field 6E.
W75-07530

THE FUTURE OF REGIONAL PLANNING IN THE UNITED STATES,
Council on Environmental Quality, Washington, D.C.
J. A. Busterud.
In: Environmental Management in the Colorado River Basin, October 15-16, 1973, Salt Lake City, Utah, Utah State University Press, Logan, 1974, p 67-74.

Descriptors: Colorado River, *Colorado River Basin, *Long-term planning, *Regional development, *Water allocation(Policy), Arizona, New Mexico, Utah, Colorado, Wyoming, Nevada, California, Water resources, Water utilization, Regional analysis.
Identifiers: Environmental management.

Regional planning is moving from questions such as 'whether or not' and 'when' to the issues of 'how much' and 'where'. This movement contains some basic trends. Land use regulation, for example, must be concrete and immediate part of politics on the local level if it is to be effective. Also, it is being recognized that public construction such as sewers can either hasten or slow growth. In many respects the water problem of the Colorado River Basin have made it a model of regional planning; seven states and two nations have been forced to find agreement on the allocation of the water. Water shortages now predicted for the future will force this region into yet more stringent planning. (See also W75-07525) (Bowden-Arizona)
W75-07531

CRITERIA FOR THE DETERMINATION OF RECREATIONAL CARRYING CAPACITY IN THE COLORADO RIVER BASIN,
Forest Service (USDA), Missoula, Mont. Northern Forest Fire Lab.
G. H. Stankey.
In: Environmental Management in the Colorado River Basin, October 15-16, 1973, Salt Lake City, Utah, Utah State University Press, Logan, 1974, p 82-101, 1 tab, 36 ref.

Descriptors: *Colorado River Basin, Recreation, *Carrying capacity, *Long-term planning, *Recreation demand, *Recreation facilities, *Land use, Arizona, New Mexico, Colorado, Wyoming, Nevada, California, Cost-benefit analysis, Environmental effects.
Identifiers: Environmental management.

Recreational use changes a site, and the number of users changes the recreational experience. Such facts force one to develop a concept of carrying capacity to determine the allocation and management of recreational resources. There are 5 categories of recreational land use: (1) Appreciative-symbolic; (2) Extractive-symbolic; (3) Passive free-play; (4) Sociable learning; (5) Active-expressive. There are five criteria for deciding which one of these uses recreational land will be put to: (1) Irreplaceability and relative abundance; (2) substitutability; (3) demand-preference relationship; (4)

complementarity-competitiveness relationship; and (5) cost. Unless some such standards and procedures are generally used in planning recreational developments long term mistakes are likely to be the result. (See also W75-07525) (Bowden-Arizona)
W75-07533

STRATEGIES FOR ENVIRONMENTAL PLANNING IN THE UPPER COLORADO RIVER REGION,
California Univ, Berkeley. Dept. of Landscape Architecture.
R. H. Twiss.
In: Environmental Management in the Colorado River Basin, October 15-16, 1973, Salt Lake City, Utah, Utah State University Press, Logan, 1974, p 102-117. 4 fig.

Descriptors: *Colorado River Basin, *Environmental engineering, *Environmental effects, *Long-term planning, *Land use, *Regional development, Arizona, Utah, Wyoming, Colorado, New Mexico, Nevada, California, Fossil fuels, Administrative agencies, Regional economics, Resource allocation.
Identifiers: Environmental management.

Will the Colorado River Basin be sacrificed to the energy crisis and molded by external pressures, or can it plan its own future. Nine levels of planning are reviewed. The environmental quality of the region will not be preserved merely by identifying and creating recreational areas. Something almost as comprehensive as a master plan is called for in the basin. Five predictions are made about the future of land planning in the basin: (1) zoning will have only a marginal success in land-use control; (2) it is not likely that the states in the basin will pass effective land use laws; (3) a federal land use policy act will pass within two years, but the law will result mainly in more studies; (4) federal agencies will continue to avoid a strong role in land use planning decisions; (5) the resultant vacuum in regional planning will be filled by public interest law firms and citizen lobbies. What is needed is a regional environmental planning agency and state laws on environmental quality. Also, regional studies should produce basic environmental inventory and constraint maps. The federal government should make the basin a single environmental unit and a single federal administrator should be appointed by the President to provide a focal point for federal activity in the region. (See also W75-07525) (Bowden-Arizona)
W75-07534

AN EXAMINATION OF THE ENVIRONMENTAL CARRYING CAPACITY CONCEPT FOR THE AGRICULTURAL SECTOR OF THE COLORADO RIVER BASIN,
New Mexico State Univ., University Park.
For primary bibliographic entry see Field 3F.
W75-07535

AGRICULTURE'S MANAGEMENT OF THE ENVIRONMENT IN THE COLORADO RIVER BASIN,
American Farm Bureau Federation, Salt Lake City, Utah. Natural Resources Dept.
For primary bibliographic entry see Field 3F.
W75-07536

FOSSIL FUELS AND POWER GENERATION IN THE COLORADO RIVER BASIN,
Brigham Young Univ., Provo, Utah. Dept. of Botany and Range Science.
For primary bibliographic entry see Field 3E.
W75-07537

POWER GENERATION AND THE COLORADO RIVER BASIN,
Utah Power and Light Co., Salt Lake City.
For primary bibliographic entry see Field 3E.
W75-07538

TRANSPORTATION AND REGIONAL ENVIRONMENTAL MANAGEMENT,
Wyoming Univ., Laramie. Dept. of Economics; and Div. of Business and Economic Research.
D. M. Blood.
In: Environmental Management in the Colorado River Basin, October 15-16, 1973, Salt Lake City, Utah, Utah State University Press, Logan, 1974, p 190-209, 23 ref.

Descriptors: *Colorado River Basin, *Transportation, *Air pollution, *Environmental effects, *Land use, Arizona, New Mexico, Utah, Colorado, Wyoming, California, Nevada, Regional development, Cost-benefit analysis, Growth rates.
Identifiers: Environmental management.

The United States has always lacked a unified transportation policy. Instead, it has had modal separatism with different funding and bureaucracies for water, rail, air, and automobiles. This diversity makes an estimate of transportation's effect on the environment difficult. The Colorado River Basin as a geographic area is not a real transportation unit since water and trade in the basin have different routes. Transportation generally impinges on the environment by shrinking distances, creating noise, generating air pollution, locating housing and by stimulating or curbing growth. The task of incorporating transportation considerations into a regional environmental framework is complicated by (1) regions outlined for one purpose do not necessarily make ideal units for analyzing function; (2) transportation decisions are hindered by the lack of national policy; (3) the base data for the interrelationship between the social, economic and environmental effects of transportation are lacking (4) transportation policy is tied to national land and water policy and cannot be pursued in regional isolation; (5) modern cost/benefit analysis of public expenditures has further complicated transportation decisions. (See also W75-07525) (Bowden-Arizona)
W75-07539

TRANSPORTATION IN THE COLORADO RIVER BASIN,
Boston Aschmann Associates, San Jose, Calif.
S. L. Hill.
In: Environmental Management in the Colorado River Basin, October 15-16, 1973, Salt Lake City, Utah, Utah State University Press, Logan, 1974, p 210-214, 1 tab.

Descriptors: *Colorado River Basin, *Roads, *Transportation, *Land management, *Environmental effects, Arizona, Utah, Nevada, New Mexico, Colorado, Wyoming, California, Access routes, Recreation.
Identifiers: Environmental Management.

Direct expenses for transportation represent 20 percent of the American Gross National Product. In the Colorado Basin, highways consitute the principal transportation investment. Most of the roads in the region are rural, and they have a direct effect on the carrying capacity of the land. The roads determine in good part the patterns of trade and housing, and have a direct effect on recreational exploitation of the region. Any concept of planning the basin based on adjusting use to the land's carrying capacity must regulate the expansion and condition of the roads. Roads in the region control access to the land. The National Environmental Policy Act, minimizing the negative environmental effects of roads, has become a major criteria in planning. Thus, in the basin, roads should not be just a response to population growth, but a tool to regulate use and exploitation of the land. (See also W75-07525) (Bowden-Arizona)
W75-07540

URBANIZATION IN THE COLORADO RIVER BASIN,
Utah State Univ., Logan. Dept. of Political Science.
For primary bibliographic entry see Field 4C.
W75-07541

URBANIZATION WITH OR WITHOUT ENVIRONMENTAL QUALITY,
United States International Univ., San Diego, Calif.
For primary bibliographic entry see Field 4C.
W75-07542

RESOURCE ALLOCATION AND MANAGEMENT IN THE COLORADO RIVER BASIN,
Utah State Univ., Logan. Dept. of Political Science.
For primary bibliographic entry see Field 6E.
W75-07543

CONCEPTS OF CARRYING CAPACITY AND PLANNING IN COMPLEX ECOLOGICAL SYSTEMS,
Colorado State Univ., Fort Collins. Dept. of Sociology and Anthropology.
For primary bibliographic entry see Field 6A.
W75-07544

THE DEVELOPMENT AND ENVIRONMENTAL PROTECTION OF THE COLORADO RIVER BASIN,
Utah Agricultural Experiment Station, Logan.
D. W. Thorne.
In: Environmental Management in the Colorado River Basin, October 15-16, 1973, Salt Lake City, Utah, Utah State University Press, 1974, Logan, p 298-313.

Descriptors: *Colorado River Basin, *Long-tern planning, *Resources development, *Urbanization, *Research priorities, Wyoming, Utah, Arizona, New Mexico, California, Nevada, Colorado, Research and development, Recreation, Transportation, Agriculture.

Various knowledge gaps hinder planning in the Colorado River Basin. A commission should be created by the various governors of the basin states to prepare goals for the region for the year 2000 and guidelines for attaining the goals. A full inventory of the region's resources must be prepared. The hydrocarbon resources of the basin should be investigated so that their potential for development in light of future technology can be assessed and the effect of exploiting them on the environment can be considered. Agricultural research is essential to mitigate the adverse effects of modern production of food and fiber, to increase the amount of this production, and to insure that the region will continue to supply such products. More data are needed on recreation so that this resources can be fully exploited for the benefit of all. Future urbanization in the basin should be considered in light of its effect on natural resources, transportation, natural beauty, and land use patterns. Future transportation needs and ways to meet than should be studied. Ways must be found for making concepts of environmental quality understandable and assessable to the public. (See also W75-07525) (Bowden-Arizona)
W75-07545

PUERTO RICO WATER RESOURCES PLANNING MODEL STUDY,
Geological Survey, Reston, Va.
For primary bibliographic entry see Field 6A.
W75-07568

RESIDENTIAL WATER USAGE CHANGE POTENTIAL RELATED TO ATTITUDES

TOWARD WATER AND KNOWLEDGE OF USAGE BEHAVIOR,
Pennsylvania State Univ., University Park. Inst. for Research on Land and Water Resources.
D. H. Carson.
Report October 1974. 6 p. OWRR B-024-PA (1). 14-31-0001-3121.

Descriptors: *Surveys, *Municipal water, *Water utilization, *Use rates, Attitudes, Water allocation(Policy), Behavior, *Pennsylvania.
Identifiers: State College(Pa).

Policies which reverse the pricing function, or which produce a U-shaped pricing function are inadequate to reduce residential water uses in locations where residential use may comprise a significant portion of total water use. In conjunction with the market and policy techniques to reduce residential water consumption, the feasibility of using direct behavioral change was explored along with attitude change potentials where change of verbal behavior was predictive of concomitant change in water use. A survey was conducted in three Pennsylvania communities, Centre Hall, a very small town which had some water problems and still was threatened by shortage; Bellefonte, a middle-sized town which has virtually no water resource problem, and State College, a small city, with no immediate water problems; the latter was the main sampling source. The survey was conducted by two series of questionnaires and monitoring devices on a continuous, 24-hour basis, combined with short interviews, and a simple diary form. Preliminary and causal questioning suggested that inidividuals would change in their awareness of water uses over the survey period. The initial evidence indicates that those uses which are generally considered inelastic--indoor domestic uses--might not change, but those which are elastic--outdoor uses--might be modified. (Auen-Wisconsin)
W75-07593

OPEN SPACE AND URBAN WATER MANAGEMENT PHASE I: GOALS AND CRITERIA,
North Carolina Univ., Chapel Hill. Dept. of City and Regional Planning.
K. Elfers, and M. Hufschmidt.
Available from the National Technical Information Service, Springfield, Va 22161 as PB-241 737, $7.25 paper copy, $2.25 microfiche. North Carolina Water Resources Research Institute, Raleigh, UNC-WRRI-Report No 104, January 1975. 197 p, 3 fig, 2 tab, 235 ref. OWRT B-073-NC(1). 14-31-0001-4156.

Descriptors: Urban hydrology, *Land use, Water resources development, *Water management(Applied), Ecosystems, Planning, *PReservation, Management, Cities, Urbanization, *Land classification, Land management, Land resources, Interfaces, Earth-water interfaces, *City planning.
Identifiers: *Open space preservation.

The key elements are a discussion of critical variables and relationships involved in open space subsystems and a very comprehensive presentation of specific goals and criteria for open space preservation and management. Also included are discussions of various historical threads which have led to the present concern for open space preservation and management; these include the conservation movement and city beautiful era in this country, Federal policies and programs with regard to environmental quality and urban development, and the open space movement in the 1960's. Open space is defined to include both open and natural areas within built up urban areas and natural areas in the countryside that have characteristics such that they are suitable to be permanently preserved in a natural state or used for various open space purposes e.g., recreation. Open space elmen ts are grouped into four basic subsystems: ecosystems such as wetlands and estuaries; land nodes such as prime agricultural lands and unusually scenic areas; water-land interfaces such as flood plains and shorelands; and urban spaces such as parks, plazas, utility corridors, and buffers. (Stewart-North Carolina State)
W75-07596

ALTERNATIVE INFORMATION AND INTERACTION APPROACHES TO PUBLIC PARTICIPATION IN WATER RESOURCES DECISION MAKING - A STATE-OF-THE-ARTS REPORT,
North Carolina State Univ., Raleigh. Dept. of Sociology and Anthropology.
A. C. Davis, J. Anderson, and R. I. Gough.
Available from the National Technical Information Service, Springfield, Va 22161 as PB-241 736, $3.75 in paper copy, $2.25 in microfiche. North Carolina Water Resources Research Institute, Raleigh, UNC-WRRI Rept No 106, March 1975. 40 p, 14 fig, 88 ref. OWRT B-075-NC(2). 14-31-0001-4158.

Descriptors: *Water resources, *Decision making, *Information exchange, Reviews, Administrative decisions, Social aspects, Model studies, *Social participation, Alternative planning.
Identifiers: *Public participation, Citizen involvement.

A state-of-the-art presentation is made on research dealing with the information and interaction approaches to public participation in water resources decision-making. Public participation has been viewed from the standpoint of public administration, with concentration on the advantage and disadvantages of the information and interaction approaches to participation for water resources agency personnel and the publics. Seven decision-participation models including the various actors, their roles, and the exemplary techniques and time requirements associated with each are discussed. A review of the literature shows the many different techniques employed by agency personnel to involve the public in the decision-making process. The information in the interaction suggests a great deal of interest in and concern for public participation; however, few practical efforts have been made to include the public beyond the limited stage of the traditional public hearing. (Stewart-North Carolina State)
W75-07598

TEACHING WATER RESOURCE MANAGEMENT WITH THE AID OF A COMPUTER-IMPLEMENTED STIMULATOR,
Virginia Polytechnic Inst. and State Univ., Blacksburg. Dept. of Fisheries and Wildlife Sciences.
R. T. Lackey.
Available from the National Technical Information Service, Springfield, Va 22161 as PB-241 753, Virginia Water Resources Research Center, Blacksburg, VPI-WRRC-Bulletin 78, March 1975. 98 p, 1 tab, 11 ref, 3 append. OWRT A-049-VA(4).

Descriptors: Water resources, *Management, Reservoir operation, *Computer programs, Reservoirs, *Multiple-purpose reservoirs, Model studies, Training, Education, Comprehensive planning.
Identifiers: Computer simulation, Teaching, Computer games, Multiple-use.

Computer-implemented learning exercises involving large system management should become an important natural resource educational tool. DAM, a computer-implemented water resource teaching game, illustrates the principles of managing a large multiple-use reservoir system. Stages in the development of DAM were: (1) model conceptualization; (2) model quantification and implementation; and (3) model refinement. The finished product is based on the use of economic and quantity numerical accumulators and a random number generating function. Management realism and role switching enhance DAM's value as a tool for acquainting students with management based on total system understanding.
W75-07601

APPROACHES TO WATER REQUIREMENT FORECASTING: A CANADIAN PERSPECTIVE,
Canada Centre for Inland Waters, Burlington (Ontario).
T. R. Lee.
Social Science Series No 9, 1972. 9 p, 1 fig, 22 ref.

Descriptors: *Canada, *Water demand, *Model studies, *Forecasting, Methodology, River basin development, Social impact, Economic impact, Water users, Economic prediction, Water quality, Competing uses, Simulation analysis.

The state of the art of water-requirement forecasting in Canada is assessed. Although Canada is fortunate in the extent and nature of her freshwater resources, there has been limited development of centralized water management. Historically, the predominant forecasting technique was a straight line projection based on previous needs per capita and estimated population. These techniques were used because of the lack of readily available information on water use. The development of an improved data base and the construction and testing of the first elaborate mathematical models of water use in specific river basins has begun. For example, the St. John River basin in New Brunswick has considered using mathematical programming and simulation models. The proposed end product is a national water forecasting model applicable to municipal, industrial, domestic, and agricultural sectors. The national model is intended to provide provincial and river basin breakdowns. Within the national model significant economic and social data will be integrated. Specifically, the future of water requirements forecasting was judged to be tied to the general relationship between overall economics and social development and water use, and the new technology available through electronic data processing and innovations in planning. (Becker-Wisconsin)
W75-07610

FORMAL PLANNING AND REPORTING SYSTEM: PROCEDURAL MANUAL,
Environmental Protection Agency, Washington, D.C. Office of Resources Management.
For primary bibliographic entry see Field 5G.
W75-07612

FISHERY RESOURCES FOR LAKE OF THE WOODS, MINNESOTA,
Minnesota Univ., St. Paul. Dept. of Entomology, Fisheries and Wildlife.
E. G. Heyerdahl, and L. L. Smith.
Available from the National Technical Information Service, Springfield, Va 22161, as COM-74-11564, $5.75 in paper copy, $2.25 in microfiche. Agricultural Experiment Station Technical Bulletin 288, 1972. 145 p, 33 fig, 30 tab, 18 ref, 1 append.

Descriptors: *Lake fisheries, *Commercial fishing, *Sport fish, *Minnesota, Fishing gear, Fish harvest, Growth rates, Sauger, Walleye, Fish management, Optimization, Economic impact, Yellow perch, Canada, Fish parasites, Fish populations.
Identifiers: *Lake of the Woods(Minn), Tullibee, Trawl fishing, Burbot, White sucker, Northern pike.

Because the commercial fishery harvests game as well as commercial species, the fishery has been criticized and suggestions have been made to discontinue commercial fishing operations entirely. The Minnesota Conservation Department has conducted a management program to effect a gradual reduction in commercial fishing by strict licensing control. This management approach was

complicated by the development of a large and important mink ranching industry which relies on the fish and an inexpensive food source. To resolve the problem of mink feed supply submerged trap net and trawl net gear were allowed under strict supervision. The concern of the local residents over the economic status of the fisheries and the related economic sector was aired at the state commission hearings. To develop management options, the Lake of the Woods commercial fishery was surveyed to determine the population structure of the various sport and commercial fish species; the catch characteristics with reference to size and age taken by various gear; whether certain commercial fish species could be exploited more heavily to the advantage of both fish protein production and sport fish yield; the effects of various commercial gear on the game fish species; and the type of utilization that will give maximum sport fishing together with maximum protein production. (Auen-Wisconsin)
W75-07613

REGIONAL GROWTH AND WATER RESOURCE INVESTMENT,
Utah State Univ., Logan. Dept. of Economics.
W. C. Lewis, J. C. Anderson, H. H. Fullerton, and B. D. Gardner.
D.C. Health and Company, Lexington, Mass. 1973. 181 p, 5 fig, 9 tab, 140 ref. AID-csd/2459.

Descriptors: *Economic impact, *Investment, *Income distribution, *Water resources development, Economic efficiency, Analytical techniques, Economic justification, Planning, Welfare(Economics), Theoretical analysis, Evaluation, Regional development.
Identifiers: *Impact analysis, *Quantitative techniques, Functional economic area, Accounting framework, Regional economic growth theory, Case studies.

The question of how investments in water resources development influence the pace and direction of regional economic growth is discussed since justification for the allocation of funds is sometimes partially based on the expectation of these influences. To evaluate the effectiveness of investments in water resources as a means to implement redistributions of wealth and income, the tools of economics, operations research and statistics are applicable. The functional economic area (FEA) delineation based on regional impacts is recommended over hydrologic delineations for use in economic analyses. Within the FEA, a complete analysis of efficiency and equity impacts for project investments should be made before project approval. The role of water resource development in regional growth was judged to be greatest in agriculture and small in nonagricultural industries, who view water as a cost factor of little importance and therefore a minor factor in location choice. A planning framework to assess the effects of an array of different kinds of water projects was developed. While this type of framework provides insights, the multidiminsional nature of regional development requires looking beyond the water-based projects investments to investment combinations, the long-run potential of economic development and national economic efficiency. (Becker-Wisconsin)
W75-07615

EEL RIVER DEVELOPMENT ALTERNATIVES. APPENDIX,
California State Dept. of Water Resources, Sacramento.
For primary bibliographic entry see Field 4A.
W75-07616

THE JOB IMPACT OF ALTERNATIVES TO CORPS OF ENGINEERS PROJECTS,
Illinois Univ., Urbana. Center for Advanced Computation.
B. M. Hannon, and R. H. Bezdek.
Available from the National Technical Information Service, Springfield, Va 22161, as PB-227 820, $3.75 in paper copy, $2.25 in microfiche. Report NSF/RA/N-73-052, 1973. 28 p, 2 fig, 8 tab, 10 ref. DAHCO4 72-C-001, NSF GI 35179X.

Descriptors: *Projects, *Alternate planning, *Employment opportunities, Budgeting, Occupations, *Illinois, Regional economics, *Input-output analysis, Social aspects, Resource allocation, Waste treatment.
Identifiers: *Social programs, National health insurance, Social Security payments, Mass transit development, General tax relief.

An economic input-output model estimates the aggregate employment and detailed occupational changes likely to result from a shift of $1.13 billion from the projected 1975 Corps of Engineers construction budget to five alternate programs: National health insurance, Social Security payments, mass transit development, construction of waste treatment facilities, and general tax relief. Tas relief would increase direct and indirect employment 10.6$, national health insurance would increase employment 57.3%, Social Security benefits would generate an employment increase of 30.5%, mass transit construction would enhance employment by 6.9%, and waste treatment construction 30.3%. Analysis of the regional employment effects of a Corps water resource development project in West Frankfort, southern Illinois indicates that unemployment rose as the project was constructed, but employment also rose on the average on southern Illinois, indicating that the West Frankfort economy is keyed more with that of the region than to a dam, 8 miles away. The rationale is that Corps construction requires special skills not likely found in a small town with a population of 9000; rather these skills are drawn from several hundred miles away for their limited time of need. (Auen-Wisconsin)
W75-07618

HUMAN ECOLOGY AND THE ECOSYSTEM, (IN JAPANESE),
Institute of Population Problems, Tokyo (Japan).
For primary bibliographic entry see Field 6G.
W75-07750

DOES CANOEING INCREASE STREAMBANK EROSION,
Forest Service (USDA), St. Paul, Minn. North Central Forest Experiment Station.
For primary bibliographic entry see Field 2J.
W75-07792

6C. Cost Allocation, Cost Sharing, Pricing/Repayment

THE CENTRAL ARIZONA PROJECT, A STAFF REPORT TO THE METROPOLITAN UTILITIES MANAGEMENT AGENCY BOARD AND THE MAYOR AND COUNCIL OF THE CITY OF TUCSON,
Tucson Metropolitan Utilities Management Agency Board, Ariz.
For primary bibliographic entry see Field 4B.
W75-07372

TEXAS WATERBORNE COMMERCE COMMODITY FLOW STATISTICS,
Texas Transportation Inst., College Station.
For primary bibliographic entry see Field 6B.
W75-07376

JAPAN: A SURVEY OF PORTS, DEEP WATER TERMINALS, AND VESSELS,
Army Engineer District, San Francisco, Calif. Economics Branch.
W. Yep.
Army Engineer Institute for Water Resources. Center Paper 73-1, June 1973. 304 p, 39 plates, 4 tab, 7 ref, append.

Descriptors: *Harbors, *Ships, Technology, Foreign countries, *Transportation, Oil, Facilities, Off-shore platforms, Dredging, Environmental effects.
Identifiers: *Japan, *Deep-water terminals, Oil tankers, Monobuoy systems, Containerships, Maritime industry, Deep-draft vessels, Container terminals.

Construction and maintenance of principal harbors and port facilities in Japan are under the jurisdiction of the Ministry of Transport. Expenditures scheduled for port development from 1971 through 1975 total $6.2 billion. As of 1972, their fleet of VLCC (very large crude carriers) consisted of five tankers, ranging from 153,685 dwt to 477,000 dwt with a draft of 28 m. Plans are drawn for 750,000 and 1,000,000 dwt tankers. The predominant means for handling the unloading of crude petroleum from VLCC are sea berths (offshore platforms). These are fixed terminals capable of handling up to 500,000 dwt. Their capital costs range between $25-40 million per platform. Operation and maintenance costs range between 1-3% of capital costs. There are also at least nine mobile single-buoy mooring systems (monobuoys) to handle VLCCs. The SBM terminal is capable of unloading, bunkering, and deballasting operations simultaneously. Their construction and installation time is usually one year or less. Capital costs for SBM for handling a 250,000 dwt tanker is approximately $2 million. However, they experience operational difficulties in adverse weather and are susceptible to high maintenance costs. The latest iron ore handling facilities and vessels, containerships and LASH (lighter aboard ships) vessels are discussed. Vessels, ports, and facilities are profusely detailed. (Auen-Wisconsin)
W75-07379

DYNAMIC PROGRAMMING FOR OPTIMAL CAPACITY EXPANSION OF WASTEWATER TREATMENT PLANTS,
Case Western Reserve Univ., Cleveland, Ohio. Systems Engineering Div.
For primary bibliographic entry see Field 5D.
W75-07390

WATER DESALTING IN HAWAII,
Holmes and Narver, Inc., Anaheim, Calif. Nuclear and Systems Sciences Group.
For primary bibliographic entry see Field 3A.
W75-07506

A NOTE ON COSTS OF COLLECTING HYDROMETRIC FLOW DATA IN THE UNITED STATES,
Geological Survey, Reston, Va.
For primary bibliographic entry see Field 7A.
W75-07578

TEN COUNTIES INVESTIGATION: MUNICIPAL, INDUSTRIAL AND ARGICULTURAL WATER DEMAND IN COLUSA, GLENN, HUMBOLDT, LAKE, MARIN, MENDOCINO, NAPA, SOLANO, SONOMA, AND YOLO COUNTIES,
California State Dept. of Water Resources, Sacramento.
For primary bibliographic entry see Field 6D.
W75-07611

REGIONAL GROWTH AND WATER RESOURCE INVESTMENT,
Utah State Univ., Logan. Dept. of Economics.
For primary bibliographic entry see Field 6B.
W75-07615

EEL RIVER DEVELOPMENT, ALTERNATIVES. APPENDIX,
California State Dept. of Water Resources, Sacramento.
For primary bibliographic entry see Field 4A.
W75-07616

THE JOB IMPACT OF ALTERNATIVES TO CORPS OF ENGINEERS PROJECTS,
Illinois Univ., Urbana. Center for Advanced Computation.
For primary bibliographic entry see Field 6B.
W75-07618

A COMPUTER PROGRAM FOR ESTIMATING COSTS OF TUNNELLING (COSTUN),
Harza Engineering Co., Chicago, Ill.
For primary bibliographic entry see Field 8B.
W75-07619

ECONOMIC FEASIBILITY OF DESALTING SYSTEMS FOR MUNICIPAL WATER SUPPLY IN IOWA,
Dewild Grant Reckert and Associates, Des Moines, Iowa.
For primary bibliographic entry see Field 3A.
W75-07631

EVALUATION OF ALTERNATIVE METHODS FOR FINANCING MUNICIPAL WASTE TREATMENT WORKS,
Meta Systems, Inc., Cambridge, Mass.
For primary bibliographic entry see Field 5D.
W75-07693

6D. Water Demand

EFFICIENT USE OF WATER - POLICY AND PROBLEMS,
Ministry of Agriculture, Tel-Aviv (Israel). Water Commission.
S. Arlosoroff.
In: Israel's Water Economy, Ministry of Agriculture, Water Commission, Tel Aviv. December 1973. p 14-20.

Descriptors: *Water utilization, *Water conservation, *Water demand, *Water consumption, *Water reuse, Efficiencies, Water costs, Marginal utility, Irrigation systems, Domestic water, Industrial water, Agriculture, Technology.
Identifiers: *Israel.

A major effort will be needed to save water, by using water more efficiently, and by using marginal waters in order to maintain a reasonable rate of growth in that part of Israel's national income dependent on irrigated agriculture. The water use sectors are evaluated from the aspect of water economy measures. First is the industrial sector which uses the smallest quantity of water but has had the largest relative growth in the last decade. Ways of reducing water consumption here include the introduction of drier industrial processes, reclamation of industrial effluents, and use of marginal waters such as urban wastes and saline water. Second is the urban and domestic sector where consumption is primarily influenced by the rise in living standards. Activity in this area is limited to technological development of appliances designed to save and more efficiently use water. Third is the agricultural sector which accounts for some 75 percent of all water used in Israel. Activities for more efficient use consist of development of more efficient irrigation systems and encouraging the introduction of these methods by granting loans at low interest rates. (Mastic-Arizona)
W75-07401

ISRAEL'S WATER ECONOMY AND ITS PROBLEMS IN THE EARLY SEVENTIES,
Tahal Consulting Engineers Ltd., Tel-Aviv (Israel). Long Range Planning Section.
E. Kally.
In: Israel's Water Economy, Ministry of Agriculture, Water Commission, Tel Aviv, December 1973. p 21-36, 1 tab.

Descriptors: *Water supply, *Water quality, *Brackish water, *Saline water, *Long term planning, Water consumption, Water demand, Desalination, Artificial precipitation, Agriculture, Industrial water, Water reuse, Sewage treatment, Groundwater mining.
Identifiers: *Israel.

Data and problems of Israel's water economy are reviewed in connection with long-range planning. Although water consumption is about 500 cu m annually per person for all uses - domestic, industrial, and agricultural, almost all of the available water that can be economically utilized is already in regular use. The problem is how to conduct and expand the country's water economy under the conditions of growing demand against a limited supply. Alternatives include limiting and better conservation of present water supplies or increasing actual yields by treating and utilizing brackish or other low quality water, by creating artificial rainfall, converting saline water, and mining the underground reservoirs. It may also become necessary to reduce the allocation of fresh water to agriculture, replacing it with water of marginal quality and transferring fresh waters to urban consumers. These changes may come about before the middle of the next decade. (Mastic-Arizona)
W75-07402

MANAGEMENT OBJECTIVES IN THE COLORADO RIVER BASIN: THE PROBLEM OF ESTABLISHING PRIORITIES AND ACHIEVING COORDINATION,
Bureau of Reclamation, Salt Lake City, Utah. Upper Colorado Region.
For primary bibliographic entry see Field 6B.
W75-07527

CRITERIA FOR THE DETERMINATION OF RECREATIONAL CARRYING CAPACITY IN THE COLORADO RIVER BASIN,
Forest Service (USDA), Missoula, Mont. Northern Forest Fire Lab.
For primary bibliographic entry see Field 6B.
W75-07533

HAS WISCONSIN ENOUGH WATER,
Geological Survey, Madison, Wis.
C. L. Holt.
Wisconsin Academy Review, Vol 21, No 1, p 30-31, Winter 1974-75.

Descriptors: *Water supply, *Wisconsin, *Water utilization, Streamflow, Groundwater, Surface waters, Water yield, *Water demand, Hydrologic budget.

The total amount of water available in Wisconsin remains essentially the same as it was more than 200 years ago. Although momentary yields of water are limited, it is a replenishing resource. Precipitation brings annually about 31 inches of water to the land's surface. Of this, about 10 inches enters streams and eventually flows out of the State. The rest returns to the atmosphere by evaporation and transpiration. A total of 6.3 billion gallons of water-about one-fifth of the average daily flow of all streams flowing from Wisconsin-is withdrawn daily from lakes, streams, and groundwater. From 1965 to 1970, water use in the State increased about 23% with much of this increase being for generation of thermoelectric power and for industrial growth. Withdrawals for municipal water-supply systems increased less than 5%, going from 440 mgd in 1965 to 480 mgd in 1970. The average daily streamflow in Wisconsin is about double the projected water requirements for the year 2000. Stored groundwater supplies are many times larger. (Knapp-USGS)
W75-07580

APPROACHES TO WATER REQUIREMENT FORECASTING: A CANADIAN PERSPECTIVE,
Canada Centre for Inland Waters, Burlington (Ontario).
For primary bibliographic entry see Field 6B.
W75-07610

TEN COUNTIES INVESTIGATION: MUNICIPAL, INDUSTRIAL AND AGRICULTURAL WATER DEMAND IN COLUSA, GLENN, HUMBOLDT, LAKE, MARIN, MENDOCINO, NAPA, SOLANO, SONOMA, AND YOLO COUNTIES,
California State Dept. of Water Resources, Sacramento.

Descriptors: *California, *Water demand, *Forecasting, Municipal water, Industrial water, Agriculture, Planning, Water supply, Water rates.
Identifiers: Colusa County(Calif), Glenn County(Calif), Humboldt County(Calif), Lake County(Calif), Mendocino County(Calif), Napa County(Calif), Solano County(Calif), Sonoma County(Calif), Yolo County(Calif).

The future economic water demands of each of the ten North San Francisco Bay counties are projected to year 2020 as a basis for determining alternative water conveyance routes from the Eel River to the Sacramento-San Joaquin Delta. The total demand for these counties, at current prices, in 1990 (in 1000-acre ft/yr) for agriculture will be 272 and for municipal and industrial uses 88; and in 2020, 455 and 535, respectively. At water rates of $20/acre foot, the demand projected for agriculture in 1990 is 93 and municipal and industrial at 88; for 2020, 154 and 535, respectively. The demands for supplemental agricultural water supplies in certain service areas would be significantly influenced by the pricing policies of the marketing agencies. The additional water supplies needed in the ten-county area in year 2020 to satisfy demands for municipal-industrial and agricultural water at prices similar to those currently prevailing within the various service areas would amount to about 990,000 acre-feet annually. The factors considered in the estimates were basic land suitability for development, population growth, urban expansion, industrial development types, unit water use values, crop marketing prospects, areal allocations of crop acreage, payment capacity limitations, and information on presently developed and utilized water supplies. (Auen-Wisconsin)
W75-07611

6E. Water Law and Institutions

ECONOMIC IMPLICATION OF PUBLIC WATER POLICY IN ARIZONA,
Arizona Univ., Tucson. Dept. of Agricultural Economics.
M. M. Kelso, D. A. Bingham, W. E. Martin, H. Padfield, and D. F. Paulsen.
Available from the National Technical Information Service, Springfield, Va 22161 as PB-241 513, $5.75 in paper copy, $2.25 in microfiche. Completion Report, October 1974. 133 p, 1 fig, 2 tab. OWRT B-003-ARIZ(15). 14-01-0001-1001.

Descriptors: *Water policy, Water law, Water rights, *Arizona, *Institutions, *Water utilization, *Organizations, Water management(Applied), Institutional constraints, Economics.
Identifiers: Tucson Metropolitan Area(Ariz), Phoenix Metropolitan Area(Ariz), Salt River Project(Ariz).

Water institutions may be broadly divided into two categories--(1) water rights law and (2) water or-

ganizations law. This research is concerned largely with the second of these. The research examined the Tucson Metropolitan Area, the Phoenix Metropolitan Area, and the Salt River Project as a major component of the latter area. The extensive and complex fractionation of water management in areas overlying separable but unified natural water systems together with restraints on the transfer of rights and of water as between uses, users, and locations of use within and between these areas are the primary sources of the economic inefficiencies and inequities in water use. To improve economic welfare in Arizona relative to water use necessitates revising water institutions to secure unified management of separable but unified natural water systems. At the same time the advantages should be retained of independent firm and household decision making relative to water use and development.
W75-07351

USE OF ENVIRONMENTAL ANALYSES ON WASTEWATER FACILITIES BY LOCAL GOVERNMENT,
Teknekron, Inc., Washington, D.C. Applied Research Div.
For primary bibliographic entry see Field 5D.
W75-07360

WATER RIGHTS,
Wisconsin Univ., Madison. School of Law.
J. B. MacDonald, and J. H. Beuscher.
American Printing and Publishing, Inc., Madison, Wis. 1973. 668 p. Second edition.

Descriptors: *Water rights, *Water law, *Riparian rights, Zoning, *Public rights, Pollution abatement, Governmental interrelations, Wisconsin, Surface waters, Drainage practices, Percolating water, Competing uses, Watercourses(Legal aspects), Water allocation(Policy), Groundwater, *Judicial decisions, Equity, Reasonable use, Navigable waters, Recreation, Prior appropriation, Interstate compacts.
Identifiers: Private rights.

Interpretations of water law by judicial decisions and further elucidated by editorial comments includes the following areas: Diffused surface water is prescribed by rulings on definition of surface waters, watercourses, and Wisconsin drainage laws. Adjudications of several state supreme courts, appelate courts, and a chancery court define the law of percolating ground water. Government levels and systems for identification of private rights in watercourses are described, followed by legal origins of the riparian theory in Anglo-American law, criteria for rationing competing water users and riparian rights, land as a basis for water allocation involving riparian vs. non-riparian land, supplemented by rulings firming up water rights in riparian states. Aquisitions of water rights under the appropriation system also delineates water adjudicative and distribution institutions in appropriation states. Limitations imposed on private water rights by assertions of public interest by both the federal and state governments are substantiated by decrees. Water allocation between states is defined by the courts, by interstate compacts, by federal legislation, and by treaty. The Supreme Court and the Western District Court of Texas rulings exemplify decisions on exportation of waters from one state to another. The final chapter discusses the role of the courts and specialized administrative agencies in pollution abatement. (Auen-Wisconsin)
W75-07378

ORIENTING STATE WATER LAWS,
Nevada Univ., Reno. Desert Research Inst.
J. C. Ohrenschall.
Available from the National Technical Information Service, Springfield, Va 22161 as PB-241 712, $3.75 in paper copy, $2.25 in microfiche. Nevada Center for Water Resources Research, Reno, Project Report No. 27, February 1975. 40 p, 31 ref. OWRT B-023-NEV(1). 14-031-0001-1921.

Descriptors: *Water law, *Riparian rights, Southwest U.S., *Nevada, *California, *Arizona, *Dual system, *Prior appropriation, Legislation, Water utilization, *Water rights, State governments.

The development of relevant legislation governing water is paramount in the Western United States because of the increasing demand upon the resource. This research investigates the water laws of California, a dual-doctrine state, and Arizona and Nevada which are appropriative in water law determinations. The three-state water systems are analyzed to determine the historical and sociopolitical bases for various legal classifications of water and the managerial framework which has evolved. Definitions of the various physical states of water are explained with emphasis on those whose poor definition may cause misuse of the resource. By relying on scientific and technological data, suggestions are made for achieving more viable legislation that can aid in the promotion of better water utilization. (Fallon-Nevada)
W75-07396

LAND AND WATER USE IN OREGON,
Oregon State Univ., Corvallis. Water Resources Research Inst.
For primary bibliographic entry see Field 6B.
W75-07507

ADJUDICATION IN LAND-WATER DISPUTES,
Oregon Div. of State Lands, Salem.
S. F. Hamilton.
In: Land and Water Use in Oregon; Seminar conducted by Oregon State University, Spring Quarter 1974, Water Resources Research Institute, Corvallis, Oregon, p 45-50, July 1974.

Descriptors: *Legislation, *Water law, *Oregon, *Law enforcement, Dredging, Channel improvement, Excavation, Channels, Banks, Shores, Shore protection, Environment, Surface waters, Rivers, Streams.
Identifiers: Oregon removal-fill law.

The organization and functions of the Division of State Lands was described. The state removal-fill law was reviewed and its effect on land management in Oregon was discussed. Current land-water disputes around the state were summarized, along with a description of the permit and enforcement procedures used in the administration of the removal-fill law. This law regulates activities affecting streams and their shorelines such as channel dredging for navigation and commercial sand and gravel, excavation projects, channelization, bank stabilization, and construction in or along the waters of Oregon. (See also W75-07507) (Sims-ISWS)
W75-07511

CONSUMER PROTECTION AND LAND USE,
Oregon Real Estate Div., Salem.
For primary bibliographic entry see Field 6B.
W75-07512

WILLAMETTE RIVER PARKS SYSTEM,
Willamette River Parks System, Salem, Oreg.
For primary bibliographic entry see Field 6B.
W75-07513

THE SEPTIC TANK'S ROLE IN LAND USE,
Oregon State Dept. of Environmental Quality, Portland.
For primary bibliographic entry see Field 5D.
W75-07514

CONSTITUTIONAL RESTRICTIONS ON COASTAL LAND USE,
Oregon State Land Conservation and Development Commission, Portland.
S. R. Schell.
In: Land and Water Use in Oregon: Seminar conducted by Oregon State University, Spring Quarter 1974, Water Resources Research Institute, Corvallis, Oregon, p 77-95, July 1974. 28 ref.

Descriptors: *Legal aspects, *Planning, *Land use, *Oregon, Administrative agencies, Judicial decisions, Comprehensive planning, Legislation, Regional development, Estuarine environment, Coasts, Wetlands, Coastal marshes, Regulation, Zoning.

The laws and court decisions relating to land use planning in the coastal areas of Oregon were examined. Cases from California and Maine were reviewed. The objectives of land use regulation were discussed. It was concluded that power does exist to control and channel growth in Oregon; however, this power must be used circumspectly. Although Oregon probably cannot say that it will not grow, it may, however, shift further population growth to relatively undeveloped portions of the state by the use of direct and indirect mechanisms. (See also W75-07507) (Sims-ISWS)
W75-07515

WATER QUALITY PLANNING FOR THE DELAWARE ESTUARY - AN EXAMPLE,
Rutgers - the State Univ., New Brunswick, N.J. Water Resources Research Inst.
For primary bibliographic entry see Field 5G.
W75-07519

BASIN-WIDE PLANNING AND THE PROBLEM OF MULTIPLE JURISDICTIONS,
Ferris, Weatherford and Brennan, San Diego, Calif.
G. D. Weatherford.
In: Environmental Management in the Colorado River Basin, October 15-16, 1973, Salt Lake City, Utah, Utah State University Press, Logan, 1974, p 1-16. 21 ref.

Descriptors: *Colorado River, *Colorado River Basin, *Water supply, *Water allocation, *Resource allocation, Arizona, Utah, New Mexico, Colorado, California, Nevada, Wyoming, Regional analysis, Jurisdiction, Environmental effects, Air pollution, Water pollution, Planning.
Identifiers: Environmental management.

Pluralism of institutions (city, county, state, regional, federal, international) presently impairs basin wide planning for environmental management of the Colorado River. Large public ownership of land in the basin does not make the area ideal for planning because the land falls under the jurisdiction of various agencies with different goals. The 7 states, 2 nations, 30 tribes, 70 counties and various cities having jurisdiction in the region only unite to exploit it. Some future developments (the Central Arizona Project, energy industries) or drought could trigger an enforced reduction in water use. Augmentation of the water supply by importation may unite diverse factions but such plans would probably create more environmental issues than they would answer. A possible solution might be to create a federal commission to oversee the basin's environment on a research and data collection level. Such a Commission would be a first step toward a basin wide planning authority. (See also W75-07525) (Bowden-Arizona)
W75-07526

COLORADO RIVER MANAGEMENT AND INTERNATIONAL LAW,
International Law Association, Mexico City.
C. Sepulveda.

In: Environmental Management in the Colorado River Basin, October 15-16, 1973, Salt Lake City, Utah, Utah State University Press, Logan, 1974, p 59-66.

Descriptors: *Colorado River, *Colorado River Basin, *International Bound. and Water Comm., *Mexico, Arizona, Utah, California, Nevada, Colorado, Wyoming, Salinity, Water law, International Waters.
Identifiers: Environmental management.

The 1944 Water Treaty between the United States and Mexico moved international river law from a concern with navigation and boundaries toward establishing a contractual basis between nations for water delivery. However, the treaty failed to foresee large Mexican developments on the Lower Colorado and may have set the level of Mexican water use too low. By examining the handling of the salinity issue by the Boundary and Water Commission since 1961, one can see the evolution of new facets of international river law. In 1961, discharge from Arizona's Wellton Mohawk area caused vast damage to downstream Mexican farmers. Mexican protest on the basis of the 1944 treaty met American evasions. Technical experts agreed that American handling of the discharge had not been correct. In 1965 the United States agreed to channel Wellton Mohawk discharge to the Gulf of California. This lowered both the salinity and amount of Mexican water. A new agreement in 1972 settled both the quality and amount of water due Mexico. Thus the legal point was made that downstream users have the same water quality rights as upstream users. (See also W75-07525) (Bowden-Arizona)
W75-07530

FUTURE DIRECTIONS IN ENVIRONMENTAL LEGISLATION,
C. Braithwait.
In: Environmental Management in the Colorado River Basin, October 15-16, 1973, Salt Lake City, Utah, Utah State University Press, Logan, 1974, p 75-81.

Descriptors: *Colorado River Basin, *Environmental effects, *Pollution abatement, *Air pollution, *Water pollution, Arizona, Utah, New Mexico, California, Nevada, Wyoming, Colorado, Legislation, Land reclamation, Regional development.
Identifiers: Environmental management.

Environmental legislation will benefit long-term growth in the Colorado River Basin. By limiting pollution, preventing environmental degradation, and protecting natural resources, such laws preserve the basis for development and growth. Put simply, pollution limits growth; laws limiting pollution enhance growth. For example, the requirement of producing an environmental impact statement before surface mining may commence protects the region on from damaged land and aquifers and thus insures that the basis for future growth will be maintained. Another virtue of pollution laws is that they threaten monopolies. Often small companies are much more flexible than huge corporations in meeting the new environmental standards. Far from being anti-technology, environmental legislation demands the invention of new technology to protect the land, air, and water. Also, such laws will not lower the standard of living if one considers the importance of the quality of life. Any successful regional effort to protect and clean up the environment will find federal money essential. (See also W75-07525) (Bowden-Arizona)
W75-07532

RESOURCE ALLOCATION AND MANAGEMENT IN THE COLORADO RIVER BASIN,
Utah State Univ., Logan. Dept. of Political Science.
J. Baden, H. H. Fullerton, and J. Neuhold.
In: Environmental Management in the Colorado River Basin, October 15-16, 1973, Salt Lake City, Utah, Utah State University Press, Logan, 1974, p 261-280, 8 ref.

Descriptors: *Colorado River Basin, *Resource allocation, *Federal government, *Administrative agencies, Arizona, New Mexico, Wyoming, Colorado, Utah, Nevada, California.
Identifiers: Environmental management.

The Colorado River Basin has natural resources of high value and there will be pressure to extract these resources for use outside the basin. The terms for this extraction have yet to be decided upon. Many of the social costs to be paid for such an exploitation of the resources will be at the point of production, but much of the power to make such decisions lie outside the Basin in Congress, federal agencies, and national corporations. Information is essential to high quality allocation decisions, and the best information seems to come from disinterested third parties. Thus, it is to be hoped that such institutions will be utilized and the plans for allocation will be flexible. (See also W75-07525) (Bowden-Arizona)
W75-07543

THE DEVELOPMENT AND ENVIRONMENTAL PROTECTION OF THE COLORADO RIVER BASIN,
Utah Agricultural Experiment Station, Logan.
For primary bibliographic entry see Field 6B.
W75-07545

ALTERNATIVE INFORMATION AND INTERACTION APPROACHES TO PUBLIC PARTICIPATION IN WATER RESOURCES DECISION MAKING - A STATE-OF-THE-ARTS REPORT,
North Carolina State Univ., Raleigh. Dept. of Sociology and Anthropology.
For primary bibliographic entry see Field 6B.
W75-07598

LANDSCAPE TENDING AND NATURE CONSERVATION AS PARTIAL TASKS FOR SOCIALISTIC LAND DEVELOPMENT,
For primary bibliographic entry see Field 4A.
W75-07707

PROJECT AQUA NORWEGIAN IB (INTERNATIONAL BIOLOGICAL PROGRAM)/PF, (IN NORWEGIAN),
Zoologisk Museum, Oslo (Norway).
For primary bibliographic entry see Field 2A.
W75-07749

NELSON V. BUTZ (ACTION SEEKING INJUNCTION AND DECLARATORY RELIEF RELATING TO CONSTRUCTION OF PROPOSED DAM).
377 F. Supp. 819 (D. Minn. 1974).

Descriptors: *Minnesota, *Judicial decisions, *Environmental effects, *Standards, Dam construction, Rivers, Water law, Legal aspects, Federal government, Federal jurisdiction, Administrative agencies, Water management(Applied), Flood protection, Reservoirs, Reservoir construction, Reservoir operation, Engineering structures, Dams, Legislation, Alternative planning, Archaeology, Cost-benefit analysis, Flooding, Comprehensive planning.
Identifiers: *Dam effects, *Environmental impact statement, Declaratory judgments, Injunctive relief, National Environmental Policy Act, Environmental policy.

The plaintiffs, individual citizens, brought action seeking declaratory and injunctive relief against the defendant federal agency (Dept. of Agriculture) with respect to the proposed construction of a dam on the Knife River, in Minnesota. The plaintiffs contended that the environmental impact statement prepared by the defendant for the project failed to comply with the National Environmental Policy Act and guidelines promulgated by the Council on Environmental Quality. The Federal District Court held that while every particular detail need not be discussed in the statement, where particularly unique aspects of the environment are affected, the statement should note them in some detail. The court ruled that the statement did not adequately discuss the environmental effects of the project on mature trees, the inundation of certain islands, the archeological sites, the alternatives to building the dam, and the cost-benefit analyses. The court enjoined the defendant from proceeding with the project until such time as an environmental statement which is in compliance with the NEPA and this decision, is properly filed. (Deckert-Florida)
W75-07757

U.S. V. STATE OF ALASKA (SUIT TO QUIET TITLE TO PART OF INLET ON ALASKAN COAST, ETC).
497 F.2d 1155 (9th Cir. 1974).

Descriptors: *Judicial decisions, *United States, *Alaska, *Boundaries(Legal aspects), *Inlets(Waterways), *Federal-state water rights conflicts, Natural resources, Land tenure, Oceans, Oil industry, Bays, International law, Measurement, Coasts, Shores, Submerged Lands Act, Jurisdiction, Leases, Oil, Exploration, State jurisdiction, Legislation.
Identifiers: Seabed mining, Territorial seas(Jurisdiction), Injunctive relief, Coastal waters, Public trust doctrine, Territorial waters, State policy.

Action was brought by the United States against the State of Alaska to quiet title to the lower part of an inlet located on the Alaskan coast. Injunctive relief was also sought to stop Alaska from offering oil and gas leases for sale in the area. The district court for Alaska held in favor of the state. On appeal the lower court's ruling that the inlet was an inland waterway and that its subsurface resources belonged to Alaska was upheld. The lower part of Cook Inlet was forty-seven miles wide at its natural entrance points. It was not an inland bay as defined in the Convention on the Territorial Sea and the Contiguous Zone which requires a distance of no more than twenty four miles between natural entrance points. The Submerged Lands Act provides that the state is entitled to natural resources of the seabed in waters up to three geographical miles seaward from the coastline or its equivalent, as drawn by connecting land openings of water inlets, and that water landward from the line forming an equivalent coastline are inland waters belonging to the state. (Sperling-Florida)
W75-07758

MIKEL V. KERR (ACTION TO QUIET TITLE TO TRACT OF LAND WHICH LAY AT THE CONFLUENCE OF TWO RIVERS).
499 F.2d 1178 (10th Cir. 1974).

Descriptors: *Land tenure, *Riparian land, *Judicial decisions, *United States, *Oklahoma, Riparian rights, Rivers, Boundaries(Property), Accretion(Legal aspects), Avulsion, Watercourses(Legal aspects), Navigable waters, Meanders, Water law, Decision-making, Adoption of practices, Boundary disputes, Adjudication procedure.
Identifiers: Water rights(Non riparians).

Appeal was made to the United States Court of Appeals from an action to quiet title to a certain tract of land which lay at the confluence of two rivers. The court held that under Oklahoma law, when real property, which is riparian and has identifiable boundaries, is submerged by gradual movement of a river, and is then subsequently

restored by gradual recession of such river, title to such property remains in the owner of record title and does not vest, pursuant to the law of accretion. Under the law of accretion ownership would vest in an adjacent owner whose land was not originally riparian, but which has become riparian by means of the river's gradual movement. This holding is not limited to cases where the river changes course by avulsion or by the fact that the river is navigable. While the navigability of a waterway may be an important factor for certain rights of riparian owners, navigability had no effect on the instant case. (Sperling-Florida)
W75-07759

GOVERNMENT VIEWS ON WATER POLLUTION CONTROL,
Federal Water Pollution Control Administration, Washington, D.C.
For primary bibliographic entry see Field 5G.
W75-07760

UNITED STATES V. RESERVE MINING CO. (ACTION ON REMAND FROM EIGHTH CIRCUIT ON SUIT TO ENJOIN MINING CO FROM DISCHARGING CARCINOGENICS INTO INTERSTATE WATERS).
For primary bibliographic entry see Field 5G.
W75-07761

SCENIC HUDSON PRESERVATION CONFERENCE V. CALLAWAY (SUIT BY CONSERVATIONISTS TO ENJOIN HYDRO-ELECTRIC PLANT CONSTRUCTION).
370 F. Supp. 162 (S.D. N.Y. 1973).

Descriptors: *Water conservation, *Judicial decisions, *Hydroelectric plants, *Dredging, *New York, Hydroelectric power, Engineering structures, Powerplants, Industrial plants, Water utilization, Excavation, Drainage engineering, Legislation, Federal Water Pollution Control Act, Rivers and Harbors Act, Water resources development, Water law, Hudson River.
Identifiers: *Injunctive relief.

Suit was brought in the United States District Court to enjoin construction of a hydroelectric plant until the defendant utility company obtained permits from the Army Corps of Engineers. Plaintiffs sought to forbid conduct consisting of dredging in the Hudson River for construction of intake facilities for the underground powerhouse and the depositing of the dredged material into the river. Plaintiffs argued that the defendant was required to obtain permits from the Army Corps of Engineers pursuant to the Rivers and Harbors Act of 1899 and the Federal Water Pollution Control Act of 1972. The defendant contended that the permit authority of the Corps was removed by the Federal Power Act of 1920. The court held that while the Corps' authority to grant permits under the Rivers and Harbors Act was preempted by the Federal Power Act, the defendant was required, nevertheless by the Federal Water Pollution Control Act to seek a permit from the Corps for discharge of dredged or fill materials into the Hudson River. (Proctor-Florida)
W75-07762

SEA BEACH ASSOCIATION, INC. V. WATER RESOURCES COMMISSION (APPEAL FROM GRANTING PERMIT TO BUILD A PILE AND TIMBER PIER, ETC.).
318 A.2d 115 (Conn. 1972).

Descriptors: *Piers, *Coastal structures, *Judicial decisions, *Connecticut, Riparian rights, Engineering structures, Permits, Piles(Foundations), Legislation, Water law, Water resources development, Environmental effects.
Identifiers: *Standing(Legal), *Coves, *State agency.

Appeal was taken from an order of the Connecticut State Water Resources Commission issuing a permit to construct a pile and timber pier into the waters of Long Island Sound. Plaintiffs, property owners, alleged that they had been aggrieved by the granting of the permit. The Commission ruled that the plaintiffs were not aggrieved parties within the statute and were therefore without standing to sue. The order of the Commission was upheld on grounds that plaintiffs had failed to show a specific personal and legal interest in the subject matter as opposed to a general interest. (Proctor-Florida)
W75-07763

A TURNING POINT,
Department of Housing and Urban Development, Washington, D.C.
For primary bibliographic entry see Field 6F.
W75-07765

WASTEWATER IRRIGATION: ITS LEGAL IMPACT,
Virginia Polytechnic Inst. and State Univ., Blacksburg. Water Resources Research Center.
W. R. Walker, and W. E. Cox.
Water Spectrum, Vol 6, No 2, p 15-22 (1974). 9 photo, 1 chart.

Descriptors: *Water demand, *Waste water disposal, *Treatment facilities, *Water supply, Water shortage, Legal aspects, Water resources, Cost analysis, Reclamation, Sewage effluents, Treatment facilities, Federal Water Pollution Control Act, Legislation, Waterpolicy, Federal government, Water pollution, Navigable waters, Aquiculture, Regulation, Administrative agencies.
Identifiers: *FWPCA Amendments of 1972.

Future world demand for production of agricultural commodities will strain available water supplies. Legal attitudes toward the role of waste water resources in the economy will need to be changed. Recycling municipally produced sludge and effluent as an alternative form of waste disposal has not had the benefit of as in-depth an evaluation as have other methods. The first comprehensive effort at waste water management at the federal level came with the passage of the Water Pollution Control Act of 1948. It was not until the 1972 Amendments to the Federal Water Pollution Control Act that a national policy was established to eliminate discharge of pollutants into navigable waters. The 1972 Amendments specifically refer to recycling potential sewage pollutants in connection with agriculture, silviculture, or aquiculture. Regulations promulgated by the Environmental Protection Agency for implementing the Amendments contain guidelines for cost effectiveness analysis that specifically include considering land or subsurface disposal techniques as feasible alternatives. (Sperling-Florida)
W75-07766

CABIN CREEK, AN ACCUMULATION OF UNPAID SOCIAL AND ENVIRONMENTAL COSTS IN APPALACHIA,
Army Engineer District, Huntington, W. Va.
For primary bibliographic entry see Field 5G.
W75-07767

SGARLATA V. CITY OF SCHENECTADY (ACTION AGAINST CITY FOR FLOOD DAMAGE WHEN COFFER DAM BURST).
353 N.Y.S.2d 603 (S. Ct. Schenectady Cty. 1974).

Descriptors: *Municipal water, *Negligence, *Judicial decisions, *Flood control, *New York, Water control, Flood routing, Dams, Civil engineering, Flood damage, Hydraulic structures, Drainage systems, Flood flow, Legal aspects, Risks, Safety, Hazards, Water law, Cofferdams.
Identifiers: *Sovereign immunity.

Plaintiffs brought suit alleging damages through the negligence of the City of Schenectady in the maintenance and operation of the City's drainage system. Heavy rainfall caused the bursting of a dam which created a drainage overflow. Defendants asserted a defense of reasonable inspection and repair. The Supreme Court of New York found for the plaintiffs, holding that defendant City failed in the exercise of due care to ascertain and correct inadequacy in the drainage system. (Proctor-Florida)
W75-07768

WATER QUALITY-BASED EFFLUENT LIMITATIONS.
For primary bibliographic entry see Field 5G.
W75-07769

DISCHARGE LIMITATIONS--FEDERAL FACILITIES.
For primary bibliographic entry see Field 5G.
W75-07770

WATER REGULATIONS--WATER QUALITY STANDARDS.
For primary bibliographic entry see Field 5G.
W75-07771

WATER REGULATIONS--STATE PROGRAM ELEMENTS NECESSARY FOR PARTICIPATION IN THE NATIONAL POLLUTANT DISCHARGE ELIMINATION SYSTEM,
For primary bibliographic entry see Field 5G.
W75-07772

WATER REGULATIONS--NPDES,
For primary bibliographic entry see Field 5G.
W75-07773

WATER REGULATIONS--PREPARATION OF WATER QUALITY MANAGEMENT BASIN PLANS,
For primary bibliographic entry see Field 5G.
W75-07774

NORMATIVE ASPECTS OF SCIENTIFIC RESEARCH IN THE OCEANS, THE CASE OF MEXICO,
Rhode Island Univ., Kingston. Law of the Sea Inst.
J. A. Vargas.
Occasional Paper No 23, October 1974. 23 p, append.

Descriptors: *Sea water, *Internal waters, *Research and development, *Continental shelf, Ships, Riparian rights, Pollutants, Navigation, Fishing, Fisheries, Coasts, Oceans, Research facilities, Management.
Identifiers: *Coastal waters, *Coastal zone, Territorial seas(Jurisdiction), Territorial waters.

The Mexican government's position regarding scientific research activities conducted within its territorial seas by foreign vessels is opposed to that adopted by the highly developed countries which believe that complete freedom of scientific research in the oceans is indispensable to scientific advancement and progress. The Montevideo, Lima, Caracas and Santo Domingo meetings developed a contrary and unified position suggested by the Latin-American nations. Mexico, in particular, does not recognize innocent passage in internal waters, identifying such sections of the oceans as integral parts of the territory of the nation itself. The Mexican government considers the 12 mile territorial sea subject to its sovereign rights, except for innocent passage, and the continental shelf a part of the ocean space under its direct domain. It is also striving for legal recognition of a patrimonial sea up to two hundred miles,

and maintains that freedom to conduct marine scientific research is one of the freedoms of the high seas. At the recent 1974 Caracas Conference on Marine Scientific Research, the Mexican statement proposed that it is not possible to accept unrestricted marine scientific research without the express consent of the coastal state. It contends that the states have the right to control such activities and that once the researching state has met bona fide requirements, the coastal state should not normally withhold authorization. (Gagliardi-Florida)
W75-07775

WATER REGULATIONS--CRITERIA FOR THE EVALUATION OF PERMIT APPLICATIONS,
For primary bibliographic entry see Field 5G.
W75-07776

GROUND-WATER PROTECTION IN PENNSYLVANIA, A MODEL STATE PROGRAM,
Geraghty and Miller, Port Washington, N.Y.
For primary bibliographic entry see Field 4B.
W75-07777

THE EMERGING RIGHT OF PHYSICAL ENFORCEMENT OF FISHERIES MEASURES BEYOND TERRITORIAL LIMITS,
Wisconsin Univ., Madison. Sea Grant Program.
R. B. Bilder.
Technical Report No 22, July 1974. 28 p, 24 ref.

Descriptors: *Fish management, *International law, *Governments, *Enforcement, Regulations, Water policy, Fish populations, Fisheries, Fishing, Legal aspects, Law of the sea, International waters, Foreign waters, Foreign trade, Treaties, United Nations, Foreign countries, Water resources development, Water law.

The Caracas Law of the Sea Conference will substantially change and limit traditional concepts of freedom of fisheries on the high seas. It is predicted that the Conference will agree upon a rather narrow territorial sea; probably twelve miles and recognize broad coastal state fisheries jurisdiction. If the Conference recognizes the right of a coastal state to establish rules governing fisheries beyond its territorial seas, the question arises whether state coastal authority will embrace broad ranging enforcement power, including the right to stop, board, search and seize foreign vessels. Various enforcement alternatives are discussed in the context of the traditional law of the sea as reflected in the Geneva Convention under existing coastal state fisheries regimes, and proposals presented to the Seabed Committee preparatory to the Law of the Sea Conference. While it is likely that conflicting concerns of coastal and other states will present substantial obstacles to uniformity, enforcement processes are not unitary but can be tailored and flexibly allocated in a way acceptable to the concerned countries. (Proctor-Florida)
W75-07778

ENVIRONMENTAL CONCERN AND POLITICAL ELITES: A STUDY OF PERCEPTIONS BACKGROUNDS AND ATTITUDES,
California Univ., Davis. Inst. of Governmental Affairs.
For primary bibliographic entry see Field 6G.
W75-07779

POSSIBLE OPTIONS FOR REDUCING THE SALINITY OF THE COLORADO RIVER WATERS FLOWING TO MEXICO (FINAL ENVIRONMENTAL IMPACT STATEMENT),
Department of State, Washington, D.C.
For primary bibliographic entry see Field 3A.
W75-07782

6F. Nonstructural Alternatives

PIMA COUNTY MOVES ON GEOLOGIC HAZARDS,
Arizona Bureau of Mines, Tucson.
H. Peirce, and J. A. Vuich.
Field Notes: From the Arizona Bureau of Mines, Vol 5, No 1, March 1975. University of Arizona, Tucson, p 1-3, 6-9. 14 fig.

Descriptors: *Arizona, *Flood protection, *Flood plains, *Groundwater recharge, *Legislation, Flood forecasting, Arid lands, Water spreading, Flood recurrence interval, Floods, Flash floods, Sheet floods, Channels, Recharge, Arroyos, Dry beds, Intermittent streams.
Identifiers: Tucson(Ariz), Pima County(Ariz), Sonoran Desert.

Pima County, Arizona, located in the Sonoran Desert, is characterized by a low rainfall and a high flood potential. This condition results from the intensity of random storms and from the high runoff from the sparsely vegetated landscape with its mountains and steep slopes. People moving into the county from other parts of the country have built housing units on the floodplains and near foothill arroyos. Periodically, such housing is threatened by erosion and occasionally destroyed. Recently, the county passed a floodplain ordinance to avoid past problems. However, the ordinance is vague and, unless enforced as part of an overall county-wide plan, could cause more problems. For example, if piecemeal development of the land continues it could lead to a demand for channelization of the arroyos and washes which in turn would achieve flood protection at the price of lowering the recharge rate of the aquifer. (Bowden-Arizona)
W75-07392

EVOLVING PATTERNS OF FLOOD PLAIN USE,
Oregon State Univ., Corvallis. Dept. of Geography.
K. W. Muckleston.
In: Land and Water Use in Oregon; Seminar conducted by Oregon State University, Spring Quarter 1974, Water Resources Research Institute, Corvallis, Oregon, p 27-44, July 1974. 4 fig, 1 tab, 26 ref.

Descriptors: *Flood plains, *Flood plain zoning, *Flood plain insurance, Non-structural alternatives, Flood damage, Insurance, Economics, Zoning, Regulation, Legal aspects, Building codes, Floodways, Dams, Riparian rights, Land use, Legislation, Flood protection, Local governments, Oregon.
Identifiers: Federal Flood Insurance Act.

Despite very large expenditures to abate flood damage, continued encroachment into riverine areas offsets these investments. In Oregon and throughout the country, present uses of the flood plains reflect their perceived advantages as sites of occupancy. Man has attempted to ensure the safe use of these riverine areas by erecting structures to control flood flows. The futility of depending almost entirely on structures was recognized by Congress in 1968 when it enacted the National Flood Insurance Program. If implemented, this program will complement the engineering approach to abating flood losses. But implementation has been slow, due largely to the value this society still places in the right of property owners to use their lands as they see fit under all but the most extradordinary circumstances. Although this view had its merits in an expanding frontier, under the present conditions it is becoming increasingly anachronistic. Evidence suggests, however, that the evolving state and federal interests in planned land management will impel local governments to more vigorously manage flood plain lands in a manner designed to achieve comprehensive, long range goals. (See also W75-07507) (Sims-ISWS)
W75-07510

quarter billion dollars and are continuing to increase, largely as a result of the improper use of the Nation's flood plains. Under the Act, the Secretary of HUD is required to notify all flood prone communities in the Nation of these tentative identifications as such by July 1, 1974. The community then must either make prompt application for participation in the program or satisfy the Secretary that it is no longer flood prone. (Sperling-Florida)
W75-07765

6G. Ecologic Impact Of Water Development

ENVIRONMENTAL QUALITY AND SAFETY, VOL. 2. GLOBAL ASPECTS OF CHEMISTRY, TOXICOLOGY AND TECHNOLOGY AS APPLIED TO THE ENVIRONMENT.
Georg Thieme Publishers: Stuttgart, West Germany. Academic Press, Inc.: New York, N.Y. 333 p, Illus. Coulston, F., Korte, F. (Ed.).

Descriptors: *Environmental effects, Environment, DDT, Atmospheric pollution, Air pollution, Potable water, Waste water, Solid wastes, Inorganie chemicals, Toxicity, Pesticides, Seawater, Sediments, Fish, Fertilizers, Ecology.

Several papers discuss man in the technological age and his environment, science in the food industry, DDT-chlorophenothene, and new technologies for the alleviation of environmental pollution. Other topics include recent air pollution problems, drinking water and waste water problems, disposal and utilization of solid waste, inorganic chemicals in the environment, chemicals in the environment, toxic microelements and therapeutica in food of animal origin, power generation chemicals and toxicological evaluation of special organochlorinated compounds. Factors to be considered in evaluating the toxicity of pesticides to birds in their environment and studies on the toxicology of nitrites and cadmium content in sea water, bottom sediment, fish, lichen and elk in Finland are presented. The economics of fertilizer use by United States farmers, economic importance of chemical crop protection in relation to its ecological impact, protection of environmental quality in Israel, and retrospective and prospective aspects in the establishment of air quality guides are studied.--Copyright 1974, Biological Abstracts, Inc.
W75-07355

USE OF ENVIRONMENTAL ANALYSES ON WASTEWATER FACILITIES BY LOCAL GOVERNMENT,
Teknekron, Inc., Washington, D.C. Applied Research Div.
For primary bibliographic entry see Field 5D.
W75-07360

SOUTHWEST ENERGY STUDY. SUMMARY REPORT.
Southwest Energy Federal Task Force.
For primary bibliographic entry see Field 6B.
W75-07380

WILDLIFE, ECOLOGY, AND PLANNING IN A PROPOSED IRRIGATION DEVELOPMENT IN NORTH DAKOTA,
North Dakota State Univ., Fargo.
G. H. Cross.
Available from the National Technical Information Service, Springfield, Va 22161 as PB-241 670, $9.50 in paper copy, $2.25 in microfiche. Ph.D. Thesis, July 1973. 222 p, 73 tab, 27 fig, 43 ref, 5 append. OWRT B-014-NDAK(1).

Descriptors: *Wildlife, *Wildlife habitats, *Wildlife conservation, *Irrigation programs, *Environmental effects, Balance of nature, Wildlife management, Habitat improvement, Shelterbelts, Carrying capacity, Windbreaks, *North Dakota, Irrigation, Irrigated land, Irrigation systems, Irrigation effects.
Identifiers: Harrison Diversion Project(NDak).

A 20,000 acre area in southeastern North Dakota will be irrigated as the first phase of the Garrison Diversion Project which will eventually irrigate 250,000 acres in central and eastern North Dakota. This study seeks to understand the impact of such land use on wildlife. Present farming practices have left a variety of odd, idle areas and shelterbelts scattered throughout the region. With the exception of the ringnecked pheasant, wildlife abounds. Irrigated agriculture will result in intensive land use. The use of sprinklers will result in a tremendous loss of wildlife habitat. The constant wetting may interfere with the nesting of some birds. Livestock forage operations will mean fall grazing of cropland; this will reduce the amount of cover and food which is important for wildlife. Soil mining (the practice of removing all grain or forage from the land) will also limit food and cover for wildlife. The problems associated with sprinkler irrigation systems are formulative and little can be done in the way of practical solutions because of the economic implications to the irrigator. The irrigated land will be almost impossible to manage for the benefit of wildlife. Any beneficial relationship between irrigation and wildlife on cultivated land will be incidental. A wildlife plan is outlined which will mitigate the negative impact of irrigated agriculture on wildlife. (Bowden-Arizona)
W75-07400

REPORT TO THE CONGRESS ON OCEAN POLLUTION, OVERFISHING, AND OFFSHORE DEVELOPMENT; JULY 1973 THROUGH JUNE 1974.
National Oceanic and Atmospheric Administration, Washington, D.C.
For primary bibliographic entry see Field 5B.
W75-07405

ENVIRONMENTAL STUDIES OF AN ARCTIC ESTUARINE SYSTEM--FINAL REPORT,
Alaska Univ., College. Marine Science Inst.
For primary bibliographic entry see Field 2L.
W75-07417

MARINE POLLUTION MONITORING: STRATEGIES FOR A NATIONAL PROGRAM,
Scripps Institution of Oceanography, La Jolla, Calif.
For primary bibliographic entry see Field 5A.
W75-07418

ENGINEERING CONSIDERATIONS FOR MARINAS IN TIDAL MARSHES,
Delaware Univ., Newark. Dept. of Civil Engineering.
For primary bibliographic entry see Field 2L.
W75-07420

BISCAYNE BAY: ENVIRONMENTAL AND SOCIAL SYSTEMS.
Miami Univ., Coral Gables, Fla.
For primary bibliographic entry see Field 2L.
W75-07427

ENVIRONMENTAL SURVEYS IN ALASKA BASED UPON ERTS DATA,
Alaska Univ., College.
For primary bibliographic entry see Field 7B.
W75-07486

THE PRACTICAL LIMITS OF POLLUTION CONTROL TECHNOLOGY,
Oregon State Univ., Corvallis. Dept. of Civil Engineering.
For primary bibliographic entry see Field 5G.
W75-07508

ENVIRONMENTAL MANAGEMENT IN THE COLORADO RIVER BASIN.
For primary bibliographic entry see Field 6B.
W75-07525

BASIN-WIDE PLANNING AND THE PROBLEM OF MULTIPLE JURISDICTIONS,
Ferris, Weatherford and Brennan, San Diego, Calif.
For primary bibliographic entry see Field 6E.
W75-07526

THE ROLE OF ENVIRONMENTAL INDICES IN REGIONAL MANAGEMENT,
Resources for the Future, Inc., Washington, D.C.
For primary bibliographic entry see Field 6B.
W75-07528

FUTURE DIRECTIONS IN ENVIRONMENTAL LEGISLATION,
For primary bibliographic entry see Field 6E.
W75-07532

STRATEGIES FOR ENVIRONMENTAL PLANNING IN THE UPPER COLORADO RIVER REGION,
California Univ., Berkeley. Dept. of Landscape Architecture.
For primary bibliographic entry see Field 6B.
W75-07534

URBANIZATION WITH OR WITHOUT ENVIRONMENTAL QUALITY,
United States International Univ., San Diego, Calif.
For primary bibliographic entry see Field 4C.
W75-07542

ENERGY FROM COAL: GUIDELINES FOR THE PREPARATION OF ENVIRONMENTAL IMPACT STATEMENTS,
Battelle Columbus Labs., Ohio.
M. L. Warner, R. C. Burke III, G. I. Nehman, G. A. Watkins, and S. Chatterjee.
Final Report to Department of the Interior, Office of Research and Development, April 30, 1975, 338 p. 14-01-0001-1933.

Descriptors: *Environmental effects, *Coals, *Energy, Mining, Economic impact, Social impact, Energy conversion, *Standards, *Research and development, Federal Government, Methodology, Alternative planning, Water quality, Groundwater, Surface water, Water utilization.
Identifiers: *Environmental Impact Statements, *Coal energy, Surface water quantity.

A comprehensive approach is presented to the preparation of environmental impact statements (EIS) on coal energy related R and D proposals. The material is organized into chapters paralleling the required EIS content points, as specified in Department of Interior guidelines. Additional chapters discuss methods of summarizing major environmental impact statements to facilitate communication to the public, and remaining research and data needs of the environmental assessment process. Guidance is offered for measuring a comprehensive set of potential physical environment, economic, and social impacts. The analysis is organized according to a hierarchy of broad impact issues, more specific aspects of the environment, and very specific measurable indices. Though much of the material presented is applicable to most coal energy related projects, coal R and D projects are of particular concern, with special techniques suggested for dealing with the unique impact assessment problems of R and D activities.

These techniques include procedures for identifying and describing the impacts of subsequent R and D steps, and for identifying, organizing, and comparing a comprehensive set of project alternatives. A special section of one chapter considers the impact of water on proposed projects, discussing factors concerned with surface water quantity, groundwater quantity and water quality.
W75-07590

DEVELOPMENT OF AN APPROACH TO IDENTIFICATION OF EMERGING TECHNOLOGY AND DEMONSTRATION OPPORTUNITIES,
Battelle Columbus Labs., Ohio.
For primary bibliographic entry see Field 5G.
W75-07617

PROCEEDINGS OF A CONFERENCE ON MANAGEMENT OF DREDGE ISLANDS IN NORTH CAROLINA ESTUARIES,
North Carolina Univ., Wilmington. Dept. of Biology.
For primary bibliographic entry see Field 2L.
W75-07716

HUMAN ECOLOGY AND THE ECOSYSTEM, (IN JAPANESE),
Institute of Population Problems, Tokyo (Japan).
N. Makoto.
Annu Rep Inst Popul Probl. Vol 17, p 70-73, 93-94. 1972, English summary.

Descriptors: *Social aspects, *Ecosystems, Social values, Environment.

Environmental problems demand a sociological theory capable of dealing with socio-environmental relationships. As a clue for understanding socio-environmental system Otis Dudley Duncan's ecosystem theory is explained. The contents of Duncan's theory follows: In order to deal with the close connection between social organization and environment, sociology must adopt a concept of ecosystem which is capable of covering broader phenomena in comparison with the concept of social system. The ecosystem is a system which is composed of 4 functionally interrelated components, i.e., population, environment, technology and social organization. In the ecosystem there are flows of 3 elements, i.e., material, energy and information, and, among these elements, information has the greatest significance for the ecosystem including the human species. Social evolution in the ecosystem can be explained by the expansion of the niches of human species, that is 'ecological expansion'. Human expansion in the ecosystem has been made possible by the subsystem of information-cumulation and application of human society. The modern stage of social evolution is called 'industrial-urban societies.' The ecological expansion in this stage is summarized into 4 interdependent facts: the accelerated cumulation of technology, the intensification of environmental development, population explosion and organizational revolution. The merit of Duncan's theory is that it adopts a comprehensive conceptual system (ecosystem) including physical environmental as an 'internal variable' and makes sociology able to deal with a socio-environmental system in principle.--Copyright 1973, Biological Abstracts, Inc.
W75-07750

NELSON V. BUTZ (ACTION SEEKING INJUNCTION AND DECLARATORY RELIEF RELATING TO CONSTRUCTION OF PROPOSED DAM),
For primary bibliographic entry see Field 6E.
W75-07757

CABIN CREEK, AN ACCUMULATION OF UNPAID SOCIAL AND ENVIRONMENTAL COSTS IN APPALACHIA,
Army Engineer District, Huntington, W. Va.
For primary bibliographic entry see Field 5G.
W75-07767

ENVIRONMENTAL CONCERN AND POLITICAL ELITES: A STUDY OF PERCEPTIONS BACKGROUNDS AND ATTITUDES,
California Univ., Davis. Inst. of Governmental Affairs.
E. Costantini, and K. Hanf.
Research Report No 21, May 1971. 40 p, 31 ref, 16 tab. OWRT A-037-CAL(1).

Descriptors: *Decision making, *Political constraints, *Political aspects, *Governments, Environment, Environmental effects, Water resources development, Regiok s Institutions, Area redevelopment, Administration, Pollutants, Governmental interrelations, Habitats, Social aspects, Water law, Regions.

Inevitably the question of what constitutes unacceptable environmental conditions is a political one. Environmental policy is not an irresistible, simple, unchallenged response to empirical or scientific fact alone, but is determined through trial by political combat. Environmental policy tends to be a function of the degree of concern for environmental problems on the part of those persons in a position to make or affect relevant decisions. The decision makers in the Latke Tahoe Basin are examined in terms of variations in their level of concern for environmental problems. The relationship between these variations and other environmental perceptions, the background, and political, social and psychological attitudes of the decision makers is discussed. A larger study is concerned with identifying and analyzing the attitudes and interests of the most significant actors concerned with environmental policy in the Lake Tahoe Basin. (Proctor-Florida)
W75-07779

BEACH EROSION CONTROL IMPROVEMENTS, WAIKIKI BEACH, OAHU, HAWAII (KAPAHULU STORM DRAIN TO THE ELKS CLUB) (FINAL ENVIRONMENTAL IMPACT STATEMENT),
Corps of Engineers, Honolulu, Hawaii. Pacific Ocean Div.
For primary bibliographic entry see Field 8A.
W75-07780

GEOTHERMAL LEASING PROGRAM, VOL IV, APPENDIX I, COMMENTS ON DRAFT IMPACT STATEMENT AND PROPOSED REGULATIONS (FINAL ENVIRONMENTAL IMPACT STATEMENT),
Department of the Interior, Washington, D.C.
For primary bibliographic entry see Field 8B.
W75-07781

POSSIBLE OPTIONS FOR REDUCING THE SALINITY OF THE COLORADO RIVER WATERS FLOWING TO MEXICO (FINAL ENVIRONMENTAL IMPACT STATEMENT),
Department of State, Washington, D.C.
For primary bibliographic entry see Field 3A.
W75-07782

FORT LAUDERDALE, FLORIDA (FINAL ENVIRONMENTAL IMPACT STATEMENT),
Environmental Protection Agency, Atlanta, Ga. Region IV.
For primary bibliographic entry see Field 5D.
W75-07783

MAINTENANCE OF BAY RIDGE AND RED HOOK CHANNELS, NEW YORK NAVIGATION PROJECT (FINAL ENVIRONMENTAL IMPACT STATEMENT),
Army Engineer District, New York.
For primary bibliographic entry see Field 8A.
W75-07784

THE MENDOTA WATERSHED PROJECT, LASALLE AND BUREAU COUNTIES, ILLINOIS (FINAL ENVIRONMENTAL IMPACT STATEMENT),
Soil Conservation Service, Champaign, Ill.
For primary bibliographic entry see Field 4D.
W75-07785

RESEARCH DEMONSTRATION PILOT STUDY OF MUNICIPAL WASTE COMPOSTING (FINAL ENVIRONMENTAL STATEMENT),
Agricultural Research Service, Washington, D.C.
For primary bibliographic entry see Field 5D.
W75-07786

NORTH BROWARD COUNTY, FLORIDA (FINAL ENVIRONMENTAL IMPACT STATEMENT),
Environmental Protection Agency, Atlanta, Ga. Region IV.
For primary bibliographic entry see Field 5D.
W75-07787

PEACOCK CREEK, LIBERTY COUNTY, GEORGIA (FINAL ENVIRONMENTAL IMPACT STATEMENT),
Army Engineer District, Savannah, Ga.
For primary bibliographic entry see Field 4A.
W75-07788

UPPER SALT CREEK WATERSHED, COOK, LAKE AND DUPAGE COUNTIES, ILLINOIS (FINAL ENVIRONMENTAL IMPACT STATEMENT),
Soil Conservation Service, Washington, D.C.
For primary bibliographic entry see Field 8A.
W75-07789

7. RESOURCES DATA

7A. Network Design

STREAM GAGING INFORMATION, AUSTRALIA -- SUPPLEMENT 1973.
Australian Water Resources Council, Canberra.
For primary bibliographic entry see Field 7C.
W75-07480

A NOTE ON COSTS OF COLLECTING HYDROMETRIC FLOW DATA IN THE UNITED STATES,
Geological Survey, Reston, Va.
W. B. Langbein, and G. E. Harbeck, Jr.
Hydrological Sciences Bulletin, Vol 19, No 2, p 227-229, June 1974.

Descriptors: *Basic data collections, *Hydrologic data, *Costs, Cost-benefit analysis, Gaging stations, Stream gages, Hydrometry, Water measurement, Streamflow.
Identifiers: *Hydrometric data.

The hydrometric program in the United States consists of 8400 full-record stations and an equal number of partial-record stations operated by 47 district offices. A sampling of four districts selected to represent the range of hydrometric conditions in the country indicated that costs (in 1972) for installation of a full-record station intended for indefinite terms of operation ranged between $5000 and $10,000. Short-term stations range between $2500 and $4000. Costs of operation for full-record stations ranged between $800 and

$1250 per year, -whereas office costs for processing the record ranged between $500 and $1250. A considerable emphasis is given in the program to partial-record stations designed to furnish specific information for floods and droughts. Annual costs in terms of full-record stations range from only 5 percent for a low-flow station, 15-20 percent for a crest-stage record, to 50 percent for a flood-hydrogram station. Publication costs average about $7 per page. This small sample survey shows considerable variations and even greater variations might be expected internationally. In any case, differences in costs nationally or internationally invite proper inquiry as to causes in the search for economy. (Knapp-USGS)
W75-07578

7B. Data Acquisition

AUTOMATED ANALYSIS OF INDIVIDUAL REFRACTORY ORGANICS IN POLLUTED WATER,
Oak Ridge National Lab., Tenn.
For primary bibliographic entry see Field 5A.
W75-07404

POTENTIAL VALUE OF EARTH SATELLITE MEASUREMENTS TO OCEANOGRAPHIC RESEARCH IN THE SOUTHERN OCEAN,
National Environmental Satellite Service Washington, D.C.
For primary bibliographic entry see Field 2C.
W75-07421

A COMPARISON OF INFRARED IMAGERY AND VIDEO PICTURES IN THE ESTIMATION OF DAILY RAINFALL FROM SATELLITE DATA,
National Environmental Satellite Service, Washington, D.C.
For primary bibliographic entry see Field 2B.
W75-07422

SNOW DEPTH AND SNOW EXTENT USING VHRR DATA FROM THE NOAA-2 SATELLITE,
National Environmental Satellite Service, Washington, D.C.
For primary bibliographic entry see Field 2C.
W75-07423

AN INEXPENSIVE MULTIPLE LEVEL WATER SAMPLER,
Toronto Univ. (Ontario). Dept. of Zoology.
M. H. Goodwin, and C. I. Goddard.
Journal of the Fisheries Research Board of Canada, Vol 31, No 10, p 1667-1668, October 1974. 1 fig.

Descriptors: *Water sampling, *Equipment, On-site investigations, *Sampling, Salinity, Dissolved oxygen, Water levels.
Identifiers: *Water samplers(Multiple level).

An inexpensive nonmetallic water sampler was designed to secure multiple samples simultaneously from different depths. The device is constructed of readily available materials and may be operated from a small boat. The sample bottle is constructed from a length of ABS drain pipe to which a nylon rope bridle is attached with plastic tape. Two rubber balls are attached to a piece of laboratory tubing passed through the pipe. Before tying, the tubing is stretched so that the balls will make a tight seal at the ends of the pipe. The desired number of sample bottles are then attached to a braided polypropylene line tied to a 25-kg weight. To prepare the units for sampling, the opposing balls are brought together at the midpoint of the pipe and the brass rings are tied together with a slip knot. All the pairs of balls are tied with the same nylon line, so that, when the end of the trip line is pulled, all knots collapse in sequence and the balls seal the pipes. (Sims-ISWS)
W75-07455

SATELLITE-TRACKED CUMULUS VELOCITIES,
Chicago Univ., Ill.
T. T. Fujita, E. W. Pearl, and W. E. Shenk.
Journal of Applied Meteorology, Vol 14, No 3, p 407-413, April 1975. 9 fig, 2 tab, 9 ref. NOAA Grant E-198-68G, NASA Grant NGR 14-001-008, NSF Grant GA-31589.

Descriptors: *Winds, *Clouds, *Satellites(Artificial), Entrainment, Evaluation, Movement, Wind velocity, Estimating, Velocity, *Remote sensing.
Identifiers: Standard deviation, *Cloud velocity, *Cumulus, Wind estimates, Updrafts, Downdrafts.

Velocities of tracer clouds have been computed by NOAA, NASA, Stanford Research Institute, University of Wisconsin, University of Chicago, and others. Despite the fact that their methods and inherent computation speeds are different from each other, the present state-of-the-art permits the computations with 1 m/s speed and 4 degrees direction in standard deviation. Such an accuracy in the cloud velocity is satisfactory for most practical purposes. The research presented warns that we have to exercise extreme caution in converting cloud velocities into winds. The motion of fair-weather cumuli obtained by tracking their shadows over Springfield, Missouri, revealed that the standard deviation in the individual cloud motion is several times the tracking error. Analysis of whole-sky images obtained near Tampa, Florida, failed to show significant continuity and stability of cumulus plumes, less than 0.3 mi in diameter. Cumulus turrets 0.3 to 2 mi in size appear to be the best target to infer the mean wind within the subcloud layers. The addition and deletion of turrets belonging to a specific cell appear to be the cause of the erratic motion of a tracer cell. It was concluded that the accuracy of wind estimates is unlikely to be better than 2 m/s unless the physical and dynamical characteristics of cumulus motion is further investigated. (Jones-ISWS)
W75-07458

A NEW HOT-WIRE LIQUID CLOUD WATER METER,
National Hurricane Research Lab., Coral Gables, Fla.
For primary bibliographic entry see Field 2B.
W75-07461

USE OF AXISYMMETRIC INFILTRATION MODEL AND FIELD DATA TO DETERMINE HYDRAULIC PROPERTIES OF SOILS,
Utah State Univ., Logan. Dept. of Civil Engineering.
For primary bibliographic entry see Field 2G.
W75-07466

TEMPERATURE MEASUREMENTS IN THE UPPER 10 M WITH MODIFIED EXPENDABLE BATHYTHERMOGRAPH PROBES,
Woods Hole Oceanographic Institution, Mass.
J. G. Bruce, and E. Firing.
Journal of Geophysical Research, Vol 79, No 27, p 4110-4111, September 20, 1974. 2 fig, 3 ref. NSF Grant GX-29051.

Descriptors: *Temperature, *Sea water, *Thermal stratification, Diffusion, Heat balance, Oceans, Oceanography, Stratification, Measurement, Surface waters, Bathythermographs, Distributions, *Atlantic Ocean.
Identifiers: Bermuda, Heat loss rate.

Observations southwest of Bermuda with modified expendable bathythermographs (XBT) of surface warming and cooling during an isolated windless day with strong insolation showed the development and, by evening, the disappearance of a shallow 1- to 2-m layer that was 2-3C warmer than the main mixed layer. (Lee-ISWS)
W75-07475

BOTTOM CURRENT MEASUREMENTS IN THE LABRADOR SEA,
Lamont-Doherty Geological Observatory, Palisades, N.Y.
For primary bibliographic entry see Field 2L.
W75-07478

THIRD EARTH RESOURCES TECHNOLOGY SATELLITE SYMPOSIUM, VOLUME II, SUMMARY OF RESULTS.
National Aeronautics and Space Administration, Greenbelt, Md. Goddard Space Flight Center.
Symposium held at Washington, D.C., December 10-14, 1973: NASA SP-356, May 1974. 179 p, append. Freden, S.C., Mercanti, E.P., and Friedman, D.B., editors.

Descriptors: *Remote sensing, *Satellites(Artificial), *Mapping, *Surveys, Cloud cover, Environment, Land use, Geology, Geological mapping, Oil wells, Exploration, Sedimentation, Fish, Strip mines, Waterfowl, Agriculture, Water resources, Data collections, Data processing.
Identifiers: *ERTS.

This symposium was the third in a series on the significant results obtained from the first Earth Resources Technology Satellite (ERTS-1). The Thursday Summary Session was designed to highlight and summarize the significant results from the first three days and also to present some typical examples of the applications of ERTS data for solving resources management problems at the national, state, and local levels. The presentations from this session are contained in Volume II of the Proceedings. The papers were grouped under the following headings: (1) selected significant aecomplishments, (2) applications and key findings, and (3) summaries in selected disciplines. (See W75-07485 thru W75-07496) (Sims-ISWS)
W75-07484

REPORT ON THE CANADIAN ERTS PROGRAM,
Canada Centre for Remote Sensing, Ottawa (Ontario).
For primary bibliographic entry see Field 7C.
W75-07485

ENVIRONMENTAL SURVEYS IN ALASKA BASED UPON ERTS DATA,
Alaska Univ., College.
J. M. Miller.
In: Third Earth Resources Technology Satellite Symposium, Vol II, Summary of Results, Washington, D.C., December 10-14, 1973: NASA SP-356, p 12-40, May 1974. 37 fig.

Descriptors: *Remote sensing, *Satellites(Artificial), *Alaska, Environment, Land use, Pipelines, Highways, Vegetation, Agriculture, Ice cover, Snow cover, Faults(Geologic), Fractures(Geologic), Magnetic studies, Glaciers, Water circulation, Sedimentation, Wildlife.
Identifiers: *ERTS, Stream icing, Lineations.

ERTS imagery is being used to map native vegetation types in Alaska to provide a guide for agricultural land inventories. ERTS data have about a 10:1 or 20:1 cost advantage over conventional aerial photography techniques for planning the best use of specific parcels of land. Stream icing has been studied with use of ERTS data. The effects of roads on snow cover melting have been measured. Magnetic anomalies have been related to

areas of lineations visible in ERTS photos. A regional ERTS mosaic of the Denali Fault in Alaska and Canada has provided corroborative evidence of a massive offset some 400 km in length along the fault. Knowledge of circulation and sedimentation in the Cook Inlet has been improved through the use of ERTS data. ERTS data have been used to map the previously unknown distribution of habitats favored by certain marine mammals. (See also W75-07484) (Sims-ISWS)
W75-07486

GEOLOGIC EVALUATION AND APPLICATIONS OF ERTS-1 IMAGERY OVER GEORGIA,
Georgia State Geological Survey, Atlanta.
S. M. Pickering, and R. C. Jones.
In: Third Earth Resources Technology Satellite Symposium, Vol II, Summary of Results, Washington, D.C., December 10-14, 1973: NASA SP-356, p 41-49, May 1974. 12 fig.

Descriptors: *Remote sensing, *Satellites(Artificial), *Geology, Geologic mapping, *Georgia, Southeast U.S., Faults(Geologic), Folds(Geologic), Structural geology, Mining, Water resources, Wetlands, Marshes, Topography.
Identifiers: *ERTS.

Geologic mapping and mineral exploration by conventional methods are very difficult in Georgia. Thick soil cover and vegetation cause outcrops of bedrock to be small, rare, and obscure. ERTS imagery, and remote sensing in general, has helped delineate major tectonic boundaries, lithologic contacts, foliation trends, topographic lineaments, and faults. Satellite imagery and other remote sensing tools and techniques have provided a powerful tool to assist geologic research; significantly increased the mapping efficiency of field geologists; shown new lineaments associated with known shear and fault zones; delineated new structural features; provided a tool to reevaluate tectonic history; helped to locate potential groundwater sources and areas of aquifer recharge; defined areas of geologic hazards; shown areas of heavy siltation in major reservoirs; and, by close interval repetition, aided in monitoring surface mine reclamation activities and the environmental protection of the intricate marshland system. (See also W75-07484) (Sims-ISWS)
W75-07487

AN EVALUATION OF THE SUITABILITY OF ERTS DATA FOR THE PURPOSES OF PETROLEUM EXPLORATION,
Earth Satellite Corp., Washington, D.C.
J. R. Everett, and G. Petzel.
In: Third Earth Resources Technology Satellite Symposium, Vol II, Summary of Results, Washington, D.C., December 10-14, 1973: NASA SP-356, p 50-61, May 1974. 16 fig.

Descriptors: *Remote sensing, *Satellites(Artificial), Geology, *Oil, Oil fields, Oil wells, Exploration, Oil industry, Geologic formations, Oil reservoirs, Sedimentary rocks, Crystalline rocks, Costs, Economics, *Oklahoma, Data collections, Data processing, *Texas.
Identifiers: *ERTS, *Anadarko Basin(Okla-Tex).

The Anadarko Basin lies in western Oklahoma and the panhandle of Texas. It was chosen as a test site because there is a great deal of published information available on the surface and subsurface geology of the area, there are many known structures that act as traps for hydrocarbons, and it is similar to several other large epicontinental sedimentary basins. MSS bands 5 and 7 together showed the greatest versatility and widest range of easily extractable information. Interpretation of ERTS imagery defined the major features of the Anadarko Basin and refined the understanding of many smaller areas within the test site. The general features of the basin can be inferred from analysis of the interpreted lithologic distribution. ERTS imagery is an excellent tool for reconnaissance exploration of large sedimentary basins or new exploration provinces. The imagery allows rapid interpretation of large features and quickly focuses attention on anomalous areas. Because of a variety of options available for obtaining reconnaissance geological and geophysical data, cost comparisons are difficult. Moreover, the types of data obtained by ERTS and that obtained by a standard program are not precisely comparable. Based on preliminary analysis, savings produced by incorporating ERTS into an exploration program might be 20 to 50% of the cost of a standard survey. The savings would be made primarily by reducing the amount of seismic and other geophysical surveys needed. (See also W75-07484) (Sims-ISWS)
W75-07488

ERTS PROGRAM OF THE U.S. ARMY CORPS OF ENGINEERS,
Corps of Engineers, Washington, D.C.
For primary bibliographic entry see Field 7C.
W75-07489

A REVIEW OF INITIAL INVESTIGATIONS TO UTILIZE ERTS-1 DATA IN DETERMINING THE AVAILABILITY AND DISTRIBUTION OF LIVING MARINE RESOURCES,
National Aeronautics and Space Administration, Bay Saint Louis, Miss. Earth Resources Lab., and National Marine Fisheries Service, Bay Saint Louis, Miss. Fisheries Engineering Lab.
W. H. Stevenson, A. J. Kemmerer, B. H. Atwell, and P. M. Maughan.
In: Third Earth Resources Technology Satellite Symposium, Vol. II, Summary of Results, Washington, D.C., December 10-14, 1973: NASA SP-356, p 76-86, May 1974. 9 fig, 2 tab, 9 ref.

Descriptors: *Remote sensing, *Satellites(Artificial), *Fish, Commercial fish, Marine fish, Fish behavior, Fisheries, Aerial photography, Monitoring, Mississippi, Data processing, Data collections, Analysis.
Identifiers: *ERTS, Menhaden, *Mississippi Sound(Miss).

The ERTS multispectral scanner band-5 imagery of August 7, 1972, was correlated with menhaden distribution patterns. A portion of this imagery was analyzed, based on surface measurements obtained on the same date. The imagery was analyzed by superimposing on it the locations of 23 photographically detected menhaden schools. Water imagery density was divided into two density ranges. All of the menhaden schools were found to lie in the less dense ranges of the imagery. These density levels were shown to correlate significantly with measurements of water transparency and depth. These parameters were also shown to correlate with menhaden distribution. Results of the analysis clearly demonstrated the feasibility of using data from environmental sensors aboard satellites to predict fish distribution under at least one set of conditions. (See also W75-07484) (Sims - ISWS)
W75-07490

AUTOMATED STRIP MINE AND RECLAMATION MAPPING FROM ERTS,
Ohio State Univ., Columbus.
W. A. Pettyjohn, R. H. Rogers, and L. E. Reed.
In: Third Earth Resources Technology Satellite Symposium Vol II, Summary of Results, Washington, D.C., Dec 10-14, 1973: NASA SP-356, p 87-101, May 1974. 22 fig, 2 tab.

Descriptors: *Remote sensing, *Satellites(Artificial), *Strip mines, Surveys, Data processing, Mapping, Automation, Strip mine wastes, Acidic water, Spoil banks, Erosion, Reclamation, *Ohio.
Identifiers: *ERTS, Strip mine reclamation, Muskingum County(Ohio).

Local, state and federal agencies must have repetitive coverage of mining areas and the capability for rapidly evaluating each situation. They must also be able to quickly determine areas of mining reclamation and progress or viability of replanted vegetation, at least on an annual basis. At present, this cannot be done economically by ground teams and aerial photographs rapidly become outdated. Although several specific areas have been examined, a very large mine in southeastern Muskingum County, Ohio, was chosen for detailed examination. Computer compatable tapes of ERTS-1 data were used as input to an automated procedure for classifying land conditions. The target classifications included stripped earth and major areas of erosion, partially reclaimed earth and minor areas of erosion, vegetation, deep (or clear) water, shallow (or turbid) water, and unclassified areas. Aerospace technology provides a ready and efficient means of monitoring strip mine operations. It also provides a technical base for decisions regarding environmental safeguards. Some months ago, Ohio let a contract to map the eastern third of the state by using aerial photography. The aerial photographic maps are to be used to develop, among other things, strip mine and reclamation maps. By using conventional techniques it will require many months or perhaps more than a year to adequately compile the information. By using ERTS data and computer processing, however, maps showing the same themes could be generated in a matter of days. It was estimated that a comparable mapping project, including field work, computer processing, and report preparation would cost only one-tenth as much. (See also W75-07484) (Sims-ISWS
W75-07491

UTILITY OF ERTS FOR MONITORING THE BREEDING HABIT OF MIGRATORY WATERFOWL,
Environmental Research Inst. of Michigan, Ann Arbor.
E. W. Work, Jr., D. S. Gilmer, and A. T. Klett.
In: Third Earth Resources Technology Satellite Symposium, Vol II, Summary of Results, Washington, D.C., December 10-14, 1973: NASA SP-356, p 102-115, May 1974. 13 fig, 13 ref.

Descriptors: *Remote sensing, *Satellites(Artificial), *Waterfowl, *Habitats, Surveys, Wildlife, Lakes, Ponds, Ducks(Wild), Migratory birds, Mallard duck, Population, Breeding, Data processing, Analytical techniques, United States, Canada.
Identifiers: *ERTS.

Waterfowl breeding-ground surveys conducted twice each year by the Bureau of Sport Fisheries and Wildlife extend over a vast region of the United States and Canada. Data from these surveys are used to estimate waterfowl production by means of a mathematical model. Counts of May and July ponds are some of the variables used in this model. Annual production estimates are used to predict fall flights of ducks. This information is then used for establishing waterfowl hunting regulations. Work to date indicates that satellite remote sensing techniques hold considerable promise for the accurate and rapid assessment of waterfowl breeding habitat, especially changes in pond numbers and distribution. Development of an operational system utilizing satellite sensors as a primary source of data appears to be a realistic goal for the future. (See also W75-07484) (Sims-ISWS)
W75-07492

AGRICULTURE, FORESTRY, RANGE RESOURCES,
National Aeronautics and Space Administration, Houston, Tex., Lyndon B. Johnson Space Center.
For primary bibliographic entry see Field 7C.
W75-07493

WATER RESOÚRCES,
National Aeronautics and Space Administration, Greenbelt, Md. Goddard Space Flight Center.
V. V. Salomonson.
In: Third Earth Resources Technology Satellite Symposium, Vol II, Summary of Results, Washington, D.C., December 10-14, 1973: NASA SP-356, p 126-137, May 1974. 20 fig.

Descriptors: *Remote sensing, *Satellites(Artificial), *Water resources, Surveys, Mapping, Watersheds(Basins), Snow cover, Lake ice, Glaciers, Surface waters, Flood plains, Wetlands, Sediments, Data processing.
Identifiers: *ERTS.

The ingredient in the ERTS-1 system that has helped to provide a fundamental advance in the monitoring of water resources is the regular repetitive coverage capability. Agreement between the ERTS-1 snow cover estimates and operational aircraft surveys is normally within 5%. In addition, the snowline or the edge of the area of significant snow cover can be mapped as precisely from ERTS as from aircraft data. The cost of acquiring and analyzing cover information in several drainage basins in the West, with use of light aircraft data, was found to be approximately two orders of magnitude larger than that required when using ERTS-1 data. ERTS-1 data continue to provide glaciologists with exciting observations as to the location, extent, and character of glaciers and their surface features. With ERTS data it is possible to see the snowlines on the glaciers, which can then be related to the mass balance of the glaciers. Several ERTS-1 images have been obtained over the Great Lakes where it has become evident that ERTS-1 provides relatively high detail, synoptic views of the ice cover on these lakes. ERTS-1 has continued to show applicability for regional surveys of flood-related features. Relative variations in water quality are dramatically illustrated in ERTS-1 imagery. There are some quantitative indications that ERTS-1 data can be used to estimate sediment load. Several investigators have utilized the ERTS data collection system in water resources monitoring and in all cases they have found that it provides excellent and reliable data in various parts of the country in near-real time. (See also W75-07484) (Sims-ISWS)
W75-07494

LAND USE AND MAPPING,
National Aeronautics and Space Administration, Bay Saint Louis, Miss., Earth Resources Lab.
A. T. Joyce.
In: Third Earth Rèsources Technology Satellite Symposium, Vol II, Summary of Results, Washington, D.C., December 10-14, 1973: NASA SP-356, p 138-146, May 1974. 10 fig.

Descriptors: *Remote sensing, *Satellites(Artificial), *Land use, *Mapping, Land classification, Planning, Urbanization, Photogrammetry, Maps, Aerial photography, Data processing.
Identifiers: *ERTS.

The ERTS program has provided data that can be used to derive information on the actual use of the land resource, in a practical and timely manner. ERTS data provide coverage of total land areas, and its repetitive nature enables the detection and monitoring of changes taking place in land use. Generally, the techniques and the procedures used to extract information from ERTS data may be categorized as pertaining to either the interpretations of ERTS imagery or to the use of digital data and computer techniques. Examples of the use of these techniques were presented. An example of a cartographic application of ERTS was also presented. There was more detail in a U-2 photomap than in the ERTS image map, but cost estimates showed that the ERTS map can be produced for one-tenth the cost of producing the U-2 photomap. (See also W75-07484) (Sims-ISWS)
W75-07495

MINERAL RESOURCES, GEOLOGICAL STRUCTURES, AND LANDFORM SURVEYS,
National Aeronautics and Space Administration, Greenbelt, Md., Goddard Space Flight Center.
N. M. Short.
In: Third Earth Resources Technology Satellite Symposium, Vol II, Summary of Results, Washington, D.C., December 10-14, 1973: NASA SP-356, p 147-167, May 1974. 22 fig, 1 tab.

Descriptors: *Remote sensing, *Satellites(Artificial), *Geologic mapping, Surveys, Geology, Monitoring, Mapping, Structural geology, Mining, Earthquakes, Rocks, Data collections, Data processing, Mineralogy.
Identifiers: *ERTS.

ERTS results in geology have shifted to an emphasis on effective applications with economic benefits and clearcut relevance to national needs. ERTS has contributed significantly to the upgrading of geologic maps. Seasonal changes in vegetation have been found to be helpful in defining and separating units for mapping purposes. Many of the small-scale maps of the world often have extensive inaccuracies. ERTS imagery has been found useful in correcting these errors. Studies of linears have revealed previously unknown faults, and have suggested the locations of likely places to explore for ore deposits and for groundwater resources. In rock identification, ERTS data have generally proved unreliable. The most promising technique consists of rationing pairs of MSS bands and reproducing images or computer printouts from the ratio signals. ERTS data have aided in locating the portions of a mining region where the probability of roof collapse is greatest. (See also W75-07484) (Sims-ISWS)
W75-07496

THIRD EARTH RESOURCES TECHNOLOGY SATELLITE SYMPOSIUM, VOLUME III, DISCIPLINE SUMMARY REPORTS,
National Aeronautics and Space Administration, Greenbelt, Md. Goddard Space Flight Center.
For primary bibliographic entry see Field 7C.
W75-07497

AGRICULTURE, FORESTRY, RANGE RESOURCES,
National Aeronautics and Space Administration, Houston, Tex., Lyndon B. Johnson Space Center.
For primary bibliographic entry see Field 7C.
W75-07498

LAND USE AND MAPPING,
National Aeronautics and Space Administration, Bay, Saint Louis, Miss. Earth Resources Lab.
A. T. Joyce.
In: Third Earth Resources Technology Satellite Symposium, Vol III, Discipline Summary Reports, Washington, D.C., December 10-14, 1973: NASA SP-357, p 15-32, May 1974. 25 ref, 3 append.

Descriptors: *Remote sensing, *Satellites(Artificial), *Land use, *Mapping, Land classification, Urbanization, Planning, Photogrammetry, Maps, Data collections, Data processing.
Identifiers: *ERTS.

Interpretation of multispectral scanner (MSS) imagery and computer-implemented classifications with MSS digital data on tapes are the two principal interpretative techniques utilized for land use classification and inventory. Surface features covering 8000 to 20,000 sq m (2 to 5 acres) have been identified, but no consistency in identification and measurement is reported below 40,000 sq m (10 acres), and minimum-sized unit area delineation of 160,000 sq m (40 acres) or larger is most common. The results of land use classifications are usually presented by recording the identification and classification of various uses of land on a format with geographical reference. Special purpose and selected area classifications in urban areas have not achieved the desired success in identification and measurement, but some data processing techniques that are not yet fully operational promise better results. ERTS images can be successfully transformed into experimental monochromatic cartographic products of standard accuracy at 1:250,000 and smaller scales in standard map format. Because of ERTS' ability to record information for a very large region during a minimum time interval, such a system can produce basic data that eliminate the discrepancies resulting from extending the collection process over long time periods as is required with aerial images. The system allows more frequent information so that changes that indicate trends in conditions can be quickly spotted and corrective action istituted when required. The broad coverage allows photomapping of large areas almost instantaneously. (See also W75-07497) (Sims-ISWS)
W75-07499

MINERAL RESOURCES, GEOLOGICAL STRUCTURE, AND LANDFORM SURVEYS,
National Aeronautics and Space Administration, Greenbelt, Md. Goddard Space Flight Center.
For primary bibliographic entry see Field 7C.
W75-07500

WATER RESOURCES,
National Aeronautics and Space Administration, Greenbelt, Md. Goddard Space Flight Center.
V. V. Salomonson.
In: Third Earth Resources Technology Satellite Symposium, Vol III, Discipline Summary Reports, Washington, D.C., December 10-14, 1973: NASA SP-357, p 52-82, May 1974. 1 tab, 34 ref, 2 append.

Descriptors: *Remote sensing, *Satellites(Artificial), *Water resources, Watersheds(Basins), Surveys, Mapping, Snow cover, Lake ice, Glaciers, Surface waters, Rivers, Flood plains, Water quality, Estuaries, Wetlands, Irrigation, Evapotranspiration, Groundwater, Soil moisture.
Identifiers: *ERTS.

The synoptic coverage of ERTS imagery permits fairly easy identification of basin extent and broad physiographic features such as drainage area, stream network character, land use, and water coverage. It is relatively easy to identify snow by using ERTS-1 MSS bands 4 and 5. Glaciers are readily observed in the ERTS imagery. Recognizable glacial features include cirques, terminal moraines, and crevassed areas. Surging glaciers can easily be distinguished from their characteristic wiggly folded moraines. Surface water is one of the most easily delineated parameters in the hydrologic cycle. Flood plain features such as natural and artificial levee systems, upland boundarics, vegetation and soil differences, flood alleviation measures, and land use and argicultural patterns are easily identified through tonal differences on ERTS-1 color composites. Indications of water quality can be observed in a limited manner through the use of ERTS-1 imagery in bands 4 and 5. Areas covered by wetlands can be measured by a variety of techniques. The presence of irrigation methods is best identified in the arid and semiarid regions of the United States with ERTS-1. Since groundwater or subsurface water cannot be seen directly from ERTS imagery, its presence must be inferred from identification of surface features that are generally correlated with or are an indication of subsurface water. Relative variations of soil moisture in unvegetated or bare-soil areas can be seen. (See also W75-07497) (Sims-ISWS)
W75-07501

MARINE RESOURCES,
National Aeronautics and Space Administration, Bay, Saint Louis, Miss., Earth Resources Lab.

E. L. Tilton, III.
In: Third Earth Resources Technology Satellite Symposium, Vol III, Discipline Summary Reports, Washington, DC, December 10-14, 1973: NASA SP-357, p 83-106, May 1974. 1 tab, 12 ref, 2 append.

Descriptors: *Remote sensing, *Satellites(Artificial), *Oceanography, Meteorology, Marine biology, Turbidity, Chlorophyll, Sea ice, Lake ice, Fish, Aquatic life, Ocean circulation, Tracers, Oceans, Coasts, Lakes, Data collections, Data processing.
Identifiers: *ERTS.

Techniques have been developed for defining coastal circulation patterns using sediment as a natural tracer, allowing the formulation of new circulation concepts in some geographical areas and, in general, better defining the seasonal characteristics of coastal circulation. An analytical technique for measurement of absolute water depth based upon the ratios of two MSS channels has been developed. In general, the problem of separating and measuring water color components such as turbidity, chlorophyll, and bottom reflection is a complex one requiring further basic research in order to understand the component properties of a total water signature. Ice features greater than 70 meters in width can be detected, and both arctic and antarctic icebergs have been identified. Because of the large daily overlap of ERTS-1 coverage at high latitudes, some tracking and quantitative measurements of ice movement are possible. In the application area of living marine resources, the use of ERTS-1 image-density patterns as a potential indicator of fish school location has been demonstrated for one coastal commercial resource, menhaden. Ocean dynamics is another area where large-scale synoptic coverage is required. ERTS-1 data have been used to locate ocean current boundaries using ERTS-1 image-density enhancement, and some techniques are under development for measurement of suspended particle concentration and chlorophyll concentration. (See also W75-07497) (Sims-ISWS)
W75-07502

ENVIRONMENT SURVEYS,
National Aeronautics and Space Administration, Langley Station, Va. Langley Research Center.
L. R. Greenwood.
In: Third Earth Resources Technology Satellite Symposium, Vol III, Discipline Summary Reports, Washington, D.C., December 10-14, 1973: NASA SP-357, p 107-122, May 1974. 34 ref, 2 append.

Descriptors: *Remote sensing, *Satellites(Artificial), *Monitoring, *Environment, Path of Pollutants, Water pollution, Strip mines, Water quality, Pollutants, Wildlife, Wildlife habitats, Surveys, Data collections, Data processing.
Identifiers: *ERTS.

Recent findings have further verified that ERTS imagery can detect smoke plumes, aircraft contrails, urban haze, atmospheric aerosols, and certain short-lived events of national and international significance. Suspended sediment is a water pollutant that occurs as a result of natural processes as well as those caused by man. The sediment load of near-surface waters can be clearly identified, and in some cases the sources can be located and current directions mapped. Manmade pollution caused by industrial chemical dumping, sewage disposal, and oil spills has been identified; pollutant location, areal extent, and even dispersal can be measured. The important identifications and measurements include delineation of strip-mining areas in which not only the stripped areas but also the reclaimed regions are measured, monitoring of construction practices, mapping to allow siting of new construction, and mapping of urban quality. Under normal population densities, terrestrial wildlife species are not resolvable on ERTS-1 imagery. However, wildlife investigators have been successful in identifying and measuring habitat factors that have both direct and indirect influences on wildlife populations. The different combinations of vegetation, soil, and surface water as affected by altitude, climate, and latitude are very meaningful indicators of supportive systems for bird and mammal populations. (See also W75-07497) (Sims-ISWS)
W75-07503

INTERPRETATION TECHNIQUES,
National Aeronautics and Space Administration, Houston, Tex. Lyndon B. Johnson Space Center.
For primary bibliographic entry see Field 7C.
W75-07504

VIBRATORY COMPACTION IN THE LABORATORY OF GRANULAR MATERIALS IN LONG COLUMNS,
Geological Survey, Reston, Va.
For primary bibliographic entry see Field 2F.
W75-07559

NASA REMOTE SENSING OF SEA ICE IN AIDJEX,
Geological Survey, Tacoma, Wash.
For primary bibliographic entry see Field 2C.
W75-07564

THREE TYPES OF REMOTE-READING DENDROGRAPHS,
Geological Survey, Reston, Va.
R. L. Phipps, and W. M. Yater, Jr.
Ecology, Vol 55, No 2, p 454-457, Early Spring 1974. 4 fig, 5 ref.

Descriptors: *Instrumentation, *Trees, *Growth rates, Dendrochronology, Plant growth.
Identifiers: *Dendrographs.

Three types of remote-reading dendrographs were developed, and all 3 are capable of registering minute changes in tree trunk radius. They are designed for remote operation, requiring periodic checks as infrequently as once a month. They are self-contained in small, lighweight, weatherproof cases, may be easily and quickly installed on a tree, and may be read with any of a variety of meters and recorders. These dendrographs are basically mechanisms for translating linear motion (change in tree trunk radius) to rotational movement which can be sensed by a continuous-rotation variable resistor. The first of the three dendrographs to be developed accomplished this by employing a machinist's dial indicator. The others convert linear to rotational movement by a lever or a lever and gear arrangement. (Knapp-USGS)
W75-07577

WATER-QUALITY STUDIES TODAY AND TOMORROW,
Geological Survey, Menlo Park, Calif.
For primary bibliographic entry see Field 5A.
W75-07579

STOCHASTIC MODELING OF GROUNDWATER SYSTEMS,
Massachusetts Inst. of Tech., Cambridge. Dept. of Civil Engineering.
For primary bibliographic entry see Field 2F.
W75-07595

A DIVER-OPERATED DREDGE FOR COLLECTING QUANTITATIVE BENTHIC SAMPLES IN SOFT SEDIMENTS,
Rice Univ., Houston, Tex.
For primary bibliographic entry see Field 2J.
W75-07614

FORMULATING CONVERSION TABLES FOR STICK-MEASURE OF SACRAMENTO PRECIPITATION STORAGE GAGES,
Forest Service (USDA), Fort Collins, Colo. Rocky Mountain Forest and Range Experiment Station.
F. R. Larson.
U.S. Department of Agriculture, Forest Service, Research Note RM-276, 2 p, December, 1974. 1 fig, 1 tab, 6 ref.

Descriptors: *Rain gages, *Calibrations, *Precipitation gages, Precipitation(Atmospheric), Instrumentation, Mathematical models, Measurement, Colorado, *Instrumentation.

Sacramento precipitation storage gages are usually built to specifications by local sheet metal companies where quality control is limited. Two mathematical models for estimating precipitation measured in locally constructed gages are presented. A calibration technique is also described. (Witt-IPC)
W75-07654

STATE OF ILLINOIS PUBLIC WATER SUPPLIES DATA BOOK,
Illinois State Government, Springfield.
January 1, 1970. 99 p, 1 tab.

Descriptors: *Municipal water, *Illinois, *Water sources, *Water works, *Water supply, *Groundwater, Pumping plants, Surface waters, Data collections, Water treatment, Treatment facilities, Fluoridation, Use rates.
Identifiers: Mineral content, Public water supplies, Population data.

Data are given on all public water supplies for Illinois. This includes a statistical summary of various aspects of water supplies such as sources, water utilities providing public service, pumpage, mineral quality of sources, types of treatment for surface and ground supplies, fluoridation, and population data. The data on the specific communities or facilities describes the population served, number of services, source of supply, capacity impounded and the plant capacity. The type of treatment used is also given. User charges and mineral content are indicated for each facility. (Poertner)
W75-07675

APPLICATION AND PROCUREMENT OF AUTOMATIC WASTEWATER SAMPLERS,
National Environmental Research Center, Cincinnati, Ohio.
For primary bibliographic entry see Field 5A.
W75-07702

INTERFACING A 24-POINT ANALOG RECORDER TO A COMPUTER CONTROLLED TELEMETRY LINE,
National Environmental Research Center, Cincinnati, Ohio.
J. M. Teuschler.
Available from the National Technical Information Service, Springfield, Va. 22161, as PB-241 086, $3.75 in paper copy, $2.25 in microfiche. Report EPA-670/4-75-002, February 1975. 25 p, 9 fig. 1HA327; ROAP 01AAD; Task 10.

Descriptors: Remote control , Control systems, Data processing, *Data transmission, *Instrumentation, Remote sensing, *Logging(Recording), *Telemetry, Electrical equipment.
Identifiers: Logic circuits, Control circuits, Timing circuits, *Analog recorders.

Interface circuitry was designed so that telemetered data originating from various remote stations could be recorded by both a digital computer and an analog recorder. The entire interface circuitry is mounted on a 3-1/2 x 2-1/2 inch printed circuit card and installed in the receiver. Data from the two methods of collection can, therefore, be collected and a comparison can be made. A switching net-

work also permits computer control with computer and recorder logging; or computer logging only; or recorder logging only. (EPA)
W75-07703

PERFORMANCE OF THE ISCO MODEL 1391 WATER AND WASTEWATER SAMPLER,
National Environmental Research Center, Cincinnati, Ohio.
For primary bibliographic entry see Field 5A.
W75-07704

EXPERIMENTS IN OCEANOGRAPHIC AEROSPACE PHOTOGRAPHY-III-SOME FILMS AND TECHNIQUES FOR IMPROVED OCEAN IMAGE RECORDING,
International Imaging Systems, Mountain View, Calif.
D. S. Ross.
Report TR-C203-5, August 1974. 60 p, 32 fig, 16 ref. NOAA Contract SOP 3-35337. Final Report.

Descriptors: *Films, *Photography, *Aerial photography, *Remote sensing, Photogrammetry.
Identifiers: *Ocean image recording, *Multispectral imagery, Aerospace photography, Multispectral cameras, Photographic films, Contrast-detection thresholds, Light transmission.

Photographic materials, equipment, and techniques are available for achieving very significant improvements in blue and green ocean image recording; a multispectral system can be standardized for operational use with a minimum of further development. Acquiring blue and green multispectral imagery of ocean subjects with films such as Royal Ortho 2569 is operationally feasible; such images contain, by several factors, more spectral and spatial information than that obtained with conventional aerial black-and-white or color films. Water penetration is significantly improved, and water color differences are much enhanced. Information is secured which is not recorded at all on standard emulsions. Contrast degradation effects of atmospheric and water hazes are greatly diminished. (NOAA)
W75-07720

WATER CURRENT OR TIDE DIRECTION-OF-FLOW INDICATOR,
H. M. Levy.
U.S. Patent No. 3,869,911, 3 p, 3 fig, 3 ref; Official Gazette of the United States Patent Office, Vol 932, No 2, p 411, March 11, 1975.

Descriptors: *Patents, *Tides, *Currents(Water), *Indicators, Flow, Equipment, Ocean currents.
Identifiers: Flow direction, Direction indicators.

A metallic coated loop is attached to a rigid float structure. An arrow indicates the direction in which the float is being dragged. The loop is a hollow tube and hence buoyant. A major mass of the float being under the water surface gains the full effect of drag of the current deterring any substantial effect of wind. (Sinha-OEIS)
W75-07823

A KINEMATIC ANALYSIS OF TROPICAL STORM BASED ON ATS CLOUD MOTIONS,
Chicago Univ., Ill. Dept. of the Geophysical Sciences.
For primary bibliographic entry see Field 2B.
W75-07824

7C. Evaluation, Processing and Publication

WATER RESOURCE OBSERVATORY WIND AND SOLAR RADIATION DATA WATER YEARS 1973 AND 1974,
Wyoming Univ., Laramie. Water Resources Research Inst.
V. E. Smith.
Available from the National Technical Information Service, Springfield, Va 22161 as PB-241 514, $4.75 in paper copy, $2.25 in microfiche. Water Resources Research Series No. 51, November 1974. 83 p. OWRT A-015-WYO(1).

Descriptors: *Wyoming, *Data collections, *Wind velocity, *Solar radiation, Winds, *Rocky Mountain region, Anemometers, Measurement, Instrumentation.
Identifiers: Laramie(Wyo), Wind data.

Wind data that have been reduced from recording anemometer charts and from readings of totalizing anemometers plus incident solar radiation data from various stations operated by the University of Wyoming in and adjacent to Laramie, Wyoming are presented in tabular form. The period covered is from October 1972 through September 1974.
W75-07354

THE INTERRELATIONSHIP OF ECONOMIC DEVELOPMENT AND ENVIRONMENTAL QUALITY IN THE UPPER COLORADO RIVER BASIN: AN INTERINDUSTRY ANALYSIS,
Colorado Univ., Boulder. Dept. of Economics.
For primary bibliographic entry see Field 6B.
W75-07377

A REVIEW AND EVALUATION OF MULTIOBJECTIVE PROGRAMMING TECHNIQUES,
Johns Hopkins Univ., Baltimore, Md. Dept. of Geography and Environmental Engineering.
For primary bibliographic entry see Field 6A.
W75-07385

WATER QUALITY MODELING BY MONTE CARLO SIMULATION,
Maine Univ., Orono. Dept. of Civil Engineering.
For primary bibliographic entry see Field 5B.
W75-07386

A GLOBAL OCEAN-ATMOSPHERE CLIMATE MODEL. PART I. THE ATMOSPHERIC CIRCULATION,
National Oceanic and Atmospheric Administration, Princeton, N.J. Geophysical Fluid Dynamics Lab.
For primary bibliographic entry see Field 2A.
W75-07446

A GLOBAL OCEAN-ATMOSPHERE CLIMATE MODEL. PART II. THE OCEANIC CIRCULATION,
National Oceanic and Atmospheric Administration, Princeton, N.J. Geophysical Fluid Dynamics Lab.
For primary bibliographic entry see Field 2A.
W75-07447

STREAM GAGING INFORMATION, AUSTRALIA -- SUPPLEMENT 1973.
Australian Water Resources Council, Canberra.
1974. 43 p, 12 tab.

Descriptors: *Gaging stations, *River basins, *Australia, *Networks, Stations, Surface waters, *Data collections, Gaging, Stream gages, Sites, Instrumentation.

This is the fourth and final supplement to 'Stream Gauging Information, Australia,' December 1969. It contains changes and additions to the stream gaging network during the 12-month period ending December 31, 1973, and it is intended for use in conjunction with the main catalog and the three preceding supplements. During 1973, a total of 119 new stations were established throughout Australia. This number of new stations included 1 station installed for flood warning purposes. Also included were 25 stream gaging stations and 1 tide recorder which were omitted in previous publications and 5 reestablished stations. Thirty-three stations have been equipped with superior instruments and were listed as upgraded stations. Eighty-seven stations were discontinued for various reasons. Details of all variations were listed and separate summaries provided information on classification of stations, types of gages installed, and organizations operating the stream gaging stations. (See also W75-01311, W74-00305, and W73-08738) (Sims-ISWS)
W75-07480

THIRD EARTH RESOURCES TECHNOLOGY SATELLITE SYMPOSIUM, VOLUME II, SUMMARY OF RESULTS,
National Aeronautics and Space Administration, Greenbelt, Md. Goddard Space Flight Center.
For primary bibliographic entry see Field 7B.
W75-07484

REPORT ON THE CANADIAN ERTS PROGRAM,
Canada Centre for Remote Sensing, Ottawa (Ontario).
L. W. Morley.
In: Third Earth Resources Technology Satellite Symposium, Vol II, Summary of Results, Washington, D.C., December 10-14, 1973: NASA SP-356, p 7-11, May 1974. 1 fig.

Descriptors: *Remote sensing, *Satellites(Artificial), *Canada, Data processing, Administrative agencies, Ice, Sea ice, Cloud cover, Reservoirs, Forest fires, Pipelines, Highways, Groundwater, Wells.
Identifiers: *ERTS.

Production statistics on Canadian ERTS imagery, a summary of several cost benefit case histories, and recommendations for the future of the international aspects of ERTS were considered. Under a four-year collaborative agreement between the United States and Canada, the Canada Centre for Remote Sensing reads out and distributes the ERTS data of Canada. The Canadian receiving station is at Prince Albert, Saskatchewan. Ice Forecasting Central, of the Department of the Environment, has recommended that April aircraft flights, which are used to determine ice conditions in the Arctic, be replaced by ERTS quick-look imagery. The flights utilize about 50 hours at a cost of approximately $50,000, compared to the ERTS imagery cost of $1500. ERTS imagery is being used in Saskatchewan to map 42 forest fire burns across the northern part of the province. A profitable application of ERTS imagery is in the mapping of large reservoirs in hydropower development projects. High benefit applications in Canada of ERTS imagery are predicted in land use mapping and in the selection of routes for pipelines, transmission lines, and highways. ERTS imagery is being used together with larger scale imagery in studies to select a route for the Polar Gas Pipeline. In spite of the fact that ERTS has been up for a year and a half, the international community has just begun to be aware of its importance. (See also W75-07484) (Sims-ISWS)
W75-07485

ENVIRONMENTAL SURVEYS IN ALASKA BASED UPON ERTS DATA,
Alaska Univ., College.
For primary bibliographic entry see Field 7B.
W75-07486

GEOLOGIC EVALUATION AND APPLICATIONS OF ERTS-1 IMAGERY OVER GEORGIA,
Georgia State Geological Survey, Atlanta.
For primary bibliographic entry see Field 7B.
W75-07487

ERTS PROGRAM OF THE U.S. ARMY CORPS OF ENGINEERS,
Corps of Engineers, Washington, D.C.
J. W. Jarman.
In: Third Earth Resources Technology Satellite Symposium, Vol II, Summary of Results, Washington, D.C., December 10-14, 1973: NASA SP-356, p 62-75, May 1974. 8 fig, 1 tab.

Descriptors: *Remote sensing, *Satellites(Artificial), *Data processing, Land use, Vegetation, Sedimentation, Dams, Snowpack, Ice, Permafrost, Coasts, Mapping, Water circulation, Hydrography, Data collections, Louisiana, Chesapeake Bay, Alaska.
Identifiers: *ERTS.

ERTS imagery was used extensively for mapping land use and vegetative cover for an atlas that was compiled as an inventory of basic environmental data for the Atchafalaya area of southern Louisiana. From ERTS data it was possible to acquire accuracy that is probably much greater than could be obtained by traditional methods. The work involved 20 man-weeks of effort, and would probably have been twice that if the ERTS data had not been available. In a study of the Chesapeake Bay area, an attempt was made to delineate the sediment content of five test areas that flowed into the bay. It was found that by visual inspection of the ERTS imagery water bodies that were less than 40,000 square meters in surface area could be located on band 7. Sediment concentrations in Cook Inlet of Alaska were investigated with ERTS imagery. Permafrost mapping, snowpack, and icing were also investigated. Digital processing and enhancement has made it possible to map the gross patterns of the coastal sedimentation, the littoral processes, the way the suspended solids are carried along the coast, where they are deposited, and where these solids come from. Hydrographic surveys of the Fiji Islands have been made with use of ERTS data. (See also W75-07484) (Sims-ISWS)
W75-07489

A REVIEW OF INITIAL INVESTIGATIONS TO UTILIZE ERTS-1 DATA IN DETERMINING THE AVAILABILITY AND DISTRIBUTION OF LIVING MARINE RESOURCES,
National Aeronautics and Space Administration, Bay Saint Louis, Miss. Earth Resources Lab., and National Marine Fisheries Service, Bay Saint Louis, Miss. Fisheries Engineering Lab.
For primary bibliographic entry see Field 7B.
W75-07490

AUTOMATED STRIP MINE AND RECLAMATION MAPPING FROM ERTS,
Ohio State Univ., Columbus.
For primary bibliographic entry see Field 7B.
W75-07491

UTILITY OF ERTS FOR MONITORING THE BREEDING HABIT OF MIGRATORY WATERFOWL,
Environmental Research Inst. of Michigan, Ann Arbor.
For primary bibliographic entry see Field 7B.
W75-07492

AGRICULTURE, FORESTRY, RANGE RESOURCES,
National Aeronautics and Space Administration, Houston, Tex., Lyndon B. Johnson Space Center.
R. B. MacDonald.
In: Third Earth Resources Technology Satellite Symposium, Vol II, Summary of Results, Washington, D.C., December 10-14, 1973: NASA SP-356, p 116-125, May 1974. 10 fig, 2 tab.

Descriptors: *Remote sensing, *Satellites(Artificial), *Surveys, *Mapping, Agriculture, Soil surveys, Soil classification, Crops, Forestry, Grasslands, Ranges, Vegetation, Data collections, Data processing.
Identifiers: *ERTS.

The imaginative use of data acquired by meteorological satellites, together with crop acreage information such as has been provided by ERTS, promises a means of estimating crop production over large areas in a cost effective and timely manner. Timely information on regional range-forage conditions is required to support sound management decisions. An important indicator of rangeland forage conditions is the biomass content. It has been found that the multitemporal data acquired by ERTS is able to provide a measure of this important indicator volume. Investigators have demonstrated that ERTS data provide a valuable means of recognizing soil association boundaries and establishing a base map for listing soils information. In-place mapping of timber volumes by district over a forest provides critical information to the forest manager. Data from ERTS, remote sensing aircraft, ground acquisition, computers, and mathematical models have been combined to develop an approach that offers a cheaper and faster method of inventorying standing timber volume. (See also W75-07484) (Sims-ISWS)
W75-07493

WATER RESOURCES,
National Aeronautics and Space Administration, Greenbelt, Md. Goddard Space Flight Center.
For primary bibliographic entry see Field 7B.
W75-07494

LAND USE AND MAPPING,
National Aeronautics and Space Administration, Bay Saint Louis, Miss., Earth Resources Lab.
For primary bibliographic entry see Field 7B.
W75-07495

MINERAL RESOURCES, GEOLOGICAL STRUCTURES, AND LANDFORM SURVEYS,
National Aeronautics and Space Administration, Greenbelt, Md., Goddard Space Flight Center.
For primary bibliographic entry see Field 7B.
W75-07496

THIRD EARTH RESOURCES TECHNOLOGY SATELLITE SYMPOSIUM, VOLUME III, DISCIPLINE SUMMARY REPORTS,
National Aeronautics and Space Administration, Greenbelt, Md. Goddard Space Flight Center.
Symposium held at Washington, D.C., December 10-14, 1973: NASA SP-357, May 1974. 155 p, append. Freden, S. C., Mercanti, E. P., and Friedman, D. B., editors.

Descriptors: *Remote sensing, *Satellites(Artificial), *Data processing, *Data collections, Agriculture, Forestry, Ranges, Land use, Mapping, Geology, Water resources, Oceanography, Environment, Analytical techniques.
Identifiers: *ERTS.

This symposium was the third in a series on the significant results obtained from the first Earth Resources Technology Satellite (ERTS-1). Volume III contains the Discipline Summary Reports. These were based on reports produced from a two-week series of intensive interviews with the individual ERTS-1 principal investigators and then updated and extended from the material presented at the symposium. The reports were written by working groups in each of the disciplines which were convened at the end of the symposium. These working groups were chaired by the respective discipline session chairmen and were composed of selected specialists in the various disciplines. Results were summarized for the following disciplines: (1) agriculture, forestry, range resources; (2) inland use and mapping; (3) mineral resources, geological structure, and landform surveys; (4) water resources; (5) marine resources; (6) environment surveys; (7) interpretation techniques. (See W75-07498 thru W75-07504)
W75-07497

AGRICULTURE, FORESTRY, RANGE RESOURCES,
National Aeronautics and Space Administration, Houston, Tex., Lyndon B. Johnson Space Center.
W. J. Crea.
In: Third Earth Resources Technology Satellite Symposium, Vol III, Discipline Summary Reports, Washington, D.C., December 10-14, 1973: NASA SP-357, p 1-14, May 1974. 33 ref, 2 append.

Descriptors: *Remote sensing, *Satellites(Artificial), *Surveys, *Mapping, Agriculture, Soil surveys, Soil classification, Crops, Land use, Forests, Forestry, Grasslands, Ranges, Vegetation, Analytical techniques, Data collections, Data processing.
Identifiers: ERTS.

Identification of major crops was accomplished by both photointerpretation and ADP techniques to accuracies ranging between 70 and 99%. Signature extension of training field data was successfully accomplished up to 80.5 km (50 mi) for major crops with very little loss in accuracy and was moderately successful for bare soil and alfalfa over a south-to-north distance of 708 km (440 mi). Investigators using multistage analysis techniques of ERTS-1 data have demonstrated the capability to economically stratify, estimate volume, and locate known tracts of discrete forested areas. Investigations to detect forest stress in early stages were basically unsuccessful due to the subtle change that accompanies most stress. Range resources have provided a formidable challenge for many years for remote sensing investigators who have attempted to classify or identify the dominant specie or plant community on ranglands or wildlands. However, it appears there are now two approaches being implemented: one for specie/plant community identification, and the other for estimation of forage products (biomass) available for livestock and wildlife. Identification of major soil associations was accomplished by both photointerpretation and ADP techniques. (See also W75-07497) (Sims-ISWS)
W75-07498

LAND USE AND MAPPING,
National Aeronautics and Space Administration, Bay, Saint Louis, Miss. Earth Resources Lab.
For primary bibliographic entry see Field 7B.
W75-07499

MINERAL RESOURCES, GEOLOGICAL STRUCTURE, AND LANDFORM SURVEYS,
National Aeronautics and Space Administration, Greenbelt, Md. Goddard Space Flight Center.
N. M. Short.
Third Earth Resources Technology Satellite Symposium, Vol III, Discipline Summary Reports, Washington, D.C., December 10-14, 1973: NASA SP-357, p 33-51, May 1974. 47 ref, 2 append.

Descriptors: *Remote sensing, *Satellites(Artificial), *Geologic mapping, *Natural resources, Mapping, Surveys, Exploration, Geomorphology, Mining, Structural geology, Faults(Geologic), Folds(Geologic), Joints(Geologic), Fractures(Geologic), Data collections, Data processing.
Identifiers: *ERTS.

In regions of sparse vegetation, good geologic reconnaissance maps can often be prepared from ERTS imagery where distinctive outcrop patterns occur. Sometimes these maps are superior to ground-based geologic maps in that contacts may be better delineated in the overview. Good mapping from ERTS can be done at scales up to

1:250,000 usually cheaper and faster than by other methods (although the relative accuracies have yet to be assessed). The major contribution of ERTS to geology continues to be the exceptional ability to show large structural features, such as folded mountain belts, major strike-slip fault systems, domes and uplifts, and crystalline shield or piedmont terrain, of regional or subcontinental size. ERTS is effective in revealing new 'linears,' many of which prove to be faults, joints, or fracture zones upon field examination. Under appropriate conditions, both metals and nonmetallic deposits should be detectable from ERTS if these have adequate surface expression. This usually involves recognition of such proven 'ore guides' as surface alteration ('gossan' or limonite stains, clays, and sulphates), structural controls (mainly intersections of fractures, foliation, and such), and surface exposures of host structures (stocks, veins, folds, and domes). ERTS has already proved capable of assessing natural conditions that could prove hazardous in road building. Regional characteristics of terrain undergoing extensive erosion accelerated by man's activities are being defined in parts of southern Arizona. ERTS is leading to a new approach in derivation of earthquake hazards maps. (See also W75-07497) (Sims-ISWS)
W75-07500

WATER RESOURCES,
National Aeronautics and Space Administration, Greenbelt, Md. Goddard Space Flight Center.
For primary bibliographic entry see Field 7B.
W75-07501

MARINE RESOURCES,
National Aeronautics and Space Administration, Bay, Saint Louis, Miss., Earth Resources Lab.
For primary bibliographic entry see Field 7B.
W75-07502

ENVIRONMENT SURVEYS,
National Aeronautics and Space Administration, Langley Station, Va. Langley Research Center.
For primary bibliographic entry see Field 7B.
W75-07503

INTERPRETATION TECHNIQUES,
National Aeronautics and Space Administration, Houston, Tex. Lyndon B. Johnson Space Center.
J. L. Dragg.
In: Third Earth Resources Technology Satellite Symposium, Vol III, Discipline Summary Reports, Washington, D.C., December 10-14, 1973: NASA SP-357, p 123-143, May 1974. 4 fig, 9 tab, 28 ref, 2 append.

Descriptors: *Remote sensing, *Satellites(Artificial), *Data processing, Data collections, Photogrammetry, Data storage and retrieval, Analytical techniques.
Identifiers: *ERTS, Enhancement, Corrections, Registration, Pattern recognition.

The image enhancement and geometric correction and registration techniques developed and/or demonstrated on ERTS data are relatively mature and greatly enhance the utility of the data for a large variety of users. Pattern recognition was improved by the use of signature extension, feature extension, and other classification techniques. Many of these techniques need to be developed and generalized to become operationally useful. Advancements in the mass precision processing of ERTS were demonstrated, providing the hope for future earth resources data to be provided in a more readily usable state. Also in evidence is an increasing and healthy interaction between the techniques developers and the user/applications investigators. (See also W75-07497) (Sims-ISWS)
W75-07504

COMPUTER SIMULATION OF LAND USE DYNAMICS,
Oregon State Univ., Corvallis. Willamette Simulation Unit.
For primary bibliographic entry see Field 6A.
W75-07509

ECONOMIC ANALYSIS OF FLOOD DETENTION STORAGE BY DIGITAL COMPUTER,
Kentucky Water Resources Inst., Lexington.
For primary bibliographic entry see Field 6F.
W75-07518

SIMULATION OF THE WATER BALANCE FOR PLANTS GROWING ON COARSE-TEXTURED SOILS,
Commonwealth Scientific and Industrial Research Organisation, Wembley (Australia). Div. of Land Resources Management.
For primary bibliographic entry see Field 2I.
W75-07523

USE OF TIME-LAPSE PHOTOGRAPHY TO ASSESS POTENTIAL INTERCEPTION IN ARIZONA PONDEROSA PINE,
Arizona Univ., Tucson. Dept. of Watershed Management.
For primary bibliographic entry see Field 2C.
W75-07547

FLOODS IN AND NEAR THE CHARLOTTE AMALIE AREA, ST. THOMAS, U.S. VIRGIN ISLANDS,
Geological Survey of Puerto Rico, San Juan.
W. J. Haire, and K. G. Johnson.
Open-file report (Puerto Rico Map Series No 3), 1973. 4 sheets, 8 fig, 1 tab, 3 maps, 1 ref.

Descriptors: *Floods, *Virgin Islands, Flood frequency, Maps, Stage-discharge relations, Flood recurrence interval.
Identifiers: *Charlotte Amalie(V.I.).

This 4-sheet map report provides information that will aid administrators, planners, engineers, and others concerned with development in areas subject to flooding in and near Charlotte Amalie on the south coast of St. Thomas. This information is useful to those responsible for formulating floodplain regulations that would minimize flood damage. St. Thomas is characterized by rugged terrain and its streams head in the volcanic uplands that form a central ridge the length of the island. The steep slopes cause rapid runoff. Most of the streamflow on St. Thomas results from direct runoff, therefore, the streams usually cease to flow several hours to a day or two after rainfall stops. Floodwaters also recede rapidly and inundation often lasts less than a day. At least four severe floods have occurred since 1867. The largest flood was that of May 8, 1960. Intense rain fell on the entire island and the U.S. Weather Bureau recorded a 2-day total of 13.25 inches at Charlotte Amalie. The second largest flood occurred on October 9, 1916, and was caused by a hurricane of great intensity, the center of which passed over the U. S. Virgin Islands. The areas inundated by the 1969 flood are shown on maps. (Knapp-USGS)
W75-07550

GEOHYDROLOGY OF BACA AND SOUTHERN PROWERS COUNTIES, SOUTHEASTERN COLORADO,
Geological Survey, Denver, Colo.
L. A. Hershey, and E. R. Hampton.
Water-Resources Investigations 16-74 (open-file report), August 1974. 1 sheet, 6 ref.

Descriptors: *Hydrogeology, *Colorado, *Water resources, *Groundwater, Water levels, Aquifer characteristics, Maps, Hydrologic data, Water yield, Withdrawal.
Identifiers: Baca County(Colo), Prowers County(Colo).

The only dependable source of water for all uses in Baca and southern Prowers Counties, Colorado, is groundwater. Groundwater is withdrawn from the three principal aquifers in the area--the Ogallala, the Dakota, and the Cheyenne-Dockum. Areas of occurrence and approximate altitude of the water table in 1967 are shown by a map. In the Ogallala, there has been little change in the altitude of the water table from 1964 to 1972. The thickness of the Ogallala Formation ranges widely throughout the area--from about 300 feet in south-central Baca County and 360 feet in eastern Prowers County to zero at many places. Approximate altitude of the potentiometric surface of the Dakota, Dockum, and Cheyenne-Dockum aquifers and their saturated thicknesses are also shown on maps. Thickness of the Dakota formation ranges from 0 to 240 feet. Saturated thickness ranges from about 230 feet in southeastern Prowers County to zero where the formation is absent. Water-level declines in wells that tap the Dakota (1956-67) were as much as 23 feet in the northern part of the area near or in areas of substantial pumpage. Water levels in Dakota wells in central Baca County have generally risen during 1947-67. Levels in wells that tap the Cheyenne-Dockum have declined as much as 285 feet during 1947-67 and 150 feet during 1962-66. The depth to the top of the Cheyenne Sandstone member is as much as 600 feet. The Cheyenne is not present in southeastern Baca County nor along the Baca-Prowers County line. (Knapp-USGS)
W75-07551

WATER QUALITY OF TAMPA BAY, FLORIDA: DRY-WEATHER CONDITIONS, JUNE 1971,
Geological Survey, Tallahassee, Fla.
For primary bibliographic entry see Field 5A.
W75-07556

GENERALIZED STREAM TEMPERATURE ANALYSIS SYSTEM,
Geological Survey, Bay Saint Louis, Miss. Gulf Coast Hydroscience Center.
For primary bibliographic entry see Field 5B.
W75-07561

NASA REMOTE SENSING OF SEA ICE IN AIDJEX,
Geological Survey, Tacoma, Wash.
For primary bibliographic entry see Field 2C.
W75-07564

HYDROLOGIC DATA OF THE HOOSIC RIVER BASIN, MASSACHUSETTS,
Geological Survey, Boston, Mass.
For primary bibliographic entry see Field 2E.
W75-07565

HYDROLOGIC RECORDS FOR LAKE COUNTY, FLORIDA, 1972-73,
Geological Survey, Tallahassee, Fla.
For primary bibliographic entry see Field 2E.
W75-07566

EXTENT AND FREQUENCY OF FLOODS ON SCHUYLKILL RIVER NEAR PHOENIXVILLE AND POTTSTOWN, PENNSYLVANIA,
Geological Survey, Harrisburg, Pa.
For primary bibliographic entry see Field 4A.
W75-07567

PUERTO RICO WATER RESOURCES PLANNING MODEL STUDY,
Geological Survey, Reston, Va.
For primary bibliographic entry see Field 6A.
W75-07568

WATER RESOURCES DATA FOR GEORGIA, 1974.
Geological Survey, Doraville, Ga.

U.S. Geological Survey, WRD 6481 Peachtree Industrial Blvd., Suite B, Doraville, Ga 30340. Data Report, 1975. 327 p, 4 fig, 4 tab, 7 ref.

Descriptors: *Basic data collections, *Georgia, *Hydrologic data, *Streamflow, *Water quality, Gaging stations, Stream gages, Stage-discharge relations, Water measurement, *Data collections.

Water resources data for the 1974 water year for Georgia include records of streamflow or reservoir storage at gaging stations, partial-record stations, miscellaneous sites, and records of water-quality data on the chemical and physical characteristics of surface water as well as records for a few pertinent gaging and water-quality stations in bordering States. These represent the Georgia portion of the National Water Data System collected by the U.S. Geological Survey and cooperating State and Federal agencies. The base data collected at gaging stations consists of records of stage and measurements of discharge of streams or canals, and stage, surface area, and contents of lakes or reservoirs. In addition, observations of factors affecting the stage-discharge relation or the stage-capacity relation, weather records, and other information are used to supplement base data in determining the daily flow or volume of water in storage. Water-quality information is presented for chemical quality, microbiological, and water temperature. (Knapp-USGS)
W75-07569

WATER RESOURCES OF THE CURLEW VALLEY DRAINAGE BASIN, UTAH AND IDAHO,
Geological Survey, Salt Lake City, Utah.
For primary bibliographic entry see Field 4A.
W75-07570

SIMULATED WATER-LEVEL CHANGES RESULTING FROM PROPOSED CHANGES IN GROUND-WATER PUMPING IN THE HOUSTON, TEXAS, AREA,
Geological Survey, Houston, Tex.
D. G. Jorgensen, and R. K. Gabrysch.
Open-file report, November 1974. 3 sheets, 6 fig, 3 ref.

Descriptors: *Subsidence, *Withdrawal, *Texas, *Analog models, *Groundwater, Hydrogeology, Water levels, Aquifer characteristics, Drawdown, Pumping.
Identifiers: *Houston(Tex).

Because of widespread interest in the hydrologic effects of decreased groundwater pumping, the Houston area analog model was programmed with anticipated decreases and increases in some areas in the rates of groundwater withdrawals and used to predict changes in the altitudes of the potentiometric surfaces in the aquifers. In general, the water-bearing units in the area consist of the Chicot aquifer and the underlying Evangeline aquifer. The Chicot is usually divided into upper and lower units, and in some parts of the area, the base of the lower unit of the Chicot is formed by a massive sand section (Alta Loma Sand of Rose, 1943), that is heavily pumped by large-capacity wells. The aquifers are underlain by a predominantly clay layer called the Burkeville confining layer. The analog model was programmed to determine the effects of proposed changes in pumping rates in terms of simulated water-level declines or recoveries in the Evangeline and Chicot aquifers. Simulated water-level declines in the aquifers are shown for 1890-1980. Because of increases in pumping in much of the Houston area, water levels in both aquifers will continue to decline after utilization of water from Lake Livingston. However, water levels will rise in southeastern Harris County and in Galveston County. Water levels in the Pasadena area will rise as much as 40 feet in the Evangeline aquifer and as much as 100 feet in the Chicot aquifer. Marked decreases in the rates of land-surface subsidence should occur in areas where the artesian heads increase. If groundwater pumping is again increased, however, to meet increasing demands in the future, the beneficial effects will be short-lived. (Knapp-USGS)
W75-07575

WATER-RESOURCES INVESTIGATIONS IN TEXAS, FISCAL YEAR 1975.
Geological Survey, Austin, Tex.
Water-Resources Investigations report, January 1975. 34 p, 1 map.

Descriptors: *Water resources, *Texas, *Projects, Hydrologic data, Data collections, Basic data collections.

The water-resources investigations of the U. S. Geological Survey in Texas consist of the collection of basic records through the hydrologic-data network, interpretive studies, and research projects. The basic-data records and the results of investigations are published by the Geological Survey or by cooperating agencies. This report describes the water-resources projects and activities of the Geological Survey in Texas for the 1975 fiscal year (July 1, 1974, to June 30, 1975). (Knapp-USGS)
W75-07583

TEACHING WATER RESOURCE MANAGEMENT WITH THE AID OF A COMPUTER-IMPLEMENTED STIMULATOR,
Virginia Polytechnic Inst. and State Univ., Blacksburg. Dept. of Fisheries and Wildlife Sciences.
For primary bibliographic entry see Field 6B.
W75-07601

A COMPUTER PROGRAM FOR ESTIMATING COSTS OF TUNNELLING (COSTUN),
Harza Engineering Co., Chicago, Ill.
For primary bibliographic entry see Field 8B.
W75-07619

USE OF MODELING FOR PLANNING STORM WATER STRATEGIES,
Florida Univ., Gainesville.
For primary bibliographic entry see Field 5G.
W75-07677

INTERFACING A 24-POINT ANALOG RECORDER TO A COMPUTER CONTROLLED TELEMETRY LINE,
National Environmental Research Center, Cincinnati, Ohio.
For primary bibliographic entry see Field 7B.
W75-07703

DIGITAL RADAR DATA AND ITS APPLICATION IN FLASH FLOOD FORECASTING,
National Weather Service Forecast Office, Pittsburgh, Pa.
For primary bibliographic entry see Field 4A.
W75-07832

HYDROGEOLOGICAL MAPS OF THE ALLUVIAL AQUIFER IN AND ADJACENT TO THE ROCKY MOUNTAIN ARSENAL, COLORADO,
Geological Survey, Denver, Colo.
L. F. Konikow.

Descriptors: *Hydrogeology, *Colorado, *Path of pollutants, Alluvium, Water table, Bedrock, Aquifers, *Maps, Groundwater movement.
Identifiers: *Rocky Mountain Arsenal(Colo), Denver(Colo).

The hydrogeologic characteristics of the alluvial aquifer in and adjacent to the Rocky Mountain Arsenal, Colo. are described on four maps that show the configuration of the bedrock surface, generalized water-table configuration, saturated thickness of alluvium, and transmissivity of the aquifer. The maps provide data needed to compute the rate and direction of groundwater movement. The alluvium forms a complex, nonuniform, sloping, discontinuous, and heterogeneous aquifer system. Groundwater contamination in the vicinity of the Rocky Mountain Arsenal is related to the disposal of liquid industrial wastes into ponds. The movement of contaminants away from the ponds or other possible sources is partly controlled by the rates and directions of groundwater flow within the shallow alluvial aquifer that underlies most of the area. The rate and direction of groundwater flow, in turn, is controlled by the hydraulic gradient, transmissivity, and boundary conditions of the aquifer. Thus, the calculation of rates of movement and flow paths followed by contaminants in the aquifer can only be accomplished if the hydrogeologic characteristics of the aquifer are known in detail. (Knapp-USGS)
W75-07836

AVAILABILITY OF GROUND WATER IN THE SACO RIVER BASIN, EAST-CENTRAL NEW HAMPSHIRE,
Geological Survey, Concord, N.H.
J. E. Cotton.
Water-Resources Investigations 39-74, 1975. 1 sheet, 1 fig, 1 map, 2 ref.

Descriptors: *Groundwater, *New Hampshire, Water yield, *Maps, Till, Glacial drift, Sands, Gravels, Glacial aquifers, Water resources, Water quality.
Identifiers: *Saco River(NH).

This map report provides a preliminary assessment of the availability of groundwater in the Saco River basin, New Hampshire, as determined by estimating the capability of the aquifers to store and transmit water. On the map aquifers are rated as having high medium, or low potential to yield groundwater. Bedrock in most of this river basin is covered by a thin veneer of unconsolidated glacial deposits of till and layered (stratified) gravel, sand, silt, and clay. The bedrock is hard and compact; it contains recoverable water only in open fractures. The size, number, distribution, and interconnection of fractures are highly variable, but the fractures commonly are so limited in these properties that wells penetrating bedrock generally do not yield enough water to sustain supplied for municipal or industrial use. Bedrock commonly yields dependable supplies of good quality water to individual wells in amounts adequate for single family domestic needs. Till is a poor aquifer and normally does not yield enough water to meet municipal, industrial, or commercial needs. In some places till will yield enough water to large diameter dug wells to supply single family domestic needs, but this yield may not be dependable during droughts when the water table declines and there is less water in storage. Stratified deposits of gravel, sand, silt, and clay occur chiefly in the valleys. These materials have abundant pore space between grains to store groundwater; these openings may amount to 30 percent or more of the total volume of the deposit. Groundwater exploration and development in New Hampshire has been most successful in thick water-saturated sand and gravel deposits. Groundwater in the Saco River basin is generally of good chemical quality. (Knapp-USGS)
W75-07837

MAPS OF SAN GORGONIO PASS-UPPER COACHELLA VALLEY AREA, CALIFORNIA, SHOWING WATER-LEVEL CONTOURS, 1936 AND 1966-17,
Geological Survey, Menlo Park, Calif.
J. J. French.
Open-File report, 1974. 3 maps.

Descriptors: *Water levels, *Water table, *Groundwater, *California, Hydrologic data, *Maps, Contours.
Identifiers: *Coachella Valley(Calif).

Maps scaled 1:62,500 show groundwater level contours in the Coachella Valley area between Beaumont and Indio, California. A table of data on more than 100 wells is included. (Knapp-USGS)
W75-07838

MAP SHOWING DRAINAGE AREAS, HADDAM QUADRANGLE, CONNECTICUT,
Geological Survey, Hartford, Conn.
M. P. Thomas, and J. E. Palmer.
Miscellaneous Field Studies Map MF-638A (Connecticut Valley Urban Area Project Contribution 119), 1975. 1 sheet, 1 map, 1 ref.

Descriptors: *Maps, *Connecticut, *Drainage area, Streams, Watersheds(Basins), Urban hydrology, River basins.
Identifiers: *Haddam quadrangle(Conn).

A map shows stream systems and drainage areas in the Haddam quadrangle, Connecticut that contribute streamflow to selected sites on streams. Drainage areas shown have not been adjusted for the manmade changes in the natural regimens such as storm sewers, diversion dams, canals, and tunnels. (Knapp-USGS)
W75-07839

MAP SHOWING DRAINAGE AREAS, GUILFORD QUADRANGLE, CONNECTICUT,
Geological Survey, Hartford, Conn.
M. P. Thomas, and J. E. Palmer.
Miscellaneous Field Studies Map MF-583B (Connecticut Valley Urban Area Project Contribution 123), 1975. 1 sheet, 1 map, 1 ref.

Descriptors: *Maps, *Connecticut, *Drainage area, River basins, Watersheds(Basins), Urban hydrology.
Identifiers: *Guilford(Conn).

This map shows stream systems and drainage areas that contribute streamflow to selected sites on streams in the Guilford quadrangle, Connecticut. Drainage areas shown have not been adjusted for the manmade changes in the natural regimens such as storm sewers, diversion dams, canals, and tunnels. (Knapp-USGS)
W75-07840

MAP SHOWING DRAINAGE AREAS, BRANFORD QUADRANGLE, CONNECTICUT,
Geological Survey, Hartford, Conn.
M. P. Thomas, and J. E. Palmer.
Miscellaneous Field Studies Map MF-560D (Connecticut Valley Urban Area Project Contribution 124), 1975. 1 sheet, 1 map, 1 ref.

Descriptors: *Maps, *Connecticut, *Drainage area, River basins, Watersheds(Basins), Urban hydrology.
Identifiers: *Branford(Conn).

This map shows stream systems and drainage areas that contribute streamflow to selected sites on streams in the Branford quadrangle, Connecticut. Drainage areas shown have not been adjusted for the manmade changes in the natural regimens such as storm sewers, diversion dams, canals, and tunnels. (Knapp-USGS)
W75-07841

MAP SHOWING DRAINAGE AREAS, NEW HAVEN-WOODMONT QUADRANGLES, CONNECTICUT,
Geological Survey, Hartford, Conn.
M. P. Thomas.
Miscellaneous Field Studies Map MF-557B (Connecticut Valley Urban Area Project Contribution 125), 1975. 1 sheet, 1 map, 1 ref.

Descriptors: *Maps, *Connecticut, *Drainage area, River basins, Watersheds(Basins), Urban hydrology.
Identifiers: *New Haven(Conn), *Woodmont(Conn).

This map shows stream systems and drainage areas that contribute streamflow to selected sites on streams in the New Haven and Woodmont quadrangles, Connecticut. Drainage areas shown have not been adjusted for the manmade changes in the natural regimens such as storm sewers, diversion dams, canals, and tunnels. (Knapp-USGS)
W75-07842

MAP SHOWING DRAINAGE AREAS, NIANTIC QUADRANGLE, CONNECTICUT,
Geological Survey, Hartford, Conn.
M. P. Thomas.
Miscellaneous Field Studies Map MF-593B (Connecticut Valley Urban Area Project Contribution 126), 1975. 1 sheet, 1 map, 1 ref.

Descriptors: *Maps, *Connecticut, *Drainage area, River basins, Watersheds(Basins), Urban hydrology.
Identifiers: *Niantic(Conn).

This map shows stream systems and drainage areas that contribute streamflow to selected sites on streams in the Niantic Quadrangle, Connecticut. Drainage areas shown have not been adjusted for the manmade changes in the natural regimens such as storm sewers, diversion dams, canals, and tunnels. (Knapp-USGS)
W75-07843

MAP SHOWING DRAINAGE AREAS, OLD LYME QUADRANGLE, CONNECTICUT,
Geological Survey, Hartford, Conn.
M. P. Thomas.
Miscellaneous Field Studies Map MF-558C (Connecticut Valley Urban Area Project Contribution 127), 1975. 1 sheet, 1 map, 1 ref.

Descriptors: *Maps, *Connecticut, *Drainage area, River basins, Watersheds(Basins), Urban hydrology.
Identifiers: *Old Lyme(Conn).

This map shows stream systems and drainage areas that contribute streamflow to selected sites on streams in the Old Lyme quadrangle, Connecticut. Drainage areas shown have not been adjusted for the manmade changes in the natural regimens such as storm sewers, diversion dams, canals, and tunnels. (Knapp-USGS)
W75-07844

GEOLOGIC MAP OF WALKER COUNTY, ALABAMA,
Geological Survey, Tuscaloosa, Ala.
K. D. Wahl, and D. M. O'Rear.
Alabama Geological Survey, University, Map 123, 1972. 1 sheet.

Descriptors: *Aquifers, *Geologic mapping, *Alabama, Stratigraphy, Geology, Water resources, Groundwater.
Identifiers: *Walker County(Ala).

The geology of Walker County, Alabama is shown on a map scaled about 2 miles to 1 inch. The entire county is underlain by the Pottsville Formation of Pennsylvanian age. There are a few outcrops of the Coker Formation of Cretaceous age in the northwest part of the county. Stream valleys have terrace deposits and alluvium. The Pottsville Formation, the principal aquifer in the county, is 1,000 to 3,000 feet thick and consists chiefly of sandstone and shale. The Pottsville also contains beds of coal which have been mined throughout the county. (Knapp-USGS)
W75-07845

WATER AVAILABILITY AND GEOLOGY OF WALKER COUNTY, ALABAMA,
Geological Survey, Tuscaloosa, Ala.
D. M. O'Rear, K. D. Wahl, and P. O. Jefferson.
Alabama Geological Survey, University, Map 120, 1972. 21 p, 3 fig, 2 plate, 5 tab, 12 ref.

Descriptors: *Water resources, *Alabama, *Groundwater, *Surface waters, Water yield, Hydrogeology, Streamflow, Water wells, Water quality, Basic data collections.
Identifiers: *Walker County(Ala).

The largest quantities of groundwater in Walker County, Alabama are obtained from sandstone beds in the Pottsville Formation, which generally yeild less than 50 gallons per minute to individual wells. The water from the Pottsville ranges from soft to very hard, and is suitable for most uses except locally where the iron and bicarbonate concentrations may be objectionable or where the water is excessively hard. The Coker Formation is tapped by only a few wells in the country, and the alluvium in the flood plain of the Mulberry Fork of the Black Warrior River provides a limited amount of water to only a few wells. The water is generally reported to be soft and satisfactory for domestic use. Parts of two large reservoirs are in Walker County--Lewis Smith Lake, with a total storage of 1,670,700 acre-feet, and Bankhead Reservoir, with a total storage of 94,100 acre-feet. Blackwater Creek near Manchester has an average flow of 196 mgd. The chemical quality of water in streams in Walker County is relatively uniform and the water should be suitable for most uses. Water use in Walker County was estimated to be 6 mgd in 1966. Groundwater sources are estimated to supply about 15 percent of the water used in the county. (Knapp-USGS)
W75-07846

PEARL RIVER BOATWAY, ROSS BARNETT RESERVOIR TO JACKSON AREA,
Geological Survey, Jackson, Miss.
C. P. Hemphreys, Jr., and F. C. Wells.
Pearl River Basin Development District, (Jackson, Mississippi), Pearl River Boatway Map No 1, 1974. 1 sheet, 1 map.

Descriptors: *Rivers, *Mississippi, *Boating, Recreation, *Maps, Water sports, Water quality.
Identifiers: *Pearl River Boatway(Miss).

The reach of the Pearl River Boatway, Mississippi, presented in this Atlas extends from the Ross Barnett Reservoir to Conway Slough, a distance of 16.4 river miles. The river flows in its natural channel from the reservoir to the Gulf, Mobile and Ohio Railroad bridge at Jackson and has been canalized from the railroad bridge to 0.4 miles upstream from the Woodrow Wilson Bridge. Snagging and clearing have been done from the canalized reach to 0.2 mile below the mouth of Conway Slough. The width in the natural channel varies from 120 feet at low stage to 200 feet at bankfull stage and in the canalized channel from 100 to 300 feet. Banks are relatively steep along this reach of the river, but there are several places where one may land his boat and stretch his legs. The sand bars exposed during periods of low flow are good picnic and rest areas. The river is relatively free of pollution, although sediment may cause it to be muddy. The water is suitable for recreation, but it should not be used for drinking. Along the reach, fishermen may catch large-mouth bass; black and white crappie; bluegill; redear; chain pickerel; warmouth; and channel, blue, flathead, and spoonbill catfish. Game that might be encountered include deer, squirrel, rabbit, beaver, raccoon, opossum, mink, otter, and muskrat. Wild turkey and various species of ducks also frequent the area. Tables may be used to estimate the time required to float with the current between points on the river. (Knapp-USGS)
W75-07847

PEARL RIVER BOATWAY MAP, MORGANTOWN TO SANDY HOOK, COLUMBIA AREA, MISSISSIPPI,
Geological Survey, Jackson, Miss.
J. K. Arthur.
Pearl River Basin Development District, (Jackson, Mississippi), Pearl River Boatway Map, 1974. 1 sheet, 1 map.

Descriptors: *Rivers, *Mississippi, *Boating, Recreation, *Maps, Water sports, Water quality.
Identifiers: *Pearl River Boatway(Miss).

The reach of the Pearl River Boatway presented in this atlas extends from Morgantown, Miss., 40.3 miles downstream to Sandy Hook. Channel width varies from 250 to 300 feet, depending upon the stage of the river, and depth varies from 2 feet at low water in shoal areas to over 30 feet at medium stage in deep areas. The banks are relatively steep along this reach of the river, but at Morgantown, Columbia, and Sandy Hook there are several sites where boats can be launched. Below Columbia there are many large sand bars that could be used for campsites or rest points. In general, the part of the reach from Morgantown to Columbia is deep and slow moving. Little difficulty should be encountered in boating except at extreme low water. From Columbia to Sandy Hook the river is shallower with higher velocities. At a stage of less than 5 feet on the Columbia gage, boating can be hazardous because of the shallow depths. The U.S. Army Corps of Engineers, Mobile District, has cleared logs and debris from the channel from the mouth of the river to 7 miles from Columbia. Submerged logs still present a hazard at low water in some places. The quality of water in the Pearl River above Columbia is good, but as the river passes through Columbia its quality is degraded by domestic and industrial wastes. Nowhere along this reach of the river should the water be used for drinking. The water is suitable for boating and fishing, but it may not be safe for swimming, especially in the Columbia vincinity. Several species of fish inhabit the river. Tables may be used to estimate the time required to float with the current between points on the river. (Knapp-USGS)
W75-07848

PEARL RIVER BOATWAY MAP, MONTICELLO TO MORGANTOWN, MISSISSIPPI,
Geological Survey, Jackson, Miss.
J. K. Arthur.
Pearl River Basin Development District, (Jackson, Mississippi), Pearl River Boatway Map, 1974. 1 sheet, 1 map.

Descriptors: *Rivers, *Mississippi, *Boating, Recreation, *Maps, Water sports, Water quality.
Identifiers: *Pearl River Boatway(Miss).

The reach of the Pearl River Boatway presented in this atlas extends from Monticello, Miss., 39.9 miles downstream to Morgantown. Channel width varies from 250 to 300 feet, depending upon the stage of the river, and depth varies from 2 feet at low water in shoal areas to more than 40 feet at medium stage in deep pools. The banks are very steep along this reach of the river and there is a limited number of sites where a boat can be launched, but there are many sand bars along the reach where boats can be put ashore and camps set up. The quality of water in the Pearl River between Monticello and Morgantown is adequate for boating and fishing, but it may not be safe for swimming and should not be used for drinking. At Monteicello and Morgantown pollutants enter the stream, but between these two sites, due to the sparse population, the water is not degraded by man. The Pearl River is a relatively deep, slow-moving stream in this area. Little difficulty should be encountered in boating except at extreme low water. The biggest hazard facing boatmen is submerged logs. Pearl River water is highly turbid, making logs and other submerged objects difficult to see. Numerous species of fish and game inhabit the river and area. Tables may be used to estimate the time required to float with the current between points on the river. (Knapp-USGS)
W75-07849

PEARL RIVER BOATWAY MAP, GEORGETOWN TO MONTICELLO, MISSISSIPPI,
Geological Survey, Jackson, Miss.
J. K. Arthur.
Pearl River Basin Development District (Jackson, Mississippi), Pearl River Boatway Map, 1974. 1 sheet, 1 map.

Descriptors: *Rivers, *Mississippi, *Boating, Recreation, *Maps, Water sports, Water quality.
Identifiers: *Pearl River Boatway(Miss).

The reach of the Pearl River Boatway presented in this atlas extends from Georgetown, Miss., 40.8 miles downstream to Monticello. Channel width in this reach varies from 250 to 300 feet, depending upon the stage of the river, and depth varies from 2 feet at low water in shoal areas to more than 30 feet at medium stage in deep pools. The banks are almost vertical along this reach of the river, but at Georgetown, Rockport, St. Regis Paper Mill, and Monticello, there are sites where boats can be launched. The Pearl also offers many large sand bars for camping or resting points. At Georgetown, Rockport, and Monticello, camping supplies can be obtained near the river. The water from the Pearl River should not be consumed unless treated, and it may not be safe for swimming, but the river is suitable for boating and fishing throughout the reach. In general, this reach of the river is moderately deep and slow moving. Little difficulty should be encountered in boating except at low water in shoal areas. Due to the high turbidity of the river water, submerged logs are difficult to spot, and one should be cautious while motoring on the river. Numerous species of fish and game inhabit the river and area. Tables may be used to estimate the time required to float with the current between points on the river. (Knapp-USGS)
W75-07850

8. ENGINEERING WORKS

8A. Structures

PORT DESIGN AND ANALYSIS METHODOLOGY,
Massachusetts Inst. of Tech., Cambridge. Sea Grant Project Office.
E. Frankel, B. Golden, P. Wilmes, R. Orner, and K. Chelst.
Sea Grant Publication, MITSG 74-31, Index No. 74-331-Nto, December 1, 1974. 2 Volumes. 341 p and 158 p, 64 fig, 6 tab, 95 ref, 8 append. (NOAA-75011403). NOAA Grant NG 43-72.

Descriptors: *Harbors, *Engineering structures, Economics, *Design, *Methodology, Model studies, *Coastal structures, Analysis.
Identifiers: *Port design.

Techniques are presented for planning and analysis of single purpose ports, multipurpose ports, multiport systems, and multiple purpose multiport systems. Novel approaches are described to multicommodity network flow analysis, port simulation and various methods of use in port system modeling. The appendices which are separately bound consist of the following: User's Manual for Linear Approximation Algorithm; The Ford-Bellman-Moor Shortest Path Algorithm; Method of Golden Search; Program Listings; Seaport Simulation (Tanker Terminal); Sample Run of Seaport Simulation; Port Simulation Program Details; and Approximate Fixed Charge Transportation Algorithm. (NOAA)
W75-07410

ENGINEERING CONSIDERATIONS FOR MARINAS IN TIDAL MARSHES,
Delaware Univ., Newark. Dept. of Civil Engineering.
For primary bibliographic entry see Field 2L.
W75-07420

GREATER TAMPA UTILITY GROUP-STANDARD UTILITIES LOCATION,
Greater Tampa Utility Group, Fla.
A. J. Hanis, D. Broome, N. Agee, N. Green, and L. Young.
February 14, 1968. 28 p, 19 fig.

Descriptors: *Utilities, *Right-of-way, *Standards, *Highways, *Planning, *Pipelines, *Construction, Sewers, Water distribution(Applied), Water management(Applied), Public utilities, Public utility districts, Water works, Electric power, Electrical networks, Facilities, Legal aspects, Easements, Florida, Roads, Coordination.
Identifiers: *Utility location, Greater Tampa Utility Group, Tampa(Florida).

In 1965 the Greater Tampa Utilities Group appointed a committee to study the possibility of coordinating all utilities in this area and to provide a pattern of standardization for the location of such utilities within the public right of way of proposed street or highway improvements. The problem was twofold in that: (1) planning standards, and their general acceptance are needed to allocate space for all the various utilities whether they are overhead or underground, and (2) coordination of construction is needed for these utilities in old as well as new areas of the community. Representatives of the City of Tampa, City of Temple Terrace, Hillsborough County, the Southwest Florida Water Management District, Florida State Road Department, General Telephone, Tampa Electric, Peoples Gas and J.E. Greiner (engineering consultants) completed their recommendations in February 1968. The recommended locations of all new utility lines (Sanitary and storm sewers; water mains; electric, gas and telephone lines; fire alarm wiring, etc.) are given, both horizontally and vertically. It should be stressed that these standards are for the general guidance of the various utilities involved and in no way should be construed as an absolute requirement. Recommended utility locations are sketched for various widths of public right-of-way and easements. (Poertner)
W75-07668

AN ARCTIC WATER SUPPLY SYSTEM,
Directorate of Construction Engineering and Design Engineering, Ottawa (Ontario).
For primary bibliographic entry see Field 5F.
W75-07684

BEACH EROSION CONTROL IMPROVEMENTS, WAIKIKI BEACH, OAHU, HAWAII (KAPAHULU STORM DRAIN TO THE ELKS CLUB) (FINAL ENVIRONMENTAL IMPACT STATEMENT),
Corps of Engineers, Honolulu, Hawaii. Pacific Ocean Div.
Available from the National Technical Information Service, U.S. Dept. of Commerce, Springfield, Va. 22161, as EIS-HI-73-0792-F, $4.75 in paper copy, $2.25 in microfiche. May 1973. 46 p, 4 fig.

Descriptors: *Groins(Structures), *Sands, *Recreation facilities, Waves(Water), Breakwaters, Recreation, Swimming, Environmental effects, *Hawaii, Beaches, Muck soils, Sea walls, Shores, Water quality, Water quality standards, Erosion, Storm drains.
Identifiers: *Environmental Impact Statements, *Waikiki Beach(HI), Oahu(HI).

The project provides for the construction of three new groins, the placement of approximately 46,000 cubic yards of sand, and the demolition of the Waikiki, Hawaii Natatorium. The sand placement will add approximately 130,000 square feet of beach, resulting in increased shoreline recreation area and improved access along the beach. The groins are designed to stabilize the reconstructed beach, allowing it to shape itself parallel to the alignment of the dominant wave front. Unavoidable adverse environmental effects include temporary impacts during the construction period, permanent loss of the Natatorium and its use, reduction of swimming area in the deep channel north of the Natatorium and increased traffic. Alternatives considered include additional sand placement protection by an offshore breakwater, retention and incorporation of the Natatorium, and preservation of the existing conditions with no beach restoration provisions. (Gagliardi-Florida)
W75-07780

MAINTENANCE OF BAY RIDGE AND RED HOOK CHANNELS, NEW YORK NAVIGATION PROJECT (FINAL ENVIRONMENTAL IMPACT STATEMENT),
Army Engineer District, New York.
Available from the National Technical Information Service, U.S. Dept. of Commerce, Springfield, Va. 22161, as EIS-NY-73-1470-F, $3.75 in paper copy, $2.25 in microfiche. September 7, 1973. 40 p, 2 map, 1 tab.

Descriptors: *Dredging, *Channel improvement, *Economic justification, *Disposal, Turbidity, Water quality, Water pollution, Water channels, *New York, Environmental effects, Environment, Transportation, Navigation, Pollutants, Discharge measurement, Oceans.
Identifiers: *Environmental Impact Statements, *Bay Ridge(NY), Red Hook(NY).

The project involves the maintenance and dredging of an existing federal channel in Bay Ridge and Red Hook, New York to its authorized project dimensions. The work is to be performed by hopper dredge with the spoil disposed of in approved dumping grounds in the New York Bight. The project will enhance the economy of commodity transportation and continue the level of navigation safety that reduces the possibility of pollutant discharge into the water due to accidents. The adverse environmental effects will entail a temporary increase in turbidity during the dredging process of affecting water quality; and spoiling in the New York Bight, which will contribute to the accumulation of materials at the disposal site and to problems associated with ocean disposal. The alternatives considered were to forego subsequent maintenance activities and to implement various alternate methods for spoil disposal. Commênt were received from the Departments of Interior, Agriculture, Commerce, Defense, Health, Education and Welfare, and Transportation and the Environmental Protection Agency and Federal Power Commission. Additional comments were submitted by the Port Authority of New York and New Jersey, the New York state Department of Environmental Conservation and the New York City Department of Health, Bureau of Sanitary Engineering. (Gagliardi-Florida)
W75-07784

PEACOCK CREEK, LIBERTY COUNTY, GEORGIA (FINAL ENVIRONMENTAL IMPACT STATEMENT),
Army Engineer District, Savannah, Ga.
For primary bibliographic entry see Field 4A.
W75-07788

UPPER SALT CREEK WATERSHED, COOK, LAKE AND DUPAGE COUNTIES, ILLINOIS (FINAL ENVIRONMENTAL IMPACT STATEMENT),
Soil Conservation Service, Washington, D.C.
Available from the National Technical Information Service, U.S. Dept. of Commerce, Springfield, Va. 22161, as EIS-IL-73-0866-F, $5.25 in paper copy, $2.25 in microfiche. May 1973. 102 p, 5 tab, 8 map, 1 fig.

Descriptors: *Watershed management, *Flood protection, *Recreation, *Channel improvement, Channels, Flood plains, Erosion, *Illinois, Flood control, Erosion control, Floods, Recreation facilities, Land development, Water control, Sediments, Environmental effects, Vegetation.
Identifiers: *Environmental Impact Statements, Cook County(Ill), Lake County(Ill), Dupage County(Ill).

Installation of a watershed is proposed over a nine-year period in Cook, Lake, and Dupage Counties, Illinois. Project purposes are watershed protection, flood prevention, and recreation. The project will include land treatment measures, a floodwater retarding-recreation structure, floodwater retarding structures, channel modification and 261 acres of flood plain preserves. The land treatment program will reduce erosion on construction sites by 29 percent, provide for storage of 40 to 50 percent of the soil eroded from these areas, reduce water runoff, and promote more efficient land use. Floodwater and sediment damages will be reduced by 88 percent, and the project will attract 1,610,000 annual visitor days of recreation. Approximately 261 acres of undeveloped floodplain will be preserved for low-hazard, low-intensity uses. Adverse environmental effects include disturbance of 208 acres of vegetation cover by construction, conversion of 649 acres from terrestrial to aquatic habitat by permanent flooding, and the temporary flooding of 851 acres by detention pools. Channel modification will temporarily disturb the vegetative cover on 26 acres of right-of-way. Alternatives include land treatment alone, restricted channel modification, flood plain management, or no action. (Gagliardi-Florida)
W75-07789

FLOOD CONTROL, SEABROOK MARINE LABORATORY, TEXAS,
Texas Parks and Wildlife Dept., Austin.
J. R. Stevens.
Completion Report, March 1975. 6 p. 2-248-C.

Descriptors: *Civil engineering, *Floodproofing, *Flood protection, *Flood control, *Flood damage, *Drainage systems, Waterproofing, Design flood, Project planning, Land forming, Land subsidence, Tidal effects, *Texas.
Identifiers: *Seabrook Marine Laboratory(TX).

A project was initiated in October 1974 to prevent the recurring problem of periodic flooding at the Texas Parks and Wildlife Department's Seabrook Marine Laboratory due to tide water. Up to six inches of water invade the first floor of the laboratory, principally during spring when high lunar tides are reinforced by strong onshore winds. A plan for solving the problem was chosen and specifications with cost estimates were developed. This report, with accompanying photographs, describes the engineering steps undertaken to stem future flooding. (NOAA)
W75-07829

SHORELINE PROTECTION GUIDE FOR PROPERTY OWNERS,
New York Sea Grant Advisory Service, Albany.
P. Sanko.
Insight No 2; NYSSGP-AS-75-001, (1975), 19 p.

Descriptors: *Erosion, *Erosion control, *Diversion structures, *Shore protection, Wind erosion, Waves, Tides, Dunes, Beach erosion, Littoral drift, Bulkheads, Sea walls, Retaining walls, Groins, Breakwaters, Vegetation regrowth, Great Lakes, Coasts.
Identifiers: *Saltwater coastlines, *Coastal processes, *Shore protection methods.

This guide reports the basic physical processes of erosion/deposition, such as wind, waves, currents, littoral drift, and tides. Common shore protection structures are explained, as well as their limitations and possible side effects. Bulkheads, revetments, seawalls, groins, breakwaters, protective beaches, dunes, and vegetative methods are examined. (NOAA)
W75-07835

8B. Hydraulics

HYDRAULIC DESIGN OF TWIN-CHAMBER TRICKLE IRRIGATION LATERALS,
Hawaii Univ., Honolulu. Dept. of Agricultural Engineering.
For primary bibliographic entry see Field 3F.
W75-07365

DETERMINATION OF SAND ROUGHNESS FOR FIXED BEDS,
Queen's Univ., Kingston (Ontario). Dept. of Civil Engineering.
J. W. Kamphuis.
Journal of Hydraulic Research, Vol 12, No 2, p 193-203, 1974. 5 fig, 1 tab, 10 ref.

Descriptors: *Roughness(Hydraulic), *Laboratory tests, *Waves(Water), *Sediment transport, *Sands, Turbulent flow, Velocity, Reynolds number.
Identifiers: *Nikuradse sand grain roughness.

The results of tests performed to determine Nikuradse's sand grain roughness were presented. This roughness parameter was expected to be used in work on shear stress and sediment transport below waves. Nikurádse assumed that the height of the roughness interfering with the flow in the pipe was equal to the diameter of the sand grain that was used to roughen the pipe. Although Nikuradse's sand grain roughness has become a standard method of describing roughness of a boundary in both pipes and channels, the results of the investigation indicated that this method may be incorrect and that some modifications should be incorporated. From these test results, it was concluded that for a natural bottom under conditions where d/D sub 90 (the ratio of water depth to the particle diameter so that 90 percent of the particles in grain size distribution is smaller) was large enough to warrant discussing the total bed rather than individual particles and where there was no viscous effect, the roughness height should be equal to twice the D sub 90 size of the bed particles. (Bhowmik-ISWS)
W75-07434

INTERACTION OF MULTIPLE JETS WITH AMBIENT CURRENT,
General Electric Co., Philadelphia, Pa. Re-entry and Environmental Systems Div.
For primary bibliographic entry see Field 5B.
W75-07467

SPARSITY ORIENTED ANALYSIS OF LARGE PIPE NETWORKS,
Waterloo Univ. (Ontario). Dept. of Systems Design.
M. Chandrashekar, and K. H. Stewart.
Journal of the Hydraulics Division, American Society of Civil Engineers, Vol 101, No HY4, Proceedings Paper 11260, p 341-355, April 1975. 10 fig, 12 ref, 1 append.

Descriptors: *Water distribution(Applied), *Pipelines, Computers, *Hydraulics, *Algorithms, Mathematical studies, Pipe flow, Reservoirs, Head loss, Data processing.
Identifiers: *Sparsity oriented matrix, Jacobian matrix.

Water distribution systems of large metropolitan centers contain several hundred nodes and pipes and a number of pumping stations and reservoirs. The size and complexity of these networks require very efficient steady-state solution techniques for analysis in large digital computer systems. In most large-scale distribution systems, the actual nonzero entries in the Jacobian matrix of nodes are only 2 to 5% total entries. Sparsity is defined as the ratio of the actual nonzero terms present to the total possible terms. Although the Jacobian matrix is sparse, its inverse is generally full. The proposed method does not compute the inverse explicitly. It is based on graph theory, sparsity oriented matrix decomposition techniques, and Newton's method of iterative solution of nonlinear algebraic equations. A Fortran coded computer program was described. Examples were given of the application of this program to several large-scale networks. (Singh-ISWS)
W75-07468

CASCADE THEORY OF TURBULENCE IN A STRATIFIED MEDIUM,
City Coll., New York.
For primary bibliographic entry see Field 2L.
W75-07481

COMPUTING BACKWATER AT OPEN CHANNEL CONSTRICTIONS,
Geological Survey, Bay Saint Louis, Miss. Gulf Coast Hydroscience Center.
V. R. Scheider, and L. A. Druffel.
ASCE Proceedings, Journal of the Hydraulics Division, Vol 100, No HY5, p 705-707, May 1974. 1 tab.

Descriptors: *Discharge(Water), *Backwater, *Stage-discharge relations, Open channel flow, Hydraulics, Estimating, Forecasting.

Excellent agreement between backwater calculations is obtainable between the U.S. Geological Survey (USGS) method, the Federal Highway Administration (FHWA) method, and the actual data when the two predictive methods are properly applied to the computation of discharge through an open channel constriction. In general, the two methods work well for a wide range of field and laboratory conditions. They were developed with laboratory experiments, were carefully verified with peak flow discharge measurements in the field, and are checked with additional data whenever possible. (Knapp-USGS)
W75-07558

EFFECT OF STREAM TURBULENCE ON HEATED WATER PLUMES,
Geological Survey, Menlo Park, Calif.
For primary bibliographic entry see Field 5B.
W75-07587

A COMPUTER PROGRAM FOR ESTIMATING COSTS OF TUNNELLING (COSTUN),
Harza Engineering Co., Chicago, Ill.
F. T. Wheby, and E. M. Cikanek.
Available from the National Technical Information Service, Springfield, Va 22161, as PB-228 740, $13.00 in paper copy, $2.25 in microfiche. Report No FRA-ORD-D-74-16, October 1973. 548 p, 49 fig, 18 ref, 8 append. DOT-FR-20007.

Descriptors: *Costs, *Tunnel design, *Estimated costs, *Computer programs, *Construction costs, *Tunnel construction, *Cost comparison, *Shafts(Excavations), Simulation analysis, Tunneling machines, Tunnel linings, Grouting, Structural shapes, Muck, Bids, Underground structures.
Identifiers: COSTUN computer program.

A computer program for estimating construction costs of tunnels and shafts is provided. The program COSTUN is intended for a variety of purposes: to provide cost estimates for planning and feasibility studies of tunnel projects; to permit the selection of a minimum cost route from a number of alternatives; to provide a means of identifying the minimum-cost construction methods for a variety of tunnel designs and site conditions; to provide a basis for comparison of alternative tunnel design features; and, in designed tunnels, to provide a check of the reasonableness of the engineer's estimate by comparison with the costs of the standard design built into the computer program. COSTUN is designed to duplicate the thought and reasoning process of an engineer. Twelve cost components are defined with each subdivided into labor, equipment, and material subcomponents: excavation setup, excavation, muck loading, muck transport, muck hoisting, muck disposal, supports, lining formwork, lining, grouting, pumping, and air conditioning. Input and adjustment procedures for the user are described for required input specifications for the project, for optional specifications and for external adjustments necessary for projects that do not fall within the range built into COSTUN. The program is only applicable to projects estimated at more than $1 million. (Becker-Wisconsin)
W75-07619

BANK AND CHANNEL PROTECTIVE LINING DESIGN PROCEDURES,
New York State Dept. of Transportation, Albany. Bureau of Soil Mechanics.
For primary bibliographic entry see Field 4A.
W75-07665

BEACH FORMS AND COASTAL PROCESSES,
Columbia Univ., New York. Teachers Coll.
For primary bibliographic entry see Field 2L.
W75-07715

THREE DIMENSIONAL TURBULENT DIFFUSION FROM POINT SOURCES OF POLLUTION IN AN OPEN CHANNEL,
Delaware Univ., Newark. Dept. of Chemical Engineering.
For primary bibliographic entry see Field 5B.
W75-07723

GEOTHERMAL LEASING PROGRAM, VOL IV, APPENDIX I, COMMENTS ON DRAFT IMPACT STATEMENT AND PROPOSED REGULATIONS (FINAL ENVIRONMENTAL IMPACT STATEMENT),
Department of the Interior, Washington, D.C.
Available from the National Technical Information Service, U.S. Dept. of Commerce, Springfield, Va. 22161, as EIS-CA-73-1681-F-4, $8.75 in paper copy, $2.25 in microfiche. October 24, 1973. 728 p, 6 map.

Descriptors: *Geothermal studies, *Wells, *Drilling, Steam, Electric power, Electric power production, Electric powerplants, Access routes, Byproducts, Grazing, Wastes, Waste disposal, Land subsidence, Wildlife, Recreation.
Identifiers: *Environmental Impact Statements.

The proposed action involves implementation of the Geothermal Steam Act of 1970 by the Secretary of the Interior. The plan entails promulgation of leasing and operating regulations pursuant to which the program is to be administered, and the leasing of federally-owned geothermal resources for development in three specific areas. Development of geothermal resources necessitates construction of access roads and well sites, drilling and testing of wells, conveyance of steam over short distances to electric power plants and by-product processing plants, construction and operation of electric power plants, by-products facilities, electrical transmission lines, and facilities for disposing of waste liquids. This action will result in preemption or restriction of land from uses such as wildlife habitat, recreational use, and grazing, as well as the modification of the terrain. Noise and noxious gas emissions may pose problems during testing and production. Other possible adverse effects include land subsidence due to production of fluids and increased seismicity due to production and reinjection of fluid wastes to producing zones. Comments were received from the departments of Agriculture, Army, Commerce, Health, Education and Welfare, and Interior and the Enviromental Protection Agency. (Gagliardi-Florida)
W75-07781

8C. Hydraulic Machinery

REVERSE OSMOSIS FOR SPACECRAFT WASH WATER RECYCLING, HIGH PRESSURE PUMP DEFINITION,
McDonnell Douglass Astronautics Co.-West, Huntington Beach, Calif.
R. E. Shook, and G. W. Wells.
Available from the National Technical Information Service, Springfield, Va. 22161, as PB-236 940, $4.75 in paper copy, $2.25 in microfiche. Report INT-OSW-RDPR-74-992, October 1974. 98 p, 4 tab, 23 fig, 28 ref. OWRT Contract 14-30-3062.

Descriptors: *Reverse osmosis, *Desalination, *Water quality, *Water temperature, *Pump testing, *Centrifugal pumps, Wa.te water treatment, *Pumps, Recycling, *Water reuse.
Identifiers: Gear pumps, Peripheral pumps, Jet pumps, Vane pumps, Rotor-screw pump, Axial-piston pumps, Radial-piston pump, Piston-valve type radial-piston pump, Wash water.

The principal objective was to continue the development of a high pressure space applicable reverse osmosis feed pump through the selection of a concept for detail design. Candidate pumping mechanisms suitable for small flow, high pressure water service were identified. Information on the efficiency, reliability, maintainability, mechanical complexity, sealing methods, valving concepts, lubrication requirements, development requirements, and projected costs was compiled from reference literature and vendor information. Summaries of the pertinent features of the various pump mechanisms were prepared. A matrix of selection criteria was prepared and a numerical comparison of the suitability of the various pump mechanisms was established. Positive displacement pumps of the vane or multi-piston types were determined to be best suited for the space vehicle RO system. Seal reliability, materials compatibility, and estimated development cost considerations resulted in the selection of a quintuplex radial piston pump for this application. (OWRT)
W75-07628

AN ARCTIC WATER SUPPLY SYSTEM,
Directorate of Construction Engineering and Design Engineering, Ottawa (Ontario).
For primary bibliographic entry see Field 5F.
W75-07684

NORTH BROWARD COUNTY, FLORIDA (FINAL ENVIRONMENTAL IMPACT STATEMENT),
Environmental Protection Agency, Atlanta, Ga. Region IV.
For primary bibliographic entry see Field 5D.
W75-07787

CONNECTION FITTING FOR WATER TREATMENT APPARATUS,
For primary bibliographic entry see Field 5F.
W75-07808

8D. Soil Mechanics

USE OF AXISYMMETRIC INFILTRATION MODEL AND FIELD DATA TO DETERMINE HYDRAULIC PROPERTIES OF SOILS,
Utah State Univ., Logan. Dept. of Civil Engineering.
For primary bibliographic entry see Field 2G.
W75-07466

BANK AND CHANNEL PROTECTIVE LINING DESIGN PROCEDURES.
New York State Dept. of Transportation, Albany. Bureau of Soil Mechanics.
For primary bibliographic entry see Field 4A.
W75-07665

8E. Rock Mechanics and Geology

TECTONIC STRESS DETERMINATIONS, NORTHERN PICEANCE CREEK BASIN, COLORADO,
Geological Survey, Reston, Va.
For primary bibliographic entry see Field 2F.
W75-07574

8F. Concrete

METHOD OF PROTECTION FOR SLOPES AND CRESTS OF RIVERS, CHANNELS, AND THE LIKE,
J. Estruco.
U.S. Patent No. 3,871,182, 2 p, 2 fig, 7 ref; Official Gazette of the United States Patent Office, Vol 932, No 3, p 817, March 18, 1975.

Descriptors: *Patents, *Shore protection, *Erosion, Rivers, Slopes, Channels, Coasts, Shores, *Casings.

A method is disclosed for protecting slopes and crests of rivers, channels, and the like by mooring flexible and permeable tubular casings filled with fresh concrete. Tubular casings may be made of synthetic fibers, burlap, canvas, etc., and are simultaneously filled with fresh concrete while being placed at the foot of surfaces which must be protected. The tubular casing is lowered by gravity to its position by means of a series of ropes tied to the tubular casing at one of their ends with the other end of the ropes being secured to an element placed at the surface of the water. The ropes provide guides for the mooring of other casings similar to the above-mentioned one with the rolls, loops or rings or any other element being used for aligning purposes through which ropes of the first casing may pass so that the following casing necessarily are placed one over the other until the rolls appear at the surface of the water. (Sinha-OEIS)
W75-07819

8G. Materials

TECTONIC STRESS DETERMINATIONS, NORTHERN PICEANCE CREEK BASIN, COLORADO,
Geological Survey, Reston, Va.
For primary bibliographic entry see Field 2F.
W75-07574

PLASTIC PIPE IN COLDER CLIMATES,
Winnipeg Waterworks, Waste and Disposal Div. (Manitoba).
For primary bibliographic entry see Field 5F.
W75-07683

CHEMICAL CONTROL OF ROOTS,
Sacramento County Dept. of Public Works, Calif.
For primary bibliographic entry see Field 5D.
W75-07685

8I. Fisheries Engineering

LITTORAL DISTRIBUTION AND DRIFT OF SELECTED RIFFLE INSECTS,
Idaho Cooperative Fishery Unit, Moscow.
D. J. Peters.
Available from the National Technical Information Service, Springfield, Va 22161 as PB-241 499, $4.25 in paper copy, $2.25 in microfiche. MS Thesis. May 1973. 56 p, 10 fig, 9 tab, 26 ref, append. OWRT A-035-IDA(1).

Descriptors: *Littoral drift, *Distribution, *Insects, *Rivers, Idaho, Benthic fauna, Currents(Water), Velocity, Biological communities, Mayflies, Caddisflies, Shores, Varieties.
Identifiers: *Insect drift, Clearwater River(Idaho).

Littoral drift and community distribution of aquatic insects were studied to assess the resiliency of specific species on subsequent diel water level fluctuations downstream from the Dworshak Dam on the Clearwater River, Idaho. Benthic samples were taken at 15, 30, and 45 cm littoral depths. Insect drift was taken on riffles at three distances from the shoreline in water depths of 30, 45 and 60 cm. Littoral variation in number and weight of riffle insects was shown to be affected by changes in depth and current velocity, interacting with the date and station of sampling. This differential distribution of riffle insects resulted in variation of the littoral community structure. In the non-fluctuating system, community diversity and diversity per individual decreased with increasing depths of 45 cm and current velocity to 1.1 m/sec. Fluctuating flows appear to reverse the order of community structure, i.e., community diversity and diversity per individual increase with increasing depth to 45 cm and current velocity to 1.1 m/sec. A flow reduction exponentially increased the number of drifting insects in zones adjacent to the exposed substrate on the shoreline. (Jones-Wisconsin)
W75-07356

REPRODUCTION AND DEVELOPMENT OF THE BAIKAL WHITEFISH COREGONUS LAVARETUS BAICALENSIS DYB. IN CONNECTION WITH THE PROBLEM OF ITS ARTIFICIAL BREEDING, (IN RUSSIAN),
Zh. A. Chernyaev.
Vopr Ikhtiol, Vol 13, No 2, p 259-274, 1973, Illus.

Descriptors: Lakes, *Fish, *Spawning, *Fish management, Breeding.
Identifiers: Coregonus-lavaretus-baicalensis, Pisciculture, USSR, *Whitefish(Baikal).

The region of reproduction of the Baikal whitefish Coregonus lavaretus baicalensis in Mukhor Bay of Lake Baikal, USSR is described. Data are given on the spawning conditions, migration routes, dynamics of the spawning run, and biological characteristics of the spawning school. The embryonic development and larval stages of the whitefish are described. The biotechniques of its artificial reproduction are considered. For artificial breeding it is necessary to establish the spawning grounds and determine the exact temperature parameters of development. Hydrclogic and hydrochemical observations of the spawning grounds should be made and experiments on hypophyseal injections, holding of spawners and regulation of the hatching time of larvae conducted.--Copyright 1974, Biological Abstracts, Inc.
W75-07711

PERIODICITY, IDENTIFICATION, AND CONTROL OF ALGAE IN MANAGED PONDS,
University of Southern Mississippi, Hattiesburg. Coll. of Science and Technology.
For primary bibliographic entry see Field 5C.
W75-07719

APPLICATION OF IMPORTED PERU FISH MEAL IN THE FISH FEED: II. STUDIES ON LIPIDS OF THE TEST DIETS, (IN JAPANESE),
Y. Shimma, and H. Shimma.
Bull Freshwater Fish Res Lab, Vol 22, No 1, p 73-98, 1972, Illus. English summary.

Descriptors: *Fish diets, *Rainbow trout, Lipids.
Identifiers: Brown lipids, Peru fish meal, *Japan.

Qualities of lipids of the test diets and supplemental extract which were fed to rainbow trout in the 1st paper of this series were checked. Although solvent treatment before feed preparation changed lipid contents of the meals, analytical data did not show much difference among their lipids. n-Hexane extractable lipids of Brown which were 30% of Brown lipids and were presumed to obstruct fish growth (Nomura et al, 1972) had relatively high carbonyl value and low TAB(2-thiobarbituric acid) absorbance ratio (450 micrometers/530 micrometers), and were contained originally in IV, V and VI fractions of Brown lipids. Remaining lipids after n-hexane extraction were major and further oxidized parts of Brown lipids of inferior qualities, but showed little ill effect on fish growth by Normura et al.--Copyright 1973, Biological Abstracts, Inc.
W75-07728

10. SCIENTIFIC AND TECHNICAL INFORMATION

10C. Secondary Publication And Distribution

A BIBLIOGRAPHY OF NUMERICAL MODELS FOR TIDAL RIVERS, ESTUARIES AND COASTAL WATERS,
Rhode Island Univ., Kingston. Dept. of Ocean Engineering.
For primary bibliographic entry see Field 02L.
W75-07409

THE EFFECTS OF EFFLUENT FROM THE CANADIAN TEXTILE INDUSTRY ON AQUATIC ORGANISMS: A LITERATURE REVIEW,
Fisheries and Marine Service, Winnipeg (Manitoba).
For primary bibliographic entry see Field 05C.
W75-07644

OIL SPILL AND OIL POLLUTION REPORTS JULY 1974 - OCTOBER 1974,
California Univ., Santa Barbara. Marine Science Inst.
For primary bibliographic entry see Field 05G.
W75-07689

10F. Preparation Of Reviews

THE EFFECTS OF EFFLUENT FROM THE CANADIAN TEXTILE INDUSTRY ON AQUATIC ORGANISMS: A LITERATURE REVIEW,
Fisheries and Marine Service, Winnipeg (Manitoba).
For primary bibliographic entry see Field 05C.
W75-07644

SUBJECT INDEX

AUTHOR INDEX

ORGANIZATIONAL INDEX

ACCESSION NUMBER INDEX

ABSTRACT SOURCES

RCE	ACCESSION NUMBER	TOTAL
CENTERS OF COMPETENCE		
Cornell University, Policy Models for Water Resources Systems	W75-07381-07391	11
Illinois State Water Survey, Hydrology	W75-07398--07399 07428--07453 07455--07478 07480--07482 07484--07504 07507--07517 07727	88
Institute of Paper Chemistry, Water Pollution from Pulp and Paper Industry	W75-07633--07644 07646--07650 07652--07660	26
University of Arizona, Arid Land Water Resources	W75-07363--07367 07369--07373 07375 07392--07393 07400--07403 07525--07548 07620	42
University of Florida, Eastern U. S. Water Law	W75-07757--07763 07765--07789	32
University of Wisconsin, Eutrophication	W75-07356--07357	2
University of Wisconsin, Water Resources Economics	W75-07359 07376--07380 07610--07613 07615--07619	15
STATE WATER RESOURCES RESEARCH INSTITUTES	W75-07351--07354 07395--07397 07518--07519 07589, 07593 07596--07601 07722--07726	22
OTHER		
Agricultural Research Service	W75-07505	1

ABSTRACT SOURCES

SOURCE	ACCESSION NUMBER	TOT
C. OTHER Continued		
BioSciences Information Service	W75-07355, 07358 07361, 07368 07374, 07394 07406, 07408 07415, 07419 07454, 07479 07483, 07552 07560, 07563 07588, 07602 07609, 07614 07645, 07651 07707, 07711 07728--07756 07764, 07791	
Commonwealth Scientific and Industrial Research Organization, Australia	W75-07520--07524	
Engineering Aspects of Urban Water Resources (Poertner)	W75-07591--07592 07661--07685 07712	
Environmental Protection Agency	W75-07360, 07362 07404, 07594 07603--07608 07686--07706 07708--07710 07790	
Forest Service (USDA)	W75-07792	
National Oceanic and Atmospheric Administration	W75-07405, 07407 07409--07414 07416--07418 07420--07427 07549 07713--07721 07824--07835	
Ocean Engineering Information Service (Patents)	W75-07805--07823	
Office of Water Research and Technology	W75-07506, 07590 07595 07621--07632	

ABSTRACT SOURCES

OURCE	ACCESSION NUMBER	TOTAL
. OTHER Continued		
U. S. Geological Survey	W75-07550--07551 07553--07559 07561--07562 07564--07587 07836--07850	50
Vanderbilt University, Metals Pollution	W75-07793--07804	12

CENTERS OF COMPETENCE AND THEIR SUBJECT COVERAGE

- Ground and surface water hydrology at the Illinois State Water Survey and the Water Resources Division of the U.S. Geological Survey, U.S. Department of the Interior.
- Metropolitan water resources planning and management at the Center for Urban and Regional Studies of University of North Carolina.
- Eastern United States water law at the College of Law of the University of Florida.
- Policy models of water resources systems at the Department of Water Resources Engineering of Cornell University.
- Water resources economics at the Water Resources Center of the University of Wisconsin.
- Eutrophication at the Water Resources Center of the University of Wisconsin.
- Water resources of arid lands at the Office of Arid Lands Studies of the University of Arizona.
- Water well construction technology at the National Water Well Association.
- Water-related aspects of nuclear radiation and safety at the Oak Ridge National Laboratory.
- Water resource aspects of the pulp and paper industry at the Institute of Paper Chemistry.

Supported by the Environmental Protection Agency in cooperation with WRSIC

- Effect on water quality of irrigation return flows at the Department of Agricultural Engineering of Colorado State University.
- Agricultural livestock waste at East Central State College, Oklahoma.
- Municipal wastewater treatment technology at the Franklin Institute Research Laboratories.

Subject Fields

- **1** NATURE OF WATER
- **2** WATER CYCLE
- WATER SUPPLY AUGMENTATION AND CONSERVATION
- WATER QUANTITY MANAGEMENT AND CONTROL
- WATER QUALITY MANAGEMENT AND PROTECTION
- WATER RESOURCES PLANNING
- RESOURCES DATA
- ENGINEERING WORKS
- MANPOWER, GRANTS, AND FACILITIES
- SCIENTIFIC AND TECHNICAL INFORMATION

INDEXES

- SUBJECT INDEX
- AUTHOR INDEX
- ORGANIZATIONAL INDEX
- ACCESSION NUMBER INDEX
- ABSTRACT SOURCES

John Littlewood
Documents Division
220 D Library
Champaign Ill. 61820

U.S. DEPARTMENT OF COMMERCE
National Technical Information Service
5285 Port Royal Road
Springfield, VA 22161

OFFICIAL BUSINESS

PRINTED MATTER

SELECTED WATER SOURCES BSTRACTS

VOLUME 8, NUMBER 16
AUGUST 15, 1975

51 – W75-08350
SWRABW

SELECTED WATER RESOURCES ABSTRACTS is published semimonthly for the Water Resources Scientific Information Center (WRSIC) by the National Technical Information Service (NTIS), U.S. Department of Commerce. NTIS was established September 2, 1970, as a new primary operating unit under the Assistant Secretary of Commerce for Science and Technology to improve public access to the many products and services of the Department. Information services for Federal scientific and technical report literature previously provided by the Clearinghouse for Federal Scientific and Technical Information are now provided by NTIS.

SELECTED WATER RESOURCES ABSTRACTS is available to Federal agencies, contractors, or grantees in water resources upon request to: Manager, Water Resources Scientific Information Center, Office of Water Research and Technology, U.S. Department of the Interior, Washington, D. C. 20240.

SELECTED WATER RESOURCES ABSTRACTS is also available on subscription from the National Technical Information Service. Annual subscription rates are: To the SWRA Journal, $75 ($95 foreign); to the Journal & Annual Index, $100 ($125 foreign); to the Annual Index only, $50 ($65 foreign). Certain documents abstracted in this journal can be purchased from the NTIS at prices indicated in the entry. Prepayment is required.

SELECTED
WATER RESOURCES ABSTRACTS

A Semimonthly Publication of the Water Resources Scientific Information Center,
Office of Water Research and Technology, U.S. Department of the Interior

VOLUME 8, NUMBER 16
AUGUST 15, 1975

W75-07851 -- W75-08350

The Secretary of the U. S. Department of the Interior has determined that the publication of this periodical is necessary in the transaction of the public business required by law of this Department. Use of funds for printing this periodical has been approved by the Director of the Office of Management and Budget through August 31, 1978.

As the Nation's principal conservation agency, the Department of the Interior has responsibility for most of our nationally owned public lands and natural resources. This includes fostering the wisest use of our land and water resources, protecting our fish and wildlife, preserving the environmental and cultural values of our national parks and historical places, and providing for the enjoyment of life through outdoor recreation. The Department assesses our energy and mineral resources and works to assure that their development is in the best interests of all our people. The Department also has a major responsibility for American Indian reservation communities and for people who live in Island Territories under U.S. administration.

FOREWORD

Selected Water Resources Abstracts, a semimonthly journal, includes abstracts of current and earlier pertinent monographs, journal articles, reports, and other publication formats. The contents of these documents cover the water-related aspects of the life, physical, and social sciences as well as related engineering and legal aspects of the characteristics, conservation, control, use, or management of water. Each abstract includes a full bibliographical citation and a set of descriptors or identifiers which are listed in the **Water Resources Thesaurus.** Each abstract entry is classified into ten fields and sixty groups similar to the water resources research categories established by the Committee on Water Resources Research of the Federal Council for Science and Technology.

WRSIC IS NOT PRESENTLY IN A POSITION TO PROVIDE COPIES OF DOCUMENTS ABSTRACTED IN THIS JOURNAL. Sufficient bibliographic information is given to enable readers to order the desired documents from local libraries or other sources.

Selected Water Resources Abstracts is designed to serve the scientific and technical information needs of scientists, engineers, and managers as one of several planned services of the Water Resources Scientific Information Center (WRSIC). The Center was established by the Secretary of the Interior and has been designated by the Federal Council for Science and Technology to serve the water resources community by improving the communication of water-related research results. The Center is pursuing this objective by coordinating and supplementing the existing scientific and technical information activities associated with active research and investigation program in water resources.

To provide WRSIC with input, selected organizations with active water resources research programs are supported as "centers of competence" responsible for selecting, abstracting, and indexing from the current and earlier pertinent literature in specified subject areas.

Additional "centers of competence" have been established in cooperation with the Environmental Protection Agency. A directory of the Centers appears on inside back cover.

Supplementary documentation is being secured from established discipline-oriented abstracting and indexing services. Currently an arrangement is in effect whereby the BioScience Information Service of Biological Abstracts supplies WRSIC with relevant references from the several subject areas of interest to our users. In addition to Biological Abstracts, references are acquired from Bioresearch Index which are without abstracts and therefore also appear abstractless in SWRA. Similar arrangements with other producers of abstracts are contemplated as planned augmentation of the information base.

The input from these Centers, and from the 51 Water Resources Research Institutes administered under the Water Resources Research Act of 1964, as well as input from the grantees and contractors of the Office of Water Research and Technology and other Federal water resource agencies with which the

Center has agreements becomes the information base from which this journal is, and other information services will be, derived; these services include bibliographies, specialized indexes, literature searches, and state-of-the-art reviews.

Comments and suggestions concerning the contents and arrangements of this bulletin are welcome.

Water Resources Scientific Information Center
Office of Water Research and Technology
U.S. Department of the Interior
Washington, D. C. 20240

CONTENTS

Identifiers: *Fragipan soils, *Freeze-thaw cycle.

Perched water table-streamflow relationships above a fragipan were studied on a forested watershed in the Valley and Ridge Province of central Pennsylvania. Automatic recording wells, a weir, and an automatic rain gage were installed to monitor perched water table changes, streamflow, and precipitation continuously. Time of year and precipitation were the most significant factors affecting perched water table and streamflow levels. In winter and early spring, streamflow and the perched water table were high and sensitive to rainfall and temperature changes. Rapid freezing and thawing affected water levesl within the recording wells and the stream. During late spring and summer, water loss due to evapotranspiration was the dominant factor in streamflow-perched water table responses. Diurnal fluctuations due to daily temperature variations were concurrently observed in both the stream and the perched water table. As the soil continued to dry in summer, streamflow ceased and water table response to rainfall declined. With heavy fall rains and low evapotranspiration, the perched water table reappeared and streamflow resumed. Increased streamflow and flooding due to large storms were greatest when the soil adjacent to the stream was saturated. (Schicht-ISWS)
W75-07946

AN INTERDISPLINARY APPROACH TO DEVELOPMENT OF WATERSHED SIMULATION MODELS,
British Columbia Univ., Vancouver. Inst. of Animal Resource Ecology.
C. Walters.
Journal of the Fisheries Research Board of Canada, Vol 32, No 1, p 177-195, January 1975. 6 fig, 3 tab, 1 ref.

Descriptors: *Simulation analysis, *Watershed management, *Multiple-purpose projects, Hydrologic systems, *Model studies, Fisheries, Fish management, Cost-benefit analysis, Forestry, Water quality, Recreation, Mathematical models, Sediment transport, Watersheds(Basins), Pacific Coast regions, *Canada.
Identifiers: Interdisciplinary studies, James Bay.

A workshop approach for the rapid development of simulation models was described. The key feature of the approach is intimate involvement of resource specialists in the model building process so that communication between resource disciplines is greatly enhanced. Two watershed models that have been developed in 1-week workshop meetings were described to show the kinds of factors that can be considered. One model is concerned with small coastal watersheds in the Pacific Northwest, and the other deals with part of the James Bay area, Quebec. Both of these models have helped scientists of Environment Canada identify major information needs that are not being considered in current research and management programs; in particular, little is known about the dynamics of recreational demand. (Terstriep-ISWS)
W75-07947

ESTIMATING LAND USE CHARACTERISTICS FOR HYDROLOGIC MODELS,
Rummel, Klepper and Kahl, Baltimore, Md.
For primary bibliographic entry see Field 4A.
W75-07982

PRECIPITATION AND STREAMFLOW ON THREE SMALL CHILEAN WATERSHEDS,
Arizona Univ., Tucson. Dept. of Watershed Management.
M. E. Jones, P. F. Ffolliott, and W. O. Rasmussen.
Progressive Agriculture in Arizona, Vol 27, No 1, p 13-16, January-February, 1975. 4 fig.

Descriptors: *Precipitation(Atmospheric), *Streamflow, *Small watersheds, *Vegetation effects, *Hydrologic data, Runoff, Sediment yeild, Water quality, Peak discharge, Land use, Rainfall, Storms, Hydrographs, Stream gauges.
Identifiers: *Chile.

Preliminary results of a small watershed project initiated by Chile's Ministry of Agriculture in 1970 are presented. Information gathered on precipitation and streamflow for single land-use and vegetation types may be used for evaluating design methods for small dams, recommending land-use procedures, and describing hydrologic events. The three watersheds instrumented and measured for this study are part of a more extensive small basin network covering diverse climatic, vegetation, and land-use conditions in Chile. Some results of this preliminary study in areas relatively unaffected by drastic vegetation manipulation indicated high water quality in terms of sediments, and low annual runoff efficiency. Peak runoff and sediment loads were more sensitive to climatic and treatment changes. Peak flow values correlated better with total storm rainfall than did flow volumes. Peak flows were as much as 90 percent higher from burned watersheds. A longer data record eventually will better define relationships between precipitation and streamflow in Chile. (Mastic-Arizona)
W75-08104

HYDROLOGIC SIMULATION OF WATERSHEDS WITH ARTIFICIAL DRAINAGE,
Florida Univ., Gainesville. Dept. of Agricultural Engineering.
K. L. Campbell, and H. P. Johnson.
Water Resources Research, Vol 11, No 1, p 120-126, February 1975. 9 fig, 1 tab, 18 ref. OWRR R-025-IA(3).

Descriptors: Hydrology, *Surface-groundwater relationships, *Soil water movement, Soil-water-plant relationships, *Simulation analysis, Subsurface drains, Mathematical models, Model studies, Evapotranspiration, Routing, Soil moisture, *Iowa, Tile drainage, Tile drains, Watersheds(Basins), *Watershed management.
Identifiers: *Artificial drainage, *Drainage simulation, Jefferson(Ia).

A deterministic hydrologic watershed model that simulates the watershed discharge and soil moisture status continuously throughout the crop season was developed for drainage watersheds with depressional storage. The model simulates the processes of interception, surface storage, infiltration, surface runoff, soil profile storage, percolation to the water table, subsurface tile drainage, soil moisture redistribution, evapotranspiration, and routing through depressions, tile mains, and the drainage ditch. The resulting outputs are daily evapotranspiration, soil moisture status in the crop root zone, and watershed discharge. The model was successfully tested on a 24-sq mi watershed near Jefferson, Iowa. (Terstriep-ISWS)
W75-08191

TEMPERATURE EFFECTS ON GREAT LAKES WATER BALANCE STUDIES,
Illinois Univ., Urbana. Water Resources Center.
For primary bibliographic entry see Field 2H.
W75-08225

ARIDITY PROBLEMS IN THE SAHEL, TWENTY YEARS OF UNESCO ACTIVITY.
Nature and Resources, Vol 10, No 1, p 8-11, January-March, 1974.

Descriptors: *Africa, *Arid lands, *Arid climates, *Climatology, *Comprehensive planning, *Data collections, *Land use, *Natural resources,

*Research and development, *United Nations, Alternative planning, Cultures, Economics, Ecosystems, Environment, Grazing, Land management, Livestock, Maps, Population, Resources development, Social aspects, Water supply.
Identifiers: *Sahelian zone.

Climatological causes of cyclical droughts, such as that devastating the Sahel in 1972-73, are still unknown, though in 1951 UNESCO set up an Advisory Committee for Arid Zone Research to study droughts in affected regions of Africa and the Mediterranean. A major interdisciplinlary project evolving from the Committee's work resulted in some 30 arid-zone study publications. Several maps on these arid regions, prepared with other international agencies, have been issued since 1962. During the last 20 years considerable data on the natural environment have been accumulated, and field studies of the affected zones have been made. Currently, multidisciplinary UNESCO activity oriented to these arid zones involves Man and the Biosphere Program and the International Hydrological Program. Through cooperation with officials in afflicted countries future UNESCO activities probably will involve emphasis on applied research with alternative life-support systems appropriate to the environment, culture, and economy. A thorough understanding of the complex interactions of this fragile ecosystem is necessary before imported technological modification of traditional land use can be instituted. Under fluctuating, marginal, climatic conditions, and given the disruptions of the drought years in this partieular socio-economic-cultural context, management of the vast Saharo-Sahelian grazing lands must be extended also to the Sudano-Sahelian area, where the migratory influx of humans and livestock has affected agriculture and sedentary activities generally, as well as crop production, grazing, and water supply. UNESCO international research programs, thus, can make a significant contribution to the Sahelian drought situation. (Gloyd-Arizona)
W75-08282

CLIMATOLOGICAL WATER BUDGET AND WATER AVAILABILITY PERIODS OF IRAQ,
Institute for Applied Research on Natural Resources, Baghdad (Iraq).
For primary bibliographic entry see Field 2B.
W75-08283

THE ANCIENT NAMIB DESERT,
E. S. Ross.
Pacific Discovery, Vol 25, No 4, p 2-13, July-August, 1972. 22 fig.

Descriptors: *Biota, *Desert plants, *Deserts, *Ecotypes, *Fog, *Xerophilie animals, Arid climates, Arid lands, Diurnal, Nocturnal, Seasonal, Temperature, Winds.
Identifiers: *Namid Desert, *South Africa, Kuiseb River, Kokerboom, Welwitschia.

Perhaps as old as the continent itself, dating from the end of the Jurassic period, the Namid Desert in southern Africa commands considerable biological interest. At Gobabeb, geographically centered astride the desert's 3 main biotypes, is the Namid Desert Research Station, the seat of the Desert Ecological Research Unit, Republic of South Africa. To the north lie extensive gravel rock plains and a thin strip of riverine forest watered by the underground flow of the Kuiseb River; to the south, vast red sand dunes. The Namid's rich biota is sustained by moisture from fog banks formed off Africa's southwestern shores and carried inland 30-40 mi by brisk west winds. Sea fog is heaviest on early winter mornings: maximum dampness occurs then, for the Namid has no regular rainy season. Plants include lichens, stone succulents, a strange gymnosperm-Welwitschia, cactus-like euphorbias and milkweeds, a tree aloe--the kokerboom, and several unique forms of the grape family. During the day only insects are in evidence, mostly beetles and wasps. Nocturnal dune animals include tenebrionids, scarabs, spiders, skinks, Palmatogeckoes, sand vipers, owls, moles, and gerbils, which avoiding hot sun and desiccating winds, appear at night to feed and mate. Studies of diurnal insects here revealed temperature adaptation is accomplished by moving from place to place in the thermal mosaic of sand, rock, and vegetation. (Gloyd-Arizona)
W75-08288

2B. Precipitation

FREQUENCY ANALYSIS OF RAINFALL INTENSITIES FOR NAGPUR (SONEGAON),
College of Agriculture, Junagadh (India).
A. I. Patel, and S. S. Vanjari.
P K V Res J, Vol 1, No 1, p 15-19, 1972.
Identifiers: *Frequency analysis, *India(Nagpur), *Rainfall intensity, Climatic data.

Autographic rainfall records of Nagpur (Sonegaon Airport), India, were analysed with a view to developing rainfall intensity duration frequency curves. For this purpose a frequency analysis of rainfall data over a period of 20 yr from 1948-1967 was carried out using Gumbels technique.-- Copyright 1973, Biological Abstracts, Inc.
W75-08000

BIOGENIC AND INORGANIC SOURCES FOR ICE NUCLEI IN THE DROUGHT-STRICKEN AREAS OF THE SAHEL--1974,
National Center for Atmospheric Research, Boulder, Colo.
R. C. Schnell.
Interim Report to the Directors, Rockefeller Foundation, New York, New York, December 1974. 18 p, 8 fig, 20 ref.

Descriptors: *Rainfall, *Africa, *Meteorology, *Weather modification, *Droughts, *Arid lands, Artificial precipitation, Cloud seeding, Water shortage, Environmental effects, Carrying capacity, Grazing.
Identifiers: *Sahel, Ice nuclei, Overgrazing.

Recent research has shown that organic decay products of tree and grass litters (i.e. biogenic nuclei) may act as atmospheric ice nuclei at relatively warm temperatures (-2 to -10 degrees C). Theory has suggested a sensitive relationship between the availability of such ice-forming nuclei and the amount of precipitation. A hypothesis is advanced that massive overgrazing in the sub-Saharan (Sahel) region of Africa which preceded the recent drought, resulted in depletion of the sources of these biogenic nuclei and a subsequent reduction in total precipitation. The hypothesis was tested by sampling the availability of surface-derived ice nuclei in the Sahel. The results show that where organic decay products were available, ice forming nuclei active at -7 degrees C were present in concentrations to 10,000 per gram. Soils relatively free of such organic decay products were found to contain no ice forming nuclei active at temperatures warmer than -14 degrees C and only 1000 per gram of material active at -18 degrees C. It is suggested that poor agricultural management contributed to the persistence and severity of the drought, and a feedback mechanism between the vegetation and local precipitation is proposed. (Bowden-Arizona)
W75-08115

ARIDITY PROBLEMS IN THE SAHEL, TWENTY YEARS OF UNESCO ACTIVITY.
For primary bibliographic entry see Field 2A.
W75-08282

CLIMATOLOGICAL WATER BUDGET AND WATER AVAILABILITY PERIODS OF IRAQ,
Institute for Applied Research on Natural Resources, Baghdad (Iraq).
M. S. Kettaneh, and M. Gangopadhyaya.
Institute for Applied Research on Natural Resources, Baghdad, Iraq. Technical Bulletin 65. July 1974. 4 fig, 2 tab, 6 ref.

Descriptors: *Hydrologic budget, *Water allocation(Policy), *Evapotranspiration, *Meteorological data, *Water zoning, *Soil moisture, *Water storage, *Agroclimatology.
Identifiers: *Iraq.

A water budget for Iraq was obtained using mean monthly rainfall and potential evapotranspiration. Soil moisture storage was also accounted for in deriving the water budget. Water availability periods were defined as humid, moist, moderately dry to dry, and very dry based on defined rainfall-potential evapotranspiration relationships. The four categories of water availability were determined for the weather stations throughout Iraq, and categories mapped to show the geographical distribution of these agroclimatic factors in Iraq. A proposal for agroclimatic zoning of the country based on these studied is being considered. (Mastic-Arizona)
W75-08283

VARIABILITY AND PROBABILITY CHARACTERISTICS OF ANNUAL RAINFALL OF IRAQ,
Institute for Applied Research on Nutural Resources, Baghdad (Iraq).
M. S. Kettaneh, M. Gangopadhyaya, and G. F. Kaka.
Institute for Applied Research on Natural Resources, Baghdad, Iraq. Technical Bulletin No 68, August 1974. 11 p, 3 fig, 2 tab, 9 ref.

Descriptors: *Rainfall, *Climatic data, *Probability, *Variability, *Isohyets, Irrigation, Agriculture.
Identifiers: *Iraq.

Data gathered from a small network of weather stations manned by the Iraq Meteorological Department were used to compile an isohyetal map of mean annual rainfall. The derivation of probability and variability factors for rainfall are important for the planning of national development activities, particularly in agriculture and irrigation. Data limited the derivation of variability and probability levels to an annual basis. Factors from the variability study show maximum and minimum rainfall, mean, median, standard deviation, coefficient of variability, sequential variability, and relative variability. Probabilities cannot be interpreted as periodicities, they only indicate an average chance of rainfall occurrence on a long-term basis. (Mastic-Arizona)
W75-08284

2C. Snow, Ice, and Frost

MACLURE GLACIER, CALIFORNIA,
Geological Survey, Sacramento, Calif.
W. W. Dean.
In: Proceedings of the Western Snow Conference, 42nd Annual Meeting, April 16-20, 1974, Anchorage, Alaska: Printed by Colorado State University, Fort Collins, p 1-8, 1974. 4 fig, 1 tab, 8 ref.

Descriptors: *Glaciers, *Glaciohydrology, *California, *Water balance, Meteorological data, Basic data collections, Hydrologic budget, Regimen.
Identifiers: *Maclure Glacier(Calif).

Maclure Glacier and other small glaciers in the Sierra Nevada of California survive in the present climatic regime because of favorable high-altitude topography and mean annual precipitation that

equals ablation on the average. The precipitation is amplified by prevailing southwest storm winds that drift snow into the steep-walled north-facing amphitheaters in which the glaciers exist. The 6 years of available data show that the present glacier mass is sensitive to changes in annual precipitation. An average depth of 1.2 m of water equivalent was added to the glacier in the heavy snow year of 1967 and 0.7 m in 1969. Precipitation both years was much above average. The 1968 and 1972 years had below-average precipitation and an average depth loss of 0.8 m of water equivalent from the glacier each year. Annual runoff from the Maclure Creek basin fluctuated much less than annual precipitation. The basin accumulated 2.0 m of snow-water equivalent in 1967 but only 0.6 m in 1968. Yet, total runoff depth was 1.5 m in 1967 when an average of 0.4 m of water was stored over the basin, and 0.9 m in 1968 because of the melting of 0.3 m of old ice and firn over the basin. The small Sierra Nevada glaciers provide natural cyclic water storage that smooths fluctuation in precipitation. Practically all runoff from the Maclure Glacier basin occurs during the June-September period when it is beneficial in sustaining downstream flow. (Knapp-USGS)
W75-07868

SOUGH CASCADE GLACIER: THE MODERATING EFFECT OF GLACIERS ON RUNOFF,
Geological Survey, Tacoma, Wash.
R. M. Krimmel, and W. V. Tangborn.
In: Proceedings of the Western Snow Conference, 42nd Annual Meeting, April 16-20, 1974, Anchorage, Alaska: Printed by Colorado State University, Fort Collins, p 9-13, 1974. 3 fig, 5 ref.

Descriptors: *Glaciers, *Glaciohydrology, *Melting, Runoff, Streamflow, *Washington, Snowmelt, Water balance, Regimen.
Identifiers: *South Cascade Glacier(Wash).

The presence of only a few small glaciers in a large drainage basin has a substantial effect on the variance of summer streamflow. This is an important factor when making streamflow forecasts, particularly during periods of low precipitation. During years of greater than normal precipitation, when nonglacier areas have high runoff, the greater snowfall occurring on glaciers retards ablation. The reverse is true during years of low precipitation and less snow accumulation. The earlier exposure of ice to radiation will cause greater glacier melt, thus compensating for the diminished streamflow from other sources. In years of high snow accumulation, a greater than average amount of avalanching and drifting occurs from the steeper slopes surrounding glaciers, producing an even greater protective blanket over the low albedo ice. The release of liquid storage from within the glacier aquifer each summer will also tend to moderate glacier runoff because this storage and release mechanism is nearly independent of any external climatic variations. Results of the South Cascade Glacier IHD program from 1965-73 can be used to exemplify these effects. (Knapp-USGS)
W75-07869

PERCHED WATER TABLE FLUCTUATION COMPARED TO STREAMFLOW,
Delaware Valley Coll. of Science and Agriculture, Doylestown, Pa.
For primary bibliographic entry see Field 2A.
W75-07946

ICE-RAFTED SEDIMENTS AS A CAUSE OF SOME THERMOKARST LAKES IN THE NOATAK RIVER DELTA, ALASKA,
Washington Univ., Seattle. Coll. of Forest Resources.
F. C. Ugolini.
Science, Vol 188, No 4183, p 51-53, April 4, 1975. 3 fig, 5 ref.

Descriptors: *Ice, *Lakes, *Deltas, Geomorphology, Ponds, Rivers, Sediments, Arctic, Cold regions, Thawing, Frozen soils, Melting, On-site investigations, *Alaska.
Identifiers: *Thermokarst, Lake forming processes, Noatak River Delta(Alas).

Irregular, barren polygonal sheets of mud scattered over the landscape of the western portion of the Noatak River Delta are derived from lake-bottom sediments, ice-rafted during flooding. The evidence suggests that the sheets of mud change the albedo and the thermal regime of the soil, induce the development of thermokarst, and lead to the formation of ponds and lakes. The angular perimeters, especially of the small ponds, support the suggested mode of formation. (Sims-ISWS)
W75-07948

A PATTERN OF HUMUS HORIZON IN TUNDRA'S LOAMY SOILS IN THE NORTHEASTERN EUROPEAN TUNDRA,
I. B. Archegova.
Ekologiya, Vol 3, No 5 p 64-67, 1972.
Identifiers: *Cryogenic-coagulative genesis, Freezing, *Humus, *Loamy soils, Soils, Thawing, *Tundra loamy soil, Tundras, *Water temperature, Soil freezing, Soil thawing, Europe.

Characteristics of humus forming conditions in tundra loamy soils are described. The most important is the water-tempe rature regime characteristic of the tundra: long freezing of the soil and slow thawing. The humus horizon has a specific cryogenic-coagulative genesis.–Copyright 1973, Biological Abstracts, Inc.
W75-07969

NAVIGATION SEASON EXTENSION DEMONSTRATION PROGRAM (FINAL ENVIRONMENTAL IMPACT STATEMENT).
Army Engineer District, Detroit, Mich.
For primary bibliographic entry see Field 4A.
W75-08044

HUNGRY HORSE CLOUD SEEDING PROJECT (FINAL ENVIRONMENTAL IMPACT STATEMENT).
Bonneville Power Administration, Portland, Oreg.
For primary bibliographic entry see Field 3B.
W75-08059

SOME EFFECTS OF EXTENDING THE NAVIGATIONAL SEASON ON THE GREAT LAKES: A NEED FOR CONGRESSIONAL ACTION,
Cleveland State Univ., Ohio. Coll. of Law.
For primary bibliographic entry see Field 6E.
W75-08072

SPECIAL FLOOD HAZARD REPORT: CHESTER CREEK, GREATER ANCHORAGE AREA,
Army Engineer District, Anchorage, Alaska.
For primary bibliographic entry see Field 4A.
W75-08173

A TECHNIQUE TO EVALUATE SNOWPACK PROFILES IN AND ADJACENT TO FOREST OPENINGS,
Arizona Univ., Tucson. Dept. of Watershed Management.
P. F. Ffolliott, and D. B. Thorud.
In: Hydrology and Water Resources in Arizona and the Southwest, Vol 4, Proceedings of the 1974 meetings of the AWRA, Arizona Section and the AAS, Hydrology Section, Flagstaff, Arizona, p 10-17. 2 fig, 10 ref. OWRR A-029-ARIZ(7). 14-31-0001-3503.

Descriptors: *Snowpacks, *Arizona, *Vegetation effects, *Ponderosa pine trees, *Snow management, Snow, Canopy, Forests, Evaluation, Estimating, Water equivalent, Water yield.
Identifiers: Strip cutting, Forest openings, Snow accumulation.

Profiles of snowpack build-up in openings in forest overstories have been widely observed; however, a quantitative characterization of such a snowpack profile would aid in developing empirical guidelines for improving water yields from snowpacks. A technique is outlined that illustrates (a) evaluating snowpack profiles in and adjacent to individual forest openings in terms of increase or decrease in water equivalent, and (b) defining trade-offs between the estimated increase or decrease in snowpack water equivalent and the forest resource removed. Snowpack water equivalent during peak seasonal accumulation was measured in and adjacent to a clearcut strip in a ponderosa pine stand in north-central Arizona. A 4-degree polynomial, which defines the snowpack profile in terms of deposition, redistribution, and ablation characteristics, was empirically selected to describe snowpack water equivalent data points. An increase of 60 percent in snowpack water equivalent was realized by removing 46 percent of the ponderosa pine in the zone of influence, using a strip equal to one and one-half the height of the adjacent overstory. (White-Arizona)
W75-08221

DEVELOPMENT OF FOREST MANAGEMENT GUIDELINES FOR INCREASING SNOWPACK WATER YIELDS IN ARIZONA,
Arizona Univ., Tucson. Dept. of Watershed Management.
P. F. Ffolliott, and D. B. Thorud.
Arizona Water Resources Project Information, Project Bulletin No. 7, 4 p, December 1974. 1 fig. OWRR A-045-ARIZ(1). 14-31-001-5003.

Descriptors: *Snowmelt, *Snowpacks, *Water yield improvement, *Forest management, *Forecasting, *Arizona, Timing, Forests, Clear-cutting, Snow management, Vegetation effects, Canopy, Interception, Snowfall, Watershed management, Runoff, Environmental effects, Geomorphology, Equations, Runoff forecasting.
Identifiers: *Salt-Verde River Basin(Ariz), Snowpack dynamics, Runoff efficiency.

Research is underway to develop operational forest management guidelines for increasing water yields from snowpacks on the Salt-Verde River Basin. Water yield improvement experiments have demonstrated that increased snowmelt runoff may result from a reduction or removal of forest overstories; however, the hydrologic mechanisms involved have not been completely identified and quantified. The investigation framework as designated by a PERT analysis has set up the required activities of the project. Steps include formulation of three inventory reports (for physiographic, climatic, and vegetation characteristics), establishment of test sites to represent these hydrologically significant features, and implementation of studies to evaluate forest overstory characteristics and the effects on snowpack dynamics. Some studies have been conducted on the snow regime as affected by different density levels and clearing patterns in the forest overstory, which has led to a time-space analytic technique to describe snowpack profiles in and adjacent to openings. Assessments of physiographic and climatic factors affecting the magnitude of snowmelt runoff have also begun. Preliminary results indicate that, although runoff efficiencies for a watershed may be unique for each year, a pattern of relatively low efficiencies at the beginning and end of runoff with relatively high efficiencies between 40 and 60 percent snowpack ablation exists. (White-Arizona)
W75-08222

2D. Evaporation and Transpiration

A SINGLE-BEAM INFRARED HYGROMETER FOR EVAPORATION MEASUREMENT,
Commonwealth Scientific and Industrial Research Organization, Aspendale (Australia). Div. of Atmospheric Physics.
P. Hyson, and B. B. Hicks.
Journal of Applied Meteorology, Vol 14, No 3, p 301-307, April 1975. 8 fig, 6 ref, 1 append.

Descriptors: *Evaporation, *Hygrometry, Infrared radiation, Instrumentation, Humidity, Eddies, Adsorption, Latent heat, Optical properties, Electronic equipment, Measurement, Remote sensing.
Identifiers: *Infrared hygrometer, Eddy correlation.

Two instruments were described which serve as humidity sensors in conjunction with existing eddy correlation techniques. The first instrument is an infrared absorption device, with a 40 cm path length, operating in a water vapor vibrational band at 6.3 micrometers. The second instrument is a development of this, operating at 2.7 micrometers with a 20 cm path length. Both devices were successfully field tested in a latent heat flux format, with a propeller anemometer as a vertical velocity sensor. Satisfactory energy balances at the surface were obtained. In the case of the 2.7 micrometer instrument, a specific advantage was its lack of sensitivity to ambient humidity levels, while both instruments were insensitive to slow variations of optical and electronic performance. (Roberts-ISWS)
W75-07901

THE MEASUREMENT OF WATER CONTENT BY AN EVAPORATOR,
National Center for Atmospheric Research, Boulder, Colo.
T. G. Kyle.
Journal of Applied Meteorology, Vol 14, No 3, p 327-332, April 1975. 4 fig, 14 ref.

Descriptors: *Ultraviolet radiation, *Clouds, *Evaporation, *Instrumentation, *Evaporators, Supercooling, Humidity, Condensation, Radar, Convection, Storms, Electronic equipment, Absorption, Moisture content, Measurement.
Identifiers: Radar reflectivity.

An instrument for measuring the condensed water content in supercooled clouds was described. The instrument operated by evaporating water and then measuring the specific humidity by ultraviolet absorption. Among the characteristics required of the instrument was the ability to operate in severe icing conditions; a response independent of the particle size, whether liquid or frozen; and the ability to measure water contents as great as 40 g/cu m. These requirements were established because the measurements were carried out inside the high radar reflectivity region of convective storms where few previous measurements had been carried out. In operation, the air and water the instrument contained flowed into a forward aperture at a rate approximately equal to the aircraft velocity, were heated, and the water evaporated. Large water drops were broken up into smaller droplets which could be more quickly evaporated and the surfaces which the water struck were not at such a high temperature as to prevent the wetting of the surface. The intake aperture was 0.8 cm in diameter, and the response time approximately 1 s. It was shown that the variance of the total water content could be used to derive the radar reflectivity with no knowledge of the drop size spectrum. Examples of data obtained inside mature convective storms were shown. (Roberts-ISWS)
W75-07902

MORPHOMETRIC CONTROL OF VARIATION IN ANNUAL HEAT BUDGETS,
Monash Univ., Clayton (Australia). Dept. of Zoology.
For primary bibliographic entry see Field 2H.
W75-07950

WINTER-REGIME SURFACE HEAT LOSS FROM HEATED STREAMS,
Iowa Univ., Iowa City. Inst. of Hydraulic Research.
For primary bibliographic entry see Field 5B.
W75-07990

THE EFFECT OF STABILITY ON EVAPORATION RATES MEASURED BY THE ENERGY BALANCE METHOD,
Macquarie Univ., North Ryde (Australia). School of Earth Science.
A. P. Campbell.
Agric Meteorol, Vol 11, No 2, p 261-267, 1973, Illus.
Identifiers: Bowen ratio, *Energy balance method, *Evaporation rates, Heat, Measurement, Stability conditions, Water vapor, Methodology, Diffusion.

Comparative lysimetric and energy balance data is examined in relation to stability conditions. Some recently published experimental relations between the eddy diffusivities for momentum, heat and water vapor are then used to determine the effect of the assumption of equal diffusivities on the calculation of the Bowen ratio. These effects are shown to support the comparative measurements.--Copyright 1973, Biological Abstracts, Inc.
W75-08088

RADIATION INDUCED THERMAL STRATIFICATION IN SURFACE LAYERS OF STAGNANT WATER,
Purdue Univ., Lafayette, Ind. School of Mechanical Engineering.
For primary bibliographic entry see Field 2H.
W75-08098

UTILIZING CLIMATE-MOISTURE-WATER USE RELATIONSHIPS IN IMPROVING SOIL MOISTURE BUDGET METHOD FOR IRRIGATION SCHEDULING,
Punjabrao Krishi Vidyapeeth, Akola (India). Dept. of Agronomy.
B. G. Bathkal, and N. F. Dastane.
P K V Res J, Vol 1, No 1, p 70-76, 1972.
Identifiers: Climates, Fodder, *Irrigation scheduling, *Soil moisture, Sorghum, Transpiration, *Water utilization, Evapotranspiration.

Two field trials were conducted. The 1st trial was aimed at working out the relationship between soil moisture and actual water use rates (ET) as well as relative evapotranspiration rates (ET/EO) of fodder sorghum under different evaporative conditions. These relationships were utilized in the next trial for predicting irrigation schedules on the same crop for 3 soil moisture regimes viz. wet regime (I sub 1), medium wet regime (I sub 2) and dry regime (I sub 3) with 100-75%, 100-50%, and 100-25%, available soil moisture, respectively, within 0-90 cm soil depth. ET was directly related to soil moisture conditions and evaporative demand of climate, while ET/EO was positively related to the available soil moisture but negatively related with EO conditions. The relationship curves gave a perfect prediction of irrigation schedules under wet and medium wet regimes, while in dry regime, predicted irrigation dates varied from the actual one by 2-3 days only. Thus, the soil-2 moisture budget method is made precise if the relationship between soil moisture and ET as well as ET/EO are worked out under different evaporative conditions.--Copyright 1973, Biological Abstracts, Inc.
W75-08275

CLIMATOLOGICAL WATER BUDGET AND WATER AVAILABILITY PERIODS OF IRAQ,
Institute for Applied Research on Natural Resources, Baghdad (Iraq).
For primary bibliographic entry see Field 2B.
W75-08283

2E. Streamflow and Runoff

HYDROGEOLOGIC AND WATER-QUALITY DATA IN WESTERN JEFFERSON COUNTY, COLORADO,
Geological Survey, Denver, Colo.
For primary bibliographic entry see Field 2F.
W75-07862

THE BIG CYPRESS SWAMP,
Geological Survey, Miami, Fla.
For primary bibliographic entry see Field 2L.
W75-07863

ANALYSIS OF ERTS-RELAYED WATER-RESOURCES DATA IN THE DELAWARE RIVER BASIN,
Geological Survey, Harrisburg, Pa.
For primary bibliographic entry see Field 7C.
W75-07871

HYDROLOGIC DATA NEEDS FOR SMALL WATERSHEDS--STREAMFLOW AND RELATED PRECIPITATION DATA,
Geological Survey, Reston, Va.
For primary bibliographic entry see Field 7A.
W75-07874

WATER RESOURCES DATA FOR NEBRASKA, 1973: PART 1. SURFACE WATER RECORDS.
Geological Survey, Lincoln, Nebr.
For primary bibliographic entry see Field 7C.
W75-07879

HARMONIC ANALYSIS OF STREAM TEMPERATURES,
Geological Survey, Reston, Va.
For primary bibliographic entry see Field 5B.
W75-07882

ONE-DIMENSIONAL STREAM EXCESS TEMPERATURE ANALYSIS,
Geological Survey, Bay Saint Louis, Miss.
For primary bibliographic entry see Field 5B.
W75-07883

INDEX OF CURRENT WATER RESOURCES PROJECTS AND DATA COLLECTION ACTIVITIES IN OHIO, 1975.
Geological Survey, Columbus, Ohio.
For primary bibliographic entry see Field 7C.
W75-07886

STATISTICS OF SURFACE LAYER TURBULENCE OVER THE TROPICAL OCEAN,
Washington Univ., Seattle. Dept. of Atmospheric Sciences.
E. Leavitt, and C. A. Paulson.
Journal of Physical Oceanography, Vol 5, No 1, p 143-156, January 1975. 18 fig, 6 tab, 28 ref, 1 append. NSF Grants GA-4091, GA-1099.

Descriptors: *Turbulence, *Winds, *Temperature, *Humidity, Tropic, Oceans, Atmosphere, Variability, Data collections, Data processing, Meteorology, Statistics, Kinetics, Energy.
Identifiers: Flip, Variances, Fluxes.

Atmospheric surface layer turbulent statistics measured during the Barbados Oceanographic and Meteorological Experiment 8 and 30 m above

mean sea level were presented. The budget equations of turbulent kinetic energy, humidity variance, and temperature variance were examined. Within discussed limitations, it was concluded that production equals dissipation in the case of turbulent kinetic energy and humidity variance. The analysis of the temperature variance budget revealed large differences between productions and dissipations computed assuming standard similarity functions derived from other data sets. Initial computation of fluxes revealed large systematic decreases with height in the shear stress and heat flux. Comparison with other results suggested corrections which would eliminate these differences. Comparison between profile fluxes and direct measurements suggested strong similarity of momentum and water vapor transfer. (Sims-ISWS)
W75-07909

SPECTRAL CHARACTERISTICS OF SURFACE LAYER TURBULENCE OVER THE TROPICAL OCEAN.
Washington Univ., Seattle. Dept. of Atmospheric Sciences.
E. Leavitt.
Journal of Physical Oceanography, Vol 5, No 1, p 157-163, January 1975. 11 fig, 1 tab, 21 ref. NSF Grants GA-4091, GA-1099.

Descriptors: *Turbulence, *Winds, *Temperature, *Humidity, Atmosphere, Boundary layers, Oceans, Tropic, Wind velocity, Variability, Meteorology, Data processing.
Identifiers: *Spectra.

Spectra of wind, temperature, and humidity fluctuations measured during BOMEX in the atmospheric surface layer were discussed. Strong similarities exist between dimensionless humidity and horizontal wind velocity spectra and between dimensionless cospectra of the water vapor flux and the momentum flux. In contrast, the peaks of the temperature spectra and the sensible heat flux cospectra occur at frequencies an order of magnitude greater than those of the other two variables. These differences are related to the mean vertical planetary boundary layer profiles of the three variables as well as to the effects of heating-cooling by divergence of radiation in the planetary boundary layer. (Sims-ISWS)
W75-07910

ROTARY CROSS-BISPECTRA AND ENERGY TRANSFER FUNCTIONS BETWEEN NON-GAUSSIAN VECTOR PROCESSES I. DEVELOPMENT AND EXAMPLE,
Oregon State Univ., Corvallis. School of Oceanography.
N-C. Yao, S. Neshyba, and H. Crew.
Journal of Physical Oceanography, Vol 5, No 1, p 164-172, January 1975. 4 fig, 1 tab, 12 ref. ONR Contract N00014-68-A-0148; NSF Grants GA-23015, GA-1589.

Descriptors: *Statistical methods, *Mathematical studies, *Oceanography, Ocean currents, Energy transfer, Methodology, Statistics, Data processing.
Identifiers: *Rotary cross-bispectra, Vector processes, Cross-bispectrum analysis.

Bispectrum and cross-bispectrum analyses of the rotary components of stationary random vector processes are more easily interpreted than similar analyses of their scalar components, and have the advantage that the bispectral estimates are invariant to coordinate rotation. Application to some wind-ocean current data showed these to be non-Gaussian and subject to significant nonlinear coupling over a wide range of interacting triplets of rotary components. A set of complex-valued energy transfer functions were developed by which the magnitudes of the linear and quadratic interactions may be compared. (Sims-ISWS)
W75-07911

A NOTE ON OBSERVATIONS OF LONG-TERM TRAJECTORIES OF THE NORTH PACIFIC CURRENT,
Texas A and M Univ., College Station. Dept. of Oceanography.
A. D. Kirwan, Jr., and G. McNally.
Journal of Physical Oceanography, Vol 5, No 1, p 188-191, January 1975. 4 fig, 7 ref.

Descriptors: *Ocean circulation, *Ocean currents, *Pacific Ocean, Tracking techniques, Currents(Water), Oceanography, Oceans.
Identifiers: *Drifter studies, North Pacific current.

Two long-term drifters were tracked for several months in the North Pacific as part of the NORPAX Pole experiment. The trajectories indicate at least one core of the North Pacific current was centered around 37N. Velocities of the drifters indicate that the current is highly variable with eastward components ranging from 0 to over 20 cm/s. After the first two weeks there was virtually no north-south movement. An analysis of the drifter separation showed that for two weeks the drifters moved together. Thereafter, the separation rate was approximately exponential. The separation was due to the eastward movement of one drifter with respect to the other. (Sims-ISWS)
W75-07913

HORIZONTAL SCALES IN THE MAIN THERMOCLINE DERIVED FROM THE TOPOGRAPHY OF A CONSTANT SOUND SPEED SURFACE BETWEEN BERMUDA AND THE ANTILLES,
Woods Hole Oceanographic Institution, Mass.
J. C. Beckerle, and J. B. Hersey.
Journal of Geophysical Research, Vol 80, No 6, p 849-855, February 20, 1975. 6 fig, 1 tab, 18 ref.

Descriptors: *Oceans, *Thermocline, *Sound waves, *Atlantic Ocean, Physical properties, On-site investigations, Spatial distribution, Temporal distribution, Temperature, Internal waves, Oceanography, Topography.
Identifiers: Rossby waves, Baroclinic waves.

Broad scale horizontal variations of the main thermocline south of Bermuda were revealed by an extensive ocean measurement program over several years. The primary physical property of the ocean sampled during these studies was the sound speed because of interest in underwater sound propagation. For the oceanographer the sound speed measurements in the main thermocline provide information similar to ocean temperature measurements except that there is also a dependence of the sound speed on the salinity and the pressure. In the summer of 1962, 31 sound speed profiles were measured. This measurement was followed in the summer of 1964 with 67 sound speed profiles. Complex horizontal variations of a surface of constant sound speed found near the depth of 800 m were the beginning indications of spatial scales of about 240 + or -60 miles of undulations in the main thermocline. In the summer of 1966, 115 sound speed profiles were measured, most of which were distributed on a rhombic grid pattern with 65 miles between stations. These observations were compared with the 1962 and 1964 measurements. The 1966 measurements confirmed the existence of a spatial scale of about 240 miles (+ or -60 miles) as well as the existence of other scales in this ocean region. The spatial variations were indicated by a contour pattern of the depth variations (approximately 300 m) of a 1502-m/s sound speed surface near the depth of 800 m in the main thermocline, where the vertical thermal gradient is large. The observations were interpreted as evidence for Rossby waves or baroclinic waves possibly of finite amplitude that show northwest-southeast alignment. (Sims-ISWS)
W75-07919

OBSERVATIONS OF OCEANIC INTERNAL AND SURFACE WAVES FROM THE EARTH RESOURCES TECHNOLOGY SATELLITE,
National Oceanic and Atmospheric Administration, Miami, Fla. Atlantic Oceanographic and Meteorological Labs.
For primary bibliographic entry see Field 7B.
W75-07920

OBSERVATION AND INTERPRETATION OF A HIGH-FREQUENCY INTERNAL WAVE PACKET AND SURFACE SLICK PATTERN,
Rosenstiel School of Marine and Atmospheric Science, Miami, Fla.
T. B. Curtin, and C. N. K. Mooers.
Journal of Geophysical Research, Vol 80, No 6, p 882-894, February 20, 1975. 15 fig, 3 tab, 14 ref. NSF Grant GX-33052.

Descriptors: *Internal waves, Oceans, Continental shelf, Acoustics, Sounding, On-site investigations, Oceanography, Temperature, Chlorophyll, *Oregon, *Pacific Ocean, *Ocean waves.
Identifiers: *Surface slicks.

A packet of high-frequency (period approximately 8 min) internal gravity waves was observed on a precision depth recorder (PDR) chart while an anchor stations was being conducted during the Cue 1 experiment off Oregon. The anchor station was located over the continental shelf and in the frontal zone associated with coastal upwelling. The packet appeared as a set of three oscillations (maximum peak-to-peak amplitude of 11 m) of an acoustic scattering layer located at a depth of about 20 m, which was immediately below the center of the permanent pycnocline (25.5-26.0 sigma t) at that time and location (water depth 80 m, 10-km offshore). The scattering layer occurred at the depth of a chlorophyll A maximum; strong temperature, salinity, and sound speed gradients; and strong vertical shear of the horizontal velocity. Simultaneously, a series of surface slicks, oriented parallel to the isobaths and propagating onshore, was observed under conditions of light winds. From the spacing of the slicks a horizontal scale of 100 m was estimated; this scale corresponded closely to the wavelength of the first internal wave mode for the observed wave period. From time series of nearby moored current and temperature sensors, bursts of high-frequency oscillations were noted on semidiurnal tidal cycles. Such bursts occurred a few hours before the internal wave packet was observed on the PDR. It was concluded that the semidiurnal baroclinic tide breaks down in the frontal zone off Oregon, forming large-amplitude high-frequency internal gravity waves. These waves can induce detectable surface slicks under light wind conditions and major perturbations of a shallow scattering layer when it is present. (Sims-ISWS)
W75-07921

COMPUTATION OF STAGE-DISCHARGE RELATIONSHIPS AFFECTED BY UNSTEADY FLOW,
National Weather Service, Silver Spring, Md. Hydrologic Research and Development Lab.
D. L. Fread.
Water Resources Bulletin, Vol 11, No 2, p 213-228, April 1975. 10 fig, 1 tab, 7 ref.

Descriptors: *Unsteady flow, *Stage-discharge relations, *Mathematical models, Open channel flow, Hysteresis, Mississippi River, Equations, Mannings equation, Floods, Discharge(Water), Hydrographs, *Louisiana.
Identifiers: Red River(La), Atchafalaya River(La).

The dynamic relationship between stage and discharge which is unique to a particular flood for a selected station along the river can be determined via a mathematical model based on the complete one-dimensional equations of unsteady flow, i.e., the equations for the conservation of mass and momentum of the flood wave and the

Manning equation. By assuming the bulk of the flood wave moves as a kinematic wave, the need for spatial resolution of the flood can be eliminated, and only the time variation of either the discharge or stage at the selected station is necessary for the computation of the other. The mathematical model can be used in river forecasting to convert the forecast discharge hydrograph into a stage hydrograph which properly reflects the unique dynamic stage-discharge relationship produced by the variable energy slope of the flood discharge. The model can be used also in stream gaging to convert a recorded stage hydrograph into a discharge hydrograph which properly accounts for the effects of unsteady flow. A simple, easily-applied graphical procedure was provided for estimating the magnitude of the effect of the unsteady flow on stage-discharge ratings. (Dawes-ISWS)
W75-07932

ON THE IMPOSSIBILITY OF A PARTIAL MASS VIOLATION IN SURFACE RUNOFF SYSTEMS,
Technion-Israel Inst. of Tech., Haifa. Faculty of Civil Engineering.
M. H. Diskin, A. Boneh, and A. Golan.
Water Resources Research, Vol 11, No 2, p 236-244, April 1975. 9 fig, 9 ref.

Descriptors: *Surface runoff, *Systems analysis, *Rainfall-runoff relationships, Hydrographs, Hydrologic cycle, Hydrology, Flood flow, Hydrologic systems, Input-output analysis, Optimization, Theoretical analysis, Model studies.
Identifiers: *Mass conservation, Kernel functions. Linear systems, Watershed response functions.

The class of nonnegative, initially relaxed, and nonanticipating systems has many applications in engineering. A proof was given to a theorem stating that in this class of systems, if the input total mass is equal to the output total mass, then for any nonnegative input-output pair, the system fulfills also a partial mass condition. By applying this theorem to systems expressed by the Volterra series it was concluded that the input functions must be bounded. Two such bounds on the input functions were considered: (1) bounds resulting from the requirement of a nonnegative output and (2) bounds resulting from the mass-conserving property of the system. The theorem mentioned above implies that the set of input functions causing nonnegative output functions is a subset of the set of input functions that do not violate the mass-conserving property of the system. It is therefore clear that the bounds of type 1 are the dominant among the two bounds for any nonnegative input function. In a system expressed by an Nth order Volterra series the bounds on the input can be evaluated by solving a polynomial inequality of order N - 1. An example was given for a system expressed by a third-order Volterra series in which the bounds on the input form two regions. Explicit equations for the bounds of type 1 and 2 were derived for a second-order system. (Lee-ISWS)
W75-07934

NONLINEAR KINEMATIC WAVE APPROXIMATION FOR WATER ROUTING,
Colorado State Univ., Fort Collins. Dept. of Civil Engineering.
R-M. Li, D. B. Simons, and M. A. Stevens.
Water Resources Research, Vol 11, No 2, p 245-252, April 1975. 8 fig, 16 ref.

Descriptors: *Flood waves, *Overland flow, *Sheet flow, *Rainfall-runoff relationships, *Surface runoff, Hydrographs, Channel flow, Open channel flow, Storm runoff, Routing, Model studies, Simulation analysis, Rainfall, *Mathematical models.
Identifiers: *Kinematic waves, *Nonlinear waves, Watershed response.

A simple numerical model for both overland and channel water routing was presented. A second-order nonlinear scheme was developed to solve the kinematic wave equation with the boundary condition of time variant inflows. The numerical solutions agreed very well with analytical solutions which were available for some particular cases. This model includes the effects of rainfall on flow resistance and simulates hydrographs which agree very well with experimental results for both constant rainfall and variable rainfall cases. The interesting phenomena of 'pip' and 'dip' in overland flow hydrographs were successfully simulated. These phenomena were found to be the results of sudden changes of flow resistance due to ceasing or starting of rainfall. The same routing procedure for overland flow was employed to route flow in natural channels. (Lee-ISWS)
W75-07935

SHORT-PERIOD INTERNAL WAVES IN THE SEA,
L. M. Brekhovskikh, K. V. Konjaev, K. D. Sabinin, and A. N. Serikov.
Journal of Geophysical Research, Vol 80, No 6, p 856-864, February 20, 1975. 14 fig, 12 ref.

Descriptors: *Internal waves, *Oceans, *Thermocline, Frequency, Wavelengths, Statistical methods, Temperature, Measurement, Atlantic Ocean.
Identifiers: Spectra, Oscillations, Black Sea, Caspian Sea, Indian Ocean.

Results of measurements of short-period internal waves(periods less than one hour) in the seasonal thermocline in the Black and Caspian Seas and some regions of the Atlantic and Indian Oceans were discussed. The line sensors of temperature (i.e., pieces of wire whose electrical resistance varies in accordance with the average temperature of the layer between the ends of the sensor) were widely used. The lengths of the line sensors used varied from 1 to 100 m. Measurements were made with arrays of such sensors in the horizontal plane and along the vertical. Records obtained were much more regular than those of point temperature sensors and were easy to analyze. It appeared often that short-period internal waves exist as groups (trains) of quasi-harmonic oscillations. The frequency and wave number in the group are nonstable. The lowest mode of the oscillations is predominant. Sometimes the waves are standing ones. (Sims-ISWS)
W75-07976

WATER RESOURCES DEVELOPMENT BY THE U.S ARMY CORPS OF ENGINEERS IN ARIZONA,
Army Engineer District, San Francisco, Calif.
For primary bibliographic entry see Field 4A.
W75-07979

A LINEAR THEORY OF INTERNAL WAVE SPECTRA AND COHERENCES NEAR THE VAISALA FREQUENCY,
Woods Hole Oceanographic Institution, Mass.
Y. J. F. Desaubies.
Journal of Geophysical Research, Vol 80, No 6, p 895-899, February 20, 1975. 6 fig, 2 tab, 11 ref.

Descriptors: *Internal waves, *Oceans, *Model studies, *Theoretical analysis, Temperature, Velocity, Mathematical models, Energy.
Identifiers: *Spectra, Coherence, *Vaisala frequency.

Various internal wave frequency spectra of temperature, velocity, and coherences were computed by using linear wave functions and the energy model of Garrett and Munk. The emphasis was on the frequency range close to the Vaisala frequency n, where it was predicted that temperature spectra and coherence have a peak before a sharp cutoff. The model was strongly dependent on the local value of n, its vertical gradient, and the wave number bandwidth of the wave field. (Sims-ISWS)
W75-07985

A BOTTOM CURRENT ALONG THE SHELF BREAK,
University of East Anglia, Norwich (England). School of Mathematics and Physics.
J. A. Johnson, and P. D. Killworth.
Journal of Physical Oceanography, Vol 5, No 1, p 185-188, January 1975. 2 fig, 4 ref.

Descriptors: *Ocean circulation, *Continental shelf, Mathematical studies, Upwelling, Continental slope, Oceanography, Currents(Water).
Identifiers: *Ekman layer.

The theory of Hill and Johnson for upwelling over the shelf break was modified to give agreement with the work of Killworth. It was shown that when upwelling occurs over a discontinuity in bottom slope, this upwelling does not penetrate into the surface Ekman layer. Associated with this upwelling is a strong current along the shelf break in the bottom Ekman layer. (Sims-ISWS)
W75-07986

ENVIRONMENTAL ASSESSMENT OF SEDIMENT SOURCES AND SEDIMENTATION DISTRIBUTIONS FOR THE LAKE LA FARGE WATERHSED AND IMPOUNDMENT,
Wisconsin Univ., Madison. Dept. of Geography.
J. C. Knox, P. J. Bartlein, and W. C. Johnson.
In: IES Report 28, Environmental Analysis of the Kickapoo River Impoundment, p 77-116. 22 fig, 15 tab, 12 ref. DACW 37-C-0130.

Descriptors: *Sediment yield, *Sedimentation, *Reservoirs, Wisconsin, Tributaries, Sediment control, Climates, Deltas, Sands, Sediment transport, Sedimenation rates, Silts, Costs, Drainage patterns, Watershed management, Land use, Channel improvement, Spawning, Dams, Streams, Runoff.
Identifiers: *Kickapoo River(Wis), *La Farge Lake(Wis), Sediment traps.

Maps of the drainage network of Wisconsin's La Farge impoundment watershed and sub-basin watersheds were used to inventory the potential sediment yield from the sub-basin tributaries, identify potential sites for sedimentation control structures, and inventory costs of sediment control measures within the impoundment drainage network. During the monitoring period, there has been below average flooding, sediment pollution, and probably nutrient pollution, and a climatic shift toward cooler, wetter weather. The average yield of sediment to the reservoir is computed to be about 390 tons/sq mile of drainage. The most critical sediment problem will be formation of deltas where tributaries enter the impoundment. Recommendations include flood retention reservoirs as sediment traps in selected tributaries; fish spawning areas in the impoundment pool to be protected by maintaining suitable water levels, low-head dams and shaping of the valley floor for Weister Creek valley bottom, upland land use management and control of stream bank erosion. Further investigations should be undertaken to better calibrate the impact of climate regimes and climate variability as they control and modify the interactions among runoff, sediment yield, and nutrient pollution. (See also W75-08158) (Buchanan-Davidson–Wisconsin)
W75-08161

COMPARISON OF INTERMITTENT AND PERMANENT STREAMS OF CALCAREOUS PROVENCE, (IN FRENCH),
Aix-Marseille-1 Univ. (France). Lab. for Animal Biology-Ecology.
P. Legier, and J. Talin.
Ann Limnol, Vol 9, No 3, p 273-292, 1973. Illus.
Identifiers: *Calcareous provence, Diptera, Intermittent streams, Permanent streams, Phreatic sheet, *Streams, Trichoptera, *France, Dry periods, Biota.

Comparison of intermittent and permanent streams in France was made to determine their affinities. Stability of physical and chemical factors was observed in the permanent streams and in the lotic period of intermittent streams. The stagnant period of intermittent streams is unstable. The biotic comparisons show the affinities between permanent lentic streams and intermittent streams. Permanent lotic streams and intermittent streams show very little similarity. Some specific populations (e.g. Trichoptera, Diptera) can maintain themselves during the dry period only when the phreatic sheet is present in depth.--Copyright 1974, Biological Abstracts, Inc.
W75-08261

2F. Groundwater

ANNUAL WATER-RESOURCES REVIEW, WHITE SANDS MISSILE RANGE, 1974, A BASIC-DATA REPORT,
Geological Survey, Albuquerque, N Mex.
For primary bibliographic entry see Field 4B.
W75-07857

SOME UPPER MIOCENE AND PLIOCENE OSTRACODA OF ATLANTIC COASTAL REGION FOR USE IN THE HYDROGEOLOGIC STUDIES,
Geological Survey, Reston, Va.
F. M. Swain.
Supt of Documents, GPO, Washington, DC 20402, for $1.85. Professional Paper 821, 1974. 50 p, 1 fig, 13 plate, 1 tab, 118 ref.

Descriptors: *Stratigraphy, *Atlantic Coastal Plain, *Aquifers, Hydrogeology, Geologic formations, Geologic time, Geologic units, Southeast US.
Identifiers: *Ostracoda.

As a part of a U.S. Geological Survey research project dealing with the permeability of sedimentary rocks in the Atlantic Coastal Plain, the Ostracoda were studied from many surface localities and well samples. Upper Miocene and Pliocene outcrop samples from North Carolina and Virginia yielded 63 species and seven subspecies of Ostracoda. The stratigraphic distribution of the species indicates the presence of an assemblage, the Aurila conradi-Thaerocythere schmidtae assemblage, that also extends into the Pliocene in southern North Carolina and South Carolina. A subassemblage, the Radimella confragosa subassemblage, represents the upper Miocene and Pliocene in southern North Carolina and in South Carolina. T. schmidtae appears to represent a cooler water subassemblage of the upper Miocene in northern North Carolina, Virginia, and southernmost Maryland. Two new genera, two new species, and one new subspecies are described. The new genera are Prodictyocythere, n. gen., and Shattuckocythere, n. gen. The new species are Murrayina macleani, n. sp., and Prodictyocythere trapezoidalis, n. sp. The new subspecies is Pontocythere agricola duopunctata, n. subsp. (Knapp-USGS)
W75-07860

HYDROGEOLOGIC AND WATER-QUALITY DATA IN WESTERN JEFFERSON COUNTY, COLORADO,
Geological Survey, Denver, Colo.
W. E. Hofstra, and D. C. Hall.
Colorado Water Resources Basic-Data Release No 36, 1975. 51 p, 2 fig, 12 tab, 8 ref.

Descriptors: *Basic data collections, *Hydrologic data, *Colorado, Surface waters, Groundwater, Water quality, Streamflow, Water wells.
Identifiers: *Jefferson County(Colo).

Information is presented on the availability of water for domestic supply in the mountainous area in Jefferson County, Colo. The area covered by the study is roughly 300 square miles of mountainous Jefferson County extending from Clear Creek on the north to the Pike National Forest boundary on the south and from the east edge of the Front Range mountains to the western boundary of the county. The population of the mountainous part of the county was roughly 20,000 in 1974. Hydrologic data were collected at 34 streamflow sites. Bacteriological and chemical analyses of surface waters are given for 32 sites. During the study, 31 springs and 727 wells were sampled. Comprehensive bacteriological and chemical analyses of samples collected from 38 wells and 1 spring are given. Eleven test wells were drilled by air-percussion. Geologic logs and hydrologic test data for these wells are given. (Knapp-USGS)
W75-07862

GROUND-WATER RESOURCES OF THE WESTERN OSWEGO RIVER BASIN, NEW YORK,
Geological Survey, Albany, N.Y.
L. J. Crain.
New York State Department of Environmental Conservation, Albany, Basin Planning Report ORB-5, 1974. 137 p, 26 fig, 3 plate, 7 tab, 54 ref.

Descriptors: *Water resources, *Groundwater, *New York, Glacial drift, Alluvial channels, Lakes, Surface-groundwater relationships, Water yield, Hydrologic data, Basic data collections.
Identifiers: *Oswego River Basin(NY).

Groundwater occurrence, aquifer yield, and geology are described for the 2,600-square mile area of the Western Oswego River basin in central New York, which includes the drainage basins of the four largest Finger Lakes: Cayuga, Seneca, Keuka, and Canandaigua. Aquifer data are summarized in geologic sections, diagrams, and maximum yield maps. Groundwater is generally available throughout the basin in quantities sufficient for domestic and farm supplies and, in many places, in quantities sufficient for municipal and industrial supplies. Nine to 12 mgd of groundwater is used in the basin, and several times this amount is available for future development. The principal aquifers are unconsolidated glacial sand and gravel deposits in the large valleys of the southern half of the basin, where well yields of 1,000 gpm or more are possible. In the northern part of the basin, the most important sources of groundwater are deposits adjacent to and in hydraulic contact with the Barge Canal. Direct groundwater recharge from precipitation ranges from about 20 million gallons per year per square mile for areas underlain by glacial till to 262 million gallons per year per square mile for areas underlain by sand and gravel in the south. (Knapp-USGS)
W75-07864

GENESIS OF HYDROGEOCHEMICAL FACIES OF GROUND WATERS IN THE PUNJAB REGION OF PAKISTAN,
Geological Survey, Washington, D.C.
For primary bibliographic entry see Field 5B.
W75-07865

KARST HYDROLOGY OF NORTHERN YUCATAN PENINSULA, MEXICO,
Geological Survey, Reston, Va.
V. T. Stringfield, and H. E. LeGrand.
In: Field Seminar on Water and Carbonate Rocks of the Yucatan Peninsula, Mexico; published for Field Trip 2, 1974 Annual Meeting, Miami, of the Geological Society of America: New Orleans Geological Society, p 26-44, 1974. 2 fig, 37 ref.

Descriptors: *Karst hydrology, *Hydrogeology, *Mexico, Water chemistry, Saline water intrusion, Surface-groundwater relationships, Groundwater movement.
Identifiers: *Yucatan(Mexico).

Northern Yucatan is underlain by nearly horizontal Tertiary formations consisting chiefly of limestone and other soluble rocks. Karst features in Yucatan may be divided into two groups: (1) surficial features that do not extend more than a few meters below the surface, and (2) deep features as sinkholes, solution shafts, and solution cavities that affect the permeability of the rocks and circulation of the water far below the surface. Many of the numerous sinkholes in the limestone are natural water wells known as cenotes which were a source of water for the Mayan cities. At Chichen Itza one cenote was used for water supply and one was used for sacrifice. Although the annual rainfall is as much as 2,000 mm, there are no surface streams because water on the surface moves freely into the underlying limestone. After reaching the zone of saturation in the limestone, the water moves laterally to the coast where part of it is discharged through cenotes and other openings. Such discharge is controlled in part by the relation of the freshwater head of the aquifer to the head of seawater. Although the altitude of the water level in the limestone aquifer away from the coast is not more than a few meters, it is sufficient to prevent seawater encroachment in the upper part of the aquifer. However, it apparently is not sufficient to keep seawater out of the lower part of the aquifer throughout the peninsula. (Knapp-USGS)
W75-07873

ENVIRONMENTAL TRITIUM IN THE EDWARDS AQUIFER, CENTRAL TEXAS, 1963-71,
Geological Survey, Reston, Va.
For primary bibliographic entry see Field 5B.
W75-07885

INDEX OF CURRENT WATER RESOURCES PROJECTS AND DATA COLLECTION ACTIVITIES IN OHIO, 1975.
Geological Survey, Columbus, Ohio.
For primary bibliographic entry see Field 7C.
W75-07886

THE RELEVANCE OF AQUIFER-FLOW MECHANISMS TO EXPLORATION AND DEVELOPMENT OF GROUNDWATER RESOURCES,
Department of Aquifer-Flow Mechanisms to Exploration and Development of Groundwater Resources,
For primary bibliographic entry see Field 4B.
W75-07896

DIGITAL SIMULATION MODEL OF AQUIFER RESPONSE TO STREAM STAGE FLUCTUATION,
California Univ., Davis. Dept. of Water Science and Engineering.
M. A. Marino.
Journal of Hydrology, Vol 25, No 1/2, p 51-58, April 1975. 6 fig, 7 ref, 1 append.

Descriptors: *Computer models, *Surface-groundwater relationships, Streams, Water table aquifers, Water level fluctuations, Numerical analysis, Groundwater movement, Hydraulic properties, Hydraulic conductivity, Boundaries(Surfaces), Equations, Aquifers, *Simulation analysis.
Identifiers: *Aquifer response, *Semipervious stream banks, Predictor-corrector scheme, Nonuniform grid, Dimensionless variables.

A digital computer model was presented that simulates the response of an unconfined aquifer to changes in stream stage. The aquifer was considered to be finite, homogeneous, and isotropic. The stream was considered to have semipervious banks. The hydraulic conductivity of the semipervious layer of the streambed was assumed smaller than that of the aquifer, and the storage capacity of the semipervious layer was assumed insignifi-

cant. Numerical solutions describing the water level fluctuation in the aquifer due to an arbitrarily varying flood pulse in the stream are obtained by a predictor-corrector scheme with a nonuniform grid spacing. The numerical scheme is unconditionally stable. (Visocky-ISWS)
W75-07897

GROUND-WATER POLLUTION BY WOOD WASTE DISPOSAL,
Oregon State Engineer's Office, Salem.
For primary bibliographic entry see Field 5B.
W75-07951

FLUORINE IN GROUND WATER AS A GUIDE TO PB-ZN-BA-F MINERALIZATION,
Toronto Univ. (Ontario). Dept. of Geology.
For primary bibliographic entry see Field 2K.
W75-07953

A STUDY OF CONVECTIVE-DISPERSION EQUATION BY ISOPARAMETRIC FINITE ELEMENTS,
State Univ. of New York, Buffalo. Faculty of Engineering and Applied Sciences.
For primary bibliographic entry see Field 5B.
W75-08009

DENITRIFICATION IN LABORATORY SANDY COLUMNS,
Soil Conservation Service, Effingham, Ill.
For primary bibliographic entry see Field 5B.
W75-08189

THE KINETICS OF MINERAL DISSOLUTION IN CARBONATE AQUIFERS AS A TOOL FOR HYDROLOGICAL INVESTIGATIONS, I. CONCENTRATION-TIME RELATIONSHIPS,
Water Planning for Israel Ltd., Tel-Aviv.
For primary bibliographic entry see Field 2K.
W75-08190

A GALERKIN-FINITE ELEMENT TECHNIQUE FOR CALCULATING THE TRANSIENT POSITION OF THE SALTWATER FRONT,
Princeton Univ., N.J. Dept. of Civil and Geological Engineering.
For primary bibliographic entry see Field 5B.
W75-08195

2G. Water In Soils

THE INFLUENCE OF WIND VELOCITY ON THE SIZE DISTRIBUTIONS OF AEROSOLS GENERATED BY THE WIND EROSION OF SOILS,
National Center for Atmospheric Research, Boulder, Colo.
For primary bibliographic entry see Field 2J.
W75-07915

MICROSCALE TRANSPORT OF SAND-SIZED SOIL AGGREGATES ERODED BY WIND,
National Center for Atmospheric Research, Boulder, Colo.
For primary bibliographic entry see Field 2J.
W75-07916

POND WATER QUALITY IN A CLAYPAN SOIL,
Illinois Univ., Urbana. Dept. of Agricultural Engineering.
For primary bibliographic entry see Field 5B.
W75-07924

FINITE ELEMENT ANALYSIS OF TWO-DIMENSIONAL FLOW IN SOILS CONSIDERING WATER UPTAKE BY ROOTS: I. THEORY,
Agricultural Research Organization, Bet-Dagan (Israel). Inst. of Soils and Water.
S. P. Neuman, R. A. Feddes, and E. Bresler.
Soil Science Society of American Proceedings, Vol 39, No 2, p 224-230, March-April 1975. 3 fig, 1 tab, 8 ref, 1 append.

Descriptors: *Finite element analysis, *Soil water movement, *Unsaturated flow, *Soil-water-plant relationships, *Root systems, Absorption, Numerical analysis, Mathematical models, Soil moisture, Porous media, Hydraulic conductivity, Flow, Air-earth interfaces, Boundaries(Surfaces), Seepage, Infiltration, Anisotropy, Equations, Evaporation.
Identifiers: *Two-dimensional flow, *Galerkin method, Soil-root interface, Weighted residuals, Iteration, Convergence.

The problem of two-dimensional nonsteady flow of water in unsaturated and partly saturates porous media was solved by a Galerkin-type finite element approach. Particular emphasis was placed on the simulation of atmospheric boundaries and on water uptake by plant roots. The finite element method was shown to have several advantages over conventional finite difference techniques. It can easily handle nonuniform flow regions having irregular boundaries and arbitrary degrees of local anisotropy. Nonlinear atmospheric boundary conditions along evaporation or infiltration surfaces and along seepage faces were handled by a unique procedure. This iterative procedure relies on the ease with which flux normal or any boundary of the flow region is assigned in the finite element approach. Experience with this method indicates that rapid rates of convergence can be achieved in many cases. (See also W75-07942) (Visocky-ISWS)
W75-07941

FINITE ELEMENT ANALYSIS OF TWO-DIMENSIONAL FLOW IN SOILS CONSIDERING WATER UPTAKE BY ROOTS: II. FIELD APPLICATIONS,
Institute for Land and Water Management Research, Wageningen (Netherlands).
R. A. Feddes, S. P. Neuman, and E. Bresler.
Soil Science Society of America Proceedings, Vol 39, No 2, p 231-237, March-April 1975. 12 fig, 6 ref.

Descriptors: *On-site tests, *Field crops, *Mathematical models, *Finite element analysis, *Soil water movement, Unsaturated flow, Soil-water-plant relationships, Root systems, Anisotropy, Absorption, Numerical analysis, Soil moisture, Hydraulic conductivity, Evapotranspiration, Ditches, Water table, Soil properties, Hydraulic gradient, Infiltration, Simulation analysis.
Identifiers: *Red cabbage.

Part I described a Galerkin-type finite element approach to the simulation of two-dimensional transient flow in saturated-unsaturated soils considering evaporation and water uptake by roots. The purpose of Part II was to verify the numerical model against field measurements, to compare the results with those obtained by a finite difference technique, and to show how the finite element method can be applied to complex but realistic two-dimensional flow situations. Two examples were given. The first concerns one-dimensional flow and it compares numerical results with those obtained experimentally in the field from water balance studies on red cabbage (Brassica oleracea L. 'Rode Herfst') grown on a clay soil in the presence of a water table. The second example describes two-dimensional flow in a complex field situation in The Netherlands where flow takes place under cropped field conditions through five anisotropic layers. Water is supplied to the system by infiltration from two unlined ditches and is withdrawn from the system by evapotranspiration and by leakage to an underlying pumped aquifer. (See also W75-07941) (Visocky-ISWS)
W75-07942

EVALUATING SURFACE-SOIL WATER CONTENT BY MEASURING REFLECTANCE,
Agricultural Research Service, Manhattan, Kans.
E. L. Skidmore, J. D. Dickerson, and H. Schimmelpfennig.
Soil Science Society of American Proceedings, Vol 39, No 2, p 238-242, March-April 1975. 7 fig, 1 tab, 24 ref.

Descriptors: *Soil moisture meters, *Soil moisture, *Instrumentation, Soil water, Soil surfaces, Reflectance, Soil erosion, Infrared radiation, Soils, Soil properties.
Identifiers: *Reflectometers, Integrating sphere, Light chopper, Infrared detectors.

Water's property to absorb certain wavelengths in the near infrared was the basis for developing a reflectometer to measure reflectance of near-infrared radiation from a soil surface. The reflectometer's essential elements include: source of infrared radiation, optical system, integrating sphere, detector, light chopper, amplifier, and meter system. The radiation from an incandescent lamp was filtered with a narrow-band pass filter, chopped, and allowed to strike the test surface where it was either absorbed or reflected onto the surface of the integrating sphere. The intensity of the reflected radiation was measured with a lead sulfide detector and appropriate amplifer and meter. The reflectance as a function of water content was measured for filter paper and several soils at 1.30, 1.45, 1.65, and 1.95 micrometers. Although at low water contents soil properties (other than water content) strongly influenced soil reflectance, at 1.95-micrometer wavelength--the most prominent absorption band of liquid water--the reflectance-water content relationship tended to be log-linear. (Sims-ISWS)
W75-07943

DRAINAGE CHARACTERISTICS OF SOILS,
Colorado State Univ., Fort Collins. Dept. of Agricultural Engineering.
A. T. Corey, and R. H. Brooks.
Soil Science Society of America Proceedings, Vol 39, No 2, p 251-255, March-April 1975. 5 fig, 12 ref.

Descriptors: *Soil moisture, *Soil water movement, *Conductivity, *Pore pressure, Drainage effects, Percolation, Moisture tension, Moisture content, Negative pore pressure, *Drainage.
Identifiers: Soil water suction.

Evidence was obtained indicating that neither water conductivity nor water content are single-valued functions of soil water suction during a period in which soil is draining continuously. Functional relationships between water conductivity and soil water suction measured during continuous drainage were found to be different from those frequently observed during steady-state experiments. During drainage, a finite suction is recorded before a soil begins to desaturate and this suction is often larger than the suction existing immediately after drainage starts. It was postulated that the reduction in suction is a result of air reaching larger (previously isolated) pores. (Gibb-ISWS)
W75-07944

PREDICTION OF INFILTRATION OF WATER INTO AGGREGATED CLAY SOIL SAMPLES,
Macdonald Coll., Ste. Anne de Bellevue (Quebec). Dept. of Soil Science.
F. A. Gumbs, and B. P. Warkentin.
Soil Science Society of America Proceedings, Vol 39, No 2, p 255-263, March-April 1975. 12 fig, 4 tab, 20 ref.

Descriptors: *Soil properties, *Infiltration, *Aggregates, Model studies, Laboratory tests, Hysteresis, Conductivity, Diffusivity, Soil pressure, Retention, Wetting, Drying, Moisture content, Percolation, Gravity, Tensiometers, Bulk density, Stability, Sampling.
Identifiers: *Soil columns, *Diffusion equation, Pore size distribution.

Physical properties--stability, water retention, diffusivity, and conductivity--relevant to the study of infiltration into aggregated media were measured for four aggregate sizes. These media were considered stable to infiltration. The hysteresis in moisture retention, equilibrium moisture retention curves, and the changes in moisture retention with time were measured for confined and unconfined samples of the aggregates. Wetting and drying diffusivities and conductivities were also measured and used in the prediction of horizontal and vertical infiltration under zero and small negative pressures into columns of each aggregate size by using the diffusion equation. Diffusivities and conductivities were larger on wetting than on drying and generally larger in unconfined than in confined samples. Horizontal and vertical infiltration were reasonably well predicted when water infiltrated under negative pressure and the diffusivities and conductivities used were calculated from infiltration profiles developed under the same water tension. For these media, the values of water tension, diffusivity, and conductivity at any water content depend on the rate of wetting. The values to be used in the prediction of infiltration must therefore be measured for times of wetting which correspond to the duration of infiltration. The classical diffusion equation can be used to predict infiltration into aggregated clay soils if the correct diffusivities and conductivities are used. (Schicht-ISWS)
W75-07945

SOIL MOISTURE MEASUREMENT AND ASSESSMENT,
Australian Water Resources Council, Canberra.
Australian Water Resources Council Hydrological Series No 9, 1974. 44 p, 2 fig, 53 ref, 1 append.

Descriptors: *Soil moisture, *Measurement, *Instrumentation, Methodology, Soil water, Capillary water, Soil moisture meters, Nuclear moisture meters, Tensiometers, Gravimetric analysis, Sampling, Australia.

Procedures for the measurement of soil moisture were discussed. Instrumentation was evaluated, and the economics of various methods were described. Some of the conclusions were: (1) Soil moisture content measurements are best made by using the gamma ray absorption method in the laboratory and the neutron thermalization method in the field. These methodss may be supplemented by gravimetric sampling. (2) Soil moisture potential is best measured by using tensiometers or thermocouple psychrometers either in the laboratory or the field. The choice of method will be determined by the range of expected values. (3) Stored soil moisture should be determined by using the neutron thermalization method in permanent access tubes. (Sims-ISWS)
W75-07952

A PATTERN OF HUMUS HORIZON IN TUNDRA'S LOAMY SOILS IN THE NORTHEASTERN EUROPEAN TUNDRA,
For primary bibliographic entry see Field 2C.
W75-07969

EFFECT OF INTERACTION OF FACTORS ON WILT OF CORIANDER CAUSED BY FUSARIUM OXYSPORUM SCHLECHT EX. FR. F. CORIANDERII KULKARNI, NIKAN ET JOSHI,
Rajasthan Agriculture Dept., Kota (India).
For primary bibliographic entry see Field 2I.
W75-07983

MOVEMENT OF TWO NONIONIC SURFACTANTS IN WETTABLE AND WATER-REPELLENT SOILS,
California Univ., Riverside. Dept. of Soil Science and Agricultural Engineering.
W. W. Miller, N. Valoras, and J. Letey.
Soil Science Society of America Proceedings, Vol 39, No 1, p 11-16, January-February 1975. 7 fig, 1 tab, 11 ref. OWRR B-072-CAL(10), B-141-CAL(1).

Descriptors: *Surfactants, *Leaching, Soil properties, *Soil water movement, Wettability, Hydrodynamics, Conductivity, Adsorption, Percolation, Infiltration, Permeability, Porous media.
Identifiers: *Nonionic surfactants, *Hydrophobic soils, *Water repellancy.

The movement of two nonionic surfactants (Soil Penetrant 3685, Aqua Gro) and their effect on water flow through wettable and water repellent soils was investigated. Surfactant concentrations of 0, 100, 500, 1000, 1600, and 3200 ppm were applied to the top of vertical soil columns and the concentration of surfactant in the column effluent was measured. When the concentration of surfactant in the effluent did not significantly change with time, leaching of the columns with tap water was initiated. Both surfactants affected the hydraulic conductivity of the hydrophobic soil. The conductivity effects appeared to be related to aggregate destabilization, micelle formation, and particle migration, all of which caused a general decrease of flow rates with time. Adsorptive characteristics were found to affect greatly the shape of the effluent concentration versus time curve. Aqua Gro was shown to be more strongly adsorbed and less subject to leaching than was Soil Penetrant. A theoretical model was tested for its ability to qualitatively predict experimental effluent concentrations. Allowing for the spreading effects of dispersion, there was reasonable agreement between most experimental and theoretical values. The behavior and movement of surfactants in soils are a function of adsorption isotherms, mixing or dispersion due to flow velocities, solute concentration, and the physical and chemical characteristics of the porous medium. (Sanderson-ISWS)
W75-07984

DISTRIBUTION OF NONIONIC SURFACTANT IN SOIL COLUMNS FOLLOWING APPLICATION AND LEACHING,
California Univ., Riverside.
W. W. Miller, and J. Letey.
Soil Science Society of America Proceedings, Vol 39, No 1, p 17-22, January-February 1975. 7 fig, 1 tab, 6 ref. OWRR B-072-CAL(11) and B-141-CAL(8).

Descriptors: *Surfactants, *Agricultural chemicals, *Infiltration, *Percolation, Wettability, Wetting, Soil physical properties, Leaching, Penetration, Seepage, Permeability, Soil properties, Adsorption, Conductivity, Distribution patterns.
Identifiers: *Water repellency, *Water drop penetration time, *Nonionic surfactants.

The distribution of 14C-tagged surfactant (Soil Penetrant) was observed in soil columns following application of various concentrations and leaching under unsaturated flow on wettable (Pachappa) and water-repellent (Morris Dam) soils. The maximum depth of surfactant penetration for a given leaching period was greater for Pachappa than for Morris Dam. Following leaching there was a more uniform distribution of surfactant throughout the column of Pachappa soil. Water drop penetration time (WDPT) experiments showed good correlation between experimental distribution as determined by 14C tracing and actual reduction of water repellency to a given depth. Consequently, the movement and distribution characteristics of a non-14C-tagged surfactant (Aqua Gro) on the Morris Dam soil following application and leaching was qualitatively examined by the WDPT method. A theoretical model was tested for its ability to qualitatively predict experimental Soil Penetrant distributions. There was reasonable agreement between experimental and calculated distributions. Specific adsorptive characteristics at low equilibrium concentrations were found to be very important to surfactant distribution in a given soil. (Sanderson-ISWS)
W75-07987

FLOW AND RETENTION OF WATER IN THE STRATIFIED SOILS OF THE OROVADA, NEVADA, AREA,
Nevada Univ., Reno. Dept. of Soil Science.
G. B. Muckel.
Available from the National Technical Information Service, Springfield, Va 22161, as PB-241 979, $5.25 in paper copy, $2.25 in microfiche. Ms Thesis, June 1974. 98 p, 32 fig, 19 tab, 39 ref, append. OWRR A-031-NEV(1).

Descriptors: *Flow, *Retention, *Water storage, *Stratification, *Soil types, *Nevada, Groundwater, Infiltration, Moisture tension, Soil moisture, Soil water, Movement, Irrigation water, Irrigation operation and maintenance, Plant growth, Soil-water-plant relationships, Laboratory tests, Permeameters, On-site data collections.
Identifiers: *Orovada area(Nev), *Neutron probes, *Alfalfa seed production, Plant yield.

Stratified soils of the Orovada area hold more water than predicted by an estimate based on uniform soils. The amount of available water held by three different soils was found. The Rebel-like soil held 21.8% by volume, the Orovada-like soil 23.2%, and the Bloor-like soil 21.4%. These values, determined by field tests, were higher than the available water contents estimated by measurements of each layer made in the laboratory. They demonstrate that the available water retained by a soil is determined by characteristics of the soil that are destroyed during sampling and sample preparation. In four instances, the greatest increase of available water per unit depth of soil was found in the soil adjacent to a coarse layer. There was not an increase adjacent to a coarse layer in three instances. Due to the area of sensitivity of the neutron probe, exact amounts of water at point locations could not be determined. Rates of water movement were determined. The unsaturated hydraulic conductivities calculated from field measurements seemed erratic, possibly because all flow was assumed vertical. Nonuniformity of soil within the basins used in the field tests could also account for some inconsistency. Measurements of water content at point locations within a soil are needed for determination of unsaturated hydraulic conductivity. The neutron probe does not measure soil water content at point locations but averages it in the probe's sphere of sensitivity. These findings are part of the basic data needed to correctly assess the frequency and dates of irrigation to provide the moisture requirements for alfalfa seed production. (Prickett-ISWS)
W75-07991

METHODS FOR CALCULATING UNSATURATED HYDRAULIC CONDUCTIVITY AND SOIL WATER DIFFUSIVITY DURING VERTICAL INFILTRATION IN A DRY SOIL,
Ghent Rijksuniversiteit (Belgium). Soil Physics, o l Conditioning and Horticultural Soil Sciences Lab.
H. Verplancke, and M. De Boodt.
Meded Fac Landbouwwet Rijksuniv Gent. Vol 38, No 2, p 440-449, 1973, Illus.
Identifiers: Dry soils, *Hydraulic conductivity, *Infiltration, *Soil water diffusivity, Methodology.

Two methods were used for calculating the unsaturated hydraulic conductivity (k) and the soil water diffusivity (D) during vertical soil water infiltration after irrigation. The values of k and D were obtained in 2 ways: according to a theory of

Gardner (1970) and according to a theory of De Boodt et al (1967). These methods are based on complete different theories. Gardner proposed a method to calculate the soil water diffusivity in the field during drainage of a wetted profile from the time rate of decrease of the matric potential at several depths in the profile. De Boodt et al. published a method where the unsaturated hydraulic conductivity can be calculated by using Darcy's law. The matric potential and volumetric water content of a field soil was determined with simply constructed electrical resistance units. The obtained soil water contents were compared with those determined with the neutron method. Both methods yield reasonably satisfactory values for the unsaturated hydraulic conductivity.–Copyright 1974, Biological Abstracts, Inc.
W75-08064

MICROMORPHOLOGY OF TWO SOIL PROFILES IN FUDHALIYAH,
Foundation of Scientific Research, Baghdad (Iraq).
A. H. Al-Rawi, and M. Knibbe.
Institute for Applied Research on Natural Resources, Abu-Ghraib, Iraq, Technical Bulletin 53, November 1973. 28 p, 3 tab, 5 fig, 3 append, 7 ref.

Descriptors: *Soil physical properties, *Soil profiles, *Salinity, Soil structure, Land reclamation, Soil formation, Irrigation, Hydraulic conductivity, Aeration, Calcite, Carbonates.
Identifiers: *Iraq(Fudhaliyah).

Micromorphology studies of soil formation in Fudhaliyah were carried out to determine reclamation potential. Two representative soil profiles were selected, one with favorable physical properties and one without. Data were collected on soil porosity, structure, salinity, and other features. Both soils developed in young alluvial deposits, mainly from irrigation water. As a result both have weak structure development, although one was considerably more saline. Soil porosity was low and although aeration was sufficient, hydraulic conductivity is expected to be too low to allow sufficient leaching of harmful salts. Recommendations include extending studies to other sample areas of large land reclamation areas of the Lower Mesopotamian Plain. (Mastic-Arizona)
W75-08118

PREDICTING VERTICAL MOVEMENT OF MANURIAL NITROGEN IN SOIL,
Cornell Univ., Ithaca, N.Y. Dept. of Agricultural Engineering.
For primary bibliographic entry see Field 5B.
W75-08192

SEASONAL VARIATION IN SOME PHYSICAL, CHEMICAL, AND MICROBIOLOGICAL CHARACTERISTICS OF A SALINE AND A NON-SALINE SOIL NEAR ABU-GHRAIB, IRAQ,
Foundation of Scientific Research, Baghdad (Iraq).
Y. Z. Ishac, and A. N. Yousef.
Institute for Applied Research on Natural Resources, Baghdad, Technical Bulletin No. 49, November 1973. 37 p, 19 tab, 30 ref.

Descriptors: *Saline soils, *Soil microbiology, *Soil bacteria, *Seasonal, *Salinization, *Soil temperature, *Soil microorganisms, *Soil physical properties, *Alkalinity, *Soil moisture.
Identifiers: *Iraq.

A comparison was made of some physicochemical and microbiological properties of a saline and a non-saline soil in order to study seasonal changes in soil properties that may be related to salinity. Non-saline cultivated soil supported higher numbers of different physiological groups of bacteria than uncultivated saline soil. Microbial activity was correlated with the amounts of organic matter present, especially in the cultivated soil. Maximum bacterial counts were recorded in the spring and autumn, while minimum counts occurred in winter and summer. Salinity proved the major factor limiting microbial activity in uncultivated soil. (Mastic-Arizona)
W75-08199

UTILIZING CLIMATE-MOISTURE-WATER USE RELATIONSHIPS IN IMPROVING SOIL MOISTURE BUDGET METHOD FOR IRRIGATION SCHEDULING,
Punjabrao Krishi Vidyapeeth, Akola (India). Dept. of Agronomy.
For primary bibliographic entry see Field 2D.
W75-08275

SOME ENZYME AND RESPIRATORY ACTIVITIES OF TROPICAL SOILS FROM NEW HEBRIDES,
Department of Scientific and Industrial Research, Lower Hutt (New Zealand). Soil Bureau.
D. J. Ross.
Soil Biol Biochem, Vol 5, No 5, p 559-567, 1973.

Descriptors: *Enzymes, *Soil chemistry, Soil bacteria, Soil moisture.
Identifiers: Amylase, Dehydrogenase, *New hebrides, Invertase, Soil enzymes, Tropical soils, Soil respiration.

Activities of invertase and amylase and respiratory activities of samples of 11 soils from New Herbrides were determined. The soils mostly were under forest and were acid with medium to low C/N ratios. Invertase activities were rather low but amylase activities were similar to those found in New Zealand soils. The ratio of invertase to amylase activities were mostly low. O_2 uptakes mostly responded markedly to glucose. Most values of respiratory quotients were about 1.0. Most, but not all, dehydrogenase activities were strongly related to O_2 uptakes. On an organic C basis, these respiratory activities declined with the depths to which the soils were sampled. Biochemical activities were mostly similar in forest soils derived from basalt and from andesite. Invertase activities were lower in soils under forest than under grassland covers. All biochemical activities were correlated significantly with contents of soil moisture and organic C, less with numbers of aerobic bacteria, and negatively with soil pH. On an organie C basis, none of the biochemical activities was significantly correlated with either soil moisture content or pH.--Copyright 1974, Biological Abstracts, Inc.
W75-08316

MOVEMENT AND PERSISTENCE OF BENSULIDE AND TRIFLURALIN IN IRRIGATED SOIL,
Agricultural Research Service, Weslaco, Tex. Lower Rio Grande Valley Research and Extension Center.
For primary bibliographic entry see Field 5B.
W75-08318

THE INFLUENCE OF SOIL WATER CONTENT ON THE UPTAKE OF IONS BY ROOTS: I. SOIL WATER CONTENT GRADIENTS NEAR A PLANE OF ONION ROOTS,
Nottingham Univ. (England). School of Agriculture.
For primary bibliographic entry see Field 2I.
W75-08330

EXTRACTION OF SOIL SOLUTION FROM FLOODED SOIL USING A POROUS PLASTIC FILTER,
Texas A and M Univ., College Station. Dept. of Soil and Crop Sciences.
For primary bibliographic entry see Field 5G.
W75-08335

IRON AND PHOSPHORUS INTERACTION IN CALCAREOUS SOILS: II. EFFECT ON CHLOROSIS DEVELOPMENT, AND SOME NUTRIENT ELEMENT CONTENTS IN SOIL AND PLANT,
Ain Shams Univ., Cairo (Egypt). Dept. of Soils.
A. M. Elgala, H. Hamdi, M. Omar, and I. Wafik.
U A R J Soil Sci, Vol 11, No 2, p 259-269, 1971.

Descriptors: Corn, Iron, Phosphorus, Soils, Soil-water-plant relationship, *Calcareous soils, *Irrigation effects.
Identifiers: *Chlorosis, Zea-mays.

In pot experiments using corn (Zea mays single cross 51), attempts were made to evaluate the interaction of iron and phosphorus in soil under high calcium carbonate and various levels of soil moisture in relation to chlorosis development and nutrient balance of growing plants. Four levels of phosphorus; P0, P1, P2 and P3 at a concentration of 0.000, 0.033, 0.066 and 1.132 g P/pot, respectively, were used and 4 levels of Fe; Fe0, Fe3, Fe2 and Fe1 at a concentration of 0, 1, 5 and 10 ppm Fe in the soil, respectively. Three levels of moisture M1, M2, M3 representing the 50%, 100% and 150% of the field capacity, respectively, were applied. The plants were harvested 1 mo. from germination. Available Fe increased by increasing the Fe level, but decreased by increasing the P rate. At any rate of Fe applied, the addition of P decreased Fe in soil. This decrease is more pronounced when Fe was applied at the Fe3 level. With respect to soil moisture, there was a slight increase and a pronounced decrease in the amounts of available Fe under M2 and M3, respectively, as compared to that under M1. Available P in the soil increased by increasing the P rate. The application of Fe had no effect on these values. Increasing soil moisture to the M2 and M3 levels generally increased available P over the M1 level. The combined effect of applied P and moisture on available P was more pronounced than that of P and Fe. Excessive irrigation may indirectly aggravate chlorosis by increasing soluble P or disturb the balance among nutrients in soil and plant.–Copyright 1973, Biological Abstracts, Inc.
W75-08344

RETENTIOS AND RELEASE OF PHOSPHORUS IN CERTAIN CALCAREOUS SOILS OF THE U.A.R. (UNITED ARAB REPUBLIC): I. THE INFLUENCE OF INCUBATION PROCESS AND CYCLES OF WETTING AND DRYING,
Ain Shams Univ., Cairo (Egypt). Dept. of Soils.
For primary bibliographic entry see Field 5B.
W75-08350

2H. Lakes

WATER BALANCE OF LAKE KERR–A DEDUCTIVE STUDY OF A LANDLOCKED LAKE IN NORTH-CENTRAL FLORIDA,
Geological Survey, Tallahassee, Fla.
G. H. Hughes.
Florida Bureau of Geology, Tallahassee, Report of Investigations No 73, 1974. 49 p, 18 fig, 6 tab, 11 ref.

Descriptors: *Water balance, *Lakes, *Florida, Evaporation, Hydrologic budget, Inflow, Precipitation(Atmospheric), Runoff, Discharge(Water).
Identifiers: *Lake Kerr(Fla).

Estimates of average yearly lake evaporation were compared with records of pan evaporation and lake-level changes as a basis for making estimates of the importance of various factors in yearly and monthly evaporation from Lake Kerr, Florida. The monthly change in lake level was computed for 1962-69 from estimates of rainfall evaporation, leakage, surface-water and groundwater inflow. Although leakage is known to vary, it was assumed to be constant at 0.1 foot per month. Sur-

face-water and groundwater inflows were estimated as zero, even though they may occur at times. The computed monthly change in level was within 0.10 foot of the observed change in level about 70 percent of the time. Errors substantially greater than 0.10 foot were somewhat erratically distributed in time. Almost all of the large errors indicated inflow not accounted for by the estimates. The absence of pronounced seasonal variation in errors less than 0.10 foot suggested that groundwater inflow played a relatively minor role in the water balance. Variations in leakage and groundwater inflow were accounted for by regression methods relating leakage and groundwater inflow to the difference between the lake stage and the level of water in a well tapping the same aquifer that underlies Lake Kerr. Lake evaporation is estimated to average about 46 inches per year. During 1962-69, leakage from Lake Kerr was about 12 inches greater than groundwater inflow. If this 12-inch difference is representative of the long-term average, surface-water inflow averaging about 4 inches per year is required to maintain the water balance. (Knapp-USGS)
W75-07881

A THEORY OF STEADY WIND-DRIVEN CURRENTS IN SHALLOW WATER WITH VARIABLE EDDY VISCOSITY,
Rochester Univ., N.Y. Dept. of Mechanical and Aerospace Sciences.
J. H. Thomas.
Journal of Physical Oceanography, Vol 5, No 1, p 136-142, January 1975. 6 fig, 2 tab, 8 ref. NSF Grant GA-32209.

Descriptors: *Currents(Water), *Winds, *Shallow water, Model studies, Mathematical models, Basins, Lakes, Lake basins, Water circulation, Limnology, Eddies, Viscosity.

A theory was given for steady wind-driven currents in shallow water (friction depth comparable to total depth) in which the vertical eddy viscosity varies linearly with depth, from zero at the bottom to a maximum at the surface. The theory was presented in a form suitable for numerical computations of currents in real, enclosed basins. The local surface value of the vertical eddy viscosity depends on the surface wind stress, the bottom roughness, and the flow itself; this leads to a quasi-linear equation for the determination of the surface slope or the vertically-integrated mass flux. Results were given for the simple case of a pure drift current in water of uniform depth, and these results were compared with those for a constant vertical eddy viscosity. (Sims-ISWS)
W75-07908

ICE-RAFTED SEDIMENTS AS A CAUSE OF SOME THERMOKARST LAKES IN THE NOATAK RIVER DELTA, ALASKA,
Washington Univ., Seattle. Coll. of Forest Resources.
For primary bibliographic entry see Field 2C.
W75-07948

MORPHOMETRIC CONTROL OF VARIATION IN ANNUAL HEAT BUDGETS,
Monash Univ., Clayton (Australia). Dept. of Zoology.
B. V. Timms.
Limnology and Oceanography, Vol 20, No 2, p 110-112, January 1975. 1 tab, 7 ref.

Descriptors: *Heat budget, *Lake morphometry, *Heat balance, Lakes, Volume, Depth, *Europe, *North America, *Australia, Inflow, Winds, Limnology, Aquatic environment, Water temperature, Physical properties, Hydrology, Hydrologic aspects, Lake morphology, Heat flow, Heat transfer, Melt water.
Identifiers: *Morphometric control.

The extent of variation in annual heat budget of 23 European, North American, and Australian lakes tends to be related to lake volume and mean depth. (Lee-ISWS)
W75-07950

CLADOPHORA DISTRIBUTION IN LAKE ONTARIO (IFYGL),
Environmental Research Inst. of Michigan, Ann Arbor.
For primary bibliographic entry see Field 5C.
W75-07968

PHOSPHORUS UPTAKE AND RELEASE BY LAKE ONTERIO SEDIMENTS,
Wisconsin Univ., Madison. Water Chemistry Program; and Wisconsin Univ., Madison. Dept. of Soils.
For primary bibliographic entry see Field 5A.
W75-07972

THE PREDATORY IMPACT OF EEL (ANGUILLA ANGUILLA L.) ON POPULATIONS OF CRAYFISH (ASTACUS ASTACUS L.),
G. Svardson.
Rep Inst Freshwater Res Drottningholm, 52 p, 149-191, 1972. Illus.

Descriptors: *Eels, Fish, Saline water fish, *Crayfish, Crustaceans, *Predation, Aquatic populations, Populations, Lakes, *Fish management, Lakes.
Identifiers: Anguilla-anguilla, Aphanomyces, Astacus-astacus, Eel, Eggs, Management, Pacifastacus-leniusculus, *Sweden, Sympatry.

Eels (Anguilla anguilla) were allowed to penetrate into the lake where they ousted crayfish (Astacus astacus) from the lake and some of its tributaries. There is a general allopatric occurrence of the 2 spp., eel dominating the western part, crayfish the eastern part of southern Sweden. Surveys from some 1600 lakes indicate that the species do have similar habitats; large eutrophic lakes being favored by both. The eel is the tougher of the 2 spp. and may live in all lakes to which it can climb. Crayfish cannot reproduce in summer-cold lakes, although older crayfish may survive and grow in them. When favorable lakes are samples, the sympatric occurrence of the 2 spp. is less frequent than it should be according to chance. The yield tends to be reversed, high eel catches occur in crayfish-free lakes and vice versa. The median annual catch of crayfish is 46 specimens/ha in lakes with no eels and 22 crayfish when eels are present but sparse. Moderate yields of both species thus may be obtained in cases of sympatry but good yields are obtained only when the species are allopatric. A number of case histories are presented where eel and crayfish have fluctuated in reversed direction. Several of the best crayfish producing lakes have had an early history of fewer crayfish and more eels. Crayfish are spontaneous and not introduced in Scandinavia by man. The impact of eel on the crayfish is compared to a number of similar cases where fish interact with crustaceans. The eel's predation on the crayfish gives a survival value to those eel having the best capacity to locate crayfish lakes from a distance. These eel are thereby led to excellent habitats sparsely populated by eel. The crayfish is a delicacy and gives a much higher economic yield/ha. The recent introduction of the Aphanomyces-resistant American crayfish Pacifastacus leniusculus in Swedish lakes has stressed the importance of a new management. Some details on how such management should be outlined are suggested.--Copyright 1974, Biological Abstracts, Inc.
W75-08010

SOME EFFECTS OF EXTENDING THE NAVIGATIONAL SEASON ON THE GREAT LAKES: A NEED FOR CONGRESSIONAL ACTION,
Cleveland State Univ., Ohio. Coll. of Law.
For primary bibliographic entry see Field 6E.
W75-08072

RADIATION INDUCED THERMAL STRATIFICATION IN SURFACE LAYERS OF STAGNANT WATER,
Purdue Univ., Lafayette, Ind. School of Mechanical Engineering.
D. M. Snider, and R. Viskanta.
Journal of Heat Transfer, Paper No 75-HT-CC, 1975, 6 p, 6 fig, 15 ref. OWRT A-029-IND(9).

Descriptors: *Thermal stratification, *Solar Radiation, *Interferometry, *Air-water interfaces, Stratification, Radiation, Heating, Energy transfer, Boundaries.
Identifiers: *Inferogram, *Radiative transfer theory.

Analysis is developed for the time dependent thermal stratification is surface layers of stagnant water by solar radiation. The transient temperature distribution is obtained by solving the one-dimensional equation for combined conduction and radiation energy transfer using a finite difference method. Experimentally, solar heating of water is simulated using tungsten filament lamps in parabolic reflectors of known spectral characteristics. The transient temperature distribution resulting from radiant heating of pure water in a glass-walled test cell is measured with a Mach-Zender interferometer. Measured and predicted temperature profiles show good agreement, thus verifying the radiation and total energy transfer models in stagnant water. The boundary condition of the air-water interface and internal radiant heating rate must be correctly specified in order to properly model stratification of water by radiation.
W75-08098

LIMNOLOGICAL CONDITIONS IN FIVE SMALL OLIGOTROPHIC LAKES IN TERRA NOVA NATIONAL PARK, NEWFOUNDLAND,
Dalhousie Univ., Halifax (Nova Scotia). Dept. of Biology.
For primary bibliographic entry see Field 5C.
W75-08131

A COMPARATIVE REVIEW OF PHYTOPLANKTON AND PRIMARY PRODUCTION IN THE LAURENTIAN GREAT LAKES,
Canada Centre for Inland Waters, Burlington (Ontario).
For primary bibliographic entry see Field 5C.
W75-08137

ON THE EFFECTS OF EUTROPHICATION ON LAKE PAIJANNE, CENTRAL FINLAND,
For primary bibliographic entry see Field 5C.
W75-08138

PHYSICAL AND CHEMICAL LIMNOLOGY OF CHAR LAKE, CORNWALLIS ISLAND (75 DEGREES N LAT.),
Fisheries Research Board of Canada, Winnipeg (Manitoba). Freshwater Inst.
For primary bibliographic entry see Field 5C.
W75-08143

REVIEW OF GEOLOGICAL RESEARCH AS IT RELATES TO AN UNDERSTANDING OF GREAT LAKES LIMNOLOGY,
Canada Centre for Inland Waters, Burlington (Ontario).
P. G. Sly, and R. L. Thomas.
Journal Fisheries Research Board of Canada, Vol 31, No 5, p 795-825, 1974. 14 fig, 5 tab, 108 ref.

Descriptors: *Quaternary period. *Geology, *Great Lakes, *Limnology, Lake sediments, Eutrophication, Lake Erie, Geochemistry, Circulation, Mercury, Water quality, Metals, Trace elements, Carbon, Nitrogen, Phosphorus, Physical properties, Chemical properties, History, Reviews.
Identifiers: Feromanganese concretions.

Geological research, as directed towards Great Lakes studies, has been developed and expanded during the last decade, nurtured by various factors, notably the impact of increased eutrophication in Lake Erie, the impact of sublethal but toxic contaminants in restricted areas, periods of extreme water level fluctuation, and a greatly increased demand for high quality water for multiple uses. A review of studies on the geology of recent sediment deposits in the Great Lakes is presented. A summary of quaternary events and a cross-correlation between each of the major basins has been attempted; in this respect it is esential to realize the control imposed upon present depositional conditions by the preceding sedimentary environments (often related to significantly different lake levels). Sediment/energy relations have. been discussed, particularly in the context of large lake limnology. Geochemical topics include major and trace metal data, formation of ferromanganese deposits, and major nutrients (C, N, and P). Published material covering these topics is, however, rather limited. Throughout this review attempt has been made to show the interrelations between geological evidence and physical, chemical, and biological processes and the application of such information to human oriented problems. (Jones-Wisconsin)
W75-08144

A REVIEW OF RESEARCH ON THE LIMNOLOGY OF WEST BLUE LAKE, MANITOBA,
Manitoba Univ., Winnipeg. Dept. of Zoology.
For primary bibliographic entry see Field 5C.
W75-08145

OXYGENATION OF LAKE HYPOLIMNIA,
Rutgers-The State Univ., New Brunswick, N.J. Water Resources Research Inst.
For primary bibliographic entry see Field 5C.
W75-08194

FISH PREDATION EFFECTS ON THE SPECIES COMPOSITION OF THE ZOOPLANKTON COMMUNITY IN EIGHT SMALL FOREST LAKES,
Goteborg Univ. (Sweden). Inst. of Zoology.
J. A. E. Stenson.
Rep Inst Freshwater Res Drottningholm. 52. p 132-148, 1972, Illus.

Descriptors: *Lakes, Europe, *Fish, *Predation, Zooplankton, *Rotenone, Fish control agents.
Identifiers: Bosmina-coregoni, Bosmina-longirostris, Bythatrephes-longimanus, Cladoceran, Daphnia-cristata, Daphnia-longispina, *Sweden(Bohuslan).

The effects of size dependent predation on the crustacean plankton fauna of 8 small forest lakes in the province of Bohuslan, S. W. Sweden were investigated. Four lakes were treated with rotenone. Three of these lakes were restocked with new fish species, the 4th was reoccupied by the original species. The physico-chemical limnology conditions were similar throughout the year and differences in the sediment composition and vegetation were very small. The lake treated with rotenone but containing the original fish fauna had the same zooplankton species composition as the untreated lakes. In the lakes with low predation intensity (i.e. those with the new fish species), the larger zooplankton species Bythotrephes longimanus and Daphnia longispina were present. These species were eliminated in the lakes with high predation intensity and D. longispina was replaced by the smaller D. cristata. A clear difference in the size distribution of the cladoceran community, between the lakes with high predation intensity (those with the original fish species) and the lakes with low predation intensity is demonstrated. The larger Bosmina coregoni replaced the smaller B. longirostris when predation intensity decreased.--Copyright 1974, Biological Abstracts, Inc.
W75-08220

TEMPERATURE EFFECTS ON GREAT LAKES WATER BALANCE STUDIES,
Illinois Univ., Urbana. Water Resources Center.
D. D. Meredith.
Water Resources Bulletin, Vol 11, No 1, p 60-68, February 1975. 2 tab, 26 ref. OWRT B-062-ILL(3). 14-31-0001-3580.

Descriptors: *Great Lakes, Hydrology, *Water balance, *Water temperature, Lakes, Monthly, Water supply, Water levels, Thermal expansion.
Identifiers: Basin supply values, Thermal contraction.

Beginning of month water temperature profiles are estimated for each lake. These water temperature profiles along with surface water temperatures are used to determine the effects of thermal expansion and contraction of water on the net basin supply values obtained from water balance studies using end of month lake levels. Net basin supply values (equivalent to precipitation on the lake minus the evaporation from the lake plus the runoff into the lake) obtained from water balance studies without accounting for the thermal expansion and contraction of water may be in error by as much as 100 percent during some months for each lake.
W75-08225

THE EPIDEMIOLOGY OF PARASITIC DISEASES FROM AKOSOMBO LAKE (GHANA) AND NASSER LAKE (SUDAN EGYPTIAN NUBIA), (IN FRENCH),
Institut Pasteur, Paris (France). Laboratoire d'Epidemiologie.
For primary bibliographic entry see Field 5C.
W75-08226

STUDIES ON THE EFFECTIVE STOCKING OF SALMONID FISH: II. ACTIVITY OF DOWN MIGRATION OF HIMEMASU, ONCORHYNCHUS NERKA, SOON AFTER STOCKING WITH SPECIAL REFERENCE TO THE FACTORS OF THEIR MIGRATION, (IN JAPANESE),
Freshwater Fisheries Research Lab., Tokyo (Japan).
Y. Shiraishi, and T. Shimada.
Bull Freshwater Fish Res Lab Tokyo, Vol 22, No 1, p 1-12, Illus, 1972. English summary.

Descriptors: *Fish migration, *Fish stocking, Salmon, Fry, *Salmonids.
Identifiers: Oncorhynchus, *Japan(Lake Chuzenji).

Down migration of the young fish of O. nerka was studied in Lake Chuzenji, Lake Yunoko (Japan) and in a rearing pond. The down migration soon after they are released is clearly different from the seaward migration of the smolt stage. In the Lake Chuzenji, fry of 0.5 g body weight were released on 1 June, 1964 at the inlet of the Lake, and traced for 2 wk. They migrated westward and eastward along the coast. The speed of the fish school in the 2 directions was very different, about 400 m/day in eastward and about 1000 m/day in westward migration. In Lake Yunoko 100,000 fry were released on 1 July, 1974 at the northern part of the lake; the fish migrating out of the lake were checked by a small net at the debouchment of the lake. On the 2nd day after they were released, a maximum number (228 fry) was trapped. After that day the fry trapped decreased daily; only 18 were trapped after a week. About 1% of total fish stocked migrated from the lake during 2 wk after they were released. The same tendency was seen in the case of the rearing pond where 50,000 fry were stocked; the number of fish migrating out of the pond at the outlet was checked. Activity of fish was accelerated at dawn and at twilight, when the light intensity changed. Migration from an experimental trough continued longer when the trough was covered with black vinyl sheet. Turbidity of water accerated the activity of down migration and the larger the fish, the lower the activity of migration. Migration was not altered by placing stones and algae in the trough. The activity of down migration was accelerated by adding some predators (O. masou) of 30 g in body weight. When O. nerka, the same species, was added, no effect was seen in the activity of down migration of the fry. (See also W75-07621)--Copyright 1973, Biological Abstracts, Inc.
W75-08237

STUDIES ON THE CARP CULTURE IN RUNNING WATER POND: VI. MORPHOMETRICAL COMPARISON OF THE COMMON CARP CULTURED IN RUNNING WATER POND, IRRIGATION POND AND FLOATING CAGE, (IN JAPANESE),
Freshwater Fisheries Research Lab., Tokyo (Japan).
For primary bibliographic entry see Field 8I.
W75-08240

THE CHANGES OF BENTHOS IN SLAPY RESERVOIR IN THE YEARS 1960-1961,
Ceskoslovenska Akademie Ved, Prague. Hydrobiologicka Laborator.
V. Hruska.
Hydrobiol Stud, 2, p 213-247, 1973, Illus.

Descriptors: *Reservoirs, *Benthos, *Europe, Oligochaetes, Diptera, *Biomass, Tubificids, Benthic fauna.
Identifiers: Chironomidae, *Czechoslovakia(Slapy reservoir), Ekman-Birge, Slapy.

The abundance and biomass were observed on 2 transects 9 km and 33km above Slapy dam(Czechoslovakia). Additional samples were taken 35 km above the dam. Experiments with the protection of 4 m2 areas of bottom against fish feeding activity were arranged on the transect of 9 km. Samples (218) were taken with the modified Ekman-Birge bottom sampler (area 225 cm2). The benthos in 1960 was quantitatively richest in the profundal of both transects (30 and 10 m, respectively). Oligochaeta were the most important components. The time of the maximal quantity of benthos at both localities differed greatly. The quantity of benthos in the littoral and the sublittoral of both transects was low. The major components were Oligochaeta and Chironomidae. In the year 1961 with the retention of river tripton in the upper Orlik Reservoir the huge quantities of Oligochaeta disappeared from the transect at 33 km. On the transect at 9 km there was a slight decrease of average biomass. The lower profundal (40 m) became quantitatively the richest zone and the changes of abundance and biomass differed from those in the preceeding year. As concerns the number of cocoons of Tubificidae in 1960 both transects revealed similar differences in the abundance and biomass of worms. In 1961 the laying of cocoons almost ceased at the 33 km transect and was greatly reduced at 9 km. The protection of 4-m2 bottom areas against fish feeding activity indicates that the differences between the quantitatively poor benthos in the littoral and sublittoral and rich benthos in the profundal must be ascribed to the better food conditions here rather than to fish feeding activity in the littoral and sublittoral. The percentage frequency for animals found in both transects is given. At 9 km, the qualitatively richest chironomid fauna was found in the littoral. The permanent fauna was qualitatively richest in

the upper and middle profundal. At 33 km, such apparent differences were not observed.--Copyright 1974, Biological Abstracts, Inc.
W75-08246

BIOLOGY AND MANAGEMENT OF SMALLMOUTH BASS IN ONEIDA LAKE, NEW YORK,
Cornell Univ., Ithaca, N.Y. Dept. of Natural Resources.
J. L. Forney.
N Y Fish Game J, Vol 19, No 2, p 132-154, 1972, Illus.
Identifiers: Age, Bass, Biology, Growth rates, Lakes, Management, *New York(Oneida Lake), Regulation, Smallmouth bass, Fish stocking, Temperature.

Age composition and growth rate of smallmouth bass (Micropterus dolomieui) in Oneida Lake, New York were determined from scales and measurements collected from 1952-1970. Dominant year classes were produced in years when mean June air temperatures were above normal. The catch of young bass in seine hauls indicated that year-class size was established by Aug., but the causal relation between June air temperature and year-class survival was not established. The long-term average growth rate of bass was stable between 1949 and 1966, but annual growth increments varied markedly. Much of this variation was attributable to differences in mean summer air temperatures and the abundance of young yellow perch which were an important forage species. Annual survival and minimum rates of exploitation were determined from tag returns reported by anglers. The mean annual survival during a 14-yr period was 0.57 which agreed closely with estimates from catch curves. A linear regression was fitted to annual survival rates and minimum rates of exploitation to obtain an estimate of natural mortality. The intercept in the event of no fishing corresponded to a natural mortality rate of 0.125. The role of regulations and stocking in the management of the population is examined.--Copyright 1973, Biological Abstracts, Inc.
W75-08250

CHARACTERISTICS OF A SMALL-LAKE FISHERY AS DETERMINED BY A CREEL CENSUS,
Cornell Univ., Ithaca, N.Y. Dept. of Natural Resources.
D. M. Green.
N Y Fish Game J, Vol 19, No 2, p 155-167, 1972. Illus.
Identifiers: *Creel census, Esox-niger, *Fisheries, Ictalurus-nebulosus, Lakes, Lepomis-gibbosus, Micropterus-salmoides, *New York, Perca-flavescens, Pomoxis-nigromaculatus, Fishing.

A creel census was conducted on a shallow 117.5-acre warm-water lake in central New York from June 1965-March 1968. Species recorded in the anglers' catch were: largemouth bass, chain pickerel, brown bullhead, yellow perch, pumpkinseed and black crappie (Micropterus salmoides, Esox niger, Ictalurus nebulosus, Perca flavescens, Lepomis gibbosus Pomoxis nigromaculatus. Catch and effort were estmated for shore, boat and ice fishermen. Effort ranged from 6887-11,874 man hours, with shore fishermen expending the greatest effort and ice fishermen the least. Monthly and daily distributions of effort was determined. Bullheads, pumpkinseeds and perch were the fish most frequently caught by shore fishermen, while pumpkinseeds, pickerel and perch sustained the boat fishermen. Boat fishermen caught over 80% of the bass taken. Perch were numerically the most important fish in the catch and comprised the bulk of the ice fishermen's catch. Ice fishermen also took a significant number of pickerel. Fish caught and released may be important in evaluating the quality of such a fishery.--Copyright 1973, Biological Abstracts, Inc.
W75-08251

DISTRIBUTION OF WALLEYE AND YELLOW PERCH FRY IN A BAY OF ONEIDA LAKE,
Cornell Univ., Ithaca, N.Y. Dept. of Natural Resources.
R. L. Noble.
NY Fish Game J, Vol 19, No 2, p 168-177, 1972. Illus.
Identifiers: Bays, *Distribution, Fry, Lakes, *New York(Oneida Lake), Perca-flavescens, *Perch, Stizostedion-vitreum-vitreum, Walleye perch, Yellow perch.

Densities of walleye (Stizostedion vitreum vitreum) and yellow perch (Perca flavescens) fry were usually greater inshore than offshore in samples taken during early June. Walleye fry concentrated at a variable depth, whereas yellow perch fry were uniformly distributed to a depth of 3.7 m except during calm weather. Although vertical and horizontal distributions of the 2 spp. did not coincide, catches were correlated within localized areas. Correlations between the abundance of yellow perch fry and their occurrence in walleye fry stomachs indicated that the association between the 2 spp. may have been caused by a predator-prey relationship. The over-all difference in distribution indicated that perch abundance was not the major influence on the distribution of walleye fry.--Copyright 1973, Biological Abstracts, Inc.
W75-08252

A RESURVEY OF THE FISH PARASITES OF WESTERN LAKE ERIE,
R. V. Bangham.
Bull Ohio Biol Surv, Vol 4, No 2, p 1-23, 1972.
Identifiers: *Lake Erie, Clinostomum-marginatum, Diplostomulum-flexicaudum, Eustrongylides-sp, *Fish parasites, Ichthyophthirius-multifiliis, Lakes, Philometra-cylindracea, Posthodiplostomum-mimimum, Proteocephalus-ambloplitis, Survey.

Parasites from fish collected from the west end of Lake Erie were identified and compared with the results of a similar study made during 1927-29 (published in 1939). In the present study 1687 fish belonging to 66 spp. were examined in 1957 of which 1589 or 94.2% were parasitized. The 1939 report cited 58.3% parasitized. No lake herring or whitefish were taken and fewer specimens of blue pike, sauger, and burbot were available in 1957, but bullheads, carp, white bass, rock bass, crappies, sunfish, bluegill and sheepshead were more readily available. Parasites (110 spp.) were encountered, including the following of economic importance: Ichthyophthirius multifiliis, Clinostomum marginatum, Diplostomulum flexicaudum, Posthodiplostomum mimimum, Proteocephalus ambloplitis, Eustrongylides sp., and Philometra cylindracea. Tables of all parasites found, as well as a comparison of the 1939 and 1957 surveys, are given.--Copyright 1973, Biological Abstracts, Inc.
W75-08253

SOME PHYSICOCHEMICAL FEATURES OF A MEROMICTIC LAKE SUIGETSU,
Nagoya Univ. (Japan). Water Research Lab.
M. Matsuyama.
J Oceanogr Soc Jap, Vol 29, No 2, p 47-52, 1973, Illus.

Descriptors: *Lakes, Meromixis, *Chemical analysis, Water temperature, *Thermal stratification, Stratification.
Identifiers: Chemocline, *Chlorinity, *Japan(Lake Suigetsu), *Meromictic lakes, Suigetsu.

Vertical distributions of temperature and chlorinity show that the lake is well stratified and no marked mixing occurs between the upper fresh water and lower salt water. In the chemocline, the vertical gradient of density is large and the vertical eddy diffusion coefficient is as low as 1.5 x 10-2 cm2 sec.-1. Dissolved O2 saturated near the surface and rapidly decreases with depth towards the chemocline, where sulfide first appears and increases towards the bottom. In the chemocline O2 comsumption is a prominent process, reaching 290 mg O2/m2/day. The oxidation of sulfide, supplied from the underlying water layer, is the main factor causing O2 consumption in the chemoeline.--Copyright 1974, Biological Abstracts, Inc.
W75-08255

ORGANIC SUBSTANCES IN SEDIMENT AND SETTLING MATTER DURING SPRING IN A MEROMICTIC LAKE SUIGETSU,
Nagoya Univ. (Japan). Water Research Lab.
M. Matsuyama.
J Oceanogr Soc Jap, Vol 29, No 2, p 53-60, 1973. Illus.

Descriptors: Asia, *Lakes, *Sediment sorting, *Sediment distribution, Meromixis, Sampling.
Identifiers: *Japan(Lake Suigetsu), *Meromictic lake, Suigetsu.

Vertical distribution of organic substances of settling matter and sediments was measured in a meromictic lake, Lake Suigetsu (Japan). Proteinaceous materials were rapidly eliminated in the early stage of settling. There was no major difference in amino acid composition of the hydrolysates of all samples, indicating that no selective decomposition of amino acids had occurred. In contrast, the decomposition of carbohydrates was sluggish. Water extractable carbohydrates were abundant in the sediments. Dissolved carbohydrates and amino acids formed in the sediments, were partly metabolized by photosynthetic sulfur bacteria, Chromatium sp. in the chemocline.--Copyright 1974, Biological Abstracts, Inc.
W75-08257

OLIGOTROPHICATION: A SELF-ACCELERATING PROCESS IN LAKES SUBJECTED TO EXCESSIVE SUPPLY OF ACID SUBSTANCES,
Institue for Water and Air Pollution Research, Stockholm (Sweden).
For primary bibliographic entry see Field 5C.
W75-08262

RATES OF OXYGEN UPTAKE BY THE PLANKTONIC COMMUNITY OF A SHALLOW EQUATORIAL LAKE (LAKE GEORGE, UGANDA),
Vienna Univ. (Austria). Limnologische Lehrkanzel.
For primary bibliographic entry see Field 5C.
W75-08263

COMMUNITIES OF OLIGOCHAETA AS INDICATORS OF THE WATER QUALITY IN LAKE HJALMAREN,
Uppsala Univ. (Sweden). Inst. of Zoology.
For primary bibliographic entry see Field 5B.
W75-08267

POTENTIAL LANDSLIDE-GENERATED WATER WAVES, LIBBY DAM AND LAKE KOOCANUSA, MONTANA; HYDRAULIC MODEL INVESTIGATION,
Army Engineer Waterways Experiment Station, Vicksburg, Miss.
For primary bibliographic entry see Field 8B.
W75-08291

RICHARD B. RUSSELL LAKE WATER QUALITY INVESTIGATION; HYDRAULIC MODEL INVESTIGATION,
Army Engineer Waterways Experiment Station, Vicksburg, Miss.
For primary bibliographic entry see Field 8B.
W75-08293

ICHTHYOFAUNA OF THE TYSMIENICA AND WLODAWKA RIVER BASINS, (IN POLISH),
Akademia Wychowania Fizycznego, Warsaw (Poland). Zaklad Nauk Biomedycznej.
Z. Danilkiewicz.
Fragm Faun (Warsaw), Vol 19, No 7, p 121-147, 1973. Illus.

Descriptors: Basins, *Lake basins, *River basins, Freshwater fish, Carp, Pike, Roach, Perches, *Populations, Rivers, Lakes, Europe, *Fish populations.
Identifiers: Carassius-auratus-bibelio, Coregonus-albula, Crucian carp, Ctenopharynogodon-idella, Ictalurus-nebulosus, Pike, *Poland, Roach, Tysmienica River, Wlodawka River, Domarzno Lake.

Freshwater fish (34 spp.) were identified in the water of the Tysmienica and Wlodawka river basins in Poland, the most common and numerous being pike, crucian carp, roach and perch. The largest number of species, 31 was found in the Tysmienica River. Of the lakes, Lake Domarzno was the richest with 23 spp., followed by Lake Biale Sosnowickie with 22 and Lake Biale Wlodawskie with 21. Coregonus albula, Carassius auratus gibelio, Ctenopharyngodon idella and Ictalurus nebulosus are fairly new in these waters. Attention is called to the damaging effect on the ichthyofauna and the environment of the region by hydrotechnical works being carried out here, and as the construction of the Wieprz-Krzna Canal. Distribution of fish in the various types of water bodies is presented in tabular form.--Copyright 1974, Biological Abstracts, Inc.
W75-08310

MUD-WATER EXCHANGE OF PHOSPHATE AND OTHER IONS IN UNDISTURBED SEDIMENT CORES AND FACTORS AFFECTING THE EXCHANGE RATES,
Copenhagen Univ. (Denmark). Freshwater Biological Lab.
For primary bibliographic entry see Field 2J.
W75-08320

THE CHEMICAL ECOLOGY OF COPEPOD DISTRIBUTION IN THE LAKES OF EAST AND CENTRAL AFRICA,
Duke Univ., Durham, N.C. Dept. of Zoology.
M. C. Labarbera, and P. Kilham.
Limnol Oceanogr, Vol 19, No 3, p 459-465, 1974, Illus.
Identifiers: *Africa, Chemical studies, Conductivity, *Copepod distribution, Ecology, Epilimnion, *Lakes, Range.

The copepods in plankton samples from 48 lakes in East and Central Africa were identified and the conductivity (k20) of the epilimnion of each lake was determined. A range, mean, and standard deviation were calculated for the conductivity of the waters in which each copepod species was found. There appears to be a definite range of conductivities in which each species can maintain a viable population.--Copyright 1974, Biological Abstracts, Inc.
W75-08321

STRATIGRAPHIC EFFECTS OF TUBIFICIDS IN PROFUNDAL LAKE SEDIMENTS,
Maine Univ., Orono. Dept. of Botany and Plant Pathology.
For primary bibliographic entry see Field 5C.
W75-08322

AGE, GROWTH, LENGTH-WEIGHT RELATIONSHIP, SEX RATIO AND FOOD HABITS OF THE ARGENTINE PEJERREY, BASILICHTHYS BONARIENSIS (CUV. AND VAL.), FROM LAKE PENUELAS, VALPARAISO, CHILE,
Universidad Catolica de Valparaiso (Chile). Laboratorio de Hidrobiologia Aplicadas.
R. G. Burbidge, M. C. Carrasco, and P. A. Brown.
J Fish Biol, Vol 6, No 3, p 299-305, 1974, Illus.
Identifiers: Age, *Argentina Pejerreys, Basilichthys-bonariensis, Bosmina-sp, *Chile(Lake Penuelas), Cladoceran, Copepods, Diaphanosoma-brachyurum, Diptera, Feeding, Food, Growth, Lakes, Length, Light, Ostracod, Sex, Simocephalus-serrulatus, Weight.

Argentine pejerreys were collected in Lake Penuelas during Jan. 1973. Calculated growth rate was maximum during the 3rd year of life. The length-weight relationship was: $\log W = -5.69395 + 3.25248 \log L$, where W = weight (g), and L = total length (mm). Age-group I was sexually mature. The sex ratio was 85 males (54%) to 73 females (46%). Young-of-the-year pejerreys fed primarily on copepods, but cladocerans (Bosmina sp., Diaphanosoma brachyurum, Simocephalus serrulatus, ostracods, and dipterans were also respresented. Feeding occurred during daylight.--Copyright 1974, Biological Abstracts, Inc.
W75-08326

SPECIES INTRODUCTION IN A TROPICAL LAKE,
Washington Univ., Seattle. Dept. of Zoology.
T. M. Zaret, and R. T. Paine.
Science, Vol 182, No 4111, p 449-455, 1973. Illus.

Descriptors: Lakes, Fish, *Predation, *Zooplankton.
Identifiers: Ceriodaphnia, Cichla, Melaniris, *Panama Canal Zone, *Gatun Lake, Lake ecosystem, *Tropical lakes.

Probably in early 1967, a piscivore from South America, Cichla ocellaris, was introduced to Gatun Lake in the Panama Canal Zone. As this predator population spread through the lake, the initial effect was dramatic reductions in almost all secondary consumers. These species reductions produced, in turn, 2nd- and 3rd-order changes at other trophic levels of the ecosystem. The resulting changes in the lake community can be seen best by examining the general Gatun Lake food web. The decrease in numbers of the important planktivore Melaniris has resulted in changes within the zooplankton community, as illustrated by the cladoceran Ceriodaphnia. The tertiary-consumer populations, such as tarpon, black terns, kingfishers and herons, formerly dependent on small fishes for food, appear less frequently in the Cichla areas of the lake. There has also been, possibly, a resurgence of the local mosquito populations (which are malaria vectors), caused by the reduction in the populations of insect-eating fishes. Even the primary producers may be affected by this introduction. Although at present the Gatun Lake ecosystem is undergoing rapid changes, an eventual return to some form of equilibrium is anticipated. However, it will be some time before the permanence or transience of the many changes produced in the trophic levels by the introduction of a single, top level predator to this lake system can be evaluated.--Copyright 1974, Biological Abstracts, Inc.
W75-08345

2I. Water In Plants

UTILITY OF BROWN COAL FROM TUROW AND KONIN MINES AS THE SEEDBED IN HYDROPONIC CULTURES, (IN POLISH),
Wroclaw Univ. (Poland). Inst. of Botany and Biochemistry.
For primary bibliographic entry see Field 3F.
W75-07853

FINITE ELEMENT ANALYSIS OF TWO-DIMENSIONAL FLOW IN SOILS CONSIDERING WATER UPTAKE BY ROOTS: I. THEORY,
Agricultural Research Organization, Bet-Dagan (Israel). Inst. of Soils and Water.
For primary bibliographic entry see Field 2G.

ON VERTICAL STRATIFICATION IN CERTAIN HYDROPHYTES,
Banaras Hindu Univ., Varanasi (India). Dept. of Botany.
K. Ram.
Trop Ecol, Vol 14, No 1, p 76-80, 1973, Illus.
Identifiers: Buoyancy, *Hydrophytes, *Specific gravity, *Vertical stratification, Aquatic plants.

Specific gravity of freshwater plants ranges from 0.17-0.9, with the exception in some plant parts (seeds, rhizomes and corms). Vertical position (buoyancy) has significant inverse correlation with specific gravity. Vertical position (buoyancy) has positive correlation with volume/weight(V/W) ratio.--Copyright 1974, Biological Abstracts, Inc.
W75-08083

SILICON DEPLETIONS IN SOME NORFOLK RIVERS,
Yorkshire River Authority, Leeds (England). Pollution Prevention Dept.
For primary bibliographic entry see Field 5C.
W75-08106

GERMINATION AND SEEDLING VIGOR OF SIX RANGE SPECIES IN RELATION TO MOISTURE STRESS AND TEMPERATURE,
Cairo Univ., Giza (Egypt). Dept. of Agronomy.
For primary bibliographic entry see Field 3B.
W75-08111

DESERT FARMERS: ANCIENT AND MODERN,
Hebrew Univ., Jerusalem (Israel). Dept. of Botany.
For primary bibliographic entry see Field 3F.
W75-08113

MAIN DEMOGRAPHIC FEATURES OBSERVED ON 50 FRENCH TROUT RIVERS: INFLUENCE OF SLOPE AND CALCIUM, (IN FRENCH),
Station d'Hydrobiologie Continentale, Biarritz (France).
R. Cuinat.
Ann Hydrobiol, Vol 2, No 2, p 187-207, Illus, 1971.

Descriptors: Europe, *Trout, *Fish populations, Aquatic populations, Statistical methods, *Mathematical studies, Rivers, *Calcium, Oxygen, *Slopes.
Identifiers: Demographic studies(Fish), *France.

Demographic data collected from 1959-1969 in 4 districts of France (Normandie, Nord-Est, Massif-central, Pyrenees-Atlantiques) were studied. A statistical study of the main demographic parameters was done. For every parameter, variation coefficients show the large diversity of trout populations. However, a large part of the variance is statistically explainable by both variables, slope and Ca. For the slope, Huet's law is confirmed by observations, with the following 2 restrictions; trout zone appears to spread onto the slope 4/1000, instead of 7/1000 (for 10 m width) and rivers studied in Normandie, although their slope is under 1.5/1000, have important trout populations. Factors other than slope (in particular temperature and O2) are also important. Ca content, expressed with a logarithmic scale, has a positive linear correlation with fish growth in length.--Copyright 1974, Biological Abstracts, Inc.
W75-08170

THE PROTECTIVE EFFECT OF SUGARS ON CHLOROPLAST MEMBRANES DURING TEMPERATURE AND WATER STRESS AND ITS RELATIONSHIP TO FROST, DESICCATION AND HEAT RESISTANCE,
Duesseldorf Univ. (West Germany). Botanical Inst.
For primary bibliographic entry see Field 3F.
W75-08242

MOISTURE MODIFICATION SHELTERS FOR EPIDEMIOLOGICAL STUDIES OF FOLIAR DISEASES,
Georgia Univ., Athen.
J. T. Reid, D. H. Smith, J. E. Hughes, and F. L. Crosby.
Plant Dis Rep, Vol 57, No 4, p 329-332, 1973, Illus.
Identifiers: *Dew, Epidemiological studies, *Foliar diseases, Moisture, *Peanut leafspot, Rain, Plant diseases, *Moisture modification shelters.

Three automatically controlled movable shelters were designed, constructed and evaluated under field conditions in a study of the effect of dew and rain on the development of peanut leafspot epidemics. The moisture modification system described, however, also can be utilized for epidemiological studies of foliar diseases in other crops. The shelters were constructed of wood-frames and covered with clear plastic film. The moving mechanism for each shelter consisted of a cable and drum, driven by a reversible electric gear motor. A moisture sensor circuit was employed to detect the onset of rainfall. The rapid response of the 'no rain' shelters prevented the accumulation of free water on plant surfaces by moving them to the 'covered plot' position within 20-40 sec after the onset of rainfall. A 24-hr time clock and the moisture sensor circuit controlled the movement of the 3 shelters to obtain the following test conditions: 'no dew', 'no dew-no rain', and 'no rain'. The system performed very satisfactorily under field conditions during 1970, 1971, and 1972.--Copyright 1973, Biological Abstracts, Inc.
W75-08245

ON THE DOWNWARD MOVEMENT OF CREOSOTE IN EUCALYPTUS POLES,
Commonwealth Scientific and Industrial Research Organization, Melbourne (Australia). Forest Products Lab.
R. Johanson.
Holzforschung, Vol 27, No 1, p 7-11, 1973, Illus.

Descriptors: *Wood preservative, *Creasote, *Eucalyptus, Fungi.
Identifiers: Transmission poles.

The downward movement under gravity of high temperature creosote was studied in sapwood of pressure impregnated eucalyptus round timers about 150 mm diameter and 2.4 m long, some of which were sealed in loosely fitted polythene tubing and others exposed without cover, and all held vertically with the butt-end down at 45C. In both E. cypellocarpa and E. obliqua the initial movement rate was similar in sealed and uncovered rounds. In some, retentions decreased within 3 mo. by more than 50% at the top of the rounds revealing a very low capacity of sapwood to hold creosote. The forces producing downward movement may contribute to the total loss of creosote in various parts of transmission poles in service. The depleted sapwood may become more susceptible to entry by fungi, through checks and cracks, into the nondurable heartwood which is resistant to pressure impregnation and which is dependent for its protection on the treated sapwood.--Copyright 1973, Biological Abstracts, Inc.
W75-08247

COMPARISON OF INTERMITTENT AND PERMANENT STREAMS OF CALCAREOUS PROVENCE, (IN FRENCH),
Aix-Marseille-1 Univ. (France). Lab. for Animal Biology-Ecology.
For primary bibliographic entry see Field 2E.
W75-08261

COMPONENTS ANALYSIS OF YIELD RESPONSES TO DROUGHT OF SORGHUM HYBRIDS,
Volcani Inst. of Agricultural Research, Bet-Dagan (Israel).
For primary bibliographic entry see Field 3F.
W75-08265

THE EFFECT OF SOIL MOISTURE TENSION AND NITROGEN SUPPLY ON NITRATE REDUCTION AND ACCUMULATION IN WHEAT SEEDLINGS,
Volcani Inst. of Agricultural Research, Bet-Dagan (Israel).
For primary bibliographic entry see Field 3F.
W75-08266

PRODUCTIVITY OF THE WATER-CONSUMPTION OF TREES, (IN GERMAN),
H. J. Braun, and P. Schmidt.
Z Pflanzenphysiol, Vol 70, No 3, p 270-275, 1973. Illus.

Descriptors: *Trees, *Water utilization, Water requirements, Measurement.

A method has been described to measure immediately and exactly the water-consumption of trees by Braun and Schmidt. To show the possibilities of this method, some results are published. The concepts 'Productivity of water consumption' and 'Coefficient of water consumption' are introduced.--Copyright 1974, Biological Abstracts, Inc.
W75-08268

CHANGE OF FEEDING OF THE GROUSE UNDER THE EFFECT OF DRAINAGE RECLAMATION, (IN RUSSIAN),
Akademiya Navuk BSSR, Minsk. Dept. of Zoology and Parasitology.
V. B. Vadkovskii.
Vyesti Akad Navuk B SSR Syer Biyal Navuk, 3 p, 122-123, 1973.

Descriptors: *Birds, Game birds, Land reclamation, Reclaimed water, *Food habits, Feeds, Pollution, Pollutants, Water pollution sources, *Diets.
Identifiers: Barley, Cottongrass, Cowberry, Cranberry, *Feeding, Fireweed, *Grouse, Hawkweed, Oats, Pine, Speedwell, *USSR(Belorussia), Wheat.

An analysis of 31 food samples and 20 fecal specimens on the feeding of grouse in Belorussia (USSR) is presented. A narrow range of food (cranberry, cottongrass inflorescences, pine needles, cowberry leaves) was characteristic for the population inhabiting an unreclaimed territory. In the case of reclamation there was a considerable change of the range of food of the birds (dock, wheat, oat, barley, hawkweed, speedwell, fireweed, etc.) toward a better food supply. Different food spectra of grouse populations living under different ecological conditions are indicated. The grouse gradually adjust to the cultivated landscape on drained territories.--Copyright 1974, Biological Abstracts, Inc.
W75-08269

OPTIMUM LEVEL OF PROTEIN IN PURIFIED DIET FOR EEL, ANGUILLA JAPONICA,
Freshwater Fish Research Lab., Tokyo (Japan).
T. Nose, and S. Arai.
Bull Freshwater Fish Res Lab Tokyo, Vol 22, No 2, p 145-155, 1972. Illus.

Descriptors: *Eels, *Diets, Proteins, Fish, *Fish diets, Freshwater fish, Testing.
Identifiers: Anguilla-japonica, Casein, Cellulose, Dextrin, Glycogen, Corn oil, Vitamins, Japan.

The protein requirement of the eel, Anguilla japonica, was studied by using a purified diet consisting of casein, dextrin, cellulose powder, vitamin mixture, mineral mixture, carboxymethylcellulose (CMC), corn oil and cod liver oil. Casein was replaced by dextrin in order to provide the different levels of protein in the diet. Thirty-five well trained eels were grouped for each diet and raised in a small aquarium at 25C. The experiment was continued for 8 wk. Body weight gain and accumulation of body protein were both linearly related to

the protein level in diet within the range of 0 approximately 44.5%, beyond which both factors were constant or decreased. Eels seem to require about 45% protein in their diet for maximum growth at 25C. A low protein and high carbohydrate diet caused accumulation of body fat and high glycogen in the liver, resulting in its enlargement. The composition of fatty acids in the body fat was slightly influenced by the levels of protein and carbohydrate in diet.--Copyright 1974, Biological Abstracts, Inc.
W75-08270

ANNOTATED CHECK-LIST OF VASCULAR PLANTS OF SAGEHEN CREEK DRAINAGE BASIN, NEVADA COUNTY, CALIFORNIA,
California State Univ., San Jose. Dept. of Biological Sciences.
W. Savage.
Madrono, Vol 22, No 3, p 115-139, 1973, Illus.
Identifiers: *California(Sageben Creek), Creeks, Drainage basins, Habitats, *Vascular plants, Sierra Nevada.

An inventory of the vascular plants of a valley in the northern Sierra Nevada was undertaken to establish a basis for comparison with other localities with a similar environment. The catalog of plants, which was compiled, includes 438 taxa, representing 217 genera and 60 families. The study area, at an elevation of approximately 2000 m, is 4.8 km by 8.9 km in size. The habitats include stream banks, bogs and wet and dry meadows interspersed among mixed coniferous forest associations. The climatic and geologic factors affecting the habitats are also discussed.--Copyright 1973, Biological Abstracts, Inc.
W75-08277

THE ANCIENT NAMIB DESERT,
For primary bibliographic entry see Field 2A.
W75-08288

GROWTH, WATER AND NUTRIENT STATUS OF PLANTS IN RELATION TO PATTERNS OF VARIATIONS IN CONCENTRATIONS OF DRY MATTER AND NUTRIENT ELEMENTS IN BASE-TO-TOP LEAVES: I. DISTRIBUTION OF CONTENTS AND CONCENTRATIONS OF DRY MATTER IN TOMATO PLANTS UNDER DIFFERENT GROWTH CONDITIONS,
Royal Veterinary and Agriculture Coll., Copenhagen (Denmark). Hydrotechnical Lab.
B. Friis-Nielsen.
Plant Soil, Vol 39, No 3, p 661-673, 1973. Illus.

Descriptors: *Plant growth, *Plant growth regulations, *Plant growth substances, Plant physiology, Tomatoes, Field crops, Water requirements, *Analytical techniques.
Identifiers: *Dry matter, Leaves, Tomato.

Patterns of variations in dry matter concentrations in tomato plants reflected production and translocation of dry matter, implying the possibility of controlling and regulating growth and development of plants by use of dry matter concentration as a useful parameter. Dry matter concentrations, analogous to nutrient concentrations, varied depending on growth conditions, and on type, age and position of plant organs. Interpretation of patterns of variations in contents and concentrations of leaf dry matter in plants, grown under widely different conditions, agreed with the source/sink hypothesis. High water applications were associated with high dry matter concentrations in upper leaves of young pot plants with low sink capacity and with low dry matter concentrations in leaves of older, through-grown plants with high sink capacity. Accumulation of dry matter in upper leaves of plants is suggested to be associated with development of secondary sinks and assumulation of dry matter in lateral shoots is considered as a possible explanation of apical dominance. Water regime and transpiration influenced distribution of contents of dry and fresh matter and of absorbed nutrient elements. Redistribution was influenced by water regime. (See also W75-08309)--Copyright 1974, Biological Abstracts, Inc.
W75-08308

GROWTH, WATER AND NUTRIENT STATUS OF PLANTS IN RELATION TO PATTERNS OF VARIATIONS IN CONCENTRATIONS OF DRY MATTER AND NUTRIENT ELEMENTS IN BASE-TO-TOP LEAVES: II. RELATIONS BETWEEN DISTRIBUTION OF CONCENTRATIONS OF DRY MATTER AND NUTRIENT ELEMENTS IN TOMATO PLANTS,
Royal Veterinary and Agriculture Coll., Copenhagen (Denmark). Hydrotechnical Lab.
B. Friis-Nielsen.
Plant Soil, Vol 39, No 3, p 675-686, 1973. Illus.

Descriptors: Tomatoes, Field crops, *Plant growth, *Plant growth regulators, *Plant growth substances, *Chemical analysis, Water requirements, *Nutrients.
Identifiers: *Dry matter, Leaves.

Patterns of distribution curves of concentrations of dry matter and of concentrations based on dry and fresh matter, of N and sum cations in base-to-top leaves were investigated in 3 cultivars of tomato plants grown under widely different conditions. The set of all 3 distribution curves reflected changes in contents of dry matter and water caused by processes underlying growth and development of the plants, and decisive for a true interpretation of the chemical plant analysis. Symmetric patterns were obtained of distribution curves of N and sum cations in leaves from base to top, provided corrections were made for irrelevant contents of dry matter and water. Positions and slopes of distribution curves of dry matter concentrations were governed by dry matter production and translocation and similar to those of nutrient concentrations by age of plants and by supplies of nutrients and water. Increasing water supplied effected increasing dry matter production associated with increasing rates of translocation of dry matter in accordance with the source/sink hypothesis. Results of the investigation demonstrate the possibility to control and regulate growth and development of plants by use of leaf dry matter concentration and leaf nutrient concentrations, the latter based on both dry and fresh matter, as important parameters, provided reference values are known. (See also W75-08308)--Copyright 1974, Biological Abstracts, Inc.
W75-08309

INLAND MANGROVES AND WATER CHEMISTRY, BARBUDA, WEST INDIES,
Cambridge Univ. (England). Dept. of Geography.
D. R. Stoddart, G. W. Bryan, and P. E. Gibbs.
J Nat Hist, Vol 7, No 1, p 33-46, 1973, Illus.
Identifiers: Calcium, Conocarpus, Inlands, Laguncularia, Magnesium, *Mangroves, Potassium, Rhizophora, Sodium, *West Indies(Barbuda), *Water chemistry, Brackish water.

Mangrove vegetation, comprising not only Laguncularia and Conocarpus, but also a closed woodland of Rhizophora, is found in inland situations in Barbuda, West Indies, having no connection with the sea and associated with geological and geomorphic features of either lat Pleistocene or possibly earlier Holocene age. These mangroves are associated with brackish water. Analyses show lowered concentrations of Na, K and Mg and higher concentrations of Ca and Sr compared with sea water having the same chloride content, the higher Ca and Sr concentrations probably resulting from diagenetic changes in the limestone. The inland mangroves are either relict from the period of formation of the lithified beach ridges, or they have more recently colonized the platin area.--Copyright 1973, Biological Abstracts, Inc.
W75-08314

BIRDS AND MAMMALS OF ANEGADA ISLAND, BRITISH VIRGIN ISLANDS,
Cornell Univ., Ithaca, N.Y. Dept. of Natural Resources.
A. Labastille, and M. Richmond.
Caribb J Sci, Vol 13, No 1/2, p 91-109, 1973, Illus.

Descriptors: *Birds, *Mammals, *Ecology, West Indies.
Identifiers: *Anegada Islands(British Virgin Islands).

Results of a recent biological reconnaissance of Anegada Island in the Greater Antilles (United Kingdom) are presented. The island is uniquely positioned between the Greater Antilles and Lesser Antilles and resembles the latter. The topography, flora, fauna and general ecology are described. All animal life, including man, is tied to small, temporary fresh-water pools and underground fresh-water reservoirs which are accessible from surface sinks and wells. Agriculture is practiced on a very limited scale and, until recently the native blacks have lived simple lives as fishermen. Birds (55 spp.) were observed and 75 small mammals were trapped or netted. Twenty-eight bird species represent 1st records for Anegada. In 1967, the DEV-CAN Corporation of England leased Anegada for development of a large resort. Construction was begun before the company abandoned the project. The government of the British Virgin Islands may take over the tourist development of Anegada. Several research and conservation needs are listed.--Copyright 1974, Biological Abstracts, Inc.
W75-08317

THE INFLUENCE OF SOIL WATER CONTENT ON THE UPTAKE OF IONS BY ROOTS: I. SOIL WATER CONTENT GRADIENTS NEAR A PLANE OF ONION ROOTS,
Nottingham Univ. (England). School of Agriculture.
R. J. Dunham, and P. H. Nye.
J Appl Ecol, Vol 10, No 2, p 585-598, 1973, Illus.
Identifiers: Allium-cepa, Ions, *Onion roots, *Roots, *Soil water, Absorption.

Water content and ion concentration gradients in soil near a plane of onion Allium cepa seedling roots were measured. Using the water content-matric potential relation for this soil, the water content gradients were transformed into matric potential gradients. Potential gradients near the roots were steeper in drier soil. In the driest soil, which was initially at -3 bar, the potential at the root surface fell to about -20 bar. However, if the root-soil geometry had been radial rather than linear, the potential at the root surface would have been about -3.5 bar, which supported the view that steep potential gradients do not normally occur near roots.--Copyright 1974, Biological Abstracts, Inc.
W75-08330

IDENTIFICATION OF TREE STUMPS, AND DRIFTWOOD ASSOCIATED WITH TEPHRA LAYERS IN ALLUVIUM, PEAT, AND DUNE SANDS,
Department of Scientific and Industrial Research, Rotorua (New Zealand). Soil Bureau.
W. A. Pullar, and Rajni N. Patel.
N Z J Bot, Vol 10, No 4, p 605-614, 1972, Illus.
Identifiers: Alluvium, Dacrydium, *Driftwood, Dunes, Leptospermum, *New Zealand, Peat, Podocarpus, Sands, *Tephra layers, *Tree stumps, Vegetation.

From 26 sites in the central and eastern parts of North Ireland, New Zealand, 37 specimens of wood have been identified botanically and their stratigraphic position established in relation to tephra layers of known age. Driftwood derived mainly from podocarp trees (Dacrydium, Podocarpus) was sampled from 5 sites associated with old shorelines and river terraces in the Waipaoa River

Catchment and from 2 sites in the Whakatane River Catchment. The results indicate times at which the corresponding vegetation was growing in the upper parts of these catchments. Stumps between tephra layers sampled from coastal lowlands were mostly from podocarp trees growing in situ during the interval 2100-1800 yr B.P. The paper also discusses the relationship of earth movement at Gisborne to other events including the Taupo Pumice eruptions, the significance of layers of preserved manuka (Leptospermum) in swamps, and changes in the coastline near Whakatane.--Copyright 1973, Biological Abstracts, Inc.
W75-08336

ANALYSES OF A FOREST DRAINAGE EXPERIMENT IN NORTHERN ONTARIO. I: GROWTH ANALYSIS,
Great Lakes Forestry Research Center, Sault Sainte Marie (Ontario).
For primary bibliographic entry see Field 4A.
W75-08337

IRON AND PHOSPHORUS INTERACTION IN CALCAREOUS SOILS: II. EFFECT ON CHLOROSIS DEVELOPMENT, AND SOME NUTRIENT ELEMENT CONTENTS IN SOIL AND PLANT,
Ain Shams Univ., Cairo (Egypt). Dept. of Soils.
For primary bibliographic entry see Field 2G.
W75-08344

2J. Erosion and Sedimentation

RECONNAISSANCE OF SEDIMENTATION IN THE UPPER RIO BERMEJO BASIN, ARGENTINA,
Geological Survey, Menlo Park, Calif.
G. Porterfield.
Open-file report, March 1972. 114 p, 17 fig, 4 tab, 9 ref, 3 append.

Descriptors: *Sediment yield, *South America, Sedimentation, Sediment load, Data collections, Hydrologic data.
Identifiers: *Rio Bermejo(Argentina).

Sediment yields in parts of the Upper Rio Bermejo basin, Argentina are among the largest recorded in the world. Thus, an important consideration in development of water resources in this basin is the effect of sediment on reservoir life and on the design and operation of dams, hydroelectric plants, and diversion structures. Sediment transport conditions were studied at 17 locations and present estimates of reservoir life at 17 proposed sites in the Upper Rio Bermejo basin. The climates in the Upper Rio Bermejo basin range from arid to subtropical. Precipitation, most of which is rainfall, ranges from less than 200 mm to more than 1,300 mm per year and about 80% of the precipitation falls from November to March. Precipitation does not vary directly with altitude but is controlled by other factors. The least precipitation (200 mm) is in the high mountains on the west side of the basin. The precipitation increases eastward to a maximum (1,300 mm) in the northcentral part of the basin, and then decreases to about 600 mm at the confluence of the Rios Bermejo and San Francisco on the east. Temperatures range from subzero minima in the mountains on the west to 50 deg C at the edge of the plains on the east. The warm season occurs at the same time as the rainy season. (Knapp-USGS)
W75-07859

NATURAL AND MODIFIED PLANT COMMUNITIES AS RELATED TO RUNOFF AND SEDIMENT YIELDS,
Geological Survey, Denver, Colo.
For primary bibliographic entry see Field 4C.
W75-07866

BIOLOGICAL AND CHEMICAL ASPECTS OF THE SAN FRANCISCO BAY TURBIDITY MAXIMUM,
Geological Survey, Menlo Park, Calif.
For primary bibliographic entry see Field 2L.
W75-07870

SOURCES OF SUSPENDED MATTER IN WATERS OF THE MIDDLE ATLANTIC BIGHT,
Geological Survey, Woods Hole, Mass.
R. H. Meade, P. L. Sachs, F. T. Manheim, J. C. Hathaway, and D. W. Spencer.
Journal of Sedimentary Petrology, Vol 45, No 1, p 171-188, March 1975. 12 fig, 3 tab, 28 ref, append.

Descriptors: *Suspended load, *Sea water, *Provenance, *Organic matter, *Atlantic Ocean, Continental shelf, Erosion, Marine geology, Waves(Water), Storms.
Identifiers: *Middle Atlantic Bight.

Suspended matter collected in the Middle Atlantic Bight (the coastal segment of the United States between Cape Cod and Cape Hatteras) in September 1969 was predominantly organic. It contained an average of 80% combustible organic matter in surface waters and 40% near bottom. Total suspended concentrations decreased between the inner shelf and the shelf break by an order of magnitude in both near-surface and near-bottom waters. The noncombustible fraction of the suspended matter decreased over the same distance by one order of magnitude in the near-bottom waters and two orders of magnitude in near-surface waters. Recently contributed river sediment is not a significant constituent of the suspended matter in the waters of the shelf, particularly the outer shelf. Most of the inorganic material in suspension represents resuspended bottom sediments (at least some of which are relict) whose suspended concentrations are increased noticeably by stotms. (Knapp-USGS)
W75-07875

MARINE PHOSPHORITE FORMATION OFF PERU,
University of South Florida, St. Petersburg. Marine Science Inst.
For primary bibliographic entry see Field 2K.
W75-07876

NET TRANSPORT OF SEDIMENT THROUGH THE MOUTHS OF ESTUARIES: SEAWARD OR LANDWARD,
Geological Survey, Woods Hole, Mass.
For primary bibliographic entry see Field 2L.
W75-07878

REMOTE SENSING TECHNIQUES FOR EVALUATION OF URBAN EROSION AND SEDIMENTATION,
Geological Survey, Reston, Va.
For primary bibliographic entry see Field 4C.
W75-07880

CHANNEL CHANGES,
Geological Survey, Boise, Idaho.
For primary bibliographic entry see Field 4C.
W75-07884

COMPUTER SIMULATION OF SEDIMENTATION IN MEANDERING STREAMS,
Queens Univ., Belfast (Northern Ireland). Dept. of Geology.
J. S. Bridge.
Sedimentology, Vol 22, No 1, p 3-43, February 1975. 25 fig, 3 tab, 69 ref, append.

Descriptors: *Sedimentation, *Meanders, *Erosion, *Computer models, *Systems analysis, Analytical techniques, Aggradation, Stratification, Particle size, Stream stabilization, Mathematical models, Streams, *Simulation analysis.
Identifiers: *Channel migration, Point bar sediments, Meander geometry, Meander movement.

A dynamic mathematical model for simulation of sedimentation in meandering streams was described. For a given physical situation and a single time increment, the following aspects of the system were included in the component models: the form of the meander, the movement of the meander in plan, the hydraulic properties of the channel in the bend, the nature and occurrence of cut-off, and a relative measure of discharge during a seasonal high period. The model in the form of a Fortran IV computer program was used to simulate various aspects of sedimentation in meandering streams under different input conditions. The model recorded the systematic distribution of sedimentary structures. It also recorded large-scale lateral changes in grain size and sedimentary strueture associated with changes in the shape of developing meanders. Wher appropriate field data exist, the model can be used in the more accurate recognition of ancient fluviatile sediments. A representative application of the model to the quantitative interpretation of an ancient point bar deposit was illustrated. (Singh-ISWS)
W75-07891

SEDIMENT DEPOSITION FROM FLOCCULATED SUSPENSIONS,
Bedford Institute of Oceanography, Dartmouth, Nova Scotia (Canada). Atlantic Oceanographic Laboratory.
K. Kranck.
Sedimentology, Vol 22, No 1, p 111-123, February 1975. 10 fig, 26 ref.

Descriptors: *Suspended load, *Flocculation, *Particle size, *Settling velocity, *Distribution patterns, Suspension, Estuaries, Salinity, Sea water, Stokes law, Deposition(Sediments), Sedimentology, *Canada.
Identifiers: *Flocculated suspensions, *Nova Scotia, Non-normal curves.

Suspended sediment in coastal environments with high inorganic content have characteristic broad size distributions and are composed of both single grains and flocculated aggregates. These flocculated suspensions have stable size distributions the model size of which is dependent on the model size of the deflocculated single grain distributions. Comparison between theoretical settling speeds of particles in natural suspensions indicates that most grains smaller than the deflocculated single grain mode settle as part of flocs, whereas the particles larger than the mode settle as single grains. As the result the size distribution curves of sediment populations which settle out during consecutive intervals are composed of a modal peak of larger grains and a low flat portion of smaller grains and resemble the asymmetrical non-normal curves common for muddy sediments. This break between the tail and the modal peak which appears on cumulative curves plotted on probability paper as a change in the slope is usually related to the presence of two log-normal sediment populations, transported by separate mechanisms. (Singh-ISWS)
W75-07892

DISTRIBUTION OF MICROBIAL ADENOSINE TRIPHOSPHATE IN SALT MARSH SEDIMENTS AT SAPELO ISLAND, GEORGIA,
Georgia Univ., Athens. Dept. of Microbiology.
For primary bibliographic entry see Field 5B.
W75-07899

SUBMERGED SOILS IN THE NORTHWESTERN MEDITERRANEAN SEA AND THE PROCESS OF HUMIFICATION,
Centre Universitaire de Perpignan, Moulin a Vent (France). Centre de Recherches de Sedimentologie Marine.
For primary bibliographic entry see Field 5B.
W75-07900

THE INFLUENCE OF WIND VELOCITY ON THE SIZE DISTRIBUTIONS OF AEROSOLS GENERATED BY THE WIND EROSION OF SOILS,
National Center for Atmospheric Research, Boulder, Colo.
D. A. Gillette, I. H. Blifford, Jr., and D. W. Fryrear.
Journal of Geophysical Research, Vol 79, No 27, p 4068-4075, September 20, 1974. 8 fig, 2 tab, 13 ref.

Descriptors: *Wind erosion, *Aerosols, *Particle size, Soil erosion, Soils, Soil physical properties, Winds, Wind velocity, On-site investigations, Filters.

The relationship of the relative size distribution of soil wind erosion aerosols to wind velocity was examined in field measurements and wind tunnel simulations. The ratio of sedimentation velocity to friction velocity, square root of (vertical momentum/air density), at which aerosol particles were significantly affected by settling was larger than 0.12 and smaller than 0.68. The shapes of the size distributions of soil wind erosion aerosols (2 micrometers less than r less than 10 micrometers) were fairly constant with wind speed. This result is evidence that the dominant mechanism of aerosol production by soil erosion is sandblasting of the soil surface. (Sims-ISWS)
W75-07915

MICROSCALE TRANSPORT OF SAND-SIZED SOIL AGGREGATES ERODED BY WIND,
National Center for Atmospheric Research, Boulder, Colo.
D. Gillette, and P. A. Goodwin.
Journal of Geophysical Research, Vol 79, No 27, p 4080-4084, September 20, 1974. 2 fig, 4 tab, 13 ref.

Descriptors: *Wind erosion, *Soil erosion, *Model studies, On-site data collections, Mathematical models, Particle size, Sediment transport, Aggregates, Soils, Aerosols, Wind velocity, Sedimentation, Diffusion.

Field measurements of the vertical profiles of horizontal fluxes of airborne, sand-sized soil aggregates were shown to be in good agreement with solutions of an equation that express the dependence of the concentration of sand at a given height on vertical diffusion and sedimentation. This approach treats sand as a diffusing agent rather than as projectiles that are affected by the wind only on the horizontal direction. The observed horizontal sand fluxes were shown to be in agreement with empirical formulas that express total horizontal flux of sand as a function of wind and soil parameters. (Sims-ISWS)
W75-07916

THE WESTERN BOUNDARY UNDERCURRENT AS A TURBIDITY MAXIMUM OVER THE PUERTO RICO TRENCH,
Lamont-Doherty Geological Observatory, Palisades, N.Y.
B. E. Tucholke, and S. Eittreim.
Journal of Geophysical Research, Vol 79, No 27, p 4115-4118, September 20, 1974. 3 fig, 15 ref. NSF Grants GA-41657, GA-27281; ONR Contract N0014-67-A-0108-0004.

Descriptors: *Turbidity, *Oceans, *Trenches, Atlantic Ocean, Suspended solids, Sediments, Temperature, Water circulation, Sounding, Depth, Exploration, Oceanography, Puerto Rico.
Identifiers: *Nephelometers, *Puerto Rico trench, Undercurrents.

Nephelometer measurements in the Puerto Rico trench record a midwater light scattering maximum at the depth of the near-bottom nepheloid layer found in the deep Atlantic basin to the northwest. This mid-water maximum is best developed near the south slope of the trench and is interpreted as a southeasterly continuation of the western boundary undercurrent, which has been documented along the continental rise of eastern North America. The eastward-advecting core of the flow overrides clearer colder antarctic bottom water that enters the trench from the east. A near-bottom nepheloid layer, best developed in the eastern part of the trench, appears to be associated with the westward-flowing antarctic bottom current. (Sims-ISWS)
W75-07918

SIMULATION OF SOIL EROSION–PART I. DEVELOPMENT OF A MATHEMATICAL EROSION MODEL,
International Rice Research Inst., Los Banos, Laguna (Philippines).
W. P. David, and C. E. Beer.
Transactions of the American Society of Agricultural Engineers, Vol 18, No 1, p 126-133, January-February 1975. 2 fig, 21 ref.

Descriptors: *Soil erosion, *Mathematical models, *Overland flow, *Precipitation intensity, *Raindrops, *Stream erosion, Sheet erosion, Rill erosion, Runoff, Suspended solids, Cultivation, Gully erosion, Model studies, Watersheds(Basins), Equations, Sediment transport, *Simulation analysis.
Identifiers: *Land slope, Wash load, Kentucky Watershed Model.

Results of a study conducted to simulate the process of sheet erosion by water were described. The primary objective of the study was to develop a mathematical model of erosion by water. The Kentucky Watershed Model was adopted to generate values of overland flow to be used in the erosion model. The other input to the model was the intensity of the precipitation. Equations expressing soil erosion from stream banks, impervious surfaces, and raindrop splash were developed. In addition, the carrying capacity of the overland flow was continuously evaluated to determine whether soil particles were being removed and transported from storage or deposited. The equations upon which the mathematical model was based are power functions with parameters that are to be evaluated during calibration runs of the model. (See also W75-07927) (Bhowmik-ISWS)
W75-07926

SIMULATION OF SOIL EROSION–PART II. STREAMFLOW AND SUSPENDED SEDIMENT SIMULATION RESULTS,
International Rice Research Inst., Los Banos, Laguna (Philippines).
W. P. David, and C. E. Beer.
Transactions of the American Society of Agricultural Engineers, Vol 18, No 1, p 130-133, January-February 1975. 2 fig, 3 tab, 8 ref.

Descriptors: *Simulation analysis, *Soil erosion, *Overland flow, *Precipitation intensity, *Sheet erosion, Mathematical models, Calibrations, Snowmelt, Suspended load, Stream erosion, Bank erosion, Scour, Streamflow, *Iowa, Model studies, Watersheds(Basins).
Identifiers: *Kentucky Watershed Model, Land slope, Four Mile Creek Watershed.

A sheet erosion model was developed to simulate sheet erosion from small agricultural watersheds. The sheet erosion model was used in conjunction with the Kentucky Watershed Model, which is a modified version of the Stanford Watershed Model. The Kentucky Watershed Model was modified and adapted to Iowa conditions. To evaluate the feasibility of the sheet erosion model, it was tested on the Four Mile Creek Watershed near Traer, Iowa. The simulated daily, monthly, and annual suspended sediment loads compared favorably to the observed values. It was mentioned that the sheet erosion model cannot be applied for large watersheds. The model also cannot predict the sediment deposition along floodplains and it lacks sufficient parameters to define the seasonal effect on some of the sheet erosion parameters. (See also W75-07926) (Bhowmik-ISWS)
W75-07927

URBAN SEDIMENT PROBLEMS: A STATEMENT ON SCOPE, RESEARCH, LEGISLATION, AND EDUCATION.
American Society of Civil Engineers, New York. Task Committee on Urban Sedimentation Problems.
For primary bibliographic entry see Field 5G.
W75-07931

NONERODIBLE AGGREGATES AND CONCENTRATION OF FATS, WAXES, AND OILS IN SOILS AS RELATED TO WHEAT STRAW MULCH,
Agricultural Research Service, Akron, Colo. Central Great Plains Field Station.
For primary bibliographic entry see Field 4D.
W75-07940

CONCENTRATION EFFECTS OF SETTLING-TUBE ANALYSIS,
Technische Hogeschool, Delft (Netherlands). Department of Civil Engineering.
C. Kranenburg, and H. J. Geldof.
Journal of Hydraulic Research, Vol 12, No 3, p 337-355, 1974. 5 fig, 15 ref, 1 append.

Descriptors: *Sediments, *Particle size, *Settling velocity, Fluid mechanics, Velocity, Reynolds number, Analysis, Convection, *Mathematical models, Hydraulics.
Identifiers: *Hindered settling, Settling tube.

A mathermatical model describing the unsteady settling of nonuniform sediment samples was developed, which accounts for the influence of sediment concentration on the fall velocity. The resulting equations were solved by using the method of integration along characteristics. An estimating procedure for the settling-tube size required was established. The procedure was based on the requirement that the relative error in the settling time of each particle, due to possible concentration effects such as hindered settling and settling convection, be less than a prescribed value. A lack of unambiguous experimental data on settling convection prevented a positive statement, this phenomenon seemed to be more severe than hindered settling. If settling convection occurred, it would apparently cause unacceptable errors in the analysis of the relatively large sample sizes (for the settling-tube dimensions) recommended in the literature. (Adams-ISWS)
W75-07949

PHOSPHORUS UPTAKE AND RELEASE BY LAKE ONTERIO SEDIMENTS,
Wisconsin Univ., Madison. Water Chemistry Program; and Wisconsin Univ., Madison. Dept. of Soils.
For primary bibliographic entry see Field 5A.
W75-07972

KAIMU BEACH HAWAII, PROPOSED SHORE PROTECTION (FINAL ENVIRONMENTAL IMPACT STATEMENT).
Corps of Engineers, Honolulu, Hawaii. Pacific Ocean Div.
For primary bibliographic entry see Field 8A.
W75-08052

VIRGINIA KEY BEACH EROSION CONTROL PROJECT, SECOND PERIODIC NOURISHMENT AND GROINS (FINAL ENVIRONMENTAL IMPACT STATEMENT).
Army Engineer District, Jacksonville, Fla.
For primary bibliographic entry see Field 8A.
W75-08053

REVIEW OF GEOLOGICAL RESEARCH AS IT RELATES TO AN UNDERSTANDING OF GREAT LAKES LIMNOLOGY,
Canada Centre for Inland Waters, Burlington (Ontario).
For primary bibliographic entry see Field 2H.
W75-08144

ENVIRONMENTAL ASSESSMENT OF SEDIMENT SOURCES AND SEDIMENTATION DISTRIBUTIONS FOR THE LAKE LA FARGE WATERHSED AND IMPOUNDMENT,
Wisconsin Univ., Madison. Dept. of Geography.
For primary bibliographic entry see Field 2E.
W75-08161

ORGANIC SUBSTANCES IN SEDIMENT AND SETTLING MATTER DURING SPRING IN A MEROMICTIC LAKE SUIGETSU,
Nagoya Univ. (Japan). Water Research Lab.
For primary bibliographic entry see Field 2H.
W75-08257

MUD-WATER EXCHANGE OF PHOSPHATE AND OTHER IONS IN UNDISTURBED SEDIMENT CORES AND FACTORS AFFECTING THE EXCHANGE RATES,
Copenhagen Univ. (Denmark). Freshwater Biological Lab.
L. Kamp-Nielson.
Arch Hydrobiol, Vol 73, No 2, p 218-237, 1974, Illus.
Identifiers: Antibiotics, *Denmark, Diffusion, Ions, Lakes, Microorganism, Mud, Oxygen, *Phosphates, *Sediment cores, *Lake sediments, *Mud-water interfaces, *Ion exchange.

The exchange rates of P,N and to a lesser extent Fe, Ca and silicate across the sediment surface were determined by experiments with undisturbed sediment cores from the profundal of a spectrum of Danish lakes. The effects of oxidation state, antibiotics and pH on the exchange rates were studied and attempts are made to relate the exhange to sediment parameters. The N exchange involves mineralization, nitrofication and denitrification and occurs by biological processes. When O2 is present the phosphate exchange is governed by adsorption, but microorganisms also seem to be involved. Under anaerobic conditions the phosphate release is linearly dependent on the concentration gradient across the mud surface and the exchange may be explained in terms of diffusion with a diffusion coefficient of 0.6 x 10 to the minus 6 power x cm2 x s to the minus 1 power. The adsorption and the concentration gradient are influenced by a pH-dependent dissolution and precipitation of Ca and Fe phosphates.--Copyright 1974, Biological Abstracts, Inc.
W75-08320

STRATIGRAPHIC EFFECTS OF TUBIFICIDS IN PROFUNDAL LAKE SEDIMENTS,
Maine Univ., Orono. Dept. of Botany and Plant Pathology.
For primary bibliographic entry see Field 5C.
W75-08322

ON RELATIONSHIPS BETWEEN THE NATURE OF THE SEDIMENT AND THE CHEMICAL PROPERTIES OF THE HYPORHEAL BIOTOPE IN THE HUNGARIAN SECTION OF THE DANUBE (DANUBIALIA HUNGARICA LIX),
Magyar Tudomanyos Akademia, Budapest. Station for Danube Research.
E. V. Kozma.
Ann Univ Sci Budap Rolando Eotvos Nominatae Sect Biol, 13. p 53-67, 1971. Illus.

Descriptors: *Rivers, Europe, Flow, Soil types, Chemical properties, Water properties, Groundwater, Physical characteristics, *Sediments.
Identifiers: *Biotopes, *Danube River, Danubialia, *Hungary, *Hyporheal biotope.

Factors influencing the properties of the hyporheal biotope in the Hungarian Danube section were studied. Such biotopes were strongly influenced by the soil composition, the chemical composition of the groundwater and of the river water, the soil permeability, and by the flow conditions. Decrease in soil temperature, pH value, and dissolved O2 content with distance from the riverbank were determined.--Copyright 1973, Biological Abstracts, Inc.
W75-08349

2K. Chemical Processes

A SUMMARY OF SELECTED CHEMICAL-QUALITY CONDITIONS IN 66 CALIFORNIA STREAMS, 1950-72,
Geological Survey, Menlo Park, Calif.
For primary bibliographic entry see Field 5A.
W75-07858

GENESIS OF HYDROGEOCHEMICAL FACIES OF GROUND WATERS IN THE PUNJAB REGION OF PAKISTAN,
Geological Survey, Washington, D.C.
For primary bibliographic entry see Field 5B.
W75-07865

GEOCHEMICAL EQULIBRIA AT LOW TEMPERATURES AND PRESSURES,
Geological Survey, Reston, Va.
B. B. Hanshaw, and W. Back.
In: Encyclopaedia Britannica, 15th Edition, p 1028-1035, 1974. 3 fig, 4 ref.

Descriptors: *Water chemistry, *Geochemistry, *Equilibrium, Aqueous solutions, Thermodynamic behavior, Thermodynamics, Chemical reactions.

Geochemical equilibria are involved in most natural geological and hydrological processes at or near the surface of the Earth. Low-temperature, low-pressure studies of chemical equilibria are concerned with the processes that take place between the lowest temperature on Earth and approximately 400C, and between near vacuum and several kilobars of pressure. The ultimate goal of low-temperature, low-pressure equlibria studies is to describe the various Earth environments that may influence Earth materials and water by reason of naturally or artificially imposed geochemical stresses. The parameters that have proven useful for environmental description are (1) the electromotive force or potential of reactions (Eh), (2) acidity (pH), (3) pressure, (4) temperature, (5) solubility of minerals, and (6) the chemistry of pore solutions in rocks. A unified description of the Earth's environments becomes possible only when the several important parameters and their variations are examined from the viewpoint of thermodynamics. Included is consideration of the principles of thermodynamics that are of special relevance to understanding geochemical equilibria at low temperatures and pressures and of geochemical diagrams that are employed to delimit environmental conditions. Additionally, there is consideration of several specific equilibria that are of significance in nature. These include carbonate, iron, and uranium systems, soil conditions, and osmotic equilibria. (Knapp-USGS)
W75-07867

MARINE PHOSPHORITE FORMATION OFF PERU,
University of South Florida, St. Petersburg. Marine Science Inst.
F. Manheim, G. T. Rowe, and D. Jipa.
Journal of Sedimentary Petrology, Vol 45, No 1, p 243-251, March 1975. 9 fig, 1 tab, 41 ref.

Descriptors: *Diagenesis, *Phosphates, Continental shelf, Connate water, Sedimentation, Water chemistry, Sea water, Carbonates, Plankton, Sedimentology.
Identifiers: *Peru, Foraminifera.

Formation of contemporary phosphorite occurs in the Peru-Chile offshore area. Synthesis occurs as a result of replacement of carbonate tests of Holocene benthonic Foraminifera in the interstitial waters of organic-rich sediments. Step-by-step phosphatization of Holocene benthic Foraminifera is demonstrated. Four simultaneous requirements for formation of phosphorites are: (a) sediments rich in organic detritus blanketed by (b) water with low concentrations of dissolved oxygen, (c) low rates of inorganic (especially terrigenous) sedimentation and (d) low but not negligible concentrations of calcium carbonate in the sediment. (Knapp-USGS)
W75-07876

WATER-RESOURCES INVESTIGATIONS OF THE U.S. GEOLOGICAL SURVEY IN THE NORTHERN GREAT PLAINS COAL REGION OF NORTHEASTERN WYOMING, 1974-75.
Geological Survey, Cheyenne, Wyo.
For primary bibliographic entry see Field 7C.
W75-07887

WATER QUALITY OF HYDROLOGIC BENCH MARKS--AN INDICATOR OF WATER QUALITY IN THE NATURAL ENVIRONMENT,
Geological Survey, Reston, Va.
For primary bibliographic entry see Field 5A.
W75-07888

NATURAL DISTRIBUTION OF TRACE METALS IN SEDIMENTS FROM A COASTAL ENVIRONMENT, TOR BAY, ENGLAND,
Imperial Chemical Industries Ltd., Brixham (England). Brixham Research Lab.
For primary bibliographic entry see Field 2L.
W75-07895

DIFFUSION COEFFICIENTS CALCULATED FROM THE MEDITERREAN SALINITY ANOMALY IN THE NORTH ATLANTIC OCEAN,
Bedford Inst. of Oceanography, Dartmouth (Nova Scotia). Atlantic Oceanographic Lab.
For primary bibliographic entry see Field 2L.
W75-07912

ELECTRONIC DIGITIZATION AND SENSOR RESPONSE EFFECTS ON SALINITY COMPUTATION FROM CTD FIELD MEASUREMENTS,
Washington Univ., Seattle. Dept. of Oceanography.
For primary bibliographic entry see Field 2L.
W75-07914

THE DETERMINATION OF THE INDEX OF REFRACTION DISTRIBUTION OF OCEANIC PARTICULATES,
Oregon State Univ., Corvallis. School of Oceanography.
J. R. V. Zaneveld, D. M. Roach, and H. Pak.
Journal of Geophysical Research, Vol 79, No 27, p 4091-4095, September 20, 1974. 3 fig, 2 tab, 17 ref. ONR Contract N00014-67-A-0369-0007.

Descriptors: *Refractivity, *Suspended solids, *Particle size, *Optical properties, Physical properties, Light, Opacity, Mathematical models, Reflectance, Sea water, Oceans, Dispersion, Turbidity, Suspension, Particle shape, Phytoplankton, Size, Distribution.
Identifiers: Mie theory, Sargasso Sea, Coulter counter, Biomodal distribution.

A method was described for determining the index of refraction distribution and the particle size distribution of suspended particles. The distributions

are obtained by breaking down an observed volume scattering function into its contributing components. The component scattering functions are calculated by using Mie theory. The component functions include all size distributions and indices of refraction that can be expected to be present. The method was applied to a volume scattering function observed in the Sargasso Sea. Forty components were used with five different indices of refraction and eight different particle size distributions. The resultant index of refraction distribution was bimodal. Components with indices of 1.05 and 1.15 dominated the calculated volume scattering function. The calculated particle size distribution fell within experimentally determined limits for the size distribution. (Henley-ISWS)
W75-07917

ANALYSIS OF LAS, ABS AND COMMERCIAL DETERGENTS BY TWO-PHASE TITRATION,
Rensselaer Polytechnic Inst., Troy, N.Y. Dept. of Chemical Engineering; and Rensselaer Polytechnic Inst., Troy, N.Y. Dept. of Environmental Engineering.
For primary bibliographic entry see Field 5A.
W75-07937

FLUORINE IN GROUND WATER AS A GUIDE TO PB-ZN-BA-F MINERALIZATION,
Toronto Univ. (Ontario). Dept. of Geology.
G. S. Graham, S. E. Kesler, and J. C. Van Loon.
Economic Geology, Vol 70, No 2, p 396-398, March-April 1975. 2 fig, 12 ref.

Descriptors: *Fluorine, *Geochemistry, *Chemical analysis, *Groundwater, *Fluorides, Inorganic compounds, Halogens, Analysis, Evaluation, Chemistry, Instrumentation, Chemical properties, Mineralogy, Exploration, Analytical techniques, Canada, Surveys.
Identifiers: *Fluorite, Fluorapatite.

Analysis of fluoride in groundwater deserves careful consideration as a method of geochemical exploration for Pb-Zn-Ba-F mineralization in the flat-lying carbonate rocks of mid-continent North America. The interpretation of analytical results was not rendered impossible by fluoride complexing, precipitation of fluoride bearing phases, or seasonal variations in groundwater fluoride content. Groundwater sampling in stratigraphically or structurally favorable areas should be useful in locating blind fluorite or fluorite-bearing mineralization at depths of several hundred feet. (Henley-ISWS)
W75-07953

CHANGE IN THE CHEMISTRY OF NATURAL WATERS IN LANDSCAPES UNDER AGRICULTURAL USE,
For primary bibliographic entry see Field 5B.
W75-07974

GROUND-WATER QUALITY RELATED TO IRRIGATION WITH IMPORTED SURFACE OR LOCAL GROUND WATER,
Agricultural Research Service, Fresno, Calif.
For primary bibliographic entry see Field 5B.
W75-07978

TEMPERATURE CONTROLLED HEATING OF THE GRAPHITE TUBE ATOMIZER IN FLAMELESS ATOMIC ABSORPTION SPECTROMETRY,
Umea Univ. (Sweden). Dept. of Analytical Chemistry.
For primary bibliographic entry see Field 5A.
W75-08079

SOME ANALYTICAL APPLICATIONS OF REACTION-RATE-PROMOTING EFFECTS--THE TRIS(1,10-PHENANTHROLINE)IRON(II)-CHROMIUM(VI) INDICATOR REACTION,
Oklahoma State Univ., Stillwater. Dept. of Chemistry.
For primary bibliographic entry see Field 5A.
W75-08080

MICRODETERMINATION OF METALS IN ORGANOMETALLIC COMPOUNDS BY THE OXINE METHOD AFTER CLOSED FLASH COMBUSTION,
Cairo Univ., Giza (Egypt). Microanalytical Unit.
For primary bibliographic entry see Field 5A.
W75-08091

ON THE CHEMICAL MASS-BALANCE IN ESTUARIES,
Massachusetts Inst. of Tech., Cambridge, Mass. Dept. of Earth and Planetary Sciences.
For primary bibliographic entry see Field 5B.
W75-08095

SOLUBILIZATION OF DIMETHYLMERCURY BY HALIDE IONS,
Missouri Univ., Rolla. Dept. of Chemistry.
For primary bibliographic entry see Field 5B.
W75-08096

REVIEW OF GEOLOGICAL RESEARCH AS IT RELATES TO AN UNDERSTANDING OF GREAT LAKES LIMNOLOGY,
Canada Centre for Inland Waters, Burlington (Ontario).
For primary bibliographic entry see Field 2H.
W75-08144

THE KINETICS OF MINERAL DISSOLUTION IN CARBONATE AQUIFERS AS A TOOL FOR HYDROLOGICAL INVESTIGATIONS, I. CONCENTRATION-TIME RELATIONSHIPS,
Water Planning for Israel Ltd., Tel-Aviv.
A. Mercado, and G. K. Billings.
Journal of Hydrology, Vol 24, No 3/4, p 303-331, February 1975. 9 fig, 2 tab, 29 ref. OWRT B-038-NMEX(1), WRRI-3109.140.

Descriptors: *Kinetics, *Geochemistry, *Carbonate rocks, *Aquifers, *Groundwater, Hydrogeology, Chemical reactions, Dating, Radioactive dating, Model studies, Mass transfer, Tracers, Carbon radioisotopes, Florida, Aqueous solutions, Thermodynamics, Calcite, Dolomite, Gypsum, Computer programs.
Identifiers: *Limestone aquifers, Concentration-time relationships, Dissolution, Aqueous species, Debye-Huckel equation.

The importance of available groundwater chemical data for hydrologic investigations has been relatively neglected. Two general courses exist for use of groundwater chemical data and dissolution kinetics in hydrologic investigations: (1) estimating relative ages according to precalibrated concentration-time relationships similar to that of tritium and C14 dating techniques; and (2) integrated study of both hydrologic and geochemical phenomena with the aid of combined hydrogeochemical models. A kinetic model for the dissolution of multimineral assemblages in porous media was derived with special emphasis on the simultaneous dissolution of calcite, dolomite, and gypsum in some carbonate aquifers. Supersaturation on groundwater samples with respect to calcite and dolomite frequently occurs and was explained by the relatively high solubility of gypsum, resulting in kinetic competition among dissolving minerals. The applicability of a computerized kinetic model was domonstrated by the evaluation of hydrogeochemical data for the limestone aquifer of central Florida. The kinetic model was calibrated with the aid of available hydrologic estimates and chemical data for part of the aquifer. Chemical age estimates based on calibrated con-

the two, or is absent where limestone crops out, whereas soil in the Everglades is usually deeper organic peat. Vegetation in the Swamp is closely associated with topography, water inundation, and soils, and is more diverse and forested than it is in the Everglades. (Knapp-USGS)
W75-07863

BIOLOGICAL AND CHEMICAL ASPECTS OF THE SAN FRANCISCO BAY TURBIDITY MAXIMUM,
Geological Survey, Menlo Park, Calif.
T. J. Conomos, and D. H. Peterson.
In: Interrelationships of Estuarine and Continenal Shelf Sedimentation; Proceedings of International Symposium, Bordeaux, France, July 9-14, 1973: Memories de l'Institut de Geologie du Bassin d'Aquitaine, No 7, p 45-52, 1974. 8 fig, 14 ref.

Descriptors: *Sedimentation, *Bays, *Estuaries, *California, Sediment load, Sediment transport, Density currents, Water circulation, Tides.
Identifiers: *San Francisco Bay(Calif).

Suspended-particle composition and distribution in the San Francisco Bay system are modulated by seasonally varying water circulation, river inflow, and phytoplankton production. Water circulation has both tidal and nontidal component. The velocity of tidal components is as much as 250 cm/sec at Golden Gate. Tidal components, often reinforced by wind mixing, resuspend particles from the relatively shallow bay floor and move these particles laterally. Nontidal components, which are generated by wind and by density differences resulting from fresh-water inflows, are responsible for advective particle movements. These nontidal components are characterized by a permanent circulation cell in the north bay typical of a partially-mixed estuary, and by seasonally reversing flow in the south bay. Seaward surface drift of low-salinity water annually averages more than 6 cm/sec while landward near-bottom drift of ocean water annually averages 5 cm/sec. The pronounced estuarine circulation in north bay maintains a turbidity maximum which changes seasonally in particle concentration and composition. In contrast to north bay, the inherent weakness of south bay nontidal circulation precludes formation of a turbidity maximum. The bay system is an effective trap for suspended particles. Approximately 4 million metric tons of suspended particles accumulate annually in the bay system. (Knapp-USGS)
W75-07870

KARST HYDROLOGY OF NORTHERN YUCATAN PENINSULA, MEXICO,
Geological Survey, Reston, Va.
For primary bibliographic entry see Field 2F.
W75-07873

SOURCES OF SUSPENDED MATTER IN WATERS OF THE MIDDLE ATLANTIC BIGHT,
Geological Survey, Woods Hole, Mass.
For primary bibliographic entry see Field 2J.
W75-07875

MOVEMENT OF SPILLED OIL AS PREDICTED BY ESTUARINE NONTIDAL DRIFT,
Geological Survey, Menlo Park, Calif.
For primary bibliographic entry see Field 5B.
W75-07877

NET TRANSPORT OF SEDIMENT THROUGH THE MOUTHS OF ESTUARIES: SEAWARD OR LANDWARD,
Geological Survey, Woods Hole, Mass.
R. H. Meade.
In: Interrelationships of Estuarine and Continental Shelf Sedimentation; Proceedings of International Symposium, Bordeaux, France, July 9-14, 1973: Memoires de l' Institut de Geologie du Bassin d' Aquitaine, No 7, p 207-213, 1974. 24 ref.

Descriptors: *Sediment transport, *Estuaries, *Provenance, Sediment yield, Continental shelf, Sedimentation, Sands, Rivers, Suspended load, Bed load.

Rivers and estuaries of the eastern U.S. may supply less sediment to the shelf than the shelf supplies to the estuaries. Evidences for transport of sediment onto the shelf from estuaries are: (1) net seaward drift of surface waters in estuaries and across the shelf; (2) plumes of turbid water that emerge from estuaries onto the shelf; and (3) measurements that suggest a net seaward transport of sediment through the mouth of Delaware Bay. Evidences of transport of shelf sediment into estuaries are: (1) net landward drift of bottom waters on the inner half of the shelf and in the estuaries, along with net longshore drift toward the mouths of the estuaries: (2) accumulation of fine sediment in estuaries in contrast with the prevalence of coarser relict material on the shelf; and (3) mineral compositions of estuarine sediments (and suspended sediment in shelf waters) that correspond more closely to older shelf sediments than to sediments being carried by rivers. The evidence that is presently available gives more support to a net landward movement of sediment from the shelf into the estuaries. (Knapp-USGS)
W75-07878

SEDIMENT DEPOSITION FROM FLOCCULATED SUSPENSIONS,
Bedford Institute of Oceanography, Dartmouth, Nova Scotia (Canada), Atlantic Oceanographic Laboratory.
For primary bibliographic entry see Field 2J.
W75-07892

EFFECTS OF SEA WATER EXTRACTS OF SEDIMENTS FROM CHARLESTON HARBOR, S.C., ON LARVAL ESTUARINE FISHES,
National Marine Fisheries Service, Beaufort, N.C. Atlantic Estuarine Fisheries Center.
For primary bibliographic entry see Field 5C.
W75-07893

HYDROCARBONS IN THE MARINE ENVIRONMENT, I. N-ALKANES IN THE FIRTH OF CLYDE,
Torry Research Station, Aberdeen (Scotland).
For primary bibliographic entry see Field 5A.
W75-07894

NATURAL DISTRIBUTION OF TRACE METALS IN SEDIMENTS FROM A COASTAL ENVIRONMENT, TOR BAY, ENGLAND,
Imperial Chemical Industries Ltd., Brixham (England). Brixham Research Lab.
D. Taylor.
Estuarine and Coastal Marine Science, Vol 2, No 4, p 417-424, October 1974. 5 fig, 3 tab, 11 ref.

Descriptors: *Trace elements, *Sediments, *Coasts, *Bays, Metals, Silts, Cadmium, Chromium, Cobalt, Copper, Lead, Manganese, Mercury, Nickel, Zinc, On-site investigations.
Identifiers: *England(Tor Bay).

The distribution of cadmium, chromium, cobalt, copper, lead, manganese, mercury, nickel, and zinc, in the sediments of Tor Bay, a coastal area relatively free of industrial pollution, was investigated. The aim of this study was to provide baseline information which could be used for comparison with similar areas receiving industrial wastes. The trace metal concentrations and the percentage of silt in each sample were tabulated. Correlations between the elements were calculated. It was found that: (1) there are no significant correlations between manganese or mercury with any other element, and (2) the metal inter-relationships are complex. (Sims-ISWS)
W75-07895

DISTRIBUTION OF MICROBIAL ADENOSINE TRIPHOSPHATE IN SALT MARSH SEDIMENTS AT SAPELO ISLAND, GEORGIA,
Georgia Univ., Athens. Dept. of Microbiology.
For primary bibliographic entry see Field 5B.
W75-07899

SUBMERGED SOILS IN THE NORTHWESTERN MEDITERRANEAN SEA AND THE PROCESS OF HUMIFICATION,
Centre Universitaire de Perpignan, Moulin a Vent (France). Centre de Recherches de Sedimentologie Marine.
For primary bibliographic entry see Field 5B.
W75-07900

STOKES TRANSPORT BY GRAVITY WAVES FOR APPLICATION TO CIRCULATION MODELS,
Connecticut Univ., Groton. Marine Scinces Inst.
J. P. Ianniello, and R. W. Garvine.
Journal of Physical Oceanography, Vol 5, No 1, p 47-50, January 1975. 2 fig, 14 ref. NSF Grant GX-33502.

Descriptors: *Ocean circulation, *Gravity waves, *Model studies, Mathematical models, Currents(Water), Ocean currents, Mass transfer, Coriolis force, Oceanography, Mathematical studies.
Identifiers: *Stokes mass transport, Lagrangian transport.

Stokes mass transport by surface gravity waves is related to the often more interesting Lagrangian transport in a manner that is complicated by the earth's rotation. The conditions under which duration- and fetch-limited gravity wave transport will be important driving mechanisms for circulation models were discussed. Curves of duration and fetch-limited Stokes transport were given as functions of dimensionless time and fetch. (Sims-ISWS)
W75-07903

MODE: IGPP MEASUREMENTS OF BOTTOM PRESSURE AND TEMPERATURE,
California Univ., San Diego, La Jolla. Inst. of Geophysics and Planetary Physics.
For primary bibliographic entry see Field 7B.
W75-07904

MODE BOTTOM EXPERIMENT,
California Univ., San Diego, La Jolla. Inst. of Geophysics and Planetary Physics.
For primary bibliographic entry see Field 7B.
W75-07905

FORMATION OF MEANDERS, FRONTS, AND CUTOFF THERMAL POOLS IN A BAROCLINIC OCEAN CURRENT,
Yale Univ., New Haven, Conn. Dept. of Geology and Geophysics.
B. Saltzman, and C-M. Tang.
Journal of Physical Oceanography, Vol 5, No 1, p 86-92, January 1975. 8 fig, 14 ref. NSF Grant GA-10555; Army Grant DAHC04-74-G-0229.

Descriptors: *Ocean currents, *Model studies, *Meanders, Ocean circulation, Mathematical models, Numerical analysis, Cyclones, Anticyclones, Oceanography.
Identifiers: *Baroclinic ocean currents, Gulf stream, Baroclinic instability, Fronts(Oceanic).

With an analytical model similar to that previously applied to the atmosphere, calculations were made showing how second-order, nongeostrophic effects can modify a two-layer baroclinic wave system that grows exponentially from a small perturbation in a uniform zonal ocean current. It was shown that many of the asymmetric features characteristic of meandering ocean currents

develop, including 'fronts' and cutoff cyclonic cold pools to the south and anticyclonic warm pools to the north of the axis of the mean current. The implication is that all of these features can be reviewed as being the simultaneous consequence of baroclinic instability (with attendant second-order finite-amplitude effects) of a broader, more uniform current that might tend to be forced externally by the wind stress and thermohaline processes. (Sims-ISWS)
W75-07906

ENTRAINMENT AND DIFFUSION IN A GULF STREAM CYCLONIC RING,
Texas A and M Univ., College Station. Dept. of Oceanography.
J. E. Schmitz, and A. C. Vastano.
Journal of Physical Oceanography, Vol 5, No 1, p 93-97, January 1975. 6 fig, 2 tab, 7 ref. ONR Contract N00014-68-0308-0002.

Descriptors: *Model studies, *Entrainment, *Diffusion, *Ocean circulation, Cyclones, Oceans, Temperature, Mathematical studies, Eddies, Oceanography, Atlantic Ocean.
Identifiers: *Cyclonic rings, Gulf Stream.

The mixing and entrainment processes present in a cyclonic ring was investigated by means of a parametric model which is fitted to serial temperature data for a North Atlantic ring. The physical model assumes an axially symmetric ring. Data from two cruises during the 1967 observation of a ring by the Woods Hole Oceanographic Institution provided estimates of the derivatives of the temperature. Upper bonds on the order of magnitudes were indicated for the diffusivities based upon near-minimum least-squares error estimates from regression analysis. An important result was that little different exists between a purely advective entrainment regime and those regimes including both entrainment and diffusion; i.e., the entrainment circulation appears to be the dominant mechanism in the temporal changes of the ring for a time scale of at least two months. The results provide streamline patterns for the transverse flow from the surface to 1000 m depth consistent with isotherm movement and changes in the ring water masses. (Sims-ISWS)
W75-07907

A THEORY OF STEADY WIND-DRIVEN CURRENTS IN SHALLOW WATER WITH VARIABLE EDDY VISCOSITY,
Rochester Univ., N.Y. Dept. of Mechanical and Aerospace Sciences.
For primary bibliographic entry see Field 2H.
W75-07908

DIFFUSION COEFFICIENTS CALCULATED FROM THE MEDITERREAN SALINITY ANOMALY IN THE NORTH ATLANTIC OCEAN,
Bedford Inst. of Oceanography, Dartmouth (Nova Scotia). Atlantic Oceanographic Lab.
G. T. Needler, and R. A. Heath.
Journal of Physical Oceanography, Vol 5, No 1, p 173-182, January 1975. 6 fig, 2 tab, 11 ref, 1 append.

Descriptors: Salinity, *Diffusion, *Atlantic Ocean, Sea water, Ocean circulation, Temperature, Model studies, On-site data collections, Oceanography.
Identifiers: *Mediterranean Sea, *Salinity anomaly, Austauch coefficients, Potential temperature, High-salinity tongue.

Vertical and horizontal austauch coefficients were obtained from standard station data on the Mediterranean high-salinity tongue by use of a simple model including advection by a constant velocity and three-dimensional diffusion. It was shown that background effects can be reduced by applying the model to the salinity anomaly relative to a linear potential temperature-salinity relationship. The analysis gave typical values for K sub H of 1.5 to 3 times 10 to the 7th power sq cm/s and for K sub V of 0.3 to 0.7 sq cm/s. It was argued that such values indicate the diffusion of potential density is not important in the main pycnocline of the North Atlantic anticyclonic gyre. (Sims-ISWS)
W75-07912

A NOTE ON OBSERVATIONS OF LONG-TERM TRAJECTORIES OF THE NORTH PACIFIC CURRENT,
Texas A and M Univ., College Station. Dept. of Oceanography.
For primary bibliographic entry see Field 2E.
W75-07913

ELECTRONIC DIGITIZATION AND SENSOR RESPONSE EFFECTS ON SALINITY COMPUTATION FROM CTD FIELD MEASUREMENTS,
Washington Univ., Seattle. Dept. of Oceanography.
G. I. Roden, and J. D. Irish.
Journal of Physical Oceanography, Vol 5, No 1, p 195-199, January 1975. 4 fig, 1 tab, 8 ref. ONR Contract N00014-67-A-0103-0014.

Descriptors: *Instrumentation, *Data processing, *Salinity, Conductivity, Temperature, Pressure, Data collections, Oceans, *Pacific Ocean, Oceanography.
Identifiers: Conductivity-temperature-depth sensors.

Spikes are often observed in salinity profiles computed from measurements of conductivity, temperature, and pressure. Many of these spikes are not real and are the result of a mismatch in the response functions of the sensors. Some of the spikes are also due to the sequential sampling technique used by most digitizers whereby the sensors are not sampled at the same time or position. Expressions were derived to linearly correct for these two causes of spikes. When the corrections were applied to measurements in the North Pacific, a significant reduction in the number and size of the spikes was observed in high gradient regions such as the thermocline. (Sims-ISWS)
W75-07914

THE WESTERN BOUNDARY UNDERCURRENT AS A TURBIDITY MAXIMUM OVER THE PUERTO RICO TRENCH,
Lamont-Doherty Geological Observatory, Palisades, N.Y.
For primary bibliographic entry see Field 2J.
W75-07918

HORIZONTAL SCALES IN THE MAIN THERMOCLINE DERIVED FROM THE TOPOGRAPHY OF A CONSTANT SOUND SPEED SURFACE BETWEEN BERMUDA AND THE ANTILLES,
Woods Hole Oceanographic Institution, Mass.
For primary bibliographic entry see Field 2E.
W75-07919

OBSERVATIONS OF OCEANIC INTERNAL AND SURFACE WAVES FROM THE EARTH RESOURCES TECHNOLOGY SATELLITE,
National Oceanic and Atmospheric Administration, Miami, Fla. Atlantic Oceanographic and Meteorological Labs.
For primary bibliographic entry see Field 7B.
W75-07920

OBSERVATION AND INTERPRETATION OF A HIGH-FREQUENCY INTERNAL WAVE PACKET AND SURFACE SLICK PATTERN,
Rosenstiel School of Marine and Atmospheric Science, Miami, Fla.
For primary bibliographic entry see Field 2E.
W75-07921

THE DISTRIBUTION OF SALINITY AND TEMPERATURE IN THE CONNECTICUT RIVER ESTUARY,
Connecticut Univ., Groton. Dept. of Mechanical Engineering.
R. W. Garvine.
Journal of Geophysical Research, Vol 80, No 9, p 1176-1183, March 20, 1975. 9 fig, 1 tab, 6 ref. NOAA Grants NG-20-72, 04-3-158-62.

Descriptors: *Estuaries, *Temperature, *Salinity, *Connecticut River, On-site investigations, Measurement, Rivers, Sounds, Saline water-freshwater interfaces, Tides, Stratification, Seasonal, Physical properties, Chemical properties, Connecticut.
Identifiers: *Long Island Sound(Conn).

Measurements of near-surface salinity and temperature were made over a period of 16 months in the Connecticut River estuary, an estuary basically of the salt wedge type. The temperature distribution was found to be very highly correlated with the salinity distribution. The horizontal salinity distribution occurred primarily in two modes, a riverine mode and a plume mode, corresponding to salinity transitions mostly within the river itself and to those mostly within Long Island Sound. Similarity variables were developed for each of the two distribution modes which render the data in compact forms that should have applications to other estuaries of a similar type. (Sims-ISWS)
W75-07922

DETERMINING AMBIENT WATER TEMPERATURES,
Stone and Webster Engineering Corp., Boston, Mass. Environmental Engineering Div.
For primary bibliographic entry see Field 5B.
W75-07929

A CONTRIBUTION TO THE ECOLOGICAL STUDY OF A MOROCCAN ATLANTIC ESTUARY: THE ESTUARY OF BOU REGREG: I,
Institut Scientifique Cherifien, Rabat (Morocco). Lab. of Zoology.
B. Elkaim.
Bull Soc Sci Nat Phys Maroc, Vol 52, No 1/2, p 131-339, 1972. Illus.
Identifiers: Atlantic Ocean, Climates, Ecological studies, Estuaries, Morocco(Bou Regreg), Salinity, Sediments, Temperature, Turbidity, Hydrogen ion concentration.

All the physiochemical parameters involved in the ecology of the estuary at Bou Regreg were studied. The underlying geology, botanical cover, climatological conditions, salinity of water, temperature range, pH, turbidity and sediments are the factors presented in this phase of the study.--
W75-07938

SHORT-PERIOD INTERNAL WAVES IN THE SEA,
For primary bibliographic entry see Field 2E.
W75-07976

A LINEAR THEORY OF INTERNAL WAVE SPECTRA AND COHERENCES NEAR THE VAISALA FREQUENCY,
Woods Hole Oceanographic Institution, Mass.
For primary bibliographic entry see Field 2E.
W75-07985

A BOTTOM CURRENT ALONG THE SHELF BREAK,
University of East Anglia, Norwich (England). School of Mathematics and Physics.
For primary bibliographic entry see Field 2E.
W75-07986

For primary bibliographic entry see Field 5B.
W75-08195

ECOLOGICAL AND ECONOMIC PRINCIPLES IN PARK PLANNING: THE ASSATEAGUE NATIONAL SEASHORE MODEL,
National Park Service, Washington, D.C.
For primary bibliographic entry see Field 6B.
W75-08216

THE BACTERIOLOGICAL CONDITIONS OF SOME BELGIAN BEACHES (IN FRENCH),
Institut Royal des Sciences Naturelles de Belgique, Brussels.
For primary bibliographic entry see Field 5B.
W75-08224

DISTRIBUTION OF PLANKTON COMMUNITIES RELATED TO ENVIRONMENTS IN ADJACENT SEAS OF JAPAN: I. PLANKTON OF MIYAKO BAY OF RIKUCHU PROVINCE, (IN JAPANESE),
Tokyo Univ. of Fisheries (Japan).
I. Yamazi, and T. Morita.
Bull Natl Sci Mus (Tokyo), Vol 15, No 2, p 347-384, 1972, Illus. English summary.

Descriptors: *Plankton, *Bays.
Identifiers: Chaetognaths, Ciliates, Cladocerans, Coelenterates, Copepods, Dinoflagellates, Ostracods, Polychaetes, Pteropods, *Japan(Miyako Bay).

The planktonic fauna and flora of Rikuchu Province of Tohoku district was studied in Miyako and Yamada Bays with different characters of topography and hydrography. Counts of populations at each station were made to obtain the quantitative estimates of number of various organisms/m3 of sea water. Both volume and number of plankton were characterized by abundance in the inner and central areas of the bays. The distribution of the communities varied and was correlated with the change of transparency, temperature, salinity and turbidity. They were also affected by the shape and depth of the sea floor, and the shape of the coast line, which produced the separate biologic?l environments. The important groups in the bay were copepods, caldocerans, pelagic tunicates, larval forms of pelagic and benthic animals, coelenterates and tintinnid ciliates. Occasional groups were chaetognaths, crustacean barnacle nauplii and cypris forms. Neritic and oceanic copepods, pelagic tunicates and dinoflagellates occurred numerously from the mouth to the east and central areas of the central part of the bay, where the inshore natives and oceanic forms were mixed together. The fauna and flora in the bay were characterized by mixed communities of coastal warm water forms and oceanic warm water ones together with some northern natives. Copepods which appeared in abundance were neritic forms, such as Paracalanus parvus, Acartia clausi, Oithona nana, O. setigera Microsetella norvegica, Centrophages abdominalis. Inlet forms P. parvus, O. nana and O. similis were predominant. Cladocera were present, such as temperate species Evadne nordmanni and Podon leuckarti. Tunicates were the inlet and coastal form, Oikopleura dioica, and the open sea form, O. longicauda. Various larval forms of a number of pelagic and benthic crustacean groups appeared. Fairly numerous larvae were polychaetes, lamellibranch and gastropod veligers. There were 16 species of dinoflagellates identified.--Copyright 1973, Biological Abstracts, Inc.
W75-08239

SEASONAL FLUCTUATIONS OF THE MEIOBENTHOS IN AN ESTUARY ON THE SWEDISH WEST COAST,
Uppsala Univ. (Sweden). Inst. of Zoology.
For primary bibliographic entry see Field 5C.
W75-08271

TRACE METAL LEVELS IN THREE SUBTIDAL INVERTEBRATES,
Stanford Univ., Pacific Grove, Calif. Hopkins Marine Station.
For primary bibliographic entry see Field 5B.
W75-08276

TILLAMOOK BAY MODEL STUDY; HYDRAULIC MODEL INVESTIGATION,
Army Engineer Waterways Experiment Station, Vicksburg, Miss.
For primary bibliographic entry see Field 8B.
W75-08294

SAN DIEGO BAY MODEL STUDY; HYDRAULIC MODEL INVESTIGATION,
Army Engineer Waterways Experiment Station, Vicksburg, Miss.
For primary bibliographic entry see Field 8B.
W75-08298

EFFECTS OF A STEADY NONUNIFORM CURRENT ON THE CHARACTERISTICS OF SURFACE GRAVITY WAVES,
Army Engineer Waterways Experiment Station, Vicksburg, Miss.
For primary bibliographic entry see Field 8B.
W75-08299

NECHES RIVER SALTWATER BARRIER,
Army Engineer Waterways Experiment Station, Vicksburg, Miss.
For primary bibliographic entry see Field 8B.
W75-08301

FOOD HABITS OF GEORGIA ESTUARINE FISHES: I. FOUR SPECIES OF FLOUNDERS (PLEURONECTIFORMES: BOTHIDAE),
Skidaway Inst. of Oceanography, Savannah, Ga.
R. R. Stickney, G. L. Taylor, and R. W. Heard, III.
U S Natl Mar Fish Serv Fish Bull, Vol 72, No 2, p 515-525, 1974, Illus.
Identifiers: Ancylopsetta-quadrocellata, Bothidae, Citharichthys-spilopterus, *Estuarine fishes, Etropus-crossotus, Fish, *Flounders, *Georgia, Neomysis-americana, Pleuronectiformes, Polychaete, Pseudodiaptomus-coronatus, Scophthalmus-aqusus, Season, Size, Species, Stomach, *Food habits.

The food habits of 4 spp. of bothid flounders from Georgia coastal waters were examined by means of stomach content analyses. Ocellated flounders, Ancylopsetta quadrocellata (Gill); bay whiff, Citharichthys spilopterus (Gunther); and windowpane, Scophthalmus aquosus (Mitchill) fed heavily on the mysid shrimp, Neomysis americana, without regard to season of the year or location within the estuary. The food habits of both A. quadrocellata and C. spilopterus changed to some extent as the fish became larger. Organisms larger than N. americana dominated the stomach contents of A. quadrocellata larger than 150 mm standard length and C. spilopterus larger than 125 mm S. aquosus, in the size range examined, fed almost exclusively on N. americana. Fringed flounder, Etropus crossotus (Jordan and Gilbert) primarily consumed the calanoid copepod, Pseudodiaptomus coronatus, during the spring, summer and fall and diversified their food habits during winter. P. coronatus dominated the stomach contents both in the rivers and sounds of Georgia estuarine waters and was the dominant organism in fishes of all sizes up to 100 mm when polychaete annelids became important. The food of E. crossotus did not appear to vary with time of day; however, E. crossotus did not actively feed at night. The difference in food habits between E. crossotus and the other 3 bothid species appears to be associated with the relative size of the mouth.--Copyright 1974, Biological Abstracts, Inc.
W75-08324

NOTES ON THE WHITEFISH OF THE COLVILLE RIVER, ALASKA,
Alaska Dept. of Fish and Game, Fairbanks. Div. of Sport Fish.
K. T. Alt, and D. R. Kogl.
J Fish Res Board Can. Vol 30, No 4, p 554-556, 1973, Illus.
Identifiers: Alaska(Colville River), Coregonus-nasus, Coregonus-sardinella, Rivers, *Whitefish, Growth rates, Age, Deltas.

Five whitefish species are present in the Colville River, Alaska. Least cisco (Coregonus sardinella) was the most common species in the Colville Delta, while the broad whitefish (C. nasus) was most abundant at test net sites near Umiat. Limited age and growth data indicate slower growth than in interior Alaska waters.--Copyright 1973, Biological Abstracts, Inc.
W75-08333

FISH POPULATIONS OF THE AVON-HEATHCOTE ESTUARY: 3. GUT CONTENTS,
Tasmanian Dept. of Agriculture, Hobart (Australia). Sea Fisheries Div.
B. F. Webb.
N Z J Mar Freshwater Res. Vol 7, No 3, p 223-234, 1973, Illus.

Descriptors: *Estuaries, *Fish populations, Fish diets, Mullets, *Food habits.
Identifiers: Aldrichetta-forsteri, Arripis-trutta, Avon-Heathcote Estuary, Gobiomorphus-basalis, *New Zealand, Peltorhamphus-novaezeelandiae, Pseudolabrus-celidotus, Rhombosolea-leporina, Rhombosolea-plebeia, Selection, Spheroides-richei, Tripterygion-nigripenne, Flounder, Sole, Bully, Globefish, *Gut-content analysis.

Details are given of gut-content analyses for 9 fish species from the Avon-Heathcote Estuary, Christchurch, New Zealand: sand flounder, Rhombosolea plebeia; yellow-bellied flounder, R. leporina; common sole, Peltorhamphus novaezeelandiae; yellow-eyed mullet, Aldrichetta forsteri; kahawai, Arripis trutta; spotty, Pseudolabrus celidotus; cockabully, Tripterygion nigripenne; common bully, Gobiomorphus basalis and globefish, Spheroides richei. The percent occurrences of each food type recorded over the sampling period (April 1965-April 1966) for each species are compared. Monthly food tables are given for those species of which suitably large samples were obtained (sand flounder, yellow-bellied flounder, common sole, yellow-eyed mullet, and globefish). Where possible, the dietary occurrence of different food types is related to environmental and other factors observed or considered likely to influence food selection.--Copyright 1974, Biological Abstracts, Inc.
W75-08340

3. WATER SUPPLY AUGMENTATION AND CONSERVATION

3A. Saline Water Conversion

PROCESS FOR PREPARING HEAVY WATER FROM SEA WATER,
H. Tabata, N. Tabata, and R. Nakajima.
U.S. Patent No 3,870,606, 7 p, 8 fig, 4 ref; Official Gazette of the United States Patent Office, Vol 932, No 2, p 629, March 11, 1975.

Descriptors: *Patents, *Heavy water, *Distillation, *Desalination, *Water quality control, *Salts, Sea water, Evaporation, Heat exchangers, Vaporization.

A process is described for preparing heavy water from sea water. It is comprised of adding 0.1-10.0 percent, calculated as Mg++/ion of a soluble halide salt to a mixture of drains produced by the evaporation of sea water in a conventional process for the manufacture of common salt. The mixture of drains is warmed to between room temperature and 40 deg C using the heat energy from the salt manufacturing process. The warmed mixture of drains is concentrated to a heavy water content of about 1 percent by exposing large surface areas of the warmed mixture to the atmosphere, removing the added halide salt from the concentrated mixture by evaporating the mixture, and collecting the condensate from the evaporation step and subjecting the condensate to distillation to yield a high concentration heavy water. (Sinha-OEIS)
W75-07854

COMBINATION SOLAR AND MANUAL DISTILLER AND RAIN CATCHER,
Minoru Sakamoto.
U.S. Patent No 3,870,605, 4 p, 16 fig, 6 ref; Official Gazette of the United States Patent Office, Vol 932, No 2, p 628, March 11, 1975.

Descriptors: *Patents, *Solar stills, *Desalination, *Distillation, Salt water, Brackish water, Separation techniques, Fresh water, Rain water, Equipment.
Identifiers: Rain catchers.

A still consists of a container that is provided with an opening on a cover that serves as a condensation surface. The cover is in the form of a hollow cone with an open base, an open apex and a rim around the base. An arcuate collecting trough is arranged adjacent the base and within the cone to receive the condensate which runs down the inner surface of the cone. The container is constructed from a heat-absorging material, and has at least its inner surface colored black. Condensate will run down the cover's inner surface under the influence of gravity and into the collecting trough. The rim of the cover is provided with a passage terminating in a lip and arranged for discharging condensate from the collecting. A vessel may be arranged on the base adjacent the terminal end of the passage for receiving condensate. (Sinha-OEIS)
W75-07856

WATER DESALINIZATION SYSTEM,
Lee (Raymond) Organization, Inc, New York. (assignee).
J. B. Swanson.
U.S. Patent No 3,871,180, 2 p, 3 fig, 7 ref; Official Gazette of the United States Patent Office, Vol 932, No 3, p 817, March 18, 1975.

Descriptors: *Patents, *Desalination, *Evaporation, *Condensation, *Water treatment, *Condensers, *Evaporators, Equipment, Salt water, Steam turbines, Electric generators.
Identifiers: Atomizers.

This desalination system consists of an atomizer, evaporator, accumulator, a steam turbine, an electric generator and a condenser. The electrical generator is coupled to and driven by the steam turbine. The atomizer, which is an air compressor, is connected to the generator. The compressed air is heated and directed at right angles to the flow of salt water. The evaporator is a circular vessel and has equiangularly spaced electodes. The consenser converts the steam to pure water after it drives the turbine. (Sinha-OEIS)
W75-07962

DESALTING TECHNIQUES FOR WATER QUALITY IMPROVEMENT.
American Water Works Association Research Foundation, Denver, Colo.
Available from the National Technical Information Service, Springfield, Va. 22161, as PB-241 977, $8.50 in paper copy, $2.25 in microfiche. Report INT-OSW-RDPR-75-1002, 1973. 257 p, 48 fig, 39 tab. O.S.W. 14-30-2864.

Descriptors: *Capital costs, *Desalination processes, *Estimated benefits, *Estimated costs, *Operating costs, *Water treatment, Brackish water, Desalination, Desalination apparatus, Desalination plants, Dissolved solids, Electrodialysis, Ion exchange, Municipal water, Reverse osmosis, Water purification, Water quality.

It is anticipated that municipal water consumption will continue to grow, and that consumers increasingly will demand improvements in water quality. The benefits of good quality water are not only reduced health hazards and greater aesthetic appeal, but also decreased operating and maintenance costs associated with the beneficial use of water connected facilities. Desalting techniques of electrodialysis, reverse osmosis and ion exchange are being used in a number of communities. These processes will not only improve the quality of a brackish water supply by removing dissolved solids, but also will remove some of the undesired minor elements which may be present in the intake water. The quality of water which is made available to the consumer can be improved by changing the municipal water supply--either by obtaining the water from a better source or by building a desalting or other water treatment plant. Information is presented which describes methods of improving the quality of brackish water supplies and which will permit preliminary estimates to be made of the tangible benefits of water quality improvement and of the capital and operating costs of conventional and desalting treatment plants. Local conditions will determine which alternative is best for each community.
W75-07998

3B. Water Yield Improvement

NATURAL AND MODIFIED PLANT COMMUNITIES AS RELATED TO RUNOFF AND SEDIMENT YIELDS,
Geological Survey, Denver, Colo.
For primary bibliographic entry see Field 4C.
W75-07866

TROUT RUN EARTHFILL DAM, BOROUGH OF BOYERTOWN, BERKS COUNTY, PENNSYLVANIA (FINAL ENVIRONMENTAL IMPACT STATEMENT).
Delaware River Basin Commission, Trenton, N.J.
For primary bibliographic entry see Field 8F.
W75-08030

HUNGRY HORSE CLOUD SEEDING PROJECT (FINAL ENVIRONMENTAL IMPACT STATEMENT).
Bonneville Power Administration, Portland, Oreg.
Available from National Technical Information Service, USDC, Springfield, Va 22161 as EIS-MT-73-2025-F, $8.75 in paper copy, $2.25 in microfiche. December 1973. 282 p, 6 fig, 14 tab, 5 chart.

Descriptors: *Energy, *Energy conversion, *Clouds, *Cloud seeding, Snowfall, Powerplants, Rain, Power operation and maintenance, *Montana, North America, River flow, *Weathe modification.
Identifiers: *Environmental impact statements, *Flathead County(Mont), Lake County(Mont).

This action involves a cloud seeding project in Flathead and Lake Counties, Montana from December 1, 1973 through April 15, 1974. The purpose is to alleviate a projected energy shortage in the Pacific Northwest by helping assure normal streamflows and hydroelectric generation through the maintenance of normal snowpack conditions in the area. Environmental impact and effects include a possible increase of up to 10% in the 1973-74 winter season over a million acre target area. This increased participation may have minor, transitory impacts on wildlife, vegetation, soil ero-

stress. Germinability and seedling vigor of Lehmann Lovegrass, Panicum, and Small Burnet were considerably reduced as moisture tension increased above 5 atm. Reduction in germination was more pronounced at 20 degrees C. than at 30 degrees C. for all species except Small Burnet. The study is part of an effort to discover drought-resistant pasture plants for revegetating depleted range lands. (Bowden-Arizona)
W75-08111

RESULTS OF SPECIES, SPACING AND IRRIGATION FREQUENCY EXPERIMENT IN HAMMAN AL-ALIL AREA,
Mosul Univ. (Iraq). Dept. of Forestry.
For primary bibliographic entry see Field 3F.
W75-08114

BRUSHY BASIN-A FORMULA FOR WATERSHED MANAGEMENT SUCCESS,
Santa Ana Watershed Planning Agency, Calif; and Santa Ana Watershed Project Authority, Riverside, Calif.
For primary bibliographic entry see Field 4C.
W75-08196

DEVELOPMENT OF FOREST MANAGEMENT GUIDELINES FOR INCREASING SNOWPACK WATER YIELDS IN ARIZONA,
Arizona Univ., Tucson. Dept. of Watershed Management.
For primary bibliographic entry see Field 2C.
W75-08222

THREE SUCCESSFUL SALT TOLERANT PLANTS,
For primary bibliographic entry see Field 3C.
W75-08280

THE ANCIENT NAMIB DESERT,
For primary bibliographic entry see Field 2A.
W75-08288

3C. Use Of Water Of Impaired Quality

FATE AND EFFECTS OF TRACE ELEMENTS IN SEWAGE SLUDGE WHEN APPLIED TO AGRICULTURAL LANDS,
California Univ., Riverside. Dept. of Soil Science and Agricultural Engineering.
For primary bibliographic entry see Field 5B.
W75-07852

POND WATER QUALITY IN A CLAYPAN SOIL,
Illinois Univ., Urbana. Dept. of Agricultural Engineering.
For primary bibliographic entry see Field 5B.
W75-07924

SPRINKLER IRRIGATION FOR LIQUID WASTE DISPOSAL,
Pennsylvania State Univ., University Park.
For primary bibliographic entry see Field 5D.
W75-07959

MUSKEGON, MICHIGAN,
Chicago Univ., Ill. Center for Urban Studies.
For primary bibliographic entry see Field 5D.
W75-07960

CHANGE IN THE CHEMISTRY OF NATURAL WATERS IN LANDSCAPES UNDER AGRICULTURAL USE,
For primary bibliographic entry see Field 5B.
W75-07974

GROUND-WATER QUALITY RELATED TO IRRIGATION WITH IMPORTED SURFACE OR LOCAL GROUND WATER,
Agricultural Research Service, Fresno, Calif.
For primary bibliographic entry see Field 5B.
W75-07978

SIMMONDSIA STUDIES AT THE NEGEV INSTITUTE,
Negev Inst. for Arid Zone Research, Beersheba (Israel).
M. Forti.
Negev Institute for Arid Zone Research, Division of Life Sciences, Beer Sheva, June, 1973. 28 p, 5 tab, 2 fig, 12 ref.

Descriptors: *Plant breeding, *Cultivation, *Industrial crops, Irrigation practices, Salt tolerance, Agriculture, Fertilization, Seeds, Ecology, Arid lands, Variability.
Identifiers: *Simmondsia chinensis, *Israel(Negev).

The possibility of cultivating Simmondsia chinensis in the arid and semi-arid area in southern Israel was studied. The plant has a promising industrial potential for producing a liquid wax from its seeds. Preliminary results show that Simmondsia, after 10 years of experimental cultivation, can survive under a variety of agricultural practices. Yields were obtained in the third or fourth year after transplating, and production was good, although supplementary irrigation did increase yields. Attempts to cultivate Simmondsia under natural conditions in sandy soils have so far proved negative, but the species is moderately salt tolerant and cultivation might be possible in brackish water. Breeding prospects appear favorable for producing species adapted to the given conditions and agricultural practices. Harvest practices will have to be improved if the plant is to be used competitively. (Mastic-Arizona)
W75-08100

SANTIAGO-NORTE DRAINAGE PROJECT (CHILE),
F. E. Schultze, and M. G. Bos.
In: International Institute for Land Reclamation and Improvement, Wageningen, The Netherlands, Annual Report 1973. p 54-63, 7 fig, 1 tab.

Descriptors: *Irrigation, *Salinity, *Drainage systems, *Drainage wells, *South America, Flood frequency, Flood damage, Saturated soils, Irrigation systems, Water management(Applied), Evapotranspiration, Irrigation effects.
Identifiers: *Chile(Santiago-Norte Drainage Project).

An area covering 42,000 hectares at the northern end of the Central Valley has been irrigated for about forty years. Because two-thirds of the irrigation water is imported, natural equilibrium of the region has been altered. Also, irrigation practices employed are inefficient since only daytime flooding of fields is followed and there is no storage capacity or night flows. Natural stream beds in the area are not adequate for the huge amounts of water used in the valley, and flooding is endemic. The result of large imports of water and little or no planned drainage has been a rising groundwater table and salinization of soils. Geologic features of the valley accentuate this problem since groundwater has no escape from the area except by evapotranspiration. (Bowden-Arizona)
W75-08109

WATERLOGGING AND SALINITY PROBLEMS IN THE INDUS PLAIN (PAKISTAN),
R. Van Aart.
International Institute for Land Reclamation and Improvement, Wageningen, The Netherlands, Annual Report 1973. p 44-53. 7 fig, 3 tab, 3 ref.

Descriptors: *Salinity, *Saturated soils, *Drainage wells, *Dewatering, Irrigation, Irrigation systems, Saline water, Drainage systems, Wells, Water storage, Water management(Applied), Canals.
Identifiers: *Pakistan(Indus Plain).

Pakistan's Indus Basin is one of the world's largest irrigated areas with 33.5 million acres within the irrigation system, although only about 25 million acres actually receive water. This tract supplies 20 percent of Pakistan's foodstuffs and almost all of its cash crops. Since the introduction of irrigation in the middle of the nineteenth century, the area's water table has risen from 60 to 100 feet to a level in some fields of five feet. This waterlogging has led to salinization of the soils. Best estimates indicate 11 million acres to be waterlogged, 6 million acres salinized. Present tactics to increase agricultural production include storing surface water in reservoirs, enlarging canals, and utilizing groundwater and improving drainage through tubewells. Horizontal drainage is also receiving attention as a way to draw off saline groundwater. Some of these solutions are highly consumptive of energy; for example, the nation's 73,000 tubewells are either deisel or electrically powered. (Bowden-Arizona)
W75-08117

SEASONAL VARIATION IN SOME PHYSICAL, CHEMICAL, AND MICROBIOLOGICAL CHARACTERISTICS OF A SALINE AND A NON-SALINE SOIL NEAR ABU-GHRAIB, IRAQ,
Foundation of Scientific Research, Baghdad (Iraq).
For primary bibliographic entry see Field 2G.
W75-08199

THREE SUCCESSFUL SALT TOLERANT PLANTS,
G. L. McPhie.
Journal of Agriculture, South Australia, Vol 76, No 1, p 5-8. February 1973. 8 fig.

Descriptors: *Halophytes, *Revegetation, *Saline soils, *Salt tolerance, *Vegetation establishment, *Australia, Erosion control, Grasses, Land reclamation, Soil stabilization, Erosion, Grazing, Saline water, Salinity, Summer, Winter, Wheatgrasses.
Identifiers: New South Wales, Seashore paspalum, Alakligrass.

Because saline areas represent an unproductive liability, susceptible to erosion and spreading, much recent research in Australia has been directed toward finding salt tolerant plants to stabilize salt-affected land. Now 3 salt tolerant perennial grasses have been found suitable for sowing in saline soils: Puccinellia capillaris; tall wheat grass, Agropyron elongatum; and salt water couch, Paspalum vaginatum. Puccinellia has been grown successfully on saline areas in South Australia, New South Wales, Western Australia, and Victoria, is a winter-growth pioneer on bare soil, self seeds easily, and once established survives moderate grazing. Tall wheat grass, a summer-growth plant in poorly drained soils, has been used not only to stabilize eroding lands but also for revegetation of salted areas in Victoria, Western Australia, and New South Wales. It withstands moderate grazing and may prove well adapted for reclamation and revegetation of salt lands in South Australia. Salt water couch is another summer-growth species well adapted to saline areas. Plant growth is creeping in habit, and plants spread rapidly by runners in moist soil. Once established, this perennial is highly resistant to grazing and has been used extensively for revegetation of saline land in South Australia, Victoria, and Western Australia, and in these regions, also, for lawns and greens irrigated with saline water. (Gloyd-Arizona)
W75-08280

WEST NUBARYA RECLAMATION PROJECT (EGYPT),
N. A. De Ridder.
In: International Institute for Land Reclamation and Improvements: Wageningen, The Netherlands. Annual Report, 1973, p 27-32. 4 fig, 1 tab.

Descriptors: *Saline water intrusion, *Irrigation systems, *Water management(Applied), *Model studies, *Drainage systems, Saline soil, Africa, Water quality, Land reclamation, Systems analysis, Cost-benefit analysis.
Identifiers: *Egypt(West Nubarya Reclamation Project).

The West Nubarya Reclamation Project, 50 kilometers southwest of Alexandria, is plagued by waterlogged fields and the intrusion of saline water into the irrigation canal. These problems must be solved if the salinity increase of the project's aquifer is to be brought under control. A systems approach is recommended for finding the optimum solution. Several subsystems (agricultural production, surface water distribution, groundwater and artificial drainage) must be incorporated into the model to enhance the predictive potential of the systems approach. From these studies, the need for artificial drainage and/or changes in the water distribution and supply systems will appear. The costs of these measures can then be compared with the benefits to the agricultural production subsystem and the optimum solution selected. (Bowden-Arizona)
W75-08285

HEMIDIEH-SHAUR PROJECT (KHUZESTAN, IRAN),
N. A. De Ridder.
In: International Institute for Land Reclamation and Improvement, Wageningen, The Netherlands, Annual Report, 1973. p 41-43, 1 fig.

Descriptors: *Irrigation systems, *Saline water, *Saline soil, *Drainage programs, Watershed management, Surveys.
Identifiers: *Iran, Mesopotamian Plain.

Although the Hamidieh-Shaur project near Ahwaz, has been irrigated for fifty years, irrigation with poor quality water from the Karkheh River, following completion of the Karkheh Dam in 1954, has turned this arid land into a saline wilderness. Only in sections of the project where water can be used abundantly and where there is good natural drainage have farmers been able to grow crops with fairly good results, and even these yields are declining as soil salinity increases. The most likely solution to the problem is a master plan for optimum land and water management based on soil surveys, piezometer data, groundwater flow, and site tests, and the installation of a field drainage system in a major part of the area. (Bowden-Arizona)
W75-08286

3D. Conservation In Domestic and Municipal Use

WATER FACTS AND FIGURES FOR PLANNERS AND MANAGERS,
Geological Survey, Menlo Park, Calif.
For primary bibliographic entry see Field 6B.
W75-07889

STATE-OF-THE-ART OF ESTIMATING FLOOD DAMAGE IN URBAN AREAS,
Colorado State Univ., Fort Collins. Dept. of Civil Engineering.
For primary bibliographic entry see Field 4A.
W75-07939

MODAL CITIES,
Dartmouth Coll., Hanover, N.H. Dept. of Geography.

Identifiers: *Irrigation runoff recovery, *Constant furrow discharge, Cut-back irrigation.

A method was presented to design an Irrigation Runoff Recovery System which will permit a constant furrow discharge throughout the irrigation set by irrigating the first set entirely from supply water, the last set entirely from pumped runoff water, and by varying the set size between the two. Since the system requires a variable number of furrows from set to set, a table and charts were presented to give the number of furrows required in successive sets, number of sets required, number of furrows in the late set irrigated entirely from stored runoff, storage volume required, potential water savings, area covered by the storage pond, and recirculating-pump flow rate. (Terstriep-ISWS)
W75-07923

WATER AND SALT TRANSFERS IN SUTTER BASIN, CALIFORNIA,
California Univ., Davis. Dept. of Water Science and Engineering.
For primary bibliographic entry see Field 5B.
W75-07925

IMPROVING PRODUCTIVITY IN LOW RAINFALL AREAS.
Food and Agriculture Organization of the United Nation, Rome (Italy). Committee on Agriculture.
Report COAG/74/4, Rev 1, April 1974. Presented at 16th Food and Agriculture Organization of the United Nations Conference, Rome, Italy, April 17-30, 1974. 82 p, 19 tab, 5 maps.

Descriptors: *Arid lands, *Agriculture, *Productivity, *Water supply, *Rainfall, Crop production, Development, Land use, Land development, Resource development, Livestock, Soils, Research and development, Arid climates, Semiarid climates, Social aspects, Economic impact.

The significance of low rainfall areas in terms of land use, productivity, and population is described. Quantitative indicators for the level of development and the socio-economic disparities as compared with the other areas of the world are presented. Indicators of the level of agricultural performance are also discussed. Some general measures for the development of these areas are considered. Proposals are presented for further FAO assistance to member countries involved. Maps of the arid and semiarid zones show types of soils; a brief description of each type is provided. A list of international agricultural research centers is given along with a description of their purposes and programs. This study is a first attempt to place the problem of improving productivity in low rainfall areas in perspective on a world-wide scale. An effort has been made to identify these areas, determine their scope and importance, identify constraints limiting production, and develop, specify and evaluate plans by which these constraints may be overcome and improvement brought about. (Mastic-Arizona)
W75-07981

FLOW AND RETENTION OF WATER IN THE STRATIFIED SOILS OF THE OROVADA, NEVADA, AREA,
Nevada Univ., Reno. Dept. of Soil Science.
For primary bibliographic entry see Field 2G.
W75-07991

A DYNAMIC WATER AND RELATED LAND RESOURCE PLANNING MODEL: ITS APPLICATION TO AN HAWAIIAN WATER SYSTEM,
Hawaii Univ., Honolulu. Water Resources Research Center.
For primary bibliographic entry see Field 6A.
W75-07993

MODEL DEVELOPMENT AND SYSTEMS ANALYSIS OF THE YAKIMA RIVER BASIN: IRRIGATED AGRICULTURE WATER USE,
Washington State Univ., Pullman. Dept. of Agricultural Engineering.
G. T. Thompson.
Available from the National Technical Information Service, Springfield, Va. 22161, as PB-241 974, $4.75 in paper copy, $2.25 in microfiche. Washington Water Research Center, Pullman, Report No 17 c, September 1974. 80 p, 7 fig, 7 tab, 22 ref. OWRT B-036-WASH(5), B-043-WASH(4), B-050-WASH(4).

Descriptors: *Model studies, *Systems analysis, Computer models, Planning, Water management(Applied), Agricultural runoff, Watershed management *Washington, Water rights, Irrigation water, Water utilization, Costs, Consumptive use, Irrigation efficiency.
Identifiers: *Yakima River basin(Wash).

A model was developed that provides a basis for determining water usage and costs of using water for irrigation of agricultural crops. The model determines monthly consumptive use and water division requirements needed to irrigate a given cropping pattern on a watershed. Provided in the model is a technique to determine the monthly return flow occurring from an irrigated watershed. The model provides for determining the irrigation needs and return flows from each of any number of sub-areas which may be used to define a watershed. The model is designed to provide options of increasing irrigation efficiencies, changing cropping patterns, or reducing irrigated areas during low flow years. The model is developed to provide the irrigation components of an overall hydrologic model of a watershed.
W75-07994

MODEL DEVELOPMENT AND SYSTEMS ANALYSIS OF THE YAKIMA RIVER BASIN: WATER QUALITY MODELING,
Washington State Univ., Pullman. Dept. of Civil Engineering.
For primary bibliographic entry see Field 5B.
W75-07995

PHYSIOLOGICAL APPROACH TO THE ANALYSIS OF SOME COMPLEX CHARACTERS OF POTATOES,
Ceskoslovenska Akademie Ved, Trebon. Lab. of Algology.
J. Necas.
Potato Res, Vol 17, No 1, p 3-23, 1974. Illus.
Identifiers: Breeding, *Genotypes, *Growth stages, *Phenotypes, *Physiological studies, *Potatoes, Transpiration, Crop production.

An attempt was made to show the possibility of analysis of the phenotypic as well as genotypic make-up of 2 complex physiological characters of cultivated potatoes. The complex characters were the yielding capacity and the water relations. The components of the 1st were analyzed for some potato varieties by the method of growth analysis. For the analysis of their water relations the ability to retain water in the plant tissues and to regulate its output by transpiration were determined. It was shown that in different potato varieties the make-up of the complex characters studied may differ. It is possible to design, for practical breeding purposes, model (type) plants with regard to the phenotypic as well as genotypic make-up of both the complex characters mentioned.--Copyright 1974, Biological Abstracts, Inc.
W75-08008

INSTITUTIONAL CONSTRAINTS ON AGRICULTURAL WATER USE,
Colorado State Univ., Fort Collins. Dept. of Agricultural Engineering.
For primary bibliographic entry see Field 6E.
W75-08013

SIMMONDSIA STUDIES AT THE NEGEV INSTITUTE,
Negev Inst. for Arid Zone Research, Beersheba (Israel).
For primary bibliographic entry see Field 3C.
W75-08100

DRIP IRRIGATION FOR REVEGETATING STEEP SLOPES IN AN ARID ENVIRONMENT,
American Smelting and Refining Co., Sahuarita, Ariz.
For primary bibliographic entry see Field 4D.
W75-08102

YIELDS AND WATER-USE EFFICIENCIES OF DRYLAND WINTER WHEAT AND GRAIN SORGHUM PRODUCTION SYSTEMS IN THE SOUTHERN HIGH PLAINS,
Southwestern Great Plains Research Center, Bushland, Tex.
O. R. Jones.
Soil Science Society of America, Proceedings, Vol 39, No 1, p 98-103, January-February, 1975. 4 tab, 2 fig, 13 ref.

Descriptors: *Water conservation, *Crop production, *Dry farming, *Farm management, *Great Plains, Texas, Water utilization, Runoff, Sorghum, Wheat, Terracing, Slopes, Erosion.

The effects of conservation bench terraces, bench terraces, and common systems on dryland production of winter wheat and grain sorghum were studied in terms of grain yields and water-use efficiencies. Grain production and water-use efficiency were highest on a bench terrace cropped in continuous grain sorghum. Conservation bench terraces with continuous grain sorghum also had higher water-use efficiencies and grain production than the common dryland systems of wheat-sorghum-fallow, continuous wheat, or wheat-fallow. In the Southern High Plains dryland grain production systems are available to increase grain production and water-use efficiencies while providing adequate control of wind and water erosion. Crop selection and land leveling are management factors that greatly influence water-use efficiencies and conserve potential runoff. (Mastic-Arizona)
W75-08105

GRAZING SYSTEMS FOR ARIZONA RANGES.
Forest Service (USDA), Tucson, Ariz. Rocky Mountain Forest and Range Experiment Station.
Arizona Interagency Range Committee, 1973. 36 p, 3 fig, 3 tab, 23 ref, 2 append.

Descriptors: *Arizona, *Forage grasses, *Grazing, *Range management, *Livestock, Ranges, Environmental effects, Land use, Plant growth, Productivity, Range grasses, Revegetation, Soil conservation, Vegetation re-growth, Water conservation, Wildlife conservation.

Since the most common grazing system now used in Arizona is yearlong or seasonal grazing, no rest is afforded the range to regain its vigor, set seed, and allow regeneration of the most favored forage plants and areas. In August 1973, a field study of 8 Arizona ranches showed that use of grazing systems is still quite limited even though research and experience have demonstrated that livestock must be forced to graze according to a carefully developed plan using all available range management techniques and skills which simultaneously will suit the needs of the rancher, the livestock, and the range itself. Proper management of Arizona's native rangeland and grazeable woodlands, which comprise the major portion of the total land area of the state, is directed now toward maximum production of desirable forage species, optimum plant density and vigor, adequate mulch cover, greater water infiltration, reduced soil-surface evaporation, minimum soil erosion, and reduced sediment pollution. Improvement of grazing lands is essential to quality environment, and increased demands for multiple use of these lands make it imperative that they be managed to yield the food, fiber, high-quality water, recreation, wildlife, and other benefits within their capability. (Gloyd-Arizona)
W75-08112

DESERT FARMERS: ANCIENT AND MODERN,
Hebrew Univ., Jerusalem (Israel). Dept. of Botany.
M. Evenari.
Natural History, Vol 83, No 7, p 42-49, August-September, 1974. 5 fig (part col), 3 ref (p 100).

Descriptors: *History, *Agricultural runoff, *Demonstration farms, *Irrigation systems, *Rainfall-runoff relationships, Crop production, Deserts, Experimental farms, Rainfall, Runoff, Alfalfa, Annual, Arid lands, Field crops, Grasses, Horticultural crops, Irrigation, Nuts, Pastures, Soil-water-plant relationships.
Identifiers: *Israel(Negev Desert).

Some 1400 years ago in the Negev Desert of Israel ancient farmers cultivated extensive crops by irrigation with runoff rainfall. In 1959, after painstaking field research, two ancient farm catchment systems at Avdat and Shivta were reconstructed to test this method. Data collections made over 15 years with modern rain-measuring instruments recorded the 1-7 inch rainfall variability typical of arid lands. Each year, however, enough catchment water was collected to keep fruit trees, perennial pasture plants and vegetables alive, though annual field crops could not be planted during 4 years when drought conditions prevailed. Certain varieties of almonds and pistachios proved the most promising vegetable crop. Annual crops grown included cereals, legumes, oil and fiber plants. Of perennial pasture plants tested, Harding grass, smilo grass, and several alfalfas proved best adapted to this type of agriculture. Loess soil was the most favorable for runoff farming; testing of microcatchments revealed surface runoff yields amounting to 62 percent of the rainfall. A third farm, established in 1970 in Wadi Mashash south of Beersheba, serves as a pilot demonstration and training center for desert runoff agriculture. Although receiving only 5-6 inches of rainfall annually for its 2000 almond, 500 olive, and 300 pistachio trees, this farm has shown that microcatchment runoff farming is practical and can be used on a large scale in other arid countries. (Gloyd-Arizona)
W75-08113

RESULTS OF SPECIES, SPACING AND IRRIGATION FREQUENCY EXPERIMENT IN HAMMAN AL-ALIL AREA,
Mosul Univ. (Iraq). Dept. of Forestry.
M. S. Kettaheh.
Mesopotamia Journal of Agriculture, Vol 8, No 2, p 171-177, 1973.

Descriptors: *Irrigation efficiency, *Water management(Applied), *Drought tolerance, *Plant growth, *Moisture stress, Irrigation, Irrigation practices, Irrigation water, Pllication methods, Water demand, Forest management, Frequency, Drought resistance, Planting management, Reforestation, Spatial distribution, Vegetation establishment, Trees, Pine trees.
Identifiers: *Iraq, Eucalyptus, Cypress, Casurina.

To aid Iraqi foresters in tree-planting programs carried out in the more arid areas of the country, studies were undertaken on the effect of irrigation frequencies on two species, Eucalyptus camaldulensis and Pinus brutia. Weekly irrigation was more beneficial for seedling survival than less frequent schedules. The eucalyptus height growth also was enhanced by weekly irrigation, although the pine reacted about the same to the three irrigation frequencies: weekly, bi-weekly, or monthly. Three plant spacings (5x2, 5x4, and 5x6 meters)

sistance, Drought resistance, Winter killing, Resistance, Environmental control.
Identifiers: Chloroplasts, Desiccation, Glucose, Heat, Phosphorylation, Spinacia-Oleracea, *Sucrose, Thylakoids, *Spinach, Trisaccharide raffinose, Disaccharide sucrose, Photophosphorylation.

Freezing, desiccation and high-temperature stress may under certain conditions result in inactivation of electron transport (DCIP reduction) and cyclic photophosphorylation of isolated chloroplast membranes of spinach (Spinacia oleracea L.). When sugars are present during temperature and water stress, the thylakoids may be partially or completely protected. This membrane stabilization depends on the concentration of sugars and their molecular size. The trisaccharide raffinose is, on a molar basis, more effective than the disaccharide sucrose and the latter more than the monosaccharide glucose. An uncoupling effect and a stimulation of electron transport can be observed during freezing, desiccation and heat treatment, e.g. electron transport reactions are less sensitive to temperature and water stress than is photophosphorylation. As sugars are known to accumulate in winter, unspecific membrane stabilization by sugars may help to explain the often reported parallel development of frost, drought and heat resistance in many plants during winter.--Copyright 1974, Biological Abstracts, Inc.
W75-08242

MOISTURE MODIFICATION SHELTERS FOR EPIDEMIOLOGICAL STUDIES OF FOLIAR DISEASES,
Georgia Univ., Athen.
For primary bibliographic entry see Field 2I.
W75-08245

COMPONENTS ANALYSIS OF YIELD RESPONSES TO DROUGHT OF SORGHUM HYBRIDS,
Volcani Inst. of Agricultural Research, Bet-Dagan (Israel).
A. Blum.
Exp Agric, Vol 9, No 2, p 159-167, 1973. Illus.
Identifiers: *Components analysis, Drought resistance, Grains, Hybrids, Panicle, Soil moisture, *Sorghum-bicolor, Tillering, *Crop production.

Drought resistance in terms of yield and its components was studied in the field in 21 agronomically-adapted high-performance grain sorghum (Sorghum bicolor Moench) hybrids. Resistance was considered to be indicated by a minimal decrease in yield under stress as compared with non-stress conditions. Water stress, imposed by a decreasing amount of stored soil moisture during the growing season, decreased grain yield and number of panicles per unit area, increased the number of grains per panicle, the number of branches per whorl and the number of grains per branch, and decreased the number of whorls per panicle. Thus, a compensatory effect was observed in some components for reduction in tillering under stress. Resistant hybrids performed better than susceptible ones under stress by producing a relatively higher number of panicles per unit area, and more grains per panicle branch. Susceptible hybrids performed better than resistant ones under nonstress (irrigated) conditions due to the relatively higher number of panicles per unit area and larger 1000-grain weight. Some of the implications regarding selection for yield performance under drought are discussed.--Copyright 1973, Biological Abstracts, Inc.
W75-08265

THE EFFECT OF SOIL MOISTURE TENSION AND NITROGEN SUPPLY ON NITRATE REDUCTION AND ACCUMULATION IN WHEAT SEEDLINGS,
Volcani Inst. of Agricultural Research, Bet-Dagan (Israel).
Z. Plaut.
Plant Soil, Vol 38, No 1, p 81-94, 1973. Illus.
Identifiers: Dry matter, Leaf, Minerals, *Nitrate reduction, *Nitrogen, Nutrition, Production, Reductase, Seedlings, *Soil moisture tension, *Wheat seedlings, Absorption.

Nitrate reductase activity was inhibited when soil moisture tension was increased to about 3.0 bars associated with a drop in leaf relative water content to about 90%. The decrease in nitrate reductase activity did not result in nitrate accumulation in short-term experiments (10 days) when plants were exposed to only 1-2 cyclies of elevated soil moisture tensions. However, when the period of different moisture regimes was extended up to the flag-leaf stage, nitrate accumulated in stressed plants. Significant increase in plant nitrate concentration as a result of increased moisture tensions was only found at the high levels of added N. On the other hand, moisture tensions had no effect on the content of total N in wheat shoots, implying that nitrate reduction was rather limiting under stress conditions. An effect of soil moisture tension and N nutrition on dry matter production by wheat seedlings was also found in the long-term experiment. At the highest dose of soil N an increase in maximal soil moisture tension from 0.1 to 0.33 bars reduced plant growth; at intermediate N doses only tension higher than 2 bars reduced growth. Under complete N deficiency, plant dry matter production was very low and was not affected by soil moisture tensions.--Copyright 1973, Biological Abstracts, Inc.
W75-08266

UTILIZING CLIMATE-MOISTURE-WATER USE RELATIONSHIPS IN IMPROVING SOIL MOISTURE BUDGET METHOD FOR IRRIGATION SCHEDULING,
Punjabrao Krishi Vidyapeeth, Akola (India). Dept. of Agronomy.
For primary bibliographic entry see Field 2D.
W75-08275

SUBDIVISION ON MALLEE FARMS,
For primary bibliographic entry see Field 4A.
W75-08281

WEST NUBARYA RECLAMATION PROJECT (EGYPT),
For primary bibliographic entry see Field 3C.
W75-08285

HEMIDIEH-SHAUR PROJECT (KHUZESTAN, IRAN),
For primary bibliographic entry see Field 3C.
W75-08286

DRIP IRRIGATION,
D. W. Armstrong, and P. J. Cole.
Journal of Agriculture, South Australia, Vol 77, No 1, p 2-9, February, 1974. 14 fig.

Descriptors: *Irrigation systems, *Soil moisture, *Soil-water-plant relationships, *Surface irrigation, Australia, Plant growth, Root zone, Costs, Fertilizers, Labor, Horticultural crops, Irrigation practices, Trickling filters, Tubes, Water conservation.
Identifiers: *Drip irrigation.

Recent experiments applying drip irrigation to fruit trees and vines in Victoria have stimulated interest in this method. Advantages lie in supplying water to plant root zones at a very low uniform rate, thus maintaining soil moisture for optimum growth. With this method, rapid growth and increased yields are noted, as well as water savings, since evaporation and runoff losses are virtually eliminated. Furthermore, weed growth is minimal, over-irrigation is avoided, and relatively saline water and saline soil, as well as low water pressure, may be utilized. Labor savings may results, particularly in comparison with portable irrigation systems. Disadvantages include limitations on fertilizer application, leaching of fertilizers from sandy soils, accumulation of salts at the edge of the wet zone, blocking of drippers and filters, and restrictions of root zone growth, especially with trees. Commercially produced systems are available in Australia, or a home-made system may be assembled by using a polyethylene microtubing, thus reducing costs. (Gloyd-Arizona)
W75-08287

GRASS FOR CONSERVATION: II. THE QUALITY OF A SECOND CUT TAKEN AFTER SIX WEEKS GROWTH,
National Inst. of Agricultural Botany, Cambridge (England).
J. W. Dent, and D. T. A. Aldrich.
J Natl Inst Agric Bot, Vol 12, No 2, p 340-346, 1971.

Descriptors: *Conservation, *Grasses, *Plant growth, *Water requirements.
Identifiers: Cocksfoot, Fescue, Italian ryegrass, Timothy, *Climatic effects.

If the 1st cut is taken under dry conditions and is followed by a period of drought, regrowth is slow, but a period of rain later in the 6-wk period may result in late and rapid growth producing material of high digestibility. The reverse may also occur with moist conditions early in the period. This may result in the early growth, deteriorating in quality towards the end of the 6-wk growth period. Climatic conditions are likely to be the main cause of site differences both in yield and quality. In most species a 2nd conservation cut taken 6 wk after the 1st cut at an estimated 63D (digestibility level) gave material at an acceptible level of quality. With the exception of Italian ryegrass and cocksfoot digestibility levels were about 65-67D. In all cases the Italian ryegrass was of low digestibility and this was probably due to the high proportion of heads in the sward. Despite site differences in digestibility, the low coefficients of variation indicated a satisfactory degree of reproducibility in variety comparisons. In 1969 significant differences between varieties were found in perennial ryegrass, timothy and meadow and tall fescue, with an average least significant difference ($P = 0.05$) of 1.9% of D-value.--Copyright 1973, Biological Abstracts, Inc.
W75-08343

IRON AND PHOSPHORUS INTERACTION IN CALCAREOUS SOILS: II. EFFECT ON CHLOROSIS DEVELOPMENT, AND SOME NUTRIENT ELEMENT CONTENTS IN SOIL AND PLANT,
Ain Shams Univ., Cairo (Egypt). Dept. of Soils.
For primary bibliographic entry see Field 2G.
W75-08344

4. WATER QUANTITY MANAGEMENT AND CONTROL

4A. Control Of Water On The Surface

IDENTIFICATION AND ANALYSIS OF SELECTED HIGH PRIORITY WATER PROBLEMS AND RELATED RESEARCH NEEDS OF THE MISSOURI RIVER BASIN,
Nebraska Univ., Lincoln. Water Resources Research Inst.
For primary bibliographic entry see Field 6B.
W75-07851

RECONNAISSANCE OF SEDIMENTATION IN THE UPPER RIO BERMEJO BASIN, ARGENTINA,
Geological Survey, Menlo Park, Calif.

For primary bibliographic entry see Field 2J.
W75-07859

FLORIDA'S WATER RESOURCES,
Geological Survey, Tallahassee, Fla.
C. S. Conover.
Reprint of paper from 'The Dare Report-1973': University of Florida Institute of Food and Agricultural Sciences Publication 11, 1973. 10 p, 5 fig, 8 ref.

Descriptors: *Water resources, *Florida, Ground-water, Surface waters, Hydrogeology, Water utilization, Water demand.

The use of freshwater in Florida in 1970 for all purposes averaged about 5.8 billion gallons per day, equivalent to about 850 gallons per day per person. The mean annual runoff of streams in Florida is about 40 billion gallons a day, equivalent to an average of 14 inches over the surface of the state. This amount is only about 7 times the amount of freshwater used in 1970 in Florida but is about 22 times the amount used consumptively. The Floridan aquifer consists essentially of solution-riddled limestone that lies beneath the land surface throughout nearly all of Florida. The aquifer is at or near land surface in the northern and central part of the peninsula, and is at depths of more than 1,000 feet in the southern part of the peninsula. The aquifer system contains a tremendous volume of freshwater in storage, about 800 cubic miles. Saltwater contamination is rather common in some areas, especially in southwestern Florida, where salty artesian water has been allowed to infiltrate, via leaky well casings, into shallow aquifers which contained fresh water, such as in the vicinity of LaBelle and in parts of Lee County. A common cause of saltwater encroachment in Florida, especially along the southeast coast, has been the construction of canals. (Knapp-USGS)
W75-07872

WATER RESOURCES DATA FOR NEBRASKA, 1973: PART 1. SURFACE WATER RECORDS.
Geological Survey, Lincoln, Nebr.
For primary bibliographic entry see Field 7C.
W75-07879

WATER BALANCE OF LAKE KERR--A DEDUCTIVE STUDY OF A LANDLOCKED LAKE IN NORTH-CENTRAL FLORIDA,
Geological Survey, Tallahassee, Fla.
For primary bibliographic entry see Field 2H.
W75-07881

WATER-RESOURCES INVESTIGATIONS OF THE U.S. GEOLOGICAL SURVEY IN THE NORTHERN GREAT PLAINS COAL REGION OF NORTHEASTERN WYOMING, 1974-75,
Geological Survey, Cheyenne, Wyo.
For primary bibliographic entry see Field 7C.
W75-07887

WATER FACTS AND FIGURES FOR PLANNERS AND MANAGERS,
Geological Survey, Menlo Park, Calif.
For primary bibliographic entry see Field 6B.
W75-07889

FLOOD PLAIN MANAGEMENT AND IMPLEMENTATION STRATEGIES FOR FPM PROGRAMS,
Iowa State Water Resources Research Inst., Ames.
For primary bibliographic entry see Field 6F.
W75-07890

OPTIMAL MONTHLY OPERATION OF INTERCONNECTED HYDROELECTRIC POWER STORAGES,
Institute of Hydrology, Wallingford (England).
A. I. McKerchar.
Journal of Hydrology, Vol 25, No 1/2, p 137-158, April 1975. 7 fig, 10 tab, 19 ref.

Descriptors: *Dynamic programming, *Hydroelectric plants, *Reservoir operation, Streamflow, *Thermal powerplants, Synthetic hydrology, Storage, Inflow, *Optimization, Computers, *Simulation analysis, Analytical techniques, *Model studies.
Identifiers: Interconnected power storages, *New Zealand, Multivariate streamflow model.

In water resource systems problems, the conceptual part consists of formulating the design of a system as a set of mathematical functions and the computational part comprises optimization of the objective function by solving the system equations recursively. A deterministic dynamic programming technique coupled with a multivariate streamflow simulation model was developed for operation of two interconnected reservoirs in the South Island of New Zealand. The releases from these reservoirs are used for hydroelectric power generation, but plants are operated in conjunction with thermal generating plants to provide a specified energy load for each month. The system objective is to minimize the expected present value of the thermal generating costs. A real-time operating policy which specifies a planned release for each month as a function of the quantities of water stored at the beginning of each month was developed. Important advantages of this particular dynamic programming approach over other optimizing techniques were illustrated; in particular, good account was taken of the stochastic nature of the inflows. (Singh-ISWS)
W75-07898

IRRIGATION RUNOFF RECOVERY IN THE DESIGN OF CONSTANT FURROW DISCHARGE IRRIGATION SYSTEMS,
Utah State Univ., Logan. Dept. of Agricultural and Irrigation Engineering.
For primary bibliographic entry see Field 3F.
W75-07923

SEISMIC RESPONSE OF RESERVOIR-DAM SYSTEMS,
Michigan Univ., Ann Arbor. Dept. of Civil Engineering.
For primary bibliographic entry see Field 8B.
W75-07930

COMPUTATION OF STAGE-DISCHARGE RELATIONSHIPS AFFECTED BY UNSTEADY FLOW,
National Weather Service, Silver Spring, Md. Hydrologic Research and Development Lab.
For primary bibliographic entry see Field 2E.
W75-07932

STATE-OF-THE-ART OF ESTIMATING FLOOD DAMAGE IN URBAN AREAS,
Colorado State Univ., Fort Collins. Dept. of Civil Engineering.
N. S. Grigg, and O. J. Helweg.
Water Resources Bulletin, Vol 11, No 2, p 379-390, April 1975. 8 fig, 19 ref.

Descriptors: *Flood damage, *Damages, *Floods, *Cities, Drainage, Flood control, Land use, Management, Planning, Zoning, Stage-discharge relations, Discharge frequency, Legislation, Estimating.

With implementation of the Flood Insurance Act of 1968 many additional local flood protection projects are being considered. Consulting engineers and local agencies need consistent methods to estimate flood damage in order to perform feasibility studies. Federal agencies have a great deal of data and long experience in making damage estimates but no comprehensive guides are available at the local level. Curves of flood damage to different residential structure types were presented. The relationships in use by the U.S. Federal Insurance Administration were shown to be reasonable and were recommended for use as approximate guides. Additional research was recommended and discussion of the paper was invited in order to make additional data available in the literature. (Dawes-ISWS)
W75-07939

DRAINAGE CHARACTERISTICS OF SOILS,
Colorado State Univ., Fort Collins. Dept. of Agricultural Engineering.
For primary bibliographic entry see Field 2G.
W75-07944

COMMENTS ON THE HISTORY OF CONTROLLED BURNING IN THE SOUTHERN UNITED STATES,
Tall Timbers Research Station, Tallahassee, Fla.
E. V. Komarek, Sr.
In: 17th Annual Arizona Watershed Symposium, Proceedings, September 19, 1973, Phoenix, p 11-17, 34 ref.

Descriptors: *Burning, *Forest management, *History, Range management, Wildlife management, Watershed management, *Southeast U.S.
Identifiers: *Controlled burning.

Controlled or prescribed burning in the Southeastern United States is used for the management of forest, range, and wildlife. Early in this century the Dixie Pioneers scientifically approached the burning question and established the modern precedents. Today the Tall Timbers Research Station operates for public, scientific, and educational purposes. Their publications, research, and seminars are designed to aid the control of an ecological balance. (McLachlan-Arizona)
W75-07977

WATER RESOURCES DEVELOPMENT BY THE U.S. ARMY CORPS OF ENGINEERS IN ARIZONA,
Army Engineer District, San Francisco, Calif.
January, 1973. 65 p, illustrated, map.

Descriptors: *Flood control, *Floodwater, *Arizona, *Historic floods, *Colorado River Basin, Engineering structures, Diversion structures, Canals, Flood plain zoning, Flood recurrence interval, Recreation, Recreation facilities, Lakes, Damsites, Dams, Watershed management.
Identifiers: Gila River Basin(Ariz), Little Colorado River Basin(Ariz).

A history of the Army Corps of Engineers activities in Arizona is given as well as brief sketches of future projects. Basically, the Corps sees its work as flood control. Recreational facilities created by the projects are also described. The Corps has been active in the state since the middle of the nineteenth century. The state is divided into three sections in the volume, Lower Main Stem Subregion, Gila Subregion, and Little Colorado Subregion. Corps participation in civil works also is described. (Bowden-Arizona)
W75-07979

ESTIMATING LAND USE CHARACTERISTICS FOR HYDROLOGIC MODELS,
Rummel, Klepper and Kahl, Baltimore, Md.
W. R. Gluck, and R. H. McCuen.
Water Resources Research, Vol 11, No 1, p 177-179, February 1975. 2 tab, 9 ref. OWRT A-025-MD(1).

Descriptors: *Land classification, *Land use, *Urban mapping, *Model studies, Watersheds(Basins), Rainfall-runoff relationships, Urban hydrology, Suburban areas, Hydrology, Equations, *Estimating.

An analytically determined general optimal policy for operating a multi-purpose reservoir is presented and depicted in graphical form. Piecewise linear cost functions are used to describe downstream flow costs, reservoir level costs, and costs incurred in meeting and not meeting power demands, the cost parameters involved in these functions being left arbitrary to allow wide applicability. Assumed are random inflows into the reservoir, known power demands, and the availability of a finite-capacity auxiliary power source. Dynamic programming is used as an analytical, as opposed to numerical, tool in determining the general form of an optimal operating policy for this model. A general solution to the problem of water allocation in a multipurpose reservoir is obtained. (Bell-Cornell)
W75-08003

FLOOD PROTECTION BENEFITS AS REFLECTED IN PROPERTY VALUE CHANGES,
Kentucky Univ., Lexington. Dept. of Economics.
For primary bibliographic entry see Field 6F.
W75-08004

RIVER BASIN WATER PLANNING ORGANIZATIONS IN THE 60'S,
Utah State Univ., Logan. Dept. of Civil Engineering.
For primary bibliographic entry see Field 6B.
W75-08011

SIXES BRIDGE DAM AND LAKE, MARYLAND AND PENNSYLVANIA (FINAL ENVIRONMENTAL IMPACT STATEMENT).
Army Engineer District, Baltimore, Md.
For primary bibliographic entry see Field 8F.
W75-08015

CORBELL HULL DAM AND RESERVOIR, CUMBERLAND RIVER, TENNESSEE (FINAL ENVIRONMENTAL IMPACT STATEMENT).
Army Engineer District, Nashville, Tenn.
For primary bibliographic entry see Field 8A.
W75-08020

GUADALUPE RIVER, TEXAS (REMOVAL OF LOG JAMS) (FINAL ENVIRONMENTAL IMPACT STATEMENT).
Army Engineer District, Galveston, Tex.
March 29, 1973. 90 p, 1 map 8 ref.

Descriptors: *Flood control, *Barriers, *Obstruction to flow, Navigation, Floods, Project planning, Project benefits, *Texas, Ecosystems, Aquatic habitats, Pollutants, Smoke, Silting, Water policy, Federal project policy.
Identifiers: *Environmental Impact statements, *Guadalupe River(Tex), Log jams.

The removal of log jams on the Lower Guadalupe River, Texas, has been examined with respect to its engineering feasibility, environmental impact, and conformity with the intent expressed by Congress. Jams now partially restrict the river flow, so that small and moderate floods overlap its banks, flooding adjacent lowlands and obstructing small boat navigation. Their removal will provide immediate benefits by preventing damage from small and frequent floods, and by increasing production and improving utilization of agricultural land. Larger and less frequent flooding will be appreciably affected. Four major log jams and a log raft, as well as any other jams which might develop, will be removed with disposal of the debris by burning at an estimated cost of $390,000. Air pollution from the burning, release of small amounts of accumulated settlement with consequent downstream siltation and elimination of spawning and feeding habitats for aquatic species will result. However, these environmental effects, which are minor and mainly temporary, are far, outweighed by the benefits expected to be received from the project. The proposed action is fully consistent with national policy, statutes, and administrative directives. (Ostapoff-Florida)
W75-08021

SHOAL CREEK CHANNEL, CHARITON-LITTLE CHARITON BASINS, MISSOURI (FINAL ENVIRONMENTAL IMPACT STATEMENT).
Army Engineer District, Kanasa City, Mo.
Available from National Technical Information Service, Springfield, Va 22161 as USDC, EIS-MO-73-0793-F, $4.25 in paper copy, $2.25 in microfiche. March 1973. 72 p, 3 map, 4 tab.

Descriptors: *Flood control, *Flood protection, *Channel improvement, Wildlife, Recreation, Flow, Drainage, Streams, Recreation facilities, Floods, Flooding, Environmental effects, Channels, *Missouri, Wetlands, Flood damage, Forestry, Forests.
Identifiers: *Environmental impact statements, *Putnam and Schuyler Counties(Mo).

The project involves construction of a flood control project, consisting of 2.4 miles of channel improvement and a high flow channel in Putnam and Schuyler Counties, Missouri. The project will provide flood protection, improve drainage, alter 2.8 miles of stream habitat, and remove wildlife habitat along the high floe channel. The loss of approximately 2.8 miles of natural character of the Shoal Creek and associated stream biota and adjacent wildlife will be the main adverse effect of the project. Additional damage to wildlife habitat will occur in the area along the high flow channel, if constructed. In addition, the provision of flood protection and drainage will encourage local farmers to encroach upon timberlands. The project will also cause temporary adverse effects on the environment during construction. The following alternatives were considered: alternate channelization alinements; small watershed flood detention developments; and no action. (Gagliardi-Florida)
W75-08024

FOURMILE RUN LOCAL FLOODPLAIN PROTECTION, CITY OF ALEXANDRIA AND ARLINGTON COUNTY, VIRGINIA (FINAL ENVIRONMENTAL IMPACT STATEMENT).
Army Engineer District, Baltimore, Md.
Available from National Technical Information Service, Springfield, Va 22161 as USDC, EIS-VA-73-06-4-F, $5.25 in paper copy, $2.25 in microfiche. April 1973. 116 p, 13 tab, 9 map, 3 fig, 7 plate.

Descriptors: *Virginia, *Flood protection, *Flood control, *Channel improvement, *Drainage systems, Channels, Walls, Levees, Drainage, Flood frequency, Flood forecasting, Flooding, Floods, Bridge design, Bridges, Aesthetics, Planting management, Recreation facilities, Recreation, Marshes, Environmental effects, Vegetation, Flood plain zoning.
Identifiers: *Environmental impact statements, Alexandria(Va), Arlington County(Va).

The project involves changes in a local flood protection project including revisions to flood frequency, channels, walls, levee dimensions and computations; alterations to interior drainage facilities; additional bridge modifications; and inclusion of recreation, beautification and enhancement programs. The revised project will enhance easthetics by elimination of portions of walls and levees and by addition of plantings. Additionally, recreational opportunities will be increased and portions of existing marshland will be preserved. Among adverse effects expected are elimination of additional streamside vegetation, reduction in the amount of active recreation space, disturbance of shallow stream bottoms and the use of 3.6 acres of low quality marshland for spoil area. The following alternatives were considered: providing a

low degree of protection with improved channel and dredge modifications; supplementary flood plain management; and walls and levees in addition to the proposed project. (Gagliardi-Florida)
W75-08025

HAMPTON CREEK NAVIGATION PROJECT (MAINTENANCE DREDGING) HAMPTON, VIRGINIA (FINAL ENVIRONMENTAL IMPACT STATEMENT).
Army Engineer District, Norfolk, Va.
Available from National Technical Information Service, Springfield, Va 22161 as USDC, EIS-VA-73-0745-F, $3.75 in paper copy, $2.25 in microfiche. November 1972. 40 p, 2 tab, 2 map, 1 fig.

Descriptors: *Dredging, *Navigation, *Virginia, *Channel improvement, Channels, Commercial fishing, Aquatic habitats, Benthic flora, Benthic fauna, Fish eggs, Water pollution sources, Waste disposal, Landfills, Recreation, Spawning, Fish populations, Commercial fish, Environmental effects.
Identifiers: *Environmental impact statements, *Hampton Creek(Va), Hampton Roads(Va).

Maintenance dredging of the 150 foot - 200 foot wide entrance channel of the Hampton Creek navigation project to the required 12-foot depth will maintain the carrying capacity of the project for the efficient movement of commercial and recreational navigation. 126,000 cubic yards of spoil will be removed from the area of Old Point Comfort to the mouth of Hampton Creek, a tidal estuary of Hampton Roads, Virginia. The spoil willbe transported 7 nautical miles to the Craney Island Disposal Area, used in 1967 in an earlier maintenance project. Turbidity from the dredging will not be sufficient to result in an increase over the normal estuarine level by any significant percentage. There will not be any notable adverse effeets on primary production, respiration, or spot attachment. However, the buoyancy of pleustonic fish eggs will be reduced by the attachment of silt particles on their outer membrane, resulting in a local reduction in fish production. Comments received on submission of the Draft Environmental Impact Statement led to the conclusion that dredging should not commence until after the spawning season terminates, in early winter. With this revision, adverse environmental effects of the project will be minimal. In view of the extensive use of the channel by the local seafood industry, the alternative of foregoing maintenance is unacceptable. (Ostapoff-Florida)
W75-08026

CENTRAL AND SOUTHERN FLORIDA PROJECT, LAKE OKEECHOBEE (FINAL ENVIRONMENTAL IMPACT STATEMENT).
Army Engineer District, Jacksonville, Fla.
Available from National Technical Information Service, Springfield, Va 22161 as USDC, EIS-FL-73-1765-F, $6.25 in paper copy, $2.25 in microfiche. November 8, 1973. 164 p.

Descriptors: *Florida, *Environmental effects, *Water supply development, Water level fluctuations, Federal government, Water supply, Water management(Applied), Lakes, Water quality, Water resources development, Water storage, Dependable supply, Multiple-purpose projects, Potential water supply, Reservoir operation, Dams, Water levels, Saline water intrusion, Levees, Potable water, Flooding.
Identifiers: *Environmental impact statements, *Lake Okeechobee(Fla), Dam effects.

This project is one of six segments of the Central and Southern Florida Project. Lake Okeechobee is a natural lake located in south-central Florida, and it is the second largest body of fresh water in the United States, having a surface area of 730 square miles. This segment consists of raising the regulation range of the lake from 14.0 to 15.5 feet, mean sea level, to 15.5 to 17.5, mean sea level. About 85% of the facilities needed to effect this raise are already completed. The remaining facilities, consisting of various levees, spillways, and locks, will be completed as part of this segment. The raise will increase the present storage capability in the lake approximately 900,000 acre-feet, providing additional water to supply all project purposes, including Everglades National Park. The raise will also periodically inundate 12,000 acres of lake bottom currently being used for pasture and agriculture, resulting in improved ground-water quality in areas adjacent to the lake and some change in location, density, and distribution of aquatic vegetation. While no significant permanent adverse environment effects are anticipated, portions of several recreational facilities will be inundated. The alternative of increasing storage capability in several other water conservation areas was rejected as impractical or not environmentally viable. Approximately 22,000 acres of upland vegetation will be convereted to marsh habitat. Concern was expressed by various groups that possible adverse environmental effects were not adequately considered. (Deckert-Florida)
W75-08027

LAKEVIEW LAKE, MOUNTAIN CREEK, TRINITY RIVER BASIN, TEXAS (FINAL ENVIRONMENTAL IMPACT STATEMENT).
Army Engineer District, Forth Worth, Tex.
For primary bibliographic entry see Field 8A.
W75-08028

SOUTH FORK WATERSHED, PAWNEE AND RICHARDSON COUNTIES, NEBRASKA (FINAL ENVIRONMENTAL IMPACT STATEMENT).
Soil Conservation Service, Washington, D.C.
For primary bibliographic entry see Field 8A.
W75-08029

ARKANSAS RIVER AND TRIBUTARIES ABOVE JOHN MARTIN DAM (FINAL ENVIRONMENTAL IMPACT STATEMENT).
Army Engineer District, Albuquerque, N.Mex.
For primary bibliographic entry see Field 8A.
W75-08033

SPRING BROOK WATERSHED, LANGLADE AND MARATHON COUNTIES, WISCONSIN (FINAL ENVIRONMENTAL IMPACT STATEMENT).
Soil Conservation Service, Washington, D.C.
Available from the National Technical Information Service, Springfield, Va. 22161, as EIS-WI-73-1416-F, $4.25 in paper copy, $2.25 in microfiche. August 28, 1973. 70 p, 1 photo, 1 graph, 4 tab, 3 map.

Descriptors: *Flood protection, *Flood control, *Watershed Protection and Flood Prevention Act, *Wisconsin, Watershed management, Flooding, Floods, Environmental effects, Sedimentation, Erosion, Erosion control, Spillways, Dams, Forests, Dikes, Trees, Vegetation, Wildlife, Channels, Flood plain zoning.
Identifiers: *Environmental impact statements, Antigo(Wisc).

The project involves watershed protection and flood prevention in Langlade and Marathon Counties, Wisconsin, to be implemented under authority of the Watershed Protection and Flood Prevention Act. The primary environmental effects of the action will be the reduction of the annual rate of erosion by up to 50 percent and the average annual sedimentation rate by about 12 percent. Additionally, average annual flood damages will be reduced by about 41 percent on agricultural land, 47 percent on roads and bridges, and 46 percent in the city of Antigo. Structural measures will reduce the frequency of flow through Skinner Dam's auxillary spillway to less than once in 50 years and will regulate the flow of Spring Brook and stabilize Antigo Lake. The proposed installation of the dam, spillway, and sediment pool will remove about 17 acres of forest and 108 acres of cropland from production. Additional adverse environmental effects include removal of trees along the channel and in the vicinity of the dike; temporary removal of 71 acres of vegetation; and the subjection of 35 acres of forest land, 385 acres of cropland, and associated wildlife habitat to occasional short duration flooding. The alternatives are to continue the present trends; accelerated the land treatment; accelerate the land treatment in connection with channel enlargements; and utilize programs of floodproofing, flood plain zoning, and structure removal in the flood plain. (Gagliardi-Florida)
W75-08035

CHANNEL EXTENSION, SIUSLAW RIVER AND BAR, LAND COUNTY, OREGON (FINAL ENVIRONMENTAL IMPACT STATEMENT).
Army Engineer District, Portland, Oreg.
For primary bibliographic entry see Field 8A.
W75-08043

NAVIGATION SEASON EXTENSION DEMONSTRATION PROGRAM (FINAL ENVIRONMENTAL IMPACT STATEMENT).
Army Engineer District, Detroit, Mich.
Available from the National Technical Information Service, Springfield, Va. 22161, as EIS-MI-73-1933-F, $8.75 in paper copy, $2.25 in microfiche. December 14, 1973. 285 p, 10 map, 9 tab.

Descriptors: *Navigation, *Great Lakes, *St. Lawrence Seaway, *Ice, Iced lakes, Ice cover, Powerplants, Ice jams, Ships, Navigable waters, Navigable rivers, Winter.
Identifiers: *Environmental impact statements, Navigability tests.

The Navigation Season Extension Demonstration Program is part of a three-year program to demonstrate the practicability of extending the commercial navigation season on the Great Lakes and St. Lawrence Seaway. The following potential extension methods were considered: bubbler systems; ice breaking activities; ice retarding heat additives in the form of power plant heat rejections; and ice stabilization and retention structures. Also investigated were modifications, vessels designed to increase ice navigation capabilities and various types of navigational aids to permit safer navigation during winter weather conditions. The purpose of the demonstration program is to establish the feasibility of this alternative to limited winter use. (Gagliardi-Florida)
W75-08044

RED RIVER WATERWAY, LOUISIANA, TEXAS ARKANSAS, AND OKLAHOMA, AND RELATED PROJECTS (FINAL ENVIRONMENTAL IMPACT STATEMENT).
Army Engineer District, New Orleans, La.
For primary bibliographic entry see Field 8A.
W75-08045

AUTHORIZED GRANITE REEF AQUEDUCT, CENTRAL ARIZONA PROJECT, ARIZONA-NEW MEXICO (FINAL ENVIRONMENTAL IMPACT STATEMENT).
Bureau of Reclamation, Denver, Colo.
For primary bibliographic entry see Field 8A.
W75-08050

VERONA DAM AND LAKE, VIRGINIA (FINAL ENVIRONMENTAL IMPACT STATEMENT).
Army Engineer District, Baltimore, Md.
For primary bibliographic entry see Field 8F.
W75-08056

CHANNEL TO NEWPORT NEWS, VIRGINIA (MAINTENANCE DREDGING) (ENVIRONMENTAL IMPACT STATEMENT).
Army Engineer District, Norfolk, Va.
For primary bibliographic entry see Field 8A.
W75-08057

SANTIAGO-NORTE DRAINAGE PROJECT (CHILE),
For primary bibliographic entry see Field 3C.
W75-08109

GRAZING SYSTEMS FOR ARIZONA RANGES.
Forest Service (USDA), Tucson, Ariz. Rocky Mountain Forest and Range Experiment Station.
For primary bibliographic entry see Field 3F.
W75-08112

AN INTEGRATED NATURAL RESOURCES SURVEY IN NORTHERN IRAQ,
Institute for Applied Research on Natural Resources, Baghdad (Iraq).
For primary bibliographic entry see Field 3F.
W75-08116

WATERLOGGING AND SALINITY PROBLEMS IN THE INDUS PLAIN (PAKISTAN),
For primary bibliographic entry see Field 3C.
W75-08117

EPA AUTHORITY AFFECTING LAND USE,
Ross, Hardies, O'Keefe, Babcock and Parsons, Chicago, Ill.
For primary bibliographic entry see Field 5G.
W75-08172

SPECIAL FLOOD HAZARD REPORT: CHESTER CREEK, GREATER ANCHORAGE AREA,
Army Engineer District, Anchorage, Alaska.
Prepared for the Greater Anchorage Area Borough, Alaska, January, 1975. 19 p, 2 tab, 24 plates.

Descriptors: *Floods, *Flooding, Flow, *Obstructions to flow, *Glaciation, *Alaska, Flood plains, Flood frequency, Flood water, Flood flow, Velocity.
Identifiers: *Chester Creek(Alas), Anchorage(Alas), Greater Anchorage Area Borough, Intermediate Regional Flood, Standard Project Flood.

The study area extends from the confluence of Chester Creek with Knik Arm to the foothills of the Chugach Mountains. Stream flows westward to and through Anchorage (population over 162,500). Flood plain has limited commercial development. Within Anchorage portions of the flood plain have been designated as a green belt for recreational development although parts of this area have been flooded previously. Rapid residential development in formerly damp and swampy areas and on both sides of the Creek is creating problems due to increased runoff and accelerated main channel flow. Floods occur in spring and winter from thaws and winter glaciation where water will freeze down to the stream bed forcing water on top of the ice sometimes creating a new water course. Culverts are a major obstruction to flow and a primary site for the glaciation process. Installation of trash racks upstream of culverts is suggested to reduce culvert plugging from debris. Regular inspection of all culverts and trash racks to remove debris is necessary. No structures or regulations exist for flood control. Latest major floods occurred in April, 1963 with others in November, 1961, April, 1966, and August, 1971, the first two due to ice conditions causing backwater effects. The Intermediate Regional flood and the Standard Project Flood would cause greater damage as channel velocities approach 12 ft/sec causing erosion and transporting materials. Glaciation or winter flooding is a constant and ever-increasing threat and should always be considered before any development near the stream. Glaciation may possibly extend beyond IRF limits shown on plates. Intended as a suitable basis for future study, no solutions to flood problems are provided. (Park-North Carolina)
W75-08173

FLOOD PLAIN INFORMATION: CROW CREEK, CHEYENNE, WYOMING,
Army Engineer District, Omaha, Nebr.
Prepared for City of Cheyenne, June, 1970. 24 p, 4 fig, 5 plates, 2 tab.

Descriptors: Floods, *Flooding, *Flood damage, *Obstructions to flow, Flood data, *Flood plains, Flood water, Maximum probable flood, Historic floods, *Wyoming.
Identifiers: *Crow Creek(Wyoming), Cheyenne(Wyoming), Intermediate Regional Flood, Standard Project Flood.

The drainage area of Crow Creek, a tributary of the South Plate River, is 253 sq mi including the southern portion of Cheyenne. The Creek provides the city with its water supply and sewage disposal. Study area extends from interstate Highway 25 downstream 6.3 miles to sewage disposal plant. Most of the channel has been straightened and confined by roads, levees, and fills and drops about 18 ft/mi in slope. Industrial, commercial and residential development in the flood plain is gradual but steady with pressures for development likely to continue. Eleven bridges cross the creek, possible obstructions to major flood flows. Elevated roadways and inadequate culverts also create problems. Intense thunderstorm rainfall during spring and summer months possibly preceded by heavy snowmelt causes most floods. Although it has been almost 40 years since the last major flood, June, 1929, future floods of the same size are still possible. Intermediate Regional Flood with a peak discharge of 5,500 cfs would overtop all bridges except on Highway 25 and the railroad bridges, covering an area about 600 ft wide upstream of Morrie Avenue. A Standard Project Flood with an estimated peak discharge of 17,000 cfs would inundate about 1,000 ft in the same reach. The depth of flood water, together with the rapidly rising waters, and high velocities can cause substantial damage to industrial, commercial, and residential areas. Recommendations for flood protection are not included. (Park-North Caolina)
W75-08174

FLOOD PLAIN INFORMATION: SAN DIEGO CREEK AND PETERS CANYON WASH, ORANGE COUNTY, CALIFORNIA,
Army Engineer District, Los Angeles, Calif.
Prepared for Orange County Flood Control District, June, 1972. 28 p, 17 fig, 6 tab, 21 plates.

Descriptors: Floods, *Flood plains, *Flood profiles, *Flood forecasting, Flood frequency, *Flooding, Flow, Obstructions to flow, Flow characteristics, Flood data, Flood damage, Tributaries, Historic floods, *California, Velocity.
Identifiers: Orange County(Cal), Newport Beach(Cal), Irvine(Cal), *San Diego Creek(Cal), *Peters Canyon Wash(Cal), Intermediate Regional Flood, Standard Project Flood.

Study area includes portions of the cities of Newport Beach and Irvine and the 80,000 acre Irvine Ranch. Development pressures have created intense demand for industrial and residential land. A planned development projected over 20 years anticipates 280,000 people and the University of California at Irvine expects an enrollment of 27,500. San Diego Creek and its major tributary, Peters Canyon Wash, drain an area of approximately 150 sq mi within Orange County ranging in elevation from sea level to about 1700 feet above mean sea level. Stream gradients range about 4 ft/mi upstream of Newport Bay to about 25 ft/mi near upstream study limits. Channels of both streams are well defined and have long reaches of improvements. Runoff is very erratic varying from almost no flow for long periods to rapid increases following heavy rains. The flood plain area currently used for agriculture is expected to become increasingly urbanized in the next decades. Most flooding has been caused by high-intensity rainfall from winter storms November through March. Trees and vegetation obstruct channels. Some channel improvements aid in flood control. An adequate system of channels and storm drains must be provided for the City of Irvine. In February, 1969, the most devastating flood of record had a peak flow of 6,700 cfs on San Diego Creek for a drainage area of 40.3 sq mi with losses on the Creek estimated at $1,157,000. The Intermediate Regional Flood and Standard Project Flood could have peak flows of 11,600 cfs. and 21,000 cfs respectively and would inundate large areas with bridges and roads rendered impassable from deposits of debris and erosion. (Park-North Carolina)
W75-08175

FLOOD PLAIN INFORMATION: MARAIS DES CYGNES RIVER, MELVERN TO OTTOWA, KANSAS, VOLUME 1.
Army Engineer District, Kansas City, Mo.
Prepared for Kansas Water Resources Board, July 1973. 32 p, 20 fig, 5 tab, 19 plates.

Descriptors: *Floods, *Flooding, *Flood plains, *Flood profiles, *Flood forecasting, Flood flow, Obstructions to flow, Flood peak, Flood discharge, Historic floods, Maximum probable flood, *Kansas.
Identifiers: *Marais Des Cygnes River(Kansas), Salt Creek(Kansas), One Hundred and Ten Mile Creek(Kansas), Ottowa(Kansas), Intermediate Regional Flood, Standard Project Flood.

Development in the flood plain of the River and two main tributaries, Salt Creek and One Hundred and Ten Mile Creek, is minimal, mostly undeveloped and agricultural. A portion of Ottowa, Kansas is in the flood plain but is protected by a system of levees and flood walls completed in 1962. Additional protection is afforded by two reservoirs, Melvern Lake and Pomona Lake controlling 650 square miles of the River's 1250 square mile basin. Past major floods occurred in November, 1928, April, 1944, and July, 1951 with peak discharges at Ottowa of 87,400, 73,000, and 142,000 cubic feet/second (cfs) respectively. Flood flows result mainly from rapid runoff from intense rainfall. Floods from local runoff below the lakes and from floodwaters through the lake spillways are possible through the entire study area. The 1973 flood on the Maria de Cygnes River had an estimated discharge or 12,500 cfs at Ottowa and was above flood stage there for 7 days. Possible future floods, the Intermediate Regional Flood (IRF) and Standard Project Flood (SPF) would have respective peak flows of 78,000 cfs and 114,000 cfs at river mile 400.7; an IRF cresting at 898.5 ft and inundating 9 bridges, an SPF cresting at 902.4 ft and inundating eight more bridges. Channel velocities could reach as high as 5.78 ft/sec in an IRF and 6.25 ft/sec in an SPF at a point on the Marais des Cygnes near Pomona, causing severe streambank erosion and eroding bridge abutments. Operation of the reservoirs, Melvern and Pomona Lakes are expected to reduce flood stage to about 3 days. No recommendations for flood control are included. (Park-North Carolina)
W75-08176

FLOOD PLAIN INFORMATION: SALT CREEK, RIVERSIDE COUNTY, CALIFORNIA.
Army Engineer District, Los Angeles, Calif.
For primary bibliographic entry see Field 4A.
W75-08177

FLOOD PLAIN INFORMATION: SALT CREEK, RIVERSIDE COUNTY, CALIFORNIA.
Army Engineer District, Los Angeles, Calif.
Prepared for Riverside County, June, 1971. 30 p, 23 fig, 3 tab, 18 plates.

Descriptors: Floods, *Flood plains, *Flood profiles, *Flood forecasting, *Flooding, *Flood damage, Maximum probable flood, Historic floods, *California.
Identifiers: *Salt Creek(Cal), Riverside County(Cal), Hemet(Cal), Sun City(Cal), Intermediate Regional Flood, Standard Project Flood.

Salt Creek, a tributary of the San Jacinto River, drains 130 sq mi from its headwaters (elevation 4500 ft) near the City of Hemet to Railroad Canyon Reservoir near Sun City. Traversing largely agricultural areas, the natural watercourse has been virtually obliterated and floods have been extensive, causing damage to agricultural and residential areas and utilities. Building codes and subdivision regulations of Hemet and Riverside County are the only controls on flood plain development. Urbanization is expected to increase. The Salt Creek Channel was designed to provide flood protection to Sun City from the 100-year flood. Hemet Channel conveys runoff to areas south of the city. Some manmade embankments affect flooding by raising roadways above the valley floor. Maximum floods of record were January, 1952 and February, 1969; the latter had a peak discharge of 2,010 cfs. An Intermediate Regional Flood (IRF) would have a peak discharge of 13,100 cfs and the Standard Project Flood (SPF) discharge would be 25,000 cfs at the Railroad Canyon Reservoir. Both floods would overtop the major highways and inundate all secondary roads in the flood plain, damaging croplands, agricultural and residential structures. General winter storms between December and April lasting several days and local thunderstorms of high intensity and short duration cause most floods. An IRF would flow at depths of 1 to 4 ft on the flood plain with an SPF ranging 1/2 ft to 2 ft higher. Severe erosion would be created by the high velocities of flow. Both floods would peak about 12 hours from the beginning of intense rainfall. In the planning of flood control facilities, consideration should be given to the whole Salt Creek Basin, otherwise the correction of a problem at one location may create a new problem at another location. (Park-North Carolina)
W75-08177

FLOOD PLAIN INFORMATION: WILSON AND WILDWOOD CREEKS, SAN BERNADINO COUNTY, CALIFORNIA,
Army Engineer District, Los Angeles, Calif.
Prepared for San Bernadino County Flood Control District, June, 1972, 33 p, 30 fig, 4 tab, 23 plates.

Descriptors: *Floods, *Flood plains, *Flooding, Flow, *Obstructions to flow, Flood water, Flood data, Flood frequency, *California.
Identifiers: San Bernadino County(Cal), *Wilson Creek(Cal), *Wildwood Creek(Cal), Yucaipo(Cal), Intermediate Regional Flood, Standard Project Flood.

January and February, 1969, were the most devastating floods of record causing $5,567,000 damage along Wilson, Wildwood, and the smaller Oak Glen Creek and Gateway Wash in the study area and adjacent land. Damage resulted from overbank flooding and high velocities causing severe erosion and bringing substantial debris downstream. This debris increased floods by jamming against bridges and other obstructions and damaged residential, commercial, and agricultural structures by depositing debris varying from 2 to 6 ft. deep over about 400 acres. Located about 15 miles southeast of the City of San Bernadino, the watershed varies in width 1 to 6 miles, is about 15 miles long. Average precipitation over the basin averages 20 inches mostly between December and March. Extreme flood peaks can rise from a nearly dry streambed in a few hours with high velocities of flow in both channel and flood plain. Lateral displacement of the streambed may occur with deposition of debris forcing cutting of a new channel, a pattern often more damaging than floodwaters. Although San Bernadino County has adopted flood plain zoning regulations, report areas have not yet been zoned except under restrictions approved by the County Planning Commission. Future floods, an Intermediate Regional Flood or a Standard Project Flood, would cause even more damage to agricultural lands and residential areas in Yucaipo, population 22,000, with problems of debris deposit, high velocity and erosion multiplied. (Park-North Carolina)
W75-08178

FLOOD PLAIN INFORMATION, ALLEGHENY RIVER, CLARION COUNTY, PENNSYLVANIA,
Army Engineer District, Pittsburgh, Pa.
Prepared for the Clarion County Planning Commission and the Commonwealth of Pennsylvania Department of Environmental Resources, June 1974, 42 p, 7 tab, 21 fig, 9 plates.

Descriptors: *Flood plains, *Flood damage, *Land use, *Flood profiles, Planning, Flood data, Snowmelt, Obstruction to flow, Ice jams, Flood control, *Pennsylvania.
Identifiers: *Allegheny River(Penn), Clarion County(Penn), Penn Central Railroad, Parker(Penn), Intermediate Regional Flood, Standard Project Flood, Flood plain management.

The flood plain of the 25.3 mile study reach of the Allegheny River through Clarion County is generally narrow and undeveloped. Damaged from past floods has not been extensive. The limited existing development is essentially residential and the main line of the Penn Central railroad which parallels the river along most of the study reach. Major floods usually occur from December through April, resulting from heavy rain and snowmelt. Although the 4 bridges in the study reach are not obstructive, the topography of the river valley causes frequent ice gorges which form temporary but effective dams, resulting in localized flood stages which can exceed those of the Intermediate Regional Flood (IRF) and Standard Project Flood (SPF). The maximum recorded flood level at Parker occurred in January, 1959, resulting from heavy rain and snowmelt and ice jamming. Despite the 5 flood control projects upstream, the peak discharge was 182,000 cfs. At Parker, peak discharge of an IRF and SPF would by 173,000 cfs and 209,000 cfs, respectively. (Diefendorf-North Carolina)
W75-08179

FLOOD PLAIN INFORMATION: BEAVERDAM CREEK, HANOVER COUNTY, VIRGINIA,
Army Engineer District, Norfolk, Va.
Prepared for Hanover County, May 1974, 28 p, 7 fig, 6 tab, 10 plates.

Descriptors: *Flood plains, *Flood damage, *Flood plain zoning, Planning, Flood profiles, Flood data, Obstruction to flow, Reservoir, Urbanization, Thunderstorms, Hurricanes, *Virginia.
Identifiers: *Beaverdam Creek(Va), Hanover County(Virginia), Totopotomoy Creek(Va), Flood plain management, Intermediate Regional Flood, Standard Project Flood.

The flood plain along Beaverdam Creek in Hanover County, five miles northeast of Richmond, Virginia, is largely undeveloped woodlands. However, Hanover County is becoming increasingly urbanized and is experiencing industrial and residential growth. Beaverdam Creek has a drainage area of 12.8 square miles. Within the 6.0 mile study reach, the stream falls an average of 12.5 feet per mile. Flooding may be caused by heavy general rains at any time, or because of the relatively small drainage area involved, flooding may occur as a result of intense rainfall during local summer thunderstorms or hurricanes. Stream heights can rise to extreme flood peaks in a relatively short time. Records of a gaging station on Totopotomoy Creek, which is located 3 miles north of Beaverdam and has similar physiographic characteristics, are indicative of flood occurrences on Beaverdam. The largest flood occurred in August, 1955. At the mouth of Beaverdam Creek, an Intermediate Regional Flood would have a peak discharge of 6,330 cfs; Standard Project Flood peak discharge would be 11,420 cfs. These floods would cause considerable damage. Five bridges cross the stream and could create obstructions to flow. The reservoir formed by an earthfill dam upstream will not significantly alter downstream flow characteristics during a large flood. (Diefendorf-North Carolina)
W75-08180

FLOOD PLAIN INFORMATION: RAPID CREEK, RAPID CITY, SOUTH DAKOTA,
Army Engineer District, Omaha, Nebr.
Prepared for City of Rapid City, June, 1973. 48 p, 24 fig, 16 plates, 6 tab.

Descriptors: Floods, *Flood damage, *Flooding, *Flood plains, Flood water, *Maximum probable flood, *Flood frequency, *Flood profiles, Obstructions to flow, Flow, Flood data, Flood protection, Flood forecasting, *South Dakota.
Identifiers: *Rapid Creek(SD), Rapid City(SD), Pennington County(SD), *June, 1972 flood, Intermediate Regional Flood, Standard Project Flood.

Rapid Creek, a Cheyenne River tributary, runs through Rapid City, second largest city in South Dakota (1970 population of 43,836). Eighteen percent of the 17 sq mi of Rapid City is in the flood plain which ranges from 2,200 to 2,900 ft wide in the business area. In the study reach, Rapid Creek channel averages 100 ft wide and 5 ft deep with an average slope of 16.5 ft/mi. Flash floods occur most frequently in May or June. Normal annual precipitation at Rapid City is 16.4 in. Pactola Dam, 14 miles upstream from Rapid City, is a multi-purpose project for irrigation, water supply and flood control with 43,00 acre-feet of storage for flood runoff. Deerfield Dam upstream from Pactola provides only incidental flood storage. Past floods were minor with one exception–the June, 1972 flood with a peak discharge of 50,000 cubic feet/second (cfs) at the Rapid City gage caused 237 deaths and $164 million damages. Pactola Dam had not the slightest effect on the outcome of the disastrous 1972 flood. Nearly every bridge between the dam and Rapid City was damaged or destroyed, due to high floodwaters, carried debris and high velocities. An Intermediate Regional Flood (IRF) would have a discharge of 14,500 cfs and the Standard Project Flood would peak at 47,000 cfs at Oshkosh Street in Rapid City. A large portion of the IRF flood plain is being cleared by the Urban Renewal Program removing highly damageable property and providing a cleared path for potential flood water to pass with less damage to remaining property. Future floods could inundate an area 2,200 - 3,000 ft wide through the city. (Park-North Carolina)
W75-08183

FLOOD PLAIN INFORMATION: VIRGIN RIVER AND FORT PIERCE WASH, VICINITY OF ST. GEORGE, WASHINGTON COUNTY, UTAH,
Army Engineer District, Los Angeles, Calif.
Prepared for Washington County Commission, April, 1973. 31 p, 22 fig, 19 plates, 6 tab.

Descriptors: Floods, *Flooding, *Flood damage, *Flood plains, *Maximum probable flood, Flood frequency, Historic floods, Flood data, Flood forecasting, Flood profile, *Utah.
Identifiers: *Virgin River(Utah), Bloomington(Utah), *Fort Pierce Wash(Utah), St. George(Utah), Washington County(Utah),

Washington(Utah); Intermediate Regional Flood, Standard Project Flood.

The Virgin River flowing southwesterly from its headwaters in Kane County, Utah, empties into Lake Mead, Arizona, draining a 6,000 sq mi area ranging in elevation from about 10,000 ft to about 1,300 ft above mean sea level. In the study reach, smooth and uniform valley lands are separated by ridges; the river gradient averages about 13 ft/mi. Fort Pierce Wash, a major tributary, flows northward from the Grand Canyon draining 1,600 sq mi between 8,000 ft to about 2,500 ft above mean sea level. Stream gradient averages 20 ft/mi through hilly areas with rock outcrops. Annual precipitation averages about 13 inches over the watershed. No major flood control projects exist or are under construction. Flash flooding with high sediment loads and severe erosion is typical. Flood plain development is minimal, most land being used for agriculture and open space. Increases in population and tourism will create pressure for development in the flood plain. Properties along the stream were severely damaged by floods of 1955, 1966, 1971. On the Virgin River, the major flood of December 1966 with a peak flow of 22,800 cubic feet per second (cfs) near Virgin, Utah caused severe erosion and destruction of bridges and roads. The greatest flood for Fort Pierce Wash was in August 1971 with an estimated flow of 15,000 cfs flooding at least 4 ft above the flood plain. Future floods predicted are the Intermediate Regional Flood (IRF) with a peak of 46,000 cfs for the Virgin River at Bloomington, a small settlement, and 104,000 cfs for a Standard Project Flood (SPF). For Fort Pierce Wash at the Virgin River, flows will reach 24,000 cfs for the IRF and 75,000 cfs, for the SPF. Both floods will cause extensive damage. (Park-North Caolina)
W75-08184

COST SHARING AS AN INCENTIVE TO ATTAIN THE OBJECTIVE OF SHORELINE PROTECTION,
National Bureau of Standards, Washington, D.C. Inst. for Applied Technology.
For primary bibliographic entry see Field 6C.
W75-08185

COLLECTION OF BASIC DATA ON REPRESENTATIVE AND EXPERIMENTAL BASINS (IN FRENCH),
For primary bibliographic entry see Field 7C.
W75-08198

MONETARY VALUES OF LIFE AND HEALTH,
Tennessee Valley Authority, Knoxville. Flood Control Branch.
B. Buehler.
Journal of the Hydraulics Division, American Society of Civil Engineers, Vol 101, No HY1, Proceedings paper No. 11047, p 29-47, January 1975. 4 fig, 7 tab, 8 ref.

Descriptors: *Economics, *Flood control, Hydraulics, *Spillways, *Public health, *Safety, *Value engineering, Human population, Investment, Estimating, Computers, Methodology, Risks, Resources.
Identifiers: *Lost earnings technique, Life expectancy.

A Task Committee of the American Society of Civil Engineers was charged with preparing standards to evaluate the adequacy of spillways of existing dams. The committee recommends standards which require appraising the consequences of dam failures. A realistic value is needed for potential death and injury; human values are needed to measure risks. Human values are needed to achieve balance in the use of the nation's resources, all of which are spent in one form or another for the welfare of its people. The use of life earnings to measure human values is demonstrated by application to a resort area which is endangered by floods and for which flood control measures are being considered. Sensible values for life and health are proposed as a substitute for the current practice of using virtually infinite value in some engineering decisions, e.g., flood control evaluation recommended human values are based on the lifestream of earnings that would be foregone in the event of death or disability. A computing procedure is illustrated, and results are compared with other sources. The technique is considered adequate for immediate use until something better is devised. (Bell-Cornell)
W75-08202

THE AMERICAN INDIAN AND MISSOURI RIVER WATER DEVELOPMENTS,
Nevada Univ., Reno. Renewable Resources Center.
For primary bibliographic entry see Field 6B.
W75-08204

USER--ORIENTED RESEARCH DESIGNS,
Nebraska Univ., Lincoln. Water Resources Research Inst.
For primary bibliographic entry see Field 6A.
W75-08206

WATERSHED MANAGEMENT WITHOUT SURFACE RUNOFF,
Nebraska Univ., Lincoln. Dept. of Agricultural Engineering.
For primary bibliographic entry see Field 4D.
W75-08207

THE IMPORTANCE OF PERCEPTIONS IN THE DETERMINATION OF INDIAN WATER RIGHTS,
Washington State Univ., Pullman. Dept. of Political Science.
For primary bibliographic entry see Field 6E.
W75-08212

LAND-BASED MODELING SYSTEM FOR WATER QUALITY MANAGEMENT STUDIES,
Gates (W. E.) and Associates, Inc., Cincinnati, Ohio.
For primary bibliographic entry see Field 5G.
W75-08218

INTERACTIVE SIMULATION FOR WATER SYSTEM DYNAMICS,
Colorado State Univ., Fort Collins. Dept. of Civil Engineering.
N. S. Grigg, and M. C. Bryson.
Journal of the Urban Planning and Development Division, American Society of Civil Engineers, Vol 101, No UP1, Proceedings paper No. 11313, p 77-92, May 1975. 6 fig, 2 tab, 2 append, 10 ref.

Descriptors: *Simulation analysis, *Water supply, *Planning, *Forecasting, Rates, Costs, Financing, Computers, Methodology, Engineering, Economics, Equations, Human population, Industries, Mathematical models, Systems analysis, Evaluation, *Colorado.
Identifiers: *Urban water systems, Environmental impact statements, *Interactive system dynamics, Fort Collins(Colo), Feedback loops, Data input, Urban engineering.

The method of simulation known as system dynamics is applied to an urban water supply problem. The technique, demonstrated by Forrester of MIT, has attracted wide interest among social scientists and the management science community. In the urban water field, the method is particularly applicable to problems concerned with the economics of supply-storage-use. Presented is an example of a rate policy simulation study for Fort Collins, Colorado. The Fort Collins model considers population, water, land, and the municipal budget as subsystems of the city. It is an economic simulation model and measures the flows of water, stocks, money, and physical plant. Input data for the water model are given. The model considers interactions among level variables and incorporates a mixture of explicit (programmed) and implicit (operator-determined) feedback loops. The use of system dynamics in conjunction with an interactive computing setup permits the use of a flexible, easily programmed, and inexpensive simulation methodology (the need for valid data, however, is not ignored). The interactive simulation is written in BASIC language and run on an office size minicomputer. The simulation can be used to evaluate the effects of a single decision or event or to observe the continuing impact of an ongoing policy. (Bell-Cornell)
W75-08219

A TECHNIQUE TO EVALUATE SNOWPACK PROFILES IN AND ADJACENT TO FOREST OPENINGS,
Arizona Univ., Tucson. Dept. of Watershed Management.
For primary bibliographic entry see Field 2C.
W75-08221

DEVELOPMENT OF FOREST MANAGEMENT GUIDELINES FOR INCREASING SNOWPACK WATER YIELDS IN ARIZONA,
Arizona Univ., Tucson. Dept. of Watershed Management.
For primary bibliographic entry see Field 2C.
W75-08222

CHARACTERIZATION OF OPTIMAL OPERATING POLICIES FOR FINITE DAMS,
California Univ., Los Angeles. Dept. of Systems Engineering.
S. Arunkumar.
Journal of Mathematical Analysis and Applications, Vol 49, No 2, February 1975. (California Water Resources Center Project UCAL-WRC-W-341). OWRT A-043-CAL(2).

Descriptors: *Computer programs, *Dynamic programming, Multiple purpose reservoirs, Model studies, Dams, *Operations, *Optimization, Water utilization, *Regulation.
Identifiers: *Finite dams.

The economical use of reservoir water for the generation of electric power as well as for irrigational and recreational uses is an important consideration at all hydro-electric installations. Characterization of optimal regulation policies is very important, whenever possible, due to the high dimensionality of the problem. Using a dynamic programming model, Gessford and Karlin (1958) were among the first to obtain the form of optimal release rules for an infinite dam, over finite periods of time, allowing the probability distributions of the input variables and the convex cost function to depend on time. Bather (1962) has investigated the asymptotic policies for a finite dam under the assumptions of time-homogeneous concave utility function and input probability distributions when the inflow at the start of a given period can be used in the same period. More recently, Gablinger (1971) has obtained the form of the optimal release rules in terms of certain critical numbers under piece-wise linear cost function. He suggests the use of simulation techniques for the determination of these critical numbers. Using the method of successive approximations, it is possible to characterize the critical numbers and return functions, associated with finite and infinite time horizons. This analytical characterization very naturally yields stopping rules for infinite time horizon and leads to substantial savings in computation time needed to solve large problems. (Snyder-California-Davis)
W75-08223

TEMPERATURE EFFECTS ON GREAT LAKES WATER BALANCE STUDIES,
Illinois Univ., Urbana. Water Resources Center.
For primary bibliographic entry see Field 2H.
W75-08225

CHANGE OF FEEDING OF THE GROUSE UNDER THE EFFECT OF DRAINAGE RECLAMATION, (IN RUSSIAN),
Akademiya Navuk BSSR, Minsk. Dept. of Zoology and Parasitology.
For primary bibliographic entry see Field 2I.
W75-08269

THE FOREST IN THE PROTECTION OF NATURE AND THE LANDSCAPE, (IN RUMANIAN),
Academia R. S. R., Cluj. Centrul de Cercetari Biologice.
E. Pop.
Ocrotirea Nat, Vol 17, No 1, p 9-16, 1973, Illus.

Descriptors: *Natural resources, *Protection, *Forests, Ecosystems, *Forest management, Europe, Conservation.
Identifiers: Pteridium-aquilinum, *Romania, Retezat Park.

The function of the forest in enriching the air in O2 is emphasized. The loss of the forest, especially in temperate and subtropical zones, has produced deserts, soil erosion of mountainous slopes, chaotic water drainage, damages to agriculture by floods and climatic changes. The destroyed forest is replaced by low bushes and Pteridium aquilinum. Modern forestry management with replanting has partly undone the damage but has created disturbances in the equilibrium of the forest life and the ecological system by destroying the manifold variety of the primitive forest to replace it with single species. The present forest regions in all parts of the world must be conserved. In Romania, there are 17 reserves of which the Retezat national park is the most important. Pictures of some of these parks are shown. The biological equilibrium on conservation areas must be investigated to clarify the ecological system. The destroyed areas must also be reclaimed. The enlargement of the forest region is necessary to satisfy the increasing O2 demand and the disequilibrium between O2 and CO2. The world population consumes 900 billion l of O2 daily which will double in a short time.--Copyright 1974, Biological Abstracts, Inc.
W75-08272

PREDICATION OF THE BALANCE OF MATTER IN STORAGE RESERVOIRS BY MEANS OF CONTINUOUS OR SEMICONTINUOUS BIOLOGICAL MODELS: II. RELIABILITY OF THE PREDICTION METHOD, (IN GERMAN),
Technische Universitaet, Dresden (East Germany). Bereich Hydrobiologie.
For primary bibliographic entry see Field 5G.
W75-08273

THE ROLE OF TRACE ELEMENTS IN MANAGEMENT OF NUISANCE GROWTHS,
Academy of Natural Sciences of Philadelphia, Pa.
For primary bibliographic entry see Field 5G.
W75-08278

SUBDIVISION ON MALLEE FARMS,
A. K. McCord, and J. S. Potter.
Journal of Agriculture, South Australia, Vol 75, No 5, p 128-135, August, 1972. 15 fig, 1 tab.

Descriptors: *Australia, *Erosion control, *Farm management, *Range management, *Soil conservation, *Water supply, *Pasture management, Land use, Carrying capacity, Cattle, Farm equipment, Grazing, Livestock, Planning, Rotations, Sheep, Stock water, Winds.
Identifiers: Fencing, Murray Mallee area(South Australia), Crop rotation.

In the Murray Mallee area of southeastern South Australia where light rainfall and various soil types present special hazards, successful management of farm property requires careful planning. Paddock size should be determined by farm property size and by the type and number of stock carried. Cattle tend to disperse, grazing areas evenly, while sheep graze favored areas bare, thus increasing erosion risk, especially in sandy soils. Such problems can be minimized by correct subdivision with appropriate fencing and by using a rotational grazing system, which in turn will aid in cropping (crop placement and rotation), cultivation, and weed control. Farm property, to achieve its livestock potential, also must have an adequate and continuous supply of drinking water within easy access of feed and so sited as to lessen the risk of uneven grazing, particularly from sheep which graze into the wind. A survey in 1970-71 of 40 farms in the Murray Mallee indicated many benefits resulted through the use of adequate subdivision, improved fencing, and careful placement of watering facilities: greater livestock carrying capacity, greater ease of erosion control, and overall ease in management were afforded. Principles applied in this region may be used with success on farm properties elsewhere. (Gloyd-Arizona)
W75-08281

PROCEEDINGS: RESEARCH PLANNING CONFERENCE ON INTEGRATED SYSTEMS OF AQUATIC PLANT CONTROL 29-30 OCTOBER 1973.
Army Engineer Waterways Experiment Station, Vicksburg, Miss.
Available from National Technical Information Service, Springfield, Va 22161. APCP (Aquatic Plant Control Program) Report, August 1974. 174 p, 44 fig, 20 tab, 6 append.

Descriptors: *Aquatic weed control, *Herbicides, *Aquatic plants, *Biocontrol, Reviews, Project, Water pollution control, Pollution abatement.

At the request of the Planning Division, Directorate Civil Works, Office, Chief of Engineers, a conference on integrated systems of aquatic plant control was held at the U.S. Army Engineer Waterways Experiment Station to review current operation activities and new research proposals, and to afford an opportunity for presentation of current research projects. (WES)
W75-08289

BIOLOGICAL CONTROL OF WATER HYACINTH WITH INSECT ENEMIES.
Army Engineer Waterways Experiment Station, Vicksburg, Miss.
Available from the National Technical Information Service, Springfield, Va 22161 as AD-775 408, $6.25 in paper copy, $2.25 in microfiche. APCP (Aquatic Plant Control Program) Technical Report 6, January 1974. 152 p, 3 fig, 3 tab, 6 append, 125 ref.

Descriptors: *Aquatic weed control, *Biocontrol, *Insects, *Water hyacinth, *Southeast U.S., Nuisance algae, Water pollution control.
Identifiers: Neochetina eichhorniae.

Present water hyacinth control programs provide at best only short-term control, and thus are of short-term benefit as far as productivity of the environment is concerned, whereas successful biological control will provide long-term benefits to productivity, with a condomitant reduction in the use of chemical or mechanical disturbances of the environment. Once a biological control agent is established, it becomes an integral part of the environment and as such may properly be considered a self-renewable resource, and a beneficial addition to our environment. It is hoped that Neochetina eichhorniae will prove to be just that, and that it will, alone or in conjunction with other native or introduced natural enemies, bring about the alleviation of the problems caused by water hyacinth in the southeastern United States. (WES)
W75-08290

NATIONAL PARKS AND NATIONAL RESERVATIONS IN THE LIGHT OF PRESENT IDEAS, (IN ROMANIAN),
Comisia Monumentelor Nationle, Bucharest (Rumania).
Val Puscariu.
Ocrotirea Nat, Vol 17, No 1, p 21-36, 1973. Illus.

Descriptors: *Parks, *National parks, Recreation facilities, Conservation, United States, Europe,
Identifiers: Czechoslovakia, France, Italy, Nymphaea-lotus-thermalis, *Romania.

The history of national parks, starting with Yellowstone Park formed in 1872 and the forest of Fontainebleau (France) in 1853 to Gran Paradiso In Italy, Retezat in Romania and Tatra in Czechoslovakia, is outlined with illustrations for scenes in these parks. There were 1204 national parks listed by the International Union for the Protection of Nature and its Resources. The parks in Romania include Retezat, Delta Dunarii, Bucegi, Ceahlau, Pietrosul Mare and others and their total area is about 100,000 ha. A scientific study of the flora and vegetation of the mountains of Retezat will be published. Detrimental human activity in these parks is also described. An alpine museum will be set up at la Sinaia in the Prahova district. Work is underway to conserve the remains of the Nymphaea lotus thermalis of the tertiary in the district of Bihor. Plans of a national conference for new national parks and reservations are described involving the creation of a park in the Apuseni Mountains in the districts of Bihor, Cluj and Alba, Romania; reservations at Piatra Craiuliu, Cheile Nerei, Muntele Cozia, Caliman and Ceahlau; a natural park connected with the hydroelectric and navigational project of Portile de Fier, Romania.--Copyright 1974, Biological Abstracts, Inc.
W75-08300

ANALYSES OF A FOREST DRAINAGE EXPERIMENT IN NORTHERN ONTARIO. I: GROWTH ANALYSIS,
Great Lakes Forestry Research Center, Sault Sainte Marie (Ontario).
B. Payandeh.
Can J For Res, Vol 3, No 3, p 387-398, 1973, Illus.

Descriptors: *Forests, Drainage, *Plant growth, *Drainage effects, *Trees, Numerical analysis, *Canada, Growth stages.

Growth analysis of the experiment carried out over 40 yr in northern Ontario (Canada) is based on remeasurement data obtained in 1969 from 38 growth plots established following drainage in 1929 and from increment cores and sectioned trees. Both annual tree diameter and height growth increased significantly after draining. Tree growth before draining was related to site quality only, while after draining it was related also to tree vigor and distance of water flow from the nearest ditch. Both stand diameter and height growth were related to site index, stand age, and initial stocking: stand basal area and volume growth were, in addition, related to a product sine function of distance of water flow from the ditch, peat moisture, decomposition and depth. Both individual tree and stand growth responded well to draining, with younger and more vigorous trees that were growing on better-quality sites showing the greatest response. For a given site, growth response was not greatest for trees and stands nearest the ditch, but for those some distance away.--Copyright 1974, Biological Abstracts, Inc.
W75-08337

Identifiers: *England, *Wales, *Permo-Triassic aquifer, Bunter sandstone.

Detailed field and laboratory investigations on four regions of the Permo-Triassic sandstones in England and Wales showed that fissure flow is of major importance in governing the yields from abstraction wells in this aquifer. The Permo-Triassic sandstones are currently the second most important source of groundwater in the United Kingdom and their extensive development is planned for the future. An understanding of the flow mechanism has enabled suggestions to be made which would act as guidelines for exploration. It was considered that the exploration and development proposals are applicable to other fissured sandstone aquifers. (Visocky-ISWS)
W75-07896

DIGITAL SIMULATION MODEL OF AQUIFER RESPONSE TO STREAM STAGE FLUCTUATION,
California Univ., Davis. Dept. of Water Science and Engineering.
For primary bibliographic entry see Field 2F.
W75-07897

CONTRIBUTIONS TO THE STUDY OF THE ALGAL FLORA OF ALGERIA. III. HYDROBIOLOGY OF CHOTT EL HODNA: AUTOECOLOGY OF THE DIATOMS,
Algiers Univ. (Algeria). Laboratoire de Botanique.
For primary bibliographic entry see Field 5C.
W75-07936

PERCHED WATER TABLE FLUCTUATION COMPARED TO STREAMFLOW,
Delaware Valley Coll. of Science and Agriculture, Doylestown, Pa.
For primary bibliographic entry see Field 2A.
W75-07946

GROUND-WATER POLLUTION BY WOOD WASTE DISPOSAL,
Oregon State Engineer's Office, Salem.
For primary bibliographic entry see Field 5B.
W75-07951

PROCEEDINGS OF THE SEMINAR ON ADVANCED WASTEWATER TREATMENT AND DISPOSAL,
Nassau-Suffolk Regional Planning Board, N. Y. Regional Marine Resources Council
For primary bibliographic entry see Field 5D.
W75-07954

THE LONG ISLAND WATER SITUATION,
Geological Survey, Mineola, N.Y. Water Resources Div.
For primary bibliographic entry see Field 5B.
W75-07955

THE STATUS OF WASTEWATER TREATMENT ON LONG ISLAND,
Suffolk County Dept. of Environmental Control, N.Y.
For primary bibliographic entry see Field 5D.
W75-07957

WASTEWATER USE AND GROUNDWATER RECHARGE IN LOS ANGELES COUNTY,
Los Angeles County Flood Control District, Calif.
For primary bibliographic entry see Field 5D.
W75-07958

SPRINKLER IRRIGATION FOR LIQUID WASTE DISPOSAL,
Pennsylvania State Univ., University Park.
For primary bibliographic entry see Field 5D.
W75-07959

MUSKEGON, MICHIGAN,
Chicago Univ., Ill. Center for Urban Studies.
For primary bibliographic entry see Field 5D.
W75-07960

SANTIAGO-NORTE DRAINAGE PROJECT (CHILE),
For primary bibliographic entry see Field 3C.
W75-08109

WATERLOGGING AND SALINITY PROBLEMS IN THE INDUS PLAIN (PAKISTAN),
For primary bibliographic entry see Field 3C.
W75-08117

DENITRIFICATION IN LABORATORY SANDY COLUMNS,
Soil Conservation Service, Effingham, Ill.
For primary bibliographic entry see Field 5B.
W75-08189

THE KINETICS OF MINERAL DISSOLUTION IN CARBONATE AQUIFERS AS A TOOL FOR HYDROLOGICAL INVESTIGATIONS, I. CONCENTRATION-TIME RELATIONSHIPS,
Water Planning for Israel Ltd., Tel-Aviv.
For primary bibliographic entry see Field 2K.
W75-08190

4C. Effects On Water Of Man's Non-Water Activities

NATURAL AND MODIFIED PLANT COMMUNITIES AS RELATED TO RUNOFF AND SEDIMENT YIELDS,
Geological Survey, Denver, Colo.
F. A. Branson.
In: An Introduction to Land-Water Interactions; International Association for Ecology Leningrad Symposium, August 1971: Springer-Verlag New York Inc, p 157-172, 1975. 13 fig, 32 ref.

Descriptors: *Water yield improvement, *Sediment yield, Clear-cutting, Watershed management, Vegetation effects, Soil treatment, Soil sealants, Brush control, Range management.

Better use of water resources, both at the point of origin and downstream, may be attempted by vegetation modifications and soil treatments. Vegetation conversions include pollution problems. In Arizona, fires have resulted in spectacular increases in sediment yields. Most conversion treatments that require exposure of much bare soil during the period of treatment result in increased erosion until vegetation becomes reestablished. Combined deforestation and use of herbicides to prevent regrowth in New Hampshire caused marked changes in chemical quality of the water but little change in sediment yield. In the Pacific Northwest neither clearcutting nor patchcutting caused nitrate levels to exceed federal water standards. Mechanical land treatments such as contour furrowing, ripping, and pitting perform several hydrologic functions, such as (1) reduction of flood peaks, (2) reduction of sediment yields, and (3) enhancement of onsite water use for forage production. Because runoff is low and much water is evaporated or returned to groundwater aquifers before reaching downstream users, the most efficient use of the water resource can be made by retention of water for increased forage production on lands that are suitable for mechanical treatments. A number of chemicals that decrease infiltration and increase water yields have been used experimentally. Runoff from sandy loams and loamy sands can be substantially increased and erosion reduced by the use of chemicals that cause the soil surface to become hydrophobic. (Knapp-USGS)
W75-07866

REMOTE SENSING: TECHNIQUES FOR EVALUATION OF URBAN EROSION AND SEDIMENTATION,

Geological Survey, Reston, Va.

H. P. Guy.

In: Effects of Man on the Interface of the Hydrological Cycle with the Physical Environment; Proceedings of Paris Symposium, September 1974: International Association of Hydrological Sciences Publication No 113, p 145-149, 1974. 2 fig, 1 tab, 7 ref.

Descriptors: *Remote sensing, *Erosion, *Sedimentation, *Urban hydrology, Storm runoff, Aerial photography, Land use, Construction, Hurricanes, Sediment yield.
Identifiers: *Reston(Va).

Low-altitude aerial photography was used to supplement ground-based measurements for the evaluation of erosion and sedimentation conditions during the construction of a large office complex at Reston, Virgina. Ground measurements included precipitation, runoff, and sediment, as well as selected measurement of sheet erosion, rill development and sediment deposition. Ground-level photographs provided additional documentation of changing basin conditions. Satellite imagery could not be used because of detail loss upon the required enlargement. Low-altitude photography (scale 1:3600) gave good delineation of land-use changes. If used within a few hours of a rainstorm, low-altitude photography provided information on erosion and sedimentation features resulting from the storm. Ground-based measurements were necessary to define the timing and magnitude of the erosion and deposition processes. Sediment yield was 91 tonnes per ha during the 2-year construction period beginning September 1971. The 5.5-ha forested part of the drainage area yielded little or no sediment relative to the 14.4-ha construction area. The maximum daily sediment yield of 1.19 tonnes per hr per ha occurred during tropical storm Agnes on 21 June 1972. (Knapp-USGS)
W75-07880

CHANNEL CHANGES,

Geological Survey, Boise, Idaho.

W. W. Emmett.

Geology, Vol 2, No 6, p 271-272, June 1974. 1 fig, 3 tab, 4 ref.

Descriptors: *Channel morphology, *Aggradation, *Urbanization, *Urban hydrology, Land use, Geomorphology, Alluvial channels.

Environmental impacts may alter the quantities of water and sediment carried in a stream and thus may increase or diminish naturally occurring rates of channel changes and the pre-impact frequency of flows. Repetitive cross-channel surveys to determine changes in channel size or location measure the response of stream to environmental impact and may provide data necessary before corrective measures can be taken to minimize the effects of the impact. One effect on stream channels from the impact of urbanization can be shown, by example from one stream, to be a loss in channel size due to deposition of sediment. After 17 years of urbanization encroching on the area, the channel was only 66 percent of the size it was at the beginning of that period. (Knapp-USGS)
W75-07884

PROCEEDINGS OF THE SEMINAR ON ADVANCED WASTEWATER TREATMENT AND DISPOSAL,

Nassau-Suffolk Regional Planning Board, N. Y. Regional Marine Resources Council

For primary bibliographic entry see Field 5D.
W75-07954

THE LONG ISLAND WATER SITUATION,

Geological Survey, Mineola, N.Y. Water Resources Div.

For primary bibliographic entry see Field 5B.
W75-07955

EROSION PROCESSES IN FELLED AREAS IN THE MOUNTAIN FORESTS OF THE CARPATHIANS,

For primary bibliographic entry see Field 4D.
W75-07975

COMMENTS ON THE HISTORY OF CONTROLLED BURNING IN THE SOUTHERN UNITED STATES,

Tall Timbers Research Station, Tallahassee, Fla.

For primary bibliographic entry see Field 4A.
W75-07977

THE ROLE OF PRESCRIBED FIRE IN WILDLIFE MANAGEMENT,

Forest Service (USDA), Albuquerque, N. Mex. Rocky Mountain Forest and Range Experiment Station.

D. A. Jones.

In: 17th Annual Arizona Watershed Symposium, Proceedings, September 19, 1973, Phoenix, p 21-22.

Descriptors: *Burning, *Chaparral, *Wildlife, management, *Watershed management, *Arizona, Conifers.
Identifiers: *Prescribed fire, Controlled burning.

Prescribed and controlled burning as a tool in wildlife habitat improvment has not been widely practiced. The carefully controlled 'hot fire' is the answer to the control of chaparral, pinyon-juniper, and mixed conifer areas. Successful burning will achieve not only successful wildlife management, but watertable control and a more complete ecological balance. Adequate financing and a technique of applying prescribed fire that will provide precision control are needed. An additional problem is getting public understanding. (McLachlan-Arizona)
W75-07980

MARKLAND LOCKS AND DAM HIGHWAY BRIDGE AND APPROACHES, KENTUCKY AND INDIANA (FINAL ENVIRONMENTAL IMPACT STATEMENT).

Army Engineer District, Louisville, Ky.

Available from the National Technical Information Service, Springfield, Va. 22161, as EIS-KY-73-2011-F, $3.75 in paper copy, $2.25 in microfiche. December 26, 1973. 32 p, 1 chart.

Descriptors: *Bridge design, *Bridge construetion, Ohio River, *Pennsylvania, Bridges, Roads, Rivers, Highways, Traffic ability, Economics, Environmental effects, Water quality, Turbidity, Pollutants.
Identifiers: *Environmental impact statements, *Pittsburg(Pa).

The proposed action entails construction of a two-lane highway bridge, supported by the Markland Dam, crossing the Ohio River 531.5 river miles below Pittsburgh, Pennsylvania. The project will also include construction of short approach roads on each side of the river to connect the proposed bridge to existing highways. The chief beneficial impact of the construction will be to facilitate traffic flow in the vicinity of the bridge, which will act as a stimulus to economic growth. Adverse environmental effects include loss of land on each side of the bridge required for construction of approach roads, and more if other road construction occurs as a result of the project; an increase in the level of air and noise pollution in the area; and temporary turbidity increases during construction and rainy weather. The only alternative to the proposed action is no action. (Gagliardi-Florida)
W75-08041

NATIONAL PARKS AND NATIONAL RESERVATIONS IN THE LIGHT OF PRESENT IDEAS, (IN ROMANIAN),
Comisia Monumentelor Nationle, Bucharest (Rumania).
For primary bibliographic entry see Field 4A.
W75-08300

URBANIZATION AND THE MICROBIAL CONTENT OF THE NORTH SASKATCHEWAN RIVER,
Alberta Univ., Edmonton. Dept. of Microbiology.
For primary bibliographic entry see Field 5C.
W75-08329

4D. Watershed Protection

RECONNAISSANCE OF SEDIMENTATION IN THE UPPER RIO BERMEJO BASIN, ARGENTINA,
Geological Survey, Menlo Park, Calif.
For primary bibliographic entry see Field 2J.
W75-07859

HYDROLOGIC DATA NEEDS FOR SMALL WATERSHEDS--STREAMFLOW AND RELATED PRECIPITATION DATA.
Geological Survey, Reston, Va.
For primary bibliographic entry see Field 7A.
W75-07874

SIMULATION OF SOIL EROSION--PART I. DEVELOPMENT OF A MATHEMATICAL EROSION MODEL,
International Rice Research Inst., Los Banos, Laguna (Philippines).
For primary bibliographic entry see Field 2J.
W75-07926

SIMULATION OF SOIL EROSION--PART II. STREAMFLOW AND SUSPENDED SEDIMENT SIMULATION RESULTS,
International Rice Research Inst., Los Banos, Laguna (Philippines).
For primary bibliographic entry see Field 2J.
W75-07927

URBAN SEDIMENT PROBLEMS: A STATEMENT ON SCOPE, RESEARCH, LEGISLATION, AND EDUCATION.
American Society of Civil Engineers, New York. Task Committee on Urban Sedimentation Problems.
For primary bibliographic entry see Field 5G.
W75-07931

NONERODIBLE AGGREGATES AND CONCENTRATION OF FATS, WAXES, AND OILS IN SOILS AS RELATED TO WHEAT STRAW MULCH,
Agricultural Research Service, Akron, Colo. Central Great Plains Field Station.
D. E. Smika, and B. W. Greb.
Soil Science Society of America Proceedings, Vol 39, No 1, p 104-107, January-February 1975. 1 fig, 4 tab, 12 ref.

Descriptors: *Wind erosion, *Cultivation, *Soil structure, Soil stabilization, Soil erosion, Rotations, Farm management, Wheat, Fallowing, Erosion, Soil conservation.

Nonerodible (greater than 0.84 mm) soil aggregates and concentration of fats, waxes, and oils in the surface 5-cm depth were determined as related to (1) rates of initial straw mulch, (2) date of initial fallow tillage, (3) removal of straw, and (4) nitrogen fertilization. Nonerodible soil aggregates were also determined as affected by tillage implements commonly used in fallow with residue removed by burning and with residue present. Soil erosion by wind in the Central Great Plains can be reduced significantly by (1) using implements that have a minimal effect on the destruction of nonerodible aggregates, (2) maintaining as much as possible of the wheat straw mulch on the soil surface, and (3) combining 1 and 2 to maintain as high as possible the concentration of fats, waxes, and oils in the soil to act as binders for soil aggregates. Increasing the concentration of fats, waxes, and oils in the soil to increase nonerodible aggregation is of greatest importance when they increase nonerodible soil aggregation to the level necessary for wind erosion control. (Sims-ISWS)
W75-07940

AN INTERDISPLINARY APPROACH TO DEVELOPMENT OF WATERSHED SIMULATION MODELS,
British Columbia Univ., Vancouver. Inst. of Animal Resource Ecology.
For primary bibliographic entry see Field 2A.
W75-07947

CONCENTRATION EFFECTS OF SETTLING-TUBE ANALYSIS,
Technische Hogeschool, Delft (Netherlands). Department of Civil Engineering.
For primary bibliographic entry see Field 2J.
W75-07949

EROSION PROCESSES IN FELLED AREAS IN THE MOUNTAIN FORESTS OF THE CARPATHIANS,
V. N. D'yakov.
Soviet Hydrology, Selected Papers No 3, p 273-276, 1973, 2 tab, 5 ref. Translated from Lesovedeniye, No 3, p 55-59, 1973.

Descriptors: *Forest management, *Soil erosion, *Lumbering, Erosion control, Sediment control, Surface runoff, Forestry, Land use, Mountain forests, Forest soils, Cutting management, Watersheds(Basins).
Identifiers: *USSR(Carpathian Mountains).

The dependence of soil erosion during logging operations in the Carpathians on felling and skidding methods, the dimensions of felled areas, the seasonality of logging operations, and other factors were examined. Data were presented on surface runoff and the dynamics of water erosion. Investigations showed that the seasonality of logging operations is very important in reducing soil erosion. For example, during logging operations in a beech forest at a site extending 200 m along the slope, soil erosion amounted to 21 cu m/hectare during logging in winter and to 68 cu m/hectare in summer. The degree of damage to the soil surface and the magnitude of erosion are directly related to the size of new growth. An average of 30% of the soil surface was damaged in an area with dense new growth and 40-50% in an area with thin new growth. The same relation was observed for erosion. Providing for good new growth is apparently one of the effective methods for controlling soil erosion. The duration of erosion processes also determines the degree of damage to the soil surface. There was no water erosion at all during winter logging, with proper logging practices and skidding with a VTU-3 skidder, or it was local and ceased the second year after felling. During the first stage of gradual felling and on small felling sites where horse skidding was used, erosion ceased in the second year after cutting and on large felling sites in the fourth year. During the second stage of gradual felling and in clear-cut areas, where the logs were tractor skidded, water erosion was observed 4-5 yrs after felling and becomes particularly severe during catastrophic rains. (Humphreys-ISWS)
W75-07975

THE ROLE OF PRESCRIBED FIRE IN WILDLIFE MANAGEMENT,
Forest Service (USDA), Albuquerque, N. Mex. Rocky Mountain Forest and Range Experiment Station.
For primary bibliographic entry see Field 4C.
W75-07980

PALATLAKAHA RIVER WATERSHED, LAKE COUNTY, FLORIDA (FINAL ENVIRONMENTAL IMPACT STATEMENT).
Soil Conservation Service, Gainesville, Fla.
For primary bibliographic entry see Field 8A.
W75-08022

SPRING BROOK WATERSHED, LANGLADE AND MARATHON COUNTIES, WISCONSIN (FINAL ENVIRONMENTAL IMPACT STATEMENT).
Soil Conservation Service, Washington, D.C.
For primary bibliographic entry see Field 4A.
W75-08035

PROPOSED HABITAT ENHANCEMENT PROJECT TOPCOCK MARSH UNIT, HAVASU NATIONAL WILDLIFE REFUGE, ETC. (FINAL ENVIRONMENTAL IMPACT STATEMENT).
Bureau of Sport Fisheries and Wildlife, Washington, D.C.
For primary bibliographic entry see Field 8D.
W75-08038

BIG RUNNING WATER DITCH WATERSHED PROJECT, LAWRENCE AND RANDOLPH COUNTIES, ARKANSAS (FINAL ENVIRONMENTAL IMPACT STATEMENT).
Soil Conservation Service, Little Rock, Ark.
Available from the National Technical Information Service, Springfield, Va. 22161, as EIS-AR-73-1501-F, $4.75 in paper copy, $2.25 in microfiche. Spetember 14, 1973. 79 p, 1 tab.

Descriptors: *Watershed management, *Channel improvement, *Sedimentation, Channels, Floodwater, Fish, *Arkansas, Agriculture, Wildlife, Vegetation, Aesthetics, Erosion, Sediments, Environmental effects, Levees, Floodways, Floodproofing.
Identifiers: *Environmental impact statements, Lawrence County(Ark), Randolph County(Ark).

The project entails construction of a small watershed in Lawrence and Randolph Counties, Arkansas. The proposed action includes land treatment measures and channel work for floodwater damage reduction and agricultural water management, with measures designed to minimize losses to fish and wildlife habitat and improve the aesthetic values of the watershed. The land treatment measures alone will reduce erosion and sediment yield into the channel system and combined with the structural measures will reduce floodwater damage an estimated 76 percent. Agricultural efficiency and fishery habitat will be improved and wildlife management will be more flexible. Adverse environmental effects include increasing sedimentation downstream during construction; channel bank erosion; destruction of present vegetation cover on one side of the channel; traffic, noise and pollution during construction; and loss of acres of agricultural land. Alternatives considered were exclusive use land treatment measures, construction of a floodway with levees, floodproofing the most seriously damaged fields or no action. (Gagliardi-Florida)
W75-08039

DIKED DISPOSAL AREA, HURON HARBOR, ERIE COUNTY, HURON, OHIO (FINAL ENVIRONMENTAL IMPACT STATEMENT).
Army Engineer District, Buffalo, NY.
For primary bibliographic entry see Field 5G.
W75-08048

PERILLA MOUNTAIN WATERSHED PROJECT, COCHISE COUNTY, ARIZONA (FINAL ENVIRONMENTAL IMPACT STATEMENT).
Soil Conservation Service, Washington, D.C.
Available from National Technical Information Service, USDC, Springfield, Va 22161 as EIS-AZ-74-0020-F, $3.75 in paper copy, $2.25 in microfiche. January 3, 1974. 41 p, 4 fig, 3 tab.

Descriptors: *Watershed management, *Land management, *Retardance, *Diversions, *Arizona, Diversion structures, Vegetation, Vegetation establishment, Watersheds(Basins), Floods, Flood water, Flood protection, Flood damage, Flood control, Flood data, Sediments, Wildlife habitats, Flood plains, Flood plain zoning, Flood plain insurance, Floodproofing.
Identifiers: *Environmental impact statements, Cochise County(Ariz).

The Perilla Mountain Watershed Project consists of conservation land treatment, two floodwater retarding structures, two floodways and one diversion. It is designed for watershed protection and flood prevention in Cochise County, Arizona. The land treatment measures will increase vegetation cover and improve range conditions. The average annual reduction in floodwater and sediment damages will be about 76%. Approximately 250 acres of vegetation will be disturbed by the construction. In addition, brush control will reduce wildlife cover for some species on approximately 600 acres. Noise and dust pollution will occur during construction. Consideration was given to implementation of the various measures in different combinations, as well as to a non-structural system including zoning, floodproofing, flood insurance and land purchase. (Denvir-Florida)
W75-08051

HIGHWAY 112 CRITICAL EROSION CONTROL RESOURCES CONSERVATION AND DEVELOPMENT PROJECT MEASURE (FINAL ENVIRONMENTAL IMPACT STATEMENT).
Soil Conservation Service, Madison, Wis.
For primary bibliographic entry see Field 8A.
W75-08055

INDIAN CREEK WATERSHED PROJECT, CITY OF CHESAPEAKE, VIRGINIA (FINAL ENVIRONMENTAL IMPACT STATEMENT).
Soil Conservation Service, Richmond, Va.
For primary bibliographic entry see Field 8A.
W75-08058

EAGLE-TUMBLEWEED DRAW WATERSHED, EDDY AND CHAVES COUNTIES, NEW MEXICO (FINAL ENVIRONMENTAL IMPACT STATEMENT).
Soil Conservation Service, Washington, D.C.
Available from National Technical Information Service, USDC, Springfield, Va 22161 as EIS-NM-73-2017-F, $4.75 in paper copy, $2.25 in microfiche. December 26, 1973. 79 p, 1 map.

Descriptors: *Watershed management, *Land management, *Retardance, *Diversion structures, Urban renewal, Vectors(Biological), Watersheds(Basins), Flood water, Flood protection, Wildlife habitats, Forages, *New Mexico.
Identifiers: *Environmental impact statements, Eddy County(NM), Chavez County(NM).

The Eagle-Tumbleweed Draw Watershed project provides for conservation land treatment measures, a floodwater retarding structure, two diversions, and an outlet channel. Its purpose is to provide watershed protection and flood prevention for Eddy and Chavez Counties, New Mexico. It is anticipated that implementation will result in the creation of a better urban environment, accelerated urban renewal and land use planning, and a reduction in health hazards such as vector breeding and water contamination. While some wildlife habitat will be disturbed or destroyed, it is expected that forage for seed-eating animals will improve and that the reduction in erosion in the long run will result in increased quantity and quality of livestock forage and wildlife habitat. Various structural and non-structural alternatives were considered. (Denvir-Florida)
W75-08060

MISSOURI RIVER GARRISON DAM TO LAKE OAHE RESERVOIR (FINAL ENVIRONMENTAL IMPACT STATEMENT).
Army Engineer District, Omaha, Nebr.
For primary bibliographic entry see Field 8A.
W75-08061

PAINT CREEK WATERSHED, HARPER COUNTY, OKLAHOMA (FINAL ENVIRONMENTAL IMPACT STATEMENT).
Soil Conservation Service, Stillwater, Okla.
Available from National Technical Information Service, USDC, Springfield, Va 22161 as EIS-OK-73-1781-F, $3.75 in paper copy, $2.25 in microfiche. November 12, 1973. 41 p, 1 tab, 2 map.

Descriptors: *Watershed management, *Oklahoma, *Environmental effects, *Dam construction, *Flood protection, Federal government, Floodways, Flood control, Multiple-purpose projects, Recreation, Water resources development, Water management(Applied), Land management, Flood plains, Dams, Levees, Erosion control, Sediment control, Wildlife habitats.
Identifiers: Dam effects, *Environmental impact statements, Harper County(Okla).

The project involves improvements to be made in the Paint Creek Watershed in Harper County, Oklahoma. The project includes: land treatment measures on 3,847 acres of agricultural land, one floodwater retarding structure, 1.1 mile of waterway, and development of 30 acres of wildlife habitat. The project area consists primarily of pastureland, with some cropland and slight urbanization. By significantly reducing floodwater, sediment, and erosion damages on the 1,478 acres of agricultural and urban floodplain, the project will enhance the economic and recreational development of the region. Adverse effects will include temporary removal of vegetation on 21 acres during construction, loss of production from 51 acres of pasture to be converted to a lake area, and rapid depletion of stored water due to the high rate of evaporation from the lake's surface. Alternatives considered unfeasible were land treatment only, land treatment with one floodwater retarding structure, floodplain zoning, a floodway with dikes, and no action. The project will enhance the long-term productivity of the floodplain. All structure sites are reclaimable, needing only a few years to re-establish cover similar to present conditions. There is no significant opposition to this project. (Deckert-Florida)
W75-08062

DRIP IRRIGATION FOR REVEGETATING STEEP SLOPES IN AN ARID ENVIRONMENT,
American Smelting and Refining Co., Sahuarita, Ariz.
S. A. Bengson.
Progressive Agriculture in Arizona, Vol 27, No 1, p 3-5, 12, January-February, 1975. 8 fig, 3 ref.

Descriptors: *Arid lands, *Vegetation establishment, *Slope stabilization, *Water conservation, *Irrigation practices, *Arizona, Erosion, Runoff, Leaching, Desert plants, Salts.
Identifiers: *Drip irrigation.

Climate, alkaline-saline soils, lack of organics, and steep slopes are major obstacles in revegetating disturbed sites in arid environments, but techniques designed to achieve revegetation have been slow to be developed. Drip irrigation has been used for farming in arid regions. The primary advantage of drip, or trickle, irrigation is conservation of water, but on steep slopes it also is important because of its capacity to apply sufficient water to a plant at a slow enough rate to alleviate runoff and subsequent erosion. Drip irrigation is also capable of leaching excess salts and other phytotoxins from the root zone. Disadvantages include costs, depending on the plant density desired, possible accumulation of salts at the edge of the wetting zone, and ineffectiveness in producing a solid vegetative cover. For extremely steep slopes or other areas difficult to revegetate, drip irrigation may be the best solution for providing vegetation to stabilize disturbed sites and improve aesthetics. (Mastic-Arizona)
W75-08102

PRECIPITATION AND STREAMFLOW ON THREE SMALL CHILEAN WATERSHEDS,
Arizona Univ., Tucson. Dept. of Watershed Management.
For primary bibliographic entry see Field 2A.
W75-08104

HYDROLOGIC SIMULATION OF WATERSHEDS WITH ARTIFICIAL DRAINAGE,
Florida Univ., Gainesville. Dept. of Agricultural Engineering.
For primary bibliographic entry see Field 2A.
W75-08191

BRUSHY BASIN-A FORMULA FOR WATERSHED MANAGEMENT SUCCESS,
Santa Ana Watershed Planning Agency, Calif; and Santa Ana Watershed Project Authority, Riverside, Calif.
For primary bibliographic entry see Field 4C.
W75-08196

THE CARRIZO-CIBECUE WILDFIRE IN RETROSPECT, WHAT IT DID AND WHAT WE ARE DOING ABOUT IT,
Arizona Univ., Tucson. Dept. of Watershed Management.
For primary bibliographic entry see Field 4C.
W75-08197

WATERSHED MANAGEMENT WITHOUT SURFACE RUNOFF,
Nebraska Univ., Lincoln. Dept. of Agricultural Engineering.
D. M. Manbeck.
Water Resources Bulletin, Vol 10, No 3, p 586-591, June 1974. 3 fig.

Descriptors: *Watershed management, *Flood control, *Agricultural engineering, *Surface runoff, *Constraints, Retention, Design, Control, *Great Plains, *Nebraska, Surface drainage, Pumping plants, Storage, Irrigation, Crops.
Identifiers: Alternatives, Water movement.

Legal, economic, and social constraints prevented the development of a surface outlet from an 878 acre watershed in the eastern Great Plains. However, frequent flooding of potentially excellent cropland within the watershed had to be controlled. The process of considering various alternatives within given constraints and utilizing natural features of the watershed to attain a water management system without surface runoff is presented. Operational and physical constraints to water management schemes for the watershed include: (1) utilization of as much of the area with uniform soils as possible for field crops production; (2) removal of excess surface water from the fields within 24 hours; (3) provision for ready access to all fields; (4) irrigation of fields by surface methods; and (5) retention of at least four inches of top soil for the soil surface. The resulting coordinated system includes surface drainage, water-holding structures, and pumping plants. The excellent water control provided permits effective

utilization of more than 115 acres of land which was previously of very low productivity. (Bell-Cornell)
W75-08207

SUBDIVISION ON MALLEE FARMS,
For primary bibliographic entry see Field 4A.
W75-08281

5. WATER QUALITY MANAGEMENT AND PROTECTION

5A. Identification Of Pollutants

A SUMMARY OF SELECTED CHEMICAL-QUALITY CONDITIONS IN 66 CALIFORNIA STREAMS, 1950-72,
Geological Survey, Menlo Park, Calif.
G. A. Irwin, and M. Lemons.
Open-file report, March 1975. 104 p, 4 fig, 1 tab, 8 ref.

Descriptors: *Water quality, *Water chemistry, *Streams, *California, Surface waters, Data collections, Hydrologic data, Regression analysis.

Water from California streams has been analyzed for concentrations of selected chemical constituents since the early 1950's. This summary includes about 1,200 water years of data from 88 sampling sites on 66 streams. About 80 percent of the sites had a mean dissolved-solids concentration of 400 milligrams per litre or less. All the sites that had mean concentrations ranging from 601 to 800 milligrams per litre were in either the South Coastal or Central Coastal subregions. Results of regression analysis between specific conductance and calcium, magnesium, sodium, bicarbonate, dissolved solids, and hardness usually indicate a high percentage of explained variance. Other constituents, such as potassium, sulfate, chloride, and particularly nitrate, were not as frequently highly associated with specific conductance. At sites where the water discharge was highly regulated, the variation in specific conductance that was explained as a function of discharge ranges from 0 to more than 90 percent, whereas at the unregulated sites, the explained variance ranges from 50 to more than 90 percent. (Knapp-USGS)
W75-07858

HYDROGEOLOGIC AND WATER-QUALITY DATA IN WESTERN JEFFERSON COUNTY, COLORADO,
Geological Survey, Denver, Colo.
For primary bibliographic entry see Field 2F.
W75-07862

WATER QUALITY OF HYDROLOGIC BENCH MARKS--AN INDICATOR OF WATER QUALITY IN THE NATURAL ENVIRONMENT,
Geological Survey, Reston, Va.
J. E. Biesecker, and D. K. Leifeste.
Circular 460-E, 1975. 21 p, 12 fig, 11 tab, 10 ref.

Descriptors: *Water quality, *Basic data collections, *Hydrologic data, Pesticides, Dissolved solids, Anions, Cations, Salts, Solutes, Baseline studies, Water quality standards.
Identifiers: *Hydrologic bench marks.

Water-quality data, collected at 57 hydrologic bench-mark stations in 37 States, allow the definition of water quality in the natural environment and the comparison of natural water quality with water quality of major streams draining similar water-resources regions. Water quality in the natural environment is generally very good. Streams draining hydrologic bench-mark basins generally contain low concentrations of dissolved constituents. Water collected at the hydrologic bench-mark stations was analyzed for the following minor metals: arsenic, barium, cadmium, hexavalent chromium, cobalt, copper, lead, mercury, selenium, silver, and zinc. Only three samples contained metals in excess of U.S. Public Health Service recommended drinking-water standards--two selenium concentrations and one cadmium concentration. Widespread but very low-level occurrence of pesticide residues in the natural environment was found--about 30 percent of all samples contained low-level concentrations of pesticidal compounds. The relationship between dissolved-solids concentration and discharge per unit area in the natural environment is a tool for approximating natural water quality. Average annual runoff and rock type can be used as predictive tools to determine the maximum dissolved-solids concentration expected in the natural environment. (Knapp-USGS)
W75-07888

HYDROCARBONS IN THE MARINE ENVIRONMENT, I. N-ALKANES IN THE FIRTH OF CLYDE,
Torry Research Station, Aberdeen (Scotland).
P. R. Mackie, K. J. Whittle, and R. Hardy.
Estuarine and Coastal Marine Science, Vol 2, No 4, p 359-374, October 1974. 10 fig, 5 tab, 20 ref.

Descriptors: *Organic compounds, *Marine biology, *Analytical techniques, *Aquatic life, *Organic matter, Benthos, Plankton, Organic wastes, Saline water, Water quality, Sediments, Fish, Chemical analysis, Chromatography, Solvents, Solvent extractions, Separation techniques, Distillation.
Identifiers: *Marine environment, *Alkanes, *Firth of Clyde, Surface film, Irving Bay, Pentane, Chloroform, Methanol.

Water, surface film, sediment, plankton and fish from the Firth of Clyde were examined to determine the amount of distribution of hydrocarbons. All samples contained hydrocarbons although at very low levels. The distribution of n-alkanes was of two types: first, a relatively smooth increase from C sub 18 to C sub 26 then a decrease to C sub 33 for water, plankton, and fish muscle; second, a strong odd carbon number predominance in the range C sub 25-C sub 33 for the sediment, benthos, and fish liver samples. No evidence was found for accretion of hydrocarbons at higher levels of the food chain. It was not possible to determine unequivocally whether the hydrocarbons present in the samples were biogenic or nonbiogenic. (Henley-ISWS)
W75-07894

MODE: IGPP MEASUREMENTS OF BOTTOM PRESSURE AND TEMPERATURE,
California Univ., San Diego, La Jolla. Inst. of Geophysics and Planetary Physics.
For primary bibliographic entry see Field 7B.
W75-07904

DIFFUSION COEFFICIENTS CALCULATED FROM THE MEDITERREAN SALINITY ANOMALY IN THE NORTH ATLANTIC OCEAN,
Bedford Inst. of Oceanography, Dartmouth (Nova Scotia). Atlantic Oceanographic Lab.
For primary bibliographic entry see Field 2L.
W75-07912

A METHOD FOR THE STEPWISE ENRICHMENT FOR THE DEMONSTRATION OF SALMONELLA IN FRESH AND SALT WATER, (IN GERMAN),
H. H. Wuthe.
Zentralbl Bakteriol Parasetenko Infektionskr Hyg Erste Abt Orig Reihe B Hyg Praev Med. Vol 157, No 4, p 328-332, 1973, English summary.

Descriptors: *Salmonella, *Fresh water, *Saline water, Bacteria, Sampling, Water pollution sources, Pollutants, Growth stages.
Identifiers: Tetrathionate, Step-wise enrichment.

A method and the results of a stepwise enrichment of Salmonella in fresh and salt water samples over a period of 6 yr are reported. The enrichment takes place via 3 stages with increasing tetrathionate concentration. At each stage olating takes place after 24 hr incubation and a further 24 h standing at room temperature. Although the most positive findings were found in the 3rd stage of enrichment, the examination of each individual stage is necessary as 27% of the positive results were obtained exclusively with 1 plate.--Copyright 1974, Biological Abstracts, Inc.
W75-07928

COMPARISON OF GELATINE AND KIEBO PLATES FOR DETERMINING THE COLONY COUNT IN DRINKING WATER: I, (IN GERMAN),
Bundesgesundheitsamt, Berlin (West Germany). Institut fuer Wasser-, Boden-, und Lufthygiene.
G. Mueller.
Zentralbl Bakteriol Parasitenkd Infektionskr Hyg Erste Abt Orig Reihe B Hyg Praev Med, Vol 157, No 4, p 376-386, 1973. (English summary).

Descriptors: *Potable water, *Water analysis, Bacteria, Water pollution sources, Pollutant identification.
Identifiers: Gelatin, Kiebo plates, Silicic-acid.

In a comparison of the colony counts obtained from about 7000 different waters (ground water, waterside filtrates, drinking water from the public supply pipes, water after phosphating and ion exchange installations, mineral waters, waters percolating through rubbish tips) using gelatin and Kiebo (= Kieselsaurenahrboden; silicic acid culture medium) pour plates by setting limiting values of less than 10/ml, over 10/ml but under 100/ml, over 100/ml but less than 1000/ml and over 10,000/ml and over 10,000/ml. 100% agreement could only be obtained for colony counts below 5/ml and over 500/ml while in the over 10 and under 100/ml range, which is relevant for the bacteriological assessment of drinking water, there was agreement in 77.8%. The greatest differences were found in phosphated waters and mineral waters (higher Kiebo Plate counts) and drainage from ion exchangers and rubbish tip waters (higher gelatin counts).--Copyright 1974, Biological Abstracts, Inc.
W75-07933

ANALYSIS OF LAS, ABS AND COMMERCIAL DETERGENTS BY TWO-PHASE TITRATION,
Rensselaer Polytechnic Inst., Troy, N.Y. Dept. of Chemical Engineering; and Rensselaer Polytechnic Inst., Troy, N.Y. Dept. of Environmental Engineering.
L. K. Wang, J. Y. Yang, R. G. Ross, and M. H. Wang.
Water Resources Bulletin, Vol 11, No 2, p 267-277, April 1975. 6 fig, 6 ref. USAMERDC Contract DAAK02-73-C-0206.

Descriptors: *Detergents, *Analytical techniques, *Surfactants, *Alkylbenzene sulfonates, *Linear alkylate sulfonates, Water analysis, Chemistry, Estimating, On-site tests, Testing, Domestic wastes, Soaps, Water quality, Waste identification, Evaluation, Reactance, *Pollutant identification, Environmental sanitation, *Volumetric analysis.
Identifiers: *Two-phase titration, Field test kit.

A two-phase titration method was developed and evaluated to determine the concentration of linear alkylate sulfonate (LAS), branched-chain alkyl benzene sulfonate (ABS), dishwashing detergents, and laundry detergents in water. This method is capable of quantitatively determining anionic sur-

factants in either fresh water or saline water and it is therefore superior to the widely used Methylene Blue Method. To simplify the titration method for adaptation to remote field utilization, a field test kit was developed. This test kit includes only a separatory funnel, a titration burette, a set of liquid measuring apparatus, and some chemicals. Emphasis was placed on compactness of the kit and simplicity in the test manipulation, so that its operation can be performed by relatively unskilled wastewater monitoring personnel. (Henley-ISWS)
W75-07937

A CONTRIBUTION TO THE ECOLOGICAL STUDY OF A MOROCCAN ATLANTIC ESTUARY: THE ESTUARY OF BOU REGREG: I,
Institut Scientifique Cherifien, Rabat (Morocco). Lab. of Zoology.
For primary bibliographic entry see Field 2L.
W75-07938

FLUORINE IN GROUND WATER AS A GUIDE TO PB-ZN-BA-F MINERALIZATION,
Toronto Univ. (Ontario). Dept. of Geology.
For primary bibliographic entry see Field 2K.
W75-07953

LOW WINTER DISSOLVED OXYGEN IN SOME ALASKAN RIVERS,
Environmental Protection Agency, Arctic Environmental Research Lab. College, Alaska.
For primary bibliographic entry see Field 5B.
W75-07966

PHOSPHORUS UPTAKE AND RELEASE BY LAKE ONTERIO SEDIMENTS,
Wisconsin Univ., Madison. Water Chemistry Program; and Wisconsin Univ, Madison. Dept. of Soils.
R. T. Bannerman, D. E. Armstrong, R. F. Harris, and G. C. Holdren.
Available from the National Technical Information Service, Springfield, Va 22161 as PB-240 614, $4.25 in paper copy, $2.25 in microfiche. Environmental Protection Agency, Report EPA-660/3-75-006, February 1975. 51 p, 4 fig, 17 tab, 33 ref. R-800609.

Descriptors: Eutrophication, *Phosphorus, *Sediments, Sediment-water interfaces, *Lake Ontario, Lakes, Great Lakes, Pollutant identification, Absorption, Water pollution sources.

Sediment cores were obtained from 15 lake stations representing the three major basins and the Inshore Zone of Lake Ontario. Cores were sectioned for characterization of the surface sediments according to inorganic P chemical mobility. Physical mobility was characterized by measurement of P release from intact cores incubated under controlled laboratory conditions. The proportions of potentially chemically mobile inorganie P were usually high (30 to 60%) in the central basin sediments and low (2 to 8%) for the inshore zone sediments. Although the amounts of inorganie P desorbed after three successive equalibrations (in .1M NaCl) of Lake Ontario sediments represented only 3 to 17% of the potentially mobile inorganic P, sufficient inorganic P was described to restore a large part of the original interstitial inorganic P concentrations. Interstitial inorganic P (mobile P) concentrations ranged from 14 to 1280 micrometers/l and were higher than dissolved inorganie P concentrations in the overlying water. Diffusion rates estimated from the range of observed interstitial inorganic P values ranged from about 0.05 to 0.6 mg m-2 day-1 and were in agreement with the range of 0.03 to 0.8 mg m-2 day-1 estimated from P release from intact cores incubated under controlled laboratory conditions. Based on an inorganic P flux of 0.2 mg m-2 day-1, the estimated annual contribution of inorganic P to Lake Ontario water is equal to about 10% of the external P loading. (EPA)
W75-07972

EFFECTS OF MIREX AND HMETHOXYCHLOR ON STRIPED MULLET, MUGIL CEPHALUS L.,
Oceanic Inst., Waimanalo, Hawaii.
For primary bibliographic entry see Field 5C.
W75-07973

LEVELS OF COPPER, NICKEL, RUBIDIUM, AND STRONTIUM IN INSTITUTIONAL TOTAL DIETS,
Food and Drug Administration, Cincinnati, Ohio.
G. K. Murthy, U. S. Rhea, and J. T. Peeler.
Environmental Science and Technology, Vol 7, No 11, p 1042-1045, November, 1973. 1 fig, 4 tab, 38 ref.

Descriptors: *Copper, *Nickel, *Strontium *Diets, *Distribution, Institutions, Sampling, Analytical techniques, Spectroscopy, *Pollutant identification, Trace elements.

The average trace element content in the diets of institutionalized children, aged 9 to 12, from 28 U.S. cities, expressed as mg/kg of food, varied as: copper, 0.438-0.873; nickel, 0.140-0.321; rubidium, 0.601-2.338; and strontium, 0.319-0.957. Similarly, the consumption of food varied from 1.18-2.55 kg/day and the milk content of diet varied from 9.5-63.8%. Minerals from drinking water were not included in the study. Statistical analyses of the data (mg/day) showed significant seasonal and geographical variations. Monthly averages for all elements showed that copper was slightly higher during summer, rubidium and strontium tended to peak during spring and autumn, and no trend could be ascribed to nickel. The low and high levels of trace elements observed in different geographical areas were briefly discussed. (Jernigan-Vanderbilt)
W75-08075

CLEAN ENVIRONMENT FOR ULTRATRACE ANALYSIS,
Baker (J.T.) Chemical Co., Phillipsburg, N.J. Research Labs.
M. Zief, and A. G. Nesher.
Environmental Science and Technology, Vol 8, No 7, p 677-678, July 1974. 2 fig, 1 tab, 11 ref.

Descriptors: *Analytical techniques, *Laboratory tests, *Trace elements, *Metals, *Air pollution, Testing procedures, Human pathology, Chromium, Nickel, *Pollutant identification.
Identifiers: *Interferences.

The inability to control ambient air blanks at levels insignificant in comparison with the constituent being determined severely restricts accuracy and precision of ultratrace metal determinations. Reduction in that portion of the blank contributed by laboratory air is discussed. Techniques were presented for upgrading a laboratory to control contamination from particulates in air. The importance of humidity control in elimination of electrostatic charges was also discussed. (Jernigan-Vanderbilt)
W75-08078

TEMPERATURE CONTROLLED HEATING OF THE GRAPHITE TUBE ATOMIZER IN FLAMELESS ATOMIC ABSORPTION SPECTROMETRY,
Umea Univ. (Sweden). Dept. of Analytical Chemistry.
G. Lundgren, L. Lundmark, and G. Johansson.
Analytical Chemistry, Vol 46, No 8, p 1028-1031, July 1974. 9 fig, 1 tab, 5 ref.

Descriptors: *Analytical techniques, *Spectroscopy, *Cadmium, *Lead, Laboratory tests, Sampling, Testing procedures, *Pollutant identification.
Identifiers: *Atomic absorption spectroscopy, Atomizer.

A temperature controller for graphite rods or tubes in flameless atomic absorption was described. An infrared detector senses the radiation from the graphite and the power is regulated by a triac. The temperature of the graphite tube is raised rapidly and then kept constant with plus or minu 10 degrees. The atomization procedure can be optimized which is important when interfering substances are present. Cadmium can be determined in sodium chloride at sea water concentrations with a detection limit of 0.03 micrograms Cd/l. at an atomization temperature of 820 degrees. The determination of lead was made both with the common constant voltage heating and with the described controller and the results were compared. (Jernigan-Vanderbilt)
W75-08079

SOME ANALYTICAL APPLICATIONS OF REACTION-RATE-PROMOTING EFFECTS--THE TRIS(1,10-PHENANTHROLINE)IRON(II)-CHROMIUM(VI) INDICATOR REACTION,
Oklahoma State Univ., Stillwater. Dept. of Chemistry.
V. V. S. E. Dutt, and H. A. Mottola.
Analytical Chemistry, Vol 46, No 8, p 1090-1094, July 1974. 3 fig, 2 tab, 24 ref.

Descriptors: *Metals, *Analytical techniques, *Oxidation, *Chemical reactions, Chromium, Vanadium, Arsenic compounds, Molybdenum, Spectroscopy, Laboratory tests, Testing procedures, Instrumentation, Rates, *Pollutant identification.

Several rate-accelerating effects on the oxidation of ferroin by Cr(VI) in sulfuric acid medium were reported. In all cases, these effects were observed in the earlier portions of the reaction profile and no catalytic cycle appeared to be associated with them. Conversion of the rate-modifying species to an inactive form by destruction or, mainly, by complexation with Cr(III) seemed to account for the lack of catalytic cycle. Judicious choice of reaction conditions allowed the determination (by initial rate measurements) of microgram amounts/milliliter or oxalic acid, citric acid, vanadium(IV), arsenic(III), chromium(VI), hexacyanoferrate(III), and mg/ml of molybdenum(VI). (Jernigan-Vanderbilt)
W75-08080

INTERNAL NORMALIZATION TECHNIQUES FOR HIGH ACCURACY ISOTOPE DILUTION ANALYSES--APPLICATION TO MOLYBDENUM AND NICKEL IN STANDARD REFERENCE MATERIALS,
National Bureau of Standards, Washington, D.C. Analytical Chemistry Div.
L. J. Moore, L. A. Machlan, W. R. Shields, and E. L. Garner.
Analytical Chemistry, Vol 46, No 8, p 1082-1089, July 1974, 1 fig, 5 tab, 24 ref.

Descriptors: *Analytical techniques, *Molybdenum, *Nickel, Instrumentation chemical reactions, Laboratory tests, *Mass spectrometry, Isotope fractionation, *Pollutant identification.

General exact equations and iteration techniques were developed for internal normalization to eliminate the effect of thermal fractionation from isotope ratio measurements, and therefore isotope dilution analyses, by thermal ionization mass spectrometry. The techniques were applicable to more than 20 elements, and have been extensively applied to the determination of Mo in ore concentrates (55% Mo) and silicate trace standards (50 and 500 ppm Mo). The standard deviations of all internally corrected Mo isotope ratio measurements were less than 0.1%. The Mo sample size was 40 micrograms, but normalization techniques should apply to microgram and smaller samples with a more sensitive ion detection system. Procedures were described for the chemical separation of Mo from matrix interferences and

for the mass spectrometric analysis of Mo. Application of the techniques to Ni in three pollution Standard Reference Materials was described. (Jernigan-Vanderbilt)
W75-08081

SPECTROPHOTOMETRIC DETERMINATION OF IRON IN ACIDS AND ACIDIC SOLUTIONS BY AN EXTRACTION--FORMATION REACTION INVOLVING 3-(2-PYRIDYL)-5,6-DIPHENYL-1,2,4-TRIAZINE AS THE CHROMOGENIC EXTRACTION REAGENT,
Northern Illinois Univ., De Kalb. Dept. of Chemistry.
C. D. Chriswell, and A. A. Schilt.
Analytical Chemistry, Vol 46, No 8, p 992-996, July 1974. 5 fig, 6 tab, 14 ref.

Descriptors: *Iron, *Analytical techniques, *Spectroscopy, *Acids, Testing procedures, Laboratory tests, Instrumentation, *Pollutant identification.

A rapid, simple, and sensitive method was developed for the spectrophotometric determination of iron in acids and acidic solutions based upon the extraction-formation of tris (3-(2-pyridyl)-5,6-diphenyl-1,2,4-triazine)iron (II) thiocyanate. The basis of the method and effect of variables were investigated and elucidated. In general, the method is suitable for acid concentrations up to 4M, applicable to iron concentrations of parts per billion, and relatively free of interferences. The iron content of some reagent grade acids were reported. (Jernigan-Vanderbilt)
W75-08082

OXIDATION OF METAL SULFIDES BY THIOBACILLUS FERRO-OXIDANS GROWN ON DIFFERENT SUBSTRATES,
Laval Univ., Quebec. Department of Biochimie.
For primary bibliographic entry see Field 5C.
W75-08085

THE EFFECT OF SILVER IONS ON THE RESPIRATORY CHAIN OF ESCHERICHIA COLI,
British Columbia Univ., Vancouver. Dept. of Biochemistry.
For primary bibliographic entry see Field 5C.
W75-08086

SYNTHESES AND SPECTROPHOTOMETRIC STUDIES OF 5(2-PYRIDYLAZO) - 2,4-DIAMINOTOLUENE AND ITS DERIVATIVES AS ANALYTICAL REAGENTS, SPECTROPHOTOMETRIC DETERMINATION OF COBALT WITH 5-(3,5-DICHLORO-2-PYRIDYL)-2,4-DIAMINOTOLUENE),
Government Industrial Research Inst., Nagoya (Japan).
S. Shibata, M. Furukawa, and E. Kamata.
Analytica Chimica Acta, Vol 73, No 1, p 107-118, November, 1974. 8 fig, 5 tab, 9 ref.

Descriptors: *Heavy metals, *Cobalt, *Spectrophotometry, *Synthesis, *Analytical techniques, *Chelation, Steel, Gold, Copper, Zinc, *Pollutant identification, Mercury, Nickel.
Identifiers: *Pyridylazo dyes, *Molar absorptivities, *Ligand, Metal ions, Color reactions, Mercury (II), Nickel (II), Palladium, Thallium, Waspaloy, Meta-tolylene diamine group.

Seven pyridylazo dyes containing the m-tolylenediamine group were synthesized and their analytical potential for the determination of cobalt was studied spectrophotometrically. The molar absorptivities and selectivity of these reagents increased compared with those of 4-(2-pyridylazo)-1,3-diaminobenzene (PADAB). Cobalt (II) and 3,5-diCl-PADAT (5- (3,5-dichloro-2-pyridyl)azo-2,4-diaminotoluene) at pH3 form a complex which is very stable even in the presence of strong mineral acids. The complex has two absorption maxima at 548 and 590 nm in hydrochloric acid (2.4 m) solution. The color is very stable and the system conforms to Beer's law; the optimal range for measurement in a one cm is 0.01-0.4 ppm cobalt. In practice, this color reaction is specific. The molar absorptivity is 138,000 liters per mol cm at 590 nm. The sensitivity is 0.00042 micrograms Co per sq cm at 590 nm for log Io/I = 0.001. The method was applied to the determination of cobalt in steel and waspaloy. (Definer-Vanderbilt)
W75-08087

A STATIC MONITOR FOR LEAD IN NATURAL AND WASTE WATERS,
Vanderbilt Univ., Nashville, Tenn. Dept. of Chemistry.
A. N. Clarke, and J. H. Clarke.
Environmental Letters, Vol 7, No 3, p 251-260, 1974. 2 tab, 13 ref.

Descriptors: *Heavy metals, *Lead, *Monitoring, Wastewater(Pollution), *Clams, Freshwater, *Spectroscopy, Adsorption pollutants, Chelation, Mollusk, Shellfish, Leaching, Acids, *Pollutant identification.
Identifiers: *Atomic absorption, Plastic ware.

The experiment was originally designed to ascertain the extent to which leaching and adsorption mechanisms affect the final lead concentrations of a fresh water mollusk shell at pH above 7. The shells of the ubiquitous fresh-water mollusk Corbicula manillensis, commonly known as the Asiatic clam, were used to monitor the relative concentration and changes in concentration of lead over extended periods of time in natural and waste waters at a pH of 7 or above. The shells not only absorb lead from background waters, but the adsorption factors increase with increasing background water levels. These shells were especially good monitors of Pb in waters at pH of 7 or higher. Commercial plastic ware that was used in the study was a source of lead contamination. (Definer-Vanderbilt)
W75-08089

A PRELIMINARY APPROACH TO THE USE OF THE ISOTOPIC RATIO 13C/12C FOR THE EVALUATION OF MINERALIZATION IN AQUATIC ENVIRONMENTS,
Istituto Italiano di Idrobiologia, Pallanza.
For primary bibliographic entry see Field 5B.
W75-08090

MICRODETERMINATION OF METALS IN ORGANOMETALLIC COMPOUNDS BY THE OXINE METHOD AFTER CLOSED FLASH COMBUSTION,
Cairo Univ., Giza (Egypt). Microanalytical Unit.
A. B. Sakla, S. W. Bishara, and P. A. Hassan.
Analytica Chimica Acta, Vol 73, No 1, p 209-212, November, 1974, 1 tab, 21 ref.

Descriptors: *Metals, *Analytical techniques, *Calcium, *Copper, *Iron, *Nickel, *Aluminum, Synthesis, *Pollutant identification, Volumetric analysis.
Identifiers: Microdeterminations, Closed flask combination, *Organoiron compound, *Organonickel compound, Bismuth, Pharmaceutical industries, Petroleum industries.

The results of using the closed flask combustion method to determine, on the micro scale, Ca, Cu, Al, Fe, Bi, and Ni, are reported. Oxine is used as the organic chemical to bind the metals. The closed flask method did not offer great advantages over the wet digestion technique for decomposition or ogranoiron or organonickel compounds, but it is advantageous for the other metals listed. This should be important for synthetic organic chemistry, pharamaceutical and petroleum industries. (Delfiner-Vanderbilt)
W75-08091

HEAD HAIR SAMPLES AS INDICATORS OF ENVIRONMENTAL POLLUTION,
University Coll., Cork (Ireland).
J. P. Corridan.
Environmental Research. Vol 8, No 1, p 12-16, Aug., 1974, 25 ref.

Descriptors: *Heavy metals, *Lead, *Mercury, *Copper, *Zinc, *Arsenic compounds, Environment, Pollution, Rural areas, Air pollution, Analytic techniques, Spectrophotometry, Colorimetry, Dusts, Public health, Spectrophotometry, *Pollutant identification, Industrial wastes.
Identifiers: *Hair *Ireland, *Atomic absorption, Wet oxidation.

A brief account is given of the problems which may arise from open cast metal mining and the value of taking head hair samples to indicate environmental pollution. In an area in rural Ireland, of note were the comparatively high arsenic levels, the normal copper and zinc levels, and the low levels of lead and mercury. Head hair can be a useful indicator of environmental pollution by metals, the analysis of hair is of epidemiological importance. (Delfiner-Vanderbilt)
W75-08092

MICRODETERMINATION OF LEAD BY A FLUORESCENT RING-OVEN TECHNIQUE,
Andrija Stampar School of Public Health, Zagreb (Yugoslavia).
Z. Skuric, F. Valic, and J. Prpic-Marecic.
Analytica Chimica Acta, Vol 73, No 1, p 213-215, November, 1974, 8 ref.

Descriptors: *Lead, *Analytical techniques, *Fluorescence, *Air pollution, Ions, Assay, *Pollutant idenfication.
Identifiers: Microdetermination, *Ring-oven technique, Lead chlorocomplexes.

A combination of techniques that can be used for the determination of lead is discussed. The efficacy of the ring-oven technique for separating and concentrating trace amounts of lead, combined with the high fluorescence intensity of the lead chloro-complex in the adsorbed state, was found to provide a simple reasonably rapid procedure adaptable for air pollution studies. A total of 29 ionic species from Groups, I, II, III, IV, V, VI, VII, VIII were studied. In determining lead in air, the sensitivity of the fluorescent ring-oven technique is quite satisfactory not only for industrial environments, but also for outdoor atmospheres. (Delfiner-Vanderbilt)
W75-08093

FLUORESCENCE REACTIONS OF ERICHROME RED B WITH METALS, PART I DETECTION OF BE, MG, AL, IN, GA, AND ZN,
Madrid Univ. (Spain). Departamento de Quimica Analitica.
C. Perez Conde, J. A. Perez-Bustamante, and F. Burrielmarti.
Analytica Chimica Acta, Vol 73, No 1, p 191-193, November, 1974, 1 tab, 4 ref.

Descriptors: *Heavy metals, *Metals, *Fluorescence, *Dye releases, Analytical techniques, Spectroscopy, Pollutant identification.
Identifiers: *Erichrome red B, Reagents, Food stuffs.

The results of a search for possible new fluorescence reagents among a considerable number of azo dye stuffs were reported. Eriochrome red B was useful for the sensitive identification of the elements, Be, Mg, Al, In, Ga, and Zn. Neither thallium (I) nor thallium (II) gave any fluorescence in any of the media investigated. The media tested were hexamine, Hcl, NaOH, acetic acid-sodium acetate buffer. Erichrome red B appeared promising for qualitative identification

and possibility for some sensitive determinations. (Delfiner-Vanderbilt)
W75-08094

SOLUBILIZATION OF DIMETHYLMERCURY BY HALIDE IONS,
Missouri Univ., Rolla. Dept. of Chemistry.
For primary bibliographic entry see Field 5B.
W75-08096

ANALYSES OF PHOSPHORUS IN LAKE ONTARIO SEDIMENT,
State Univ. Coll., Buffalo, N.Y. Great Lakes Lab.
For primary bibliographic entry see Field 5C.
W75-08122

KEYS TO WATER QUALITY INDICATIVE ORGANISMS (SOUTHEASTERN UNITED STATES),
Georgia State Coll., Atlanta.
For primary bibliographic entry see Field 5C.
W75-08146

FUNGI,
Georgia State Coll., Atlanta. Dept. of Biology.
For primary bibliographic entry see Field 5C.
W75-08147

ALGAE,
Robert A. Taft Sanitary Engineering Center, Cincinnati, Ohio. Cincinnati Water Research Lab.
For primary bibliographic entry see Field 5C.
W75-08148

OLIGOCHAETA,
Toronto Univ. (Ontario). Dept. of Zoology.
For primary bibliographic entry see Field 5C.
W75-08150

EPHEMEROPTERA,
Florida Univ., Gainesville. Dept. of Biological Science.
For primary bibliographic entry see Field 5C.
W75-08152

PLECOPTERA,
Massachusetts Univ., Amherst. Dept. of Entomology and Plant Pathology.
For primary bibliographic entry see Field 5C.
W75-08153

TRICHOPTERA,
Georgia Univ., Athens. Dept. of Entomology.
For primary bibliographic entry see Field 5C.
W75-08154

CHIRONOMIDAE,
Florida State Board of Health, Jacksonville.
For primary bibliographic entry see Field 5C.
W75-08155

FRESHWATER FISHES,
Auburn Univ., Ala.
For primary bibliographic entry see Field 5C.
W75-08156

DATA REQUIREMENTS OF A WATER QUALITY MANAGEMENT PROGRAM,
Colorado State Univ., Fort Collins. Dept. of Agricultural Engineering.
For primary bibliographic entry see Field 5G.
W75-08213

SUSPENDED SOLIDS MONITOR,
Newark Coll. of Engineering, N.J.
J. W. Liskowitz, G. J. Franey, and J. Tarczynski.

Available from the National Technical Information Service, Springfield, Va 22161 as PB-241 581, $3.75 in paper copy, $2.25 in microfiche. Environmental Protection Agency, Cincinnati, Ohio, Report EPA-670/2-75-002, April 1975. 39 p, 14 fig, 6 tab, 6 ref. 1BB034/ROAP 21-ASY/TASK 037. 11024DZB (14-12-494).

Descriptors: Measurement, *Measuring instruments, Automatic control, Remote sensing, Flow control, Flow measurement, Remote control, *Water analysis, Monitoring, *Chemical analysis, *Instrumentation, Flow characteristics, Waste identification, Suspended solids.
Identifiers: Multiple light scatter, In situ measurement, *Suspended solids meter, Depolarization.

A method for measuring concentration of suspended solids in liquid media, based on depolarization of backscattered polarized light, has been developed and instrumented. Feasibility studies and field evaluation of the instrument, using sewage influent, effluent and sludge, showed that there is a specific relationship between concentration of solid particles and polarization ratio. The relationship is independent of size distribution and density of particles, color of particles or solution, sludge consistency, velocity, and build-up of solids on the optical window. The field evaluation results indicate that this instrument provides a continuous instantaneous in situ measurement of suspended solids concentrations in combined sewers and other wastewater flows. (EPA)
W75-08227

FORTRAN PROGRAMS FOR ANALYZING COLLABORATIVE TEST DATA, PART I: GENERAL STATISTICS,
National Environmental Research Center, Cincinnati, Ohio.
For primary bibliographic entry see Field 7C.
W75-08230

FORTRAN PROGRAMS FOR ANALYZING COLLABORATIVE TEST DATA, PART II: SCATTER DIAGRAMS,
National Environmental Research Center, Cincinnati, Ohio.
For primary bibliographic entry see Field 7C.
W75-08231

DETECTION OF SHIGELLA IN WATERS USING AN IMMUNOFLUORESCENCE TECHNIQUE AND THE IMMUNO-INDIA-INK REACTION (GECK REACTION), (IN FRENCH),
Institute of Hygiene and Epidemiology, Hanoi (North Vietnam).
D. D. Nguyen.
Rev Epidemiol Med Soc Sante Publique, Vol 21, No 4, p 337-347, 1973, Illus.

Descriptors: *Analytical techniques, *Fluorescence, *Shigella sampling, Water pollution, Pollutants, Water pollution sources, Europe, Epidemiology, Water pollution effects, *Pollutant identification.
Identifiers: *Geck reaction, Hungary, India-Ink technique, *Immunofluorescence technique.

Detection of shigellae in Hungarian waters, using an immunofluorescence technique and the immuno-india-ink reaction (Geck reaction) is reported. This investigation was carried out on smears of centrifugation sediment, of filtration sediment and of enriched cultures obtained from 60 water samples. The fluorescent antibody tests revealed the presence of shigellae in 38.3% of the water samples, and the Geck reaction revealed their presence in 41.1%; shigellae were isolated in only 3.3% of the samples with the direct bacteriological method. The 3 types of samples gave similar results. Compared with the immunofluorescene and the direct bacteriological methods, the Geck reaction was very accurate and as specific as the 2 other methods, but essentially quicker than the classical techniques. The Geck reaction has a great epidemiological value. It is simple, inexpensive and could easily be used in all bacteriological laboratories.--Copyright 1974, Biological Abstracts, Inc.
W75-08244

SPECTROPHOTOMETRIC DETERMINATION OF CYCLOHEXANONE IN BODIES OF WATER,
Nauchno-Issledovatelskii Institut Gigieny, Moscow (USSR).
K. O. Lastochkina.
Gig Sanit, Vol 38, No 1, p 68-70, 1973.

Descriptors: *Water pollution, Analytical techniques, *Spectrophotometry, Sampling, Infrared radiation, *Pollutant identification.
Identifiers: IR spectrophotometry, *Cyclohexanone.

Apparatus and methods for the determination of cyclohexanone in polluted water by IR spectrophotometry are described. The water samples are distilled from 500 - 100 ml of sample and CCl_4 is added during the extraction. The extract is transferred into a cuvette with KBr. The method is suitable for the determination of cyclohexanone in a concentration range of 0.1-10 mg/l.--Copyright 1974, Biological Abstracts, Inc.
W75-08248

THE DETERMINATION OF 2H2O IN WATER AND BIOLOGICAL FLUIDS BY GAS CHROMATOGRAPHY,
Ceskoslovenska Akademie Ved, Brno. Ustav Instrumentalni Analyticke Chemie.
For primary bibliographic entry see Field 2K.
W75-08264

COMMUNITIES OF OLIGOCHAETA AS INDICATORS OF THE WATER QUALITY IN LAKE HJALMAREN,
Uppsala Univ. (Sweden). Inst. of Zoology.
For primary bibliographic entry see Field 5B.
W75-08267

CHANGE OF FEEDING OF THE GROUSE UNDER THE EFFECT OF DRAINAGE RECLAMATION, (IN RUSSIAN),
Akademiya Navuk BSSR, Minsk. Dept. of Zoology and Parasitology.
For primary bibliographic entry see Field 2I.
W75-08269

MEASUREMENT OF MICROBIAL OXIDATION OF METHANE IN LAKE WATER,
Manitobe Univ., Winnipeg. Dept. of Microbiology.
J. W. M. Rudd, R. D. Hamilton, and N. E. R. Campbell.
Limnol Oceanogr, Vol 19, No 3, p 519-530, 1974, Illus.
Identifiers: Cells, Lakes, Measurement, *Methane, Microbial oxidation, Oxygen, *Radioactive, Tracers.

A radiotracer method which measures rates of oxidation of methane to cell material, extracellular products, and carbon dioxide was applied to 2 lakes and indicates that methane oxidation occurs in a narrow band where methane and O_2 occur together in the water column. Oxidation rates of 1.0 micromolar/hr were recorded in a eutrophic lake; rates in a meromictic lake reached 0.15 micromolar/hr. Usually 1/3 of the C from oxidized methane was found in cell material and extracellular products and the rest was converted to CO_2. This ratio changed at very low O_2 concentrations.--Copyright 1974, Biological Abstracts, Inc.
W75-08323

SOME OBSERVATIONS ON DIRECT COUNTS OF FRESHWATER BACTERIA OBTAINED WITH A FLUORESCENCE MICROSCOPE,
Freshwater Biological Association, Ambleside (England).
J. G. Jones.
Limnol Oceanogr, Vol 19, No 3, p 540-543, 1974.
Identifiers: Acridine, *Bacteria, Counts, Cyanates, Dyes, Euchrysine, Fluorescence, Microscopes, *Fluorescein microscope, *Pollutant identification.

The use of different fluorochromes for direct counts of bacteria in water was compared. The 2 dyes in most common use, acridine orange (AO) and fluorescein isothiocyanate (FITC) were compared with an acridine derivative, euchrysine 2GNX (E-2GNX). Minor changes in technique could produce significant differences in counts. The acridine based dyes were easier to apply than FITC, and of these, E-2GNX gave consistently higher counts all at a final dye concentration of 5 mg 1-1 with a contact time of 3 min. Details of the method should be consulted since changes can produce opposite results.--Copyright 1974, Biological Abstracts, Inc.
W75-08325

ACCUMULATION, RELEASE AND RETENTION OF PETROLEUM HYDROCARBONS BY THE OYSTER CRASSOSTREA VIRGINICA,
Woods Hole Oceanographic Institution, Mass. Dept. of Biology.
For primary bibliographic entry see Field 5C.
W75-08331

EFFECTS OF WATER HARDNESS ON THE TOXICITY OF SEVERAL ORGANIC AND INORGANIC HERBICIDES TO FISH,
For primary bibliographic entry see Field 5C.
W75-08332

5B. Sources Of Pollution

FATE AND EFFECTS OF TRACE ELEMENTS IN SEWAGE SLUDGE WHEN APPLIED TO AGRICULTURAL LANDS,
California Univ., Riverside. Dept. of Soil Science and Agricultural Engineering.
A. L. Page.
Available from the National Technical Information Service, Springfield, Va. 22161, as PB-231 171, $5.25 in paper copy, $2.25 in microfiche. National Environmental Research Center, Cincinnati, Ohio, EPA Report No EPA-670/2-74-005, January, 1974, 106p, 33 tab, 107 ref. .

Descriptors: *Reviews, *Trace elements, *Sewage sludge, Agriculture, *Soil amendments, Sludge disposal, *Path of pollutants, Soil contamination, Soil chemical properties, Toxicity, Molybdenum, Manganese, Copper, Zinc, Nickel, Cadmium, Cobalt, Chromium, Lead, Boron, Mercury, Arsenic compounds, Heavy metals.

An evaluation was made of potential problems associated with the long-term (decades) application of sewage treatment plant wastes on land resulting in the accumulation of toxic concentrations of trace elements. This evaluation was based on published information, and included the following trace elements: Mo, Mn, Ba, Cu, Zn, Ni, Cd, Co, Sn, Cr, Pb, V, B, Hg, As, Se, and Ag. Total concentrations of trace elements in sewage sludges vary widely as determined from the ranges reported from approximately 300 treatment plants in the U.S.A., Canada, Sweden, England, and Wales. Trace element concentrations in the aqueous phase of sludges may exceed those predicted from solubility product considerations indicating that soluble trace element-organic complexes occur in liquid sludges. Field and greenhouse studies demonstrated that yields and trace element concentrations of higher plants grown on sludge amended soils are dependent on the amount of sludge applied trace element composition of the sludge, soil pH, and plant species. Applications of most sludges at a rate of 400 m tons/ha if mixed uniformly thoughout the surface 15 cm will add more Cd, Cu, Hg and Zn than is normally present in natural soils. The mobility of the various elements was also discussed. (Pulliam-Vanderbilt)
W75-07852

GENESIS OF HYDROGEOCHEMICAL FACIES OF GROUND WATERS IN THE PUNJAB REGION OF PAKISTAN,
Geological Survey, Washington, D.C.
P. R. Seaber, W. Back, C. T. Rightmire, and R. N. Cherry.
In: Proceedings of International Symposium on Development of Ground Water Resources, Nov. 26-29, 1973, Madras, India, Vol 6, p 9-20, 1974. 5 fig, 7 ref.

Descriptors: *Water pollution sources, *Geochemistry, *Return flow, *Evaporation, *Water chemistry, Carbon radioisotopes, Calcium, Sodium, Magnesium, Chlorides, Sulfates.
Identifiers: *Punjab(Pakistan).

Principles and techniques of hydrogeochemistry and isotopic hydrology were applied to a selected area of the Punjab Region of Pakistan. The distribution of the deuterium and oxygen isotopic composition permits delineation of areas in Rechna Doab in which either the Ravi River or the Chenab River contributes to the groundwater today, on the basis of the Ravi River water being isotopically heavier. Mid-Doab waters show the results of mixing and evaporation of the two river waters. Carbon-14 concentrations show the waters to have a modern age. Most of the groundwater is recycled irrigation water, and the chemical reactions resulting from transpiration and evaporation are a major control in its chemical composition. Calcium has three sources: (1) river water draining calcareous rocks at higher elevations; (2) solution of calcareous minerals; and (3) original evaporites in the Punjab Alluvium of the Indus Plain. Sodium is derived chiefly from solution of evaporites and secondarily from dissolution of silicates. The major source of magnesium is the dissolution of calcite and dolomite. Chloride is derived primarily from solution of evaporites, evaporite dust particles, and rainfall. Bicarbonate is derived from five major sources: (1) infiltration of river water; (2) dissolution of secondary soil evaporites; (3) dissolution of calcareous minerals; (4) sulfate reduction; and (5) silicate buffering. Sulfate is derived almost entirely from the solution of gypsum and anhydrite. (Knapp-USGS)
W75-07865

NATURAL AND MODIFIED PLANT COMMUNITIES AS RELATED TO RUNOFF AND SEDIMENT YIELDS,
Geological Survey, Denver, Colo.
For primary bibliographic entry see Field 4C.
W75-07866

BIOLOGICAL AND CHEMICAL ASPECTS OF THE SAN FRANCISCO BAY TURBIDITY MAXIMUM,
Geological Survey, Menlo Park, Calif.
For primary bibliographic entry see Field 2L.
W75-07870

KARST HYDROLOGY OF NORTHERN YUCATAN PENINSULA, MEXICO,
Geological Survey, Reston, Va.
For primary bibliographic entry see Field 2F.
W75-07873

MOVEMENT OF SPILLED OIL AS PREDICTED BY ESTUARINE NONTIDAL DRIFT,
Geological Survey, Menlo Park, Calif.
T. J. Conomos.
Limnology and Oceanography, Vol 20, No 2, p 159-173, March 1975. 5 fig, 1 tab, 37 ref.

Descriptors: *Path of pollutants, *Oily water, *California, *Oil spills, Oil pollution, Water pollution, Currents(Water), Water circulation, Estuaries, Bays, Aquatic drift.
Identifiers: *San Francisco Bay(Calif).

The movement of oil spills was studied using information on water movement obtained from bimonthly releases of surface and seabed drifters in the San Francisco Bay and adjacent Pacific Ocean. River-induced nontidal estuarine circulation was the dominant factor controlling net movement of oil accidentally spilled at the entrance of the bay system, reinforcing ebbing tidal currents and causing the seaward movement of floating oil, which followed paths taken by surface drifters released 3 weeks before the spill. Some oil formed globules which sank to the near-bottom waters, had the same relative buoyancy as seabed drifters, and moved similarly, beaching in eastern San Pablo Bay after being transported landward in the near-bottom waters. No oil or surface drifters floated into the south bay because surface waters were drifting seaward, away from the south bay. Notable seasonally modulated phenomena which must be considered in predicting surface and near-bottom oil drifts include a summer (low-river discharge period) diminution of the estuarine circulation mechanism in the north and central bay-adjacent ocean region and a seasonal reversal in two-layer drift in the south bay. (Knapp-USGS)
W75-07877

HARMONIC ANALYSIS OF STREAM TEMPERATURES,
Geological Survey, Reston, Va.
T. D. Steele.
Availability from NTIS, Springfield, Va 22161 as PB-239 016. Price $4.25 printed copy; $2.25 microfiche. Computer Contribution, December 1974. 53 p.

Descriptors: *Computer programs, *Water temperature, Statistics, Water quality, Regression analysis, Fourier analysis.
Identifiers: *Harmonic analysis.

This computer program is one of a series of programs in the USGS SYSLAB system for data analysis of water-quality records. This special-purpose program was developed for harmonic analysis of water-quality constituent records, primarily stream-temperature data. It includes certain alternative-input and data-analysis capabilities not normally contained in more general statistical-analysis systems. The program, by means of a simple-harmonic regression function, is used to depict graphically and analytically the annual seasonal cycle of stream-temperature variability. Additionally, it may be applicable to characterize other water-quality time-dependent variables. The data-input alternatives to the program include options for analysis of both periodic (intermittent) measurements and daily (continuous) records. Appropriate adjustments are made in the harmonic curve-fitting procedure to compensate for missing values or gaps in a given record. Harmonic functins may be determined for either single- or multiple-year records, and alternatives in terms of detail of computer output are described and illustrated. Options are also available for calculating and graphically depicting correlograms or for determining Hurst coefficients of the constituent or harmonic-residuals time series. A source-deck listing, alternative data-set cluster options, and resultant line-printer outputs depicting the several operational modes and options of modes and options of the program are provided as attachments to this computer-program documentation. (Knapp-USGS)
W75-07882

ONE-DIMENSIONAL STREAM EXCESS TEMPERATURE ANALYSIS,
Geological Survey, Bay Saint Louis, Miss.
D. P. Bauer, and E. Mackenroth.
Available from NTIS, Springfield, Va 22161 as PB-238 965 Price $3.75 printed copy, $2.25 in microfiche. Computer Contribution, November 1974. 35 p.

Descriptors: *Computer programs, *Mathematical models, *Path of pollutants, *Thermal pollution, Mixing, Heated water, Water temperature, Water cooling.

A one-dimensional stream excess temperature model predicts the decay of waste heat in natural streams for the so-called 'far region' of stream temperature analysis. The technique, which is most useful in situations where the waste heat is approximately well mixed laterally and vertically, may also be used to describe the distribution of other soluble contaminants. The computer program is based on a one-dimensional stream excess temperature model. A general surface exchange equation is used in the model. (Knapp-USGS)
W75-07883

ENVIRONMENTAL TRITIUM IN THE EDWARDS AQUIFER, CENTRAL TEXAS, 1963-71,
Geological Survey, Reston, Va.
F. J. Pearson, Jr., P. L. Rettman, and T. A. Wyerman.
Open-file report 74-362, January 1975. 32 p, 8 fig, 4 tab, 13 ref.

Descriptors: *Tritium, *Tracers, *Groundwater movement, *Texas, Aquifers, Hydrogeology, Hydrologic data.
Identifiers: *Edwards aquifer(Texas).

Tritium concentrations of samples from 50 wells and springs in the Edwards aquifer in the San Antonio area of Texas were analysed. Tritium now in the aquifer is partly natural tritium, but most is tritium produced by thermonuclear tests in the 1950's and early 1960's. The tritium levels in precipitation and streams recharging the Edwards were also determined for comparison with the groundwater data. In general, tritium distribution within the Edwards confirms the accepted pattern of water flow within the aquifer. Concentrations of greater than 20 tritium units occur in the recharge areas, while less than 1 tritium unit is present along the aquifer's southern and southeastern boundary. (Knapp-USGS)
W75-07885

NATURAL DISTRIBUTION OF TRACE METALS IN SEDIMENTS FROM A COASTAL ENVIRONMENT, TOR BAY, ENGLAND,
Imperial Chemical Industries Ltd., Brixham (England). Brixham Research Lab.
For primary bibliographic entry see Field 2L.
W75-07895

DISTRIBUTION OF MICROBIAL ADENOSINE TRIPHOSPHATE IN SALT MARSH SEDIMENTS AT SAPELO ISLAND, GEORGIA,
Georgia Univ., Athens. Dept. of Microbiology.
R. R. Christian, K. Bancroft, and W. J. Wiebe.
Soil Science, Vol 119, No 1, p 89-97, January 1975. 2 fig, 5 tab, 32 ref. NSF Grant GA-35793X.

Descriptors: *Sediments, *Salt marshes, *Biomass, Marsh plants, Coastal marshes, Aquatic environment, Soils, Soil chemical properties, Soil analysis, Soil chemistry, Sedimentology, Carbon, Nitrogen, Nutrients, *Georgia, *Path of pollutants.
Identifiers: Adenosine triphosphate, Sapelo Island(Geo).

The vertical distribution of microbial adenosine triphosphate (ATP) was determined seasonally for sediments of the salt marsh at Sapelo Island, Georgia. Two study areas were chosen representing major differences in productivity of the marsh grass, Spartina alterniflora. The streamside zone represented an area of greater production of S. alterniflora than did the high marsh zone. In all cases the concentration of ATP was greatest in the surface 1 cm and decreased with increasing depth. ATP varied seasonally in both regions. A comparison was made of the sediments organic carbon and total nitrogen within the sediments and the calculated carbon and nitrogen associated with the microbial community. The contribution of these elements within the microbial community was at most a few percent of the total pools. The surface sediment ATP values reported were within the range of those for water-logged sediments from various diverse environments. (Sims-ISWS)
W75-07899

SUBMERGED SOILS IN THE NORTHWESTERN MEDITERRANEAN SEA AND THE PROCESS OF HUMIFICATION,
Centre Universitaire de Perpignan, Moulin a Vent (France). Centre de Recherches de Sedimentologie Marine.
F. Gadel, G. Cahet, and A. J. M. Bianchi.
Soil Science, Vol 119, No 1, p 106-112, January 1975. 1 fig, 20 ref.

Descriptors: *Sediments, *Organic matter, *Lagoons, Sedimentology, Benthic fauna, Humic acids, Marine geology, Chemistry, Soils, Estuaries, Biology, Geochemistry, Geography, Soils, Oceans, Water pollution sources.
Identifiers: *Mediterranean Sea, France.

Detailed information was given on the analysis of accumulation and humification of organic material in marine and lagoonal sediments in various areas of the northwestern Mediterranean Sea. Typical geographic and hydrodynamical conditions such as the absence of tides, sudden climatic variations, and discharge of low-water rivers and strong floods govern the geological situation. In contrast to the coastal and lagoonal sediments, the sediments of the open sea are only slowly accumulating without a major contribution by deposition and humification of organic substances. Abundant biological activity directly influencing the geochemical situation in the sediment takes place only in lagoons (such as the Etang de St. Nazaire and the Bages-Sigean complex), and certain parts of the coastal zone (including the Bay of Port Vendres, the Gulf of Marseille, and the Banyuls region). Geochemical analysis on carbon content, sulfur compounds present, nitrogen content, and humus characterization, as well as biomass estimation and bacterial counts from the investigated areas, were reported. Major biopedological factors involved were found to be temperature, presence or absence of oxygen, activity of benthic organisms, and concentration of organic matter. With increasing depths of burial, the biogeochemical alterations were found to slow down. (Sims-ISWS)
W75-07900

THE DISTRIBUTION OF SALINITY AND TEMPERATURE IN THE CONNECTICUT RIVER ESTUARY,
Connecticut Univ., Groton. Dept. of Mechanical Engineering.
For primary bibliographic entry see Field 2L.
W75-07922

POND WATER QUALITY IN A CLAYPAN SOIL,
Illinois Univ., Urbana. Dept. of Agricultural Engineering.
E. C. Dickey, and J. K. Mitchell.
Transactions of the American Society of Agricultural Engineers, Vol 18, No 1, p 106-110, January-February 1975. 8 fig, 2 tab, 14 ref.

Descriptors: *Farm ponds, *Water quality, *Pollutants, Ponds, Water supply, Domestic water, Runoff, Vegetation, Bacteria, Nitrates, Ammonia, Nitrogen, Livestock, Sampling, On-site investigations, *Illinois.

A field inspection was made of Washington County, Illinois, ponds having three basic types of watersheds: (1) those containing ungrazed pasture or trees, (2) those having cultivated land, and (3) those consisting primarily of a livestock exercise area. Ten watersheds were selected for this study. Watershed types greatly influence the amount of nitrate nitrogen occurring in farm pond water. Grassed and cultivated watershed pond water reached a maximum nitrate nitrogen level of 2.84 mg/l. Ponds having livestock on the watershed exceeded the public health standard of 10 mg/l nitrate nitrogen with one pond reaching a maximum level of 22.0 mg/l on one occasion. Ponds having few nutrients applied in the form of animal wastes on the watershed reached maximum levels of nitrate during early spring. Ponds with dense livestock concentrations on the watershed reached maximum levels in late fall after intense runoff events. Pond water for human consumption would need some type of treatment for bacteria. Pond water is at present the most reliable source for drinking water for animals in Washington County. Farm ponds having grassed or cultivated watersheds could provide water of acceptable quality to replace existing high-nitrate wells or low-yielding wells. (Sims-ISWS)
W75-07924

WATER AND SALT TRANSFERS IN SUTTER BASIN, CALIFORNIA,
California Univ., Davis. Dept. of Water Science and Engineering.
K. K. Tanji, D. W. Henderson, S. K. Gupta, M. Iqbal, and A. F. Quek.
Transactions of the American Society of Agricultural Engineers, Vol 18, No 1, p 111-121, January-February 1975. 8 fig, 3 tab, 10 ref. UCAL W-438.

Descriptors: *Water transfer, *Surface-groundwater relationships, *Saline water intrusion, *Salt balance, *Hydrogeology, *Irrigation effects, Saline water-freshwater interfaces, Hydrology, Salinity, Irrigation, Water quality, Connate water, Geohydrologic units, Geology, *California, Model studies, Water table, Return flow.
Identifiers: *Sutter Basin(Calif), Crop root zone.

An analysis of water and salt transfers was conducted in Sutter Basin, California. The average drainage index for the hydrologic years 1964-1972 was estimated as 0.42 + or -0.08 and the average salt balance index for the hydrologic years 1970-1972 as 2.59 + or -1.25. For the 1970 hydrologic year, the flow-weighted average surface input of salts (precipitation and irrigation water) was 0.74 tons per ha-m and the surface output (return flow) was 5.08 tons per ha-m. About 40% of the water and 70% of the salt load in the return flow was estimated to have originated from subsurface origins, mainly rising connate water. (Terstriep-ISWS)
W75-07925

DETERMINING AMBIENT WATER TEMPERATURES,
Stone and Webster Engineering Corp., Boston, Mass. Environmental Engineering Div.
M. Markofsky, and R. C. Binkerd.
Journal of the Hydraulics Division, American Society of Civil Engineers, Vol 101, No HY3, Proceedings Paper 11171, p 361-366, March 1975. 2 fig, 1 tab, 1 append.

Descriptors: *Water quality control, *Water temperature, *Hydrography, *Powerplants, Heated water, Mixing, Solar radiation, Statistical methods, *Thermal pollution, Thermal water, Water pollution control, Water quality standards, Hydraulics, Regulation, Lakes, Estuaries.

Regulations concerning discharge of condenser cooling water from power plants frequently refer

to temperature rises above ambient temperature. Some ambiguities are attached to the definition of 'ambient' if both time and space factors for a given control region are not considered. A method to determine ambient temperature from statistical analysis of preoperational temperature records and the uncertainty of determining ambient temperature expressed in confidence limits was reviewed in regard to temperature criteria. Temporal and spatial variations in temperature records were examined. Data from an application to an estuary, including preoperational estimates and post operational measurements, were presented. (Harmeson-ISWS)
W75-07929

GROUND-WATER POLLUTION BY WOOD WASTE DISPOSAL,
Oregon State Engineer's Office, Salem.
H. R. Sweet, and R. H. Fetrow.
Ground Water, Vol 13, No 2, p 227-231, March-April 1975. 6 fig, 1 tab, 10 ref.

Descriptors: *Groundwater, *Water pollution, *Groundwater movement, *Unconsolidated aquifers, Malenclaves, Leachate, Industrial wastes, *Wood wastes, Lignins, *Oregon.
Identifiers: Mid-Willamette Valley, Lignin-tannins.

Timber production and wood products industries in the Mid-Willamette Valley of Oregon annually dispose of about 547,000 tons of wood and bark wastes. Land storage or disposal of these wastes can result in the generation of significant volumes of leachate. Wood waste leachates are commonly characterized by lignin-tannin (measured as tannic acid), oxygen demanding materials, color, and odor. In this study, lignin-tannin concentrations in the groundwater ranged as high as 7.5 mg/l; iron and manganese were also shown to increase markedly relative to natural background concentrations, ranging as high as 13 mg/l and 106 mg/l, respectively. In August 1972 the area affected by the contaminated groundwater covered about 4 acres and extended nearly 1000 feet downgradient from the disposal site. By late January 1973 the plume had migrated latterally to affect an area of about 15 acres while extending over 1500 feet downgradient. The lateral migration was attributed to a seasonal change in the local flow system. At least eleven existing domestic water-supply wells have been rendered nonpotable by this pollution. (Gibb-ISWS)
W75-07951

PROCEEDINGS OF THE SEMINAR ON ADVANCED WASTEWATER TREATMENT AND DISPOSAL,
Nassau-Suffolk Regional Planning Board, N. Y. Regional Marine Resources Council
For primary bibliographic entry see Field 5D.
W75-07954

THE LONG ISLAND WATER SITUATION,
Geological Survey, Mineola, N.Y. Water Resources Div.
P. Cohen.
In: Proceedings of the Seminar on Advanced Wastewater Treatment and Disposal, June 10, 1971 at Hauppauge, N.Y., p 5-17, (1972) 5 fig, 1 tab.

Descriptors: Groundwater, Areal hydrology, *Groundwater resources, *Saline water intrusion, *Natural recharge, *Water quality, Groundwater recharge, Glacial aquifers, Aquifer characteristics, Groundwater availability, Recharge, Water source, Water supply, Groundwater movement, Water table, Water level fluctuations, *New York.
Identifiers: *Long Island(NY), Nassau County(NY), Suffolk County(NY).

Rapid population growth to nearly 7 million, especially at the western end of 120-mile by 20-mile Long Island, has caused significant deterioration in both quality and quantity of groundwater resources. The Island has a tremedous groundwater supply, accumulated over centuries from the average annual precipitation of 44 inches. Water percolates into the glacial deposits of fine sand, silt, clay, and some coarse sand and gravel which underlie the island at an average rate of approximately 1 mgd (million gallons per day) square mile. It gradually flows down gradient from the central hills toward the edges of the island where fresh water in contact with salty groundwater forms a zone of diffusion. Lacation of this zone depends on the height of the water table above sea level and the rate of subsurface outflow of fresh water. Man has decreased the groundwater reservoir, causing salt water intrusion, by pumping and discharge of sewage water directly to tidewater. These developments, along with construction of impermeable surfaces which prevent aquifer recharge, accompany urbanization. Contamination has come from agriculture, industrial discharges, and the nearly one half million septic tanks. Synthetic detergents and increased quantities of nitrates are now found in drinking water. Increased sewering and decreasing agriculture will probably decrease pollution of the groundwater, although these gains may be partially offset by contamination from lawn fertilizers in suburban developments. (See also W75-07954) (Herr-North Carolina)
W75-07955

THE STATUS OF WASTEWATER TREATMENT ON LONG ISLAND, N.Y.
Suffolk County Dept. of Environmental Control, N.Y.
For primary bibliographic entry see Field 5D.
W75-07957

SPRINKLER IRRIGATION FOR LIQUID WASTE DISPOSAL,
Pennsylvania State Univ., University Park.
For primary bibliographic entry see Field 5D.
W75-07959

LOW WINTER DISSOLVED OXYGEN IN SOME ALASKAN RIVERS,
Environmental Protection Agency, Arctic Environmental Research Lab. College, Alaska.
E. W. Schallock, and F. B. Lotspeich.
For sale by the Superintendent of Documents, U.S. Government Printing Office, Washington, D.C. 20402 Price $0.85. Environmental Protection Agency, Report EPA-660/3-74-008, April 1974. 33 p, 11 fig, 3 tab, 36 ref.

Descriptors: *Dissolved oxygen, *Alaska, *Rivers, Winter, *Seasonal, Conductivity, Alkalinity, Hydrogen ion concentration, Water temperature, Water quality standards, Arctic, Subarctic, *Pollutant identification, *Water pollution sources.
Identifiers: Low dissolved oxygen, Yukon-River(Alas), Sagawanirktok River(Alas), Chena River(Alas).

Water samples collected during the years 1969 through 1972, from 36 selected Alaskan rivers were analyzed for dissolved oxygen, pH, conductivity and alkalinity. Dissolved oxygen (D.O.) ranged from 0.0 to 15.3 ml/l (106 percent saturation); pH from 6.2 to 8.4; conductivity varied from 105 to 3000 (umho/cm); and alkalinity from 28 to 410 (mg/l). Severe D.O. depletion during winter was found in many river systems large and small, and located in a range of latitudes (70 degrees N to 61 degrees N). Sufficient data were collected on the Chena, Chatanika, and Salcha Rivers to reveal annual D.O. trends: near saturation during spring 'breakup' and fall 'freezeup when water temperatures are near 0C; somewhat lower D.O. concentrations during warm water summer periods; and yearly minimum concentrations during the winter (January-March) interval. D.O. depression begins in October and continues into February. D.O. from stations near the mouth of a river were generally depressed more than at upper stations. The latter trend was observed in the Yukon River which contained 10.5 mg/l (73 percent saturation) at the Canadian Border but only 1.9 mg/l (13 percent) near the mouth. pH gradually decreased in some rivers although alkalinity and conductivity increased. The depressed winter D.O. concentrations and low winter discharge in many Alaskan rivers are more severe and widespread than present literature indicates. Winter conditions may already limit aquatic organisms in some systems. (EPA)
W75-07966

MICROBIAL DEGRADATION AND ACCUMULATION OF PESTICIDES IN AQUATIC SYSTEMS,
Environmental Protection Agency, Athens, Ga. Southeast Environmental Research Lab.
D. F. Paris, D. L. Lewis, J. T. Barnett, Jr., and G. L. Baughman.
Available from the National Technical Information Service, Springfield, Va. 22161, as PB-241 293, $4.25 in paper copy, $2.25 in microfiche. Report EPA-660/3-75-007, March 1975. 45 p, 9 fig, 5 tab, 55 ref. 1BA023.

Descriptors: *Biodegradation, *Sorption, *2,4-D, Aquatic microorganisms, Pesticide kinetics, *Pesticide residues, Hydrolysis, Metabolism, Bacteria, Fungi, *Microbial degradation, Water pollution sources, Water pollution effects.
Identifiers: *Malathion, *Methoxychlor, *Toxaphene, *Carbaryl.

The microbial degradation and sorption of carbaryl, malathion, butoxyethyl ester of 2,4-dichlorophenoxyacetic acid (2,4-DBE), methoxychlor, atrazine, diazinon, captan, parathion, and toxaphene were investigated. Malathion and 2,4-DBE were found to undergo transformation readily in both bacterial and fungal cultures. Degradation of malathion and 2,4-DBE at low concentrations (< 1 mg/l) in batch cultures of bacteria followed second-order kinetics as predicted by the Michaelis-Menten theory. A single isomer, beta-monoacid of malathion, was the primary metabolite in transformation of malathion by both bacterial and fungal populations. The major metabolite found in 2,4-DBE studies was 2,4-D. Carbaryl underwent chemical hydrolysis to alpha-naphthol in both heterogeneous bacterial cultures and uninoculated controls. In the cultures alpha-naphthol was metabolized to 1,4-naphthoquinone and two unidentified compounds. Bacterial degradation of methoxychlor was slower than bacterial degradation of malathion or 2,4-DBE. The insecticide was metabolized to methoxychlor-DDE. Rapid and extensive sorption of pesticides to fungi, bacteria, and algae was observed and methoxychlor and toxaphene, but not with any of the other pesticides investigated. Distribution coefficients for methoxychlor ranged from 1.2 x 1000 to 4.8 x 10,000 for the different organisms whereas the coefficients for toxaphene ranged from 3.4 x 1000 to 1.7 x 10,000. Captan underwent neither microbial degradation nor sorption because of its rapid hydrolysis in water. (EPA)
W75-07970

PHOSPHORUS UPTAKE AND RELEASE BY LAKE ONTERIO SEDIMENTS,
Wisconsin Univ., Madison. Water Chemistry Program; and Wisconsin Univ., Madison. Dept. of Soils.
For primary bibliographic entry see Field 5A.
W75-07972

CHANGE IN THE CHEMISTRY OF NATURAL WATERS IN LANDSCAPES UNDER AGRICULTURAL USE,
G. S. Shil'krot.

Soviety Hydrology, Selected Papers No 3, p 258-264, 1973, 2 tab, 26 ref. Translated from Izvestiya Akad, nauk SSSR, Ser geograf No 3, p 42-50, 1973.

Descriptors: *Water quality, *Drainage effects, *Water pollution sources, Agricultural chemicals, Fertilizers, Groundwater, Nitrogen, Phosphorus, Runoff, Precipitation(Atmospheric), Surface runoff, Surface waters, Soil water, Agricultural runoff, Chlorides, Sulfates, Carbonates.
Identifiers: *USSR.

Some characteristic changes in the chemical composition of groundwater and surface runoff and precipitation, produced by human activity and leading to an increase in the content of phosphorus and nitrogen compounds and also of chlorides and sulfates in the natural waters of landscapes under agricultural use, were investigated. The changing role of soils in the composition of natural waters as a result of intense chemical action of agriculture was analyzed along with the effect of domestic and industrial wastes. The content of nitrogen and phosphorus compounds increased in the surface runoff from fields after prolonged application of large amounts of mineral fertilizers. The nitrogen content increased sharply in groundwaters under plowed and fertilized fields. The mineral content of groundwaters increased sharply near populated points as did the content of chlorides, sulfates, and the concentration of biogenic substances. The content of nitrogen, phosphorus, and sulfur also increased in precipitation because of human activity; this resulted in an increased supply of individual chemicals to natural waters in areas remote from large populated areas. All these unfavorable changes in the chemical composition of natural waters demand a reduction of anthropogenic effects. Domestic and industrial wastes, in which the concentration of water pollutants is especially high, must be completely purified. As for agricultural return waters, their removal of nitrogen and phosphorus compounds from fertilized fields can be reduced by proper agricultural practices, i.e., soil cultivation, selection of crops under rotation, times of fertilizer application, etc., which reduce losses of fertilizers added to the soil. (Humphreys-ISWS)
W75-07974

GROUND-WATER QUALITY RELATED TO IRRIGATION WITH IMPORTED SURFACE OR LOCAL GROUND WATER,
Agricultural Research Service, Fresno, Calif.
H. I. Nightingal, and W. C. Bianchi.
Journal of Environmental Quality, Vol 3, No 4, October-December, 1974. p 356-361, 2 tab, 7 fig, 13 ref.

Descriptors: *Imported water, *Irrigation water, *Groundwater, Surface waters, *Arid lands, *Irrigation, *Water quality, Irrigation wells, Electrical conductance, Chlorine, Nitrates, Salinity, Sampling, Statistical methods, Water reuse, Irrigation canals, Water sources.

Groundwater quality in an arid irrigated area that imports high quality surface water was compared with an adjacent up-gradient area that uses local pumped groundwater. Intensive sampling of the groundwater in irrigation and domestic wells done in fall, 1972, showed that the electrical conductivity, NO3- and Cl- concentrations had not significantly changed since 1967. Results of nonparametric statistical tests show that continued use of local groundwater for irrigation has resulted in electrical conductivity, NO3- and Cl- concentrations 9.5, 18.6, and 91.8 percent higher, respectively, than the area using mostly high quality surface water for irrigation. Areas of higher groundwater NO3- and Cl- were generally related to soil drainge-recharge and agricultural use . The use of supplemental surface water supplies will be necessary to reduce increases in electrical conductivity, NO3-, and Cl- concentrations caused by the exclusive use of low quality local groundwater (Mastic-Arizona)
W75-07978

WINTER-REGIME SURFACE HEAT LOSS FROM HEATED STREAMS,
Iowa Univ., Iowa City. Inst. of Hydraulic Research.
P. P. Paily, E. O. Macagno, and J. F. Kennedy.
Available from the National Technical Information Service, Springfield, Va 22161 as PB-241 941, $6.25 in paper copy, $2.25 in microfiche. ITHR Report No 155, March 1974. 137 p, 23 fig, 18 tab, 207 ref, 1 append. OWRT B-018-IA(3).

Descriptors: *Evaporation, *Solar radiation, *Radiation, *Heat flow, *Air-water interfaces, Equations, *Thermal pollution, Heat, Winter, Climatic data, Humidity, Model studies, Heat transfer, Streams.
Identifiers: Empirical analysis.

Evaluation of the rate of surface heat exchange between the water and air has become very significant because of the need to determine the thermal response of streams to heat inputs. The different mechanisms of heat exchange that contribute to the total heat exchange were discussed and the various empirical formulas to compute each of the components, as developed by various investigators, were presented and discussed. The suitability of each empirical formula was examined. The methods to linearize the total heat exchange rate were reviewed and a new linearized relation was proposed. General equations, suitable for winter-regime conditions, were presented to compute the coefficients of the linearized heat loss model. (Adams-ISWS)
W75-07990

MODEL DEVELOPMENT AND SYSTEMS ANALYSIS OF THE YAKIMA RIVER BASIN: WATER QUALITY MODELING,
Washington State Univ., Pullman. Dept. of Civil Engineering.
W. B. Betchart.
Available from the National Technical Information Service, Springfield, Va. 22161, as PB-241 940, $4.25 in paper copy, $2.25 in microfiche. Washington Water Research Center, Pullman, Report No 17D, November 1974. 50 p, 3 fig, 6 tab, 15 ref. OWRT B-036-WASH(5), B-043-WASH(5), B-050-WASH(5).

Descriptors: *Model studies, Systems analysis, Watershed management, River basin development, Water quality, *Mathematical models, Water resources, Planning, Dissolved oxygen, Temperature, *Washington.
Identifiers: *Yakima River basin(Wash), *Water quality models.

A study of water quality modeling as a planning tool has been conducted with specific reference to the Yakima River in central Washington. Four different water quality models have been developed for use in planning of the Yakima Water Quality. Each model permits progressively more parameters to describe river water quality. Available data were found to be the limiting factor in model development and calibration. A particularly important limitation was precise data on the hydraulic characteristics of the river at various specific low flows. Two general types of use for models have been identified: (1) as a description of a real world situation or expected situation which constitutes a water quality problem (problem definition) or (2) to predict the results of a possible problem-solving action. These models indicate relative rather than absolute response of water quality to various action unless the extensive input data requirements can be satisfied. Each of the four models is applied to the Yakima in the problem definition mode and their strengths and weaknesses in this use are assessed. A general strategy for obtaining and using such models is also described.
W75-07995

OPTIMAL COST DESIGN OF BRANCHED SEWER SYSTEMS,
Illinois Univ., Urbana. Dept. of Civil Engineering.
For primary bibliographic entry see Field 5D.
W75-07999

WATER QUALITY CONTROL BY ARTIFICIAL AERATION OF STREAM RECEIVING THERMAL AND ORGANIC WASTE DISCHARGES,
Kansas State Univ., Manhattan. Inst. for Systems Design and Optimization.
For primary bibliographic entry see Field 5G.
W75-08005

DIGITAL SIMULATION OF THE EFFECT OF THERMAL DISCHARGE ON STREAM WATER QUALITY,
Kansas State Univ., Manhattan. Inst. for Systems Design and Optimization.
S. H. Lin, L. T. Fan, and C. L. Hwang.
Water Resources Bulletin, Vol 9, No 4, p 689-702, August 1973. 9 fig, 1 tab, 11 ref. OWRT-B-030-KAN(2).

Descriptors: *Water quality control, Streams, *Thermal pollution, *Simulation analysis, *Dissolved oxygen demand, Effects, Digital computers, Powerplants, Water temperature, Upstream, Downstream, Velocity, Equations, Systems analysis, Mathematical models.
Identifiers: *Streeter-Phelps model, Waste heat discharge, Energy balance equation, Method of characteristics, Heated cooling water, Heat loss.

A modified tansient version of the Streeter-Phelps model along with the energy balance equation is employed to analyze the effects of waste heat discharge from power plants on the concentration distributions of BOD and DO along a stream. Also examined are the effects of the upstream water quality and stream velocity on the downstream DO concentration level. The resulting coupled non-linear hyperbolic partial differential equations representing the energy, BOD, and DO concentrations are solved by the method of characteristics and simulated on a digital computer. Results indicate that increased biochemical reaction rate and decreased reaeration and photosynthetic rates at a high temperature contribute significantly to the DO deficit. The upstream condition is an important factor in determining the allowable thermal discharge from a power plant. (Bell-Cornell)
W75-08006

A STUDY OF CONVECTIVE-DISPERSION EQUATION BY ISOPARAMETRIC FINITE ELEMENTS,
State Univ. of New York, Buffalo. Faculty of Engineering and Applied Sciences.
M-S. Wang, and R. T. Cheng.
Journal of Hydrology, Vol 24, No 1-2, p 45-56, January 1975. 9 fig, 20 ref. OWRT C-4026(No 9006)(3), 14-31-0001-9006.

Descriptors: *Path of pollutants, *Groundwater movement, *Convection, *Dispersion, *Mathematical models, Finite element analysis, Water pollution control, Mixing.
Identifiers: Convective-dispersion equation.

The transport of pollutants in groundwater aquifers was studied by means of a mathematical model. The governing equation for the movement of impurities takes the form of a convective-dispersion equation which is solved numerically using isoparametric, quadrilateral finite element method. The mixed boundary conditions and irregular distribution of the nodes can be handled easily by the finite element technique. The numerical model can be used as a means to predict the distribution of contaminants and to plan pollution control. (Knapp-USGS)
W75-08009

PHYTOPLANKTON CONCENTRATIONS IN THE MALAMOCCO CHANNEL OF THE LAGOON OF VENICE,
Istituto di Biologia del Mare, Venice (Italy).

For primary bibliographic entry see Field 5C.
W75-08063

CLEAN ENVIRONMENT FOR ULTRATRACE ANALYSIS,
Baker (J.T.) Chemical Co., Phillipsburg, N.J. Research Labs.
For primary bibliographic entry see Field 5A.
W75-08078

A PRELIMINARY APPROACH TO THE USE OF THE ISOTOPIC RATIO 13C/12C FOR THE EVALUATION OF MINERALIZATION IN AQUATIC ENVIRONMENTS,
Istituto Italiano di Idrobiologia, Pallanza.
R. Bertoni, U. Melchiorri-Santolini, R. Letolle, M. Lugrin, and P. Olive.
Int Rev Gesamten Hydrobiol, Vol 59, No 1, p 65-68, 1974.
Identifiers: Aquatic environment, Carbon-12, Carbon-13, *Isotopic carbon, Microbes, *Mineralization, *Traces, *Pelagic bacteria, *Bacteria, Organic matter.

The ratio 12C/13C is used as natural tracer for the estimation of the mineralizing acitivity of pelagic bacteria. Attention is particularly given to the variations of the isotopic ratio of the inorganic C produced by the microbial oxidation in comparison with ratio of the dissolved organic matter.-Copyright 1974, Biological Abstracts, Inc.
W75-08090

HEAD HAIR SAMPLES AS INDICATORS OF ENVIRONMENTAL POLLUTION,
University Coll., Cork (Ireland).
For primary bibliographic entry see Field 5A.
W75-08092

ON THE CHEMICAL MASS-BALANCE IN ESTUARIES,
Massachusetts Inst. of Tech., Cambridge, Mass. Dept. of Earth and Planetary Sciences.
E. Boyle, R. Collier, A. T. Dengler, J. M. Edmond, and A. C. Ng.
Geochemica et Cosmochimica Acta, Vol 38, p 1719-1728, 1974, 2 tab, 2 fig, 26 ref.

Descriptors: *Model studies, *Iron, *Heavy metals, *Estuaries, *Chemicals, Rivers, River-flow, Silica, Reviews, River basin, Oceans, *Mixing, Dissolved solids, Salinity, Eddies, Sea water, Tributaries.
Identifiers: *Chemical mass-balance, Concentration gradients, Diffusion gradients, Sea salt, Diffusive flux, Coastal seawater.

A general model is presented for mixing processes between river and ocean water in which are established criteria for the identification of any non-conservative behavior of the dissolved constituents involved. A review of previous data shows that in no case has removal of silica been demonstrated unambiguously in estuarine regimes. New data for iron which show highly non-conservative behavior are used in an example of the application of the model. (Delfiner-Vanderbilt)
W75-08095

SOLUBILIZATION OF DIMETHYLMERCURY BY HALIDE IONS,
Missouri Univ., Rolla. Dept. of Chemistry.
L. E. Smith, and G. L. Bertrand.
Environmental Letters, Vol 4, p 273-279, 1973. 2 tab, 2 ref. OWRR A-045-MO(2).

Descriptors: *Mercury, *Solubility, Aqueous solutions, *Electrolytes, Organic compounds, Ions, Laboratory tests, Analytical techniques, Chemical reactions, Spectroscopy, *Pollutant identification.
Identifiers: *Methylmercury, *Atomic absorption analysis.

The solubility of dimethylmercury in water and aqueous electrolyte solutions at 25C was investigated with flameless atomic absorption analysis. Solubility was determined as the total concentration of all forms of mercury in an aqueous phase which results from prolonged contact with an excess amount of dimethylmercury. No attempt was made to differentiate between the various chemical states of mercury which might exist in the aqueous phase, nor to analyze the denser liquid phase composed primarily of dimethylmercury. The solubility in water (4 ppm) was generally decreased by addition of electrolyte, except in the case of halides, with which the solubility was greatly increased. (Jernigan-Vanderbilt)
W75-08096

RADIATION INDUCED THERMAL STRATIFICATION IN SURFACE LAYERS OF STAGNANT WATER,
Purdue Univ., Lafayette, Ind. School of Mechanical Engineering.
For primary bibliographic entry see Field 2H.
W75-08098

INTEGRATING CHEMICAL FACTORS WITH WATER AND SEDIMENT TRANSPORT FROM A WATERSHED,
Agricultural Research Service, Chickasha, Okla.
M. H. Frere.
Journal of Environmental Quality, Vol 4, No 2, p 12-17, Jan-Mar 1975. 3 fig, 3 tab, 18 ref.

Descriptors: *Mathematical models, *Water pollution sources, Sediment transport, Agricultural runoff, *Path of pollutants, Chemicals, Pesticides, Leaching, Soil erosion, Nutrients, Watershed management, Model studies.

A mathematical model that calculates the movement of a chemical as it is transported through or off of an agricultural watershed is described. Loss of the chemical between storms by degradation or volatilization is described by a first-order rate equation. Simple chromatographic theory is used to describe the chemical distribution in the soil during leaching, assuming a linear adsorption relation and dispersion that is proportional to the square root of the distance moved. The concentration at the surface during the storm is calculated to estimate the amounts lost in runoff water and with interrill erosion. It is assumed that rill erosion removes the chemical in proportion to the fraction of the area in rills and to the fraction of the chemical distribution in the soil intercepted by the rills. Mineralization and uptake are an additional source and sink for nitrate between storms. Lithium bromide movement on a microplot was used to examine some features of the model. (ARS)
W75-08099

RECREATION USES CHANGE MOGOLLON RIM ECONOMY,
Forest Service (USDA), Tucson, Ariz. Rocky Mountain Forest and Range Experiment Station; and Arizona Univ., Tucson.
For primary bibliographic entry see Field 6B.
W75-08108

WATER POLLUTION BY TANNERY WASTES: THE POSSIBLE CAUSES OF MASS KILLING OF FISH AT MOSUL, IRAQ,
Mosul Univ. (Iraq). Dept. of Biology.
S. A. Rahim, A. N. Bhatnagar, A. N. Memon, and A. Alsarau.
Mesopotamia Journal of Agriculture, Vol 8, No 2, p 211-218, 1973. 3 tab, 1 map, 3 ref.

Descriptors: *Water pollution, *Fishkill, *Tannery wastes, Water pollution treatment, Water pollution sources, *Water pollution effects, Sulfur compounds, Dissolved solids, Killifishes, *Industrial wastes.
Identifiers: *Iraq, Orophon, Papain.

Tannery wastes discharged into the Tigris River near Mosul, Iraq, were determined to be the cause of a massive fish kill in the summer of 1972, following a team investigation into circumstances associated with the event. Analyses of water samples, sulfur compounds, dissolved oxygen, and toxic elements established that the sulfur compounds contributed most directly to the fishkill. In addition, the use of Orophon by the tanneries for treatment of animals skins may have been a factor, inasmuch as it has proved lethal on an experimental basis, although the exact nature of its physiological action is not known. The soluble sulphites appear to be the major cause, leading to a recommendation that the tanneries undertake certain chemical treatments to remove these substances which play such an important role in the depletion of dissolved oxygen. (Bowden-Arizona)
W75-08110

DENITRIFICATION IN LABORATORY SANDY COLUMNS,
Soil Conservation Service, Effingham, Ill.
L. A. Davenport, Jr., W. D. Lembke, and B. A. Jones, Jr.
Transactions of the ASAE American Society of Agricultural, Vol 18, No 1, p 95-105, January-February 1975. 8 fig, 2 tab, 12 ref. OWRT A-044-ILL(2).

Descriptors: *Denitrification, *Laboratory tests, *Soil water movement, *Groundwater, Water analysis, Chemical reactions, Nitrates, Model studies, Hydraulic models, Subsurface waters, Confined water, Tile drains, Nutrient removal, Moisture content.
Identifiers: Sand columns, *Substrate effects, *Methanol, Breakthrough curves, Gas production.

Nitrate was effectively reduced when methanol was added as a substrate material to a slowly moving solution in porous columns. Applied nitrate was removed at a rate of 87.4% during 24 days at 24C and 62% during 27 days at 13C. The use of sawdust as an oxidizable material had little effect upon nitrate removal. The flux was maintained at approximately 0.23 cm/hr. The production of gases which accompanied the denitrification process desaturated the methanol columns and influenced the flow rate. The breakthrough curves observed indicated that there may have been significantly different effective diffusion coefficient for nitrate as compared with chloride. The passage of nitrate and chloride through the columns was accompanied by an increase in redox potential and, in some cases, a discoloration of the effluent. The removal of a high percentage of nitrate at relatively large pore velocities was encouraging for the prospect of removing excess nitrate from soil water in the vicinity of tile drains. While a technique was not described, it could involve a system for water table control with additions of substrate material introduced by surface application or deep plowing. (Prickett-ISWS)
W75-08189

PREDICTING VERTICAL MOVEMENT OF MANURIAL NITROGEN IN SOIL,
Cornell Univ., Ithaca, N.Y. Dept. of Agricultural Engineering.
M. F. Walter, G. D. Bubenzer, and J. C. Converse.
Transactions of the American Society of Agricultural Engineers, Vol 18, No 1, p 100-105, January-February 1975. 10 fig, 4 tab, 14 ref. OWRT B-076-WIS(2).

Descriptors: *Farm wastes, *Soil water movement, *Nitrates, *Leachate, *Mathematical models, Water pollution sources, Feed lots, Groundwater, Denitrification, Soil temperature, Soil-water-plant relationships, Ammonium compounds, Equations, Solutes, Laboratory tests, Computer models, *Path of pollutants.
Identifiers: *Manure storage, Nitrate accumulation, *Nitrate transport, Solute movement.

A quantitative computer model to predict the vertical nitrate distribution in soil resulting from heavy land applications of anaerobic liquid dairy manure applied to a coarse textured soil was developed. The model predicted net nitrogen transformations to nitrate as a function of temperature. Nitrate movement was based on predicted one-dimensional unsaturated flow and solute dispersion. Dispersion was assumed dependent on solute displacement but not on soil water velocity. Parameters used in the model were developed for (1) soil with a deep water table, (2) soil temperatures of 0 to 20C, and (3) soil matric potentials of 0 to -0.3 bars. (Prickett-ISWS)
W75-08192

RUNOFF FROM AN INTERTIDAL MARSH DURING TIDAL EXPOSURE - RECESSION CURVES AND CHEMICAL CHARACTERISTICS,
South Carolina Univ., Columbia. Belle W. Baruch Coastal Research Inst.
For primary bibliographic entry see Field 2L.
W75-08193

A GALERKIN-FINITE ELEMENT TECHNIQUE FOR CALCULATING THE TRANSIENT POSITION OF THE SALTWATER FRONT,
Princeton Univ., N.J. Dept. of Civil and Geological Engineering.
G. Segol, G. F. Pinder, and W. G. Gray.
Water Resources Research, Vol 11, No 2, p 343-347, April 1975. 7 fig, 13 ref. OWRT C-5224(No 4214)(1).

Descriptors: *Saline water intrusion, *Groundwater movement, *Finite element analysis, *Mathematical models, Simulation analysis, Mass transfer, Path of pollutants, Convection, Mixing.
Identifiers: *Galerkin method.

The set of nonlinear partial differential equations that describe the movement of the saltwater front in a coastal aquifer may be solved by the Galerkin-finite element method. Pressure and velocities are obtained simultaneously in order to guarantee continuity of velocities between elements. A layered aquifer may be modeled either with a functional representation of permeability or by a constant value of permeability over each element. (Knapp-USGS)
W75-08195

SEASONAL VARIATION IN SOME PHYSICAL, CHEMICAL, AND MICROBIOLOGICAL CHARACTERISTICS OF A SALINE AND A NON-SALINE SOIL NEAR ABU-GHRAIB, IRAQ,
Foundation of Scientific Research, Baghdad (Iraq).
For primary bibliographic entry see Field 2G.
W75-08199

THE CONTRIBUTION OF AGRICULTURE TO EUTROPHICATION OF SWISS WATERS: II. EFFECT OF FERTILIZATION AND SOIL USE ON THE AMOUNT OF NITROGEN AND PHOSPHOROUS IN THE WATER,
Eidgenoessische Forschungsanstalt fuer Agrikulturchemie, Bern.
For primary bibliographic entry see Field 5C.
W75-08200

THE BACTERIOLOGICAL CONDITIONS OF SOME BELGIAN BEACHES (IN FRENCH),
Institut Royal des Sciences Naturelles de Belgique, Brussels.
Z. Dartevelle.
Bull Inst R Sci Nat Belg Biol. Vol 49, No 2, p 1-27, 1973, Illus.

Descriptors: Europe, *Beaches, *Water pollution, *Bacteria, Microorganisms, *Coliforms, E. coli, *Public health.
Identifiers: Salmonella-paratyphi, Shigella, *Belgium.

The contamination of certain Belgian beaches and of the Nieuwpoort Channel with coliforms and Escherichia coli was studied to determine the effects of the season of the year, tides, human or animal presence and effluent discharge on the contamination level. The mean concentration of coliform bacteria was significantly higher in summer than in the spring. High or low tide did not affect the concentration of bacteria, and the exposed beach zone occupied by vacationers was as polluted as the intertidal zone. The discharge of coliforms by sewers was considerable. The only pathogenic organism detected was Salmonella paratyphi B; Shigella was not identified in spite of the presence of shigaphages.--Copyright 1974, Biological Abstracts, Inc.
W75-08224

DETECTION OF SHIGELLA IN WATERS USING AN IMMUNOFLUORESCENCE TECHNIQUE AND THE IMMUNO-INDIA-INK REACTION (GECK REACTION), (IN FRENCH),
Institute of Hygiene and Epidemiology, Hanoi (North Vietnam).
For primary bibliographic entry see Field 5A.
W75-08244

METHEMOGLOBIN LEVELS IN INFANTS IN AN AREA WITH HIGH NITRATE WATER SUPPLY,
California State Dept. of Public Health, Sacramento.
For primary bibliographic entry see Field 5C.
W75-08256

BENTHIC DIATOMS AS INDICATORS OF MINING POLLUTION IN THE NORTH WEST MIRAMICHI RIVER SYSTEM, NEW BRUNSWICK, CANADA,
Fisheries Research Board of Canada, St. Andrews (New Brunswick). Biological Station.
W. K, Besch, M. Ricard, and R. Cantin.
Int Rev Gesamten Hydrobiol, Vol 57, No 1, p 39-74, 1972. Illus.
Identifiers: *Canada(Miramichi River NB), *Diatoms, Indicators, Mining pollution, Miramichi, *Acid mine wastes, *Benthos, *Bioindicators, Heavy metals.

Effects of acid heavy metal mining pollution on diatom communities from polyethylene and natural substrata were studied in a river system free of any other kind of pollution. a total of 169 species was recorded, many of them for the 1st time from the Atlantic provinces of Canada. Diatom communities were reliable indicators of the average pH. The presence of heavy metals is shown not by indicator species byt by the dominance of species of a corresponding tolerance with the simultaneous lack of less tolerant forms. A preliminary indicator system is proposed for this sort of pollution.--Copyright 1973, Biological Abstracts, Inc.
W75-08259

NEMATODES FOUND IN TAP WATER FROM DIFFERENT LOCALITIES IN PUERTO RICO,
Puerto Rico Univ., Rio Piedras. Dept. of Entomology.
J. Roman, and X. Rivas.
J Agric Univ PR, Vol 56, No 2, p 187-191, 1972.
Identifiers: *Nematodes, Plant parasites, *Puerto Rico, *Potable water, Water supply.

A total of 17 genera of known and suspected plant parasitic nematodes and 14 genera of free-living and particulate feeders were found in 12 localities. Presence of the nematodes presents a source of contamination for experiments and could interfere

sity guidelines, pretreatment regulations for industry, control of heavy metal pollution and control of oil, grease and phenols discharged to the Missouri River. (Katz)
W75-08307

ICHTHYOFAUNA OF THE TYSMIENICA AND WLODAWKA RIVER BASINS, (IN POLISH),
Akademia Wychowania Fizycznego, Warsaw (Poland). Zaklad Nauk Biomedycznej.
For primary bibliographic entry see Field 2H.
W75-08310

SOME ENZYME AND RESPIRATORY ACTIVITIES OF TROPICAL SOILS FROM NEW HEBRIDES,
Department of Scientific and Industrial Research, Lower Hutt (New Zealand). Soil Bureau.
For primary bibliographic entry see Field 2G.
W75-08316

MOVEMENT AND PERSISTENCE OF BENSULIDE AND TRIFLURALIN IN IRRIGATED SOIL,
Agricultural Research Service, Weslaco, Tex. Lower Rio Grande Valley Research and Extension Center.
R. M. Menges, and S. Tamez.
Weed Sci, Vol 22, No 1, p 67-71, 1974, Illus.

Descriptors: *Irrigated soil, *Pesticide kinetics, Herbicides, Sorghum, *Path of pollutants.
Identifiers: *Bensulide, *Trifluralin.

Bensulide (0,0-diisopropyl phosphorodithioate S-ester with N-(2-mercaptoethyl)benzenesulfonamide) and trifluralin (a,a,a-trifluoro-2,6-dinitro-N,N-dipropyl-p-toluidine) were incorporated to a depth of 2.5 and 7.5 cm in sandy loam soil on the same plots in 3 annual applications to study the effect of incorporation depth on movement and persistence of the herbicides in furrow-irrigated soil. Bioassays and gas-liquid chromatographic assays indicated that, regardless of rainfall, both herbicides remained within the original soil zones of incorporation. Trifluralin persisted longer in soil as depth of incorporation was increased. Neither bensulide at 4.5 or 9.0 kg/ha nor trifluralin at 1.1 kg/ha persisted in appreciable amounts of 12 mo. after treatment. At these rates, significant residues of bensulide and trifluralin were detected after 6 mo. only when tillage was restricted. Herbicide concentrations that persisted 6 mo. as determined in laboratory assays caused severe reduction in growth of field-grown sorghum (Sorghum bicolor (L.) Moench).--Copyright 1974, Biological Abstracts, Inc.
W75-08318

THE BREACH IN THE FLOW OF MINERAL NUTRIENTS,
G. Borgstrom.
Ambio, Vol 2, No 5, p 129-135, 1973, Illus.

Descriptors: *Ecosystems, *Urbanization, Effeets, Fertilizers, *Nutrients, *Minerals, Sewage effluents, Water pollution, Nitrogen, Phosphates, Industrial effluents, Waste disposal, Waste water disposal.

The urban ecosystem is analyzed as affected by the increasing urban congestion. Attention is focused on 1 key feature, the breach in the cycling of mineral nutrients via food. As no device was adequate to bridge this gap the fertilizer industry became the logical response. No corresponding countermeasure has been taken to tackle the sewage accumulation with the concomitant water pollution, which is further aggravated by this repeat fertilizing. Compounding this effect is: the increasing outtake of water, reducing the volume of lakes, rivers and similar recipients; and the separation of plant and animal production (accumulation of manure). Factors that have been instrumental in making the N and phosphate loads excessive are discussed. City sewage and waste disposal system for food and pulp factories urgently need to be transformed into food and feed raising centers, supplementary to conventional agriculture and fisheries.--Copyright 1974, Biological Abstracts, Inc.
W75-08319

URBANIZATION AND THE MICROBIAL CONTENT OF THE NORTH SASKATCHEWAN RIVER,
Alberta Univ., Edmonton. Dept. of Microbiology.
For primary bibliographic entry see Field 5C.
W75-08329

RETENTIOS AND RELEASE OF PHOSPHORUS IN CERTAIN CALCAREOUS SOILS OF THE U.A.R. (UNITED ARAB REPUBLIC): I. THE INFLUENCE OF INCUBATION PROCESS AND CYCLES OF WETTING AND DRYING,
Ain Shams Univ, Cairo (Egypt). Dept. of Soils.
A. H. El-Damaty, A. E. E-Leboudi, and H. Hamdi.
U A R J Soil Sci. Vol 11, No 1, p 89-97, 1971, Illus.

Descriptors: *Calcareous soils, *Phosphorus, Soils, *Soil chemical properties, *Soil physical properties, *Alluvial soils, Wetting, Drying.
Identifiers: *United Arab Republic, Wetting-drying cycles.

Available P was found to decrease, opposite to its retention percentage, with the increase of either the period of incubation or the number of wetting and drying cycles in the soil. However, wetting and drying processes had a more pronounced effeet than that of incubation, soils of alluvial nature being more affected than those of calcareous origin. Values representing the percentages of retention within the soil samples were lower, opposite to those of available P, as the amounts of applied phosphates were higher.--Copyright 1973, Biological Abstracts, Inc.
W75-08350

5C. Effects Of Pollution

FATE AND EFFECTS OF TRACE ELEMENTS IN SEWAGE SLUDGE WHEN APPLIED TO AGRICULTURAL LANDS,
California Univ., Riverside. Dept. of Soil Science and Agricultural Engineering.
For primary bibliographic entry see Field 5B.
W75-07852

EFFECTS OF SEA WATER EXTRACTS OF SEDIMENTS FROM CHARLESTON HARBOR, S.C., ON LARVAL ESTUARINE FISHES,
National Marine Fisheries Service, Beaufort, N.C. Atlantic Estuarine Fisheries Center.
D. E. Hoss, L. C. Coston, and W. E. Schaaf.
Estuarine and Coastal Marine Science, Vol 2, No 4, p 323-328, October 1974. 1 fig, 4 tab, 14 ref. Army Contract DACW60-71-C-0011.

Descriptors: *Sediments, *Water pollution effeets, *Fishkill, Laboratory tests, Estuaries, Dredging, Spoil banks, Waste disposal, Mortality, Fish toxins, Larvae, Larval growth stage, Estuarine environment, Estuarine fisheries, *South Carolina.
Identifiers: Charleston Harbon(SC), Cooper River(SC).

Larvae of seven species of estuarine fishes (Atlantic menhaden, Brevoortia tyrranus; pinfish, Lagodon rhomboides; flounder, Paralichthys dentatus, P. albigutta, P. lethostigma; spot, Leiostomus xanthurus; and Atlantic croaker, Micropogon undulatus) were exposed to sea water extracts of sediments from Charleston Harbor, South Carolina, for periods of time up to 14 days. Survival of the larvae in various concentrations of

the extracts was measured. Survival of the larvae was affected at the highest concentrations of extract tested and indications are that different species of fish have different survival rates. In the selection of disposal areas for dredged material, consideration should be given to its relative toxicity to organisms. (Sims-ISWS)
W75-07893

A METHOD FOR THE STEPWISE ENRICHMENT FOR THE DEMONSTRATION OF SALMONELLA IN FRESH AND SALT WATER, (IN GERMAN),
For primary bibliographic entry see Field 5A.
W75-07928

CONTRIBUTIONS TO THE STUDY OF THE ALGAL FLORA OF ALGERIA. III. HYDROBIOLOGY OF CHOTT EL HODNA: AUTOECOLOGY OF THE DIATOMS,
Algiers Univ. (Algeria). Laboratoire de Botanique.
R. Baudrimont.
Bull Soc Hist Nat Afr Nord, Vol 62, No 3/4, p 39-49, 1971, Illus.
Identifiers: Algal flora, *Algeria(Chott el Hodna), Carbonates, Chlorides, *Diatoms, Ecology, Hydrobiology, *Sulfates, *Artesian wells, *Alkalinity, Bicarbonates, Halobios, Anions.

Artesian well waters of the western zone of Chott et Hodna are alkaline, beta-mesohaline, rich in sulfates and bicarbonates and low in chlorides. A study of the diatoms has resulted in a characterization of species associated with these different anions, and a definition of their position in the halobios. (See also W73-10399)--Copyright 1973, Biological Abstracts, Inc.
W75-07936

CLADOPHORA DISTRIBUTION IN LAKE ONTARIO (IFYGL),
Environmental Research Inst. of Michigan, Ann Arbor.
C. T. Wezernak, D. R. Lyzenga, and F. C. Polcyn.
Available from the National Technical Information Service, Springfield Va. 22161, as PB-240 307, $4.75 in paper copy, $2.25 in microfiche. Environmental Protection Agency, Grosse Ile, Michigan, Report EPA-660/3-74-028, December 1974. 76 p, 54 fig, 8 tab, 5 ref. 1B1026, 800778.

Descriptors: *Cladophora, *Distribution, Lakes, *Remote sensing, Great Lakes, *Lake Ontario, Standing crops, Eutrophication, Growth rates, Temperature, Thermal pollution, Water pollution effects.

Multispectral remote sensing data were collected along the U.S. shoreline of Lake Ontario, under the sponsorship of the Environmental Protection Agency, as part of the International Field Year on the Great Lakes (IFYGL) program in Lake Ontario. Data were processed to show the distribution of Cladophora in the nearshore zone and to estimate the standing crop. Additionally, thermal data in the study area were displayed. The results show an extensive growth and development of Cladophora in the study area. Approximately 66% of the nearshore zone in the western portion of the lake and 79% in the eastern portion is covered by Cladophora. Several major and minor thermal features and thermal discharges were evident at several locations along the U.S. shoreline. (EPA)
W75-07968

MICROBIAL DEGRADATION AND ACCUMULATION OF PESTICIDES IN AQUATIC SYSTEMS,
Environmental Protection Agency, Athens, Ga. Southeast Environmental Research Lab.
For primary bibliographic entry see Field 5B.
W75-07970

EFFECTS OF MIREX AND HMETHOXYCHLOR ON STRIPED MULLET, MUGIL CEPHALUS L.,
Oceanic Inst., Waimanalo, Hawaii.
J. H. Lee, C. E. Nash, and J. R. Sylvester.
Available from the National Technical Information Service, Springfield, Va 22161 as PB-241 635, $3.75 in paper copy, $2.25 in microfiche. Environmental Protection Agency, Gulf Breeze, Florida, Report EPA-660/3-75-015, May 1975. 18 p, 10 tab, 29 ref. OI-120. 1EA077. R802348.

Descriptors: *Chlorinated hydrocarbon pesticides, Mortality, Pesticide toxicity, Bioassay, Pesticide residues, Water pollution effects, Fish, *Mullets Fiskill, Fish eggs, Pollutant identification.
Identifiers: *Mirex, *Methoxychlor, Larval survival(Mullet), Striped mullet.

The effects of two chlorinated insecticides, mirex and methoxychlor, on striped mullet, Mugil cephalus L., were studied. Test concentrations of both insecticides used were 0.01, 0.1, 1.0 and 10.0 ppm in dynamic bioassay. Young juveniles were more susceptible to mirex exposure than older juveniles or adults. No mortalities occurred in older juveniles and adults exposed to mirex for 96 hours. For young juveniles, mortalities were highest in concentrations of 0.1 and 1.0 ppm and were less in concentrations of 0.01 and 10.0 ppm. Significant amounts of mirex residues were accumulated in the body tissues of the test fish; concentrations increased with increased environmental concentrations. Methoxychlor was more toxic to mullet than mirex. Mortalities were greater than 90 percent over a 96-hour period for all life stages studied at concentrations of 0.1, 1.0 and 10.0 ppm. Mortality at a concentration of 0.01 was 5.1 percent or less for 96 hours. Relative to mirex, small amounts of methoxychlor residues accumulated in the tissues of the test fish. Results of the experiments on eggs and larvae were inconclusive. Egg survival was slightly better in mirex than in methoxychlor over a 96-hour period. Larval survival was generally better in mirex than methoxychlor. (EPA)
W75-07973

DEVELOPING BIOLOGICAL INFORMATION SYSTEMS FOR WATER QUALITY MANAGEMENT,
Virginia Polytechnic Inst. and State Univ., Blacksburg. Center for Environmental Studies; and Virginia Polytechnic Inst. and State Univ., Blacksburg. Dept. of Biology.
For primary bibliographic entry see Field 5G.
W75-08002

DIGITAL SIMULATION OF THE EFFECT OF THERMAL DISCHARGE ON STREAM WATER QUALITY,
Kansas State Univ., Manhattan. Inst. for Systems Design and Optimization.
For primary bibliographic entry see Field 5B.
W75-08006

PHYTOPLANKTON CONCENTRATIONS IN THE MALAMOCCO CHANNEL OF THE LAGOON OF VENICE,
Istituto di Biologia del Mare, Venice (Italy).
D. Voltolina.
Arch Oceanogr Limnol. Vol 18, No 1, p 1-18, 1973, Illus.
Identifiers: Channels, *Diatoms, *Flagellates, *Italy(Lagoon of Venice), Lagoons, Microorganisms, Peridinians, *Phytoplankton, Seasons, Estuaries.

The phytoplanktological data of a research program carried out in the central basin of the lagoon of Venice (Italy) are presented. The data collected during a yearly period of observations show that the phytoplankton populations of lagoonar origin are not, on average, quantitatively different from those coming from the sea, being distinguishable only from a qualitative point of view. Diatoms and

THE EFFECT OF SILVER IONS ON THE RESPIRATORY CHAIN OF ESCHERICHIA COLI,
British Columbia Univ., Vancouver. Dept. of Biochemistry.
P. D. Bragg, and D. J. Rainnie.
Canadian Journal of Microbiology, Volume 20, No 6, p 883-889, June 1974. 6 fig, 17 ref.

Descriptors: *Silver, *Respiration, *Microorganisms, *Inhibitors, Microbiology, Cytological studies, Chromosomes, Laboratory tests, Cultures, Ions, Metabolism, Water pollution effects, *E. coli, Pollutant identification.

Silver ions inhibited the oxidation of glucose, clycerol, fumarate, succinate, D- and L-lactate, and endogenous substrates by intact cell suspensions of Escherichia coli. Silver ions reacted with the respiratory chain at two levels. The site most sensitive to inhibition was located between the b-cytochromes and cytochrome a sub 2. The second level of inhibition was in the NADH and succinate dehydrogenase regions of the respiratory chain, and was situated on the substrate side of the flavin components. (Jernigan-Vanderbilt)
W75-08086

EFFECTS OF POLLUTANTS ON MARINE LIFE PROBED.
Chemical and Engineering News, Vol 51, No 51, p 17, 18, 23, December, 1973, 1 fig, 1 photo.

Descriptors: Water pollution, *Oceans, *Plankton, *Pesticide toxicity, *Oil wastes, On-site investigations, Testing procedures, Marine life, *Heavy metals, Copper, Mercury, *Canada, *Water pollution effects, Lethal limit.
Identifiers: Vancouver, B.C., Sublethal effects.

An international team of scientistis from seven institutions began attacking the problem of the effects of low concentrations of pollutants on the marine environment. In a Controlled Ecosystem Pollution Experiment (CEPEX) sponsored by the National Science Foundation, scientists from the U.S, Canada, and the United Kingdom were attempting to determine the long-term effects on natural marine ecosystems of low levels of three types of chemical pollutants: heavy metals, certain synthetic hydrocarbons, and petroleum hydrocarbons. In particular, they were examining the sublethal effects of pollution on the stability of plankton communities. The key to the CEPEX effort is the establishment of a large-scale but controlled replica of the natural environment. This will be accomplished by using a system of large plastic cylinders, 10 meters in diameter and 30 meters in height, that will be closed at the bottom, open to the atmosphere at the top, and suspended in the natural ocean environment of Vancouver Island, BC. They will enclose about 2400 cubic meters of sea water including the natural plant and animal populations. (Jernigan-Vanderbilt)
W75-08097

SEASONAL CHANGES IN THE BIOMASS OF THE MACRO-BENTHOS OF A TIDAL FLAT AREA IN THE DUTCH WADDEN SEA,
Nederlands Instituut voor Onderzoek der Zee, Texel.
J. J. Beukema.
Neth J Sea Res, Vol 8, No 1, p 94-107, 1974. Illus.
Identifiers: Arenicola-marina, *Benthos, *Biomass, Birds, Fish, Food, Growth rates, Mya-arenaria, Seas, *Seasonal, Shellfish, Tidal, *Netherlands(Wadden Sea).

Macrofauna benthos has been sampled frequently during 6 yr at 3 intertidal stations on a tidal flat area in the westernmost part of the Wadden Sea. Biomass, expressed as ash-free dry weight, fluctuated with a regular annual pattern. Maximal amounts were observed every year at each station during the July-Sept. periods, minimal amounts during the Dec.-March periods. The steep increases during spring were for the greater part due to fast growth of animals already present in winter. Spat fall generally contributed only a minor part to the annual biomass increases. The declines during autumn were attributable both to decreases in numbers and to individual weight losses. The latter dominated in the big and deep-living specimen of 2 spp. (Mya arenaria and Arenicola marina) which comprised about half of the total biomass of the benthos. Among the predators feeding on the benthos at the tidal flats, fish, just as the shellfish, are most numerous during summer, but monthly numbers of birds are unrelated to seasonal changes in availability of food.--Copyright 1974, Biological Abstracts, Inc.
W75-08103

SILICON DEPLETIONS IN SOME NORFOLK RIVERS,
Yorkshire River Authority, Leeds (England). Pollution Prevention Dept.
A. M. C. Edwards.
Freshwater Biol, Vol 4, No 3, p 267-274, 1974. Illus.
Identifiers: Depletions, *Diatoms, *Magnesium, Productivity, Rivers, Seasonal, *Silicon depletion, *United Kingdom(Norfolk rivers), *Dissolved solids.

Water samples collected weekly from the rivers Yare, Tud, Wensum and Tas in Norfolk, England, displayed marked depletions in the spring and summer of the concentration of dissolved silicon. These were unconnected with any hydrological event and were assumed to be due to the assimilation of silicon by diatoms. Equilibrium concentrations were maintained in the Yare and Tud during the weeks prior to and following the spring bloom. It was estimated that 35 Mg (51%) of the predicted load were removed from the Yare during the 11 wk of this depletion and 6.0 Mg (45%) from the Tud. The lowest observed concentration (0.4 mg/l) occurred during the 1st week in May when over 90% of the silicon had been removed. However, the maximum amount of removal and hence maximum diatom productivity occurred earlier at a time of higher water discharge. A similar pattern was observed in the Yare during the spring of 1971. Two small blooms occurred later in the summer of 1970 in the Yare and Tud. It was estimated that 15% of the Yare's dissolved silicon load of 263 Mg was in the assimilated form and 12.5% of the Tud's output of 56.6 Mg. The weathering of silicate minerals was probably the source of almost all the silicon and the outputs represented a silicon erosion rate of 1.15 Mg/km2/yr for the Yare and 0.77 Mg/km2/yr for the Tud.--Copyright 1974, Biological Abstracts, Inc.
W75-08106

INVESTIGATIONS ON THE TOXICITY OF SEAWATER-EXTRACTS OF THREE CRUDE OILS ON EGGS OF COD (GADUS MORHUA),
Kiel Univ. (West Germany). Institut fuer Meereskunde.
W. W. Kuehnhold.
Ber Dtsch Wiss Komm Meeresforsch, Vol 23, No 2, p 165-180, 1974.
Identifiers: Abnormalities, *Cod eggs, *Crude oil, *Embryonic stages, Gadus-morrhua, Gastrulation, Hatching, Larvae, Sea water, *Toxicity, Water pollution effects, *Oil wastes, Oil pollution, Fish eggs.

The influence of the water-soluble fractions of 3 crude oils (Tia Juana/Venezuela, Agha Jari/Iran, Sarir/Libya) upon embryogenesis was studied. At continuous and at short term influence the crude oils exerted different rates of mortality. The water-soluble fraction was extracted from 2.5, 25 and 250 ml of oil using 25 l seawater under slow stirring, resulting in concentrations of 0.015-3.5 ppm of total-hydrocarbon. The 48 LC50 and 96 LC50 were in the order of 1-12 ppm. The retarding effect of the Iran extract during development was particularly obvious during gastrulation and before hatching. The broadest spectrum of embryonic abnormalities was found after the gastrula stage. The rate of distorted, non-viable larvae was high in certain experiments after treatment of eggs with crude oils.--Copyright 1974, Biological Abstracts, Inc.
W75-08107

WATER POLLUTION BY TANNERY WASTES: THE POSSIBLE CAUSES OF MASS KILLING OF FISH AT MOSUL, IRAQ,
Mosul Univ. (Iraq). Dept. of Biology.
For primary bibliographic entry see Field 5B.
W75-08110

GJERSJOEN--A EUTROPHIC LAKE IN NORWAY,
H. Holtan.
Verhandlungen Internationale Vereinigung Limnologie, Vol 18, p 349-354, 1972. 3 fig, 2 tab, 8 ref.

Descriptors: *Eutrophication, *Lakes, Water pollution effects, Anaerobic conditions, Agricultural runoff, Dissolved oxygen, Nutrients, Organic matter, Stratification, Cyanophyta, Diatoms, Chlorophyta, Sewage effluents, Industrial wastes, Oxidation-reduction potential, Europe, Conductivity, Physicochemical properties, Primary productivity, Dystrophy.
Identifiers: *Lake Gjersjoen(Norway).

Eutrophication of Lake Gjersjoen is an example of destruction of lakes receiving wastes. About 19% of its drainage area is agricultural land. Untreated or mechanically-treated sewage from the population is discharged into the lake or its tributaries. Oxygen consumption, normal for dystrophic lakes, was clearly perceptible in the deeper layers during stratification periods. Since 1960, waste discharged into Lake Gjersjoen has doubled resulting in a markedly eutrophic state. In the fall of 1964, water blooms of blue-green algae suddenly developed and have been steadily increasing. Corresponding to changes in biological conditions is the marked change in chemical composition. Shortly after the spring circulation period, a heavy diatom population develops; later the green and blue-green algae dominate. The accelerating eutrophic development in this lake during the last decade is due to use of the lake as a recipient for sewage and industrial wastes. In this connection, it is important to remember that the lake in its original state contained a heavy concentration of allochthonous organic material; also that dystrophic lakes are unsuitable as recipients of polluted water. (Jones-Wisconsin)
W75-08119

SEASONAL VARIATION OF NITROGEN, PHOSPHORUS, AND CHLOROPHYLL A IN LAKE MICHIGAN AND GREEN BAY, 1965,
National Marine Fisheries Service, Ann Arbor, Mich. Great Lakes Fishery Lab.
H. E. Allen.
Technical Papers 70, June 1973 (Contribution 471 of the Great Lakes Fishery Laboratory). 23 p, 10 fig, 9 tab, 16 ref.

Descriptors: *Nitrogen, *Phosphorus, *Chlorophyll, *Lake Michigan, Seasonal, Nutrients, Michigan, Wisconsin, Phosphates, Nitrates, Eutrophication, Aphotic zone, Euphotic zone, Littoral.
Identifiers: *Green Bay(Wis).

Phosphorus and nitrate content of Lake Michigan and its relation to phytoplankton abundance were determined. The data help to establish a base for evaluation of future changes in nutrient content. Total and dissolved phosphorus, nitrate, and chlorophyll-a were measured at four stations (inshore Michigan, offshore Michigan, offshore Wisconsin, and inshore Wisconsin) and one station in southern Green Bay. Nutrients were measured at 2,- 5,- and 10-meter depths and

chlorophyll-a at 2 meters. In Green Bay total phosphorus was about five times as high and dissolved phosphorus more than twice as high as the averages for the four Lake Michigan stations, but nitrate nitrogen concentration was only about one-third that in the lake. Total and dissolved phosphorus were about 50% higher in the inshore Lake Michigan area than in the other three. Concentration and seasonal trends in nitrates differed relatively little among the stations. Nitrate at all areas and depths sampled decreased to almost nondectable levels during September. Chlorophyll-a was 70% higher at the two inshore stations than at the two offshore areas and was more than four times higher in Green Bay than any other portion of lake. (Jones-Wisconsin)
W75-08120

NITROGEN CYCLE AND BLUE-GREEN ALGAE (2),
H. L. Golterman.
H2O, Tijdschrift voor Watervoorziening en Afvalwaterbehandeling, Vol 7, No 8, p 152-155, 1974. 2 fig, 77 ref.

Descriptors: *Nitrogen cycle, *Cyanophyta, Plant physiology, Nitrogen fixation, Eutrophication, Light intensity, Migration, Algal toxins, Nitrification.
Identifiers: Light inhibition.

In addition to the N-fixing abilities of blue-green algae several other physiological differences between them and other algal groups may separately or jointly be the cause of the 'bloom' phenomenon. They can grow in dim light which allows them to inhabit two completely different niches of the lake. Various species of blue-green algae contain gas vacuoles; by varying their number the algae are able to migrate between suitable light conditions and the dark, more nutrient-rich layers. Some blue-green algae often occur simultaneously with high concentrations of organic matter, often organic pollutants. The question of whether or not toxin production by blue-green algae does stimulate their blooms under natural conditions is still open to doubt. There is no evidence that the blue-green algal cells have a lower than average N or P content. A nitrogen cycle can be composed in a similar form to that for the summary of the phosphate process (Golterman 1973). Analysis of the nitrification phenomenon can be carried out using a generalized steady state multidimensional feedback model. (Jones-Wisconsin)
W75-08121

ANALYSES OF PHOSPHORUS IN LAKE ONTARIO SEDIMENT,
State Univ. Coll., Buffalo, N.Y. Great Lakes Lab.
R. K. Wyeth.
International Association Great Lakes Research, Proceedings 16th Conference on Great Lakes Research, p 345-348, 1973. 4 tab, 10 ref.

Descriptors: *Analytical techniques, *Phosphorus, *Lake Ontario, *Lake sediments, Technology.
Identifiers: Ascorbic acid.

Since phosphorus is an element of major importance to the growth of aquatic organisms, it is essential to have precise and accurate methods to determine its concentrates. In an attempt to ascertain a rapid reproducible and accurate method for determining the phosphorus content in sediment from the Great Lakes, two methods of digestion were examined, persulfate and nitric acid-sulfuric acid. The sediment was collected from Lake Ontario during the spring and summer of 1972. Phosphorus analyses on the digested samples were made according to vandomolybophosphoric acid colorometry, stanous chloride and two variations of the ascorbic acid method, combined reagent and combined reagent plus alcohol. The data presented were statistically analyzed. The ascorbic acid method using combined reagent and alcohol following nitric acid-sulfuric acid digestion yielded the most accurate results, 92-96% recovery, as determined by the use of spiked and split dilution samples, and the least deviation (less than 0.010-0.017) at concentration between 0.35 and 1.67 mg P/g. The nitric acid-sulfuric acid digestion procedure is very rigorous, where the sediment is boiling in the concentrated acid mixture for up to 24 hours. Despite this time period, many samples can be digested simultaneously. (Jones-Wisconsin)
W75-08122

THE CONDITION OF LAKES AND PONDS IN RELATION TO THE CARRYING OUT OF TREATMENT MEASURES,
Institut National de la Recherche Agronomique, Thonon-les-Bains (France). Station d'Hydrobiologie Lacustre.
P. J. Laurent, J. Garaucher, and P. Vivier.
In: Advances in Water Pollution Research, Pergamon Press, Oxford and New York, 1972, p III-23/1-III-23/10. 6 fig, 3 tab, 11 ref.

Descriptors: *Lakes, *Pollution abatement, Waste water treatment, Physicochemical properties, Dissolved oxygen, Phytoplankton, Eutrophication, Sewerage, Lake sediments, Europe.
Identifiers: Lake Leman(France), Lake Annecy(France), Lake of Nantua(France).

Some aspects of pollution and associated eutrophication occurring in the three largest freshwater lakes in eastern France and remedial measures are described. Studies were commenced on Lake Leman in 1957 and on Lake Annecy in 1966. Wastewater treatment programs have been applied either before or simultaneously with the investigations. Results show response to remedial measures and permit an initial judgment of their efficacy. Considered as 'becoming eutrophic' in 1937, Lake Annecy after construction of part of the peripheral sewer and discharge of treated sewage effluent downstream seems to have stopped its eutrophication trend. Lake Leman, despite installation of mechanical and biological wastewater treatment plants similar to those at Lake Annecy, has, since 1937, undergone an unfavorable chemical and biological evolution. The Lake of Nantua is known for its advanced state of eutrophication. It seems that the only appropriate remedy lies in diverting all wastewater contributions from the lake and discharging these downstream. This remedial action is being carried out. Because of the combined sewerage in the Town of Nantua, a storm overflow will have to be installed at the head of the main diverting canalization. (Jones-Wisconsin)
W75-08123

ECOSYSTEM STUDIES IN CONNECTION WITH THE RESTORATION OF LAKES,
S. Bjork.
Verhandlungen Internationale Vereinigung Limnologie, Vol 18, p 379-387, 1972. 7 fig, 2 tab, 6 ref.

Descriptors: *Pollution abatement, *Lakes, Eutrophication, Shallow water, Submerged plants, Water pollution effects, Waterfowl, Lake sediments, Phosphorus, Dredging, Phosphates, Nitrates, Nutrients, Hydrogen ion concentration, Phytoplankton, Primary productivity, Sedimentation, Detritus, Plant populations, Europe.
Identifiers: *Lake rehabilitation, Lake Trummen(Sweden), Lake Hornborga(Sweden).

Lake Trummen (Central South Sweden) and Lake Hornborga (between Lakes Vattern and Vannern), characterized as having been irreversibly damaged by man, are described before, during, and after intervention. Until 1958 Lake Trummen received town sewage and wastewater from a flax factory. Intensive limnologic studies were started in 1968, a detailed restoration plan was developed in 1969, and the restoration process begun in 1970-1971. In unrestored Lake Trummen no submerged vegetation was able to develop. Prior to pollution the regionally characteristic plant species, Isoetes lacustris and Myriophyllum alterniflorum, were common. At the early stage of restoration there are unmistakable indications of considerable improvement. Lake Hornborga has been lowered five times between 1802-1933. From 1933 to 1954 the whole lake area was dry during summer. Since 1954 part of the lake is diked-in. Water depth is maximally 80 cm. Lake Hornborga was considered an important waterfowl lake in Western Europe, but lowerings resulted in a rapid decrease in ornithologic value. Lowerings have caused an almost complete overgrowth of emergent macrophyte vegetation, mainly Phragmites communis, resulting in voluminous detritus deposition. In some areas it is possible to remove the emergent vegetation by mechanical treatment and allow submerged vegetation to flourish. (Jones-Wisconsin)
W75-08124

LIMNOLOGICAL OBSERVATIONS ON AN ULTRA-OLIGOTROPHIC LAKE IN OREGON, USA,
K. W. Malueg, J. R. Tilstra, D. W. Schultz, and C. F. Powers.
Verhandlungen Internationale Vereinigung Limnologie, Vol 18, p 292-302, 1972. 7 fig, 4 tab, 11 ref.

Descriptors: *Baseline studies, *Oligotrophy, *Lakes, Oregon, Physicochemical properties, Limnology, Temperature, Light penetration, Biological properties, Hydrogen ion concentration, Dissolved oxygen, Conductivity, Nitrogen, Phosphorus, Chlorophyll, Phytoplankton, Zooplankton, Productivity, Bacteria, Submerged plants.
Identifiers: *Waldo Lake(Ore).

Waldo Lake, Oregon, is located in the Cascade Mountain Range at an altitude 1650 m. It is the headwater of North Fork of Willamette River, and is surrounded by coniferous forests, predominately Douglas fir, pine, and hemlock. It has been accessible only by trail or four-wheel drive vehicle, until, in 1969, a paved road was built linking it with a major highway. This investigation was designed to elaborate on an earlier survey and comprehensively document the unusual limnology of this body of water. Results would serve as a baseline for future investigations. Data are reported from only one station, located at maximum depth. Temperature, light penetration, water transparency, pH, dissolved oxygen and specific conductance were measured. Samples for nitrogen and phosphorus analyses were preserved. Biological measurements included chlorophyll-a, phytoplankton, zooplankton, primary productivity, and bacteria. Plankton net haul samples revealed no zooplankton at any time. Two plants were growing luxuriously on the sediment at 127 m depth, a hepatic, Jungermannia triris and a moss, Hygrohypnum (molle.); both appeared in excellent physiological condition. Limnological data from 1969 and 1970 indicate Waldo Lake as one of the most oligotrophic lakes in the world. (Jones-Wisconsin)
W75-08125

SEASONAL BIOLOGICAL STRUCTURE OF LAKE ONEGA,
I. I. Nikolaev.
Verhandlungen Internationale Vereinigung Limnologie, Vol 18, p 542-547, 1972. 4 fig.

Descriptors: *Lakes, *Seasonal, *Biological communities, Oligotrophy, Biomass, Cycles, Productivity, Distribution, Temperate, Stratification.
Identifiers: *Lake Onega(USSR).

The annual cycle of structural and functional changes in Lake Onega, USSR, as well as other lakes, is generally determined by cycle of incoming solar radiation. The significance of hydrological processes in biological cycles is clearly revealed in productivity and distribution of pelagic

density for its environment. The superficial sediments contain high concentrations of viable phytoplankton; since there is a frequent exchange of material between sediments and open water it is suggested that a more realistic mean algal biomass is about 1000 mg chl-a/sq m instead of about 600 mg/sq m. This may be sustained by the observed daily values of integral photosynthesis only because the photosynthesis and respiration components of the phytoplankton are vertically separated. (Jones-Wisconsin)
W75-08128

LOSS RATES FROM A LAKE PHYTOPLANKTON COMMUNITY,

California Univ., Davis. Inst. of Ecology.
A. D. Jassby, and C. R. Goldman.
Limnology and Oceanography, Vol 19, No 4, p 618-627, 1974. 3 fig, 44 ref. NSF GB-6422X and GB-35371.

Descriptors: *Fluctuation, *Population, *Phytoplankton, Primary productivity, Biomass, California, Standing crops, Lakes, Temporal distribution, Mortality.
Identifiers: *Algal losses, Castle Lake(Calif).

The discrepancy between primary productivity and actual biomass changes in a water column in Castle Lake has been analyzed. Castle Lake lies in a protected cirque basin at a 1700 m altitude in northern California. Measurements of primary productivity and phytoplankton biomass are presented for an 8-month period. Primary productivity and phytoplankton carbon content under a square meter of lake surface exhibit similar seasonal trends and achieve maximum values in July. Phytoplankton loss rates are calculated by subtracting the rate of change of carbon content from the primary productivity, and specific loss rates are estimated by dividing loss rates by phytoplankton carbon. Specific loss rates range from more than 0.80 per day in May to less than 0.20 per day in midsummer and in December. Loss rates in the spring cannot be attributed to water transport, sinking, or grazing. Cell mortality and decomposition when environmental tolerances are exceeded may be significant causes of phytoplankton loss in the lake. Mathematical models of primary productivity should include phytoplankton mortality unrelated to grazing. (Jones-Wisconsin)
W75-08129

GROWTH OF SELENASTRUM CAPRICORNUTUM IN NATURAL WATERS AUGMENTED WITH DETERGENT PRODUCTS IN WASTEWATERS,

Lake George Limnological Research Center, Inc., Troy, N.Y.
J. J. Ferris, S. Kobayashi, and N. L. Clesceri.
Water Research, Vol 8, No 12, p 1013-1020, 1974. (Rensselaer FWI Report 74-21). 4 fig, 3 tab, 8 ref.

Descriptors: *Eutrophication, *Detergents, *Phosphorus, Growth rates, Algae, New York, Lakes, Waste water treatment, Sewage effluents, Phosphates, Phosphorus compounds.
Identifiers: *Selenastrum capricornutum, Snyders Lake(NY), Lake George(NY), Saratoga Lake(NY).

To determine whether removal of phosphates from detergents would significantly alter the ability of domestic secondary sewage effluent to stimulate algal growth in receiving waters, growth of the alga Selenastrum capricornutum was tested in waters of different trophic states: receiving water alone or with sewage effluent containing non-phosphate detergent or soap, sewage effluent containing phosphate detergent, sewage effluent chemically treated to remove nutrients (especially phosphorus), or treated effluent plus added phosphorus. The three lakes located in northeastern New York used as sources of test water had total phosphorus concentrations ranging from 0.01-0.04 mg P/l. Algal growth was stimulated in the lake waters by secondary sewage containing detergents with or without phosphate. Significant algal growth occurred in two samples with a concentration of 60 microgram P/l, but concentrations up to 110 microgram P/l did not induce such a response in the third sample. It is difficult to attach more significance to the effect of detergent products on algal growth than to secondary sewage alone. Tertiary treatment by alum precipitation of secondary sewage containing phosphorus formed an effluent which did not enhance algal growth when added to lake waters. Agents other than phosphorus are partly responsible for the algal growth observed. (Buchanan-Davidson-Wisconsin)
W75-08130

LIMNOLOGICAL CONDITIONS IN FIVE SMALL OLIGOTROPHIC LAKES IN TERRA NOVA NATIONAL PARK, NEWFOUNDLAND,

Dalhousie Univ., Halifax (Nova Scotia). Dept. of Biology.
J. J. Kerekes.
Journal Fisheries Research Board of Canada, Vol 31, No 5, p 555-581, 1974. 17 fig, 13 tab, 67 ref.

Descriptors: *Lake morphometry, *Oligotrophy, *Physicochemical properties, Lakes, Phytoplankton, Depth, Salinity, Phosphorus, Chlorophyll, Nutrients, Solar radiation, Light penetration, Color, Primary productivity, Canada, Water temperature, Dissolved oxygen, Oxygen sag, Turbidity, Hydrogen ion concentration, Alkalinity, Carbon, Nitrates.
Identifiers: Terra Nova Natl Park(Newfoundland), Water renewal rate.

Selected physicochemical characteristics and morphometric factors are described and related to phytoplankton production in five small lakes in eastern Newfoundland. The lakes, varying in mean depth, in water renewal rate, in salinity, in total phosphorus, and in chlorophyll-a concentrations, were investigated during 1969 and 1970. Hypolimnetic oxygen deficits ranged between 111 and 217 mg oxygen/sq m/day. Low nutrient levels, reduced solar radiation, and low underwater light penetration, owing to excessive cloudiness and high water color, seriously limited planktonic primary production. The relation between primary production at optimum light, and water renewal per annum, appeared to be curvilinear when the rate of primary production began to decline above an optimum water renewal rate. The seasonal and annual variations in water color and salinity were dependent on the rate of water renewal, but other lakes on the catchment areas modified that relation. Winter road salting operations within the catchment area caused a considerable increase in salinity, total phosphorus concentration, and primary production in one lake. Anew morphometric index which reflects the littoral effect on the lake basin volume is proposed. (Jones-Wisconsin)
W75-08131

VERTICAL DISTRIBUTION OF PLANT NUTRIENTS,

Oklahoma Cooperative Fishery Unit, Stillwater.
D. W. Toetz.
Completion Report Oklahoma Proj F-27-1, 1972. 3 tab, 6 ref.

Descriptors: *Cycling nutrients, *Spatial distribution, *Nutrients, Oklahoma, Destratification, Stratification, Nitrates, Reservoirs, Phosphates, Hypolimnion, Epilimnion, Nitrification, Nitrogen, Aeration, Denitrification, Nitrites.
Identifiers: Lake Eufaula(Okla).

An attempt was made to destratify the central pool of Lake Eufaula, Oklahoma, and nutrient cycling during destratification was studied. In stratified lakes, nitrate is absent from bottom waters, while phosphate concentrations are higher in the hypolmnion than in the epilimnion. It was hypothesized that destratification would lead to an

orthograde distribution of these nutrients. Total and total dissolved phosphorus were many times higher near the bottom than in the surface. Phosphorus depletion was never evident. It is not possible to learn from these data if the sediments were a source or a sink for phosphorus during destratification. The data indicate that the destratification effort did not bring about complete mixing of phosphorus. It appears that during June, only two processes were affecting nitrate concentration: nitrate assimilation and nitrification. In general, nitrate-nitrogen was lower at the surface than near the bottom during July, implying a high uptake there or intense nitrification close to the sediments. After aeration began, chlorophyll-a concentrations decreased at all stations, but later the concentrations rose. No nitrate could be detected and only 12 micrograms nitrate-nitrogen was observed in the water samples. (Jones-Wisconsin)
W75-08132

PRIMARY REPRODUCTION STUDIES IN SHALLOW AQUATIC ENVIRONMENTS IN SOUTHERN ILLINOIS,
M. Munawar, J. Verduin, and I. Fatima.
Verhandlungen Internationale Vereinigung Limnologie, Vol 18, p 113-120, 1972. 2 fig, 6 tab, 25 ref.

Descriptors: *Primary productivity, *Shallow water, Illinois, On-site investigations, Carbon dioxide, Biological communities, Cladophora, Cyanophyta, Diurnal, Respiration, Photosynthesis, Variability.
Identifiers: Campus Lake(Ill), Carbondale(Ill).

Primary production studies were made in shallow aquatic environments (about 1 decimeter), sampling at least three times weekly and three time daily for an extensive period. Two techniques were followed simultaneously: a pH meter for carbon dioxide changes and an oxygen probe for oxygen changes. Significant differences were revealed for communities dominated by different species. Lowest rates (70 micromoles/gram dry weight of algae per hour) were observed for communities dominated by Cladophora; highest rates (580) for communities dominated by Cyanophyta. A pronounced diurnal trend was established with the highest rates in the morning, declining to rates one-half or less in the late afternoon. Respiration rates were one-fourth to one-sixth as high as gross photosynthesis, and did not show consistent diurnal trends. Experiments utilizing carbon dioxide-fertilized waters revealed enhanced photosynthetic rates in communities dominated by filamentous algae, but not in blue-green communities. In all communities an interesting phenomenon of carbon dioxide-uptake was encountered in dark bottles, exhibiting dark carbon dioxide-absorption similar to that attributable to photosynthesis. Photosynthetic rates under natural conditions average 8 micromoles/l of water per hour, agreeing closely with data reported for less shallow environments. (Jones-Wisconsin)
W75-08133

DIURNAL MIXING AND THE VERTICAL DISTRIBUTION OF PHYTOPLANKTON IN A SHALLOW EQUATORIAL LAKE (LAKE GEORGE, UGANDA),
Freshwater Biological Association, Ambleside (England); and Royal Society African Freshwater Biological Team, Lake Katwe (Uganda).
G. G. Ganf.
Ecology, Vol 62, No 2, p 611-629, 1974. 7 fig, 4 tab, 38 ref.

Descriptors: *Diurnal, *Mixing, *Spatial distribution, *Phytoplankton, Shallow water, Thermal stratification, Density, Velocity, Chlorophyta, Cyanophyta.
Identifiers: *Lake George(Uganda), Species stratification, Gas vacuoles, Sinking rates.

The diurnal changes of thermal stratification and vertical phytoplankton distribution which occur in the African Lake George are illustrated and these changes are analyzed in terms of sinking rates, density gradients, and water velocity. Lake George, shallow equatorial lake, stratifies diurnally. During the night and early morning the column is isothermal, over mid-day it is thermally stratified but isothermal conditions return with the onset of light evening winds. Phytoplankton is usually evenly distributed during the night and early morning. During mid-day the majority of the community sinks to deeper water and marked chlorophyll-a gradients occur. Towards evening the phytoplankton resumes uniform distribution, concurrent with the return to isothermal conditions. Surface accumulations of Microcystis, during calm mid-day periods, were noted. Algal counts revealed difference of behavior between species. Strong winds may resuspend previously settled phytoplankton. Algal counts suggest that the survival ability of chlorophytes within the anoxic lake sediments is poor when compared with the survival of blue-green algae and Synedra sp. Diurnal changes of the vertical phytoplankton distribution are interpreted as a function of diurnal and depth variations of Richardson's number and of the influence of excess algal density during periods of minimum turbulence. (Jones-Wisconsin)
W75-08134

CHANGES IN LAKE NORRVIKEN AFTER SEWAGE DIVERSION,
I. Ahlgren.
Verhandlungen Internationale Vereinigung Limnologie, Vol 18, p 355-361, 1972. 4 fig, 3 tab, 5 ref.

Descriptors: *Sewage effluents, *Diversion, *Pollution abatement, Yeasts, Nitrogen, Phosphorus, Eutrophication, Water quality, Phytoplankton, Biomass, Primary productivity, Sedimentation, Lake sediments, Carbon, Limiting factors, Europe.
Identifiers: *Lake Norrviken(Sweden).

Lake Norrviken in central Sweden has for many years received sewage of both domestic and industrial origin. A yeast factory was by far the largest contributor of nitrogen and phosphorus, thus the lake has become strongly eutrophic. In 1969 all sewage effluents were diverted from the lake. In two years following this diversion slight improvements of water quality have been noted. Total N concentration has decreased from 5-6 to 2-3 mg/l, and there is evidence that N was a limiting factor for phytoplankton growth in 1970. P concentration has decreased very slowly from 300-400 to 200-300 micrograms/l. Phytoplankton biomass was much smaller in 1970 than previous years, but primary production was larger than that measured in 1961/62. Sedimentation of P in 1970 was estimated to be 3.1 g/sq m and the release of P from the sediments 2.7 g/sq m. This means that sedimentation and release of P approximately counterbalance each other. Further recovery of the lake is not expected unless the P concentration in the main tributary decreases to much lower values. (Jones-Wisconsin)
W75-08135

ZOOPLANKTON OF THE ST. LAWRENCE GREAT LAKES--SPECIES COMPOSITION, DISTRIBUTION, AND ABUNDANCE,
Canada Centre for Inland Waters, Burlington (Ontario).
N. H. F. Watson.
Journal Fisheries Research Board of Canada, Vol 31, No 5, p 783-794, 1974. 3 fig, 2 tab, 45 ref.

Descriptors: *Zooplankton, *Great Lakes, *Distribution, Seasonal, Lake Erie, Lake Huron, Lake Ontario, Lake Superior, Biomass, Crustaceans, Varieties, Rotifers, Migration, On-site investigations, Sampling.

Descriptors: *Oligotrophy, *Water pollution effects, *Eutrophication, *Biological communities, Europe, Domestic wastes, Industrial wastes, Zooplankton, Distribution, Fish, Benthic fauna, Primary productivity, Organic loading, Bioindicators.
Identifiers: Lake Paijanne(Finland).

The reactions of an aquatic biocoenose, an oligotrophic and oligohumic lake, into which different kinds of waste waters are discharged are described. Paijanne is the central lake of the Kymijoki watercourse, the second largest watercourse in Finland. The total effluent load up to 1969 was calculated to be equal to the wastes of about 1.7 million people. In the central parts of Lake Paijanne waste waters from the wood-processing industry predominate. The lake contains areas ranging from oligotrophic to eutrophic. Eutrophication seems to affect the zooplankton species composition through chemical environmental factors and through food organisms (algae and bacteria), and by lack of planktivorous fishes in some areas. The number of species of bottom fauna is smallest in the most polluted areas and different species occur most evenly in the cleanest areas. In the areas loaded by the wood-processing industry the percentage of roach is clearly lower and the percentage of perch higher than in those loaded by urban wastes. In eutrophic areas vendace is almost totally absent and smelt is most important pelagic species. In clean areas the abundance of perch is prominent. (Jones-Wisconsin)
W75-08138

AVAILABILITY OF PHOSPHORUS-32, ADSORBED ON CLAY PARTICLES, TO A GREEN ALGA,

Michigan Agricultural Experiment Station, East Lansing.
L. A. Helfrich, and N. R. Kevern.
Michigan Academician, Vol 6, No 1, p 71-81, 1973. 5 fig, 21 ref.

Descriptors: *Phosphorus, *Adsorption, *Clays, *Chlorophyta, Runoff, Kaolinite, Sediments.
Identifiers: *Phosphorus sources, Clay particles, Pandorina morum.

Whether phosphate adsorbed on clay particles, as representative of drainage water sediments is available to phosphate-limited Pandorina morum is determined and some parameters influencing phosphorus availability are examined. Effects of light on uptake of adsorbed P-32 by algal cells are described. Kaolinite, a clay mineral whose role in phosphate fixation in soils has been established, was used to represent typical suspended and settleable sediments in aquatic systems. Centrifugation and density gradient separation procedures were used to fractionate water samples into three categories: culture media, clay particles, and algal cells. Initially all phosphorus introduced to the cultures was adsorbed on clay particles. Mean percentage of the total amount of P-32 present in the algal cells and clay particles for each day is shown. Results serve to emphasize the potential role of clay particles in supplying phosphorusnecessary for algal nutrition. That phosphate-limited P. morum can obtain this nutrient adsorbed to clay particles was demonstrated. The relatively high concentrations of radiophosphorus found in the algal cells demonstrates movement of the isotope from the tagged clay to the cells. (Jones-Wisconsin)
W75-08139

INFLUENCE OF EFFLUENTS OF SULPHITE CELLULOSE FACTORY ON ALGAE IN CULTURES AND RECEIVING WATERS,

Jyvaskyla Univ. (Finland). Dept. of Biology.
P. Eloranta.
Vattern, Vol 30, No 1, p 36-48, 1974. 13 fig, 2 tab, 22 ref.

Descriptors: *Industrial wastes, *Sulfite liquors, *Pulp wastes, *Water pollution effects, Bleaching wastes, Toxins, Bioassay, Phytoplankton, Eutrophication, Acidity, Europe, Inhibition, Chlorides, Calcium, Pulp and paper industry.
Identifiers: Ankistrodesmus falcatus, Jyvaskyla(Finland).

Effect of effluents from a sulphite cellulose factory on growth of pure cultures of Ankistrodesmus falcatus v. acicularis was studied. Effluents were taken from three main lake outfalls discharging wastes of barking works, cellulose factory, bleaching works, and other factory processes. Results were compared with observations on phytoplankton occuring in nature in waters receiving factory effluents. The effluents had toxic and growth-inhibiting and -stimulating effects on algae. Effluents with clearest toxic and inhibitory effects were from the factory processes and from its main waste conduit. Toxicity is probably attributable to acidity. The effluent from the main concuit occasioned an initial inhibition of growth, the duration of which depended on the amount of algae in the culture. This growth-inhibiting effect is presumably attributable to the sulphur compounds contained in the effluent. The barking works effluent promoted algal growth evidently due to its phosphorus content. The bleaching works effluent did not have any particular effect on algal growth. Effluent from the main conduit of the cellulose factory also had a growth-stimulating effect. At their highest concentrations, the effluents exerted an inhibiting effect on all algal groups, decreasing species numbers and total biomass. (Jones-Wisconsin)
W75-08140

THE DISTRIBUTION OF EPIPHYTIC DIATOMS IN YAQUINA ESTUARY, OREGON (U.S.A.),

Wartburg Coll., Waverly, Iowa. Dept. of Biology.
S. P. Main, and C. D. McIntire.
Botanica Marina, Vol 17, No 2, p 88-89, 1974. 4 fig, 6 tab, 35 ref. NSF GB18591, GA33231.

Descriptors: *Spatial distribution, *Periphyton, *Diatoms, *Estuaries, Oregon, Aquatic plants, Seasonal, Varieties, Intertidal areas, Biological communities, Salinity, Hosts.
Identifiers: *Epiphytic diatoms, Yaquina Estuary(Ore), Zostera marina, Fucus evanescens, Enteromorpha, Polysiphonia, Ulva.

A qualitative and quantitative analysis of diatom flora associated with selected macrophytes in the Yaquina Estuary, Oregon, is reported. These assemblages were examined in relation to vertical, horizontal, and seasonal environmental gradients and to the host macrophytes. The diatom assemblages were epiphytic on host plants, except for one endophytic taxon. Information about the systematics of estuarine diatoms and hypotheses related to host-epiphyte interactions are contributed. Epiphytic diatom assemblages in the intertidal zone were sampled from the host macrophytes Zostera marina, Fucus evanescens, and Enteromorpha species, Polysiphonia, and Ulva. In general, host-epiphyte specificity was not apparent. The structure of diatom assemblages on adjacent host macrophytes of the same species often differed as greatly as the community structures of assemblages from nearby host macrophytes of different species. Differences in community structure between assemblages in September and May were correlated with horizontal salinity gradients, to vertical exposure, and insolation gradients. In January, differences between assemblages apparently were also related to biological factors involving host-epiphyte interactions, and thc condition of the host macrophyte was probably the basis for this interaction. The epiphytic diatom flora was similar in species composition to the epilithic flora described in an earlier study. (Jones-Wisconsin)
W75-08141

COMPLEXING CAPACITY OF THE NUTRIENT MEDIUM AND ITS RELATION TO INHIBITION OF ALGAL PHOTOSYNTHESIS BY COPPER,

Canada Centre for Inland Waters, Burlington (Ontario).
R. Gachter, K. Lum-Shue-Chan, and Y. K. Chau.
Schweizerische Zeitschrift fur Hydrologic, Vol 35, No 2, p 252-261, 1973. 2 fig, 3 tab, 35 ref.

Descriptors: *Chelation, *Algal control, *Copper, *Toxicity, *Inhibition, Chlorella, Ions, Inorganic compounds, Photosynthesis.
Identifiers: *Copper detoxification, Ligands.

How much ionic copper could be masked by filtered lake waters and by aged culture medium in which Chlorella had been grown and to relate this masking ability to a capacity to buffer further additions of copper without adversely affecting phytoplankton production was investigated. Natural waters have the property to mask added copper ions. This complexing capacity is attributed to ligands forming copper complexes. It is possible to measure this complexing capacity with relatively high accuracy. The complexing capacity of a water sample does not guarantee that the equivalent amount of copper could be tolerated by the system without adversely affecting phytoplankton production. It is not possible now either to measure the concentration of free copper ions in equilibrium with ligands or to estimate it indirectly by calculation, since the nature of ligands and therefore the formation constants with other metals are not known. If only ionic and not complexed copper is toxic, it is most probable that it inhibits photosynthesis of planktonic algae at concentrations of about 1 million mole/1. Seasonal variations of natural copper concentration in concert with the complexing property of the water might have an influence on phytoplankton succession. (Jones-Wisconsin)
W75-08142

PHYSICAL AND CHEMICAL LIMNOLOGY OF CHAR LAKE, CORNWALLIS ISLAND (75 DEGREES N LAT.),

Fisheries Research Board of Canada, Winnipeg (Manitoba). Freshwater Inst.
D. W. Schindler, H. E. Welch, J. Kalff, G. J. Brunskill, and N. Kritsch.
Journal Fisheries Research Board of Canada, Vol 31, No 5, p 585-607, 1974. 15 fig, 6 tab, 44 ref.

Descriptors: *Physical properties, *Chemical properties, *Limnology, Canada, Polar regions, Lakes, Evaporation, Conductivity, Ice, Snow, Solar radiation, Freezing, Phosphorus, Nitrogen, Precipitation(Atmospheric), Nutrients, Silica, Chlorides, Sulfates, Bicarbonates, Arctic.
Identifiers: *Char Lake(Canada).

Although limnological research has been carried out in the arctic for several decades, data on high arctic lakes are few. Seasonal data for several physical and chemical variables in Char Lake are given. Lake temperatures were measured at 1-m intervals and ice thickness near the center of the lake. Snow measurements were made at irregular intervals and surface irradiance at lake-side. Light energy entering the water was calculated. Annual cycles of major solutes are influenced primarily by freeze-thaw cycles. Concentrations of most substances are increased by freezing-out during winter. Because the lake does not circulate during maximum spring meltwater flow, this freezing-out maintains concentrations above those in inflow streams. Concentration of phosphorus and nitrogen are low throughout the year. Precipitation contains little phosphorus or nitrogen. Inputs of phosphorus and nitrogen are calculated to be 0.016 and 0.314 g/sq m, respectively. Retention of nutrients is lower than in temperature regions, although quite efficient. With the exception of silica, return of ions from sediments during winter was negligible. Disturbance of one inflow stream due to airstrip constuction caused great increases in concentrations of nitrogen, silica, chloride,

sulfate, and bicarbonate in the stream. (Jones-Wisconsin)
W75-08143

A REVIEW OF RESEARCH ON THE LIMNOLOGY OF WEST BLUE LAKE, MANITOBA,
Manitoba Univ., Winnipeg. Dept. of Zoology.
F. J. Ward, and G. G. C. Robinson.
Journal Fisheries Research Board of Canada, Vol 31, No 5, p 977-1005, 1974. 11 fig, 12 tab, 52 ref.

Descriptors: *Limnology, *Productivity, Reviews, Canada, Phytoplankton, Diatoms, Anabaena, Zooplankton, Carbon, Varieties, Bacteria, Dominant organisms, Fish populations, Perches, Walleye, Organic compounds, Copepods, Daphnia, Fish diets, Biomass.
Identifiers: *West Blue Lake(Manitoba).

Previously unpublished data, information from theses, and data abstracted from published papers are reviewed. In spring 'net' phytoplankton diversity and abundance were highest with diatoms predominating. In summer Anagena spiroides and Aphanizomenon flos aquae were a major component. Cyclotella bodanica dominated in winter. Average summer phytoplankton primary productivity approximated 320 mg C/sq m/day. Average daily estimates (exclusive of zooplankton) of organic carbon in the euphotic zone during summer were, respectively, 5 and 8 g C/sq m. Kinetic parameters for bacterial uptake of 11 dissolved organie substrates are reported. Evidence for proliferation and adaptation of bacteria in sample bottles is presented and the absence of photoheterotrophy is described. Generally, Cyclops bicuspidatus was more abundant than Diaptomus siciloides; both were relatively scarce in summer. Daphnia pulicaria was usually most abundant in spring and early summer, and persisted at low levels during winter. Largest animals with high relative caloric content predominated in fall, winter, and early spring when reproduction was minimal. Northern pike, brook stickleback, lake trout, yellow perch and walleye inhabit the lake with the latter two most abundant. Perch are an important food for walleye consequently the feeding habits and general biology of perch were investigated. (Jones-Wisconsin)
W75-08145

KEYS TO WATER QUALITY INDICATIVE ORGANISMS (SOUTHEASTERN UNITED STATES),
Georgia State Coll., Atlanta.
FWPCA, November 1968. 197 p, 203 fig, 2 tab, 166 ref. FWPCA ITT1-WP-19-01.

Descriptors: *Water quality, *Systematics, *Biology, *Southeast U.S., Aquatic fungi, Algae, Mollusks, Oligochaetes, Crustaceans, Aquatic insects, Mayflies, Stoneflies, Caddisflies, Midges, Freshwater fish, Freshwater, Bioindicators.

This manual was prepared as a reference for biologists in southeastern United States involved in water quality studies. In order to accurately identify those organisms most important in water quality surveys, illustrated keys of fungi, algae, Mollusca, Oligochaeta, Crustacea, Ephemoroptera, Plecoptera, Trichoptera, Chironomidae, and fish are presented, with labeled figures for each couplet, except in three sections. The section on fungi is merely an introduction indicating their occurence in nature and including a guide to the literature. Illustrated keys to algae and fish are available thus are not given in this publication, although a guide and key to the most commonly encountered algae is included. The freshwater biota of southeastern United States is not as well-known as those for other areas; much of the existing literature concerning life histories and ecological requirements is based on forms from other areas which are often not applicable to this region. Suggestions for reference materials with descriptions of the forms which have been keyed, for seeking information from specialists, and for preserving speciemens are made. Additional references are given in bibliographies for each section. Each key also includes information on known ecological requirements, distribution, etc., as an aid to water quality evaluations. (See W75-08147 thru W75-08156) (Buchanan-Davidson--Wisconsin)
W75-08146

FUNGI,
Georgia State Coll., Atlanta. Dept. of Biology.
D. G. Ahearn.
In: Keys to Water Quality Indicative Organisms (Southeastern United States), p C1-C8, FWPCA, November 1968. 21 ref. FWPCA ITT1-WP-19-01.

Descriptors: *Aquatic fungi, *Systematics, Yeasts, Degradation (Decomposition), Bioindicators, Sewage bacteria, Sphaerotilus, Bacteria.
Identifiers: Sewage fungi.

A general introduction to fungi is given. Traditionally true fungi are classified as Eumycotina of phylum Mycota of the plant kingdom, but some consider fungi an esentially monophyletic group distinct from plants and animals. Most fungi have broad enzymic capacities, degrading polysaccharides, proteins, hydrocarbons, and pesticides. Most possess oxidative or microaerophilic metabolism, but some have anaerobic catabolism or metabolism. Fungi are ubiquitous in aquatic habitats, are important in mineralization of organic wastes, and may be used as indicator organisms. The most common 'sewage fungi' are Sphaerotilus natans and Leptomitus lacteus, but S. natans is actually a sheath bacterium. Both thrive in organically rich water, do not grow well above 30C, have oxidative metabolism and appear as reddish -brown flocs or stringy slimes. Deuteromycetes and phycomycetes may be more ecologically important than 'sewage fungi'. Usually classifications are based on morphology of sexual and zoosporic stages; however many fungi do not demonstrate these stages, thus classification should be based on morphological and/or physiological characteristics. A synopsis of fungi classification is presented. (See also W75-08146) (Buchanan-Davidson–Wisconsin)
W75-08147

ALGAE,
Robert A. Taft Sanitary Engineering Center, Cincinnati, Ohio. Cincinnati Water Research Lab.
C. M. Palmer.
In: Keys to Water Quality Indicative Organisms (Southeastern United States), p E1-E27, EWPCA, November 1968. 50 fig, 2 tab, 13 ref. FWPCA ITT1-WP-19-01.

Descriptors: *Algae, *Bioindicators, *Systematics, Eutrophication, Water quality, Water pollution effects, Varieties.

Most algae are aquatic, are found in surface water exposed to sunlight, and can produce large quantities of organic matter. Algae and other aquatic plants and animals grow on dissolved and suspended nutrients and affect water quality. Algae may be unattached, grow collectively as plankton, or accumulate as blooms or blankets. Some aquatic, pigmented forms containing chlorophyll can swim or crawl, but are listed here as algae. Most algae important in sanitary science can be classified in four main groups: blue-green, pigmented flagellates, greens, and diatoms. Algal growth can be adversely affected by gross pollution with organic wastes, with the survivors useful as pollution indicators. Over 600 species and genera of pollution-tolerant algae were reported by 110 workers which are arranged in order of pollution tolerance. Twenty-two most tolerant algae genera and 20 most tolerant species are listed as aids for individuals engaged in stream pollution surveys or related projects. They represent a general consensus as to the relative significance of algae tolerant of organic wastes which have been reported. Particular care can thus be taken in biological surveys to check for the presence of these algae during sample examination. A taxonomic key to algae important in water pollution is given. (See also W75-08146) (Buchanan-Davidson-Wisconsin)
W75-08148

MOLLUSCA,
Florida State Univ., Tallahassee. Dept. of Biological Science.
W. H. Heard.
In: Keys to Water Quality Indicative Organisms (Southeastern United States), p G1-G26, FWPCA, November 1968. 42 fig, 23 ref. FWPCA ITT1-WP-19-01.

Descriptors: *Systematics, *Mollusks, *Southeast U.S., Gastropods, Snails, Clams, Analytical techniques, Freshwater, Speciation, Aquatic animals.

Distribution of gastropods (snails) and pelecypods (clams) found in southeastern United States freshwater varies and is sometimes inadequately known. Because taxonomic characteristics used to identify mollusks are somewhat inconsistent, separate keys for snails (univalved) and clams (bivalved) are presented in which the most striking shell characteristics are used, except when soft-part characteristics along are applicable. Snails are subdivided into those without an operculum (Subclass Pulmonata) and those with an operenlum (Subclass Prosobranchia). Prosobranchia are subdivided into families Bythinidae, Neritidae, Pilidae, Pleuroceridae, Valvatidae, and Viviparidae and the Pulmonata into families Ancylidae, Lymnaeidae, Physidae, and Planorbidae,. Four families (Corbiculidae, Margaritiferidae, Sphaeridae, and Unionidae) of clams inhabit North America. Distribution of certain species vary widely, with the family Unionidae being the most widespread and abundant in southeastern United States. Careful narcotization to relax living animals in life-like positions, fixation to kill the animals, and preservation must be done to obtain a specimen showing minimal contraction and withdrawal into the shell, unharmed shell, and with soft-parts available for dissection of the reproductive system or preparation of radular mounts. Marsupial conditions found in the Unionidae are described. (See also W75-08146) (Buchanan-Davidson–Wisconsin)
W75-08149

OLIGOCHAETA,
Toronto Univ. (Ontario). Dept. of Zoology.
R. O. Brinkhurst.
In: Keys to Water Quality Indicative Organisms (Southeastern United States), p I1-I17, FWPCA, November 1968. 14 fig, 6 ref. FWPCA ITT1-WP-19-01.

Descriptors: *Oligochaetes, *Systematics, Worms, Tubificids, Freshwater, Speciation, Analytical techniques.

Oligochaeta can be classified into eight families which are found in freshwater habitats east of the Rocky Mountains: Aeolosomatidae, Naididae, Tubificidae, Enchytraeidae, Lumriculidae, Haplotaxidae, Opistocystidae, and Branchiobdellidae. The most important family, the Tubificidae, can be identified from simple whole-mounts, without keying out the genera; about half can be identified from immature specimens. Fewer than forty important species are known east of the Rockies. New species must be dissected for placement in genera, but can then be identified by superficial characteristics. Most Lumbriculidae must be dissected, but they are of limited importance. Worms may be killed and preserved in 70% alcohol, except for Branchiura sowerbyi which must be narcotized in 5% magnesium chloride before preservation. The first segment of oligochaetes is devoid of setae which are otherwise arranged in

four bundles on each segment (two dorsolateral and two ventrolateral). Detached as exually-produced forms differ as the dorsal setae is located in more anterior segments and the prostomium is absent. Setae are the principal features to study; they may be hair setae, bifid crotchets, pectinate setae, or genital setae. The commonest combinations of setae found in the various families are described. Taxonomic keys to freshwater oligochaetes and tubificids of Eastern North America is included. (See also W75-08146) (Buchanan-Davidson--Wisconsin)
W75-08150

CRUSTACEA: MALACOSTRACA,
Smithsonian Institution, Washington, D.C. Dept. of Invertebrate Zoology.
H. H. Hobbs.
In: Keys to Water Quality Indicative Organisms (Southeastern United States), p K1-K36, FWPCA, November 1968. 33 fig, 30 ref. FWPCA ITT1-WP-19-01.

Descriptors: *Crustaceans, *Systematics, Speciation, Amphipods, Isopods, Crayfish, Shrimp, Distribution, Southeast U.S.
Identifiers: *Malacostraca, Mysids, Decapods.

An illustrated key to freshwater Malacostraca occurring in southeastern United States contains descriptions of four orders: Isopoda, Amphipoda, Mysidacea, and Decapoda. The order Decapoda contributes the most species to epigean waters, with Astacidae (crayfish) outnumbering the Palaemonidae (shrimp). A number of undescribed species occur in the area and some may seem to fit couplets in the key, but identifications based on the key should be considered tentative until comparisons are made with full descriptions or with authoritatively determined specimens. Blue crab (Callinectes sapidus), typically marine forms which may invade freshwater in some localities, the introduced Saber crab (Platychirograpsus typicus), and albinistic (trogloditic) forms found in epigean waters near springs or streams issuing from underground water courses are not included in the key. Methods of collecting, preservation, preparation, and equipment for the examination of specimens are described in detail. The genus Macrobrachium can be identified only if males with the second pair of pereiopods intact are available. The key to crayfish is applicable only to first form males. Figures are given to illustrate the major characteristics used in identifcation, especially the first pleopod. Lists are given for species belonging to each genus with their known ranges. (See also W75-08146) (Buchanan-Davidson--Wisconsin)
W75-08151

EPHEMEROPTERA,
Florida Univ., Gainesville. Dept. of Biological Science.
L. Berner.
In: Keys to Water Quality Indicative Organisms (Southeastern United States), p M1-M10, FWPCA, November 1968. 9 fig, 7 ref. FWPCA ITT1-WP-19-01.

Descriptors: *Mayflies, *Aquatic insects, *Systematics, Speciation, Larvae, Varieties, Southeast U.S., Habitats.
Identifiers: Ephemeroptera.

A key is presented for the Ephemeroptera, listing only those genera known to occur in the southeastern United States. Mayfly nymphs are characterized by having chewing mouthparts, noticeable wing pads developing on the mesothorax, single larval claws, gills on abdominal segments 1-7 (some may be modified to form gill covers, others are vestigial, and some may be missing from certain segments), and an abdomen terminating in two or three long tails. All species require fresh water for development, although one Florida form tolerates a certain amount of salinity. The key should only be used with older insects since nymphs in their early instars are difficult to identify because distinctive traits have not developed. Since it may be hard to identify the first abdominal segment, counting should start with the most posterior or tenth segment and count anteriorly. Segment number is important to counting gills. Determination of the presence or absence of hind wing pads may also be difficult. The forewing pad must often be lifted to observe the hindwing pad. A brief statement of the most frequently encountered habitats in which the insect lives and the frequency of occurrence are given for each genus. Sketches of pertinent taxonomic characteristics are given. (See also W75-08146) (Buchanan-Davidson--Wisconsin)
W75-08152

PLECOPTERA,
Massachusetts Univ., Amherst. Dept. of Entomology and Plant Pathology.
J. F. Hanson.
In: Keys to Water Quality Indicative Organisms (Southeastern United States), p P1-P6, FWPCA, November 1968. 13 fig, 3 ref. FWPCA ITT1-WP-19-01.

Descriptors: *Stoneflies, *Systematics, *Aquatic insects, Bioindicators, Speciation.
Identifiers: *Plecoptera, Naiads.

The key to identify genera and subgenera to stoneflies by their most conspicuous characters and characters that are present in all or most of the stages of naiad growth is not a natural key. As presented, the characters are in decreasing order of importance. Because of high oxygen requirements, stonefly naiads live only in moving water and are often used to indicate lack of organic pollution. This may be true for species with long life cycles whose naiads spend two to four years in the water. Most species have a one year life cycle and often spend most of the year in the egg stage which is probably quite resistant to pollutants and tolerant of relatively low oxygen contents. Because many species have long egg stages, sampling may be difficult. In the summer it may be difficult to find stonefly naiads in streams that may have a varied and abundant fauna. Stoneflies are mobile, especially when the naiads are nearly full-grown and ready for emergence as adults, and may be carried downstream to emerge from polluted waters. Caution must be exercised in interpreting sample collections. More information is needed on stoneflies before they can be reliably used as pollution indicators. (See also W75-08146) (Buchanan-Davidson--Wisconsin)
W75-08153

TRICHOPTERA,
Georgia Univ., Athens. Dept. of Entomology.
J. B. Wallace.
In: Keys to Water Quality Indicative Organisms (Southeastern United States), p S1-S19, FWPCA, November 1968. 26 fig, 8 ref. FWPCA ITT1-WP-19-01.

Descriptors: *Caddisflies, *Aquatic insects, *Systematics, *Speciation, Varieties, Analytical techniques, Southeast U.S., Larvae, Habitats.
Identifiers: Trichoptera.

A taxonomic key is given for Trichoptera (caddisflies) which are found in southeastern United States, especially the southern Appalachians and their foothills. Most of the 19 families found in the United States are represented. Caddisfly larvae are found in habitats ranging from spring seeps and ponds to mountain streams. Larvae and pupae should be preserved in 80% ethyl alcohol, which should be changed after one week. Killing larvae in boiling water before preservation results in well extended specimens. Caddisfly larvae are of various types: free living forms (no cases or nets), net spinning forms (nets attached to plants, rocks, etc., which collapse when taken from the water), tube making forms (some psychomyiid larvae burrow into sandy bottoms of stream beds and cement tube walls), saddle case makers (Glossosomatidae live in tortoise-like cases of gravel), purse case makers (have a slit at each end of case for head and anal legs, found in many microcaddisflies or Hydroptilidae), and case makers (a variety of cases made from plant materials to sand grains). Some of the more important morphological characteristics used in larval identification are illustrated. The sclerites and/or setae may or may not be present, depending on the group. (See also W75-08146) (Buchanan-Davidson--Wisconsin)
W75-08154

CHIRONOMIDAE,
Florida State Board of Health, Jacksonville.
W. M. Beck.
In: Keys to Water Quality Indicative Organisms (Southeastern United States), p V1-V22, FWPCA, November 1968. 16 fig, 7 ref. FWPCA ITT1-WP-19-01.

Descriptors: *Diptera, *Aquatic insects, *Systematics, Analytical techniques, Southeast U.S., Florida, Larvae, Varieties, Midges.
Identifiers: *Chironomids, Tendipes, Pelopia, Tanypus.

The taxonomy of chironomids is based largely on adult morphology, but there is a need for knowledge of the identification and distribution of larvae. An estimated 400 species of chironomids are found in Florida, of which 275 adult species are named and fewer than 200 larvae are known. Many conflicts exist in the scientific nomenclature and several revisions of groups are currently being prepared which will necessitate revisions in portions of the key. Detailed directions are given for the preparation of slide mounts of specimens for larvae identification. The most important part for identification purposes is the head capsule which should be mounted ventral side up. The posterior portion bearing the posterior prolegs, supra-anal papillae, supra-anal bristles, anal gills, and blood gills is also important. Abdominal segments bearing lateral hair fringes, large setae, hair pencils. and special integument characteristics are of interest, but those of large larvae may be discarded. The key as presented has intentionally omitted a subfamily which is not found in the southeast, marine inter-tidal midges, and midges confined to highly specialized habitats. Suggestions are made for using the key: short cuts, calculation of the antennal ratio, and counting the number of teeth. (See also W75-08146) (Buchanan-Davidson--Wisconsin)
W75-08155

FRESHWATER FISHES,
Auburn Univ., Ala.
J. S. Ramsey.
In: Keys to Water Quality Indicative Organisms (Southeastern United States), p Y1-Y15, FWPCA, November 1968. 35 ref. FWPCA ITT1-WP-19-01.

Descriptors: *Freshwater fish, *Varieties, *Southeast U.S, *Bioindicators, Analytical techniques, Water pollution effects, Eutrophication, Bibliographies, Fish types, Fish behavior, Streams, Darters, Yellow perch, Rainbow trout, Brook trout, Pikes, Shiners, Minnows, White bass, Suckers, Channel catfish, Bass, Lake trout, Catfishes, Carp, Salmon, Cisco, Smelt, Walleye, Sculpins, Perches, Sunfishes, Lampreys.
Identifiers: Goldfish, Bluegills, Mountain whitefish, Mosquitofish, Swampfishes, Shad.

Methods of collection, preservation, labeling, and identification of freshwater fishes are described in detail. A bibliography containing useful modern references for identification of Eastern fishes containing 31 references is given as well as several references on fish distribution relative to the presence or absence of pollution. An attempt was

being made to determine tolerance levels or ecological requirements for 20 representative fish species and a number of fish were being tested against overall and specific pollutants. Possibly the only species which consistently thrives in polluted waters in Central and Southern U.S. is the mosquitofish (Gambusia affinis). In the Southern states three species seem to adapt to or tolerate a variety of pollutants that eliminate other fish, especially in small streams: the mosquitofish, the green sunfish (Lepomis cyanellus) and the bluegill (Lepomis macrochirus). In larger streams the fathead minnow (Pimephales promelas) also survives. If only one or a combination of these four species occurs pollution may be indicated. Several species of non-sessile habit are indicators of good water quality in Southern or Coastal Plain waters. A complete survey of fishes in a locality is desirable for proper pollution analysis. Knowledge of the normal habitat and natural fish limitation is essential for determining water quality. (See also W75-08146) (Auen-Wisconsin)
W75-08156

PHYTOPLANKTON GROWTH, DISSIPATION AND SUCCESSION IN ESTUARINE ENVIRONMENTS,
Johns Hopkins Univ., Baltimore, Md. Dept. of Biology.
H. H. Seliger.
Available from the National Technical Information Service, Springfield, Va 22161 as COO-3278-27, $4.00 in paper copy, $2.25 in microfiche. Progress report through April 1974. 35 p, 5 fig, 18 ref. AEC AT(11-1)3278.

Descriptors: *Estuaries, *Chesapeake Bay, *Plankton, Phytoplankton, Model studies, Primary productivity, Light, Nutrients, Secondary productivity, Sampling, Instrumentation, Succession, Microorganisms, Maryland.
Identifiers: *Rhode River(Maryland).

A progress report covering three years of research of the plankton dynamics at the Rhode River, a subestuary of Chesapeake Bay, briefly describes the scope and theoretical approach of the following research areas: Light- and nutrient-dependent physiology of estuarine phytoplankton; the relative contributions of phytoplankton primary production and bacterial (detrital) secondary production to the nutrition of the microzooplankton and possible filter feeders; instrumentation techniques, diagnostic parameters and sampling procedures for analyzing phytoplankton growth, dissipation and species succession; and development of a plankton model for comparable sections of subestuaries which can define the system's stability in relation to its response to nutrient, biocide, or thermal loading. Comprehensive details of each research phase are given in the parenthetically numbered documents, available separately under the following titles: Investigations of the light environment in Rhode River (COO-3278-24), Natural phytoplankton community and the requirement for in situ diffusible containers (COO-3278-16), Rotifer biomass and predation rates (COO-3278-3), Carbon limitations in Chesapeake Bay (COO-3278-21), Cooperative studies on baywide phytoplankton distributions (COO-3278-26), In vivo fluorescence of chlorophyll-a (COO-3278-22), and, The effects of Trophical Storm Agnes on the phytoplankton in the Rhode River (COO-3278-23). (Auen-Wisconsin)
W75-08157

ALGAL BIOMASS PROJECTIONS FOR THE PROPOSED KICKAPOO RIVER IMPOUNDMENT,
Wisconsin Univ., Madison. IBP Lake Wingra Project.
E. H. Dettman.
In: IES Report 28, Environmental Analysis of the Kickapoo River Impoundment, p 117-124. 4 fig, 4 ref. DACW 37-C-0130.

Descriptors: *Reservoirs, *Cyanophyta, *Biomass, Eutrophication, Nuisance algae, Wisconsin, Aquatic plants, Absorption, Nutrients, Computer models, Nitrogen, Diatoms, Phosphorus.
Identifiers: *Kickapoo River(Wis), *La Farge Lake(Wis).

Computer simulations of algal biomass in Lake La Farge, Wisconsin, the proposed Kickapoo River impoundment, between April to mid-September were made with a model of biomass, nitrogen, and phosphorus dynamics in freshwater lakes to indicate the general range of actual lake behavior. Simulations showed that nutrients would support a mean algal biomass of 6.1-9.5 g dry weight/sq m. Macrophyte uptake would reduce mean algal density 4-8% thus should not cause a major reduction of algal abundance. Reduced nutrient loading would lower algal biomass; a reduction of 28% would decrease biomass by 19%. Investigation of model behavior for buoyant blue-green algae indicated the potential for densities in the range of 12-18 g dry weight/sq m. The simulations indicate a trend toward a decrease in algal biomass in July, August, and September when blue-green species are present. The algae developing a deep system like Lake La Farge would probably be the more buoyant, scum-forming species. Simulated blue-green algal levels appear to be partially limited by the algal sinking rate and not phosphorus, consequently the late summer algal biomass may be higher than computed. Large blooms of noxious species may occur in late summer. (See also W75-08158) (Buchanan-Davidson--Wisconsin)
W75-08162

RUNOFF FROM AN INTERTIDAL MARSH DURING TIDAL EXPOSURE - RECESSION CURVES AND CHEMICAL CHARACTERISTICS,
South Carolina Univ., Columbia. Belle W. Baruch Coastal Research Inst.
For primary bibliographic entry see Field 2L.
W75-08193

OXYGENATION OF LAKE HYPOLIMNIA,
Rutgers-The State Univ., New Brunswick, N.J. Water Resources Research Inst.
W. Whipple, J. V. Hunter, F. B. Trama, and J. R. Westman.
Research report, April 1973. 5 p, 5 fig. OWRT B-050-NJ(1).

Descriptors: *Oxygenation, *Lakes, *Hypolimnion, *Methodology, Eutrophication, Fisheries, Nutrients, Reservoirs, *New Jersey.
Identifiers: *Spruce Run(NJ).

The hypothesis to be tested is that, if the cycle of annual algal growth can once be broken for a two year period, it is probable that in many cases the eutrophication process would be arrested, and in such cases the lake would remain aerobic (oligotrophic) until a surplus nutrient supply is again introduced. The presumption is that by oxygenating the hypolimnion, without destratifying the lake, trout and their food fish can be successfully raised in the lake the year round. The experimental lake is Spruce Run, a water supply reservoir located near Clinton, N.J. on the South Branch of the Raritan River. Year round trout culture in the reservoir is marginal and algal growth is prolific in summer, despite the very high quality of incoming water. Three deep water oxygenators will be installed in a test area and only the hypolimnion will be oxygenated during the summers of 1973 and 1974. Methods are illustrated and described. The reduction in dissolved phosphate due to the oxygenation will be the most direct measure of success of the project. Biological changes will be monitored. (Jones-Wisconsin)
W75-08194

THE CHANGES OF BENTHOS IN SLAPY RESERVOIR IN THE YEARS 1960-1961,
Ceskoslovenska Akademie Ved, Prague. Hydrobiologicka Laborator.
For primary bibliographic entry see Field 2H.
W75-08246

SOME PHYSICOCHEMICAL FEATURES OF A MEROMICTIC LAKE SUIGETSU,
Nagoya Univ. (Japan). Water Research Lab.
For primary bibliographic entry see Field 2H.
W75-08255

METHEMOGLOBIN LEVELS IN INFANTS IN AN AREA WITH HIGH NITRATE WATER SUPPLY,
California State Dept. of Public Health, Sacramento.
L. A. Shearer, J. R. Goldsmith, C. Young, O. A. Kearns, and B. R. Tamplin.
Am J Public Health, Vol 62, No 9, p 1174-1180, 1972. Illus.
Identifiers: *Bacteria, *Nitrates, *Water supply, *Methemoglobin levels(Human infants), Water pollution effects, Water pollution sources, Public health.

A study of methemoglobin levels in infants from birth through 6 mo. showed that even healthy babies not exposed to excessive nitrate levels in diets have higher levels when young. Babies with diarrhea or respiratory illness had the highest levels in this population. Ingestion of water or formula high in nitrates appears to increase the frequency of elevated methemomoglobin. More than 60% of formulae showed bacterial contamination. Long-term consequences should be investigated.--Copyright 1973, Biological Abstracts, Inc.
W75-08256

ORGANIC SUBSTANCES IN SEDIMENT AND SETTLING MATTER DURING SPRING IN A MEROMICTIC LAKE SUIGETSU,
Nagoya Univ. (Japan). Water Research Lab.
For primary bibliographic entry see Field 2H.
W75-08257

THE EFFECTS OF TEMPERATURE AND RADIATION STRESS ON AN AQUATIC MICROECOSYSTEM,
Virginia Commonwealth Univ., Richmond. Dept. of Biology.
G. L. Samsel, Jr.
Trans Ky Acad Sci, Vol 33, No 1/2, p 1-12, 1972. Illus.
Identifiers: Aquatic life, Cyclops-viridis, Cypris-virens, *Ecosystems, *Radiation stress, *Temperature, *Ostracods, Production, Water pollution effects.

The effects of temperature and ionizing radiation on population density and net production of clonal strains of an ostracod (Cypris virens) and a copepod (Cyclops viridis growing separately and together in aquatic microecosystems were studied. At 10, 20, and 35C, copepods consistently achieved greater adult population densities when accompanied by ostracods. Total net production (all immature forms), adult population densities, and maximum longevities of both crustaceans were greatest at 10C and greater at 20C than at 35C. Three replicates were cultured at 10, 20, and 35C, after exposure to 0, 24, 48, and 96 kR of gamma rays. Adult survival of copepods was nuaffected immediately after radiation exposure of 24 and 48 and 96 kR level. Copepod reproduction was inhibited at 16, 24, 48 and 96 kR; but reproduction did occur at 8 kR. The adult population density and life span of the copepod was similar at all radiation levels not exposed to temperature stress. Ostracod survival immediately decreased 7% after exposure to 24 kR, 23% after exposure to 48 kR, and 47% after exposure to 96 kR. Adult population density and net production of both organisms exposed to 24, 48, and 96 kR varied insignificantly when cultured at 20C. Net production, life span, and adult population density or irradiated organisms cultured at 35C were considerably lower than those at 20 or 10C. Net production of irradiated organisms was significantly lower than controls, but varied very little among exposure doses.--Copyright 1973, Biological Abstracts, Inc.
W75-08258

OLIGOTROPHICATION: A SELF-ACCELERATING PROCESS IN LAKES SUBJECTED TO EXCESSIVE SUPPLY OF ACID SUBSTANCES,
Institue for Water and Air Pollution Research, Stockholm (Sweden).
O. Grahn, H. Hultberg, and L. Landner.
Ambio, Vol 3, No 2, p 93-94, 1974. Illus.
Identifiers: *Acids, Lakes, *Oligotrophication, Hydrogen ion concentration, Eutrophication, Ecosystems.

The dynamics of the ecosystems of acidified lakes were investigated by integrated studies directed at all trophic levels in 6 acid lakes with pH values between 4.4 and 5.4. The primary biological effects on individuals and populations of a continuous supply of acid substances to a lake may induce profound, long-term changes, forcing the lake into an increasingly more oligotrophic state. This general oligotrophication of lakes tends-by means of a feedback mechanism-to further accelerate the process of acidification.--Copyright 1974, Biological Abstracts, Inc.
W75-08262

RATES OF OXYGEN UPTAKE BY THE PLANKTONIC COMMUNITY OF A SHALLOW EQUATORIAL LAKE (LAKE GEORGE, UGANDA),
Vienna Univ. (Austria). Limnologische Lehrkanzel.
G. G. Ganf.
Oecologia (Berl), Vol 15, No 1, p 17-32, 1974. Illus.
Identifiers: Algae, Bacteria, Equatorial lakes, Lakes, *Oxygen absorption(Plankton), Photosynthesis, Phytoplankton, Planktonic communities, Respiration, *Uganda(Lake George), Zooplankton, Shallow lakes.

Community respiration rates of the plankton in the upper meter of a shallow equatorial lake (Lake George, Uganda) show diurnal fluctuations within the range 1-4.5 mg O2/mg chlorophyll a h. In the deeper water, below the euphotic zone, rates show less variation and approximate a value of 1 mg O2/mg chl a h. Comparative field and laboratory measurements of the relationship between community respiration and temperature indicate that the dirunal variation observed is not a simple function of temperature variation. Field measurements suggest that the rate of community respiration tends to increase, in a non-linear manner, as the daily cumulative photosynthesis/unit population increases. A series of laboratory experiments are described which attempt to fractionate, by chemical means, the O2 uptake due to phytoplankton, bacteria and zooplankton. Although the results were variable they indicate that somewhere between 10 and 50% of the total O2 uptake is due non-algal material. The influence of these findings on calculations of net daily photosynthesis is discussed.--Copyright 1974, Biological Abstracts, Inc.
W75-08263

SEASONAL FLUCTUATIONS OF THE MEIOBENTHOS IN AN ESTUARY ON THE SWEDISH WEST COAST,
Uppsala Univ. (Sweden). Inst. of Zoology.
K.-G. Nyholm, and I. Olsson.
Zoon, Vol 1, No 1, p 69-76, 1973, Illus.

Descriptors: *Benthos, *Coasts, Europe, *Estuaries, Sewage, Pollution, Water pollution, *Organic wastes, Waste water, Ecosystems.

Identifiers: Cyclopidea, Foraminifera, Halacarida, Harpacticoidea, Hydroidea, Kinorhyncha, *Meiobenthos, Nematoda, Ostracoda, *Sweden.

The investigation was carried out 1961-65 in the inner part of the Kungsbackafjorden, an estuary on the Swedish west coast in a region where an increase of sewage can be expected. Samples were taken on 9 occasions during about 1 yr in order to study the hydrography and the meiobenthos (0.2-2 mm) at 3 localities at 3, 4 and 16 m. The salinity may in all cases be classified as polyhalin. At the deeper station more decomposed organic debris is accumulated and here the content of organic C is very high. The O2 content of the bottom water is not a critical factor but saturation values below 50% were intermittently obtained. The meiobenthos samples were taken with a 'Bodensauger' (100cm2) and only the upper-most cm of the sediment was studied. Meiobenthos ranged from 4000-150,000/m2 in number of individuals and from 0.002-0.7 g/m2 in wet weight. Maximum abundances were obtained in the autumn. The following groups were included: Foraminifera, Hydroidea, Nematoda, Kinorhyncha, Ostracoda, Harpacticoidea, Cyclopidea and Halacarida. All the data concerning these faunal groups were statistically treated by analysis of variance. The data of the 2 shallower stations were compared with regard to both time and space and the interaction effect of these quantities was examined. The comparison between localities gave significant differences for monothalamous foraminifers, Rotaliidae, Ostracoda and Harpacticoidea. With regard to time, there were significant differences for all groups except Hydroidea and Kinorhyncha. As to the deepest station, with regard to time, there were significant differences for monothalamous foraminifers, Nematoda, Kinorhyncha and Harpacticoidea. The pattern in the quantitative fluctuations of the group. Kinorhyncha was very similar to that of Nematoda, which indicates an important role in the estuarine ecosystem for the former group.--Copyright 1974, Biological Abstracts, Inc.
W75-08271

NATURAL RESOURCES IN MODERN WORLD AND THE PROBLEM OF THEIR CONSERVATION, (IN ROMANIAN),
Academia R. S. R., Cluj. Centrul de Cercetari Biologice.
For primary bibliographic entry see Field 6G.
W75-08274

THE ROLE OF TRACE ELEMENTS IN MANAGEMENT OF NUISANCE GROWTHS,
Academy of Natural Sciences of Philadelphia, Pa.
For primary bibliographic entry see Field 5G.
W75-08278

MODELING DYNAMICS OF BIOLOGICAL AND CHEMICAL COMPONENTS OF AQUATIC ECOSYSTEMS,
Environmental Protection Agency, Athens, Ga. Southeast Environmental Research Lab.
R. R. Lassiter.
Available from the National Technical Information Service, Springfield, Va 22161 as PB-241 987, $4.25 in paper copy, $2.25 in microfiche. Report EPA-660/3-75-012, May, 1975. 54 p, 11 fig, 43 ref. 1BA023.

Descriptors: *Simulation analysis, Photosynthesis, *Growth rates, Phytoplankton, Zooplankton, *Ecosystems, Water chemistry, *Model studies, Nitrogen cycle, Computer models, Limnology, Algae.
Identifiers: Predator-prey models, Inhibition models, Microbial growth rate, Algal growth rate, *Aquatic ecosystem models, Temperature related growth.

To provide capability to model aquatic ecosystems or their sub-systems as needed for particular research goals, a modeling strategy was developed. Submodels of several processes common to aquatic ecosystems were developed or adapted from previously existing ones. Included are submodels for photosynthesis as a function of light and depth, biological growth rates as a function of temperature, dynamic chemical equilibrium, feeding and growth, and various types of losses to biological populations. These submodels may be used as modules in the construction of models of subsystems or ecosystems. A preliminary model for the nitrogen cycle subsystem was developed using the modeling strategy and applicable submodels. (EPA)
W75-08279

A REVIEW OF THE LITERATURE ON THE USE OF BAYLUSCIDE IN FISHERIES,
National Marine Fisheries Service, Ann Arbor, Mich. Great Lakes Fishery Lab.
S. E. Hamilton.
Available from the National Technical Information Service, Springfield, Va. 22161, as PB-235 441, $4.25 in paper copy, $2.25 in microfiche. National Marine Fisheries Service, July 1974. 54 p, 1 tab, 114 ref.

Descriptors: *Reviews, *Pest control, *Pesticides, *Lamphreys, Bibliographies, Freshwater fish, Fisheries, Surveys, Sport fish, Mode of Action, Toxicity.
Identifiers: *Bayluscide, *Lampricides.

A review of the literature on the uses and applications of Bayluscide is presented. Bayluscide has been tested against freshwater snails and has been used in field trials as a fish toxicant. In the 5% granular formation, Bayluscide has been used since 1966 to survey populations of larval sea lampreys in Great Lakes estuaries and deepwater tributaries. At present, in the United States, the registration restricts use to population surveys only. (Katz)
W75-08303

BEHAVIOR OF ULTRASONIC TAGGED CHINOOK SALMON AND STEELHEAD TROUT MIGRATING PAST HANFORD THERMAL DISCHARGES(1967),
Battelle-Pacific Northwest Labs., Richland, Wash.
C. C. Coutant.
Available from the National Technical Information Service, Springfield, Va. 22161, as BNWL-1530, $4.00 in paper copy, $2.25 in microfiche. Report BNWL-1530, prepared for the US Atomic Energy Commission, under Contract AT (45-1): 1830, July 1973. 15 p, 2 tab, 5 fig, 11 ref.

Descriptors: *Thermal pollution, *Fish behavior, *Trout, *Migration, *Chinook Salmon, Aquatic environment, Fish migration, Columbia River, Tracking techniques, Temperature, Nuclear reactors, Movement.
Identifiers: *Oncorhynchus tshawytscha, *Steelhead trout.

Ultransonic tagged, adult chinook and steelhead were tracked in 1967 during upstream migration past cooling water discharges from nuclear reactors. All fish migrated near shorelines, showing preference for the river bank opposite reactors. Clear responses to local temperature differences were exhibited by few fish, these responses being to small shoreline seepages rather than to main center-channel outfalls. (Katz)
W75-08304

MAMMALIAN TOXICOLOGY AND TOXICITY TO AQUATIC ORGANISMS OF WHITE PHOSPHORUS AND 'PHOSSY WATER", A WATERBORNE MUNITIONS MANUFACTURING WASTE POLLUTANT - A LITERATURE EVALUATION FINAL COMPREHENSIVE REPORT,
Associated Water and Air Resources Engineers, Inc., Nashville, Tenn.
D. Burrows, and J. C. Dacre.
Available from the National Technical Information Service, Springfield, Va. 22161, as AD-777 901, $3.75 in paper copy, $2.25 in microfiche. Report to US Army Medical Research and Development Command, Washington, DC, 20315, November 1973. 50 p, 1 fig, 7 tab, 189 ref.

Descriptors: *Phosphorus, *Toxicity, *Lethal limit, *Reviews, Fish, Molluscs, Lobsters, Mortality, Water pollution sources, Pollutants, Aquatic life.
Identifiers: Phossy water, Phosphine, Munitions.

A review of the literature on the toxicology and toxicity of white phosphorus is presented. Elemental white phosphorus is highly toxic to experimental animals and man causing gastrointestinal irritation, liver damage and eventual coma, convulsions and death. The fatal dose for man is about 1-1.4 mg/kg. Biochemical studies are reported and summarized. White phosphorus is also highly toxic to aquatic animals. The 96 hr LC50's are less than 50 ppb for all fish studied, and the incipient lethal level is probably less than 1 ppb for most fish. Crustaceans and many molluscs are more tolerant, but still succumb to phosphorus concentrations of 1 ppm or less. Phosphorus poisoning appears to be cumulative and irreversible for fish and lobsters. The cause of mortality in fish has not been determined. Recommendations for studies on white phosphorus and phossy water in experimental animals and in wastewaters are outlined. (Katz)
W75-08305

A REVIEW OF THE LITERATURE ON THE USE OF ANTIMYCIN IN FISHERIES,
Bureau of Sport Fisheries and Wildlife, LaCrosse, Wis. Fish Control Lab.
R. A. Schnick.
Available from the National Technical Information Service, Springfield, Va. 22161, as PB-235 440, $4.75 in paper copy, $2.25 in microfiche. April 1974. 85 p, 5 tab, 70 ref.

Descriptors: *Pesticides, *Piscicides, Antibiotics(Pesticides), *Pest control, *Reviews, *Antimycin A, *Aquiculture, Fishes, Freshwater fish, Mode of action, Toxicity.

Literature on the use of antimycin in fisheries in reviewed. Antimycin can be used very selectively, and can be detoxified by potassium permanganate or chlorine. Piscicidal concentrations of antimycin are relatively harmless to other aquatic life. However, on-site bioassays should be conducted to ensure that an overdose of antimycin is not applied. A sensitive assay method is available for determining levels in the water and current research may soon provide a sensitive method for tissues. (Katz)
W75-08306

THE CHEMICAL ECOLOGY OF COPEPOD DISTRIBUTION IN THE LAKES OF EAST AND CENTRAL AFRICA,
Duke Univ., Durham, N.C. Dept. of Zoology.
For primary bibliographic entry see Field 2H.
W75-08321

STRATIGRAPHIC EFFECTS OF TUBIFICIDS IN PROFUNDAL LAKE SEDIMENTS,
Maine Univ., Orono. Dept. of Botany and Plant Pathology.
R. B. Davis.
Limnol Oceanogr, Vol 19, No 3, p 466-488, 1974, Illus.
Identifiers: Alimentation, Feces, Lakes, Limnodrilus, Mathematical models, Pollen, Sediments, *Stratigraphic effects, *Tubificids, *Lake sediments(Profundal), *Maine(Messalonskee Lake).

Experiments conducted with natural mixed populations of 800 and 1800 tubificids (Limnodrilus) m to minus 2 power in sediment from Messalonskee Lake, Maine, showed average sediment transport by alimentation at 10C 2-3 times greater than highest rates previously reported. More than 95% of feeding on introduced pollen was at depths above 7 cm, with greatest feeding at 3-4 cm. Small amounts of pollen were raised to the surface from as deep as 15 cm. Downward transport was 14 and 19% of upward. Small pollen grains (< 40 micrometers) were fed upon and displaced at higher rates than large grains. Organic matter was less in the surface layer of feces than in sediment from feeding depths and in surface sediment where no worms were present. A mathematical model was used to appraise the stratigraphic effects of the worms by deriving age-frequency composition of sediment at various depths.--Copyright 1974, Biological Abstracts, Inc.
W75-08322

THE EFFECTS OF DISSOLVED ZINC ON THE GILLS OF THE STICKLEBACK GASTEROSTEUS ACULEATUS (L.),

Queen Elizabeth Coll., London (England). Dept. of Biology.
P. Matthiessen, and A. E. Brafield.

J Fish Biol, Vol 5, No 5, p 607-613, 1973, Illus.
Identifiers: Cytoplasmic, Excretion, Gasterosteus-aculeatus, Gills, Ions, Pollution, *Stickleback, Water pollution effects, *Zinc(Dissolved).

Concentrations of 0.5-1.0 mg Zn2+/dm3 distilled water killed sticklebacks after 103 days, producing detachment and sloughing of epithelial cells and coalescing of adjacent secondary lamellar epithelia. Cytoplasmic abnormalities included extensive vacuolation, followed by swelling of nuclei and mitochondria leading to cellular disintegration. Many acutely poisoned fish recovered in Zn-free hard water, regeneration of epithelia being accompanied by a temporary appearance of chloride cells on the secondary lamellae. Concentrations of 2.0-6.0 mg Zn2+/dm3 hard water were not toxic over periods of up to 600 h. Extensive cytoplasmic abnormalities appeared including the formation of membrane-bound vesicles and dense accumulations of metabolites. The most pronounced effect was the appearance of active chloride cells on the secondary lamellae. The possible involvement of chloride cells in the excretion of ions other than Cl- is briefly discussed.--Copyright 1974, Biological Abstracts, Inc.
W75-08327

STUDIES ON UPTAKE AND LOSS OF METHYLMERCURY-203 BY BLUEGILLS (LEPOMIS MACROCHIRUS RAF.),

Associated Water and Air Resources Engineers, Inc., Nashville, Tenn.
W. D. Burrows, and P. A. Krenkel.

Environ Sci Technol, Vol 7, No 13, p 1127-1130, 1973, Illus.
Identifiers: *Bluegills, Kidney, Lepomis-macrochirus, Liver, *Mercury-203, *Methylmercury, Pollution, Water pollution effects, Absorption.

The uptake of methylmercury-203 directly from water by bluegills was nearly constant after 5 days at about 20%/g of fish/l of water. Transferred to Hg-free water at 24C, bluegills exhibited a rapid loss of about 40% of the Hg, followed by a slow loss with a half-time of about 5 mo. Hg levels in the liver and kidneys were 2-7 times higher than whole fish levels, but there was no discernible trend in this ratio with time. The proportion of Hg present as methylmercury in the whole remained at 73 plus or minus 10% throughout the course of the experiment. The proportion of methylmercury in the liver and kidneys fell rapidly in the 1st few weeks after exposure, ultimately leveling off at about 10%. This suggests that biochemical demethylation is taking place in these organs.--Copyright 1974, Biological Abstracts, Inc.
W75-08328

URBANIZATION AND THE MICROBIAL CONTENT OF THE NORTH SASKATCHEWAN RIVER,

Alberta Univ., Edmonton. Dept. of Microbiology.
R. N. Coleman, J. N. Campbell, F. D. Cook, and D. W. S. Westlake.

Appl Microbiol, Vol 27, No 1, p 93-101, 1974, Illus.

Descriptors: *Urbanization, Rivers, *Microorganisms, Bacteria, *Canada, E. coli.
Identifiers: Salmonella, *North Saskatchewan River.

The effect of urbanization on the microbial content of the North Saskatchewan River, Canada was determined by following the changes in the numbers of total bacteria, total eosin methylene blue (EMB) plate count, and Escherichia coli as the river flowed from its glacial source, through parklands, and out into the prairies. Changes in physical parameters such as pH, temperature, salt concentration, and the amount and nature of the suspended material were also determined to evaluate their effect on the microbial parameters being measured. The level of all 3 microbial parameters studied slowly increased as the river flowed from its glacial source out into the prairies. The major effect of small hamlets, with or without sewage treatment facilities, is to supply nutrients which supports the growth of the indigenous river flora but not E. coli. In contrast, the effect of a large urban center, with a population of approximately 500,000 which utilizes primary and secondary sewage processes in disposing of sewage, is to provide the nutrients and an inoculum of E. coli which results in a marked increase in the numbers of all 3 microbial groups studied. The effect of this urban center was still discernible 300 miles downstream. The river was also monitored for the presence of Salmonella sp. Only 1 positive isolation was achieved during this study, and this isolate was characterized as being Salmonella alachua.--Copyright 1974, Biological Abstracts, Inc.
W75-08329

ACCUMULATION, RELEASE AND RETENTION OF PETROLEUM HYDROCARBONS BY THE OYSTER CRASSOSTREA VIRGINICA,

Woods Hole Oceanographic Institution, Mass. Dept. of Biology.
J. J. Stegeman, and J. M. Teal.

Mar Biol (Berl). Vol 22, No 1, p 37-44, 1973, Illus.
Identifiers: Carbons, Chromatography, Crassostrea-virginica, *Oysters, Petroleum, *Petroleum hydrocarbons, Absorption, Water pollution effects.

Two C. virginica populations, differing in fat content, were experimentally exposed to a complex petroleum-hydrocarbon fraction. The hydrocarbons in this mixture were accumulated by both groups of oysters and their lipid content, as well as the concentration of hydrocarbon in the water, affected the rate and extent of accumulation. Hydrocarbons accumulated were rapidly, although incompletely, discharged when the oysters were transferred to an uncontaminated system. Amounts of hydrocarbons discharged and amounts retained after discharge are probably related to the level of contamination. The data indicate that equilibration and the occurrence of multiple compartments where hydrocarbons can reside are factors involved in the uptake and retention of nonbiogenic hydrocarbons by oysters. The petroleum hydrocarbons contained in the oysters differed from the contaminating oil by displaying a greater aromatic content. In addition, gas-liquid chromatograms of aliphatic fractions of the hydrocarbons in the oysters rapidly showed a degraded appearance. The oysters themselves may modify the oil.--Copyright 1974, Biological Abstracts, Inc.
W75-08331

EFFECTS OF WATER HARDNESS ON THE TOXICITY OF SEVERAL ORGANIC AND INORGANIC HERBICIDES TO FISH,

A. Inglis, and E. L. Davis.

US Bur Sport Fish Wildl Tech Pap. 67, p 1-22, 1972, Illus.
Identifiers: Arsenite, Black, Bluegills, Bullheads, Copper sulfate, Dichlobenil, Endothall, Fish, Goldfish, Hardness, *Herbicides, Inorganic pesticides, Organic pesticides, Phenol, Rainbow trout, Redear, Silvex, Sodium, Sunfish, *Toxicity, *Water hardness, *Bioassay, Calcium carbonate, Water pollution effects.

Effects of water hardness on the acute toxicity of organic and inorganic herbicides were determined in static bioassays. Concentrations of total hardness (calculated as CaCO3) of 13.0, 52.2, 208.7, and 365.2 ppm were tested in water containing Ca/Mg ion ratios of 1:1 and 5:1. Bluegills were the principal test species; rainbow trout, bluespotted sunfish, goldfish, redear sunfish, and black bullheads were also tested. Organic herbicides tested included 3 formulations of 2,4-D (butoxy ethanol ester (BEE), propylene glycol butyl ether ester (PGBEE), dimethylamine salt (DMS)), 3 formulations of endothall (Na salt, and 2 dimethylalkylamine derivatives), and 1 formulation each of silvex (BEE), pentachlorophenol, and dichlobenil; inorganic herbicides included technical grades of sodium arsenite and CuSO4. Hardness had no significant effect on toxicity of the organic herbicides or that of sodium arsenite; the toxicity of copper sulfate decreased in the harder waters. The significance of the results is discussed.--Copyright 1974, Biological Abstracts, Inc.
W75-08332

STUDIES ON THE SKIN OF PLAICE (PLEURONECTES PLATESSA L.). III. THE EFFECT OF TEMPERATURE ON THE INFLAMMATORY RESPONSE TO THE METACERCARIAE OF CRYPTOCOTYL LINGUA (CREPLIN, 1825) (DIGENEA:HETEROPHYIDAE),

Glasgow Univ. (Scotland). Dept. of Dermatology.
A. McQueen, K. MacKenzie, R. J. Roberts, and H. Young.

J Fish Biol, Vol 5, No 2, p 241-247, 1973, Illus.
Identifiers: *Bacteria, *Cryptocotyle-lingua, Digenea, Fibrillar, Heterophyidae, Inflammatory, *Metacercariae, Necrosis, *Plaice, Pleuronectes-platessa, Skin, Temperature.

O-group plaice (89) from a natural population were exposed at 15C to heavy infection by C. lingua cercariae. Subsequently 45 fish were retained at 15C, while 44 were held at 5C. Both groups were sample by killing individual fish at intervals of 6, 18, 42 h and daily thereafter up to 710 h. Entire fish were fixed immediately in formol saline, transversely sectioned and stained by H and E (hematoxylin eosin), PAS (Periodic-acid Schiff), PAS-diastase, JSDB 109, Picro-Mallory, Masson's trichrome, Gram-Weigert and Alcian blue. Histopathological observations showed: epidermal lesions associated with encysted metacercariae in adjacent tissues; myofibrillar necrosis associated with bacteria possibly introduced by the parasite and a reactive swelling of the intermuscular septa. The progressive development of the parasite cyst and host capsule is described. Development of both was markedly inhibited at the lower temperature, but the inflammatory response at either temperature was slight. This may be evidence of a long-standing host-parasite relationship which has evolved to an advanced state of adaptation on the part of the parasite and tolerance on the part of the host.--Copyright 1973, Biological Abstracts, Inc.
W75-08334

TUBERCULOSIS OF FISH AND OTHER HETEROTHERMIC VERTEBRATES (IN POLISH),

Polskie Towarzystwo Nauk Weterynaryjnych, Warsaw (Poland).
Z. Jara.

Med Weter, Vol 28, No 12, p 705-710, 1972. Illus.

Descriptors: *Fish diseases, Fish diets, Amphibians, Reptiles.
Identifiers: *Heterothermic vertebrates, Mycobacterium, *Tuberculosis.

Tuberculosis in fish was described for the 1st time in carp in 1897. It was thought at the time that a new type of tuberculosis was discovered. Since then tuberculosis symptoms were found in 151 spp. of fish, 11 spp. of amphibians and 23 spp. of reptiles. Fish are usually infected through feed. The disease in general develops slowly, the only external symptoms being loss of weight at times accompanied by changes on the skin consisting of paleness, loss of scales and injury of fins. Treatment is difficult and only prophylactic measures can be recommended. Several types of Mycobacterium infecting fish were distinguished. Tubercular infection in amphibians and reptiles is noted.--Copyright 1974, Biological Abstracts, Inc.
W75-08346

PARASITES OF THE NINE-SPINED STICKLEBACK PUNGITIUS PUNGITIUS (L.),
Nature Conservancy, Abbots Ripton (England). Monks Wood Experimental Station.
H. J. G. Dartnall.
J Fish Biol, Vol 5, No 4, p 505-509, 1973. Illus.

Descriptors: *Parasitism, Europe, Water pollution sources, Pollutants, *Sticklebacks, Fish, Fish diseases, *Fish parasites, *Animal parasites.
Identifiers: Anodonta-cygnea, Cryptocotyle-lingua, Diplostomum-spathaceum, Epistylis, Gyrodactylus-spp, Proteocephalus-filicollis, Pungitius-pungitius, Schistocephalus-solidus, Thersitina-gasterostei, Trichodina-domerguei, Trichodina-tenuidens, Vorticella-sp, Great Britain.

Eleven species of parasite are reported from the nine-spined stickleback P. pungitius. Of these, Trichodina domerguei, T. tenuidens, Vorticella sp., Epistylis, Diplostomum spathaceum, Cryptocotyle lingua, Proteocephalus filicollis, Schistocephalus solidus and glochidia of Anodonta cygnea, are new host records for Great Britain. Gyrodactylus spp. and Thersitina gasterostei were also found.--Copyright 1974, Biological Abstracts, Inc.
W75-08347

5D. Waste Treatment Processes

PROCEEDINGS OF THE SEMINAR ON ADVANCED WASTEWATER TREATMENT AND DISPOSAL,
Nassau-Suffolk Regional Planning Board, N. Y. Regional Marine Resources Council
Held on June 10, 1971 at Hauppauge, N.Y., (1972) 167 p.

Descriptors: *Waste water treatment, *New York, *Tertiary treatment, *Waste water disposal, Waste disposal, Management, Groundwater, Water pollution, Regional analysis, Water quality control, Water reuse, Recycling, Reviews, Irrigation, Water pollution sources, Path of pollutants.
Identifiers: *Long Island(NY), Nassau-Suffolk region(NY).

The seminar was intended to present current views and experience in wastewater-groundwater management to those persons responsible for developing public policy decisions in the Nassau-Suffolk region. The program was not designed for general public information, but rater as an exchange of ideas and expertise for administrators charged with the responsibility of managing water resources. One of the major problems identified by the Regional Marine Resources Council (MRC) of the Nassau-Suffolk Regional Planning Board is the treatment and disposal of wastewater and groundwater management. These problems are part of the MRC's ongoing research activities funded by both the National Sea Grant Program and the Nassau-Suffolk Regional Planning Board. (See W75-07955 thru W75-07961)
W75-07954

THE LONG ISLAND WATER SITUATION,
Geological Survey, Mineola, N.Y. Water Resources Div.
For primary bibliographic entry see Field 5B.
W75-07955

STATUS OF ADVANCED WASTE TREATMENT,
National Environmental Research Center, Cincinnati, Ohio. Advanced Waste Treatment Research Lab.
I. J. Kugelman.
In: Proceedings of the Seminar on Advanced Wastewater Treatment and Disposal, June 10, 1971 at Hauppauge, N.Y. p 19-98, (1972) 25 fig, 34 tab, 59 ref.

Descriptors: *Waste water treatment, *Municipal wastes, *Sewage treatment, *Waste treatment, Sanitary engineering, Aeration, Coagulation, Filtration, Flocculation, Oxidation, Reverse osmosis, Activated carbon, Sewage effluents, Organic matter, Pollutants, Denitrification, Biological treatment, *Tertiary treatment, Separation techniques.

Advanced wastewater treatment techniques are described with emphasis on those ready for full-scale engineering application. Six major contaminants which exist at presently measurable levels are discussed: suspended solids, organics, (biological oxygen demand (BOD), chemical oxygen demand (COD), total organic carbon (TOC)), phosphorous compounds, nitrogen compounds, microorganisms, and salts. Although conventional primary plus secondary treatment removes suspended solids, biodegradable organics, and microorganisms from wastewater, it is no longer sufficient with rising water quality standards and increasing generation of contaminants. Performance can be upgraded, especially in the removal of suspended solids and BOD, with biological-physical treatments including microstainers and deep bed filtration. Chemical coagulants can cause flocculation into removable particles. But to remove phosphorous, nitrogen, organic carbon, or TDS (total dissolved salts) requires additional processes. Phosphorous can be removed by adding iron or aluminum salts or lime. Nitrogen, particularly organic-N and ammonia-N, exert BOD (biological oxygen demand) on receiving waters unless biologically mediated oxidation reactions are used to change them to nitrate-N or nitrite-N. Ammonia-N can also be removed by ion exchange, air stripping, or a breakpoint chlorination process. Refractory organics, not removed by other processes, can be removed with activated carbon, ozonation, or pure oxygen activated sludge treatment. Reverse osmosis, still experimental, may someday remove virtually all TDS as well as every other pollutant. Cost functions and experimental results are given. (See also W75-07954) (Herr-North Carolina)
W75-07956

THE STATUS OF WASTEWATER TREATMENT ON LONG ISLAND,
Suffolk County Dept. of Environmental Control, N.Y.
J. Flynn.
In: Proceedings of the Seminar on Advanced Wastewater Treatment and Disposal, June 10, 1971 at Hauppauge, N.Y. p 99-104, (1972).

Descriptors: *Waste water treatment, *Municipal wastes, *Sewage treatment, Waste treatment, *Water quality, Groundwater recharge, Groundwater availability, Water table, Groundwater movement, Groundwater, Saline water intrusion, *New York.
Identifiers: *Suffold County(NY), Nassau County(NY).

The wastewater treatment systems of Suffolk County, New York are compared to those of neighboring Nassau County. Nassau is now sewering 55 to 60 percent of its population, and expects to be serving over 85 percent by the year 2000. Suffolk has had difficulty passing the required referendum measures and is now sewering only 7 percent. The Southwest Sewer District, approved in 1969, will serve 25 to 30 percent of the population when completed. Suffolk's 1970 Subdivision Program will also require developers to either construct sewers and sewage plants to county specifications, install sewers (in additional to cesspools) for later connection to a sewage plant, or contribute per lot toward eventual plant construction. The groundwater level must be maintained to prevent salt water instrusion at the coastline and maintain the flow of freshwater streams. Groundwater recharge in the past has been increased by the county's 300,000 cesspools. A less polluted source of recharge using communal wastewater systems instead of individual systems must be developed, though it will be costly and inconvenient to construct. Consultants are currently studying the types of waste treatment, the levels of treatment, and the timing and location of recharge that will be rquired to maintain groundwater levels and quality. (See also W75-07954) (Herr-North Carolina)
W75-07957

WASTEWATER USE AND GROUNDWATER RECHARGE IN LOS ANGELES COUNTY,
Los Angeles County Flood Control District, Calif.
A. E. Bruington.
In: Proceedings of the Seminar on Advanced Wastewater Treatment and Disposal, June 10, 1971 at Hauppauge, N.Y., p 105-127, (1972) 12 fig.

Descriptors: Water resource development, *Groundwater barriers, *Groundwater recharge, *Recharge wells, *Water reuse, *Saline water intrusion, Artificial recharge, Water wells, Groundwater resources, Water sources, Water table, Injection wells, Recharge ponds, Groundwater movement, Groundwater, *California.
Identifiers: *Los AngelesCounty(Calif), West Coast Basin Barrier Project.

Injection well groundwater recharge of the West Coast Basin Barrier Project, in operation for over ten years, has successfully halted saltwater intrusion into the water table in Los Angeles County. Paralleling the Coast at an average distance of 30 miles is a mountain range which receives 40 inches of rain per year while the coast averages 9 inches. Runoff from the mountains enters the very large groundwater basin of the coastal plain composed of accumulated marine sediments. In spite of water imported from the Colorado River, the county continues to depend on groundwater for about one third of its supply. Artificial spreading basins formed on flat land and in river beds to increase groundwater recharge tend to become clogged with silt and recharge at very slow rates. The nine mile long row of 97 wells at the coastline has been more successful. Injection of 35,000 acre feet of Colorado River industrial and commercial water per year has raised the groundwater surface, forming a ridge which salt water won't penetrate. Experiments with thoroughly treated wastewater injection show no transfer of virus to test wells only 20 feet away. Biological oxygen demand (BOD) is not a problem if the water is injected with oxygen. Costs are competitive with Colorado River water. Reclaimed water hasn't been used on a large scale due to potential hazards from exotic new chemical wastes, capital outlay costs, and public opinion. (See also W75-07954) (Herr-North Carolina)
W75-07958

SPRINKLER IRRIGATION FOR LIQUID WASTE DISPOSAL,
Pennsylvania State Univ., University Park.
E. A. Myers.
In: Proccedings of the Seminar on Advanced Wastewater Treatment and Dispoal, June 10, 1971, at Hauppauge, N.Y., p 129-141, (1972) 1 fig, 9 ref.

Descriptors: *Groundwater recharge, *Irrigation engineering, *Water reuse, *Water spreading, *Waste water treatment, Irrigation, Irrigation design, Artificial recharge, Waste disposal, Waste assimilative capacity.
Identifiers: Center pivot and traveler irrigation, Solid-set irrigation, Wastewater renovation-conservation concept.

There is increasing acceptance of the use of land irrigation for final disposal of municipal and industrial effluent after primary and secondary treatment and chlorination. The renovation-conservation concept involves return, renovation, recharge, and reuse of water. After considering soil type and current water content, treated water is returned to the soil over a wide area in a properly timed sequence. As it percolates through the soil profile the nutrients are chemically fixed in the soil and the water is naturally renovated. The water is then recharged into the groundwater supply. Both water and nutrients are then available for reuse; the water by man and the hydrologic cycle, the nutrients by plants grown on the soil. When the plants are harvested the nutrients are removed in them so that the soil's capacity to renovate water continues. The basic objective of the system is to add as much water to the land as possible while maintaining thorough renovation so that water below a depth of four feet is potable. Water should be applied at a rate between 1/8 and 1/4 inch per hour, depending on soil, season, and type of waste. Municipal wastes should be applied at an average of 100 inches per year, while some industrial and cannery wastes, containing only organic matter, may be applied much more rapidly. Because these water applications are not always consistent with good agricultural practices, municipalities or industries should own their irrigation land. Costs of Installing a solid-set system average from $2500 to $4000 per acre. Travelers and center pivot irrigation systems, if appropriate, are considerably less expensive to install but operating costs are somewhat higher and wind drift can be a nuisance. (See also W75-07954) (Herr-North Carolina)
W75-07959

MUSKEGON, MICHIGAN,
Chicago Univ., Ill. Center for Urban Studies.
J. R. Sheaffer.
In: Proceedings of the Seminar on Advanced Wastewater Treatment and Disposal, June 10. 1971 at Hauppauge, N.Y., p 145-160, (1972) 2 fig, 1 tab.

Descriptors: *Waste water treatment, *Tertiary treatment, *Irrigation design, *Water reuse, *Irrigation parctices, Artificial recharge, Water quality, Groundwater recharge, Waste disposal, Water spreading, Water purification, *Michigan.
Identifiers: *Muskegon County(Mich).

The Muskegon County National Pilot Program utilizes a 6-element effluent irrigation system to provide low cost tertiary treatment with significant benefits. Raw sewage is transported 15 miles inland, processed in aerated treatment cells, and transformed to an odorless liquid. Capacity has been developed to store this secondary treatment liquid for up to 150 days. Before being sprayed on 6000 acres of agricultural land it is chlorinated and dechlorinated. Percolation through the aerobic soil zone provides the equivalent of tertiary treatment. Reclaimed water flows to the monitoring sites along a complete system of drainage wells and drainage tiles. Reliability is increased by flexibility at several points. Treatment cells can be operated in series or parallel, handling shock loads more easily than conventional physical-chemical treatment plants. Blowing vapor from spray irrigation is minimized by holding water during cold and rainy times and using pivot irrigation where effluent can be delivered downward from overhead pipes in large droplet size. Operation and maintenance costs are about 9 cents/1000 gallons, compared to 17 cents/1000 gallons in comparable activated sludge secondary treatment plants. Counting the costs of 10,000 acres of land acquisition, the cost will still be less than traditional treatment: $37.72 compared to $48.25 per year for a family of four. Income from crop yield will offset these costs. Additional benefits include removal of treatment plants from urban locations, planned permanent agricultural land which could be positioned as a greenbelt, and additional land between irrigation rings which could be used for sanitary landfill. (See also W75-07954) (Herr-North Carolina)
W75-07960

WASTEWATER MANAGEMENT ACTIVITIES AT THE BROOKHAVEN NATIONAL LABORATORY,
Brookhaven National Lab., Upton, N.Y.
M. M. Small.
In: Proceedings of the Seminar on Advanced Wastewater Treatment and Disposal, June 10, 1971, at Hauppauge, N.Y., p 160-167, (1972).

Descriptors: *Waste water treatment, *Acral hydrology, Water resources development, *Sewage treatment, *Computer simulation, Groundwater resources, Pollutants, Landfills, Nuclear wastes, Groundwater movement, Water level fluctuations, Water sources, Groundwater, Aquifer characteristics, *New York.
Identifiers: Long Island(NY).

Brookhaven National Laboratory on Long Island would be an excellent site for exploration of wastewater recharge problems. Located on 5,200 acres with 2500 resident employees, it is a microcosm of all of Nassau and Suffolk Counties in terms of waste-water treatment. All variations of geological, geographical, topological, and ecological contrasts of the counties are represented. There is already in operation a 3 mgd (million gallons per day) water treatment plant for removal or iron from water supplied to the domestic distribution system. Total well pump capacity is 12 mgd. The Laboratory's sewage treatment plant is capable of providing secondary treatment to 3 mgd and has 20 acres of sand filtration beds which could be modified for experiments with settling lagoons and filtering media. The Laboratory is also developing a computer assisted hydrological model to show rates, quantities, and directions of flow in the underlying aquifers so that changes in hydrology due to Laboratory withdrawal and recharge can be predicted. Sixty sampling wells are already in operation and additional ones will be drilled to study underground migration of water and contaminants. Areas to study include groundwater around the sewage treatment plant, an old burning dump, a sanitary landfill, and radioactive materials processing areas. Data from these wells will assist in developing a prototype model which could be expanded into a long-term water use and reuse predictive model for the entire island, an invaluable engineering planning tool for the future management of water use and recharge facilities of Long Island. (See also W75-07954) (Herr-North Carolina)
W75-07961

HIGH-OXYGEN TREATMENT OF WASTE WITH SELECTIVE OXYGEN RECIRCULATION,
Chicago Bridge and Iron Co., Aurora, Ill. (assignee)
J. D. Walker.
U.S. Patent No 3,872,003, 7 p, 2 fig, 8 ref; Official Gazette of the United States Patent Office, Vol 932, No 3, p 1075, March 18, 1975.

Descriptors: *Patents, *Waste water treatment, *Oxygenation, *Water pollution control, *Pollution abatement, Bubbles, Dissolved oxygen, Water quality control.

The method of treating waste liquid with gas richer than air in oxygen includes flowing the waste liquid through a retention tank. A gas-lift rolling action of the tank contents is maintained with the gas-lifted contents forming a horizontal stream flowing away from the gas-lift zone in surface-exposed position by liberating and allowing to rise immediately by buoyancy the gas at submerged locations along selected zones of the tank. A small portion of its total horizontal cross section holds sufficient quantities to create and maintain the rolling action and thereby cause the contents to carry small entrained bubbles to remote areas. Oxygen from a source of nearly pure oxygen is constantly added to the repumped gas. The quantity of this enrichment is determined automatically, in response to a meter determining the dissolved oxygen content in the tank liquid, to supply just the amount neede to maintain a desired dissolved oxygen content. In some forms of the invention the waste liquid to be treated flows through successive isolated or semi-isolated cells, and the oxygen enrichment supplied to each cell is automatically regulated to provide the desired oxygen content of that cell. (Sinha-OEIS)
W75-07963

OPTIMAL COST DESIGN OF BRANCHED SEWER SYSTEMS,
Illinois Univ., Urbana. Dept. of Civil Engineering.
L. W. Mays, and B. C. Yen.
Water Resources Research, Vol 11, No 1, p 37-47, February 1975. 7 fig, 3 tab, 19 ref. OWRT C-4123(No 9023)(1).

Descriptors: *Sewers, *Cost analysis, *Design, *Pipes, *Dynamic programming, *Methodology, Size, Elevation, Optimization, Storms, Constraints, Hydrology, Hydraulics, Systems analysis, Mathematical models, Equations.
Identifiers: *Branched sewer systems, *Cost minimization, Serial sewer systems, Decomposition technique.

Methodologies for the least cost design of large storm sewer systems are presented. The methods utilize dynamic programming (DP) and discrete differential dynamic programming (DDDP) to achieve optimal cost design of pipe sizes and elevations of branched sewer systems. The basic strategy is to decompose the branched system into equivalent serial subsystems for solutions. For sake of clarity, to demonstrate the optimization techniques, only simple hydraulic model and cost equations are used. The DP approach is discussed first for an easy understanding of the DDP approach, and serial sewer systems are discussed as a prelude to the branched systems. The DDP approach is usually preferred to DP for large systems because of its savings in computer time, although it cannot guarantee global optimization. Major factors affecting the efficiency in using DDP are the location and width of the initial trial trajectory corridor, the number of states (lattice points) used, and the reduction rate of the state increment during iterations. (Bell-Cornell)
W75-07999

UPPER THOMPSON SANITATION DISTRICT, PROJECT NO. C 080322 (FINAL ENVIRONMENTAL IMPACT STATEMENT).
Environmental Protection Agency, Denver, Colo. Region VIII.
Available from National Technical Information Service, Springfield, Va 22161 as USDC, EIS-CO-73-1531-F-1, $7.00 in paper copy, $2.25 in microfiche. Volume 1, September 21, 1973. 177 p, 12 tab, 10 map, 3 fig, 1 graph.

Descriptors: *Interceptor sewers, *Sewage, Sewage disposal, Environmental effects, Water

quality, *Colorado, Septic tanks, Sewage effluents, Sewage treatment, Sewerage, Sewers, Recreation, Fishing, Water supply, Wildlife, Aesthetics, Vegetation, Odor, Effluents.
Identifiers: *Environmental impact statements, *Olympus Dam, Colo., *Rocky Mountain National Park(Colo).

The proposed project would construct interceptor sewers in the major subdrainages of the Big Thompson River above Olympus Dam, Colorado. The interceptors would transport sewage from residences presently using septic tanks, from several small package sewage treatment plants, and from some present facilities in Rocky Mountain National Park. The interceptors would transport the sewage to a proposed new tertiary sewage treatment plant to be located on publicly-owned land administered by the U.S. Bureau of Reclamation below Olympus Dam. Favorable environmental impacts included protection of the surface and ground water quality of the Big Thompson River Drainage from inadequately treated sewage effluent from septic tanks and small sewage treatment plants; protection of the waters for recreation, fishing and water supply; and assurance of flexible and reliable sewage treatment service. Adverse environmental effects will entail short-term construction impacts on water quality, vegetation, wildlife, aesthetics, and solitude. Additionally, the sewage treatment plant's operation could result in occastional odors in the immediate vicinity of the plant. Other potential problems are possible plant breakdown, with accompanying raw sewage discharge into the river and slight degradation of water quality due to the nutrient release. The following alternatives are considered: design sizing of the systems; timing of interceptor construction; interceptor location; treatment plant location; effluent disposal; and basin-wide wastewater treatment systems. (Gagliardi-Florida)
W75-08016

SOUTH DADE COUNTY FLORIDA, C120377 (FINAL ENVIRONMENTAL IMPACT STATEMENT).
Environmental Protection Agency, Atlanta, Ga. Region IV.
Available from the National Technical Information Service, Springfield, Va. 22161, as EIS-FL-73-1490-F, $6.25 in paper copy, $2.25 in microfiche. September 11, 1973. 326 p, 15 tab, 8 map, 1 graph, 1 photo.

Descriptors: *Waste water disposal, *Waste water treatment, *Sewage treatment, Sewage effluents, Effluents, Canals, Septic tanks, Waste water(Pollution), Waste treatment, Wastes, *Florida, Sewage disposal, Sewers, Sewage, Sewerage, Deep wells, Environmental effects, Construction, Outfall sewers, Sludge, Sludge disposal.
Identifiers: *Environmental impact statements, *Dade County(Fla).

The project entails construction of major waste water treatment facilities for the South District of Dade County, Florida. Essential features of the overall project are a sewage transmission system intercepting flows from nine sewage systems in the county, a single regional secondary treatment plant which will replace nine smaller plants, and a deep well disposal system for the treated and disinfected effluent. Major beneficial impacts of the proposed action include the elimination of nine waste water treatment plants that are currently discharging inadequately treated effluent into four canals and Biscayne Bay; elimination of septic tanks; diversion of all sewage to a single efficiently-run secondary treatment plant; collection of sewage from areas which are presently unrecovered or undeveloped; and possible recovery and reuse of waste water from the builder zone. Adverse environmental impacts are primarily short-term and associated with the initial construction of the facilities. The following alternative methods of effluent disposal were considered: deep well disposal, disposal through an ocean outfall, alternative methods of sewage treatment, and different plant locations and sludge disposal techniques. (Gagliardi-Florida)
W75-08032

NORTH DADE COUNTY REGIONAL COLLECTION, TREATMENT AND DISPOSAL SYSTEM (FINAL ENVIRONMENTAL IMPACT STATEMENT).
Environmental Protection Agency, Atlanta, Ga. Region IV.
Available from the National Technical Information Service, Springfield, Va. 22161, as EIS-FL-73-1600-F, $4.75 in paper copy, $2.25 in microfiche. October 10, 1973. 460 p, 22 tab, 6 map, 2 fig, 1 graph, 2 photo.

Descriptors: *Treatment facilities, *Waste water disposal, *Water quality, Water quality control, Atlantic Ocean, Environmental effects, Treatment, *Florida, Waste water treatment, Waste water(Pollution), Odor, Septic tanks, Effluents, Marine biology, Beaches, Sludge treatment, Sludge disposal, Sludge.
Identifiers: *Environmental impact statements, North Dade County(Fla).

The proposed project consists of an 80 million gallons per day secondary treatment facility to be constructed at the Interama site east of Biscayne Boulevard in North Dade County, Florida. The method of wastewater disposal will be via a 22,850 foot long, 90-inch diameter ocean outfall, terminating in the Atlantic Ocean. The beneficial environmental effects of the water quality management program include elimination of small wastewater treatment plants; reduction of health hazards; enhancement of water quality; elimination of existing nuisances; and the reduction of individual septic tank systems. Additionally, the discharge of adequately treated effluent into the ocean at the edge of the Florida current, rather than into shallower water closer to shore, will result in improvement of ocean water quality, protection of marine life, enhancement of the beaches, and reduction of health hazards. Adverse impacts which cannot be avoided should the projcet be implemented include both long and short term deleterious effects on land, water, air and social resources. Several alternatives to the proposed action were considered; different treatment techniques; different treatment sites; different wastewater collection schemes; and several sludge treatment disposal techniques. (Gagliardi-Florida)
W75-08036

CONSTRUCTION OF WASTEWATER FACILITIES, FORT WORTH, TEXAS (FINAL ENVIRONMENTAL IMPACT STATEMENT).
Environmental Protection Agency, Dallas, Tex. Office of Grants Coordination.
Available from the National Technical Information Service, Springfield, Va. 22161, as EIS-TX-74-0116-F, $9.25 in paper copy, $2.25 in microfiche. January 16, 1974. 312 p, 15 tab, 5 map, 6 graph.

Descriptors: *Texas, *Waste water treatment, *Sewage effluents, *Sewage treatment, Water quality, Water quality control, Water Quality Act, Environmental effects, Waste treatment, Sewage, Water pollution control, Water pollution treatment, Water law, Water policy.
Identifiers: *Environmental impact statements, *Ft. Worth(Tex).

The project consists of constructing additional wastewater treatment facilities at the Village Creek Wastewater Treatment Facility site. The proposed facilities are expected to reduce health hazards in the area, to enhance water quality in the Trinity River, and to aid in the orderly physical development of local communities. Minor, unavoidable adverse effects include increased noise levels and the possible emanation of odors from the facility, but such drawbacks are to be minimized by modern design techniques and efficient operation. No serious adverse effects are anticipated. Alternatives considered included taking no action; improving the existing 45 MGD Village Creek plant so that it can achieve capability of the required effluent control with odor suppression while upgrading the 30 MGD Riverside plant to achieve the same desired level of effluent control, thus maintaining present capacity but improving the quality of effluent so as to meet current Texas Water Quality Board permit requirements; upgrading the 30 MGD Riverside plant to achieve the required effluent control quality while expanding the Village Creek plant capacity by 20 MGD to a new capacity of 66 MGD (sic), with necessary improvements to achieve required effluent quality, and thus resulting in a total plant capacity of 96 MGD. Under the current, preferred proposal the Riverside plant will be abandoned and the Village Creek plant capacity will be enlarged from 45 MGD to 96 MGD with additions and improvements to meet the effluent quality requirements. (Gerlach-Florida)
W75-08042

UPPER THOMPSON SANITATION DISTRICT, ESTES PARK, COLORADO PROJECT NO. C0803222 (FINAL ENVIRONMENTAL IMPACT STATEMENT).
Environmental Protection Agency, Denver, Colo. Region VIII.
Availabile from the National Technical Information Service, Springfield, Va. 22161, as EIS-CO-73-1531-F-2, $9.25 in paper copy, $2.25 in microfiche. September 21, 1973. 306 p, 5 tab, 3 map, 1 fig, 6 graph, 1 photo.

Descriptors: *Sanitary engineering, *Discharge measurement, *Nutrient removal, Nitrates, *Colorado, Environmental effects, Phosphorus, Sludge disposal, Interceptor sewers, Disposal, Economics, Engineering, Water quality, Aesthetics, Odor.
Identifiers: *Environmental impact statements, Estes Park(Colo).

This second and final volume of the Upper Thompson Sanitation District, Estes Park, Colorado, environmental impact statement contains an extensive listing and chronology of individual and agency comments and Environmental Protection Agency response raised in public discussion of relevant issues. The statement contains a detailed consideration of the siting for the plant and the location of discharge, the reliability of plant operation, nutrient removal (both phosphates and nitrates), the design and sizing of the system's growth, sludge disposal, and interceptor routings. The following factors were considered in determining the proper plant siting: engineering, economics, water quality, aesthetic values, odor, biotic resources, legal and time delays, cultural and archaeological. (Gagliardi-Florida)
W75-08047

LAKE QUINAULT SEWAGE COLLECTION AND TREATMENT FACILITY, OLYMPIC NATIONAL FOREST, OLYMPIA, WASHINGTON (FINAL ENVIRONMENTAL IMPACT STATEMENT).
Available from National Technical Information Service, USDC, Springfield, Va 22161 as EIS-WA-74-0233-F, $4.75 in paper copy, $2.25 in microfiche. February 11, 1974. 80 p, 3 fig, 2 plate.

Descriptors: *Washington, *Sewage treatment, *Recreation facilities, *Sewage disposal, *Spoil banks, Odor, Pollution abatement, Surface waters, Recreation, Groundwater, Construction, Environmental effects, Environmental sanitation, Drainage area, Sites.
Identifiers: *Environmental impact statements, *Olympia(Wash).

In an effort to abate water pollution emanating from U.S. Forest Service facilities, the Forest Service proposes to construct a sewage collection and treatment facility along the south shore of Lake Quinault on the west side of the Olympic Peninsula in western Washington State. The project will eliminate ground and surface water pollution emanating from the Forest Service facilities, which will assure the continued use of the facilities in the future. Construction of the facility will not generate greater recreational use, but will make the current level of use safer. Only minimal adverse environmental effects associated with the digging of trenches is anticipated. In addition the location of the drainfield and sewage treatment facility will require clearing approximately 5 1/2 acres of land. Among alternatives considered were no action, or relocation of the recreation facilities at a site removed from the lake. (Denvir-Florida)
W75-08054

ENVIRONMENTAL PROTECTION AGENCY'S 1974 NEEDS SURVEY.
Hearing--Subcomm. on Environmental Pollution--Comm. on Public Works, U.S. Senate, 93d Cong, 2d Sess, September 11, 1974. 61 p, 8 tab, 2 append.

Descriptors: *Treatment facilities, *Construction costs, *Federal Water Pollution Control Act, *Sewage treatment, Wastes, Waste treatment, Construction, Treatment, Water pollution control, Water pollution, Water pollution treatment, Sewage, Sewerage, Infiltration, Seepage, Water quality, Water quality control, Water quality standards, Effluents, Environmental effects, Environment.
Identifiers: Administrative regulations, Effluent limitations.

Preliminary state estimates of the cost of construction of publicly-owned treatment works needed to meet the 1983 goals of the Federal Water Pollution Control Act Amendments (FWPCA) of 1972 are presented. The survey asked the states to report their cost estimates in five major categories: costs for facilities which would provide a legally required level of secondary treatment; costs for treatment facilities that must achieve more stringent levels of treatment; costs for correction of sewer system infiltration/inflow problems; costs for construction of collector sewer systems designed to correct violations caused by raw discharge and seepage; and costs to prevent periodic bypassing of untreated wastes. The costs reported in 1974 for the traditional water quality program of treatment plants and interceptors are $17 billion greater than the $36 billion reported in the 1973 survey. Major variations have been identified in the criteria and methodology used by the states in making their estimates. These variances have prompted the EPA to announce that it has reservations about using the preliminary estimates reported in the 1974 survey for future allocation of construction funds among the states. (Gagliardi-Florida)
W75-08065

AREA-WIDE COMPREHENSIVE WATER AND SEWER PLAN: VOLUME 1, GENERAL REPORT,
Caldwell (Robert W.) and Associates, Bryan, Tex.
R. W. Caldwell, C. W. Caldwell, G. Barber, and W. Merriman.
Prepared for Panhandle Regional Planning Commission, Amarillo, Texas, Final report No GEN-73-31, April, 1973. 225 p, 28 maps, 49 tab. 50-88-23-124.

Descriptors: *Regional analysis, *Sewerage, *Sewers, *Water supply, Water consumption, Irrigation, Water wells, Septic tanks, Systems analysis, *Texas, Agriculture, Feed lots, Population, Income distribution, *Comprehensive planning.
Identifiers: Gas fields, Oil fields, Amarillo(Tex), *Panhandle Region(Tex), Swisher County(Tex), Wheeler County(Tex), Supply lines, Pipelines, Electric service, Area economic condition.

Topics of general concern based on the Regional Area of 25 counties under the jurisdiction of the Panhandle Regional Planning Commission (PRPC) and a Study Area of 18 counties within the PRPC Region are discussed in Volume I of a 2 part plan. Technical data are presented in Volume II. Population increased significantly in 10 counties between 1940-1970 with greatest increases in Deaf Smith (44%), Hartley (28%, attributable to City of Dalhart growth), Randall (15% due to South Amarillo and Canyon growth), and Sherman (40%). Closing of Amarillo Air Force Base, depleting oil and gas reserves, mechanization of agriculture and diminishing job opportunities contributed to decreases in population. An overall increase in population of 13.5% is projected over the next 20 years (to 1990). Area economic conditions are discussed in terms of the financial conditions of local governments, per capita buying power, income, labor force. Projections to 1990 are made for wages, manufacturing, retail/wholesale trade, and bank deposits. Basic information is given on physical and natural characteristics which influence the ability to provide water and sewer services. Discussions of agriculture, a major topic, include farm characteristics, irrigation, value of agricultural production, and employment. Description of existing public utilities and facilities and a brief discussion of existing methods of obtaining water and disposal of sewage precedes a summary of city and county water and sewer plans. Now 63 water systems exist. Between 1972-1980 eighty-two are proposed for construction, 70 more by 1990. There are now 46 sewer systems. Construction of 61 more before 1980, 49 for the period 1980-1990 are proposed. (See also W75-08182) (Hufschmidt-North Carolina)
W75-08181

AREA-WIDE COMPREHENSIVE WATER AND SEWER PLAN: VOLUME 2, TECHNICAL REPORT,
Caldwell (Robert W.) and Associates, Bryan, Tex.
R. W. Caldwell, C. W. Caldwell, G. Barber, and W. Merriman.
Prepared for Panhandle Regional Planning Commission, Amarillo, Texas, Final report No GEN 73-31, April, 1973. 623 p, 180 maps, 8 tab. 50-88-123-124.

Descriptors: *Water supply, Water pollution, Sewage, *Sewage treatment, *Sewage disposal, Water resources, *Water consumption, Distribution systems, *Capital costs, Rural areas, Water distribution, Water treatment, *Texas.
Identifiers: *Panhandle Region(Tex), Amarillo(Tex), Dalhart(Tex), Canyon(Tex), Perryton(Tex), Capital improvement program.

General discussions of water and sewer planning criteria and technique, and a summary discussion of the Regional Water and Sewer Plan precede a presentation of present status and projections to 1990 of water and sewage flows and needed facilities. Each of 18 counties in the study area is considered separately. Items covered include country aggregates of population projections, water resources, pollution control. With in each county individual communities are discussed in terms of water consumption, water supply, distribution system, sewage system, capital improvement program, with cost estimates usually based on on 1973 prices and very preliminary engineering studies. Rural water systems are proposed where there is or will be enough population to serve economically or where the availability of potable ground water is doubtful. Rural sewerage systems were generally determined as infeasible where population is or will be insufficient to support a central system. Septic tanks are considered the logical alternative. Each individual system is mapped. In addition to the smaller communities (under 5,500 populations) and rural areas, four cities are included: Dumas, Dalhart, Canyon, and Perryton, and also the Amarillo SMSA. The time period for the population and water and sewer system projections is 1972-1990, broken down into two periods 1972-1980 and 1980-1990. Cost estimates are listed in the Capital Improvements Program only for the first period. (See also W75-08181) (Park-North Carolina)
W75-08182

ANALYSIS OF COST-SHARING PROGRAMS FOR POLLUTION ABATEMENT OF MUNICIPAL WASTEWATER,
National Bureau of Standards, Washington, D.C. Inst. for Applied Technology.
H. E. Marshall, and R. T. Ruegg.
Prepared for Office of Research and Monitoring, US Environmental Protection Agency, Washington, DC Final Report NBSIR 74-479, September, 1974. 137 p, 10 fig, 11 tab, 34 ref.

Descriptors: *Cost sharing, Cost-benefit analysis, *Water utilization, *Pollution abatement, *Water Quality Act, *Water pollution control, *Project planning, *Cost analysis, Economic efficiency, Sewage treatment, *Waste water treatment, Treatment facilities.
Identifiers: Federal Water Pollution Control Act Amendments of 1972, EPA, Plant treatment, Non-plant treatment.

An evaluation of existing and alternative cost-sharing programs for water pollution abatement deals primarily with their national efficiency and equity effects. The existing cost-sharing program described in the Federal Water Pollution Control Act Amendments of 1972 and implemented by EPA regulations is discussed. The analysis identifies theoretical relationships between cost sharing and its incentive effect on community decisions regarding size of abatement projects and techniques used therein. Two types of efficiency issues, the least-cost techniques and the efficient scale, are examined. Case examples illustrate the biasing effects of current rules that apply different cost-sharing percentages to different techniques and cost categories. To eliminate the bias, the study identifies action to increase local share of abatement costs, reduce cost-sharing bias toward capital-intensive, land-intensive projects, reduce the cost-sharing bias for plant over non-plant techniques, increase the degree of abatement per national dollar spent and, in general, result in more efficient and equitable projects. By changing the effective-cost shares, user fees influence community government's choice of abatement programs. Also, to include an interest charge in user fees collected from industry would help assure that industry paid its full share of costs. (Salzman-North Carolina)
W75-08186

WATER QUALITY MANAGEMENT PLAN--SUMMARY REPORT,
Department of Metropolitan Development, Indianapolis, Ind. Div of Planning and Zoning.
610: Water Quality Control Program, 1970-76, for the Indianapolis-Marion County Metropolitan Area, May, 1973. 168 p, 32 fig, 35 tab.

Descriptors: Water quality, *Water quality control, Water pollution control, Water allocation(Policy), *Planning, Economic efficiency, *Water management(Applied), *Alternate planning, *Comprehensive planning, *Sewage systems, Cost analysis, Multiple purpose projects, Abatement, Pollution control, *Indiana, Treatment facilities.
Identifiers: Non-point source treatment, Multiple management.

To improve and maintain water quality in the 8-county Indianapolis SMSA, a cost-effective and environmentally sound program of water quality management has been developed. After examining demographic, economic and land use factors for the area, the study developed immediate and long term structural and nonstructural measures for abating pollution from point and nonpoint sources. A collection system conveying the flow from com-

bined sewer overflows singularly, or in combination with storm sewer discharges, to a single treatment location provides the most cost-effective solution to urban runoff pollution. Rural runoff pollution may be abated through implementation of good conservation practices. The plan identifies the present water quality situation, existing and anticipated pollution sources and the necessary actions to provide and maintain adequate water quality. A range of management structures and possible financial programs are outlined. Environmental assessment of the plan considers the impact of new treatment facilities on the water quality, land uses and the total region. Final recommendations suggest that (1) a comprehensive regional water quality sampling and monitoring network be established, (2) a regional system as the most cost-effective and environmentally sound approach be established, (3) treatment facilities be upgraded with proper state and federal regulatory agencies, and (4) a multiple management structure for program implementation be developed. (See also W75-08188) (Salzman-North Carolina)
W75-08187

WATER QUALITY MANAGEMENT PLAN (APPENDIX E - VOLUME 3), WASTEWATER COLLECTION AND TREATMENT RECOMMENDATIONS FOR BOONE AND HAMILTON COUNTIES,
Department of Metropolitan Development, Indianapolis, Ind. Div. of Planning and Zoning.
610: Water Quality Control Program of the Unifed Planning Program, 1970-76, for the Indianapolis-Marion County Metropolitan Area, May, 1973. 90 p, 2 fig.

Descriptors: Cost-benefit analysis, *Economic efficiency, *Project planning, *Water utilization, *Sewage treatment, *Sewage districts, Sewage disposal, Pollution abatement, *Indiana, Treatment facilities, *Cost analysis.
Identifiers: Boone County(Ind), Hamilton County(Ind), Indianapolis-Marion County Metropolitan Area(Ind).

One of six volumes, this study defines the general sewage collection system and sewage treatment plant improvements required for each community in Boone and Hamilton Counties. Facility requirements are delineated on an individual community basis and in combination with other population centers. Feasibility of the community combining with another entity to achieve savings in wastewater handling is evaluated and the combination which would provide the most economical regional collection and treatment system is defined. Combining sewerage facilities through regionalization indicates cost savings in many areas. Cost allocations to the entities involved in regionalization plans are calculated as proportions of peak hour flows for sewage collection systems and average day flows for sewage treatment facilities. Values are only illustrative of one allocation approach. Equitable cost allocations must be negotiated between the parties in each regionalization system. Specific recommendations are given for each community for the sewage collection system and for sewage treatment facility after alternatives have been set forth. (See also W75-08187) (Salzman-North Carolina)
W75-08188

THE RECLAMATION OF SULFURIC ACID FROM WASTE STREAMS,
New Jersey Zinc Company, Palmerton, Pennsylvania. Research Department.
H. C. Peterson, and P. L. Kern.
Available from the National Technical Information Service, Springfield, Va 22161 as PB-241 791, $3.75 in paper copy, $2.25 in microfiche. Environmental Protection Agency, Cincinnati, Ohio. Report EPA-670/2-75-016, April 1975. 44 p, 12 fig, 12 tab, 8 ref. 1BB036; ROAP 21AZQ; Task 07/08. S-801349.

Descriptors: *Sulfuric acid, Reclamation, *Waste treatment, Operating costs, *Evaporation, Titanium, Byproducts, *Industrial wastes, Recycling, *Pennsylvania.
Identifiers: *Sulfuric acid reclamation, *Titanium dioxide manufacture, Titanium dioxide byproducts, Acid recovery.

The New Jersey Zinc Company process for acid recovery employs spray evaporation to separate sulfuric acid from metallic sulfates. The salts are removed as dry, free-flowing solids and the acid-laden off-gas is directly cooled to partially condense product acid having a concentration in excess of 85% H2SO4. The process was piloted at Palmerton, Pennsylvania, at a rate of two tons per day of sulfuric acid (100% basis) using as feed the waste stream of a titanium dioxide pigment plant. On the basis of the pilot work, a commercial plant was designed to process 345,000 metric tons annually of 19.5% H2SO4 waste end liquor from a 38,100-metric-ton-per-year pigment plant. The estimated investment (as of January 1, 1975) is $7,800,000. Operating costs (including depreciation at 10%) would be approximately $77 per metric ton of 100% H2SO4 recovered. This cost includes neutralization of the dried solids and disposal in a landfill site. (EPA)
W75-08228

COPPER RECOVERY FROM BRASS MILL DISCHARGE BY CEMENTATION WITH SCRAP IRON,
Anaconda American Brass Co., Waterbury, Conn.
O. P. Case.
Available from the National Technical Information Service, Springfield, Va 22161 as PB-241 822, $3.75 in paper copy, $2.25 in microfiche. Environmental Protection Agency, Cincinnati, Ohio, Report EPA-670/2-75-029, April 1975. 50 p, 7 fig, 8 tab, 6 ref. 1BB036; ROAP 21AZO; Task 23. S-803226-01-0.

Descriptors: Water pollution, Industrial wastes, *Waste water treatment, Pollution abatement, Waste treatment, Recycling, Iron, Copper.
Identifiers: *Copper recovery, *Hexavalent chromium reduction, Metal finishing wastes, *Metals recovery, Cementation, Iron reductant.

Results are presented of studies of copper recovery (and incidental reduction of hexavalent chromium) in brass mill discharge by passage of the discharge over scrap iron in a rotating drum. The drum feed consisted of normal production discharge of combined pickle rinse water and spent sulfuric acid and sulfuric acid - bichromate pickle. About half of the total mill waste discharge over a period of 16 weeks was processed. Four modes of drum operation were studied: (1) continuous rotation, (2) no rotation, (3) intermittent rotation (1 hr off - 5 min on), and (4) intermittent rotation (2-1/2 hr off - 10 min on). Each mode was studied at two flow levels and two scrap iron surface area levels. Data were evaluated in terms of percent cementation of available copper, excess iron consumption over theoretical, and completeness of chromium reduction. Results indicate that the over-riding factor in the efficiency of copper cementation is the level of copper in the feed solution. Hexavalent chromium is effectively reduced providing the pH is below 2.5. (EPA)
W75-08229

LIME STABILIZED SLUDGE: ITS STABILITY AND EFFECT ON AGRICULTURAL LAND,
Battelle Pacific Northwest Lab, Richland, Wash.
C. A. Counts, and A. J. Shuckrow.
Available from the National Technical Information Service, Springfield, Va. 22161 as PB-241 809, $4.75 in paper copy, $2.25 in microfiche. Environmental Protection Agency, Cincinnati, Ohio, Report EPA-670/2-75-012, April 1975. 87 p, 33 fig, 30 tab, 16 ref. 1BB043;ROAP-21ASD;Task-16. EPA Contract 68-03-0203.

Descriptors: Calcium hydroxide, Lime, Sludge disposal, Disinfection, Odors, *Sludge treatment, Sewage sludge, Crop response, *Waste water treatment.
Identifiers: *Sludge stabilization, *Lime treatment, Liquid phase lime demands, Solid phase lime demands, Agricultural land, *Odor control.

An optimum system for the lime stabilization of municipal sewage sludge was developed and evaluated. The primary objectives were: (1) to determine the degree of stability induced in a sludge by lime addition and (2) to determine the effects of spreading lime-stabilized sludge on agricultural land. Lime doses and contact times required to eliminate the pathogenic bacteria and odors from a raw sludge were determined by laboratory studies, and the information obtained was translated into design and operational parameters for a pilot scale, continuous flow process. Physical, chemical, and biological characteristics of both the raw and stabilized sludges were measured. Soil and crop studies, both in a greenhouse and on controlled outdoor plots, were performed to determine the effects of spreading lime-stabilized sludge. Effective lime stabilization of sludge was accomplished by elevating the pH to 12.0 with lime addition and maintaining this pH level for at least 30 minutes. From 102 to 208 g of Ca(OH)2 was needed to stabilize 1.0 kg of sludge solids. The average amount required was 150 g. Total operation and maintenance costs for lime stabilization were estimated to be $10 per metric ton. (EPA)
W75-08232

CHLOR-ALKALI PRODUCERS SHIFT TO DIAPHRAGM CELLS,
For primary bibliographic entry see Field 3E.
W75-08235

EPIDEMIOLOGICAL CONSEQUENCES OF VIRUS CONTAMINATION OF WATERS, (IN FRENCH),
Hopital Mileırie, Poitiers (France). Laboratoire C. Nicolle.
For primary bibliographic entry see Field 5C.
W75-08243

PERFORMANCE OF REGIONALLY RELATED WASTEWATER TREATMENT PLANTS,
McGill Univ., Montreal (Quebec). Dept. of Civil Engineering and Applied Mechanics.
B. J. Adams, and R. S. Gemmell.
J Water Pollut Control Fed, Vol 45, No 10, p 2088-2103, 2237, 1973, Illus.

Descriptors: *Treatment facilities, *Waste water treatment, Regional analysis, *Performance, Effluents.
Identifiers: Decentralization.

Statistical analyses of the performances of regionally related wastewater treatment plants indicated that little linear trend could be discerned in individual plant results. In analysis for cyclical variation, only the 1st harmonic appeared influential for influent and effluent parameters, and the 1st and 4th for discharge. Non-random forces had some significance in long-term records, whereas sequences of monthly means were random. Among plants, only a weak correlation among influent and effluent quality variables was noted, but discharge correlation was much stronger. Decentralized treatment systems can lessen high peaks in waste load variability; many relatively independently performing plants will tend to result in combined performance with less variance than will a single plant.--Copyright 1974, Biological Abstracts, Inc.
W75-08315

SUGAR MILL EFFLUENT TREATMENT WITH NUTRIENT ADDITION,
National Inst. for Water Research, Congella (South Africa). Regional Lab.

D. E. Simpson, and J. Hemens.
J Water Pollut Control Fed, Vol 45, No 10, p 2194-2243, 1973, Illus.

Descriptors: *Waste water treatment, *Activated sludge, *Industrial wastes, Oxygen demand, Dewatering.
Identifiers: Sugar mill wastes.

Laboratory studies showed that efficient activated sludge treatment of sugar mill effluent is possible if supplementary N and P are provided. Nutrient addition can approximately double the rate of chemical oxygen demand (COD) removal and is essential for proper sludge settlement and low effluent/turbidity. Minimum satisfactory supplementary COD : N : P in input was 100 : 2 : 0.4, and optimum load factor was 0.6 g COD/-day/g mixed liquor suspended solids with average sludge volume index of 53. Average effluent COD and biochemical oxygen demand were 97 and 13 mg/l, respectively. Dewatering of excess sludge can be achieved on a conventional drying bed with pretreatment.--Copyright 1974, Biological Abstracts, Inc.
W75-08348

5E. Ultimate Disposal Of Wastes

NORTH DADE COUNTY REGIONAL COLLECTION, TREATMENT AND DISPOSAL SYSTEM (FINAL ENVIRONMENTAL IMPACT STATEMENT).
Environmental Protection Agency, Atlanta, Ga. Region IV.
For primary bibliographic entry see Field 5D.
W75-08036

LIME STABILIZED SLUDGE: ITS STABILITY AND EFFECT ON AGRICULTURAL LAND,
Battelle Pacific Northwest Lab., Richland, Wash.
For primary bibliographic entry see Field 5D.
W75-08232

5F. Water Treatment and Quality Alteration

COMPARISON OF GELATINE AND KIEBO PLATES FOR DETERMINING THE COLONY COUNT IN DRINKING WATER: I, (IN GERMAN),
Bundesgesundheitsamt, Berlin (West Germany). Institut fuer Wasser-, Boden-, und Lufthygiene.
For primary bibliographic entry see Field 5A.
W75-07933

STATUS OF ADVANCED WASTE TREATMENT,
National Environmental Research Center, Cincinna i, Ohio. Advanced Waste Treatment Research Lab.
For primary bibliographic entry see Field 5D.
W75-07956

DESALTING TECHNIQUES FOR WATER QUALITY IMPROVEMENT.
American Water Works Association Research Foundation, Denver, Colo.
For primary bibliographic entry see Field 3A.
W75-07998

EPIDEMIOLOGICAL CONSEQUENCES OF VIRUS CONTAMINATION OF WATERS, (IN FRENCH),
Hopital Miletrie, Poitiers (France). Laboratoire C. Nicolle.
For primary bibliographic entry see Field 5C.
W75-08243

5G. Water Quality Control

REMOTE SENSING TECHNIQUES FOR EVALUATION OF URBAN EROSION AND SEDIMENTATION,
Geological Survey, Reston, Va.
For primary bibliographic entry see Field 4C.
W75-07880

WATER FACTS AND FIGURES FOR PLANNERS AND MANAGERS,
Geological Survey, Menlo Park, Calif.
For primary bibliographic entry see Field 6B.
W75-07889

WATER AND SALT TRANSFERS IN SUTTER BASIN, CALIFORNIA,
California Univ., Davis. Dept. of Water Science and Engineering.
For primary bibliographic entry see Field 5B.
W75-07925

DETERMINING AMBIENT WATER TEMPERATURES,
Stone and Webster Engineering Corp., Boston, Mass. Environmental Engineering Div.
For primary bibliographic entry see Field 5B.
W75-07929

URBAN SEDIMENT PROBLEMS: A STATEMENT ON SCOPE, RESEARCH, LEGISLATION, AND EDUCATION.
American Society of Civil Engineers, New York. Task Committee on Urban Sedimentation Problems.
Journal of the Hydraulics Division, American Society of Civil Engineers, Vol 101, No HY4, Proceedings Paper 11256, p 329-340, April 1975. 1 tab, 7 ref, 1 append.

Descriptors: *Soil erosion, *Accelerated erosion, *Sediment yield, *Cities, Construction, Education, Erosion, Land use, Legislation, Sediments, Sedimentation rates, Sediment control, Research and development, Streams, Urbanization, Urban runoff, Urban drainage, Environmental control, Urban hydrology, Storms, Erosion control, Costs.
Identifiers: *Environmental protection, Soil loss, Urban impacts.

The present system of coping with accelerated erosion and sediment movement in areas of urban development tends towards application of a large array of control techniques, mostly borrowed from rural settings. But too little is known of their control effectiveness, or whether they represent the optimum treatment, or whether they are needed in the first place. A systematic method is needed for estimating sediment movement that can be coupled with a specifically designed set of controls to minimize the adverse effects of sediment movement. This should be done in a manner that would insure that the probable reduction in damages would exceed the cost of application of such control. The need for legislative, educational, and research activities to stimulate progress in solving the many different kinds of urban sediment problems was examined. (Lee-ISWS)
W75-07931

WASTEWATER USE AND GROUNDWATER RECHARGE IN LOS ANGELES COUNTY,
Los Angeles County Flood Control District, Calif.
For primary bibliographic entry see Field 5D.
W75-07958

WASTEWATER MANAGEMENT ACTIVITIES AT THE BROOKHAVEN NATIONAL LABORATORY,
Brookhaven National Lab., Upton, N.Y.
For primary bibliographic entry see Field 5D.
W75-07961

USE OF MICROORGANISMS TO DISPERSE AND DEGRADE OIL SPILLS,
Exxon Research and Engineering Co., Linden, N.J. (assignee)
R. R. Mohan, G. H. Byrd, Jr., J. Nixon, and E. R. Bucker.
U. S. Patent No 3,871,957, 14 p, 28 tab, 3 ref; Official Gazette of the United States Patent Office, Vol 932, No 3, p 1065, March 18, 1975.

Descriptors: *Patents, *Oil spills, *Oil pollution, *Water pollution control, Shore protection, *Microorganisms, Biological treatment, *Pollution abatement, Beaches, Coasts, Bacteria.
Identifiers: Arthobacter, Micrococcus, Achromobacter.

A new method is described for the preparation and application of specified microoganisms for the rapid dispersal of oil spills found in open seas, along beaches, in coastal areas and along the shore lines and also for protecting beaches and solid surfaces against oil contamination. The process of preparing freeze-dried cultures of selected bacterial species of hydrocarbon consuming microorganisms involves growing the mixed population in a suitable aqueous medium containing high inorganic phosphate concentration and a suitable easily assimiable inorganic nitrogen source, trace metals and a hydrocarbon containing C8 to C18 carbons as the only carbon source. The preparation is generally reconstituted in suitable aqueous medium such as water or sea water and applied onto the oil or hydrocarbon surfaces or sprayed on the solid surfaces such as beaches, rocks, shore lines, to prevent oil contaminating the solid surfaces. (Sinha-OEIS)
W75-07964

MODAL CITIES,
Dartmouth Coll., Hanover, N.H. Dept. of Geography.
For primary bibliographic entry see Field 6B.
W75-07967

LAND USE FORMS AND THE ENVIRONMENT - AN EXECUTIVE SUMMARY,
Chicago Univ., Ill. Dept. of Geography; and Chicago Univ., Ill. Center for Urban Studies.
For primary bibliographic entry see Field 6G.
W75-07971

GROUND-WATER QUALITY RELATED TO IRRIGATION WITH IMPORTED SURFACE OR LOCAL GROUND WATER,
Agricultural Research Service, Fresno, Calif.
For primary bibliographic entry see Field 5B.
W75-07978

WINTER-REGIME SURFACE HEAT LOSS FROM HEATED STREAMS,
Iowa Univ., Iowa City. Inst. of Hydraulic Research.
For primary bibliographic entry see Field 5B.
W75-07990

ECONOMIC AND INSTITUTIONAL ANALYSIS OF COLORADO WATER QUALITY MANAGEMENT,
Colorado State Univ., Fort Collins. Dept. of Economics.
R. A. Young, G. Radiosevich, S. L. Gray, and K. L. Leathers.
Available from the National Technical Information Service, Springfield, Va. 22161, as PB-241 946, $5.25 in paper copy, $2.25 in microfiche. Colorado Environmental Resources Center, Fort Collins, Completion Report Series No 61, March 1975. 105 p, 6 fig, 22 tab, 28 ref. OWRT B-042-COLO(3).

Descriptors: *Colorado, *Water quality, *Management, *Water pollution control,

*Economic impacts, *Institutions, Evaluation, Legal aspects, *Waste dilution, *Return flow, Irrigation water, Salinity, Water pollution sources, Legislation, Administration, Forecasting, Regional analysis.
Identifiers: *Grand Valley(Colo).

Waste products of production and consumption activities are often discharged into the nation's watercourses. The objective of this study was to develop information on economic and institutional aspects of water quality management in Colorado. An economic conceptualization of the water quality management problem is presented. The legal and institutional settings within which the present water pollution control program operates is reviewed and described. Two economic case studies are presented. One provides estimates of the economic value of water for waste dilution and the other examines economic impacts of programs for control of saline irrigation return flows in western Colorado.
W75-07992

MODEL DEVELOPMENT AND SYSTEMS ANALYSIS OF THE YAKIMA RIVER BASIN: WATER QUALITY MODELING,
Washington State Univ., Pullman. Dept. of Civil Engineering.
For primary bibliographic entry see Field 5B.
W75-07995

THE IMPACT OF HIGH INTEREST RATES ON OPTIMUM MULTIPLE OBJECTIVE DESIGN OF SURFACE RUNOFF URBAN DRAINAGE SYSTEMS,
Purdue Univ., Lafayette, Ind. Dept. of Agricultural Economics.
W. L. Miller, and S. P. Erickson.
Water Resources Bulletin, Vol 11, No 1, p 49-59, February 1975. 2 fig, 4 tab, 18 ref. OWRT C-3277(No 3713)(6), 14-31-0001-3713.

Descriptors: *Economic impact, *Interest rates, *Design, *Urban drainage, *Surface runoff, *Water quality, Methodology, Linear programming, Assessment, Economic efficiency, Water pollution control, *Indiana, Optimization, Costs, Rainfall, Mathematical models, Systems analysis.
Identifiers: *Multiple objectives, Cost minimization, Integer programming, Cost effective, Discount, Treatment plants, Environmental quality Equilibrium analysis, Sensitivity.

Studied is the impact of high interest rates on the least cost system design of urban drainage systems when water quality is a critical parameter. Twelve alternative system designs in a case study watershed in Indiana are examined. Objectives considered are economic efficiency and environmental quality. Linear integer programming is used to determine the cost of the alternative system designs and the sensitivity of the optimal solution to varying levels of interest rates and water pollution. Results indicate that the least cost study design is highly sensitive to the rate of interest but not sensitive to the water quality parameters. When the high rates of interest currently prevalent are introduced into the model, those systems containing open channel collection components are selected as the minimum cost system. At low rates of interest, pipeline collection components are selected as the least cost system. Holding pond components of the system design are cost effective at several levels of water quality. They are neutral to the rate of interest so they are incorporated in least cost systems at all levels of interest rates. Results show that at the current high rates of interest, open channel collection systems and holding ponds are cost effective system components to achieve selected levels of water quality in urban drainage system design. (Bell-Cornell)
W75-08001

DEVELOPING BIOLOGICAL INFORMATION SYSTEMS FOR WATER QUALITY MANAGEMENT,
Virginia Polytechnic Inst. and State Univ., Blacksburg. Center for Environmental Studies; and Virginia Polytechnic Inst. and State Univ., Blacksburg. Dept. of Biology.
J. Cairns, Jr., G. R. Lanza, R. E. Sparks, and W. T. Waller.
Water Resources Bulletin, Vol 9, No 1, p 81-99, February 1973. 10 fig, 6 tab, 10 ref. OWRT A-039-VA(3).

Descriptors: *Water pollution control, *Industrial wastes, *Management, Aquatic environment, *Monitoring, *Quality control, Streams, Fish, Diatoms, Bioindicators, Rivers, Measurement, Efficiency, Toxicity, Time lag, Simulation analysis.
Identifiers: *Biological monitoring, Aquatic ecosystems, Industrial plants, Laser holography, Information feedback, Waste discharge.

Management of aquatic ecosystems requires a clear understanding of the goals to be achieved, appropriate information and the means to achieve the goals. Control measures applied to aquatic ecosystems, in the absence of information on the condition of the system, are apt to be in appropriate and thus may overprotect the receiving system at times and underprotect it at other times since the ability of ecosystems to receive wastes is not constant. A major determinant of the effectiveness and efficiency of ecological quality control is the lag time in the feedback of information. If the lag is too great, the control measures may repeatedly overshoot or undershoot the desired goal. Present techniques for measuring the responses of aquatic organisms and communities require days or weeks, whereas information for ecosystem quality control and prevention of ecological crises should be generated in minutes or hours. Two biological monitoring systems developed to generate information rapidly are presented. One system measures changes in the movement and breathing of fish in order to provide an early warning of developing toxicity in the wastes of an industrial plant. The other system measures changes in the diversity of algal communities in streams by means of laser holography. The incorporation and use of these systems in industrial plants is discussed. (Bell-Cornell)
W75-08002

WATER QUALITY CONTROL BY ARTIFICIAL AERATION OF STREAM RECEIVING THERMAL AND ORGANIC WASTE DISCHARGES,
Kansas State Univ, Manhattan. Inst. for Systems Design and Optimization.
S. H. Lin, L. T. Fan, and C. L. Hwang.
Water Resources Bulletin, Vol 9, No 5, p 874-883, October 1973. 6 fig, 1 tab, 17 ref. OWRT-B-030-KAN(3).

Descriptors: *Water quality control, Streams, *Thermal pollution, *Organic wastes, *Dissolved oxygen, *Simulation analysis, Velocity, Biochemical oxygen demand, Aquatic life, Upstream, Systems analysis, Mathematical models.
Identifiers: *Artificial aeration, *Diffusor aerators, *Streeter-Phelps equation, Waste discharges.

The installation of artificial aerators for water quality control of a stream which receives thermal and organic waste discharges is investigated. Considered are diffusor aerators, which use compressed air as a means of maintaining stream DO content. The modified Streeter-Phelps model including an energy balance equation is used to determine the location and number of diffusor aerators to be installed along the stream so as to maintain the stream DO concentration above a minimum requirement (4 mg/l or 5 mg/l) for normal aquatic life. Effects of stream velocity, upstream BOD concentration, amount of thermal discharge, and rates of thermal and organic waste discharges to the stream are examined. Results indicate that the waste discharge as well as thermal

W75-08014

MAINTENANCE OF BUTTERMILK CHANNEL, NEW YORK (FINAL ENVIRONMENTAL IMPACT STATEMENT).
Army Engineer District, New York.
For primary bibliographic entry see Field 8A.
W75-08017

PROPOSED 1973 OUTER CONTINENTAL SHELF OIL AND GAS GENERAL LEASE SALE, OFFSHORE MISSISSIPPI, ALABAMA AND FLORIDA (FINAL ENVIRONMENTAL IMPACT STATEMENT).
Bureau of Land Management, Washington, D.C.
Available from the National Technical Information Service, Springfield, Va 22161 as USDC, EIS-MS-73-1651-F-1, $9.50 in paper copy, $2.25 in microfiche. Volume 1, Description of the Proposal, etc., October 17, 1973. 327 p, 40 tab, 45 map, 23 fig, 7 graph.

Descriptors: *Gasoline, *Oil, *Oil pollution, *Oil spills, *Gulf of Mexico, Continental shelf, Wastes, Mississippi, Alabama, Florida, Oil industry, Environmental effects, Shoreline cover, Shore protection, Shores.
Identifiers: *Environmental impact statements, Energy crisis, Oil Pollution Act.

The project involves a proposed oil and gas lease sale on the outer continental shelf of the Gulf of Mexico. One hundred and forty-seven tracts (817,338 acres) of outer continental shelflands are to be included in the leasing action. The tracts are located offshore Mississippi, Alabama, and Florida. All tracts offered pose some degree of pollution risk to the environment and adjacent shoreline. The risk potential is related to adverse effects on the environment and other resource uses which may result from accidental or chronic oil spillage. Each tract offered is subjected to a matrix analytical technique in order to evaluate significant environmental impacts should leasing and subsequent oil and gas exploration and production ensue. The following alternatives to the proposed action were considered: hold the sale in modified form; withdraw the sale; or delay the sale. (Gagliardi-Florida)
W75-08018

BLUE MARSH LAKE PROJECT, TULPEHOCKEN CREEK, PENNSYLVANIA (FINAL ENVIRONMENTAL IMPACT STATEMENT).
Army Engineer District, Philadelphia, Pa.
For primary bibliographic entry see Field 8D.
W75-08019

SOUTH DADE COUNTY FLORIDA, C120377 (FINAL ENVIRONMENTAL IMPACT STATEMENT).
Environmental Protection Agency, Atlanta, Ga. Region IV.
For primary bibliographic entry see Field 5D.
W75-08032

MAINTENANCE DREDGING, BRONX RIVER, NEW YORK (FINAL ENVIRONMENTAL IMPACT STATEMENT).
Army Engineer Districts, New York.
For primary bibliographic entry see Field 8A.
W75-08037

DIKED DISPOSAL AREA, HURON HARBOR, ERIE COUNTY, HURON, OHIO (FINAL ENVIRONMENTAL IMPACT STATEMENT).
Army Engineer District, Buffalo, NY.
Available from the National Technical Information Service, Springfield, Va. 22161, as EIS-OH-73-1857-F, $4.75 in paper copy, $2.25 in microfiche. November 28, 1973. 88 p, 6 fig, 7 tab, 2 append.

Descriptors: *Sediment control, *Lake Erie, *Dredging, *Sedimentary structures, Sediments, Sedimentation, Pollution abatement, Pollutants, Aesthetics, Water quality, Water pollution control, Recreation facilities, Recreation, Turbidity, Sites, *Ohio.
Identifiers: *Environmental impact statements, Huron(Ohio).

The project is designed to remove polluted harbor sediment from Lake Erie which has resulted from annual dredging operations. An offshore contained spoil disposal structure to receive the sediment will be constructed which will abate pollution from the dredging for a period of ten years, at which time it is expected that the pollutants reaching the Lake and Harbor will be controlled at their sources. Construction and operation of the spoil area will cause some local convenience and unsightly conditions but water quality enhancement, long term recreational benefits associated with fishing and waterfront opportunities are expected to improve. Some turbidity will result during construction, and thereafter annually during dredging operations. Continued open lake dumping, discontinuance of maintenance dredging, disposal at alternate sites, and treatment of polluted dredge spoil were considered, but rejected. (Denvir-Florida)
W75-08048

RICHMOND INNER HARBOR, MAINTENANCE DREDGING, CONTRA COSTA COUNTY, CALIFORNIA (FINAL ENVIRONMENTAL IMPACT STATEMENT).
Army Engineer District, San Francisco, Calif.
Available from the National Technical Information Service, Springfield, Va. 22161, as EIS-CA-73-1830-F, $4.25 in paper copy, $2.25 in microfiche. 26 November 1973. 61 p, 8 tab, 4 map.

Descriptors: *Dredging, *Channel improvement, Shoals, Channels, Harbors, Disposal, Channeling, *California, Benthic fauna, Maintenance, Turbidity, Benthic flora, Silts, Environmental effects, Sessile algae, Oxygen, Oxygen sag.
Identifiers: *Environmental impact statements, Contra Costa County(Calif), *Alcatraz Island(Calif).

The proposed action involves the maintenance dredging of shoal areas in the port of Richmond and the maintenance of other channels and disposition of dredged materials at Alcatraz, California. These maintenance operations are deemed necessary to provide for the continued vessel use of the harbor. There will be an increase in turbidity during dredging and disposal and the accompanying displacement of benthic organisms. The resuspension of silt will possibly adversely affect fishlife and plankton by increasing turbidities. Other adverse environmental effects are the removal of sessile benthic organisms in areas to be dredged, a temporary oxygen sag in the area, a temporary disruption of benthic fauna in areas adjacent to the dredge site and in the disposal area, and a temporary reduction in mean population numbers. The alternatives available for consideration were ocean disposal, land disposal, or no action. (Gagliardi-Florida)
W75-08049

LAKE QUINAULT SEWAGE COLLECTION AND TREATMENT FACILITY, OLYMPIC NATIONAL FOREST, OLYMPIA, WASHINGTON (FINAL ENVIRONMENTAL IMPACT STATEMENT).
For primary bibliographic entry see Field 5D.
W75-08054

COMMONWEALTH, DEPARTMENT OF ENVIRONMENTAL RESOURCES V. BOROUGH OF CARLISLE (APPEAL FROM ORDER PROHIBITING DISCHARGES INTO SANITARY SEWER SYSTEM WITHOUT DER APPROVAL).
330 A.2d 293-300 (Pa. Cmwlth. 1974).

Descriptors: *Environmental control, *Sewage treatment, *Permits, Streams, Water quality control, *Pennsylvania, Environmental effects, Environment, Resources, Discharge(Water), Pollution abatement, Pollutants, Sewers, Sewerage, Sewage, Sewage disposal, Water quality, Water, Water quality standards, Water pollution, Water pollution control.
Identifiers: Administrative regulations, Hazardous substances(Pollution).

The Pennsylvania Department of Environmental Resources (DER) issued an order prohibiting additional discharges without DER approval into a sanitary sewer system tributary to a borough sewer system. Both the borough and the borough sewer authority appealed. The Environmental Hearing Board (EHB) then amended the order to allow the issuance of four new permits per month, prompting all parties to appeal. The Commonwealth Court held that the EHB afforded a proper statutory hearing even though the DER had not provided a hearing prior to the issuance of its order and that the evidence sustained its finding that the sewer authority's plant was polluting the river into which it discharged. However, the court found that in view of the fact that a new plant would be built within three years and that even a non-polluting plant at the current site could not restore the stream to an unpolluted state within three years, the decision of the EHB to amend the order should be sustained. (Gagliardi-Florida)
W75-08069

SHELL OIL CO. V. POLLUTION CONTROL BOARD (PETITION BY OIL CO. TO REVIEW DENIAL OF VARIANCE FOR DISCHARGE OF WASTE WATER CONTAINING CYANIDE).
321 N.E.2d 170-174 (App. Ct. Ill. 1974).

Descriptors: *Oil pollution, *Pollution abatement, *Pollutants, *Illinois, Discharge measurement, Oil industry, Oil, Oil wastes, Water, Wastes, Waste water(Pollution), Waste water treatment, Waste treatment, Waste identification.
Identifiers: Administrative regulations, Evidence.

Plaintiff oil refinery petitioned for review of an order of the Illinois Pollution Board denying the refinery's motion for reconsideration of an order denying a petition for variance from the Board rule governing the discharge of waste water containing cyanide. The Illinois Appellate Court, Fifth District, held that denial of the petition for variance was not against the manifest weight of evidence that the oil refinery refused to comply with the Board's request for a showing of firm assurance of compliance or attempted compliance with the rule. The court refused to consider evidence presented by affidavit in support of the motion for reconsideration since it was untimely and improper under Board rules. Additionally, the court held that the oil refinery was not denied equal protection because other oil refineries which had instituted good-faith programs to correct excessive cyanide discharges were granted variances. (Gagliardi-Florida)
W75-08070

VILLAGE OF GLENCOE V. METROPOLITAN SANITARY DISTRICT OF GREATER CHICAGO (ACTION TO REVIEW DISTRICT'S WASTE CONTROL ORDINANCE WHICH PROHIBITED ANY DISCHARGE OF SEWAGE, INDUSTRIAL OR OTHER WASTE INTO LAKE MICHIGAN).
For primary bibliographic entry see Field 6E.
W75-08071

THE ENVIRONMENTAL PROTECTION AGENCY AND COASTAL ZONE MANAGEMENT: STRIKING A FEDERAL-STATE BALANCE OF POWER IN LAND USE MANAGEMENT,
H. A. Cassidy, and S. Kladis.
Houston Law Review, Vol 11, p 1152-1193 (1974). 52 p, 408 ref.

Descriptors: *Environmental control, *Protection, *Land use, *Texas, *Federal government, Coasts, Planning, Legislation, Constitutional law, Land development, Land management, Land resources, Conservation, Administrative agencies, Pollution abatement, Water pollution control, Clean Air Act.
Identifiers: *Coastal zone management, *National Environmental Policy Act, *Environmental Protection Agency, Coastal Zone Management Act, Environmental policy.

Traditionally, a balance has existed between landowners' rights and public controls, but today a quiet revolution in land use laws is effecting radical changes. Numerous federal regulations are discussed, with particular emphasis on coastal zone management. Today, there are two major sources of activity in land use controls: the National Environmental Policy Act as enforced by the Environmental Protection Agency (EPA) and the recently enacted Coastal Zone Management Act. The accretion of power in the EPA through congressional enactments and executive directives and the potential for the exertion of the EPA's power in land use management are discussed. Federal and state interactions in environmental control are examined in light of the experience in Texas with the EPA under the provisions of the Clean Air Amendments of 1970. Also discussed are the Coastal Zone Management Act, its legislative history, accompanying guidelines, grant qualifications, and the required interagency coordination at the federal, state, and local levels. Special emphasis is placed on Texas and its current effort to qualify for Coastal Zone Management Act funding. States must plan and control land uses according to federal guidelines or forfeit their local options to federal decision making. (Fernandez-Florida)
W75-08073

MEDICAL ASPECTS OF CHILDHOOD LEAD POISONING.
U.S. Health Service and Mental Health Administration Health Reports, Vol 86, No 2, p 140-143, February 1971. 16 ref.

Descriptors: *Lead, *Toxicity, *Public health, *Testing procedures, Human pathology, Sampling, Analytical techniques, Administrative agencies.

Medical aspects of and recommendations regarding childhood lead poisoning were discussed. The Public Health Service made the following recommendations: (1) screening programs for the prevention and treatment of lead poisoning (plumbism) in children include all those who are 1 to 6 years of age and living in old, poorly maintained houses; (2) blood lead determinations be used in screening for the detection of lead poisoning and excessive absorption of lead; (3) all children found to have a blood lead concentration of 80 micrograms or more per 100 ml of whole blood, regardless of the presence or absence of clinical symptoms or of other laboratory findings, be considered as having unequivocal cases of lead poisoning and that they be handled as medical emergencies (they should be hospitalized immediately for chelation therapy); (4) all children who are found in screening programs to have lead values of 50-79 micrograms per 100 ml of whole blood should be referred immediately for evaluation as having possible cases of lead poisoning; (5) where resources permit, all children who in screening programs are found to have blood values of 40-49 micrograms/100 ml of whole blood should be recalled immediately for evaluation; (6) sources of lead must be removed from the environment of children who have lead poisoning or who have absorbed hazardous amounts of the poison in their blood. (Jernigan-Vanderbilt)
W75-08077

SELECTIVE WITHDRAWAL FROM THE LA FARGE RESERVOIR FOR DOWNSTREAM TEMPERATURE CONTROL,
Wisconsin Univ., Madison. Water Resources Center.
P. D. Uttormark, J. W. Mason, and T. L. Wirth.
In: IES Report 28, Environmental Analysis of the Kickapoo River Impoundment, p 45-76. 6 fig, 3 tab, 8 ref, 3 append.

Descriptors: *Water temperature, *Downstream, *Reservoir releases, Wisconsin, Rivers, Hydrogen sulfide, Control systems, Reservoir operation, Stream fisheries, Theoretical analysis, Hypolimnion, Streams, Zone of aeration.
Identifiers: *Kickapoo River(Wis), *La Farge Lake(Wis).

To determine the feasibility of utilizing selective water withdrawal from the proposed La Farge Reservoir on the Kickapoo River in Wisconsin to control temperatures in the river below in a manner beneficial to cold-water fish and other aquatic life, water temperature, streamflow data, and time of travel studies were made on the Kickapoo River and eight tributary streams which merge with the main stream below the dam site. Using a temperature release schedule developed with the Army Corps of Engineers to predict downstream temperature effects, it was estimated that water temperatures suitable for cold-water fish species can be maintained in the river from the damsite to at least Viola or to the confluence with the west branch of the Kickapoo above Readstown, but there are some potential detrimental effects associated with a bottom-water discharge from the impoundment--dissolved oxygen sag and prevention of hydrogen sulfide releases. Selective withdrawal of water should be utilized to control water temperature, and a release schedule of water is proposed. A small power dam located 1.3 miles below the dam should be removed. A hypolimnetic aeration system for the reservoir would be beneficial. A post-impoundment monitoring system should be undertaken. (See also W75-08158) (Buchanan-Davidson--Wisconsin)
W75-08160

COST OF ESTABLISHMENT AND OPERATION OF WATER IMPROVEMENT PROCEDURES,
Wisconsin Univ., Madison. Inst. for Environmental Studies.
For primary bibliographic entry see Field 6G.
W75-08169

EPA AUTHORITY AFFECTING LAND USE,
Ross, Hardies, O'Keefe, Babcock and Parsons, Chicago, Ill.
F. P. Bosselman, D. A. Feurer, and D. L. Callies.
Available from the National Technical Information Service, Springfield, Va. 22161, as PB-235 331, $7.00 in paper copy, $2.25 in microfiche. Prepared for Office of Planning and Evaluation, Environmental Protection Agency, Washington, D.C., Final report No EPA 230/3-74-012, March 12, 1974, 194 p, 2 tab. BOA 68-01-1560.

Descriptors: *Land use, *Land management, *Environmental effects, *Legislation, *Clean Air Act, Environmental control, Governmental interrelations, Water Quality Act.
Identifiers: *Noise Control Act, *Solid Waste Disposal Act.

Evaluation of the legislative basis for involvement of EPA with land use decision making and control processes of the states is presented. By use of land control measures, EPA could achieve their statutory goals set forth in the Clean Air Act, the Marine Protection Research and Sanctuaries Act, the Noise Control Act, the Solid Waste Disposal Act. The direct relationship between land utilization and environmental impacts is evident; the challenge to EPA is to establish a flexible program to integrate their objectives with state and local environmental and land use regulations and agen-

Research, Regulation, Streams, Standards, Projects.
Identifiers: *Data needs, *Data requirements, Data acquisition, Routine surveillance data, Legal enforcement, Technical assistance, Water programs.

Routine data collection currently consumes a large amount of the total resources devoted to water quality management. Too often, data collection becomes an end in itself, with little thought given to the purpose of the data collection. The problem usually stems from a lack of proper routine surveillance system design and a failure on the part of the designers to initially identify the data needs of the management program. This study attempts, in a general way, to delineate the data needs of a water quality management program. This first required an identification of the activities involved in water quality management; these were broken down into the broad functions of prevention and abatement. The activities were then discussed in terms of the types of information needed to successfully complete their assigned tasks. Several detailed examples are given. Discussion results are summarized and several strategies are proposed to relate the results to surveillance system design. (Bell-Cornell)
W75-08213

A NOTE ON COST-EFFECTIVENESS IN DATA ACQUISITION IN WATER QUALITY MANAGEMENT,
Vandkvalitetsinstitut, Soborg (Denmark).
K. S. Nielsen, N. Friborg, and M. Bundgaard-Nielsen.
Water Resources Research, Vol 11, No 2, p 357-358, April 1975. 2 fig, 1 ref.

Descriptors: *Water quality, *Management, *Sampling, *Costs, Equations, Effluents, Monitoring, River basins, Optimization, Constraints, Algorithms, Systems analysis, Mathematical models.
Identifiers: *Cost-effectiveness, Data acquisition, Uncertainty, Denmark, Independent variables, Sensitivity, *Mixed integer programming, Cost minimization.

An iterative procedure for sampling in water quality management is presented. The procedure, which utilizes constrainted mixed integer programming, establishes a relationship between cost of sampling and relative uncertainty in total discharge into the water system and at the same time provides an optimal frequency matrix for sampling. The frequency of sampling at each discharge is treated as an independent variable. (Bell-Cornell)
W75-08214

SALINITY CONTROL AND FEDERAL WATER QUALITY ACT,
Bureau of Reclamation, Denver, Colo. Water Quality Office.
M. B. Bessler, and J. T. Maletic.
Journal of the Hydraulics Division, American Society of Civil Engineers, Vol 101, No HY5, Proceedings paper No. 11321, p 581-594, May 1975. 6 fig, 1 tab, 17 ref.

Descriptors: *Salinity, *Water quality control, *Colorado River, *Water management(Applied), Water resources development, *Comprehensive planning, Standards, Economic impact, Evaluation, River basins, Simulation analysis, Computer models, Constraints, Mathematical models, Systems analysis, Federal jurisdiction, Southwest US.
Identifiers: *Salinity control.

Salinity as a mineral pollutant is receiving increased attention in the Western U.S. in terms of economic impacts. The salinity control problem on the Colorado River is examined in relation to the Federal Water Quality Act, PL 92-500. Even basin-wide salinity controls as presently envisioned will not be able to meet anticipated salinity standards and the 'zero discharge' goals of the Act. Described is the Colorado River Water Quality Improvement Program (CRWQIP), only one element of an entire matrix of management plans in the Colorado River Basin. CRWQIP has five categories of control under present study: river system management; point source control; diffuse source control; irrigation source control; and return flow utilization. Options that may be required for the present nondegradation policy are: minimize deep percolation losses from irrigation; desalt return flow and divert brine stream from the system; desalt water prior to select use; divert and reuse saline flows for nonagricultural use; and combinations of foregoing. Discussed is the use of the Colorado River Simulation Model. A new planning strategy of total water management is suggested to identify and evaluate water needs, water resources, physical technology, management technology, and other nonphysical constraints. Thus, specific economic limitations and institutional constraints identified under the various management options will assist in setting attainable salinity levels within a river basin in lieu of meeting rigid zero discharge limitations for each user. Systems analysis tools are advocated for comprehensive basinwide management. (Bell-Cornell)
W75-08217

LAND-BASED MODELING SYSTEM FOR WATER QUALITY MANAGEMENT STUDIES,
Gates (W. E.) and Associates, Inc., Cincinnati, Ohio.
W. M. Grayman, R. M. Males, W. E. Gates, and A. W. Hadder.
Journal of the Hydraulics Division, American Society of Civil Engineers, Vol 101, No HY5, Proceedings paper No. 11327, p 567-580, May 1975. 6 fig, 4 ref.

Descriptors: *Water quality control, *Management, *Computer models, *Comprehensive planning, *Land use, Design, *Treatment facilities, Sewers, Networks, Waste water(Pollution), Environmental control, Rivers, Costs, Alternative planning, Optimization, Simulation analysis, Systems analysis, *Virginia.
Identifiers: *James River(Virginia), Least cost.

Only recently has water quality planning begun to focus on the relationship between land use and waste management. The system of land use/development, waste generation transport-treatment, and the aquatic environment must be considered as a whole in water quality planning for which comprehensive planning tools are required. In response to this need, a computer system called ADAPT (Areal Design and Planning Tool) has been developed. ADAPT is composed of a highly accessible large data file and a series of mathematical submodels which facilitate the storage and use of spatially arrayed data. Though originally implemented as part of a large water quality management study of the lower James River in Virginia where it was used in a variety of land-use/development and sewer/treatment plant design tasks, its flexible structure makes it broadly applicable to a wide range of environmental planning concerns. The basic structure of ADAPT is described together with a discussion of its application to the James River. (Bell-Cornell)
W75-08218

THE RECLAMATION OF SULFURIC ACID FROM WASTE STREAMS,
New Jersey Zinc Company, Palmerton, Pennsylvania. Research Department.
For primary bibliographic entry see Field 5D.
W75-08228

COPPER RECOVERY FROM BRASS MILL DISCHARGE BY CEMENTATION WITH SCRAP IRON,
Anaconda American Brass Co., Waterbury, Conn.
For primary bibliographic entry see Field 5D.
W75-08229

THOSE ELUSIVE 1985 WATER QUALITY GOALS.
Professional Engineer, Vol 44, No 3, p 30-31, March 1974. 2 p, 3 fig.

Descriptors: *Water pollution control, Pollution treatment, *Water quality control, *Government finance, Federal government, Federal Water Pollution Control Act, Industrial wastes, Industrial water, Costs, Cost analysis, Cost trends, Research and development, Research priorities.
Identifiers: Federal Water Pollution Control Act Amendments of 1972, Estimated costs, *Installation costs.

It is doubtful that the federal government will meet the 1985 water quality goals incorporated into the 1972 amendments to the Federal Water Pollution Act. The prime cause is an under expenditure of funds for research and developmenta, a shortchanging which will lead to a technological inability to achieve these water quality goals. There are seven areas in which improvements are required if the goals are to be reached: (1) research to determine how pollutants get into the water, what happens to them, and what is their effect; (2) minimizing the cost of treating municipal sewage; (3) necessary technology to control pollution from industrial and nonpoint sources; (4) need for a water pollution reseach and development strategy; (5) making the research and development program of the Environmental Protection Agency more responsive to operating programs; (6) need for national plans to improve coordination of water pollution research and development; and (7) need for a federal focal point to coordinate the dissemination of research information. The office of Management and Budget should attempt to obtain the full cooperation and support of all federal agencies engaged in water pollution research in the development and implementation of a comprehensive national research and development plan. (Gerlach-Florida)
W75-08233

CHLOR-ALKALI PRODUCERS SHIFT TO DIAPHRAGM CELLS,
For primary bibliographic entry see Field 3E.
W75-08235

JAPAN'S FISHERMEN FORCE CHLORINE MAKERS TO SWITCH.
Chemical Week, Vol 113, No 5, p 31-32, August, 1973. 2 photos.

Descriptors: *Mercury, *Industrial wastes, *Regulations, *Public health, Toxicity, Fish, Chlorides, Legal aspects.
Identifiers: *Japan.

As a result of the latest fish poisoning furor in Japan, the government ordered chlorine producers to end all discharges from mercury-cell plants and switch to diaphragm cells by September, 1975. The Japanese Ministry of International Trade and Industry's order came after investigation of an outbreak of organic mercury poisoning on the coast of the Sea of Ariake. Protest marches in Tokyo and a blockade by fishing boats of the port used by the Chisso Corporation acetylene plant were instrumental in prompting government action. The Japanese industries are now seeking U.S. technology and assistance in order to comply with the new regulations. (Jernigan-Vanderbilt)
W75-08236

THE PROTECTION OF NATURE AS REFLECTED IN THE WORK OF THE FIRST UNITED NATIONS CONFERENCE OF THE ENVIRONMENT (STOCKHOLM, 1972), (IN ROMANIAN),
Consiliul National al Apelor, Bucharest (Rumania).
For primary bibliographic entry see Field 6G.
W75-08241

STANDARDS FOR FAECAL COLIFORM BACTERIAL POLLUTION: COMMENT AND REPLY,
Otago Univ., Dunedin (New Zealand). Dept. of Microbiology.
I. L. Vidal, A. A. Collins, and M. Loutit.
N Z J Mar Freshwater Res, Vol 6, No 1/2, p 214-219, 1972.
Identifiers: *Bacteria, Coliforms, *Fecal coliforms, *New Zealand, *Water quality standards, Water pollution, Recreation.

Vidal and Collins argue in favor of separate standards for recreational water of various regions in New Zealand. This suggestion is disputed by Loutit in a short commentary; and then refuted in a reply by Vidal and Collins.--Copyright 1973, Biological Abstracts, Inc.
W75-08254

PREDICATION OF THE BALANCE OF MATTER IN STORAGE RESERVOIRS BY MEANS OF CONTINUOUS OR SEMICONTINUOUS BIOLOGICAL MODELS: II. RELIABILITY OF THE PREDICTION METHOD, (IN GERMAN),
Technische Universitaet, Dresden (East Germany). Bereich Hydrobiologie.
J. Benndorf.
Int Rev Gesamten Hydrobiol, Vol 58, No 1, p 1-18, 1973, Illus.

Descriptors: Model studies, *Reservoirs, Reservoir storages, *Forecasting, *Balance of nature, Reliability, *Mathematical analysis, Phosphates.
Identifiers: Asterionella-formosa, Biological models, Nitzschia-acicularis, Phytoplankton.

The phosphate removal in small, completely mixed storage reservoirs (preimpoundment basins) mainly is a function of the production of biomass by the phytoplankton. The knowledge of the critical detention time of the water is the most important premise to the prediction. The critical detention time is computed from a derived equation. A comparison of the predicted results from semicontinuous cultures and from the preimpoundment basin of the Weida reservoir revealed a satisfactory degree of conformity.--Copyright 1974, Biological Abstracts, Inc.
W75-08273

NATURAL RESOURCES IN MODERN WORLD AND THE PROBLEM OF THEIR CONSERVATION, (IN ROMANIAN),
Academia R. S. R., Cluj. Centrul de Cercetari Biologice.
For primary bibliographic entry see Field 6G.
W75-08274

THE ROLE OF TRACE ELEMENTS IN MANAGEMENT OF NUISANCE GROWTHS,
Academy of Natural Sciences of Philadelphia, Pa.
R. Patrick.
Available from the National Technical Information Service, Springfield, Va. 22161 as PB-241 985, $7.50 in paper copy, $2.25 in microfiche. Environmental Protection Agency, Ada, Oklahoma, Report EPA-660/2-75-008, April 1975. 250 p. Task 1BB045 (ROAP 21-ASJ, 02), R-800731, (Formerly 16080 FQK).

Descriptors: *Trace elements, *Algal control, Bioindicators, *Nuisance algae, Diatoms, Cyanophyta, Chlorophyta, Water pollution control, Productivity, Standing crops, *Aquatic weed control, Water pollution effects.
Identifiers: Species diversity, Aquatic ecosystems.

The purpose was to examine the effects of various kinds and amounts of trace metals on the structure of algal communities and their possible subsequent effect upon the productivity of the aquatic ecosystem. The following trace metals were examined: vanadium, Chromium, Selenium, boron, nickel, and rubidium. The results of these experiments indicate the concentration and form of a trace metal may have a definite effect upon which algal species can out-compete others. These shifts may greatly reduce the productivity of the system as a whole. If the shift is to species which have lower predator pressure, large standing crops which may be nuisances may develop. (EPA)
W75-08278

PROCEEDINGS: RESEARCH PLANNING CONFERENCE ON INTEGRATED SYSTEMS OF AQUATIC PLANT CONTROL 29-30 OCTOBER 1973.
Army Engineer Waterways Experiment Station, Vicksburg, Miss.
For primary bibliographic entry see Field 4A.
W75-08289

BIOLOGICAL CONTROL OF WATER HYACINTH WITH INSECT ENEMIES.
Army Engineer Waterways Experiment Station, Vicksburg, Miss.
For primary bibliographic entry see Field 4A.
W75-08290

A BACTERIOLOGICAL SURVEY OF THE LITTLE RIVER, SOUTH CAROLINA- CALABASH CREEK, NORTH CAROLINA AREA.
Environmental Protection Agency, Athens, Ga. Surveillance and Analysis Div.
For primary bibliographic entry see Field 5B.
W75-08302

WATER QUALITY AND WASTE SOURCE INVESTIGATIONS. MISSOURI RIVER AND KANSAS RIVER, KANSAS CITY, KANSAS.
Environmental Protection Agency, Kansas City, Mo. Region VII.
For primary bibliographic entry see Field 5B.
W75-08307

THE BREACH IN THE FLOW OF MINERAL NUTRIENTS,
For primary bibliographic entry see Field 5B.
W75-08319

EXTRACTION OF SOIL SOLUTION FROM FLOODED SOIL USING A POROUS PLASTIC FILTER,
Texas A and M Univ., College Station. Dept. of Soil and Crop Sciences.
L. R. Hossner, and D. P. Phillips.
Soil Sci, Vol 115, No 1, p 87-88, 1973, Illus.
Identifiers: *Extraction, Filter, *Flooded soils, *Iron, *Manganese, *Phosphorus, Plastics, Porous filters, Soil solution.

The concentration of Fe, Mn and P extracted from a series of soils with varying concentration of these elements is shown. These data are plotted against those values obtained by pulling solution from the soils on the same day using a Buchner funnel and vacuum flask. In general, concentrations of Fe, Mn and P obtained by the 2 methods were comparable. There was a tendency for slightly lower Fe concentrations in solution when the solution was extracted with the plastic filter particularly when the Fe concentration exceeded about 40 ppm. This method of extraction allows for periodic sampling of the same container for an element over an extended period of time. Concentrations of Fe, Mn and P in the soil solution of an Edna clay loam during 36 days of flooding are shown. The characteristic increases in the solution concentration of Fe and Mn with time can be seen. Mn is reduced at a higher reduction potential than Fe and increases in solution first followed by a rapid increase in the concentration of soluble Fe. P concentration in this soil was low throughout the flooding period and never increased above 0.10 ppm.--Copyright 1973, Biological Abstracts, Inc.
W75-08335

6. WATER RESOURCES PLANNING

6A. Techniques Of Planning

OPTIMAL MONTHLY OPERATION OF INTERCONNECTED HYDROELECTRIC POWER STORAGES,
Institute of Hydrology, Wallingford (England).
For primary bibliographic entry see Field 4A.
W75-07898

AN INTERDISPLINARY APPROACH TO DEVELOPMENT OF WATERSHED SIMULATION MODELS,
British Columbia Univ., Vancouver. Inst. of Animal Resource Ecology.
For primary bibliographic entry see Field 2A.
W75-07947

A STOCHASTIC DYNAMIC PROGRAMMING MODEL FOR THE OPTIMUM OPERATION OF A MULTI-PURPOSE RESERVOIR,
California Univ., Los Angeles.
For primary bibliographic entry see Field 4A.
W75-07988

ON THE MOISTURE BETWEEN DATA AND MODELS OF HYDROLOGIC AND WATER RESOURCE SYSTEMS,
Arizona Univ., Tuscon. Dept. of Management.
J. E. Weber, C. C. Kisiel, and L. Duckstein.
Water Resources Bulletin, Vol 9, No 6, p 1075-1088, December 1973. 1 fig, 26 ref. OWRT C-3259(No 3708)(5) NSF Grants GK34014, GK35915.

Descriptors: *Model studies, *Data collections, *Regression analysis, *Forecasting, *Planning, Water resources development, Hydrology, Estimating, Evaluation, Analytical techniques.
Identifiers: *Multiobjective problem, Secondary data, Proxy variables, Multicriterion problem.

Many difficulties exist in the matching of models with data. Elements of this problem were identified and considerations involved in model evaluation were discussed. The well known multivariate linear regression model was used to illustrate the distinctions between accuracy and precision and between estimation and prediction (because the model is commonly misused). No amount of additional data will improve the accuracy of a poor model. A high correlation coefficient, while indicative of a good matching between the observed data and model estimates, is a poor criterion for judging adequacy of the model to make good predictions of future events. Model evaluation also includes the problem of introducing secondary data and proxy variables into a model. Secondary data frequently enter, for example, the mass, energy, and budget equations, because of difficulties in measuring the primary variables. Proxy variables arise because of a desire to collapse a vector of incomparable values, say, of water quality into a single number. Review of the above issues indicated that model evaluation is a multicriterion problem, often imbedded in a larger framework where models are intended to

meet multiple objectives. The mismatch of models and data has increasing legal and social consequences. (Singh-ISWS)
W75-07989

A DYNAMIC WATER AND RELATED LAND RESOURCE PLANNING MODEL: ITS APPLICATION TO AN HAWAIIAN WATER SYSTEM,
Hawaii Univ., Honolulu. Water Resources Research Center.
T. Liang, W.-Y. Huang, and I-P. Wu.
Available from the National Technical Information Service, Springfield, Va. 22161, as PB-241 937, $4.25 in paper copy, $2.25 in microfiche. Technical Report No 81, July 1974. 55 p, 14 fig, 18 ref. OWRT A-038-HI(1), 14-31-0001-3811 and 14-31-0001-4011.

Descriptors: *Computer models, *Linear programming, *Land use, Water resources, Crops, *Irrigation, Management, Reservoirs, *Hawaii, Planning, *Optimum development plans, Land resources, Model studies, Optimization, Water distribution(Applied).
Identifiers: Multiple cropping, Efficient land use.

Planning an optimal system of activities for generating economic goods and services within an existing natural resource capacity is a difficult problem. A mathematical programming model with the capacity to check multiple resource demand and supply compatibility over many time periods was developed as a solution to this type of problem. The characteristics of natural resource supply and the demand of activities were utilized to reduce the number of time periods and to minimize the loss of the dynamic reality of the problem. Reduction in the number of time periods extended the capability of the model in solving complex resource planning problems without oversimplification. The advance in computer memory size and speed has made multi-period mathematical programming models a practical and desirable tool in planning optimal production scheduling and optimal allocation of resources. However, the construction of a large constraint matrix generated by multi-period models remains an obstacle to the use of multi-period linear programming (LP) models. A matrix generator capable of dividing time span according to resource characteristics and IBM-MPS output compatible matrix for LP otimization was developed.
W75-07993

MODEL DEVELOPMENT AND SYSTEMS ANALYSIS OF THE YAKIMA RIVER BASIN: IRRIGATED AGRICULTURE WATER USE,
Washington State Univ,. Pullman. Dept. of Agricultural Engineering.
For primary bibliographic entry see Field 3F.
W75-07994

WATER RESOURCES PLANNING, SOCIAL GOALS AND INDICATORS: METHODOLOGICAL DEVELOPMENT AND EMPIRICIAL TEST.
Utah State Univ., Logan. Technical Committee of the Water Resources Research Center of the Thirteen Western States.
For primary bibliographic entry see Field 6B.
W75-07997

OPTIMAL COST DESIGN OF BRANCHED SEWER SYSTEMS,
Illinois Univ., Urbana. Dept. of Civil Engineering.
For primary bibliographic entry see Field 5D.
W75-07999

THE IMPACT OF HIGH INTEREST RATES ON OPTIMUM MULTIPLE OBJECTIVE DESIGN OF SURFACE RUNOFF URBAN DRAINAGE SYSTEMS,
Purdue Univ., Lafayette, Ind. Dept. of Agricultural Economics.
For primary bibliographic entry see Field 5G.
W75-08001

DEVELOPING BIOLOGICAL INFORMATION SYSTEMS FOR WATER QUALITY MANAGEMENT,
Virginia Polytechnic Inst. and State Univ., Blacksburg. Center for Environmental Studies; and Virginia Polytechnic Inst. and State Univ., Blacksburg. Dept. of Biology.
For primary bibliographic entry see Field 5G.
W75-08002

AN OPTIMAL POLICY FOR OPERATING A MULTIPURPOSE RESERVOIR,
Clemson Univ., S.C.
For primary bibliographic entry see Field 4A.
W75-08003

FLOOD PROTECTION BENEFITS AS REFLECTED IN PROPERTY VALUE CHANGES,
Kentucky Univ., Lexington. Dept. of Economics.
For primary bibliographic entry see Field 6F.
W75-08004

WATER QUALITY CONTROL BY ARTIFICIAL AERATION OF STREAM RECEIVING THERMAL AND ORGANIC WASTE DISCHARGES,
Kansas State Univ., Manhattan. Inst. for Systems Design and Optimization.
For primary bibliographic entry see Field 5G.
W75-08005

DIGITAL SIMULATION OF THE EFFECT OF THERMAL DISCHARGE ON STREAM WATER QUALITY,
Kansas State Univ., Manhattan. Inst. for Systems Design and Optimization.
For primary bibliographic entry see Field 5B.
W75-08006

WATER QUALITY MANAGEMENT AND INFORMATION SYSTEMS,
Krannert Graduate School of Industrial Administration, Lafayette, Ind.
For primary bibliographic entry see Field 5G.
W75-08007

PEAK LOAD PRICING AND URBAN WATER MANAGEMENT: VICTORIA, B.C., A CASE STUDY,
Victoria Univ. (British Columbia). Dept. of Economics.
For primary bibliographic entry see Field 3B.
W75-08074

PLANNING THE TEHACHAPI CROSSING,
Burns and Roe, Inc., Sacramento, Calif.
A. R. Golze.
Journal of the Hydraulics Division, American Society of Civil Engineers, Vol 101, No HY1, Proceedings paper No. 11052, p 1-16, January 1975. 7 fig, 1 tab, 10 ref.

Descriptors: *Planning, *Hydraulic models, California, *Aqueducts, *Pumps, *Earthquakes, Pumping, Projects, Water delivery, Water supply, Design, Construction.
Identifiers: *California Water Project, *Water tunnels, Tehachapi Mountains(California).

The Tehachapi Crossing of the California Water Project represents a definite advancement in the art of planning, designing, and constructing high-head pumping facilities in North America; it demonstrates the benefits obtainable from a well-planned and-executed research and development program in water transportation. The planning of the California Aqueduct crossing of the Tehachapi Mountains in California north of Los Angeles involved 10 years of intensive research and study in the United States and Europe to design a 4,100-cfs (116,112 l/s), 2,000-ft (610m) high-head pump lift, the largest in the U.S. Engineering examination of alternate aqueduct routes over the high mountain ranges ended in selection of a crossing at El. 3100 (945.5m). Study of the number of pump lifts was resolved in favor of a single-lift on the Ridge Route. Model tests of various types of European and American pump designs identified as most suitable a vertical four-stage single-flow centrifugal pump 33 ft (10.065m) in height, 16 ft (4.88m) in diameter. Ten miles of 23.5-ft (7.18m) diameter tunnel convey the pumped water through the mountain range. The Tehachapi Crossing has been in operation since October 1971. (Bell-Cornell)
W75-08201

ON THE MEASUREMENT OF ENVIRONMENTAL IMPACTS OF PUBLIC PROJECTS FROM A SOCIOLOGICAL PERSPECTIVE,
East Texas State Univ., Commerce. Dept. of Sociology and Anthropology.
For primary bibliographic entry see Field 6G.
W75-08203

CREATIVITY AND RATIONALITY IN PLAN FORMULATION,
Hydrologic Engineering Center, Davis, Calif. Planning Analysis Branch.
For primary bibliographic entry see Field 6B.
W75-08205

USER-ORIENTED RESEARCH DESIGNS,
Nebraska Univ., Lincoln. Water Resources Research Inst.
W. Viessman, Jr., and K. E. Stork.
Water Resources Bulletin, Vol 10, No 3, p 440-446, June 1974.

Descriptors: *Water resources, *Research, Design, Planning, Technology, Social aspects, Projects, Priorities.
Identifiers: *User-oriented research, *Technology transfer.

The traditional approach to water resources problem solving has been technical. Today, however, problems originate more often from ineffective institutions or techniques for planning, management and regulation than from inadequacies or lack of physical works. A user-oriented research plan for water resources is presented. Its principal components are: (1) a mechanism for identifying social goals and translating them into research objectives; (2) procedures for setting priorities; (3) a program planning technique for designing projects to have impact on important research objectives; (4) a mechanism for coordinating research activities of important research producers; (5) a structure for encouraging and establishing interdisciplinary team efforts when they are required; (6) a well-coordinated technology transfer plan; and (7) an effective method for promoting and sustaining user-researcher cooperation. Both basic and applied research designs are examined and criteria presented. The implementation of research plans is also discussed and various factors which play a role in implementation are outlined, including: coordination, goal interpretation and priority setting, project planning, project review, interdisciplinary considerations and the user-researcher interface. (Bell-Cornell)
W75-08206

A NOTE ON COST-EFFECTIVENESS IN DATA ACQUISITION IN WATER QUALITY MANAGEMENT,
Vandkvalitetsinstitut, Soborg (Denmark).
For primary bibliographic entry see Field 5G.
W75-08214

ECOLOGICAL AND ECONOMIC PRINCIPLES IN PARK PLANNING: THE ASSATEAGUE NATIONAL SEASHORE MODEL,
National Park Service, Washington, D.C.
For primary bibliographic entry see Field 6B.
W75-08216

SALINITY CONTROL AND FEDERAL WATER QUALITY ACT,
Bureau of Reclamation, Denver, Colo. Water Quality Office.
For primary bibliographic entry see Field 5G.
W75-08217

LAND-BASED MODELING SYSTEM FOR WATER QUALITY MANAGEMENT STUDIES,
Gates (W. E.) and Associates, Inc., Cincinnati, Ohio.
For primary bibliographic entry see Field 5G.
W75-08218

INTERACTIVE SIMULATION FOR WATER SYSTEM DYNAMICS,
Colorado State Univ., Fort Collins. Dept. of Civil Engineering.
For primary bibliographic entry see Field 4A.
W75-08219

6B. Evaluation Process

IDENTIFICATION AND ANALYSIS OF SELECTED HIGH PRIORITY WATER PROBLEMS AND RELATED RESEARCH NEEDS OF THE MISSOURI RIVER BASIN,
Nebraska Univ., Lincoln. Water Resources Research Inst.
Available from the National Technical Information Service, Springfield, Va. 22161, as PB-241 945, $5.25 in paper copy, $2.25 in microfiche. Completion Report, Missouri River Basin Water Institute Consortium, March 1975, 125 p. OWRT X-135(No 9079)(1), 14-31-0001-9079.

Descriptors: Evaluation, Research and development, Cost analysis, *Research priorities, *Regional analysis, Planning, *Missouri River, Riber basin development, *Coordination, *Alternative planning, Water resources development, Reservoir operation.
Identifiers: *Research needs, Research problems.

In 1972 the Water Institutes in the ten states of the Missouri River Basin formed a Consortium for coordinating research planning and implementation with regard to regional problems. The objectives were to: (1) identify principal water resources problems of the Missouri River Basin; (2) determine the most reasonable alternatives for solving these problems; (3) identify research needed to permit cost-effective solutions; (4) evaluate mechanisms to implement the needed research; and (5) assign priorities, estimate costs and evaluate funding opportunities. During 1973 each state in the Basin was requested to conduct a state workshop to determine regional research needs and problem identification. A regional workshop was held, during which 23 research problem areas in the Basin were identified. This list was revised and evaluated during 1974 meetings of MRBWIC Directors, and a list of 10 problem areas was delineated. Each Institute Director was assigned to analyze one problem area. Again state workshops were held on many of the specific problem areas. These results were again tabulated by MRBWIC Directors and a final reassessment of research priorities for the Missouri River Basin showed six principal categories as follows: (1) source and adequacy of water for energy production; (2) irrigation systems; (3) evapotranspiration; (4) flood plain management; (5) sediment; and (6) reservoir management.
W75-07851

WATER FACTS AND FIGURES FOR PLANNERS AND MANAGERS,
Geological Survey, Menlo Park, Calif.
J. H. Feth.
Circular 601-I, 1973. 30 p, 9 fig, 8 tab, 22 ref.

Descriptors: *Water management(Applied), *Urban hydrology, Hydrology, *Water resources, Thesauri, Water properties, Water measurement, Surface waters, Groundwater, Water quality, Education, *Documentation, *Classification.

This circular is intended to provide the basic information that goes into management considerations of water. It is concerned mostly with the language used in dealing with water. Terminology, numbers, and equivalents are mainly presented; theory and principles are briefly mentioned. Water terms are presented together with a suggestion of their significance and interrelations. (Knapp-USGS)
W75-07889

FLOOD PLAIN MANAGEMENT AND IMPLEMENTATION STRATEGIES FOR FPM PROGRAMS,
Iowa State Water Resources Research Inst., Ames.
For primary bibliographic entry see Field 6F.
W75-07890

MODAL CITIES,
Dartmouth Coll., Hanover, N.H. Dept. of Geography.
J. W. Sommer, and G. B. Pidot, Jr.
Available from the National Technical Information Service, Springfield, Va. 22161, as PB-239 719, $4.25 in paper copy, $2.25 in microfiche. Environmental Protection Agency, Report EPA-600/5-74-027, October 1974. 55 p, 9 fig, 9 tab. EPA Program Element 1HA096, 801226.

Descriptors: *Cities, Analytical techniques, Urbanization, Regional analysis, Model studies, Human population.
Identifiers: *Modal cities, *Components analysis, Modalities, Standard metropolitan statistical area.

Model cities are representative cities based on a specific set of criteria. Using principal components analysis, 224 U.S. SMSA's (Standard Metropolitan Statistical Areas) were examined in terms of 48 selected variables. This analysis yielded 14 dimensions, of which 7 explained 67% of the variance. The 224 cities were then grouped using a method that minimizes the differences among cities within a group and maximizes the differences across groups. This procedure allowed for a confident selection of 9 modalities of the U.S. metropolitan system. Each city fell into a modality and was ranked relative to its distance from the mean. The two cities closes to the mean were taken as representative of that group. One unforeseen result of this research was the distinct regional character of the different groupings. (EPA)
W75-07967

IMPROVING PRODUCTIVITY IN LOW RAINFALL AREAS,
Food and Agriculture Organization of the United Nation, Rome (Italy). Committee on Agriculture.
For primary bibliographic entry see Field 3F.
W75-07981

ECONOMIC AND INSTITUTIONAL ANALYSIS OF COLORADO WATER QUALITY MANAGEMENT,
Colorado State Univ., Fort Collins. Dept. of Economics.
For primary bibliographic entry see Field 5G.
W75-07992

A DYNAMIC WATER AND RELATED LAND RESOURCE PLANNING MODEL: ITS APPLICATION TO AN HAWAIIAN WATER SYSTEM,
Hawaii Univ., Honolulu. Water Resources Research Center.
For primary bibliographic entry see Field 6A.
W75-07993

THE LITERATURE CITED IN THE WISCONSIN DEPARTMENT OF NATURAL RESOURCES PUBLICATIONS ON WATER RELATED SUBJECTS, 1964-1973,
Wisconsin Univ., Madison. Library School.
For primary bibliographic entry see Field 10D.
W75-07996

WATER RESOURCES PLANNING, SOCIAL GOALS AND INDICATORS: METHODOLOGICAL DEVELOPMENT AND EMPIRICIAL TEST.
Utah State Univ., Logan. Technical Committee of the Water Resources Research Center of the Thirteen Western States.
Available from the National Technical Information Service, Springfield, Va. 22161, as PB-242 025, $8.50 in paper copy, $2.25 in microfiche. Report PRWG-131-1, Utah Water Research Laboratory, Utah State University, Logan, December 31, 1974. 261 p, 43 fig, 18 tab, 114 ref. OWRT C-4330(No 9049)(1).

Descriptors: *Planning, *Social Values, *Decision making, *Water policy, *Welfare(Economics), *Evaluation, Social aspects, Federal government, Model studies, Intangible benefits, Conservation, Recreation, Aesthetics, Water resources development, Policies, Environment, Methodology, Attitudes, Social participation.
Identifiers: *Social indicators, *Social goals, Well-being, Policy action, Public participation.

A methodology for comprehensive evaluation of water resources development and use (TECHCOM) has been developed and partially field tested. A model of 3 societal goals consists of nine primary goals successively articulated into increasingly specific subgoals consists of nine primary goals successively articulated into increasingly specific subgoals. Achievement of subgoals is perceived as affected by measurable social indicators whose values are perturbed by water resources actions. Linking the elements of the goal taxon by connectives results in an evaluation system. Historical, political and philosophical considerations of the proposed system are discussed in Part I. Part II describes the results of the Rio Grande of New Mexico test including public perception and weighting of the subgoals and goals, and development of specific connectives. Future values of 128 social indicators for 5 action plans for four five-year intervals to 1987 are estimated using a computerized system based on an inversion of an input-output model interacting with social and environmental indicator connectives. A computerized system for quantified planning inquiry provides comparisons of relative goal achievement and permits review of all planning information through a simple retrieval procedure providing visual display or hard copy. The methodology is conceived as applicable generally to natural resources actions.
W75-07997

AN OPTIMAL POLICY FOR OPERATING A MULTIPURPOSE RESERVOIR,
Clemson Univ., S.C.
For primary bibliographic entry see Field 4A.
W75-08003

WATER QUALITY MANAGEMENT AND INFORMATION SYSTEMS,
Krannert Graduate School of Industrial Administration, Lafayette, Ind.
For primary bibliographic entry see Field 5G.
W75-08007

RIVER BASIN WATER PLANNING ORGANIZATIONS IN THE 60'S,
Utah State Univ., Logan. Dept. of Civil Engineering.
D. H. Hoggan.
Water Resources Bulletin, Vol 10, No 6, p 1173-1186, December, 1974. 1 fig, 2 tab, 11 ref. OWRT C-2089(No 3671)(2).

Descriptors: *River basins, *River basin commissions, *River basin development, *Inter-agency cooperation, *Planning, Organizations, Comprehensive planning, Rivers, U.S. Water Resources Council.
Identifiers: Inter-agency river basin planning, Regional planning studies.

The experience of 15 state-federal interagency river basin studies is examined. The Water Resources Council envisioned framework studies (Type 1) for large multi-state areas while Type 2 studies were to provide a basis for authorization for projects to begin during the next 10-15 years. Essentially Army Corps of Engineer studies, Type 2 studies represent a significant step in coordination with other agencies. Usually with the Corps as lead agency, study contributors collected large amounts of unused data without formulating objectives or early hypotheses. Growing public interest in citizen participation and multi-objective planning complicated the task, as did the 1969 requirement of Environmental Impact Statements. A general lack of commitment to cooperative comprehensive planning and a lack of central administration and funding increased organizational difficulties. Type 2 studies, unable to plan in sufficient detail to provide specific plans due to organizational, time, and financial constraints, were classified Level B studies (preliminary or reconnaissance level) by the Council in 1970 under a new policy which established levels of planning in lieu of types of planning. Conclusions: (1) Focus should be on the total system of a geographically designed planning area instead of on separate development purposes, with a centralized planning staff and centralized funding. (2) Conceptual plans and public participation should be included in early planning stages. (3) Planning should be a continuous process with adjustment for dynamic conditions and mechanisms for comprehensive implementation. (4) Guidelines for organizing river basin studies and criteria for evaluating planning are badly needed. (5) Formal training programs in planning skills will improve leadership and staff capabilities. (Herr-North Carolina)
W75-08011

A BASIS FOR ASSESSING DIFFERENTIAL PARTICIPATION IN WATER-BASED RECREATION,
Washington State Water Resources Center, Pullman.
D. R. Field, and N. H. Cheek, Jr.
Water Resources Bulletin, Vol 10, No 6, p 1218-1227, 1974. 5 tab, 22 ref. OWRR A-047-WASH(3).

Descriptors: *Recreation, *Psychological aspects, *Attitudes, Social aspects, *Social participation, Alternative planning, Evaluation.
Identifiers: Public participation.

Participation in water-based recreation activities does not arise in random fashion nor is it simply the result of having a water resource immediately available. Neither do individuals and groups engage in the same activities or a specific activity in the same way. This study describes an alternative framework whereby differences among recreation users can be identified as opposed to studies assuming that recreation activity is site specific. Investigations of designated activity spots disclosed that the largest proportion of human action observed was not related to, or dependent on the recreational activity for which the area might have been designed. Rather recreation areas are defined by users as leisure places instead of activity sites. Similarities are noted of leisure places in terms of the presence or absence of specific recreation activities. It is when recreation sites are considered as leisure settings where people gather in groups, distinguishing features of recreation activities become evident. The study was based on social groups subdivided into friendship groups, family units, and mixed, a combination of family and friends, and utilized a portion of the data compiled by the National Park Service and the Washington State Water Resources Center. (Auen-Wisconsin)
W75-08012

WRINGING OUT THE WEST, REMEMBER THE MISSOURI AND THE COLORADO,
For primary bibliographic entry see Field 6D.
W75-08101

RECREATION USES CHANGE MOGOLLON RIM ECONOMY,
Forest Service (USDA), Tucson, Ariz. Rocky Mountain Forest and Range Experiment Station; and Arizona Univ., Tucson.
R. S. Boster, P. F. O'Connell, and J. C. Thompson.
Arizona Review, Vol 23, Nos 8-9, August-September, 1974. 5 p, 3 fig, 1 tab.

Descriptors: *Water supply, *Land use, *Recreation demand, *Arizona, *Environmental effects, Economic impact, Water pollution, Waste water treatment, Land development, Recreation wastes.
Identifiers: *Mogollon Rim(Ariz).

Located less than 100 miles from Phoenix, Arizona, the Mogollon Rim country is experiencing rapid and uncontrolled growth and development. Private lands in the area have historically been used for grazing and crop production. Recently, these practices have become uneconomical and land owners are turning to residential development, particularly summer home construction and facilities for transient recreationists. Development of these private lands is creating management problems for adjacent National Forests through increased demands for services such as fire protection and water supplies. In addition, evidence of environmental degradation is present, primarily water pollution resulting from inadequate or nonexistent waste treatment systems. Land use planning along with private land and Forest Service cooperation are viewed as steps to the solution of a complex problem. (Mastic-Arizona)
W75-08108

AN INTEGRATED NATURAL RESOURCES SURVEY IN NORTHERN IRAQ,
Institute for Applied Research on Natural Resources, Baghdad (Iraq).
For primary bibliographic entry see Field 3F.
W75-08116

IMPACT OF A PROPOSED IMPOUNDMENT OPERATION ON THE INVERTEBRATE ASSEMBLAGES IN THE KICKAPOO RIVER, LA FARGE (VERNON CO.), WISCONSIN,
Wisconsin Univ., Madison. Dept. of Zoology.
R. Hall, J. J. Magnuson, and W. Shaffer.
In: IES Report 28, Environmental Analysis of the Kickapoo River Impoundment, p. 129-159. 5 fig, 2 tab, 26 ref, 2 append.

Descriptors: *Benthos, *Pre-impoundment, *Invertebrates, *Post-impoundment, Aquatic insects, Oligochaetes, Wisconsin, Hypolmnion, Crustaceans, Stoneflies, Water beetles, Caddisflies, Mayflies, Diptera, Worms, Reservoirs, Snails, Rivers, Fish food organisms, Water temperature, Biomass, Stream improvement, Varieties.
Identifiers: *Kickapoo River(Wis), *La Farge Lake(Wis).

Seasonal fluctuations in invertebrate species, abundance, distribution, and diversity were examined at sites at the proposed La Farge impoundment of the Kickapoo River. Mayflies, stoneflies, caddisflies, beetles, and Diptera (true flies) were the most common organisms on the river bottom. True bugs were present along the bank. Aquatic oligochaete worms and chireonomids were in the stream. Gammarus was the most abundant crustacean. The reservoir will change the environment thus inducing changes in the benthos from lotic species to lentic fauna. Most of the present aquatic insects and crustacea will persist upstream from the impoundment. In the impoundment, some lake species will become abundant, but fluctuating water levels and possible anoxic conditions in the hypolimnion will restict distribution. Plankton will develop in the limnetic zone. Below the impoundment, some insects and plankton may appear in the discharge, many species will disappear, diversity will decline, but food supply will increase. Biomass and invertebrate production may improve near the dam. Stream improvement may be needed to insure substrates for macroinvertebrates and cover for trout. Due to the small size of the chironomids and simuliids, a viable forage fish population may reduce the smaller organisms and provide food particle sizes more suitable for trout. (See also W75-08158) (Buchanan-Davidson--Wisconsin)
W75-08164

INITIAL COASTLINE PLAN FOR THE SAN DIEGO REGION,
Duncan and Jones, Berkeley, Calif. and San Diego County Comprehensive Planning Organization, Calif.
For primary bibliographic entry see Field 6F.
W75-08171

AREA-WIDE COMPREHENSIVE WATER AND SEWER PLAN: VOLUME I, GENERAL REPORT,
Caldwell (Robert W.) and Associates, Bryan, Tex.
For primary bibliographic entry see Field 5D.
W75-08181

WATER QUALITY MANAGEMENT PLAN--SUMMARY REPORT,
Department of Metropolitan Development, Indianapolis, Ind. Div of Planning and Zoning.
For primary bibliographic entry see Field 5D.
W75-08187

THE AMERICAN INDIAN AND MISSOURI RIVER WATER DEVELOPMENTS,
Nevada Univ., Reno. Renewable Resources Center.
B. D. Shanks.
Water Resources Bulletin, Vol 10, No 3, p 573-579, June 1974. 18 ref.

Descriptors: *Missouri River, *Water resources development, *Social aspects, *Economic impact, Land resources, Costs, Benefits, History.
Identifiers: *American Indians, *Social costs, *Cultural costs.

Considered are the social costs to the American Indian occasioned by construction of three Missouri River main stem dams (Garrison, Oahe, and Fort Randall) and related reservoir taking. Socioeconomic changes have occurred on five Indian reservations: Fort Berthold, Cheyenne River, Standing Rock, Crow Creek and Lower Brule. Inundation of Missouri River riparian lands caused the loss of important cultural, social and economic environments. Ninety percent of the reservations' timber, seventy-five percent of the wildlife and most of the fertile cropland were in the reservoir taking area. Urban and more fertile environments downstream and to the east received most of the projects benefits. The Indian minority on the five reservations received few economic and social

benefits after bearing a disproportionate share of the social and economic costs of the developments. Relocation was forced upon those who had the longest historic and cultural claim to the land. The social costs to the American Indian occasioned by the Missouri River water developments illustrate two broad areas seldom considered during the decision process: First, the unique historic, cultural or religious values of minorities affected by developments; second, the disproportionate spatial allocation of both benefits and costs. The second item includes social, economic and cultural considerations in not just a geographic framework but in a cultural framework as well. (Bell-Cornell)
W75-08204

CREATIVITY AND RATIONALITY IN PLAN FORMULATION,
Hydrologic Engineering Center, Davis, Calif. Planning Analysis Branch.
W. K. Johnson.
Water Resources Bulletin, Vol 10, No 3, p 478-485, June 1974. 3 fig, 10 ref.

Descriptors: *Planning, *Creativity, *Decision making, *Water resources development, Model studies, Alternative resources, Management, Forecasting, Systems analysis.
Identifiers: Planning process, *Plan formulation, Production function, Inventory, Rationality.

Plan formulation is both art and science; to improve formulation and to develop better alternatives, the planner needs to improve his creative capability and to think more systematically. Research into creativity by psychologist and social scientist has identified four aspects of creativity: the creative process, the creative product, the creative person, and the creative situation. A review of research results on each aspect suggests several ways in which planners can improve the creative dimension of plan formulation. To improve the rational aspects of plan formulation, a way of thinking is presented in the form of a conceptual model to assist the planner in systematically developing a broader range of plans. The major components are inventory, forecast and synthesis. The model utilizes the concept of a production function to provide information about the water resource, management practices, and the resource use. Creativity is difficult for the planner/engineer educated in the scientific method to fully appreciate, yet it is a very real factor. (Bell-Cornell)
W75-08205

USER--ORIENTED RESEARCH DESIGNS,
Nebraska Univ., Lincoln. Water Resources Research Inst.
For primary bibliographic entry see Field 6A.
W75-08206

WATERSHED MANAGEMENT WITHOUT SURFACE RUNOFF,
Nebraska Univ., Lincoln. Dept. of Agricultural Engineering.
For primary bibliographic entry see Field 4D.
W75-08207

WATER RESOURCE MANAGEMENT-PLANNING FOR ACTION,
Stanley Consultants, Inc., Muscatine, Iowa.
R. G. Paulette, and W. R. Klatt.
Water Resources Bulletin, Vol 10, No 2, p 384-388, April 1974.

Descriptors: *Water resources, *Management, *Planning, *Decision making, River basin development, Methodology, Institutional constraints, Organizations, Inter-agency cooperation.

Effective decision making in water resource management programs necessitates effective planning, planning which encourages that programs get off the shelf and are acted upon. There is a gap between intentions for and results from the planning process. Failures should be examined and the causes identified. A primary cause is neglecting to identify the potentials of the implementing agencies early in the planning process. These agencies constitute a hierarchy of governmental units at national, state, regional and local levels. Each of these levels has its own interests, point of view, capabilities and constraints. A technically and functionally sound plan can fail as a program if these conflicting interests are not accounted for. The implementation mechanisms must be identified as an initial phase of the planning process. All levels of the governmental hierarchy must be involved throughout the planning process. The successful plan must also provide for suitable assignment of responsibilities which are accepted by the executing agency and monitored for satisfactory fulfillment; consistency and continuity of the advocate agency are further essential elements to plan success. Experience in water resource management planning has shown that these strategies will produce programs which are accepted and implemented and which accomplish the goals and objectives of the planning process. (Bell-Cornell)
W75-08209

WATER AND THE ENERGY CRISIS,
Nebraska Univ., Lincoln. Water Resources Research Inst.
W. Viessman, Jr., and K. E. Stork.
Water Resources Bulletin, Vol 10, No 2, p 220-228, April 1974. 6 ref.

Descriptors: *Water resources, *Energy, *Planning, *Water utilization, *Decision making, Management, Social aspects, Political aspects, Economics, Conservation, Technology, Priorities, Environmental effects, Research, Water quality, Agriculture, Irrigation.
Identifiers: *Water use efficiency, Water-energy impacts, Energy crisis.

Water and energy are inextricably bound. Energy is consumed and sometimes produced by every form of water resources system. Opportunities for future development and production of energy resources abound as well as those for significant reductions in energy consumption through wise water development and management. Technological, political, social, economic and environmental factors interrelate in the energy-water mix. The role of the water resources planner will have to be expanded to include assessment of water-energy impacts in addition to traditional planning considerations. An energy conservation account may well have to be added to the dimensions of national economic development and environmental quality in water resources planning. Ways must be found to reduce amounts and rates of water used and energy consumed through new manufacturing processes, improved irrigation practices, better management, new or altered social-political-economic arrangements, and other procedures. To do this will require setting priorities and making difficult management decisions. The water fraternity can play a major role in alleviating the energy crisis. (Bell-Cornell)
W75-08210

THE IMPORTANCE OF PERCEPTIONS IN THE DETERMINATION OF INDIAN WATER RIGHTS,
Washington State Univ., Pullman. Dept. of Political Science.
For primary bibliographic entry see Field 6E.
W75-08212

ECOLOGICAL AND ECONOMIC PRINCIPLES IN PARK PLANNING: THE ASSATEAGUE NATIONAL SEASHORE MODEL,
National Park Service, Washington, D.C.
P. Gaskin, and J. R. Stottlemyer.
Coastal Zone Management Journal, Vol 1, No 4, p 395-413, 1974. 5 fig.

Descriptors: *National parks, *Planning, *Economics, *Ecology, *Seashores, *Barrier islands, Management, Recreation, Preservation, Environmental effects, Economic impact, Construction costs, Land management, Beaches, Water utilization, Water quality, Storms, Damages, Erosion, Vegetation, Decision making, Maryland, Virginia.
Identifiers: Maintenance costs, Animal life, Visitor use, *Assateague National Seashore(Md-Va).

The National Park Service is required by law to conserve nationally significant resources for public benefit. Susceptibility to local short-term economic pressures and a lack of understanding of resource dynamics can jeopardize mandate compliance. Assateague National Seashore is an example of a dynamic barrier island where early understanding of ecologic factors should have preceded its establishment and must precede its management and development. Research conducted on a similar system has demonstrated the dramatic environmental impacts and high maintenance costs associated with an inappropriate recreation management scheme. Alternatives are available which minimize resource degradation and maintenance costs without restricting visitation. To better ensure incorporation of long-run ecologic and economic criteria into the decision-making process, a proposal is made which recognizes the need for an expanded research effort and close adherence to early planning steps. Required is the identification of a minimally acceptable basic data package for decision making and the determination of who is responsible for its preparation. (Bell-Cornell)
W75-08216

INTERACTIVE SIMULATION FOR WATER SYSTEM DYNAMICS,
Colorado State Univ., Fort Collins. Dept. of Civil Engineering.
For primary bibliographic entry see Field 4A.
W75-08219

6C. Cost Allocation, Cost Sharing, Pricing/Repayment

LAND USE FORMS AND THE ENVIRONMENT - AN EXECUTIVE SUMMARY,
Chicago Univ., Ill. Dept. of Geography; and Chicago Univ., Ill. Center for Urban Studies.
For primary bibliographic entry see Field 6G.
W75-07971

MODEL DEVELOPMENT AND SYSTEMS ANALYSIS OF THE YAKIMA RIVER BASIN: IRRIGATED AGRICULTURE WATER USE,
Washington State Univ., Pullman. Dept. of Agricultural Engineering.
For primary bibliographic entry see Field 3F.
W75-07994

THE IMPACT OF HIGH INTEREST RATES ON OPTIMUM MULTIPLE OBJECTIVE DESIGN OF SURFACE RUNOFF URBAN DRAINAGE SYSTEMS,
Purdue Univ., Lafayette, Ind. Dept. of Agricultural Economics.
For primary bibliographic entry see Field 5G.
W75-08001

ENVIRONMENTAL PROTECTION AGENCY'S 1974 NEEDS SURVEY.
For primary bibliographic entry see Field 5D.
W75-08065

A NOTE ON COST-EFFECTIVENESS IN DATA ACQUISITION IN WATER QUALITY MANAGEMENT,
Vandkvalitetsinstitut, Soborg (Denmark).
For primary bibliographic entry see Field 5G.
W75-08214

ON THE PEAK-LOAD PRICING OF URBAN WATER SUPPLY,
Clark Univ., Worcester, Mass. Graduate School of Geography.
S. L. Feldman.
Water Resources Research, Vol 11, No 2, p 355-356, April 1975. 10 ref.

Descriptors: *Peak loads, *Pricing, *Water supply, Operating costs, Design, Equity, Seasonal, Sprinkling, Systems analysis, Mathematical models, Demand, Peak loads.
Identifiers: *Urban water systems, Design capacity, Meters.

Peak-load pricing through seasonal price increases without changes in metering and billing practices may produce distortions in efficiency and equity in urban water systems. Demand management models using parameters to evaluate the effect of seasonal price policy upon maximum day sprinkling demands may be misleading because of behavioral constraints to price responsiveness. Proposed are alternative pricing schemes that are likely candidates for improving the operating cost structure and design capacity of water supply systems without violating popular notions of equity. (Bell-Cornell)
W75-08215

6D. Water Demand

FLORIDA'S WATER RESOURCES,
Geological Survey, Tallahassee, Fla.
For primary bibliographic entry see Field 4A.
W75-07872

PEAK LOAD PRICING AND URBAN WATER MANAGEMENT: VICTORIA, B.C., A CASE STUDY,
Victoria Univ. (British Columbia). Dept. of Economics.
For primary bibliographic entry see Field 3B.
W75-08074

WRINGING OUT THE WEST, REMEMBER THE MISSOURI AND THE COLORADO,
J. McCaull.
Environment, Vol 16, No 7, p 10-17, September 1974. 1 tab, 1 fig, 5 photos.

Descriptors: *Salinity, *Colorado River, *Missouri River, *Water demand, *Industrial water, Water allocation(Policy), Water requirements, Water shortage, Water utilization, Irrigation, River basins, Great Plains, Rocky Mountain Region.
Identifiers: Energy development.

Federal studies reveal that future energy development projects in the western states will require more water than is available. The Missouri and Colorado Rivers are in greatest jeopardy from this development. The industrial plans could reduce the flow of the lower Missouri to a rate that will barely float a barge, and the lower Colorado River may become too small and too salty to support irrigation demands in California and the Southwest. With little or no public awareness, water used since 1972 have been directed toward energy conversion and development projects instead of irrigation, wildlife management, or municipal and industrial purposes. As a result, the development of the entire energy industry must be evaluated in assessing future water requirements in the West. (Mastic-Arizona)
W75-08101

ON THE PEAK-LOAD PRICING OF URBAN WATER SUPPLY,
Clark Univ., Worcester, Mass. Graduate School of Geography.
For primary bibliographic entry see Field 6C.
W75-08215

6E. Water Law and Institutions

URBAN SEDIMENT PROBLEMS: A STATEMENT ON SCOPE, RESEARCH, LEGISLATION, AND EDUCATION,
American Society of Civil Engineers, New York. Task Committee on Urban Sedimentation Problems.
For primary bibliographic entry see Field 5G.
W75-07931

ECONOMIC AND INSTITUTIONAL ANALYSIS OF COLORADO WATER QUALITY MANAGEMENT,
Colorado State Univ., Fort Collins. Dept. of Economics.
For primary bibliographic entry see Field 5G.
W75-07992

RIVER BASIN WATER PLANNING ORGANIZATIONS IN THE 60'S,
Utah State Univ., Logan. Dept. of Civil Engineering.
For primary bibliographic entry see Field 6B.
W75-08011

INSTITUTIONAL CONSTRAINTS ON AGRICULTURAL WATER USE,
Colorado State Univ., Fort Collins. Dept. of Agricultural Engineering.
R. C. Ward, G. V. Skogerboe, and W. R. Walker.
Presented at Winter Meetings of the American Society of Agricultural Engineers, December 11-14, 1973. Chicago, Illinois. 18 p, 18 ref. (ASAE Paper No 73-2545). OWRR B-071-COLO(7).

Descriptors: *Water utilization, *Agriculture, *Institutional constraints, Law enforcement, Water allocation(Policy), Colorado, River basins.

Scarcity of water in the western U.S. has resulted in the development of a vast institutional framework to insure its just allocation. The institutions are briefly reviewed, and their impact on agriculture's water use is discussed. (Skogerboe-Colorado State)
W75-08013

ENVIRONMENTAL PROTECTION AGENCY'S 1974 NEEDS SURVEY.
For primary bibliographic entry see Field 5D.
W75-08065

DUDLEY SPECIAL ROAD DISTRICT OF STODDARD COUNTY V. HARRISON (ACTION BY UPSTREAM LANDOWNERS FOR REMOVAL OF LEVEE CONSTRUCTED BY DOWNSTREAM OWNERS NEAR UPSTREAM BORDER OF PROPERTY).
517 S.W.2d 170-182 (Mo. Ct. App. 1974).

Descriptors: *Levees, *Judicial decisions, *Natural flow doctrine, *Natural streams, *Obstruction to flow, Land tenure, *Missouri, Check structures, Retaining walls, Flood control, Legal aspects, Public rights, Riparian land, Water law, Water rights, Riparian rights, Streams, Floods, Alteration of flow, Diversion.
Identifiers: Injunctive relief, Nuisance(Legal aspects), Absolute liability.

Upstream landowners brought an action against downstream landowners seeking removal of a levee constructed by downstream landowners near

the upstream border of their property. Running through the lands of the plaintiffs was a natural watercourse, which also flowed through the land of the defendants prior to construction of the levee. Plaintiffs contended that the levee 'blocked the natural flow of water' causing it to collect north of the levee, and inundate the plaintiffs' lands. Defendants conceded the effect of changing the course of the water but argued that it did not reduce the drainage benefits which plaintiffs had derived. The court held it unlawful for a downstream landowner to obstruct a natural watercourse in a manner causing waters to overflow and inflict damage to the land of upstream landowners, whether or not the conduct was intentional or negligent. In granting injunctive relief, the court further held that the defendants must restore the natural course of the water, or make alternative provision to discontinue flooding of plaintiffs' lands. (Fernandez-Florida)
W75-08066

KURRLE V. WALKER (ACTION BY LANDOWNERS TO ENJOIN BARRIER FENCE AND COMMERCIAL MARINA CONSTRUCTED BY OTHER LANDOWNER INTO BAYOU).
224 N.W.2d 99-103 (Ct. App. Mich. 1974).

Descriptors: *Bayous, *Barriers, *Marinas, *Navigable waters, *Riparian rights, *Michigan, Ponds, Bodies of water, Structures, Sea walls, Judicial decisions, Water law, Navigation, Legal aspects, Trespass, Water rights, Obstruction to flow.
Identifiers: Injunctive relief, Nuisance(Legal aspects).

Plaintiff landowners sued for damages and injunetion relief for removal of a barrier fence and commercial marina constructed in a bayou by defendant, adjacent landowner. The respective properties are bordered on one side by a navigable pond. Defendant began construction of a marina on his property and erected a wall which effectively precluded plaintiffs from access to and use of the pond. The main issue was whether the defendant's construction of docks and piers on the navigable inlet was such an interference with plaintiffs' riparian rights that an injunction should issue ordering removal of the structures from the water. In upholding the equitable power of a court to enjoin a nuisance, where legal remedies are inadequate, the court ordered the removal of the barrier fence, which would be sufficient to restore to plaintiffs their access to the bayou for navigational purposes. Balancing the equities, the court further held that the remedy for maintenance of the marina should be damages. (Fernandez-Florida)
W75-08067

STATE V. DEETZ (ACTION BY STATE AGAINST DEVELOPER TO ENJOIN DEPOSIT OF MATERIALS IN LAKE WISCONSIN).
224 N.W.2d 407-419 (Wis. 1974).

Descriptors: *Judicial decisions, *Deposition(Sediments), *Lakes, *Surface runoff, *Soil erosion, *Wisconsin, Water law, Legal aspects, Silting, Runoff, Erosion, Bank erosion, Adjacent landowners, Public rights, Riparian land, Water rights, Riparian rights.
Identifiers: Common enemy rule, Nuisance(Legal aspects), Injunctive relief, Public trust doctrine, Standing(Legal), Reasonable use doctrine.

The State of Wisconsin brought an action against a property developer and others seeking to enjoin them from permitting the deposit of materials in Lake Wisconsin. Defendants purchased a large area of land on a bluff overlooking the lake and platted and developed a residential area. This development disturbed the topsoil causing erosion and runoff resulting in the formation of substantial sand deltas which impaired fishing, boating, and swimming. Plaintiff contended that under the 'public trust' doctrine any interference with the public's right to use the State's navigable waters is a nuisance and must be abated. Defendants argued that the 'common enemy doctrine' is applicable, whereby a possessor of land has an unlimited right to deal with the surface water on his land. Plaintiff responded that the common enemy rule should be overruled in view of the 'reasonable use' doctrine which imposes liability for unreasonable interference with the flow of surface waters. The court abandoned the common enemy doctrine with respect to surface waters and prospectively adopted the reasonable use doctrine, holding that the public trust doctrine merely gives the State standing as trustee to vindicate any rights that are infringed by existing law. (Fernandez-Florida)
W75-08068

COMMONWEALTH, DEPARTMENT OF ENVIRONMENTAL RESOURCES V. BOROUGH OF CARLISLE (APPEAL FROM ORDER PROHIBITING DISCHARGES INTO SANITARY SEWER SYSTEM WITHOUT DER APPROVAL).
For primary bibliographic entry see Field 5G.
W75-08069

SHELL OIL CO. V. POLLUTION CONTROL BOARD (PETITION BY OIL CO. TO REVIEW DENIAL OF VARIANCE FOR DISCHARGE OF WASTE WATER CONTAINING CYANIDE).
For primary bibliographic entry see Field 5G.
W75-08070

VILLAGE OF GLENCOE V. METROPOLITAN SANITARY DISTRICT OF GREATER CHICAGO (ACTION TO REVIEW DISTRICT'S WASTE CONTROL ORDINANCE WHICH PROHIBITED ANY DISCHARGE OF SEWAGE, INDUSTRIAL OR OTHER WASTE INTO LAKE MICHIGAN).
320 N.E.2d 524-529 (App. Ct Ill 1974).

Descriptors: *Sewage, *Sewage disposal, *Waste disposal, Waste treatment, Wastes, Industrial wastes, *Illinois, Sewage treatment, Sewerage, Sewers, Lake Michigan, Pollution abatement, Pollutants, Water pollution, Water, Water pollution control, Water pollution treatment, Water supply, Lakes.
Identifiers: Hazardous substances(Pollution).

The Village of Glencoe, Illinois, brought an action for review of an order of the board of trustees of the Metropolitan Sanitary District of Greater Chicago requiring the Village to cease and desist from violating the District's sewage and waste control ordinance. The Circuit Court for Cook County affirmed tne order and the Village appealed. The first District, Fourth Division, Appelate Court held that the District's enactment of an ordinance providing that 'no sewage, industrial wastes or other waste of any kind may be discharged into the waters of Lake Michigan' did not exceed the District's statutory authority. The court reasoned that such ordinances did not bar a discharge without regard to whether it constituted pollution, and that the ordinance bore a rational relation to the legitimate public interest of preventing pollution of water supplies. Even if the Village's discharge into Lake Michigan of alum and particles previously filtered out of raw lake water was not an 'industrial waste' within the meaning of the statute, such discharge was an 'other waste' within the statutory provision granting the District the power to prevent 'other wastes'. (Gagliardi-Florida)
W75-08071

SOME EFFECTS OF EXTENDING THE NAVIGATIONAL SEASON ON THE GREAT LAKES: A NEED FOR CONGRESSIONAL ACTION,
Cleveland State Univ., Ohio. Coll. of Law.
W. C. Hain.
Cleveland State Law Review, Vol 23, p 295-318 (1974). 24 p, 131 ref.

W75-07890

STATE-OF-THE-ART OF ESTIMATING FLOOD DAMAGE IN URBAN AREAS,
Colorado State Univ., Fort Collins. Dept. of Civil Engineering.
For primary bibliographic entry see Field 4A.
W75-07939

FLOOD PROTECTION BENEFITS AS REFLECTED IN PROPERTY VALUE CHANGES,
Kentucky Univ., Lexington. Dept. of Economics.
D. M. Soule, and C. M. Vaughan.
Water Resources Bulletin, Vol 9, No 5, p 918-922, October 1973. 2 tab, 4 ref. OWRT A-006-KY(14).

Descriptors: *Flood protection, *Benefits, *Economic impact, *Property values, *Measurement, Flood damage, Annual, Land use, Real property, Methodology, Lakes, Reservoirs, Dams, Rates, Prices, Statistical models, Systems analysis, *Kentucky.
Identifiers: *Covariance analysis, *Lake Cumberland(Ky), Depressed land value, Shoreline, Regression coefficients.

Measuring flood control benefits from estimated property damage in prior floods omits losses in the form of depressed values of land put to less valuable uses because of annual flooding. Herein, economic benefits from flood protection are measured by differences in property value changes in a period following introduction of flood protection. A statistical analysis of covariance compares differences in rates of change in average selling price per urban sale of real property over a 15-year period among three urban areas differently situated around Lake Cumberland, Kentucky. The three regions considered were: an area below a dam, which receives flood control benefits; a region above the dam, including areas inundated by the lake; and a contiguous region not directly affected by the reservoir. The analysis shows a much larger rate of increase in real property value for the area receiving flood protection. This suggests that the economic benefits from a flood protection facility include these additional property value increases as well as the prevented property value increases as well as the prevented peoperty damage. Moreover, the greater rate of increase in value of property in the region protected from flooding may be regarded as flood control benefits that would not be indicated by a study merely of property damage in prior floods. (Bell-Cornell)
W75-08004

FOURMILE RUN LOCAL FLOODPLAIN PROTECTION, CITY OF ALEXANDRIA AND ARLINGTON COUNTY, VIRGINIA (FINAL ENVIRONMENTAL IMPACT STATEMENT).
Army Engineer District, Baltimore, Md.
For primary bibliographic entry see Field 4A.
W75-08025

PROPOSED CHASSAHOWITZKA WILDERNESS AREA, FLORIDA (FINAL ENVIRONMENTAL IMPACT STATEMENT).
Bureau of Sport Fisheries and Wildlife, Washington, D.C.
For primary bibliographic entry see Field 6G.
W75-08034

INITIAL COASTLINE PLAN FOR THE SAN DIEGO REGION,
Duncan and Jones, Berkeley, Calif. and San Diego County Comprehensive Planning Organization, Calif.
April, 1974. 85 p, 4 maps, 5 append.

Descriptors: *Comprehensive planning, Coasts, *Planning, Shores, *Shore protection, *California, Beaches, *Beach erosion, Environment, *Lagoons, Bays, Estuaries.
Identifiers: *San Diego(Calif), *Coastal planning, San Diego County(Calif), Coastal zone, Camp Pendleton(Calif), Lagoon buffers.

Basic goals, objectives and policies primarily directed at preserving the coast for public use with emphasis on conservation as opposed to development are set forth. Integration of the natural and urban environment and preservation and enhancement of distinct, identifiable communities throughout the region are goals for the physical form of the region. Other goals are: (1) development of open space, needed to preserve natural resources and to provide land for agriculture, parks, and outdoor recreation; (2) retention of natural benefits of flood plains and estuaries; (3) beneficial utilization and conservation of soil; (4) elimination of billboards; and (5) adoption of a land ethic for a balanced coexistence of man and nature. For coastal areas of regional significance, ocean beach, shoreline lagoons, and lagoon buffers, establishment of a special regional review procedure including a cost/benefit evaluation and environmental impact analysis of any proposed development project is recommended. Beach and lagoon resource management concerned with erosion and stabilization of lagoon openings and ocean estuaries should investigate technology and methods of control in cooperation with state, federal and regional agencies. Financing proposals stress regional/local funding (2:1), and promote general obligation bonds for facility construction and land acquisition. Specific recommendations for local coastal jurisdictions, while emphasizing coastal natural resources, do not give reduced priority to industrial, commercial or recreational uses. Cities and unincorporated coastal areas are described and policies are recommended for each area. (Park-North Carolina)
W75-08171

FLOOD PLAIN INFORMATION: CROW CREEK, CHEYENNE, WYOMING,
Army Engineer District, Omaha, Nebr.
For primary bibliographic entry see Field 4A.
W75-08174

FLOOD PLAIN INFORMATION: SAN DIEGO CREEK AND PETERS CANYON WASH, ORANGE COUNTY, CALIFORNIA,
Army Engineer District, Los Angeles, Calif.
For primary bibliographic entry see Field 4A.
W75-08175

FLOOD PLAIN INFORMATION: MARAIS DES CYGNES RIVER, MELVERN TO OTTOWA, KANSAS, VOLUME 1.
Army Engineer District, Kansas City, Mo.
For primary bibliographic entry see Field 4A.
W75-08176

FLOOD PLAIN INFORMATION: SALT CREEK, RIVERSIDE COUNTY, CALIFORNIA.
Army Engineer District, Los Angeles, Calif.
For primary bibliographic entry see Field 4A.
W75-08177

FLOOD PLAIN INFORMATION: WILSON AND WILDWOOD CREEKS, SAN BERNADINO COUNTY, CALIFORNIA,
Army Engineer District, Los Angeles, Calif.
For primary bibliographic entry see Field 4A.
W75-08178

FLOOD PLAIN INFORMATION, ALLEGHENY RIVER, CLARION COUNTY, PENNSYLVANIA,
Army Engineer District, Pittsburgh, Pa.
For primary bibliographic entry see Field 4A.
W75-08179

FLOOD PLAIN INFORMATION: BEAVERDAM CREEK, HANOVER COUNTY, VIRGINIA,
Army Engineer District, Norfolk, Va.
For primary bibliographic entry see Field 4A.
W75-08180

FLOOD PLAIN INFORMATION: RAPID CREEK, RAPID CITY, SOUTH DAKOTA,
Army Engineer District, Omaha, Nebr.
For primary bibliographic entry see Field 4A.
W75-08183

FLOOD PLAIN INFORMATION: VIRGIN RIVER AND FORT PIERCE WASH, VICINITY OF ST. GEORGE, WASHINGTON COUNTY, UTAH,
Army Engineer District, Los Angeles, Calif.
For primary bibliographic entry see Field 4A.
W75-08184

AN APPLICATION OF DISCRIMINANT ANALYSIS TO PREDICT INDUSTRIAL/COMMERCIAL FLOOD PLAIN LOCATION,
Missouri Univ., St. Louis.
C. F. Meyer, and A. B. Corbeau.
Water Resources Bulletin, Vol 10, No 3, p 426-439, June 1974. 2 fig, 10 tab, 24 ref.

Descriptors: *Flood plains, *Data collections, *Statistical methods, Locating, Industries, Surveys, Costs, Computers, Research, Missouri.
Identifiers: *Discriminant analysis, Factor analysis, Commercial firms, Manufacturing, Prediction, St. Louis(Missouri), Data management, Software.

Described are the techniques of factor and discriminant analyses to isolate and quantify the statistical differences between firms located on flood plains and those located off flood plains. The research effort described consists of three segments: data collection, isolation of potential classification variables, and the determination of the appropriate discriminant functions to classify a given firm as either on or off the flood plain. Significant classification functions are developed for both manufacturing and commercial establishments, whose arguments include dollar sales volume, total shipping cost, total employee cost, dollar valuations on the building and inventories, all on an annual basis, and the square footage of the site. (Bell-Cornell)
W75-08208

6G. Ecologic Impact Of Water Development

LAND USE FORMS AND THE ENVIRONMENT - AN EXECUTIVE SUMMARY,
Chicago Univ., Ill. Dept. of Geography; and Chicago Univ., Ill. Center for Urban Studies.
B. J. L. Berry.
Available from the National Technical Information Service, Springfield, Va 22161 as PB-241 093, $3.75 paper copy, $2.25 microfiche. Environmental Protection Agency, Report EPA-600/5-75-003, March 1975. 36 p, 4 fig, 2 tab. EPA Program Element 1HA098, 801419.

Descriptors: *Land use, *Environmental effects, Spatial distribution, Pollutants, Cities, Regional analysis, Water quality, Comparative, Comparative benefits, Human population.

This executive summary contains highlights of the full study which focused on the relationship between land use forms and environmental quality. It investigated the influence of the spatial distribution of land rises on the pollutants generated and the resulting environmental quality. The investigation was assisted by the preparation of a 'sorting table' in which the 'rows' are the various urban forms and land use patterns and the 'columns' are the several classes, types and elements of environmental pollution. A comparative analysis of the materials assembled for the table determined trends across the urban forms and land use types, focusing particularly on the identification of those land use forms that naturally generate the least pollution. Also, parallel investigation of national trends in population distribution and land use was performed, so that some expectations could be developed as to the likely impacts on pollution of current patterns of regional growth and change. (EPA)
W75-07971

SIXES BRIDGE DAM AND LAKE, MARYLAND AND PENNSYLVANIA (FINAL ENVIRONMENTAL IMPACT STATEMENT).
Army Engineer District, Baltimore, Md.
For primary bibliographic entry see Field 8F.
W75-08015

UPPER THOMPSON SANITATION DISTRICT, PROJECT NO. C 080322 (FINAL ENVIRONMENTAL IMPACT STATEMENT).
Environmental Protection Agency, Denver, Colo. Region VIII.
For primary bibliographic entry see Field 5D.
W75-08016

MAINTENANCE OF BUTTERMILK CHANNEL, NEW YORK (FINAL ENVIRONMENTAL IMPACT STATEMENT).
Army Engineer District, New York.
For primary bibliographic entry see Field 8A.
W75-08017

PROPOSED 1973 OUTER CONTINENTAL SHELF OIL AND GAS GENERAL LEASE SALE, OFFSHORE MISSISSIPPI, ALABAMA AND FLORIDA (FINAL ENVIRONMENTAL IMPACT STATEMENT).
Bureau of Land Management, Washington, D.C.
For primary bibliographic entry see Field 5G.
W75-08018

BLUE MARSH LAKE PROJECT, TULPEHOCKEN CREEK, PENNSYLVANIA (FINAL ENVIRONMENTAL IMPACT STATEMENT).
Army Engineer District, Philadelphia, Pa.
For primary bibliographic entry see Field 8D.
W75-08019

CORBELL HULL DAM AND RESERVOIR, CUMBERLAND RIVER, TENNESSEE (FINAL ENVIRONMENTAL IMPACT STATEMENT).
Army Engineer District, Nashville, Tenn.
For primary bibliographic entry see Field 8A.
W75-08020

GUADALUPE RIVER, TEXAS (REMOVAL OF LOG JAMS) (FINAL ENVIRONMENTAL IMPACT STATEMENT).
Army Engineer District, Galveston, Tex.
For primary bibliographic entry see Field 4A.
W75-08021

PALATLAKAHA RIVER WATERSHED, LAKE COUNTY, FLORIDA (FINAL ENVIRONMENTAL IMPACT STATEMENT).
Soil Conservation Service, Gainesville, Fla.
For primary bibliographic entry see Field 8A.
W75-08022

APPLICATION FOR PERMIT TO CONSTRUCT A DAM ON MURDERERS CREEK GREEN COUNTY, NEW YORK (FINAL ENVIRONMENTAL IMPACT STATEMENT).
Army Engineer District, New York.
For primary bibliographic entry see Field 8D.
W75-08023

MARKLAND LOCKS AND DAM HIGHWAY BRIDGE AND APPROACHES, KENTUCKY AND INDIANA (FINAL ENVIRONMENTAL IMPACT STATEMENT).
Army Engineer District, Louisville, Ky.
For primary bibliographic entry see Field 4C.
W75-08041

CONSTRUCTION OF WASTEWATER FACILITIES, FORT WORTH, TEXAS (FINAL ENVIRONMENTAL IMPACT STATEMENT).
Environmental Protection Agency, Dallas, Tex. Office of Grants Coordination.
For primary bibliographic entry see Field 5D.
W75-08042

CHANNEL EXTENSION, SIUSLAW RIVER AND BAR, LAND COUNTY, OREGON (FINAL ENVIRONMENTAL IMPACT STATEMENT).
Army Engineer District, Portland, Oreg.
For primary bibliographic entry see Field 8A.
W75-08043

NAVIGATION SEASON EXTENSION DEMONSTRATION PROGRAM (FINAL ENVIRONMENTAL IMPACT STATEMENT).
Army Engineer District, Detroit, Mich.
For primary bibliographic entry see Field 4A.
W75-08044

RED RIVER WATERWAY, LOUISIANA, TEXAS ARKANSAS, AND OKLAHOMA, AND RELATED PROJECTS (FINAL ENVIRONMENTAL IMPACT STATEMENT).
Army Engineer District, New Orleans, La.
For primary bibliographic entry see Field 8A.
W75-08045

NEW ROCHELLE AND ECHO BAY HARBORS, NEW YORK (FINAL ENVIRONMENTAL IMPACT STATEMENT).
Army Engineer District, New York.
For primary bibliographic entry see Field 8A.
W75-08046

UPPER THOMPSON SANITATION DISTRICT, ESTES PARK, COLORADO PROJECT NO. C0803222 (FINAL ENVIRONMENTAL IMPACT STATEMENT).
Environmental Protection Agency, Denver, Colo. Region VIII.
For primary bibliographic entry see Field 5D.
W75-08047

DIKED DISPOSAL AREA, HURON HARBOR, ERIE COUNTY, HURON, OHIO (FINAL ENVIRONMENTAL IMPACT STATEMENT).
Army Engineer District, Buffalo, NY.
For primary bibliographic entry see Field 5G.
W75-08048

RICHMOND INNER HARBOR, MAINTENANCE DREDGING, CONTRA COSTA COUNTY, CALIFORNIA (FINAL ENVIRONMENTAL IMPACT STATEMENT).
Army Engineer District, San Francisco, Calif.
For primary bibliographic entry see Field 5G.
W75-08049

AUTHORIZED GRANITE REEF AQUEDUCT, CENTRAL ARIZONA PROJECT, ARIZONA-NEW MEXICO (FINAL ENVIRONMENTAL IMPACT STATEMENT).
Bureau of Reclamation, Denver, Colo.
For primary bibliographic entry see Field 8A.
W75-08050

PERILLA MOUNTAIN WATERSHED PROJECT, COCHISE COUNTY, ARIZONA (FINAL ENVIRONMENTAL IMPACT STATEMENT).
Soil Conservation Service, Washington, D.C.
For primary bibliographic entry see Field 4D.
W75-08051

KAIMU BEACH HAWAII, PROPOSED SHORE PROTECTION (FINAL ENVIRONMENTAL IMPACT STATEMENT).
Corps of Engineers, Honolulu, Hawaii. Pacific Ocean Div.
For primary bibliographic entry see Field 8A.
W75-08052

VIRGINIA KEY BEACH EROSION CONTROL PROJECT, SECOND PERIODIC NOURISHMENT AND GROINS (FINAL ENVIRONMENTAL IMPACT STATEMENT).
Army Engineer District, Jacksonville, Fla.
For primary bibliographic entry see Field 8A.
W75-08053

LAKE QUINAULT SEWAGE COLLECTION AND TREATMENT FACILITY, OLYMPIC NATIONAL FOREST, OLYMPIA, WASHINGTON (FINAL ENVIRONMENTAL IMPACT STATEMENT).
For primary bibliographic entry see Field 5D.
W75-08054

HIGHWAY 112 CRITICAL EROSION CONTROL RESOURCES CONSERVATION AND DEVELOPMENT PROJECT MEASURE (FINAL ENVIRONMENTAL IMPACT STATEMENT).
Soil Conservation Service, Madison, Wis.
For primary bibliographic entry see Field 8A.
W75-08055

VERONA DAM AND LAKE, VIRGINIA (FINAL ENVIRONMENTAL IMPACT STATEMENT).
Army Engineer District, Baltimore, Md.
For primary bibliographic entry see Field 8F.
W75-08056

CHANNEL TO NEWPORT NEWS, VIRGINIA (MAINTENANCE DREDGING) (ENVIRONMENTAL IMPACT STATEMENT).
Army Engineer District, Norfolk, Va.
For primary bibliographic entry see Field 8A.
W75-08057

INDIAN CREEK WATERSHED PROJECT, CITY OF CHESAPEAKE, VIRGINIA (FINAL ENVIRONMENTAL IMPACT STATEMENT).
Soil Conservation Service, Richmond, Va.
For primary bibliographic entry see Field 8A.
W75-08058

HUNGRY HORSE CLOUD SEEDING PROJECT (FINAL ENVIRONMENTAL IMPACT STATEMENT).
Bonneville Power Administration, Portland, Oreg.
For primary bibliographic entry see Field 3B.
W75-08059

EAGLE-TUMBLEWEED DRAW WATERSHED, EDDY AND CHAVES COUNTIES, NEW MEXICO (FINAL ENVIRONMENTAL IMPACT STATEMENT).
Soil Conservation Service, Washington, D.C.
For primary bibliographic entry see Field 4D.
W75-08060

MISSOURI RIVER GARRISON DAM TO LAKE OAHE RESERVOIR (FINAL ENVIRONMENTAL IMPACT STATEMENT).
Army Engineer District, Omaha, Nebr.
For primary bibliographic entry see Field 8A.

W75-08061

PAINT CREEK WATERSHED, HARPER COUNTY, OKLAHOMA (FINAL ENVIRONMENTAL IMPACT STATEMENT).
Soil Conservation Service, Stillwater, Okla.
For primary bibliographic entry see Field 4D.
W75-08062

THE ENVIRONMENTAL PROTECTION AGENCY AND COASTAL ZONE MANAGEMENT: STRIKING A FEDERAL-STATE BALANCE OF POWER IN LAND USE MANAGEMENT,
For primary bibliographic entry see Field 5G.
W75-08073

ENVIRONMENTAL ANALYSIS OF THE KICKAPOO RIVER IMPOUNDMENT.
Wisconsin Univ., Madison. Inst. for Environmental Studies.
IES Report 28, November 1974. 291 p, 95 fig, 97 tab, 198 ref. DACW 37-C-0130.

Descriptors: *Environmental effects, *Reservoir construction, *Water quality, *Nutrients, Agricultural watersheds, Runoff, Sedimentation, Water release, Algae, Eutrophication, Aquatic plants, Wildlife habitats, Watersheds(Basins), Vegetation, Forests, Grazing, Economics, Stream fishing, Tailwater, Water temperature, Recreation, Land use, Stream improvement, Reservoir operation, Wisconsin.
Identifiers: *Kickapoo River(Wis), *La Farge Lake(Wis).

A multidisciplinary investigation to determine water quality in the proposed impoundment to be constructed on the Kickapoo River north of La Farge, Wisconsin is described. The La Farge Reservoir is expected to be eutrophic and will support a large growth of macrophytes and algae. An environmental assessment was made of the sources and availability of nitrogen and phosphorus. Downstream temperature will be able to be controlled by selective water withdrawal to maintain cold-water fisheries. Sediments and their distributions were investigated. The present population of fish, invertebrates, birds, mammals, and terrestrial vegetation was determined and predictions made of the probable impact of the impoundment on the algal biomass, fish, invertebrates, birds, mammals, terrestrial vegetation, and macrophytes. Land use and development trends for the area surrounding the Kickapoo River Valley near the proposed impoundment were studied. Estimates were made of the costs for establishing and operating water improvement procedures in the lake. Specific recommendations are made to ensure the best possible water quality: such as encouragement of marsh vegetation, sewage treatment, hypolimnetic aeration, water level control, selective planting and harvesting of macrophytes, control of land use practices, watershed management, construction of sediment trap dams, use of algicides, and fencing. (See W75-08159 thru W75-08169) (Buchanan-Davidson-Wisconsin)
W75-08158

ENVIRONMENTAL ASSESSMENT OF THE SOURCES AND AVAILABILITY OF NITROGEN AND PHOSPHORUS TO LAKE LA FARGE,
Wisconsin Univ., Madison. Dept. of Soil Science.
D. R. Keeney, D. S. Nichols, and K. W. Lee.
In: IES Report 28, Environmental Analysis of the Kickapoo River Impoundment, p 1-44, November 1974. 36 fig, 33 tab, 20 ref. DACW 37-C-0130.

Descriptors: *Reservoirs, *Nitrogen, *Phosphorus, *Water pollution control, *Reservoir operation, Algal control, Aquatic weed control, Sewage disposal, Farm wastes, Costs, Fertilization, Wisconsin, Sewage treatment, Eutrophication, Water pollution sources, Base flow, Rivers, Regression analysis, Soil surveys, Agricultural watersheds.
Identifiers: *Kickapoo River(Wis), La Farge Lake(Wis), Nutrient load.

The nitrogen and phosphorus loadings in the proposed La Farge Impoundment on the Kickapoo River in Wisconsin are predicted to be high. The severity of the water quality problems will depend on the light penetration depth. The river drains on agricultural watershed with moderately fertile soils; thus a large portion of the nutrients will be from non-point sources which are difficult to control. Runoff is the most important source, followed by base points, sewage treatment plants, and farmyards. The river contains sufficient silica dioxide and carbon to support aquatic weed and algal populations. Water quality will be similar to that of other area impoundments. If the impoundment is completed, sound reservoir management should be practiced to control algal blooms and provide weed-free recreational areas. Sewage treatment plants should provide at least secondary treatment and land disposal of effluents and sludge to recycle the nutrients and provide tertiary treatment should be considered. Control of animal wastes from farmyards and elimination of manure spreading on frozen ground should be encouraged. Control measures should be initiated as soon as possible. The reservoir will have significant effects on downstream water, especially if hypolimnion withdrawal is practiced during the summer. Nutrient control costs are estimated. (See also W75-08158) (Buchanan-Davidson--Wisconsin)
W75-08159

SELECTIVE WITHDRAWAL FROM THE LA FARGE RESERVOIR FOR DOWNSTREAM TEMPERATURE CONTROL,
Wisconsin Univ., Madison. Water Resources Center.
For primary bibliographic entry see Field 5G.
W75-08160

ENVIRONMENTAL ASSESSMENT OF SEDIMENT SOURCES AND SEDIMENTATION DISTRIBUTIONS FOR THE LAKE LA FARGE WATERHSED AND IMPOUNDMENT,
Wisconsin Univ., Madison. Dept. of Geography.
For primary bibliographic entry see Field 2E.
W75-08161

ALGAL BIOMASS PROJECTIONS FOR THE PROPOSED KICKAPOO RIVER IMPOUNDMENT,
Wisconsin Univ., Madison. IBP Lake Wingra Project.
For primary bibliographic entry see Field 5C.
W75-08162

FISH POPULATION INVESTIGATIONS,
Wisconsin Dept. of Natural Resources, Madison.
For primary bibliographic entry see Field 8I.
W75-08163

IMPACT OF A PROPOSED IMPOUNDMENT OPERATION ON THE INVERTEBRATE ASSEMBLAGES IN THE KICKAPOO RIVER, LA FARGE (VERNON CO.), WISCONSIN,
Wisconsin Univ., Madison. Dept. of Zoology.
For primary bibliographic entry see Field 6B.
W75-08164

BIOLOGICAL ASPECTS--BIRDS AND MAMMALS,
Wisconsin Univ., Madison. Dept. of Wildlife Ecology.
R. L. Jurewicz, and O. J. Rongstad.
In: IES Report 28, Environmental Analysis of the Kickapoo River Impundment, p. 160-189. 5 fig, 14 tab, 32 ref. DACW 37-C-0130.

Descriptors: *Wildlife, *Impoundments, Wisconsin, Hunting, Birds, Mammals, Game birds, Non-game birds, Song birds, Waterfowl, Furbearers, Habitats, Varieties, Deer, Small game, Wildlife management, Reservoirs, Cultivated lands, Forests, Marshes, Water levels.
Identifiers: *Kickapoo River(Wis), *La Farge Lake(Wis).

The effect of the proposed impoundment at La Farge on the Kickapoo River, Wisconsin, on wildlife of the related watershed is evaluated based on an inventory of bird and mammal species. Management recommendations are made, including hunter use. Vegetation of tall grass fields, short grass forb fields, sedge meadows, low-land hardwood, oak-maple-elm woodlot, and hemlock-birch stands was identified and small mammals trapped. Meadow voles, shrew, and mice, red squirrels, and chipmunks were found. White-tailed deer, cottontail rabbits, gray, red and fox squirrels, otter, beaver, muskrat, mink, raccoon, red and gray fox, skunk, opossum, waterfowl, ruffed grouse, bobwhite quail, pheasants, woodcocks, and songbirds were counted. The impoundment should prove beneficial to the wildlife. White-tailed deer could pose a problem, but can be controlled by the project management. Openings should be maintained by cultivation, burning, or mowing, and some crops and cover fields rotated periodically. To avoid detrimental effects on the furbearing population, water levels should be as constant as possible during the fall and winter. Shallow water areas that will become marshes and perhaps act as silt ponds should be created. Small game hunting should be allowed unless conflicting uses develop and should be controlled by the project's governing agency. (See also W75-08158) (Buchanan-Davidson--Wisconsin)
W75-08165

BIOTIC ASPECTS--TERRESTRIAL VEGETATION,
Wisconsin Univ., Madison. Dept. of Botany.
V. M. Kline.
In: IES Report 28, Environmental Analysis of the Kickapoo River Impoundment, p 190-210. 1 fig, 10 tab, 7 ref. DACW 37-C-0130.

Descriptors: *Vegetation, *Plant populations, *Impoundments, Land use, Wisconsin, Roads, Forests, Runoff, Watersheds(Basins), Plant groupings, Varieties, Erosion control, Conservation, Water resources development, Grazing.
Identifiers: *Kickapoo River(Wis), *La Farge Lake(Wis).

A survey of vascular plants growing without cultivation in the watershed of the proposed La Farge impoundment on the Kickapoo River identified 488 species. Some rare species were observed. One ridge top was an example of a dry prairie and should be preserved. On the cliffs along the river there were four plant species on the rare or endangered list. Three of these will be lost during filling and the fourth species will be substantially reduced. Aerial photographs used to estimate the amount of vegetative cover showed that approximately one-third was cultivated, one-third pasture and open woods, and one-third woods. A grazing index was calculated and identified 28 species of trees, 44 shrubs, and 173 herbs and vines. Natural forest vegetation can provide steep slopes with protection from erosion, but cattle grazing and the presence of plowed fields and roads above wooded slopes increased erosion. It is recommended that cattle be excluded from woodlots in the watershed; a buffer strip of grass or permanent vegetation be maintained between the cultivated fields and the woods; and that roads be engineered so that runoff is not channelled down wooded slopes. (See also W75-08158) (Buchanan-Davidson--Wisconsin)
W75-08166

Lands designated as development districts in a proposed zoning ordinance should be adequate to accomodate anticipated lot development. Prime agricultural lands must be protected. The area can develop the recreation industry but should protect the scenic bluffs, woodlands, and agricultural enterprises. Land use zoning should be strengthened. New commercial development should be guided to the villages. Overgrazing of pastures and woodlots and removal of fencerows must be controlled by zoning and establishment of soil and water conservation districts. The economic viability of the valley depends on both agriculture and recreation, the latter contingent on the water quality of the impoundment. (See also W75-08158) (Buchanan-Davidson--Wisconsin)
W75-08168

COST OF ESTABLISHMENT AND OPERATION OF WATER IMPROVEMENT PROCEDURES,
Wisconsin Univ., Madison. Inst. for Environmental Studies.
G. Cottam.
In: IES Report 28, Environmental Analysis of the Kickapoo River Impoundment, p 288-291. DACW 37-C-0130.

Descriptors: *Water quality control, *Impoundments, *Estimated costs, Wisconsin, Algal control, Algicides, Stream improvement, Aquatic weed control, Operation and maintenance, Farm management, Aeration, Monitoring, Waste treatment, Projections, Harvesting, Land management, Cost analysis, Reservoirs, Earth dams.
Identifiers: *Kickapoo River(Wis), *La Farge Lake(Wis).

Estimates of some of the costs related to the maintenance of water quality in the La Farge Impoundment on the Kickapoo River were made, assuming that Lake La Farge will support a large macrophyte biomass in places less than seven feet deep, that there will be extensive algal blooms, and that the hypolimnion will become anoxic. A minimal management plan to enhance the use of the lake as a swimming-fishing-boating lake would require $25,000 to $57,000 annual costs and includes the use of copper sulfates or organic copper compounds as algicides; limited harvesting of macrophytes adjacent to beaches, land access points, and intense use areas; and monitoring to determine when and where to initiate control procedures. Cost estimates are also given for a more comprehensive management program, which would involve the use of aeration structures to add oxygen to the hypolimnion without destratifying the lake. Hypolimnetic aerators would displace the hydrogen sulfide odor from the outlet to the middle of the lake and prevent nighttime downstream oxygen sag. Additionally, municipal sewage plants should be improved, farmstead management programs established, sediment dams erected in fourth order streams, reservoirs contoured to encourage marshes and macrophytes, flood retarding structures constructed downstream and fensing built. (See also W75-08158) (Buchanan-Davidson--Wisconsin)
W75-08169

ON THE MEASUREMENT OF ENVIRONMENTAL IMPACTS OF PUBLIC PROJECTS FROM A SOCIOLOGICAL PERSPECTIVE,
East Texas State Univ., Commerce. Dept. of Sociology and Anthropology.
R. N. Singh, and K. P. Wilkinson.
Water Resources Bulletin, Vol 10, No 3, p 415-425, June 1974. 1 fig, 2 tab, 45 ref.

Descriptors: *Measurement, *Projects, *Watersheds(Basins), *Attitudes, Data collections, River basins, Environment, Reservoirs, Dams, *Texas, Planning, Cost-benefit ratio, Political aspects, Psychological aspects, Social aspects.
Identifiers: *Environmental impact, Development programs, Sociological approach, Residents, Physical sciences, Guttman scale, Correlation matrix, Cooper Reservoir(Tex).

Objectives are to (1) identify the problems involved in measuring the environmental impacts of public projects from selected perspectives, and (2) elaborate a sociological approach used in an empirical investigation in that respect. The construct of environmental impact of a planned action is generally operationalized from different perspectives and with different methodological emphases in the various disciplines. Although there has been a steady increase in the number of studies from a sociological perspective concerning environmental problems, there is lack of sociological counsel in writing environmental impact statements, sociological methodology and operational procedures for that purpose are wanting. Attitudinal measures employed to find how residents of a river basin perceived negative and positive environmental impacts of a proposed watershed development project are reviewed. These come from a study of creation of the Cooper Reservoir and Dam in Texas. Data on 343 heads of households in the selected areas were collected through structured questionnaires with items on personal information, a vested interest scale, a knowledge of the project scale, and an environmental impact scale. Data show that perception of impacts by residents is influenced significantly by degree of their vested interests involved. Four categories of variables for inclusion in a sociological model of environmental impact are suggested: economic development; provision of services and amenities; human welfare; and collective viability. (Bell-Cornell)
W75-08203

WATER AND THE ENERGY CRISIS,
Nebraska Univ., Lincoln. Water Resources Research Inst.
For primary bibliographic entry see Field 6B.
W75-08210

THE PROTECTION OF NATURE AS REFLECTED IN THE WORK OF THE FIRST UNITED NATIONS CONFERENCE OF THE ENVIRONMENT (STOCKHOLM, 1972), (IN ROMANIAN),
Consililul National al Apelor, Bucharest (Rumania).
C. Radescu.
Ocrotirea Nat, Vol 17, No 1, p 37-44, 1973, Illus.

Descriptors: *Pollution, Water pollution, *Environmental control, Environment protection, Flora, Fauna, Water pollution, Oceans, Seas, *Conferences, Conservation, Natural resources, Water resources.
Identifiers: *United Nations.

A description of the organization and results of the conference are given. The most important subjects studied included the management of human habitation and natural resources from the point of view of the environment and the determination of pollutants of international importance. The protection of nature, including flora, fauna soil, water and genetic resources, was also a major theme. The conference recommended national natural reservations and protected zones and national laws for the protection of wildlife. Supervision of the introduction of new species to avoid displacing indigenous species was also mentioned. International action recommendations included the publication of an annual assessment of fauna by the United Nations, and international programs for the protection of genetic resources, forests and water resources. Pollution was emphasized as an international danger affecting soil and water resources and climate. International supervision of the effect of pollution, especially of the oceans and seas, was recommended.--Copyright 1974, Biological Abstracts, Inc.
W75-08241

NATURAL RESOURCES IN MODERN WORLD AND THE PROBLEM OF THEIR CONSERVATION, (IN ROMANIAN),
Academia R. S. R., Cluj. Centrul de Cercetari Biologice.
V. Soran.
Octrotirea Nat, Vol 17, No 1, p 51-57, 1973. English summary.

Descriptors: *Natural resources, *Conservation, *Protection, Pollution, Pesticide toxicity, Ecosystems, Balance of nature, Water pollution effects, Effects, Environmental effects.

The problem of natural resources and their conservation in the modern world are discussed, starting from the idea that Earth and its goods are limited and that during the past 3000 or 4000 yr of history all the main natural resources (soil, water and air) were successively transformed into wares. The pollution problem and the effects of different chemicals, especially pesticides, on natural ecosystems are also presented. Stressed are the measures which must be taken to avoid ecological disaster, with emphais on the new era in man-nature relationships grounded on a rational equilibrium between the development of human society and the real possibilities of the environment to support it.--Copyright 1974, Biological Abstracts, Inc.
W75-08274

ARIDITY PROBLEMS IN THE SAHEL, TWENTY YEARS OF UNESCO ACTIVITY.
For primary bibliographic entry see Field 2A.
W75-08282

BIRDS AND MAMMALS OF ANEGADA ISLAND, BRITISH VIRGIN ISLANDS,
Cornell Univ., Ithaca, N.Y. Dept. of Natural Resources.
For primary bibliographic entry see Field 2I.
W75-08317

THE BREACH IN THE FLOW OF MINERAL NUTRIENTS,
For primary bibliographic entry see Field 5B.
W75-08319

7. RESOURCES DATA

7A. Network Design

ANALYSIS OF ERTS-RELAYED WATER-RESOURCES DATA IN THE DELAWARE RIVER BASIN,
Geological Survey, Harrisburg, Pa.
For primary bibliographic entry see Field 7C.
W75-07871

HYDROLOGIC DATA NEEDS FOR SMALL WATERSHEDS--STREAMFLOW AND RELATED PRECIPITATION DATA.
Geological Survey, Reston, Va.
Office of Water Data Coordination, Interagency Advisory Committee on Water Data, December 1974. 58 p, 4 fig, 52 tab, 56 ref.

Descriptors: *Basic data collections, *Hydrologic data, *Small watersheds, *Network design, Streamflow, Floods, Design flow, Discharge measurement, Precipitation(Atmospheric).
Identifiers: Data needs.

A Federal Interagency Work Group, impaneled in 1971 by the Office of Water Data Coordination, Geological Survey, recommends a data-collection system to provide the streamflow information needed for planning and designing water resources related projects on small watersheds. The recommended data-collection system was designed to provide sufficient base data for estimating selected flow characteristics at those ungaged sites having a drainage area less than 50 square miles, where the flow is virtually natural, where runoff from urban basins occurs in open channels, and where any upstream reservoirs or diversions have fixed control structures. The selected flow characteristics are those commonly used in planning and designing projects on small streams, and include the magnitude and frequency of flood peaks and of flood volumes for durations of 1 to 15 days, the mean and variability of annual and monthly flows, and the time and shape characteristics of flood hydrographs. The recommended system is expected to provide sufficient data for estimating flow characteristics at ungaged sites with a reliability equivalent to the reliability of determinations from 10 years of observed flow records. (Knapp-USGS)
W75-07874

DATA REQUIREMENTS OF A WATER QUALITY MANAGEMENT PROGRAM,
Colorado State Univ., Fort Collins. Dept. of Agricultural Engineering.
For primary bibliographic entry see Field 5G.
W75-08213

7B. Data Acquisition

INTERPRETATION--APOLLO 9 PHOTOGRAPHY OF PARTS OF SOUTHERN ARIZONA AND SOUTHERN NEW MEXICO,
Geological Survey, Denver, Colo.
For primary bibliographic entry see Field 7C.
W75-07861

REMOTE SENSING TECHNIQUES FOR EVALUATION OF URBAN EROSION AND SEDIMENTATION,
Geological Survey, Reston, Va.
For primary bibliographic entry see Field 4C.
W75-07880

A SINGLE-BEAM INFRARED HYGROMETER FOR EVAPORATION MEASUREMENT,
Commonwealth Scientific and Industrial Research Organization, Aspendale (Australia). Div. of Atmospheric Physics.
For primary bibliographic entry see Field 2D.
W75-07901

THE MEASUREMENT OF WATER CONTENT BY AN EVAPORATOR,
National Center for Atmospheric Research, Boulder, Colo.
For primary bibliographic entry see Field 2D.
W75-07902

MODE: IGPP MEASUREMENTS OF BOTTOM PRESSURE AND TEMPERATURE,
California Univ., San Diego, La Jolla. Inst. of Geophysics and Planetary Physics.
F. Snodgrass, W. Brown, and W. Munk.
Journal of Physical Oceanography, Vol 5, No 1, p 63-74, January 1975. 15 fig, 1 tab, 7 ref. ONR Contract N00014-69-A-0200-6008, NSF Grant GX-29052.

Descriptors: *Instrumentation, *Temperature, *Pressure, *Oceans, Measurement, Equipment, Oceanography, On-site investigations, Laboratory tests, Electrical equipment.
Identifiers: *Ocean bottom pressure, *Instrument noise, Mid-Ocean Dynamics Experiment, Temperature sensors, Underwater pressure sensors.

The Mid-Ocean Dyanmics Experiment (MODE) deployment of the Institute of Geophysics and Planetary Physics bottom instruments was reviewed, together with preliminary tests on the Pacific seafloor and in the laboratory. Pressure and temperature were measured with quartz-crystall transducers in different configurations. Spectra of instrument noise in the laboratory and on the seafloor were estimated from duplicate transducers. These estimates are prerequisite to the forthcoming discussions of MODE tides, and bottom experiment, and internal waves. There are two puzzling features: (1) the temperature noise continuum on the seafloor is generally 20 dB above that in the laboratory, and (2) the pressure noise spectrum has a tidal line structure. Instrument drifts during MODE are of the order of a few millibars and a millidegree Celcius, respectively. (Sims-ISWS)
W75-07904

MODE BOTTOM EXPERIMENT,
California Univ., San Diego, La Jolla. Inst. of Geophysics and Planetary Physics.
W. Brown, W. Munk, F. Snodgrass, H. Mofjeld, and B. Zetler.
Journal of Physical Oceanography, Vol 5, No 1, p 75-85, January 1975. 15 fig, 7 ref, 1 append. ONR Contract N00014-69-A-0200-6008; NSF Grant GX-29052.

Descriptors: *Oceans, *Pressure, *Temperature, Oceanography, Measurement, On-site investigations, Model studies, Mathematical models, Ocean circulation, Atmospheric pressure, Atlantic Ocean.
Identifiers: *Ocean bottom pressure, Mid-Ocean Dynamics Experiment.

Pressure fluctuations on the deep seafloor at frequencies below inertial and tidal were measured. Between 0.1 and 1 cycle per ay the variance is about 2 sq mb, spectra diminish with increasing frequency as omega to the (-n) power, n = 1.5 to 2, and a signal-to-instrument noise ratio of 10 dB is achieved. Fluctuations are in phase and highly coherent within the MODE area (greater than 0.9 at 200 km) and even with inferred (atmosphere plus sea level) Bermuda subsurface pressures (0.8 at 700 km). Station differences (to which MODE-sized eddies would make the principal contribution) are relatively small. The large horizontal scale of the recorded bottom pressure fluctuation resembles that of atmospheric pressure, yet the coherence locally between atmospheric and bottom pressure is slight; and recorded fluctuations may be related to a barotropic ocean response to a variable wind stress on the subtropical gyre. Bottom temperature records show 'sudden' (1 day) changes of order 30 millidegrees Celsius separated by long intervals (20 days) of uniform temperatures. The changes are much larger than have been observed in the Pacific. They are correlated at horizontal separations of 2 km, but uncorrelated to bottom pressure and to temperatures 1 km above the seafloor. (Sims-ISWS)
W75-07905

ELECTRONIC DIGITIZATION AND SENSOR RESPONSE EFFECTS ON SALINITY COMPUTATION FROM CTD FIELD MEASUREMENTS,
Washington Univ., Seattle. Dept. of Oceanography.
For primary bibliographic entry see Field 2L.
W75-07914

OBSERVATIONS OF OCEANIC INTERNAL AND SURFACE WAVES FROM THE EARTH RESOURCES TECHNOLOGY SATELLITE,
National Oceanic and Atmospheric Administration, Miami, Fla. Atlantic Oceanographic and Meteorological Labs.
J. R. Apel, H. M. Byrne, J. R. Proni, and R. L. Charnell.
Journal of Geophysical Research, Vol 80, No 6, p 865-881, February 20, 1975. 17 fig, 14 ref.

Descriptors: *Internal waves, *Remote sensing, Satellites(Artificial), Oceans, Seashores, Con-

INTERPRETATION--APOLLO 9 PHOTOGRAPHY OF PARTS OF SOUTHERN ARIZONA AND SOUTHERN NEW MEXICO,
Geological Survey, Denver, Colo.
J. R. Owen, and L. M. Shown.
Open-file report, February 1973. 18 p, 4 fig.

Descriptors: *Remote sensing, *Aerial photography, *Vegetation effects, *New Mexico, *Arizona, Arid lands, Deserts, Mapping, Terrain analysis.

Examination of small-scale (approximately 1:650,000) multispectral photographs obtained on the Apollo 9 mission in March 1969 revealed that in semiarid regions features due to differences in soils or quantity of vegetation could most easily be discriminated on the color infrared photographs. Where there is sufficient ground truth, it is possible to delineate regional wildland plant communities on the basis of tone. The precision of the method may be improved by using photographs obtained two or more times during the year. Sites where vegetation-improvement practices have been completed are not always discernible. For example, where waterspreaders have been constructed, there was sufficient change in the density of vegetation to be readily detected on the photographs; however, pinyonjuniper to grass conversions or contour furrowing did not always produce a sufficient change in the vegetation to be detected on the photographs. (Knapp-USGS)
W75-07861

ANALYSIS OF ERTS-RELAYED WATER-RESOURCES DATA IN THE DELAWARE RIVER BASIN,
Geological Survey, Harrisburg, Pa.
R. W. Paulson.
In: Management and Utilization of Remote Sensing Data; Proceedings of Symposium, October 29-November 1, 1973, Sioux Falls, S Dak: American Society of Photogrammetry, p 191-205, 1973. 8 fig, 1 tab.

Descriptors: *Delaware River, Delaware River Basin Commission, *Data collections, *Data transmission, *Telemetry, Satellites(Artificial), Hydrologic data, Water wells, Water levels, Floods, Water quality, Gaging stations, Monitoring, *Remote sensing.
Identifiers: *ERTS.

The U.S. Geological Survey, in cooperation with the National Aeronautics and Space Administration, the Earth Resources Observations System Program of the Department of the Interior, and the Delaware River Basin Commission, studied the feasibility of relaying hydrologic data operationally from water-resources stations in the Delaware River basin, using the Data Collection System on the Earth Resources Technology Satellite. Battery-operated radios, called Data Collection Platforms, transmit data to the satellite from 20 hydrologic stations in the basin. These stations include groundwater observation wells, streamgaging stations, and water-quality monitors. Analysis of these data indicates that the Data Collection System works well, and that such a system has the potential for being used as an operational tool by water-data collection agencies. (Knapp-USGS)
W75-07871

HYDROLOGIC DATA NEEDS FOR SMALL WATERSHEDS--STREAMFLOW AND RELATED PRECIPITATION DATA.
Geological Survey, Reston, Va.
For primary bibliographic entry see Field 7A.
W75-07874

WATER RESOURCES DATA FOR NEBRASKA, 1973: PART 1. SURFACE WATER RECORDS.
Geological Survey, Lincoln, Nebr.
Data Report, 1974. 200 p, 2 fig, 1 tab, 3 ref.

Descriptors: *Basic data collections, *Nebraska, *Hydrologic data, Streamflow, Stage-discharge relations, Lakes, Reservoirs, Gaging stations.

The surface-water records for the 1973 water year for gaging stations, partial-record stations, and miscellaneous sites within the State of Nebraska are given in this report. The base data collected at gaging stations consists of records of stage and measurements of discharge of streams or canals, and stage, surface area, and contents of lakes or reservoirs. In addition, observations of factors affecting the stage-discharge relation or the stage-capacity relation, weather records, and other information are used to supplement base data in determining the daily flow or volume of water in storage. The description of the gaging station gives the location, drainage area, period of record, type and history of gages, average discharge, extremes of discharge or contents, and general remarks. (Knapp-USGS)
W75-07879

HARMONIC ANALYSIS OF STREAM TEMPERATURES,
Geological Survey, Reston, Va.
For primary bibliographic entry see Field 5B.
W75-07882

ONE-DIMENSIONAL STREAM EXCESS TEMPERATURE ANALYSIS,
Geological Survey, Bay Saint Louis, Miss.
For primary bibliographic entry see Field 5B.
W75-07883

INDEX OF CURRENT WATER RESOURCES PROJECTS AND DATA COLLECTION ACTIVITIES IN OHIO, 1975.
Geological Survey, Columbus, Ohio.
Project report, January 1975. 26 p.

Descriptors: *Basic data collections, *Hydrologic data, *Ohio, Projects, Water resources.

The water-resources program of the U.S. Geological Survey in Ohio consists of the collection of basic information through its research projects, areal hydrologic studies, and hydrologic data stations. This index consists of two parts; Part A--a listing of current projects and Part B--a listing of hydrologic data-collection stations. Tables show station numbers and names, types of data collected, and projects benefiting from the data collected at the site. (Knapp-USGS)
W75-07886

WATER-RESOURCES INVESTIGATIONS OF THE U.S. GEOLOGICAL SURVEY IN THE NORTHERN GREAT PLAINS COAL REGION OF NORTHEASTERN WYOMING, 1974-75.
Geological Survey, Cheyenne, Wyo.
Open-file report, March 1975. 28 p, 9 fig, 27 ref.

Descriptors: *Water resources, Bibliographies, *Wyoming, *Coal mines, *Investigations, Surveys, Data collections, Hydrologic data, Exploration, *Great Plains.

The U.S. Geological Survey has four data-collection activities and five water-resource appraisal projects in the Northern Great Plains coal region of northeastern Wyoming (the Powder River structural basin). The data-collection activities include: (1) streamflow measurements; (2) measurements of water levels in wells; (3) sampling and chemical analysis of water from streams and wells; and (4) sampling and sediment analysis of water from streams. The water-resource appraisal projects include: (1) water resources of Weston County, Wyoming; (2) measurement of water losses to the Madison Limestone and associated rocks from streams in northeastern Wyoming; (3) hydrology of Paleozoic rocks in the Powder River basin and adjacent areas, northeastern Wyoming; (4) water

resources of the Powder River structural basin in Wyoming in relation to energy development; and (5) availability of groundwater from the Cretaceous and Tertiary aquifers of the Fort Union Coal Region. A listing of selected reports by USGS authors is included to give an indication of what has been done in the past. (Knapp-USGS)
W75-07887

WATER QUALITY OF HYDROLOGIC BENCH MARKS--AN INDICATOR OF WATER QUALITY IN THE NATURAL ENVIRONMENT,
Geological Survey, Reston, Va.
For primary bibliographic entry see Field 5A.
W75-07888

COMPUTER SIMULATION OF SEDIMENTATION IN MEANDERING STREAMS,
Queens Univ., Belfast (Northern Ireland). Dept. of Geology.
For primary bibliographic entry see Field 2J.
W75-07891

DIGITAL SIMULATION MODEL OF AQUIFER RESPONSE TO STREAM STAGE FLUCTUATION,
California Univ., Davis. Dept. of Water Science and Engineering.
For primary bibliographic entry see Field 2F.
W75-07897

ROTARY CROSS-BISPECTRA AND ENERGY TRANSFER FUNCTIONS BETWEEN NON-GAUSSIAN VECTOR PROCESSES I. DEVELOPMENT AND EXAMPLE,
Oregon State Univ., Corvallis. School of Oceanography.
For primary bibliographic entry see Field 2E.
W75-07911

WASTEWATER MANAGEMENT ACTIVITIES AT THE BROOKHAVEN NATIONAL LABORATORY,
Brookhaven National Lab., Upton, N.Y.
For primary bibliographic entry see Field 5D.
W75-07961

ESTIMATING LAND USE CHARACTERISTICS FOR HYDROLOGIC MODELS,
Rummel, Klepper and Kahl, Baltimore, Md.
For primary bibliographic entry see Field 4A.
W75-07982

A STOCHASTIC DYNAMIC PROGRAMMING MODEL FOR THE OPTIMUM OPERATION OF A MULTI-PURPOSE RESERVOIR,
California Univ., Los Angeles.
For primary bibliographic entry see Field 4A.
W75-07988

ON THE MOISTURE BETWEEN DATA AND MODELS OF HYDROLOGIC AND WATER RESOURCE SYSTEMS,
Arizona Univ., Tuscon. Dept. of Management.
For primary bibliographic entry see Field 6A.
W75-07989

WATER RESOURCES PLANNING, SOCIAL GOALS AND INDICATORS: METHODOLOGICAL DEVELOPMENT AND EMPIRICIAL TEST.
Utah State Univ., Logan. Technical Committee of the Water Resources Research Center of the Thirteen Western States.
For primary bibliographic entry see Field 6B.
W75-07997

DEVELOPING BIOLOGICAL INFORMATION SYSTEMS FOR WATER QUALITY MANAGEMENT,
Virginia Polytechnic Inst. and State Univ., Blacksburg. Center for Environmental Studies; and Virginia Polytechnic Inst. and State Univ., Blacksburg. Dept. of Biology.
For primary bibliographic entry see Field 5G.
W75-08002

DIGITAL SIMULATION OF THE EFFECT OF THERMAL DISCHARGE ON STREAM WATER QUALITY,
Kansas State Univ., Manhattan. Inst. for Systems Design and Optimization.
For primary bibliographic entry see Field 5B.
W75-08006

SPECIAL FLOOD HAZARD REPORT: CHESTER CREEK, GREATER ANCHORAGE AREA,
Army Engineer District, Anchorage, Alaska.
For primary bibliographic entry see Field 4A.
W75-08173

FLOOD PLAIN INFORMATION: CROW CREEK, CHEYENNE, WYOMING,
Army Engineer District, Omaha, Nebr.
For primary bibliographic entry see Field 4A.
W75-08174

FLOOD PLAIN INFORMATION: SAN DIEGO CREEK AND PETERS CANYON WASH, ORANGE COUNTY, CALIFORNIA,
Army Engineer District, Los Angeles, Calif.
For primary bibliographic entry see Field 4A.
W75-08175

FLOOD PLAIN INFORMATION: MARAIS DES CYGNES RIVER, MELVERN TO OTTOWA, KANSAS, VOLUME 1.
Army Engineer District, Kansas City, Mo.
For primary bibliographic entry see Field 4A.
W75-08176

FLOOD PLAIN INFORMATION: WILSON AND WILDWOOD CREEKS, SAN BERNADINO COUNTY, CALIFORNIA,
Army Engineer District, Los Angeles, Calif.
For primary bibliographic entry see Field 4A.
W75-08178

FLOOD PLAIN INFORMATION, ALLEGHENY RIVER, CLARION COUNTY, PENNSYLVANIA,
Army Engineer District, Pittsburgh, Pa.
For primary bibliographic entry see Field 4A.
W75-08179

FLOOD PLAIN INFORMATION: BEAVERDAM CREEK, HANOVER COUNTY, VIRGINIA,
Army Engineer District, Norfolk, Va.
For primary bibliographic entry see Field 4A.
W75-08180

FLOOD PLAIN INFORMATION: RAPID CREEK, RAPID CITY, SOUTH DAKOTA,
Army Engineer District, Omaha, Nebr.
For primary bibliographic entry see Field 4A.
W75-08183

FLOOD PLAIN INFORMATION: VIRGIN RIVER AND FORT PIERCE WASH, VICINITY OF ST. GEORGE, WASHINGTON COUNTY, UTAH,
Army Engineer District, Los Angeles, Calif.
For primary bibliographic entry see Field 4A.
W75-08184

COLLECTION OF BASIC DATA ON REPRESENTATIVE AND EXPERIMENTAL BASINS (IN FRENCH),
P. Dubreuil, Chaperon, P. J. Guiscafre, and J. Herbaud.
Office de la Recherche Scientifique et Technique Outre-Mer: Paris, France, 1972. 916 p, illus.

Descriptors: *Africa, Rainfall, Hydrology, *Basins, River basins, Lake basins, *South America, *Tropical regions, Geomorphology, Topography, Climate, Geology, Vegetation, Soils, Drainage patterns, *Basic data collections.
Identifiers: Brazil, Climates, Drainage, Equatorial, Geology, Guadeloupe, Guiana, Hydrology, Madagascar, New-Caledonia, Rainfall, Representative, Soils, Vegetation, Water.

This volume contains data on areas surrounding bodies of water or rivers situated mainly in West and Equatorial Africa, with some additional data from Madagascar, New Caledonia, French Guyana, Guadeloupe and Brazil. For each region the material is classified under 10 headings, including observations and measures of water levels, rainfall, hydrology, geomorphology, physical characteristics, topographic maps and equipment, regional climate, geology, vegetation, soils and drainage. Each basin represents an area of various size surrounding a river or a chain of lakes. In most cases the basin is only a small part of the country.--Copyright 1974, Biological Abstracts, Inc.
W75-08198

AN APPLICATION OF DISCRIMINANT ANALYSIS TO PREDICT INDUSTRIAL/COMMERCIAL FLOOD PLAIN LOCATION,
Missouri Univ., St. Louis.
For primary bibliographic entry see Field 6F.
W75-08208

DATA REQUIREMENTS OF A WATER QUALITY MANAGEMENT PROGRAM,
Colorado State Univ., Fort Collins. Dept. of Agricultural Engineering.
For primary bibliographic entry see Field 5G.
W75-08213

CHARACTERIZATION OF OPTIMAL OPERATING POLICIES FOR FINITE DAMS,
California Univ., Los Angeles. Dept. of Systems Engineering.
For primary bibliographic entry see Field 4A.
W75-08223

FORTRAN PROGRAMS FOR ANALYZING COLLABORATIVE TEST DATA, PART I: GENERAL STATISTICS,
National Environmental Research Center, Cincinnati, Ohio.
E. C. Julian.
Available from the National Technical Information Service, Springfield, Va 22161 as PB-241 707, \$3.75 in paper copy, \$2.25 in microfiche. Report EPA-670/4-75-004a, April 1975. 38 p, 2 ref. 1HA327 ROAP 24EL; Task 006.

Descriptors: Laboratory tests, Statistics, *Computer programs, Testing, *Programming languages, *Analytical techniques, *Statistical methods, Pollutant identification, Data processing.
Identifiers: *Collaborative tests, *Fortran computer programs, Scatter diagrams.

A FORTRAN program for IBM 1130 is described by which general statistics on inter-laboratory studies of chemical analytical methods may be obtained. Data screening followed by a statistical t-test for identifying outliers is included. A histogram of data in ascending order is provided. (See also W75-08231) (EPA)
W75-08230

FORTRAN PROGRAMS FOR ANALYZING COLLABORATIVE TEST DATA, PART II: SCATTER DIAGRAMS,
National Environmental Research Center, Cincinnati, Ohio.
E. C. Julian.
Available from the National Technical Information Service, Springfield, Va 22161 as PB-241 708 $3.75 in paper copy, $2.26 in microfiche. Report EPA-670/4-75-0046, April 1975. 29 p, 1 fig, 3 ref. 1HA327, ROAP 24AEL; Task 006.

Descriptors: *Computer programs, Statistical methods, Data processing, Testing, Programming language, Pollutant identification, Analytical techniques, Laboratory tests.
Identifiers: *Collaborative tests, *Scatter diagrams, *Fortran computer program.

A FORTRAN program for IBM 1130 designed to plot three pairs of data sets in three scatter diagrams on one page is described. These data stem from interlaboratory studies of chemical analytical methods. (See also W75-08230) (EPA)
W75-08231

PREDICATION OF THE BALANCE OF MATTER IN STORAGE RESERVOIRS BY MEANS OF CONTINUOUS OR SEMICONTINUOUS BIOLOGICAL MODELS: II. RELIABILITY OF THE PREDICTION METHOD, (IN GERMAN),
Technische Universitaet, Dresden (East Germany). Bereich Hydrobiologie.
For primary bibliographic entry see Field 5G.
W75-08273

8. ENGINEERING WORKS

8A. Structures

SEISMIC RESPONSE OF RESERVOIR-DAM SYSTEMS,
Michigan Univ., Ann Arbor. Dept. of Civil Engineering.
For primary bibliographic entry see Field 8B.
W75-07930

WATER RESOURCES DEVELOPMENT BY THE U.S ARMY CORPS OF ENGINEERS IN ARIZONA,
Army Engineer District, San Francisco, Calif.
For primary bibliographic entry see Field 4A.
W75-07979

UPPER THOMPSON SANITATION DISTRICT, PROJECT NO. C 080322 (FINAL ENVIRONMENTAL IMPACT STATEMENT).
Environmental Protection Agency, Denver, Colo. Region VIII.
For primary bibliographic entry see Field 5D.
W75-08016

MAINTENANCE OF BUTTERMILK CHANNEL, NEW YORK (FINAL ENVIRONMENTAL IMPACT STATEMENT).
Army Engineer District, New York.
Available from National Technical Information Service, Springfield, Va 22161 as USDC, EIS-NY-73-1872-F, $3.75 in paper copy, $2.25 in microfiche. November 28, 1973. 43 p, 3 map, 5 tab.

Descriptors: *Dredging, *Disposal, *Channels, Excavation, Navigation, Turbidity, *New York, Environmental effects, Channeling, Oceans, Incineration, Aerobic conditions.
Identifiers: *Environmental impact statements, *Buttermilk Channel(NY).

The project entails the dredging of Buttermilk Channel to authorized federal project dimensions. Disposal of the excavated material will be in the approved dumping ground in the New York Bight. The environmental impacts of the proposed project consist of the excavation and disposal of 500,000 cubic yards of bottom materials, continuation of the economy of commodity transportation, and increased safety in navigation. Adverse environmental effects include construction disturbance due to the disruption of channel bottom or associated life and the generation of turbidity and the disposal of excavated material at the already degraded approved dumping area in the New York Bight. Alternatives to the enlargement include the continued use of the present channel or use of other modes of commodity transportation. The alternatives to ocean disposal of the dredged materials are placement in upland areas, high temperature incineration, aerobic stabilization, placement in leveed areas in open waters and disposal of materials farther out to sea than the approved location. (Gagliardi-Florida)
W75-08017

CORBELL HULL DAM AND RESERVOIR, CUMBERLAND RIVER, TENNESSEE (FINAL ENVIRONMENTAL IMPACT STATEMENT).
Army Engineer District, Nashville, Tenn.
Available from National Technical Information Service, Springfield, Va 22161 as USDC, EIS-TN-73-1620-F, $4.25 in paper copy, $2.25 in microfiche. October 11, 1973. 62 p, 6 tab, 3 map, 8 ref.

Descriptors: *Hydroelectric plants, *Environmental effects, *Multiple-purpose reservoirs, Reservoirs, Reservoir operation, Impoundments, Impounded waters, Water management(Applied), Cost-benefit analysis, Project planning, Project benefits, Dams, Economic impact, Ecosystems, *Tennessee, Recreation, Fishing.
Identifiers: *Cordell Hull Dam and Reservoir(Tenn), *Environmental impact statements, Carthage(Tenn), *Cumberland River(Tenn).

Construction of the dam, now 89% complete, on the Cumberland River near Carthage, Tennessee, will constitute a major unit in the comprehensive plan for the development of the Cumberland River Basin. Completion of the dam, including an 84 x 400 foot navigation lock, a 100-megawatt power facility, a spillway, and the 12,209 acre reservoir, will provide a cheap and efficient source of power, introduce new industrial potential to the area, enhance navigation and outdoor recreation, and attract attention to several historical points of interest. Adverse environmental effects will be experienced, in a potential threat of cold-water fisheries by introduction of warm-water lake-type fishes, loss of 9,428 acres of terrestrial space, loss of 750 man-days of hunting, conversion of 72 miles of free-flowing stream to impoundment, introduction of new industry with potential for industrial sprawl, temporary adverse effects due to construction activity, and downstream bank erosion. However, these effects are not considered of major importance and are outweighed by the beneficial results expected on completion of the dam. Suggested alternatives were found unhelpful, particularly in light of the present stage of construction. (Ostapoff-Florida)
W75-08020

PALATLAKAHA RIVER WATERSHED, LAKE COUNTY, FLORIDA (FINAL ENVIRONMENTAL IMPACT STATEMENT).
Soil Conservation Service, Gainesville, Fla.
Available from National Technical Information Service, U.S. Dept. of Commerce, as EIS-FL-73-0959-F, $5.25 in paper copy, $2.25 in microfiche. April 1973. 123 p, 4 map, 1 tab, 5 fig.

Descriptors: *Watershed management, *Water control, *Flood damage, *Floodwater, Erosion, Sediments, Water, Water management(Applied), *Florida, Channels, Recreation, Velocity, Fishing, Irrigation, Citrus fruits, Marshes, Wildlife, Wetlands, Sedimentation, Flood plains, Flood plain zoning, Fish, Flood plain insurance.
Identifiers: *Environmental impact statements, Lake County(Fla).

The action involves implementation of a watershed project to be carried out with federal assistance in Lake County, Florida. The project includes the installation of needed conservation land treatent measures, 6.2 miles of channel improvement, eight structures for water control and five grade stabilization structures with water control features. The project will reduce floodwater damages; reduce areas of erosion and sediment production; create an additional 370 acres of water; improve water management; reduce excessive velocities; improve recreational and fishing opportunities; add 45 acres for future recreation sites; provide front abatement and increased irrigation resources; improve income prospects for the citrus industry; protect 1350 acres of marshland from future development; recharge isolated marshes; assure continuation of wildlife production and use of the wetlands; divert 81 acres of rangeland to recreation and spoil areas; and create temporary sedimentation problems and erosion of bare areas. The following alternatives were considered: a system of channel improvements; grade stabilization and water control structures; additional storage of floodwater; floodplain zoning; public ownership of flood damage areas; additional funds for expansion of fish and wildlife and recreational resources; land treatment without structural measures; flood insurance; and no project. (Gagliardi-Florida)
W75-08022

SHOAL CREEK CHANNEL, CHARITON-LITTLE CHARITON BASINS, MISSOURI (FINAL ENVIRONMENTAL IMPACT STATEMENT).
Army Engineer District, Kanasa City, Mo.
For primary bibliographic entry see Field 4A.
W75-08024

FOURMILE RUN LOCAL FLOODPLAIN PROTECTION, CITY OF ALEXANDRIA AND ARLINGTON COUNTY, VIRGINIA (FINAL ENVIRONMENTAL IMPACT STATEMENT).
Army Engineer District, Baltimore, Md.
For primary bibliographic entry see Field 4A.
W75-08025

HAMPTON CREEK NAVIGATION PROJECT (MAINTENANCE DREDGING) HAMPTON, VIRGINIA (FINAL ENVIRONMENTAL IMPACT STATEMENT).
Army Engineer District, Norfolk, Va.
For primary bibliographic entry see Field 4A.
W75-08026

CENTRAL AND SOUTHERN FLORIDA PROJECT, LAKE OKEECHOBEE (FINAL ENVIRONMENTAL IMPACT STATEMENT).
Army Engineer District, Jacksonville, Fla.
For primary bibliographic entry see Field 4A.
W75-08027

LAKEVIEW LAKE, MOUNTAIN CREEK, TRINITY RIVER BASIN, TEXAS (FINAL ENVIRONMENTAL IMPACT STATEMENT).
Army Engineer District, Forth Worth, Tex.
Available from National Technical Information Service, Springfield, Va as USDC, EIS-TX-73-1760-F, $5.25 in paper copy, $2.25 in microfiche. November 7, 1973. 126 p, 31 tab, 5 map.

Descriptors: *Texas, *Dam construction, *Multiple-purpose projects, *Reservoir construction, *Flood control, Environmental effects, Recreation, Water supply, Water resources development, Water supply development, Conservation, Wildlife conservation, Fish conservation,

Federal government, Economics, Regional development, Lakes.
Identifiers: *Environmental impact statements, Forth Worth(Tex), Dallas(Tex), Dam effects, Open space preservation.

This project calls for the construction of Lakeview Dam on Mountain Creek, approximately 10 miles southwest of Dallas, Texas, and the creation of Lakeview Lake, in order to provide flood control, water supply, recreation, and fish and wildlife conservation for the Fort Worth-Dallas metropolitan area. Approximately 10 miles of Mountain and Walnut Creeks will be inundated, as will 7500 acres of moderately productive agricultural land. Extensive land use changes around the lake can be expected and there will be social imposition and possible economic loss to individuals forced to relocate. In all the project will entail the acquisition and subsequent change in land-use of about 17,600 acres. Marginal fish and wildlife habitat will be inundated and income presently derived from lands to be flooded will be permanently lost. The proposed project is considered the most feasible among the various water supply and flood control alternatives considered. The enhancement of long-term productivity is deemed to greatly offset any benefits to be derived from present short-term uses of the land. The land to be inundated, which includes some known archaeological sites will be irretrievably committed to the project. (Deckert-Florida)
W75-08028

SOUTH FORK WATERSHED, PAWNEE AND RICHARDSON COUNTIES, NEBRASKA (FINAL ENVIRONMENTAL IMPACT STATEMENT).
Soil Conservation Service, Washington, D.C.
Available from the National Information Service, Springfield, Va 22161 as USDC, EIS-NB-73-1802-F, $4.25 in paper copy, $2.25 in microfiche. November 14, 1973. 70 p.

Descriptors: *Nebraska, *Reservoir construction, *Watershed management, *Multiple-purpose projects, *Flood control, Environmental effects, Recreation, Land management, Erosion control, Land use, Economics, Soil stabilization, Flood protection, Engineering structures, Habitat improvement, Flood plain zoning, Area redevelopment.
Identifiers: Dam effects, *Environmental impact statements, Pawnee County(Neb), Richardson County(Neb).

This project, located in southern Nebraska, proposes conservation land treatment measures within the watershed supplemented by 14 grade stabilization structures. Also included are two floodwater retarding structures, a multiple-purpose reservoir, and recreational facilities. The project is to be carried out by the Nemaha Natural Resources District with federal assistance under Public Law 566. Besides reducing erosion and sediment damage, the project will provide flood control and reduce flood damage to over 2000 acres of agricultural land. Water based recreation will also be provided. The project will eliminate agricultural use of 425 acres, temporarily eliminate wildlife use of 33 acres during construction, and convert 311 acres from private agricultural land to publicly owned land for recreational use. Alternatives considered were land treatment measures alone, flood plain zoning and public purchase, present plan without land and water for public use, and no action. The project will greatly enhance the long-term economic development of the region. Approximately 175 acres of land will be permanently inundated, and another 170 acres will be subject to occasional flooding. (Deckert-Florida)
W75-08029

NAWILIWILI SMALL BOAT HARBOR, KAUAI, HAWAII (FINAL ENVIRONMENTAL IMPACT STATEMENT).
Corps of Engineers, Honolulu, Hawaii.
Available from the National Technical Information Service, Springfield, Va. 22161, as EIS-HI-73-0753-F, $3.75 in paper copy, $2.25 in microfiche. March 29, 1973. 41 p, 2 tab, 3 map.

Descriptors: *Harbors, *Hawaii, Boating, *Marinas, Navigation, Environmental effects, Dikes, Breakwaters, Barriers, Recreation facilities, Aquatic habitats, Intertidal areas, Wetlands, Crabs, Dredging.
Identifiers: *Environmental impact statements, *Nawiliwili Bay(Hawaii).

Creation of a small boat harbor in the inner Nawiliwili Bay on the Island of Kauai, Hawaii, will require construction of a breakwater, revetted tide, stub breakwater, and navigational channel. Such action will result in the dredging of 71,000 cubic yards of spoil and the conversion of 18.4 acres of tidal flat areas to harbor structures and deeper water. A commercial harbor is located in the central portion of the Bay, the principle such facility on Kauai. The small boat harbor will eliminate the hazard to smallcraft from the surge action and backwash of deepdraft vessels, as well as providing needed mooring and launching facilities. Adverse environmental effects include an increase in turbidity, during construction, which will be minimized through dredging techniques and settling basin provisions. In addition, the project has been designed so that floating debris, oil and fuel spills connected with boating activity will float by action of the prevailing winds, against the dike for easy removal. Reduction of the tidal flat area should have no significant effect on the extent of local flooding. However, the flats presently provide habitat for crab species which will experience only limited recovery from the effects of the dredging. This destruction of marine habitat is unavoidable. Study has shown alternative plans untenable, and the present project will provide an urgently needed harbor for light-draft vessels and long term benefits to recreational boating and fishing and commercial fishing. (Ostapoff-Florida)
W75-08031

ARKANSAS RIVER AND TRIBUTARIES ABOVE JOHN MARTIN DAM (FINAL ENVIRONMENTAL IMPACT STATEMENT).
Army Engineer District, Albuquerque, N.Mex.
Available from the National Technical Information Service, Springfield, Va. 22161, as EIS-CO-73-1376-F, $5.75 in paper copy, $2.25 in microfiche. August 20, 1973. 140 p, 2 tab, 3 fig.

Descriptors: *Flood protection, *Flood control, *Dam construction, Fish, Wildlife, Levees, *Colorado, Flooding, Floods, Dams, Dam design, Lakes, Environmental effects, Floodwaters, Eutrophication, Reservoirs, Tributaries, Streams, Channels.
Identifiers: *Environmental impact statements, *Arkansas River Floodway(Colo), *Fountain Dam and Lake(Colo).

The project consists of a general investigation study comprised of four major aspects: (1) the Arkansas River Floodway, Colorado; (2) additional local flood protection projects; (3) construction of Fountain Dam and Lake; and (4) a restudy of the Arkansas River prior to authorization, considering all appropriate structural and non-structural alternatives for flood control and allied purposes and the environmental impact of such alternatives. The floodway will provide flood protection to 49 urban areas, 930 cultivated acres, and 121 transportation areas. 1090 acres of irrigated land will also be drained with resulting damage to the habitat of fish and wildlife. Additionally, land between the levees will provide greenbelt. Adverse environmental effects of the total project will entail detriment to fish and wildlife, detractions from scenic qualities, and a possibility of excessive eutrophication of Fountain Lake. The following alternatives were considered: single and multiple-purpose reservoirs on the main stream and tributaries; alteration of stream channels to increase flood carrying capacity; diversions, intercepting channels, levees, and floodwalls; bank protection works; combinations of the foregoing; and management of flood prone areas and resettlement. (Gagliardi-Florida)
W75-08033

SPRING BROOK WATERSHED, LANGLADE AND MARATHON COUNTIES, WISCONSIN (FINAL ENVIRONMENTAL IMPACT STATEMENT).
Soil Conservation Service, Washington, D.C.
For primary bibliographic entry see Field 4A.
W75-08035

MAINTENANCE DREDGING, BRONX RIVER, NEW YORK (FINAL ENVIRONMENTAL IMPACT STATEMENT).
Army Engineer Districts, New York.
Available from the National Technical Information Service, Springfield, Va. 22161, as EIS-NY-73-1349-F, $8.50 in paper copy, $2.25 in microfiche. August 15, 1973. 34 p, 1 map, 3 tab.

Descriptors: *Navigation, *Dredging, *New York, *Wildlife habitats, Environmental efaects, Water pollution, Waste disposal, Channels, Channel improvement, Landfills, Oceans, Commercial fishing.
Identifiers: *Environmental impact statements, *Bronx River(NY), New York Bight, Ocean dumping, Bronx County(NY).

The Bronx River, running a highly urbanized section of Bronx County, New York requires maintenance dredging of the federal channel and turning basin to the authorized project dimensions. This area is highly polluted, offering only nominal wildlife habitat, but to minimize the impact on fish, dredging will be scheduled during the winter months. Disposal of 83,000 cubic yards of spoil has been planned in the New York Bight. Past dumping has resulted in severe depreciation of environmental quality of the Bight, which has recovered only slowly. An alternate disposal site may exist at Coven Point in Jersey City, New Jersey, where a large industrial development is being planned, requiring land fill. The Corps of Engineers will continue investigation of this alternative, which will minimize the adverse environmental effects of ocean disposal. Abandonment of the navigation project would deprive the area of industry access by water requiring use of rail and trucks which would increase the level of noise and air pollution. (Ostapoff-Florida)
W75-08037

BIG RUNNING WATER DITCH WATERSHED PROJECT, LAWRENCE AND RANDOLPH COUNTIES, ARKANSAS (FINAL ENVIRONMENTAL IMPACT STATEMENT).
Soil Conservation Service, Little Rock, Ark.
For primary bibliographic entry see Field 4D.
W75-08039

HANNIBAL LOCKS AND DAM, OHIO RIVER, OHIO AND WEST VIRGINIA (FINAL ENVIRONMENTAL IMPACT STATEMENT).
Army Engineer District, Pittsburgh, Pa.
Available from the National Technical Information Service, Springfield, Va. 22161, as EIS-OH-73-1142-F, $4.75 in paper copy, $2.25 in microfiche. July 1973. 80 p, 4 map, 5 fig, 1 tab.

Descriptors: *Locks, *Dam construction, *Dams, Navigation, Navigable rivers, *Ohio River, Ohio, West Virginia, Rivers, Dredging, Channeling, Channels, Environmental effects, Oxygen, Recreation, Turbidity, Sedimentation.
Identifiers: *Environmental impact statements, *Hannibal Locks and Dams(Ohio-WVa).

The project's purpose is to replace the badly deteriorated Hannibal Locks and Dams, and bring this branch of the Ohio River, in Ohio and West

NAVIGATION SEASON EXTENSION DEMONSTRATION PROGRAM (FINAL ENVIRONMENTAL IMPACT STATEMENT).
Army Engineer District, Detroit, Mich.
For primary bibliographic entry see Field 4A.
W75-08044

RED RIVER WATERWAY, LOUISIANA, TEXAS ARKANSAS, AND OKLAHOMA, AND RELATED PROJECTS (FINAL ENVIRONMENTAL IMPACT STATEMENT).
Army Engineer District, New Orleans, La.
Available from the National Technical Information Service, Springfield, Va. 22161, as EIS-LA-73-0800-F, $8.50 in paper copy, $2.25 in microfiche. April 2, 1973. 260 p, 19 map, 8 fig.

Descriptors: *Channel improvement, *Bank stabilization, *Flood protection, Surface waters, Recreation facilities, Flood damage, Locks, Dams, Dam design, Banks, Texas, Construction, Navigation, Mississippi River, Channels, Dam sites, Louisiana, Arkansas, Recreation, Floods, Flood control, Environmental effects, Forests, Agriculture, Wildlife, Turbidity.
Identifiers: *Environmental impact statements, *Shreveport(La), *Daingerfield(Tex), *Index(Ark).

The proposed project involves the construction and maintenance of the Red River Waterway project, which consists of a navigation channel, with five locks and dams and related bank stabilization from the Mississippi River to Shreveport, Louisiana, and continuation of a navigation channel from Shreveport to Daingerfield, Texas, utilizing four locks and dams. In addition, the water project incorporates a bank stabilization feature between Shreveport and Index, Arkansas, which provides for channel realignment and bank stabilization works where necessary. The development of recreational facilities is included as a co-feature to both navigation and bank stabilization. The projects will halt the continuing loss, concommitant to the meandering of the Red River, of valuable lands and improvements located thereon. Flood damages will be reduced, the security and integrity of existing flood protection works will be increased, and the availability of surface water will be enhanced. The following adverse environmental effects are unavoidable: dedication of agricultural and forest lands to project purposes; modification or alteration of existing resources or land areas to be committed to project purposes; changes in ground water levels adjacent to slack water pools; loss of wildlife habitats; introduction and increases in turbidity; modification of water bottoms; and modification of aesthetic attributes. (Gagliardi-Florida)
W75-08045

NEW ROCHELLE AND ECHO BAY HARBORS, NEW YORK (FINAL ENVIRONMENTAL IMPACT STATEMENT).
Army Engineer District, New York.
Available from the National Technical Information Service, Springfield, Va. 22161, as EIS-NY-73-1780-F, $3.75 in paper copy, $2.25 in microfiche. November 12, 1973. 32 p, 1 map, 1 fig, 1 tab.

Descriptors: *New York, Federal government, *Environmental effects, *Dredging, *Harbors, Navigable waters, Non-consumptive use, disposal, Water resources development, Recreation, Bays, Recreation facilities, Navigation, Boating, Channel improvement.
Identifiers: New Rochelle(NY), *Echo Bay Harbor(NY), *Environmental impact statements, Spoil disposal.

This project consists of construction of a 34.8 acre anchorage area and access channel in Echo Bay Harbor in New Rochelle, New York. The minimum depth in the anchorage area will vary between 6 and 7 feet and the access channel will measure 6 feet deep and 100 feet wide for a distance of 0.11 mile. The spoil from this project will probably be disposed of in the approved dumping grounds in the nearby New York Bight, although alternative disposal methods are available. The area surrounding Echo Bay is generally urban in character and the harbor primarily recreational. This project will enhance the long-term value of the bay as a recreational boating resource. A temporary increase in turbidity during dredging is expected, but the impact, if any, on fish life should be localized and of shor duration. Alternative plans considered included a smaller anchorage area, no action, and alternative spoil disposal methods. The purpose action would not have any significant impact on the aquatic uses of the harbor by existing marine life, and it would preserve the productivity of the harbor as a recreational resource. Ocean disposal of the spoil would have a long-term detrimental effect on the biological productivity of the disposal site. Comments were received from various government agencies, but there is no known opposition to this project. (Deckert-Florida)
W75-08046

UPPER THOMPSON SANITATION DISTRICT, ESTES PARK, COLORADO PROJECT NO. C0803222 (FINAL ENVIRONMENTAL IMPACT STATEMENT).
Environmental Protection Agency, Denver, Colo. Region VIII.
For primary bibliographic entry see Field 5D.
W75-08047

DIKED DISPOSAL AREA, HURON HARBOR, ERIE COUNTY, HURON, OHIO (FINAL ENVIRONMENTAL IMPACT STATEMENT).
Army Engineer District, Buffalo, NY.
For primary bibliographic entry see Field 5G.
W75-08048

RICHMOND INNER HARBOR, MAINTENANCE DREDGING, CONTRA COSTA COUNTY, CALIFORNIA (FINAL ENVIRONMENTAL IMPACT STATEMENT).
Army Engineer District, San Francisco, Calif.
For primary bibliographic entry see Field 5G.
W75-08049

AUTHORIZED GRANITE REEF AQUEDUCT, CENTRAL ARIZONA PROJECT, ARIZONA-NEW MEXICO (FINAL ENVIRONMENTAL IMPACT STATEMENT).
Bureau of Reclamation, Denver, Colo.
Available from the National Technical Information Center, Springfield, Va. 22161, as EIS-AZ-74-0124-F, $12.50 in paper copy, $2.25 in microfiche. January 22, 1974. 548 p, 72 fig, 9 tab.

Descriptors: *Aqueducts, *Colorado River, *Pumping plants, Environmental effects, Environment, *Arizona, Water, Pumping canals, Reefs, Siphons, Tunnels, Biota, Migration, Migration patterns.
Identifiers: *Environmental impact statements, *Phoenix(Ariz).

The project involves the construction of an aqueduct to convey Colorado River water from the Havasu diversion facilities at Lake Havasu, Yuma County, to the bifurcation works at the start of the Salt-Gila Aqueduct near Phoenix, Maricopa County, Arizona. The water will enter the aqueduct at the outlet portal of the Buckskin Mountains Tunnel, be raised 388 feet in the aqueduct by a series of pumping plants, and then conveyed by an open concrete-lined canal, siphons and tunnels for approximately 183 miles. The action will result in a long-term average of 1.1 million acre-feet of water pumped annually from Lake Havasu and conveyed through the aqueduct to the service area in central Arizona for multiple-purpose uses. The adverse environmental effects

of the project include alteration of the environment within the alinement route of the Granite Reef Aqueduct; damage to the aesthetic value of the immediate area due to construction of the pumping plants and the canal; disturbance of biota in the area; alteration of migration patterns of certain species of animals; and animal losses due to drowning. The following proposals were also considered: alternative water sources; alternative power sources; alternatives to the selected route of the Granite Reef Aqueduct; and no action. (Gagliardi-Florida)
W75-08050

PERILLA MOUNTAIN WATERSHED PROJECT, COCHISE COUNTY, ARIZONA (FINAL ENVIRONMENTAL IMPACT STATEMENT).
Soil Conservation Service, Washington, D.C.
For primary bibliographic entry see Field 4D.
W75-08051

KAIMU BEACH HAWAII, PROPOSED SHORE PROTECTION (FINAL ENVIRONMENTAL IMPACT STATEMENT).
Corps of Engineers, Honolulu, Hawaii. Pacific Ocean Div.
Available from National Technical Information Service, USDC, Springfield, Va 22161 as EIS-HI-74-0188-F, $5.75 in paper copy, $2.25 in microfiche. January 31, 1974. 134 p, 5 plate, 3 tab, 1 append.

Descriptors: *Shore protection, *Excavation, *Sands, *Breakwaters, Beach erosion, Beaches, Surf-boarding, Benthic fauna, Benthic flora, Shores, Structures, Structural design, National seashores, *Hawaii.
Identifiers: Black sand, *Environmental impact statements, Kaimu Beach(Hawaii).

The Kaimu Beach Shore Protection Plan provides for excavation and stockpiling of about 5800 cubic yards of black sand from Kaimu Beach and placement of approximately 38,000 cubic yards of new sand, followed by a two year monitoring program. Included in the plan are construction of a submerged breakwater, placement of about 10,800 cubic yards of beach sand and topping of the beach with the 5800 cubic yards of stockpiled black sand. The sand placement will result in a widened and restored beach, and the breakwater will reduce erosion of the natural black sand. The breakwater will add a permanent man-made element to the natural environment and disrupt waves presently suitable for surfing. The project will also disturb some benthic life. Alternatives considered consists of various structural alternatives or no action. (Denvir-Florida)
W75-08052

VIRGINIA KEY BEACH EROSION CONTROL PROJECT, SECOND PERIODIC NOURISHMENT AND GROINS (FINAL ENVIRONMENTAL IMPACT STATEMENT).
Army Engineer District, Jacksonville, Fla.
Available from National Technical Information Service, USDC, Springfield, Va 22161 as EIS-FL-73-1952-F, $4.25 in paper copy, $2.25 in microfiche. December 17, 1973. 65 p, 6 plate, 4 chart.

Descriptors: *Erosion control, *Beach erosion, *Berms, *Groins(Structures), Benthic fauna, Benthic flora, Vegetation regrowth, Vegetation, Erosion, Beaches, Vegetation establishment, Invertebrates, Sands, Water quality, Borrow pits, Construction, Structures, Environmental effects, *Florida.
Identifiers: *Environmental impact statements, *Virginia Key(Fla).

The Virginia Key Beach Erosion Control Project consists of excavation and placement of 100,000 cubic yards of sand on 1.8 miles of Virginia Key ocean shore and construction of 1 impermeable and 12 permeable groins. Implementation will create 70 feet of level beach berm. Some vegetation, benthic organisms, and invertebrates will be destroyed during excavation and construction, but should reestablish on suitable portions of the beach, and will assist in preventing erosion. Dredging and distributing sand fill will temporarily degrade water quality at the borrow and beach fill sites. The groins will cover some bottom habitats and change to some extent the composition of species in the area. Consideration was given to alternate borrow sites, varying number of groins and construction of other structures. The plan selected was assessed as the most beneficial entailing the least environmental costs. (Denvir-Florida)
W75-08053

LAKE QUINAULT SEWAGE COLLECTION AND TREATMENT FACILITY, OLYMPIC NATIONAL FOREST, OLYMPIA, WASHINGTON (FINAL ENVIRONMENTAL IMPACT STATEMENT).
For primary bibliographic entry see Field 5D.
W75-08054

HIGHWAY 112 CRITICAL EROSION CONTROL RESOURCES CONSERVATION AND DEVELOPMENT PROJECT MEASURE (FINAL ENVIRONMENTAL IMPACT STATEMENT).
Soil Conservation Service, Madison, Wis.
Available from National Technical Information Service, USDC, Springfield, Va 22161 as EIS-WI-73-2013-F, $4.25 in paper copy, $2.25 in microfiche. December 26, 1973. 54 p, 3 fig, 6 photo.

Descriptors: *Erosion control, *Erosion, *Gully erosion, *Gullies, Slope protection, Grading, Mulching, Seed treatment, Tiles, Sediments, Sedimentation, Vegetation establishment, Surface runoff, Surface waters, *Wisconsin.
Identifiers: *Environmental impact statements, *White River(Wis).

The project is aimed at controlling erosion in a gully in White River, Wisconsin by means of sod waterways, sloping, grading, seeding, mulching, and tiling. Implementation will control the rate of erosion from a single site as well as decrease the volume of sediment being deposited in the White River. The project will change the type of vegetative cover in the area and increase the exposure of unprotected soil until the new vegetation becomes established. Alternatives such as installation of a closed conduit, diversion of surface runoff to another watercourse, or diversion to the White River via three watercourses were considered. (Denvir-Florida)
W75-08055

CHANNEL TO NEWPORT NEWS, VIRGINIA (MAINTENANCE DREDGING) (ENVIRONMENTAL IMPACT STATEMENT).
Army Engineer District, Norfolk, Va.
Available from National Technical Information Service, USDC, Springfield, Va 22161 as EIS-VA-73-1871-F, $3.75 in paper copy, $2.25 in microfiche. November 28, 1973. 40 p, 2 fig, 3 tab.

Descriptors: *Dredging, *Channels, Turbidity, Harbors, Shoals, Neritic, Environmental effects, *Virginia, Navigation, Oysters, Channeling, Channel improvement, Clams, Benthic fauna, Benthic flora.
Identifiers: *Environmental impact statements, Newport News(Va).

The project involves dredging required to maintain the 800-foot wide channel to Newport News, Virginia at the project depth of 45 feet. This channel extends westwardly approximately 4.8 miles from Norfolk Harbor Channel to the Chesapeake and Ohio Railway Company coal piers. Maintenance dredging will require removal of about 300,000 cubic yards of shoal material over the entire channel length while maintaining the carrying capacity of the channel for efficient movement of commercial navigation. The action will remove or disrupt some neritic and benthic organisms and will result in a temporary increase in turbidity near the dredge area. The environment will be adversely affected by removal or disturbance of resident benthic organisms such as oysters and clams and will result in the temporary increase in turbidity. The only alternative considered was to forego further maintenance. (Gagliardi-Florida)
W75-08057

INDIAN CREEK WATERSHED PROJECT, CITY OF CHESAPEAKE, VIRGINIA (FINAL ENVIRONMENTAL IMPACT STATEMENT).
Soil Conservation Service, Richmond, Va.
Available from National Technical Information Service, USDC, Springfield, Va 22161 as EIS-VA-74-00016-F, $4.25 in paper copy, $2.25 in microfiche. January 2, 1974. 67 p, 2 map, 6 tab, 3 append.

Descriptors: *Watershed management, *Flood protection, *Drainage, *Watershed Protect. and Flood Prev. Act, Turbidity, Vegetation, Flooding, Floods, *Virginia, Channels, Water, Pastures, Crops, Mosquitoes, Flood control.
Identifiers: *Environmental impact statements, Chesapeake(Va), Indian Creek watershed(Va).

The project entails watershed protection, flood prevention and drainage in Chesapeake, Virginia, to be implemented under authority of the Watershed Protection and Flood Prevention Act, as amended. The proposed action will reduce net crop and pasture damage by about 25 percent with a resulting improvement in crop quality. Additionally, the removal of excess water through adequate outlets for farm drainage systems will reduce mosquito breeding areas and provide benefits to 2,375 acres on 40 farms now in cropland and pasture. Farm operators will be able to use the modern production methods needed to maintain their competitive marketing position. Planned construction will disturb about 17 acres on 8 farms which will create turbidity for a few weeks during construction and prior to vegetation cover being established. The following alternatives were considered: land treatment and additional channel work, acquisition of land, and no action. (Gagliardi-Florida)
W75-08058

EAGLE-TUMBLEWEED DRAW WATERSHED, EDDY AND CHAVES COUNTIES, NEW MEXICO (FINAL ENVIRONMENTAL IMPACT STATEMENT).
Soil Conservation Service, Washington, D.C.
For primary bibliographic entry see Field 4D.
W75-08060

MISSOURI RIVER GARRISON DAM TO LAKE OAHE RESERVOIR (FINAL ENVIRONMENTAL IMPACT STATEMENT).
Army Engineer District, Omaha, Nebr.
Available from National Technical Information Service, USDC, Springfield, Va 22161 as EIS-NB-73-1866-F, $4.25 in paper copy, $2.25 in microfiche. November 28, 1973. 70 p, 6 plate, append.

Descriptors: *Bank protection, *Bank erosion, *Erosion control, *Trenches, Dikes, Aesthetics, Flood plains, Flood protection, Flooding, Erosion, Habitats, Wildlife habitats, *North Dakota, *Missouri River.
Identifiers: *Environmental impact statements, Dry Point(ND), *Bismark(ND).

The 88th and 90th Congress authorized the Corps of Engineers to provide for bank protection or rectification works on the Missouri River at or below Garrison Dam as may be found necessary. To data erosion control measures have been taken

lattice nodes. The latticework model was calibrated to assure accurate predictions of the transient response. Comparisons with exact solutions of the two-dimensional hydrodynamic problem were presented for a step function input and for actual earthquake excitations. The temporal variation of hydrodynamics forces were computed on a vertical faced dam in a confined reservoir and in a semi-infinite reservoir. The interaction between a flexible tapered concrete gravity dam, which was modeled as a shear-beam, and a confined reservoir was studied. (Adams-ISWS)
W75-07930

COMPUTATION OF STAGE-DISCHARGE RELATIONSHIPS AFFECTED BY UNSTEADY FLOW,
National Weather Service, Silver Spring, Md. Hydrologic Research and Development Lab.
For primary bibliographic entry see Field 2E.
W75-07932

NONLINEAR KINEMATIC WAVE APPROXIMATION FOR WATER ROUTING,
Colorado State Univ., Fort Collins. Dept. of Civil Engineering.
For primary bibliographic entry see Field 2E.
W75-07935

OPTIMAL COST DESIGN OF BRANCHED SEWER SYSTEMS,
Illinois Univ., Urbana. Dept. of Civil Engineering.
For primary bibliographic entry see Field 5D.
W75-07999

POTENTIAL LANDSLIDE-GENERATED WATER WAVES, LIBBY DAM AND LAKE KOOCANUSA, MONTANA; HYDRAULIC MODEL INVESTIGATION,
Army Engineer Waterways Experiment Station, Vicksburg, Miss.
D. D. Davidson, and R. W. Whalin.
Available from the National Technical Information Service, Springfield, Va. 22161. Technical Report H-74-15, December 1974. 102 p, 2 fig, 3 tab, 6 photo, 51 pl, 4 append, 7 ref.

Descriptors: *Hydraulic models, *Landslides, *Waves(Water), *Montana.
Identifiers: *Lake Koocanusa(Mont), *Libby Dam(Mont).

A hydraulic model, constructed at an undistorted scale of 1:120, reproduced about 1 mile upstream of the dam and about 1200 ft downstream of the dam for the purpose of determining the magnitude of wave heights, runup, and over-topping of the dam for four potential landslides. The model landslide material primarily consisted of 1/18-cu-ft bags of iron ore and lead mixed to reproduce the correct rock mass density. These bags were hand-stacked up the inclined plane slope to obtain the correct elevation-volume-shape relationship, held in place mechanically, and then released to slide into the model under the influence of gravity. A few tests also were conducted with gravel and concrete cubes as the landslide material for comparison with the results of the bag tests. Results of the model study showed the wave amplitudes, runup, and downstream water expected at various reservoir pool elevations as a function of landslide parameters. Two important conclusions were that: (a) full volume landslides caused unacceptable conditions at the dam for pool elevations tested, depending on the landslide velocity; and (b) partial landslide failure (both upper and lower portions) also generated unacceptable conditions at the dam. (WES)
W75-08291

PRACTICAL GUIDANCE FOR DESIGN OF LINED CHANNEL EXPANSIONS AT CULVERT OUTLETS; HYDRAULIC MODEL INVESTIGATION,
Army Engineer Waterways Experiment Station, Vicksburg, Miss.
B. P. Fletcher, and J. L. Grace, Jr.
Available from the National Technical Information Service, Springfield, Va. 22161. Technical Report H-74-9, October 1974. 90 p, 38 fig, 3 tab, 8 pl, 8 photo, 2 append, 14 ref.

Descriptors: *Culverts, *Discharge(Water), *Scour, Froude number, Open channel flow, Design.
Identifiers: *Channel lining, *Channel expansion, Tailwater elevation.

Detailed results are presented of research conducted to develop practical guidance for design of lined channel expansions at culvert outlets. Results of related research efforts during the past decade to develop practical guidance for estimating and controlling erosion downstream of culvert and storm-drain outlets are summarized. Empirical equations and charts are presented for estimating the extent of localized scour to be anticipated downstream of culvert and storm-drain outlets the size and extent of various natural and artificial type revetments and energy dissipators that may be used to control localized scour. With these results, designers can estimate the extent of scour to be expected and select appropriate and alternative schemes of protection for controlling erosion downstream of culvert and stormdrain outlets. (WES)
W75-08292

RICHARD B. RUSSELL LAKE WATER QUALITY INVESTIGATION; HYDRAULIC MODEL INVESTIGATION,
Army Engineer Waterways Experiment Station, Vicksburg, Miss.
D. G. Fontane, and J. P. Bohan.
Available from the National Technical Information Service, Springfield, Va. 22161. Technical Report H-74-14, December 1974. 51 p, 25 pl, 5 ref.

Descriptors: *Mathematical models, *Model studies, Reservoirs, *Water quality, *Hydraulic models, Lakes, *Georgia, Oxygen, Thermal pollution, Path of pollutants.
Identifiers: Oxygen regimes, *Richard B. Russell Lake(Ga).

The thermal and dissolved oxygen regimes of the proposed Trotters Shoals (Richard B. Russell) Reservoir were simulated using a combination of physical and mathematical models. The effects of the Trotters Shoals Reservoir upon the thermal and dissolved oxygen regimes of a downstream impoundment, Clark Hill, were also evaluated. Both conventional power generation and pumped-storage power operations at Trotters Shoals Reservoir were studied. Three physical models were used to describe the expected hydrodynamics in Trotters Shoals and Clark Hill Reservoirs. The withdrawal characteristics of the intakes and the entrainment, dilution, placement, and travel time of the inflow and pumpback density currents were determined. The results of the physical model tests were incorporated into a mathematical model capable of simulating the physical and chemical characteristics of an impoundment. This mathematical model was further modified to include a routine to predict the dissolved oxygen structure of an impoundment. The mathematical model was calibrated with observed thermal and dissolved oxygen data on the existing Hartwell and Clark Hill impoundments, which are immediately upstream and downstream, respectively, of the proposed Trotters Shoals Reservoir. The model was then used to simulate the thermal and dissolved oxygen regimes of Trotters Shoals Reservoir. (WES)
W75-08293

TILLAMOOK BAY MODEL STUDY; HYDRAULIC MODEL INVESTIGATION,
Army Engineer Waterways Experiment Station, Vicksburg, Miss.
G. M. Fisackerly.
Available from the National Technical Information Service, Springfield, Va. 22161. Technical Report H-74-11, November 1974. 22 p, 8 fig, 1 tab, 6 photo, 117 pl, 2 append.

Descriptors: *Hydraulic models, Salinity, Tides, Flow, *Shoals, *Jetties, Estuaries, *Oregon, *Saline water intrusion, Bays.
Identifiers: *Tidal currents, *Tillamook Bay(Ore).

The Tillamook Bay model was of the fixed-bed type, constructed to scales of 1:500 horizontally and 1:100 vertically, and reporduced Tillamook Bay, Oregon, in its entirety and a suitable area of the Pacific Ocean. The model was equipped for accurate reporduction and measurement of tides, tidal currents, salinity intrusion, freshwater inflow, shoaling distribution, and other significant prototype phenomena. The purpose of the model study was to determine the optimum alignment and length of south jetty at the entrance to Tillamook Bay. Model verification tests indicated that the model hydraulic and salinity regimens were in satisfactory agreement with those of the prototype for comparable conditions. It therefore can be assumed that the model provided quantitative answers concerning the effect of the proposed plans on the hydraulic and salinity regimens of the bay. The optimum plan consisted of existing conditions plus a 7000-ft south jetty located 1200 ft from the north jetty. Lengths greater than this do not modify the shoaling pattern to an great degree and should be considered only if additional protection for navigation is required. (WES)
W75-08294

UNSTEADY FLOW COMPUTATIONS ON THE OHIO-CUMBERLAND-TENNESSEE-MISSISSIPPI RIVER SYSTEM,
Army Engineer Waterways Experiment Station, Vicksburg, Miss.
B. H. Johnson.
Available from the National Technical Information Service, Springfield, Va. 22161. Technical Report H-74-8, September 1974. 44 p, 2 fig, 2 tab, 11 pl, 3 append.

Descriptors: *Flood control, *Mathematical models, *Mississippi River, *Ohio River, *Tennessee River, *Unsteady flow.
Identifiers: *Cumberland River, Barkley Reservoir, Kentucky Reservoir.

The U.S. Army Engineer Division, Ohio River, directs the operation of Barkley and Kentucky Reservoirs on the Cumerland and Tennessee Rivers, respectively, during periods of flooding on the lower Ohio and lower Mississippi Rivers. Flood control regulation by these reservoirs is met by controlling, to some degree, the Ohio River stage at Cairo, Illinois. A mathematical model, SOCHMJ, capable of accurately preidcting Ohio River stages as a result of reservoir operations at Barkley and Kentucky Reservoirs has been developed. SOCHMJ provides the capability of modeling a system containing an unlimited number of junctions. The physical limits of the Ohio-Cumberland-Tennessee-Mississippi system modeled are Golconda, Illinois, on the Ohio River; Barkley Dam on the Cumberland River; Kentucky Dam on the Tennessee River; Cape Girardeau on the upper Mississippi River; and Caruthersville on the lower Mississippi River. Three applications of SOCHMJ were made in the study. These were (a) an application using 1950 flood data, (b) an application using 1973 flood data, and (c) an application using data from a 3-day period in February 1974. (WES)
W75-08295

SPILLWAY FOR COLUMBUS LOCK AND DAM TOMBIGBEE RIVER, ALABAMA; HYDRAULIC MODEL INVESTIGATION,
Army Engineer Waterways Experiment Station, Vicksburg, Miss.
N. R. Oswalt, and G. A. Pickering.
Available from the National Technical Information Service, Springfield, Va. 22161. Technical Report H-74-13, November 1974. 29 p, 5 fig, 1 tab, 5 photo, 7 pl.

Descriptors: *Hydraulic models, *Open channel flow, *Riprap, *Spillways, *Stilling basins, Flow, *Alabama.
Identifiers: Columbus Lock and Dam(Ala), *Tombigbee River(Ala).

Tests were conducted on a 1:36-scale model of the Columbus Lock and Dam spillway to determine discharge characteristics of the spillway, stilling basin performance, and riprap requirements downstream from the structure for both normal and single-gate operations. The proposed spillway will consist of five 60-ft-wide bays through which flow will be regulated by tainter gates. An unsteady flow condition was detected with gated flows when a trench to be excavated during construction was left more than 10 ft lower than the crest of the spillway. Therefore, it is recommended that this area be filled to at least el 128. The stilling basin as originally designed resulted in satisfactory performance during normal operation. However, with only one gate one-half or fully open, performance of the basin was unsatisfactory. Several modifications to the basin were tested in an effort to improve energy dissipation and a stilling basin that provided satisfactory flow conditions was developed. Tests to determine the riprap requirements in the exit channel indicated that the coverage of protection needed was the same whether the gate was one-half or fully open. (WES)
W75-08296

SPILLWAY FOR ALICEVILLE LOCK AND DAM TOMBIGBEE RIVER, ALABAMA; HYDRAULIC MODEL INVESTIGATION,
Army Engineer Waterways Experiment Station, Vicksburg, Miss.
N. R. Oswalt.
Available from the National Technical Information Service, Springfield, Va. 22161. Technical Report H-74-10, October 1974. 35 p, 7 fig, 7 photo, 8 plates.

Descriptors: Energy dissipation, *Hydraulic models, *Open channel flow, *Riprap, *Spillways, *Stilling basins, *Alabama.
Identifiers: Aliceville Lock and Dam(Ala), *Tombigbee River(Ala).

Tests were conducted on a 1:36-scale model of the Aliceville spillway to develop an energy dissipator and plan of riprap that would provide adequate protection of the exit channel both for normal operating conditions and for the condition of one gate opened full with minimum tailwater conditions. A stilling basin was developed to provide satisfactory flow conditions for both normal and emergency operating conditions. The following changes from the original design were recommended: Eliminate a 90-deg end-section of the left stilling basin training wall, shorten the length of the right training wall between the gated and ungated spillways from 115 to 40 ft, reduce the original excavation requirements along the downstream right bank, and decrease the approach depth immediately upstream of the spillway. Tests to determine the minimum riprap requirements for the exit channel indicated the necessity to develop a plan of protection for about 600 ft downstream of the basin. To eliminate undesirable eddy patterns in the lower lock approach downstream of the spillway a vane dike was constructed, and the riprap requirements for stability of the dike were determined. (WES)
W75-08297

SAN DIEGO BAY MODEL STUDY; HYDRAULIC MODEL INVESTIGATION,
Army Engineer Waterways Experiment Station, Vicksburg, Miss.
G. M. Fisackerly.
Available from the National Technical Information Service, Springfield, Va. 22161. Technical Report H-74-12, November 1974. 144 p, 10 fig, 4 tab, 6 photo, 113 pl.

Descriptors: *Hydraulic models, *Tides, *Estuaries, *California.
Identifiers: *San Diego Bay(Cal), Tidal currents.

The San Diego Bay model was a fixed-bed model constructed of concrete to scales of 1:500 horizontally and 1:100 vertically. The model was equipped for the accurate reproduction of tides, tidal currents, and other significant prototype phenomena. The purpose was to determine the effects of a second entrance into the bay on the hydraulic and flushing characteristics of the bay. Model verification tests indicated that hydraulic phenomena reproduced in the model were in satisfactory agreement with those of the prototype for comparable conditions. Tests were conducted with plans for two different second entrance locations near the south end of the bay installed in the model. Maximum current velocities throughout the northern half of the bay were generally reduced by about 70 percent by both plans. The results of dye tracer tests showed that both plans would appreciably improve the overall flushing characteristics of the bay, with the northernmost second entrance producing the most improvement in flushing. With either second entrance in the model, the nodal point of the incoming tide was somewhat to the south of the nodal point of the outgoing tide, thus creating a circulation pattern with a net flow into the bay through the existing entrance and a net outflow through the proposed second entrance. (WES)
W75-08298

EFFECTS OF A STEADY NONUNIFORM CURRENT ON THE CHARACTERISTICS OF SURFACE GRAVITY WAVES,
Army Engineer Waterways Experiment Station, Vicksburg, Miss.
L. Z. Hales, and J. B. Herbich.
Available from the National Technical Information Service, Springfield, Va. 22161. Miscellaneous Paper H-74-11, December 1974. 186 p, 64 fig, 13 tab, 34 ref, append.

Descriptors: *Gravity waves, *Waves(Water).
Identifiers: *Surface waves(Water), *Tidal currents, *Tidal inlets.

This study investigated the manner in which nonuniform currents affect characteristics of a superimposed surface gravity wave train. The work was conducted in a three-dimensional wave basin in which was simulated a tidal inlet through which could be created nonuniform currents in both an ebb and flood direction. Current was required to build up on its own accord from essentially zero velocity in the ocean, reach a maximum value in the inlet throat and decay to essentially zero velocity in the bay region, for the flood condition. The ebb condition was similar except the current opposed the direction of the wave motion. For a variety of steady-state flow conditions through the facility, a range of wave trains with initial characteristics representative of those found in nature were superimposed. Measurements of velocity, wave height, and wave length were determined at selected points along the axis of the facility. Spectral analyses of the generated wave form justified the assumption of constancy of the wave period; hence, theoretically the change in wave length was expected to vary with a current parameter in a linear fashion. Analysis indicated that in addition to the current parameter, the relative depth and initial wave steepness were statistically highly significant parameters affecting the changes in both wave length and wave height. (WES)
W75-08299

tion, Turbidity, Reservoirs, Control structures, Wildlife, Landscaping, Channels, Outlet works, Water quality, Flood protection, Industrial water, Pollutants.
Identifiers: *Environmental impact statements, Berks County(Penn).

The proposed project, located on Tulpehocken Creek in Berks County, Pennsylvania, includes an earth and rockfill embankment and three nearby dikes to contain the reservoir during high pool levels. Also, an unlined open channel spillway will be excavated across a natural saddle approximately 1,000 feet south of the embankment. Outlet works and a levee will also be constructed. The proposed action will result in the following environmental effects: a decrease in potential damage from flooding; an increase in industrial and municipal water supply; increased recreation and wildlife potential; improvement of water quality; and increased turbidity of Tulpehocken Creek. The most important long-term adverse effect is the potential arsenic and biological pollution in the proposed reservoir. There are indications, however, that these concentrations can be controlled. Adverse aesthetic effects will hopefully be mitigated by restorative landscaping, intended to blend the project structures into the present environment. The following alternatives were considered: non-structural projects, such as flood plain management; a different locale for the project; and no action. (Gagliardi-Florida)
W75-08019

APPLICATION FOR PERMIT TO CONSTRUCT A DAM ON MURDERERS CREEK GREEN COUNTY, NEW YORK (FINAL ENVIRONMENTAL IMPACT STATEMENT).
Army Engineer District, New York.
Available from National Technical Information Service, Springfield, Va 22161 as USDC, EIS-NY-73-0835-F, $8.50 in paper copy, $2.25 in microfiche. December 7, 1972. 254 p, 20 tab, 3 graph, 4 fig, 10 map.

Descriptors: *Dam construction, *Recreation facilities, *Land use, Environmental effects, Impoundments, Dam design, Dams, Lakes, Forests, *New York, Hudson River, Recreation, Water quality, Eutrophication, Wildlife, Construction, Air, Turbidity, Erosion, Streams.
Identifiers: *Environmental impact statements, *Murderers Creek(NY).

The project entails construction of an earth fill dam on Murderers Creek, New York, just upstream of its confluence with tidewater of the Hudson River. The dam will create a 323 acre lake that would be the central feature of a recreational-residential development. The overall development will beneficially affect the local economy, land use, water quality and biological resources. Adverse environmental effects include removal of forestation, conversion of an open creek into an impoundment with the potential for eutrophication and an adverse effect on local wildlife. Construction activities would generate temporary noise and air pollution and accelerate erosion with resulting increases in turbidity and nutrient loads in the stream. The alternative to the proposed action is not to issue the permit for construction of the dam. The alternatives relevant to the overall development are building at another site, providing a series of small impoundments instead of a single large one, or varying the size of the dam and lake. (Gagliardi-Florida)
W75-08023

PROPOSED HABITAT ENHANCEMENT PROJECT TOPCOCK MARSH UNIT, HAVASU NATIONAL WILDLIFE REFUGE, ETC. (FINAL ENVIRONMENTAL IMPACT STATEMENT).
Bureau of Sport Fisheries and Wildlife, Washington, D.C.
Available from the National Technical Information Service, Springfield, Va. 22161, as EIS-AZ-73-1643-F, $5.25 in paper copy, $2.25 in microfiche. October 15, 2973. 110p, 9 map, 1 fig.

Descriptors: *Dikes, *Water management(Applied), *Channels, *Water circulation, Habitats, Habitat improvements, *Arizona, Marshes, Channeling, Canals, Fishing, Fisheries, Fish, Wildlife, Canal construction, Levees, Sediments, Sedimentation, Silts, Turbidity.
Identifiers: *Environmental impact statements, Mohave County(Ariz), Wilderness areas.

The project, proposed by the Bureau of Sport Fisheries and Wildlife of the Department of Interior, involves habitat enhancement within the Topcock Marsh Unit of Havusu National Wildlife Refuge, Mohave County, Arizona. The proposed project would include diking to permit water management; channeling to improve water circulation; levees and management units to provide habitat for the endangered Yuma clapper rail; construction of a sediment basin to trap silt from the marsh inlet canal; and diking to isolate water from Fort Mohave Indian land. Adverse environmental effects entail a possible reduction in microorganisms, short-term disturbance of wildlife use during construction, and a short-term increase in local turbidity within the marsh during construction. The following alternatives were considered: continuation under the present management; increase of the water diversion to the marsh; development of a system of cross dikes to control water distribution; implementation only of the diking portion of the project; and further reduction of the size of the marsh. (Gagliardi-Florida)
W75-08038

8F. Concrete

SIXES BRIDGE DAM AND LAKE, MARYLAND AND PENNSYLVANIA (FINAL ENVIRONMENTAL IMPACT STATEMENT).
Army Engineer District, Baltimore, Md.
Available from National Technical Information Service, Springfield, Va 22161 as U.S.D.C. EIS-MD-73-1914-F. December 11, 1973. 229 p, 4 map, 4 photo, 24 tab, 1 graph.

Descriptors: *Water supply, *Stream improvement, *Dam construction, *Recreation, *Concrete dams, Maryland, Dams, Lakes, Wildlife, Flow, Flow profiles, Streams, Pennsylvania, Dam design, Flow control, Environmental effects, Biota, Reservoirs, Rivers.
Identifiers: *Environmental impact statements, *Keysville(Md), Monocracy River(Md).

The proposed project is designed to enhance water supply, stream quality, and recreation opportunities. A concrete gravity dam with earth wings will be constructed on the Monocacy River, two miles due west of Keysville, Maryland. The recreation pool of the lake, at an elevation of 375 feet above mean sea level, will have an area of 3500 acres. A total of 10,880 acres of land will be acquired, including 2,380 acres for the replacement of wildlife habitat. The project will increase the dependable flow of the Monocacy River by 85 million gallons per day, provide adequate flow to meet the maximum day water supply needs of the area, projected for the year 2020, and support an ultimate recreation of 625,000 visitor-days annually. Adverse environmental effects include inundation of 3,500 acres of land, eliminating habitat for all associated terrestrial biota and certain stream dwelling aquatic organisms and damage to historic and archaeological sites within the project area. Alternatives to the proposed project include additional dam and reservoir projects, withdrawals of water from the Potomac Estuary, and importation of water from other river basins. (Gagliardi-Florida)
W75-08015

TROUT RUN EARTHFILL DAM, BOROUGH OF BOYERTOWN, BERKS COUNTY, PENNSYLVANIA (FINAL ENVIRONMENTAL IMPACT STATEMENT).
Delaware River Basin Commission, Trenton, N.J.
Available from National Technical Information Service, Springfield, Va 22161 as USDC, EIS-PA-73-1176-F, $5.25 in paper copy, $2.25 in microfiche. July 1973. 117 p, 17 tab, 8 fig, 8 ref.

Descriptors: *Delaware River Basin Commission, *Earth dams, *Ecosystems, *Water management(Applied), Environmental effects, Habitats, Wildlife habitats, Wildlife, Impoundments, Water supply, Water demand, Reservoirs, Project planning, Project benefits, Water resources development, *Pennsylvania.
Identifiers: *Environmental impact statements, *Berks County(Pa).

Construction of an earth-fill dam on Trout Run, a tributary to Manatawney Creek entering the Schuylkill River in the Southeastern section of Berks County, Pennsylvania, will generate the new water supply required for this area because of a projected population increase and the presently diminishing reservoir supply. Relocation of about 1 mile of highway LR 06053 will be required in the creation of this 42 acre, 330 million gallon water supply reservoir. Ecological impact of the work will be neutral, since the loss of habitat to existing terrestrial species will be balanced by the concomitant gain to aquatic and wetland wildlife. Cost is estimated at $1,010,000 over 600 days of construction. Suggested alternatives to the proposed project included no action, expansion of the existing source, an impoundment on Ironstone Creek, alternative sites on Trout Run, a diversion dam on Trout Run, importation of water supply and use of ground water. These were found either untenable or less satisfactory than the Trout Run Dam planned. (Ostapoff-Florida)
W75-08030

VERONA DAM AND LAKE, VIRGINIA (FINAL ENVIRONMENTAL IMPACT STATEMENT).
Army Engineer District, Baltimore, Md.
Available from National Technical Information Service, Springfield, Va 22161 as EIS-VA-73-1932-F, $6.25 in paper copy, $ 2.25 in microfiche. December 12, 1973. 167 p, 3 fig, 1 plate, 20 tab.

Descriptors: *Dams, *Water supply, *Water supply development, *Stream improvement, Rivers, Environmental effects, *Virginia, Lakes, Recreation, Concrete dams, Damsites, Estuaries, Fishing, Reservoirs, Headwaters.
Identifiers: *Environmental impact statements, Staunton(Va), Verona(Va).

The action involves the reformulation of the proposed Verona Dam and Lake, Virginia, for water supply, stream enhancement, and recreation. The concrete gravity dam with earth wing will be located on Middle River, a tributary to South Fork Shenandoah River, about 9 miles northeast of Staunton, Virginia. The project will increase the dependable flow in Middle River by approximately 110 million gallons per day, a flow sufficient to meet the water supply needs of the Verona-Staunton area through the year 2000, and to provide for the environmental enhancement of the stream from the damsite through the Shenandoah and Potomac River Basin to the Potomac Estuary. The 3,900 acre lake formed by the project will support an ultimate recreation visitation of 700,000 user-days annually and an estimated 98,400 fisherman-days of lake related fishing opportunity. Adverse environmental effects include elimination of about 12 miles of free-flowing streams in the project area, along with an estimated 10,900 fisherman-days of stream fishing use and 12,000 user days of stream-related recreation use. Additionally, approximately 7,850 acres of farm-game habitat will be foregone and an estimated 1,170 hunter days of existing hunting use in the project area will be eliminated. The following alternative water supply concepts were considered: use of new reservoirs; use of hardwater reservoirs; withdrawal of water from the Potomac Estuary; importation of water; development of ground water; use of existing reservoirs; institution of water use restrictions; and no action. (Gagliardi-Florida)
W75-08056

8I. Fisheries Engineering

APPARATUS FOR SUCKING UP AND TRANSFERRING FISHES,
Kyoei Zoki Kabushiki Kaisha, Naruto (Japan) (assignee).
T. Hayashi.
U. S. Patent No 3,871,332, 11 p, 20 fig, 2 ref; Official Gazette of the United States Patent Office, Vol 932, No 3, p 866, March 18, 1975.

Descriptors: *Patents, *Fish handling facilities, Equipment, Conveyance structures, Fish populations, Industry.
Identifiers: *Fisheries engineering, Fish transfer.

An apparatus is described for sucking up fishes caught by a fishing net at a fishing ground or fishes bred in a fish breeding farm into a tank and then transferring the fishes to a given place such as a fish tank. The apparatus comprises a hermetically closed tank that has an air opening at its upper portion, and a fish water suction opening at its lower part. There is a special control device for alternately changing the air extracting and air supplying means. A control valve is arranged for communication the fish water suction pipe with the closed tank and closing the fish transfer pipe during the air extracting step and closing the fish water suction pipe and communicating the fish transfer pipe with the closed tank during the air supplying step. (Sinha-OEIS)
W75-07965

FISH POPULATION INVESTIGATIONS,
Wisconsin Dept. of Natural Resources, Madison.
T. L. Wirth, and J. W. Mason.
In: IES Report 28, Environmental Analysis of the Kickapoo River Impoundment, p 125-128. 1 fig, 2 tab, 3 ref. DACW 37-C-0130.

Descriptors: *Cold-water fishing, *Reservoirs, *Fish populations, Wisconsin, Trout, Rough fish, Forage fish, Tributaries, Dissolved oxygen, Fish barriers, Dams, Aeration.
Identifiers: *Kickapoo River(Wis), *La Farge Lake(Wis).

Fish populations were sampled by electro-fishing in three reaches of the Wisconsin Kickapoo River and seven sections of the tributary streams flowing into the Kickapoo below La Farge. Below the La Farge dam site, the game fish population was very sparse and rough and forage fish predominated. The increased number of carp in the summer suggested a large scale seasonal movement. Trout were found in five of the streams; some natural reproduction occurred. Thirty-five different species of rough and forage fish but no endangered species were found in these waters, with white suckers the most common, then creek chub, hog sucker, bluntnose minnow, blacknose dace, common shiner, and Johnny and fantail darters. The La Farge Dam should benefit the fishery downstream. Siltation could occur behind the old power dam, carp may be attracted to the dam in spring and summer, and dissolved oxygen problems may occur. The Kickapoo River should be managed as trout water, existing fish populations eradicated, a fish barrier built to prevent rough fish reinvasion, the old power dam near La Farge removed, and the hypolimnion of the lake aerated to reduce the biochemical oxygen demand and increase dissolved oxygen in the downstream reach. (See also W75-08158) (Buchanan-Davidson-Wisconsin)
W75-08163

fish of lot V, fed untreated Peru meal, resulted in the lowest growth and feeding efficiency. Though the solvents used for the extraction of lipids from the meal were different in Lot I and II, the fish in both lots showed about the same growth and feed efficiency. These values were intermediate between those of white meal and untreated Peru meal. Digestibility of the protein of each diet was measured twice during the experimental period. In both cases, the white fish meal showed the highest value and the untreated Peru meal the lowest. The treatment of Peru meal with solvent increased the digestibility about 4% in both lot I and II. A significant correlation was noted within the 5 lots between digestibility of protein and final body weight. Although Peru meals has some negative factors such as low digestibility and low feed efficiency for the growth of rainbow trout, the meal could be used for fish feed after appropriate.--Copyright 1973, Biological Abstracts, Inc.
W75-08238

STUDIES ON THE CARP CULTURE IN RUNNING WATER POND: VI. MORPHOMETRICAL COMPARISON OF THE COMMON CARP CULTURED IN RUNNING WATER POND, IRRIGATION POND AND FLOATING CAGE, (IN JAPANESE),
Freshwater Fisheries Research Lab., Tokyo (Japan).
K. Chiba.
Bull Freshwater Fish Res Lab, Vol 22, No 1, p 25-38, 1972, Illus. English summary.

Descriptors: *Carp, Farm ponds, *Fish farming.
Identifiers: Japan.

The morphological differences between common carp cultured in running and standing water culture ponds are clarified. Carp cultured in running water were sampled from 2 ponds of T Fish Farm in Gumma prefecture (Japan). Fish cultured in stagnant water conditions were collected from an irrigation pond and a floating culture cage in Lake Suwa in Nagano Prefecture. Analysis by covariance tests of various biometrical characters in these 6 ponds and chemical analysis of carp muscle in all but the floating cage were studied. When compared with carp cultured in the irrigation pond samples from running water ponds were larger in each of the following: body height, body height at the anal position, height of the peduncle, body width, snout-anal fin length, pectoral fin-anal fin length, the weights of body, viscera, visceral adispose tissue and hepatopancreas, and the condition factor. Specimens from the floating cage were similar to those of M Fish Farm in almost all body characters measured. Chemical analysis showed that fat content in the muscle of running water carp was much higher than that of the irrigation pond. Characteristics of carp in running pond water were: larger body height and body width, larger condition factor and heavier viscera and visceral adispose tissue. In some specimens from T-1 visceral adispose tissue was 10% of body weight. The heavy storage of adipose tissues in the viscera seems to be caused by over-feeding of silkworm pupae. Morphometrical differences observed among the carp from 6 ponds is dependent on practices of feeding, especially the amount and composition of diets.--Copyright 1973, Biological Abstracts, Inc.
W75-08240

VARIABILITY OF JUVENILE GRASS CARP CTENOPHARYNGODON IDELLA (VAL.) AND CARP (CYPRINUS CARPIO L. RAISED AT A SOUTH UKRAINIAN FISH HATCHERY, (IN RUSSIAN),
Akademiya Nauk SSSR, Moscow. Inst. of Evolutionary Morphology and Animal Ecology.
D. T. Lekhoa.
Vopr Ikhtiol, Vol 13, No 2, p 367-371, 1973, Illus.

Descriptors: Fish, *Carp, Freshwater fish, *Juvenile fish, *Juvenile growth stages, *Fish management, *Fish hatcheries, Spawning.
Identifiers: Ctenopharyngodon-Idella, *Grass carp, USSR(Ukraine).

The larvae and fry (less than 1 yr old) of the grass carp C. idella and carp C. carpio were raised in experimental and rearing ponds in the Kherson region of the Ukraine, USSR in the summer of 1970. The average water temperature in May was 19.2C, in June 23.5, in July 25.3, and in the 1st half of Aug. 25.2. Owing to unfavorable meteorological conditions and food shortage the juvenile grass carp grew poorly. The maximum retardation of growth was in mid-summer. The juvenile carp, obtained from naturally spawned eggs and fed in a rearing pond on silkworm pupae, reached 17.2 g in 2.5 mo. Retardation of growth was observed between late June and mid-July. The juvenile carp obtained from artifically incubated eggs and reared in a small experimental pond on the same natural food reached a weight of 10.2 g during the same period. With the lack of food, the growth rate of the juveniles decreased steadily, reaching a minimum at the end of summer. Despite this, the juveniles were quite fit and were not inferior to the juveniles obtained from natural spawning with respect to condition and relative length of the intestine. Retardation of the juvenile fishes was accompanied by an increased variability of size and weight and increased positive skewness of the distribution by size-weight classes. The variability indices, especially the skewness coefficient, can serve as a reliable criterion for evaluating the living and biological conditions of juvenile fishes in spawning and rearing ponds. During a period of deterioration of living conditions and retardation of growth, the relative length of the intestine of the juvenile grass carp and carp can decrease considerably.--Copyright 1974, Biological Abstracts, Inc.
W75-08249

BIOLOGY AND MANAGEMENT OF SMALLMOUTH BASS IN ONEIDA LAKE, NEW YORK,
Cornell Univ., Ithaca, N.Y. Dept. of Natural Resources.
For primary bibliographic entry see Field 2H.
W75-08250

CHARACTERISTICS OF A SMALL-LAKE FISHERY AS DETERMINED BY A CREEL CENSUS,
Cornell Univ., Ithaca, N.Y. Dept. of Natural Resources.
For primary bibliographic entry see Field 2H.
W75-08251

OPTIMUM LEVEL OF PROTEIN IN PURIFIED DIET FOR EEL, ANGUILLA JAPONICA,
Freshwater Fish Research Lab., Tokyo (Japan).
For primary bibliographic entry see Field 2I.
W75-08270

THE CONTENT OF AMINO ACIDS IN THE PROTEINS OF LOWER AQUATIC ANIMALS AND ITS SIGNIFICANCE FOR FISH NUTRITION,
Institut fuer Binnenfischerei, Berlin (East Germany).
M. L. Albrecht, and J. Wuensche.
Arch Tierernaehr, Vol 22, No 6, p 423-430, 1972.

Descriptors: Fish, *Aquatic animals, *Chemical analysis, *Proteins, Carp, Trout, Fish diets, Feeds, *Animal growth, *Growth rates.
Identifiers: *Amino acids, Cystine, Methionine, Oncorhynchus-tshawytscha.

The essential amino acid content in the proteins of lower aquatic animals (28 spp. or genera) was determined microbiologically. The methionine content of these proteins reaches only about 62% of that of fish while the average cystine content is twice as high. Calculations of the amino acid content of 2 populations of fish (carp and trout) revealed that the 2 populations were comparatively well-balanced with regard to crude protein although there were great differences in species composition. The qualitative requirements of fish for amino acids are largely equivalent to those of higher vertebrates. Quantitative data were obtained only for salmon (Oncorhynchus tshawytscha). Poor growth in salmon is due to unfavorable ecological factors rather than poor feed quality.--Copyright 1974, Biological Abstracts, Inc.
W75-08311

RESEARCH ON A POPULATION MODEL OF SOCKEYE ONCORHYNCHUS NERKA (WALB.) UNDER CONDITIONS OF VARIABLE FOOD SUPPLY, (IN RUSSIAN),
Akademiya Nauk SSSR, Leningrad. Institut Evolyutsionoi Fiziologii i Biokhimii.
V. V. Sukhanov.
Vopr Ikhtiol, Vol 13, No 4, p 626-632, 1973, Illus.

Descriptors: *Animal growth, *Growth, *Fish management, *Mathematical models, Populations, Fish populations, *Sockeye salmon, Environmental effects, *Analytical techniques.
Identifiers: Oncorhynchus-nerka.

The effect of a fishery, nutritive conditions and variability of the environment on population dynamics and growth pattern of Oncorhynchus nerka (Walb.) was studied with the aid of a mathematical model. The algorithm ALGOL-60 was employed on a BESM-3M electronic calculating machine. The applicability of the Ricker 'stock recruitment' curve for approximation of empirical and model data is considered.--Copyright 1974, Biological Abstracts, Inc.
W75-08312

THE GROWTH AND CHEMICAL COMPOSITION OF THE BODY OF THE JUVENILE CARP CYPRINUS CARPIO L. IN RELATION TO THE QUALITY OF PARENTS AND TEMPERATURE CONDITIONS IN NURSERY PONDS, (IN RUSSIAN),
Sibirskii Nauchno-Issledovatelskii Institut Zhivotnovodstva, Novosibirsk (USSR).
V. A. Korovin, and N. P. Mitskevich.
Vopr Ikhtiol, Vol 13, No 4, p 655-661, 1973, Illus.

Descriptors: *Carp, Juveniles, Fish, Growth, Fish reproduction, Life cycles, Growth stages, Fish management, Fish hatcheries.
Identifiers: Cyprinus-carpio.

The effect of water temperature and the quality of derivation on the growth and fattening of young carp was studied. A combination of paratypic and genotypic factors had maximal influence on growth time, while young from the best quality parents under the best conditions have an advantage in growth over young of the same age derived from parents rated lower with respect to a complex of indices. The chemical composition of the body of newly hatched fish and yearlings is entirely determined by the quality of the parents. The process of accumulation of fat during the 1st yr occurs evenly. Loss of weight and reserve fat in the wintering period in superior young occurs less intensely than in contemporaries of the 1st and 2nd class. The necessity for selective breeding is indicated.--Copyright 1974, Biological Abstracts, Inc.
W75-08313

MATERIAL ON THE MATURATION AND FECUNDITY OF FISH (GENUS SALVELINUS) FROM LAKES IMANDRA AND UMBOZERO (IN RUSSIAN),
Polyarnyi Nauchno-Issledovatelskii i Proektnyi Institut Morskogo Rybnogo Khozyaistva i Okeanografii, Murmansk (USSR).
A. I. Kolyushev.
Vopr Ikhtiol, Vol 13, No 4, p 633-646, 1973, Illus.

Descriptors: Fish, Lakes, Fish populations, *Fish management, *Fish reproduction.
Identifiers: Eubotrium-crassum, Salvelinus, Salvelinus-alpinus, Salvelinus-fontinalis, Salvelinus-leppechini, Salvelinus-malma, *USSR(Lake Imandra), *USSR(Lake Umbozero).

Maturation of the sex glands and fertility were studied in the following species of fish from Lakes Imandra and Umbozero: Salvelinus alpinus, S. leppechini, S. fontinalis, Eubotrium crassum, S. malma (Walb.). The specific of the sexual cycle, which determines the size of a population of fish of the genus Salvelinus in reservoirs is considered. Commercial stocks of these fish can be maintained at a relatively high level by rational organization of fisheries and effective artificial breeding.--Copyright 1974, Biological Abstracts, Inc.
W75-08338

THE UTILIZATION OF THE KAYRAKKUM RESERVOIR FOR FISHERIES (IN RUSSIAN),
Akademiya Nauk Tadzhikskoi SSR, Dushanbe. Institut Zoologii i Parazitologii.
V. A. Maksuniv.
Vopr Ikhtiol. Vol 13, No 4, p 618-625, 1973, Illus.

Descriptors: *Fisheries, *Reservoirs, Fish migration, *Fish management, Crustaceans, Mollusks, Reservoirs.
Identifiers: Abramis-brama, Capoetobrama-kuschakewitschi, Chalcalburnus-chalcoides, Ictiobus-cyprinellus, Mysidae, Pelecus-cultratus, Rutilus-rutilus-aralensis, Tadzhik-SSR, *USSR(Kayrakkuma reservoir).

On the basis of size-weight and age composition of catches of the most important commercial fish of the Kayrakkuma water storage basin (Tadzhik SSR, USSR), an analysis of stocks and migration routes is presented. Abramis brama, Pelecus cultratus, Rutilus rutilus aralensis and Capoetobrama kuschakewitschi are emphasized. An increase in fattening of certain species of fish was noted after settling of Mysidae in 1963. The prognosis for reserves over the next 5 yr is given. The primary measures for ensuring the indicated growth of the fish productivity of the reservoir should be: prevention of catching young valuable fish with an enclosed structure; acclimitization in the water storage basin of crustacea (e.g., Cumacea) mollusks (Monodacna, Corbicula, etc.) and fish (Chalcalburnus chalcoides and possibly Ictiobus cyprinellus); selective catching of unprotected species of fish in the shallow upper reaches of the water storage basin; and introduction of new instruments and fishing methods.--Copyright 1974, Biological Abstracts, Inc.
W75-08339

BEHAVIOR OF PERCH FINGERLINGS, PERCA FLUVIATILIS L., OF DIFFERENT ECOLOGICAL GROUPS IN THE PROGENY OF ONE PAIR OF BREEDERS,
Akademiya Nauk SSSR, Moscow. Institut Biologii Vnutrennykh Vod.
L. K. Il'ina.
Vopr Ikhtiol, Vol 13, No 2, p 350-361, 1973, Illus.

Descriptors: Ponds, Fish handling facilities, *Fish behavior, *Perch, *Fry.
Identifiers: Perca-fluviatilis, Fish tanks.

Investigations were carried out in small ponds (20 x 40 m) and concrete fish tanks (4 x 4 m) in 1966-1968. One pair of breeders was placed in each tank. After spawning, 2 approximately equal ribbons of eggs were selected, 1 of which was transferred to the pond. Three ecological groups formed in the progeny of a single pair of breeders during rearing of the fingerlings: predators, bottom feeders and plankton feeders. The behavior of the fingerlings of each group during their summer growth are discussed. Remaining in the same body of water, these groups occupied independent ecological niches. This enabled the species to utilize the food resources more fully.--Copyright 1974, Biological Abstracts, Inc.
W75-08341

THE SCOPE OF UTILIZING PADDY FIELDS AS FISH HATCHERIES,
University of Agricultural Sciences, Bangalore (India). Fishery Research Station.
V. Muddanna, K. V. Rajagopal, and H. N. Chandrasekhariah.
Mysore J Agric Sci, Vol 5, No 4, p 447-460, 1971.

Descriptors: Fish management, *Fish hatcheries, Fish reproduction, *Fish-rice rotations, *Rice-fish rotations, *Cultivated lands, Plankton, *Fish farming, Cultures, Phosphates.
Identifiers: Insect larvae, *Paddy fields, Rogor, *Culture media.

The plankton, insect larvae, plant residues and physicochemical factors like dissolved O2, pH and phosphate offered a conducive medium for culture of fish in paddy fields. Rescue pits provided in each of the plots were more useful in giving safe refuge to fish both during reduction of water and at the time of harvest. In spite of spraying pesticides (Rogor 0.1%), a certain percentage of fish survived. Plots not sprayed with pesticide gave better survival than those that were sprayed. Though stocking rate was high (100,000/ha spawn, 50,000/ha fry and 4000/ha fingerlings) the rate of survival, growth of fish and fish production was encouraging. While the rate of fish production ranged from 87,574 to 447,500 kg/ha, the rate of recovery was 6.6-52.5%. There was a slight increase in paddy yield in plots stocked with fish. The wide scope prevalent for paddy-cum-fish culture warrants immediate improvement of cultural techniques to overcome present hurdles like supply of water, damage by pesticides and escape through improper bunds.--Copyright 1973, Biological Abstracts, Inc.
W75-08342

TUBERCULOSIS OF FISH AND OTHER HETEROTHERMIC VERTEBRATES (IN POLISH),
Polskie Towarzystwo Nauk Weterynaryjnych, Warsaw (Poland).
For primary bibliographic entry see Field 5C.
W75-08346

PARASITES OF THE NINE-SPINED STICKLEBACK PUNGITIUS PUNGITIUS (L.),
Nature Conservancy, Abbots Ripton (England). Monks Wood Experimental Station.
For primary bibliographic entry see Field 5C.
W75-08347

10. SCIENTIFIC AND TECHNICAL INFORMATION

10C. Secondary Publication And Distribution

THE LITERATURE CITED IN THE WISCONSIN DEPARTMENT OF NATURAL RESOURCES PUBLICATIONS ON WATER RELATED SUBJECTS, 1964-1973,
Wisconsin Univ., Madison. Library School.
For primary bibliographic entry see Field 10D.
W75-07996

ORD PUBLICATIONS SUMMARY.
Environmental Protection Agency, Washington, D.C. Office of Research and Development.
For primary bibliographic entry see Field 5G.
W75-08014

MAMMALIAN TOXICOLOGY AND TOXICITY TO AQUATIC ORGANISMS OF WHITE PHOSPHORUS AND 'PHOSSY WATER", A WATERBORNE MUNITIONS MANUFACTURING WASTE POLLUTANT - A LITERATURE EVALUATION FINAL COMPREHENSIVE REPORT,
Associated Water and Air Resources Engineers, Inc, Nashville, Tenn.
For primary bibliographic entry see Field 5C.
W75-08305

10D. Specialized Information Center Services

THE LITERATURE CITED IN THE WISCONSIN DEPARTMENT OF NATURAL RESOURCES PUBLICATIONS ON WATER RELATED SUBJECTS, 1964-1973,
Wisconsin Univ., Madison. Library School.
R. D. Walker, and G. J. Zuck.
Available from the National Technical Information Service, Springfield, Va. 22161, as PB-241 981, $4.75 in paper copy, $2.25 in microfiche. Wisconsin Water Resources Center, Madison, Technical Report WIS-WRC-75-03, 1975. 87 p, 6 graphs, 34 tab, 31 ref. OWRT B-083-WIS(1), 14-31-0001-4183.

Descriptors: *Documentation, *Publications, *Information Exchange, *Wisconsin, Water quality, Water supply, Water cycle, Planning.
Identifiers: Technical writing, *Information transfer, Information dissemination.

This study is part of a more comprehensive research study to examine the transfer of information in the area of water resources. It deals with the use of literature cited in the Wisconsin Department of Natural Resources publications on topics of water resources, such as, water quality and quantity, water supply, water cycle, planning, and other water subjects. Citations to the literature in all water related publications issued during the period, 1964-73, are analyzed by subject, age, form, and publisher of cited material. Dispersion of cited journal titles is given and comparative analyzes with other relevant studies are made.
W75-07996

USER--ORIENTED RESEARCH DESIGNS,
Nebraska Univ., Lincoln. Water Resources Research Inst.
For primary bibliographic entry see Field 06A.
W75-08206

10F. Preparation Of Reviews

A REVIEW OF THE LITERATURE ON THE USE OF BAYLUSCIDE IN FISHERIES,
National Marine Fisheries Service, Ann Arbor, Mich. Great Lakes Fishery Lab.
For primary bibliographic entry see Field 05C.
W75-08303

A REVIEW OF THE LITERATURE ON THE USE OF ANTIMYCIN IN FISHERIES,
Bureau of Sport Fisheries and Wildlife, LaCrosse, Wis. Fish Control Lab.
For primary bibliographic entry see Field 05C.
W75-08306

SUBJECT INDEX

E

E

AUTHOR INDEX

ORGANIZATIONAL INDEX

ACCESSION NUMBER INDEX

ABSTRACT SOURCES

URCE	ACCESSION NUMBER	TOTAL
CENTERS OF COMPETENCE		
Cornell University, Policy Models for Water Resources Systems	W75-07999 08001--08007 08201--08210 08212--08219	26
Illinois State Water Survey, Hydrology	W75-07891--07927 07929--07932 07934--07935 07937 07939--07953 07974--07976 07982 07984--07991 08189--08193	76
University of Arizona, Arid Land Water Resources	W75-07977--07981 08100--08102 08104--08105 08108--08118 08196--08197 08199 08280--08288	33
University of Florida, Eastern U. S. Water Law	W75-08015--08062 08065--08074 08233	59
University of North Carolina, Metropolitan Water Resources Planning and Management	W75-07954--07961 08011 08171--08188	27
University of Wisconsin, Eutrophication	W75-08119--08126 08128--08169 08194	51
University of Wisconsin, Water Resources Economics	W75-08012	1
. STATE WATER RESOURCES RESEARCH INSTITUTES	W75-07992--07996 08013, 08098 08221--08223 08225	11

ABSTRACT SOURCES

SOURCE	ACCESSION NUMBER	TO
C. OTHER		
Agricultural Research Service	W75-08099	
Army Engineer Waterways Experiment Station	W75-08289--08299 08301	
BioSciences Information Service	W75-07853, 07928 07933, 07936 07938, 07969 07983, 08000 08008, 08010 08063--08064 08076, 08083 08088, 08090 08103 08106--08107 08127, 08170 08198, 08200 08211, 08220 08224, 08226 08237--08277 08300 08308--08350	
Effects of Pollutants on Aquatic Life (Katz)	W75-08302--08307	
Environmental Protection Agency	W75-07966--07968 07970--07973 08014 08227--08232 08278--08279	
Ocean Engineering Information Service (Patents)	W75-07854--07856 07962--07965	
Office of Water Research and Technology	W75-07851, 07890 07997--07998	
U. S. Geological Survey	W75-07857--07889 08009, 08195	
Vanderbilt University, Metals Pollution	W75-07852, 08075 08077--08082 08084--08087 08089 08091--08097 08234--08236	

* U. S. GOVERNMENT PRINTING OFFICE: 1975 O - 210-951 (3)

CENTERS OF COMPETENCE AND THEIR SUBJECT COVERAGE

- Ground and surface water hydrology at the Illinois State Water Survey and the Water Resources Division of the U.S. Geological Survey, U.S. Department of the Interior.
- Metropolitan water resources planning and management at the Center for Urban and Regional Studies of University of North Carolina.
- Eastern United States water law at the College of Law of the University of Florida.
- Policy models of water resources systems at the Department of Water Resources Engineering of Cornell University.
- Water resources economics at the Water Resources Center of the University of Wisconsin.
- Eutrophication at the Water Resources Center of the University of Wisconsin.
- Water resources of arid lands at the Office of Arid Lands Studies of the University of Arizona.
- Water well construction technology at the National Water Well Association.
- Water-related aspects of nuclear radiation and safety at the Oak Ridge National Laboratory.
- Water resource aspects of the pulp and paper industry at the Institute of Paper Chemistry.

Supported by the Environmental Protection Agency in cooperation with WRSIC

- Effect on water quality of irrigation return flows at the Department of Agricultural Engineering of Colorado State University.
- Agricultural livestock waste at East Central State College, Oklahoma.
- Municipal wastewater treatment technology at the Franklin Institute Research Laboratories.

Subject Fields

1 NATURE OF WATER

2 WATER CYCLE

3 WATER SUPPLY AUGMENTATION AND CONSERVATION

4 WATER QUANTITY MANAGEMENT AND CONTROL

5 WATER QUALITY MANAGEMENT AND PROTECTION

6 WATER RESOURCES PLANNING

7 RESOURCES DATA

8 ENGINEERING WORKS

9 MANPOWER, GRANTS, AND FACILITIES

10 SCIENTIFIC AND TECHNICAL INFORMATION

INDEXES

SUBJECT INDEX

AUTHOR INDEX

ORGANIZATIONAL INDEX

ACCESSION NUMBER INDEX

ABSTRACT SOURCES

SELECTED WATER SOURCES BSTRACTS

VOLUME 8, NUMBER 17
SEPTEMBER 1, 1975

W75-08351 -- W75-08850
CODEN: SWRABW

SELECTED WATER RESOURCES ABSTRACTS is published semimonthly for the Water Resources Scientific Information Center (WRSIC) by the National Technical Information Service (NTIS), U.S. Department of Commerce. NTIS was established September 2, 1970, as a new primary operating unit under the Assistant Secretary of Commerce for Science and Technology to improve public access to the many products and services of the Department. Information services for Federal scientific and technical report literature previously provided by the Clearinghouse for Federal Scientific and Technical Information are now provided by NTIS.

SELECTED WATER RESOURCES ABSTRACTS is available to Federal agencies, contractors, or grantees in water resources upon request to: Manager, Water Resources Scientific Information Center, Office of Water Research and Technology, U.S. Department of the Interior, Washington, D. C. 20240.

SELECTED WATER RESOURCES ABSTRACTS is also available on subscription from the National Technical Information Service. Annual subscription rates are: To the SWRA Journal, $75 ($95 foreign); to the Journal & Annual Index, $100 ($125 foreign); to the Annual Index only, $50 ($65 foreign). Certain documents abstracted in this journal can be purchased from the NTIS at prices indicated in the entry. Prepayment is required.

SELECTED
WATER RESOURCES ABSTRACTS

A Semimonthly Publication of the Water Resources Scientific Information Center,
Office of Water Research and Technology, U.S. Department of the Interior

VOLUME 8, NUMBER 17
SEPTEMBER 1, 1975

W75-08351 -- W75-08850

The Secretary of the U. S. Department of the Interior has determined that the publication of this periodical is necessary in the transaction of the public business required by law of this Department. Use of funds for printing this periodical has been approved by the Director of the Office of Management and Budget through August 31, 1978.

As the Nation's principal conservation agency, the Department of the Interior has responsibility for most of our nationally owned public lands and natural resources. This includes fostering the wisest use of our land and water resources, protecting our fish and wildlife, preserving the environmental and cultural values of our national parks and historical places, and providing for the enjoyment of life through outdoor recreation. The Department assesses our energy and mineral resources and works to assure that their development is in the best interests of all our people. The Department also has a major responsibility for American Indian reservation communities and for people who live in Island Territories under U.S. administration.

FOREWORD

Selected Water Resources Abstracts, a semimonthly journal, includes abstracts of current and earlier pertinent monographs, journal articles, reports, and other publication formats. The contents of these documents cover the water-related aspects of the life, physical, and social sciences as well as related engineering and legal aspects of the characteristics, conservation, control, use, or management of water. Each abstract includes a full bibliographical citation and a set of descriptors or identifiers which are listed in the **Water Resources Thesaurus.** Each abstract entry is classified into ten fields and sixty groups similar to the water resources research categories established by the Committee on Water Resources Research of the Federal Council for Science and Technology.

WRSIC IS NOT PRESENTLY IN A POSITION TO PROVIDE COPIES OF DOCUMENTS ABSTRACTED IN THIS JOURNAL. Sufficient bibliographic information is given to enable readers to order the desired documents from local libraries or other sources.

Selected Water Resources Abstracts is designed to serve the scientific and technical information needs of scientists, engineers, and managers as one of several planned services of the Water Resources Scientific Information Center (WRSIC). The Center was established by the Secretary of the Interior and has been designated by the Federal Council for Science and Technology to serve the water resources community by improving the communication of water-related research results. The Center is pursuing this objective by co-ordinating and supplementing the existing scientific and technical information activities associated with active research and investigation program in water resources.

To provide WRSIC with input, selected organizations with active water resources research programs are supported as "centers of competence" responsible for selecting, abstracting, and indexing from the current and earlier pertinent literature in specified subject areas.

Additional "centers of competence" have been established in cooperation with the Environmental Protection Agency. A directory of the Centers appears on inside back cover.

Supplementary documentation is being secured from established discipline-oriented abstracting and indexing services. Currently an arrangement is in effect whereby the BioScience Information Service of Biological Abstracts supplies WRSIC with relevant references from the several subject areas of interest to our users. In addition to Biological Abstracts, references are acquired from Bioresearch Index which are without abstracts and therefore also appear abstractless in SWRA. Similar arrangements with other producers of abstracts are contemplated as planned augmentation of the information base.

The input from these Centers, and from the 51 Water Resources Research Institutes administered under the Water Resources Research Act of 1964, as well as input from the grantees and contractors of the Office of Water Research and Technology and other Federal water resource agencies with which the

Center has agreements becomes the information base from which this journal is, and other information services will be, derived; these services include bibliographies, specialized indexes, literature searches, and state-of-the-art reviews.

Comments and suggestions concerning the contents and arrangements of this bulletin are welcome.

Water Resources Scientific Information Center
Office of Water Research and Technology
U.S. Department of the Interior
Washington, D. C. 20240

CONTENTS

WATER RESOURCES ABSTRACTS

2. WATER CYCLE

2A. General

THE ESTIMATION OF (RHO) IN THE FIRST-ORDER AUTOREGRESSIVE MODEL: A BAYESIAN APPROACH,
Massachusetts Inst. of Tech., Cambridge. Dept. of Civil Engineering.
R. L. Lenton, I. Rodriguez-Iturbe, and J. C. Schaake, Jr.
Water Resources Research, Vol 10, No 2, p 227-241, April 1974. 11 fig, 5 tab, 13 ref. OWRR C-4118(9021)(3).

Descriptors: *Regression analysis, *Stochastic processes, *Markov processes, Synthetic hydrology, Systems analysis, Probability, Variability, Design criteria, Model studies.
Identifiers: Bayes methods.

Three general approaches are given to derive marginal posterior probability density functions for the autocorrelation coefficient of the first-order normal autoregressive model. Bayes estimators can be obtained for a given loss function. The different approaches are based on varying assumptions about the incidental parameters of the model and are shown numerically to be approximately equivalent with respect to their mean and variance. A comparison is made between the Bayes estimator and some classical estimators on the basis of the risk function and the expected risk. The risk functions are determined by Monte Carlo methods for quadratic, symmetric linear, and various asymmetric linear loss functions. The Bayes estimators are shown to be considerably advantageous, especially when the sample size is small. The Bayes estimators are shown to be extremely robust under changes of the loss function. (Knapp-USGS)
W75-08387

SOME COMMENTS ON TESTING RANDOM TOPOLOGY STREAM NETWORK MODELS,
State Univ. of New York, Buffalo. Dept. of Geography.
For primary bibliographic entry see Field 2E.
W75-08437

PARAMETERIZATION OF SURFACE MOISTURE AND EVAPORATION RATE IN A PLANETARY BOUNDARY LAYER MODEL,
National Oceanic and Atmospheric Administration, Oak Ridge, Tenn. Air Resources Atmospheric Turbulence and Diffusion Lab.
For primary bibliographic entry see Field 2D.
W75-08451

EROSION MODELING ON A WATERSHED,
Agricultural Research Service, Morris, Minn. North Central Soil Conservation Research Center.
For primary bibliographic entry see Field 2J.
W75-08459

PROCESS IN DATA COLLECTION AND DISSEMINATION IN WATER RESOURCES, 1964-1974,
Geological Survey, Reston, Va. Office of Water Data Coordination.
For primary bibliographic entry see Field 7A.
W75-08505

EFFECT OF ATMOSPHERIC STABILITY AND WIND DIRECTION ON WATER TEMPERATURE PREDICTIONS FOR A THERMALLY-LOADED STREAM,
Pennsylvania State Univ., University Park. School of Forest Resources.
For primary bibliographic entry see Field 5B.
W75-08576

ASPECTS OF HYDROLOGICAL EFFECTS OF URBANIZATION.
American Society of Civil Engineers, New York. Task Committee on the Effects of Urbanization on Low Flow, Total Runoff, Infiltration, and Ground-Water Recharge.
For primary bibliographic entry see Field 4C.
W75-08697

DYNAMIC BEHAVIOR MODEL OF EPHEMERAL STREAM,
Agricultural Research Service, Tucson, Ariz. Southwest Watershed Research Center.
For primary bibliographic entry see Field 2E.
W75-08699

THE SEASONAL VARIATION OF THE HYDROLOGIC CYCLE AS SIMULATED BY A GLOBAL MODEL OF THE ATMOSPHERE,
National Oceanic and Atmospheric Administration, Princeton, N.J. Geophysical Fluid Dynamics Lab.
S. Manabe, and J. L. Holloway, Jr.
Journal of Geophysical Research, Vol 80, No 12, p 1617-1649, April 20, 1975. 32 fig, 1 tab, 42 ref.

Descriptors: *Model studies, *Atmosphere, *Hydrologic cycle, *Simulation analysis, Evaporation, Temperature, Winds, Water vapor, Moisture, Soil moisture, Snow cover, Arid lands, Snow, Seasonal, Numerical analysis, Hydrology, Climates, Precipitation(Atmospheric), Snowmelt, Wet climates, Runoff, Tropical regions, Mountains, Water balance, Latitudinal studies.
Identifiers: *Global model, Insolation, Grid network, Continents, Koppen climate types.

A numerical model was demonstrated to be capable of reproducing many of the basic features of the seasonal variation of hydrology and climate on a global scale. The model of the atmosphere with a seasonal variation of insolation and sea surface temperature was integrated for over 3 simulation years on a finite difference grid network having a nearly uniform horizontal resolution of about 265 km. There were 11 levels in the model from 80 m to 31 km above the ground, with realistic continents having smoothed topography. In addition to wind, temperature, pressure, and water vapor, the model simulated rainfall, snowfall, and evaporation at the surface. The simulated precipitation and other hydrologic quantities were compared with those derived from observed data. In addition, the correspondence between the distribution of precipitation rate and those of other relevant quantities, such as sea level pressure and kinetic energy of transient disturbances, was examined. Sensitivity studies of this character can help determine the strategy for further improvements of the parameterization of hydrologic processes. (Roberts-ISWS)
W75-08704

THE TIDAL ENERGETICS OF NARRAGANSETT BAY,
Rhode Island Univ., Kingston. Graduate School of Oceanography.
For primary bibliographic entry see Field 2L.
W75-08705

DEVELOPMENT OF A WATER PLANNING MODEL FOR MONTANA,
Montana State Univ., Bozeman. Dept. of Industrial Engineering and Computer Science.
For primary bibliographic entry see Field 6A.
W75-08811

WINTER STORM AND FLOOD ANALYSES, NORTHWEST INTERIOR,
Agricultural Research Service, Boise, Idaho. Northwest Watershed Research Center.
For primary bibliographic entry see Field 2E.
W75-08818

CALIBRATION OF WATERSHED WETNESS AND PREDICTION OF FLOOD VOLUME FROM SMALL WATERSHEDS IN HUMID REGION,
Pennsylvania Dept. of Environmental Resources, Harrisburg.
S. L. Chiang.
In: Hydraulic Engineering and the Environment; Proceedings of the 21st Annual Hydraulic Division Specialty Conference, Montana State University, Bozeman, August 15-17, 1973. American Society of Civil Engineers, New York, p 371-382, 1973. 6 fig, 13 ref.

Descriptors: *Flood discharge, *Runoff, *Moisture content, Floods, Volume, Forecasting, Equations, Watersheds(Basins), Precipitation(Atmospheric), Antecedent precipitation, Antecedent moisture content, Temperature, Evapotranspiration, Vegetation effects, Hydrology, Meteorology, Pennsylvania.

Given a storm total, the runoff volume of a watershed is mainly determined by the antecedent wetness of the watershed. Various investigations have shown that there is no relationship between the return period of a rainfall and the return period of the peak resulting from the rainfall. Since the peak is directly related to runoff volume, it can be concluded that the antecedent watershed wetness is mostly responsible for the difference. Calibration of watershed wetness is fundamental to volume prediction which is, in turn, a prerequisite to peak prediction. The objective of the study was to develop storm runoff volume prediction equations through a process by which watershed wetness can be calibrated. For comparison, another approach requiring a direct correlation between the runoff volume and its causal factors was developed. (See also W75-08786) (Sims-ISWS)
W75-08819

THE IHD--TEN YEARS OF PROGRESS,
National Committe for the International Hydrological Decade, Washington, D.C.
L. A. Heindl.
In: A Decade of Progress in Water Resources: American Water Resources Association Proceedings Series No 19, p 10-16, March 1974. 1 ref.

Descriptors: *International Hydrological Decade, *Reviews, *Hydrology, Foreign countries, Data collections, Information exchange, Long-term planning, Water resources, Economics, Education.
Identifiers: *IHD accomplishments.

The International Hydrological Decade (IHD) ends this year (1974). Its principal international success appears to have been its use to enhance and enlarge hydrological services in many countries around the globe. As a result, there will be greatly increased sources of water data for scientific studies and social and economic applications. In North America, the outstanding success has been the International Field Year for the Great Lakes, conducted together with Canada. The Decade worked a gradual but definite shift in emphasis from scientific research to beneficial applications of scientific technology, particularly in developing countries. Recognizing the overall accomplishments of the Decade, the United Nations Educational, Scientific and Cultural Organization (UNESCO) will launch an open-ended International Hydrological Program (IHP) beginning in 1975. The United States has voted to participate in the IHP. The main objectives of the IHP paraphrase those of the Decade. (Woodard-USGS)
W75-08829

2B. Precipitation

PRECIPITATION CHARACTERISTICS IN THE NORTHEAST BRAZIL DRY REGION,
Colorado State Univ., Fort Collins. Dept. of Atmospheric Science.
R. P. L. Ramos.
Journal of Geophysical Research, Vol 80, No 12, p 1665-1678, April 20, 1975. 17 fig, 5 tab, 24 ref. NSF Grants GA-32589X2, GA-29147.

Descriptors: *Precipitation(Atmospheric), *Climatology, *Rainfall disposition, *Meteorology, Cloud cover, Temperature, Pressure, Winds, South America, Geographical regions, Atmosphere, Moisture content, Satellites(Artificial), Rainfall, Tropical regions.
Identifiers: *Diurnal rainfall distribution, *Brazil.

The general meteorological conditions and precipitation characteristics in the Northeast Brazil dry region during its rainy season from December through April were discussed. It was found that most of the yearly rainfall comes in six to eight episodes from organized weather systems which move from east to west with about the same speed (approximately 5 m/s) as the lower tropospheric wind flow. These systems appear not to be of local origin. Rainfall was shown to be inversely correlated with the regional subsidence. An interesting and previously unknown diurnal rainfall variation was found. Orographic influences appear to act to modulate the weather systems and develop upslope and downslope winds. This produces rainfall in the morning over the lowland regions and in the afternoon over the hills and more elevated regions. Extensive comparisons of the rain systems with other tropical regions were made. Other characteristics were discussed. (Huff-ISWS)
W75-08421

OPTICAL CONSTANTS OF WATER IN THE INFRARED,.
Kansas State Univ., Manhattan. Dept. of Physics.
For primary bibliographic entry see Field 1A.
W75-08422

EXTREME WAVE CONDITIONS DURING HURRICANE CAMILLE,
Naval Oceanographic Office, Washington, D.C.
For primary bibliographic entry see Field 2L.
W75-08427

A STOCHASTIC ANALYSIS OF EXTREME DROUGHTS,
Arizona Univ., Tucson. Dept. of Hydrology and Water Resources.
V. K. Gupta, and L. Duckstein.
Water Resources Research, Vol 11, No 2, p 221-228, April 1975. 9 fig, 1 tab, 19 ref. NSF Grants GK-35915, GK-35791.

Descriptors: *Stochastic processes, *Droughts, *Model studies, Dry seasons, Probability, Rainfall, Hydrology, Precipitation(Atmospheric), Theoretical analysis, Numerical analysis, Rainfall intensity, Regional analysis, Statistical model, Statistical methods.
Identifiers: Poisson process.

A stochastic analysis was performed on the extreme drought duration defined to be the maximum dry interval for a point rainfall process. The assumptions underlying previous analyses were generalized to those of a nonhomogeneous Poisson process. Analytical results, which seem intractable in general, were derived for two particular forms of the intensity function of the Poisson process; for a general intensity function, simulation was recommended. Next, small time intervals such as the growing season of a crop were considered so that the assumption of a homogeneous Poisson rainfall process could be made and the effect of parameter estimation on the theoretical results could be studied qualitatively. To illustrate this point, four estimates of the intensity parameter were calculated by using precipitation data from Chicago and Austin. A good agreement was found between the theoretical and empirical distribution functions for the two parameter estimates calculated by use of the developed model; on the other hand, a substantial bias was present for parameters calculated directly from the data. Finally, an approach was schematically indicated to extend the model to regional droughts by using stochastic superposition. (Dawes-ISWS)
W75-08433

EVALUATION OF THE REPRESENTATIVENESS OF THE PRECIPITATION NETWORK IN RELATION TO THE SPATIAL INTERPOLATION OF PRECIPITATION,
V. A. Rumyantsev, and S. V. Shanochkin.
Soviet Hydrology, Selected Papers No. 3, p 199-206, 1973. 3 fig, 8 ref. Translated from Transactions of the State Hydrologic Institute (Trudy GGI), No. 196, p 215-227, 1973.

Descriptors: *Regional analysis, *Networks, *Precipitation(Atmospheric), *Statistical methods, Least squares method, Statistics, Hydrologic aspects, Spatial distribution, Rainfall disposition, Diurnal distribution, Seasonal.
Identifiers: *USSR, Network density.

One major obstacle to improving the accuracy of hydrologic computations and forecasts is the low density of the precipitation network. The representativeness of the network with respect to the problem of spatial interpolation was evaluated from corrected views on the statistical structure of precipitation fields. The least squares principle, in which the average of the sum of squares of deviations is interpolated from actual values, was taken as a measure of dispersion. The representativeness of the precipitation network was evaluated from the data for two regions: the Valdai Hills and the Central regions. Investigated was precipitation over semidiurnal, diurnal, 10-day, and seasonal summation periods. The estimated correlation functions for the interpolation of precipitation values at points having observational data and a comparison of the reconstructed with the actual values showed that, with the exception of small number of cases, the root-mean-square errors obtained by computation are close to the actual errors. This indicates that the estimates of the correlation functions are adequate and that it is possible to use them to interpolate precipitation values at points where direct observations are not obtained. Results showed that the optimum network density required one station per 16 sq km for diurnal precipitation and one station per 550 sq km for seasonal precipitation. Such a dense precipitation network would be difficult to justify economically. It was recommended that several experimental precipitation measuring areas be created and coordinated with radar methods and meteorological satellites to study the statistical structure of precipitation fields. (Humphreys-ISWS)
W75-08444

PARAMETERIZATION OF SURFACE MOISTURE AND EVAPORATION RATE IN A PLANETARY BOUNDARY LAYER MODEL,
National Oceanic and Atmospheric Administration, Oak Ridge, Tenn. Air Resources Atmospheric Turbulence and Diffusion Lab.
For primary bibliographic entry see Field 2D.
W75-08451

A DIRECT SOLUTION OF THE SPHERICAL-HARMONICS APPROXIMATION TO THE TRANSFER EQUATION FOR A PLANE-PARALLEL, NONHOMOGENEOUS ATMOSPHERE,
California Univ., Livermore. Lawrence Livermore Lab.
For primary bibliographic entry see Field 5A.
W75-08661

THE SEASONAL VARIATION OF THE HYDROLOGIC CYCLE AS SIMULATED BY A GLOBAL MODEL OF THE ATMOSPHERE,
National Oceanic and Atmospheric Administration, Princeton, N.J. Geophysical Fluid Dynamics Lab.
For primary bibliographic entry see Field 2A.
W75-08704

METEOROLOGY AND HYDROLOGY OF RAPID CITY FLOOD,
Corps of Engineers, Omaha, Nebr. Hydrology and Meteorology Section.
For primary bibliographic entry see Field 2E.
W75-08824

2C. Snow, Ice, and Frost

ECOLOGY OF THE GREEN KRYOPHILIC ALGAE FROM BELANSKE TATRY MOUNTAINS (CZECHOSLOVAKIA),
Ceskoslovenska Akademie Ved, Trebon. Inst. of Microbiology.
For primary bibliographic entry see Field 5C.
W75-08393

CONCERNING THE EFFECT OF ANISOTROPIC SCATTERING AND FINITE DEPTH OF THE DISTRIBUTION OF SOLAR RADIATION IN SNOW,
High Altitude Observatory, Boulder, Colo.
B. R. Barkstrom, and C. W. Querfeld.
Journal of Glaciology, Vol 14, No 70, p 107-124, 1975. 6 fig, 1 tab, 23 ref, 1 append.

Descriptors: *Snow, *Model studies, *Solar radiation, Reflectance, Mathematical models, analysis, Albedo, Depth, Optical properties, Anisotropy, Radiation, Diffusivity, Isotropy.

It was shown that anisotropic scattering with a strong forward peak can give reasonable agreement with angular reflectance data for snow. As a result of the forward peak, solar radiation penetrates deeper into the medium, when measured in terms of photon mean free paths, than it does for isotropic scattering. The radiation transmitted directly through finite slabs can be seen to an optical depth of seven, and decreases much more rapidly with optical depth than does the diffusely transmitted (scattered) radiation. It was suggested that measurements of the flux extinction coefficient using the light transmitted through finite layers of snow (under 2.5 cm thick) may lead to serious errors if extrapolated to effectively semi-infinite layers below the boundary layer in the latter. An appendix contains mathematical analysis that can be used to develop working numerical routines for computers. (Humphreys-ISWS)
W75-08405

QUATERNARY GLACIATIONS IN THE ANDES OF NORTH-CENTRAL CHILE,
Saskatchewan Univ., Regina. Dept. of Geography.
C. N. Caviedes, and R. Paskoff.
Journal of Glaciology, Vol 14, No 70, p 155-170, 1975. 7 fig, 1 tab, 44 ref.

Descriptors: *Glaciation, *South America, *Quaternary period, Glaciology, Geologic history, Geomorphology, Topography, Mountains, Valleys, Cirques, Glacial drift, Climates, Geology.
Identifiers: *Chile, Andes Mountains, Laguna, Tapado, Portillo, Guardia Vieja, Salto del Soldado.

The extension of the Quaternary glaciations was studied in the semi-arid Andes of north-central Chile, where the glacial modeling is striking. In the Elqui valley (latitude 30S), two glacial advances were identified reaching down to 3100 m (Laguna glaciation) and 2500 m (Tapado glaciation). In the Aconcagua valley (latitude 33S), moraines from three major glacial advances were found, at 2800 m (Portillo glaciation), 1600 m (Guardia Vieja glaciation), and 1300 m (Salto del Soldado glaciation). The Quaternary glaciations were linked with a decrease of temperature, but more significantly with a marked increase of precipitation probably related to an equatorward shift of 5-6 degrees of the austral polar front. The results obtained in the semi-arid Chilean Andes were correlated with those recently reported from other sectors of the southern Andes. Glacial advances in the Andes of central Chile between latitudes 30S and 41S were tabulated. (Humphreys-ISWS)
W75-08406

LIQUID BRINE IN ICE SHELVES,
Scott Polar Research Inst., Cambridge (England).
R. H. Thomas.
Journal of Glaciology, Vol 14, No 70, p 125-136, 1975. 5 fig, 13 ref, 1 append.

Descriptors: *Ice, *Saline water, *Model studies, *On-site investigations, *Brines, Temperature, Mathematical studies, Flow, Flow rates, *Antarctic, Thermocline, Firn, Percolation, Heat flow.
Identifiers: *Brunt Ice Shelf(Ant).

Holes drilled into thin areas of the Brunt Ice Shelf encounter a layer of liquid brine less than 1 m thick approximately at sea-level. Assuming the brine to be moving horizontally, analysis of its effects on thermal equilibrium gives an estimate of steady-state annual brine flow that is in good agreement with the value deduced from a percolation model. The effect of firn density on percolation rates is such that the slope of an active brine layer increases rapidly as ice thickness increases. However, the heat transport model predicts that brine layers are unlikely to be active in both very thick and very thin ice shelves. An appendix contains mathematical analysis for temperature gradient in the firn, temperature gradient in impure ice, and significance of brine trapped within the superimposed ice. (Humphreys-ISWS)
W75-08407

THE FORMATION OF BRINE DRAINAGE FEATURES IN YOUNG SEA ICE,
Washington Univ., Seattle. Dept. of Oceanography.
L. I. Eide, and S. Martin.
Journal of Glaciology, Vol 14, No 70, p 137-154, 1975. 10 fig, 1 tab, 23 ref, 1 append. NR307-252 ONR Contract N00014-67-A-0103-0007.

Descriptors: *Sea ice, *Laboratory tests, *Brines, Laboratory equipment, Saline water, Ice-water interfaces, Boundaries(Surfaces), Instrumentation, Ice, Channels, Flow, Drainage, Drainage systems, Thermal properties, Freezing.
Identifiers: *Brine pockets.

Laboratory experiments on the growth of sea ice in a very thin plastic tank filled with salt water, cooled from above, and insulated with thermopane, clearly show the formation and development of brine drainage channels. The sea-water freezing cell is 0.3 cm thick by 35 cm wide by 50 cm deep; the thermopane insulation permits the ice interior to be photographed. Experimental observation showed that vertical channels with diameters of 1 to 3 mm and associated smaller feeder channels extend throughout the ice sheet. Close examination of the brine channels show that their diameter at the icewater interface is much narrower than higher up in the ice, so that the channel has a 'neck' at the interface. Further, oscillations occur in the brine channels, in that brine flows out of the channel followed by a flow of sea-water up into the channel. Theoretically, a qualitative theory based on the difference in pressure head between the brine inside the ice and the sea-water provides a consistent explanation for the formation of the channels, and the onset of a convective instability explains the existence of the neck. An analysis based on the presence of the brine-channel neck provides an explanation for the observed oscillations. An appendix contains an analysis of the thermal consequences of brine movement inside the ice. (Humphreys-ISWS)
W75-08408

STEAM, HOT-WATER AND ELECTRICAL THERMAL DRILLS FOR TEMPERATE GLACIERS,
Centre National de la Recherche Scientifique, Grenoble (France). Laboratoire de Glaciologie.
F. Gillet.
Journal of Glaciology, Vol 14, No 70, p 171-179, 1975. 6 fig, 18 ref.

Descriptors: *Glaciers, *Boreholes, *Drilling equipment, *Exploration, Glaciology, Temperate, Drilling, Steam, On-site investigations.
Identifiers: Hot-water drills, Electro-thermal drills.

The study of temperate glaciers has led to the development of three drilling processes. The steam drill used for ablation stakes is easily portable and its speed is 30-40 m/h for the first 10 m. A fairly large but irregular hole can be drilled to a depth of 100 m in less than 5 h with the hot-water drill. The electro-thermal drill, usable to great depths, is particularly suitable for rapid drilling (15 m/h and more) of small diameter holes (25 mm) with easily portable equipment. Design of the electro-thermal drill was described. (Humphreys-ISWS)
W75-08409

THE ORIGIN OF FOLIATION IN GLACIERS: EVIDENCE FROM SOME NORWEGIAN EXAMPLES,
Eidgenoessische Technische Hochschule, Zurich (Switzerland). Geologisches Institut.
M. J. Hambrey.
Journal of Glaciology, Vol 14, No 70, p 181-185, 1975. 3 fig, 14 ref.

Descriptors: *Glaciers, Europe, *Stratification, Ice, Stratigraphy, On-site investigations, Geomorphology.
Identifiers: *Norway(Okstindan), *Foliation, Basal foliation.

Studies of Norwegian glaciers indicate that foliation is frequently derived from sedimentary stratification. Shearing and accompanying recrystallization of the ice is most likely to occur in the planes of the sedimentary layers, particularly where they are steeply dipping and have a longitudinal trend. Foliation not related to pre-existing layering is uncommon. Steeply dipping transverse layers, often referred to as foliation, are believed to be simply the traces of former crevasses. Studies of other glaciers are necessary to determine whether or not this is an isolated occurrence. (Humphreys-ISWS)
W75-08410

DROP STONES RESULTING FROM SNOW-AVALANCHE DEPOSITION ON LAKE ICE,
University of Western Ontario, London. Dept. of Geography.
B. H. Luckman.
Journal of Glaciology, Vol 14, No 70, p 186-188, 1975. 1 fig, 9 ref.

Descriptors: *Avalanches, *Geomorphology, *Lake ice, Snow, Lakes, Rocks, Ablation, *Canada, Erosion, Debris avalanches, Deposition(Sediments).
Identifiers: Scree, Lake Helen, Drop stones.

Dirty snow avalanches have been observed to carry considerable amounts of rock debris onto lake ice at the foot of scree slopes. As ice breaks up in the spring thaw, this material is carried back

and forth on ice floes and is gradually deposited in the lake. In some areas this produces typical drop stones of rock debris in predominantly fine-grained deposits. Most avalanche debris is very angular which enables avalanche drop stones to be differentiated from those of glacial or other drift-ice origins. However, where avalanches incorporate glacial debris, such deposits may be indistinguishable from those formed by floating glacier ice. (Humphreys-ISWS)
W75-08411

RADIO SOUNDINGS ON TRAPRIDGE GLACIER, YUKON TERRITORY, CANADA,
Department of the Environment, Calgary (Alberta). Inland Waters Directorate.
R. H. Goodman, G. K. C. Clarke, G. T. Jarvis, and S. G. Collins.
Journal of Glaciology, Vol 14, No 70, p 79-84, 1975. 4 fig, 2 tab, 10 ref.

Descriptors: *Glaciers, *Sounding, On-site investigations, Radar, Depth, Surveys, Measurement, Evaluation, Temperate, *Canada.
Identifiers: *Trapridge Glacier(Yukon Territory), Surge glaciers.

As part of a program to study surge-type glaciers, a radar-depth survey, using a frequency of 620 MHz, was made of Trapridge Glacier, Yukon Territory. Soundings were taken at 26 locations on the glacier surface and a maximum ice thickness of 143 m was measured. A rapid change in surface slope in the lower ablation region marks the boundary between active and stagnant ice and is suggestive of an 'ice dam' or the water 'collection zone' postulated by Robin and Weertman for surging glaciers. (Humphreys-ISWS)
W75-08412

EFFECT OF INVERSION WINDS ON TOPOGRAPHIC DETAIL AND MASS BALANCE ON INLAND ICE SHEETS,
Ohio State Univ. Research Foundation, Columbus. Inst. of Polar Studies; and Ohio State Univ., Columbus. Dept. of Geology and Mineralogy.
I. M. Whillans.
Journal of Glaciology, Vol 14, No 70, p 85-90, 1975. 1 fig, 20 ref. NSF Grant GV-26137X.

Descriptors: *Glaciers, *Mathematical studies, *Snow, *Antarctic, Ice, Winds, Snowpacks, Topography, Slopes, Profiles, Surfaces, Analysis, Temperature.
Identifiers: Marie Byrd Land, Inversion winds, Accumulated snow, Mass balance.

Steady-state gravity flow of air (inversion wind) on sloping snow-covered ice sheets was analyzed for sensitivity to local topography. Topographic features of the order of a few kilometers or less in length are too small to affect the direction and speed of this air flow. Air flow on a larger scale should, however, conform closely to topography. Surface roughness on ice sheets is consistent with these results. Features of length shorter than a few kilometers (drifts and sastrugi) are transient, but longer features (surface undulations) remain essentially unaltered for many years. On the longer scale, inversion wind speed and therefore the amount of drifting and blowing snow should vary with the surface slope even where slope changes by as little as 0.1%. Observed variations in surface mass balance (accumulated snow) in upper Marie Byrd Land, Antarctica, support this hypothesis. Snow drift and inversion winds thus constitute a feed-back mechanism on the form of ice sheets and some of the topographic detail, formerly attributed to ice-flow character alone, may be in large part due to this mechanism. (Humphreys-ISWS)
W75-08413

WIND REGIMES AND HEAT EXCHANGE ON GLACIER DE SAINT-SORLIN,
Centre National de la Recherche Scientifique, Grenoble (France). Laboratoire de Glaciologie.
S. Martin.
Journal of Glaciology, Vol 14, No 70, p 91-105, 1975. 11 fig, 2 tab, 14 ref.

Descriptors: *Glaciers, *Winds, *On-site investigations, On-site data collections, Measurement, Evaluation, Analysis, Heat balance, Temperature, Velocity, Meteorological data, Humidity, Radiation, Snowmelt, Runoff, Ablation, Profiles.
Identifiers: *France(Glacier de Saint-Sorlin), Katabatic flow, Glacier wind.

During the summers of 1969 and 1970, data recorded in the ablation zone of the Glacier de Saint-Sorlin (Massif des Grandes Rousses, France) included temperature, air moisture, and wind profiles, as well as the radiation balance and the daily ablation. Numerous profiles characterize a katabatic flow following the line of greatest slope, and there appears to be a correlation between the speed of the 'glacier wind' and the corresponding temperature gradients. Computed according to Prandtl's theory of turbulent transfers, the flux of sensible and latent heat added to the radiation flux lead to theoretical values for the daily melting in good agreement with the measured values. The relative importance of the radiation balance on the melting of snow is 57%; that of the sensible heat flux is 43%; the latent heat flux is very weak and negative. (Humphreys-ISWS)
W75-08414

TEMPERATURE MEASUREMENTS IN A TEMPERATE GLACIER,
Washington Univ., Seattle. Geophysics Program.
W. D. Harrison.
Journal of Glaciology, Vol 14, No 70, p 23-30, 1975. 2 fig, 3 tab, 17 ref, 1 append. NSF Grants GU 2655, GA 28544.

Descriptors: *Glaciers, *Temperature, *On-site investigations, Ice, *Washington, Measurement, Instrumentation, On-site tests, Spatial distribution, Temperate, Thermometers.
Identifiers: *Blue Glacier(Wash), Thermistor.

Temperatures were measured at two sites in a temperate glacier (Blue Glacier, Washington) to depths of 192 and 76 m. The accuracy, which varies between about 0.002 and 0.005C, is about an order of magnitude better than previously obtained. Except near the surface, temperatures vary linearly with depth but are in disagreement with the simplest model of a temperate glacier, being about 0.02C colder near the surface and 0.04C colder at 192 m depth. (Humphreys-ISWS)
W75-08415

A MEASUREMENT OF SURFACE-PERPENDICULAR STRAIN-RATE IN A GLACIER,
Washington Univ., Seattle. Geophysics Program.
W. D. Harrison.
Journal of Glaciology, Vol 14, No 70, p 31-37, 1975. 2 fig, 1 tab, 9 ref. NSF Grants GU 2655, GA 28544.

Descriptors: *Glaciers, *Strain measurement, *On-site tests, *Theoretical analysis, On-site investigations, Strain, Rates, Velocity, Instrumentation, Measurement, Temperate, *Washington, Deformation, Ice.
Identifiers: *Blue Glacier(Wash), Surface-perpendicular components, Cables.

The surface-perpendicular components of velocity and strain-rate were determined at one site in the ablation area of Blue Glacier, Washington, where the total depth is about 250 m. The strain-rate is near zero at the surface but increases with depth to about 4% per year at 175 m. The results were obtained with the help of a finite deformation theory from the measured stretch of 9 cables frozen into the ice. (Humphreys-ISWS)
W75-08416

RADIO ECHO SOUNDINGS AND ICE-TEMPERATURE MEASUREMENTS IN A SURGE-TYPE GLACIER,
British Columbia Univ., Vancouver. Dept. of Geophysics.
G. K. C. Clarke, and R. H. Goodman.
Journal of Glaciology, Vol 14, No 70, p 71-78, 1975. 6 fig, 12 ref.

Descriptors: *Glaciers, *Sounding, *On-site investigations, Radar, Ice, Temperature, Temperate, Measurement, Evaluation, Depth, *Canada, Surveys.
Identifiers: *Rusty Glacier(Yukon Territory), Basal ice, *Surge-type glaciers.

Radio echo soundings on Rusty Glacier, a small surge-type glacier in Yukon Territory, reveal that the ice is considerably thicker than previously believed. A reinterpretation of deep ice-temperature measurements made in 1969 and 1970 suggested that a large zone of temperate basal ice exists. This result supports thermal instability as the surge mechanism for Rusty Glacier. (Humphreys-ISWS)
W75-08417

INVESTIGATION OF POLAR SNOW USING SEISMIC VELOCITY GRADIENTS,
Wisconsin Univ., Madison. Dept. of Geology and Geophysics; and Wisconsin Univ., Middleton. Geophysical and Polar Research Center.
J. D. Robertson, and C. R. Bentley.
Journal of Glaciology, Vol 14, No 70, p 39-48, 1975. 2 fig, 3 tab, 14 ref. NSF Grants GV-27044, GV-32873.

Descriptors: *Snow, *Seismic waves, *Antarctic, *Glaciology, On-site investigations, Velocity, Seismic studies, Exploration, Polar regions, Ice, Depth, Temperature, Regression analysis.
Identifiers: *Velocity gradients, Snow accumulation.

Compressional wave velocity gradients at 43 of 50 Antarctic traverse stations plot as sequences of straight lines on semilogarithmic graph paper. Intersections of the lines appear to correlate with depths at which the predominant metamorphic mechanism in polar snow changes. The seismic pattern supports a three-layer interpretation of snow densification. The base of the upper layer (8.4 + or -2.3 m) corresponds to the 'critical depth' of Anderson and Benson (1963) at which snow grains settle into a 'random close-packed' arrangement. The base of the lower layer may correspond to the firn : ice transition depth, but more data are needed to confirm this conclusion. It is unclear what densification phenomenon is marked by the base of the middle layer (27.7 + or -4.4 m). The distinction between the middle and lower layers tends to disappear and the velocity gradient at a fixed depth increases as mean annual accumulation decreases. (Humphreys-ISWS)
W75-08418

RADIO ECHO SOUNDING ON TEMPERATE GLACIERS,
Water Management Service, Calgary (Alberta).
R. H. Goodman.
Journal of Glaciology, Vol 14, No 70, p 57-69, 1975. 14 fig, 1 tab, 21 ref.

Descriptors: *Glaciers, *Sounding, *Remote sensing, *On-site investigations, Glaciology, Ice, Depth, Instrumentation, Radar, Surveys, Temperate, Attenuation, *Canada, Data processing.
Identifiers: *Wapta Icefield, *Athabasca Glacier.

A high-resolution radio echo sounder operating at a frequency of 620 MHz was developed for studies of temperate glaciers. Excellent spatial resolution

was obtained through the use of a short pulse length (70 ns) and an antenna beam width of 5.2 degrees. Large amounts of high-quality data may be rapidly collected since the sounder incorporates an automatic positioning system and an on-line computer. Real time analysis of the echoes facilitates the understanding of complex reflecting horizons observed in temperate glaciers. Results obtained during field trials of the echo sounder on both the Wapta Icefield and Athabasca Glacier were given. The depth measurements obtained by radio echo soundings agreed with the seismic and borehole measurements of Savage and Paterson (1963) on Athabasca Glacier to within 14 m. Intraglacial structures which may be due to water levels within the ice were detected. Remote sensing of ice depths has applications to the analysis of gravity surveys in glaciated areas, to iceberg-scouring studies, and potentially to permafrost investigations. (Humphreys-ISWS)
W75-08419

DEDUCING THICKNESS CHANGES OF AN ICE SHEET FROM RADIO-ECHO AND OTHER MEASUREMENTS,
Bristol Univ. (England). H. H. Wills Physics Lab.
J. F. Nye.
Journal of Glaciology, Vol 14, No 70, p 49-56, 1975. 1 fig, 2 tab, 9 ref, 1 append.

Descriptors: *Glaciers, *Ice, *Model studies, *Analysis, Velocity, Depth, Glaciology, Measurement, Theoretical analysis, Evaluation, Radar, Arctic.
Identifiers: *Greenland(Jarl-Joset station), Ice sheet, Thickness, Accumulation rate.

The displacement of the surface of an ice sheet and of markers set in its top layers can be measured geodetically, and also, it is expected, by radio-echo methods. Discussed were how such measurements could be interpreted as showing long-term changes in the thickness of the ice sheet and how an experiment might be designed so as to avoid unwanted effects due to short-term changes in rate of accumulation. The analysis, similar to that of Federer and others (1970), corrects an error, so that when applied to their results for central Greenland it gives a different result for the lowering of the surface. Federer and others have already concluded that the average accumulation rates during the past 100 years have been below those needed to keep in balance with the velocity of the ice sheet as a whole. With the developed model, it was found that this has resulted in the surface lowering at a mean rate of 0.050 m/yr between 1871 and 1968, and a mean rate of 0.140 m/yr between 1959 and 1968. An analysis of the effect of thinning of the annual layers by lateral flow was given in an appendix. (Humphreys-ISWS)
W75-08420

THE STEADY DRIFT OF AN INCOMPRESSIBLE ARCTIC ICE COVER,
Washington Univ., Seattle. Dept. of Atmospheric Sciences.
D. A. Rothrock.
Journal of Geophysical Research, Vol 80, No 3, p 387-397, January 20, 1975. 9 fig, 1 tab, 32 ref. ONR Contract N00014-67-A-0103-0007, NSF Grant GV 28807.

Descriptors: *Ice cover, *Arctic, Movement, Model studies, Mathematical models, Arctic Ocean, Sea ice, Pressure, Velocity, *Compressibility, Mechanical properties.
Identifiers: Ridging, Vorticity.

The steady drift of pack ice in an idealized arctic basin was calculated by assuming that the ice is incompressible and inviscid. The momentum and continuity equations for the ice were solved for the velocity and the ice pressure. The divergence of velocity was assumed to be 0.33 x 10 to the minus 8th power/s. The boundary conditions required that no ice flows across coastal boundaries but that ice flows out of the basin into the Greenland Sea and into the basin from the Kara Sea. The patterns of calculated velocities and vorticities were realistic, but their magnitudes were too high. The maximum calculated ice pressure of about 10 to the 8th power dyn/cm (pressure integrated through the ice thickness) was marginally able to ridge thick ice, according to the ridging model of Parmerter and Coon. These maximum values occur near Greenland, where Wittmann and Schule report intense ridging. When the wind stress was reduced to one third of the strength first assumed, realistic speeds and vorticities were obtained, and the maximum pressures were reduced to one third of the above value. Coastal shear zones of the order of 100 km wide can be represented by the added assumption of a shear viscosity of about 6 x 10 to the 12th power g/s and a no-slip condition on coastal boundaries. (Sims-ISWS)
W75-08423

OBSERVATIONS OF STAGE, DISCHARGE, PH, AND ELECTRICAL CONDUCTIVITY DURING PERIODS OF ICE FORMATION IN A SMALL SUBARCTIC STREAM,
Alaska Univ., College. Geophysical Inst.
T. E. Osterkamp, R. E. Gilfilian, and C. S. Benson.
Water Resources Research, Vol 11, No 2, p 268-272, April 1975. 6 fig, 16 ref. NSF Grant GA-30748.

Descriptors: *Ice, *Streamflow, *Electrical conductance, Conductivity, Frazil ice, Freezing, Permafrost, Discharge(Water), Flow profiles, Discharge measurement, Water levels, Hydrogen ion concentration, *Subarctic, Streams, *Alaska.

Ice formation in a small subarctic stream modified the stage, velocity profiles, discharge, and electrical conductivity, while the pH remained nearly constant. Frazil ice crystals suspended in the flow reduced the velocity profiles and increased the stage. Anchor ice and border ice growth decreased the discharge by 31 and 55% for two periods of underwater ice production. These reductions in discharge may be attributed to storage in the form of ice and to upstream water storage caused by increased flow resistance in the stream. The increase in the electrical conductivity of the stream water during periods of ice production was related to the concentration of ice in the stream. Ice concentrations calculated from this increase in conductivity were 1.8, 0.9, and 4.7% (by volume) for the first 150 min of three different periods of ice production. (Sims-ISWS)
W75-08440

A THEORY FOR WATER FLOW THROUGH A LAYERED SNOWPACK,
Cold Regions Research and Engineering Lab., Hanover, N.H.
S. C. Colbeck.
Water Resources Research, Vol 11, No 2, p 261-266, April 1975. 4 fig, 11 ref. DA 4A161102B52E.

Descriptors: *Snowpacks, *Flow, *Permeability, Ice, Snow, Flow rates, Fluid mechanics, Anisotropy, Stratification, Snowmelt, Slopes, Hydrology, Stratigraphy, Model studies, Cold regions.

A natural snowpack with ice layers was described in terms of an equivalent anisotropic porous medium. The anisotropic permeability was represented as a diagonalized matrix whose principal values can be calculated from a small amount of information about the prototype snowpack. Ice layers increase the transit time for water movement by a factor equal to the ratio of the principal values of permeability. The flow path, volume flux, and wave speed were determined by the slope of the snowpack and principal values of permeability. When a snowpack is assumed to be isotropic, the error in calculating transit time increases with the difference between the principal values of permeability. Uusual variations in slope introduce a small change in the transit time. (Sims-ISWS)
W75-08441

SOME CHARACTERISTICS OF THE ALBEDO OF SNOW,
Utah State Univ., Logan. Dept. of Soil Science and Biometeorology.
I. Dirmhirn, and F. D. Eaton.
Journal of Applied Meteorology, Vol 14, No 3, p 375-379, April 1975. 6 fig, 17 ref.

Descriptors: *Albedo, *Snow cover, *Remote sensing, Radiation, Solar radiation, Reflectance, Optical properties, Satellites(Artificial), Instrumentation, Anisotropy.
Identifiers: Snow cover metamorphism, Radiometers, Pyranometers, Specular reflectance, Diffuse reflectance.

Spring snowcovers exhibit a substantial contribution of a specular component to their reflection of solar radiation. This anisotropy can be measured with radiometers with small aperture, such as a TIROS radiometer. Indicatrices thus determined are dependent on solar angle. They are of importance for interpreting albedo values and for reducing airborne or spaceborne reflectance data taken under distinct nadir angles. (Sims-ISWS)
W75-08452

SALVAGE OF HEAVY CONSTRUCTION EQUIPMENT BY A FLOATING ICE BRIDGE,
Foundation of Canada Engineering Corp. Ltd., Calgary (Alberta). Arctic Div.
For primary bibliographic entry see Field 8G.
W75-08461

A FIRST SIMPLE MODEL FOR PERIODICALLY SELF-SURGING GLACIERS,
Department of Science, Melbourne (Australia). Antarctic Div.
W. F. Budd.
Journal of Glaciology, Vol 14, No 70, p 3-21, 1975. 7 fig, 2 tab, 36 ref.

Descriptors: *Model studies, *Glaciers, *Movement, Mathematical models, Ice, Glaciology, Ablation, Flow rates, Velocity, Flow characteristics, Frequency.
Identifiers: Self-surging glaciers, Two-dimensional model, *Glacier advance, Glacier retreat.

A two-dimensional model of glacier flow was presented which includes periodical surging as a natural phenomenon for a certain class of glaciers. The input consists of the bedrock and balance profiles along the glacier, ice flow properties and a frictional lubrication factor. The basal stress is determined from the condition of gross equilibrium for the whole glacier and the distribution of the frictional lubrication from energy dissipation along the glacier. The difference between the basal stress and the down-slope stress of the glaciers produces longitudinal strain-rates which determine the basal sliding velocity. Since the velocity is also involved in the frictional lubrication, feedback develops between the basal stress and sliding velocity. For a given lubrication factor, a critical stage can be reached for which the velocity becomes sufficiently high to lower the basal stress enough to cause high velocities to develop. The model gives rise to three classes of glaciers with two modes of flow. 'Ordinary' glaciers do not have sufficient mass flux, for the given bedrock profile, to go beyond the 'slow mode' in which the basal stress and velocity increase together as the glacier builds up to steady state. 'Fast' glaciers have sufficient flux to remain continuously in the 'fast mode' with high velocities and relatively low basal stress. 'Surging' glaciers have sufficient flux to reach the fast mode but not to maintain it, and thus develop a periodically oscillating state between the fast and slow modes with gradual build up and rapid drainage. Results were presented for models of a typical large valey surging glacier and for a very high-speed surging glacier. (Humphreys-ISWS)

W75-08713

METHOD FOR CONSTRUCTING ICE ISLANDS IN COLD REGIONS,
Union Oil Co. of California, Los Angeles. (assignee)
For primary bibliographic entry see Field 8C.
W75-08734

RESERVOIR OPERATION USING SNOW SURVEY DATA,
Soil Conservation Service, Bozeman, Mont.
For primary bibliographic entry see Field 4A.
W75-08809

2D. Evaporation and Transpiration

CONCERNING THE EFFECT OF ANISOTROPIC SCATTERING AND FINITE DEPTH OF THE DISTRIBUTION OF SOLAR RADIATION IN SNOW,
High Altitude Observatory, Boulder, Colo.
For primary bibliographic entry see Field 2C.
W75-08405

WIND REGIMES AND HEAT EXCHANGE ON GLACIER DE SAINT-SORLIN,
Centre National de la Recherche Scientifique, Grenoble (France). Laboratoire de Glaciologie.
For primary bibliographic entry see Field 2C.
W75-08414

RESPONSE OF AN UNSATURATED SOIL TO FOREST TRANSPIRATION,
Connecticut Agricultural Experiment Station, New Haven.
J-Y. Parlange, and D. E. Aylor.
Water Resources Research, Vol 11, No 2, p 319-323, April 1975. 3 fig, 12 ref, 1 append.

Descriptors: *Transpiration, *Discharge(Water), *Forest watersheds, Evaporation, Diurnal, Saturated soils, Soil water, Soil moisture, Hydrologic aspects, Water consumption, Seepage, Deep percolation, Cycles, Gravimetric analysis, Connecticut, Forests, Moisture content, Movement, *Connecticut.
Identifiers: Sandy loam.

Diurnal cycles in water outflow from a small watershed due to forest transpiration were observed 4 times during August 1973. Each time the daytime outflow was reduced significantly below that during the following night. The recovery of the outflow to the steady night level took place for several hours after sunset, and this time of recovery was shown to be controlled by the unsaturated soil water movement in the root zone. The observations of transpiration were made on a small area of a 5-acre forested watershed in North Madison, Connecticut, surrounding a lake. Water seeped from the lake into the observation plot and emerged on the other side where it passed through a weir and was monitored continuously. The difference between the amount of water seeping into the test plot from the lake and the measured outflow determined the evapotranspiration from the plot. (Roberts-ISWS)
W75-08436

PERSISTENCE OF SELECTED ANTITRANSPIRANTS,
Colorado Univ., Boulder. Dept. of Chemical Engineering.
F. Kreith, A. Taori, and J. E. Anderson.
Water Resources Research, Vol 11, No 2, p 281-286, April 1975. 5 fig, 15 ref. NSF Grant GK-17184.

Descriptors: *Antitranspirants, *Persistence, *Tobacco, Water vapor, Phenols, Sprays, Leaves, Water loss, Transpiration, Transpiration control, Analytical techniques, Ecology, Laboratory tests.
Identifiers: *Experimental conditions, Phenylmercuric acetate, Wilt Pruf, Monoglycerol ester, Mobileaf, Metabolic agents, Wind tunnel.

The short- and long-term effectiveness of two film-forming and two physiologically active antitranspirants was evaluated on tobacco leaves under controlled experimental conditions. The physiologically active antitranspirants (phenylmercuric acetate and monoglycerol ester of n-decenyl succinic acid) initially reduced water loss to less than 40% of controls, but their effectiveness diminished sharply within 2-3 days. Treatment with the film-forming antitranspirants (Wilt Pruf and Mobileaf) resulted in initial transpiration reductions to 50-65% of controls, but the duration of effectiveness was longer with these than with the metabolic agents. The results were compared with those of previous studies, and implications for large-scale antitranspirant applications were discussed. Since the cost of water varied considerably in different parts of the world, the economic viability of using antitranspirants could not be ascertained by a technical study alone. Under conditions for which water is expensive or not available, the use of antitranspirants may be economical provided no adverse ecological effects occur. (Roberts-ISWS)
W75-08439

THE EVAPORATION OF INTERCEPTED RAINFALL FROM A FOREST STAND: AN ANALYSIS BY SIMULATION,
Duke Univ., Durham, N.C. School of Forestry.
C. E. Murphy, Jr., and K. R. Knoerr.
Water Resources Research, Vol 11, No 2, p 273-280, April 1975. 8 fig, 1 tab, 36 ref. NSF AG-199, BMS69-01147-A09.

Descriptors: *Evaporation, *Evapotranspiration, *Rainfall, *Forests, Interception, Canopy, Rain, Simulation analysis, Energy transfer, Radiation, Hydrologic cycle, Latent heat, Absorption, Vegetation, Atmosphere.
Identifiers: *Forest stand, Sensible heat.

Both evapotranspiration and the evaporation of intercepted precipitation are evaporative losses. They generally have been expressed as separate terms in the hydrologic cycle because they were believed to be independent of each other. A model was described of the energy exchange between the atmosphere and a vegetated surface which was developed and used to investigate the sources of energy available for evaporation of precipitation intercepted by a forest canopy. Simulations of this model demonstrated that a forest canopy wetted by rainfall partitions more of the absorbed radiant energy into latent heat exchange than an unwetted canopy in the same environment. This energy diversion creates a decrease in sensible heat transfer from the canopy to the atmosphere and a smaller decrease in a long-wave radiation emitted by the canopy. From this analysis, it was clear that precipitation intercepted by vegetation evaporated at a greater rate than transpiration from the same type of vegetation in the same environment. The model demonstrated that the enhanced evaporation of intercepted water can occur for forests of large areal extent, where horizontal advection may be negligible. (Roberts-ISWS)
W75-08442

PARAMETERIZATION OF SURFACE MOISTURE AND EVAPORATION RATE IN A PLANETARY BOUNDARY LAYER MODEL,
National Oceanic and Atmospheric Administration, Oak Ridge, Tenn. Air Resources Atmospheric Turbulence and Diffusion Lab.
C. J. Nappo, Jr.
Journal of Applied Meteorology, Vol 14, No 3, p 289-296, April 1975. 7 fig, 1 tab, 20 ref.

Descriptors: *Model studies, *Evaporation, *Moisture, Meteorology, Mathematical models, Air-earth interfaces, Soils, Soil moisture, Boundary layers, Boundary processes, Soil surfaces, Soil types, Temperature, Water vapor.

Two methods of parameterizing expressions for ground surface evaporation rate that are used in planetary boundary layer models were examined. In one method (Method A) the surface evaporation rate is proportional to M(Q sub s - Q sub 1). In the other (Method B) the surface evaporation rate is proportional to hQ sub s - Q sub 1. Here Q sub s is the surface saturation mixing ratio, Q sub 1 the mixing ratio at the lowest level of the atmospheric model, M the moisture availability parameter, and h the relative humidity immediately above the ground. The analysis was performed by running a planetary boundary layer numerical model several times, using at each time either Method A or B with different specifications of M and h. The calculated diurnal surface temperature and surface latent heat flux were examined. Specific results were: (1) for equal M and h, Method B results in higher surface temperatures than Method A; (2) the surface evaporation rate calculated using Method A is less sensitive to changes in M, than the surface evaporation rate calculated using Method B is to changes in h; (3) negative surface evaporation rates can occur much more easily using Method B than Method A; and (4) calculation of h by calculating the flux of moisture below the ground surface does not improve the model. (Sims-ISWS)
W75-08451

SPRINKLER AND SOAKER IRRIGATION OF PEACH TREES TO REDUCE PLANT WATER STRESS AND INCREASE FRUIT SIZE,
Florida Univ., Gainesville. Dept. of Fruit Crops.
For primary bibliographic entry see Field 3F.
W75-08596

SIMULATION MODEL FOR EVAPOTRANSPIRATION OF WHEAT: EMPIRICAL APPROACH,
Agricultural Research Organization, Bet Dagan (Israel). Inst. of Soils and Water.
D. Shimshi, D. Yaron, E. Bresler, M. Weisbrod, and G. Strateener.
Journal of the Irrigation and Drainage Division, American Society of Civil Engineers, Vol 101, No IR1, Proceedings Paper 11170, p 1-12, March 1975. 2 fig, 4 tab, 16 ref, 2 append.

Descriptors: *Evapotranspiration, *Wheat, *Simulation analysis, Agriculture, *Soil water, Root zone, Irrigation, Rain water, Arid lands, Infiltration, Soil surfaces, Wetting, Field capacity, Water loss, Root systems, Soil profiles, Canopy, Evaporation, *Model studies.
Identifiers: *Israel(Neveg).

A simulation model was described for predicting the changes in the soil-water content of the root zone of wheat growing under various irrigation regimes in a semi-arid region. The model was based on the following assumptions: (1) irrigation water and rainwater infiltrates from the soil surface, wetting each successive soil layer as the overlying one is wetted in excess of the field capacity (as conventionally defined); and (2) the rate of water loss from the soil changes with time and with depth of soil. Parameters were determined empirically from soil moisture data collected from a series of wheat irrigation experiments carried out over a 4-year period in northern Negev, Israel. The average relative deviation between computed and observed values of soil moisture ranged from 8.8 to 13.5%. The changes in parameters reflected the development of the root system in the soil profile and the changes in time of canopy cover and evaporation conditions. (Roberts-ISWS)
W75-08712

ACOUSTIC MINIPROBING FOR OCEAN MICROSTRUCTURE AND BUBBLES,
Naval Postgraduate School, Monterey, Calif. Dept. of Physics and Chemistry.
For primary bibliographic entry see Field 2L.
W75-08425

MAXIMUM HEIGHTS OF OCEAN WAVES,
MPR Associates, Inc., Washington, D.C.
For primary bibliographic entry see Field 2L.
W75-08426

THE BERING SLOPE CURRENT SYSTEM,
Washington Univ., Seattle. Dept. of Oceanography.
For primary bibliographic entry see Field 2L.
W75-08431

SOME COMMENTS ON TESTING RANDOM TOPOLOGY STREAM NETWORK MODELS,
State Univ. of New York, Buffalo. Dept. of Geography.
R. S. Jarvis, and A. Werritty.
Water Resources Research, Vol 11, No 2, p 309-318, April 1975. 6 fig, 3 tab, 16 ref.

Descriptors: *Channel morphology, *Distribution patterns, *Statistical methods, Analytical techniques, *Model studies, Drainage, Data collections, Probability, Algorithms, Tributaries, Geomorphology, Streams.
Identifiers: *Stream network models, *Random topology, Stream-ordering systems, Bifurcation ratios, Morphometry.

Various methods of classifying stream networks were examined in terms of their attendant information losses. Grouping networks according to their mean source height scored well in this respect because it retains a considerable amount of the original topologic detail present in each individual topologically distinct channel network. Stream set values determine the structural properties of the network and the degree to which a given network is 'compact' or 'lineated.' Because of difficulties in interpretation, tests of random topology hypotheses are best conducted on networks sampled at a constant magnitude. A means of comparing the topologic structure of the main stem of two or more networks was developed, based on the absolute limits and the expectation of the parameter mean source height. (Singh-ISWS)
W75-08437

PROPERTIES OF THE THREE-PARAMETER LOG NORMAL PROBABILITY DISTRIBUTION,
Washington Univ, Seattle. Dept. of Civil Engineering.
S. J. Burges, D. P. Lettenmaier, and C. L. Bates.
Water Resources Research, Vol 11, No 2, p 229-235, April 1975. 4 fig, 3 tab, 8 ref.

Descriptors: *Statistical models, *Synthetic hydrology, *Analytical techniques, *Frequency analysis, *Reliability, Mathematics, Estimating, Monte Carlo method, Variability, Hydrology.
Identifiers: *Three-parameter lognormal distribution, Skew coefficient.

Mathematical properties of the three-parameter log normal probability distribution were detailed. Two methods for estimation of the third parameter a were compared. The estimator of a using sample mean, median, and standard deviation was found to be more variable and to have larger bias for distributions of interest in operational hydrology than the estimator using sample mean, standard deviation, and skew. Graphical solutions for the third parameter a were presented; a single feasible value of a was shown to result when the skew estimator was used; two feasible solutions result when the median estimator was used. The smaller of the two solutions was shown to correspond to skews of less than 5.87 and hence is the desired solution in most hydrologic applications. (Singh-ISWS)
W75-08438

OBSERVATIONS OF STAGE, DISCHARGE, PH, AND ELECTRICAL CONDUCTIVITY DURING PERIODS OF ICE FORMATION IN A SMALL SUBARCTIC STREAM,
Alaska Univ., College. Geophysical Inst.
For primary bibliographic entry see Field 2C.
W75-08440

A THEORY FOR WATER FLOW THROUGH A LAYERED SNOWPACK,
Cold Regions Research and Engineering Lab., Hanover, N.H.
For primary bibliographic entry see Field 2C.
W75-08441

WELSH FLOODPLAIN STUDIES: THE NATURE OF FLOODPLAIN GEOMETRY,
University Coll. of Wales, Aberystwyth.
J. Lewin, and M. M. M. Manton.
Journal of Hydrology, Vol 25, No 1/2, p 37-50, April 1975. 6 fig, 1 tab, 16 ref.

Descriptors: *Flood plains, *Braiding, *On-site investigations, Meanders, Geomorphology, Surveys, Evaluation, Channel morphology, Flood profiles, Discharge measurement, Aggradation, Photogrammetry, Topography, Terrain analysis.
Identifiers: *Floodplain geometry, Wales.

Field studies of floodplain geometry are necessary if the extent and patterns of inundation are to be related to discharge magnitudes. This was considered in relation to the floodplain geometry of parts of the three Welsh rivers—the Ystwyth, the Rheidol, and the Tywi. A photogrammetric approach was used and tested, together with the development of computer procedures for automated plotting of floodplain profiles on any required scale. The complex and locally variable relief (1.7 to 3.3 m) of the floodplains studied was shown to be related to former braided and meandering river activity, some of it within the past 130 years for which reasonable historical evidence is forthcoming. Relief results dominantly from the presence of abandoned channel loops, from point bars, and from former channel bedforms now incorporated into the floodplain surface. Local aggradation and incision are also evident. Variation along the rivers is such that a single discharge-related flood-stage is not identifiable; instead there are sequences of flooding and emptying beginning at relatively low discharges and related to floodplain relief. Some consequences for flood studies and floodplain management were suggested. (Dawes-ISWS)
W75-08448

ESTIMATING STREAMFLOW CHARACTERISTICS FOR STREAMS IN UTAH USING SELECTED CHANNEL-GEOMETRY PARAMETERS,
Geological Survey, Salt Lake City, Utah.
For primary bibliographic entry see Field 4A.
W75-08494

EMPIRICAL DATA ON LONGITUDINAL DISPERSION IN RIVERS,
Geological Survey, Denver, Colo.
For primary bibliographic entry see Field 5B.
W75-08495

POTENTIAL FLOOD HAZARD--NORTH AVENUE AREA, DENVER FEDERAL CENTER, LAKEWOOD, COLORADO,
Geological Survey, Denver, Colo.
For primary bibliographic entry see Field 4A.
W75-08496

REPORT OF THE ANNUAL YIELD OF THE ARKANSAS RIVER BASIN FOR THE ARKANSAS RIVER BASIN COMPACT, ARKANSAS-OKLAHOMA, 1972: 1974 WATER YEAR,
Geological Survey, Little Rock, Ark.
For primary bibliographic entry see Field 4A.
W75-08497

FLOOD ON BUFFALO CREEK FROM SAUNDERS TO MAN, WEST VIRGINIA,
Geological Survey, Reston, Va.
For primary bibliographic entry see Field 7C.
W75-08508

RECONNAISSANCE OF THE UPPER AU SABLE RIVER, A COLD-WATER RIVER IN THE NORTH-CENTRAL PART OF MICHIGAN'S SOUTHERN PENINSULA,
Geological Survey, Reston, Va.
For primary bibliographic entry see Field 7C.
W75-08512

ANNUAL PEAK DISCHARGES FROM SMALL DRAINAGE AREAS IN MONTANA, THROUGH SEPTEMBER 1974,
Geological Survey, Helena, Mont.
For primary bibliographic entry see Field 7C.
W75-08516

MAGNITUDE AND FREQUENCY OF FLOODS IN WASHINGTON,
Geological Survey, Tacoma, Wash.
For primary bibliographic entry see Field 4A.
W75-08520

DESIGN AND IMPLEMENTATION OF A HYDROLOGIC DATA PROCESSING SYSTEM IN BRAZIL, 1971-74,
Geological Survey, Reston, Va.
For primary bibliographic entry see Field 7A.
W75-08523

A COMPUTATIONAL MODEL FOR PREDICTING THE THERMAL REGIMES OF RIVERS,
Iowa Univ., Iowa City. Inst. of Hydraulic Research.
For primary bibliographic entry see Field 5B.
W75-08683

DETERMINATION OF URBAN WATERSHED RESPONSE TIME,
Colorado State Univ., Fort Collins. Dept. of Civil Engineering.
For primary bibliographic entry see Field 4C.
W75-08685

NORMAL MODES OF THE ATLANTIC AND INDIAN OCEANS,
Chicago Univ., Ill. Dept. of the Geophysical Sciences.
For primary bibliographic entry see Field 2L.
W75-08686

TIDAL CHARTS OF THE CENTRAL PACIFIC OCEAN,
Massachusetts Inst. of Tech., Cambridge. Dept. of Earth and Planetary Sciences.
For primary bibliographic entry see Field 2L.
W75-08687

SOME PROPERTIES OF THE WARM EDDIES GENERATED IN THE CONFLUENCE ZONE OF THE KUROSHIO AND OYASHIO CURRENTS,
Hokkaido Regional Fisheries Research Lab., Yoichi (Japan).
For primary bibliographic entry see Field 2L.
W75-08688

MICROSTRUCTURE AND INTRUSIONS IN THE CALIFORNIA CURRENT,
Scripps Institution of Oceanography, La Jolla, Calif.
For primary bibliographic entry see Field 2L.
W75-08689

INTERNAL WAVE REFLECTION BY A VELOCITY SHEAR AND DENSITY ANOMALY,
Naval Research Lab., Washington, D.C. Ocean Sciences Div.
R. P. Mied, and J. P. Dugan.
Journal of Physical Oceanography, Vol 5, No 2, p 279-287, April 1975. 5 fig, 1 tab, 29 ref.

Descriptors: *Internal waves, *Reflectance, *Shear, *Density, Thermocline, Velocity, Waves(Water), Energy, Oceans, Ocean waves, Oceanography, Numerical analysis.

Numerical solutions were obtained for the reflection of upward propagating internal waves by simple pycnocline and current shear models. Results for a simple monotonic shear and a velocity jet, with and without a pycnocline, led to the conclusions that: (1) significant portions of an internal wave spectrum generated in the deep ocean can be reflected back downward by changing Brunt-Vaisala frequency and shear, even in situations not involving critical layers; (2) reflections by shear usually reinforce those from density variations; and (3) under some propagation conditions, a portion of the wave energy is leaked through the velocity jet, even when the fluid within the jet will not support wave motion of the impinging frequency. (Sims-ISWS)
W75-08690

A NUMERICAL STUDY OF TIME-DEPENDENT TURBULENT EKMAN LAYERS OVER HORIZONTAL AND SLOPING BOTTOMS,
Florida State Univ., Tallahassee. Dept. of Oceanography, and Florida State Univ., Tallahassee. Geophysical Fluid Dynamics Inst.
G. L. Weatherly.
Journal of Physical Oceanography, Vol 5, No 2, p 288-299, April 1975. 11 fig, 17 ref. ONR Contract N000-14-75-C-201.

Descriptors: *Oceans, *Turbulent boundary layers, *Numerical analysis, Profiles, Velocity, Model studies, Time, Tides, Ocean currents, Currents(Water), Oceanography, Florida.
Identifiers: *Ekman layers, Logarithmic layers, Time-dependence, *Straits of Florida.

A numerical study was made of a time-dependent turbulent Ekman bottom boundary layer. Parameters for the model were chosen to simulate conditions near the bottom of the Florida Current in the Straits of Florida. The model allows the coefficient of turbulent viscosity v to vary with time t and height z and permits the effects of an imposed stable stratification and sloping bottom to be included. The variation of v with t and z was not present but was determined in the course of solving the problem. The results of this preliminary study were compared to the author's observations. The agreement was good for the friction velocity values as well as for the mean total Ekman veering. However, most of the computed Ekman veering occurred above the logarithmic layer while most of the measured veering occurred within the logarithmic layer. The results suggest, as do the observations, that turbulent Ekman bottom layers varying on time scales of order the local inertial period are not quasi-stationary. Allowing the bottom to be inclined at a small angle transverse to the flow was found to modify significantly the temperature profile near the bottom, leading at times either to the formation of a homogeneous layer of depth order 10 m or to conditions marginally suitable for the formation of convectively mixed layer of comparable depth. (Sims-ISWS)
W75-08691

COASTAL TRAPPED WAVES IN A BAROCLINIC OCEAN,
Rosenstiel School of Marine and Atmospheric Science, Miami, Fla.
For primary bibliographic entry see Field 2L.
W75-08692

THE INFLUENCE OF LONGITUDINAL VARIATIONS IN WIND STRESS CURL ON THE STEADY OCEAN CIRCULATION,
Scripps Institution of Oceanography, La Jolla, Calif.
K. E. Kenyon.
Journal of Physical Oceanography, Vol 5, No 2, p 334-346, April 1975. 11 fig, 20 ref.

Descriptors: *Ocean circulation, *Winds, *Model studies, Mathematical models, Oceans, Temperature, Wind pressure, *Pacific Ocean, Oceanography.
Identifiers: *Wind stress curl, Longitudinal variations, Mean ocean temperatures.

The influence of longitudinal variations in wind stress curl on the steady circulation in a rectangular ocean basin was investigated analytically in a linear barotropic model. It was shown that longitudinal variations in the interior circulation are produced by longitudinal variations in the magnitude of a wind stress curl of constant (negative) sign. If friction is small in the interior, the east-west variation in southward flow is directly proportional to that of the applied wind stress curl in accordance with the Sverdrup vorticity balance. Examples showed that when the wind stress curl has a maximum in the center of the basin, the southward flow is also concentrated in the center of the basin. When the wind stress curl has a minimum in the center of the basin, the soutward flow is concentrated in two regions, one on either side of the minimum curl. This variation in southward flow causes a concentration in east-west flow along the northern and southern boundaries of the basin, which is not obvious from the Sverdrup balance. If the minimum value of the wind stress curl term is smaller than the friction term in the vorticity equation, there is northward flow in the center of the basin which is part of a closed anticyclonic gyre in the eastern half of the basin. Longitudinal variations in wind stress curl can also produce differences in the northward flow in the western boundary current compared to the case of a wind stress curl which is independent of longitude. The longitudinal distribution in mean sea surface temperature was consistent with the circulation in the dynamical model which is produced by a qualitatively realistic longitudinal variation in mean wind stress curl. (Sims-ISWS)
W75-08693

DYNAMIC HEIGHT FROM TEMPERATURE PROFILES,
Hawaii Univ., Honolulu. Dept. of Oceanography.
W. J. Emery.
Journal of Physical Oceanography, Vol 5, No 2, p 369-375, April 1975. 6 fig, 1 tab, 11 ref.

Descriptors: *Temperature, *Salinity, *Oceans, Sounding, Hydrography, Curves, *Pacific Ocean, Water temperature, Oceanography, On-site investigations.
Identifiers: *Dynamic height, Temperature-salinity relationships, Weatherships, Inversions.

A method was developed for the computation of dynamic height from temperature data alone by using a mean temperature-salinity relationship to provide salinity values. This method was tested at three Pacific weathership locations where a large number of hydrographic stations were available. At weatherships Victor (34N, 164E) and November (30N, 140W), the difference between dynamic height found by this method and dynamic height computer from temperature and salinity observations was smaller (0.2 sq m/sq s) than either the theoretical measurement error (0.4 sq m/sq s)

or observed variation in dynamic height. At location Papa (50N, 145W), however, the difference was greater than the uncertainties in dynamic height, due to a thermal inversion. The small difference at Victor and November means that when the temperature-salinity relationship is 'tight', as it is at these locations, dynamic height can be computed from temperature data along. (Sims-ISWS)
W75-08696

DYNAMIC BEHAVIOR MODEL OF EPHEMERAL STREAM,
Agricultural Research Service, Tucson, Ariz. Southwest Watershed Research Center.
K. G. Renard, and E. M. Laursen.
Journal of the Hydraulics Division, American Society of Civil Engineers, Vol 101, No HY5, Proceedings Paper 11315, p 511-528, May 1975. 16 fig, 15 ref, append.

Descriptors: *Mathematical models, *Sedimentation, *Erosion, *Rainfall-runoff relationships, Sediment transport, Surface runoff, Hydrology, Ephemeral streams, Analytical techniques, Open channel flow, Sediments, Hydraulics, Hydrology, Sediment load, Stream erosion, Peak discharge, River beds, River flow, Geomorphology, Storm runoff, Model studies, Watersheds(Basins), Demonstration watersheds, *Arizona.
Identifiers: Runoff-sediment relationships, *Walnut Gulch Experimental Watershed(Ariz).

Ephemeral stream hydraulic features are dynamic and respond to the variable streamflow available to move sediment. Streamflow varies both from the runoff-producing storms and transmission losses that decrease the runoff volume and peak. The channel profile in an ephemeral stream tends to be concave up because of the transmission losses and concave down because there is more flow downstream due to tributary inflow. These phenomena were modeled for the main channel of the Walnut Gulch Experimental Watershed using a geomorphic approach to describe the channel and its tributaries and a hydraulic-hydrologic model for the runoff-sediment movement. Runoff and sediment transport were synthesized using the Diskin-Lane stochastic runoff model with a deterministic sediment transport relationship using the Manning and Laursen equations. (Lee-ISWS)
W75-08699

NONEQUILIBRIUM RIVER FORM,
Colorado State Univ., Fort Collins. Dept. of Civil Engineering.
For primary bibliographic entry see Field 2J.
W75-08700

A TWO LAYER FLOW THROUGH A CONTRACTION,
New South Wales Univ., Kensington (Australia). Water Research Lab.
For primary bibliographic entry see Field 8B.
W75-08701

CIRCULATION IN CENTRAL LONG ISLAND SOUND,
Yale Univ., New Haven, Conn. Dept. of Geology and Geophysics.
For primary bibliographic entry see Field 2L.
W75-08702

PROPAGATION OF TIDAL WAVES IN THE JOSEPH BONAPARTE GULF,
Wollongong Univ., Coll. (Australia). Dept. of Mathematics.
For primary bibliographic entry see Field 2L.
W75-08706

THE EFFECT OF ROUGHNESS STRIPS OF TRANSVERSE MIXING IN HYDRAULIC MODELS,
California Univ., Berkeley. Dept. of Civil Engineering.
For primary bibliographic entry see Field 8B.
W75-08708

THE DETERMINATION OF CURRENT VELOCITIES FROM DIFFUSION/ADVECTION PROCESSES IN THE IRISH SEA,
University Coll. of North Wales, Bangor. Dept. of Physical Oceanography.
J. R. Hunter.
Estuarine and Coastal Marine Science, Vol 3, No 1, p 43-55, January 1975. 3 fig, 15 ref.

Descriptors: *Water circulation, *Oceans, *Currents(Water), *Model studies, Mathematical models, Velocity, Tidal waters, Tidal streams, Distribution patterns, Diffusion, Flow, Advection, Movement, Salinity.
Identifiers: *Irish Sea.

The validity of estimations of current velocity from the distribution of a property subject to diffusion and advection was discussed. The observed salinity distribution in the Irish Sea, observed values of the diffusion coefficient, and the results of a tidal numerical model were used to investigate the water circulation pattern. The results showed a residual Northward transport through the center of the Irish Sea, with southward flowing transports to the east and west of the main stream. It was shown that a numerical model of the diffusion/advection processes together with a knowledge of the salinity, diffusivity coefficients, precipitation, and evaporation can yield useful information concerning the vertically-integrated velocity field. The input data was not of sufficient quality to calculate the actual vector field, but only one component of the required vector. *Humphreys-ISWS)
W75-08717

ANALYSIS OF FLOW IN CHANNELS WITH GRAVEL BEDS,
Washington State Univ., Pullman. Dept. of Civil Engineering.
For primary bibliographic entry see Field 8B.
W75-08793

DISCHARGE, SLOPE, BED ELEMENT RELATIONS IN STREAMS,
Sargent and Lundy, Chicago, Ill.
J. K. Virmani, D. F. Peterson, and G. Z. Watters.
In: Hydraulic Engineering and the Environment; Proceedings of the 21st Annual Hydraulic Division Specialty Conference, Montana State University, Bozeman, August 15-17, 1973. American Society of Civil Engineers, New York, p 73-84, 1973. 3 fig, 5 tab, 10 ref, 1 append. USDA Grant 12-11-204-3.

Descriptors: *Discharge(Water), *Slopes, *Beds, Drainage area, Discharge frequency, Streamflow, Hydraulics, Roughness(Hydraulic), Flow, Channel flow, Flood frequency, Channel erosion, Rocks, Gravels, On-site investigations, Mathematical models.
Identifiers: Bed materials, Bear River Basin.

Throughout the world in mountainous and hilly terrain, flow occurs in both natural and man-made channels with large slopes. In many of these streams, the beds are composed of large elements where the ratio of depth to average bed element size is less than 30. The hydraulic roughness and size distribution of bed elements and the random behavior of the spatial distribution of these elements have not been studied in sufficient depth. A better understanding of the formation of these streams, the size distribution of their roughness elements, and their hydraulic behavior could lead to useful practical applications in predicting stream erosion and the effects of alterations of natural conditions caused by road construction, dam construction, etc. With these objectives in mind extensive data were collected in the Bear River Basin in Utah, Idaho, and Wyoming on discharges, drainage areas, channel slopes, channel cross-section shapes, and bed material size distribution. Hydraulic geometry equations were used and the power relationships of width, depth, velocity, and area to discharge were established. The relationship between discharge, drainage area, and frequency of occurrence of discharges was found. A method for relating slope, bed roughness, size, and discharge was presented which is based on the distribution of stream power. An example was presented which illustrates the application of the work to a typical engineering situation. (See also W75-08786) (Sims-ISWS)
W75-08794

FLOOD PLAIN MANAGEMENT IN MONTANA,
Montana Dept. of Natural Resources and Conservation, Helena. Floodway Management Bureau.
For primary bibliographic entry see Field 6F.
W75-08795

WINTER STORM AND FLOOD ANALYSES, NORTHWEST INTERIOR,
Agricultural Research Service, Boise, Idaho. Northwest Watershed Research Center.
C. W. Johnson, and R. P. McArthur.
In: Hydraulic Engineering and the Environment; Proceedings of the 21st Annual Hydraulic Division Specialty Conference, Montana State University, Bozeman, August 15-17, 1973. American Society of Civil Engineers, New York, p 359-369, 1973. 7 fig, 4 tab, 6 ref, 1 append.

Descriptors: *Floods, *Winter, *Mountains, *Runoff, Watersheds(Basins), Precipitation(Atmospheric), Snowfall, Snowmelt, Instrumentation, Precipitation gages, Winds, Temperature, Frozen soils, Storm runoff, Flood frequency, Peak discharge, On-site investigations, Hydrology, Meteorology, *Idaho, Demonstration watersheds.
Identifiers: *Reynolds Creek(Ida).

In the Northwestern United States, severe winter floods occur frequently and have produced the greatest peak discharges of record at many runoff stations. Winter flooding has been reported at some locations in southern Idaho about once in 2 years, and two or more events have been reported during some years. The Reynolds Creek Experimental Watershed in southwest Idaho was chosen for a detailed investigation of winter floods. This watershed represents a variety of rangeland conditions in Idaho, Nevada, and Oregon. A network of nearly 100 recording raingages have been maintained on and adjacent to the watershed since 1961. Temperature, humidity, and wind direction and velocity were recorded at three climatological stations. Snow depth and density measurements were made twice each month at eight snow courses. Additional snow measurements were made regularly at raingage locations when snow was on the ground. The depths of frost penetration and thawing were measured and noted regularly at raingage sites. Continuous records of runoff were obtained from a network of 13 weirs. Results of a runoff evaluation procedure show the extrme variability in watershed areas that contribute to winter storm runoff and indicate that large errors are associated with the common assumption that all areas of a watershed contribute equally. (See also W75-08786) (Sims-ISWS)
W75-08818

CALIBRATION OF WATERSHED WETNESS AND PREDICTION OF FLOOD VOLUME FROM SMALL WATERSHEDS IN HUMID REGION,
Pennsylvania Dept. of Environmental Resources, Harrisburg.
For primary bibliographic entry see Field 2A.

W75-08819

PREDICTING LOW FLOWS AND FLOODS FROM UNGAGED DRAINAGE BASINS,
Washington State Univ., Pullman. Dept. of Civil Engineering.
For primary bibliographic entry see Field 4A.
W75-08820

ESTIMATION FLOODS SMALL DRAINAGE AREAS IN MONTANA,
Montana State Univ., Bozeman. Dept. of Civil Engineering and Engineering Mechanics.
For primary bibliographic entry see Field 4A.
W75-08821

METEOROLOGY AND HYDROLOGY OF RAPID CITY FLOOD,
Corps of Engineers, Omaha, Nebr. Hydrology and Meteorology Section.
K. A. Johnson.
In: Hydraulic Engineering and the Environment; Proceedings of the 21st Annual Hydraulic Division Specialty Conference, Montana State University, Bozeman, August 15-17, 1973. American Society of Civil Engineers, New York, p 451-455, 1973. 4 tab.

Descriptors: *Floods, *Hydrology, *Meteorology, Rainfall, Cloudbursts, Runoff, Peak discharge, Flood discharge, Dam failure, Dams, Spillways, Flash floods, Historic floods, Disasters, *South Dakota.
Identifiers: *Rapid City(SD).

The June 1972 storm and flood that struck City. It should be recognized, however, that the sheer magnitude and intensity of the storm and resulting flood event were the major causative factors of the disaster. The pertinent meteorological and hydrologic features of the June flood in Rapid City were briefly described. (See also W75-08786) (Sims-ISWS)
W75-08824

INDEX TO MAPS TO FLOOD-PRONE AREAS IN INDIANA,
Geological Survey, Indianapolis, Ind.
For primary bibliographic entry see Field 7C.
W75-08834

2F. Groundwater

AN APPLICATION OF PARAMETRIC STATISTICAL TESTS TO WELL-YIELD DATA FROM CARBONATES OF CENTRAL PENNSYLVANIA,
Pennsylvania State Univ,. University Park.
For primary bibliographic entry see Field 4B.
W75-08388

DRAWDOWN DISTRIBUTION DUE TO WELL FIELDS IN COUPLED LEAKY AQUIFERS: 2. FINITE AQUIFER SYSTEM,
Illinois Univ., Chicago. Dept. of Geological Sciences.
Z. A. Saleem, and C. E. Jacob.
Water Resources Research, Vol 10, No 2, p 336-342, April 1974. 1 fig, 14 ref.

Descriptors: *Drawdown, *Artesian aquifers, *Withdrawal, *Water table, Groundwater movement, Equations, Mathematical studies, Leakage, Water wells.
Identifiers: *Leaky aquifers.

Solutions are given for the drawdown distribution due to the operation of wells fields in coupled leaky aquifers of finite areal extent. A transform to solve the flow problem was obtained by modification of the zero-order Hankel transform. Two cases of the problem are analyzed. Case 1 concerns the upper aquifer when it is confined or unconfined and the drawdown on it is very small compared with its saturated thickness. Case 2 concerns the upper unconfined aquifer when the drawdown in it can be significant in relation to its saturated thickness. Approximate solutions and solutions for special cases were obtained in additou to the exact solutions. The solutions are in the form of series that can readily be evaluated. (See also W74-02773) (Knapp-USGS)
W75-08389

HYDROGEOLOGY OF THE EDMONTON AREA (NORTHWEST SEGMENT), ALBERTA,
Alberta Research, Edmonton.
For primary bibliographic entry see Field 4B.
W75-08398

HYDROGEOLOGY OF THE GLEICHEN AREA, ALBERTA,
Alberta Research, Edmonton.
For primary bibliographic entry see Field 4B.
W75-08399

ANALYSIS OF PUMPING TEST DATA FROM ANISOTROPIC UNCONFINED AQUIFERS CONSIDERING DELAYED GRAVITY RESPONSE,
Agricultural Research Organization, Bet Dagan (Israel). Inst. of Soils and Water.
S. P. Neuman.
Water Resources Research, Vol 11, No 2, p 329-342, April 1975. 9 fig, 2 tab, 22 ref.

Descriptors: *Groundwater, *Aquifers, *Aquifer characteristics, *Aquifer testing, *Mathematical studies, Pump testing, Testing, Drawdown, Specific yield, Water wells, Unsteady flow, Equations, Anisotropy, Analysis, Observation wells.
Identifiers: Delayed yield, Gravity drainage, Type-curve solutions, Partial penetration effects.

A new analytical model was proposed for the delayed response process characterizing flow to a well in an unconfined aquifer. The new approach was based only on well-defined physical parameters of the aquifer system. As such, it can be used to develop methods for determining the hydraulic properties of anisotropic unconfined aquifers from field drawdown data. Two methods of analysis were described, one based on the matching of field data with theoretical type curves and the other based on the semi-logarithmic relationship between drawdown and time. These methods were illustrated by applying them to field pumping tests. Similar procedures can be used to analyze data from partially penetrating wells, but this requires that a special set of theoretical curves be developed for each field situation. Such theoretical curves can easily be developed with the aid of a computer program. An explicit mathematical relationship was derived between Boulton's delay index and the physical characteristics of the aquifer. It was shown that contrary to the assumption of Boulton the delay index is not a characteristic constant of the aquifer but decreases linearly with the logarithm of the radial distance from the pumping well. This discovery makes it possible to reinterpret the results of pumping tests that were previously obtained with the aid of Boulton's theory without necessarily reexamining the original drawdown data. Results from pumping tests were used to illustrate this last point. (Prickett-ISWS)
W75-08434

A STOCHASTIC MODEL OF DISPERSION IN A POROUS MEDIUM,
Ecole Polytechnique, Montreal (Quebec).
P. Todorovic.
Water Resources Research, Vol 11, No 2, p 348-354, April 1975. 4 fig, 10 ref.

Descriptors: *Stochastic processes, *Dispersion, *Porous media, *Groundwater, Equations, Mathematical studies, Diffusion, Groundwater movement, Diffusivity, Statistical methods, Saturated flow, Mass transfer, Model studies, Hydraulics, Probability.
Identifiers: *Kinematic motion, *Random walk.

A set of tagged particles released in a flow through a porous medium is subject to random dispersion. For a statistically homogeneous and isotropic porous medium a stochastic model of longitudinal dispersion was determined, provided the fluid flow was steady and no mass transfer occurs between the solid phase and the fluid. A stochastic model was presented to describe longitudinal dispersion of a set of tagged particles released continuously (but not necessarily at uniform rate) in a flow through a porous structure. The model depends on two constant parameters which in turn depend on the properties of the porous medium and hydraulic conditions. It was emphasized that the model presented was kinematic in the sense that it treated only the statistical properties of the law of motion of a tagged particle in a flow through a porous medium and did not go into particulars of dynamic conditions. Consequently, it did not explicitly contain parameters of the hydraulic forces leading to this motion. (Prickett-ISWS)
W75-08435

A STUDY BY THE FINITE-ELEMENT METHOD OF THE INFLUENCE OF FRACTURES IN CONFINED AQUIFERS,
Dundee Univ. (Scotland).
A. B. Gureghian.
Society of Petroleum Engineers Journal, Vol 15, No 2, p 181-191, April 1975. 15 fig, 1 tab, 17 ref, 1 append.

Descriptors: *Groundwater, *Fracture permeability, *Finite element analysis, *Model studies, *Anisotropy, Cracks, Fissures(Geologic), Mathematical studies, Numerical analysis, Analog models, Borehole geophysics, Subsurface investigations, Limestones, Wells, Confined water.
Identifiers: *Electrolytic model, *Fracture flow capacity, Three-dimensional flow.

A treatment was presented of the effect of sand-filled fractures in a confined aquifer on the flow behavior, particularly flow to a fully penetrating well. The mathematical study was based on the variational method and the computation was carried out by using the finite-element method. A new governing equation was derived based on the variational principle applicable to the fracture problem and its form was explained. Experimental checks were carried out with an electrolytic tank. The investigations determined the potential distribution and the borehole discharge in relation to the fracture flow capacity (that is, the ratio of the permeability of the fracture to the permeability of the surrounding formation), length, position, and orientation of fractures. The effect of horizontal and vertical anisotropy was also investigated. (Prickett-ISWS)
W75-08443

GEOCHEMISTRY OF GROUNDWATERS IN THE CHAD BASIN,
Geological Survey of Israel, Jerusalem.
For primary bibliographic entry see Field 2K.
W75-08445

DISPERSION EFFECT ON BUOYANCE-DRIVEN CONVECTION IN STRATIFIED FLOWS THROUGH POROUS MEDIA,
Oslo Univ. (Norway). Inst. of Mathematics.
J. E. Weber.
Journal of Hydrology, Vol 25, No 1/2, p 59-70, April 1975. 16 ref, 1 append.

Descriptors: *Groundwater, *Porous media, *Geothermal studies, *Dispersion, *Mathematical

studies, Water temperature, Thermal stratification, Convection, Heated water, Mass transfer, Buoyancy, Gravitational water, Equations, Darcys law, Hydrodynamics, Heat flow, Solutes.
Identifiers: *Thermally driven flow, *Peclet numbers.

The effect of hydrodynamic dispersion on the onset of convection in flows through porous media was theoretically studied. The medium was isotropic, and bounded by two horizontal impermeable planes having a constant concentration difference. Pressure-driven as well as thermally-driven basic flows were considered. The investigations were valid in the limit of small and large Peclet numbers. The analysis showed that the onset of convection is independent of the longitudinal dispersion coefficient, while lateral dispersion always has a stabilizing effect. The preferred mode of instability is stationary, two-dimensional disturbances with axes aligned in the direction of the basic flow (longitudinal rolls). (Prickett-ISWS)
W75-08447

THE CHALK GROUNDWATER TRITIUM ANOMALY--A POSSIBLE EXPLANATION,
Institute of Geological Sciences, London (England). Dept. of Hydrogeology.
S. S. D. Foster.
Journal of Hydrology, Vol 25, No 1/2, p 159-165, April 1975. 2 fig, 10 ref.

Descriptors: *Groundwater, *Groundwater movement, *Saturated flow, *Tritium, Diffusion, Dispersion, Permeability, Porosity, Pore water, Carbonate rocks, Fissures(Geologic).
Identifiers: *British Chalk aquifer, Thermonuclear tritium.

Attention was drawn to a mechanism which could profoundly complicate the interpretation of tritium determinations in investigations of the rate of groundwater movement in the British Chalk and other physically-comparable formations. It could explain the anomalously low levels of thermonuclear tritium currently observed in the saturated zone of the Chalk aquifer, with important implications for pollution control. (Gibb-ISWS)
W75-08449

INVESTIGATION OF VERTICAL GROUND-WATER FLOW IN BOREHOLES,
International Hydrological Decade, New Delhi (India). Indian National Committee.
M. Bardhan.
Journal of Hydrology, Vol 25, No 1/2, April 1975. 2 fig, 9 ref.

Descriptors: *Groundwater, *Groundwater movement, *Wells, *Logging(Recording), *Radioactive well logging, Boreholes, Neutron absorption, Flow, Seepage, Sinks.
Identifiers: Vertical flow, Gamma-gamma logs, Neutron-neutron logs.

An integrated nuclear approach involving conjunctive application of gamma--gamma and neutron--neutron depth gages and a strong neutron-absorbent tracer (boron) was followed to locate the source and sink zones supporting vertical groundwater flow as well as quantifying the flow volume in uncased sub-artesian borewells sunk in trappean terrains. The results were utilized in calculating the seepage loss from the saturated zone into the unsaturated zone through the well bore, which in turn aided in decision-making relating to the design of production wells in the areas studied. (Gibb-ISWS)
W75-08450

NON-EQUALIBRIUM THERMODYNAMIC TREATMENT OF TRANSPORT PROCESSES IN GROUND-WATER FLOW,
Nevada Univ., Reno. Desert Research Inst.
C. L. Carnahan.
Available from the National Technical Information Service, Springfield, Va 22161 as PB-242 311, $4.75 in paper copy, $2.25 in microfiche. Water Resources Research Center, Publication No 24, May 1975. 83 p, 2 fig, 2 tab, 49 ref. OWRT B-067-NEV(2). 14-31-0001-4103.

Descriptors: *Chemical potential, Chemical reactions, Chemistry, Groundwater, *Thermodynamics, *Base flow, *Groundwater movement, Porous media, *Dispersion, Equations, Model studies, *Path of pollutants.

The theory of non-equilibrium thermodynamics is applied to transport processes in ground-water flow systems. The theory and the manner in which it can be applied to natural processes are described. The theory is postulated to be applicable to a continuum model of porous medium in which fluxes and forces at points in the fluid phase are averaged over a representative elementary volume. Phenomenological equations appropriate to ground-water flow systems are derived to illustrate the presence of coupled phenomena in dispersive processes and simultaneous transport of heat and matter. It is proposed that phenomenological coefficients for coupled and direct dispersive processes be formed of the product of a fourth-rank tensor, dispersivity of the medium, with the dyadic product of solute velocities, rather than with fluid flow velocities. Group theory is applied to resulting coefficients, and new results are obtained for the forms assumed by the coefficients in certain anisotropic media. (Fallon-Nevada)
W75-08488

MEASUREMENT OF THE HORIZONTAL COMPONENT OF GROUND WATER FLOW USING A VERTICALLY POSITIONED IN-SITU THERMAL PROBE,
New Mexico Inst. of Mining and Technology, Socorro. Dept. of Geoscience.
S. G. McLin, M. A. Reiter, and A. R. Sanford.
Available from the National Technical Information Service, Springfield, Va 22161 as PB-242 312, $4.25 in paper copy, $2.25 in microfiche. New Mexico Water Resources Research Institute, Las Cruces, Report No 055, May 1975. 34 p, 13 fig, 3 tab, 3 ref. OWRT A-044-NMEX(1).

Descriptors: *Instrumentation, *Groundwater movement, *Base flow, *Measurement, Thermal conductivity, Isotherms, *Calibration, *Flow rates, Boreholes.
Identifiers: *Thermal probe.

A thermal probe for the in-situ measurement of groundwater flow rates in a borehole was calibrated in a vertical position. The probe is a long slender metal rod having a heat source along its entire length and a temperature sensor at its midpoint. When a constant quantity of heat is applied to the probe, the rise in temperature is inversely related to the rate of water flowing past the probe. Full scale calibration of the probe was considered necessary because theoretical studies over-simplify the interaction between the heated probe and the horizontal flow of groundwater. Fifty eight calibration runs of the thermal probe were made; most of these tests were used to perfect the experimental techniques of data gathering and the design of the calibration tank. Fourteen of the calibration tests were selected to construct preliminary calibration curves. The selection of specific tests was based on a statistical analysis of the A1 coefficients from a third order polynomial fit of the experimental data. Final calibration curves were constructed on the basis of the ten calibration tests. These curves show that if a temperature difference of 0.1 degree Centegrade can be measured at the end of a two hour test, the probe is capable of distinguishing small differences in specific discharges when the flow exceeds 120 cm/day. (Hain-New Mexico State)
W75-08490

EVALUATION OF RECHARGE POTENTIAL NEAR INDIO, CALIFORNIA,
Geological Survey, Menlo Park, Calif.
For primary bibliographic entry see Field 4B.
W75-08493

BASIC GROUND-WATER DATA FOR THE MOSCOW BASIN, IDAHO,
Geological Survey, Boise, Idaho.
E. G. Crosthwaite.
Open-file report, 1975. 96 p, 7 fig, 2 tab, 23 ref, append.

Descriptors: *Basic data collections, *Hydrologic data, *Idaho, *Groundwater, Aquifers, Basalts, Water wells, Water levels, Water yield, Groundwater basins.
Identifiers: *Moscow basin(Idaho).

The Moscow basin encompasses an area of 65 square miles in Latah County and borders the Idaho-Washington State line. The basin is along the eastern edge of the 'Palouse Country' where the rolling Palouse hills merge with the low mountains of northern Idaho. All water supplies for the basin are derived from wells and springs. Virtually all large-capacity wells are owned by the city of Moscow and the University of Idaho. These wells are open to the basalt of the Columbia River Group and the interbedded sands in the Latah Formation. Presented are a table of well records, well logs, a table of annual groundwater withdrawals, water levels in observation wells, a contour map showing the approximate elevation of the water level in the upper series of basalt flows and interbedded sediments in the southern part of the area, and a bibliography of the more important reports pertaining to groundwater in the area. (Knapp-USGS)
W75-08499

CHEMISTRY OF SUBSURFACE WATERS,
Geological Survey, Menlo Park, Calif.
For primary bibliographic entry see Field 2K.
W75-08506

ESTIMATED YIELD OF FRESH-WATER WELLS IN FLORIDA,
Geological Survey, Tallahassee, Fla.
For primary bibliographic entry see Field 7C.
W75-08507

GROUND-WATER CONDITIONS IN THE FRANKLIN AREA, SOUTHEASTERN VIRGINIA,
Geological Survey, Reston, Va.
For primary bibliographic entry see Field 7C.
W75-08509

GROUND-WATER FAVORABILITY AND SURFICIAL GEOLOGY OF THE CHERRYFIELD-JONESBORO AREA, MAINE,
Geological Survey, Reston, Va.
For primary bibliographic entry see Field 7C.
W75-08510

SALINE GROUND-WATER RESOURCES OF LEE COUNTY, FLORIDA,
Geological Survey, Tallahassee, Fla.
D. H. Boggess.
Open-file report FL 74-247, 1974. 62 p, 10 fig, 5 tab, 7 ref, append.

Descriptors: *Saline water, *Florida, *Groundwater, Hydrogeology, Groundwater movement, Hydrologic data, Withdrawal, Water levels, Saline water intrusion.
Identifiers: *Lee County(Fla).

Lee County, Florida is underlain at depths greater than 400 feet by formations containing saline water. Two saline water-bearing zones occur

within the depth interval 400 to 1,200 feet; the upper zone is termed the lower Hawthorn aquifer and the lower zone is termed the Suwannee aquifer. Fresh water infiltrates into the aquifers in the central highlands regions of Florida where water levels are as much as 130 feet above sea level. The water subsequently moves southwestward becoming progressively more saline toward the coast. Both aquifers are under sufficient artesian pressure to cause wells tapping them to flow at land surface. Artesian pressure in the aquifers has been reduced along the Caloosahatchee River by heavy withdrawal and this reduction in pressure is a major factor in deterioration of water quality in the McGregor Isles area, south of Fort Myers. The saline water from the lower Hawthorn and Suwannee aquifers is hard and sulfurous. The dissolved solids range from 700 to 3,300 mg/litre. (Knapp-USGS)
W75-08517

SOIL MOISTURE MOVEMENT UNDER TEMPERATURE GRADIENTS,
Department of Irrigation, Colombo (Sri Lanka). Land Use Div.
For primary bibliographic entry see Field 2G.
W75-08597

GEOELECTRICAL POSSIBILITIES OF DETECTING STREAM CHANNELS IN CARBONATE ROCKS,
Missouri Univ., Rolla.
R. K. Frohlich.
Arkansas Academy of Science Proceedings, Vol 26, p 71-72. 1972, 3 fig, 3 ref. OWRR A-046-Mo(4) 14-01-0001-3825.

Descriptors: Karst, Streams, Channels, *Resistivity, *Underground streams, Electrical networks, *Carbonate rocks, *Karst hydrology, *Subsurface flow.

Several geoelectrical resistivity methods that may be used to determine the position and flow characteristics of underground water associated with carbonate bedrock and karst development are considered. The most promising method studied employs depth soundings patterned after Sehlumberger. The plotting of half electrode separation against apparent resistivity yields a curve which may be used to discriminate between lateral and vertical inhomogeneities in bedrock. A network of depth soundings of this type ultimately may lead to a map that will show geoelectrical anisotropies that may be used to analyze subsurface water courses in carbonate rock.
W75-08603

CARBON 14 DATING OF GROUNDWATER FROM CLOSED AND OPEN SYSTEMS,
Waterloo Univ. (Ontario). Dept. of Mechanical Engineering.
T. M. L. Wigley.
Water Resources Research, Vol 11, No 2, p 324-328, April 1975. 2 fig, 1 tab, 14 ref.

Descriptors: *Isotope studies, *Carbon radioisotopes, *Radioactive dating, *Groundwater recharge, Stable isotopes, Isotope fractionation, Geochemistry, Temperature, Aquifer systems, Hydrogeology, *Florida, Groundwater, Aquifers.
Identifiers: Mass balance method, *Arcadia aquifer(Fla).

Groundwaters may be dated by using carbon 14, provided that the raw data are properly adjusted. However, adjustment factors determined from geochemical or isotopic measurements and based on simple models of carbonate dissolution do not always agree with adjustment factors obtained by independent means. Established adjustment methods were reinterpreted in terms of closed and open system models of carbonate dissolution, and it was suggested that these models provide a sounder framework for determining adjustment factors. Hypothetical and real examples were considered, and it was shown that some otherwise anomalous results may be explained in terms of the closed and open system models. (Schicht-ISWS)
W75-08707

AN APPROXIMATE INFINITE CONDUCTIVITY SOLUTION FOR A PARTIALLY PENETRATING LINE-SOURCE WELL,
Bureau de Recherches Geologiques et Minieres, Orleans (France).
For primary bibliographic entry see Field 4B.
W75-08715

RESEARCH AND ADVANCES IN GROUNDWATER RESOURCES STUDIES, 1964-1974,
Florida Water Management District, Brooksville.
G. G. Parker, and A. I. Johnson.
In: A Decade of Progress in Water Resources: American Water Resources Association, Proceedings, Series No 19, p 42-75, March 1974.

Descriptors: *Bibliographies, *Publications, *Groundwater, *Groundwater resources, Information retrieval, Groundwater availability, Groundwater movement, Model studies, Hydrologic data, Aquifer characteristics, Water quality, Water pollution sources, Legal aspects, State governments, Federal government, Water law.

Approximately 800 bibliographic entries including most of the published works on groundwater research in the United States, both basic and applied, during the period 1964-1974, are listed in alphabetical order by author. In the past 10 years there has been a predominant shift to the inclusion of groundwater studies and other aspects of water resources including surface water and soil moisture, and the influences of the entire environmental framwork in which water occurs. Further, the trend is away from the descriptive and qualitative to the evaluative and quantitative. Most current reports are made in the context of systems analysis and commonly include modeling, either digital or electric analogue models and in a growing number of studies use is made of hybrid models. Because water law is currently undergoing changes both in the State and Federal governments, important water-law entries have been included. (Woodard-USGS)
W75-08825

ONE-DIMENSIONAL SIMULATION OF AQUIFER SYSTEM COMPACTION NEAR PIXLEY, CALIFORNIA: 1. CONSTANT PARAMETERS,
Geological Survey, Sacramento, Calif.
D. C. Helm.
Water Resources Research, Vol 11, No 3, p 465-478, June 1975. 8 fig, 4 tab, 20 ref.

Descriptors: *Land subsidence, *Aquifer characteristics, *Pumping, *Mathematical models, Forecasting, Water levels, *California, Geomorphology, Hydrogeology, Evaluation, Water level fluctuations, Compaction, Soil physical properties, Model studies, Aquitards, Simulation analysis.
Identifiers: *Pixley(Calif).

One of the major problems facing groundwater hydrologists is how to predict subsidence of the land surface due to extraction of underground fluid. Aggregate one-dimensional compaction (consolidation) of a series of aquitards in a compacting aquifer system has been simulated through use of a finite difference representation of the vertical stress distribution within an idealized aquitard. Among the parameters affecting the simulated compaction are two storage coefficients (compressibility values), one for recoverable and the other for nonrecoverable compression. These two storage coefficients introduce a transient heterogeneity within an aquitard that is generally ignored by hydrologists. A computer program with two sets of constant coefficients calculates the daily deformation due to observed changes in applied stress near Pixley, California. Although water levels fluctuate annually, no long-term water level decline occurred near Pixley between January 1, 1959, and February 4, 1971. During this period, 3.19 ft to compaction was observed. The net difference between simulated and observed compaction on February 4, 1971, was 1.3% of the observed value. Maximum deviation occurred in mid-1964 and equaled 7% of the observed compaction. (Woodard-USGS)
W75-08826

BOUGUER GRAVITY ANOMALY MAP OF THE TEMECULA AREA, RIVERSIDE COUNTY, CALIFORNIA,
Geological Survey, Garden Grove, Calif.
For primary bibliographic entry see Field 7C.
W75-08831

2G. Water In Soils

REPORT AND INTERPRETATIONS FOR THE GENERAL SOIL MAP OF PIMA COUNTY, ARIZONA,
Soil Conservation Service, Portland, Oreg.
M. L. Richardson, and M. L. Miller.
USDA Soil Conservation Service and Pima County Natural Resource Conservation District, July 1973, 49 p, 3 tab, 2 append, 1 map, 4 refs.

Descriptors: *Soil groups, *Soil properties, *Soil temperature, *Soil surveys, *Maps, Water management, Soil classification, Arid lands, Recreation, Soil structure, Soil texture, Drainage, Depth, Slopes, Gravels, *Arizona, Regional analysis, Flood plains, Alluvial channels.
Identifiers: Pima County(Arizona).

Fifteen major soil associations found in Pima County, Arizona, are described, giving the setting in which the soils occur, the proportion of major and important minor soils present, and a brief description of the major soils classified according to the national classification system. Tables list not only estimated soil properties and suitability for selected uses, but also soil limitation ratings and soil features affecting select engineering, nonfarm, recreational, and water management uses for the major soil components. The soil map was designed for use in general planning, showing general locations of soils suitable for particular uses, but on-site investigations are recommended for more detailed planning. (Mastic-Arizona)
W75-08373

RESPONSE OF AN UNSATURATED SOIL TO FOREST TRANSPIRATION,
Connecticut Agricultural Experiment Station, New Haven.
For primary bibliographic entry see Field 2D.
W75-08436

GEOCHEMICAL FACIES OF SEDIMENTS,
Geologisch-Palaeontologisches Institut der Universitat (West Germany).
For primary bibliographic entry see Field 2J.
W75-08462

NITRATE AND NITRITE REDUCTION IN FLOODED GAMMA-IRRADIATED SOIL UNDER CONTROLLED PH AND REDOX POTENTIAL CONDITIONS,
Ghent Rijksuniversiteit (Belgium). Faculteit Landbouwwetenschappen.
For primary bibliographic entry see Field 5G.
W75-08470

HEAT AND MOISTURE CONDUCTION IN UNSATURATED SOILS,
Arkansas Univ., Fayetteville. Dept. of Chemical Engineering.
For primary bibliographic entry see Field 5B.
W75-08477

WATER AND SOLUTE TRANSPORT IN LAKELAND FINE SAND,
Florida Univ., Gainesville. Dept. of Soil Sciences.
For primary bibliographic entry see Field 5B.
W75-08480

WATER INTAKE RATES ON A SILT LOAM SOIL WITH VARIOUS MANURE APPLICATIONS,
Nebraska Univ., Lincoln. Dept. of Agricultural Engineering.
O. E. Cross, and P. E. Fischbach.
Transactions of the ASAE (American Society of Agricultural Engineers), Vol 16, No 2, p 282-284, March-April, 1973. 9 fig, 5 ref.

Descriptors: *Irrigation practices, *Permeability, Soil Physics, Soil structure, Soil ammendments, Soil density, Soil management, Soil texture, Organic matter, *Farm wastes, Water pollution control.

Feedlot manure was applied to and incorporated into a sharpsburg silt loam soil. Four levels of manure were applied and the plots disk plowed to three depths. During 1970 the crops were irrigated three times and during 1971, four times. Water infiltration rates were determined from data of the inflow-outflow method. The initial water intake rate increased as the quantity of manure application increased. The basic water intake rate increased as more time from date of manure application had elapsed. Manure application decreased the basic intake rate as compared to the basic intake rate of non-manured silt loam soil. Depth of plowing did not appreciably affect the basic intake rate. (Skogerboe-Colorado State)
W75-08574

MICROBIAL AVAILABILITY OF PHOSPHORUS IN LAKE SEDIMENTS,
Wisconsin Univ., Madison. Water Chemistry Lab.
For primary bibliographic entry see Field 5B.
W75-08578

SOIL MOISTURE MOVEMENT UNDER TEMPERATURE GRADIENTS,
Department of Irrigation, Colombo (Sri Lanka). Land Use Div.
W. D. Joshua, and E. De Jong.
Can J Soil Sci, Vol 53, No 1, p 49-57, 1973.

Descriptors: Soil moisture, *Soil water movement, *Thermocline, *Sands, Loam, Thermodynamics, *Analytical techniques.
Identifiers: Temperature gradients, Sandy loam, Irreversible thermodynamic theory.

Temperature gradients of 0.5, 1.0, and 1.5 degree C/cm were imposed on sealed soil columns of a fine sandy loam at various moisture contents. When steady state was reached, heat flux, temperature distribution, and moisture content or moisture tension distribution were measured. The coupling between heat and moisture flux was calculated using the theory of irreversible thermodynamics. The coupling between heat and moisture flux was negligible for tensions less than 0.1 bar or higher than 15 bars. Coupling increased as the temperature increased. Within experimental error, Onsager's relation for the interaction between heat and moisture flow was valid. The agreement between the thermodynamic approach and the 'series-parallel' theory was satisfactory between 0.3- and 15 bar tension. At tensions above 15 bars or below 0.1 bar, the series-parallel theory predicted more interaction between heat and moisture flow than was observed. The coupling between heat and moisture flow was significant only when the moisture flow occurred in the liquid phase and when soil-water interaction was pronounced.--Copyright 1973, Biological Abstracts, Inc.
W75-08597

RESPONSE OF THREE CORN HYBRIDS TO LOW LEVELS OF SOIL MOISTURE TENSION IN THE PLOW LAYER,
Agricultural Research and Educational Center, Quincy, Fla.
For primary bibliographic entry see Field 3F.
W75-08600

EMITTER VALVE FOR SOIL IRRIGATION,
Salco Products, Inc., Los Angeles, Calif. (assignee)
For primary bibliographic entry see Field 3F.
W75-08614

MOISTURE RESPONSIVE APPARATUS FOR CONTROLLING MOISTURE CONTENT OF SOIL,
For primary bibliographic entry see Field 3F.
W75-08615

SIMULATION MODEL FOR EVAPOTRANSPIRATION OF WHEAT: EMPIRICAL APPROACH,
Agricultural Research Organization, Bet Dagan (Israel). Inst. of Soils and Water.
For primary bibliographic entry see Field 2D.
W75-08712

POLLUTION OF OPEN WATERS BY PESTICIDES ENTERING FROM AGRICULTURAL AREAS, (IN RUSSIAN),
Kiev Research Inst. of General Communal Hygiene (USSR).
For primary bibliographic entry see Field 5B.
W75-08729

2H. Lakes

THE CONTRIBUTION OF AGRICULTURE TO EUTROPHICATION OF SWISS WATERS: I. RESULTS OF DIRECT MEASUREMENTS IN THE DRAINAGE AREA OF VARIOUS MAIN DRAINAGE CHANNELS,
Eidgenoessische Technische Hochschule, Kastienbaum (Switzerland). Hydrobiology Lab.
For primary bibliographic entry see Field 5B.
W75-08376

TEMPERATURES SELECTED SEASONALLY BY FOUR FISHES FROM WESTERN LAKE ERIE,
Ohio State Cooperative Fishery Unit, Columbus.
For primary bibliographic entry see Field 5C.
W75-08381

NEMATODES OF LAKE BALATON: III. THE FAUNA IN LATE-SUMMER,
Research Inst. for Water Resources Development, Budapest (Hungary). Water Quality and Technology Dept.
For primary bibliographic entry see Field 5C.
W75-08385

THE SPECIFIC SURFACE AREA OF CLAYS IN LAKE SEDIMENTS--MEASUREMENT AND ANALYSIS OF CONTRIBUTORS IN LAKE KINNERET, ISRAEL,
Hebrew Univ., Rehovoth (Israel). Dept. of Soil and Water Science.
For primary bibliographic entry see Field 2J.
W75-08428

PHOSPHORUS SOURCES FOR LOWER GREEN BAY, LAKE MICHIGAN,
Wisconsin Univ., Green Bay. Ecosystems Analysis.
For primary bibliographic entry see Field 5B.
W75-08467

DEVELOPMENT OF A MANAGEMENT FRAMEWORK OF THE GREAT SALT LAKE,
Utah Water Research Lab., Logan.
For primary bibliographic entry see Field 6A.
W75-08473

WATER QUALITY OF THE LAKE SISKIYOU AREA AND A REACH OF UPPER SACRAMENTO RIVER BELOW BOX CANYON DAM, CALIFORNIA, MAY 1970 THROUGH SEPTEMBER 1971,
Geological Survey, Menlo Park, Calif.
For primary bibliographic entry see Field 5B.
W75-08521

EVALUATION OF BACTERIAL PRODUCTION IN A POND IN SOLOGNE, (IN FRENCH),
Centre National pour l'Exploitation des Oceans, Paris (France).
For primary bibliographic entry see Field 5C.
W75-08534

GROWTH OF THE BLUE-GREEN ALGA MICROCYSTIS AERUGINOSA UNDER DEFINED CONDITIONS,
Nebraska Univ., Lincoln. Dept. of Chemical Engineering.
For primary bibliographic entry see Field 5C.
W75-08579

STATUTORY DEFINITIONS OF FRESHWATER WETLANDS.
For primary bibliographic entry see Field 6E.
W75-08594

RADIOLOGICAL AND ENVIRONMENTAL RESEARCH DIVISION ANNUAL REPORT, ECOLOGY, JANUARY - DECEMBER 1973.
Argonne National Lab., Ill.
For primary bibliographic entry see Field 5B.
W75-08670

NUMERICAL ANALYSIS OF WARM, TURBULENT SINKING JETS DISCHARGED INTO QUIESCENT WATER OF LOW TEMPERATURE,
Iowa Univ., Iowa City. Inst. of Hydraulic Research.
For primary bibliographic entry see Field 5B.
W75-08684

TRAJECTORIES AND SPEEDS OF WIND-DRIVEN CURRENTS NEAR THE COAST,
Louisiana State Univ., Baton Rouge. Coastal Studies Inst.
S. P. Murray.
Journal of Physical Oceanography, Vol 5, No 2, p 347-360, April 1975. 15 fig, 1 tab, 28 ref. NR 388 002. ONR Contract N00014-69-A-0211-0003.

Descriptors: *Rheotropism, *Coasts, *Lake breezes, *Sea breezes, Ocean currents, Drift bottles, Flow, Movement, Water circulation, Coriolis force, Eddies, Winds, Currents(Water), On-site investigations.
Identifiers: Drogues.

Detailed observation of drogue movements within 800 m of a straight shoreline indicates the primary current generated by local winds to be directed within a few degrees of parallel to the shore nearly independently of wind direction. Subtle vertical structure in the onshore-offshore speed com-

ponent is dependent on vertical stratification such that unstratified water produces a two-layer flow (onshore in the surface layer, off-shore in the bottom layer), and moderately stratified water produces a three-layered flow (onshore in surface and bottom layers, offshore at intermediate depths). Theoretical conclusions from Jeffreys' constant eddy viscosity theory support the unstratified velocity profile and accurately predict the alongshore current speeds. Numerical solutions with a depth-dependent eddy viscosity indicate that the three-layered flow pattern is a direct result of the density gradient. Even in these shallow waters the inclusion of Coriolis effects in the theory is necessary for a complete understanding of the current observations. Simple theoretical calculations on the response characteristics of various sized surface-tracked drogues as a function of wind speed indicate that drogue size should be carefully selected in terms of expected magnitudes of wind and current speeds. (Jess-ISWS)
W75-08694

THE EFFECT OF WIND AND SURFACE CURRENTS ON DRIFTERS,
Texas A and M Univ., College Station. Dept. of Oceanography.
A. D. Kirwan, Jr., G. McNally, M-S., Chang, and R. Molinari.
Journal of Physical Oceanography, Vol 5, No 2, p 361-368, April 1975. 8 fig, 2 tab, 1 ref.

Descriptors: *Rheotropism, *Ocean currents, *Lake breezes, *Sea breezes, Drift bottles, Flow, Movement, Water circulation, Coriolis force, Winds, Theoretical analysis, Velocity, Currents(Water).
Identifiers: Drifters, Wind currents, Surface currents.

The motion of a drifter acted on by wind, surface, and subsurface currents was analyzed. From the condition of static equilibrium of all drag forces acting on the drifter, the effects of wind and surface current of arbitrary direction and magnitude and drogue characteristics were examined parametrically. Specific application was made to a recently developed drifter with 9.2 and 11.85 m parachute drogues and a window shade drogue. The calculations show that for some environmental conditions the deviation between the magnitudes of the drifter velocity and the water parcel velocity may exceed 50%. Furthermore, the direction of velocity vectors may differ by as much as 45 degrees. Drifter data from an experiment conducted by the Atlantic Oceanographic and Meteorological Laboratories and the NOAA Data Buoy Office in the Gulf of Mexico Loop Current were examined in light of the theoretical results. The wind effects predicted by the theory were observed in the field. Thus, wind corrections to the drifter velocity records which are based on the theory can significantly improve the velocity records. (Jess-ISWS)
W75-08695

ON THE TIME-DEPENDENT FLOW IN A LAKE,
Case Western Reserve Univ., Cleveland, Ohio.
A. Haq, and W. Lick.
Journal of Geophysical Research, Vol 80, No 3, p 431-437, January 20, 1975. 6 fig, 16 ref.

Descriptors: *Lakes, *Flow, *Mathematical models, *Circulation, Model studies, Computer models, Equations, Surface waters, *Lake Erie, Great Lakes, Hydrodynamics, Path of pollutants.

The time-dependent flow in a constant depth basin was investigated. Various time scales of interest were explicitly identified and simple analytical formulas for these time scales were derived. In addition, the rigid lid and free surface models were compared. The results were verified by comparison with numerical calculations. (Sims-ISWS)
W75-08703

CHEMICAL AND BIOLOGICAL INDICES OF EUTROPHICATION OF THE LUBACHOW RESERVOIR,
Panstwowy Instytut Hydrologiozno-Meteorologiczny, Wroclaw (Poland).
For primary bibliographic entry see Field 5C.
W75-08765

EUTROPHICATION OF BAIKAL LAKE,
For primary bibliographic entry see Field 5C.
W75-08766

RELATIONS BETWEEN NUTRIENT BUDGET AND PRODUCTIVITY IN PONDS,
Ceskoslovenska Akademie Ved, Prague. Hydrobiologicka Laborator.
For primary bibliographic entry see Field 5C.
W75-08767

LIMNOLOGICAL MODELS OF RESERVOIR ECOSYSTEM,
Ceskoslovenska Adademie Ved, Prague. Hydrobiologicka Laborator.
For primary bibliographic entry see Field 5C.
W75-08770

DRAWING OFF OF HYPOLIMNION WATERS AS A METHOD FOR IMPROVING THE QUALITY OF LAKE WATERS,
For primary bibliographic entry see Field 5C.
W75-08771

MODELING WIND INDUCED WATER CURRENTS,
Worcester Polytechnic Inst., Mass. Alden Research Labs.
For primary bibliographic entry see Field 5B.
W75-08816

PRIMARY PRODUCTION IN A GREAT PLAINS RESERVOIR,
For primary bibliographic entry see Field 5C.
W75-08846

2I. Water In Plants

CLASSIFICATION AND WORLD DISTRIBUTION OF VEGETATION RELATIVE TO V/STOL AIRCRAFT OPERATIONS,
Army Engineer Topographic Labs., Fort Belvoir, Va.
For primary bibliographic entry see Field 7B.
W75-08366

STUDIES ON FLOATING RICE: IV. EFFECTS OF RAINSING WATER LEVEL ON THE NITROGENOUS COMPOUNDS OF THE TOPS, (IN JAPANESE),
Kobe Univ. (Japan). Faculty of Agriculture.
T. Yamaguchi.
Proc Crop Sci Soc Jap, Vol 42, No 1, p 35-40, 1973. Illus. English summary.

Descriptors: *Rice, Nitrogen compounds.

Cultivars of floating and non-floating rice were grown under submerged condition by raising the water level. Total-, protein-, total soluble-, and amide plus ammonia-N of the floating and non-floating rice plants were compared with those under ordinary conditions. In another experiment, rice plants were grown under submerged condition by raising the water level and then lowering it. The various fractions of nitrogenous compounds of the leaf blade, leaf sheath and internode grown under submerged condition were compared with those under ordinary conditions. Under ordinary conditions, there were no significant differences in the contents of total-, protein-, and amide plus ammonia-N between the non-floating and floating rice, but the content of total soluble-N was slightly higher in floating rice, while concentrations of total-, protein-, and total soluble-N were higher in non-floating rice. The content of protein-N of non-floating rice was decreased, but that of floating rice was increased under submerged conditions. Concentration of protein-N decreased in both types with the submerging treatment. Total soluble-N in the non-floating rice was increased under submerged condition, while that of the floating rice showed no appreciable change. The content of amide plus ammonia-N increased markedly under sumberged conditions in both types of rice. Amide plus ammonia-N concentration of the non-floating rice was increased more markedly than that of the floating rice. The nitrogenous compounds of the leaf sheath and internode were more affected by submerging treatment than that of leaf blade. The ratios of total soluble-N or amide plus ammonia-N to protein-N became larger under submerged condition in the non-floating rice, while the change of the ratios remained narrow in the floating rice. Floating rice seems to maintain normal N metabolism under both ordinary and submerged conditions. (See also W75-02722)--Copyright 1974, Biological Abstracts, Inc.
W75-08375

THE EVAPORATION OF INTERCEPTED RAINFALL FROM A FOREST STAND: AN ANALYSIS BY SIMULATION,
Duke Univ., Durham, N.C. School of Forestry.
For primary bibliographic entry see Field 2D.
W75-08442

NITRATE UPTAKE EFFECTIVENESS OF FOUR PLANT SPECIES,
Purdue Univ., Lafayette, Ind. Dept. of Agronomy.
For primary bibliographic entry see Field 5B.
W75-08607

SEASONAL VARIATION OF SIEVING EFFICIENCY IN LOTIC HABITAT,
Commonwealth Scientific and Industrial Research Organization, Deception Bay (Australia). Div. of Fisheries and Oceanography.
For primary bibliographic entry see Field 5A.
W75-08609

DYNAMICS OF HIGHER PLANT WATER METABOLISM AND ITS INFORMATION SIGNIFICANCE, (IN RUSSIAN),
Agrofizicheskii Nauchno-Issledovatelskii Institut, Leningrad (USSR).
V. G. Karmanov, O. O. Lyalin, G. G. Mamulashvili, S. N. Meleshchenko, and V. A. Nikishin.
Fiziol Biokhim Kul't Rast. Vol 6, No 1, p 69-75, Illus, 1974. (English summary).

Descriptors: *Plant physiology, *Beans, Vegetable crops, Crops, *Consumptive use, Water utilization.
Identifiers: USSR, Kidney beans.

A comparative study of hydrodynamic and bioelectric reactions occurring in a transpiring plant (kidney bean) in response to different external effects showed that hydrodynamic reactions are one of possible mechanisms of rapid information transfer from 1 organ of the plant to another. The dynamic parameters of the water regime were studied for obtaining information on physiological processes in the plant organisms without disturbing its integrity.--Copyright 1975, Biological Abstracts, Inc.
W75-08789

DYNAMICS OF FREE AMINO ACID CONTENT IN LEAVES OF WINTER WHEAT UNDER

law for fragmented materials were discussed. (Sims-ISWS)
W75-08424

THE SPECIFIC SURFACE AREA OF CLAYS IN LAKE SEDIMENTS–MEASUREMENT AND ANALYSIS OF CONTRIBUTORS IN LAKE KINNERET, ISRAEL,
Hebrew Univ., Rehovoth (Israel). Dept. of Soil and Water Science.
A. Banin, M. Gal, Y. Zohar, and A. Singer.
Limnology and Oceanography, Vol 20, No 2, p 278-282, March 1975. 1 fig, 3 tab, 17 ref.

Descriptors: *Lake sediments, *Sediment-water interfaces, *Nutrients, Adsorption, Chemical precipitation, Urbanization, Carbonates, Clay minerals, Chemical analysis, Ion exchange, X-ray analysis, Electron microscopy, Suspended solids, Water circulation, Particle size.
Identifiers: *Specific surface area, *Israel(Lake Kinneret), *Jordan River.

The specific surface area of recent sediments of Lake Kinneret was measured and the contributions of various sediment components to it were evaluated. Most of the lake sediments had specific surface areas (SSA) larger than 100 sq m/g. Average SSA of the sediments is 181.8 + or -59.7 sq m/g, whereas that of the noncarbonate fraction, constituting on the average 54.8 + or -12.3% by weight of the sediment, is 374.6 + or -106.9 sq m/g. Despite their high proportion in the sediment, carbonates contribute only a very small fraction of the SSA; clay minerals in the 0-2 micron size fraction, particularly smectite, contribute most of it. (Visocky-ISWS)
W75-08428

WELSH FLOODPLAIN STUDIES: THE NATURE OF FLOODPLAIN GEOMETRY,
University Coll. of Wales, Aberystwyth.
For primary bibliographic entry see Field 2E.
W75-08448

EROSION MODELING ON A WATERSHED,
Agricultural Research Service, Morris, Minn. North Central Soil Conservation Research Center.
C. A. Onstad, and G. R. Foster.
Transactions of the American Society of Agricultural Engineers, Vol 18, No 2, p 288-292, March-April 1975. 2 fig, 3 tab, 7 ref.

Descriptors: *Erosion rates, *Rill erosion, *Model studies, *Soil erosion, *Sediment yield, Watersheds(Basins), Sediment transport, Mathematical models, Runoff, Slopes, Sheet erosion, Surface runoff, Storm runoff, Deposition(Sediments), Iowa, Ohio.
Identifiers: *Universal Soil Loss Equation, Interrill erosion, Soil detachment.

An erosion-deposition model was described based on a modified form of the Universal Soil Loss Equation incorporating hydrologic variables. The sediment yield concept and computations involve calculating soil detachment potential and transport potential on a storm by storm basis and then comparing the two, resulting in sediment yields and deposition. All computations were made on a unit width basis and extended to the entire watershed, using an appropriate watershed transformation scheme. Calculations along the slope length were made on slope segments, each with different length and steepness. A procedure for estimating the relative contributions of rill and interrill erosion was also presented. The final result was an estimate of the rill and interrill erosion distribution on a watershed, indicating areas of severe erosion and deposition. The model was used to simulate the soil movement during 11 storms on two Midwest watersheds planted to contour corn. Predictions on the 82.8-acre Iowa watershed were better than those on the smaller 1.5-acre Ohio watershed. (Lee-ISWS)
W75-08459

GEOCHEMICAL FACIES OF SEDIMENTS,
Geologisch-Palaeontologisches Institut der Universitat (West Germany).
K. Krejci-Graf.
Soil Science, Vol 119, No 1, p 20-23, January 1975. 11 ref.

Descriptors: *Geochemistry, *Facies(Sedimentary), *Physicochemical properties, *Sediments, *Soils, Nitrates, Calcareous soils, Methane, Dolomite, Phosphates, Quartz, Aluminum, Clay minerals, Sedimentology, Petrology, Soil profiles, Diagenesis, Potassium compounds, Magnesium compounds, Iodine, Oil shales, Sodium chloride, Gypsum, Silica, Carbon, Fluorescence, Bromine, Calcium compounds, Manganese, Coals.
Identifiers: *Fossil bionomy, *Paleobiochemistry, *Lithified sediments, Chemical facies, Metamorphism.

Geochemical facies of sediments and soils (the chemical indicators of the environment) provide geologists with a means to reconstruct fossilized environments of past ages. Facies diagnosis may be based on analysis of fossil bionomy, paleobiochemistry, or geochemistry. Geochemical facies diagnosis may be based on main constituents (lithology, sedimentology, and soil profile); minor components (concentrations in the order of 0.01 or 0.001, or less: salinity, ion conceentrations of C1, Br, I, F, and P; Ca: Sr and 12C: 13C as well as 180: 160 ratios, and indications on redox potentials), or the type and nature of organic substances preserved (C : N ratios, biochemistry of carbohydrates, and enrichment in certain elements of coals, oil, and gas). Analysis of chemical facies from remains in lithified sediments should incorporate the physical chemistry of the compounds studied, as well as the changes that will take at high burial pressures and possible increase in temperature. (Sanderson-ISWS)
W75-08462

REDOX PROCESSES IN DIAGENESIS OF SEDIMENTS IN THE NORTHWEST PACIFIC OCEAN,
Akademiya Nauk SSSR, Moscow. Institut Okeanologii.
For primary bibliographic entry see Field 2K.
W75-08463

HANS A. EINSTEIN'S CONTRIBUTIONS IN SEDIMENTATION,
Colorado State Univ., Fort Collins. Dept. of Civil Engineering.
H. W. Shen.
Journal of the Hydraulics Division, American Society of Civil Engineers, Vol 101, No HY5, Proceedings Paper 11290, p 469-488, May 1975. 1 fig, 74 ref, 2 append.

Descriptors: *Sedimentation, *Sediment transport, *Bed load, *Suspended load, Roughness(Hydraulic), Channels, Erosion, Flow resistance, Hydraulics, Hydraulic models, Boundary processes, *History.
Identifiers: *Hans A. Einstein.

Some of Einstein's major contributions (See W769-02690; W71-03995; W72-03851; W72-06482; and W74-03788) to the field of sedimentation were examined. Einstein established many firsts in his research on bed load and wash load, alluvial bed roughness, form resistance, bed load motion, application of stochastic analysis to sediment transport, instantaneous lift force on particles, and suspended load. Einstein also made significant contributions on secondary currents, erosion and deposition of cohesive material, flow fluctuation in a viscous sublayer, transport of bed particles due to oscillating flow motion, vorticity, deposition of suspended particles in a gravel bed, and sediment transport in pipes. (Visocky-ISWS)
W75-08466

SEDIMENT TRANSPORT THROUGH HIGH MOUNTAIN STREAMS OF THE IDAHO BATHOLITH,
Idaho Univ., Moscow. Dept. of Agricultural Engineering.
D. R. Neilson.
Available from the National Technical Information Service, Springfield, Va 22161 as PB-242 344, $4.75 in paper copy, $2.25 in microfiche. M S Thesis, April 1974. 83 p, 36 ref. OWRT B-025-IDA(2).

Descriptors: Streambeds, Aquatic habitats, *Sediment transport, Chinook salmon, *Carrying capacity, Aquatic life, Methodology, Measurement.
Identifiers: *Idaho Batholith, Bedload transport, Steelhead runs, Mountain streams.

The objectives were to determine the carrying capacity, allowable amounts of sediment and methods to measure levels of fine sediments of 0.25 inches or finer in mountain streams in the Idaho Batholith. The sources and the effects of the sand size sediments once they leave the mountain Batholith streams are not considered. Sediment discharge during the high water event of 1973, a year of minimal peak discharge, was insignificant. Projected transport rates using the Meyer-Peter, Muller formula, which shows good agreement with empirical data for Batholith streams, are presented. The allowable amount of fine sediments to enter these streams was determined by a sediment budget within limits established by the aquatic managers. A method of visually classifying the streambed, used by aquatic entomologists, correlated well with core samples for determining streambed composition.
W75-08483

ANALYSIS AND DESIGN OF SETTLING BASINS FOR IRRIGATION RETURN FLOW,
Idaho Univ., Moscow. Dept. of Civil Engineering.
For primary bibliographic entry see Field 5G.
W75-08484

RECONNAISSANCE STUDY OF SEDIMENT TRANSPORT BY SELECTED STREAMS IN THE YAKIMA INDIAN RESERVATION, WASHINGTON, 1974 WATER YEAR,
Geological Survey, Tacoma, Wash.
P. R. Boucher.
Open-file report 75-67, 1975. 12 p, 1 fig, 1 tab, 5 ref.

Descriptors: *Sediment yield, *Sediment transport, *Washington, Sediment load, Mass wasting, Floods, Erosion, *Indian reservations.
Identifiers: *Yakima Indian Reservation(Wash).

Suspended-sediment concentrations and basin yields were measured at 21 sites on selected streams in the Yakima Indian Reservation in Washington, and two sites on nearby streams. Suspended-sediment yields were generally low relative to those of other streams in southeastern Washington, the southern Cascade Range, and the upper Columbia River basin. The highest annual sediment yield on the reservation probably is about 150 tons per square mile. The suspended sediment transported by this stream is largely from glacial outwash from Mount Adams. Other yields in the basin were estimated to be from 10 to 50 tons per square mile. Mass wasting is the principal cause of sediment transport in the streams studied. Some evidence of accelerated sediment production due to road construction was found along Surveyor Creek. During the flood of January 1974, which has a calculated recurrence interval of more than 100 years, the maximum observed suspended-sediment concentration was 7,830 milligrams per litre. An estimated 70,000 tons of sediment was transported from the upper Toppenish Creek basin; this was nearly 600 tons per square mile. However, the long-term average annual yield was estimated to be only about 30 tons per square mile. (Knapp-USGS)
W75-08518

THE ELECTRODEPOSITION AND DETERMINATION OF RADIUM BY ISOTOPIC DILUTION IN SEA WATER AND IN SEDIMENTS SIMULTANEOUSLY WITH OTHER NATURAL RADIONUCLIDES,
Scripps Institution of Oceanography, La Jolla, Calif. Geological Research Div.
For primary bibliographic entry see Field 5A.
W75-08538

EXCHANGEABLE INORGANIC PHOSPHATE IN LAKE SEDIMENTS,
Wisconsin Univ., Madison. Water Chemistry Program.
For primary bibliographic entry see Field 5B.
W75-08577

MICROBIAL AVAILABILITY OF PHOSPHORUS IN LAKE SEDIMENTS,
Wisconsin Univ., Madison. Water Chemistry Lab.
For primary bibliographic entry see Field 5B.
W75-08578

MODULAR EROSION CONTROL DEVICE,
For primary bibliographic entry see Field 8A.
W75-08611

CAVITATION DAMAGE SCALE EFFECTS--STATE OF ART SUMMARIZATION.
International Association for Hydraulic Research, Delft (Netherlands). Section for Hydraulic Machinery, Equipment and Cavitation.
For primary bibliographic entry see Field 8B.
W75-08698

DYNAMIC BEHAVIOR MODEL OF EPHEMERAL STREAM,
Agricultural Research Service, Tucson, Ariz. Southwest Watershed Research Center.
For primary bibliographic entry see Field 2E.
W75-08699

NONEQUILIBRIUM RIVER FORM,
Colorado State Univ., Fort Collins. Dept. of Civil Engineering.
M. A. Stevens, D. B. Simons, and E. V. Richardson.
Journal of the Hydraulics Division, American Society of Civil Engineers, Vol 101, No HY5, Proceedings Paper 11334, p 557-566, May 1975. 9 fig, 13 ref, 1 append.

Descriptors: *Channel morphology, *Channel erosion, *Sedimentation, *River systems, Channels, Erosion, Flood plains, Floods, Floodways, Geomorphology, Meanders, Width, Alluvial channels, Regime, Streamflow, Hydraulics.
Identifiers: *Nonequilibrium river form, Regime theory.

In the absence of man-induced changes and climatic changes and in the engineering time scale, the form of many rivers is primarily a result of the flood history of the river. Evidence of the effects of floods on river channel width is found in the scientific literature. The extreme event flood is the erosional agent that widens the river channels; in some cases the entire river valley has been gutted by the extreme event flood. Succeeding floods of lesser magnitude result in channel deposits that narrow the river channel. The problem is to recognize river systems that are changing form or are susceptible to change in form. If the ratio of each individual flood-peak discharge to the average annual peak-flood discharge is small, the river form can be in equilibrium or 'in regime'. If the ratio of some individual peak discharge to the average annual peak discharge is large, the river channel can exhibit nonequilibrium river form, i.e., the form will change with time. (Lee-ISWS)
W75-08700

MEASUREMENT OF INSTANTANEOUS BOUNDARY SHEAR STRESS,
Agricultural Research Service, Fort Collins, Colo.
For primary bibliographic entry see Field 8G.
W75-08791

WALL SHEAR STRESS MEASUREMENTS WITH HOT-FILM SENSORS,
Lehigh Univ., Bethlehem, Pa. Fritz Engineering Lab.
For primary bibliographic entry see Field 8G.
W75-08792

WAVE REFRACTION ANALYSIS: AID TO INTERPRETATION OF COASTAL HYDRAULICS,
Massachusetts Univ., Amherst. Dept. of Civil Engineering.
For primary bibliographic entry see Field 8B.
W75-08800

PHYSICAL AND BIOLOGICAL REHABILITATION OF A STREAM,
Montana State Univ., Bozeman. Dept. of Fisheries.
For primary bibliographic entry see Field 4A.
W75-08810

SEDIMENT TRANSPORT SYSTEM IN A GRAVEL-BOTTOMED STREAM,
Washington State Dept. of Ecology, Olympia.
R. T. Milhous, and P. C. Klingeman.
In: Hydraulic Engineering and the Environment; Proceedings of the 21st Annual Hydraulic Division Specialty Conference, Montana State University, Bozeman, August 15-17, 1973. American Society of Civil Engineers, New York, p 293-303, 1973. 2 fig, 1 tab, 7 ref.

Descriptors: *Sediment transport, *Gravels, *Streams, Suspended solids, Sediment load, Beds, Streambeds, Bed load, Streamflow, Model studies, On-site investigations, Stream erosion, Oregon.
Identifiers: *Armour layers.

The sediment transport system in a coarse-bedded mountain stream in the Oregon Coast Range has been studied for three years. The stream bed is nonhomogenous, with an armour layer of larger particles on top of finer material. A conceptual model of the sediment transport system in an armoured stream was developed to better describe the suspended sediment component of the total transport system. The use of existing bed load calculation procedures for determining the bed load in an armoured stream was examined. It was found that there is an important interaction between the armour layer and the movement of material as bed load and as suspended load. Use of the existing bed load equations is made quite tenuous when an armour layer exists. The armour layer is the single most important factor in limiting the availability of stream bed sediment and in controlling the relationship of streamflow and sediment load in a gravel-bottomed stream. The armour layer controls the sediment transport system by regulating the reservoir of sand and finer particles in the stream bed and by protecting the bed material from entrainment in the flow. At high flows the armour layer controls the rate of release of material to the bed load and suspended load of the stream; at intermediate flows it prevents fine sand in the bed from being entrained in the flow; at low flows it filters out fine material. (See also W75-08786) (Sims-ISWS)
W75-08812

CLARKS FORK YELLOWSTONE RIVER REMOTE SENSING STUDY,
Colorado State Univ., Fort Collins. Dept. of Civil Engineering.
J. F. Ruff, J. W. Keys, III, and M. M. Skinner.

In: Hydraulic Engineering and the Environment; Proceedings of the 21st Annual Hydraulic Division Specialty Conference, Montana State University, Bozeman, August 15-17, 1973. American Society of Civil Engineers, New York, p 305-313, 1973. 2 fig, 1 ref, 1 append.

Descriptors: *Remote sensing, *Sediments, *Aerial photography, Infrared radiation, Photography, On-site data collections, Erosion, Irrigation, Agriculture, Sedimentology, *Montana.
Identifiers: Clarks Fork Yellowstone River(Mont).

In an effort to define sediment problems and their causes in the Clarks Fork Yellowstone River, the 1971 Montana State Legislature established the Clarks Fork Siltation Study Committee. The Clarks Fork Yellowstone River is located in south-central Montana and northwestern Wyoming. The river drains an area of approximately 2783 square miles extending from the northeast cornor of Yellowstone National Park northeastward to its confluence with the Yellowstone River near Laurel, Montana. Aerial reconnaissance of the Clarks Fork Yellowstone River Basin was conducted on September 13, 1972, and covered the main stem of the river and its tributaries in Montana. The ground-truth data program for the aerial remote sensing study of sediment in the river was designed to provide information on flow conditions of the river and its tributaries during the time when remote sensing flights were in progress. The aerial photography for the Clarks Fork Yellowstone River and Red Lodge and Rock Creeks was taken on August 18, 1972. From results of this investigation, the following conclusions were drawn on sediment in the Clarks Fork Yellowstone River: (1) only a small amount of active erosion of surface material is being caused by irrigation; (2) the majority of suspended material being transported by the river is being obtained from the bed and banks of the river and its tributaries; (3) the erodible bed and bank materials were probably deposited in the river as a result of the highly erosive soils of the basin and runoff from high intensity storms of the area; and (4) irrigation return flows contribute to the sediment problems of the river by providing the water to carry the material. (See also W75-08786) (Sims-ISWS)
W75-08813

CHANNEL AGGRADATION IN WESTERN UNITED STATES AS INDICATED BY OBSERVATIONS AT VIGIL NETWORK SITES,
Geological Survey, Boise, Idaho. Water Resources Div.
W. W. Emmett.
Zeitschrift fur Geomorphologie (Federal Republic of Germany), Vol 21, p 52-62, December 1974. 2 fig, 2 tab, 17 ref.

Descriptors: *Sedimentation, *Aggradation, *Alluvial channels, *Geomorphology, Land use, Erosion, Climatology, Alluvium.
Identifiers: Western US.

In the semiarid and arid western United States channels at locations ranging from Montana to New Mexico are aggrading. This aggradiation may signify a reversal of the widespread trend of arroyo cutting, which began about A.D. 1880. Observed rates of valley alluviation indicate that valley bottoms would fill to a level of the old valley floor within a period of 200 to 700 years. The data suggest that epicycles of valley trenching and alluviation are related to changes in climate, but these changes in climate may be subtle and difficult to detect. Land use practices may aggravate or enhance naturally occurring rates of geomorphic processes. (Knapp-USGS)
W75-08830

WATER RESOURCES DATA FOR NEBRASKA, 1973: PART 2. WATER QUALITY RECORDS.
Geological Survey, Lincoln, Nebr.
For primary bibliographic entry see Field 5A.
W75-08833

2K. Chemical Processes

A HIGHLY SENSITIVE AUTOMATED TECHNIQUE FOR THE DETERMINATION OF AMMONIUM NITROGEN,
Ruakura Soil Research Station, Hamilton (New Zealand).
For primary bibliographic entry see Field 5A.
W75-08382

RELATIONSHIP OF VARIOUS INDICES OF WATER QUALITY TO DENITRIFICATION IN SURFACE WATERS,
Purdue Univ., Lafayette, Ind. Dept. of Agronomy.
For primary bibliographic entry see Field 5A.
W75-08384

WATER VOL. 39. A YEARBOOK FOR HYDROCHEMISTRY AND WATER PURIFICATION TECHNIQUE,
For primary bibliographic entry see Field 5F.
W75-08390

INDUSTRIAL WATER RESOURCES OF CANADA, THE HUDSON BAY, LABRADOR AND ARCTIC DRAINAGE BASINS, 1959-65,
Department of the Environment, Ottawa (Ontario). Water Quality Branch.
For primary bibliographic entry see Field 5A.
W75-08395

GEOCHEMISTRY OF GROUNDWATERS IN THE CHAD BASIN,
Geological Survey of Israel, Jerusalem.
A. Arad, and U. Kafri.
Journal of Hydrology, Vol 25, No 1/2, p 105-127, April 1975. 11 fig, 2 tab, 8 ref.

Descriptors: *Geochemistry, *Salinity, *Groundwater movement, Lake basins, Structural geology, Drainage, Aquifers, Unconfined aquifers, Water table, Potentiometric level, Chemical analysis, Bicarbonates, Sulfates, Sodium chloride, Cation exchange, Calcium, Magnesium, Geologic control, Underflow, Chemicals.
Identifiers: *Chad Basin, *Lake Chad.

The prevailing chemical patterns of groundwater in the Chad Basin coincide with its present hydrodynamics. The geochemistry of these waters indicates that their salinity is of non-marine origin and is the result of thorough flushing downgradient of the basinfill sediments, mainly of continental origin. The hydrochemical evolutionary trend is from calcium-bicarbonate isotopically light waters in the intake area in the south and southwestern fringe of the basin toward progressively distinct chemical groups to the northeast. (Visocky-ISWS)
W75-08445

THE NA'AMAN SPRINGS, NORTHERN ISRAEL: SALINATION MECHANISM OF AN IRREGULAR FRESHWATER-SEAWATER INTERFACE,
Geological Survey of Israel, Jerusalem. Hydrogeology Div.
For primary bibliographic entry see Field 2L.
W75-08446

POLYNUCLEAR AROMATIC HYDROCARBONS IN RAW, POTABLE AND WASTE WATER,
Imperial Coll. of Science and Technology, London (England). Dept. of Public Health Engineering.
For primary bibliographic entry see Field 5A.
W75-08453

A SIMPLE RESPIROMETER FOR MEASURING OXYGEN AND NITRATE CONSUMPTION IN BACTERIAL CULTURES,
Agricultural Univ., Wageningen (Netherlands). Dept. of Microbiology.
For primary bibliographic entry see Field 5A.
W75-08458

REDOX PROCESSES IN DIAGENESIS OF SEDIMENTS IN THE NORTHWEST PACIFIC OCEAN,
Akademiya Nauk SSSR, Moscow. Institut Okeanologii.
I. I. Volkov, A. G. Rozanov, and V. S. Sokolov.
Soil Science, Vol 119, No 1, p 28-35, January 1975. 3 fig, 20 ref.

Descriptors: *Diagenesis, *Sediments, *Pacific Ocean, *Decomposing organic matter, *Geochemistry, Bottom sediments, Physiocochemical properties, Cores, Manganese, Sulfur, Iron.
Identifiers: *Redox processes.

Redox processes are quite widespread in bottom sediments of modern water bodies. Decomposition of organic matter in the mass of sediments, taking place as a result of micro-biological and chemical processes, changes the physicochemical conditions, thereby bringing about a decrease in the redox potential of pore liquids. Under the reducing conditions created by the decomposition of organic material, the valencies, forms, and geochemical mobility of compounds of certain elements become changed. A possibility is thus created for the redistribution and concentration of certain elements in bottom sediment. Based on geochemical measurements in some 27 sediment cores collected from bottom sediments in the northwest section of the Pacific Ocean, information on the forms of iron, manganese, and sulfur, as well as organic carbon, was given. The sediments studied can be divided into three major categories: (1) reduced sediments of the continental slope; (2) transitional sediments of the marginal oceanic zone; and (3) pelagic sediments of the open ocean (red oozes). Apart from data on the areal distribution of the geochemical factors measured, profiles of element distribution versus depth of sediment core were given. (Sanderson-ISWS)
W75-08463

NITRATE AND NITRITE REDUCTION IN FLOODED GAMMA-IRRADIATED SOIL UNDER CONTROLLED PH AND REDOX POTENTIAL CONDITIONS,
Ghent Rijksuniversiteit (Belgium). Faculteit Landbouwwetenschappen.
For primary bibliographic entry see Field 5G.
W75-08470

SPECTRAL STUDIES OF MONILIFORMIN AND AFLATOXIN B1,
Auburn Univ., Ala. Dept. of Chemistry.
For primary bibliographic entry see Field 5A.
W75-08475

ANALYSES OF SELECTED CONSTITUENTS IN NATIVE WATER AND SOIL IN THE BAYOU BOEUF-CHENE-BLACK AREA NEAR MORGAN CITY, LOUISIANA, INCLUDING A MODIFIED STANDARD ELUTRIATE TEST,
Geological Survey, Baton Rouge, La.
For primary bibliographic entry see Field 5A.
W75-08501

CHEMISTRY OF SUBSURFACE WATERS,
Geological Survey, Menlo Park, Calif.
I. Barnes, and J. D. Hem.
Annual Review of Earth and Planetary Sciences, Vol 1, F. A. Donath, editor: Annual Reviews Inc, Palo Alto, Calif, p 157-181, 1973. 178 ref.

Descriptors: *Water chemistry, *Groundwater, *Reviews, Hydrogeology, Geochemistry, Subsurface waters, Bibliographies, Soil water, Connate water, Magmatic water.

This review concentrates on processes and reactions that control compositions of groundwaters because causal relations have greater transfer value than mere reports of compositions. A four part classification of waters is used: (1) waters not noteworthy for either their temperatures or their compositions; (2) waters noted for both their temperatures and their compositions; (3) waters noted primarily for their temperatures; and (4) waters noted primarily for their compositions. (Knapp-USGS)
W75-08506

GROUND-WATER FAVORABILITY AND SURFICIAL GEOLOGY OF THE CHERRYFIELD-JONESBORO AREA, MAINE,
Geological Survey, Reston, Va.
For primary bibliographic entry see Field 7C.
W75-08510

WATER RESOURCES OF THE CROW RIVER WATERSHED, SOUTH-CENTRAL MINNESOTA,
Geological Survey, Reston, Va.
For primary bibliographic entry see Field 7C.
W75-08511

RECONNAISSANCE OF THE UPPER AU SABLE RIVER, A COLD-WATER RIVER IN THE NORTH-CENTRAL PART OF MICHIGAN'S SOUTHERN PENINSULA,
Geological Survey, Reston, Va.
For primary bibliographic entry see Field 7C.
W75-08512

WATER RESOURCES OF THE BLUE EARTH RIVER WATERSHED, SOUTH-CENTRAL MINNESOTA,
Geological Survey, Reston, Va.
For primary bibliographic entry see Field 7C.
W75-08513

WATER RESOURCES OF THE CLINTON RIVER BASIN, SOUTHEASTERN MICHIGAN,
Geological Survey, Reston, Va.
For primary bibliographic entry see Field 7C.
W75-08514

CHEMICAL QUALITY OF GROUND WATER IN THE WESTERN OSWEGO RIVER BASIN, NEW YORK,
Geological Survey, Albany, N.Y.
For primary bibliographic entry see Field 5B.
W75-08515

DISCHARGE DATA AT WATER-QUALITY MONITORING STATIONS IN ARKANSAS,
Geological Survey, Little Rock, Ark.
For primary bibliographic entry see Field 7A.
W75-08519

WATER QUALITY OF THE LAKE SISKIYOU AREA AND A REACH OF UPPER SACRAMENTO RIVER BELOW BOX CANYON DAM, CALIFORNIA, MAY 1970 THROUGH SEPTEMBER 1971,
Geological Survey, Menlo Park, Calif.
For primary bibliographic entry see Field 5B.
W75-08521

NON-FLAME ATOMIZATION IN ATOMIC ABSORPTION SPECTROMETRY,
Auckland Univ. (New Zealand). Dept. of Chemistry.
For primary bibliographic entry see Field 5A.
W75-08529

STANDARDIZATION OF METHODS FOR THE DETERMINATION OF TRACES OF MERCURY -- PART I. DETERMINATION OF TOTAL INORGANIC MERCURY IN INORGANIC SAMPLES.
Bureau International Technique du Chlore, Brussels (Belgium). Mercury Analysis Working Party.
For primary bibliographic entry see Field 5A.
W75-08530

SOME OBSERVATIONS ON THE DETERMINATION OF COPPER WITH THIOCYANATE,
Loughborough Univ. of Technology (England). Dept. of Chemistry.
For primary bibliographic entry see Field 5A.
W75-08532

DETERMINATION OF NANOGRAM QUANTITIES OF MERCURY IN SEA WATER,
Marine Research Inst., Reykjavik (Iceland).
For primary bibliographic entry see Field 5A.
W75-08535

SPECTROPHOTOMETRIC DETERMINATION OF TUNGSTEN IN ROCKS BY AN ISOTOPE DILUTION PROCEDURE,
Geological Survey, Washington, D.C.
E. G. Lillie, and L. P. Greenland.
Journal of Research of the U.S. Geological Survey, Vol 1, No 5, p 555-558, September-October, 1973. 3 tab, 8 ref.

Descriptors: *Metals, *Analytical techniques, *Spectroscopy, *Rocks, Chemical reactions, Tracers, Radioisotopes, Separation techniques.
Identifiers: *Tungsten.

A method for the determination of tungsten which gives a reliable tungsten thiocyanate color owing to the prior separation from most other sample constituents was described. Samples were decomposed with hydrofluoric acid in the presence of W181 tracer. Molybdenum was extracted from a hydrochloric acid solution with tributyl phosphates. Tungsten was separated from most other elements by extraction of the alpha-benzoinoximate into chloroform. Stannous chloride in concentrated hydrochloric acid was used to strip tungsten and reduce it to W(+5). The amount of tungsten was determined spectrophotometrically after extraction as the thiocyanate complex into amyl alcohol. The correction for chemical losses was determined by counting W181. (Jernigan-Vanderbilt)
W75-08536

DETERMINATION OF SELENIUM IN WATER AND INDUSTRIAL EFFLUENTS BY FLAMELESS ATOMIC ABSORPTION,
Calgon Corp., Pittsburgh, Pa.
For primary bibliographic entry see Field 5A.
W75-08541

SPECTROPHOTOMETRIC DETERMINATION OF DISSOLVED OXYGEN CONCENTRATION IN WATER,
Simon Fraser Univ., Burnaby (British Columbia). Dept. of Biological Sciences.
For primary bibliographic entry see Field 5A.
W75-08551

SINGLE-SWEEP POLAROGRAPHIC TECHNIQUES USEFUL IN MICROPOLLUTION STUDIES OF GROUND AND SURFACE WATERS,
Naval Weapons Center, China Lake, Calif.
For primary bibliographic entry see Field 5A.
W75-08554

THE USE OF MEMBRANE ELECTRODES IN THE DETERMINATION OF SULPHIDES IN SEA WATER,
For primary bibliographic entry see Field 5A.
W75-08558

DETERMINATION OF NITRATE IN WATER WITH AN AMMONIA PROBE,
Brussels Univ. (Belgium). Laboratorium Analytische Chemie.
For primary bibliographic entry see Field 5A.
W75-08561

ZETA-POTENTIAL CONTROL FOR ALUM COAGULATION,
Fertilizer Corp. of India, Sindri.
For primary bibliographic entry see Field 5F.
W75-08565

KRAMERS-KRONIG ANALYSIS OF RATIO REFLECTANCE SPECTRA MEASURED AT AN OBLIQUE ANGLE,
Missouri Univ., Kansas City. Dept. of Physics.
For primary bibliographic entry see Field 1A.
W75-08601

WATER TURBIDITY MEASURING APPARATUS,
Fishmaster Products, Inc., Tulsa, Okla. (assignee)
For primary bibliographic entry see Field 7B.
W75-08626

QUANTITATIVE DETERMINATION OF FREON 12 AND FREON 22 IN WATER, (IN RUSSIAN),
For primary bibliographic entry see Field 5A.
W75-08682

CARBON 14 DATING OF GROUNDWATER FROM CLOSED AND OPEN SYSTEMS,
Waterloo Univ. (Ontario). Dept. of Mechanical Engineering.
For primary bibliographic entry see Field 2F.
W75-08707

STANDARD CONDUCTIVITY CELL FOR MEASUREMENT OF SEA WATER SALINITY AND TEMPERATURE,
Westinghouse Electric Corp., Pittsburgh, Pa. (Assignee).
For primary bibliographic entry see Field 7B.
W75-08760

QUALITY OF PUBLIC WATER SUPPLIES OF NEW YORK, MAY 1972-MAY 1973.
Geological Survey, Albany, N.Y.
For primary bibliographic entry see Field 5A.
W75-08832

WATER RESOURCES DATA FOR NEBRASKA, 1973: PART 2. WATER QUALITY RECORDS.
Geological Survey, Lincoln, Nebr.
For primary bibliographic entry see Field 5A.
W75-08833

STREAM RECONNAISSANCE FOR NUTRIENTS AND OTHER WATER-QUALITY PARAMETERS, GREATER PITTSBURGH REGION, PENNSYLVANIA,
Geological Survey, Carnegie, Pa.
For primary bibliographic entry see Field 5A.
W75-08835

2L. Estuaries

THE RESPONSE OF MASSACHUSETTS BAY TO WIND STRESS,
Massachusetts Inst. of Tech., Cambridge.
B. B. Parker, and B. R. Pearce.
Report No MITSG 75-2, February 1975. 107 p, 21 fig, 5 tab, 48 ref. NOAA Grant 04-5-158-1.

Descriptors: *Winds, *Wind pressure, *Tides, Wind velocity, Transportation, Pollutants, Sea level, Storm surges, Waves, Atmospheric physics, Atmosphere, Massachusetts, Thermal stratification, Bays.
Identifiers: *Wind stress, *Quadratic law, *Transport mechanisms, *Massachusetts Bay(Mass), Boston(Mass), 'Wind set-up' method, Filtered tidal records.

The effect of atmospheric stability on the wind stress coefficient (or drag coefficient), (CD), of the commonly used quadratic law is demonstrated. The method of determining values for CD is essentially a 'wind set-up' method using Doodson filtered tidal records from Boston and Sandwich, Massachusetts and similarly filtered wind and barometric pressure data. The mean values for CD for the three stability groups are: 1.10x10-3 for stable conditions, 1.40x10-3 for neutral conditions, and 1.84x10-3 for unstable conditions. Correlation exists not only between Boston-Sandwich sea level differences and the component of wind stress along the longitudinal axis of the bay, but also between Boston-Portsmouth sea level differences and the onshore component of wind stress. Analyzing Boston, Sandwich, Portsmouth, and Eastport, Maine tidal records results in very similar non-tidal sea level curves even after pressure correction. This implies that the Gulf of Maine has been an important effect on Massachusetts Bay. Wind data at Boston is used for this study but it is corrected for the frictional effect of land using the result of comparisons with other wind stations around the bay. Wind stress was generally much greater in the winter of 1971 than in the summer, not only because of generally higher wind speeds, but also because of greater atmospheric instability and denser air. Current data off Salem harbor indicate the existence of internal waves. (NOAA)
W75-08358

THREE NEW SPECIES OF PARACINETA (PROTOZOA: SUCTORIA) FROM MOBILE BAY, ALABAMA,
University of South Alabama, Mobile. Dept. of Biological Sciences.
E. E. Jones.
Journal Marine Science Alabama, (1973), Vol 2, No 3, p 31-40, 6 fig, 1 tab, 9 ref. OWRT A-021-ALA(3).

Descriptors: Bays, *Protozoa, Estuaries, Surveys, *Alabama.
Identifiers: New species, *Suctoria, *Mobile Bay(Ala), *Paracineta spp.

Substrates (microscope slides) were immersed in Mobile Bay for a one-week period. They were stained with Grenacher's Borax Carmine and Lyon's Blue. This technique has been used monthly for the past two years to study the protozoa of the Bay. Three new species of suctoria, Paracineta lineata n. sp., P. meridionalis n. sp., and P. estuarina n. sp., are described.
W75-08363

NEW SPECIES OF PROTOZOA FROM MOBILE BAY, ALABAMA,
University of South Alabama, Mobile. Dept. of Biological Sciences.
E. E. Jones, and G. Owen.
Journal Marine Science Alabama, (1973), Vol 2, No 3, p 41-56, 15 fig, 1 chart, 19 ref. OWRT A-021-ALA(4).

Descriptors: Bays, *Protozoa, Estuaries, Surveys, *Alabama, Systematics, Salinity.
Identifiers: New species, *Mobile Bay(Ala).

Mobile Bay is the third largest drainage basin in the country. Salt water from the Gulf of Mexico enters the moutn of the bay and flows upward along the eastern shore where it mixes with the fresh water from the nine rivers which drain into the bay. The flow pattern is counter-clockwise so that the water along the western shore is less saline than that of the eastern shore. More than two hundred and fifty free-living species of protozoa have been identified in the bay. Four new and undescribed species were collected there: Cienkowskya arborenscens n. sp., Stephanopogon mobilensis n. sp., S. colpoda Entz, 1884, var., and Microgromia biportalis n. sp.
W75-08364

SEAWEEDS: THEIR PRODUCTIVITY AND STRATEGY FOR GROWTH,
Dalhousie Univ., Halifax (Nova Scotia). Dept. of Biology.
For primary bibliographic entry see Field 5C.
W75-08377

REDESCRIPTION OF GAETANUS INTERMEDIUS CAMPBELL (CALANOIDA: COPEPODA) FROM THE TYPE LOCALITY,
Washington Univ., Friday Harbor. Friday Harbor Lab.
T. Park.
Journal of the Fisheries Research Board of Canada, Vol 30, No 10, p 1597-1600, October 1973. 2 fig, 6 ref.

Descriptors: *Systematics, *Copepods, Speciation, Pacific Ocean.
Identifiers: *Gaetanus intermedius, Vancouver Island, Washington Sound.

Gaetanus intermedius Campbell 1930, is redescribed from specimens taken in the type locality, the Vancouver Island region in the northeastern Pacific. Gaetanus simplex Brodsky 1950, is found to be a junior synonym of G. intermedius. (Little-Battelle)
W75-08380

A SCHEMATIZATION OF ONSHORE-OFFSHORE TRANSPORT,
Waterloopkundig Laboratorium, Delft (Netherlands).
D. H. Swart.
Publication 134, September 1974. 17 p, 12 fig, 10 ref.

Descriptors: *Beaches, *Waves(Water), *Equilibrium, *Profiles, *Sediment transport, *Coasts, Laboratory tests, Model studies, Particle size, Equations, Hydraulics.
Identifiers: *Onshore-offshore transport, Deepwater waves.

The results of a physically-based schematic model of the onshore-offshore profile development on small scale and full scale model tests were described. The investigation covered two aspects of the schematization of coastal processes on sandy beaches in a direction perpendicular to the coastline: (1) the prediction of equilibrium beach profiles and (2) the corresponding offshore sediment transport due to wave action. Physically-based empirical relationships were derived to enable the application of the model results to both small-scale and prototype conditions. It was concluded that the proposed equilibrium profile is effected by particle diameter and absolute value of deepwater wave heights. It was also shown that the rate of offshore transport under three-dimensional conditions was higher than under corresponding two-dimensional conditions. (Bhowmik-ISWS)
W75-08401

EQUILIBRIUM PROFILES OF COARSE MATERIAL UNDER WAVE ATTACK,
Waterloopkundig Laboratorium, Delft (Netherlands).
E. van Hijum.
Publication 133, September 1974. 19 p, 19 fig, 3 tab, 7 ref.

Descriptors: *Beaches, *Waves(Water), *Gravels, *Equilibrium, *Profiles, Band protection, Sediment transport, Laboratory tests, Scaling, Froude number, Model studies, Hydraulics.
Identifiers: *Progressive waves, Wave run-up, Critical velocity.

The results of a laboratory investigation of equilibrium beach profiles under wave attack were presented. The beach materials were composed of gravels and rubbles. The aim of the study was to determine the dimensions, form, and way of formation of an equilibrium profile under regular, perpendicular wave attack. It was concluded that gravel with D sub 90 sizes less than 0.006 meter is sensitive to scale effects. (Bhowmik-ISWS)
W75-08402

SIZE SPECTRA OF BIOGENIC PARTICLES IN OCEAN WATER AND SEDIMENTS,
Physical Research Lab., Ahmedabad (India).
For primary bibliographic entry see Field 2J.
W75-08424

ACOUSTIC MINIPROBING FOR OCEAN MICROSTRUCTURE AND BUBBLES,
Naval Postgraduate School, Monterey, Calif. Dept. of Physics and Chemistry.
H. Medwin, J. Fitzgerald, and G. Rautmann.
Journal of Geophysical Research, Vol 80, No 3, p 405-413, January 20, 1975. 11 fig, 2 tab, 15 ref.

Descriptors: *Oceans, *Bubbles, *Acoustics, On-site data collections, Instrumentation, Measurement, Sound waves, Hydrophones, Oceanography, Statistics.
Identifiers: *Ocean microstructure, Sound speed.

Analysis of sound phase and amplitude fluctuations over a 1-m range has provided in situ statistics that can be used to infer the statistics of the ocean microstructure. A particularly fruitful use of such a simple acoustic miniprobe is the study of the sound phase fluctuations near the sea surface. With the aid of simultaneous statistics of temperature and wave height the observed sound phase fluctuations were used to calculate bubble statistics at sea. At sound frequencies less than about 25 kHz the sound speed dispersion and its fluctuations reveal the bubble volume fraction and its standard deviation, respectively. At higher sound frequencies a large resonant bubble population can be identified by a cross correlation of sound phase and ocean wave height. In this case the predominant part of the sound phase modulation is caused by the changing bubble radius due to the fluctuating wave height. The spectrum of the sound phase modulation then mimics the ocean wind wave spectrum, and its change with depth can be used to infer the change of number of resonant bubbles with depth. (Sims-ISWS)
W75-08425

MAXIMUM HEIGHTS OF OCEAN WAVES,
MPR Associates, Inc., Washington, D.C.
F. Sellars.
Journal of Geophysical Research, Vol 80, No 3, p 398-404, January 20, 1975. 5 fig, 3 tab, 22 ref, 1 append.

Descriptors: *Ocean waves, *Height, Waves(Water), Standing waves, Wavelengths, Winds, Laboratory tests, Model studies, On-site investigations, *Atlantic Ocean, Oceanography.
Identifiers: *Wave steepness, Irregular waves, Wave spectra, Traveling waves, Breaking waves.

Laboratory and field measurements of maximum wave amplitudes of irregular waves were reported. Few measurements of maximum irregular wave heights have been available previously, and the results in this paper will aid in evaluating limiting wave proportions. The data cover observations of breaking waves in a laboratory irregular wave system and results for the largest waves in field observations for severe weather conditions in the North Atlantic. The data were compared with theoretical predictions based on the assumption that wave breaking is the predominant factor limiting wave height. These results may be used to estimate maximum wave conditions for design purposes when field data for maximum wave conditions are not available. Differences in wave spectra for equilibrium wave conditions were investigated, and it was concluded that the proportion of breaking waves in an irregular wave record explains the variations observed. (Sims-ISWS)
W75-08426

EXTREME WAVE CONDITIONS DURING HURRICANE CAMILLE,
Naval Oceanographic Office, Washington, D.C.
M. D. Earle.
Journal of Geophysical Research, Vol 80, No 3, p 377-379, January 20, 1975. 3 fig, 2 tab, 7 ref.

Descriptors: *Waves(Water), *Hurricanes, *Frequency, *Height, Ocean waves, Wavelengths, Storms, Winds, Gulf of Mexico, Offshore platforms, On-site investigations, Measurement, Oceanography, Meteorology.
Identifiers: *Hurricane Camille.

Ten hours of wave data recorded from a fixed platform during hurricane Camille were analyzed to determine wave heights and periods. Wave conditions were severe with a maximum measured wave height of 23.6 m. The analysis results indicate that a Rayleigh distribution can be used to compute wave height relationships for large hurricane-generated waves. (Sims-ISWS)
W75-08427

EVOLUTION OF GULF STREAM EDDIES AS SEEN IN SATELLITE INFRARED IMAGERY,
National Environmental Satellite Service, Washington, D.C.
H. G. Stumpf, and P. K. Rao.
Journal of Physical Oceanography, Vol 5, No 2, p 388-393, April 1975. 5 fig, 9 ref.

Descriptors: *Remote sensing, Satellites(Artificial), *Eddies, *Meanders, *Atlantic Ocean, Infrared radiation, Ocean circulation, Ocean currents, Oceanography.
Identifiers: *Gulf Stream.

Pronounced eddies along the western edge of the Gulf Stream were again observed by the Very High Resolution Radiometer aboard the NOAA-2 satellite. A rare sequence of infrared images obtained over a period of seven days shows for the first time the complete evolution of meanders through the eddy stage. (Sims-ISWS)
W75-08429

SATELLITE DETECTION OF UPWELLING IN THE GULF OF TEHUANTEPEC, MEXICO,
National Environmental Satellite Service, Washington, D.C.
H. G. Stumpf.
Journal of Physical Oceanography, Vol 5, No 2, p 383-388, April 1975. 4 fig, 4 ref.

Descriptors: *Remote sensing, *Satellites(Artificial), *Upwelling, Pacific Ocean, *Mexico, Infrared radiation, Ocean circulation, Meteorology, Oceanography, Ocean currents.
Identifiers: *Gulf of Tehuantepec(Mex), Gyres.

The daily acquisition of thermal infrared imagery from the NOAA-2 satellite permitted the delineation and monitoring of a series of upwellings in the Gulf of Tehuantepec during December 1973. Following the upwelling, a large anticyclonic gyre was detected in the imagery as the coastal currents returned to their historical positions. (Sims-ISWS)
W75-08430

THE BERING SLOPE CURRENT SYSTEM,
Washington Univ., Seattle. Dept. of Oceanography.
T. H. Kinder, L. K. Coachman, and J. A. Galt.
Journal of Physical Oceanography, Vol 5, No 2, p 231-244, April 1975. 18 fig, 1 tab, 18 ref. NSF Grant GA 11147 A 3.

Descriptors: *Ocean currents, *Continental slope, *Temperature, *Salinity, Continental shelf, On-site investigations, Ocean circulation, Ships, Surveys, Eddies, Topography, Oceanography.
Identifiers: *Bering Sea, Drogues, Geostrophic calculations, Planetary waves.

The Bering Slope Current flows from southeast to northwest across the Aleutian Basin of the Bering Sea, parallel to the continental slope of the eastern Bering Sea shelf. The water mass characteristics and distributions and the flow field were investigated in August 1972 during T.G. Thompson Cruise 071. Water mass analysis revealed a southeast-flowing countercurrent bounded by two northwest-flowing bands. The countercurrent was clearly delineated by analyses of a temperature-minimum layer between approximately 50-300 m and a temperature-maximum layer between approximately 300-800 m. The description of the current as comprised of three bands was supported by parachute drogue measurements and geostrophic calculations along six salinity-temperature-depth sections normal to the slope. The dynamic topographies showed an alternative description of the current as a system of eddies, and an interpretation based on incident and reflected planetary waves with a period of one year was presented. The generating mechanism may be related to the strong annual variation in Bering Sea weather. (Sims-ISWS)
W75-08431

THE NA'AMAN SPRINGS, NORTHERN ISRAEL: SALINATION MECHANISM OF AN IRREGULAR FRESHWATER-SEAWATER INTERFACE,
Geological Survey of Israel, Jerusalem. Hydrogeology Div.
A. Arad, U. Kafri, and E. Fleisher.
Journal of Hydrology, Vol 25, No 1/2, p 81-104, April 1975. 10 fig, 5 tab, 18 ref.

Descriptors: *Springs, *Saline water-freshwater interfaces, *Saline water intrusion, Salinity, Geologic control, Faults(Geologic), Water pollution, Brackish water, Watersheds(Basins), Aquifers, Structural geology, Karst hydrology, Limestones, Dolomite, Groundwater movement, Chemical analysis, Geochemistry, Radioisotopes, Oxygen isotopes.
Identifiers: *Israel(Na'aman Springs), Judea Group, Horst, Graben, Ratios.

In the Na'aman catchment area, the water in the Judea Group aquifer varies from freshwater to dilute seawater. It was previously assumed that high salinities in this area were due to fossil brackish water or connate seawater. However, the chemical composition of the water indicates contamination by present seawater. The irregular distribution of high salinities along the main E-W faults in the area points to the possibility that these faults are the main conduit for active contamination of the aquifer by seawater. (Visocky-ISWS)
W75-08446

SALINE GROUND-WATER RESOURCES OF LEE COUNTY, FLORIDA,
Geological Survey, Tallahassee, Fla.
For primary bibliographic entry see Field 2F.

W75-08517

ENVIRONMENTAL REQUIREMENTS OF SELECTED ESTUARINE CILIATED PROTOZOA,
New Hampshire Univ., Durham. Dept. of Zoology.
For primary bibliographic entry see Field 5C.
W75-08592

PHYSICAL CRITERIA IN COMPUTER METHODS FOR PARTIAL DIFFERENTIAL EQUATIONS,
Rutgers - the State Univ., New Brunswick, N.J. Dept. of Computer Science.
For primary bibliographic entry see Field 5G.
W75-08593

STATUTORY DEFINITIONS OF FRESHWATER WETLANDS.
For primary bibliographic entry see Field 6E.
W75-08594

MODULAR EROSION CONTROL DEVICE,
For primary bibliographic entry see Field 8A.
W75-08611

NORMAL MODES OF THE ATLANTIC AND INDIAN OCEANS,
Chicago Univ., Ill. Dept. of the Geophysical Sciences.
G. W. Platzman.
Journal of Physical Oceanography, Vol 5, No 2, p 201-221, April 1975. 11 fig, 6 tab, 23 ref, 2 append. NSF Grant GA-15995.

Descriptors: Oceans, *Resonance, *Tides, Water level fluctuations, Ocean circulation, Oceanography, Model studies, Computer models, *Atlantic Ocean, *Indian Ocean, Coriolis force, Energy transfer, Hydrodynamics.
Identifiers: Modes, Oscillations, Gravity modes, Rotational modes.

Normal modes were calculated for a homogeneous ocean occupying a connected domain consisting of the North Atlantic, South Atlantic, and Indian Oceans. Coastal configuration and bathymetry were resolved on a grid of 675 six-degree Mercator squares. The calculation was based upon the Lanczos process and was more efficient than resonance iteration. Twenty-six gravity modes were found with periods greater than 8 h, the slowest being a fundamental mode of about 67 h. The North Atlantic co-oscillates with the South Atlantic at a period of about 42 h, and has strong resonances at 23, 21, 14.4, 12.8, 8.6, and 8.3 h. Eleven topographically-induced modes of rotational type were found with periods less than 100 h; the fastest of these is a 44 h mode in the Weddell Sea. In the 6-degree model the fastest rotational mode of the North Atlantic is a 55 h topographic wave most prominent near the Grand Banks of Newfoundland. (Sims-ISWS)
W75-08686

TIDAL CHARTS OF THE CENTRAL PACIFIC OCEAN,
Massachusetts Inst. of Tech., Cambridge. Dept. of Earth and Planetary Sciences.
D. S. Luther, and C. Wunsch.
Journal of Physical Oceanography, Vol 5, No 2, p 222-230, April 1975. 11 fig, 2 tab, 26 ref. NSF Grant GA 32979.

Descriptors: *Tides, *Pacific Ocean, *Charts, Oceans, Oceanography, Water level fluctuations, Time series analysis.
Identifiers: Cotidal charts, Co-amplitude charts, Modes, Amphidromes.

New co-amplitude and cotidal charts of the central Pacific Ocean were constructed for constituents M

sub 2, S sub 2, N sub 2, K sub 1 and O sub 1. The charts exhibit some significant differences from previous attempts. Admittance curves, calculated where possible, do not show any rapidly varying characteristics in contrast to the North Atlantic. (Sims-ISWS)
W75-08687

SOME PROPERTIES OF THE WARM EDDIES GENERATED IN THE CONFLUENCE ZONE OF THE KUROSHIO AND OYASHIO CURRENTS,
Hokkaido Regional Fisheries Research Lab., Yoichi (Japan).
K. Kitano.
Journal of Physical Oceanography, Vol 5, No 2, p 245-252, April 1975. 11 fig, 1 tab, 19 ref.

Descriptors: *Ocean currents, *Eddies, Temperature, Currents(Water), On-site investigations, Oceanography, Isotherms, Mapping, *Pacific Ocean, *Water temperature.
Identifiers: *Warm eddies, Fronts(Oceanic), Japan.

The size, movement, and maximum core temperature of warm eddies off Japan were discussed on the basis of 154 examples of warm eddies from various sources during the 17 year period 1957-1973. The warm eddies generated in the confluence zone of the Kuroshio and the Oyashio Currents are distributed in a rather restricted area of the sea and have an elliptical form with an average diameter of about 70 n mi. The eddies usually move to north or northeast with speeds of 0.3-2.0 n mi/day along the contours of the continental slope. As the eddies move north their size and the maximum core temperature gradually decrease. (Sims-ISWS)
W75-08688

MICROSTRUCTURE AND INTRUSIONS IN THE CALIFORNIA CURRENT,
Scripps Institution of Oceanography, La Jolla, Calif.
M. C. Gregg.
Journal of Physical Oceanography, Vol 5, No 2, p 253-278, April 1975. 21 fig, 3 tab, 21 ref. ONR Contracts N00014-69-A-0200-6049, N00014-69-A-0200-6039.

Descriptors: *Ocean currents, Temperature, *Salinity, Density, Profiles, Oceanography, Currents(Water), Pacific Ocean, Sounding, On-site data collections, California, *Water temperature.
Identifiers: Microstructure, *Intrusions(Oceanic), Cox number, Potential density, *Baja California, *California Current.

Two microstructure records taken at shallow depths off Cabo San Lucas, at the southern tip of Baja California, were compared. One was similar to records previously taken in the mid-gyre, and had an 'irregularly steppy' appearance, a linear T-S relation, and a Cox number of approximately 10. It was suggested that this type of profile may represent the background condition of the ocean in which the levels of vertical turbulence are quite low and the principal dissipation occurs by small-scale shear instabilities at the 'step' structures. The other record exhibited a very irregular T-S relation, due to multiple interleavings of the water masses present in the area. Coupled with this was an average Cox number of at least 6000 and a much greater variability in the local microstructure levels along the record; half-meter averages of the dissipation rate of temperature fluctuations showed a range greater than 1,000,000. In some cases these differences occurred over vertical separations of a few meters. In general, the regions of intense microstructure activity occur at the vertical boundaries of the intrusions and seem to be the result of shears and double diffuse phenomena associated with the spreading motion of the intrusion and the vertical T-S differences. These processes act to dissipate the intrusion as an identifiable feature. The presence of similar intrusive features in other locations suggests that they are major factors in the dissipation of fluctuations in the ocean, but microstructure profiles, by themselves, are not sufficient to assess the vertical heat flux associated with them. (Sims-ISWS)
W75-08689

INTERNAL WAVE REFLECTION BY A VELOCITY SHEAR AND DENSITY ANOMALY,
Naval Research Lab., Washington, D.C. Ocean Sciences Div.
For primary bibliographic entry see Field 2E.
W75-08690

A NUMERICAL STUDY OF TIME-DEPENDENT TURBULENT EKMAN LAYERS OVER HORIZONTAL AND SLOPING BOTTOMS,
Florida State Univ., Tallahassee. Dept. of Oceanography, and Florida State Univ., Tallahassee. Geophysical Fluid Dynamics Inst.
For primary bibliographic entry see Field 2E.
W75-08691

COASTAL TRAPPED WAVES IN A BAROCLINIC OCEAN,
Rosenstiel School of Marine and Atmospheric Science, Miami, Fla.
D-P. Wang.
Journal of Physical Oceanography, Vol 5, No 2, p 326-333, April 1975. 6 fig, 27 ref, 1 append. CUEA GX 33052: ONR N00014-67-A-0201-0013.

Descriptors: *Ocean waves, *Coasts, *Continental shelf, Internal waves, Waves(Water), Model studies, Mathematical models, Channeling, Stratification, Oceans, Oceanography.
Identifiers: *Trapped waves, Baroclinic oceans, Internal Kelvin waves.

Coastal-trapped waves were studied in a two-layered, non-flat shelf model. Internal Kelvin wave and quasi-geostrophic waves appear as eigenmodes of the system. The latter reduce to the familiar barotropic shelf waves only in the limit of vanishing stratification. With strong stratification, i.e., where the internal Kelvin wave phase speed is larger than the phase speed of the quasi-geostrophic wave, quasi-geostrophic waves are bottom-trapped. Resonant coupling occurs when the two types of waves have compatible phase speeds; in this case, the relative amplitude distribution of the resonant modes is very sensitive to the change of the baroclinic radius of deformation. Implications of this work for the study of shelf water response to external disturbances were briefly discussed. (Sims-ISWS)
W75-08692

THE INFLUENCE OF LONGITUDINAL VARIATIONS IN WIND STRESS CURL ON THE STEADY OCEAN CIRCULATION,
Scripps Institution of Oceanography, La Jolla, Calif.
For primary bibliographic entry see Field 2E.
W75-08693

TRAJECTORIES AND SPEEDS OF WIND-DRIVEN CURRENTS NEAR THE COAST,
Louisiana State Univ., Baton Rouge. Coastal Studies Inst.
For primary bibliographic entry see Field 2H.
W75-08694

THE EFFECT OF WIND AND SURFACE CURRENTS ON DRIFTERS,
Texas A and M Univ., College Station. Dept. of Oceanography.
For primary bibliographic entry see Field 2H.
W75-08695

DYNAMIC HEIGHT FROM TEMPERATURE PROFILES,
Hawaii Univ., Honolulu. Dept. of Oceanography.
For primary bibliographic entry see Field 2E.
W75-08696

CIRCULATION IN CENTRAL LONG ISLAND SOUND,
Yale Univ., New Haven, Conn. Dept. of Geology and Geophysics.
R. B. Gordon, and C. C. Pilbeam.
Journal of Geophysical Research, Vol 80, No 3, p 414-422, January 20, 1975. 11 fig, 2 tab, 12 ref.

Descriptors: *Sounds, *Currents(Water), *Water circulation, *On-site investigations, Tidal effects, Streamflow, Wind tides, Rainfall, River flow, Saline water-freshwater interfaces, Salinity, Convection, Gravity, Tides, Tidal waters, On-site data collections, Density currents, Estuaries, Flow measurement, *Connecticut, Evaluation.
Identifiers: *Long Island Sound(Conn).

Current meter records from 28 stations were used to define the flow of water near the bottom of central Long Island Sound. Records were made at two of the stations for over 1 year and for 10 days or more at most of the others. Tidal and nontidal flow components were separated. Random fluctuations of up to 10 day's duration occur in the non-tidal flow; they are not directly influenced by wind, rainfall, river runoff, or variations in sea level along the shore. Salinity observations showed the presence of well-defined surface and bottom water layers. Mixing between these is confined to shore side zones where the water is less than 10 m deep and to shoals where strong turbulence is generated. The current meter data showed the bottom water at depths greater than 20 m to be flowing upstream at a rate that decreases toward the head of the estuary. At depths less than 20 m there is a shoreward flow of bottom water toward the mixing zone. The salinity and current data were used to construct a circulation model for the sound. The large-scale flow is apparently due to gravitational convection associated with salinity differences. However, response to changes in the freshwater inflow is delayed by about 2 months because of the large volume of surface water relative to the freshwater supply. (Dawes-ISWS)
W75-08702

THE TIDAL ENERGETICS OF NARRAGANSETT BAY,
Rhode Island Univ., Kingston. Graduate School of Oceanography.
E. R. Levine, and K. E. Kenyon.
Journal of Geophysical Research, Vol 80, No 12, p 1683-1688, April 20, 1975. 3 fig, 16 ref. EPA Grant WP-252-02.

Descriptors: *Tidal energy, *Energy budget, *Energy dissipation, Estuaries, Tidal waters, Tidal effects, Energy loss, Energy gradient, Tides, Height, *Rhode Island, Bays.
Identifiers: *Tidal dissipation, Stratified estuary, *Narragansett Bay(RI), Tidal currents, Energy sink, Vertical mixing.

The average tidal energy budget of Narragansett Bay, a weakly stratified estuary, was determined from observations of tidal height and current. For average conditions the tidal energy influx to the bay is balanced by the bay's energy sinks, and within the error limits the energy budget balances completely. The average energy inputs to the three bay channels, the West Passage, the East Passage, and the Sakonnet River, are 4.3, 6.4, and 1.1 x 10 to the 13th power ergs/s, respectively. Tidal energy is dissipated on the bottom of the bay at the average rate of 8.8 x 10 to the 13th power ergs/s, mostly in a few localized areas of high dissipation. The bay does work on the moon at an average rate of 1.8 x 10 to the 13th power ergs/s. The energy required for vertical mixing is 0.3 x 10 to the 13th power ergs/s. Phase adjustment between tidal

height and current was suggested as a mechanism contributing to the instantaneous balance of the tidal energy budget over the lunar cycle. (Lee-ISWS)
W75-08705

PROPAGATION OF TIDAL WAVES IN THE JOSEPH BONAPARTE GULF,
Wollongong Univ., Coll. (Australia). Dept. of Mathematics.
J. P. Louis, and J. R. M. Radok.
Journal of Geophysical Research, Vol 80, No 12, p 1689-1690, April 20, 1975. 3 fig, 8 ref.

Descriptors: *Tidal bores, *Tidal waters, *Surges, *Water circulation, *Ocean waves, Waves(Water), Gulfs, *Australia, Estuaries, Ocean currents, Model studies, Bays.
Identifiers: Tidal waves, Wave propagation, *Joseph Bonaparte Gulf(Australia), Tidal phase, Phase angles, Semidiurnal tides, Circular gulf mode.

It was conjectured that tidal phase lags around large bays and gulfs can be explained in terms of simple harmonic shelf waves propagating around a constant depth circular region. The Joseph Bonaparte Gulf was considered as an example, and the observed phase trends were shown to be well correlated with those predicted for a circular gulf with a radius of 190 km and a depth of 80 m. (Lee-ISWS)
W75-08706

DREDGED SPOIL DISPOSAL ON THE NEW JERSEY WETLANDS: THE PROBLEM OF ENVIRONMENTAL IMPACT ASSESSMENT,
Rutgers - The State Univ., New Brunswick, N.J. Marine Science Center.
For primary bibliographic entry see Field 5C.
W75-08716

THE DETERMINATION OF CURRENT VELOCITIES FROM DIFFUSION/ADVECTION PROCESSES IN THE IRISH SEA,
University Coll. of North Wales, Bangor. Dept. of Physical Oceanography.
For primary bibliographic entry see Field 2E.
W75-08717

COASTAL POWER PLANT HEAT DISPOSAL CONSIDERATIONS,
Southern California Edison Co., Rosemead, Calif.
For primary bibliographic entry see Field 5G.
W75-08719

FLOATING BREAKWATER,
Bridgestone Tire Co. Ltd., Tokyo (Japan). (assignee)
For primary bibliographic entry see Field 8B.
W75-08746

FLOATING BREAKWATER SYSTEM,
Reid, Middleton and Associates, Inc., Edmonds, Wash. (Assignee).
For primary bibliographic entry see Field 8B.
W75-08756

ON ENVIRONMENTAL FACTORS AFFECTING THE PRIMARY PRODUCTION IN SHALLOW WATER BODIES,
Deutsche Akademie der Wissenschaften zu Berlin (East Germany). Institut fuer Meereskunde.
For primary bibliographic entry see Field 5C.
W75-08769

THE RADIOACTIVE, METALLIC AND BACTERIAL POLLUTANTS IN THE ESTUARY OF THE ESCAUT (SCHELT) RIVER AND ON THE COAST OF BELGIUM, (IN FRENCH),
Institut Royal des Sciences Naturelles de Belgique, Brussels. Lab. for Oceanographic Physics.
For primary bibliographic entry see Field 5A.
W75-08774

MARINE TRADES AND THE COASTAL CRISIS,
Rhode Island Univ., Kingston. Coastal Resources Center.
For primary bibliographic entry see Field 6B.
W75-08784

WAVE REFRACTION ANALYSIS: AID TO INTERPRETATION OF COASTAL HYDRAULICS,
Massachusetts Univ., Amherst. Dept. of Civil Engineering.
For primary bibliographic entry see Field 8B.
W75-08800

3. WATER SUPPLY AUGMENTATION AND CONSERVATION

3A. Saline Water Conversion

REVERSE OSMOSIS MAKES HIGH QUALITY WATER NOW,
Universal Oil Products Co., San Diego, Calif.
S. S. Kremen.
Environmental Science and Technology, Vol 9, No 4, p 314-318, April 1975. 5 fig, 3 tab.

Descriptors: *Reverse osmosis, *Water supply, *Reclaimed water, Membrane processes, Separation techniques, Economics, Capital costs, Operating costs, Costs, Municipal wastes, Industrial wastes, Waste water treatment, Water purification, *Desalination, Water treatment, Brackish water, Energy.

The concept of reverse osmosis is reviewed, followed by a brief discussion of its effectiveness in purifying different types of water (brackish water, municipal and industrial waste waters). The economics (capital and operating costs) of reverse osmosis treatment, both as a means of water purification from a brackish source and as part of a municipal waste effluent treatment sequence, are discussed. Reverse osmosis installations in the United States and other parts of the world are listed, and the energy requirements for converting sea water to potable water by the distillation and reverse osmosis processes are compared. (Witt-IPC)
W75-08564

RESEARCH ON REVERSE OSMOSIS MEMBRANES FOR PURIFICATION OF WASH WATER AT STERILIZATION TEMPERATURE (165F), REPORT NO 2,
General Electric Co., Lynn, Mass. Direct Energy Conversion Programs.
M. E. Nolan, and A. B. LaConti.
Available from the National Technical Information Service, Springfield, Va. 22161, as PB-242 521, $4.25 in paper copy, $2.25 in microfiche. Report INT-OSW-RDPR-75-1003, June 1975. 53 p, 9 fig, 19 tab, 12 ref. Contract 14-30-2752.

Descriptors: Reclamation, *Waste water treatment, *Reverse osmosis, *Desalination, *Membranes, *Water reuse.
Identifiers: *Wash water, Sulfonated polyphenylene oxide, Sterilization, Tubular reverse osmosis, Polour polysulfone.

The goal was to develop viable reverse osmosis (RO) modules and systems of tubular design of approximately 80 gpd capacity to recover wash water at sterilization temperatures. An 80 gpd RO system was fabricated for recovering wash water at sterilization temperatures. The performance characteristics of ancillary components including particulate filters, gauges, meters, RO pump, accumulator carbon polishing column were verified by integrating the components into a suitable subsystem containing the RO module and life testing with wash water. The twenty tube module was used to define the total system and identify/correct some of the life limiting problems, and was tested under simulated mission conditions with wash water. It appears a viable 80 gpd sulfonated PPO RO system for recycling wash water at sterilization temperatures and meeting the National Academy of Science (NAS) specifications if feasible. Some further work should be conducted to improve reliability and obtain a more weight/volume effective system.
W75-08575

LABORATORY PROGRAM TO STUDY FLASHING AND SCALING CHARACTERISTICS OF GEOTHERMAL BRINES,
Dow Chemical Co., Midland, Mich.
J. S. Wilson, and G. R. Warren.
Available from the National Technical Information Service, Springfield, Va. 22161, as PB-233 051, $4.75 in paper copy, $2.25 in microfiche. Report INT-OSW-RDPR-74-969, June 1973. 87 p, 30 fig, 11 tab, 1 ref. OSW Contract 14-30-2936.

Descriptors: Geothermal studies, *Brines, Hydrogen sulfide, Flocculation, Silica, Scaling, Corrosion, Oxidation, Desalination processes, Desalination plants, California, Solid wastes.
Identifiers: *Geothermal brines, Imperial Valley(Calif), *Flashing, Boric acid.

The purpose was to identify and study problems associated with the production of desalted water in a dual-purpose geothermal flash plant. The investigation was carried out by controlled flashing of a brine, prepared to simulate the geothermal brine expected to be found in the Imperial Valley of California. Anticipated problem areas were boric acid and hydrogen sulfide carry-over into the product water, solids in the waste stream, scaling in the flash equipment and corrosion. On unexpected problem, low pH of the product water, was encountered. Scaling did not occur but may be a problem in a continuous plant. Corrosion of 316 stainless steel, nickel, and monel did occur but no rates were determined.
W75-08590

METHOD OF DESALINATING SALT WATER,
Atomic Energy Commission, Washington, D.C. (Assignee).
M. R. Fox, and E. S. Grimmett.
U.S. Patent No 3,872,909, 3 p, 1 fig, 6 ref; Official Gazette of the United States Patent Office, Vol 932, No 4, p 1382, March 25, 1975.

Descriptors: *Patents, *Desalination processes, *Water treatment, Steam, Temperature, Sea water, *Saline water.
Identifiers: Critical temperature, Critical pressure.

A method for desalinating salt water is described in which a fluidized bed of salt particles is established and maintained at a pressure above the critical pressure of water. Steam is passed upward through the fluidized bed heating it to above the critical temperature of water. Salt water is introduced into the bed and steam is taken off from the fluidized bed. The fluidized bed is formed of salt particles having a size range between about 0.3 and 0.6 mm and is operated at 3500 psia and about 705 deg F. (Sinha-OEIS)
W75-08631

METHOD OF DISTILLING SEA WATER ON SMALL SHIPS AND MARINE PLATFORMS HAVING INTERNAL COMBUSTION ENGINE,
A. J. Arnold.

U.S. Patent No. 3,864,215, 2 p, 1 fig, 11 ref; Official Gazette of the United States Patent Office, Vol 931, No 1, p 318, February 4, 1975.

Descriptors: *Patents, *Distillation, *Water treatment, *Desalination, Sea water, Heat exchangers, Condensation, Saline water, Ships, Offshore platforms, Separation techniques.
Identifiers: Demister, Internal combustion engine, Heat of condensation, Vaporization, Flash vaporization.

Vaporization and condensation are carried on in a closed chamber at pressures reduced to permit flash vaporization at temperatures available from the water jacket of an internal combustion main engine. Heating tubes are mounted adjacent the bottom of the closed chamber and connected to the water jacket. Condenser tubes are mounted in the top of the closed chamber and connected to cool circulating sea water. Spray nozzles are mounted above the heater tubes and connected with a supply of heated sea water. A demister is mounted above the spray nozzles for detraining sea water droplets carried upward by vapor rising from the heater tubes. A collector for condensate is secured below the condenser tubes and connected to an exterior condensate line. Pressure in the closed chamber is reduced by connecting it to a low pressure area of a venturi installed in a cool sea water circulating line to the condenser tubes. A first branch of this sea water circulating line goes to a first heat exchanger that is also connected in the exterior condensate line for cooling the condensate. A second branch carries sea water, warmed by heat of condensation absorbed in the condenser tubes, to be further preheated by hot condensate which in turn is cooled in a second heat exchanger also connected in the condensate line ahead of the first heat exchanger. The preheated sea water is utilized by feeding to the spray nozzles for spraying on the heater tubes for flash vaporization of part and recirculation of the rest back to the spray nozzles and overboard. (Sinha-OEIS)
W75-08737

SEA WATER DESALTING APPARATUS,
Pioneer Science Ltd., Kowloon (Hong Kong). (assignee)
W. Hsiao.
U.S. Patent No. 3,864,932, 5 p, 11 fig, 2 ref; Official Gazette of the United States Patent Office, Vol 931, No 2, p 562, February 11, 1975.

Descriptors: *Patents, *Crystallization, *Desalination apparatus, Salt water, Potable water, Condensation, Sea water.
Identifiers: Partial vacuum, Subatmospheric pressure.

The invention is an apparatus for separating potable water from salt water by forcing salt water under pressure through one or more spray nozzles to reduce the water to a fine mist or fog. The salt water is introduced into a treatment chamber having a subatmospheric pressure or partial vacuum which permits potable water to be separated from the salt water by crystallization in which the potable water is frozen into crystalline form or by condensing portions of the mist or fog to recover potable water. (Sinha-OEIS)
W75-08747

APPARATUS FOR EVAPORATING LIQUIDS,
Aktiebolaget Atomenergi, Stockholm (Sweden). (Assignee).
P. H. E. Margen.
U S Patent No 3,879,265, 4 p, 3 fig, 5 ref; Official Gazette of the United States Patent Office, Vol 933, No 4, p 1735, April 22, 1975.

Descriptors: *Patents, *Desalination apparatus, *Evaporation, Sea water, Salt water, Separation techniques, Equipment, Steam, Water treatment.

An apparatus for evaporating liquids, particularly for evaporating salt water under low pressure in a desalination plant, comprises a liquid emitter, a guide surface along which the liquid flows, and a means for collecting the liquid. The guide surface consists of at least two guide vanes, each having only one curve, arranged one after the other. The generatrices have substantially the same direction. The adjacent guide vanes are oppositely curved. The liquid emitter is arranged to conduct the liquid towards the concave side of the first guide vane and the means for collecting liquid is arranged to conduct the water from the concave surface of the last guide vane. A film of liquid flowing along the guide vanes is subjected to oppositely directed centrifugal force fields on neighboring guide vanes and exposure on opposite surfaces to produce steam and separate it. (Sinha-OEIS)
W75-08762

DISTILLATION APPARATUS,
G. C. Sorensen.
U S Patent No 3,879,266, 3 p, 3 fig, 4 ref; Official Gazette of the United States Patent Office, Vol 933, No 4, p 1736, April 22, 1975.

Descriptors: *Patents, *Distillation, *Desalination apparatus, *Water treatment, *Evaporation, *Heat exchangers, Equipment, Salt water, Sea water, Fresh water.

A distillation report is provided which includes a raw fluid submerged device for spraying raw fluid upward against the under surface of a splash shield to be greatly atomized providing an immense total raw fluid surface are for evaporation. A combination pump and compressor draws vapor from the splash shield protected atomized raw fluid urged and heated for evaporation by the mingling commonly wasted heat from a cooperating combustion engine. The resultant mixture of vapor is compressed and condensed in a heat exchanger submerged in the included raw fluid sump. The resultant condensate is accumulated for biological production while a concentrated raw fluid is drained for further process or waste and the dehydrated gas is expanded through a fueling system turbo blower than recycled for further condensate entrainment. (Sinha-OEIS)
W75-08763

3C. Use Of Water Of Impaired Quality

ANALYSIS AND DESIGN OF SETTLING BASINS FOR IRRIGATION RETURN FLOW,
Idaho Univ., Moscow. Dept. of Civil Engineering.
For primary bibliographic entry see Field 5G.
W75-08484

3D. Conservation In Domestic and Municipal Use

URBAN WATER DEVELOPMENT AND MANAGEMENT IN ARID ENVIRONMENTS, VOLUME I: COMPLETION REPORT,
Rockwell International Corp., Canoga Park, Calif. Rocketdyne Div.
For primary bibliographic entry see Field 6A.
W75-08352

URBAN WATER DEVELOPMENT AND MANAGEMENT IN ARID ENVIRONMENTS, VOLUME II: THE WATER GAME--GAMING SIMULATION FOR URBAN WATER RESOURCES PLANNING,
Rockwell International Corp., Canoga Park, Calif. Rocketdyne Div.
For primary bibliographic entry see Field 6A.
W75-08353

EFFECTS OF PRICE CHANGE UPON THE DOMESTIC USE OF WATER OVER TIME,
Clemson Univ., S.C. Dept. of Agricultural Economics.
For primary bibliographic entry see Field 6C.
W75-08355

WATER CONSERVATION BY THE USER,
General Dynamics Corp., Groton, Conn. Electric Boat Div.
H. E. Bostian, S. Cohen, and H. Wallman.
Paper presented at the International Public Works Congress and Equipment Show, Denver, Colorado, September 16-20, 1973. 13 p, 1 fig, 3 tab.

Descriptors: *Water conservation, *Domestic water, *Municipal water, *Impaired water use, *Water supply, *Water demand, Conservation, Water utilization, Water users, Surveys, Water reuse, Reclaimed water, Recirculated water, Urbanization, Economic impact.
Identifiers: *Water fixtures.

Conservation of water can extend the reserves of our treated and natural water supplies and will obviously lower per capita costs of water supply and wastewater treatment. Where the reduction of sewage flow is important, reduction of infiltration is probably the best approach. However, when water supply is the problem, water conservation is the only way to reduce demand. Two aspects of water conservation are considered: (1) reducing the domestic use of water, and (2) recycling water in the home. Domestic water is but a small percentage of total water use, but it accounts for a fairly large percentage of water obtained from public water supplies. Domestic water conservation can be directly reduced by plumbing fixtures that require less water, as well as a conceptualized and tested fixtures that can recycle a portion of household waste water for uses not requiring drinking water quality. A user survey showed high acceptance of proposed water conservation and recycling systems. Included were flow-limiting shower heads, shallow-trap toilets, and dural-flush devices. Because of numerous factors involved in using these devices, it is also necessary to examine sociological, economic and technical problems. Total municipal use patterns may offer greater potential for water conservation. (Poertner)
W75-08360

URBAN STORM RUNOFF, PUGET SOUND REGION, WASHINGTON,
Washington Univ., Seattle. Coll. of Forest Resources.
For primary bibliographic entry see Field 5G.
W75-08492

TOTAL URBAN WATER POLLUTION LOADS: THE IMPACT OF STORM WATER,
Enviro Control, Inc., Rockville, Md.
For primary bibliographic entry see Field 5B.
W75-08677

ASPECTS OF HYDROLOGICAL EFFECTS OF URBANIZATION.
American Society of Civil Engineers, New York. Task Committee on the Effects of Urbanization on Low Flow, Total Runoff, Infiltration, and Ground-Water Recharge.
For primary bibliographic entry see Field 4C.
W75-08697

ARTIFICIAL RECHARGE IN THE URBAN ENVIRONMENT--SOME QUESTIONS AND ANSWERS,
California Univ., Davis. Dept. of Water Science and Engineering.
For primary bibliographic entry see Field 4B.
W75-08822

WASTEWATER RECLAMATION AND RECHARGE, BAY PARK, N.Y.,
Geological Survey, Mineola, N.Y.
For primary bibliographic entry see Field 5D.
W75-08827

STREAM RECONNAISSANCE FOR NUTRIENTS AND OTHER WATER-QUALITY PARAMETERS, GREATER PITTSBURGH REGION, PENNSYLVANIA,
Geological Survey, Carnegie, Pa.
For primary bibliographic entry see Field 5A.
W75-08835

THE IMPACT OF WATER QUALITY OBJECTIVES ON URBAN WATER SUPPLY PLANNING,
Colorado State Univ., Fort Collins. Dept. of Agricultural Engineering.
For primary bibliographic entry see Field 5D.
W75-08845

EVALUATION AND IMPLEMENTATION OF URBAN DRAINAGE PROJECTS,
Colorado State Univ, Fort Collins. Dept. of Civil Engineering.
For primary bibliographic entry see Field 4A.
W75-08847

CONTRASTS IN COMMUNITY ACTION AND OPINION,
Oregon State Univ, Corvallis. Dept. of Anthropology.
For primary bibliographic entry see Field 5G.
W75-08848

3E. Conservation In Industry

ENERGY PRODUCTION AND WATER SUPPLY,
Utah State Univ., Logan.
For primary bibliographic entry see Field 6B.
W75-08369

ENERGY-WATER RELATIONSHIPS: MANAGEMENT AND CONSERVATION IN THE CALIFORNIA-COLORADO RIVER - GREAT BASIN REGIONS,
Nevada Univ., Reno.
For primary bibliographic entry see Field 6B.
W75-08370

INDUSTRIAL WATER RESOURCES OF CANADA, THE HUDSON BAY, LABRADOR AND ARCTIC DRAINAGE BASINS, 1959-65,
Department of the Environment, Ottawa (Ontario). Water Quality Branch.
For primary bibliographic entry see Field 5A.
W75-08395

FEEDING CATTLE AT THE PULP MILL,
Tampella A.B., Tampere (Finland).
For primary bibliographic entry see Field 5D.
W75-08539

ENVIRONMENTAL PROTECTION IN KRAFT PULP MILLS,
Munksjo A.B., Jonkoping (Sweden).
For primary bibliographic entry see Field 5D.
W75-08566

ECOLOGICAL APPROACH TO POWER GENERATION UNDER ENVIRONMENTAL CONSERVATION,
Kansas State Univ., Manhattan. Dept. of Chemical Engineering.
For primary bibliographic entry see Field 6G.
W75-08604

GEOTHERMAL EXPLORATION,
Atlantic Richfield Co., New York. (assignee)
For primary bibliographic entry see Field 4B.
W75-08616

GEOTHERMAL HEAT EXHANGE METHOD AND APPARATUS,
For primary bibliographic entry see Field 4B.
W75-08618

METHOD OF RECOVERING GEOTHERMAL ENERGY,
Mobil Oil Corp., New York. (assignee)
For primary bibliographic entry see Field 4B.
W75-08736

SLIME CONTROL COMPOSITIONS AND THEIR USE,
Betz Labs., Inc., Trevose, Pa. (assignee)
For primary bibliographic entry see Field 5D.
W75-08739

ECONOMIC ANALYSIS OF EFFLUENT GUIDELINES--FLAT GLASS INDUSTRY,
Little (Arthur D.), Inc., Cambridge, Mass.
For primary bibliographic entry see Field 5G.
W75-08781

ECONOMIC ANALYSIS OF EFFLUENT GUIDELINES: RUBBER PROCESSING INDUSTRY,
Little (Arthur D.), Inc., Cambridge, Mass.
For primary bibliographic entry see Field 5G.
W75-08782

ECONOMIC ANALYSIS OF EFFLUENT GUIDELINES FOR SELECTED SEGMENTS OF THE SEAFOOD PROCESSING INDUSTRY. (CATFISH, CRAB, SHRIMP AND TUNA),
Development Planning and Research Associates, Inc., Manhattan, Kans.
For primary bibliographic entry see Field 5G.
W75-08783

3F. Conservation In Agriculture

EFFECT OF BEAN POD MOTTLE VIRUS ON YIELD COMPONENTS AND MORPHOLOGY OF SOYBEANS IN RELATION TO SOIL WATER REGIMES: A PRELIMINARY STUDY,
Mississippi State Univ., State College.
For primary bibliographic entry see Field 5C.
W75-08359

A MODEL FOR ESTIMATING DESIRED LEVELS OF NITRATE-N CONCENTRATION IN COTTON PETIOLES,
California Univ., Davis. Dept. of Water Science and Engineering.
D. W. Grimes, W. L. Dickens, H. Yamada, and R. J. Miller.
Agron J. Vol 65, No 1, p 37-41, 1973, Illus.

Descriptors: *Cotton(Field), Soils, *Soil-water-plant relationships, Semiarid climates, *Nitrogen, *Density, Fertilizers, *Nutrient requirements, *Water requirements, *Plant populations.
Identifiers: Gossypium-Hirsutum, Petioles.

Field studies were conducted on 2 widely different soils over a 3-yr period in a semiarid irrigated region to establish functional relations between responses of cotton (Gossypium hirsutum L.) plants and the major production input factors: water, N and plant density. The nitrate-N concentrations of petioles from the most recently matured leaves were influenced by N-fertilization level, time of sampling in the season and water management. Plant population did not alter the nitrate-N levels of petioles. High concentrations were associated with large amounts of N applied in side-dress soil applications. On a fine-textured soil with a high water-retention capacity N side-dressed after emergence was not taken up by the plant until the 1st irrigation was added. Concentrations of nitrate-N in petioles at critical times in the season were characterized by a 2nd-degree polynomial model having water and N quantities as independent variables (0.54 less than or equal to R2 less than or equal to 0.94). A 2nd model was subsequently developed that incorporates time as an independent variable in addition to water and N quantities. Using a yield equation and model 2, a procedure was developed that enables time-dependent 'desired' levels of plant nutrient concentrations to be established that are dependent on commodity price and production factor costs.--Copyright 1973, Biological Abstracts, Inc.
W75-08396

EFFECTS OF FRUIT LOAD, TEMPERATURE AND RELATIVE HUMIDITY ON BOLL RETENTION OF COTTON,
Agricultural Research Service, Brawley, Calif. Imperial Valley Conservation Research Center.
C. F. Ehlig, and R. D. Mert.
Crop Sci. Vol 13, No 2, p 168-171, 1973, Illus.

Descriptors: *Cotton(Field), Field crops, *Environmental effects, *Plant growth, Temperature, Humidity.
Identifiers: Boll retention, Climatological effects, Fruit load, Gossypium-Hirsutum.

Climatological factors and the boll load from the 1st fruiting cycle were evaluated as primary causes for low boll retention by cotton (Gossypium hirsutum L.) during midseason. Boll retention was permitted from incipient flowering, or after June 26, July 15, July 30 or Aug. 14, by the daily removal of flowers. Boll retention was greater than 75% initially, but decreased to less than 50% after bolls equivalent to 500-1200 kg lint/ha (1-2 bales/acre) were retained and less than 20% after bolls equivalent to 700-1300 kg lint/ha (1.25-2.25 bales/acre) were retained. The fruit load was the primary cause for low boll retention and cessation of flowering during midseason. No direct relationship between low boll retention and high maximum or minimum temperatures or high relative humidity was observed.--Copyright 1973, Biological Abstracts, Inc.
W75-08397

PERSISTENCE OF SELECTED ANTITRANSPIRANTS,
Colorado Univ., Boulder. Dept. of Chemical Engineering.
For primary bibliographic entry see Field 2D.
W75-08439

AN ECONOMIC ANALYSIS OF CHANGES IN IRRIGATION PRACTICES IN JEFFERSON COUNTY, IDAHO,
Idaho Univ., Moscow. Department of Agricultural Economics.
J. E. Milliner.
Available from the National Technical Information Service, Springfield, Va 22161 as PB-242 343, $5.25 in paper copy, $2.25 in microfiche. M S Thesis, August 1974. 100 p, 5 fig, 24 tab, 22 ref, 4 append. OWRT B-033-IDA(2).

Descriptors: *Irrigation practices, *Idaho, Feasibility studies, *Water table, Economics, *Linear programming, *Sprinkler irrigation, Crop rotation, Model studies, *Cost analysis, Cost comparison.
Identifiers: Parametric analysis, Rotation policy, Center-pivot sprinkler systems.

Economic effects of solving a high water table problem in southeastern Idaho near Rigby were analyzed. The objectives were to analyze the farm situation and to determine the feasibility of solving

the problem by decreasing water use at the farm level. Two methods were used: one involved a theoretical decrease of water availability without alterations to the present farm irrigation system while the second involved a water decrease by incorporating sprinkler systems to the area. Primary and secondary information was collected and representative budgets were used for 80, 160, and 320 acre farms. An optimum organization of farms was achieved through linear programming. A parametric routine was entered into the linear model, reducing the water in five percent intervals. This substantially affected income at both 25 and 50 percent reduction levels, primarily because the water reductions made tillable land unproductive. Budgets were developed for hand-moved, wheel-moved and a center-pivot sprinkler system; costs were then deducted from the linear programming solution and analyzed. The cost comparison showed that the sprinkler system was more profitable.
W75-08481

METHODOLOGY FOR OBTAINING LEAST COST IRRIGATION STEM SPECIFICATIONS,
Idaho Univ., Moscow. Dept. of Agricultural Engineering.
J. R. Busch.
Available from the National Technical Information Service, Springfield, Va 22161 as PB-242 386 $7.50 in paper copy, $2.25 in microfiche. Ph D Thesis, December 1974. 214 p, 28 fig, 18 tab, 76 ref, 3 append. OWRT B-028-IDA(2). B-033-IDA(3).

Descriptors: *Irrigation systems, *Methodology, Model studies, *Linear programming, Dynamic programming, Water wells, Cost analysis, *Idaho, Pumping.
Identifiers: *Least cost irrigation, High lead pipelines, *Parametric programming, Handline sprinklers, Sideroll sprinklers.

A methodology for obtaining least cost irrigation systems specifications was developed and applied. Irrigation systems as defined, consisted of application system and distribution components and did not include reservoirs of any type. An analytical model employing a two-stage dynamic linear-programming technique was used to select and arrange system such that a least cost overall system would result. Based on cost function, more costly and less efficient distribution system component combinations were eliminated. Linear and parametric programming were applied to the model in North Rigby Irrigation District, Jefferson County, Idaho to determine least cost rehabilitation schemes for various specified conditions. Results showed that the analytical model is a valid tool.
W75-08482

EFFECTS OF DATE AND DEPTH OF PLANTING ON THE ESTABLISHMENT OF THREE RANGE GRASSES,
Colorado State Univ., Fort Collins. Dept. of Range Science.
W. J. McGinnies.
Agron J. Vol 65, No 1, p 120-123. 1973.

Descriptors: *Grasses, *Wheat grasses, Range grasses, *Forage grasses, Soil moisture, *Plant growth, *Soil-water-plant relationships, Plant physiology, Seasonal, Spring, Summer, Crop response.
Identifiers: Agropyron-Desertorum, Agropyron-Trichophorum, Depth of planting, Elymus-Junceus, Planting depth.

Crested wheatgrass (Agropyron desertorum (Fisch. ex Link) Schult.), pubescent wheatgrass (A. trichophorum (Link) Richt.) and Russian wildrye (Elymus junceus Fisch.) were planted at depths of 1.3, 2.5, 3.8, and 5.1 cm on average dates of planting of April 4, April 18, May 4, May 20, and June 9, 1967 through 1970 north of Fort Collins, Colorado. Crested wheatgrass and Russian wildrye were also planted at the same depths on average dates of planting of April 20, May 3, May 18, and June 8, 1968 through 1970 on Central Plains Experimental Range (CPER) near Nunn, Colorado. Establishment was evaluated from seedling counts made in Sept. of the year of planting. At Fort Collins the greatest average number of seedlings was obtained from the April 18, May 4, and May 20 dates of seeding. Although year-to-year variations were great, the most reliable establishment was from the April 18 planting. At CPER, establishment from the June 8 planting was markedly poorer than for the 3 earlier dates of planting. Number of seedlings per meter of row was essentially the same for 1.3- and 2.5-cm planting depths within species and locations except that crested wheatgrass averaged 12% more seedlings from 1.3-than from 2.5-cm depths at Fort Collins. At 3.8 cm, numbers declined to about 50% of those in the shallower depths and declined still more at 5.1 cm. The decline was about 50% as much for pubescent wheatgrass as for crested wheatgrass and Russian wildrye. Soil moisture in the zone 2.5-5.1 cm deep appeared to be most critical for establishment. When moisture at this soil depth averaged less than 12% following seeding, stands contained only 53% as many seedlings as when the soil moisture averaged above 12%.--Copyright 1973, Biological Abstracts, Inc.
W75-08546

WATER INTAKE RATES ON A SILT LOAM SOIL WITH VARIOUS MANURE APPLICATIONS,
Nebraska Univ., Lincoln. Dept. of Agricultural Engineering.
For primary bibliographic entry see Field 2G.
W75-08574

SPRINKLER AND SOAKER IRRIGATION OF PEACH TREES TO REDUCE PLANT WATER STRESS AND INCREASE FRUIT SIZE,
Florida Univ., Gainesville. Dept. of Fruit Crops.
P. L. Ryan, J. F. Bartholic, and D. W. Buchanan.
Proceedings of the Florida State Horticultural Society, Vol 86, November 6-8, 1973, p 311-315. 3 fig, 1 tab, 4 ref. OWRR B-014-FLA(1). 14-31-0001-3868.

Descriptors: *Evapotranspiration, Evapotranspiration control, Energy budget, Water balance, Fruit crops, *Peaches, *Sprinkler irrigation, Soil moisture, Orchards.

'Early Amber' peach trees were irrigated using intermittent daily sprinkling, soaker hoses, and recommended overhead sprinklers. The first 2 systems were designed to maintain a constant soil moisture level near field capacity. The intermittent sprinkling, in addition, modified the trees' environment through evaporative cooling. On trees with about 300 fruit, sprinkling produced the largest fruit yielding 47% that were 2 inches or larger in diameter, while trees irrigated with soaker hoses yielded approximately 18% and the controls 10%. (Morgan-Florida)
W75-08596

RESPONSE OF THREE CORN HYBRIDS TO LOW LEVELS OF SOIL MOISTURE TENSION IN THE PLOW LAYER,
Agricultural Research and Educational Center, Quincy, Fla.
F. M. Rhoads, and R. L. Stanley, Jr.
Agron J, Vol 65, No 2, p 315-318, 1973, Illus.

Descriptors: *Corn(Field), *Soil moisture, Soil-water-plant relationships, *Irrigation effects, Crops, Field crops, Grains(Crops), Plant growth.
Identifiers: Hybrids(Corn).

The response of 3 corn (Zea mays L.) hybrids to irrigation treatments that were designed to maintain soil moisture tension at low levels (less than 1-bar) in plow layer rather than the entire root zone was evaluated. Flowering date, plant height and grain yield were used as indexes of response. Irrigation was applied at 4 levels (0.3, 0.6, 2.0 and 5.0 bars) of soil moisture tension in 1970 and at 3 levels (0.2, 0.4, and 0.6 bars) in 1971. N was applied in 336 and 560 kg/ha, in 1971, to treatments irrigated at 0.2 bar of soil moisture tension. Each irrigation treatment was replicated 4 times and consisted of applying water at a selected value of soil moisture tension. A tensiometer was placed in each plot to be irrigated at soil moisture tensions below 1 bar in order to monitor soil moisture tension at a depth of 15 cm. Electrical resistance units were used in 1970 to monitor soil moisture tension in plots irrigated at tensions above 1 bar. Flowering occurred earlier and plant height increased as soil moisture tension at irrigation decreased. Grain yields were increased significantly (5% level) each year when plots were irrigated at 0.2 and 0.3 bar soil moisture tension instead of 0.6 bar. Irrigation at 0.6 bar did not increase grain yields in comparison with no irrigation in 1970. Each corn variety gave an inverse linear grain yield response to soil moisture tension values between 0.2 and 0.6 bar in 1971. There was a significant difference (5% level) between varieties in magnitude of grain yield response to irrigation in 1971. Highest grain yields were produced each year when soil moisture tension in the plow layer was maintained below 1/3 bar.--Copyright 1973, Biological Abstracts, Inc.
W75-08600

NITRATE UPTAKE EFFECTIVENESS OF FOUR PLANT SPECIES,
Purdue Univ., Lafayette, Ind. Dept. of Agronomy.
For primary bibliographic entry see Field 5B.
W75-08607

EMITTER VALVE FOR SOIL IRRIGATION,
Salco Products, Inc., Los Angeles, Calif. (assignee)
D. Werner.
US Patent No 3,874,591, 7 p, 12 fig, 12 ref; Official Gazette of the United States Patent Office, Vol 933, No 1, p 197, April 1, 1975.

Descriptors: *Patents, *Irrigation systems, *Surface irrigation, *Soil moisture, *Water distribution(Applied), Equipment, Valves.

The emitter valve, which is useful for irrigation of soil, includes a valve body placed intermediate the ends of a supply conduit and provided with a valve head. The head has an inlet connected to the supply conduit and one or more outlets opening to the valve exterior for supply of controlled amounts of water to the soil. The valve outlet are unobstructed by the deformable cylinder regardless of operational pressures exerted thereon by a set screw except when great set screw pressure is exerted to purposely shut off flow of water. The amount of water released by the valve is determined by the pressure of water in the supply conduit which overcomes the applied pressure of the set screw and cylinder in order to deform the cylinder and to allow water to pass around the cylinder, its grooves, and the shell-shaped opening to the soil. (Sinha-OEIS)
W75-08614

MOISTURE RESPONSIVE APPARATUS FOR CONTROLLING MOISTURE CONTENT OF SOIL,
W. H. Gibson.
US Patent No 3,874, 590, 11 p, 10 fig, 5 ref; Official Gazette of the United States Patent Office, Vol 933, No 1, p 197, April 1, 1975.

Descriptors: *Patents, *Irrigation system, *Surface irrigation, *Water distribution(Applied), *Soil moisture, Valves.
Identifiers: Pilot values, Sensors.

A moisture responsive apparatus is disclosed for automatically controlling the operation of a soil ir-

rigation system. The apparatus includes a moisture sensor having a perforated tubular sensing element adapted to be placed in contact with or in proximity to the soil and made of a material, such as nylon, that absorbs moisture and expands in accordance with the amount of moisture absorbed. The expansion and contraction of the sensing element relative to a menber whose dimensions are unaffected by moisture are used to operate a pilot valve which in turn supplies a small control flow that actuates an irrigation system valve. The sensing element and related member may have the same coefficient of thermal expansion to compensate for dimensional changes due to temperature variations, and may be adjustably coupled to permit setting the moisture content operating limits of the pilot valve. The sensing element may comprise a plurality of concentric, serially connected sensing tubes to increase the sensitivity of the sensing element for a given overall length. The sensing element may also include reinforcing ribs projecting from the exterior surface and may also be isolated from direct contact with the soil by means of a moisture-permeable screen placed about the element but not contacting it. (Sinha-OEIS)
W75-08615

IRRIGATION CONTROL,
R. E. Shettel.
US Patent No 3,874,176, 5 p, 17 fig, 7 ref; Official Gazette of the United States Patent Office, Vol 933, No 1, p 62, April 1, 1975.

Descriptors: *Patents, *Irrigation systems, *Water distribution(Applied), Equipment, Open channel flow, Conduits.
Identifiers: *Open channel irrigation.

A balancing assembly for controlling the diversion of water in a channel comprises a dam positioned in a channel, the top surface of which includes a depression adapted to receive an opening spill segment, and a pivot permitting pivotal movement of the dam relative to the channel. It has a seal depending from the perimeter of the dam for bearing agains the channel when the dam is in the closed position. Controls for pivoting the dam are attached to the dam and permit relative movement between the controls and the dam. On extremity of the controls extend downward from the attachment to bear against the channel for support and another extremity of the controls extends upward from the attachment to permit the actuation of the controls to selectively space the dam apart from the channel. (Sinha-OEIS)
W75-08617

WEEPER IRRIGATION SYSTEM AND METHOD,
W. C. Reeder, and N. D. Batterson.
US Patent No 3,873,031, 7 p, 14 fig, 10 ref; Official Gazette of the United States Patent Office, Vol 932, No 4, p 1423, March 25, 1975.

Descriptors: *Patents, *Irrigation systems, *Surface irrigation, Equipment, Mist irrigation, Water distribution(Applied), Distribution system.
Identifiers: *Weeper irrigation system.

A weeper type irrigation system and method features unusual flexibility of use and mode of assembly. The weeper proper is installable in a self-sealing manner in the side of a plastic water distributing manifold or tube. It is operable to provide either a misty spray discharge into the air of weeper flow at more than one selected rate. The weeper flow may be directed laterally into the air or conducted to a more remote discharge point or along the exterior of the weeper. The weepers are readily installable remote from or in close proximity to one another and each is individually operable at will to dispense water in a selected manner and at a selected rate. A protective cap is installable with a snap fit over the outer end and selectively adjustable thereon to provide fast or slow weeper flow as well as to convert the discharge between a confined flow at either a slow or fast rate and into a widely dispersed mistly spray or a confined flow. (Sinha-OEIS)
W75-08621

ONE-PIECE DRIP IRRIGATION DEVICE,
J. S. Barragan.
US Patent No 3,873,030, 2 p, 3 fig, 3 ref; Official Gazette of the United States Patent Office, Vol 932, No 4, p 1423, March 25, 1975.

Descriptors: *Patents, *Irrigation system, *Surface irrigation, Equipment, Water distribution(Applied), Distribution system.
Identifiers: *Drip irrigation.

A one-piece drip irrigation device is attached to a perforated wall of an irrigation liquid supply pipe. The device comprises a casing having side and bottom walls and a flange extending outwardly from the edges of an open wall of the casing. The flange when attached to the pipe wall constitutes an enclosed housing having a multiplicity of alternate walls that form a passage provided with a multiplicity of obstacles to free flow of liquid. Included in one of its ends is a perforation for liquid exit at lowered pressure. (Sinha-OEIS)
W75-08622

DRIP-TYPE IRRIGATION EMITTER,
BPG Co., Inc., Mission, Tex. (assignee)
R. R. Ruben.
US Patent No 3,876,155, 8 p, 19 fig, 5 ref; Official Gazette of the United States Patent Office, Vol 933, No 2, p 714, April 8, 1975.

Descriptors: *Patents, *Irrigation systems, *Water distribution(Applied), Equipment, Mist irrigation, Surface irrigation, Distribution systems, Automation.
Identifiers: *Drip irrigation, Emitter units.

A basic emitter unit is designed for automatic self-flushing and drip operation, but it can be readily modified by adding parts to convert it to a combination drip irrigation emitter and mister for spraying finely divided particles of heated water into the air to warm the air to prevent frost damage to plants, trees, ets. By the substitution of differently designed orifice discs, the basic emitter unit can be made self-flushing and to provide misting only, or to be self-flushing and function as an unlimited-pressure mister. By alternative minor disc modification, the basic emitter unit can be connected at the end of an irrigation line to effect flushing of the line only. The basic emitter unit is further characterized by its capability of (1) automatically compensating for variations in line pressure and changes in elevation of terrain; (2) maintaining a uniform flow rate regardless of variations in line pressure; (3) eliminating the necessity of water filtration; (4) when connected with other emitters in an irrigation line taking advantage of line friction and enabling flushing and seating of the emitters progressively under very low line pressure; and (5) eliminating the need for a dual pump system. (Sinha-OEIS)
W75-08628

SIMULATION MODEL FOR EVAPOTRANSPIRATION OF WHEAT: EMPIRICAL APPROACH,
Agricultural Research Organization, Bet Dagan (Israel). Inst. of Soils and Water.
For primary bibliographic entry see Field 2D.
W75-08712

2020 HINDSIGHT: ANOTHER FIFTY YEARS OF IRRIGATION,
Committee on Interior and Insular Affairs (U.S. Subcommittee on Water and Power Resources.
D. A. Dreyfus.
Journal of the Irrigation and Drainage Division, ASCE, Vol 101, No IR2, Proceedings paper No 11363, p 87-94, June 1975. 4 ref.

Descriptors: *Irrigation, *Planning, *Water resources, *Water supply, Regional development, Reclamation, Agriculture, Management, Decision making, Water policy, Colorado River.
Identifiers: *Government agencies, Western U.S.

Water resources management has been a concern of governments from the time of the earliest recorded civilizations. In the United States, policies that have evolved over several decades to guide the Federal role in water resources planning and development are no longer relevant to national problems and goals. Water resources planning presently is in disarray because mechanical analysis has been subsitituted for continued policy guidance. The nation appears to be approaching a major reevaluation of governmental water resources policy. New objectives and a new Federal role will be defined. Recent social and economic conditions indicate that there will be renewed national interest in the management of western water resources and that irrigated agriculture will continue to be a significant function in Federal water policy. (Bell-Cornell)
W75-08721

APPARATUS FOR SUBSOIL IRRIGATION,
T. J. Frazier.
U.S. Patent No. 3,865,057, 9 p, 13 fig, 8 ref; Official Gazette of the United States Patent Office, Vol 931, No 2, p 605, February 11, 1975.

Descriptors: *Patents, *Irrigation systems, *Subsurface irrigation, *Agricultural engineering, Wells, Conduits, Distribution systems, Water distribution(Applied), Water delivery.

The irrigation system includes a translatable vehicle having a number of horizontally spaced soil splitting shanks. The translatable vehicle is adapted to be progressively maneuvered over an area to be irrigated in alternate, adjacent parallel paths of movement, with water used for irrigation being pumped through reelable conduit from a stationary water supply source to pressure pumps located on the translatable vehicle. The water is delivered from the pressure pump through conduit operatively associated with each of the soil splitting shanks and is ejected into the subsoil of the area through openings located adjacent the lower portions of the soil splitting shanks. (Sinha-OEIS)
W75-08748

DYNAMICS OF HIGHER PLANT WATER METABOLISM AND ITS INFORMATION SIGNIFICANCE, (IN RUSSIAN),
Agrofizicheskii Nauchno-Issledovatelskii Institut, Leningrad (USSR).
For primary bibliographic entry see Field 21.
W75-08789

DYNAMICS OF FREE AMINO ACID CONTENT IN LEAVES OF WINTER WHEAT UNDER VARIABLE CONDITIONS OF SOIL MOISTURE, (IN RUSSIAN),
Akademiya Nauk URSR, Kiev. Institut Fiziologii Rastenii i Agrokhimii.
S. I. Slukhai, and O. P. Opanasenko.
Fiziol Biokhim Kul't Rast, 6(1): 47-53, 1974. English summary.

Descriptors: Plant physiology, *Wheat, Crops, Cereal crops, Agronomic crops, *Leaves, *Soil moisture, Water requirements, *Amino acids, Nitrogen compounds.
Identifiers: Asparagine, Proline, Winter wheat, *USSR.

A 2 yr study of free amino acid content in the winter wheat leaves in ontogenesis under green-

Hydrologic, geographic, engineering, socio-economic, and other feasibility conditions were investigated for the concept of regional water exchanges. As a drought alleviation alternative, it was determined that regional water exchanges, with bi-directional pipe-line networks, have some advantages over the other drought alleviation measures, external to users. The exchange systems have the advantage of being free from inter-regional controversies commonly involved with the uni-directional water transfer. The partial substitution for the required storage capacity is an important advantage of exchange systems. To measure the magnitude of this effect, the maximum reduction ratio of the sum of ranges was introduced and its implication and practical use were demonstrated by using the river basin systems of the west-central part of the United States as a case study. (Dawes-ISWS)
W75-08403

EFFICIENT SEQUENTIAL OPTIMIZATION IN WATER RESOURCES,
Iowa Univ., Iowa City. Inst. of Hydraulic Research.
T. E. Croley, II.
Colorado State University Hydrology Papers No. 69, September 1974. 31 p, 12 fig, 13 tab, 48 ref, 5 append. NSF Grant GK-11564.

Descriptors: *Optimization, *Stochastic processes, *Dynamic programming, *Analytical techniques, Simulation analysis, Operations research, Statistical methods, Optimum development plans, Mathematical studies, Reservoir operation, Water resources.
Identifiers: *Sequential optimization.

Reduction of computation effort in water resource optimization problems can be made through a modification of the optimization technique instead of limiting development of the system models. Considerations were presented which lead to the development of a heuristic application of deterministic optimization techniques. Stochastic optimization techniques that are used in water resource systems engineering were presented. A heuristic alternate stochastic optimization technique was then described and suggested as an improvement. For a single reservoir system, the techniques were applied and compared. Computation costs were reduced and system performance was improved with the use of the alternate. (Jess-ISWS)
W75-08404

THE FORMATION OF BRINE DRAINAGE FEATURES IN YOUNG SEA ICE,
Washington Univ., Seattle. Dept. of Oceanography.
For primary bibliographic entry see Field 2C.
W75-08408

SEEPAGE CHARACTERISTICS OF FOUNDATIONS WITH A DOWNSTREAM CRACK,
Madras Univ., Guindy (India). Coll. of Engineering.
For primary bibliographic entry see Field 8D.
W75-08432

PROPERTIES OF THE THREE-PARAMETER LOG NORMAL PROBABILITY DISTRIBUTION,
Washington Univ., Seattle. Dept. of Civil Engineering.
For primary bibliographic entry see Field 2E.
W75-08438

WELSH FLOODPLAIN STUDIES: THE NATURE OF FLOODPLAIN GEOMETRY,
University Coll. of Wales, Aberystwyth.
For primary bibliographic entry see Field 2E.
W75-08448

ANALYSIS OF RUNOFF FROM SOUTHERN GREAT PLAINS FEEDLOTS,
Agricultural Research Service, Bushland, Tex. Southwestern Great Plains Research Center.
For primary bibliographic entry see Field 5B.
W75-08460

MECHANICAL HARVESTING OF AQUATIC VEGETATION: DEVELOPMENT OF A HIGH SPEED PICKUP UNIT,
Wisconsin Univ., Madison. Dept. of Mechanical Engineering.
H. F. Link.
Available from the National Technical Information Service, Springfield, Va 22161 as PB-242 338, $4.75 in paper copy, $2.25 in microfiche. M.S. Thesis, 1974. 82 p, 37 fig, 10 ref, 4 append. OWRR B-018-WIS(5). 14-01-0001-1957.

Descriptors: Aquatic plants, *Rooted aquatic plants, *Harvesting, *Productivity, *Costs, *Wisconsin, *Aquatic weed control, Mechanical equipment.
Identifiers: Dane County lakes(Wis).

The unit described gathers and picks up cut vegetation floating on the water surface. The gathering system consists of two horizontal arms approximately one foot above the water arranged in a 'V' configuration with the open end forward and the vertex just ahead of the barge onto which they are mounted. Steel tines attached at approximately 5 inch intervals to chains extend vertically into the water, travel rearwards along the bottom of the arm to the vertex of the 'V' and then return forward along the top. If the forward velocity of the barge and the rearward component of tooth velocity are matched, the floating vegetation contacted by the teeth is concentrated sideways into a windrow, passes through a gap at the vertex of the 'V' and is elevated onto the barge by a slatted conveyor, the bottom end of which extends just below the water surface. Tests were run using various forward velocities and angles between the arms. Power requirements were measured and collection performance was evaluated. While the collection performance was deemed satisfactory, power requirements indicated that friction losses in the arms were high. Consequently, a redesign of the arm mechanism was indicated. In addition to the collecting arms the barge which carried them was designed and built using two aluminum military bridge pontoons. Dewatering rolls used in conjunction with the pickup conveyor were ineffective, while a pinch-off roll with radial blades appeared promising for reducing the vegetation to short lengths which were easily handled. (Koegel-Wisconsin)
W75-08471

DEVELOPMENT OF A MANAGEMENT FRAMEWORK OF THE GREAT SALT LAKE,
Utah Water Research Lab., Logan.
For primary bibliographic entry see Field 6A.
W75-08473

URBAN STORM RUNOFF, PUGET SOUND REGION, WASHINGTON,
Washington Univ., Seattle. Coll. of Forest Resources.
For primary bibliographic entry see Field 5G.
W75-08492

ESTIMATING STREAMFLOW CHARACTERISTICS FOR STREAMS IN UTAH USING SELECTED CHANNEL-GEOMETRY PARAMETERS,
Geological Survey, Salt Lake City, Utah.
F. K. Fields.
Available from NTIS, Springfield, Va 22161 as PB-241 541, $3.25 in paper copy, $2.25 in microfiche. Water-Resources Investigations 34-74, February 1975. 19 p, 2 fig, 10 tab, 7 ref.

Descriptors: *Flood recurrence interval, *Channel morphology, *Utah, *Streamflow, Alluvial channels, Sand bars, Flow characteristics.
Identifiers: *Channel geometry.

Channel-geometry parameters were studied in relation to mean annual streamflow and the 25- and 50-year recurrence-interval flood discharges of Utah streams. Channel width and depth between depositional bars can be used to estimate mean annual streamflow for perennial streams with a standard error of estimate of 34 percent. The standard error of estimate of mean annual streamflow for ephemeral streams is 73 percent. The 25- and 50-year floods on perennial and ephemeral streams can be estimated from the channel width between depositional bars with standard errors of estimate ranging from 28 to 43 percent. (Knapp-USGS)
W75-08494

POTENTIAL FLOOD HAZARD--NORTH AVENUE AREA, DENVER FEDERAL CENTER, LAKEWOOD, COLORADO,
Geological Survey, Denver, Colo.
R. U. Grozier, J. F. McCain, and G. L. Ducret, Jr.
Open-file report 75-45, 1975. 12 p, 1 fig, 1 plate, 1 tab, 5 ref.

Descriptors: *Floods, *Colorado, *Urbanization, *Urban hydrology, Urban runoff, Storm runoff, Hazards.
Identifiers: *Denver(Colo), *Flood hazards.

A potential flood hazard has been created on the Denver Federal Center by development of property adjacent to the northwest corner of the Center. Prior to development of the property, the 100-year 1-hour rainfall of 2.10 inches produced a peak discharge of 140 cubic feet per second at the west side of Union Street. This discharge entered Welch Ditch and the combined discharge of 205 cfs flowed south into McIntyre Gulch without overflowing the east bank of the ditch. Under developed basin conditions, the same rainfall would produce a peak discharge of 212 cfs. The total storm runoff would enter the Center through a 54-inch corrugated metal pipe recently constructed under Union Street and Welch Ditch. The 100-year flood discharge for developed basin conditions would cause damages to Buildings 67, 56, and 48. (Knapp-USGS)
W75-08496

REPORT OF THE ANNUAL YIELD OF THE ARKANSAS RIVER BASIN FOR THE ARKANSAS RIVER BASIN COMPACT, ARKANSAS-OKLAHOMA, 1972: 1974 WATER YEAR,
Geological Survey, Little Rock, Ark.
T. E. Lamb.
Open-file report, 1974. 26 p, 1 fig, 3 tab, 4 ref.

Descriptors: *Water yield, *Streamflow, *Arkansas, *Oklahoma, *Interstate compacts, Withdrawal, Data collections, Hydrologic data.
Identifiers: *Arkansas River Basin Compact.

The computed annual yield of subbasins in the Arkansas River basin as defined in the Arkansas River Basin Compact, Arkansas-Oklahoma, 1972, are presented. The annual yield and deficiency were computed for each subbasin. Actual runoff was compiled for the subbasins. Annual depletion caused by major reservoirs was computed for the four major reservoirs in the basin. (Knapp-USGS)
W75-08497

HYDROLOGIC RECORDS FOR VOLUSIA COUNTY, FLORIDA: 1972-73,
Geological Survey, Tallahassee, Fla.
P. E. Meadows, and D. M. Hughes.
Open-file report 74021, 1974. 47 p, 28 fig, 8 tab, 6 ref.

Descriptors: *Basic data collections, *Hydrologic data, *Surface waters, *Groundwater, *Florida, Water wells, Streamflow, Aquifers, Precipitation(Atmospheric).
Identifiers: *Volusia County(Fla).

Hydrologic conditions in Volusia County, Florida are summarized. The data are presented in tabular and graphic form. Data on wells, springs, and lakes are for May 1972 to May 1973; data on streams are for the 1972 water year, October 1, 1971 to September 30, 1972. Groundwater is the principal source of potable water in Volusia County. The major source of groundwater is the Floridan aquifer, an artesian system comprised of a thick sequence of limestone and dolomite; all observation wells for which data are included in this report tap the Floridan aquifer. A shallow aquifer consisting of sand and shell beds is a source of domestic water supply along parts of the east coast where the Floridan aquifer contains saline water. Average groundwater levels in the artesian aquifer have not declined appreciably in recent years over most of the county. Surface drainage in Volusia County is poorly developed, resulting in large swampy areas in much of the county. In the De Land Ridge area, both north and south of De Land, karst topography is well developed and drainage is internal by downward seepage to the Floridan aquifer. Streamflow leaving the county averages about 590 million gallons per day. (Knapp-USGS)
W75-08498

AN EVALUATION OF THE ERTS DATA COLLECTION SYSTEM AS A POTENTIAL OPERATIONAL TOOL,
Geological Survey, Harrisburg, Pa.
For primary bibliographic entry see Field 7C.
W75-08503

FLOOD ON BUFFALO CREEK FROM SAUNDERS TO MAN, WEST VIRGINIA,
Geological Survey, Reston, Va.
For primary bibliographic entry see Field 7C.
W75-08508

WATER RESOURCES OF THE CROW RIVER WATERSHED, SOUTH-CENTRAL MINNESOTA,
Geological Survey, Reston, Va.
For primary bibliographic entry see Field 7C.
W75-08511

RECONNAISSANCE OF THE UPPER AU SABLE RIVER, A COLD-WATER RIVER IN THE NORTH-CENTRAL PART OF MICHIGAN'S SOUTHERN PENINSULA,
Geological Survey, Reston, Va.
For primary bibliographic entry see Field 7C.
W75-08512

WATER RESOURCES OF THE BLUE EARTH RIVER WATERSHED, SOUTH-CENTRAL MINNESOTA,
Geological Survey, Reston, Va.
For primary bibliographic entry see Field 7C.
W75-08513

WATER RESOURCES OF THE CLINTON RIVER BASIN, SOUTHEASTERN MICHIGAN,
Geological Survey, Reston, Va.
For primary bibliographic entry see Field 7C.
W75-08514

ANNUAL PEAK DISCHARGES FROM SMALL DRAINAGE AREAS IN MONTANA, THROUGH SEPTEMBER 1974,
Geological Survey, Helena, Mont.
For primary bibliographic entry see Field 7C.
W75-08516

MAGNITUDE AND FREQUENCY OF FLOODS IN WASHINGTON,
Geological Survey, Tacoma, Wash.
J. E. Cummans, M. R. Collings, and E. G. Nassar.
Open-file report 74-336, 1975. 46 p, 3 plate, 4 tab, 19 ref.

Descriptors: *Floods, *Washington, Flood frequency, Peak discharge, Regression analysis, Rainfall-runoff relationships.

Relations are provided to estimate the magnitude and frequency of floods on Washington streams. Annual-peak-flow data from stream gaging stations on unregulated streams having 10 years or more of record were used to determine a log-Pearson Type III frequency curve for each station. Flood magnitudes having recurrence intervals of 2, 5, 10, 25, 50, and 100 years were then related to physical and climatic indices of the drainage basins by multiple-regression analysis. These regression relations are useful for estimating flood magnitudes of the specified recurrence intervals at ungaged or short-record sites. Peak flows are related most significantly in western Washington to drainage-area size and mean annual precipitation. In eastern Washington they are related most significantly to drainage-area size, mean annual precipitation, and percentage of forest cover. (Knapp-USGS)
W75-08520

DESIGN AND IMPLEMENTATION OF A HYDROLOGIC DATA PROCESSING SYSTEM IN BRAZIL, 1971-74,
Geological Survey, Reston, Va.
For primary bibliographic entry see Field 7A.
W75-08523

COMPUTER PROCESSING HYDROLOGIC DATA IN BRAZIL,
Geological Survey, Reston, Va.
For primary bibliographic entry see Field 7A.
W75-08524

THE IMPLEMENTATION OF A HYDROLOGIC DATA PROCESSING SYSTEM IN BRAZIL,
Geological Survey, Reston, Va.
For primary bibliographic entry see Field 7A.
W75-08526

MANAGEMENT STUDY OF SOME ASPECTS OF SISTEMA DE INFORMACOES HIDROLOGICAS,
Geological Survey, Reston, Va.
For primary bibliographic entry see Field 7A.
W75-08527

EFFECTS OF DATE AND DEPTH OF PLANTING ON THE ESTABLISHMENT OF THREE RANGE GRASSES,
Colorado State Univ., Fort Collins. Dept. of Range Science.
For primary bibliographic entry see Field 3F.
W75-08546

A CASE STUDY OF THE APPLICATION OF COST-BENEFIT ANALYSIS TO WATER SYSTEM CONSOLIDATION BY LOCAL GOVERNMENT,
Delaware Univ., Newark. Div. of Urban Affairs; and Delaware Univ., Newark. Water Resources Center.
For primary bibliographic entry see Field 6B.
W75-08573

EFFECT OF ATMOSPHERIC STABILITY AND WIND DIRECTION ON WATER TEMPERATURE PREDICTIONS FOR A THERMALLY-LOADED STREAM,
Pennsylvania State Univ., University Park. School of Forest Resources.

Although extensive surveys have been made in search of diseases with biocontrol potential on this noxious plant, this spot disease differed from the others that had been thus far noted during these surveys. Leaf spots caused by Cerocospora piaropi were oval and ranged from approximately 1.5 to 4.0 mm in size. Smaller ones were uniformly purplish-black but developed a tan center as they enlarged. Spots were more concentrated on the distal portion of the leaf blade. In this area there was often confluence of lesions resulting in a general necrosis of the distal part of the leaf. Large lesions were often faintly zonate in the tan center. (Morgan-Florida)
W75-08610

LAND USE AND NUCLEAR POWER PLANTS - CASE STUDIES OF SITING PROBLEMS,
Directorate of Regulatory Standards (AEC), Washington, D.C.
For primary bibliographic entry see Field 6G.
W75-08654

NEWPORT--MAIN DRAINAGE SCHEME TAKES SHAPE,
For primary bibliographic entry see Field 5D.
W75-08675

A TWO LAYER FLOW THROUGH A CONTRACTION,
New South Wales Univ., Kensington (Australia). Water Research Lab.
For primary bibliographic entry see Field 8B.
W75-08701

SEEPAGE THROUGH OPENING IN CUTOFF WALL UNDER WEIR,
Bengal Engineering Coll., Howrah (India). Dept. of Civil Engineering.
For primary bibliographic entry see Field 8D.
W75-08711

CHANNELIZATION: A SEARCH FOR A BETTER WAY,
North Carolina Univ., Charlotte. Dept. of Geography and Earth Sciences.
For primary bibliographic entry see Field 8B.
W75-08714

ENVIRONMENTAL GEOLOGY--AN AID TO GROWTH AND DEVELOPMENT IN LAUDERDALE, COLBERT AND FRANKLIN COUNTIES, ALABAMA,
Geological Survey of Alabama, University. Environmental Div.
For primary bibliographic entry see Field 7C.
W75-08718

2020 HINDSIGHT: ANOTHER FIFTY YEARS OF IRRIGATION,
Committee on Interior and Insular Affairs (U.S. Subcommittee on Water and Power Resources.
For primary bibliographic entry see Field 3F.
W75-08721

ENGINEERING ECONOMICS OF RURAL SYSTEMS: A NEW U S APPROACH,
National Water Well Association, Columbus, Ohio; and Rice Univ., Houston, Tex.
M. D. Campbell, and J. H. Lehr.
Journal American Water Works Association, Vol 67, No 5, p 225-231, May 1975. 20 ref.

Descriptors: *Water supply, *Rural areas, *Engineering, *Economics, Standards, Water quality, Operation and maintenance, Costs, Water policy, Wells, Projects, Alternative planning, Design, Safety factors.
Identifiers: Safe water.

Rural areas in the United States have always had difficulty in receiving services from public or private utilities. This discusses engineering principles and problems with regard to providing adequate, safe water supply services to rural areas. The public-private approach being used by the National Demonstration Water Project (NDWP) and the Com. on Rural Water is considered; the NDWP approach is discussed in detail. Local conditions and system design are explored and defined in both quantitative and qualitative terms. Weaknesses in the U.S. National delivery system are identified. Future funding agencies need to be less restrictive about the types of water systems they will finance. According to NDWP, the centrality of a water system may lie in (1) its water source and treatment configurations, (2) its type of management, or (3) both. NDWP assesses the degree of impact of the local conditions on the ultimate design of the system and then translates the impact into the system's design. System alternative types are evaluated in terms of system costs over project life. The effects of local field parameters are translated into estimated dollars in terms of their effect on construction, operation, and maintenance costs. Considered are central well systems vs. cluster well systems. (Bell-Cornell)
W75-08723

SAMPLE UNCERTAINTY IN FLOOD LEVEE DESIGN: BAYESIAN VERSUS NON-BAYESIAN METHODS,
Arizona Univ., Tucson. Dept. of Systems and Industrial Engineering; and Arizona Univ., Tucson. Hydrology and Water Resources Interdisciplinary Program.
For primary bibliographic entry see Field 8A.
W75-08724

APPLICATION OF A HYDROLOGIC MODEL FOR LAND USE PLANNING IN FLORIDA,
Florida Univ., Gainesville. Dept. of Environmental Engineering Sciences.
P. B. Bedient, W. C. Huber, and J. P. Heaney.
Water Resources Bulletin, Vol 11, No 3, p 469-482, June 1975. 6 fig, 1 tab, 4 equ, 15 ref.

Descriptors: *River basins, *Land use, *Planning, Hydrology, *Ecology, *Simulation analysis, *Management, Mathematical models, Equations, Methodology, Reservoirs, Flood control, Environmental engineering, Vegetation, Water balance, Linear programming, Agriculture, Irrigation, Flood plains, Systems analysis, *Florida, Forecasting.
Identifiers: *Upper St. Johns River Basin(Fla).

An environmental simulation model of the Upper St. Johns River Basin in Florida has been developed in order to predict hydrologic responses under proposed management plans. Land use projections for each of 19 hydrologic planning units are provided by a linear programming analysis of agricultural activities. Inputs to the model include rainfall, runoff, evapotranspiration (ET), aquifer properties, topography, soil types, and vegetative patterns. A water balance is developed in the uplands based on infiltration, ET, surface runoff, and groundwater. Valley continuity is based on stage-volume relationship for inflows and outflows and a variable roughness coefficient dependent on vegetative patterns. Land use changes form the basis for predicting hydroperiod variation under alternative management schemes. Plans are ranked according to two criteria: deviation from a natural hydroperiod, and flood or drought control provided. Results indicate that (1) a single reservoir without irrigation and (2) floodplain preservation plans are superior to (3) multiple reservoir with irrigation and (4) uncontrolled floodplain plans with regard to both criteria. The next generation of simulation models in water resources planning should unite concepts from systems hydrology, systems ecology, and land use planning in order to achieve a more balanced view of the interacting dynamic processes. (Bell-Cornell)

W75-08727

OPTIMAL CAPACITIES OF WATER SUPPLY RESERVOIRS IN SERIES AND PARALLEL,
Wharton School of Finance and Commerce, Philadelphia, Pa. Dept. of Regional Science.
M. Wathne, C. S. ReVelle, and J. C. Liebman.
Water Resources Bulletin, Vol 11, No 3, p 536-545, June 1975. 1 fig, 9 equ, 7 ref.

Descriptors: *Water supply, *Reservoirs, *Dynamic programming, Size, *River systems, *Water demand, Algorithms, Streams, Sites, Monthly, Construction costs, Alternative planning, Design, Optimization, Volume, Decision making, Inflow, Withdrawal, Hydrology, Operation research, Equations, Mathematical models.
Identifiers: *Optimal capacity, Sequent peak method, *Cost minimization.

Water supply reservoir planning has traditionally been based on the Rippl or sequent peak analysis which applies to the design of a single reservoir. This paper incorporates the sequent peak method as the central feature is establishing a procedure for determining the sizes of several potential reservoirs located in a system of one or more rivers. Separate algorithms are developed for sites on parallel streams and for sites on the same stream. In both cases, the approach is to find the combination of reservoirs which can satisfy a given constant monthly demand at a minimum total construction cost. It is shown that both problems can be solved as a dynamic programming problem. A more complex system, then is a combination of reservoirs in parallel and in series. An extension is given if the monthly demand is not constant but each reservoir satisfies a constant fraction of the monthly demand. (Bell-Cornell)
W75-08728

THE CIVIL ENGINEER AND FIELD DRAINAGE,
Ministry of Agriculture, Fisheries and Food. Lincoln (England).
R. H. Miers.
Journal of the Institution of Water Engineers, Vol 28, No 4, p 211-223, June 1974. 9 fig, 11 tab, 3 ref.

Descriptors: *Drainage systems, *Flooding, *Design, *Optimum development plans, *Civil engineering, *Standards, Agriculture, Water levels, Depth, Soils, Pumping, Fen, Marshes, Ditches, Natural streams, Runoff, Mole drainage, Rivers, Flow, Flood plains, Design criteria, Design flood, Flood frequency, Crop production, Topography, Outlets.
Identifiers: *Arterial drainage, *Field drainage, Underdrainage, Upland, Water gradients, Land level, Flood valleys.

Considered are the standards which the civil engineer should aim for in his design of arterial drainage so as to provide optimum conditions in different types of topography: fens and marshes, upland valleys, and flood valleys. The need to design for normal conditions as well as for peak flows is emphasized. The author remarks that arterial drainage in agricultural areas has hitherto been based on an arbitrary flood flow and a freeboard, for which design values have no basis. Needed for any satisfactory drainage project is provision for underdrainage. Underdrainage is successful in most soils only if there are sufficient cracks through which the water can flow. Particularly under arable farming, these cracks often must be made artificially under appropriate soil moisture conditions. Even in flood times, the cracks must not become waterlogged. With the aid of a block-up underdrainage outfall taken from the side of a ditch in which there had been regular fluctuations in water level, the need to keep the normal water level below the underdrainage is emphasized. Two examples of how to grade and site field drains are considered. This paper is intended to enable civil engineers to design arterial drainage schemes giving optimum conditions for field drainage without acquiring a comprehensive knowledge of that subject. (Bell-Cornell)
W75-08731

A 'RATIONAL' POLICY FOR THE ENERGY AND ENVIRONMENTAL CRISES,
Calgary Univ. (Alberta). Dept. of Civil Engineering.
For primary bibliographic entry see Field 6D.
W75-08732

APPARATUS FOR SUBSOIL IRRIGATION,
For primary bibliographic entry see Field 3F.
W75-08748

CONTROL APPARATUS FOR A WATER SUPPLY SYSTEM,
Weil-McLain Co., Inc., Dallas, Tex. (assignee)
For primary bibliographic entry see Field 8C.
W75-08749

MECHANICAL ELIMINATION OF AQUATIC GROWTHS,
For primary bibliographic entry see Field 5G.
W75-08761

COMPUTER USE FOR RIVER REGULATION,
Corps of Engineers, Portland, Oreg. Reservoir Control Center.
C. E. Abraham.
Journal of the Hydraulics Division, Proceedings of the American Society of Civil Engineers, Vol 101, No HY2, p 291-297, 1974. 3 fig, 6 ref.

Descriptors: *Reservoir releases, *Regulated flow, *Reservoir operation, *Computer programs, *Automation, Hydrologic systems, Streamflow forecasting, Routing, Reservoir storage, Simulation analysis, Data processing, *Columbia River, *River regulation.
Identifiers: SSARR computer program, HYSYS computer program, SYSREG computer program, Target elevation technique.

Computer programs, primarily mathematical models that represent the physical conditions of hydrologic, reservoir, and river systems, developed for the Columbia River area, have greatly advanced the ability to analyze hydrologic and reservoir systems. As opposed to planning study applications, real-time reservoir regulation and streamflow forecasting require answers to day-to-day operating problems. Some of the most important criteria for real-time scheduling programs are: (1) automation and flexibility with input and output functions, (2) ability to adjust the model within a simulation or from day-to-day, (3) generalized watershed, river and reservoir model including streamflow routing, and (4) convenience in application. A family of computer programs--the Streamflow Synthesis and Reservoir Regulation (SSARR) package--that meets these criteria is described. This package includes the SSARR program, and the Hydro-Power System Regulation Analysis (HYSYS) and System Reservoir Regulation (SYSREG) programs. The various hydrometeorological functions necessary in the package are computed by the storage routing procedure using short reaches or subreaches. Reservoir regulation is based on the target elevation technique, which is useful for carrying out optimum multi-purpose operations policies given actual constraints. It is impractical to provide logic that considers all operating contingencies, such as construction work, fish requirements, navigation accidents, etc. (Becker-Wisconsin)
W75-08776

STREAM CHANNELIZATION: THE ECONOMICS OF THE CONTROVERSY,
Cornell Univ., Ithaca, N.Y. Dept. of Economics.
For primary bibliographic entry see Field 6C.

of Civil Engineers, New York, p 249-258, 1973. 3 fig, 2 tab.

Descriptors: *Reservoirs, *Reservoir operation, *Snowmelt, *Regulated flow, Multiple-purpose reservoirs, Reservoir storage, Management, Hydraulics, Inflow, Reservoir releases, Floods, Snow surveys, Forecasting, Snowpacks, Runoff, Melt water, Precipitation(Atmospheric), *Montana.
Identifiers: Hebgen Lake(Mont).

Measurements of the snowpack stored on the mountainous watersheds of the West are used to forecast the amount of streamflow expected from snowmelt. Forecasts can be improved by including the ammount of moisture stored in the soil beneath the snowpack and an estimate of subsequent precipitation. A combination of the three variables–snow water equivalent, soil moisture, and spring precipitation–in their proper weight provides a method for making an accurate prediction of runoff 3 to 6 months in advance. The forecasts are used by irrigators, reservoir operators, municipalities, industry, and many others to evaluate the potential water supply. The use of these procedures was illustrated by a discussion of the operation of the Hebgen Lake on the Madison River in southwestern Montana. Flows during the 1972 runoff were kept within desirable limits below the dam. Without the benefit of a reservoir management plan, flood damages could have been excessive and one of the largest experienced on the Madison River. (See also W75-08786) (Sims-ISWS)
W75-08809

PHYSICAL AND BIOLOGICAL REHABILITATION OF A STREAM,
Montana State Univ., Bozeman. Dept. of Fisheries.
R. J. Luedtke, F. J. Watts, M. A. Brusven, and T. E. Roberts.
In: Hydraulic Engineering and the Environment; Proceedings of the 21st Annual Hydraulic Division Specialty Conference, Montana State University, Bozeman, August 15-17, 1973. American Society of Civil Engineers, New York, p 259-267, 1973. 9 ref.

Descriptors: *Streams, *Sediment transport, *Benthic fauna, *Gabions, Insects, Gravels, Sands, Silts, Streamflow, Stream improvement, Rehabilitation, Structures, Hydraulic structures, Scour, Sediments, On-site investigations, *Idaho.
Identifiers: Log jams, Log drops, Riffles, *Emerald Creek(Ida).

This study was conducted on the East Fork and main stem of Emerald Creek, a tributary of the St. Maries River in northern Idaho. The lower reach of Emerald Creek is rather heavily polluted with sand and silt as a result of private and commercial mining of garnets and garnet sand. Gabions were constructed in the lower reaches of the main stem of Emerald Creek. Both test sites were located in heavily silted runs extending over 300 feet in length. The structures were built to contrict channel width, thereby increasing current velocity, riffle length, sediment transport, and insect drift. In general, the net effect of the gabion constrictors was positive. Riffle conditions were extended for about 75 feet. Species and diversities were effective indicators of physical changes in the bed. There was a rapid and pronounced faunal shift from slow water forms of insects to riffle species in the high velocity zone created by the gabions. Trout were observed to move into the scoured areas. Fluorescent tagging techniques were used to determine sediment transport during the winter-spring high flow regime in Emerald Creek. Transport of sand and fine gravel, pebble and cobble was studied at four sites. Results of tagged sediment studies indicate that Emerald Creek has the capability of transporting large quantities of sediments, and would readily return to premining conditions if the sources of excess sediment were eliminated. (See also W75-08786) (Sims-ISWS)
W75-08810

SEDIMENT TRANSPORT SYSTEM IN A GRAVEL-BOTTOMED STREAM,
Washington State Dept. of Ecology, Olympia.
For primary bibliographic entry see Field 2J.
W75-08812

PREDICTING LOW FLOWS AND FLOODS FROM UNGAGED DRAINAGE BASINS,
Washington State Univ., Pullman. Dept. of Civil Engineering.
J. F. Orsborn.
In: Hydraulic Engineering and the Environment; Proceedings of the 21st Annual Hydraulic Division Specialty Conference, Montana State University, Bozeman, August 15-17, 1973. American Society of Civil Engineers, New York, p 383-394, 1973. 8 fig, 1 tab, 14 ref, 1 append.

Descriptors: *Low flow, *Flood flow, *Streamflow forecasting, Regression analysis, Correlation analysis, Forecasting, Runoff forecasting, Floods, Hydrology, Streamflow, Surface waters, Flood forecasting, Design flood, Geomorphology, Methodology, Washington.

A study was conducted to develop methodology for determining the quantity (hydrologic), quality, and economic procedures for establishing minimum streamflows. The resultant hydrologic-geomorphic method of determining not only the average low flow value at a particular point, but also the natural discharge-recurrence interval graph for ungaged streams was presented. The relationships developed are valid for both small and large drainage basins. Some anomalies still exist but these can be exposed by balancing predicted flows against downstream gaged flows, by field checking and/or by miscellaneous streamflow records. The predicted values are generally very accurate compared with stream gaging records which were not used to generate the prediction graphs. A similar method of analysis was applied to flood flows from ungaged basins with equally good results. Intermediate steps for determining relationships of flood flows to geomorphic parameters are not yet as well defined as for low flows. (See also W75-08786) (Sims-ISWS)
W75-08820

ESTIMATION FLOODS SMALL DRAINAGE AREAS IN MONTANA,
Montana State Univ., Bozeman. Dept. of Civil Engineering and Engineering Mechanics.
E. R. Dodge.
In: Hydraulic Engineering and the Environment; Proceedings of the 21st Annual Hydraulic Division Specialty Conference, Montana State University, Bozeman, August 15-17, 1973. American Society of Civil Engineers, New York, p 395-407, 1973. American Society of Civil Engineers, New York, p 395-407, 1973. 5 fig, 3 tab, 11 ref, 1 append.

Descriptors: *Floods, *Flood forecasting, *Streamflow forecasting, *Estimating equations, Estimating, Regression analysis, Correlation analysis, Runoff forecasting, Hydrology, Streamflow, Flow, Design flood, Methodology, Watersheds(Basins), *Montana, Small watersheds.

The estimation of flood magnitudes for various recurrence intervals which may be expected from small ungaged rural watersheds is a rather common problem in engineering practice. A study to provide a method for predicting the magnitude and frequency of floods from small drainage areas in Montana for culvert design practice was described. The highway engineer needs a method of flood prediction which is based upon data readily available to him and which can be applied with relative ease in a routine manner. It was decided to use a combination of regional analysis to estimate flood frequency curves for flood regions of the state and a stepwide multiple regression analysis technique to relate flood peaks for a given recurrence interval to watershed parameters for each region. It appeared that this method would produce the most reliable results since it would be based on actual flood records, hopefully with their reliability optimized through regional analysis. Flood records through 1969 were available for 230 watersheds which had at least 10 years of record with upstream diversion not affecting flood peaks. The primary focus of this study was on small watersheds. The equations developed for flood prediction are as valid as 1969 data permit for drainage areas in Montana within the range of about 1 to 1000 sq mi. (See also W75-08786) (Sims-ISWS)
W75-08821

CHANNEL AGGRADATION IN WESTERN UNITED STATES AS INDICATED BY OBSERVATIONS AT VIGIL NETWORK SITES,
Geological Survey, Boise, Idaho. Water Resources Div.
For primary bibliographic entry see Field 2J.
W75-08830

INDEX TO MAPS TO FLOOD-PRONE AREAS IN INDIANA,
Geological Survey, Indianapolis, Ind.
For primary bibliographic entry see Field 7C.
W75-08834

WATER RESOURCES OF INDIAN RIVER COUNTY, FLORIDA,
Geological Survey, Tallahassee, Fla.
L. J. Crain, G. H. Hughes, and L. J. Snell.
Open-file report 75-66, 1975. 98 p, 38 fig, 5 tab, 14 ref.

Descriptors: *Water resources, *Florida, *Surface waters, *Groundwater, Aquifers, Water supply, Hydrologic data, Water yield, Streamflow.
Identifiers: *Indian River County(Fla).

The water resources of Indian River County, on the Atlantic coast in southern Florida, are described. About half the county is developed; pasture and citrus groves predominate. The population tripled during 1950-70, from 11,872 to 35,992. Water use, largely for agriculture, is about four times the average per capita use in Florida. About 135 mgd was withdrawn in 1970 from ground- and surface-water bodies in the county. Only 3 mgd was for public water supply. Rainfall at Vero Beach averages 51.3 inches, almost two-thrids of it during the summer and early autumn. Large streams do not exist. A shallow aquifer consisting of sand, shell, and some silt and clay, is present in all of the county, its base reaching depths of 150 feet. The aquifer is underlain by the Hawthorn Formation which acts as a confining bed to retard upward movement of water from the underlying Floridan aquifer. Water from the shallow aquifer is of good quality. The Floridan aquifer underlies the county at a depth of 300 to 600 feet. Throughout much of the county withdrawals of water for irrigation use appear to have caused a decline of 10 to 15 feet in the level of the potentiometric surface of the Floridan aquifer over a 20-year period. A high chloride concentration is the common objectionable characteristic of Floridan-aquifer water. In spite of its high chloride concentration, the water has proved valuable; water having chloride concentrations as high as 2,000 mg/liter has been used for irrigation. About 420 million gallons per day surface water is available for development in the county. (Knapp-USGS)
W75-08836

EVALUATION AND IMPLEMENTATION OF URBAN DRAINAGE PROJECTS,
Colorado State Univ., Fort Collins. Dept. of Civil Engineering.
N. S. Grigg.

Journal of the Urban Planning and Development Division, ASCE, Vol. 101, No. UP1, Proceedings paper No 11324, p 61-75, May 1975. 6 fig, 1 tab, 32 ref. OWRT B-086-COLO(2).

Descriptors: *Urban drainage, *Projects, *Planning, *Flood control, *Economics, *Social participation, Cost-benefit analysis, Evaluation, Optimization, Expenditures, Water quantity, Decision making, Methodology, Rainfall, Intangible costs, Intangible benefits, Systems analysis.
Identifiers: Cost minimization, Benefit maximization, Public works, Public funds, Social benefits, Implementation.

Public works problems associated with evaluation and implementation situations are described. By clarifying criteria and evaluation methodologies, a large amount of uncertainty can be eliminated and public dollars can be saved. Urban drainage and flood control (UDFC) must compete for funding from the limited public purse. Evaluation problems include: (1) determination of the merit of individual projects; (2) ranking of competing UDFC projects to determine priorities; (3) determination of optimal investment timing; and (4) determination of the incidence of costs and benefits on different population sectors so that project costs can be equitably apportioned. UDFC systems are identified as minor and major. The former provides substantial flood damage reduetion benefits, and the latter furnishes intangible benefits. Economic evaluation procedures must provide necessary information for financing and implementation. The state-of-the-art of evaluation capability is discussed and the use of minimum cost and benefit maximization criteria in the selection of UDFC projects for implementation is considered. In the case of the major flood control project, attention has been focused on the potential reduction in flood damages. All public programs, e.g., public safety, water supply library services, urban drainage and flood control, and others should be subjected to the type of analysis presented to identify precisely the benefits from expenditures of public funds and the recipients of the benefits. (Bell-Cornell)
W75-08847

4B. Groundwater Management

REGIONAL PROBLEM ANALYSIS IN THE PACIFIC NORTHWEST: PART A-INSTREAM FLOW NEEDS; PART B-BASALT AQUIFERS; PART C-WILD AND SCENIC RIVERS.
Washington State Water Research Center, Pullman.
For primary bibliographic entry see Field 6B.
W75-08356

WATER RESOURCES DEVELOPMENT IN THE MULLICA RIVER BASIN,
Rutgers - the State Univ., New Brunswick, N.J. Dept. of Zoology.
J. B. Durand, M. L. Granstrom, and N. S. Rudolph.
Water Resources Bulletin, Vol 10, No 2, p 272-282, April 1974. 4 fig, 1 tab, 4 ref. OWRR A-018-NJ(5), B-014-NJ(7), and B-018-NJ(5).

Descriptors: River basins, Estuaries, *Withdrawal, *Linear programming, *Water supply, *Conjunctive use, Environmental effects, *Salinity, Simulation analysis, Groundwater, Surface waters, Water utilization, Streamflow, Fish, Humid areas, *New Jersey, Droughts, Long-term planning, Biology, Mathematical models, Systems analysis.
Identifiers: Chance-constrained programming, *Mullica River-Great Bay Estuary(New Jersey).

The potentiality of withdrawing water from the Mullica River-Great Bay Estuary in southern New Jersey prompted a joint study of biologists and engineers to determine the maximum supply of water that could be diverted from the basin without causing harmful environmental effects. The consequence of removing water from the basin over long periods of time was simulated by review records of a severe drought. It was proposed to develop a salinity regime for the estuary such that minimal disturbance of the estuary would result. Based on the analysis of streamflows and salinities during the drought conditions, minimum mean monthly streamflows were determined corresponding to the maximum salinities tolerable by the fish and shellfish communities, important sources for revenue and recreation in the region. Engineering consideration was given only to possibilities of conjunctive use, either by direct diversions of flow from the streams, pumping from wells, or a combination of these. A physically-optimized, chance-constrained linear programming model was developed for the conjunctive use of ground and surface waters. Adjusting water withdrawal from streamflow and groundwater sources according to physical and seasonal criteria would permit maximum use of the basin's resources with no additional burden on the ccology of the estuary. While the model was applied to the Mullica River Basin, it could also be applied to other areas of humid climatology. (Bell-Cornell)
W75-08386

AN APPLICATION OF PARAMETRIC STATISTICAL TESTS TO WELL-YIELD DATA FROM CARBONATES OF CENTRAL PENNSYLVANIA,
Pennsylvania State Univ., University Park.
S. H. Siddiqui, and R. R. Parizek.
Journal of Hydrology, Vol 21, No 1, p 1-14, January 1974. 1 fig, 4 tab, 11 ref. OWRR A-005-PA(7).

Descriptors: *Water yield, *Hydrogeology, *Statistical methods, Carbonate rocks, Fractures(Geologic), Structural geology, *Pennsylvania, Aquifer characteristics.
Identifiers: Factor analysis.

Variation in productivity (yield in gallons per minute per foot of drawndown per foot of saturated thickness) of 80 water wells located in folded and faulted carbonate rocks and shales of Cambro-Ordovician age in central Pennsylvania, was studied in relation to six hydrogeologic factors. Parametric and nonparametric statistical techniques were applied. Productivity values were transformed to common logarithms, and it was assumed that a long-normal model would reasonably describe the variation in productivity, especially as the sample size was increased. The variations in number of fracture traces, rock type, dip of bedrock strata and topography were significant, and variation in depth to water table was not significant in accounting for variation in well yield. Student t-test showed that anticlinal wells were significantly different from synclinal wells. However, wells in the same rock type but different structural settings were not significantly different. This shows that variations in rock type and number of fracture traces are more important than other structural variations. Both parametric and nonparametric tests gave identidal results, which justifies the use of parametric tests which require normally distributed data. (Knapp-USGS)
W75-08388

HYDROGEOLOGY OF THE EDMONTON AREA (NORTHWEST SEGMENT), ALBERTA,
Alberta Research, Edmonton.
R. Bibby.
Report 74-10, 1974. 10 p, 1 fig, 55 ref.

Descriptors: *Hydrogeology, *Maps, *Groundwater, Areal hydrogeology, Topography, Geologic mapping, Drainage, Climates, Meteorology, Geology, Aquifers, Water chemistry, *Canada.
Identifiers: *Edmonton area(Alberta).

The topography of the Edmonton area is predominantly level to gently rolling. The area is drained by the North Saskatchewan and Sturgeon Rivers. The area has a cold, humid continental climate, receiving 17.5 inches of precipitation on average each year, 70% as rain. Most of the area is covered by glacial materials (mainly till), clay, and silt. Buried valleys are coincident with the two main rivers and contain sand and gravel deposits which are in hydraulic connection with the rivers. Yields are fairly high in the sand and gravel aquifers of the drift, particularly those in connection with the rivers. Groundwater flow systems in the upper 300 feet are largely controlled by the connection between the rivers and buried valley sand and gravel deposits, and by the incised nature of the valleys. The chemistry of the groundwaters shows a marked correlation with soil type and drift lithology. Groundwaters in areas covered by till, clay, and silt are typified by the presence of sulfate and higher total dissolved solids. The exchange of calcium for sodium as flow passes from the drift to the bedrock is pronounced and some sulfate reduction occurs in the bedrock. (Sims-ISWS)
W75-08398

HYDROGEOLOGY OF THE GLEICHEN AREA, ALBERTA,
Alberta Research, Edmonton.
G. F. Ozoray, and A. T. Lytviak.
Report 74-9, 1974. 16 p, 1 fig, 58 ref, 1 append.

Descriptors: *Hydrogeology, *Maps, *Groundwater, Areal hydrogeology, Geologic mapping, Topography, Drainage, Climates, Meteorology, Geology, Aquifers, Water chemistry, *Canada.
Identifiers: *Gleichem area(Alberta).

The hydrogeology of the uppermost 1000 feet of strata in the Gleichem area was described. Maps and profiles were constructed from existing data and from data collected by a field survey and drilling and testing operations. The 20-year safe yields range from 1 igpm (about 5 1/min) to more than 100 igpm (about 450 1/min). The best aquifers are Quaternary sands and gravels and Upper Cretaceous Belly River sandstones. Water quality varies: total dissolved solids range from less than 1000 to more than 5000 ppm, and the general chemical character of the water varies from Ca/HCO3 type to Na/SO4 type. In the deep Milk River sandstones in the southeast corner of the map area, Na/C1 type waters are present. (Sims-ISWS)
W75-08399

ANALYSIS OF PUMPING TEST DATA FROM ANISOTROPIC UNCONFINED AQUIFERS CONSIDERING DELAYED GRAVITY RESPONSE,
Agricultural Research Organization, Bet Dagan (Israel). Inst. of Soils and Water.
For primary bibliographic entry see Field 2F.
W75-08434

INVESTIGATION OF VERTICAL GROUNDWATER FLOW IN BOREHOLES,
International Hydrological Decade, New Delhi (India). Indian National Committee.
For primary bibliographic entry see Field 2F.
W75-08450

DISTRIBUTION, CULTIVATION AND CHEMICAL DESTRUCTION OF GALLIONELLA FROM ALABAMA GROUND WATER,
Alabama Univ., University. Dept. of Microbiology.
For primary bibliographic entry see Field 5B.
W75-08479

GROUND-WATER FAVORABILITY AND SURFICIAL GEOLOGY OF THE CHERRYFIELD-JONESBORO AREA, MAINE,
Geological Survey, Reston, Va.
For primary bibliographic entry see Field 7C.
W75-08510

WATER RESOURCES OF THE CROW RIVER WATERSHED, SOUTH-CENTRAL MINNESOTA,
Geological Survey, Reston, Va.
For primary bibliographic entry see Field 7C.
W75-08511

WATER RESOURCES OF THE BLUE EARTH RIVER WATERSHED, SOUTH-CENTRAL MINNESOTA,
Geological Survey, Reston, Va.
For primary bibliographic entry see Field 7C.
W75-08513

WATER RESOURCES OF THE CLINTON RIVER BASIN, SOUTHEASTERN MICHIGAN,
Geological Survey, Reston, Va.
For primary bibliographic entry see Field 7C.
W75-08514

CHEMICAL QUALITY OF GROUND WATER IN THE WESTERN OSWEGO RIVER BASIN, NEW YORK,
Geological Survey, Albany, N.Y.
For primary bibliographic entry see Field 5B.
W75-08515

SALINE GROUND-WATER RESOURCES OF LEE COUNTY, FLORIDA,
Geological Survey, Tallahassee, Fla.
For primary bibliographic entry see Field 2F.
W75-08517

GEOELECTRICAL POSSIBILITIES OF DETECTING STREAM CHANNELS IN CARBONATE ROCKS,
Missouri Univ., Rolla.
For primary bibliographic entry see Field 2F.
W75-08603

GEOTHERMAL EXPLORATION,
Atlantic Richfield Co., New York. (assignee)
J. E. Hardison.
US Patent No 3,874,232, 4 p, 5 fig, 3 ref; Official Gazette of the United States Patent Office, Vol 933, No 1, p 81, April 1, 1975.

Descriptors: *Patents, *Geothermal studies, *Thermal studies, *Temperature, Geology, Borehole geophysics, Exploration, Subsurface investigations, Thermal conductivity.
Identifiers: *Probes, Thermisters.

A uranium prospecting system is based on the determination of temperature anomalies in the earth's crust. The earth heat flux is measured at preselected points in shallow boreholes in order to detect heat given off as a result of radioactive decay. Localized anomalies are indicative of concentrations of radioactive materials. The temperature measuring apparatus is comprised of a tubular probe having temperature sensors at vertically spaced positions. The temperature sensors are thermistors contained in discs that extend laterally about the probe. Decentralizer means are attached to the probe and are designed to be remotely actuated from the surface. When the decentralizer is actuated, the sensors are forced into contact with the walls of the borehole at preselected sample points. The probe is left in position until thermal equilibrium is established with the sensors and then the desired temperature readings are taken. The temperature measuring apparatus can also be used to make conductivity measurements. (Sinha-OEIS)
W75-08616

GEOTHERMAL HEAT EXHANGE METHOD AND APPARATUS,
C. K. Greene.
US Patent No 3,874,174, 4 p, 2 fig, 3 ref; Official Gazette of the United States Patent Office, Vol 933, No 1, p 62, April 1, 1975.

Descriptors: *Patents, *Geothermal studies, *Brines, *Heat exhangers, Powerplants, Electric powerplants.
Identifiers: Sonic energy.

A method of generating power includes establishing two deep wells adjacent each other into a pool of hot brine beneath the earth's surface. Heat exchange apparatus is enclosed within each of the wells. Hot brine is circulated upward in one of the wells and thence downward in the other well. Vapor is created within each of the heat exchange units from the hot brine and is utilized to produce power by appropriate power generating equipment. The vapor is condensed during and after the power generation and returned to the heat exchange unit. Sonic energy is directed into each of the wells so as to constantly agitate the interior so as to dispel any scale which may bend to form on either the interior of the well casing or on the heat exchange apparatus. (Sinha-OEIS)
W75-08618

GEOLOGY OF GEOTHERMAL TEST HOLE GT-2, FENTON HILL SITE, JULY 1974,
Los Alamos Scientific Lab., N. Mex.
For primary bibliographic entry see Field 5A.
W75-08649

DEEP ROCK NUCLEAR WASTE DISPOSAL TEST: DESIGN AND OPERATION,
Sandia Labs., Albuquerque, N. Mex.
For primary bibliographic entry see Field 5E.
W75-08656

ON THE SELECTION OF A GROUND DISPOSAL SITE FOR RADIOACTIVE WASTES BY MEANS OF A COMPUTER,
Kyoto Univ. (Japan). Dept. of Sanitary Engineering.
For primary bibliographic entry see Field 5G.
W75-08665

ASPECTS OF HYDROLOGICAL EFFECTS OF URBANIZATION.
American Society of Civil Engineers, New York. Task Committee on the Effects of Urbanization on Low Flow, Total Runoff, Infiltration, and Ground-Water Recharge.
For primary bibliographic entry see Field 4C.
W75-08697

CARBON 14 DATING OF GROUNDWATER FROM CLOSED AND OPEN SYSTEMS,
Waterloo Univ. (Ontario). Dept. of Mechanical Engineering.
For primary bibliographic entry see Field 2F.
W75-08707

AN APPROXIMATE INFINITE CONDUCTIVITY SOLUTION FOR A PARTIALLY PENETRATING LINE-SOURCE WELL,
Bureau de Recherches Geologiques et Minieres, Orleans (France).
A. C. Gringarten, and H. J. Ramey, Jr.
Society of Petroleum Engineers Journal, Vol 15, No 2, p 140-148, April 1975. 4 fig, 4 tab, 35 ref, 2 append.

Descriptors: *Wells, *Pressure head, *Unsteady flow, *Mathematical studies, Equations, Subsurface investigations, Artesian wells, Hydraulics,

Groundwater potential, Flow, Pumping, Analytical techniques, Steady flow, Laminar flow, Boundaries(Surfaces).
Identifiers: Partial penetrating wells, Line-source well, Restricted entry wells, Wellbore.

A review of previous studies of transient flow to partially penetrating wells was made. All analytical studies involved the assumption of a constant flux along the open interval. This analytical study was a new solution that closely approximates an infinite-conductivity line source (constant pressure along the producing interval). (Prickett-ISWS)
W75-08715

ENVIRONMENTAL GEOLOGY--AN AID TO GROWTH AND DEVELOPMENT IN LAUDERDALE, COLBERT AND FRANKLIN COUNTIES, ALABAMA,
Geological Survey of Alabama, University. Environmental Div.
For primary bibliographic entry see Field 7C.
W75-08718

ENGINEERING ECONOMICS OF RURAL SYSTEMS: A NEW U S APPROACH,
National Water Well Association, Columbus, Ohio; and Rice Univ., Houston, Tex.
For primary bibliographic entry see Field 4A.
W75-08723

METHOD OF RECOVERING GEOTHERMAL ENERGY,
Mobil Oil Corp., New York. (assignee)
J. L. Fitch.
U.S. Patent No. 3,863,709, 5 p, 4 fig, 8 ref; Official Gazette of the United States Patent Office, Vol 931, No 1, p 159, February 4, 1975.

Descriptors: *Patents, *Groundwater, *Geothermal studies, Energy, Wells, Heated water, Thermal water, Heat flow.

A method and system is disclosed for recovering geothermal energy from a subterranean geothermal formation having a preferred vertical fracture orientation. At least two deviated wells are provided which extend into the geothermal formation in a direction transversely of the preferred vertical fracture orientation and a plurality of vertical fractures are hydraulically formed to intersect the deviated wells. A fluid is injected via one well into the fractures to absorb heat from the geothermal formation and the heated fluid is recovered from the formation via another well. (Sinha-OEIS)
W75-08736

PITLESS WATER SYSTEM,
For primary bibliographic entry see Field 8B.
W75-08750

ARTIFICIAL RECHARGE IN THE URBAN ENVIRONMENT--SOME QUESTIONS AND ANSWERS,
California Univ., Davis. Dept. of Water Science and Engineering.
V. H. Scott, W. E. Johnston, and J. C. Scalmanini.
In: Hydraulic Engineering and the Environment; Proceedings of the 21st Annual Hydraulic Division Specialty Conference, Montana State University, Bozeman, August 15-17, 1973. American Society of Civil Engineers, New York, p 409-415, 1973.

Descriptors: *Artificial recharge, *Multiple-purpose projects, *Recreation facilities, *Recharge ponds, Recharge, Induced infiltration, Water management(Applied), Multiple-purpose reservoirs, Groundwater recharge, Cities, Groundwater, Surface waters, Infiltration rates, Aquifers, Ponds, Recreation, Management, Maintenance, California.
Identifiers: *Recharge ponds maintenance.

In many areas, comprehensive management of urban water supplies requires that surface and groundwater supplies be integrated. An essential component of management programs can be artificial recharge for aquifer replenishment while minimizing land subsidence and preventing impairment of water quality. All the design variables which affect a potential multipurpose facility must be considered. Artificial recharge pond design can accommodate both good infiltration and other purposes. If alternate sources of water with various solids content are available for recharge, use of the water with the lowest solids content will give the best infiltration and longest cycles between pond maintenance. The attitudes of water districts, managers, and homeowners sampled tend to favor multiple-use facilities, especially in urban areas; and a good, positive attitude can be maintained if designs are both aesthetic and functional. Effective management of water resources as it relates to artificial recharge, especially in urban areas, requires a mutual understanding of objectives by both water agencies and other interests. Funds may be available from state and federal agencies to assist or support the multipurpose aspects of an artificial recharge facility, and aid of this type should both promote consideration and increase the attractivness of potential multipurpose projects. (See also W75-08786) (Sims-ISWS)
W75-08822

RESEARCH AND ADVANCES IN GROUNDWATER RESOURCES STUDIES, 1964-1974,
Florida Water Management District, Brooksville.
For primary bibliographic entry see Field 2F.
W75-08825

ONE-DIMENSIONAL SIMULATION OF AQUIFER SYSTEM COMPACTION NEAR PIXLEY, CALIFORNIA: 1. CONSTANT PARAMETERS,
Geological Survey, Sacramento, Calif.
For primary bibliographic entry see Field 2F.
W75-08826

WASTEWATER RECLAMATION AND RECHARGE, BAY PARK, N.Y.,
Geological Survey, Mineola, N.Y.
For primary bibliographic entry see Field 5D.
W75-08827

BOUGUER GRAVITY ANOMALY MAP OF THE TEMECULA AREA, RIVERSIDE COUNTY, CALIFORNIA,
Geological Survey, Garden Grove, Calif.
For primary bibliographic entry see Field 7C.
W75-08831

WATER RESOURCES OF INDIAN RIVER COUNTY, FLORIDA,
Geological Survey, Tallahassee, Fla.
For primary bibliographic entry see Field 4A.
W75-08836

4C. Effects On Water Of Man's Non-Water Activities

EFFECTS OF URBANIZATION ON WATER QUALITY,
Water Resources Engineers, Inc., Springfield, Va. and DeKalb County Planning Dept., Decatur, Ga.
For primary bibliographic entry see Field 5B.
W75-08351

REGIONAL WATER EXCHANGE FOR DROUGHT ALLEVIATION,
Colorado State Univ., Fort Collins. Dept. of Civil Engineering.
For primary bibliographic entry see Field 4A.
W75-08403

IMPACTS OF FOREST MANAGEMENT PRACTICES ON THE AQUATIC ENVIRONMENT-PHASE II,
Washington Cooperative Fishery Unit, Seattle.
For primary bibliographic entry see Field 5B.
W75-08468

POTENTIAL FLOOD HAZARD--NORTH AVENUE AREA, DENVER FEDERAL CENTER, LAKEWOOD, COLORADO,
Geological Survey, Denver, Colo.
For primary bibliographic entry see Field 4A.
W75-08496

DETERMINATION OF URBAN WATERSHED RESPONSE TIME,
Colorado State Univ., Fort Collins. Dept. of Civil Engineering.
E. F. Schulz, and O. G. Lopez.
Hydrology Papers, No 71, December 1974. 41 p, 6 fig, 11 tab, 74 ref, 2 append. Contract DACWO 5-73-C-0029.

Descriptors: *Unit hydrographs, *Urbanization, *Statistical methods, *Watersheds(Basins), Time lag, Time of concentration, Parametric hydrology, Small watersheds, Regression analysis, *Colorado, Hydrualics, Hydrology, Rainfall, Floods, Runoff, Channels, Peak discharge, Drainage systems, Data processing, Discharge(Water), Hydrologic aspects.
Identifiers: *Response time, *Denver(Colo), Hydraulic capacity, *Urban watersheds.

A brief review of previous work was presented. Different methods for quantifying urbanization were discussed. A stepwise multiple regression technique was used to select the best parameter of urbanization. The rainfall and flood events from nine urban watersheds in the Denver Metropolitan region were analyzed. Unit hydrographs were derived from the measured floods on these watersheds. The unit hydrograph parameters were correlated with storm and physical watershed parameters. It was found that the changes in the unit hydrograph in the urban region were related to the decrease in the watershed response time. The best way of defining the response time was the lag time. The lag time was found to be sensitive to the increase in the hydraulic capacity to the decrease in the ratio of pervious watershed and the shape of the watershed. (Dawes-ISWS)
W75-08685

ASPECTS OF HYDROLOGICAL EFFECTS OF URBANIZATION,
American Society of Civil Engineers, New York. Task Committee on the Effects of Urbanization on Low Flow, Total Runoff, Infiltration, and Ground-Water Recharge.
Journal of the Hydraulics Division, American Society of Civil Engineers, Vol 101, No HY5, Proceedings Paper 11301, p 449-468, May 1975. 2 fig, 89 ref, append.

Descriptors: *Urban hydrology, *Hydrologic cycle, *Urban runoff, *Infiltration, *Groundwater recharge, *Urbanization, Water resources development, Low flow, Runoff, Infiltration rates, Saline water intrusion, Hydrologic aspects, Social aspects, Water supply, Land use.

Urbanization both alters and complicates the natural hydrologic cycle. However, the effects are often not consistent, but depend on the nature and magnitude of the urban influence. The effects of urbanization on four aspects of the hydrologic cycle were examined: (1) low flow, (2) total runoff, (3) infiltration, and (4) groundwater recharge. Both supporting data and a selected bibliography were provided. Inherent in the alteration of the hydrologic cycle by urbanization is the contamina-

tion by urban wastes, and the consequent pollution of the water resource. (Prickett-ISWS)
W75-08697

REHABILITATION OF A CHANNELIZED RIVER IN UTAH,
Brigham Young Univ., Provo, Utah. Dept. of Civil Engineering.
For primary bibliographic entry see Field 8A.
W75-08787

4D. Watershed Protection

WATERSHED ORGANIZATIONS - IMPACT ON WATER QUALITY MANAGEMENT, AN ANALYSIS OF SELECTED MICHIGAN WATERSHED COUNCILS,
Michigan State Univ., East Lansing. Dept. of Resources Development.
For primary bibliographic entry see Field 5G.
W75-08354

EROSION MODELING ON A WATERSHED,
Agricultural Research Service, Morris, Minn. North Central Soil Conservation Research Center.
For primary bibliographic entry see Field 2J.
W75-08459

RESERVOIR OPERATION USING SNOW SURVEY DATA,
Soil Conservation Service, Bozeman, Mont.
For primary bibliographic entry see Field 4A.
W75-08809

WINTER STORM AND FLOOD ANALYSES, NORTHWEST INTERIOR,
Agricultural Research Service, Boise, Idaho. Northwest Watershed Research Center.
For primary bibliographic entry see Field 2E.
W75-08818

CALIBRATION OF WATERSHED WETNESS AND PREDICTION OF FLOOD VOLUME FROM SMALL WATERSHEDS IN HUMID REGION,
Pennsylvania Dept. of Environmental Resources, Harrisburg.
For primary bibliographic entry see Field 2A.
W75-08819

ESTIMATION FLOODS SMALL DRAINAGE AREAS IN MONTANA,
Montana State Univ., Bozeman. Dept. of Civil Engineering and Engineering Mechanics.
For primary bibliographic entry see Field 4A.
W75-08821

5. WATER QUALITY MANAGEMENT AND PROTECTION

5A. Identification Of Pollutants

PROBIT TRANSFORMATION: IMPROVED METHOD FOR DEFINING SYNCHRONY OF CELL CULTURES,
Carnegie Institution of Washington, Stanford, Calif. Dept. of Plant Biology.
W. G. Hagar, and T. R. Punnett.
Science, Vol 182, No 4116, p 1028-1030, December 7, 1973. 1 fig, 1 tab, 15 ref.

Descriptors: *Cultures, *Cytological studies, *Statistical methods, Computer programs, Data processing, Equations.
Identifiers: *Synchrony, *Chlorella pyrenoidosa, Data interpretation, *Probit transformation.

Cell numbers can be converted to probits that are used to compare the degree and timing of synchronized cell cultures. The solution follows from the fact that the change in the rate of cell division follows a normal distribution function, with the maximum rate of cell divison at the midpoint of the curve. The time curve for the total cell number is the integral of the cell division rates up to that time and, therefore, has the same shape as the integral of a normal probability curve. For this reason, the sigmoidal growth curves from various experiments can be easily compared by converting the cell numbers to probits. In the case of cell division, and plot of probit against time produces a straight line having a midpoint corresponding to the peak of the cell division rate with reciprocal of the slope equaling the standard deviation of the cell release rate. These two parameters are all that are needed to define degree of synchrony. Data from synchronous cultures of Chlorella pyrenoidosa have been analyzed by this method by means of a readily available computer program. The method can be used with any biological system that generates normal sigmoidal data. (Little-Battelle)
W75-08378

REDESCRIPTION OF GAETANUS INTERMEDIUS CAMPBELL (CALANOIDA: COPEPODA) FROM THE TYPE LOCALITY,
Washington Univ., Friday Harbor. Friday Harbor Lab.
For primary bibliographic entry see Field 2L.
W75-08380

TEMPERATURES SELECTED SEASONALLY BY FOUR FISHES FROM WESTERN LAKE ERIE,
Ohio State Cooperative Fishery Unit, Columbus.
For primary bibliographic entry see Field 5C.
W75-08381

A HIGHLY SENSITIVE AUTOMATED TECHNIQUE FOR THE DETERMINATION OF AMMONIUM NITROGEN,
Ruakura Soil Research Station, Hamilton (New Zealand).
M. W. Brown.
Journal of the Science of Food and Agriculture, Vol 24, No 9, p 1119-1123, September 1973. 1 fig, 2 tab, 6 ref.

Descriptors: *Ammonium compounds, *Soils, *Automation, *Chemical analysis, Fertilizers, Water analysis, Soil analysis.
Identifiers: *Ammonium nitrogen, Phenol hypochlorite reaction, Autoanalyzer, Catalytic methods, Reproducibility, Sample preparation, Method validation.

The catalytic action of nitroprusside on the phenol hypochlorite reaction has been utilized to design a more sensitive automated technique for determining ammonium nitrogen in soil extracts. The method gives reproducible results in close agreement with manual methods. Sensitivity is such that as little as 0.1 ppm of N in solution can be determined without the use of recorder range expansion. Using this procedure, 10 g of air-dried soil were shaken for one hour with 100 ml 2 M-potassium chloride. The supernatant extract was fed into the analyzer without prior filtration, along with standard solutions. Where the anticapated level of nitrogen was greater than 4 ppm, the soil extract was first suitably diluted with 2 M-potassium chloride. Agreement between the two sets of results is very good. Statistical tests, Student's t, show there is no significant difference between the two sets of results even at the 20 percent probability level. Experience with the basic phenol hypochlorite method strongly suggests that the method would also be suitable for the analysis of fertilizers and natural waters. (Mortland-Battelle)
W75-08382

STEREO-SCANNING ELECTRON MICROSCOPY OF DESMIDS,
Colorado Univ., Boulder. Dept. of Molecular, Cellular and Developmental Biology.
J. D. Pickett-Heaps.
Journal of Microscopy, Vol 99, No 1, p 109-116, September 1973. 8 fig, 12 ref.

Descriptors: *Systematics, *Chlorophyta, Electron microscopy, Speciation.
Identifiers: *Scanning electron microscopy, *Sample preparation, Staurastrum manfeldtii, Staurastrum gracile, Staurastrum pingue, Cosmarium botrytis, Micrasterias thomasiana, Micrasterias sol, Fixation, Sample preservation, *Desmids.

Stereo-pairs of scanning electron micrographs are presented of two species of Staurastrum, one species of Cosmarium and two species of Micasterias, including the triradiate, diploid variant of M. thomasiana. Some specimens were treated with a relatively broad range polysaccharidase preparation called 'Glusulase', washed, and allowed to stand at room temperature for 1-1/2 h in culture medium before fixation. Cells were normally fixed in 1 percent glutaraldehyde made up in culture medium, for about 1 h at room temperature; after washing, they were post-fixed for up to 1 h in 1 percent osmium tetroxide, also made up in the culture medium. After post-fixation, the cells were suspended in water and collected on a small 'Millipore' filter. A suitable choice is the 'Solvinert' series of filter pads with pore sizes around 1.5 micrometers. The filter pad served as a mount for the cells. The material and mount were slowly dehydrated in acetone and then passed through the critical point drying (CPD) procedure. The dried specimens were mounted on specimen stubs using transfer or double-sided sticky tape. Thy were then coated quite heavily and omnidirectionally with 5.0 nm carbon and then 15.0 nm gold. Specimens were examined at 20 kV. For taking stereo-pairs, a difference in tilt of 12 degrees between successive micrographs was found empirically to give good results. Some typical morphological variations encountered in cultures are illustrated; the methods are reasonably quick and reliable and may prove useful in taxonomic studies of desmids. (Little-Battelle)
W75-08383

RELATIONSHIP OF VARIOUS INDICES OF WATER QUALITY TO DENITRIFICATION IN SURFACE WATERS,
Purdue Univ., Lafayette, Ind. Dept. of Agronomy.
L. B. Owens, and D. W. Nelson.
Proceedings of the Indiana Academy of Science, Vol 82, p 404-413, 1972 (published 1973). 8 fig, 17 ref. OWRR A-019-IND(2).

Descriptors: *Surface waters, *Water chemistry, Rivers, Ponds, *Indiana, *Denitrification, *Nitrates, *Water quality, Waste water(Pollution), Dissolved oxygen, Bacteria, Phosphorus, Temperature, Hydrogen ion concentration, Nitrogen, Effluents, Water pollution sources, Waste assimilative capacity, Self-purification, Kinetics, Carbon, Municipal wastes, Industrial wastes.
Identifiers: *Wabash River(Indiana).

Water samples were collected monthly from 3 farm ponds and from 3 locations on the Wabash River near Lafayette, Indiana, to determine the actual and potential rates of denitrification in such water systems. Denitrification may serve as an important mechanism for nitrate removal from surface waters. Water parameters which may affect denitrification were estimated at the time of sampling and then related to the observed denitrification rates. Actual and potential denitrification rates were normally small unless an energy source was added, indicating that the low amount of dissolved carbon plus a high dissolved oxygen content may be the factors limiting denitrification in surface waters. Water temperature, pH, nitrate concentration, and number of denitrifying bacteria

appeared suitable for denitrification during most of the year. Higher levels of bacteria, nitrate, and phosphorus existed in the river than in the ponds, but the ponds contained slightly more dissolved carbon. The nitrate-N levels did not exceed the 10 ppm standard of the U.S. Public Health Service, and the river and pond surface waters remained aerobic throughout the year. Contaminant levels were little affected by the municipal and industrial effluents discharged between the river locations sampled. (Brown-IPC)
W75-08384

BIOLOGICAL METHODS FOR THE ASSESSMENT OF WATER QUALITY.
ASTM Special Technical Publication No. 528, 1973. 256 p, Illus, Maps.

Descriptors: *Bioassay, *Monitoring, Pollutant identification, Water quality, Biology.

This book contains the contributed papers presented at the symposium covering a variety of aspects involving biological methods for the assessment of water quality. One paper discusses the interaction of engineers and biologists in water quality management. Others discuss: pollutant bioassay using fish and mixing zone concepts; biological monitoring of the aquatic environment, bacteria and the assessment of water quality and the use of algae, especially diatoms, in the assessment of water quality; the use of aquatic invertebrates in the assessment of water quality; continuous-flow bioassays with aquatic organisms. A tentative proposal for a rapid in-plant biological monitoring system, rapid biological monitoring systems for determining aquatic community structure in receiving systems and use of toxicity tests with fish in water pollution control are studied. Several papers cover the following topics: assessment of fish flesh tainting substances; use of histologic and histochemical assessments in the prognosis of the effects of aquatic pollutants; stabilization oxygen demand; and microbiological inhibition testing procedure. The use of artificial substrate samplers to assess water pollution and mobile bioassay laboratories is discussed. Numerous illustrations are included throughout, and each contribution ends with a list of references.--Copyright 1974, Biological Abstracts, Inc.
W75-08392

INDUSTRIAL WATER RESOURCES OF CANADA, THE HUDSON BAY, LABRADOR AND ARCTIC DRAINAGE BASINS, 1959-65,
Department of the Environment, Ottawa (Ontario). Water Quality Branch.
J. F. J. Thomas, and R. M. Gale.
Water Survey Report No. 15, 1973. 147 p, 3 fig, 6 tab, 7 ref, 3 append.

Descriptors: *Water quality, *Chemical anallysis, *Canada, Surveys, Sampling, Water chemistry, Surface waters, Groundwater, Municipal water, Chemical properties, Hardness(Water), Basins, Arctic, Pollutant identification, Industrial wastes.
Identifiers: *Hudson Bay(Labrador).

This, the final part of the series of Water Survey Reports of the industrial water resources of Canada, dealt with the Hudson's Bay, Labrador, and Arctic drainage basins. Chemical analyses of waters from 216 stations were recorded, with descriptions of 49 municipal and 17 other water supplies. Records between 1947 and 1961 were included. The geology of the drainage basins, the procedures used, and the analytical techniques employed were summarized briefly. Two maps of the areas dealt with were supplied. The waters vary widely in hardness; mineral content is mainly alkaline earth bicarbonates; alkalies, sulphates and chlorides are for the most part low. (Sims-ISWS)
W75-08395

POLYNUCLEAR AROMATIC HYDROCARBONS IN RAW, POTABLE AND WASTE WATER,
Imperial Coll. of Science and Technology, London (England). Dept. of Public Health Engineering.
R. M. Harrison, R. Perry, and R. A. Wellings.
Water Research, Vol 9, No 4, p 331-346, April 1975. 2 fig, 20 tab, 147 ref.

Descriptors: *Pollutant identification, *Aromatic compounds, *Organic compounds, Water quality control, *Organic matter, *Water analysis, Analytical techniques, Organic wastes, Waste treatment, Water quality, Analysis, Chemistry, Evaluation, Monitoring, Sewage treatment, *Potable water, Public health, Reclaimed water, Water utilization, Aquatic environment, Trace elements, Separation techniques, Domestic wastes.
Identifiers: *Polynuclear aromatic hydrocarbons, Carcinogen compounds, Fused ring compounds, Pyrolysis systems, Activated carbon filters.

A review was given of the analytical techniques available for monitoring polynuclear aromatic hydrocarbons (PAH) in raw, potable, and wastewaters. In addition, the effects of water and wastewater treatment processes upon levels of PAH were reviewed and consideration was given to the probable sources of such compounds in the aqueous environment. Analytical results have shown that PAH derived from drinking water contribute only a small proportion to the average total human intake. However, there are still many aspects of the occurrence, formation, and degradation of these compounds which need clarification. The reliability of much of the information concerning the removal of PAH by conventional water treatment processes is open to considerable doubt. Further analytical work is required in this field, and fundamental studies of the chemical changes that occur with chlorination of these compounds at low concentrations are necessary. Increasing water reuse makes the need for this type of information particularly acute. (Henley-ISWS)
W75-08453

AN EXAMINATION OF THE CONCENTRATION OF ORGANIC COMPONENTS WATER-EXTRACTED FROM PETROLEUM PRODUCTS,
Naval Research Lab., Washington, D.C.
P. J. Sniegoski.
Water Research, Vol 9, No 4, p 421-423, April 1975. 1 fig, 2 tab, 4 ref.

Descriptors: *Pollutant identification, *Oil wastes, *Oily water, Organic compounds, *Analytical techniques, *Organic wastes, Solvent extractions, Organic matter, Water pollution sources, Chemical wastes, Water pollution, Water quality, Oil, Fuels, Oil spills, Oil-water interfaces, Waste water(Pollution), Ships, Separation techniques.
Identifiers: *Dissolved organics, Total carbon analysis, Polar compounds.

Overboard discharge of effluent water resulting from the usual methods used to separate ships' oily waste water may present a pollution problem since the dissolved organics are present. By means of total carbon analysis the solubility characteristics of petroleum products commonly found in naval vessels were investigated. Special emphasis was given to the dependence of the organic concentration in the water phase to the water-oil ratio of the system. By means of various abstractive treatments an estimate was made of the relative amounts of polar compounds and hydrocarbons that are present in the water phase. (Henley-ISWS)
W75-08454

CONCENTRATION OF ADENOVIRUS FROM SEAWATER,
New Hampshire Univ., Durham. Dept. of Microbiology.
H. A. Fields, and T. G. Metcalf.
Water Research, Vol 9, No 4, p 357-364, April 1975. 8 tab, 15 ref. NSF Grant GI 38976.

Descriptors: *Viruses, *Sea water, *Aquatic microorganisms, *Analytical techniques, *Water pollution, Microorganisms, Biology, Water pollution sources, Oceans, Salinity, Membranes, Filters, Chemistry, Water quality, Analysis, Assay, Monitoring, Microbiology.
Identifiers: *Adenovirus, Virology, Aqueous polymer phase separation.

Factors influencing adenovirus 5 recovery from seawater by virus concentrator methods were determined. A 19,000-fold concentration of 25 gal samples with a theoretical recovery efficiency of 90% was possible with input multiplicities of 1000 TCID sub 50 units/ml. Pretreatment of orlon and cellulose acetate filters with beef extract or between 80 solutions promoted adenovirus passage during sample clarification. Adenovirus adsorbed to textile and epoxy fiberglass filters at acid pH. Adsorption to textile filters was enhanced by 0.05 M MgC12. No salt enhancement was necessary for adsorption to epoxy fiberglass filters. Adenovirus was recovered from adsorbent filters following elution with 3% beef extract solution adjusted to pH 9.0. Adenovirus was reconcentrated from beef extract eluates by aqueous polymer phase separation. Actual recovery of 106 PFU of adenovirus from 50 gal of a waste treatment plant effluent was made with the modified virus concentrator procedure developed in the study. (Henley-ISWS)
W75-08455

NITRIFICATION IN RIVERS IN THE TRENT BASIN,
Water Pollution Research Lab., Stevenage (England).
For primary bibliographic entry see Field 5B.
W75-08456

A SIMPLE RESPIROMETER FOR MEASURING OXYGEN AND NITRATE CONSUMPTION IN BACTERIAL CULTURES,
Agricultural Univ., Wageningen (Netherlands). Dept. of Microbiology.
J. F. van Kessel.
Water Research, Vol 9, No 4, p 417-419, April 1975. 4 fig, 4 ref.

Descriptors: *Pollutant identification, *Denitrification, *Microorganisms, *Oxygen, *Nitrates, *Analytical techniques, Chemistry, Instrumentation, Respiration, Oxygen requirements, Dissolved oxygen, Nitrogen compounds, Nitrites, Nitrogen cycle, Chemical reactions, Pseudomonas, Cultures, Bacteria.
Identifiers: *Respirometer, Specific ion electrode, Polarographic sensor, Terminal electron acceptor.

A simple respirometer was described to measure simultaneously oxygen and nitrate concentrations. It proved to be an easy tool in denitrification studies. This was tested with Pseudomonas acruginosa. (Henley-ISWS)
W75-08458

ANALYSIS OF RUNOFF FROM SOUTHERN GREAT PLAINS FEEDLOTS,
Agricultural Research Service, Bushland, Tex. Southwestern Great Plains Research Center.
For primary bibliographic entry see Field 5B.
W75-08460

SPECTRAL STUDIES OF MONILIFORMIN AND AFLATOXIN B1,
Auburn Univ., Ala. Dept. of Chemistry.
J. A. Lansden.
Available from the National Technical Information Service, Springfield, Va 22161 as PB-242 339, $4.25 in paper copy, $2.25 in microfiche. MS Thesis, December 1973. 49 p, 18 fig, 16 ref. OWRT A-035-ALA(3).

Descriptors: *Pollutants, Water quality, Bioassay, Fluorescence, *Pollutant identification, Volumetric analysis, *Spectrophotometry, Chemical analysis.
Identifiers:. Southern corn blight, Fungus metabolites: Fluorescence excitation, Emission spectra, Phosphorescence emission spectrum, *Moniliformin, *Aflatoxin B1.

The spectroanalytical parameters of moniliformin were investigated. The fluorescence and phosphorescence spectra were reported as well as the quantum efficiency of fluorescence and the phosphorescence lifetime. An hypothesis was expounded to explain anomalies occurring in the work. The interaction of desoxynuclaic acid (DNA) with moniliformin was investigated using fluorescence titration techniques. Moniliformin was found to interact with a linear dependency on the concentration of DNA. Interactions of bovine serum albumin and nucleic acid histone with moniliformin were not observed. The triplet-triplet absorption spectrum of aflatoxin B1 was reported using kinetic flash techniques. The T-T absorption bands in aflatoxin B1 were assigned. Investigation of triplet-triplet absorption spectra for moniliformin was also performed and negative results were reported.
W75-08475

THE PHOTOSENSITIZING ACTION OF 2-NAPHTHYLAMINE ON ESCHERICHIA COLI, K-12,
Auburn Univ., Ala. Dept. of Chemistry.
A. F. Osteen.
Available from the National Technical Information Service, Springfield, Va 22161 as PB-242 340, $4.25 in paper copy, $2.25 in microfiche. MS Thesis, November 1973. 45 p, 10 fig, 3 tab, 12 ref. OWRT A-035-ALA(2).

Descriptors: *Pollutants, Water quality, Assay, Industrial wastes, *Toxicity, Coliforms, *E. coli, Bacteria, *Pollutant identification, *Bioassay, Water pollution effects.
Identifiers: Carcinogens, *Phototoxicity, Photodynamic assay, *Amines.

2-naphthylamine is an industrial carcinogen which has been under study since 1930. Biological investigators have tested for tumor incidence caused by injections, oral doses, or vapor inhalation, of the amine and its metabolites. In this study the phototoxicity of the amine is investigated by conducting binding studies and measuring the energy transferred from the amine to Escherichia coli, a coliform bacteria. Detection of a photoproduct of the amine formed within timed periods of the kill zone has been accomplished and preliminary study of its spectra has been made.
W75-08476

ANALYSES OF SELECTED CONSTITUENTS IN NATIVE WATER AND SOIL IN THE BAYOU BOEUF-CHENE-BLACK AREA NEAR MORGAN CITY, LOUISIANA, INCLUDING A MODIFIED STANDARD ELUTRIATE TEST,
Geological Survey, Baton Rouge, La.
F. C. Wells, and A. J. Gogel.
Open-file report 75-176, April 1975. 23 p, 1 fig, 6 tab, 4 ref, 2 append.

Descriptors: *Water quality, *Dredging, *Bayous, *Louisiana, Data collections, Chemical analysis, Sampling, Soils, Core drilling, Sediments, Inland waterways, Evaluation, Water pollution effects.
Identifiers: *Chene Bayou(La), *Black Bayou(La), Dredging effects.

A series of analytical tests, including a modified standard elutriate test, were performed on native water, cores of shallow sediments, marsh soil, and core-water mixtures collected from nine sites along Bayous Chene and Black near Morgan City, La. The work was done at the request of the U.S. Army Corps of Engineers to provide data on possible influences that dredging might have on water quality in the area. Results of the analyses indicate that the native waters are well oxygenated, alkaline, and low in concentrations of dissolved solids. Concentrations of heavy metals in the native waters are low in the dissolved, suspended, and total phases; and concentrations of dissolved metals in the core-water mixture show little or no increase over dissolved metals in the native water. However, in the total phase, concentrations of metals in the core-water mixture are much greater than in the native water, due to the greater quantities of suspended matter, with adsorbed metals, in the mixture. Concentrations of volatile solids, nutrients, and chemical oxygen demand are low in the native waters. High concentrations of these constituents in the core material, marsh soil, and subsequently in the core-water mixture are probably due to the presence of large amounts of organic material. Concentrations of oil and grease and pesticides were low in all samples. (Woodard-USGS)
W75-08501

DISCHARGE DATA AT WATER-QUALITY MONITORING STATIONS IN ARKANSAS,
Geological Survey, Little Rock, Ark.
For primary bibliographic entry see Field 7A.
W75-08519

MICROBIOLOGICAL STUDY OF THE INFLUENCE OF CHALK ON POND MUD, (IN FRENCH),
Station d'Hydrobiologie Continentale, Biarritz (France).
For primary bibliographic entry see Field 5B.
W75-08522

NON-FLAME ATOMIZATION IN ATOMIC ABSORPTION SPECTROMETRY,
Auckland Univ. (New Zealand). Dept. of Chemistry.
J. Aggett, and A. J. Sprott.
Analytica Chimica Acta, Vol 72, No 2, p 49-56, September, 1974. 6 tab, 13 ref.

Descriptors: *Spectroscopy, *Analytical techniques, Instrumentation, *Metals, Chemical analysis, Testing procedures, Oxices, Chemical reactions, *Pollutant identification, Cobalt, Tin, Iron, Nickel.
Identifiers: *Atomic absorption spectroscopy.

The role of the metal oxides and the graphite in non-flame atomizers was examined. Graphite probably acts as a reducing agent in the atomization of cobalt, iron, nickel and tin. Interferences may originate both on the surface of the graphite rod and in the vapor phase immediately above the rod. The origin of these interferences is discussed. A non-flame atomizer modified to use tantalum filaments was used in combination with a Unicam SP90A atomic absorption spectrophotometer in the experiments. (Pulliam-Vanderbilt)
W75-08529

STANDARDIZATION OF METHODS FOR THE DETERMINATION OF TRACES OF MERCURY -- PART I. DETERMINATION OF TOTAL INORGANIC MERCURY IN INORGANIC SAMPLES.
Bureau International Technique du Chlore, Brussels (Belgium). Mercury Analysis Working Party.
Analytica Chimica Acta, Vol 72, No 2, p 37-48, September, 1974. 3 fig, 3 tab, 14 ref.

Descriptors: *Spectroscopy, *Analytical techniques, *Mercury, *Inorganic compounds, Metals, Chemical analysis, Testing procedures, Instrumentation, Industrial plants, Trace elements, *Pollutant identification.
Identifiers: Sample preparation, Atomic absorption spectroscopy.

Flameless atomic absorption spectrometry was selected as the best method to determine mercury. To carry out the determination, all mercury compounds are converted into metallic mercury. A method is described for the determination of total inorganic mercury in inorganic samples. The method can be used for the routine determination of mercury in process streams and wastes of a chlor alkali electrolysis plant (excluding chlorine). In general, the procedure should be capable of detecting 0.01 microgram of Hg in a solution with a (maximum) volume of 40 ml. Results for interlaboratory trials involving up to 37 participating laboratories were presented. Samples with Hg contents between 20 micrograms/kg and 20 mg/kg were analyzed. Statistical evaluation of the results gave a value of 4-8% for repeatability and 6-22% for reproducibility. (Pulliam-Vanderbilt)
W75-08530

PB IN PARTICULATES FROM THE LOWER ATMOSPHERE OF THE EASTERN ATLANTIC,
Liverpool Univ. (England). Dept. of Oceanography.
R. Chester, and J. H. Stoner.
Nature, Vol 245, No 5419, p 27-28, September 7, 1973. 1 tab, 1 fig, 8 ref.

Descriptors: *Lead, *Air pollution effects, *Spatial distribution, *Atlantic Ocean, Sampling, On-site data collections, Industrial wastes, Water pollution, *Path of pollutants, *Pollutant identification.

Particulates were collected from seawater and from the lower atmosphere (approximately 15m above the sea surface) over large tracts of the world ocean. There was a marked decrease in the lead contents of the particulates southwards from the Westerlies to the Inter-Tropical Convergence Zone (ITCZ) in the northern hemisphere, and a decrease from the variable winds of the South African coast to the ITCZ in the southern hemisphere. This offers evidence of anthropogenic effects on the lead concentrations of particulates from oceanic regions. The effects were geographically dependent, the highest lead concentrations being found in particulates originating from relatively heavily populated source areas such as Western Europe, which can supply solids to the Westerlies in this region of the North Atlantic, and South Africa. (Jernigan-Vanderbilt)
W75-08531

SOME OBSERVATIONS ON THE DETERMINATION OF COPPER WITH THIOCYANATE,
Loughborough Univ. of Technology (England). Dept. of Chemistry.
W. P. Hayes, A. H. Sasa, V. S. Farced, and D. T. Burns.
Analytica Chimica Acta, Vol 71, No 1, p 210-214, July, 1974. 20 ref.

Descriptors: *Copper, *Chemical precipitation, *Potentiometers, *Volumetric analysis, Analytical techniques, Iron, Testing procedures, Gravimetric analysis, Oxidation, Reduction(Chemical), *Pollutant identification, Chemical analysis.
Identifiers: Thiocyanates.

The relative merits of various reducing agents in gravimetric procedures, the interferences caused by diverse ions, and the conditions under which thiocyanate acts as reductant were investigated. Also described are studies of the titration of copper in the presence of thiocyanate. Determination of copper in solution by reduction from copper (II) to copper (I) and precipitating as copper (I) thiocyanate was achieved by using a variety of reducing agents. The titration of copper (II) by the ascorbic acid procedure was preferred to the hydroquinone procedure. In the potentiometric titrations the potential change with ascorbic acid was much greater than found with hydroquinone, making the endpoint determination simpler and more precise. No suitable visual in-

dicator was found to use with hydroquinone but 2,6-dichlorophenol was satisfactory with ascorbic acid. (Jernigan-Vanderbilt)
W75-08532

THE DISTRIBUTION OF INTRAPERITONEALLY INJECTED CADMIUM-115M IN CHICKENS,
Purdue Univ., Lafayette Ind. Dept. of Bionucleonics.
R. D. Dyer, G. S. Born, and W. V. Kessler.
Environmental Letters, Vol 7, No 2, p 119-124, June, 1974, 1 tab, 20 ref. (5-TO1-RL00064-09) USPHS (5 TO1-ES00071-05).

Descriptors: *Cadmium, *Radioisotopes, *Poultry, *Distribution, Tracers, Toxicity, Inorganic compounds, Laboratory tests, Testing procedures, Absorption, Trace elements, *Pollutant identification.

Cadmium was injected into Leghorn chickens in trace quantities over a 12-week period. Six chickens were given weekly for 12 weeks intraperitoneal injections containing trace quantities of cadmium acetate labeled with Cd-115m. After the 12-week injection period, the chickens were maintained for 3 additional weeks. During this time they began laying eggs which were collected. The chickens were sacrificed and the cadmium levels in various tissues were determined. The liver and kidneys showed the largest percentages of whole body cadmium. Small percentages were found in eggs. (Jernigan-Vanderbilt)
W75-08533

DETERMINATION OF NANOGRAM QUANTITIES OF MERCURY IN SEA WATER,
Marine Research Inst., Reykjavik (Iceland).
J. Olafsson.
Analytica Chimica Acta, Vol 68, No 1, p 207-211, January, 1974. 2 fig, 1 tab, 17 ref.

Descriptors: *Mercury, *Sea water, *Analytical techniques, *Spectroscopy, Gold, Sampling, Inorganic compounds, Tin, Testing procedures, *Pollutant identification.
Identifiers: *Atomic absorption spectroscopy.

A flameless atomic absorption procedure coupled to amlgamation on gold for the determination of nanogram quantities of mercury in samples from North Atlantic waters was described. Early results showed that after inorganic mercury salts in deionized water had been reduced with tin (II) chloride, the mercury vapor could be collected from a stream of argon by amalgamation with gold. Moreover, the mercury could be completely released from the gold by heating and then carried with a stream of argon into the optical cell for measurement. However, when this procedure was applied to sea water spiked with mercury, low and irreproducible recoveries were found. This was remedied by greatly reducing the argon flow rate and simultaneously increasing the time of aeration. At fast argon flow rates, droplets of sea water were carried over to the mercury collector, and their chloride content greatly reduces the extent of amalgamation. (Jernigan-Vanderbilt)
W75-08535

SPECTROPHOTOMETRIC DETERMINATION OF TUNGSTEN IN ROCKS BY AN ISOTOPE DILUTION PROCEDURE,
Geological Survey, Washington, D.C.
For primary bibliographic entry see Field 2K.
W75-08536

THE ELECTRODEPOSITION AND DETERMINATION OF RADIUM BY ISOTOPIC DILUTION IN SEA WATER AND IN SEDIMENTS SIMULTANEOUSLY WITH OTHER NATURAL RADIONUCLIDES,
Scripps Institution of Oceanography, La Jolla, Calif. Geological Research Div.
M. Koide, and K. W. Bruland.
Analytica Chimica Acta, Vol 75, No 1, p 1-19, March, 1975. 7 fig, 3 tab, 34 ref.

Descriptors: *Radium radioisotopes, *Sea water, *Sediments, *Water analysis, Analytical techniques, Radioisotopes, Uranium radioisotopes, Tracers, Water pollution sources, Trace elements, Lead, Isotope studies, Lead radioisotopes, Background radiation, *Radiochemical analysis, Aluminum, Phosphates, Nitrates, Radiation, *Pollutant identification.

An isotopic dilution method has been developed for the determination of Ra226 and Ra228 in sea water and sediments with Ra223 as a yield tracer. An alternative procedure which obviates the need for Ra223 is demonstrated for sediments by the assay of Ra224 and Th228 which occur naturally in sediments. In addition, a direct method for beta-counting Ra228-Ac228 is proposed. Radium, polonium, thorium, and uranium isotopes and Pb210 are co-precipitated from sea water with aluminum phosphate carrier. The radium and Pb210 are co-precipitated with lead nitrate in sediment leachings. All radium procedures utilize identical chemical isolation and the cathodic electrodeposition of radium. Subsequently, the alpha-radiation emitted by Ra226, Ra223, and Ra224 is determined by pulse-height analysis; the Ra228-Ac228 and Pb210-Bi210 are measured by low background anticoincidence beta-counting techniques. The Ra226 method is applicable to all environmental samples, whereas Ra228 determinations are limited to applications where the Ra228/Ra226 activity ratio is greater than 0.1. This method is especially attractive for studies of parent-daughter disequilibria. (Witt-IPC)
W75-08538

DETERMINATION OF SELENIUM IN WATER AND INDUSTRIAL EFFLUENTS BY FLAMELESS ATOMIC ABSORPTION,
Calgon Corp., Pittsburgh, Pa.
E. L. Henn.
Analytical Chemistry, Vol 47, No 3, p 428-432, March, 1975. 4 fig, 3 tab, 12 ref.

Descriptors: *Water analysis, *Industrial wastes, *Spectrophotometry, *Pollutant identification, Analytical techniques, Water pollution sources, Chemical analysis, Cation exchange, Metals, Cations, Ions, Trace elements, Chemicals, Colorimetry, Molybdenum, Inorganic compounds, Resins.
Identifiers: *Selenium.

A procedure for determining selenium in water and industrial effluents is described. The method utilizes flameless atomic absorption preceded by treatment with a cation exchange resin to eliminate interference from metallic cations and the addition of molybdenum to enhance sensitivity and suppress interference from inorganic anions. Advantages and limitations of the method are discussed, and analytical results on real samples are compared with those obtained using the colorimetric diaminobenzidine method. The range of the test is 1.0 to 50 microgram/liter selenium. (Witt-IPC)
W75-08541

ARTIFICIAL FOG PRODUCED BY INDUSTRIAL EMISSION OF WATER VAPOR (BROUILLARDS ARTIFICIELS PRODUITS PAR EMISSION INDUSTRIELLE DE VAPEUR D'EAU),
Quebec Univ., Chicoutimi. Centre de Recherche du Moyen Nord.
L. P. Cong, and J. Dessens.
Journal de Recherches Atmospheriques, Vol 7, No 2, p 109-116, April/June, 1973. 4 fig, 1 tab, 4 ref.

Descriptors: *Fog, *Water vapor, *Industrial wastes, *Air pollution effects, *Pulp and paper industry, Gases, Atmopshere, Condensation, Solar radiation, Chemical analysis, Foreign countries, Europe, Climates, Pollutants, Air pollution, Air environment, Pollution abatement.

Water vapor is not considered an atmospheric pollutant and is usually ignored in studies related to air pollution. However, under particular conditions, water vapor emitted by industrial plants can give rise to stable artificial fog and thus influence the local climate. This is the case for the Saint-Gaudens (Haute-Garonne) mill of La Cellulose d'Aquitaine, located a short distance from the river in an enclosed valley characterized by the absence of wind and by frequent inversions. Recently a significant increase in fog frequency was observed, coinciding with a production increase at the mill. The higher frequency as well as persistence of the fog until the noon hours prompted a study of the origin and nature of the emission. Studied were the visibility, the spectrum of droplets, and the chemical composition of the fog. The results of these studies established the contribution of the mill to the formation of fog. Due to nocturnal inversion, the water vapor emitted from the mill can form a fog that can cover tens of sq km, the solar radiation maintaining the inversion conditions by heating the upper layer of the fog. The high water content of the fog and its small droplets account for the low visibility. The fog could be controlled either by condensing the water vapor at its source or by a treatment which would increase the size of the droplets and accelerate the dissipation of the fog. (Stapinski-IPC)
W75-08545

PRECONCENTRATION AND X-RAY FLUORESCENCE DETERMINATION OF COPPER, NICKEL, AND ZINC IN SEA WATER,
Georgia Univ., Athens. Dept. of Zoology.
D. E. Leyden, T. A. Patterson, and J. J. Alberts.
Analytical Chemistry, Vol 47, No 4, p 733-735, April, 1975. 1 fig, 1 tab, 10 ref.

Descriptors: *Copper, *Nickel, *Zinc, *Sea water, *Water analysis, *X-ray fluorescence, Ion exchange, Trace elements, Water pollution sources, Metals, Water pollution, Analytical techniques, .Resins, Separation techniques, Chemical analysis, *Pollutant identification.
Identifiers: Tetraethylenepentamine, Toluene diisocyanate.

Copper, nickel, and zinc in 500 ml sea water samples were concentrated on an ion-exchange resin prepared from tetraethylenepentamine and toluene diisocyanate. The resin containing the Cu, Ni, and Zn was then compressed into a pellet which was used for the x-ray fluorescence determination. The recovery of Cu, Ni, and Zn from sea water at pH 8.2 when their concentrations ranged from 2 to 24 micrograms/liter was 92, 97, 93%, respectively. (Witt-IPC)
W75-08549

PRELIMINARY RESULTS ON THE USE OF TENAX UOR THE EXTRACTION OF PESTICIDES AND POLYNUCLEAR AROMATIC HYDROCARBONS FROM . SURFACE AND DRINKING WATERS FOR ANALYTICAL PPRPOSES,
Rome Univ. (Italy). Istituto d'Igiene.
V. Leoni, G. Puccetti, and A. Grella.
Journal of Chromatography, Vol 106, No 1, p 119-124, March 19, 1975. 3 tab, 15 ref.

Descriptors: *Pesticides, *Water analysis, *Pollutant identification, Analytical techniques, Potable water, Surface waters, Trace elements, Water pollution sources, Wastes, Pollutants, Separation techniques, Chromatography, Gas chromatography, Organophosphorus pesticides, Organic pesticides, Chlorinated hydrocarbon pesticides, Water pollution, Surfactants, Oil, Lipids, Organic compounds.
Identifiers: *Tenax, Thin-layer chromatography, Acetone, Dibutyl ether.

propylene glycol dinitrate, 2,4,6-trinitrotoluene (TNT), 1,3,5-trinitro-1,3,5-hexahydrotriazine, diethyl phthalate, and dibutyl sebacate are also presented and discussed. (Witt-IPC)
W75-08554

ORGANIC SUBSTANCES IN POTABLE WATER AND IN ITS PRECURSOR. III. THE CLOSED-LOOP STRIPPING PROCEDURE COMPARED WITH RAPID LIQUID EXTRACTION,

Eidgenoessische Technische Hochschule, Zurich (Switzerland). Gas Chromatography Lab.
K. Grob, K. Grob, Jr., and G. Grob.

Journal of Chromatography, Vol 106, No 2, p 299-315, March 26, 1975. 6 fig, 4 tab, 18 ref.

Descriptors: *Organic compounds, *Gas chromatography, *Water analysis, Analytical techniques, Chemical analysis, Chromatography, Potable water, Separation techniques, Water pollution sources, Organic wastes, Trace elements, Water chemistry, Water properties, Water quality, Water pollution, Pollutants, Water types, *Pollutant identification.

An attempt is made to define the role of gas cbromatography in the investigation of organic substances in water, which is important because the handling of water samples before gas chromatographic analysis depends entirely on the information expected from the subsequent separation, identification, and quantification. Practical long-term experience with the previously published closed-loop stripping procedure (with intermediate adsorption on activated carbon) is described, and further refinements are reported. A rapid and simple liquid extraction method is described, based on shaking 1 liter of water with a small volume (0.5-1 ml) of solvent and subsequent high-resolution gas chromatographic analysis of the extract. Qualitative and semiquantitative information at the parts per trillion level is easily obtained. Further studies of recovery rates under conditions where the volatility and polarity of extracted organic substances are varied are described for both methods. The suitability of both methods for the analysis of different types of water samples is discussed. The final decision in favor of one or other method probably depends in most instances on two fundamental conditions: (1) availability of the equipment for stripping; (2) the relative importance of the volatility range for light and medium versus heavy pollutants. (Witt-IPC)
W75-08556

THE USE OF MEMBRANE ELECTRODES IN THE DETERMINATION OF SULPHIDES IN SEA WATER,

E. Mor, V. Scotto, G. Marcenaro, and G. Alabiso.

Analytica Chimica Acta, Vol 75, No 1, p 159-167, March 1975. 5 fig, 1 tab, 14 ref.

Descriptors: *Sulfides, *Sea water, *Water analysis, Thermodynamics, Water pollution sources, Pollutants, Analytical techniques, *Electrodes, Potentiometers, Hydrogen ion concentration, Membranes, Inorganic compounds, Sulfur compounds.
Identifiers: *Membrane electrodes(Sulfide-selective).

The direct potentiometric determination of sulfides in natural sea water with a sulfide-selective membrane electrode is proposed. The experimental evaluation of the apparent mixed dissociation constants and the thermodynamic activity coefficient in spiked sea water samples, by means of the electrode, permits direct calibration in terms of activity. Alternatively, it is possible to establish, for natural sea water, an experimental equation for the correction of the electrode potentials in terms of pH; this allows direct calibration of the electrodes in terms of total sulfide concentration. This criterion can be applied to any aqueous solution. (Witt-IPC)
W75-08558

DETERMINATION OF NITRATE IN WATER WITH AN AMMONIA PROBE,

Brussels Univ. (Belgium). Laboratorium Analytische Chemie.
J. Mertens, Winkel P. Van den, and D. L. Massart.

Analytical Chemistry, Vol 47, No 3, p 522-526, March 1975. 6 fig, 6 tab, 24 ref.

Descriptors: *Nitrates, *Water analysis, Ammonia, Reduction(Chemical), Analytical techniques, Chemical analysis, Water pollution sources, Water, Water chemistry, Water properties, Trace elements, *Inorganic compounds, Nitrogen compounds, Nitrites, Chemicals, Water quality, *Pollutant identification.
Identifiers: *Ammonia probe, Devarda alloy.

Manual and automatic procedures are described for the determination of nitrates in water containing ammonia by means of an ammonia probe. The nitrates are determined by measuring the ammonia produced during a heterogeneous reduction by means of Devarda alloy powder. The yield of the nitrate reduction with the Devarda alloy was quantitative. The method shows good accuracy and reproducibility and can be applied in waters ranging from mineral water to sewage. Procedures for the elimination of excess ammonium and nitrite are proposed. Other reduction methods, which did not yield good results, are also discussed. (Witt-IPC)
W75-08561

FLOW-THROUGH APPARATUS FOR ACUTE TOXICITY BIOASSAYS WITH AQUATIC INVERTEBRATES,

Fisheries and Marine Service, Winnipeg (Manitoba). Aquatic Toxic Studies Div.
H. D. Maciorowski, and P. M. Kondra.

Canadian Department of the Environment, Fisheries and Marine Service, Technical Report No. CEN/T-75-2, 1975. 20 p, 1 fig, 4 tab, 5 ref.

Descriptors: *Aquatic life, *Bioassay, Equipment, *Toxicity, Water pollution effects, Water quality, Invertebrates.
Identifiers: *Mount-Brungs diluter.

A description is given of a modified Mount-Brungs proportional diluter used as an acute toxicity bioassay system for aquatic invertebrates. Differences between the original and modified models are outlined, and construction problems associated with modifying the Mount-Brungs diluter are discussed. (Witt-IPC)
W75-08563

DETECTION OF GB, VX AND PARATHION IN WATER,

Edgewood Arsenal, Aberdeen Proving Ground, Md.
R. M. Gamson, D. W. Robinson, and A. Goodman.

Available from the National Technical Information Service, Springfield, Va. 22161, as AD-784 079, $3.25 in paper copy, $2.25 in microfiche. Technical Report ED-TR-74015, June, 1974. 18 p, 1 tab, 2 fig, 10 ref.

Descriptors: *Monitoring *Pesticides, Technology, *Organophosphorus compounds, *Enzymes, *Inhibitors, Water pollution, *Pollutant identification, Toxicants.
Identifiers: *Parathion, Agent GB, Agent VX, *Cholinesterase.

A simple device containing paper impregnated with cholinesterase is reported for detection of organophosphorus agents in the ppb to ppm range in water. Parathion is included for comparison. Optimum performance is obtained at 20C and pH 8. Under these conditions, the enzyme is completely inhibited in 20 minutes or less by 10 ppb up to 1 ppm depending on the inhibitor. Comparison of inhibition data with rate constants indicates that the sensitivity of the device to any given inhibitor can be estimated if the rate constant value is known

for that inhibitor with horse serum cholinesterase. (Katz)
W75-08582

APPARATUS AND PROCEDURE FOR MEASURING SUBLETHAL TOXICITY OF WASTEWATER DISCHARGES,
New Mexico Univ., Albuquerque. Eric H. Wang Civil Engineering Research Facility.
R. A. Callahan.
Available from the National Technical Information Service, Springfield, Va. 22161, as AD-787 456, $6.25 in paper copy, $2.25 in microfiche. Air Force Weapons Laboratory (DEE), Kirtland Air Force Base, New Mexico Report AFWL-TR-74-55, July 1974. 94 p, 16 fig, 14 tab, 56 ref, 4 append.

Descriptors: *Toxicity, Waste water(Pollution), Waste water disposal, *Monitoring, Control systems, *Respiration, *Bioassay, *Design, Measurement, *Pollutant identification, Equipment, Animal physiology, Fish, Trout, Rainbow trout, Brook trout, Computer programs.
Identifiers: Sublethal toxicity, Salvelinus fontinalis.

A screening test to detect the presence of sublethal toxicity was developed. Changes in respiration rates were used as the criteria for toxicity to aquatic life in wastewater effluents. An aquatic respirometry system and a data acquisition system were designed, constructed, and tested. Respiration rates are determined by electronically measuring the current used by a demand-type electrolysis cell which generates oxygen by the electrolysis of water. The oxygen concentrations within the respirometers vary less than plus or minus 0.05 mg/l; measurements of oxygen consumption exceed 98 per cent accuracy. The respirometers are connected to a toxicant metering system which automatically dispenses up to 13 different concentrations of toxicants. Normal operation consists of three cycles: toxicant renewal, equilibration, and data acquisition, all performed automatically. A holding facility producing large numbers of animals suitable for bioassay testing was also designed and constructed. Data are presented showing the growth rates of rainbow trout (Salmo gairdneri) and brook trout (Salvelinus fontinalis) in this holding facility. The routine respiration rates of these species measured in the respirometry system are compared with rates reported in the literature. Preliminary experiments determined the effects of ammonia and two fire fighting foams on trout respiration. A computer program was written which tests the data for interaction between time and treatment effects, graphs the data according to several formats, and performs various tests for significance. (Katz)
W75-08586

METHODS FOR ACUTE TOXICITY TESTS WITH FISH, MACROINVERTEBRATES, AND AMPHIBIANS.
National Water Quality Lab., Duluth, Minn.
For primary bibliographic entry see Field 5C.
W75-08591

THE OCCURRENCE OF BENTHOS DEEP IN THE SUBSTRATUM OF A STREAM,
Waterloo Univ. (Ontario). Dept. of Biology.
D. D. Williams, and H. B. N. Hynes.
Freshwater Biol. Vol 4, No 3, p 233-256. 1974, Illus.

Descriptors: *Benthos, *Benthic fauna, Canada, *Rivers, *Streams, *Sampling, *Analytical techniques, *Connate water, Chemical analysis, Biomass, *Samplers.
Identifiers: Chironomide Hyporheos, Ontario, Parameters, Sampler, Stream, Substratum, Temperature, Hyporheal, Hyporheic, *Interstitial sampling methods, *Speed River(Ont).

The vertical distribution of the benthic fauna of the Speed River, Ontario was studied over a 13-mo. period from Oct. 1970-Oct. 1971. Various physical and chemical parameters of this interstitial environment were also measured. Several new techniques for sampling the interstitial environment of rivers were devised. These methods and their relative efficiencies are considered. The validity of the terms 'hyporheal' and 'hyporheic' are discussed and the term 'hyporheos' is offered to replace the former. A brief resume of interstitial sampling methods is given with comments on their limitations for sampling deep heterogeneous substrates. Chemical parameters are more important in the control and distribution of the fauna than physical parameters. Many larvae of stream-dwelling chironomids have overwintering stages when they penetrate deep into the substrate to: actively feed on the trapped organic detritus; and follow an optimum temperature for development. The shape of an organisms probably determines its success as a hyporheic form. The numbers of animals occurring in the sub-benthic populations are very large. For the Speed River, estimates of between 184, 760 and 797,960 animals/m3 are made for different times of the year. Dry weight biomass is estimated to vary between 30.9 and 253-2 g/m3 throughout the year. Sub-benthic or hyporheic populations exist in at least 3 other Canadian rivers. Some of the animals found are common to 2 or more of these rivers. The inefficiencies of many conventional benthic samplers is sampling the total biomass of certain streams with hyporheic populations is discussed.--Copyright 1974, Biological Abstracts, Inc.
W75-08602

SEASONAL VARIATION OF SIEVING EFFICIENCY IN LOTIC HABITAT,
Commonwealth Scientific and Industrial Research Organization, Deception Bay (Australia). Div. of Fisheries and Oceanography.
W. E. Barber, and N. R. Kevern.
Freshwater Biol, Vol 4, No 3, p 293-300, Illus, 1974.

Descriptors: *Diptera, Biomass, *Lotic environment, Aquatic environment, *Insects, *Aquatic insects, *Sieve analysis, *Seasonal sieves, Mayflies.
Identifiers: Chironomid, Coleoptera, Mite, Plecoptera, Simuliid, Trichoptera.

Sieving efficiency, defined as the percent increase in yield of numbers or biomass of organisms, obtained by use of a sieve with 0.25-mm mesh openings instead of a 0.50-mm meshed sieve, was investigated in a lotic habitat over a 12 mo. period. Greatest efficiencies obtained were 300-600% for mayflies, chironomids, simuliids, 'other dipterans,' water mites and plecopterans and 90 and 190% for trichopterans and coleopterans, respectively. For the fauna as a whole, efficiency varied from 95-325% over the study period. Efficiency in estimating biomass was not as great as that with numbers and generally was below 10% for trichopterans, mayflies, 'other dipterans,' coleopterans and the fauna taken as a whole. For chironomids, simuliids and water mites efficiencies generally were higher than 10% and reached as high as 174%, 60% and 80%, respectively. In all groups efficiency varies throughout the year with lowest occurring during winter months. The findings are compared with data found in the literature and discussed in relation to structural, behavioral, and life history characters.--Copyright 1974, Biological Abstracts, Inc.
W75-08609

WATER TURBIDITY MEASURING APPARATUS,
Fishmaster Products, Inc., Tulsa, Okla. (assignee)
For primary bibliographic entry see Field 7B.
W75-08626

REDUCTION OF ATMOSPHERIC POLLUTION BY THE APPLICATION OF FLUIDIZED-BED COMBUSTION AND REGENERATION OF SULFUR CONTAINING ADDITIVES,
Argonne National Lab., Ill.
G. J. Vogel, W. M. Swift, J. F. Lenc, P. T. Cunningham, and W. I. Wilson.
Available from the National Technical Information Service, Springfield, Va 22161 as Rept. No ANL/ES-CEN-1007, and EPA-650/2-74-104, $5.45 in paper copy, $2.25 in microfiche. Annual Report, July 1973-June 1974. ANL/ES-CEN-1007 and EPA-650/2-74-104, (1974). 135 p, 31 fig, 25 tab, 26 ref.

Descriptors: *Burning, *Chemical reactions, *Coals, *Effluents, *Trace elements, Environment, Soil chemical properties, Water chemistry, Water properties, Kinetics, Transfer, Movement, Sulfur compounds, Mercury, Lead, Beryllium, Fluorine.
Identifiers: *Combustion, *Fluidized-bed.

The program for developing and demonstrating the feasibility of fluidized-bed combustion for possible use in power and steam-plant applications is divided into three studies: (a) the combustion of coal in a pressurized combustor; (b) a determination of the distribution of trace elements in the combustion products; and (c) a fundamental investigation of the kinetics of additive sulfation and regeneration reactions. A bench-scale, fluidized-bed combustion pilot plant capable of operating at 10-atm pressure was used to evaluate the effects of operating variables on response variables such as SO2 and NO levels in the flue gas, combustion efficiency, additive utilization, and heat-transfer coefficients. High retentions of sulfur (>90%) and low NO levels (<150 ppm) were achieved. The combustor was also successfully tested using a variety of coals: a highly caking, high-volatile bituminous coal, a high ash subbituminous coal, and a low-heating-value lignite. (Houser-ORNL)
W75-08642

DISPERSION AND MOVEMENT OF TRITIUM IN A SHALLOW AQUIFER IN MORTANDAD CANYON AT THE LOS ALAMOS SCIENTIFIC LABORATORY,
Los Alamos Scientific Lab., N. Mex.
For primary bibliographic entry see Field 5B.
W75-08645

AERIAL RADIOLOGICAL MEASURING SURVEY OF THE COOPER NUCLEAR STATION AUGUST 1972.
EG and G, Inc., Las Vegas, Nev.
Available from the National Technical Information Service, Springfield, Va 22161 as ARMS-72.6.5., $4.00 in paper copy, $2.25 in microfiche. Report No ARMS-72.6.5, August 1974. 22 p, 3 fig, 3 tab, 3 ref.

Descriptors: *Surveys, *Monitoring, *Measurement, *Radioactivity, *Remote sensing, *Aerial sensing, Aircraft, Data collections, Nuclear powerplants, Effluents, Sites, Fallout, Public health, Background radiation.
Identifiers: *Cooper Nuclear Station, Gamma radiation.

The Aerial Radiological Measuring System (ARMS) was used to survey the area surrounding the Cooper Nuclear Station during August 1972, prior to reactor start-up. The survey measured terrestrial gamma radiation. A high-sensitivity detection system collected gamma-ray spectral and gross-count data. The data were then computer processed into a map of 700 square mile area showing isoexposure contours three feet above the ground. Exposure rates and isotopes identified are consistent with normal terrestrial background radiation. (Houser-ORNL)
W75-08648

GEOLOGY OF GEOTHERMAL TEST HOLE GT-2, FENTON HILL SITE, JULY 1974,
Los Alamos Scientific Lab., N. Mex.
W. D. Purtymun, F. G. West, and R. A. Pettitt.
Available from the National Technical Information Service, Springfield, Va 22161 as LA-5780-MS, $4.00 in paper copy, $2.25 in microfiche. Rept No LA-5780-MS, November 1974. 15 p, 3 fig, 5 tab, 13 ref.

Descriptors: *Geology, *Testing, *Test wells, *Geothermal studies, *Borehole geophysics, Temperature, *Thermal properties, Hydrologic data, Well logging.

The test hole GT-2, drilled at the Fenton Hill Site, was completed at a depth of 6346 ft (1934.3 m) below land surface. The hole penetrated 450 ft (137.2 m) of Cenozoic volcanics, 1945 ft (592.8 m) of sediments of Permian and Pennsylvanian age and 3951 ft (1204.3 m) of granitic rocks of Precambrian age. The field geologic log of the hole and hydrologic data compiled during the drilling phase of the program are presented. (Houser-ORNL)
W75-08649

TRITIUM AND NOBLE GAS FISSION PRODUCTS IN THE NUCLEAR FUEL CYCLE. I. REACTORS,
Argonne National Lab., Ill.
L. E. Trevorrow, B. J. Kullen, R. L. Jarry, and M. J. Steindler.
Available from the National Technical Information Service, Springfield, Va. 22161, as Rept No ANL-8102, $5.45 in paper copy, $2.25 in microfiche. Rept No ANL-8102, October 1974. 88 p, 24 fig, 25 tab, 130 ref, append.

Descriptors: *Nuclear reactors, *Effluents, *Tritium, *Fuels, Behavior, Toxins, *Path of pollutants, Gases, Liquids.
Identifiers: *Noble gas, *Fuel cycle, Fission products.

A review of the behavior of tritium and noble-gas fission products in nuclear reactors is presented. The sources of tritium considered include fission and activation of poisons and impurities in coolants. The noble gases included in this review are limited to fission products, with emphasis on the long-lived species. Reactor types surveyed include light water reactors, high-temperature gas-cooled reactors, and liquid-metal-cooled fast breeder reactors. Data indicative of the normal operating procedures have been expanded to provide estimates of the quantities of tritium and noble gases and their diluents expected at various points along the flow path for both gaseous and liquid waste streams. Data are normalized to an energy of 1000 MWe-yr to permit comparison with present-generation reactors. (Houser-ORNL)
W75-08652

LIQUID PLUGGING IN IN-SITU COAL GASIFICATION PROCESSES,
California Univ., Livermore. Lawrence Livermore Lab.
D. W. Gregg.
Available from the National Technical Information Service, Springfield, Va. 22161, as Rept No UCRL-51686, $4.00 in paper copy, $2.25 in microfiche. Rept No UCRL-51686, October 1974. 9 p, 1 fig, 7 ref.

Descriptors: *Coals, *Burning, *Chemical reactions, *Oxidation, *Research and development, Fossil fuels, Liquids, Condensation, Gases, Flow, Air demand, Flow system, Kinetics, Hydraulic design, Hydraulics.
Identifiers: *Coal gasification, Energy research.

The presence of liquids can severely alter the spacial propagation characteristics of the flame front in an in-situ coal gasification process. In a cocurrent burn, the liquids, water, and coal tars will be baked or pyrolyzed out of the coal in the hot zone near the flame front and will condense on cooler coal further downstream from the flame front. In the region where condensation is taking place, the liquids can plug the formation and thus alter or stop the gas flow pattern necessary for maintaining a spacially controlled flame front. Liquid plugging effects and their relationship to the permeability and the absolute crack sizes in the formation are discussed in a semiquantitative manner. The calculations presented are a rough guide to the requirements for preparing the coal seam with hydraulic or explosive fracturing, when such fracturing is needed. (Houser-ORNL)
W75-08657

A NEW IN-SITU COAL GASIFICATION PROCESS THAT COMPENSATES FOR FLAME-FRONT CHANNELING, RESULTING IN 100% RESOURCE UTILIZATION,
California Univ., Livermore. Lawrence Livermore Lab.
D. W. Gregg.
Available from the National Technical Information Service, Springfield, Va. 22161, as Rept No UCRL-51676, $4.00 in paper copy, $2.25 in microfiche. Rept No UCRL-51676, October 1974. 8 p, 2 fig, 9 ref.

Descriptors: *Coals, *Burning, *Oxidation, *Liquids, Theoretical analysis, Evaluation, Gases, Flow, Gravity flow, Boreholes, Mining engineering.
Identifiers: *Coal gasification, Energy development.

Flame-front channeling and liquid plugging are important, if not the dominant, merchanisms that will limit the fractional resource recovery for many proposed concepts for in-situ gasification of coal. A method is described to gasify coal in situ, using gravitational forces and a specified drill hole pattern, to compensate for flame-front channeling along both the vertical and horizontal axes (elevation and plan views). The theoretical resource utilization for this method of coal gasification is 100%. (Houser-ORNL)
W75-08658

PROJECT DIAMOND ORE, PHASE IIA: CLOSE-IN MEASUREMENTS PROGRAM,
California Univ., Livermore. Lawrence Livermore Lab.
C. J. Sisemore, D. E. Burton, and J. B. Bryan.
Available from the National Technical Information Service, Springfield, Va. 22161, as Rept No UCRL-51620, $5.45 in paper copy, $2.25 in microfiche. Rept No UCRL-51620, August 1974. 61 p, 12 fig, 6 tab, 7 ref.

Descriptors: *Nuclear explosions, *Beneficial use, *Craters, *Rock mechanics, *Instrumentation, *Measurement, Seismology, Seismographs, Seismic waves, Vibrations, Sound waves, Stress, Velocity, *Montana.
Identifiers: Project Diamond Ore(Mont).

Project Diamond Ore was designed to determine the effects of . temming, depth of burial, and geology on nuclear and high explosive cratering phenomena. Phase IIA included three multition chemical explosive cratering events. The close-in instrumentation for these events provided data to further code development work and to determine detonation histories. The instrumentation plan and emplacement procedures are described, and the recorded waveforms are reported, summarized, and interpreted in detail. (Houser-ORNL)
W75-08659

FURTHER NUMERICAL MODEL STUDIES OF THE WASHOUT OF HYGROSCOPIC PARTICLES IN THE ATMOSPHERE,
California Univ., Livermore. Lawrence Livermore Lab.
G. J. Stensland.
Available from the National Technical Information Service, Springfield, Va. 22161, as Rept No UCRL-51614, $4.00 in paper copy, $2.25 in microfiche. Rept No UCRL-51614, July 2, 1974. 24 p, 13 fig, 2 tab, 18 ref.

Descriptors: *Washouts, *Fallout, *Hygroscopic water, *Sediment load, Suspended load, Particle size, Raindrops, Rain, Rainfall, Rain water, Evaporation, Model studies.

Numerical and analytical methods are used to study rainout and washout of hygroscopic particles in the atmosphere. The variation in concentration of hygroscopic material in rain water was investigated as a function of raindrop size class, changing radius of released particles due to drop evaporation, and time from initiation of rainfall. (Houser-ORNL)
W75-08660

A DIRECT SOLUTION OF THE SPHERICAL-HARMONICS APPROXIMATION TO THE TRANSFER EQUATION FOR A PLANE-PARALLEL, NONHOMOGENEOUS ATMOSPHERE,
California Univ., Livermore. Lawrence Livermore Lab.
J. V. Dave.
Available from the National Technical Information Service, Springfield, Va. 22161, as Rept No UCRL-51581, $4.00 in paper copy, $2.25 in microfiche. Rept No UCRL-51581, June 17, 1974. 54 p, 1 append.

Descriptors: *Radioactivity, *Radiation, *Transfer, *Model studies, Atmosphere, Air environment, Diffusion, Gases, Aerosols, Clouds, Meteoric water, Mathematical studies.

In recent years, the method of obtaining a direct solution of the spherical harmonics approximation to the equation of radiative transfer has been shown to be a very efficient and powerful one for the evaluation of diffuse fluxes at various levels of a plane-parallel, nonhomogeneous atmosphere containing arbitrary height distributions of absorbing gases, aerosol particles, and cloud water drops. Presented are (a) a detailed derivation of the spherical harmonics equations starting with the basic transfer equation, and (B) a description of the method for the numerical solution of the resultant system of linear equations. To be consistent with the other published work in this field, the zenith angle is measured relative to the negative normal-optical-thickness axis. Furthermore, to provide a full treatment of the planetary radiation problem, earlier derivations have been extended to include isotropic illumination of the atmosphere from below. (Houser-ORNL)
W75-08661

NUCLEAR CHEMICAL COPPER MINING AND REFINING: RADIOLOGICAL CONSIDERATIONS,
California Univ., Livermore. Lawrence Livermore Lab.
For primary bibliographic entry see Field 5C.
W75-08662

ENVIRONMENTAL RADIOACTIVITY IN THE FAROES IN 1973,
Danish Atomic Energy Commission, Risoe. Research Establishment.
A. Aarkrog, and J. Lippert.
Available from the National Technical Information Service, Springfield, Va. 22161, as Rept No Riso 306, $4.00 in paper copy, $2.25 in microfiche. Report No Riso 306, July 1974. 21 p, 9 fig, 17 tab, 5 ref.

Descriptors: *Environment, *Monitoring, *Measurement, *Radioactivity, *Fallout, Cesium, Strontium, Sampling, Precipitation(Atmospheric), Grasses, Milk, Fish, Sea Water, Food chains, Vegetable crops, Potatoes, Biology, Domestic water, Diets.

Identifiers: *Faroes.

Measurements of fall-out radioactivity in the Faroes in 1973 are presented. Sr 90 (and Cs 137 in most instances) was determined in regularly collected samples of precipitation, grass, milk, fish, sea water, bread, and drinking water. In addition, analyses of spot samples of lamb, potatoes, sea plants, vegetables, eggs, and human bone were carried out. Estimates of the mean contents of Sr 90 and Cs 137 in the human diet in the Faroes in 1973 are given. (Houser-ORNL)
W75-08663

ENVIRONMENTAL RADIOACTIVITY IN GREENLAND IN 1973,
Danish Atomic Energy Commission, Risoe. Research Establishment.
A. Aarkrog, and J. Lippert.
Available from the National Technical Information Service, Springfield, Va. 22161, as Rept No Riso-307, $4.00 in paper copy, $2.25 in microfiche. Report No Riso 307, July 1974. 20 p, 7 fig, 11 tab, 4 ref.

Descriptors: *Environment, *Monitoring, *Measurement, *Radioactivity, *Fallout, Cesium, Strontium, Precipitation(Atmospheric), Sea water, Vegetation, Domestic water, Aquatic animals, Diets, Human pathology.
Identifiers: *Greenland.

Measurements of fall-out radioactivity in Greenland in 1973 are reported. Strontium-90 (and Caesium-137 in most instances) was determined in samples of precipitation, sea water, vegetation, animals, and drinking water. Estimates of the mean contents of Sr 90 and Cs 137 in the human diet in Greenland in 1973 are given. (Houser-ORNL)
W75-08664

NATURAL RADIATION EXPOSURE IN THE UNITED STATES,
Office of Radiation Programs, Washington, D.C.
D. T. Oakley.
Available from the National Technical Information Service, Springfield, Va. 22161, as Rept No PB-235 795, $4.75 in paper copy, $2.25 in microfiche. June 1972. 68 p, 17 fig, 23 tab, 134 ref.

Descriptors: *Environment, *Radioactivity, *Background radiation, Population, Human population, Geology, Elevation, Assessment, Surveys, Measurement.
Identifiers: *Dosimetry, Natural radiation, *Population exposure, *Cosmic radiation.

The exposure of man to natural radiation sources in the United States has been estimated by considering the distribution of the population with respect to certain factors, principally geology and elevation, which influence exposure to terrestrial and cosmic radiation. Data obtained by aerial surveys in the United states have been used to calculate an average dose equivalent (DE) estimate of 40 mrem/yr. to the population. The results also indicate three distinct areas of terrestrial radioactivity in the United States - (1) the Coastal Plain, which consists of all or portions of States from Texas to New Jersey (23 mrem/yr.); (2) a portion of the Colorado Front Range (90 mrem/yr.); and (3) the rest of the United States not included in '1' or '2' (46 mrem/yr.). Since elevation is the primary determinant of cosmic ray DE in the United States, the population distribution with respect to elevation was determined. The average population elevation in the United States was determined to be approximately 700 feet, and the average cosmic ray DE was estimated to be 44 mrem/yr. To arrive at an estimate of the gonadal DE, the influence of housing, biological shielding, and DE contribution of internal emitters was also considered. The first two factors serve to attenuate man's gonadal DE due to terrestrial radiation by about the same amount that is contributed by internal emitters. The average gonadal DE to the U.S. Population was calculated to be 86 mrem/yr. (Houser-ORNL)
W75-08669

STORMWATER POLLUTION--SAMPLING AND MEASUREMENT,
Trent Polytechnic, Nottingham (England). Dept. of Building and Civil Engineering.
C. G. J. Tucker.
Journal of the Institution of Municipal Engineers, Vol 101, No 10, p 269-273, October, 1974. 6 fig, 1 tab, 10 ref.

Descriptors: *Urban runoff, *Storm water, *Measurement, *Storm runoff, Flow, Automation, *Pollutant identification, *Sampling, Hydrographs, Installation, Manholes, Dilution, Water pollution sources, *Path of pollutants, Control.
Identifiers: Dilution gauging, Gulp injection, Lithium tracer.

Assessment of the nature of urban runoff pollutants requires the measurement of both flow and composition throughout a storm. It is important that automatic equipment measure the initial flow, where a first flush of pollutant often occurs. Various types of automatic control may be used, such as floats, static head transducers and pressure switches. Sampling may be done on a continuous or discrete basis at variable time intervals. Two methods of dilution gauging, constant rate injection and gulp injection, are used for measuring storm water. A lithium tracer is used since rainfall and runoff do not contain natural lithium. Described is the method of gulp injection, controlled by an interval sampler which is activated by an automatic float switch. A mass of tracer solution is added to the flow in a gulp dose. The passage of the resultant pulse is measured downstream. Equipment is detailed; its installation in manholes is simple, so long as space is sufficient for sampler and doser to pass through a 21-inch manhole ring. Results are given by storm hydrographs and concentration-time curves which are plotted to determine the polluting constituents. The integrated or Total Storm Load (TSL) value is found. This TSL is derived from a sum of the sampling intervals and represents the quantity of a pollutant which is washed by a storm from the surface water catchment. (Prague-FIRL)
W75-08678

QUANTITATIVE DETERMINATION OF FREON 12 AND FREON 22 IN WATER, (IN RUSSIAN),
N. A. Petrova, and G. S. Salyamon.
Gig Sanit. Vol 38, No 10, 68-71, Illus, 1973.

Descriptors: *Analytical techniques, *Colorimetry, *Oxygen, *Pollutant identification.
Identifiers: Alkali, *Freon, Pyridine, Organohalogen compounds, USSR.

The colorimetric reaction of organohalogen compounds with pyridine and alkali is suitable for analyzing Freon 22 in water. The determinable minimum is 2 microgram of Freon 22 in the sample (or 0.2 mg/1). However, the reaction is not recommended for analyzing Freon 12 in water, since accompanying impurities have a strong effect on the color. To analyze Freon 12 in water, a method was developed which is based on blowing it out of the water with a stream of O2 and igniting it in a quartz tube over a Pt screen with subsequent colorimetry of the F ion. The range of analysis is 4-280 mg/1.--Copyright 1975, Biological Abstracts, Inc.
W75-08682

RESPONSES OF THE THREE TEST ALGAE OF THE ALGAL ASSAY PROCEDURE: BOTTLE TEST,
Procter and Gamble Co., Cincinnati, Ohio. Environmental Water Quality Research Dept.
A. G. Payne.
Water Research, Vol 9, No 4, p 437-445, April 1975. 13 fig, 7 ref, 3 append.

Descriptors: *Algae, *Bioassay, *Nutrients, *Sewage, *Analytical techniques, Phytoplankton, Microorganisms, Assay, Testing, Water analysis, Water chemistry, Water quality, Sewage treatment, Nutrient requirements, Productivity, Water properties, Growth rates, *Pollutant identification.
Identifiers: Selenastrum capricornutum, Microcystis aeruginosa, Anabaena flos-aquae.

The Algal Assay Procedure (AAP): Bottle Test utilizes three test organisms which, under standardized culture conditions, give a range of responses to the physical and nutritional states of test waters. The test algae of the AAP are Selenastrum capricornutum, Microcystis aeruginosa, and Anabaena flos-aquae. The responses of these organisms to light intensities and to micro- and macronutrients were described. Phosphate spikes as low as 1-2 micrograms P/1 were shown to give a measurable bioassay response in highly oligotrophic waters. The AAP test algae were used to assess the effects of nutrient enrichment with sewage in waters from a cross section of U.S. lakes. Enrichment of oligotrophic waters with primary or secondary sewage effluent results in significant growth of the three algae, while sewage additions to eutrophic waters cause little or no significant increase in algal growth rate or maximum standing crop. The response of the AAP algae also indicate the nutrient removal by tertiary treatment greatly reduces the stimulatory properties of sewage. In the presence of tertiary sewage, growth rate and maximum standing crop of the three test organisms are near those of lake water controls. The AAP test protocol was shown to be useful in the determination of limiting nutrients and in the comparison of the algal growth potential of natural waters to that of defined media. (Henley-ISWS)
W75-08710

STANDARD CONDUCTIVITY CELL FOR MEASUREMENT OF SEA WATER SALINITY AND TEMPERATURE,
Westinghouse Electric Corp., Pittsburgh, Pa. (Assignee).
For primary bibliographic entry see Field 7B.
W75-08760

THE RADIOACTIVE, METALLIC AND BACTERIAL POLLUTANTS IN THE ESTUARY OF THE ESCAUT (SCHELT) RIVER AND ON THE COAST OF BELGIUM, (IN FRENCH),
Institut Royal des Sciences Naturelles de Belgique, Brussels. Lab. for Oceanographic Physics.
E. Peeters, and M. Mertens.
Bull Inst R Sci Nat Belg Biol. Vol 49, No 12, 1-10. Illus. 1973.

Descriptors: Rivers, *Europe, *Pollutants, *Estuaries, Water pollution sources, *Sampling, Analysis, Analytical techniques, Uranium, Radiochemical analysis, Bacteria, Radioactive wastes, Spectrophotometry, *Pollutant identification.
Identifiers: Bacteria pollution, *Belgium, Escaut River, Metallic pollution, Radioactive pollution, Schelde, Spectrophotometry, Schelt River, Spectro-photometric methods.

The Institute of Natural Sciences (Belgium) conducted a study of the different kinds of pollution, using the newest techniques of sampling, treatment and protection of samples for analysis in the laboratory. Activities in microCi/kg for radioactive Cs137, Ce144, and Bi214/T1208 were recorded and charted from samplings at several different stations at high and low tides and in sediments. Gamma-spectrophotometry of suspended material retained on filters are reported. Clay sediments have the highest radioactive Cs content. Samples from the Schelt estuary show a Bi214/T1208 ratio in excess of 1, indicating U contamination from the river itself.--Copyright 1975, Biological Abstracts, Inc.
W75-08774

QUALITY OF PUBLIC WATER SUPPLIES OF NEW YORK, MAY 1972-MAY 1973.
Geological Survey, Albany, N.Y.
Open-file report, 1975. 8 fig, 2 tab, 11 ref.

Descriptors: *Water quality, *Chemical analysis, *Water supply, *New York, Sampling, *Data collections, Sites, Inorganic compounds, Nutrients, Coliforms, Trace elements, Hydrologic data, Pollutant identification.

This report is the second in a series that presents analytical results of water samples collected in a continuing study of the quality of public water supplies in the State of New York. From May 16, 1972, to May 3, 1973, samples were collected from 233 public water supply and 13 industrial systems. The general locations of the systems are shown on maps. A total of 739 samples were collected: 498 raw-water samples, 52 treated-water samples, and 189 distribution-system samples. Paired raw and treated or distribution samples were collected from 17 systems. Thirty-two sites were selected for repetitive sampling. Raw water samples were collected from 16 systems at about 2-week intervals. Raw and treated samples were collected from 13 systems and from three New York City distribution sampling sites at about 3-month intervals. Analyses are arranged in three columns. Major constituents, selected physical properties, and minor constituents determined in the Albany laboratory are in the first column. Minor constituents determined by spectrographic analysis in the Denver laboratory and total coliform bacteria colony counts made in the field by USGS personnel are in the second column. Pesticide and related constituents determined in the Washington laboratory are in the third column. (Woodard-USGS)
W75-08832

WATER RESOURCES DATA FOR NEBRASKA, 1973: PART 2. WATER QUALITY RECORDS.
Geological Survey, Lincoln, Nebr.
Data Report, 1975. 212 p, 1 fig, 4 tab, 25 ref.

Descriptors: *Pollutant identification, *Water quality, *Chemical analysis, *Nebraska, Surface waters, Groundwater, Physical properties, Sediment transport, Particle size, Inorganic compounds, Biological properties, Water temperature, Sampling, Sites, *Data collections, Hydrologic data, Well data.

Water-resources data for the 1973 water year for Nebraska include records of data for the chemical and physical characteristics of surface and groundwater. Data on the quality of surface water (chemical, biological, temperature, and sediment) were collected from 64 sampling sites. Chemical quality data are reported for 57 of these sites; water temperature for 16; and sediment analyses for 10 of the sites. Records of chemical analyses and well data are given for about 700 groundwater sites. Records for pertinent water-quality stations in border States are included. (Woodard-USGS)
W75-08833

STREAM RECONNAISSANCE FOR NUTRIENTS AND OTHER WATER-QUALITY PARAMETERS, GREATER PITTSBURGH REGION, PENNSYLVANIA,
Geological Survey, Carnegie, Pa.
R. M. Beall.
Available from the National Technical Information Service, Springfield, Va 22161 as PB-241 493, $3.75 in paper copy, $2.25 in microfiche. Water-Resources Investigations 50-74, February 1975. 47 p, 7 fig, 2 plate, 4 tab, 30 ref.

Descriptors: *Pollutant identification, *Wnter quality, *Streams, *Regional analysis, *Nutrients, *Pennsylvania, Chemical analysis, Data collections, Chemical properties, Inorganic compounds, Water pollution sources, Sampling.

Eighty-five stream sites in and near the six-county Greater Pittsburgh Region were sampled in mid-June 1971 and again in mid-October 1972. Data are reported for 89 sites (including 4 substitute sites sampled in the second period). Drainage areas of the basins sampled ranged from 4.1 to 19,500 square miles (10.6 to 50,500 square kilometers). The chemical analyses include constituents of three general classes: (1) nutrients, (2) activity indicators, and (3) dominant anions. Nutrient concentrations were high enough to indicate potential problems at about a quarter of the sampling sites. Temperature, dissolved oxygen, and pH values indicated a generally favorable capacity for regeneration or recovery from degradation, although a number of streams east of the Allegheny and Monongahela Rivers are marginal or lacking in that capacity. Regionally, sulfate is the dominant ion and was observed in concentrations of 40 milligrams per litre or more at 90% of the sites. Bicarbonate exceeded 100 milligrams per litre at 22 sites. A moderate to high degree of mineralization, as indicated by conductance readings of more than 500 micromhos per centimeter at half of the sampling sites, is a characteristic of the region's surface waters. (Woodard-USGS)
W75-08835

EVALUATION OF METHODS FOR ESTIMATING STREAM WATER QUALITY PARAMETERS IN A TRANSIENT MODEL FROM STOCHASTIC DATA,
Kansas State Univ., Manhattan. Dept. of Chemical Engineering.
For primary bibliographic entry see Field 5B.
W75-08849

5B. Sources Of Pollution

EFFECTS OF URBANIZATION ON WATER QUALITY,
Water Resources Engineers, Inc., Springfield, Va. and DeKalb County Planning Dept., Decatur, Ga.
R. P. Shubinski, and S. N. Nelson.
Available from the National Technical Information Service, Springfield, Va. 22161, as PB-242 297, $3.75 in paper copy, $2.25 in microfiche. American Society of Civil Engineers, Urban Water Resources Research Program Technical Memorandum No 26, New York, NY, March, 1975, 34 p, 11 tab, 7 fig, 29 ref. OWRT C-5045(No 4224)(2), OWRT 14-31-0001-4224.

Descriptors: *Comprehensive planning, *Urbanization, *Water pollution sources, *Land use, *Environmental effects, *Impaired water quality, Pollutants, Erosion, Hydrologic aspects, Drainage effects, Aquatic environment, Project planning, *City planning.
Identifiers: *Metropolitan studies, *Receiving waters, Storm sewer discharges, Combined sewer overflows, Stormwater treatment.

The intended audience for this Technical Memorandum is urban planners. Numerical values are given whenever available. Land use and water quality relationships are outlined, including the relations between source and type of water pollution. Effects of land use on point discharges are enumerated, for residential, commercial, industrial and power generation land uses. A parallel evaluation is made of nonpoint discharges from urban storm runoff, agricultural drainage, construction runoff and resource extraction. Also, effects of land use are categorized within environmentally sensitive areas, such as flood-plains and shorelines, aquifer recharge areas and estuaries and wetlands. (McPherson-ASCE)
W75-08351

THE CONTRIBUTION OF AGRICULTURE TO EUTROPHICATION OF SWISS WATERS: I. RESULTS OF DIRECT MEASUREMENTS IN THE DRAINAGE AREA OF VARIOUS MAIN DRAINAGE CHANNELS,
Eidgenoessische Technische Hochschule, Kastienbaum (Switzerland). Hydrobiology Lab.
R. Gaechter, and O. J. Furrer.
Schweiz Z Hydrol, Vol 34, No 1, p 41-70, 1972. Illus.

Descriptors: Europe, *Eutrophication, Agriculture, *Drainage area, Erosion, Algae, Nitrogen, Nutrients, *Lakes, Phosphorous, Essential nutrients, Nitrogen compounds, Phosphorus compounds, *Aquatic algae, *Drains, *Channels, *Measurement.
Identifiers: Alpine, *Switzerland.

In Swiss lakes, the growth of algae is generally limited by the supply of P but sometimes also by that of N. This nutrient supply into waters originates from the atmosphere (rainfall, fixation and N), from the soils in the drainage area (leaching and erosion) and from wastewater. The P and N loss in soil dependent on the method of cultivation, climatic conditions and topography was assessed. The increased loss of P in the Lower Alpine regions used for agricultural purposes accounts for the greater amount of specific run-off (m3/km2. year) and for the steep positions favoiring erosion. It is assumed that the higher rate of N in soils of the lowland regions where the climate is milder, is caused on the one hand by the more intensive microbiological mobilization and on the other by the more frequent application of nitrogenous fertilizers. The agricultural contribution to the total nutrient load of a lake depends on the cultivation method in the drainage area, as well as on the population density and the effectiveness of wastewater purification. As a rule, it is assumed that for conditions prevailing in Switzerland, more than 70% of N, but less than 50% of P discharged into the lakes, originate from the soil of drainage areas. In the case of balanced growth, N and P are assimilated by algae in a weight ratio of about 7:1. The N/P ratio in receiving water bodies of the Lower Alpine region, not influenced by wastewater, amounts to about 30, in the lowland region to about 80 and would only decrease to about 7 when mixed with untreated sewage (N/P = 4 : 1) from a population of 200-300 inhabitants/km2. From those 2 macro-elements one can infer that in most cases there is a nitrogen surplus, while the P supply is the growth limiting element in algae. A tolerable supply of P from the drainage area dependent on the mean depth of a lake and the surrounding factor fU (fU = drainage area/lake surface) is given. The danger exists that in many cases this critical value is attained or even exceeded through P depletion in soil alone.--Copyright 1974, Biological Abstracts, Inc.
W75-08376

MODELLING PRIMARY PRODUCTIN IN WATER BODIES: A NUMERICAL APPROACH THAT ALLOWS VERTICAL INHOMOGENEITIES,
Fisheries Research Board of Canada, Winnipeg, (Manitoba). Freshwater Inst.
For primary bibliographic entry see Field 5C.
W75-08379

RELATIONSHIP OF VARIOUS INDICES OF WATER QUALITY TO DENITRIFICATION IN SURFACE WATERS,
Purdue Univ., Lafayette, Ind. Dept. of Agronomy.
For primary bibliographic entry see Field 5A.
W75-08384

EGGSHELL THINNING, CHLORINATED HYDROCARBONS, AND MERCURY IN INLAND AQUATIC BIRD EGGS, 1969 AND 1970,
Wisconsin Univ., Madison. Dept. of Wildlife Ecology.
For primary bibliographic entry see Field 5C.
W75-08391

LIQUID BRINE IN ICE SHELVES,
Scott Polar Research Inst., Cambridge (England).
For primary bibliographic entry see Field 2C.
W75-08407

THE FORMATION OF BRINE DRAINAGE FEATURES IN YOUNG SEA ICE,
Washington Univ., Seattle. Dept. of Oceanography.
For primary bibliographic entry see Field 2C.
W75-08408

A STOCHASTIC MODEL OF DISPERSION IN A POROUS MEDIUM,
Ecole Polytechnique, Montreal (Quebec).
For primary bibliographic entry see Field 2F.
W75-08435

POLYNUCLEAR AROMATIC HYDROCARBONS IN RAW, POTABLE AND WASTE WATER,
Imperial Coll. of Science and Technology, London (England). Dept. of Public Health Engineering.
For primary bibliographic entry see Field 5A.
W75-08453

NITRIFICATION IN RIVERS IN THE TRENT BASIN,
Water Pollution Research Lab., Stevenage (England).
E. J. C. Curtis, K. Durrant, and M. M. I. Harman.
Water Research, Vol 9, No 3, p 255-268, March 1975. 4 fig, 13 tab, 15 ref.

Descriptors: *Nitrification, *Rivers, *Microbial degradation, Microorganisms, Aquatic microorganisms, Bacteria, Nitrites, Nitrates, Oxidation, Biochemical oxygen demand, Water pollution, Biochemistry, Sediments.
Identifiers: *River Trent basin, River Tame.

The presence of autotrophic nitrifying bacteria in the waters and sediments of both the River Trent and its polluted tributary the River Tame was established and their concentrations determined. Nitrification was shown to occur mainly in the sediments, where it was estimated that at least 80% of the oxidation of ammonia occurred. (Sims-ISWS)
W75-08456

THE EFFECT OF WEATHERING ON A CRUDE OIL RESIDUE EXPOSED AT SEA,
University Coll. of North Wales, Bangor. Dept. of Marine Biology.
S. J. Davis, and C. F. Gibbs.
Water Research, Vol 9, No 3, p 275-285, March 1975. 7 fig, 3 tab, 25 ref.

Descriptors: *Oil wastes, *Weathering, *Sea water, Emulsions, Oil spills, Biodegradation, Degradation(Decomposition), Chemical degradation, Chemical analysis, Chromatography, Chemical properties, Physical properties, Viscosity, Oil, Oily water, Water pollution.

Kuwait crude oil residues have been exposed to weathering at sea (Langstone Harbour, Portsmouth) for 2 yr, in the form of a water-in-oil emulsion ('chocolate mousse') in a floating layer about 1.4 cm thick. One batch of oil was exposed in a tank open to tidal flushing below the water line, and a second batch was exposed in a closed tank. A number of chemical and physical properties of the oil were measured at intervals, as were the concentrations of mineral nutrients and bacterial numbers in the sea water. Asphaltenes, specific gravity, and viscosity all increased, as did the 'polar' fraction from liquid chromatography. The n-alkanes decreased to about half the original levels in the open tank but were little altered in the closed tank. The constancy of vanadium and nickel concentrations suggest that no net loss of oil occurred, the substantial changes in properties deriving from chemical modification (probably oxidation arid polymerization) of oil components, rather than mineralization (conversion to carbon dioxide and water) of some componenets leaving a residue of altered composition. It was not determined which of several processes predominated in causing these changes, but it is thought likely that in this thick layer of mousse auto-oxidation predominated over biodegradation. (Sims-ISWS)
W75-08457

ANALYSIS OF RUNOFF FROM SOUTHERN GREAT PLAINS FEEDLOTS,
Agricultural Research Service, Bushland, Tex. Southwestern Great Plains Research Center.
R. N. Clark, A. D. Schneider, and B. A. Stewart.
Transactions of the American Society of Agricultural Engineers, Vol. 18, No. 2, p 319-322. March-April 1975. 6 fig. 7 ref.

Descriptors: *Feed lots, *Surface runoff, *Water quality, *Agricultural runoff, Farm wastes, Great Plains, Runoff, Confinement pens, Cattle, *Texas, Path of pollutants, Pollutant identification.
Identifiers: *Feedlot runoff.

Runoff amounts and chemical quality were measured from a Southern Great Plains cattle feedlot at Bushland, Texas. The rainfall-runoff relationship for runoff-producing storms was linear, with about one-third of the rainfall in excess of 10 mm ending up as runoff. Runoff amounts were smaller but concentrations of various runoff constituents were higher than those found for cattle feedlots elsewhere. Low rainfall, high evaporation rates, and high stocking rates cause the manure pack in the feedlots to contain more salts, thus allowing increased concentrations in runoff. A dilution factor of about five parts well water to one part feedlot runoff would reduce the salinity hazard for irrigation from very high to medium for most holding ponds in the Southern Great Plains. Runoff caught in playas where the area of the feedlot is one-fifth or less of the total watershed could be considered as having a low or medium salinity hazard. (Jess-ISWS)
W75-08460

ENVIRONMENTAL EFFECTS OF DREDGING AND SPOIL DISPOSAL,
Washington State Dept. of Ecology, Olympia.
For primary bibliographic entry see Field 5C.
W75-08465

PHOSPHORUS SOURCES FOR LOWER GREEN BAY, LAKE MICHIGAN,
Wisconsin Univ., Green Bay. Ecosystems Analysis.
P. E. Sager, and J. H. Wiersma.
Journal of Water Pollution Control Federation, Vol 47, No 3, p 504-514, March 1975. 3 fig, 2 tab, 18 ref.

Descriptors: *Water pollution sources, *Phosphorus, *Lake Michigan, Effluents, Eutrophication, Nutrients, Phosphates, Phosphorus compounds, Wastewater(Pollution), Water quality, Path of pollutants, Farm wastes, Algae, Water pollution, Sewage treatment, Runoff, Wisconsin.
Identifiers: *Green Bay(Wis), *Fox River(Wis), Orthophosphate.

The major sources of phosphorus for lower Green Bay were quantified and the significance of nonpoint sources in the lower Fox River drainage basin were determined. Sources examined included municipal waste treatment plants, surface runoff from rural and urban areas, industrial discharges, and Lake Winnebago. The relative importance of the major sources (rural runoff, Lake Winnebago, municipal treatment plants) varies considerably on a seasonal basis. Nonpoint sources (rural runoff and Lake Winnebago), in the absence of controls, were expected to maintain high levels of phosphorus in Green Bay, despite control measures being implemented for municipal treatment plants in the drainage basin. (Sims-ISWS)
W75-08467

IMPACTS OF FOREST MANAGEMENT PRACTICES ON THE AQUATIC ENVIRONMENT-PHASE II,
Washington Cooperative Fishery Unit, Seattle.
R. R. Whitney, and T. E. Wright.
Available from the National Technical Information Service, Springfield, Va. 22161, as PB-242 432, $3.75 in paper copy, $2.25 in microfiche. Annual Report, Quinault Resources Development Project, Quinault Tribal Council, Taholak, Washington, (April 30, 1975). 38 p, 16 fig, 2 tab. OWRT C-5336(no 4223)(2).

Descriptors: *Acid streams, *Salmonids, *Water pollution sources, Clear-cutting, Reforestation, Organic acids, Decomposing organic matter, Aquatic insects, Aquatic productivity, Drainage effects, Soil chemistry, Path of pollutants, Acidic soils, Lysimeter, Wood wastes, *Washington, Land use, Forest management, Environment.
Identifiers: *Gel permeation chromatography, *Cedar leachates, Quinault Indian Reservation(Wash), High water tables.

An investigation of stream quality as related to land use variables was undertaken on the Quinault Reservation. Low pH conditions and cedar leachates have been shown to play a part in low salmonid productivity. Investigations indicate that iron and other heavy metals in the soil matrix play important roles in stream pH levels. Lower pH resulting from the release of iron oxides has also been associated with chemical reactions occurring during groundwater movement through areas with different redox potentials. Laboratory analyses indicate that tropolones are the principal toxic substances in Western Red Cedar. Lethal effects of tropolones as related to temperature, iron concentration, acclimatization time, and pH were investigated in laboratory experiments using fish stocks of different genetic composition. No differences were found between genetic stocks or pH variations. Temperature, iron concentrations, and acclimatization times were significant factors in tropoline toxicity. No lethal levels of tropolones were found in study area streams. (See also W74-12355).
W75-08468

HEAT AND MOISTURE CONDUCTION IN UNSATURATED SOILS,
Arkansas Univ., Fayetteville. Dept. of Chemical Engineering.
J. A. Havens, and R. E. Babcock.
Available from the National Technical Information Service, Springfield, Va 22161 as PB-242 328, $5.25 in paper copy, $2.25 in microfiche. Arkansas Water Resources Research Center, Fayettevills, Publication No 25, May 1975. 108 p, 21 fig, 4 tab, 77 ref, 2 append. OWRT A-014-ARK(2), 74-31-0001-3804.

Descriptors: *Thermal pollution, *Heat transfer, Moisture, *Mathematical models, Soils, Soil moisture, Conduction, Forecasting, Pipes, Soil temperature, Soil profiles, Cooling water.
Identifiers: Waste heat, *Soil warming, *Moisture transfer, Underground pipes.

Mathematical models are developed for the prediction of heat transfer from hot water pipes buried in the soil. Heat transfer in the absence of moisture transfer is described as a function of the difference between the temperatre of the pipe and the temperature of the soil surface. The energy balance is used to determine the longitudinal temperature distribution of the water. The method is extended to describe a system of equally spaced, parallel buried pipes. Soil temperature profiles

around the pipes are presented. The model is used to calculate the land area that can be heated by an underground piping system carrying cooling water from the condensers of a 1000 MW nuclear-electric plant. A new development of the phenomenological equations for coupled heat and moisture flow, based on the theory of irreversible thermodynamics, is presented. Solutions of the equations for boundary conditions representative of buried piping systems designed for simultaneous soil heating and irrigation are presented.
W75-08477

DISTRIBUTION, CULTIVATION AND CHEMICAL DESTRUCTION OF GALLIONELLA FROM ALABAMA GROUND WATER,
Alabama Univ., University. Dept. of Microbiology.
R. D. Christian, Jr.
Available from the National Technical Information Service, Springfield, Va 22161 as PB-242 341, $6.25 in paper copy, $2.25 in microfiche. M S Thesis, 1975. 145 p, 25 tab, 15 fig, 62 ref, 2 append. OWRT B-045-ALA(1). 1431-0001-3855.

Descriptors: *Iron bacteria, *Groundwater, *Microbiology, *Hydrogeology, *Alabama, Water wells, Disinfection, Water treatment, Ammonium compounds, Water pollution sources.
Identifiers: *Gallionella.

Results of hydrogeologic and microbiologic studies were combined to determine the ecology of the iron bacteria, Gallionella, in water systems in Alabama and to find a 'chemical cure' for water wells contaminated with this organism. Treatment of laboratory strains of Gallionella with disinfectants indicated that a chemical cure is possible; however, only field experiments can determine if permanent cures occur. Success in the future will probably depend on the effectiveness of quaternary ammonium compounds which have several advantages over chlorine compounds.
W75-08479

WATER AND SOLUTE TRANSPORT IN LAKELAND FINE SAND,
Florida Univ., Gainesville. Dept. of Soil Sciences.
A. A. Elzeftaway.
Available from the National Technical Information Service, Springfield, Va 22161 as PB-242 342, $5.25 in paper copy, $2.25 in microfiche. PH D Thesis, 1974. 104 p, 18 fig, 5 tab, 78 ref, append. OWRT A-026-FLA(1). 14-31-0001-5009.

Descriptors: *Infiltration, *Herbicides, Fertilizers, Soils, *Sands, *2-4-D, *Chlorides, Solutes, Soil water, *Path of pollutants, Adsorption, Soil analysis.
Identifiers: Lakeland fine sand.

The objective was to investigate effects of three water supply rates--2,4 and 8 cm/hr--and three initial soil water contents--1,2, 10.9, and 20.2% by volume--upon the simultaneous transport of water and solutes--2,4-D herbicide and chloride--in vertical columns of Lakeland fine sand. Columns were prepared by packing air-dry soil into cylinders 7.6 cm diameter and 107 cm long. A specific volume of aqueous solution containing 57.9 ppm chloride and 5 ppm 2,4-D was introduced and displaced through each column. Gamma-ray attenuation and pressure-transducer-tensiometers were used to precisely monitor soil-water content and pressure distributions with time. Soil solution was extracted at selected depth intervals along the soil columns and extracted samples were then analyzed for 2,4-D and chloride content. Depths to which chloride and 2,4-D moved for a given quantity of water infiltrated into the surface of the soil was found to depend upon the surface water flux. Increasing water application rates resulted in an increased water content in surface soil and in shallower displacement of chloride and 2,4-D for equal quantities of accumulative infiltration. For a given quantity of water infiltrated, initial soil-water content did not influence depths of chloride or 2,4-D transport. Adsorption caused 2,4-D distributions to lag behind those for chloride for all experiments. (Morgan-Florida)
W75-08480

ANALYSIS AND DESIGN OF SETTLING BASINS FOR IRRIGATION RETURN FLOW,
Idaho Univ., Moscow. Dept. of Civil Engineering.
For primary bibliographic entry see Field 5G.
W75-08484

NON-EQUALIBRIUM THERMODYNAMIC TREATMENT OF TRANSPORT PROCESSES IN GROUND-WATER FLOW,
Nevada Univ., Reno. Desert Research Inst.
For primary bibliographic entry see Field 2F.
W75-08488

EMPIRICAL DATA ON LONGITUDINAL DISPERSION IN RIVERS,
Geological Survey, Denver, Colo.
C. F. Nordin, Jr., and G. V. Sabol.
Available from NTIS, Springfield, Va 22161 as PB-240 740, $7.50 in paper copy, $2.25 in microfiche. Water-Resources Investigations 20-74, August 1974. 332 p, 58 fig, 5 tab, 35 ref, 2 append.

Descriptors: *Dispersion, *Streams, *Mixing, Data collections, Hydrologic data, Diffusion, Path of pollutants.

Empirical data on longitudinal dispersion processes in rivers are compiled from published and unpublished sources. Fifty-one sets of data, covering flows from about 30 cubic feet per second to 241,000 cubic feet per second are analyzed graphically. For a few cases, the empirical data agree very well with the one-dimensional Fickian-type diffusion theory, but for many of the data, the dispersion processes exhibit a non-Fickian behavior with the properties that the variance of the concentration distribution of a conservative dispersant increases with time. The one-dimensioual Fickian-type diffusion equation does not adequately describe longitudinal dispersion processes in some rivers. (Knapp-USGS)
W75-08495

WASTE-LOAD ALLOCATION STUDIES FOR ARKANSAS STREAMS, WHITE RIVER BASIN, SEGMENT 4A,
Geological Survey, Little Rock, Ark.
J. E. Terry, B. F. Lambert, E. E. Morris, and A. H. Ludwig.
Open-file report, 1975. 72 p, 2 fig, 4 tab, 5 ref, 3 append.

Descriptors: *Low flow, *Path of pollutants, *Arkansas, Waste dilution, Model studies, Mathematical models, Water pollution control, *Waste assimilative capacity, Water quality standards.
Identifiers: *White River(Ark), *Waste-load allocation.

Data and the results of a waste-load allocation study are presented for Segment 4A of the White River water-quality management planning basin. The water-quality model was calibrated for dissolved oxygen, total dissolved solids, chlorides, and sulfates, by using existing waste-load data and streamflow and water-quality data collected during summer low-flow conditions. Waste-load analyses were made by adjusting the calibrated model to include waste loads expected to exist 5 years from the present time (1974), in combination with the minimum average flow for 7 consecutive days that is expected to occur on the average of once in 10 years (Q7-10). The segment includes a 101-mile reach of the White River and selected reaches of its principal and minor tributaries. Dischargers in the segment consist of 8 municipalities and 5 industries. Plots of dissolved oxygen (DO), total dissolved solids (TDS), chlorides (Cl), and sulfates (SO4) resulting from 5-year waste-load projection and Q7-10 low-flow conditions are given. The plots show that under the specified conditions the concentration of dissolved oxygen, total dissolved solids, chlorides, and sulfates in the White River meet standards set by the State of Arkansas. Carbonaceous waste discharge in terms of 5-day biochemical oxygen demand (CBOD5), nitrogenous oxygen demand as ammonia nitrogen (NH3-N), chlorides (Cl), and sulfates (SO4) for each discharger are summarized. (Knapp-USGS)
W75-08500

WASTE-LOAD ALLOCATION STUDIES FOR ARKANSAS STREAMS, WHITE RIVER BASIN, SEGMENT 4D,
Geological Survey, Little Rock, Ark.
J. E. Reed, J. E. Terry, M. E. Broom, and J. W. Stephens.
Open-file report, 1975. 55 p, 2 fig, 4 tab, 5 ref, 3 append.

Descriptors: *Low flow, *Path of pollutants, *Arkansas, Waste dilution, Model studies, Mathematical models, Water pollution control, *Waste assimilative capacity, Water quality standards.
Identifiers: *White River(Ark), *Waste-load allocation.

Data and the results of a waste-load allocation study are presented for Segment 4D of the White River water-quality management planning basin. The water-quality model was calibrated for dissolved oxygen, total dissolved solids, chlorides, and sulfates, by using existing waste-load data and streamflow and water-quality data collected during summer low-flow conditions. Waste-load analyses were made by adjusting the calibrated model to include waste loads expected to exist 5 years from the present time (1974), in combination with the minimum average flow for 7 consecutive days that is expected to occur on the average of once in 10 years (Q7-10). The segment consists chiefly of a 78-mile reach of the White River, a 38-mile reach of the Cypress Bayou, a 58-mile reach of Bayou Des Arc, and a 48-mile reach of Wattensaw Bayou. Dischargers in the segment consist of six municipalities. Plots of dissolved oxygen (DO), total dissolved solids (TDS), chlorides (Cl), and sulfates (SO4) resulting from 5-year waste-load projection and Q7-10 low-flow conditions are given. The plots show that under the specified conditions the concentration of dissolved oxygen, total dissolved solids, chlorides, and sulfates in the White River, Segment 4D, meet standards set by the State of Arkansas. Carbonaceous waste discharge in terms of 5-day biochemical oxygen demand (CBOD5), nitrogenous oxygen demand as ammonia nitrogen (NH3-N), chlorides (Cl), and sulfates (SO4) for each discharger are summarized. (Knapp-USGS)
W75-08502

WASTE-LOAD ALLOCATION STUDIES FOR ARKANSAS STREAMS, OUACHITA RIVER BASIN, SEGMENT 2E,
Geological Survey, Little Rock, Ark.
J. E. Terry, E. E. Morris, and J. W. Stephens.
Open-file report, 1975. 24 p, 2 fig, 4 tab, 5 ref, append.

Descriptors: *Low flow, *Path of pollutants, *Arkansas, Waste dilution, Model studies, Mathematical models, Water pollution control, *Waste assimilative capacity, Water quality standards.
Identifiers: *Ouachita River(Ark), *Waste-load allocation.

Data and the results of a waste-load allocation study are presented for Segment 2E of the Ouachita River water-quality management planning basin. Data for Segment 2E were not sufficient to apply the water-quality model. Instead, a method for determining target loads (maximum-waste load a stream can assimilate before dissolved oxygen is depleted below standards) was

used for all tributaries. The segment consists chiefly of a 69-mile reach of Cornie Creek and a 65-mile reach of Bayou de Loutre, and the principal tributaries along the reaches of these two streams. Dischargers in the segment consist of 2 municipalities and 6 industries. Waste-load conditions, present and 5-year projected, for each discharger in the segment are given. Carbonaceous waste discharge in terms of 5-day biochemical oxygen demand (CBOD5), nitrogenous oxygen demand as ammonia nitrogen (NH3-N), chlorides (Cl), and sulfates (SO4) from each discharger on the streams in Segment 2E are summarized. (Knapp-USGS)
W75-08504

CHEMISTRY OF SUBSURFACE WATERS,
Geological Survey, Menlo Park, Calif.
For primary bibliographic entry see Field 2K.
W75-08506

GROUND-WATER CONDITIONS IN THE FRANKLIN AREA, SOUTHEASTERN VIRGINIA,
Geological Survey, Reston, Va.
For primary bibliographic entry see Field 7C.
W75-08509

CHEMICAL QUALITY OF GROUND WATER IN THE WESTERN OSWEGO RIVER BASIN, NEW YORK,
Geological Survey, Albany, N.Y.
L. J. Crain.
New Uork Department of Environmental Conservation, Albany, Basin Planning Report ORB-3, 1975. 69 p, 17 fig, 4 tab, 21 ref.

Descriptors: *Water quality, *Groundwater, *New York Water chemistry, Sampling, Hydrologic data, Data collections, Hydrogeology.
Identifiers: *Oswego River basin(NY), Finger Lakes(NY).

The Western Oswego River basin is an area of about 2,600 square miles in central New York. Within the boundaries of the area is all the drainage into (1) the four largest Finger Lakes (Cayuga, Seneca, Keuka, and Canandaigua) and (2) part of the New York State Barge Canal. The geology of the basin generally consists of glacial deposits overlying bedrock of Silurian and Devonian age. The bedrock consists of shale, siltstone, and sandstone, in the southern half of the basin, and limestone, dolomite, and gypsiferous shale in the northern half. The dissolved-solids concentration of precipitation in the Western Oswego River basin is about 10 mg/liter, whereas that of overland flow and high streamflow generally ranges from 50 to 300 mg/liter. The dissolved-solids concentration of the water commouly tapped by wells in the southern half of the basin generally ranges from 150 to 500 mg/liter; in the area north of the outcrop of the Onondaga Limestone, it generally ranges from 500 to more than 1,000 mg/liter. Highest concentrations were found in deeper wells and in the low-lying areas that are points of groundwater discharge. Heavy pumping in the northern part of the basin is likely to result in a deterioration of the chemical quality of the water except in those areas adjacent to the New York State Barge Canal, where better quality water may be induced to replace that pumped. No major groundwater quality problems are anticipted in the southern half of the basin. (Knapp-USGS)
W75-08515

SALINE GROUND-WATER RESOURCES OF LEE COUNTY, FLORIDA,
Geological Survey, Tallahassee, Fla.
For primary bibliographic entry see Field 2F.
W75-08517

WATER QUALITY OF THE LAKE SISKIYOU AREA AND A REACH OF UPPER SACRAMENTO RIVER BELOW BOX CANYON DAM, CALIFORNIA, MAY 1970 THROUGH SEPTEMBER 1971,
Geological Survey, Menlo Park, Calif.
A. E. Dong, and R. L. Tobin.
Available from National Technical Information Service, Springfield, Va. 22161, as PB-241 673, $3.75 in paper copy, $2.25 in microfiche. Water-Resources Investigations 15-73, September 1973. 40 p, 5 fig, 12 tab, 8 ref.

Descriptors: *Water quality, *Lakes, *California, Data collections, Chemical analyses, Water properties, Streams, Specific conductance, Dissolved oxygen, Nitrogen, Phosphorus, Coliforms, Water temperature, Streamflow, Water pollution sources, Thermocline.
Identifiers: *Lake Siskiyou area(Calif).

Periodic field and laboratory measurements of water quality in samples from streams tributary to Lake Siskiyou, from the lake itself, and from selected downstream sites near three sewage-disposal ponds indicated that water in most of the inflows, in the lake, and in the downstream reach of the Sacramento River contains low concentrations of nitrogen and phosphorus. Water samples from Wagon Creek and Cold Creek contain higher concentrations of nitrogen and phosphorus and have higher counts of total and fecal coliform bacteria than the water in samples from the other tributary streams. Analyses of samples from above and below the fish hatchery on Big Spring Creek (tributary to Cold Creek) indicate that the water downstream from the hatchery is higher in coliform bacteria counts, lower in dissolved oxygen, and higher in nitrogen and phosphorus concentrations. Thermal and dissolved oxygen stratification occur in Lake Siskiyou during the summer. In the Sacramento River below Lake Siskiyou, samples collected at sites downstream from the sewage effluent exhibit higher average concentrations of total phosphorus than samples from the upstream site. Concentrations of other constituents and coliform bacteria counts are similar in samples from sites upstream and downstream from the sewage effluent. (Woodward-USGS)
W75-08521

MICROBIOLOGICAL STUDY OF THE INFLUENCE OF CHALK ON POND MUD, (IN FRENCH),
Station d'Hydrobiologie Continentale, Biarritz (France).
M. Laurent, and J. Sechet.
Ann Hydrobiol. Vol 4, No 2, p 143-168, 1973. Illus. English summary.

Descriptors: Europe, *Mud, *Analyses, *Pollutant identification, *Industrial wastes, Bioindicators, Analytical techniques, Biological communities, Pollutants, *Sewage bacteria, Microorganisms, Chemical analysis.
Identifiers: Algae, Calcium carbonate, *Chalk, Characeae, *France(Leon Pond), Saprophobous organisms, Saproxeneous organisms, Saprophilous organisms.

The biological mechanisms resulting from the influence of CaCO3 on mud were studied. Research was carried out in the field, at Leon Pond (Landes, Frances), in relation to different kinds of factory wastes and municipal sewage being determined. The zones of pollution were determined according to the communities of indicator organisms and on the basis of chemical investigations. A number of species or organisms were classified into ecological groups: 1. saprophobous organisms, 2. saproxenous organisms, 3. saprophilous organisms and 4. saprobiontic organisms.--Copyright 1974, Biological Abstracts, Inc.
W75-08522

PB IN PARTICULATES FROM THE LOWER ATMOSPHERE OF THE EASTERN ATLANTIC,
Liverpool Univ. (England). Dept. of Oceanography.
For primary bibliographic entry see Field 5A.
W75-08531

ARTIFICIAL FOG PRODUCED BY INDUSTRIAL EMISSION OF WATER VAPOR (BROUILLARDS ARTIFICIELS PRODUITS PAR EMISSION INDUSTRIELLE DE VAPEUR D'EAU),
Quebec Univ., Chicoutimi. Centre de Recherche du Moyen Nord.
For primary bibliographic entry see Field 5A.
W75-08545

EFFECT OF ATMOSPHERIC STABILITY AND WIND DIRECTION ON WATER TEMPERATURE PREDICTIONS FOR A THERMALLY-LOADED STREAM,
Pennsylvania State Univ., University Park. School of Forest Resources.
D. R. DeWalle.
Available from the National Technical Information Service, Springfield, Va. 22161, as PB=242 531, $3.75 in paper copy, $2.25 in microfiche. Pennsylvania Institute for Research on Land and Water Resources, University Park, Completion Report, January 1975. 29 p, 5 fig, 5 tab, 14 ref. OWRT C-4199(No 9032)(1).

Descriptors: *Heat balance, Air circulation, Fetch, Temperature, Downstream, River flow, *Water temperature, *Thermal pollution, *Forecasting, *Pennsylvania, Equations, *Numerical analysis, Path of pollutants, River forecasting.
Identifiers: Thermal discharge, Downstream water temperature, *Heat exchange rate, *Evaporative heat exchange, Thermally loaded water bodies, Motion of the stream, Free convection, Numerical integration, direct integration, One-dimensional equation, *Susqehanna River(Penn).

A steady-state, one-dimensional equation was used to predict water temperatures in the West Branch Susquehanna River at a point 5.4-km downstream from a thermal discharge for 131 time intervals. Two methods were employed to integrate the equation to predict downstream water temperature: direct integration assuming a constant water surface heat exchange rate calculated from upstream water temperature and numerical integration with the heat exchange rate varying with temperature. Two equations were also used to compute evaporative heat exchange: the Jobson form of the familiar Lake Hefner equation derived under conditions of near-neutral stability and a Russian equation modified after Shulyakovskiy which included a correction for free convection. The direct integration method produced overestimates of heat loss and consequently underestimates of downstream water temperatures. Downstream water temperature prediction errors when the Hefner equation--numerical integration was used were large and well correlated with an index to atmospheric stability ($R2 > 46\%$). Prediction errors were smallest with the Russian equation--numerical integration combination and were not correlated with atmospheric stability ($R2 < 1\%$). (Sink-Penn State)
W75-08576

EXCHANGEABLE INORGANIC PHOSPHATE IN LAKE SEDIMENTS,
Wisconsin Univ., Madison. Water Chemistry Program.
W. C. Li.
Available from the National Technical Information Service, Springfield, Va. 22161, as PB-242 509, $5.75 in paper copy, $2.25 in microfiche. Ph.D. Thesis, 1974. 125 p, 15 tab, 6 fig, 67 ref. OWRT B-022-WIS(10), 14-01-0001-1961.

Descriptors: Sediments, *Phosphorus, *Nutrients, *Rooted aquatic plants, Phosphates, *Lake sediments, *Wisconsin, Water pollution sources.
Identifiers: *Myriophyllum spicatum, *Macrophytes.

The quantity of available P in selected sediments was evaluated by measurement of the amounts of P removed from sediments by Myriophyllum spicatum L. grown in columns containing sediment as the sole P source and amended with other essential nutrients. The relationships between the amount of sediment inorganic P added, the yield and P content of the plants, and the uptake of sediment inorganic P were evaluated. Available P comprised from 12.3 to 17.2% of total sediment inorganic P for the eight lake sediments investigated. Relationships between P uptake by Myriophyllum plants (micrograms phosphorus/gram of sediment) and the total inorganic phosphate, nonoccluded inorganic phosphate and total exchangeable inorganie phosphate contents of sediments were evaluated. Correlation coefficients were 0.99, 0.98, 0.97, respectively, for the dependent variables, namely, total inorganic phosphate, noncclucled inorganic phosphate and total exchangeable inorganic phosphate, indicating that each of these measurements provided a good index of available P in lake sediments. However, the uptake of sediment P by Myriophyllum plants arose mainly from the nonoccluded inorganic phosphate fraction (sodium hydroxide phosphate in calcareous sediments and ammonium fluoride plus sodium hydroxide phosphate in noncalcareous sediments), and most of the exchangeable inorganic P was contained in the nonoccluded inorganic phosphate fraction, indicating that available P was obtained mainly from the exchangeable inorganic P fraction. (Armstrong-Wisconsin)
W75-08577

MICROBIAL AVAILABILITY OF PHOSPHORUS IN LAKE SEDIMENTS,
Wisconsin Univ., Madison. Water Chemistry Lab.
A. Sagher.
Available from the National Technical Information Service, Springfield, Va. 22161, as PB-242 510, $5.75 in paper copy, $2.25 in microfiche. MS Thesis, 1974. 122 p, 18 fig, 24 tab, 48 ref. OWRT A-040-WIS(2), 14-31-0001-3550, 14-31-0001-3850.

Descriptors: Aquatic microorganisms, *Soil bacteria, *Phosphates, Lakes, *Soils, Phosphorus, *Wisconsin, *Scenedesmus, *Lake sediments, Water pollution sources.
Identifiers: *Selenastrum.

The microbial availability of phosphorus (P) in surficial sediments from diverse Wisconsin lakes was evaluated using Selenastrum and Scenedesmus and indigenous sediment populations as test organisms. Phosphorus-deficient algal cells were inoculated into monsterile sediment-water systems amended with all growth nutrients except phosphorus so that the sediment was the sole source of phosphorus (0.6 millegrams phosphorus per liter). The inoculated systems were incubated with intermittent shaking under standard light conditions until microbial biomass increases ceased (3 to 4 weeks), with periodic analysis for : (1) algal cell counts and ATP to provide data on microbial growth responses; (2) levels of dissolved ortho-inorganic phosphate (Pi), sodium hydroxide-extractable Pi, and hydrochloric acid-extractable Pi to provide information on the utilization of different sediment Pi forms. Appropriate controls were included to establish phosphorus deficiency in the test system and assess sediment organic phosphorus mineralization. All sediments supplied sufficient phosphorus to increase microbial biomass about two orders of magnitude. Between 51 and 80% of the sediment Pi was available to the microorganisms. Between 55 and 100% of the nonoccluded iron-bound fraction extracted with sodium hydroxide, but essentially none of the hydrochloric acid-extractable calcium-bound Pi fraction was available. Mineralization of sediment organic phosphorus was minimal.
W75-08578

BIOLOGICAL FEATURES OF INTERTIDAL COMMUNITIES NEAR THE U.S. NAVY SEWAGE OUTFALL, WILSON COVE, SAN CLEMENTE ISLAND, CALIFORNIA,
For primary bibliographic entry see Field 5C.
W75-08585

HEAT TRANSFER AND FLUID MECHANICS OF THE THERMAL POLLUTION PROBLEM,
Virginia Polytechnic Inst. and State Univ., Blacksburg. Dept. of Aerospace and Ocean Engineering.
J. A. Schetz, C. J. Chien, and B. L. Sill.
A paper for the 5th International Heat Transfer Conference, (1974). 5 p, 5 fig, 14 ref. OWRR B-041-VA(4).

Descriptors: *Heat transfer, *Fluid mechanics, *Thermal pollution, Jets, Specific heat, Velocity, Viscosity, Thermal conductivity, Channel flow, Mixing.
Identifiers: Trajectory, Drag coefficient.

The results of a coordinated, three-pronged study of the development of the three-dimensional mixing zone produced by a heated discharge in a waterway are presented. An approximate analysis and a detailed computer solution procedure are developed, and the resulting predictions are compared with laboratory experiments.
W75-08599

THE OCCURRENCE OF BENTHOS DEEP IN THE SUBSTRATUM OF A STREAM,
Waterloo Univ. (Ontario). Dept. of Biology.
For primary bibliographic entry see Field 5A.
W75-08602

NITRATE UPTAKE EFFECTIVENESS OF FOUR PLANT SPECIES,
Purdue Univ, Lafayette, Ind. Dept. of Agronomy.
D. D. Warncke and S. A. Barber.
Journal of Environmental Quality, Vol 3, No 1, p 28-30, Jan-Mar 1974. 2 tab, 5 ref. OWRR-B-026-IND(4).

Descriptors: *Soil-water-plant relationships, *Root systems, *Nitrates, Water quality, Absorption, Nutrients, Forage sorghum, Grain sorghum, Corn(Field), Soybeans, Bromegrass.
Identifiers: *Nitrate uptake.

The effectiveness of nitrate uptake of corn, soybeans, sorghum, and bromegrass intact roots were investigated in nutrient solution culture. The maximum uptake rate per centimeter of root for corn occurred at 10mM, for sorghum at 2.4mM, and for bromegrass at 0.8 mM. Increasing the nitrate level above 1.0 mM did not increase the growth rate during the first 3 weeks for any of these species. The minimum level to which the plant roots reduced the nitrate concentration was 1.7, 2.7, 2.4, and 1.4 micrometer for forage sorghum, grain sorghum, soybeans, and bromegrass, respectively. Three cultivars of corn were compared. Two reduced the nitrate level to 2 micrometer and the third to 4 micrometer. The results of this research indicate that the roots of the species investigated absorbed nitrate of maximum rates from relatively low nitrate concentrations provided the concentration was maintained. Also, the degree of reduction in nitrate level where nitrate in solution was not maintained indicated that these plant roots had the absorptive capacity to reduce solution nitrate to concentrations of 4 micrometer or less.
W75-08607

PLUTONIUM AND OTHER TRANSURANIUM ELEMENTS: SOURCES, ENVIRONMENTAL DISTRIBUTION AND BIOMEDICAL EFFECTS.
Atomic Energy Commission, Washington, D.C.
For primary bibliographic entry see Field 5C.
W75-08640

EFFECT OF INDIVIDUAL FACTORS ON THE FORMATION OF WATER QUALITY OF THE KARA KUM CANAL AS A WATER SUPPLY SOURCE OF THE TURKMEN SSR, (IN RUSSIAN),
Institute of General and Municipal Hygiene, Moscow (USSR).
G. I. Ovsyannikova.
Gig Sanit, 38(12): 99-100, 1973.

Descriptors: *Potable water, *Analysis, Canals, Conduits, Water pollution sources, *Water quality, *Pollutants, *Water supply, Water treatment.
Identifiers: Bacteriological studies, Dredging, Kara-Kum canal, *USSR(Turkman-SSR).

Investigations established that, with respect to physicochemical and sanitary-bacteriological indices, the quality of the water of the Kara-Kum canal (USSR) is suitable for use as a centralized drinking water supply after treatment and decontamination (2-fold chlorination at water works). Mineralization of the canal's water increases with distance from the intake, which was ascertained by the increase of chlorides, total hardness and alkalinity. The water quality of the canal is affected by the quality of the initial water (Amu-Darya River), its use for recreational purposes (swimming, fishing, boating, etc.), presence of cattle watering sites near banks, and by the operation of dredges.--Copyright 1975, Biological Abstracts, Inc.
W75-08644

DISPERSION AND MOVEMENT OF TRITIUM IN A SHALLOW AQUIFER IN MORTANDAD CANYON AT THE LOS ALAMOS SCIENTIFIC LABORATORY,
Los Alamos Scientific Lab., N. Mex.
W. D. Purtymun.
Available from the National Technical Information, Springfield, Va 22161 as LA-5716-MS, $4.00 in paper copy, $2.25 in microfiche. Rept No LA-5716-MS, September 1974. 10 p, 5 fig, 2 tab, 2 ref.

Descriptors: *Tritium, *Effluents, *Water pollution, *Aquifers, Movement, *Dispersion, Groundwater reservoir, Measurement, Canyons, Radioactive tracer, Evapotranspiration, Soil moisture, *Path of pollutants.

Twenty (20) Ci of tritium discharged into Mortandad Canyon in November 1969 were used to determine the dispersion and movement of the tritium in a shallow aquifer in the alluvium. It took 388 days for the peak concentration to move 3 027 m from the effluent outfall to the eastern end of the aquifer. The concentration decreased from 77 700 pCi/ml to 310 ρCi/ml in that distance. Ground water is transit storage contained about 0.9 Ci of tritium prior to the release of the 20Ci. About 3.9 Ci of tritium remained in transit storage at the end of 1970. The remaining 17.0 Ci were lost with evapotranspiration, infiltration with ground water into the underlying tuff or suspended with soil moisture above the aquifer. (Houser-ORNL)
W75-08645

STUDIES OF PLUTONIUM, AMERICIUM, AND URANIUM IN ENVIRONMENTAL MATRICES,
Los Alamos Scientific Lab., N. Mex.
W. H. Adams, J. R. Buchholz, C. W. Christenson, G. L. Johnson, and E. B. Fowler.
Available from the National Technical Information Service, Springfield, Va 22161 as LA-5661, $4.00 in paper copy, $2.25 in microfiche. Rept No LA-5661, January 1975. 24 p, 16 tab, 36 ref.

Descriptors: *Environment, *Plutonium, *Uranium, Acids, Oxides, Dissolved solids, Salts, Soils, Separation techniques, Anion adsorption, Ion exchange, Absorption, Field crops, Environmental effects.

Identifiers: *Matrices, *Americium.

A nitric acid-hydrofluoric acid treatment for dissolution of plutonium oxides in soils has been developed; its adaption to other biological matrices is discussed. Plutonium recoveries of 94 to 99% from 1 - g samples of spiked and heated soils are reported. Adaptation of the acid solution to subsequent anion exchange separation of plutonium, followed by coupling to known electroplating techniques, is described. The uptake of plutonium, americium, and uranium from spiked soils by alfalfa, beans, radishes, lettuce, tomatoes, and barley is reported. The 'apparent' solubility of 238PuO2 in tap water was measured, and the deposition of plutonium in fish, algae, and snails in aquaria containing 238PuO2 microspheres is reported. (Houser-ORNL)
W75-08646

AERIAL RADIOLOGICAL MEASURING SURVEY OF THE COOPER NUCLEAR STATION AUGUST 1972.
EG and G, Inc., Las Vegas, Nev.
For primary bibliographic entry see Field 5A.
W75-08648

COMMERCIAL ALPHA WASTE PROGRAM QUARTERLY PROGRESS REPORT JULY - SEPTEMBER 1974.
Hanford Engineering Development Lab., Richland, Wash.
For primary bibliographic entry see Field 5D.
W75-08651

TRITIUM AND NOBLE GAS FISSION PRODUCTS IN THE NUCLEAR FUEL CYCLE. I. REACTORS,
Argonne National Lab, Ill.
For primary bibliographic entry see Field 5A.
W75-08652

ANALYSIS OF POPULATION, BIRTH, AND DEATH STATISTICS IN THE COUNTIES SURROUNDING THE BIG ROCK POINT NUCLEAR POWER STATION, CHARLEVOIX COUNTY, MICHIGAN,
Argonne National Lab., Ill.
For primary bibliographic entry see Field 5C.
W75-08653

LIQUID PLUGGING IN IN-SITU COAL GASIFICATION PROCESSES,
California Univ., Livermore. Lawrence Livermore Lab.
For primary bibliographic entry see Field 5A.
W75-08657

PROJECT DIAMOND ORE, PHASE IIA: CLOSE-IN MEASUREMENTS PROGRAM,
California Univ., Livermore. Lawrence Livermore Lab.
For primary bibliographic entry see Field 5A.
W75-08659

FURTHER NUMERICAL MODEL STUDIES OF THE WASHOUT OF HYGROSCOPIC PARTICLES IN THE ATMOSPHERE,
California Univ., Livermore. Lawrence Livermore Lab.
For primary bibliographic entry see Field 5A.
W75-08660

A DIRECT SOLUTION OF THE SPHERICAL-HARMONICS APPROXIMATION TO THE TRANSFER EQUATION FOR A PLANE-PARALLEL, NONHOMOGENEOUS ATMOSPHERE,
California Univ., Livermore. Lawrence Livermore Lab.
For primary bibliographic entry see Field 5A.
W75-08661

ENVIRONMENTAL RADIOACTIVITY IN THE FAROES IN 1973,
Danish Atomic Energy Commission, Risoe. Research Establishment.
For primary bibliographic entry see Field 5A.
W75-08663

ENVIRONMENTAL RADIOACTIVITY IN GREENLAND IN 1973,
Danish Atomic Energy Commission, Risoe. Research Establishment.
For primary bibliographic entry see Field 5A.
W75-08664

NATURAL RADIATION EXPOSURE IN THE UNITED STATES,
Office of Radiation Programs, Washington, D.C.
For primary bibliographic entry see Field 5A.
W75-08669

RADIOLOGICAL AND ENVIRONMENTAL RESEARCH DIVISION ANNUAL REPORT, ECOLOGY, JANUARY - DECEMBER 1973.
Argonne National Lab., Ill.
Available from the National Technical Information Service, Springfield, Va. 22161, as Rept No ANL-8060, Part III, $7.60 in paper copy, $2.25 in microfiche. Rept No ANL-8060, Part III, (1973), 187 p.

Descriptors: *Environmental effects, Ecology, Ecological distribution, *Radioecology, *Great Lakes, *Radioactivity, *Research and development, *Thermal pollution, Nuclear powerplants, Effluents, Water pollution, Tritium, Thermal stress, Trace elements, Radioisotopes, Fish migration, Air pollution, Crop response, Economic impact.
Identifiers: *Terrestrial ecology, Terrestrial ecosystems, Thermal discharges, Radiotelemetry, Sulfur dioxide, Biogeochemical cycling.

The Ecology Section, comprising the Great Lakes Radioecology, Thermal Studies, and Terrestrial Ecology Groups, has the overall objective of predicting the environmental behavior and ecological effects of energy-related effluents in the Great Lakes region. The Great Lakes Radioecology Group continued investigations of toxic trace elements and of radionuclides in the Great Lakes, with emphasis on natural radionuclides and long-lived artificial ones in Lake Michigan. This program on the biogeochemical cycling of these elements in a joint effort between Argonne and the University of Michigan's Great Lakes Research Division. The Great Lakes Thermal Studies Group continued studies of the effects of heated discharges from the Point Beach Nuclear Power Plant on Lake Michigan fish. The group recently has concentrated its efforts on development of radiotelemetry methods for tracking the movements of fish in the vicinity of thermal discharges. The Terrestrial Ecology Group completed studies of tritium behavior and radiation stress in terrestrial ecosystems, and began redirecting efforts toward assessment of the economic impact of air pollutants upon agricultural crops in the Great Lakes region. Sulfur dioxide was chosen for initial study because of its current and projected importance as an air pollutant in the northeastern part of the United States. (Houser-ORNL)
W75-08670

TOTAL URBAN WATER POLLUTION LOADS: THE IMPACT OF STORM WATER,
Enviro Control, Inc., Rockville, Md.
A. M. Vitale, and P. M. Sprey.
Available from the National Technical Information Service Springfield, Va. 22161, as PB-231 730. $7.00 in paper copy, $2.25 in microfiche. Report submitted to Council on Environmental Quality, Washington, D.C. 1974. 183 p, 87 tab, 81 fig, 24 ref, 2 append.

Descriptors: *Storm water, *Storm runoff, *Water pollution sources, Water quality, Cities, Surface runoff, Urban runoff, Storm drains, Combined sewers, Separated sewers, *Delaware River.

This analysis of engineer survey data from eight cities and the effects of storm events on water quality in the Delaware river estuary, estimates the quantities of pollutants entering receiving waters from cities, determines the portions that can be attributed to other than sewage treatment plants, especially storm water related sources, compares the cost and effectiveness of alternative methods of reducing pollution from storm water, and discusses the implication for policy decisions. Major findings of the study included: a large part of the water pollution load created by urban areas results from storm associated surface runoff, storm sewer discharges, sewer overflows, sewer leaks and treatment plant bypasses; pollutant materials include oxygen demanding material, settleable solids, nutrients, heavy metals and other toxic substances, and pathogens and bacteria; urban storm water has a severe impact on dissolved oxygen content in the receiving water; the pattern of storm events is such that the oxygen demand from urban runoff occurs both infrequently and intensely; and the average oxygen depletion due to typical storm events reaches 2 ppm, and the depletion lasts for substantial periods of time--from 8 to 12 days. Policy implications of this study include: both water quality planning and water pollution abatement programs need to be based on an analysis of the total urban pollution loads; municipalities need more federal incentive to identify and perform the comparatively inexpensive and cost effective sewer inspection, cleaning, and maintenance programs which could significantly reduce the discharge of pollutants; and, sewer separation is not a cost effective approach to the storm water problem. (Orr-FIRL)
W75-08677

STORMWATER POLLUTION--SAMPLING AND MEASUREMENT,
Trent Polytechnic, Nottingham (England). Dept. of Building and Civil Engineering.
For primary bibliographic entry see Field 5A.
W75-08678

THE CONFIGURATION OF THE HYDROCHEMICAL RELATIONSHIPS IN THE HUNGARIAN SECTION OF THE DANUBE DURING THE YEAR 1971: DANUBIALIA HUNGARICA LXVI, (IN GERMAN),
Magyar Tudomanyos Akademia, Budapest (Hungary). Station for Danube Research.
Z. T. Dvihally.
Ann Univ Sci Budap Rolando Eotvos Nominatae Sect Biol. 15: 23-30. 1973.

Descriptors: *Rivers, Europe, *Analysis, *Pollutants, Water pollution sources, *Path of pollutants, Nitrates, Nitrites, Dissolved oxygen, Iron.
Identifiers: *Danube River, *Hungary.

While the amounts of O_2 consumption, nitrite, ammonium, dissolved CO_2 and dissolved Fe have steadily grown since 1965, the amount of dissolved O_2, the O_2 saturation and the absolute values of the nitrate and silicate ions have diminished, indicating a qualitative deterioration of the Danube water below Budapest. Comparisons are made between the O_2 balance of non-polluted Hungarian sections of the Danube and the German Rhine, Main and Danube Rivers. The O_2 production in the upper water layers of the Hungarian Danube is 6-14 g O_2/m^3 or 1100-1740 tons O_2 daily, whereas the average primary production of the German rivers is 3-4 g O_2/m^3.--Copyright 1975, Biological Abstracts, Inc.
W75-08680

CHARACTERISTICS OF THE ORGANIZATION OF SANITARY CONTROL OF WATER SUPPLY

SOURCES AND DRINKING WATER QUALITY IN THE OIL AND GAS-BEARING REGIONS IN THE NORTHERN OBTERRITORY, (IN RUSSIAN),
Tyumenskii Gosudarstvennyi Meditsinskii Institut (USSR).
For primary bibliographic entry see Field 5F.
W75-08681

A COMPUTATIONAL MODEL FOR PREDICTING THE THERMAL REGIMES OF RIVERS,
Iowa Univ., Iowa City. Inst. of Hydraulic Research.
P. P. Paily, and J. F. Kennedy.
Report 169, November 1974. 61 p, 2 fig, 7 ref, 2 append.

Descriptors: *Thermal pollution, *Numerical analysis, *Rivers, *Unsteady flow, *Heat budget, Analysis, Energy, Duffusion, Convection, Equations, Temperature, Distribution, Inflow, Heat flow, Analytical techniques, *Path of pollutants.
Identifiers: Convective-diffusion equation, Implicit predictor-corrector method.

A predictor-corrector type of numerical procedure for solving the unsteady one-dimensional convective-diffusion equation was developed to predict unsteady streamwise temperature distributions in natural and thermally loaded rivers. Input data required for the computations included river flow rates, channel characteristics, climatic conditions, tributary inflows, and thermal discharges. The model was developed for application in cases with unsteady thermal input rates and climatic conditions. (Adams-ISWS)
W75-08683

NUMERICAL ANALYSIS OF WARM, TURBULENT SINKING JETS DISCHARGED INTO QUIESCENT WATER OF LOW TEMPERATURE,
Iowa Univ., Iowa City. Inst. of Hydraulic Research.
J. M. Pena, and S. C. Jain.
Report 154, February 1974. 76 p, 9 fig, 8 ref, 1 append.

Descriptors: *Jets, *Numerical analysis, *Design data, *Thermal pollution, Diffusion, Temperature, Velocity, Froud number. Turbulent flow, Winter, Density, Outlets, Profiles, Water temperature, *Path of pollutants.
Identifiers: *Sinking jets.

A numerical analysis of sinking jets in quiescent water of low temperature was conducted. Jets from circular nozzles and two-dimensional slots were considered. The integral approach and similarity conditions for velocity and temperature profiles were used in the analysis. Results were presented in graphical form for jet trajectory, width, and dilution. These graphs were to be used in predicting the behavior of warm, submerged jets discharging into lakes during the winter season when the lake water temperature is near the freezing point. (Adams-ISWS)
W75-08684

ON THE TIME-DEPENDENT FLOW IN A LAKE,
Case Western Reserve Univ., Cleveland, Ohio.
For primary bibliographic entry see Field 2H.
W75-08703

THE EFFECTS OF DOMESTIC AND INDUSTRIAL EFFLUENTS ON A LARGE TURBULENT RIVER,
Alberta Univ., Edmonton. Dept. of Zoology.
C. G. Paterson, and J. R. Nursall.
Water Research, Vol 9, No 4, p 425-435, April 1975. 6 fig, 8 tab, 34 ref.

Descriptors: *Rivers, *Pollutants, *Effluents, Limnology, Climates, Flow, Ice cover, Chemical analysis, Benthic fauna, Fish populations, Temperature, Biochemical oxygen demand, *Path of pollutants, On-site investigations, *Canada.
Identifiers: *North Saskatchewan River.

The North Saskatchewan River receives effluents largely from its south bank. Consequently the north side of the river is little affected and useful N-S comparisons can be made along transects. Dissolved oxygen values stay high in all parts of the river at all seasons. BOD is low and steady along the north side, higher and variable along the south side. Nitrogen, phosphorus, and other chemical parameters generally measured higher along the south side. There was much more benthic variety along the north side of the river. Fish stayed to the north side. There was a general biomass increase through the region affected by effluents, demonstrating a pollutional eutrophication. It was suggested that the oligochaete-chironomid biota of the south side of the river is governed by short term, restricted area pollutional events, which are difficult to anticipate to measure. (Sims-ISWS)
W75-08709

COASTAL POWER PLANT HEAT DISPOSAL CONSIDERATIONS,
Southern California Edison Co., Rosemead, Calif.
For primary bibliographic entry see Field 5G.
W75-08719

POLLUTION OF OPEN WATERS BY PESTICIDES ENTERING FROM AGRICULTURAL AREAS, (IN RUSSIAN),
Kiev Research Inst. of General Communal Hygiene (USSR).
Ya. I. Kostovetskii, G. V. Tolstopyatova, and G. Ya. Chegrinets.
Gig Sanit, 38(10): 99-100, 1973.

Descriptors: *Water pollution sources, *Pesticides, Runoff, Surface runoff, *Agricultural runoff, DDT, *Soil contamination, Pollutants, *Path of pollutants, Soil analysis.
Identifiers: Arylam, Cresol, Lindane, Malathion, Parathion, Trichlorfon, USSR, Sevin.

A determination was made of the content of DDT, lindane, Sevin (arylam), 4,6-dinitro-o-cresol, methyl parathion, malathion and trichlorfon in soils of fields and orchards and in waters and bottom deposits of ponds and rivers adjacent to them. Of 456 analyses (soil), 224 water analyses, and 216 analyses of bottom deposits, pesticides were found respectively in 97 (21.3%), and 16 (7.1%) and 54 (25%) of the cases. Primarily organochlorine pesticides were found in the soil and bottom deposits (in 92.9% and 85.2% of the cases) and organophosphorus compounds in the waters (in 75% of the cases). These differences were evidently due to the investigated agricultural areas being treated more often with organophosphorus pesticides which probably entered the waters with the surface runoff.--Copyright 1975, Biological Abstracts, Inc.
W75-08729

THE RADIOACTIVE, METALLIC AND BACTERIAL POLLUTANTS IN THE ESTUARY OF THE ESCAUT (SCHELT) RIVER AND ON THE COAST OF BELGIUM, (IN FRENCH),
Institut Royal des Sciences Naturelles de Belgique, Brussels. Lab. for Oceanographic Physics.
For primary bibliographic entry see Field 5A.
W75-08774

ECONOMIC AND ENVIRONMENTAL EVALUATION OF NUCLEAR WASTE DISPOSAL BY UNDERGROUND IN SITU MELTING,
California Univ., Livermore. Lawrence Livermore Lab.
For primary bibliographic entry see Field 5E.
W75-08785

MODELING WIND INDUCED WATER CURRENTS,
Worcester Polytechnic Inst., Mass. Alden Research Labs.
G. E. Hecker, and G. A. Yale.
In: Hydraulic Engineering and the Environment; Proceedings of the 21st Annual Hydraulic Division Specialty Conference, Montana State University, Bozeman, August 15-17, 1973. American Society of Civil Engineers, New York, p 335-348, 1973. 7 fig, 14 ref, 1 append.

Descriptors: *Model studies, *Currents(Water), *Winds, Hydraulic models, Hydraulic similitude, Waves(Water), Froude number, Reynolds number, Scaling, Shear stress, Research facilities, Hydraulics, Path of pollutants.
Identifiers: Surface slope.

The movement and concentration of surface contaminants in slow moving water bodies may be affected by wind induced currents. Modeling of wind-water interaction may also be relevant to other studies such as the effects of ambient circulation patterns on surface vortices at intakes and changes of flow patterns in cooling ponds. A review of the available literature indicated that considerable scale effects would occur when simulating wind induced currents by small Froude scale models. In addition, it was shown that simulation of surface slopes and shear stresses does not guarantee scaling of wind induced currents. Experiments were conducted to evaluate the induced surface current relative to the wind at low Reynolds numbers, and information was presented which allows the proper model wind speed to be selected without the need for field data. Of three basic methods used to simulate wind induced currents, the approach based on available laboratory versus field data on the ratio of surface currents to wind speed is most useful since it requires no additional field data. However, any simulation of wind induced currents in small Froude models involves scale effects. Such scale effects were evaluated and data were presented which allow the proper model wind speed to be selected. (See also W75-08786) (Sims-ISWS)
W75-08816

POLLUTION POTENTIAL OF A SANITARY LANDFILL NEAR TUCSON,
Arizona Water Resources Research Center, Tucson.
L. G. Wilson, and G. G. Small.
In: Hydraulic Engineering and the Environment; Proceedings of the 21st Annual Hydraulic Division Specialty Conference, Montana State University, Bozeman, August 15-17, 1973. American Society of Civil Engineers, New York, p 427-436, 1973. 1 fig, 3 tab, 16 ref, 1 append.

Descriptors: *Landfills, *Water quality, *Water pollution sources, Leachate, *Path of pollutants, Waste disposal, Solid wastes, Water pollution, Pollutant identification, Ephemeral streams, Water analysis, Perched water, Groundwater, *Arizona.
Identifiers: Tucson(Ariz), Santa Cruz River(Ariz).

A study was started in July 1972 to determine the quality of leachate produced in the Ina Rd sanitary landfill, near Tucson, and to monitor the effect of such leachate on groundwater quality. The landfill site lies along the Santa Cruz River, an ephemeral stream. The first few months of study involved conducting a geophysical investigation, determining river intake rates during low flows of sewage effluent, monitoring water level changes in wells, and analyzing samples of river and well water. A

shallow clay lens was inferred at the site, based on the geophysical survey. Apparently, groundwater mounds develop on this lens, but interactions with landfill deposits occur only during recharge from storm runoff events. Leachate generated within the fill closely reflected the quality of river water. The total soluble salt levels were less than 700 mg/l; nitrate and BOD levels were low. Concentrations of certain trace metals were above recommended levels, but presumably sorption would inhibit the movement of these metals into water bearing materials at 70 ft. Concentrations of certain constituents within samples from a 100 ft well were higher than corresponding levels in other wells. It was concluded that, to date, the leachate produced in the landfill near the sampling well does not represent a pollution hazard. Further observations are required, however, to follow the quality of leachate during the 'aging' of the deposits at the well site. (See also W75-08786) (Sims-ISWS)
W75-08823

WASTEWATER RECLAMATION AND RECHARGE, BAY PARK, N.Y.,
Geological Survey, Mineola, N.Y.
For primary bibliographic entry see Field 5D.
W75-08827

STREAM RECONNAISSANCE FOR NUTRIENTS AND OTHER WATER-QUALITY PARAMETERS, GREATER PITTSBURGH REGION, PENNSYLVANIA,
Geological Survey, Carnegie, Pa.
For primary bibliographic entry see Field 5A.
W75-08835

WASTE-LOAD ALLOCATION STUDIES FOR ARKANSAS STREAMS, RED RIVER BASIN, DORCHEAT BAYOU, SEGMENT 1A,
Geological Survey, Little Rock, Ark.
J. E. Reed, E. E. Morris, B. F. Lambert, and M. S. Hines.
Open-file report, 1975. 107 p, 2 fig, 4 tab, 5 ref, 3 append.

Descriptors: *Low flow, *Path of pollutants, *Arkansas, Waste dilution, Model studies, Mathematical models, Water pollution control, *Waste assimilation capacity.
Identifiers: *Dorcheat Bayou(Ark), *Waste-load allocation.

Data and the results of a waste-load allocation study are presented for Segment 1A of the Red River water-quality management planning basin. The water-quality model was calibrated for disssolved oxygen, total dissolved solids, chlorides, and sulfates, by using existing waste-load data and streamflow and water-quality data collected during summer low-flow conditions. Waste-load analyses were made by adjusting the calibrated model to include waste loads expected to exist 5 years from the present time (1974), in combination with the minimum average flow for 7 consecutive days that is expected to occur on the average of once in 10 years (Q7-10). The segment consists of a 49-mile reach of Dorcheat Bayou and its principal tributaries. Dischargers in the segment consist of 9 municipalities, including Southern State College, and 4 industries. Plots of dissolved oxygen (DO), total dissolved solids (TDS), chlorides (Cl), and sulfates (SO4) resulting from 5-year waste-load projection and Q7-10 low-flow conditions are given. The plots show that under the specified conditions the concentrations of all the above mentioned chemical constituents in Dorcheat meet standards by the State of Arkansas. Carbonaceous waste discharge in terms of 5-day biochemical oxygen demand (CBOD5), nitrogenous oxygen demand as ammonia nitrogen (NH3-N), chlorides (Cl), and sulfates (SO4) for each discharger are summarized. (Knapp-USGS)
W75-08837

WASTE-LOAD ALLOCATION STUDIES FOR ARKANSAS STREAMS, RED RIVER BASIN, SEGMENT 1B,
Geological Survey, Little Rock, Ark.
J. E. Reed, J. E. Terry, J. W. Stephens, and M. E. Broom.
Open-file report, 1975. 63 p, 2 fig, 4 tab, 5 ref, 3 append.

Descriptors: *Low flow, *Path of pollutants, *Arkansas, Waste dilution, Model studies, Mathematical models, Water pollution control, *Waste assimilative capacity.
Identifiers: *Red River(Ark), *Waste-load allocation.

Data and the results of a waste-load allocation study are presented for Segment 1B of the Red River water-quality management planning basin. The water-quality model was calibrated for dissolved oxygen, total dissolved solids, chlorides, and sulfates, by using existing waste-load data and streamflow and water-quality data collected during summer low-flow conditions. Waste-load analyses were made by adjusting the calibrated model to include waste loads expected to exist 5 years from the present time (1974), in combination with the minimum average flow for 7 consecutive days that is expected to occur on the average of once in 10 years (Q7-10). The segment consists of about a 163-mile reach of the Red River, and its principal tributaries in this reach. Dischargers in the segment consist of 5 municipalities and 3 industries. Plots of dissolved oxygen (DO), total dissolved solids (TDS), chlorides (Cl), and sulfates (SO4) resulting from 5-year waste-load projection and Q7-10 low-flow conditions are given. The plots show that under the specified conditions the concentrations of all the above chemical constituents in the Red River meet standards set by the State of Arkansas. Carbonaceous waste discharge in terms of 5-day biochemical oxygen demand (CBOD5), nitrogenous oxygen demand as ammonia nitrogen (NH3-N), chlorides (Cl), and sulfates (SO4) for each discharger are summarized. (Knapp-USGS)
W75-08838

WASTE-LOAD ALLOCATION STUDIES FOR ARKANSAS STREAMS, OUACHITA RIVER BASIN, BOEUF RIVER AND BAYOU MACON, SEGMENT 2A,
Geological Survey, Little Rock, Ark.
J. E. Terry, E. E. Morris, B. F. Lambert, and R. Sniegocki.
Open-file report, 1975. 120 p, 2 fig, 4 tab, 5 ref, 3 append.

Descriptors: *Low flow, *Arkansas, *Path of pollutants, Waste dilution, Model studies, Mathematical models, Water pollution control, *Waste assimilative capacity.
Identifiers: *Boeuf River(Ark), *Waste-load allocation.

Data and the results of a waste-load allocation study are presented for Segment 2A of the Ouachita River water-quality management planning basin. The water-quality model was calibrated for dissolved oxygen, total dissolved solids, chlorides, and sulfates, by using existing waste-load data and streamflow and water-quality data collected during summer low-flow conditions. Waste-load analyses were made by adjusting the calibrated model to include waste loads expected to exist 5 years from the present time (1974), in combination with the minimum average flow for 7 consecutive days that is expected to occur on the average of once in 10 years (Q7-10). The segment consists of the upper reaches of Boeuf River and Bayou Macon. Including their main-stem tributaries, Boeuf River and Bayou Macon in this segment are, respectively, about 125 miles and 76 miles in length. Dischargers in the segment consist of 9 municipalities and 2 industries. Plots of dissolved oxygen (DO), total dissolved solids (TDS), chlorides (Cl), and sulfates (SO4) resulting from 5-year waste-load projection and Q7-10 low-flow conditions are given. Carbonaceous waste discharge in terms of 5-day biochemical oxygen demand (CBOD5), nitrogenous oxygen demand as ammonia nitrogen (NH3-N), chlorides (Cl), and sulfates (CO4) for each discharger are summarized. (Knapp-USGS)
W75-08839

WASTE-LOAD ALLOCATION STUDIES FOR ARKANSAS STREAMS, OUACHITA RIVER BASIN, BAYOU BARTHOLOMEW, SEGMENT 2B,
Geological Survey, Little Rock, Ark.
J. E. Reed, J. E. Terry, B. F. Lambert, and E. E. Morris.
Open-file report, 1975. 70 p, 2 fig, 4 tab, 5 ref, 3 append.

Descriptors: *Low flow, *Path of pollutants, *Arkansas, Waste dilution, Model studies, Mathematical models, Water pollution control, *Waste assimilative capacity.
Identifiers: *Bayou Bartholomew(Ark), *Waste-load allocation.

Data and the results of a waste-load allocation study are presented for Segment 2B of the Ouachita River water-quality management planning basin. The water-quality model was calibrated for dissolved oxygen, total dissolved solids, chlorides, and sulfates, by using existing waste-load data and streamflow and water-quality data collected during summer low-flow conditions. Waste-load analyses were made by adjusting the calibrated model to include waste loads expected to exist 5 years from the present time (1974), in combination with the minimum average flow for 7 consecutive days that is expected to occur on the average of once in 10 years (Q7-10). The segment consists chiefly of a 284-mile reach of Bayou Bartholomew, a 21-mile reach of Overflow Creek, and a 24-mile reach of Chemin-a-Haut Creek. Dischargers in the segment consist of seven municipalities. Plots of dissolved oxygen (DO), total dissolved solids (TDS), chlorides (Cl), and sulfates (SO4) resulting from 5-year waste-load projection and Q7-10 low-flow conditions are given. Carbonaceous waste discharge in terms of 5-day biochemical oxygen demand (CBOD5), nitrogenous oxygen demand as ammonia nitrogen (NH3-N), chlorides (Cl), and sulfates (SO4) for each discharger are summarized. (Knapp-USGS)
W75-08840

WASTE-LOAD ALLOCATION STUDIES FOR ARKANSAS STREAMS, OUACHITA RIVER BASIN, SEDMENT 2D,
Geological Survey, Little Rock, Ark.
J. E. Reed, J. E. Terry, J. W. Stephens, and C. T. Bryant.
Open-file report, 1975. 189 p, 2 fig, 4 tab, 5 ref, 3 append.

Descriptors: *Low flow, *Path of pollutants, *Arkansas, Waste dilution, Model studies, Mathematical models, Water pollution control, *Waste assimilative capacity.
Identifiers: *Ouachita River(Ark), *Waste-load allocation.

Data and the results of a waste-load allocation study are presented for Segment 2D of the Ouachita River water-quality management planning basin. The water-quality model was calibrated for dissolved oxygen, total dissolved solids, chlorides, and sulfates, by using existing waste-load data and streamflow and water-quality data collected during summer low-flow conditions. Waste-load analyses were made by adjusting the calibrated model to include waste loads expected to exist 5 years from the present time (1974), in combination with the minimum average flow for 7 consecutive days that is expected to occur on the average of once in 10 years (Q7-10). The segment consists chiefly of a 148-mile reach of the Ouachita River, and its principal tributaries in this

reach including the Little Missouri River and Smackover Creek. Dischargers in the segment consist of nineteen municipalities and seven industries. Plots of dissolved oxygen (DO), total dissolved solids (TDS), chlorides (Cl), and sulfates (SO4) resulting from 5-year waste-load projection and Q7-10 low-flow conditions are given. The plots show that under the specified conditions the concentrations of all the above chemical constituents in the Little Missouri River meet standards set by the State of Arkansas. (Knapp-USGS)
W75-08841

WASTE-LOAD ALLOCATION STUDIES FOR ARKANSAS STREAMS, OUACHITA RIVER BASIN, SALINE RIVER, SEGMENT 2C,
Geological Survey, Little Rock, Ark.
J. E. Reed, B. F. Lambert, E. E. Morris, and J. W. Stephens.
Open-file report, 1974. 75 p, 2 fig, 4 tab, 5 ref, 3 append.

Descriptors: *Low flow, *Path of pollutants, *Arkansas, Waste dilution, Model studies, Mathematical models, Water pollution control, *Waste assimilative capacity.
Identifiers: *Ouachita River(Ark), *Waste-load allocation.

Data and the results of a waste-load allocation study are presented for Segment 2C of the Ouachita River water-quality management planning basin. The water-quality model was calibrated for dissolved oxygen, total dissolved solids, chlorides, and sulfates, by using existing waste-load data and streamflow and water-quality data collected during summer low-flow conditions. Waste-load analyses were made by adjusting the calibrated model to include waste loads expected to exist 5 years from the present time (1974), in combination with the minimum average flow for 7 consecutive days that is expected to occur on the average of once in 10 years (Q7-10). The segment includes the complete 202-mile reach of the Saline River and selected reaches of its principal and minor tributaries. Dischargers in the segment consist of 7 municipalities and 6 industries. Plots of dissolved oxygen (DO), total dissolved solids (TDS), chlorides (Cl), and sulfates (SO4) resulting from 5-year waste-load projection and Q7-10 low-flow conditions are given. (Knapp-USGS)
W75-08842

WASTE-LOAD ALLOCATION STUDIES FOR ARKANSAS STREAMS, OUACHITA RIVER BASIN, SEGMENT 2F,
Geological Survey, Little Rock, Ark.
C. T. Bryant.
Open-file report, 1975. 216 p, 3 fig, 4 tab, 5 ref, 3 append.

Descriptors: *Low flow, *Path of pollutants, *Arkansas, Waste dilution, Model studies, Mathematical models, Water pollution control, *Waste assimilative capacity.
Identifiers: *Ouachita River(Ark), *Waste-load allocation.

Data and the results of a waste-load allocation study are presented for Segment 2F of the Ouachita River water-quality management planning basin. The water-quality model was calibrated for dissolved oxygen, total dissolved solids, chlorides, and sulfates, by using existing waste-load data and streamflow and water-quality data collected during summer low-flow conditions. Waste-load analyses were made by adjusting the calibrated model to include waste loads expected to exist 5 years from the present time (1974), in combination with the minimum average flow for 7 consecutive days that is expected to occur on the average of once in 10 years (Q7-10). The segment consists chiefly of a 220-mile reach of the Ouachita River, a 40-mile reach of the South Fork Ouachita River, and a 70-mile reach of the Caddo River. Dischargers in the segment consist of 8 municipalities and 34 industries. Plots of dissolved oxygen (DO), total dissolved solids (TDS), chlorides (Cl), and sulfates (SO4) resulting from 5-year waste-load projection and Q7-10 low-flow conditions are given. The plots show that under the specified conditions the concentration of dissolved oxygen, total dissolved solids, chlorides, and sulfates in Caddo River meet standards set by the State of Arkansas. Carbonaceous waste discharge in terms of 5-day biochemical oxygen demand (CBOD5), nitrogenous oxygen demand as ammonia nitrogen (NH3-N), chlorides (Cl), and sulfates (SO4) for each discharger are summarized. (Knapp-USGS)
W75-08843

WASTE-LOAD ALLOCATION STUDIES FOR ARKANSAS STREAMS, ST. FRANCIS RIVER BASIN, SEGMENT 5A,
Geological Survey, Little Rock, Ark.
J. E. Terry, E. E. Morris, B. F. Lambert, and M. S. Hines.
Open-file report, 1975. 52 p, 2 fig, 4 tab, 5 ref, 3 append.

Descriptors: *Low flow, *Path of pollutants, *Arkansas, Waste dilution, Model studies, Mathematical models, Water pollution control, *Waste assimilative capacity.
Identifiers: *St. Francis River(Ark), *Waste-load allocation.

Data and the results of a waste-load allocation study are presented for Segment 5A of the St. Francis River water-quality management planning basin. The water-quality model was calibrated for dissolved oxygen, total dissolved solids, chlorides, and sulfates, by using existing waste-load data and streamflow and water-quality data collected during summer low-flow conditions. Waste-load analyses were made by adjusting the calibrated model to include waste loads expected to exist 5 years from the present time (1974), in combination with the minimum average flow for 7 consecutive days that is expected to occur on the average of once in 10 years (Q7-10). The segment consists chiefly of a 64-mile reach of the St. Francis River, and its principal tributaries in this reach. Dischargers in the segment consist of three municipalities. Plots of dissolved oxygen (DO), total dissolved solids (TDS), chlorides (Cl), and sulfates (SO4) resulting from 5-year waste-load projection and Q7-10 low-flow conditons are given. The plots show that under the specified conditions the concentrations of all the above chemical constituents in the St. Francis River meet standards set by the State of Arkansas. Carbonaceous waste discharge in terms of 5-day biochemical oxygen demand (CBOD5), nitrogenous oxygen demand as ammonia nitrogen (NH3-N), chlorides (Cl), and sulfates (SO4) for each discharger are summarized. (Knapp-USGS)
W75-08844

EVALUATION OF METHODS FOR ESTIMATING STREAM WATER QUALITY PARAMETERS IN A TRANSIENT MODEL FROM STOCHASTIC DATA,
Kansas State Univ., Manhattan. Dept. of Chemical Engineering.
K. P. R. Krishnan, J. J. Lizcano, L. E. Erickson, and L. T. Fan.
Water Resources Bulletin, Vol 10, No 5, p 899-913, October 1974. 6 fig, 8 tab, 10 equ, 15 ref. OWRT B-021-KAN(10).

Descriptors: *Streams, *Water quality, *Estimating, Stochastic processes, Water pollution control, Measurement, Computers, Evaluation, Data collections, Equations, Biochemical oxygen demand, Wastes, Mathematical models, Systems analysis.
Identifiers: *Parameter estimation, *Bard's method, *Simplex search method, Transient model, Input-output data, Least square criterion function, Minimization, Standard deviation.

The estimation of parameters in water quality models represented by linear first order partial differential equations is investigated. Two sets of simulated input-output data, one with input noise and the other with output measurement error, were used. BOD parameters from simulated data measured at two locations along a stream were estimated by a gradient technique (Bard's method) and a pattern search technique. The results indicate that the output measurement error significantly affects the values of parameter estimates as compared to the noise added to the input. Bard's method consistently gave results with a smaller sum of square value. (Bell-Cornell)
W75-08849

METER FOR SEWER FLOW MEASUREMENT,
Illinois Univ., Urbana. Dept. of Civil Engineering.
For primary bibliographic entry see Field 7B.
W75-08850

5C. Effects Of Pollution

EFFECT OF BEAN POD MOTTLE VIRUS ON YIELD COMPONENTS AND MORPHOLOGY OF SOYBEANS IN RELATION TO SOIL WATER REGIMES: A PRELIMINARY STUDY,
Mississippi State Univ., State College.
D. L. Mynre, H. N. Pitre, M. Haridasan, and J. D. Hesketh.
Plant Dis Rep, Vol 57, No 12, p 1050-1054, 1973. Illus.

Descriptors: *Soybeans, *Soil moisture, *Plant diseases, Plant fungi, Crop production, *Viruses.
Identifiers: Bean pod mottle virus.

The yield components and morphology of 'Bragg' soybeans naturally infected with bean pod mottle virus (BPMV) prior to bloom and grown under different soil water regimes were compared with those of healthy plants growing adjacent to a diseased plant under the same conditions in field plots. Healthy plants yielded higher than diseased plants, irrespective of the soil water regimes. BPMV infection reduced yield by 29%. BPMV infection was more detrimental than the imposed soil water stress during the growing season. A soil water stress coupled with BPMV infection further decreased yield. Lower yields caused by infection were reflected in a reduction in total dry matter and total number of fruiting sites and pods per plant. Plant height, number of pods per fruiting site, number of seeds per pod, and mean weight of seeds were not affected by BPMV infection.--Copyright 1974, Biological Abstracts, Inc.
W75-08359

BEHAVIORAL RESPONSES OF NORTHERN PIKE, YELLOW PERCH AND BLUEGILL TO OXYGEN CONCENTRATIONS UNDER SIMULATED WINTERKELL CONDITIONS,
Ichthyological Associates, Inc., Middletown, Del.
B. R. Petrosky, and J. J. Magnuson.
Copeia, Vol 1973, No 1, p 124-133, Illus. 1973.

Descriptors: Oxygen, *Pikes, Yellow perch, Perches, Sunfiches, *Fish physiology, Winter killing, *Environmental effects, *Fish, *Cold regions, *Fish behavior, Fishkill, Morbidity, Fish management, Water pollution effects.
Identifiers: Bluegill, Esox-lucius, Lepomis-macrochirus, Perca-flavescens.

Northern pike (Esox lucius), yellow perch (Perca flavescens), and bluegill (Lepomis macrochirus) were exposed to successively lower O2 concentrations 4.0, 2.0, 1.0, 0.5 and 0.25 mg/1) each day for 5 days in aquaria sealed above with simulated 'ice'. Water temperature varied from 2.5-4.0C, and light intensity and photoperiod simulated conditions in an ice-covered lake. Gill ventilation rates increased in response to lowered O2, doubling for bluegill and yellow perch but quadrupling for

northern pike. Maximum ventilation rates occurred at 0.5 mg/l D.O. (dissolved oxygen) for northern pike and yellow perch and at 1.0 mg/l D.O. for bluegill. Locomotory activity was greatest at 0.25 mg/l D.O. for northern pike but at 0.5 mg/l D.O. for yellow perch and bluegill. Northern pike and yellow perch began to move toward the ice at 0.5 mg/l D.O. At 1.0 mg/l D.O, bluegill kept sinking to the bottom of the aquaria; they continually made forays upward only to sink again. Northern pike and yellow perch nosed at the under surface at the ice at the lowest O_2 coneentrations while bluegill seldom did. The fish never aggregated more than 10% of the time even at the lowest concentrations of dissolved O_2. Almost all northern pike and yellow perch were still alive at 0.25 mg/l D.O. while all bluegill were dead. Evidently northern pike are best adapted for survival in winterkill lakes and bluegill the least. The upward movement takes the fish to the highest O_2 available in the immediate vicinity. Detection of an O_2 gradient is not a requirement of this response because in the aquaria the fish move to the ice at low O_2 concentrations in absence of a gradient. High free CO_2 and dissolved H_2S are also not necessary to stimulate or orient the upward movement. Increased locomotory activity, coupled to reduced activity when respiratory distress is alleviated, also provides an effective mechanism for locating higher O_2.--Copyright 1973, Biological Abstracts, Inc.
W75-08361

THREE NEW SPECIES OF PARACINETA (PROTOZOA: SUCTORIA) FROM MOBILE BAY, ALABAMA,
University of South Alabama, Mobile. Dept. of Biological Sciences.
For primary bibliographic entry see Field 2L.
W75-08363

NEW SPECIES OF PROTOZOA FROM MOBILE BAY, ALABAMA,
University of South Alabama, Mobile. Dept. of Biological Sciences.
For primary bibliographic entry see Field 2L.
W75-08364

THE CONTRIBUTION OF AGRICULTURE TO EUTROPHICATION OF SWISS WATERS: I. RESULTS OF DIRECT MEASUREMENTS IN THE DRAINAGE AREA OF VARIOUS MAIN DRAINAGE CHANNELS,
Eidgenoessische Technische Hochschule, Kastienbaum (Switzerland). Hydrobiology Lab.
For primary bibliographic entry see Field 5B.
W75-08376

SEAWEEDS: THEIR PRODUCTIVITY AND STRATEGY FOR GROWTH,
Dalhousie Univ., Halifax (Nova Scotia). Dept. of Biology.
K. H. Mann.
Science, Vol 182, No 4116, p 975-981, December 7, 1973. 5 fig, 2 tab, 57 ref.

Descriptors: *Primary productivity, *Biomass, *Kelps, Water temperature, Predation, Seasonal, Growth rates, Light, Nutrients, Marine plants, Plant ecology, Food chains, Lobsters, Food habits, Population, Standing crops, *Canada.
Identifiers: *Growth strategy, Laminaria longicruris, Laminaria digitata, Agarum cribrosum, Nova Scotia, Seaweeds, Sea urchins, *St. Margaret's Bay(NS).

As part of a multidisciplinary study at St. Margaret's Bay, Nova Scotia, a systematic study of the seaweed zone along approximately 50 km of the shoreline was carried out with the aid of a research submarine and scuba gear. It was found that algal zones dominated by Laminaria and Agarum accounted for over 80 percent of the total biomass of seaweeds in the bay. To investigate the rate of biomass turnover, 180 plants (L. longicuris, L. digitata, A. cribrosum) at five sites with different water depths and wave actions were tagged for identification, and holes punched in the blades. The movement of these holes showed that all growth in length occurred at the junction of the stipe and the blade. Over a 2-yr period, all three species completely renewed the tissue between one and five times a year. The biomass of the new tissue was up to 20 times the initial biomass of the blade. Furthermore, peak growth occurred in late winter or early spring when the water temperature was close to 0C. Primary productivity was estimated to be 1750 g C/sq m/yr, and in the Bay, seaweed production was about 3 times that of phytoplankton. Comparison of results from other areas shows that the productivity of seaweeds is as high or higher than that of the most productive terrestrial systems. Study of the growth strategy of seaweeds, especially at low light and temperature levels seems to indicate that kelps are capable of storage, translocation, and mobilization of carbon reserves. However, the theory of energy translocation from an old frond to a new one does not describe the growth of species in eastern Canada since these plants replace old fronds at least once in the winter. It is suggested that the anaerobic mud surrounding the roots provides nitrogen in sufficient amounts to make the plants independent of atmospheric N. Less than 10 percent of the kelp production normally enters grazing food chains; the remainder enters detritus food chains, having been released as particulate or dissolved organic matter. It is postulated that human predation on lobsters has allowed sea urchin populations to increase which in turn destroy portions of kelp forests. (Little-Battelle)
W75-08377

PROBIT TRANSFORMATION: IMPROVED METHOD FOR DEFINING SYNCHRONY OF CELL CULTURES,
Carnegie Institution of Washington, Stanford, Calif. Dept. of Plant Biology.
For primary bibliographic entry see Field 5A.
W75-08378

MODELLING PRIMARY PRODUCTIN IN WATER BODIES: A NUMERICAL APPROACH THAT ALLOWS VERTICAL INHOMOGENEITIES,
Fisheries Research Board of Canada, Winnipeg, (Manitoba). Freshwater Inst.
E. J. Fee.
Journal of the Fisheries Research Board of Canada, Vol 30, No 10, p 1469-1473, October 1973. 4 fig, 11 ref.

Descriptors: *Algae, *Primary productivity, *Mathematical models, Photosynthesis, Light, Biomass, Depth, Equations, Phytoplankton, Mathematical studies, Model studies, Eutrophication.

A new model for computing integral daily phytoplankton primary production is described. The model incorporates vertical variations of algal biomass, complex photosynthesis vs light responses, nonexponential extinction of light vs depth, and any distribution of surface light over a day. The basic approach is to combine measured relations for photosynthetic rate vs light, light vs depth, and light vs time in an interpolative scheme rather than attempting to fit equations to the data and using the resulting equations to obtain a mathematical solution. The model is general and should have wide applicability. Model predictions agreed well with in situ measurements of production. (Little-Battelle)
W75-08379

TEMPERATURES SELECTED SEASONALLY BY FOUR FISHES FROM WESTERN LAKE ERIE,
Ohio State Cooperative Fishery Unit, Colu- us.
C. A. Barans, and R. A. Tubb.
Journal of the Fisheries Research Board of Canada, Vol 30, No 11, p 1697-1703, November 1973. 2 fig, 22 ref.

Descriptors: *Water temperature, *Thermal pollution, *Yellow perch, *White bass, Seasonal, Water pollution effects, Bioassay, Shiners, *Lake Erie.
Identifiers: Temperature selection, Acclimatization, *Smallmouth bas, *Emerald shiner.

When four species of fish were taken from western Lake Erie in each of four seasons and held usually for less than 7 days at ambient lake temperatures, the temperatures they selected during 2-3 days in a horizontal temperature gradient differed seasonally. The differences were largely attributable to the conditions at which the fish had been acclimatized in the lake and were modified by acclimation during 2-3 days in the gradient. The selected temperatures provided insights into the temperatures that might be selected by these species each season if the lake basin or other waters with similar seasonal ambient temperatures were subjected to thermal discharges. Temperatures selected were above ambient lake temperatures except for emerald shiners (Notropis atherinoides) in summer and fall. In general, white bass (Morone chrysops) and smallmouth bass (Micropterus dolomieui) selected a high range in temperatures throughout the year (18-30 C and 18-31 C, respectively), yellow perch (Perca flavescens) an intermediate range (10-29 C) and emarald shiners the lowest range (6-23 C). Three of the species were distributed within a relatively precise temperature range in the summer and within a larger range during other seasons; emarald shiners selected a narrow range during all seasons. A fairly stable temperature preference was usually reached within several hours in summer, but the temperatures selected by three species generally increased with time in the gradient during the other seasons; emerald shiners selected constant temperatures in all seasons. Temperatures selected by young and adults differed mainly in yellow perch and emerald shiners in summer and winter, when the lake temperatures fluctuated least. (Little-Battelle)
W75-08381

NEMATODES OF LAKE BALATON: III. THE FAUNA IN LATE-SUMMER,
Research Inst. for Water Resources Development, Budapest (Hungary). Water Quality and Technology Dept.
Kalman Biro.
Ann Inst Biol (Tlhany) Hung Acad Sci, 39 p 89-100, 1972. Illus.
Identifiers: Achromadora-terricola, Biomass, *Bottom sediments, Dorylaimus-helveticus, *Fauna, *Hungary(Lake Balaton), Ironus-tenuicaudatas, Lakes, Microlaimus-globiceps, Monhystera-paludicola, *Nematodes, Paraphanolaimus-anistsi, Paraphanolaimus-behningi, Paraplectonema-pedunculatum, Summer, Theristus-setosus, Tobrilus-helveticus.

The qualitative and quantitative composition of nematodes in the bottom sediment of the open water of Lake Balaton (Hungary) in late-summer, 1968, was studied. Two new species were found for the Hungarian fauna: Microlaimus globiceps De Man and Paraphanoliamus anisitsi (Dad.) Andrassy. Achromadora terricola De Man, Dorylaimus helveticus Steiner, Tobrilus helveticus Hofm. found in the collections are new species for Lake Balaton. The most frequent 5 nematodes were: Paraplectonema pedunculatum S., Paraphanolaimus behningi M., Monhystera paludicola Dm., Theristus setosus B., Ironus tenuicaudatus Dm., their distribution, however, in the bottom sediment of the open water was not uniform. The number of nematodes was greater in the north-east-basin of Lake Balaton (15,000/m2) than in the south-west (10,000/m2). Greater numbers, above 23,000/m2, were generally found near the northern shore. Along the longitudinal axis of the lake a minimum was observable: 5000/m2. Lowest

Arch Hydrobiol Supplementb. Vol 41, No 4, p 427-449. 1973, Illus.

Descriptors: Europe, Mountains, *Algae, *Ecology, *Snow cover, Snowpacks, Photosynthesis, Photosynthetic bacteria, *Cold regions, Subarctic.
Identifiers: Green algae, Belanske, Tatry Mts., Carbon-14, Chlamydomonas-Sp, *Kryophilic, Algae, Czechoslovakia, Koliella-tatrae, Tatry Mountains, Biotopes.

The ecology of kryophilic algae of the permanent snowfield (1340 m) was studied in Belanske Tatry Mountains (Tatra National Park, north Slovakia, Czechoslovakia). The main components of the algal community were Koliella tatrae and 1 green species of Chlamydomonas. The vegetation lasted from May to the end of Oct., reaching its maximal development from the end of Aug. to the beginning of Oct. During the entire cycle of vegetation, the temperature was about 0C. The concentrations of main nutrients in the surface snow layer were comparable with eutrophic water reservoirs and were not a limiting factor. K. tatrae seems to be shade adapted, as it follows from its distribution over the snowfield and on its flanks. The field is situated on a rocky gorge, facing NNE and during the whole year it is protected against the direct sunshine. The maximal coloration of snow was found in the noon light intensities (0.2-0.6-(1.0).10-2 cal.cm-2.min-1. The abundance, biomass of algae, chlorophyll-a concentrations and photosynthesis in situ by means of 14CO2 gas chambers are given. The mean chlorophyll content in the shaded snow algal population is low and corresponds with values found for the 'sun phytoplankton' of mesotrophic water bodies. The net photosynthesis in the range (0.04)-0.13-088(1.85)Cass(assimilated) microgram (mm3 of algae)-1.h-1, and photosynthetic activity in the range (0.26)0.9-6.1(12.9) Cass microgram.Cbm (in biomass)mg-1.h-1, were determined. Results are comparable with those given by Fogg (1967) and Thomas (1969) from the similar biotopes. As the entire life cycles of kryophilic algae run close to the lower temperature limit of photosynthesis, they have a special importance for the recognition of photosynthetic potentiality in extremely cold biotopes.--Copyright 1974, Biological Abstracts, , Inc.
W75-08393

CONCENTRATION OF ADENOVIRUS FROM SEAWATER,
New Hampshire Univ., Durham. Dept. of Microbiology.
For primary bibliographic entry see Field 5A.
W75-08455

ENVIRONMENTAL EFFECTS OF DREDGING AND SPOIL DISPOSAL,
Washington State Dept. of Ecology, Olympia.
G. S. Jeane, II, and R. E. Pine.
Journal Water Pollution Control Federation, Vol 47, No 3, p 553-561, March 1975. 2 fig, 5 tab, 2 ref.

Descriptors: *Dissolved oxygen, *Dredging, *Toxicity, *Fish, Salmon, Water quality, Settling basins, Conductivity, Salinity, Temperature, Environmental effects, Organic matter, Industrial wastes, Breakwaters, Turbidity, Soil engineering, Sands, Bioassay, Waste disposal, Hydraulics, *Washington.
Identifiers: *Everett Harbor(Wash), *Spoil disposal, Ship docking, Berthing areas, Supernatant.

The Washington State Department of Ecology instituted a study of the effects of hydraulic dredging on water quality at the Port of Everett Hewitt Avenue Terminal project in October 1972. In addition to water quality parameters, toxicity to juvenile chinook salmon (O. tshawytscha) was investigated. The settling basin effluent weir had a maximum of 0.21 ppb of mercury, a Pearl-Benson Index of 41 mg/l, 18% volatile solids, and no detectable sulfides. The in situ bioassay demonstrated no toxicity. Dissolved oxygen was depressed more than 50% in the area of dredging and supernatant return during sludge material removal. The dredging portion of the project was accomplished with a cutter suction-type hydraulic dredge. The dredge had a pumping capability of 25,000 gpm of water containing 15-18% solids. The dredge spoils were transported through a 24-inch floating pipeline to a two-cell settling basin with a 200-foot long effluent weir. The material consisted of sand, organic material, and industrial waste. (Roberts-ISWS)
W75-08465

PHOSPHORUS SOURCES FOR LOWER GREEN BAY, LAKE MICHIGAN,
Wisconsin Univ., Green Bay. Ecosystems Analysis.
For primary bibliographic entry see Field 5B.
W75-08467

IMPACTS OF FOREST MANAGEMENT PRACTICES ON THE AQUATIC ENVIRONMENT-PHASE II,
Washington Cooperative Fishery Unit, Seattle.
For primary bibliographic entry see Field 5B.
W75-08468

THE PHOTOSENSITIZING ACTION OF 2-NAPHTHYLAMINE ON ESCHERICHIA COLI, K-12,
Auburn Univ., Ala. Dept. of Chemistry.
For primary bibliographic entry see Field 5A.
W75-08476

HYDROGEN SULFIDE EFFECTS ON SELECTED LARVAL AND ADULT MARINE INVERTEBRATES,
Oregon State Univ., Corvallis. Water Resources Research Inst.
R. S. Caldwell.
Available from the National Technical Information Service, Springfield, Va 22161 as PB-242 313, $3.75 in paper copy, $2.25 in microfiche. Completion Report WRRI-31, April 1975. 22 p, 2 fig, 4 tab, 16 ref. OWRT A-020-ORE(1).

Descriptors: Hydrogen sulfide, Invertebrates, Water pollution effects, Crabs, Oysters, Sea water, Lethal limit, Toxicity, Embryonic growth stage, Larvae, Juvenile growth stage.
Identifiers: Marine invertebrates, Dungeness crabs, Pacific oysters, Anoxic conditions.

Six species of marine invertebrates including larval and juvenile Dungeness crab, Cancer magister, and Pacific oyster, Crassostrea gigas, were examined for their tolerance to dissolved hydrogen sulfide in sea-water. In tests lasting up to 4 days, the sulfide tolerances of organisms ranged from a low of 0.2 mg/l for Anisogammarus confervicola to 6.0 mg/l for Macoma balthica. The range of tolerances appeared to correlate with the expected degree of anoxic conditions that would be encountered by each species in its natural habitat. Early embryos of C. gigas were very sensitive to hydrogen sulfide since an exposure to 0.32 mg/l for only 2 h. drastically affected the normal development of this stage. Seven day old veliger larvae of this species were not affected by 2 h. exposures of up to 0.56 mg/l hydrogen sulfide but were inactivated by 1.0 and 3.2 mg/l. However, recovery, even after exposure to the highest concentration, was complete after 24 h. Dungeness crab zoeae exposed for 74 h. to 0.56 mg/l sulfide were less able to tolerate a 15 or 90 min. period of heat shock at 29.0 deg C than were control organisms or those exposed to 0.18 mg/l. However, zoeae exposed for 48 h. to either 0.5 or 1.0 mg/l sulfide survived as well as controls at temperatures of 25.0 - 28.0 deg C. It is suggested that estuarine organisms live very close to their tolerance limits for hydrogen sulfide.

W75-08491

ANALYSES OF SELECTED CONSTITUENTS IN NATIVE WATER AND SOIL IN THE BAYOU BOEUF-CHENE-BLACK AREA NEAR MORGAN CITY, LOUISIANA, INCLUDING A MODIFIED STANDARD ELUTRIATE TEST,
Geological Survey, Baton Rouge, La.
For primary bibliographic entry see Field 5A.
W75-08501

A COMPARISON OF THE LETHALITY OF VARIOUS COMBINATIONS OF HEAVY METALS AND WATER TEMPERATURE TO JUVENILE RAINBOW TROUT.
Available from the National Technical Information Service, Springfield, Va. 22161, as BNWL SA4704, $4.00 in paper copy, $2.25 in microfiche. (1973), 5 p.

Descriptors: Water pollution, *Mercury, *Bioassay, *Heavy metals, *Rainbow trout, Water temperature, Water quality standards, Baseline studies, Environmental effects, *Toxicity, Water pollution effects, Fish reproduction, Animal growth, Thermal pollution, *Lethal limit.

This research project attempted to define and quantify the combined action of potential chemical pollutants with various water temperatures on fish and fish food organisms. Effects of a toxicant at different water temperatures were compared using the 96 hour TL50 continuous flow bioassay. Also included were studies on the growth and reproduction of the fish and fish food organisms wich survive sublethal pollutant exposures. The pollutants were mercury and chlorine at temperatures of 10C, 15C and 20C. Rainbow trout exhibited a three-fold difference in resistance to both mercury and chlorine depending upon the ambient temperature. Fish at 15C were the most resistant to the pollutant concentrations while either an increase or decrease of temperature from 15C caused a decreased resistance. The chlorine studies were hampered by analytical techniques which would not detect chlorine sufficiently at low levels. (Jernigan-Vanderbilt)
W75-08528

THE DISTRIBUTION OF INTRAPERITONEALLY INJECTED CADMIUM-115M IN CHICKENS,
Purdue Univ., Lafayette Ind. Dept. of Bionucleonics.
For primary bibliographic entry see Field 5A.
W75-08533

EVALUATION OF BACTERIAL PRODUCTION IN A POND IN SOLOGNE, (IN FRENCH),
Centre National pour l'Exploitation des Oceans, Paris (France).
J. Hussenot, and M. Laurent.
Ann Hydrobiol. Vol 4, No 2, p 169-181. 1973, (English summary).

Descriptors: *Bacteria, Ponds, *Analytical techniques, *Water pollution, *Measurement, Statistical methods, Numerical analysis, *Approximation techniques, *Growth rates, Mud, *Reproduction, Benthic fauna, *Algae, Microorganisms, Chara.
Identifiers: Dialysis, Bag, *France(Sologne), Chalk, Characeae, Zaika's formula.

A method for the measurement of bacterial production was developed by means of a bag meant for long incubations, the dialysis bag. The wall of the bag usually used for perfusion studies allows the passage of gas and ions of molecules. The confinement of bacteria during incubation is thus avoided. Bacteria are counted by the suspension-dilution method, using successive 50% dilutions, with 8 tubes for each dilution, which allows enough precision for evaluating the doubling of the number of germs. After a critical study of the various formulas for the estimation of bacterial production, Zaika's formula was chosen. The adding of chalk to the mud, in an intimate mixture in the laboratory, involves the development of benthic algae, mainly Characeae there was also an increase in the number of ammonifying microorganisms and a decrease in the organic matter content. The adding of chalk to these samples, in which the mud layers are not disturbed, provokes the same phonomena as the intimate mixture and a slight decrease in the mud level. The results observed in the field corroborate those obtained in the laboratory. The CaCO3 seems then to be a stimulating factor in organic matter mineralization.--Copyright 1974, Biological Abstracts,Inc.
W75-08534

FLOW-THROUGH APPARATUS FOR ACUTE TOXICITY BIOASSAYS WITH AQUATIC INVERTEBRATES,
Fisheries and Marine Service, Winnipeg (Manitoba). Aquatic Toxic Studies Div.
For primary bibliographic entry see Field 5A.
W75-08563

GROWTH OF THE BLUE-GREEN ALGA MICROCYSTIS AERUGINOSA UNDER DEFINED CONDITIONS,
Nebraska Univ., Lincoln. Dept. of Chemical Engineering.
S. Goto.
Available from the National Technical Information Service, Springfield, Va. 22161, as PB-242 511, $4.75 in paper copy, $2.25 in microfiche. M Sc Thesis, September 1972, 93 p, 7 fig, 34 tab, 60 ref, 4 append. OWRR A-020-NEB(2), 14-31-0001-3527.

Descriptors: *Eutrophication, Algae, Eutrophication, Lakes, *Cyanophyta, Bacteria, Cultures, Phosphates, Nitrates.
Identifiers: *Microcystis aeruginora.

There has been considerable speculation that eutrophication is aggravated by phosphates and nitrates released from fertilized fields and incompletely treated sewage. This research attempts to determine the limiting factors for growth of the blue-green alga, Microcystis aeruginosa, which causes massive algal blooms in lakes, by growing it in continuous culture under controlled conditions on a synthetic medium. Eventually, this project will evaluate the symbiotic growth of a typical species of bacteria with M. aeruginosa. By monitoring and controlling medium flow rate, feed nutrient concentrations of phosphate and nitrate, light intensity, and air or enriched carbon dioxide flow rate, and by employing two-species as well as one-species culture it is possible to determine the limiting concentrations of each component for the algae or the algae and bacteria. Results from continuous cultures of the alga as well as preliminary work on both the bacteria and algae are reported.
W75-08579

ACID TOLERANCE IN THE BROWN BULLHEAD ICTALURUS NEBOLOSUS (LE SUEUR),
West Virginia Univ., Morgantown. Dept. of Biology.
B. E. Sprague.
Available from the National Technical Information Service, Springfield, Va. 22161, as PB-242 513, $5.25 in paper copy, $2.25 in microfiche. MSC Thesis, 1974, 98 p, 26 fig, 34 tab, 14 ref. OWRT A-017-WV(3).

Descriptors: *Acidic waters, *Bullheads, *Bioassay, *Lethal limit, Hydrogen ion concentration mine wastes, Water pollution sources, Water pollution effects, Acid mine wastes, Freshwater fish, Mortality, Laboratory tests, *West Virginia, Temperature.
Identifiers: *Brown Bullhead, Ictalurus nebulosus, *Monongahela River(WV).

TL50 bioassays were conducted to determine the tolerance of the brown bullhead to minimum pH and maximum acidity in a chemically constituted water simulating the mine acid polluted environment of the Monogahela River. An intermittent flow-through system was used with sulphuric acid as the toxicant. The TL 50 bioassays were classified as a warm water experiment and two cold water experiments because of temperature variation during the research. The 72 hour estimates for the warm water bioassay, mean water temperature 25.9C, were TL 50 values of pH 3.32, hot total acidity 44.8 mg/l (as Ca CO3) and cold total acidity 42.1 mg/l. The 72 hour estimates in the cool water bioassay, mean water temperature 18.5C were based on a combination of treatments in the two experiments. The cool water temperature 72 hour TL 50 values were pH 3.21, hot total acidity 51.7 mg/l and cold total acidity 54.9 mg/l. The toxicity of sulphuric acid appears to be dependent on the hydrogen ion concentration. The apparent cause of the mortality was asphyxiation from coagulation of mucus on the gill filaments. The TL 50 results tend to support the hypothesis that the brown bullhead is one of the most acid tolerant species in the Monongahela River. (Katz)
W75-08581

THE EFFECTS OF POLLUTANTS ON MARINE MICROBIAL PROCESSES: A FIELD STUDY,
Harvard Univ., Cambridge, Mass. Div. of Engineering and Applied Physics.
R. Mitchell.
Available from the National Technical Information Service, Springfield, Va. 22161, as AD-787 602, $3.75 in paper copy, $2.25 in microfiche. Technical Report No 6, Sept 1974 45 p, 2 fig, 6 tab.

Descriptors: *Water pollution effects, *Mathematical models, *Bacteria, *Coral, Laboratory tests, *Electron microscopy, Lethal limit, Methodology, Oil, Phosphates, Oxygen, Toxins.
Identifiers: *Sub-lethal effects, Mucus, *Microbial processes, Tissue cultures, Beggiota.

Red Sea corals were used as a model for describing the effects of low concentrations of chemical pollutants on microbial processes in seawater. Low concentrations of crude oil, copper, and available organic matter, which were insufficient to kill the corals directly, upset the microbiological balance on the coral surface. Mucus production by the coral was stimulated and bacteria were attracted to the mucus and grew on it. Three factors associated with bacteria growth were responsible for the death of the coral colonies: (1) oxygen depletion; (2) chemical toxins; and (3) bacterial predators, particularly, Beggiota. Described is the development of a mathematical model to stimulate the destruction of corals by bacteria when the corals are under pollution stress. The model will be used to determine feedback between microbial processes involved in coral death. The model will be extended to provide predictive curves of the effeet of combinations of low level pollutants on microbial kill of corals and on other microbial processes in the ocean. (Katz)
W75-08583

BIOLOGICAL FEATURES OF INTERTIDAL COMMUNITIES NEAR THE U.S. NAVY SEWAGE OUTFALL, WILSON COVE, SAN CLEMENTE ISLAND, CALIFORNIA,
Available from the National Technical Information Service, Springfield, Va. 22161, as AD-783 029, $4.75 in paper copy, $2.25 in microfiche. Naval Undersea Center, San Diego, California, Report NVC TP396, July 1974, 85 p, 17 tab, 18 fig, 84 ref. Murray, S. N. and Littler, M. M., eds.

Descriptors: *Intertidal areas, *Sewage effluents, *Biological communities, *Benthos, *California, Water pollution sources, Water pollution effects, Algae, Invertebrates, Cyanophyta, Chlorophyta, Stratification, Domestic wastes, Primary productivity, Growth rates.

Identifiers: *San Clemente Island(Calif), Acmaea limatula.

Studies on the effects of a low-volume discharge of raw sewage on rocky marine intertidal communities near Wilson Cove, San Clemente Island, California included taxonomic surveys and quantitative assessments of standing stock, community structure and primary production for the sewage-affected area and nearby unpolluted (control) areas. Additionally, a comparative populational study of the limpet Acmaea limatula revealed that only larger individuals were present in the outfall area. Near the outfall pipe, intertidal communities were characterized by lower species diversity, reduced standing stocks of large, canopy-forming intertidal macrophytes (which largely had been replaced by a low-growing algal turf) and an abundance of suspension-feeding animals. The most productive macrophytes were among those most abundant in the outfall area. Additional manipulative studies revealed that the outfall area consisted of disclimax communities. (Katz)
W75-08585

APPARATUS AND PROCEDURE FOR MEASURING SUBLETHAL TOXICITY OF WASTEWATER DISCHARGES,
New Mexico Univ., Albuquerque. Eric H. Wang Civil Engineering Research Facility.
For primary bibliographic entry see Field 5A.
W75-08586

A REVIEW OF THE LITERATURE ON THE USE OF 2,4-D IN FISHERIES,
Southeastern Fish Control Lab., Warm Springs, Ga.
D. P. Schultz, and P. D. Harman.
Available from the National Technical Information Service, Springfield, Va. 22161, as PB-235 457, $4.75 in paper copy, $2.25 in microfiche. March 1974. 90 p, 201 ref.

Descriptors: *Reviews, *2,4-D, Publications, *Herbicides, Effects, *Bibliographies , Chlorinated hydrocarbon pesticides, Pesticides, Regulation, *Toxicity, Irrigation canals, Water pollution effects.

The herbicide 2,4-D was adapted from terrestrial to aquatic use. Recommended treatment rates vary from 2.24 kg/ha to 22.4 kg/ha or even higher for submersed species. The most commonly used formulation is the dimethylamine salt of 2,4-D (DMA-2,4-D). The ester formulations are also used, but are 10 to 20 times as toxic to fish and other aquatic organisms as the dimethylamine salt. A tolerance of 0.1 mg/liter has been issued for DMA - 2,4-D that occurs in potable water as a result of applications of DMA - 2,4-D to ditch banks in the western United States. Several federal agencies are presently pursuing the registration of 2,4-D for use in irrigation canal banks and for use in moving water. Most of the research necessary for registration of 2,4-D has been completed. A review is presented of the literature concerning the use of 2,4-D in fisheries. (Katz)
W75-08587

A REVIEW OF THE LITERATURE ON THE USE OF TFM-BAYLUSCIDE IN FISHERIES,
National Marine Fisheries Service, Ann Arbor, Mich. Great Lakes Fishery Lab.
S. E. Hamilton.
Available from the National Technical Information Service, Springfield, Va. 22161, as PB-235 442, $4.25 in paper copy, $2.25 in microfiche. March 1974. 53 p, 54 ref, 1 tab.

Descriptors: *Reviews, *Publications, *Bibliographies, *Lampreys, *Pest control, *Pesticides, Water pollution effects, Freshwater fish, Fisheries, Bioassay, Toxicity, Testing, Fishes.
Identifiers: *Bayluscide, *Lampricides, *TFM, 3-triflouromethyl-4-nitrophenol.

In a search for a selective larvicide that would control lampreys without destroying fish and other aquatic organisms, about 6,000 chemicals were tested by the U.S. Fish and Wildlife Service, largely during the mid 1950's. One compound, TFM, which is selectively toxic to sea lampreys was developed for field use. In 1963 Bayluscide (R) was discovered to be extremely toxic to sea lampreys. Because Bayluscide is also very toxic to fish, being virtually non-selective between lampreys and rainbow trout, only 3% by weight can be added to TFM without losing the selective toxicity of TFM. Addition of Bayluscide to TFM, however, effects substantial savings by greatly reducing the amount of TFM needed for effective treatment of lamprey populations. A complete review of literature concerning TFM-Bayluscide's use in fisheries is presented. (Katz)
W75-08588

THE ROLE OF PLANKTONIC PROTOZOA IN THE MARINE FOOD CHAIN: SEASONAL CHANGES, RELATIVE ABUNDANCE, AND CELL SIZE DISTRIBUTION OF TINTINNIDA,
New York Aquarium, Brooklyn. Osborn Labs. of Marine Sciences.
K. Gold.
Available from the National Technical Information Service, Springfield, Va. 22161, as C00 3390 14, $4.00 in paper copy, $2.25 in microfiche. Prepared for the Atomic Energy Commission (1974). 26 p, 15 fig, 13 ref. AEC-AT (11-1)-3390.

Descriptors: *Plankton, *Primary productivity, *Seasonal, *Protozoa, Measurement, *Water temperature, Size, *Growth rates, Population, Water pollution effects, *Food chains, Microorganisms, Environmental effects, *New York.
Identifiers: *Tintinnida.

Tintinnida in local waters were identified throughtout the year to relate species occurrences to water temperature. Maximum number of species was found in the fall; minimum number in the winter. The dimensions of Tintinnida were used for taxonomic purposes and also as an index to physiological processes. Length reflected cell growth and division, and could be used to identify newly divided juveniles and loricae of older generations in the same population. Length of certain species varied according to the temperature during the year: loricae were smaller in warmer waters than at lower temperature, probably due to different rates of fission by the protozoa seasonally. The natural variability of lorica sizes and shapes, much of which is due to environmental factors, was identified for a number of species in the plankton. (Katz)
W75-08589

METHODS FOR ACUTE TOXICITY TESTS WITH FISH, MACROINVERTEBRATES, AND AMPHIBIANS.
National Water Quality Lab., Duluth, Minn.
Available from the National Technical Information Service, Springfield, Va 22161 as PB-242 105, $4.25 in paper copy, $2.25 in microfiche. Environmental Protection Agency, Report EPA-660/3-75-009, April 1975. 61 p, 6 tab, 55 ref. EPA Program Element 1BA021.

Descriptors: Water pollution effects, Fish, Amphibians, Methodology, Aquatic animals, Invertebrates, *Bioassay, *Test procedures, *Toxicity, Diseases, Effluents, *Pollutant identification.
Identifiers: *Acute toxicity, Median lethal coneentration, Macroinvertebrates, *Toxicity tests.

Four detailed methods for conducting acute toxicity tests with freshwater, estuarine, and marine fish, macroinvertebrates, and amphibians are presented in an integrated format. Nomenclature is consistent with that used in other branches of toxicology. Concepts incorporated into the methods are applicable to toxicity tests with most aquatic organisms. This report was prepared by the Committee on Methods for Toxicity Tests with Aquatic Organisms. (EPA)
W75-08591

ENVIRONMENTAL REQUIREMENTS OF SELECTED ESTUARINE CILIATED PROTOZOA,
New Hampshire Univ., Durham. Dept. of Zoology.
A. C. Borror.
Available from the National Technical Information Service, Springfield, Va 22161 as PB-242 125, $4.25 in paper copy, $2.25 in microfiche. Environmental Protection Agency, Report EPA-660/3-74-031, May 1975. 49 p, 14 tab, 62 ref. 18080 FBW.

Descriptors: *Estuarine environment, Protozoa, *Tidal marshes, Distribution, Ecology, Oxygen, Hydrogen sulfide, Salinity, Cycles, Bacteria, Hydrogen ion concentration, Water temperature, *New Hampshire, Water pollution effects, Estuaries.
Identifiers: Tidal cycles, Spartina patens, Spartina alterniflora.

Measurements of temperature, pH, oxygen concentration, H2S concentration, salinity, bacterial concentration, occurrence of micrometazoa, and distribution and abundance of ciliated protozoa were recorded during the summers of 1970 and 1971 in a tidal marsh at Adams Pt., Durham, New Hampshire. Numerous differences in ciliate distribution occurred between the upper (Spartina patens) marsh and the lower (Spartina alterniflora) marsh. Physical and biological parameters of a patens-panne pond were measured during a 2-week period involving the initial flushing of the pool by a session of full moon spring tides. Effects of a full moon spring tide cycle, a neap tide cycle, and a new moon spring tide cycle for one station in the lower marsh were evaluated. During 1970 and 1971, 103 species of ciliates, representing 41 families and 10 orders were identified, including 4 new species. Several instances of correlations between ciliate abundance and oxygen concentration, H2S concentration, and salinity were observed. Contribution of tidal marsh ciliates in general to estuarine food webs probably occurs through their association with particulate detritus. (EPA)
W75-08592

PLUTONIUM AND OTHER TRANSURANIUM ELEMENTS: SOURCES, ENVIRONMENTAL DISTRIBUTION AND BIOMEDICAL EFFECTS.
Atomic Energy Commission, Washington, D.C.
Available from the National Technical Information Service, Springfield, Va 22161 as Rept No WASH-1359, $10.60 in paper copy, $2.25 in microfiche. Rept. No WASH-1359, Dec 1974. p 332, 48 fig, 36 tab, 247 ref.

Descriptors: *Plutonium, *Uranium, *Energy, *Energy transfer, Assessment, Environment, Distribution, Radioactivity effects, Public health, Safety, Evaluation, Biology, Biodegradation, Biological control, Standards, Administration, Governments.
Identifiers: *Transuranium elements.

This material was prepared at the request of the Division of Biomedical and Environmental Research, U.S. Atomic Energy Commission, in response to a notice appearing in the Federal Register, October 24, 1974. This notice stated the intent of the U. S. Environmental Protection Agency to hold public hearings to evaluate the environmental impact of plutonium and the other transuranium elements and to consider whether new guidelines or standards are needed to assure adequate protection of the general ambient environment and of the public health from potential contamination of the environment by radionuclides of these elements. This report is a compilation of Testimony presented before an EPA hearing board, December 10-11, 1974, Washington, D.C. (Houser-ORNL)
W75-08640

DEMOLITION OF BUILDING 12, AN OLD PLUTONIUM FILTER FACILITY,
Los Alamos Scientific Lab., N. Mex.
For primary bibliographic entry see Field 5E.
W75-08643

STUDIES OF PLUTONIUM, AMERICIUM, AND URANIUM IN ENVIRONMENTAL MATRICES,
Los Alamos Scientific Lab., N. Mex.
For primary bibliographic entry see Field 5B.
W75-08646

ANALYSIS OF POPULATION, BIRTH, AND DEATH STATISTICS IN THE COUNTIES SURROUNDING THE BIG ROCK POINT NUCLEAR POWER STATION, CHARLEVOIX COUNTY, MICHIGAN,
Argonne National Lab., Ill.
D. Grahn.
Available from the National Technical Information Service, Springfield, Va. 22161, as Rept No ANL-8149, $4.00 in paper copy, $2.25 in microfiche. Rept No ANL-8149, January 1975. 35 p, 5 fig, 5 tab, 7 ref.

Descriptors: *Monitoring, *Nuclear powerplants, *Effluents, *Environmental effects, Public health, *Mortality, Toxins, Water pollution, Statistics, Census, Population, Radioactivity, Data collections, Surveys, Data processing, *Michigan.

Allegations that changes in the frequency of infant mortality, cancer mortality, and immature births might be associated with releases of radioactive gases from the 75 MWe nuclear power station at Big Rock Point, Charlevoix, Michigan, are evaluated. Examined are the level of radiation exposures attributable to the station, the demographic and vital statistics of Charlevoix County and seven additional surrounding counties, and the implications of the allegations in view of existing knowledge of radiation effects. The allegations are not supported by this conjoint analysis of population and vital statistics. (Houser-ORNL)
W75-08653

REACTOR SAFETY STUDY - AN ASSESSMENT OF ACCIDENT RISKS IN U.S. COMMERCIAL NUCLEAR POWER PLANTS. APPENDIX VII - RELEASE OF RADIOACTIVITY IN REACTOR ACCIDENTS (DRAFT),
Battelle Columbus Labs., Ohio.
R. L. Ritzman, P. C. Owzarski, A. K. Postma, D. L. Lessor, and D. L. Morrison.
Available from the National Technical Information Service, Springfield, Va. 22161, as Rept No WASH-1400, $7.60 in paper copy, $2.25 in microfiche. Rept No WASH-1400, August 1974. 67 p, 6 fig, 15 tab, 44 ref, 11 append.

Descriptors: *Nuclear powerplants, *Safety, *Assessment, *Radioactivity, Research and development, Atmospheric pollution, Methodology, Environmental effects.
Identifiers: *Reactor safety, *Reactor accidents, *Containment boundary, *Fission products, Containment, Boiling water reactor, Pressurized water reactor.

Results are described of the Fission Product Source Term Task which has been conducted as part of the U.S. Atomic Energy Commission's Reactor Safety Study. The objective of the Reactor Safety Study is the evaluation of postulated accidents in large water-cooled power reactors with respect to the probability of occurrence and the magnitude of resulting consequences. The primary purpose of the Fission Product Source Term Task has been to specify the size of the fission product source which would escape the containment boundary as a function of time for various accident conditions defined by the Reactor Safety Study. A dominant portion of the effort on the task concerned fission product behavior under reactor core meltdown conditions. The Reactor Core Meltdown Task provided data on physical events and conditions that were essential in developing the definitions and procedures used to specify fission product movement within and loss from the containment boundary. The methodology that was evolved to enable the performance of calculations of fission product escape to the atmosphere for various accident sequences in a large pressurized water reactor or boiling water reactor is presented. (Houser-ORNL)
W75-08655

NUCLEAR CHEMICAL COPPER MINING AND REFINING: RADIOLOGICAL CONSIDERATIONS,
California Univ., Livermore. Lawrence Livermore Lab.
H. A. Tewes, H. B. Levy, and L. L. Schwartz.
Available from the National Technical Information Service, Springfield, Va. 22161, as Rept No UCRL-51345 Rev 1, $4.00 in paper copy, $2.25 in microfiche. Rept No UCRL-51345, Rev 1, June 3, 1974. 37 p, 4 fig, 13 tab, 24 ref, append.

Descriptors: *Mining, Copper, *Chemical reaction, *Nuclear energy, *Safety, *Evaluation, Assessment, Hazards, Safety factors, Public health, Environmental effects, Standards, Path of pollutants, Air pollution, Water pollution.
Identifiers: Nuclear chemical, *Copper mining.

A preliminary radiological safety analysis of the proposed nuclear chemical mining and refining process for copper has been carried out. Exposure sources and paths, exposed populations, and dose levels are discussed. Existing data were utilized in the formulation of the safety analysis, and conservative (i.e., 'worst case') assumptions were used where data were unavailable. Despite the 'upper limit' formulation of hypothetical radiological exposures to members of the public, all such exposures were found to be far below (much less than 1% of) current radiation protection guides. (Houser-ORNL)
W75-08662

RADIOLOGICAL AND ENVIRONMENTAL RESEARCH DIVISION ANNUAL REPORT, ECOLOGY, JANUARY - DECEMBER 1973.
Argonne National Lab., Ill.
For primary bibliographic entry see Field 5B.
W75-08670

THE CONFIGURATION OF THE HYDROCHEMICAL RELATIONSHIPS IN THE HUNGARIAN SECTION OF THE DANUBE DURING THE YEAR 1971: DANUBIALIA HUNGARICA LXVI, (IN GERMAN),
Magyar Tudomanyos Akademia, Budapest (Hungary). Station for Danube Research.
For primary bibliographic entry see Field 5B.
W75-08680

THE EFFECTS OF DOMESTIC AND INDUSTRIAL EFFLUENTS ON A LARGE TURBULENT RIVER,
Alberta Univ., Edmonton. Dept. of Zoology.
For primary bibliographic entry see Field 5B.
W75-08709

DREDGED SPOIL DISPOSAL ON THE NEW JERSEY WETLANDS: THE PROBLEM OF ENVIRONMENTAL IMPACT ASSESSMENT,
Rutgers - The State Univ., New Brunswick, N.J. Marine Science Center.
N. P. Psuty, K. F. Nordstrom, R. W. Hastings, and S. Bonsall.
Shore and Beach, Vol 42, No 1, p 25-30, April 1974. 3 fig, 4 ref.

Descriptors: *Dredging, *Spoil banks, *Environmental effects, Shoals, Bays, Lagoons, *Wetlands, Shellfish, Environmental control, Navigable waters, Channels, Depth, Maintenance, Economic feasibility, Disposal, *New Jersey, Cost-benefit ratio.
Identifiers: *Environmental impact, Intercoastal waterways, Inland water route.

The problems of maintenance dredging in a 177 mile section of the New Jersey Intracoastal Waterway from Manasquan River to Delaware Bay via the Cape May Canal were discussed. The waterway had been used mainly by pleasure crafts and commercial and sport fishing vessels. Previous dredging had been done with little attention to environmental impacts. Expediency had determined the location of dredge spoil disposal sites. The basic question was whether dredging should be continued in this waterway. Boat operators wanted dredging continued; but environmentalists and others were concerned with protecting the wetlands, shellfish areas, and fish habitats from misuse. It was concluded that the continuation of maintenance dredging could not be accomplished without some environmental destruction. The alternatives to dredge disposal on the marsh included creation of tidal marshlands, development of shoals for shellfish, beach nourishment, and an improvement of the sandy soils of the adjacent coastal uplands. Several studies were recommended to gather environmental data that is required for formation of a new cost-benefit ratio. (Roberts-ISWS)
W75-08716

THE CASCADE TYPE OF DAM RESERVOIRS AND THE EUTROPHICATION,
Polish Academy of Science, Krakow. Zaklad Biologii Wod.
S. Wrobel, and M. Bombowna.
In: International Symposium on Eutrophication and Water Pollution Control, October 16-20, 1973, Castle Reinhardsbrunn, DDR, sponsored by the Hydrobiological Section of the Biological Society of DDR and the Hydrology Section of the Technical University of Dresden, p 19-25. 3 fig, 1 ref.

Descriptors: *Dams, *Reservoirs, *Eutrophication, Water quality, Rivers, Primary productivity, Chlorophyll, Phytoplankton, Zooplankton, Benthic fauna, Watersheds(Basins), Detention reservoirs, Electric power, Thermal properties.
Identifiers: Cascade reservoirs(Poland), Sola River(Poland).

As dam reservoirs serve many purposes it is necessary to investigate the influence of the cascade type of dam reservoirs on eutrophication of the water bodies situated below them as well as the quality of water in the rivers below the dams. This problem was considered in relation to the dam reservoirs on the Carpathian rivers. The investigations were carried out during two years, at least three times in a season. Besides the primary production and chlorophyll content, the analyses of phyto- and zooplankton as well as of the bottom fauna were carried out. The chlorophyll was determined spectrophotometrically in an acetone extract from the filtrate obtained on membrane filters and the primary production by using light and dark bottles. The influence of reservoirs on a river is many sided and depends on many factors. The size and depth of the reservoir, the ratio of the volume of the reservoir to the mean yield of rivers, the depth of flood-gates in the dams, the management of the catchment basins of the rivers, the degree of their pollution and the state of banks all play a role. (Jones-Wisconsin)
W75-08764

CHEMICAL AND BIOLOGICAL INDICES OF EUTROPHICATION OF THE LUBACHOW RESERVOIR,
Panstwowy Instytut Hydrologiozno-Meteorologiczny, Wroclaw (Poland).
H. Florczyk, S. Golowin, and A. Solski.

water bloom was due to Aphanizomenon flos-aquae, Anabaena, Ceratium hirundinella. Bacterioplankton increased. Cladocera and Copepoda prevailed instead of Rotaroria. The profundal of the upper part of the Bratsk reservoir is characterized by bottom deposits of suspended materials from industrial and agrarian sewages. (Jones-Wisconsin)
W75-08766

RELATIONS BETWEEN NUTRIENT BUDGET AND PRODUCTIVITY IN PONDS,
Ceskoslovenska Akademie Ved, Prague. Hydrobiologicka Laborator.
J. Hrbacek.
In: International Symposium on Eutrophication and Water Pollution Control, October 16-20, 1973, Castle Reinhardsbrunn, DDR, sponsored by the Hydrobiological Section of the Biological Society of DDR and the Hydrology Section of the Technical University of Dresden, p 59-62. 5 ref.

Descriptors: *Cycling nutrients, *Ponds, *Productivity, Eutrophication, Fertilization, Fish farming, Phosphorus, Nitrogen, Bottom sediments, Energy transfer, Equilibrium, Fluctuations, Ammonia.
Identifiers: Blatna(Czechoslovakia), Nutrient budget.

The study of eutrophication could profit considerably if the knowledge of the effects and the mechanism of intentional fertilization were compiled. Data are reported from fishponds west of the town of Blatna, Czechoslovakia. The ponds were fertilized with superphosphate and pig manure. The average amount of total dissolved and dispersed phosphorus was 0.16 mg/l P, which is less than a fifth of the phosphorus applied yearly to the ponds by superphosphate. The maximum values found were only slightly above one third of the amount of phosphorus applied. The average amount of total dissolved and dispersed nitrogen was 1.4 mg/l N; this is more than twice the amount added to the pond in manure. The fish production showed fairly good correlations with the seasonal mean of the total nitrogen in ponds and poorer correlation with total phosphorus. There were low values in total nitrogen in April and May and high values from June through September, with the highest value in August. In phosphate and total phosphorus, values higher than the yearly means were found only in April and May and in phosphate phosphorus also in September. (Jones-Wisconsin)
W75-08767

CHEMICAL AND BIOLOGICAL ASPECTS OF THE EUTROPHICATION OF A TROUT BROOK,
Brno Univ. (Czechoslovakia). Hydrobiologicka Laborator.
F. Kubicek.
In: International Symposium on Eutrophication and Water Pollution Control, October 16-20, 1973, Castle Reinhardsbrunn, DDR, sponsored by the Hydrobiological Section of the Biological Society of DDR and the Hydrology Section of the Technical University of Dresden, p 80-83. 7 ref.

Descriptors: *Chemical properties, *Biological properties, *Eutrophication, *Streams, Water pollution sources, Water pollution effects, Municipal wastes, Bioindicators, Agriculture, Oxygen sag, Self-purification.
Identifiers: Trout streams, Czechoslovakia.

A trout brook which receives a waste water load from a community of 2,500 inhabitants in its upper reach was studied. Pollution sources are untreated slope waters from household and public facilities, going directly into the stream. Most houses are provided with privy pits. A periodic pollution source is runoff from fertilized fields. The character of the brook changes markedly after several hundred meters and in station 2 there are clearly different chemical and biological indices. Oxygen conditions improve especially and clean water fauna are more numerous. Periphyton consists mainly of diatoms. In the microbenthos Ciliata are still dominant. The third section assumes the character of a natural trout brook. Quantity of nutrients is higher than that found in other trout brooks, but the biological composition of the bottom is characterized by a wide range of diatom species, by the occurrence of filamentous algae and by more clean water animal species othan other groups. The proportion of Ciliata in the microbenthos is much lower than in preceding station. Length of the zone with its decisive phase of self-purification and change in nutrient contents depends on conditions. (Jones-Wisconsin)
W75-08768

ON ENVIRONMENTAL FACTORS AFFECTING THE PRIMARY PRODUCTION IN SHALLOW WATER BODIES,
Deutsche Akademie der Wissenschaften zu Berlin (East Germany). Institut fuer Meereskunde.
G. Schellenberger.
In: International Symposium on Eutrophication and Water Pollution Control, October 16-20, 1973, Castle Reinhardsbrunn, DDR, sponsored by the Hydrobiological Section of the Biological Society of DDR and the Hydrology Section of the Technical University of Dresden, p 89-91.

Descriptors: *Primary productivity, *Shallow water, *Mathematical models, Estuaries, Radiation, Photosynthesis, Biomass, Phytoplankton, Detritus, Seston, Light intensity.

In developing mathematical models of estuarine ecosystems, it is necessary to elaborate models of the involved subsystems. An important one deals with representation of primary productivity. Gross production rate per unit volume at depth z depends on such environmental properties as light field in the water, temperature, and nutrients. A preliminary model has been constructed under the assumption that nutrients are not lacking and water temperature does not change. In this case the photosynthesis depends only on biomass primary producers and light conditions. Since the water bodies are relatively shallow and well mixed, phytoplankton is homogenously distributed throughout the whole basin. The attenuation coefficient of natural water is the sum of its components (pure water, dissolved organic substances, particles). Particles, especially effective optically, are phytoplankton and detritus. Although a linear relationship is assumed between production rate per unit volume and phytoplankton biomass, the total production rate per unit column -- depending on the ratio of phytoplankton to seston – seems hardly affected by the total amount of phytoplankton biomass. Considering a production inhibition at high light intensities, total production rate can be favorably influenced by a certain content of dead suspended matter, protecting bioseston against excess light. (Jones-Wisconsin)
W75-08769

LIMNOLOGICAL MODELS OF RESERVOIR ECOSYSTEM,
Ceskoslovenska Adademie Ved, Prague. Hydrobiologicka Laborator.
M. Straskraba.
In: International Symposium on Eutrophication and Water Pollution Control, October 16-20, 1973, Castle Reinhardsbrunn, DDR, sponsored by the Hydrobiological Section of the Biological Society of DDR and the Hydrology Section of the Technical University of Dresden, p 110-110d.

Descriptors: *Mathematical models, *Reservoirs, *Eutrophication, Analytical techniques, Statistical methods, Stratification, Phytoplankton, Productivity, Mixing, Depth, Nutrients, Reservoir storage.
Identifiers: Empirical models, Czechoslovakia.

Two kinds of limnological models are of particular interest relative to eutrophication--empirical and analytical. Empirical models are derived by statistical techniques from direct measurements of dependent and corresponding independent variables. Analytical models, expressed as sets of differential equations, are based on combinations of general quantitative expressions of basic relationships among dominating variables. Particular values for individual water bodies (parameters of the model) are derived either from direct observations or from literary data. For prediction of new conditions, e.g., prediting the effect of the given nutrient supply into an existing water body or predicting water quality in a new reservoir, both approaches have their limitations. A major drawback of the empirical models is the limitation of the validity, for particular sets of conditions, from which they were derived. The analytical models are up to now severely limited by implying constant structure, behavior, and parameters of the system during major changes of trophic status. Two approaches are followed for minimizing drawbacks of both models: empirically determining the relationships of the parameters of analytical models to environmental variables; treating model structure and parameters as a function of major controlling variables. (Jones-Wisconsin)
W75-08770

DRAWING OFF OF HYPOLIMNION WATERS AS A METHOD FOR IMPROVING THE QUALITY OF LAKE WATERS,
P. Olszewski, and A. Sikorowa.
In: International Symposium on Eutrophication and Water Pollution Control, October 16-20, 1973, Castle Reinhardsbrunn, DDR, Sponsored by the Hydrobiological Section of the Society of DDR and the Hydrology Section of the Technical University of Dresdon, p 136-141, 1 tab.

Descriptors: *Hypolimnion, *Oxygenation, *Water treatment, *Lakes, Thermal properties, Chemical properties, Biological properties, Thermal stratification, Bottom sediments, Epilimnion, Thermocline, Primary productivity, Zooplankton, Microorganisms, Bacteria, Benthic fauna.
Identifiers: *Lake Kortowe(Poland).

The thermal, chemical and biological phenomena of Lake Kortowe, Poland resulting from the withdrawal of hypolimnetic waters is presented. The lake has two depressions considerably removed from one another, a southern and a northern 'control,' divided by a shoal with an average depth of 6 m. As a result of pumping from the hypolimnion in the experimental part of the lake, the number of oxygen-free days over the bottom averaged 97 per year, and 124 in the control for 16 years. Hypolimnetic withdrawal in the southern part was begun in 1956. Drawing off the deeper waters was usually begun about May and June, and as a result differences were noted in the two parts of the lake: the epilimnion in the experimental part increased, the thermocline deepened, and autumnal circulation began on an average four weeks earlier and at higher temperatures compared with the control part. An enormous growth in zooplankton numbers was noted. Microorganisms occurred in greater numbers at both sites under study during the summer stagnation period in 1966 and 1967 at a depth of 0.3 to 1 m, in the thermal transition layer, and at the bottom. (Jones-Wisconsin)
W75-08771

DISTURBANCE OF WATER SUPPLY DUE TO SECONDARY BIOLOGICAL CONTAMINANTS, (IN RUSSIA),
Institutul de Sanatate Publica si Cercetare Medicale, Iasi (Rumania).
G. Zamfir, and S. Apostol.
Gig Sanit. 38(9): 73-75. 1973.

Descriptors: *Water quality control, *Water pollution sources, *Water pollution effects, Microorganisms, Bacteria, Fungi, Algae, Benthos, Benthic fauna, Benthic flora, Potable water, Industrial water, *Water supply, Water treatment.
Identifiers: Chlorination, Contaminants, Corrosives.

The effect of secondary biological contaminants (bacteria, fungi, algae, macrophytes, protoza worms, mollusks, crustaceans, insects, fish, etc.) which can increase in number and affect the hygienic and organoleptic properties of water, plug pipes, filters, and pumps and in general make the water unfit for drinking and industrial purposes are discussed. The measures used for controlling contamination (chlorination, ozonation, anti-corrosion coatings, ultrasound, UV and ionizing irradiations, algicides, fungicides, herbicides, insecticides, etc), should be used very judiciously, since all these organisms are also active participants in water self-purification processes. Copyright 1975, Biological Abstracts, Inc.
W75-08773

SWIMMING PERFORMANCE OF ARCTIC GRAYLING,
Idaho Univ., Moscow. Dept. of Civil Engineering.
For primary bibliographic entry see Field 8A.
W75-08788

PRIMARY PRODUCTION IN A GREAT PLAINS RESERVOIR,
G. R. Marzolf, and J. A. Osborne.
Verhandlungen Internationale Vereinigung Limnologie, Vol 18, p 126-133, 1972. 1 fig, 4 tab, 15 ref. OWRR A-032-KAN(2). NSF GB 4560.

Descriptors: *Primary productivity, *Reservoirs, *Great Plains, Oligotrophy, Photosynthesis, Physicochemical properties, *Kansas, Shallow water, Wind, Chlorophyll, Light penetration, Turbidity, Lake morphology, Eutrophication.
Identifiers: *Tuttle Creek Reservoir(Kans).

The investigation of the photosynthetic production of Tuttle Creek Reservoir, Kansas, was motivated predominantly to understand the dynamics of higher trophic levels in this ecosystem. The reservoir is a result of the damming of the Big Blue River 16 kilometers upstream from its confluence with the Kansas River. The features which combine to make this reservoir intriguing are its relatively shallow water and long fetch to winds which constitue a major feature of the prairie environment. It is very likely that the annual mean rate of primary production is light limited in Tuttle Creek Reservoir. It is not clear that seasonal variation under that limitation is totally energy dependent. There are instances when the production rate is not commensurate with chlorophyll concentration. The correlation of primary production with the light extinction coefficient is not sufficiently suggestive to stimulate a search for casusality though cause and effect cannot be denied. It is concluded that primary production is light limited and that the mechanisms of the limitation are likely to be related to the morphology of the basin and to wind which serves to maintain turbid conditions and to limit the time available for photosynthesis by vertical mixing. (Jones-Wisconsin)
W75-08846

5D. Waste Treatment Processes

FORMATION OF HALOGENATED ORGANICS BY CHLORINATION OF WATER SUPPLIES,
Harvard Univ., Cambridge, Mass. Dept. of Sanitary Engineering.
For primary bibliographic entry see Field 5F.
W75-08357

FACTORS AFFECTING COLOR DEVELOPMENT DURING TREATMENT OF TNT WASTE,
Air Force Academy, Colo.
M. W. Nay, Jr, C. W. Randall, and P. H. King.
Paper presented at the 27th Annual Purdue Industrial Waste Conference, Purdue University, Lafayette, Indiana, May 2-4, 1972. 8 p, 5 tab, 7 fig, 8 ref.

Descriptors: *Explosives, *Waste water treatment, *Industrial wastes, *Color reactions, *Lime, *Colorimetry, Spectrophotometry, Light, Activated carbon, Temperature, Ambient light, Temperature control, Organic wastes, Waste treatment, Organic compounds.
Identifiers: *Trinitrotoluene(TNT), Color removal, Nitroaromatic compounds.

Experiments have demonstrated that color development in TNT waste does occur as the pH increases and that the developed color has a derogatory effect on subsequent waste treatment, both biological and physical-chemical. The color development during pH adjustment is a function of the light intensity, temperature, type of neutralizing agent, chemical dosage and the time since chemical adjustment. Obviously, if the waste is to be treated biologically or discharged to a biological system, the pH must be adjusted first. The first color development experiment consisted of raising the pH of the raw TNT waste to selected values with both neutralizing agents and observing the immediate color development. Typical results show that lime contributes to a greater immediate increase in color than does soda ash at all pH values. Experimental results have shown that a photochemical enhancement of color development does occur and temperature also affects color development. Excessive dosages of neutralizing agents can increase color development. The prevention of color development, rather than the removal of developed color is emphasized. Neutralization facilities should be designed to eliminate sunlight, to provide a stable pH, to permit cooling of the waste before chemical adjustment and to avoid overdose situations. (Poertner)
W75-08362

REMOVAL OF 2,4-D AND OTHER PRESISTENT ORGANIC MOLECULES FROM WATER SUPPLIES BY REVERSE OSMOSIS,
Cornell Univ., Ithaca, N.Y. School of Chemical Engineering.
V. H. Edwards, and P. F. Schubert.
Journal of the American Water Works Association, Vol 66, No 10, p 610-614, October 1974. 1 tab, 28 ref. OWRR A-032-NY(2).

Descriptors: *Reverse osmosis, *Water quality control, *Experiments, *Water chemistry, Water analysis, Pesticides, Waste treatment, Adsorption, Aqueous solutions, Water reuse, *Waste water treatment.
Identifiers: *Organic chemicals, Water purification.

Reverse osmosis is still one of the most promising techniques for removal of many refractory organics of intermediate to high molecular weight from water, and reuse of recovered byproducts is simpler than with carbon adsorption. Presented is a review of thé ways in which these techniques are used. First, recalcitrant organic chemicals, reverse osmosis for waste treatment and water purification, and pesticide analysis are discussed. Next, the following experimental methods and their results are discussed: reverse osmosis experiments; adsorption experiments; 2,4 dichlorophenoxyacetic acid (2,4-D) analysis; preparation of cellulose triacetate membranes; and preparation of iron-complex 2,4-D derivative. Considered also are aqueous solutions of a single organic, anionic polyelectrolyte complexes, and aqueous mixtures of several organics. Reverse osmosis shows varying selectivity for pesticide residues depending on the residue, residue concentration, membrane, and the presence of other solutes. Reverse osmosis membranes remove bacteria and viruses quantitatively in the absence of membrane defects. (Bell-Cornell)
W75-08365

WATER VOL. 39. A YEARBOOK FOR HYDROCHEMISTRY AND WATER PURIFICATION TECHNIQUE,
For primary bibliographic entry see Field 5F.
W75-08390

ALGAE REMOVAL BY UPFLOW FILTRATION,
Nebraska Univ., Lincoln. Dept. of Civil Engineering.
J. H. Forbes, Jr.
Available from the National Technical Information Service, Springfield, Va 22161 as PB-242 369, $4.75 in paper copy, $2.25 in microfiche. M S Thesis, December 1974. 86 p, 19 fig, 3 tab, 38 ref, 3 append. OWRT A-027-NEB(7). 14-31-0001-5027.

Descriptors: *Algae, *Oxidation ponds, *Suspended solids, *Filtration, *Waste water treatment, Design criteria, Operations.
Identifiers: *Algae removal, Upflow filtration.

Upflow filtration of oxidation ponds has shown promise of being an effective and economical method of removing suspended solids. This preliminary investigation determined some design and operating criteria which should be incorporated in a further study. Some conclusions found: (1) suspended solids removals of 50% are obtainable on influents in the 110 mg/l range; (2) the upflow unit provided an average 40% BOD and 16% COD reduction; (3) effluent was always of higher quality than the influent with maximum removals occurring during the first hour; (4) the minimum backwash time is five minutes; (5) filamentous algae are consistently removed while smaller algae pass through indicating expansion controls should be initiated; and (6) upflow filtration shows promise of being an effective and economical means of algae removal from oxidation ponds.
W75-08474

EFFECT OF HOLDING TIME ON RETENTION POND EFFLUENT,
Kansas State Univ., Manhattan. Dept. of Civil Engineering.
L. A. Schmid, and K. W. Mueldener.
Available from the National Technical Information Service, Springfield, Va 22161 as PB-242 351, $4.25 in paper copy, $2.25 in microfiche. Kansas Water Resources Research Institute, Manhattan, Contribution Number 162, April 1975. 67 p, 22 tab, 10 fig, append. OWRT A-057-KAN(1). 14-31-0001-3816.

Descriptors: Water quality, *Retention, Settling basins, Effluents, *Waste water treatment, *Tertiary treatment, Lagoons, Sewage treatment, Copper.
Identifiers: *Polishing ponds, Algae control, Flow equalization.

Polishing ponds are often required following extended aeration activated sludge sewage treatment. These polishing ponds are installed to further treat the secondary effluent by sedimentation and flow equalization. The quiescent pond conditions combined with the readily available nutrients in the secondary effluent often results in profuse algal blooms which can result in a lowering of the overall water quality through the pond. Two polishing ponds were monitored for one year to evaluate their effectiveness. One pond, with a detention time of 10 days, received a well treated secondary effluent. This pond lowered the water quality in the summer, while improving it in the winter. For the entire year on an average, there was no water quality improvement through the pond. Sludge build-up was not a problem in this 10 day pond. Coliform reduction was poor through the pond. Copper was effective as an algicide from 0.3 to 1 mg/l. Copper residuals were detected for several weeks indicating little precipitation of copper as copper carbonate. The second polishing pond folowed an inefficient treatment plant. This pond, detention time of 4 days, provided emergency treatment that would not have been available without the pond. The pond reduced, BOD5, COD, and suspended solids by about 50 percent. It was concluded that polishing ponds serve a useful purpose simply by providing emergency treatment during periods of plant upset.
W75-08487

WATER REUSE: RESOURCE OF THE FUTURE,
Dallas Water Utilities Dept., Tex.
H. J. Graeser.
American Water Works Association Journal, Vol 66, No 10, p 575-578, October, 1974. 1 fig.

Descriptors: *Water reuse, *Water resources, *Waste water treatment, *Water treatment, Viruses, Public health, Chemical precipitation, Organic compounds, Pesticides, Nitrification, Heavy metals.

This paper presented the opinion that water reuse may soon be the only alternative available to the water-supply industry if it is to maintain its present supply of water resources. The author noted that American wastefulness is putting an increasing burden on our streams. A recent Gallup poll indicated that the concept of water reuse is acquiring more acceptability. The author also presented brief descriptions of three areas of investigation in water reuse by the Dallas Reclamation Research Center. Alum treatment at doses three to four times greater than those required for clarification with filtration can produce an effluent that can be successfully disinfected for virus. Activated carbon filtration was found to be most effective in removing potentially dangerous organics, such as pesticides. In addition, when the activated sludge process was operated in a nitrifying mode, effluent organics were markedly reduced and heavy metals removal also apparently increased. The removal of heavy metals by carbon adsorption decreased very markedly as the effluent ammonia concentration increased. The researchers found the most difficult metals to remove are lead, cadmium and barium. (Pulliam-Vanderbilt)
W75-08537

FEEDING CATTLE AT THE PULP MILL,
Tampella A.B., Tampere (Finland).
H. Romantschuk.
Unasylva, Vol 26, No 106, p 15-17, Autumn, 1974. 2 fig, 1 tab.

Descriptors: *Sulfite liquors, *Proteins, *Fermentation, *Pulp wastes, Industrial wastes, Wastes, Fungi, Foreign research, Foreign countries, Europe, Water pollution sources, Feeds, Water pollution control, Waste water treatment, Cattle, *Recycling.
Identifiers: *Pekilo process, Pekilo protein, Finland.

A brief description is given of the 'Pekilo' process, development in Finland, for converting the spent liquor of a sulfite pulp mill into single-cell protein through fermentation by fungi. The process is also applicable to other carbohydrate-containing wastes. Animal feeding tests showed that Pekilo protein can be used as a partial substitute for soybean meal, fish meal, or skim milk powder. United Paper Mills Ltd. is building a Pekilo plant with a capacity of 10,000 tons annually at its Jamsankoski (Finland) pulp mill. The advantages of the Pekilo process over other carbohydrate fermentation processes are given. (Witt-IPC)
W75-08539

PURIFICATION OF WASTEWATERS AND GASEOUS EMISSIONS IN THE U.S.A. (OCHISTKA STOCHNYKH VOD I GAZOVYKH VYBROSOV NA PREDPRIYATIYAKH S.SH.A.),
Ministerstvo Bumazhnoi i Derevoobrabatyvayushchei Promyshlennost, Moscow (USSR).
A. M. Pristupa.
Bumazhnaya Promyshlennost, No 12, p 23-26, December, 1974. 4 fig, 1 tab.

Descriptors: *Water pollution control, *Air pollution, *Pulp and paper industry, *United States, Research and development, Chemicals, Ozone, Chlorine, Sludge, Economics, Wastes, Industrial wastes, Water pollution sources, Water pollution control, Effluents, Waste water treatment, Organizations, Bleaching wastes, Pulp wastes, Foreign countries.
Identifiers: USSR(Soviet Union).

Within the frame of the USSR-U.S.A. agreement on cooperation in the area of environment protection, a group of Soviet specialists visited several U.S. mills and paper industry organizations to learn about water and air pollution control. This report on the visit discusses recent progress in pollution control, describes control measures at individual mills, and reviews research conducted in this field. Increased attention is paid to the use of bleaching agents other than chlorine (e.g., ozone) and to the economical utilization of sediments from effluent purification. (Stapinski-IPC)
W75-08540

SIMPLE AERATOR SOLVES PROBLEMS.
Processing, Vol 21, No 1, p 6-7, January, 1975. 2 fig.

Descriptors: *Aeration, *Equipment, *Treatment facilities, Sewage treatment, Oxygenation, Water purification, Water quality control, Industrial wastes, *Waste water treatment.
Identifiers: *Helixor aerator.

The Helixor aeration device, developed by Polcon Corporation of Canada, consists of a rigid polyethylene pipe (18 inches in diameter) incorporating an internal helix element. The Helixor is anchored in vertical position on the bottom of a tank, basin, lagoon, or the like, and air is supplied at the base of the unit on either side of the helix component by means of a plastic tube. The air bubbles generated create an upward draft which carries water into and up through the pipe, creating good circulation and providing maximum oxygen transfer. Possible applications of the Helixor for treating industrial wastes are indicated. (Witt-IPC)
W75-08542

ABILITY OF LIGNIN TO BIND IONS OF CERTAIN HEAVY METALS (ISSLEDOVANIE SPOSOBNOSTI LIGNINA SBYAZYVAT' IONY NEKOTORYKH TYAZHELYKH METALLOV),
Stavropolskii Gosudarstvennyi Pedagogicheskii Institut (USSR).
D. G. Garkusha, P. M. Kuznetsov, and R. S. Fogileva.
Zhurnal Analiticheskoi Khimii, Vol 29, No 11, p 2295-2298, November, 1974. 5 fig, 1 tab, 5 ref.

Descriptors: *Lignins, *Waste water treatment, *Ion exchange, *Copper, *Cobalt, *Iron, *Nickel, Metals, Alkalinity, Activated carbon, Hydrogen ion concentration, Separation techniques, Cation exchange, Water pollution sources, Yeasts, Wastes, Industrial wastes, Waste treatment, Water pollution treatment, Water purification, Adsorption, Ions, Heavy metals.

Wastes from a feed yeast plant were used as the source of lignin for studying its ability to remove traces of Fe(III), Co(II), Ni(II), and Cu(II) ions from 29 solutions of alkali metal salts as functions of ion concentration and pH. Chromatographic columns were packed with lignin or with layers of lignin and activated charcoal separated by a filter paper disk. At concentrations of 0.01 to 0.00001 molar the removal of Cu was almost complete over the entire range, while only approximately 50% of the Ni was removed. The removal of Fe ions decreased with increasing concentration. How-

ever, with the lignin-charcoal column the Fe was removed at the same high level over the entire concentration range. Removal of the heavy metal ions increased with increasing pH, reaching a maximum at pH 4-5. Further increases in the pH did not increase the adsorption of the metal ions from the solutions. The sharp rise in the pH of filtrates after passage of the solutions through the lignin indicated that H ions were being exchanged for the metal ions, i.e., the lignin was acting as a cation-exchange resin. The ion-exchange capacity of the lignin at pH 4-5 for the metal ions was determined. Analyses of the filtrates indicated that the amount of lignin washed out decreased rapidly with increasing amounts of solution passing through it. (Chern-IPC)
W75-08543

APPLICATION OF ACID/PRESSURE FLOTATION TO THE THICKENING OF EXCESS ACTIVATED SLUDGE (ZASTOSOWANIE FLOTACJI KWASNOCISNIENIOWEJ DO ZAGESZCZANIA NADMIERNEGO OSADU CZYNNEGO),
Prosan (B.P.), Warsaw (Poland).
A. Olezczyk.
Prace Naukowe Instytutu Inzynierii Ochrony Srodowiska Politechniki Wroclawskiej, No 20, p 115-129, 1973. 6 fig, 4 tab, 11 ref.

Descriptors: *Activated sludge, *Dewatering, *Sludge treatment, Air, Acids, Sludge, Neutralization, Lime, Ammonia, Laboratory tests, Foreign research, Hydrogen ion concentration, Industrial wastes, Water pollution sources, Water pollution control, Wastes, *Waste water treatment, Polyelectrolytes.
Identifiers: *Acid/pressure flotation, Sulfuric acid, Sodium hydroxide.

Flotation experiments were carried out in the laboratory with two samples of excess sludge from the purification plants at the Ostroleka and Swiecie mills. The concentration of the sludge was 0.55%, the pH about 7.5. Neither sludge could be thickened by gravitation, even at high doses of polyelectrolytes or other additives. In preliminary experiments, attempts were made to achieve flotation by air pressure (0.5-3.5 kg/sq cm) or by the addition of concentrated sulfuric acid (0.1-1 ml/250 ml sludge). Both were unsuccessful. Pressure increased the concentration to 1.7%, but a part of the suspension sedimented and the liquid discharged contained a considerable amount of suspended solids. There was no sedimentation in chemical flotation and the concentration was increased to over 2%, but the process was slow, requiring long residence time. A combination of air pressure and chemical treatment gave satisfactory results. Within 20 minutes, about 80% reduction of the sludge volume was obtained, and the thickened sludge sedimented only with difficulty. The maximum acid needed was 1 ml/liter sludge. The thickened sludge can be neutralized with lime, NaOH, or ammonia, depending on the method of further processing. The combined flotation method reduces the filtration resistance of the sludge, so that it is dewatered easily in vacuum filters, filter presses, or drying beds. (Stapinski-IPC)
W75-08544

STATISTICAL ANALYSIS OF THE PROCESS OF EFFLUENT PURIFICATION AT THE BAIKAL PULP MILL FOR THE PURPOSE OF CONTROL (STATISTICHESKII ANALIZ PROTSESSA OCHISTKI STOCHNYKH VOD BAIKAL'SKOGO TSELLYULOZNOGO ZAVOD DLYA TSELEI UPRAVLENIYA),
N. E. Milagina, V. Z. Ponizovskii, A. Ya. Rudomir, and V. M. Khushutdinova.
Sbornik Trudov Vsesoyuznyi Nauchno-Issledovatel'skii Institut Tsellyulozno-Bumazhnoi Promyshlennosti No 62, p 59-69, 1973. 7 fig, 2 tab.

Descriptors: *Statistical methods, *Waste water treatment, *Pulp wastes, Treatment facilities, Computer models, Biological treatment, Chemical precipitation, Aeration, Temperature, Hydrogen ion concentration, Biochemical oxygen demand, Chemical oxygen demand, Suspended solids, Color, Nitrogen, Phosphorus, Water pollution sources, Water pollution, Water pollution control, Industrial wastes, Wastes, Waste treatment.
Identifiers: Lake Baikal(USSR).

A statistical analysis was made, with the help of a computer, of the effluent purification process at the Baikal pulp mill, based on daily and two-hour data from the purification plant laboratory for a period of 8 months. Calculations were made of the means of the parameters and of standard deviations, and tests were conducted of normal distribution. The samples analyzed were taken at various points of the purification equipment which consists of biological purification, chemical purification, mechanical treatment, and final aeration treatment. A diagram is given of the purification plant on which the sampling points are indicated. The parameters studied included temperature, pH, BOD, COD, oxidizability, suspended solids content, color, and nitrogen and phosphorus contents. The results of the analysis are discussed in terms of the effect of the individual variable fluctuations on the process and the levelling action of the equipment units. (Stapinski-IPC)
W75-08547

FOR A CLEAN DIGESTER (FUR EINEN SAUBEREN KOCHER).
Allgemeine Papier-Rundschau, No 35, p 990, 992, September 5, 1974. 2 fig.

Descriptors: *Activated sludge, *Pulp wastes, *Waste water treatment, Wastes, Industrial wastes, Water pollution sources, Water pollution treatment, Water pollution control, Water purification, Biological treatment, Foreign countries, Europe.
Identifiers: *Bio-sedimat clarifiers.

The biological clarification plant installed at Papierfabrik Palm KG (West Germany) is briefly described. The system consists essentially of Bio-Sedimat activated sludge clarifiers. (Speckhard-IPC)
W75-08548

TREATMENT AND DISPOSAL OF WASTEWATER SLUDGES,
Duke Univ., Durham, N.C. Dept. of Civil Engineering.
P. A. Vesilind.
Ann Arbor Science Publishers, Ann Arbor, Michigan, 1974. 236 p.

Descriptors: *Sludge disposal, *Sludge treatment, Volume, Stabilization, Pumping, Dewatering, Drying, Incineration, Water pollution sources, Sludge, Solid wastes, Wastes, Sewage sludge, *Waste water treatment, *Waste treatment.

This graduate-level text discusses effluent sludge sources, volumes, characteristics, stabilization, pumping, thickening, dewatering, conditioning, drying, combustion, and ultimate disposal. Laboratory exercises are appended. (Brown-IPC)
W75-08552

ROLE AND CHARACTERISTICS OF THE BIOSORPTION PROCESS IN THE PURIFICATION OF EFFLUENTS FROM HYDROLYSIS FACTORIES (ROL' I ZAKONOMERNOSTI PROTSESSA BIOSORBTSIIPRI OCHISTKE STOKOV GIDROLIZNOGO PROIZVODSTVA),
Vsesoyuznyi Nauchno-Issledovatelskii Institut Gidroliznoi Promyshlennosti, Moscow (USSR).
T. V. Zharova, Yu. S. Sedova, and N. A. Skachkova.
Gidroliznaya i Lesokhimicheskaya Promyshlennost, No 8, p 13-14, 1974. 4 fig, 3 ref, 1 tab.

Descriptors: *Waste water treatment, *Biological treatment, *Yeasts, Activated sludge, Waste water(Pollution), Wastes, Industrial wastes, Water pollution sources, Aeration, Biochemical oxygen demand, Chemical oxygen demand, Biodegradation, Liquid wastes, Water pollution treatment, Hydrogen ion concentration, Effluents, Oxidation, Waste treatment, Foreign countries.
Identifiers: USSR, Hydrolysis industry.

In the biological purification process, the first stage, which is quite rapid, is the adsorption (biosorption) of effluent components on the surface of activated sludge cells. This process was studied on samples of residual liquor from yeast production. The samples were aerated in the presence of activated sludge for varying times, and determinations were made of the 5- and 20-day BOD and COD. According to data obtained, up to 30% impurities are removed within the first minute of contact with the sludge. The biosorption continues for about 30 minutes, but at a low rate, so that the final amount of impurities removed corresponds to a maximum of about 50% 5-day BOD. During the next 1.5-2 hr the BOD remains constant, then the biooxidation process begins. The amount of impurities sorbed depends on the concentrations of the sludge and the effluent and on the pH. The amount sorbed increases linearly with the concentration of the sludge up to 1.5-2 g/liter, then increases only slightly with concentration. Biosorption is reduced by lowering the pH to 4.2-4.35, is higher and approximately constant at pH 5-7, and increases again at pH 8. The sorption power of activated sludge regenerated after full oxidation of effluents was lower than that of sludge from the aeration tank. Biosorption can be recommended as the first independent stage in biological purification of effluents. (Stapinski-IPC)
W75-08553

STUDIES ON ACTIVATED-SLUDGE BIOLOGICAL TREATMENT OF PAPER MILL EFFLUENT (STUDIO SUL TRATTAMENTO BIOLOGICO A FANGHI ATTIVI APPLICATO AD UN EFFLUENTE DI CARTIERA),
V. Scarlata, and E. Porrozzi.
Cellulosa e Carta, Vol 25, No 10, p 51-59, Oct., 1974. 2 fig, 17 ref, 2 tab, English summary.

Descriptors: *Activated sludge, *Pulp wastes, *Waste water treatment, *Biological treatment, Industrial wastes, Wastes, Waste treatment, Water pollution sources, Water pollution control, Pilot plants, Foreign countries, Europe, Foreign research, Phosphorus, Nitrogen, Water purification, Chemical oxygen demand, Biochemical oxygen demand, Nutrients.
Identifiers: Waste paper, Corrugating medium.

Activated-sludge tests in a 24-liter/day pilot plant were carried out at ENCC (Ente Nazionale per la Cellulosa e per la Carta) on the effluent from a mill producing corrugating medium from waste paper. The biological treatment reduced COD and BOD to satisfactory levels. The effect of phosphorus and nitrogen on the purification capacity was also examined. (Speckhard-IPC)
W75-08555

TREATMENTS OF BASIC DYES BY MICROBIAL POPULATIONS IN ACTIVATED SLUDGE (IN JAPANESE),
Gifu Univ. (Japan). Faculty of Engineering.
T. Ogawa, E. Idaka, and Y. Yamada.
Journal of the Society of Fiber Science and Technology, Japan (Sen-i Gakkaishi), Vol 30, No 11, p T516-T522, 1974. 7 fig, 2 tab, 13 ref, English summary.

Descriptors: *Dyes, *Microorganisms, *Activated sludge, *Waste water treatment, Water pollution sources, Wastes, Industrial wastes, Biochemical oxygen demand, Flocculation, Water pollution treatment, Water purification, Biological treatment, Microbial degradation, Sewage treatment.

Identifiers: Basic Violet 1, Basic Orange 22, Acid dyes, Basic dyes, Direct dyes.

To elucidate the cultural conditions and the inhibitive mechanism in the biological treatment of basic dyes, the dye concentration, cell concentration, and uptake of oxygen in the medium were measured in cultures on a reciprocating shaker. The cultures were maintained at 30C in a medium of peptone, meat extract, glucose, and mineral salts. To treat the dye solution effectively at 20 ppm, the media should contain 100 times the BOD of the average sewage sample at pH 7.5. Ninety percent of the Basic Violet 1 was removed in 24 hr because of the high bioflocculation capacity despite strong toxicity, while only 10% of Basic Orange 22 was removed because of low bioflocculation capacity. Repeated inoculation of a medium with the same composition resulted in a reduction of the lag phase of the growth curve. When the microorganisms acclimated to Basic Violet 1 were inoculated to the medium containing other dyes, acclimatization of microorganisms was maintained for the basic dyes of the homologous series, but not for the basic dyes of other series, acid dyes, or direct dyes. (Witt-IPC)
W75-08557

AMINE TREATMENT PROCESS FOR THE DECOLORIZATION OF PULP MILL EFFLUENTS. PART I. LABORATORY STUDIES,
Pulp and Paper Research Inst. of Canada, Pointe Claire (Quebec).
S. Prahacs, A. Wong, and H. G. Jones.
AICHE (American Institute of Chemical Engineers), Symposium Series, Vol 70, No 139, p 11-22, 1974. 13 fig, 15 ref, 5 tab.

Descriptors: *Pulp wastes, *Waste water treatment, *Color, Water pollution sources, Wastes, Industrial wastes, Economics, Capital costs, Operating costs, Bleaching wastes, Water pollution, Water pollution control, Waste treatment, Laboratory tests, Foreign research, Research facilities, *Canada, Foreign countries, North America.
Identifiers: *Amines.

Studies on the applicability and possible improvements in the technical performance and economics of using high-molecular weight amines for the removal of color from kraft pulp mill effluents are described. The laboratory investigations with effluents from Canadian mills confirmed the high degree of decolorization (90-99%) attainable with this technique. Process improvements resulting from the study are described. Preliminary economic estimates for a 500 ton/day bleached kraft pulp mill indicate that the treatment of the caustic extraction stage effluent, the principal source of color in a typical bleached kraft mill, would require a capital cost of $600,000 and an operating cost of approximately $1.40/ton of pulp. (Witt-IPC)
W75-08559

LA CELLULOSE DU PIN REDUCES ITS SOURCES OF POLLUTION (LA CELLULOSE DU PIN REDUIT SES SOURCES DE POLLUTION),
D. Ladmiral.
La Papeterie, Vol 96, No 12, p 814-822, December 1974. 17 fig, 1 tab.

Descriptors: *Pulp wastes, *Waste water treatment, *Treatment facilities, Biological treatment, Activated sludge, Aerated lagoons, Water purifications, Odor, Sulfite liquors, Industrial wastes, Wastes, Waste treatment, Pulp and paper industry, Foreign countries, Europe, Forestry, Fertilization, Forest management, Waste disposal, Irrigation, Waste disposal.

Described are the effluent treatment facilities (activated sludge treatment plus aerated lagooning) at a bisulfite pulp mill at Tartas (France), the effluent treatment facilities (biological treatment plus spreading over forest stands for highly colored effluent and biological treatment plus clarification for less colored effluent) at the kraft mill at Roquefort, and the overall operations for the pulp and paper mill at Facture (including effluent and odor treatment facilities). Some woodland plantation and fertilization operations are also briefly covered. (Speckhard-IPC)
W75-08560

HIGH-PURITY OXYGEN APPLICATION AT THE CHESAPEAKE CORPORATION OF VIRGINIA,
Chesapeake Corp. of Virginia, West Point.
B. Djordjevic, A. W. Plummer, and W. D. South.
TAPPI Annual Meeting (New York), Preprinted Proceedings (TAPPI, Atlanta, Ga.), p 99-111, Feb. 24-26, 1975. 4 fig, 4 tab, 7 ref.

Descriptors: *Oxygenation, *Waste water treatment, *Bleaching wastes, *Pulp wastes, Waste treatment, Water pollution sources, Industrial wastes, Oxygen, Water pollution treatment, Oxidation, Wastes, Water pollution control, Water purification, Pulp and paper industry, Virginia.
Identifiers: *Kraft mills, *Black liquors, *MoDo-CIL bleaching process, UNOX oxygenation system.

Chesapeake Corporation of Virginia recently started up an on-site cryogenic oxygen generation plant at its West Point, Virginia, pulp and paper mill. The oxygen is used for kraft pulp bleaching, for waste water treatment, and for oxidation of black liquor to reduce odorous emissions. Descriptions are given of the oxygen-generating plant, the MoDo-CIL oxygen bleach plant, the effluent treatment plant with its UNOX system, and the black liquor oxidation system. Initial operating problems and typical operating results with these units are given. (Brown-IPC)
W75-08562

REVERSE OSMOSIS MAKES HIGH QUALITY WATER NOW,
Universal Oil Products Co., San Diego, Calif.
For primary bibliographic entry see Field 3A.
W75-08564

ENVIRONMENTAL PROTECTION IN KRAFT PULP MILLS,
Munksjo A.B., Jonkoping (Sweden).
A. Knuts, U. Albertsson, and S-O. Sandberg.
Journal Water Pollution Control Federation, Vol 47, No 4, p 783-788, April 1975.

Descriptors: *Pulp wastes, *Waste water treatment, Industrial wastes, Effluents, Water pollution sources, Foreign countries, Europe, Pulp and paper industry, Wastes, Sludge, Water pollution control, Waste water(Pollution), Waste treatment, Chemical precipitation, Closed conduits.
Identifiers: Sweden, Cross recovery, Spills, Clarifiers, Evaporator condensates, Digester condensates, Closed pulping system, Kraft mills.

A survey is given of environmental protection techniques in the pulp industry. The applications of these techniques are exemplified by a description of environmental protection practices at two kraft mills of Munksjo AB. (Sweden). The description includes pulping in a completely closed liquor system, treatment of condensates, systems for handling temporary discharges, chemical treatment of waste water in a clarifier, sludge handling, and cross recovery. (Witt-IPC)
W75-08566

A SURVEY OF THE YOKOHAMA MUNICIPAL NANBU SEWAGE TREATMENT PLANT (YOKOHAMA-SHI HANBU GESUI SHORIJO NO GAIYO),
S. Ogura.
Gesuido Kyokaishi, Vol 11, No 123, p 54-61, August 1974. 8 fig, 1 tab.

Descriptors: *Planning, *Municipal wastes, *Sewage treatment, Construction, Equipment, Design criteria, Sludge, Waste treatment, Biochemical oxygen demand, Suspended solids, *Treatment facilities.
Identifiers: Sewage treatment plants, Japan, Nanbu Sewage Plant.

A sewage works and treatment plan was initiated in 1962 in Yokohama. One plant, the Nanbu plant, covers 2965 ha, and services a population of 670,000. Construction was started in 1962 and operation was begun in July, 1965. With subsequent gradual expansion, the plan is to be completed during 1974. The plant's constituents are 32 percent commercial, 8 percent industrial or sub-industrial, and 60 percent residential. The sewage BOD is about 200 mg/liter, and suspended solids are about 300 mg/liter, of which 200 mg/liter is settled. The step anaerobic digestion sludge treatment is designed to eliminate 90 percent of BOD--down to 20 mg/liter, and 85 percent of suspended solids--down to 45 mg/liter. In the adjacent area is a city refuse incinerator with a maximum capacity of 450 ton/day; part of its steam production is used for heating the sludge digestion tank. After the digestion gas is desulfurized, part of it can be used as supplementary fuel for the incinerator. Scrub water for the incinerator is supplied by treated sewage water, and the waste water is returned to the plant. The main facilities of the plant are: settling ponds, electrical machinery rooms, initial precipitation ponds, aeration tanks, final precipitation tanks, chlorine mixture tanks, return sludge pump rooms, sludge condensation pump rooms, sludge condensate tanks, blowers, sludge treatment rooms with deodorization systems, sludge digestion tanks, sludge scrubbers, and sludge dryers. (Seigle-FIRL)
W75-08567

SPLIT CHLORINATION: YES-NO,
V. Kothandaraman, and D. B. Beuscher.
Water and Sewage Works, Vol 121, No 7, p 90-92, July 1974. 3 tab, 9 ref.

Descriptors: *Water pollution, *Waste water treatment, *Effluent control, *Disinfection, *Chlorination, Water purification, Sampling, Bacteria, Membrane processes, Coliforms.
Identifiers: *Split-chlorination, Secondary waste effluents.

Continuous disinfection of wastewater effluents likely to contain fecal coliform bacteria has become mandatory in Illinois. The principal method used for disinfection is chlorination. Since chlorination practices in wastewater treatment are expensive, greater efforts are being directed to improve process efficiency. The split chlorination process consists of administering a portion of the total applicable chlorine dosage at the head end of the contact chamber and the remainder of another location along the contact basin. The efficiency of the split chlorination of secondary waste effluents was investigated. The extent of bacterial kill with split chlorination, under both quiescent and air agitated conditions, were evaluated separately and compared with the bacterial kill obtained from single point chlorination under quiescent conditions, all in batch reactors. Based on the results obtained, split chlorination does not appear to be an advantageous procedure in wastewater chlorination practice. (FIRL)
W75-08568

SYSTEMS ANALYSIS OF CENTRALIZED REACTIVATION OF EXHAUSTED CARBON IN WASTEWATER TREATMENT,
Michigan Univ., Ann Arbor.
J. S-y. Hsu.
Available from University Microfilms, Inc., Ann Arbor, Michigan 48106. Order No. 74-15,756. PhD Dissertation, 1973. 137 p.

Descriptors: *Waste water treatment, *Activated carbon, *Tertiary treatment, Regional economics, Mathematical studies, Model studies, Numerical analysis, Estimated costs, *Systems analysis.
Identifiers: *Carbon reactivation.

A system in which industrial and/or municipal waste water treatment plants of a region transport their exhausted carbon to one or more central furnaces for reactivation can result in savings in the total cost of carbon reactivation. Such a system is described. Based on empirical data, four major costs are estimated and expressed as mathematical functions of the reactivation demand. From these cost functions two location models were constructed. Some numerical results were obtained based on a region of 150-mile radius. (Sandoski-FIRL)
W75-08569

MATHEMATICAL MODELING OF UNSTEADY-STATE THICKENING OF COMPRESSIBLE SLURRIES,
Clemson Univ., S.C.
K. D. Tracey.
Available from University Microfilms, Inc., Ann Arbor, Michigan 48106. Order No. 74-16,117. PhD Dissertation, 1973. 202 p.

Descriptors: *Mathematical models, *Sludge treatment, *Sedimentation, Performance, Simulation analysis, Activated sludge, Treatment facilities, Design criteria, Model studies, *Waste water treatment, Slurries.
Identifiers: *Sludge thickening.

A dynamic mathematical model of the sludge thickening process has been formulated and the model is verified by conducting laboratory scale continuous thickening experiments. The model was based on the assumption that the downward movement of solids in a thickener was the result of two factors, gravitational sedimentation and bulk flow resulting from the withdrawal of the underflow. The model was used to simulate the performance of the secondary clarifier in the activated sludge process. Such simulations served to illustrate the utility of the model as a tool in the design and operation of water and waste water treatment facilities. The thickener model should be coupled with other process models to simulate unit interactions. (Sandoski-FIRL)
W75-08570

MATHEMATICAL MODELING OF HETEROGENEOUS SORPTION IN CONTINUOUS CONTRACTORS FOR WASTEWATER DECONTAMINATION,
Clemson Univ., S.C.
R. P. Carnahan.
Available from Univ. Microfilms, Inc. Ann Arbor, Mich. 48106. Order No 74-16,113. PhD Dissertation, 1973. 172 p.

Descriptors: *Mathematical models, *Adsorption, *Waste water treatment, Activated carbon, Model studies, Kinetics.

Because of strict water quality standards legislation, interest has increased in the use of activated carbon to remove trace contaminants. An analytical description of multi-solute adsorption equilibrium and a description of contractor dynamics as it effects mass transfer were derived. These were prerequisite in the development of a predictive model for adsorption of multisolutes of activated carbon by a differential contacting system. Results of the model studies indicated that the use of the film diffusion expression for adsorption kinetics as the semi-competitive Langmuir expression provided good agreement with experimental data at low concentrations. (Sandoski-FIRL)
W75-08571

RESEARCH ON REVERSE OSMOSIS MEMBRANES FOR PURIFICATION OF WASH WATER AT STERILIZATION TEMPERATURE (165F), REPORT NO 2,
General Electric Co., Lynn, Mass. Direct Energy Conversion Programs.
For primary bibliographic entry see Field 3A.
W75-08575

INVESTIGATION OF RATIONAL EFFLUENT AND STREAM STANDARDS FOR TROPICAL COUNTRIES,
Asian Inst. of Tech., Bangkok (Thailand).
For primary bibliographic entry see Field 5G.
W75-08584

PURIFYING APPARATUS FOR PURIFYING CONTAMINATED WATER,
Sanaqua S.A., Geneva (Switzerland). (assignee)
S. Nordgard.
US Patent No, 3,875,058, 4 p, 6 fig, 7 ref; Official Gazette of the United States Patent Office, Vol 933, No 1, p 340, April 1, 1975.

Descriptors: *Waste water treatment, *Patents, *Microorganisms, *Water purification, *Aeration, Equipment, Baffles.
Identifiers: Helical baffles.

Water purifying apparatus has a cylindrical casing rotatably supported in a tank containing contaminated water. The casing contains a helical baffle and is rotated so that contaminated water flowing in a through one end of the casing is displaced to an outlet at the other end by the helical baffle and thereby brought into contact with microorganisms on the helical baffle. The apparatus is provided with a buoyancy jacket or pontoons for buoyantly supporting the apparatus on the contaminated water. (Sinha-OEIS)
W75-08613

SEPARATION OF LIQUIDS FROM WET SOLIDS,
Harleyford Hydrosand Equipment Co. Ltd., Marlow (England). (assignee)
A. T. Lovegreen.
US Patent No 3,873,450, 6 p, 12 fig, 12 ref; Official Gazette of the United States Patent Office, Vol 932, No 4, p 1554, March 25, 1975.

Descriptors: *Patents, *Waste water treatment, Pollution abatement, *Sewage treatment, Solid wastes, Equipment, Animal wastes(Wildlife), Effluents, *Separation techniques.
Identifiers: Wet solids.

A water/solid mixture such as sewage or animal effluent is separated on a perforated moving endless belt with the addition of a compression stage for retained material. The perforations may be transverse slits. There may be an oversize indicator and/or water disintegration step prior to pressing, and/or a scraper and/or belt cleaning air supply after pressing, together with brushes and water sprays on the belt return flight. Compression may be effected by a roller but preferably by a second belt optionally provided with individually biassed pressing rollers inside. (Sinha-OEIS)
W75-08619

METHOD OF RECOVERING NOIL FIBRES AND SOLUBLE WOOD MATERIAL FROM WASTE WATER,
Savo Oy, Kuopio (Finland). (assignee)
E. K. Brax.
US Patent No 3,873,418, 6 p, 10 ref; Official Gazette of the United States Patent Office, Vol 932, No 4, p 1545, March 25, 1975.

Descriptors: *Patents, *Waste water treatment, *Wood wastes, Pulp and paper industry, *Pulp wastes, *Pollution abatement, Water pollution control, Water reuse, Reclaimed water.
Identifiers: Noil fibers, White water.

A method of recovering noil fibres and soluble wood material in white water from a manufacturing process involves the formation of a pulp web by separating flocked out material from water to produce cleared water and returning the material flocked out to the pulp web for retention has a beneficial constituent of the manufactured product. The method comprises adding a sufficient quantity of an alkaline substance to white water to prevent premature coagulation of suspended material; then adding as a coagulating agent a material whose presence in the pulp web formed is beneficial. It is selected from the group consisting of phenolformaldehyde resin, carboxymethylcellulose, urea resin, melamine, linseed oil emulsion, polyvinylchloride-latex emulsion and acrylic latex emulsion. The white water is thoroughly mixed with the coagulating agent to obtain a substantially homogeneous suspension. After mixing, a sufficient quantity of an acidic substance is added to the suspension to lower the pH to form flocks incorporating the coagulating agent, noil fibres and soluble wood material from the white water. Water is separated from the flocks by gravity separation to obtain cleared water which is recycled for use in manufacturing processes. The flocks are returned to the pulp web to form constituent material in the final product of the manufacturing process. (Sinha-OEIS)
W75-08620

AEROBIC SEWAGE TREATMENT SYSTEM,
Coate Burial Vault, Inc., West Milton, Ohio. (assignee)
K. J. Yost.
US Published Patent Application B 340,833, 4 p 3 fig, 9 ref; Official Gazette of the United States Patent Office, Vol 930, No 4, p 1613, January 28, 1975.

Descriptors: *Patents, *Waste water treatment, *Aerobic treatment, *Sewage treatment, Treatment facilities, Pollution abatement, Water pollution control, Water quality control, Organic wastes, Dissolved oxygen.

Water containing organic solid material is directed into one end of a shallow rectangular tank having a cover and a series of internal walls defining a series of longitudinally disposed treating chambers. The water is maintained within each chamber at a level slightly below the cover, and low pressure air is continuously injected from an air supply pump into each chamber. This produces circulation of the water around a baffle projecting downward from the cover and causes diffusion of the air into the water for dissolving the solid material. Air supply and exhaust passages for each chamber are formed within the cover, and air is also directed in series through the chambers. The purest water within each chamber at the water surface is directed into the water within the adjacent chamber below the surface to provide a series of successive aerobic treatments which result in producing a progressively purer water and a clear discharge effluent having a high percentage of dissolved oxygen. (Sinha-OEIS)
W75-08625

WASTE OXIDATION PROCESS,
Sterling Drug, Inc., New York. (assignee)
L. A. Pradt, and J. A. Meidl.
US Patent No 3,876,536, 3 p, 2 fig, 2 ref; Official Gazette of the United States Patent Office, Vol 933, No 2, p 831, April 8, 1975.

Descriptors: *Patents, *Waste water treatment, *Sewage sludge, *Oxidation, *Activated carbon, Pollution abatement, Biomass, Organic wastes, *Biological treatment.
Identifiers: Wet air oxidation.

A process is described for treating raw sewage sludge or night soil by wet air oxidation at a temperature between 150 deg and 375 deg C, and a pressure between 150 and 4,000 psig. A reduction

of between 30 and 70 percent in chemical oxygen demand is obtained, separating the gaseous, liquid and solid phases from the oxidation, and biologically oxidizing the liquid phase in an aeration contact tank containing a biomass suitable to effect biological oxidation of the organic solutes present in the liquid phase. Powdered activated carbon is maintained in the aeration contact tank in an amount sufficient to enhance the bio-oxidation and substantially reduce the odor and color of the liquid phase. The biological oxidation is carried out until excess biomass builds up and the activated carbon becomes spent. A mixture of the excess biomass and spent carbon is transferred to a wet oxidation reactor and the mixture is oxidized under conditions similar to those used for wet air oxidation of the raw sewage sludge so as to regenerate the powdered activated carbon for further use in the biological oxidation step and at the same time disposing of the excess biomass. (Sinha-OEIS)
W75-08627

INSTALLATION FOR SEPARATION ON THE SEABED OF THE EFFLUENTS FROM UNDERWATER OIL WELLS,
Entreprise de Recherches et d'Activities Petrolieres, Paris (France).
For primary bibliographic entry see Field 5G.
W75-08629

FOUR-MEDIA FILTER,
Neptune Microfloc, Inc., Corvallis, Oreg. (Assignee).
A. K. Hsiung, and W. R. Conley.
U S Patent No 3,876,546, 6 p, 8 fig, 9 tab, 6 ref; Official Gazette of the United State Patent Office, Vol 933, No 2, p 834, April 8, 1975.

Descriptors: *Patents, *Specific gravity, *Water treatment, *Waste water treatment, Pollution abatement, *Filters, Coals, Silica, Equipment, Water pollution control, *Filtration.
Identifiers: Garnet, Ilmenite.

A filter bed comprises four filter media of different specific gravities and sizes. The media are intermixed in such a manner that the number of particles continually increases in the direction of fluid flow through the bed. The media comprise coal of two different size ranges and specific gravities, plus silica sand and garnet. The first filter medium comprises coal having a specific gravity in the range between about 1.30 and 1.50. The second filter medium comprises coal having a specific gravity in the range between about 1.60 and 1.80. The third filter medium comprises silica sand having a specific gravity in the range between about 2.60 and 2.65 and the fourth filter medium comprises particles selected from the group consisting of garnet particles and ilmenite particles. (Sinha-OEIS)
W75-08632

APPARATUS FOR PHYSICALLY AND BIOLOGICALLY PURIFYING SEWAGE,
A. Schreiber, B. Schreiber, and E. Schreiber.
U S Patent No 3,876,543, 6 p, 4 fig, 6 ref; Official Gazette of the United States Patent Office, Vol 933, No 2, p 833, April 8, 1975.

Descriptors: *Waste water treatment, *Patents, *Filters, *Sewage treatment, *Aeration, Microorganisms, *Biological treatment, Pollution abatement, Equipment, Sludge treatment, Filtration.
Identifiers: Biological filters, Compressed air.

A combination filter-biofilter containing a bed of artificially aerated filler material is used for physically and biologically purifying sewage. The sewage is preliminary clarified and distributed evenly over the filler material and is caused to flow through the latter for a limited time until the sewage has coated the surfaces of the filler material with sludge and microorganisms to an extent that the passage of air through the filler bed is substantially decreased because of encrustation of the interstices of the filler material. At this point the flow of sewage through the filler material is halted and the bulk of the sludge is removed from the filler material by turning the same over with air. Then, the flow of sewage through the filler material is reinstituted. An abrasion resistant filler material is used and for purposes of turning-over the filler material, the bed of the latter is filled with water and the water and the filler material are turned over within the filter-biofilter by means of blown-in compressed air. At the same time the released sludge is drawn off. The turning-over of the filler material and water are accomplished gradually in a horizontal direction through the contents of the filter-biofilter. (Sinha-OEIS)
W75-08633

LIQUID WASTES REDISTRIBUTION APPARATUS,
Neptune Microfloc, Inc., Corvallis, Oreg. (Assignee).
E. R. Carlson.
U S Patent No 3,876,542, 6 p, 6 fig, 8 ref; Official Gazette of the United States Patent Office, Vol 933, No 2, p 833, April 8, 1975.

Descriptors: *Patents, *Liquid wastes, *Waste water treatment, Pollution abatement, Water pollution control, *Biological treatment, *Filters, Equipment, *Filtration.
Identifiers: Biological filters.

The apparatus is comprised of a liquid wastes distribution media positioned between the top of biological filter media and distribution discharge outlets. The redistribution media is formed with vertically spaced and superimposed layers of upward facing horizontal surfaces with openings for downward flow of the liquid wastes to the filter media. The horizontal surfaces are formed and arranged to interrupt, retard and redistribute the liquid wastes and may include a maze-like flow channel to reduce surges in filter loading. Lath-like horizontally oriented, relatively spaced, side-by-side members preferably provide the redistribution media, and the layers of members may be relatively staggered and/or oriented in an intersecting manner to eliminate vertical channels. (Sinha-OEIS)
W75-08634

PACKED BED REACTOR APPARATUS FOR WASTEWATER TREATMENT,
General Filter Co., Ames, Iowa. (Assignee).
M. H. Anderson, and J. J. Scholten.
U S Patent No 3,876,541, 5 p, 5 fig, 4 ref; Official Gazette of the United States Patent Office, Vol 933, No 2, p 832, April 8, 1975.

Descriptors: *Patents, *Waste water treatment, *Aerobic bacteria, *Pollution abatement, Equipment, Organic wastes, *Biological treatment.

'Packed Bed' reactor apparatus for treatment of wastewater by aerobic bacterial action includes a tank containing a horizontally and vertically extending bed of particulate medium capable of supporting aerobic bacterial growth, and an outlet for removing the treated wastewater from the upper portion of the tank. The improvement is characterized by providing the lower portion of the tank with combined water and air inlets. The air distribution pipes extend within the water distribution pipes with releasable connections interposed between the air header and the ends of the air pipes. Access is also provided so that the releasable air connections can be reached from outside of the tank, permitting the air pipes to be disconnected and removed from the water pipes for inspection and servicing without disturbing the bacterial treatment bed and permitting cleaning the interior of the water distribution pipes which may foul with organic growths. (Sinha-OEIS)
W75-08635

SKIMMING DEVICE,
Societe Nationale des Petroles d'Aquitaine, Paris (France). (Assignee).
H. Falxa.
U S Patent No 3,876,540, 3 p, 4 fig, 5 ref; Official Gazette of the United States Patent Office, Vol 933, No 2, p 832, April 8, 1975.

Descriptors: *Patents, *Waste water treatment, *Skimming, *Pollution abatement, Brines, Ponds, Oil fields, Chemical wastes, Oil pollution, Pulp and paper industry, Separation techniques.
Identifiers: Oil refineries.

A floating devices is described to skim still liquids without disturbing the lower depths. The device consists of a shallow funnel, submerged in the liquid and equipped with means for draining off the extracted liquid. The level of submersion, governing the amount of liquid drawn off, is regulated by a set of floats, which are either ballasted or adjusted in height, possibly by remote control. The main applications of this appliance are in the treatment of open-air brine ponds and tanks for residual water in oil fields, refineries, paper mills and other chemical industries. (Sinha-OEIS)
W75-08636

MULTI-TANK ION EXCHANGE WATER TREATMENT SYSTEM,
Rock Valley Water Conditioning, Inc., Rockford, Ill. (Assignee).
For primary bibliographic entry see Field 5F.
W75-08637

PROCESS FOR DISPOSING OF AQUEOUS SEWAGE AND PRODUCING FRESH WATER,
Texaco, Inc., New York. (Assignee).
H. V. Hess, W. F. Franz, and E. L. Coleman.
U S Patent No 3,876,538, 3 p, 1 fig, 4 ref; Official Gazette of the United States Patent Office, Vol 933, No 3, p 831, April 8, 1975.

Descriptors: *Patents, *Pollution abatement, *Sewage treatment, Water pollution control, *Waste water treatment, Freshwater, Oxidation, Brines, Gravity separation, Chemical oxygen demand, *Biochemical oxygen demand, Organic compounds, *Sewage treatment, Waste disposal.
Identifiers: Coke.

The process involves coking sewage or sewage sludges in the liquid phase in the absence of added free oxygen under a pressure of 300 to 3500 psi at a temperature of 400 deg to 700 deg F for 0.5 minutes to 6 hours to form gases, coke and an effluent having a reduced COD and BOD as compared with that of the charge. The effluent is oxidized with O2 to further reduce its COD and BOD and contacted with a hot hydrocarbon liquid characterized by its ability to extract a greater amount of water at a high temperature than at a lower temperature. This contact results in a substantial amount of the water dissolving in the hot hydrocarbon and in the production of a concentration 'brine' phase containing dissolved inorganic salts which are physically separated. The hot hydrocarbon-water solution is cooled by an amount sufficient to produce a water phase and a hydrocarbon phase which are separated by gravity. (Sinha-OEIS)
W75-08638

METHOD OF INSOLUBILIZING DEMINERALIZER AND COOLING TOWER BLOWDOWN WASTES,
Industrial Resources, Inc., Chicago, Ill. (Assignee).
J. M. Dulin, E. C. Rosar, H. S. Rosenburg, and J. M. Genco.
U S Patent No 3,876,537, 10 p, 5 fig, 6 tab, 5 ref; Official Gazette of the United States Patent Office, Vol 933, No 2, p 831, April 8, 1975.

Descriptors: *Patents, *Demineralization, *Cooling tower, *Pollution abatement, Water pollution control, Aeration, Chemical wastes, Bacteria, Hydrogen ion concentration, Waste treatment.
Identifiers: *Sulfate wastes, Sodium sulfur oxides, Sodium sulfite.

A process for insolubilizing water soluble sodium sulfur oxide wastes resulting from backwash of process feed-water demineralizers and cooling tower blowdown wastes is disclosed. The sodium sulfur oxide wastes, typically sodium sulfate and sulfite, are reacted in solution with ferric ions and sulfuric acid to produce insoluble, basic hydrous or anhydrous sodium hydroxy ferric sulfate or sulfite compounds. The principal insoluble compounds include Natrojarosite, Metasideronatrite, Sideronatrite, Depegite which is a mixture of Sideronatrite, Rosarite and Iriite, and mixtures thereof. The reaction takes place at an acid pH in a temperature ranging from about 50 deg - 300 deg F and may occur in single or multistage reactors. Air and/or bacterial activation at a pH of less than about 5.5 may be employed. The end-product basic, sodium hydroxy ferric sulfate and sulfite compounds are substantially water insoluble, having a solubility of less than the standard calcium sulfate, and may be disposed of by simple landfill without the water pollution hazards inherent with landfilling of wet or dry sodium sulfite or sulfate wastes. (Sinha-OEIS)
W75-08639

WASTE TREATMENT AND HANDLING PROCESSES ANNUAL REPORT,
Battelle-Pacific Northwest Labs., Richland, Wash.
L. K. Mudge, R. A. Walter, and G. F. Schiefelbein.
Available from the National Technical Information Service, Springfield, Va 22161 as Rept No BNWL-1861, $5.45 in paper copy, $2.25 in microfiche. BNWL-1861, UC-70, September 1974. 41 p, 12 fig, 11 tab, 4 ref.

Descriptors: *Radioactive waste disposal, *Management, *Waste treatment, *Nuclear wastes, Research and development, Assessment, Evaluation, Model studies, Design criteria.
Identifiers: *Waste handling.

Laboratory scale studies were conducted to evaluate pyrolysis and gasification processes for the volume reduction of combustible components found in typical alpha waste mixtures. Volume reduction obtained on pyrolysis of a simulated alpha waste mixture at 700 degrees C was by an approximate factor of 2, while volume reduction of simulated feed with air was by a factor of about 20. Gasification of simulated wastes produced an inert stable ash, while prolysis produced a combustible carbonaceous residue. Both gasification and pyrolysis (700 degrees C) of simulated wastes produced about 40% by weight of condensate. The lab studies also showed that fluxes of NaOH and Na2CO3 were effective in retaining chloride in the residue during pyrolysis of PVC. Results obtained on pyrolysis of individual components typically present in alpha wastes are presented. (Houser-ORNL)
W75-08641

TRANSURANIC SOLID WASTE MANAGEMENT RESEARCH PROGRAMS, PROGRESS REPORT FOR APRIL-JUNE, 1974.
Los Alamos Scientific Lab., N. Mex. Health Div.
Available from the National Technical Information Service, Springfield, Va 22161 as LA-5762-PR, $4.00 in paper copy, $2.25 in microfiche. Rept No LA-5762-PR, October 1974. 18 p, 6 fig, 5 tab, 16 ref.

Descriptors: *Radioactive waste disposal, *Nuclear waste, *Management, Research and development, *Transporation, Corrosion, Inhibition, Corrosion control, Acids, Pressure, Design criteria, Facilities, Incineration.
Identifiers: *Transuranics.

Progress is reported on three transuranic solid waste management research programs funded by the AEC Division of Waste Management and Transportation. The report covers the period of April-June 1974. Corrosion of mild steel drums and the effectiveness of potential corrosion inhibitors are undergoing continued investigation in a variety of humid environs. One 11-year-old waste container was opened and examined. Exterior corrosion was negligible but substantial interior corrosion had resulted from acid residues in the contained waste materials. Total pressurization rate from radiolytic gases appears to diminish as the total absolute pressure increases. Almost no Cl or HCL was detected in gas samples from radiolysis of chlorinated plastics. The reasons for these phenomena are being investigated. The Facility Design Criteria Report for the waste treatment development facility has been published and an architect-engineer selected for Title I design work. An incinerator was selected and ordered for prefacility testing with nonradioactive materials; it is anticipated that the same type of incinerator will ultimately be installed in the facility. (Houser-ORNL)
W75-08647

COMMERCIAL ALPHA WASTE PROGRAM QUARTERLY PROGRESS REPORT JULY - SEPTEMBER 1974.
Hanford Engineering Development Lab., Richland, Wash.
Available from the National Technical Information Service, Springfield, Va. 22161, as Rept No HEDL-TME 74-61, $4.00 in paper copy, $2.25 in microfiche. Rept No HEDL TME 74-61, November 1974. 35 p, 4 fig, 12 tab, 6 ref.

Descriptors: *Radioactive waste disposal, Research and development, *Management, *Radioactive wastes, Waste treatment, Waste identification, Waste storage, Waste disposal, Transportation, Fuels, Fabrication.
Identifiers: *Fuel reprocessing.

This is the second Quarterly Progress Report on the Commercial Alpha Waste Program being conducted for the Division of Waste Management and Transportation, USAEC. Progress to date on identification and classification of fuel fabrication and fuel reprocessing wastes is discussed, as well as work on development of the acid digestion process and development work on product storage and disposal of wastes. Data on HEPA (High Efficiency Particulate Air) filter usage throughout the United States also are discussed. (Houser-ORNL)
W75-08651

REPORT TO CONGRESS - DISPOSAL OF HAZARDOUS WASTES.
Environmental Protection Agency Programs. Washington, D.C. Office of Solid Waste Management.
Available from the US Government Printing Office, Washington, DC, as Rept No SW-115, for $1.55. Report No SW-115, 1974. 122 p, 17 fig, 17 tab, 68 ref, 7 append.

Descriptors: *Management, *Waste disposal, *Radioactive waste disposal, *Waste storage, *Federal government, *Administration, Regulation, Public health, Technology, Economics, Research and development, Waste treatment, Transportation, State governments, Toxicity, Legal aspects.

A comprehensive investigation was undertaken of the storage and disposal of hazardous wastes. This document represents Environmental Protection Agency's Report to the President and the Congress summarizing the Agency's investigations and recommendations in response to a congressional mandate. The report is organized into a summary, five major sections, and appendixes. The congressional mandate and the Agency's response to it are discussed. The public health, technological, and economic aspects of the problem of disposing of hazardous wastes are reviewed. Hazardous waste regulation is discussed. A discussion of implementation issues and a presentation of findings and recommendations are included. (Houser-ORNL)
W75-08666

REMOVAL OF CESIUM AND STRONTIUM FROM FUEL STORAGE BASIN WATER,
Allied Chemical Corporation, Idaho Falls, Idaho. Idaho Chemical Programs Operations Office.
M. W. Wilding, and D. W. Rhodes.
Available from the National Technical Information Service, Springfield, Va. 22161, as Rept No ICP-1048, $4.00 in paper copy, $2.25 in microfiche. Rept No ICP-1048, August 1974. 23 p, 10 fig, 7 tab, 9 ref.

Descriptors: *Water pollution, *Cesium, *Strontium, *Separation techniques, *Waste treatment, Ion exchange, Waste storage, Evaluation, Assessment.
Identifiers: Fuel rods, Spent fuel.

Spent fuel from nuclear reactors is stored underwater at the Idaho Chemical Processing Plant for cooling and shielding before processing. The fuel storage basin water becomes contaminated with fission products, primarily cesium 137 and strontium 90, from fuel elements that 'leak' and from cut pieces of fuel and miscellaneous scrap contained in cans, which are vented to release gases. Laboratory research and plant-scale tests are described of candidate ion-exchange materials for removing cesium 137 and strontium 90 from the contaminated storage basin water, which contains moderate quantities of nonradioactive dissolved solids. Cesium 137 is removed by a zeolitic ion-exchange material; strontium 90 is removed by an organic ion-exchange resin. Operational experience with plant-size ion-exchange columns indicate that both cesium 137 and strontium 90 are removed effectively by ion exchange. (Houser-ORNL)
W75-08667

NUCLEAR WASTE MANAGEMENT AND TRANSPORTATION QUARTERLY PROGRESS REPORT JULY-SEPTEMBER, 1974.
Battelle-Pacific Northwest Labs., Richland, Wash. Nuclear Waste Technology Dept.
Available from the National Technical Information Service, Springfield, Va. 22161, as Rept No BNWL-1876, $5.45 in paper copy $2.25 in microfiche. Rept No BNWL-1876, November 1974. 92 p, 28 fig, 12 tab.

Descriptors: *Management, *Waste disposal, *Radioactive waste disposal, *Waste treatment, Waste storage, Transportation, Monitoring, Assessment, Safety, Evaluation, Analytical techniques, Tritium, Separation analysis, Facilities.
Identifiers: *Actinides.

Reported are studies of methods for waste management and disposal of radioactive wastes. Included are separation techniques of actinide elements and tritium, waste treatment and handling, characterization of ground burial, and disposition of retired facilities. (Houser-ORNL)
W75-08668

STORMWATER CONTROL KEY TO BAY POLLUTION SOLUTION.
Engineering News-Record, Vol 193, No 25, p 17-18, December 12, 1974. 4 fig.

Descriptors: *Combined sewers, *Storm runoff, *Flooding, *Overflow, Sewers, Treatment facilities, Computers, Effluents, Planning, Costs, *Waste water treatment, Tunnels, Flood control, *California.

Identifiers: *Retention basins, *San Francisco(Calif).

A thirty-year master plan for the San Francisco Bay Area for collection and treatment works has been designed. The San Francisco system combines both sanitary sewage and stormwater, and each year an estimated six billion gallons of waste water escape treatment during storms. Out of $700 million allotted for the 30-year project, about $500 million would go for stormwater control. The total plan calls for over forty retention basins capable of holding up to 7 million cu ft of overflow for subsequent treatment. These basins will counteract uneven patterns of flooding and pollutant loading that are caused by Pacific storms. Severe storms increase dry weather flow more than ten times. A computer system would control basin gates to match flow from the basins with treatment capacity. The overall plan aims at reducing the number of overflows by 90%. It includes: a new 1000 mgd treatment plant near Lake Merced to provide split-flow treatment (250 mgd of secondary capacity and 750 mgd for primary capacity) for stormwater; a five mile long dual conduit ocean outfall to discharge wet weather effluent 8000 ft offshore from the Lake Merced plant; and a tunnel of up to 32 ft in diameter to move sewage eight miles across town. Problems on the San Francisco side of the Bay involve buying public lands and receiving sufficient Federal funding. (Prague-FIRL)
W75-08671

HURRICANE SPURS SEWER RENOVATION.
Water and Wastes Engineering, Vol 11, No 10, p 14, October, 1974.

Descriptors: *Sewers, *Floods, Drainage, Repairing, Data, Flood damage, Planning, Cleaning, Manholes, Installation, *Pennsylvania.
Identifiers: *Wilkes-Barre(Penn), *Hurricane Agnes, *Closed-circuit television inspection.

Under the auspices of the Wilkes-Barre Redevelopment Authority, the city of Wilkes-Barre, Pennsylvania is as well as reevaluating renovating its sanitary and storm sewage system. Cleaning, closed-circuit television inspection, and repair of existing sewers were done in the South Wilkes-Barre disaster urban renewal project area. As a result of data gathered by the southern Line Cleaning of Casselberry, Florida, a new, updated drainage system for South Wilkes-Barre will be plotted. This is part of an overall $11 million public improvements program to serve the residential area for several decades. The closed-circuit television inspection of existing sewer lines will allow for the inspection of conditions with the highest degree of accuracy possible. These planned programs will result in the first cleaning of existing lines since the flooding caused by Hurricane Agnes in 1972. In cases where crushed lines and non-existent manholes prohibit working on a particular length of line, reconstruction of these collapsed lines and installation of manholes will take place. (Prague-FIRL)
W75-08672

PUMPS FOR POLLUTION CONTROL,
J. A. Edwards.
Pollution Engineering, Vol 6, No 11, p 26-35, November, 1974. 33 fig.

Descriptors: *Pumps, *Construction materials, *Design criteria, *Centrifugal pumps, Centrifugation, Waste treatment, Sludge treatment, Costs, *Waste water treatment, Water pollution control.

Design and construction materials for over thirty waste treatment pumps are described. These include the centrifugal pump used for transferring solutions between reaction tanks, the proportioning pump for accurate control of chemical addition, the diaphragm pump for slurries, the screw pump for high viscosity solutions and the gear pump for hydraulic systems. Criteria for choosing the proper pump for a system are detailed. Factors to be considered in selecting a centrifugal pump are total discharge head, net positive suction head, motor RPM, seal design, equipment location, construction materials, solution temperature, and equipment application. A pump may use a packed stuffing box seal or a mechanical seal or may be designed to use no seal at all. Impeller design is usually related to size of housing and type of liquids or solids pumped; impellers described include open and semi-enclosed impellers and shrouded impellers. Sludge handling pumps in pollution control systems are also discussed. Two distinct varieties are the progressive cavity pump and the diaphragm pump. Pump designs may be single-stage, multi-stage, turbine, diaphragm, in-line or vertical and horizontal centrifugal. Each type fills a specific need, and should be chosen by factors of efficiency and economy. (Prague-FIRL)
W75-08674

NEWPORT--MAIN DRAINAGE SCHEME TAKES SHAPE,
P. Millbank.
Civil Engineering, p 24-25, 38 December, 1974. 2 fig.

Descriptors: *Rivers, *Water pollution control, *Sewerage, Sewers, Organic matter, Dissolved oxygen, Pipelines, Drainage, Water treatment, Sewage treatment, *Waste water treatment.
Identifiers: *River Usk(Newport South Wales).

The development of a scheme for pollution control on the River Usk at Newport, South Wales is described. The major part of the existing sewerage system carries both sewage water and surface water and was designed over a century ago. In 1960, control of new or altered outlets for the discharge of sewage and trade effluent came within jurisdication of the river authorities under a Clean Rivers (Estuaries and Tidal Waters) Act. River analysis confirmed that the estuary of the Usk was heavily polluted by decomposing organic matter, that a belt of polluted water swings to and fro with the tide, and that the expected twice daily flushing of the estuary as a result of a large tidal difference of 40 feet does not occur. It was recommended that sewage be discharged into the river below the town of Newport after partial treatment; it was estimated that this would keep the dissolved oxygen in the river over 50%, contrasted with the 30% or less that it had been. Work was begun on a large trunk sewer on each side of the river, to carry up to six times the dwf drawn from existing outfall pipelines. Local relief sewers were proposed to alleviate drainage in problem areas. A final three-stage proposal included stage one as an internal drainage works and a new pumping station, design for a stage two Nash treatment works and a pumping main to connect it with the Liswerry pumping station, and a stage three sewage works in the Duffryn area to be connected across the Usk to Nash. (Prague-FIRL)
W75-08675

DAVENTRY SEWERAGE SCHEME COMPLETED AHEAD OF SCHEDULE.
Water Services, Vol 78, No 941, p 252, July, 1974.

Descriptors: *Construction, *Sewage treatment, Municipal wastes, Industrial wastes, Underground streams, *Treatment facilities, Tunnels, *Wastewater treatment, Waste disposal.
Identifiers: Great Britain(Daventry), Combined municipal-industrial wastes.

A new sewage disposal works at Daventry, Great Britain, has been designed to treat both industrial and domestic effluents. The works is capable of handling a population of 30,000, which is the estimate for 1980. Engineers have designed the works for 100 percent extention of capacity, with available land for even further expansion. Over eight miles of cast iron pipes, up to 30 inches in diameter, have been laid to connect sewerage purification equipment within the plant. A sludge treatment area, administration buildings, a sludge press house, two pumping stations, a land treatment area, pipework chambers, and access and site roads have been constructed. In order not to disrupt motor or rail traffic, excavation was done by a thrust boring technique. The greatest problem faced was underground water found in the tunnel section. Continuous deep well pumping during construction was necessary at three bore holes to remove 250,000 gallons per 24 hours. (Prague-FIRL)
W75-08676

TOTAL URBAN WATER POLLUTION LOADS: THE IMPACT OF STORM WATER,
Enviro Control, Inc., Rockville, Md.
For primary bibliographic entry see Field 5B.
W75-08677

SELF-CLEANING STORM OVERFLOW BASINS WITH MEANDER DUCT (SELBSTREINIGENDE REGENUBERLAUFBECKEN MIT SCHLANGENRINNE),
J. Koral, and C. Saatci.
Wasserwirtschaft, Vol 64, No 10, p 301-306, October, 1974. 11 fig, 4 ref.

Descriptors: *Storm water, *Storm runoff, Precipitation(Atmospheric, Construction, Planning, *Design, Pilot plants, Waste water treatment.
Identifiers: Pilot tests, *Switzerland, *Storm water tanks.

The construction of a new, self-cleaning storm water tank is described. Solids which have settled during the precipitation are removed by dry weather flow, which crosses the bottom of the tank like a meander. This reduces the work required to clean the tank. This construction has been pilot tested for six years continuously in Switzerland. The dimensions and application possibilities are detailed. Other examples are presented; specialists' opinions about possible problems with the method are given. (Prague-FIRL)
W75-08679

STOCHASTIC ANALYSIS OF TRICKLING FILTER,
Texas Univ. at Austin. Dept. of Chemical Engineering.
K. J. Mistry, and D. M. Himmelblau.
Journal of the Environmental Engineering Division, ASCE, Vol 101, No EE3, Proceedings paper No 11362, p 333-350, June 1975. 5 fig, 1 tab, 19 equ, 17 ref.

Descriptors: *Water quality, *Waste water treatment, *Trickling filters, *Stochastic processes, *Environmental engineering, Design, Model studies, Simulation analysis, Monte Carlo method, Statistical methods, Flow rates, Probability, Distribution, Oxygen, Biochemical oxygen demand, Measurement, Safety factors, Equations, Mathematical models, Systems analysis, *Risks.
Identifiers: Random variables, Tolerances(Mechanics), Mass balance, Numerical values, Deterministic models, Mean, Standard deviation.

In most conventional methods of analysis and design for wastewater processes, the stochastic nature of the process inputs and parameters is ignored. Stochastic treatment of a process is more difficult than a deterministic treatment but can provide more significant information concerning the design parameters. A stochastic approach to trickling filter design is described based on a two-phase two-component model of the filter. Random variables were introduced to represent random BOD inputs and flow rates as well as uncertainty in the model coefficients. The study results demonstrate how to use a stochastic analysis as a

supplement to the usual deterministic design and to achieve a more quantitative specification of uncertainty. Indicated is under what circumstances the sample estimate of the expected value of the output of a stochastic model of a trickling filter differs from the output of the related deterministic model based on replacing the random variables by their expected values. Also, the study shows how to use the measurements of sample dispersion of the output BOD to compute safety factors for design. Although application has been to a trickling filter, the methods of stochastic analysis described herein can be applied to most other wastewater treatment apparatus. (Bell-Cornell)
W75-08720

DYNAMIC MODELING AND CONTROL STRATEGIES FOR THE ACTIVATED SLUDGE PROCESS,
Clemson Univ., S.C. Dept. of Environmental Systems Engineering; and Environmental Dynamics, Inc., Greenville, S.C.
J. B. Busby, and J. F. Andrews.
Journal Water Pollution Control Federation, Vol 47, No 5, p 1055-1080, May 1975. 22 fig, 3 tab, 23 equ, 45 ref.

Descriptors: *Activated sludge, *Waste water treatment, *Water quality, *Simulation analysis, Biological treatment, Wastes, Computers, Suspended solids, Systems analysis, Mathematical models, Recycling.
Identifiers: *Process control, Dynamic models, Feeding, Step-feed process, Ratio control.

Conventional activated sludge processes may be controlled by sludge recycle rate, waste sludge flow rate, and aeration rate. In a multistage reactor system such as the step-feed process, variations in wastewater feed patterns are another control technique. A wide-spectrum activated sludge process model was developed that considers the storage capability of the sludge, incorporates the active and inert fractions of the mixed liquor volatile suspended solids in separate mass balances, and in coupled with a dynamic model of the final clarifier. Control strategies investigated include various sludge wasting and recycle control techniques and hydraulic methods. Computer simulation results indicate that the model satisfactorily describes the different process versions and that dynamic variations in wastewater feed pattern are valuable for control. (Bell-Cornell)
W75-08725

MADAM I--A NUMERIC METHOD FOR DESIGN OF ADSORPTION SYSTEMS,
Michigan Univ., Ann Arbor. Dept. of Environmental and Water Resources Engineering.
W. J. Weber, Jr., and J. C. Crittenden.
Journal Water Pollution Control Federation, Vol 47, No 5, p 924-940, May 1975. 11 fig, 27 equ, 20 ref.

Descriptors: *Adsorption, *Design, *Water quality control, *Waste water treatment, Mathematical models, Numerical analysis, Computers, Evaluation, Equations, Systems analysis, Treatment facilities, Separation techniques.

Considered are the development of a numeric method for adsorber design and the critical evaluation and comparison of this and other modeling techniques for adsorption processes in packed and expanded beds. The numeric model described herein is the Michigan Adsorption Design and Applications Model--I (MADAM I). It can accomodate the dynamic aspects of fluid dispersion, solids mixing, multisolute interactions, and biological growth on activated carbon surfaces. The numeric solution solves for the values of dependent variables at discrete points in the domain of the independent variables. In the case of adsorption, the solid-phase concentration is predicted at any new point in time by using prior values of solid- and liquid-phase concentrations. Then, the equations governing liquid-phase concentrations are solved at the current time level. Breakthrough curves may be obtained by proceeding through time. Results agree well with experimental data. The method has advantages over conventional modeling techniques. The aim of the authors in constructing MADAM I has been to develop a general modeling scheme that describes the dynamics of the adsorption treatment process, provides an optimum design, and reduces costs and planning time required at both the pilot and full-scale plant levels. (Bell-Cornell)
W75-08726

GRAVITY OIL-WATER SEPARATOR WITH TWO INTERCONNECTED SINGULAR CELLS HAVING AUTOMATIC FREE OIL DISCHARGE,
R. L. Summers.
U.S. Patent No. 3,862,039, 3 p, 3 fig, 4 ref; Official Gazette of the United States Patent Office, Vol 930, No 3, p 1332, January 21, 1975.

Descriptors: *Patents, Oily water, *Waste water treatment, Pollution abatement, Water pollution control, *Separation techniques, Equipment, Gravity, *Oil wastes, *Oil pollution.
Identifiers: Gravity separation.

A gravity separator comprises a tank assembly including side-by-side first and second tank components. The tank components are closed at their lower ends. The first tank component includes an upper inlet opening at a level below the upper end while the second tank component includes an upper outlet opening outward at a level below the upper end and horizontally aligned with the inlet of the first component. The second component includes an upstanding lift passage in closed communication with the outlet of this component which opens downward into a lower interior portion. At its lower end a transfer passage is provided which communicates with a lower portion of the interior of the first tank component. The first tank component includes an oil outlet placed slightly above the level on the inlet. As water enters the tank component it falls to the bottom and moves upward through the inlet pipe, through the transfer pipe and into the interior of the second tank component through the vertical outlet portion of the transfer pipe. Any oil remaining in the liquid flowing through the transfer pipe will be elevated and there will be substantially no oil with the liquid entering the lower end of the lift pipe for discharge from the second tank component. (Sinha-OEIS)
W75-08735

METHOD OF APPARATUS FOR TREATING SEWAGE,
Trans-Continental Purification Research and Development Ltd., North Bay (Ontario). (assignee)
A. Z. Morin, and T. H. Boyd.
U.S. Patent No. 3,864,252, 4 p, 3 fig, 4 ref; Official Gazette of the United States Patent Office, Vol 931, No 1, p 329, February 4, 1975.

Descriptors: *Patents, *Sewage treatment, *Distillation, *Waste water treatment, Pollution abatement, Equipment, Evaporation, Septic tanks, Condensation, Water vapor, Domestic wastes, *Incineration.

The treatment of wastes such as domestic sewage is disclosed for the method of and apparatus for handling the run-off from a septic tank or other separating unit including the evaporation and/or burning of the outflow of such unit. In the case of a septic tank the solids progressively settle in a series of connected tanks where the eventual run-off is a relatively clear liquid. It is proposed to heat this fluid, discharging the water vapour to the atmosphere, and subject any combustible gases that are present to an open flame. The liquid, heated in one or more stages to a high temperatures, is preferably sprayed as steam or gaseous vapour into an open flame to further raise the temperature of the steam and to ignite and burn off the combustibles. The steam in part may then be condensed and drained off as mainly distilled water while the remaining gaseous vapours are treated to a second open flame to burn off any residual combustile volatiles, with the products of combustion and reheated steam or water vapour being discharged to the atmosphere. (Sinha-OEIS)
W75-08738

SLIME CONTROL COMPOSITIONS AND THEIR USE,
Betz Labs., Inc., Trevose, Pa. (assignee)
B. F. Shema, R. H. Brink, Jr., and P. Swered.
U.S. Patent No. 3,864,253, 5 p, 1 tab, 5 ref; Official Gazette of the United States Patent Office, Vol 931, No 1, p 329, February 4, 1975.

Descriptors: *Patents, *Waste water treatment, Microorganisms, *Slime, Bacteria, Fungi, Algae, Pulp and paper industry, Cooling water, *Industrial water, *Pulp wastes.
Identifiers: *Chemical treatment, Aerobacter aerogens.

This invention relates to certain processes and compositions useful for inhibiting the growth of slime in water and, in particular, water used for industrial purposes; for example, in the manufacture of pulp paper, in the manufacture of paper, in cooling water systems and in effluent water treatment. The processes or mixtures show unexpected synergistic activity against microorganisms, including bacteria, fungi, and algae which produce slime in aqueous systems of bodies which are objectionable from either an operational or aesthetic point of view. Specifically, the invention is directed to the use of compositions comprising a combination of 2,2-Dibromo-3-nitrilopropionamide and Sodium linear dodecyl benzene sulfonate. (Sinha-OEIS)
W75-08739

SEWAGE TREATMENT UNIT,
Texaco Inc., New York. (assignee)
H. V. Hess, W. F. Franz, and E. L. Cole.
U.S. Patent No. 3,864,254, 3 p, 1 fig, 6 ref; Official Gazette of the United States Patent Office, Vol 931, No 1, p 329, February 4, 1975.

Descriptors: *Patents, *Waste water treatment, *Sewage treatment, Pollution abatement, Water quality control, Water pollution control, Domestic wastes, Sewage sludge, Chemical oxygen demand.
Identifiers: *Hydrogen peroxide.

A sewage treatment unit for the disposal of aqueous waste sewage from a small installation includes a primary settling zone receiving the sewage and separating raw sludge from the water. A first pump conveys the water to a storage zone and actuates a second pump which meters in hydrogen peroxide from a supply thereof into the storage zone to reduce the COD of the water. A pump forces the settled sludge to a coking zone where it is coked in the liquid phase. The coke thus formed then passes to a pressure settling device where it is separated from the coking effluent which is recycled to the storage zone. (Sinha-OEIS)
W75-08740

METHOD AND APPARATUS FOR SURFACE SKIMMING,
Ecodyne Corp., Lincolnshire, Ill. (assignee)
R. L. Shaffer.
U.S. Patent No. 3,864,257, 4 p, 4 fig, 6 ref; Official Gazette of the United States Patent Office, Vol 931, No 1, p 330, February 4, 1975.

Descriptors: *Patents, *Flotsam, *Water treatment, Water pollution control, Pollution abatement, *Skimming, Industrial wastes, *Waste water treatment, Separation techniques.
Identifiers: Clarification, Surface skimming.

A surface skimming system is provided which in its simplest form includes a rotating arm, a fixed anti-rotation arm, and an airlift pumping device. The rotating arm is mounted tangentially to a rotating stilling well or a centrally disposed shaft and positioned so that it projects above the surface of the clarifier. The anti-rotation arm is positioned so that it breaks the surface of the clarifier. The bottom portion of the anti-rotation arm is of a flexible material, such as rubber, so that it may deflect and allow the rotating arm to pass under it. The airlift is positioned under the outer periphery so that it draws water from the surface. The rotating arm sweeps the surface of the clarifier, pushing the floating matter ahead of it. As the rotating arm approaches the fixed anti-rotation arm, a 'wedge' is formed therebetween which traps the floating matter. As the rotating arm continues to rotate, the 'wedge' is made smaller and moves outward, forcing the floating matter to the airlift pump which removes it along with some water. (Sinha-OEIS)
W75-08741

APPARATUS FOR TREATING SEWAGE,
RSC Industries, Inc., Opa-Locka, Fla. (assignee)
J. M. Richardson, and G. W. Reid.
U.S. Patent No. 3,864,258, 4 p, 2 fig, 10 ref; Official Gazette of the United States Patent Office, Vol 931, No 1, p 330, February 4, 1975.

Descriptors: *Patents, *Waste treatment, Pollution abatement, *Sewage treatment, Water pollution control, Equipment, Domestic wastes, Filtration, *Separation techniques.

The process of using the apparatus of this invention comprises separating the sewage solids present in an aqueous medium immediately on generation, avoiding the inclusion of liquid with solids, which is costly to treat, by accumulation as a layer on a movable porous medium through which the aqueous medium passes to a filtered liquid accumulation reservoir, then transporting the accumulated sewage solids through a thermal destruction chamber wherein the solids are converted to inert ashes and gases, discharging gases produced at temperatures sufficient to destroy odors and then withdrawing the accumulated inert ash solids. The apparatus comprises a moving porous element, a filtered liquid accumulator tank positioned below a limited area of the porous element, means for delivering sewage solids to the limited area of the porous element present above the accumulator reservoir, means for the thermal destruction of the solids by radiant heat, means for actuating the moving porous element to carry the solids through the thermal destructor and finally means for withdrawing inert ash separately from vented gases. (Sinha-OEIS)
W75-08742

APPARATUS FOR THE TERTIARY TREATMENT OF LIQUIDS,
Hendrick Mfg. Co., Carbondale, Pa. (assignee)
G. Spohr, and V. R. Sparham.
U.S. Patent No. 3,864,264, 5 p, 3 fig, 9 ref; Official Gazette of the United States Patent Office, Vol 931, No 1, p 332, February 4, 1975.

Descriptors: *Patents, *Tertiary treatment, *Waste water treatment, *Waste treatment, Water quality control, Chlorine, Solid wastes, Sludges, Pollution abatement.
Identifiers: Clarifiers.

A tertiary treatment apparatus comprises a chlorine contact tank into which is compactly assembled an upflow clarifier adapted to receive water to be treated. The clarifier is equipped with a septum in the form of a single sheet or layer or metallic wires which promotes the formation of a flimsy sludge blanket above the septum. The flimsy blanket represents solids, mostly of a colloidal nature, which have escaped the secondary treatment but which, being entrapped in the blanket, are rendered accessible for removal. The apparatus includes a downflow treatment means assembled in the upflow clarifier and above its septum. The downflow treatment means receive clarified water and after treatment, discharge into the chlorine contact tank. Removal of the sludge blanket before it reaches the downflow treatment means is accomplished by means of drainage devices associated with the upflow clarifier and operative, without appreciable disturbance to the progressive operation of the entire apparatus, to withdraw the liquid in above the septum so as to collapse the flimsy blanket downward through the septum and thus remove the blanket contents from the water being treated. (Sinha-OEIS)
W75-08744

DIFFUSED AERATION PIPE APPARATUS FOR USE WITH AN AERATION TANK,
Nigata Engineering Co. Ltd., Tokyo (Japan). (assignee)
S. Suzuki.
U.S. Patent No. 3,864,441, 4 p, 10 fig, 5 ref; Official Gazette of the United States Patent Office, Vol 931, No 1, p 375, February 1975.

Descriptors: *Patents, *Aeration, *Piping systems(Mechanical), *Waste water treatment, *Pollution abatement, Equipment, Pipes, Water treatment.
Identifiers: *Aeration tanks.

A diffused aeration pipe apparatus for use with an aeration tank is comprised of air supply pipes pivotably connected to each other by way of swivel joints and an air diffusion pipe at the lower end of the air supply pipe system. A guide member for pulling a hoisting rope is provided along the vertical bent portion of an upper most air supply pipe for reducing the moment of rotation required for hoisting the piping system. Each adjacent two air supply pipes in the piping system have a projection piece and a projection lever engaging respectively for restricting the rotation of the two adjacent pipes within a predetermined angle. A movable carriage having an electric motor, a speed retarder for the motor, a winding up wheel pivotally connected to the power shaft of the retarder and a control panel is provided for enabling the successive hoisting and descending of the diffused aeration pipe apparatus. (Sinha-OEIS)
W75-08745

PURIFICATION CONTROL UNIT,
Camper and Nicholsons Ltd., Gosport (England). (Assignee).
For primary bibliographic entry see Field 5F.
W75-08751

APPARATUS FOR REMOVAL OF DISSOLVED OR SUSPENDED SOLIDS IN WASTE WATER,
Swift and Co., Chicago, Ill. (Assignee).
H. T. Anderson.
U S Patent No 3,865,711, 5 p, 2 fig, 3 ref; Official Gazette of the United States Patent Office, Vol 931, No 2, p 810-811, February 11, 1975.

Descriptors: *Patents, *Oil wastes, *Oil pollution, Oily water, *Water pollution treatment, *Waste water treatment, Emulsions, Electric currents, Dissolved solids, Suspended solids, Separation techniques, Hydrogen ion concentration.
Identifiers: Water-oil emulsion, Anolyte stream.

Waste water containing oil and water emulsions and dissolved or suspended solids is de-emulsified and clarified by creating a three dimensional anolyte stream resulting from the careful placement of anodes and impressing direct or galvanic current through the water. Waste water is first contacted with an anode system in a restricted zone so as to give substantially all of the waste water a rapid pH change of several units and is then conveyed to a second zone wherein a three dimensional anolyte stream is formed causing the oily particles to float to the surface of the water where they can be skimmed off. The apparatus consists of a container having an entry conduit and an exit conduit and having a baffle across the width of the container and positioned nearer the inlet end than the discharge end thereby dividing the container into an inlet zone and a discharge zone. The lower section of the baffle is parallel to the inlet end and the upper section of the baffle is inclined toward the discharge end of the container. Cylindrical anodes in the inlet zone are spaced transverse to the longitudinal axis of the container, and cylindrical anodes in the discharge zone are spaced parallel to the longitudinal axis of the container at about nearly equal distance apart in the discharge zone. (Sinha-OEIS)
W75-08752

AERATORS WITH DE-ICING MEANS,
For primary bibliographic entry see Field 5G.
W75-08755

SYSTEM FOR SEPARATING HYDROCARBONS FROM WATER,
Fram Corp., East Providence, R.I. (Assignee).
For primary bibliographic entry see Field 5G.
W75-08757

CONTAMINATED WATER TREATING APPARATUS,
T. Mochizuki, and K. Kawada.
U S Patent No 3,878,097, 5 p, 12 fig, 5 ref; Official Gazette of the United States Patent Office, Vol 933, No 3, p 1341, April 15, 1975.

Descriptors: *Patents, *Waste water treatment, Pollution abatement, *Biological treatment, *Oxidation, *Sewage treatment, Industrial wastes, Water quality control, Equipment.

An apparatus for biologically improving the quality of contaminated water comprises of at least three side by side oxidation compartments spaced at intervals from each other and each being open at the top and bottom. The compartments have end walls vertically extending aeration compartments. Aeration means at the lower end of each aeration compartment feeds a flow of air into the bottom of the aeration compartments for lifting contaminated water up through the aeration compartments and over the upper ends of the compartment walls. Partitions extend upward to the bottoms of the biological oxidation sections in each oxidation compartment which lies between two aeration compartments to define sludge collection compartments beneath each aeration compartment and a portion of the oxidation compartment. An overflow passage extends upward from the sludge collection compartment. Contaminated water is introduced and circulated through the biological oxidation section repeatedly until purity of the water is improved. (Sinha-OEIS)
W75-08758

SEWAGE TREATMENT APPARATUS,
S. R. Kennedy.
U S Patent No 3,878,101, 6 p, 3 fig, 5 ref; Official Gazette of the United States Patent Office, Vol 933, No 3, p 1342, April 15, 1975.

Descriptors: *Patents, *Sewage treatment, Pollution abatement, *Waste water treatment, Water quality control, *Aeration, Equipment, Weirs, Skimming, Sludge.

The sewage treatment apparatus comprises a primary liquid circulation chamber in which sewage is circulated around a curved circulation guide barrier that shields an outlet port. The sewage circulates due to the introduction of pressurized air in the chamber liquid. The air is directed along a predetermined path thereby influencing liquid circulation. The circulation guide barrier extends between opposite walls of the primary chamber to prevent the liquid from crossing over the barrier to

the outlet port. An entry opening is provided in the barrier leading to the outlet port to ensure that liquid passes into the outlet port along a predetermined path. The outlet port is located substantially central of the circulating liquid, and sludge that is present in the liquid tends to move radially away from the outlet port. Liquid entering the outlet port is thus rendered substantially free of sludge. The radially moving sludge tends to sink to the bottom of the primary ciruclation chamber and is drawn our by suction apparatus placed at the bottom of the chamber. The collection chamberfpools the circulated liquid from a second circulation chamber and includes weirs for skimming the surface layer of the pooled water. (Sinha-OEIS)
W75-08759

THE PROTECTION OF THE QUALITY OF WATERS, AN IMPORTANT ELEMENT IN THE CONSERVATION OF NATURE, (IN ROMANIAN),
Consililul National al Apelor, Bucharest (Rumania).
For primary bibliographic entry see Field 5G.
W75-08775

DESIGN OF COOLING TOWER RETURN CHANNEL FOR TVA'S BROWNS FERRY NUCLEAR PLANT,
Tennessee Valley Authority, Norris. Engineering Lab.
S-T. Hsu, and R. A. Elder.
In: Hydraulic Engineering and the Environment; Proceedings of the 21st Annual Hydraulic Division Specialty Conference, Montana State University, Bozeman, August 15-17, 1973. American Society of Civil Engineers, New York, p 179-187, 1973. 7 fig, 2 ref.

Desc.iptors: Structures, *Model studies, *Flow control, *Nuclear powerplants, *Cooling towers, Water cooling, Heated water, Outlet works, Channels, Gates, Hydraulic gates, Gate control, Engineering structures, Hydraulic models, Hydraulic structures, Spillways, Spillway gates, Tennessee Valley Authority, *Thermal pollution, *Waste water treatment.

TVA's Browns Ferry Nuclear Plant is located on the Tennessee River about 12 miles northwest of Decatur in northern Alabama. A diffuser-pipe system was orginally designed for purposes of heat dissipation. The design of this diffuser-pipe system satisfied the water temperature standards proposed by Alabama for compliance with the Water Quality Act of 1965. These criteria, however, were revised after December 1971. To comply with the new criteria, TVA is building six mechanical-draft cooling towers to supplement the diffuser pipes. There will be three possible modes of operation for the combined cooling tower-diffuser pipe system: (1)open-mode cooling using the diffuser pipes, (2)closed-mode cooling using the cooling towers, and (3) helper-mode cooling using the towers and the pipes in series. In order to achieve the three modes of operation, three structures were designed to control the flow in the return channel. Model studies and transient computations were conducted to ensure proper performance of the return channel and the three associated structures. The hydraulic problems associated with the designs originally proposed and the modifications found necessary for optimal use were described. The results of these studies showed the effect of vortex formation on the headloss due to Gate Structure No. 1, the importance of conducting hydraulic transient computations in the design of Gate Structure No. 2, and the flow characteristics downstream from Gate Structure No. 2 and Discharge Control Structure prior to and after installations of the floor strue-tures in the stilling basins. (See also W75-08786) (Sims-ISWS)
W75-08803

TRANSIENT COOLING POND BEHAVIOR,
Oak Ridge National Lab., Tenn.
P. J. Ryan, and D. R. F. Harleman.
In: Hydraulic Engineering and the Environment; Proceedings of the 21st Annual Hydraulic Division Specialty Conference, Montana State University, Bozeman, August 15-17, 1973. American Society of Civil Engineers, New York, p 191-201, 1973. 7 fig, 1 tab, 5 ref.

Descriptors: *Ponds, *Cooling water, *Powerplants, Model studies, Mathematical models, Laboratory tests, Unsteady flow, Skimming, Temperature, Heat transfer, Winds, Behavior, *Thermal pollution, *Waste water treatment.
Identifiers: *Cooling ponds, Skimmer walls, Transient response.

An analytical and experimental study of transient cooling pond behavior was conducted. The characteristics of an efficient type of cooling pond were defined, and the performance of this type of pond was examined in the laboratory. A new expression for surface heat loss from an artificially heated water surface was developed and tested in the field and the laboratory. The expression explicitly includes the effect of free (buoyancy driven) convection. The effects of entrance mixing and density currents on cooling pond performance were studies. A predictive mathematical model, which incorporates transient temperature variations in both the horizontal and vertical planes, was developed and tested against data from a laboratory cooling pond and against five years of data from two different types of field cooling ponds. (See also W75-08786) (Sims-ISWS)
W75-08804

WATER POLLUTION CONTROL BY HYDRAULIC AERATION,
Toronto Univ. (Ontario). Dept. of Mechanical Engineering.
For primary bibliographic entry see Field 5G.
W75-08814

CHARACTERISTICS OF AN AIR-WATER MIXTURE IN A VERTICAL SHAFT,
Georgia Inst. of Tech., Atlanta. Dept. of Civil Engineering.
For primary bibliographic entry see Field 8B.
W75-08815

WASTEWATER RECLAMATION AND RECHARGE, BAY PARK, N.Y.,
Geological Survey, Mineola, N.Y.
J. Vecchioli, J. A. Oliva, S. E. Ragone, and H. F. H. Ku.
ASCE Proceedings, Journal of the Environmental Engineering Division, Vol 101, No EE2, Paper 11232, p 201-214, April 1975. 9 fig, 4 tab, 21 ref.

Descriptors: *Water reuse, *Reclaimed water, *Artificial recharge, *Injection wells, *New York, Tertiary treatment, Water quality, Groundwater.
Identifiers: *Long Island(NY).

A water-conservation method currently under study by Nassau County, New York, involves reclamation of wastewater and its return to the groundwater reservoir. Since 1968, the Nassau County Department of Public Works has operated an advanced waste-treatment plant at Bay Park, N.Y., near the south shore of Nassau County. Reclaimed water from this plant has been used in a series of deep-well artificial-recharge experiments. About 600,000 gal/day of effluent from an activated-sludge sewage treatment plant was further purified by clarification, filtration, activated-carbon adsorption, and chlorination. Significant quality parameters of the reclaimed water and their usual concentrations were: Chemical oxygen demand approx. 10 mg/litre; phosphorus approx. 0.1 mg/litre, methylene blue active substances <0.1 mg/litre, and turbidity <1 mg/litre. Reclaimed water was injected intermittently in a series of tests into the Magothy aquifer through a well screened at a depth of 418 ft to 480 ft below land surface. The rate of excessive head buildup observed during the recharge of 41,700,000 gal averaged 3 ft per 1,000,000 gal. Operation and maintenance costs (1972) of further purifying the secondary-stage effluent to rechargeable quality, but without nitrogen removal, are estimated to be about $0.27 per 1,000 gal on a 3-mgd scale. (Knapp-USGS)
W75-08827

THE IMPACT OF WATER QUALITY OBJECTIVES ON URBAN WATER SUPPLY PLANNING,
Colorado State Univ., Fort Collins. Dept. of Agricultural Engineering.
W. R. Walker, and G. V. Skogerboe.
Water Resources Bulletin, American Water Resources Association, Vol 9, No 5, p 861-873, October 1973. 6 fig, 1 tab, 5 ref. OWRR B-071-COLO(6).

Descriptors: *Municipal water, *Water supply, *Water quality, *Management, *Alternative planning, *Water reuse, *Waste water treatment, Optimization, Costs, Algorithms, Operation and maintenance, Construction costs, Dissolved solids, Biochemical oxygen demand, Activated sludge, Electrodialysis, Equations, Mathematical models, Operations research, Constraints, Colorado.
Identifiers: *Urban effluent, *Cost minimization, Nonlinear programming, Denver(Colo).

Economically optimum policies for supplying rapidly expanding urban centers with additional water supplies are shown to be dependent on water quality goals for the urban effluent. A nonlinear elimination algorithm has been developed and applied to the wastewater treatment system of a typical urban water supply network to delineate minimum-cost treatment procedures under a wide variety of effluent standards. To define the feasibility of new water sources as opposed to reuse, a comparison of costs with and without various levels of reuse are made, and unit costs of water under these conditions are determined. Data from the Denver metropolitan area are used to derive cost information. It is shown that as effluents are required to meet increasingly higher standards, the unit costs associated with wastewater treatment system capacity expansion for water recycling decrease substantially. The model considers primary, secondary (activated sludge), and tertiary treatment, as well as desalting (electrodialysis). The water quality vector is limited to the inorganic concentration of total dissolved solids and the five-day Biochemical Oxygen Demand concentration. (Bell-Cornell)
W75-08845

5E. Ultimate Disposal Of Wastes

TREATMENT AND DISPOSAL OF WASTEWATER SLUDGES,
Duke Univ., Durham, N.C. Dept. of Civil Engineering.
For primary bibliographic entry see Field 5D.
W75-08552

WASTE TREATMENT AND HANDLING PROCESSES ANNUAL REPORT,
Battelle-Pacific Northwest Labs., Richland, Wash.
For primary bibliographic entry see Field 5D.
W75-08641

DEMOLITION OF BUILDING 12, AN OLD PLUTONIUM FILTER FACILITY,
Los Alamos Scientific Lab., N. Mex.
E. L. Christensen, R. Garde, and A. M. Valentine.

Available from the National Technical Information Service, Springfield, Va 22161 as Rept No LA-5755, $4.00 in paper copy, $2.25 in microfiche. Rept No LA-5755, January 1975. 20 p, 38 fig, 5 tab.

Descriptors: *Radioactive waste disposal, *Plutonium, *Environmental effects, *Filters, *Facilities, Air pollution, Soil contamination, Water pollution, Public health, Safety, Evaluation, Transportation, Comprehensive planning, Alternative planning, Engineering, Monitoring, Air, Soils, Sampling.
Identifiers: *Demolition, *Decontamination.

The decommissioning and disposal of a plutonium-contaminated air filter facility that provided ventilation for the main plutonium processing plant at Los Alamos from 1945 until 1973 are described. The health physics, waste management, and environmental aspects of the demolition are also discussed. (Houser-ORNL)
W75-08643

TRANSURANIC SOLID WASTE MANAGEMENT RESEARCH PROGRAMS, PROGRESS REPORT FOR APRIL-JUNE, 1974.
Los Alamos Scientific Lab., N. Mex. Health Div.
For primary bibliographic entry see Field 5D.
W75-08647

DEEP ROCK NUCLEAR WASTE DISPOSAL TEST: DESIGN AND OPERATION,
Sandia Labs., Albuquerque, N. Mex.
R. D. Klett.
Available from the National Technical Information Service, Springfield, Va. 22161, as Rept No SAND 74-0042, $5.45 in paper copy, $2.25 in microfiche. Rept No SAND 74-0042, September 1974. 144 p, 57 fig, 9 tab, 38 ref.

Descriptors: *Radioactive waste disposal, *Liquid, *Nuclear waste, *Model studies, *Research and development, *Geological formations, *Bedrock, Granites, Design criteria, Operations, Simulation analysis, Feasibility.

An electrically heated test of nuclear waste simulant in granitic rock was conducted to demonstrate the feasibility of the concept of deep rock nuclear waste disposal and to obtain design data. The deep rock disposal systems study and the design and operation of the first concept feasibility test are described. (Houser-ORNL)
W75-08656

REPORT TO CONGRESS - DISPOSAL OF HAZARDOUS WASTES.
Environmental Protection Agency Programs. Washington, D.C. Office of Solid Waste Management.
For primary bibliographic entry see Field 5D.
W75-08666

REMOVAL OF CESIUM AND STRONTIUM FROM FUEL STORAGE BASIN WATER,
Allied Chemical Corporation, Idaho Falls, Idaho. Idaho Chemical Programs Operations Office.
For primary bibliographic entry see Field 5D.
W75-08667

NUCLEAR WASTE MANAGEMENT AND TRANSPORTATION QUARTERLY PROGRESS REPORT JULY-SEPTEMBER, 1974.
Battelle-Pacific Northwest Labs., Richland, Wash. Nuclear Waste Technology Dept.
For primary bibliographic entry see Field 5D.
W75-08668

DAVENTRY SEWERAGE SCHEME COMPLETED AHEAD OF SCHEDULE.
For primary bibliographic entry see Field 5D.
W75-08676

DREDGED SPOIL DISPOSAL ON THE NEW JERSEY WETLANDS: THE PROBLEM OF ENVIRONMENTAL IMPACT ASSESSMENT,
Rutgers - The State Univ., New Brunswick, N.J. Marine Science Center.
For primary bibliographic entry see Field 5C.
W75-08716

ECONOMIC AND ENVIRONMENTAL EVALUATION OF NUCLEAR WASTE DISPOSAL BY UNDERGROUND IN SITU MELTING,
California Univ., Livermore. Lawrence Livermore Lab.
J. J. Cohen, R. L. Braun, L. L. Schwartz, and H. A. Tewes.
Available from the National Technical Information Service, Springfield, Va. 22161 as UCRL-51713. $4.00 in paper copy, $2.25 in microfiche. UCRL-51713, (TID-4500 UC-11) November 1974. 14 p, 6 fig, 2 tab, 19 ref. AEC W-7405-Eng-48.

Descriptors: *Ultimate disposal, *Radioactive waste disposal, *Nuclear wastes, *Cost-benefit analysis, Rock excavation, Waste treatment, Underground waste disposal, Liquid wastes.
Identifiers: *Underground melting, Nuclear fuel reprocessing wastes, DUMP.

A Deep Underground Melt Process (DUMP) for the management of high level nuclear waste is reviewed and evaluated relative to other proposed waste management methods. The concept calls for direct placement of liquid radioactive waste from fuel reprocessing operations deep underground into rubble-filled void spaces. The process consists of the following general phases: waste and water addition to the void space--less than 1 month; self boiling period--1 month through 25 years; rubble, followed by surrounding rock melts--25 through 90 years; and rock begins to resolidify--after 90 years. The heat from the radioactive decay melts rock in situ deep underground and an insoluble rock matrix eventually encapsulates the nuclear waste. The advantages of DUMP are elimination or reduction of many interim processes (and their associated risks) considered necessary with methods of disposal involving transportation; its applicability to all levels of liquid waste; and the permanent elimination of the waste from the biosphere. These advantages weigh favorably against AEC regulations requiring retrievability of wastes and storage at a single site. While the implementation of DUMP does not provide a significantly lesser health hazard than other proposed disposal methods, the resultant economic savings could be up to 80%. (Becker-Wisconsin)
W75-08785

5F. Water Treatment and Quality Alteration

FORMATION OF HALOGENATED ORGANICS BY CHLORINATION OF WATER SUPPLIES,
Harvard Univ., Cambridge, Mass. Dept. of Sanitary Engineering.
J. C. Morris.
Available from the National Technical Information Service, Springfield, Va. 22161, as PB-241 511, $4.25 in paper copy, $2.25 in microfiche. Environmental Protection Agency, Washington, DC, Report EPA-600/1-75-002, March 1975. 54 p, 166 ref. 1CA046 (PEMP), P5-01-1805-J.

Descriptors: Toxicity, Activated carbon, *Chlorination, Aeration, Catalysis, Chemical reactions, Coagulation, *Water treatment, *Water supply, *Reviews, *Waste water treatment, *Organic compounds, Phenols.
Identifiers: *Halogenated organic compounds, Chloroform, Acetones, Enolacetone.

Literature on the formation of halogenated organic compounds during the chlorination of water supplies has been reviewed critically. Types of organic compounds likely to be encountered in natural waters have been surveyed and various known or prospective reactions of dilute aqueous chlorine with these types of compounds have been discussed. Two principal types of chlorination reaction are expected: (1) electrophilic aromatic chlorination as in the long-known formation of chlorophenols; and (2) electrophilic chlorine addition to activated double bonds like that of enolacetone. Chloroform or other haloforms may occur as end products of exhaustive chlorination in either case. General substitution reactions of chlorine are unlikely however. So carbon tetrachloride or fully chlorinated higher hydrocarbons are not probable products of water chlorination. Possible methods for minimizing the concentrations of halogenated organic compounds in municipal supplies have been outlined. These include pretreatment methods, such as coagulation or preozonation to reduce amounts of precursors to the halogenated compounds, and posttreatment methods, such as carbon adsorption or aeration to remove halogenated compounds after their formation. (EPA)
W75-08357

WATER VOL. 39. A YEARBOOK FOR HYDROCHEMISTRY AND WATER PURIFICATION TECHNIQUE,
W. Husmann.
Symposium, Marburg, W Germany, 1972. Verlag Chemie GMBH: Weinheim/Bergstr, W Germany. 1972. 393 p, Illus. Pr DM 68.

Descriptors: *Water purification, *Chemicals, Water pollution, Potable water, Waste water(Pollution), Water treatment, *Water pollution sources, *Chemical wastes, *Water management(Applied), *Water quality control, Conferences.
Identifiers: *Hydrochemistry.

This book contains contributed papers on hydrochemistry, covering water pollution and drinking water treatment, waste water problems in the chemical industry and modern procedures for water treatment in power plants. The 1st group of papers includes the following specific topics: simultaneous continuous determination of the chemical O2 requirement and organic carbon; physiochemical data and testing possibilities for using polyphosphates in water; purification and disinfection processes in treatment of swimming pool water; and technical measures against eutrophication of surface waters in Germany. The next group of papers includes the following specific topics: identification of pollutants which are not readily biodegradable; studies on the mechanism of flocculation by polyelectrolytes; studies on the behavior of trace elements in treatment of drinking water; and recent aspects of water and sewage treatment. The next group of papers covers the following specific topics: test of purification of production waste water from the chemical industry; measures for the purification of petrochemical waste waters; the methylation of mercury; and experiences with waste water from chemical and physical institutes. The final group of papers covers the following specific subjects: bases for the valuation of sewage taxes dependent upon the amount of pollutants; procedure for the maintenance of water purity in the water system of power stations; perspectives in condensate treatment; and operating experiences with continuous ion exchange plants. Numerous graphs, diagrams and other illustrations are included throughout, and each paper ends with a pertinent list of references. (See also W72-08483)--Copyright 1973, Biological Abstracts, Inc.
W75-08390

DISTRIBUTION, CULTIVATION AND CHEMICAL DESTRUCTION OF GALLIONELLA FROM ALABAMA GROUND WATER,
Alabama Univ., University. Dept. of Microbiology.

For primary bibliographic entry see Field 5B.
W75-08479

WATER REUSE: RESOURCE OF THE FUTURE,
Dallas Water Utilities Dept., Tex.
For primary bibliographic entry see Field 5D.
W75-08537

ZETA-POTENTIAL CONTROL FOR ALUM COAGULATION,
Fertilizer Corp. of India, Sindri.
V. S. Gupta, S. K. Bhattacharjya, and B. K. Dutta.
Journal American Works Association, Vol 67, No 1, p 21-23, January 1975. 13 fig, 5 ref.

Descriptors: *Montomorillonite, *Kaolinite, *Zeta potential, Surface waters, Aluminum, Sulfates, *Coagulation, Chemical reactions, *Water treatment, Chemical precipitation, Clays, Clay minerals, Inorganic compounds, Hydrogen ion concentration, Cation exchange, Water quality, Suspended solids, Flocculation, Water properties, Water purification.
Identifiers: *Fuller's earth, Isoelectric point.

The zeta potential of different clays such as kaolinite, montomorillonite, and fuller's earth at 100, 250, 500, and 1000 mg/liter in 0.0000145, 0.000058, 0.000145, and 0.00058 molar aluminum sulfate at various pH was studied and compared with results for a surface water. The clays were selected on the basis of cation exchange capacity. The results are discussed with respect to the isoelectric point as an indicant for achieving optimum destabilization with an economically efficient coagulant dose. (Witt-IPC)
W75-08565

AUTOMATION OF FILTERS IN PURIFYING DEVICES IN WATER PIPES (AVTOMATIZATSIYA FIL'TROV NA VODOPROVODNYKH OCHISTNYKH SOORUZHENIYAKH),
V. B. Shimkovich.
Vodosnabzheniye i Sanitarnaya Tekhnika, No 4, p 9-11, 1974. 2 fig, 4 ref.

Descriptors: *Filters, *Automation, Hydraulics, Flow rates, Water purification, Filtration, Turbidity, Equipment, Pipes, Valves, Water treatment.
Identifiers: *Water pipes, Rotary valves.

Automatic control systems for water filters in municipal and industrial water ply systems are critically reviewed. The rates of filtration are controlled primarily by the water levels or by the flow rates of the filtrates, by means of electric or hydraulic, and sometimes pneumatic automatic control systems. The automatic control systems act upon electrically or hydraulically powered sluice valves. Poor hydraulic characteristics of of conventional sluice valves make their replacement by rotary valves necessary. The automatic sequential switchover of the filters to flushing is possible by a pulse from a limit switch. Switchover is a function of the limit value of the pressure loss, and a function of the turbidity which is controlled by a turbidimeter. (Takacs-FIRL)
W75-08572

FOUR-MEDIA FILTER,
Neptune Microfloc, Inc., Corvallis, Oreg. (Assignee).
For primary bibliographic entry see Field 5D.
W75-08632

MULTI-TANK ION EXCHANGE WATER TREATMENT SYSTEM,
Rock Valley Water Conditioning, Inc., Rockford, Ill. (Assignee).
C. H. Yocum.
U S Patent No 3,876,539, 6 p, 5 fig, 5 ref; Official Gazette of the United States Patent Office, Vol 933, No 2, p 832, April 8, 1975.

Descriptors: *Patents, *Water treatment, *Ion exchange, Water pollution control, Pollution abatement, Treatment facilities, Equipment, Waste water treatment.

The general aim is to interconnect exchangers with unique and relatively simple means for taking exchanger out of service when the exchanger begins its regenerating cycle, for keeping the exchanger out of service and in a standby status after the exchanger completes its regenerating cycle, and for bringing the standby exchanger back into service when another exchanger begins its regenerating cycle. A novel interconnecting means enables construction of the exchangers as virtually identical modular units and enables a given exchanger to be used interchangeably in treatment systems equipped with two, three or even more exchangers. Hydraulic interconnecting means switch a newly regenerating exchanger out of service and a standby exchanger into service in response to the initial flow of liquid through the drain line of the newly regenerating exchanger. (Sinha-OEIS)
W75-08637

EFFECT OF INDIVIDUAL FACTORS ON THE FORMATION OF WATER QUALITY OF THE KARA KUM CANAL AS A WATER SUPPLY SOURCE OF THE TURKMEN SSR, (IN RUSSIAN),
Institute of General and Municipal Hygiene, Moscow (USSR).
For primary bibliographic entry see Field 5B.
W75-08644

CHARACTERISTICS OF THE ORGANIZATION OF SANITARY CONTROL OF WATER SUPPLY SOURCES AND DRINKING WATER QUALITY IN THE OIL AND GAS-BEARING REGIONS IN THE NORTHERN OBTERRITORY, (IN RUSSIAN),
Tyumenskii Gosudarstvennyi Meditsinskii Institut (USSR).
V. I. D'yachkov.
Gig Sanit. 38(9): 88-89. 1973.

Descriptors: *Water quality control, *Potable water, *Public health, Water quality, Pathogenic bacteria, Arctic regions, Water treatment, *Water supply.
Identifiers: *USSR(Ob River).

An important social factor influencing man's adaptation to the rigorous natural and climatic conditions of the northern region of the Ob river (USSR) for the purpose of developing and exploiting oil deposits is the organization of an industrial and drinking water supply. The local characteristics of the region with reference to sanitary control of water sources and quality of drinking water (with reference to microbial pathogens) and the duties of sanitary and epidemiological stations in protecting these sources are discussed.--Copyright 1975, Biological Abstracts, Inc.
W75-08681

METHOD AND APPARATUS FOR SURFACE SKIMMING,
Ecodyne Corp., Lincolnshire, Ill. (assignee)
For primary bibliographic entry see Field 5D.
W75-08741

PURIFICATION CONTROL UNIT,
Camper and Nicholsons Ltd., Gosport (England). (Assignee).
R. J. Phipps.
U S Patent No 3, 865,710, 5 p, 4 fig, 5 ref; Official Gazette of the United States Patent Office, Vol 931, No 2, p 810, February 11, 1975.

Descriptors: *Patents, *Water purification, *Water treatment, Polarity, Coagulation, Swimming pools, *Control systems.
Identifiers: *Electronic control circuit, Multivibrator circuit.

A water purification control circuit has a pair of supply terminals; first and second pairs of unidirectional output terminals; a network including controlled rectifiers and interconnecting the supply and output terminals for supplying to the first and second pairs of output terminals purification and coagulation currents respectively; a multivibrator circuit connected with the network; and a circuit controlling the operation of the multivibrator circuit. The arrangement is such that a change in state of the multivibrator circuit changed the conducting state of the controlled rectifiers to reverse the polarity of both pairs of the output terminals. (Sinha-OEIS)
W75-08751

DISTURBANCE OF WATER SUPPLY DUE TO SECONDARY BIOLOGICAL CONTAMINANTS, (IN RUSSIA),
Institutul de Sanatate Publica si Cercetare Medicale, Iasi (Rumania).
For primary bibliographic entry see Field 5C.
W75-08773

QUALITY OF PUBLIC WATER SUPPLIES OF NEW YORK, MAY 1972-MAY 1973.
Geological Survey, Albany, N.Y.
For primary bibliographic entry see Field 5A.
W75-08832

5G. Water Quality Control

WATERSHED ORGANIZATIONS - IMPACT ON WATER QUALITY MANAGEMENT, AN ANALYSIS OF SELECTED MICHIGAN WATERSHED COUNCILS,
Michigan State Univ., East Lansing. Dept. of Resources Development.
E. Dersch, and E. Hood.
Available from the National Technical Information Service, Springfield, Va. 22161, as PB-242 298, $9.50 in paper copy, $2.25 in microfiche. Completion Report, Institute of Water Research, Michigan State University, (May 1975), 329 p, 47 fig, 25 tab, 285 ref. OWRT A-069-MICH(1), 14-31-0001-4022.

Descriptors: *Watershed management, *Organizations, Water quality, *Water quality control, *Management, *Legislation, *Michigan, Watersheds(Basins), Planning, Model studies, Institutional constraints, Local governments.
Identifiers: *Watershed councils(Mich).

Utilizing a case study approach, eight Michigan Watershed Councils were evaluated to determine the degree to which they could have an effective impact on planning for water quality management within constraints imposed by existing state legislation. Methods chosen to measure the extent and type of this impact included first the development of a weighted index of effectiveness. Models established from this index were tested against organization operation, as revealed through council records and activities and through results of questionnaires and interviews of key individuals, representatives and government officials associated with the individual councils. Results of this procedure revealed watershed councils have, in varying degrees, contributed to water quality management planning through their advisory, planning and information-education functions. The variation was traced largely to problems associated with statutory weaknesses and deficiencies as well as structural and operational difficulties concerning internal organization, orientation and approach. Recommendations developed focused on more complete application of current

statutory responsibilities and opportunities and on more frequent contact, interaction and role-sharing with state agencies and local government units.
W75-08354

THE POLLUTION ENVIRONMENT,
Utah State Univ., Logan.
J. M. Neuhold.
In: Energy, Environment and Water Resources, Proceedings of Universities Council on Water Resources Meeting, July 28-31, 1974, Logan, Utah. p 341-343, (1974).

Descriptors: *Environmental effects, *Water pollution, *Colorado River basin, *Energy, *Water shortage, Air pollution, Thermal pollution, Power plants, Saline soils, Saline water, Irrigation, Arizona, Colorado, Utah, New Mexico, Wyoming, California, Nevada, Mexico, Land use, Water utilization, Planning, *Regional analysis.

The Colorado River Basin is characterized by light rainfall and surface water scarcity. White civilization over the past century has lowered both the amount and the quality of available water. Development of energy resources will constitute yet another impact on an overtaxed, increasingly saline water supply. Oil shale and coal exploitation could be major contributors to the dewatering of the basin. Pressure to increase food supplies will accentuate the current salinity problems of agriculture. A land use/water use planning function is called for on a regional basis. Limits have to be set in terms of population increases and in terms of industrial and resource development within the region so that the resources of the region can be maintained not only for the regional population but for the nation at large. (Bowden-Arizona)
W75-08371

A MODEL FOR ESTIMATING DESIRED LEVELS OF NITRATE-N CONCENTRATION IN COTTON PETIOLES,
California Univ., Davis. Dept. of Water Science and Engineering.
For primary bibliographic entry see Field 3F.
W75-08396

AN EXAMINATION OF THE CONCENTRATION OF ORGANIC COMPONENTS WATER-EXTRACTED FROM PETROLEUM PRODUCTS,
Naval Research Lab., Washington, D.C.
For primary bibliographic entry see Field 5A.
W75-08454

THE EFFECT OF WEATHERING ON A CRUDE OIL RESIDUE EXPOSED AT SEA,
University Coll. of North Wales, Bangor. Dept. of Marine Biology.
For primary bibliographic entry see Field 5B.
W75-08457

OIL SPILL PROTECTION IN THE BALTIC SEA,
Institute for Water and Air Pollution Research, Stockholm (Sweden). Project on Ecological Effects of Oil Pollution in the Baltic Sea.
L. Ladner, and A. Hagstrom.
Journal Water Pollution Control Federation, Vol 47, No 4, p 796-809, April 1975. 7 fig, 4 tab, 23 ref.

Descriptors: *Oil spills, *Legislation, *Research and development, Oil pollution, Water pollution control, Water pollution effects, Toxicity, Toxins, Microbial degradation, Pollutant identification, Analytical techniques, Water pollution sources.
Identifiers: *Baltic Sea, Sweden.

Pursuant to an agreement among Baltic Sea countries, Sweden has enacted strict legislation regarding the discharge of oil into its territorial waters and instituted a new control system. However, accidental or illegal discharges from tankers in the Baltic is still unacceptably high. A program to combat such spills was undertaken and is partially complete, and an oil spill research group was formed by the Swedish Coast Guard, the National Environmental Protection Board, the Swedish Petroleum Institute, and the Water and Air Pollution Research Laboratory. During the first few years of existence, the research group carried out in detail the following studies: (1) determination of the acute toxicity in brackish water of different oil dispersants, oils, and combinations of both, as well as identification of most toxic components in oils; (2) studies on composite effects of oil spills on faunal communities in the littoral zone of the Baltic; (3) studies on transformation and eventual decomposition of an oil spill as a result of microbial activity; and (4) development of analytical procedures for oil analysis, which are more relevant from an ecological point of view than traditional analytical methods are. Progress on these studies was reported. (Sims-ISWS)
W75-08464

NITRATE AND NITRITE REDUCTION IN FLOODED GAMMA-IRRADIATED SOIL UNDER CONTROLLED PH AND REDOX POTENTIAL CONDITIONS,
Ghent Rijksuniversiteit (Belgium). Faculteit Landbouwwetenschappen.
O. Van Cleemput, and W. H. Patrick, Jr.
Soil Biol Biochem. Vol 6, No 2, p 85-88, 1974, Illus.
Identifiers: Denitrifyication, Enzymes, *Flooded soils, Gamma-Irradiated soils, *Nitrate reduction, *Nitrite reduction, Organisms, Potential, Radiation, *Redox, Reduction, Resistant, Soil, Hydrogen ion concentration.

Nitrate and nitrite reduction was studied in a waterlogged soil after gamma irradiation with 2.5 Mrad. Before irradiation and mineral-N addition the pH was controlled at 4.5, 6 and 8, and the redox potential controlled at 0, +200 and +400 mV. Nitrate reduction rate increased with increasing pH as well as with decreasing redox potential. Nitrate reduction rate was doubled by decreasing the redox potential from +400 to 0 mV. At pH 4.5 almost no nitrite accumulated regardless of redox potential, while at pH 6 and 8 marked nitrite accumulation occurred at low redox potential. In relation to nonirradiation, gamma irradiation had a stimulating effect on nitrate reduction at pH 6 and 8 but a retarding effect at pH 4.5; nitrite reduction proceeded slower at pH 6 and 8 but at the same rate at 4.5. Nitrate and nitrite reduction can be carried out by radiation-resistant enzyme systems of non-proliferating cells of denitrifying organisms.--Copyright 1974, Biological Abstracts, Inc.
W75-08470

MECHANICAL HARVESTING OF AQUATIC VEGETATION: DEVELOPMENT OF A HIGH SPEED PICKUP UNIT,
Wisconsin Univ., Madison. Dept. of Mechanical Engineering.
For primary bibliographic entry see Field 4A.
W75-08471

ANALYSIS AND DESIGN OF SETTLING BASINS FOR IRRIGATION RETURN FLOW,
Idaho Univ., Moscow. Dept. of Civil Engineering.
F. L. Ballard.
Available from the National Technical Information Service, Springfield, Va 22161 as PB-242 345, $4.75 in paper copy, $2.25 in microfiche. M S Thesis, January 1975. 66 p, 14 fig, 10 tab, 14 ref, append. OWRR A-042-IDA(2).

Descriptors: *Sediments, *Sediment yield, *Settling basins, Irrigation, *Return flow, Erosion, Tailwater, Ponds, *Design criteria, *Regression analysis, Mathematical models, Phosphates, Nitrogen.

Nine fields under furrow irrigation were studied to determine sediment yield to ponds as a function of crop type, soil type and topography. Data were collected from seven farm settling ponds located on these fields to gain insight into the factors which affect pond removal efficiency. To determine design criteria for on-farm settling ponds, regression analysis was used to develop predictive equations for sediment yield. Independent variables included flow onto field, slope, furrow length, time of run, and the irrigated area. During an irrigated season 0.339 to 37.00 tons of sediment per acre were eroded. When regression analysis was used to find how pond efficiency was affected by parameters overflow rate, length to width ratio, sediment size and detention time, little was learned. However, a mathematical model was a useful tool for pond design; efficiencies ranged from 43.0%-100% for sediment and 28.6%-77.7% for phosphate and nitrogen.
W75-08484

ENVIRONMENT: A BIBLIOGRAPHY ON SOCIAL POLICY AND HUMANISTIC VALUES,
Nevada Univ., Reno. Desert Research Inst.
For primary bibliographic entry see Field 10C.
W75-08489

URBAN STORM RUNOFF, PUGET SOUND REGION, WASHINGTON,
Washington Univ., Seattle. Coll. of Forest Resources.
D. D. Wooldridge, G. M. Mack, and J. Veasey.
Available from the National Technical Information Service, Springfield, Va 22161 as PB-242 304, $7.00 in paper copy, $2.25 in microfiche. Washington Water Research Center, Pullman, Completion Report, February 1975. 182 p, 11 fig, 43 tab, 22 ref. OWRT B-042-WASH(1).

Descriptors: *Urban runoff, Storm runoff, *Washington, Land use, Regional development, Legal aspects, *Peak discharge, Small watersheds, *Runoff forecasting, Regulation.
Identifiers: Urban watersheds, *Puget Sound(Wash), *Storm runoff control.

Peak storm discharge had flood flow of a 225 year storm on an intensely developed small urban watershed when other streams with lesser urbanization had usual winter runoff. Mathematical relationships which predict mean daily discharge from precipitation show storm flow yields have increased from 130 to 185% over the past decade. These increases in flow range from 0.5 to 0.9 cubic feet per second per square mile per year, based on current trends. In area inches these range from 0.6 to 1.86 inches of increased runoff from small basins. Common law of surface water rights of the State of Washington has established that owners of lower land have the right to prevent upper land owners from burdening a natural watercourse with a quantity or velocity of water beyond its capacity. Governmental entities are subject to the same rights and liabilities in their public works. Governmental entities may constitutionally exercise regulatory or policy powers to impose burdens on land ownership and on construction of improvements where such regulation preserves or promotes public health, safety or general welfare. Counties and cities have statutory and constitutional power relating to both flood and surface waters. Considerable progress has been made in recent years in regulation and assessment of responsibilities for control of storm runoff. Improved control of storm runoff could be achieved by requirements for clearing and grading permits accompanied by an environmental assessment of the impacts of the proposed action on quantity, quality, and timing of storm flow. On site storage of stormwater in excess of natural flow must be provided in all development.
W75-08492

WASTE-LOAD ALLOCATION STUDIES FOR ARKANSAS STREAMS, WHITE RIVER BASIN, SEGMENT 4A,
Geological Survey, Little Rock, Ark.
For primary bibliographic entry see Field 5B
W75-08500

WASTE-LOAD ALLOCATION STUDIES FOR ARKANSAS STREAMS, WHITE RIVER BASIN, SEGMENT 4D,
Geological Survey, Little Rock, Ark.
For primary bibliographic entry see Field 5B.
W75-08502

WASTE-LOAD ALLOCATION STUDIES FOR ARKANSAS STREAMS, OUACHITA RIVER BASIN, SEGMENT 2E,
Geological Survey, Little Rock, Ark.
For primary bibliographic entry see Field 5B.
W75-08504

PURIFICATION OF WASTEWATERS AND GASEOUS EMISSIONS IN THE U.S.A. (OCHISTKA STOCHNYKH VOD I GAZOVYKH VYBROSOV NA PREDPRIYATIYAKH S.SH.A.),
Ministerstvo Bumazhnoi i Derevoobrabatyvayushchei Promyshlennost, Moscow (USSR).
For primary bibliographic entry see Field 5D.
W75-08540

STATISTICAL ANALYSIS OF THE PROCESS OF EFFLUENT PURIFICATION AT THE BAIKAL PULP MILL FOR THE PURPOSE OF CONTROL (STATISTICHESKII ANALIZ PROTSESSA OCHISTKI STOCHNYKH VOD BAIKAL'SKOGO TSELLYULOZNOGO ZAVOD DLYA TSELEI UPRAVLENIYA),
For primary bibliographic entry see Field 5D.
W75-08547

WATER INTAKE RATES ON A SILT LOAM SOIL WITH VARIOUS MANURE APPLICATIONS,
Nebraska Univ., Lincoln. Dept. of Agricultural Engineering.
For primary bibliographic entry see Field 2G.
W75-08574

INVESTIGATION OF RATIONAL EFFLUENT AND STREAM STANDARDS FOR TROPICAL COUNTRIES,
Asian Inst. of Tech., Bangkok (Thailand).
M. B. Pescod.
Available from the National Technical Information Service, Springfield, Va. 22161, as AD-782 199, $4.25 in paper copy, $2.25 in microfiche. US Army Research and Development Group, Far East, APO San Fransisco, Calif. Report No FE-476-2, May 1974. 60 p, 6 fig, 16 tab, 10 ref.

Descriptors: *Dissolved oxygen, *Water quality standards, *Asia, *Irrigation, *Fishing, *Waste water treatment, Water quality, Standards, Water pollution, Surface waters, Water pollution treatment, Potable water, Public health, Toxicants, Heavy metals, Temperature, Water pollution, Sources, Food chains, Dissolved solids, Oxidation lagoons.
Identifiers: *Stream standards.

Water quality standards were reviewed and tentative stream standards proposed for use in developing countries of Southeast Asia on the basis of legitimate water uses and adaptation of available data to local conditions. A survey of stream standards and water uses applied in the Southeast Asian region indicated that few countries had adopted standards and practically no attempt had been made to adjust to suit local conditions. Experimental studies suggested that oxidation pond effluent would have a beneficial effect on the oxygen balance of a stream under tropical conditions provided that the algal concentration was not more than 1x105 cells/ ml after dilution in the stream. Oxidation ponds were assessed as being more attractive than either trickling filter or activated sludge treatment plants for populations less than 175,000 and land rental costs of U.S. $0.10 per square meter per year or less. (Katz)
W75-08584

PHYSICAL CRITERIA IN COMPUTER METHODS FOR PARTIAL DIFFERENTIAL EQUATIONS,
Rutgers - the State Univ., New Brunswick, N.J. Dept. of Computer Science.
R. Vichnevetsky.
Proceedings of the International Association for Analog Computation, Vol 16, No 1, 1974, p 3-15. 15 fig, 47 ref. Paper was presented at the 7th International Congress, Prague, Aug 1973. OWRT B-045-NJ(1), B-049-NJ(1).

Descriptors: *Approximation method, *Model studies, Systems analysis, Simulation analysis, Estuaries.
Identifiers: *Numerical analysis, *Estuary quality models, Simulation.

Physical or problem related criteria are used to measure quantitatively certain aspects of numerical accuracy. Case studies involving partial differential equations commonly found in estuarial analysis are presented. (Davidson-Rutgers)
W75-08593

PROCESSING AND STORAGE OF WATER-HYACINTH SILAGE,
Florida Univ., Gainesville. Dept. of Agricultural Engineering.
For primary bibliographic entry see Field 4A.
W75-08595

A NEW DORATOMYCES FROM WATER-HYACINTH,
Florida Univ., Gainesville. Dept. of Plant Pathology.
For primary bibliographic entry see Field 4A.
W75-08606

ENVIRONMENTAL LOBBYING: TAKING THE RIGHT ISSUE TO THE RIGHT PLACE AT THE RIGHT TIME,
Clemson Univ., S.C.
For primary bibliographic entry see Field 6G.
W75-08608

OCCURRENCE OF CEROCOSPORA PIAROPI ON WATER HYACINTH IN FLORIDA,
Florida Univ., Gainesville. Water Resources Research Center.
For primary bibliographic entry see Field 4A.
W75-08610

DEVICE FOR CLEANING WATER POLLUTED BY OIL,
J. Rafael.
US Patent No. 3,875,062, 3 p, 2 fig, 4 ref; Official Gazette of the United States Patent Office, Vol 933, No 1, p 341, April 1, 1975.

Descriptors: *Patents, *Oil spills, *Oil pollution, Water pollution control, Water quality control, *Pollution abatement, *Separation techniques, Equipment, Skimming.

A device for cleaning water polluted by oil comprises a floating body which contains an inlet opening and a collecting chamber for the polluted water. The collecting chamber has a cover and the water surface polluted by oil that is inside the collecting chamber is fully or partly in contact with the cover. The cover is arched so that the oil accumulates at the highest point of the arch. Oil removal means are provided on the cover and the inside of the cover is below the minimum skimming height of the inlet opening. The rear end of the collecting chamber is connected to two ducts through which the water flows out of the collecting chamber. The outlet ends of the ducts are constricted to a slit so that the speed of the emerging surface layer of the water is reduced and residual oil particles dragged along the roof of the ducts rise upwards. (Sinha-OEIS)
W75-08612

DEVICE FOR RECEIVING WATER SURFACE FLOATING IMPURITIES,
A. Y. Derzhavets, P. G. Kogan, and S. M. Nunuparov.
US Patent No 3,862,902, 4 p, 3 fig, 7 ref; Official Gazette of the United States Patent Office, Vol 930, No 4, p 1874, January 28, 1975.

Descriptors: *Patents, *Flotsam, *Oil spills, *Oil pollution, *Pollution abatement, Water pollution control, Skimming, Jetsam, Domestic wastes, Boats, Bodies of water.

A device for receiving water surface floating impurities in the collecting receptacle of an oil and garbage skimmer craft is comprised of a gate installed at the inlet to the collecting receptacle. The upper horizongal edge of the gate forms a weir above which the upper layer of water together with floating impurities is overflowing. The gate is rigidly connected to a float. Both the gate and the float are fixed with a possibility for free rocking around a horizontal axis, thus providing for a constant depth of immersion of the upper horizontal edge of the gate in relation to the water level. The gate has an outside surface facing a water basin being cleaned and is given the shape of a portion of cylinder whose axis coincides with a horizontal axis around which the gate and float are rocking. (Sinha-OEIS)
W75-08623

OIL POLLUTION TOTALIZER,
J. O. Moreau, and R. A. Halko.
US Published Patent Application B 369,563, 4 p, 2 fig, 3 ref; Official Gazette of the United States Patent Office, Vol 930, No 4, p 1484, January 28, 1975.

Descriptors: *Patents, *Oil spills, *Oil pollution, Water pollution control, *Pollution abatement, Sensors, Filters, *Separation techniques.
Identifiers: Ballast, Deballasting, Refinery wastes.

An oil pollution totalizer is provided for accumulating all of the oil from a sample stream at a rate which is directly proportional to the rate of oil being discharged, e.g., in a stream from a tanker during a deballasting operation or in an effluent stream from a refinery operation. The totalizer comprises means for removing the oil from the sample stream and means for controlling the sample flow rate in proportion to the stream flow rate, and then finally, means for storing the oil for analysis such as by a continuous oil monitoring device or by standard laboratory techniques. (Sinha-OEIS)
W75-08624

INSTALLATION FOR SEPARATION ON THE SEABED OF THE EFFLUENTS FROM UNDERWATER OIL WELLS,
Entreprise de Recherches et d'Activities Petrolieres, Paris (France).
P. Charpentier.
US Patent No 3,875,998, 4 p, 7 fig, 8 ref; Official Gazette of the United States Patent Office, Vol 933, No 2, p 661, April 8, 1975.

Descriptors: *Patents, *Oil wells, *Oil spills, *Pollution abatement, Water pollution control, Equipment, Effluents, *Separation techniques.
Identifiers: Underwater wells.

An installation for separation on the seabed of the effluents from underwater oil wells consists of a base with negative buoyancy anchored on the seabed, and a hermetic caisson attached to this base and preferably articulated on it. It is equipped with at least one gas/liquid separator which is connected by pipes to each underwater well and from which one pipe leads to a burner, with another pipe to draw off the liquid phase. A buoyant tubular column surmounts the caisson and is connected to it. The upper end of this column which is above water, supports a platform, and means inside the caisson control the operation of the separator. (Sinha-OEIS)
W75-08629

SKIMMING DEVICE,
Societe Nationale des Petroles d'Aquitaine, Paris (France). (Assignee).
For primary bibliographic entry see Field 5D.
W75-08636

REDUCTION OF ATMOSPHERIC POLLUTION BY THE APPLICATION OF FLUIDIZED-BED COMBUSTION AND REGENERATION OF SULFUR CONTAINING ADDITIVES,
Argonne National Lab., Ill.
For primary bibliographic entry see Field 5A.
W75-08642

A REVIEW OF EXPLOSIVES USED IN EXPLOSIVE EXCAVATION RESEARCH LABORATORY PROJECTS SINCE 1969,
Army Engineer Waterways Experiment Station, Livermore, Calif. Explosive Excavation Research Lab.
For primary bibliographic entry see Field 8H.
W75-08650

LAND USE AND NUCLEAR POWER PLANTS - CASE STUDIES OF SITING PROBLEMS,
Directorate of Regulatory Standards (AEC), Washington, D.C.
For primary bibliographic entry see Field 6G.
W75-08654

DEEP ROCK NUCLEAR WASTE DISPOSAL TEST: DESIGN AND OPERATION,
Sandia Labs., Albuquerque, N. Mex.
For primary bibliographic entry see Field 5E.
W75-08656

ON THE SELECTION OF A GROUND DISPOSAL SITE FOR RADIOACTIVE WASTES BY MEANS OF A COMPUTER,
Kyoto Univ. (Japan). Dept. of Sanitary Engineering.
S. Morisawa, and Y. Inoue.
Health Physics, Vol 27, No 5, p 447-457, November 1974. 9 fig, 1 tab, 10 ref.

Descriptors: *Radioactive waste disposal, *Sites, *Computer program, *Nuclear powerplants, *Effluents, *Model studies, *Strontium, Environmental effects, Safety, Evaluation, Assessment, Public health, Groundwater, Water table, Water flow, Porosity.
Identifiers: *Site selection, *Population exposure, *Human dose, Internal dose.

Processes of selecting optimum locations for the disposal of radioactive wastes by means of a computer are discussed. A program for site selection is based on some reasonable assumptions and includes the data required to estimate the dose of radioactivity in the human body due to the disposed wastes of a nuclear facility along a coast. The calculations were made for a model nuclear facility that was chosen to show the general method of selecting a ground disposal site. An optimum location for a ground disposal site is defined as a location with minimum internal dose caused by the disposed wastes. Four locations were selected using a computer, each location having a minimum internal dose based on the assumption of 0.1 Ci/yr leakage of Sr 90. The minimum internal dose for the four locations was estimated to be lower than 10(-80) mrem/yr. The method of selecting optimum locations is resonably promising for solving current problems of site selection for disposal. A chart to compare the safety of sites by evaluating each with reference to eighteen environmental factors is included. (Houser-ORNL)
W75-08665

STORMWATER CONTROL KEY TO BAY POLLUTION SOLUTION.
For primary bibliographic entry see Field 5D.
W75-08671

PUMPS FOR POLLUTION CONTROL,
For primary bibliographic entry see Field 5D.
W75-08674

COASTAL POWER PLANT HEAT DISPOSAL CONSIDERATIONS,
Southern California Edison Co., Rosemead, Calif.
D. M. Golden.
Journal of the Environmental Engineering Division, ASCE, Vol 101, No EE3, Proceedings paper No 11359, p 365-380, June 1975. 1 tab, 11 ref.

Descriptors: *Water pollution control, *Environmental engineering, *Energy, *Thermal pollution, *California, Coasts, Oceanography, Legislation, Underwater, Pipelines, Conduits, Water resources, Environmental effects, Environmental control, Demand, Costs, Planning, Evaluation, Design.
Identifiers: *Environmental impact statements, *Thermal diffusion.

Presented is an overview of some of the engineering and ecological considerations that need to be evaluated in the selection of optimal once-through waste heat disposal systems. The review focuses on open ocean discharges along the southern California coast, but the information should have wide application. Examination of cooling system alternatives for powerplants in coastal areas indicates that once-through cooling is the most favorable from an overall environmental standpoint. Preliminary evaluation of the year-long Thermal Effect Studies conducted at all California coastal powerplants indicates that existing thermal discharges are exerting only localized environmental impacts. With proper oceanographic and biological surveys to determine the aquatic inhabitants and hydraulic characteristics of a potential site, a criterion can be developed to discharge the thermal effluent safely into the ecosystem. However conceptually attractive geothermal, hydroelectric, solar, tidal, and fusion power may be, it would appear that none of them has the capability of providing sufficient amounts of power to meet the projected demands for electrical energy during the next two decades. (Bell-Cornell)
W75-08719

OPTIMAL PRICING AND INVESTMENT IN COMMUNITY WATER SUPPLY,
Tennessee Univ., Knoxville. Dept. of Finance.
For primary bibliographic entry see Field 6C.
W75-08722

GRAVITY OIL-WATER SEPARATOR WITH TWO INTERCONNECTED SINGULAR CELLS HAVING AUTOMATIC FREE OIL DISCHARGE,
For primary bibliographic entry see Field 5D.
W75-08735

CORONA DISCHARGE TREATMENT OF AN OIL SLICK,
P. C. Stoddard.
U S Patent No 3,865,722, 5 p, 5 fig, 2 ref; Official Gazette of the United States Patent Office, Vol 931, No 2, p 813, February 11, 1975.

Descriptors: *Patents, *Oil spills, *Oil pollution, *Pollution abatement, *Water pollution control, Electrical coronas, Extra high voltage, *Separation techniques.
Identifiers: Corona discharge.

A process is described in which an oil slick floating on a water surface is subjected to a high voltage corona discharge for a time sufficient to effect a change in its physical properties. The oil is then allowed to congeal and preferably conglomerate after which it is removed from the water surface by conventional techniques such as, for example, with the air of a surface suction pump. Because the oil becomes cohesive and tends to conglomerate when subjected to the corona, it is far easier to handle during removal operations. A corona discharge is the ionization of the gas surrounding an electrical lead raised to a high electrical potential. The physical properties of the oil change such that the oil in the slick tends to become cohesive and the slick itself not only stops spreading but may even conglomerate. (Sinha-OEIS)
W75-08753

OIL SPILL CLEANUP,
Shell Oil Co., Houston. Tex. (Assignee).
R. R. Ayers, and D. P. Hemphill.
U S Patent No 3,865,730, 3 p, 5 fig, 9 ref; Official Gazette of the United States Patent Office, Vol 931, No 2, p 815, February 11, 1975.

Descriptors: *Patents, *Skimming, *Oil spills, Oil pollution, *Pollution abatement, *Water pollution control, Equipment, *Separation techniques.

An apparatus for removing oil from the surface of water comprises a rotatable drum immersed in the water up to about its axis of rotation, and compartments arranged around the periphery of the drum for admitting oil and water to an axial chamber in the drum. The compartments have spiraling funnels diminishing in cross-sectional area from the periphery of the drum to the axial chamber. The axial chamber is divided into upper and lower rooms, the lower room providing an exit for the water-rich effluent, and the upper room providing an exit for an oil-rich effluent. (Sinha-OEIS)
W75-08754

AERATORS WITH DE-ICING MEANS,
B. E. Hirshon.
U S Patent No 3,865,908, 4 p, 13 fig, 5 ref; Official Gazette of the United States Patent Office, Vol 931, No 2, p 858, February 11, 1975.

Descriptors: *Patents, *Waste water treatment, *Pollution abatement, *Aeration, *Deicers, *Water pollution control, Conduits, Water circulation, Equipment.
Identifiers: Ice formation.

An aerator is placed in a body of open water such as a lake, pond, river, or bay, where ice formation is to be expected. The aerator has an inflow and outflow conduit with their upper ends interconnecting in part below the surface level of the body of water and with their lower ends so disposed relative to each other as to inhibit circulation between them. Also included is a wall structure extending above the water level to bar the inflow of surface water, means to effect the flow of water upward through the inflow portion through the interconnecting portion, and downward through the outflow portion as a continuous stream and to aerate the circulating water before its entry into the outflow portion. The interconnecting porting is oriented to provide a time delay in the flow of the elevated water into the outflow portion to permit the escape of air. The aerator is inclined upward and outward to provide sufficient draft to facilitate

the freeing of the ice as an incident to the operation of the aerator. (Sinha-OEIS)
W75-08755

SYSTEM FOR SEPARATING HYDROCARBONS FROM WATER,
Fram Corp., East Providence, R.I. (Assignee).
J. D. Conley, D. E. Belden, and R. D. Terhune.
U S Patent No 3,878,094, 3 p, 2 fig, 9 ref; Official Gazette of the United States Patent Office, Vol 933, No 3, p 1340, April 15, 1975.

Descriptors: *Patents, *Oil pollution, *Pollution abatement, *Waste water treatment, *Water quality control, Emulsions, *Separation techniques, Organic compounds, *Emulsifiers.
Identifiers: Emulsified hydrocarbons.

The invention features a mechanical emulsion breaker for removing emulsified hydrocarbon from the water stream, and, upstream of the emulsion breaker, a separator for removing from the stream free and entrained hydrocarbon. A preconditioner upstream of the emulsion breaker removes solids and initiates the separation of hydrocarbon. Controls maintain the hydrocarbon-water interface levels in the separator and the emulsion breaker within predetermined limits despite variation of the hydrocarbon concentration in the incoming stream. This prevent re-mixing of water and hydrocarbon. The controls operate in a closed, pressurized system by sensing the interfaces and adjusting the hydrocarbons and water discharge rates. A monitor continuously measures hydrocarbon concentration in the treated water discharge and provides a signal to recycle that discharge in the event effluent quality is too low. (Sinha-OEIS)
W75-08757

MECHANICAL ELIMINATION OF AQUATIC GROWTHS,
M. P. Chaplin.
U S Patent No 3,878,669, 8 p, 43 fig, 2 ref; Official Gazette of the United States Patent Office, Vol 933, No 4, p 1546, April 22, 1975.

Descriptors: *Patents, *Eutrophication, *Pollution abatement, *Water quality control, Lakes, Rivers, Streams, Rooted aquatic plants, *Aquatic weed control, Water utilization.

The apparatus and method for eliminating upstanding, floating and other aquatic growths from lakes, rivers and streams, including much of their root structure are described. It comprises of mechanically moving the upstanding and floating aquatic growths generally downward to a zone automatically controlled as to its position relative to the root structure of the growths. Suction is applied to draw the growths and roots through a cutting zone where the growths and roots are cut into short pieces. They are moved into a vacuum chamber where entrained air and growths juices are removed from their stems and leaves and the growths structure collapsed. The cut and collapsed growths and roots may then be subjected to a second cutting operation, with or without pressure, to further destroy their growth identity, and reduce the growths and roots to a finely divided inert mass. They may then be spread as a blanket on the water bottom from which the growths and roots were originally removed, or delivered to a remote location. (Sinha-OEIS)
W75-08761

THE PROTECTION OF THE QUALITY OF WATERS, AN IMPORTANT ELEMENT IN THE CONSERVATION OF NATURE, (IN ROMANIAN),
Consililul National al Apelor, Bucharest (Rumania).
M. Lazarescu.
Ocrotirea Nat. Vol 17, No 1, p 45-52, Illus, 1973, Rom. and Fr. summ.).

Descriptors: Water reuse, Waste water treatment, Water pollution, Water quality, *Water pollution control, *Water quality control, Water pollution sources, Fertilizers, Detergents, Pesticides, Water temperature, Organic compounds, Water pollution effects, Industrial wastes, Chemical industry, Pulp and paper industry, Oil industry.
Identifiers: Romania.

The actions taken in Romania to prevent water pollution and to develop water resources of good quality necessary for development are outlined. A 1972 law limits water pollution and a special program approved in 1971 provides for research in water quality and pollution. Various factors such as fertilizers, detergents, pesticides, hydrocarbons and changes in water temperature are analyzed with respect to their specific effects on water quality, flora and fauna. Experimental water protection units associated with a paper plant and an antibiotic factory are illustrated. In the years 1960-1970, 1000 water purification installations were constructed and installations are currently being added at the chemical works of Fagaras and Tirnaveni, at the petroleum refineries of Ploesti and at the paper factories of Suceava. The quality of water needed for various uses is defined. Water reuse in industrial units and processes to recover valuable products formerly discharged into polluted waters are discussed.--Copyright 1975, Biological Abstracts, Inc.
W75-08775

SHORT-RUN EFFECTS OF AN INCREASED EFFLUENT CHARGE IN A COMPETITIVE MARKET,
North Carolina Univ., Chapel Hill.
K. L. Wertz.
Canadian Journal of Economics, Vol 7, No 4, p 676-682, 1974. 8 ref.

Descriptors: *Pollution taxes(Charges), *Elasticity of demand, *Equilibrium prices, *Model studies, *Industrial wastes, Industrial production, Assessments, Profit, Effluents, Economics.
Identifiers: Short-term economic effects, Competitive markets, Statics analysis, *Effluent charges, Partial equilibrium model, Sensitivity indicators(Economic), Marginal product.

Relationships between the magnitude of effluent charges, production levels, prices, pollution and profits in competitive industries are investigated. A firm subject to increased charges usually abates by transferring resources from production to control, where the value of the marginal product of each factor has increased relative to its value in production. A simple partial equilibrium model of a charge-paying firm is developed around a general specification of the firm's emission control function that permits an interaction of variable factors of emissions control and levels of production to generate a level of emissions. Other equations assume the level of a firm's pollutant emissions to be governed either by the employment of variable factors to emissions control or by its choice of production level. A comparative statics analysis identifies characteristics of industries in which increased effluent charges would lead to changes in short-run output, price, and emissions levels. The elasticities of various cost functions and the price elasticity of demand are combined to give indicators of the sensitivity of short-run levels of output, price and emissions to increased effluent charges. Competitive producers as a group, after effluent charges are increased, may enjoy higher profits prior to new firms entering the market. (Becker-Wisconsin)
W75-08778

ENVIRONMENTAL ECONOMICS: A THEORETICAL INQUIRY,
Stockholm Univ. (Sweden). Dept. of Economics.
K-G. Maler.
The Johns Hopkins University Press, Baltimore and London. 1974. 267 p, $15.00.

Descriptors: *Welfare(Economics), *Pollutants, *Compensation, *Resources, *Value engineering, *Theoretical analysis, Social values, *Pollution taxes(Charges), Effluents.
Identifiers: Materials-balance model, Externalities, Effluent charges, General equilibrium, Partial equilibrium, Pareto optimality, Economic growth.

Problems connected with payment for discharge of residuals into the environment are approached from both theoretical and practical points of view. The natural environment is a public good with no market in which buyers and sellers reveal preferences. A simple materials-balance, general equilibrium model is constructed with five flow sites--environment, production, consumption, capital accumulation and environmental management--connected by the exchange of goods, services and residuals. A Pareto optimal equilibrium exists where the markets are cleared and profits and utilities are maximized. Charges, bribes and compensation are considered in a discussion of the determination of optimal policy connected with waste discharges. Bribes and charges are equivalent from a purely theoretical point of view, but differ in the area of administration and enforecement. Compensation of consumers for environmental degradation may have income effects. Economic growth and the quality of the environment are tied to questions of resource allocation over time. The demand for environmental services, although important in the consideration of resource allocation, is not revealed through a market structure. Alternative methods for determining consumer preferences are discussed. The notion that it is possible to support an optimum with prices on waste disposal is considered in relation to alternative environmental policies. (Becker-Wisconsin)
W75-08780

ECONOMIC ANALYSIS OF EFFLUENT GUIDELINES--FLAT GLASS INDUSTRY,
Little (Arthur D.), Inc., Cambridge, Mass.
W. Lee.
Available from the National Technical Information Service, Springfield, Va. 22161 as PB-234 845, $4.25 in paper copy, $2.25 in microfiche. Report No. EPA-230/2-74-013, August 1974. 71 p, 20 tab. 68-01-1541.

Descriptors: *Pollution abatement, *Waste water treatment, Standards, *Economic impact, *Industrial wastes, Effluents, Pricing, Unit costs, Employment, Fabrication, *Water quality standards.
Identifiers: *Flat glass industry, Sheet glass industry, Plate glass industry, Float glass industry, Automotive glass industry.

An analysis of the economic impact of EPA water pollution control requirements on the flat glass industry is provided. Initial segmentation of the industry into sheet glass, plate glass and float glass was revised when it was determined that the waste water treatment costs associated with meeting anticipated guidelines were small for sheet glass and float glass fabricators. Rolled and polished glass segments were excluded since they represent a relatively small fraction of the total glass industry. Final impact assessment was made on the plate glass, solid tempered automotive glass, and laminated windshield fabrication industry segments. Impact was analyzed for three levels of treatment: (1) Best Practicable Technology (BPT), (2) Best Available Technology (BAT), (3) New Source Performance Standards (NSPS). The economic impacts analyzed are: (1) price, (2) profitability, growth and capital availability, (3) employment, (4) community effects, (5) balance of payments, (6) related industries. The economic impacts of the BPT and BAT levels of treatment on each industry segment are presented (the proposed control technology of NSPS is identical to BAT for the float glass, solid tempered automotive glass and laminated windshield fabircation segments). Little or no impact is expected in any of the flat

glass industry segments at either level of treatment. (BeckercWisconsin)
W75-08781

ECONOMIC ANALYSIS OF EFFLUENT GUIDELINES: RUBBER PROCESSING INDUSTRY,
Little (Arthur D.), Inc., Cambridge, Mass.
J. T. Howarth, J. A. Carter, and K. R. Sidman.
Available from the National Technical Information Service, Springfield, Va. 22161 as PB-235 691 $3.75 in paper copy, $2.25 in microfiche. Report No. EPA-230/2-74-024, August 1974. 61 p, 7 fig, 22 tab, 2 append. 68-01-1541.

Descriptors: Standards, *Industrial wastes, *Effluents, *Economic impact, *Pollution abatement, Synthetic rubber, Capital costs, Operating costs, Prices, Waste water treatment, *Water quality standards.
Identifiers: Rubber processing industry, Tires and tubes.

Waste treatment costs associated with the Best Practical Technology and Best Available Technology Economically Achievable for the synthetic rubber and tires and tubes segments of the rubber processing industry are analyzed. The investment, annual costs and estimated price increases as a percent of sales are summarized and averaged for the two segments. The additional costs are not expected to exert a significant impact on the market and prices of the respective products. It is not anticipated that any plants will be closed in either the synthetic rubber or tire and tube sectors. However, there may be a short period of plant shutdown, particularly in the older plants, while effluent lines are segregated. No adverse effects on the industry's growth due to BPT, BAT, and New Source Performance Standrds are indicated. Costs should not significantly affect either the domestic market competitiveness or the international market. The conclusions are based on the guidelines as proposed in the Effluent Guideline Development Documents, the associated technology to meet these limits, and the related cost. The calculated price increases for these pollution guidelines are the maximum expected increases. Certain companies and certain plants already meet BPT guidelines and may not increase their prices at all. (Auen-Wisconsin)
W75-08782

ECONOMIC ANALYSIS OF EFFLUENT GUIDELINES FOR SELECTED SEGMENTS OF THE SEAFOOD PROCESSING INDUSTRY. (CATFISH, CRAB, SHRIMP AND TUNA),
Development Planning and Research Associates, Inc., Manhattan, Kans.
D. L. Jordening.
Available from the National Technical Information Service, Springfield, Va 22161 as PB-234 214, $5.75 in paper copy, $2.25 in microfiche. Report No EPA-230/2-74-025, July 1974. 127 p, 3 fig, 40 tab. 68-01-1533.

Descriptors: *Waste treatment, *Fish handling facilities, *Economic impact, Standards, Economic efficiency, Shrimp, Crabs, Catfishes, Industrial wastes, Canneries, Pollution abatement, *Water quality standards.
Identifiers: Seafood processing plants, Tuna.

The economic impacts of EPA proposed effluent guidelines for the tuna, shrimp, crab and catfish industries are assessed. Specialty item plants, reprocessing plants, and plants where less than 80% of the total value of all output is from shrimp, crab, tuna, or catfish are excluded from this analysis. Except for the tuna processing sector, the industry can be characterized as a composite of many small, underutilized, old plants. Each segment is analyzed separately for financial characteristics, and a segment profitability range is estimated. Return on sales analysis with profitability measures are used in assessing the severity of the effluent restrictions. The impact methodology includes five basic parts: (1) industry segmentation, (2) pollution abatement cost conversion, (3) preliminary impacts with cost of pollution abatement as a percent of sales, (4) price effects induced by abatement standards, and (5) estimated impacts of standards on viability of plants. Effects of effluent controls on financial status, production, employment, community, and balance of trade are analyzed. The Best Practicable Technology effluent control level was estimated to have an insignificant impact on the evaluated segments of the seafood industry. In general, the availability of municipal wastewater treatment systems will be important in the number of closures of processing plants. (Becker-Wisconsin)
W75-08783

HYDRAULIC ENGINEERING AND THE ENVIRONMENT.
For primary bibliographic entry see Field 8B.
W75-08786

REGULATION OF LOW STREAMFLOWS,
Environmental Protection Agency, Cincinnati, Ohio.
For primary bibliographic entry see Field 4A.
W75-08808

PHYSICAL AND BIOLOGICAL REHABILITATION OF A STREAM,
Montana State Univ., Bozeman. Dept. of Fisheries.
For primary bibliographic entry see Field 4A.
W75-08810

DEVELOPMENT OF A WATER PLANNING MODEL FOR MONTANA,
Montana State Univ., Bozeman. Dept. of Industrial Engineering and Computer Science.
For primary bibliographic entry see Field 6A.
W75-08811

WATER POLLUTION CONTROL BY HYDRAULIC AERATION,
Toronto Univ. (Ontario). Dept. of Mechanical Engineering.
H. J. Leutheusser, and F. J. Resch.
In: Hydraulic Engineering and the Environment; Proceedings of the 21st Annual Hydraulic Division Specialty Conference, Montana State University, Bozeman, August 15-17, 1973. American Society of Civil Engineers, New York, p 315-321, 1973. 6 fig, 10 ref.

Descriptors: *Hydraulic jump, *Aeration, *Aerobic treatment, *Water pollution control, Water pollution, Water quality, Bubbles, Turhulent flow, Critical flow, Hydraulics, Fluid mechanics, Biochemical oxygen demand, Sluice gates, Flumes, Laboratory tests.

An important process involved in the natural purification of streams is the removal of biodegradable pollutants by the action of aerobic microorganisms. This exerts a biochemical oxygen demand which must be satisfied by the atmosphere in order to maintain the water quality at an acceptable level. The familiar phenomenon of hydraulic jump is beginning to receive attention as a potentially well-suited hydraulic aeration device. The investigation of entrainment characteristics was carried out in the bubbly two-phase flow region of jumps created in a horizontal, 15.25 m long and 0.39 m wide laboratory flume. The findings suggest that hydraulic jumps with both undeveloped and with fully developed inflow will function well as effective aerators. The size of air bubbles occuring is small, but the large number of bubbles provides a large effective interfacial contact area between air and water. There was clear evidence, however, that the jump with fully developed inflow retains its air content far longer than does its undeveloped counterpart. It would thus appear that this type of hydraulic jump, which is also characterized by especially intense mixing, ought to be particularly well suited for applications as a hydraulic aeration device. (See also W75-08786) (Sims-ISWS)
W75-08814

POLLUTION POTENTIAL OF A SANITARY LANDFILL NEAR TUCSON,
Arizona Water Resources Research Center, Tucson.
For primary bibliographic entry see Field 5B.
W75-08823

WASTE-LOAD ALLOCATION STUDIES FOR ARKANSAS STREAMS, RED RIVER BASIN, DORCHEAT BAYOU, SEGMENT 1A,
Geological Survey, Little Rock, Ark.
For primary bibliographic entry see Field 5B.
W75-08837

WASTE-LOAD ALLOCATION STUDIES FOR ARKANSAS STREAMS, RED RIVER BASIN, SEGMENT 1B,
Geological Survey, Little Rock, Ark.
For primary bibliographic entry see Field 5B.
W75-08838

WASTE-LOAD ALLOCATION STUDIES FOR ARKANSAS STREAMS, OUACHITA RIVER BASIN, BOEUF RIVER AND BAYOU MACON, SEGMENT 2A,
Geological Survey, Little Rock, Ark.
For primary bibliographic entry see Field 5B.
W75-08839

WASTE-LOAD ALLOCATION STUDIES FOR ARKANSAS STREAMS, OUACHITA RIVER BASIN, BAYOU BARTHOLOMEW, SEGMENT 2B,
Geological Survey, Little Rock, Ark.
For primary bibliographic entry see Field 5B.
W75-08840

WASTE-LOAD ALLOCATION STUDIES FOR ARKANSAS STREAMS, OUACHITA RIVER BASIN, SEDMENT 2D,
Geological Survey, Little Rock, Ark.
For primary bibliographic entry see Field 5B.
W75-08841

WASTE-LOAD ALLOCATION STUDIES FOR ARKANSAS STREAMS, OUACHITA RIVER BASIN, SALINE RIVER, SEGMENT 2C,
Geological Survey, Little Rock, Ark.
For primary bibliographic entry see Field 5B.
W75-08842

WASTE-LOAD ALLOCATION STUDIES FOR ARKANSAS STREAMS, OUACHITA RIVER BASIN, SEGMENT 2F,
Geological Survey, Little Rock, Ark.
For primary bibliographic entry see Field 5B.
W75-08843

WASTE-LOAD ALLOCATION STUDIES FOR ARKANSAS STREAMS, ST. FRANCIS RIVER BASIN, SEGMENT 5A,
Geological Survey, Little Rock, Ark.
For primary bibliographic entry see Field 5B.
W75-08844

CONTRASTS IN COMMUNITY ACTION AND OPINION,
Oregon State Univ., Corvallis. Dept. of Anthropology.
C. L. Smith.

Water Resources Bulletin, Vol 10, No 5, p 877-883, October 1974. 2 fig, 11 ref. OWRT B-023-ORE(4).

Descriptors: *Surveys, *Attitudes, Waste water(Pollution), Management, Decision making, Rural areas, Surburban areas, Community development, Data collections, Sewage, Organizations, Sampling, Water pollution control.
Identifiers: *Population growth, Human behavior, Environmental quality.

Opinion or attitude surveys and observations of people's actions are complementary research tools, but they often provide different results. This was the case where two communities, one rural and one suburban, made waste water management decisions which would promote population growth while survey data indicated that community attitudes were neutral or slightly opposed to population growth. Observation of action, and expanding the range of survey response variation, revealed that the structure of both community opinion and action was primarily influenced by small groups of people with very strong feelings favoring and disfavoring population growth. Those with very strong feelings were the ones observed to be acting to promote or retard growth. (Bell-Cornell)
W75-08848

6. WATER RESOURCES PLANNING

6A. Techniques Of Planning

URBAN WATER DEVELOPMENT AND MANAGEMENT IN ARID ENVIRONMENTS, VOLUME I: COMPLETION REPORT,
Rockwell International Corp., Canoga Park, Calif. Rocketdyne Div.
W. Unterberg, A. L. Mindling, J. A. Dracup, J. W. Bulkley, and G. L. Widman.
Available from the National Technical Information Service, Springfield, Va. 22161, as PB-242 300, $6.25 in paper copy, $2.25 in microfiche. Report R-9625-1, March 1975. 165 p, 5 fig, 32 tab, 19 ref. OWRT C-1734(No 3395)(1), and C-3151(No 9000)(1). 14-31-0001-3393 and-9000.

Descriptors: Water resources development, *Management, Planning, Arid climates, Semiarid climates, Decision making, *Computer models, Political aspects, Water law, *City planning, Urbanization, Cities, *Simulation analysis, *Model studies, *Arid lands, Environment, Computer programs.
Identifiers: *Urban water resources, Strategic planning, Case studies, *Gaming simulation, Multi-disciplinary constraints, Las Vegas(NV), Oxnard(CA), Salt Lake City(UT), San Bernardino(CA), San Diego(CA), Tucson(AZ), Carson City(NV), Goleta County Water District(CA), Alamogordo(NM).

In Phase I (Project C-1734), an appraisal was made of urban water development and management in arid and semiarid environments by means of case studies of key historic water decisions in six cities. In each city alternative solutions to water resource problems and organizations and factors that affected the decisions were identified and researched through interviews. These data were inputs to a Political Interaction Simulation computer program (PISP), which was used to model the decision-making processes. The results of the case studies led to guidelines that were applied, during Phase II (Project C-3151) in three arid and semiarid cities having to make key water decisions in the near future. This included the use of PISP as a predictive decision-making tool, validated by election results, and the development of a Gaming Simulation tool entitled 'The Water Game', as a strategic arid urban water resources planning tool. This Game was played and is available for dissemination. (See also W75-08353)
W75-08352

URBAN WATER DEVELOPMENT AND MANAGEMENT IN ARID ENVIRONMENTS, VOLUME II: THE WATER GAME--GAMING SIMULATION FOR URBAN WATER RESOURCES PLANNING,
Rockwell International Corp., Canoga Park, Calif. Rocketdyne Div.
W. Unterberg, J. A. Dracup, W. J. Trott, and M. E. Mulvihill.
Available from the National Technical Information Service, Springfield, Va. 22161, as PB-242 301, $5.75 in paper copy, $2.25 in microfiche. Report R-9625-2, March 1975. 146 p, 8 fig, 13 tab. OWRT C-1734(No 3395)(1), and C-3151(No 9000)(1), 14-31-0001-3393 and 9000.

Descriptors: Water resources development, *Management, Planning, Arid climates, Semiarid climates, Decision making, *Computer models, Political aspects, Water law, *City planning, Urbanization, Cities, *Simulation analysis, *Model studies, *Arid lands, Environment, Computer programs.
Identifiers: *Urban water resources, Strategic planning, Case studies, *Gaming simulation, Multi-disciplinary constraints, Las Vegas(NV), Oxnard(CA), Salt Lake City(UT), San Bernardino(CA), San Diego(CA), Tucson(AZ), Carson City(NV), Goleta County Water District(CA), Alamogordo(NM).

Volume 2 deals with the generation and practice of The Water Game, a Gaming Simulation for Urban Water Resources Planning. Part 1, 'Game Description' deals with the development and detailed features of The Water Game. It includes the documentation and listing of the digital computer program that forms part of the gaming simulation. Part 2 constitutes the 'Players' Manual,' which is the actual document used by the participants during the playing of the game. Because both parts are paginated separately, is Players' Manual can be removed from this volume and bound separately for practical use. Part 1 is written for the reader, and Part 2 for the player. Where the interests of the two are identical (e.g., introduction to gaming simulation, water supply alternatives, and elsewhere), identical prose has been used, although the coverage may be more detailed in one part than the other. (See also W75-08352)
W75-08353

THE ESTIMATION OF (RHO) IN THE FIRST-ORDER AUTOREGRESSIVE MODEL: A BAYESIAN APPROACH,
Massachusetts Inst. of Tech., Cambridge. Dept. of Civil Engineering.
For primary bibliographic entry see Field 2A.
W75-08387

EFFICIENT SEQUENTIAL OPTIMIZATION IN WATER RESOURCES,
Iowa Univ., Iowa City. Inst. of Hydraulic Research.
For primary bibliographic entry see Field 4A.
W75-08404

DEVELOPMENT OF A MANAGEMENT FRAMEWORK OF THE GREAT SALT LAKE,
Utah Water Research Lab., Logan.
J. P. Riley, C. G. Clyde, W. J. Grenney, Y. Y. Haimes, and C. T. Jones.
Available from the National Technical Information Service, Springfield, Va 22161 as PB-242 327, $4.25 in paper copy, $2.25 in microfiche. Utah Water Research Laboratory, Logan, Publication JEW116-1, March 1975. 70 p, 19 fig, 3 tab, 62 ref, append. OWRT A-019-UTAH(1). 14-31-0001-3545.

Descriptors: Water resources, Planning, *Management, Systems analysis, Simulation analysis, *Brine shrimp, *Great Salt Lake, *Utah, *Model studies, Environmental effects, Coordination, Lakes, Legal aspects, Social values, Water supply, Recreation, Tourism, Transporation.
Identifiers: Oil drilling, Mineral extraction.

The development of a comprehensive management framework of the Great Salt Lake is a complex process involving the cooperation and close coordination of many groups, disciplines, and activities. The study was divided into three separate phases. Phase I provides the overall structural framework for management of the Great Salt Lake, identifies the data needs, and establishes priorities for the development of submodels (both structural and non-structural) for incorporation into the overall framework. The submodels can be developed both from basic considerations and through the modifications of existing models. Results of Phase I are summarized. Phase II involves the process of developing submodels, and Phase III is concerned with the application of the framework of models to specific management problems. The management framework developed here takes into account the major societal and economic uses of the Great Salt Lake. These uses are (1) recreation and tourism, (2) mineral extraction, (3) transportation, (4) brine shrimp harvesting, (5) oil drilling, and (6) fresh water supply. On the basis of these six major uses, a chart was prepared which lists the potential impacts on cultural and social factors, biological conditions, and physical and chemical characteristics resulting from alterations to the existing lake system.
W75-08473

EVALUATION OF A PROBABILITY APPROACH TO UNCERTAINTY IN BENEFIT-COST ANALYSIS,
California Univ., Santa Barbara. Dept. of Economics.
For primary bibliographic entry see Field 6B.
W75-08478

STOCHASTIC ANALYSIS OF TRICKLING FILTER,
Texas Univ. at Austin. Dept. of Chemical Engineering.
For primary bibliographic entry see Field 5D.
W75-08720

MADAM I--A NUMERIC METHOD FOR DESIGN OF ADSORPTION SYSTEMS,
Michigan Univ., Ann Arbor. Dept. of Environmental and Water Resources Engineering.
For primary bibliographic entry see Field 5D.
W75-08726

APPLICATION OF A HYDROLOGIC MODEL FOR LAND USE PLANNING IN FLORIDA,
Florida Univ., Gainesville. Dept. of Environmental Engineering Sciences.
For primary bibliographic entry see Field 4A.
W75-08727

OPTIMAL CAPACITIES OF WATER SUPPLY RESERVOIRS IN SERIES AND PARALLEL,
Wharton School of Finance and Commerce, Philadelphia, Pa. Dept. of Regional Science.
For primary bibliographic entry see Field 4A.
W75-08728

A TECHNIQUE FOR THE PREDICTION OF WATER DEMAND FROM PAST CONSUMPTION DATA,
Sheffield Univ. (England). Dept. of Control Engineering.
For primary bibliographic entry see Field 6D.
W75-08730

THE CIVIL ENGINEER AND FIELD DRAINAGE,
Ministry of Agriculture, Fisheries and Food. Lincoln (England).
For primary bibliographic entry see Field 4A.
W75-08731

DEVELOPMENT OF A WATER PLANNING MODEL FOR MONTANA,
Montana State Univ., Bozeman. Dept. of Industrial Engineering and Computer Science.
D. W. Boyd, and T. T. Williams.
In: Hydraulic Engineering and the Environment; Proceedings of the 21st Annual Hydraulic Division Specialty Conference, Montana State University, Bozeman, August 15-17, 1973. American Society of Civil Engineers, New York, p 269-278, 1973. 3 fig, 1 tab.

Descriptors: *Model studies, *Water resources, *Planning, Computer models, Numerical analysis, Hydrologic aspects, Hydrology, Surface waters, Groundwater resources, Water storage, Water utilization, *Montana.
Identifiers: *Yellowstone River Basin(Mont).

A water planning research effort resulted in a series of three models, each one more refined than the previous one. The three modeled hydrologic systems were (1) Montana, (2) the Yellowstone River Basin in Montana, and (3) a sub-basin of the Yellowstone. Although a particular basin and sub-basin were used in the development, each version of the model is completely general, and may be calibrated for two or more sub-basins. These models may be subsequently linked to permit the study of any combination of sub-basins. Any version of the model could be applied easily to any drainage basin whereever located. It is not limited to Montana. Although the model is hydrologic in scope, it is capable of receiving a water-quality overlay, or of providing the constraints for the optimization of an economic objective function. (See also W75-08786) (Sims-ISWS)
W75-08811

THE IMPACT OF WATER QUALITY OBJECTIVES ON URBAN WATER SUPPLY PLANNING,
Colorado State Univ., Fort Collins. Dept. of Agricultural Engineering.
For primary bibliographic entry see Field 5D.
W75-08845

6B. Evaluation Process

EFFECTS OF URBANIZATION ON WATER QUALITY,
Water Resources Engineers, Inc., Springfield, Va. and DeKalb County Planning Dept., Decatur, Ga.
For primary bibliographic entry see Field 5B.
W75-08351

URBAN WATER DEVELOPMENT AND MANAGEMENT IN ARID ENVIRONMENTS, VOLUME I: COMPLETION REPORT,
Rockwell International Corp., Canoga Park, Calif. Rocketdyne Div.
For primary bibliographic entry see Field 6A.
W75-08352

URBAN WATER DEVELOPMENT AND MANAGEMENT IN ARID ENVIRONMENTS, VOLUME II: THE WATER GAME--GAMING SIMULATION FOR URBAN WATER RESOURCES PLANNING,
Rockwell International Corp., Canoga Park, Calif. Rocketdyne Div.
For primary bibliographic entry see Field 6A.
W75-08353

REGIONAL PROBLEM ANALYSIS IN THE PACIFIC NORTHWEST: PART A-INSTREAM FLOW NEEDS; PART B-BASALT AQUIFERS; PART C-WILD AND SCENIC RIVERS.
Washington State Water-Research Center, Pullman.
Available from the National Technical Information Service, Springfield, Va. 22161, as PB-242 280, $5.25 in paper copy, $2.25 in microfiche. Completion Report, March 1975. 122 p, 1 fig, 3 tab, OWRT B-056-WASH(1).

Descriptors: *Regional analysis, *Research priorities, Interstate, *Wild rivers, Water allocation, Basalts, Aquifers, Conjunctive use, *Pacific Northwest US, Water resources, Planning, *Water requirements, *Water utilization, Social aspects.
Identifiers: Scenic rivers, *Basalt aquifers.

A four-state project engaged the states of Alaska, Idaho, Oregon, and Washington to jointly undertake a regional problem-research analysis of water resources problems in the Pacific Northwest. Activities are summarized of the three contiguous states to identify, analyze the structure, evaluate alternatives for resolution, and assess the knowledge and understanding required for the resolution of three water-related problems of the Pacific Northwest. The three regional problems analyzed were: (1) instream flow needs methodology to determine how much water is required for various water uses; (2) study of the basalt aquifers in Washington, Oregon, and Idaho to determine the extent, boundaries, capacity, and potential uses; (3) the impact of designation of Wild and Scenic rivers on other values, including social, economic, and political values, and upon alternative uses for water and adjacent land resources. Selection of these three areas for in depth analysis was based on a survey of state and federal agency representatives and legislators in the three states. A series of workshops with a combination of university faculties and agency representatives was the primary method used for analyzing the problems. The results of the problem analyses for each of the problem areas are reported in detail.
W75-08356

ENERGY PRODUCTION AND WATER SUPPLY,
Utah State Univ., Logan.
C. G. Clyde.
In: Energy, Environment and Water Resources, Proceedings of the Universities Council on Water Resources Meeting, July 28-31, 1974. Logan Utah. p 319-331, (1974) 9 fig, 3 tab, 7 ref.

Descriptors: *Resources development, *Powerplants, *Energy, *Electric power production, *Colorado River, *Water shortage, Coals, Colorado River Basin, *Water supply, Nuclear powerplants, Environmental effects, Arizona, Colorado, Wyoming, California, Nevada, Mexico, New Mexico, Utah, Agriculture, Irrigation, Air pollution, Water pollution, Regional analysis.
Identifiers: Project independence.

The Colorado River Basin is rich in energy resources and poor in its water supply. An overview is given of how the region's energy and water future fits into national patterns. Fifteen questions are directed at participants of the conference to aid them in discovering how additional energy reserves can be developed in a region where water is already totally committed, if not over-committed. (Bowden-Arizona)
W75-08369

ENERGY-WATER RELATIONSHIPS: MANAGEMENT AND CONSERVATION IN THE CALIFORNIA-COLORADO RIVER - GREAT BASIN REGIONS,
Nevada Univ., Reno.
G. F. Cochran.
In: Energy, Environment and Water Resources, Proceedings of Universities Council on Water Resources Meeting, July 28-31, 1974. Logan, Utah. p 332-340, (1974) 4 ref.

Descriptors: *Colorado River Basin, *Great Basin, *Electric power production, *Energy, *Environmental effects, *Water shortage, *California, Colorado, Arizona, New Mexico, Mexico, Utah, Nevada, Wyoming, Institutional constraints, Flanning, Regions, Regional analysis.
Identifiers: Project Independence.

Water and energy resources of the Colorado River Basin, California, and the Great Basin are reviewed. The Colorado River, under the existing plan of development, is a bankrupt stream in terms of both quality and commitments for use of its waters. Because Project Independence will increase demand for water from this overtaxed flow, the need for systematic planning is stressed. For example: if energy production retires agricultural land in the region because there is insufficient water for both, additional crop production must be planned for some other part of the country, if shortages are to be avoided. Conservation must be considered as a way to lower both water and energy demands. (Bowden-Arizona)
W75-08370

INSTITUTIONAL ASPECTS OF ENERGY-WATER DECISIONS IN THE PACIFIC SOUTHWEST REGION,
Arizona Univ., Tucson.
H. M. Ingram.
In: Energy, Environment and Water Resources, Proceedings of Universities Council on Water Resources Meeting, July 28-31, 1974. Logan, Utah. p 344-353, (1974), 4 tab, 3 ref.

Descriptors: *Colorado River Basin, Watershed management, *Colorado River Compact, *Legal aspects, *Energy, Arizona, Nevada, California, Utah, New Mexico, Wyoming, Powerplants, Water shortage, Institutional constraints, Electric power, Production, Environmental effects, *Southwest U.S., *Regional analysis.

The Pacific Southwest Region is fragmented into states and cities competing with each other for water resources. Traditionally, water decisions have been made at the federal level; the states, long resentful of this fact, are now fighting to have a larger role in such decisions. However, energy development now promises to be a major factor in future water allocation plans, and the states lack any institutional framework adequate for competing with federal agencies in this area. Thus, without clear energy policies, the states face renewed pressure in their efforts to make their own water resource allocation decisions. (Bowden-Arizona)
W75-08372

APPLICATIONS OF HYDROLOGY TO WATER RESOURCES MANAGEMENT (PLANNING AND DESIGN LEVEL),
Department of the Environment, Ottawa (Ontario). Hydrology Research Div.
V. Klemes.
Operational Hydrology Report No. 4, World Meteorological Organization Publication No. 356, Geneva (Switzerland), 1973. 104 p, 20 fig, 9 tab, 52 ref.

Descriptors: *Water resources development, *Planning, *Design, Analytical techniques, Hydrologic aspects, *Hydrology, Surface waters, *Management, Runoff, Surface runoff, Statistical methods, Stochastic processes, Streamflow, Storm runoff, Droughts, Water shortage, Regulated flow, Simulation analysis, Numerical analysis, Floods, Flood routing, Flood control, Hydrographs, Maximum probable flood, Channels, Reservoirs, Flood frequency, Flood discharge.

Discussed were the different methods and concepts involved in the practical applications of hydrology and the effective use of hydrological techniques in the planning, design, and management of projects in the field of surface water resources. Groundwater resources were not considered. A general discussion was presented of new trends, conceptual changes, and the gradual

broadening of the scope of water resources management involving the adoption of systems analysis, statistical and probabilistic concepts, and extensive use of high-speed digital computers. Discussed were techniques of extracting the maximum amount of information obtainable from single station records, methods of assessing its reliability, extending streamflow records of a single station, and indirect determination of streamflow. Various interpretations of droughts were reviewed, and objectives of analysis, methods of analysis, and streamflow regulation by means of storage reservoirs were discussed. Techniques of flood analysis, flood synthesis, flood routing and flood control were described. (Humphreys-ISWS)
W75-08400

ECONOMIC VALUE OF WATER-ORIENTED RECREATION QUALITY,
Utah State Univ., Logan. Dept. of Economics.
E. B. Wennergren, H. H. Fullerton, J. E. Keith, and R. Meale.
Available from the National Technical Information Service, Springfield, Va. 22161, as PB-242 368, $3.75 in paper copy, $2.25 in microfiche. Utah Water Research Laboratory, Logan Publication PRRAE 805-1, January 1975. 27 p, 7 fig, 12 tab, append. OWRT C-4371(no 9064)(2). 14-31-0001-9064.

Descriptors: *Boating, Economics, *Economic rent, *Recreation, Linear programming, Recreation demand, *Utah, *Idaho, *Evaluation, Recreation facilities, Lakes, Regression analysis.
Identifiers: *Recreation site quality, Consumers surplus, Transportation algorithm.

A linear programming system was developed to segregate total site values into location and quality components. Empirical value estimates, both aggregate and quality, were made for 42 boating sites in Utah and 69 sites in Idaho. The estimated aggregate value for Utah, based on the rent model, was $1,113,577, and for Idaho $4,601,125. Quality values accounted for approximately 82 percent of total value in Utah and 74 percent in Idaho. In Utah, differences in site quality were significantly related to lake size and campsite facilities. The partial regression coefficient was positive and statistically significant at the 1 percent level. The model R2 was .81. In Idaho, site quality differences were significantly related to variation in boat launching ramps. The partial regression coefficient was positive and statistically significant at the 1 percent level. The model R2 was .76. A mathematical comparison of the estimates of site value b based on the concepts of economic rent and consumer surplus revealed that rent estimates typically exceed those of consumer surplus. However, the empirical estimation procedures can cause the relationship to fluctuate depending upon the expansion methodology used to derive population estimates from sample data.
W75-08469

UNIVERSITY OF NEBRASKA FACULTY WITH COMPETENCE IN WATER RESOURCES - SECOND EDITION.
Nebraska Univ., Lincoln. Water Resources Research Inst.
For primary bibliographic entry see Field 10D.
W75-08472

DEVELOPMENT OF A MANAGEMENT FRAMEWORK OF THE GREAT SALT LAKE,
Utah Water Research Lab., Logan.
For primary bibliographic entry see Field 6A.
W75-08473

EVALUATION OF A PROBABILITY APPROACH TO UNCERTAINTY IN BENEFIT-COST ANALYSIS,
California Univ., Santa Barbara. Dept. of Economics.
L. J. Mercer, and W. D. Morgan.
Available from the National Technical Information Service, Springfield, Va. 22161 as PB-242 370, $4.25 in paper copy, $2.25 in microfiche. California Water Resources Center, Davis. Contribution No 149, April 1975. 61 p, 6 fig, 23 tab, 23 ref. OWRT A-053-CAL(1).

Descriptors: *Cost-benefit analysis, *Cost-benefit ratio, *Probability, *Risks, Evaluation, Feasibility studies, Cost analysis, Stochastic processes.
Identifiers: *Weibull probability distribution.

Application of the Weibull probability distribution to the problem of uncertainty in benefit-cost analysis was tested. While there is no formal theoretical basis for describing the stochastic behavior of variables in benefit-cost analysis as Weibull distributions, the economy of information, versatility with regard to shape, ability to incorporate objcetive information, and ease of mathematical manipulation, support the use of the distribution. Compared to range sensitivity tests, the only additional pieces of information required are the probabilities that the actual values of the variables will be less than the low or exceed the high of the range. The Weibull probability assignment technique is applied for four separate benefit-cost studies. The standard deviation and central tendeney measures of the outcome distribution (net benefits, benefit-cost ratio, etc.), as well as the probability of an outcome indicating the project is not feasible, are among the valuable new information provided. The results obtained indicate that the technique tested is a significant improvement over range sensitivity tests to resolve uncertainty in benefit-cost analysis. (Snyder-California, Davis)
W75-08478

DIRECTORY OF KENTUCKY WATER RESEARCH PERSONNEL,
Kentucky Water Resources Inst., Lexington.
For primary bibliographic entry see Field 10D.
W75-08485

A CASE STUDY OF THE APPLICATION OF COST-BENEFIT ANALYSIS TO WATER SYSTEM CONSOLIDATION BY LOCAL GOVERNMENT,
Delaware Univ., Newark. Div. of Urban Affairs; and Delaware Univ., Newark. Water Resources Center.
M. R. Brams.
The Engineering Economist, Vol 17, No 2, p 99-114, 1972. 2 fig, 3 tab, 8 ref. OWRR-A-003-DEL(8).

Descriptors: *Water distribution(Applied), *Water works, *Economic feasibility, *Cost-benefit analysis, Benefits, Local governments, Public utilities, Cost-benefit ratios, Investment, Decision making, *Delaware.
Identifiers: *Water system consolidation, New Castle County(Del), Private companies, Acquisition costs, Case study.

The economic and engineering feasibility of county ownership of all municipal and private water systems serving the northern area of New Castle County, Delaware, is tested using cost-benefit analysis. The present value of the quantifiable anticipated benefits of this plant for physical and administrative unification of the county's water system are computed for various alternative discount rates and time periods. The benefits estimated include changes in efficiency, improved allocation of resources, and financial impacts. On the basis of these estimated present values, alternative costs of purchasing the private water companies as based on their capitalized earnings, original cost, replacement cost, or fair value are evaluated. Keeping in mind that many specified benefits and costs could not be estimated, it was concluded that unification might be justified in instances when the benefit-cost ratio exceeded one. Thus, benefit-cost analysis can only provide a perspective for public decision-making. (Weaver-Wisconsin)
W75-08573

MODEL DEVELOPMENT AND SYSTEMS ANALYSIS OF THE YAKIMA RIVER BASIN: FISHERIES,
Washington Univ., Seattle. Coll. of Fisheries.
M. C. Bell, and B. W. Mar.
Available from the National Technical Information Service, Springfield, Va. 22161, as PB-242 512, $3.75 in paper copy, $2.25 in microfiche. State of Washington Water Research Center, Pullman, Partial Completion Report No 17F, November 1974. 34 p, 6 fig, 11 tab, 12 ref. OWRT B-036-WASH(7), B-043-WASH(6), B-050-WASH(6).

Descriptors: *Washington, *Model studies, *Systems analysis, *Fish reproduction, *Fish management, Salmon, Rainbow trout, Computer models, Runoff, Water management(Applied), Water resources, Planning, Water rights, Watersheds(Basins), *Fisheries, River basins.
Identifiers: *Yakima River basin(Wash).

The fisheries model is a simple analytical statement of fish production as a function of wetted area in any given reach. A major limitation of model development is the high cost of information. Physical characteristics of each reach are costly to define and fish production is difficult to measure. Sensitivity of fish production to drift in water quality and fishing effort and difficult to formulate. Based on the simple analysis it was demonstrated that the capacity of the river to produce fish cannot be increased more than a factor of 2-4. Furthermore, increase of salmon and steelhead may not be cost effective since major investments in fish passage and screening are required. The release of flows to achieve minimum low flows below diversions can produce significant increases in sport fish, but ponds or other man-made impoundments may be required in the long run.
W75-08580

2020 HINDSIGHT: ANOTHER FIFTY YEARS OF IRRIGATION,
Committee on Interior and Insular Affairs (U.S. Subcommittee on Water and Power Resources.
For primary bibliographic entry see Field 3F.
W75-08721

APPLICATION OF A HYDROLOGIC MODEL FOR LAND USE PLANNING IN FLORIDA,
Florida Univ., Gainesville. Dept. of Environmental Engineering Sciences.
For primary bibliographic entry see Field 4A.
W75-08727

A MANAGEMENT PROGRAM FOR THE OYSTER RESOURCE IN APALACHICOLA BAY, FLORIDA,
Florida State Univ., Tallahassee. Dept. of Economics.
For primary bibliographic entry see Field 6C.
W75-08772

TAX WEDGES AND COST-BENEFIT ANALYSIS,
Virginia Univ., Charlottesville. Dept. of Economics.
R. N. McKean.
Public Finance, Vol 29, No 1, p 105-109, 1974. 1 fig, 6 ref.

Descriptors: *Evaluation, *Cost-benefit analysis, *Taxes, *Economic efficiency, Resource mix.
Identifiers: *Tax wedges, Excise tax, Income tax, Sales tax, Shadow prices.

Observed prices for taxed items reflect the wedge driven between the marginal rates of substitution in consumption and marginal rates of transforma-

W75-08822

THE IHD--TEN YEARS OF PROGRESS,
National Committe for the International Hydrological Decade, Washington, D.C.
For primary bibliographic entry see Field 2A.
W75-08829

EVALUATION AND IMPLEMENTATION OF URBAN DRAINAGE PROJECTS,
Colorado State Univ., Fort Collins. Dept. of Civil Engineering.
For primary bibliographic entry see Field 4A.
W75-08847

CONTRASTS IN COMMUNITY ACTION AND OPINION,
Oregon State Univ., Corvallis. Dept. of Anthropology.
For primary bibliographic entry see Field 5G.
W75-08848

6C. Cost Allocation, Cost Sharing, Pricing/Repayment

EFFECTS OF PRICE CHANGE UPON THE DOMESTIC USE OF WATER OVER TIME,
Clemson Univ., S.C. Dept. of Agricultural Economics.
R. M. Pope, Jr., J. M. Stepp, and J. S. Lytle.
Available from the National Technical Information Service, Springfield, Va. 22161, as PB-242 279, $5.75 in paper copy, $2.25 in microfiche. South Carolina Water Resources Research Institute, Clemson Report No 56, March 1975. 129 p, 21 fig, 30 tab, 48 ref, 4 append. OWRT B-032-SC(3).

Descriptors: Water demand, *Pricing, *Water rates, *Elasticity of demand, *South Carolina, Cities, Municipale water, Water uses, Water utilization.
Identifiers: *Price changes, Temporal analysis, *Residential water users.

This research is based upon mail-survey data and monthly water-use records for a randomized sample of 1464 households in four South Carolina municipalities which increased the price of water during the period 1966-1969. In each case the data were for 12 months before the price change and 24 months thereafter. It was hypothesized that the residential water-use effect of a price increase (i.e. elasticity of demand) would tend to decrease over time as people become accustomed to paying the higher price, and it would be hoped that a 'turning point' could be identified. Non-comparability of 'monthly' water-use records precluded meaningful analysis of monthly differences in water use, but demand elasticity coefficients computed on an annual basis for the first and second years following the price increases supported the hypothesis stated above. For 820 non-irrigators, whose water use was presumably not affected by the amount and timing of rainfall, the 4-city average elasticity of demand coefficient was -0.26 the first year and -0.11 the second year following the price change. For all 1464 respondents the comparable figures were -0.33 and -0.14.
W75-08355

AN ECONOMIC ANALYSIS OF CHANGES IN IRRIGATION PRACTICES IN JEFFERSON COUNTY, IDAHO,
Idaho Univ., Moscow. Department of Agricultural Economics.
For primary bibliographic entry see Field 3F.
W75-08481

METHODOLOGY FOR OBTAINING LEAST COST IRRIGATION STEM SPECIFICATIONS,
Idaho Univ., Moscow. Dept. of Agricultural Engineering.
For primary bibliographic entry see Field 3F.
W75-08482

MODEL DEVELOPMENT AND SYSTEMS ANALYSIS OF THE YAKIMA RIVER BASIN: FISHERIES,
Washington Univ., Seattle. Coll. of Fisheries.
For primary bibliographic entry see Field 6B.
W75-08580

ALLOCATING ENVIRONMENTAL RESOURCES,
Virginia Univ., Charlottesville.
A. H. Barnett, and B. Yandle, Jr.
Public Finance, May 1973. 16 p, 2 fig, 9 ref. S-038-SC.

Descriptors: *Economics, *Resource allocation, *Decision making, Water management, Marginal costs, Marginal benefits, Optimization, Economic efficiency.
Identifiers: *Contrived markets, Bidding scheme, Property rights, Externalities.

A contrived market process is outlined for the allocation of environmental resources. Making the assumption that the particular resource to be allocated has been previously a part of the common wealth of the community, a governmental authority claims title to the resource and develops a bidding scheme whereby allocation to competing users occurs. In the process the 'optimal' level of quality is determined, these quality shares are allocated, and all parties bidding are paid for their losses of the previous common wealth and pay for their newly acquired rights to quality. A critique of the process is also given.
W75-08598

OPTIMAL PRICING AND INVESTMENT IN COMMUNITY WATER SUPPLY,
Tennessee Univ., Knoxville. Dept. of Finance.
W. Goolsby.
Journal American Water Works Association, Vol 67, No 5, p 220-224, May 1975. 6 fig, 2 equ, 20 ref.

Descriptors: *Water supply, *Pricing, *Investment, *Demand, *Economies of scale, Water distribution(Applied), Water treatment, Costs, Marginal costs, Estimating, Peak loads, Optimization, Mathematical models, Equations, Systems analysis.
Identifiers: Production function, Production plant, Capacity, Plant expansion.

Presented in a discussion emphaizing the two cycles of concern to water suppliers -- the demand cycle and the investment cycle. An attempt is made to show the interaction of pricing and investment policies under conditions of indivisibilities, cyclical demand, demand that grows over time, and economies of scale. All of these factors should be accounted for by a metropolitan water supplier, with the possible exception of demand that grows over time. Moreover, these factors should be considered simultaneously since they are inextricably bound together. The response of water prices to the demand and the investment cycles should be that prices rise with increased demand, whether the increase in demand occurs because of weather, population or income growth, or whatever, and that prices fall with increases in excess capacity, whether an increase in excess capacity occurs as the result of an expansion of the existing plant or a slackening of demand. Water suppliers should not require subsidies, but losses experienced in slack periods should be covered by profits in periods when the capacity of the water facility is fully utilized. In effect, slack periods may extend over several years as well as seasonally. Water suppliers should consider both cycles when establishing price. (Bell-Cornell)

W75-08722

ENGINEERING ECONOMICS OF RURAL SYSTEMS: A NEW U S APPROACH,
National Water Well Association, Columbus, Ohio; and Rice Univ., Houston, Tex.
For primary bibliographic entry see Field 4A.
W75-08723

SAMPLE UNCERTAINTY IN FLOOD LEVEE DESIGN: BAYESIAN VERSUS NON-BAYESIAN METHODS,
Arizona Univ., Tucson. Dept. of Systems and Industrial Engineering; and Arizona Univ., Tucson. Hydrology and Water Resources Interdisciplinary Program.
For primary bibliographic entry see Field 8A.
W75-08724

A 'RATIONAL' POLICY FOR THE ENERGY AND ENVIRONMENTAL CRISES,
Calgary Univ. (Alberta). Dept. of Civil Engineering.
For primary bibliographic entry see Field 6D.
W75-08732

A MANAGEMENT PROGRAM FOR THE OYSTER RESOURCE IN APALACHICOLA BAY, FLORIDA,
Florida State Univ., Tallahassee. Dept. of Economics.
C. E. Rockwood.
Available from the National Technical Information Service Springfield Va 22161 as COM-74-11640 $10.00 in paper copy, $2.25 in microfiche. Report No. NOAA-74100803, May 1973. 352 p. 4 fig, 42 tab, 96 ref. N-042-44-72(N).

Descriptors: *Management, *Commercial shellfish, *Oysters, *Shellfish farming, *Economic impact, *Social impact, Employment opportunities, Marketing, Reefs, Harvesting, *Florida.
Identifiers: *Oyster industry, Franklin County(Fla.), Apalachicola Bay(Fla.).

The Apalachicola oyster industry needs a community-approved program of change and development. All oyster resource management changes in the relatively small oyster based economy of Apalachicola and of Franklin County have important long range consequences for local employment patterns, family structure, and community life. Three specific management objectives are developed in conjunction with an economic analysis of alternatives and an assessment of sociological consequences of the proposed changes: (1) productivity improvement--by the mechanization and modernization of the harvesting process and of the oyster industry in general, and by the establishment of regulations on minimum harvestable size and on selective closing of oyster bars; (2) output enhancement--by reef planting and cultivation and by the control of water pollution and oyster predation and disease; and (3) marketing promotion--by improving the quality and packaging of the delivered product and by promoting the wholesomeness and tastiness of Apalachicola oysters. A management policy that does not encompass all three of these objectives is less likely to be of net social benefit to Apalachicola and probably would be opposed strongly for that reason. A rank ordering of management alternatives for each objective based on economic and sociological or community preference points of view is provided. (Becker-Wisconsin)
W75-08772

STREAM CHANNELIZATION: THE ECONOMICS OF THE CONTROVERSY,
Cornell Univ., Ithaca, N.Y. Dept. of Economics.
J. P. Brown.
Natural Resources Journal, Vol 14, No 4, p 557-576, 1974. 9 ref.

Descriptors: *Cost allocation, Rivers, *Channel improvement, *Jurisdication, Environmental effects, Decision making, Alteration of flow, Relative rights, Financing, Welfare(Economics).
Identifiers: *Stream channelization, Externalities.

The merits of stream channelization must be evaluated on the level of the individual project since each project contains different private and social costs and benefits. Outdoor recreationists emphasize the externalities associated with stream channelization--the effects on fish and wildlife--while private citizens or groups are concerned with maximizing the difference between private costs and private benefits. Three methods of stream channelization are discussed: (1) increasing the channel cross-section by excavation, (2) by building levees, and (3) increasing the velocity of the stream by lowering frictional drag. The major benefits of stream channelization are flood probability reduction and drainage of wetlands. Alternatives to channelization are also presented. Stream channelization externalities, including downstream effects, effects on other users of the rivers, and the effects on later generations, should be included in any computation of costs and benefits associated with a project. If externalities exist, then the private individual wealth maximizer should not make final allocation decisions, but rather jurisdiction should be at a local governmental level, such as Water Conservation District. The appropriate role of the Federal Government is to represent the otherwise unrepresented interests and restict rather than encourage the construction of these projects. (Becker-Wisconsin)
W75-08777

SHORT-RUN EFFECTS OF AN INCREASED EFFLUENT CHARGE IN A COMPETITIVE MARKET,
North Carolina Univ., Chapel Hill.
For primary bibliographic entry see Field 5G.
W75-08778

TAX WEDGES AND COST-BENEFIT ANALYSIS,
Virginia Univ., Charlottesville. Dept. of Economics.
For primary bibliographic entry see Field 6B.
W75-08779

ECONOMIC ANALYSIS OF EFFLUENT GUIDELINES--FLAT GLASS INDUSTRY,
Little (Arthur D.), Inc., Cambridge, Mass.
For primary bibliographic entry see Field 5G.
W75-08781

ECONOMIC ANALYSIS OF EFFLUENT GUIDELINES: RUBBER PROCESSING INDUSTRY,
Little (Arthur D.), Inc., Cambridge, Mass.
For primary bibliographic entry see Field 5G.
W75-08782

6D. Water Demand

EFFECTS OF PRICE CHANGE UPON THE DOMESTIC USE OF WATER OVER TIME,
Clemson Univ., S.C. Dept. of Agricultural Economics.
For primary bibliographic entry see Field 6C.
W75-08355

ECONOMIC VALUE OF WATER-ORIENTED RECREATION QUALITY,
Utah State Univ., Logan. Dept. of Economics.
For primary bibliographic entry see Field 6B.
W75-08469

larger appetites. Another economic justification for C.P. is that it would certainly delay a utility's capacity expansion requirements, lowering the use of resources and long run supply costs. An example of the effect of C.P. in the water supply industry is given. Conservational Pricing could offer short term easing of the energy and environmental crises by lowering per capita demand. Administrators responsible for resources allocation should consider C.P. in addition to searching for new supplies in the race to lower demand-supply differentials. (Bell-Cornell)
W75-08732

MARINE TRADES AND THE COASTAL CRISIS,
Rhode Island Univ., Kingston. Coastal Resources Center.
For primary bibliographic entry see Field 6B.
W75-08784

6E. Water Law and Institutions

WATERSHED ORGANIZATIONS - IMPACT ON WATER QUALITY MANAGEMENT, AN ANALYSIS OF SELECTED MICHIGAN WATERSHED COUNCILS,
Michigan State Univ., East Lansing. Dept. of Resources Development.
For primary bibliographic entry see Field 5G.
W75-08354

INSTITUTIONAL ASPECTS OF ENERGY-WATER DECISIONS IN THE PACIFIC SOUTHWEST REGION,
Arizona Univ., Tucson.
For primary bibliographic entry see Field 6B.
W75-08372

OIL SPILL PROTECTION IN THE BALTIC SEA,
Institute for Water and Air Pollution Research, Stockholm (Sweden). Project on Ecological Effects of Oil Pollution in the Baltic Sea.
For primary bibliographic entry see Field 5G.
W75-08464

A CASE STUDY OF THE APPLICATION OF COST-BENEFIT ANALYSIS TO WATER SYSTEM CONSOLIDATION BY LOCAL GOVERNMENT,
Delaware Univ., Newark. Div. of Urban Affairs; and Delaware Univ, Newark. Water Resources Center.
For primary bibliographic entry see Field 6B.
W75-08573

STATUTORY DEFINITIONS OF FRESHWATER WETLANDS.
Chapter 818, Acts of the Great and General Court of Massachusetts, p 2-4, (1974). OWRT B-023-MASS(12). 14-31-0001-3596.

Descriptors: *Wetlands, Northeast U.S., *Massachusetts, Bogs, Swamps, Marshes, *Water law, *Legislation.

The first legal definitions of bogs, swamps, wet meadows and marshes in Massachusetts legislation are provided. These definitions facilitate the implementation of the state's Wetland Protective Act, Chapter 131, Section 40, General Laws of the Commonwealth of Massachusetts.
W75-08594

ENVIRONMENTAL LOBBYING: TAKING THE RIGHT ISSUE TO THE RIGHT PLACE AT THE RIGHT TIME,
Clemson Univ., S.C.
For primary bibliographic entry see Field 6G.
W75-08608

THE PROTECTION OF THE QUALITY OF WATERS, AN IMPORTANT ELEMENT IN THE CONSERVATION OF NATURE, (IN ROMANIAN),
Consililul National al Apelor, Bucharest (Rumania).
For primary bibliographic entry see Field 5G.
W75-08775

STREAM CHANNELIZATION: THE ECONOMICS OF THE CONTROVERSY,
Cornell Univ., Ithaca, N.Y. Dept. of Economics.
For primary bibliographic entry see Field 6C.
W75-08777

ECONOMIC ANALYSIS OF EFFLUENT GUIDELINES FOR SELECTED SEGMENTS OF THE SEAFOOD PROCESSING INDUSTRY. (CATFISH, CRAB, SHRIMP AND TUNA),
Development Planning and Research Associates, Inc., Manhattan, Kans.
For primary bibliographic entry see Field 5G.
W75-08783

RESEARCH AND ADVANCES IN GROUND-WATER RESOURCES STUDIES, 1964-1974,
Florida Water Management District, Brooksville.
For primary bibliographic entry see Field 2F.
W75-08825

THE IHD--TEN YEARS OF PROGRESS,
National Committe for the International Hydrological Decade, Washington, D.C.
For primary bibliographic entry see Field 2A.
W75-08829

6F. Nonstructural Alternatives

FLOOD PLAIN MANAGEMENT IN MONTANA,
Montana Dept. of Natural Resources and Conservation, Helena. Floodway Management Bureau.
C. Parrett.
In: Hydraulic Engineering and the Environment; Proceedings of the 21st Annual Hydraulic Division Specialty Conference, Montana State University, Bozeman, August 15-17, 1973. American Society of Civil Engineers, New York, p 85-91, 1973. 2 fig, 4 ref, 1 append.

Descriptors: *Flood protection, *Flood plain zoning, *Management, Flood plains, Floodways, Land use, River basin development, Non-structural alternatives, Flood damage, Flood frequency, Flood recurrence interval, Legislation, Legal aspects, *Montana.

Although floodplain management has just started in Montana, the eventual implementation of floodplain regulations will hopefully have a significant effect on flood-damage prevention. Montana's floodplain law is based on an established and workable law in Nebraska and seems to offer a sound legal basis for floodplain land-use restrictions. In addition, Montana's proposed minimum standards for regulation are based on workable models used elsewhere. Two signficant problems, however, could seriously limit the overall success of Montana's floodplain management program. One major problem is the length of time and expense required to prepare the technical floodplain delineation data. Sound data are needed for effective regulation, but floodplain development often takes place much more rapidly than the data can be supplied. The second significant problem concerns local opposition to land-use regulation. Regulatory programs require local people to pay the costs for flood-damage prevention, and this is often opposed if communities are not fully aware of the potential benefits. Not only is engineering expertise required to help administer a management program, but engineering activities on floodplain areas can significantly affect potential flood hazard. The engineer thus has a responsibility to insure that his floodplain works are compatible with periodic flooding and that they do not increase potential flood damages. (See also W75-08786) (Sims-ISWS)
W75-08795

FLOODLAND MANAGEMENT: THE ENVIRONMENTAL CORRIDOR CONCEPT,
Southeastern Wisconsin Regional Planning Commission, Waukesha.
S. G. Walesh.
In: Hydraulic Engineering and the Environment; Proceedings of the 21st Annual Hydraulic Division Specialty Conference, Montana State University, Bozeman, August 15-17, 1973. American Society of Civil Engineers, New York, p 105-111, 1973. 8 ref, 1 append.

Descriptors: *Flood plain zoning, *Regulation, *Beneficial use, Flood plains, Legal aspects, Zoning, River basin development, Non-structural alternatives, Planning, Management, Regional development, Social aspects, Recreation facilities, Scenery, *Wisconsin.

The primary objective of floodland management in contemporary engineering and planning practice is to accomplish the single purpose objective of tailoring urban development to riverine areas in such a manner so as to mitigate flood damages. It was maintained that, in the context of regional land and water resource planning, floodland management should incorporate a second, equally important objective: protection of environmental corridors and recreational, scenic, ecological, and cultural values inherent in them. The environmental corridor concept as applied by the Southeastern Wisconsin Regional Planning Commission in its regional land and water resources planning programs consists of identifying the corridors--using delineated floodlands for the basic form--and recommending various means whereby much of the corridor lands can be retained in natural or partly developed open space for public use and enjoyment. (See also W75-08786) (Sims-ISWS)
W75-08797

PILOT STUDY IN FLOOD PLAIN MANAGEMENT,
Washington State Univ, Pullman. R. L. Albrook Hydraulic Lab.
A. C. Mueller, and J. E. Hoffman.
In: Hydraulic Engineering and the Environment; Proceedings of the 21st Annual Hydraulic Division Specialty Conference, Montana State University, Bozeman, August 15-17, 1973. American Society of Civil Engineers, New York, p 113-120, 1973. 2 fig, 1 tab, 2 ref, 1 append.

Descriptors: *Hydraulic models, *Model studies, *Flood plains, Flooding, River flow, Flow around objects, Land use, City planning, Roughness(Hydraulic), Flow resistance, Erosion, *Washington.
Identifiers: *Pullman(Wash).

A pilot study in floodplain management with the Washington Department of Ecology was undertaken at the Albrook Hydraulic Laboratory. The study consisted of basic data gathering, analyzing, and interpreting the needed investigation of statewide flooding and related problems. The construction of a physical hydraulic model to investigate many of the problems was a significant portion of the study. It was decided to model approximately one mile (1.6 km) of the river in Pullman, Washington, including the downtown floodplain. Small improvements such as modification of the channel and man-made structures in partcularly bothersome areas were observed to ascertain their effects. The full range of flows were checked for each change tested from a minor flood of 10-yr return frequency to the 100-yr frequency flood. The model was used as a pilot project to demonstrate and test many types of management and

control features. The outstanding feature of this type of model is visualization. Engineers and laymen can get a better grasp of the situation. The physical model provides an overview of flooding problems which is difficult to convey through words and tabulated data. (See also W75-08786) (Sims-ISWS)
W75-08798

6G. Ecologic Impact Of Water Development

THE POLLUTION ENVIRONMENT,
Utah State Univ., Logan.
For primary bibliographic entry see Field 5G.
W75-08371

ENVIRONMENTAL EFFECTS OF DREDGING AND SPOIL DISPOSAL,
Washington State Dept. of Ecology, Olympia.
For primary bibliographic entry see Field 5C.
W75-08465

IMPACTS OF FOREST MANAGEMENT PRACTICES ON THE AQUATIC ENVIRONMENT-PHASE II,
Washington Cooperative Fishery Unit, Seattle.
For primary bibliographic entry see Field 5B.
W75-08468

ENVIRONMENT: A BIBLIOGRAPHY ON SOCIAL POLICY AND HUMANISTIC VALUES,
Nevada Univ., Reno. Desert Research Inst.
For primary bibliographic entry see Field 10C.
W75-08489

ANALYSES OF SELECTED CONSTITUENTS IN NATIVE WATER AND SOIL IN THE BAYOU BOEUF-CHENE-BLACK AREA NEAR MORGAN CITY, LOUISIANA, INCLUDING A MODIFIED STANDARD ELUTRIATE TEST,
Geological Survey, Baton Rouge, La.
For primary bibliographic entry see Field 5A.
W75-08501

ENVIRONMENTAL PROTECTION IN KRAFT PULP MILLS,
Munksjo A.B., Jonkoping (Sweden).
For primary bibliographic entry see Field 5D.
W75-08566

ECOLOGICAL APPROACH TO POWER GENERATION UNDER ENVIRONMENTAL CONSERVATION,
Kansas State Univ., Manhattan. Dept. of Chemical Engineering.
L. T. Fan, C. L. Hwang, S. H. Lin, and R. Shojalashkari.
Kansas Water Resources Research Institute, Manhattan Contribution Number 114. In: Energy 73, First International Seminar and Exhibition, Palais du Centenaire, Brussels, September 10-14, 1973, p 127-161, (1973) , 12 fig, 2 tab, 47 ref. OWRR B-030-KAN(7), 14-31-0001-3592.

Descriptors: Thermal pollution, *Environmental control, Conservation, Water quality, *Systems analysis, Operations research.
Identifiers: *Thermal pollution control, *Power generation, *Environmental conservation, System engineering.

Power generation and environmental conservation are two human activities of the utmost importance and yet their requirements are diametrically opposed. It is highly desirable that an interdisciplinary or systems approach be employed to find an optimal solution which satisfies such requirements. Several examples of systems engineering approaches to thermal pollution control are illustrated. However, a need for non-technological approaches is also emphasized.
W75-08604

ENVIRONMENTAL LOBBYING: TAKING THE RIGHT ISSUE TO THE RIGHT PLACE AT THE RIGHT TIME,
Clemson Univ., S.C.
H. E. Albert.
Paper Presented in Rural Sociology Section, ASAW, Proceedings for 1973. 16 p, 2 fig, 16 ref. OWRR B-034-SC(8).

Descriptors: *Administration, *Local governments, Water pollution, Economic development, Environment, South Carolina, State governments, Environmental effects.
Identifiers: Victoria Bluff(So Car).

A particularly bitter struggle between certain segments of the private sector and the state and local governments of South Carolina occurred in 1969 and 1970. The conflict was precipitated by the announcement that Badische Anilin und Soda Fabrik Corporation (BASF) would build a $200 million petrochemical plant at Victoria Bluff in Beaufort County, South Carolina. The private sector was unique in its ability to organize and oppose public policy ans was ultimately effective in preventing the state and industry from locating the plant at Victoria Bluff. The decisive factor was reception at the national level of the private sector complaints. This reception was enhanced by the fact that many of the leaders of the opposition against BASF were personal friends of high level government personnel, were active in the Republican Party at the national level (which happened to be in control of the executive branch of the national government), and had long practiced the skills of interest groups. Research methods consisted primarily at structured interviews, and search public and private files.
W75-08608

ANALYSIS OF POPULATION, BIRTH, AND DEATH STATISTICS IN THE COUNTIES SURROUNDING THE BIG ROCK POINT NUCLEAR POWER STATION, CHARLEVOIX COUNTY, MICHIGAN,
Argonne National Lab., Ill.
For primary bibliographic entry see Field 5C.
W75-08653

LAND USE AND NUCLEAR POWER PLANTS - CASE STUDIES OF SITING PROBLEMS,
Directorate of Regulatory Standards (AEC), Washington, D.C.
R. Ramsey, and P. R. Reed.
Available from the Superintedent of Documents, Government Printing Office, Washington, DC, for $0.95. Rept No WASH-1319, October 1974. 58 p, 12 fig, 3 tab.

Descriptors: *Nuclear powerplants, *Sites, *Environmental effects, *Land use, Wetlands, Urban sociology, Agriculture, Forest soils, Land.

Until recently, public concern with nuclear power plants had concentrated on the impact of thermal effluents on nearby water bodies. But since the water problem has changed increasingly from an impact assessment problem to a problem of meeting strict government standards, concern has shifted to other types of impacts from power plant siting. In particular, a great deal of interest has developed in the impacts of siting a nuclear power plant on surrounding land use. Four cases are discussed involving nuclear plants (built, proposed, or under construction). These cases are intended to illustrate direct land use impacts on four different types of land: in terms of U. S. Geological Survey Land Classification System these are 'Urban and Built-up Lands,' 'Agricultural Land,' 'Wetlands,' and 'Forest Land.' Also, an indirect effect on another land

DISCHARGE DATA AT WATER-QUALITY MONITORING STATIONS IN ARKANSAS,
Geological Survey, Little Rock, Ark.
R. K. Knott.
Open-file report, April 1975. 19 p, 1 tab.

Descriptors: *Discharge(Water), *Discharge measurement, *Streamflow, *Arkansas, *Basic data collections, Hydrologic data, Monitoring, Water quality.

Discharge data are presented for a network of water-quality monitoring stations operated throughout Arkansas. Most of the stations are at points where discharge records are not otherwise collected. (Knapp-USGS)
W75-08519

DESIGN AND IMPLEMENTATION OF A HYDROLOGIC DATA PROCESSING SYSTEM IN BRAZIL, 1971-74,
Geological Survey, Reston, Va.
M. D. Edwards, W. L. Isherwood, and R. N. Eicher.
Open-file report, April 1975. 201 p.

Descriptors: *Data processing, *Basic data collections, *Data storage and retrieval, *Hydrologic data, Data collections, Streamflow, Computer programs, South America, Information retrieval.
Identifiers: *Brazil.

Streamflow records have been collected intermittently for over a half a century by numerous Brazilian organizations, both governmental and private. The responsibility for the national hydrological data collection program is vested in the Projeto Hidrologia, Departmento Nacional de Aguas e Energia Eletrica (DNAEE), Ministerio das Minas e Energia (MME). The DNAEE requested assistance of the U.S. Geological Survey (USGS) in the design and implementation of a hydrologic information system for automatic processing of Brazilian streamflow records. The plans and procedures for the design and implementation of a hydrologic-data processing system of high transfer value that can be adapted to similar hydrologic environments elsewhere are described. (See W75-08524 thru W75-08527) (Knapp-USGS)
W75-08523

COMPUTER PROCESSING HYDROLOGIC DATA IN BRAZIL,
Geological Survey, Reston, Va.
W. L. Isherwood.
In: Design and Implementation of a Hydrologic Data Processing System in Brazil, 1971-74: Geological Survey open-file report, p 1-11, April 1975. 3 append.

Descriptors: *Data processing, *Data storage and retrieval, *Hydrologic data, Computer programs, South America.
Identifiers: *Brazil.

For computer processing of hyhydrologic data in Brazil, techniques developed by the USGS in the United States were adapted to conditions prevailing in Brazil. A system of numerical indentification for sites of hydrologic data collection for both on-stream sites and off-stream sites and generalized format for computer based storage for hydrologic data were recommended. In addition, it was recommended that an exchange of computer trained personnel both from the USA to Brazil and from Brazil to the USA, be planned in order to carry out the conversions of computer programs to a form useful in Brazil. (See also W75-08523) (Knapp-USGS)
W75-08524

HYDROLOGIC DATA PROCESSING SYSTEM FOR BRAZIL,
Geological Survey, Reston, Va.
M. D. Edwards.
In: Design and Inplementation of a Hydrologic Data Processing System in Brazil, 1971-74: Geological Survey open-file report, p 12-98, April 1975. 9 fig, 3 append.

Descriptors: *Data storage and retrieval, *Hydrologic data, Data processing, Computer programs, South America.
Identifiers: *Brazil.

Recommendations are given for the establishment of a processing system for hydrologic data in the Ministerio das Minas e Energia, Brazil. A primary effort in the use of this system is the processing of large volumes of historical hydrologic data in the Departamento Nacional de Aguas e Energia Eletrica. (See also W75-08523) (Knapp-USGS)
W75-08525

THE IMPLEMENTATION OF A HYDROLOGIC DATA PROCESSING SYSTEM IN BRAZIL,
Geological Survey, Reston, Va.
M. D. Edwards.
In: Design and Implementation of a Hydrologic Data Processing System in Brazil, 1971-74: Geological Survey open-file report, p 99-157, April 1975. 6 fig, 2 ref.

Descriptors: *Data storage and retrieval, *Hydrologic data, Data processing, Computer programs, South America.
Identifiers: *Brazil.

The formats and file structures of the National Water Data Storage and Retrieval System of the U.S. Geological Survey were used in the implementation of the Hydrologic Information System (HIS) in Brazil. In addition to the Daily Values File, the system contains a Station Inventory File which contains pertinent information related to the geographic location, period of record available and types of data available for each station. (See also W75-08523) (Knapp-USGS)
W75-08526

MANAGEMENT STUDY OF SOME ASPECTS OF SISTEMA DE INFORMACOES HIDROLOGICAS,
Geological Survey, Reston, Va.
R. N. Eicher.
In: Design and Implementation of a Hydrologic Data processing System in Brazil, 1971-74: Geological Survey open-file report, p 158-201, April 1975. 6 fig, 5 tab.

Descriptors: *Data processing, *Data storage and retrieval, *Hydrologic data, Basic data collections, Computer programs, South America, Information retrieval.
Identifiers: *Brazil.

A management study was made of the flow of data between the several organizations that are concerned with the collection, compilation, processing, analysis and publication of the basic hydrologic data in Brazil. (See also W75-08523) (Knapp-USGS)
W75-08527

THE SEASONAL VARIATION OF THE HYDROLOGIC CYCLE AS SIMULATED BY A GLOBAL MODEL OF THE ATMOSPHERE,
National Oceanic and Atmospheric Administration, Princeton, N.J. Geophysical Fluid Dynamics Lab.
For primary bibliographic entry see Field 2A.
W75-08704

CHANNEL AGGRADATION IN WESTERN UNITED STATES AS INDICATED BY OBSERVATIONS AT VIGIL NETWORK SITES,
Geological Survey, Boise, Idaho. Water Resources Div.
For primary bibliographic entry see Field 2J.
W75-08830

7B. Data Acquisition

CLASSIFICATION AND WORLD DISTRIBUTION OF VEGETATION RELATIVE TO V/STOL AIRCRAFT OPERATIONS,
Army Engineer Topographic Labs., Fort Belvoir, Va.
W. C. Robison, and J. Viletto, Jr.
Report No ETL-SR-74-4, December, 1973. 30 p, 8 fig, 1 map, 18 ref.

Descriptors: *Vegetation, *Distribution, *Deserts, *Aquatic plants, *Irrigation, *Aircraft, Climatic zones, Trees, Shrubs, Tundra, Cultivated lands, Classification, Grassland.

Vegetation was considered in regard to effects on the operation of V/STOL aircraft and classified into nine formation-classes: closed forest, open forest and woodland, savanna, treeless grassland, closed shrubs, sparse woodland and scrub, vegetation sparse to absent (without trees), aquatic vegetation and cultivated vegetation in short planting cycles. The sparse or absent vegetation category occupies the most extensive area of the earth and includes the low latitude deserts, the Arctic tundra, the entire Antarctic continent, and all the other areas that for some reason have little or no vegetation. This class is also least affected by cultivation. In addition to the development of a vegetation classification for V/STOL aircraft operations, this study produced a world vegetation map using the developed classification. (Mastic-Arizona)
W75-08366

ARIZONA SCANNED BY ERTS-1.
Geotimes, Vol 19, No 9, p 24, September 1974. 1 fig.

Descriptors: *Arizona, *Remote sensing, *Terrain analysis, *Aerial reconnaissance, Infrared radiation, Colorado River, Satellites(Artificial).
Identifiers: ERTS-1.

A mosaic of Arizona was assembled by U.S. Geological Survey scientists using 24 images tqken by NASA's Earth Resources Technology Satellite. Boundaries between land and water are especially sharp. Desert land appears white; forests dark. The Colorado River can be traced along its course through the state. Prominent features such as the Black Mesa in the northeast, the White Mountains and Baldy Peak in the eastern portion of the state, Phoenix, Tucson, and the Santa Cruz and Gila Rivers in the South central part of the state are distinct. (Mastic-Arizona)
W75-08367

REMOTE SENSING OF NATURAL RESOURCES, THE ROLE OF UNESCO'S RESOURCES RESEARCH PROGRAMME.
Nature and Resources, Vol 10, No 1, p 18-20, January-March 1974.

Descriptors: *Remote sensing, *Aerial photography, *Satellites(Artificial), *Data collections, International Hydrological Decade, Hydrologic data, Surveys.

The use of remote sensing from satellites and rockets constitutes a new tool of environmental and natural resources research, particularly when it is necessary to survey or monitor large areas of the Earth's surface. While it seems unlikely that Unesco can contribute to design of satellite-borne remote sensing equipment, a more significant role may be the interpretation of satellite data and their use for practical purposes. Contributions may be made toward problems that cannot be solved without cooperation and collaboration between launching countries and those countries covered by satallite surveys. Unesco has a definite interest in the development of space techniques such as remote sensing, and could provide input for establishing and maintaining international cooperation in order to promote their use. Hydrological studies, small-scale mapping of soils and vegetation types, mapping and studies of geological and geomorphological features, measurement of ocean temperature, turbidity, pollution, etc., are examples. (Mastic-Arizona)
W75-08368

STEAM, HOT-WATER AND ELECTRICAL THERMAL DRILLS FOR TEMPERATE GLACIERS,
Centre National de la Recherche Scientifique, Grenoble (France). Laboratoire de Glaciologie.
For primary bibliographic entry see Field 2C.
W75-08409

RADIO SOUNDINGS ON TRAPRIDGE GLACIER, YUKON TERRITORY, CANADA,
Department of the Environment, Calgary (Alberta). Inland Waters Directorate.
For primary bibliographic entry see Field 2C.
W75-08412

A MEASUREMENT OF SURFACE-PERPENDICULAR STRAIN-RATE IN A GLACIER,
Washington Univ., Seattle. Geophysics Program.
For primary bibliographic entry see Field 2C.
W75-08416

RADIO ECHO SOUNDING ON TEMPERATE GLACIERS,
Water Management Service, Calgary (Alberta).
For primary bibliographic entry see Field 2C.
W75-08419

EVOLUTION OF GULF STREAM EDDIES AS SEEN IN SATELLITE INFRARED IMAGERY,
National Environmental Satellite Service, Washington, D.C.
For primary bibliographic entry see Field 2L.
W75-08429

SATELLITE DETECTION OF UPWELLING IN THE GULF OF TEHUANTEPEC, MEXICO,
National Environmental Satellite Service, Washington, D.C.
For primary bibliographic entry see Field 2L.
W75-08430

THE CHALK GROUNDWATER TRITIUM ANOMALY--A POSSIBLE EXPLANATION,
Institute of Geological Sciences, London (England). Dept. of Hydrogeology.
For primary bibliographic entry see Field 2F.
W75-08449

INVESTIGATION OF VERTICAL GROUNDWATER FLOW IN BOREHOLES,
International Hydrological Decade, New Delhi (India). Indian National Committee.
For primary bibliographic entry see Field 2F.
W75-08450

SOME CHARACTERISTICS OF THE ALBEDO OF SNOW,
Utah State Univ., Logan. Dept. of Soil Science and Biometeorology.
For primary bibliographic entry see Field 2C.
W75-08452

A SIMPLE RESPIROMETER FOR MEASURING OXYGEN AND NITRATE CONSUMPTION IN BACTERIAL CULTURES,
Agricultural Univ., Wageningen (Netherlands). Dept. of Microbiology.
For primary bibliographic entry see Field 5A.
W75-08458

meter for use in sewer flow measurement. The meter consists of a constriction in the pipe which produces critical flow under open channel flow conditions and acts as a conventional Venturi meter under full flow conditions. The constriction is constructed using cylindrical segments, the diameter of which is larger than that of the pipe, leaving the invert and crown clear. Head loss characteristics and experimental rating curves for both open channel and full flow conditions are described. Information is presented to permit the selection of geometrical parameters for optimum performance for a specific installation. A Venturi type flow meter for measurement of sewer flows under both open channel and full flow conditions is feasible. Its advantages are low cost and simple operation. (Bell-Cornell)
W75-08850

7C. Evaluation, Processing and Publication

URBAN WATER DEVELOPMENT AND MANAGEMENT IN ARID ENVIRONMENTS, VOLUME I: COMPLETION REPORT,
Rockwell International Corp., Canoga Park, Calif. Rocketdyne Div.
For primary bibliographic entry see Field 6A.
W75-08352

URBAN WATER DEVELOPMENT AND MANAGEMENT IN ARID ENVIRONMENTS, VOLUME II: THE WATER GAME--GAMING SIMULATION FOR URBAN WATER RESOURCES PLANNING,
Rockwell International Corp., Canoga Park, Calif. Rocketdyne Div.
For primary bibliographic entry see Field 6A.
W75-08353

REPORT AND INTERPRETATIONS FOR THE GENERAL SOIL MAP OF PIMA COUNTY, ARIZONA,
Soil Conservation Service, Portland, Oreg.
For primary bibliographic entry see Field 2G.
W75-08373

PROBIT TRANSFORMATION: IMPROVED METHOD FOR DEFINING SYNCHRONY OF CELL CULTURES,
Carnegie Institution of Washington, Stanford, Calif. Dept. of Plant Biology.
For primary bibliographic entry see Field 5A.
W75-08378

HYDROGEOLOGY OF THE EDMONTON AREA (NORTHWEST SEGMENT), ALBERTA,
Alberta Research, Edmonton.
For primary bibliographic entry see Field 4B.
W75-08398

HYDROGEOLOGY OF THE GLEICHEN AREA, ALBERTA,
Alberta Research, Edmonton.
For primary bibliographic entry see Field 4B.
W75-08399

EFFICIENT SEQUENTIAL OPTIMIZATION IN WATER RESOURCES,
Iowa Univ., Iowa City. Inst. of Hydraulic Research.
For primary bibliographic entry see Field 4A.
W75-08404

TEMPERATURE MEASUREMENTS IN A TEMPERATE GLACIER,
Washington Univ., Seattle. Geophysics Program.
For primary bibliographic entry see Field 2C.
W75-08415

EMPIRICAL DATA ON LONGITUDINAL DISPERSION IN RIVERS,
Geological Survey, Denver, Colo.
For primary bibliographic entry see Field 5B.
W75-08495

REPORT OF THE ANNUAL YIELD OF THE ARKANSAS RIVER BASIN FOR THE ARKANSAS RIVER BASIN COMPACT, ARKANSAS-OKLAHOMA, 1972: 1974 WATER YEAR,
Geological Survey, Little Rock, Ark.
For primary bibliographic entry see Field 4A.
W75-08497

HYDROLOGIC RECORDS FOR VOLUSIA COUNTY, FLORIDA: 1972-73,
Geological Survey, Tallahassee, Fla.
For primary bibliographic entry see Field 4A.
W75-08498

BASIC GROUND-WATER DATA FOR THE MOSCOW BASIN, IDAHO,
Geological Survey, Boise, Idaho.
For primary bibliographic entry see Field 2F.
W75-08499

AN EVALUATION OF THE ERTS DATA COLLECTION SYSTEM AS A POTENTIAL OPERATIONAL TOOL,
Geological Survey, Harrisburg, Pa.
R. W. Paulson.
In: Third Earth Resources Technology Satellite-1 Symposium, Vol 1: Technical Presentations, Section B, Goddard Space Flight Center, Dec 10-14, 1973, Washington, D.C.: National Aeronautics and Space Administration Report SP-351, p 1099-1111, Paper W8, 1974. 5 fig, 4 ref.

Descriptors: *Data transmission, *Telemetry, *Satellites(Artificial), *Data collections, Instrumentation, Monitoring, Streamflow, Water quality, Water levels.
Identifiers: *ERTS.

The Earth Resources Technology Satellite (ERTS) data collection system is a reliable and simple system for collecting data from U.S. Geological Survey operational field instrumentation. It is technically feasible to expand the ERTS system into an operational polar-orbiting data-collection system to gather data from the Geological Survey's hydrologic data network. This could permit more efficient internal management of the network, and could enable the Geological Survey to make data available to cooperating agencies in near-real time. The Geological Survey is conducting an analysis of the costs and benefits of satellite data-relay systems. (Knapp-USGS)
W75-08503

PROCESS IN DATA COLLECTION AND DISSEMINATION IN WATER RESOURCES, 1964-1974,
Geological Survey, Reston, Va. Office of Water Data Coordination.
For primary bibliographic entry see Field 7A.
W75-08505

ESTIMATED YIELD OF FRESH-WATER WELLS IN FLORIDA,
Geological Survey, Tallahassee, Fla.
C. A. Pascale.
Florida Bureau of Geology, Tallahassee, Map Series No 70, 1975. 1 sheet, 1 fig, 1 map, 15 ref.

Descriptors: *Groundwater resources, *Aquifers, *Groundwater availability, *Florida, Aquifer characteristics, Wells, Geology, *Maps, Pumping, Water supply, Groundwater movement.

This one-sheet map report depicts the great geographical variation of well yield for four major

aquifers used to supply potable water in Florida. (1) Wells that tap the Floridan aquifer--the most extensive and widely used aquifer--generally yield at least 250 gal/min throughout the State except for a few areas. In general wells that yield at least 1,000 gal/min tap limestone containing interconnected solution cavities. In northwest Florida, wells inland have greater yields because the Floridan aquifer along the coast contains much limey clay and sand, which reduce its transmissivity. (2) The Biscayne aquifer, underlying Dade and Broward and part of Palm Beach Counties, is the prime source of water for populous southeast Florida. The aquifer is composed mainly of limestone, coquina, coralline reef rock, and sand, and is highly productive; well yields commonly exceed 2,000 gal/min. (3) Except along the coast, in Escambia and Santa Rosa Counties, wells tapping the sand-and-gravel aquifer generally yield 250 gal/min or more. Along the coast the aquifer is less than 250 feet thick and contains clay beds that reduce the transmissivity. Wells there yield less than 250 gal/min. (4) Wells that tap the shallow aquifer along the east coast generally yield less than 250 gal/min because the aquifer in that area consists of sediments of low permeability. The shallow aquifer in northern Collier and southern Hendry Counties is composed of highly permeable limestone; wells in this area generally yield at least 2,000 gal/min. (Woodard-USGS)
W75-08507

FLOOD ON BUFFALO CREEK FROM SAUNDERS TO MAN, WEST VIRGINIA,
Geological Survey, Reston, Va.
G. S. Runner.
For sale by US Geol. Survey, Reston, Va 22092 - Price $1.50 per set. Hydrologic Investigations Atlas HA-547, 1974. 2 sheets, 13 fig, 4 tab, 2 ref.

Descriptors: *Floods, *Coal mine wastes, *West Virginia, *Dam failure, Disasters, Water quality, Water levels, Damages, *Maps.
Identifiers: *Buffalo Creek(W Va).

On February 26, 1972, at approximately 8 a.m., a coal mine refuse dam collapsed on Middle Fork, a tributary to Buffalo Creek, West Virginia. This 1-sheet hydrologic atlas report documents the hydrologic events associated with the Buffalo Creek disaster as an aid in planning remedial measures to reduce potential flood hazards from similar dams and impoundments. This most destructive flood in West Virginia's history swept through 15.3 miles of the Buffalo Creek valley at an average speed of 7 feet per second (5 miles per hour) and reached the town of Man at the mouth of Buffalo Creek around 11 a.m. The travel time for the 15.3 miles was about 3 hours. During the 3-hour cascade down the valley at least 118 lives were lost, 500 homes were destroyed, 4,000 people were left homeless, property damage exceeded $50 million and highway damage exceeded $15 million. (Knapp-USGS)
W75-08508

GROUND-WATER CONDITIONS IN THE FRANKLIN AREA, SOUTHEASTERN VIRGINIA,
Geological Survey, Reston, Va.
G. A. Brown, and O. J. Cosner.
For sale by U.S. Geol. Survey, Reston, Va 22092 - $1.25 per set. Hydrologic Investigations Atlas HA-538, 1974. 3 sheets, 13 ref.

Descriptors: *Drawdown, *Saline water intrusion, *Aquifers, *Virginia, Withdrawal, Water yield, Salinity, Path of pollutants, Groundwater movement, Hydrogeology, *Maps.
Identifiers: *Franklin(Va).

During the past 30 years large quantities of groundwater have been withdrawn at Franklin, Virginia, and a cone of depression has formed in the water level of the Lower Cretaceous aquifer. This cone extends westward to the Fall Line, coalesces to the north and east with other small cones caused by pumping, and reaches southward into North Carolina. The water-level decline has caused concern about the future groundwater supplies. This 3-sheet hydrologic atlas presents the results of a field investigation of geology and hydrology and an interpretation of the aquifer systems in the Franklin area. Water levels have declined as much as 185 feet near the center of the cone since 1937-39. Water with relatively high concentrations of chloride is known to be present in the aquifer in the southeastern corner of the study area and to the east. Movement of water in the aquifer is toward Franklin. Water in the Lower Cretaceous aquifer in most of the Franklin area is of excellent quality for domestic, municipal, and most industrial uses. (Knapp-USGS)
W75-08509

GROUND-WATER FAVORABILITY AND SURFICIAL GEOLOGY OF THE CHERRYFIELD-JONESBORO AREA, MAINE,
Geological Survey, Reston, Va.
G. C. Prescott, Jr.
For Sale by USGS, Reston, Va 22092 - Price $1.00. Hydrologic Investigations Atlas HA-529, 1974. 1 sheet, 27 ref.

Descriptors: *Groundwater, *Water resources, *Maine, *Maps, Hydrogeology, Water yield, Water quality, Hydrologic data.
Identifiers: *Cherryfield(Maine), *Jonesboro(Maine).

This 1-sheet hydrologic atlas describes the geologic and hydrologic conditions governing the occurrence of groundwater in the Cherryfield-Jonesboro area, Maine. The magnitude of yields that might be expected from properly located and constructed wells or from springs is indicated by the map showing groundwater-favorability areas and surficial geology. This map gives a generalized interpretation of observed geologic and hydrologic data and provides a logical basis for directing detailed exploration for groundwater. The quality of groundwater is generally good for most purposes. It is normally soft, low in dissolved solids and in most areas is free from constituents that would limit its usefulness. The depth of 487 bedrock wells ranged from 27 to 600 feet. The average was 150 feet and the median 145 feet. A few of the wells were drilled for industrial or commercial use, but most were drilled for domestic purposes. The yield of wells ranged from less than 1 to 250 gpm. About 5 percent of the wells yielded more than 30 gpm, and yields exceeding 50 gpm were reported from several depth ranges. The largest reported yield, 250 gpm, was from a well 130 feet deep. (Knapp-USGS)
W75-08510

WATER RESOURCES OF THE CROW RIVER WATERSHED, SOUTH-CENTRAL MINNESOTA,
Geological Survey, Reston, Va.
G. F. Lindholm, D. F. Farrel, and J. O. Helgesen.
For Sale by U.S. Geological Survey, Reston, Va 22092, Price $2.25 per set. Hydrologic Investigations Atlas HA-528, 1974. 3 sheets, 17 ref.

Descriptors: *Water resources, *Groundwater, *Surface waters, *Minnesota, Hydrogeology, Hydrologic data, *Maps, Water quality, Water yield, Aquifers.
Identifiers: *Crow River(Minn).

The water resources of the Crow River watershed, Minnesota, an area of about 2,760 square miles are discussed in a 3-sheet hydrologic atlas. The area is covered entirely by glacial deposits. A topographically high, east-west-trending end moraine divides most of the watershed into two drainage areas of approximately equal size. The North Fork Crow River drains a mixture of glacial outwash and till deposits, whereas the South Fork Crow River drains chiefly till deposits. Cambrian and Precam-

The water resources of Blue Earth River watershed in Minnesota are described in a 3-sheet hydrologic atlas. The watershed includes 3,106 square miles of land surface, which varies from fairly flat to gently rolling. The western, southern, and eastern boundaries are end moraines formed by Pleistocene glaciers. In their lower reaches major streams have cut through glacial deposits and into underlying bedrock. Water supplies are obtained from wells tapping Pleistocene glacial deposits, Ordovician and Cambrian sedimentary rocks, and Precambrian crystalline rocks. In the western part of the watershed, glacial sand and gravel (generally buried) form the most accessible and widely used aquifers. Toward the east, increasing numbers of wells obtain water from Ordovician and Cambrian rocks. Most of the Blue Earth River watershed is an area of groundwater recharge. The use of groundwater in the watershed is estimated at 6,428 million gallons per year. At present, no areas of significant groundwater decline are known, indication that only part of the available groundwater has been developed. Surface water provides excellent year-round recreational facilities and habitat for fish and wildlife. Sites for large storage reservoirs are limited to lower reaches of the rivers. The small tributary streams in the watershed go dry during the fall and winter in may years because they have little natural storage and little groundwater contribution. (Knapp-USGS)
W75-08513

WATER RESOURCES OF THE CLINTON RIVER BASIN, SOUTHEASTERN MICHIGAN,
Geological Survey, Reston, Va.
J. O. Nowlin.
For sale by U.S. Geological Survey, Reston, Va. 22092 Price $1.00 per set. Hydrologic Investigations Atlas HA-469, 1973. 2 sheets, text, 10 ref.

Descriptors: *Water resources, *Surface waters, *Groundwater, *Michigan, Hydrologic data, Hydrogeology, Water yield, *Maps, Water quality, Aquifers.
Identifiers: *Clinton River(Mich).

This hydrologic atlas provides information on the physical features of the Clinton River, Michigan, and its tributaries, the characteristics of streamflow, the quality of ground and surface water, and the availability of groundwater. The Clinton River rises in a chain of lakes near the northwest edge of the basin. The drainage system in the undulating uplands of the headwaters area is poorly developed, consisting of a series of interconnected lakes and marshes draining to the south. About 670 lakes and ponds are within the Clinton River basin, ranging in size from 1,280 acres to less than an acre. The population of the Clinton River basin is primarily urban and suburban. The population in 1970 was about 900,000, of which 760,000 (about 84 percent) was concentrated in incorporated cities of 14,000 or more. The largest city is Warren, with a 1970 population of 179,260. The surficial features of the Clinton River basin were formed by the action of glacial ice and melt waters on rock debris deposited by the ice sheets of the last glacial period. Outwash and deltaic deposits are generally well sorted and coarse grained and generally are excellent sources of water. Wells completed in the bedrock generally yield only small supplies of water, although large supplies may be obtained occasionally. (Knapp-USGS)
W75-08514

ANNUAL PEAK DISCHARGES FROM SMALL DRAINAGE AREAS IN MONTANA, THROUGH SEPTEMBER 1974,
Geological Survey, Helena, Mont.
M. V. Johnson, and R. J. Omang.
Open-file report, 1975. 170 p, 2 fig, 1 tab.

Descriptors: *Peak discharge, *Small watersheds, *Montana, *Basic data collections, Hydrologic data, Floods, Discharge(Water).

A program to investigate the magnitude and frequency of floods from small drainage areas in Montana was begun July 1, 1955. A total of 191 stations were in operation at the end of the 1974 water year. This, the twentieth annual report, is primarily a tabulation, of water year, of the annual peak stage and discharge at each crest-stage gaging station. Also, activities and progress made during the 1974 water year are summarized. Substantial peak flows occurred during the 1974 water year, however, storm patterns varied greatly. West of the divide record high flows in January were caused by combined snowmelt and rain. Peak flows in mountain areas east of the divide during January were caused by snowmelt without contributions from rain. In the prairie area peak flows were mostly caused by isolated rainstorms during the summer and spring. Peak flow of record was equaled or exceeded at 12 sites. (Knapp-USGS)
W75-08516

DISCHARGE DATA AT WATER-QUALITY MONITORING STATIONS IN ARKANSAS,
Geological Survey, Little Rock, Ark.
For primary bibliographic entry see Field 7A.
W75-08519

DESIGN AND IMPLEMENTATION OF A HYDROLOGIC DATA PROCESSING SYSTEM IN BRAZIL, 1971-74,
Geological Survey, Reston, Va.
For primary bibliographic entry see Field 7A.
W75-08523

COMPUTER PROCESSING HYDROLOGIC DATA IN BRAZIL,
Geological Survey, Reston, Va.
For primary bibliographic entry see Field 7A.
W75-08524

HYDROLOGIC DATA PROCESSING SYSTEM FOR BRAZIL,
Geological Survey, Reston, Va.
For primary bibliographic entry see Field 7A.
W75-08525

THE IMPLEMENTATION OF A HYDROLOGIC DATA PROCESSING SYSTEM IN BRAZIL,
Geological Survey, Reston, Va.
For primary bibliographic entry see Field 7A.
W75-08526

MANAGEMENT STUDY OF SOME ASPECTS OF SISTEMA DE INFORMACOES HIDROLOGICAS,
Geological Survey, Reston, Va.
For primary bibliographic entry see Field 7A.
W75-08527

ENVIRONMENTAL GEOLOGY--AN AID TO GROWTH AND DEVELOPMENT IN LAUDERDALE, COLBERT AND FRANKLIN COUNTIES, ALABAMA,
Geological Survey of Alabama, University. Environmental Div.
P. H. Moser, and L. W. Hyde.
Atlas Series 6, 1974. 45 p, 25 fig, 1 tab, 63 ref, 72 photo.

Descriptors: *Environmental engineering, *Geology, Water resources, *Energy, *Mineralogy, *Alabama, Environmental effects, Community development, Topography, Industries, Engineering geology, Surface waters, Groundwater, Water utilization, Water quality.
Identifiers: Lauderdale County(Ala), Colbert County(Ala), Franklin County(Ala).

A pictorial and graphical presentation of Lauderdale, Colbert, and Franklin Counties in northwestern Alabama was presented in conjunction with an explanatory text and tabular data on the geology, water and mineral resources, engineering geology, and associated factors. These are to be used by planners and developers for implementing immediate and long-range plans for the effective and orderly development of the area. (Scott-ISWS)
W75-08718

MADAM I--A NUMERIC METHOD FOR DESIGN OF ADSORPTION SYSTEMS,
Michigan Univ., Ann Arbor. Dept. of Environmental and Water Resources Engineering.
For primary bibliographic entry see Field 5D.
W75-08726

OPTIMAL CAPACITIES OF WATER SUPPLY RESERVOIRS IN SERIES AND PARALLEL,
Wharton School of Finance and Commerce, Philadelphia, Pa. Dept. of Regional Science.
For primary bibliographic entry see Field 4A.
W75-08728

A TECHNIQUE FOR THE PREDICTION OF WATER DEMAND FROM PAST CONSUMPTION DATA,
Sheffield Univ. (England). Dept. of Control Engineering.
For primary bibliographic entry see Field 6D.
W75-08730

COMPUTER USE FOR RIVER REGULATION,
Corps of Engineers, Portland, Oreg. Reservoir Control Center.
For primary bibliographic entry see Field 4A.
W75-08776

BOUGUER GRAVITY ANOMALY MAP OF THE TEMECULA AREA, RIVERSIDE COUNTY, CALIFORNIA,
Geological Survey, Garden Grove, Calif.
W. R. Moyle, Jr., and D. J. Downing.
Santa Margarita-San Luis Rey Watershed Planning Agency Map, 1975. 1 sheet, 1 map, 1 tab, 6 ref.

Descriptors: *Groundwater resources, *Water wells, *Maps, *California, Pumping, Water yield, Sedimentology, Aquifer characteristics, Gravity, Depth, Well data, Contours.
Identifiers: *Temecula area(Calif), Anomaly, Bouguer anomaly.

A Bouguer gravity anomaly map of the Temecula, Calif., area shows the general shape of the sedimentary basin, which is nearly surrounded by basement complex. The deepest part of the sedimentary basin exceeds 4,000 feet, but well drillers' logs indicate that the most permeable sedimentary deposits probably do not exceed 1,250 feet in thickness. A groundwater barrier across Buck Mesa is located between test wells. The pump-test data show that a dramatic change in permeability occurs across this barrier. One well has a specific capacity of 0.4 gallon per minute per foot, indicative of the low permeability of the material on the northeast side of the barrier. The specific capacity of wells on the southwest side of the barrier ranges between 5.8 and 31 gpm per foot and indicates a higher permeability of the material on this side of the barrier compared to that on the northeast side. (Woodard-USGS)
W75-08831

QUALITY OF PUBLIC WATER SUPPLIES OF NEW YORK, MAY 1972-MAY 1973,
Geological Survey, Albany, N.Y.
For primary bibliographic entry see Field 5A.
W75-08832

WATER RESOURCES DATA FOR NEBRASKA, 1973: PART 2. WATER QUALITY RECORDS.
Geological Survey, Lincoln, Nebr.
For primary bibliographic entry see Field 5A.
W75-08833

INDEX TO MAPS TO FLOOD-PRONE AREAS IN INDIANA,
Geological Survey, Indianapolis, Ind.
W. G. Weist, Jr.
Available from the National Technical Information Service, Springfield, Va 22161 as PB-241 860, $3.75 in paper copy, $2.25 in microfiche. Water-Resources Investigations 48-74, March 1975. 27p.

Descriptors: *Floods, *Maps, *Indiana, Documentation, Information retrieval, Flood data, Flood frequency, Flood profiles.
Identifiers: *Flood-map index(Ind).

A listing of 487 flood maps for Indiana prepared by the U.S. Geological Survey through July 1974 is presented by county. The list provides information on the type of flooding depicted and the reliability of the delineation. The list was prepared from a computer file, and an available program allows retrieval of data by landline location, State and county, and Standard Metropolitan Statistical Area (SMSA). The file will be continuously updated. The landline location of a mapped flood area is referred to the standard Geological Survey quadrangle (nominally 7-1/2 or 15-minute quad) in which this area lies. The landline identification includes the mapping scale and latitude and longitude of the southeast corner of the quadrangle, as well as the quadrangle name. If the flood area lies in part of several quadrangles, the name, latitude-longitude, and scale of each quadrangle is listed in the computer file and in the index. The type of flood information available within the quadrangle area is described either by: the year in which the mapped area was flooded, 1937, for instance, or the frequency at which the delineated area is expected to be flooded, expressed as a recurrence interval in years (100-year, for example). (Woodard-USGS)
W75-08834

EVALUATION OF METHODS FOR ESTIMATING STREAM WATER QUALITY PARAMETERS IN A TRANSIENT MODEL FROM STOCHASTIC DATA,
Kansas State Univ., Manhattan. Dept. of Chemical Engineering.
For primary bibliographic entry see Field 5B.
W75-08849

8. ENGINEERING WORKS

8A. Structures

FLOOD ON BUFFALO CREEK FROM SAUNDERS TO MAN, WEST VIRGINIA,
Geological Survey, Reston, Va.
For primary bibliographic entry see Field 7C.
W75-08508

MODULAR EROSION CONTROL DEVICE,
H. Campbell.
US Patent No 3,875,750, 3 p, 9 fig, 8 ref; Official Gazette of the United States Patent Office, Vol 933, No 2, p 576, April 8, 1975.

Descriptors: *Patents, *Shore protection, *Erosion control, Deposition, Sedimentation, Bank protection, Diversion structures.
Identifiers: *Wave action.

A modular unit for marine use for preventing and reversing erosion of water from land subject to wave action is provided. The device has a central peak with at least one additional peak located forward (toward the water) and of a lower height. The peaks are separated by depressions or valleys and are directed toward the water. The forward faces of the peaks are sloped toward the rear and the devices are placed adjacent the shoreline. Under the action of the waves, even heavy waves, the sloped configuration directs and deflects the waves generally upward and over the devices while the rear parts and the peak and valley configuration traps the sand and other solid material carried by the waves as it retreats thus preventing the washing away of sand from the shoreline area and in fact trapping incoming sand and thereby not only preventing additional erosion but actually building up additional ground by virture of the trapped solid material. (Sinha-OEIS)
W75-08611

IRRIGATION CONTROL,
For primary bibliographic entry see Field 3F.
W75-08617

STORMWATER CONTROL KEY TO BAY POLLUTION SOLUTION.
For primary bibliographic entry see Field 5D.
W75-08671

HURRICANE SPURS SEWER RENOVATION.
For primary bibliographic entry see Field 5D.
W75-08672

SELF-CLEANING STORM OVERFLOW BASINS WITH MEANDER DUCT (SELBSTREINIGENDE REGENUBERLAUFBECKEN MIT SCHLANGENRINNE),
For primary bibliographic entry see Field 5D.
W75-08679

SAMPLE UNCERTAINTY IN FLOOD LEVEE DESIGN: BAYESIAN VERSUS NON-BAYESIAN METHODS,
Arizona Univ., Tucson. Dept. of Systems and Industrial Engineering; and Arizona Univ., Tucson. Hydrology and Water Resources Interdisciplinary Program.
L. Duckstein, I. Bogardi, F. Szidarovszky, and D. R. Davis.
Water Resources Bulletin, Vol 11, No 3, p 425-435, June 1975. 3 fig, 2 tab, 6 equ, 13 ref. 2 append.

Descriptors: *Flood control, *Levees, *Design, *Probability, *Hydraulic structures, *Hydrology, *Water resources, Safety factors, Cost-benefit analysis, Optimization, Sampling, Algorithms, Equations, Mathematical models, Systems analysis, *Risks.
Identifiers: *Economic analysis, *Bayesian methods, *Bayesian decision theory, Benefit-risk analysis.

Bayesian and non-Bayesian flood levee design methods that account for the uncertainty due to limited record length are compared using a case study. Flood protection is not a purely economic problem; however, the approach taken by the ASCE Task Force Committee (1973) is followed, whereby the vector character of flood damage is eliminated by assigning a dollar value to human life, suffering and inconvenience. The specific flood levee problem concerns determining the optimum design or redesign level of a levee which results from the trade-off between construction, maintenance, and operations costs, and expected flood losses, while explicity considering uncertainty. The first method, Bayesian decision theory (BDT), imbeds the uncertainty in the parameters of the yearly peak stage into a loss function. The optimum design of the flood levee, called Bayes design, corresponds to the minimum expected loss, called Bayes risk. The second method, induced safety algorithm (ISA), computes a margin of safety to be added to either an existing levee or a levee designed by classical benefit-cost analysis. The design decision is shown to fluctuate as different record lengths are considered. For short record lengths, BDT, which takes small sample bias into account, appears to yield a more conservative design than ISA. On the other hand, ISA, which is simple to implement, seems to be preferable to BDT for longer record lengths. (Bell-Cornell)
W75-08724

HYDRAULIC ENGINEERING AND THE ENVIRONMENT.
For primary bibliographic entry see Field 8B.
W75-08786

REHABILITATION OF A CHANNELIZED RIVER IN UTAH,
Brigham Young Univ., Provo, Utah. Dept. of Civil Engineering.
J. R. Barton, and P. V. Winger.
In: Hydraulic Engineering and the Environment; Proceedings of the 21st Annual Hydraulic Division Specialty Conference, Montana State University, Bozeman, August 15-17, 1973. American Society of Civil Engineers, New York, p 1-10, 1973. 8 fig, 19 ref.

Descriptors: *Channel improvement, *Rehabilitation, *Fish, Habitats, Check structures, Hydraulic structures, Gabions, Rocks, Channel flow, Water chemistry, Water temperature, Structures, Fish populations, Fish food organisms, Vegetation, Rivers, *Utah.

On a recent highway construction contract in Utah where the construction of Highway I-80 resulted in the channelization of several stretches of the Weber River, various types of instream rehabilitation structures were installed in the altered sections in an attempt to alleviate some of the detrimental effects of channelization. The influence of these structures on the hydrology and biology of the Weber River was evaluated. Six types of instream rehabilitation structures were installed in the altered sections of the river. Gabion deflectors (wire baskets filled with rocks) and check dams were placed in three sections and rock deflectors and check dams were placed in two sections. A concrete diversion dam used for irrigation purposes was placed in one section. Random rocks were installed in all sections. Water chemistry data were collected from water samples collected above and below the channelized areas. Macroinvertebrate (fish food) organisms were collected monthly. Fish population data were collected with use of electrofishing equipment. After a relatively short time, fish populations were the same in changed and unchanged areas. Fish food organisms colonized the channeled areas within a few months. The construction itself and the initially unstable substrate of the altered section caused a marked increase in erosion and turbidity but these were of relatively short duration and seemed to have little long term effect on the biology of the area. The water chemistry and water temperature were not altered by the channelization. (See also W75-08786) (Sims-ISWS)
W75-08787

SWIMMING PERFORMANCE OF ARCTIC GRAYLING,
Idaho Univ., Moscow. Dept. of Civil Engineering.
F. J. Watts, and C. MacPhee.
In: Hydraulic Engineering and the Environment; Proceedings of the 21st Annual Hydraulic Division Specialty Conference, Montana State University, Bozeman, August 15-17, 1973. American Society of Civil Engineers, New York, p 11-20, 1973. 3 fig, 1 tab.

Descriptors: *Culverts, *Fish migration, *Fish behavior, Hydraulic structures, Fish barriers, Fish passages, Fish populations, Anadromous fish, Structures, Habitats, *Alaska, *Design criteria.
Identifiers: *Arctic Grayling.

Design criteria were established for culverts which will insure the maintenance of fish populations in streams traversed by the proposed Alaska Pipe Line and its supporting highway. Poorly designed culverts can block or impede fish movement upstream. A diversion dam, a headgate and approach conduit, and a tiltable 24-inch diameter culvert and associated head box and tail box were constructed on Poplar Grove Creek in south central Alaska. The general procedure used for the culvert part of the study was to block the upstream migration of fish with the dam, seine or trap the fish in the creek, place the fish in the tail box below the culvert, record the number of successes or failures per size group for a holding period of not longer than one day for a particular slope and flow condition, then collect all fish and release them in the stream above the facility. Only preliminary data were reported, along with a general discussion of design considerations which would allow free passage of fish. (See also W75-08786) (Sims-ISWS)
W75-08788

GENERAL CONSIDERATIONS OF FLOW IN BRANCHING CONDUITS,
Bureau of Reclamation, Denver, Colo.
For primary bibliographic entry see Field 8B.
W75-08805

COMBINING FLOW IN BRANCHES AND WYES,
Beck (R. W.) and Associates, Seattle, Wash.
For primary bibliographic entry see Field 8B.
W75-08806

FLOW THROUGH TRIFURCATIONS AND MANIFOLDS,
British Columbia Univ., Vancouver. Dept. of Civil Engineering.
For primary bibliographic entry see Field 8B.
W75-08807

OVERFLOW SPILLWAY ENERGY DISSIPATION BY JET ASSISTED HYDRAULIC JUMP,
Kentucky Univ., Lexington. Dept. of Civil Engineering.
For primary bibliographic entry see Field 8B.
W75-08817

8B. Hydraulics

THE ESTIMATION OF (RHO) IN THE FIRST-ORDER AUTOREGRESSIVE MODEL: A BAYESIAN APPROACH,
Massachusetts Inst. of Tech., Cambridge. Dept. of Civil Engineering.
For primary bibliographic entry see Field 2A.
W75-08387

ANALYSIS OF RESISTANCE OVER STAGGERED ROUGHNESS,
Colorado State Univ., Fort Collins. Dept. of Civil Engineering.
H. W. Shen, and R.-M. Li.
ASCE Proceedings, Journal of the Hydraulics Division, Vol 99, No HY11, p 2169-2174, November 1973. 3 fig, 2 tab, 5 ref. OWRR B-014-COLO(8), Grant 14-01-0001-1435.

Descriptors: *Roughness(Hydraulic), Regression analysis, Chezy equation, *Roughness coefficient, Open channel flow.

A general relationship satisfactorily predicts the resistance factor for a given combination of flow and roughness properties. The only pattern considered in this study is the staggered pattern. (Knapp-USGS)
W75-08394

A SCHEMATIZATION OF ONSHORE-OFFSHORE TRANSPORT,
Waterloopkundig Laboratorium, Delft (Netherlands).
For primary bibliographic entry see Field 2L.
W75-08401

EQUILIBRIUM PROFILES OF COARSE MATERIAL UNDER WAVE ATTACK,
Waterloopkundig Laboratorium, Delft (Netherlands).
For primary bibliographic entry see Field 2L.
W75-08402

HEAT TRANSFER AND FLUID MECHANICS OF THE THERMAL POLLUTION PROBLEM,
Virginia Polytechnic Inst. and State Univ., Blacksburg. Dept. of Aerospace and Ocean Engineering.
For primary bibliographic entry see Field 5B.
W75-08599

REDUCING FLUID FRICTION WITH OKRA,
Clemson Univ., S.C.
For primary bibliographic entry see Field 8G.
W75-08605

NUMERICAL ANALYSIS OF WARM, TURBULENT SINKING JETS DISCHARGED INTO QUIESCENT WATER OF LOW TEMPERATURE,
Iowa Univ., Iowa City. Inst. of Hydraulic Research.
For primary bibliographic entry see Field 5B.
W75-08684

CAVITATION DAMAGE SCALE EFFECTS--STATE OF ART SUMMARIZATION.
International Association for Hydraulic Research, Delft (Netherlands). Section for Hydraulic Machinery, Equipment and Cavitation.
Journal of Hydraulic Research, Vol 13, No 1, p 1-17, 1975. 50 ref.

Descriptors: *Cavitation, *Velocity, *Pressure, *Fluid mechanics, *Powerplants, Laboratory tests, Vapor pressure, Damages, Temperature, Surface tension, Flow, Hydraulics, *Reviews, Erosion, *Scaling.
Identifiers: *Scale effects, Cavitation index, Suppression pressure.

A state-of-the-art review of cavitation damage scale effects was made. The only general conclusion that could be drawn was that damage rate increases very strongly in most cases with increased velocity, pressure, or size when sigma is maintained constant. Damage rates in general are more sensitive to these parameters than to any others. The velocity damage exponent usually lies in the range 4-6, and the diameter exponent in the range 3-4. Considerable further systematic experimentation is required before these effects can be evaluated more precisely. Uncertainty in erosion scale effects is also due to the lack of any universally accepted criteria in the measure of damage parameters. Only damage intensities from rather identical eroding environments can really be compared at this time. (Singh-ISWS)
W75-08698

NONEQUILIBRIUM RIVER FORM,
Colorado State Univ., Fort Collins. Dept. of Civil Engineering.
For primary bibliographic entry see Field 2J.
W75-08700

A TWO LAYER FLOW THROUGH A CONTRACTION,
New South Wales Univ., Kensington (Australia). Water Research Lab.
K. K. Lai, and I. R. Wood.
Journal of Hydraulic Research, Vol 13, No 1, p 19-33, 1975. 5 fig, 8 ref.

Descriptors: *Density stratification, *Flow, *Withdrawal, *Pressure, Reservoirs, Flow control, Energy equation, Analytical techniques, Discharge(Water), Interfaces, Numerical analysis, Froude number, Hydraulics.
Identifiers: *Two-layer flow, Selective withdrawal, Stationary layers, Flow contractions.

The withdrawal from a reservoir of two layers through separate valves which are downstream of a contraction was described. The fluid was considered as inviscid and the flow gradually varied. The variations of flow profiles obtained were shown and the limitation that the contraction places on the total discharge and on the ratio of discharge from each layer was discussed. The total withdrawal rate for a given discharge ratio was limited and some particular discharge ratios were not attainable. The flow profile for the possible cases showed considerable variety. (Singh-ISWS)
W75-08701

THE EFFECT OF ROUGHNESS STRIPS OF TRANSVERSE MIXING IN HYDRAULIC MODELS,
California Univ., Berkeley. Dept. of Civil Engineering.
H. B. Fischer, and T. Hanamura.
Water Resources Research, Vol 11, No 2, p 362-364, April 1975. 2 fig, 1 tab, 3 ref. NSF Grant GI-34932.

Descriptors: *Mixing, *Roughness(Hydraulic), *Prototypes, *Laboratory tests, *Turbulence, Flumes, Shear stress, Velocity, *Hydraulic models, Rhodamine, Open channel flow, Analysis, Model studies.
Identifiers: *Transverse mixing coefficient.

Most physical models are constructed with distorted scales, or different horizontal and vertical scales. For open channel flows in the prototype, the shear stress is primarily from the bottom. In distorted models, however, the resistance to flow is provided mainly by vertical strips because the bottom resistance is not sufficient to counteract the distorted slope. An experiment in a laboratory flume was conducted to measure the rate of transverse mixing in a flow with frictional resistance caused by strips. The transverse mixing coefficient was found to depend on the strip arrangement, the width of the strip, and the flow velocity. Agreement of transverse mixing between model and prototype is possible through a proper combination of strip widths and velocities, but such agreement needs to be investigated in each case. (Singh-ISWS)
W75-08708

SEEPAGE THROUGH OPENING IN CUTOFF WALL UNDER WEIR,
Bengal Engineering Coll., Howrah (India). Dept. of Civil Engineering.
For primary bibliographic entry see Field 8D.
W75-08711

CHANNELIZATION: A SEARCH FOR A BETTER WAY,
North Carolina Univ., Charlotte. Dept. of Geography and Earth Sciences.
E. A. Keller.
Geology, Vol 3, No 5, p 246-248, May 1975. 3 fig, 16 ref.

Descriptors: *Channel improvement, *Beds, *Depth, Stream improvement, Channels, Channeling, Shape, Alluvial channels, Slopes, Width, Thalweg, Channel morphology, Erosion, Sedimentation, Flow, Riprap, Design criteria.
Identifiers: *Riffles, Channelization.

A reproduction of channel forms produced by natural fluvial processes will minimize some adverse effects of channelization. Design criteria intended to improve drainage or control flooding should, in many cases, include the construction of pools (deeps) and riffles (shallows). An optimal spacing of pools and riffles, averaging about six times the channel width, will improve the modified stream by providing a channel morphology that is relatively stable, biologically productive, and aesthetically pleasing. (Sims-ISWS)
W75-08714

AN APPROXIMATE INFINITE CONDUCTIVITY SOLUTION FOR A PARTIALLY PENETRATING LINE-SOURCE WELL,
Bureau de Recherches Geologiques et Minieres, Orleans (France).
For primary bibliographic entry see Field 4B.
W75-08715

THE CIVIL ENGINEER AND FIELD DRAINAGE,
Ministry of Agriculture, Fisheries and Food. Lincoln (England).
For primary bibliographic entry see Field 4A.
W75-08731

METHOD OF RECOVERING GEOTHERMAL ENERGY,
Mobil Oil Corp., New York. (assignee)
For primary bibliographic entry see Field 4B.
W75-08736

FLOATING BREAKWATER,
Bridgestone Tire Co. Ltd., Tokyo (Japan). (assignee)
S. Tazaki, and Y. Ishida.
U.S. Patent No. 3,864,920, 4 p, 16 fig, 6 ref; Official Gazette of the United States Patent Office, Vol 931, No 2, p 558, February 11, 1975.

Descriptors: *Patents, *Breakwaters, *Shore protection, Specific gravity, Floating.
Identifiers: *Floating breakwaters, *Wave action, Synthetic resin foam.

A floating breakwater assembly is comprised of a number of substantially equally dimensioned, elongated, floating bodies each comprising a rigid hollow upper shell and a rigid hollow lower shell bonded together. Each upper shell projects upward and out of the water along its entire length to a height of at least one half of the average height of waves to be broken. Floatation material is contained within each hollow upper shell and ballast material is contained within each hollow lower shell in order to submerge them. Spaced elongated, rigid cylindrical members extend transversely of and between the floating bodies for bonding them together in a spaced assembly. Means are provided for mooring the assembly to the sea bottom so that the floating bodies are generally perpendicular to the direction of movement of the waves. The specific gravity of the overall assembly is from 0.15 to 0.75. (Sinha-OEIS)
W75-08746

PITLESS WATER SYSTEM,
T. B. Clark.
U.S. Patent No. 3,865,513, 4 p, 4 fig, 7 ref; Official Gazette of the United States Patent Office, Vol 931, No 2, p 756, February 11, 1975.

Descriptors: *Patents, *Water supply, *Water wells, Frost, Groundwater, Casings, Pumps, Valves.
Identifiers: *Well casings, Submersible pumps, Constant pressure valve units.

A hidden water system has an open-ended nonpressurized shell buried in the ground with only the removable top above ground. The bottom portion is below the frost line and connected to a casting which in turn is connected to a well casing. A constant pressure valve unit is mounted in the bottom portion of the shell in fluid communication with a submersible pump in the well casing and also in fluid communication with a demand pipe through a spool-type adapter mounted within the casting, and with pump and valve controls at the top of the shell for controlling operation of the valve and the pump. (Sinha-OEIS)
W75-08750

FLOATING BREAKWATER SYSTEM,
Reid, Middleton and Associates, Inc., Edmonds, Wash. (Assignee).
J. O. Olsen.
U S Patent No 3,877,233, 5 p, 6 fig, 7 ref; Official Gazette of the United States Patent Office, Vol 933, No 3, p 1072, April 15, 1975.

Descriptors: *Patents, *Breakwaters, *Shore protection, Erosion, Equipment, Marinas, Pontoons.
Identifiers: *Wave action.

A floating breakwater array to dissipate wave action in a body of water comprises a plurality of individual similarly shaped pontoon modules secured and held in the array by a network of structural members to collectively form a grid pattern of vertical walls and openings. The grid pattern has a plurality of regularly spaced openings in mutually transverse first and second horizontal directions of the array. Anchoring means connected to the array secure it in a desired position in the body of water. The vertical walls and openings extend into the upper portion of the wave to interfere with the movement of fluid in the orbital flow under the wave crest. The pontoon modules each comprise vertical walls which form a generally rectangular central portion having oppositely disposed protuberant end sections. The vertical walls also form at least one protuberant side section which is located between the protuberant end sections and which extend laterally away from the central portion. (Sinha-OEIS)
W75-08756

HYDRAULIC ENGINEERING AND THE ENVIRONMENT.
Proceedings of the 21st Annual Hydraulics Division Specialty Conference, Montana State University, Bozeman, August 15-17, 1973. American Society of Civil Engineers, New York. 1973. 466 p.

Descriptors: *Conferences, *Hydraulic engineering, *Environment, *Environmental effects, Hydraulic structures, Fish, Channel flow, Flow characteristics, Sedimentation, Sediment transport, Management, Flood plains, Reservoirs, Waves(Water), Streamflow, Flood peak, Water quality, Surface waters, Groundwater, Cooling water, Hydraulics, Aeration, Water temperature, Watersheds(Basins), Disasters.
Identifiers: Branching conduits, Urban environment.

The conference aim was to develop an awareness of the effects of new hydraulic information on the environment. The twelve broad subject areas discussed were channel flow requirements for fish, sedimentation related flow characteristics, environmental impact of flood plain management and reservoirs, flow and wave hydromechanics, stream temperature and cooling water research, branching conduits, surface water environmental factors, determination of sediment loads, water quality and hydraulics, predicting flood peaks and volumes, groundwater and the urban environment, and the June 1972 Rapid City flood disaster. (See W75-08787 thru W75-08824) (Humphreys-ISWS)
W75-08786

REHABILITATION OF A CHANNELIZED RIVER IN UTAH,
Brigham Young Univ., Provo, Utah. Dept. of Civil Engineering.
For primary bibliographic entry see Field 8A.
W75-08787

SWIMMING PERFORMANCE OF ARCTIC GRAYLING,
Idaho Univ., Moscow. Dept. of Civil Engineering.
For primary bibliographic entry see Field 8A.
W75-08788

HYDRAULICS OF A GRAVEL CORE FISH SCREEN,
Washington Univ., Seattle. Dept. of Civil Engineering.
For primary bibliographic entry see Field 8I.
W75-08790

MEASUREMENT OF INSTANTANEOUS BOUNDARY SHEAR STRESS,
Agricultural Research Service, Fort Collins, Colo.
For primary bibliographic entry see Field 8G.
W75-08791

WALL SHEAR STRESS MEASUREMENTS WITH HOT-FILM SENSORS,
Lehigh Univ., Bethlehem, Pa. Fritz Engineering Lab.
For primary bibliographic entry see Field 8G.
W75-08792

ANALYSIS OF FLOW IN CHANNELS WITH GRAVEL BEDS,
Washington State Univ., Pullman. Dept. of Civil Engineering.
J. A. Roberson, and S. J. Wright.
In: Hydraulic Engineering and the Environment; Proceedings of the 21st Annual Hydraulic Division Specialty Conference, Montana State University, Bozeman, August 15-17, 1973. American Society of Civil Engineers, New York, p 63-72, 1973. 2 fig, 1 tab, 13 ref, 2 append.

Descriptors: *Channel flow, *Roughness(Hydraulic), *Mathematical models, *Flow resistance, Channels, Beds, Gravels, Drag, Shear stress, Boundaries(Surfaces), Velocity, Model studies.

The problem of predicting the resistance of flow in channels with rough surfaces has faced practicing engineers for many years. The common solution to this problem has been to perform experimental tests which model the actual flow situation. A mathematical model previously used to predict the resistance to flow in conduits with a low concentration of roughness was modified to consider completely roughened boundaries. The resistance to flow in streams with a natural type of roughness can be adequately predicted. The larger roughness elements contribute a relatively greater proportion of resistance; therefore, when using this method for modeling other types of roughness, more attention should be directed to the characteristics of the largest elements. (See also W75-08786) (Sims-ISWS)
W75-08793

DISCHARGE, SLOPE, BED ELEMENT RELATIONS IN STREAMS,
Sargent and Lundy, Chicago, Ill.
For primary bibliographic entry see Field 2E.
W75-08794

FLOOD PLAIN MANAGEMENT IN MONTANA,
Montana Dept. of Natural Resources and Conservation, Helena. Floodway Management Bureau.
For primary bibliographic entry see Field 6F.
W75-08795

ENVIRONMENTAL IMPACTS OF RESERVOIRS--A CASE STUDY,
Stanford Univ., Calif. Dept. of Civil Engineering.

The relative ease of preparing wave refraction diagrams with digital computer and automatic plotting routines allows their convenient application to a wide variety of engineering and geologic problems of the coastline. Two examples of such applications to New England coastal problems were discussed. For these problems, the wave refraction diagrams corresponding to many possible wave conditions were the primary analytical tool, with computations of various wave parameters along the shore being used for more detailed estimates of coastal process activity. The limitations and benefits of such analyses were emphasized. Substantiation of conclusions drawn from theoretical wave refraction studies obtained through field observations. (See also W75-08786) (Sims-ISWS)
W75-08800

CAVITATION CHARACTERISTICS OF 18-INCH BUTTERFLY VALVE,
For primary bibliographic entry see Field 8C.
W75-08801

WAVE FORCES ON CYLINDERS NEAR A PLANE BOUNDARY,
Oregon State Univ., Corvallis. Dept. of Civil Engineering.
T. Yamamoto, J. H. Nath, and L. S. Slotta.
In: Hydraulic Engineering and the Environment; Proceedings of the 21st Annual Hydraulic Division Specialty Conference, Montana State University, Bozeman, August 15-17, 1973. American Society of Civil Engineers, New York, p 155-165, 1973. 7 fig, 8 ref. NOAA Contract 2-35187.

Descriptors: *Waves(Water), *Loads(Forces), *Drag, *Boundaries(Surfaces), Pipelines, Laboratory tests, Hydraulic models, Hydraulics, Oceanography.
Identifiers: *Wave forces, *Cylinders, Lift forces, Horizontal forces, Acceleration, Underwater pipes.

Only rigid cylinders subjected to flow which is perpendicular to the central axis were considered. In addition, the cylinders were circular and horizontal at a varying distance from a horizontal plane boundary and at a relatively large distance from the free water surface. Experimentally, the cylinders were subjected to waves and the total horizontal and vertical forces were measured. Theoretically, the steady flow was considered as well as the unsteady flow characterized by surface waves. Acceleration and velocity dependent forces can be considered separately, and then superimposed for determining wave forces on horizontal cylinders with good results for engineering purposes, provided the proper coefficient values are used. The coefficients can be properly evaluated from potential flow theory if the drag forces and vortex forces are negligible with respect to the added mass effects and the circulation lift forces. Experimental results with waves agreed fairly well with the theory that the horizontal and vertical acceleration forces are equal for a cylinder close to a plane boundary. The convective acceleration should not be neglected in some cases when determining the horizontal force due to fluid acceleration. For one case investigated it was equal to 30% of the total acting horizontal acceleration force. Lift forces on horizontal cylinders from circulation can be accurately estimated for waves. (See also W75-08786) (Sims-ISWS)
W75-08802

DESIGN OF COOLING TOWER RETURN CHANNEL FOR TVA'S BROWNS FERRY NUCLEAR PLANT,
Tennessee Valley Authority, Norris. Engineering Lab.
For primary bibliographic entry see Field 5D.
W75-08803

TRANSIENT COOLING POND BEHAVIOR,
Oak Ridge National Lab., Tenn.
For primary bibliographic entry see Field 5D.
W75-08804

GENERAL CONSIDERATIONS OF FLOW IN BRANCHING CONDUITS,
Bureau of Reclamation, Denver, Colo.
T. J. Rhone.
In: Hydraulic Engineering and the Environment; Proceedings of the 21st Annual Hydraulic Division Specialty Conference, Montana State University, Bozeman, August 15-17, 1973. American Society of Civil Engineers, New York, p 205-214, 1973. 3 fig, 7 ref, 1 append.

Descriptors: *Conduits, *Flow, *Pipe flow, *Flow characteristics, Fluid mechanics, Hydraulics, Head loss, Cavitation, Pipes, Hydraulic models, *Reviews.
Identifiers: *Branching conduits, Dividing flow, Combining flow, Wyes, Manifolds, Branch spacing, Flow disturbance.

A review of the literature shows that the configurations of branches and manifolds used to combine or divide flows are many and diverse. The terminology and definitions used in describing the structure and the flow phenomena are equally varied and the attempts of experimenters to generalize on design criteria show complex the problem is. One thesis that was repeated over and over was that the published information is adequate for preliminary designs but model investigations are essential to assure a satisfactorily operating structure. Well documented information on prototype operation is almost nonexistent and every attempt should be made to further the knowledge in this field. It was hoped that the work of the Task Committee on Branching Conduits of the ASCE will be of some aid in reducing the confusion in nomenclature and definition as well as providing some consistency in presenting the previously published experimental data. Recommended head loss coefficients curves developed from an analysis of this data should be of significant assistance to the practicing design engineer. (See also W75-08786) (Sims-ISWS)
W75-08805

COMBINING FLOW IN BRANCHES AND WYES,
Beck (R. W.) and Associates, Seattle, Wash.
J. V. Williamson.
In: Hydraulic Engineering and the Environment; Proceedings of the 21st Annual Hydraulic Division Specialty Conference, Montana State University, Bozeman, August 15-17, 1973. American Society of Civil Engineers, New York p 215-226, 1973. 7 fig, 11 ref, 2 append.

Descriptors: *Conduits, Flow, *Pipe flow, *Flow characteristics, Fluid mechanics, Hydraulics, Head loss, Pipes, Hydraulic models.
Identifiers: *Branching conduits, *Wyes, Combining flow, Conical junctions, Cylindrical junctions.

A progress report on the activities of the Task Committee on Branching Conduits was presented. It gave the results of investigations on the subject of head losses for combining flow with special reference to large hydraulic conduits. In general, circular conduits were analyzed. Results of experiments were plotted and compared on the same basis for the various conditions of branch junction geometry. Based on these comparisons, recommended values for head loss coefficients were developed and were included as illustrations. (See also W75-08786) (Sims-ISWS)
W75-08806

FLOW THROUGH TRIFURCATIONS AND MANIFOLDS,
British Columbia Univ., Vancouver. Dept. of Civil Engineering.
E. Ruus.

In: Hydraulic Engineering and the Environment; Proceedings of the 21st Annual Hydraulic Division Specialty Conference, Montana State University, Bozeman, August 15-17, 1973. American Society of Civil Engineers, New York, p 227-239, 1973. 4 fig, 11 ref, 2 append.

Descriptors: *Conduits, *Flow, *Pipe flow, Flow characteristics, Fluid mechanics, Head loss, Pipes, Hydraulics, Fluid friction, Friction.
Identifiers: *Branching conduits, *Trifurcations, *Manifolds, Combining flow, Dividing flow.

The total head losses in a piping system are generally considered to consist of losses due to pipe wall friction and those due to local changes in flow pattern. The local or form losses caused by the local flow pattern changes in trifurcations and manifolds were considered. The term form loss includes the head loss measured across the branching configuration (trifurcation or manifold) and the additional losses occurring over a distance up to 30 diameters in the branches downstream. These additional losses are caused by the junction and appear as an increase in regular losses due to branch wall friction. Many investigations were reviewed. The state of art presented and the conclusions drawn were based primarily on the results of those applicable for large diameter installations, at which the total form loss includes the additional losses in branches, but excludes losses due to wall friction. (See also W75-08786) (Sims-ISWS)
W75-08807

REGULATION OF LOW STREAMFLOWS,
Environmental Protection Agency, Cincinnati, Ohio.
For primary bibliographic entry see Field 4A.
W75-08808

RESERVOIR OPERATION USING SNOW SURVEY DATA,
Soil Conservation Service, Bozeman, Mont.
For primary bibliographic entry see Field 4A.
W75-08809

PHYSICAL AND BIOLOGICAL REHABILITATION OF A STREAM,
Montana State Univ., Bozeman. Dept. of Fisheries.
For primary bibliographic entry see Field 4A.
W75-08810

DEVELOPMENT OF A WATER PLANNING MODEL FOR MONTANA,
Montana State Univ., Bozeman. Dept. of Industrial Engineering and Computer Science.
For primary bibliographic entry see Field 6A.
W75-08811

SEDIMENT TRANSPORT SYSTEM IN A GRAVEL-BOTTOMED STREAM,
Washington State Dept. of Ecology, Olympia.
For primary bibliographic entry see Field 2J.
W75-08812

CLARKS FORK YELLOWSTONE RIVER REMOTE SENSING STUDY,
Colorado State Univ., Fort Collins. Dept. of Civil Engineering.
For primary bibliographic entry see Field 2J.
W75-08813

WATER POLLUTION CONTROL BY HYDRAULIC AERATION,
Toronto Univ. (Ontario). Dept. of Mechanical Engineering.
For primary bibliographic entry see Field 5G.
W75-08814

CHARACTERISTICS OF AN AIR-WATER MIXTURE IN A VERTICAL SHAFT,
Georgia Inst. of Tech., Atlanta. Dept. of Civil Engineering.
C. S. Martin.
In: Hydraulic Engineering and the Environment; Proceedings of the 21st Annual Hydraulic Division Specialty Conference, Montana State University, Bozeman, August 15-17, 1973. American Society of Civil Engineers, New York, p 323-334, 1973. 4 fig, 13 ref.

Descriptors: *Aeration, *Bubbles, *Flow, Pipes, Froude number, Laboratory tests, Hydraulics, Piezometers, Instrumentation, Hydraulic models, Pipe flow, Hydraulic structures, Sewers.
Identifiers: *Air-water mixtures, *Vertical shafts, Bubbly flow, Slug flow, Transport concentration.

In addition to the need for the understanding of flow in a vertical shaft spillway, recently built and futuristically planned engineering projects that entail the dropping of storm water down vertical shafts of great height necessitate the study of the flow processes in greater detail. Slug-flow conditions are of special concern because of the attendant problem of vibration as well as possible blowout or blowback of huge air pockets. A test apparatus included a 140 mm ID Plexiglass test pipe. This vertically mounted pipe was 8.01 m long and had a well-streamlined entrance at the top. Piezometers were mounted at frequent intervals along the pipe. Provisions were made to control the flow and to provide air to the water flow either by natural entrainment, or by forced aeration under pressure. Transition from bubbly flow to slug flow in a vertically downward air-water mixture was found to occur if the flowing volumetric concentration was greater than 0.235. The difference in entrance conditions between the cases of natural aeration and forced aeration had no apparent effect on transition. The slugs can be quite irregular in shape, possessing a tendency to ride the wall of the conduit. (See also W75-08786) (Sims-ISWS)
W75-08815

MODELING WIND INDUCED WATER CURRENTS,
Worcester Polytechnic Inst., Mass. Alden Research Labs.
For primary bibliographic entry see Field 5B.
W75-08816

OVERFLOW SPILLWAY ENERGY DISSIPATION BY JET ASSISTED HYDRAULIC JUMP,
Kentucky Univ., Lexington. Dept. of Civil Engineering.
T-Y, Kao, and D. L. Shoemaker.
In: Hydraulic Engineering and the Environment; Proceedings of the 21st Annual Hydraulic Division Specialty Conference, Montana State University, Bozeman, August 15-17, 1973. American Society of Civil Engineers, New York, p 349-358, 1973. 4 fig, 5 ref, 1 append.

Descriptors: *Spillways, *Hydraulic jump, *Energy dissipation, Supercritical flow, Model studies, Hydraulic models, Jets, Structures, Hydraulic structures, Dams, Discharge(Water), Hydraulics.

High overflow spillways produce a water jet at the toe which contains a tremendous amount of kinetic energy due to the high velocity supercritical flow. Unless the energy contained in this flow is effectively dissipated before the flow enters the natural stream bed, severe erosion and, possibly, undermining of the structure will result. The most common energy dissipation methods are those which employ the hydraulic jump. To help stabilize the jump, various devices which create internal friction and turbulence are usually used. A new approach to control of the hydraulic jump is by using a submerged cross jet. The principles involved in the application of a submerged water jet to control the hydraulic jump are similar to those of chute blocks, end sills, and baffle piers. The water jet acts as a chute block to divert the high velocity bottom flow upward. In this study, a three foot high overflow spillway was used as the control structure which provides the supercritical flow and maintains the operating head for the siphon jet. The results indicated that, for this particular model, at higher Froude number range the siphon-jet system requires smaller tailwater depth compared to that required by all other types of hydraulic jump control arrangement. On the other hand, at the lower Froude number region, the cross jet does not appear to be as effective as the solid control appurtenances. The comparison of the energy dissipation characteristics of the jet system to stilling basins revealed approximately the same general trend. For the most part, the jet controlled jump has higher efficiency than that provided by the Bureau of Reclamation type II stilling basin. (See also W75-08786) (Sims-ISWS)
W75-08817

WINTER STORM AND FLOOD ANALYSES, NORTHWEST INTERIOR,
Agricultural Research Service, Boise, Idaho. Northwest Watershed Research Center.
For primary bibliographic entry see Field 2E.
W75-08818

CALIBRATION OF WATERSHED WETNESS AND PREDICTION OF FLOOD VOLUME FROM SMALL WATERSHEDS IN HUMID REGION,
Pennsylvania Dept. of Environmental Resources, Harrisburg.
For primary bibliographic entry see Field 2A.
W75-08819

PREDICTING LOW FLOWS AND FLOODS FROM UNGAGED DRAINAGE BASINS,
Washington State Univ., Pullman. Dept. of Civil Engineering.
For primary bibliographic entry see Field 4A.
W75-08820

ESTIMATION FLOODS SMALL DRAINAGE AREAS IN MONTANA,
Montana State Univ., Bozeman. Dept. of Civil Engineering and Engineering Mechanics.
For primary bibliographic entry see Field 4A.
W75-08821

ARTIFICIAL RECHARGE IN THE URBAN ENVIRONMENT--SOME QUESTIONS AND ANSWERS,
California Univ., Davis. Dept. of Water Science and Engineering.
For primary bibliographic entry see Field 4B.
W75-08822

POLLUTION POTENTIAL OF A SANITARY LANDFILL NEAR TUCSON,
Arizona Water Resources Research Center, Tucson.
For primary bibliographic entry see Field 5B.
W75-08823

METEOROLOGY AND HYDROLOGY OF RAPID CITY FLOOD,
Corps of Engineers, Omaha, Nebr. Hydrology and Meteorology Section.
For primary bibliographic entry see Field 2E.
W75-08824

EVALUATION AND IMPLEMENTATION OF URBAN DRAINAGE PROJECTS,
Colorado State Univ., Fort Collins. Dept. of Civil Engineering.
For primary bibliographic entry see Field 4A.
W75-08847

8C. Hydraulic Machinery

STEAM, HOT-WATER AND ELECTRICAL THERMAL DRILLS FOR TEMPERATE GLACIERS,
Centre National de la Recherche Scientifique, Grenoble (France). Laboratoire de Glaciologie.
For primary bibliographic entry see Field 2C.
W75-08409

SALVAGE OF HEAVY CONSTRUCTION EQUIPMENT BY A FLOATING ICE BRIDGE,
Foundation of Canada Engineering Corp. Ltd., Calgary (Alberta). Arctic Div.
For primary bibliographic entry see Field 8G.
W75-08461

MECHANICAL HARVESTING OF AQUATIC VEGETATION: DEVELOPMENT OF A HIGH SPEED PICKUP UNIT,
Wisconsin Univ., Madison. Dept. of Mechanical Engineering.
For primary bibliographic entry see Field 4A.
W75-08471

AUTOMATION OF FILTERS IN PURIFYING DEVICES IN WATER PIPES (AVTOMATIZATSIYA FIL'TROV NA VODOPROVODNYKH OCHISTNYKH SOORUZHENIYAKH),
For primary bibliographic entry see Field 5F.
W75-08572

NEW DIAPHRAGM PUMP UTILIZES OLD PRINCIPLE,
Chemical Processing, Vol 20, No 9, p 44, September, 1974. 1 fig.

Descriptors: *Pumps, *Venturi, Pressure, Valves, Liquids, Operation, Equipment, Liquids, Corrosion.
Identifiers: *Diaphragm pumps.

A new air pressure, diaphragm-operated pump has been designed to handle a wide range of liquids. Its operating principle is the adaptation of the venturi effect to create low pressure and actuate the suction cycle; it may be driven by compressed air, either from mains supply or from a portable compressor. The pump operation is the same as conventional diaphragm pumps but its new feature centers around the control of the cycle of pressurization and evacuation. Air supply and exhaust are controlled by a poppet valve, moved between two end positions by a control rod attached to the diaphragm membrane. The diaphragm is flexible and the pressure of the liquid in the pumping compartment is the same as that in the air compartment throughout the operation of the pump. The applications of this pump range from handling viscous liquids to dealing with various corrosive fluids. (Prague-FIRL)
W75-08673

PUMPS FOR POLLUTION CONTROL,
For primary bibliographic entry see Field 5D.
W75-08674

METHOD FOR CONSTRUCTING ICE ISLANDS IN COLD REGIONS,
Union Oil Co. of California, Los Angeles. (assignee)
P. J. Durning.
U.S. Patent No. 3,863,456, 4 p, 3 fig, 4 ref; Official Gazette of the United States Patent Office, Vol 931, No 1, p 73, February 4, 1974.

Descriptors: *Patents, *Cold regions, Offshore platforms, Drilling, Ice.
Identifiers: Artificial islands, *Ice islands.

This invention relates to the construction of ice islands, and more particularly to a method for forming artificial ice island in cold regions to serve as a base for operations. Construction of the ice island is commenced by depositing water directly onto the surface of the ice sheet at the desired location. Sea water can be used to form the ice island, however, fresh water is preferred, if available, since fresh water forms higher strength ice upon freezing. Water is placed upon the ice sheet either by flooding or by spraying. The water is discharged onto the surface of the natural ice at the center of the portion to be thickened in an oval or circular pattern having its thickest portion at the middle and tapering outwardly to the edges. The application of water is continued until the mass of the ice body is such that its draft is greater than the depth of the water body so that the ice body becomes grounded and anchored in place. Flooding is continued until the mass of ice island is sufficient to securely anchor the island to the marine bottom and to obtain an elevated working platform. (Sinha-OEIS)
W75-08734

MARINE WATER INLET DEVICE MEANS,
P. M. Banner.
U.S. Patent No. 3,864,260, 4 p, 11 fig, 1 ref; Official Gazette of the United States Patent Office, Vol 931, No 1, p 331, February 4, 1975.

Descriptors: *Patents, *Boats, *Water supply, Pipes, Pipe flow.
Identifiers: Inlet pipes, *Pipe cleaning devices.

A water inlet cleaning device for marine craft and fluid supply systems is disclosed that will clean out the inlet pipe and inlet fitting from foreign matter allowing liquid to flow. The device can operate manually or automatically, having a signal responsive means to indicate a clogging condition and the subsequent operation of the device. (Sinha-OEIS)
W75-08743

DIFFUSED AERATION PIPE APPARATUS FOR USE WITH AN AERATION TANK,
Nigata Engineering Co. Ltd., Tokyo (Japan). (assignee)
For primary bibliographic entry see Field 5D.
W75-08745

APPARATUS FOR SUBSOIL IRRIGATION,
For primary bibliographic entry see Field 3F.
W75-08748

CONTROL APPARATUS FOR A WATER SUPPLY SYSTEM,
Weil-McLain Co., Inc., Dallas, Tex. (assignee)
E. M. Deters.
U.S. Patent No. 3,865,512, 7 p, 10 fig, 2 ref; Official Gazette of the United States Patent Office, Vol 931, No 2, p 756, February 11, 1975.

Descriptors: *Patents, *Water supply, Pressure, Pumps, Equipment, *Control systems.

A control apparatus for a water supply system has a motor operated pump for pumping water through a delivery line to one or more valved outlets. The control apparatus includes a pressure switch responsive to the pressure in the delivery line and operable at preselected upper and lower pressure limits to respectively stop and start the pump motor. It also includes a control valve for controlling flow from the pump to the delivery line operable during normal flow from the delivery line to maintain the delivery line pressure in a regulated pressure range below the upper switch operating pressure and operable when flow from the delivery line is terminated to cause the pressure in the delivery line to rapidly build up to the upper switch operating pressure. The control valve also has provision for shutting off flow to the delivery line when the pressure rises above the upper switch operating pressure, to prevent further increase in pressure in the delivery line. (Sinha-OEIS)
W75-08749

PURIFICATION CONTROL UNIT,
Camper and Nicholsons Ltd., Gosport (England). (Assignee).
For primary bibliographic entry see Field 5F.
W75-08751

CAVITATION CHARACTERISTICS OF 18-INCH BUTTERFLY VALVE,
S. M. Cho, W. J. Carlson, and M. J. Tessier.
In: Hydraulic Engineering and the Environment; Proceedings of the 21st Annual Hydraulic Division Specialty Conference, Montana State University, Bozeman, August 15-17, 1973. American Society of Civil Engineers, New York, p 141-154, 1973. 10 fig, 1 tab, 9 ref, 2 append. AEC Contract AT(04-3)-700.

Descriptors: *Valves, *Cavitation, *Hydraulics, Fluid mechanics, Butterfly valves, Hydraulic valves, Flow, Equipment, Systems analysis, Laboratory tests, Head loss, Hydraulic equipment, Damage, Erosion.
Identifiers: *Incipient cavitation index.

Test data were presented for the head-loss coefficients and the incipient cavitation indexes as a function of the valve disk position for an 18-inch butterfly valve in water. The test results for the incipient cavitation index, when compared to other experimental data, showed reasonable agreement at lower valve openings, but increasing discrepancy with an increasing valve opening. It appeared that the discrepancy is due mainly to the differences in the size of the valve, the system pressure, and the quality of the test water. The effects of different fluids, of room temperature test water versus high temperature liquid sodium, on the incipient cavitation index and cavitation damage were discussed. For the incipient cavitation index, the information obtained in the water system may be extended to the sodium system conservatively. However, as for cavitation damage, unilateral conservatism cannot be stated. The cavitation information obtained in the water system was applied to a sodium flow loop in which a number of butterfly valves are to be installed. A method of optimizing the valve disk positions to minimize cavitation potential in the loop was discussed. (See also W75-08786) (Sims-ISWS)
W75-08801

DESIGN OF COOLING TOWER RETURN CHANNEL FOR TVA'S BROWNS FERRY NUCLEAR PLANT,
Tennessee Valley Authority, Norris. Engineering Lab.
For primary bibliographic entry see Field 5D.
W75-08803

TRANSIENT COOLING POND BEHAVIOR,
Oak Ridge National Lab., Tenn.
For primary bibliographic entry see Field 5D.
W75-08804

METER FOR SEWER FLOW MEASUREMENT,
Illinois Univ., Urbana. Dept. of Civil Engineering.
For primary bibliographic entry see Field 7B.
W75-08850

8D. Soil Mechanics

SEEPAGE CHARACTERISTICS OF FOUNDATIONS WITH A DOWNSTREAM CRACK,
Madras Univ., Guindy (India). Coll. of Engineering.
R. Sakthivadivel, and S. Thiruvengadachari.

Journal of Hydraulic Research, Vol 13, No 1, p 57-77, 1975. 5 fig, 5 tab, 5 ref.

Descriptors: *Seepage, *Foundations, *Uplift pressure, *Mathematical studies, *Cracks, Underseepage, Flow nets, Hydraulic structures, Dams, Equations, Flow around objects, Flow, Distribution patterns, Model studies, Pipe flow.
Identifiers: *Conformal transformations, *Electrolytic tank models.

The seepage characteristics of foundations with a downstream crack were analyzed with the use of a conformal transformation technique. Two cases were investigated: a downstream vertical crack in a finite depth of pervious stratum and a downstream inclined crack of finite depth in a pervious stratum of infinite depth. Experimental verification of the flow lines with an electrolytic tank model showed satisfactory agreement with the theory. It was shown that a downstream foundation crack, irrespective of its length and inclination, has negligible effect on the seepage characteristics when the crack is at a distance equal to or greater than the depth of the previous stratum from the downstream end of the hydraulic strueture. (Prickett-ISWS)
W75-08432

SEEPAGE THROUGH OPENING IN CUTOFF WALL UNDER WEIR,
Bengal Engineering Coll., Howrah (India). Dept. of Civil Engineering.
S. P. Brahma.
Journal of the Geotechnical Engineering Division, American Society of Civil Engineers, Vol 101, No GT3, Proceedings Paper 11204, p 329-340, March 1975. 4 fig, 7 ref, 2 append.

Descriptors: *Cutoff walls, *Graphical analysis, *Seepage, *Uplift pressure, Weirs, Soil mechanics, Walls, Hydraulics, Cutoffs, Porous media, Groundwater.
Identifiers: *Conformal mapping.

A solution to the problem of seepage through an opening in a cutoff wall under an impervious strueture lying on the ground level was presented with the use of the conformal transformation technique. The cutoff extends from the base of the structure to the impervious layer, which is overlaid by an isotropic and homogeneous porous stratum. The solution was found to agree with established solutions for a partial cutoff wall and for a partial cutoff wall under a weir sitting on the ground level. Graphical presentation of the solution, which takes into account the geometry, was made for ready use by designers. (Lee-ISWS)
W75-08711

8E. Rock Mechanics and Geology

GEOLOGY OF GEOTHERMAL TEST HOLE GT-2, FENTON HILL SITE, JULY 1974,
Los Alamos Scientific Lab., N. Mex.
For primary bibliographic entry see Field 5A.
W75-08649

PROJECT DIAMOND ORE, PHASE IIA: CLOSE-IN MEASUREMENTS PROGRAM,
California Univ., Livermore. Lawrence Livermore Lab.
For primary bibliographic entry see Field 5A.
W75-08659

8G. Materials

SEEPAGE CHARACTERISTICS OF FOUNDATIONS WITH A DOWNSTREAM CRACK,
Madras Univ., Guindy (India). Coll. of Engineering.
For primary bibliographic entry see Field 8D.
W75-08432

SALVAGE OF HEAVY CONSTRUCTION EQUIPMENT BY A FLOATING ICE BRIDGE,
Foundation of Canada Engineering Corp. Ltd., Calgary (Alberta). Arctic Div.
H. R. Kivisild, G. D. Rose, and D. M. Masterson.
Canadian Geotechnical Journal, Vol 12, No 1, p 58-69, February 1975. 12 fig, 2 tab, 7 ref, 1 append.

Descriptors: *Ice, *Cold weather construction, *Bridge construction, Civil engineering, Construction materials, Construction equipment, Engineering structures, Freezing, Bearing strength, Strength of materials, Tides, Salinity, Temperature, On-site data collections, *Canada.
Identifiers: *Floating ice bridges, *James Bay.

During the summer of 1972, a barge load of heavy construction equipment under tow to the James Bay Project on the eastern shore of James Bay became grounded on a shoal at the mouth of the Fort George River, only a few miles from its intended destination. Federal Commerce and Navigation Limited retained Foundation of Canada Engineering Corporation Limited (FENCO) to study the feasibility of removing the heavy equipment from the barge by an overice crossing. FENCO personnel visited the site in November and December 1972, compiled the necessary environmental data, and designated a crossing consisting of ice built up by flooding. Following the completion of the 100 foot wide and 74 inch thick bridge by Sainte-Marie Construction, the ice bridge was instrumented and tested prior to and during the unloading process. Parameters measured were thickness, width, temperature, ice soundness, and deflections. Tide readings were also taken. Loads of 70 tons and heavy trucks were removed with no problem. Deflections were very small and cracking was confined to the tidal zone. (Sims-ISWS)
W75-08461

REDUCING FLUID FRICTION WITH OKRA,
Clemson Univ., S.C.
W. E. Castro, and J. G. Neuwirth, Jr.
Chemtech, p 697-701, November 1971. 10 fig, 15 ref. OWRR A-009-SC(4).

Descriptors: *Fluid friction, Polymers, Flow resistance, Turbulent flow, Pipe flow.
Identifiers: Okra gum, Polysaccharides, Bovine blood.

The use of high polymer additives to reduce flow friction in turbulent pipe flow has been well documented. For engineering applications, polymers which are more resistant to shear degradation are needed. Okra gum, a natural occurring polysaccharide, was investigated as a potential friction reducing additive. Pheological studies in the literature indicate that this material is suitable for this purpose. Okra gum in saline has also been used successfully as a plasma expander suggesting its use in blood flow. Experimental results show that Okra gum, in dilute aqueous solution is a very effective friction reducer in turbulent pipe flow with overall behavior comparable to polyethylene oxide. Preliminary experiments on friction reduction of bovine blood with Okra gum show the same general behavior as obtained in aqueous solutions and suggest other applications of this phenomenon.
W75-08605

MEASUREMENT OF INSTANTANEOUS BOUNDARY SHEAR STRESS,
Agricultural Research Service, Fort Collins, Colo.
P. H. Blinco, and D. B. Simons.
In: Hydraulic Engineering and the Environment; Proceedings of the 21st Annual Hydraulic Division Specialty Conference, Montana State University, Bozeman, August 15-17, 1973. American Society of Civil Engineers, New York, p 43-54, 1973. 5 fig, 18 ref, 1 append.

Descriptors: *Shear stress, *Streamflow, *Sediment transport, Flow, Flumes, Beds, Channels, Erosion, Channel erosion, Scour, Anemometers, Turbulent flow, Turbulent boundary layers, Laboratory tests.
Identifiers: Hot-film anemometers.

Measurement of the instantaneous boundary shear stress was made for several flow conditions in a smooth open channel. Comparison with related previous work suggested that the flush surface hot-film sensor is capable of measuring the turhulent boundary shear stress in hydraulically smooth flows. Statistical inference from time series analysis revealed the following information: (1) The relative turbulence intensity of the shear stress decreased with increasing Reynolds number. (2)The probability density function of the shear stress is positively skewed. (3)The spectral density function of the boundary shear stress process indicated that most of the energy was found to be associated with frequencies less than 3 hertz. (See also W75-08786) (Sims-ISWS)
W75-08791

WALL SHEAR STRESS MEASUREMENTS WITH HOT-FILM SENSORS,
Lehigh Univ., Bethlehem, Pa. Fritz Engineering Lab.
O. Yucel, and W. H. Graf.
In: Hydraulic Engineering and the Environment; Proceedings of the 21st Annual Hydraulic Division Specialty Conference, Montana State University, Bozeman, August 15-17, 1973. American Society of Civil Engineers, New York p 55-61, 1973. 8 ref.

Descriptors: *Shear stress, *Instrumentation, *Sediment transport, Laboratory tests, Anemometers, Pipe flow, Sands, Heat transfer, Hydraulics.
Identifiers: *Hot-film shear sensors, Wall shear stress.

Experiments conducted in both clear-water and sand-water mixture flow experiments indicated that the flush-mounting hot-film shear sensors can be used for the measurement of the wall shear stress. However, a modification of the clear-water calibration equation is necessary for each sensor to account for the increased heat transfer due to suspended sand particles. (See also W75-08786) (Sims-ISWS)
W75-08792

8H. Rapid Excavation

A REVIEW OF EXPLOSIVES USED IN EXPLOSIVE EXCAVATION RESEARCH LABORATORY PROJECTS SINCE 1969,
Army Engineer Waterways Experiment Station, Livermore, Calif. Explosive Excavation Research Lab.
H. H. Reed.
Available from the National Technical Information Service, Springfield, Va 22161. Miscellaneous Paper-E-74-6, December 1974. 54 p, 1 fig, 3 tab, 17 ref, 1 bib, 1 append.

Descriptors: *Beneficial use, *Nuclear explosions, *Exploration, *Excavation, Safety, Evaluation, Surveys, Design criteria, Construction, Constraints, Research and development, Materials, Specifications, *Reviews.

Since 1969 the Explosive Excavation Research Laboratory has been engaged primarily in using commercially developed explosives and blasting agents in a variety of explosives excavation jobs and experiments. Dry and wet (slurry) explosives and blasting agents have comprised the bulk of these products, which are generally fuel-oxidizer mixes with an ammonium nitrate base. General properties of these explosives are covered. The specific products used by EERL are discussed in detail as are the media in which they were used. Techniques available for procuring explosives are also discussed. (Houser-ORNL)

W75-08650

8I. Fisheries Engineering

BEHAVIORAL RESPONSES OF NORTHERN PIKE, YELLOW PERCH AND BLUEGILL TO OXYGEN CONCENTRATIONS UNDER SIMULATED WINTERKELL CONDITIONS,
Ichthyological Associates, Inc., Middletown, Del.
For primary bibliographic entry see Field 5C.
W75-08361

MODEL DEVELOPMENT AND SYSTEMS ANALYSIS OF THE YAKIMA RIVER BASIN: FISHERIES,
Washington Univ., Seattle. Coll. of Fisheries.
For primary bibliographic entry see Field 6B.
W75-08580

METHOD FOR PROVIDING COOLED AERATED WATER,
L. E. Gallup.
U.S. Patent No. 3,863,605, 4 p, 4 fig, 2 ref; Official Gazette of the United States Patent Office, Vol 931, No 1, p 124, February 4, 1975.

Descriptors: *Patents, *Aquiculture, *Aeration, *Fish management, *Water temperature, Fish, Trout, Oxygen, Temperature control.
Identifiers: *Aquaculture, Heat exchange.

The invention is directed to a trout growing system which enables the maintenance of water conditions suitable for the growth of trout year round in climates normally incapable of providing adequately low water temperatures in combination with sufficiently high levels of oxygen in the water in which the trout are maintained. The method comprises the steps of taking quantities of oxygen-rich warm water from near the surface of the body of water and moving it into a heat exchange relationship with the cooler oxygen-poor water without intermixing the oxygen-rich warm water with the oxygen-poor cooler water. A conduit extends through the deeper portion of a body of water. The oxygen-rich warm water enters the conduit through an inlet and flows along the length of the conduit and is discharged into a separate storage area. (Sinha-OEIS)
W75-08733

SWIMMING PERFORMANCE OF ARCTIC GRAYLING,
Idaho Univ., Moscow. Dept. of Civil Engineering.
For primary bibliographic entry see Field 8A.
W75-08788

HYDRAULICS OF A GRAVEL CORE FISH SCREEN,
Washington Univ., Seattle. Dept. of Civil Engineering.
R. E. Nece, and M. C. Bell.
In: Hydraulic Engineering and the Environment; Proceedings of the 21st Annual Hydraulic Division Specialty Conference, Montana State University, Bozeman, August 15-17, 1973. American Society of Civil Engineers, New York, p 31-41, 1973. 6 fig, 3 tab, 6 ref.

Descriptors: *Gravels, *Head loss, *Fish barriers, Screens, Breakwaters, Hydraulic structures, Trout, Salmon, Fish behavior, Intakes, Structures.

Screens are needed to prevent fish or other aquatic life from entering diversions located on lakes, rivers, or estuaries. A possible alternative to the more conventional screens was considered. The concept is that of a gravel core screen placed within a rubble mound breakwater enclosing the intake structures. The proposed idea involved questions for which limited data were readily available. Consequently, a two-phase study was initiated to: (1) determine head losses associated with flow through gravel core screens, and (2) determine the behavior of small fish with respect to penetrating gravel screens. The tests gave lower friction factors than are obtained from flows through rubble. Fanning friction factors f between 3.0 and 10 can be used as suitable limits in design calculations. A limited number of fish penetration tests were run in a laboratory flume. Some correlation between a calculated minimum opening size and fish size was indicated by these limited data. Results were too restricted to draw numerical conclusions. (See also W75-08786) (Sims-ISWS)
W75-08790

9. MANPOWER, GRANTS AND FACILITIES

9A. Education (Extramural)

UNIVERSITY OF NEBRASKA FACULTY WITH COMPETENCE IN WATER RESOURCES - SECOND EDITION.
Nebraska Univ., Lincoln. Water Resources Research Inst.
For primary bibliographic entry see Field 10D.
W75-08472

DIRECTORY OF KENTUCKY WATER RESEARCH PERSONNEL,
Kentucky Water Resources Inst., Lexington.
For primary bibliographic entry see Field 10D.
W75-08485

10. SCIENTIFIC AND TECHNICAL INFORMATION

10B. Reference and Retrieval

WATER RESOURCES: A BIBLIOGRAPHIC GUIDE TO REFERENCE SOURCES,
Connecticut Univ., Storrs. Inst. of Water Resources.
For primary bibliographic entry see Field 10C.
W75-08486

10C. Secondary Publication And Distribution

WATER RESOURCES: A BIBLIOGRAPHIC GUIDE TO REFERENCE SOURCES,
Connecticut Univ., Storrs. Inst. of Water Resources.
V. H. Ralston.
Available from the National Technical Information Service, Springfield, Va 22161 as PB-242 310, $5.25 in paper copy, $2.25 in microfiche. Institute Report No 23, (University of Connecticut Library Storrs Bibliography Series, No 2). January 1975. 123 p. OWRT A-999-CONN(16).

Descriptors: *Information retreival, Water resources, *Libraries, *Bibliographies, *Publications, *Abstracts, Information exchange, Indexing, Documentation.
Identifiers: *Bibliographic guide, *Reference sources, Statistics sources, Encyclopedias, Information services.

A detailed study has been made of water resources literature materials; and an inventory of reference sources available and a guide facilitating their location and use have been compiled. Initially undertaken as an attempt to classify the publications of the various water resources research institutes and organizations, emphasis was placed, as the research progressed, on providing a guide to reference materials, and in this way outlining the literature of the field, rather than producing a subjcet approach to individual items in the University of Connecticut collection. Sections on water resource-related Guides to the literaute, Dictionaries, Encyclopedias, Statistics sources, Standards, Bibliographies and Information services are included. In addition to reference titles, pertinent material such as editors or authors' names, publishers and addresses, dates of publication and availability are mentioned. Of the 411 references to individual publications of services, 46% are sponsored by government agencies, emphasizing the importance of both federal and state governments in the support of research and the resulting literature. (deLara-Connecticut)
W75-08486

ENVIRONMENT: A BIBLIOGRAPHY ON SOCIAL POLICY AND HUMANISTIC VALUES,
Nevada Univ., Reno. Desert Research Inst.
R. T. Roelofs, and W. Jenkins.
Available from the National Technical Information Service, Springfield, Va 22161 as PB-242 303, $5.75 in paper copy, $2.25 in microfiche. Center for Water Resources Research, Project Report No 31, May 1975, 136 p. OWRT A-039-NEV(1). 14-31-0001-3228.

Descriptors: *Environment, *Bibliographies, Social aspects, *Social values, Evaluation, Indexing, *Environmental effects, Water quality, Water policy.

This comprehensive bibliography contains over 3,000 items covering publishing material on and related to the environment as it pertains to social policy and humanistic values. Material was selected if it was substantively, methodologically or theoretically relevant to man and his activities in relation to the environment. This bibliography is compiled alphabetically by author with a cross-referenced category index of fifty-six subjects. (Fallon-Nevada)
W75-08489

RESEARCH AND ADVANCES IN GROUND-WATER RESOURCES STUDIES, 1964-1974,
Florida Water Management District, Brooksville.
For primary bibliographic entry see Field 2F.
W75-08825

INDEX TO MAPS TO FLOOD-PRONE AREAS IN INDIANA,
Geological Survey, Indianapolis, Ind.
For primary bibliographic entry see Field 7C.
W75-08834

10D. Specialized Information Center Services

UNIVERSITY OF NEBRASKA FACULTY WITH COMPETENCE IN WATER RESOURCES - SECOND EDITION.
Nebraska Univ., Lincoln. Water Resources Research Inst.
Available from the National Technical Information Service, Springfield, Va 22161 as PB-242 381, $4.75 in paper copy, $2.25 in microfiche. Publication No 6, February 1975, 70 p. OWRT A-999-NEB(15). 14-31-0001-5027.

Descriptors: *Specialization, *Nebraska, Water resources institute, *Personnel, *Scientific personnel, Research and development.

Information was prepared to provide a basis for identifying individuals with special competence and expertise for research and/or teaching in the water resources field at the University of Nebraska. It is espected that this listing will be useful in the future development of both individual and interdisciplinary research project activities.
W75-08472

DIRECTORY OF KENTUCKY WATER RESEARCH PERSONNEL,
Kentucky Water Resources Inst, Lexington.
R. R. Huffsey.
Available from the National Technical Information Service, Springfield, Va 22161 as PB-242 309, $4.25 in paper copy, $2.25 in microfiche. Technical Series No 100, March 1975. 46 p. OWRT A-999-KY(2). 14-31-0001-5017.

Descriptors: *Personnel, Manpower, *Scientific personnel, Human resources, *Kentucky, Organizations, Water resources Institute, *Specialization.
Identifiers: *Directories, Water research personnel.

The Directory is a tabulation of Interest Profiles that were distributed throughout the Commonwealth of Kentucky. The Directory section consists of an alphabetic list of water and water-related keywords. Below the keyword is a list of individuals who have indicated a degree of expertise in specific water-related areas in the Interest Profile. The Directory also includes a list of the Kentucky Water Resources Research Institute's State Advisory Council. The primary function of this group is to identify significant water research needs throughout the Commonwealth. The University Advisory Council, which aids the Institute in generating and evaluating water research proposals, is also included. Addresses of the Institute officers are also provided.
W75-08485

10F. Preparation Of Reviews

FORMATION OF HALOGENATED ORGANICS BY CHLORINATION OF WATER SUPPLIES,
Harvard Univ., Cambridge, Mass. Dept. of Sanitary Engineering.
For primary bibliographic entry see Field 05F.
W75-08357

A REVIEW OF THE LITERATURE ON THE USE OF 2,4-D IN FISHERIES,
Southeastern Fish Control Lab., Warm Springs, Ga.
For primary bibliographic entry see Field 05C.
W75-08587

A REVIEW OF THE LITERATURE ON THE USE OF TFM-BAYLUSCIDE IN FISHERIES,
National Marine Fisheries Service, Ann Arbor, Mich. Great Lakes Fishery Lab.
For primary bibliographic entry see Field 05C.
W75-08588

CAVITATION DAMAGE SCALE EFFECTS--STATE OF ART SUMMARIZATION.
International Association for Hydraulic Research, Delft (Netherlands). Section for Hydraulic Machinery, Equipment and Cavitation.
For primary bibliographic entry see Field 08B.
W75-08698

SUBJECT INDEX

AUTHOR INDEX

ORGANIZATIONAL INDEX

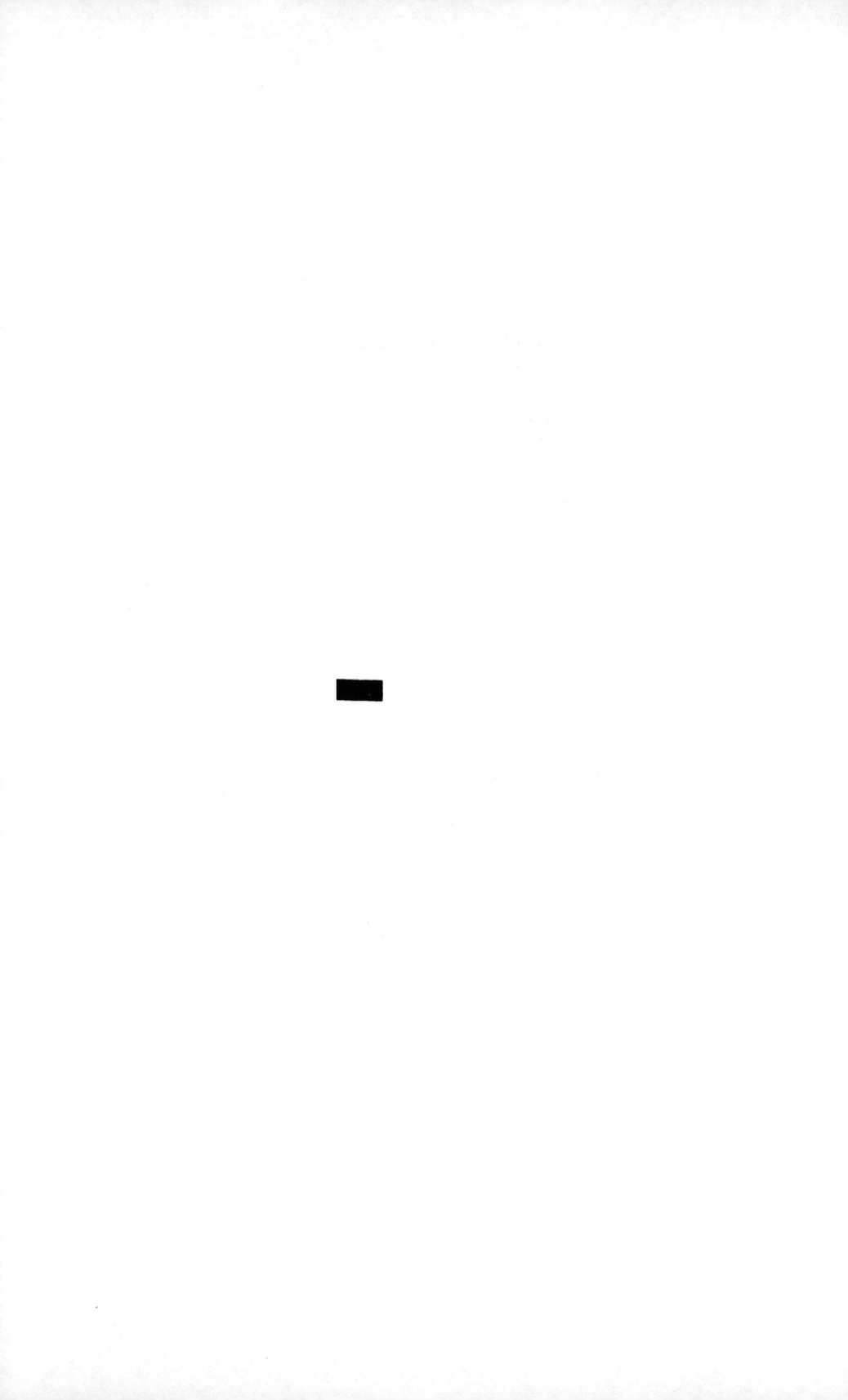

ACCESSION NUMBER INDEX

ABSTRACT SOURCES

SOURCE	ACCESSION NUMBER	TOTAL
A. CENTERS OF COMPETENCE		
Colorado State University, Irrigation Return Flow Quality	W75-08574	1
Cornell University, Policy Models for Water Resources Systems	W75-08386 08719--08728 08730--08732 08845--08850	20
ERDA Oak Ridge National Laboratory, Nuclear Radiation and Safety	W75-08640--08643 08645--08670	30
Franklin Institute (FIRL), Municipal Wastewater Treatment Technology	W75-08567--08572 08671--08679	15
Illinois State Water Survey, Hydrology	W75-08395 08398--08467 08683--08718 08786--08788 08790--08824	145
Institute of Paper Chemistry, Water Pollution from Pulp and Paper Industry	W75-08384 08538--08545 08547--08566	29
University of Arizona, Arid Land Water Resources	W75-08366--08373	8
University of Wisconsin, Eutrophication	W75-08764--08771	8
University of Wisconsin, Water Resources Economics	W75-08573, 08772 08776--08785	12
B. STATE WATER RESOURCES RESEARCH INSTITUTES	W75-08354--08356 08363--08365 08471--08492 08577--08580 08593--08596 08598--08599 08601 08603--08608 08610	46

SOURCE	ACCESSION NUMBER	TOTAL
C. OTHER		
BioSciences Information Service	W75-08359, 08361 08374--08376 08385 08390--08393 08396--08397 08470, 08522 08534, 08546 08597, 08600 08602, 08609 08644 08680--08682 08729 08773--08775 08789, 08828	30
Effects of Pollutants on Aquatic Life (Katz)	W75-08581--08589	9
Engineering Aspects of Urban Water Resources (Poertner)	W75-08360, 08362	2
Environmental Protection Agency	W75-08357 08591--08592	3
National Oceanic and Atmospheric Administration	W75-08358	1
Ocean Engineering Information Service (Patents)	W75-08611--08639 08733--08763	60
Office of Water Research and Technology	W75-08351--08353 08468--08469 08575--08576 08590	8
U. S. Geological Survey	W75-08387--08389 08394 08493--08521 08523--08527 08825--08827 08829--08844	57
Vanderbilt University, Metals Pollution	W75-08528--08533 08535--08537	9

U. S. GOVERNMENT PRINTING OFFICE : 1975 O - 210-961 (3)

CENTERS OF COMPETENCE AND THEIR SUBJECT COVERAGE

- Ground and surface water hydrology at the Illinois State Water Survey and the Water Resources Division of the U.S. Geological Survey, U.S. Department of the Interior.
- Metropolitan water resources planning and management at the Center for Urban and Regional Studies of University of North Carolina.
- Eastern United States water law at the College of Law of the University of Florida.
- Policy models of water resources systems at the Department of Water Resources Engineering of Cornell University.
- Water resources economics at the Water Resources Center of the University of Wisconsin.
- Eutrophication at the Water Resources Center of the University of Wisconsin.
- Water resources of arid lands at the Office of Arid Lands Studies of the University of Arizona.
- Water well construction technology at the National Water Well Association.
- Water-related aspects of nuclear radiation and safety at the Oak Ridge National Laboratory.
- Water resource aspects of the pulp and paper industry at the Institute of Paper Chemistry.

Supported by the Environmental Protection Agency in cooperation with WRSIC

- Effect on water quality of irrigation return flows at the Department of Agricultural Engineering of Colorado State University.
- Agricultural livestock waste at East Central State College, Oklahoma.
- Municipal wastewater treatment technology at the Franklin Institute Research Laboratories.

Subject Fields

1 NATURE OF WATER

2 WATER CYCLE

3 WATER SUPPLY AUGMENTATION AND CONSERVATION

4 WATER QUANTITY MANAGEMENT AND CONTROL

5 WATER QUALITY MANAGEMENT AND PROTECTION

6 WATER RESOURCES PLANNING

7 RESOURCES DATA

8 ENGINEERING WORKS

9 MANPOWER, GRANTS, AND FACILITIES

10 SCIENTIFIC AND TECHNICAL INFORMATION

INDEXES

SUBJECT INDEX

AUTHOR INDEX

ORGANIZATIONAL INDEX

ACCESSION NUMBER INDEX

ABSTRACT SOURCES

U.S. DEPARTMENT OF COMMERCE
National Technical Information Service
5285 Port Royal Road
Springfield, VA 22161

SELECTED WATER RESOURCES ABSTRACTS

VOLUME 8, NUMBER 18
SEPTEMBER 15, 1975

W75-08851 -- W75-09350
CODEN: SWRABW

SELECTED WATER RESOURCES ABSTRACTS is published semimonthly for the Water Resources Scientific Information Center (WRSIC) by the National Technical Information Service (NTIS), U.S. Department of Commerce. NTIS was established September 2, 1970, as a new primary operating unit under the Assistant Secretary of Commerce for Science and Technology to improve public access to the many products and services of the Department. Information services for Federal scientific and technical report literature previously provided by the Clearinghouse for Federal Scientific and Technical Information are now provided by NTIS.

SELECTED WATER RESOURCES ABSTRACTS is available to Federal agencies, contractors, or grantees in water resources upon request to: Manager, Water Resources Scientific Information Center, Office of Water Research and Technology, U.S. Department of the Interior, Washington, D. C. 20240.

SELECTED WATER RESOURCES ABSTRACTS is also available on subscription from the National Technical Information Service. Annual subscription rates are: To the SWRA Journal, $75 ($95 foreign); to the Journal & Annual Index, $100 ($125 foreign); to the Annual Index only, $50 ($65 foreign). Certain documents abstracted in this journal can be purchased from the NTIS at prices indicated in the entry. Prepayment is required.

SELECTED
WATER RESOURCES ABSTRACTS

A Semimonthly Publication of the Water Resources Scientific Information Center,
Office of Water Research and Technology, U.S. Department of the Interior

VOLUME 8, NUMBER 18
SEPTEMBER 15, 1975

W75-08851 -- W75-09350

The Secretary of the U. S. Department of the Interior has determined that the publication of this periodical is necessary in the transaction of the public business required by law of this Department. Use of funds for printing this periodical has been approved by the Director of the Office of Management and Budget through August 31, 1978.

As the Nation's principal conservation agency, the Department of the Interior has responsibility for most of our nationally owned public lands and natural resources. This includes fostering the wisest use of our land and water resources, protecting our fish and wildlife, preserving the environmental and cultural values of our national parks and historical places, and providing for the enjoyment of life through outdoor recreation. The Department assesses our energy and mineral resources and works to assure that their development is in the best interests of all our people. The Department also has a major responsibility for American Indian reservation communities and for people who live in Island Territories under U.S. administration.

FOREWORD

Selected Water Resources Abstracts, a semimonthly journal, includes abstracts of current and earlier pertinent monographs, journal articles, reports, and other publication formats. The contents of these documents cover the water-related aspects of the life, physical, and social sciences as well as related engineering and legal aspects of the characteristics, conservation, control, use, or management of water. Each abstract includes a full bibliographical citation and a set of descriptors or identifiers which are listed in the **Water Resources Thesaurus.** Each abstract entry is classified into ten fields and sixty groups similar to the water resources research categories established by the Committee on Water Resources Research of the Federal Council for Science and Technology.

WRSIC IS NOT PRESENTLY IN A POSITION TO PROVIDE COPIES OF DOCUMENTS ABSTRACTED IN THIS JOURNAL. Sufficient bibliographic information is given to enable readers to order the desired documents from local libraries or other sources.

Selected Water Resources Abstracts is designed to serve the scientific and technical information needs of scientists, engineers, and managers as one of several planned services of the Water Resources Scientific Information Center (WRSIC). The Center was established by the Secretary of the Interior and has been designated by the Federal Council for Science and Technology to serve the water resources community by improving the communication of water-related research results. The Center is pursuing this objective by coordinating and supplementing the existing scientific and technical information activities associated with active research and investigation program in water resources.

To provide WRSIC with input, selected organizations with active water resources research programs are supported as "centers of competence" responsible for selecting, abstracting, and indexing from the current and earlier pertinent literature in specified subject areas.

Additional "centers of competence" have been established in cooperation with the Environmental Protection Agency. A directory of the Centers appears on inside back cover.

Supplementary documentation is being secured from established discipline-oriented abstracting and indexing services. Currently an arrangement is in effect whereby the BioScience Information Service of Biological Abstracts supplies WRSIC with relevant references from the several subject areas of interest to our users. In addition to Biological Abstracts, references are acquired from Bioresearch Index which are without abstracts and therefore also appear abstractless in SWRA. Similar arrangements with other producers of abstracts are contemplated as planned augmentation of the information base.

The input from these Centers, and from the 51 Water Resources Research Institutes administered under the Water Resources Research Act of 1964, as well as input from the grantees and contractors of the Office of Water Research and Technology and other Federal water resource agencies with which the

Center has agreements becomes the information base from which this journal is, and other information services will be, derived; these services include bibliographies, specialized indexes, literature searches, and state-of-the-art reviews.

Comments and suggestions concerning the contents and arrangements of this bulletin are welcome.

Water Resources Scientific Information Center
Office of Water Research and Technology
U.S. Department of the Interior
Washington, D. C. 20240

CONTENTS

SELECTED WATER RESOURCES ABSTRACTS

2. WATER CYCLE

2A. General

FEEDBACK COUPLING OF ABSORBED SOLAR RADIATION BY THREE MODEL ATMOSPHERES WITH CLOUDS,
State Univ. of New York, Buffalo. Dept. of Biophysical Sciences.
For primary bibliographic entry see Field 2B.
W75-08982

COMPARATIVE EVALUATION OF THREE URBAN RUNOFF MODELS,
Canada Centre for Inlands Waters, Burlington (Ontario).
J. Marsalek, T. M. Dick, P. E. Wisner, and W. G. Clarke.
Water Resources Bulletin, Vol 11, No 2, p 306-328, April 1975. 3 fig, 7 tab, 13 ref, 1 append.

Descriptors: *Urban hydrology, *Urban runoff, *Urban drainage, *Mathematical models, Simulation analysis, Hydrology, Hydraulics, Hydrologic systems, Hydrographs, Hydraulic models, Computer models, Model studies, Evaluation, Watersheds(Basins).

Three urban runoff models, the Road Research Laboratory Model (RRLM), the Storm Water Management Model (SWMM), and the University of Cincinnati Urban Runoff Model (UCURM), were examined by comparing the model simulated hydrographs with the hydrographs measued on several instrumented urban watersheds. This comparison was done for the hydrograph peak points as well as for the entire hydrographs by using such statistical measures as the correlation coefficient, the special correlation coefficient, and the integral square error. The results indicated that, when applying the three selected noncalibrated models on small urban catchments, the SWM model performed marginally better than the RRL model and both these models were more accurate than the UCUR model. On larger watersheds, the comparisons between the SWM model and the other two models would be likely even more favorable for the SWM model, because it has the most advanced flow routing scheme among the studied models. (Terstriep-ISWS)
W75-08988

OPTIMIZING PARAMETERS FOR A WATERSHED MODEL,
Virginia Polytechnic Inst. and State Univ., Blacksburg. Dept. of Agricultural Engineering.
For primary bibliographic entry see Field 2E.
W75-09077

A DISCRETE KERNEL GENERATOR FOR STREAM-AQUIFER STUDIES,
Colorado State Univ., Fort Collins. Dept. of Civil Engineering.
For primary bibliographic entry see Field 4B.
W75-09078

STREAMFLOW DEPLETION RESULTING FROM UPSTREAM SURFACE-WATER IMPOUNDMENT,
Geological Survey, Bay Saint Louis, Miss. Water Resources Div.
For primary bibliographic entry see Field 4A.
W75-09175

A NUMERICAL STUDY OF BOUNDARY EFFECTS ON CONCENTRATED VORTICES WITH APPLICATION TO TORNADOES AND WATERSPOUTS,
Edinburgh Univ. (Scotland). Dept. of Applied Mathematics.
For primary bibliographic entry see Field 2B.
W75-09194

SYSTEMS ANALYSIS OF HYDROLOGIC PROBLEMS.
Proceedings of the Second International Seminar for Hydrology Professors, August 2-14, 1970, Utah State University, Logan. 452 p.

Descriptors: *Conferences, *Hydrology, *Systems analysis, *Hydrologic systems, *Model studies, Simulation analysis, Stochastic processes, Statistical models, Synthesis, Synthetic hydrology, Water resources development, Estimating, Reservoir operation, Multiple-purpose reservoirs, Computer models, Analog models, Mathematical models, Urban drainage, Storm water, Probable maximum precipitation, Runoff, Streamflow, Statistical methods, Hydrologic aspects.

The seminar objectives were to study and examine the interrelationships between the various hydrologic processes and to emphasize application of the systems approach to hydrology. The broad subject areas discussed were: (1) nature of hydrologic systems, (2) description of hydrologic systems, (3) hydrologic system modeling techniques and devices, and (4) applications. (See W75-09211 thru W75-09228) (Humphreys-ISWS)
W75-09210

AN INTRODUCTION TO SYSTEMS ANALYSIS OF HYDROLOGICAL PROBLEMS,
Illinois Univ., Urbana. Dept. of Civil Engineering.
V. T. Chow.
In: Systems Analysis of Hydrologic Problems; Proceedings of the Second International Seminar for Hydrology Professors, August 2-14, 1970, Utah State University, Logan, p 15-41. 4 fig, 1 tab, 7 ref, 2 append.

Descriptors: *Systems analysis, *Rainfall-runoff relationships, *Analytical techniques, *Storage, *Decision making, Unit hydrographs, Hydrologic systems, Model studies, Hydrologic data, River basins.
Identifiers: *Nonlinear systems, Objective function.

Systems anslysis provides a modem tool for interpreting complex hydrological phenomena. Once a hydrologic system is identified, the hydrologic processes may be simulated theoretically or conceptually by mathematical models. Modeling is only a part of systems analysis, which should include other important processes such as design and decision. Systems analysis comprises system identification, system elements modeling, system objectives and constraints, and alternatives to system objectives. An example was given of the development of a generalized deterministic hydrologic system of a watershed response. The system storage was represented by a mathematical function of the input, rainfall, and the output, discharge, and their derivatives with respect to time. For a particular rainstrorm and its runoff, the coefficients were assumed constant, reducing the nonlinear equation to a linear form. After effecting a solution for the linear equation, the watershed storage was considered as nonlinear by expressing the coefficients as functions of the characteristic values of input and output. The proposed model was shown to produce satisfactory results from an analysis of hydrologic data for a number of watersheds. (See also W75-09210) (Singh-ISWS)
W75-09211

USE OF SYSTEM ANALYSIS APPROACH IN THE HYDROLOGICAL PROJECTS OF THE WORLD METEOROLOGICAL ORGANIZATION,
World Meteorological Organization, Geneva (Switzerland). Dept. of Hydrology and Water Resources.
J. Nemec.
In: Systems Analysis of Hydrologic Problems; Proceedings of the Second International Seminar for Hydrology Professors, August 2-14, 1970, Utah State University, Logan, p 47-54. 10 ref.

Descriptors: *Systems analysis, *International Hydrological Decade, *Model studies, *Hydrology, Network design, Hydrologic aspects, Forecasting, Research and development, Research priorities, Foreign countries.

Application of systems analysis within the framework of World Meteorological Organization activities was discussed in general terms. These activities include network design for data collection, economic aspects of establishing and operating data collection networks, hydrological models for real-time forecasting, and intercomparison of conceptual hydrological models which are operational and use electonic computers (either digital, analog, or hybrid). (See also W75-09210) (Humphreys-ISWS)
W75-09212

THE UNITED STATES IHD PROGRAM,
National Committee for the International Hydrological Decade, Washington, D.C.
C. E. Downs.
In: Systems Analysis of Hydrologic Problems; Proceedings of the Second International Seminar for Hydrology Professors, August 2-14, 1970, Utah State University, Logan, p 55-68.

Descriptors: *International Hydrological Decade, *Hydrology, *United States, Foreign countries, Research and development, Research priorities, Hydrologic aspects.

The history and structure of the International Hydrological Decade (IHD) at the international and national levels were reviewed, and examples of the U.S. program activities of some of the U.S. IHD work groups were discussed. The IHD program consists of: (1) studies of regional, continental, hemispheric, and global phenomena and processes; (2) studies in international basins polar regions, and/or involving orbiting satellites; (3) joint or coordinated work in two or more countries; and (4) studies of specific phenomena and processes of fundamental interest and wide usefulness. A major long-term objective of IHD is an estimate of the world water balance. Twelve international working groups were formed to study specific aspects of hydrology. The five catagories of the US IHD program are: (1) studies and investigations of national and regional large-scale water balances to be summarized in the National Water Atlas; (2) studies of hydrological processes in river, lake, and groundwater basins in differing environmental provinces, including those under progressively increasing human influence; (3) research in a variety of specific fields related to hydrological phenomena, processes, and methodology; (4) education and training, exchange of students, research scientists and professors, programs in graduate fellowships, and on the job training; and (5) supporting activities, including scientific communication, documentation, and liaison with participating countries, and the secretariat of the IHD coordinating council (UNESCO). The U.S./IHD program is centered around 13 work groups. (See also W75-09210) (Humphreys-ISWS)
W75-09213

HYDROLOGIC INSTRUMENTATION,
Utah Water Research Lab., Logan.
For primary bibliographic entry see Field 7B.
W75-09214

SYSTEM EVALUATION - RELIABILITY OF DATA AND EXTRAPOLATION AND CORRELATION OF DATA,
Utah Water Research Lab., Logan.
For primary bibliographic entry see Field 7A.

W75-09215

STOCHASTIC PROCESSES AND MODELS IN HYDROLOGY,
Colorado State Univ., Fort Collins. Dept. of Civil Engineering.
V. Yevjevich.
In: Systems Analysis of Hydrologic Problems; Proceedings of the Second International Seminar for Hydrology Professors, August 2-14, 1970, Utah State University, Logan, p 109-170. 32 fig.

Descriptors: *Stochastic processes, *Hydrologic systems, *Systems analysis, *Analytical techniques, *Time series analysis, Solar radiation, River flow, Flood data, Correlation analysis, Water resources, Hydrology, Model studies.
Identifiers: *Deterministic models, *Periodicities, Stationarity.

By changing the space scale on which a phenomenon is observed, the randomness may be either clearly shown or masked. Hydrologic phenomena are mostly stochastic although some contain systematic components of nature in the form of short-term periodicities. The era of determinism in hydrology can be seen by the search for deterministic functions to relate hydrologic random variables. The classical hydrologic research approach consisted of studying an individual environment as a system and its parts as subsystems. It is almost impossible to find a pure deterministic hydrologic process in nature. Hydrologic processes in time and space characteristics of hydrologic environments, are either stochastic processes or a combination of stochastic and deterministic components, mainly as periodic-stochastic or trend-stochastic processes. These stochastic processes for solar radiation and daily river flows were discussed as examples. The smaller the stochastic component in a process, the easier it is for studying, planning, and developing water resources. A study of the structure of a hydrologic process comprises three essentials: process analysis, process description in a concise mathematical form, and prediction. The stationarity of stochastic components of a process was stressed. Various estimators and indicators for incorporating stochastic components in models were described. (See also W75-09210) (Singh-ISWS)
W75-09216

MATHEMATICAL PROGRAMMING IN WATER RESOURCES,
Case Western Reserve Univ., Cleveland, Ohio. Systems Research Center.
Y. Y. Haimes.
In: Systems Analysis of Hydrologic Problems; Proceedings of the Second International Seminar for Hydrology Professors, August 2-14, 1970, Utah State University, Logan, p 171-222. 9 fig, 4 tab, 4 ref.

Descriptors: *Systems analysis, *Simulation analysis, *Synthetic hydrology, Analytical techniques, *Dynamic programming, Hydrologic systems, *Linear programming, Operations research, Stochastic processes, Synthesis, Hydrology, Mathematical models, Water resources.

Following a general discussion of systems analysis, specific items were discussed. Topics covered in various degrees of detail included: linear, nonlinear, deterministic, probabilistic, static, and dynamic programming techniques; simulation techniques; and distributed versus lumped parameters. Several examples illustrated the discussion. (See also W75-09210) (Jess-ISWS)
W75-09217

GAME THEORY,
Utah State Univ., Logan. Dept. of Civil Engineering.
For primary bibliographic entry see Field 6A.
W75-09218

THE USE OF INPUT-OUTPUT (TRANSFER FUNCTION) MODELS IN HYDROLOGY,
California Univ., Davis. Dept. of Water Science and Engineering.
J. Amorocho.
In: Systems Analysis of Hydrologic Problems; Proceedings of the Second International Seminar for Hydrology Professors, August 2-14, 1970, Utah State University, Logan, p 231-248. 3 fig, 16 ref.

Descriptors: *Input-output analysis, *Mathematical studies, *Hydrology, Mathematical models, Operations research, Systems analysis, Rainfall-runoff relationships, Statistical methods, Equations, Analytical techniques.

Summarized were the main principles involved in the use of hydrologic models of the input-output, or 'black box' type, as they are often called. It can be stated that so far it has never been possible to formulate any real hydrological situation in strictly deterministic terms because there is time variability of hydrologic systems due to man-made changes and to the natural processes of weathering erosion, climatic changes, etc., which constitute the geomorphological evolution of the land; there is uncertainty with respect to the magnitudes and the space and time distribution of the inputs and outputs of hydrologic systems, and with respect to the states and properties of their interior elements; and there are difficulties in the mathematical formulation of the complex nonlinear processes of mass and energy transfer that constitute the hydrologic cycle. The use of 'black box' analysis in hydrology is a very powerful method for modeling the behavior of natural-catchments, provided it is applied with an adequate understanding of its limitations. The principal of these is the structure of the rainfall field, and the degree to which it can be described by a lumped index function. When this description is plausible, the methods of nonlinear analysis provide a large improvement over the unit hydrograph concept for the prediction of runoff from rainfall. (See also W75-09210) (Jess-ISWS)
W75-09219

COMPUTER SIMULATION OF WATER RESOURCE SYSTEMS,
Utah Water Research Lab., Logan.
J. P. Riley.
In: Systems Analysis of Hydrologic Problems; Proceedings of the Second International Seminar for Hydrology Professors, August 2-14, 1970, Utah State University, Logan, p 249-274. 13 fig, 14 ref.

Descriptors: *Simulation analysis, *Mathematical models, *Calibrations, *Computer models, *Water resources, Systems analysis, Hydrologic data, Runoff, Overland flow, Snowfall, Hydrology, Model studies.
Identifiers: *Sensitivity analysis, Distributed parameter model.

The problems of managing water resource systems are basically those of decision-making based on a consideration of the physical, economic, and sociological processes which are strongly interrelated and form a continuous, dynamic system. Once a prototype system is identified, the various processes in the system may be simulated by either physical or mathematical models. The mathematical representation of natural hydrologic systems may be achieved by means of either a lumped parameter model or a distributed parameter model. Computer simulation of water resource systems or models is a form of sysystems analysis. The systems approach is defined as a technique for examining the responses of a particular component complex which is subject to certain constraints and input functions. The development of a model for a system requires creation of a conceptual model and its transformation to a working mathematical model. Model verification, calibration, and testing form an integral part of the systematic development of a computer simulation model. A clear delineation of different purposes and objectives is a must for this approach. The effect of various management strategies and the sensitivity of system variables can be easily evaluated on the computer model. Some examples of computer simulation studies were given. (See also W75-09210) (Singh-ISWS)
W75-09220

THE SYNTHESIS OF HYDROLOGIC SYSTEMS ON THE ANALOG AND HYBRID COMPUTERS,
City Univ., London (England).
For primary bibliographic entry see Field 7C.
W75-09221

A PROBLEM ORIENTED LIBRARY FOR HYDROLOGY,
McMaster Univ., Hamilton (Ontario). Dept. of Civil Engineering and Engineering Mechanics.
For primary bibliographic entry see Field 7C.
W75-09222

PRACTICAL APPLICATIONS OF HYDROLOGIC SIMULATION,
Hydrocomp International, Palo Alto, Calif.
For primary bibliographic entry see Field 4A.
W75-09223

CONTROL RULES FOR MULTIPLE-USE RESERVOIRS AND MULTI-RESERVOIR SYSTEMS,
Water Research Association, Marlow (England).
For primary bibliographic entry see Field 4A.
W75-09224

A MATHEMATICAL MODEL OF URBAN STORM DRAINAGE,
Water Resources Engineers, Inc., Walnut Creek, Calif.
For primary bibliographic entry see Field 5D.
W75-09225

SOME PROBLEMS IN THE APPLICATION OF SYSTEMS ANALYSES IN WATER RESOURCES SYSTEMS,
Office of Science and Technology, Washington, D.C.
For primary bibliographic entry see Field 3B.
W75-09226

DESIGN TYPHOON MODEL FOR ESTIMATION OF PROBABLE MAXIMUM PRECIPITATION AND PROBABLE MAXIMUM FLOOD IN TAIWAN,
National Taiwan Univ., Taipei. Dept. of Civil Engineering.
For primary bibliographic entry see Field 2B.
W75-09227

SOCIAL ISSUES IN WATER RESOURCES DEVELOPMENT,
Utah State Univ., Logan. Dept. of Sociology.
For primary bibliographic entry see Field 6B.
W75-09228

BIBLIOGRAPHY OF HYDROLOGY, CANADA, 1971-1973,
National Research Council of Canada, Ottawa, Associate Committee on Feodesy and Geophysics.
For primary bibliographic entry see Field 10C.
W75-09288

2B. Precipitation

CLIMATIC MODIFICATION BY AIR POLLUTION, II: THE SAHELIAN EFFECT,

Wisconsin Univ., Madison. Inst. for Environmental Studies.
R. A. Bryson.
Wisconsin University, Madison, Institute for Environmental Studies. Report 9, August, 1973. 12 p, 4 fig, 12 ref.

Descriptors: *Air pollution effects, *Arid climates, *Climatology, *Droughts, *Monsoons, *Africa, Deserts, Thermocline, Weather modification, Air pollution, Air temperature, Arid lands, Carbon dioxide, Climatic data, Dusts, Earth-air interfaces, Livestock, Mortality, Population, Rainfall, Seasonal, Turbidity, Variability, *Monsoons.
Identifiers: *Sahelian Zone, West Africa.

Severe drought has persisted more than 5 years within the Sahelian Zone, a broad belt of arid land some 3000 km along the southern edge of the Sahara Desert. Sharing the zone are the 6 countries of Mauritania, Senegal, Mali, Upper Volta, Niger, and Chad. Losses of human life and livestock have been staggering, for most of the population lives in the zone's southern region where formerly rainfall amounted to over 19 inches annually. Monsoon rains did not materialize in 1972 in West Africa, nor in any of the monsoon lands or lands with monsoon-like climates. Unfortunately, knowledge of the dynamics of the monsoons is still inadequate, and climatic data for the Sahel is rather limited. Technical data support the thesis that when the natural equator-to-pole and surface-to-upper air temperature differences are greater, desert-making climates move farther south, displacing the monsoons. Both carbon dioxide content and the amount of particulate matter suspended in the atmosphere (turbidity) affect these two gradients, and such pollutants have increased substantially over the last century, acting to supress the monsoons. In recent times the human contribution to temperature variance has amounted to perhaps 30 percent. With expected increasing volcanic activity, carbon dioxide, dust, and turbidity pollution from the rapidly industrializing human world population, it is not likely the monsoons will return with any regularity in this century. (Gloyd-Arizona)
W75-08949

THE OPACITY OF ACCRETED ICE,

Western Australia Univ., Nedlands. Dept. of Physics.
J. N. Carras, and W. C. Macklin.
Quarterly Journal of the Royal Meteorological Society, Vol 101, No 428, p 203-206, April 1975. 3 fig, 5 ref.

Descriptors: *Instrumentation, Ice, *Hail, *Opacity, Optical properties, Bubbles, Freezing, Temperature, Laboratory equipment, Analytical techniques, Meteorology.
Identifiers: Wet growth(Hail), Dry growth(Hail), Ice layers, Light transmittance, Accreted ice.

A technique which yields quantitative measurement of the opacity of accreted ice deposits was described. This consists of determining the attenuation of a light beam as it passes through a thin section of the deposit, with the use of a photovoltaie cell as the detector. The transmittance of the deposits is related to the air bubble concentration, and the technique provides a useful supplementary method for analyzing the air bubble structures of hailstones. (Sims-ISWS)
W75-08974

CRYSTAL SIZE IN ACCRETED ICE,

Western Australia Univ., Nedlands. Dept. of Physics.
P. J. Rye, and W. C. Macklin.
Quarterly Journal of the Royal Meteorological Society, Vol 101, No 428, p 207-215, April 1975. 6 fig, 16 ref.

Descriptors: *Ice, *Crystals, *Size, Crystallography, Crystal growth, Freezing, Temperature, Laboratory equipment, Drops(Fluids), Hail, Meteorology, Cloud physics.
Identifiers: *Crystallographic orientation, Accreted ice, Substrates.

Studies were made of the crystallographic orientation of 100 micrometer-radius supercooled droplets frozen on ice substrates whose c-axis orientations varied from 0 to 90 degrees to the surface normal. For a given droplet temperature and substrate orientation, there is a critical substrate temperature below which a frozen droplet has a high (greater than 0.8) probability of having an orientation which differes from that of the substrate. Above this critical substrate temperature there is a small (less than 0.2) residual probability of reorientation which is dependent on the droplet temperature and substrate orientation but independent of the substrate temperature. The lengths and maximum widths of ice crystals in accreted ice deposits have also been determined. In the dry growth regime there is a general decrease in the mean length from about 8 to 0.25 mm, and in the mean maximum width from about 1 to 0.2 mm, as the ambient temperature decreases from -5 to -30C. At ambient temperatures above -15C there is no dependence of the crystal dimensions on the temperature of the deposit. At ambient temperatures below this value, the crystal dimensions vary with deposit temperature in a manner consistent with the individual droplet studies. Consequently, measurements of the crystal dimensions in hailstone layers may give useful indications of their growth conditions. (Sims-ISWS)
W75-08975

A MEASUREMENT OF THE MIXING RATIO OF WATER VAPOUR FROM 15 TO 45 KM,

British Meteorological Office, Bracknell (England).
C. G. DeJonckheere.
Quarterly Journal of the Royal Meteorological Society, Vol 101, No 428, p 217-226, April 1975. 4 fig, 1 tab, 18 ref, append.

Descriptors: *Water vapor, *Instrumentation, *Infrared radiation, Measurement, Attenuation, Light, Meteorology, *Remote sensing.
Identifiers: *Stratosphere, Rockets, Mixing ratio.

The stratospheric water vapor altitude profile was derived from a measurement of the attenuation of solar infrared radiation at 2.61 micrometers by using a rocket-borne sensor. The solar zenith angle during the flight, which was made from Woomera in April 1970, was 98 degrees. The water vapor to air mixing ratio obtained was in the range 0.5 to 2 micrograms/gram in the lower stratosphere, with an upper limit of 4 micrograms/gram at 45 km. An appendix contains details of the calculation of theoretical attenuation. (Sims-ISWS)
W75-08976

FEEDBACK COUPLING OF ABSORBED SOLAR RADIATION BY THREE MODEL ATMOSPHERES WITH CLOUDS,

State Univ. of New York, Buffalo. Dept. of Biophysical Sciences.
R. L. Temkin, B. C. Weare, and F. M. Snell.
Journal of the Atmospheric Sciences, Vol 32, No 5, p 873-880, May 1975. 6 fig, 1 tab, 22 ref. N.I.H. Training Grant 5T01 GM00718.

Descriptors: *Models studies, *Atmosphere, *Clouds, Absorption, Solar radiation, Radiation, Cloud cover, Cloud physics, Mathematical models, Albedo, Optical properties, Meteorology, Temperature.

A study of the amount of solar radiation absorbed by the earth-atmosphere system as a function of the surface temperature was made comparing three model atmospheres with clouds. The atmospheres were generated by a model that involves a quasi-isentropic expansion of moist surface air of given relative humidity. 'Rainout' of condensate and the lapse rate were parameterized. The three atmospheres compared were a horizontally homogeneous diffuse thin cloud structure, a half-cloud half-clear structure, and a variable fractional cloud cover, each normalized to give the upper albedo at a reference point representative of global annual average conditions. Radiative transfer calculations were made by using the modified two-stream approximation and/or the Eddington approximation. The results indicate that with the diffuse thin cloud the magnitude of the feedback coupling of solar radiation absorbed to surface temperature lies intermediate to that of the other structures, with the variable fractional cloud showing the largest negative feedback. The negativity decreases with increasing surface reflectivity and may become positive at reflectivities representative of snow or ice. The negativity also decreases slightly with a decrease in zenith angle of the sun and with an increase in surface relative humidity. Implications of these results in global climatic modeling were discussed. (Sims-ISWS)
W75-08982

MEAN MERIDIONAL CIRCULATION IN THE SOUTHERN HEMISPHERE STRATOSPHERE BASED ON SATELLITE INFORMATION,

Colorado State Univ., Fort Collins. Dept. of Atmospheric Sciences.
R. F. Adler.
Journal of the Atmospheric Sciences, Vol 32, No 5, p 893-898, May 1975. 7 fig, 2 tab, 12 ref. NASA Grant NGR 06-002-098, AEC Contract AT(11-1)-1340.

Descriptors: *Remote sensing, *Circulation, *Satellites(Artificial), Heat transfer, Heat budget, Winter, Radiation, Air circulation, Meteorology.
Identifiers: *Stratosphere, Southern Hemisphere, Vertical motion.

Atmospheric structure derived from satellite, multi-channel radiance data was used to calculate zonally-averaged vertical motions in the wintertime stratosphere of both hemispheres with a heat budget approach. The Northern Hemisphere calculations based on the satellite data were shown to compare favorably with a computation carried out with conventional data, and with results of previous studies. The mean Southern Hemisphere pattern for July 1969 indicates a high-latitude cell with the axis of sinking motion at approximately 50 degrees S, while the rising motion is centered at 70 degrees S. Thus, the antarctic stratospheric jet stream is associated with an indirect cell. Two individual 10-day periods from July 1969 were examined to compare the mean meridional circulation and eddy heat flux patterns in the Southern Hemisphere during a minor midwinter warming and during a quiet period. Large eddy fluxes at 60 degrees S and a strong indirect cell in the meridional circulation are associated with the minor warming. During the quiet period, eddy fluxes at 60 degrees S are relatively small and the mean meridional circulation appears to develop an additional cell in very high latitudes with sinking motion over the South Pole. (Sims-ISWS)
W75-08983

A THREE-DIMENSIONAL NUMERICAL MODEL OF AN ISOLATED DEEP CONVECTIVE CLOUD: PRELIMINARY RESULTS,

Wisconsin Univ., Madison. Dept. of Meteorology.
R. E. Schlesinger.
Journal of the Atmospheric Sciences, Vol 32, No 5, p 934-957, May 1975. 14 fig, 48 ref, 1 append. NSF Grant GI-31278X.

Descriptors: *Model studies, *Storms, *Convection, Clouds, Atmosphere, Air circulation, Thunderstorms, Cloud physics, Mathematical models, Computer models, Shear, Winds, Temperature, Advection, Meteorology, Buoyancy.
Identifiers: Veering, Liquid water content, Downdrafts.

The development of an isolated convective storm in a sheared environment was studied with an anelastic three-dimensional numerical model. Each grid cell has horizontal dimensions of Delta x = Delta y = 3.2 km and a vertical dimension of Delta z = 0.7 km. Although it is ultimately planned to use at least a 31x31x20 grid with turbulence and liquid precipitation included, an 11x11x8 trial grid was used with both of these processes suppressed, simulating only early cloud growth. Comparative experiments were run for three vertical profiles of ambient wind: no ambient wind, positive speed shear but no directional shear, and positive speed shear with veering. The cases were compared with regard to airflow, pressure, and thermal patterns. It was found that: (1) A vortex doublet develops at middle levels when ambient shear is present. A contributing factor may be tilting of horizontal vorticity into the vertical by differential vortex-tube lifting. (2) Shear introduces asymmetry, with upshear dominance of perturbation outflow and horizontal gradients of physical properties. (3) The perturbed pressure field exhibits a meso-low under the cloud, and a meso-high near its top. With shear, the meso-low is displaced downshear of the meso-high. (4) Thermal buoyancy and the vertical perturbed pressure gradient force are the dominant vertical forces, but strongly oppose each other. (5) With directional shear, the middle-level horizontal pressure gradient force is directed to the right of the direction of cloud motion, suggesting a potential propagation mechanism. (Sims-ISWS)
W75-08?94

FIELD GENERATION AND DISSIPATION CURRENTS IN THUNDERCLOUDS AS A RESULT OF THE MOVEMENT OF CHARGED HYDROMETEORS,

State Univ. of New York, Albany. Atmospheric Sciences Research Center.
R. F. Griffiths, and J. Latham.
Journal of the Atmospheric Sciences, Vol 32, No 5, p 958-964, May 1975. 1 fig, 8 tab, 22 ref. NSF Grant AO 41166

Descriptors: *Electric fields, *Thunderstorms, *Hail, *Raindrops, Cloud physics, Precipitation(Atmospheric), Atmospheric physics, Electrical properties, Electrical coronas, Lightning, Meteorology, Storms.
Identifiers: *Atmospheric electricity, Cloud droplets, Current density, Charging current, Hydrometeors.

Calculations of the terminal velocities of charged hydrometeors in the presence of electric fields have formed the basis of computations of the charging current density flowing through a thundercloud as a result of the operation of a precipitative mechanism of cloud electrification. Values of the charging density were calculated for a range of values of field strength, precipitation rate, precipitation content, cloud water content, charge distribution, total separated charge, and the fraction of the small particles that have undergone a charging event. It was found that the estimated field required for the initiation of a lightning stroke (about 3.5 kV/cm) can be achieved only over a narrow range of conditions. The ease with which precipitative mechanisms can produce breakdown fields is considerably increased, however, if account is taken of spatial inhomogeneities in the field. (Sims-ISWS)
W75-08985

PACIFIC NORTHWEST LABORATORY ANNUAL REPORT FOR 1973 TO THE USAEC DIVISION OF BIOMEDICAL AND ENVIRONMENTAL RESEARCH, PART 3 ATMOSPHERIC SCIENCES.

Battelle-Pacific Northwest Labs., Richland, Wash.
For primary bibliographic entry see Field 5A.
W75-09069

REMOVAL AND RESUSPENSION PROCESSES - WET REMOVAL PROCESSES.

Battelle-Pacific Northwest Labs., Richland, Wash.
For primary bibliographic entry see Field 5A.
W75-09073

CHARGE SEPARATION DUE TO WATER DROP AND CLOUD DROPLET INTERACTIONS IN AN ELECTRIC FIELD,

Durham Univ. (England). Dept. of Physics.
S. G. Jennings.
Quarterly Journal of the Royal Meteorological Society, Vol 101, No 428, p 227-233, April 1975. 3 fig, 1 tab, 14 ref.

Descriptors: *Electric fields, *Electrical studies, *Drops(Fluids), Electricity, Coalescence, Cloud physics, Electrical properties, Atmosphere, Clouds.
Identifiers: *Drop interactions.

Measurements were made of the electric charge acquired by drops of mean radius of about 750 microns, in the presence of a vertical electric field, the value of which could be varied from 4.5 to 27kV/m. It was found that the average charge acquired by the water drop as a consequence of the inductive process increased from 0.1fC to about 0.25fC as the electric field strength increased from 5kV/m to about 15kV/m, but thereafter decreased with increasing values of electric field. It was suggested that the collisions between polarized raindrops and cloud droplets in natural clouds could give rise, very effectively, to the production of electric fields of about 30kV/m; but that significantly larger fields could not be produced because all collisions in the higher fields would result in permanent coalescence. (Jones-ISWS)
W75-09193

A NUMERICAL STUDY OF BOUNDARY EFFECTS ON CONCENTRATED VORTICES WITH APPLICATION TO TORNADOES AND WATERSPOUTS,

Edinburgh Univ. (Scotland). Dept. of Applied Mathematics.
L. Bode, L. M. Leslie, and R. K. Smith.
Quarterly Journal of the Royal Meteorological Society, Vol 101, No 428, p 313-324, April 1975. 6 fig, 2 tab, 20 ref.

Descriptors: *Numerical analysis, *Boundary processes, *Vortices, *Tornadoes, Stress, Velocity, Flow friction, Drag.
Identifiers: *Flow parameters, *Waterspouts, Surface roughness.

The important role of boundaries on vortex behavior was investigated. Particular interest was focused on the boundary which is normal to the vortex core and 'behind' the body force. On this boundary the surface stress is related to the surface velocity by a drag coefficient C sub D and experiments were performed in which C sub D was infinite, unity, and zero, corresponding with a no-slip, a partially yielding, and a free-slip boundary, respectively. These calculations were motivated by the desire to assess what differences, if any, between tornadoes (which develop over land) and waterspouts (which develop over the sea) can be attributed to the different surface constraint. The effect on a vortex due to an abrupt change in surface condition was also studied as this is relevant to the behavior of a tornado which crosses a water surface, or even one which traverses ground with varying roughness characteristics, and conversely to the behavior of a waterspout which moves over land. The results accord with the behavior of laboratory vortices formed in air over surfaces of different roughness. They also appear consistent with observations concerning the behavior of a waterspout whose circulation decreased rapidly and visible funnel expanded during a traverse of about a kilometer over land and which subsequently reformed on moving back over water. (Jones-ISWS)
W75-09194

THE NATURE OF OROGRAPHIC RAIN AT WINTERTIME COLD FRONTS,

Royal Radar Establishment, Malvern (England). Meteorological Office Research Unit.
K. A. Browning, C. W. Pardoe, and F. F. Hill.
Quarterly Journal of the Royal Meteorological Society, Vol 101, No 428, p 333-352, April 1975. 15 fig, 1 tab, 13 ref.

Descriptors: *Precipitation(Atmospheric), *Orography, *Distribution patterns, Winter, Rainfall, Radiosondes, Topography, Ice, Crystals, Clouds, Cloud seeding, Forecasting, Radar, On-site investigations.
Identifiers: *Cold fronts, *Pre-frontal low-level jets, Liquid water content, Wales, England, British Isles.

Some of the largest falls of orographic rain in the western parts of the British Isles are associated with wintertime cold fronts. Four case studies of wet cold fronts were presented. They were all characterized by southwesterly prefrontal low-level jets but were widely different in other respects. The distribution of rainfall in England and Wales was analyzed by using a network of autographic raingages, specially augmented near the coast and over the hills of south Wales, and the orographic effects were explained by data from series of hourly rawinsonde ascents from a single station. The rain was considered in three distinct regions: pre-frontal, the surface cold front, and post-frontal. Behind the front, orographic effects were found to be well defined but rather slight. At the surface front, orographic effects were negligible, heavy rain tending to occur regardless of topography. Ahead of the front, orographic effects varied from small to very large, depending on the existence of a moist low-level feeder cloud and seeding particles. (Jones-ISWS)
W75-09195

COMPUTERIZED RAIN ASSESSMENT AND TRACKING OF SOUTH FLORIDA WEATHER RADAR ECHOES,

National Oceanic and Atmospheric Administration, Coral Gables, Fla. Experimental Meteorology Lab.
V. Wiggert, and S. Ostlund.
Bulletin American Meteorological Society, Vol 56, No 1, p 17-26, January 1975. 9 fig, 17 ref.

Descriptors: *Radar, *Precipitation(Atmospheric), *Instrumentation, Measurement, Computers, Rainfall, Cloud seeding, *Florida, Weather, Data collections, Data processing, Weather forecasting.

Weather radar power can be electronically assessed and digitally quantified within many small 'range bins.' The tape recorded output from a radar digitizer linked to the Miami WSR-57 is being processed post hoc by a sequence of computer programs written at the Experimental Meteorology Laboratory. One program assesses radar-derived rainfall rates and total rain volumes over preselected areas and for preselected time periods; another isolates and tracks radar echoes and, while so doing, calculates the rainfall from each echo as it grows, moves, splits, merges, or dies. Sample results were displayed and future applications discussed. (Jones-ISWS)

W75-09208

USE OF SYSTEM ANALYSIS APPROACH IN THE HYDROLOGICAL PROJECTS OF THE WORLD METEOROLOGICAL ORGANIZATION,
World Meteorological Organization, Geneva (Switzerland). Dept. of Hydrology and Water Resources.
For primary bibliographic entry see Field 2A.
W75-09212

DESIGN TYPHOON MODEL FOR ESTIMATION OF PROBABLE MAXIMUM PRECIPITATION AND PROBABLE MAXIMUM FLOOD IN TAIWAN,
National Taiwan Univ., Taipei. Dept. of Civil Engineering.
C. M. Wu.
In: Systems Analysis of Hydrologic Problems; Proceedings of the Second International Seminar for Hydrology Professors, August 2-14, 1970, Utah State University, Logan, p 418-445. 12 fig, 8 tab, 7 ref, 3 append.

Descriptors: *Probable maximum precipitation, *Typhoons, *Orography, *Moisture content, *Circulation, Maximum probable flood, Unit hydrographs, Depth-area-duration analysis, Infiltration, Storm runoff, Model studies.
Identifiers: *Horizontal convergence, *Taiwan, Linear reservoir model.

At any watershed, peak flow caused by a typhoon depends upon the characteristics of the typhoon rainfall, especially the peak intensity and the rate of change in rainfall intensity near the peak, the moisture content, and the motion of the typhoon. A typhoon rainfall results from the ascending of saturated air induced by low-level horizontal convergence. In the mountainous region of Taiwan, orographic lifting plays a more important part than horizontal convergence in causing rainfall. Typhoon rainfall can be decomposed into two components: (1) circulation rainfall predicted from the continuity of moisture, and (2) orographic rainfall evaluated by dividing the atmosphere into several layers. The probable maximum flood is obtained by first estimating the probable maximum precipitation from the typhoon model, then computing the runoff volume by considering the infiltration factor, and finally preparing the hydrograph shape by applying the unit hydrograph principle. A linear reservoir model is adopted for deriving the unit hydrograph shape. The depth-duration-area curve is used for summarizing the quantitative characteristics of the recorded storms. (See also W75-09210) (Singh-ISWS)
W75-09227

WEATHER MODIFICATION GRANTS.
For primary bibliographic entry see Field 3B.
W75-09259

STUDY ON A SIGNIFICANT PRECIPITATION EPISODE IN THE WESTERN UNITED STATES,
National Weather Service, Salt Lake City, Utah. Western Region.
I. S. Brenner.
Available from National Technical Information Service, Springfield, Va 22161. NOAA Technical Memorandum NWS WR-98, April 1975. 36 p, 29 fig, 1 tab, 7 ref.

Descriptors: *Precipitation(Atmospheric), *Storms, *Clouds, *Dry seasons, Climatology, Atmosphere, Vortices, Satellites, Weather forecasting, Model studies, California.
Identifiers: *Extratropical system, *Subtropical system, Case analysis, Tropospheric perturbations, Troughs.

This synoptic study for the period 22 September to 3 October 1974 involves a case analysis of an unforeseen major precipitation episode associated with the merging of an inactive upper tropospheric perturbation that moved east-northeastward out of the subtropics and an inactive extratropical low, moving southeastward. The amalgamation of the two systems caused a major surface storm within 24 hours. The major impact of this storm was to bring an abrupt end to the California dry season. Effects of these systems can be disastrous if they occur 'unexpectedly' during the raisin-drying season. More documentation is needed to better define the characteristics and possible forecasting procedures required. (NOAA)
W75-09267

STORM TIDE FREQUENCY ANALYSIS FOR THE GULF COAST OF FLORIDA FROM CAPE SAN BLAS TO ST. PETERSBURG BEACH,
National Weather Service, Silver Spring, Md.
F. P. Ho, and R. J. Tracey.
Available from National Technical Information Service, Springfield, Va 22161. NOAA Technical Memorandum NWS HYDRO-20, April 1975. 34 p, 8 fig, 7 tab, 21 ref.

Descriptors: *Storms, *Tides, *Storm surge, Tropical cyclones, Water levels, Hurricanes, Hydrodynamics, Climatology, Model studies, *Florida, *Gulf of Mexico, *Frequency analysis.
Identifiers: *Storm tides, Tide frequency analysis, Storm surge models, Coastal profiles.

Storm tide height frequency distributions are developed for the Gulf coast of Florida from Cape San Blas to St. Petersburg Beach for the National Flood Insurance program. Storm tides are computed from a full set of climatologically representative hurricanes, using the National Weather Service hydrodynamic storm surge model. Tide levels are shown in coastal profile between annual frequencies of 0.10 and .002. This report is to be used in estimating actuarial risk to buildings from coastal floods and in land use management. (NOAA)
W75-09268

PARAMETERIZED MOISTURE AND HEAT FLUX THROUGH TOP OF BOMEX VOLUME,
National Weather Service, Silver Spring, Md.
V. A. Myers.
Available from the National Technical Information Service, Springfield, Va. 22161. NOAA Technical Memorandum EDS BOMAP-15, May 1975. 39 p, 13 fig, 7 tab, 11 ref.

Descriptors: *Oceans, *Tropical regions, *Moisture, *Enthalpy, *Mass, Fluctuations, Atmosphere, Thermodynamics, Oceanography, Meteorology.
Identifiers: BOMEX volume, Barbados, *Tropical oceans, Moisture flux, Enthalpy flux, Parameterization.

A prime objective of the Barbados Oceanographic and Meteorological Experiment (BOMEX) in 1969 was to determine the budgets of moisture, enthalpy, and mass in a fixed atmospheric volume over a tropical ocean. The fluxes through the top of the volume, approximately at 500 mb, were not measured directly. A parameterization scheme is developed to estimate the top-of-volume moisture flux as a ratio to rainfall produced. The enthalpy flux is also treated briefly. (NOAA)
W75-09272

QUANTIZING 3- AND 5-CM RADAR HURRICANE PRECIPITATION DATA,
Miami Univ., Coral Gables, Fla. Remote Sensing Lab.
For primary bibliographic entry see Field 7C.
W75-09276

HURRICANES ON THE TEXAS COAST: DESCRIPTION AND CLIMATOLOGY (1),
Texas A and M Univ., College Station. Center for Applied Geosciences.
W. K. Henry, and J. P. McCormack.
Report TAMU-SG-75-501, March 1975, 29 p. TAMU-SG-75-501.

Descriptors: *Hurricanes, *Tropical cyclones, *Coasts, Tornadoes, Winds, Storms, Floods, Storm surge, Precipitation, Climatology, Meteorology, Erosion, *Texas.
Identifiers: Wind damage, Cyclonic circulation.

This booklet is the first in a series of three prepared for publication by Texas A and M's Sea Grant Program. The series is designed to help Texans understand, prepar for, and recover from the harmful effects of hurricanes. Various types of tropical cyclones and hurricanes are described. The characteristics of hurricanes and their frequency of occurrence over sections of the Texas coast also are analyzed. (See also W75-09284) (NOAA)
W75-09283

HURRICANES ON THE TEXAS COAST: THE DESTRUCTION (2),
Texas A and M Univ., College Station. Center for Applied Geosciences.
W. K. Henry, D. M. Driscoll, and J. P. McCormack.
Report TAMU-SG-75-502, March 1975, 16 p. TAMU-SG-75-502.

Descriptors: *Hurricanes, *Tropical cyclones, *Coasts, *Disasters, Tornadoes, Winds, Storms, Floods, Storm surge, Precipitation, Erosion, Climatology, Meteorology, *Texas.
Identifiers: Wind damage, Hurricane-spawned tornadoes.

This booklet is the second in a series of three discussing tropical storms and hurricanes, and their effects. Types of damage a hurricane can cause along the Texas coast and adjacent, inland areas are described. Hurricane-related events, such as storm surge, heavy rains, high winds, tornadoes, and resulting hazards, such as floods and downed electrical wires, are discussed. Special emphasis is given to types of destruction that occurred during previous hurricanes. (See also W75-09283) (NOAA)
W75-09284

RIVER FORECASTS PROVIDED BY THE NATIONAL WEATHER SERVICE.
National Weather Service, Silver Spring, Md.
Available from National Climatic Center, Asheville, NC 28801, for $0.75. Volume 2, 1973, 1974, 67 p.

Descriptors: *River forecasting, *Hydrologic data, *Rivers, *Forecasting, *Flood forecasting, Hydrology, Tables(Data), Warning systems, Floods, Water supply, Data aquisition, Surface waters, Flood control, *United States.

River forecasts and warnings, as well as other National Weather Service hydrologic services are described and information is given on: Hydrologic operations, forecasts and services; River Forecast Centers; NWS Field Offices; other hydrologic services; Data Acquisition Networks; Flash Flood Warning Program; Water Supply Forecasting Program; River Forecast Center addresses; River Forecast points and micellaneous information; Highest stages at National Weather Service gages; and Record high stages prior to Gage Records. Indexes are arranged by states, stations, and by rivers. A list of water supply forecast points is included. Illustrations included are: Map of River Forecast Centers, Map of Local NWS Offices, Map of Radar Network, Hydrologic Forecast System Chart, and Operations Chart - River and Flood Forecast and Warning Program. (NOAA)
W75-09285

WEATHER CONDITIONS AND SCREWWORM ACTIVITY,
National Weather Service, University Park, Pa.
For primary bibliographic entry see Field 3F.
W75-09318

2C. Snow, Ice, and Frost

HYDROLOGY OF PATCH CUTS IN LODGEPOLE PINE,
Colorado State Univ., Fort Collins. Dept. of Earth Sciences.
For primary bibliographic entry see Field 3B.
W75-08947

THE OPACITY OF ACCRETED ICE,
Western Australia Univ., Nedlands. Dept. of Physics.
For primary bibliographic entry see Field 2B.
W75-08974

CRYSTAL SIZE IN ACCRETED ICE,
Western Australia Univ., Nedlands. Dept. of Physics.
For primary bibliographic entry see Field 2B.
W75-08975

ISOTHERMS UNDER ICE,
For primary bibliographic entry see Field 2H.
W75-09011

HYDROLOGY OF PATCH CUTS IN LODGEPOLE PINE,
Colorado State Univ., Fort Collins. Dept. of Earth Resources.
For primary bibliographic entry see Field 3B.
W75-09198

A CONCEPTUAL MODEL OF OFFSHORE PERMAFROST,
Alaska Univ., College. Geophysical Inst.
For primary bibliographic entry see Field 2J.
W75-09266

EFFECTS OF ICE COVER ON DISSOLVED OXYGEN IN SILVER LAKE, ONTARIO,
Department of the Environment, Ottawa (Ontario). Water Quality Branch.
R. J. Maguire, and N. Watkin.
Technical Bulletin No 89, 3 p, 1975. 2 fig, 1 tab, 8 ref.

Descriptors: *Ice cover, *Dissolved oxygen, Ice-water interfaces, Chemicals, Investigations, Research, Iced lakes.
Identifiers: Silver lake, Ontario, Ice cover effects.

Weekly sampling was performed at the deepest point (23 m) of Silver Lake for a few chemical parameters during the late fall and winter of 1973-74. The amount of dissolved oxygen in most of the water column decreased by about 2 ppm during the winter. At the bottom, the decrease in dissolved oxygen amounted to 4-5 ppm, and the level of hydrogen sulfide increased signficantly. This decrease in the amount of dissolved oxygen is probably due to the prevention of atmospheric mixing by the ice and snow cover. In general, the amounts of orthophosphate, nitrate, chloride and total organic carbon remained constant during the winter, as did the values of specific conductance and pH. (Envir-Canada)
W75-09291

FLOATING ICE THICKNESS AND STRUCTURE DETERMINATION - HEATED WIRE,
Department of the Environment, Ottawa (Ontario). Water Resources Branch.
R. O. Ramseier, and R. J. Weaver.
Technical Bulletin No 88, 16 p, 1975. 10 fig, 8 ref.

Descriptors: *Ice cover, Methodology, Analytical techniques, Measurement, Instrumentation, Gages, Ice.
Identifiers: *Ice thickness, *Ice structure, *Heated wire technique.

The thickness of floating ice is one of the most important general parameters to be measured for many applications in the fields of transportation, engineering and climatology. The requirement for accurate thickness information, with details on the ice structure, led to the development and use of the heated wire ice thickness gauge. Once installed, the gauge provides a means of making in situ thickness measurements on fresh and salt water ice quickly and accurately. This report describes the measurement methods of determining ice structure from readings obtained, and details of construction of the gauge complete with engineering drawings. (Envir-Canada)
W75-09293

2D. Evaporation and Transpiration

EFFECTS OF ROOT MEDIUM AND WATERING ON TRANSPIRATION, GROWTH AND DEVELOPMENT OF GLASSHOUSE CROPS: I. EFFECTS OF COMPRESSION AT VARYING WATER LEVELS ON PHYSICAL STATE OF ROOT MEDIA AND A TRANSPIRATION AND GROWTH OF TOMATOES,
State Experiment Station Landvik, Grimstad (Norway).
G. Guttormsen.
Plant Soil. Vol 40, No 1, p 65-81, 1974, Illus.

Descriptors: *Plant growth, *Transpiration, Tomatoes, *Root systems, *Soil-water-plant relationships, Peat, Clays, Compaction, *Irrigation effects.
Identifiers: *Glasshouse crops, Montmorillonite.

The effect of adding clay, moisture and the compaction on the physical properties of peat as well as the effect on transpiration and growth of tomato plants were investigated during short term laboratory experiments. The effect of 6, 12 and 20 cm peat height in beds with constant water level was investigated in a 5-mo. tomato crop. Admixture of clay reduced the porosity of the peat. Adding the clay at moderate pressures (10, 100 g sq cm) decreased the amount of large pores (equivalent to pores emptied at pF 2.0) and to an increase of smaller pores (equivalent to pores emptied in the pF intervals 2.0-4.2). The reduction in the amount of large pores was greater with admixture of montmorillonite than with a soil clay. An increase of the soil clay content from 50 to 70% had an insignificant effect on the amount of large pores. Increasing the moisture content of the peat resulted in that fewer pores were emptied at pF 1.3. At a pressure of 1000 g sq cm the decrease of large pores was more marked for pure peat than for mixtures of peat and soil clay. Increasing the pressures from 10 to 100 g sq cm had only a slight effect. For a mixture of peat and montmorillonite a linear relationship was found between the clay content and bulk density, while a curvilinear relationship existed for a mixture of peat and soil clay. In short term laboratory experiments with tomato seedlings transpiration and growth rate were at a maximum at a pF equivalent to 20-30% airfilled pores. In a glasshouse experiment with tomatoes an increase was recorded in yield, size of fruit, leaf area and total dry matter production with increasing peat heights above a constant water level. Porous root media, such as peat, should be treated to counteract the existence of zones having suboptimal air content by use of sub-irrigation.--Copyright 1974, Biological Abstracts, Inc.
W75-09162

SIMULATION MODEL FOR EVAPOTRANSPIRATION OF WHEAT: EFFECT OF EVAPORATIVE CONDITIONS,
Hebrew Univ., Jerusalem (Israel).
G. Strateener, D. Yaron, E. Bresler, and D. Shimshi.
Journal of the Irrigation and Drainage Division, Proceeding of American Society of Civil Engineers, Vol 101, No IR1, Proceedings Paper 11169, p 13-19, March 1975. 4 tab, 3 ref, 2 append.

Descriptors: *Evapotranspiration, *Simulation analysis, *Agriculture, *Irrigation, *Wheat, Consumptive use, Soil moisture, Evaporation, Computers, Computer programs, Field capacity, Regression analysis, Plant growth, Root systems, Soil profiles, Model studies, Evaporation pans, Canopy.
Identifiers: *Israel(Negev).

A simulation model for tracing soil moisture fluctuations under irrigated wheat in a semi-arid climate was presented. The model was based on a function relating evapotranspiration to soil moisture and evaporative conditions as measured by means of a class A pan. The recharge of soil moisture by rain or irrigation was predicted by this model on the basis of a simplified infiltration scheme with the conventional concept of 'field capacity' as the upper limit of soil moisture content following the redistribution of moisture in the soil profile. By means of an iterative procedure, the 'best fitting' parameters were computed for each soil layer and each month from data on a wheat irrigation experiment in the arid Negev region in the year 1967-1968. The average relative deviation of the predicted soil moisture from the observed soil moisture was 9.3% for the five soil layers and 6.2% for the upper three soil layers. The reliability of the model was presented by these and other data and its performance was examined. (Roberts-ISWS)
W75-09196

RELATION OF SOIL WATER POTENTIAL TO STOMATAL RESISTANCE OF SOYBEAM,
Kansas State Univ., Manhattan. Evapotranspiration Lab.
R. A. Brady, S. M. Goltz, W. L. Powers, and E. T. Kanemasu.
Agronomy Journal, Vol 67, p 97-99, Jan-Feb 1975. 5 fig, 13 ref. OWRT A-049-KAN(9). 14-31-0001-3516.

Descriptors: *Evapotranspiration, *Soybeans, Soil water, Stomata, Measurement, Irrigation practices, Growth stages, Canopy, Leaves.
Identifiers: Water stress, *Stomatal resistance, *Soil water potential.

This research was undertaken to establish a meaningful relationship between stomatal resistance of soybeans and soil water potential. The main objectives were to establish this relationship and examine some of the factors affecting measurements of stomatal resistance of soybeans. Stomatal resistance in the soybean leaves was measured with a stomata porometer and plotted against soil water potential. A definite relationship was determined in two consecutive growing seasons between the soil water potential and stomatal resistance. Adaxial stomatal resistance increased rapidly when soil water potentials decrease to near -4 bars. Stomatal resistance of upper canopy leaves was not affected by the physiological stage of growth of the whole plant. The difference in stomatal resistance of well-irrigated and nonirrigated soybeans was distinct, and stomatal resistance showed promise in determining irrigation schedules.
W75-09235

ON CHANGES OF TRANSPIRATIONAL RESISTANCE IN LEAVES OF FITTONIA AS A RESULT OF DIFFERENT HUMIDITY, (IN GERMAN),
Basel Univ. (Switzerland). Botanisches Institut.
J. Burckhardt.
Ber Schweiz Bot Ges, Vol 82, No 4, p 309-338, 1972. Illus. English summary.

Descriptors: Transpiration, *Plant physiology, Environmental effects, Plant growth, *Stomata, *Transpiration control.
Identifiers: Fittonia-argyroneura, Mesophyll.

Formulas were devised for water vapor and heat transfer coefficients as functions of wind velocity, and length and width of a filter paper leaf-model. Fittonia argyroneura Coem., cuttings with adventitious roots, cultivated in nutrient solution were used for the experiments. The measurements were all performed in the dark. (30C, wind velocity = 0.4 m/s). The plants were exposed to selected antecedents, (A) induced wind velocity 0 m/s, relative air humidity 25%, air temperature 30C, liminious flux density 3000 Lux or 0 Lux, and (B) induced wind velocity 0 m/s, relative air humidity greater than 80%, air temperature 30C, luminious flux density 3000 Lux or 0 Lux. Their effects on the single transpiration resistances were examined. According to their antecedents the plants reached similar final values for the total diffusion resistances Sigma R regardless of the initial values. (Antecedents A) produced relatively high, antecedents B) relatively low total resistances.) These processes were reversible. Sudden changes of the total resistance were interpreted as a regulatory function of the stomata. On the other hand the principal level of the transpiration was adjusted by the 'cuticular' possible to prove the variability of RMIu directly. There is considerable evidence that the plant tries to keep it transpiration-level constant by changing its resistances, e.g. antecedents B), by opening the stomata in the dark. The observed oscillations of Sigma R were discussed as a regulatory function of the stomata, the oscillation was induced by the water economy. Exposing the leaves to light superimposed an 'opening order' to the stomata upon the 'order' of the water economy. The periodic opening and closing of the stomata was explained by the alternating requirements of the CO2- and O2-exchanges and the water economy.--Copyright 1974, Biological Abstracts, Inc.
W75-09330

2E. Streamflow and Runoff

HYDROLOGIC UNIT MAP--1974, STATE OF MICHIGAN.
Geological Survey, Reston, Va.
For primary bibliographic entry see Field 7C.
W75-08916

HYDROLOGIC UNIT MAP--1974, STATE OF SOUTH CAROLINA.
Geologic Survey, Reston, Va.
For primary bibliographic entry see Field 7C.
W75-08917

HYDROLOGIC UNIT MAP--1974, STATE OF VIRGINIA.
Geological Survey, Reston, Va.
For primary bibliographic entry see Field 7C.
W75-08918

HYDROLOGIC UNIT MAP--1974, STATE OF ALABAMA.
Geological Survey, Reston, Va.
For sale by USGS, Reston, Va 22092, Price $1.00. Hydrologic Unit Map of Alabama, 1974. 1 sheet, 1 map.

Descriptors: *Maps, *Hydrology, *Alabama, Water resources, Data collections, Planning.
Identifiers: *Hydrologic unit maps.

This map and accompanying table show Hydrologic Units in Alabama that are basically hydrographic in nature. The Cataloging Units shown will supplant the Cataloging Units previously used by the U.S. Geological Survey in its Catalog of Information on Water Data (1966-72). The Regions, Subregions and Accounting Units are aggregates of the Cataloging Units. The Regions and Subregions are currently (1974) used by the U.S. Water Resources Council for comprehensive planning, including the National Assessment, and as a standard geographical framework for more detailed water and related land-resources planning. The Accounting Units are those currently (1974) in use by the U.S. Geological Survey for managing the National Water Data Network. (Woodard-USGS)
W75-08919

HYDROLOGIC UNIT MAP--1974, STATE OF NEW YORK.
Geological Survey, Reston, Va.
For primary bibliographic entry see Field 7C.
W75-08920

A NEW DEVELOPMENT IN FLOOD FREQUENCY ESTIMATION,
Queensland Irrigation and Water Supply Commission, Brisbane (Australia).
W. C. Boughton.
In: Hydrology Symposium, Armidale, Australia, 1975. The Institution of Engineers Australia, Preprints of Papers, p 31 - 35, May 1975. 5 fig, 3 tab, 8 ref.

Descriptors: *Flood frequency, *Daily hydrographs, *Frequency analysis, Estimating, Peak discharge, Flood recurrence intervals, Rainfall-runoff relationships, Watersheds(Basins), *Australia.
Identifiers: *Queensland(Australia).

Peak flood flows are highly correlated with the daily flows in which they occur, and this relationship is used to develop a method of extending short flood records. The frequency distribution of daily flows, estimated from daily rainfalls by a rainfall-runoff model, is used with the short flood record to estimate the long term distribution of floods. Tests were made on 8 catchments, 67 to 505 square miles in area, in Queensland, Australia, using 10 years of streamflow record in each case with daily rainfalls to estimate 30 to 35 years of floods. Log-normal and Log-Pearson III distributions were fitted to both estimated and actual flood series. The estimated 1 in 50 years and 1 in 100 years floods differed on average by less than 8% from the actual records. (CSIRO)
W75-08957

COMPARISON OF UNIT HYDROGRAPH AND RUNOFF ROUTING METHODS OF FLOOD ESTIMATION,
Monash Univ., Clayton (Australia).
E. M. Laurenson, and R. G. Mein.
In: Hydrology Symposium, Armidale, Australia, 1975. The Institution of Engineers Australia, Preprints of Papers, p 36 - 40, May 1975. 4 fig, 9 ref.

Descriptors: *Unit hydrographs, *Routing, *Runoff forecasting, Hydrograph analysis, Streamflow forecasting, Rainfall-runoff relationships, Design flood, Watersheds(Basins), *Australia.
Identifiers: Yarra River(Vic), Thomson River(Vic), South Creek(NSW).

The unitgraph method of flood estimation is highly respected, but it nevertheless shows some inherent difficulties: notably, it neglects both areal variability of rainfall and losses over a catchment, and non-linearity of catchment response over a range of excess rainfall. The runoff routing method overcomes these and other limitations at the expense only of more extensive catchment analysis and computation. These points are explained and demonstrated with particular reference to the results of comparative applications of the two methods on three Australian catchments. (CSIRO)
W75-08958

DEVELOPMENT OF REGIONAL FLOOD ESTIMATION PROCEDURES,
Cameron, McNamara and Partners, Brisbane (Australia).
For primary bibliographic entry see Field 4A.
W75-08959

A FLOW AND SALT TRANSPORT SIMULATION SYSTEM FOR THE RIVER MURRAY IN SOUTH AUSTRALIA,
South Australia Engineering and Water Supply Dept., Adelaide.
For primary bibliographic entry see Field 7C.
W75-08960

ELECTROMAGNETIC FLOW SENSORS,
Woods Hole Oceanographic Institution, Mass.
For primary bibliographic entry see Field 7B.
W75-08987

OPTIMIZING PARAMETERS FOR A WATERSHED MODEL,
Virginia Polytechnic Inst. and State Univ., Blacksburg. Dept. of Agricultural Engineering.
V. O. Shanholtz, and J. C. Carr.
Transactions of the ASAE (American Society of Agricultural Engineers), Vol 18, No 2, p 307-311, March-April 1975. 4 fig, 3 tab, 9 ref. OWRT A-018-VA(7).

Descriptors: *Model studies, *Simulation analysis, *Computer models, Optimization, Hydrology, Analytical techniques, Hydrologic aspects, Runoff, Mathematical models, Mathematics, Watersheds(Basins), Parametric hydrology.
Identifiers: *Kentucky Watershed Model.

Use of the Kentucky Watershed Model and experimentation with various land phase parameters were discussed. Examples were presented demonstrating the year-to-year parameter variation and the effect of including additional records. Potential errors due to unrepresentative, short periods of record were also discussed. When longer historical records were available, new criteria for selecting representative input data were presented. (Jess-ISWS)
W75-09077

FLOOD PLAIN INFORMATION; TUCKAHOE CREEK, HENRICO COUNTY, VIRGINIA.
Army Engineer District, Norfolk, Va.
July 1965, 11 p, 3 plates, 3 fig; append, 24 p, 6 plates, photos, 2 tab, 24 ref.

Descriptors: *Flood plains, *Flood damage, *Flood plain zoning, Flood profiles, Flood stages, Flood proofing, Obstruction to flow, Land use, Planning, Urbanization, *Virginia.
Identifiers: *Tuckahoe Creek(Va), *Deep Run(Va), Stony Run(Va), Henrico County(Va), Flood plain management, '50-year flood', Standard Project Flood.

Although now sparsely populated, the portion of Henrico County, Virginia, in the study area is being rapidly developed as Richmond expands to the west. Much of the flood plain is low and swampy. The stream channels are relatively shallow and overgrown with dense vegetation. During a flood, the vegetation along with 7 bridges would create obstructions to flow. Rainfall averages 43 inches per year and is greatest in the summer. Based on rainfall and flow records of surrounding streams, peak flows for a '50-year flood' and a Standard Project Flood (SPF) were computed. At the C and O Railroad, the point of highest peak discharge, a '50-year flood' would produce 11,360 cfs and an SPF 29,200 cfs. Guidelines for use of floodplains and reducing future flood losses are discussed, including floodplain zoning, building codes, subdivision regulations, floodplain evacuation, flood proofing, flood control works, and alternative sites and alternative uses. (Diefendorf-North Carolina)

W75-09115

FLOODS IN WAIAHOLE-WAIKANE AREA, OAHU, HAWAII,
Geological Survey, Reston, Va.
C. J. Ewart, and R. Lee.
For sale by US Geological Survey, Reston, Va. 22092 - $1.25. Hydrologic Investigations Atlas HA-531, 1974. 1 sheet, 7 fig, 1 map, 8 ref.

Descriptors: *Floods, *Flood frequency, *Flood data, *Maps, *Hawaii, Flood profiles, Flood peak, Flood plains, Flood protection, Flood forecasting, Hydrograph analysis, Streamflow.
Identifiers: *Oahu(Hawaii), Waiahole-Waikane area.

This one-sheet atlas presents hydrologic data concerning the extent and frequency of flooding in the Waiahole-Waikane area of windward Oahu, Hawaii. The data provide a technical basis for the formulation of flood-plain regulations, building and zoning ordinances, the design and location of flood-control projects, and modification or improvement of the existing drainage system. The three main streams in the study area are Waiahole, Waikane, and a smaller unnamed stream, which is located between these two. Waiahole and Waikane Streams head near the crest of the Koolau Range and are perennial; the unnamed stream heads at about the 700-foot elevation and is intermittent. The stream gradients are steep in the upper reaches and fairly flat on the coastal flood plain. The approximate area subject to inundation by a flood having an estimated recurrence interval of 50 years is outlined on a topographic map. The major part of the inundated area is the lowland between Waiahole and Waikane Streams. (Woodard-USGS)
W75-09169

FLOODS IN EAST BATON ROUGE PARISH AND ADJACENT AREAS, LOUISIANA, FOR THE PERIOD 1953-74,
Geological Survey, Baton Rouge, La.
For primary bibliographic entry see Field 4A.
W75-09173

STREAMFLOW DEPLETION RESULTING FROM UPSTREAM SURFACE-WATER IMPOUNDMENT,
Geological Survey, Bay Saint Louis, Miss. Water Resources Div.
For primary bibliographic entry see Field 4A.
W75-09175

WATER RESOURCES DATA FOR KANSAS, 1974: PART 1. SURFACE WATER RECORDS.
Geological Survey, Lawrence, Kans.
For primary bibliographic entry see Field 7C.
W75-09180

AN INTRODUCTION TO SYSTEMS ANALYSIS OF HYDROLOGICAL PROBLEMS,
Illinois Univ., Urbana. Dept. of Civil Engineering.
For primary bibliographic entry see Field 2A.
W75-09211

MATHEMATICAL MODELING OF NEAR COASTAL CIRCULATION,
Massachusetts Inst. of Tech., Cambridge.
For primary bibliographic entry see Field 2L.
W75-09273

RIVER FORECASTS PROVIDED BY THE NATIONAL WEATHER SERVICE.
National Weather Service, Silver Spring, Md.
For primary bibliographic entry see Field 2B.
W75-09285

FLOOD OF JUNE 1972 IN THE SOUTHERN PEACE (SMOKY RIVER) BASIN, ALBERTA,
Department of the Environment, Calgary (Alberta). Water Resources Branch.
For primary bibliographic entry see Field 4A.
W75-09292

2F. Groundwater

AVAILABILITY AND QUALITY OF GROUND WATER IN THE SUTHERLIN AREA, DOUGLAS COUNTY, OREGON,
Geological Survey, Portland, Oreg.
For primary bibliographic entry see Field 7C.
W75-08910

SOURCES OF EMERGENCY WATER SUPPLIES IN SAN MATEO COUNTY, CALIFORNIA,
Geological Survey, Menlo Park, Calif.
For primary bibliographic entry see Field 6D.
W75-08911

GROUND WATER IN GRAY COUNTY, SOUTHWESTERN KANSAS,
Geological Survey, Reston, Va.
For primary bibliographic entry see Field 7C.
W75-08915

MODELLING A GROUNDWATER AQUIFER IN THE GRAND PRAIRIE OF ARKANSAS,
Arkansas Univ., Fayetteville. Dept. of Agricultural Engineering.
C. L. Griffis.
Transactions of the American Society of Agricultural Engineers, Vol 15, No 2, p 261-263, March-April 1972. 6 fig, 5 ref. OWRR A-020-ARK(1).

Descriptors: *Groundwater, *Computer models, *Mathematical models, Aquifer management, Groundwater recharge, Recharge wells, Artificial recharge, Water yield, Surface-groundwater relationships, Aquifers, *Arkansas, Model studies.
Identifiers: Quaternary aquifer(Ark), Grand Prairie(Ark).

Most of the irrigation water for the Grand Prairie of Arkansas comes from the Quaternary aquifer lying beneath the area. Constant pumping has lowered the water table and shortened the water supply. A model was developed to investigate the possibility of artificial recharging of the aquifer. The area was divided into sections of one square mile. The flow equations were then solved for each section. Various methods of recharge were then evaluated using the model. Recharge wells were found to provide the best solution. (Skogerboe-Colorado State)
W75-08923

THE APPLICATION OF THE DSDT HYBRID COMPUTER METHOD TO WATER RESOURCES PROBLEMS,
California Univ., Los Angeles. School of Engineering and Applied Science.
W. J. Karplus, and J. A. Dracup.
Paper at Proceedings, 8th Annual Water Resource Conference, Rollo, Missouri, October, 1972. 7 ref. (California Water Resources Center Project UCAL-WRC-W-340). OWRR B-150-CAL(9).

Descriptors: *Computer models, *Simulation analysis, *Mathematical models, Reviews, *Hybrid computers, Analog models, *Groundwater.

The progressive evolution of the Discrete-Space-Discrete-Time Hybrid Computer System and application of the system in simulating ground-water systems is reviewed. The review demonstrates that a variety of hydrology problems can be treated successfully using the analog subroutine approach. Advantages and disadvantages of the system are presented together with literature citations of the specific applications of the system. (Snyder-California, Davis)
W75-08929

THE USE OF THE DIGITAL SIMULATION LANGUAGE PDEL IN HYDROLOGIC STUDIES,
California Univ., Los Angeles. Dept. of Computer Science.
W. C. Tam, and W. J. Karplus.
Water Resources Bulletin, Vol 9, December 1973, p 1100-1111. 10 fig, 5 ref. (California Water Resources Center Project UCAL-WRC-W-340). OWRR B-150-CAL(12).

Descriptors: *Simulation analysis, *Hydrologic models, Mathematical models, *Groundwater, *Programming language, Digital computers, Computer programs, Aquifers, Percolation.

Digital simulation languages have become popular means for the simulation and analysis of systems on a digital computer. However, the use of these languages for the simulation of systems characterized by partial differential equations has been very limited. In hydrologic studies, mathematical models involving elliptic and parabolic partial differential equations are most common. This paper describes the application of the digital simulation language PDEL to analyze problems in hydrologic studies. PDEL is designed specifically to solve partial differential equations of the elliptic, parabolic, and hyperbolic types. The language provides convenient and easy-to-learn statements for the description of problem to the computer. A computer program is automatically generated to solve the problem and the numerical solution printed and plotted. Two important hydrologic problems are used for illustration. The first is the analysis of ground-water table recession in large unconfined aquifers and the second is the growth of ground-water mounds in response to uniform percolation. (Snyder-California, Davis)
W75-08930

ESTIMATION OF THE WATER RESOURCES OF A PORTION OF THE GAMBIER PLAIN SOUTH AUSTRALIA USING A NEW METHOD FOR EVALUATING LOCAL RECHARGE,
Commonwealth Scientific and Industrial Research Organization, Adelaide (Australia). Div. of Soils.
G. B. Allison.
In: Hydrology Symposium, Armidale, Australia, 1975. Institution of Engineers Australia, Preprints of Papers, p 1 - 5, May 1975. 3 fig, 1 tab, 19 ref.

Descriptors: *Groundwater recharge, *Tritium, *Vegetation effects, *Soil types, Estimating, Radioisotopes, Pasture, Forests, Planning, Water resources development, *Australia.
Identifiers: Gambier Plain(SA).

A technique for estimating local recharge to an unconfined aquifer using environmental tritium is outlined. For four different soil types in the same climatic regime, local recharge was found to vary between 50 and 180 mm per year beneath pasture. Lesser recharge occurs by a different mechanism beneath native forest. The estimates of local recharge together with an approximate soil map are used to estimate that the mean local recharge to the aquifer is approximately 150,000,000 cu. m. per year. Some implications for future planning of the variation in local recharge with soil type are discussed. (CSIRO)
W75-08953

INVESTIGATION OF SENSITIVITY AND ERROR PROPAGATION IN NUMERICAL MODELS OF GROUNDWATER BASINS,
James Cook Univ. of North Queensland, Townsville (Australia).
R. E. Volker, and B. E. Guvanasen.

In: Hydrology Symposium, Armidale, Australia, 1975. The Institution of Engineers Australia, Preprints of Papers, p 16 - 20, May 1975. 6 fig, 1 tab, 10 ref.

Descriptors: *Mathematical models, *Groundwater movement, Numerical analysis, Model studies, Equations, Aquifer characteristics.

A description is given of a series of numerical experiments to study patterns of error propagation produced by inaccuracy of data in digital models of groundwater basins. The results show that errors in initial head data will usually be of most significance in short term predictions although the consequent discrepancies will decrease with time. Errors in predicted heads resulting from incorrect transmissivity and storage coefficient data tend to increase with time and will therefore cause problems in using models for long term predictions of aquifer response. (CSIRO)
W75-08954

TECHNIQUES FOR HANDLING INPUT DATA FOR FINITE ELEMENT ANALYSIS OF REGIONAL GROUNDWATER FLOW,
New South Wales Univ., Kensington (Australia). Water Research Lab.
P. S. Huyakorn, and C. R. Dudgeon.
In: Hydrology Symposium, Armidale, Australia, 1975. The Institution of Engineers Australia, Preprints of Papers, p 21-25, May 1975. 10 fig, 14 ref.

Descriptors: *Finite element analysis, *Data processing, *Computer programs, *Groundwater movement, Groundwater basins, Numerical analysis.

Techniques are presented which enable a significant proportion of the input data for finite element analysis of regional groundwater flow problems to be automatically generated. A computer program incorporating these techniques is described. Salient features of the program include subroutines which plot the generated input data and computed results. Through visual inspection of the plots, errors in the input data can be readily detected and rectified. (CSIRO)
W75-08955

FACTORS CONTROLLED POROSITY AND PERMEABILITY IN THE CURDSVILLE MEMBER OF THE LEXINGTON LIMESTONE,
Kentucky Water Resources Inst. Lexington.
W. C. MacQuown, Jr.
Available from the National Technical Information Service, Springfield, Va 22161 as PB-242 987, $4.75 in paper copy, $2.25 in microfiche. Research Report No 7, 1967. 80 p, 19 fig, 5 tab, 13 ref. OWRR A-003-KY. 14-01-0001-911.

Descriptors: *Porosity, *Permeability, *Kentucky, *Carbonates, Carbonate rocks, *Limestones, Hydrogeology, Aquifers, Groundwater.
Identifiers: Carbonate porosity, Carbonate permeability, Carbonate aquifer, Limestone aquifer, Curdsville limestone, Carbonate petrology, Carbonate lithology, Carbonate bank facies.

Factors controlling the porosity and peameability of the Curdsville Limestone Member of the Lexington Limestone of Middle Ordovician Age in the Blue Grass Region of Kentucky are geological. Microstratigraphic analysis has led to the division of the lower Lexington Limestone, consisting principally of the Curdsville Member into three beds which may be subdivided into 'zones' made up of several lithological types and sub-types. Lower, middle, and upper bed characteristics are helpful in determining the regional dispositional history in the progressively transgressing Curdsville sea. Paleogeography of Curdsville time has been determined by delineation of two local facies: (1) a carbonate bank--shoal area facies, and (2) a shelf--channel area facies. Permeable carbonate bank--shoal facies are best developed on the structurally high Jessamine Dome Shoal Area where the Curdsville Limestone is found at shallow depth. Ground waters of meteoric origin have created sink holes, solution valleys, and caverns through solution enlargement of fractures comprising an extensive intersecting joint system. (Huffsey-Kentucky)
W75-09051

A DISCRETE KERNEL GENERATOR FOR STREAM-AQUIFER STUDIES,
Colorado State Univ., Fort Collins. Dept. of Civil Engineering.
For primary bibliographic entry see Field 4B.
W75-09078

GEOPHYSICAL EXPLORATION OF GROUNDWATER IN SOFT FORMATIONS AND ITS UTILIZATION IN MINOR IRRIGATION,
Indian Inst. of Tech., Kharagpur. Dept. of Geology and Geophysics.
For primary bibliographic entry see Field 4B.
W75-09103

DIGITAL MODEL ANALYSIS OF THE PRINCIPAL ARTESIAN AQUIFER, GLYNN COUNTY, GEORGIA,
Geological Survey, Doraville, Ga.
For primary bibliographic entry see Field 7C.
W75-09171

A GALERKIN-FINITE ELEMENT ANALYSIS OF THE HYDROTHERMAL SYSTEM AT WAIRAKEI, NEW ZEALAND,
Geological Survey, Reston, Va.
J. W. Mercer, G. F. Pinder, and I. G. Donaldson.
Journal of Geophysical Research, Vol 80, No 17, p 2608-2621, June 10, 1975. 15 fig, 3 tab, 64 ref.

Descriptors: *Geothermal studies, *Mathematical studies, *Numerical analysis, *Finite element analysis, Foreign research, Borehole geophysics, Thermal water, Confined water, Forecasting, Heat flow, Thermal properties, Preesure, Temperature, Porous media, Aquifer characteristics, Correlation analysis, Groundwater movement.
Identifiers: *New Zealand, Two-dimensional areal analysis, Three-dimensional flow.

A single-phase simulation model was applied to the hot-water hydrothermal field at Wairakei, New Zealand. A two-dimensional areal analysis was made of the production aquifer under steady state and transient flow conditions, allowing vertical flow of heat and fluid through an overlying confining bed. Calculated temperature and pressure patterns correlate well with observed patterns until approximately 1963, when increasing quantities of stream in the production aquifer invalidated the assumption of single-phase flow. For futher simulation of the Wairakei reservoir the numerical model will need to be extended to incorporate phase change and three-dimensional flow. Preliminary results, however, indicate that the response of hot-water hydrothermal systems to exploitation can be simulated by using a mathematical reservoir model based on a Galerkin-finite element approach. (Woodard-USGS)
W75-09176

HYDRAULIC CHARACTERISTICS AND WATER-SUPPLY POTENTIAL OF THE AQUIFERS IN THE VICINITY OF THE WASTEWATER TREATMENT PLANT, SOUTH BEND, INDIANA,
Geological Survey, Indianapolis, Ind.
For primary bibliographic entry see Field 4B.
W75-09179

PROBLEMS IN C-14 DATING OF WATER FROM AQUIFERS OF DELTAIC ORIGIN--AN EXAMPLE FROM THE NEW JERSEY COASTAL PLAIN,
Geological Survey, Reston, Va.
I. J. Winograd, and G. M. Farlekas.
In: Isotope Techniques in Groundwater Hydrology 1974, Vol 2; Proceedings of Symposium organized by International Atomic Energy Agency, March 11-15, 1974, Vienna: International Atomic Energy Agency Publication, Vienna, p 69-93, August 1974. 8 fig, 2 tab, 28 ref.

Descriptors: *Radioactive dating, *Carbon radioisotopes, *Groundwater, *Aquifers, *New Jersey, Dating, Methodology, Geologic time, Geochemistry, Groundwater movement, Sedimentology, Evaluation, Coastal plains.
Identifiers: *Potomac-Raritan-Magothy aquifer(NJ), Deltaic sediments, Marginal marine sediments.

Major assumptions common to interpretive studies of C-14 in groundwater systems are: (a) no CO_2 is introduced after recharge; (b) the C-13 of carbonate phases in the aquifer is known and taken to be zero per mil; and (c) interformational flow can be neglected. None of these assumptions are fulfilled in deltaic and marginal marine sediments comprising the Potomac-Raritan-Magothy aquifer system of New Jersey; and it is likely that the first two cannot be met in most aquifers of deltaic to marginal marine origin because: (1) variations of pH, H_2CO_3, HCO_3, and Ca+Mg in the groundwater show a significant amount of CO_2 being generated within the Potomac-Raritan-Magothy aquifer to distances of 45 kilometers down the hydraulic gradient. The hypothesis that coalification of ubiquitous lignitic detritus is the source of CO_2 described in other deltaic aquifers is tentatively accepted here; (2) the C-13 of common carbonate mineral phases in deltaic and marginal marine sediments ranges from 0 to -20 per mil; (3) the aquifer is recharged both by infiltration on its outcrop areas and by leakage from overlying marine strata; the leakage is significantly more mineralized than the aquifer water; the C-14 content probably also differs. For these reasons, and despite regular variations of C-14 and C-13 down the hydraulic gradient, meaningful interpretation of even relative C-14 ages and groundwater velocities cannot be made in the New Jersey aquifer. (Woodard-USGS)
W75-09183

HYDROLOGIC CONSEQUENCES OF USING GROUND WATER TO MAINTAIN LAKE LEVELS AFFECTED BY WATER WELLS NEAR TAMPA, FLORIDA,
Geological Survey, Tallahassee, Fla.
For primary bibliographic entry see Field 4B.
W75-09184

GROUND-WATER RESOURCES OF THE HOLLYWOOD AREA, FLORIDA,
Geological Survey, Tallahassee, Fla.
For primary bibliographic entry see Field 6D.
W75-09185

DESCRIPTIONS AND CHEMICAL ANALYSES FOR SELECTED WELLS IN THE TEHAMA-COLUSA CANAL SERVICE AREA, SACRAMENTO VALLEY, CALIFORNIA,
Geological Survey, Menlo Park, Calif.
For primary bibliographic entry see Field 4B.
W75-09187

ESTIMATED GROUND-WATER FLOW, VOLUME OF WATER IN STORAGE, AND POTENTIAL YIELD OF WELLS IN THE POJOAQUE RIVER DRAINAGE BASINS, SANTA FE COUNTY, NEW MEXICO,
Geological Survey, Albuquerque, N.Mex.
For primary bibliographic entry see Field 4B.
W75-09188

THE INFLUENCE OF LATE CENOZOIC STRATIGRAPHY ON DISTRIBUTION OF IMPOUNDMENT-RELATED SEISMICITY AT LAKE MEAD, NEVADA-ARIZONA,
Geological Survey, Denver, Colo.
For primary bibliographic entry see Field 8G.
W75-09192

2G. Water In Soils

CONTENT OF THE TRACE ELEMENTS COPPER AND MANGANESE IN STREAM WATER, SOIL, AND PLANTS IN SOUTHERN UKRAINE, (IN RUSSIAN),
Odesskii Meditinskii Institut (USSR).
For primary bibliographic entry see Field 5B.
W75-08907

CHARACTERIZATION OF THE FOREST FLOOR IN STANDS ALONG A MOISTURE GRADIENT IN SOUTHERN NEW MEXICO,
North Carolina State Univ., Raleigh. Dept. of Soil Science.
A. G. Wollum, II.
Soil Science Society of America, Proceedings, Vol 37, No 4, p 637-640, July-August, 1973. 5 tab, 13 ref.

Descriptors: *New Mexico, *Forest watersheds, *Soil moisture, *Moisture availability, *Soil physical properties, *Soil chemical properties, Potassium, Nutrients, Vegetation effects, Leaching, Limestones, Pinyon pine trees, Juniper trees, Ponderosa pine trees.
Identifiers: Moisture gradient.

Forest floor properties along a moisture gradient ranging from dry, represented by a pinyon-juniper stand, to wet, represented by a white fir stand, were studied. Dry weights and amounts of nutrients were directly related to the moisture gradient. Nutrient concentrations were not related to the moisture gradient except for potassium. Sufficent water appears to have been present to allow substantial leaching of potassium from the forest flow in the more mesic stands. Other factors that influence forest floor properties include moisture regime, vegetation types, and parent material. Stand composition is influenced by the moisture gradient as evidenced by the stands at the drier elevations which have open areas that exceed 15 percent. As moisture becomes less of a limiting factor, a greater amount of space may be occupied and utilized. As available moisture increased, there was a tendency for stands to become multilayered. (Mastic-Arizona)
W75-08948

CONTROLLED SUBSURFACE DRAINAGE FOR SOUTHERN COASTAL PLAINS SOIL,
Agricultural Research Service, Florence, S.C. Coastal Plains Soil and Water Conservation Research Center.
C. W. Doty, S. T. Currin, and R. E. McLin.
Journal of Soil and Water Conservation, Vol 30, No 2, p 82-84, March-April 1975. 5 fig, 1 tab, 9 ref.

Descriptors: *Water table, *Subsurface drains, *Silage, *Drainage, Rainfall, Soil types, Pervious soils, Soil moisture, Crops, Crop response, Ditches, Hydraulic gradient, Regulation, Costs, Soil profiles, Capillary fringe, Regression analysis, *Southeast US, Coastal Plains.

A field study of water table control through subsurface conduits on a typical Southern Coastal Plains soil showed that in these sandy soils the water table must be kept at 42 inches or less from the soil surface. Silage yields from a field under controlled drainage were greater than those from a nondrained field. For each additional day, between 25 and 55 days, that the water table was less than 42 inches from the soil surface, silage yields increased 0.3 to 0.6 ton per acre. (Visocky-ISWS)
W75-08972

STUDIES ON SOIL INSECTICIDES: XII. EFFECT OF TEMPERATURE AND SOIL MOISTURE ON THE BIOACTIVITY OF SOIL INSECTIDES,
Higher Agricultural Inst., Mushtuhur (Egypt). Dept. of Plant Protection.
A. A. A. Gawaar, A-R. El-Bery, E-S. Abdel-Karim, and F. A. El-Lakwah.
Z Angew Entomol, Vol 75, No 1, p 98-103, 1974.

Descriptors: *Insecticides, *Soil moisture, *Temperature, *Toxicity, Cotton.
Identifiers: Bioactivity, *Lindane, Soil insecticides, Spodoptera-littoralis, *Thimet.

The effects of temperature (26, 30, 35, 40C) and moisture contents (10, 20, 30%) on toxicity of 2.37 ppm of Thimet and lindane were investigated. Thimet had a positive temperature coefficient against prepupae and pupae of the cotton leaf worm Spodoptera littoralis, while lindane showed a negative temperature coefficient. Differences in mortalities due to Thimet at different degrees of temperature were highly significant in contrast to lindane that induced insignificant differences in mortalities as indicated by the analysis of variances. The prepupae were more sensitive to increase in temperature than the pupae. Toxicities of both lindane and Thimet at 20% moisture content were generally higher than at 30% but the differences were not statistically significant.--Copyright 1974, Biological Abstracts, Inc.
W75-08999

ENZYMATIC ACITIVITY OF ERODED SOILS, (IN RUSSIAN),
For primary bibliographic entry see Field 2I.
W75-09105

PREDICTION OF WATER SOLUBLE ARSENIC IN SEWAGE-SOIL SYSTEMS,
Missouri Univ., Columbia. Dept. of Agronomy.
For primary bibliographic entry see Field 5A.
W75-09127

A SIMPLE SOIL WATER SIMULATION MODEL FOR ASSESSING THE IRRIGATION REQUIREMENTS OF WHEAT,
Israel Meteorological Service, Bet-Dagan.
For primary bibliographic entry see Field 3F.
W75-09152

MAP SHOWING DEPTH TO BEDROCK, PLAINFIELD QUADRANGLE, MASSACHUSETTS,
Geological Survey, Boston, Mass.
For primary bibliographic entry see Field 7C.
W75-09165

MAP SHOWING DEPTH TO BEDROCK, HEATH QUADRANGLE, MASSACHUSETTS-VERMONT,
Geological Survey, Boston, Mass.
For primary bibliographic entry see Field 7C.
W75-09166

CONTOUR MAP OF THE BEDROCK SURFACE, BRISTOL QUADRANGLE, CONNECTICUT,
Geological Survey, Hartford, Conn.
For primary bibliographic entry see Field 7C.
W75-09167

CONTOUR MAP OF THE BEDROCK SURFACE, SOUTHINGTON QUADRANGLE, CONNECTICUT,
Geological Survey, Hartford, Conn.
For primary bibliographic entry see Field 7C.
W75-09168

NON-EQUILIBRIUM THERMODYNAMICS OF ELECTRO-OSMOSIS OF WATER THROUGH COMPOSITE CLAY MEMBRANES, 1. THE PARALLEL ARRANGEMENT,
Harcourt Butler Technological Inst., Kanpur (India). Dept. of Chemistry.
For primary bibliographic entry see Field 2K.
W75-09200

NON-EQUILIBRIUM THERMODYNAMICS OF ELECTRO-OSMOSIS OF WATER THROUGH COMPOSITE CLAY MEMBRANES, 2. THE SERIES ARRANGEMENT,
Harcourt Butler Technological Inst., Kanpur (India). Dept. of Chemistry.
For primary bibliographic entry see Field 2K.
W75-09201

NON-EQUILIBRIUM THERMODYNAMICS OF ELECTRO-OSMOSIS OF WATER THROUGH COMPOSITE CLAY MEMBRANES, 3. THE ELECTRO-KINETIC ENERGY CONVERSION,
Harcourt Butler Technological Inst., Kanpur (India). Dept. of Chemistry.
For primary bibliographic entry see Field 2K.
W75-09202

QUANTITATIVE INVESTIGATIONS ON MOISTURE ATTRACTION IN HYGROSCOPIC SALINE SOIL SURFACES IN THE KUCUK MENDERES PLAIN, TURKEY,
W. Andriesse.
Versl Landbouwkd Onderz (Agric Res Rep). 785. 175-179. Illus. 1972.

Descriptors: *Soil moisture, *Saline soils, *Salts, *Soil surfaces, *Chlorides, *Hygroscopic water, Hygrometry, Humidity, Calcium chloride, Magnesium compounds, Plains.
Identifiers: *Turkey(Kucuk Menderes plain).

Saline surfaces with hygroscopic salts (especially $MgCl_2$ and $CaCl_2$) have a moisture content which at night is twice as high as by day, when relative air humidity is lower. In ordinary salt crusts the increase is slight. The hygroscopic surfaces change in color with water content.--Copyright 1974, Biological Abstracts, Inc.
W75-09262

HYGROSCOPIC SURFACES OF SALINE SOILS IN THE KUCUK MENDERES PLAIN, TURKEY: OCCURRENCE, DESCRIPTION AND CHEMICAL ANALYSIS,
W. Andriesse.
Versl Landbouwkd Onderz (Agric Res Rep). 785. 165-174. Illus. 1972.

Descriptors: Saline soils, Hygrometry, Salts, Hygroscopic water, Soil surfaces, Chlorides, Magnesium compounds, Calcium chloride, Chemical analysis.
Identifiers: *Turkey(Kucuk Menderes plain).

Saline soils occur with usually moist and dark surfaces of a puffed nature due to the hygroscopicity of the salts (especially $MgCl_2$ and $CaCl_2$) which are present in higher amounts than in the adjoining dry and pale-colored ordinary salt crusts. Both are rich in NaCl.--Copyright 1974, Biological Abstracts, Inc.
W75-09263

2H. Lakes

CONTRIBUTION TO ECOLOGY OF INDIAN AQUATICS: V. SEASONAL CHANGES IN BIOMASS AND RATE OF PRODUCTION OF 2 PERENNIAL SUBMERGED MACROPHYTES (HYDRILLA VERTICILLATA ROYLE AND

NAIAS GRAMINEA DEL) OF RAMGARH LAKE OF GORAKHPUR (INDIA),
Saint Andrew's Coll., Gorakhpur (India). Dept. of Botany.
For primary bibliographic entry see Field 5C.
W75-08932

MECHANISMS FOR DEEP WATER RENEWAL IN LAKE NITINAT, A PERMANENTLY ANOXIC FJORD,
Washington Univ., Seattle. Dept. of Oceanography.
For primary bibliographic entry see Field 2L.
W75-08969

AN EMPIRICAL METHOD OF ESTIMATING THE RETENTION OF PHOSPHORUS IN LAKES,
Toronto Univ. (Ontario). Dept. of Zoology.
For primary bibliographic entry see Field 5B.
W75-08970

A SUBMERGED HYPOLIMNION AERATOR,
Union Carbide Corp., Tarrytown, N.Y. Aquatic Environmental Sciences.
For primary bibliographic entry see Field 5G.
W75-08971

A TEST OF A SIMPLE NUTRIENT BUDGET MODEL PREDICTING THE PHOSPHORUS CONCENTRATION IN LAKE WATER,
Toronto Univ. (Ontario). Dept. of Zoology.
For primary bibliographic entry see Field 5C.
W75-08986

LIMNOLOGY OF WESTERN SPRINGS, AUCKLAND, NEW ZEALAND,
Kansas Univ., Lawrence. Dept. of Botany.
For primary bibliographic entry see Field 5C.
W75-09000

PIGMENT CYCLES IN TWO HIGH-ARCTIC CANADIAN LAKES,
For primary bibliographic entry see Field 5C.
W75-09002

EVALUATION OF PRIMARY PRODUCTION PARAMETERS IN LAKE KINNERET (ISRAEL),
For primary bibliographic entry see Field 5C.
W75-09003

BACTERIAL PRODUCTIVITY OF A HIGH MOUNTAIN LAKE,
Innsbruck Univ. (Austria). Inst. of Zoology.
For primary bibliographic entry see Field 5C.
W75-09004

METABOLISM OF THE DOMINANT AUTOTROPHS OF THE NORTH AMERICAN GREAT LAKES,
For primary bibliographic entry see Field 5C.
W75-09005

PRINCIPLES OF TYPOLOGY OF STRATIFIED LAKES IN RELATION TO VERTICAL EXCHANGE,
W. R. Khomskis, and T. N. Filatova.
Verhandlungen Internationale Vereinigung Limnologie, Vol 18, p 528-536, 1972. 3 fig, 2 tab, 8 ref.

Descriptors: *Stratification, *Lakes, Water temperature, Estimating, Estimating equations.
Identifiers: *Lake stratification typology.

Stratification of water in the majority of lakes depends on thermal heterogeneity. When observation data on temperature are available during the summer phase the character of thermal stratification of a lake can be determined by: duration of continuous metalimnion existence; maximum and mean vertical temperature gradient for every phase of the summer period; depth of metalimnion expansion, its upper and lower boundaries during different phases of a summer period; mean velocity of variation for the position of upper and lower boundaries of metalimnion during different phases of summer periods; maximum and mean stability of water mass for every summer phase; coefficient of turbulent heat conductivity; variations of water temperature at bottom layer of hypolimnion during its existence or variations of water temperature at the bottom layer during the annual cycle if the beginning and the end of stagnation are not quite evident. If lake typification is carried out on the basis of these characteristics it is necessary to analyze the data for a deep water area of the lake by means of average observations and take into account extreme values. (Jones-Wisconsin)
W75-09006

THE KINETICS OF EXTRACELLULAR RELEASE OF SOLUBLE ORGANIC MATTER BY PLANKTON,
For primary bibliographic entry see Field 5C.
W75-09007

ESTIMATION OF AQUATIC ECOSYSTEM PARAMETERS,
For primary bibliographic entry see Field 5C.
W75-09008

THE BENTHIC CARBON BUDGET OF A SOUTHERN MICHIGAN MARL LAKE,
For primary bibliographic entry see Field 5C.
W75-09009

THE BIOLOGICAL CYCLE OF MOLYBDENUM IN RELATION TO PRIMARY PRODUCTION AND WATERBLOOM FORMATION IN A EUTROPHIC POND,
For primary bibliographic entry see Field 5C.
W75-09010

ISOTHERMS UNDER ICE,
K. M. Stewart.
Verhandlungen Internationale Vereinigung Limnologie, Vol 18, p 303-311, 1972. 7 fig, 9 ref.

Descriptors: *Isotherms, *Ice cover, *Lakes, *New York, *Wisconsin, Thermal stratification, Density currents, Advection, Convection, Springs, Seepage, Subsurface flow, Heat flow.
Identifiers: McCargo Lake(NY), White Clay Lake(Wis), Lake Wingra(Wis), Tub Lake(Wis), Lime Lake(NY), Conesus Lake(NY).

The thermal stratification and density differences beneath the ice of frozen lakes are usually slight in comparison to those during summer. There is an increase in viscosity in colder water, but the energy requirements for water motion are still less. A variety of frozen lakes in New York and Wisconsin were investigated and checked for water motion as inferred from the distribution of isotherms. Thermal transects were made across the ice of each lake to sampling positions determined by direct measurement or sextant triangulation. Holes were drilled in the ice and temperatures were measured at half-meter depth intervals, or to specific isotherms or fractions thereof. This investigation indicates that the variability and irregularity in isotherm patterns beneath ice are probably greater than heretofore considered. Some apparent thermal instabilities may be countered by chemical contributions arising from reducing conditions in the sediments. Information concerning advection, convection, subsurface springs, heat flux, density currents, and the tracing of effluents can be inferred from the slope and distribution of isotherms in frozen lakes. Isotherms may be essentially horizontal at all levels in some lakes and surprisingly irregular and difficult to interpret in others. (Jones-Wisconsin)
W75-09011

THE RADIATION BALANCE OF LAKES ON THE TERRITORY OF THE USSR,
For primary bibliographic entry see Field 5C.
W75-09012

HYDROLOGICAL FEATURES OF LAKE ONEGA IN THE ANNUAL CYCLE,
For primary bibliographic entry see Field 5C.
W75-09013

SEASONAL CHANGES IN DISSOLVED ORGANIC NITROGEN IN SIX MICHIGAN LAKES,
For primary bibliographic entry see Field 5C.
W75-09014

BIOLOGICAL ASPECTS ON THE LARGE LAKES IN SOUTH SWEDEN,
For primary bibliographic entry see Field 5C.
W75-09015

A COMPARISON OF SEDIMENT OXYGEN UPTAKE, HYPOLIMNETIC OXYGEN DEFICIT AND PRIMARY PRODUCTION IN LAKE ESROM, DENMARK,
For primary bibliographic entry see Field 5C.
W75-09017

PHYTOPLANKTONIC PRIMARY PRODUCTION DURING THE SUMMER STAGNATION IN THE EUTROPHICATED LAKES LOVOJARVI AND ORMAJARVI, SOUTHERN FINLAND,
Helsinki Univ. (Finland). Dept. of Botany.
For primary bibliographic entry see Field 5C.
W75-09018

ALGAE IN ALKALINE WATERS OF KANEM (TCHAD): I, (IN FRENCH),
Office de la Recherche Scientifique et Technique Outre-Mer, Fort Lamy (Chad).
For primary bibliographic entry see Field 5C.
W75-09020

SIMULATION OF URBAN RUNOFF, NUTRIENT LOADING, AND BIOTIC RESPONSE OF A SHALLOW EUTROPHIC LAKE,
Wisconsin Univ., Madison. Inst. for Environmental Studies.
For primary bibliographic entry see Field 5C.
W75-09022

THE PHOSPHORUS BUDGET OF CAMERON LAKE, ONTARIO: THE IMPORTANCE OF FLUSHING RATE TO THE DEGREE OF EUTROPHY OF LAKES,
Toronto Univ. (Ontario). Dept. of Zoology.
For primary bibliographic entry see Field 5C.
W75-09023

SOME RELATIONSHIPS BETWEEN ALGAL STANDING CROP, WATER CHEMISTRY, AND SEDIMENT CHEMISTRY IN THE ENGLISH LAKES,
Minnesota Univ., Minneapolis. Dept. of Botany.
For primary bibliographic entry see Field 5C.
W75-09024

DISTRIBUTION OF BENTHIC INVERTEBRATES IN THE SOUTH END OF LAKE MICHIGAN,
Michigan Univ., Ann Arbor. Great Lakes Research Div.
For primary bibliographic entry see Field 5C.

W75-09025

CHEMICAL AND HYDROLOGICAL CHARACTERISTICS OF THE WISCONSIN-LAKE SUPERIOR DRAINAGE BASIN: EASTERN SECTOR,
Northland Coll., Ashland, Wis.
For primary bibliographic entry see Field 5C.
W75-09026

POSSIBLE ACCELERATED EUTROPHICATION THRESHOLDS IN THE GREAT LAKES RELATIVE TO HUMAN POPULATION DENSITY,
State Univ. Coll., Brockport, N.Y. Dept. of Biological Sciences.
For primary bibliographic entry see Field 5C.
W75-09027

CHANGES IN ZOOPLANKTON POPULATIONS IN LAKE ONTARIO (1939-1972),
State Univ. of New York, Albany. Dept. of Biological Sciences.
For primary bibliographic entry see Field 5C.
W75-09028

THE INFLUENCE OF WATER RENEWAL ON THE NUTRIENT SUPPLY IN SMALL, OLIGOTROPHIC (NEWFOUNDLAND) AND HIGHLY EUTROPHIC (ALBERTA) LAKES,
Canadian Wildlife Service, Halifax (Nova Scotia).
For primary bibliographic entry see Field 5C.
W75-09029

EUTROPHIC LAKES IN THE MACKENZIE DELTA: THEIR USE BY WATERFOWL,
Alberta Univ., Edmonton. Dept. of Geography.
For primary bibliographic entry see Field 5C.
W75-09031

CHANGES IN WATER CHEMISTRY ACCOMPANYING SUMMER FISH KILLS IN SHALLOW EUTROPHIC LAKES OF SOUTHWEST MANITOBA,
Fisheries Research Board of Canada, Winnipeg (Manitoba). Freshwater Inst.
For primary bibliographic entry see Field 5C.
W75-09032

EUTROPHICATION AND RECREATIONAL FISHES IN TWO LARGE LAKE BASINS IN BRITISH COLUMBIA,
British Columbia Univ., Vancouver. Inst. of Animal Resource Ecology.
For primary bibliographic entry see Field 5C.
W75-09033

ENGINEERING ASPECTS OF POLLUTED LKE RECLAMATION,
Notre Dame Univ., Indiana. Dept. of Civil Engineering.
For primary bibliographic entry see Field 5G.
W75-09034

RELATIONS BETWEEN MICROBIAL HETEROTROPHIC ACTIVITY, ORGANICS, AND DEOXYRIBONUCLEIC ACID IN OLIGOTHROPHIC LAKE SEDIMENTS,
Rensselaer Polytechnic Inst., Troy, N.Y. Fresh Water Inst.
For primary bibliographic entry see Field 5C.
W75-09035

EFFECTS OF THE DISCHARGE OF THERMAL EFFLUENT FROM A POWER STATION ON LAKE WABAMUN, ALBERTA, CANADA: THE EPIPELIC AND EPIPSAMMIC ALGAL COMMUNITIES,
Alberta Univ., Edmonton. Dept. of Botany.
For primary bibliographic entry see Field 5C.
W75-09036

SPATIAL AND TEMPORAL DISTRIBUTION OF CHLORPHYLL, AND PHEOPIGMENTS IN SURFACE WATERS OF LAKE ERIE,
Canada Centre for Inland Waters, Burlington (Ontario).
For primary bibliographic entry see Field 5C.
W75-09039

THE EFFECT OF CITRATE ON PHYTOPLANKTON IN LAKE ONTARIO,
Canada Centre for Inland Waters, Burlington (Ontario).
For primary bibliographic entry see Field 5C.
W75-09040

ORGANIC PRODUCTION STUDIES IN HIGH ALTITUDE LAKES OF INDIA: II. ZOOPLANKTON, PHYTOPLANKTON AND PEDON OF HIGH ALTITUDE KASHMIR LAKES, KOUNSARNAG AND ALPATHER, WITH CORRELATION OF PLANKTONVOLUME, PH AND TEMPERATURE OF DAL LAKE,
Kashmir Univ., Srinagar (India). Dept. of Zoology.
For primary bibliographic entry see Field 5C.
W75-09041

ABUNDANCE AND PRODUCTION OF BACTERIA IN LATVIAN LAKES,
For primary bibliographic entry see Field 5C.
W75-09042

DYNAMICS AND PRODUCTION OF SIMOCEPHALUS SERRULATUS (KOCH) IN TWO LARGE NATURAL AND MAN-MADE PONDS IN EASTERN CANADA,
For primary bibliographic entry see Field 5C.
W75-09044

A DIURNAL ZOOPLANKTON MIGRATION STUDY IN LAKE MEAD,
Arizona Univ., Tucson.
For primary bibliographic entry see Field 5C.
W75-09059

THE EFFECTS OF DIURON ON BACTERIAL POPULATIONS IN AQUATIC ENVIRONMENTS,
Clemson Univ., S.C. Dept. of Microbiology; and Clemson Univ., S.C. Dept. of Zoology.
For primary bibliographic entry see Field 5C.
W75-09079

PHYTOPLANKTON DISTRIBUTION AND WATER QUALITY INDICES FOR LAKE MEAD (COLORADO RIVER),
Arizona Univ., Tucson. Dept. of Biological Sciences.
For primary bibliographic entry see Field 5C.
W75-09083

THE INFLUENCE OF LATE CENOZOIC STRATIGRAPHY ON DISTRIBUTION OF IMPOUNDMENT-RELATED SEISMICITY AT LAKE MEAD, NEVADA-ARIZONA,
Geological Survey, Denver, Colo.
For primary bibliographic entry see Field 8G.
W75-09192

THE LAKE DILEMMA,
For primary bibliographic entry see Field 6E.
W75-09265

PRELIMINARY REPORT ON WIND ERRORS ENCOUNTERED DURING AUTOMATIC PROCESSING OF IFYGL LORAN-C DATA,
National Oceanic and Atmospheric Administration, Washington, D.C. Environmental Data Service.
For primary bibliographic entry see Field 7A.
W75-09270

IFYGL PHYSICAL DATA COLLECTION SYSTEM: INTERCOMPARISON DATA,
National Oceanic and Atmospheric Administration, Washington, D.C. Environmental Data Service.
For primary bibliographic entry see Field 7C.
W75-09271

EFFECTS OF ICE COVER ON DISSOLVED OXYGEN IN SILVER LAKE, ONTARIO,
Department of the Environment, Ottawa (Ontario). Water Quality Branch.
For primary bibliographic entry see Field 2C.
W75-09291

PLANKTON, CHEMISTRY, AND PHYSICS OF LAKES IN THE CHURCHILL FALLS REGION OF LABRADOR,
Waterloo Univ. (Ontario). Dept. of Biology.
H. C. Duthie, and M. L. Ostrofsky.
J Fish Res Board Can, Vol 31, No 6, p 1105-1117, 1974. Illus.

Descriptors: *Canada, *Lakes, Plankton, Reservoirs, *Diatoms, Phytoplankton, Eutrophication, Water chemistry.
Identifiers: Asterionella-formosa, Bosmina-coregoni, Churchill Falls, Cyclops-scutifer, Daphnia-galeata-mendotae, Daphnia-longiremis, Diaptomus-minutus, Dinobryon, Holopedium-gibberum, Labrador, Rhizosolenia-eriensis, Tabellaria-fenestrats, Michikaman Lake, Ossokmanuan Reservoir.

Of 10 lakes and a reservoir in the Churchill Falls region of western Labrador (Canada) studied in 1970-71, 9 lakes were 12 m or less deep, humic, thermally unstratified and had Secchi disc transparencies between 3.5 and 8.25 m. Maximum surface temperatures of 16-17 C in the 9 lakes were generally reached by mid-Aug. Michikamau Lake (area 1980 km2, depth 84 m) rarely exceeded 12 C and had a Secchi disc transparency of 13 m. Conductivities and alkalinities (as $CaCO_3$) ranged from about 13 micro-mho/cm and less than 6.5 mg/l, for lakes draining granite, gneiss, or quartz bedrock, to about 30 and 15, for those draining gabbro or slate. Maximum live phytoplankton biomasses in 1970 ranged 70 mg/m3, in Michikamau Lake, to 739 mg/m3, in Ossokmanuan Reservoir, and, in general, there was a positive correlation with conductivity. Diatoms were the most abundant group, in particular Asterionella formosa, Tabellaria fenestrata and Rhizosolenia eriensis; however, flagellated Chysophta, mainly species of Dinobryon, were more abundant in the reservoir than in the natural lakes. Predominant zooplankters included Diaptomus minutus, Cyclops scutifer, Holopedium gibberum, Daphnia longiremis, D. galeata mendotae and Bosmina coregoni. Maximum seasonal standing crops ranged from 1600 to 8910 individuals/m3, with the highest densities being found in the reservoir. The reservoir, 8 yr after filling, showed little evidence of trophic upsurge and was possibly entering a period of trophic depression.--Copyright 1974, Biological Abstracts, Inc.
W75-09317

Identifiers: Bone ash, Hematocrit levels, Ictalurus-punctatus.

Channel catfish (Ictalurus punctatus) fingerlings were fed diets containing varying dietary levels and ratios of Ca (0.5-2.0%) and P (0.5-1.2%). Results from 2 studies indicated that the available P requirement of catfish is approximately 0.8% of diet. In both experiments gains were maximal in fish fed diets containing 1.5% Ca and were reduced when higher levels were fed. This hypercalcemia effect could not be prevented by adjusting the Ca/P ratio by the addition of P to the diet. A P deficiency characterized by reduced growth, poorer food efficiency and lower bone ash and hematocrit levels occurred in fish fed 0.5 or 0.6% available P. The absence of a growth response to 0.4% supplemented P in the form of calcium phytate suggested that catfish are not able to fully utilize phytin P. Bone ash values from skull and vertebrae samples indicated that the Ca requirement for maximal bone mineralization may be higher than that for optimal growth.--Copyright 1973, Biological Abstracts, Inc.
W75-09299

PATTERNS OF SOIL MOISTURE DEPLETION IN A MIXED OAK STAND,
Rhode Island Univ., Kingston.
J. H. Brown, Jr., and T. G. Bourn.
For Sci, Vol 19, No 1, p 23-30, 1973. Illus.
Identifiers: *Moisture depletion, Neutron, *Oak, Patterns, *Quercus-alba, *Quercus-coccinea, *Soil moisture, Stemflow, Throughfall.

Soil moisture regimes were studied under 5 white oak trees (Quercus alba L.) and 5 scarlet oak trees (Q. coccinea Muench.) in a mixed-oak stand. Locations under canopies (near trunk, mid-crown and crown-edge) were monitored with a neutron probe. Soil water losses for each location were calculated for the 1968 growing season, taking into consideration inputs of throughfall and stemflow. Although overall patterns of depletion and accretion were similar between species, significant differences in depletion existed at the 2.0 and 2.5 ft depths near tree trunks. Soil moisture depletion near tree trunks was greater under scarlet oaks than under white oaks. Similarly, seasonal water losses for locations near tree trunks were greater for scarlet oaks; losses averaged 24.2 in. for scarlet oaks and 18.4 in. for white oaks. This difference was due to a greater amount of estimated stemflow reaching soil under scarlet oaks.--Copyright 1973, Biological Abstracts, Inc.
W75-09320

ECOLOGY OF INDIAN DESERT: VIII. ON THE WATER RELATIONS AND ASSIMILATE BALANCE OF SOME DESERT PLANTS,
Jodhpur Univ. (India). Dept. of Botany.
For primary bibliographic entry see Field 3B.
W75-09322

STUDIES ON THE BIOLOGY OF DANISH STREAM FISHES: III. ON SEASONAL FLUCTUATIONS IN THE STOCK DENSITY OF YELLOW EEL IN SHALLOW STREAM BIOTOPES, AND THEIR CAUSES,
Danmarks Fiskeri- og Havundersogelser, Charlottenlund.
K. Larsen.
Medd Dan Fisk Havunders, Vol.7, No 2, p 23-46, 1972. Illus.

Descriptors: *Eels, Europe, Fish, Marine fish, Lampreys, Populations, *Fish populations, Shallow water, *Temperature, *Vegetation effects.
Identifiers: *Denmark, Lellinge stream, Ejby stream, Yellow eel.

Stock analyses were bade over a 4-yr period on eels in the shallow biotopes of the Lellinge and the Ejby streams. The density of eels fluctuates greatly and in a distinctly seasonal rhythm. In accordance with the marked direct relation between the fluctuations in the stock density of eel on one hand and the changes in the water temperature on the other, the conclusion can be drawn that the stock fluctuations are directly temperature-conditioned. High water temperatures cause a high density of eels, while at low water temperatures the density is low, and the extreme cases there is even a total absence of eels. The consequence is, therefore, a high density of eels in summer, and a low density in winter. On biotopes as those selected for the present investigation, where various kinds of shelters for eels are found, the overgrowing of the stream by water plants has no or at least no apparent-influence on the stock density, while the opposite may be assumed to be the case in streams, where eels can only hide in the vegetation, and where consequently the percentage vegetation cover may be a decisive factor as to how many eels can actually hide there. The majority of the yellow eels in the shallow localities of a stream is of a size which is below the prescribed minimum legal size, i.e., 35 cm. Those biotopes are therefore important growth localities and only to a very limited extent catch localities.--Copyright 1974, Biological Abstracts, Inc.
W75-09328

PROCEEDINGS TALL TIMBERS CONFERENCE ON ECOLOGICAL ANIMAL CONTROL BY HABITAT MANAGEMENT, NO. 4.
Tall Timbers Research Station, Tallahassee, Fal.
Tallahassee, Fla, Feb 24-25, 1972, 244 p. Tall Timbers Research Station: Tallahassee, Fla, 1973.

Descriptors: *Animal control, Habitats, Wildlife habitats, *Conferences, Insects, Biocontrol, Insect populations, Hosts, Parasites, Water hyacinth, Nematodes, Plant breeding, *Pest control, *Insect control, *Predation, *Management.
Identifiers: Argentina, Labauchena-daguerrei, Neodiprion, Solenopsis, Trichogramma, Biometeorology, Ants, Flies, Mites, Pests, Symposiums.

This volume contains the contributed papers presented at the symposium covering a variety of aspects involving animal control by habitat management. The content begins with a paper on interfield and interplant spacing in tropical insect control, followed by a discussion on private enterprise pest management based on biological control. The next several papers cover the following specific topics: the application of biometeorology for determining the microenvironment of insect populations; influence of host-origin feeding inhibitors on Neodiprion (sawfly) feeding behavior; animals associated with the Solenopsis (fire ants) complex, with special reference to Labauchena daguerrei; and potential for water hyacinth management based on studies in Argentina. A group of papers is then included covering the following specific topics: managing nematodes by plant breeding; management of nematode populations in Great Britain; management of plant-parasitic nematode populations; and utilization of parasites and predators in nematode pest management ecology. A group of papers follows on the following specific topics: nematode parasites of insects; the use of Trichogramma in the USSR; integrated control of insect pests of cotton; and management of insect pests of soybeans. Finally, a paper is included on agroecological factors influencing the biology and management of predaceous mites, followed by a paper on the International Biological Program work on the strategies and tactics of pest management. Numerous tables, diagrams and photographs are included throughout, and each paper ends with a list of literature cited.--Copyright 1973, Biological Abstracts, Inc.
W75-09333

2J. Erosion and Sedimentation

ENVIRONMENTAL ASPECTS--SACRAMENTO BANK PROTECTION,
Hydrologic Engineering Center, Davis, Calif. Water Resources Planning Branch.
For primary bibliographic entry see Field 4D.
W75-08981

TECHNIQUES FOR TRACING SEDIMENT MOVEMENT,
Canada Centre for Inland Waters, Burlington (Ontario).
D. E. Nelson, and J. P. Coakley.
Scientific Series No. 32, 1974. 2 fig, 3 tab, 61 ref.

Descriptors: *Analytical techniques, *Tracking techniques, *Sediment transport, *Tracers, Movement, Clays, Silts, Sands, Coarse sediments, Data collections, Raioactive tracers, Fluorescent dye, Tagging, Neutron activation analysis, X-ray fluorescence, Synoptic analysis, Radioactivity techniques, Fluorometry, Sedimentation, Bed load.
Identifiers: *Mass transport, Thermoluminescence, Radio-photoluminescence.

Methods using artificial tracers to quantitatively determine sediment movement are described and the principles of tagging sediment, injection, detection, and interpretation of data are discussed. Radioactive tracing is probably the most effective for synoptic or near-synoptic surveys of large, rapidly evolving systems, but involves some hazards. Fluorescent tracers are non-hazardous, inexpensive, and simple to inject. Several tracers can be used simultaneously, but quantitative detection is difficult on quickly evolving systems. Their long life makes repeated studies difficult and may cause unfavorable public reaction; this technique is most useful on slowly-evolving systems. Neutron activation, x-ray fluorescence, atomic absorption, and atomic emission tracing methods require unit sampling, but offer some advantages over fluorescent tracers. Thermoluminescence and radio-photoluminescence can be used to mark clays, silts, and sands inexpensively. Labelled sediment is harmless and indistinguishable from unmarked material except when heated. Sediment could be mass labelled in situ, have several different tags, and be measured over a period of time. This method requires unit sampling. The best tracing techniques for sediments containing various particle sizes are discussed. The Oak Ridge National Laboratory radioisotope sand tracing system (RIST) and a simplified data acquisition device for sediment transport studies are described. A bibliography containing 349 references is appended. (Buchanan-Davidson--Wisconsin)
W75-08995

A COMPARISON OF SEDIMENT OXYGEN UPTAKE, HYPOLIMNETIC OXYGEN DEFICIT AND PRIMARY PRODUCTION IN LAKE ESROM, DENMARK,
For primary bibliographic entry see Field 5C.
W75-09017

SOME RELATIONSHIPS BETWEEN ALGAL STANDING CROP, WATER CHEMISTRY, AND SEDIMENT CHEMISTRY IN THE ENGLISH LAKES,
Minnesota Univ., Minneapolis. Dept. of Botany.
For primary bibliographic entry see Field 5C.
W75-09024

RELATIONS BETWEEN MICROBIAL HETEROTROPHIC ACTIVITY, ORGANICS, AND DEOXYRIBONUCLEIC ACID IN OLIGOTHROPHIC LAKE SEDIMENTS,
Rensselaer Polytechnic Inst., Troy, N.Y. Fresh Water Inst.
For primary bibliographic entry see Field 5C.
W75-09035

ENZYMATIC ACITIVITY OF ERODED SOILS, (IN RUSSIAN),
B. N. Simonyan, and A. S. Galstyan.
Biol Zh Arm, Vol 27, No 4, p 60-67, 1974.

Descriptors: *Enzymes, Erosion, *Erosion rates, Soils, *Soil erosion, Chenozems, Brown soils, Chestnut soils, Deserts, *Biological communities.
Identifiers: Catalase, Dehydrogenase, *Invertase, Phosphatase, Urease, Armenia, USSR, Semidesert regions, Meadowland, Steppes, *Enzymatic activity.

The activity of enzymes (invertase, phosphatase, urease, catalase and dehydrogenases) was studied according to the degree of erosion of chernozems, mountain-meadow, brown forest-steppe, chestnut and brown semidesert soils of the Armenian SSR. The method of enzymatic reactions made it possible to characterize the biological activity of the eroded soils and to reveal features of the soil erosion processes. Eroded soils had a lower biological activity than the uneroded ones. The most suitable enzyme for diagnosis is of eroded soils was invertase.--Copyright 1975, Biological Abstracts, Inc.
W75-09105

WATER RESOURCES DATA FOR KANSAS, 1974: PART 2. WATER QUALITY RECORDS.
Geological Survey, Lawrence, Kans.
For primary bibliographic entry see Field 7C.
W75-09181

PROGRESS IN WATERSHED DEVELOPMENT IN THE AWR BASINS AREA UNDER USDA PROGRAMS - SEPTEMBER 1974.
Soil Conservation Service, Wichita, Kans.
For primary bibliographic entry see Field 4D.
W75-09246

A CONCEPTUAL MODEL OF OFFSHORE PERMAFROST,
Alaska Univ., College. Geophysical Inst.
T. E. Osterkamp.
Geophysical Institute Report No. UAG R-234, Sea Grant Report No. 75-3, April 1975. 23 p, 8 fig, 12 ref. OSG 40-3-158-41.

Descriptors: *Model studies, *Permafrost, *Coasts, *Erosion, Climatology, Thermodynamics, Oceanography, *Alaska.
Identifiers: *Conceptual models, *Offshore permafrost, Coastal erosion, Thermal boundary conditions, Chemical boundary conditions, Transport equations, Vertical soil profiles.

The coastal erosion process has been examined for the northern Alaskan coast for the purpose of developing a conceptual model of offshore permafrost. A series of as many as five stages of coastal erosion, characterized by different thermal and chemical boundary conditions, is necessary to describe the physical setting of the offshore permafrost. The seasonal variations of thermal and chemical boundary conditions are discussed, and incorporation of these varying boundary conditions into a model of offshore permafrost, consisting of the generalized transport equations from non-equilibrium thermodynamics, is suggested. This can be accomplished by successive application of the transport equations to the five stages experienced by a vertical soil profile during the erosion process. (NOAA)
W75-09266

ENVIRONMENTAL STUDY OF THE MARINE ENVIRONMENT NEAR NOME, ALASKA,
Alaska Univ., College. Inst. of Marine Science.
For primary bibliographic entry see Field 2L.
W75-09275

BELWOOD RESERVOIR, 1971 SEDIMENTATION STUDY.
Department of the Environment, Ottawa (Ontario). Water Resources Branch; and Ontario Ministry of Natural Resources, Toronto. Conservation Authorities Branch.
29 p, 1975, Inland Waters Directorate, Environment Canada, Ottawa, Canada, 48 fig, 6 append.

Descriptors: *Sedimentation, *Sedimentation rates, *Reservoirs, Deposition(Sediments), Beds, Bank erosion, Data collections, Analytical techniques.
Identifiers: *Grand River, Reservoir lifetime, Sectional sedimentation rates, Belwood Reservoir.

A 1971 Sediment Survey of the Belwood Reservoir is described. This was the first of a series of at least three surveys which are to be conducted at this reservoir. Thirty-three cross-sections were established within the reservoir and their profiles were surveyed. Sampling of bed material and suspended sediment was also carried out. The results are illustrated by tables and graphs in the Appendixes. Recommendations include a plan for subsequent surveys of the reservoir and an outline of methods to be utilized for determining densities of the deposited sediment. The computed density patterns and volumetric assumulation rates will form the basis for estimating sedimentation rates within all sections of the reservoir. This information should help pinpoint future problem areas thereby enabling preventive measures to be taken in some cases. Additionally the above sectional sedimentation rates will determine the overall reservoir sedimentation rate and therefore anticipated reservoir lifetime. (Env. Canada)
W75-09286

AN ANALYSIS OF THE DYNAMICS OF DDT IN MARINE SEDIMENTS,
Stanford Univ., Pacific Grove, Calif. Hopkins Marine Station.
For primary bibliographic entry see Field 5B.
W75-09300

2K. Chemical Processes

SHORT-TERM VARIATIONS IN ESTIMATES OF CHLOROPHYLL ABUNDANCE,
National Marine Fisheries Service, Woods Hole, Mass. Northeast Fisheries Center.
J. B. Colton.
Available from the National Technical Information Service, Springfield, Va. 22161, as COM-73-10850, $3.25 in paper copy, $2.25 in microfiche. International Commission for the Northwest Atlantic Fisheries Research Bulletin No 9, p 81-84, 1972. 2 fig, 16 ref. (Report No NOAA-73050414).

Descriptors: *Chlorophyll, *Fluctuations, *Continental Shelf, Canada, New York, Water temperature, Tidal effects, Internal waves, Sampling, Depth, Thermocline.
Identifiers: Nova Scotia(Canada), Long Island(NY).

Quarterly surveys were made of Continental Shelf waters between Nova Scotia and Long Island. Changes in chlorophyll abundance observed within a given water mass during June 1966 are illustrated and the variation examined in relation to hydrographic conditions and sampling techniques. Chlorophyll was determined by fluorescence of sea water extracts. Although tidal forces undoubtedly were instrumental in generating interal waves, turbulent forces due to winds and bottom topography tended to mask the semidiurnal periodicity in the vertical oscillations. Hourly bathythermograph observations revealed the presence of internal waves of a shorter period than indicated by the 2-hr sampling interval. Average 'chlorophyll depth' (determined by multiplying concentration of chlorophyll by depth sampled, summing the weighted samples, and dividing by

point sources of dissolved constituents as did solutions equilibrated with soil and rock samples. Analyses of stream hydrographs suggest four flow components: overland, 'interflow', rapid-groundwater system, and long-term, low-flow system. Estimated flow percentages of each on a long-term basis are 30%, 11%, 51%, and 8% respectively. Water chemistry of each component appears to be distinctive. Effective porosity of rocks appears to be very low (.05%). Chert dominates the soil mineralogy with particle sizes ranging from a micron to centimeters and may be dense to very porous. Properties of cherty residuum from the Fort Payne and other formations are important in determining soil properties and stability. Aluminum may be a key to the diagenetic redistribution of silica in silica rich sediments.
W75-09129

DISCHARGE MEASUREMENTS AND CHEMICAL ANALYSES OF WATER IN NORTHWESTERN WYOMING,
Geological Survey, Cheyenne, Wyo.
For primary bibliographic entry see Field 7C.
W75-09172

SALT-BALANCE STUDY OF PAUBA VALLEY, UPPER SANTA MARGARITA RIVER AREA, RIVERSIDE COUNTY, CALIFORNIA,
Geological Survey, Menlo Park, Calif.
For primary bibliographic entry see Field 5B.
W75-09177

WATER RESOURCES DATA FOR KANSAS, 1974: PART 2. WATER QUALITY RECORDS.
Geological Survey, Lawrence, Kans.
For primary bibliographic entry see Field 7C.
W75-09181

PROBLEMS IN C-14 DATING OF WATER FROM AQUIFERS OF DELTAIC ORIGIN--AN EXAMPLE FROM THE NEW JERSEY COASTAL PLAIN,
Geological Survey, Reston, Va.
For primary bibliographic entry see Field 2F.
W75-09183

GROUND-WATER RESOURCES OF THE HOLLYWOOD AREA, FLORIDA,
Geological Survey, Tallahassee, Fla.
For primary bibliographic entry see Field 6D.
W75-09185

DESCRIPTIONS AND CHEMICAL ANALYSES FOR SELECTED WELLS IN THE TEHAMA-COLUSA CANAL SERVICE AREA, SACRAMENTO VALLEY, CALIFORNIA,
Geological Survey, Menlo Park, Calif.
For primary bibliographic entry see Field 4B.
W75-09187

NON-EQUILIBRIUM THERMODYNAMICS OF ELECTRO-OSMOSIS OF WATER THROUGH COMPOSITE CLAY MEMBRANES, 1. THE PARALLEL ARRANGEMENT,
Harcourt Butler Technological Inst., Kanpur (India). Dept. of Chemistry.
R. C. Srivastava, and A. K. Jain.
Journal of Hydrology, Vol 25, No 3/4, p 307-324, May 1975. 9 fig, 4 tab, 11 ref.

Descriptors: *Membranes, *Electro-osmosis, *Clays, *Thermodynamics, Kaolinite, Bentonite, Electric currents, Zeta potential, Permeability, Model studies, Pressure, Flow, Isotropy, Hydraulic conductivity.
Identifiers: Irreversible processes, Streaming potential, Streaming current, Water flux, Parallel arrangements, Mass flux, Phenomenological coefficients.

Electro-osmosis of water through composite clay membranes consisting of kaolinite and bentonite in parallel arrangement was studied, and the form of the phenomenological relations for the simultaneous transport of water and electricity was derived. The phenomenological relation for the electrical flux was found to be the usual linear and homogeneous equation, while the relationship between the water flux and the thermodynamic forces was found to be represented by a nonlinear exponential type of relationship. Relationships among the phenomenological coefficients characterizing the parallel arrangement as a whole and its constituent membrane elements were investigated. The combination rules given by Kedem and Katchalsky were found to be valid for the phenomenological coefficients representing the streaming current and ordinary electrical conductivity but not in the case of the other two coefficients representing the hydraulic conductivity and the electro-osmotic velocity, for which modifications in the combination rules were suggested. Study of directional characteristics of the phenomenological coefficients revealed the isotropic character of the composite parallel clay membrane. (See also W75-09201 and W75-09202) (Visocky-ISWS)
W75-09200

NON-EQUILIBRIUM THERMODYNAMICS OF ELECTRO-OSMOSIS OF WATER THROUGH COMPOSITE CLAY MEMBRANES, 2. THE SERIES ARRANGEMENT,
Harcourt Butler Technological Inst., Kanpur (India). Dept. of Chemistry.
R. C. Srivastava, and A. K. Jain.
Journal of Hydrology, Vol 25, No 3/4, p 325-337, May 1975. 5 fig, 5 tab, 4 ref.

Descriptors: *Membranes, *Electro-osmosis, *Clays, *Thermodynamics, Kaolinite, Bentonite, Electric currents, Zeta potential, Permeability, Model studies, Pressure, Flow, Anisotropy.
Identifiers: *Irreversible processes, *Streaming potential, *Streaming currents, Water flux, Series, Mass flux, Phenomenological coefficients.

The electro-osmosis of water through a composite clay membrane consisting of kaolinite and bentonite clay-membrane elements in a series array was studied and the form of the phenomenological relations ascertained. The electrical flux in the presence of both pressure difference and electrical-potential difference was found to be represented by the usual linear equation. The phenomenological relation for the water flux, though linear, was different from the usual one, because the graphs between water flux and pressure difference, and electro-osmotic velocity and applied electrical-potential difference were found to be straight lines having definite intercepts on the x-axis. The combination rules for membranes in series were found to be valid only for the phenomenological coefficients representing the hydraulic permeability and not in the case of the other three coefficients representing the electro-osmotic velocity, streaming current, and electrical conductivity. The study of directional characteristics of the phenomenological coefficients revealed the anisotropic character of the composite clay membrane in a series arrangement. (See also W75-09200 and W75-09202) (Visocky-ISWS)
W75-09201

NON-EQUILIBRIUM THERMODYNAMICS OF ELECTRO-OSMOSIS OF WATER THROUGH COMPOSITE CLAY MEMBRANES, 3. THE ELECTRO-KINETIC ENERGY CONVERSION,
Harcourt Butler Technological Inst., Kanpur (India). Dept. of Chemistry.
R. C. Srivastava, and A. K. Jain.
Journal of Hydrology, Vol 25, No 3/4, p 339-351, May 1975. 8 fig, 2 tab, 9 ref.

Descriptors: *Thermodynamics, *Electro-osmosis, *Membranes, *Kinetics, Clays, Kaolinite, Efficiencies, Zeta potential, Energy transfer, Membrane processes, Pressure head, Flow, Equations.
Identifiers: *Nonequilibrium conditions, Streaming potential, Composite membranes, Parallel membranes, Series membranes.

The efficiencies of electro-kinetic energy conversion in the cases of kaolinite, bentonite, and composite clay membranes, consisting of kaolinite and bentonite membrane elements in a parallel array and in a series array, were calculated. The conversion efficiencies in the case of composite clay membrane systems were found to be linearly related to the conversion efficiencies of the constituent membrane elements. This result was experimentally supported in the case of the parallel membranes. The maximum values of the conversion efficiency for both modes of conversion, i.e., electro-osmotic flow and streaming potential were found to be equal to each other and also independent of the applied input forces. However, the efficiency of energy conversion was found to be dependent on the direction of the input force in the case of a series clay membrane system. The optimum values predicted by the respective figures of merit agree with those experimentally found. Conversion efficiency would be maximum if the output force equals half of the value of the electro-osmotic pressure. (See also W75-09200 and W75-09201) (Visocky-ISWS)
W75-09202

CHANGE IN POTENTIAL OF REFERENCE FLUORIDE ELECTRODE WITHOUT LIQUID JUNCTION IN MIXED SOLVENTS,
Missouri Univ., Columbia. Dept. of Chemistry.
K. M. Stelting, and S. E. Manahan.
Analytical Chemistry, Vol 46, No 4, p 592-594, April 1974. 3 fig. OWRR A-049-MO(6). 14-31-0001-3525.

Descriptors: Potentiometers, Fluorides, Analysis, Electrodes, Instrumentation.
Identifiers: Liquid junction potentials, Acetonitrile, Silver, Organic solvents, Complexation, Potentiometry.

A major problem with potentiometric measurements is liquid junction potentials at the reference electrode. To eliminate this effect the fluoride electrode was used as a reference in a cell without liquid junction. It was a less suitable reference than the calomel electrode for complexation studies in systems where addition of an organic ligand appreciably alters the properties of the solvent. The relatively large negative shift in potential of the fluoride reference electrode in going from an aqueous medium 0.100 M in acetonitrile to a similar medium 4.0 M in acetonitrile can be explained entirely upon the basis of decreased solubility of the lanthanum fluoride electrode membrane in the partially organic medium.
W75-09239

QUANTITATIVE INVESTIGATIONS ON MOISTURE ATTRACTION IN HYGROSCOPIC SALINE SOIL SURFACES IN THE KUCUK MENDERES PLAIN, TURKEY,
For primary bibliographic entry see Field 2G.
W75-09262

HYGROSCOPIC SURFACES OF SALINE SOILS IN THE KUCUK MENDERES PLAIN, TURKEY: OCCURRENCE, DESCRIPTION AND CHEMICAL ANALYSIS,
For primary bibliographic entry see Field 2G.
W75-09263

2L. Estuaries

SOME FACTORS AFFECTING THE SURVIVAL OF COLIFORM BACTERIA IN SEAWATER (IN JAPANESE),
Tokai Univ., Tokyo (Japan). Coll. of Marine Science Technology.
For primary bibliographic entry see Field 5C.
W75-08884

SALINITY-TEMPERATURE PROFILES IN THE PANAMA CANAL LOCKS,
Smithsonian Institution, Washington, D.C. Dept. of Invertebrate Zoology.
M. L. Jones, and C. E. Dawson.
Mar Biol (Berl), Vol 21, No 2, p 86-90, 1973, Illus.

Descriptors: *Canals, *Turbulence, *Temperature, Mixing, Salinity, Biota, Barriers, Lakes.
Identifiers: Canal locks, Gatun Lake, Marine animals, *Panama, Sea, *Salanity-temperature profiles.

In discussions concerning the possible construction of a Panama sea-level canal it was assumed that Gatun Lake, part of the present canal, acts as a fresh-water barrier to the migration of marine animals from either end of the Canal to the other. Methodical documentary salinity determinations were not made previously and only a few surface salinity observations were recorded. Determinations of salinity-temperature profiles made in spring and fall, 1972, show essentially fresh water to be present from Miraflores Lake, through the Pedro Miguel Locks, through Gatun Lake, to, and including, the upper chambers of the Gatun Locks. With the exception of those of the lower chamber of the Miraflores Locks, and profiles indicate homogeneity and thorough vertical mixing of all water masses in the lock systems and lakes of the canal. Homogeneity of the water in the lock chambers is thought to be due to turbulence during filling of the chambers, to the 'piston-effect' of large ships moving into the chambers, to the action of ships' propellers and to density currents established as the lock gates are opened. Water in the approach channel at the Pacific end appears to be more homogeneous than that at the Atlantic end. The Panama Canal constitutes a fresh-water barrier to the migration of the stenohaline marine biota of the Pacific and Atlantic Oceans.--Copyright 1974, Biological Abstracts, Inc.
W75-08927

INTERTIDAL MACROBIOLOGY OF SELECTED STUDY BEACHES IN SOUTHERN CALIFORNIA,
University of Southern California, Los Angeles. Allan Hancock Foundation.
M. M. Patterson.
Available from the National Technical Information Service, Springfield, Va 22161 as COM-74-11551, $3.75 in paper copy, $2.25 in microfiche. Sea Grant Program, September 1974. 41 p, 9 tab, 8 fig, 20 ref.

Descriptors: *Beaches, *Invertebrates, *Numerical analysis, *Distribution, *Population, *Geomorphology, *Habitats, Benthos, Intertidal areas, Sands, Amphipods, Isopods, Mollusks, Insects, Slopes, Waves(Water), Sampling, Seasonal, Crabs, Environment, *California.
Identifiers: *Macrofauna.

Nine study beaches in southern California were sampled for an analysis of macroscopic fauna over a one year period. Statistical analysis was employed to elucidate the effects of zonation, seasonality and site physiography on the beach macrofauna. At the nine study beaches, there were more species and individual organisms associated with fine, homogeneous sand than with coarse, heterogeneous sand. Intertidal zonation is well-developed at the sheltered beach type, where

Estuarine and Coastal Marine Science, Vol 3, No 1, p 95-102, 1975. 6 fig, 7 ref.

Descriptors: *Estuaries, *On-site investigations, *Hydrography, *Tidal waters, Surveys, Measurement, Evaluation, Exploration, Currents(Water), Velocity, Salinity, Water temperature, Dissolved oxygen, Distribution patterns, Flow, *Washington, Sounds.
Identifiers: *Puget Sound(Wash), Bottom water flushing.

Currents were measured 2 m off the bottom on a 100-m deep sill of a basin within Puget Sound for a period of two months. During this time bottom water in the basin was replaced resulting in the older water being raised to shallower depths. Net motion into the estuary occurred during four intervals each of about five days duration. In-flow corresponded with minimum variance in the velocity fluctuations and minimum tidal currents. Out-flow occurred during maximum variance and tidal currents. The average speed during each of three of the five-day in-flow periods was about 6 cm/s and was approximately sufficient to replace all water below sill depth during the five days. (Humphreys-ISWS)
W75-08967

ANTIMONY IN THE COASTAL MARINE ENVIRONMENT, NORTH ADRIATIC,
Institut Rudjer Boskovic, Rovinj (Yugoslavia). Center for Marine Research.
For primary bibliographic entry see Field 5A.
W75-08968

MECHANISMS FOR DEEP WATER RENEWAL IN LAKE NITINAT, A PERMANENTLY ANOXIC FJORD,
Washington Univ., Seattle. Dept. of Oceanography.
R. J. Ozretich.
Estuarine and Coastal Marine Science, Vol 3, No 2, p 189-200, April 1975. 8 fig, 15 ref. NSF Grants GA-10084, GA-24875.

Descriptors: *Fjords, *Fishkill, *Anaerobic conditions, *Ocean circulation, *Structural geology, Oceans, Mortality, Water pollution effects, Fish, Wildlife conservation, Hydrographs, Meteorological data, Climatic data, Local precipitation, Nitrates, Sulfates, Hydrogen sulfide, *Canada, Tidal effects, Weather, Wind velocity, Salinity.
Identifiers: *Anoxic fjords, *Lake Nitinat(Brit Col), Renewal process.

Major deep water renewals, manifest by fish kills, were investigated. Meteorological and hydrographic observations of Lake Nitinat were made to separate the factors influencing renewal processes. Below average precipitation was found to be primarily responsible for renewals of 10-30% of the deep water volume between July 1968 and October 1970. (Henley-ISWS)
W75-08969

USE OF REMOTE SENSING FOR MAPPING WETLANDS,
Georgia Univ., Sapelo Island. Marine Inst.
R. J. Reimold, and R. A. Linthurst.
Transportation Engineering Journal, American Society of Civil Engineers, Vol 101, No TE2, Proceedings Paper 11293, p 189-198, May 1975. 4 fig, 14 ref, 1 append. National Sea Grant 04-3-158-6.

Descriptors: *Remote sensing, *Mapping, *Wetlands, *Estuaries, Aquatic plants, Land use, Natural resources, Oceanography, Photogrammetry, Tides, Transportation, Coasts, *Georgia, Water pollution, Beaches, Coastal engineering, Conservation, Dredging, Highways, Hydrology, Flow, Water quality, Water resources, Channels.

Contemporary remote sensing methodology and its application in wetlands was summarized. Using color, color infrared, black-and-white, and black-and-white infrared photography, multiband imagery, and infrared imagery, various applications were examined as they relate to wetlands use. Boundary mapping, vegetation differentiation, and plant primary production patterns have all been demonstrated with remote sensing. A new approach was presented for determination of intertidal water movement by infrared imagery in place of more costly time-consuming dye studies. Remote sensing also has been used in wetlands for location and field orientation, comparative analysis, landform analysis, and water pollution analysis. In terms of documenting baseline conditions for future litigation as well as planning purposes, remote sensing techniques afford the most reliable, least expensive, and least time-consuming means of accomplishing these tasks. (Dawes-ISWS)
W75-08977

ELECTROMAGNETIC FLOW SENSORS,
Woods Hole Oceanographic Institution, Mass.
For primary bibliographic entry see Field 7B.
W75-08987

ACTINOMYCETALES ISOLATED FROM SAINT LOUIS BAY, MISSISSIPPI,
Mississippi Univ., University. Dept. of Biology.
For primary bibliographic entry see Field 5C.
W75-08993

INHIBITION OF DIATOM PHOTOSYNTHESIS BY GERMANIC ACID: SEPARATION OF DIATOM PRODUCTIVITY FROM TOTAL MARINE PRIMARY PRODUCTIVITY,
California Univ., San Diego, La Jolla. Inst. of Marine Resources.
For primary bibliographic entry see Field 5C.
W75-09001

PHYTOPLANKTON ENRICHMENT EXPERIMENTS AND BIOASSAYS IN NATURAL COASTAL SEA WATER AND IN SEWAGE OUTFALL RECEIVING WATERS OFF SOUTHERN CALIFORNIA,
California Univ., San Diego, La Jolla. Inst. of Marine Resources.
For primary bibliographic entry see Field 5C.
W75-09019

THE USE OF ARTIFICIAL SUBSTRATES IN SAMPLING ESTUARINE BENTHOS,
York Univ., Downsview (Ontario). Dept. of Biology.
For primary bibliographic entry see Field 5B.
W75-09149

TOXICITY OF KRAFT MILL WASTES TO AN ESTUARINE PHYTOPLANKTER,
North Carolina State Univ., Raleigh. Dept. of Zoology.
For primary bibliographic entry see Field 5C.
W75-09159

TISSUE HYDROCARBON BURDEN OF MUSSELS AS POTENTIAL MONITOR OF ENVIRONMENTAL HYDROCARBON INSULT,
Naval Biomedical Research Lab., Oakland, Calif.
For primary bibliographic entry see Field 5B.
W75-09163

PROBLEMS IN C-14 DATING OF WATER FROM AQUIFERS OF DELTAIC ORIGIN--AN EXAMPLE FROM THE NEW JERSEY COASTAL PLAIN,
Geological Survey, Reston, Va.
For primary bibliographic entry see Field 2F.
W75-09183

NET PRIMARY PRODUCTIVITY OF PERIPHYTIC ALGAE IN THE INTERTIDAL ZONE, DUWAMISH RIVER ESTUARY, WASHINGTON,
Geological Survey, Menlo Park, Calif.
For primary bibliographic entry see Field 5C.
W75-09189

NITROGEN CONTENT OF SHALLOW GROUND WATER IN THE NORTH CAROLINA COASTAL PLAIN,
North Carolina State Univ., Raleigh. Dept. of Soil Science.
For primary bibliographic entry see Field 5B.
W75-09232

TRANSIENT ANALYSIS OF WATER QUALITY IN THE DELAWARE ESTUARY SYSTEM VIA ONE-DIMENSIONAL INTRA-TIDAL TIME VARYING MODELS WITH APPLICATION TO THE IDENTIFICATION OF THE TIDAL DISPERSION COEFFICIENT USING DISCRETE SPACE CONTINUOUS TIME OCEAN SALINITY DATA,
Rutgers - the State Univ., New Brunswick, N.J. Dept. of Chemical and Biochemical Engineering.
For primary bibliographic entry see Field 5B.
W75-09233

STORM TIDE FREQUENCY ANALYSIS FOR THE GULF COAST OF FLORIDA FROM CAPE SAN BLAS TO ST. PETERSBURG BEACH,
National Weather Service, Silver Spring, Md.
For primary bibliographic entry see Field 2B
W75-09268

MATHEMATICAL MODELING OF NEAR COASTAL CIRCULATION,
Massachusetts Inst. of Tech., Cambridge.
J. D. Wang, and J. J. Connor.
Report No MITSG 75-13, April 1975 272 p, 90 fig, 16 tab, 81 ref.

Descriptors: *Mathematical models, *Model studies, *Coasts, *Ocean circulation, Discharge(Water), Hydrodynamics, Oceanography, Finite element analysis, Numerical analysis, *Boundary processes.
Identifiers: *Hydrodynamic circulation, One layered situation, Two layered situation, Boundary conditions, Variational statements.

Hydrodynamic circulation in coastal waters is formulated in terms of mathematical models. The derivation of a set of governing equations, expressing conservation of mass and momentum is discussed. A simplification is introduced by integrating all variables and equations over the total water depth. The derivation of the vertically integrated formulation for one and two layered situations is discussed along with the underlying assumptions and closure problems. The treatment of boundaries and boundary conditions is given particular attention. By analogy to the mechanics of a particle, it is postulated that the admissible boundary conditions must either be in terms of forces or discharges. (NOAA)
W75-09273

VARIATIONS IN THE HYDROGRAPHIC STRUCTURE OF PRINCE WILLIAM SOUND,
Alaska Univ., College. Inst. of Marine Science.
R. D. Muench, and C. M. Schmidt.
IMS Report R75-1, Sea Grant Report R75-1, (1975). 135 p, 72 fig, 15 ref. 04-3158-41(OSG).

Descriptors: *Estuarine environment, *Hydrography, *Measurements, *Surveys, Temperature, Density, Salinity, Circulation, Mixing, Meteorology, Estuaries, Management, Data collections, *Alaska.
Identifiers: *Prince William Sound(Alas), *Hydrographic data, *Gulf of Alaska, Trans-Alaskan pipeline, Deep-water renewal processes.

Prince William Sound, a complex fjord-type estuarine system located off the northern Gulf of Alaska, is one of the larger North American estuarine systems not presently influenced by metropolitan activities. However, within the next decade, the Sound faces major development as the receiving-loading area for the trans-Alaskan pipeline, recreational and urban stresses from Anchorage, and increasing pressure from commercial fishermen. Physical oceanographic conditions in the Sound are analyzed to provide information which can be used in making management decisions and planning specific research in the region. Described are the distribution of temperature, salinity, and density; mixing processes and circulation; deep-water renewal processes; and seasonal variations in hydrographic conditions. (NOAA)
W75-09274

ENVIRONMENTAL STUDY OF THE MARINE ENVIRONMENT NEAR NOME, ALASKA,
Alaska Univ., College. Inst. of Marine Science.
D. W. Hood, V. Fisher, D. Nebert, H. Feder, and G. J. Mueller.
Institute of Marine Science Report 74-3, Sea Grant Report 73-14, July 1974, 265 p. NSF GD-31610, OSG 04-3-1581-41.

Descriptors: *Aquatic environment, *Sedimentation, Aquatic life, Hydrography, Water circulation, Trace elements, Marine biology, Oceanography, Data collections, Economics, *Baseline data studies, *Alaska, Metals.
Identifiers: *Marine environment, *Nome(Alas), Water column primary productivity, Trace metals.

The purpose was to collect baseline data to define the sedimentary, biological, and physical-chemical environments in the vicinity of Nome. The investigation included: a determination of the surficial bottom sediments including suspended sediment loads and trace metal content of the sediments; the collection and identification of bottom dwelling organisms; a few estimates of water column primary productivity; studies of the hydrography circulation patterns and oxygen distributions, the nutrient levels and trace metal content of the water column, and the socio-economic status of the town of Nome. (NOAA)
W75-09275

NEW YORK BIGHT PROJECT, WATER COLUMN SAMPLING CRUISES NO 6-8 OF THE NOAA SHIP FERREL, APRIL - JUNE 1974,
National Oceanic and Atmospheric Administration, Boulder, Colo. Marine EcoSystems Analysis Program.
J. B. Hazelworth, B. L. Kolitz, R. B. Starr, R. L. Charnell, and G. A. Berberian.
NOAA Data Report MESA-1, January 1975. 177 p, 7 fig, 2 tab, 9 ref.

Descriptors: *Data collections, *Marine biology, *Marine geology, Chemistry, Physics, Oceanography, Instrumentation, *Sampling, Remote sensing, Cruises, New York.
Identifiers: *Marine ecosystem, *New York Bight, Satellite monitoring, Water column, Sediment chemistry.

During the period April-June 1974, three oceanographic cruises, denoted 6, 7, and 8, were made by the NOAA ship Ferrel in the New York Bight. The objective of the cruises was to supply data to provide a base for analysis of the water movements on the highly impacted ecosystem. The corrected physical and chemical data from these cruises are presented and the parameters measured, the measurement methods, and the corrections applied to the data are described. (NOAA)
W75-09277

ASSESSMENT OF OFFSHORE DUMPING; TECHNICAL BACKGROUND: PHYSICAL

high potential for water yield increase by small patch cuts from sites similar to those studied. (Roberts-ISWS)
W75-09198

THE PARADOX OF PLANNED WEATHER MODIFICATION,
Illinois State Water Survey, Urbana.
S. A. Changnon, Jr.
Bulletin American Meteorological Society, Vol 56, No 1, p 27-37, January 1975. 2 fig, 1 tab, 73 ref. NSF Grant GI-37859.

Descriptors: *Weather modification, *Federal project policy, Fog, Snow, Tropical regions, Rain, Cloud seeding, Precipitation(Atmospheric), Social aspects, Economics, Climatology, Weather.

A paradox has developed involving sizable reductions during the last two years in federal support of weather modification as opposed to major scientific-technical advances in and strong recommendations for increased federal support from the scientific community. Many possible causes for the paradox appear, including fear of weather changes, lack of scientific commitment, and a series of public, scientific, political, and military controversies. The three basic issues are that weather modification is still an immature technology, the socio-economic impacts are ill defined, and its management has been uncertain. Proper resolution of the paradox is more apt to occur either because of a dramatic scientific breakthrough or from growing concerns about weather and climate-related environmental changes. (Jones-ISWS)
W75-09209

SOME PROBLEMS IN THE APPLICATION OF SYSTEMS ANALYSES IN WATER RESOURCES SYSTEMS,
Office of Science and Technology, Washington, D.C.
W. A. Hall.
In: Systems Analysis of Hydrologic Problems; Proceedings of the Second International Seminar for Hydrology Professors, August 2-14, 1970, Utah State University, Logan, p 407-417. 15 ref.

Descriptors: *Systems analysis, *Optimization, *Mexico, *Agricultural engineering, *Water resources, *Surface-groundwater relationships, Hydrology, Infiltration, Precipitation(Atmospheric), Infiltrometers, Arid lands, Agricultural watersheds, Runoff.
Identifiers: Risk minimization, Micro watersheds.

A general discussion of systems analysis of water resources problems was presented as well as specific problems to which systems analysis is applied. The general discussion included comparisons of scientific approaches versus engineering approaches. Example was made of an arid portion of Mexico in which the goal was to increase the per capita income. The development of a simple idea, i.e., as a watershed decreases in size the percent of precipitation appearing as runoff increases, was carried through a series of experiments into actual practice. Optimization by maximizing profit was demonstrated, but it was also shown that minimizing risk in a marginal economy may be more important. (See also W75-09210) (Terstriep-ISWS)
W75-09226

PREAUTHORIZATION PLANNING ACTIVITIES OF THE BUREAU OF RECLAMATION, THE CORPS OF ENGINEERS AND THE SOIL CONSERVATION SERVICE FOR FISCAL YEAR 1975.
For primary bibliographic entry see Field 4A.
W75-09244

POST AUTHORIZATION PROJECT ACTIVITIES ANNUAL STATUS REPORT - BUREAU OF RECLAMATION.
For primary bibliographic entry see Field 4A.
W75-09245

WEATHER MODIFICATION GRANTS.
Hearing--Subcomm. on Agricultural Research and General Legislation, Comm. on Agriculture and Forestry, U.S. Senate, 93d Cong, 2d Sess, August 19, 1974. 139 p, 20 fig, 6 map, 1 tab, 9 chart, 32 ref.

Descriptors: *Weather modification, *Droughts, *Water shortage, *Grants, Crops, Artificial precipitation, Artificial storms, Cloud seeding, Agroclimatology, Climatology, Cloud physics, Meteorology, Precipitation(Atmospheric), Rain, Storms, Water supply, Weather, Weather data, Legislation, Climatic data, Federal government, Research and development, Livestock, Programs.
Identifiers: Weather modification grants, Congressional hearings.

Hearings were held on S.3313 which is a bill to authorize the administrator of the Environmental Protection Agency to carry out an emergency assistance program to assist states in relieving severe drought conditions that threaten to destroy livestock or crops. Further, the bill authorizes financial grants to states for the purpose of assisting and initiating weather modification measures. Statements of numerous commentators representing government, public, and private interest groups are presented. Miscellaneous documents reprinted from articles on weather modification programs to alleviate drought are included. Proponents of the bill suggest that it will improve present programs by providing for coordinating and monitoring as well as cost sharing of operational weather modification programs. The central concern is to avoid economic disasters which accompany droughts by preventing droughts before they occur. (Fernandez-Florida)
W75-09259

DECENTRALIZED WATER REUSE SYSTEMS IN A WATER SCARCE ENVIRONMENT: THE TOURIST INDUSTRY IN ST. THOMAS, VIRGIN ISLANDS,
Clark Univ., Worcester, Mass.
For primary bibliographic entry see Field 5D.
W75-09297

ECOLOGY OF INDIAN DESERT: VIII. ON THE WATER RELATIONS AND ASSIMILATE BALANCE OF SOME DESERT PLANTS,
Jodhpur Univ. (India). Dept. of Botany.
T. Mathur, and D. N. Sen.
Ann Arid Zone, Vol 11, No 1/2, p 18-30, 1972.

Descriptors: Asia, *Plant ecology, Deserts, Water balance, *Desert plants, Soil moisture.
Identifiers: Calotropis-procera, *India(Rajasthan), Prosopis-cineraria, Prosopis-juliflora, Tephrosia-purpurea, Polysaccharides, Monosaccharides.

A study on the water relations and the assimilate balance of 4 desert plant species has been made after the rains were over and the dry period started in Western Rajasthan (India) for a period of 4-6 mo. It was observed that a reduction in the water loss and stomatal openings took place when the soil water decreased. The percentage of absolute moisture in Calotropis procera were found to be the maximum among the 4 spp., probably because of latex. It was minimum in Prosopis cineraria. The percentage of relative water content of P. cineraria, Prosopis juliflora and Tephrosia purpurea decreased, but in C. procera increased with decrease in soil moisture. The polysaccharides were detected only in Nov. and the presence of monosaccharides in summer months had led to a high osmotic potential, resulting in an echanced water uptake. The values of total N do not appear to show any particular trend in relation to the sur-

vival or otherwise of these desert plant species.--
Copyright 1974, Biological Abstracts, Inc.
W75-09322

3C. Use Of Water Of Impaired Quality

IRRIGATION WITH WASTE WATER AT BOARD OF WORKS FARM, WERRIBEE,
Melbourne and Metropolitan Board of Works (Australia).
For primary bibliographic entry see Field 5D.
W75-08941

RESPONSE OF ASPEN TO IRRIGATION BY MUNICIPAL WASTE WATER,
Pennsylvania State Univ., University Park. School of Forest Resources.
W. K. Murphey, and J. J. Bowier.
Tappi, Vol 58, No 5, p 128-129, May 1975. 4 ref, 2 tab.

Descriptors: *Aspen, *Municipal wastes, *Crop response, *Irrigation effects, Waste disposal, Water pollution sources, Irrigation, Fibers(Plant), Forest management, Irrigation practices, Water reuse, Forestry.
Identifiers: *Populus tremuloides, Fiber length, Specific gravity, Pulpwood.

American quaking aspen (Populus tremuloides), viewed as a pulpwood species, responded favorably to treatment with effluent from municipal sewage treatment plants. Average annual increment and fiber length were different for irrigated and control samples at the 1% level of significance. Differences did not occur among annual increments at the same height within treatment groups, but height in the bole did show an effect. Average annual increment in the crown was significantly larger than at either mid-bole or base. Specific gravity at the base of the bole was greater than at the other two locations. Fiber length in irrigated trees was greater in the crown than at the other locations. In the control trees, the length of fibers in the base was lower than in the two upper regions. The increase in fiber length in the irrigated trees produced a better fiber length-to-width ratio which is considered advantageous to pulp strength. (Sykes-IPC)
W75-09342

3D. Conservation In Domestic and Municipal Use

SOURCES OF EMERGENCY WATER SUPPLIES IN SAN MATEO COUNTY, CALIFORNIA,
Geological Survey, Menlo Park, Calif.
For primary bibliographic entry see Field 6D.
W75-08911

RECONNAISSANCE OF THE WATER RESOURCES OF THE OKLAHOMA CITY QUADRANGLE, CENTRAL OKLAHOMA,
Geological Survey, Oklahoma City, Okla.
For primary bibliographic entry see Field 7C.
W75-08912

PLANT SCALE STUDIES OF THE MAGNESIUM CARBONATE WATER TREATMENT PROCESS,
Black, Crow and Eidsness, Inc., Montgomery, Ala.
For primary bibliographic entry see Field 5F.
W75-08939

COMPARATIVE EVALUATION OF THREE URBAN RUNOFF MODELS,
Canada Centre for Inlands Waters, Burlington (Ontario).
For primary bibliographic entry see Field 2A.
W75-08988

STUDIES IN ENVIRONMENT - VOLUME III, POLLUTION AND THE MUNICIPALITY,
Homer Hoyt Inst., Washington, D.C.
For primary bibliographic entry see Field 6G.
W75-09055

COLLIER COUNTY WATER MANAGEMENT ORDINANCE.
For primary bibliographic entry see Field 6E.
W75-09260

3E. Conservation In Industry

THE BASIC TECHNOLOGY OF THE PULP AND PAPER INDUSTRY AND IT'S WASTE REDUCTION PRACTICES,
Lakehead Univ., Port Arthur (Ontario).
For primary bibliographic entry see Field 5D.
W75-09334

3F. Conservation In Agriculture

BIOLOGICAL FERTILIZER PRODUCTION - BY TREATMENT OF SEWAGE SLUDGES WITH SULFITE LIQUORS.
For primary bibliographic entry see Field 5D.
W75-08863

ON THE DIRUNAL VARIATION OF LEAF WATER CONTENT ON AN AREA BASIS IN THE RICE PLANT, IN JAPANESE,
Tokyo Uniur of Agriculture and Technology (Japan). Faculty of Agriculture.
Kuni Ishihara, Yasuyuki Ishida, and Tadaharu Ogura.
Proc Crop Sci Soc Jpn, 43(1): 77-82, Illus. 1974. English summary.

Descriptors: *Rice, Leaves, Cerea crops, Field crops, *Diurnal, *Consumptive use, Diurnal distribution, *Environmental effects, *Biorhythms.

An investigation was undertaken to clarify the diurnal variation of leaf water content on an area basis in some developmental stages of rice plants under various weather conditions. Maximal water content was obtained for the 12th and 13th leaves, fully expanded just at the panicle formation stage. The water content decreased more and more for both upper and lower leaves further from the relevant leaves. The water content of each successive leaf followed the diurnal variation pattern of reaching the maximal value in early morning and decreasing towards noon, but the range of variation was wider at the tillering stage, becoming narrower after the booting stage. The midday decrease of water content was rather remarkable on fine days accompanied with intense transpiration, but the difference of diurnal variation between fine and cloudy days was small as was expected. It is suggested that the water content of rice plants grown in submerged conditions did not decrease below a certain limit, owing perhaps to the increase of water absorption in accordance with intensive transpiration or stomatal closure due to the decrease of water content. In the afternoon of fine days, stomatal aperture became much smaller than on cloudy days. It was considered that the slight variation of water content had much influence upon stomatal aperture when water content on leaf blade decreased to a certain limit and that this influence became more prominent after the booting stage with a narrower range of the variation of water content. The dry weight/leaf area was much larger in fine days compared with cloudy days, suggesting the effect of dry weight increase upon the decrease of customary leaf water content on a dry weight or fresh weight basis.--Copyright 1975, Biological Abstracts, Inc.

dicted soil moisture and wheat yield values were found to agree with measured values, and the model was used to calculate the probability of different levels of yield for a number of irrigation treatments, on the basis of long-term rainfall data.--Copyright 1974, Biological Abstracts, Inc.
W75-09152

EFFECTS OF ROOT MEDIUM AND WATERING ON TRANSPIRATION, GROWTH AND DEVELOPMENT OF GLASSHOUSE CROPS: I. EFFECTS OF COMPRESSION AT VARYING WATER LEVELS ON PHYSICAL STATE OF ROOT MEDIA AND A TRANSPIRATION AND GROWTH OF TOMATOES,
State Experiment Station Landvik, Grimstad (Norway).
For primary bibliographic entry see Field 2D.
W75-09162

SIMULATION MODEL FOR EVAPOTRANSPIRATION OF WHEAT: EFFECT OF EVAPORATIVE CONDITIONS,
Hebrew Univ., Jerusalem (Israel).
For primary bibliographic entry see Field 2D.
W75-09196

EFFECT OF FERTILIZER APPLICATION ON REGENERATION OF NATURAL GRASSLANDS IN COASTAL PARTS OF MAHARASHTRA,
College of Agriculture, Poona (India). Botany Section.
For primary bibliographic entry see Field 2I.
W75-09231

RELATION OF SOIL WATER POTENTIAL TO STOMATAL RESISTANCE OF SOYBEAM,
Kansas State Univ., Manhattan. Evapotranspiration Lab.
For primary bibliographic entry see Field 2D.
W75-09235

WEATHER CONDITIONS AND SCREWWORM ACTIVITY,
National Weather Service, University Park, Pa.
J. J. Rahn, and G. L. Barger.
Agric Meteorol, Vol 11, No 2, p 197-211, 1973. Illus.
Identifiers: Cochliomyia-hominivorax, *Screwworms, Temperature, *Weather, *Pest eradication, *Pest control.

The screwworm (Cochliomyia hominivorax) has been a serious economic pest in southean sections of the USA for many years. Recently, USA Department of Agriculture eradication program significantly reduced the number of reported infestations in the Southwest, although periodic outbreaks continue to occur. The relationship between reported screwworm cases and weather conditions was investigated, with the objective of establishing guidelines for the use of real-time weather data as input to the eradication program. Because of several complicating factors the results were larely qualitative. The screwworm activity/rainfall relationship was quite variable. Periods of moderate or heavy precipitation were often followed within several weeks by an increase in reported screwworm cases. In other instances, there were wet periods with no resulting increase in screwworm activity. Some of this believed due to a temperature factor, since insect activity appeared to be diminshed by extremely high temperatures. A critical threshold temperature of approximately 95F was suggested. Palmer Crop Moisture Index (CMI) values were useful indicator of screwworm activity, with above normal CMI values often, but not always, associated with increased infestation reports in following weeks. Periods of moderate or heavy rainfall, or persistent light precipitation, accompanied by temperatures remaining below the mid-90's should be a signal to the eradication program of an increased potential for screwworm outbreaks.--Copyright 1973, Biological Abstracts, Inc.
W75-09318

EFFECT OF GYPSUM AND MANURE ON THE GROWTH OF WHEAT IRRIGATED WITH BICARBONATE RICH WATER,
Rajasthan Salinity Lab., Jodhpur (India).
S. S. Puntamkar, P. C. Mehta, and S. P. Seth.
J Indian Soc Soil Sci, Vol 20, No 3, p 281-285, 1972.

Descriptors: *Irrigation effects, *Wheat, *Gypsum, Calcium compounds, Sulfur compounds, Inorganic compounds, *Farm wastes, *Crop production, Cereal crops, Field crops.
Identifiers: Bicarbonate-rich water.

A field experiment was conducted to study the effect of gypsum at 5, 10 and 20 tons/ha and manure at 15 and 30 tons/ha, respectively, alone or with irrigation with bicarbonate rich water. Gypsum and manure increased the yield of wheat ('Sonora 64'); the highest yield of wheat was recorded with 20 tons of gypsum alone. Combined gypsum and manure were less valuable than the highest dose of gypsum alone. Exchangeable Na decreased by 1.6-10.9% while exchangeable Ca increased up to 17.7%.--Copyright 1973, Biological Abstracts, Inc.
W75-09321

COMPARING THE EFFECTS OF IRRIGATION AND NITROGENOUS FERTILIZERS ON THE YIELD, QUALITATIVELY AND QUANTITATIVELY, OR VARIOUS VARIETIES OF MAIZE: II. YIELD OF PROTEIN, (IN FRENCH),
Institut National de la Recherche Agronomique, Toulouse (France). Station d'Agronomie.
J. Decau, and B. Pujol.
Ann Agron (Paris), Vol 24, No 3, p 359-373, 1973. English summary.

Descriptors: Corn(Field), *Irrigation effects, *Fertilizers, *Nitrogen compounds, Nutrients, *Crop production, *Proteins, *Yield equations, Grains(Crops), Field crops, Crops.
Identifiers: Maize, Yield.

An opaque mutant maize 2(O sub 2), subjected to various nitrogenous feeding conditions, chiefly in dry crops, reacts more markedly than natural maizes (+) and has a higher protein content (N x 6.25). However, the yield of both grains and nitrogenous matter per acre of maize (+) remains higher than the mutant's. The range of protein content in the mutant is larger, (Fertilizing variations being comparable) in dry than in wet crops, 8.6-12.6 and 8.9-11.8, respectively. When both maizes are equally heavily fertilized, the protein content of the irrigated-maize grain is lower than that of the dry crop. To explain this, the relative effects of nitrogenous fertilizing and of irrigation on N absorption on the plant yield of both protein and the total dry matter, and the same irrigation effects on the compared migration of the proteins and the other substances to the grain are dealt with. The comparatively lower capability of nitrogenous substances to shift towards the grain, compared with that of ternary compounds apparently stems from the different nitrogenous enrichment of the grain that was observed.--Copyright 1974, Biological Abstracts, Inc.
W75-09331

PROCEEDINGS TALL TIMBERS CONFERENCE ON ECOLOGICAL ANIMAL CONTROL BY HABITAT MANAGEMENT, NO. 4.
Tall Timbers Research Station, Tallahassee, Fal.
For primary bibliographic entry see Field 2I.
W75-09333

4. WATER QUANTITY MANAGEMENT AND CONTROL

4A. Control Of Water On The Surface

WATER RESOURCES INVENTORY OF CONNECTICUT--PART 5, LOWER HOUSATONIC RIVER BASIN,
Geological Survey, Hartford, Conn.
W. E. Wilson, E. L. Burke, and C. E. Thomas, Jr.
Connecticut Water Resources Bulletin No 19, 1974. 79 p, 60 fig, 4 plate, 29 tab, 110 ref.

Descriptors: *Water resources, *Connecticut, Surface waters, Groundwater, Hydrologic data, Data collections, Water yield, Hydrogeology, Streamflow, Glacial drift, Aquifers, Maps.
Identifiers: *Housatonic River(Conn).

The lower Housatonic River basin in western Connecticut includes the basins of two major tributaries, the Pomperaug and Naugatuck Rivers. Almost half the precipitation--21.6 inches--was lost from the basin by evapotranspiration. Except for small amounts exported, the remainder dicharged as runoff and underflow into Long Island Sound. Variations in streamflow at 6 long-term continuous-record gaging stations are summarized in standardized graphs and tables. Of the 37 principal lakes, ponds, and reservoirs in the basin, 6 have usable storage of more than 1 billion gallons. Water can be obtained from three aquifers underlying the basin--stratified drift, till, and bedrock. Groundwater supplies generally range in yield from several millions tof gallons per day from large well fields to 1 gpm from single wells. Large supplies, with yields of 100 gpm or more from individual wells, are most commonly obtained from stratified drift. Small to moderate water supplies can be obtained from any of the aquifers under suitable conditions. Where unaffected by man's activities, water in the basin is generally low in dissolved-solids concentration, is of the calcium magnesium bicarbonate type, and is soft to moderately hard. Man's activities have degraded the quality of water in streams in much of the basin, except in the Pomperaug subbasin. The quantity and quality of water in the basin are satisfactory for a wide variety of uses, and, with suitable treatment, the water may be used for most purposes. (Knapp-USGS)
W75-08905

SUMMARY OF HYDROLOGIC DATA COLLECTED DURING 1973 IN DADE COUNTY, FLORIDA,
Geological Survey, Tallahassee, Fla.
For primary bibliographic entry see Field 7C.
W75-08908

SUMMARY STATEMENTS OF WATER RESOURCES INVESTIGATIONS IN FLORIDA, 1974-75.
Geological Survey, Tallahassee, Fla.
For primary bibliographic entry see Field 7C.
W75-08909

WATER RESOURCES OF WISCONSIN, LOWER WISCONSIN RIVER BASIN,
Geological Survey, Reston, Va.
For primary bibliographic entry see Field 7C
W75-08913

WATER RESOURCES OF HAMILTON COUNTY, SOUTHWESTERN KANSAS,
Geological Survey, Reston, Va.
For primary bibliographic entry see Field 7C.
W75-08914

HYDROLOGIC UNIT MAP--1974, STATE OF MICHIGAN.
Geological Survey, Reston, Va.
For primary bibliographic entry see Field 7C.
W75-08916

HYDROLOGIC UNIT MAP--1974, STATE OF SOUTH CAROLINA.
Geologic Survey, Reston, Va.
For primary bibliographic entry see Field 7C.
W75-08917

HYDROLOGIC UNIT MAP--1974, STATE OF VIRGINIA.
Geological Survey, Reston, Va.
For primary bibliographic entry see Field 7C.
W75-08918

HYDROLOGIC UNIT MAP--1974, STATE OF NEW YORK.
Geological Survey, Reston, Va.
For primary bibliographic entry see Field 7C.
W75-08920

EROSION-PROOFING DRAINAGE CHANNELS,
Connecticut Univ., Storrs. Dept. of Civil Engineering.
For primary bibliographic entry see Field 4D.
W75-08925

OPTIMAL TIMING, SEQUENCING, AND SIZING OF MULTIPLE RESERVOIR SURFACE WATER SUPPLY FACILITIES,
California Univ., Los Angeles. Dept. of Engineering Systems.
L. Becker, and W. W-G. Yeh.
Water Resources Research, Vol 10, No 1, February 1974, p 57-62. 3 fig, 4 tab, 18 ref. (California Water Resources Center Project UCAL-WRC-W-338). OWRR A-040-CAL(2).

Descriptors: *Time series analysis, Timing, Water supply, Surface waters, *California, *Optimization, *Multiple-purpose reservoirs.
Identifiers: *Eel River(Calif).

A method is outlined whereby the timing, sequeneing, and sizing of a water supply development is validly performed. The method takes care of the vital fact that although it is firm water that is demanded or sold, it is reservoir capacity at a particular site that is costed, and the two are not simply related, nor is the relationship independent of previously constructed reservoirs and the stream-reservoir configuration. A feature of this method is a simple firm water determination concept that is applicable to any stream-reservoir configuration and that uses rational and reasonable operating rules at each basic time period for the calculations of reservoir storage changes resulting from excess or deficit streamflows relative to demand in those periods. Details of interchanges of water between reservoirs are not relevant to this concept. Streamflows are taken to be the subnormal flow hydrographs that would correspond to a critical period analysis method, but no advantage is taken of any supposed knowledge about future flows. (Snyder-California, Davis)
W75-08928

A STUDY TO EXPLORE THE USE OF ORBITAL REMOTE SENSING TO DETERMINE NATIVE ARID PLANT DISTRIBUTION,
Arizona Univ., Tuson. Office of Arid-Lands Studies.
For primary bibliographic entry see Field 7B.
W75-08945

ESTIMATION OF THE WATER RESOURCES OF A PORTION OF THE GAMBIER PLAIN

UROS4: URBAN FLOOD SIMULATION MODEL PART 1. DOCUMENTATION AND USERS MANUAL,

Georgia Inst. of Tech., Atlanta. School of Civil Engineering.
A. M. Lumb.
Available from the National Technical Information Service, Springfield, Va. 22161, as PB-242 936, $7.50 in paper copy, $2.25 in microfiche. March 1975. 225 p, 30 fig, 48 tab, 17 ref.

Descriptors: Urban runoff, *Urban drainage, Hydrographs, *Georgia, *Urban hydrology, *Model studies, Flood control, *Simulation analysis, *Flood stages, Flood peak, Computer programs.
Identifiers: Runoff files, DeKalb County(Geo).

An Urban Flood Simulation Model was developed for use by DeKalb County, Georgia, in evaluating the hydrologic effects of tributary area land use, constricting culverts, detention storage, and channel conditions. The Model was formulated as a working tool for tributary land use planning, structural design, and flood plain management to deal with a widespread drainage problem along small urban creeks. Rainfall, streamflow, and soils data were analyzed with the Stanford Watershed Model to develop an historic data file of rainfall excess or runoff for the range of land surface conditions found in DeKalb County. The Urban Flood Simulation Model simulates 25 years of annual flood peaks given the data file and prescribed physical characteristics of as many as 100 area, channel, and storage segments in a selected drainage area. The model will calculate flood elevations and associated probabilities for specified points. Though collecting, coding, and checking the physical data may take a man-month, once the coding is complete it is relatively easy to explore the effects of changing land-use, altering the drainage system, or adding detention storage. The procedures used in developing the file of runoff data, selecting equations to incorporate within the model, the computer programming, and the recommended procedures for collecting and coding data on drainage characteristics are described in detail. The computer program is listed. (See also W75-09047) (James-Georgia Tech)
W75-09046

UROS4: URBAN FLOOD SIMULATION MODEL PART 2. APPLICATIONS TO SELECTED DEKALB COUNTY WATERSHEDS,

Georgia Inst. of Tech., Atlanta. School of Civil Engineering.
L. D. James, and A. M. Lumb.
Available from the National Technical Information Service, Springfield, Va. 22161, as PB-242 937, $7.50 in paper copy, $2.25 in microfiche. May 1975. 237 p, 37 fig, 106 tab.

Descriptors: *Georgia, Urban drainage, *Urban hydrology, *Urbanization, *Channelization, Detention storage, Culverts, Model studies, Flood control, *Simulation analysis.
Identifiers: DeKalb County(Geo).

The Urban Flood Simulation Model developed for use by DeKalb County, Georgia, to evaluate the hydrologic effects of tributary land use, constricting culverts, detention storage, and channel conditions was applied to eight watersheds within the county. For each watershed, the basic physical characteristics, the nature of the flooding problem, the data collected for flood hydrograph simulation, and the results of the studies are described. On one 1058-acre watershed, a number of simulation runs were used to study the effects of impervious tributary area and channel improvement on flood flows. These runs showed urbanization to multiply flood peaks by a factor of about three, channelization to multiply flood peaks by a factor that increased from 1.06 to 1.23 as drainage area increased from 1 to 1000 acres, and six different storms as critical in different parts of the watershed. The hydrologic analyses of the eight watersheds found that sites suitable for flood retardation dams generally were not effective except in very small watersheds, that existing culverts were causing sufficient ponding to significantly reduce downstream flooding, and that sediment and debris deposits were a major problem. The Model was very useful for quick estimation of the hydrologic effects of land use and channel changes and for estimating flood flows for various purposes. (See also W75-09046)
W75-09047

A LAND USE PROGRAM FOR ARIZONA.

Arizona Environmental Planning Commission, Phoenix.
For primary bibliographic entry see Field 6B.
W75-09058

OPTIMIZING PARAMETERS FOR A WATERSHED MODEL,

Virginia Polytechnic Inst. and State Univ., Blacksburg. Dept. of Agricultural Engineering.
For primary bibliographic entry see Field 2E.
W75-09077

BENEFITS AND LAND USE CHANGE CONNECTED WITH A FLOOD CONTROL PROJECT,

Dayton Univ., Ohio. Dept. of Economics.
D. B. Oyen, and J. R. Barnard.
Water Resources Bulletin, Vol 11, No 3, p 483-490, June 1975. 2 tab, 11 ref. OWRT A-038-IA(2).

Descriptors: *Water resources, *Projects, *Land use, *Estimating, Benefits, Regression analysis, Flood plains, Dams, Agriculture, Economics, Mathematical models, Systems analysis, Iowa.
Identifiers: *Iowa River, *Land use changes.

To insure that expenditures on water resources projects are justified, more accurate predictions of land use change are needed; this in turn requires more information on the factors that influence land use change. This study examines agricultural land use change in the flood plain of the Iowa River as a result of building the Coralville Dam. Estimates of land use change and the benefits realized from the project are compared to the original project study benefits estimated by the Corps of Engineers. An analysis of the factors affecting land use change is carried out through a regression model to determine those variables that explain observed land use change. It has been contended that net benefits from flood control projects are overstated because the anticipated land conversion does not take place, because of the low discount rate applied to the benefits stream of public projects, and because agricultural prices have been influenced by government programs to bolster farm prices. Results of the ex post evaluation of the actual agricultural benefits originating from the Coralville Dam indicate that actual benefits, even when adjusted downward to account for the above three factors, were one-third greater than the projected benefits from the original Corps of Engineers feasibility study. The biggest error in the Corps' projection of benefits came from underestimating yields. The probability of land use change increases with increases in the number of acres available for conversion, the age of the landowner, and the number of years of education of the landowner. (Bell-Cornell)
W75-09081

FLOOD PLAIN INFORMATION: SANTA CLARA RIVER AND SESPE CREEK, FILLMORE, CALIFORNIA.

Army Engineer District, Los Angeles, Calif.
Prepared for the County of Ventura, June 1972. 31 p, 21 fig, 23 plates, 6 tab.

Descriptors: *Floods, *Flood plains, *Flooding, *Flood profiles, Flow, *Flood forecasting, Flood data, Flood frequency, *California.

Identifiers: Santa Clara River(Calif), Sespe Creek(Calif), Fillmore(Calif), Ventura County(Calif), Intermediate Regional Flood, Standard Project Flood.

Ninety percent of the watershed of the Santa Clara River which begins in the San Gabriel mountains consists of high rugged mountains; the remainder, valley floor and coastal plain. In the study reach where the average gradient is 24.4 ft/mi, the river is a wide, sandy watercourse with a floodplain about 1 mile wide, containing citrus orchards, about 80 structures, the Fillmore sewage disposal plant, the California State fish hatchery, and a mobile home park. Construction of a proposed freeway on the north side of the river may stimulate development. Erosion of river banks during large floods with formation of sand bars has had a significant effect in changing the river's channel cross section. The Santa Clara River had a peak discharge of 68,000 cfs at the Ventura-Los Angeles County line in the record flood of January, 1969. Sespe Creek, with a study reach gradient of 40 ft/mi, joins it near Fillmore, California, about 15 miles downstream, it crested at 60,000 cfs. This flood was followed by another damaging flood a month later which again washed out roads, bridges, and orchards. An Intermediate Regional Flood (IRF) would have peak discharges of 165,000 cfs on the Santa Clara River at the downstream limit of the study and 85,000 cfs on Sespe Creek at the confluence with the Santa Clara River. A Standard Project Flood (SPF) would have discharges at those points of 250,000 cfs and 109,000 cfs. Severe damages would be sustained by orchards, commercial establishments, and residential sections, and related streets and utilities. Stream velocities would erode banks in the channel and cause hazardous overbank flooding. High velocities could also cause damage due to transportation of debris, which, when deposited, forms a barrier that intensifies lateral flooding. (Park-North Carolina)
W75-09084

SPECIAL FLOOD HAZARD INFORMATION REPORT: ATLANTA, GEORGIA, INCLUDING PEACHTREE CREEK BASIN IN DEKALB COUNTY.
Army Engineer District, Mobile, Ala.
Prepared for Atlanta Region Metropolitan Planning Commission, October 1971. 16 p, 2 fig, 35 plates, 3 tab.

Descriptors: *Floods, *Flooding, *Flood control, *Flood protection, *Flood plains, *Control structures, *Georgia, Flood plain zoning, Warning systems, Flood forecasting.
Identifiers: Atlanta(Geo), Peachtree Creek Basin(Geo), DeKalb County(Geo), Fulton County(Geo), Intermediate Regional Flood, Greater Probable Flood, Standard Project Flood.

Twenty-one streams and tributaries contribute to the floodplain area of Atlanta which is hilly with relatively steep streams with elevations ranging from 750 to 1,100 ft above mean sea level. This report covers 85 1/2 stream miles. The watersheds of all streams lie within Fulton County with the exception of the Peachtree Creek basin which extends into Gwinnett and Dekalb Counties. Data on each stream include length, width, and height of channel and the average slope; individual plates show extent of flooding in an Intermediate Regional Flood (IRF) and Greater Probable Flood (GPF). A floodplain management program in Atlanta can be based on data collected in seven preceding floodplain information reports and in this report. Past floods have caused damages to floodplain development. Increased urbanization demands further land development which could restrict the flow of water and increase flood heights and damages upstream. Profiles give specific stream peak elevations for an IRF and GPF which mark the limits of the flood. Corrective measures such as flood proofing, construction regulations for floodplains, land filling, and land use regulations, could be implemented to increase flood protection in the Atlanta Area. (Salzman-North Carolina)
W75-09085

FLOOD PLAIN INFORMATION: EAST FORK BIG WOOD RIVER, GIMLET TRIUMPH, IDAHO.
Army Engineer District, Walla Walla, Wash.
Prepared for Blaine County, Idaho, November 1973. 18 p, 4 fig, 13 plates, 2 tab.

Descriptors: *Floods, *Flood plain zoning, *Idaho, Flooding, Flood control, Flood protection, Flood plains, Flood frequency, Flood plain insurance, Flood profiles.
Identifiers: *East Fork Big Wood River(Ida), Gimlet(Ida), Triumph(Ida), Intermediate Regional Flood, Standard Project Flood.

East Fork, a tributary of Big Wood River, drains an area of 81 square miles in South Central Idaho east of Ketchum. The East Fork channel slopes through steep mountainous terrain at 74 feet per mile, varies in width from about 30 to 70 feet and has a maximum depth of about 5 feet. The floodplain has little development, but pressure from the resort industry in nearby Ketchum will probably spur future development. East Fork has no streamflow records but its flooding parallels the flooding on Warm Springs Creek to the east and Big Wood River to the South. Flood flows above bankfull occur on the average every 3 to 4 years. Flood season is from late April to early June resulting from melting of snowpack. Winter rain plus snowmelt floods also can occur. Natural and manmade obstructions including 2 bridges restrict flood flow. Blaine County has enacted a floodplain zoning ordinance, and is eligible for federal flood insurance. Either an Intermediate Regional Flood or a Standard Project Flood could result from a combination of rainfall and snowmelt causing a 3.5 foot rise or a 7.0 foot rise respectively in the East Fork Big Wood River and inundating the floodplain for up to 3 weeks. (Salzman-North Carolina)
W75-09086

FLOOD PLAIN INFORMATION: PORTNEUF RIVER, INKOM, IDAHO, AND VICINITY.
Army Engineer District, Walla Walla, Wash.
Prepared for the Bannock County Board of Commissioners, April 1974. 30 p, 10 fig, 11 plates, 3 tab.

Descriptors: *Flood plains, *Flood, *Flooding, Flood control, Flood protection, Historic floods, *Idaho.
Identifiers: *Portneuf River(Ida), Inkom(Ida), Standard Project Flood(SPF), Intermediate Regional Flood(IRF).

Inkom, a railroad transport town, has numerous industries surrounded by agricultural land. The Portneuf River Basin, a semi-arid area which includes Inkom and several other towns, is formed by the 97 mile long river emptying into the Snake River. Its slope ranges from 37 ft/mi in the upper reaches to 4 ft/mi in the Inkom area. Residential and commercial developments in Inkom as well as railroad tracks running parallel to the stream are in the floodplain. A stream gage at Pocatello, downstream from Inkom, has recorded data since 1912. The greatest flood, on February 14, 1962, crested at 11.3 feet where an overbank flood height is 7 feet and had peak discharge of 2,990 cfs. Damages were estimated at $3 million. Major floods occur during winter and spring resulting from rainfall runoff combined with snowmelt. Winter rainstorm flooding above bankfull lasts for several days. Spring snowmelt floods rise slowly and last much longer up to several weeks. Natural and manmade obstructions including 7 bridges restrict flood flow. No flood ordinances exist. Extreme combinations of rainfall and snowmelt could result in the severe flooding of an Intermediate Regional Flood (IRF) or Standard Project Flood

hazardous overbank velocity of 5 feet per second. To avoid damage, this report should be used as a basis for floodplain management ordinances, floodproofing of endangered structures, and delineation of an area for warning and evacuation procedures. Structural solutions are not recommended. (Herr-North Carolina)
W75-09091

FLOOD PLAIN INFORMATION: DEEP RIVER, TURKEY CREEK, DUCK CREEK, LAKE COUNTY, INDIANA.
Army Engineer District, Chicago, Ill.
Prepared for the Lake-Porter County Regional Transportation and Planning Commission, March 1973. 37 p, 12 fig, 25 plates, 8 tab.

Descriptors: *Floods, *Flooding, *Flood plains, *Flood plain zoning, Flood control, Flood protection, Historic floods, *Indiana, Flood forecasting, Flood profiles.
Identifiers: *Deep River(Ind), Turkey Creek(Ind), Duck Creek(Ind), Lake County(Ind), Intermediate Regional Flood, Standard Project Flood.

Deep River drains 138 square miles of Lake County in northwest Indiana. Turkey and Duck Creeks, tributaries of Deep River, have slopes of 3.20 feet per mile and 6.70 feet per mile respectively. Deep River, including an artificial lake created by construction of Hobart Dam, slopes at an average of 3.75 feet per mile. Cities of Hobart, Crown Point and Merrillville mark the land development on the floodplain and are surrounded by residential and agricultural land. Pressure for development of floodplain land stems from intense urbanization of Gary. Floods occur during all seasons and can rise to extreme flood peaks in a relatively short period of time. The streams are spanned by 51 bridges and culverts which increase flood flow restrictions. Hobart Dam has little flood control capacity and no flood reduction projects exist. Under state law, any floodway construction must be approved. The largest flood occurred on October 11, 1954, cresting at 606.61 feet mean sea level datum (msld). The most recent flood, in May 15, 1970, crested at 603.57 feet msld and caused significant property damage due to the increased development in the floodplain. Both an Intermediate Regional Flood and a Standard Project Flood would result in inundation of agricultural, residential, commercial, and industrial sites cresting at 610.6 feet msld and 621 feet msld respectively. (Salzman-North Carolina)
W75-09092

POLICY ALTERNATIVES IN FLOOD PLAINS.
East Central Florida Regional Planning Council, Winter Park.
For primary bibliographic entry see Field 6F.
W75-09094

FLOOD PLAIN INFORMATION: SANTA ANA RIVER (IMPERIAL HIGHWAY TO PRADO DAM), ORANGE AND RIVERSIDE COUNTIES, CALIFORNIA.
Army Engineer District, Los Angeles, Calif.
Prepared for Orange County Flood Control District, June, 1971. 35 p, 27 fig, 13 plates, 6 tab.

Descriptors: *Floods, *Flooding, *Flood plains, Flow, Flood frequency, Flood recurrence interval, Flood profile, *California.
Identifiers: *Santa Ana River(Calif), Orange County(Calif), Riverside County(Calif), Intermediate Regional Flood, Standard Project Flood, Prado Dam(Calif).

The 10.84-mile reach of the Santa Ana River from Prado Dam to the Imperial Highway is analyzed for flood history and potential. Existing development is primarily agricultural, using the river for irrigation of citrus groves, but residential pressures from the City of Anaheim are increasing floodplain development of both a residential and transportation nature. Gage records have been kept for a number of years and the major flood record was in March, 1938, which had a peak discharge of 100,000 cubic feet/second (cfs) below Prado Dam. November to April is the major flood season. Obstructions to flow, both natural and manmade, increase flood damages causing backwater flooding and eorsion. A flood in February, 1969, had a discharge of only 5,000 cfs due to Prado Dam but damage was still extensive. Prado Dam is the only flood control facility but the two possible future floods would exceed the basin storage capacity of 198,200 acre-feet. These floods, the Intermediate Regional Flood (IRF) and the Standard Project Flood (SPF), would have flows of 48,000 and 150,000 cfs, respectively, and velocities exceeding 20 feet/second in canyon sections capable of severe erosion and movement of material up to large boulder size. (Park-North Carolina)
W75-09096

FLOOD PLAIN INFORMATION--COASTAL FLOODING, PORTSMOUTH, VIRGINIA.
Army Engineer District, Norfolk, Va.
51 p, 14 fig, 14 plates, 2 tab, glossary.

Descriptors: *Tidal waters, *Floods, *Flood waves, *Flood control, *Sea walls, Evacuation, Flood damage, Flood frequency, Flood peak, Flood protection, Flooding, *Virginia.
Identifiers: Standard Project Tidal Flood, Intermediate Regional Tidal Flood, Portsmouth(Va), *Elizabeth River(Va).

Portsmouth, Virginia, stands at the confluence of the James and Elizabeth Rivers. Bounded on the east by the Elizabeth River and on the north by the waters of Hampton Roads and penetrated by several tidal estuaries, it is subject to frequent serious tidal flooding of residential as well as commercial and industrial property. Tidal gage records as well as newspaper records indicate that severe flooding often accompanies autumn hurricanes, usually lasting for one tide cycle. Hydrological and meteorological data show that Portsmouth averages one hurricane per year, with a more serious storm averaging every ten years. Portsmouth also experiences winter and spring northeasters, powerful winds and heavy rains that have caused widespread flooding and damage, intensified by their long duration and wind-driven waves. In August, 1933, a hurricane flooded Portsmouth to a depth of 8 feet above mean sea level, and the northeaster in March, 1962, flooded to 7.4 feet, causing $1.4 million damages in 5 days of flooding. Studies show that even deeper floods are possible: an Intermediate Regional Tidal Flood (100-year flood) would crest at 8.5 feet, a Standard Project Tidal Flood would crest at 13.0 feet. Since this represents the reasonable upper limit of flooding, it should be used for regulations, evacuation plans, and floodplain management. The 1800-foot Crawford Redevelopment Project sea wall should be extended to connect with high ground. (Herr-North Carolina)
W75-09097

FLOOD PLAIN INFORMATION: TOMS RIVER, UNION BRANCH, RIDGEWAY BRANCH AND LONG SWAMP CREEK, OCEAN COUNTY, NEW JERSEY,
Army Engineer District, Philadelphia, Pa.
Prepared for the Ocean County Planning Board, June, 1972. 26 p, 10 fig, 19 plates, 19 tab.

Descriptors: *Flood plains, *Flood damage, *Flood plain zoning, Planning, Land use, Historic floods, Obstruction to flow, Flood discharge, Flood data, Floodways, Urbanization, *New Jersey, Marshes, Hurricanes.
Identifiers: *Toms River(NJ), Union Branch(NJ), Ridgeway Branch(NJ), Long Swamp Creek(NJ), Ocean County(NJ), *Flood plain management, Floodway Design Flood, Flood Hazard Area Design Flood, Standard Project Flood, Fluvial flooding, Tidal flooding, Barnegat Bay.

The portion of Ocean County covered by this report is subject to flooding from Toms River and its 3 tributaries. Properties along these streams are primarily residential and commercial. Continued industrial and commercial activity and subsequent increase in population will probably occure in the area, intensifying development in the floodplain. Because of the flat gradient and low relief of surrounding land, Toms River and its tributaries have formed a broad, poorly-drained floodplain with abundant swamp and marshland. Floods resulting from tropical hurricanes comprise the majority of the most severe floods and usually occur in the late summer and fall. The area is also subject to flooding from northwestern storms occurring throughout the year; to fluvial flooding from Toms River, and to tidal flooding from Barnegat Bay. Floods generally rise slowly and stay out of the banks for long periods. The largest stage of record for Toms River was estimated at 12.50 feet and 2000 cfs from a flood mark set in September 1938, but the actual gage reading was not available. Four of the 5 highest flows occurred within the last 3 years. Future floods discussed are Floodway Design Flood (FDF), Flood Hazard Area Design Flood (FHADF), and Standard Project Flood (SPF). At the gage on river mile 8.8, the peak flows for these floods would be 2800 cfs, 3600 cfs and 10,500 cfs, respectively. Of the 45 bridges and culverts crossing the streams in the study area, most of them are obstructive to FDG and FHADF and even more are obstructive to SPF. Floatable materials and small craft may cause additional hazards to life and property. (Diefendorf-North Carolina)
W75-09098

FLOOD PLAIN INFORMATION: POMPESTON CREEK BURLINGTON COUNTY, NEW JERSEY.
Army Engineer District, Philadelphia, Pa.
Prepared for Burlington County Planning Board and New Jersey Department of Environmental Protection, June 1971. 33 p, 6 fig, 11 plates, 3 tab.

Descriptors: *Flood plains, *Flood control, *Urbanization, Planning, Land use, Flood data, Flood stages, Obstruction to flow, *New Jersey, Delaware River.
Identifiers: Pompeston Creek(NJ), Burlington County(NJ), Flood plain management, Intermediate Regional Flood(IRF), Standard Project Flood(SPF), Encroachment law, Tidal flooding, Fluvial flooding.

Pompeston Creek and its major and minor tributaries are discussed. The surrounding area is part of a large commercial and industrial complex which is affected greatly by improvements in Delaware River Port facilities. There has been extensive development in the relatively narrow floodplain, which has increased the flooding potential by altering stream runoff characteristics. Three types of floods occur in this area: tidal flooding from high tides on the Delaware River, fluvial flooding due to storms of high intensity, and flooding from inadequate drainage due to urbanization. Summer and fall are the main flood seasons. The greatest flood occurred in August 1933 resulting from tidal flooding on the Delaware River. Stages of 8.8 feet, m.s.l.d. were recorded at the mouth of Pompeston Creek. An Intermediate Regional Flood (IRF) would reach a height of 1.6 feet above the 1933 flood, and a Standard Project Flood (SPF) would reach 5 feet above an IRF. There are 2 dams with no flood control capacity and 23 crossings which may cause obstruction to flow. At present, there are no gaging stations, no floodplain regulations, and no existing, authorized or proposed control measures. However, New Jersey does have an Encroachment Law which is essentially a preventive flood loss measure. (Diefendorf-North Carolina)
W75-09099

FLOOD PLAIN INFORMATION: ANIMAS RIVER AND TRIBUTARIES, DURANGO, COLORADO.
Army Engineer District, Sacramento, Calif.
Prepared for the Animas Regional Planning Commission, La Plata County, and the City of Durango, Colorado, June, 1974. 43 p, 20 fig, 29 plates, 8 tab.

Descriptors: *Flooding, *Flood plains, *Flood profiles, *Floods, *Flood data, Flood frequency, *Colorado, Flood recurrence interval, Gages, Rivers, Tributaries.
Identifiers: *Animas River(Colo), Durango(Colo), La Plata County(Colo), Intermediate Regional Flood(IRF), Standard Project Flood(SPF).

Portions of Durango, Colorado, and adjoining lands covered in this report are subject to flooding from the Animas River and Lightner, Junction, and Dry Gulch Creeks. The study area consists of 24% urban land uses, 47% agricultural use or vacant, and 29% public facilities and rights of way, with additional urbanization projected. Floods have occurred on an average of once every 3 years. A major flood occurred in October, 1911 on the Animas River (25,000 cfs discharge) and as recently as June, 1973 (7,590 cfs discharge). Future floods projected include the Intermediate Regional Flood (IRF) with an estimated discharge of 28,500 cfs at the Durango gage of the Animas River and the Standard Project flood (SPF) with a discharge of 42,000 cfs at the gage. The area inundated would include 1270 acres of agricultural or open land and 330 acres of urban land in an IRF. An SPF would not cover appreciably more land but the velocity of flow could be more hazardous than the estimated 13 ft/sec channel velocity on the Animas River for an IRF. Two reservoir sites and a channel modification project have been proposed but found uneconomical at this time. Non-structural alternatives are urged. (Park-North Carolina)
W75-09100

FLOOD PLAIN INFORMATION: VICINITY OF AUSTELL, GEORGIA, SWEETWATER CREEK.
Army Engineer District, Mobile, Ala.
Prepared for Atlanta Regional Commission, Janurary 1972. 19 p, 4 fig, 13 plates, 9 tab.

Descriptors: *Floods, *Flooding, *Flood plains, *Flood plain zoning, Historic floods, Flood control, Flood protection, *Georgia.
Identifiers: Austell(Ga), Sweetwater Creek(Ga), Cobb County(Ga), Intermediate Regional Flood, Standard Project Flood.

Sweetwater Creek, a 40-mile-long tributary of the Chattahoochee River, is located northwest of Atlanta, Georgia. The upper reach is characterized by numerous waterfalls and rapids and agricultural uses on the floodplain. For a 7-mile reach in the vicinity of Austell the floodplain is about 1,000 to 3,000 feet wide. Development there includes residential, commercial and industrial property. Below Austell, the floodplain is narrow and wooded. Data from a staff gage installed in 1904 were supplemented by interviews, newspaper files and historical records. Floods are most numerous in winter and spring, caused by extensive frontal type storms lasting 2 to 4 days. Natural and manmade obstructions including bridges and their approach fills restrict flood flow. Flood control includes zoning ordinances which require structures located in the floodplain to be elevated. Greatest flooding occurred July, 1916, resulting from a tropical storm. The latest flood, in February 1961, with a discharge of 10,100 cfs, caused severe property damages. Both an Intermediate Regional Flood (IRF) and a Standard Project Flood (SPF) would cause severe damage with estimated peak discharges of 15,340 cfs 31,260 cfs, respectively. (Salzman-North Carolina)
W75-09101

high rate of rise and velocity of flood flow. (Park-North Carolina)
W75-09109

FLOOD PLAIN INFORMATION: BIG WOOD RIVER, BELLEVUE-HAILEY, IDAHO AND VICINITY.
Army Engineer District, Walla Walla, Wash.
Prepared for Blaine County, Idaho. June 1971 33 p, 8 fig, 20 plates, 2 tab.

Descriptors: *Floods, *Flooding, *Flood plains, Flood control, Flood protection, Levees, Historic floods, *Idaho, Flood forecasting, Snowmelt.
Identifiers: Bellevue(Ida), Hailey(Ida), *Big Wood River(Ida), Standard Project Flood, Intermediate Regional Flood.

During a flood the floodplain of Big Wood River in South Central Idaho would be inundated to depths that would greatly damage flood vulnerable facilities. The drainage area covers 741 square miles of steep mountainous terrain. Big Wood River slopes at approximately 36 ft/mi and varies in width from 60 to 360 feet. The resort at Sun Valley has caused increased residential and recreational development. Much of the floodplain is rural except for portions of Bellevue and Hailey. Flood season from snowmelt and rain is from late April to early June. Floods can last for a month or more. Man-made and natural obstructions impede flood flow. Flood damage prevention measures are limited to local removal of debris, channel improvements, and levees, which are inadequate to protect against severe flooding. Stream gages at Hailey and 10 miles southwest of Bellevue show that the largest known flood occurred on May 25, 1967 cresting at 5.59 feet, lasting 12 days. Both an Intermediate Regional Flood (IRF) and a Standard Project Flood (SPF) would cause inundation of a large part of the floodplain. They would be about 1.5 and 2.5 feet higher, respectively, than the flood of 1967. Floodway limits wide enough to convey the IRF with a maximum of 1 ft of backwater effect in rural areas and 0.5 ft backwater effect in urban areas are detailed on plates. (Salzman-North Carolina)
W75-09110

FLOOD PLAIN INFORMATION: LOWER SANTIAGO CREEK, ORANGE COUNTY, CALIFORNIA.
Army Engineer District, Los Angeles, Calif.
Prepared for Orange County Flood Control District, June 1973. 57 p, 49 fig, 27 plates, 5 tab.

Descriptors: *Floods, *Flood plains, *Flood profiles, *Flooding, *Flood damage, Maximum probable flood, Historic floods, Flood data, Flood forecasting, Flood frequency, *California, Erosion.
Identifiers: Orange County(Calif), Orange(Calif), Santa Ana(Calif), Lower Santiago Creek(Calif), Handy Creek(Calif), Intermediate Regional Flood, Standard Project Flood.

Flooding on the Santiago Creek with its fairly level floodplain and a major tributary, Handy Creek, can be caused by general winter storms, local thunderstorms, or intense general summer storms. Runoff in the basin is very eratic with long dry spells and intense runoff and flash flooding after excessive rainfall. Damages have occurred throughout the 9.4 mile study reach including the cities of Santa Ana and Orange with a combined population of 253,000, and agricultural lands within the county. Flood damage reduction projects include channel improvements, Villa Park Dam constructed in 1963, Santiago Reservoir constructed in 1933, and county floodplain zoning ordinance. The largest flood was probably in 1862 although the greatest flood damage was in 1969 involving over $3 million in physical damages, with severe damage due to lateral erosion to both the natural and improved channel. Most of these areas have been restored to pre-1969 conditions. Future floods could be larger; an Intermediate Regional Flood (IRF) would cover approximately 646 acres including 198 acres of built-up area and have an estimated peak discharge of 10,400 cfs, compared to the 6,000 cfs discharge in 1969. A Standard Project Flood utilizing a wider floodplain would crest at 17,000 cfs. Many bridges would be in danger, causing damming of flood waters and increasing flood depths. Velocities could reach 6-19 ft/sec. in the channel and 2-10 ft/sec. on the floodplain, making the creek capable of transporting large materials and causing substantial erosion. Structures along the creek banks would be in danger of both water damage and severe undercutting. (Park-North Carolina)
W75-09111

FLOOD PLAIN INFORMATION, MULBERRY CREEK, DRY CREEK, SALINA, KANSAS.
Army Engineer District, Kansas City, Mo.
Prepared for the City of Salina, Kansas, March 1972. 26 p, 8 fig, 13 plates, 4 tab.

Descriptors: *Flood plains, *Floods, *Flooding, *Flood control, Flood protection, Flood damage, Channel improvement, Diversion structures, Levees, *Kansas, Flood forecasting.
Identifiers: Mulberry Creek(Kan), Dry Creek(Kan), Salina(Kan), Intermediate Regional Flood, Standard Project Flood.

Characterized by a serpentine stream with a wide floodplain averaging 1.5 to 2 miles in width, Mulberry Creek drains an area of 271 square miles and slopes at an average of 3 ft/mi. Portions of the lower basin near Salina, Kansas, are becoming urbanized but most of the land is in agricultural use. Dry Creek flows into Mulberry Creek from the south along the western edge of Salina, and has a drainage area of 27 square miles not diverted to Smokey Hill River by Salina Flood Project. The remaining portion has been altered by the project and channel realignment. Most of the basin is agricultural with about 5 square miles used by airport and surrounding buildings. Flood season begins with spring rains and continues through early summer with generalized storms over the basin. Flows are characterized by high stages and high velocities. An effective flood damage prevention program has been initiated which includes channel improvement, diversion of Dry Creek to Smokey Hill River, channel straightening, and levee construction to protect the downtown part of Salina. New development of the floodplain encouraged by highways I-70 and I-35 will be vulnerable to even moderate floods. The most recent flood on May 22, 1971 discharged 7,800 cfs. An Intermediate Regional Flood and Standard Project Flood with peak discharges of 37,000 cfs and 54,000 cfs respectively could severely damage the Salina area. (Salzman-North Carolina)
W75-09112

FLOOD PLAIN INFORMATION: SMOKY HILL RIVER, SALINE RIVER, DRY CREEK DIVERSION, SALINA, KANSAS.
Army Engineer District, Kansas City, Mo.
Prepared for the City of Salina, Kansas, June 1972. 25 p, 7 fig, 4 tab, 21 plates.

Descriptors: *Floods, *Flood control, *Flood protection, *Flood plains, Flooding, Channel improvement, Levees, *Kansas, Diversion structure.
Identifiers: *Smoky Hill River(Kan), *Saline River(Kan), Dry Creek(Kan), Saline(Kan), Intermediate Regional Flood, Standard Project Flood.

Situated in wide valleys of well-developed agricultural lands, the Saline and Smoky Rivers drain a total area of 12,478 square miles of which 1,683 are uncontrolled by reservoirs. Width of channels average 90 ft and 100 to 200 ft on the Saline and Smoky Hill Rivers respectively in the city area. Floodplains vary from 2.5 to 3 miles. East of Saline (population 37,700) the two rivers share a common floodplain abnormally wide for a river of

this size. Dry Creek Diversion channel, created by the Salina Flood Protection Project along with 14 miles of levees and other channel improvements, is 2 miles long and about 120 feet wide and diverts Dry Creek into Smoky Hill River south of the city. Flood season begins with spring rains and continues through early summer. Flood flows are characterized by high stages, high velocities and long durations. Manmade encroachments obstruct flood flows. In Salina a planned flood damage program includes channel cutoffs, diversion channels and levees to be constructed along Smoky Hill River, Saline River and Dry Creek. The greatest flood on Smoky Hill River on May 29, 1903, had a peak discharge of 32,000 cfs and crested at 26.5 ft. The most recent flood, May 25, 1969, crested at 18.2 ft. An Intermediate Regional Flood and Standard Project Flood, with peak discharges of 32,000 cfs and 73,400 cfs respectively, would cause extensive inundation of the floodplain. A sewage disposal plant, a camp, and highway businesses are the only developments susceptible to flooding from an IRF due to the Salina Flood Protection Project. An SPF would cause much widespread flooding, overflowing the protective structures. (Salzman-North Carolina)
W75-09113

FLOOD PLAIN INFORMATION, KANSAS AND BIG BLUE RIVERS, MANHATTAN, KANSAS.
Army Engineer District, Kansas City, Kans.
Prepared for the City of Manhattan, Kansas, May 1972. 25 p, 8 fig, 12 plates, 4 tab.

Descriptors: *Flood data, *Flood control, *Flood plains, Floods, Flooding, Flood protection, Flood damage, Levees, Historic floods, *Kansas, Flood forecasting, Flood profiles.
Identifiers: *Kansas River(Kan), *Big Blue River(Kan), Manhattan(Kan), Standard Project Flood, Intermediate Regional Flood.

The Kansas River Basin drains an area of 45,465 square miles of which 39,929 square miles are controlled by reservoirs. Width of its floodplains vary from 5 to 3 miles. The river slope averages 2 feet per mile. Big Blue River, flowing southward east of the city of Manhattan, enters Kansas River 2 miles downstream from Manhattan. Although much of Manhattan's business district lies in the floodplain, the Central Business District is protected by a 1963 control project. Much of the floodplain land is agriculture slowly being replaced by mobile home parks. Major floods are caused by high intensity storms following a protracted period of general rains. With completion of Tuttle Creek Lake, part of a flood damage protection plan on Big Blue River, flooding in the eastern section of Manhattan will only be caused by backwater from the Kansas River. The flood of 1844 appears to have produced the maximum flood stage cresting at 40 feet on the Kansas River. An Intermediate Regional Flood would discharge 140,000 cfs on the Kansas River and 35,000 cfs on Big Blue River. For a Standard Project Flood, peak discharges would be 250,000 cfs for the Kansas River, 100,000 cfs for Big Blue River. Floodplain areas including commercial and residential land would be inundated by flood waters. (Salzman-North Carolina)
W75-09114

FLOOD PLAIN INFORMATION; TUCKAHOE CREEK, HENRICO COUNTY, VIRGINIA.
Army Engineer District, Norfolk, Va.
For primary bibliographic entry see Field 2E.
W75-09115

FLOOD PLAIN INFORMATION: PLUM CREEK, CUYAHOGA AND LORAIN COUNTIES, OHIO.
Army Engineer District, Buffalo, N.Y.
Prepared for Ohio Department of Natural Resources, Division of Planning, Flood Plain Management Section, June 1973. 32 p, 31 fig, 10 plates, 3 tab.

Descriptors: *Flood plains, *Flood damage, *Land use, *Planning, Flood stages, Flood profiles, Flood forecasting, Obstruction to flow, Floodplain utilization, *Ohio, Flood plain zoning.
Identifiers: *Plum Creek(Ohio), Cuyahoga County(Ohio), Lorain County(Ohio), Flood plain management, Intermediate Regional Flood(IRF), Standard Project Flood(SPF), Columbia Township(Ohio).

The downstream 9.8 miles of Plum Creek in Cuyahoga and Lorain Counties, Ohio, are discussed. Major floods have occurred in late winter or early spring caused by melting snow coincident with moderate amounts of precipitation. Along Plum Creek a principal obstruction to flow is dense growth of brush and trees along the stream channel. Of the 33 bridges within the study reach, 4 would probably wash out during flood flow and the rest would obstruct flow. Widespread residential development on the floodplain would also be subject to damage. As there are no stream gaging stations, it was estimated that the thunderstorm rainfall in September 1972 resulted in a flood with a discharge of 2650 cfs. This flood, approximating a 100-year frequency discharge, resulted in contamination of the water supply and damage to homes. Along the reach, an Intermediate Regional Flood (IRF) would range from 1730 to 2760 cfs, and a Standard Project Flood (SPF) would range from 3070 to 7120 cfs. The elevation of a SPF outlined on maps is considered to be the upper limit of the floodplain and may be used to help develop land use regulations. Columbia Township adopted a floodplain zoning ordinance in December 1964 which restricts the use of floodplains to agricultural, park, and recreational facilities. (Diefendorf-North Carolina)
W75-09116

FLOOD PLAIN INFORMATION: NUECES RIVER AND TURKEY CREEK, CRYSTAL CITY, TEXAS.
Army Engineer District, Fort Worth, Tex.
Prepared for the City of Crystal City, June 1974. 34 p, 9 fig, 17 plates, 5 tab.

Descriptors: *Flood plains, *Flood damage, *Planning, *Land use, Flood data, Flood profiles, Floodplain zoning, Historic floods, Obstruction to flow, *Texas, Flood proofing.
Identifiers: *Nueces River(Tex), Turkey Creek(Tex), Crystal City(Tex), *Flood plain management, Intermediate Regional Flood, Standard Project Flood.

Information is provided on the flood hazard at the south Texas town of Crystal Creek posed by the Nueces River, Turkey Creek (a major tributary of the Neuces) and an unnamed creek. The area is sparsely developed with communities scattered throughout the upper watershed. Above the study area, the Nueces River is confined in a gorge. Where the study area begins, the gorge section changes rather abruptly into a wide valley section, and the stream channel decreases in size and capacity. There are 11 bridges which could cause obstruction to flow. Most flood-producing storms occur in spring and fall and are caused by heavy rain or intense thunderstorms. The storm in June 1935 produced the maximum flood of record on the Nueces River. At Uvalde, about 25 miles upstream, the peak discharge was 616,000 cfs. On the Nueces River with averaged maximum conditions, the peak discharge of an Intermediate Regional Flood (IRF) would be 274,000 cfs, and of a Standard Project Flood (SPF) 495,000 cfs. For both types of future floods, main channel velocity would be approximately 3 feet per second and flood waters would spread over much of the study area. (Diefendorf-North Carolina)
W75-09117

FLOOD PLAIN INFORMATION: SMITH CREEK - CLIFTON FORGE AND ALLEGHANY COUNTY, VIRGINIA.
Army Engineer District, Norfolk, Va.
Prepared for the City of Clifton Forge, January, 1971. 41 p, 9 fig, 7 tab, 9 plates.

Descriptors: *Flood forecasting, *Flood profiles, *Flood data, Floodways, Watershed management, Flood peak, *Flood plains, Flood protection, Flood recurrence interval, *Virginia, Flood flow, Floodwater, Warning systems, Flow duration, Flood damage, Floodproofing, Water levels, River forecasting, Maximum probable flood.
Identifiers: *Smith Creek(Va), Clifton Forge(Va), Alleghany County(Va), Intermediate Regional Flood(IRF), Standard Project Flood(SPF), Gathright Dam(Va).

In Clifton Forge, Virginia, residential, public, and commercial development is concentrated on both sides of Smith Creek. While most development is on high ground above flood danger, there are properties in low-lying areas. Greatest flooding occurred in August, 1969, and in December, 1950. Intermediate Regional Floods (IRF) on Smith Creek would be from 2 to 7 feet higher than the 1969 flood, and Standard Project Floods (SPF) would be from 4 to 12 feet higher. Flood damage would be significant, especially with an SPF. Main flooding season for larger floods is during the summer and fall due to intense local thunderstorms and tropical disturbances. IRF velocities range from 13 feet per second in natural channels to 18 feet per second at restricted stream sections. During an SPF, channel velocities would range from 4 to 24 feet per second and up to 20 feet per second at restricted sections. Flood duration is short, lasting a few hours. No protection through flood plain regulations exists in Clifton Forge or Alleghany County, although Gathright Dam, when constructed, will reduce flood heights by 3 feet. A flood warning system for Smith Creek is not provided. (Grden-North Carolina)
W75-09118

FLOOD PLAIN INFORMATION: REPUBLICAN RIVER, FRANKLIN, NEBRASKA.
Army Engineer District, Kansas City, Mo.
Prepared for the City of Franklin, Nebraska, March 1973. 25 p, 12 fig, 7 plates, 4 tab.

Descriptors: *Floods, *Flood protection, *Flood forecasting, Flooding, *Flood plains, Flood plain zoning, Flood control, *Nebraska.
Identifiers: *Republican River(Neb), Franklin(Neb), Harlan County Lake(Neb), Intermediate Regional Flood, Standard Project Flood.

Width of the flood plain fo the Republican River at Franklin, Nebraska, averages 1 1/2 miles. Since Harlan County Lake went into operation upstream, the total drainage runoff area is 440 square miles. Width of the channel averages 150 feet and it slopes about 4 feet per mile. Center, Ewing and Beauty Creeks, with a combined drainage area of 88 square miles, contribute to the flood-prone areas surrounding Franklin. Franklin flood plain areas have been left relatively free from encroachment through local zoning which restricts land to agricultural and other open space use. Flood season begins with spring rains and continues through early summer causing high river stages and floods of long duration. The short tributary creeks are characterized by flash flooding. On the river, bridges obstruct the flood flows. The creeks are overgrown with trees and brush. The greatest known flood in the upper Republican River Basin occurred in 1935 with a peak discharge of 260,000 cfs at Bloomington, Nebraska. Even with the completion of Harlan County Lake in 1952 flood hazards still exist. Estimated peak discharges for an Intermediate Regional Flood and Standard Project Flood on the Republican River at Franklin would be 34,000 cfs and 110,400 cfs respectively. Plates detail flood plain areas that would be inundated. (Salzman-North Carolina)
W75-09119

FLOOD PLAIN INFORMATION: MILL CREEK, NEW CASTLE COUNTY, DELAWARE.
Army Engineer District, Philadelphia, Pa.
Prepared for New Castle County Department of Planning, May 1973. 27 p, 10 fig, 19 tab, 11 plates.

Descriptors: *Flood plains, *Flood damage, *Planning, *Delaware, Flood data, Flood stages, Obstructions to flow, Historic floods, Hurricanes, Thunderstorms, Flood profiles.
Identifiers: *Mill Creek(Del), New Castle County(Del), White Clay Creek(Del), Delaware Park Race Track, Standard Project Flood, Intermediate Regional Flood, Floodplain management, Hockessin(Del).

Most of Mill Creek's floodplain is sparsely developed, although the gently rolling floodplain in the southern portion of the watershed is occupied by some development, including the Delaware Park Race Track. The study area covers Mill Creek from its confluence with White Clay Creek upstream 9.3 miles to its headwaters. Information on past floods is available from records of the gaging station at Hockessin which has been in operation since 1966. The greatest flood of record occurred in July 1969, reached 225.1 ft m.s.l. and had a peak discharge of 2100 cfs. An Intermediate Regional Flood (IRF) and a Standard Project Flood (SPF) would reach 226.8 and 227.0 ft. m.s.l. and would produce 2300 and 2500 cfs respectively. Both of these planning floods would inundate development in the area, causing considerable damage. Floods generally occur in July, August, and September--the season of hurricane and thunderstorm activity. They generally rise slowly and stay out of banks for long periods of time. There are natural and man-made obstructions to flow, including 27 bridges. The 2 dams within the study reach have no flood control capacity. (Diefendorf-North Carolina)
W75-09120

FLOOD PLAIN INFORMATION: ANTIETAM CREEK, WASHINGTON COUNTY, MARYLAND.
Army Engineer District, Baltimore, Md.
Prepared for Washington County Planning and Zoning Commission, June 1972. 31 p, 2 fig, 14 plates, 8 tab.

Descriptors: *Flood plains, *Flood damage, *Flood profiles, Planning, Land use, Flood data, Historic floods, Obstruction to flow, *Maryland, Flood forecasting, Potomac River.
Identifiers: *Antietam Creek(Md), Washington County(Md), Hagerstown(Md), Intermediate Regional Flood, Standard Project Flood, Floodplain management, Little Antietam Creek(Md).

The watershed of Antietam Creek is long and narrow, ranging in width from 4 to 12 miles. The floodplain is also narrow, averaging 520 feet in width within the 36-mile study reach from Route 60 downstream to the Potomac River. The land adjacent to the stream is mostly wooded or agricultural. Urban development is concentrated in and around the city of Hagerstown, Md. Flood occur throughout the year, generally caused by heavy, basin-wide rains or intense thunderstorms, and are usually of short duration. Within the study reach there are 23 bridges, many of which would be overtopped by a Standard Project Flood (SPF). A July 1956 thunderstorm produced the largest recorded flood, 12,600 cfs at the gaging station, approximately the same size as an Intermediate Regional Flood (IRF). An IRF would have a peak discharge of 12,300 cfs and a channel velocity of 12 feet per second. An SPF would be 25 feet higher, producing a peak discharge of 63,000 cfs and a channel velocity of 18 feet per second. At present there are no flood control measures, although an ordinance restricts development in the floodplain. The 4 proposed headwater reservoirs on Little Antietam Creek will have no appreciable effect on flood flows on Antietam Creek. (Diefendorf-North Carolina)
W75-09121

AN EVALUATION OF STATE LAND USE PLANNING AND DEVELOPMENT CONTROL IN THE ADIRONDACKS,
Cornell Univ., Ithaca, N.Y.
M. K. Heiman.
Available from the National Technical Information Service, Springfield, Va 22161 as PB-243 015, $8.75 in paper copy, $2.25 in microfiche. M S Thesis, January 1975. 277 p, 2 fig, 4 tab, 199 ref. OWRT A-049-NY(1).

Descriptors: *Comprehensive planning, Administration, *Regional development, *Land management, City planning, Project planning, Coordination, State jurisdiction, Land classification, Rural areas, Environmental effects, *Land use, Parks, *New York, Evaluation.
Identifiers: *Adirondack Park(NY), Adirondack Park Agency(NY), State-local governmental cooperation.

In the late '60's, strong tourist, recreational, and second home development became increasingly significant in the Adirondack Park region of upstate New York. Land use controls were in part needed because shallow soils were unsuitable to cope with increasing waste disposal. The Adirondack Park Agency (APA) was formed to develop and administer regional land use planning for this six million acre park spread over twelve hilly-to-mountainous counties which includes the headwaters of five major drainage basins. Efforts of the APA to gain local compliance with state and regional development goals for the Adirondack Park are examined. National and other state land use planning efforts and the history of APA are summarized. The APA's land use regulations, some of the most stringent enacted by a state, are set forth, including shoreline development intensities, setback standards, and vegetation removal controls. The APA must approve local land use plans before they can be locally administered. Local governmental compliance and involvement are analyzed to determine the extent and type of local cooperation and what the APA should do to increase local acceptance of a regional perspective, a necessary component of the long-run protection of the Adirondack environment. (Herr-North Carolina)
W75-09122

MULTIOBJECTIVE WATER RESOURCES PLANNING, A BIBLIOGRAPHY.
Office of Water Research and Technology, Washington, D.C.
For primary bibliographic entry see Field 6B.
W75-09123

ECOLOGICAL STUDIES OF TWO SWAMP WATERSHEDS IN NORTHEASTERN NORTH CAROLINA - A PRECHANNELIZATION STUDY,
North Carolina State Univ., Raleigh. Dept. of Zoology.
For primary bibliographic entry see Field 5C.
W75-09130

VEGETATION OF SWAMPS RECEIVING REACTOR EFFLUENTS,
Savannah River Ecology Lab., Arken, S.C.
For primary bibliographic entry see Field 5C.
W75-09137

WATER IN THE GREAT BASIN REGION; IDAHO, NEVADA, UTAH, AND WYOMING,
Geological Survey, Reston, Va.
For primary bibliographic entry see Field 7C.
W75-09170

DISCHARGE MEASUREMENTS AND CHEMICAL ANALYSES OF WATER IN NORTHWESTERN WYOMING,
Geological Survey, Cheyenne, Wyo.
For primary bibliographic entry see Field 7C.
W75-09172

FLOODS IN EAST BATON ROUGE PARISH AND ADJACENT AREAS, LOUISIANA, FOR THE PERIOD 1953-74,
Geological Survey, Baton Rouge, La.
A. S. Lowe.
Water-Resources Investigations 44-74, March 1975. 12 p, 12 fig, 16 plate, 4 ref.

Descriptors: *Floods, *Maps, *Flood profiles, *Louisiana, Flood damage, Stage-discharge relations, Flood stages, Peak discharge, Flood frequency, Flood plain zoning, Flood recurrence interval, Flood control, Flood discharge, Economics, Planning.
Identifiers: East Baton Rouge Parish(La).

Flood damage resulting from development in flood plains in East Baton Rouge Parish. La., and adjacent areas has caused economic losses, making governmental officials and planners aware of the need for flood maps. Flood maps for 7 1/2-minute topographic quadrangles show the interpretative delineation of the highest flood elevation that occurred between the years 1953 and 1974. The flood boundaries were mapped on the following quadrangles: Port Hudson, Zachary, Fred, Pride, Pine Grove, Walls, Scotlandville, Comite, Watson, Baton Rouge West, Baton Rouge East, Denham Springs, Plaquemine, St. Gabriel, and Prairieville. The flood data provide a technical base on which responsible officials can make decisions for developing building and zoning regulations, locating waste-disposal facilities, developing recreational areas, and for evaluating the economic development of flood plains. (Woodard-USGS)
W75-09173

STREAMFLOW DEPLETION RESULTING FROM UPSTREAM SURFACE-WATER IMPOUNDMENT,
Geological Survey, Bay Saint Louis, Miss. Water Resources Div.
S. P. Sauer.
In: Proceedings of the Irrigation and Drainage Division Specialty Conference on Agricultural-Urban Considerations, held at Fort Collins, Colo, April 22-24, 1973: American Society of Civil Engineers, p 593-617, 1973. 8 fig, 3 tab, 16 ref.

Descriptors: *Reservoirs, *Diversion losses, *Water losses, *Texas, Mathematical models, Reservoir evaporation.
Identifiers: *Streamflow depletion.

A model was developed for use in evaluating site depletions to be expected from systems of small reservoirs similar to those constructed by the U.S. Soil Conservation Service for flood control and water conservation. The depletions range from 0 to 100 percent in a given year, depending on the physical characteristics of the impoundments and the combination of climatic and hydrologic conditions for that year. The model provides information from upstream surface water impoundments in a monthly time frame. Information required for assessing depletions includes physical characteristics of impoundments, soil maps of the area, runoff, and meteorological information collected at first order weather stations. The hydrologic response model was applied to several basins in Texas having diverse climatic and physical characteristics, with ranges in average annual runoff from 1.37 to 6.50 inches and average annual rainfall from 27 to 38 inches. (Knapp-USGS)
W75-09175

OAK GLEN WATER-RESOURCES DEVELOPMENT STUDY USING MODELING TECHNIQUES, SAN BERNARDINO COUNTY, CALIFORNIA,
Geological Survey, Menlo Park, Calif.
For primary bibliographic entry see Field 4B.
W75-09178

WATER RESOURCES DATA FOR KANSAS, 1974: PART 1. SURFACE WATER RECORDS.
Geological Survey, Lawrence, Kans.
For primary bibliographic entry see Field 7C.
W75-09180

HYDROLOGIC CONSEQUENCES OF USING GROUND WATER TO MAINTAIN LAKE LEVELS AFFECTED BY WATER WELLS NEAR TAMPA, FLORIDA,
Geological Survey, Tallahassee, Fla.
For primary bibliographic entry see Field 4B.
W75-09184

A GENERAL OUTLINE OF THE WATER RESOURCES OF THE TOPPENISH CREEK BASIN, YAKIMA INDIAN RESERVATION, WASHINGTON,
Geological Survey, Tacoma, Wash.
D. O. Gregg, and L. B. Laird.
Open-file report 75-19, 1975. 37 p, 17 fig, 32 ref.

Descriptors: *Water resources, *Washington, *Indian reservations, Surface waters, Groundwater, Irrigation water, Water supply, Water levels, Water balance, Hydrologic data.
Identifiers: *Yakima Indian Reservation(Wash), *Toppenish Creek(Wash).

An accounting of the overall availability of water on the Yakima Indian Reservation broadly outlines the water resources of the Toppenish Creek basin. Precipitation averages about 20 inches a year over the basin but only about 2 inches fall during the April-September growing season. However, diversions from the Yakima River make the Toppenish Creek valley one of the best agricultural areas in the State. Groundwater in the basin occurs in three distinct units: the basalt, old valley fill deposits, and young valley fill deposits. Each unit is capable of yielding more than 1,000 gallons per minute to properly constructed wells. Water levels in wells tapping the young valley fill are higher under present (1974) irrigation conditions than they were in the past, but some-water-level declines have occurred in the old valley fill in response to pumping. Water levels in the basalt wells in some areas have been lowered as much as 80 feet by pumping during the past 15 years. Some additional pumping in these areas can be allowed without lowering the water level more than a few feet. The young valley fill in the eastern part of the lower valley is the best source of groundwater in the basin. The zones of coarse sand and gravel to depths of about 150 feet in this area can produce large quantities of water. Irrigation water from the Yakima River seeps into the ground and builds up this groundwater supply. About 120,000 acre-feet of water goes into temporary storage each irrigation season in the young valley fill. (Knapp-USGS)
W75-09186

GENERALIZED NOMOGRAPHIC SOLUTION OF HOOGHOUDT EQUATIONS,
Public Power Corp., Athens (Greece). Hydroelectric Project Design Branch.
For primary bibliographic entry see Field 8B.
W75-09197

HYDROLOGY OF PATCH CUTS IN LODGEPOLE PINE,
Colorado State Univ., Fort Collins. Dept. of Earth Resources.
For primary bibliographic entry see Field 3B.
W75-09198

SOLUTIONS FOR UNCONFINED NON-DARCY SEEPAGE,
James Cook Univ. of North Queensland, Townsville (Australia). Dept. of Engineering.
R. E. Volker.
Journal of the Irrigation and Drainage Division, Proceedings of American Society of Civil Engineers, Vol 101, No IR1, Proceedings Paper 11203, p 53-65, March 1975. 8 fig, 1 tab, 17 ref, 2 append.

Descriptors: *Porous media, *Darcys law, *Model studies, Digital computers, Hydraulic conductivity, Reynolds number, Wells, *Seepage, Transmissivity, Permeameters, Flow nets, Drainage, Rock fill, Boundary processes, Piezometers, Head loss.
Identifiers: *Finite difference solution, Forcheimer solution.

Numerical and experimental studies of non-Darcy flow in porous media were examined. Laboratory experiments with a screened gravel included radial flow to a simulated well and a sector and two-dimensional flow through a bank with vertical sides in a flume. Permeameter tests on the gravel were used to estimate coefficients in the nonlinear relation between head loss and velocity. Results were presented of analyses performed by a finite difference solution of the appropriate partial differential equation boundary value problem. The flow nets and discharges obtained were compared with the experimental results and the corresponding solutions for Darcy flow. (Schicht-ISWS)
W75-09199

ENGINEERING CHALLENGES OF DREDGED MATERIAL DISPOSAL,
Army Engineers Waterways Experiment Station, Vicksburg, Miss. Office of Dredged Material Research.
For primary bibliographic entry see Field 5G.
W75-09205

ANALYTICAL MODEL OF HYDRAULIC PIPELINE DREDGE,
Texas A and M Univ., College Station.
For primary bibliographic entry see Field 8C.
W75-09206

SYSTEMS ANALYSIS OF HYDROLOGIC PROBLEMS.
For primary bibliographic entry see Field 2A.
W75-09210

THE SYNTHESIS OF HYDROLOGIC SYSTEMS ON THE ANALOG AND HYBRID COMPUTERS,
City Univ., London (England).
For primary bibliographic entry see Field 7C.
W75-09221

PRACTICAL APPLICATIONS OF HYDROLOGIC SIMULATION,
Hydrocomp International, Palo Alto, Calif.
N. H. Crawford.
In: Systems Analysis of Hydrologic Problems; Proceedings of the Second International Seminar for Hydrology Professors, August 2-14, 1970, Utah State University, Logan, p 326-342. 6 fig, 1 tab, 5 ref.

Descriptors: *Simulation analysis, *Mathematical models, *Calibrations, *Algorithms, *Flood forecasting, *Flood plains, Urbanization, Rainfall, Runoff, Hydrologic data, Computers, Model studies, Hydrology, California, Illinois.
Identifiers: *Parameter adjustment, Santa Ynez River(Calif), Skokie River(Ill).

Hydrologic simulation is defined as the development and application of mathematical models to represent the time variant interaction of natural processes. A mathematical model consists of algorithms that are coded for execution on a computer. These algorithms contain parameters that can be varied to fit the model to a prototype. Parameter adjustment is called calibration of the model and may require a trial and error approach. A valid simulation model reproduces the time behavior of the prototype. The model includes functions which represent the physical processes. A physically based model will have physically defined parameters and these parameters can be adjusted easily for actual or planned changes. Two examples were given of hydrologic simulation as applied to flood forecasting and reservoir management, and flood plain mapping. Computer results were shown for real-time flood forecasting on the Santa Ynez River in California. Flood plain storage and watershed changes affect the hydrologic response of a basin to rainfall. Simulated and observed flood stages on the Skokie River near Chicago were shown. The progressive effect of urbanization on the flood peaks can be studied by using simulation. (See also W75-09210) (Singh-ISWS)
W75-09223

CONTROL RULES FOR MULTIPLE-USE RESERVOIRS AND MULTI-RESERVOIR SYSTEMS,
Water Research Association, Marlow (England).
J. A. Cole.
In: Systems Analysis of Hydrologic Problems; Proceedings of the Second International Seminar for Hydrology Professors, August 2-14, 1970, Utah State University, Logan, p 343-378. 9 fig, 43 ref.

Descriptors: *Multiple-purpose reservoirs, *Systems analysis, *Dynamic programming, *Cost analysis, *Synthetic hydrology, Linear programming, Low-flow augmentation, Water supply, Flood control, Recreation, Algorithms, Reservoirs, Mathematical studies.
Identifiers: *Out-of-kilter algorithm, System decomposition.

A complex system of rivers, reservoirs, diversions, and returns can be arbitrarily decomposed into subsystems of tractable size for analysis. Where a particular need dominates, it may be possible to take some empirical shortcuts to simplify the problem. Stochastic dynamic programming can be used for certain subsystems to identify optimal control rules. Implicit cost weighting of water supply failure and water quality shortfall, given by the incremental cost of alternative measures to remedy such shortcomings, were discussed. Various mathematical programming techniques, such as linear programming, out-of-kilter algorithm, and dynamic programming for solving multi-reservoir problems were described. (See also W75-09210) (Singh-ISWS)
W75-09224

DESIGN TYPHOON MODEL FOR ESTIMATION OF PROBABLE MAXIMUM PRECIPITATION AND PROBABLE MAXIMUM FLOOD IN TAIWAN,
National Taiwan Univ., Taipei. Dept. of Civil Engineering.
For primary bibliographic entry see Field 2B.
W75-09227

GUARDING OUR WATER RESOURCES, 1974 ANNUAL REPORT.
Virginia Polytechnic Inst. and State Univ., Blacksburg. Water Resources Research Center.
For primary bibliographic entry see Field 9D.
W75-09243

PREAUTHORIZATION PLANNING ACTIVITIES OF THE BUREAU OF RECLAMATION, THE CORPS OF ENGINEERS AND THE SOIL CONSERVATION SERVICE FOR FISCAL YEAR 1975.
Report for Arkansas-White-Red Basins Interagency Committee, September 1974. 119 p, 12 map.

Descriptors: *Dams, *Watershed management, *Erosion control, *Flood control, *River basin development, *Water yield improvement, Water storage, Water supply, Water yield, Watersheds(Basins), Drainage, Floods, Multiple-

purpose projects, River basins, Federal government, Administrative agencies, Water resources development, Dams, Reservoirs, Fish conservation, Wildlife conservation, Irrigation, Water management(Applied), Basins, Water supply development.
Identifiers: Dam effects, Arkansas-White-Red River Basins.

A consolidated report is presented on watershed preauthorization planning activities of the Bureau of Reclamation, the Corps of Engineers, and the Soil Conservation Service for fiscal year 1975. Activities are located in the Arkansas-White-Red Basins (AWR Basins) and include the Arkansas River Basin above Keystone Dam, Cimarron and Canadian River Basins; Arkansas River Basin below Keystone Dam, White River Basin; Red River Basin above Denison Dam; and Red River Basin below Denison Dam. Numerous maps are presented. The function of the presentation is to acquaint each agency with the plans of others and achieve coordination of programs, and to assist each agency in better comprehending the inter-related planning activities, and to recognize areas where further coordination is desirable. The Buréau of Reclamation primarily appraises available municipal and industrial water resources with some consideration of irrigation, pollution abatement, flood control, recreation, and fish and wildlife conservation. Flood control is the main concern of the Corps of Engineers, while the Soil Conservation Service focuses on watershed protection. (Fernandez-Florida)
W75-09244

POST AUTHORIZATION PROJECT ACTIVITIES ANNUAL STATUS REPORT - BUREAU OF RECLAMATION.
Arkansas-White-Red-Basins Inter-Agency Committee, October 1974. 6 p.

Descriptors: *Land reclamation, *Reclamation states, *Reclaimed water, *Flood control, *River basins, Arkansas, Reclamation, Recreation, Federal Reclamation Law, Irrigable land, Conservation, Crops, Wildlife, Fish, Fish conservation, Basins, Water conservation, Multiple-purpose reservoirs, Reservoirs, Federal government, Water supply, Water yield improvement, Aqueducts, Canals, Diversion.
Identifiers: *Arkansas-White-Red-River Basins, Dam effects.

This presentation is the annual status report, as of October 1974, on post authorization project activities in the Arkansas-White-Red Basins conducted by the Bureau of Reclamation. Projects include those presently in operation and those under construction. The Bureau has ten projects in the basin on which construction is now complete; these are the Vermejo, Tucumcari, W.C. Austin, Fort Cobb and Foss Divisions of the Washita Basin Project, Norman, Cheney Division of the Wichita Project, Arbuckle, Canadian River, and Upper Colorado River Storage Project, Transmission Division. These projects furnish municipal and industrial water and provide flood control, fish, wildlife, and recreation benefits. Proposed projects will serve similar functions. These include the Fryingpan-Arkansas, Upper Colorado River Storage, and Mountain Park Projects. (Fernandez-Florida)
W75-09245

BELLE FOURCHE DAM AND GLENDO DAM-RESERVOIR ROADWAY.
For primary bibliographic entry see Field 6E.
W75-09257

CIBOLO, TEXAS, AND FRYINGPAN-ARKANSAS, COLORADO, PROJECTS.
For primary bibliographic entry see Field 6E.
W75-09258

COLLIER COUNTY WATER MANAGEMENT ORDINANCE.
For primary bibliographic entry see Field 6E.
W75-09260

RIVER FORECASTS PROVIDED BY THE NATIONAL WEATHER SERVICE.
National Weather Service, Silver Spring, Md.
For primary bibliographic entry see Field 2B.
W75-09285

FLOOD OF JUNE 1972 IN THE SOUTHERN PEACE (SMOKY RIVER) BASIN, ALBERTA,
Department of the Environment, Calgary (Alberta). Water Resources Branch.
L. A. Warner, and W. C. Thompson.
Technical Bulletin No 87, 51 p, 1974. 16 fig, 3 tab, 4 ref, 3 append.

Descriptors: *Floods, *Flood damage, Streamflow, Meteorology, Data collections, Gaging stations, Discharge measurement, Flood discharge.
Identifiers: *Smoky River, *Peace River basin.

In June 1972, more than six inches of rain fell over parts of the Peace River basin southwest of Grande Prairie, resulting in record flows in nearly all streams in that area. The rain occurred with the passage of a cold low over Central Alberta, which permitted a northeasterly upslope of warm, moist air to prevail over the southern Peace River basin for about 26 hours. Flood damage was reported in Grande Prairie, Grande Cache, Watino, and the town of Peace River. Calculations indicate that the influence of the W.A.C. Bennett Dam and a diking operation in the town probably reduced the severity of flooding at Peace River townsite. The effect of the diking operation on water levels associated with an ice jam in April 1973 is discussed. Details on agricultural flood damage incurred by farmers along Peace River system have been excerpted from 'Flood Damage Estimation, June, 1972, Athabasca, North Saskatchewan and Peace River Basins' by J.L. Knapp of Alberta Department of Agriculture. The present report contains a brief account of the flood damage, a description of the Southern Peace (Smoky River) basin, and a location map which shows the area affected by the flood, the various stream gauging and meteorological observation stations, as well as an isohyet analysis of the rainfall event. The description of the flood covers the following: meteorological analysis, flood hydrographs, maximum discharges, and maximum unit discharges. The analysis of the flood includes flood frequency analyses for two of the gauging sites and an explanation of streamflow data tables. Hourly discharge determinations are provided for seven gauging sites, and peak flow for two miscellaneous sites. (Envir-Canada)
W75-09292

STATE FINANCIAL ASSITANCE OF FLOOD CONTROL PROJECTS.
Arizona Water Commission, Phoenix.
For primary bibliographic entry see Field 6B.
W75-09301

DRAINAGE SYSTEM,
For primary bibliographic entry see Field 4B.
W75-09329

LAND USE AND WATER RESOURCES IN TEMPERATURE AND TROPICAL CLIMATES,
For primary bibliographic entry see Field 6D.
W75-09343

4B. Groundwater Management

DISPOSING OF LIQUID WASTES UNDERGROUND.
For primary bibliographic entry see Field 5E.
W75-08881

WATER RESOURCES INVENTORY OF CONNECTICUT--PART 5, LOWER HOUSATONIC RIVER BASIN,
Geological Survey, Hartford, Conn.
For primary bibliographic entry see Field 4A.
W75-08905

WASTEWATER INFILTRATION NEAR THE CITY OF MOUNT SHASTA, SISKIYOU COUNTY, CALIFORNIA,
Geological Survey, Menlo Park, Calif.
For primary bibliographic entry see Field 5B.
W75-08906

SUMMARY OF HYDROLOGIC DATA COLLECTED DURING 1973 IN DADE COUNTY, FLORIDA,
Geological Survey, Tallahassee, Fla.
For primary bibliographic entry see Field 7C.
W75-08908

SUMMARY STATEMENTS OF WATER RESOURCES INVESTIGATIONS IN FLORIDA, 1974-75,
Geological Survey, Tallahassee, Fla.
For primary bibliographic entry see Field 7C.
W75-08909

AVAILABILITY AND QUALITY OF GROUND WATER IN THE SUTHERLIN AREA, DOUGLAS COUNTY, OREGON,
Geological Survey, Portland, Oreg.
For primary bibliographic entry see Field 7C.
W75-08910

WATER RESOURCES OF WISCONSIN, LOWER WISCONSIN RIVER BASIN,
Geological Survey, Reston, Va.
For primary bibliographic entry see Field 7C.
W75-08913

WATER RESOURCES OF HAMILTON COUNTY, SOUTHWESTERN KANSAS,
Geological Survey, Reston, Va.
For primary bibliographic entry see Field 7C.
W75-08914

GROUND WATER IN GRAY COUNTY, SOUTHWESTERN KANSAS,
Geological Survey, Reston, Va.
For primary bibliographic entry see Field 7C.
W75-08915

AN ECONOMIC ANALYSIS OF THE EFFECTS OF A DECLINING GROUND WATER LEVEL IN THE RAFT RIVER BASIN, CASSIA COUNTY, IDAHO,
Idaho Univ., Moscow. Dept. of Agricultural Economics.
H. L. Schatz.
Available from the National Technical Information Service, Springfield, Va 22161 as PB-242 865, $6.25 in paper copy, $2.25 in microfiche. MS Thesis, March 1974. 162 p, 11 fig, 21 tab, 11 ref, 8 append. OWRR B-019-IDA(1).

Descriptors: *Groundwater resources, *Crop reduction, *Economic impact, *Overdraft, *Return(Monetary), *Groundwater basins, Farm management, *Idaho, Irrigation wells, Agriculture, Grains(Crops), Withdrawal.
Identifiers: Opportunity costs, Groundwater decline, *Raft River Basin(Idaho).

Several strategies are available for groundwater management. An economic analysis of four alternatives and their consequences is presented as part of a study to: (1) estimate the economic value of water pumped from the aquifer system in the Raft River, (2) estimate the benefits and costs as-

sociated with varying rates of groundwater decline in the basin on returns to farms, and (3) estimate the opportunity cost by not pumping the groundwater. Data pertaining to costs of production, returns from crops, and agricultural practices, and cropping patterns were gathered in 1972 to provide the information base for this study. Linear programming analysis using information from the activity budgets for producing crops was applied to estimate returns to operator labor and management. The impact from various rates of water level decline on the 20 year accumulated present value of net returns and annual annuity values for a farm were also estimated. Ground water decline affects farm returns, but by relatively minor amounts compared to the location of the farm and crop mix produced. The results indicate that administration of the groundwater resource to achieve 'full economic development of the resource would be more appropriate than administration to maintain reasonable pumping levels.' (Becker-Wisconsin)
W75-08921

MODELLING A GROUNDWATER AQUIFER IN THE GRAND PRAIRIE OF ARKANSAS,
Arkansas Univ., Fayetteville. Dept. of Agricultural Engineering.
For primary bibliographic entry see Field 2F.
W75-08923

SALT WATER DETECTION IN THE CIMARRON TERRACE, OKLAHOMA.
Oklahoma Water Resources Board, Oklahoma City.
For primary bibliographic entry see Field 5A.
W75-08936

ESTIMATION OF THE WATER RESOURCES OF A PORTION OF THE GAMBIER PLAIN SOUTH AUSTRALIA USING A NEW METHOD FOR EVALUATING LOCAL RECHARGE,
Commonwealth Scientific and Industrial Research Organization, Adelaide (Australia). Div. of Soils.
For primary bibliographic entry see Field 2F.
W75-08953

INVESTIGATION OF SENSITIVITY AND ERROR PROPAGATION IN NUMERICAL MODELS OF GROUNDWATER BASINS,
James Cook Univ. of North Queensland, Townsville (Australia).
For primary bibliographic entry see Field 2F.
W75-08954

TECHNIQUES FOR HANDLING INPUT DATA FOR FINITE ELEMENT ANALYSIS OF REGIONAL GROUNDWATER FLOW,
New South Wales Univ., Kensington (Australia). Water Research Lab.
For primary bibliographic entry see Field 2F.
W75-08955

A DISCRETE KERNEL GENERATOR FOR STREAM-AQUIFER STUDIES,
Colorado State Univ., Fort Collins. Dept. of Civil Engineering.
H. J. Morel-Seytoux, and C. J. Daly.
Water Resources Research, Vol 11, No 2, p 253-260, April 1975. 5 fig, 3 tab, 22 ref, 2 append. OWRT B-109-COLO(2). Grant 14-31-0001-4067.

Descriptors: *Surface-groundwater relationships, *Mathematical models, *Cost comparisons, *Aquifer management, *Computer models, *Conjunctive use, Economics, Water rights, Drawdown, Water wells, Porosity, Transmissivity, Regulation, Alluvial aquifers, Model studies, Finite element analysis.
Identifiers: Dupuit assumption, Boussinesq equation.

A finite difference model of the behavior of an aquifer without stream interaction was developed as a first-stage component of a management model of a stream-aquifer system. The model was not built as a usual simulator but as a discrete impulse response generator. Once the basic response coefficients were generated, the finite difference model was no longer necessary to simulate the behavior of the aquifer. Any aquifer response (e.g., return flow to a given reach for a given week) was expressed as an explicit function of the pumping rates. A complete description of the 'discrete kernel generator' was provided including the basic equations, truncation error propagation, accuracy, and run costs. (Schicht-ISWS)
W75-09078

POLICY ALTERNATIVES IN WATER RECHARGE AREAS.
East Central Florida Regional Planning Council, Winter Park.
Preliminary Report ECFRPC 74-7, July, 1974. 100 p, 14 fig, 8 tab, 18 ref, append. CPA-FL-04-29-1040.

Descriptors: *Alternative planning, Alternative water use, *Aquifer management, *Groundwater recharge, *Hydrologic budget, Recharge wells, Potentiometric level, Geology, Hydrologic aspects, Saline water intrusion, Infiltration rates, Water supply, *Florida, Water policy.
Identifiers: Floridan Aquifer, Orlando(Fla).

East central Florida is experiencing rapid population growth with the attendant increase in demand for water, supplied primarily from wells into the Floridan Aquifer. Urbanization can decrease water supply if natural recharge areas are not properly managed. At present rates of development, this region could be using 10% more water per year than naturally recharged by 1990, causing salt water intrusion and diminished well and spring flows. Water demand projections, geologic and hydrologic aspects, and recent trends in groundwater use are presented as background. Current land use controls as well as the legal bases of local, state, and regional policies which may be used for recharge area management are presented. There is currently no widespread regulatory authority for this purpose in east central Florida, though concern is increasing as the magnitude of the water supply problem becomes apparent. State designation of a large portion of Green Swamp as an Area of Critical State Concern will eventually specify development regulations to protect its recharge function. Other state and federal action is certain to have considerable effect. Sixteen widely applicable policy alternatives for local or regional governments are presented with benefits and drawbacks of each. In spite of imperfect knowledge about recharge functions, action must be taken to insure the long-range prosperity and livability of the area. (Herr-North Carolina)
W75-09095

GEOPHYSICAL EXPLORATION OF GROUNDWATER IN SOFT FORMATIONS AND ITS UTILIZATION IN MINOR IRRIGATION,
Indian Inst. of Tech., Kharagpur. Dept. of Geology and Geophysics.
H. P. Patra.
Indian J Agric Sci, Vol 42, No 10, p 883-886, 1972. Illus.

Descriptors: Exploration, Geophysics, Borehole geophysics, *Groundwater availability, Aquifers, Resistivity, Electrodes, Irrigation wells.

Geophysical exploration methods, including logging techniques, are useful in the selection of appropriate location of boreholes and in the estimation of groundwater reserve. Direct-current geoelectric sounding has been found to be the most suitable and convenient surface geophysical method for the detection of water-bearing aquifers in soft formation. Electrical-resistivity sounding with Schlumberger configuration of electrodes is usually preferred for the purpose. The electrode arrangement is outlined, and a brief discussion is given on the instrumentation, field procedure and interpretation of resistivity data leading to assessment of groundwater potential in an area. Electrical-resistivity sounding is important in the selection of drilling sites for irrigation wells.--Copyright 1974, Biological Abstracts, Inc.
W75-09103

MAP SHOWING DEPTH TO BEDROCK, PLAINFIELD QUADRANGLE, MASSACHUSETTS,
Geological Survey, Boston, Mass.
For primary bibliographic entry see Field 7C.
W75-09165

MAP SHOWING DEPTH TO BEDROCK, HEATH QUADRANGLE, MASSACHUSETTS-VERMONT,
Geological Survey, Boston, Mass.
For primary bibliographic entry see Field 7C.
W75-09166

CONTOUR MAP OF THE BEDROCK SURFACE, BRISTOL QUADRANGLE, CONNECTICUT,
Geological Survey, Hartford, Conn.
For primary bibliographic entry see Field 7C.
W75-09167

CONTOUR MAP OF THE BEDROCK SURFACE, SOUTHINGTON QUADRANGLE, CONNECTICUT,
Geological Survey, Hartford, Conn.
For primary bibliographic entry see Field 7C.
W75-09168

WATER IN THE GREAT BASIN REGION; IDAHO, NEVADA, UTAH, AND WYOMING,
Geological Survey, Reston, Va.
For primary bibliographic entry see Field 7C.
W75-09170

DIGITAL MODEL ANALYSIS OF THE PRINCIPAL ARTESIAN AQUIFER, GLYNN COUNTY, GEORGIA,
Geological Survey, Doraville, Ga.
For primary bibliographic entry see Field 7C.
W75-09171

A GALERKIN-FINITE ELEMENT ANALYSIS OF THE HYDROTHERMAL SYSTEM AT WAIRAKEI, NEW ZEALAND,
Geological Survey, Reston, Va.
For primary bibliographic entry see Field 2F.
W75-09176

SALT-BALANCE STUDY OF PAUBA VALLEY, UPPER SANTA MARGARITA RIVER AREA, RIVERSIDE COUNTY, CALIFORNIA,
Geological Survey, Menlo Park, Calif.
For primary bibliographic entry see Field 5B.
W75-09177

OAK GLEN WATER-RESOURCES DEVELOPMENT STUDY USING MODELING TECHNIQUES, SAN BERNARDINO COUNTY, CALIFORNIA,
Geological Survey, Menlo Park, Calif.
W. R. Powers, III, and W. F. Hardt.
Available from the National Technical Information Service, Springfield, Va. 22161, as PB-242 429, \$4.25 in paper copy, \$2.25 in microfiche. Water-Resources Investigations 31-74, December 1974. 59 p, 13 fig, 9 tab, 24 ref.

Descriptors: *Mathematical models, *Computer models, *Water resources, *Imported water, Water demand, *California, Economic feasibility, Groundwater resources, Surface waters, Surface water availability, Hydrologic data, *Conjunctive use.
Identifiers: Oak Glen area(Calif), San Bernardino County(Calif).

In the Oak Glen area, San Bernardino County, California, hydrologic, digital-model and economic analyses were made to determine the most efficient balance of conjunctive use of local groundwater and surface water--specifically, whether additional groundwater supplies could be developed for local use and also for export to the adjacent Yucaipa area, and what would be the effeets of imported water available in 1980. Transmissivity values of the aquifer ranged from 1,000 to 6,750 gallons per day per foot or their equivalent 134 to 902 square feet per day (12 to 84 metres squared per day) and that net annual recharge was about 1,940 acre-feet (2.39 cubic hectometres) per year. The volume of groundwater in storage in 1970 was about 86,000 acre-feet (106 cubic hectometres). The economic evaluation suggests: (1) increase groundwater pumping for local use, (2) reduce well-water import to the lower parts of the Oak Glen study area from adjacent areas to the west, (3) short term prior to 1980 overdevelopment appears to be feasible with export to Yucaipa, and (4) tunnel development or new shallow wells at the higher altitudes could help alleviate the water problem. (Woodard-USGS)
W75-09178

HYDRAULIC CHARACTERISTICS AND WATER-SUPPLY POTENTIAL OF THE AQUIFERS IN THE VICINITY OF THE WASTE-WATER TREATMENT PLANT, SOUTH BEND, INDIANA,
Geological Survey, Indianapolis, Ind.
J. R. Marie.
Available from the National Technical Information Service, Springfield, Va. 22161, as PB-242 238, $3.75 in printed copy, $2.25 in microfiche. Water-Resources Investigations 49-74, February 1975. 26 p, 13 fig, 9 ref.

Descriptors: *Groundwater resources, *Water supply, *Aquifer characteristics, *Indiana, Model studies, Water yield, Forecasting, Wells, Pumping, Dewatering, Construction, Treatment facilities, Waste water treatment, Hydrologic data, Transmissivity, Groundwater recharge.
Identifiers: *South Bend(Ind).

An intensive study was made of a 24-square mile area surrounding the South Bend, Indiana waste-water treatment plant. This was done to (1) document the effects of dewatering about 40 feet of the 130-ft thick aquifer during construction at the plant; (2) define the hydrologic system in order to allow development of a predictive model; and (3) select and evaluate one possible water-supply development plan as a model demonstration. Model-simulated water levels agree very well with those observed, both before and during dewatering. Consequently, the model was used to predict effects of developing 28 million gallons per day from three hypothetical well fields. Model results indicate that the hydrologic system can sustain this withdrawal indefinitely with little effect on groundwater levels. The quantity diverted from the St. Joseph River is less than 10 percent of the estimated minimum daily flow. (Woodard-USGS)
W75-09179

HYDROLOGIC CONSEQUENCES OF USING GROUND WATER TO MAINTAIN LAKE LEVELS AFFECTED BY WATER WELLS NEAR TAMPA, FLORIDA,
Geological Survey, Tallahassee, Fla.
J. W. Stewart, and G. H. Hughes.
Florida Bureau of Geology, Tallahassee, Report of Investigations No 74, 1974. 41 p, 20 fig, 2 tab, 3 ref.

Descriptors: *Lakes, *Water levels, *Water transfer, *Groundwater, *Florida, Water wells, Pumping, Aquifers, Water yield, Limnology, Chemical properties, Hydrologic data.
Identifiers: *Tampa area(Fla), Groundwater supplement to lakes, Lake level maintenance.

Lake levels about 12 miles north of Tampa, Florida, have been lower than normal in recent years owing to less-than-normal rainfall and a lowering of groundwater levels by large withdrawals from the Floridan Aquifer. By pumping Floridan Aquifer water into the lakes, local residents have stabilized the levels of Round Lake since mid-1966 and of Saddleback and Charles Lakes since mid-1968. Total pumpage into the lakes ranged from 217 million gallons in 1969 to 401 million gallons in 1971; the large increase in pumpage is attributed to weather conditions which were drier in 1971 than in 1969. In 1971 pumpage averaged 143,000 gpd at Round Lake; 468,000 gpd at Saddleback Lake; and 492,000 gpd at Lake Charles. These values represent the water required to maintain lake levels at a nearly constant level which generally was above the level that would have occurred naturally. (Woodard-USGS)
W75-09184

A GENERAL OUTLINE OF THE WATER RESOURCES OF THE TOPPENISH CREEK BASIN, YAKIMA INDIAN RESERVATION, WASHINGTON,
Geological Survey, Tacoma, Wash.
For primary bibliographic entry see Field 4A.
W75-09186

DESCRIPTIONS AND CHEMICAL ANALYSES FOR SELECTED WELLS IN THE TEHAMA-COLUSA CANAL SERVICE AREA, SACRAMENTO VALLEY, CALIFORNIA,
Geological Survey, Menlo Park, Calif.
R. P. Fogelman.
Open-file report, April 1975. 52 p, 3 fig, 28 map, 4 tab.

Descriptors: *Chemical analysis, *Water quality, *Groundwater, *Wells, *California, Data collections, Hydrologic data, Sampling, Sites, Well data, Water levels, Pumping, Water yield, Drawdown

The Tehama-Colusa Canal Service Area is in the Northwestern part of the Sacramento Valley, in parts of Yolo, Colusa, Glenn, and Tehama Counties, Calif. The area includes 450 square miles (1,160 square km). The boundaries are: West, the eastern slopes of the Coast Ranges; north, Elder Creek; northeast, the Sacramento River and the Glenn-Colusa Canal; east and southeast, the Colusa Basin Drainage Canal; and south, Oat Creek. Between August and October 1974, water samples were collected for chemical analysis from 222 wells. Field determinations of alkalinity, conductance, pH, and temperature were made on the site at the time of sampling. The samples were then field prepared for shipment and analysis for individual constituents at the Geological Survey Central Laboratory, Salt Lake City, Utah. Descriptive data for water wells, chemical data, and location of the wells are included. (Woodard-USGS)
W75-09187

ESTIMATED GROUND-WATER FLOW, VOLUME OF WATER IN STORAGE, AND POTENTIAL YIELD OF WELLS IN THE POJOAQUE RIVER DRAINAGE BASINS, SANTA FE COUNTY, NEW MEXICO,
Geological Survey, Albuquerque, N.Mex.
F. C. Koopman.
Open-file report, May 1975. 33 p, 7 fig, 2 tab, 5 ref.

Descriptors: *Groundwater resources, *Aquifer characteristics, *Well data, *New Mexico, Pumping, Water yield, Specific capacity, Drawdown, Groundwater recharge, Surface-groundwater relationships.
Identifiers: *Pojoaque River basin(NMex).

The hydrology of a major part of the Pojoaque River drainage basin, a tributary of the Rio Grande in north-central New Mexico, was studies by the U.S. Geological Survey at the request of the Bureau of Indian Affairs. The flow of groundwater in the alluvium and Tesuque Formation was estimated (after constructing a resistance model, drilling exploratory holes, and conducting tests) to be about 2.7 cubic feet per second toward the Rio Grande for each section 1 mile wide. The volume of groundwater in storage, estimated from geologic information and assumed values of porosity, is about 5.5 x 10 to the 7th power acre-feet for the Tesuque Formation, and about 13,300 acre-feet for the alluvium. Shallow wells constructed in the alluvium yield 10 gallons per minute per foot of drawdown. Wells in the alluvium have a specific capacity about 200 times that of wells in the Tesuque Formation. Wells penetrating 1,000 feet of aquifer of the Tesuque Formation may yield several hundred gallons per minute with long-term depletion effects on both the overlying alluvium and surface-water sources. (Woodard-USGS)
W75-09188

UPWARD MIGRATION OF DEEP-WELL WASTE INJECTION FLUIDS IN FLORIDAN AQUIFER, SOUTH FLORIDA,
Geological Survey, Tallahassee, Fla.
For primary bibliographic entry see Field 5B.
W75-09190

PRELIMINARY FINDINGS OF A LEACHATE STUDY ON TWO LANDFILLS IN SUFFOLK COUNTY, NEW YORK,
Geological Survey, Mineola, N.Y.
For primary bibliographic entry see Field 5B.
W75-09191

GENERALIZED NOMOGRAPHIC SOLUTION OF HOOGHOUDT EQUATIONS,
Public Power Corp., Athens (Greece). Hydroelectric Project Design Branch.
For primary bibliographic entry see Field 8B.
W75-09197

SOLUTIONS FOR UNCONFINED NON-DARCY SEEPAGE,
James Cook Univ. of North Queensland, Townsville (Australia). Dept. of Engineering.
For primary bibliographic entry see Field 4A.
W75-09199

SOME PROBLEMS IN THE APPLICATION OF SYSTEMS ANALYSES IN WATER RESOURCES SYSTEMS,
Office of Science and Technology, Washington, D.C.
For primary bibliographic entry see Field 3B.
W75-09226

OPTIMAL OPERATION OF SURFACE AND GROUNDWATERS FOR POLLUTION DILUTION,
Colorado State Univ., Fort Collins. Dept. of Civil Engineering.
For primary bibliographic entry see Field 5B.
W75-09230

NITROGEN CONTENT OF SHALLOW GROUND WATER IN THE NORTH CAROLINA COASTAL PLAIN,
North Carolina State Univ., Raleigh. Dept. of Soil Science.
For primary bibliographic entry see Field 5B.
W75-09232

COLLIER COUNTY WATER MANAGEMENT ORDINANCE.
For primary bibliographic entry see Field 6E.
W75-09260

DRAINAGE SYSTEM,
D. A. Alsberg, and G. R. Alsberg.
United States Patent 3,837,168. Issued September 24, 1974. Official Gazette of the United States Patent Office, Vol 926, No 4, p 1181, September, 1974. 1 fig.

Descriptors: *Patents, *Flooding, *Groundwater recharge, *Drainage systems, *Flood proofing, Flood control, Drainage wells, Drainage programs, Drainage water, Groundwater resources.

A drainage system will reduce flooding and simultaneously recharge underground water supplies. The system consists of dry wells which connect to underground water sources, structures for carrying the water to the dry wells, and storage basins where excess water can be stored temporarily until the dry wells can discharge it to the water supplies. (Orr-FIRL)
W75-09329

4C. Effects On Water Of Man's Non-Water Activities

COST ANALYSIS OF EXPERIMENTAL TREATMENTS ON PONDEROSA PINE WATERSHEDS,
Forest Service (USDA), Tucson, Ariz. Roey Mountain Forest and Range Experiment Station.
J. M. Turner, and F. R. Larson.
USDA Forest Service, Research Paper RM-116, March, 1974, 12 p, 8 fig, 8 tab, 4 ref.

Descriptors: *Forest watersheds, *Costs, *Ponderosa pine trees, *Slopes, *Regression analysis, Watersheds(Basins), Cost analysis, Watershed management, Timber sites, Forecasting, Harvesting, *Arizona.
Identifiers: Sensitivity analysis, Basal area.

Treatments were prescribed for five ponderosa pine watersheds in order to develop a cost prediction model for experimental and operational applications. A sensitivity analysis was used to test effects of labor, equipment, materials, slope steepness, and stand density on treatment of cost. Types of watershed treatments subjected to cost analysis included a regular one-third stripcut, clearcut, irregular one-third stripcut, irregular one-half stripcut, and a severe thin. Regression models were developed which predict various logging costs as a function of the timber basal area removed. The use of basal area removals as a cost indicator averages out a number of forest conditions such as slope steepness, which might affect costs. (Mastic-Arizona)
W75-08940

HYDROLOGY OF PATCH CUTS IN LODGEPOLE PINE,
Colorado State Univ., Fort Collins. Dept. of Earth Sciences.
For primary bibliographic entry see Field 3B.
W75-08947

COMPARATIVE EVALUATION OF THREE URBAN RUNOFF MODELS,
Canada Centre for Inlands Waters, Burlington (Ontario).
For primary bibliographic entry see Field 2A.
W75-08988

UROS4: URBAN FLOOD SIMULATION MODEL PART 1. DOCUMENTATION AND USERS MANUAL,
Georgia Inst. of Tech., Atlanta. School of Civil Engineering.
For primary bibliographic entry see Field 4A.
W75-09046

UROS4: URBAN FLOOD SIMULATION MODEL PART 2. APPLICATIONS TO SELECTED DEKALB COUNTY WATERSHEDS,
Georgia Inst. of Tech., Atlanta. School of Civil Engineering.
For primary bibliographic entry see Field 4A.
W75-09047

CHANGES IN STORM HYDROGRAPHS DUE TO ROADBUILDING AND CLEARCUT LOGGING ON COASTAL WATERSHEDS IN OREGON,
Oregon State Univ., Corvallis. Water Resources Research Inst.
J. T. Krygier, and R. D. Harr.
Available from the National Technical Information Service, Springfield, Va. 22161, as PB-242 942, $4.25 in paper copy, $2.25 in microfiche. Project Termination Report, August 1972. 57 p, 3 fig, 11 tab, 41 ref, append. OWRT A-001-ORE(15).

Descriptors: *Clearcutting, *Lumbering, *Peak discharge, *Oregon, Hydrology, Watersheds(Basins), Drainage, Coasts, Small watersheds, Hydrographs, *Forest watersheds, *Road construction.
Identifiers: *Alsea watershed(Ore), Coastal watersheds, Storm hydrographs.

Construction of roads in the Alsea forested watershed, lead to an increase in peak discharge as much as 50 percent in the fall months and 21 percent in winter. No volume changes from road construction were detected among the watersheds. The influence of roads on peak discharge at the outlet of a larger watershed was not detectable. Clearcutting without effects of roads and slash burning induced changes in peak discharge of 128 percent for fall months and 22 percent for the winter 'recharged' period. Clearcutting increased peaks by 90 percent in fall and 28 percent in winter. The results of this study cannot be extrapolated to peak discharges beyond a 10-year return period. (See also W71-04968)
W75-09048

POLICY ALTERNATIVES IN FLOOD PLAINS.
East Central Florida Regional Planning Council, Winter Park.
For primary bibliographic entry see Field 6F.
W75-09094

POLICY ALTERNATIVES IN WATER RECHARGE AREAS.
East Central Florida Regional Planning Council, Winter Park.
For primary bibliographic entry see Field 4B.
W75-09095

ROCK VALLEY METROPOLITAN COUNCIL REGIONAL DEVELOPMENT GUIDE.
Rock Valley Metropolitan Council, Rockford, Ill.
For primary bibliographic entry see Field 6B.
W75-09106

AN EVALUATION OF STATE LAND USE PLANNING AND DEVELOPMENT CONTROL IN THE ADIRONDACKS,
Cornell Univ., Ithaca, N.Y.
For primary bibliographic entry see Field 4A.
W75-09122

A MATHEMATICAL MODEL OF URBAN STORM DRAINAGE,
Water Resources Engineers, Inc., Walnut Creek, Calif.
For primary bibliographic entry see Field 5D.
W75-09225

BIOLOGICAL VIEW OF PROBLEMS OF URBAN HEALTH,
John Curtin School of Medical Research, Canberra (Australia). Dept. of Human Biology.
For primary bibliographic entry see Field 6G.
W75-09332

4D. Watershed Protection

EROSION-PROOFING DRAINAGE CHANNELS,
Connecticut Univ., Storrs. Dept. of Civil Engineering.
C. J. Posey.
Journal of Soil and Water Conservation, Vol 28, No 2, March-April, 1973, p 93-95, 3 p, 5 fig, 7 ref. OWRR A-035-CONN(3). 14-31-0001-3807.

Descriptors: *Erosion, *Soil erosion, *Drainage effects, Urbanization, Concretes, Gullies, Gully erosion.
Identifiers: *Erosion-proofing, *Drainage channels, Rock linings, Reverse filters.

A large portion of soil eroded from land is scoured from the beds and banks of natural channels that are dry much of the time. As urbanization spreads, storm runoff peaks exceed the capacity of natural channels more frequently. To improve channels, methods of preventing erosion include lining with grass, concrete drop structures, lining with asphalt or concrete or rock linings. Rock linings have the problems of staying in place and fine-material wash. The use of reverse filter techniques developed by Terzaghi may be used to prevent this type of failure. Erosion-proofing of water channels also serves to prevent the growth of gullies and gully erosion. (Deitchman-Connecticut)
W75-08925

CONSTRUCTION REQUIREMENTS AND COST ANALYSIS OF GRASSED BACKSLOPE TERRACE SYSTEMS,
Nebraska Univ., Lincoln. Dept. of Agricultural Engineering.
H. D. Wittmuss.
Transactions of ASAE, Vol 16, No 5, 1973. p 970-972, 1 fig, 4 tab, 10 ref. OWRT A-029-NEB(1). 14-31-0001-4027.

Descriptors: *Terracing, Grassed waterways, Conservation, *Erosion control, *Construction costs, *Cost analysis, Systems analysis, *Nebraska, *Installation costs, Computer programs, Maps.

A method of terrace system analysis has been developed which can be used to predict the cost of parallel grassed backslope terrace systems with grassed or underground waterways. This analysis is based on the length of waterway and the area of land positioned above the bottom terrace in the field. The cost and construction requirements of four parallel grassed backslope terrace systems constructed over a 5-year period (1966-1970) were analyzed. The average cost of the grassed backslope terrace systems installed at Lincoln, Nebraska was $37.22 per acre terraced for each moving and $1.11 per ft. for clay tile waterway for a total of $82.25 per acre terraced. The use of a topographic map and a computer program to design the terrace system and plastic tubing for waterways reduced the technical input time requirement and installation costs of the parallel storage type terrace systems.
W75-08926

ENVIRONMENTAL ASPECTS--SACRAMENTO BANK PROTECTION,
Hydrologic Engineering Center, Davis, Calif. Water Resources Planning Branch.
C. S. Mifkovic, and M. S. Petersen.
Journal of the Hydraulics Division, American Society of Civil Engineers, Vol 101, No HY5, Proceedings Paper 11326, p 543-555, May 1975. 7 fig, 5 ref, 1 append.

Descriptors: *Bank protection, *Environmental effects, *Erosion, *Flood control, Hydraulics, Levees, Riparian plants, Wildlife habitats, Design, *California, Retaining walls, Rivers, Erosion control, Aesthetics.
Identifiers: *Sacramento River(Calif).

Studies show that bank protection can include environmental measures and can preserve environmental values from erosion. Reclamation of the Sacramento Valley, California, included Federal construction of a leveed flood-control project. Erosion has threatened the integrity of the levee system and a program of revetment construction at critical sites was authorized in 1960. Early construction was on a least-cost basis and seriously reduced riparian vegetation which supplies important wildlife habitat in the semi-arid valley. Alternative revetment designs and construction procedures have been developed to minimize adverse environmental effects. (Dawes-ISWS)
W75-08981

PREAUTHORIZATION PLANNING ACTIVITIES OF THE BUREAU OF RECLAMATION, THE CORPS OF ENGINEERS AND THE SOIL CONSERVATION SERVICE FOR FISCAL YEAR 1975.
For primary bibliographic entry see Field 4A.
W75-09244

POST AUTHORIZATION PROJECT ACTIVITIES ANNUAL STATUS REPORT - BUREAU OF RECLAMATION.
For primary bibliographic entry see Field 4A.
W75-09245

PROGRESS IN WATERSHED DEVELOPMENT IN THE AWR BASINS AREA UNDER USDA PROGRAMS - SEPTEMBER 1974.
Soil Conservation Service, Wichita, Kans.
Presented at Meeting--Arkansas-White-Red Basins Inter-Agency Committee, Wichita, Kansas, October 1974. 18 p, 1 tab.

Descriptors: *Watershed Protect and Flood Prev. Act, *Watershed management, *Erosion control, *Flood control, *Sediment control, Legislation, Control, Land management, Soil management, Water management(Applied), Floods, Flow, Water control, Water policy, Agriculture, Flood protection, Investigations, Surveys, Programs, Soil conservation, Federal government, Administrative agencies.
Identifiers: *Administrative regulations, Environmental policy.

Four congressional enactments authorize participation of the Department of Agriculture in watershed programs. The first watershed program was initiated under the Flood Control Act of 1944 for the purpose of soil erosion prevention, waterflow retardation, and other improvements to prevent floodwater and sediment damage. Existing authority in 1953 provided for the second program which involved the installation of improvements on 60 pilot watersheds throughout the country. The Watershed Protection and Flood Prevention Act authorized the third program in 1954, providing for Federal assistance in the installation of improvements, and authorizing the Secretary of Agriculture to make investigations and surveys of the watersheds of rivers and other waterways as a basis for the development of coordinated programs. A fourth watershed program was made possible by the Food and Agriculture Act of 1962 and authorized the Secretary to provide technical assistance to sponsors of Resource Conservation and Development projects. A progress report is presented of watershed development in the Department of Agriculture, and includes construction status as well as information relating to land treatment which is vital to the watershed protection and flood prevention program. (Fernandez-Florida)
W75-09246

5. WATER QUALITY MANAGEMENT AND PROTECTION

5A. Identification Of Pollutants

OXYGEN CONTENT AND B. O. D. OF EFFLUENTS MEASUREMENT.
German Patent 55341V/31. Applied May 9, 1973. Issued July 25, 1974. Derwent German Patents Report, Vol 5, No 31, p 2-3, July, 1974.

Descriptors: *Patents, *Biochemical oxygen demand, *Effluents, Measurement, *Oxygenation, Electrodes, Activated sludge, *Pollutant identification, Instrumentation.

A patent was granted for measurement of oxygen content and BOD of effluents. This involves an electrode with a movable collar which prevents fresh liquor from entering a cell during BOD determination. The electrode measures both the effectiveness of the oxygenation of an activated sludge process and the residual BOD. Oxygenation is measured by pumping the aqueous effluent past the cell. To measure biochemical oxygen demand, a collar is slid down, sealing on O-rings, and traps a sample within the cell. As the oxygen is consumed, the signal given declines and the BOD can be calculated from this rate of decline. (Prague-FIRL)
W75-08851

FLOW PHOTOMETER (DURCHFLUSS-PHOTOMETER).
Galvanotechnik, Vol 65, No 9, p 611, July, 1974. 1 fig.

Descriptors: *Analytical techniques, *Instrumentation, *Turbidity, Photometry, Design, Waste water, Calibrations, Water analysis, *Pollutant identification.
Identifiers: *Flow photometer.

A flow photometer was designed by the Bruno Large Company of Duesseldorf, West Germany, for the continuous control of the turbidity of water and waste water. Based on the light scattering principle, the photometer uses a beam deviated by 90 degrees for the detection of turbidity-generating particles by the Tyndall effect. The possible soiling of the cuvette is compensated for by an extra beam going directly through the cuvette. Kieselguhr or formacin solution can be used for calibration. (Takacs-FIRL)
W75-08858

AUTONOMOUS, AUTOMATIC APPARATUS FOR WATER POLLUTION CONTROL (APPARECCHIO PER IL CONTROLLO AUTOMATICO DEGLI INQUINAMENTI DELL ACQUA CON AUTONOMIA DI FUNZIOAMENTO).
Inquinamento Acqua Aria Suolo, Vol 16, No 6, p 11, June, 1974.

Descriptors: *Automation, *Measurement, *Dissolved oxygen, *Water temperature, Instrumentation, Data collections, Water pollution control, Measurement, *Pollutant identification.

An automatic apparatus developed by a British company for the continuous measurement and recording of the dissolved oxygen content and the water temperature in rivers, sewers, canals, lakes and basins is described. The battery-powered unit is suitable for autonomous operation for up to six weeks, with the battery having to be changed once a week. The apparatus is portable and can be implanted at depths of up to 30 meters. The measuring intervals can be selected between one minute and two hours by means of a built-in timer. The measurement data is recorded numerically. (Takacs-FIRL)
W75-08859

MUNICIPAL WASTEWATER BACTERIA CAPABLE OF SURVIVING CHLORINATION,
Texas Univ., Houston. School of Public Health.
For primary bibliographic entry see Field 5D.
W75-08876

TLC FINDS HEXANE SOLUBLES,
Western Electric Co., Inc., Chicago, Ill. Hawthorne Works.
H. Atanus.
Water and Wastes Engineering, Vol 11, No 10, p 26, 28, October 1974. 4 fig, 1 tab.

Descriptors: *Analytical techniques, *Pollutant identification, *Oil wastes, *Chromatography, Sampling, *Industrial wastes, Costs, Illinois, Oil pollution.
Identifiers: *Hexane solubles, Thin-layer chromatography, Chicago(Ill).

An analysis by thin layer chromatography of hexane solubles is described, for the detection of oil wastes in outfalls from plant discharges. The Metropolitan Sanitary District of Chicago conducts source sampling, direct measurement of waste water from each industrial complex in its area. If wastes are to be discharged into the sewage system, the limit of the amount of oil must be under 100 mg/liter. Oil is usually removed by standard techniques, such as skimming settling tanks and filtration before releasing treated sewer effluents. To identify and separate some of the hexane solubles (those relatively non-volatile organie material soluble in hexane), the thin layer chromatography method is utilized. A small quantity of hexane solubles is placed near the edge of a plastic or glass sheet coated with silica gel sorbent. When the glass is placed in an appropriate mixture of solvents, the solvents travel up the coated sheet with different affinities of the sample constituents travelling different distances. Separated components may be visualized with ultraviolet light or color-forming chemical reactions. Spotter solvents for detecting specific organic mixtures were: petroleum ether, ethyl acetate, acetic acid; petroleum ether, ethyl acetate, ammonium hydroxide; and benzene, methyl alcohol, ammonium hydroxide. Good separations were obtained by this method, without the use of costly or sophisticated equipment. Concentrations were measurable at the nanogram to the milligram level, and the technique is portable. (Prague-FIRL)
W75-08885

DETERMINATION OF THE AMMONIUM CONTENT IN WASTE WATERS BY MEANS OF THE AIR GAP ELECTRODE,
Technical Univ. of Denmark, Lyngby. Dept. of Chemistry.
J. Ruzicka, E. H. Hansen, P. Bisgaard, and E. Reymann.
Analytica Chimica Acta, Vol 72, No 1, p 215-219, September 1974. 1 tab, 11 ref.

Descriptors: *Analytical techniques, *Ammonia, Equipment, *Water analysis, *Pollutant identification, *Electrodes, Electrolytes, Water quality control.
Identifiers: Air-gap electrode, Indophenol method.

The indophenol method has been recommended for the determination of ammonia in an aqueous solution. However, this method is time-consuming and subject to serious interference from mercury and iron ions and soluble sulphides. To minimize sample handling and the likelihood of contamination and to avoid the interferences of the indophenol method, ammonia-specific electrodes have been developed. The basic principle of these electrodes is the use of a hydrophobic gas-permeable membrane which separates the alkaline test solution from an internal solution of ammonium chloride of fixed molarity and the immersion of a glass pH electrode and a reference electrode in the internal solution. The air-gap electrode is similar to other gas sensors but the gas-permeable membrane is replaced by the air gap which separates the electrolyte layer from the sample solution. The greatest advantage of the air-gap electrode is that the electrode is never in direct contact with the sample solution. Instead the electrolyte is adsorbed as a very thin film on the surface of the indicator electrode. Additional advantages include simplicity of design, ease of renewal of the electrolyte, and fast response. (Orr-FIRL)
W75-08886

TWO NEW WATER MONITORS AVAILABLE.
Chemical and Engineering News, Vol 52, No 42, p 33-34, October 21, 1974.

Descriptors: *Monitoring, *Instrumentation, *Water quality control, *Chlorine, Aquatic environments, Water treatment, Waste water treatment, Regional analysis, *Pollutant identification, Measurement.
Identifiers: Ultrasonic cleaning, Chlorine detectors.

Two new water pollution monitoring instruments have recently been developed. The first is a portable, inexpensive chlorine detector, used for measuring instantaneous chlorine levels in all aquatic environments. It was produced by the National Bureau of Standards, and will detect total chlorine in the parts-per-billion range, an extremely sensitive measurement. This NBS chlorine monitor may be used for wildlife protection as well as to measure effectiveness of municipal water treatment plants and waste water plants. The second water pollution monitoring instrumentation is an elaborate system introduced by Philips Electronic Instruments. This system automatically provides for continuous surveillance of up to seven water quality parameters, including redox potential, pH, pCl, dissolved oxygen concentration, electrical conductivity, temperature, and turbidity. The station can be programmed to operate unattended for up to five weeks, or it can feed data directly into a processing station by way of a communications network. The Philips water monitoring station has the unusual feature of automatic cleaning of its sensors regularly with an ultrasonic cleaner. In addition to the use of this monitoring system by itself, it is suggested that greater potential might be achieved in water quality control with an integrated network of stations to monitor regional and perhaps national water characteristics. (Prague-FIRL)
W75-08887

OCCURRENCE AND DETERMINATION OF INORGANIC POLLUTING AGENTS (IN GERMAN),
Munich Univ. (West Germany). Institut fuer Wasserchemie und Chemische Balneologie.
K.-E. Quentin, and H. A. Winkler.
Zentralbl Bakteriol Parasitenkd Infektionskr Hyg Erste Abt Orig Reihe B Hyg Praev Med. 158(6): 514-523, 1974. (In Ger. with Ger. and Engl. summ.).

Descriptors: Pollutants, *Water pollution sources, *Inorganic compounds, Phosphorus, Eutrophication, Water pollution effects, *Sampling, *Analytical techniques, Rivers, Lakes, Europe, *Heavy metals, Metals, Potable water, *Water treatment.
Identifiers: Drinking water, *Germany, West Germany, Danube River, Lake Constance.

The definition of a polluting agent applied to all solid or gaseous substances or organisms in the water which directly or indirectly impair biocoenosis and utilization of the water. They can be inconvenient, impair health or have a toxic effect. Phosphorous which becomes active indirectly is an inorganic polluting agent. The eutrophication of waters caused by phosphorus demonstrates the effect on aquatic life and on the purity of drinking water. The heavy metals, for which various countries and organizations have established limiting values, are cationic inorganic polluting agents. Sampling methods and apparatus for monitoring heavy metals are described. Results of a research project on heavy metals in the Bavarian part of the Danube River and in Lake Constance near Linaur, West Germany, are described. Water tests are concerned with dissolved substances and also with metals bound to substances causing turbidity or to sediments. These metals may remobilize. Procedures for elimination of such substances in the preparation of drinking water are discussed.--Copyright 1975, Biological Abstracts, Inc.
W75-08888

DETERMINATION OF NON-IONOGENIC SURFACTANTS IN WASTEWATERS BY THIN-LAYER CHROMATOGRAPHIC METHOD (OPREDELENIYE NEIONOGENNYKH POVERKHNOSTNO AKTIVNYKH VESHCHESTV V STOCHNYKH VODAKH METODOM KHROMATOGRAFII V TONKOM SLOYE),
N. M. Yudina, and A. A. Cherkasskiy.
Zavodskaya Laboratoriya, Vol 40, No 6, p 642-644, 1974. 1 fig, 2 tab, 4 ref.

Descriptors: *Extraction, *Surfactants, *Analytical techniques, Waste water, *Chromatography, *Pollutant identification.
Identifiers: Thin-layer chromatography, Eluents.

Extraction and a thin-layer chromatographic method for the quantitative determination of non-ionogenic surfactants, such as oxyethylated dodecyl alcohol, oxyalkylated dodecyl alcohol, polyoxyethylated polyoxypropylene glycol, polyoxyethylated polyoxyethylene diamine, and oxyethylated amides of synthetic fatty acids of the C10-C16 fraction, in industrial as well as other waste waters are described. Following extractive enrichment by means of chloroform at a recovery rate of 95-98%, the extract is applied on alumina layer, and 50:1.5 ratio of chloroform and ethanol is used as eluent. The spots are visualized by means of Draggendorf's reagent. (Takacs-FIRL)
W75-08889

DETERMINATION OF HEAVY METALS IN MUNICIPAL SEWAGE PLANT SLUDGES BY NEUTRON ACTIVATION ANALYSIS,
North Carolina State Univ., Raleigh. Nuclear Services Lab.
J. N. Weaver, A. Hanson, J. McGaughey, and F. J. Steinkruger.
Water, Air, and Soil Pollution, Vol 3, No 3, p 327-335, September, 1974. 5 fig, 3 tab, 10 ref.

Descriptors: *Analytical techniques, *Sewage sludge, *Neutron activation analysis, Municipal wastes, Urban runoff, Water pollution effects, Sewage treatment, *Pollutant identification, North Carolina, Treatment facilities, *Heavy metals.
Identifiers: *Trace metals.

Six North Carolina cities of varying sizes and degrees of industrialization were compared in terms of trace metals content of their sewage sludges. The method used was Neutron Analysis, using a Low Energy Photon Detector. The knowledge of trace metal concentrations has application in: determining whether industralized municipal sludge is polluted by industrial sources which are exceeding the effluent limits on heavy metals set up by the EPA; determining the effect of urban runoff by analysis of a basically rural municipal sludge; detecting the gradual build-up of heavy metals which could indicate future inhibition of the bacterial action on the sewage treatment; assessing the potential environmental hazards posed by use of such sludges by farmers; and determining possible air pollution problems associated with final disposal of such sludges by burning in sludge incinerators. The metals of particular interest were Hg, Se, Cr, Sb, Co and Fe. It was found that high levels of trace metals, including heavy metals, do exist in certain sewage sludges from North Caolina municipal treatment plants,and are likely to exist in other United States cities. With the use of Neutron Activation Analysis as a multi-element analytical scanning tool, however, most of the pollution problems associated with these sludges could be traced and removed. (Prague-FIRL)
W75-08891

F2 COLIPHAGE AS TRACER IN WASTEWATER BASIN,
Johns Hopkins Univ., Baltimore, Md. Dept. of Environmental Health.
For primary bibliographic entry see Field 5D.
W75-08893

CONTAMINATION OF WATER BY SYNTHETIC POLYMER TUBES,
Iowa State Univ., Ames. Dept. of Chemistry.
G. A. Jung, H. J. Svec, R. D. Vick, and M. J. Avery.
Environmental Science and Technology, Vol 8, No 13, p 1100-1106, December, 1974. 4 fig, 3 tab, 44 ref.

Descriptors: *Gas chromatography, *Mass spectrometry, *Polymers, *Plastics, Water pollution, Analytical techniques, Construction materials, *Pollutant identification.
Identifiers: *Organic contamination, Polyethylene, Polyvinylchloride.

An accurate method for testing polymer tubes intended for use in situations which require flowing water or water solutions is described. Identifications of polymer additives such as plasticizers were made by a combination of gas chromatography-mass spectrometry. Contaminants in effluent water were isolated by sorption on macroreticular resin beads, contained in a small glass column. These sorbed organic compounds were then eluted with diethylether, the eluate was concentrated by evaporation, and the organic contaminants were separated and measured quantitatively by gas chromatography. The results showed detection of organic contamination ranging from one to 5000 parts per billion by weight where water had flowed through tubes of polyethylene, polypropylene, black latex, six different formulations of polyvinylchloride, and plastic garden hose. (Prague-FIRL)
W75-08894

WASTE WATER LEVEL MEASUREMENT.
Process Biochemistry, p 22, October, 1974.

Descriptors: *Instrumentation, *Sewers, *Waste water(Pollution), *Measurement, Automation, Manholes, Analytical techniques, Equipment, Planning, *Pollutant identification.
Identifiers: *Waste water levels, Dipper.

A new precision instrument has been designed for measurement of waste water levels in sewers. Portacel, Limited is marketing the Dipper, which relies for its measurement accuracy on an electrically-activated non-corroding thin steel probe. The probe is lowered into a manhole on a 25-ft length of wire until it touches the surface of the water.

Concern has been expressed that chlorination of effluents from sewage treatment plants for disinfection may yield stable chlorine-containing organie compounds which have undesirable environmental effects. To study the effects of chlorination on sewage and sewage treatment plant effluents, an investigation was conducted. This method involved combining radioactive tracer (36Cl) chlorination with high-resolution chromatography. By this technique, over 40 chlorine-containing organic compounds were separated from a chlorinated primary effluent (chlorine residual 2 mg/liter) of a domestic sanitary sewage treatment plant. Secondary effluents were investigated separately, and appear to have lower concentrations of these organic constituents. Toxicity effects of the organic compounds on both microorganisms and higher organisms have yet to be determined. (Prague-FIRL)
W75-08898

STATISTICAL AIDS TO BACTERIOLOGICAL APPRAISAL OF EFFLUENTS. PART I--DIRECT COUNT METHOD,
G. v. R. Marais.
The Civil Engineer in South Africa, Vol 16, No 7, p 227-237, July, 1974. 9 fig, 6 tab, 10 ref.

Descriptors: *Statistical methods, *Sewage effluents, Bacteria, Microorganisms, Rivers, Water purification, Effluents, *Bioindicators, *Pollutant identification.
Identifiers: Poisson, Direct count method.

Bacteriological tests on sewage effluents have yielded variable results, due to both the method of determination and to the process itself. The variability must be understood in terms of statistical analysis. The two most commonly used methods for enumeration of microorganisms are the Most Probable Number method and the Direct Count method. The latter is detailed, in terms of statistical behavior. The properties of the Poisson distribution, its form, standard deviation, and the sum of two Poisson distributions are explained. Precision and accuracy of this method are examined. Observations were made as to confidence intervals. In application of the Direct Count method, both small field counts and large field counts are necessary, in order to assure a broad-based sample. In the cases where microorganisms grow in clumps, chains or clusters, a large field direct count assures the counting of the individual organisms in a given clump. Theoretical and experimental distributions for density of algal counts with clumping are given. This method has been chosen by many research engineers for use in measuring the bacteriological processes in rivers and in purification works. (Prague-FIRL)
W75-08902

RECONNAISSANCE OF THE WATER RESOURCES OF THE OKLAHOMA CITY QUADRANGLE, CENTRAL OKLAHOMA,
Geological Survey, Oklahoma City, Okla.
For primary bibliographic entry see Field 7C.
W75-08912

WATER RESOURCES OF WISCONSIN, LOWER WISCONSIN RIVER BASIN,
Geological Survey, Reston, Va.
For primary bibliographic entry see Field 7C.
W75-08913

WATER RESOURCES OF HAMILTON COUNTY, SOUTHWESTERN KANSAS,
Geological Survey, Reston, Va.
For primary bibliographic entry see Field 7C.
W75-08914

GROUND WATER IN GRAY COUNTY, SOUTHWESTERN KANSAS,
Geological Survey, Reston, Va.
For primary bibliographic entry see Field 7C.
W75-08915

MERCURY IN WATER, A BIBLIOGRAPHY, VOLUME 2.
Office of Water Research and Technology, Washington, D.C.
For primary bibliographic entry see Field 5C.
W75-08934

DETAILED COST ESTIMATED FOR ADVANCED EFFLUENT DESULFURIZATION PROCESSES,
Tennessee Valley Authority, Muscle Shoals, Ala.
G. G. McGlamery, R. L. Torstrick, W. J. Broadfoot, J. P. Simpson, and L. J. Henson.
Available from the National Technical Information Service, Springfield, Va. 22161, as PB-242 541, $11.25 in paper copy, $2.25 in microfiche. Environmental Protection Agency, Report EPA-600/2-75-006, January 1975. 417 p, 93 fig, 85 tab, 62 ref. 1AB013, EPA EPA IAG-134(D) Part A.

Descriptors: *Air pollution, Chemical reactions, *Economic analysis, *Capital costs, *Operating costs, Design, Fuels, Sulfur compounds.
Identifiers: Air pollution control, Scrubbing-regeneration, Limestone slurry, Lime slurry, Magnesia slurry - regeneration, Sodium solution - SO2 reduction, Catalytic oxidation, *Desulfurization.

A detailed, segmented, highly visible cost comparison of the five leading stack gas desulfurization processes was conducted. Using data available in late 1973, complete economic evaluations were prepared for limestone slurry scrubbing, lime slurry scrubbing, magnesia slurry - regeneration to sulfuric acid, sodium solution scrubbing - SO2 reduction to sulfur, and catalytic oxidation (Cat-Ox). Assuming the process technology to be proven in application, a prescribed set of representative power plant, process design, and economic premises was established. For each process design, projections are included for a base case (500-MW, 3.5% S in coal, new unit) and 16 other variations in power unit size, fuel type (coal or oil), sulfur in fuel, unit status (new vs. existing), solids disposal method (off-site vs. on-site ponding), and SO2 removal (80% vs. 90%). Capital investment, annual operating costs (7,000 hr/yr) and lifetime operating costs (overa 30-year declining operating profile) were estimated for the base case and each variation. Using sensitivity analysis, effects of variations in energy costs, raw material costs,. maintenance costs, cost of capital, operating labor cost escalation, and net sales revenue were studied. A 3-year construction schedule ending in mid-1975 is assumed for a midwestern location. Investment costs (mid-1974 dollars) can be scaled or altered to reflect any predictable project schedule, escalation rate, or location. Definition of the systems estimated, sources of cost data, and recommended equipment size-cost scale factors are given. The ranges in estimated capital cost of these processes are substantial. For example, the installed costs of the limestone slurry system were estimated to range from $23/kW to about $113/kW, depending on unit size, unit status, fuel type, sulfur content of fuel, solid disposal method, and overall project scope. Furthermore, due to high level of construction cost inflation in recent years, these estimates probably would be subject to substantial escalation for a project initiated now or in future years. (EPA)
W75-08935

SALT WATER DETECTION IN THE CIMARRON TERRACE, OKLAHOMA.
Oklahoma Water Resources Board, Oklahoma City.
Available from the National Technical Information Service, Springfield, Va. 22161, as PB-242 269, $7.00 in paper copy, $2.25 in microfiche. Environmental Protection Agency, Ada, Oklahoma, Report EPA-660/3-74-033, April 1975, 166 p, 28 fig, 5 tab, 22 ref. EPA 1BA024, Grant No S-800994.

Descriptors: Groundwater, *Brines, *Oklahoma, *Resistivity, Aquifers, *Saline water, Water pollution sources, *Alluvial aquifers, *Pollutant identification.
Identifiers: Natural brines, Wenner spread, Barnes layer.

The objectives were to demonstrate the applicability of surface resistivity techniques to delineate salt water contamination in a shallow alluvial aquifer, to outline areas of salt water contamination in a valuable terrace aquifer, to permit safe future development, and to identify the sources of such contamination. Surface resistivity using the Wenner spread and both Barnes layer and apparent resistivity interpretive methods was useful in outlining areas of major water quality changes where the geologic environment was simple and the terrace composed of sand. However, where clay was present in the terrace or where the bedrock relief was large, surface resistivity was not an accurate definitive tool. Two large areas of salt water contamination were intensively studied by test drilling. In one of these areas resistivity was extensively used. Brine contamination of one of these areas was attributed to oil field brine evaporation pits while the other area was contaminated by natural brines from the underlying bedrock. The sodium-chloride ratio was used to identify the source of brines. (EPA)
W75-08936

PHARMACOKINETICS OF TOXIC ELEMENTS IN RAINBOW TROUT, I. UPTAKE, DISTRIBUTION AND CONCENTRATION OF METHYLMERCURY BY RAINBOW TROUT (SALMO GAIRDNERI) TISSUES, II. THE MECHANISM OF METHYLMERCURY TRANSPORT AND TRANSFER TO THE TISSUES OF THE RAINBOW TROUT (SALMO GAIRDNERI),
State Univ. of New York, Buffalo.
For primary bibliographic entry see Field 5C.
W75-08938

CLIMATIC MODIFICATION BY AIR POLLUTION, II: THE SAHELIAN EFFECT,
Wisconsin Univ., Madison. Inst. for Environmental Studies.
For primary bibliographic entry see Field 2B.
W75-08949

ANTIMONY IN THE COASTAL MARINE ENVIRONMENT, NORTH ADRIATIC,
Institut Rudjer Boskovic, Rovinj (Yugoslavia). Center for Marine Research.
P. Strohal, D. Huljev, S. Lulic, and M. Picer.
Estuarine and Coastal Marine Science, Vol 3, No 2, p 119-123, April 1975. 3 tab, 17 ref.

Descriptors: *Pollutant identification, *Analytical techniques, *Neutron activation analysis, *Chemical properties, *Water quality, *Sea water, Marine biology, Chemical analysis, Spectroscopy, Limestones, Dolomite, Quartz, Sediments, Water pollution, Water pollution sources, Non-destructive tests, Salinity, Suspended solids, Nuclear powerplants.
Identifiers: *Antimony, *Adriatic Sea coast.

Concentration of stable antimony in the North Adriatic coastal waters was investigated by the neutron activation technique. The following concentrations were obtained: 0.31 microgram Sb/cu dm in the case of 0.45 micron filtered sea water and 45 micrograms Sb/cu dm for nonfiltered sea water, respectively. The concentrations of stable antimony in a number of North Adriatic organisms and sediments were also reported. Laboratory tracer experiments on the sorption of Sb125 by limestone, dolomite, quartz, and marine sediments were performed in order to have a better knowledge of the fate of antimony in the marine environment. The results obtained were discussed from a standpoint of pollution. (Henley-ISWS)
W75-08968

CIVIL ENGINEERING APPLICATIONS OF REMOTE SENSING,
Missouri Univ., Rolla. Dept. of Geological Engineering.
For primary bibliographic entry see Field 7B.
W75-08978

TECHNIQUES FOR TRACING SEDIMENT MOVEMENT,
Canada Centre for Inland Waters, Burlington (Ontario).
For primary bibliographic entry see Field 2J.
W75-08995

SUSPENDED SOLIDS ANALYSER.
Australian Patent 453,333. Issued September 26, 1974. Offical Journal of Patents, Trade Marks and Designs, Vol 44, No 36, p 3993, September, 1974.

Descriptors: *Patents, *Suspended solids, Analytical techniques, *Pollutant identification, Measurement, Sensing.
Identifiers: Sensor devices, Power photocells.

A system for detecting and measuring the coneentration of suspended solids in a liquid is described. A sensing device is adapted for submersion in a liquid containing suspended solids, and a power sources is connected with this device. The sensing device consists of a housing with a light source and several photocells; each photocell is located at a different distance from the light source and is positioned to sense only light scattered backwards from the suspended solids. Conversion means are connected with the output terminals of the photocells for taking the logarithmic ratio of the photocell output signals to provide a single output, which is linearly representative of the solids concentration. (Prague-FIRL)
W75-09064

APPENDIX - HEALTH AND SAFETY LABORATORY FALLOUT PROGRAM QUARTERLY SUMMARY REPORT, MARCH 1, 1974 THROUGH JUNE 1, 1974.
Health and Safety Lab. (AEC), New York.
Available from the National Technical Information Service, Springfield, Va 22161 as HASL-284, Appendix, $13.60 in paper copy, $2.25 in microfiche. Report No HASL-284, Appendix, July 1974. 465 p, 4 fig, 6 tab, 7 ref.

Descriptors: *Fallout, *Radioisotopes, *Sampling, *Analysis, *Measurement, *Assay, *Assessment, Sites, Strontium, Lead, Food chains, Milk, Domestic water, Data collections, Publications, Public health.
Identifiers: Conversion factors.

Appendices, mostly tabular data, are presented for: Sr-90 and Sr-89 in Monthly Deposition at World Land Sites; Radionuclides and Lead Surface Air; Radiostrontium in Milk and Tap Water; Table of Conversion Factors; and Table of Radionuclides. (See W75-09066 thru W75-09068).
W75-09065

STRONTIUM-90 AND STRONTIUM-89 IN MONTHLY DEPOSITION AT WORLD LAND SITES.
Health and Safety Lab. (AEC), New York.
In: Report No HASL-284, Appendix, p A-1 - 332, July 1974. 2 fig, 1 tab.

Descriptors: *Monitoring, *Measurement, *Fallout, *Strontium, *Sites, Publications, Sampling, Analysis, Data collections, Data processing, Data storage and retrieval, Networks, Computers, Public health, Laboratories.

Detail fallout deposition data are given for Sr 90 and Sr 89 at 116 sampling points located in the United States and other countries. Sampling methods and analytical techniques are reported. To facilitate the accurate storage, retrieval and handling of the data generated from the monthly fallout collection network, all data have been transcribed to punched cards. The data printed out from the punched cards are presented in tables. (See also W75-09065). (Houser-ORNL)
W75-09066

RADIONUCLIDES AND LEAD IN SURFACE AIR,
Health and Safety Lab. (AEC), New York.
H. L. Volchok, L. Toonkel, and M. Schonberg.
In: Report No HASL-284, Appendix, p B-1 - 124, July 1974. 2 tab, 7 ref.

Descriptors: *Monitoring, *Measurement, *Radioactivity, *Lead, *Sites, *Aquatic environment, Data collections, Publications, Sampling, Analysis, Quality control, Gross gamma, Radiochemical analysis, Beryllium, Plutonium, Manganese, Iron, Cadmium.
Identifiers: *Surface air.

The primary objective is to study the spatial and temporal distribution of nuclear weapons debris and lead in the surface air. Other special studies of surface air contamination have been added. Many of the original Naval Research Laboratory (NRL) sites, which grouped roughly along the 80th Meridian (West), have been continued in the current program. Since 1963 a number of other sites were added to investigate the possible effects of longitude, elevation and proximity to coastlines, and from late 1965 through March 1969, samplers were placed on four Atlantic Ocean weather ships to extend the surface air study over the marine environment. The present network extends from about 76 degrees North to 90 degrees South. Sampling stations along with their coordinates and elevations are listed. (See also W75-09065). (Houser-ORNL)
W75-09067

RADIOSTRONTIUM IN MILK AND TAP WATER.
Health and Safety Lab. (AEC), New York.
For primary bibliographic entry see Field 5B.
W75-09068

PACIFIC NORTHWEST LABORATORY ANNUAL REPORT FOR 1973 TO THE USAEC DIVISION OF BIOMEDICAL AND ENVIRONMENTAL RESEARCH, PART 3 ATMOSPHERIC SCIENCES.
Battelle-Pacific Northwest Labs., Richland, Wash.
Available from the National Technical Information Service, Springfield, Va 22161 as BNWL-1850, Pt 3, $7.60 in paper copy, $2.25 in microfiche. Rept No BNWL-1850 Pt 3, April 1974. 293 p, 97 fig, 45 tab, 189 ref.

Descriptors: *Atmosphere, *Precipitation(Atmospheric), *Air pollution, *Water pollution, *Radiation, *Radioactivity, Environment, Fallout, Aerosols, Human population, Winds, Storms, Dynamics, Diffusion, Turbulence, Ion transport, Ecology, Ecosystems.
Identifiers: Decontamination, Resuspension.

The Atmospheric Sciences Program is focused on atmospheric cleansing and reinsertion processes. Studies of pollutant interaction with cloud and precipitation droplets and with the earth's surface are being conducted. Accompanying them are the necessary related investigations of aerosol description and behavior, air trajectories, cloud and storm dynamics, turbulence and diffusion. The program is aimed at providing a continually improving capability to describe the transport of contaminants released from nuclear facilities which are ultimately delivered to human populations and ecological systems. Emphasis of the program is on pollutant removal and resuspension processes, but research on all aspects of the at-

desire to assess low-level radiation effects is requiring more realistic atmospheric models where conservative models were adequate before. (See also W75-09069) (Houser-ORNL)
W75-09071

ATMOSPHERIC TRANSFORMATION PROCESSES.
Battelle-Pacific Northwest Labs., Richland, Wash.
In: Rept. No. BNWL-1850, Pt. 3, p 87 - 107, April 1974. 9 fig, 1 tab, 4 ref.

Descriptors: *Atmosphere, *Environment, *Radioactivity, Movement, *Aerosols, *Trace elements, *Gases, Tracers, Tracking techniques, Diffusion, Air pollution, Winds, Meteorology, Model studies, Aircraft.

Contaminants, once released to the atmosphere, can be altered in many ways. Gases may become adsorbed on particles and particles may coagulate. Many chemical processes occur, frequently promoted by light and catalyzed by trace substances in the air. Understanding of transformation is essential in making material balances of air pollutants and accounting for observed downwind concentrations. During the past two years the program on atmospheric transformations has proceeded essentially through three stages of development. The first began with acquisition of the Cessna 411 aircraft, where the primary task was to acquire trace gas and aerosol instrumentation and incorporate it for airborne analysis. The second stage of the program was to utilize this newly developed facility for airborne observation and to relate these observations qualitatively to atmospheric transformation phenomena. The third stage of this program - beginning at the present time - is to develop mathematical models for quantitative diagnosis and analysis of atmospheric phenomena observed using the aircraft facility. It is anticipated that subsequent comparison between transformations models and observation will result in improved models which will be useful as input to other programs - particularly those involving wet- and dry-deposition processes. (See also W75-09069) (Houser-ORNL)
W75-09072

REMOVAL AND RESUSPENSION PROCESSES - WET REMOVAL PROCESSES.
Battelle-Pacific Northwest Labs., Richland, Wash.
In: Rept. No. BNWL-1850, Pt. 3, p 109 - 155, April 1974. 14 fig, 4 tab, 48 ref.

Descriptors: *Precipitation(Atmospheric), *Atmosphere, Environment, *Monitoring, *Radioactivity, Fallout, Aerosols, Gases, Trace elements, Tracers, Tracking techniques, *Air pollution.
Identifiers: *Scavenging.

Washout and in-cloud scavenging are important processes by which air pollutant particles and gases are removed from the atmosphere. The primary objective of the precipitation scavenging research is to develop methods for modeling and predicting wet removal processes in the atmosphere. Several significant new findings in the precipitation scavenging program have substantially altered research emphasis. These have also resulted in a reassessment of the program. Some important findings are: (a) It has been demonstrated mathematically that field and laboratory experiments of washout using polydisperse aerosols, while suitable for determining the washout characteristics of certain well defined aerosols, are of limited value as tests of particulate washout theory; below-cloud scavenging efforts are being revised accordingly. (b) An in-cloud tracer scavenging experiment performed at Quillayute resulted in removal rates much lower than anticipated from previous results. This finding appears to indicate that inter- and intra-cloud transport is more significant to scavenging than expected previously. Consequent modifications of experiment plans are being made. (c) Substantial evidence suggests that under some conditions scavenged gases may desorb significantly subsequent to the raindrops' impact on the surface. This finding has strong implications to delivery-rate assessment and sampler design. As a result, a no-resuspension sampler is being fabricated and future tests of this effect are anticipated. (See also W75-09069) (Houser-ORNL)
W75-09073

REMOVAL AND RESUSPENSION PROCESSES - DRY DEPOSITION OF PARTICLES.
Battelle-Pacific Northwest Labs., Richland, Wash.
In: Rept. No. BNWL-1850, Pt. 3, p 157 - 199, April 1974. 7 fig, 3 tab, 52 ref.

Descriptors: *Radioisotopes, *Volatility, *Particle shape, *Particle size, Fallout, Diffusion, Ion transport, Environmental effect, Cooling towers, Cooling water, Ponds, Regulation, Air pollution.
Identifiers: Deposition, Decontamination, Resuspension.

An important mechanism by which an atmosphere is depleted of particulate material is by gravity settling and by turbulent eddy diffusion processes. Historically research has been directed to deposition studies with monodisperse particles, first in tubes transporting particles, then in wind tunnel studies. Some field studies were undertaken much earlier to determine by mass balance the depletion of particles from a plume. Recent work in the wind tunnel has shown the relationship of deposition velocity to particulate size, average velocity, friction velocity, and the unique characteristics of surfaces. Models have been developed which take into account these variables, and a large body of data has been made available. Wind tunnel studies are to be implemented with field studies using well characterized aerosols. The studies in 1973 were concerned with deposition to crushed rock surfaces, shallow water, and vegetation canopies. Ongoing field studies have utilized comparisons of depositing with nondepositing tracers for evaluating deposition. This technique as well as direct turbulent flux measurements of pollutants should provide expanded capability for future investigation of deposition over larger regions and onto varied surfaces of wider range of interest. (See also W75-09069) (Houser-ORNL)
W75-09074

REMOVAL AND RESUSPENSION PROCESSES - RESUSPENSION OF PARTICLES.
Battelle-Pacific Northwest Labs., Richland, Wash.
In: Rept. No. BNWL-1850, Pt. 3, p 201 - 233, April 1974. 10 fig, 10 tab, 22 ref.

Descriptors: *Atmosphere, *Environment, *Radioactivity, *Particle size, *Particle shape, Aerosol, *Air pollution, Soil contamination, Air movement, Winds, Sands, Radioisotopes, Ion transport.
Identifiers: Deposition, Decontamination, Resuspension.

Particles, once airborne and deposited, can again become airborne when wind stresses are sufficiently high. Research in this area is undertaken to help establish the important variables and their interrelationships. The ultimate use for data of this kind is to determine the exposure to man from such secondary sources and to set permissible limits on ground contamination. An important variable is the wind speed, but the interaction between the primary particle of interest and the bulk soil particles is also very important. Areas contaminated inadvertently with radioisotopes from various processes are being used; but also initial studies using a tracer placed on an instrumented plot of prairie-like terrain were performed.

An important part of this work is to develop models which account for particles resuspended and deposited. Diffusion and dispersion in the atmosphere, once particles are resuspended, are important in diluting the airborne material; hence, this work interfaces directly with diffusion studies. The physics of wind blown sand and fine particles is also studied to determine the mechanisms of resuspension and transport. Studies on the nature and release of radioactive particle in local Hanford project areas during fires are also described. (See also W75-09069) (Houser-ORNL)
W75-09075

SPECIAL STUDIES - COOLING TOWER RESEARCH - BIOMETEOROLOGY.
Battelle-Pacific Northwest Labs., Richland, Wash.
In: Rept. No. BNWL-1850, Pt. 3, p 235 - 270, April 1974. 16 fig, 3 tab, 26 ref.

Descriptors: *Cooling towers, *Effluents, *Chromium, *Measurement, *Nuclear powerplants, *Thermal pollution, Water quality, Water quality control, Assessment, Environmental effects, Micrometeorology, Meteorology, Model studies, Ecology, Ecosystems, Climatology.

The number of cooling towers being constructed in the U.S. is rapidly increasing due to the expansion of electrical generating capacity demand, water quality thermal limits, and competition for fresh water resources. In addition, the localization of electrical demand in coastal areas is encouraging wide utilization of salt water cooling towers. With this trend and the trend for progressively larger power plants on the same site, immediate attention must be given to establishing the basic information necessary to assess the impact of such actions. The data base available for predicting salt water cooling drift amounts and the potential for inadvertent weather modification is meager and far behind plans for future development. It was with this background that cooling tower studies were initiated. In the first year, emphasis has been placed upon both theoretical and experimental studies of drift modeling and scoping the effects of waste heat releases to the atmosphere. The results to date and the trends in utility developments have not only confirmed and reinforced the initial motivation for these investigations, but have injected a sense of urgency to such research if the scientific community is to keep pace with the requirements for its product. Cooling tower studies will continue to address the need for drift models, and increased emphasis will be placed on obtaining cooling tower plume data and evaluating potential effects on weather from multi-unit reactor sites. (See also W75-09069) (Houser-ORNL)
W75-09076

STOCHASTIC VARIATION OF WATER QUALITY OF THE PASSAIC RIVER,
Rutgers - the State Univ., New Brunswick, N.J. Dept. of Chemical and Biochemical Engineering.
B. M. Mehta, R. C. Ahlert, and S. L. Yu.
Water Resources Research, Vol 11, No 2, p 300-308, April 1975. 2 fig, 12 tab, 10 ref. OWRT A-035-NJ(4).

Descriptors: *Water quality control, *Stochastic processes, *Time series analysis, *Simulation analysis, Streamflow, Water temperature, Biochemical oxygen demand, Dissolved oxygen, Fluctuations, Discharge(Water), Rainfall, Mathematical models, Equations, Systems analysis, *New Jersey.
Identifiers: *Passaic River(NJ), Arima models, Prediction, Oxygen regime, Oxygen deficit, Daily.

Most receiving water quality models are steady state, deterministic, one-dimensional structures. Yet it is clear that stream quality varies in time and is non-deterministic; receiving water quality is a stochastic variable. A rational approach to the problem is to consider stochastic variation as an important aspect of water quality and to incorporate some form of this concept into water quality standards. In addition to aiding the development of manageable standards, stochastic modeling is especially important to successful quality forecasting. The stochastic structures of some water quality times series are examined. These time series include daily observations in streamflow, water temperature, BOD, and dissolved oxygen deficit. Autoregressive integrated moving average (Arima) models have been used to describe the random components of these time series. Except for the BOD, the Arima models provide very satisfactory results. (Bell-Cornell)
W75-09080

PHYTOPLANKTON DISTRIBUTION AND WATER QUALITY INDICES FOR LAKE MEAD (COLORADO RIVER),
Arizona Univ., Tucson. Dept. of Biological Sciences.
For primary bibliographic entry see Field 5C.
W75-09083

HIGH SENSITIVITY LASER ABSORPTION SPECTROSCOPY OF LABORATORY AQUEOUS SOLUTIONS AND NATURAL WATERS, (PHASE II OF) A FEASIBILITY STUDY,
Missouri Univ., Kansas City. Dept. of Physics.
M. R. Querry, W. C. Holland, R. C. Waring, and G. M. Hale.
Available from the National Technical Information Service, Springfield, Va 22161 as PB-243 123, $4.75 in paper copy, $2.25 in microfiche. Missouri Water Resource Research Center Completion Report, March 31, 1975. 84 p, 12 fig, 8 ref, 3 append. OWRT A-058-MO(4). 14-31-0001-4025.

Descriptors: Measurement, Optical properties, Sulfates, Ion compounds, *Spectroscopy, Absorption, *Chlorophyll, *Lasers, Aqueous solutions, Feasibility studies, Non-destructive tests, Analytical techniques, *Chemical analysis, *Pollutant identification.
Identifiers: *Absorption spectroscopy, Ferrous sulfate.

Investigations conducted have shown that the quantity of both chlorophyll types a and b can be nondestructively measured in solution by use of laser enhanced absorption spectroscopy (LEAS) at 1/100 the concentration easily detectable by use of ordinary spectrophotometric methods; this is a 100 times increase in sensitivity. It is estimated with considerable confidence that the ultimate sensitivity for the LEAS technique is 10,000 times greater than that for ordinary spectrophotometric methods. During the first phase (1 July 1972 - 30 June 1973) narrow-band dye-laser enhanced absorption was measured. (See W74-01658). During the second phase of the project (1 July 1974 - 31 December 1974) preparations were made on laboratory apparatus to measure broad-band dye-laser enhanced absorption spectra of chlorophyll. The optical properties of water were also investigated in the spectral region 200 micrometer.
W75-09125

PORTABLE DEVICE FOR THE QUANTITATIVE DETERMINATION OF TRACE ELEMENTS IN WATER IN THE SUB-NANO GRAM SENSITIVITY RANGE,
Missouri Univ., St. Louis. Dept. of Physics.
C. C. Foster, and R. Hight.
Available from the National Technical Information Service, Springfield, Va 22161 as PB-243 132, $5.25 in paper copy, $2.25 in microfiche. Missouri Water Resources Research Center Completion Report, April 18, 1975. 75 p, 29 fig, 7 tab, 55 ref, 2 append. OWRT A-064-MO(2). 14-31-0001-3825 and 4025.

Descriptors: Radioisotopes, *X-ray fluorescence, *Trace elements, *Pollutant identification, Water analysis, Analytical techniques, *Radiochemical analysis, *X-ray analysis.

Alpha particles and protons from charged particle accelerators and photons from both x-ray tubes and radioactive sources have been shown to be useful for the excitation of characteristic x-rays for multi-element energy dispersive trace analysis of environmental samples to the few ppm range. The use of 4.5 MeV alpha particles from a thin window Po-210 source (t1/2=138.4d) of 5 mCi effective strength to directly excite x-rays from trace elements in 1 cc water samples evaporated on 1.75mg/sq cm thick mylar backings in a helium atmosphere in a lucite enclosure was investigated. Minimum detectable amounts (MDA's) were established for 20 elements ($22<Z<82$) using K-, L- and M- radiation and 50 minute counting times. The smallest MDA determined was 0.14 microgram for Vanadium. Other representative MDA's, in microgram, are Fe-0.57, Mo- 0.33 and Pb - 0.5. Radioalpha induced x-ray trace element analysis offers the same advantages of portability, ease of operation, low maintenance and cost, and 'in house' availability as radiophoton induced analysis. Because of the availability of more intense sources (up to 10 Ci), the fact that the detected radiation (x-rays) differs from the excitation radiation (alpha-particles) and that K, L, and M x-ray emission cross sections depend essentially only on the emitted x-ray energy, lower MDA's are obtainable for many elements in thin samples for comparable counting times, as well.
W75-09126

PREDICTION OF WATER SOLUBLE ARSENIC IN SEWAGE-SOIL SYSTEMS,
Missouri Univ., Columbia. Dept. of Agronomy.
R. Hess, and R. Blanchar.
Available from the National Technical Information Service, Springfield, Va 22161 as PB-243 127, $9.25 in paper copy, $2.25 in microfiche. Missouri Water Resources Center Completion Report, June 1, 1975. 287 p, 46 fig, 86 tab, append. OWRT A-068-MO(1). 14-31-0001-4025 and 5025.

Descriptors: *Arsenic compounds, *Soil chemistry, Soil water, Oxidation, Reduction(Chemical), Aeration, Sewage, *Missouri, Land use, *Soil contamination, *Loam, Soil analysis, *Soil chemical properties, Lead, *Oxidation-reduction potential, Pollutant identification.

Fifteen g samples of Sharpsburg silty clay loam and a Menfro silt loam soil containing 320 and 160 ug As/g, respectively, were equilibrated for 21 days with 30 ml of distilled water or 1% dextrose. After 21 days the samples were freeze dried, divided into 2 groups, one air dry and the other at 26.7% water and exposed to the atmosphere. Eh, pH, As, Fe, Al, Mn, Ca and Pb in solution were determined periodically. After an initial Eh drop in the 1% dextrose equilibration, the As in solution increased rapidly in both soils, but was constant after 12 days. The As in solution increased more slowly in the water equilibration, but also remained constant after 12 days. At 4 days after freeze drying the As level was near the level observed before reduction. Both soils were equilibrated with dilute HCl and NaOH for 7 days at 25 degrees at values of pAl + 3pOH, pAl + pAsO sub 4, pFe + 3pOH, pFe + pAsO sub 4, 3pMn + 2pAsO sub 4, 3pCa + 2pAsO sub 4 and 3pPb + 2pAsO sub 4, computed and compared to those of synthesized arsenates. Both soils were undersaturated with respect to aluminum, ferric, and calcium arsenates, and near equilibrium concentrations of As predicted from lead and manganese arsenates.
W75-09127

HYDRO-GEOCHEMISTRY IN A CARBONATE BASIN - GEOMORPHIC AND ENVIRONMENTAL IMPLICATION,
Vanderbilt Univ., Nashville, Tenn. Dept. of Geology.
For primary bibliographic entry see Field 2K.
W75-09129

tion with suitable organic solvents. The level of chlorine varies from about 20-650 ppm in the samples investigated. The larger part of this lipid-soluble organic-bound chlorine can hardly be accounted for by known substances. They may in part be synthesized by natural means in the marine environment. The absorption of unidentified chlorinated pollutants is another possible source. Bromine and iodine have also been determined to allow comparison with previously obtained data. (Katz)
W75-09147

ACCUMULATION OF 3,4,3',4'-TETRACHLOROBIPHENYL AND 2,4,5,2',4',5'-AND 2,4,6,2',4',6' - HEXACHLOROBIPHENYL IN JUVENILE COHO SALMON,

National Marine Fisheries Service, Seattle, Wash.
E. H. Gruger, Jr., N. L. Karrick, A. I. Davidson, and C. T. Hruby.

Environmental Science and Technology, Vol 9, No 2, p 121-127, February 1975. 5 tab, 27 ref.

Descriptors: *Salmon, *Polychlorinated biphenyls, *Growth rates, *Bioassay, Chlorinated hydrocarbon pesticides, Stress, Laboratory tests, Food chains, Analysis, Analytical technique, *Absorption, Water pollution effects, *Pollutant identification.
Identifiers: *Bioaccumulation, Oncorhynchus kisutch, Chlorobiphenyls, *Coho salmon.

Coho salmon parr were fed 10 micrograms of equal proportions of 3,4,3',4'-tetrachlorobiphenyl, 2,4,5,2',5'-hexachlorobiphenyl, and 2,4,6,2',4',6'-hexachlorobiphenyl per gram of food pellets. Analyses at various time intervals indicated that significant differences in accumulated body concentrations of the chlorobiphenyls occurred only after 108 days of feeding. At this time, three fish averaged 1.4 plus or minus 0.35 micrograms of each hexachlorobiphenyl and 0.65 plus or minus 0.32 micrograms of the tetrachlorbiphenyl per gram wet whole body tissues. Analyses before and after a final 48 days of starvation showed different concentrations for the tetrachlorobiphenyl compared to the hexachlorobiphenyls in various tissues. Before starvation, concentrations of the tetrachlorobiphenyl ranged from a low of 0.09 micrograms/g wet white muscle to a high of 10.8 micrograms/g wet adipose tissues; concentrations of hexachlorobiphenyls were about twice as high. After starvation concentrations of the hexachlorobiphenyls were three to four times greater than the those of the tetrachlorobiphenyls. (Katz)
W75-09148

BIOASSAY METHODS OF THE NATIONAL SWEDISH ENVIRONMENT PROTECTION BOARD,

National Swedish Environment Protection Board, Stockholm. Research Lab.
T. B. Hasselrot.

Journal Water Pollution Control Federation, Vol 47, No 4, p 851-857, April 1975. 12 ref.

Descriptors: *On-site investigations, *Bioassay, *Bioindicators, *Testing procedures, *Pollutant identification, Water pollution effects, Water pollution control, Toxicants, Tagging, Industrial wastes, Water waste treatment, Organoleptic properties, *Pulp wastes, Cellulose, Fish eggs.
Identifiers: *Salmo spp., Bioaccumulation, Dimethyl sulfide.

The bioassay methods used by the research laboratory of the National Swedish Environment Protection Board for testing toxicants and polluted waters from industries and communities are described. Field investigations are the main task of the research laboratory. To study toxicological and accumulative effects of water pollution, cages containing fish and bivalves have been stationed in lakes, water courses and coastal waters. The purpose was to follow the effect of a known source of water pollution or to trace an unknown one. Results of the cage investigations are presented. Also, free-swimming fish have been tagged to compare the concentration of a certain water pollutant in these fish and in the caged specimens. Biotests at industries and wastewater treatment plants determine the toxicological and cumulative effects of polluted water so that action may be taken at an early stage to prevent fish death in the receiving water. (Katz)
W75-09155

OIL SPILL PROTECTION IN THE BALTIC SEA,

Institute for Water and Air Pollution Research, Stockholm (Sweden).
For primary bibliographic entry see Field 5G.
W75-09156

A FILTER AND CHILLER FOR AN OPEN SEA-WATER SYSTEM,

National Marine Fisheries Service, Beaufort, N.C. Atlantic Estuarine Fisheries Center.
For primary bibliographic entry see Field 7B.
W75-09158

CONTAMINATION BY 51CR AND 109CD OF CULTURES OF THE ALGA DUNALIELLA BIOCULATA (CONTAMINATION PAR LE 51CR ET LE 109CD DE CULTURES DE L'ALGUE DUNALIELLA BIOCULATA), (IN FRENCH),

Institut Oceanographique, Paris (France).
M. C. Saraiva, and A. Fraizier.

Marine Biology, Vol 29, No 4, p 343-350, 1975. 6 fig, 9 tab, 16 ref. English abstract.

Descriptors: *Metals, *Absorption, *Algae, *Chromium, Cadmium, *Cadmium radiosiotopes, Radioisotopes, Analytical techniques, Bioassay, *Pollutant identification, Water pollution effects.
Identifiers: *Dunaliella bioculata, Uptake mechanisms, Bioaccumulation.

Contamination of Dunaliella bioculata by 51Cr and 109Cd was observed experimentally to determine the possible uptake mechanisms of the metals by this alga. Despite slight contamination by 51Cr, it was not possible to demonstrate any active mode of absorption of the radionuclide. In the case of 109Cr, however, the various tests revealed that uptake did occur, the concentration factor being about 300 for a contact time of 15 days. (Katz)
W75-09160

DISCHARGE MEASUREMENTS AND CHEMICAL ANALYSES OF WATER IN NORTHWESTERN WYOMING,

Geological Survey, Cheyenne, Wyo.
For primary bibliographic entry see Field 7C.
W75-09172

WATER RESOURCES DATA FOR KANSAS, 1974: PART 2. WATER QUALITY RECORDS.

Geological Survey, Lawrence, Kans.
For primary bibliographic entry see Field 7C.
W75-09181

DETERMINATION OF TRACE ELEMENTS IN WATER AND AQUATIC BIOTA BY NEUTRON ACTIVATION ANALYSIS,

Geological Survey, Denver, Colo.
L. L. Thatcher, and J. O. Johnson.

In: Bioassay Techniques and Environmental Chemistry: Ann Arbor Science Publishers, Inc, Ann Arbor, Mich, p 277-298, 1973. 3 fig, 5 tab, 9 ref.

Descriptors: *Trace elements, *Neutron activation analysis, *Pollutant identification, Water analysis, Chemical analysis, Sampling.

Advantages offered by neutron activation for water pollution analysis include positive identifi-

cation of elements, high sensitivity, elimination of contamination from reagents, and minimization of exchange between the water sample and container. Contamination is minimized by use of a special sampling procedure using a pre-analyzed polyethylene bag. Quartz ampoules are also used. Both containers eliminate transfer of sample prior to irradiation. Mercury is determined by a post-irradiation carrier precipitation. Fourteen other elements are determined by a post-irradiation mixed carrier hydroxide-sulfide precipitation. Rare earths have been detected in many water samples. Even with radiochemistry, it is essential to use a high resolution lithium-drifted germanium detector to eliminate rare earth interference. The principal disadvantage of the method is failure to determine lead. (Knapp-USGS)
W75-09182

GROUND-WATER RESOURCES OF THE HOLLYWOOD AREA, FLORIDA,
Geological Survey, Tallahassee, Fla.
For primary bibliographic entry see Field 6D.
W75-09185

LENGTH OF INCUBATION FOR ENUMERATING NITRIFYING BACTERIA PRESENT IN VARIOUS ENVIRONMENTS,
Rutgers - The State Univ., New Brunswick, N.J. Dept. of Environmental Science.
V. A. Matulewich, P. F. Strom, and M. S. Finstein.
Applied Microbiology, Vol 29, No 2, p 265-268, February 1975. 2 tab, 18 ref. OWRT A-030-NJ(4), 14-01-0001-3230.

Descriptors: *Nitrification, Water pollution effects, *New Jersey, *Incubation, Bacteria, *Pollutant identification.
Identifiers: *Nitrosomonas, *Nitrobacter, *Nitrifying bacteria, Microbial ecology, Passaic River(NJ), Mine Brook(NJ).

The effect of incubation time on most-probable-number (MPN) estimates of autotrophic nitrifying bacteria was investigated using water, rooted aquatic plants, muds, and slimes as inoculum sources. Maximum MPNs of the NH sub 4 + -oxidizing group were attained in 20 to 55 days (median, 25). Estimates of NO sub -2 -oxidizers were highest at termination (103-113 days). (Whipple-Rutgers)
W75-09234

THE USE OF PHYSIOLOGICAL INDICATORS OF STRESS IN MARINE INVERTEBRATES AS A TOOL FOR MARINE POLLUTION MONITORING,
Virginia Inst. of Marine Science, Gloucester Point.
M. P. Lynch.
In: Marine Technology Society Tenth Annual Conference Proceedings, (1974), p 881-890, Contribution No. 625 of the Virginia Institute of Marine Science. 4 fig, 4 tab, 17 ref.

Descriptors: Water pollution effects, Water pollution sources, *Crabs, *Pesticide residues, Pollutants, Aquatic environments, Marine animals, Red tide, DDT, Thermal stress, *Monitoring, *Bioindicators, *Pollutant identification.
Identifiers: *Blue crab(Callinectes sapidus), *Glucose, Synergistic effects, Ionic composition, Physiological criteria, Ninhydrin positive substances, Osmotic concentration, Sea Grant Program.

Present techniques for monitoring pollution in aquatic environments rely heavily upon measuring the concentration of a given pollutant. In marine environments, because of the possibility of synergistic effects brought about by the ionic composition of the medium, physiological criteria would be a much more sensitive measure of pollution effects than a determination of the pollutant itself. Selected serum constituents of the blue crab, Callinectes sapidus, subjected to natural stresses (red tide and holding) and pollution related stresses (DDT and thermal shock) were compared to 'baseline' concentrations of the same constituents in crabs from unstressed environments. Glucose in new year class females and serum protein in both males and females were higher in red tide stressed crabs. Protein and total osmotic concentration were lower in DDT stressed crabs. Thermal stress resulted in higher total ninhydrin positive substances, total osmotic concentration and glucose and lower chloride in female crabs. Comparing serum constituents of animals offers promise as a tool for assessing the effects of pollutants on marine animals and for monitoring pollution effects in natural environments. (NOAA)
W75-09269

IGOSS MARINE POLLUTION MONITORING PILOT PROJECT,
National Oceanic and Atmospheric Administration, Rockville, Md.
R. A. Zachariason.
Mariners Weather Log, Vol 18, No 6, p 370-373, November 1974. 4 fig, 1 tab, 3 ref.

Descriptors: *Oil spills, *Oil pollution, *Monitoring, *Oceans, Pollutants, Flotsam, Plastics, Environmental control, Beaches, Organic compounds, Pollutant identification.
Identifiers: *Monitoring pollution, *Marine pollution, Oil slicks, Ocean environments, Tar balls, Floating particulates, Global scale, *Petroleum hydrocarbons.

A worldwide system for monitoring petroleum in the oceans is scheduled to begin in January 1975. This Pilot Project is aimed toward the development of organizational machinery and experience needed in the formulation of any coordinated exercise on marine pollution monitoring. The selected vehicle for the project is petroleum-derived oils, since currently they are being monitored to some degree by various national authorities and within several regional frameworks. The following pollutant types will be included: (1) Oil slicks and other floating pollutants; (2) Floating particulate petroleum residues or 'tar balls'; (3) Tar on beaches; and (4) Dissolved/dispersed petroleum hydrocarbons in the surface waters (1 m; additional depths are optional) of the ocean. The basic components of the Pilot Project are outlined. (NOAA)
W75-09280

IN SITU COLOUR MEASUREMENTS ON THE GREAT LAKES,
Canada Centre for Inland Waters, Burlington (Ontario).
K. P. B. Thomson, and J. Jerome.
Scientific Series, No 51, 8 p, 1975. 3 fig, 5 tab, 10 ref.

Descriptors: *Color, *Productivity, Lake Ontario, Algae, Lake Superior, Sediment load, Effluents, Upwelling, Limnology, Measurements, Analytical techniques, Water analysis, Optical properties.
Identifiers: Spectral irradiance, Downwelling.

Measurement of upwelling and downwelling spectral irradiance have been used to compute in situ color for Lakes Ontario and Superior. The computations of the color are based on the CIE (Committee on Colorimetry, 1953) chromaticity system. Tristimulus values for a network of stations and a number of different time periods are analysed with reference to limnological parameters. The analysis shows that suspended inorganic material and biological activity affect the in situ color in characteristic ways. In effect, three principal water regimes can be identified by their characteristic or dominant wavelength. These are clear water with little dissolved or suspended substances, water that is biologically productive, and water with heavy sediment loading. The in situ color also indicates basic differences between the two lakes that are related to their productivity. (Envir-Canada)
W75-09294

INTERLABORATORY QUALITY CONTROL STUDY NO 9, COPPER, CADMIUM, ALUMINUM, STRONTIUM AND MERCURY,
Canada Centre for Inland Waters, Burlington (Ontario).
D. J. McGirr, and R. W. Wales.
Report Series No 34, 13 p, 1975. 10 tab, 16 ref, 1 append.

Descriptors: *Cations, *Water analysis, *Trace elements, Water quality, Cadmium, Copper, Aluminum, Strontium, Mercury, Water pollution, Methodology.
Identifiers: *Atomic absorption, Manual methods, Precision, metals.

Twenty-six laboratories participated in a quality control study on the determination of copper, cadmium, aluminum, strontium and mercury in water. Copper and cadmium are determined frequently by most participants in this study, and results for these two metals were satisfactory as for a previous study using standard atomic absorption techniques. Precision for aluminum was fair, with a non-zero blank reading, likely picked up from the glassware. Most participants determine aluminum rarely; some had switched methods recently. Satisfactory results for strontium were obtained by seven laboratories using atomic absorption and by five laboratories using flame emission spectroscopy. The automated method used by the Water Quality Branch (WQB) demonstrated greatly improved precision and accuracy for mercury compared to a previous study, whereas the variety of manual methods used produced many outliers. (Envir-Canada)
W75-09295

INTERLABORATORY QUALITY CONTROL STUDY NO 10, TURBUDITY AND FILTERABLE AND NONFILTERABLE RESIDUE,
Canada Centre for Inland Waters, Burlington (Ontario).
D. J. McGirr.
Report Series No 37, 10 p. 4 fig, 6 tab, 14 ref.

Descriptors: *Turbidity, *Residues, Suspended load, Suspended solids, Water quality, Water analysis, Sewage, Sludge.
Identifiers: Nonfilterable residue, Filterable residue.

The turbidity and filterable and nonfilterable residue determinations were evaluated by means of an interlaboratory study and by additional studies on storage stability and reproducibility conducted at the Canada Centre for Inland Waters. Although none of these tests can be considered very precise, reasonably useful data can be obtained from the use of the appropriate test under carefully controlled conditions. Turbudity measured by the turbidimeter is shown to be the most precise measurement of suspended matter at the levels normally encountered in natural waters, and it is the preferred test if the analysis is done immediately. The most serious problem affecting turbidity measurements is limited storage stability. In the case of samples which have to be shipped to the laboratory, the negative bias generally introduced by storage instability can be at least partly overcome by shaking the samples very vigorously before the determination. Preservatives such as mercuric chloride are of no value. Nonfilterable residue is less affected by storage instability but is less precise than turbidity at all levels tested and has a detection limit of the order of 2 mg/l assuming that a sample of 100 ml to 250 ml is used. Although the fixed filterable residue and fixed nonfilterable residue determinations may be useful for sewage and sludge samples, they contributed little useful additional information for natural waters. It is suggested that they could be eliminated from Water Quality Branch (WQB) tests. (Envir-Canada)
W75-09296

United States Patent 3,831,432. Issued August 27, 1974, Official Gazette of the United States Patent Office, Vol 925, No 4, p 1153, August 1974. 1 fig.

Descriptors: *Patents, *Monitoring, Control systems, Equipment, Environmental control, Adsorption, *Pollutant identification.
Identifiers: Sensors.

A monitoring system for determining the presence and concentration of selected substances in an environment includes a set of sensors providing outputs responsive to substances adsorbed from the environment. One of the sensors has a output differing from the others in the set in its response to at least one monitored substance. The sensors consist of adsorption field effect transistors respectively having chemically specific films in the gate region for the capability of preferential adsorption of preselected substances. (Leibowitz-FIRL)
W75-09305

EXHAUSTIVE ELECTROLYSIS METHOD FOR DETERMINATION OF OXYGEN DEMAND,
Honeywell, Inc., Minneapolis, Minn. (assignee).
J. P. Cummings.
United States Patent 3,857,761. Issued December 31, 1974. Official Gazette of the United States Patent Office, Vol 929, No 5, p 2044, December, 1974. 1 fig.

Descriptors: *Patents, *Electrolysis, Cathodes, Anodes, Analytical techniques, Samples, Liquids, Membranes, *Oxygen demand, *Pollutant identification.

An exhaustive electrolysis method for determination of oxygen demand consists of placing an aqueous sample into an electrolytic cell having a pair of electrodes in contact with the sample. This includes an anode within an anode compartment, a cathode remote from the anode compartment, and an ion permeable membrane in contact with the sample to provide an electrolytic bridge between the anode and the cathode. An alkali metal hydroxide is added to the sample until the pH of the sample is greater than ten. An electrolyzing current is then applied across the electrodes at a potential suitable for the generation of oxygen along the sample contacting surface of the anode, until the sample is electro-inactive and maintains a substantially constant temperature. Finally, measurement is made of the partial pressure of oxygen evolved from the anode-sample interface during the period when the sample is substantially electro-inactive. (Prague-FIRL)
W75-09311

MEASURE EFFLUENT COD WITH RAPID PERMANGANATE TEST,
Saskatchewan Univ., Saskatoon.
M. S. Nasr, and D. G. MacDonald.
Pulp and Paper Canada, Vol 76, No 3, p 91-93, (T87-89), March 1975. 4 fig, 11 ref.

Descriptors: *Bleaching wastes, *Chemical oxygen demand, *Pulp wastes, *Indicators, Industrial wastes, Wastes, Water pollution sources, Chemical analysis, Effluents, Water pollution, Water pollution control, Alkalinity, Catalysts, Oxidation, Canada, *Pollutant identification.
Identifiers: *Permanganate number, Alkaline extraction, Dichromates, Manganese sulfate.

The permanganate number method used to determine the relative hardness (lignin content) of pulp can be modified to determine the COD of effluents produced by the pulpaper industry. The test takes about 10 min to complete, and the results can be reported as a Permanganate Value (PV) or as ppm of COD if a correlation with the standard dichromate method is established. Effluent from the caustic extraction stage of a bleach plant was used to study the parameters affecting the permanganate method, and modifications were made. More sulfuric acid than is normally used was added because of the alkalinity of the effluent, and manganese sulfate was added to catalyze the reaction. This study showed a typical correlation between the permanganate number and the COD for the caustic extraction effluent. When the COD of the effluent is changed by dilution, a straight-line relationship through the origin exists. COD changes due to treatment of the effluent (e.g., lime treatment) results in a straightline relationship, but with the COD non-zero when the PV is zero, because the permanganate does not oxidize all of the organic compounds that the dichromate does. For this reason, it is necessary to correlate the PV with the dichromate method for each application. Once the correlation is established, the permanganate method is a simpler and faster method of measuring COD. (Sykes-IPC)
W75-09344

5B. Sources Of Pollution

SOME FACTORS AFFECTING THE SURVIVAL OF COLIFORM BACTERIA IN SEAWATER (IN JAPANESE),
Tokai Univ., Tokyo (Japan). Coll. of Marine Science Technology.
For primary bibliographic entry see Field 5C.
W75-08884

OCCURRENCE AND DETERMINATION OF INORGANIC POLLUTING AGENTS (IN GERMAN),
Munich Univ. (West Germany). Institut fuer Wasserchemie und Chemische Balneologie.
For primary bibliographic entry see Field 5A.
W75-08888

METALS AND METALLOIDS IN WATER: THEIR IMPORTANCE TO MAN (IN GERMAN),
Mainz Univ. (West Germany). Hygiene Institut.
For primary bibliographic entry see Field 5G.
W75-08890

WASTEWATER INFILTRATION NEAR THE CITY OF MOUNT SHASTA, SISKIYOU COUNTY, CALIFORNIA,
Geological Survey, Menlo Park, Calif.
G. L. Bertoldi.
Water-Resources Investigations 20-73, September 1973. 31 p, 7 fig, 6 tab, 5 ref, 2 append.

Descriptors: *Water pollution sources, *Sewage effluents, *Waste water disposal, Ponds, *Infiltration rates, Groundwater, Hydrogeology, *Path of pollutants, Seepage, Soil physical properties, Glacial aquifers, Water table, Groundwater movement, *California.
Identifiers: Mount Shasta(Calif), Lake Siskiyou area, Upper Sacramento River, Box Canyon Dam.

Disposal of waste discharged from the city of Mount Shasta, Calif., is by use of sewage-disposal ponds. The Siskiyou County Flood Control and Water Conservation District, under order from the California Regional Water Quality Control Board is required to stop discharging effluent from the ponds to the Sacramento River during the recreation season. Sewage discharge at the input to the disposal ponds is about three times the quantity that should be expected from a city the size of Mount Shasta. The input to the ponds probably includes a large quantity of groundwater leaking into the sewage system. The area where the ponds are located is underlain by glacial material containing several thin intercalated layers of nearly impermeable tuff. The layers of tuff, found from the surface downward, are barriers to vertical movement of water and prevent the disposal ponds from operating at the design level of efficiency. Infiltration rates, calculated and measured, at the existing ponds are about one-third the design capacity of the ponds. The first layer of tuff was found at depths ranging from 1.5 to 8 feet below land sur-

face and apparently is contiguous throughout the glacial material. (Woodward-USGS)
W75-08906

CONTENT OF THE TRACE ELEMENTS COPPER AND MANGANESE IN STREAM WATER, SOIL, AND PLANTS IN SOUTHERN UKRAINE, (IN RUSSIAN),
Odesskii Meditinskii Institut (USSR).
V. G. Kolesnikova, L. A. Kasatkina, O. P. Malakhova, V. I. Muzychenko, and D. M. Babov.
Gig Sanit. 38(3): 110-111, 1973.

Descriptors: *Copper, *Manganese, *Trace elements, *Soil chemical properties, Running waters, Soil-water-plant relationships, Crops, *Irrigation effects, Apples, Carrots, Potatoes.
Identifiers: Beets, Cabbage, Corn(Field), Grapes, Plants, *USSR(Ukraine).

Cu and Mn concentrations were determined in soil and in Dnestr stream water, USSR, used for irrigation and in plants (potatoes, beets, cabbage, carrots, corn, grapes, apples) of irrigated and unirrigated fields. Soil and water samples were obtained in the summer, autumn and spring over a 4 yr period. A photocolorimetric method was used. Cu concentration in crops from unirrigated soil was 1-1/2-2 times higher than in irrigated crops. Similar results were obtained for Cu concentrations in soil. Mn concentration in crops from irrigated and unirrigated soil did not vary significantly.--Copyright 1975, Biological Abstracts, Inc.
W75-08907

STUDY OF THE EFFECTIVENESS OF WATER TREATMENT PLANTS IN REMOVING BENZO(A)PYRENE, (IN RUSSIAN),
Institute of General and Municipal Hygiene, Moscow (USSR).
For primary bibliographic entry see Field 5D.
W75-08924

MERCURY IN WATER, A BIBLIOGRAPHY, VOLUME 2.
Office of Water Research and Technology, Washington, D.C.
For primary bibliographic entry see Field 5C.
W75-08934

SALT WATER DETECTION IN THE CIMARRON TERRACE, OKLAHOMA.
Oklahoma Water Resources Board, Oklahoma City.
For primary bibliographic entry see Field 5A.
W75-08936

RADIOECOLOGY OF BOMBAY HARBOR--A TIDAL ESTUARY,
Bhabha Atomic Research Centre, Bombay (India). Health Physics Div.
B. Patel, C. D. Mulay, and A. K. Ganguly.
Estuarine and Coastal Marine Science, Vol 3, No 1, p 13-42, January 1975. 10 fig, 13 tab, 61 ref.

Descriptors: *Radioecology, *Radioactive waste disposal, *Nuclear wastes, *Radioactivity, *Environmental effects, Waste disposal, Radioactive wastes, Chemical wastes, *Radioisotopes, Ecology, Biology, Estuaries, Fish, Estuarine environment, Plankton, Aquatic habitats, Water pollution effects, Aquatic environment, Sediments, Biota, *Path of pollutants.
Identifiers: *Bombay Harbor(India).

Low level liquid radioactive waste from nuclear facilities at Bhabha Atomic Research Centre, Bombay, are released into Bombay harbor after monitoring and dilution. The interactions of gamma-emitting fission product nuclides, especially cesium-137, with sedimentary particles and biota were studied during 1968-1971. Cesium-137 is first scavenged by the sedimentary particles, followed by cerium-144 and ruthenium-106. Zirconium/niobium-95, though present in the effluent, was not sorbed. Cesium-137 was distributed throughout the harbor, whereas cerium and ruthenium deposition were limited to a few stations off Trombay coast. Maximum deposition of activity was found in the upper 5-cm layer of the sediment column; decreasing thereafter either intermittently or exponentially with depth. The occurrence of artificial radioactivity in fish and shellfish of economic importance in 1965 before regular discharge began was below detection limit. Analysis since then showed accumulation of cesium-137 only. The absolute concentration as such, however, varied from species to species. The radiation dose through the contaminated environment to the benthic communities was far below the limits required to produce any detectable radiation damage. The radiation dose to fishermen, both internally through the consumption of contaminated marine products and externally through fishing over the contaminated bed, was also well below the permissible dose limit. (Henley-ISWS)
W75-08964

NITRIFICATION IN THE SCHELDT ESTUARY (BELGIUM AND THE NETHERLANDS),
Brussels Univ. (Belgium). Laboratorium voor Ekologie en Systematiek.
G. Billen.
Estuarine and Coastal Marine Science, Vol 3, No 1, p 79-89, January 1975. 6 fig, 28 ref.

Descriptors: *Nitrification, *Nitrogen cycle, *Bacteria, *Organic matter, *Nitrogen, Ammonium, Nitrates, Nitrites, Nitrogen compounds, Water quality, Fungi, Microorganisms, Sediments, Analytical techniques, Hydrogen ion concentration, Oxidation-reduction potential, Inorganie compounds, Estuaries.
Identifiers: *Scheldt Estuary(Belgium-The Netherlands), Redox potential.

Nitrification and repartition of nitrifying bacteria were investigated in the autoepuration zone of the Scheldt Estuary. Measurements of vertical profiles of nitrate and nitrite concentration in the interstitial water of sediments showed that nitrification in sediments is very low, implying that most of the nitrate and nitrite production occurs in the water of the river itself. Nitrifying bacteria, probably of terresterial origin, are present throughout the water along a longitudinal profile of the estuary, with a regular decrease in numbers downstream. However, nitrification occurs only in a zone of favorable oxidation-reduction conditions, which coincides with the thermodynamic stability fields of nitrate and nitrite with respect to ammonium. (Henley-ISWS)
W75-08966

OBSERVATIONS OF BOTTOM-WATER FLUSHING IN A FJORD-LIKE ESTUARY,
National Science Foundation, Washington, D.C. Oceanography Section.
For primary bibliographic entry see Field 2L.
W75-08967

AN EMPIRICAL METHOD OF ESTIMATING THE RETENTION OF PHOSPHORUS IN LAKES,
Toronto Univ. (Ontario). Dept. of Zoology.
W. B. Kirchner, and P. J. Dillon.
Water Resources Research, Vol 11, No 1, p 182-183, February 1975. 1 fig, 1 tab, 7 ref.

Descriptors: *Nutrients, *Phosphorus, *Model studies, *Lakes, Water balance, Surface waters, Hydrologic systems, *Canada, *Estimating.

The relationship between phosphorus retention and several other lake and watershed parameters was examined for 15 Canadian lakes. Multiple linear regressions were first attempted, but the model developed from the best correlation would

PACIFIC NORTHWEST LABORATORY ANNUAL REPORT FOR 1973 TO THE USAEC DIVISION OF BIOMEDICAL AND ENVIRONMENTAL RESEARCH, PART 3 ATMOSPHERIC SCIENCES.
Battelle-Pacific Northwest Labs., Richland, Wash.
For primary bibliographic entry see Field 5A.
W75-09069

CHARACTERIZATION OF SOURCES AND AMBIENT POLLUTANTS.
Battelle-Pacific Northwest Labs., Richland, Wash.
For primary bibliographic entry see Field 5A.
W75-09070

TRANSPORT, DIFFUSION, AND TURBULENCE.
Battelle-Pacific Northwest Labs., Richland, Wash.
For primary bibliographic entry see Field 5A.
W75-09071

ATMOSPHERIC TRANSFORMATION PROCESSES.
Battelle-Pacific Northwest Labs., Richland, Wash.
For primary bibliographic entry see Field 5A.
W75-09072

REMOVAL AND RESUSPENSION PROCESSES - DRY DEPOSITION OF PARTICLES.
Battelle-Pacific Northwest Labs., Richland, Wash.
For primary bibliographic entry see Field 5A.
W75-09074

REMOVAL AND RESUSPENSION PROCESSES - RESUSPENSION OF PARTICLES.
Battelle-Pacific Northwest Labs., Richland, Wash.
For primary bibliographic entry see Field 5A.
W75-09075

SPECIAL STUDIES - COOLING TOWER RESEARCH - BIOMETEOROLOGY.
Battelle-Pacific Northwest Labs., Richland, Wash.
For primary bibliographic entry see Field 5A.
W75-09076

MODEL FOR ACCUMULATION OF METHYL MERCURY IN NORTHERN PIKE ESOX LUCIUS,
Institute for Water and Air Pollution Research, Stockholm (Sweden).
T. Fagerstrom, B. Asell, and A. Jernelov.
Oikos, Vol 25, No 1, p 14-20, 1974. 1 fig, 35 ref.

Descriptors: *Mercury, *Mathematical Models, *Pikes, *Model studies, Bioassay, Heavy metals, Absorption, Metabolism, Statistical models, Size, Animal growth, Growth rate, Food chains, Path of pollutants, Water pollution effects.
Identifiers: *Methyl mercury, *Bioaccumulation, *Esox lucius, Tissue analysis, Body burden.

A compartmental model of mercury residue accumulation in individual fishes is presented. The model assumes a single residue pool that acquires methyl mercury from respired water and with the diet. Uptake and clearance of residue are treated as functions of metabolic rate, which is itself size-dependent. The parameters for the model are estimated from a release-recapture experiment and from Literature data, and the solutions produced by the model when using these estimates are compared with real-world data where the latter set of data is independent of the set that was used for parameter estimation. The correspondence between the calculated concentration of methyl mercury in lateral muscle tissue and empirically observed values is acceptable though the calculated values in the lower weight range are somewhat high. The possibility that the model may apply to other substances is discussed. (Katz)
W75-09145

EXPERIMENTAL STUDIES ON THE EFFECTS OF COPPER ON A MARINE FOOD CHAIN,
Marine Lab., Aberdeen (Scotland).
For primary bibliographic entry see Field 5C.
W75-09146

PRESENCE OF LIPID-SOLUBLE CHLORINATED HYDROCARBONS IN MARINE OILS,
Central Inst. for Industrial Research, Oslo (Norway).
For primary bibliographic entry see Field 5A.
W75-09147

THE USE OF ARTIFICIAL SUBSTRATES IN SAMPLING ESTUARINE BENTHOS,
York Univ., Downsview (Ontario). Dept. of Biology.
C. I. Goddard, M. H. Goodwin, and L. A. Greig.
21Transactions of the American Fisheries Society, Vol 104, No 1, p 50-52, 1975. 1 fig, 1 tab, 12 ref.

Descriptors: *Model studies, *Benthos, *Aquatic productivity, Aquatic animals, *Estuarine environment, *Biomass, Benthic fauna, Marine animals, Aquatic habitats, Aquatic environment, Estuaries, Scuba divers, Sediments, Detritus, Canada.
Identifiers: *St. Croix River(New Brunswick), *Artificial substrate, Species density, Placopeten magellanicus, Buccinum undatum, Strongylocentrotus droebachiensis, Cucumaria frondosa, Asterias vulgaris.

A comparison was made between density estimates of estuarine benthos based on artificial substrate sampling and direct observation by divers in St. Croix River estuary, New Brunswick. Of six species occurring in the sample area - giant scallop, waved whelk, sea urchin, sea cucumber, starfish and sea anemone, the latter four were collected on artificial substrates. Density of these four species was significantly higher on artificial substrates than on natural surfaces. Differences suggest that artificial substrates may preferentially sample certain portions of the fauna. (Katz)
W75-09149

SWEDISH PERSPECTIVES ON MERCURY POLLUTION,
Institute for Water and Air Pollution Research, Stockholm (Sweden). Dept. of Biology.
For primary bibliographic entry see Field 5C.
W75-09157

STUDIES ON THE CYTOLYTIC EFFECTS OF SEASTAR (MARTHASTERIAS GLACIALIS) SAPONINS AND SYNTHETIC SURFACTANTS IN THE PLAICE PLEURONECTES PLATESSA,
Institute of Marine Biochemistry, Aberdeen (Scotland).
For primary bibliographic entry see Field 5C.
W75-09161

TISSUE HYDROCARBON BURDEN OF MUSSELS AS POTENTIAL MONITOR OF ENVIRONMENTAL HYDROCARBON INSULT,
Naval Biomedical Research Lab., Oakland, Calif.
L. H. DiSalvo, H. E. Guard, and L. Hunter.
Environmental Science and Technology, Vol 9, No 3, p 247-251, March 1975. 4 fig, 3 tab, 12 ref.

Descriptors: *Bioindicators, *Mussels, *Monitoring, Indicators, Water quality, Analytical

techniques, Organic compounds, Invertebrates, Estuaries, Path of pollutants, *Oil, Pollutants, *California, Water pollution effects.
Identifiers: Mytilus edulis, Mytilus californianus, *Tissue analysis, Hydrocarbon burden, Bioaccumulation, *San Francisco Bay(Calif).

A simplified method for the analysis of total tissue hydrocarbon burden was used to measure hydrocarbon concentrations in the mussels Mytilus edulis and M. californianus as an indicator of chronic hydrocarbon insult. Mussels transferred from cleanwater stations to polluted water stations took up hydrocarbons, and when they were replaced in clean waters, their hydrocarbon content approached cleanwater baseline values. Mussels transferred from polluted water to clean water lost a minor fraction of their hydrocarbon burden over a 10-week period. The mussels were useful as systems monitors of chronic hydrocarbon pollution, although initial results obtained with other San Francisco invertebrates suggest that certain of these may also be of value as hydrocarbon monitors. (Katz)
W75-09163

TWO-DIMENSIONAL EXCESS TEMPERATURE MODEL FOR A THERMALLY LOADED STREAM,
Geological Survey, Bay Saint Louis, Miss.
D. P. Bauer, and N. Yotsukura.
Available from the National Technical Information Service, Springfield, Va. 22161, as PB-238 126, $5.25 in printed copy, $2.25 in microfiche. Computer Contribution, November 1974. 91 p, 2 fig.

Descriptors: *Thermal pollution, *Mathematical models, *Water temperature, Streams, Hydroelectric plants, Forecasting, *Path of pollutants, Dispersion, Diffusion, Computer models, Analytical techniques.
Identifiers: Excess temperature, Convective diffusion.

A digital model which calculates distribution of excess temperature (temperature in excess of natural water temperature) or soluble contaminant concentration in a steady flow natural stream is described. The program is based on approximate solutions to a convective diffusion equation combined with an exponential decay equation. The program is useful for prediction purposes in a stream region where the waste is uniformly mixed with depth while still markedly nonuniform in the transverse and longitudinal directions. (Woodard-USGS)
W75-09174

SALT-BALANCE STUDY OF PAUBA VALLEY, UPPER SANTA MARGARITA RIVER AREA, RIVERSIDE COUNTY, CALIFORNIA,
Geological Survey, Menlo Park, Calif.
J. W. Warner.
Availabile from the National Technical Information Service, Springfield, Va. 22161, as PB-242 252, $3.75 in printed copy, $2.25 in microfiche. Water-Resources Investigations 43-74, February 1975. 44 p, 3 fig, 14 tab, 26 ref, 4 append.

Descriptors: *Salt balance, *Irrigation, *Waste water disposal, *Water pollution, Water quality, Saline water, Salinity, Groundwater, Hydrogeology, Groundwater movement, *California, Sewage disposal.
Identifiers: *Pauba Valley(Calif).

The salt balance was calculated in the groundwater in the shallow aquifer in Pauba Valley, Calif., in two steps: (1) solution of the hydrologic-balance equation; and (2) solution of the salt-balance equation. Solution of these equations yielded a negative salt balance of about 500 tons of salt per year. Local areas within the valley may be accumulating salt in the groundwater. The salt balance was calculated for the 23-year time period from 1950 through 1972. Proposed sewage-disposal ponds in Pauba Valley should not cause any major effects on the salt balance of the shallow aquifer. Disposal of the sewage effluent either by irrigation or by direct recharge to the groundwater should be feasible. If the sewage effluent is used to irrigate crops, more salt will be retained within the system than would be retained by disposal of the effluent by direct recharge. The salt load on the hydrologic system from disposal of sewage effluent will be partly reduced by the increase in discharge out of the groundwater system and the salt associated with it. (Knapp-USGS)
W75-09177

UPWARD MIGRATION OF DEEP-WELL WASTE INJECTION FLUIDS IN FLORIDAN AQUIFER, SOUTH FLORIDA,
Geological Survey, Tallahassee, Fla.
M. I. Kaufman, and D. J. McKenzie.
Available from Superintendant of Documents, US Government Printing Office, Washington, DC 20402, for $3.15 in paper copy, $2.25 in microfiche. Journal of Research of the US Geological Survey Vol 3, No 3, p 261-271, May-June 1975. 11 fig, 3 tab, 13 ref.

Descriptors: *Waste disposal wells, *Injection wells, *Geochemistry, *Path of pollutants, *Florida, Water pollution sources, Groundwater movement, Aquifer characteristics, Industrial wastes, Hydrogeology, Water levels, Sampling, Chemical analysis, Hydrologic data, Chemical reactions, Chemical properties, Water quality.
Identifiers: *Lake Okeechobee area(Fla).

Geochemical data from an industrial deep-well waste injection system southeast of Lake Okeechobee, Fla., indicate a decrease in sulfate concentration concomitant with an increase in hydrogen sulfide concentration, a result of oxidation of injected organic waste by anaerobic bacteria. Subtle decreases in the sulfate-chloride ratio suggest that the waste migrated upward to a shallow monitor well about 27 months after waste injection began and again within 15 months of the resumption of waste injection after the injection well was deepened. The possibility of a hydraulic connection between the injection zone and overlying monitoring zone is implied. The decrease in the sulfate-chloride ratio appears to be a sensitive indicator of waste migration. Potential conflicts exist in the use of the Floridan aquifer for waste disposal and subsequent use as a natural resource. (Woodward-USGS)
W75-09190

PRELIMINARY FINDINGS OF A LEACHATE STUDY ON TWO LANDFILLS IN SUFFOLK COUNTY, NEW YORK,
Geological Survey, Mineola, N.Y.
G. E. Kimmel, and O. C. Braids.
Journal available from Sup Doc, U.S. Gov't. Print. Off. 20402 for $3.15. Journal of Research of the US Geological Survey, Vol 3, No 3, p 273-280, May-June 1975. 5 fig, 7 ref.

Descriptors: *Landfills, *Water quality, *Path of pollutants, *Groundwater movement, *Solid wastes, *New York, Water pollution sources, Geochemistry, Chemical reactions, Soil properties, Leachate, Infiltration, Soil chemistry, Sampling, Hydrologic data, Chemical analysis.
Identifiers: Babylon(NY), Islip(NY).

Plumes of leachate-enriched groundwater extend 10,600 and 5,000 ft downgradient from landfills in the towns of Babylon and Islip, N.Y., respectively, and extend vertically beneath the landfills to the base of the upper glacial aquifer, whose thickness ranges from 71 to 77 ft at the Babylon site and is 170 ft at the Islip site. The Babylon and Islip landfills were started in 1947 and 1933, respectively. The quantities of groundwater in the plumes are 2 billion gal at Babylon and 1 billion gal at Islip. Differences in quantity of water in the

stationary-state quality profile under a wide variation of conditions were investigated. Results made it possible to estimate the effective longitudinal dispersion coefficient using time-varying salinity data at several gaging stations in the Upper Delaware Estuary System. The methodology was put into the form of a distributed parameter identification scheme.
W75-09233

STUDIES OF THE BEHAVIOR OF HEAVY PARTICLES IN A TURBULENT FLUID FLOW,
Illinois Univ., Urbana. Nuclear Engineering Lab.
For primary bibliographic entry see Field 8B.
W75-09237

LINEARIZED NON-STOKESIAN DRAG IN TURBULENT FLOW,
Illinois Univ., Urbana. Nuclear Engineering Lab.
For primary bibliographic entry see Field 8B.
W75-09238

ENVIRONMENTAL STUDY OF THE MARINE ENVIRONMENT NEAR NOME, ALASKA,
Alaska Univ., College. Inst. of Marine Science.
For primary bibliographic entry see Field 2L.
W75-09275

ASSESSMENT OF OFFSHORE DUMPING; TECHNICAL BACKGROUND: PHYSICAL OCEANOGRAPHY, GEOLOGICAL OCEANOGRAPHY, CHEMICAL OCEANOGRAPHY.
National Oceanic and Atmospheric Administration, Boulder, Colo. Environmental Research Labs.
NOAA Technical Memorandum ERL MESA-1, April 1975. 83 p, 15 ref. Robert L. Charnell (Ed).

Descriptors: *Waste disposal, *Oceanography, *Ocean currents, Ocean circulation, Marine geology, Chemistry, Sludge disposal, Sedimentation, Sewage sludge, Sampling, New York.
Identifiers: *New York Bight, Water columns, ERTS data.

Physical, geographical, and chemical oceanographic features of the New York Bight and their relationship to waste and sewage disposal in the area are examined. The investigation includes studies of ocean currents, sea floor topography, sedimentation, methods of sewage disposal, and the chemical composition of sewage. Data from sampling in the area are presented. (NOAA)
W75-09278

DISPERSION OF GRANULAR MATERIAL DUMPED IN DEEP WATER,
Canada Centre for Inland Waters, Burlington (Ontario).
B. G. Krishnappan.
Scientific Series No 55, 114 p, 1975, 9 fig, 1 tab, 1 append.

Descriptors: *Dispersion, *Dredging, *Entrainment, Waste dumps, Sludge, Settling velocity, Deep water, Physical properties, Particle size, Spoil banks.
Identifiers: *Granular material, Lake dumping, Ocean dumping.

The motion of dredged material when dumped near the surface of deep water is formulated using the principle of superposition. The dredged material is considered to consist of various fractions of uniform-size particles and each fraction exerts an influence on the total behaviour of the dredged material in the same proportion as its negative buoyancy. The behaviour of uniform-size particles has been formulated using the theory of dimensions and laboratory experiments. The results show that the motion of the particles can be treated in two distinct phases, namely, the initial 'entrainment' phase and the final 'settling' phase. During the entrainment phase, the size of the 'cloud' grows owing to the incorporation of external fluid, while the vertical downward velocity diminishes. During the settling phase, when the vertical downward velocity is the same as the fall velocity of the individual solid particles constituting the cloud, the increase in the cloud size is due solely to ambient turbulence. The method developed permits the evaluation of vertical height and horizontal size of the 'mound' formed by the deposition of the dredged material at the bottom of deep water. It also indicates how the above characteristics of the mound depend on the volume of the dump, the size distribution of the dredged material and height of the deep water, therby providing guidance for the selection of optimum dump size and the location for dispoal of the dredged material. (Envir-Canada)
W75-09290

AN ANALYSIS OF THE DYNAMICS OF DDT IN MARINE SEDIMENTS,
Stanford Univ., Pacific Grove, Calif. Hopkins Marine Station.
J. H. Phillips, E. E. Haderlie, and W. L. Lee.
Available from the National Technical Information Service, Springfield, Va 22161 as PB-238 511, $5.25 in paper copy, $2.25 in microfiche. Environmental Protection Agency, Report EPA-660/3-75-013, May 1975. 98 p, 8 fig, 24 tab, 11 ref.

Descriptors: Degradation, *DDT, DDD, DDE, Coasts, Assay, Pollution, Bays, *California, Nitrates, *Sediments, *Analytical techniques, *Microbial degradation, *Chemical degradation, Pesticide residues, Chlorinated hydrocarbon pesticides, Organic pesticides, Aerobic conditions.
Identifiers: Rates of change, *Monterey Bay(Calif).

The concentrations of DDT, DDD and DDE were measured in sediments at 57 stations in Monterey Bay on the Central California coast during 1970-1971. Mean concentrations in parts per billion were DDT 3.1, DDD 2.3, and DDE 5.4. During 1973 nineteen of the original stations were sampled. Mean concentrations were DDT 15.5, DDD 2.3, and DDE 5.4 ppb. Two approaches to the estimation of annual system rates for input, I, output, 0, decay, D, and internal translocation, T sub I and T sub 0 expressed as decimal fractions of existing concentrations were developed, and fraction programs that permit rapid estimations were written. The mean annual rates in South Monterey Bay obtained were for DDT, I + 1.30, O 0.59, 0 -0.036 T sub I and T sub 0 plus or minus 0.80 with a residence time of 11 years and life time of 29 years. An I of 1.30 means the amount of input is 130% of the existing concentration per year. Rates for DDD were, I +0.25, 0 -0.11, D -0.025, T sub I and T sub 0 plus or minus 0.20 with residence time of 7 years and life time of 44 years. Rates for DDE were I +0.28, O 0.10, D -0.027, T sub 0 and T sub I plus or minus 0.22 with residence time of 8 years and life time of 39 years. Laboratory assays were developed to determine the relative rate of decomposition in sediment under conditions selective for various physiologically different kinds of microorganisms. Decay under aerobic conditions was greater than under anaerobic conditios. Nitrate increased the rate of decomposition under anaerobic conditions. The Q10 for decay was 2.5 (EPA)
W75-09300

ASBESTOS IN POTABLE WATER SUPPLIES,
Johns-Manville Sales Corp., Denver, Colo. Public Water Pipe Div.
For primary bibliographic entry see Field 5A.
W75-09302

THE STUDY ON THE AQUATIC INSECT FAUNA OF THE MATSUKAWA AND YONAKO RIVERS (MINERAL ACID POLLUTED RIVER), (IN JAPANESE),
Rissho Women's Coll., Koshigaya (Japan).
Y. Ide.

Bull Inst Nat Educ Shiga Heights, 10 p, 11-24, 1971. Illus.

Descriptors: Asia, *Rivers, *Insects, Water quality, *Acidic water, *Aquatic insects, Aquatic populations, Water pollution sources.
Identifiers: Ephemeroptera, *Japan, Matsukawa River, Protonemoura, Trichoptera, Yonako River.

Relations between the water quality and the aquatic insects fauna were investigated at 24 places: 15 strongly acidic places along the Matsukawa and Yonago Rivers (Japan) and 9 neutral areas along their tributaries. Only 8 spp. were found at the 15 acidic sites while 40 were found at the 9 neutral sites. Water of the acidic places contained significant amounts of Fe++, Fe+++ and SO4--; especially the concentration of SO4-- being from 49 ppm (lowest)-87 ppm (highest). At the acidic sites the dominant species of aquatic insects was Protonemoura spp. Ephemeroptera spp. were rare at the acidic places. At the neutral places most of the dominant species were those of Trichoptera or Ephemeroptera. When the percentages of appearance at the 90% confidence level of the main aquatic insects were put in order of dominancy in a table or a graph, if a smooth gradually decreasing curve was obtained, the river would be normal and clean. If the curve was of the type decreasing sharply between the 1st and 2nd dominant species, the river would be somewhat abnormal. The all acidic sites of the rivers investigated belonged to this type. When the aquatic insects were classified by order to obtain a species distribution table, if Trichoptera or Ephemeroptera were most numerous, the area of river would be normal and clean. The 9 neutral sites of the rivers investigated belonged to this type.--Copyright 1973, Biological Abstracts, Inc.
W75-09316

PLANKTON, CHEMISTRY, AND PHYSICS OF LAKES IN THE CHURCHILL FALLS REGION OF LABRADOR,
Waterloo Univ. (Ontario). Dept. of Biology.
For primary bibliographic entry see Field 2H.
W75-09317

MIXING ZONE STUDIES OF THE WASTE WATER DISCHARGE FROM THE CONSOLIDATED PAPER COMPANY INTO THE WISCONSIN RIVER AT WISCONSIN RAPIDS, WISCONSIN,
Wisconsin Univ., Madison. Dept. of Civil and Environmental Engineering.
J. A. Hoopes, D.-S. Wu, and R. Ganatra.
Available from the National Technical Information Service, Springfield, Va 22161 as N74-26871, $4.25 in paper copy, $2.25 in microfiche. Report of 1969 Summer Field Surveys to Wisconsin, Dept. of Natural Resources and National Aeronautics and Space Administration, DNR, March 1973. 24 fig, 2 tab, 14 ref.

Descriptors: *Pulp wastes, *Mixing, *Waste dilution, Rivers, *Industrial wastes, Wastes, Water pollution sources, Wisconsin, On-site investigations, Effluents, Dispersion, Water pollution, Temperature, Velocity, River flow, Laboratory tests, Mathematical models, Outlets, Buoyancy, *Path of pollutants.
Identifiers: *Wisconsin River(Wis).

Consolidated Paper Company discharges effluent from its Wisconsin Rapids kraft pulp mill into the Wisconsin River. A field survey was conducted on September 12, 1969, of the effluent concentration distributions in the river. Effluent concentrations were determined from measurements of the temperature distribution; measurements of the velocity distribution in the vicinity of the outfall were also made. Horizontal and vertical concentration patterns of the waste discharge, developed from the data, are analyzed and compared with the results of laboratory experiments and of several mathematical models to determine the macroscopic characteristics and relations governing the effluent spreading and dilution for the effluent discharge, river and weather conditions during the survey. These characteristics include the centerline concentration variation, the centerline trajectory, and the lateral and vertical spreads of the effluent discharge. Due to limitations in the extent of the field observations, the analysis and comparison of the measurements is limited to the region within about 300 ft from the outfall. The effects of outfall submergence, of buoyance and momentum of the effluent, and of the pattern and magnitude of river currents on these characteristics are discussed. Finally, using the field observations, with results from the laboratory experiments and mathematical models, the extent and shape of the mixing zone is estimated for the effluent and river conditions on September 12, 1969. (Witt-IPC)
W75-09338

THE BOD AND TOXICITY OF EFFLUENTS FROM SULFITE PULPING FOR NEWSPRINT,
Pulp and Paper Research Inst. of Canada, Pointe Claire (Quebec).
G. J. Kubes, and A. Wong.
Preprint Canadian Pulp and Paper Association, Annual Meeting (Montreal), 1975, p A149-153. 7 fig, 5 ref, 9 tab.

Descriptors: *Pulp wastes, *Sulfite liquors, *Toxicity, *Biochemical oxygen demand, Industrial wastes, Water pollution sources, Foreign research, Foreign countries, Canada, Legislation, Laboratory tests, Effluents, Organic loading.
Identifiers: Pulp yield, Sulfite mills, High-yield pulps, Newsprint mills.

High-yield bisulfite pulp mills, which are integrated with many eastern Canadian newsprint operations, produce acutely toxic effluents with extremely high organic loadings. The results of an experimental program, sponsored by Environment Canada and done at the Pulp and Paper Research Institute of Canada, to measure the toxicity and 5-day BOD of laboratory-produced sodium-base bisulfite pulps in the yield range of 60 to 80% are reported. Significant reductions in toxicity and 5-day BOD loadings were achieved by increasing pulp yield, but it was not possible to comply with Environment Canada's regulation for a 5-day BOD of 37.5 kg/air-dry ton solely by increasing yield. The properties of pulps prepared during this investigation seem to indicate that 75% is the maximum yield at which pulps can be obtained that are compatible with the needs of newsprint production. Ultrahigh-yield bisulfite pulps (80% plus) with adequate strength properties may be obtained by refining at high consistency. (Witt-IPC)
W75-09348

5C. Effects Of Pollution

SOME FACTORS AFFECTING THE SURVIVAL OF COLIFORM BACTERIA IN SEAWATER (IN JAPANESE),
Tokai Univ., Tokyo (Japan). Coll. of Marine Science Technology.
K. Ogawa.
J Oceanogr Soc Jpn. 30(2): 54-60, Illus, 1974, English summary.

Descriptors: *Estuaries, Shores, Analysis, *Coliforms, Microorganisms, *Bacteria, *Sea water, Saline water, Nutrients, *E. coli, Seashores.

Experiments were carried out to explain why the number of coliform organisms decreased rapidly from estuaries to offshore, and also in deeper layers, and why the appearance of the coliform types varied. In natural seawater, results did not show that Escherichia coli was eliminated by the self-purification or anti-biosis action of seawater. This organism decreased mainly because of starvation. Although the decreasing rate of bacterial density was delayed to enriched seawater, addition of nutrients even at the time of bacterial extinction promoted the appearance of a variant form of this bacteria with floc formation. Flocculation of bacterial cells was influenced by quality and quantity of added nutrients. Temperature affected floc formation, but the appearance of a variant form in flocculated cells of E. coli was not affected by temperature. Flocculated particles of coliform bacteria were absorbed on suspended particles in seawater and precipitated rapidly. This phenomenon seems to be a cause of the rapid disappearance of coliform bacteria in coastal waters. In bottom deposits the coliform bacteria probably survive longer in physiologically variant forms when suitable nutrients were supplied.--Copyright 1975, Biological Abstracts, Inc.
W75-08884

CONTRIBUTION TO ECOLOGY OF INDIAN AQUATICS: V. SEASONAL CHANGES IN BIOMASS AND RATE OF PRODUCTION OF 2 PERENNIAL SUBMERGED MACROPHYTES (HYDRILLA VERTICILLATA ROYLE AND NAIAS GRAMINEA DEL) OF RAMGARH LAKE OF GORAKHPUR (INDIA),
Saint Andrew's Coll., Gorakhpur (India). Dept. of Botany.
A. B. Sinha, and R. Sahai.
Trop Ecol, Vol 14, No 1, p 19-28, 1973. Illus.

Descriptors: *Seasonal, Ecology, Lakes, *Biomass, *Production, Aquatic plants.
Identifiers: Gorakhpur, Hydrilla-verticillata, *India(Ramgarh Lake), *Macrophytes, Najas-graminea, Perennials, Photosynthesis, Rain.

The maximum above ground, photosynthetic biomass of H. verticillata and N. graminea was found during Aug. (4.52 plus or minus 0.34 and 4.60 plus or minus 0.22 mt(metric tons) dry matter/ha respectively). The maximum underground biomass of these plants was 0.81 plus or minus 0.12 and 0.95 plus or minus 0.12 mt dry matter/ha respectively. The percentage of ash in dry matter of their biomass was only 18.0 to 22.0%. Highest production rate was 39.6 dry matter/m2 day (H. verticillata) and 52.6 g dry matter/m2/day (Naias graminea) during July-Aug., just after a few heavy showers of rain. The net dry and organic matter production during 1 yr growth was found as 3.64 mt/ha and 3.28 mt/ha respectively in H. verticillata and 3.24 mt/ha and 3.00 mt/ha respectively in N. graminea (values are exclusive of losses suffered by these plants during their respiration, physical damage and decay of their older parts).--Copyright 1974, Biological Abstracts, Inc.
W75-08932

MERCURY IN WATER, A BIBLIOGRAPHY, VOLUME 2.
Office of Water Research and Technology, Washington, D.C.
Available from the National Technical Information Service, Springfield, Va. 22161, as PB-242 940, $9.25 in paper copy, $2.25 in microfiche. Water Resources Scientific Information Center, Report OWRT/WRSIC 75-203, May 1975, 308 p.

Descriptors: *Mercury, *Bibliographies, *Path of pollutants, Analytical techniques, Bioassay, Chemical analysis, Environmental effects, *Heavy metals, *Industrial wastes, *Pollutant identification, Toxicity, Trace elements, Water pollution effects.
Identifiers: Atomic absorption spectroscopy, Detection limits, *Mercury compounds.

This report, containing over 900 abstracts, is another in a series of planned bibliographies in water resources to be produced from the information base comprising SELECTED WATER RESOURCES ABSTRACTS (SWRA). Volume 1 (see W72-04440) covered material announced in SWRA from 1968 through 1971. At the time of

Descriptors: *Toxicity, *Water pollution sources, *Lakes, *Recreation wastes, Boating, *Oil wastes, Water pollution effects, Environmental effects, Adsorption, Evaporation, Sediments, Microbial degradation, Populations, Benthos, Chemical analysis, Bioassay, Organic compounds, Bibliographies.
Identifiers: *Exhaust emissions, Outboard engines, Lake George(NY).

A combined laboratory and field study has been made to determine the extent of pollution arising from the operating of two-cycle outboard engines in an oligotrophic/mesotrophic lake. The fate of the exhaust products discharged to a lake environment has been studied. Three bays having different boat usage were compared. Attempts have been made to examine the quantities of exhaust products found in the water column, the water surface, and in the bottom sediments. The role of such mechanisms as microbial decomposition, evaporation and adsorption has been studied. Results of these studies have shown very low levels of hydrocarbons, other than from natural sources, in sediments and the water column. Somewhat greater quantities were found in surface films. The microbiological studies and evaporative studies indicate that these mechanisms play a significant role in the dispersion of engine exhaust products. The relatively low levels of exhaust products found appear to be related to both purification mechanisms and to low levels of boating stress. Such indicators as surface film concentrations and threshold odor numbers follow boating usage patterns rather closely in the bays studied. (Katz)
W75-08950

MECHANISMS FOR DEEP WATER RENEWAL IN LAKE NITINAT, A PERMANENTLY ANOXIC FJORD,
Washington Univ., Seattle. Dept. of Oceanography.
For primary bibliographic entry see Field 2L.
W75-08969

A TEST OF A SIMPLE NUTRIENT BUDGET MODEL PREDICTING THE PHOSPHORUS CONCENTRATION IN LAKE WATER,
Toronto Univ. (Ontario). Dept. of Zoology.
P. J. Dillon, and F. H. Rigler.
Journal of the Fisheries Research Board of Canada, Vol 31, No 11, p 1771-1778, November 1974. 1 fig, 4 tab, 10 ref.

Descriptors: *Budgeting, *Nutrients, *Phosphorus, *Lakes, Eutrophication, Epilimnion, Hypolimnion, Chlorophyll, Lake morphometry, Mixing, Oligotrophy, Mesotrophy, Sedimentation rates, Stratification, Trophic level, Model studies, Retention, Water balance, Surface waters, *Canada.
Identifiers: *Haliburton-Kawartha region(Ontario).

The total phosphorus budgets for a number of lakes in the Haliburton-Kawartha region of southern Ontario were measured over a 20-month period. Phosphorus loadings, phosphorus retention coefficients, mean depths, and water replenishment coefficients were used to test a simple nutrient budget model similar to that proposed by Vollenweider (1969) to predict the total phosphorus concentration in lakes. Mean lake depths ranged from 0.73 to 27.2 meters and, except in the case of two very shallow lakes whose mean depths were less than 1 meter, the concentrations predicted by the model were very close to those measured at spring overturn. Additional data from the literature supported the belief that this model could be used effectively for oligotrophic and mesotrophic lakes. The model's value lies in the fact that quantitative changes in phosphorus loadings can be interpreted in terms of changes in phosphorus concentration, which in turn can be related to changes in parameters that reflect a lake's trophic state, such as summer concentration of chlorophyll alpha. (Harmeson-ISWS)
W75-08986

WATER QUALITY FEATURES OF THE UPPER ILLINOIS WATERWAY,
Illinois State Water Survey, Urbana. Water Quality Section.
For primary bibliographic entry see Field 5B.
W75-08991

SHORT-TERM VARIATIONS IN ESTIMATES OF CHLOROPHYLL ABUNDANCE,
National Marine Fisheries Service, Woods Hole, Mass. Northeast Fisheries Center.
For primary bibliographic entry see Field 2K.
W75-08992

ACTINOMYCETALES ISOLATED FROM SAINT LOUIS BAY, MISSISSIPPI,
Mississippi Univ., University. Dept. of Biology.
D. H. Roush.
Available from the National Technical Information Service, Springfield, Va. 22161, as COM-74-10042, $3.75 in paper copy, $2.25 in microfiche. Sea Grant Publication No MSGP-72-014, December 1972. 32 p, 1 fig, 7 tab, 24 ref.

Descriptors: *Bays, *Actinomycetes, *Soil bacteria, *Mississippi, Water pollution, Mycobacterium, Tributaries, Sediments, Surface waters, Gulf of Mexico, Laboratory tests, Salinity.
Identifiers: *Saint Louis Bay(Miss), Streptomyces, Micronomospora, Nocardia.

Samples taken from Saint Louis Bay were examined for the presence of actinomycetes immediately after collection and in the laboratory. The majority of organisms isolated were found in surface water, bottom water, and sediment or core samples. All actinomycetes isolated were of the genus Streptomyces. Eight different types were isolated on the original plates and four on secondary plates. Salinity and position of the collecting stations were the most influential factors affecting isolation. The higher the salinity, the lower the number of actinomycetes and the fewer types isolated. Only one isolate grew well in salt water media. There was a slight increase in the number of different types of actinomycetes from secondary samples in months with the lowest salinity. Micromonospora and Nocardia were not isolated. The distribution of actinomycetes indicated soil pollution from incoming freshwater sources. Water temperature had only a minor influence. A study should be made to determine whether the Streptomyces isolated were of soil or marine origin and what ecological role they play in the Saint Louis Bay environment. (Buchanan-Davidson--Wisconsin)
W75-08993

PUBLICATIONS AND REPORTS RESULTING FROM RESEARCH GRANTS FUNDED THROUGH COASTAL POLLUTION BRANCH, PACIFIC NORTHWEST ENVIRONMENTAL RESEARCH LABORATORY.
National Environmental Research Center, Corvallis, Oreg.
1974. 15 p, 156 ref.

Descriptors: *Publications, *Bibliographies, *Coasts, *Water pollution, Continental margin, Aerial photography, Photogrammetry, Algae, Dispersion, Estuaries, Heavy metals, Water pollution sources, Hydrodynamics, Marine bacteria, Marine fish, Oxygen demand, Phytoplankton, Inhibitors, Pollutants, Outlets, Turbulence, Diffusion, Waste disposal, Sediments, Tidal marshes, Dredging, Pesticide residues, Bacteria, Thermal pollution, Reservoirs, Outfall sewers, Baseline studies, Model studies, Fish diseases, Biocontrol, Benthos, Sulfides, Saline water intrusion.

A list of 156 extramural publications, indicating sources where they are available, relating to coastal pollution discuss various aspects of the subject. Among the areas discussed are aerial photography, algae, dispersion of pollutants, estuaries, floatables, heavy metals, hydrodynamics, marine bacteria, marine fish, mixing of stratified impoundments, oxygen consumption, phytoplankton growth inhibitors, various pollutants, including pesticide residues, submarine outfalls, turbulent diffusion of small particles, viruses, thermal pollution, saline water intrusion, waste disposal, and baseline studies. (Buchanan-Davidson--Wisconsin)
W75-08994

WATER QUALITY AND WASTE TREATMENT REQUIREMENTS ON THE UPPER HOLSTON RIVER, KINGSPORT, TENNESSEE, TO CHEROKEE RESERVOIR.
Environmental Protection Agency, Athens, Ga. Surveillance and Analysis Div.
Available from the National Technical Information Service, Springfield, Va. 22161, as PB-227 573, $5.75 in paper copy, $2.25 in microfiche. Technical Study TS-03-71-208-97, July 1972. 143 p, 11 fig, 14 tab, 2 ref, 8 append.

Descriptors: *Water quality, *Waste treatment, *Pollution abatement, *Reservoirs, Rivers, *Tennessee, Biochemical oxygen demand, Dissolved oxygen, Nitrogen compounds, Aquatic weed control, Hydroelectric plants, Cooling water, Flow augmentation, Nutrient removal, Water pollution sources, Thermal pollution, Flow rates, Flow control, Reservoir releases, Tennessee Valley Authority.
Identifiers: *Holston River(Tenn), *Cherokee Reservoir(Tenn), Kingsport(Tenn).

Wastes with approximately 137,500 pounds/day of 5-day BOD were discharged into the Holston River near Kingsport, Tennessee. The ultimate oxygen demand from nitrification of total Kjeldahl nitrogen was 84,000 pounds. Sludge beds covered about 25% of the total bottom area between the confluence of the Holston River and the Cherokee Reservoir. Total benthic oxygen consumption for 22.8 miles of the River was over 31,200 pounds/day. An estimated 170 tons of attached aquatic weeds (primarily Potamogeton pectinates) covered the river bottom. The plants were beneficial to the dissolved oxygen of the system, but there was excessive variation in diurnal dissolved oxygen levels. Water temperature increased due to cooling water discharges. Water releases from the reservoir for a power plant affected river flow and dissolved oxygen levels. Pollution abatement schedules and limits should be implemented immediately. A minimum of 6.0 mg/l dissolved oxygen should be maintained in releases from the Fort Patrick Henry Dam. Total pollutional loads discharged should be limited to a maximum of 14,040 pounds/5-day BOD and 1940 pounds/day total Kjeldahl nitrogen. A minimum flow release of 750 cubic feet per second should be maintained. (Buchanan-Davidson--Wisconsin)
W75-08996

THE OHIO RIVER-MCALPINE POOL REPORT: KENTUCKY-INDIANA,
Environmental Protection Agency, Athens, Ga. Surveillance and Analysis Div.
D. W. Hill.
Available from the National Technical Information Service, Springfield, Va. 22161, as PB-227 061, $5.75 in paper copy, $2.25 in microfiche. Report June 1973. 137 p, 17 fig, 7 tab, 6 ref, 6 append.

Descriptors: *Water quality, *Dissolved oxygen, *Ohio River, *Kentucky, *Indiana, Ohio, Interstate rivers, Rivers, Thermal pollution, Standards, Sewage effluents, Sewage treatment, Industrial wastes, Municipal wastes, Water pollution, Water pollution control, Alkalinity, Analytical techniques, Water pollution sources, Water treatment, Enteric bacteria, Hydrogen ion concentration, Biochemical oxygen demand, Dissolved solids, Specific conductivity, Salmonella, River flow, Carbon, Ammonia, Nitrification, Organic compounds, Nitates, Nitrites, Phosphorus, Turbidity, Coliforms, Disinfection.
Identifiers: *McAlpine Pool(Ohio River).

Wastewater discharges into the McAlpine Pool reach of the Ohio River are comparatively small but tend to retard recovery of the river from effects of the Cincinnati area waste load. Waste discharges from municipal and industrial sources were not enough to cause the low dissolved oxygen problems observed, although waste treatment was inadequate in several cases. No cause and effect relationships were established between any waste discharge and low oxygen levels. Low reaeration rates in sluggish impoundments caused little oxygenation. Dissolved oxygen levels increased downstream for 25 miles, then declined downstream to McAlpine Dam. This trend correlated with factors affecting reaeration: river velocity and cross-sectional area. Total organic carbon, ammonia, and the five-day BOD profiles were similar and inversely proportional to nitrite-nitrate concentrations. Most of the oxygen demand appeared due to ammonia oxidation. Phosphorus concentrations were essentially constant. Specific conductance (dissolved solids) and pH values were within acceptable limits. Turbidity gradually declined through the McAlpine Pool. Coliform counts were excessive in certain areas. It is recommended that all municipal and industrial sanitary waste discharges receive adequate secondary treatment and disinfection. Upstream water sources, especially in the Cincinnati area, must provide better waste treatment; nitrification will probably be necessary. (Buchanan-Davidson--Wisconsin)
W75-08997

A WATER QUALITY INVESTIGATION OF THE CODORUS CREEK WATERSHED,
Environmental Protection Agency, Philadelphia, Pa. Field Investigation Section.
E. A. Kaeufer.
Available from the National Technical Information Service, Springfield, Va. 22161, as PB-227 635, $5.25 in paper copy, $2.25 in microfiche. Report March 1972. 119 p, 12 fig, 11 tab, append.

Descriptors: *Sewage districts, *Water quality, *Watersheds(Basins), *Pennsylvania, *Baseline studies, Self-purification, Water quality control, Waste water treatment, Agricultural runoff, Industrial wastes, Municipal wastes, Waste assimilative capacity, Eutrophication, Watershed management, Water utilization, Metals, Coliforms, Sewage treatment, Water pollution sources, Sewage effluents, Drainage area, Effluents, Water quality standards, Nutrients, Physical properties, Chemical properties, Biological properties.
Identifiers: *Codorus Creek Basin(Pa), York County(Pa).

A water quality study of the Condorus Creek Watershed in York County, Pennsylvania, a subbasin of the Susquehanna River, was made to establish a wastewater management plan. The watershed has a drainage area of 294 square miles and its waters are used for water supplies, recreation, treated waste assimilation, and power. There are forty reported industrial pollution sources and six municipal wastewater treatment facilities. The seven wastewater discharges sampled did not comply with effluent standards established by the Pennsylvania Implementation Plan (December 1967). Concentrations of toxic materials exceeded state water quality standards and were of the type normally found in industrial discharges. Nutrient concentrations exceeded levels which stimulate growth of algae and aquatic weeds and promoted eutrophication but stream discoloration, caused by effluent discharges from a paper company, limited light penetration and retarded aquatic plant growth. High counts of indicator microorganisms

Identifiers: Mountain lakes, *Vorderer Finstertaler See(Austria).

The importance of bacterial productivity in the production process of lakes had been emphasized. Bacteria are not only the final stage of the food chain but also play a considerable role for subsequent producers. The Vorderer Finstertaler See, Austria, is situated in the Central Alps at an elevation of 2237 m asl, above the timber line. Photosynthesis reaches the bottom of the lake due to the high transparency of the water. Bacterial cell numbers as determined by direct counts on membrane filters were unexpectedly high. As a consequence of the high turbulence of the water, bacterial biomass is almost unstratified, while phytoplankton, composed predominantly of motile forms, shows distinct vertical stratification. In the mean, heterotrophic carbon dioxide uptake amounts 35% of photosynthesis but is extremely high during winter and low after ice thaw. During the winter, heterotrophic productivity is due to bacteria only, while in summer algae also seem to be of some importance. This can be explained by the differences in the uptake mechanisms for organie substances. There is experimental evidence of a close connection between autotrophic and heterotrophic processes during the day which makes possible short-way cycles of nutrients. (Jones-Wisconsin)
W75-09004

METABOLISM OF THE DOMINANT AUTOTROPHS OF THE NORTH AMERICAN GREAT LAKES,
J. Verduin.
Verhandlungen Internationale Vereinigung Limnologie, Vol 18, p 105-112, 1972. 3 fig, 5 tab, 13 ref.

Descriptors: *Productivity, *Metabolism, *Dominant organisms, *Great Lakes, Photosynthesis, Respiration, Littoral, Biological communities, Phytoplankton, Shallow water, Deep water, Euphotic zone, Growth rates.

Photosynthetic and respiratory rates for both the littoral zone communities and the phytoplankton communities of the Great Lakes are presented. An interesting contrast among the lakes and between enriched near-shore areas and offshore areas is revealed. Lake Superior with its soft water and its low nutrient supply shows the lowest yields. Lake Michigan's yields are about 3-fold higher. Lake Huron exhibits a photosynthetic yield intermediate between that of Michigan and Superior. As the water enters western Lake Erie they receive spectacular nutrient influx from Detroit, and from agricultural and urban areas of southeastern Michigan and northwestern Ohio. The western basin yields are similar to those of enriched nearshore areas of the upper lakes such as Green Bay, Wisconsin and Saginaw Bay, Michigan. The last lake in the system, Ontario, exhibits yields closely similar to eastern Lake Erie. The filamentous algal communities found on the shores exhibit photosynthetic yields of about 50 micromoles of carbon dioxide absorbed per ml of algal biomass per hour, regardless of species composition or of locality, excepting western Lake Erie. Respiration rates of the filamentous community were about 6 micromoles of carbon dioxide evolved per ml of algae/hour except in western Lake Erie, where the rate was about doubled. (Jones-Wisconsin)
W75-09005

THE KINETICS OF EXTRACELLULAR RELEASE OF SOLUBLE ORGANIC MATTER BY PLANKTON,
G. W. Saunders, Jr.
Verhandlungen Internationale Vereinigung Limnologie, Vol 18, P 140-146, 1972. 6 fig, 5 ref.

Descriptors: *Kinetics, *Organic matter, *Plankton, Phytoplankton, Lakes, Light intensity, Diurnal, Carbon, Bicarbonates, Transpiration, Biochemistry, Photosynthesis.
Identifiers: *Soluble organic matter.

The kinetics of extracellular release of soluble organie matter by phytoplankton communities in different types of lakes were examined under conditions approximating natural changes in light intensity during a 24-hour period from sunrise to sunrise. Lake water was placed in gallon bottles to which radioactive sodium bicarbonate was added. The bottles were resuspended at the depth of sampling and were shaken and sampled frequently from sunrise of one day until sunrise of the following day. Radioactivity as soluble organic matter was determined by acidifying the filtrate, degassing, and drying the soluble organic matter in cupped plates. The net cumulative soluble organic carbon accumulation is a result of the differential between the release rate of soluble organic matter by the phytoplankton and the assimilation rate of that material by the bacterial community. There are three patterns of extra-cullular release that occur. The data presented here are suggestive of a continuous spectrum of release patterns ranging from simple organic molecules to large polymers and from release throughout the day to release only during daylight. Any specific pattern will depend on environmental conditions, the structure of the phytoplankton community, and the growth states of the phytoplankton populations in that community. (Jones-Wisconsin)
W75-09007

ESTIMATION OF AQUATIC ECOSYSTEM PARAMETERS,
R. A. Parker.
Verhandlungen Internationale Vereinigung Limnologie, Vol 18, p 257-263, 1972. 3 fig, 1 tab, 9 ref.

Descriptors: *Estimating, *Ecosystems, *Mathematical models, Physicochemical properties, Biological properties, Equations, Systems analysis, *Canada.
Identifiers: *Kootenay Lake(British Columbia), Parameter estimation.

The development of parameter estimation techniques which rely on field data to optimize model fit is presented and was prompted in part by prior study of Kootenay Lake, British Columbia. This lake has been subject to low level nutrient enrichment for nearly two decades (primarily inorganic phosphate effluent from a fertilizer plant as well as occassional influxes of nitrate from other sources). Physicochemical data included seasonal changes in river inflow and outflow, inorganic phosphate concentration in the river, temperature and inorganic phosphate concentration in the lake, nitrate and solar radiation. Of the biological components, phytoplankton were subdivided into two groups based primarily on seasonal occurrence; zooplankters were divided into cladocerans and copepods. Their growth rates in the model were determined by grazing activity modified by a reduction in the presence of large quantities of algae. Natural mortality and displacement were included as well as predation. The model represents a compromise between reality and mathematical expediency. The differential equation model utilized for simulation is described; it involves 18 parameters. Simulation output is vastly improved over that produced by the earlier model. (Jones-Wisconsin)
W75-09008

THE BENTHIC CARBON BUDGET OF A SOUTHERN MICHIGAN MARL LAKE,
P. H. Rich, and R. G. Wetzel.
Verhandlungen Internationale Vereinigung Limnologie, Vol 18, p 157-161, 1972. 3 fig, 2 tab.

Descriptors: *Productivity, *Benthos, *Carbon, *Detritus, *Lakes, *Michigan, Respiration, Seasonal, Submerged plants, Aquatic plants, Marl, Bottom sediments, Food chains, Periphyton.
Identifiers: *Carbon budget, *Lawrence Lake(Mich).

Assuming that benthic production and permanent loss of carbon to the sediments are known, rates of benthic respiration during decomposition of detritus determine the efficiency of detrital production and the ultimate amount of detrital material available to the open water community may be estimated by the difference. Measurements made of the benthic production of Lawrence Lake, Michigan, a small, hardwater lake, are described. Benthic production was partitioned into macrophyte productivity, epiphytic productivity, sedimentation of phytoplankton, epipelic productivity and terrestrial inputs. Losses of carbon from the benthos were partitioned into loss to the permanent sediments, loss as respiration of carbon dioxide, and utilization of detritus. Maximal values for benthic respiration were found in the spring and seasonal variations corresponded closely with littoral and pelagic productivity. The vertical variations in rates of benthic respiration correlated directly with the biomass production curves of submersed macrophytes in all cases during the ice-free period. The results of the carbon budget for Lawrence Lake gave a positive balance and indicate that 8.9 g C sq m/yr leave the benthos of this lake as a detrital contribution to the open water community. (Auen-Wisconsin)
W75-09009

THE BIOLOGICAL CYCLE OF MOLYBDENUM IN RELATION TO PRIMARY PRODUCTION AND WATERBLOOM FORMATION IN A EUTROPHIC POND,
H. J. Dumont.
Verhandlungen Internationale Vereinigung Limnologie, Vol 18, p 84-92, 1972. 3 fig, 2 tab, 28 ref.

Descriptors: *Trace elements, Cycles, *Molybdenum, *Primary productivity, *Eutrophication, *Cycling nutrients, Freshwater, Food chains, Cyanophyta, Europe.
Identifiers: *Lake Donk(Belgium).

The molybdenum needs of aquatic environments, the dynamics of this element in Lake Donk, Belgium and its flow through the food chain were studied. In feshwater, soluble Mo is usually present at sub-microgram/l levels. The phytoplankton absorbs considerable quantities of Mo from solution, without really concentrating it. The zooplankton, supposedly stocking Mo with its algal food contains quantities one or two orders of magnitude lower than pure blue-green cultures. This indicates an active and very rapid recreation of the element, perhaps because high levels might act as poison. This rapid recretion was crucial in keeping the element in solution. The phenomenon, in which the ferro/ferri system operates apparently governs the molybdenum system as well. If Lake Donk is taken as a yardstick, it would appear that, in order to obtain top-production (all other factors, except light, not being limiting), 10 mg Mo/sq m would approximately meet the algal needs (5 micrograms/l for a depth of 2 m in Lake Donk). A trace element deficiency, and not impossibly a Mo deficiency, might help to explain causality of blue-green water blooms ascribed to an abundant N and P supply along. (Jones-Wisconsin)
W75-09010

THE RADIATION BALANCE OF LAKES ON THE TERRITORY OF THE USSR,
T. V. Kirillova, and N. P. Smirnova.
Verhandlungen Internationale Vereinigung Limnologie, Vol 18, p 554-562, 1972. 4 fig, 2 tab.

Descriptors: *Albedo, *Solar radiation, *Lakes, *Estimating, Europe, Equations, Light penetration.
Identifiers: *Radiation balance, *USSR.

The solar radiation reaching lake surfaces is the energy source of all the processes occurring in the lakes. It determines the thermal regime, the evaporation from the lake surface and provides for photosynthesis and life in the water masses. Different formulae are often used for estimation of radiation balance and its components over water surfaces. Monthly charts of radiation balance are derived for the land on the basis of observation data from a network of actinometric stations. The main differences between water and land radiation balance values are determined from the differences in albedo and surface temperature values. A formula is given for the lake radiation balance calculation. In deriving the formula, the global radiations both over the lake and the land surfaces are considered to be equal and the difference in the effective radiation can be evaluated from the difference in the longwave radiation flows from the surface. The radiation balance in USSR lakes is estimated by two main factors: physicogeographical conditions and morphometric peculiarities. An attempt was made to evaluate changes in the radiation balance values in lakes of different depths and sizes. (Jones-Wisconsin)
W75-09012

HYDROLOGICAL FEATURES OF LAKE ONEGA IN THE ANNUAL CYCLE,
T. I. Malinina.
Verhandlungen Internationale Vereinigung Limnologie, Vol 18, p 537-541, 1972. 2 tab.

Descriptors: *Hydrology, *Lakes, *Cycles, Europe, Hydrogeology, Clay, Mud, Sands, Sedimentation, Silts, Oxidation-reduction potential, Hydrogen ion concentration, Carbon, Nitrogen, Trace elements, Phosphorus, Iron, Copper, Heat balance, Rainfall, Solar radiation, Productivity, Chemical properties, Physical properties.
Identifiers: *Lake Onega(USSR).

Lake Onega, USSR is the second largest lake in Europe. Average depth is 30 m, the maximum depth is 120 m. For the most part, the bottom is covered with claylike mud overlying limnoglacial clays, mainly banded clays. The bands become narrower towards the surface due to the decrease of the sedimentation rate after the glacier had melted. The southern part of the lake is covered with sand; the sublittoral zone abounds in silts; the bottom of profundal zone is covered with a very fine layer of clayey mud. There is the tendency to common concentration of carbon, phosphorus, iron and copper in the sediments. The climate of the territory is characterized by a mean annual air temperature of 1.9C, average rainfall of 450 mm and an ice-free period of about 200 days. The annual period of sunshine is on the average 1600 hrs, which corresponds to a value of solar radiation of 74.2 kcal; 73% of the annual solar radiation occurs between May and October. The natural conditions of Lake Onega, its thermal regime, its dynamics, and its hydrochemical peculiarities exert considerable influence upon the composition of the organisms in the lake and its biological productivity. (Jones-Wisconsin)
W75-09013

SEASONAL CHANGES IN DISSOLVED ORGANIC NITROGEN IN SIX MICHIGAN LAKES,
B. A. Manny.
Verhandlungen Internationale Vereinigung Limnologie, Vol 18, p 147-156, 1972. 10 fig, 2 tab, 15 ref.

Descriptors: *Fluctuations, *Seasonal, *Nitrogen cycle, *Lakes, Michigan, Ultraviolet radiation, Hardness(Water), Nitrates, Nitrites, Aquatic plants, Primary productivity, Chlorophyta, Chrysophyta.
Identifiers: *Dissolved organic nitrogen, Particulate organic nitrogen, Lawrence Lake(Mich), Wintergreen Lake(Mich), Purdy Lake(Mich), Cassidy Lake(Mich), Duck Lake(Mich), Gull Lake(Mich).

Dissolved organic nitrogen (DON) occurs in lakes in concentrations six times higher than particulate organic nitrogen which can be measured by UV combustion. Seasonal measurements of UV-labile dissolved organic nitrogen (LDON) and UV-

Identifiers: *Finland, *Lake Lovojarvi(Finland), *Lake Ormajarvi(Finland), *Lake Paajarvi(Finland).

Primary production, biomass, species composition, and chemistry of Lakes Lovojarvi and Ormajarvi in southern Finland were studied during summer stagnation eutrophic and thermally stratified. Lake Lovojarvi showed meromictic features, earlier summer stagnation, a much greater increase in electrolytic conductivity and potassium permanganate consumption, and higher concentrations of nitrogen, phosphorus, calcium, and magnesium in the hypolimnion. The chemical properties were nearly the same in the epilimnion of both lakes. Primary production was relatively high. During the period of high primary production, oxygen concentration increased, surface layer pH increased, and inorganic carbon content decreased very little in Lovojarvi and could be used to estimate the lake productivity stage. Total nitrogen and phosphorus could not be correlated with seasonal variations in phytoplankton production. In both lakes production was maximum when stratification was most stable, and decreased towards autumn. Biomass could be correlated with production. Cyanophytes were predominant during high production (2/3 of total biomass) and diatoms were low. Phytoplanktonic production was high compared to Paajarvi. Productive ability of Ormajarvi was higher than that of Lovojarvi. The production/biomass ratio and renewal time varied widely. (Buchanan-Davidson--Wisconsin)
W75-09018

PHYTOPLANKTON ENRICHMENT EXPERIMENTS AND BIOASSAYS IN NATURAL COASTAL SEA WATER AND IN SEWAGE OUTFALL RECEIVING WATERS OFF SOUTHERN CALIFORNIA,

California Univ., San Diego, La Jolla. Inst. of Marine Resources.
W. H. Thomas, D. L. R. Seibert, and A. N. Dodson.
Estuarine and Coastal Marine Science, Vol 2, p 191-206, 1974. 8 fig, 4 tab, 26 ref. NSF GA 27545 and GA 32529X.

Descriptors: *Limiting factors, *Phytoplankton, *Sea water, *Outfall sewers, *Bioassay, *California, Inhibition, Pacific Coast Region, Nitrogen, Eutrophication, Growth rates, Fluorescence, Red tide, Upwelling.

Nutrient enrichment experiments using diatoms and a dinoflagellate with near-shore Southern California surface water showed that nitrogen was the principal nutrient limiting phytoplankton growth. Secondary limitations were shown for phosphate, silicate, iron, trace metals (molybdenum, zinc, manganese, cobalt, copper) and vitamins (vitamin B12, biotin, thiamin). Addition of Point Loma sewage was stimulatory and a complete nutritive additive. Bioassays showed that receiving waters were sometimes stimulatory and at other times inhibitory to algal growth. In some cases there was little or no growth, even on enrichment; this inhibition varied with the test organism, season, and water sample tested. Red tides were probably not caused by sewage enrichment but by any process (advection or upwelling) which enriched surface sea waters. Water near outfalls was eutrophic with a balance between inhibition and stimulation of phytoplankton by sewage input. These studies used in vivo fluorescence to measure algal growth. A comparison of growth rates obtained by fluorescence with cell division rates showed that fluorescence was rapid, sensitive, could be used with all types of phytoplankton, and measured chlorophyll increase, but may vary with light intensity and cellular nutritional status. (Buchanan-Davidson--Wisconsin)
W75-09019

ALGAE IN ALKALINE WATERS OF KANEM (TCHAD): I, (IN FRENCH),

Office de la Recherche Scientifique et Technique Outre-Mer, Fort Lamy (Chad).
A. Iltis.
Cah ORSTOM Ser Hydrobiol. Vol 6, No 3/4, p 173-246, 1972, Illus, English summary.

Descriptors: *Algae, Phytoplankton, Lakes, Ponds, Cyanophyta, Chlorophyta, Diatoms, Pyrrophyta, Euglenophyta, *Alkaline water, Salinity.
Identifiers: Chad, Cryptophyta, *Tchad(Kanem).

Samples of phytoplankton collected in 22 alkaline ponds and lakes have been qualitatively analyzed. The salinity varies from 1- > 100 g/l according to the stations. Five hundred fourteen taxa were determined; among them, 97 Cyanophyta, 52 Euglenophyta, 209 diatoms, 149 Chlorophyta and 7 Pyrrophyta and Cryptophyta were presented.--Copyright 1974, Biological Abstracts, Inc.
W75-09020

ECOLOGY OF BLUE-GREEN ALGAL VIRUSES,

North Carolina Univ., Greensboro. Dept. of Biology.
R. E. Cannon, M. S. Shane, and E. DeMichele.
Journal of the Environmental Engineering Division, Proceedings of the American Society of Civil Engineers, Vol 100, No EE6, p 1205-1211. 1974. 19 ref.

Descriptors: *Algal control, *Ecological distribution, *Cyanophyta, *Viruses, Hosts, Water pollution, *Delaware, Sea water, Salinity, Protozoa, Reviews, Algae.
Identifiers: LPP-group Cyanophages, Christina River(Dela), Plectonema boryanum, Hartmanella glebae, Amoeba.

Studies of ecology of blue-green algal viruses, specifically LPP-group, are reviewed. LPP-viruses can be isolated from both artificial and natural aquatic environments and are isolated only from organically polluted areas, according to Delaware's Christina River survey. The LPP-cyanophage has been found in marine environments and laboratory study has shown that virus and host can interact at high salinity. Laboratory investigations have demonstrated LPP-viruses can lysogenize their host blue-green alga, Plectonema boryanum, when the alga is 'stressed' by antibiotics, heavy metals, or nutrient limitation, that may occur in natural environment. An amoeba, Harmanella glebae, has been isolated which appears to act as reservoir for the LPP-cyanophage while feeding on infected Plectonema filaments. The nonblooming nature of this blue-green alga might be hypothetically explained through control of algal populations with temperate viruses via the lysis-lysogeny decision in conjunction with a protozoan reservoir that would move the virus efficiently to better grazing areas. Cyanophages may control blue-green algal blooms and may serve as more reliable indicators of organic and cultural pollution than other microorganisms. (Jones-Wisconsin)
W75-09021

SIMULATION OF URBAN RUNOFF, NUTRIENT LOADING, AND BIOTIC RESPONSE OF A SHALLOW EUTROPHIC LAKE,

Wisconsin Univ., Madison. Inst. for Environmental Studies.
D. D. Huff, J. F. Koonce, W. R. Ivarson, P. R. Weikv, and E. H. Dettman.
Eastern Deciduous Forest Biome-IBP Contribution No. 114, (1974). 53 p, 25 fig, 4 tab, 14 ref. NSF AG-199, 40-193-69.

Descriptors: *Ecosystems, *Model studies, *Urban runoff, *Nutrients, *Biota, Shallow water, Eutrophication, Lakes, Watersheds(Basins), Precipitation(Atmospheric), Groundwater,

*Wisconsin, Hydrology, Productivity, Path of pollutants.
Identifiers: *Lake Wingra(Wis).

Through orderly progression of process model synthesis, testing, and new synthesis, a solid model structure can be built and extended for simulating whole ecosystem response to natural and man-made perturbations. Multi-disciplinary research and team modeling efforts have provided the opportunity to conduct detailed whole ecosystem simulation studies. The lake water balance was analyzed, followed by estimated nutrient loading from precipitation, dryfall, runoff, and groundwater flow. Simulations of lake response, from April to September, 1970, were compared with observations. In a first attempt to link terrestrial and aquatic ecosystem models, a six month period was selected for simulating both water and nutrient loading from the terrestrial system and the associated response of the Lake Wingra, Wisconsin ecosystem. Hydrologic simulations appear equally as accurate as field measurements, and serve as reliable means for estimating nutrient loading from storm drains in an urban watershed. The simulated response to a wide range of nutrient influx indicates that Lake Wingra is less sensitive to nutrient influx than to regeneration within the pelagic system. This implies that already productive lake systems will be less responsive to nutrient diversion than those with lower productivity. (Jones-Wisconsin)
W75-09022

THE PHOSPHORUS BUDGET OF CAMERON LAKE, ONTARIO: THE IMPORTANCE OF FLUSHING RATE TO THE DEGREE OF EUTROPHY OF LAKES,

Toronto Univ. (Ontario). Dept. of Zoology.
P. J. Dillon.

Limnology and Oceanography, Vol 20, No 1, p 28-39, 1975. 8 fig, 6 tab,.31 ref.

Descriptors: *Phosphorus, *Discharge(Water), Depth, *Trophic level, *Canada, Lakes, *Eutrophication, Mathematical models, Nutrient removal.
Identifiers: *Flushing rate, *Cameron Lake(Ontario), Phosphorus budget, Vollenweider's trophic model.

Studies of the total phosphorus budgets of several lakes in southern Ontario showed that a number of lakes were not accurately depicted by Vollenweider's phosphorus loading-mean depth relationship. Cameron Lake, described here, is an example of such a lake. Cameron Lake is clearly not a highly eutrophic lake, as the simple model would suggest. The reason for this discrepancy is the high flushing rate--the lake's water volume is replaced 13.8 and 18.9 times per year. The total phosphorus budget of this lake is described for two 12-month periods. Although the phosphorus loadings were high (1.70 and 2.21 g/sq m/yr) the lake is not eutrophic because the high flushing rate counteracts the high loading. A plot with the phosphorus loading, the retention coefficient of phosphorus in the lake, and the hydraulic flushing rate, vs. the mean depth, is suggested as a means of relating lake trophic state to phosphorus loading. This formulation accurately predicted that nearby Four Mile Lake would be almost identical to Cameron Lake in terms of degree of eutrophy despite the fact that Four Mile Lake's phosphorus load is 20 times less than that of Cameron Lake. (Jones-Wisconsin)
W75-09023

SOME RELATIONSHIPS BETWEEN ALGAL STANDING CROP, WATER CHEMISTRY, AND SEDIMENT CHEMISTRY IN THE ENGLISH LAKES,

Minnesota Univ., Minneapolis. Dept. of Botany.
E. Gorham, J. W. G. Lund, J. E. Sanger, and W. E. Dean.

Limnology and Oceanography, Vol 19, No 4, p 601-617, 1974. 13 fig, 5 tab, 45 ref. NSF 2448 and GB 6018.

Descriptors: *Trophic level, *Algae, *Standing crops, *Water chemistry, *Lake sediments, Pigments, Cyanophyta, Ions, Calcium, Bicarbonates, Vitamins, Sulfur, Agricultural runoff, Carbon, Nitrogen, Cycling nutrients.
Identifiers: *English Lake District.

This investigation reveals that algal standing crops vary significantly with a number of environmental properties which themselves are interrelated. For example, the sediments of productive lakes are much higher in both sulfur and sedimentary carotenoids than the sediments of unproductive lakes. Estimates of standing crop, derived approximately from algal counts, have been used to separate the English Lakes into three groups of low, intermediate, and high fertility. The fertile lakes are proportionally poorer than the infertile lakes in micro-algae, but richer in 'large algae' and Cyanophyta. The fertile lakes are richer in dissolved ions, especially calcium and bicarbonate, in filter-passing and particulate vitamin B-12, in sedimentary sulfur, and in sedimentary chlorophyll derivatives and carotenoids. The relationship noted by Pearsall between lake fertility and agricultural activity is shown by a strong correlation between algal standing crop and the percentage of the drainage basin under cultivation. Sediment ratios of carbon to sulfur and of chlorophyll derivatives to carotenoids decline with increasing fertility, whereas the ratio of carbon to nitrogen shows little change. This study lends support to the use of sedimentary pigments as indices to lake productivity. The pigment data also indicate that much of the organic matter in sediments of productive lakes comes from autochthonous sources within the lakes. (Jones-Wisconsin)
W75-09024

DISTRIBUTION OF BENTHIC INVERTEBRATES IN THE SOUTH END OF LAKE MICHIGAN,

Michigan Univ., Ann Arbor. Great Lakes Research Div.
S. C. Mozley, and W. P. Alley.

In: International Association Great Lakes Research, Proceedings 16th Conference Great Lakes Research, p 87-96, 1973. 8 fig, 3 tab, 23 ref. FWPCA WP-00311.

Descriptors: *Ecological distribution, *Benthic fauna, *Invertebrates, *Lake Michigan, Water pollution effects, Oligochaetes, Amphipoda, Sediments, Habitats, Path of pollutants.

Large areas of the south end of Lake Michigan have been considered very polluted. Pollution-sensitive Amphipoda occur in large populations over much of the south end. Abundant Oligochaeta occur at stations 15 km away from major shoreline sources of pollution, while some stations near harbors and river mouths support few Oligochaeta, on the average. Very profuse oligochaetes, which are good evidence of pollution, occur sporadically at most stations shallower than 20 m. While the regional differences in average amphipod and oligochaete abundances between the central and southern parts of the lake indicate some deterioration of the south end, very few areas can definitely be called polluted on the basis of data now available. Irregular, high abundances of oligochaetes at many inshore stations suggest that polluted sediments are not evenly or permanently deposited at depths exposed to wave action and coastal currents, but are probably dispersed gradually over wide areas. The more pronounced regional differences occur between 9 and 40 m, which suggests that enriching materials from shoreline sources ultimately come to rest in a band which follows these depth contours. (Jones-Wisconsin)
W75-09025

oligotrophic lakes lying in an area with a high water surplus in Newfoundland indicates that both primary production at optimum light and total phosphorus concentration per unit volume representative of the whole lake, bear a relationship to water renewal coefficient that is curvilinear, with primary production and total phosphorus beginning to decline when water renewal exceeds an optimum rate. In five highly eutrophic lakes with minimal or no water surplus near Edmonton, Alberta, basins with higher evaporation coefficients have higher nutrient supply and higher salinities. The relationship between primary production and evaporation coefficient is curvilinear. Once an optimal salinity level is reached, further increase in salinity will inhibit primary production. (Jones-Wisconsin)
W75-09029

EUTROPHICATION AND ITS ALLEVIATION IN THE UPPER QU'APPELLE RIVER SYSTEM, SASKATCHEWAN,
Saskatchewan Univ. (Saskatoon). Dept. of Biology.
U. T. Hammer.
In: Proceedings, Symposium on the Lakes of Western Canada, 1972, Water Resources Center, University of Alberta, Edmonton, p 352-368, 1973. 6 fig, 4 tab, 23 ref.

Descriptors: *Water quality control, *Eutrophication, *Multiple-purpose reservoirs, *Canada, *Cyanophyta, Nutrients, Sewage effluents, Agriculture, Runoff, River basins, Oxygen sag, Fish, Dissolved solids, Ions, Phosphates, Nitrogen, Standing crops, Stratification, Light penetration, Primary productivity.
Identifiers: Qu'Appelle River System(Saskatchewan), Buffalo Pound Lake(Saskatchewan), Echo Lake(Saskatchewan), Katepwa Lake(Saskatchewan), Last Mountain Lake(Saskatchewan), Pasqua Lake(Saskatchewan), Nutrient budget, Dilution.

Blue-green algae blooms have been prominent in the lakes of the Upper Qu'Appelle River system during the last two decades. These blooms are associated with high nutrient levels in the lakes as well as high nutrient loadings derived from domestic sewage and from agricultural runoff. The lakes are important for recreation, commercial fishing, agricultural uses, a source of water for Moose Jaw and Regina, and as cesspools for sewage effluent from these two cities. They are sites of significant waterfowl habitats and are important in flood control. Buffalo Pound Lake, uppermost in the system and a water supply source, has received, since 1967, an intermittent supply of water from Lake Diefenbaker, a large oligotrophic reservoir on the South Saskatchewan River which has resulted in a decrease in total dissolved solids and major ions to less than half former levels; the orthophosphate was reduced to one-tenth of former levels; total inorganic nitrogen was also reduced to some extent. Algal blooms were absent in 1971 and 1972 in this lake, whereas the lakes further downstream contained very heavy blooms. Legislative action, public cooperation, and stringent guidelines to control nutrient influx are suggested as approaches to mitigate eutrophication in these lakes. (Jones-Wisconsin)
W75-09030

EUTROPHIC LAKES IN THE MACKENZIE DELTA: THEIR USE BY WATERFOWL,
Alberta Univ., Edmonton. Dept. of Geography.
D. Gill.
In: Proceedings, Symposium on the Lakes of Western Canada, 1972, Water Resources Center, University of Alberta, Edmonton, p 196-201, 1973.

Descriptors: *Eutrophication, *Lakes, *Waterfowl, *Canada, Deltas, Sediment transport, Aquatic plants, Habitats, Geomorphology, Water levels.
Identifiers: *Mackenzie Delta(Canada), Thermokarst lakes, Delta lakes.

The geomorphology and plant succession of lakes in the Mackenzie River Delta and their use by waterfowl are described and the interaction that occurs between vegetation and waterfowl in this type of ecologic niche is traced. Because of their position within an alluvial environment, most delta lakes are eutrophic and harbor much aquatic vegetation. Delta lakes are not equally eutrophic, particularly within deltas underlain by permafrost. In the Mackenzie River Delta, one-third of the lakes are bounded by high levees and receive an input of nutrients through sediment transport only during high floods, thus reducing aquatic vegetation. Most of these lakes are subject to bank recession through thermokarst action, thus littoral plant succession is absent; such lakes are not frequented by waterfowl. Another third of the lakes are highly eutrophic, maintained in this condition through transport of nutrient-rich sediment by small channels during flood stages, and during channel flow reversals. Within this type of lake miniature deltas are formed near lake-channel junction, and shoals are constructed from incoming sediment by wave action. These isolated geomorphic features provide relatively predator-free resting habitat for waterfowl. The successional vegetation that establishes on them provides high-quality waterfowl grazing. (Jones-Wisconsin)
W75-09031

CHANGES IN WATER CHEMISTRY ACCOMPANYING SUMMER FISH KILLS IN SHALLOW EUTROPHIC LAKES OF SOUTHWEST MANITOBA,
Fisheries Research Board of Canada, Winnipeg (Manitoba). Freshwater Inst.
J. Barica.
In: Proceedings, Symposium on the Lakes of Western Canada, 1972, Water Resources Center, University of Alberta, Edmonton, p 228-241, 1973. 4 fig, 2 tab, 13 ref.

Descriptors: *Water chemistry, *Summer, *Fishkill, *Shallow water, *Eutrophication, Salinity, *Canada, Cyanophyta, Oxygen sag, Ammonia, Phosphates, Nitrogen, Carbon, Phosphorus, Chlorophyll, Carbon dioxide, Fish farming, Rainbow trout.
Identifiers: *Manitoba, Aphanizomenon flos-aquae.

Fish mortalities resulting from excessive growth of Cyanophyta and their degradation products represent the most advanced stage of lake eutrophication. Four cases of summer fish kills following the collapse of heavy blooms of Aphanizomenon flos-aquae in shallow eutrophic lakes located in the Erickson area of Southwestern Manitoba are described. The sequence of events was similar in each case. Partial die-off of algae preceded the fish kills. Rapid degradation of algal cells and their metabolites played a crucial role in the subsequent chemical changes. Dissolved oxygen dropped from supersaturation levels to below those required by fish. Ammonia and orthophosphate concentrations increased rapidly, while changes in dissolved organic nitrogen, carbon and phosphorus were slight. On the average, particulate CNP fell on one-third and chlorophyll-a to one fifth of their concentrations proceding the blooms. Total inorganic carbon dioxide concentrations reached their maxima before the fish kills. The recovery of normal chemical conditions and the algal succession following the collapse of the Aphanizomenon bloom varied from lake to lake. An evaluation of the fish kill mechanism from the viewpoint of water chemistry as a part of broader studies of aquaculture in Canadian winterkill lakes currently in progress is presented. (Jones-Wisconsin)
W75-09032

EUTROPHICATION AND RECREATIONAL FISHES IN TWO LARGE LAKE BASINS IN BRITISH COLUMBIA,
British Columbia Univ., Vancouver. Inst. of Animal Resource Ecology.

T. G. Northcote.
In: Proceedings, Symposium on the Lakes of Western Canada, 1972, Water Resources Center, University of Alberta, Edmonton, p 175-188, 1973. 3 fig, 2 tab, 14 ref.

Descriptors: *Eutrophication, *Sport fish, *Productivity, Water pollution effects, *Canada, Growth rates, Phosphates, Agricultural runoff, Zooplankton, Salmonids, Sewage effluents, Spawning, Habitats, Nitrogen.
Identifiers: *British Columbia, Kootenay Lake(British Columbia), Okanagan Lake(British Columbia), Skaha Lake(British Columbia), Wood Lake (British Columbia).

Two large lake basins in British Columbia--the Kootenay and the Okangan--are compared relative to the causes and sequence of eutrophication and its impact on recreational fishes. In Kootenay Lake high phosphate loading was due largely from operation of a fertilizer plant nearly 400 km upstream on the Kootenay River. Increased algal production, zooplankton abundance and growth of some salmonoids are probably attributable to this source, but not the sharply increased catch of sport fish. The largest lake in the Okanagan drainage basin, Okanagan Lake, receives a major portion of its phosphate load from two domestic sewage plants but, except for localized areas, does not exhibit serious effects of eutrophication. Intermediate-sized Skaha Lake receives high nutrient loads from a domestic sewage treatment plant and has shown characteristic eutrophication effects including algal blooms and enhanced salmonoid growth. On the other hand, Wood, one of the smaller lakes in the system, has shown more intense eutrophication effects for several decades and recent deterioration of recreational fishing. In balance, effects of eutrophication in both major systems probably have not had such deleterious effects on recreational fishes as have losses of spawning stream habitats through various other man-induced disturbances. (Jones-Wisconsin)
W75-09033

ENGINEERING ASPECTS OF POLLUTED LKE RECLAMATION,
Notre Dame Univ., Indiana. Dept. of Civil Engineering.
For primary bibliographic entry see Field 5G.
W75-09034

RELATIONS BETWEEN MICROBIAL HETEROTROPHIC ACTIVITY, ORGANICS, AND DEOXYRIBONUCLEIC ACID IN OLIGOTHROPHIC LAKE SEDIMENTS,
Rensselaer Polytechnic Inst., Troy, N.Y. Fresh Water Inst.
L. S. Cresceri, and M. Daze.
FWI Report 74-14, (1974). (EDFB-IBP No 173) 17 p, 8 fig, 7 ref. AEC AG 199, 40-193-69.

Descriptors: *Bacteria, *Microbial degradation, *Lake sediments, *Biomass, Organic matter, Hydrogen ion concentration, *New York, Fluctuations, Lakes, Water temperature, Rates, Algae.
Identifiers: *Deoxyribonucleic Acid, *Lake George(NY).

Microbial decomposition dynamics in sediments of bays in Lake George, New York were studied by relating rate measurements to microbial biomass. In a developed bay in a mesotrophic basin, organic content varied widely. Deoxyribonucleic acid (measure of living cellular material) and microbial activity followed each other closely in a diphasic plot, due to variable allochthonous inputs and wave action which decreased with depth. The macroalga, Nitella flexilis, showed spring and summer growth surges. Soluble organics and plant material probably contributed to the diphasic activity. At all depths, there was decreased microbial activity at the beginning and end of the growing season, probably due to temperature in the spring and nutrition in the fall. Over the winter there was probably an accumulation of microbial biomass which showed less activity per milligram DNA at low temperatures. In Warner Bay microbial activity could be expressed as a function of the sediment DNA content and percent organic content. In the minimally developed oliogtrophic Hearts Bay, activity was expressed as a function of DNA content, percent organic content, and temperature. DNA measurements have applicability as a biomass indicator in lake sediments, since rapid biodegradability in natural systems and correlation with microbial activity measurements have been shown. (Buchanan-Davidson--Wisconsin)
W75-09035

EFFECTS OF THE DISCHARGE OF THERMAL EFFLUENT FROM A POWER STATION ON LAKE WABAMUN, ALBERTA, CANADA: THE EPIPELIC AND EPIPSAMMIC ALGAL COMMUNITIES,
Alberta Univ., Edmonton. Dept. of Botany.
M. Hickman.
Hydrobiologia, Vol 45, No 2-3, p 199-215, 1974. 6 fig, 4 tab, 17 ref.

Descriptors: *Biological communities, *Algae, *Thermal pollution, Powerplants, Varieties, Standing crops, Light penetration, Diatoms, Lake sediments, Water temperature, Littoral, Waves(Water), *Canada, Ice cover, Deep water.
Identifiers: *Lake Wabamun(Alberta).

Epipelic algal standing crops were increased by the discharge of thermal effluent into Lake Wabamun, particularly in the discharge canal. The increase in the standing crop size of the epipelon was due to Oscillatoria amoena and O. borneti in the heated area, while the discharge canal provided the inoculum of algae for the heated area of the lake. In the discharge canal the increase of algal standing crops was also due to increased light penetration to the sediment, because the heated effluent kept that area of the lake free of ice. The species composition of the diatoms was similar at all stations except in the discharge canal where there was a reduction in the number of diatom species. Navicula cuspidata developed best in the canal in the summer. Amphora ovalis var. pediculus was the dominant diatom during the winter under ice cover. The heated effluent had no effect on the standing crop or species composition of the epipsammon. Study of sediment cores showed that the shallow littoral zone of the lake was very disturbed by wind-induced wave action thus affecting the epipelic algal communities. (Buchanan-Davidson--Wisconsin)
W75-09036

SOLUBILITY EQUILIBRIUM CONSTANT OF ALPHA-HOPEITE,
Canada Centre for Inland Waters, Burlington (Ontario).
J. O. Nriagu.
Geochimica et Cosmochimica Acta, Vol 37, No 11, p 2357-2561, 1973. 1 tab, 18 ref.

Descriptors: *Solubility, *Zinc, *Phosphates, Model studies, Lake sediments, Ions.
Identifiers: *Alpha-hopeite, Zinc phosphates.

Precipitation of zinc phosphates may play an important role in regulating the levels of Zn and P in natural water systems. The 25C saturation curve of alpha-hopeite in dilute phosphoric acid solutions and the solubility equilibrium constant derived therefrom are presented. The composition of the supernatant solutions saturated with respect to alpha-hopeite is tabulated along with the solubility product constants derived from each set of data. The saturation curve for synthetic alpha-hopeite in dilute phosphoric acid solutions has been determined at 25C as a function of pH. Interpretation of the data in terms of a model which assumes the formation of the ion-pairs zinc hypophosphate and ZnH2PO4 ions in these solu-

den rise from middle of April to a maximum volume in June which is directly proportional to the water temperature during the period. However, the pH shows only a slight rise from April to June. The plankton volume drops off sharply during July and Aug.; while the water temperature is still rising to a peak in Aug. Therefore, temperature and light could not be limiting factors for plankton production, which is usually the case in temperate lakes. The only possible factors for this reduction in plankton appear to be: intensive grazing by fish larvae and frogs which are abundant in the lake after June, and a sharp falloff in phosphate and silicate values. A list of the various species composing plankton and pedon of these lakes is given. The significance of this study to organic production and high altitude fisheries is stressed.--Copyright 1973, Biological Abstracts, Inc.
W75-09041

ABUNDANCE AND PRODUCTION OF BACTERIA IN LATVIAN LAKES,
V. I. Romanenko.
Mitteilungen Internationalen Vereiningung Limnologie, Vol 18, Part 3, p 1306-1310, 1973. 5 ref.

Descriptors: *Productivity, *Bacteria, *Lakes, Decomposing organic matter, Trophic level, Oxygen, Phytoplankton, Reproduction, Oxidation-reduction potential, Hydrogen ion concentration.
Identifiers: *Latvia.

Of eight Latvian lakes studied, two were oligotrophic, two mesotrophic with macrophyte growths in the littoral zone, two eutrophic, and two dystrophic. The oligotrophic lakes have a depth of 65 m and water transparency of 3.9 m. The other lakes are shallower, with a transparency in the eutrophic lakes of 0.3 m. The lakes were examined for oxygen (by Winkler's method), bicarbonates (by direct titration), the production of phytoplankton (by radiocarbon technique), decomposition of organic matter (from oxygen consumption in dark bottles), the abundance of bacteria (by direct counts in membrane filters), heterotrophic assimilation of carbon dioxide by microorganisms (by C-14 technique). The reproduction rate and production of bacteria were calculated from the heterotrophic assimilation of carbon dioxide. The bacterial groups were identified in elective incubation media. The oxidation-reduction potential was determined with a platinum electrode in the mud sampled with a plexiglass tube. The lakes poor in organic matter produce 16-37 micrograms of C/l per day in the bacterial biomass, the rich lakes give 490-1190 micrograms of C. The generation time of bacteria varies from 6 to 40 hours. (Jones-Wisconsin)
W75-09042

THE CONTRIBUTION OF INDIVIDUAL SPECIES OF ALGAE TO PRIMARY PRODUCTIVITY OF CASTLE LAKE, CALIFORNIA,
E. A. Stull, E. de Amezaga, and C. R. Goldman.
Mitteilungen Internationalen Vereiningung Limnologie, Vol 18, Part 3, p 1776-1783, 1973. 4 fig, 1 tab, 11 ref. NSF GB 6422X.

Descriptors: *Algae, *Primary productivity, California, Biological communities, Photosynthesis, Carbon fixation, Biomass, Radioactivity techniques.
Identifiers: *Individual algal species, Castle Lake(Calif), Autoradiography.

Quantitative autoradiography was used to measure the contribution of individual algal species to primary productivity of Castle Lake, California, and demonstrated the types of information available with the use of this technique. Sar.:ples for autoradiographic analysis of primary productivity were an integral part of the extensive sampling program. At O m the most abundant organism was the diatom Cyclotella meneghiana with 353 cells per milliliter. At 1 m Cyclotella meneghiniana and Microcystis aeruginosa had the largest biomass and were large contributors to community primary productivity. The most interesting aspect of the comparison between biomass and primary productivity is the observation that some minor species contribute more heavily to primary productivity than to algal biomass. Autoradiography measurements of the primary productivity of individual species yields much information that can be used to interpret the nature of phytoplankton communities. Studies of the relationship between abundance and productivity of algal species will provide more information on the structure of phytoplankton communities and a reanalysis of the meaning of diversity and seasonal sucession. (Jones-Wisconsin)
W75-09043

DYNAMICS AND PRODUCTION OF SIMOCEPHALUS SERRULATUS (KOCH) IN TWO LARGE NATURAL AND MAN-MADE PONDS IN EASTERN CANADA,
K-J. Ang, and C. H. Fernando.
Mitteilungen Internationalen Vereiningung Limnologie, Vol 18, Part 3, p 1448-1456, 1973. 8 fig, 1 tab, 8 ref.

Descriptors: *Dynamics, *Productivity, *Zooplankton, *Littoral, Canada, Reproduction, Mortality, Predation.
Identifiers: *Simocephalus serrulatus, Waterloo(Ontario), Columbia Lake Reservoir(Ontario), Miller's Lake(Ontario).

Field and laboratory studies were combined in investigating the dynamics and production of littoral zooplankton populations. Simocephalus serrulatus, the dominant littoral species in large ponds near Waterloo, Ontario, was chosen. Both these ponds have a high proportion of their total area covered by rooted vegetation during the summer accounting for about 30% in Columbia Lake reservoir and about 50% in Miller's Lake. Experiments were conducted to determine the rate of egg development, population growth in the absence of predation, physiological death, number of instars, and duration of juvenile and adult. The best turnover rate of S. serrulatus and the high rate of predation indicate that practically all the biomass produced by this species is passed on rapidly to the next trophic level. The logistic growth curve of the population is typical of many zooplankters. This pattern of growth may be interpreted as a reflection of a food limited system in which food becomes abundant as the result of increased nutrients in spring. Population size in summer is probably regulated more by predator pressure than by food scarcity. (Jones-Wisconsin)
W75-09044

SUMMER PHYTOPLANKTON BLOOMS IN AUKE BAY, ALASKA, DRIVEN BY WIND MIXING OF THE WATER COLUMN,
Oregon State Univ., Corvallis. School of Oceanography.
R. L. Iverson, H. C. Curl, H. B. O'Connors, D. Kirk, and K. Zakar.
Limnology and Oceanography, Vol 19, No 2, p 271-278, 1974. 8 fig, 24 ref.

Descriptors: *Bays, *Phytoplankton, *Eutrophication, *Winds, *Mixing, Alaska, Nitrates, Summer, Nitrogen, Chlorophyll, Density.
Identifiers: *Auke Bay(Alaska).

A mechanism for producing major summer phytoplankton blooms in Auke Bay, Alaska based on wind mixing of nitrate-rich water from deeper layers into the photic zone, is proposed. Temperature, salinity, and chlorophyll-a were measured. Nitrate was determined in samples, frozen and analyzed. Surveys to determine the spatial variability of chlorophyll-a and water density in Auke Bay showed that the density structure was uniform over the bay. Density was largely a func-

tion of salinity with temperature effects secondary. Both temperature and salinity were stratified most of the summer. Tidal-induced turbulence was not sufficient to destroy the near surface density structure. At 27 m, nitrate showed a general decrease over summer, accelerating during the first few days of June after a period of strong wind mixing. Winds blowing from the southeast along the only significant entrance into Auke Bay mixed nitrate into the photic zone from deeper in the water column, resulting in major summer phytoplankton blooms. The wind-mixing effect could be monitored by measuring salinity changes caused by mixing of freshwater from the glacially originating Mendenhall River down into the water column. (Jones-Wisconsin)
W75-09045

A DIURNAL ZOOPLANKTON MIGRATION STUDY IN LAKE MEAD,
Arizona Univ., Tucson.
R. D. Staker.
Journal of Arizona Academy of Science, Vol 9, No 3, p 85-88, October 1974. 6 fig, 1 tab, 25 ref. OWRT A-036-ARIZ(4).

Descriptors: *Zooplankton, *Migration patterns, *Migration, *Diurnal, *Water temperature, Depth, Sampling, Thermal stratification, Lakes, Freshwater, Thermal properties, *Arizona, Water pollution effects.
Identifiers: *Lake Mead(Ariz).

The purpose was to find out whether nocturnal migration patterns occur in the zooplanktonic fauna of Lake Mead under isothermal conditions and to determine the extent of this migration. The principal organisms sampled and analyzed were calanoid, cyclopoid, nauplii, Bosmina longirostris, Keratella cochlearis, and Polyartha sp. An analysis of variance on the data comparing the variation in the mean depth during the daylight hours to the night hours was performed to test whether variations were due to change alone. The results obtained show that the rotifers Keratella cochlearis and Polyartha sp. and the Bosmina longisostris do migrate. The analysis also indicates that variations seen in Calanoida, Cyclopoida, and nauplii are due to change variation. The depth of the three migrating organisms changed less than 5 m between day and night. Since the study was performed under the isothermal conditions of winter, it is believed that migration is not a function of temperature. (Mastic-Arizona)
W75-09059

THE EFFECTS OF DIURON ON BACTERIAL POPULATIONS IN AQUATIC ENVIRONMENTS,
Clemson Univ., S.C. Dept. of Microbiology; and Clemson Univ., S.C. Dept. of Zoology.
R. K. Guthrie, D. S. Cherry, and R. N. Ferebee.
Water Resources Bulletin, Vol 10, No 2, p 304-310, April 1974. 1 fig, 2 tab, 7 ref. OWRT A-022-SC(9).

Descriptors: *Bacteria, *Herbicides, *Aquatic environment, *Reservoirs, Lakes, Laboratories, Runoff, Waste water(Pollution), Water treatment, Drainage water, Food chains, Water quality, Water pollution effects.
Identifiers: *Diuron, Chromagenic bacteria, Natural aquatic bacteria, Impounded ecosystems.

The naturally occurring, aerobic, heterotrophic bacterial populations of two impounded ecosystems were studied in a laboratory tank system. One reservoir received runoff from a rural drainage basin only, while the second received treated municipal sewage, industrial waste and heavy recreational use. Water from each reservoir was treated with 1.4 ppm final concentration of diuron and studied for total bacterial counts and nutritional source types. Control tanks were studied concurrently. Total counts increased shortly after diuron addition; however, this was followed by a decrease to a level below the control. Reduction in diversity was significantly greater in water from the polluted reservoir, but chromagenic bacteria were significantly reduced in the non-polluted reservoir. Starch utilizers were most affected by herbicide addition. Bacteria growing on protein or glucose salts were essentially unaffected. (Bell-Cornell)
W75-09079

PHYTOPLANKTON DISTRIBUTION AND WATER QUALITY INDICES FOR LAKE MEAD (COLORADO RIVER),
Arizona Univ., Tucson. Dept. of Biological Sciences.
R. D. Staker, R. W. Hoshaw, and L. G. Everett.
Journal of Phycology, Vol 10, No 3, p 323-331, 1974. 2 fig, 4 tab, 39 ref. OWRT A-036-ARIZ(5). NSF 25130.

Descriptors: *Reservoirs, *Eutrophication, *Bioindicators, *Phytoplankton, Diatoms, Chlorophyta, Pyrrophyta, Cyanophyta, Euglenophyta, Dinoflagellates, Varieties, *Colorado River, Water pollution effects, Pollutant identification, *Arizona.
Identifiers: *Lake Mead(Ariz), Bacillariophyta, Chrysophyta, Cryptophyta.

Phytoplankton samples were collected at varying stations, times, and depths from September 1970 to June 1971 at Lake Mead, Arizona, then processed through a millipore filter apparatus and 79 planktonic algae identified. Species of Bacillariophyta were most numerous (42), followed by Chlorophyta (18), Cyanophyta (9), Chrysophyta (3), Cryptophyta (3), Pyrrophyta (2), and Euglenophyta (2). Bacillariophyta were present at all times and stations, with maximum occurrence during winter and late summer. Chlorophyta were present at all stations and depths throughout the year with the highest percentage composition in April. Of 18 green algae, 10 were chlorococcalean species. Cyanophyta were the major phytoplanktons in September and November. Cryptophyta were high in February-April. Ceratium hirundinella was the most important dinoflagellate. Thirty-three of the 60 most pollution-tolerant algae genera according to Palmer's pollution-tolerant algae index and at least one species of each of five of Palmer's and Nygaard's indices calculated from the phytoplankton data indicated eutrophic conditions in Lake Mead, especially Boulder Basin. (Buchanan-Davidson-Wisconsin)
W75-09083

ECOLOGICAL STUDIES OF TWO SWAMP WATERSHEDS IN NORTHEASTERN NORTH CAROLINA - A PRECHANNELIZATION STUDY,
North Carolina State Univ., Raleigh. Dept. of Zoology.
G. B. Pardue, M. T. Huish, and H. R. Perry, Jr.
Available from the National Technical Information Service, Springfield, Va 22161 as PB-243 126, $11.50 in paper copy, $2.25 in microfiche. North Carolina Water Resources Research Institute, Raleigh, UNC-WRRI Rept No 105, April 1975. 455 p, 29 fig, 51 tab, 120 ref, 4 append. OWRT B-049-NC(1). 14-31-0001-3626.

Descriptors: Fish, Wildlife, Channel improvement, *Wildlife habitats, *Baseline studies, *Fish populations, Stream improvement, *Swamps, Wetlands, Drainage effects, *Watersheds(Basins), *North Carolina, Ecology, *Ecosystems.
Identifiers: *Preconstruction, *Stream channelization, Swamp ecosystem, Wildlife population, Prechannelization.

Indices to the abundances of fish and wildlife of two eastern North Carolina wooded swamp stream environments were developed during 1972, 1973, and 1974, as a preconstruction study of the effects of stream channelization on fish and wildlife. In addition, the relationships of physical, chemical and vegetative parameters to the faunal components of the study sites were evaluated. Indices were obtained for some fish, bird and mammal populations (mourning dove, quail, ducks, woodcock, songbirds, breeding songbirds, gray squirrel, raccoon, opossum, small mammals and deer). Hunter use studies were also conducted. Statistical tests were utilized when applicable to test year and area differences. The results are considered to be essential as baseline information to future studies of stream alteration and also provide useful information regarding faunal and floral diversity as well as seasonal relationships within the swamp ecosystem. (Stewart-North Carolina State)
W75-09130

EFFECTS OF REDUCED OXYGEN CONCENTRATIONS ON THE EARLY LIFE STAGES OF MOUNTAIN WHITEFISH, SMALLMOUTH BASS AND WHITE BASS,
National Water Quality Lab., Duluth, Minn.
R. E. Siefert, A. R. Carlson, and L. J. Herman.
The Progressive Fish-Culturist, Vol 36, No 4, p 186-190, October 1974. 3 tab, 10 ref.

Descriptors: *White bass, *Dissolved oxygen, *Bioassay, *Immature growth stage, *Laboratory tests, Temperature, Juvenile fish, Viability, Larval growth stage, Freshwater fish, Bass, Oxygen, Water pollution effects.
Identifiers: *Micropterus dolomieui, *Mountain whitefish.

As a part of a study to determine the dissolved oxygen requirements of some freshwater fish species, mountain whitefish (Prosopium williamsoni, smallmouth bass (Micropterus dolomieui), and white bass (Morone chyrsops) at various early growth stages were raised in conditions of reduced dissolved oxygen. A reduction of oxygen concentration of 50% saturation at 4C and 7C did not affect the survival of young mountain whitefish but developmental delays did occur. A reduction to 35 percent saturation of dissolved oxygen appears to harm the survival of mountain whitefish. Smallmouth bass embryos require a dissolved oxygen concentration of greater than 50% at optimal temperature for proper survival. There was poor survival of young white bass at 20 percent saturation. Larvae reared at 35 percent saturation appeared normal except for an apparent inhibition of yolk-sac absorption. (Katz)
W75-09132

FISH KILL DUE TO 'COLD SHOCK' IN LAKE WABAMUN, ALBERTA,
Alberta Univ., Edmonton. Dept. of Zoology.
G. H. Ash, N. R. Chymko, and D. N. Gallup.
Journal of the Fisheries Research Board of Canada, Vol 31, No 11, p 1822-1824, November 1974. 2 fig, 6 ref.

Descriptors: *Fishkill, *Heated water, Temperature, *Shiners, Mortality, Thermal water, Discharge(Water), Thermal powerplants, Clams, Powerplants, *Canada, *Pikes, Thermal stress, Lakes, Thermal pollution, Water pollution effects.
Identifiers: *Cold shock, *Lake Wabamun(Alberta).

A thermal fish kill due to 'cold shock' caused by a mechanical failure in the steam electric generating unit was observed in Lake Wabamun, Alberta, on February 8, 1973 in the region of the discharge canal. The most rapid temperature decline occurred in the initial 30 minutes after shutdown when the temperature dropped 16.9C (21.8 to 4.9C). The major fish species affected included spottail shiners (Notropis hudsonius and Northern pike (Esox lucius). The freshwater clam Anodonta sp. did not appear to be affected. (Katz)
W75-09133

RETARED BEHAVIORAL DEVELOPMENT AND IMPAIRED BALANCE IN ATLANTIC SAL-

Vegetational properties of mixed hardwood swamps of the Savannah River exposed to different thermal regimes from the release of nuclear reactor effluents were compared on the bases of floristic similarity, importance values of the dominant species, and diversity. Floristic composition was greatly altered by high water temperatures and by increased flooding and silting associated with the discharge of reactor effluents. Although the forest canopy was destroyed, diversity of the herbaceous flora remained high under conditions of thermal loading and post-thermal recovery. Trees comprise 40% of the species present in the undisturbed swamp habitat and less than 10% in the stressed areas. Successional recovery of the swamp following removal of stress is slow. (Katz)
W75-09137

A TECHNIQUE TO PROLONG THE INCUBATION PERIOD OF BROWN TROUT OVA,
Imperial Chemical Industries Ltd., Brixham (England). Brixham Research Lab.
For primary bibliographic entry see Field 5A.
W75-09138

TOXICITY OF COPPER AT TWO TEMPERATURES AND THREE SALINITIES TO THE AMERICAN LOBSTER (HOMARUS AMERICANUS),
Fisheries Research Board of Canada, St. Andrews (New Brunswick). Biological Station.
D. W. McLeese.
Journal of the Fisheries Research Board of Canada, Vol 31, No 12, p 1949-1952, December 1974. 2 tab, 17 ref.

Descriptors: *Lobsters, *Copper, *Salinity, *Water temperature, *Lethal limit, *Toxicity, *Heavy metals, Environmental effects, Mortality, Water pollution effects.
Identifiers: *LT50.

Toxicity of copper to lobsters (Homarus americanus) was studied to provide a measure of lethal concentrations and to observe whether the toxicity is affected by temperature and salinity. The time to 50% mortality at a particular lethal concentration of copper was longer at 5C than at 13C but it was not affected by salinities of 20-30%. The lethal copper threshold was close to 56 micrograms/liter. (Katz)
W75-09139

THERMAL TOLERANCE OF EGGS AND LARVAE OF HAWAIIAN STRIPED MULLET, MUGIL CEPHALUS L.,
Oceanic Inst., Waimanalo, Hawaii.
J. R. Sylvester, and C. E. Nash.
Transactions of the American Fisheries Society, Vol 104, No 1, p 144-147, 1975. 1 fig, 3 tab, 24 ref.

Descriptors: *Mullets, *Incubation, *Temperature control, Fish, *Water temperature, *Larval growth stage, *Fish eggs, *Environmental effects, Reproduction, Graphical analysis, Graphical methods, Life cycles, Water Quality, Heated water, Water cooling, Marine fish, Metabolism, Spawning, Hatching, Mortality, Breeding, Fertilization, Model studies, Nutrient requirements, Zooplankton, Productivity, Dissolved oxygen, Sea water, Aquatic Environment, Equations, Equipment, Aquaria, Design, Statistical analysis, Water pollution effects.
Identifiers: Mugil cephalus, *Thermal tolerance, Logarithmic transformations, Hypohysation, Technique.

Relationships between temperature and mortaility of eggs and survival of the larvae are described for the striped mullet Mugil cephalus. Eggs were incubated at temperatures between 1.0 and 40.5C. Mortalities were least (4.2%) within the range 22.7-23.3C. Hatching time was inversely related to temperature. The equation $Y=3.6674 - 1.5240X$ describes the relation between incubation time and temperature over the range of 11-30C. Larvae were exposed to temperatures between 2.7 and 32.9C. Survival up to 12 days was greatest (19.9%) at a mean temperature of 24.9 (range 24.5-25.3C). Results suggest that optimum temperatures for egg development and hatching occur at temperature. levels which are inefficient or inimical for larvae growth and development. (Katz)
W75-09140

EFFECT OF DISSOLVED OXYGEN CONCENTRATION ON THE ACUTE TOXICITY OF CADMIUM TO THE MUMMICHOG, FUNDULUS HETEROCLITUS (L.), AT VARIOUS SALINITIES,
National Marine Water Quality Lab., West Kingston, R.I.
R. A. Voyer.
Transactions of the American Fisheries Society, Vol 104, No 1, p 129-134, 1975. 1 fig, 3 tab, 18 ref.

Descriptors: *Heavy metals, *Cadmium, *Dissolved oxygen, *Lethal limit, *Toxicity, *Salinity, Freshwater fish, Water pollution sources, Chemical wastes, Environmental effects, Laboratory studies, Structural design, Statistical analysis, Tissue analysis, Mortality, Fish physiology, Oxygen demand, Chlorides, Inorganic compounds, Water pollution effects.
Identifiers: *Fundulus heteroclitus, *TL50, Mummichogs.

The resistance of mummichogs, Fundulus heteroclitus, to acute cadmium poisoning was not influenced by reductions in dissolved oxygen levels to about 4 mg/liter at selected salinities. Fish were acclimated to either test salinities (10, 20, and 32%) or to 32% and then exposed to 10 and 20%. Results suggest cadmium as being the only source of significant variance influencing response. Histological response of mummichogs' exposure to cadmium is discussed. (Katz)
W75-09141

ACUTE TOXICITIES OF A POLYCHLORINATED BIPHENYL (PCB) AND DDT ALONE AND IN COMBINATION TO EARLY LIFE STAGES OF COHO SALMON (ONCORHYNCHUS KISUTCH),
Michigan State Univ., East Lansing. Dept. of Fisheries and Wildlife.
M. T. Halter, and H. E. Johnson.
Journal of the Fisheries Research Board of Canada, Vol 31, No 9, p 1543-1547, 1974. 2 tab, 15 ref.

Descriptors: Fry, *Aroclor, *Polychlorinated biphenyls, Hatching, *Fish eggs, *Toxicity, *Pesticides, *Salmon, *DDT, Clorinated Hydrocarbon pesticides, Lethal limit, Water pollution effects.
Identifiers: Synergistic effects, *Coho salmon.

Egg hatchability, mean time to hatching, and alevin survival and growth decreased when coho salmon eggs and alevins were exposed at 12-14C to 4.4 mg/liter Aroclor 1245 or higher until 4 weeks after hatching, and to 15 mg/liter or more until 2 days before hatching. Premature hatching occurred in all egg groups exposed to the PCB. The median survival times of fry exposed to Aroclor 1254-DDT combinations for two weeks were similar to those after exposure to the various concentrations of DDT alone. The more rapid reaction time to DDT is suggested as the basis for lack of additive toxicity. (Katz)
W75-09142

VERTEBRAL DAMAGE TO MINNOWS PHOXINUS PHOXINUS EXPOSED TO ZINC,
Umea Univ. (Sweden). Dept. of Biology.
B-E. Bengtsson.
Oikos, Vol 25, No 2, p 134-139, 1974. 7 fig, 2 tab, 17 ref.

Descriptors: *Zinc, *Minnows, *Animal pathology, Metals, Pollutants, Lethal limit, Mortality, Growth rates, Reproduction, Fish behavior, Toxicants, Water pollution effects, Organophosphorus pesticides, Symptomology.
Identifiers: *Phoxinus phoxinus, *Sublethal effects, *Vertebral damage(Fish).

Adult minnows exposed to different concentrations of Zn(NO3)2 in fresh water developed hemorrhages and lesions. Vertebral damage occurred between 0.20 and 2.4ppm Zn2+ which is below the 96-hr LC50 dosage. The similarity between the symptomology of zinc and organophosphates is discussed. (Katz)
W75-09144

MODEL FOR ACCUMULATION OF METHYL MERCURY IN NORTHERN PIKE ESOX LUCIUS,
Institute for Water and Air Pollution Research, Stockholm (Sweden).
For primary bibliographic entry see Field 5B.
W75-09145

EXPERIMENTAL STUDIES ON THE EFFECTS OF COPPER ON A MARINE FOOD CHAIN,
Marine Lab., Aberdeen (Scotland).
D. Saward, A. A. Stirling, and B. G. Topping.
Marine Biology, Vol 29, No 4, p 351-361, 1975. 11 fig, 1 tab, 34 ref.

Descriptors: *Copper sulfate, *Food chains, *Path of pollutants, *Bioassay, Environmental effects, Copper, Toxicants, Pollutants, Photosynthesis, Growth rates, Metabolism, Food webs, Copper compounds, Biomass, Inorganic pesticides, Phytoplankton, Laboratory tests, Absorption, Adsorption, Sands, Crustaceans, Water pollution effects, Methodology, Lethal limit, Water pollution effects.
Identifiers: *Plaice, Pleuronectes platessa, *Tellina tenuis, Bioaccumulation, Tissue analysis, Sublethal effects.

Effects of copper sulfate on a marine food chain were investigated in a laboratory test. The food chain consisted of phytoplankton, the bivalve Tellina tenuis and the plaice Pleuronectes platessa. Copper dose rates of 10, 30 and 100 micrograms Cu/l were investigated. Copper levels in water, sand, algae, T. tenuis shell and flesh, and plaice muscle and viscera were measured. Copper accumulated in sand, T. tenuis flesh and shell, and plaice viscera. Accumulations were dose-dependent and no plateau concentrations were reached. The effects of copper on phytoplankton metabolism and on growth and condition of T. tenuis and plaice were investigated. (Katz)
W75-09146

ACCUMULATION OF 3,4,3',4'-TETRACHLOROBIPHENYL AND 2,4,5,2',4',5'-AND 2,4,6,2',4',6' - HEXACHLOROBIPHENYL IN JUVENILE COHO SALMON,
National Marine Fisheries Service, Seattle, Wash.
For primary bibliographic entry see Field 5A.
W75-09148

REPRODUCTIVE CYCLES OF LARGEMOUTH BASS (MICROPTERUS SALMOIDES) IN A COOLING RESERVOIR,
Savannah River Ecology Lab., Aiken, S.C.
D. H. Bennett, and J. W. Gibbons.
Transactions of the American Fisheries Society, Vol 104, No 1, p 77-82, 1975. 1 fig, 2 tab, 17 ref.

Descriptors: *South Carolina, *Environmental effects, *Heated water, *Fish reproduction, *Bass, Water temperature, *Fish physiology, Reservoirs, Gonads, Freshwater fish, Sexual maturity, Heat flow, Temperature control, *Thermal pollution, Fish behavior, Animal metabolism, Growth stages, Life Cycles, Biorhythms, Photoperiod, Nuclear powerplants, Water pollution effects.
Identifiers: *Centrarchid, *Micropterus salmoides, Gonosomadic indices, Savannah River Plant(SC).

Annual reproductive cycles of largemouth bass collected in the heated area of a 1120-hectare reservoir on the Savannah River Plant, South Carolina, receiving thermal effluent were similar to cycles from bass collected in unheated waters during 1969 and 1970. Average maximum monthly temperatures at the heated area exceeded those in unheated waters by greater than 10C for 2 years. Few monthly differences in gonosomatic indices were found between heated and unheated areas. Earlier attainment of maximum gonadal size and the presence of significantly larger juvenile bass at the heated area suggested that reproduction might be accelerated by thermal discharge. However, gonadal condition indicated that the reproductive period started in March and continued through April in both areas. Reproduction may have been advanced in some heated-area bass, although this was not obvious from overall changes in the reproductive cycles of bass from unheated areas. (Katz)
W75-09150

SURVIVAL OF LARGEMOUTH BASS EMBRYOS AT LOW DISSOLVED OXYGEN CONCENTRATIONS,
New York Cooperative Fishery Unit, Ithaca.
R. G. Dudley, and A. W. Eipper.
Transactions of the American Fisheries Society, Vol 104, No 1, p 122-128, 1975. 2 fig, 2 tab, 18 ref.

Descriptors: *Bass, *Sunfishes, Hatching, *Mortality, *Embryonic growth stage, *Larval growth stage, Environmental effects, *Dissolved oxygen, Movement, Water circulation, *Biomass, Water temperature, Temperature control, Structural design, Construction material, Construction, Instrumentation, Dissolved oxygen analyzers, Fish reproduction, Fish physiology, Water quality, Fertilization, Fish eggs, Mathematics, Life cycles, Growth stages, Graph analysis, Nutrient requirements, Equipment, Laboratory tests, Equations.
Identifiers: Micropterus salmoides, Survival rates.

Low oxygen concentrations were identified that significantly decreased survival of largemouth bass (Micropterus salmoides) embryos incubated at three temperatures in both stationary and moving containers. Embryos developed and hatched at oxygen concentrations of 1.0, 1.1 and 1.3 mg/liter at temperatures of 15, 20 and 25C, respectively, but concentrations below 2.0, 2.1 and 2.8 mg/liter significantly lowered survival. Most mortality at these oxygen concentrations occurred during hatching. At oxygen concentrations below 1.0 mg/liter, survival during the pre-hatching period was higher among those groups of embryos that were moved slowly up and down during incubation than among unmoved embryos; however, moved embryos suffered nearly complete mortality during hatching at all oxygen concentrations. Possible explanations of results were expressed. (Katz)
W75-09151

USE OF A SUDDEN TEMPERATURE DECREASE TO REDUCE THE EXCITABILITY OF CHANNEL CATFISH DURING HANDLING,
Southern Illinois Univ., Carbondale. Fisheries Research Lab.
W. K. Anderson, and W. M. Lewis.
The Progressive Fish-Culturist, Vol 36, No 4, p 213-215, October 1974. 3 tab, 2 fig, 2 ref.

Descriptors: *Channel catfish, *Commercial fish, *Heated water, *Temperature, *Aquiculture, Fish behavior, Mortality, Respiration, *Fish harvest, *Fish farming, Catfishes, Cooling, Water pollution effects.
Identifiers: *Thermal shock, *Fish handling.

damage to the gill epithelium, death resulting from a disturbance in the levels of oxygen, carbon dioxide, and sodium ions in the tissues and blood. Histological examination showed that solutions of the synthetic surfactants caused less damage to the gill epithelium than did the M. glacialis saponins. There was a linear relationship between the logarithm of the median hemolytic concentration and the logarithm of the median lethal concentration for the synthetic surfactants. Hemolytic inhibition experiments suggest that the M. glacialis saponins damage cell membranes by interacting with membrane cholesterol. (Katz)
W75-09161

TISSUE HYDROCARBON BURDEN OF MUSSELS AS POTENTIAL MONITOR OF ENVIRONMENTAL HYDROCARBON INSULT,
Naval Biomedical Research Lab., Oakland, Calif.
For primary bibliographic entry see Field 5B.
W75-09163

EFFECTS OF LOWERED DISSOLVED OXYGEN CONCENTRATIONS ON CHANNEL CATFISH (ICTALURUS PUNCTATUS) EMBRYOS AND LARVAE,
National Water Quality Lab., Duluth, Minn.
A. R. Carlson, R. E. Siefert, and L. J. Herman.
Transactions of the American Fisheries Society, Vol 103, No 3, p 623-626, July 1974. 1 tab, 11 ref.

Descriptors: *Dissolved oxygen, *Channel catfish, *Larval growth stage, *Embryonic growth stage, Freshwater fish, Laboratory tests, Temperature, Water pollution effects.

Channel catfish embryos and larvae were exposed to several reduced dissolved oxygen concentrations and control concentrations near air saturation at 25 and 28C (7.8 and 7.3 mg/liter respectively). At 25C survival was similar but slightly reduced at 60% and 70% saturation and was statistically less at 30% and 50% saturation. No embryos hatched at 20% and 25C. Survival to the end of the test at 28C was slightly reduced at 50%, 60% and 70% saturation and was statistically less at 30% saturation. At all reduced oxygen concentrations at 25 and 28C embryonic pigmentation was lighter, duration of hatch was extended, feeding was delayed and growth was reduced. (Katz)
W75-09164

NET PRIMARY PRODUCTIVITY OF PERIPHYTIC ALGAE IN THE INTERTIDAL ZONE, DUWAMISH RIVER ESTUARY, WASHINGTON,
Geological Survey, Menlo Park, Calif.
L. J. Tilley, and W. L. Haushild.
Available from Superintendent of Documents, US Government Printing Office, Washington, DC, 20402, for $3.15 in paper copy, $2.25 in microfiche. Journal of Research of the US Geological Survey, Vol 3, No 3, p 253-259, May-June 1975. 3 fig, 4 tab, 16 ref.

Descriptors: *Algae, *Estuaries, *Tidal waters, *Washington, Growth rates, Data collections, Sessile algae, Analytical techniques, Environmental effects, Waste water disposal, Dredging, Tidal effects, Water quality, Evaluation, Water pollution sources, Water pollution effects.
Identifiers: *Periphytic algae, *Duwamish River estuary(Wash).

In a comprehensive study of the Duwamish River estuary, Seattle, Wash., investigations of the amount of algal biomass produced or deposited in the estuary included an estimation of the rate of growth of attached algae. New primary productivity of periphyton in the intertidal zone was determined. This productivity, measured as chlorophyll a concentration in the periphyton on fixed glass substrates, was 0.11 mg/sq m per week. The low productivity of attached algae on the substrates was attributed to out-of-water desiccation, and part of the variability in accumulation of periphytic algae was attributed to the time out-of-water exposure, which varied greatly from week to week owing to the irregularity of tides in the estuary. (Woodard-USGS)
W75-09189

LENGTH OF INCUBATION FOR ENUMERATING NITRIFYING BACTERIA PRESENT IN VARIOUS ENVIRONMENTS,
Rutgers - The State Univ., New Brunswick, N.J. Dept. of Environmental Science.
For primary bibliographic entry see Field 5A.
W75-09234

THE PEOPLE'S LAKE,
Save Lake Superior Association, Duluth, Minn.
K. T. Carlson.
Environment, Vol 17, No 2, p 16-20, 25-26, March 1975. 5 photo, 19 ref.

Descriptors: *Judicial decisions, *Water pollution, *Mine wastes, *Environmental effects, *Lake Superior, Minnesota, Legal aspects, Water law, Public health, Waste disposal, Solid wastes, Industrial wastes, Wastes, Aquatic environment, Water injury, Water pollution sources, Water quality, Water supply, Lakes.
Identifiers: Hazardous substances(Pollution), Injunctive relief, Coastal waters, Coastal zone management.

A mining company in Minnesota dumps 750 million gallons of wastewater, containing 67,000 tons of taconite waste and 60,000 pounds of dissolved solids into Lake Superior daily. In order to prevent pollution of the lake, a local environmental group sought to curtail the dumping operations. The problems and concerns of the group are described, as well as the history of the litigation. The plaintiffs fought a long and tedious battle to prove that the particular form of pollution was harmful. Concern was expressed that the company's operations were causing the irreparable harm to aquatic life and the drinking water supply. Central to the controversy was whether asbestos fibers in the waste material were cancer causing. Balanced against the factors of environmental protection and public health was the fate of 3,200 workers who faced loss of their jobs if the plant were closed. The district court ordered immediate curtailment of the discharge, but was reversed by the circuit court. The Supreme Court, without comment refused to reinstate the order. (Fernandez-Florida)
W75-09247

THE USE OF PHYSIOLOGICAL INDICATORS OF STRESS IN MARINE INVERTEBRATES AS A TOOL FOR MARINE POLLUTION MONITORING,
Virginia Inst. of Marine Science, Gloucester Point.
For primary bibliographic entry see Field 5A.
W75-09269

APPLICATION OF THE PHOSPHORUS-LOADING CONCEPT TO EUTROPHICATION RESEARCH,
Canada Centre for Inland Waters, Burlington, (Ontario).
P. J. Dillon.
Scientific Series No 46, 14 p, 1975, 5 fig, 8 tab, 45 ref.

Descriptors: *Phosphorus, *Chlorophyll, *Primary productivity, *Eutrophication, Water pollution, Ecosystems, Great Lakes.
Identifiers: *Phosphorus-loading, Water retention time.

Recent advances in the study of eutrophication include the improvement of Vollenweider's (The Scientific Basis of Lake and Stream Eutrophication, with Particular Reference to Phosphorus and Nitrogen as Eutrophication Factors, Technical Re-

port OECD, Paris DAS/CS1/68, Vol 27, p 1-182, 1968) original phosphorus-loading-mean depth relationship to take into account the water retention time of the lake. The relationship between phosphorus loading and phosphorus concentration has been investigated, and correlations between phosphorus loading and primary production for the Great Lakes and between spring phosphorus concentration and summer chlorophyll concentration for a wide variety of lakes have been developed. A number of lakes have undergone reductions in phosphorus load; in those where the reduction was significant, the lakes have responded favorably. (Env. Canada)
W75-09287

HUCHO HUCHO L. IN MARAMURES WATERS, (IN ROMANIAN),
Institutul Pedagogic Baia-Mare (Rumania).
For primary bibliographic entry see Field 5G.
W75-09304

THE STUDY ON THE AQUATIC INSECT FAUNA OF THE MATSUKAWA AND YONAKO RIVERS (MINERAL ACID POLLUTED RIVER), (IN JAPANESE),
Rissho Women's Coll., Koshigaya (Japan).
For primary bibliographic entry see Field 5B.
W75-09316

PLANKTON, CHEMISTRY, AND PHYSICS OF LAKES IN THE CHURCHILL FALLS REGION OF LABRADOR,
Waterloo Univ. (Ontario). Dept. of Biology.
For primary bibliographic entry see Field 2H.
W75-09317

BIOLOGICAL VIEW OF PROBLEMS OF URBAN HEALTH,
John Curtin School of Medical Research, Canberra (Australia). Dept. of Human Biology.
For primary bibliographic entry see Field 6G.
W75-09332

5D. Waste Treatment Processes

PURIFICATION OF INDUSTRIAL AND MUNICIPAL WASTE WATER.
French Patent 36854V/20. Applied October 25, 1973. Issued June 28, 1974. Derwent French Patents Report, Vol 5, No 35, p 4, 1974.

Descriptors: *Patents, *Waste water treatment, *Carbon, *Organic compounds, *Municipal wastes, Dissolved oxygen, Color, Water purification.
Identifiers: *Total organic carbon.

A process for the purification of industrial and municipal waste water was patented. It reduces total organic carbon content and improves the color of water contaminated by organic compounds. The process is performed at 0 to 100C. An amount of the contaminated water is introduced into a tank, adding active carbon to form a suspension. The mixture is stirred and contacted with an 02 containing gas, preferably by setting up a 1 to 9 mg/liter dissolved oxygen content. The amount of active carbon added provides a 50 to 200 g/liter suspension density of the contaminated water. After treatment active carbon may be separated from the water and reused for treating a further charge of water. Waste water color can be reduced from 500 to 1000 to less than 100 APHA color units. (Prague-FIRL)
W75-08852

SEWAGE PROCESSING,
I. S. Turovskii, L. L. Goldfarb, and B. L. Gordon.
Soviet Patent SU 403632. Applied October 26, 1973. Issued March 20, 1974. Soviet Inventions Illustrated, Vol 5, No 37, p 1, 1974. 1 fig.

Descriptors: *Patents, *Sewage treatment, *Sludge treatment, Capital costs, Operating costs, *Storage tanks, Aeration, Storage, Dewatering, *Waste water treatment, *Coagulation.

A sewage treatment process was patented which coagulates chemicals, reduces emergency sludge areas, and eliminates a dehelminthisation chamber. Precipitates are fermented in a reservoir-storage tank, with aeration for 2.5 to 3.2 cu m/hr/cu m of precipitate for 12 to 48 hours, and then heated at 60 to 70 degrees c. These are then coagulated and dewatered. The sewerage supply pipes go from settlers and a sludge thickener to an aeration and storage tank. Pipes supply air to the latter. A heater, a mixer, a coagulant doser, a distributer, a combustion chamber, a drum vacuum filter, a belt conveyor, and a container for dewatered precipitate are illustrated. There is an emergency aerator-storage tank supplied with one cu m/cu m/hour of air. Heating and aeration make the materials non toxic and cut viscosity so that less ferric chloride must be added. After dewatering to 57% H2O, the resultant liquid can then be stored. Capital costs are cut 2.5 fold and operating costs are cut by 15 percent. (Prague-FIRL)
W75-08853

AUTOMATIC PRIMING OF WASTE-WATER PUMP.
French Patent 65042V/37. Applied November 13, 1973. Issued July 12, 1974. Derwent French Patents Abstracts, Vol 5, No 37, p 3, 1974.

Descriptors: *Patents, Equipment, *Waste water treatment, *Pumps, Automation, Drainage, Hydraulic machinery, Valves, Tanks.
Identifiers: *Waste water tanks.

An automatic priming system for a waste water pump was patented which will overcome siphoning due to failures in downstream drainage. This pumping unit is used to evacuate a waste water tank, especially one associated with a domestic unit, under level control, into a drainage system. The system has an inclined side-arm, branching below the non-return valve downstream of the pump, fitted with a valve which permits flow of air in either direction, but closes under pressure when the pump is in operation. The unit has a vertical Mono pump, below which is a rotary disc mill disintegrator. Backflow from the drainage system is prevented by a non-return valve. Should there be pressure loss in the drainage system due to leakage, siphoning through the non-return valve occurs, but it is prevented from de-priming the pump by entry of air or liquid through the sidearm. This serves to bleed away air during the initial start-up of the pump, and to equilibriate pressure in the pump when the non-return valves is closed, so that re-starting is facilitated. (Prague-FIRL)
W75-08854

AUTOMATIC CHAMBER FILTER PRESSES FOR WASTEWATER TREATMENT, (AUTOMATISCHE KAMMERFILTERPRESSEN ZUR ABWASSERBEHANDLUNG).
Galvanotechnik, Vol 65, No 7, p 612, July, 1974. 1 fig.

Descriptors: *Waste water treatment, Automation, Industrial wastes, Municipal wastes, Sewage sludge, Design, Filters, *Filtration, *Dewatering.
Identifiers: *Filter presses, *Filter cokes.

Netzsch type chamber filter presses for the dewatering of industrial and municipal sewage sludge are described. The filter presses are designed for filter pressures of up to 15 atm, and are also available in fully automatic design. With a filter surface of 4 sq m per chamber, one filter press accomodate up to 120 chambers. The filtrate obtained is clear and can be discharged into the sewer system, while the filter cake has a dry content of 40 percent. (Takacs-FIRL)
W75-08855

BIOLOGICAL FERTILIZER PRODUCTION - BY TREATMENT OF SEWAGE SLUDGES WITH SULFITE LIQUORS.
Belgian Patent 56760V/32. Applied March 2, 1973. Issued July 1, 1974. Derwent Belgian Patents Report, Vol 5, No 32, p 4, September, 1974.

Descriptors: *Patents, *Fertilizers, *Sewage sludge, *Sulfite liquors, *Waste water treatment, Industrial wastes, Hydrogen ion concentration, Farm wastes, Recycling.
Identifiers: Biological fertilizer production, Clarification.

Biological fertilizer production by treatment of sewage sludges with sulphite liquors is described. Fertilizer is produced using waste waters, such as agglomerated sewage, industrial waste waters, or agricultural waste liquors. These sewage sludges, obtained when the waste waters are clarified, are mixed with a residual sulphite liquor and reacted at an optimum pH of less than 6 in the presence of an oxidising agent. The treated sludges are then mixed with ground vegetable material and left to be transformed into a biological fertilizer by traditional methods. (Prague-FIRL)
W75-08863

UNDERDRAIN STRUCTURE FOR WASTE EFFLUENT FILTER AND METHOD OF USING SAME,
Hydro-Clear Corp., Avon Lake, Ohio. (Assignee).
D. S. Ross.
United States Patent 3,840,117. Applied April 30, 1973. Issued October 8, 1974. Official Gazette of the United States Patent Office, Vol 927, No 2, p 526, October, 1974. 1 fig.

Descriptors: *Patents, *Filtration, *Sewage effluents, Drains, Liquids, Equipment, Tanks, *Waste water treatment, Filters.
Identifiers: Underdrains.

An underdrain structure and method for waste effluent filtration is described. A waste effluent filter is included in a tank with a filter bed of particulate material, an underdrain cavity, and a lower portion. Means for draining from the underdrain cavity filtered effluent after the filtered effluent has passed through the bed, means for allowing air to enter the underdrain cavity, and means for forcing liquid into the underdrain cavity where the air is compressed are provided. One feature of this equipment is an air distribution device secured in the underdrain cavity which defines several vertically extending chambers below the bed. Each chamber has an inner cavity, a lower open end opening into the underdrain cavity and at least one means for forming an aperture in the upper end where liquid is forced into the underdrain cavity. The apertures have a second area substantially smaller than the first area, and liquid closes the open ends and then forces air entrapped in the chambers up through the aperture and then through the bed. (Prague-FIRL)
W75-08864

SEWAGE AND MUNICIPAL REFUSE LIQUID PHASE COKING PROCESS,
Texaco Development Corp., New York.
H. V. Hess, R. F. Wilson, and E. L. Cole.
Canadian Patent 954,810. Applied June 15, 1971. Issued September 17, 1974. Patent Office Record, Vol 102, No 38, p 33-34, September, 1974.

Descriptors: *Municipal wastes, *Patents, Sewage, Solid wastes, Water clarification, Liquids, Sewage sludge, *Waste water treatment.
Identifiers: *Coking process.

A combination process for treating both municipal refuse and sewage was patented. Solid refuse is shredded and the shredded material obtained is mixed with a recycle stream of water resulting from a subsequent coking step to form a slurry. Non-combustible materials are removed from this slurry. The slurry is then mixed with sewage sludge, and the resulting mixture is coked under sufficient pressure to prevent the vaporization of water. Thus, grease, clean water, and clean coke are produced. (Prague-FIRL)
W75-08865

SLUDGE SETTLING DEVICE FOR SEWAGE FILTER SYSTEMS (OSUI ROKA SOCHI NI OKERU SURAJJI NO CHINKO BURNRI SHORI SOCHI),
J. Sasaki.
Japanese Patent 49-19659. Applied June 21, 1968. Issued May 25, 1974.

Descriptors: *Patents, Pumps, *Filters, *Sewage treatment, Equipment, Flocculation, Water purification, *Filtration, *Waste water treatment.
Identifiers: Sludge settling, Sewage filters, Japan.

A sludge settling device for sewage filter systems is reported. In the treatment tank, sewage water is supplied by a pipe submerged deep in the sludge settling chamber. The sewage rises above to reach multi-filter material installed at the top of the chamber. The sludge settling device is a funnel shaped receptacle with a small outlet into the sludge removal channel. Between the filter material at the upper part of the sludge treatment tank and the sludge settling chamber is a frame bar with many slits through which the sewage water rises into the filter material. Many thin wire-like fibers are suspended from the frame bar over the entire cross section of the sludge settling chamber. Fibrous material accelerate sludge flocculation around them while sewage water moves up the tank between the hanging fibers. The flocculated sludge, growing in size and weight, can drop and slip into the outlet of the settling chamber and is drawn out by a suction pump. The purified water above the filter is emitted into the purification tank through a magnetic valve and is discharged by a pump. (Seigle-FIRL)
W75-08866

OXIDATION DITCH FOR WASTE TREATMENT.
Australian Patent 452,527. Applied September 21, 1971. Issued September 5, 1974. Official Journal of Patents, Trade Marks and Designs, Vol 44, No 33, p 3641, September, 1974.

Descriptors: *Patents, *Aeration, *Liquid wastes, Jets, Waste water treatment, *Oxidation lagoons, Aerated lagoons, Waste treatment.
Identifiers: *Oxidation ditch.

A method for the aeration treatment of waste liquid was patented. First the waste liquid is introduced into a ditch defining a continuous, substantially closed cource for liquid movement with a surface level well above the ditch bottom. This waste liquid is then impacted with high velocity jets of a mixture of air and water, which is admitted below the surface level. This process imparts a velocity of at least about 0.3 foot per second to the waste liquid while mixing the air with the liquid. The treated liquid is thus removed from the oxidation ditch. (Prague-FIRL)
W75-08867

WASTE WATER PURIFICATION SYSTEM (OSUI JOKA SOCHI),
Electric Industrial Co. Ltd., Osaka (Japan). Matsushita.
T. Jomoto, K. Shinogi, M. Oshibi, and T. Terada.
Japanese Patent 49-26661. Applied July 13, 1970. Issued July 11, 1974. p 91-96, 1974. 4 fig.

Descriptors: *Patents, *Sewage treatment, *Aeration, Disinfection, Equipment, *Waste water treatment, Settling basins.
Identifiers: *Settling tanks, *Aeration chambers.

A sewage purification system was patented in which the circulation of sewage current in the aeration chamber moves only along the walls of the tank. The system contains a settling tank within an aeration tank in order to save space. The unit has a separation room, an aeration chamber, a settling chamber, and a disinfection chamber. The separation room has a sewage pipe which supplies the sewage water while the aeration room has air dispersion pipes. The settling chamber has a narrow upper part and a flared middle; near the top is an overflow opening. A sediment exit near its bottom returns the sludge to the aeration tank. There is a space between the settling chamber partition wall and the aeration room wall in which sewage water can circulate and oxidize well. Since the settling chamber has a flared bottom and a narrow top, the supernatant liquid forms a deep layer at the top and does not receive the effects of the circulation in the aeration chamber. The sediment returns to the aeration chamber from the exit near the bottom. The supernatant liquid overflows into the disinfection chamber were a disinfectant is supplied. The cleaned liquid is then emitted from the discharge pipe. (Seigle-FIRL)
W75-08868

BIOLOGICAL PURIFICATION OF SEWAGE WATER.
Belgian Patent 61825V/35. Applied February 2, 1974. Issued August 12, 1974. Derwent Belgian Patents Abstracts, Vol 5, No 36, p 2, 1974.

Descriptors: *Patents, *Sewage treatment, *Biological treatment, Bacteria, Tanks, *Waste water treatment.
Identifiers: *Rotating discs.

A method of biological purification of sewage water is recorded. The installation for the secondary processing of this sewage water has a tank divided into a series of compartments. In each of these there are partly submerged rotating discs, so that the fluid passes through the tank divisions at a controlled rate of flow. The bacteria propagate themselves while exposed alternately to the sewage and to atmospheric oxygen on the disc surfaces. The area of these disc surfaces are compared to the volume of the liquid being processed as held at its optimum ratio. (Prague-FIRL)
W75-08869

SEWAGE TREATMENT TANK SCREENING STRUCTURE (OSHUI SHORISO YO SUKURIN KOZO),
T. Sugimoto.
Japanese Patent 49-28359. Applied December 28, 1970. Issued August 2, 1974. p 87-89. 4 fig.

Descriptors: *Patents, *Sewage treatment, Filters, Tanks, Equipment, Screens, *Waste water treatment, Filtration.
Identifiers: *Rotation drum screens.

A sewage purification device is described. In the system, sewage water led into a digestion tank or separation tank must first be filtered to remove solids. A simple filter screen quickly becomes clogged with the solids and requires frequent removal and washing. The use of sweeper does not solve this clogging problem. A rotation drum screen also solves the clogging very little. This device was designed to remove screen-clogging solids periodically or at a desired time. The structure has several semi-circular segments joined by an inclined common axis. Each segment has a stable screen with a semi-circular bottom and teeth that will fit into the gaps of the semicircular screen perfectly. The rotation drum screen also provides a sweeper for the solids. The sewage water is supplied from a high level by a pipe at the top of the inclination, so that the solid will be screened and swept. As the drum rotates, the swept solid gradually is pushed toward the lower part, and finally pushed off into the solid receptacle. (Seigle-FIRL)
W75-08870

SEWAGE TREATMENT METHOD UPS CAPACITY.
Chemical and Engineering News, Vol 52, No 33, p 6-7, August 1974.

Descriptors: *Bacteria, *Sewage treatment, *Sewers, *Digestion, Anaerobic conditions, Anaerobic digestion, Biochemical oxygen demand, Nutrient removal, Pipelines, California, *Waste water treatment.

Lathrop Laboratories, Fresno, California, has developed a sewage treatment process that uses a newly developed bacterial isolate and the sewage lines themselves as partial digesters. The bacterial isolate is not a normal constituent of feces. However, it multiplies in the anaerobic environment of most sewage lines and degrades waste without producing offensive odors. Tests of the process showed that it can achieve a great reduction in BOD, ammonia and nitrates concentration and hydrogen sulfide levels. The cost of treating one mgd was about $400 per month. The bacteria were developed from normal 'earth bacteria' and present no health or safety problems. They were grown in 2000 gallon nonpressurized tanks and metered into the sewage lines in appropriate amounts. The bacterial isolates could also be applied to rivers, lakes, and ponds, using crop dusting aircraft, to improve the ability of these bodies of water to assimilate sewage and other effluents. (Orr-FIRL)
W75-08871

GET READY FOR UNI-FLOW FILTERS,
Western Regional Research Lab., Berkeley, Calif.
W. M. Camirand, and K. Popper.
Water and Wastes Engineering, Vol 11, No 10, p 31-34, October 1974. 4 fig, 3 tab.

Descriptors: *Filters, *Municipal wastes, *Waste water treatment, Settling, Lime.
Identifiers: *Physical-chemical treatment, Uni-flow filters.

The uni-flow filter for the physical-chemical treatment of municipal waste water is described. This filter was invented as an inexpensive alternative to a settling tank for concentration of calcium hydroxide and magnesium hydroxide slurries in connection with an ion exchange desalination process. It has been tested as a solid liquid separator in a municipal sewage treatment scheme using modular mobile equipment. The filter itself is a vertical cloth tube between four and twenty feet long, which might be seen as a settling tank with permeable canvas walls. Input is at the top and a sludge discharge valve and a filtrate collector are located at the bottom. Solids are retained on the inside of the porous tube. Hydrostatic pressure forces the filtrate through the porous walls, and gravity effects the settling of solids within the tube. The simplified steps of the process are: comminution; liming; solid liquid separation; carbonation; additional solid liquid separation; and activated carbon treatment. Carbonation may be supplanted by ion exchange and the activated carbon treatment by reverse osmosis. In a 32-hour filtration of lime-treated municipal waste water with the uni-flow filter, biochemical oxygen demand was reduced by 78%, and suspended solids and E. coli were cut by 100%. Dissolved oxygen was increased from one ppm to 7.7 ppm. (Prague-FIRL)
W75-08872

SLUDGE DEWATERING,
K. G. Barnhill.
Industrial Water Engineering, Vol 11, No 5, p 21-24, September/October, 1974.

Descriptors: *Waste disposal, *Dewatering, Costs, Equipment centrifugation, Filtration, Sewage sludge, *Waste water treatment.
Identifiers: *Sludge dewatering.

Union Canal and its branches as a main aqueduct to convey reclaimed effluent to points of demand. The scheme could provide 50 mgd raw water for public supply at a capital cost of between 60,000 and 70,000 pounds per million gallons, as well as providing water for second class industrial supply purposes. The costs of supplies by this scheme compare favorably with present costs of raw water supplied by conventional methods of water conservation. The plan also uses minimal land and creates minimal environmental disturbance. (Prague-FIRL)
W75-08877

HOW TO OPTIMIZE AN ACTIVATED SLUDGE PLANT,
R. J. Joyce, C. Ortman, and C. Zickefoose.
Water and Sewage Works, Vol 121, No 10, p 96-99, October 1974. 15 fig.

Descriptors: *Municipal wastes, *Waste water treatment, *Treatment facilities, *Activated sludge, Effluents, Hydraulic capacity, *Industrial wastes, Standards, *Oregon, Water quality standards.
Identifiers: Hillsboro(Ore), *Combined treatment.

The Hillsboro Oregon waste treatment plant treats both municipal wastes from its community and industrial wastes from four food plants. Until July, 1973, the treatment plant had trouble meeting effluent standards, due to large and random variations in plant loading. In order to control effluent standards, it was necessary to make fast measurements of organic loading, as well as other key variables. The activated sludge process is reviewed, in terms of its contact and stabilization steps, and the sludge conditioning time. The Hillsboro plant has a nominal hydraulic capacity of 2 MGD and a complete-mixing aeration tank, which is divided into four quadrants. Sludge conditioning time is quite flexible. The measurement and control actions for the plant are illustrated. Parameters considered for optimal ranges are the food/biomass ratio (F/M), the effluent organic pollutant (BOD5), the return sludge flow (RSF) and the waste sludge (WS). Control strategy is applied so that the F/M ratio, the settling volume for 5 minutes, and the respiration rate interact with each other. These bring corrective action in terms of increases or decreases in sludge conditioning time, returned sludge flow, and waste return flow. (Prague-FIRL)
W75-08878

FULL-SCALE TRIALS OF POLYELECTROLYTES FOR CONDITIONING OF SEWAGE SLUDGES FOR FILTER PRESSING,
M. J. D. White, and R. C. Baskerville.
Water Pollution Control, Vol 73, No 5, p 486-504, 1974. 6 fig, 4 tab, 21 ref.

Descriptors: *Polyelectrolytes, *Sewage treatment, *Filtration, Operation, Treatment facilities, Drainage, *Waste water treatment, Filters.
Identifiers: *Filter pressing.

Sewage sludge is known to be conditioned in the laboratory using polyelectrolytes. Full-scale operation was successfully tried by the Oadby sewage works, with pressing periods from two to five hours. The reasons for failures and disappointing results in the use of polyelectrolytes is discussed. The difficulties associated with the filter pressing of sludge after polyelectrolyte conditioning seems to be due mainly to blinding of the filter medium, to inadequate provision for the discharge of filtrate at a high rate, or to incorrect mixing techniques. Some of the difficulties of blinding the filter medium can be overcome by use of an in-line mixing system; the use of the press feed pump as an in-line mixer may be applied in certain cases. Regular cleaning of the drainage surfaces and the backs of the cloths is necessary to maintain a high rate of filtration flow associated with polymer-conditioned sludges. Thus, if precautions are taken to ensure that satisfactory conditioning is achieved, and that this sludge can then be transported to the press without breaking down the flocs excessively, and if the cloth and drainage surfaces are kept clean and clear, this method can be carried out, offering savings in both costs and time. (Prague-FIRL)
W75-08879

CONTROL SYSTEM FOR TOTSUKA-DAINI SEWAGE TREATMENT PLANT (IN JAPANESE),
Y. Hattori, H. Matsumoto, Y. Matsuzaki, M. Endo, and Y. Negoro.
Toshiba Review, Vol 29, No 11, p 937-941, November 1974. 3 fig, 20 ref. English summary.

Descriptors: *Sewage treatment, *Treatment facilities, Urban areas, Management, Computers, *Control system, Pumps, *Waste water treatment.
Identifiers: *Japan.

Management and control of sewage treatment plants are becoming necessary with an increased amount of construction to cope with pollution of rivers adjacent to large cities. The control system of the Totsuka-Daini Sewage Treatment Plant in Japan is described. It features the collective automatic management of multiple sewage treatment plants in block, the automatic operation of waste and storm sewage pumps by means of the computer CLEARAC, the separation of pumping rooms, and a tele-control system which connects these pumping rooms to a central control for supervisory control. In addition, contacts in the sequence circuit are eliminated, and sequence change is accomplished by the use of the computer PROSEC. Automatic and interlocked operation of individual treatment plants is practiced in addition to the centralized supervisory control of the overall plant. (Prague-FIRL)
W75-08880

EXPANDING CLEVELAND'S SOUTHERLY WASTEWATER TREATMENT PLANT.
Water and Sewage Works, Vol 121, No 11, p 86-88, November 1974. 3 fig, 5 tab.

Descriptors: *Waste water treatment, *Treatment facilities, Design criteria, *Sewage treatment, Municipal wastes, Sludge, Biological treatment, Waste disposal, *Ohio.
Identifiers: Cleveland(Ohio).

The city of Cleveland, Ohio has three waste water treatment plants; of these, the Southerly plant has not met water quality standards. The City of Cleveland, the United States Environmental Protection Agency, and the state of Ohio are now working on the design of systems to solve three problems: to eliminate discharges of untreated industrial wastes; to minimize combined sewer discharge effects; and to upgrade the level of treatment at the Southerly Wastewater Treatment Center. The basis of a new design was that all flow to the plant up to 400 mgd be given complete treatment and that all flows in excess of 400 mgd up to 735 mgd be given the equivalent of primary treatment and disinfection with provisions available for the addition of organic and/or inorganic flocculants. A treatment system has been selected consisting of primary sedimentation, two-stage activated sludge system, and effluent polishing by filtration and disinfection. A wet-stream process system requires the construction of additional headworks, screening and grit removal facilities, additional primary treatment facilities, modification of an existing aeration system, construction of additional first-stage clarifiers, construction of effluent filtration and disinfection systems. Sludge handling consists of degritting and thickening of the sludges; storage; dewatering; and incineration. An on-site disposal system is presently used, but future land disposal is also feasible. (Prague-FIRL)
W75-08882

WHEN TO USE CONTINUOUS FILTRATION HARDWARE,
Envirotech Corp., Salt Lake City, Utah.
R. C. Emmett, and C. E. Silverblatt.
Chemical Engineering Progress, Vol 70, No 12, p 38-42, December 1974. 3 fig, 1 tab, 7 ref.

Descriptors: *Filtration, *Equipment, *Waste water treatment, Slurries, Sludge, Capital costs, Operating costs, Construction, *Filters.

Selection of the proper filtration equipment for a particular application requires guidelines. Detailed are the types of slurries that can be handled by continuous filtration, the factors that must be considered in a flowsheets, and the costs and benefits involved. Feed slurry properties include: suspended solids concentration, particle size distribution, system composition, liquid viscosity, liquid volatility, degree of liquid saturation, temperature, special properties of solids or liquid, required materials of construction, and feed rate. Filtration requirements analysis should consider several facets of operation. One can never obtain a high filtration rate, an absolutely clear filtrate, a completely washed cake, and an extremely low residual cake liquor content. Requirements should include minimum performance which can be reasonably tolerated and take capital and operating costs into account. These requirements include: filtrate clarity, cake washing, cake moisture, filtrate dilution, end use of solids, capital limitation, total process flowsheet, product value and in-process inventory, chemical conditioning, and pretreatment of slurry. Bench scale testing begins with choice of a filter medium and should be designed to determine the rate of its operations as applied to possible type of continuous filtration equipment. In considering the available solid-liquid separation methods, economics should be the final decision, with flexibility and dependibility for a practical system. (Prague-FIRL)
W75-08883

DETERMINATION OF HEAVY METALS IN MUNICIPAL SEWAGE PLANT SLUDGES BY NEUTRON ACTIVATION ANALYSIS,
North Carolina State Univ., Raleigh. Nuclear Services Lab.
For primary bibliographic entry see Field 5A.
W75-08891

FIELD TESTING OF CENTRIFUGAL WASTE-WATER PUMPS,
Clinton Bogert Associates, Fort Lee, N.J.
P. E. Cardillo, and W. Eakins.
Public Works, Vol 105, No 12, p 55-57, December, 1974. 2 fig, 2 tab.

Descriptors: *Pumps, *Waste water treatment, *On-site tests, *Centrifugal pumps, Equipment, Pumping.

The preparation and procedures for testing centrifugal waste water pumps at the site of installation are described. Field performance of the pumps must be made by qualified personnel and in accordance with the test code of the Hydraulic Institute Standards. Variations should be expected between field test results and the manufacturer's shop test results because of the conditions of instrumentation and the degree of accuracy. Troubles which may occur with the pump and their probable causes are outlined; problems include failure of the pump to deliver liquid, insufficient capacity, insufficient discharge pressure, pump overloading driver, pump vibrating, and noise in the pump. Preparation for testing involves checking the alignment of the pump and driver, checking the motor rotor for binding, and priming the pump. Instruments such as the pressure gauges, rpm counter, and watt-megger should be calibrated for accuracy. In the actual field test of the pump, it should be started with a closed discharge valve; then the valve should be slowly opened. Observations of proper stuffing box location, noises in pump or motor, vibrations in the pump, motor, or piping, and leaks in piping should be made. Readings should then be taken of vertical distance between suction and discharge gauges, suction gauge reading, discharge gauge reading, flow, and the power input to the motor measured at the motor. A standard for this entitled 'Centrifugal Pumps Test Code' is available from the Hydraulic Institute to record data for each pump tested. (Prague-FIRL)
W75-08892

F2 COLIPHAGE AS TRACER IN WASTE-WATER BASIN,
Johns Hopkins Univ., Baltimore, Md. Dept. of Environmental Health.
K. Kawata, and V. P. Olivieri.
Journal of the Environmental Engineering Division, Procedings of ASCE, Vol 100, No EE6, p 1307-1310, December, 1974. 1 fig, 6 ref.

Descriptors: *Tracers, *Waste water treatment, Basins, Sedimentation basins(Waste disposal), Municipal wastes, Viruses, *Bioindicatiors, Pollutant identification.
Identifiers: *f2 Coliphage, Biological tracers.

Various types of chemical tracers have been used to determine actual rather than theoretical flow-through times in sedimentation basins for waste water treatment. As an alternative, the use of the biological tracer, f2 coliphage was investigated. This virus is often used as a model virus and can be grown in the laboratory with little difficulties to very high concentrations. Its assay is relatively uncomplicated, and there are normally very few male strains of the host of this virus to be found in community waste water. It was concluded that f2 is a suitable tracer to determine virus flow-through in a basin. When virus study was conducted in waste water unit processes, the use of the f2 coliphage for determination of flow-through time was convenient and gave little difficulty. (Prague-FIRL)
W75-08893

FILM TRANSPORT COEFFICIENT IN AGITATED SUSPENSIONS OF ACTIVATED CARBON,
Northwestern Univ., Evanston, Ill. Environmental Health Engineering.
R. D. Letterman, J. E. Quon, and R. S. Gemmell.
Journal Water Pollution Control Federation, Vol 46, No 11, p 2536-2546, November, 1974. 7 fig, 2 tab, 13 ref.

Descriptors: *Activated carbon, *Adsorption, *Phenols, Organic compounds, Kinetics, Mathematical studies, *Waste water treatment, Waste disposal.
Identifiers: *Film transport coefficient.

Adsorption equilibrium and kinetics must be understood for effective application of the activated carbon process for the removal of dissolved organic substances from water and waste water. The rate of uptake of phenol from dilute aqueous solutions by activated carbon particles was studied by using an agitated batch system. The effects of the initial phenol concentration and particle size on the uptake rate when extra-particle resistance to mass transfer is controlling were noted. Film transport coefficients were determined. The uptake of phenol may be described by the dimensionless expressions of either the Gilliland-Sherwook or the Froessling type. The film transport coefficient and its relationship to variables in the system, when it is correlated by the use of the Sherwood, Schmidt, and the specific power numbers was found to be independent of vessel geometry, impeller geometry, and impeller rotational speed. For the phenol carbon system, the film transport coefficient was shown to vary with the specific power input to the 0.149 power and with the particle diameter to the -0.348 power. (Prague-FIRL)
W75-08895

INSTRUMENTATION FOR FILTRATION TESTS,
Coulter Electronics, Inc., Hialeah, Fla.
For primary bibliographic entry see Field 5A.
W75-08897

DETERMINATION OF CHLORINE-CONTAINING ORGANICS IN CHLORINATED SEWAGE EFFLUENTS BY COUPLED 36CL TRACER--HIGH RESOLUTION CHROMATOGRAPHY,
Oak Ridge National Lab., Tenn.
For primary bibliographic entry see Field 5A.
W75-08898

ALGAE REMOVAL BY CHEMICAL COAGULATION,
M. A. Al-Layla, and E. J. Middlebrooks.
Water and Sewage Works, Vol 121, No 9, p 76-80, September, 1974. 9 fig, 2 tab, 12 ref.

Descriptors: *Algae, Surface waters, *Water purification, *Temperature, Regression analysis, Mathematical models, *Coagulation, Alum, Flocculation, Settling, *Waste water treatment, Nutrient removal.
Identifiers: Analysis of variance, Algal coagulation, *Algal removal, Chemical coagulation.

Algae in surface waters and waste water stabilization pond effluents cause problems such as the shortening of filter runs in water purification plants, and clogging of distribution pipes and other water conduits. During the warm seasons, waste water stabilization pond effluents contain particularly high concentrations of algal cells which are discharged to a watercourse. These algae necessitate further treatment to meet newly legislated effluent guidelines. As a method of algal removal prior to discharge, chemical coagulation is proposed. This study investigated the effect of temperature on algal cell coagulation a variable which had not been previously analyzed. Interactions between five independent variables--temperature, alum dosage, mixed speed, flocculation time, and settling time--were mathematically studied. In an analysis of variance test, the most significant variable was alum dosage, followed by temperature, then flocculation time, paddle (mixing) speed, and settling time. Step-wise multiple regression analysis indicated the relationship between the percentage removal of algae and the other independent variables; a linear mathematical model was the most successful. Additional factors that might account for the effect of temperature on algae coagulation include the hydrophilic characteristics of algal colloidal material. (Prague-FIRL)
W75-08900

BOUNDARY LAYER SEPARATION CONCEPT OF SETTLING TANKS,
George Washington Univ., Washington, D.C. Dept. of Civil, Mechanical and Environmental Engineering.
Y. Chiu.
Journal of the Environmental Engineering Division, Proceedings of ASCE, Vol 100, No EE6, p 1213-1218, December, 1974. 1 fig, 2 ref.

Descriptors: *Separation techniques, *Sedimentation, Mathematical models, Solids, Settling basins, *Waste water treatment.
Identifiers: Circular tanks, Rectangular tanks, *Settling tanks.

An investigation of the inefficiency in sedimentation of using a circular tank as compared with a rectangular sedimentation tank was conducted. Theoretical flow characteristics of each type of settling tank were determined mathematically. Because of convenience of operation and other factors, more circular tanks than rectangular tanks have recently been used. However, it was demonstrated that separation will occur in the conventional horizontal-flow central-feed circular tank, but not in the rectangular tank. This separation

control method for a wide range of operating conditions. In particular, proportional control with measurement of the substrate flow rate and manipulation of the rate of return sludge was an effective as much more complex combinations of feed forward and feed back controllers. There was some indication that on-off control would be highly effective. (Huffsey-Kentucky)
W75-08931

REMOVAL OF PESTICIDES FROM WATER BY VARIOUS WATER TREATMENT METHODS, (IN RUSSIAN),
K. K. Vrochinskii.
Gig Sanit, Vol 38, No 11, p 76-78, 1973.

Descriptors: *Reviews, *Water treatment, Coagulation, Sedimentation, Filtration, Chlorination, Separation techniques, Pollutants, *Pesticides, Water pollution sources, DDT, Waste water treatment.
Identifiers: Adsorbents, BHC Methyl, Oxidizing agents, Parathion, Phosphamide.

A review of the literature established that the conventional methods of water treatment-coagulation, sedimentation, filtration and chlorination-did not remove pesticides from water or reduce their quantity significantly. The exception was DDT. Removal of pesticides from water generally required special methods of treatment with the use of oxidizing agents (ozone, K permanganate, etc.) or adsorbents (activated C, etc.). Intermediate substances more toxic than the initial substances (parathion, phosphamide) or substances adversely affecting the organoleptic properties of water (Malathion, methyl parathion, hexachlorocyclohexane) can form in the case of small doses of oxidizing agents.--Copyright 1975, Biological Abstracts, Inc.
W75-08933

LIVESTOCK AND THE ENVIRONMENT: A BIBLIOGRAPHY WITH ABSTRACTS, VOLUME II,
East Central State Coll., Ada, Okla. School of Environmental Science.
For primary bibliographic entry see Field 5G.
W75-08937

IRRIGATION WITH WASTE WATER AT BOARD OF WORKS FARM, WERRIBEE,
Melbourne and Metropolitan Board of Works (Australia).
C. F. Kirby.
Paper presented at Water Research Foundation Sumposium, August, 1967, 5 p.

Descriptors: *Waste water disposal, *Watste water treatment, *Irrigation practices, *Australia, *Livestock, Irrigation water, Range grasses, Soils, Drainage, Channels, Sedimentation, Oxidation, Farm wastes.

Near the end of the 19th century, the Australian government established a Board of Works farm outside the city of Melbourne of utilize treated human and industrial waste carried by a waterborne waste disposal system for irrigation of the prepared land. A study of this land some 70 years later shows that farm pastures are in good condition, the grazing livestock healthy, and the 170 people residing on the farm enjoying normal health and freedom from disease. Other than aesthetic ones, results show no reason why present irrigation methods cannot continue with a greater portion of the city waste water being put to similar productive use. With suitable treatment this water could also by used for more valuable crops where first-use water becomes inadequate. (Mastic-Arizona)
W75-08941

EVALUATION OF POTENTIAL SPACECRAFT WASH WATER PRETREATMENT SYSTEMS,
Abcor, Inc., Cambridge, Mass. Walden Research Div.
D. C. Grant, A. Gollan, and R. L. Goldsmith.
Available from the National Technical Information Service, Springfield, Va. 22161, as PB-242 984, $5.25 in paper copy, $2.25 in microfiche. OWRT Report INT-OSW-RDPR-75-1005, June 1975. 91 p, 30 fig, 12 tab, 14 ref, 4 append. 14-30-3275.

Descriptors: *Waste water treatment, *Reverse osmosis, *Water purification, *Membranes, *Filtration, Adsorption, Filters.
Identifiers: *Carbon adsorption, Glass fiber filtration, Spacecraft wash water recycle system, Depth filters, Cellulose acetate, *Ultrafiltration, Sand filtration.

The studies evaluated several treatment processes for use in the purification of recycle wash waters generated aboard spacecrafts. The unit processes investigated included: regenerable filtration, ultrafiltration, regenerable sand depth filtration, regenerable glass fiber depth filtration, carbon adsorption and reverse osmosis. The regenerable filtration studies have shown that ultrafiltration is far superior to the other filtration methods investigated from all aspects. Superiority was demonstrated in product water quality, system compactness, reliability, maintainability and safety.
W75-09050

A STUDY OF THE REMOVAL OF PESTICIDES FROM WATER,
Kentucky Water Resources Inst., Lexington.
J. D. Whitehouse.
Available from the National Technical Information Service, Springfield, Va 22161 as PB-242 971, $7.00 in paper copy, $2.25 in microfiche. Research Report No 8, 1967. 175 p, 64 fig, 5 tab, 51 ref. OWRR A-002-KY(3). 14-01-0001-911.

Descriptors: *Pesticide removal, *Pesticides, Water treatment, *Aeration, Adsorption, Form separation, *Waste water treatment, Pesticide residues, *Activated carbon, Clays, DDT, Coagulation, 2,4-D, Aldrin, Dieldrin, 2,4,5-T.
Identifiers: Chemical coagulation, Malathion, Captan, Benzene haxachloride.

The purpose was to investigate some of the properties of pesticides as they exist in water, and to determine the effectiveness of several water treatment processes in the removal of pesticides from water. Among the pesticides investigated were malathion, DDT, aldrin, dieldrin, captan, benzene hexachloride (BHC), 2,4-D, and 2,4,5-T. The water treatment processes include aeration, chemical coagulation, adsorption on activated carbons and clays, and foam separation. The removal of pesticides from water by aeration was significant. Dieldrin was removed almost 100 percent, while aldrin, DDT, and BHC were removed to a lesser extent. There was no loss of 2,4,5-T and captan through aeration. Chemical coagulation alone was ineffective in the removal of pesticides from water. Several coagulant aids were investigated but all proved ineffective with the possible exception of one which increased the apparent removal slightly. Of the processes investigated adsorption with activated carbon was the most effective in removing pesticides from water. The removals obtained were--malathion near 100 percent; 2,4-D, 90 percent; DDT, 95 percent; aldrin, 100 percent; dieldrin 90 percent. (Huffsey-Kentucky)
W75-09052

RANDOM PLASTICS MEDIA ARE KEY TO HIGH-QUALITY EFFLUENT,
I. Rodgers.
Process Engineering, p 68-69, August, 1974. 2 ref.

Descriptors: *Plastics, *Filters, Effluents, *Biological treatment, Costs, Materials, Filtering systems, Electric power costs, *Waste water treatment, *Filtration.
Identifiers: Flocor RC, Random plastic media, Polyvinyl chloride, Stone media(Filtering), Plastic filters.

The use of random media for filtering both domestic and industrial effluents has been applied to biological effluent treatment. In the past, stone filters were the only type used. Recently however, the use of plastics as percolating filters has been investigated. The major problem, which was overcome, was to devise a shape with the highest surface possible, consistent with the requirements of adequate void space and resistance to compression. The necessary plastic media has to give a surface three times that of stone, or 300 sq m/cu m, in order to be economical. One such product derived from PVC is Flocor RC, developed by ICI. It is tubular in shape with corrugations running around the circumference. The material is inert and highly resistant to chemical, biological, and photochemical degradation. PVC also has strength of compression. New random plastic filters may be used in older systems to replace stone filters, thus relieving hydraulic and organic overload. They may also be used in new installations. Flocor RC filters have two advantages: they are light in weight--one seventh that of stone media--and thereby require lower-cost structures; and percolating filters have negligible power cost, representing another savings. (Prague-FIRL)
W75-09060

CONTROLS DRY UP WET WEATHER POLLUTION,
Metcalf and Eddy, Inc., Mass.
J. A. Lager.
Water and Wastes Engineering, Vol 11, No 9, p 35-37, September 1974. 2 fig.

Descriptors: *Storm runoff, *Combined sewers, *Waste water treatment, *Storm water, Cities, Water storage, Storm drains, Pollution control, Pollution abatement, Equipment, Conduits, Sanitary engineering, Treatment facilities.

One of the most challenging tests of sanitary engineering skills is the development of methods for wet weather pollution control and abatement. System control and storage with feedback to existing plants, independent facilities and modified existing plants have been developed to meet these problems. The goal of system control is to optimize the containment and treatment of storm runoff. The actions taken are dependent upon the storm pattern, treatment and storage availability, and projected storm and system behavior. Mathematical models can be an important asset in the development and fine-tuning of these systems. Storage is one of the most cost-effective tools for the reduction of pollution resulting from combined sewage overflow. Storage can be in-line damming, gating or otherwise restricting the flow passage in combined sewers that are designed to carry maximum flows that might occur once every five years. Storage can be offline through the use of basins, controlled ponding, tunnels, and silos. The total systems approach may be impractical in some situations; immediate solutions may then be relatively limited purpose, independent facilities which will either be integrated or made obsolete by future construction. Examples of these facilities include: fine screening; microstraining; swirl concentrating; dissolved air flotation; physical-chemical treatment; and, disinfection. The storm runoff treatment processes of many United States cities are described. (Orr-FIRL)
W75-09061

PRESSURE FILTER FOR WATER TREATMENT - FROM PRE-STRESSED CONCRETE RINGS WITH INTEGRAL FILTER PLANTS.
German Patent 74441V/43. Issued October 17, 1974. Derwent German Patents Report, Vol 5, No 43, p 1, December 3, 1974.

Descriptors: *Patents, *Filters, Concrete, Construction materials, Pressure, Water treatment, Filtration.
Identifiers: Concrete rings, Pressure filters.

A pressure filter for water treatment was designed from pre-stressed concrete rings with integral filter plates. A closed horizontal pressure vessel with filter plates, fitted with filter nozzles, consists of a series of adjacently situated pre-stressed concrete rings with two end closures. These are clamped together by tensioning members running along inside the wall of the vessel. The concrete rings have parallel vertial side walls and curved arcuate upper and lower wall parts, with at least two integrally-formed filter plates extending over the full width of the ring between the parallel side walls. (Prague-FIRL)
W75-09062

SMALL-SCALE SEWAGE TREATMENT PLANT-WITH DETACHABLE AERATION AND ACTIVATED SLUDGE RECYCLING FITMENTS.
German Patent 63255V/36. Issued August 29, 1974. Derwent German Patents Report, Vol 5, No 36, p 3, October 15, 1974.

Descriptors: *Patents, *Sewage treatment, *Activated sludge, *Aeration, Recycling, Clarification, Treatment facilities, Biological treatment, *Waste water treatment, *Treatment facilities.

A small-scale sewage treatment plant with detachable aeration and activated sludge recycling fittings is described. It consists of an inner tank, which acts as the final clarification basin, and an annular space surrounding it. This space is divided by segments into two mechanical precleaning chambers in series and one chamber which can be converted into an activated basin by an aeration device. An activated sludge discharge pipe and an activated sludge recycling arrangement can be readily removed or inserted from the third chamber. The plant can cope with widely fluctuating input rates and can be operated as an activated sludge plant for mechanical-biological clarification. It can also be utilized as a mechanical settling basin with good clarification efficiency. (Prague-FIRL)
W75-09063

REMOVAL AND RESUSPENSION PROCESSES - DRY DEPOSITION OF PARTICLES.
Battelle-Pacific Northwest Labs., Richland, Wash.
For primary bibliographic entry see Field 5A.
W75-09074

SPECIAL STUDIES - COOLING TOWER RESEARCH - BIOMETEOROLOGY.
Battelle-Pacific Northwest Labs., Richland, Wash.
For primary bibliographic entry see Field 5A.
W75-09076

OPTIMAL RISK-BASED DESIGN OF STORM SEWER NETWORKS,
Illinois Univ., Urbana. Dept. of Civil Engineering.
W. H. Tang, L. W. Mays, and B. C. Yen.
Journal of the Environmental Engineering Division, American Society of Civil Engineers, Vol 101, No EE3, Proceedings paper No. 11360, p 381-398, June 1975. 7 fig, 3 tab, 14 ref. OWRT C-4123(No 9023)(2).

Descriptors: *Dynamic programming, *Environmental engineering, *Risks, *Sewers, Networks, Design, Probability, Costs, Drainage, Optimization, Sanitary engineering, Evaluation, Safety factors, Hydraulic models, Flooding, Constraints, Computers, Damages, Methodology, Equations, Mathematical models, Systems analysis.
Identifiers: *Economic analysis, *Storm sewers, Uncertainty principle, Cost minimization.

Rapid population growth is causing severe problems in urban storm sewer management. Despite this situation, existing design methods fail both to account explicitly for the cost interaction of the various components of sewer systems and to consider systematically the uncertainties that are unavoidable in sewer network design, such as precipitation rate, insufficient data, and errors in design equations. Presented is a least-cost, optimization method for the design of storm sewersystems that considers risk due to uncertainties in the design parameters. The optimal choice of slopes and diameters of the entire sewer network is based on a tradeoff between risk due to potential flood losses and the cost of installation of the sewers. Two models, ranging in the degree of sophistication, are suggested to account for the costs of expected flood damages. These are incorporated into a dynamic programming solution procedure; discrete differential dynamic programming is successfully applied to make the design optimization procedure of a large storm sewer network become feasible by significantly reducing the computer time and storage involved. This method provides a rational yet practical approach to design storm sewer systems, particularly when considerable flood damages are expected or when differential damage costs will be incurred between regions of the same storm sewer system. (Bell-Cornell)
W75-09082

ENVIRONMENTAL SYSTEMS APPRAISALS AND DEVELOPMENT GUIDES.
Harza Engineering Co., Chicago, Ill.
Prepared for Rock Valley Metropolitan Council, Rockford, Illinois, December, 1973. 226 p, 23 fig, 25 tab, 140 ref, 6 append.

Descriptors: *Regional development, *Water supply development, *Waste water disposal, *Regional analysis, Water treatment, Water quality control, *Waste water treatment, Environmental sanitation, *Illinois, Landfills, Septic tanks, Storm runoff, Air pollution, *Wisconsin, River basin development.
Identifiers: *Rock Creek Metropolitan Council(Ill-Wis), Open space development, *Rock River basin(Ill-Wis).

Rock Valley Metropolitan Council (RVMC) serves 3 counties in the Rock River Basin--Winnebago and Boone in Illinois, and Rock County, Wisconsin. These regional guides for water supply, sewerage and open space, and appraisals of storm drain, solid waste, and air pollution control systems were done for RVMC. Water Supply: 72% of the region is served by central supply systems which are generally adequate but lack sufficient storage capacity. The other 18% is served by private systems, some of which are threatened by septic tank sewage disposal and/or poorly constructed or located wells. Sanitary Sewage: Four priority categories are defined. The immediate need is to eliminate health hazards. First priority is to provide sewage collection and treatment for areas currently served by septic tanks. Second priority is expansion of present treatment capacities where needed. Third priority is expansion for future needs. Fourth priority areas show no apparent need up to the year 2000. Open Space: Land should be acquired to preserve the form of the urban areas and for aesthetic, recreation, or wildlife qualities. Air Pollution and Storm Drain Appraisals show no serious present problem. Solid Waste: New and better-managed landfill sites are

Descriptors: *Urban hydrology, *Drainage systems, *Storm water, *Mathematical models, *Storm runoff, Urban drainage, Urban runoff, Water quality, Design, Rainfall-runoff relationships, Hydrologic systems, Hydrology, Routing, Management, Water pollution treatment, Optimization, Systems analysis, Computer models, Watersheds(Basins), Model studies.

A stormwater model under development was described. The model is capable of representing urban runoff phenomena, both quantity and quality, from the onset of precipitation on the basin through collection, conveyance, storage, and treatment systems to points downstream from outfalls which are significantly affected by storm discharges. Each of the three parts, urban runoff, storm water transport, and receiving water, were described and the composite model was demonstrated on four basins. (See also W75-09210) (Terstriep-ISWS)
W75-09225

STRIP-MINED LAND RECLAMATION WITH SEWAGE SLUDGE: AN ECONOMIC SIMULATION,
Illinois Univ., Urbana. Dept. of Agricultural Economics.
W. D. Seitz.
American Journal of Agricultural Economics, Vol 56, No 4, p 799-804, November 1974. 1 fig, 1 tab, 14 ref. OWRT A-061-ILL(2). 14-31-0001-3813.

Descriptors: *Reclamation, Sewage sludge, Economics, *Illinois, *Simulation analysis, *Land reclamation, Mine wastes, Cost analysis, Performance, *Recycling, Waste treatment.
Identifiers: *Chicago(Ill).

The economic aspects of a land reclamation, sludge utilization project being operated by the Metropolitan Sanitary District of Greater Chicago are simulated. The variables influencing performance most were sludge transport costs, site preparation costs, the nitrogen budget, cropping system, and source of labor in site preparation.
W75-09236

CANNED AND PRESERVED SEAFOOD PROCESSING POINT SOURCE CATEGORY--PROPOSED EFFLUENT LIMITATION GUIDELINES, STANDARDS OF PERFORMANCE AND PRETREATMENT STANDARDS.
Environmental Protection Agency, Washington, D.C.
For primary bibliographic entry see Field 5G.
W75-09250

TEXTILE INDUSTRY POINT SOURCE CATEGORY--PROPOSED EFFLUENT LIMITATIONS GUIDELINES.
Environmental Protection Agency, Washington, D.C.
For primary bibliographic entry see Field 5G.
W75-09251

WATER POLLUTION CONTROL--CONSTRUCTION GRANTS FOR WASTE TREATMENT WORKS.
Environmental Protection Agency, Washington, D.C.
Federal Register, Vol 39, No 29, Part III, p 5252-5270, February 11, 1974.

Descriptors: *Construction, *Grants, *Administrative agencies, *Environmental control, *Waste treatment, Water pollution control, Government finance, Contracts, Projects, Research and development, Federal government, Environment, Environmental engineering, Environmental effects, Environmental sanitation, Waste water(Pollution), Waste water(Treatment), Wastes, Water pollution, Legislation, Projects.
Identifiers: Administrative regulations, FWPCA Amendments of 1972, Environmental policy, Hazardous substances(Pollution).

Tital II of the Federal Water Pollution Control Act Amendments of 1972 authorizes the award of construction grants for waste treatment works. This regulation attempts to conform the procedures and requirements of the new grant system to the construction grants program established under section eight of the prior Federal Water Pollution Control Act, as well as to ensure that new statutory requirements will be met. The three-step grant process provides that a basic grant application is submitted for the initial award of grant assistance, and that subsequent related projects will be funded through amendment of this grant. Section 35.915 has been revised and expanded to explain more clearly Environmental Protection Agency requirements under applicable statutory provisions for state priority systems. Facilities planning requirements are set forth and new procedures have been established to assure that the infiltration/inflow requirements are met without unnecessary documentation and expense. New provisions state the Agency's position with respect to the initiation of project construction, and a considerable number of technical revisions have been made throughout. (Fernandez-Florida)
W75-09256

A PROPOSED METHOD OF WASTE MANAGEMENT IN CLOSED-CYCLE MARICULTURE SYSTEMS THROUGH FOAM-FRACTIONATION AND CHLORINATION,
Delaware Univ., Newark. Dept. of Agricultural Engineering.
R. C. Dwivedy.
In: 1973 Proceedings of the National Shellfish Association. Vol 64, p 111-117, 1974. 4 fig, 1 tab, ref. Report DEL-SG-8-75.

Descriptors: *Waste treatment, *Aquaculture, *Foam fractionation, *Chlorination, Filtration, Carbon filters, Animal wastes(Wildlife), Ammonia, Marine biology, Biochemistry, Waste water treatment.
Identifiers: *Closed-cycle mariculture systems, Bacterial filters, Non-bacterial filters, Biological filters.

A scheme of waste management independent of bacterial filters in closed-cycle mariculture systems was presented. Foam-fraction was recommended for organic removal to prevent build-up of high ammonia levels in the system. Breakpoint chlorination was recommended for the removal of remaining low levels of ammonia. Dechlorination was achieved through carbon filtration. An algal production system can easily be coupled in the system if mollusks are to be cultured. Non-bacterial filters remove contaminant more rapidly and completely and are not limited by disadvantages associated with bacterial filters, such as excessive space requirements and build-up of high nitrate in the system. (NOAA)
W75-09279

DECENTRALIZED WATER REUSE SYSTEMS IN A WATER SCARCE ENVIRONMENT: THE TOURIST INDUSTRY IN ST. THOMAS, VIRGIN ISLANDS,
Clark Univ., Worcester, Mass.
R. E. Kasperson, C. Schepart, J. Sorensen, and R. Simpson.
Government of the Virgin Islands, Department of Health, Division of Environmental Health, Water Pollution Report No 13, commissioned by Caribbean Research Institute, College of the Virgin Islands. May 1971. 39 p, 9 fig, 7 ref, 1 append.

Descriptors: *Water reuse, *Reclaimed water, *Water supply development, *Virgin Islands, Salvage value, Water costs, Supply development, Consumptive use, Dependable supply, Storage requirements, Impaired water use, Irrigation

water, Cisterns, *Water treatment, Waste water treatment, Desalination, Potable water.
Identifiers: Dual water supply systems, Charlotte Amalie, St. Thomas(Virgin Islands).

Substantial economic savings appear possible through water reclamation and reuse on St. Thomas, Virgin Islands, at least for high volume tourist industry users remote from the municipal system at Charlotte Amalie. This system, faced with unreliable rainfall and rapidly growting demand for potable water, has added three desalinization plants to provide the needed supply. Remote resorts on the island also have used rainwater collected from roof runoff and large catchment structures, stored in cisterns with total capacity up to 1,205,000 gallons at one large resort. Unreliable rainfall and high per capita use have led to supply augmentation, primarily by trucking in water from Charlotte Amalie. Costs can be up to ten times the cost in the city, depending on distance. Use of high cost water is lessened with dual supply systems which use water of impaired quality for flushing and irrigation (up to 50% of demand). Guests are not often asked to conserve water. Poor soils and irregular terrain make the 1250 septic tanks at various facilities costly to operate. Development has tended toward package plants. Cost of package plant treatment with dual water supply system using reclaimed water for irrigation is compared to the present combination of less expensive septic tank disposal combined with more expensive water supply. Decentralized integrated reuse systems are less expensive. (Herr-North Carolina)
W75-09297

REMOVAL OF PHOSPHATE FROM WATER BY ALUMINUM,
Rutgers - The State Univ., New Brunswick, N.J. Dept. of Soils and Crops.
W. L. Yuan.
PhD Thesis, January 1972, 79 p. 8 fig, 14 tab, 34 ref. OWRT A-031-NJ(5). 14-31-0001-3530.

Descriptors: Phosphates, *Waste water treatment, *Nutrient removal, *Aluminum, Chemical precipitation, *Coagulation, Anions, Chemical reactions.
Identifiers: Reactants mixing, *Phosphate removal.

Two factors governing the effectiveness of aluminum to precipitate phosphate from solution were investigated: (1) Effect of foreign components: The effectiveness of OH-Al polymers to precipitate phosphate was greatly influenced by the ratio of phosphate to aluminum and also by the nature and concentration of foreign components present. In the presence of sulfate, montmorillonite or kaolinite, phosphate removal was greatly improved. Also, the dosage of coagulant and the acidity did not need critical control in order to attain the optimum phosphate removal. Some anions, such as F-, however, had serious detrimental effects. (2) Effect of the order of reactants mixing: A change in the order of reactants mixing resulted in a different degree of phosphate removal in many cases, evidently due to the lack of equilibrium. Little change toward equilibrium state occurred during aging up to at least two years when the experimentation was terminated. (Hsu-Rutgers)
W75-09298

RECIRCULATING SEWERAGE SYSTEM,
Koehler-Dayton, Inc., New Britain, Conn. (Assignee).
A. H. Cornish, G. W. Foster, and A. J. Campbell.
United States Patent 3,828,372. Issued August 13, 1974. Official Gazette of the United States Patent Office, Vol 925, No 2, p 353, August 1974. 1 fig.

Descriptors: *Sewage treatment, *Effluents, *Waste water treatment, *Patents, Equipment, Domestic wastes, Recycling, Water reuse.
Identifiers: *Recriculating sewerage system, Water closet.

A recirculating sewerage system consists of at least one water closet, a recirculating tank, including effluent receiving and pumping chambers divided by a common wall, and a drainage opening in the bottom of the recirculating tank. Included also was a pump with a filtering element for drawing liquid from the pumping chamber and for directing that liquid to the water closet for flushing. The separating common wall includes a filter to restrict the flow of bulk waste, such as paper products, from the chamber receiving effluent to the pumping chamber. There is also a sealing means to prevent effluent from passing from the effluent receiving chamber when a drainage value is at its first position. Both chambers are drained by the displacement of the drainage valve to its second position which allows direct passage from each of the chambers to the drainage opening. (Leibowitz-FIRL)
W75-09306

SYSTEM FOR SEPARATING HYDROCARBONS FROM WATER,
Fram Corp., East Providence, R.I. (Assignee).
For primary bibliographic entry see Field 5G.
W75-09307

SEDIMENTATION APPRATUS WITH PLURAL SLUDGE DISCHARGE FEATURE,
General Signal Corp., Rochester, N.Y. (Assignee).
E. J. Smith.
United States Patent 3,857,788. Issued December 31, 1974. Official Gazette of the United States Patent Office, Vol 929, No 5, p 2052, December 1974. 1 fig.

Descriptors: *Patents, *Sedimentation, Tanks, Sludge treatment, Waste discharge, Conduits, *Waste water treatment.

A sedimentation apparatus includes a tank having a base and an encircling side wall. It also contains means for supplying sludge-containing influent to the tank, which has a sludge hopper in its base, means for maintaining a predetermined fluid level in the tank, and means within the tank for collecting and transporting sludge settling on the base to a common location in the sludge hopper. These means include a rotary raking structure supported in the tank for rotation about the central vertical axis of the tank. Sludge pick-up means remove sludge of uniform consistency from a common location. A rotating spout, connected to the sludge pick-up means discharges sludge of uniform consistency to a place of distribution from a first and a second conduit. (Prague-FIRL)
W75-09309

EFFLUENT TREATMENT,
Cadborough Engineering Co. Ltd., Hertford (England). (Assignee).
W. E. Scragg.
United States Patent 3,817,848. Issued June 18, 1974. Official Gazette of the United States Patent Office, Vol 923, No 3, p 1064-1065, June 1974. 1 fig.

Descriptors: *Waste water treatment, *Effluents, *Activated sludge, *Patents, *Sludge removal, Water pollution, Solid wastes, Agricultural wastes, *Aeration, Screens, *Filters.

A method and apparatus to treat effluent are described. Farm effluent containing solids and fibrous matter is stored in a storage container, then passed into an aeration compartment after a portion of the treated effluent has been removed. Fibrous material with entrained activated sludge is removed by a rotary screen filter over the edge of an aeration compartment. (Leibowitz-FIRL)
W75-09310

METHOD AND APPARATUS FOR SEPARATING PARTICLES FROM A LIQUID,
E. Condolios, and U. Van Essen.
United States Patent 3,849,310. Issued November 19, 1974. Official Gazette of the United States Patent Office, Vol 928, No 3, p 1224, November, 1974. 1 fig.

Descriptors: *Patents, *Separation techniques, Liquids, Tanks, Equipment, Waste water treatment, Waste discharge.
Identifiers: Collecting tanks.

An apparatus for separating particles from a liquid consists of a basin which from top to bottom is composed of four parts, one on top of the other. These are: a cylindrical upper front part forming an overflow edge and surrounded by a discharge gutter; a downwardly diverging second part; a third part having a cylindrical section which is greater in diameter than that of the upper part, in which a screen divides the third part into a portion over and a portion under the screen, the solids being able to pass through the perforations of the screen; and, a lower part composed of several funnels, each funnel constituting a collecting tank and having a discharge outlet for particles separated from the liquid. (Prague-FIRL)
W75-09312

WASTEWATER TREATMENT UNIT,
K. L. Rost.
United States Patent 3,825,119. Issued July 23, 1974. Official Gazette of the United States Patent Office, Vol 924, No 4, p 886, July, 1974. 1 fig.

Descriptors: *Patents, *Waste water treatment, Domestic wastes, *Aeration, Water pollution, Tanks, Equipment, *Filters, *Trickling filters, Filtration.

A unit for waste water treatment with a tank to receive the waste water and a chamber above the tank is adaptable to domestic use. Within the chamber is a filter with a downwardly and inwardly tapering fabric bag holding a trickling filter body, having its bottom end open and communicating with the tank. A pump in the tank pushes the waste water through a conduit which as a distributor or diffuser above the filter body, as well as a return pipe in communication with the tank with an aspirator for returning waste water to draw air into the tank. The return pipe next to the distributor is smaller in diameter than the distributor so that pressure can build in the distributor. This forces some circulating water through lengthwise slits and into the filter with solids continuing with the rest of the water into and through the return pipe. Water which passes through the trickling filter body down to the bottom of the bag returns to the tank. Water filtered by the bag is discharged from the unit. Time control may be exercised for use in aerating the tank contents by circulation of the contents. (Leibowitz-FIRL)
W75-09313

DENSE SOLVENT DEMULSIFICATION METHOD FOR BITUMINOUS PETROLEUM WATER EMULSIONS,
Texaco Exploration Canada Ltd., Calgary (Alberta). (assignee).
D. A. Redford.
United States Patent 3,878,090. Issued April 15, 1975. Official Gazette of the United States Patent Office, Vol 933, No 3, p 1339, April, 1975.

Descriptors: *Patents, *Oily water, Emulsions, Waste water treatment, Solids contact processes, Emulsifiers.
Identifiers: Bituminous petroleum.

A process is described for resolving an emulsion of water and bituminous petroleum, the specific gravity of the bituminous petroleum being essentially the same as the specific gravity of water. The method consists of contacting the emulsion with a

THE BASIC TECHNOLOGY OF THE PULP AND PAPER INDUSTRY AND IT'S WASTE REDUCTION PRACTICES,
Lakehead Univ., Port Arthur (Ontario).
A. J. Bruley.
Canadian Department of the Environment, Training Manual EPS 6-W-74-3. May 1974. 148 p, 60 fig, 13 tab, 11 ref.

Descriptors: *Pulp and paper industry, *Waste treatment, *Technology, Training, Publications, Foreign countries, Canada, Economics, Effluents, Water reuse, Water treatment, *Waste water treatment, Water pollution, Water pollution treatment, History, Industrial wastes, Wastes, Chemistry.
Identifiers: Wood, Pulping, Papermaking.

This training manual is intended for Canadian Environmental Protection Service field representatives whose responsibility involves surveillance of effluents from pulp and paper mills. It reviews the national and regional importance, general pollution abatement picture, and economic outlook of the Canadian pulp and paper industry, and outlines briefly the historical development of paper and papermaking. This is followed by a comprehensive survey of pulp and paper technology, describing processes and materials used, with emphasis on the waste produced from individual operations (wood procurement and preparation, pulping, pulp screening, cleaning, thickening, and bleaching, stock preparation, paper manufacture, and finishing and converting operations). A section devoted to waste reduction practices discusses effluents from a typical kraft mill, water reuse and recycling, external water treatment practices, and waste treatment economics. A bibliography and glossary of pulp and paper terms and an appendix on wood chemistry are included. (Witt-IPC)
W75-09334

DEVELOPMENT AND EVALUATION REPORT: PHYSICAL-CHEMICAL MARINE SANITATION SYSTEM,
General American Transportation Corp., Niles, Ill.
J. M. Heeney, R. B. Neveril, E. K. Krug, and G. A. Remus.
Available from the National Technical Information Service, Springfield, Va 22161 as PB-231 846, $4.75 in paper copy, $2.25 in microfiche. Environmental Protection Agency, Report EPA-670/2-74-043, May 1974. 78 p, 18 fig, 10 tab.

Descriptors: *Waste water treatment, *Sewage treatment, *Ships, Suspended solids, Biochemical oxygen demand, Activated carbon, Chlorination, Disinfection, Treatment facilities, Economics, Capital costs, Costs, Filtration, Water pollution sources, Water pollution control, Coagulation, Wastes, Adsorption, Filters, Cellulose, Polymers, Coagulation.
Identifiers: *Marine sewage treatment, Cellulose sponge, Polypropylene, Coagulants.

A physical-chemical system for the onboard treatment of shipboard wastes has been developed. The system is capable of removing suspended solids from raw sewage using the capillary properties of cellulose sponge to draw liquid through a polypropylene filter. The use and effectiveness of a pressure-bed filter and coagulants as filtering techniques are also demonstrated. A series of activated carbon adsorption beds were evaluated for the removal of dissolved organic materials, and a chlorination unit with no moving parts was shown to be suitable for disinfection. Evaluation tests of the overall system indicated a range of BOD reductions between 30 and 90% and suspended solids removals between 50 and 90%. The study indicated the operating characteristics of the major components of the treatment system and showed a need for auxiliary filtering or coagulation techniques to handle small particles (below 30 microns). The total cost of such a system suitable for treating wastes onboard a marine vessle with a crew of 12 to 20 members, generating up to 2650 liters of wastes/day, is estimated to be $14,500-15,000. (Witt-IPC)
W75-09337

A SELECT BIBLIOGRAPHY ON ACTIVATED SLUDGE PLANTS,
British Steel Corp., Sheffield (England).
D. G. Brinn.
Available from the National Technical Information Service, Springfield, Va 22161 as PB-236 358, $3.25 in paper copy, $2.25 in microfiche. Aug 1974, 20 p, 140 ref.

Descriptors: *Bibliographies, *Activated sludge, *Treatment facilities, Sewage treatment, Waste treatment, Design, Operations, Costs, Industrial plants, Water pollution treatment, Water pollution control.
Identifiers: Coke plants.

This bibliography lists about 140 briefly annotated references to the literature on activated sludge plants from 1960 to date. The references are organized under 5 sections, including theory and general design aspects, operation and control, plant descriptions and specific applications, treatment of coke plant effluent, and costs of activated sludge plant operation. (Witt-IPC)
W75-09339

EXPERIMENTAL INVESTIGATION OF THE WET OXIDATION DESTRUCTION OF SHIPBOARD WASTE STREAMS,
Naval Ship Research and Development Center, Annapolis, Md.
P. Schatzberg, D. F. Jackson, and C. M. Kelly.
Available from the National Technical Information Service, Springfield, Va 22161 as AD-787 061, $4.25 in paper copy, $2.25 in microfiche. Report 4416 (AD 787061), Oct 1974. 38 p, 24 fig, 10 tab, 12 ref, 4 append.

Descriptors: *Waste water treatment, *Sewage treatment, Burning, Chemical reactions, Organic wastes, Kinetics, Laboratory tests, Catalysts, Chemical oxygen demand, Reverse osmosis, Water pollution sources, Water pollution treatment, Wastes, Ships, Oxidation, Disinfection, Water pollution control.
Identifiers: *Marine sewage treatment, *Wet oxidation.

Increasingly stringent water quality regulations anticipate the need for treating all shipboard waste streams containing combustible matter. Ultimate disposal/destruction must include laundry, shower, galley, bilge, and sanitary (human) wastes as well as garbage and refuse. Wet air oxidation or pressurized aqueous combustion conducted at 475-600 F at operating pressures from 600 to 1850 lb/sq inch gage was investigated as one means for the ultimate destruction of organic wastes. This process was investigated by conducting experiments in a 1-gallon pressure vessel with a variety of wastes (sanitary, food, oil, municipal sludge, glucose, and cellulose) under different conditions. Results showed that the wet oxidation process obeys first-order kinetics with an initial fast reduction followed by a slower second reaction. Catalysts have their main influence on the fast reaction, increasing its rate by a factor of three. Applying wet oxidation to destroy waterborne organic wastes consists of taking advantage of the fast reaction. Reduction in organic waste content, expressed as COD, ranged from 60 to 85%, depending on the waste material, after 15 min of reaction time. The use of catalysts can increase this figure to 95%. Additional removal of organic matter can be achieved by further processing the wet oxidation effluent through a reverse osmosis membrane. The wide range of materials capable of being destroyed by wet air oxidation, the innocuous sterile nature of the effluent, and its potential to be recycled with little or no post-treatment make this process a candidate for the ultimate destruction of shipboard wastes. (Witt-IPC)
W75-09340

RESPONSE OF ASPEN TO IRRIGATION BY MUNICIPAL WASTE WATER,
Pennsylvania State Univ., University Park. School of Forest Resources.
For primary bibliographic entry see Field 3C.
W75-09342

GULF STATES PAPER MAKES BIG MOVE TOWARDS ZERO POLLUTION,
K. E. Lowe.
Pulp and Paper, Vol 49, No 4, p 54-58, April 1975. 6 fig, 3 tab.

Descriptors: *Pulp wastes, *Treatment facilities, *Waste water treatment, Industrial wastes, Wastes, Water purification, Suspended solids, Activated sludge, Color, Lagoons, Sludge, Dewatering, Incineration, Nutrients, Phosphorus, Nitrogen, Inorganic compounds, Water reuse, Water pollution sources, Water pollution treatment, Sewage treatment, Tertiary treatment, Alabama, Pulp and paper industry, Water pollution control, Oxygenation, Effluents, Biochemical oxygen demand, Sludge treatment.
Identifiers: Ash, Unox oxygenation system, Aluminum oxide, Aluminum silicate, Kraft mills.

The effluent treatment system at Gulf States Paper Corporation's 100 ton/day kraft mill in Tuscaloosa, Alabama, is described. The combined effluent from the pulp and paper mills is first clarified in a primary clarifier to settle out suspended solids, treated in a 4-stage Unox activated sludge plant to remove 85-90% of the BOD, decolored by reacting with an alum-silica slurry (alum mud), and finally clarified to remove the organic precipitate and discharged to a holding lagoon. The sludges from the primary, Unox clarifier, and the color reactor are combined and dewatered in a Beloit-Passavant filter press, and the resulting high-solids sludge is incinerated without auxiliary fuel in a multi-hearth Nichols-Herreshoff furnace. The ash from the furnace, which contains a mixture of aluminum oxide and silicates, is regenerated with sulfuric acid and reused in the color-removal step. Nutrients (1 lb P/11 lb BOD and 1 lb N/15 lb BOD) are added to the effluent as it enters the Unox units. Gulf States eventually plans to reuse most of the purified effluent. (Witt-IPC)
W75-09345

OZONIZATION OF EFFLUENTS OF A KRAFT PULP MILL (OZONIROVANIE STOCHNYKH VOD SUL'FATNO-TSELLYULOZNOGO PROIZVODSTVA),
Moskovskii Inzhenerno-Stroitelnyi Institut (USSR).
Ya. A. Karelin, and Yu. P. Salamatov.
Izvestiya Vysshikh Uchebnykh Zavedenii Stroitel'stuvo i Arkhitektura, Vol 16, No 7, p 136-141, 1973. 1 fig, 6 ref, 3 tab.

Descriptors: *Pulp wastes, *Ozone, *Waste water treatment, *Water purification, Industrial wastes, Wastes, Waste treatment, Water pollution sources, Pulp and paper industry, Biochemical oxygen demand, Chemical oxygen demand, Suspended solids, Color, Sulfur compounds, Phenols, Effluents, Oxidation, Oxidation lagoons, Water pollution treatment, Biological treatment, Coagulation, Filtration, Sedimentation, Separation techniques, Saturation, Foreign countries, Water reuse, Recycling, Tertiary treatment.
Identifiers: Alumina, Polyacrylamide, Kraft mills, Soviet Union(USSR), Baikal kraft mill.

Ozonization as an additional means of effluent purification was studied on effluents of the Baikal kraft mill producing viscose-grade bleached kraft pulp. The effluent purification system at the mill includes 4 stages, viz., biochemical purification, coagulation with alumina or polyacrylamide, mechanical treatment (sand filter, sedimentation pond), and saturation with oxygen in an aeration pond. The process reduces 5-day BOD to 6-8 mg/liter, COD to 100-150 mg/liter, the suspended solids content to 8-10 mg/liter, and the color index to 80-100. This is considered insufficient. Ozonization experiments, carried out under laboratory conditions, were aimed at determining whether further purification could be achieved, especially the removal of sulfur compounds and phenols. Even under stationary conditions, ozonization was found to be effective in increasing the degree of purifity of biologically treated effluent and of the evaporation condensate. Ozoinzation under dynamic conditions (in a bubbling column) and higher ozone concentrations (up to 120 mg/liter) gave a 65% reduction in COD of the biologically purified effluent, entirely eliminated sulfur compounds and phenols from the evaporation condensate, and reduced the COD of effluent from the filtration stage by 80%. Consequently, ozonization could eliminate the coagulation stage after biochemical purification, and give the possibility of recycling the evaporation condensate. (Stapinski-IPC)
W75-09346

DISSOLVED AIR FLOTATION FOR WOODROOM EFFLUENT TREATMENT,
Kruger Pulp and Paper, Ltd., Bromptonville (Quebec).
Y. Valiquette.
Preprint Canadian Pulp and Paper Association, Annual Meeting (Montreal), 1975, p A-41-44. 3 fig, 9 tab.

Descriptors: *Wood wastes, *Pulp wastes, *Waste water treatment, *Flotation, Water pollution treatment, Industrial wastes, Wastes, Waste treatment, Water pollution sources, Water purification, Bark, Suspended solids, Temperature, Viscosity, Pilot plants, Coagulation, Separation techniques, Biochemical oxygen demand, Canada.
Identifiers: White water, Woodroom effluents.

The dissolved air flotation process has been evaluated at Kruger Pulp and Paper Ltd.'s Bromptonville, Quebec, mill for the removal of suspended solids from woodroom effluent. The woodroom effluent is composed of white water and bark fines and has a suspended solids concentration of 1000-6000 ppm (average 2500-3000 ppm), a temperature of 28-36 C, and a viscosity of between 1.5 and 3.0 centipoises. The main elements of the flotation pilot plant are listed, along with the variables studied (feed rate of raw influent, recirculation rate, initial suspended solids concentration, solids loading rate, initial BOD concentration, influent temperature, and coagulant concentration). The results indicate an 85% removal of suspended solids at a feed rate of 2.3-3.0 U.S. gal/min/sq ft. Adding 1 ppm of a coagulant (anionic polymer) increased this to 93%. The initial BOD load was reduced by 30-45%. (Witt-IPC)
W75-09347

SELECTION OF EFFLUENT TREATMENT SYSTEMS FOR WAUSAU PAPER MILLS COMPANY,
Van Luven Consultants Ltd., Montreal (Quebec).
R. Van Soest, and J. Scott.
Preprint Canadian Pulp and Paper Association, Annual Meeting (Montreal), 1975, p A35-39. 2 fig, 3 tab.

Descriptors: *Pulp wastes, *Treatment facilities, *Waste water treatment, Industrial wastes, Wastes, Water pollution sources, Biological treatment, Water purification, Water pollution control, Water pollution treatment, Sewage treatment, Wisconsin, Operating costs, Operations, Capital costs, Activated sludge, Effluents, Sulfite liquors, Pulp and paper industry *Pilot plants.
Identifiers: *Zurn-Attisholz effluent treatment process, Sulfite mills.

After extensive pilot plant testing of various effluent treatment systems, Wausau Paper Mills Company (Brokaw, Wisconsin) has decided to in-

ASSESSMENT OF OFFSHORE DUMPING; TECHNICAL BACKGROUND: PHYSICAL OCEANOGRAPHY, GEOLOGICAL OCEANOGRAPHY, CHEMICAL OCEANOGRAPHY.
National Oceanic and Atmospheric Administration, Boulder, Colo. Environmental Research Labs.
For primary bibliographic entry see Field 5B.
W75-09278

HUMAN WASTE PYROLYZER,
Franklin Inst. Research Labs., Philadelphia, Pa.
D. Pindzola.
Available from the National Technical Information Service, Springfield, Va 22161 as AD-784 552, $3.25 in paper copy, $2.25 in microfiche. U.S. Army Land Warfare Laboratory, Aberdeen Proving Ground (Maryland), Technical Report No LWL-CR-02B74, June 1974. 22 p, 4 fig, 5 ref.

Descriptors: *Waste disposal, *Incineration, Urine, Solid wastes, Liquid wastes, Water pollution sources, Ultimate disposal, Waste water(Pollution), Water pollution, *Waste water treatment, Odor.
Identifiers: *Human wastes, *Pyrolysis, Field waste disposal, Feces.

A simple and effective system for thermally reducing and inerting human waste products (feces and urine) has been successfully demonstrated. The modular unit tested should service up to 14 men in its present form. Basic components consist of a 5 gallon collector pail, a liquid-fueled weed burner, and a 30 or 55-gallon openhead drum lined with a mineral fiber blanket of insulation to serve as the furnace enclosure. A 2.5 hr burning period will completely reduce a 37 lb (4 gallon) daily waste load to less than 0.5 lb of dry sterile non-polluting residue. Only 1.7 gallons of liquid fuel are required for the complete operation. The only problems are odor (over a 300 ft radius) and occasional burner flame-out. (Witt-IPC)
W75-09335

5F. Water Treatment and Quality Alteration

GERMFREE WATER PRODUCED BY OZONIZERS (KEIMFREIES WASSER DURCH OZONANLAGEN),
D. Blankenfeld.
CZ Chemie-Technik, Vol 1, No 11, p 527-528, 1972.

Descriptors: *Ozone, *Potable water, *Water treatment, Municipal water, Public health, Rivers, Viral removal, Waste water treatment.
Identifiers: River water, *Ozonizers.

The possible uses of ozone in water preparation are outlined, and preparation of potable water from percolated river water by ozonization is described. Ozone can be used to kill germs, to improve the organoleptic properties, and to oxidize iron, manganese and organic compounds in water. In the Wittlaer waterworks which prepares drinking water from polluted Rhine water, ozone is generated from liquid oxygen, and is used in a closed cycle. Ozone is contacted with a partial stream which is later united with the raw water to avoid bubbling. In the waterworks of the city of Ulm, which extracts water from the Danube and other rivers, ozone is generated from air in a fully automatic ozonization plant. Quantitative oxidation of iron, manganese and phenols, and total destruction of the germs were observed along with a very significant improvement of the organoleptic properties of the drinking water. The activated charcoal consumption for the subsequent final filtration decreased from 30-40 to 3 g/cu m by the use of ozonization. (Takacs-FIRL)
W75-08856

VIRUS INACTIVATION DURING TERTIARY TREATMENT,
Texas A and M Univ., College Station.
For primary bibliographic entry see Field 5D.
W75-08874

OCCURRENCE AND DETERMINATION OF INORGANIC POLLUTING AGENTS (IN GERMAN),
Munich Univ. (West Germany). Institut fuer Wasserchemie und Chemische Balneologie.
For primary bibliographic entry see Field 5A.
W75-08888

REMOVAL OF PESTICIDES FROM WATER BY VARIOUS WATER TREATMENT METHODS, (IN RUSSIAN),
For primary bibliographic entry see Field 5D.
W75-08933

PLANT SCALE STUDIES OF THE MAGNESIUM CARBONATE WATER TREATMENT PROCESS,
Black, Crow and Eidsness, Inc., Montgomery, Ala.
A. P. Black, and C. G. Thompson.
Available from the National Technical Information Service, Springfield, Va. 22161, as PB-241 884, $6.25 in paper copy, $2.25 in microfiche. Environmental Protection Agency, Report EPA-660/2-75-006, May 1975. 140 p, 26 fig, 25 tab, 15 ref. EPA Program Element 1BB036, 12120 HMZ.

Descriptors: Water purification, Florida, Coagulation, Magnesium, Alabama, *Sludge treatment, Recycling, *Magnesium carbonate, *Water treatment, Water reuse.
Identifiers: Carbonation, Chemical recovery, Treatment comparison, Alum treatment process.

The magnesium carbonate process of water treatment has replaced alum in a portion of two water plants in full scale studies conducted over the past two and one-half years. This new water treatment technology was compared to the presently used alum process in parallel treatment using identical units in Montgomery, Alabama and Melbourne, Florida. The results indicate a number of significant advantages; primarily that the existing problem of sludge disposal in Melbourne's case is completely eliminated and at Montgomery is greatly reduced. All water is recycled within the process along with the three basic water treatment chemicals - lime, magnesium bicarbonate, and carbon dioxide. Other advantages were increased floc settling rates, simplicity of operation and control, reduced costs when sludge treatment and disposal costs are considered, and more complete disinfection. In Melbourne's case, considerable energy would be conserved by on-site lime recovery. (EPA)
W75-08939

ENVIRONMENTAL SYSTEMS APPRAISALS AND DEVELOPMENT GUIDES.
Harza Engineering Co., Chicago, Ill.
For primary bibliographic entry see Field 5D.
W75-09107

DECENTRALIZED WATER REUSE SYSTEMS IN A WATER SCARCE ENVIRONMENT: THE TOURIST INDUSTRY IN ST. THOMAS, VIRGIN ISLANDS,
Clark Univ., Worcester, Mass.
For primary bibliographic entry see Field 5D.
W75-09297

FILTER APPARATUS,
A. M. Timpe.
United States Patent 3,814,252. Issued June 4, 1974. Official Gazette of the United States Patent Office, Vol 923, No 1, p 156, June 1974. 1 fig.

Descriptors: *Patents, *Water treatment, Water pollution, Water supply, *Filters, Equipment, Screens, *Filtration.

From a source of supply, water is added to a first chamber, and from an exit opening in the lower part of the first chamber is welled up into a second chamber through a filter element. From the second chamber, water overflows on the filtered side through a fine screening element into a third chamber which is smaller in volume. It then flows to an outlet connecting with uulization pipes and a further inlet where such products as fertilizer may be admixed with the water. A low sidewall of the second chamber below the filter element may pivot to an open position, making removal of sediment possible by the water pressure entering from the first chamber. (Leibowitz-FIRL)
W75-09308

COMPARISON OF WATER CHLORINATING PROCESSES FOR ARMY FIELD APPLICATIONS,
Life Systems, Inc., Cleveland, Ohio.
K. K. Kacholia, and R. A. Wynveen.
Available from the National Technical Information Service, Springfield, Va 22161 as AD-786 672, $11.25 in paper copy, $2.25 in microfiche. U S Army Medical Research and Development Command (Washington, DC), Final Report ER-197-6, May 1974. 120 p, 45 fig, 12 tab, 19 ref.

Descriptors: *Chlorination, *Potable water, *Water treatment, Chemicals, Calcium compounds, Disinfection, Water purification, Design criteria, Design, Maintenance, Reliability, Operations, Performance, Size, Weight, Water chemistry, Chlorine, Equipment.
Identifiers: *Hypochlorite generator, Calcium hypochlorite, Sodium hypochlorite, Chlorine dioxide, Mechanical feeders, Military.

A study was successfully completed which compared chlorination of field potable water with aqueous calcium hypochlorite metered with chemical feeding pumps and sodium hypochlorite or chlorine generated on-site. Current Army chlorination practices were first investigated, and all types of on-site hypochlorinators were surveyed. Utilizing this information, design data were developed for an on-site hypochlorite generator sized to meet current military needs. Criteria for comparing mechanical feeders and on-site generators included maintainability/reliability, ease of operation, performance, size, and weight. On a scale from zero to 100%, where 100% represents an ideal chlorination source, the mechanical feeder system and the on-site hypochlorinator system were rated at 87.7 and 87%, respectively. These ratings are based on answers of 6 military and civilian personnel to a questionnaire. Answers of another group of 36 military sanitary and health engineers led to ratings of 88.6 and 84.3%, respectively. Thus, it is concluded that the two systems compare favorably with an ideal system and both are satisfactory for field application. (Witt-IPC)
W75-09336

5G. Water Quality Control

METALS AND METALLOIDS IN WATER: THEIR IMPORTANCE TO MAN (IN GERMAN),
Mainz Univ. (West Germany). Hygiene Institut.
J. Borneff.
Zentralbl Bakteriol Parasitenkd Infektionskr Hyg Erste Abt Orig Reihe B Hyg Praev Med. 158(6): 524-529, 1974, English summary.

Descriptors: Metals, *Trace metals, *Potable water, Water quality control, Surface water, Industrial wastes, Pollutants, Water pollution sources, Rivers, Europe.
Identifiers: Germany, *Metalloids, Rhine River, West Germany.

Trace metals in drinking water can impair health. Health can also be endangered through the biological food chain. Certain substances in water are essential for the syntheses of enzymes. Excessive metal concentrations should be avoided. The standards are determined by values of the natural, average ground water. Better control of water is essential because trace elements have rarely been included in drinking water analysis. A continuous surface water control is important in order to deteet discharge of dangerous industrial wastes. Standards of quality of the Rhine (West Germany) water are set up to guarantee that water pollution is kept within limits.--Copyright 1975, Biological Abstracts, Inc.
W75-08890

WASTEWATER INFILTRATION NEAR THE CITY OF MOUNT SHASTA, SISKIYOU COUNTY, CALIFORNIA,
Geological Survey, Menlo Park, Calif.
For primary bibliographic entry see Field 5B.
W75-08906

LIVESTOCK AND THE ENVIRONMENT: A BIBLIOGRAPHY WITH ABSTRACTS, VOLUME II,
East Central State Coll., Ada, Okla. School of Environmental Science.
R. H. Ramsey, M. L. Rowe, and L. Merryman.
Available from the National Technical Information Service, Springfield, Va. 22161, as PB-242 545, $10.00 in paper copy, $2.25 in microfiche. Environmental Protection Agency, Ada, Oklahoma, Report EPA-660/2-75-003, April 1975. 139, 360 ref. R-801454.

Descriptors: *Bibliographies, Cattle, Sheep, Hogs, Poultry, Fish farming, *Feed lots, *Confinement pens, *Research and development, *Farm wastes, Waste identification, Waste treatment, Waste storage, Waste disposal, Agricultural runoff.
Identifiers: *Waste management, Title index, Author index, Keyword index, Animal waste information categories index.

Management and research information on animal wastes has expanded rapidly in recent years. This material has appeared in such diverse sources as journal articles, conference proceedings papers, university publications, government publications, magazine articles, books, and theses. This bibliography was compiled in order to speed the flow of information on findings in one segment of the livestock industry to other segments that could benefit from this technology. Included in this publication are the following indexes: (1) title, (2) author, (3) keyword, (4) animal information categories. These indexes are followed by a section of abstracts of each reference entry found in the bibliography. Single copies of most articles can be obtained in hard copy or microfiche form at cost from the Animal Waste Technical Information Center, School of Environmental Science, East Central Oklahoma State University, Ada, Oklahoma 74820. (EPA)
W75-08937

A REVIEW OF THE LITERATURE ON THE USE OF CALCIUM HYPOCHLORITE IN FISHERIES,
Bureau of Sport Fisheries and Wildlife, Cortland, N.Y. Tunison Lab. of Fish Nutrition.
H. A. Podoliak.
Available from the National Technical Information Service, Springfield, Va 22161 as PB-235 444, $3.25 in paper copy, $2.25 in microfiche. Bureau of Sport Fisheries and Wildlife, U.S. Fish and Wildlife Service, Division of Population Regulation Research, Report FWS-LK-74-05, March 1974. 281 p, 2 tab, approx. 1130 ref.

Descriptors: *Reviews, *Bibliographies, Publications, *Algicides, *Aquiculture, *Disinfection,

For primary bibliographic entry see Field 5D.
W75-09082

DELAWARE RIVER BASIN COMMISSION ANNUAL REPORT, 1974.
Delaware River Basin Commission, Trenton, N.J.
For primary bibliographic entry see Field 6E.
W75-09093

MULTIOBJECTIVE WATER RESOURCES PLANNING, A BIBLIOGRAPHY.
Office of Water Research and Technology, Washington, D.C.
For primary bibliographic entry see Field 6B.
W75-09123

OIL SPILL PROTECTION IN THE BALTIC SEA,
Institute for Water and Air Pollution Research, Stockholm (Sweden).
L. Landner, and A. Hagstrom.
Journal Water Pollution Control Federation, Vol 47, No 4, p 796-809, April 1975. 4 tab, 7 fig, 22 ref.

Descriptors: *Oil pollution, *Pollutant identification, Oil, Water quality control, *Oil spills, *Oil wastes, *Water pollution control, *Legislation, Analytical techniques, Toxicity, Environmental effects, Water pollution sources, Brackish water, Biodegradation, Crustaceans, Molluscs, Fish.
Identifiers: Oil tagging, *Baltic Sea, Sweden, Sticklebacks, Mytilus, Gammarus, Neomysis, Corexit.

Persuant to an agreement among Baltic Sea countries, Sweden has enacted strict legislation regarding the discharge of oil into its territorial waters and instituted a new control system. However, the number of accidental or illegal discharges from tankers in the Baltic is still unacceptably high. A program to combat such spills has been undertaken and is partially complete, and an oil spill research group has been formed by the Swedish Coast Guard, the National Environmental Protection Board, the Swedish Petroleum Institute, and the Water and Air Pollution Research Laboratory. Oil tagging, research on the environmental effects of oil spills, and analytical techniques are integrated into the new control system. (Katz)
W75-09156

SALT-BALANCE STUDY OF PAUBA VALLEY, UPPER SANTA MARGARITA RIVER AREA, RIVERSIDE COUNTY, CALIFORNIA,
Geological Survey, Menlo Park, Calif.
For primary bibliographic entry see Field 5B.
W75-09177

ASSESSMENT OF EFFICIENCY IN DIGESTIBILITY OF MOSQUITO LARVAE BY LARVICIDAL FISHES,
Taraporewala Marine Biological Research Station, Bombay (India).
G. A. Shirgur.
J Anim Morphol Physiol. 19(2): 166-180. Illus. 1972.

Descriptors: *Mosquitos, *Fish, *Larvae, *Digestion, *Insect control, Larvicides, Evaluation.
Identifiers: Carassius-auratus, Digestibility, Panchax-panchax, Rasbora-daniconius.

Studies were made on chitinolytic activity in alimentary canals of 9 spp. of larvicidal fishes, to ascertain their efficiency in digesting mosquito larvae possessing a chitinous exoskeleton. Initial in vivo studies were made and the rate of food passage was the fastest in Panchax panchax and the lowest in Carassius auratus. Chitinous remains from fecal pellets in different larvicidal fishes were analyzed, showing that exoskeletons were crumpled and loose textured. Subsequent in vitro studies showed that C. auratus had maximum chitinolytic activity, whereas Rasbora daniconius had the least. Correlation between rates of passage of chitinous food in different fishes and respective strengths of chitinolytic activity indicated that P. panchax was the most efficient in chitin digestion and the fastest in rate of food passage, whereas C. auratus was the least in such a capacity.--Copyright 1974, Biological Abstracts, Inc.
W75-09203

FUTURE OF SANITARY LANDFILL,
Schlitz (Joseph) Brewing Co., Milwaukee, Wis.
B. Thompson, and I. Zandi.
Journal of the Environmental Engineering Division, Proceedings of American Society of Civil Engineers, Vol 101, No EE1, Proceedings Paper 11113, p 41-54, February 1975. 9 fig, 2 tab, 37 ref, 1 append.

Descriptors: *Landfills, *Solid wastes, *City planning, *Area redevelopment, Costs, Environmental engineering, Forecasting, Municipal wastes, Waste disposal, Land use, Social aspects, Aerial photography, Parks, Incineration, Leachate.
Identifiers: *Vacant land, Capital improvement costs, Hauling.

A new policy was offered and examined which, upon adoption, could: (1) reduce people's objection to sanitary landfill as a neighbor, (2) significantly increase the amount of land eligible for use as sanitary landfill, (3) reduce to some degree inequity between rich and poor, and (4) provide a more desirable land-use policy. The proposed policy has four salient features: (1) it allows the use of only small sites (20 acres or less); (2) it allows utilization of each site for a short period of time (1 to 3 years); (3) it guarantees that at the end of the designated period, the site will be converted into a community asset, such as a park; and (4) it allows only the most advanced engineering design, construction, and operation to eliminate temporary nuisances as much as possible. The data and analysis presented indicate that (1) in Philadelphia, sufficient vacant land exists within the city limits to operate sanitary landfills for more than 40 years; and (2) the cost of such a plan is within the acceptable range. (Visocky-ISWS)
W75-09204

ENGINEERING CHALLENGES OF DREDGED MATERIAL DISPOSAL,
Army Engineers Waterways Experiment Station, Vicksburg, Miss. Office of Dredged Material Research.
R. M. Meccia, W. C. Allanach, Jr., and F. H. Griffis.
Journal of the Waterways, Harbors and Coastal Engineering Division, Proceedings of American Society of Civil Engineers, Vol 101, No WW1, Proceedings Paper 11096, p 1-13, February 1975. 2 fig, 1 tab, 5 ref, 1 append.

Descriptors: *Dredging, *Waste disposal, *Channels, *Water quality, *Dikes, Environmental effects, Harbors, Research priorities, Sediment load, Spoil banks, Turbidity, Waste disposal, Wildlife habitats, Pipelines, Pumping, Slurries, Pollutants, Sediments, Wetting, Dewatering, Particle size, Mineralogy, Clays, Silts, Planning, Maintenance, Density.
Identifiers: Agglomeration.

The U.S. Army Corps of Engineers has been concerned with the development of navigable waterways in the United States since 1824. In fulfilling its mission, the Corps has been responsible for the annual dredging of approximately 380,000,000 cu yd of bottom sediments. Increasing concern has developed over the impacts of the disposal of these materials. The U.S. Army Engineer Waterways Experiment Station is conducting a nationwide research program to develop alternatives, including consideration of dredged material as a

manageable resource. Problem identification and assessments were summarized, and program progress with emphasis on engineering aspects of the study was examined. This research effort provided solutions to many problems within 2 years and to some of the more difficult and complex ones within 5 years. Of 47 separate projects currently underway or in advanced planning stages in 1974, 30 projects representing approximately 15% of the total anticipated funding were scheduled for completion by the end of fiscal year 1974. (Roberts-ISWS)
W75-09205

ANALYTICAL MODEL OF HYDRAULIC PIPELINE DREDGE,
Texas A and M Univ., College Station.
For primary bibliographic entry see Field 8C.
W75-09206

INDIANA STREAM POLLUTION CONTROL BOARD V. U.S. STEEL CORP (APPEAL FROM ORDER SETTING ASIDE BOARD'S ORDER AGAINST CORPORATION, BOARD APPEALS FROM DETERMINATION THAT ITS FINDINGS WERE INSUFFICIENT).
For primary bibliographic entry see Field 6E.
W75-09240

GUARDING OUR WATER RESOURCES, 1974 ANNUAL REPORT.
Virginia Polytechnic Inst. and State Univ., Blacksburg. Water Resources Research Center.
For primary bibliographic entry see Field 9D.
W75-09243

THE PEOPLE'S LAKE,
Save Lake Superior Association, Duluth, Minn.
For primary bibliographic entry see Field 5C.
W75-09247

REVIEW OF NPDES PERMITS.
Corps of Engineers, Washington, D.C.
Federal Register, Vol 39, No 191, p 35369-35373, October 1, 1974.

Descriptors: *Administrative agencies, *Federal government, *Permits, *Water pollution, *Navigation, Administration, Regulation, Coordination, Legal aspects, Legislation, Water Quality Act, Federal Water Pollution Control Act, Navigable rivers, Navigable waters, Obstruction to flow, Solid wastes, Wastes, Disposal, Suspended solids, Water pollution sources.
Identifiers: Administrative regulations, Navigation obstructions, *National Pollutant Discharge Elimination System, Effluent limitations, Environmental policy, Hazardous substances(Pollution).

The proposed regulation, 402(b)(6) of the Federal Water Pollution Control Act of 1972, prescribes the policy, practice, and procedures to be followed by all District and Division Offices in their review of proposed National Pollutant Discharge Elimination System (NPDES) permit applications as to their effect on navigation and anchorage. In order to promote coordination with the Environmental Protection Agency (EPA) and states with approved NPDES programs, the regulation requires that the District Engineer meet with appropriate Regional Administrators or states. To insure that the interests of navigation and anchorage are protected in the administration of the NPDES permit program the District Engineer may issue permits only if the applicant will not substantially impair navigation and anchorage. In reviewing a proposed NPDES discharge as to its effect on navigation and anchorage, and in developing appropriate terms and conditions to granting permits, the District Engineer must consider the nature, characteristics, and average daily discharge by weight of any suspended solids to be discharged by the applicant. (Fernandez-Florida)
W75-09248

EFFLUENT GUIDELINES AND STANDARDS--GENERAL PROVISIONS.
Environmental Protection Agency, Washington, D.C.
Federal Register, Vol 39, No 24, Part II, p 4532-4533, February 4, 1974.

Descriptors: *Administrative agencies, *Standards, *Effluents, *Waste treatment, *Federal Water Pollution Control Act, Water quality, Water quality control, Federal government, Water pollution, Legislation, Water pollution control, Water pollution sources, *Water quality standards, Control, Wastes, Industrial wastes, Regulation, Treatment facilities, Waste water(Pollution).
Identifiers: Administrative regulations, Effluent limitations, FWPCA Amendments of 1972, Pretreatment standards(Effluent), Environmental policy, Hazardous substances(Pollution).

This notice amends 40 CFR Chapter I, by adding a new Subchapter N and new Part 401. These regulations provide effluent limitations guidelines for existing sources, standards of performance for new sources, and pretreatment standards for new and existing sources for particular categories of point sources to be issued under 40 CFR Parts 402 through 699. Part 401 is intended to provide a description of the applicable legal authorities and definitions which will apply throughout the series of individual regulations. General definitions have been expanded to include certain additional terms such as process waste water, process waste water pollutants, non-contact cooling water, noncontact cooling water pollutants, and blowdown. The authority under the Federal Water Pollution Control Act, as amended, for promulgation of these rules is described; and provision is made for future revision to update the list of terms, definitions, abbreviations and parameters. (Fernandez-Florida)
W75-09249

CANNED AND PRESERVED SEAFOOD PROCESSING POINT SOURCE CATEGORY--PROPOSED EFFLUENT LIMITATION GUIDELINES, STANDARDS OF PERFORMANCE AND PRETREATMENT STANDARDS.
Environmental Protection Agency, Washington, D.C.
Federal Register, Vol 39, No 26, Part II, p 4708-4728, February 6, 1974.

Descriptors: *Administrative agencies, *Regulation, *Aeration, *Oxidation, *Recycling, Standards, Federal government, Water pollution, Environmental engineering, Environmental sanitation, Federal Water Pollution Control Act, Industrial wastes, Liquid wastes, Solid wastes, Treatment facilities, Waste treatment, Waste water(Pollution), Waste water treatment, Wastes, Water pollution control, Water pollution sources.
Identifiers: Administrative regulations, Effluent limitations, FWPCA Amendments of 1972, Environmental policy, Hazardous substances(Pollution), Pretreatment standards(Effluent).

Pursuant to the Federal Water Pollution Control Act, as amended, the Environmental Protection Agency gives notice of proposed effluent limitations guidelines, standards of performance, and pretreatment standards for the canned and preserved seafood processing point source category. Regulations are proposed for the following subcategories of processing: farm-raised catfish, conventional and mechanical blue crab, Alaskan crab meat and crab section, dungeness and tanner crab, Alaskan shrimp, Northern shrimp, Southern nonbreaded shrimp, breaded shrimp, and tuna. Waste water treatment and control technologies are discussed in terms of the best practicable control technology currently available; the best available

regulations by the Environmental Protection Agency, the following changes have been made in the regulations: limitations have been increased for leached dust; provision has been made for the discharge into navigable waters of storage pile runoff as an alternative to complete containment; a provision allowing flexibility in the application of the limitations representing the best practicable control technology available has been added to each subpart of the Federal Water Pollution Control Act for special circumstances that may not have been previously adequately accounted for. Implementing the effluent limitations guidelines will substantially reduce the environmental harm which would otherwise be attributable to the continued discharge of polluted waste water from existing and newly constructed plants in the cement industry. (Gagliardi-Florida)
W75-09254

RUBBER PROCESSING POINT SOURCE CATEGORY--TIRE AND INNER TUBE PLANTS EMULSION CRUMB RUBBER, SOLUTION CRUMB RUBBER, AND LATEX RUBBER SUBCATEGORIES.
Environmental Protection Agency, Washington, D.C.
Federal Register, Vol 39, No 36, Part II, p 6660-6667, February 21, 1974.

Descriptors: *Industrial wastes, *Environmental control, *Effluents, *Federal Water Pollution Control Act, *Water pollution sources, Water pollution control, Water pollution, Environment, Environmental effects, Rubber pollutants, Pollutant identification, Pollution abatement, Water pollution effects, Water pollution treatment, Waste water(Pollution), Waste water disposal.
Identifiers: Administrative regulations, Effluent limitations.

The Environmental Protection Agency has proposed effluent limitations guidelines for existing sources and standards of performance and pretreatment standards for new sources within the tire and rubber processing category of point sources. As a result of public comment and continuing review and evaluation, the following changes have been made: the older tire and inner tube plants subcategory and the newer tire and inner tube plants subcategory have been combined and designated as the tire and inner tube plants subcategory; the subparts of the regulation have been numbered to reflect a total of four subcategories instead of five; and provision has been added to the Federal Water Pollution Control Act allowing flexibility in the application of the limitations representing the best practicable control technology currently available. Implementing the effluent limitations guidelines will substantially reduce the environmental harm which would otherwise be attributable to the continued discharge of polluted waste waters from existing and newly constructed plants in the rubber processing industry. (Gagliardi-Florida)
W75-09255

WATER POLLUTION CONTROL--CONSTRUCTION GRANTS FOR WASTE TREATMENT WORKS.
Environmental Protection Agency, Washington, D.C.
For primary bibliographic entry see Field 5D.
W75-09256

STATE OF OREGON NAVIGABLE WATER QUALITY STANDARDS.
Environmental Protection Agency, Washington, D.C.
Federal Register, Vol 39, No 24, p 4486, February 4, 1974.

Descriptors: *Oregon, *Navigable waters, Water quality, *Water quality control, *Sewage disposal, *Gases, Administrative agencies, Federal government, Water, Water law, Water pollution, Legislation, Water pollution control, Water pollution sources, Control, Quality control, *Water quality standards, Sewage, Wastes, Industrial wastes, Sewage treatment.
Identifiers: Administrative regulations, FWPCA Amendments of 1972, Environmental policy, Hazardous substances(Pollution).

Regulations setting forth standards of water quality applicable to the navigable waters of the State of Oregon, pursuant to section 303 (b) of the Federal Water Pollution Control Act, as amended are proposed. Under section 303 (a) of the Act, the Administrator of the U.S. Environmental Protection Agency (EPA) is required to review water quality standards for interstate and intrastate waters adopted and submitted by the states. If the state does not adopt provisions in compliance with the requirements of the Act, the EPA Administrator may publish proposed revised water quality standards. The State of Oregon adopted water quality standards for both interstate and intrastate waters, but failed to adopt a total dissolved gas criterion which is consistent with the applicable criteria adopted by the bordering states of Idaho and Washington. Evidence indicates that the proposed Oregon total gas criterion is unreasonably stringent and generally unachievable. The proposed new EPA regulation thus provides that the concentrations of total dissolved gas relative to atmospheric pressure at the point of sample collection shall not exceed one hundred percent of saturation except when stream flows are less than the average minimum seven days low flow which occurs once in ten years. (Fernandez-Florida)
W75-09261

OIL POLLUTION ACT AMENDMENTS OF 1973.
Law and Policy in International Business, Vol 6, No 4, p 1251-1261, 1974. 78 ref.

Descriptors: *Oil pollution, *Oil spills, *Legislation, *Oceans, *Design standards, Water pollution, Water pollution sources, Oily water, Fuels, Oil, International waters, Legal aspects, Penalties(Legal), Regulation, Water law, Ships, Transportation, Control, Standards, Specifications, Federal government.
Identifiers: Hazardous substances(Pollution), *Oil Pollution Act, Coastal waters, Environmental policy, International agreements, Liability(Legal aspects), Non-point sources(Pollution).

The 1973 Amendments to the 1961 Oil Pollution Act were adopted as a positive step toward the elimination of maritime oil pollution caused by oil tankers and other vessels. The rigorous standards of the Amendments in regulating the discharge of oil at sea and new tanker construction requirements designed to minimize oil outflow in the event of collision or stranding are discussed. Weaknesses, loopholes, and ineffective enforcement of antipollution standards under the 1961 Act are considered. Ramifications of the 1973 Amendments and their impact upon discharge standards, exemptions, tanker construction, criminal penalties, and various additional enforcement mechanisms are analyzed. Collateral effects on tanker operation and construction costs are reviewed in terms of higher carriage rates, and resultant higher prices for gasoline, home heating oil, lubricants, and other petroleum products. Although the Amendments represent no more than a limited step in the effort to eliminate oil pollution of the seas, this legislation demonstrates considerable progress. (Fernandez-Florida)
W75-09264

A PROPOSED METHOD OF WASTE MANAGEMENT IN CLOSED-CYCLE MARICULTURE SYSTEMS THROUGH FOAM-FRACTIONATION AND CHLORINATION,
Delaware Univ., Newark. Dept. of Agricultural Engineering.
For primary bibliographic entry see Field 5D.

W75-09279

COMPUTER PROGRAMS IN USE IN THE WATER QUALITY BRANCH, VOL 5, WATER QUALITY DATA: POWER SPECTRUM (HARMONIC) ANALYSES AND FREQUENCY,
Department of the Environment, Ottawa (Ontario). Water Quality Branch.
For primary bibliographic entry see Field 7C.
W75-09289

HUCHO HUCHO L. IN MARAMURES WATERS, (IN ROMANIAN),
Institutul Pedagogic Baia-Mare (Rumania).
R. Frank.
Ocrotirea Nat, Vol 16, No 1, p 13-20, 1972, Illus.

Descriptors: *Fish reproduction, Spawning, *Water quality standards, Water pollution control, Distribution, *Growth rates, Water pollution effects.
Identifiers: *Hucho-hucho, Pisciculture, *Romania(Maramures), Roe.

By the end of the last century, Hucho hucho occurred in the major watercourses in Romania. Currently, it occurs only in Moldova, Bistrita and some tributaries, Tisa, ans some rivers in Maramures. Among the causes of reduction of the species, some are biological matters, H. hucho has a rapid growth rate, almost 10 times faster than that of the carp. Consequently, it became an item of attraction and profit for the residents of the areas involved. However, the reproductive rates is slow (the 1st roe are deposited at the age of 4-5 yr). Snow thawing coincides with the spawning period, and consequently torrents are destructive. Environmental deterioration as a result of irrational timber cutting, dams, water pollution, and rafting had a negative effect which in some cases irreversibly altered the environmental setup. The measures suggested for providing adequate conditions include strengthening piscicultural regulations, establishing preserves, replanting some river banks, afforsting and fighting water pollution.--Copyright 1974, Biological Abstracts, Inc.
W75-09304

SYSTEM FOR SEPARATING HYDROCARBONS FROM WATER,
Fram Corp., East Providence, R.I. (Assignee).
J. D. Conley, D. E. Belden, and R. D. Terhune.
United States Patent 3,878,094. Issued April 15, 1975. Official Gazette of the United States Patent Office, Vol 933, No 3, p 1340, April 1975. 1 fig.

Descriptors: *Patents, Waste water treatment, *Separation techniques, *Oil wastes, Oily wastes, Pollution abatement, Oil pollution, Water pollution control.
Identifiers: Oil-water separation.

A system is described for removing hydrocarbon pollutants from a water stream to provide a purified effluent stream. A separator removes free and entrained hydrocarbons from the stream; this separator has separate hydrocarbon and water outlets and a mechanical emulsion breaker for removing emulsified hydrocarbon from the stream. The emulsion breaker consists of an inlet connected to the separator water outlet, a control mounted to continuously sense the hydrocarbon-water interface in the separator, and valves for controlling the flow rates through the outlets. Controls are connected to the valves for adjustment of flow rates in response to changes in the position and the interface to counteract changes therein. Thus the system is closed and pressurized. A fluid analyzer and an associated conduit continuously sample water effluent from the emulsion breaker and recycle the sample to the effluent stream. (Prague-FIRL)
W75-09307

APPARATUS FOR PREVENTING OIL POLLUTION,
Texaco Development Corp., New York. (assignee).
R. Tuggle, R. H. Graves, and R. J. DeRouen.
Canadian Patent 964,475. Issued March 18, 1975. Patent Office Record, Vol 103, No 11, p 16, March, 1975.

Descriptors: *Oil pollution, *Water pollution control, *Patents, Equipment, *Pollution abatement.

An oil pollution control device isolates a segment of a substantial body of water into which oil may be then introduced. The isolated portion extends from above the surface to near the bottom of such a water body. For example, a vertical caisson with its base extending into the bottom of the body of water and with openings just above the bottom may be utilized, permitting circulation of water at that level. (Prague-FIRL)
W75-09314

APPARATUS FOR IMPROVED SHIPPING OF CRUDE OIL RELATIVE TO ENVIRONMENTAL DAMAGE AND ECOLOGICAL PROBLEMS,
J. M. Elson.
United States Patent 3,864,935. Issued February 11, 1975. Official Gazette of the United States Patent Office, Vol 931, No 2, p 563-564, February, 1975. 1 fig.

Descriptors: *Patents, *Oil, *Transportation, *Oil spills, Equipment, Environmental effects, *Water pollution control.
Identifiers: Shipping.

Equipment is described for use in shipping crude oil between two geographical locations, in order to avoid oil spills. Equipment is included to freeze the oil into molds in the shape of geometrical forms for transportation. The tranportation means include a tube through which the units of oil are transported; the tube's cross-section corresponds to the geometrical forms of the molds. The freezing apparatus also has the function of freezing water or a fluid other than oil. Means for pouring oil into the containers, and for closing the containers also are described. (Prague-FIRL)
W75-09319

TRAP TO CLEANSE OIL-POLLUTED WATER,
M. S. Kharchenko.
Soviet Patents 410,998. Issued May 30, 1974. Derwent Soviet Patents Report, Vol 5, No 42, p 1. November 26, 1974 1 fig.

*Patents, *Oil spills, Water treatment, Pollution abatement, Flotation, Equipment, Oil pollution, Separation techniques, Waste water treatment.
Identifiers: *Traps(Pollution).

A trap to cleanse oil-polluted water has a protective grid, injectors, flotation, and foam chambers. To increase effectiveness of operation, each oil trap is in the form of a hull of varying sections with protective grills, consisting of, in sequence, a flotation chamber with air distribution injectors, a foam-forming chamber, a foam pumping-out chamber and a chamber for ejecting cleansed liquid. Fluid passes through a protective grid, entering a flotation chamber, where air from a compressor via injectors saturates the polluted liquid. Foam from a chamber is directed into the restricting chamber and then with the aid of a froth-suction manifold and a fan, it is directed onto a pollutant collecting tank. The cleansed fluid then passes through a chamber and is ejected. (Prague-FIRL)
W75-09323

COALESCENCE OF SMALL SUSPENDED DROPS E. G. OIL FROM WATER.
Netherlands Patent 73745V/42. Issued October 2, 1974. Derwent Netherlands Patents Report, Vol 5, No 42, p 1, Novermber 26, 1974.

Descriptors: *Patents, *Suspensions, *Oil pollution, Equipment, Waste water treatment, Lime, Water pollution control, Pollution abatement.
Identifiers: Floating plastic balls.

A system was described for the coalescence of small suspended drops of oil from water. Liquid containing a finely divided contaminant such as suspended oil drops, is passed through a bed containing floating plastic balls, one to ten mm in diameter. The balls should be wetted by the oil. The flow should be in the direction in which the contaminant settles, upwards for oil in water. The oil drops collide with each other and the balls and coalesce. Abrasion best removes deposits of lime, and the bed may be agitated for this purpose. The bed operates longer than conventional equipment without blocking. (Prague-FIRL)
W75-09325

METHOD AND APPARATUS FOR FLUID COLLECTION AND/OR PARTITIONING,
Corning Glass Works, N.Y. (assignee).
C. M. Lawhead.
United States Patent 3,814,248. Issued June 4, 1974. Official Gazette of the United States Patent Office, Vol 923, No 1, p 155, June, 1974. 1 fig.

Descriptors: *Patents, *Water quality control, *Sampling, Equipment, *Separation techniques, Centrifugation, Water analysis, Instrumentation, Homogeneity.
Identifiers: Spools.

Spools or partitioning assemblies have been designed to be used with rigid tubular containers for effecting the physical or the complete physical and chemical partitioning of the heavier fluid phase from the lighter fluid phase of a centrifugally separated fluid sample. Each spool has a central axial orifice and a resilient annular wiper portion. The wiper portion includes a container-contacting surface and is adapted to engage the inner surface of the container and an integral annular skirt portion. Because the specific gravities of the spools are between the specific gravities of the fluid phases, the spools move downward in the containers to the vicinity of the fluid phase interface. The lighter fluid phase flows upward through the central orifice. Physical partitioning occurs by the combination of a spool or spool-diaphragm with a natural plub of the heavy phase fluid, which acts to retain the heavy fluid phase. Complete physical and chemical partitioning is accomplished by combining a float apparatus and a spool to form a continuous line contact seal on the inner surface of the spool skirt portion. The partitioning assemblies can be used in evacuated fluid collection tubes or in atmospheric pressure tubes. (Leibowitz-FIRL)
W75-09327

PROCEEDINGS TALL TIMBERS CONFERENCE ON ECOLOGICAL ANIMAL CONTROL BY HABITAT MANAGEMENT, NO. 4.
Tall Timbers Research Station, Tallahassee, Fal.
For primary bibliographic entry see Field 2I.
W75-09333

FOREST PRODUCTS POLLUTION CONTROL ANNOTATED BIBLIOGRAPHY (EXCLUDING PULP AND PAPER),
Western Forest Products Lab., Vancouver (British Columbia).
For primary bibliographic entry see Field 10C.
W75-09341

GULF STATES PAPER MAKES BIG MOVE TOWARDS ZERO POLLUTION,
For primary bibliographic entry see Field 5D.
W75-09345

helpful in analyzing the problem, describing the alternatives and selecting an optimum strategy. The examples presented were of rather simple games, i.e., two person zero-sum games with pure and mixed strategies. Each was carried through to its optimum conclusion. (See also W75-09210) (Jess-ISWS)
W75-09218

COMPUTER SIMULATION OF WATER RESOURCE SYSTEMS,
Utah Water Research Lab., Logan.
For primary bibliographic entry see Field 2A.
W75-09220

A PROBLEM ORIENTED LIBRARY FOR HYDROLOGY,
McMaster Univ., Hamilton (Ontario). Dept. of Civil Engineering and Engineering Mechanics.
For primary bibliographic entry see Field 7C.
W75-09222

PRACTICAL APPLICATIONS OF HYDROLOGIC SIMULATION,
Hydrocomp International, Palo Alto, Calif.
For primary bibliographic entry see Field 4A.
W75-09223

CONTROL RULES FOR MULTIPLE-USE RESERVOIRS AND MULTI-RESERVOIR SYSTEMS,
Water Research Association, Marlow (England).
For primary bibliographic entry see Field 4A.
W75-09224

SOME PROBLEMS IN THE APPLICATION OF SYSTEMS ANALYSES IN WATER RESOURCES SYSTEMS,
Office of Science and Technology, Washington, D.C.
For primary bibliographic entry see Field 3B.
W75-09226

6B. Evaluation Process

AN ECONOMIC ANALYSIS OF THE EFFECTS OF A DECLINING GROUND WATER LEVEL IN THE RAFT RIVER BASIN, CASSIA COUNTY, IDAHO,
Idaho Univ., Moscow. Dept. of Agricultural Economics.
For primary bibliographic entry see Field 4B.
W75-08921

RECREATION REIMBURSEMENT FOR WYOMING'S NORTH PLATTE RIVER BASIN,
Wyoming Univ., Laramie. Div. of Agricultural Economics.
A. S. Hersch.
Available from the National Technical Information Service, Springfield, Va 22161 as PB-242 814, $5.25 in paper copy, $2.25 in microfiche. MS Thesis, February 1974. 112 p, 6 fig, 11 tab, 55 ref, 2 append. OWRR C-4351(9063)(1).

Descriptors: *Recreation, *Pricing, *Payment, *Evaluation, Benefits, *Wyoming, Marginal costs, Average costs, Taxes, Government finance, Permits, Economic efficiency, Social aspects, Income, Economic impact, Indirect benefits, Average costs.
Identifiers: *North Platte River Basin(Wyo), User charges, Reimbursement options.

Development of feasible pricing and reimbursement mechanisms for recreation in Wyoming's North Platte River Basin were based on identification of groups likely to benefit from water resource development projects and conceptualization of the nature of such benefits. Reimbursement mechanisms that might be utilized in project financing are proposed and defined, and alternative reimbursement mechanisms are evaluated utilizing the efficiency, equity, administrative feasibility, and revenue raising ability criteria, with consideration of the various beneficiary groups and the multi-dimensional nature of the project benefits. The selected sites for the study were Glendo Reservoir, Alcova Reservoir, and the 'Miracle Mile.' An attempt was made to ascertain the incidence and direction (positive or negative) of economic impacts of recreation projects upon certain beneficiary sectors and groups. Three accounts--(1) development or economic efficiency, (2) environmental/recreational quality, and (3) social factor effects--were utilized in conceptualizing recreation project impacts. A recommended set of reimbursement mechanisms for each area is proposed with emphasis on a marine fuel tax. Federal-local transfer payments, and facility use fees. (Auen-Wisconsin)
W75-08922

STUDIES IN ENVIRONMENT - VOLUME I-SUMMARY REPORT,
Homer Hoyt Inst., Washington, D.C.
For primary bibliographic entry see Field 6G.
W75-09053

STUDIES IN ENVIRONMENT - VOLUME II - QUALITY OF LIFE,
Homer Hoyt Inst., Washington, D.C.
For primary bibliographic entry see Field 6G.
W75-09054

STUDIES IN ENVIRONMENT - VOLUME IV - CONSUMPTION DIFFERENTIALS AND THE ENVIRONMENT,
Homer Hoyt Inst., Washington, D.C.
For primary bibliographic entry see Field 6G.
W75-09056

STUDIES IN ENVIRONMENT - VOLUME V - OUTDOOR RECREATION AND THE ENVIRONMENT,
Homer Hoyt Inst., Washington, D.C.
For primary bibliographic entry see Field 6G.
W75-09057

A LAND USE PROGRAM FOR ARIZONA.
Arizona Environmental Planning Commission, Phoenix.
Final Report to the Governor and the Legislature of Arizona, January 15, 1975. 226 p, 2 fig.

Descriptors: *Arizona, *Land use, *Comprehensive planning, *Legal aspects, Legislation, Environment, Natural resources, State governments, Real property.

Responding to a legislative act of 1973, the Arizona Environmental Planning Commission and the Governor's Office of Environmental Planning undertook a 2-year comprehensive and coordinated land use planning program, which reviewed existing roles and responsibilities of relevant State, Federal, and local agencies, land use laws, and the general pattern of court decisions relating to land use regulation in Arizona and other states, relevant federal laws, and the American Law Institute's Model Land Development Code(draft). Recommendations are presented for new legislation and amendments to existing legislation, basic needs are discussed, and background information used in the preparation of the report is presented. Specific geographic areas of state concern are analyzed with respect to special needs for planning at that level. (Paylore-Arizona)
W75-09058

BENEFITS AND LAND USE CHANGE CONNECTED WITH A FLOOD CONTROL PROJECT,
Dayton Univ., Ohio. Dept. of Economics.
For primary bibliographic entry see Field 4A.
W75-09081

ROCK VALLEY METROPOLITAN COUNCIL REGIONAL DEVELOPMENT GUIDE.
Rock Valley Metropolitan Council, Rockford, Ill.
June, 1972. 57 p, 12 fig, 7 tab, 1 append.

Descriptors: *Regional development, *Planning, *Land use, *Urbanization, Regions, Land classification, Natural development, Land development, Rural areas, Zoning, *Illinois, *Wisconsin, River basin development.
Identifiers: *Rock Valley Metropolitan Region(Ill-Wis), Rock River basin(Ill-Wis).

Long-range development of the coalescing urban complex in the Rock Valley Metropolitan Region is considered and recommendations are made. Boone and Winnebago counties in northern Illinois and Rock county in southern Wisconsin, which make up the RVMR, are part of the Chicago-Milwaukee Industrial District. The entire Region is with the Rock River drainage basin. Most of the urban development is located near the river and Interstate 90 which traverse the Region from north to south. Population and economic projections indicate an increasing need for land for housing and employment. The Development Guide expresses regional goals for land and resource use, including preservation of prime land in agriculture, establishment of 'environmental corridors', e.g. floodplains, wetlands, and undeveloped stream shorelines, and the use of areas for urban development soils are suitable and public sewer and water are available. Major region-shaping elements are also considered. Four alternative regional growth patterns are analyzed: continuation of present trends, radial-corridor concept, local planning without regional guidance, and coordinated multiple centers. The last is found most suitable as it preserves the individuality of various communities while conforming best to the regional development goals. (Herr-North Carolina)
W75-09106

AN EVALUATION OF STATE LAND USE PLANNING AND DEVELOPMENT CONTROL IN THE ADIRONDACKS,
Cornell Univ., Ithaca, N.Y.
For primary bibliographic entry see Field 4A.
W75-09122

MULTIOBJECTIVE WATER RESOURCES PLANNING, A BIBLIOGRAPHY.
Office of Water Research and Technology, Washington, D.C.
Available from the National Technical Information Service, Springfield, Va 22161 as PB-243 115, $7.00 in paper copy, $2.25 in microfiche. Water Resources Scientific Information Center, Report OWRT/WRSIC 75-206, May 1975, 176 p. Edited by Daniel P. Loucks, Cornell University, Ithaca, New York.

Descriptors: *Systems analysis, *Bibliographies, *Water resources, Abstracts, Alternative planning, Decision making, Methodology, Project planning, Optimum development plans, *Planning, Multiple purpose.
Identifiers: *Multiobjective planning.

This annotated bibliography contains 112 abstracts of selected documents published since 1968 pertaining to multiobjective water resources planning. Both subject and author indexes are provided. Descriptors are listed with each abstract. The abstracted material emphasizes the theory as well as the application of methods for assisting in the planning and management of water resource systems that must satisfy more than one objective. This report is another in a series of planned bibliographies in water resources produced from the information base comprising SELECTED WATER RESOURCES ABSTRACTS (SWRA). At the time of search for this bibliography, the data base had 82,687 abstracts covering SWRA through March 1, 1975 (Volume 8, Number 5).
W75-09123

LANDSCAPE AESTHETICS NUMERICALLY DEFINED (LAND SYSTEM): APPLICATION TO FLUVIAL ENVIRONMENTS,
Purdue Univ., Lafayette, Ind. Dept. of Geosciences.
W. N. Melhorn, E. A. Keller, and R. A. McBane.
Available from the National Technical Information Service, Springfield, Va 22161 as PB-243 122, $6.25 in paper copy, $2.25 in microfiche. Purdue University Water Resources Research Center, Technical Report No 37, April 1975. 149 p, 12 fig, 13 tab, 11 plates, 53 ref, 2 append. OWRT A-018-IND(1).

Descriptors: *Aesthetics, Geomorphology, Rivers, *Streams, Psychological aspects, Value, *Landscaping, Recreation, Wild rivers, Computer programs, *Social values, *Evaluation, Data processing, *River systems.
Identifiers: *Matrix techniques, Scenic environment.

There is developed a quantitative method for objectively assessing the aesthetic values of a fluvial landscape. The LAND (Landscape Aesthetics Numerically Defined) System is an extension of the matrix technique of Leopold. A parametric, computerized data sorting process provides an easy to use method to objectively evaluate natural fluvial landscapes. Landscape evaluation indices, e.g. Uniqueness, Aesthetic, Scenic, Recreational, and Wild are arbitrarily defined or taken from statutory definitions. Preliminary testing of the system suggests that personnel doing the evaluation tend to arrive at essentially the same numerical values regardless of education, background, etc. LAND has been only tested in the evaluation of fluvial systems in terms of physical, biological, water quality, and human factors. However, the system can be adapted to produce a different set of evaluation indices to rank non-fluvial landscapes. The basic computer program for the system is included in an appendix.
W75-09128

THE PARADOX OF PLANNED WEATHER MODIFICATION,
Illinois State Water Survey, Urbana.
For primary bibliographic entry see Field 3B.
W75-09209

THE UNITED STATES IHD PROGRAM,
National Committee for the International Hydrological Decade, Washington, D.C.
For primary bibliographic entry see Field 2A.
W75-09213

GAME THEORY,
Utah State Univ., Logan. Dept. of Civil Engineering.
For primary bibliographic entry see Field 6A.
W75-09218

SOCIAL ISSUES IN WATER RESOURCES DEVELOPMENT,
Utah State Univ., Logan. Dept. of Sociology.
W. H. Andrews.
In: Systems Analysis of Hydrologic Problems; Proceedings of the Second International Seminar for Hydrology Professors, August 2-14, 1970, Utah State University, Logan, p 446-452.

Descriptors: *Water resources development, *Social aspects, *Social values, Social needs,

OAK GLEN WATER-RESOURCES DEVELOPMENT STUDY USING MODELING TECHNIQUES, SAN BERNARDINO COUNTY, CALIFORNIA,
Geological Survey, Menlo Park, Calif.
For primary bibliographic entry see Field 4B.
W75-09178

GROUND-WATER RESOURCES OF THE HOLLYWOOD AREA, FLORIDA,
Geological Survey, Tallahassee, Fla.
H. W. Bearden.
Florida Bureau of Geology, Tallahassee Report of Investigations No 77, 1974. 35 p, 17 fig, 5 tab, 21 ref.

Descriptors: *Groundwater resources, *Water supply, *Water quality, *Florida, Aquifer characteristics, Water yield, Water wells, Well data, Drawdown, Groundwater recharge, Saline water intrusion, Water demand, Population, Hydrologic data, Chemical analysis, Water level fluctuations.
Identifiers: *Hollywood(Fla).

Population in the Hollywood, Fla., area increased more than 200% from 1960 to 1970 (35,237 to 106,873). This explosion in population is the source of most of the area's water problems. Fresh water for all purposes in Hollywood is derived from the highly permeable Biscayne aquifer. The aquifer is composed chiefly of permeable beds of limestone, sandstone, and sand that extend from land surface to a depth of about 200 feet. Water levels in the aquifer fluctuate chiefly in response to rainfall, the major source of recharge. The water table slopes gently from the west and averages about 1.0 foot higher in the western part of the city than in the eastern part. The configuration of the water table is greatly influenced by Hollywood Canal and the ocean. Because the permeability of the aquifer is high, the effect of pumping wells is dispersed over a large area and drawdowns are about 0.1 foot. Salt-water intrusion from Hollywood Canal is the chief threat to the groundwater supply. When discharge is low, the chloride concentration of water in the canal has reached levels greater than 10,000 milligrams per litre. Salt water has been detected in the aquifer at depth within 0.1 mile of the municipal wells. (Woodard-USGS)
W75-09185

LAND USE AND WATER RESOURCES IN TEMPERATURE AND TROPICAL CLIMATES,
H. C. Pereira.
Cambridge University Press: London, England; New York, NY, 1973, 246 p.
Identifiers: Animals, Books, Climates, Human populations, *Land use, Resources, Temperature, *Tropical climates, *Water resources.

Problems arising from increasing demands made by rapidly growing human populations on their water supplies and on the load from which these flow are described. Chapters discuss: the world's water resources and the growing demand, development of a watershed discipline, achievement of hydrological information, and recorded experience of the effects of forests on watersheds. Other chapters discuss: research on forested watersheds, watershed experiments in tropical forests, effects of grazing animals on watersheds, effects of croplands on water resources, the roles of irrigation and drainage in water resources, and problems and priorities. A list of recommended reading and a list of references are included. Technical terms are used sparingly, but references are given through to specialized source material. The book is intended for use by students of resource management, conservation, water engineering, ecology, agriculture and geography.--Copyright 1973, Biological Abstracts, Inc.
W75-09343

6E. Water Law and Institutions

A LAND USE PROGRAM FOR ARIZONA.
Arizona Environmental Planning Commission, Phoenix.
For primary bibliographic entry see Field 6B.
W75-09058

DELAWARE RIVER BASIN COMMISSION ANNUAL REPORT, 1974.
Delaware River Basin Commission, Trenton, N.J.
1975. 20 p, 3 fig, 22 photos, 1 tab.

Descriptors: *Delaware River Basin Commission, *Delaware River, Comprehensive planning, River basin development, Water supply, Recreation, Project feasibility, Flood control, Environmental effects, Energy, Delaware, New Jersey, New York, Pennsylvania.
Identifiers: *Tocks Island Lake, Environmental Impact Statements.

The 12th annual report of the Delaware River Basin Commission (DRBC) describes actions of this interstate-federal organization in areas of water supply, flood loss reduction, environmental protection, project reviews, pollution abatement, and program planning in the 13,000 square mile Delaware River valley (DL., NJ, NY, and PA). Althogh streamflows were 35% above average in 1974, there was no extensive flooding. Future flood damages will be lessened through wiser land use based on floodplain delineations DRBC is undertaking in 119 municipalities. The relatively undeveloped upper river was closely examined in studies of pollution control, water supply, recreation needs, and nonpoint pollution. A basinwide siting plan for petroleum company facilities is in process, as well as an updated electricity generator site plan. One hundred and thirty projects were cleared after public hearings and DRBC analysis showed no conflict with the Comprehensive Plan. The Tocks Island Lake project is undergoing intensive further study. Wastewater discharge permits, allocating the permissible waste load, have made some improvement in the estuary water quality, but further improvement is required from a majority of dischargers. New and increased water use will no longer be free under a program to offset reservoir costs. (Herr-North Carolina)
W75-09093

FLOOD PLAIN INFORMATION: TOMS RIVER, UNION BRANCH, RIDGEWAY BRANCH AND LONG SWAMP CREEK, OCEAN COUNTY, NEW JERSEY,
Army Engineer District, Philadelphia, Pa.
For primary bibliographic entry see Field 4A.
W75-09098

OIL SPILL PROTECTION IN THE BALTIC SEA,
Institute for Water and Air Pollution Research, Stockholm (Sweden).
For primary bibliographic entry see Field 5G.
W75-09156

THE PARADOX OF PLANNED WEATHER MODIFICATION,
Illinois State Water Survey, Urbana.
For primary bibliographic entry see Field 3B.
W75-09209

THE UNITED STATES IHD PROGRAM,
National Committee for the International Hydrological Decade, Washington, D.C.
For primary bibliographic entry see Field 2A.
W75-09213

SOCIAL ISSUES IN WATER RESOURCES DEVELOPMENT,
Utah State Univ., Logan. Dept. of Sociology.

For primary bibliographic entry see Field 6B.
W75-09228

INDIANA STREAM POLLUTION CONTROL BOARD V. U.S. STEEL CORP (APPEAL FROM ORDER SETTING ASIDE BOARD'S ORDER AGAINST CORPORATION, BOARD APPEALS FROM DETERMINATION THAT ITS FINDINGS WERE INSUFFICIENT).
313 N E 2d 693 (Indiana 1974).

Descriptors: *Pollution abatement, *Water pollution control, *Water pollution, *Water pollution sources, Steel, Waste water, Effluents, Waste water treatment, Rivers, Lake Michigan, Indiana, Water quality control, Water law, Water resources development, Waste water disposal, Waste water(Pollution), Treatment facilities, Administrative decisions, Legal review, Adjudication procedure, Environmental control, Judicial decisions.
Identifiers: *State policy, *Environmental policy, Administrative regulations.

An appeal was made from the order of the Lake Superior Court reversing an order of the Indiana Stream Pollution Control Board against United States Steel Corporation. The appellee owns and operates an integrated steel manufacturing facility along the banks of the Grand Calumet River and the shoreline of Lake Michigan. In the processes of manufacturing steel, it uses great quantities of water from Lake Michigan. Appellee discharges its waste water back into the river. The appellant is an administrative board charged with the responsibility of controlling the preventing the pollution of state waters with deleterious substances. The appellant conducted hearings to determine if U.S. Steel was discharging excessive quantities of impurities into the Grand Calumet River and Lake Michigan. The Board gave U.S. Steel notice of the hearing. The court found that the findings of fact made by the Board were insufficient to require U.S. Steel to install pollution abatement facilities. The evidence did not support the conclusion that the effluents discharged were violative of the Board's regulations. (Proctor-Florida)
W75-09240

COUNTY OF OCEAN V. STOCKHOLD (APPEAL BY LANDOWNERS FROM JUDGEMENT UPHOLDING COUNTY'S RIGHT TO CONDEMN PROPERTY FOR PURPOSE OF A DRAINAGE EASEMENT).
323 A2d 515 (N J App 1974).

Descriptors: *Eminent domain, *Condemnation, *Drainage systems, *Drainage programs, *Judicial decisions, Drainage, Drainage engineering, Ditches, Adjacent landowners, New Jersey, Governments, Water law, Social aspects, Public benefits, Public health, Local governments, Adjudication procedure, State governments, Water policy, Surface water runoff, Water management(Applied), Legal review, Legal aspects.

Defendent landowners appealed from a judgement of the Superior Court holding that the county has the authority to condemn a portion of landowner's property for a drainage easement. Defendents contend that since there are reasonable alternative drainage routes, the necessity of the present condemnation is questionable and therefore the County lacks authority. The Court held that the County has a responsibility to provide adequate drainage systems in order to protect the public from flood waters. The condemnation, sought by the County for a drainage easement was for this public purpose, and was not initiated primarily for benefit of private individuals. Since the requisite public purpose is evident the condemnation is valid. Appellants finally contend that the matter should have been determined in a plenary hearing. The court held that no hearing was required by the summary procedure application to the action. (Proctor-Florida)
W75-09241

WOODLAWN MEMORIAL PARK OF NASHVILLE, INC. V. L AND N RAILROAD CO., INC. (SUIT FOR DAMAGES CAUSED BY COLLECTION AND DIVERSION OF RAINWATER).
377 F Supp 932 (M D Tenn 1974).

Descriptors: *Tennessee, *Judicial decisions, *Surface runoff, *Adjacent land owners, *Legal aspects, Suburban areas, Subsurface drains, Land tenure, Water law, Federal jurisdiction, Floods, Drainage effects, Drainage, Drainage water, Rainfall-runoff relationships, Rain, Storm runoff, Runoff, Urban runoff, Floodwater, Land development, Repulsion(Legal aspects), Riddance(Legal aspects), Surface waters, Adjudication procedure.
Identifiers: Common enemy rule, Nuisance(Legal aspects), Water rights(Non-riparians).

Plaintiff corporate landowner sued the defendant corporation, owner of adjacent higher lands, for damages allegedly caused by the collection and diversion of rainfall on the defendant's property in such manner as to cause water to flow onto plaintiff's property in greater quantities and at a place other than normal drainage shed. The plaintiff contended that certain improvements made upon defendant's property constituted an interference with the natural drainage of surface water and as such was an actionable nuisance under Tennessee law. A Federal District Court ruled that the flooding of the plaintiff's land was not caused by the improvments made by the defendant and that any loss suffered by the plaintiff was caused by the increase in surface water due to commercial and industrial development of surrounding property and the inability of the plaintiff's underground drainage system to accommodate heavy and intense rainfall. Judgement was entered for the defendant. (Deckert-Florida)
W75-09242

PROGRESS IN WATERSHED DEVELOPMENT IN THE AWR BASINS AREA UNDER USDA PROGRAMS - SEPTEMBER 1974.
Soil Conservation Service, Wichita, Kans.
For primary bibliographic entry see Field 4D.
W75-09246

THE PEOPLE'S LAKE,
Save Lake Superior Association, Duluth, Minn.
For primary bibliographic entry see Field 5C.
W75-09247

REVIEW OF NPDES PERMITS.
Corps of Engineers, Washington, D.C.
For primary bibliographic entry see Field 5G.
W75-09248

EFFLUENT GUIDELINES AND STANDARDS--GENERAL PROVISIONS.
Environmental Protection Agency, Washington, D.C.
For primary bibliographic entry see Field 5G.
W75-09249

CANNED AND PRESERVED SEAFOOD PROCESSING POINT SOURCE CATEGORY--PROPOSED EFFLUENT LIMITATION GUIDELINES, STANDARDS OF PERFORMANCE AND PRETREATMENT STANDARDS.
Environmental Protection Agency, Washington, D.C.
For primary bibliographic entry see Field 5G.
W75-09250

TEXTILE INDUSTRY POINT SOURCE CATEGORY--PROPOSED EFFLUENT LIMITATIONS GUIDELINES.
Environmental Protection Agency, Washington, D.C.
For primary bibliographic entry see Field 5G.
W75-09251

Descriptors: *Bodies of water, *Banks, *Classification, *Accretion(Legal aspects), *Ownership of beds, Legal aspects, Judicial decisions, Water law, Streams, Running waters, Lakes, Navigable waters, High water mark, Low water mark, Riparian rights, Streambeds, Beds under water, Boundaries(Property), Lake beds, Riparian land, Louisiana.
Identifiers: Reliction, Equal footing doctrine.

Discussed is a recent decision of the Supreme Court of Louisiana which renovated the test for determining the legal classification of bodies of water. Classification of a body of water as a stream gives ownership of its bank to the riparian owners, while labelling the body a lake vests ownership up to the high-water mark in the state. The history of decisions in this area is traced by discussing the approaches utilized by the court in determining ownership of beds and categorization of bodies of water. A 'vast expanse' test, which was the prevailing rule, has been abandoned in favor of a broader 'multifactor test'. The multifactor test is a more realistic approach to the problem of waterbody classification because it allows determination based upon a balancing of facts rather than on a stringent judicial standard. It is concluded that this approach is sound from both legal and practical standpoints. (Fernandez-Florida)
W75-09265

PUBLIC RIGHTS IN GEORGIA'S TIDELANDS,
Georgia Univ., Athens. Inst. of Government.
J. Owens Smith, and J. L. Sammons.
Georgia Law Review, Vol 9, No 1, p 79-114, 1974.
OSG 1-36009 and 04-3-158-6.

Descriptors: *Public rights, *Coastal marshes, *Water law, Coasts, Intertidal areas, Tides, Boundaries(Property), Legal aspects, Common law, *Georgia.
Identifiers: *Tidelands, *Public trust doctrine, Private property.

The importance of coastal marshlands and other intertidal areas to both commercial and environmental interests precludes application of traditional concepts of private property ownership to their use. Although the necessity for state regulation has been established and to some extent implemented, the theoretical basis for such regulation is highly determinative of its effectiveness in protecting the interests of the public. The evolution of the public trust doctrine is traced. Proper interpretation of Georgia law in this area requires that the role of the state be controlled by the public trust doctrine. (NOAA)
W75-09281

FEDERAL PLAN FOR ENVIRONMENTAL DATA BUOYS.
National Oceanic and Atmospheric Administration, Rockville, Md. Federal Coordinator for Marine Environmental Prediction.
For primary bibliographic entry see Field 7A.
W75-09282

STATE FINANCIAL ASSITANCE OF FLOOD CONTROL PROJECTS.
Arizona Water Commission, Phoenix.
For primary bibliographic entry see Field 6B.
W75-09301

6F. Nonstructural Alternatives

FLOOD PLAIN INFORMATION: SANTA CLARA RIVER AND SESPE CREEK, FILLMORE, CALIFORNIA.
Army Engineer District, Los Angeles, Calif.
For primary bibliographic entry see Field 4A.
W75-09084

SPECIAL FLOOD HAZARD INFORMATION REPORT: ATLANTA, GEORGIA, INCLUDING PEACHTREE CREEK BASIN IN DEKALB COUNTY.
Army Engineer District, Mobile, Ala.
For primary bibliographic entry see Field 4A.
W75-09085

FLOOD PLAIN INFORMATION: EAST FORK BIG WOOD RIVER, GIMLET TRIUMPH, IDAHO.
Army Engineer District, Walla Walla, Wash.
For primary bibliographic entry see Field 4A.
W75-09086

FLOOD PLAIN INFORMATION: PORTNEUF RIVER, INKOM, IDAHO, AND VICINITY.
Army Engineer District, Walla Walla, Wash.
For primary bibliographic entry see Field 4A.
W75-09087

FLOOD PLAIN INFORMATION: OROFINO CREEK-WHISKEY CREEK, OROFINO, IDAHO, AND VICINITY.
Army Engineer District, Walla Walla, Wash.
For primary bibliographic entry see Field 4A.
W75-09088

SPECIAL FLOOD HAZARD INFORMATION: SOUTH FORK PALOUSE RIVER, MOSCOW, IDAHO, AND VICINITY.
Army Engineer District, Walla Walla, Wash.
For primary bibliographic entry see Field 4A.
W75-09089

FLOOD PLAIN INFORMATION: THREE MILE CREEK, LEAVENWORTH, KANSAS.
Army Engineer District, Kansas City, Kans.
For primary bibliographic entry see Field 4A.
W75-09090

FLOOD PLAIN INFORMATION--MECHUMS RIVER, ALBEMARLE COUNTY, VIRGINIA.
Army Engineer District, Norfolk, Va.
For primary bibliographic entry see Field 4A.
W75-09091

FLOOD PLAIN INFORMATION: DEEP RIVER, TURKEY CREEK, DUCK CREEK, LAKE COUNTY, INDIANA.
Army Engineer District, Chicago, Ill.
For primary bibliographic entry see Field 4A.
W75-09092

POLICY ALTERNATIVES IN FLOOD PLAINS.
East Central Florida Regional Planning Council, Winter Park.
Preliminary Report ECFRPC 74-8, July 1974. 103 p, 5 fig, 5 tab, 16 ref, 2 append. CPA-FL-04-29-1040.

Descriptors: *Alternative planning, Water policy, *Flood plain insurance, *Flood plain zoning, *Non-structural alternatives, *Tidal water, Legal aspects, Building codes, Condemnation, Easements, Legislation, Flood protection, Flood forcasting, *Florida, Hurricanes.
Identifiers: *National Flood Disaster Protection Act of 1973, 100-year floods, Beach and Shore Preservation Act.

In east central Florida the last 14 years have been without the normal heavy rains, hurricanes, and floods. Consequently, rapid urbanization has encroached on flood prone land on the coast and along rivers and lakes. This guide examines federal, state, and local legislation and policies available to minimize flood damage through non-structural alternatives. Guidelines and examples of necessary ordinances and forms are presented.

Major federal legislation includes the National Flood Disaster Protection Act of 1973 written to help flood victims and to discourage investment in vulnerable improvements. Federally subsidized flood insurance, required for mortgages on affected properties, is available to residents of communities which undertake floodplain land use controls. Of the 48 east central Florida communities designated as flood prone (20 on the coast), 18 (including 15 on the coast) qualified for this insurance by August, 1974. State action includes the Beach and Shore Preservation Act, the Flood Water Resources Act of 1972, and the establishment of the Coastal Coordinating Council. Local officials have a range of flood protection tools available including flood plain zoning, subdivision regulations, building codes, transfers of development rights, land acquisition, tax incentives, and 8 others which are described. (Herr-North Carolina)
W75-09094

FLOOD PLAIN INFORMATION: SANTA ANA RIVER (IMPERIAL HIGHWAY TO PRADO DAM), ORANGE AND RIVERSIDE COUNTIES, CALIFORNIA.
Army Engineer District, Los Angeles, Calif.
For primary bibliographic entry see Field 4A.
W75-09096

FLOOD PLAIN INFORMATION--COASTAL FLOODING, PORTSMOUTH, VIRGINIA.
Army Engineer District, Norfolk, Va.
For primary bibliographic entry see Field 4A.
W75-09097

FLOOD PLAIN INFORMATION: POMPESTON CREEK BURLINGTON COUNTY, NEW JERSEY.
Army Engineer District, Philadelphia, Pa.
For primary bibliographic entry see Field 4A.
W75-09099

FLOOD PLAIN INFORMATION: ANIMAS RIVER AND TRIBUTARIES, DURANGO, COLORADO.
Army Engineer District, Sacramento, Calif.
For primary bibliographic entry see Field 4A.
W75-09100

FLOOD PLAIN INFORMATION: VICINITY OF AUSTELL, GEORGIA, SWEETWATER CREEK.
Army Engineer District, Mobile, Ala.
For primary bibliographic entry see Field 4A.
W75-09101

FLOOD PLAIN INFORMATION: WARM SPRINGS CREEK, KETCHUM, IDAHO, AND VICINITY.
Army Engineer District, Walla Walla, Wash.
For primary bibliographic entry see Field 4A.
W75-09102

FLOOD PLAIN INFORMATION: LOYALSOCK CREEK, LYCOMING COUNTY, PENNSYLVANIA.
Army Engineer District, Baltimore, Md.
For primary bibliographic entry see Field 4A.
W75-09104

FLOOD PLAIN INFORMATION, PIGEON RIVER, CLINTONVILLE, WISCONSIN.
Army Engineer District, Chicago, Ill.
For primary bibliographic entry see Field 4A.
W75-09108

FLOOD PLAIN INFORMATION: TURKEY CREEK, METROPOLITAN KANSAS CITY.
Army Engineer District, Kansas City, Mo.
For primary bibliographic entry see Field 4A.
W75-09109

FLOOD PLAIN INFORMATION: BIG WOOD RIVER, BELLEVUE-HAILEY, IDAHO AND VICINITY.
Army Engineer District, Walla Walla, Wash.
For primary bibliographic entry see Field 4A.
W75-09110

FLOOD PLAIN INFORMATION: LOWER SANTIAGO CREEK, ORANGE COUNTY, CALIFORNIA.
Army Engineer District, Los Angeles, Calif.
For primary bibliographic entry see Field 4A.
W75-09111

FLOOD PLAIN INFORMATION, MULBERRY CREEK, DRY CREEK, SALINA, KANSAS.
Army Engineer District, Kansas City, Mo.
For primary bibliographic entry see Field 4A.
W75-09112

FLOOD PLAIN INFORMATION: SMOKY HILL RIVER, SALINE RIVER, DRY CREEK DIVERSION, SALINA, KANSAS.
Army Engineer District, Kansas City, Mo.
For primary bibliographic entry see Field 4A.
W75-09113

FLOOD PLAIN INFORMATION, KANSAS AND BIG BLUE RIVERS, MANHATTAN, KANSAS.
Army Engineer District, Kansas City, Kans.
For primary bibliographic entry see Field 4A.
W75-09114

FLOOD PLAIN INFORMATION: PLUM CREEK, CUYAHOGA AND LORAIN COUNTIES, OHIO.
Army Engineer District, Buffalo, N.Y.
For primary bibliographic entry see Field 4A.
W75-09116

FLOOD PLAIN INFORMATION: NUECES RIVER AND TURKEY CREEK, CRYSTAL CITY, TEXAS.
Army Engineer District, Fort Worth, Tex.
For primary bibliographic entry see Field 4A.
W75-09117

FLOOD PLAIN INFORMATION: SMITH CREEK - CLIFTON FORGE AND ALLEGHANY COUNTY, VIRGINIA.
Army Engineer District, Norfolk, Va.
For primary bibliographic entry see Field 4A.
W75-09118

FLOOD PLAIN INFORMATION: REPUBLICAN RIVER, FRANKLIN, NEBRASKA.
Army Engineer District, Kansas City, Mo.
For primary bibliographic entry see Field 4A.
W75-09119

FLOOD PLAIN INFORMATION: MILL CREEK, NEW CASTLE COUNTY, DELAWARE.
Army Engineer District, Philadelphia, Pa.
For primary bibliographic entry see Field 4A.
W75-09120

FLOOD PLAIN INFORMATION: ANTIETAM CREEK, WASHINGTON COUNTY, MARYLAND.
Army Engineer District, Baltimore, Md.
For primary bibliographic entry see Field 4A.
W75-09121

6G. Ecologic Impact Of Water Development

THE ENVIRONMENT OF OFFSHORE AND ESTUARINE ALABAMA,
Geological Survey of Alabama, University. Environmental Div.
For primary bibliographic entry see Field 2L.
W75-08961

STUDIES IN ENVIRONMENT - VOLUME I-SUMMARY REPORT,
Homer Hoyt Inst., Washington, D.C.
M. Selden, and L. G. Llewellyn.
Available from the National Technical Information Service, Springfield, Va 22161 as PB-240 786, $5.25 in paper copy, $2.25 in paper copy. Environmental Protection Agency, Report EPA-600/5-73-012a, December 1973. 112 p, 1 tab, 675 ref. Program Element 1 HA098. 801473.

Descriptors: *Environment, Measurement, Indicators, *Social values, Industrial wastes, Municipal wastes, *Legislation, *Management, *Recreation, Governmental interrelations, Air pollution, Water pollution, *Environmental effects.

Twenty-five students who participated as EPA summer fellows were selected from among 800 applicants responding to a national recruitment program. The students majored in a wide range of environmentally related studies on university and college campuses across the U.S. Select research topics were undertaken to bring fresh, hopefully unbiased, viewpoints on existing environmental problems in the anticipation that contributions would suggest new avenues for the development of current long-range environmental strategy. The students, composing 5 investigative teams, concentrated their efforts on: a possible approach toward quantifying the concept 'quality-of-life'; development of an accounting system for allocating pollution produced by industry as a result of consumer demands for goods and the environment; investigating the realm of environmental management; and lastly, how the generation of pollution differs as a characteristic of a community's location within large metropolitan areas. This volume, the first in a series, presents a synopsis of the full length reports published as separate reports. The other reports are: (Vol. 2) Quality of Life; (Vol. 3) Pollution and the Municipality; (Vol. 4) Consumption Differentials and the Environment; (Vol. 5) Outdoor Recreation and the Environment; (Vol. 6) Environmental Management. (See W75-09054 thru W75-09057) (EPA)
W75-09053

STUDIES IN ENVIRONMENT - VOLUME II - QUALITY OF LIFE,
Homer Hoyt Inst., Washington, D.C.
K. Hornback, J. Guttman, H. Himmelstein, A. Rappaport, and R. Reyna.
Available from the National Technical Information Service, Springfield, Va 22161 as PB-240 787, $5.75 in paper copy, $2.25 in microfiche. Environmental Protection Agency Report EPA-600/5-73-012b, February 1974. 112 p, 2 fig. 801473.

Descriptors: Social aspects, Economic impact, Indicators, Measurement, Environment, Social values, Envi ronmental effects, Water pollution, Air pollution.
Identifiers: Quality of life, Social indicators.

The concept of the Quality of Life (QOL) is investigated and a development methodology for constructing a measurement scheme to assess the QOL is presented. A brief synopsis is given of research done to data including various guidelines and rationale used in attempting to develop a meaningful social indicator for the QOL, and the current state-of-the-art and the research concerning attempts to adequately define and assess

the consuming public. The model studies consumer behavior patterns from three viewpoints: income of family, age of head of family, and regional location of family within the United States. The methodology relates 126 final consumption industry groupings to 48 consumer item (product) groupings of the National Conference Board's taxonomy. The methodology employs the Resources for the Future's 'National Pollution Model', basically an input-output plus residual technique. Findings focus on most polluting industries, and the pollution associated characteristics of subgroups of the U.S. population. (See also W75-09053) (Gerba-EPA)
W75-09056

STUDIES IN ENVIRONMENT - VOLUME V - OUTDOOR RECREATION AND THE ENVIRONMENT,
Homer Hoyt Inst., Washington, D.C.
B. Kimmelman, K. Bildstein, P. Bujak, W. Horton, and M. Savina.
Available from the National Technical Information Service, Springfield, Va 22161 as PB-240 790, $4.75 in paper copy, $2.25 in microfiche. Environmental Protection Agency, Report EPA-600/5-73-012e, February 1974. 91 p, 19 tab. 801473.

Descriptors: Recreation, Environment, *Recreation demand, *Social mobility, *Social participation, *Environmental effects, Social needs, Recreation facilities, National parks, *Forecasting, Water pollution, Air pollution.
Identifiers: *Leisure activities.

Increases in discretionary time (time free from 'earning a living') over the past number of years have dramatically increased the pursuit of leisure activities. Reductions in the length of the work week, increases in paid holidays, longer vacations, and early retirement all foster increases in leisure activities, as do the rise in personal disposable income and higher levels of educational attainment. Add to these factors the increase in mobility, and the resulting boom in recreation is almost obvious. The increasing tendency toward recreational activity has notably placed a heavy demand on existing facilities and has also created a shortage of recreational facilities during peak vacation periods. This potential strain on the ecological carrying capacity of recreational areas is an ever-increasing environmental concern. This study focuses on the problems and potentials between outdoor recreation and the environment. The areas studied include recreation on private land, along coastal areas, national parks and urban areas. All of the factors contributing to recreational demand--leisure time, education, disposable income, population growth and mobility--are forecasting to increase and will result in increased participation in recreational activities. (See also W75-09053) (EPA)
W75-09057

DELAWARE RIVER BASIN COMMISSION ANNUAL REPORT, 1974.
Delaware River Basin Commission, Trenton, N.J.
For primary bibliographic entry see Field 6E.
W75-09093

ENVIRONMENTAL SYSTEMS APPRAISALS AND DEVELOPMENT GUIDES.
Harza Engineering Co., Chicago, Ill.
For primary bibliographic entry see Field 5D.
W75-09107

AN EVALUATION OF STATE LAND USE PLANNING AND DEVELOPMENT CONTROL IN THE ADIRONDACKS,
Cornell Univ., Ithaca, N.Y.
For primary bibliographic entry see Field 4A.
W75-09122

ECOLOGICAL STUDIES OF TWO SWAMP WATERSHEDS IN NORTHEASTERN NORTH CAROLINA - A PRECHANNELIZATION STUDY,
North Carolina State Univ., Raleigh. Dept. of Zoology.
For primary bibliographic entry see Field 5C.
W75-09130

BIOLOGICAL VIEW OF PROBLEMS OF URBAN HEALTH,
John Curtin School of Medical Research, Canberra (Australia). Dept. of Human Biology.
S. Boyden.
Hum Biol Oceania, Vol 1, No 3, p 159-169, 1972.

Descriptors: *Public health, Diseases, Urbanization, *Environmental effects, *Biology, Cities.

The pattern of health and disease in any community of animals, including mankind, is determined by the quality of the total environment. Disease patterns are changing and approaches to the problem of public health may be outdated and inappropriate today. Although severe forms of phylogenetic maladjustment, such as neoplastic disease and injury through motor accidents will undoubtedly continue to be a cause for concern, the main health problem will lie in the universality of relatively mild subthreshold conditions. The new components of the environment are so numerous and varied that it will be very difficult to identify the causes of chronic and low grade illnesses resulting from these changes. The insights provided by the study of human biology can contribute substantially to an understanding of society's attempts to overcome these difficulties. Since health depends on the quality of the total environment, a broadly based integrative approach in education, research and administration will be absolutely essential, involving the active cooperation of the representatives of many different academic disciplines.--Copyright 1973, Biological Abstracts, Inc.
W75-09332

7. RESOURCES DATA

7A. Network Design

USE OF SYSTEM ANALYSIS APPROACH IN THE HYDROLOGICAL PROJECTS OF THE WORLD METEOROLOGICAL ORGANIZATION,
World Meteorological Organization, Geneva (Switzerland). Dept. of Hydrology and Water Resources.
For primary bibliographic entry see Field 2A.
W75-09212

SYSTEM EVALUATION - RELIABILITY OF DATA AND EXTRAPOLATION AND CORRELATION OF DATA,
Utah Water Research Lab., Logan.
R. W. Jeppson.
In: Systems Analysis of Hydrologic Problems; Proceedings of the Second International Seminar for Hydrology Professors, August 2-14, 1970, Utah State University, Logan, p 78-105. 5 fig, 4 tab, 9 ref.

Descriptors: *Reliability, *Correlation analysis, *Hydrologic data, *Measurement, Digital computers, Statistical methods, Mathematical studies, *Evaluation, Systems analysis, Data processing, Evaporation, Least squares method, Analytical techniques.
Identifiers: *Extrapolation, *Orthogonal least squares method, Multivariate analysis, Analysis of variance.

System evaluation was interpreted as defining the natural system through judicious analyses and in-

terpretation of available hydrologic data. Since the description of a hydrologic system includes the interactions of many variables and processes, whose magnitudes are subject to measurement and extrapolation errors, multivariate statistical methods are among the most useful tools available to hydrologists. Two-variate correlation and regression analyses were the first tools used in extending short records at one station by relating them to another station with longer records. With the advent of high speed digital computer, multiple correlation and regression analyses and statistical methods such as principal component analysis, autocorrelation, and spectral analysis of ten or more variables can easily and economically be obtained. Of a number of statistical parameters and tests available for ascertaining the significance of the regression fit, and multiple correlation coefficient and the coefficient of determination represent the most widely used parameters. Analysis of variance is used in conjunction with regression analysis to show contribution to the corrected sum of variance by each of the independent variables. (See also W75-09210) (Singh-ISWS)
W75-09215

PRELIMINARY REPORT ON WIND ERRORS ENCOUNTERED DURING AUTOMATIC PROCESSING OF IFYGL LORAN-C DATA,
National Oceanic and Atmospheric Administration, Washington, D.C. Environmental Data Service.
J. Sullivan, and J. Matejceck.
Available from National Technical Information Service, U.S. Department of Commerce, Sills Building, 5385 Port Royal Road, Springfield, Va 22161. NOAA Technical Memorandum EDS CEDDA-4, May 1975. 9 p, 6 fig, 2 tab, 1 ref.

Descriptors: *Winds, *Data collections, *Instrumentation, *Lake Ontario, Computers, Atmospheric physics, Meteorology.
Identifiers: LORAN-C, *Rawinsondes, *Wind data, Upper air, Errors, Noise(Data).

Upper air winds were measured by tracking rawinsondes over Lake Ontario during the International Field Year for the Great Lakes. The rawinsonde time-delay data, from which winds were computed, contained four primary types of errors. The frequency of errors and the correction procedures are discussed. The most frequent source of error, noisy data presumably generated from sky-wave interference, was corrected entirely by automatic procedures. Also shown is the effect of correction procedures on vertical resolution of the wind data. (NOAA)
W75-09270

IFYGL PHYSICAL DATA COLLECTION SYSTEM: INTERCOMPARISON DATA,
National Oceanic and Atmospheric Administration, Washington, D.C. Environmental Data Service.
For primary bibliographic entry see Field 7C.
W75-09271

IGOSS MARINE POLLUTION MONITORING PILOT PROJECT,
National Oceanic and Atmospheric Administration, Rockville, Md.
For primary bibliographic entry see Field 5A.
W75-09280

FEDERAL PLAN FOR ENVIRONMENTAL DATA BUOYS.
National Oceanic and Atmospheric Administration, Rockville, Md. Federal Coordinator for Marine Environmental Prediction.
Available from Superintendent of Documents, US Government Printing Office, Washington, DC 20402, for $1.00. Federal Plan for Environmental Data Buoys; Fiscal Year 1975, November 1974.

Descriptors: *Buoys, *Gaging stations, *Monitoring, *Control systems, *Data collections, *Instrumentation, Meteorological data, Climatic data, Weather data, Weather patterns, Forecasting, Programs, Planning, Warning systems, Oceanography, Oceans.
Identifiers: *Environmental data buoys, *Ocean monitoring, Federal plans, Ocean observations, Surface observations, Climate studies.

Buoys are supplying surface meteorological observations and limited surface and subsurface oceanographic data under all weather conditions. The environmental data buoy represents a ready technological opportunity to enhance ocean monitoring capability and make available additional information to support the rational development of the ocean and its resources. This plan represents a phased schedule for the deployment of 36 environmental data buoys. These include the purchase of new buoys and the retro-fitting of 6 existing deep ocean buoys with improved payload systems. Included are details of the technological development effort that will be pursued to achieve optimum capability and reliability of buoy systems and components. Three areas of buoy application are discussed: buoys for basic monitoring to monitoring to support climate studies and other scientific research, and buoy technology development. (NOAA)
W75-09282

7B. Data Acquisition

OXYGEN CONTENT AND B. O. D. OF EFFLUENTS MEASUREMENT.
For primary bibliographic entry see Field 5A.
W75-08851

FLOW PHOTOMETER (DURCHFLUSS-PHOTOMETER).
For primary bibliographic entry see Field 5A.
W75-08858

AUTONOMOUS, AUTOMATIC APPARATUS FOR WATER POLLUTION CONTROL (APPARECCHIO PER IL CONTROLLO AUTOMATICO DEGLI INQUINAMENTI DELL ACQUA CON AUTONOMIA DI FUNZIOAMENTO).
For primary bibliographic entry see Field 5A.
W75-08859

TWO NEW WATER MONITORS AVAILABLE.
For primary bibliographic entry see Field 5A.
W75-08887

WASTE WATER LEVEL MEASUREMENT.
For primary bibliographic entry see Field 5A.
W75-08896

INSTRUMENTATION FOR FILTRATION TESTS,
Coulter Electronics, Inc., Hialeah, Fla.
For primary bibliographic entry see Field 5A.
W75-08897

A STUDY TO EXPLORE THE USE OF ORBITAL REMOTE SENSING TO DETERMINE NATIVE ARID PLANT DISTRIBUTION,
Arizona Univ., Tuson. Office of Arid-Lands Studies.
W. G. McGinnies, E. F. Haase, L. K. Lepley, J. S. Conn, and H. B. Musick.
Final report, August, 1974, 36 p, 2 tab, append, 3 ref. NASA NAS5-21812.

Descriptors: *Remote sensing, *Desert plants, *Aerial photography, *Mapping, Vegetation, Arid lands, Arizona, Soils, Soil types.
Identifiers: *ERTS, Orbital imagery.

dies, Electronics, Flow rates, Theoretical analysis, Instrumentation.
Identifiers: *Electromagnetic flow rate transducer.

A mathematical analysis was made using tensor calculus to obtain detailed output expressions for an electromagnetic flow rate transducer in terms of flow and the externally influenced 'hum' voltages along with other parameters. An electromagnetic flow rate transducer was fabricated and various output parameters were measured. A comparison of the computed and measured parameters showed good agreement. (Bhowmik-ISWS)
W75-08989

TECHNIQUES FOR TRACING SEDIMENT MOVEMENT,
Canada Centre for Inland Waters, Burlington (Ontario).
For primary bibliographic entry see Field 2J.
W75-08995

A SIMPLE AIRLIFT-OPERATED TANK FOR CLOSED-SYSTEM CULTURE OF DECAPOD CRUSTACEAN LARVAE AND OTHER SMALL AQUATIC ANIMALS,
South Carolina Wildlife and Marine Resources Dept., Charleston. Marine Resources Center.
P. A. Sandifer, P. B. Zielinski, and W. E. Castro.
Available from the National Technical Information Service, Springfield, Va. 22161, as COM-74-11452, $3.25 in paper copy, $2.25 in microfiche. Helgolander wissenschaftiche Meeresunters, Vol 26, p 82-87, 1974. 3 fig, 3 ref.

Descriptors: Design, *Aquaria, Technology, *Larval growth stages, *Aquiculture, *Crustaceans, Aquatic animals, Crustaceans.
Identifiers: *Macrobrachium, Decapod crustacea.

A rectangular tank for culture of decapod crustacean larvae with continuous water recirculation is described. The tank has a sloped bottom and an attached gravel filter unit. Water circulation through the filter serves at the same time for maintaining food particles in suspension and for dispersing the larvae; it is accomplished by airlift pumps. Tanks of this design have been successfully used for closed-system culture of the larvae of the prawn Macrobrachium rosenbergii and are expected to be satisfactory for other small aquatic animals. (Katz)
W75-09143

A FILTER AND CHILLER FOR AN OPEN SEAWATER SYSTEM,
National Marine Fisheries Service, Beaufort, N.C. Atlantic Estuarine Fisheries Center.
W. F. Hettler, Jr.
The Progressive Fish-Culturist, Vol 36, No 4, p 234-238, October 1974. 2 fig, 2 ref.

Descriptors: *Design, *Equipment, *Temperature, *Sea water, Filtration, *Filters, Technology, Laboratory equipment, Pollutant identification, Instrumentation.
Identifiers: *Chillers.

A reliable filtration and chilling system for seawater pollution research and marine aquaculture is described. The filter system is constructed of nonmetallic materials and is designed to operate in parallel, to provide a large volume of water, or in series, to provide multiple filtration. The seawater chiller is able to chill seawater to the freezing point for experiments on temperature tolerance and metabolic responses of estuarine organisms. (Katz)
W75-09158

COMPUTERIZED RAIN ASSESSMENT AND TRACKING OF SOUTH FLORIDA WEATHER RADAR ECHOES,
National Oceanic and Atmospheric Administration, Coral Gables, Fla. Experimental Meteorology Lab.
For primary bibliographic entry see Field 2B.
W75-09208

HYDROLOGIC INSTRUMENTATION,
Utah Water Research Lab., Logan.
D. G. Chadwick.
In: Systems Analysis of Hydrologic Problems; Proceedings of the Second International Seminar for Hydrology Professors, August 2-14, 1970, Utah State University, Logan p 69-77. 6 fig.

Descriptors: *Instrumentation, *Telemetry, *Measurement, *Data transmission, Electronic equipment, Automatic control, Equipment, Manometers, Hydrologic data, Hydrology.
Identifiers: Actinometer, Microbarograph.

Described was a hydrologic instrumentation and telemetering system designed to incorporate desired precision, simplicity of design, and economical cost. The system is for unattended, remote use in mountainous terrain. It can operate for long periods without loss of accuracy. Specifically, a microbarograph, actinometer, and a manometer for measuring water content of snow have been developed. (See also W75-09210) (Jess-ISWS)
W75-09214

QUANTIZING 3- AND 5-CM RADAR HURRICANE PRECIPITATION DATA,
Miami Univ., Coral Gables, Fla. Remote Sensing Lab.
For primary bibliographic entry see Field 7C.
W75-09276

ENVIRONMENT MONITORING DEVICE AND SYSTEM,
Texas Instruments, Inc., Dallas. (Assignee).
For primary bibliographic entry see Field 5A.
W75-09305

7C. Evaluation, Processing and Publication

WATER RESOURCES INVENTORY OF CONNECTICUT--PART 5, LOWER HOUSATONIC RIVER BASIN,
Geological Survey, Hartford, Conn.
For primary bibliographic entry see Field 4A.
W75-08905

SUMMARY OF HYDROLOGIC DATA COLLECTED DURING 1973 IN DADE COUNTY, FLORIDA,
Geological Survey, Tallahassee, Fla.
J. E. Hull, and D. J. McKenzie.
Open-file report 74029, 1974. 122 p, 43 fig, 8 tab, 12 ref.

Descriptors: *Basic data collections, *Groundwater, *Surface waters, *Florida, *Hydrologic data, Streamflow, Water levels, Saline water intrusion, Withdrawal.
Identifiers: Dade County(Fla), *Miami(Fla).

This report is eighth in a series documenting the annual hydrologic conditions in Dade County, Florida. The general hydrologic data in Dade County for the 1973 water year (October 1, 1972) to September 30, 1973) are summarized in tables, graphs, and maps. During the 1973 calendar year rainfall was 9.19 inches below the long-term average. Groundwater levels ranged from 0.3 foot above to 9.0 foot below average. In the 1973 water year, the combined average daily discharge from

seven major streams and canals that flow into Biscayne Bay was 1,120 cfs, 296 cfs below the combined average daily flow for the 1972 water year. The combined average daily flow through the Tamiami Canal outlets was 602 cfs, 80 cfs below that of the 1972 water year. The 1973 position of the salt front in the coastal part of the Biscayne aquifer was about the same as that in 1971 and 1972, except at Miami International Airport and Homestead Air Force Base where the salt front had encroached inland. (Knapp-USGS)
W75-08908

SUMMARY STATEMENTS OF WATER RESOURCES INVESTIGATIONS IN FLORIDA, 1974-75,
Geological Survey, Tallahassee, Fla.
Project Summaries Report, September 1974. 139 p.

Descriptors: *Water resources, *Investigations, *Florida, *Data collections, *Hydrologic data, Surveys, Water quality, Groundwater, Surface waters.

This report contains summary statements for water resources investigations by the U.S. Geological Survey in Florida during 1974-75. In Florida, water resources appraisals are highly diversified, ranging from hydrologic records networks to interpretative appraisals of water resources and applied research to develop investigative techniques. The interpretative reports, map, diagrams, and records that are products of the investigations are a principal hydrologic foundation upon which the plans and development of Florida's water resources may be based. (Knapp-USGS)
W75-08909

AVAILABILITY AND QUALITY OF GROUND WATER IN THE SUTHERLIN AREA, DOUGLAS COUNTY, OREGON,
Geological Survey, Portland, Oreg.
J. H. Robison.
Water-Resources Investigations 32-74, 1974. 2 sheets, 16 ref.

Descriptors: *Groundwater, *Oregon, Hydrogeology, Aluvium, *Maps, Water yield, Water supply, Hydrologic data.
Identifiers: Sutherlin(Oreg), Douglas County(Oreg).

This 2-sheet map report presents information in a form that will enable water users, potential water users, and planners to estimate the likelihood of obtaining groundwater in adequate quantity and of suitable quality at desired locations in the Sutherlin area, Douglas County, southwestern Oregon. The city of Sutherlin obtains its municipal water supply from Cooper and Calapooya Creeks; Oakland also uses Calapooya Creek. The Umpqua Basin Water Association withdraws water from the North Umpqua River. The city of Roseburg serves the area south of Winchester with water obtained from the North Umpqua River. Water levels of wells range from slightly above land surface to as deep as 300 feet below land surface. Quantities of water obtainable from wells within the study area are not adequate for irrigation, municipal, nor large industrial use. (Knapp-USGS)
W75-08910

SOURCES OF EMERGENCY WATER SUPPLIES IN SAN MATEO COUNTY, CALIFORNIA,
Geological Survey, Menlo Park, Calif.
For primary bibliographic entry see Field 6D.
W75-08911

RECONNAISSANCE OF THE WATER RESOURCES OF THE OKLAHOMA CITY QUADRANGLE, CENTRAL OKLAHOMA,
Geological Survey, Oklahoma City, Okla.
For primary bibliographic entry see Field 7C.
W75-08912

RECONNAISSANCE OF THE WATER RESOURCES OF THE OKLAHOMA CITY QUADRANGLE, CENTRAL OKLAHOMA,
Geological Survey, Oklahoma City, Okla.
R. H. Bingham, and R. L. Moore.
Oklahoma Geological Survey Hydrologic Atlas 4, 1975. 4 sheets, 12 fig, 4 tab, 3 ref.

Descriptors: *Maps, *Hydrologic data, *Water resources, *Water quality, *Oklahoma, Hydrogeology, Groundwater resources, Surface waters, Rivers, Lakes, Ponds, Water supply, Water utilization, Chemical analysis, Aquifer characteristics, Surface-groundwater relationships, Precipitation(Atmospheric).
Identifiers: *Oklahoma City quadrangle.

This 4-sheet atlas describes the water resources of the Oklahoma City quadrangle which includes about 7,800 square miles in central Oklahoma. Most of the quadrangle is underlain by rocks of Pennsylvanian and Permian age. Approximately 1.5 to 3.5 inches of the annual precipitation is available to recharge the groundwater reservoir. Groundwater in most parts of the quadrangle is hard or very hard and locally contains sulfate and chloride in excess of 250 mg/litre. In some areas water from shallow wells contains more than 45 mg/litre nitrate, indicating possible pollution. In the western half of the quadrangle the terrace deposits yeild water of good quality, less than 500 mg/litre dissolved solids. The greatest potential sources of surface water include the Cimarron, North Canadian, Deep Fork, and Little Rivers and manmade ponds and lakes. The total amount of water used in 1970 is estimated at 50.7 billion gallons. Approximately 66% of this was taken from the lakes and rivers of the area; the remaining 17.4 billion gallons was provided from groundwater sources. The major use of water was for municipal purposes. (Woodard-USGS)
W75-08912

WATER RESOURCES OF WISCONSIN, LOWER WISCONSIN RIVER BASIN,
Geological Survey, Reston, Va.
S. M. Hindall, and R. G. Borman.
For sale by USGS, Reston Va 22092, $2.50 per set. Hydrologic Investigations Atlas HA-479, 1974. 3 sheets, 46 ref.

Descriptors: *Water resources, *Surface water availability, *Groundwater resources, *Water quality, *Wisconsin, River basin development, Hydrologic data, Water utilization, *Maps, Streamflow, Discharge(Water), Water wells, Water data, Aquifer characteristics, Water yield, Water supply, Surface-groundwater relationships.
Identifiers: *Lower Wisconsin River basin(Wisc).

This 3-sheet map report describes the physical environment, availability, characteristics, distribution, movement, and quality of water in the lower Wisconsin River basin. In addition, water use and water problems are summarized to aid in water management within the basin. The lower basin, as used in this report, has an area of approximately 3,780 square miles, 6.7 percent of the State, and consists of all or parts of 11 counties in southwestern Wisconsin. The 1970 population of the basin was estimated to be 133,000, a decrease of about 1,500 persons since 1960. The economy of the area is primarily agricultural. Dairy farming and beef production are of primary importance. Large amounts of good-quality water are available. Of the 32.1 inches of average annual precipitation that falls on the basin, 8.9 inches, an average of 2,200 billion gallons, leaves the basin as streamflow each year. This represents the amount of surface water available for use. More surface water is used than groundwater. Surface water is used for hydroelectric power generation (3,620 mgd), industrial and commercial (47.3 mgd), irrigation (0.1 mgd), waste transport, and recreation. Groundwater is used for all municipal supplies and most rural supplies (13.9 mgd), many industrial purposes (8.7 mgd), and irrigation (0.5 mgd). (Woodard-USGS)
W75-08913

WATER RESOURCES OF HAMILTON COUNTY, SOUTHWESTERN KANSAS,
Geological Survey, Reston, Va.
D. H. Lobmeyer, and C. G. Sauer.
For sale by USGS, Reston, Va 22092 and Denver, Colo 80225 $1.50 per set. Hydrologic Investigations Atlas HA-516, 1974. 2 sheets, 11 ref.

Descriptors: *Water resources, *Surface water availability, *Groundwater resources, *Water quality, *Kansas, Hydrologic data, Water yield, Water utilization, Streamflow, Discharge(Water), Well data, Aquifer characteristics, Precipitation(Atmospheric), Groundwater recharge, Surface-groundwater relationships, *Maps, Geology, Hydrogeology.
Identifiers: *Hamilton County(Kans).

This 2-sheet atlas describes water resources of Hamilton County, Kansas. The average annual precipitation is about 16 inches. Of this amount, 83% occurs during the growing season (March 15 to October 15). The average groundwater recharge from precipitation is estimated to be 0.1 inch per year. In the upland area of the county, dryland farming and grazing are the predominant land uses. The Arkansas River supplies water for irrigation along the valley. Average annual diversion by the Alamo Canal is 1,430 acre-feet and 4,740 acre-feet by the Fort Aubrey Canal. The Frontier Ditch, which diverts water from the river west of the Kansas State line, returns an average of 3,960 acre-feet annual about 4 miles downstream from Coolidge. Groundwater in the unconsolidated Tertiary and Quaternary deposits in Hamilton County occurs in three general areas: (1) The upland area in the northern part of the county; (2) the valley of the Arkansas River; and (3) the area south of the Bear Creek fault. Outside of these areas, little water is available. In the valley of the Arkansas River, wells commonly yield more than 1,000 gpm. The dissolved-solids content of groundwater in most of the county ranges from 500 to 800 mg/litre. (Woodard-USGS)
W75-08914

GROUND WATER IN GRAY COUNTY, SOUTHWESTERN KANSAS,
Geological Survey, Reston, Va.
H. E. McGovern, and W. A. Long.
For sale by USGS, Denver, Colo 80225 and Reston, Va 22092, $1.50 per set. Hydrologic Investigations Atlas HA-517, 1974. 2 sheets, 14 ref.

Descriptors: *Groundwater resources, *Water quality, *Aquifer characteristics, *Kansas, Hydrogeology, Water wells, Water supply, Groundwater movement, Chemical analysis, Water yield, *Maps, Hydrologic data, Transmissivity, Hydraulic conductivity, Storage coefficient, Geology.
Identifiers: *Gray County(Kans).

This 2-sheet atlas describes the hydrogeology and chemical quality of groundwater in Gray County, Kansas. Unconsolidated deposits of Tertiary and Quaternary age form the principal aquifer. The water-yielding characteristics of the aquifer differ greatly from one area to another, and the groundwater may occur under unconfined or semiconfined conditions. Water having concentrations of dissolved solids less than 50 mg/litre is available in most of the county. Water having concentrations of 500 to 1,000 mg/litre occurs in an area north of the river valley in the western part of the county. In the Arkansas River Valley, concentrations of dissolved solids in water from the alluvium decrease from 1,600 mg/litre at the western county line to about 500 mg/litre at the eastern county line. In the same reach of the river valley, coneentrations in water from the undifferentiated Pleistocene deposits decrease from 800 to about 200 mg/litre. Concentrations of more than 500 mg/litre of dissolved solids generally are as-

National Assessment, and as a standard geographical framework for more detailed water and related land-resources planning. The Accounting Units are those currently (1974) in use by the U.S. Geological Survey for managing the National Water Data Network. (Woodard-USGS)
W75-08918

HYDROLOGIC UNIT MAP–1974, STATE OF NEW YORK.
Geological Survey, Reston, Va.
For sale by USGS, Reston, Va 22092, price $1.25. Hydrologic Unit Map of State of New York, 1974. 1 sheet, 1 map.

Descriptors: *Maps, *Hydrology, *New York, *Water resources, Data collections, Planning.
Identifiers: *Hydrologic unit maps.

This map and accompanying table show Hydrologic Units in New York State that are basically hydrographic in nature. The Cataloging Units shown will supplant the Cataloging Units previously used by the U.S. Geological Survey in its Catalog of Information on Water Data (1966-72). The Regions, Subregions and Accounting Units are aggregates of the Cataloging Units. The Regions and Subregions are currently (1974) used by the U.S. Water Resources Council for comprehensive planning, including the National Assessment, and as a standard geographical framework for more detailed water and related land-resources planning. The Accounting Units are those currently (1974) in use by the U.S. Geological Survey for managing the National Water Data Network. (Woodard-USGS)
W75-08920

MODELLING A GROUNDWATER AQUIFER IN THE GRAND PRAIRIE OF ARKANSAS,
Arkansas Univ., Fayetteville. Dept. of Agricultural Engineering.
For primary bibliographic entry see Field 2F.
W75-08923

THE APPLICATION OF THE DSDT HYBRID COMPUTER METHOD TO WATER RESOURCES PROBLEMS,
California Univ., Los Angeles. School of Engineering and Applied Science.
For primary bibliographic entry see Field 2F.
W75-08929

THE USE OF THE DIGITAL SIMULATION LANGUAGE PDEL IN HYDROLOGIC STUDIES,
California Univ., Los Angeles. Dept. of Computer Science.
For primary bibliographic entry see Field 2F.
W75-08930

INVESTIGATION OF SENSITIVITY AND ERROR PROPAGATION IN NUMERICAL MODELS OF GROUNDWATER BASINS,
James Cook Univ. of North Queensland, Townsville (Australia).
For primary bibliographic entry see Field 2F.
W75-08954

TECHNIQUES FOR HANDLING INPUT DATA FOR FINITE ELEMENT ANALYSIS OF REGIONAL GROUNDWATER FLOW,
New South Wales Univ., Kensington (Australia). Water Research Lab.
For primary bibliographic entry see Field 2F.
W75-08955

VARIATIONS IN ESTIMATES OF DESIGN FLOODS,
New South Wales Univ., Kensington (Australia). School of Civil Engineering.
For primary bibliographic entry see Field 4A.
W75-08956

A NEW DEVELOPMENT IN FLOOD FREQUENCY ESTIMATION,
Queensland Irrigation and Water Supply Commission, Brisbane (Australia).
For primary bibliographic entry see Field 2E.
W75-08957

COMPARISON OF UNIT HYDROGRAPH AND RUNOFF ROUTING METHODS OF FLOOD ESTIMATION,
Monash Univ., Clayton (Australia).
For primary bibliographic entry see Field 2E.
W75-08958

DEVELOPMENT OF REGIONAL FLOOD ESTIMATION PROCEDURES,
Cameron, McNamara and Partners, Brisbane (Australia).
For primary bibliographic entry see Field 4A.
W75-08959

A FLOW AND SALT TRANSPORT SIMULATION SYSTEM FOR THE RIVER MURRAY IN SOUTH AUSTRALIA,
South Australia Engineering and Water Supply Dept., Adelaide.
P. J. Manoel, and I. E. Laing.
In: Hydrology Symposium, Armidale, Australia, 1975. The Institution of Engineers Australia, Preprints of Papers, p 51 - 55, May 1975. 4 fig, 2 ref, append.

Descriptors: *Computer models, *River flow, *Salinity, Model studies, River forecasting, River regulation, Operations research, Planning, Water resources development, *Australia, Saline water, Data processing.
Identifiers: *Murray River(SA).

The salinity of the River Murray in South Australia has been recognised as an important constraint on the ultimate development of the river as a water resource. A computer model consisting of a flow model to compute river discharges and a salt transport model using the flow model to compute salinities is described, with examples of its use. The theoretical basis and evaluation of the parameters is explained for each of the component models, and the data processing system designed to support the model is outlined. The system allows the model to find application both in the real time operation of the river, in operations research and in planning for the use of the water resource. (CSIRO)
W75-08960

CURRENT SURGES IN THE ST. GEORGES CHANNEL,
Institute of Oceanographic Sciences, Birkenhead (England).
For primary bibliographic entry see Field 2L.
W75-08965

COMPARATIVE EVALUATION OF THREE URBAN RUNOFF MODELS,
Canada Centre for Inlands Waters, Burlington (Ontario).
For primary bibliographic entry see Field 2A.
W75-08988

RBAD, RELATIVE BASAL AREA DETERMINATION, A FORTRAN PROGRAM TO DETERMINE BASAL AREA BY SPECIES AND PLOT FROM IBP STANDARD FORMAT FOREST SERVICE PLOT TAPES,
Oak Ridge National Lab., Tenn.
F. G. Goff.
Report EDFB-IBP 74-6, December 1974. 31 p, 4 ref, 3 append. NSF AG-199, 40-193-69.

Descriptors: *Computer programs, *Data processing, *Vegetation, *Distribution patterns, Data storage and retrieval, Information retrieval, Trees, Forests, Spatial distribution, Coniferous trees, Deciduous trees.

The purpose of this program is to summarize plot data from IBP standard format (i.e., reformatted) tree detail tapes obtained from the Forest Service. A deck of species code names and numbers is read by the program and used to label output. Output consists of: (1) a list of all species present on one or more of the plots that are read, with the number of plots on which each occurs; and (2) a table for each plot that shows the actual basal area (sq ft/acre) and relative basal area (percent) by species and size class (reproduction - stems less than 5.0 inches dbh; and tree - stems equal to or greater than 5.0 inches dbh). Species present on the plot are ranked in decreasing order of total (tree + reproduction) basal area. Appendixes included: (1) a Fortran listing of the main program and the subroutines; (2) a sample output; and (3) a listing of the Species Name Deck. (Humphreys-ISWS)
W75-08990

WATER QUALITY FEATURES OF THE UPPER ILLINOIS WATERWAY,
Illinois State Water Survey, Urbana. Water Quality Section.
For primary bibliographic entry see Field 5B.
W75-08991

UROS4: URBAN FLOOD SIMULATION MODEL PART 1. DOCUMENTATION AND USERS MANUAL,
Georgia Inst. of Tech., Atlanta. School of Civil Engineering.
For primary bibliographic entry see Field 4A.
W75-09046

UROS4: URBAN FLOOD SIMULATION MODEL PART 2. APPLICATIONS TO SELECTED DEKALB COUNTY WATERSHEDS,
Georgia Inst. of Tech., Atlanta. School of Civil Engineering.
For primary bibliographic entry see Field 4A.
W75-09047

A DISCRETE KERNEL GENERATOR FOR STREAM-AQUIFER STUDIES,
Colorado State Univ., Fort Collins. Dept. of Civil Engineering.
For primary bibliographic entry see Field 4B.
W75-09078

FLOOD PLAIN INFORMATION: SANTA CLARA RIVER AND SESPE CREEK, FILLMORE, CALIFORNIA.
Army Engineer District, Los Angeles, Calif.
For primary bibliographic entry see Field 4A.
W75-09084

SPECIAL FLOOD HAZARD INFORMATION REPORT: ATLANTA, GEORGIA, INCLUDING PEACHTREE CREEK BASIN IN DEKALB COUNTY.
Army Engineer District, Mobile, Ala.
For primary bibliographic entry see Field 4A.
W75-09085

FLOOD PLAIN INFORMATION: EAST FORK BIG WOOD RIVER, GIMLET TRIUMPH, IDAHO.
Army Engineer District, Walla Walla, Wash.
For primary bibliographic entry see Field 4A.
W75-09086

FLOOD PLAIN INFORMATION: PORTNEUF RIVER, INKOM, IDAHO, AND VICINITY.
Army Engineer District, Walla Walla, Wash.
For primary bibliographic entry see Field 4A.
W75-09087

FLOOD PLAIN INFORMATION: OROFINO CREEK-WHISKEY CREEK, OROFINO, IDAHO, AND VICINITY.
Army Engineer District, Walla Walla, Wash.
For primary bibliographic entry see Field 4A.
W75-09088

SPECIAL FLOOD HAZARD INFORMATION: SOUTH FORK PALOUSE RIVER, MOSCOW, IDAHO, AND VICINITY.
Army Engineer District, Walla Walla, Wash.
For primary bibliographic entry see Field 4A.
W75-09089

FLOOD PLAIN INFORMATION: THREE MILE CREEK, LEAVENWORTH, KANSAS.
Army Engineer District, Kansas City, Kans.
For primary bibliographic entry see Field 4A.
W75-09090

FLOOD PLAIN INFORMATION--MECHUMS RIVER, ALBEMARLE COUNTY, VIRGINIA.
Army Engineer District, Norfolk, Va.
For primary bibliographic entry see Field 4A.
W75-09091

FLOOD PLAIN INFORMATION: DEEP RIVER, TURKEY CREEK, DUCK CREEK, LAKE COUNTY, INDIANA.
Army Engineer District, Chicago, Ill.
For primary bibliographic entry see Field 4A.
W75-09092

FLOOD PLAIN INFORMATION: SANTA ANA RIVER (IMPERIAL HIGHWAY TO PRADO DAM), ORANGE AND RIVERSIDE COUNTIES, CALIFORNIA.
Army Engineer District, Los Angeles, Calif.
For primary bibliographic entry see Field 4A.
W75-09096

FLOOD PLAIN INFORMATION--COASTAL FLOODING, PORTSMOUTH, VIRGINIA.
Army Engineer District, Norfolk, Va.
For primary bibliographic entry see Field 4A.
W75-09097

FLOOD PLAIN INFORMATION: TOMS RIVER, UNION BRANCH, RIDGEWAY BRANCH AND LONG SWAMP CREEK, OCEAN COUNTY, NEW JERSEY,
Army Engineer District, Philadelphia, Pa.
For primary bibliographic entry see Field 4A.
W75-09098

FLOOD PLAIN INFORMATION: POMPESTON CREEK BURLINGTON COUNTY, NEW JERSEY.
Army Engineer District, Philadelphia, Pa.
For primary bibliographic entry see Field 4A.
W75-09099

FLOOD PLAIN INFORMATION: ANIMAS RIVER AND TRIBUTARIES, DURANGO, COLORADO.
Army Engineer District, Sacramento, Calif.
For primary bibliographic entry see Field 4A.
W75-09100

FLOOD PLAIN INFORMATION: VICINITY OF AUSTELL, GEORGIA, SWEETWATER CREEK.
Army Engineer District, Mobile, Ala.
For primary bibliographic entry see Field 4A.
W75-09101

FLOOD PLAIN INFORMATION: WARM SPRINGS CREEK, KETCHUM, IDAHO, AND VICINITY.
Army Engineer District, Walla Walla, Wash.
For primary bibliographic entry see Field 4A.
W75-09102

FLOOD PLAIN INFORMATION: LOYALSOCK CREEK, LYCOMING COUNTY, PENNSYLVANIA.
Army Engineer District, Baltimore, Md.
For primary bibliographic entry see Field 4A.
W75-09104

FLOOD PLAIN INFORMATION, PIGEON RIVER, CLINTONVILLE, WISCONSIN.
Army Engineer District, Chicago, Ill.
For primary bibliographic entry see Field 4A.
W75-09108

FLOOD PLAIN INFORMATION: TURKEY CREEK, METROPOLITAN KANSAS CITY.
Army Engineer District, Kansas City, Mo.
For primary bibliographic entry see Field 4A.
W75-09109

FLOOD PLAIN INFORMATION: BIG WOOD RIVER, BELLEVUE-HAILEY, IDAHO AND VICINITY.
Army Engineer District, Walla Walla, Wash.
For primary bibliographic entry see Field 4A.
W75-09110

FLOOD PLAIN INFORMATION: LOWER SANTIAGO CREEK, ORANGE COUNTY, CALIFORNIA.
Army Engineer District, Los Angeles, Calif.
For primary bibliographic entry see Field 4A.
W75-09111

FLOOD PLAIN INFORMATION, MULBERRY CREEK, DRY CREEK, SALINA, KANSAS.
Army Engineer District, Kansas City, Mo.
For primary bibliographic entry see Field 4A.
W75-09112

FLOOD PLAIN INFORMATION: SMOKY HILL RIVER, SALINE RIVER, DRY CREEK DIVERSION, SALINA, KANSAS.
Army Engineer District, Kansas City, Mo.
For primary bibliographic entry see Field 4A.
W75-09113

FLOOD PLAIN INFORMATION, KANSAS AND BIG BLUE RIVERS, MANHATTAN, KANSAS.
Army Engineer District, Kansas City, Kans.
For primary bibliographic entry see Field 4A.
W75-09114

FLOOD PLAIN INFORMATION: PLUM CREEK, CUYAHOGA AND LORAIN COUNTIES, OHIO.
Army Engineer District, Buffalo, N.Y.
For primary bibliographic entry see Field 4A.
W75-09116

FLOOD PLAIN INFORMATION: NUECES RIVER AND TURKEY CREEK, CRYSTAL CITY, TEXAS.
Army Engineer District, Fort Worth, Tex.
For primary bibliographic entry see Field 4A.
W75-09117

FLOOD PLAIN INFORMATION: SMITH CREEK - CLIFTON FORGE AND ALLEGHANY COUNTY, VIRGINIA.
Army Engineer District, Norfolk, Va.
For primary bibliographic entry see Field 4A.

shown are a generalization of localized highly variable conditions and do not include any weathered (decomposed) bedrock. (Woodard-USGS)
W75-09166

CONTOUR MAP OF THE BEDROCK SURFACE, BRISTOL QUADRANGLE, CONNECTICUT,
Geological Survey, Hartford, Conn.
E. H. Handman, and D. B. Meade.
Miscellaneous Field Studies Map MF-665 A (Connecticut Valley Urban Area Project Environmental Geologic and Hydrologic Studies Contribution 134), 1975. 1 sheet, 1 map, 3 ref.

Descriptors: *Soil surveys, *Connecticut, *Geologic mapping, *Bedrock, Geologic investigations, Overburden, Soils, Sediments, Rocks.
Identifiers: *Bristol(Conn), *Bedrock surface map.

Contours show the altitude of the bedrock surface in the Bristol quadrangle, Connecticut. The position of the contours is based largely on data from wells, test holes, and published geologic maps supplemented by knowledge of the geologic history of the region. The map shows the configuration of the bedrock surface if all unconsolidated earth materials were removed. (Woodard-USGS)
W75-09167

CONTOUR MAP OF THE BEDROCK SURFACE, SOUTHINGTON QUADRANGLE, CONNECTICUT,
Geological Survey, Hartford, Conn.
D. L. Mazzaferro.
Miscellaneous Field Studies Map MF-660 A (Connecticut Valley Urban Area Project Environmental Geologic and Hydrologic Studies Contribution 133), 1975. 1 sheet, 1 map, 4 ref.

Descriptors: *Soil surveys, *Connecticut, *Geologic mapping, *Bedrock, Geologic investigations, Overburden, Soils, Sediments, Rocks.
Identifiers: *Southington(Conn), *Bedrock surface map.

Contours show the altitude of the bedrock surface in the Southington quadrangle, Connecticut. The position of the contours is based largely on data from wells, test holes, and published geologic maps supplemented by knowledge of the geologic history of the region. The map shows the configuration of the bedrock surface if all unconsolidated earth materials were removed. (Woodard-USGS)
W75-09168

WATER IN THE GREAT BASIN REGION; IDAHO, NEVADA, UTAH, AND WYOMING,
Geological Survey, Reston, Va.
D. Price, and T. E. Eakin.
For sale by U.S. Geological Survey, Reston, Va. 22092 - Price $2.25 per set. Hydrologic Investigations Atlas HA-487, 1974. 4 sheets, 82 ref.

Descriptors: *Hydrologic data, *Maps, *Great Basin, Idaho, Nevada, Utah, Wyoming, Great Salt Lake, Standing waters, Saline lakes, Playas, Mud flats, Precipitation(Atmospheric), Runoff, Water supply, Water yield, Hydrogeology, Groundwater resources, Water utilization, Water wells, Surface-groundwater relationships, Water quality, Hydrographs.

The Great Basin Region includes the drainage of the Great Basin physiographic section in Idaho, Nevada, Utah, and Wyoming. This 3-sheet atlas describes the hydrologic data (including a general appraisal) that were compiled for a comprehensive framework study completed in June 1971. The Great Basin Region has no surface drainage to the sea. Streams in the region end in lakes or in sinks, including playas, mudflats, and salt marshes. The largest terminal lakes or sinks, all of which are saline, include Great Salt Lake, Sevier Lake (usually dry), Walker Lake, Pyramid Lake, and Carson Sink. Altitudes in the region range from about 2,200 feet in the Amargosa Desert to more than 10,000 feet above mean sea level in the highest mountain ranges. The climate is arid to semiarid in the valleys and subhumid to humid in the mountains. The highest mountains in the east, west, and north-central parts of the region receive the largest amounts of precipitation and are the headwater areas for the principal river systems. The region is subdivided into six hydrologic subregions, largely on the basis of drainage, as follows: Bear River, Great Salt Lake, Sevier Lake, Humboldt, Central Lahontan, and Tonopah, for a total of 136,659 sq mi. (Woodard-USGS)
W75-09170

DIGITAL MODEL ANALYSIS OF THE PRINCIPAL ARTESIAN AQUIFER, GLYNN COUNTY, GEORGIA,
Geological Survey, Doraville, Ga.
R. E. Krause, and H. B. Counts.
Water-Resources Investigations 1-75 (open-file report), 1975, 4 sheet, 11 ref.

Descriptors: *Drawdown, *Water resources development, *Artesian aquifers, *Georgia, *Simulation analysis, Mathematical models, Withdrawal, Water levels, Groundwater.
Identifiers: *Glynn County(Geo).

A digital model is a useful tool for managing the groundwater supply from the principal artesian aquifer in the Glynn County area of Georgia. Computations may be extended in time, thus indicating what the water-level configuration is likely to be in the future, showing comparisons of different management alternatives. Groundwater users in the Brunswick area withdraw about 105 mgd of water from the aquifer. This high usage has caused some problems of water-level decline and deterioration of the water quality. Maps show both the measured and computed water-level contours for the Brunswick area in 1960 and 1970. Hydrographs show the measured water-level trend from 1940 to 1970 for four wells in the Brunswick area tapping the principal artesian aquifer, and also water-level trends for four hypothetical wells located in those nodes corresponding to the actual wells. The maps indicate good areal match of computed to actual water level, and the hydrographs show that the computed trend matches the trend of the measured water levels. The transient model was extended from 1970 to the year 2000. This projection assumes that the pumping rate for 1970-2000 will be the same rate as in the 1963-70 period, and that all other hydrologic parameters used in the model remain unchanged. The 2000 water level is virtually the same as for 1970. Any added discharge from the aquifer, however, will lower the water level, and by use of the transient model, this lowering and new water level may be calculated. (Knapp-USGS)
W75-09171

DISCHARGE MEASUREMENTS AND CHEMICAL ANALYSES OF WATER IN NORTHWESTERN WYOMING,
Geological Survey, Cheyenne, Wyo.
E. R. Cox.
Wyoming Water Planning Report No 14 (Basic-Data Report), 1975. 20 p, 1 fig, 5 tab.

Descriptors: *Discharge(Water), *Chemical analysis, *National parks, *Wyoming, Surface waters, Groundwater, Basic data collections, Sampling, Sites, Hydrologic data, Water quality, Well data, Streamflow, Lakes.
Identifiers: *Yellowstone National Park(Wyo), Grand Teton National Park(Wyo).

Discharge measurements and water samples for chemical analysis were obtained from 1959 through 1972 in and near Yellowstone and Grand Teton National Parks as part of studies made in cooperation with the National Park Service. Data

were collected in areas outside the National Parks in 1973 in cooperation with the Wyoming State Engineer. The data are tabulated in five tables. A map shows location sites where samples were collected from 122 wells, 50 springs, 83 streams, and 6 lakes in about 5,500 square miles of northwestern Wyoming. The data supplement interpretive reports by the U.S. Geological Survey on water resources of the area. (Woodward-USGS)
W75-09172

FLOODS IN EAST BATON ROUGE PARISH AND ADJACENT AREAS, LOUISIANA, FOR THE PERIOD 1953-74,
Geological Survey, Baton Rouge, La.
For primary bibliographic entry see Field 4A.
W75-09173

WATER RESOURCES DATA FOR KANSAS, 1974: PART 1. SURFACE WATER RECORDS.
Geological Survey, Lawrence, Kans.
Data Report, 1975. 202 p, 2 fig, 3 ref.

Descriptors: *Basic data collections, *Hydrologic data, *Kansas, Streamflow, Stage-discharge relations, Lakes, Reservoirs, Gaging stations.

Water resources data for the 1974 water year for Kansas including records of streamflow or reservoir storage at gaging stations, partial-record stations, and miscellaneous sites are given. Records are included for 163 gaging stations of which 143 are streamflow discharge stations and 20 are reservoir or lake stations; also are included records for 23 low-flow partial-record stations, 127 crest-stage partial-record stations, and 2 flood-hydrograph stations. Locations of gaging stations are shown. The base data collected at gaging stations consist of records of stage and measurements of discharge of streams or canals, and stage, surface area, and contents of lakes or reservoirs. In addition, observations of factors affecting the stage-discharge relation or the stage-capacity relation, weather records, and other information are used to supplement base data in determining the daily flow or volume of water in storage. The description of the gaging stations gives the location, drainage area, period of record, type and history of gages, average discharge, extremes of discharge or contents, general remarks, and notations of revisions of previously published records. (See also W75-09181) (Knapp-USGS)
W75-09180

WATER RESOURCES DATA FOR KANSAS, 1974: PART 2. WATER QUALITY RECORDS.
Geological Survey, Lawrence, Kans.
Data Report, 1974. 188 p, 2 fig, 5 tab, 25 ref.

Descriptors: *Water quality, *Chemical analysis, *Kansas, Surface waters, Groundwater, Physical properties, Sediment transport, Inorganic compounds, Biological properties, Water temperature, Sampling, Sites, Data collections, Hydrologic data.

Water-resources data for the 1974 water year for Kansas include records of data for the chemical and physical characteristics of surface and groundwater. Data on the quality of surface water (chemical, biological, temperature, and sediment) were collected from designated sampling sites once daily, weekly, monthly, or less frequently, and at some sites data were recorded on punched paper tape at 60-minute intervals. Records are given for 69 sampling stations. Miscellaneous temperatures of streamflow are given for 82 gaging stations, and records of chemical analyses are given for 219 groundwater sites. Locations of the sampling stations are shown. Records for pertinent water-quality stations in bordering States are also included. (See also W75-09180) (Woodard-USGS)
W75-09181

DESCRIPTIONS AND CHEMICAL ANALYSES FOR SELECTED WELLS IN THE TEHAMA-COLUSA CANAL SERVICE AREA, SACRAMENTO VALLEY, CALIFORNIA,
Geological Survey, Menlo Park, Calif.
For primary bibliographic entry see Field 4B.
W75-09187

SIMULATION MODEL FOR EVAPOTRANSPIRATION OF WHEAT: EFFECT OF EVAPORATIVE CONDITIONS,
Hebrew Univ., Jerusalem (Israel).
For primary bibliographic entry see Field 2D.
W75-09196

SYSTEMS ANALYSIS OF HYDROLOGIC PROBLEMS.
For primary bibliographic entry see Field 2A.
W75-09210

SYSTEM EVALUATION - RELIABILITY OF DATA AND EXTRAPOLATION AND CORRELATION OF DATA,
Utah Water Research Lab., Logan.
For primary bibliographic entry see Field 7A.
W75-09215

STOCHASTIC PROCESSES AND MODELS IN HYDROLOGY,
Colorado State Univ., Fort Collins. Dept. of Civil Engineering.
For primary bibliographic entry see Field 2A.
W75-09216

THE USE OF INPUT-OUTPUT (TRANSFER FUNCTION) MODELS IN HYDROLOGY,
California Univ., Davis. Dept. of Water Science and Engineering.
For primary bibliographic entry see Field 2A.
W75-09219

COMPUTER SIMULATION OF WATER RESOURCE SYSTEMS,
Utah Water Research Lab., Logan.
For primary bibliographic entry see Field 2A.
W75-09220

THE SYNTHESIS OF HYDROLOGIC SYSTEMS ON THE ANALOG AND HYBRID COMPUTERS,
City Univ., London (England).
W. J. Morris.
In: Systems Analysis of Hydrologic Problems; Proceedings of the Second International Seminar for Hydrology Professors, August 2-14, 1970, Utah State University, Logan, p 275-301. 8 fig.

Descriptors: *Systems analysis, *Hybrid computers, *Analytical techniques, *Flood routing, *Infiltration rates, Digital computers, Analog computers, Mathematics, Reservoirs, Flow, Hydrologic systems.
Identifiers: *Circuit diagrams, Machine equations.

A hybrid computer combines the capabilities of both the digital and analog computers. The analog computer is a parallel device in that all operations are performed simultaneously, while the digital computer is a sequential device with all operations performed in series. The hybrid computer retains the speed advantage, man-machine capability (for changing parameters and verification studies), and instant display of results in grapical form on an oscilloscope or a plotter of the analog computer. It also takes advantage of the greater precision, dynamic range, and storage capability of the digital computer for arithmetical computations. Basic programming for analog computers comprises development of mathematical system equations, simple block diagrams, and machine equations. Solutions by the hybrid computer of flood routing through a reservoir and Horton's infiltration curve for a storm were presented. (See also W75-09210) (Singh-ISWS)
W75-09221

A PROBLEM ORIENTED LIBRARY FOR HYDROLOGY,
McMaster Univ., Hamilton (Ontario). Dept. of Civil Engineering and Engineering Mechanics.
A. A. Smith.
In: Systems Analysis of Hydrologic Problems; Proceedings of the Second International Seminar for Hydrology Professors, August 2-14, 1970, Utah State University, Logan, p 305-325. 13 fig, 1 append.

Descriptors: *Computer programs, *Hydrology, *Libraries, Digital computers, Open channel flow, Hydraulics, Fluid mechanics, Engineering.
Identifiers: *Problem-oriented language, *FORTRAN-HYDRO computational modules.

A problem-oriented library was described and compared with problem-oriented languages. Advantages and disadvantages of each were described. A specific problem was illustrated by FORTRAN-HYDRO and by the determination of a surface water profile in a natural channel. The basic internal structure of all computational modules or subroutines necessary to solve such problems were described. The standard documentation of a subroutine was described and an example was presented. (See also W75-09210) (Terstriep-ISWS)
W75-09222

STUDY ON A SIGNIFICANT PRECIPITATION EPISODE IN THE WESTERN UNITED STATES,
National Weather Service, Salt Lake City, Utah. Western Region.
For primary bibliographic entry see Field 2B.
W75-09267

PRELIMINARY REPORT ON WIND ERRORS ENCOUNTERED DURING AUTOMATIC PROCESSING OF IFYGL LORAN-C DATA,
National Oceanic and Atmospheric Administration, Washington, D.C. Environmental Data Service.
For primary bibliographic entry see Field 7A.
W75-09270

IFYGL PHYSICAL DATA COLLECTION SYSTEM: INTERCOMPARISON DATA,
National Oceanic and Atmospheric Administration, Washington, D.C. Environmental Data Service.
J. Foreman.
Available from National Technical Information Service, Springfield, Va. 22161. NOAA Technical Memorandum EDS CEDDA-3, May 1975. 7 p, 16 tab, 1 ref.

Descriptors: *Data collections, *Instrumentation, *Lake Ontario, Wind velocity, Water temperature, Air temperature, Data processing, Buoys, Great Lakes, Meteorology.
Identifiers: *Physical Data Collection System, *Data intercomparison, *International Field Year for the Great Lakes.

During the International Field Year for the Great Lakes (IFYGL) 1972-73, 14 buoys and towers (equipped with automatic recording devices) were deployed in Lake Ontario as the major segment of the Physical Data Collection System (PDCS). Data from buoy intercomparisons before deployment indicate that measurements by the PDCS sensors were accurate. During the field year, the buoy system was compared with sensors aboard the U.S. S/V (survey vessel) Johnson, and the data obtained confirmed the reliability of the air- and water-temperature sensors. The wind-speed and wind-direction sensors apparently functioned properly throughout the field year, but the quality

8. ENGINEERING WORKS

8A. Structures

CONSTRUCTION REQUIREMENTS AND COST ANALYSIS OF GRASSED BACKSLOPE TERRACE SYSTEMS,
Nebraska Univ., Lincoln. Dept. of Agricultural Engineering.
For primary bibliographic entry see Field 4D.
W75-08926

COMPUTER ASSISTED DESIGN OF DIVERGING BRANCH FLUID NETWORK: A DYNAMIC PROGRAMMING APPROACH,
Hawaii Univ., Honolulu. Dept. of Agricultural Engineering.
For primary bibliographic entry see Field 8B.
W75-09124

ECOLOGICAL STUDIES OF TWO SWAMP WATERSHEDS IN NORTHEASTERN NORTH CAROLINA - A PRECHANNELIZATION STUDY,
North Carolina State Univ., Raleigh. Dept. of Zoology.
For primary bibliographic entry see Field 5C.
W75-09130

WAVE INDUCED PRESSURES ON SUBMERGED PLATES,
Worcester Polytechnic Inst., Mass. Alden Research Labs.
For primary bibliographic entry see Field 8B.
W75-09207

PREAUTHORIZATION PLANNING ACTIVITIES OF THE BUREAU OF RECLAMATION, THE CORPS OF ENGINEERS AND THE SOIL CONSERVATION SERVICE FOR FISCAL YEAR 1975.
For primary bibliographic entry see Field 4A.
W75-09244

POST AUTHORIZATION PROJECT ACTIVITIES ANNUAL STATUS REPORT - BUREAU OF RECLAMATION.
For primary bibliographic entry see Field 4A.
W75-09245

BELLE FOURCHE DAM AND GLENDO DAM-RESERVOIR ROADWAY.
For primary bibliographic entry see Field 6E.
W75-09257

CIBOLO, TEXAS, AND FRYINGPAN-ARKANSAS, COLORADO, PROJECTS.
For primary bibliographic entry see Field 6E.
W75-09258

8B. Hydraulics

EXPERIMENTAL STUDY OF INTERMITTENT PIPE FLOW USING PITOT-TUBE PROBES WITH HIGH FREQUENCY RESPONSE,
J. Meseth.
Archives of Mechanics, Vol 26, No 3, p 319-400, 1974. 9 fig, 5 ref.

Descriptors: *Pitot tubes, *Pressure, *Model studies, *Pressure measuring instruments, *Reynolds number, Measurement, Laminar flow, Turbulent flow, *Pipe flow.
Identifiers: *Flow velocity.

Special Pitot-tube probes have been designed to measure pressure fluctuations of water flow up to a frequency of 1 kHz. A model was presented to interpret experimental observations on intermittent pipe flow up to a Reynolds-number of about 20,000. Disturbances were introduced by injections of a thin water jet at the pipe entrance over a short period of time. This resulted in a turbulent slug of pipe flow, which increases with time. The result was intermittent flow in the pipe without significant change in mean flow velocity. Measurements were then taken in the regions where the laminar flow was followed by turbulent flow and vice versa. In such regions, fluctuations in velocity are significantly larger than in a developed turbulent pipe flow. (Prague-FIRL)
W75-08899

GROSS PARAMETER SOLUTIONS OF JETS AND PLUMES,
Chalmers Univ. of Technology, Goteborg (Sweden).
K. Cederwall.
Journal of the Hydraulics Division, American Society of Civil Engineers, Vol 101, No HY5, Proceedings Paper 11285, p 489-509, May 1975. 4 fig, 2 tab, 14 ref, 2 append.

Descriptors: *Jets, *Dimensional analysis, *Momentum equation, *Continuity equation, *Density, Equations, Submergence, Turbulent flow, Froude number, Diffusion, Stratification, Outlets, Entrainment, Hydraulics, Buoyancy, Water pollution, Discharge(Water), *Path of pollutants.
Identifiers: *Plumes.

Gross parameter solutions were developed for turbulent jets, plumes, and buoyant jets in stagnant, homogeneous, or linearly stratified environments. The results were presented in a form that facilitates comparisons of the effects of various assumptions that could be made concerning hydraulic conditions in a design situation. The solutions were obtained by use of dimensional analysis, geometric relations for jet trajectory, and conservation equations for mass and momentum. Mathematical point and line sources were used consistently. This simplified the procedures of normalizing and solving the governing equations, and also, presenting the results. (Adams-ISWS)
W75-08980

ENVIRONMENTAL ASPECTS--SACRAMENTO BANK PROTECTION,
Hydrologic Engineering Center, Davis, Calif. Water Resources Planning Branch.
For primary bibliographic entry see Field 4D.
W75-08981

ANALYSIS OF AN ELECTROMAGNETIC FLOW RATE TRANSDUCER,
Central Scientific Instruments Organization, Chandigarh (India).
For primary bibliographic entry see Field 7B.
W75-08989

COMPUTER ASSISTED DESIGN OF DIVERGING BRANCH FLUID NETWORK: A DYNAMIC PROGRAMMING APPROACH,
Hawaii Univ., Honolulu. Dept. of Agricultural Engineering.
K-P. Yang.
Available from the National Technical Information Service, Springfield, Va 22161 as PB-243 133, $4.75 in paper copy, $2.25 in microfiche. Ms Thesis, December 1973. 85 p, 16 fig, 3 tab, 12 ref, 4 append. OWRT B-029-HI(1) and B-034-HI(1).

Descriptors: *Dynamic programming, *Pipelines, *Computer models, *Mathematical studies, Computer programs, Numerical analysis, Simulation analysis, Piping systems(Mechanical), Pipes, Distribution systems, Hydraulic design, Networks, Pipe flow, Conduits.
Identifiers: *Diverging branch networks.

The dynamic programming technique has been successfully applied previously in solving serial type fluid systems. This technique was expanded to application to nonserial diverging branch type fluid networks. An interactive computer program based on a more efficient optimization method was developed. Pressure loss between pipe segments due to change of conduit sizes was incorporated into the design. The computer program was discussed with flow charts and a sample run of the program was presented. Results from this example demonstrated that the dynamic programming method is applicable to the solution of diverging branch type fluid system problems. Appendixes contain the Fortran listing of the program and the program output for the sample run. (Sims-ISWS)
W75-09124

GENERALIZED NOMOGRAPHIC SOLUTION OF HOOGHOUDT EQUATIONS,
Public Power Corp., Athens (Greece). Hydroelectric Project Design Branch.
J. G. Sakkas.
Journal of the Irrigation and Drainage Division, Proceedings of American Society of Civil Engineers, Vol 101, No IR1, Proceedings Paper 11182, p 21-39, March 1975. 4 fig, 8 tab, 16 ref, 2 append.

Descriptors: *Drainage, *Drains, *Groundwater, *Water table, Dupuit-Forchheimer theory, Hydraulic conductivity, Rainfall, Irrigation water, Graphical analysis.
Identifiers: *Drain spacing, *Nomographs, Steady-state theory.

The equation of drain spacing developed by Hooghoudt has gained considerable popularity among drainage design engineers because it is sufficiently accurate and possesses a simple mathematical expression. The latter is due to the notion of equivalent depth which he introduced. On the contrary, the application of the equation is quite cumbersome, requiring a trial-and-error procedure. In recent years drainage design for unsteady flow conditions also utilized the notion of equivalent depth. To simplify the use of both the drain spacing and the equivalent depth equations, they were put into dimensionless form containing fewer independent variables. An array of values suffices for quick and inexpensive determination of the equivalent depth. Tables of dimensionless equivalent depth also were prepared. A unique dimensionless nomographic solution of the drain spacing equation was obtained and was displayed in a set of five graphs. Work relevant to Hooghoudt equations by two investigators was analyzed with the aid of this analysis. (Schicht-ISWS)
W75-09197

SOLUTIONS FOR UNCONFINED NON-DARCY SEEPAGE,
James Cook Univ. of North Queensland, Townsville (Australia). Dept. of Engineering.
For primary bibliographic entry see Field 4A.
W75-09199

WAVE INDUCED PRESSURES ON SUBMERGED PLATES,
Worcester Polytechnic Inst., Mass. Alden Research Labs.
W. W. Durgin, and J. C. Shiau.
Journal of the Waterways, Harbors and Coastal Engineering Division, Proceedings of American Society of Civil Engineers, Vol 101, No WW1, Proceedings Paper 11098, p 59-71, February 1975. 7 fig, 7 ref, 2 append.

Descriptors: *Waves(Water), *Hydrodynamics, *Model studies, *Intakes structures, Intakes, Coastal engineering, Velocity, Analysis, Laboratory tests, Pressure, Distribution, Hydraulic models.
Identifiers: *Wave forces, *Submerged intakes, Vortex sheet.

A submerged plate was assumed to be rigidly suspended at an arbitrary fixed depth. For analysis, the plate was replaced by a vortex sheet with strength which varied both temporally and spatially. The velocity potential of this vortex sheet was adjusted so that in combination with the velocity potential of the oncoming waves, the boundary conditions on the plate, the free surface, and the bottom were approximately satisfied. The final vortex strength distribution was determined and the velocity field and pressure distribution on each side of the plate were calculated. An experimental program was conducted in a 4 ft by 4 ft by 40 ft flume equipped with a wave generator of the piston type. A flat plate of sandwich construction was instrumented with small pressure transducers. The transducer outputs were processed and recorded on an oscillograph. Two plates, one 1.1 ft wide spanning the flume and one 1.1 ft wide octagon, were tested. Results of analytical and experimental investigations were presented as instantaneous differential pressure distributions for various wave positions as a wave progressed over the plate. (Adams-ISWS)
W75-09207

STUDIES OF THE BEHAVIOR OF HEAVY PARTICLES IN A TURBULENT FLUID FLOW,
Illinois Univ., Urbana. Nuclear Engineering Lab.
C. C. Meek, and B. G. Jones.
Journal of Atmospheric Sciences, Vol 30, No 2, p 239-244, March 1973. 3 fig, 1 tab, 13 ref. OWRT B-067-ILL(3). 14-31-0001-3582.

Descriptors: Sedimentation, Turbulent flow, Diffusion, *Flow, Dispersion, *Path of pollutants, Turbulence, Fluid mechanics.
Identifiers: *Particle dispersion, Particle suspensions.

A statistical analysis has been made of individual particle transport in a homogeneous, turbulent fluid flow. Expressions for dispersion, correlation coefficients, and turbulent energy content have been obtained. Two parameters were found to characterize particulate transport, one of which relates to inertial effects acting on the particle, while the other describes the effects of crossing trajectories. As in previous studies by others, crossing-trajectories effects are found to be of particular importance; inertial effects, however, even for heavy particles, are not insignificant. Comparison of theoretical predictions with experimental data shows good agreement.
W75-09237

LINEARIZED NON-STOKESIAN DRAG IN TURBULENT FLOW,
Illinois Univ., Urbana. Nuclear Engineering Lab.
B. G. Jones, R. J. Ostensen, and C. C. Meek.
Journal of the Engineering Mechanics Division, American Society of Civil Engineering, Technical Notes, Vol 99, No EM-1, Proc. Paper 9528, p 233-243, February 1973. 4 fig, 10 ref. OWRT A-019-ILL(3). 14-01-0001-1632.

Descriptors: *Turbulent flow, *Turbulence, *Path of pollutants, *Drag, Fluid mechanics, Analytical techniques, Reynolds number.
Identifiers: Drag coefficient, Non-stokesian drag, Particle free fall.

One of the vexing problems related to the analytical description of particle motion in a fluid medium is the departure from linearity of the viscous drag force acting on the particle as its Reynolds number is increased appreciably beyond unity. This nonlinear characteristic in many treatments is only approximately considered or neglected entirely. It is felt that the linearization of this nonlinear term will prove to be useful. An analytical technique is presented which retains both the effects of nonlinear viscous drag and the linear form

system factors (horsepower, cavitation, plugging velocity, and material dislodgement) which limit output were identified and examined. A model incorporating these factors was developed for computer computation of dredge system performance. (Adams-ISWS)
W75-09206

8D. Soil Mechanics

EARTH-DAM SEEPAGE AND RELATED LAND WATER PROBLEMS,
Dames and Moore, Phoenix, Ariz.
For primary bibliographic entry see Field 4A.
W75-08973

THE INFLUENCE OF LATE CENOZOIC STRATIGRAPHY ON DISTRIBUTION OF IMPOUNDMENT-RELATED SEISMICITY AT LAKE MEAD, NEVADA-ARIZONA,
Geological Survey, Denver, Colo.
For primary bibliographic entry see Field 8G.
W75-09192

8F. Concrete

PRESSURE FILTER FOR WATER TREATMENT - FROM PRE-STRESSED CONCRETE RINGS WITH INTEGRAL FILTER PLANTS.
For primary bibliographic entry see Field 5D.
W75-09062

8G. Materials

CONTAMINATION OF WATER BY SYNTHETIC POLYMER TUBES,
Iowa State Univ., Ames. Dept. of Chemistry.
For primary bibliographic entry see Field 5A.
W75-08894

RANDOM PLASTICS MEDIA ARE KEY TO HIGH-QUALITY EFFLUENT,
For primary bibliographic entry see Field 5D.
W75-09060

THE INFLUENCE OF LATE CENOZOIC STRATIGRAPHY ON DISTRIBUTION OF IMPOUNDMENT-RELATED SEISMICITY AT LAKE MEAD, NEVADA-ARIZONA,
Geological Survey, Denver, Colo.
R. E. Anderson, and R. L. Laney.
Journal available from Sup Doc, U.S. Gov't. Print. Off. 20402 for $3.15. Journal of Research of the US Geological Survey, Vol 3, No 3, p 337-343, May-June 1975. 4 fig, 18 ref.

Descriptors: *Seismic studies, *Lakes, *Lake beds, *Faults(Geologic), *Nevada, *Arizona, Cenozoic era, Hydrogeology, Structural geology, Geomorphology, Earthquakes, Reservoirs, Stratigraphy, Geologic units, Impounded water, Aquifer characteristics.
Identifiers: *Lake Mead(Nev-Ariz), Impounded water-earthquake relationships.

The impoundment of water in some reservoirs stimulates the release of seismic energy. At Lake Mead, Nevada-Arizona, contrasts in permeability of upper Cenozoic sediments show a better correlation with irregularly distributed impoundment-related seismicity than do contrasts in structure. An evaluation of structures developed during the late Cenozoic fails to explain the erratic distribution of seismicity. An evaluation of the late Cenozoic stratigraphy, however, shows a coneentration of relatively impermeable evaporite beds and fine-grained clastic strata in the less seismic part of the lake basin; therefore, the authors conclude that a hydraulic connection between the lake water and the deep aquifer system that includes buried faults is needed in the Lake Mead area to cause the release of seismic energy. Where hydraulic connection is prevented by continuous or quasi-continuous upper Cenozoic basin-fill strata of low permeability, as in the eastern basin area, seismicity does not occur. (Woodard-USGS)
W75-09192

8I. Fisheries Engineering

A REVIEW OF THE LITERATURE ON THE USE OF CALCIUM HYPOCHLORITE IN FISHERIES,
Bureau of Sport Fisheries and Wildlife, Cortland, N.Y. Tunison Lab. of Fish Nutrition.
For primary bibliographic entry see Field 5G.
W75-08952

USE OF A SUDDEN TEMPERATURE DECREASE TO REDUCE THE EXCITABILITY OF CHANNEL CATFISH DURING HANDLING,
Southern Illinois Univ., Carbondale. Fisheries Research Lab.
For primary bibliographic entry see Field 5C.
W75-09153

9. MANPOWER, GRANTS AND FACILITIES

9D. Grants, Contracts, and Research Act Allotments

GUARDING OUR WATER RESOURCES, 1974 ANNUAL REPORT.
Virginia Polytechnic Inst. and State Univ., Blacksburg. Water Resources Research Center.
Bulletin No 83, 1974. 64 p, 45 fig. OWRT A-999-VA(22).

Descriptors: *Water resources institute, *Water management(Applied), *Water resources development, *Water Research Act, *Research and development, *Flood protection, Water conservation, Water policy, Water pollution, Water resources, Water pollution control, Planning, Projects, Resources development, Water supply, *Virginia, Non-structural alternatives, Flood control, Flood damage, Flood routing, Land use, Land management, Waste treatment, State governments, Federal government.
Identifiers: *Virginia Water Resources Research Center, State policy.

The Virginia Water Resources Research Center was established in response to the need for effective action through sound research on water resources problems in Virginia. The Center serves three purposes: it surveys the state's water resource problems, it sponsors and administers water resources research, and it collects and distributes information on water resources. This publication is the Center's 1974 Annual Report. Seven developments and trends over the past year are discussed to demonstrate the Center's expanding activities and increased effectiveness. Major categories of water resource problems receiving priority research attention are identified. Capsule descriptions of forty-three research projects currently in progress under Center sponsorship are included. Case histories are presented of projects producing information of direct and immediate value in solving important water resource problems, in Virginia and elsewhere. (Fernandex-Florida)
W75-09243

10. SCIENTIFIC AND TECHNICAL INFORMATION

10C. Secondary Publication And Distribution

MERCURY IN WATER, A BIBLIOGRAPHY, VOLUME 2.
Office of Water Research and Technology, Washington, D.C.
For primary bibliographic entry see Field 5C.
W75-08934

LIVESTOCK AND THE ENVIRONMENT: A BIBLIOGRAPHY WITH ABSTRACTS, VOLUME II,
East Central State Coll., Ada, Okla. School of Environmental Science.
For primary bibliographic entry see Field 5G.
W75-08937

EFFECTS OF EXHAUST FROM TWO-CYCLE OUTBOARD ENGINES,
Rensselaer Polytechnic Inst., Troy, N.Y. Bio-Environmental Engineering Div.
For primary bibliographic entry see Field 5C.
W75-08950

A REVIEW OF THE LITERATURE ON THE USE OF CALCIUM HYPOCHLORITE IN FISHERIES,
Bureau of Sport Fisheries and Wildlife, Cortland, N.Y. Tunison Lab. of Fish Nutrition.
For primary bibliographic entry see Field 05G.
W75-08952

PUBLICATIONS AND REPORTS RESULTING FROM RESEARCH GRANTS FUNDED THROUGH COASTAL POLLUTION BRANCH, PACIFIC NORTHWEST ENVIRONMENTAL RESEARCH LABORATORY.
National Environmental Research Center, Corvallis, Oreg.
For primary bibliographic entry see Field 05C.
W75-08994

TECHNIQUES FOR TRACING SEDIMENT MOVEMENT,
Canada Centre for Inland Waters, Burlington (Ontario).
For primary bibliographic entry see Field 02J.
W75-08995

MULTIOBJECTIVE WATER RESOURCES PLANNING, A BIBLIOGRAPHY.
Office of Water Research and Technology, Washington, D.C.
For primary bibliographic entry see Field 06B.
W75-09123

BIBLIOGRAPHY OF HYDROLOGY, CANADA, 1971-1973.
National Research Council of Canada, Ottawa, Associate Committee on Feodesy and Geophysics.
1974, 410 p.

Descriptors: *Hydrology, Water resources, Rivers, Lakes, Ice, Snow, Groundwater, Moisture, Instrumentation, Water utilization, Analytical techniques, Water quality, Model studies, Tracking techniques, Tracers, Water balance, Water pollution, Meteorology, Precipitation, Runoff, Evaporation.

The bibliography 1596 references on hydrology includes listings covering; general hydrology, hydrometeorology, surface water, sub-surface water, related sciences and miscellaneous topics;

Also included are listings on water quality and water pollution. An author index is provided. (Envir-Canada)
W75-09288

A SELECT BIBLIOGRAPHY ON ACTIVATED SLUDGE PLANTS,
British Steel Corp., Sheffield (England).
For primary bibliographic entry see Field 05D.
W75-09339

FOREST PRODUCTS POLLUTION CONTROL ANNOTATED BIBLIOGRAPHY (EXCLUDING PULP AND PAPER),
Western Forest Products Lab., Vancouver (British Columbia).
M. E. Johnson.
Available from the National Technical Information Service, Springfield, Va 22161 as PB-235 025, $3.25 in paper copy, $2.25 in microfiche. June 1974, 11 p, 66 ref.

Descriptors: *Bibliography, *Lumbering, *Air pollution, *Water pollution, Environmental effects, Lumber, Wood wastes, Disposal, Industrial wastes, Water pollution sources, Wastes, Saw mills, Forest management.
Identifiers: *Forest products industry, Noise, Plywood.

This bibliography lists 66 publications which deal with water, air, noise, or scenic pollution caused by logging, log handling, or the manufacture of lumber, plywood and other forest products. Several publications on residue disposal as related to the energy crisis are included. (Witt-IPC)
W75-09341

SUBJECT INDEX

AUTHOR INDEX

ORGANIZATIONAL INDEX

ACCESSION NUMBER INDEX

ABSTRACT SOURCES

URCE	ACCESSION NUMBER	TOTAL
CENTERS OF COMPETENCE		
Cornell University, Policy Models for Water Resources Systems	W75-09079--09082	4
ERDA Oak Ridge National Laboratory, Nuclear Radiation and Safety	W75-09065--09076	12
Franklin Institute (FIRL), Municipal Wastewater Treatment Technology	W75-08851--08883 08885--08887 08889 08891--08903 09060--09064 09302--09303 09305--09315 09319 09323--09327 09329	75
Illinois State Water Survey, Hydrology	W75-08961--08991 09077--09078 09124 09193--09202 09204--09228	69
Institute of Paper Chemistry, Water Pollution from Pulp and Paper Industry	W75-09333--09342 09344--09350	17
University of Arizona, Arid Land Water Resources	W75-08940--08949 09058--09059 09301	13
University of Florida, Eastern U. S. Water Law	W75-09240--09261 09264--09265	24
University of North Carolina Metropolitan Water Resources Planning and Management	W75-09084--09102 09104 09106--09122 09297	38
University of Wisconsin, Eutrophication	W75-08992--08998 09001--09019 09021--09040 09042--09045 09083	51
University of Wisconsin, Water Resources Economics	W75-08921--08922	2

ABSTRACT SOURCES

SOURCE	ACCESSION NUMBER	TOTAL
B. STATE WATER RESOURCES RESEARCH INSTITUTES	W75-08923 08925--08926 08928--08931 09046--09048 09051--09052 09125--09131 09229--09230 09232--09239 09298	30
C. OTHER		
BioSciences Information Service	W75-08884, 08888 08890, 08904 08907, 08924 08927 08932--08933 08999--09000 09020, 09041 09103, 09105 09152, 09162 09203, 09231 09262--09263 09299, 09304 09316--09318 09320--09322 09328 09330--09332 09343	34
Commonwealth Scientific and Industrial Research Organization, Australia	W75-08953--08960	8
Effects of Pollutants on Aquatic Life (Katz)	W75-08950--08952 09132--09151 09153--09161 09163--09164	34
Environmental Protection Agency	W75-08935--08939 09053--09057 09300	11
Environment Canada	W75-09286--09296	11
National Oceanic and Atmospheric Administration	W75-09266--09285	20
Office of Water Research and Technology	W75-08934 09049--09050 09123	4
U. S. Geological Survey	W75-08905--08906 08908--08920 09165--09192	43

☆ U. S. GOVERNMENT PRINTING OFFICE : 1975 O - 210-951 (4)

CENTERS OF COMPETENCE AND THEIR SUBJECT COVERAGE

- Ground and surface water hydrology at the Illinois State Water Survey and the Water Resources Division of the U.S. Geological Survey, U.S. Department of the Interior.
- Metropolitan water resources planning and management at the Center for Urban and Regional Studies of University of North Carolina.
- Eastern United States water law at the College of Law of the University of Florida.
- Policy models of water resources systems at the Department of Water Resources Engineering of Cornell University.
- Water resources economics at the Water Resources Center of the University of Wisconsin.
- Eutrophication at the Water Resources Center of the University of Wisconsin.
- Water resources of arid lands at the Office of Arid Lands Studies of the University of Arizona.
- Water well construction technology at the National Water Well Association.
- Water-related aspects of nuclear radiation and safety at the Oak Ridge National Laboratory.
- Water resource aspects of the pulp and paper industry at the Institute of Paper Chemistry.

Supported by the Environmental Protection Agency in cooperation with WRSIC

- Effect on water quality of irrigation return flows at the Department of Agricultural Engineering of Colorado State University.
- Agricultural livestock waste at East Central State College, Oklahoma.
- Municipal wastewater treatment technology at the Franklin Institute Research Laboratories.

Subject Fields

1 NATURE OF WATER

2 WATER CYCLE

3 WATER SUPPLY AUGMENTATION AND CONSERVATION

4 WATER QUANTITY MANAGEMENT AND CONTROL

5 WATER QUALITY MANAGEMENT AND PROTECTION

6 WATER RESOURCES PLANNING

7 RESOURCES DATA

8 ENGINEERING WORKS

9 MANPOWER, GRANTS, AND FACILITIES

10 SCIENTIFIC AND TECHNICAL INFORMATION

INDEXES

SUBJECT INDEX

AUTHOR INDEX

ORGANIZATIONAL INDEX

ACCESSION NUMBER INDEX

ABSTRACT SOURCES

U.S. MAIL

POSTAGE AND FEES PAID
U.S. DEPARTMENT OF COMMERCE
COM 211

AN EQUAL OPPORTUNITY EMPLOYER

U.S. DEPARTMENT OF COMMERCE
National Technical Information Service
5285 Port Royal Road
Springfield, VA 22161

OFFICIAL BUSINESS

PRINTED MATTER

Lightning Source UK Ltd.
Milton Keynes UK
UKHW012353210119
335965UK00006B/111/P